Routledge
Encyclopedia of
PHILOSOPHY

General Editor
EDWARD CRAIG

London and New York

First published 1998
by Routledge
11 New Fetter Lane, London EC4P 4EE
Simultaneously published in the USA and Canada
by Routledge
29 West 35th Street, New York, NY 10001

©1998 Routledge

Typeset in Monotype Times New Roman by
Routledge

Printed in England by
T J International Ltd, Padstow, Cornwall, England

Printed on acid-free paper which conforms to ANS1.Z39, 48-1992 and ISO 9706 standards

British Library Cataloguing-in-Publication Data
A catalogue record for this book is available from the British Library

The Library of Congress Cataloguing-in-Publication data is given in volume 10.

ISBN: 0415-07310-3 (10-volume set)
ISBN: 0415-18706-0 (volume 1)
ISBN: 0415-18707-9 (volume 2)
ISBN: 0415-18708-7 (volume 3)
ISBN: 0415-18709-5 (volume 4)
ISBN: 0415-18710-9 (volume 5)
ISBN: 0415-18711-7 (volume 6)
ISBN: 0415-18712-5 (volume 7)
ISBN: 0415-18713-3 (volume 8)
ISBN: 0415-18714-1 (volume 9)
ISBN: 0415-18715-X (volume 10)

ISBN: 0415-16916-X (CD-ROM)
ISBN: 0415-16917-8 (10-volume set and CD-ROM)

Contents

Using the *Encyclopedia*

List of entries

Using the *Encyclopedia*

The *Routledge Encyclopedia of Philosophy* is designed for ease of use. The following notes outline its organization and editorial approach and explain the ways of locating material. This will help readers make the most of the *Encyclopedia*.

SEQUENCE OF ENTRIES

The *Encyclopedia* contains 2,054 entries (from 500 to 19,000 words in length) arranged in nine volumes with a tenth volume for the index. Volumes 1–9 are arranged in a single alphabetical sequence, as follows:

Volume 1: A posteriori *to* Bradwardine, Thomas

Volume 2: Brahman *to* Derrida, Jacques

Volume 3: Descartes, René *to* Gender and science

Volume 4: Genealogy *to* Iqbal, Muhammad

Volume 5: Irigaray, Luce *to* Lushi chunqiu

Volume 6: Luther, Martin *to* Nifo, Agostino

Volume 7: Nihilism *to* Quantum mechanics, interpretation of

Volume 8: Questions *to* Sociobiology

Volume 9: Sociology of knowledge *to* Zoroastrianism

Alphabetical order

Entries are listed in alphabetical order by word rather than by letter with all words including *and*, *in*, *of* and *the* being given equal status. The exceptions to this rule are as follows:

- biographies: where the forenames and surname of a philosopher are inverted, the entry takes priority in the sequence, for example:

  Alexander, Samuel (1859–1938)
  Alexander of Aphrodisias (*c.* AD 200)
  Alexander of Hales (*c.* 1185–1245)

- names with prefixes, which follow conventional alphabetical placing (see Transliteration and naming conventions below).

A complete alphabetical list of entries is given in each of the Volumes 1 to 9.

Inverted titles

Titles of entries consisting of more than one word are often inverted so that the key term (in a thematic or signpost entry) or the surname (in a biographical entry) determines the place of the entry in the alphabetical sequence, for example:

  Law, philosophy of *or*
  Market, ethics of the *or*
  Hart, Herbert Lionel Adolphus (1907–93)

Conceptual organization

Several concerns have had a bearing on the sequence of entries where there is more than one key term.

In deciding on the sequence of entries we have tried, wherever possible, to integrate philosophy as it is known and studied in the USA and Europe with philosophy from around the world. This means that the reader will frequently find entries from different philosophical traditions or approaches to the same topic close to each other, for example, in the sequence:

  Political philosophy [signpost entry]
  Political philosophy, history of
  Political philosophy in classical Islam
  Political philosophy, Indian

Similarly, in entries where a philosophical tradition or approach is surveyed we have tried, whenever appropriate, to keep philosophical traditions from different countries together. An example is the sequence:

  Confucian philosophy, Chinese
  Confucian philosophy, Japanese
  Confucian philosophy, Korean
  Confucius (551–479 BC)

Finally, historical entries are usually placed with contemporary entries under the topic rather than the historical period. For example, in the sequence:

  Language, ancient philosophy of
  Language and gender
  Language, conventionality of
  Language, early modern philosophy of
  Language, Indian theories of
  Language, innateness of

DUMMY TITLES

The *Encyclopedia* has been extensively cross-referenced in order to help the reader locate their topic of interest. Dummy titles are placed throughout the alphabetical sequence of entries to direct the reader to the actual title of the entry where a topic is discussed. This may be under a different entry title, a synonym or as part of a larger entry. Wherever useful we have included the numbers of the sections (§§) in which a particular topic or subject is discussed. Examples of this type of cross-reference are:

AFRICAN AESTHETICS *see*
AESTHETICS, AFRICAN

CANGUILHEM, GEORGES *see*
FRENCH PHILOSOPHY OF SCIENCE §§3–4

TAO *see* DAO

GLOSSARY OF LOGICAL AND MATHEMATICAL TERMS

A glossary of logical and mathematical terms is provided to help users with terms from formal logic and mathematics. 'See also' cross-references to the glossary are provided at the end of entries where the user might benefit from help with unfamiliar terms. The glossary can be found in Volume 5 under L (LOGICAL AND MATHEMATICAL TERMS, GLOSSARY OF).

THE INDEX VOLUME

Volume 10 is devoted to a comprehensive index of key terms, concepts and names covered in Volumes 1–9, allowing readers to reap maximum benefit from the *Encyclopedia*. A guide to the index can be found at the beginning of the index. The index volume includes a full listing of contributors, their affiliations and the entries they have written. It also includes permission acknowledgements, listed in publisher order.

STRUCTURE OF ENTRIES

The *Routledge Encyclopedia of Philosophy* contains three types of entry:

- 'signpost' entries, for example, METAPHYSICS; SCIENCE, PHILOSOPHY OF; EAST ASIAN PHILOSOPHY. These entries provide an accessible overview of the sub-disciplines or regional coverage within the *Encyclopedia*; they provide a 'map' which directs the reader towards and around the many entries relating to each topic;
- thematic entries, ranging from general entries such as KNOWLEDGE, CONCEPT OF, to specialized topics such as VIRTUE EPISTEMOLOGY;
- biographical entries, devoted to individual philosophers, emphasizing the work rather than the life of the subject and with a list of the subject's major works.

Overview

All thematic and biographical entries begin with an overview which provides a concise and accessible summary of the topic or subject. This can be referred to on its own if the reader does not require the depth and detail of the main part of the entry.

Table of contents

All thematic and biographical entries over 1000 words in length are divided into sections and have a numbered table of contents following the overview. This gives the headings of each of the sections of the entry, enabling the reader to see the scope and structure of the entry at a glance. For example, the table of contents in the entry on HERACLITUS:

1 Life and work
2 Methodology
3 Unity of opposites and perspectivism
4 Cosmology
5 Psychology, ethics and religion
6 Influence

Cross-references within an entry

Entries in the *Encyclopedia* have been extensively cross-referenced in order to indicate other entries that may be of interest to the reader. There are two types of cross-reference in the *Encyclopedia*:

1. 'See' cross-references

Cross-references within the text of an entry direct the reader to other entries on or closely related to the topic under discussion. For example, a reader may be directed from a conceptual entry to a biography of the philosopher whose work is under discussion or vice versa. These internal cross-references appear in small capital letters, either in parentheses, for example:

> Opponents of naturalism before and since Wittgenstein have been animated by the notion that the aims of social science are not causal explanation and improving prediction, but uncovering rules that make social life intelligible to its participants (see EXPLANATION IN HISTORY AND SOCIAL SCIENCE).

or sometimes, when the reference is to a person who

has a biographical entry, as small capitals in the text itself, for example:

> Thomas NAGEL emphasizes the discrepancy between the objective insignificance of our lives and projects and the seriousness and energy we devote to them.

For entries over 1,000 words in length we have included the numbers of the sections (§) in which a topic is discussed, wherever useful, for example:

> In *Nicomachean Ethics*, Aristotle criticizes Plato's account for not telling us anything about particular kinds of goodness (see ARISTOTLE §§ 21–6).

2. 'See also' cross-references

At the end of the text of each entry, 'See also' cross-references guide the reader to other entries of related interest, such as more specialized entries, biographical entries, historical entries, geographical entries and so on. These cross-references appear in small capitals in alphabetical order.

References

References in the text are given in the Harvard style, for example, Kant (1788), Rawls (1971). Exceptions to this rule are made when presenting works with established conventions, for example, with some major works in ancient philosophy. Full bibliographical details are given in the 'List of works' and 'References and further reading'.

Bibliography

List of works

Biographical entries are followed by a list of works which gives full bibliographical details of the major works of the philosopher. This is in chronological order and includes items cited in the text, significant editions, dates of composition for pre-modern works (where known), preferred English-language translations and English translations for the titles of untranslated foreign-language works.

References and further reading

Both biographical and thematic entries have a list of references and further reading. Items are listed alphabetically by author's name. (Publications with joint authors are listed under the name of the first author and after any individual publications by that author). References cited in the text are preceded by an asterisk (*). Further reading which the reader may find particularly useful is also included.

The authors and editors have attempted to provide the fullest possible bibliographical information for every item.

Annotations

Publications in the 'List of works' and the 'References and further reading' have been annotated with a brief description of the content so that their relevance to readers' interests can be quickly assessed.

EDITORIAL STYLE

Spelling and punctuation in the *Encyclopedia* have been standardized to follow British English usage.

Transliteration and naming conventions

All names and terms from non roman alphabets have been romanized in the *Encyclopedia*. Foreign names have been given according to the conventions within the particular language.

Arabic

Arabic has been transliterated in a simplified form, that is, without macrons or subscripts. Names of philosophers are given in their Arabic form rather than their Latinate form, for example, IBN RUSHD rather than AVERROES. Arabic names beginning with the prefix 'al-' are alphabetized under the substantive part of the name and not the prefix, for example:

> KILWARDBY, ROBERT (d. 1279)
> AL-KINDI, ABU YUSUF YAQUB IBN ISHAQ (d. *c*.866–73)
> KNOWLEDGE AND JUSTIFICATION, COHERENCE THEORY OF

Arabic names beginning with the prefix 'Ibn' are alphabetized under 'I'.

Chinese, Korean and Japanese

Chinese has been transliterated using the Pinyin system. Dummy titles in the older Wade–Giles system are given for names and key terms; these direct the reader to the Pinyin titles.

Japanese has been transliterated using a modified version of the Hepburn system.

Chinese, Japanese and Korean names are given in Asian form, that is, surname preceding forenames, for example:

> WANG FUZHI
> NISHITANI KEIJI

The exception is where an author has chosen to present their own name in conventional Western form.

Hebrew

Hebrew has been transliterated in a simplified form, that is, without macrons or subscripts.

Russian

Cyrillic characters have been transliterated using the Library of Congress system. Russian names are usually given with their patronymic, for example, BAKUNIN, MIKHAIL ALEKSANDROVICH.

Sanskrit

A guide to the pronunciation of Sanskrit can be found in the INDIAN AND TIBETAN PHILOSOPHY signpost entry.

Tibetan

Tibetan has been transliterated using the Wylie system. Dummy titles in the Virginia system are given for names and key terms. A guide to Tibetan pronunciation can be found in the INDIAN AND TIBETAN PHILOSOPHY signpost entry.

European names

Names beginning with the prefixes 'de', 'von' or 'van' are usually alphabetized under the substantive part of the name. For example:

BEAUVOIR, SIMONE DE
HUMBOLDT, WILHELM VON

The exception to this rule is when the person is either a national of or has spent some time living or working in an English-speaking country. For example:

DE MORGAN, AUGUSTUS
VON WRIGHT, GEORG HENRIK

Names beginning with the prefix 'de la' or 'le' are alphabetized under the prefix 'la' or 'le'. For example:

LA FORGE, LOUIS DE
LE DOEUFF, MICHÈLE

Names beginning with 'Mc' or 'Mac' are treated as 'Mac' and appear before Ma.

Historical names

Medieval and Renaissance names where a person is not usually known by a surname are alphabetized under the forename, for example:

GILES OF ROME
JOHN OF SALISBURY

List of entries

Below is a complete list of entries in the order in which they appear in the *Routledge Encyclopedia of Philosophy*.

An alphabetical list of contributors, their affiliations and the entries they have written can be found in the index volume (Volume 10).

LUTHER, MARTIN (1483–1546)

Martin Luther was an Augustinian monk who found the theology and penitential practices of his times inadequate for overcoming fears about his salvation. He turned first to a theology of humility, whereby confession of one's own utter sinfulness is all that God asks, and then to a theology of justification by faith, in which human beings are seen as incapable of any turning towards God by their own efforts. Without preparation on the part of sinners, God turns to them and destroys their trust in themselves, producing within them trust in his promises made manifest in Jesus Christ. Regarding them in unity with Christ, God treats them as if they had Christ's righteousness: he 'justifies' them. Faith is produced in the sinner by the Word of God concerning Jesus Christ in the Bible, and by the work of the Holy Spirit internally showing the sinner the true subject matter of the Bible. It is not shaped by philosophy, since faith's perspective transcends and overcomes natural reason. Faith, through the working of God's Holy Spirit within the believer, naturally produces good works, but justification is not dependent upon them – they are free expressions of faith in love. Nevertheless, secular government with its laws and coercion is still necessary in this world because there are so few true Christians. Luther's theology brought him into conflict with the Church hierarchy and was instrumental in the instigation of the Reformation, in which the Protestant churches split from Rome.

1 Life
2 Theology of humility
3 Justification by faith
4 Ethics and politics
5 Theological method: philosophy and revelation
6 Theological method: biblical interpretation

1 Life

Martin Luther was born in Eisleben, Germany. While studying at the University of Erfurt in 1505, he was nearly struck by lightning in a storm. In terror he vowed to become a monk. Against the advice of friends and family, he entered the local monastery of Observant Augustinians shortly afterwards.

Over the next few years he found himself assailed by doubts as to his salvation and the forgiveness of his sins, which the nominalist theology and penitential practices current at that time did little to assuage. On becoming a Bible professor at Wittenberg in Electoral Saxony in 1512, Luther began to develop his own theological response to these trials through his lectures on the Psalms (1513–15) and on Romans (1515–16), eventually producing a theology of justi-

fication by faith (see §§2–3). In the process, he began to criticize the selling of 'indulgences' (reductions of one's punishment and guilt by authority of the Pope), publishing his *Disputatio pro declaratione et vitutis indulgentiarum* (Disputation on the Power and Efficacy of Indulgences, the 'Ninety-five Theses') explaining this disagreement in 1517. Trouble with Rome ensued, and escalated in 1519 when Luther, in a debate in Leipzig, was forced to shift the debate to the issue of papal authority.

In 1520 Luther began working out the implications of his theology. Such works as *Von der Freiheit eines Christenmenschen* (The Freedom of a Christian) and *An den christlichen Adel deutscher Nation* (To the Christian Nobility of the German Nation) outline a programme of reform for the Church. However, the Pope soon threatened him with excommunication, and at the Diet of Worms in 1521 Emperor Charles V confirmed the sentence, forcing Luther into hiding. While there he began work on a German translation of the Bible, a task which was to occupy him until 1534. The Emperor was unable to enforce his edict, however, and Luther was able to return to Wittenberg in 1522.

Meanwhile, others had been pursuing the reformation of the Church, and on his emergence Luther became embroiled in controversy with them. He rejected iconoclastic reform, and later opposed the Peasants' Revolt, in which radical reformers played a key role. His main debate with moderate reformers was over the Eucharist. At Marburg in 1529, attempts to forge a consensus broke down, with Luther sticking fiercely to his belief in the real presence of Jesus Christ in the Lord's Supper. Another significant debate was with ERASMUS (§1) over free will, leading to the publication in 1525 of Luther's *De servo arbitrio* (The Bondage of the Will).

In 1530 Charles V made another attempt to enforce the quashing of the Reformation, but he was not in a position to clamp down on those German princes (the 'Protestants') who refused to carry out his wishes. Luther was left with the freedom to refine and disseminate his theology, pursue controversies, and influence – in Saxony and beyond – those reforms of education, monasticism, the liturgy, preaching and ecclesial organisation in which he had been engaged since 1517. He died while visiting Eisleben in 1546.

2 Theology of humility

Luther was educated in a tradition of voluntaristic theology stemming from WILLIAM OF OCKHAM (§10) and refined by such thinkers as Gabriel BIEL (see VOLUNTARISM). They taught that God in his absolute power has freely ordained a covenant with human beings by which he promises to save those who 'do what is in them' (*facere quod in se est*). Biel, for instance, claimed that it is possible for human beings of their own natural powers to love God supremely, at least for an instant, and that God has covenanted to respond to this with his merciful acceptance.

Luther's earliest theology, in his 1513–15 lectures on the Psalms, retained a *quod in se est* position, albeit one which had been significantly reinterpreted. For Luther, doing *quod in se est* is not a heroic moral achievement, but the acknowledgement of one's sin, the recognition that one has no power to do good. This self-accusation and confession is the fitting disposition for the reception of God's grace. God, according to the covenant that he has ordained, will save those who cast themselves upon his mercy in this way, even though they have done nothing which from a human perspective merits salvation ([1513–15] 1974–6: 267, 373; compare [1515–16] 1972: 135). It was this view which led Luther to begin criticizing the sale of indulgences, which in his view did little to inculcate this humility, perhaps even militating against it (a view found throughout the 'Ninety-five Theses').

3 Justification by faith

From 1515 to 1518 or 1519, catalysed by reading some of Augustine of Hippo's writings, Luther moved away from the theology of humility and developed an understanding of 'justification by faith' which was to remain largely unchanged for the rest of his life (see AUGUSTINE §§6, 13). He came to believe that the *quod in se est* position was wrong, and that sinners are passive with respect to their justification ([1525] 1972: 267). That is, the faith to which God responds by saving the sinner is itself a work of God in the sinner, and not the sinner's achievement. The salvation of some and not others is related not to the fact that some and not others do *quod in se est*, but to God's ineffable predestination (1517b: thesis 29; [1525] 1972: 292).

Central to this theology is an understanding that human beings are, apart from God's active grace working in them, not free to choose to fulfil God's law (1517b: theses 4, 5, 7, 16; 1518: thesis 13). The law which defines righteousness and unrighteousness is not one which could be fulfilled by external obedience; it is a spiritual law which requires a right orientation of the 'inner person' ([1522] 1960: 367). It is not that one becomes righteous by performing righteous acts, but that one can only perform truly righteous acts if one has already become righteous (1517b: thesis 40). Since the Fall, when Adam and Eve ate the forbidden fruit in Eden, human beings have been 'turned in on themselves' and require God's

intervention to break their self-reliance and turn them to him.

God awakens faith in the sinner by the power of his Word given in the Bible and communicated through preaching, and by the power of his Spirit at work in the sinner (1536a: thesis 28). The Word both condemns, leading sinners to despair of their own righteousness, and inculcates trust in the promises of God made evident in the life of Jesus Christ. In response to this faith that he himself has awoken, God 'justifies' the sinner: he refuses to impute sin to the sinner's account. To put it positively, God decides to impute righteousness to sinners, to treat them as if they were righteous. God does this because of the intercession of his son, Jesus Christ, who in the Incarnation identified himself with sinners, and to whom sinners are joined in faith. Luther speaks of a marriage between sinners and Jesus, with God in his mercy choosing to regard the sinners as participating in Christ's own righteousness. Faith is both the acceptance of this relationship to Christ and the refusal to attempt to stand outside this relationship when confronted by God (1536a).

In and of itself this justification does not remove actual sin from believers, but leaves them paradoxically 'at one and the same time righteous and sinners' – sinners according to what is in them, righteous according to God's decision. Nevertheless, as he justifies believers, God gives them the gift of the Holy Spirit, who, in a secondary process, works in them to remove actual sin, and to produce righteousness within them by making them conform to Christ. This process is a continual one, and is not finished until the believer is taken into heaven ([1522] 1960: 370).

4 Ethics and politics

Faith is in one sense the fulfilment of the law. Luther called it the fulfilment of the First Commandment, which is to have no other gods before God ([1520a] 1966: 23–4), but stressed that faith itself is not a work but a gift from God. Whatever is done in faith is righteous, because faith by the power of God's Holy Spirit naturally expresses itself in love for God and for other people, and naturally works to remove the actual sin remaining in the believer ([1520a] 1966: 27). In this sense the believer is entirely free from all constraints. No law is needed for the believer ([1520a] 1966: 34).

However, true Christians are few and far between in this world, and God has ordained coercive secular government in order to restrain the excesses of sinners. Luther thus claimed that there are two 'kingdoms': one of Christians, in which there is complete freedom and love is the basis of action, and to which Jesus' injunction to 'turn the other cheek' is appropriate; and another 'of the world', in which justice is the basis of action and punishment is necessary. Luther argued that obedience to secular authority is a necessary service on the part of Christians who value peace, even when that authority is deemed unjust (unless the authority tries to coerce a rejection of faith, in which case resistance in such internal matters is proper) (1523). Spiritual authorities, set up by the community of believers for its own good order, should exercise no secular or coercive power – and Luther thus raged against the peasants when they (to his understanding) tried to coerce spiritual changes in the Peasants' Revolt of 1525. In his antagonism, he did little justice to their genuine grievances.

Nevertheless, in the absence of an accepted ecclesial authority after the break with Rome, Luther called upon Elector Frederick the Wise – who, although one believer among many, had certain resources – to help in establishing Luther's reforms of the Church in Saxony. This development paved the way for the later establishment of a State Church.

5 Theological method: philosophy and revelation

According to Luther, philosophy is able to identify and describe things in their worldly relations. It can even partially identify God – as the source of the world's ordering. Yet it can know nothing of God as gracious and merciful. Philosophy is therefore incompetent to describe anything in its full relationship to God, because God can only be properly identified through his self-identification in Jesus Christ. Even with regard to things in the world, then, philosophy is only partially adequate (see, for example, [1536b] 1960: 137–8).

God's self-identification is grasped only in faith, since it is a self-identification 'hidden' in weakness and suffering. Only by the Holy Spirit's illumination of the scriptural Word can this revelation be grasped. Faith then construes everything on the basis of the revelation of God in Christ (1518: thesis 20). The perspective of faith is dual, however, incorporating both a Law perspective and a Gospel perspective. The two are dialectically related. Law is the instrument of God's 'alien work', by which he judges and condemns the world, and philosophy can contribute to an understanding of Law. Law is, however, wholly in the service of God's 'proper work', about which philosophy knows nothing, which is to save the world by bringing it to faith and justifying it. God's proper work is 'hidden' within his alien work, and both are shown forth (to

the eyes of faith) in the cross of Christ, where God's saving intention is hidden beneath suffering and condemnation ([1525] 1972: 140).

Only true faith in Jesus Christ opens up this true dual perspective of Law and Gospel, which is the complete interpretive perspective for any worldly or spiritual reality, and which incorporates within it those insights of philosophy which it does not destroy. For instance, Luther was happy that Aristotle's *Logic* should continue to be taught in the universities as long as the inability of syllogistic logic to deal with God's proper work was acknowledged, but he railed against the use of Aristotle as a foundation for theology, and considered the *Ethics* in particular to be antithetical to the doctrine of justification by faith (1517b: thesis 41).

6 Theological method: biblical interpretation

Rather than philosophy, Luther put biblical exegesis at the heart of his project. In his lectures on the Psalms, he used a complex system which involved a distinction between historical and spiritual interpretation (the former relating the Psalms to ancient Israel and the Jews, the latter viewing them with the eyes of faith, and treating them as prophetic of God's work in Jesus Christ), and combined that with the medieval scheme of the four senses of Scripture (literal, allegorical = doctrinal, tropological = moral, and anagogical = relating to the end-times). Luther rejected historical interpretation in favour of spiritual interpretation, and agreed with the medieval consensus in privileging the literal sense ([1513–15] 1974–6: 3–5).

As time went on, however, he simplified this system greatly, concentrating on a combined literal–tropological sense and spiritual interpretation, according to which the whole Bible is taken to have as its subject matter Christ's work for us, and our response ([1513–15] 1974–6: 402). More precisely, the Bible is both Law and Gospel (the former predominating in the Old Testament, the latter in the New, but both found in each), which correspond respectively to God's alien work of condemnation and humiliation and his proper work of justification ([1520b] 1957: 348). Those with eyes of faith (that is, with the knowledge and experience of what Christ has done for them, conveyed by the Holy Spirit) can see that the message of the whole Bible is that Christ died for sinners; this message is hidden in Law and revealed in Gospel (1521).

See also: CALVIN, J.; HUS, J.; JUSTIFICATION, RELIGIOUS; MELANCHTHON, P.; WYCLIF, J.

List of works

Luther, M. (1483–1546) *D. Martin Luthers Werke: Kritische Gesamtausgabe* (Martin Luther's Works: Complete Critical Edition), Weimar: Hermann Böhlhaus Nachfolger, 1883–1986, 97 vols. (The most complete and most commonly cited of several original-language editions; of the 97 volumes, 12 are devoted to the *Deutsche Bibel* (German Bible), 18 to *Briefwechsel* (Letters), 6 to *Tischreden* (Table Talk), and the remaining 61 to essays, lectures, treatises and other works.)

—— (1483–1546) *Luther's Works*, ed. J. Pelikan and H.T. Lehmann, St Louis, MO: Concordia, and Philadelphia, PA: Fortress/Muhlenberg, 1955–86, 55 vols. (A thorough selection, normally the best or only available English translations, with short introductions to each piece.)

—— (1513–15) *Dictata super Psalterium*, in *D. Martin Luthers Werke*, vols 3–4 and 55; trans. H.J.A. Bouman, *First Lectures on the Psalms*, in *Luther's Works*, vols 10 and 11, ed. H.C. Oswald, St Louis, MO: Concordia, 1974–6. (Luther's earliest lectures, exploring a theology of humility. The English translation does not contain Luther's glosses.)

—— (1515–16) *Divi Pauli apostoli ad Romanos Epistola*, in *D. Martin Luthers Werke*, vol. 56; trans. W.G. Tillmanns and J.A.O. Preuss, *Lectures on Romans: Glosses and Scholia*, in *Luther's Works*, vol. 25, ed. H.C. Oswald, St. Louis, MO: Concordia, 1972. (Easier to follow than the Psalms lectures, these mark the move towards a theology of justification by faith.)

—— (1517a) *Disputatio pro declaratione et vitutis indulgentiarum*, in *D. Martin Luthers Werke*, vol. 1; trans. C.M. Jacobs and H.J. Grimm, *Ninety-five Theses, or Disputation on the Power and Efficacy of Indulgences*, in *Luther's Works*, vol. 31, *Career of the Reformer I*, ed. H.J. Grimm, Philadelphia, PA: Fortress/Muhlenberg, 1957. (Began the controversy that led to Luther's break with Rome: a seminal document of the Reformation.)

—— (1517b) *Disputatio contra scholasticam theologiam*, in *D. Martin Luthers Werke*, vol. 1; trans. H.J. Grimm, *Disputation Against Scholastic Theology*, in *Luther's Works*, vol. 31, *Career of the Reformer I*, ed. H.J. Grimm, Philadelphia, PA: Fortress/Muhlenberg, 1957. (Luther's break with the late-medieval theology in which he was educated.)

—— (1518) *Disputatio Heidelbergae habita*, in *D. Martin Luthers Werke*, vol. 1; trans. H.J. Grimm, *Heidelberg Disputation*, in *Luther's Works*, vol. 31, *Career of the Reformer I*, ed. H.J. Grimm, Philadelphia, PA: Fortress/Muhlenberg, 1957. (A first programmatic statement of Luther's theology, contrasting the perspective of the cross with human perspectives.)

—— (1520a) *Von den guten Werken*, in *D. Martin Luthers Werke*, vol. 6; trans. W.A. Lambert and J. Atkinson, *A Treatise on Good Works*, in *Luther's Works*, vol. 44, *The Christian in Society I*, ed. J. Atkinson, Philadelphia, PA: Fortress/Muhlenberg, 1966. (Luther defends himself against the charge that he has rejected the doing of good works.)

—— (1520b) *Von der Freiheit eines Christenmenschen*, in *D. Martin Luthers Werke*, vol. 7; trans. W.A. Lambert and H.J. Grimm, *The Freedom of a Christian*, in *Luther's Works*, vol. 31, *Career of the Reformer I*, ed. H.J. Grimm, Philadelphia, PA: Fortress/Muhlenberg, 1957. (The best introduction to Luther's ethics.)

—— (1520c) *An den christlichen Adel deutscher Nation von des christlichen Standes Besserung*, in *D. Martin Luthers Werke*, vol. 6; trans. C.M. Jacobs and J. Atkinson, *To the Nobility of the German Nation Concerning the Reform of the Christian Estate*, in *Luther's Works*, vol. 44, *The Christian in Society I*, ed. J. Atkinson, Philadelphia, PA: Fortress/Muhlenberg, 1966. (One of several calls to reform that Luther issued at this time, this one informative on the relationship between secular and ecclesial power.)

—— (1521) *Ein klein Unterricht, was man in den Evangeliis suchen und gewarten soll*, in *D. Martin Luthers Werke*, vol. 10.1; trans. E.T. Bachmann, *A Brief Instruction on What to Look for and Expect in the Gospels*, in *Luther's Works*, vol. 35, *Word and Sacrament I*, ed. E.T. Bachmann, Philadelphia, PA: Fortress/Muhlenberg, 1960. (A simple introduction to the structure of Luther's hermeneutics.)

—— (1522) 'Vorrede auff die Epistel S. Paul an die Römer', in *D. Martin Luthers Werke, Deutsche Bibel*, vol. 7; trans. E.T. Bachmann, 'Preface to the Epistle of St Paul to the Romans', in *Luther's Works*, vol. 35, *Word and Sacrament I*, ed. E.T. Bachmann, Philadelphia, PA: Fortress/Muhlenberg, 1960. (An influential summary of Luther's understanding of justification by faith.)

—— (1523) *Von weltlicher Oberkeit, wie weit man ihr Gehorsam schuldig, ist*, in *D. Martin Luthers Werke*, vol. 11; trans. H. Höpel, *On Secular Authority, How Far it Must be Obeyed*, in *Luther and Calvin on Secular Authority*, ed. H. Höpel, Cambridge: Cambridge University Press, 1991. (Luther's 'two kingdoms' doctrine of secular and spiritual power.)

—— (1525) *De servo arbitrio*, in *D. Martin Luthers Werke*, vol. 18; trans. P.S. Watson and B. Drewery, *The Bondage of the Will*, in *Luther's Works*, vol. 33, *Career of the Reformer III: The Bondage of the Will*, ed. P.S. Watson, Philadelphia, PA: Fortress/

Muhlenberg, 1972. (Luther's longest exposition of his understanding of humanity's lack of freedom.)

—— (1536a) *Die Disputation 'de iustificatione'*, in *D. Martin Luthers Werke*, vol. 39.1; trans. L.W. Spitz, *The Disputation Concerning Justification*, in *Luther's Works*, vol. 34, *Career of the Reformer IV*, ed. L.W. Spitz, Philadelphia, PA: Fortress/Muhlenberg, 1960. (A clearly defined, mature presentation of the doctrine of justification.)

—— (1536b) *Die Disputation 'de homine'*, in *D. Martin Luthers Werke*, vol. 39.1; trans. L.W. Spitz, *The Disputation Concerning Man*, in *Luther's Works*, vol. 34, *Career of the Reformer IV*, ed. L.W. Spitz, Philadelphia, PA: Fortress/Muhlenberg, 1960. (A clear presentation of Luther's theological anthropology, and his attitude towards philosophy.)

References and further reading

Aland, K., Reichert, E.O. and Jordan, G. (1970) *Hilfsbuch zum Lutherstudium* (Guide to Luther Studies), Witten/Ruhr: Luther-Verlag. (A list of all Luther's works, and an introduction to all major editions.)

Althaus, P. (1963) *Die Theologie Martin Luthers*, Gütersloh: Gütersloher Verlag; trans. R.C. Schultz, *The Theology of Martin Luther*, Philadelphia, PA: Fortress Press, 1966. (Dated, but very clear and comprehensive.)

Bainton, R.H. (1950) *Here I Stand: A Life of Martin Luther*, New York: Abingdon-Cokesbury Press. (Still the most readable single-volume life of Luther, dated and hagiographic but basically reliable.)

Brecht, M. (1981–7) *Martin Luther*, vol. 1, *Sein Weg zur Reformation 1483–1521*, vol. 2, *Ordnung und Abgrenzung der Reformation 1521–1532*, vol. 3, *Die Erhaltung der Kirche 1532–1545*, Stuttgart: Calwer Verlag; trans. J.L. Schaaf, *Martin Luther*, vol. 1, *His Road to Reformation 1483–1521*, vol. 2, *Shaping and Defining the Reformation 1521–1532*, Minneapolis, MN: Fortress Press, 1985–90. (The best detailed biography of Luther around, although the translation makes it heavy going.)

Cargill Thompson, W.D.J. (1984) *The Political Thought of Martin Luther*, ed. P. Broadhead, Brighton: Harvester Press. (A thorough survey.)

Dalferth, I.U. (1988) 'The Law–Gospel Model', in *Theology and Philosophy*, Oxford: Blackwell. (An excellent and very clear account of the relationship of theology and reason in Luther.)

Lohse, B. (1980) *Martin Luther – Eine Einfuhrung in sein Leben und sein Werk*, Munich: Verlag C.H. Beck; trans. R.C. Schultz, *Martin Luther: An Introduction to his Life and Work*, Edinburgh: T. & T. Clark, 1987. (The place to begin in studying Luther: an introduction to contemporary and historical debates, to Luther's life and work, and a survey of the primary texts.)

McGrath, A.E. (1985) *Luther's Theology of the Cross: Martin Luther's Theological Breakthrough*, Oxford: Blackwell, 1985. (Good on the medieval background, and on the stages of Luther's development.)

McSorely, H.J. (1969) *Luther: Right or Wrong? An Ecumenical-Theological Study of Luther's Major Work, The Bondage of the Will*, New York: Newman Press, and Minneapolis, MN: Augsburg Publishing House. (A Roman Catholic defence of the orthodoxy and coherence of Luther's denial of the freedom of the will, if not of all his arguments.)

Oberman, H.A. (1986) *The Dawn of the Reformation: Essays in Late Medieval and Early Reformation Thought*, Edinburgh: T. & T. Clark. (Important and careful articles trying to sort out the precise nature and role of Luther's innovations and contributions.)

Steinmetz, D.C. (1980) *Luther and Staupitz: An Essay in the Intellectual Origins of the Protestant Reformation*, Durham, NV: Duke University Press. (Contains a sensitive account of Luther's theology of humility.)

—— (1986) *Luther in Context*, Bloomington, IN: Indiana University Press. (A good selection of articles, including on the hidden God and free will.)

M.A. HIGTON

LUXEMBURG, ROSA (1871–1919)

Rosa Luxemburg, of Polish-Jewish origins, was for most of her life a prominent activist and theorist on the radical left of the German Social Democratic Party. She defended revolutionary Marxism against the 'revisionist' critique of Eduard Bernstein; she developed an original and controversial Marxist theory of imperialism; and she advocated direct revolutionary action by the masses, as contrasted with Lenin's insistence on 'democratic centralism' and the leading role of the Party.

1   **Beginnings**
2   **The analysis of capitalism**
3   **Last years**

1   Beginnings

Rosa Luxemburg was born in Zamość near Lublin in eastern Poland, then part of Russia. Her father was a merchant of Jewish extraction. Two years later the family moved to Warsaw where she spent her childhood. While still at school she engaged in illegal political activities and, in 1889, had to flee to Zurich, where she attended the university. When, shortly afterwards, the Social Democratic Workers Party of Poland was founded, she joined and soon became a leading member. From the beginning, she took the view that, with the emergence of the world market, nationalism had become regressive and dangerously disruptive and that, in particular, the growing integration of the Polish and Russian economies had rendered the demand for Polish independence (advanced by many Polish radicals) redundant. This launched a controversy in which she crossed swords with, among others, KAUTSKY and Liebknecht. In 1897 she submitted her doctoral dissertation, *Die industrielle Entwicklung Polens* (The Industrial Development of Poland), still regarded by many as a seminal work. A year later she participated in a marriage of convenience with Gustav Lübeck, a German citizen. This gave her the right to live in Germany and enabled her to take part in the activities of the German Social Democratic Party (SPD).

She lost no time in seizing the opportunity. The 'revisionist' debate was in full spate and, in the summer of 1898, she went to Berlin where she wrote a comprehensive refutation of Bernstein's position (see BERNSTEIN, E.). The result appeared as a series of articles in the *Leipziger Volkszeitung*. In these she argued that transnational cartels, sophisticated credit systems and improved means of communication, far from providing the 'means of adaptation' enabling the capitalist system to soften the impact of economic crises, merely enhanced the system's self-destructive tendencies and hastened the day of its inevitable economic collapse. She agreed that social reforms had a place in the party's programme, but only in so far as they raised the revolutionary consciousness and combat readiness of the working class. Finally, she suggested that Bernstein's basic position was that of philosophical idealism, and that this meant that he had defected to the camp of the reformist *petit bourgeoisie*. It was a case presented with remarkable intellectual acumen. Bernstein himself described her arguments as 'true examples of false dialectics, but handled at the same time with great talent' – a rare compliment. Her collected articles against Bernstein were published as a book, *Sozialreform oder Revolution? (Social Reform or Revolution?)*, in 1899.

In the following years, she consolidated her position in the German socialist movement as a leading theorist and agitator, becoming associated in particular with Kautsky and Franz Mehring. In 1904 she added to her credentials by spending three months in prison for slandering the crown (*Majestätsbeleidi-*

gung); and in the same year, she wrote two substantial articles criticizing Lenin's democratic centralism as applied to party organization (see LENIN, V.I.). In these, as in all her subsequent writings on party organization and tactics, she took a strong stand on a principle Marx and Engels had always insisted upon; namely, that the liberation of the working class can be achieved only by the working class itself. In her view, this meant that the revolution had to be a matter of direct spontaneous action by the workers and that the party as such should act in an enabling rather than in a directing role. 'Historically', she declared, 'the errors committed by a truly revolutionary movement are infinitely more fruitful than the infallibility of the cleverest Central Committee' ([1903/4] 1961: 108).

This view was reinforced when, in 1905, she went to Warsaw to take part in the revolutionary upheavals which followed Russia's defeat in its war with Japan. Her experiences inspired one of her best political works, *Gewerkschaftskamp und Massenstreik* (The Mass Strike, The Political Party and The Trade Unions) (1906). Here she elaborated her 'spontaneity theory' and argued that democratic proletarian organizations are not the precondition of revolutionary action but rather the consequence of it.

2 The analysis of capitalism

Luxemburg's most important contribution to Marxist theory was her *Die Akkumulation des Kapitals* (The Accumulation of Capital), published in 1913. In it, she pointed out that a capitalist economy can expand only if it can realize surplus value by finding purchasers for the goods it produces. Since the workers in a capitalist economy receive only the value of their labour power, but not the surplus value which they produce, they are unable to repurchase their whole product, thus leaving a surplus product. If the capitalists themselves purchase the surplus product, they gain nothing. No capital is accumulated. The surplus product must therefore find a market beyond the boundaries of capitalism, that is to say, in the non-industrial or pre-capitalist world. Hence the competition for markets in the peasant economies of Asia and Africa, and hence the struggle for political control of those markets – a phenomenon known as imperialism. When, in due course, all non-capitalist areas of the world market have been conquered and absorbed into the capitalist economy, the accumulation of capital will, of necessity, come to a halt and capitalism itself will collapse.

Rosa Luxemburg's analysis carried three important implications. First, it vindicated the claim that the terminal crisis of capitalism was inevitable. Second, it meant that imperialism was, not (as Lenin, for instance, would have it) the 'final stage of capitalism', but a structural feature of capitalism as such. Finally, it meant that war on a worldwide scale between capitalist states was unavoidable.

3 Last years

At the outbreak of war, Luxemburg was among the few who resisted the wave of patriotic war fever which swept the German SPD. In 1916 she was imprisoned and remained so for the rest of the war. Her last significant work, written while she was still in prison and published posthumously, was *Die russische Revolution* (The Russian Revolution) (1922). Once again she voiced her doubts about Lenin's notion of party organization and tactics. His 'Jacobin' style of organization might have been appropriate in the bourgeois revolution, but (she argued) it could not be employed in the very different circumstances of the proletarian revolution. The danger was that the dictatorship of the proletariat could easily be replaced by the dictatorship of a party or clique. For her, the dictatorship of the proletariat implied direct rule by the proletariat and therefore the active participation of the mass of the people. It was, she insisted, no paradox to think of the dictatorship of the proletariat as taking the form of 'unrestricted democracy'.

Upon her release from prison at the end of the war, she joined the leadership of the radical Spartacus group. Following the ill-timed and unsuccessful Spartacist insurrection in 1919, she was arrested and, together with Karl Liebknecht, murdered on her way to prison.

See also: REVOLUTION; MARXISM, WESTERN

List of works

Luxemburg, R. (1898) *Die industrielle Entwicklung Polens* (The Industrial Development of Poland), Leipzig: Duncker & Humblot. (Her first serious contribution to Marxist socio-economic analysis.)
—— (1899) 'Organisationsfragen der russischen Sozialdemokraten' *Die Neue Zeit* 2: 484–92 and 529–35; repr. in *Iskra* 69, 10 July 1904; *Sozialreform oder Revolution*, Leipzig: G. Heinisch; repr. *Social Reform or Revolution?*, New York: Three Arrows, 1937; trans. and ed. D. Howard, *Selected Political Writings of Rosa Luxemburg*, New York and London: Monthly Review Press, 1971. (Her famous critique of Edward Bernstein's revisionism.)
—— (1906) *Gewerkschaftskamp und Massenstreik* (The Mass Strike, The Political Party and the Trade Unions), New York: Harper & Row, 1971, 52–135.

(Luxemburg's reassessment of social democratic tactics following the upheavals in Russia in 1905.)
—— (1913) *Die Akkumulation des Kapitals* (The Accumulation of Capital), London: Routledge, 1951. (Her main work on imperialism and its relation to capitalist development.)
—— (1903/4) trans. and ed. with intro. by B.D. Wolfe, 'Leninism or Marxism?', in *The Russian Revolution and Leninism or Marxism?*, Ann Arbor, MI: University of Michigan Press, 1961. (Her critique of Leninism and the direction the Bolshevik revolution was taking.)
(1922) *Die russische Revolution: Eine kritische Wurdigung*, ed. with intro. by P. Levi, Berlin: Verlag Gesellschaft; trans. and ed. with intro. by B.D. Wolfe, 'Leninism or Marxism?', in *The Russian Revolution and Leninism or Marxism?*, Ann Arbor, MI: University of Michigan Press, 1961. (A critique of the direction taken by the Bolshevik revolution in Russia: her last significant work.)
—— (1971) *Selected Political Writings of Rosa Luxemburg*, ed. D. Howard, New York and London: Monthly Review Press. (A useful selection of her main writings.)

References and further reading

Bronner, S.E. (1987) *Rosa Luxemburg: A Revolutionary for our Times*, New York: Monthly Review Press. (A sympathetic but not uncritical account.)
Frohlich, P. (1972) *Rosa Luxemburg*, New York: Monthly Review Press. (Well-known work, originally published for the Left Book Club.)
Geras, N. (1976) *The Legacy of Rosa Luxemburg*, London: Humanities Press. (A subtle and perceptive analysis.)
Nettl, J.P. (1966) *Rosa Luxemburg*, London: Oxford University Press. (An excellent and, indeed, authoritative intellectual and political biography.)

H. TUDOR

LYCEUM *see* ARISTOTLE; PERIPATETICS; THEOPHRASTUS

LYELL, CHARLES *see* GEOLOGY, PHILOSOPHY OF

LYOTARD, JEAN-FRANÇOIS (1924–)

Jean-François Lyotard is a prominent French philosopher who is generally considered the leading theorist of postmodernism. His work constitutes an insistent critique of philosophical closure, historical totalization and political dogmatism and a re-evaluation of the nature of ethics, aesthetics and politics after the demise of totalizing metatheories.

In his early works, Lyotard confronts the limitations of dialectical philosophy and structuralist linguistics and analyses the disruptive, extradiscursive force of desire and the nonrepresentational or figurative dimensions of art and literature. In La Condition postmoderne *(1979a) (*The Postmodern Condition, *1984), he treats narrative pragmatics and language games as the bases for a critical approach to postmodern art and politics, as well as to the problem of justice. Recent texts insist on the obligation of philosophy, politics and writing to bear witness to heterogeneity and to what is repressed or forgotten in all representations of the past. His work questions the limits of philosophy, aesthetics and political theory in terms of problems linked to the irreducible complexities of art and literature and the nonrepresentational affects of historical-political events.*

1   Phenomenology, structuralism and the question of art
2   Postmodernism, narratology and critical judgment
3   The *différend* and the unrepresentable in history and memory

1   Phenomenology, structuralism and the question of art

Jean-François Lyotard was born in Versailles in 1924 and educated in Paris. After passing the 'Agrégation' in philosophy in 1950, he taught for one year in a lycée in Constantine, Algeria, and for seven years in La Flèche, France. He was a member of the radical political group 'Socialism or Barbarism' from 1954 to 1964 and regularly contributed articles to the journal it published and later to *Pouvoir Ouvrier* (*Worker Power*). He has taught at the Sorbonne, at Nanterre, where he played an important role in 'the events of May '68', and at the University of Paris at Vincennes and then Saint-Denis, until his retirement in France in 1987. He was a founding member of the International College of Philosophy in Paris and its second director. He has also been associated with various universities in the United States, including the University of California, San Diego, Johns Hopkins University,

Emory University and the University of California, Irvine, where for eight years he was Professor of French and Critical Theory. He has also been a visiting professor in Germany.

Lyotard's first works offer critical perspectives on phenomenology, structuralism, Hegelian dialectics and Marxist political theory. In *La Phénoménologie* (1954) (*Phenomenology*, 1991), which reveals the influence of both Heidegger and Merleau-Ponty on his early thinking, Lyotard analyses phenomenology's radical notion of historicity and the possibilities phenomenology offers for uncovering and moving beyond the limitations of objectivism, subjectivism and idealism.

In *Discours, figure* (1971), phenomenology, Marxism and structuralism are treated as ideological restrictions or deformations of the forces and constructs that underlie ordered reality and thought. Lyotard proposes a deconstructive approach to aesthetics to open the way for new forms of political practice (see DECONSTRUCTION). He insists on the radical differences between the linguistic or philosophical determination of meaning and the pictorial, spatial displacement of meaning in painting and experimental forms of poetry. He criticizes philosophy for the way it has attempted to master the sensible by making it discursive or meaningful and thus transform art into a form of philosophy.

Lyotard attacks the structuralist model for language and especially the Lacanian interpretation of Freud as serious restrictions and repressions of desire. He insists on the transgressive effects of desire, whose traces are manifest in the productive-disruptive *force* and not the completed *form* or structure of the figure. The exteriority and resistance of the figural to the discursive are for Lyotard also signs of the resistance of historical-political events to philosophical or historical totalizations. A libidinal aesthetics points to the possibility of a libidinal politics.

économie libidinale (1974) (*Libidinal Economy*, 1993) attacks the dogmatism of Marxist theory in an attempt to uncover the disruptive traces of libidinal drives that resist being systematized within the dialectic and that are signs of the possibility of alternate forms of political practice. What Lyotard himself calls 'the metaphysics of desire' at the base of his 'libidinal works' produces a humorous and at times outrageous satire of Marx and other political theorists and dramatically indicates the limitations of theory in general and its inability to foster or account for radical, unprogrammed actions or creations.

2   Postmodernism, narratology and critical judgment

In *La Condition postmoderne* (1979a) (*The Post-*

modern Condition, 1984), Lyotard defines the post-modern as an era characterized by its incredulity concerning the ability of foundational, totalizing metanarratives – whether liberal or Marxist – to effectively legitimate the sciences and the arts. Lyotard argues that the self-legitimating pragmatics of 'little narratives' break with the forms of philo-sophical and political totalization characteristic of modernism. He defends a concept of language games he derives from Wittgenstein and the principle that the specificity of the rules governing each game must be respected and the different games not confused with or derived from each other. Postmodernism is presented as the basis for a politics rooted in heterogeneity and dissension which 'would respect both the desire for justice and the desire for the unknown' (1984: 67).

The central problem posed by Lyotard's later work is how to create links among the heterogeneous realms and discourses constituting postmodernity without negating their specificity. His innovative readings of Kant bring to light the radical, post-modern implications of Kant's refusal to derive critical judgment from the cognitive faculty (see KANT, I. §12). Lyotard argues that the form of universalization related to critical (reflective) judg-ment can never be more than a demand and that Kant's notion of a universal *sensus communis* does not therefore imply consensus and a predetermined notion of community, as it does for communicational theorists such as Habermas and Rorty, but 'dissensus' and an open, conflictual, always undetermined community.

Lyotard argues that the problem of judgment should be considered essential to both the aesthetic and political realms, because it is in them that representation, conceptual knowledge and ethical determination are confronted with their own limita-tions. The derivation of either realm from any concept or predetermined system constitutes the form of aesthetic and political dogmatism against which Lyotard's entire critical enterprise is aimed.

3   The *différend* and the unrepresentable in history and memory

In *Le Différend* (1983) (*The Differend*, 1988), Lyotard defines the political in terms of the conflict of fundamental 'differends' (disputes), which, unlike forms of litigation that can be judged according to a determined set of rules or laws, cannot be equitably resolved for lack of a universal rule of judgment applicable to all of the arguments. He makes the problem of the linkage between conflicting idioms, phrases and faculties the primary obligation of critical

thinking and of a politics rooted in diversity and disputation. To be judicious in terms of differends is to acknowledge the heterogeneity of the discursive universe and the incommensurability of different genres and idioms. It is to bear witness to the injustice occurring whenever 'a plaintiff is deprived of the means of arguing and by this fact becomes a victim' (1988: 24).

In *L'Enthousiasme: la critique kantienne de l'his-toire* (Enthusiasm: The Kantian Critique of History) (1986a) and *Leçons sur l'analytique du sublime* (1991) (*Lessons on the Analytic of the Sublime*, 1994), Lyotard develops further the postmodern implica-tions of Kant's *Critique of Judgment* and particularly his concept of the sublime. He argues that the Kantian sublime makes possible a critical approach to history based on the recognition of the limitations of presentation and a respect for the fundamental and irreducible heterogeneity of the sociopolitical realm.

In *The Differend* and other recent works, Lyotard appropriates Adorno's analysis of the status of art and culture 'After Auschwitz' (in *Negative Dialektik*, 1966) and emphasizes what he calls the agony of art and its responsibilities to memory (see ADORNO, T.). In *Heidegger et 'les juifs'* (1988a) (*Heidegger and 'the Jews'*, 1990), which is Lyotard's contribution to the debate in France over the philosophical and political implications of Heidegger's relation to National Socialism and of his silence on the subject of the Shoah, Lyotard argues that writing and philosophy have a fundamental obligation both to those who have been excluded from or marginalized in history and to 'the Forgotten' or what has not and cannot be represented in thought, history and memory.

It would be possible to connect different texts of Lyotard to the later works of the phenomenologist Merleau-Ponty, to Levinas's radical reformulation of the ethical, to Adorno's work on aesthetics and politics, and finally to the work of other contempor-ary French philosophers such as Deleuze and Derrida. Lyotard's treatment of the links between aesthetics and politics, his provocative analyses of Marx, Freud, postmodernism and the Kantian notion of the sublime, as well as what Derrida has called 'the categorical challenge' he has made to his contempor-aries to make the problem of judgment a primary concern (*La Faculté de juger*, 1985), all give his work a unique place within contemporary French critical philosophy.

See also: POSTMODERNISM; POST-STRUCTURALISM IN THE SOCIAL SCIENCES §§4–5

List of works

Lyotard, J.-F. (1954) *La Phénoménologie*, Paris: Presses Universitaires de France, Collection 'Que sais-je?'; trans. B. Beakley, *Phenomenology*, Albany, NY: State University of New York Press, 1991. (A presentation and critical analysis of phenomenology's notion of historicity and its critique of objectivism, subjectivism and idealism.)

—— (1971) *Discours, figure* (Discourse, Figure), Paris: Klincksieck. (A radical deconstructive approach to aesthetics which criticizes the structuralist model for language and especially the Lacanian interpretation of Freud as serious restrictions and repressions of desire.)

—— (1973a) *Dérive à partir de Marx et Freud*, Paris: Union Générale des Éditions, Collection '10/18'; trans. S. Hanson, A. Knab, R. Lockwood, J. Maierand R. McKeon, *Driftworks*, New York: Semiotext(e), 1984. (The translation contains five chapters from *Dérive* and other essays dealing with Marx, Freud and the politics of the student movement of May '68 that attack the dogmatic, systematic restrictions of different versions of Marxism and psychoanalysis in the name of disruptive libidinal drives and politics.)

—— (1973b) *Des Dispositifs pulsionnels* (Mechanisms of the Drives), Paris: Union Générale des Éditions, Collection '10/18'. (A collection of essays on art, music, cinema, politics, Adorno and Nietzsche which demonstrate the subversive effects of libidinal politics.)

—— (1974) *économie libidinale*, Paris: Éditions de Minuit; trans. I. Hamilton Grant, *Libidinal Economy*, London: Athlone, 1993. (A humorous and at times outrageous satire of the dogmatism of Marxist theory which attempts to uncover the disruptive traces of libidinal drives that resist being systematized within the dialectic and that are signs of the possibility of alternate forms of political practice.)

—— (1979a) *La Condition postmoderne: rapport sur le savoir*, Paris: Éditions de Minuit; trans. G. Bennington and B. Massumi, *The Postmodern Condition: A Report on Knowledge*, Minneapolis, MN: University of Minnesota Press. (A critical approach to the conditions of knowledge which defends the self-legitimating pragmatics of 'little narratives' in a postmodern era when the foundational, totalizing metanarratives used to legitimate the sciences and the arts have collapsed and are no longer credible.)

Lyotard, J.-F. with Thébaud, J.-L. (1979b) *Au juste: conversations*, Paris: Christian Bourgois; trans. W. Godzich, *Just Gaming*, Minneapolis, MN: University of Minnesota Press, 1985. (A series of 'conversations' which deal with topics such as pagan philosophy, Plato, Kant and Wittgenstein and stress the fundamental importance of dissension and a critical notion of justice in an era when there exist no universally acknowledged criteria to determine judgment.)

Lyotard, J.-F. (1983) *Le Différend*, Paris: Éditions de Minuit; trans. G. Van Den Abbeele, *The Differend: Phrases in Dispute*, Minneapolis, MN: University of Minnesota Press, 1988. (In this work Lyotard defines the political in terms of the conflict of fundamental 'differends' (disputes), which cannot be equitably resolved for lack of a universal rule of judgment applicable to all of the arguments, and treats the problem of the linkage between conflicting idioms, phrases and faculties as the primary obligation of critical thinking and of a politics rooted in diversity and disputation.)

—— (1985) *La Faculté de juger* (The Faculty of Judging), with J. Derrida, V. Descombes, G. Kortian, P. Lacoue-Labarthe, and J.-L. Nancy, Paris: Éditions de Minuit; Lacoue-Labarthe's essay trans. as 'Talks', in *The Work of Jean-François Lyotard*, special issue of *Diacritics* 14 (3), 1984. (A collection of essays having to do with Lyotard's work and the problem of judgment which were chosen from papers given at the Cérisy-la-Salle Colloquium on Lyotard of July-August 1982 entitled 'Comment juger?' (How to Judge?).)

—— (1986a) *L'Enthousiasme: la critique kantienne de l'histoire* (Enthusiasm: The Kantian Critique of History), Paris: Éditions Galilée. (A critical reading of the significance of Kant's notion of the sublime in the *Critique of Judgment* and in his texts on history which propose a notion of politics and justice that cannot be derived from knowledge or any predetermined idea.)

—— (1986b) *Le Postmoderne expliqué aux enfants: correspondance, 1982-1985*, Paris: Éditions Galilée; trans. and ed. J. Pefanis and M. Thomas, *The Postmodern Explained: Correspondence, 1982-1985*, Minneapolis, MN: University of Minnesota Press, 1992. (A collection of short essays in which Lyotard defends his notion of the postmodern in art and politics.)

—— (1988a) *Heidegger et 'les juifs'*, Paris: Éditions Galilée; trans. A.. Michel and M.S. Roberts, *Heidegger and 'the Jews'*, Minneapolis, MN: University of Minnesota Press, 1990. (Lyotard's contribution to the debate in France over the philosophical and political implications of Heidegger's relation to National Socialism and of his silence on the subject of the Shoah in which Lyotard argues that writing and philosophy have a fundamental obligation to 'the Forgotten' or what has not and cannot be represented in thought, history and memory.)

—— (1988b) *Peregrinations: Law, Form, Event*, New York: Columbia University Press. (A series of lectures given at the University of California, Irvine in May 1986 in which Lyotard describes his own intellectual formation and the development of his approach to ethics, politics, art and history. These essays are followed by 'A Memorial of Marxism', which analyses his own *'différend'*. Includes an excellent bibliography of texts by and about Lyotard compiled by E. Yeghiayan.)

—— (1989a) *La Guerre des Algériens: écrits, 1956-1963* (The Algerians' War: Writings, 1956-1963), Paris: Éditions Galilée; 11 of 13 chapters trans. in *Political Writings*, ed. B. Readings, Minneapolis, MN: University of Minnesota Press. (A collection of essays written by Lyotard on the Algerian War for the radical Marxist journal *Socialisme ou barbarie* and preceded by a short preface written in 1989.)

—— (1989b) *The Lyotard Reader*, ed. A. Benjamin, Cambridge, MA: Blackwell. (A representative selection of chapters from Lyotard's books and other essays on art, literature and politics.)

—— (1991) *Leçons sur l'analytique du sublime*, Paris: Éditions Galilée; trans. E. Rottenberg, *Lessons on the Analytic of the Sublime*, Stanford, CA: Stanford University Press, 1994. (A rigorous analysis of the Analytic of the Sublime in Kant's *Critique of Judgment* which deals with the limits of presentation in philosophy, art and politics and emphasizes the necessity of reflexive thinking.)

—— (1993a) *Political Writings*, ed. B. Readings, Minneapolis, MN: University of Minnesota Press. (Contains essays from *Tomb of the Intellectual and Other Papers* (1984), *The Algerians' War* (1989) and recent essays from various sources.)

—— (1993b) *Toward the Postmodern / Lyotard*, ed. R. Harvey and M.S. Roberts, Atlantic Highlands NJ: Humanities Press. (Contains essays from *Dérive à partir de Marx et Freud* and *Des dispositifs pulsionnels*, as well as more recent essays on art and literature.)

—— (1996) *Signé Malraux*, Paris: Grasset. (A biography of André Malraux.)

References and further reading

* Adorno, T. (1966) *Negative Dialektik*, Frankfurt: Suhrkamp; trans. E.B. Ashton, *Negative Dialectics*, New York: Continuum, 1983. (The last section, 'Meditations on Metaphysics', which includes 'After Auschwitz', is an important reference for Lyotard's recent thinking on art and culture.)

L'Arc (1976) *Lyotard*, special issue of *L'Arc* 64. (A collection of essays in French on the aesthetic and psychoanalytical implications of Lyotard's early work.)

Benjamin, A. (ed.) (1992) *Judging Lyotard*, London and New York: Routledge. (A good collection of essays from different critical perspectives focused on the implications of Lyotard's approach to postmodernity, of his differences with Habermas and of his approach to aesthetic and political judgment.)

Bennington, G. (1988) *Lyotard: Writing the Event*, New York: Columbia University Press. (A good introduction and insightful analysis of three of Lyotard's most important works, *Discourse, Figure, Libidinal Economics* and *The Different*. Special emphasis is given to Lyotard's affinities with Derrida.)

Carroll, D. (1987) *Paraesthetics: Foucault, Lyotard, Derrida*, London and New York: Methuen. (A critical analysis of Lyotard's strategic use of art and literature to indicate the limits of politics and theory. It focuses on Lyotard's recasting of politics in terms of the problem of critical judgment and an aesthetics of the sublime.)

—— (1990) 'The Memory of Devastation and the Responsibilities of Thought: "And let's not talk about that"', foreword to *Heidegger and 'the Jews'*. (An analysis of Lyotard's philosophical and political critique of Heidegger and of his own paradoxical relation to deconstruction.)

Diacritics (1984) *The Work of Jean-François Lyotard*, special issue of *Diacritics* 14 (3). (A collection of essays dealing with issues raised by *The Postmodern Condition, Just Gaming* and *The Differend*. Includes an interview with Lyotard.)

* *La Faculté de juger* (The Faculty of Judging). (1985) Paris: Éditions de Minuit. (Collection of essays from the Cérisy-la-Salle Colloquium of July–August 1982 which was devoted to Lyotard.)

Jameson, F. (1984) 'Foreword' to *The Postmodern Condition: A Report on Knowledge*. (A presentation of this work from a critical Marxist position.)

Lingis, A. (1994) 'Some Questions About Lyotard's Postmodern Legitimation Narrative', *Philosophy & Social Criticism* 20 (1–2). (A critique of Lyotard's postmodern notion of narrative and performance as the bases for legitimation.)

Rorty, R. (1985) 'Habermas and Lyotard on Post-Modernity', *PRAXIS INTERNATIONAL* 4 (1). Republished in R. Bernstein (ed.) *Habermas and Modernity*, London: Polity Press, 1985, and in R. Rorty, *Essays on Heidegger and Others*, Cambridge: Cambridge University Press. (An analysis of the differences between Habermas and Lyotard from a liberal, communicational perspective which focuses on the problem of consensus and its implications for democracy.)

—— (1991) 'Cosmopolitanism without Emancipation: A Response to Jean-François Lyotard', in *Objectivity, Relativism, and Truth*, Cambridge: Cambridge University Press; originally appeared in *Critique* 41 (456), 1985, trans. P. Saint-Amand. (A critique of Lyotard's reading of Wittgenstein and of his notion of differends from a liberal, pragmatist position that defends the notion of universal history.)

Tomiche, A. (1994) 'Rephrasing the Freudian Unconscious: Lyotard's Affect-Phrase', *Diacritics* 24 (1). (A clear and insightful analysis of Lyotard's recent work on Freud and the problem of the affect.)

Weber, S. (1985) 'Literature – Just Making It', an Afterword to *Just Gaming*, trans. W. Godzich, Minneapolis, MN: University of Minnesota Press. (A critical analysis of the prescriptive dimensions of Lyotard's use of language games and the postmodern notion of justice he advocates.)

Yeghiayan, E. (1988) 'Checklist of Writings By and About Jean-François Lyotard: A Selected Bibliography', in *Peregrinations: Law, Form, Event*, New York: Columbia University Press. (Most complete bibliography of works by and on Lyotard through 1987.)

DAVID CARROLL

M

MACH, ERNST (1838–1916)

Mach was an Austrian physicist and philosopher. Though not one of the great philosophers, he was tremendously influential in the development of 'scientific philosophy' in the late nineteenth and early twentieth centuries. A vigorous opponent of 'metaphysics', he was celebrated as a progenitor of logical positivism. His work is regarded as a limiting case of pure empiricism; he stands between the empiricism of Hume and J.S. Mill, and that of the Vienna Circle.

Mach's positivist conception of science saw its aims as descriptive and predictive; explanation is downgraded. Scientific laws and theories are economical means of describing phenomena. Theories that refer to unobservable entities – including atomic theory – may impede inquiry. They should be eliminated where possible in favour of theories involving 'direct descriptions' of phenomena. Mach claimed to be a scientist, not a philosopher, but the 'Machian philosophy' was 'neutral monism'. Close to phenomenalism, it saw the world as functionally related complexes of sensations, and aspired to anti-metaphysical neutrality.

1 Life
2 Positivism, rejection of metaphysics, thought-economy
3 Scientific methodology: laws, theories and explanation
4 Neutral monism

1 Life

Born in Moravia, Ernst Mach studied at Vienna, and became professor of mathematics at Graz in 1864. In 1867 he was appointed professor of physics at Prague. From 1895 until 1901 he was professor of history and theory of inductive science at Vienna, before becoming a member of the upper house of the Austrian parliament. Mach's scientific interests were extraordinarily wide. He contributed to acoustics, theory of electricity, hydrodynamics, mechanics, optics, thermodynamics, and the physiology and psychology of perception.

2 Positivism, rejection of metaphysics, thought-economy

Mach was the leading positivist of the later nineteenth century, and the most important progenitor of the Vienna Circle (see VIENNA CIRCLE; LOGICAL POSITIVISM). Positivism originates with Comte. Central to it is the celebration of scientific knowledge and corresponding hostility to 'metaphysics'; the aim of philosophy is to understand the dominant, scientific mode of thought of the age. Science is seen as descriptive and predictive; scientific knowledge is exclusively of the correlations between phenomena. Comte and Mach differed in the *extent* of their hostility to metaphysics. Comte believed that speculation about the underlying, real nature of things was unwarranted; Mach held that no such nature, the 'things-in-themselves' behind the phenomena, exists.

This rejection separates Mach from 'two-worlds' Kantianism; but he is closer to late nineteenth-century scientific Neo-Kantians who favoured a 'dual aspect' account (see NEO-KANTIANISM §3). Mach's professed idealist origins (see §4 below), and the labels 'empirio-criticism' and 'critical positivism' bestowed on his position, indicate some affinity to Neo-Kantianism and a corresponding distance from earlier empiricism. Positivism does not imply inductivism, the view that theories are churned out mechanically from the data (see INDUCTIVE INFERENCE; MILL, J.S. §5). None the less, for Mach all genuine knowledge is scientific knowledge. Although the logical positivists may have rejected merely the transcendental underpinnings of the synthetic a priori, Mach seems to reject it completely, regarding space and time as given, and not as forms of intuition (for which he was criticized by Schlick). Hence there is some truth, but not complete truth, in the traditional view of Mach as the purest empiricist.

Mach's work predated intellectually and for the most part chronologically the 'linguistic turn'. He was innocent of Frege's revolution in logic, central to the outlook of members of the Vienna Circle such as Carnap and Reichenbach. Mach's concern with 'analysis' in *Die Analyse der Empfindungen* (*The Analysis of Sensations*) (1886a) was ontological, not the 'logical' or 'conceptual' analysis foundational to analytic philosophy (see §4). Likewise his 'verificationism' was not the developed semantic thesis it

13

became with the Vienna Circle. It was Mach's vigorous hostility to 'metaphysics', more than his detailed views, that was influential.

Central to Mach's philosophy is 'economy of thought', influenced by the economist Emanuel Herrman. Scientific laws and theories are economical descriptions of phenomena. The order science imposes on experience is a biological process of adaptation that overcomes limitations of memory; it does not reflect anything intrinsic to nature. *Die Mechanik in ihrer Entwicklung historisch-critisch dargestellt* (The Science of Mechanics) (1883) is a history of the evolution of science; its origins in 'the manual arts' are emphasized, and false abstraction and 'misplaced rigour' are debunked. 'All so-called axioms are...instinctive knowledge', the funded experience of the human race. The economy of thought is at the root of Mach's so-called 'sensationalism'. Talk of 'bodies' or 'objects' results from a 'partly instinctive, partly voluntary and conscious economy of mental presentation'.

3 Scientific methodology: laws, theories and explanation

Science, for Mach, is 'the compendious representation of the actual'. Known laws of nature – that is, regularities or interconnections between appearances – are explained and new laws discovered by the construction of theories. Explanation is downgraded, on the grounds that it makes a misguided appeal to metaphysical causes of things. The positivist account of scientific theorizing, with its anti-explanatory bias, is nowadays regarded as moribund. However, as Laudan has argued, Mach's own account of theory is more subtle than is often acknowledged. He was not hostile to the speculative construction of theories, as such. None the less, even if theories are required for the integration of data, they remain *about* the data; given that the correlation of the data takes one beyond them, entities should not be postulated beyond what is strictly necessary for that correlation.

In *Populärwissenschaftliche Vorlesungen* (Popular Scientific Lectures) (1894) Mach distinguishes 'direct' and 'indirect' descriptions. The former involves terms that have acquired 'a fixed significance independent of every object and connexion', taking on 'an "abstract" or "conceptual" import': for example, 'red' or 'straight'. (It has been said that direct descriptions are given in terms of sensations, but Mach is not explicit.) A 'theory' or 'theoretical idea' involves *indirect* description – the extension of analogy – and hence unfamiliar phenomena are made comprehensible. (In talking of 'auxiliary' and 'transitional theories', Mach later implies that there are

theories that consist simply in direct descriptions; there is ambiguity here.)

But the picture expressed in an indirect description may impede further inquiry, Mach believes. Black's discovery of specific heat was guided by the picture of thermal processes as the flow of a substance from one body to another; which, however, impeded the realization that heat is produced by friction, for which the picture of heat as a form of motion is more appropriate. Either picture may be heuristically valuable, but neither should be regarded as constituting the reality behind the observable phenomena.

Hence a theory may be heuristically and predictively useful; but the difference between theory and observation is purely quantitative. What is essential is that the theory contain the correct quantitative relations between work done and heat generated, between heat disappearing in one place and appearing in another, etc. Once we have established the functional dependence at the level of appearances, the theoretical model has done its work and should be jettisoned: 'as the new facts grow familiar, [one should] substitute for indirect description *direct* description, which contains nothing that is unessential and restricts itself absolutely to the abstract apprehension of facts'.

Laudan terms this the 'thesis of positivistic elimination'; 'purely observational' and 'mixed theories' (which refer in part to entities beyond the reach of experimentation) should have a different methodological status, and the latter eliminated where practicable in favour of the former. Hence one reason for Mach's notorious opposition to atomic theory, namely that it has outlived its usefulness; rather than, as customarily imputed, that atoms are 'unobservable'. In so far as Dalton discovered new connections between phenomena, the theory, properly interpreted as a heuristic device, had been acceptable, Mach believed. Many of Mach's opponents in the atomist debate accepted his methodology and defended atomic theory on its terms.

Mach's deflationary attitude towards theoretical entities is also expressed in his view that theory-choice is underdetermined by empirical evidence. In *Erktenntnis und Irrtum* (Knowledge and Error) (1905) he writes that concepts 'must be consistent with observation and...must be logically consistent with one another. These two requirements are satisfiable in *numerous* ways'. Thus, despite his biological determinism, there is a conventionalist element in Mach's scientific methodology. The pervasive role of the 'economy of thought' implies a more thoroughgoing instrumentalism than for Mill, for whom inductive proof was still central (see CONVENTIONALISM).

4 Neutral monism

'There is above all *no* Machian philosophy but at most a scientific methodology and a psychology of knowledge...I am by no means a philosopher, but only a scientist' (1905). In one sense, Mach's disclaimer was disingenuous. His philosophical standpoint was one shared with positivists and non-positivists around the turn of the century – namely, neutral monism (a term coined by Russell, though Mach himself referred to both 'monism' and 'neutrality') (see NEUTRAL MONISM).

The Science of Mechanics introduced a constant theme, leading to the alternative characterization of his position as 'sensationalism':

> Sensations are not signs of things; but on the contrary, a thing is a thought-symbol for a compound sensation of relative fixedness. Properly speaking the world is not composed of 'things'... but of colours, tones, pressures, spaces, times, in short what we ordinarily call individual sensations. ([1883] 1974: 579)

Mach was greatly influenced by Fechner's 'psychophysics', and worked on the physiological basis of sensation, while opposing Fechner's mechanistic reduction of mental phenomena to a concourse of physical atoms (see FECHNER, G.T. §2). What is required for developing psychophysical investigation, Mach believed, is a *sensational* atomic basis. He aspired to 'the gathering up of the sciences into a single whole', but this early version of the 'unity of science' was not materialistic. In *The Analysis of Sensations*, Mach traces his idealist roots. In adolescence he was a Kantian, but then he reacted against the thing-in-itself: 'the world...suddenly appeared to me as one coherent mass of sensations, only more strongly coherent in the ego'. He still shared Berkeley's belief in an ego not identical with sensations, before finally rejecting that too. Mach concluded that the useful habit of regarding complexes as unities generates the notion 'at first impressive, but subsequently recognized as monstrous, of a "thing-in-itself", different from its "appearance", and unknowable'. The idea of a transcendental, unknowable Ego is for Mach the last remnant of the detested 'thing-in-itself'.

Mach emphasizes that the 'elements' are neither mental nor physical, subjective nor objective, but 'neutral'. The title 'neutral monism' is therefore more appropriate than 'sensationalism', since it implies a rejection of two dualisms, mental–physical and subject–object. The complexes of elements, Mach claims, are functionally interdependent. The green of a leaf is a physical element in its dependence on other properties of the leaf and its environment, and a psychical element in its dependence on my perceptual processes. Which it should be regarded as depends simply on whether one's interest is that of the physicist or the psychologist.

Mach's account of the subject prefigures twentieth-century eliminative accounts of the self. But his analysis of objects more strongly anticipates an often complementary phenomenalism. For its originator, J.S. Mill, phenomenalism is the seemingly *non*-neutral view that physical objects are constructions from sensations (see PHENOMENALISM). Despite protestations of neutrality, does Mach's view of objects as actual and possible sensations and his rejection of any full-blooded distinction between appearance and reality simply amount to phenomenalism?

Mill's is the ontological thesis that physical objects are collections of actual and possible sensations, construed as mental, or at least subjective, items. Mach wants to resist this, but claims both that: (1) 'another's sensations are no more directly given to me than mine to him' (1905), yet (2) there is no 'essential distinction' between my sensations and those of another person; 'the same elements are connected at different points of attachment, namely those of the Ego'. (1) implies a subjective interpretation of the elements. Mach recognizes the pressure to go in this direction; but since the ego is, he thinks, a mere thought-economical pseudo-unity, he believes he is entitled to (2), which implies an objective interpretation. His vacillation is understandable but unsatisfactory.

But this ambivalence in neutral monism itself determined the structure of twentieth-century linguistic phenomenalism. Mach was followed by later phenomenalists when he tried to correct Mill's subjectivism, but he was unable to take Carnap's further 'neutralizing' or anti-metaphysical step of replacing (or perhaps implementing) the ontological thesis with a semantic one – that physical objects are *logical* constructions from sense data (see CARNAP, R.). This became possible only after the 'linguistic turn' of analytic philosophy.

Neutral monism, then, is the 'Machian philosophy'. But the scientific methodology was more important, and Mach wrote ten times as much on it as he did on sensationalist epistemology. In another sense, Mach's disclaimer of any 'Machian philosophy' is an important precursor of Carnap's view of philosophy as the 'logic of science'. Mach's attempt to generate a unified science on the basis of ontological neutrality was combined with a circumscribed role for philosophy – the dissolution of 'pseudoproblems' – as adjunct to that science. His disclaimer is echoed in Carnap's positive claim in

Logische Syntax der Sprache (The Logical Syntax of Language) (1937) that 'the logic of science takes the place of the inextricable tangle of problems which is known as philosophy'.

See also: SCIENCE, NINETEENTH-CENTURY PHILOSOPHY OF; RELATIVITY THEORY, PHILOSOPHICAL SIGNIFICANCE OF §6

List of works

Mach, E. (1883) *Die Mechanik in ihrer Entwicklung historisch-critisch dargestellt*, Prague; trans. T. McCormack (1893) *The Science of Mechanics*, La Salle, IL: Open Court, 1974. (A history of the evolution of science, including a comprehensive attempt to reconstruct classical mechanics on positivist lines.)
—— (1886a) *Beiträge zur Analyse der Empfindungen*, Jena; 5th edn, *Die Analyse der Empfindungen*, Jena, 1906; trans. C. Williams (1914) *Contributions to the Analysis of Sensations*, La Salle, IL: Open Court, 1986. (Mach's most developed statement of his neutral monism.)
—— (1886b) *Die Prinzipien der Wärmelehre*, Leipzig; trans. T. McCormack, P. Jourdain and A. Heath, *Principles of the Theory of Heat*, Dordrecht: Reidel, 1986. (Influential account of the history of the theory of heat.)
—— (1894) *Populärwissenschaftliche Vorlesungen*, Leipzig; trans. T. McCormack (1894) *Popular Scientific Lectures*, La Salle, IL: Open Court, 1986. (Exposition of familiar Machian scientific themes for a more general audience.)
—— (1905) *Erktenntnis und Irrtum*, Leipzig; trans. T. McCormack and P. Foulkes, *Knowledge and Error*, Dordrecht: Reidel, 1976. (A collection of essays which constitutes Mach's most mature statement of his scientific epistemology.)
—— (1906) *Space and Geometry*, Chicago, IL, trans. and collected by T. McCormack, La Salle, IL: Open Court, 1984. (Treatment of the concepts of 'physiological' and 'geometrical' space, and of the history of geometry. Collected from three essays originally published in *The Monist*, 1901–3.)

References and further reading

Blackmore, J. (1972) *Ernst Mach – His Life, Work and Influence*, Berkeley, CA: University of California Press. (Pedestrian, but the only full-length biography.)
—— (ed.) (1992) 'Ernst Mach – A Deeper Look', in *Boston Studies in the Philosophy of Science* vol. 143, Dordrecht: Kluwer. (Useful correspondence, some good articles and an invaluable bibliography.)
* Carnap, R. (1934) *Logische Syntax der Sprache*, Vienna: Springer; trans. A. Smeaton, *The Logical Syntax of Language*, London: Kegan Paul, Trench, Trubner & Co., 1937. (Carnap's presentation of his conventionalism.)
Cohen, R. and Seeger, R. (eds) (1970) 'Ernst Mach, Physicist and Philosopher', *Boston Studies in the Philosophy of Science* vol. 6, Dordrecht: Reidel. (Useful collection.)
Haller, R. (1982) 'Poetic Imagination and Economy: Ernst Mach as Theorist of Science', in J. Agassi and R. Cohen (eds) *Scientific Philosophy Today – Essays in Honour of Mario Bunge, Boston Studies in the Philosophy of Science* vol. 67, Dordrecht: Reidel; also in J. Blackmore (ed.) *Boston Studies in the Philosophy of Science* vol. 143, Dordrecht: Kluwer. (Useful corrective to the received picture of Mach.)
Hamilton, A. (1990) 'Ernst Mach and the Elimination of Subjectivity', *Ratio* (new series) 3 (2): 117–35. (Expansion of the material of §4.)
Holton, G. (1970) 'Mach, Einstein and the Search for Reality', in *Thematic Origins of Scientific Thought – Kepler to Einstein*, Cambridge, MA: Harvard University Press, 1972; also in Cohen and Seeger (eds). (Discussion of Mach's influence on Einstein.)
* Laudan, L. (1981) 'Ernst Mach's Opposition to Atomism', in *Science and Hypothesis: Historical Essays on Scientific Methodology*, Dordrecht: Reidel. (Pellucidly relates Mach's anti-atomism to his central concerns. An outstanding article of a different level of sophistication to most writing on Mach and positivism.)
Mandelbaum, M. (1971) *History, Man and Reasons: A Study in Nineteenth-Century Thought*, Baltimore, MD: Johns Hopkins Press, chaps 1, 14. (A classic treatment of nineteenth-century intellectual history.)
* Schlick, M. (1985) *General Theory of Knowledge*, La Salle, IL: Open Court, 194–233. (A penetrating critique of Mach's neutral monism by a leading member of the Vienna Circle; first published 1925.)
Skorupski, J. (1993) *English-Language Philosophy 1750–1945*, Oxford: Oxford University Press, ch. 3. (Introductory though not particularly easy.)
Smith, B. (1987) 'Austrian Origins of Logical Positivism', in B. Gower (ed.) *Logical Positivism in Perspective*, London: Croom Helm. (Authoritative historical enquiry.)

ANDY HAMILTON

MACHIAVELLI, NICCOLÒ (1469–1527)

Florentine diplomat, dramatist and political thinker, Machiavelli's treatise, Il principe *(The Prince) (1532a), has earned him notoriety as a political immoralist (or at least an amoralist) and a teacher of evil. In* The Prince, *Machiavelli posits a complex relationship between ethics and politics that associates princely* virtù *with the capacity to know and act within the political world as it 'is', and with the beastly abilities to dispense violence and practise deception. Behind this argument dwells the distinctly Machiavellian insight that politics is a realm of appearances where the practice of moral or Christian virtues often results in a prince's ruin, while knowing 'how not to be good' may result in greater security and wellbeing for both prince and people. Machiavelli warns that the prince's possibilities for success in this matter are always mediated by fortune; hence the prudent prince is one who is prepared to resist fortune by adapting his procedure to the times and his nature to 'the necessity of the case'.*

A less notorious but equally influential text is the Discorsi sopra la prima deca di Tito Livio *(Discourses on the First Ten Books of Titus Livy) (1531), in which Machiavelli offers a defence of popular liberty and republican government that takes the ancient republic of Rome as its model and emphasizes the role of the people in the 'public administration' of the city. However, Machiavelli also argues that a republic is only as successful in self-governance as its citizens are infused with civic* virtù *and therefore not corrupted. Accordingly, he praises the work of political founders who craft republican laws and institutions, and religious founders who fuse God and* patria *as one in the people's hearts. The apparent tension between Machiavelli's republican sympathies in* Discourses *and his elitist proclivities in* The Prince *has helped to fuel a vast interpretive literature concerning his political attitudes, his theory of politics, and the nature and meaning of 'machiavellianism' in Western political thought.*

1   Machiavelli in politics

From the beginning Niccolò Machiavelli's life, like the city of Florence itself, was caught in the ebb and flow of power that characterized the fortunes of the great banking and ruling house of the Florentine Medici. Machiavelli was born into the Florence of Lorenzo the Magnificent, a Medici prince who ruled the city until his death in 1492. When Piero de' Medici fled Florence at the approach of the French army in 1494, the family's hold on power was temporarily broken. After the short-lived regime of the charismatic friar Savonarola, the Florentine republic was restored, and Machiavelli was positioned to begin a career in politics. As Second Chancellor and Secretary to the Ten of War, he worked as a government functionary in affairs of state, travelling widely on diplomatic missions to various secular and ecclesiastical courts, as well as to the campaign headquarters of Cesare Borgia. As a result, Machiavelli became intimately acquainted with the strategies that are a part of 'the art that is necessary to one who commands' ([1532a] 1950: 53).

The Florentine republic was relatively short-lived. With the aid of the Spanish army, the Medici recaptured the city in 1512. Machiavelli was arrested, imprisoned and tortured, under suspicion as a co-conspirator in a plot to assassinate the Medici brothers. In 1513, he was released from prison and sent to rural isolation on his farm in the Tuscan countryside. 'To-day fortunate, tomorrow ruined,' was Machiavelli's succinct summation later. He would never again participate actively in the political affairs of Florence.

Like many displaced political actors, Machiavelli turned to writing. Within the first year of his exile, he produced a short treatise on *l'arte dello stato* wherein, he reported to his friend Francesco Vettori, 'I go as deeply as I can into considerations on this subject, debating what a princedom is, of what kinds they are, how they are gained, how they are kept, why they are lost' ([1498–1527] 1961: 142). Under this seemingly prosaic description smoulders the book that ignited a firestorm of invective in the sixteenth century, a book that continues to be one of the most controversial texts in the history of Western political thought.

2   *Il principe* (The Prince)

In terms of its formal structure, *Il principe* (The Prince) consists of a dedication (to Lorenzo the Magnificent, son of Piero de' Medici), and twenty-six chapters that can be divided into five general sections: chapters I–XI: a typology of states and how they are acquired; chapters XII–XIV: observations on militia and military command; chapters XV–XIX: advice to a prince regarding character and conduct; chapters XX–XV: advice to a prince regarding circumstances and conditions (fortresses, favours, functionaries and fortune); and chapter XVI: an exhortation to Italy that reconfigures the credo of Pope Julius II: *Fuori i Barbari!* (Put the barbarians out!). The formal structure of the treatise belies its substantive complexity, however, and the magnitude of rival interpretations that attend it. (There are now well over 3,000 commentaries.)

The notoriety of *The Prince* rests primarily upon the nature of Machiavelli's advice concerning the 'methods and rules' that a leader must follow in order to exhibit strength (*virtù*), gain and maintain his position within a particular territory (*lo stato*), and secure the state itself. On these matters, Machiavelli crafts a perspective that aligns politics with warfare, and justifies the deployment of force, the exercise of cruelties, the practice of deceit and the manipulation of appearances in the service of a political mentality that is 'disposed to adapt itself according to the wind' and 'able to do evil if constrained' ([1532a] 1950: 65). In the opening paragraph of chapter XV, in which this perspective on politics crystallizes, Machiavelli dismisses the usefulness of those writers who imagine 'republics and principalities which have never been seen or known to exist in reality', and declares that he will go 'to the real truth of the matter' (*verità effettuale*) ([1532a] 1950: 56). The real truth is that in politics, a ruler must be ready to play upon falsehoods and appearances, 'being often obliged, in order to maintain the state, to act against faith, against charity, against humanity, and against religion' ([1532a] 1950: 65). Accordingly, a prince must 'learn how not to be good,' and 'use this knowledge and not use it, according to the necessity of the case' ([1532a] 1950: 56).

In producing this perspective, *The Prince* forcefully deviates from and craftily subverts an entire genre of Renaissance advice-books that traditionally had aligned princely *virtù* (those qualities that enable a ruler to acquire honour, glory and fame) with the Platonic and Ciceronian 'cardinal' virtues of wisdom, justice, courage and moderation, and with the Christian ethic of goodness and righteousness. Machiavelli's treatise may not have 'revolutionized' the genre of advice-books, as Skinner (1978) contends, but it surely constitutes an unprecedented Renaissance challenge both to moral philosophy and to Christianity as normative bases for a theory of politics. This challenge may have earned the Florentine the admiration of 'anti-philosophers' and 'anti-Christs' of later ages (Nietzsche foremost among them), but more immediately it induced the Roman papacy to place all of Machiavelli's writings on the Index, where they remained for almost 300 years. *The Prince* also set in train its author's long-lived reputation as an atheistic, evil and satanic 'Machiavel', a man 'inspired by the Devil to lead good men to their doom' (Berlin 1982: 35). In contemporary vocabulary, the terms 'machiavellian' and 'machiavellianism' capture an understanding of politics as a domain that embraces naked self-interest, the maintenance of rulership at all costs, the utility of unethical behaviour and the centrality of power as an end that justifies any means.

3 The politics of princes

Despite the durability of these characterizations, Machiavelli posits a more complex relation between value (or ethics) and politics in *The Prince* than either an immoralist, 'teacher of evil', or an amoralist, *realpolitik*, rendering of his views allow. It is true that, unlike any other humanist writer, he openly associates princely *virtù* not with law (which he deems often insufficient to the combat that is ineliminable in politics), but with the abilities to dispense violence, or imitate the lion, and practise deception, or imitate the fox. Behind this argument dwells the distinctively Machiavellian insight that, in matters of state, 'some things which seem virtues would, if followed, lead to one's ruin, and some others which appear vices result in one's greater security and wellbeing' ([1532a] 1950: 57). Goodness is sometimes disastrous in politics, and cruelty less ruinous than clemency. Thus knowledge of beastly abilities and when and how to use them is essential, and it is acquired in two ways: by action, and by the historical study of the good and bad fortunes of 'eminent men'. The men Machiavelli admires and recommends for study are unexcelled in their capacity to exert coercive power and trick others into doing what they want, and thus bring fortune (*fortuna*) under control: the bloody Pope Alexander VI, and the warring and impetuous Pope Julius II, the ruthless Cesare Borgia, the scheming Roman emperor Severus, the more humane Marcus, the wily *condottiere* Francesco Sforza, and Scipio, Cyrus and Alexander the Great.

Yet there are also apparently effective rulers that Machiavelli introduces and condemns: Agathocles the Sicilian, Oliverotto da Fermo, and a host of nefarious Roman emperors. In proffering these examples, *The Prince* appears to formulate a standard of right, or at least prudential, conduct that is appropriate to *virtù*. Thus it throws into question the standard view that machiavellianism celebrates politics as a sphere of unrestrained evil, and power as the exercise of unremitting violence. Machiavelli's most notable condemnation concerns Agathocles, who arrived at his position as prince in Syracuse through the cold-blooded slaughter of the senators and richest men of the city. Machiavelli remarks: 'it cannot be called virtue to kill one's fellow-citizens, betray one's friends, be without faith, without pity and without religion; by these methods one may indeed gain power but not glory' ([1532a] 1950: 32). The comment on glory (*gloria*) introduces a crucial qualification, because it suggests that the truly *virtù*ous prince is not one who uses his power simply for self-aggrandizement, but in order to construct something that will outlast him, and sanctify his name.

Even in political situations where glorious deeds are unlikely, however, and pure power reigns supreme, Machiavelli distinguishes between ferocious and contemptible conduct, and praises as *virtù*ous those leaders who are feared but not hated. At issue here is a deeper distinction that does not obviate conflict and cruelty as inescapable aspects of political action, but nevertheless differentiates cruelties that are 'well-committed' from those that are 'ill-committed', and therefore increase rather than diminish with time. It is precisely Machiavelli's refusal to disentangle conflict and cruelty from politics that has led some commentators to configure him as a teacher of evil who divorces politics from ethics (Strauss 1958). For others, however, his thought represents a powerful reconstitution of an action concept that, even as it withdraws politics from the domain of purely moral or Christian judgment, reinvests it as a value sphere with its own peculiar and demanding configurations of good and evil, and hence its own norms and standards of ethical evaluation (Berlin 1982).

4 *Virtù* and *fortuna*

Whatever their ethical implications, neither Machiavelli's action concept of politics nor his notion of princely *virtù* can be fully appreciated without considering the role he assigns to *fortuna* in human affairs. The metaphysical picture behind his account of politics is that of an all-pervading necessity that forms the fabric of the world, but wherein freedom, as the exercise of human control over circumstances, is a real possibility at least half of the time. Thus princely *virtù* also presupposes a capacity to master fortune and navigate within the inherent flux and turmoil of political affairs. It is perhaps this elusive capacity that Machiavelli struggled hardest to comprehend, in response to a phenomenological puzzle about action, character, circumstance and method. Strategically, he cast the solution to this problem as the ability to be prudent (*prudente*), and thereby read circumstances, anticipate probabilities and master events. In terms of character, he presented it as the ability to be

inherently flexible, the willingness to deviate from what comes naturally and the determination to exercise a steely self-control. Thus, Machiavelli writes: '[the prince] is happy whose mode of procedure accords with the needs of the times, and similarly he is unfortunate whose mode of procedure (*modo di procedere*) is opposed to the times' ([1532a] 1950: 92).

Readers should note, following Pitkin (1984), that Machiavelli's 'metaphysics' is decisively gendered, in so far as he represents *fortuna* not only as a river, but also as a woman, or an engulfing female power that threatens to overwhelm and crush the man of *virtù*. 'Fortune varies and commands men, and holds them under her yoke'; but if the prince is impetuous and willing 'to conquer her by force', he can subdue fortune and thereby use her to his advantage (1498–1527: 99, 94). The symbolic gendering of action, chance and circumstance that Machiavelli effects on a state level in *The Prince* is recapitulated on a domestic level in his play *Mandragola* (c.1518 (1957)), where the oppositional erotics of instrumental violence is delivered as comedy. Both *The Prince* as politics, and *Mandragola* as domestics, allow us to see the limits of a world that is constructed as a struggle between *virtù* and *fortuna*, a world wholly devoid of human mutuality, reciprocity and genuine civic life.

5 *Discorsi* (The Discourses)

Discorsi sopra la prima deca di Tito Livio (*Discourses on the First Ten Books of Titus Livy*) appears to redress, if not repudiate, the uncivic orientation of *The Prince* and its comedic counterpart *Mandragola* by directing its political attentions elsewhere. In this work (probably completed in 1518 although not printed until 1531), Machiavelli distances himself from 'those who generally dedicate their works to some prince' and resolves to undertake the dangerous task of introducing 'new principles and systems' like the explorers of 'unknown seas and continents' in order to 'open a new route, which has not yet been followed by any one'. The new route is discoverable only by way of a return to the past or to 'examples of antiquity' ([1531] 1950: 102–4). Although he implies at the start that the subject matter of his treatise will encompass a vast array of historical and political topics, *Discourses* in fact concentrates upon one singular historical example, the Roman republic, and one singular type of ruler: 'the sagacious legislator of a republic . . . whose object is to promote the public good, and not his private interests, and who prefers his country to his own successors' ([1531] 1950: 138). Thus *Discourses* is best read as illuminating the presence of the past, in order to assess what is necessary if modern republics are to flourish and endure like ancient Rome. More indirectly but no less decisively, *Discourses* is also a biting condemnation of the corruption of Florence, a subject that Machiavelli addressed more subtly in *Istorie Fiorentine* (The History of Florence), a work commissioned in 1520 (although not published until 1532) by a new Medicean court that, at long last, rewarded his literary if not his diplomatic talents.

Discourses is divided into three books (of 60, 33 and 49 chapters respectively) that span an impressive array of political topics concerning the early history of Rome and the Romans: origins and founders, religion, armies, conquests and colonies, the constitution, institutions of government, customs, laws (civil and agrarian), character, warfare and diplomacy, notable leaders (including a tribute to Cincinnatus) and citizens. A careful look at the chapter titles reveals the question that is central to Machiavelli's investigation of Rome: What makes republican regimes stable and enduring? Pocock (1975) argues that in *Discourses* Machiavelli configures the relationship between the all-too-human 'republic' and the unremitting forces of 'time' as a historical confrontation that cannot be deferred. But Machiavelli also attempts to mediate the confrontation through a careful study of the conditions and civic qualities that are necessary if republics are to have even a minimal chance of effectively countering the ordinances of *fortuna* and 'achieving greatness like that of Rome'. Machiavelli's study of civic *virtù* is at the heart of his republican theory of citizenship (see REPUBLICANISM §2).

6 The politics of republics

If we approach Machiavelli's classical republican theory as a complex of elements, then four emerge as primary. The first, which can hold for either principalities or republics, is *libertà*, or the condition of being free from subjection to a foreign power and governed by one's own laws. The significance that Machiavelli attaches to liberty cannot be overstated, for he argues that only a city free from servitude is potentially capable of achieving greatness, whether in power, or wealth, or both. For this reason he cautions against attempts to establish republics in countries not suited to them lest the government 'lack proper proportions and have but little durability' ([1531] 1950: 257). Nevertheless and in general, the institutions that are essential to civic liberty are better perfected in republics than in monarchies.

If republics are better safeguards of liberty than monarchies, then republics which entrust their liberty to the people are even more likely to retain freedom than those who favour the nobility. The second element of Machiavellian republicanism involves a defence of the people (*popolo*), as the active guardians of public liberty. As usual, Machiavelli's reasoning on this matter is complex and contextual, and it does not denote an absolute rule. In Sparta and Venice for example, where power was entrusted to the nobility, liberties endured far longer than in Rome. Nevertheless, a republic that desires to extend its empire, rather than merely seek its own preservation, would do well to follow Rome and entrust liberty to the people. A republic that emulates Rome recognizes that its liberty depends upon admitting its people 'to a share of its glory', for the people are superior in maintaining the 'institutions, laws and ordinances' upon which the freedom of the republic rests.

Machiavelli recognizes, however, that a self-governing republic that is animated by ordinary citizens is only as *virtù*ous as its laws and institutions (*ordini*) allow. Thus the third element of his republican theory places great emphasis upon the talents of the founders of republics, like Romulus, and even more emphasis upon those founders who recognize God and religion 'as the most necessary and assured support of any civil society' and use them to divinize the republic's laws and institutions before an awe-struck people, as Numa did in Rome. The welfare of a republic does not consist, then, 'in having a prince who governs it wisely during his lifetime, but in having one who will give it such laws that it will maintain itself even after his death' ([1531] 1950: 146, 148). Among the specific institutions that Machiavelli recommends as most beneficial to republican liberty is a government that combines 'a prince, a nobility and the power of the people' under the same constitution. This was the case in ancient Rome, where the consuls, the senate and the tribunes maintained a tense equilibrium, and kept each other in check. The significance of Machiavelli's advice on this matter has less to do with the later 'separation of powers' doctrine than with his insistence that 'all the laws that are favourable to liberty' result from partisan struggles between the nobility and the people ([1531] 1950: 119).

The emphasis on struggle which, as we have seen, is an indelible aspect of Machiavellian politics, leads to the fourth and most audacious element of Machiavellian republicanism. This element forwards a view of civic participation (*participazione*) as the inevitable clash of interests within and among diverse competing political forces, and it embraces a view of the republic as a 'theatre of turbulence'. From this perspective, the prosperity of republics hinges not upon quelling turbulence or repressing divisiveness, but rather on finding ways of channelling the energies and agitations within the state to good effect. This is particularly true with regard to the people. Accordingly, Machiavelli insists that: 'every free state ought to afford the people the opportunity of giving vent, so to say, to their ambition' ([1531] 1950: 120). Behind this remark rests an even deeper conviction: when civic disturbances generate *ordini* that give the people 'a share in the public administration', they also establish the most assured guardians of liberty, as the tribunes were in Rome.

From the complex of elements (*libertà*, *popolo*, *ordini* and *participazione*) that constitutes the republican orientation of *Discourses* arises a host of secondary issues that are no less important to Machiavelli's analysis of how republics can survive the test of time and fortune. Primary among these is the issue of vulnerability, or what threatens a republic's stability from within and from outside. Since he is well aware of the vulnerability of republics to threats from within, Machiavelli is alert to the problem of corruption (or the disintegration of civic *virtù*), especially as it manifests itself in ambition (*ambizione*) and in factions that threaten to turn productive conflict into internecine warfare (see CORRUPTION §1, 3). Book III, chapter 6 of *Discourses*, 'Of Conspiracies', unmasks the motives and methods that induce individuals, whether alone or in groups, to engage in such warfare, and plot against princes and republics. In true Machiavellian fashion, it also instructs potential conspirators about what works and what does not.

Machiavelli is also aware of the vulnerability of republics to threats from outside, and on this score he repeats and develops an admonition that is found in *The Prince* and elaborated at great length in *Arte della guerra* (The Art of War) (1521): if glory is to be attained, a state must rely upon its own armies and cultivate in its citizens a military *virtù*, as the Romans did. Thus: 'any republic that adopts the military organization and discipline of the Romans... will always and under all circumstances find [her soldiers] to display a courage and dignity similar to that of the Romans' ([1531] 1950: 504). Without good military organization there can be neither 'good laws nor anything else good', and a republic is left prey to the vicissitudes of fortune. Although Machiavelli is in this instance comparing the 'wretched military organization' of Venice to that of Rome, it is hard not to see Florence in this depiction. Read in this light, *Discourses* intones a dirge for Florence, even as it strikes symbols of tribute to ancient Rome.

7 The motives of Machiavelli

Almost inevitably, the comparison of the subject matter of *The Prince* and *Discourses* gives rise to the intriguing question of Machiavelli's motives and his political attitudes. For several centuries, commentators have found it difficult to overlook what seems to be a glaring contrast between the Medicean sympathies of *The Prince*, in which Machiavelli extols princes and insists that all that the people want is not to be oppressed, and the republican convictions of *Discourses*, in which the people are elevated as the guardians of liberty, and the lives of princes are short. In essence, the interpretive question seems to be this: How is it possible to hail Machiavelli as a defender of republican citizenship and liberty, self-government and civic *virtù*, when these appear to be the very regimes and values he teaches his Medici protégé to subvert'?

In response, some critics (such as Hans Baron and J.R. Hale) argue that Machiavelli was in fact less a republican and more of a realist who adjusted his advice as political conditions warranted. Thus *The Prince* can be read as a clear-sighted, if opportunistic, attempt to gain favour with the ruling regime. Other critics insist upon Machiavelli's unwavering commitment to republicanism (as SPINOZA did), and reconfigure the notorious advice-book as (a) a subversive handbook for republicans (an interpretation favoured by Rousseau); (b) a satire on princely governance (provided by Garrett Mattingly); or (c) a masterful act of political deception, intended for and against the Medici (offered by Mary Dietz). Still others, including Sheldon Wolin, suggest that there are no real dissimilarities between the two texts at all; thus the republicanism of the *Discourses* can be taken as the salutary result of the political acts of a well-advised, *virtù*ous prince. Whatever else, these debates over Machiavelli the man are proof that Machiavelli the theorist of politics sought and perhaps mastered the ability to be simultaneously deceptive and truthful, realistic and ethical, cruel and humane.

See also: HUAINANZI; POLITICAL PHILOSOPHY, HISTORY OF §4

List of works

Machiavelli, N. (1960–5) *Opere*, in *Bibliotheca di classici italiani*, ed. S. Bertelli, Milan: Feltrinelli, 8 vols.

—— (1883) *Lettere familiare*, Florence: Edordo Alvisi G.C. Sansone.

—— (1498–1527) *The Letters of Machiavelli*, trans. A. Gilbert, New York: Capricorn, 1961. (Machiavelli's wide-ranging correspondence and commentary on affairs public and private, cultural and literary, international and domestic.)

—— (c. 1518) *Mandragola*, trans. A. Paolucci and H. Paolucci, New York: Bobbs-Merrill, 1957. (A domestic comedy of sexual intrigue, deception and gender transgression.)

—— (1521) *Arte della guerra* (The Art of War), trans. E. Farneworth, New York: Washington Square Press, 1965. (A military classic in the form of a dialogue. Subjects range from matters concerning ancient and contemporary arms and armour, battalion formations, and Greek and Roman methods of war, to giving commands, dividing spoils and avoiding battles and traps.)

—— (1531) *Discorsi sopra la prima deca di Tito Livio* (Discourses on the First Ten Books of Titus Livy), in *The Prince and The Discourses*, trans. L. Ricci, New York: Modern Library, 1950.

—— (1532a) *Il principe* (The Prince), in *The Prince and The Discourses*, trans. L. Ricci, New York: Modern Library, 1950. (The famous treaty on power, conduct, effectiveness and princely *virtù* in politics that earned Machiavelli his reputation as a political 'immoralist'.)

—— (1532b) *Istorie Fiorentine* (History of Florence), trans. H.A. Rennart, Washington, DC, and London: Walter Dunne, 1901. (A historical study of transformation and change in Florentine domestic and international politics from the Middle Ages (1010) until the late Renaissance (1492).)

References and further reading

* Berlin, I. (1982) 'The Originality of Machiavelli', in *Against the Current: Essays in the History of Ideas*, New York: Penguin. (A classic survey of the existing literature on Machiavelli and his motives also makes a case for the 'pagan' morality of his politics.)

Grazia, S. de (1989) *Machiavelli in Hell*, Princeton, NJ: Princeton University Press. (Pulitzer Prize-winning biography.)

* Pitkin, H.F. (1984) *Fortune is a Woman: Gender and Politics in the Thought of Niccolò Machiavelli*, Berkeley, CA: University of California Press. (Insightful analysis of the psycho- and sociological dimensions of feminine/masculine symbolics in Machiavelli's writings and their implications for his political thought.)

* Pocock, J.G.A. (1975) *The Machiavellian Moment: Florentine Republic Thought and the Atlantic Republican Tradition*, Princeton, NJ: Princeton University Press. (An innovative study of Florentine thought in the era of Machiavelli, and its anglicization as 'neo-Machiavellian' in the eighteenth century.)

Schevill, F. (1936) *History of Florence from the Founding of the City Through the Renaissance*, New York: Ungar Publishing Company. (A classic study of Florence and Florentine culture.)

* Skinner, Q. (1978) *The Foundations of Modern Political Thought*, vol. 1, *The Renaissance*, Cambridge: Cambridge University Press. (A pathbreaking work that situates and analyses Machiavelli's writings in the context of Florentine and Renaissance humanist traditions.)

—— (1981) *Machiavelli*, New York: Hill & Wang. (An accessible and instructive introduction to Machiavelli's political thought.)

* Strauss, L. (1958) *Thoughts on Machiavelli*, Chicago, IL: University of Chicago Press. (A textual reading of the blasphemous and dangerously seductive nature of Machiavelli's political writings as deviations from the Platonic-Christian tradition.)

MARY G. DIETZ

MACINTYRE, ALASDAIR (1929–)

Alasdair MacIntyre has contributed to the diverse fields of social, moral and political philosophy. He is one of the leading proponents of a virtue ethical approach in moral philosophy, part of a wider attempt to recover an Aristotelian conception of both morality and politics. His return to ancient sources has been powered by a critical indictment of the modern moral predicament, which MacIntyre regards as theoretically confused and practically fragmented; only a return to a tradition which synthesizes Aristotelian and Augustinian themes will restore rationality and intelligibility to contemporary moral and political life.

MacIntyre's long career culminated in the trilogy of works *After Virtue, Whose Justice? Which Rationality?* and *Three Rival Versions of Moral Enquiry*. These works claim that contemporary moral and political philosophy analyses incoherent fragments of a Judaeo-Christian theistic ethic that has lost its point with the increasing secularization of modern culture, leading to practical fragmentation and theoretical incoherence. MacIntyre's aim is to reconstruct a purpose and context for moral thought from the fragments of coherent moral life that survive only in marginal communities alienated from the main currents of the modern world.

This project draws on both philosophy and history. MacIntyre argues that the philosophical justification of rival positions in both theoretical and practical contexts involves narrative explanation. Such narratives set out how competing traditions of inquiry develop from, and are opposed to, each other. A theory is demonstrably superior to another if it explains both the successes and the failures of the previous theory. This form of justification requires an evaluatively engaged historical inquiry, whether applied to scientific theories or moral views.

Underpinning this methodology is MacIntyre's view of rationality and agreement. Rational agreement or disagreement is only possible in the context of a fixed framework of inquiry sharing paradigm uses of concepts and rational procedures. This kind of framework is socially and historically embedded in traditions of inquiry. Thus within or across traditions that can re-interpret each other's terms, rational disagreement is possible. When this is not so, there is interminable disagreement, a failure of rationality, and 'incommensurability'.

MacIntyre's methodology sets the stage for his distinctive history of moral philosophy in the West. Moral life was once rational and unified, in the ancient Greek *polis*, as described in the ethical and political works of Aristotle. This was guaranteed by the relation Aristotle envisaged between his account of human beings as they are, the set of prescriptions directing them as to how to realize their essential nature, and the ideal of human excellence that would be the result (see ARISTOTLE). The discrediting of Aristotle's teleological metaphysics led to the loss of a sense that a human life had a unified purpose which could ground the value of that life. Thus all subsequent moral philosophy in the West is in MacIntyre's view a fruitless search for a means to connect the original elements of Aristotle's tripartite schema, once the idea of the purpose of an individual life has been lost.

This analysis culminates in MacIntyre's apocalyptic account of the contemporary moral situation, which he views as in complete intellectual disorder. The reasons for this disorder are threefold. First, some traditions of thought are just incoherent: they fail to achieve the internal integrity and coherence required in MacIntyre's account of inquiry. Second, even if forms of inquiry are coherent, conflicts among them are pointless since without a matrix of commensurability disagreement across traditions is in principle irresoluble. Third, the contemporary world fails to recognize the intellectual authority of the Neo-Augustinian Catholicism MacIntyre views as uniquely privileged in its relation to other traditions. MacIntyre criticizes contemporary liberalism for vainly aspiring to this role of adjudicating disputes within moral and political culture from a privileged standpoint. Liberalism attempts to regulate this disagreement in the name of higher ideals or privileged procedures, but in MacIntyre's view

liberalism has no such intellectual authority over other traditions.

MacIntyre proposes that we resurrect Aristotelian ethics in the modern world. The key element is a new account of the overall purpose of a human life, which permits the restoration of an ethic of virtue, and the cultivation of appropriate forms of community. Politically, MacIntyre is a utopian, seeking the development of small communities analogous to the ancient *polis*, united by a common conception of the good life.

MacIntyre's project has met with a mixed reception in contemporary philosophy; his sharply critical tone, particularly directed against liberalism, has met with robust criticism in its turn. The first line of criticism challenges the methodological underpinnings of MacIntyre's account: it is argued that MacIntyre has no principled way of distinguishing between the disagreement to which he assigns a positive role within moral traditions and the 'incommensurable' disagreement between traditions he criticizes. In response to this charge MacIntyre has developed a distinctive account of the relation between translation and interpretation, arguing that partial failures of translatability across languages illustrate the type of incommensurability he is concerned with (see RADICAL TRANSLATION AND RADICAL INTERPRETATION).

Second, MacIntyre's account of morality has been accused of being both reductive and foundationalist: we should not see our task in moral philosophy as constrained by MacIntyre's tripartite schema, fitting moral injunctions as a whole to a non-moral foundation in 'human nature'. MacIntyre views the relation between the three elements of the tripartite schema as internally related, unintelligible in isolation; but this internal connection would only be possible in an ideal life. Similarly, MacIntyre's argument does not rest on a prior conception of human nature that constrains possible developments of morality: reflective moral life may be a partial determinant of this 'essence'.

The third criticism is that MacIntyre is actually far more modern than he seems, and rhetoric aside he is as committed to the values of modern moral and political philosophy as any modern liberal. These critics point out that MacIntyre is committed to such values as autonomy and positive freedom, and exaggerates the difference between ancient and modern ethical outlooks.

Their case is strengthened by the final line of criticism, which challenges MacIntyre's historical narrative, and presents an alternative account of the history of moral thought in the West that offers a better explanation than MacIntyre's version. Philosophers such as Charles Larmore and J.B. Schneewind have presented a view of modern moral life more hospitable to the rise of modern liberalism, and Charles Taylor's *Sources of the Self* (1989) offers an alternative view of modern morality far more sympathetic than MacIntyre to the values of the modern world. This third line of criticism is the most powerful since it matches MacIntyre's strengths of combining philosophical insight with wide historical learning.

See also: VIRTUE ETHICS (§5)

List of works

MacIntyre, A. (1977) 'Epistemological Crises, Dramatic Narrative, and the Philosophy of Science', *The Monist* 60: 433–72. (An indispensable guide to MacIntyre's early methodology.)

—— (1981) *After Virtue: A Study in Moral Theory*, London: Duckworth, 2nd edn, with Postscript, 1985. (Clearest statement of the whole project and the account of virtue and the good life. Postscript is a valuable clarification.)

—— (1984) 'The Relationship of Philosophy to Its Past', in R. Rorty, J.B. Schneewind, Q. Skinner (eds) *Philosophy in History*, Cambridge: Cambridge University Press. (Further methodological reflections on the creative synthesis envisaged between philosophy and history.)

—— (1985) 'Relativism, Power, and Philosophy', *Proceedings and Addresses of the American Philosophical Association*, Newark, DE: American Philosophical Association, 5–22. (Argues for a principled distinction between the disagreement internal to, and between, traditions. Contests the challenge to this view from Donald Davidson's views on language and translation.)

—— (1988) *Whose Justice? Which Rationality?*, London: Duckworth. (Extended the scope of the argument from the theory of the good to the theory of practical reasoning. Contains the clearest statement of MacIntyre's criticism of liberalism.)

—— (1990) *Three Rival Versions of Moral Enquiry*, London: Duckworth. (A return to more methodological reflections, contrasting MacIntyre's methodology with that of post-Enlightenment political rationalism and Nietzschean genealogy.)

References and further reading

Horton, R. and Mendus, S. (1994) *After MacIntyre*, Cambridge: Polity Press. (Multi-author collection of critical essays on MacIntyre's work. Also contains an invaluable reply from MacIntyre clarifying several misunderstandings of his project.

Valuable bibliography of MacIntyre's published work.)

Larmore, C. (1987) *Patterns of Moral Complexity*, Cambridge, Cambridge University Press. (Contains an extended discussion of MacIntyre's project, and criticizes both MacIntyre's epistemological foundationalism and political romanticism. The latter claim should be balanced by a reading of MacIntyre's 'Reply' in the Horton and Mendus volume.)

O'Neill, O. (1989) 'Kant After Virtue', in *Constructions of Reason*, Cambridge: Cambridge University Press. (A criticism of MacIntyre's reading of Kant, typical of corrections of MacIntyre's treatment of individual figures. Also contains a valuable discussion of MacIntyre's attitude to modernity.)

Schneewind, J.B. (1982) 'Virtue, Narrative and Community: MacIntyre and Morality', *Journal of Philosophy* 79: 653–63. (Schneewind's papers are critical but constructive, and suggest the outlines of Schneewind's alternative narrative of the moral philosophy of the modern period.)

—— (1983) 'Moral Crisis and the History of Ethics', *Midwest Studies in Philosophy*, 8: 525–39. (See Schneewind (1982) above.)

* Taylor, C. (1989) *Sources of the Self*, Cambridge: Cambridge University Press. (A magisterial survey of the historical development of the modern moral identity, indebted to MacIntyre for its general methodology, but very different in its assessment of modern moral philosophy and its resources. An optimistic work which is an essential counterweight to MacIntyre's views.)

ALAN THOMAS

McTAGGART, JOHN McTAGGART ELLIS (1866–1925)

McTaggart was one of the last of the 'British Idealists', the group of British philosophers, such as B. Bosanquet and F.H. Bradley, who took their inspiration from Hegel. In his early writings from the 1890s, McTaggart gave a critical exposition of themes from Hegel's logic before advancing his own distinctive idealist positions concerning time, the mind, and reality in general. But in his writings from 1910 he developed an independent account of the structure of existence from which he then argued for the same idealist positions as before.

The thesis for which McTaggart is now most famous is that of the unreality of time; what is even more difficult to come to terms with is his thesis that the ultimate reality of the world comprises a community of selves wholly constituted by their loving perceptions of each other. This thesis is a manifestation of a mysticism that is an essential element in McTaggart's philosophy; yet this mysticism is combined with a rationalist determination, reminiscent of Spinoza, to vindicate mystical insights by the light of pure reason alone.

1   Hegelian dialectic
2   Time
3   Idealist metaphysics
4   Error and love

1   Hegelian dialectic

John McTaggart Ellis McTaggart's curious name arises from the fact that his father, Francis Ellis, having named his son 'McTaggart' after an uncle of that name, then took the name himself as a surname in order to inherit his uncle's wealth, and thereby passed the name again to his son. McTaggart studied at Cambridge and then taught there throughout his life. In his first work, *Studies in the Hegelian Dialectic* (published in 1896 but largely based on his 1891 Fellowship Dissertation), he defends the use of the Hegelian dialectic as the primary tool of philosophical argument. According to McTaggart, the great strength of Hegel's dialectic is that, by starting from minimal presumptions about the concepts to be applied on the basis of experience, it is possible to unravel significant conclusions concerning the structure of that which experience reveals — reality itself (see HEGEL, G.W.F.).

McTaggart's emphasis on the dialectical method is indicative of the fact that he seeks to base his metaphysics on premises that are in a broad sense 'logical'. But he also thinks that there is something essentially mystical about the truths of metaphysics. These two fundamental presumptions of his philosophy are held together by the fact that he holds that the dialectical method itself leads one to recognize the fundamental reality of a domain which transcends ordinary experience. Following Hegel, McTaggart calls that which is thus fundamentally real 'The Absolute', but goes on to make it clear that his detailed conception of the Absolute is not that of Hegel. Thus he insists that the Absolute is not the culmination of a historical process, since the dialectic is not a temporal process whereby the Absolute realizes itself in the world – it is only a method of reasoning whereby we make explicit to ourselves what has always been the only fundamental reality. Instead, McTaggart argues in his *Studies in Hegelian Cosmology* (1901), the Absolute comprises a community of selves wholly occupied in loving perceptions of

each other; for only within a structure of this kind are the formal requirements of the dialectic fully satisfied. It is not easy to follow McTaggart's reasoning on this issue, and even more difficult to grasp how one can suppose that the loving perceptions of such a community are, in fact, absolutely the only things that there really are. But the challenge of explaining himself on these issues is, in effect, that to which McTaggart dedicated the rest of his life (see ABSOLUTE, THE §1).

2   Time

The thesis of the unreality of time is one that McTaggart endorses in his early Hegelian writings. In 1908, however, he published a paper on 'The Unreality of Time' in which he argued for this thesis from an independent starting-point.

He starts from the fact that we have two ways of indicating the time of an event such as the Battle of Hastings: we can either just indicate its relation to present experience, by noting that it is in the past; or we can give its date – 1066 AD – and thereby indicate its relationship as earlier or later than the event which is taken as the origin for the system of dates. Where events are ordered in accordance with a system of tenses McTaggart says that they form an 'A-series'; where they are ordered by a system of dates he says that they form a 'B-series'. The first part of his argument is intended to establish that the A-series is more fundamental than the B-series to the conception of such series of events as a series ordered in time. McTaggart argues first that change is essential to time and that while the A-series conception includes change (in so far as that which was future becomes past), the B-series relations are immutable; second, he argues that time is essentially directed from past to future in a way which involves the A-series but not the B-series. The second part of McTaggart's argument revolves around the claim that the A-series does not after all provide a coherent temporal ordering of events: for the way in which the A-series allows for change leads to the contradiction of supposing that one and the same event is both past and future. Hence, McTaggart concludes, neither A-series nor B-series yields a coherent conception of a temporal ordering of events, and we must conclude that our very conception of events as ordered in time is illusory. In reality, the events are ordered in some other way (as the 'C-series'), and it is this real ordering which we erroneously perceive as a temporal ordering.

McTaggart's critics maintain that the appearance of contradiction inherent in the A-series arises only because McTaggart moves illegitimately from the coherent thought that the Battle of Hastings *was* future and *is now* past to the contradictory thought that it *is* (tenselessly) both future and past. McTaggart was aware of this response, but argued that the use of tenses here merely postpones the difficulty; for not only was the battle future, it was also present and past, so that the same contradiction arises even when tenses are used. Or does it? McTaggart's critics urge that it does not; and, further, that an A-series theorist need never assent to whatever combinations of tenses are incompatible.

Other critics seek to defend the status of the B-series. They argue that although the B-series does not allow for changes in the truth-value of judgments concerning temporal order, it does not follow that no conception of change can be included in such a scheme. Thus Russell (1903) urged that we can say that an object *a* has changed where the judgment that *a* has the property *F* at one date is true and the judgment that *a* has the property *F* at some different date is false. This is perhaps too simple, for it implies that things themselves change when, for example, people alter their attitudes to them; but if some restriction is placed on the relevant properties *F* that occur here (for example, that they be such that losing or gaining such a property has immediate effects for the thing in question), Russell's account looks plausible. Similarly, McTaggart's other claim, that the B-series does not yield an account of the direction of time, is disputed by those who argue that the temporal structure of causation gives time its unique direction.

Whether one wants to be an A-series or a B-series theorist, then, it looks as though there are positions that are preferable to McTaggart's denial of the unreality of time. Perhaps the most commonly held position these days embodies a compromise: it is argued that McTaggart's mistake lay in not recognizing that these two conceptions of time are interdependent – in that the A-series captures the tensed temporal perspective of the subject which is an essential ingredient of practical thought, whereas the B-series captures the tenseless truth-conditions of these A-series judgments, which cannot be coherently captured in A-series terms (see Mellor 1981 for a classic statement of this position) (see TIME §1).

3 Idealist metaphysics

McTaggart's 1908 discussion of time shows him already arguing for his idealist conclusions without direct reference to Hegelian dialectic. In 1910 he completed a critical study of Hegel's logic, *A Commentary on Hegel's Logic*, which, although not at all hostile to Hegel's method, revealed substantial

defects in the details of his arguments. Hence, McTaggart realized, if he was to secure the idealist conclusions of his earlier work, he needed to find new foundations for them. This was the task that occupied him for the rest of his life, and which he brought to fruition in his final, two-volume work, *The Nature of Existence* (1921, 1927).

In the first volume, McTaggart develops three fundamental ontological principles which, he argues, are a priori conditions of any acceptable metaphysics. McTaggart's account of these principles is obscure, but we can identify them as: (1) the identity of indiscernibles; (2) the infinite divisibility of substances; (3) the principle of 'ontological determinacy' – that is, the principle that the properties possessed by a substance must be fully determinate. In the second volume, McTaggart then argues that these principles can only be satisfied if his previous idealist convictions are correct (see IDENTITY OF INDISCERNIBLES).

McTaggart's line of thought is best approached by considering why he thinks that material substances fail to satisfy his a priori conditions. His claim is that once one has satisfied conditions (1) and (2) by supposing that a material substance is infinitely divisible into ever smaller parts, each of which differs descriptively from any other part, one will violate condition (3) since it will no longer be wholly determinate, at any stage in the division, just what properties a substance possesses – for the precise determination of these properties will depend on the properties of its distinct parts *ad infinitum*. There is much here that might be questioned, including each of McTaggart's principles; but it is worth noting in passing that although McTaggart denies the reality of matter ('the result is that matter is in the same position as the Gorgons or the Harpies'), he is quite explicit that he does not dispute the propriety of common-sense talk of hands and so on. So, *pace* G.E. Moore (1939), he cannot be refuted by a simple appeal to the propriety of such talk.

It remains to be seen why McTaggart thinks that a community of at least two selves does satisfy his a priori conditions. The key point is that he takes it that condition (2) is satisfied because perceptions are 'parts' of a self, and the possibility of indefinitely reiterated perceptions of perceptions constitutes, therefore, the possibility of infinite 'division' of a self. Because these ever more complex perceptions are generated by reiteration, condition (1) is satisfied; and he holds that condition (3) is also satisfied because the content of simpler perceptions does not depend on that of the more complex perceptions of perceptions which are their 'parts'. Solipsism is ruled out in favour of a community of selves and their mutual perceptions of each other because a self whose only 'part' was its perception of itself would not have a proper part at all and would therefore violate condition (2); whereas once two or more selves are introduced, each self will have perceptions of the other as well as of itself and thereby introduce a structure of mutually self-reflecting perceptions of perceptions which McTaggart calls 'determining correspondence' and which, he thinks, is the only structure that can satisfy his a priori conditions.

4   Error and love

Because McTaggart's account of this community of selves and their perceptions of each other is supposed to be an account of the only things that there really are, he holds that our ordinary experience is almost entirely erroneous or misunderstood. It is not just that we misconstrue our perceptions of our hands as perceptions of a material world; we also radically mistake the nature of our own experience. We seem to ourselves to have mental states other than perceptions; but in fact we have *only* perceptions – and these perceptions are *only* perceptions of selves and their perceptions. How, then, is this massive error possible?

The conceptual possibility of massive error of this kind is allowed for by the 'perceiving as' idiom: what are in fact just perceptions of selves and their perceptions are perceived as material objects, choices and the like. Furthermore, according to McTaggart, the illusion of time is the ground of these errors. This illusion rests on our misperceiving the ordering of the members of the timeless C series (which can only be selves and their perceptions) as a temporal ordering. McTaggart expends much ingenuity in setting out the structure of this C-series and suggesting how, once the illusion of time arises, other errors follow; but he acknowledges that he can give no reason why the illusion arises in the first place (in *Studies in the Hegelian Dialectic* he had observed that even the appearance of evil and error poses a deep challenge to the Hegelian dialectic; the deep reason for his abandonment of that method was probably a growing conviction that this challenge is unanswerable).

What, finally, of love? McTaggart's basic thought is that love is the emotion which manifests a sense of intimate union with a self; and since perceptions of ourselves and others provide precisely this sense of intimate union, the community of mutual perceivers is also a city of love. But there is also an element of residual Hegelian teleology here. McTaggart acknowledges that our ordinary perceptions of each other rarely, if ever, give rise to the appropriate sense of intimate union, but he looks forward to a kind of immediate awareness of others which resembles our awareness of ourselves. This possibility requires,

however, an extension to our lives, a kind of immortality whereby we exist indefinitely into the future – or rather throughout the C-series, which we mistake for time. At the final stage of this series, McTaggart holds, all perceptions will be clear and distinct; hence here at last the city of love will be realized. We are not now at this stage, for the C-series is real and progress along it appears to us as the passage of time; but in the final ecstatic sentences of *The Nature of Existence* McTaggart looks forward to this ultimate consummation:

> We know that it is a timeless and endless state of love – love so direct, so intimate, and so powerful that even the deepest mystic rapture gives us but the slightest foretaste of its perfection.
>
> (1927: 479)

List of works

McTaggart, J.M.E. (1896) *Studies in the Hegelian Dialectic*, Cambridge: Cambridge University Press. (A critical discussion of the metaphysical significance of Hegel's dialectic.)

—— (1901) *Studies in Hegelian Cosmology*, Cambridge: Cambridge University Press. (Discusses topics in ethics and political theory and argues that the Hegelian Absolute is the city of love.)

—— (1906) *Some Dogmas of Religion*, London: Arnold; 2nd edn, 1930, with intro. by C.D. Broad. (McTaggart rejects conventional religion but defends immortality and mysticism.)

—— (1908) 'The Unreality of Time', *Mind* 17: 457–74. (McTaggart's first statement of his classic argument for the unreality of time; the argument is slightly modified in McTaggart (1927).)

—— (1910) *A Commentary on Hegel's Logic*, Cambridge: Cambridge University Press. (A critical study of the details of Hegel's dialectic.)

—— (1921) *The Nature of Existence*, vol. 1, Cambridge: Cambridge University Press. (McTaggart sets out his a priori conditions for the existence of substances.)

—— (1927) *The Nature of Existence*, vol. 2, ed. C.D. Broad, Cambridge: Cambridge University Press. (Published posthumously; McTaggart argues that only his idealism satisfies the a priori conditions of vol. 1.)

—— (1934) *Philosophical Studies*, ed. S.V. Keeling, London: Arnold. (A valuable collection of McTaggart's papers, including McTaggart (1908).)

References and further reading

Broad, C.D. (1933, 1938) *Examination of McTaggart's*

Philosophy, Cambridge: Cambridge University Press, 2 vols. (A commentary on *The Nature of Existence*; mostly tedious but sometimes helpful; also includes some intrinsically interesting discussions.)

Dickinson, G.L. (1931) *J. McT. E. McTaggart*, Cambridge: Cambridge University Press. (A personal memoir which conveys McTaggart's strange personality.)

Dummett, M.A.E. (1960) 'A Defence of McTaggart's Proof of the Unreality of Time', *Philosophical Review* 69: 497–504; repr. in *Truth and Other Enigmas*, London: Duckworth, 1978. (An idiosyncratic defence of McTaggart.)

Geach, P.T. (1979) *Truth, Love and Immortality*, London: Hutchinson. (A critical exposition of *The Nature of Existence*; much shorter and more helpful than Broad (1933, 1938).)

* Mellor, D.H. (1981) *Real Time*, Cambridge: Cambridge University Press. (Defends McTaggart on the unreality of the A-series and expounds the standard A/B compromise.)

* Moore, G.E. (1939) 'Proof of an External World', *Proceedings of the British Academy* 25: 273–300; repr. in G.E. Moore: *Selected Writings*, ed. T. Baldwin, London: Routledge, 1993. (A classic attempt at a refutation of McTaggart's idealism.)

* Russell, B.A.W. (1903) *The Principles of Mathematics*, London: Allen & Unwin. (See 469–70 for Russell's account of change.)

Stern, R. (1994) 'British Hegelianism: A Non-Metaphysical view?', *European Journal of Philosophy* 2: 293–321. (Sets McTaggart's early work on Hegel in its historical context, and argues that his account resembles recent 'non-metaphysical' approaches to Hegel.)

THOMAS BALDWIN

MADAME DE STAËL *see* STAËL-HOLSTEIN, ANNE-LOUISE-GERMAINE, MME DE

MĀDHAVA (d. 1386)

Mādhava was a minister, scholar and philosopher in India in the fourteenth century. He gave support and advice at the founding of the Vijayanagara Empire in southern India, which lasted 300 years. He is best known for his Sarvadarśanasaṃgraha *(Survey of the Major Philosophical Systems). In it, he presented sixteen systems of philosophy, starting with the materialists, discussing the Buddhists, Jainas, several Hindu schools and the school of Logic (Nyāya), and ending with Advaita Vedānta. To him and to many scholars at that time, Advaita Vedānta was the most complete and sophisticated philosophy. Mādhava is often identified with other people, especially Vidyārāya, the saint and abbot of a monastery in Śṛṅgeri. The general view now is that Mādhava may have become a monk, receiving as a religious name that of Vidyāraṇya. This Vidyāraṇya was also an accomplished philosopher. His* Pañcadaśī *(Fifteen Chapters), a digest of Advaita Vedānta, is still popular today.*

1   **Mādhava and his times**
2   **Mādhava's works**
3   **Advaita Vedānta refined and restated**

1   Mādhava and his times

Mādhava was a statesman, philosopher and polyhistor who lived in southwest India in the fourteenth century. Four names are associated with this one person. After examination of the various hypotheses regarding these names, the most frequent solution seems to be to regard two of them, Mādhava and Vidyāraṇya, as the civil and religious names respectively of the same person, and to treat Bhāratītīrtha as the name of his teacher and Sāyaṇa as the name of his brother. This opinion ignores the indigenous tradition.

By the fourteenth century, the Muslims were well settled in the north of India and were making almost continuous efforts to occupy the south as well. The Vijayanagara empire, founded by the brother kings Bukka I and Harihara I in the fourteenth century, resisted the invasions for a long time, flourishing until the middle of the seventeenth century. It was based in a region south of the rivers Krishna and Tungabhadra. At that time the empire was a bastion of the best of Hindu culture, the intellectual strength and growth of which was reflected in architecture, a variety of arts, and learning.

Mādhava was one of the primary instigators of this cultural tradition. He spent part of his life at the court as an advisor to the brother kings. It is speculated that he may have left to become a monk at the monastery in Śṛṅgeri ('The Mountain Peak'), a few miles south of the capital, Vijayanagara ('The Victorious City'). When he entered the monastery, he received the religious name Vidyāraṇya ('The Forest of Wisdom or Knowledge'). Adding a religious name to a civil one was unusual.

Traditional Indian sources do not identify the two

personages. On the contrary, they insist on their difference. The abbots at Śṛṅgeri entered the monastery as celibate young men. It would be exceptional that a mature person like Mādhava, who had spent his life engaged in worldly affairs, should later have become an abbot.

2 Mādhava's works

The ascription 'Mādhavīya' ('of Madhava') occurs in the titles of a number of works. We know from inscriptions that grants were given to learned men (pandits) to help produce commentaries on the Vedic tradition. Mādhava, acting at his kings' behest to propagate the Hindu tradition, appointed several capable scholars to produce works, such as commentaries on the Vedas. Among them was Sāyaṇa, who seems to have been a leader of a writing guild. Mādhava was the mastermind and 'purse' behind this voluminous body of work. His name lent authority, and he himself could also have contributed to these works. It is virtually impossible to determine their exact authorship or date.

Because of the uncertainty of authorship, it is also difficult to make a definitive list of works. It is possible that Mādhava co-authored chapters or even whole works. In the case of the *Sarvadarśanasaṃgraha* (Survey of the Major Philosophical Systems), he may have shared a chapter with his brother, Sāyaṇa. Of the several works that are ascribed to Vidyāraṇya, the *Pañcadaśī* (Fifteen Chapters) may have been written by, or at least in collaboration with, Vidyāraṇya's teacher, the abbot Bhāratītīrtha. The *Jīvanmuktiviveka* (Correct Insight into the Concept of Liberation-while-Alive) is attributed to Vidyāraṇya.

Of some thirty works that are ascribed to Mādhava, Vidyāraṇya, Sāyaṇa and Bhāratītīrtha, several are still only in manuscript form. A number were edited either in part or in full in the nineteenth century and at the beginning of the twentieth century. Some were translated into various Indian languages and several also exist in English today.

Some of the best-known works that have proved to be important for the development and preservation of the Hindu tradition are the *Sarvadarśanasaṃgraha*, the *Jīvanmuktiviveka*, the *Pañcadaśī* and the *Vivaraṇaprameyasaṃgraha* (Compendium of Objects of Knowledge in the Vivaraṇa Tradition), to mention just a few. In the *Sarvadarśanasaṃgraha*, the author discusses sixteen philosophical systems, which he arranges according to their relation (or lack of it) with Vedānta philosophy. He starts with the materialists, who are the most alien to Vedānta, and ends with the Vedānta teaching. The materialists praise immediate enjoyment and have no appreciation for

spiritual striving and growth, whereas Vedānta aims at spiritual accomplishment, with its final goal of liberation from repeated physical existences. Between these two systems, he presents, among others, those of the Buddhists, the Jainas and the Naiyāyikas (Logicians). The author shows himself here as an erudite scholar of philosophy, skilled in logic.

The *Jīvanmuktiviveka* deals with the state of being-liberated-while-still-alive. It is well known that the Buddha attained such a state of enlightenment and continued to teach for almost five more decades before he died. The idea that it is not only possible, but quite likely that a person will live for a long time after attaining full enlightenment is explained here. In this state, a person still functions normally, but is not subject to the usual desires and passions, and does not accumulate karmic impressions – either good or bad – that will result in future rebirth. After gaining the insightful experience, the person still lives on, just as a potter's wheel keeps turning even though the pot is already completed. The author supports his statements with a number of quotations from the most essential sources of Hindu ideology: the *Bhagavad Gītā*, the Upaniṣads, the *Yogasūtra*, and so on. Many consider this work highly eclectic.

The *Pañcadaśī* presents in an accessible manner the main teachings of Vedānta and is still well liked and much revered. It is divided into three sections consisting of five chapters each. The first set deals with correct insight (*viveka*) leading to knowledge of reality, the second with consciousness which illuminates, and the third with the bliss experienced in the state of trance.

Vidyāraṇya's *Vivaraṇaprameyasaṃgraha* is a work of the greatest importance to Advaita dialectics. Vidyāraṇya shows himself here as an erudite philosopher arguing against his opponents' views. Although his is considered a commentary on Prakāśātman's commentary on Padmapāda's work, each of these is not a commentary as such, but rather an expansion and elaboration of the previous work in the same *vivaraṇa* ('laying out bare' – in other words, 'analysis') tradition of Vedānta. Padmapāda is considered the father of the Vivaraṇa school. His exposition is based on the first four sections of Śaṅkara's *Brahmasūtrabhāṣya*.

Vidyāraṇya's *Vivaraṇaprameyasaṃgraha* deals with the method by which it is possible to examine true objects and distinguish between empirical and philosophical knowledge. In order to make these distinctions, it is essential that the objects of knowledge (*prameya*) be properly established. Vidyāraṇya was also a philosopher of language and had particular interpretations of traditional terms in Vedānta. He departed from the usual Vedāntic understanding of concepts such as self (*ātman*); according to him, Vedānta does not teach that the self continues to exist after the death of the physical body.

3 Advaita Vedānta refined and restated

Although many of these works show a thorough knowledge of all the schools of Indian philosophy, their primary focus is on the nondualist Vedānta of ŚAṄKARA. This philosophy was concerned with finding the true nature of reality, and liberation. In general, medieval Indian thinkers did not aim at originality and innovation. Only those with strong minds and personalities changed the course of the teachings, giving rise to new varieties of Vedānta, such as the dualist school (see VEDĀNTA §3). We tend to single out these thinkers and teachers, whereas we often do not know the names of those who stayed in the fold of the old tradition. We know of Mādhava and Vidyāraṇya because of their significant activities besides teaching Śaṅkara's Vedānta. Mādhava, for instance, is notable for his well-rounded knowledge and active life as a statesman. Although they did not necessarily formulate original thoughts, Mādhava, Vidyāraṇya and numerous others contributed to keeping alive the Vedānta tradition by restating and refining it. Mādhava's activities helped to preserve the Hindu traditions by building a cultural and political stronghold against attacks and foreign influences.

List of works

Mādhava (14th century) *Sarvadarśanasaṃgraha* (Survey of the Major Philosophical Systems), trans. E.B. Cowell and A.E. Gough, *The Sarva-darśana-saṃgraha or Review of the Different Systems of Hindu Philosophy*, Chowkhamba Sanskrit Series 10, Varanasi: Chowkhamba, 6th edn, 1961. (An excellent overview of the main ideas of the various philosophical schools. The work exercised considerable influence in the study of Indian philosophies.)

Vidyāraṇya (14th century) *Jīvanmuktiviveka* (Correct Insight into the Concept of Liberation-while-Alive), ed. and trans. S. Subrahmanya Sastri and T.R. Srinivasa Ayyangar, Madras: The Adyar Library and Research Centre, 1978. (The text and translation deal with the issues of attaining freedom from rebirth and place emphasis on yogic practices.)

—— (14th century) *Vivaraṇaprameyasaṃgraha* (Compendium of Objects of Knowledge in the Vivaraṇa Tradition), trans. S.S. Suryanarayana Sastri and Saileswar Sen, Kumbakonam: The Sri Vidya Press, 1941. (An accessible translation of an important philosophical work so far neglected. Among other things, the main focus is on establishing the objects of knowledge according to Vedānta and refuting the notions of the Buddhists and others.)

—— (14th century) *Pañcadaśī* (Fifteen Chapters), trans. Hari Prasad Shastri, *Panchadasi: A Treatise on Advaita Metaphysics by Swami Vidyaranya*, London: Shanti Sadan, 1956. (A popular and authoritative guide to the teachings of Advaita Vedānta.)

—— (14th century) *Praṇavamīmāṃsā*, ed. and trans. P. Olivelle, '*Praṇavamīmāṃsā*: A Newly Discovered Work of Vidyāraṇya', *Annals of of the Bhandarkar Oriental Research Institute* 62, 1981. (Translation of a text on the sacred syllable OM, after the *Praṇavakalpa* of the Skandapurāṇa.)

References and further reading

Fort, A. (1996) 'Liberation While Living in the *Jīvanmuktiviveka*: Vidyāraṇya's "Yogic Advaita"', in A. Fort and P. Mumme (eds) *Living Liberation in Hindu Thought*, Albany, NY: State University of New York Press. (Points to the focus on the use of yoga and also shows the dependence on the *Laghu Yogavāsiṣṭha* (The Abridged *Yogavāsiṣṭha*), almost functioning as a commentary on this text.)

Hacker, P. (1978) 'Zur Geschichte und Darstellung des Hinduismus' (On the History and Interpretation of Hinduism), in *Kleine Schriften* (Minor Works), Wiesbaden: Franz Steiner. (The new hypothesis here is that it was Vidyāraṇya who started the 'Śaṅkara' monasteries.)

Kripacharyulu, M. (1986) *Sāyaṇa and Mādhava-Vidyāraṇya: A Study of Their Lives and Letters*, Guntur: Rajyalakshmi Publications. (A challenge to the prevailing opinions. The author amasses a lot of information, especially epigraphic, but references and annotations are inadequate.)

Mahadevan, T.M.P. (1957) *The Philosophy of Advaita with Special Reference to Bhāratītīrtha-Vidyāraṇya*, Madras: Ganesh & Co. (A clear account of Vidyāraṇya's metaphysics and epistemology.)

Mishra, G. (1984) 'Vidyāraṇya on Method, Object and Limit of Philosophical Investigation', *Indian Philosophical Quarterly* 11 (3). (A study of Vidyāraṇya's philosophical method in the *Vivaraṇaprameyasaṃgraha* showing that his is a logico-linguistic analysis.)

Sprockhoff, J.F. (1964, 1970) 'Der Weg zur Erlösung bei Lebzeiten, ihr Wesen und ihr Wert, nach dem *Jīvanmuktiviveka* des Vidyāraṇya' (The Path to Liberation-while-Alive, its Nature and Significance, in the *Jīvanmuktiviveka* of Vidyāraṇya), *Wiener Zeitschrift für die Kunde Süd- und Ostasiens* 8

(1964), 14 (1970). (A summary of the text and an excellent analysis of the ideas.)

EDELTRAUD HARZER CLEAR

MADHVA (1238?–1317?)

Madhva, Hindu theologian and ascetic, founded the philosophical school commonly called Dvaita Vedānta, but which Madhva and his followers termed tattvavāda, *or realism. The name Dvaita refers to Madhva's dualistic interpretation of the Hindu canonical texts known as the Upaniṣads, also known as Vedānta. In contrast to the monist and semi-monist systems of his two major Vedāntin predecessors, Śaṅkara and Rāmānuja, Madhva asserted the absolute difference between God (*īśvara*) and human souls (*jīva*), claiming that they were uncreated, eternal principles with fundamentally distinct natures. Madhva delineated the respective natures of God and souls so as to assert God's complete transcendence of the world and to legitimate the practice of devotion as the principal means of attaining liberation from the cycle of rebirth (*saṃsāra*). Madhva's realist epistemology served as the foundation for this ontological emphasis on difference (*bheda*).*

Our knowledge of Madhva's life comes from hagiographical literature and from scattered references to personal experience in his works. While traditions differ regarding his dates, inscriptional evidence corroborated with statements by Madhva make the dates 1238–1317 most likely. Madhva was born near Udupi in the present-day Indian state of Karnataka, where he established a monastic compound which continues to function as the ritual centre of modern Mādhvaism. Madhva presented himself as an incarnation of the Hindu god Vāyu who would save humankind through correct knowledge. This unique claim for a Hindu thinker has prompted some scholars to speculate that Madhva was influenced by Christianity. In fact, Madhva's milieu was heavily Jaina and his epistemology and ontology arguably reflect this influence.

Madhva's emphasis on the ontological significance of difference and its counterpart, individuality, was supported by his realist epistemology, which asserted the inherent validity of experience wherein difference is presented as an undeniable fact. Madhva used this ontological framework to support his sectarian devotion to the Hindu god Viṣṇu and articulated in many of his writings those unique qualities which, he believed, render Viṣṇu superior to all other Hindu gods.

Madhva's emphasis on the ontological significance of difference (*bheda*) was a direct challenge to his famous predecessor ŚAṄKARA, a monist who claimed that the individual human soul was completely identical with the Godhead at the level of ultimate truth. By contrast, Madhva divided reality into two separate, uncreated principles, God (*īśvara*) and matter (*prakṛti*), and further subdivided matter into sentient matter, or souls (*jīva*), and insentient matter (*jaḍa*). Differences exist between these three categories and between individual members of the same category, resulting in a fivefold schema of difference: souls–God, souls–souls, souls–insentient matter, insentient matter–insentient matter, insentient matter–God; God cannot differ from himself. According to this view, no two things are identical, although their difference might be extremely subtle. Madhva rejected the Nyāya-Vaiśeṣika position on universals (*sāmānya*), arguing that universalized conceptions ultimately rest on perceived similarities (*sādṛśya*) between particular objects (see UNIVERSALS, INDIAN THEORIES OF §2).

Madhva saw this particularity as resulting from the fact that qualities are completely identical with their substances. However, Madhva wanted to avoid taking the Buddhist position, which states that since all entities are nothing more than their qualities, they are impermanent and inessential. To distinguish between qualities and substances while upholding the notion that qualities are essential to the substance, Madhva posited the concept of *viśeṣa*, often translated as distinction. In Madhva's system, these distinctions exist between the entity and its attributes in such a way that the attributes are nevertheless integrated into the entity. Thus, the concept of *viśeṣa* allows an entity to possess different, often changing attributes without compromising the object's inherent unity or ontological validity. This challenging doctrine engaged many of Madhva's commentators.

Viśeṣas play an important role in the relationship between God and the world. One of God's permanent attributes is his independence (*svatantratva*), whereas souls and insentient matter are permanently dependent (*paratantra*) upon God. While insentient matter is beginningless, God transforms it from an original chaos into an ordered reality, and finally returns it to its original form. God, however, remains unaffected due to his transcendence.

Souls, although eternal in nature and generally free in agency, depend upon God for their destinies, since God governs the law of karma and grants liberation through grace. While the recognition of one's dependence upon God inspires one to acts of devotion (*bhakti*) which can lead to liberation, ignorance can lead to eternal damnation. Fatalistically, Madhva asserted that a given soul's capacity to recognize its dependence upon God was a result of its permanent attributes and thus predetermined. In accordance with the three traditional Hindu locales for rebirth, Madhva asserted a threefold gradation of souls: those destined for eternal liberation, those destined for eternal *saṃsāra*, and those damned to eternal hell. While God oversees this structure, he is not implicated in its apparent injustices, since it is the souls' inherent properties which bring these about. God merely metes out destinies in accordance with behaviour. Thus Madhva maintained God's supremacy both by removing him from the presence of evil and placing him in charge of retribution.

The most crucial element of Madhva's epistemology was the role he gave to the 'witnessing subject' (*sākṣin*), which coordinates the senses and illuminates their data. Madhva posited the *sākṣin* as infallible and able to pass final judgment on the validity of the data presented to it, thereby asserting the self-validation of experiential knowledge. Indeed, while Madhva advocated three means of knowledge (*pramāṇas*) – perception, inference and verbal testimony (especially sacred scripture) – he insisted that the latter two *pramāṇas* never be so construed as to contradict perception. This position was one of his principal attacks upon the Advaitins, who looked to statements in the sacred texts declaring the identity of the soul with God as proof of the unreality of ordinary experience. However, Madhva fiercely defended the sanctity of the revealed literature (Veda) due to its ability to grant access to privileged domains of knowledge such as the nature of duty (*dharma*) and liberation (*mokṣa*).

See also: KNOWLEDGE, INDIAN VIEWS OF; MONISM, INDIAN; VEDĀNTA

List of works

Madhva (1238?–1317?) *Sarvamūlagranthāḥ* (Collected Works), ed. Bannanje Govindacarya, Udupi: Akhila Bharata Madhva Maha Mandala Publication, 1980. (A Sanskrit edition of Madhva's collected works; translations of the most important of these are listed below.)

—— (1238?–1317?) *Anuvyākhyāna* (Commentary [on the *Brahmasūtra*]), trans. S. Siauve, *Les Noms védiques de Viṣṇu dans l'Anuvyākhyāna de Madhva, Brahma Sūtra I.1.1, adhikaraṇa 2 à 12*, Pondicherry: Institut Français d'Indologie, 1959; trans. S. Siauve, *Les Hierarchies spirituelles selon l'Anuvyākhyāna de Madhva III.2.121–167; III.3.68–123, 193–203; III.4.4–51, 75–111, 232–278*, Pondicherry: Institut Français d'Indologie, 1971. (Siauve 1959 is a translation of those portions of the *Anuvyākhyāna* that discuss Viṣṇu's Vedic names; Siauve 1971 is a translation of those portions bearing on the topic of the gradation of souls.)

—— (1238?–1317?) *Brahmasūtrabhāṣya* (Commentary on the *Brahmasūtra*), in B.N.K. Sharma, *The Brahmasūtras and their Principal Commentaries: A Critical Exposition*, Bombay: Bharatiya Vidya Bhavan, 1978. (Provides translations of key sections of Madhva's *Brahmasūtrabhāṣya* and places these in comparative perspective with other Vedāntin commentaries.)

—— (1238?–1317?) *Daśaprakaraṇāni* (Ten Treatises), ed. P.P. Lakshminarayana Upadhyaya, Madras: Dharmaprakash Press, 1969, 4 vols. (A Sanskrit edition of Madhva's ten works that are not commentaries but independent treatises; includes commentaries by Vyāsatīrtha, Rāghavendratīrtha, Srinivāsatīrtha, Jayatīrtha and Vedeśabhikṣu, important followers of Madhva.)

—— (1238?–1317?) *Mahābhāratatātparyanirṇayaḥ*, trans. K.T. Pandurangi, Chirtanur: Sriman Madhva Siddhantonnahini Sabha, 1993. (Translation of portions of Madhva's commentary on the central story of the *Mahābhārata*.)

—— (1238?–1317?) *Srimadviṣṇutattvavinirṇaya*, trans. S.S. Raghavachar, *An Examination of the Truth of Vishnu*, Mangalore: Sharada Press, 1971. (Very clear translation of an accessible Madhva text that outlines his basic philosophy; one of the 'Ten Treatises'.)

—— (1238?–1317?) *Upaniṣadbhāṣyāḥ* (Commentaries on the Upaniṣads), esp.: Rai Bahadur Sris Chandra Vasu (trans.) *Bṛhadāraṇyaka Upaniṣad with the Commentary of Śrī Madhvācārya, Called also Anandatīrtha*, Allahabad: The Panini Office, 1916; Major B.D. Basu (trans.) *The Aitareya Upaniṣad (with Madhva's Commentary)*, Sacred Books of the Hindus, Allahabad: The Panini Office, 1925. (Translations of Madhva's commentaries on selected Upaniṣads, the later Vedic texts that form the ideological basis for the Brahmasūtras.)

References and further reading

Sharma, B.N.K. (1961) *The History of the Dvaita School of Vedānta and its Literature*, Delhi: Motilal Banarsidass. (Crucial survey of almost all known literature of the Dvaita school.)

—— (1961) *Sri Madhva's Teachings in his own Words*, Bombay: Bharatiya Vidya Bhavan. (Provides clear translations of portions of Madhva's important works in explanatory contexts.)

—— (1962) *The Philosophy of Sri Madhvācārya*,

Bombay: Bharatiya Vidya Bhavan. (Survey of Madhva's teachings.)

Siauve, S. (1968) *La Doctrine de Madhva*, Pondicherry: Institut Français d'Indologie. (Clear explanation of Madhva's central teachings.)

Viṣṇudāsācārya (1390?) *Vādaratnāvali*, trans. E. Gerow, *The Jewel Necklace of Argument (The Vādaratnāvali of Viṣṇudāsācārya)*, New Haven, CT: American Oriental Society, 1990. (Thorough translation of a later Dvaita work.)

Zydenbos, R. (1991) 'On the Jaina Background of Dvaita Vedānta', *Journal of Indian Philosophy* 19: 250–71. (Well-documented discussion of the Jaina influence on Dvaita.)

VALERIE STOKER

MĀDHYAMIKA BUDDHISM IN INDIA AND TIBET *see*

BUDDHISM, MĀDHYAMIKA: INDIA AND TIBET

MAHĀVĪRA (6th–5th century BC)

Mahāvīra's significance for Jaina philosophy is comparable to that of his contemporary, Buddha, for Buddhist philosophy. Both are regarded as the source of ideas, concepts and categories with far-reaching implications for later philosophical activity. In their respective traditions, both Mahāvīra and Buddha are recognized as enlightened or omniscient beings because they grasped the essential nature of reality, human life and the world. The teachings ascribed to them were at first passed on orally and were compiled into their present form several centuries later.

Despite similarities between Mahāvīra and Buddha, both in their biographies and in their rules for ascetics, Jainism is clearly an independent stream which has made its own valuable contribution to the development of Indian philosophy. One significant difference between Buddha and Mahāvīra is that Mahāvīra was not the founder of a new movement, but rather a reformer of the teachings of his predecessor, Pārśva.

'Mahāvīra' (literally 'Great Hero') is an epithet used especially for the Jaina saviour Vardhamāna. His dates are a matter of considerable debate, partly because they are related to those of the Buddha's, which are also problematic; neither wrote any works, which otherwise might have helped with deciding their dates. According to the Śvetāmbara sect of Jainism, Mahāvīra died at the age of seventy-two in 527 BC, whereas the Digambara sect gives the date as 510 BC, and recent research suggests 477 BC. The source of Mahāvīra's teachings is a body of scripture which was redacted in its present canonical form by a council held in Valabhī, Gujarat, around the fifth century AD. The Digambara sect rejects this Śvetāmbara version, believing the original canon to have been irretrievably lost, although it does have texts regarded as procanonically sacred. The style of both sets of texts is very repetitive, and whatever has a direct bearing on philosophy has to be extracted from a huge volume of material on a wide range of other themes, such as the religious practices of ascetics and the conduct of monks and nuns. The teachings are generally in the form of questions put by disciples and answers given by Mahāvīra or one who has heard his teaching, with little, if any, philosophical discussion of the concepts.

The authority which Mahāvīra's teaching enjoys in the Jaina tradition is inextricably related to the position given to him and twenty-three others as universal teachers. Historicity is ascribed only to the last two, Pārśva and Mahāvīra. All have the epithet 'Jina', meaning 'Victor' or 'Conqueror' of the passions fettering an individual. The tradition acknowledges them as omniscient beings who have obtained enlightenment through extreme asceticism. Their teachings are like a ford that enables others to cross to the other side of human existence, and hence they are called 'Tīrthaṃkaras', 'Fordmakers'.

Mahāvīra's teaching and biography represent an ascetic (*śramaṇa*) tradition that was already well established during his lifetime, one to which even his predecessor Pārśva belonged 250 years earlier. The exact origins of Indian asceticism are difficult to trace, but it is possible that there were world-renouncers before the arrival of the Aryans around 1700 BC. Mahāvīra's teaching characterizes this ascetic tradition in that he too holds that life in the world intrinsically entails suffering, ignorance and pain, which may be overcome through the knowledge of reality and of one's essential nature that is attainable in an ascetic life. This basic teaching is associated with the theory of karma, whereby karma is responsible for the cycles of existence (*saṃsāra*) that living beings have to undergo until they realize how, through Mahāvīra's teachings, accumulated karma may be destroyed and future ones avoided. In its simplest form, the theory, as it applies to human beings, is presented through an agricultural metaphor: one's actions, including thoughts and words, are said to leave behind traces which, like seeds, bear fruit in an appropriate environment either in one's present existence or a future one, the former being also determined by previous karma. This theory, shared by Buddha and the Upaniṣad thinkers, is the hallmark and essential starting point of all soteriological Indian systems and seems to have been pan-Indian during Mahāvīra's time, which is perhaps why no philosophical justification is offered for its acceptance in his teachings (see KARMA AND REBIRTH, INDIAN CONCEPTIONS OF).

Mahāvīra's interpretation of karma is unique, in that it is seen as particles of subtle matter which attach themselves to the soul, hindering the development of what later thinkers called the three jewels of Jainism, namely the soul's innate powers of right belief, right knowledge and right conduct. Mahāvīra mentions killing or violence (hiṃsā) as the cause of karma and says that the practice of nonviolence (ahiṃsā) is the common doctrine of all Jaina fordmakers: 'The Arhats and Bhagavats of the past, present, and future, all say thus, speak thus, declare thus, explain thus: all breathing, existing, living, sentient creatures should not be slain, nor treated with violence, nor tormented, nor driven away.'

It was not until around the fourth century AD that Mahāvīra's metaphysics, epistemology, ethics and cosmology, unsystematically scattered around in the various canonical works, were presented in a manner comparable to the basic philosophical texts of the Hindu systems. This was done by Umāsvāti (also called Umāsvāmī) in his Tattvārthasūtra.

See also: JAINA PHILOSOPHY; MANIFOLDNESS, JAINA THEORY OF

References and further reading

Deleu, J. (1970) Viyāhapannatti (Bhagavaī): the Fifth Aṅga of the Jaina Canon, Brugge: De Tempel. (A philological analysis of the Prakrit work also known as the Bhagavatī, which is an important source for early Jaina philosophy.)

Dundas, P. (1992) The Jains, London: Routledge. (An excellent modern survey of the history of Jainism to the present time, based on original sources.)

Glasenapp, H. von (1925) Der Jainismus: Eine indische Erlösungsreligion (Jainism: An Indian Liberation Religion), Berlin: Alf Häger Verlag. (One of the earliest general surveys of Jainism in the West and still a standard basic work; not yet translated into English.)

Jacobi, H. (trans.) (1884) Jaina Sūtras: Part I, Sacred Books of the East, Oxford: Oxford University Press; repr. Delhi: Motilal Banarsidass, 1964. (Translation from the Prakrit of two Jaina canonical works, the Ākārāṅga Sūtra (or Ācārāṅga Sūtra) and the Kalpa Sūtra, with an introduction on the origin and development of Jainism.)

—— (trans.) (1895) Jaina Sūtras: Part II, Sacred Books of the East, Oxford: Oxford University Press; repr. Delhi: Motilal Banarsidass, 1964. (Translation from the Prakrit of two Jaina canonical works, the Uttarādhyayana Sūtra and the Sūtrakritāṅga Sūtra, with an introduction on the Jaina records of the philosophical doctrines of the heretics.)

Jain, H. and Upadhye, A.N. (eds) (1939–59) Ṣaṭkhaṇḍāgama (Scripture in Six Parts), Solapur: Jaina Samskṛti Samrakṣaka Saṅgha, revised 3rd edn, 1992, 16 vols. (An important eighth-century Digambara work, the composition of which is based on the preaching of Mahāvīra; also includes Vīrasena's commentary, Dhavalā.)

Ohira, S. (1994) A Study of the Bhagavatīsūtra. A Chronological Analysis, Ahmedabad: Prakrit Text Society. (The Bhagavatīsūtra is a Jaina canonical work; this book is a systematic and historical analysis of the first half of the text – chapters 1–20, regarded as the oldest part – and includes a survey of currents of thought in the canonical period.)

Punyavijaya, Muni. et al. (eds) (1971) Pàavanāsuttam Jain Agama Series 9.2 (Prajñāpanā Sūtra), Bombay: Mahāvīra Jaina Vidyālaya. (A more systematic presentation of the contents of the fifth Aṅga above.)

Schubring, W. (1926) Worte Mahāvīras. Kritische Übersetzung aus dem Kanon der Jaina (Mahāvīra's Words. Critical Translation from the Jaina Canon), Göttingen: Vandenhoeck & Ruprecht. (Mahāvīra's teachings presented on the basis of original sources.)

—— (1935) Die Lehre der Jainas, Berlin and Leipzig: Walter de Gruyter & Co.; trans. W. Beurlen, The Doctrine of the Jainas. Described after the Old Sources, Delhi: Motilal Banarsidass, 1962. (This standard work is a survey of Jaina doctrine based on original sources.)

—— (ed.) (1974) Isibhāsiyāiṃ, A Jaina Text of the Early Period: Ahmedabad: L.D. Institute of Indology. (A relatively ignored ancient work, perhaps of the fourth century BC, the title of which literally means 'Sayings of the Ṛṣis'; it records the views of Mahāvīra and his predecessor Pārśva, together with the views of over forty others, many of whom are legendary figures.)

Upadhye, A.N. et al. (eds) (1977) Mahāvīra and his Teachings, Bombay: Bhagavān Mahāvīra 2500th Nirvāṇa Mahotsava Samiti. (Contains a series of articles by eminent scholars, not only on Mahāvīra, but also on Jaina philosophy, religion, literature, history and art.)

JAYANDRA SONI

MAIMON, ABRAHAM BEN MOSES *see* MAIMONIDES, ABRAHAM BEN MOSES

MAIMON, MOSES BEN *see* MAIMONIDES, MOSES

MAIMON, SALOMON (1753/4–1800)

Educated as a rabbi in Lithuania, Shlomo (Salomon) ben Yehoshua migrated to Germany and adopted the surname Maimon in honour of Maimonides. His criticism of Kant's dualism and his monistic account of the human mind as an imperfect expression of God's infinite mind influenced Fichte, Schelling and Hegel. Kant regarded him as the critic who understood him best.

Maimon's system combines rational dogmatism with empirical scepticism. As a rational dogmatist, he argues that cognition requires the absolute unity of subject and object. Maimon therefore criticizes Kant's dualistic divisions between the mental form and extra-mental matter of knowledge, and between the faculties of sensibility and understanding. Experience in Kant's sense – empirical knowledge – is possible only if these dualisms are merely apparent. Our finite minds must be imperfect expressions of an infinite, divine mind that produces the form and matter of knowledge. Through scientific progress, our minds become more adequate expressions of the infinite mind. Kant has not refuted Hume's scepticism, which could be refuted only if science became perfect. Perfect science is an ideal for which we must strive but which we will never reach.

Maimon is deeply indebted to Maimonides, but he reformulates Maimonidean ideas in light of modern mathematical physics and deploys them within a Kantian investigation of the possibility of experience. The result is a unique encounter between medieval and modern philosophy that decisively influenced German idealism and remains philosophically interesting.

1 Life and works

Maimon was born in Sukoviborg, Lithuania, and educated in the Talmud. He studied Kabbalah, was attracted then repelled by early Hasidism (see HASIDISM); and, under the influence of Maimonides, migrated to Germany in search of secular wisdom (see MAIMONIDES, M.). Turned away from Berlin, he became a wandering beggar and then taught at Posen, where he composed several Hebrew works. Maimon finally entered Berlin *c.*1780 and was befriended by enlightened Jews associated with Mendelssohn (see MENDELSSOHN, M.; ENLIGHTENMENT, JEWISH). However, Mendelssohn advised him to leave Berlin because of the tensions arising from Maimon's reluctance to earn a livelihood and from his sensuous lifestyle. Maimon studied German and contemporary philosophy and science. After returning to Berlin, Maimon's critical notes on Kant's *Critik der Reinen Vernunft* (Critique of Pure Reason) were forwarded to Immanuel KANT by Markus Herz, Kant's student, physician and friend in 1789. Kant realized the work's excellence. The notes were published (1790), followed a year later by a Hebrew commentary on Maimonides (1791). These works laid the foundations for a decade of publication, during which Maimon contributed to almost every area of contemporary philosophy. Influenced by Maimonides's naturalistic account of prophecy, Maimon pioneered the scientific study of parapsychology (see PARAPSYCHOLOGY). He also argued that Maimonides's ideas could solve contemporary philosophical problems. Maimon polemicized against REINHOLD and Schulze, and exercised great influence upon FICHTE. His financial problems were alleviated when Count Kalkreuth offered to house him, and he died in 1800 at Kalkreuth's estate in Nieder-Siegersdorf, where he was buried outside the Jewish cemetery. His autobiography (1792/3) provides important testimony about eighteenth-century Jewish life.

2 Criticism of Kant's dualism

Maimon severely criticized Kant's attempt to refute Hume's scepticism. Hume had argued that our claims to find necessary (for example, causal) connections between events are justified neither by logic (because there is no contradiction in denying such connections) nor by experience (because we experience what is, not what must be) (see HUME, D.). Kant responded that experience is impossible unless we regard such connections as necessary, which cannot be derived from logic or experience but are justified as necessary conditions for the possibility of experience. These necessary conditions are the categories of the understanding (see KANT, I.). However, Maimon argues that Kant understands experience differently from Hume. For Kant, experience is empirical knowledge – organized information about the sensible world. But for Hume, experience is an unorganized body of sensory impressions. Kant has not refuted Hume because Hume need not concede that we have experience in Kant's sense, so he need not concede that its necessary conditions are justified.

Furthermore, Maimon argues that Kant has failed to specify necessary and sufficient conditions for applying the categories to sensory impressions. Kant cannot explain how we apply the categories, whereas Hume explains that we claim necessary connections because we become accustomed to associations among events of certain types.

In Maimon's view, Kant's failure arises from the twofold dualism he attributes to the human mind. First, the mind is divided from the things in themselves that produce the matter of sensation. Second, the mind is divided into two faculties, each supplying its own form. Sensibility supplies space and time, while the understanding supplies the categories. Maimon argues that the categories can be justifiably applied only if the mind produces sensations, matter as well as form – thus, only if sensibility and understanding are not distinct. Empirical knowledge is possible if Kant's dualisms are overcome, if Kant's divergent mental faculties are only apparent features of the human mind, which is in reality an imperfect expression of the divine mind, generating both the form and the matter of experience.

To explain how experience is possible, then, Maimon rethinks Kant's central notions. He understands the thing-in-itself not as an extra-mental reality but as the reality known by the infinite mind. The thing-in-itself is the goal of scientific progress and not, as Kant thinks, the unknowable substratum of experience.

To overcome the dualism between sensibility and understanding, Maimon rejects Kant's view that space and time are non-conceptual forms of sensibility. Instead, he regards them as the minimal conceptual conditions for thinking diverse objects. Diverse objects must be the same in one respect and different in another, so two forms are required: the objects might occupy the same space at different times or different spaces at the same time. Whereas Kant takes space and time to be objects of intuition, Maimon regards them as concepts, misleadingly represented as objects of intuition by the imagination.

Maimon overcomes the dualism between sensations and the categories by drawing on the infinitesimal calculus as developed by LEIBNIZ. He regards sensations as composed, not of passive affections, but rather of differentials or infinitesimal degrees of mental activity below the threshold of consciousness. Instead of pertaining to a distinct faculty of sensibility, these differentials are ideas of understanding: they are the elements that the understanding would ideally reach if it carried out an infinite analysis. For its part, the understanding seeks to know objects in their genesis, and its categories are rules for the production of objects. To categorize a sensation is to grasp the law-like relationship between its differentials (dy/dx) through which a sensed object is produced. There is no gulf between sensations and the understanding, so the categories can be applied to sensible objects – and experience is possible.

3 Rational dogmatism and empirical scepticism

To some of Maimon's contemporaries, these monistic revisions of Kant suggested a way to refute Hume. But Maimon thinks Hume cannot be refuted, for although empirical knowledge is possible, it is not actual. This empirical scepticism follows from Maimon's rational dogmatism about knowledge, which in turn arises from his unique combination of Maimonides's medieval Aristotelianism with an understanding of mathematics based on the modern accomplishments of Leibniz and Newton (see MAIMONIDES, M.; LEIBNIZ, G.W.; NEWTON, I.).

Maimon is dogmatic about the conditions prescribed by reason for the attainment of knowledge: knowledge requires the absolute unity of the subject, the object and the act of knowing. Thus in arithmetic, he claims, we produce mathematical objects (numbers) without any input from outside the mind; and there is no real distinction between our number-generating minds, the numbers generated, and the rules by which we generate them. Maimon combines this modern understanding of mathematics as creation with a medieval understanding of God. Maimonides attributed to the philosophers the (Aristotelian) dictum that God is the intellect as well as the intellectually cognizing subject and the intellectually cognized object. He also said that God is always engaged in actual knowing and is therefore always absolutely one, whereas we attain absolute unity only if we actualize our potential for knowledge. On Maimon's interpretation, God is the mathematical mind that generates the world, and we can know the world in so far as we understand the mathematical rules of its generation. Experience (empirical knowledge) is possible if we are made in God's image or, in Maimon's formulation, if the finite mind is the schema of the infinite mind. When we engage in mathematics, we are divine.

So Maimon rejects Kant's dualisms, not only because Kant's response to Hume is inadequate, but also because dualism is incompatible with knowledge. He believes experience can be actual only if we eliminate dualism from science and become one with God. However, this is an ideal, for which we must strive but which we can never attain. So Hume is right to be sceptical about our claims to actual empirical knowledge.

Maimon's remarks about mathematics suggest that even mathematics is tainted by dualism and must be transformed before experience is actual. Symbolic proofs explain why premises imply a conclusion, but they may employ unreal concepts, such as 'regular dodecahedron'. In contrast, constructions in intuition, such as geometric figures, can show that a concept is real, but not why. The dualism of symbol and intuition must be eliminated, creating a mathematics that, at present, cannot even be imagined.

The moral of Maimon's scepticism is not despair but a commitment to scientific progress and intellectual honesty. We must strive for perfection without pretending we are already perfect (see SCEPTICISM).

4 The categories and the principle of determinability

As rules of production, Maimon's categories differ from Kant's, which are empty forms derived from the forms of logical judgment. Dissatisfied with Kant's reliance on traditional logic, Maimon reconsiders Aristotle's pioneering account of the categories and logic. He undertakes to derive the categories and the forms of judgment from a first principle, rendering logic a systematic science at last.

He proposes the principle of determinability: in a judgment determining a real object, the subject can be thought without the predicate but not the predicate without the subject. The infinite mind may be conceived as a single chain of judgments, beginning with the principle of determinability, determining every subject by a unique predicate, and culminating in the thing-in-itself as the fully determinate object of experience. This monistic system is akin to that of SPINOZA. But we cannot complete it – only approximate it as science progresses.

5 Practical philosophy

Maimon rejects Kant's doctrine of the primacy of the practical. This is the doctrine that reason seeks an absolute ground, but entangles itself in contradictions and illusions when it seeks that absolute ground through the scientific pursuit of knowledge, whereas reason finds an absolute ground in the practical pursuit of moral action. In Maimon's view, reason can find an absolute ground through the scientific pursuit of knowledge, if dualism is eliminated. Contradictions and illusions arise only when reason conflicts with imagination. Maimon's ethics are closer to Maimonides and Aristotle than to Kant, and he undertakes to derive morality from theoretical reason (see MAIMONIDES, M.; ARISTOTLE).

Maimon is committed only to religious doctrines reconcilable with reason. He finds Jewish monotheism more rational than Christianity and praises rabbinic morality, but criticizes the artificial development of Jewish law since the destruction of the Temple and does not oppose conversion to Christianity, if it is pursued for the sake of one's intellectual development. Maimon himself attempted conversion but, when he declared himself committed to rationalizing Christianity and uninterested in it for its own sake, he was rejected as too much of a philosopher to be become a Christian.

See also: ENLIGHTENMENT, JEWISH; GERMAN IDEALISM; HUME, D.; JEWISH PHILOSOPHY IN THE EARLY 19TH CENTURY; KANT, I.; MAIMONIDES, M.

List of works

Maimon, S. (1965–76) *Gesammelte Werke* (Collected Works), ed. V. Verra, Hildesheim: G. Olms, 7 vols. (A photoreproduction of all Maimon's German publications. No critical edition exists.)

—— (1790) 'Versuch über die Transcendentalphilosophie mit einem Anhang über die symbolische Erkenntnis und Anmerkungen' (Essay on Transcendental Philosophy with an Appendix on Symbolic Cognition and Annotations), in *Gesammelte Werke* (Collected Works), ed. V. Verra, Hildesheim: G. Olms, 1965–76, vol. 2. (Maimon's most influential work, written in admiration and sharp criticism of Kant's *Critik der Reinen Vernunft* (Critique of Pure Reason).)

—— (1791) *Giv'at ha-More* (The Hill of the Guide), ed. S.H. Bergmann and N. Rotenstreich, Jerusalem: Israel Academy of Sciences and Humanities, 1965. (Introduction to the history of philosophy and an incomplete commentary on Maimonides's *Guide to the Perplexed*, the text that most influenced Maimon's life and work. Develops Maimon's central thoughts, such as the absolute unity of subject, act and object in knowledge, and criticizes Maimonides's Aristotelian physics.)

—— (1792/3) *Salomon Maimons Lebensgeschichte: Von ihm selbst geschrieben und herausgegeben von K. P. Moritz*, trans. J. Clark Murray, *The Autobiography of Solomon Maimon*, London: East and West Library, 1954. (An abridged translation, omitting ten chapters on Maimonides's philosophy. Includes an essay on Maimon's philosophy by S.H. Bergman, which provides a clear, short introduction.)

—— (1794) 'Briefe des Philaletes an Aenesidemus', trans. and annotated by G. di Giovanni, 'Letters of Philaletes to Aenesidemus', in G. di Giovanni and H.S. Harris (eds and trans.) *Between Kant and Hegel: Texts in the Development of Post-Kantian Idealism*, Albany, NY: State University of New York Press, 1985. (A partial translation of Maimon's reply to Aenesidemus-Schulze's sceptical attack on Kant's philosophy. Provides an excellent sketch of Maimon's system and the distinctiveness of his scepticism.)

References and further reading

Altmann, A. (1973) *Moses Mendelssohn: A Biographical Study*, Philadelphia, PA: Jewish Publication Society, 360–4. (An excellent study of the enlightened Jewish circles in which Maimon moved in Berlin, with important details about Maimon's relationship with Mendelssohn.)

Atlas, S. (1965) *From Critical to Speculative Idealism: The Philosophy of Salomon Maimon*, The Hague: Martinus Nijhoff. (A clear and comprehensive account of Maimon's philosophy.)

—— (1970) 'Salomon Maimon's Doctrine of Fiction and Imagination', *Hebrew Union College Annual* 40/41: 363–89. (A clear account of a difficult but central area of Maimon's philosophy.)

Baumgardt, D. (1963) 'The Ethics of Salomon Maimon (1753–1800)', *Journal of the History of Philosophy* 1(2): 199–210. (The only English article on the sadly neglected topic of Maimon's ethics, exploring his increasingly sceptical attitude towards Kant's critical philosophy.)

Beiser, F. (1988) *The Fate of Reason: German Philosophy from Kant to Fichte*, Cambridge, MA: Harvard University Press. (A clear and indispensable account of Maimon's philosophy and his pivotal role in development of German idealism.)

Bergman, S.H. (1967) *The Philosophy of Salomon Maimon*, trans. N. Jacobs, Jerusalem: The Magnes Press. (The best comprehensive book on Maimon in English. An excellent introduction.)

Zac, S. (1988) *Salomon Maimon: critique de Kant*, Paris: Les Éditions du Cerf. (A useful study, particularly for its emphasis on Maimon's conception of philosophy and his relation to Spinoza.)

PAUL FRANKS

MAIMONIDES, ABRAHAM BEN MOSES (1186–1237)

Jewish theologian, mystical pietist, physician, and the only son of Moses Maimonides, with whom he studied rabbinics, philosophy and medicine. Upon his father's death, Abraham became the spiritual and temporal head of Egyptian Jewry and a leading rabbinical authority. Using this position, he propagated a form of Jewish pietism, introducing ideas and ritual practices inspired by Islamic mysticism. Moving beyond defence of his father's legal and philosophical writings, Abraham's most important work, Kifayat al-'Abidin *(Complete Guide for Devotees) – a monumental compendium of jurisprudence and religious philosophy – develops his own pietist interests. It attracted something of a following in its time but also met with concerted Jewish opposition to its Sufi-inspired ideals.*

Born in Fustat, Egypt, Abraham showed exceptional gifts that were noted from an early age. In 1204, a time of temporal and spiritual upheavals, he was chosen, a youth of eighteen, to lead Egyptian Jewry, the first of his family to occupy the office of *rayyis al-yahud*, which would become hereditary and remain in the family for two centuries, in large part because of the prestige of their distinguished ancestor Moses Maimonides. An able administrator and a constructive activist as well as a theorist, Abraham enjoyed close relations with the Muslim authorities as court physician to the Ayyubid ruler al-Malik al-Kamil. Much of his writing, perforce, was devoted to defending his father's works against their rabbinical and philosophical detractors. His *Milhamot ha-Shem* (Wars of the Lord), written after 1235, responded in particular to the criticisms of the rabbis of Provence.

Abraham wholeheartedly espoused his father's philosophical system and was seen as a continuator of the Arabic Aristotelian tradition. But his mature views diverged widely and creatively from such ideas. Moses Maimonides had considered the ultimate human aim to be knowledge of God, but the son stressed ethical perfection. His ascetic mysticism earned him the epithet by which he is consistently cited in later literature, Abraham *he-hasid* ('the Pious'). Identifying with a pietistic circle who were dissatisfied with the rationalism of some contemporary peripatetics, Abraham brought Sufi ideals into traditional Judaism, inspired by Abraham Abu'l-Rabi'a (d. 1223), also known as *he-hasid*, whom he calls 'our master in the Way'. He became the leader of this circle, whose adepts included his father-in-law, Hanan'el ben Samuel, and his own son 'Obadyah (1228–65), author of the mystical *al-Maqala al-Hawdiyya* (The Treatise of the Pool).

Pressing his prerogative as *nagid* (communal leader), he tried to enforce pietistic practices on the larger community, much as his father had sought to introduce various ritual reforms. Abraham's far-reaching measures included such Islamic-influenced practices as ablutions of the feet before prayer, sitting in a dignified posture during prayer, standing in rows, raising the hands in supplication, and punctuating prayer with profuse prostrations.

Abraham defended his pietism in the *Kifayat al-'Abidin* (Complete Guide for Devotees) (written *circa* 1230). This monumental legal and ethical treatise is not extant *in toto*, but substantial manuscripts survive in Genizah collections. Regrettably, the final section, dealing with *wusul* (the mystical goal), seems to be lost.

Written in Arabic in a warm and attractive style, the work is well constructed. The early parts rehearse the legal rulings of Abraham's father, albeit in a distinctively spiritualized vein. But the fourth and final section, on the 'special way', highlights the virtues of *tariq* (the path): sincerity, mercy, generosity, gentleness, humility, faith, contentedness, abstinence, mortification and solitude. These are *maqamat* (stages or stations), well known in the classical Sufi manuals. The goal, *wusul* ('arrival'), is in both cases encounter with God and the certitude of his light.

Abraham openly admires the Muslim Sufis, whose practices, he claims, derive originally from the prophets of Israel (see MYSTICAL PHILOSOPHY IN ISLAM). He even finds a Jewish origin for Sufi self-mortifications – combating sleep, solitary retreats in dark places, weeping, nightly vigils and daily fasts. Notable is the obligation of the novice to take as his guide an experienced teacher who has traversed all the stages of the path and will initiate the novice in the intricacies of mystical discipline before bestowing on him his mantle, as Elijah did on Elisha.

Departing from the juridical mode of his father's legal code, the *Mishneh Torah*, Abraham stresses the spiritual significance of the traditional Jewish precepts (*mitzvot*, divine commandments) and the 'mysteries' they conceal, in much the same manner of al-Ghazali's classic Islamic summa, the *Ihya' 'ulum al-din* (Revival of the Religious Sciences) (see AL-GHAZALI). The idea that Abraham Maimonides had rediscovered lost mysteries of Jewish provenance in traditions preserved by the Sufis but long forgotten by the Jews in the tribulations of their exile allowed his

circle to justify their adoption of Muslim customs and symbolisms. Calling themselves 'the disciples of the prophets', the Jewish pietists confidently awaited the imminent renewal of prophecy in Israel. The ancient Jewish traditions recovered from the Sufis were integral to the 'prophetic discipline'. Restoration of that discipline would hasten the return of prophecy itself, which Moses Maimonides had predicted in principle, but for a seemingly remote and certainly unspecifiable date.

Abraham had intended to compose a biblical commentary, but only the sections on Genesis and Exodus seem to have been completed, some time after 1231. Here, as in the *Kifayat*, he gives free reign to his mystical predilections, often, for polemical reasons, projecting into the patriarchal past his own innovations, depicting ancient biblical figures as pietists in much the way that Sufi literature clothes Muhammad and his companions in the garb of the early Sufis. He often alludes to an esoteric interpretation of the 'subtle mysteries' of the Pentateuch. These are not mentioned in his father's system. They typically point to pietist doctrines.

Although intended to enhance the spiritual ambience of Jewish worship with new forms of decorum like those to be observed among the Muslim neighbours of the Egyptian Jews, the novel practices Abraham Maimonides championed did not go unchallenged. Despite his office and familial prestige, which furthered pietist aims immensely, Abraham confronted fierce opponents, who went as far as to denounce him to the Muslim authorities, accusing the Jewish pietists of introducing 'false ideas', 'unlawful changes' and 'gentile customs' into the synagogue.

This opposition, and the spiritual elitism that had characterized the movement from its inception, may explain why it never gained universal approval. With the general decline of Oriental Jewry, Abraham Maimonides' construction of a Sufi-influenced Jewish pietism, gradually sank into oblivion.

See also: MAIMONIDES, M.; MYSTICAL PHILOSOPHY IN ISLAM

List of works

Maimonides, Abraham ben Moses (*c.*1230) *Kifayat al-'Abidin* (Complete Guide for Devotees), trans. Y. Duri, *Sefer ha-Maspiq le-'Ovdey ha-Shem*, Jerusalem, 1973; trans. N. Dana, *Kitab Kifayat al-'Abidin (Part Two, Volume Two), The Arabic Original with an Introduction and an Annotated Hebrew Translation*, Ramat-Gan: Bar-Ilan University, 1989; ed. and trans. S. Rosenblatt, *The High Ways to Perfection of Abraham Maimonides*,

New York and Baltimore, MD: Johns Hopkins University Press, 1927–38. (The *Kifayat* is a code of laws with pietistic leanings. It is incompletely preserved. Dana's edition provides the Judaeo-Arabic original and Hebrew translation of the liturgical section of the work; Rosenblatt's edition comprises the Judaeo-Arabic text of the ethical section of the work, with English translation.)

—— (after 1235) *Milhamot ha-Shem* (Wars of the Lord), ed. R. Margaliot, Jerusalem: Mossad ha-Rav Kook, 1953. (Abraham Maimonides' defence of his father's work.)

—— (before 1237) *Birkhat Abraham* (Responsa of Abraham), trans. B. Goldberg, Lyck, 1859; ed. A. Freimann and S.D. Goitein, *Abraham Maimuni, Responsa*, Jerusalem: Mekize Nirdamin, 1937. (Legal correspondence of Abraham. The Freimann and Goitein edition comprises the Arabic text with Hebrew translation.)

—— (before 1237) 'A Treatise in Defence of the Pietists', trans. S.D. Goitein, *Journal of Jewish Studies* 16, 1965: 105–114. (Polemical tract by Abraham.)

—— (before 1237) *Ma'aseh Nissim* (The Act of Miracles), trans. B. Goldberg, Paris: Brill, 1867. (Polemical. Abraham Maimonides' reply to Daniel ha-Babli's strictures on Moses Maimonides' code of laws, the *Mishneh Torah*.)

—— (c.1237) *Abraham Maimonides Commentary on Genesis and Exodus*, trans. E. Wiesenberg, ed. S.D. Sassoon, London, 1958. (A pietistic commentary, infused with Sufi ideas and terminology. The Wiesenberg-Sassoon edition consists of a Hebrew translation of the work and the Arabic original.)

References and further reading

* al-Ghazali (1096–7) *Ihya' 'ulum al-din* (Revival of the Religious Sciences), Cairo: Matba'ah Lajnah Nashr al-Thaqafah al-Islamiyyah, 1937–8, 5 vols; partial translations can be found in E.E. Calverley, *Worship in Islam: al-Ghazali's Book of the Ihya' on the Worship*, London: Luzac, 1957; N.A. Faris, *The Book of Knowledge, Being a Translation with Notes of the Kitab al-'Ilm of al-Ghazzali's Ihya' 'ulum al-din*, Lahore: Shaykh Muhammad Ashraf, 1962. (Close in spirit to the *Kifayat*, of which it may have served as a model.)

Cohen, G. (1967–8) 'The Soteriology of Abraham Maimuni', *Proceedings of the American Academy for Jewish Research* 35: 75–98, 36: 33–56. (An account of Abraham's thought in its socio-religious context.)

Eppenstein, S. (1914) *Abraham Maimuni: sein Leben und seine Schriften*, Berlin: Louis Lamm Verlag.

(The first modern account of Abraham's life and works.)

Fenton, P.B. (1981) 'Some Judaeo-Arabic fragments by Rabbi Abraham he-Hasid, the Jewish Sufi', *Journal of Semitic Studies* 26: 47–72. (Discusses the writings of Abraham's close companion.)

—— (1987) *Deux Traités de mystique juive* (Two Essays on Jewish Mysticism), Lagrasse: Verdier. (Survey of Sufi influences on Judaism and translation of two pietist texts.)

Goitein, S.D. (1967) 'Abraham Maimonides and his Pietist Circle', in A. Altmann (ed.) *Jewish Medieval and Renaissance Studies*, Cambridge, MA: Harvard University Press, 145–64. (Account of Abraham's activities based on Genizah documents.)

—— (1988) *A Mediterranean Society*, Berkeley, CA: University of California Press, vol. 5, 476–96. (Portrait of Abraham Maimonides.)

* Maimonides, 'Obadayah (c.1250) *al-Maqala al-Hawdiyya* (The Treatise of the Pool), trans. and ed. P. Fenton, *The Treatise of the Pool, al-Maqala al-Hawdiyya by 'Obadyah Maimonides*, London: Octagon Press, 1981. (A pietist, Judaeo-Arabic vade-mecum for the mystical way, based on rabbinical teachings and Sufi asceticism, written by Abraham's son. As well as giving a translation and notes on the text, Fenton's edition includes the original Arabic text, edited from a manuscript in the Bodleian Library, Oxford and Genizah fragments.)

Wieder, N. (1948) *Islamic Influences on the Jewish Worship*, London: Phaidon. (Study of Abraham's ritual innovations.)

PAUL B. FENTON

MAIMONIDES, MOSES (1138–1204)

*Called the Rambam in the Hebrew sources, an acronym on his name, and known in Islamic texts as Musa ibn Maimun, Rabbi Moses ben Maimon is best known in the West as Moses Maimonides and generally recognized as the greatest of the medieval Jewish philosophers. Maimonides lived his mature life in Egypt and earned his living as a physician. He was the author of ten medical works but gained fame in his own lifetime from his work on Jewish law (*halakhah*), chiefly the* Kitab al-Fara'id *(Sefer ha-Mitzvot, that is, the Book of the Commandments), cataloguing the traditional 613 commandments of the Pentateuch;* Kitab al-Siraj *(Sefer ha-Maor, Perush ha-Mishnah,* Commentary on the Mishnah*); and, above all, the* Mishneh Torah

(The Law in Review), a comprehensive and still authoritative code of rabbinic law. The clarity and definitiveness of the Mishneh Torah led to its criticism and (after Maimonides' death) even condemnation by some rabbis, who prized the ongoing dialectic of Talmudic disputation and felt suspicious of Maimonides' rationalism.

Maimonides' philosophic masterpiece, the Dalalat al-Ha'irin *or* Guide to the Perplexed, *was written in Arabic, with a view to helping the more intellectually inquisitive readers of the Torah, who were troubled by the apparent disparity between biblical and scientific/philosophical ideas. The work frames a powerful but not supercilious rationalism that locates and accommodates many biblical postulates and profits from the instruction of the rabbinic (Talmudic) sources and from critical appropriation of the achievements of Muslim philosophers and theologians and their Greek predecessors. It defends the doctrine of the world's creation against the eternalism of Neoplatonic Aristotelians but rejects the notion that creation (or eternity) is subject to proof. Rather, Maimonides argues, creation is preferable to its alternative, and more plausible, because it preserves the idea of divine volition as an explanation for the emergence of complexity from divine simplicity, and because it marks the difference God's act made to the existence and nature of the world.*

God is pure perfection and absolute simplicity. The Torah's anthropomorphisms themselves lead us to that realization, if we follow the dialectic by which prophetic language directs us to ever higher conceptions of divine transcendence. Biblical poetry and the concrete demands of the Law are accommodations to our creaturely limitations. Such accommodations are made possible by the material side of the prophet's nature, as manifested in language and imagination, which are, no less than intellect, expressions of God. For matter in general is an expression of God, apprehensible to us through what seems wilful or arbitrary in nature. It is not a positive principle or hypostasis, but it is a necessary concomitant of the act of creation itself. For without it nothing other than God would exist. Our task as humans is to discipline our material natures – not to battle or seek to destroy them but to put them to work in behalf of our self-perfection, through which our inner, intellectual affinity to God will be realized.

Maimonides' synthetic approach, accommodating to one another the insights of reason and the teachings of Scripture and tradition, was highly valued by Aquinas, who frequently cites him, and by other European philosophers such as Jean Bodin. Leibniz warmly appreciated Maimonides' thought, as his reading notes reveal. Among subsequent Jewish thinkers, Maimonides' work became the paradigm of Jewish rationalism for his admirers and detractors alike. His philosophy was at the core of the philosophic tradition that Spinoza addressed. Even today practitioners of Jewish philosophy stake out their positions in reference to Maimonides and formulate their own views as appropriations, variants or interpretations of the elements of his thought.

1   Life and works

Called the Rambam in the Hebrew sources, an acronym on his name, and known in Islamic texts as Musa ibn Maimun, Rabbi Moses ben Maimon is best known in the West as Moses Maimonides and generally recognized as the greatest of the medieval Jewish philosophers. A physician and jurist as well as a philosopher, Maimonides was born in Cordoba, but his family fled the forced conversions of the Almohad invasion in 1148. From about 1160 they lived quietly in Fez, the heart of the Almohad movement, but came to public attention with the youthful Maimonides' publication of a defence of a rabbinic ruling his father had made promulgating full acceptance by the Jewish community of those who had undergone a nominal conversion. Journeying to Palestine in 1165, the family were nearly lost in a storm at sea but made their way to Acre. Maimonides prayed at the ruined Temple site and fulfilled a shipboard vow of pilgrimage to Hebron, burial site of the biblical patriarchs. Abraham bore a special significance for Maimonides. In keeping with the biblical and midrashic tradition, he viewed the patriarch as a natural theologian whose religion was formed not in the tradition of his fathers but by reason confronting nature and experience.

Finding permanent residence impossible in the undeveloped land, then under the Crusader kingdom of Jerusalem, the family settled in Cairo, where Maimonides was prostrated with grief by the death of his younger brother David, a jewel merchant, in a shipwreck on the Indian Ocean. Recovering and taking over the support of the family, Maimonides turned to medicine. Like the ancient Talmudic sages, he disdained making his livelihood from his Judaic learning and judicial authority. He developed an active medical practice and became court physician to the *wazir* of Saladin, who overthrew the Fatimid dynasty in 1171. Late in life Maimonides wrote ten medical treatises, but it was his work in rabbinic law that gave him fame and made him a leader of the Egyptian Jewish community as early as 1167.

Three works secure his place among the greatest rabbinic jurists: his *Kitab al-Fara'id*, known in Hebrew as the *Sefer ha-Mitzvot*, cataloguing and classifying the traditional 613 biblical laws, lays the foundations; his Arabic *Kitab al-Siraj* or *Book of the Lamp*, known in Hebrew as the *Sefer ha-Maor, Perush ha-Mishnah* (1168), expounds the rational purposes of the ancient rabbinic code; and his *Mishneh Torah* (*c.*1185), written in rabbinic Hebrew and popularly known as the *Yad Hazakah* (The Strong Hand), or simply the *Yad*, an allusion to its fourteen volumes, since the numerical value of the letters of the Hebrew word *yad*, or hand, is fourteen. This work organizes the vast complexity of Talmudic and post-Talmudic Jewish law in a still authoritative codification, allowing clear access to definitive legal rulings on matters of *halakhah* (see HALAKHAH).

Despite the prestige of these works – in part because of it – Maimonides' jurisprudence was not universally hailed. The *Mishneh Torah* in particular was criticized: its title, which might be rendered 'The Law in Review', and which echoes a title traditionally assigned to the biblical book of Deuteronomy, seemed almost to promise a second revelation. The economy of the work, which placed a premium on stating clear-cut practical decisions, demanded the omission of rabbinic citations and dispensed with the voluminous dialectic which for many was the heartsblood of the Law as an intellectual discipline, even a way of life.

Maimonides was in fact sometimes impatient with the digressive and midrashic (homiletical) methods of rabbinic discourse. His insistence on juridical clarity, determinateness and Socratic conceptual organization (as sharply contrasted with the associative exposition of the Talmud) were clearly much on his mind when he turned from writing commentaries on parts of the Talmud to his more distinctive commentary on the Mishnah. The notion that study of the law could somehow supplant the robust life that the law meant to regulate seemed especially unwholesome to him – as it had to his Andalusian predecessor Judah HALEVI.

A brilliant and faithful jurist, Maimonides drew the axioms of his theology from scriptural rather than rabbinic sources; he worked eclectically and creatively with the rabbinic responses to biblical ideas to forge a coherent and appropriable framework of thought – just as his rabbinic predecessors had done. But traditionalists, legal positivists and fideists could not fail to note that where Maimonides could not find room to cite his legal authorities (and some of them are still being found, giving the lie to long-standing claims that he based some of his legal doctrines sheerly on his own opinions) he did make room, in the first volume of his code, to frame a thematic ethics and to elaborate a natural theology and cosmology – and, in the last volume, to develop a biblically grounded theory of sovereignty and public law. Similarly, he does not regard it as digressive in

discussing the laws of penitence to include a defence of human freedom of will. Reacting against what they viewed as an excessive rationalism, a number of rabbis condemned the *Mishneh Torah*, although others defended it vigorously. Denounced to Church authorities by Jewish adversaries, the first and most thematic volume of Maimonides' code, the *Sefer ha-Mada* (Book of Knowledge), was burnt at Montpellier in 1232, along with the seemingly heretical *Guide to the Perplexed*. Despite the reservations of some Jewish traditionalists to this day about the rationalism of his philosophical and jurisprudential work, Maimonides remains a towering figure in *halakhah*. His work is the cornerstone of all subsequent Jewish philosophy, and it has had a significant impact on philosophy at large. His synthetic approach, accommodating to one another the insights of reason and the teachings of Scripture and tradition, was highly valued by Aquinas, who frequently cites him, and by other European philosophers such as Jean Bodin. Leibniz warmly appreciated Maimonides' thought, as his reading notes reveal. Maimonides' work became the paradigm of Jewish rationalism for his admirers and detractors alike. It was a major philosophic backstop to the thinking of Spinoza, providing a clear paradigm of the committed Jewish philosophy that Spinoza would address, whether by way of refutation, accommodation or revision. Even today practitioners of Jewish philosophy stake out their positions in reference to Maimonides and formulate their own views as appropriations, variants or interpretations of the elements of his thought.

2 *Guide to the Perplexed*: its literary form and intent

Maimonides' philosophic masterpiece, *Dalalat al-Ha'irin* (Guide to the Perplexed) (*c.*1190), was written in Arabic but widely circulated in Hebrew translations as the *Moreh Nevukhim*. Aiming to mediate between the scriptural and philosophic idioms, it opens by deriving a sophisticated negative theology from a subtle deconstruction of the anthropomorphisms that had long troubled thoughtful readers of the Torah. This discussion, filling the first seventy chapters of the *Guide*, is widely but erroneously read as a refutation of anthropomorphism. I say erroneously, because Maimonides assumes that the falsity of anthropomorphism is well established by argument and well known to his reader. But Maimonides does not do much to prevent such misprision. He does not state the objective of his discussions in this extended section of the first part of the *Guide* but leaves casual readers to fend for themselves. One natural outcome is the commonplace assumption that what Maimonides takes for granted is what he is seeking to prove.

That, in Maimonides' view, is better than allowing his philosophic work to do more harm than good.

The difficulty that Maimonides confronts is this: the *Guide* is written to aid a reader who is confused by the seeming disparity between biblical and scientific/philosophical ideas. To mention only the most obvious issues: Scripture tells us that the world is created, but Aristotelian philosophers present numerous proofs to show that the world has always existed with the same, invariant nature that we observe today. Scripture speaks of God as the ruler of nature and the lawgiver of humanity in general and of Israel in particular. But the philosophical tradition argues that the divine transcends all knowledge of particulars, let alone concern for them. Indeed, it is readily enough argued that chance seems to rule, in this life at least, and that sufferings outweigh happiness. So where are the divine justice and judgment that loom so large in the vision of the Torah and the prophets? How is prophecy even possible, if God is so far above us as philosophy seems to teach? And how can we relate the philosophical teaching of divine transcendence to the vivid concreteness of prophetic imagination?

Maimonides unifies these problems about transcendence and immanence, providence and revelation, creation and eternity, finitude and privation under the rubrics of two rabbinic problematics: the account of creation and the account of the chariot. The first rubric alludes to the opening of Genesis, the second to that of Ezekiel, in whose epiphany, despite all his reverent periphrasis, God seems to take human form. Voicing a sense of the paradox or mystery surrounding these two passages, the rabbis of the Talmud (Haggigah 11b, 13a) forbade public instruction in the issues they involve. Only in private teaching were these to be discussed, and then only the subject headings were to be broached.

Interpreting this ruling, Maimonides understands 'the account of Genesis' as the rabbis' name for cosmology, the principles of nature or physics, understood in relation to God; 'the account of the Chariot' is, by metonymy, the entire realm of theology, that is, metaphysics understood in relation to God. The core issue in both cases: how can the Infinite be manifest in finite terms?

The cosmological side of this question is evident in the Neoplatonists' problematic of the Many and the One – why is there anything other than God? It crops up polemically in the sensitive and vexed area of creation, where philosophers of Aristotelian stamp find it incongruous to ascribe an origin to the world, in part because their naturalism balks at subjecting the cosmos to external interference but in part because they wish to avoid compromising divine transcendence in temporality.

Viewed in this light, creation itself appears to be an instance of theophany. The problem of evil and that of prophetic revelation reflect the same issue: why does divine creation content itself with a world as flawed as this one? Why would revelation single out one people or individual to hear God's word, leaving others dependent or unenlightened altogether; and why should God's expression, as epiphany or as law, take the precise form ascribed to it by individual prophets, with all their human weaknesses and differences of outlook and circumstance?

The ordinary mind, Maimonides finds, is generally content to accept what is familiar, not noticing the difficulties a tradition may contain. But such faith, if faith it may be called, is of limited value and entirely dependent on the veracity and coherence of those who establish a tradition. In the strictest sense, such unreflective acceptance is not faith at all. For belief is commitment to what one understands; it cannot be confined to mere conformity.

To the more questioning, especially those who have read scientific and philosophical literature, theological problems are apparent. Responsible intellectual leaders must work creatively to discover for themselves and show others how these problems can be addressed. Progress here, as in other areas of intellectual inquiry, is possible. Indeed, our progress towards God can be asymptotic, Maimonides argues, invoking the geometrical image of two lines that grow ever closer together, even though they will never meet. But progress, to be cumulative, requires writing and teaching, and that presents a difficulty; it is not responsible to introduce others to problems whose solutions they might not grasp. Maimonides takes this issue very seriously, holding a teacher responsible even for the misinterpretations of followers and disciples.

Taking a hint from the language of the ancient Talmudic restriction, Maimonides adopts an 'esoteric' mode of writing in the *Guide*. Not that he writes obscurely or treats his subject as occult or hermetic. He simply does not state the problems to be addressed. A reader who has grappled with the same questions will readily enough discover the relevance of the discussions in the *Guide*. But that relevance is not spelled out – let alone promoted in the mercantile manner of twentieth-century pedagogy. The order of exposition, moreover, as with the texts that Maimonides studied most closely – the Hebrew Bible, the Talmud, the Aristotelian corpus – demands that one read well into the text before being able to make much of it, since every part is relevant to the rest, and no passage is wholly self-explanatory or transparent.

Maimonides' work, like Aristotle's, and the Jewish canonical sources, is clearly not part of the Cartesian modernist project, with its Euclidean pyramidal structure, designed to move upwards from foundational axioms, postulates and definitions to theorems, scholia and lemmas. Rather, the work is bound together like a Gordian knot – not impenetrable, but resistant to simple unravelling by the teeth and fingers of the unprepared.

Uncritical thinking is probably just as common today as it was in Maimonides' time, but exposure to doubt and (somewhat conventional) lines of objection to biblical categories and assumptions is far more widespread. Today's unexamined faith is often a form of scepticism. So the *Guide to the Perplexed*, although written to address specific issues at a very particular historical juncture, has the character of a classic – not only because it is synthetic, original and insightful, but also because readers today find its approach and many of its arguments as relevant as when first set down.

Following the rabbinic injunction that the problems of creation and theophany are to be taught not publicly but in a direct and idividual communication, Maimonides adapts to his purposes the Arabic literary genre of the epistolary essay (*risala*). The *Guide* is written in the form of a letter addressed to a particular disciple, whose needs and questions can be addressed in an informal, dialectical style, rather than the formal, systematic style of a treatise like the *Mishneh Torah*. Having sketched the background, skills and uncertainties of this first intended reader, Maimonides has created a persona, not in the authorial voice but in the figure of the reader, clearly alerting others to the scope and relevance to their own concerns of the arguments they will encounter.

In keeping with his expository strategy, Maimonides never calls the *Guide* a book. He moves with seemingly casual, conversational rhythms from exegetical remarks to philosophical observations, arguments, typologies and critiques, relying on sensitive readers to follow his hints, supply the unstated problematic, and piece together the larger argument. He well understands that the broader impact of the opening chapters will be fully felt only by readers who take the time and trouble to read them once again after having progressed through the work as a whole.

It might seem that Maimonides has simply employed a legal fiction, and a thin one at that, to skirt the rabbinic restriction on the sort of teaching he wants to pursue. But his strategy is far subtler than that. He has successfully kept the *Guide*'s problematic within the circle of its intended audience. Casual readers typically emerge from an encounter with the *Guide* without any knowledge of its subject matter; most casual readers do not finish it, let alone begin

again, so as to be able to piece together the scattered elements of its larger argument.

3 *Guide to the Perplexed*: creation and eternity

If we begin not where Maimonides did, with the deconstruction of biblical anthropomorphism, but where Genesis does, with the beginning, we find Maimonides in a spirited defence of the idea of creation against the eternalism of AL-FARABI, IBN SINA, ARISTOTLE, and the whole Neoplatonic Aristotelian tradition (see ETERNITY OF THE WORLD, MEDIEVAL VIEWS OF). The problem is not, Maimonides argues, that philosophical proof contradicts scriptural dogma. On the contrary, if we had proof that creation was impossible, as Aristotelian philosophers long argued, we would simply allegorize the biblical account of creation, just as we allegorize biblical anthropomorphism. But Aristotle knew that he had no such proof. That is why he speaks so emphatically when he tries to assure us of the world's eternity. After all, it was he who taught us the difference between proof and mere persuasion.

What the philosophers of the Aristotelian tradition have done is simply read into the metaphysics of being the familiar character of nature: no event without a prior event, no process without potentiality, no potentiality without matter as its substrate. Of course assumptions like these will generate an eternal cosmos. But they amount to nothing more than an aprioristic attempt to generalize the conditions of the settled order of nature and impose the assumptions we derive from study of that order on the wholly unknown conditions of the world's disputed origin – as if a brilliant young man who knew nothing of sex or procreation were to infer the impossibility of embryogenesis and foetal development from his knowledge of the biology of mature adults: how could a human live in an enclosed sac, without breathing, moving about, ingesting solid food, or excreting bodily wastes?

Rejecting efforts to demonstrate the world's eternity, Maimonides even-handedly rejects creationist attempts of the same sort. If it is really true, he argues, that the world must reflect God's timelessness, as eternalists suppose, then change itself becomes impossible, and the argument has proved too much. If the claim is that God, to be a creator, must be a constant creator, then creation becomes not impossible but necessary. Those who try to demonstrate creation, not surprisingly, produce a similar result: the world is new at every instant. The radical occasionalism of Arabic dialectical theology that results from such thinking, Maimonides argues, renders nature unintelligible and divine governance irrational (see ISLAMIC THEOLOGY §§1–2; OCCASIONALISM). Creation, in that case, to be the outcome of a clear proof, must cease to be God's choice and become a sheer necessity and unending chore.

But, although efforts to demonstrate the world's creation or its eternity fail, there are grounds for choosing between the rival cosmological visions. Creation is more plausible conceptually and preferable theologically: more plausible, because a free creative act allows differentiation of the world's multiplicity from divine simplicity, as the seemingly mechanical necessitation of emanation, strictly construed, cannot do; preferable, because Avicennan claims that God is author of the world and determiner of its contingency are undercut by the assertion that at no time was nature other than it is now (see IBN SINA). Without the notion of creation at a particular time, one cannot say that atheism ensues, as AL-GHAZALI had supposed. The view of the Neoplatonic Aristotelians is neither incoherent nor insincere. But it does unduly attenuate the world's dependence on God's act, and it does leave unexplained the emergence of complexity from simplicity – problems which the human idea of a will that is not simply reducible to intellect or understanding far more readily addresses.

4   *Guide to the Perplexed*: God's governance of nature

In discussing God's governance of nature, Maimonides adopts and adapts the emanative ideas of the Neoplatonic philosophers (see NEOPLATONISM). But he modifies their notion that emanation is a necessary progression, poetically compared to the radiation of light from the sun (which, after all, cannot help but shine) but more perspicuously described in terms of the necessitation of theorems by their axioms. In place of such deductivist, intellectualist models, Maimonides uses a more voluntaristic model, allowing for creativity and novelty in nature's unfolding, while rejecting the more radical voluntarism of the occasionalists, who make God the immediate author of all events, without the intervention of natural causes or human volitions (see VOLUNTARISM). If persons and things do not act and react, Maimonides argues, was it not otiose of God to create foodstuffs that play no role in our sustenance, or to ordain commandments that we have no power to obey or disobey?

Taking the Neoplatonists to task for not exploiting adequately the resources of their own ontology for addressing the problem of evil, Maimonides couches his response to the Epicurean dilemma in a gloss on the Book of Job. The Satan (or 'adversary') responsible for Job's sufferings, he notes, is not called one of the 'sons of God' but is said only to have come along with them, 'in their midst'. One might suppose, with

the Talmudic sage Resh Lakish, that Job's adversary was sin – equating sin and death with the adversary (see SIN). Maimonides likes the allegory but rejects its application here. For it is a premise of the Book of Job (which Maimonides, like Resh Lakish, quite clearly takes to be a fiction, although he regards it as one with considerable verisimilitude) that Job was without sin (see EVIL, PROBLEM OF).

The Satan, then, would be Job's vulnerability, that is, his materiality, the physical nature that makes us all subject to sufferings and loss. For, as GALEN explained, one should not expect bodies of the sort of matter that makes our own to last forever. Here we see the weight of Scripture's saying that the Satan came 'in the midst of' the sons of God: matter, that is, otherness, alienation from the unity of the Divine, is not a positive principle, a hypostasis, angel or Form, but a concomitant to the emergence of finite being, a requisite of creation and createdness. The existence we enjoy has vulnerability as its price; divine generosity could not be expressed and vouchsafed to lesser beings at all unless those beings were indeed made other, given a reality that is at once their own and (by the same token) inevitably deficient. Matter is that independence and deficiency. It is at once the good woman of Proverbs 31, constantly active on our behalf, and the married harlot of Proverbs 7, never contented but constantly changing forms/partners.

Our human task is to overcome the limitations of matter, but we can do so through its strengths. Thus mortification of the flesh is not a worthy but an unwholesome ideal, based on the illusion that if a little medicine is good for us a lot will be that much better. Medical arts, politics, and otherworldly endeavours are precious but instrumental efforts, since they sustain the human individual and community, allowing us the necessary time and opportunity to seek and reach the human goal.

What is that goal? Maimonides categorically agrees with Plato (*Theaetetus* 176b) and Leviticus (19:2): it is to become as like to God as humanly possible, to emulate and pursue God's holiness, to realize and fulfil what is divine and holy in ourselves. Job's reward is not in the restoration of his family and possessions but in the epiphany he is granted, a communion with God that is not the recompense of his sufferings but an emblem of the sort of human attainment that makes all sufferings if not bearable then at least outweighed.

It is not true, as Muhammad ibn Zakariyya'AL-RAZI and even SAADIAH GAON supposed, that sufferings overbalance good fortune in this life. But the deeper flaw in the emotively appealing notion that life is a vale of tears is that it assays human life in terms of pain and suffering, whereas the ultimate coin is not hedonic at all but intellectual. Reason is the surest guide to the good life and test of sound and unsound norms and precepts; but it is also our closest bond with God, our purchase on immortality, and the focus of divine providence within us. For providence, in the human case, is not confined to the level of the species and its generalized nature. Indeed, it was Aristotle, once again, who taught us that only individuals are real, not species as such.

Contrary to the Aristotelian teaching (expounded by Peripatetics such as Alexander of Aphrodisias in the face of the Stoic doctrine of providence – see ALEXANDER OF APHRODISIAS; STOICISM §20), providence does extend to the individual, through our capacity to perfect the mind, realize our inner affinity to God, and grasp the immortality that lies so close at hand. This is symbolized in the biblical account of Adam, whose ready access to the fruit that would give him eternal life represents not a long vanished moment of apotheosis in the mythic past (and still less a damning fall) but the universal human condition, of an immortal intelligence strapped to a body that is at once its trap and its springboard to the divine.

5   *Guide to the Perplexed*: anthropomorphism and the human connection with God

Quietly celebrating the human affinity with God, Maimonides (as noted by the medieval commentator Narboni) begins his survey of biblical anthropomorphisms with 'image and likeness' (see Narboni's *Be'ur le-Sefer Moreh Nevukhim* (Commentary on the *Guide*): I 1). Maimonides explains that some Hebrew words (as, for example, when we read that Joseph was fair of form) denote only physical appearance; but 'likeness' can refer to spiritual affinities. Thus in Psalms (102:6), the psalmist likens himself to a pelican in the desert: not that he looks like a pelican, but that he is as desolate as a pelican would be in such a place. As his survey proceeds, Maimonides unfolds a hierarchy of meanings, with the most physical at the bottom, social and other senses rising higher, and the spiritual/intellectual surmounting the rest: wherever the Torah applies to God a term that bears physical (or other privative) connotations, that term can always be taken in a higher, spiritual/intellectual sense, and that is the sense we must pursue.

Maimonides does not here refute anthropomorphism but assumes it to have been refuted by well-known arguments based on the incompatibility of divinity with privation. Correspondingly, he pursues the idea of perfection, the opposite of privation, as the notion that orients this hierarchy, as it orients the ladder of love in Plato's *Symposium* – or Jacob's ladder in the Book of Genesis. What Maimonides finds here is an ontic hierarchy that fuses higher degrees of reality with higher degrees of intellectuality. He shows that none of the Torah's anthropomorphisms need be taken literally ('jealousy' refers to exclusivity, 'coming and going' to manifestation in a human awareness), but in the process he vindicates the legitimacy of conceptualizing the Divine in terms of the human mind (and will).

We begin to see how prophecy is possible, as a human response to the exigency of relating to others the sheer power of Perfection. The Torah, using human language, speaks of action in terms of motion, of existence in terms of matter. Only the Tetragrammaton signifies God directly, signalling nothing more (but nothing less) than the absoluteness of God's being – 'I am that I am'. All other epithets only point towards Perfection, assigning to God some notion humanly regarded as a perfection, while other passages systematically exclude the privations concomitant with the perfections known to us. Thus the deconstruction of biblical anthropomorphism is the work of Scripture itself; the Torah teaches of divine transcendence through the medium of ordinary human language. It uses terms intelligible to us through their generality to convey the idea of divine uniqueness. This was what the rabbis meant in saying, 'Great is the boldness of the prophets' to speak of the Creator in the language of his creations.

Prophets are historically situated human beings, but they are not and cannot be mere ignoramuses whose minds are magically filled with divine words; nor can they be immoralists, simply plucked up to be inspired. They are and must be wise individuals, filled with the kind of philosophic insight that can grow only within an upright character. But they are gifted also through the material side of their nature, with the language and imagination to body forth these ideas in concrete visions, laws, rituals, poetic and rhetorical symbols, to speak of them persuasively and act on them with conviction.

Prophets themselves learn nothing new from revelation, although it may bring to the surface ideas that were only latent in their minds. The ignorant remain ignorant; but the gift of imagination in the wise, if they are disciplined by the moral virtues, especially courage and contentment, gives wing to ideas, rendering them accessible to the masses and setting them into practice. The message of all true prophets is thus coherent and universal, an expression of the truth itself.

In principle, any philosopher of character and imagination might be a prophet; but in practice the legislative, ethical and mythopoetic imagination that serves philosophy finds fullest articulation in Judaism.

Its highest phase, where imagination yields to pure intellectual communion, was unique to Moses, elaborated in Judaism and its daughter religions. This judgment, that the burden of prophetic teaching finds its epitome in the Torah, is no mere subjective preference: it is grounded in intensive study of the means by which the biblical commandments, read thematically, serve to inform human character and understanding. The most general summary of the outcome of that study is in the Maimonidean thesis that the Mosaic law is no mere personal code, private vision or closely held teaching like Abraham's; nor is it a mere derivative faith. Rather, it is a systematic way of life based on sustained, intellectual contact with the Divine. When courage and contentment – read here 'self-confidence and independence' – return, with the restoration of Israel to her land, prophecy will resume among this people, to the great benefit of the nations of the world, who will observe the peace and prosperity of Israel living under God's law and will flock to follow not her religion but her example. It is this that is to be understood by the lion's lying down with the lamb: the nations will learn the ways of peace, and Israel will be the little child that leads them (see PROPHECY).

God governs through nature. The forms of things are the objective manifestations of his wisdom, intelligible through their fit with the subjective rationality of our own divinely imparted intelligence. Where a human discoverer must take apart the waterclock to understand its workings, the inventor knows it first: his knowledge does not follow but anticipates the design. The same is true with God, whose knowledge is prior to the realities we know, since it is their cause.

But the matter of things, readily enough associated with chance and the irrational, is another aspect of God's manifestation in nature, the aspect that we would link, through its seeming arbitrariness, with the human faculty of willing. In God's ultimate and absolute unity, will and wisdom are united; their multiplicity is subjective. So in biblical parlance all the operations of nature but also the workings of sheer chance are ascribed to God. But we humans must always think in human categories, so it is not possible for us, while we live, to grasp the absoluteness of God's unity and hold in one mental breath what we can conceptualize only as the wisdom and the will of God.

Human finitude, accordingly, denied Moses the vision he requested, of God's face; but a perfect mind allowed him to see God's 'back' – what follows from God, the effects of God in nature, where divine absoluteness becomes specific and can be apprehended as if in attributes like those of a person. God, of course, in his infinitude, transcends personality, as even little children should be taught. Attributes belong only to composite beings. But Moses' request, after all, was a practical one: he wanted to know God so that he would know how to govern; and for practical purposes, we have knowledge of what God is like by examining the attributes that should be perfected in ourselves, the very attributes named in Moses' epiphany: mercy, compassion, justice – and, of course, the human power that all of these presuppose, that of reason, our direct link with the Divine.

See also: ARISTOTELIANISM, MEDIEVAL; ARISTOTELIANISM IN ISLAMIC PHILOSOPHY; BIBLE, HEBREW; CREATION AND CONSERVATION, RELIGIOUS DOCTRINE OF; GOD, CONCEPTS OF; HALAKHAH; MAIMONIDES, A.; MIDRASH; NAHMANIDES, M.; RELIGION, PHILOSOPHY OF; THEOLOGY, RABBINIC

List of works

Maimonides, Moses (1168) *Kitab al-Siraj* (Commentary on the Mishnah), complete translation available in Hebrew only, *Sefer ha-Maor, hu Perush ha-Mishnah*, ed. M.D. Rabinowitz, Tel Aviv: Rishonim, 1948; English translation of the part of the work entitled *Shemonah Perakim* (Eight Chapters), trans. J. Gorfinkle, *The Eight Chapters of Maimonides on Ethics*, New York, 1912; repr. New York. AMS, 1966. (Expounds the rational purposes of the ancient rabbinic code. *Shemonah Perakim* is a thematic introduction to the mishnaic collection of ethical aphorisms known as *Pirkei Avot* (The Sayings of the Fathers). It develops a capsule virtue ethics and sketches a theory of action aiming to rebut determinism.)

—— (c.1185) *Mishneh Torah* (The Law in Review), Books I and II trans. M. Hyamson, *The Book of Knowledge and the Book of Adoration*, Jerusalem: Feldheim, 1974; Books III–XIV trans. as *The Code of Maimonides*, Yale Judaica Series, New Haven, CT: Yale University Press, 1949–72. (Maimonides's authoritative fourteen-volume code of rabbinic law, written in mishnaic Hebrew with a view to providing lucid and comprehensive guidance to the requirements of *halakhah*. The work opens with detailed discussions (in the first volume) of the intellectual and moral foundations of rabbinic law. It closes with an exposition of public law and a description of the Messianic age of Israel's political restoration. The intervening volumes discuss each requirement of the civil, criminal and ritual law of Israel.)

—— (c.1190) *Dalalat al-Ha'irin* (*Moreh Nevukhim*, Guide to the Perplexed), ed. S. Munk, *Le Guide des*

Égarés, Arabic text, critically edited, with annotated French translation, Paris, 1856–66, 3 vols; repr. Osnabrück: Zeller, 1964; trans. S. Pines, with an introductory essay by L. Strauss, *The Guide of the Perplexed*, Chicago, IL: University of Chicago Press, 1969; *Rambam*, extensive selections from the *Guide* with commentary by L.E. Goodman, New York: Viking, 1976; reissued, Los Angeles, CA: Gee Tee Bee, 1984. (Maimonides' philosophic masterwork, written in Arabic in the form of a letter to a disciple who has confronted the apparent disparities between philosophic/scientific and biblical ideas.)

—— (before 1204) *Millot ha-Higgayon* (On Logic), ed. Y. Satnov, with commentary by M. Mendelssohn, Berlin: B. Cohen, 1927. (Maimonides' work on logic.)

—— (before 1204) *Kitab al-Fara'id* (*Sefer ha-Mitzvot*, Book of the Commandments), trans. with notes by C.B. Chavel, *The Commandments (Sefer ha-Mitzvot)*, London and New York: Soncino, 1967. (Maimonides' listing of the 613 commandments traditionally held to be conveyed in the Pentateuch. In keeping with his thematic approach, Maimonides lists first among the 248 positive commandments 'I am the Lord thy God' and first among the negative commandments 'Thout shalt have no other gods before me'. These are the two commandments that were rabbinically said to have been learned from God himself, as Maimonides explains, citing the Babylonian Talmud, Makkot 23 b.)

—— (before 1204) *Iggerot ha-Rambam* (Maimonides' Epistles), trans. with notes by A. Halkin and discussions by D. Hartman, *Epistles of Maimonides: Crisis and Leadership*, Philadelphia, PA: Jewish Publication Society, 1993. (Comprises 'The Epistle on Martyrdom', 'The Epistle to Yemen' and 'Essay on the Resurrection'.)

References and further reading

Baron, S.W. (ed.) (1941) *Essays on Maimonides: an Octocentennial Volume*, New York: Columbia University Press. (Papers of the historic Maimonides conference held in the 1930s in Cordoba for the 800th anniversary of the philosopher's birth, then dated in 1135.)

Buijs, J. (1988) *Maimonides: A Collection of Critical Essays*, Notre Dame, IN: Notre Dame University Press. (Includes studies by Harry Wolfson, Alexander Altmann, Seymour Feldman, Larry Berman, and others, including some reprinted classics.)

Hartman, D. (1976) *Maimonides, Torah and Philosophic Quest*, Philadelphia, PA: Jewish Publication Society, 1976. (Seeks to overcome the polarity some find between Maimonides' rabbinic and his philosophical work.)

Katz, S. (ed.) (1980) *Maimonides: Selected Essays*, New York: Arno Press. (Reprints a number of classic essays, some of them now fairly inaccessible.)

Kellner, M. (1990) *Maimonides on Human Perfection*, Atlanta, GA: Scholars Press. (A careful examination of Maimonides' conception of the ultimate goal of human existence.)

Kraemer, J. (ed.) (1991) *Perspectives on Maimonides: Philosophical and Historical Studies*, Oxford: Oxford University Press. (Includes essays by Alfred Ivry, Warren Harvey, Arthur Hyman, Tzvi Langermann and others on Maimonides' logic, theology and jurisprudence, along with historical studies of his environment.)

Leibowitz, Y. (1987) *The Faith of Maimonides*, trans. J. Glucker, New York: Adama Books. (Monograph by a well-known exponent of Jewish legal positivism and fideism.)

* Narboni, Moses (1355–62) *Be'ur le-Sefer Moreh Nevukhim* (Commentary on Maimonides' *Guide to the Perplexed*), French trans. M.R. Hayoun, *Moshe Narboni*, Tübingen: J.C.B. Mohr, 1986. (The French translation is marred by an excessive attempt at literalism, but this volume provides valuable information about Narboni and a valuable text.)

Pelaez, J. (ed.) (1991) *Sobre la Vida y Obra de Maimonides*, Cordoba: Ediciones El Almendro. (Proceedings of a major international conference celebrating the 850th anniversary of Maimonides' birth.)

Pines, S. and Yovel, Y. (eds) (1986) *Maimonides and Philosophy*, Dordrecht: Kluwer. (Proceedings of an anniversary conference with papers by a number of distinguished scholars.)

Robinson, I., Kaplan, L. and Bauer, J. (1990) *The Thought of Maimonides: Philosophical and Legal Studies*, Queenston, Ont.: Edwin Mellen. (Another anniversary symposium gathering a representative sampling of recent work on Maimonides.)

Sarachek, J. (1935) *Faith and Reason: the Conflict over the Rationalism of Maimonides*, repr. New York: Hermon Press, 1970. (Wide-ranging study of the figures and issues of the 'Maimonidean controversy'.)

Silver, D.J. (1965) *Maimonidean Criticism and the Maimonidean Controversy, 1180–1240*, Leiden: Brill, 1965. (Reviews the same ground.)

Strauss, L. (1952) *Persecution and the Art of Writing*, Glencoe, IL: Free Press. (This brief collection of essays, including chapters on Maimonides, al-Farabi, and Spinoza, was the manifesto of Strauss' approach to the reading of esoteric texts. It spawned a cottage industry of exegesis, the lesser examples of which link laboured and mannered readings of texts with inferences or innuendoes about the cynical insincerity of their authors, among whom Maimonides remains a focal point of interest.)

Twersky, I. (1991) *Studies in Maimonides*, Cambridge, MA: Harvard University Center for Judaic Studies. (Papers by Shlomo Pines, Aviezer Ravitzky, Jacob Levinger, Moshe Idel, and Gerald Blidstein on the relationship of Maimonides' thought to law and mysticism and on his literary impact and communal role.)

L.E. GOODMAN

MAINE DE BIRAN, PIERRE-FRANÇOIS (1766–1824)

Maine de Biran claimed that the starting point for our understanding of human beings lay in introspective psychology: it was the awareness of willed effort. A proper understanding of the will should be the foundation of all work in psychology, including empirical psychology, as well as in the human sciences in general, which should work together towards a coordinated 'anthropology'. Contrary to the assumptions of associationist psychology, mental facts were essentially relational, and language was a constitutive feature of them, rather than being a secondary device intended to represent them. But conscious mental life arose from and was influenced by a subconscious underlayer which could be studied only by the joint use of physiological and introspective methods. Biran rejected the view that mental states can be reduced to, or are nothing other than, physical states. There was a partial 'symbolic' correspondence between them, which meant that physical accounts and mental accounts could not be translated into each other without loss. Later in his life, though still maintaining the belief that psychology was primary, he held that it was necessary to accommodate questions of metaphysics, morality and religion. He published very little during his lifetime, and many of the 'works' found in editions are (sometimes conjectural) editorial restitutions made from a jumbled mass of much corrected manuscripts. His failure to complete a single work on what the eighteenth century had called the 'Science of Man' (which he said was the greatest interest of his entire life) reflects the times: this eighteenth-century project was fragmenting into the multiplicity of human sciences which were emerging as the nineteenth century came. But his insistence on the primacy of the will remains a major challenge for the human sciences of today.

1 Life and works
2 Problems of the manuscript tradition
3 The mature position
4 Later views

1 Life and works

Pierre-François Gont(h)ier de Biran, French philosopher and public figure, was born at Bergerac in 1766. His father was a doctor. In 1785, after his schooling in Périgueux, he became a royal guardsman and in 1789 was wounded at the defence of Versailles. Though the Guards were dissolved in 1791, Biran (who by now was called 'Maine', a name acquired from a family estate at his majority) still envisaged a career in the military engineers, but this came to nothing. At the end of 1792, he retired to the estate of Grateloup, near Bergerac. At this time, reading was a main occupation and he wrote mainly notes or meditations, rather than works. He did begin a translation of Beccaria with a commentary and somewhat later a memoir on signs. But both these works were left incomplete, setting a pattern repeated throughout his life of intellectual work only sometimes carried to the point of completion.

Gouhier (1948) said of him that 'he was a one-book man – but he never wrote the book'. This book would have been an attempt to fulfil the eighteenth-century project of a 'Science of Man', and he worked at it constantly, once calling it 'the greatest interest of my entire life'. In earlier stages, his attention was focused on psychological topics. His memoir on habit (*Mémoire sur l'influence de l'habitude sur la faculté de penser*, 1803) received a prize from the Institut de France in 1802, and another reflecting the conception of mental science held by the *idéologues* (*Mémoire sur la décomposition de la pensée*, 1804) was awarded the prize in 1805. Publication of this work was stopped at the page-proof stage for mysterious reasons. A memoir on the data immediately present to consciousness (*De l'aperception immédiate*, 1807), replying to a question set by the Academy of Berlin, was awarded a prize in 1807. There followed a series of memoirs on much more specific topics delivered to the Medical Society of Bergerac, which Biran founded, the first on unconscious perception, the second on phrenology, and the third on sleep, dreams and somnambulism. Biran then returned to larger-scale work, with the memoir on the relations between body and mind (*Mémoire sur les rapports du physique et du moral de l'homme*, 1811), submitted to the Royal Academy of Copenhagen, which awarded him the first prize in 1811. In the same year, he signed a contract with a Paris publisher for the publication of revised versions of the memoirs of Berlin and Copenhagen. But he quickly changed his mind, speaking now of a single 'large work'. We know that he regarded this in 1811–12 as 'almost finished'. It concerned the foundations of psychology and its relations to the natural sciences (*Essai sur les fondements de la psychologie, et sur ses rapports avec l'étude de la nature*). But Biran came to think that metaphysical questions of a kind which he formerly disqualified now needed to be treated. This already emerges in a work allied in subject matter to the *Essai* (*Les rapports des sciences naturelles avec la psychologie*), which may have arisen as a reworking of the second part of the *Essai* and may be dated to around 1814. Within a year or two, Biran began to take a much stronger interest than before in questions to do with the nature of morality, and this further extension of interest put completion at a greater distance. In 1819, he congratulated himself in his diary on not having published 'anything definitive' yet, since the spiritual life now needed to be taken into account. In 1820, a specific project intervened. He revised the memoir of Copenhagen for the use of a doctor, Antoine-Athanase Royer Collard, who had consulted him in connection with a course on insanity (*aliénation mentale*) which Royer Collard was to give in the asylum of Charenton in the following year. At the same time, he signed another contract with the same publisher as before for the publication of this revised work, together with the memoir of Berlin, thereby reinstating the plan of ten years earlier. But the publication did not take place, and in 1822 Biran wrote in his diary of going back to his manuscripts and making a work from them which could shortly be published. Among his last attempts at this was a work on 'anthropology' in the broadest sense, with the title *Nouveaux essais d'anthropologie* (1823), now making explicit in the title itself the nature of Biran's ambition; but he died in 1824 without fulfilling his lifelong goal.

2 Problems of the manuscript tradition

The many thousands of surviving folios, often much corrected, present a fascinating spectacle of a mind at work, and a headache for subsequent editors, one of whom wrote in exasperation a generation after Biran's death of this 'atrocious scribble' ('affreux barbouillage'). The first editor was Victor Cousin (delegated by Biran's literary executor). He was careless and unscholarly, publishing only four volumes. The second initiative came from François-Marc Louis Naville, a Protestant pastor from Geneva who had met and admired Biran, and who was helped by his son Ernest. They collected about 12,000 pages of manuscript, and Ernest wrote 'what a task to bring light into this chaos!'. They did a considerable amount of work, recruiting various helpers, and published a version of Biran's *Essai sur les fondements de la psychologie*. The third editor was Pierre Tisserand, who produced between 1920 and 1949 an edition of Biran's works in fourteen volumes. Though incomplete and not very scholarly, it made available for the first time a wide and representative collection of texts. Henri Gouhier produced an edition of the philosopher's diaries between 1954 and 1957. Finally, a more scholarly thirteen-part edition (consisting of seventeen volumes) of the collected works was started in 1984, under the direction of François Azouvi. This edition, for the first time, makes it sufficiently clear to the reader that many of the 'works' of Biran were never regarded by him as complete, and that texts have often had to be established by editorial conjecture.

Why Biran completed (and published) so little has been a subject of discussion. A simple answer is that he was too busy with other things. He led an active public life, holding regional and national offices during the revolutionary period, under the consulate of Bonaparte, under the Empire of Napoleon and after the Restoration of the monarchy. Yet this answer seems too simple. Voutsinas diagnosed a deep narcissism in Biran: he avoided publication since he feared the wound of his work not being esteemed. Despite the somewhat obsessive character of Biran's constant revisions, additions, deletions and reorderings, it may be more enlightening to place his work in its broader intellectual context. For the 'Science of Man' was already being fragmented. Biran was thinking about these questions during the birth-pangs of neurophysiology, empirical psychology, social anthropology, economics, political science, linguistics and so on. He was well aware that his project demanded some way of coordinating all these emerging disciplines. He himself made a serious study of some of them. We also find attempts at tabulation. The core should be a reflective psychology which would recognize the will in a way which the British empiricists and their successors had failed to do, and the multiple empirical disciplines studying human nature should be related to and should depend upon this core. But he was never satisfied with his own attempts at seeing how they should fit together. In short, he was pursuing an objective which ran against the temper of the times. Arguably, he was trying to complete a task which, by its nature, could never be completed.

3 The mature position

Biran's philosophical work stands at a time of transition from the certainties of classical thought. Its character and content permit it to be seen in the context of the meditative tradition of such as Montaigne and Pascal, a tradition which gives prominence to the intimate workings of one's own mind. This is clear not only from the philosopher's personal diaries, but also in the central role which he gives to introspection or reflection in his mature theory. Those who see him in this light regard him as part of a lineage which leads to late nineteenth-century French 'spiritualism', illustrated by authors like Ravaisson. On the other hand, Biran allies himself strongly with the eighteenth-century empiricist tradition illustrated by authors like David Hartley, Condillac and Charles Bonnet. This emerges not only from his own avowals, but also from his account of the mind which, though diverging from those of his predecessors, is nevertheless clearly a successor to them. It is also associated with Biran's detailed interest in a variety of fields of empirical study, attested both by the contents of his library, and by the references made in his works. He was interested in physiology, psychiatry, penology, experimental psychology, hypnotism, linguistics, phrenology, ethnography, medicine, pedagogy. In the latter case, it may be noted that he corresponded with Pestalozzi, and appointed one of Pestalozzi's pupils to establish and run a school on Pestalozzian principles in Bergerac (see EDUCATION, HISTORY OF PHILOSOPHY OF §8). It would be insufficient however to give Biran only this double lineage, from the empiricist and the meditative traditions, for he also took an interest in the rationalists, writing on Leibniz. In addition, he read and reckoned with Kant.

It is the works of the first decade of the nineteenth century, culminating in the Essai, which develop the position in and about psychology for which Biran is especially known. He accepted what was regarded as a commonplace, that John LOCKE was the pioneer of mental science. But he held that Locke had made a number of crucial errors. Locke was right to hold reflection to be one of the two sources of knowledge, but wrong to think that it consisted in awareness of 'ideas' (a term newly adapted to mean 'mental representations'). This was to give rise to an essentially passive model of the mind. Perception became the simple reception of data, and action would be either the mechanical result of reception of such data (together with any internal mechanisms at work), or an arbitrary event mysteriously outside the world of causality (see PERCEPTION). This view gave rise to a series of problems which Biran thought that no one could answer, or had answered (including Kant). He held that the primary datum of consciousness was the awareness of willed effort (and, in particular, muscular effort) (see ACTION §4).

The inability of classical empiricism to give an adequate account of the will was illustrated by Hume's claim that the will is 'nothing but *the internal impression we … are conscious of, when we knowingly give rise to any new motion of our body*'. The circularity of this account is frequently criticized by Biran, who insists that what is given to consciousness is essentially relational. An example of a primary fact would be the awareness of raising one's arm. This cannot properly be decomposed into two elements – awareness of a volition and awareness of the arm going up – for then the relation will escape us. 'The inner sense has no object'. What is given is a *fact*, not an object. Of course, we can express our understanding of the fact by referring to the terms of a relation; but the relation is prior to these terms. When I raise my arm, the relation already exists in the effort exerted. It is not that there are two successive components of the experience, either of which might exist without the other.

It may seem that problems arise here. Is there not a causal process capable of empirical study, which consists of successive events in the nervous system which result in the arm going up? Biran conceded this: indeed, he took an active interest in physiology. But he rejected the reductionist view of mental events (see REDUCTIONISM IN THE PHILOSOPHY OF MIND). The relation between the awareness of raising one's arm and the physiological story was, he said, 'symbolic'. That is, the one story corresponded systematically but only partially to the other. Neither could be translated into the other without loss.

But if I can be aware of raising my arm, it seems that this presupposes knowledge. I must know that it is my arm that I am raising. This leads to another important difference between Biran and Locke. For Locke thought that ideas were prior to language, and that the function of language was simply to communicate them. Biran, by contrast, held that ideas could not exist without language. Thus a first deliberate raising of the arm is itself the birth of language, since it must bring into being the awareness of the arm. In so far as the movement itself expresses this awareness, it is a sign in the making.

But how can some creatures raise themselves by their bootstraps into a conscious life? Here, Biran departs both from the rationalist and from the empiricist traditions. For he maintains the existence of a passive underlayer of our experience, a great range of affective states which are capable of being drawn up into our conscious life, and which influence it. His interest in this is evidenced not only in his diaries, but also in his philosophical writings, where he discusses at length phenomena such as dreams. There was 'an inner New World to be discovered some day by a Columbus of metaphysics' (*Maine de Biran: Journal*, vol. 1: 176). Physiology and introspection would be needed to 'plunge into the underground caverns of the soul' (*Maine de Biran: Journal*, vol. 1: 240).

These, then, are the main features of Biran's mature position. The awareness of willed effort, a new distinction between passive and active, the crucial role of language, the relational nature of mental phenomena.

4 Later views

While elaborating these views, Biran usually held on to the rejection of 'metaphysics'; but he found increasingly that questions about the 'primitive facts' could not be properly treated without approaching metaphysical, moral and religious questions. His attempts at dealing with these questions can be seen in the generally more fragmentary works of the last decade of his life.

Near the end of his life, Biran reviewed what he had been doing in his diary, saying that he had come to:

> scorn everything that had previously been my main concern, and to which I had attached some importance and some glory, and I reproached myself for spending my life in erecting a mere scaffold...However, giving today the chief importance to man's relations with God and with the society of his fellows, I still think that a thorough knowledge of the relations of the *self* ... with the concrete person must precede in order of time or study all theoretical or practical research on these two first relations; it is experimental *psychology*, or a science at first purely reflective, that should lead us in due order to the determination of our moral relations with our fellows, and our religious ones with the infinite and higher being....
>
> (*Maine de Biran: Journal*, vol. II: 376)

Biran's partial disillusionment with his own work must be taken seriously: it plays a part in understanding why he completed so little. Yet it opened many very different paths to the future. His claim that mental states are essentially relational ('rien n'est dans la conscience qu'à titre de rapport',) prefigures phenomenology (see PHENOMENOLOGY, EPISTEMIC ISSUES IN). His claim that there is an internal relation between language and ideas prefigures contemporary critiques by analytic philosophers of the older empiricist tradition. His work coincided with and influenced the early development of empirical psychology. His meditative style prefigures French spiritualism. His claim that there is a new world of the unconscious to be explored by some Columbus versed in physiology and introspection prefigures Freud. And these are not merely points of historical interest. For the central role which he gives to the will, and the way in which he pursues it, are of great current importance, given that late twentieth-century debates about the nature of the mind, including those concerning the development of cognitive science, still often make assumptions which Biran decisively challenged two centuries earlier.

See also: INTROSPECTION, PSYCHOLOGY OF; WILL, THE

List of works

Most of the works of Maine de Biran were not published during his lifetime, and some were published for the first time more than a century and a half after his death.

Maine de Biran, P. F. (1766–1824) *Œuvres de Maine de Biran*, ed. F. Azouvi, Paris: Vrin, 1984–, 13 vols. (The most complete collection of Maine de Biran's works.)

—— (1766–1824) *Œuvres de Maine de Biran*, ed. P. Tisserand, Paris: Alcan and Presses Universitaires de France, 14 vols, 1920–49. (This was the first attempt at a comprehensive edition of the works of Biran. It is useful but unscholarly.)

—— (1766–1824) *Maine de Biran: Journal*, ed. H. Gouhier. Neuchâtel: Éditions de la Baconnière, 3 vols. (A valuable edition of most of Biran's surviving diaries. It does not include some 'private' materials which the Naville family in Geneva considered that they could not release, even many years after the death of Biran's last surviving blood relative.)

—— (1803) *Mémoire sur l'influence de l'habitude sur la faculté de penser*, Paris: Henrichs; trans. M.D. Boehm, *The influence of habit on the faculty of thinking*, Westport, CT: Greenwood Press, 1970. (A discussion of habit and thought.)

—— (1807) *De l'aperception immédiate* (On immediate awareness); repr. ed. J. Echeverria, *Maine de Biran: de l'aperception immédiate (mémoire de Berlin 1807)*, Paris: Vrin, 1963. (A work which emphasizes the priority of phenomenology in the 'study of man'.)

References and further reading

Azouvi, F. (1995) *Main de Biran: la science de l'homme* (Main de Biran: The Science of Man), Paris: Vrin. (A thorough treatment of Biran's approach to the 'science of man'.)

Baertschi, B. (1992) *Les rapports de l'âme et du corps: Descartes, Diderot et Maine de Biran* (The relationships between mind and body: Descartes, Diderot et Maine de Biran), Paris: Vrin. (A useful work, setting Biran's treatment of the mind/body question in a wider context.)

—— (1982) *L'Ontologie de Maine de Biran* (The Ontology of Maine de Biran), Fribourg: Éditions Universitaires. (An interesting but not elementary study of the ontological questions which arise from Biran's mature position.)

Boas, G. (1925) *French Philosophies of the Romantic Period*, Baltimore, MD: Baltimore. (One of the few studies in English. Approachable but superficial.)

Cresson, A. (1950) *Maine de Biran, sa vie, son œuvre* (Maine de Biran: His Life and Work), Paris. (An acceptable introductory work.)

Delbos, V. (1931) *Maine de Biran et son œuvre philosophique* (Maine de Biran and his Philosophical Work), Paris: Vrin. (A standard scholarly study.)

Fessard, G. (1938) *La Méthode de réflexion chez Maine de Biran* (The Reflective Method of Maine de Biran), Paris: Bloud. (A worthwhile exploration of the reflective method.)

Ghio, M. (1962) *Maine de Biran e la tradizione biraniana in Francia* (Maine de Biran and the Biran Tradition in France), Turin: Edizioni di Filosofia. (A fair introductory work for readers with good Italian.)

* Gouhier, Henri (1948) *Les Conversions de Maine de Biran*, Paris: Vrin. (The best overall study of Biran's work. It is not intended as introductory reading.)

—— (1970) *Maine de Biran par lui-même* (Maine de Biran by Himself), Paris: Editions du Seuil. (An excellent introduction to Biran for the interested layman.)

Hallie, P.P. (1959) *Maine de Biran, Reformer of Empiricism, 1766–1824*, Cambridge, MA: Harvard University Press. (An adequate introduction to Biran's philosophy for the reader who requires a text in English.)

Henry, M. (1965) *Philosophie et phénoménologie du corps (essai sur l'ontologie biranienne)* (Philosophy and Phenomology of the body (Essay on the Ontology of Biran)), Paris: Presses Universitaires de France. (An essay of some interest written from a phenomenological point of view.)

Lacroze, R. (1970) *Maine de Biran*, Paris: Presses Universitaires de France. (This overview need not be neglected.)

La Valette Monbrun, A. de (1914) *Maine de Biran: essai de biographie*, Paris: Fontemoing. (This is the only biography, and is therefore mentioned here in spite of the fact that it is unscholarly and unsatisfactory.)

Lemay, P. (1936) *Maine de Biran et la Société Médicale de Bergerac* (Maine de Biran and the Medical Society of Bergerac), Paris, Liège. (A worthwhile study of Biran's Medical Society, and his contributions to it.)

Le Roy, G. (1937) *L'Expérience de l'effort et de la grâce chez Maine de Biran* (The Experience of Effort and of Grace in Maine de Biran), Paris: Boivin. (Takes up Biran's later interest in the spiritual life as a higher passivity.)

Montebello, P. (1994) *La décomposition de la pensée: dualité et empirisme transcendantal chez Maine de Biran* (The Deconstruction of Thought: Duality and Transcendental Empiricism in Maine de Biran), Grenoble: Millon. (Interprets Biran's position as a form of transcendental empiricism.)

Moore, F.C.T. (1970) *The Psychology of Maine de Biran*, Oxford: Clarendon Press. (A critical review of Biran's mature position, from a broadly analytic perspective. Contains a useful bibliography.)

Paliard, J. (1925) *Le Raisonnement selon Maine de Biran* (Reasoning according to Maine de Biran), Paris: Alcan. (A useful study of Biran's view of reasoning.)

Rhomeyer-Dherbey, G. (1974) *Maine de Biran, penseur de l'immanence radicale* (Maine de Biran, Thinker of Radical Immanence), Paris: Segers. (This study may be read with some profit.)

Truman, N.E. (1904) *Maine de Biran's Philosophy of Will*, New York: Macmillan. (This, in spite of various defects, is a quite useful and approachable work for the reader requiring a text in English.)

Vancourt, R. (1944) *La Théorie de la connaissance chez Maine de Biran* (The Theory of Knowledge in Maine de Biran), Paris: Aubier, 2nd edn. (A good study of Biran's epistemology.)

Voutsinas, D. (1964) *La Psychologie de Maine de Biran* (The Psychology of Maine de Biran), Paris: SIPE. (A somewhat eccentric diagnosis of Biran, which nevertheless has points of interest.)

F.C.T. MOORE

MAIR, JOHN *see* MAJOR, JOHN

MAJOR, JOHN (1467–1550)

John Major was one of the last great logicians of the Middle Ages. Scottish in origin but Parisian by training, he continued the doctrines and the mode of thinking of fourteenth-century masters like John Buridan and William of Ockham. Using a resolutely nominalist approach, he developed a logic centred on the analysis of terms and their properties, and he applied this method of analysis to discourse in physics and theology. Although he came to oppose excessive dependence on logical subtlety in theology and maintained the authority of Holy Scripture, Major's work was stubbornly independent of the growing influence of humanism in Europe. Later, he would be regarded as representative of the heavily criticized 'scholastic spirit', being referred to disparagingly by Rabelais as well as by later historians such as Villoslada (1938), but at the beginning of the sixteenth century, his teaching influenced an entire generation of students in the fields of logic, physics and theology.

1　Life
2　Logic
3　Natural philosophy, theology and history
4　Influence

1　Life

John Major (or Mair) was born in 1467 at Gleghornie near Haddington in Scotland. He began his studies at Haddington, and after a period at Cambridge, went to Paris. He received his MA in 1494, and in 1495 began to teach as a regent master at the College of Montaigu. In 1506 he became a Doctor of Theology. In 1518 he returned to Scotland where he was principal of the University of Glasgow, as well as teaching logic and theology. From 1523 to 1526 he taught logic and theology at the University of St Andrews. Returning to Paris in 1526, he re-edited his works on logic, as well as publishing commentaries on Aristotle's *Physics* (1526) and *Nicomachean Ethics* (1530), and on the four Gospels (1529). In 1533 he became Provost of St Salvator's College at St Andrews, and remained there until his death in 1550.

2　Logic

Although in the last period of his life at St Andrews Major was regarded as a great authority in theology, he first became famous as a logician. Between 1499 and 1506 he published a large number of logical works, later published as a collection. These works included commentaries on Aristotle and on PETER OF SPAIN, treatises on terms and their properties, on

exponibles, consequences, insolubles and obligations (see LOGIC, MEDIEVAL).

John Major was trained by the masters who had taken part in the revival of nominalism in the last twenty-five years of the fifteenth century, especially Thomas Bricot, who edited the logic of John BURIDAN (§2). John Major himself edited John Dorp's early fifteenth-century commentary on Buridan in 1504, and he also edited the logic of the young Spaniard Jerónimo Pardo (d. 1502 or 1505). In his own logical works, his approach was that of a terminist. He accorded a central place to the study of the properties of terms in propositions, particularly their different types of reference, a subject which was thought to be indispensable for avoiding errors of reasoning. This approach goes back to the great synthesizers of the thirteenth century, especially Peter of Spain who was the favourite reference point for the Parisian masters, but it culminated at Paris with the work of John Buridan who placed the study of terms in a nominalist context. In this Major remained faithful to Buridan, often referring to and explicitly adopting 'the solution of the nominalists'.

Major's logic presupposes a theory of spoken and conceptual signs which owed a great deal to WILLIAM OF OCKHAM (§§6–7). In his treatises on terms, John Major assumed the fundamental presupposition of late medieval logico-linguistic analysis: a term is a sign, and as a logico-linguistic sign, it can only be contemplated in the context of a general semiotic theory. Having defined a sign generally as that which is taken in place of a thing, Major departed from Buridan to assume a position closer to that of Ockham or ALBERT OF SAXONY. For him, a spoken sign refers in a proper and primary way to a thing and not, as Buridan had held, to a concept. It is none the less necessary to take into account the properly conceptual components of signification, and so John Major gave a very detailed analysis of the different types of referential relation between the word, the concept, and the thing signified. In this context, he gave a long analysis of the *sophisma* or puzzle case, *debeo tibi equum* ('I owe you a horse'), explaining the different positions which had become standard, namely those of William of Ockham, William HEYTESBURY, and the one Major preferred, that of John Buridan. This involves distinguishing between the contexts in which a thing is owed under a certain description (the 'appellation of reason'), and those contexts in which direct reference is made to a particular object.

There were very lively debates during this period about the structure of mental language, and John Major developed a theory of mental language close to that of Pierre d'Ailly (see AILLY, P. D'), in which signifying, thinking and representing have a tendency to be assimilated to one another. Following an idea due to GREGORY OF RIMINI, Major admitted that there were two types of mental language, one of which is the image of spoken language, while the other forms mental language properly so-called. He criticized Ockham's view that synonymy as well as some accidental characteristics, such as grammatical gender, could form no part of mental language.

John Major is a witness to the continued life and capacity for innovation of logic at the University of Paris at the beginning of the sixteenth century. He sometimes shows a tendency to wordiness, and in his hands theories become over-refined and over-complicated. However, this complication primarily shows his desire to take into account the difficulties which had become apparent in the course of the two previous centuries, while continuing to make use of terminist and nominalist principles of analysis.

3 Natural philosophy, theology and history

In his commentary on the *Physics* of Aristotle (see ARISTOTLE §8), John Major followed the initiatives of John BURIDAN (§4) and MARSILIUS OF INGHEN (§3) by reformulating problems of natural philosophy on the basis of an analysis of propositions. At the same time, he showed an interest in gathering observations of natural phenomena. In his treatise *De l'infini* (On the Infinite), added to his logical works in 1506, he took up the distinction between categorematic and syncategorematic senses of the term 'infinite' which had been popularized by Buridan, and he defended the existence of an actual infinite (see NATURAL PHILOSOPHY, MEDIEVAL).

John Major was also a theologian. His commentary on the *Sentences* of Peter LOMBARD, published in various versions from 1509, was considered by the humanists as representative of a theology which used logic too broadly, introduced too many properly philosophical considerations, and made too regular appeal to Aristotle and Averroes (see IBN RUSHD §§2, 5). It is true that Major, who relied heavily on the commentary by GREGORY OF RIMINI did, like Gregory, include a great deal of logic and philosophy in his theological discussion. None the less, he recommended a moderate attitude on this point. He affirmed the primacy of Holy Scripture, and criticized the excessive use of dialectical subtleties in the study of Scripture. He himself distinguished scholastic theology from positive theology, by which he seems to have meant the more legalistic and moralistic developments of religious teaching.

In religion Major seems to have been animated by the desire to reconcile orthodoxy with the critical approach of nominalism. He regretted the fact that some of his students turned towards the Reformation, and for his part he defended fidelity to dogma and submission to the Catholic Church. In his *In Mattheum ad literam expositio* (Literal Exposition of Matthew) (1518), and then in his commentary on the four Gospels (In quator evangelia expositiones) (1529), he firmly defended the Roman Catholic Church against the theories of WYCLIF, HUS (§4) and LUTHER.

In his politico-ecclesiastical works, however, he showed the influence of the Gallican and conciliarist traditions. He limited the power of the Pope in temporal matters, and above all he defended the superiority of church councils over the Pope on the grounds that the fullness of power resides in the church itself, as represented by a council (see POLITICAL PHILOSOPHY, HISTORY OF §§4, 8).

His *History of Greater Britain*, published in 1521, studies the history of Scotland as parallel to the history of England, and recommends a bringing together of the two kingdoms. The work is written in a critical manner, rejecting a number of traditional stories.

4 Influence

Major's teaching gave birth to a whole school. His pupils (the Spaniards Luis and Antonio Coronel, Gaspar Lax, the Scotsmen Robert Cuubralth, David Cranston, George Lokert, the Belgian Peter of Brussels and John Dullaert, among others) carried on the teaching they had received at Montaigu. While in theology some of them, such as Patrick Hamilton (who was burned for heresy at St Andrews in 1527) and the famous reformer John Knox, embraced Protestantism, in logic most were faithful to nominalism. However, the intellectual climate was to change, especially in Paris, becoming hostile to logical subtleties. Not only did interest develop in languages and rhetoric, but polemical texts called into question the very principles of the logical and scientific developments of the preceding centuries. The work of John Major was done just before this break in tradition, and his merit is that he assured the last hours of glory for the old forms of thought at the University of Paris, with a force that allowed it to continue for a while in Scotland and in Spain.

See also: BURIDAN, J. §§2–3; LANGUAGE, MEDIEVAL THEORIES OF; LANGUAGE, RENAISSANCE PHILOSOPHY OF §§1–2; LOGIC, MEDIEVAL; LOGIC, RENAISSANCE; NOMINALISM §2

List of works

Major, J. (1506a) *Le Traité 'De l'infini' de Jean Mair* (John Major's Treatise 'On the Infinite'), ed. H. Élie, Paris: Vrin, 1938. (Modern edition of *De l'infini* with translation into French.)

—— (1506b) *Libri quos in artibus in collegio Montis acuti parisius regentendo compilavit* (The books which John Major put together while teaching arts at the College of Montaigu in Paris), Paris. (This collection of nineteen logical works was reprinted, with some additions and changes, in 1508, 1513 and 1516. There are also a great many early editions of individual works: for details see Farge 1980.)

—— (1518) *In Mattheum ad literam expositio* (Literal Exposition of Matthew), Paris: Jean Granjon.

—— (1521) *A History of Greater Britain, as well England as Scotland*, trans. A. Constable, Edinburgh: Scottish History Society, 1892. (English translation.)

—— (1529) *In quator evangelia expositiones* (Commentary on the Four Gospels), Paris: Josse Bade.

References and further reading

Biard, J. (1986) 'La logique de l'infini chez Jean Mair' (The Logic of the Infinite in John Major), *Études philosophiques* 3: 329–48. (Study of the relations between logic and physics in Major's treatise *De l'infini*.)

Broadie, A. (1985) *The Circle of John Mair: Logic and Logicians in Pre-Reformation Scotland*, Oxford: Clarendon Press. (Thematic study of logical theories at the time of John Major and his pupils.)

Burns, J.H. (1954) 'New Light on John Major', *Innes Review* 5: 83–100. (Detailed bibliography of Major's works.)

Élie, H. (1951) 'Quelques Maîtres de l'université de Paris vers 1500' (Some Masters of the University of Paris Around 1500), *Archives d'histoire doctrinale et littéraire du moyen âge* 18: 193–242. (Presents the life and career of fifteenth- and sixteenth-century philosophers, with special emphasis on Major.)

Farge, J.F. (1980) *Biographical Register of Paris Doctors of Theology 1500–1536*, Toronto, Ont.: Pontifical Institute of Mediaeval Studies. (A very useful reference work for the biography of many early sixteenth-century philosophers. Includes a biography and bibliography of Major on pages 304–11.)

Oakley, F. (1961–2) 'On the Road from Constance to 1688: the Political Thought of John Major and George Buchanan', *The Journal of British Studies* 1 (2): 1–31. (Discusses parallels between Major's conciliarism and the case of secular rulers.)

—— (1965) 'Almain and Major: Conciliar Theory on the Eve of the Reformation', *The American Historical Review* 70: 673–90. (Study of the theory of the primacy of a general council over the pope.)

Renaudet, A. (1918) *Préréforme et humanisme à Paris (1497–1517)* (The Pre-Reformation Movement and Humanism in Paris), Paris: Libraire d'Argences; 2nd edn, 1953; repr. Geneva: Slatkine, 1981. (Contains a chapter on John Major, in the context of a study of the general evolution of ideas at the end of the fifteenth century and the beginning of the sixteenth century.)

* Villoslada, R. (1938) *La universidad de Paris durante los estudios de Francisco de Vitoria, O.P. (1507–1522)* (The University of Paris during the Studies of Francisco de Vitoria), Rome: Gregorianum. (Referred to in the introduction. Chapter 6 is devoted to John Major, from a point of view very critical of scholastic thought.)

Translated by E.J. ASHWORTH

JOËL BIARD

MALEBRANCHE, NICOLAS (1638–1715)

Nicolas Malebranche (1638–1715), a French Catholic theologian, was the most important Cartesian philosopher of the second half of the seventeenth century. His philosophical system was a grand synthesis of the thought of his two intellectual mentors: Augustine and Descartes. His most important work, De la recherche de la vérité *(The Search After Truth), is a wide-ranging opus that covers various topics in metaphysics, epistemology, ethics, physics, the physiology of cognition, and philosophical theology. It was both admired and criticized by many of the most celebrated thinkers of the period (including Leibniz, Arnauld and Locke), and was the focus of several fierce and time-consuming public debates. Malebranche's philosophical reputation rests mainly on three doctrines. Occasionalism – of which he is the most systematic and famous exponent – is a theory of causation according to which God is the only genuine causal agent in the universe; all physical and mental events in nature are merely 'occasions' for God to exercise his necessarily efficacious power. In the doctrine known as 'vision in God', Malebranche argues that the representational ideas that function in human knowledge and perception are, in fact, the ideas in God's understanding, the eternal archetypes or essences of things. And in his theodicy, Malebranche justifies God's ways and explains the existence of evil and sin in the world by appealing to the simplicity and universality of the laws of nature and grace that God has established and is compelled to follow. In all three doctrines, Malebranche's overwhelming concern is to demonstrate the essential and active role of God in every aspect – material, cognitive and moral – of the universe.*

1   Life and works
2–3 Vision in God
4   Occasionalism
5   Ethics
6   Philosophical theology
7   Influence

1 Life and works

Nicolas Malebranche was born in Paris on 6 August 1638, one of the many children of Catherine de Lauzon and Nicolas Malebranche, a royal secretary. Because of a malformation of the spine which caused lifelong pain, he was kept at home for his education, under the direction of his mother, until the age of sixteen. In 1656, he graduated from the Collège de la Marche. The education he received there, and from three years studying theology at the Sorbonne, was heavily laden with Aristotelianism, and it left Malebranche highly dissatisfied. After rejecting the offer of a canonry at Notre-Dame de Paris, Malebranche entered the Oratory in 1660 and was ordained in 1664.

His four years in the Oratory proved to be of great intellectual consequence. While studying the Bible, ecclesiastical history and Hebrew, Malebranche, like other Oratorians, immersed himself in the writings of AUGUSTINE. There were also Cartesians among his teachers, who introduced him to the doctrines of DESCARTES. He did not read any of Descartes' works, however, until 1664 when he happened upon a copy of Descartes' *Treatise on Man* (*L'homme*) in a bookstall. The event was life-changing: according to his biographer, Father André, the joy of becoming acquainted with so many discoveries 'caused him such palpitations of the heart that he had to stop reading in order to recover his breath'. Malebranche devoted the next ten years of his life to studying mathematics and philosophy. He was particularly taken by Descartes' critique of the Aristotelian philosophy that he had earlier found so stultifying and sterile (see MEDIEVAL PHILOSOPHY).

Those ten years of study culminated in the publication in 1674–5 of *De la recherche de la vérité* (The Search After Truth), Malebranche's first and most ambitious work and a synthesis of the systems of Augustine and Descartes. Malebranche's stated goal

in the *Recherche* is to investigate the sources of human error and to direct us towards the clear and distinct perception of truth – truth about ourselves, about the world around us and about God. His motives are deeply theological, and he is ultimately concerned to demonstrate the essential and active role of God in every aspect – material, cognitive and moral – of the created world. The *Recherche*, quickly supplemented by seventeen *Eclaircissements*, contains early but solidly-argued presentations of Malebranche's three most famous doctrines: the vision in God, occasionalism and his theodicy.

While the Abbé Simon Foucher, canon of Sainte Chapelle of Dijon, was the first in a long line of critics of Malebranche's doctrines, the Jansenist theologian and Cartesian philosopher Antoine Arnauld was undoubtedly the harshest and most acute (see FOUCHER, S.; ARNAULD, A. §3). Arnauld approved of the *Recherche* upon first reading it. But when he later learned of Malebranche's views on grace and divine providence – sketchily presented in the *Recherche* but more fully expounded in the *Traité de la Nature et de la Grace* (Treatise on Nature and Grace) in 1680 – he embarked on a detailed critique of the major theses of the *Recherche*. Arnauld's *Des vraies et des fausses idées* (1683), and Malebranche's reply, *Réponse du Père Malebranche au livre des vraies et des fausses idées* (1684), were only the opening salvos in what would come to be a long, often bitter public battle on both philosophical and (to the participants more importantly) theological matters. Although Arnauld's allies succeeded in having the *Traité* put on the Index Librorum Prohibitorum in 1690 (the *Recherche* was added in 1709), their exchanges – public and private – continued until Arnauld's death in 1694. The debate, one of the great intellectual events of the seventeenth century, attracted the attention of Leibniz, Spinoza, Bayle, Locke, Newton and many others.

After the publication of the *Recherche*, Malebranche turned to a 'justification' of the Catholic religion and morality, presented in suitably Malebranchian terms and published as the *Conversations Chrétiennes* in 1676. This was followed in 1683 by the *Médiations Chrétiennes et Métaphysiques*, which consists of dialogues in which 'the Word' explains and defends Malebranche's system. That same year Malebranche also published his *Traité de Morale* in which he undertakes a rigorous demonstration of a true Christian ethics.

By the mid-1680s, Malebranche was widely regarded as the most important, if highly unorthodox, representative of the Cartesian philosophy. His regular correspondents included Leibniz and the physicist Pierre-Sylvain Régis. With Leibniz he debated the

Cartesian account of the laws of motion (Malebranche published his *Traité des lois de la communication du mouvement* in 1692), as well as occasionalism and the nature of causal relations. With Régis, who defended a more orthodox brand of Cartesianism, he discussed natural philosophy and the nature of ideas (see LEIBNIZ, G.W. §11; RÉGIS, P.-S.).

Having been forced in his arguments with Arnauld, Régis and others to clarify, develop and even modify his doctrines, Malebranche decided, at the urging of friends, to compose a treatise in which he would both present an up-to-date and concise picture of his theories and defend them as a proper Augustinian (and Catholic) system. The *Entretiens sur la métaphysique* (Dialogues on Metaphysics) were published in 1688 and were supplemented in 1696 by the *Entretiens sur la mort*, which Malebranche wrote after an illness from which he did not expect to recover. In 1699, he was elected to the Académie Royale des Sciences.

During the last fifteen years of his life, Malebranche remained actively engaged in philosophical, theological, and scientific matters, publishing the *Entretien d'un philosophe chrétien et d'un philosophe chinois, sur l'existence et la nature de Dieu* in 1708 and his *Réflexions sur la prémotion physique* in 1715. He also continued to work on the *Recherche*, producing the sixth edition, the last to appear in his lifetime, in 1712. In June 1715, Malebranche became ill while visiting a friend in Villeneuve St. Georges. He was taken back to the Oratory in Paris, where he died on October 13.

2 Vision in God

Malebranche's system is fundamentally Augustinian, and he was inspired by Descartes' philosophy not just because of the scientific and mathematical discoveries he found there but especially because of its own Augustinian nature. He tried to be as faithful as possible to Augustine's thought while at the same time incorporating into his doctrines what he took to be the important metaphysical and epistemological insights of the new mechanistic science. This is particularly evident in his theory of ideas and account of human knowledge.

Nearly all philosophers in the seventeenth century agreed that perception and knowledge is mediated by immaterial representations immediately present to the mind, after Descartes generally called 'ideas'. There was much disagreement, however, over the origin and ontological status of these ideas: How do ideas become present to the mind? Are ideas 'modifications' of the mind? Are they *acts* of the mind or the *objects* of perception? Malebranche's doctrine of the vision in God was the most unorthodox and controversial

theory of ideas in the period. He looked back to the Christian-Platonic and Augustinian model, according to which ideas proper are archetypes or essences in the divine understanding. Human beings have access to these ideas, which serve as the ground of all eternal truths, through a continuous process of illumination that informs their cognitive powers.

Malebranche orients his discussion of ideas and knowledge in the *Recherche* around the problem of error, particularly the errors that arise when we base our judgments on the testimony of the senses and the imagination, rather than on reason and understanding. He relies in his analysis of error on what is probably the most comprehensive and systematic account of the physiology of sense and imagination in the seventeenth century. For example, based upon a detailed investigation into the structure of the eye and the geometry of optics, he argues that our sight does not present to us the extension of external bodies as it is in itself, but rather only as it is in relation to our body. He describes the eye as a kind of 'natural spectacles', and examines the ways in which the material images conveyed into the brain (and thus the sensory images these stimulate in the soul) are variously affected by the distance between the eyes, the different humours in the eyes, the shape of the crystalline lens and its distance from the retina, and other factors. The difference between sensation and imagination is due simply to the fact that in imagination the tiny fibres in the centre of the brain are agitated not by the impressions made by external objects on the exterior surface of the nerves, but by the flow of the animal spirits initiated by the soul itself. These animal spirits are easily affected by the changing state of the body and by external things, as well as by 'moral' causes (prejudices, 'conditions of living'). The imagination thus represents a second important source of the differences between minds and how things are represented to them. Malebranche's goal in highlighting how the senses and the imagination 'lead us into error' is to warn us not to allow their images to serve as a basis for judgment about the truth of things. We should rely, rather, on the testimony of reason and the perfect evidence of clear and distinct ideas.

Malebranche's account of the nature of ideas is grounded in the basic dualist framework of Cartesian ontology. Mind, or thinking substance, is unextended thought, and has absolutely nothing in common with matter, defined as extension. A material body has only the mathematical properties of shape, size, divisibility and mobility. All other sensible qualities – colour, heat, cold, taste, odour and so on – are really only sensations in the mind, mental modifications occasioned by external material objects. While such sensations may indicate to us the presence of bodies to our own body, they cannot provide us with clear and distinct knowledge of those bodies. Sensations can only inform us of what is presently taking place in our own minds; they have no representational value with respect to the external world. Malebranche claims, however, that in addition to our own inner sensations we have access to representative ideas. Ideas, unlike qualitative sensations, have a clear and distinct representational content – generally of a quantitative nature – and provide us with unambiguous and complete knowledge about objects and their properties. The idea of the square, for example, presents with perfect evidence all the information needed for full knowledge of the geometric properties of squares. On the other hand, the heat one feels when near a fire is simply an obscure sensation that reveals nothing about the nature of fire itself as an extended reality. Malebranche's ideas are pure concepts, and their content has no sensory component whatsoever. They just are the logical essences of things or kinds. His epistemological distinction between ideas and sensations derives from Descartes' distinction between clear and distinct ideas and obscure, confused ideas. It roughly corresponds to the distinction made famous by Boyle and Locke between primary quality ideas and secondary quality ideas (see BOYLE, R.; DESCARTES, R. §8; LOCKE, J. §4).

This epistemological difference between ideas and sensations is, for Malebranche, grounded in an ontological one. While sensations are mental, ideas are not. Representative ideas are 'present to the mind', but they are not modifications of the mind's substance. (Their presence is what allows them to represent extended beings to the mind.) Rather, they are in God, and finite minds have access to them because God wills to reveal them to those minds, all of which exist in a perpetual union with God. That ideas do not belong to the mind becomes clear from the fact that some of our ideas are infinite, and it is impossible for a finite mind to have an infinite modification. Likewise, our ideas are all general – they only become particular or specific when combined with some sensory components – and a particular substance such as the mind cannot have a modification that is general.

Ideas function in all of the mind's cognitive activities; most importantly, in conception and perception. In conception, the mind apprehends a pure idea by itself, without any sensations to particularize the experience (for example, conceiving a geometric circle). In perception, ideas are present but are accompanied by various sensory elements. Thus, when we perceive the sun, the pure idea of a geometric circle is accompanied by colour (yellow) and heat sensations.

Malebranche offers two kinds of argument to demonstrate that representative ideas are required for knowledge and perception. First, he argues that there is generally an unbridgeable distance between the mind and its objects. He sometimes appears to mean this literally, and to be relying on the fact that the mind is not locally present to the external bodies it knows and sees, and that in cognition it is neither the case that objects travel to the mind or that the mind leaves the body to 'travel across the great spaces' that separate it from its objects. His more considered intention, however, is probably to draw our attention to the metaphysical, rather than the physical gulf that separates mind from matter: bodies, being extended, cannot be united with, and thus present to, the unextended mind in the way required for direct cognitive acquaintance. Thus, what is required are intermediary entities that can both represent extended bodies and be immediately present to the mind: ideas.

Second, it is often the case that we have a perceptual experience of an object when in fact the object itself does not actually exist (for example, in hallucinations and dreams). But Malebranche insists upon the truth of the principle of intentionality, or the claim that every perception must be object-directed – 'to perceive is to perceive something' (see INTENTIONALITY). As Malebranche understands this principle, every perception must be the direct and immediate apprehension of some really present object. As the illusory cases illustrate, however, the intentional objects of the mind cannot be really existing material bodies; for if they were, we could never have perceptual experiences of objects that do not exist. Thus, it must be that we directly apprehend ideas, non-material representations, even though sometimes there is no external body corresponding to the idea.

3 Vision in God (cont.)

Malebranche's position is that the ideas that function in human perception and knowledge are simply the ideas – the eternal essences and archetypes – in the divine understanding: that 'we see all things in God'. In the *Recherche* itself, he relies mainly on an argument from elimination. He shows how all other accounts of the source of our ideas – the Scholastic and Epicurean doctrines, various Cartesian theories (innatism, self-production by the soul) – are untenable, thus leaving the vision in God as the only viable alternative (see EPICUREANISM). But in this work and others, he also marshals more positive considerations in support of his doctrine. His account, he insists, is simpler than any other hypothesis (hence more worthy of God's ways), and best fosters a proper and pious sense of our ontological and epistemological dependence upon our creator: we as knowers and perceivers are not self-sufficient, no more than we as beings are self-sufficient substances.

In the *Eclaircissements* appended to the *Recherche*, Malebranche's debt to Augustine becomes more overt. For Augustine, what we see in God are eternal and immutable truths. Truth is, by its nature, changeless, universal and uncreated. Moreover, truth is higher than, and common to, many minds. Hence, it can be nowhere but in the divine reason, in God himself (in Augustine's words, truth *is* God) (see AUGUSTINE §§6–7). For Malebranche, too, truth is necessarily universal, immutable and infinite. But the truths we know just are relations between ideas. Thus, the ideas themselves must be universal, immutable, and infinite. And such ideas can only be those in God's understanding. The vision in God is the only possible explanation for our common knowledge of necessary truth – we are all similarly united with one universal, infinite Reason, in which we perceive the same ideas.

Malebranche's doctrine of the vision in God is motivated, then, not just by the problem of how we perceive bodies in the external world – a specifically Cartesian concern – but primarily by the problem of how we have knowledge of eternal truths. And behind it all lies Malebranche's deep fear of the dangers of scepticism. The vision in God represents for Malebranche the most effective countersceptical strategy available. First, we can be sure that the ideas we apprehend in sense-perception really do represent bodies in the world because these ideas just are the archetypes that served and directed God in creating those bodies. Thus, they cannot fail to reveal the nature of extended things as they are. On the other hand, if ideas were, as many Cartesians insist, merely fleeting and subjective modifications of the soul, there would be no justification for believing that what they represent about bodies in the world really characterizes those bodies. This would seriously undermine the certainty of physics. Second, any sceptical worries about the necessity, universality and objectivity of mathematical and moral knowledge are forestalled by showing that the ideas upon which such knowledge is based are mind-independent (non-subjective) realities, accessible to all knowers in a universal Reason.

To be sure, there are many relevant questions that the doctrine of vision in God cannot, and is not intended to, answer. For example, while the ideas we apprehend in God inform us as to the essences of things, they cannot provide any evidence about the existence of things. Certainty in this regard can only come about through a combination of faith and sensory experience. This is not to say that Malebranche is a sceptic when it comes to the existence of the external world. Although he claims that we cannot have rational and demonstrative certainty about the existence of a world of things, we still have no good reasons to doubt of it, as well as a natural propensity to believe in it. Nor does the vision in God provide us with a clear and distinct idea of the soul, which would make possible a science of the soul as certain as our science of bodies (physics) based on the idea of body. Our knowledge of the soul is limited to the testimony of *sentiment intérieur*, to what we actually experience in consciousness, and Malebranche rejects Descartes' claim that we know the soul as well as (or even better than) the body.

The vision in God is a systematic attempt to combine the doctrine of divine illumination that Malebranche found in Augustine with a somewhat deviant Cartesian metaphysics and philosophy of mind. The theory is deeply Augustinian in inspiration, but is geared also to answer certain epistemological questions that really only arise in the seventeenth century.

As Malebranche's contemporary critics were quick to point out, the doctrine was fraught with ambiguities and inconsistencies. For example, if there is a single immutable idea in God for each object or kind of object he created, how is it that we perceive change and motion in extended things? In the *Eclaircissements* Malebranche denies that he ever meant that there is a plurality of individual, discrete ideas in God. He insists that there is in God an 'infinite intelligible extension', and that by applying our minds to this extension in various ways we apprehend representations of different extended bodies in different states of being.

Foucher, in one of his criticisms of Malebranche, focused on the ontological status of ideas. If ideas are spiritual, but are not substances, then they must be modifications of some spiritual substance. Malebranche denies that they are (he insists that they are neither modifications of our minds nor of the divine substance), but then what else can they be? And if they are not 'ways of being' of our minds, then they must be as external to our minds as anything else and not 'present' to the mind in the manner required for direct cognition. Foucher also asks how immaterial ideas could possibly represent material bodies that they do not resemble (see FOUCHER, S. §3).

Arnauld argued that the whole notion of ideas as representative beings, distinct from the mind's perceptions and which are in fact the mind's objects in perception, is false and even incoherent. Ideas, Arnauld insisted, are not distinguished from the mental acts (he calls them *perceptions*) which represent objects to the mind but are not themselves distinct objects. He claims that Malebranche's theory, far from explaining how we perceive bodies external to us, actually demonstrates that we never perceive such bodies, and that the mind is surrounded by a 'palace of ideas' beyond which it has no cognitive access. Arnauld also focused in his attack on Malebranche's doctrine of the infinite intelligible extension, and wonders how Malebranche can avoid the charge of materialism, of having placed extension really (that is, 'formally') in God and thus making God himself extended (see AR-NAULD, A. §3). This point is taken up in Spinozistic terms by Dortuous de Mairan, a young man whom Malebranche had once tutored. Mairan was impressed by Spinoza, and he challenged Malebranche both to refute Spinoza's arguments and to show how the relationship between the infinite intelligible extension in God and the material extension of bodies differs from the substance/affection (or mode) relationship that for Spinoza characterizes the relationship between infinite extension and particular bodies (see SPINOZA, B. §§2–3).

4 Occasionalism

Just as the doctrine of the vision in God demonstrates the epistemological dependence that we as knowers have upon God, so the causal doctrine of occasionalism demonstrates the ontological dependence that we and *all* beings have upon an omnipotent God (see OCCASIONALISM). Nothing, it claims, exists or happens in the universe that is not a direct and immediate effect of the divine will. Although occasionalism has its ancestry in certain medieval Islamic, Jewish and Christian theories of causation and divine omnipotence, especially the voluntarist tradition (see AL-GHAZALI; DAMIAN, P.), as well as in Descartes' metaphysics; and while there were others before Malebranche who were, to one degree or another, occasionalists (see CLAUBERG, J.; CORDEMOY, G. DE; GEULINCX, A.; LA FORGE, L. DE), Malebranche was the first to argue systematically for a thoroughgoing and rigorous version of the doctrine.

Occasionalism is the doctrine that all finite created entities are absolutely devoid of causal efficacy and that God is the only true causal agent. God is directly, immediately and solely responsible for bringing about all phenomena. When a needle pricks the skin, the physical event is merely an occasion for God to cause the appropriate mental state (pain); a volition in the soul to raise an arm or to think of something is only an occasion for God to cause the arm to rise or the idea to be present to the mind; and the impact of one billiard ball upon another is an occasion for God to

move the second ball. In all three contexts – mind–body, mind alone and body–body – God's ubiquitous causal activity proceeds in accordance with certain general laws, and (except in the case of miracles) he acts only when the requisite material or psychic conditions obtain.

Far from being an *ad hoc* solution to a Cartesian mind–body problem as it has traditionally been portrayed, occasionalism is argued for by Malebranche (and others) from general philosophical considerations of the nature of causal relations, from an analysis of the Cartesian concept of matter and, perhaps most importantly, from theological premises about the essential ontological relationship between an omnipotent God and the created world that he sustains in existence.

Malebranche's first argument that there are no real causal powers in finite created substances and that God is the sole causal agent, focuses on the motion of bodies. He begins with the causal principle that in order for one thing, A (which can be a substance or a state of being of a substance), to count as the cause of another thing, B, there must be a necessary connection between the existence of A and the existence of B. 'A true cause as I understand it is one such that the mind perceives a necessary connection [*liaison nécessaire*] between it and its effects' (1674–5 vol. 2: 316). But we can find no such connection between any two physical events, nor between any human mental event and a corresponding physical event. For example, it is certainly conceivable that one can will to raise one's arm but the arm will not rise. 'When we examine our idea of all finite minds, we do not see any necessary connection between their will and the motion of any body whatsoever. On the contrary, we see that there is none and that there can be none' (1674–5 vol. 2: 313). When we consider God, however, as an infinitely perfect being, we see that there *is* such a necessary connection between the divine will and the motion of bodies, since it is logically impossible that an omnipotent God should will to move a body and it does not move; such is the nature of omnipotence. God, therefore, is the only true cause of the motion of bodies.

Malebranche's second argument is based on the 'inconceivability' that any natural cause, any finite mind or material body, should have 'a force, a power, an efficacy to produce anything' (1674–5 vol. 3: 204). First, an idea of body – that is, the clear and distinct idea of extension – represents it as having only one property: the entirely passive faculty of 'receiving various figures and various movements' (1688: 148). It certainly does not represent body as having any active power. Here Malebranche is drawing out the ramifications of Descartes' conception of matter: a Cartesian material body, *qua* pure extension, is essentially passive and inert, and devoid of any motive force. In fact, such a force or power is perceived as *incompatible* with the notion of extension, since it cannot be reduced to or explained in terms of relations of shape, divisibility and distance. Thus, bodies cannot *act*, whether on minds or other bodies. Second, whatever minimal knowledge I have of my soul does not involve the perception of any power, whether to move the body or even to produce its own ideas. All I perceive through inner consciousness is an actual volition to move my arm upwards, and all I notice in my body is that my arm subsequently rises. But I do not perceive, either by inner consciousness or by reason, any power on the part of the soul by means of which it might effect this motion. It is in this sense that 'those who maintain that creatures have force and power in themselves advance what they do not clearly perceive' (1674–5 vol. 3: 204). Indeed, according to Malebranche, I perceive a general incompatibility between the idea of a created finite being and such a power or productive faculty. Only in my idea of the will of an infinite being do I clearly and distinctly recognize any element of power whatsoever.

The third argument is based on a supposedly intuitive premise which (echoing an argument for occasionalism introduced by Geulincx) sets an epistemic condition on the notion of 'cause': in order to count as the cause of an effect, a thing must know how to bring about that effect. Malebranche then appeals to the evident fact that this condition is not satisfied by our minds in order to show that we do not, in fact, cause those motions that we consider voluntary: 'There is no man who knows what must be done to move one of his fingers by means of animal spirits' (1674–5 vol. 2: 315). This same condition rules out the mind's ability to produce its own ideas. It also rules out, *a fortiori*, the possession of causal efficacy by bodies.

Malebranche's most general argument against real interaction appeals to God's role as creator and sustainer of the universe. The argument – which has its roots in both medieval and Cartesian doctrines – purports to show that it is an 'absolute contradiction' that anything besides God should move a body. God's activity is required not only to create the world, but, since creatures are absolutely dependent on God, to sustain it in existence as well. Indeed, for God there is no essential difference between creating and sustaining: 'If the world subsists, it is because God continues to will that the world exist. On the part of God, the conservation of the creatures is simply their continued creation' (1688: 316). When God conserves/recreates a body, he must recreate it in some particular place and in some relation of distance to other bodies. If God conserves it in the same relative place from moment to moment, it remains at rest; if God conserves it successively in different places, it is in motion. But this means that God is and can be the *only* cause of motion: 'The moving force of a body, then, is simply the efficacy of the volition of God who conserves it successively in different places…. Hence, bodies cannot move one another, and their encounter or impact is only an occasional cause of the distribution of their motions' (1688: 162). And finite minds are no more causes of motion than bodies are.

Thus, God is the direct and efficacious cause of every event in nature; finite beings are only 'secondary' or 'occasional' causes. Malebranche's doctrine can be seen as embedded within a voluntarist tradition that extends from certain medieval thinkers – many of whom attacked the Aristotelian theory of nature in the name of safeguarding God's omnipotence – up through Descartes (see VOLUNTARISM).

This does not mean that for Malebranche natural philosophy has been reduced to a single theocratic claim. At the level of physics proper, the task of the scientist is still to uncover regularities in nature and formulate the laws that govern the correlations between events. The programme of the mechanical philosophy, to which Malebranche enthusiastically subscribes, remains the same: to discover the hidden mechanisms that underlie observed phenomena and to frame such explanations (referring to secondary causes) solely in terms of matter and motion. What Malebranche's occasionalism does is to give an account of the metaphysical foundations of Cartesian physics. Motion, the primary explanatory element in the new science, must ultimately be grounded in something higher than the passive inert extension of Cartesian bodies; it needs a causal ground in an active power or force. Because a body consists in extension alone, motive force cannot be an inherent property of bodies. Malebranche accordingly – and his account seems to be a logical extension of the role Descartes gives to God as the 'universal and primary cause of motion' (see DESCARTES, R. §§6, 11) – places the locus of force in the will of God, and bodies behave the way they do because that is how God moves them around, following the laws of nature he has established.

Malebranche did, in fact, use his metaphysics of motion to modify some details of Descartes' physics, particularly the rules governing bodily impact. This led to an extended debate with Leibniz over the laws of motion. In the *Recherche* Malebranche insists, contrary to Descartes, that bodies at rest do not have a force to remain at rest (unlike bodies in motion, which have a force to remain in motion). This conclusion follows directly from his occasionalist account of motion: although God does need to will positively to put a body in motion, he does not need to apply any force to keep it at rest; all he needs to do is will that it continue to exist, that is, recreate it in the same relative place. Thus, the tiniest body in motion will contain more force than the largest body at rest. And this means that three of Descartes' seven rules of impact are wrong. Leibniz, in his general critique of Cartesian physics, praised Malebranche for recognizing Descartes' errors. He insisted, however, that because Malebranche was still wedded to Descartes' conservation law (where what is conserved is quantity of motion, rather than the quantity of motive force that Leibniz proposed), Malebranche has failed to see that *all* except the first of Descartes' rules, along with the new rules he had substituted for the ones he rejected, were wrong (see LEIBNIZ, G.W. §11). In 1692, Malebranche published his *Des lois de la communication des mouvements*, in which he concedes that Leibniz is right about the rules themselves, but continues to maintain the old conservation law. It was not until a letter to Leibniz in 1699 and the 1700 edition of the *Recherche* (which contains a revised version of *Des lois*) that Malebranche admits that Descartes' conservation law is false.

5 Ethics

For Malebranche, God's ubiquitous causal activity does not eliminate freedom of the will in human beings. God is the direct source of an invincible inclination or 'natural motion' in the soul towards good in general. We cannot not will to be happy, and we necessarily love what we 'clearly know and vividly feel' to be good. But it is in our power to allow or to refuse to allow this general determination towards good given to us by God to rest upon one or another of the particular things we believe to be good. All minds, he notes, love God 'by the necessity of their nature', and if they love anything else, it is by a free choice of their will. We sin when, rather than directing the will by a clear and distinct perception of the supreme good to the love of God, we allow it to be directed away from God towards the pleasing but false goods presented to us by our senses.

In the *Traité de morale* (1683b), Malebranche elaborates on just what this love of God involves, providing a fuller account of our ethical duties. Within God, there lies an immutable order or law which God consults when acting. This order is constituted by what Malebranche calls 'relations of perfection', which in turn entail a hierarchy of value among beings. Order dictates, for example, that a

beast is more perfect, hence more worthy or 'estimable' than a rock, and a human being more perfect and worthy than a beast. A human being is thus to be treated with more consideration than a horse. Through our 'union with the eternal word, with universal reason' we can have rational knowledge of order. Our duty, then, consists in 'submitting ourselves to God's law, and in following order'. We ought, like God, to regulate our actions and esteem by consulting it. In this way, 'there is a true and a false, a just and an unjust' that is binding upon *all* intelligent beings. Malebranche insists that our principal duty and our 'fundamental and universal virtue' is to love order and obey its precepts.

6 Philosophical theology

Malebranche's occasionalism takes on greater importance in the context of his theodicy, or justification of God's ways in the realms of nature and grace. In his *Traité de la nature et de la grace* (1680), Malebranche undertakes the task of explaining how God's omnipotence, benevolence and perfection can be reconciled with the persistence of evil and imperfections in the natural world (including human suffering and sin) and with the apparent unfairness and inefficiency in the distribution of divine grace and everlasting happiness.

Our concept of God tells us that God is infinitely wise, good, powerful and perfect. And yet the world which God has created certainly appears to us to be quite imperfect in its details and full of disorders of every variety. As Theodore, Malebranche's spokesman in the *Entretiens sur la métaphysique*, exclaims, 'The Universe then is the most perfect that God can make? But really! So many monsters, so many disorders, the great number of impious men – does all this contribute to the perfection of the universe?' (1688: 211). Aristes, his interlocutor, is led thereby to wonder either about the efficacy of God's will or the benevolence of God's intentions.

The resolution of this conundrum, as presented in both the *Entretiens* and the *Traité*, is to be found in the consideration not just of the particular, superficial and obvious details of the universe, but also of the means undertaken to achieve and sustain the whole. God, according to Malebranche, looks not only to the final result of his creative act (that is, to the goodness and perfection of the world *per se*), but also to his work or ways of operation. And the activity or means most expressive of God's nature are of maximum simplicity, uniformity, fecundity and universality. God does not accomplish by complex means that which can be accomplished by simple means; and God does not execute with many particular volitions that which can be executed by a few general volitions. This holds true even if it means that the world created by God could be spared some imperfections were God to compromise the simplicity and generality of his operations. Thus, the perfection of the world in its details as a product is completely relative to the mode of activity that is most worthy of God. God might increase the absolute perfection of the world, perhaps by decreasing the number of defects or evils therein. But this would entail greater complexity in the divine ways and constant departures from the general laws of nature established at creation.

Thus, the world that God has created is the one of the infinitely many possible worlds that best reconciles perfection of design with simplicity and generality of means of production and conservation. By a number of 'particular volitions' – that is, volitions that are *ad hoc* and not occasioned by some prior event in accordance with some law of nature – God could correct deformities of birth, keep fruit from rotting on trees, prevent physical disasters about to occur by the regular course of the laws of nature, and forestall sin and wickedness. But, Malebranche insists, 'we must be careful not to require constant miracles from God, nor to attribute them to him at every moment' (1680: 34). God, in other words, acts only by 'general volitions' – that is, volitions that are in accordance with some law and whose operation is occasioned by a prior event, as dictated by that law – and the most simple ways.

Similar considerations apply to the problem of grace. A benevolent God wills, with what Malebranche calls a 'simple volition', that sinners convert and that all humans should be saved. But clearly not all humans are saved; many are lost. And not all those who are saved appear to be worthy of salvation or ready to receive grace. The anomaly is again explained by the generality of God's volitions. The distribution of grace is governed by certain general laws willed by God, and the occasional causes responsible for the actual distribution of grace in accordance with those laws are the thoughts and desires in the human soul of Jesus Christ. Because Jesus *qua* human has finite cognitive capacities, he cannot at any given time attend to all the relevant facts about the agent upon whom grace is to be bestowed – for example, whether they are ready to make the best use of it – or actually think of all who deserve to be saved. Thus, as with the distribution of evil and imperfection in the natural world, God *allows* grace to be distributed unevenly and even inequitably by the laws of grace in combination with the occasional causes that activate them.

It was the *Traité*, with its claim that God wills to save all humans and the implication that God's volitions are not always efficacious (since not everyone is saved), that initially aroused Arnauld's ire and occasioned his attack on Malebranche's whole system. Arnauld, as a Jansenist, was committed first and foremost to a strong doctrine of predestination and to the efficacy of divine volitions, particularly in the matter of grace. Pierre BAYLE rallied to Malebranche's defence on this and other issues, and the pages of Bayle's *Nouvelles de la république des lettres* in the 1680s became an important battleground for the debates instigated by Malebranche's works.

7 Influence

Malebranche's influence in the seventeenth and eighteenth centuries was significant, but subtle and often unacknowledged. There is no question that his contemporaries recognized him as *the* major representative of the Cartesian system, however unorthodox his Cartesianism may have been. Leibniz's arguments against 'the Cartesians', for example, are often directed at Malebranche. And yet, despite his criticisms of occasionalism, Leibniz was himself impressed by Malebranche's discussion of causation and critique of interaction between substances. Moreover, Leibniz's own theodicy and solution to the problem of evil were clearly influenced by what he read in Malebranche. Like Malebranche, Leibniz insists that God in creation chooses from an infinity of possible worlds, and that God pays particular attention not just to the created theatre itself, but especially to its relationship with the laws of nature and grace. Malebranche considers the laws as separate from 'the world', and gives them a higher value. He grants that the world God created may not be, absolutely speaking, the best of all possible worlds, but it is the best that can be done given the absolute simplicity of means God employs. Leibniz, on the other hand, considers the laws and the universe they govern together as 'the world', and insists that the combination *is* the best world overall. But they agree that evil and sin occur because God *allows* them to occur as a result of the ordinary course of nature as governed by the laws God has chosen. They agree that God could diminish the imperfections of the created world, but only by violating the simplicity of the divine ways (as Malebranche would put it), or by detracting from the *overall* optimality of the world (as Leibniz would say). Leibniz even goes so far as to suggest to Malebranche that, in the end, their accounts are the same, although Malebranche disagrees.

Malebranche's influence extended across the Channel (and not just to such overt followers as John

NORRIS). Despite Berkeley's indignant claim that 'there are no principles more fundamentally opposed than his [Malebranche's] and mine', there are obvious echoes of Malebranche's doctrines in Berkeley's works (see BERKELEY, G. §2). For example, Berkeley's ideas, like Malebranche's ideas, are not modifications of the finite mind but are independent of it. They are also in the mind of God, since it is 'an infinite spirit who contains and supports' the world of ideas. Similarly, with respect to causation, Berkeley denies that our ideas of bodies provide us with any notion of causal power or efficacy. And while Berkeley departs from Malebranche's doctrine and grants real causal power to the human soul (and thus is not a complete occasionalist), he insists, like Malebranche, that the ordinary course of natural phenomena, the regularities and correspondences in our ideas of things, are the result of the causal activity of the will of a governing spirit, that is, God.

HUME was more forthcoming in acknowledging his debt to Malebranche in his conclusions about causality. His arguments denying that our idea of body affords us any notion of causal power and his insistence that all that experience reveals is a constant conjunction between events seem to come right out of Malebranche's *Recherche*. Both Hume and Malebranche stress the centrality of the concept of necessary connection to our understanding of causation, and both deny that such necessity can be discovered (by reason or experience) between any things in nature. The difference is that Malebranche held that we can perceive a necessary connection between the will of God and any event willed by God, while Hume rejected any such claim.

List of works

Malebranche, N. (1958–67) *Oeuvres complètes de Malebranche* (Complete works of Malebranche), ed. A. Robinet, Paris: J. Vrin, 20 vols. (The standard edition of Malebranche's writings. The main philosophical works are in the volumes listed below.)

—— (1674–5) *De la recherche de la vérité*, in *Oeuvres*, vols 1–3, 6th edn, 1712; trans. T. Lennon and P.J. Olscamp as *The Search After Truth/Elucidations of the Search After Truth*, Columbus, OH: Ohio State University Press, 1980. (Malebranche's most important philosophical work. Vol. 3 of the *Oeuvres* contains the *Éclaircissements*.)

—— (1676) *Conversations chrétiennes* (Christian conversations), in *Oeuvres*, vol. 4. (A 'justification' of the Catholic religion and morality.)

—— (1680) *Traité de la nature et de la grace*, in *Oeuvres*, vol. 5; trans. P. Riley as *Treatise on Nature and Grace*, Oxford: Oxford University Press, 1992.

(Malebranche's theodicy and account of human freedom.)

—— (1683a) *Méditations chrétiennes et métaphysiques* (Christian and metaphysical meditations), in *Oeuvres*, vol. 10. (A reworking of his metaphysical and epistemological doctrines including the vision of God.)

—— (1683b) *Traité de morale* (Treatise on morality), in *Oeuvres*, vol. 11. (A treatise in Christian ethics and human happiness.)

—— (1684–94) *Recueil de toutes les réponses à M. Arnauld* (Collection of all the responses to M. Arnauld), in *Oeuvres*, vols 6–9. (Contains correspondence related to the Malebranche–Arnauld debate, as well as Malebranche's *Réponse* to Arnauld's *Des vraies et des fausses idées*, and some other pieces.)

—— (1688) *Entretiens sur la métaphysique et sur la religion*, in *Oeuvres*, vol. 12; trans. W. Doney as *Dialogues on Metaphysics*, New York: Abaris, 1980. (A presentation, in dialogue form, of Malebranche's doctrines c. 1688, after some development since the *Recherche* in the light of various debates.)

—— (1692) *Traité des lois de la communication du mouvement*, in *Oeuvres*, vol. 2. (A critique of Descartes' account of the rule of impact.)

—— (1696) *Entretiens sur la mort*, in *Oeuvres*, vol. 13. (A continuation of the dialogues on metaphysics concentrating on death and the soul.)

—— (1708) *Entretien d'un philosophe chrétien et d'un philosophe chinois* (Dialogue between a Christian philosopher and a Chinese philosopher), in *Oeuvres*, vol. 15. (Christian apologetics.)

—— (1715) *Réflexions sur la prémotion physique* (Reflections on physical premotion), in *Oeuvres*, vol. 16. (Malebranche's response to Abbé Boursier on God's action on creatures.)

References and further reading

Alquié, F. (1974) *Le Cartésianisme de Malebranche* (The Cartesianism of Malebranche) , Paris: J. Vrin. (An examination of what Malebranche inherits from orthodox Cartesianism and what he modifies or rejects.)

André, Y. (1886) *La vie du R. P. Malebranche, prêtre de l'Oratoire, avec l'histoire de ses ouvrages* (The life of Father Malebranche, priest of the oratory, with the history of his works), Paris; Geneva: Slatkine Reprints, 1970. (Written in the first half of the eighteenth century; still the standard source on Malebranche's life.)

* Arnauld, A. (1683) *Des vraies et des fausses idées*; trans. E. Kremer as *On True and False Ideas*, Lewiston, NY: Edwin Mellon Press, 1990; also

trans. S. Gaukroger, Manchester: Manchester University Press, 1990. (Arnauld's attack on Malebranche's theory of ideas and doctrine of the vision in God.)

Brown, S. (ed.) (1991) *Nicolas Malebranche: His Philosophical Critics and Successors*, Assen: Van Gorcum. (A collection of essays on Malebranche, his influence, and his contemporary and later critics.)

Church, R.W. (1931) *A Study in the Philosophy of Malebranche*, London: Allen & Unwin. (A valuable general study of Malebranche's philosophy.)

Dreyfus, G. (1958) *La volonté selon Malebranche* (The will according to Malebranche), Paris: J. Vrin. (A thorough account of Malebranche on the divine will and the human will.)

Easton, P., Lennon, T. and Sebba, G. (1991) *Bibliographia Malebranchiana: A Critical Guide to the Malebranche Literature 1638–1988*, Edwardsville, IL: Southern Illinois University Press. (A comprehensive bibliography covering both Malebranche and his friends and critics.)

Gouhier, H. (1948) *La philosophie de Malebranche et son expérience religieuse (The philosophy of Malebranche and his religious experience)*, Paris: J. Vrin. (An examination of some essential Malebranchian doctrines and their theological aspects.)

Gueroult, M. (1955) *Malebranche*, Paris: Aubier, 3 vols. (An exhaustive and masterly study of Malebranche's system.)

Jolley, N. (1990) *The Light of the Soul: Theories of Ideas in Leibniz, Malebranche, and Descartes*, Oxford: Clarendon Press. (Examines Malebranche's theory of ideas, especially in comparison to Descartes' and Leibniz's accounts.)

McCracken, C. (1983) *Malebranche and British Philosophy*, Oxford: Clarendon Press. (Looks at the way Malebranche's philosophy was variously assimilated and criticized in early modern British philosophy; chapters on Locke, Berkeley and Hume.)

Nadler, S. (1992) *Malebranche and Ideas*, New York: Oxford University Press. (An analysis of Malebranche's theory of ideas and doctrine of the vision in God.)

Prost, J. (1907) *Essai sur l'atomisme et l'occasionalisme dans la philosophie cartésienne* (Essay on atomism and occasionalism in Cartesian philosophy), Paris: Henry Paulin. (A fine study of occasionalism and its roots in Descartes' philosophy, with several chapters on Malebranche.)

Radner, D. (1978) *Malebranche: A Study of a Cartesian System*, Assen: Van Gorcum. (A useful general and analytical presentation of Malebranche's doctrines.)

Robinet, A. (1955) *Malebranche et Leibniz: relations personelles* (Malebranche and Leibniz: personal relations), Paris: J. Vrin. (A valuable resource that contains correspondence and other documents concerning the mutual relations between Malebranche and Leibniz.)

—— (1965) *Système et existence dans l'oeuvre de Malebranche* (System and existence in the work of Malebranche), Paris: J. Vrin. (One of the most important studies of Malebranche's philosophy, with emphasis on its development.)

Rodis-Lewis, G. (1963) *Nicolas Malebranche*, Paris: Presses Universitaires de France. (A general account of Malebranche's life and thought.)

Walton, C. (1972) *De la recherche du bien: A Study of Malebranche's Science of Ethics*, The Hague: Martinus Nijhoff. (An analysis of Malebranche's moral philosophy, concentrating on his account of virtue and duty.)

STEVEN NADLER

MAMARDASHVILI, MERAB KONSTANTINOVICH (1930–90)

Merab Mamardashvili was one of the Soviet Union's most influential thinkers in the fields of phenomenology and philosophy of consciousness. Although he preferred the Socratic genres of the dialogue, interview and philosophical meditation to the abstract rigours of more systematic philosophy, he left substantial published work on Descartes, Hegel, Kant and French literature (especially Proust).

Mamardashvili began his career as a historian of philosophy, with a series of close readings of Karl Marx. By the 1970s he had evolved his own distinctive style of 'philosophizing out loud', addressing the foundations of European philosophy based on Descartes and Kant, at the core of which was the search for the 'free phenomenon' (svobodnyi fenomen) or the 'event of a thought' (sobytie mysli). In Kantian fashion, Mamardashvili attended to those a priori conditions of lived experience which govern that moment when reality enters the transcendental realm – but he switched the emphasis: rather than the mental problems presented by the a priori moment, Mamardashvili concentrated on what he called a 'metaphysics of the a posteriori', that is, on the actual event, or advent, of a thought. Perhaps the single motivating question of his life was: 'How is a new thought possible?' Among his many answers, developed in public lectures and interviews during the last twenty years of his life, was the notion that the very processes of thought provoke 'hearing a thought' in another. From this follows his concern with dialogic forms and his interest in the Cartesian dualism of soul and body – not as a necessary truth but as a 'productive tautology' that makes internal reason and a 'grammatical' analysis of thinking possible on a palpable basis.

1 Life
2 Critical works
3 'Philosophizing' versus 'Russian' philosophy
4 Contribution to the performing arts and practical aesthetics

1 Life

Mamardashvili was born in Gori, Soviet Georgia (the birthplace of Stalin), to a military family. After residence in Leningrad and Kiev, the family resettled in Tbilisi in 1941, where he finished high school; he then entered the Department of Philosophy at Moscow State University, graduating in 1954 and receiving his candidate's degree (Ph.D.) in 1957. Always more interested in the nature of human consciousness as *experience* rather than as system or theory, Mamardashvili did not immediately attach to an academic institution. After working as editor for the journal *Voprosy filosofii* (Questions of Philosophy), he spent 1961–6 in Prague as editor of *Problems of Peace and Socialism*; upon his return to Moscow he lost his rights to travel (managing to visit his beloved France only in 1988). At this time Mamardashvili began delivering lectures (or *besedy*, 'conversations', as he preferred to call them) in various institutes to students of philosophy, psychology, pedagogy, theatre and cinematography. In 1970 he defended his doctoral dissertation in Tbilisi; he worked in that city and in Moscow until his sudden death at the age of 60.

Disciples of his thought are very active in post-communist Russia, especially in the Laboratory for Post-Classical Studies (of the Institute of Philosophy, Russian Academy of Sciences), pursuing questions of symbolic consciousness, history of science and theory of creativity. Among his most prominent students are Aleksandr Piatigorskii, Mikhail Ryklin, Anatolii Akhutin and Mamardashvili's archivist Iurii Senokosov.

2 Critical works

Mamardashvili's genre was the interview, the lecture series, the roundtable discussion, which enabled what he called '*filosofstvovanie vslukh*', 'philosophizing out loud'. In his meditations on Kant, Mamardashvili defined *filosofstvovanie* as a 'sensual and palpable turn of the soul, a feeling for ideas', which was always

prompted by an 'element of life, not of theory' ([1982b] 1991: 150). As one of Mamardashvili's most prolific students, Mikhail Ryklin, has remarked, oral speech for Mamardashvili was like improvisation for a jazz musician: to emerge at all, his most creative ideas needed a live listener present. Mamardashvili did not write 'for the drawer' because, in his words, he 'utterly lacked any consciousness of persecution' and preferred talking to writing (1990a: 178).

3 'Philosophizing' versus 'Russian' philosophy

Mamardashvili did not believe that one could be a 'national philosopher'. He was no partisan of the Russian Religious-Philosophical Renaissance (in this he resembles Pëtr Chaadaev rather than Nikolai Berdiaev or Vladimir Solov'ëv); in his lectures on Proust, he remarked that 'one of the ideas that had ruined Russian culture at the beginning of the century was the theurgical idea, the notion that the world had been created so that life itself could be constructed like a work of art' (Kruglikov 1994: 111). He charged the radical intelligentsia with '"dirty", littered consciousness and slovenly thinking' (1990a: 132); and even the *Vekhi* (Signposts) opposition, in his opinion, was too partial to endless acts of repentance. Mamardashvili's attitude towards religion was complex. In his 'Besedy o myshlenii' (Conversations about Thinking) (1986–7), discussing the sophisticated forms of French secular and sacred language, he remarked that 'the language of religion is necessary in order to distinguish a person striving towards the good from a [simply] good person' – a distinction that arrives very late in 'infantile cultures' such as the Russian, and when it does (Mamardashvili says, agreeing with Dostoevskii), it goes unnoticed, causes anguish and often generates evil ([1986–7] 1991: 25).

In general we do not think enough about *how we think*, nor about the consequences of an act of thought. Russia was especially deficient in this talent, eager to use words but unwilling to accept results; thus it has been in the 'hellish condition' of a country of 'eternal pregnancy' ([1987] 1990: 372). Descartes and Pushkin were exemplarily honest thinkers in this sense, Mamardashvili believed, as men who became free by accepting responsibility for control over their own words and gestures (Kruglikov 1994: 20–3); Dostoevskii was less so, for, in some of his preconceptions – his odd assumption, for example, that to be poor was *ipso facto* to be simple and honest – he challenged the sensible workings of the mind ([1986–7] 1991: 26). Ideas themselves, in the structure of consciousness, are so 'complex, delicate and multi-layered' that we should 'tremble from fear before the responsibility' of handling them (1990a: 130). As

Ryklin sums up his teacher's position: on the one hand, 'in his work, all of philosophy becomes ethics'; on the other, 'ethics itself is presented exclusively in the form of a theory of cognition' (*Voprosy filosofii* (1991) 5: 21).

Mamardashvili did not believe that ideas were ever produced by the 'masses'. For culture is assimilated individually and cannot be collectivized or generalized. By 'culture', Mamardashvili understood not a set of guidelines or fixed values, but rather a 'definitiveness of *form* within which people were capable (and prepared), through their acts, to practise *complexity*' (1990a: 173). Accordingly, Mamardashvili's recurring concerns were individual autonomy; the necessity to keep separate the empirical and the non-empirical worlds (Mamardashvili resisted all utopian and apocalyptic models of history); a more modest societal role for art and the literary word ('art for art's sake' is more democratic, he felt, than prophetic or socially committed art (1990a: 127)); how to achieve 'civilization', the major binding force or grammar uniting highly independent and particularized minds; and, underlying all these concerns, the mechanism of thinking itself.

Mamardashvili's major questions and modes of thought nevertheless reflect the Russian philosophical tradition in three ways. First, like his heroes Descartes and Tolstoi, he directs his insights on consciousness and morality not to academic philosophers but to untrained minds seeking clarification in everyday language. Second, he draws on great literature as primary material for philosophical speculation – and indeed, he sees no firm boundary between art and this type of 'science'. And third, his subject matter is grounded not in formal logic or abstract systems but rather evolved under the inspiration of several exemplary creative figures in European culture: Hegel, Kant, the early Marx, Descartes, Husserl, Proust, Kafka and Mandelstam.

Mamardashvili devoted dozens of 'conversations' to the meaning of philosophy itself. It is not a science, he claimed, nor is it a picture of the world. In an interview near the end of his life (1990), published under the title 'Solitude is my Profession', Mamardashvili defines the philosophical moment as 'a shard from the broken mirror of universal harmony, fallen into the eye or the soul', 'an allegory for the passion of freedom' (Kruglikov 1994: 64). Elsewhere Mamardashvili explains that such freedom is in fact a necessity: for only the rational epiphany of a newly coalesced thought can reverse natural law and move from death to life (otherwise, the cosmos would have long ago contained only inert matter). But this epiphany is not religious; religion elicits from us a worshipful response and we can suspend its acts passively, indefinitely, within a system of faith. Philosophy, on the other hand, is an interval, a 'pause that is essential to the structure of the life of consciousness, essential to human acts'.

Thus philosophy is a place – or an attitude – that we occupy when we have the courage to say 'I do not understand'. It does not judge content (good and evil, right or wrong), and it does not 'fill up'; like moral conscience, it is best defined as a form and a dynamics, an inner reflex that, once stimulated, will *not turn away*; and thus it exists eternally and its problems repeat forever. (Following Socrates, Mamardashvili insists that to exist, philosophy – like virtue – must be accomplished again and again; whereas evil can register its effects by happening only once.) We philosophize when our consciousness is exacerbated by a sudden break or discontinuity between itself and its surroundings; in order to mend that break we must commit to an effort to think honestly or honourably (*myslit' chestno*). This is extremely difficult to do; and for this reason, Mamardashvili considered Descartes and Kant among the greatest European philosophers.

When Mamardashvili delivered his *Kartezianskie razmyshleniia* (Cartesian Meditations) in Moscow in the winter of 1981, it marked, according to one eyewitness, the rebirth of professional philosophical thought in the Soviet Union. Through the medium of Descartes, these fifteen meditations reintroduced the themes of faith, the possibility of God within a rationalist universe, the 'miracle of individual thought', and the centrality of epistemology to any primary philosophy. In his opening lectures, Mamardashvili declared that 'for thought, the worst enemy is the *past*'; knowing that every mental image becomes more concrete, precise and manageable the less it is actually present, Descartes filled his own 'Meditations' and 'method' with the word 'now'. This was welcome balm to his Soviet audience, weary of Marxist-Leninist surrogates for the present tense. In his final lecture, Mamardashvili gently chided both the Russian tradition of the radical intelligentsia and the revived clichés of Russian religious thought through the sobering lens of Cartesian thinking – with its methodical doubt, its separation of body and spirit, its assumption (and here Mamardashvili also drew on Proust) that too many 'serious conversations' were a 'waste of time' and better worked out in solitude. On Christ's crucifixion, Mamardashvili remarked that

> 'the cross is an ironic reminder to us that we need not herd people into an image, inasmuch as this image, within our heads, is capable of killing. And there are cultures and even whole epochs when

MAMARDASHVILI, MERAB KONSTANTINOVICH

people love the dead most of all, because the dead can no longer exit from their own image and thus they speak only that which we speak ourselves'

([1991] 1993: 341)

4   Contribution to the performing arts and practical aesthetics

This fascination with the rights and possible reconstitution of a genuine *present* lies behind Mamardashvili's interest in the theatre and visual temporal art (he was a frequent lecturer at theatre training institutes); and, as he wrote in *Teatr* magazine in 1989, 'the theatrical stage is a place for the "presence of absent reality"' (1990a: 138). It also permeates his 1982–4 lectures on Proust. Among the major themes in those lectures are the 'indivisibility of presence' (Kruglikov 1994: 114), the nature and degree of energy required to awaken ourselves from habit, and the phenomena of 'aroused attention' and memory. How, indeed, does a 'thought' or a 'desire' start? What does it mean to actualize a part of the past towards this end?

'Spontaneous memory' occurs in us in response to an apparently arbitrary summons. But, Mamardashvili asks, can we *command* ourselves to experience something strongly, to love, to be aroused, to be upset or to be riveted in place? The Proustian moment – being triggered by a present triviality into re-experiencing a profound past reality – Mamardashvili calls the 'zone of helplessness' (Kruglikov 1994: 94). It is a finicky and subtle state. If we try to force it, then the memory-experience is almost always negative: it feels empty, and we feel at a loss. For any mental gesture that does not provide the potential for a free supplement from the present, that is only a forced calling-up of the past, is a void that will be filled with illusion. Mamardashvili interprets the folksaying *'Sviato mesto pusto ne byvaet'* ('A sacred space is never empty') to mean that evil always settles in emptiness; the Good demands fullness, that is, a responsive act from us in return. When this condition is not met, we have negative memory: that which summons us in the absence of an active and sentient present. Mamardashvili concludes that for Proust (and for him), our life is real to the extent that a precious event in it is *created anew by thought* (Kruglikov 1994: 97). Ending one of his lectures on 'What is Philosophy?' with a discussion of Proust's novel, Mamardashvili noted:

(The text of the novel is the means by which feelings can be experienced.) Not those that *you* experience... but you-as-an-other, recreated, fixed in time and space, posited by a movement of

decoding, which does not depend on the chance happenings of life and in which you can establish yourself as a person of fate who controls his own fate. For you there will be no other fate. But that which will be, you already control.

(*Voprosii filosofii* (1991) 5: 10)

Certain general statements can now be made. In Proust – and in philosophy in general – Mamardashvili investigated 'sudden beginnings', or what he called 'surprise': those experiences, thoughts and events that seem to arise 'out of nothing'. Unlike Russian apocalyptic and messianic thinkers (who studied collective ends), and unlike his senior colleague in the philosophy of consciousness, Bakhtin (who exclusively studied middles), Mamardashvili made a point of studying the miraculous surprise of *individualized beginnings*. Culture itself is defined as that set of specific forms within which individuals could realize increasing complexity.

All true philosophizing has a phenomenological aspect, Mamardashvili taught, although the impulse for his own questioning came not from Husserl but from Marx (in his own words, he moved from Marx to an 'intuition of "bodies"', that is, to "structures of palpable agency"' in the world, and then to the 'concrete object-ness of a thought' as the 'living, extra-mental reality of the soul' (1990a: 102)). Mamardashvili was not a political philosopher, nor a social one. He was, rather, a personalist and intentionalist of the sort that has special resonance in a culture like Soviet Russia, so familiar with political abuse and collective utopia: while greatly admiring Kant and considering him not part of that 'epoch of strictly German philosophy, so repulsive to me' ([1982b] 1991: 121), Mamardashvili distrusted the power that moral norms held over an individual and worried about the proper procedures for stitching ourselves into them ('In a broad sense', Mamardashvili writes, 'for Kant, a norm is a grimace, a going to church... Grimaces of the spirit' ([1982b] 1991: 145)). Individual will is integrated into norms, he believed, but all social and spiritual creativity is dependent upon the participation of 'a sufficient number of adult, non-infantile people who rely on their own individual minds' ([1987] 1990: 374). In a lengthy excursus on memory and its role in the poet Mandelstam's famed *'toska po mirovoi kul'ture'* (longing for world culture), Mamardashvili remarked, again in the spirit of Chaadaev, that Russians have never achieved a secure sense of continuity, of belonging, of having authentic organs of birth ([1986–7] 1991: 40–4); and for this reason, perhaps, Russians are so familiar with the terror at possible non-being which fuels philosophy.

In the late 1980s, Mamardashvili elaborated his 'Principle of the Three Ks': Karteziia (Cartesianism, Descartes), Kant and Kafka ([1984b] 1990: 109–12). The Cartesian 'I' asserts its own first-person-singular existence and doubts every other thing. The Kantian 'I' is subordinated to a third-person transcendental point of view; its strength lies in its attention to the real-world conditions and coordinates that shape an act. The Kafkaesque 'I' knows neither first nor third person; it is a zombie, a humanoid without agency functioning in the realm of the absurd. Curiously, Mamardashvili suggested that it was only in the *glasnost'* period – for he did not live to see the end of Soviet communism – that the third, Kafkaesque 'I' was in fact recognized as such on Russian soil: before that time, absurdity was blamed on politics, on Stalinism, and thus explained away not as a spiritual option (which it is) but as a brutal imposition by politics. In laying out his taxonomy of the three types of self, Mamardashvili reveals himself to be an unsentimental phenomenologist in the Stoic vein. 'A philosopher is not surprised at evil, destruction, chaos or disorder, although usually we, people, are surprised at that....What is surprising and remarkable is that there is good....Just a tiny island of order in the chaos – that's remarkable' ([1979] 1992: 31).

List of works

Mamardashvili, M.K. (1968) *Formy i soderzhanie myshleniia* (The Forms and Content of Thinking), Moscow. (Survey of phenomenological and Kantian paradigms for the production of thought; academic in approach.)

—— (1979) 'O poniatii filosofii' (On the Concept of Philosophy), lecture at Rostov State University, in *Novyi Krug* (Kiev) 1992: 1. (Mamardashvili's discussion of 'two categories of things': those that happen, and those that do not happen, 'by themselves'; the notion of freedom as that which happens 'without choice'; the difference between philosophy and culture.)

—— (1982a) *Simvol i soznanie (metafizicheskie rassuzhdeniia o soznanii, simvolike i iazyke)* (Symbol and Consciousness: Metaphysical Speculations on Consciousness, Symbolic Structures and Language), with A. Piatigorskii, Jerusalem. (Non-technical discussion of the structure of consciousness, the sign, the symbol, the natural versus the artificed in language, as part of a search for the epistemological basis for semiotics.)

—— (1982b) *Kantianskie variiatsii* (Kantian Variations), lectures delivered in Moscow; fragments published in *Kvintessentsiia: Filosofskii almanakh 1991*, Moscow, 120–57. (An examination of Kant's

sentiment that 'a soul overfilled with feelings, and not speech, is the highest of all perfections'; the role of words for Rousseau and of meaning for Kant.)

—— (1984a) *Klassicheskii i neklassicheskii idealy ratsional'nosti* (Classic and Non-Classic Ideals of Rationality), Tbilisi. (Investigations of a relatively non-technical nature into the problem of observation, the notion of a phenomenon and its multiple dimensions; and the symbolic element in all rational thought.)

—— (1984b) 'Soznanie i tsivilizatsii' (Consciousness and Civilization), lecture delivered in Batumi, published in *Kak ya ponimayu filosofiiu* (How I Understand Philosophy), 1990, 107–21. (Includes Mamardashvili's 'three Ks' as ways of organizing the world: Decartes, Kant and Kafka.)

—— (1986–7) 'Besedy o myshlenii' (Conversations about Thinking), lecture series delivered at Tbilisi University, in V.A. Kruglikov (ed.) *'Mysl' izrechennaia...': sbornik nauchnykh statei*, Moscow, 1991, 13–50. (Meditations on the unexpected origins of a thought; on the difficulty of willing a desire versus willing an insight; the responsibilities that accrue to thinking.)

—— (1987) 'Filosofiia i svoboda' (Philosophy and Freedom) (lecture), in *Kak ya ponimayu filosofiiu* (How I Understand Philosophy), Moscow 1990, 365–74. (The Good as a productive state, not as an attribute or a product, because freedom can only produce more of itself; Russia as a land of 'eternal pregnancy'.)

—— (1990a) *Kak ya ponimayu filosofiiu* (How I Understand Philosophy) Moscow. (A collection of sixteen seminal lectures and interviews, and fifteen formal articles, from the 1970s to 1990s.)

Mamardachvili [Mamardashvili] (1990b) *'La pensée empêchée (Entretien avec Annie Epelboin)'*, Editions de l'Aube. (Biographical material.)

—— (1991) *Kartezianskie razmyshleniia* (Cartesian Meditations), lectures delivered in Moscow, expanded and published in book form, Moscow, 1993. (On Descartes the man and his masks; the desirability of thinking in the present; thought and epiphany; the responsibilities of becoming conscious.)

References and further reading

* Kruglikov, V. (1994) *Kongenial'nost' mysli: o filosofe Merabe Mamardashvili* (The Congeniality of Thought: On the Philosopher Merab Mamardashvili), Moscow. (A posthumous collection in three parts, containing primary material (an essay and interview by Mamardashvili), appreciations by

fellow philosophers, biographical information and summaries of his thought.)

Murchland, B. (1991) 'The Mind of Mamardashvili', Ohio: Kettering Foundation. (Monograph prepared after several days of conversation with Mamardashvili during the last year of his life.)

* 'Pamiati filosofa' (In Commemoration of the Philosopher), special forum devoted to Mamardashvili in *Voprosy filosofii* (1991) 5: 3–25. (Memoiristic and eulogistic articles by seven scholar-disciples, including Iu. Senokosov, M. Ryklin, A. Piatigorskii and A. Akhutin.)

CARYL EMERSON

MANDEVILLE, BERNARD (1670–1733)

Bernard Mandeville's Fable of the Bees *(1714) scandalized contemporaries by arguing that the flourishing commercial society they valued depended on vices they denounced. It resulted not only from the complementary satisfaction of appetites but was also based upon pride, envy and shame, which Mandeville traced to 'self-liking'. Numerous individuals, driven by their own desires, acted independently to produce goods which required extensive, cooperative operations   an idea central to the economic concept of a market.*

Mandeville initially appeared to credit 'skilful politicians' with originating morality and society. However, in defending and expounding his views, he set out 'conjectural histories' of the gradual development of many complex social activities and institutions, including language and society itself, thereby denying that they had been invented by public spirited heroes. Throughout his works, Mandeville adopted a strict criterion of virtue, repeatedly denying that he was advocating, rather than exposing, the vices he identified as inherent in human society.

1   **Early writings**
2   **Human nature and morality**
3   **Economics**
4   **Later writings**

1   Early writings

Bernard Mandeville studied philosophy and medicine at Leiden, qualifying in 1691. In the mid-1690s he settled in England, specializing in nervous and digestive disorders. His early verse works included *Some Fables after the Easie and Familiar Method of Monsieur de la Fontaine* (1703; enlarged into *Aesop*

Dress'd 1704), two tales from which were by Mandeville himself. In 1705 he published a longer original verse fable, *The Grumbling Hive: or, Knaves Turn'd Honest*, whose bees continually complain of the vices and faults of their society, despite its power and prosperity. Granted virtue and honesty by Jove, they decline into contented, impoverished simplicity.

Mandeville then turned to female dialogues. In *The Virgin Unmask'd* (1709) 'an elderly maiden lady' advises her niece against the servility of marriage and lectures about the danger to Europe posed by Louis XIV. In the period 1709–10, Mandeville wrote thirty-two 'Lucinda' and 'Artesia' papers for the *Female Tatler*, an imitator of Richard Steele's *Tatler*. Mandeville ridiculed Steele's encomiums on the dignity of human nature and his advocacy of quasi-aristocratic 'politeness'; his 'Oxford gentleman' maintained that both sociability and prosperity were based on vice – on pride, flattery and the invention and satisfaction of luxurious desires. His 'sisters' debated honour, the advisability of military service in Marlborough's wars and the possibility of living to make money. Eight papers contended that women are fully capable of all the traditional male virtues, giving numerous historical, biblical and mythical examples (Goldsmith 1985).

2   Human nature and morality

The Fable of the Bees: or, Private Vices, Publick Benefits (1714), Mandeville's best-known work, reprinted *The Grumbling Hive*, adding extensive remarks and essays which analysed human conduct, finding it motivated by avarice, prodigality, envy, pride, honour, shame and luxury   with contrary passions balancing each other. 'Skilful politicians', moralists and lawgivers had socialized human beings by persuading them to restrain their immediate self-interested desires in return for the praise accorded to their noble self-sacrifice, thereby gratifying their desires to think well of themselves and be admired by others.

Much of this account of human nature was derived from the French *moralistes* and Pierre Bayle (see BAYLE, P. §1; Mandeville 1714; Horne 1978; Hundert 1994), who had also pointed out the worldly benefits of unregenerate human conduct. Defining virtue as requiring self-denial for the good of others or one's own rational improvement enabled Mandeville to claim that he condemned the vicious passions to which he traced all human conduct, including apparently religious or virtuous conduct. Contemporary critics (for example, William LAW and George BERKELEY) accused Mandeville of advocating vice and subverting the standards of right conduct; Adam

SMITH, in his *Theory of Moral Sentiments* (1759, part VII, sect. ii, ch. 4), calls Mandeville's a 'licentious system' because it removes the distinction between vice and virtue. Kaye (Mandeville 1714) argued that Mandeville tended towards a consequentialist acceptance of the benefits of vice thereby implying a *reductio* of his professed strict (or 'rigourist') standard of virtue. None the less some commentators have accepted Mandeville's claim, reiterated in his last work *A Letter to Dion* (1732), that Dion's book *Alciphron* so misrepresented the *Fable of the Bees* that Berkeley could not have read that work (Monro 1975). Mandeville's satiric analysis of human nature along with his scorn for reformers and standards of 'politeness' and virtue have puzzled subsequent commentators as well as his contemporaries (Castiglione 1986).

Originally aimed at Steele (in the *Female Tatler* papers and the first edition of the *Fable*) and at the proselytizing Societies for the Reformation of Manners, 'A Search into the Nature of Society', added to the second edition of the *Fable* (1723), extended the attack to the Third Earl of Shaftesbury. Also added to that edition was the 'Essay on Charity and Charity-Schools', which resulted in the *Fable*'s notoriety. In it Mandeville distinguished true charity from natural pity or compassion, discovered pride behind magnificent charitable bequests, asserted that charity schools were promoted by parish busybodies to confirm their sense of self-importance, and denied that the schools were socially beneficial in decreasing irreligion and crime, claiming rather that they were harmful in providing poor children with education and aspirations incompatible with the life of drudgery required of them by a prosperous commercial society. This provoked the *Fable*'s being presented as a public nuisance by a Middlesex Grand Jury and incited numerous refutations, most notably William Law and Francis Hutcheson (see HUTCHESON, F. §§2–3).

It seems likely that a materialist and naturalist theory underlay Mandeville's ridicule of the dignity of human nature. The *Fable* treats humans as similar to other mammals in their anatomy, feelings, motives and behaviour – a rejection of the Cartesianism Mandeville learned at university. Its discussion of the slaughter and eating of higher animals and the debate between a lion and a man about superiority support that hypothesis, as do the methodological views expressed in Mandeville's *Treatise of the Hypocondriack and Hysterick Passions* (1711, 1730). This *Treatise* is a set of medical dialogues in which the doctor (clearly Mandeville) talks his patients into cures based on simpler diets, more exercise and fewer, milder medicines; he advocates the empirical study of diseases, sceptically rejecting fashionable and fanciful medical theories.

3 Economics

The paradox of private vices creating public benefits was illustrated by showing how natural and moral evils, such as disasters like the Great Fire of London, crimes like theft, vices like prostitution and harmful activities like the liquor trade, benefited society by providing work, circulating wealth, preserving chastity and, through taxes, by supporting the state. Thus Mandeville extended his 'selfish' conception of human nature, which has reminded commentators of Hobbes (see HOBBES, T. §6), into the thesis that human needs and vices produce social wellbeing. By serving the desires of others in order to satisfy their own desires, individuals acting independently produce complex social processes and institutions (including brewing, baking and, in 1723, the worldwide activity necessary to provide the luxury of scarlet coats for common soldiers). HAYEK (1966) therefore credited Mandeville with the basic insight involved in the theory of the free market; namely, the social importance of the unintended consequences of individual actions. But claims that Mandeville was a conscious precursor of classical economics are exaggerated (Goldsmith 1985). Despite some passages advocating free trade, rejecting sumptuary laws, defending luxury, accepting the export of specie (gold and silver) and insisting that a nation must buy foreign goods if it expects to sell its goods abroad, Mandeville also states typically mercantilist views without expounding a clear economic theory (Horne 1978). Government must maintain a system of justice, provide defence and also regulate internal and external trade. Only *A Modest Defence of Public Stews* (1724), usually attributed (without definite proof) to Mandeville, provides a clear example of a self-regulating system of supply and demand – a scheme for a system of public houses of prostitution.

4 Later writings

In 1720, before the *Fable*'s notoriety, Mandeville published the moderate, whiggish *Free Thoughts on Religion*. Relying on Bayle to the point of plagiarism, Mandeville sceptically advocated irenic tolerance while expressing anticlerical views (also found in the *Fable*). *Free Thoughts* supported the Protestant succession, the Hanoverian dynasty and the British mixed constitution.

In two later works, signed 'by the author of the Fable of the Bees', Mandeville supplemented and defended his views. Both were dialogues between the same principal interlocutors: Cleomenes, who combines Christianity with advocacy of Mandeville's doctrines, and the worldly, sceptical Horatio. *The Fable of the Bees. Part II* (1729) explicitly distinguishes between two types of self-gratification: self-love (satisfying self-preservatory desires) and self-liking (satisfying the desires for superiority, admiration and one's good opinion of oneself). (Rousseau later used the same distinction.) *An Enquiry into the Origin of Honour and the Usefulness of Christianity in War* (1732) not only pursues Mandeville's discussion of honour and contrasts true with nominal religion, but also further refines the analysis of self-liking in showing that it causes both shame and pride. The *Fable Part II* is especially notable for elaborating the historical thesis suggested in Mandeville's earlier remarks on the development of artefacts, processes and institutions (Goldsmith 1985). The designs of ships and clocks are the result of the labour and experience of many ages. So too are the elaborate laws and the complex institutions of government which – contrary to some previous views – have not been invented by heroic individual benefactors and law-givers. The conjectural history of the stages of human development from animal existence through savagery to commercial society, already indicated as early as the *Female Tatler*, shows that the Fable's story of the civilizing of humans by skilful politicians and moralists is not to be taken literally. In holding that the development of language itself must have taken many ages, Mandeville implicitly rejected literal, biblical chronology.

Mandeville's views were widely known and extensively used and commented on in the eighteenth century, by thinkers such as Hutcheson, Voltaire and Rousseau among others; David HUME and Adam Smith clearly knew Mandeville's discussion of human nature, the utility of vice and the beneficial results of complex social interaction (Goldsmith 1988; Hundert 1994).

List of works

Mandeville, B. (1703) *Some Fables after the Easie and Familiar Method of Monsieur de la Fontaine*, London: Richard Wellington; enlarged edn, *Aesop Dress'd; or a Collection of Fables Writ in Familiar Verse,* London: Richard Wellington, 1704; reset edn of *Aesop Dress'd*, London: 'sold at Lock's-Head adjoyning to Ludgate', 1727[?]; reprint of reset edn of *Aesop Dress'd*, intro. J.S. Shea, Augustan Reprint Society Publication no. 120, Los Angeles, CA: Augustan Reprint Society, 1966. (Verse fables, based on La Fontaine's version of *Aesop*, but containing two original fables composed by Mandeville.)

—— (1705) *The Grumbling Hive: or, Knaves Turn'd Honest,* London: printed for S. Ballard and sold by A. Baldwin. (The verse fable used in *The Fable of the Bees.*)

—— (1709) *The Virgin Unmask'd: or, Female Dialogues Bewixt an Elderly Maiden Lady, and Her Niece,* London: sold by J. Morphew and J. Woodward; reprinted, intro. S.H. Good, Delmar, NY: Scholars' Facsimiles, 1975. (Dialogues on mores, manners and political affairs.)

—— (1709–10) *The Female Tatler.* (Thirty-two issues between numbers 52, 2 November 1709, and 111, 29 March 1710, signed 'Lucinda' and 'Artesia', discussing topics including the origin and development of society, honour and female virtue.)

—— (1711) *A Treatise of the Hypocondriack and Hysterick Passions,* London: printed for the author, D. Leach, W. Taylor and J. Woodward; enlarged 3rd edn, *A Treatise of the Hypocondriack and Hysterick Diseases,* London: printed for J. Tonson, 1730; reprinted 1st edn and reprinted 3rd edn, intro. S.H. Good, Delmar, NY: Scholars' Facsimiles, 1976. (Dialogues between doctor and patients on the causes and cures of nervous and digestive diseases.)

—— (1714) *The Fable of the Bees: or, Private Vices, Publick Benefits,* London: printed for J. Roberts; 2nd edn, enlarged, London: printed for E. Parker, 1723; 3rd edn, enlarged, London: printed for J. Roberts, 1724; reprinted, ed. F.B. Kaye, Oxford: Clarendon Press, 1924. (Mandeville's best-known work. Kaye's classic critical edition includes life, bibliography, annotations, discussions of Mandeville's thought, its background and influence, brief summaries of contemporary critics and a chronological list of references to Mandeville's work to 1923.)

—— (1729) *The Fable of the Bees. Part II*, London: printed for J. Roberts; reprinted, ed. F.B. Kaye, Oxford: Clarendon Press, 1924, vol. 2; reprinted, Indianapolis, IN: Liberty Classics, 1988. (Dialogues expanding, explaining and refining the *Fable's* doctrines; included in Kaye's classic edition.)

—— (1720) *Free Thoughts on Religion, the Church, and National Happiness,* London: sold by T. Jauncy and J. Roberts; reprinted, intro. S.H. Good, Delmar, NY: Scholars' Facsimiles, 1981; 2nd edn, London: printed for John Brotherton, 1729; reprinted, Stuttgart-Bad Cannstatt: Frommann, 1969. (Discussion of religion heavily indebted to Pierre Bayle, otherwise relatively straightforward advocacy of toleration, anticlericalism and political whiggism.)

—— (1724) *A Modest Defence of Public Stews: or, An Essay upon Whoring, as it is now practis'd in these Kingdoms,* London: printed by A. Moore; rep-

73

rinted, intro. R. I. Cook, Los Angeles, CA: Augustan Reprint Society, no. 162, 1973. (Standardly attributed to Mandeville; advocates public houses of prostitution to preserve chastity.)

—— (1732) *An Enquiry into the Origin of Honour and the Usefulness of Christianity in War*, London: printed for J. Brotherton, 1732; reprinted, intro. M.M. Goldsmith, London: F. Cass, 1972. (Dialogues on honour and the distinction between real and nominal Christianity.)

—— (1732) *A Letter to Dion, Occasion'd by his Book call'd Alciphron, or the Minute Philosopher*, London: printed for J. Roberts; reprinted, intro. J. Viner, Los Angeles, CA: Augustan Reprint Society, no. 41, 1953. (Defends the *Fable of the Bees* on the grounds that it advocates strict morality and exposes vice; Viner denies that Mandeville advocated *laissez-faire* while favouring mercantilist government intervention.)

References and further reading

* Castiglione, D. (1986) 'Considering Things Minutely: Reflections on Mandeville and Eighteenth-Century Science of Man', *History of Political Thought* 7 (3): 463–88. (A subtle discussion of Mandeville's satiric critique of eighteenth-century values: his enigmatic views resisted 'moralization'.)
* Goldsmith, M.M. (1985) *Private Vices, Public Benefits: Bernard Mandeville's Social and Political Thought*, Cambridge: Cambridge University Press. (Considers Mandeville's views, §§2–3, 4, on the operation and development of social institutions; emphasizes the importance of the *Female Tatler*; rejects the contention that Mandeville was an economic thinker; argues that he accepted modes of life rejected by the 'polite' aristocratic ethic of the early eighteenth century; extensive bibliography.)
* Hayek, F.A. (1966) 'Dr Bernard Mandeville', *Proceedings of the British Academy* 52: 125–41. (Classic attribution to Mandeville (§3) of laissez-faire individualism and the notion of 'unintended consequences'.)
* Horne, T.A. (1978) *The Social Thought of Bernard Mandeville: Vice and Commerce in Early Eighteenth-Century England*, New York: Columbia University Press. (Emphasizes Mandeville's relations to the 'reformation of manners', the French *moralistes*, Shaftesbury and mercantilism, and sees him as justifying commercial society, §§2–3.)
* Hundert, E.J. (1994) *The Enlightenment's Fable: Bernard Mandeville and the Discovery of Society*, Cambridge: Cambridge University Press. (Extensive treatment of both the British and continental

Europe intellectual context and and the sources of Mandeville's views; emphasizes Mandeville's importance for many Enlightenment thinkers and for the development of several areas of Enlightenment thought; extensive bibliography.)
* Monro, H.D. (1975) *The Ambivalence of Bernard Mandeville*, Oxford: Clarendon Press. (Discusses most aspects of Mandeville's life and works: comprehensive review of moral positions attributed to Mandeville and extensive examination of him as an ethical theorist; critically annotated select bibliography, including works on Mandeville 1924–72.)
* Primer, I. (ed.) (1975) *Mandeville Studies: New Explorations in the Art and Thought of Dr Bernard Mandeville*, The Hague: Nijhoff. (Essays on many aspects of Mandeville's writings, mainly by literary scholars; useful bibliography.)
* Smith, A. (1759) *The Theory of Moral Sentiments*, ed. D.D. Raphael and A.L. Macfie, Oxford: Clarendon Press, 1976. (Smith's moral philosophy, developing the theory of the 'impartial spectator' and denouncing Mandeville's 'wholly pernicious views', which eliminated the distinction between virtue and vice.)

M.M. GOLDSMITH

MANICHEISM

Manicheism is a defunct religion, born in Mesopotamia in the third century AD and last attested in the sixteenth century in China. Its founder, Mani (c.216–76), had some familiarity with Judaism, Christianity, Zoroastrianism and Buddhism, and aimed to supplant them all. He taught a form of dualism, influenced by earlier Gnostics: God is opposed by forces of darkness; they, not God, created human beings, who nevertheless contain particles of light which can be released by abstemious living. Two points of contrast with Catholic Christianity are particularly striking. First, in Manicheism, sinfulness is the natural state of human beings (because of their creators), and does not stem from Adam's Fall. Second, the Manichean God did not create and does not control the forces of darkness (although he will eventually triumph); hence the problem of evil does not arise in as stark a form as it does for the all-powerful Christian God.

Although Mani's own missionary journeys took him eastwards, it was in the Roman Empire to the west that the main impact of his teaching was first felt; Augustine of Hippo was an adherent for nine years. The religion was eventually suppressed in the Roman Empire, and driven east by the Arab conquest of Mesopotamia. In the West, various Christian heresies were loosely called Manichean throughout the Middle Ages.

1   The background
2   Mani
3   Augustine and the Manichees
4   Dualism in Christianity

1   The background

Dualism emerges into history with the Persian prophet Zoroaster (or Zarathustra), who lived perhaps as early as the thirteenth century BC, and who taught that the High God Zervan or his son Ormuzd (Mazda) battles with Ahriman, the Spirit of Darkness, and will one day send a Saviour to redeem mankind. Here we have the seeds of Mani's religion, seeds that may have been nourished by the Zoroastrian state cult of the Sassanian dynasty which came to power in Persia during Mani's lifetime. But a stronger affinity was with Gnosticism. Gnostic tenets, perhaps originating among certain 'God-fearing' Judaic communities (and perhaps themselves owing something to much more ancient Zoroastrian influence on Judaism), become known to us around the end of the first century AD. Many of the groups they affected, such as the followers of Marcion (d. c.160), absorbed enough Christianity to be attacked as Christian heretics.

Within much diversity the common features of Gnosticism were these. God the First Principle emanated divine associates or 'Aeons'. Among them was one who through pride or curiosity fell. It was this one, the Demiurge, who created the visible world and human beings in it. Human beings contain a spark of divinity, which it became God's purpose to rescue by imparting knowledge, gnosis, through his messenger Jesus. Gnostics repudiated the Old Testament, sometimes identifying the Demiurge with Yahweh and honouring Yahweh's opponents such as the Serpent and the Sodomites. Jesus was not born, or was born through Mary's ear, and he stood by the cross while a surrogate phantom suffered and died in his place. Gnosis is imparted only to the initiated. It teaches that the human body is evil, and it therefore enjoins ascetic practices and deplores procreation (see GNOSTICISM).

2   Mani

Mani (or Manes or Manichaeus) was born around 216 and brought up near Ctesiphon on the Tigris among a sect of baptists apparently founded a century earlier by a Jew named Elchasai. The sect observed the Sabbath, washed a great deal, and expected the imminent end of the world following the appearance of a final prophet. At the age of 12, and again at 24, Mani saw visions which he came to compare with the apostle Paul's. Like Paul he felt called to renounce the legalism of his upbringing and to take a message to the world; unlike Paul's, his message included a complete cosmological story. With the favour of the Sassanian king Shapur I he preached in Persia, organized missions as far west as Alexandria, and himself travelled eastwards, perhaps to India. After the death of Shapur's successor in 273 Mani fell out with the next king and was confined to prison, where he died in 276.

Mani held that God, the father of truth, exists before all things and persists after all things, and that everything exists through his power (*Concerning the Origin of His Body*, 66.4–15; Cameron and Dewey 1979: 52–3). But he also warned against those who 'teach that good and bad come from the same source, and introduce a single principle, not distinguishing or dividing darkness from light and good from bad ... as we preach' ([Hegemonius] v). In prosaic summary, the story he preached was this. When first the Lord of Darkness and his demons invaded the realm of light, God sent Primeval Man attired in bright elements to resist them. But Primeval Man was defeated and stripped of his attire, which the demons swallowed. In his quest to retrieve this stolen light God emanated seductive Messengers, the sight of whom caused emissions and abortions among the demons, from which sprang plants and beasts. Some of the light being thus trapped anew, a demon couple engendered Adam as a repository for most of the remainder. With Jesus' help we, as Adam's descendants, can by breathing and belching release our light upwards, feeding the moon as it waxes, which as it wanes feeds the sun in turn; but both eating and procreation have the contrary effect of trapping light. In the end Jesus will come again and light will triumph.

Mani's church was organized, with grand books, music, bishops and eventually monasteries, for the purpose of assisting God in this cosmic struggle. Its membership was divided between Elect and Hearers. Even Hearers (such as Augustine was) must not eat meat, or kill, must fast on Sundays, avoid procreation, and above all sustain the Elect – men and women – who were additionally forbidden to drink wine, copulate, farm, or prepare their own food.

The Manichees were interested in natural, especially celestial, phenomena and offered explanations of them which had to be consistent with Mani's cosmology.

3 Augustine and the Manichees

Perhaps in emulation of Paul, Mani signed his letters 'Apostle of Jesus Christ'. In Augustine's day the African Manichees claimed Christianity for their own and called Catholics *semichristiani*. One thing that underlay this surprising pretension was the Manichees' refusal to compromise the austerity they discerned in Paul's primitive Christian communities. Another may have been Mani's dualism, which not only could offer comfort to sensitive and frightened people in the thought that their sins and shortcomings stemmed from the machinations of superior powers, but could easily in the third and fourth centuries find heralds of that thought among Gnosticizing Christians. Manicheism is not strictly dualistic: its God is above all, and there is assurance that he will win in the end. Besides, Christians and Manichees shared a common cosmological concern with the problem of evil, agreeing both that it is a problem (why should there be any?) and that the solution lies in the past, when an originally happy state was upset by some fall from good behaviour.

What at this high level chiefly marks off Manicheism from Catholic Christianity, as the latter emerged in the councils and apologetics of the fourth century, is Mani's conception of human evils, sin and suffering, as tracing their origin back to an act – creation by demons – which unlike the biblical Fall was not the act of any human. Thus the two religions differ in their anthropology: for Manichees, sin and suffering are our natural state, not an Adam-induced lapse from it (see SIN §2). Augustine saw that difference, and used it to frame the risky charge that Manichean metaphysics leaves no room for human responsibility – risky because he was later to find the same charge brought against his own Catholic metaphysics by the Pelagians (see AUGUSTINE (§§6, 9, 12); PELAGIANISM §1–2). Manichees also, of course, seemed to have a readier means than Catholics of exculpating God from complicity in evil; for their God had not created and did not control the powers of darkness.

4 Dualism in Christianity

Augustine wrote of the time when Manicheism was losing its grip on him, 'It still seemed to me that it is not we who sin, but some other nature within us' (*Confessions*, 5.10.18); here was one comfort he would lose by resuming Catholic Christianity. Another was freedom to criticize the Bible, for the early Manichees won much of their missionary success by an aggressive policy of mocking the Old Testament and exposing inconsistencies in the Catholic canon of the New (their own New Testament canon was more Gnostic). But aggressiveness faded under persecution in the West, till the religion was exterminated from Christendom by about 600. It continued in Mesopotamia until driven east by the Arab conquest in the seventh century. For a time it was the state religion of the Uighur Turks in Sinkiang, and from the T'ang period it established a lasting presence in China, being last attested on the Fukien coast in the sixteenth century.

In Christendom, 'Manichee' became an opprobrious epithet for heresies that pronounced human nature evil (so excluding redemption) and harboured a class of Elect (so rejecting infant baptism). Paulicians, who flourished in Armenia and the eastern confines of the Roman Empire in the eighth and ninth centuries, believed that the Demiurge, not God, made the world and Jesus only seemed to die. In tenth-century Bulgaria, Bogomil (Theophilus, 'God-beloved') echoed much of Mani's cosmology and ethics. His views guided the thirteenth-century Sclavonian church of Bosnia, called Patarene by the West. During the twelfth century there were Poblicans in Flanders, perhaps inheritors of Paulicianism through itinerant weavers. And the Cathars of the same period, powerful in southern France until de Montfort's 'crusade' overthrew them, joined Manichean dietary and sexual proscriptions with the old Gnostic rejection of Christ's humanity. All of these sects, while attracting support from simple people, had leaders who knew history and tried to model their lives on past practice: not indeed on the outlandish Mani, about whom they probably knew little and cared less, but on primitive Christianity as transmitted through early Gnosticism. They succumbed to Catholic persecution in the West, and many in the Balkans converted to Islam after the Turkish conquests of the fifteenth century. But even in modern times like-minded movements arise now and again, nourished by certain books of the Bible, especially Daniel and Revelation.

See also: EVIL; EVIL, PROBLEM OF

References and further reading

Mani is credited with seven works in Syriac, and one in Middle Persian addressed to King Shapur, but only fragments survive. Traditions were preserved by Muhammad ben Ishâk's 'Doctrines of the Manicheans' in the *Fihrist*, a history of Arabic literature to 987 compiled by an-Nadîm, and less reliably in various hostile writings from the fourth and fifth centuries by Christians and others. Further Manichean writings have come to light during the twentieth century in Chinese and other languages (Turfan 1904–15, Tun-huang 1905), Coptic (Egypt, Medinet Madi 1930), Greek (Cologne 1969) and Latin. The greater part of the Coptic collection, including letters of Mani himself, went to the Berlin Academy from where it disappeared in 1945 before publication was complete; most of the remainder, including homilies edited by Polotsky and a Psalm Book edited by Allberry, is in the Chester Beatty Collection in Dublin. Many of these texts are collected in Adam (1969). The Cologne manuscript edited by Koenen and Römer is a gospel-cum-apocalypse in Greek from a Syriac original, some of it presented as autobiography by Mani. It dates from about 400.

Adam, A. (1969) *Texte zum Manichäismus* (Manichean Texts), Kleine Texte für Vorlesungen und Übungen, vol. 175, enlarged edn, Berlin: de Gruyter. (Contains the basic texts, apart from the Cologne manuscript, in Greek, Latin or German translation.)

Allberry, C.R.C. (ed.) (1938) *A Manichaean Psalm Book, Part II*, Manichaean Manuscripts in the Chester Beatty Collection 2, Stuttgart: W. Kohlhammer. (Sumptuous edition with English translation. From the Coptic find.)

* Augustine (397–401) *Confessions*, Corpus Scriptorum Ecclesiasticorum Latinorum, vol. 33, Vienna: Tempsky, 1896, and elsewhere; trans. H. Chadwick, Oxford: Oxford University Press, 1991, and elsewhere. (One of the many works in which Augustine as a Catholic bishop responded to charges of lingering Manicheism.)

—— (400) *Contra Faustum Manichaeum*, Corpus Scriptorum Ecclesiasticorum Latinorum, vol. 25.1, Vienna: Tempsky, 1891; trans. R. Stothert, in P. Schaff (ed.) (1886–9) *A Select Library of the Nicene and Post-Nicene Fathers*, vol. 4, Grand Rapids, MI: Eerdmans, 1974. (A lengthy polemic against the most celebrated local Manichee.)

* Cameron, R. and Dewey, A.J. (1979) *The Cologne Mani Codex 'Concerning the Origin of His Body'*, Society of Biblical Literature, Texts and Translations 15, Early Christian Literature Series 3, Missoula, MT: Scholars Press. (Incomplete text and translation of the work later edited by Koenen and Römer.)

Chadwick, H. (1989) 'The Attractions of Mani', *Compostellanum* 34: 203–22; reprinted in H. Chadwick, *Heresy and Orthodoxy in the Early Church*, Aldershot: Variorum, 1991. (Describes Manicheism as it presented itself to Augustine and his contemporaries.)

* [Hegemonius] (*c.*320) *Acta disputationis Archelai cum Manete haeresiarcha*, ed. C.H. Beeson, Leipzig: Hinrichs, 1906. (A hostile biography of Mani, but using Manichean material. Forged in Syriac and preserved only in Latin. The chief early source in the West.)

Koenen, L. and Römer, C. (eds) (1985) *Der Kölner Mani-Kodex* (The Cologne Mani Codex), diplomatic edition, Papyrologische Texte u. Abhandlungen, vol. 35, Bonn: Habelt. (Edition of the Cologne manuscript, a tiny codex measuring 4.5 by 3.5 cm.)

Lieu, S.N.C. (1992) *Manichaeism in the Later Roman Empire and Medieval China: A Historical Survey*, Tübingen: Mohr, revised 2nd edn. (An excellent study of the religion's history, West and East.)

Polotsky, H.J. (1934) *Manichäische Homilien* (Manichean Homilies), Manichaean Manuscripts in the Chester Beatty Collection 1, Stuttgart: W. Kohlhammer. (Sumptuous edition with German translation. From the Coptic find.)

Runciman, S. (1947) *The Medieval Manichee*, Cambridge: Cambridge University Press. (Traces the Christian heresies that were lumped together as Manichean.)

CHRISTOPHER KIRWAN

MANIFOLDNESS, JAINA THEORY OF

The Sanskrit term anekāntavāda *literally means 'not-one-sided doctrine', and refers to the Jaina epistemological theory of manifold standpoints from which an object may be considered and the manifold predications that can be made with regard to it. It evolved out of Mahāvīra's ethical emphasis on nonviolence – the multidimensional nature of objects should not be violated by single, absolutist (*ekānta*) predications about them. Respect for life is thus transformed in its philosophical application into a principle of respect for other views. The theory has come to be called the central philosophy of Jainism and was developed in a milieu of intensive debate between the various Indian philosophical schools. Though the theory was based on Mahāvīra's teaching, it implicitly presupposed, in its later highly developed form, various philosophical alternatives (representing the views of other schools of thought), which it sought to syncretize. Each standpoint and predication presents a partial truth and, according to Jainism, only the theory of manifoldness does justice to the complex nature of entities. While it can be seen as an attempt to practice intellectual nonviolence, it is evident that the Jainas adhered to it zealously and defended it as vehemently as the others did their own views.*

77

1   Historical background
2   The significance of *syāt*
3   The seven standpoints

1   Historical background

There is an obvious similarity between the Jaina theory of manifold predication (*anekāntavāda*) and its precursor, the theory of analysis or differentiation (*vibhajyavāda*), which is more famous as Buddha's method of dealing with questions, but was also employed by Mahāvīra. Buddha is renowned for not categorically answering metaphysical questions and for seeking an appropriate answer by breaking up (*vibhajya*) a question into its component parts, often thereby demonstrating it to be a pseudo-question. B.K. Matilal (1981: 11) refers to two types of this theory: the first 'operates by dividing the subject class into sub-classes' (to the question 'Will all beings be reborn?' the answer is 'Only those with defilements'); the second 'operates by specifying or relativizing the predicate' (the answer to the question 'Is man superior or inferior?' is 'Man is inferior to gods and superior to the lower beings'). According to Matilal, it was the second type that Mahāvīra adopted and which was developed into the *anekānta* method.

The *Bhagavatī Sūtra*, part of the Jaina canon, has examples of this style of teaching that are comparable with the better-known ones of Buddha (for example, IX, 33, 485b; Deleu: 164). To quote Matilal again:

> The Buddha's method was one of withdrawal from philosophical disputes, for he avoided committing himself to any extreme view. But Mahāvīra's method was one of commitment, for he attempted to understand the points of view of the fighting parties (in a philosophical dispute) so that their dispute could be resolved and reconciled. Thus, the essence of the *anekānta-vāda* lies in exposing and making explicit the standpoints or presuppositions of the different philosophical schools.
>
> (1981: 23)

Both Jaina and Buddhist sources refer to one Gośāla, a contemporary of Mahāvīra and Buddha and founder of the Ājīvaka sect, which disappeared very soon after his death. He is reputed to have asserted that all entities have a triple character: existent, nonexistent, and both existent and nonexistent (or living, nonliving, and both living and nonliving). The Jaina theory seems to interpret these as positive, negative, and both positive and negative; when they were combined with the possibility that an entity can have an inexpressible nature, a sevenfold formula emerged (see §3).

Just as the Buddhists used the famous fourfold alternative to establish the doctrine of the void (Nāgārjuna's alternatives are: everything is true; not everything is true; both everything is true, and not everything is true; or neither everything is true nor is everything not true), so the Jaina developed the theory of standpoints and sevenfold predication to defend the doctrine of manifoldness (see NĀGĀRJUNA §3). The key to the Jaina position is the need to qualify an assertion or to make it conditionally true in order to leave open other possibilities. This represents the Jaina respect for the views of other schools and at the same time implicitly criticizes their absolutist stands, which have the potential for dogmatism and intolerance. The way to overcome one-sided doctrines is to adopt Mahāvīra's method of accepting metaphysical theories with a qualified affirmation. The philosophic attempt to come as close as possible to capturing the true, multidimensional nature of an entity is to qualify one's assertion with the particle *syāt*.

2   The significance of *syāt*

The Jaina theory of the manifoldness of reality has two aspects: the doctrine of standpoints (*nayavāda*) and the sevenfold predication (*saptabhaṅgī*) associated with it, whereby each type of predication is an epistemological assertion from a certain viewpoint (*syāt*). The theory of manifoldness (*anekāntavāda*) is often used as a synonym for the theory of viewpoints (*syādvāda*). The word *syāt* is identical with a verbal form (the third person singular of the optative mood) of the Sanskrit root 'to be' (*as*), and means things like 'perhaps, possibly, maybe it is or exists'. This has led to a description of the theory as agnostic, giving the impression of doubt, uncertainty and indeterminacy and an inability definitely to determine an object of investigation. The crucial point of the theory is missed, however, if the word is interpreted as a verbal form. Each of the seven statements (see §3) which may be explicitly made with respect to an entity has, in addition to the word *syāt*, a finite form of the same root 'to be', the third person singular present indicative (*asti*, implicit in the fourth case). The technical sense in which it is employed by the Jainas, which semantically does justice to its use, requires an analysis of *syāt* as an indeclinable word meaning 'from a point of view' or 'in a certain sense', with the obvious extension 'from another point of view' or 'in another sense'. Thus, the Jaina theory does not imply that it is epistemologically difficult to determine the nature of an object, but rather that it can be definitely determined from several particular points of view, even though some assertions have a negative structure or express indescribability.

3 The seven standpoints

The two aspects of the theory of manifoldness mentioned at the beginning of §2 relate to two different but theoretically related contexts in which it is employed. The doctrine of standpoints (*naya-vāda*) is the general framework indicating seven ways of considering an object or entity, and the theory of viewpoints (*syādvāda*) represents the seven assertions which may be made regarding an object or entity. Both aspects are intended to demonstrate how partial truths about entities are presented. Jainism makes a clear distinction between knowledge of an entity as a whole and knowledge of a part or an aspect of an entity. This is the epistemological distinction implicit in the terms *pramāṇa*, which signifies complete knowledge of an entity in all its qualities and modes of appearance, and *naya*, which signifies partial knowledge with reference to an entity as it appears to be in the present time and place, having a particular quality and mode which may later change. Complete knowledge of an entity, simultaneously grasping it in all its modes and in all possible ways, occurs only in the case of beings unhindered by karma and is a sign of omniscience. In the case of human knowledge, which is restricted to the functions of the sense organs whose capacities are impeded by karma, only partial knowledge is posssible. The doctrine of standpoints thus represents the various kinds of partial knowledge accessible to human beings. It serves two functions: it facilitates analyses of objects of inquiry and, when applied to other schools of thought, it enables Jainism to classify the partial truths of those schools in terms of one or the other standpoint.

Jainism evinces what may be called a passion for enumeration, classification and categorization of practically all the major philosophical terms: the single term 'karma', for instance, is divided into eight important kinds with a further 148 others; and knowledge is deemed to be derived in two ways, each with its own specific kinds (see JAINA PHILOSOPHY §2). Theoretically, an infinite number of standpoints are possible when considering an entity, but traditionally Jainism enumerates the following seven in the context of the theory of manifoldness:

(1) The common or nondistinguished standpoint (*naigamanaya*) refers to an entity without taking its general and specific characteristics or qualities into consideration. The words 'jar' and 'cloth', for example, can be used in two senses according to this standpoint. They may refer to specific objects within one's view or they may refer to the class of objects that they denote. The example of 'cooking' is also mentioned here; ambiguity can arise when no clear distinction is made between the activity of actually cooking and the preliminary preparations. The general and particular properties of an object or activity are not explicitly distinguished in this standpoint, yet statements concerning 'jar' and 'cooking' are easily understandable. This standpoint represents what is understood conventionally; it is emphasized, according to the Jainas, by the Nyāya-Vaiśeṣika school. The fifth-century Jaina philosopher Siddhasena Divākara does not recognize this as a separate standpoint.

(2) The general or collective standpoint (*saṅgrahanaya*) takes into consideration the class to which an entity belongs, as, for example, when one refers to fruit trees in general. This point is indirectly related to the problem of universals and treats class properties as but one way among others of referring to entities. Class properties like 'fruitness' and 'treeness' are treated as representing a partial truth about an entity. With reference to the all-encompassing category 'being', this standpoint represents the Vedānta school, with its notion of Brahman as the only ultimately real substance. Whereas the first standpoint may be ambiguous in that it can refer to both a particular object as well as a class of objects, this standpoint represents the partial knowledge of an entity because it emphasizes the general aspect alone.

(3) The practical standpoint (*vyavahāranaya*) is a complement to the second and a corollary to the first in that it refers to something specific. When one asks for a fruit, the reference is to something specific, for fruit in general cannot be brought. It is a standpoint which implicitly particularizes an entity and, like the first standpoint, is generally understood. The practical standpoint implies classification and differentiation and is said to represent the view of the materialist Cārvāka school. Like the second standpoint, it avoids the ambiguity of the first, but is no less a partial standpoint, an emphasis on which can furnish only partial knowledge of an entity, because it emphasizes a single, particular object.

(4) The 'straight thread' standpoint (*rjusūtranaya*) considers an entity as it appears at the present moment, ignoring both its previous form and the one it will have in future. An emphasis on this partial truth leads to the metaphysical conclusion of existence as momentary. The Jaina theory includes the Buddhist doctrine of universal flux here as an example of the kind of partial truth furnished by this standpoint (see MOMENTARINESS, BUDDHIST DOCTRINE OF §1).

(5) The verbal standpoint (*śabdanaya*) represents the method of referring to an entity in terms of the syntactic relations between the words used in a sentence where the meaning is determined by grammatical inflections which can offer different

semantic interpretations. The analysis of this standpoint is inextricably related to Sanskrit grammar. The meaning of a sentence is dependent on the relations between its words and these relations are grammatically governed. The partial knowledge is represented by the specific interpretation given to the relations, which then furnish a meaning relative to it.

(6) The subtle standpoint (*samabhirūḍhanaya*) makes a subtle distinction between synonyms in terms of their etymology. This standpoint represents a partial truth in which only etymological differences are emphasized, whereas the object referred to is the same. Thus the same person may be referred to as a king, regent, or sovereign; the Sanskrit equivalents of these words can produce different meanings depending on their derivations. A partial view is represented according to this standpoint when the meaning of synonymous words is explained *only* on the basis of their etymology.

(7) The 'thus-happened' standpoint (*evambhūta-naya*) is an extension of the above in that it restricts the meaning of a word to a particular occasion of use. Thus the word 'cook' should be used, according to this standpoint, only when a person is actually cooking. The restriction of the use of words to actual cases gives only a partial truth because it either ignores a person's other activities, or could imply that a person is not a cook by occupation (say) when doing something else.

The second aspect of the Jaina theory of manifoldness, which is correlated with the theory of standpoints, represents statements or predications about an object that can be made from only one specific point of view. As with the seven standpoints, the seven viewpoints – which constitute the framework of the Jaina theory of sevenfold predication – are intended to apply to any specific entity. One can make the following assertions about any entity:

(i) From one point of view it exists (*syād asti*).
(ii) From one point of view it does not exist (*syān nāsti*).
(iii) From one point of view it exists and from another point of view it does not exist (*syād asti syān nāsti*). This assertion, combining (i) and (ii) into a single unit, does not apply simultaneously, thereby avoiding an apparent contradiction. The assertion may be fully expressed as, for example: 'from one point of view a pot exists (as a pot) and from another point of view it does not exist (as a tree).'
(iv) From one point of view it is inexpressible (*syād avaktavyam*).
(v) From one point of view it both exists and is inexpressible (*syād asti cāvaktavyam*).
(vi) From one point of view it both does not exist and is inexpressible (*syān nāsti cāvaktavyam*).
(vii) From one point of view it exists, does not exist and is also inexpressible (*syād asti ca nāsti cāvaktavyam*).

Jainism ascribes validity to the need for these kinds of assertions about an entity on the basis of lists of factors mentioned in the Jaina canon which were employed when investigating the nature of an entity. The lists originally served as tools for investigating words, especially the titles and chapter titles of canonical texts, but later took on an epistemological significance when applied to assertions about entities in general. They were 'gateways of investigation' (*anuyogadvāra*) which served to 'set down' or 'bring forward' (*nikṣepa*) the context in which the investigation of an object applies. Of the several lists (containing up to thirteen items) that feature in the canonical texts, the list of four is the most popular. According to this list, clarity about an entity can be achieved if there is an analysis that considers it in terms of: the name or the word used to designate the entity; the form or the way in which it can be illustrated; the substance out of which it is constituted; and its specific state or condition at the moment of investigation. Other factors, such as place, time and the means by which an object is known, were also used, with analyses taking on complex dimensions when repetitively (and often futilely) applied to the objects with which an entity is compared. However, this method of analysis directly influenced the later form of the theory of manifoldness and served, in the last resort, as its justification. The historical background and traditional application of the theory were generally ignored by its critics when assessing its contribution.

The Jaina theory of manifoldness was regarded by the other schools of Indian philosophy as generally representing the entire Jaina philosophy, so much so that it was what they attacked above all. It was asserted that the theory is self-contradictory, and that it demonstrates an uncertain and vague standpoint, with equivocality as its greatest error. Jainism was criticized for not being in a position clearly to describe reality. This explains why the majority of Jaina thinkers take every opportunity to justify the theory (which thus features in practically all Jaina philosophical studies) and to vindicate the nonabsolutism of Jainism. One of the most insightful and even independent thinkers within Jainism is Vidyānandin (ninth century), who belonged to the Digambara tradition of Jainism. Accepting three basic kinds of predicates, the positive, the negative, and the neutralized or indescribable, he concludes that only seven combinations are possible, which shows that the Jaina theory of manifoldness takes all cases into consideration when analysing an entity.

See also: EPISTEMOLOGY, INDIAN SCHOOLS OF; KNOWLEDGE, INDIAN VIEWS OF; MAHĀVĪRA

References and further reading

Alsdorf, L. (1973) 'Nikṣepa – A Jaina Contribution to Scholastic Methodology', *Journal of the Oriental Institute (Baroda)* 22: 455–63; repr. in *Ludwig Alsdorf Kleine Schriften*, ed. A Wetzler, Wiesbaden: Franz Steiner Verlag, 1974, 257–65. (Explains the significance and practical use of the term, mentioned in the second last paragraph of the entry.)

Bhatt, B. (1978) *The canonical Nikṣepa. Studies in Jaina Dialectics*, Leiden: Brill. (Deals in detail with the term mentioned in the second last paragraph of the entry, using Jaina canonical sources.)

Malliṣeṇa (13th century) *Syād-vāda-mañjarī*, trans. F.W. Thomas, *The Flower-Spray of the Quodammodo Doctrine*, Delhi: Motilal Banarsidass, 1968. (An annotated translation of a technical work by a Jaina logician who defends the sevenfold standpoint against attacks by other schools of Indian philosophy. The work is a commentary which made famous Hemacandra's *Anyayogavyavacchedikā*.)

* Matilal, B.K (1981) *The Central Philosophy of Jainism (Anekānta-Vāda)*, Ahmedabad: L.D. Institute of Indology. (More extended discussion of the material covered in §§1, 3. Comparison with Buddhist standpoint dealt with in detail, on the basis of original texts.)

Mookerjee, S. (1978) *The Jaina Philosophy of Non-Absolutism*, Delhi: Motilal Banarsidass, 2nd edn. (Discusses the theory of manifoldness and allied problems, like universals and particulars, to demonstrate the basic non-absolutist standpoint of the Jainas.)

Padmarajiah, Y.J. (1963) *A Comparative Study of the Jaina Theories of Reality and Knowledge*, Delhi: Motilal Banarsidass, repr. 1986. (Discusses Jaina ontology, and to a lesser degree, Jaina epistemology, in comparison with other schools of Indian thought.)

JAYANDRA SONI

MANY-VALUED LOGICS

Many-valued logics may be distinguished from classical logic on purely semantic grounds. One of the simplifying assumptions on which classical logic is based is the thesis of bivalence, which states that there are only two truth-values – true and false – and every sentence must be one or the other. Many-valued logics reject the thesis of bivalence and permit more than two truth-values.

1 Motivations
2 An example
3 Technical matters

1 Motivations

Bivalence, in conjunction with some plausible assumptions about the nature of time, seems to lead to determinism. It seems plausible that no matter what I do now, I cannot change what was the case yesterday. This fact suggests that statements about the past are not contingent in the way most of us feel that statements about the future are. Suppose we want to know whether Charles will go sailing tomorrow, Saturday. We think Charles is a free agent, and his going sailing tomorrow is dependent on how he feels, his view of the weather, and other such factors. Consider the sentence 'Yesterday it was the case that Charles will go sailing on Saturday'. Since yesterday is past, the truth-value of this sentence is fixed, even if we do not now know what it is. If the sentence is true, then it must be the case that Charles is going to go sailing tomorrow; and if the sentence is false, then it must be the case that Charles is not going to go sailing tomorrow. Either way, it seems that whether or not Charles is going sailing tomorrow is already determined, so the notion of future contingency is an illusion.

One way of escaping this argument for determinism is to reject the thesis of bivalence. The most obvious first approach would be to insist on three truth-values: 'true', 'false' and 'indeterminate'. This problem was discussed by Aristotle (in *De Interpretatione*), although his position on the issue of bivalence remains a matter of debate. Indeterminists, such as the Epicureans, rejected the thesis of bivalence; determinists, such as the Stoics, advocated it. In the modern era, the Polish logician Łukasiewicz developed several many-valued logics as a means to escape the determinist argument (see ŁUKASIEWICZ, J. §3).

Many other motivations for many-valued logics have been advanced. In every case, there is much debate over the extent to which many-valued logic solves the problems which motivated its advocacy.

Another ancient motivation for expanding the stock of truth-values was the consideration of modalities. Some sentences, for example, 'Two plus two is four', seem to be not just true, but *necessarily* true. 'The sun is shining today', however, may well be true, but is not necessarily true since we can imagine an alternative. Such considerations suggest having at least four truth-values: 'necessarily true', 'contingently true', 'contingently false', 'necessarily false'. However, it has been shown that most important systems of modal logic do not correspond to any finite-valued semantics.

Another common motivation for many-valued logics is the consideration of uncertainty. Uncertainty from many sources has been considered: from the incompleteness of human knowledge; from the lack of termination of machine computations; from the conflicting judgment of expert opinion; from true statistical fluctuations in nature; and from accumulating error. A major problem is that uncertainties do not combine in a truth-functional way, but many-valued logics are generally truth-functional.

Many attributions which we commonly make every day (for example, 'Charles is ugly') seem to be vague, that is, subject to degree, rather than being black or white (see VAGUENESS). Investigations of many-valued logics have been motivated by attempts to deal with inherently vague aspects of natural language. Considerations of vagueness have led to interest in so-called 'fuzzy logic' in computing science and electrical engineering (see FUZZY LOGIC).

Many-valued logics have been advocated as a means of avoiding various paradoxes, including the usual semantic paradoxes (see SEMANTIC PARADOXES AND THEORIES OF TRUTH), such as the liar paradox, as well as paradoxes associated with the comprehension axiom of set theory (see PARADOXES OF SET AND PROPERTY). For the semantic paradoxes, unless the syntax of the language is unnaturally restricted so that crucial aspects of the semantics cannot even be expressed, versions of the paradoxes simply reappear. For example, suppose we have three truth-values, and consider the sentence 'This sentence is either false or has indeterminate truth-value'. If its value is false, then what it says is true; if its value is indeterminate then what it says is true; but if its value is true, then it is either false or indeterminate. Similarly, the paradoxes of adopting the unrestricted comprehension axiom in axiomatic set theory cannot be avoided solely by adopting a many-valued logic.

2 An example

As a simple example, suppose that instead of the classical semantic range of just 'true' and 'false', we use the following.

T: logically true

t: empirically true

U: undeterminable

f: empirically false

F: logically false

The values T and t are said to be 'designated' values, or ways of being true. The other values are said to be 'undesignated'. We could give semantic characterizations for a great number of connectives, but here are just a few examples.

A	$J_T(A)$	$J_t(A)$	$J_U(A)$	$J_f(A)$	$J_F(A)$	$\sim A$	$\neg A$
T	T	F	F	F	F	F	F
t	F	T	F	F	F	f	F
U	F	F	T	F	F	U	T
f	F	F	F	T	F	t	T
F	F	F	F	F	T	T	T

$\supset$	T	t	U	f	F
T	T	t	U	f	F
t	t	t	U	f	f
U	U	U	U	U	U
f	U	U	U	U	U
F	U	U	U	U	U

$\rightarrow$	T	t	U	f	F
T	T	t	f	f	F
t	T	t	t	f	f
U	T	t	t	t	t
f	T	t	t	t	t
F	T	T	T	T	T

$\vee$	T	t	U	f	F
T	T	T	T	T	T
t	T	t	t	t	t
U	T	t	U	U	U
f	T	t	U	f	f
F	T	t	U	f	F

The J_i connectives have the property that $J_i(A)$ has the value T if and only if A has the value i. They are known as 'autodescriptive' operators; they allow the expression in the syntax of the underlying semantic motivation. While $\neg$ corresponds to 'is not designated', the connective $\sim$ is the more usual complement negation. The conditional $\supset$ reflects the view that if the antecedent is not true, then we cannot tell the value of the conditional. However, $\rightarrow$ parallels the usual material conditional. The disjunction operator $\vee$ is the usual 'max'.

The connectives $\neg$, $\rightarrow$ and $\vee$ are 'pseudo-classical' operators; if we map all the designated values to 'true' and the undesignated values to 'false', then the truth-conditions for these operators correspond to the classical connectives. The connectives $\sim$ and $\supset$ are not pseudo-classical.

Given our semantic account, we may inquire about an appropriate proof theory. Note that if we restrict our language to $\sim$ and $\supset$, then there will be no logical truths (formulas that are always designated); any formula composed with just these two connectives will take the undesignated value U when all atomic formulas take value U. Hence a proof theory for tautologies would not be appropriate were our language so restricted. However, an axiomatization of the consequence relation would still be of interest, and would include such sequents as $A, A \supset B \vdash B$.

Although often presented as restrictions of classical systems, many-valued logics can almost always be formulated as conservative extensions of classical logic. The trick is to include pseudo-classical connectives in the language. A classical proof theory may be stated using the pseudo-classical connectives. Then using the autodescriptive operators, the additional required principles can be formulated. For example, some principles arise simply by stating the truth-conditions for each connective. The last entry on the table for $\supset$, above, corresponds to $J_F(A) \to (J_F(B) \to J_U(A \supset B))$ for an axiomatic system or to $J_F(A), J_F(B) \vdash J_U(A \supset B)$ for a sequent system.

3 Technical matters

All the metatheoretical concerns raised with classical logic also arise with respect to many-valued logics. The model theory of many-valued logics can be developed in much the same way as that of classical logic. Depending on the specifics of the syntax, proof theories are formulated in all the usual varieties: axiomatic, natural deduction, single- and multiple-conclusion consequence relations. Many-valued extensions of non-classical logics may be constructed, and many-valued versions of standard identity theory have been formulated.

Two frequently encountered questions warrant special mention, though we provide only partial answers here. (1) Given an arbitrary semantic theory, can we always find a corresponding proof theory? For the finite-valued case, the answer is affirmative, providing the syntax has appropriate connectives; but if the syntax is limited, it may be impossible to formulate an appropriate proof theory for a single-conclusion consequence relation. For the infinite-valued case, most interesting quantificational systems will not be axiomatizable; even for propositional logics it will be impossible to formulate a finitistic proof theory if the syntax is rich enough (for example, including autodescriptive operators). (2) Given a proof theory, can we always find a corresponding many-valued semantics? If we are concerned only with logical truth (not consequence in general) and if the proof theory admits a rule of substitution, then there will always be an infinite-valued semantics,

though the designated values may turn out not to be decidable.

See also: LOGICAL AND MATHEMATICAL TERMS, GLOSSARY OF; MODAL LOGIC

References and further reading

Belnap, N.D. (1977) 'A Useful Four-Valued Logic', in J.M. Dunn and G. Epstein (eds) *Modern Uses of Multiple-Valued Logic*, Boston, MA: Reidel. (Uncertainty due to conflicting opinion.)

Black, M. (1937) 'Vagueness: An Exercise in Logical Analysis', *Philosophy of Science* 427–55. (Logic of vagueness.)

Chang, C.C. (1965) 'Infinite-Valued Logic as a Basis for Set Theory', in Y. Bar-Hillel (ed.) *Logic, Methodology and Philosophy of Science*, Amsterdam: North Holland. (Paradoxes of set theory.)

Chang, C.C. and Keisler, H.J. (1966) *Continuous Model Theory*, Princeton, NJ: Princeton University Press. (Many-valued model theory.)

Dugundji, J. (1940) 'Note on a Property of Matrices for Lewis and Langford's Calculi of Propositions', *Journal of Symbolic Logic* 5: 370–99. (Important modal systems do not have finite-valued semantics.)

Fitting, M.C. (1992) 'Many-Valued Modal Logics', parts 1 and 2, *Fundamenta Informaticae* 15: 235–54, 17: 55–73. (Many-valued extensions of modal logics.)

Fraassen, B.C. van (1971) *Formal Semantics and Logic*, New York: Macmillan. (Finding a semantics for a given proof theory.)

Kleene, S.C. (1952) *Introduction to Metamathematics*, Princeton, NJ: Van Nostrand. (Uncertainty due to lack of termination of computation.)

Martin, R.L. (ed.) (1970) *The Paradox of the Liar*, New Haven, CT: Yale University Press. (On many-valued logics as a response to the liar paradox.)

McCall, S. (ed.) (1967) *Polish Logic 1920–1939*, London: Oxford University Press. (Source for papers of Łukasiewicz.)

Morgan, C.G. (1974) 'A Theory of Equality for a Class of Many-Valued Logics', *Zeitschrift für mathematische Logik* 20: 427–32. (Many-valued identify theory.)

—— (1975) 'Similarity as a Theory of Graded Equality for a Class of Many-Valued Logics', in *Proceedings of the 1975 International Symposium of Multiple-Valued Logic*, Long Beach, CA: IEEE Society, 436–49. (Many-valued identity theory.)

—— (1976) 'Many-Valued Propositional Intuitionism', in *Proceedings of the Sixth International Symposium on Multiple-Valued Logic*, Long Beach,

CA: IEEE Society, 150–6. (Many-valued extension of intuitionistic logic.)

—— (1979) 'Local and Global Operators and Many-Valued Modal Logics', *Notre Dame Journal of Formal Logic* 20: 401–11. (Many-valued extensions of common modal logics.)

Morgan, C.G. and Pelletier, F.J. (1976) 'Some Notes concerning Fuzzy Logics', *Linguistics and Philosophy* 1: 79–97. (Finding proof theory for infinite-valued semantics.)

Putnam, H. (1957) 'Three-Valued Logic', *Philosophical Studies* 8: 73–80. (On uncertainty due to the incompleteness of human knowledge.)

Reichenbach, H. (1944) *Philosophic Foundations of Quantum Mechanics*, Berkeley, CA: University of California Press. (On uncertainty due to statistical fluctuations in nature.)

Rescher, N. (1969) *Many-Valued Logic*, New York: McGraw-Hill. (Survey of historically important systems.)

Rosser, J.B. and Turquette, A.R. (1952) *Many-Valued Logics*, Amsterdam: North Holland. (Finding proof theory for finite-valued semantics.)

Scarpellini, B. (1962) 'Die Nicht-Axiomatisierbarkeit des unendlichwertigen Prädikatenkalküls van Łukasiewicz', *Journal of Symbolic Logic* 27: 159–70. (Finding proof theory for infinite-valued semantics.)

Scott, D. (1974) 'Completeness and Axiomatizability in Many-Valued Logic', in *Proceedings of the Tarski Symposium, Proceedings of Symposia in Pure Mathematics*, vol. 25, Providence, RI: American Mathematical Society, 411–35. (On uncertainty due to accumulating error.)

Shoesmith, D.J. and Smiley, T.J. (1978) *Multiple-Conclusion Logic*, Cambridge: Cambridge University Press. (Proof theory for a given semantics.)

Thomason, S.K. (1978) 'Possible Worlds and Many Truth Values', *Studia Logica* 37: 195–204. (Many-valued extensions of indexical logics.)

Urquhart, A. (1986) 'Many-Valued Logic', in D. Gabbay and F. Guenthner (eds) *Handbook of Philosophical Logic*, vol. 3, Dordrecht: Reidel, 71–116. (Survey of important technical results.)

CHARLES G. MORGAN

MANY-VALUED LOGICS, PHILOSOPHICAL ISSUES IN

The first philosophically-motivated use of many-valued truth tables arose with Jan Łukasiewicz in the 1920s. What exercised Łukasiewicz was a worry that the principle of bivalence, 'every statement is either true or false', involves an undesirable commitment to fatalism. Should not statements about the future whose eventual truth or falsity depends on the actions of free agents be given some third status – 'indeterminate', say – as opposed to being (now) regarded as determinately true or determinately false? To implement this idea in the context of the language of sentential logic (with conjunction, disjunction, implication and negation), we need to show – if the usual style of treatment of such connectives in a bivalent setting is to be followed – how the status of a compound formula is determined by the status of its components.

Łukasiewicz's decision as to how the appropriate three-valued truth-functions should look is recorded in truth tables in which (determinate) truth and falsity are represented by '1' and '3' respectively, with '2' for indeterminacy (see tables in the main body of the entry). Consider the formula $A \vee B$ ('A or B'), for example, when A has the value 2 and B has the value 1. The value of $A \vee B$ is 1, reasonably enough, since if A's eventual truth or falsity depends on how people freely act, but B is determinately true already, then $A \vee B$ is already true independently of such free action. There are no constraints as to which values may be assigned to propositional variables. The law of excluded middle is invalidated in the case of indeterminacy: if p is assigned the value 2, then $p \vee \neg p$ also has the value 2. This reflects Łukasiewicz's idea that such disjunctions as 'Either I shall die in a plane crash on January 1, 2030 or I shall not die in a plane crash on January 1, 2030' should not be counted as logical truths, on pain of incurring the fatalistic commitments already alluded to.

Together with the choice of designated elements (which play the role in determining validity played by truth in the bivalent setting), Łukasiewicz's tables constitute a (logical) matrix. An alternative three-element matrix, the 1-Kleene matrix, involves putting $2 \rightarrow 2 = 2$, leaving everything else unchanged. And a third such matrix, the 1,2-Kleene matrix, differs from this in taking as designated the set of values $\{1,2\}$ rather than $\{1\}$. The 1-Kleene matrix has been proposed for the semantics of vagueness. In the case of a sentence applying a vague predicate, such as 'young', to an individual, the idea is that if the individual is a borderline case of the predicate (not definitely young, and not definitely not young, to use our example) then the value 2 is appropriate, while 1 and 3 are reserved for definite truths and falsehoods, respectively. Łukasiewicz also explored, as a technical curiosity, n-valued tables constructed on the same model, for higher values of n, as well as certain infinitely many-valued tables. Variations on this theme have included acknowledging as many values as there are real numbers, with similar applications to vagueness and approximation in mind.

1   Second thoughts on some popular applications

Motivated by a concern that the principle of bivalence ('every statement is either true or false') involves an undesirable commitment to fatalism, Łukasiewicz introduced truth tables involving the value 'indeterminate' in addition to 'true' and 'false' in the 1920s (see Łukasiewicz 1970). His decision as to how these three truth-values should be combined is shown in the following tables:

$\land$	1	2	3		$\lor$	1	2	3
*1	1	2	3		1	1	1	1
2	2	2	3		2	1	2	2
3	3	3	3		3	1	2	3

$\to$	1	2	3		A	$\neg A$
1	1	2	3		1	3
2	1	1	2		2	2
3	1	1	1		3	1

The asterisk flagging the first occurrence of '1' in the tables is the conventional way of indicating that this value is 'designated': in other words, that this value plays the role, in defining validity, played by truth in the bivalent setting.

The formal apparatus introduced by these tables is a special case of the notion of a matrix M with which are associated an algebra (a non-empty set – here, the set of matrix elements – closed under some specified operations), that we may call $A(M)$; and a set of matrix elements which are to count as the designated elements, which we will call $D(M)$. An alternative three-element matrix, the 1-Kleene matrix, differs from Łukasiewicz's only in having $2 \to 2 = 2$. A third such matrix, the 1,2-Kleene matrix, differs from this in taking as designated the set of values $\{1, 2\}$ rather than $\{1\}$.

One might expect the term 'matrix' to apply to the individual tables for the connectives depicted in such diagrams, but the standard logical usage, reflected in the definition just given, means that it is the whole set of tables that depicts a single matrix. If we call this matrix M, then the set of M-elements is $\{1, 2, 3\}$ and the algebra $A(M)$ has operations '$\land$', '$\lor$', '$\to$', '$\neg$', behaving as depicted in the tables. (When more care is called for, we distinguish these operations from the connectives, writing something like '$\land^M$', '$\lor^M$' and so on.) Finally, $D(M) = \{1\}$. A logic which is – to use

terminology defined in §2 below – 'determined by' a matrix with n elements but by no matrix with fewer than n elements – is called an n-valued logic.

From the table for '$\lor$' we can see that $1 \lor 2 = 1$. While this seems satisfactory (if A is true then $A \lor B$ will be true regardless of the value assigned to B), we can see that all is not well by looking at another case. The table for '$\land$' tells us that $2 \land 2 = 2$: a result which is suggested by the case in which the two conjuncts concerned are independent ('I shall die in a plane crash', 'Britain will become a republic'), as well as by the case in which the conjuncts are identical, but which goes obviously wrong otherwise ('I shall die in a plane crash', 'I shall not die in a plane crash' – to take an extreme case). The falsity of the conjunction 'I shall die in a plane crash and I shall not die in a plane crash' is fixed regardless of how anyone decides to act. Thus it should receive the value 3. But of course we cannot simply emend Łukasiewicz's matrix and insert a '3' in the middle box of the '$\land$' table, since we shall then have the wrong result for the other cases. Similar reasoning applies in the case of disjunction: the disjunction of 'I shall die in a plane crash' and its negation is not something whose eventual truth can be prevented, so it should have the value 1. So we cannot acquiesce in Łukasiewicz's $2 \lor 2 = 2$. The only conclusion possible is that treating the threefold classification Łukasiewicz had in mind as a range of values with respect to which the familiarly truth-functional connectives could indeed be taken as truth-functional is misconceived. Not every threefold classification of statements gives us a three-valued logic.

It seems appropriate to return a similarly negative verdict on the proposed application of 3- (and more) element matrices, including the 1-Kleene matrix (see Cleave 1974), to vagueness (see VAGUENESS §3). In these and other cases the truth-functional paradigm is simply inappropriate for the notions being modelled (Geach 1949). The problem of failed truth-functionality which afflicts these approaches arises out of the fact that there is a linear ordering of the truth-values with respect to which '$\land$' and '$\lor$' are interpreted as *min* and *max*. In the case of Łukasiewicz's three-valued tables – contrary to what is suggested by the labelling – we are taking 1 as the greatest and 3 as the least, with 2 intermediate. Not all many-valued tables exhibit this kind of linear ordering, however, including some that Łukasiewicz himself proposed for treating modal notions; typically, though, there are more suggestive ways of developing the semantics for such applications than by the laying down of such tables (see Prior 1955). We return in §4 to other applications; we shall also have occasion to observe that the above talk of rejecting the principle of bivalence turns out on reflection to be somewhat dubious – even apropos of certain more promising applications of matrix semantics than those touched on above.

2   Logic

Suppose we have a matrix M and a formal language whose primitive connectives are in one-to-one correspondence with the operations of $A(M)$. Then an assignment of elements of M to the formulas of that language, in which $A(M)$ is used to compute the value of compounds on the basis of their components, will be called an M-evaluation. This generalizes the idea of a 'valuation', which term we shall always reserve for the bivalent case (so a valuation assigns either T or F to every formula), and we wish now to adapt the familiar idea of validity as preservation of truth. The resulting notion is to apply to sequents, and we begin by distinguishing three conceptions of what a sequent is to look like – three (as we shall say) 'logical frameworks'.

The most general framework we call SET-SET, and it takes a sequent of a given language to be something of the form $\Gamma >- \Delta$ (read 'Γ, therefore Δ' or 'Γ yields Δ'), where Γ and Δ are arbitrary sets of formulas of that language (Blamey 1986). If we impose the condition that Δ has to be $\{B\}$ for some formula B, we have the more restricted logical framework SET-FMLA, and write $\Gamma >- B$ rather than $\Gamma >- \{B\}$. Finally, if we impose, in addition to this condition on Δ, the further condition that Γ must be empty, we have the framework we call FMLA, and when no confusion arises we identify the sequents $>- B$ (that is, $\emptyset >- B$) which this framework provides with the formulas B themselves.

Early approaches to logic (Frege, Hilbert) used the framework FMLA, syntactically codifying a logic with the axiomatic method. The provable formulas were formal analogues of the 'logical truths' of that area of natural language being formalized. The sequents of SET-FMLA are formal analogues of arguments with premises on the left of the ' $>-$ ', and the conclusion to the right. For SET-SET, we have a generalization in which, roughly speaking, we may say that sets of formulas on the right are understood disjunctively, just as those on the left are (as in SET-FMLA) understood conjunctively. More precisely, in the bivalent setting, we say that a sequent $\Gamma >- \Delta$ of SET-SET holds on a valuation v (for the language in question) just in case if $v(A) = \text{T}$ for every $A \in \Gamma$, then $v(B) = \text{T}$ for some $B \in \Delta$. Since the other logical frameworks simply restrict the class of sequents, we may use this same definition in connection with them. A set of sequents which contains all substitution

instances of any of its elements will be what we have in mind as a *logic* in that framework. The set of sequents determined by a class of valuations is the set comprising precisely those sequents holding on each valuation in the class. This set may or may not constitute a logic, on the definition just given, depending on what class of valuations is chosen.

It remains to provide a 'matrix semantics' version of the above. We simply make clear the intention that the designated values are those which play the role of truth. Suppose, then, that h is an M-evaluation, for some matrix M; we say that the sequent $\Gamma >- \Delta$ holds on h just in case

$$\text{If } h(\Gamma) \subseteq D(M) \text{ then } h(\Delta) \cap D(M) \neq \emptyset,$$

where $h(\Gamma)$ denotes $\{h(A)\,|\,A \in \Gamma\}$. Again, this definition fixes what it is for a sequent of SET-FMLA or FMLA to hold on an evaluation. Finally, a sequent is *valid* in a matrix M if it holds on every M-evaluation. We will not use the term 'tautologous sequent' (or 'tautology', in the case of FMLA) except for the special case of validity in the familiar two-element matrix. For this special case, also, we do not need the distinction between valuations and evaluations. The set of sequents determined by a class of matrices comprises precisely those sequents valid in each matrix in the class: such a set will always be a logic (as defined above). A logic determined by the class $\{M\}$ will be said to be determined by the matrix M. Notice that the logic in FMLA determined by the 1-Kleene matrix (which differs only from Łukasiewicz in that $2 \to 2 = 2$) is just the empty set, the assignment of the value 2 to every formula being an evaluation for this matrix. Since Łukasiewicz worked in FMLA, this is one reason that in his tables we have $2 \to 2 = 1$ (rather than $= 2$). (The logics determined by the Kleene matrices in the other frameworks are of course non-empty.)

3   Logic (cont.)

We say a logic is 'many-valued in the narrow sense' when it is determined by some matrix, and 'many-valued in the broad sense' when it is determined by some class of matrices. In FMLA this is a distinction without a difference, an early result of Lindenbaum and Tarski having established that in this framework every logic is many-valued in the narrow sense. However, in the case of the other frameworks, the distinction is a real one.

In SET-FMLA, for example, every logic closed under certain structural rules ('overlap', 'dilution' and 'cut' (for sets) – see Shoesmith and Smiley 1978) is broadly many-valued. We call a relation '⊢' between sets of formulas and individual formulas (of some given language) a consequence relation (on that language) when there is some collection Σ of sequents of SET-FMLA which is closed under the SET-FMLA structural rules and for which we have $\Gamma \vdash A$ if and only if the sequent $\Gamma >- A$ belongs to Σ. (This means that '$\Gamma >- A$' is treated as an alternative notation for $\langle \Gamma, A \rangle$.) Closure under these structural rules is a necessary condition for a logic to be determined by any class of valuations. These same rules must be satisfied by any logic determined by a class of matrices for the following reason. Given an M-evaluation h (for some matrix M), we define the (bivalent) valuation v_h induced by h thus: $v_h(A) = T$ if and only if $h(A) \in D(M)$, for all formulas A. Then a sequent holds in the many-valued sense on h just in case it holds, in the bivalent sense, on v_h. Accordingly a set of sequents is determined (many-valued sense) by a class C of matrices precisely when it is determined (bivalent sense) by the class of valuations $\{v_h : h$ is an M-evaluation for some $M \in C\}$. Thus the structural rules must also be satisfied by any SET-FMLA logic which is many-valued in the broad sense. Now while a necessary and sufficient condition for a logic in SET-FMLA to be many-valued in the broad sense is that it should be a consequence relation, there is a further condition to be satisfied in the case of the narrow sense, which is called the cancellation condition in Shoesmith and Smiley (1978). (See also Wójcicki 1974.) This further condition is not satisfied in the case of the consequence relation determined by the pair comprising the 1-Kleene matrix and the 1,2-Kleene matrix, for example, which is not, therefore, a many-valued logic in the narrow sense.

Note that the narrow sense could be further narrowed to exclude determination by a two-element matrix: it is only on such a usage that Łukasiewicz could be counted a pioneer of many-valued logic, for example. A further narrowing in the 'opposite' direction comes by disallowing determination by an infinite matrix to suffice for many-valuedness. The motivation for excluding infinite matrices comes from more than one source. Philosophically, there may be a feeling that such a case involves too many distinctions for the values so distinguished to represent a plausible generalization of the idea of truth-values (Haack 1978: 214). Perhaps the assignment made by an evaluation in this case is better thought of as the assignment of a 'proposition' to a formula (see Dunn 1975). There is also a technical pressure tending towards excluding the infinite case, coming from the Lindenbaum–Tarski result mentioned above together with an early concentration on the framework FMLA: since *every* logic is many-valued in the absence of the restriction to finite determining matrices, we might impose this restriction to avoid

making the term 'many-valued' vacuous. However, since (again) this threat of vacuity does not arise for other logical frameworks, we prefer not to narrow further the above narrow sense of 'many-valued'. It is better to have a separate word for the property of being determined by a finite matrix; the usual word is 'tabular'.

The first demonstration that a logic was not tabular came when Gödel (1932) addressed this question for intuitionistic sentential logic in FMLA. We can introduce the argument he gave for this conclusion by considering a well-known puzzle. Suppose you have a drawer containing (only) twenty socks, ten of which are blue and ten of which are green. You have to choose a pair of the same colour to wear, but because the room is dark, you cannot see the colours. The question is: what is the smallest number of socks you need to remove in order to be sure that among them there will be a matching pair? And the answer is: (not *eleven* but) *three*. The reason is that, since there are only two colours involved, three socks cannot all be of different colours, so you are guaranteed a matching pair. This is a special case of what is sometimes called the 'pigeonhole principle': if a number of pigeons are to be placed in a smaller number of pigeonholes, then at least one pigeonhole must have more than one pigeon in it.

With the example of the socks in mind, consider the question of whether or not the following formula is a (two-valued) tautology:

$$Pigeon_3 \quad (p \leftrightarrow q) \vee (p \leftrightarrow r) \vee (q \leftrightarrow r)$$

It should not be necessary to construct the eight-line truth table to answer this question. Since there are only two truth-values (T, F) to go round, no valuation can assign different truth-values to all three propositional variables p, q and r. (The variables here are playing the role of the pigeons – whence the labelling of the formula – with the truth-values being the pigeonholes.) So each valuation must assign the value T to at least one of the disjuncts of the above formula, thus assigning T to the whole disjunction, which is therefore a tautology.

We turn to Gödel's argument that intuitionistic logic in FMLA – which we shall denote by IL – is not determined by any finite matrix. Let CL denote classical sentential logic in FMLA (alias the set of tautologies in two-valued logic). To begin with, let us see how considerations such as those of the preceding paragraph reveal IL to be determined by no three-element matrix, when supplemented by three additional facts: (1) IL $\subseteq$ CL; (2) IL has the 'disjunction property': for all formulas A, B, if $A \vee B \in$ IL, then either $A \in$ IL or $B \in$ IL; and (3) if C is a disjunction one of whose disjuncts is a formula of the form

$A \leftrightarrow A$, then $C \in$ IL. (We take '$\leftrightarrow$' as a primitive connective for simplicity here; in fact the whole argument goes through if this is replaced by '$\rightarrow$'.) Now consider the formula

$Pigeon_4 \quad (p \leftrightarrow q) \vee (p \leftrightarrow r) \vee (p \leftrightarrow s) \vee (q \leftrightarrow r)$
$\vee (q \leftrightarrow s) \vee (r \leftrightarrow s).$

This formula is not provable in IL, in view of facts (1) and (2) above. Now suppose that some three-element matrix M determines IL. For any M-evaluation h, fact (3) and the pigeonhole principle imply that $Pigeon_4$ holds on h, since h cannot assign distinct M-elements to all four propositional variables. Thus, though not IL-provable, $Pigeon_4$ is M-valid: so IL is not determined by M. The same argument shows (by analogous consideration of the formula we naturally call $Pigeon_n$) that, for any finite number n, IL is not determined by any matrix having n elements: IL is not tabular.

4   From evaluations to valuations

Our introduction, in §3, of the valuation v_h induced by a matrix evaluation h, serves as a reminder of the twofold division which is always present in the background of the many-valued setting, in the form of the ubiquitous designated/undesignated distinction. The notion of validity for sequents is always a matter of invariable possession or preservation of truth: of T as a value of the functions v_h. Distinctions within the classes of designated and undesignated matrix-values do not matter for validity, and enter the semantic account only because the connectives concerned cannot be seen as simply 'designation-functional': in the case of Łukasiewicz's and Kleene's three-valued tables, for example, while $h(\neg A)$ is uniquely determined by $h(A)$, there is no such unique determination of $v_h(\neg A)$ by $v_h(A)$. So we do our compositional semantics at the level of evaluations, and then modulate to valuations for talk of validity.

Here is an analogy: imagine that chemistry were concerned in the first instance with the colours of chemical compounds. We would like to know what colour a compound of substances of given colours will be. The trouble is that just knowing what colour the constituents are is not enough to tell us what colour the compound will be. We also need to know about their chemical composition, so that this extra information can be used to predict the eventual colour of the compound, via its chemical composition. Similarly, even if all we are interested in knowing about a composite formula $A \# B$ (where $\#$ is some binary connective) is whether or not it has a designated value on evaluation h, we cannot obtain

this information – that is, the value of $v_h(A \# B)$ – just from knowing $v_h(A)$ and $v_h(B)$ (the 'colours' of A and B). Rather, we need to know $h(A)$ and $h(B)$, so that we can apply our matrix operation $\#$ to these values and obtain $h(A \# B)$, and then, eventually, $v_h(A \# B)$. This is precisely to acknowledge the possibility of a failure of what was called designation-functionality above.

But are the subdivisions effected by the apparatus of many-valued logic of merely instrumental interest? Such a suggestion has been elaborated over a long period by Michael Dummett, beginning with his article 'Truth' in 1959. The problem Dummett noted is that when we consider the point of the true/false dichotomy as applied to whole sentences (of an interpreted language such as English) which might be used to make assertions, there does not seem to be room for alleging any particular sentence to fall on neither side:

> We need to distinguish those states of affairs such that if the speaker envisaged them as possibilities he would be held to be either misusing the statement or misleading his hearers, and those of which this is not the case: and one way of using the words 'true' and 'false' would be to call states of affairs of the former kind those in which the statement was false, and the others those in which the statement was true.

([1959] 1978: 11–12)

Dummett went on to describe in the light of this criterion how particular cases in which statements have been described as neither true nor false should be classified as true or as false, depending on the nature of the case. The various values of many-valued matrices are then seen as subdivisions of the true (the designated values) and the false (the undesignated) – different ways of being true or of being false, the difference between which needs to be taken into account for settling how the fundamental binary true/false distinction is to apply to compounds into which they enter as components. We repeat one of Dummett's illustrations:

> I once imagined a case in which a language contained a negation operator '−' which functioned much like our negation save that it made '$-(A \rightarrow B)$' equivalent to '$A \rightarrow -B$', where '$\rightarrow$' is the ordinary two-valued implication. In this case, the truth or falsity of '$-(A \rightarrow B)$' would not depend solely on the truth or falsity of '$A \rightarrow B$', but on the particular way in which '$A \rightarrow B$' was true (whether by the truth of both constituents or by the falsity of the antecedent). This would involve the use of three-valued truth tables, distinguishing

two kinds of truth. In the same way, it might be necessary to distinguish two kinds of falsity.

([1963] 1978: 155)

Indeed, Dummett (1959) suggested this last possibility as the appropriate gloss on the response of those who describe sentences containing non-denoting singular terms as 'neither true nor false'. The response is a natural one if one thinks of falsity of a sentence as the truth of its negation (supposing the identification of a sentence's negation is not itself problematic), but since it would be equally erroneous ('misleading') to assert either the given afflicted sentence or its negation, in terms of the more fundamental true/false dichotomy, both sentences fall alike on the false side. The two undesignated values of Łukasiewicz's three-valued logic can be regarded in the same light: as cases in which a sentence having either value are not, the facts being what they are, fit for assertion. They differ in respect of whether the negation of the sentence in question suffers the same fate (according to Łukasiewicz's metaphysical assumptions, that is, and setting to one side the problems about truth-functionality mentioned in §1).

It is for reasons such as this that Dummett speaks of 'the legitimate but comparatively superficial character of the rejection of the law of bivalence involved in the use of a many-valued logic' (1973: 448). In the same work, Dummett draws a distinction between the 'assertoric content' and the 'ingredient sense' of a statement, introduced in terms of the distinction between knowing the meaning of a statement 'in the sense of grasping the content of an assertion of it' and 'in the sense of knowing the contribution it makes to determining the content of a complex statement in which it is a constituent' (1973: 447). Sentences (or statements) which are alike in respect of assertoric content are true (that is, have some designated value) under the same conditions, which does not imply that the replacement of one by the other in some complex sentence will secure a similar likeness for the two complex sentences produced. When the complex sentences differ in respect of designation in this way, the components in respect of which they differ themselves differ in ingredient sense, their similarity of assertoric content notwithstanding. Thus, in terms of our formal notation, and slightly oversimplifying, equality of ingredient sense, for A and B, corresponds to having $h(A) = h(B)$ for every matrix-evaluation h, while equality of assertoric content corresponds to having $v_h(A) = v_h(B)$ for each such evaluation h.

Dummett's rationale for many-valued (that is, k-valued for $k > 2$) logic, then, is that there is sometimes a need to record differences in ingredient sense among statements which do not differ in assertoric content. Without going into too much technical detail, though, we can see that this is not quite accurate. We call a consequence relation '⊢' 'extensional' if for all formulas A, B, with $C(A)$ and $C(B)$ the results of putting formulas A and B into some context C, and for all sets Γ of formulas, we have

If Γ, $A \vdash B$ and Γ, $B \vdash A$, then Γ, $C(A) \vdash C(B)$;

and we call '⊢' 'congruential' when the above condition is satisfied by all A, B, C for the special case in which $\Gamma = \emptyset$. Congruentiality is strictly weaker than extensionality (consider normal modal logics, for example) and, as the end of the last paragraph makes clear, the need to distinguish ingredient sense from assertive content arises precisely when the logic (in SET-FMLA, for expository convenience) is not congruential. Yet, as the reader may care to check, it is failures of the stronger condition, extensionality, rather than just failures of congruentiality, that force a matrix treatment to involve more than two values.

5   From evaluations to valuations (cont.)

We end by briefly taking up one further issue raised by the above exposition: the case of intuitionistic logic. A perusal of Dummett (1959) reveals that his talk (quoted above) of the 'superficial character of the rejection of the law of bivalence' in many-valued logic is intended to contrast with the 'deeper' character of such a rejection in the case of intuitionistic logic. One reason for not considering intuitionistic logic to be many-valued seems hardly to the point here: namely the fact that, as we saw in §3, intuitionistic logic in FMLA is not determined by any finite matrix. (Nobody questions the classification of Łukasiewicz's infinite-valued logic as many-valued, for example.) By the Lindenbaum–Tarski result cited in that section, this ceases to be the case if 'finite' is deleted. Turning to SET-FMLA, the consequence relation associated with intuitionistic logic satisfies the cancellation condition (alluded to in §3) and so here too there is a single determining matrix. On formal grounds, then, we have to say that intuitionistic logic in either of these frameworks is indeed many-valued in the narrow sense of the term. Cardinality of determining matrices aside, are there any good reasons for not regarding IL as many-valued? There is a sense of 'many-valued' which we have not touched on, which allows an affirmative answer to this question: but it has more to do with what its adherents say about a logic than with the logic itself. The usual sort of reason for denying that IL is many-valued is that it would be inconsistent, according to IL itself, for an intuitionist to claim of some given statement that it was neither true nor false – at least when the falsity of A is identified with the truth of $\neg A$. (This use of 'falsity' is of course not that focused on in the quotation from Dummett (1959).) For such a claim would then be of the form $\neg(A \vee \neg A)$, or, IL-equivalently, of the form $\neg A \wedge \neg\neg A$: but the negation of anything of this form is itself IL-provable. So the claim is not one an intuitionist could consistently make. The trouble with this as a way of distinguishing IL from a paradigmatically many-valued logic such as Łukasiewicz's three-valued logic is that dangerously similar moves can be made in the context of the latter logic also. If, instead of adopting an external perspective and saying that A is a statement which is neither true nor false, we think of representing such a claim as the claim that for the given A (which concerns, say, someone's later free actions), $\neg(A \vee \neg A)$, then again we have the equivalence with $\neg A \wedge \neg\neg A$, and this time the further equivalence with $\neg A \wedge A$. And while the negation of the latter is not provable in Łukasiewicz's logic (so that here we have a disanalogy with the case of IL) it remains the case that nothing of that form can receive the designated value on any matrix evaluation: so it is presumably after all not the kind of claim anyone attracted to Łukasiewicz's revision of classical logic ought to be making. As in the case of IL, such a theorist is distinguished from an adherent of classical logic by refraining from making certain claims (for example, some having the form $A \vee \neg A$), rather than by trying to make contrary claims. Further work, then, is called for on the part of anyone wishing to maintain that in some philosophically significant sense Łukasiewicz's logic is many-valued while that of the intuitionists is not.

See also: INTUITIONISM; LOGICAL AND MATHEMATICAL TERMS, GLOSSARY OF; ŁUKASIEWICZ; MANY-VALUED LOGICS

References and further reading

* Blamey, S.R. (1986) 'Partial Logic', in D. Gabbay and F. Guenthner (eds) *Handbook of Philosophical Logic*, vol. 3, *Alternatives to Classical Logic*, Dordrecht: Reidel, 1–70. (The logic in SET-SET determined by the 1-Kleene and 1,2-Kleene matrices taken together is the $\{\wedge, \vee, \neg, \rightarrow\}$-fragment of the 'partial logic' presented here, although Blamey urges us to take the 'indeterminate' not as a truth-value on a par with the other two, but as representing undefinedness in respect of truth-value.)

* Cleave, J.P. (1974) 'The Notion of Logical Consequence in the Logic of Inexact Predicates', *Zeitschrift für mathematische Logik und Grundlagen der Mathematik* 20: 307–24. (Proposes an application of the Kleene matrices to the logic of vagueness.)

Czelakowski, J. (1981) 'Equivalential Logics (I), (II)' *Studia Logica* 40: 227–36, 355–72. (Includes a discussion bearing on what we call 'extensionality' in §4.)

* Dummett, M.A.E. (1959) 'Truth', *Proceedings of the Aristotelian Society* 59: 141–62; repr. with post-script (1972) in *Truth and Other Enigmas*, London: Duckworth, 1978. (Distinguishes deep from superficial grounds for rejecting the principle of bivalence.)

* —— (1963) 'Realism', in *Truth and Other Enigmas*, London: Duckworth, 1978, 145–65. (Further elaboration of the distinction between deep and superficial grounds for rejecting the principle of bivalence.)

* —— (1973) *Frege: Philosophy of Language*, London: Duckworth. (See the appendix to chapter 12 for a critical review of some central concepts of matrix semantics, using some traditional terminology not employed here.)

* Dunn, J.M. (1975) 'Intensional Algebras', in A.R. Anderson and N.D. Belnap, *Entailment: The Logic of Relevance and Necessity*, vol. 1, Princeton, NJ: Princeton University Press, 1975, 180–206. (A gentle introduction to algebraic semantics.)

Fine, K. (1975) 'Vagueness, Truth, and Logic', *Synthese* 30: 265–300. (This paper, like Kamp's (1975), includes a good formulation of the 'failed truth-functionality' argument, as in §1 above, and an explanation of the appeal of a different treatment of vagueness, in terms of 'supervaluations'.)

* Geach, P.T. (1949) 'If's and And's', *Analysis* 9: 58–62. (First published appearance of the 'failed truth-functionality' argument.)

* Gödel, K. (1932) 'Zum intuitionistischen Aussagenkalkül', *Anzeiger der Akademie der Wissenschaften Wien, mathematisch-naturwissenschaftliche Klasse* 69: 65–6; trans. 'On the Intuitionistic Propositional Calculus', in *Kurt Gödel: Collected Works*, vol. 1, *Publications 1929–1936*, ed. S. Feferman, J.W. Dawson Jr, S.C. Kleene, G.H. Moore, R.M. Solovay and J. van Heijenoort, Oxford: Oxford University Press, 1986, 223–5. (In this paper Gödel shows that intuitionistic logic in FMLA is not tabular. A by-product of the argument is a proof of the existence of an infinite sequence of distinct logics intermediate between classical and intuitionistic propositional logic.)

* Haack, S. (1978) *Philosophy of Logics*, Cambridge: Cambridge University Press. (Chapter 11 provides a short survey of some intended applications of many-valued logic.)

* Łukasiewicz, J. (1970) *Jan Łukasiewicz: Selected Works*, ed. L. Borkowski, Amsterdam: North Holland. (See especially 'On Three-Valued Logic' (1920), 'On Determinism' (Łukasiewicz's inaugural address at Warsaw University; 1922) and 'Philosophical Remarks on Many-Valued Systems of Propositional Logic' (1930).)

* Prior, A.N. (1955) 'Many-Valued and Modal Systems: An Intuitive Approach', *Philosophical Review* 64: 626–30. (Shows how to relate certain many-valued matrices to the possible world's semantics for modal logic later popularized by Kripke.)

Rescher, N. (1969) *Many-Valued Logic*, New York: McGraw-Hill. (Provides extensive historical information on the subject, including more on the Kleene matrices, which are versions of Kleene's 'strong' three-valued truth tables, the 'weak' ones being associated with Bochvar.)

Scott, D.S. (1974) 'Completeness and Axiomatizability in Many-Valued Logic', in L. Henkin *et al.* (eds) *Proceedings of the Tarski Symposium*, Providence, RI: American Mathematical Society. (This work provides a useful introduction to semantics in terms of valuations, and proposes a treatment of many-valued logic in which the 'many values' are replaced by 'many valuations'; the logical framework is a finitized version of SET-SET.)

—— (1976) 'Does Many-Valued Logic Have Any Use?', in S. Körner (ed.) *Philosophy of Logic*, Oxford: Blackwell, 64–74. (A less technical discussion of the philosophical underpinnings of Scott 1974.)

Seeskin, K.R. (1971) 'Many-Valued Logic and Future Contingencies', *Logique et Analyse* 14: 759–73. (Includes the 'failed truth-functionality argument' mentioned in §1.)

* Shoesmith, D.J. and Smiley, T.J. (1978) *Multiple-Conclusion Logic*, Cambridge: Cambridge University Press. (Includes a general discussion of many-valued logic and the theory of consequence relations. The cancellation conditions for SET-FMLA and SET-SET appear in chapter 15.)

Urquhart, A. (1986) 'Many-Valued Logic', in D. Gabbay and F. Guenthner (eds) *Handbook of Philosophical Logic*, vol. 3, *Alternatives to Classical Logic*, Dordrecht: Reidel, 71–116. (Good for information about certain aspects of many-valued logic, such as fundamental completeness, but makes the mistake of claiming that there is no distinction between – as we would put it – the broad and narrow senses of 'many-valued' in the framework SET-SET. See Wroński 1987 for correction.)

* Wójcicki, R. (1974) 'Note on Deducibility and Many-Valuedness', *Journal of Symbolic Logic* 39: 563–6.

(Traces the history of the Shoesmith–Smiley cancellation principle.)

* —— (1988) *Theory of Logical Calculi*, Dordrecht: Kluwer. (A comprehensive survey of matrix methodology. Congruentiality, mentioned in §4, is treated under the name 'self-extensionality'.)

Wroński, A. (1987) 'Remarks on a Survey Article on Many Valued Logic by A. Urquhart', *Studia Logica* 46: 275–8. (Corrects a serious error in Urquhart 1986.)

LLOYD HUMBERSTONE

MAO TSE-TUNG/MAO ZEDONG *see* MARXISM, CHINESE

MAOISM *see* MARXISM, CHINESE

MARC-WOGAU, K. *see* SCANDINAVIA, PHILOSOPHY IN (§2)

MARCEL, GABRIEL (1889–1973)

Marcel was a distinguished French playwright and music critic as well as philosopher. It was he who coined the term 'existentialism', although he was reluctant to be pigeon-holed a 'Christian existentialist'. Born into a well-off family of civil servants, Marcel – never a healthy man – worked for the Red Cross during the First World War, an experience which shaped his view of human relationships and confirmed a religious conviction that led to conversion to Roman Catholicism in 1929. After an early flirtation with F.H. Bradley's idealism, Marcel independently developed a phenomenology of human existence and a religious conception of being similar, in several respects, to those of Karl Jaspers and Martin Buber. He was much in demand as a lecturer in his later years.

Marcel was an idiosyncratic writer. Disavowing any 'system', his early writings were ruminative diaries, while his later lectures largely consisted in 'orchestrating', as he put it, the themes tentatively announced in those diaries. The personal anecdotes, of his wartime work for example, testified to his belief that reflection on certain experiences – of 'homelessness' and 'hope', for instance – is a key to understanding our place in the universe. Indeed, they reflect his sense, shared with other existentialists, of 'the primacy of being over knowledge' ([1933] 1949: 8), and his denunciation of 'the execrable habit of considering problems ... in abstraction from ... the very texture of life' ([1935] 1949: 102). Marcel describes his philosophy as a 'concrete' one, and as a true empiricism distinguished by a refusal to follow most empiricists in their myopic focus on *perceptual* experience.

Marcel's ambition was 'to restore its ontological weight to human experience' ([1935] 1949: 103). Restoration is required because human beings now live in – to cite the title of his best-known play – 'a broken world', where they have been reduced to mere 'functions' by the levelling processes of modern technology and politics. As such, while people feel alienated or homeless, they have all but lost the capacity to reflect on their existence and its relation to being at large. A main reason is the predominance of scientific thinking, which reduces all questions to 'problems' with 'technical' solutions, thereby obscuring the sphere of the 'metaproblematic' or 'mysterious'. A 'mystery' is something I am so 'caught up' in that objective analysis, which presupposes a sharp distinction between myself and what is 'in front of me', is inappropriate. For being is precisely what 'withstands ... exhaustive analysis ... [into] elements ... devoid of intrinsic significance' ([1933] 1949: 5), so scientific thought is hostile to ontology, to inquiry into being.

A main culprit behind the hegemony of problem-centred thinking has been philosophies, like Cartesianism, which portray the self as an inner, closed-in sphere 'spectating' a world outside it. This has encouraged the views that the mind is distinct from the body, that we perceive internal data which 'translate' external stimuli, and that 'other minds' need to be inferred from perceptual data. The general effect is to promote the image of myself standing to the world as a 'subject' to an array of 'objects'. Against this, Marcel insists that 'I am not watching a show', that 'ours is a being whose ... essence is to be in every way *involved*' ([1935] 1949: 21, 116-17). I am not distinct from my body as a participating agent in the world. Perception is not awareness of inner data, but active 'reception' of the world, a 'power of opening oneself' to it ([1940] 1964: 29). And in relations like love, other persons are directly 'present' to me, not phantoms whose existence I infer from their behaviour. Marcel's is 'a metaphysic of *we are* as opposed to a metaphysic of *I think*' ([1950b] 1951: 9).

While Cartesianism and its relatives are philosophical errors, it is depressingly familiar in our 'broken world' to live as if they were true, like the solipsistic figures in Proust's later volumes. Marcel's task is to summon us to a 'secondary reflection' which 'reconquers [our] unity' ([1950a] 1950: 103) with the world and each other, one broken by the 'primary reflection' of analytical science, and thereby to free us from the 'sclerosis' which confines us within narrow 'concentric zones'. In particular, he summons people to be 'available' (*disponible*), a stance best manifested in absolute 'fidelity' or commitment to others. Far from sacrificing individuality and freedom through being 'available' to others, this is the only way to achieve them. Not only can I 'really know myself only when I have committed myself' to others ([1940] 1964: 163), but it is only through 'collaboration with his freedom' – through our mutual acknowledgement of one another as 'Thou' – that I myself attain freedom ([1935] 1949: 107). (Marcel, predictably, is acutely critical of Sartre's bleak and agonistic portrait of human relations in *Being and Nothingness*).

Marcel indicates, however, a potential paradox in the making of absolute commitments to others. Given the uncertainty of the future, how for example can a man, unless naïve or disingenuous, commit himself to a lasting loving relationship with his wife? The solution is that he must place hope and faith, if not precisely in God 'as someone other', then at least in a mysterious and co-operative process of being. Thus mundane fidelities only 'become possible ... with that absolute fidelity which [is] faith' ([1940] 1964: 167). Indeed, in the intimations of hope and confidence for the future resides the best testimony to a divine, mysterious order. The traditional proofs for God's existence are of little interest to Marcel, since even if they cannot be logically faulted, they clearly have no power to convince people not already predisposed to belief. He remains hesitant, however, over the need for specifically Christian belief for the possibility of 'availability' and 'fidelity'. On the one hand, this does not logically 'presuppose the data of Christianity'; on the other, we are the legatees of a rich Christian tradition which may, as a matter of fact, provide us moderns with our only viable resources for full and undespairing participation in the world and the lives of our fellows ([1933] 1949: 29f).

See also: BUBER, M.; EXISTENTIALISM; EXISTENTIALIST ETHICS; EXISTENTIALIST THEOLOGY; JASPERS, K., SARTRE, J.-P.

List of works

Marcel, G. (1927) *Journal métaphysique*, Paris: Gallimard; trans. B. Wall, *Metaphysical Journal*, Chicago, IL: Regnery, 1952. (A diary of early reflections on Marcel's staple themes of mystery and human relationships.)

—— (1933) 'On the Ontological Mystery', trans. M. Harari in *The Philosophy of Existence*, London: Harvill, 1949. (Seminal essay on the distinction between the 'problems' addressed by science and the 'mysteries' explored by existential philosophy. This book also contains Marcel's critique of Sartre, 'Existence and Human Freedom'. The essays in this book are arguably the best introduction to Marcel's thinking.)

—— (1935) *Être et avoir: philosophie de l'esprit*, Paris: Aubier; trans. K. Farrer, *Being and Having: An Existentialist Diary*, London: Dacre, 1949. (Like the *Metaphysical Journal*, a loose collection of reflections on human experience and relations.)

—— (1940) *Du refus à l'invocation*, Paris: Gallimard; trans. R. Rosthal, *Creative Fidelity*, New York: Noonday, 1964. (Marcel's most thorough discussion of the theme of 'availability'.)

—— (1945) *Homo Viator: prolégomènes à une métaphysique de l'espérance*, Paris: Aubier; trans. E. Crauford, *Homo Viator: Introduction to a Metaphysic of Hope*, New York: Harper & Row, 3rd edn, 1965. (Focuses on the intimations of the eternal and the divine which are to be found in our everyday lives.)

—— (1950a) *Le Mystère de l'être*, Paris: Aubier, 2 vols; trans. G. Fraser, *The Mystery of Being*, vol. 1, *Reflection and Mystery*, London: Harvill, 1950. (The two volumes of *The Mystery of Being* are Marcel's Gifford Lectures of 1949–50 and are the most complete representation of his increasingly religious concerns.)

—— (1950b) *The Mystery of Being*, vol. 2, *Faith and Reality*, trans. R. Hague, London: Harvill, 1951. (The two volumes of *The Mystery of Being* are Marcel's Gifford Lectures of 1949–50 and are the most complete representation of his increasingly religious concerns.)

—— (1963) *The Existential Background of Human Dignity*, Cambridge, MA: Harvard University Press. (Marcel's William James Lectures at Harvard in 1961–2; the most socially and politically aware of Marcel's works.)

References and further reading

Gallagher, K.T. (1962) *The Philosophy of Gabriel Marcel*, with a Foreword by G. Marcel. New York: Fordham University Press, 3rd edn, 1975. (General and lucid introduction to Marcel's thought.)

McCown, J. (1978) *Availability: Gabriel Marcel and the Phenomenology of Human Openness*, Missoula, MT: Scholars Press. (Short and rewarding study of Marcel on human relationships and the divine.)

Troisfontaines, R. (1953) *De l'existence a être: la philosophie de Gabriel Marcel*, 2 vols, Paris: Vrin. (Gigantic study of Marcel by a sympathetic fellow Catholic.)

DAVID E. COOPER

MARCUS AURELIUS
(AD 121–80)

Marcus Aurelius Antoninus, Emperor of Rome, was the author of a book of philosophical reflections written in Greek and known as the Meditations. *These reflections are based primarily on Stoicism, but also reveal the influence of other currents of thought and of his experience as emperor. Marcus was deeply influenced by Epictetus and shares his interest in the inner mental life and the psychology of moral improvement. He combines a deep commitment to the providential cosmology traditional in the Stoic school with a more pronounced religious sensibility and a frequent emphasis on the insignificance of human life in space and time. The Stoic recognition of the irreducibly social character of human nature is obviously pertinent to an emperor whose career consisted largely of self-sacrificing public service.*

1 Life
2 The *Meditations*

1 Life

Marcus was born in Rome in AD 121, was adopted by the future emperor Antoninus Pius in 138, and succeeded to the throne (jointly with Lucius Verus) in 161. In 169 Verus died, leaving Marcus sole emperor until 177 when his son Commodus joined him. Marcus died on campaign.

Marcus was the last in a series of efficient and humane emperors chosen by adoption whose reigns made the second century AD the high point of Roman imperial culture. The stability of this culture was threatened, however, by military challenges, and Marcus' reign was beset by wars on its borders. (It was during these campaigns, late in his life, that Marcus composed the notebooks which were published after his death.) The reign of his son Commodus was unsuccessful; his assassination in 192 ushered in a period of uncertainty which ended with the consolidation of the rule of Septimius Severus in 197. It is tempting to regard Marcus' reign as the acme of the Roman system and to assign Marcus much of the credit. But the seeds of decay were already present and Marcus did little to prevent the decline.

As a member of the ruling elite, Marcus was educated in Latin oratory and in law, but he also had Greek tutors, including the 'sophist' Herodes Atticus. Marcus' mentor in Latin was Marcus Cornelius Fronto, one of the most famous literary figures in Rome. Fronto's influence on Marcus was personal as well as literary and the correspondence (in Latin) between them rounds out the picture of Marcus which we get from his philosophical writings.

To the disappointment of Fronto, Marcus chose the study of philosophy (which he had begun under the Stoic Apollonius) over law and oratory. The catalyst for this choice was Quintus Junius Rusticus, who not only provided a model of philosophical principle applied in public life, but also introduced Marcus to the *Discourses* of EPICTETUS (*Meditations* I 7). Marcus' personal circle included philosophers of various schools, some of them active in the administration of the empire. He describes Claudius Severus, a Peripatetic, as 'brother' and credits him with inspiration in the area of political theory and practice; Severus introduced Marcus to the ideas of Thrasea Paetus and other figures of the philosophical opposition to Nero (I 14). Severus may be responsible for Marcus' acceptance of the un-Stoic denial of the equality of moral errors (II 10) (see STOICISM). Another influence was Marcus' friend Claudius Maximus, a political and military leader as well as a (possibly Peripatetic) philosopher (I 15); yet another friend, Cinna Catulus, was probably a Stoic (I 13). A certain Alexander, a Platonist, was given a key political post (Greek secretary) at a time of crisis (I 12). Perhaps the best insight into Marcus' philosophical formation comes from reflection on his relationship with Sextus of Chaeronea, a professional philosopher and nephew of Plutarch of Chaeronea. Marcus continued to attend Sextus' lectures even while emperor; in the *Meditations* (I 9.1) Marcus says that he learned from this Platonist the meaning of 'life according to nature' – the defining slogan of the Stoic school (see STOICISM §17). This same philosophical breadth is reflected in Marcus' establishment of the first ever chairs of philosophy. In AD 176 he endowed four chairs at Athens, one for each of the recognized major schools – Platonism, Aristotelianism, Stoicism and Epicureanism.

2   The *Meditations*

The *Meditations* reflects this lack of school dogmatism. While Stoicism provides the framework, Platonic and other ideas are also accommodated. Marcus' philosophical importance does not lie in the preservation or development of the Stoic system but rather in his demonstration of its adaptability to various circumstances and philosophical temperaments.

The framework for Marcus' thought is providential cosmology. The cosmos is an organic whole; each individual is not just a part of that whole, but a limb or organ of the living universe (VII 13). Our well-being is inseparable from that of the whole; he frequently calls humans mere 'fragments' of it. We are similarly related to human society: our private benefit can never conflict with that of the collectivity. Our human nature is fundamentally social; personal fulfilment can never be achieved at the cost of the welfare of the whole. This idea is made into a test of what counts as harm to an individual: 'what is not harmful to the city does not harm the citizen either' (V 22). Civic welfare subsumes, but does not negate, that of the individual. Marcus emphasizes the Stoic claim that whatever happens by nature is in the best interests of each rational agent, that nothing genuinely bad can befall anyone except by way of their own failings. The conjunction of providential determinism with an emphasis on our role as parts of an organic whole brings Marcus close to the *amor fati* ('love of fate') of which Stoics are often accused.

Marcus' conception of the true interests of each person rests on the Socratic idea that nothing bad can happen to any good person. Also Socratic are his determination to teach, not punish, the wrong-doer (everyone should be forgiven, since all are aiming at their own good – XI 16) and the notion that a happy life is based on critical examination of one's convictions. This reveals, he thinks, that nothing unexpected or unbearable ever happens to a rational person (V 18). Like Epictetus, he emphasizes the role of mental reservation (IV 1, V 20), the analysis of impressions, and impersonal detachment; the one thing which ultimately matters is our mental life, our desires, beliefs and convictions.

If the cosmos subsumes individual well-being, then each of us is transient, important only for the rationality we embody, a rationality identified with an indwelling divinity. Hence Marcus emphasizes the smallness of human life, that we are a mere point in space and time (for example, XII 32). The inevitabilty of material change and the cyclical certainty of birth and death are themes to which Marcus returns repeatedly, often drawn from HERACLITUS imagery; nothing as predictable as our own deaths can be regarded as important. Hence there are no surprises for anyone who has spent even half a lifetime in critical reflection on the world (XI 1.2); the most important thing is to structure one's beliefs around the rationally inevitable. Another link between cosmology and ethics emerges from Marcus' repeated reflection on Epicurean atomism – a system opposed to the providential cosmology shared by Platonists and Stoics (see X 6). He states the case tersely at XI 18.1: 'If not atoms, then there is a nature which organizes the universe; and if this is the case, then the inferior exist for the sake of the superior, and the superior [that is, rational beings] for the sake of each other.'

Marcus' views on the composition of human beings can be singled out as an illustration of his openness to non-Stoic influences. We are made up of three components (XII 3): body, 'spirit' or *pneumation*, and intelligence (Nous, identifiable with an internal divinity); although we must care for all three aspects of ourselves, only the third is really our own. The separation of *pneuma*, the stuff of the entire soul according to traditional Stoic theory (see Pneuma), from our rationality is a mark of Platonic influence; this *pneuma* is associated by Marcus with automatic, puppet-like responses. If our reason is separable from the rest of our soul and from our body, then our personal identity has been detached from our empirical selves and the early Stoic unity of the person has been abandoned. Hence Marcus says: 'Wipe out impression; stop your impulse; extinguish desire; keep your commanding-faculty (*hēgemonikon*) in your own control' (IX 7). The similarity to Epictetus is limited. For Marcus, to set impulse, impression and desire in opposition to the commanding faculty appears as a step on the road to Neoplatonism (see Neoplatonism).

But Marcus never abandons the foundations of Stoic physical theory. He repeatedly claims that everything is either 'material' or 'causal' (V 13, VII 29, VIII 11, IX 37, XII 29). Though the terminology is new (it is also reflected in Seneca, *Letters* 65.2), this is the same physical dualism which Zeno of Citium and Chrysippus employed when they divided the universe into the active and passive principles and identified the former with a rational divinity (see Stoicism §§3, 5). Building on this, the founders of Stoicism had outlined a cosmology in which divine guidance and rational coherence were integral parts of the natural world. Despite the appeal of Peripatetic and especially Platonic thought, Marcus retained a Stoic commitment to a unified and physicalist conception of the natural world. Marcus the emperor clung tenaciously to the political and military stability of the second century AD, but he was the last to do so. Similarly, Marcus the philosopher clung to his Stoic tradition.

List of works

Marcus Aurelius (AD 121–80) Meditations in A.S.L. Farquharson, *The Meditations of the Emperor Marcus Antoninus*, Oxford: Clarendon Press, 1944; trans. *The Meditations of Marcus Aurelius Antoninus*, Oxford: Oxford University Press, 1990. (Text, translation and commentary.)

References and further reading

Arnold, E.V. (1911) *Roman Stoicism*, Cambridge: Cambridge University Press (Standard work, somewhat dated but still useful.)

Asmis, E. (1989) 'The Stoicism of Marcus Aurelius', in W. Haase (ed.) *Aufstieg und Niedergang der römischen Welt*, Berlin and New York: de Gruyter, II 36 3: 2,228–52. (A thorough survey of influences on Marcus, both personal and philosophical; emphasis on his openness to other schools and the impact of his own moral reflection.)

Birley, A. (1987) *Marcus Aurelius: A Biography*, revised edn, New Haven, CT and London: Yale University Press. (Reliable biography and history.)

* Fronto (c. AD 95–166) *The Correspondence of Marcus Cornelius Fronto*, trans. C.R. Haines, Loeb Classical Library, Cambridge, MA: Harvard University Press and London: Heinemann, 2 vols, 1919–20. (Latin text with English translation of the letters between Fronto and various friends and figures at court, including Marcus both before and after he became emperor.)

Rutherford, R.B. (1989) *The Meditations of Marcus Aurelius: A Study*, Oxford: Clarendon Press. (Thoughtful literary study of the *Meditations*.)

BRAD INWOOD

MARCUSE, HERBERT (1898–1979)

Herbert Marcuse endured a brief moment of notoriety in the 1960s, when his best-known book, One-Dimensional Man *(1964), was taken up by the mass media as the Bible of the student revolts which shook most Western countries in that decade. Though Marcuse's actual political influence was uneven, his public image was not wholly misleading. On the one hand, he popularized the critique of post-war capitalism that he, with the other theorists of the Frankfurt School, had helped develop: the Western liberal democracies were, they argued, 'totally administered societies' permeated by the values of consumerism, in which the manufacture and satisfaction of 'false needs' served to prevent the working class from gaining any genuine insight into their situation. On the other hand, Marcuse never fully subscribed to the highly pessimistic version of Marxism developed by the central figures of the Frankfurt School, Adorno and Horkheimer. He hoped that revolts by an underclass of 'the outcasts and the outsiders, the exploited and persecuted of other races and other colours, the unemployed and unemployable' would stimulate a broader social transformation. Underlying this affirmation of revolutionary possibilities was a conception of Being as a state of rest in which all conflicts are overcome, where rational thought and sensual gratification are no longer at war with one another, and work merges into play. Intimations of this condition – which could only be fully realized after the overthrow of capitalism (and perhaps not even then) – were, Marcuse believed, offered in art, 'the possible Form of a free society'. Imagination could thus show politics the way.*

1   Life
2   Eros and capitalism
3   Art and Being

1   Life

Marcuse was born in Berlin. Like many young intellectuals of his generation, he was radicalized by his experience of the First World War, and, as a soldier stationed in Berlin, took part in the Revolution of November 1918. Though he studied Marxism during and after the war (when he went to Freiburg University), Marcuse was never involved in the Communist movement. After reading *Being and Time* soon after its publication in 1927 Marcuse returned to Freiburg to work under Martin HEIDEGGER. His early philosophical writings represented a remarkable attempt, as he later put it, 'to combine existentialism and Marxism', though Marcuse later turned against what he came to think of as the 'false concreteness' of Heidegger's philosophy (see EXISTENTIALISM). The main work of this period was Marcuse's *Habilitationsschrift*, the dissertation submitted to obtain the right to teach in German universities. Originally called *Hegel's Ontology and the Foundations of the Theory of Historicity* and completed in 1932, this text was (accounts differ) either never formally submitted or rejected by Heidegger on political grounds.

Marcuse left Germany in December 1932, a few weeks before Hitler came to power. Thanks to the help of, among others, Edmund HUSSERL (another of his teachers at Freiburg), he was invited to join the Institute for Social Research, which had left its

base at Frankfurt University to take refuge in Geneva. Marcuse followed the Institute to Paris and then, in July 1934, to New York, and became one of its most active theorists, publishing a series of major essays in its journal, the *Zeitschrift für Sozialforschung*. Marcuse's active collaboration in the collective work of the Frankfurt School culminated in his second major study of HEGEL, *Reason and Revolution* (1941).

Somewhat ironically, in the light of his later notoriety, Marcuse worked in the Office of Strategic Services, the predecessor of the Central Intelligence Agency, between 1942 and 1950. Unlike Horkheimer and Adorno, he did not return to Frankfurt after the Second World War, but became a US citizen. After holding research posts at Columbia and Harvard, Marcuse taught at Brandeis University from 1954 till his retirement in 1965. During these years he wrote *Soviet Marxism* (1958) and his two most influential books, *Eros and Civilization* (1955) and *One-Dimensional Man* (1964). Between 1965 and 1970 Marcuse held a series of temporary appointments at the University of California at San Diego. It was then that he became an international figure, thanks to his depiction in the mass media as the intellectual author of the radical student movement of the late 1960s. Though this was grossly exaggerated (two leaders of the French student revolt in May 1968 declared, 'None of us have read Marcuse'), Marcuse did make clear his sympathy with the students. In this respect he was quite different from Horkheimer and Adorno, who became increasingly conservative as they grew older. Marcuse's most important later works were perhaps *An Essay on Liberation* (1969) and *The Aesthetic Dimension* (1978). Taken ill during a lecture tour of Germany, he died at Starnberg.

2   Eros and capitalism

Marcuse's starting point, like that of the other leading figures in the Frankfurt School, was provided by the two decisive moves taken by Georg LUKÁCS in *History and Class Consciousness* (1923). First, he developed Marx's theory of commodity fetishism into a general critique of reification (see MARX, K.). Capitalist society, Lukács claimed, seemed to its participants to be a collection of fragments; while individuals might adopt the instrumentally rational means to achieve their particular ends, they lacked any well-founded understanding of the social whole. Second, Lukács identified a unique vantage-point from which such understanding could be gained – that of the proletariat, conceived less as an empirical social class than as the 'identical subject–object' of history, able because of its reduction to the status of a commodity to grasp the meaning of the whole as it strove towards the revolutionary overthrow of capitalism.

The Frankfurt School was enormously influenced by Lukács's theory of reification, but found the idea of the proletariat as a stand-in for the Hegelian Absolute quite implausible. The result was the radical pessimism of Horkheimer's and Adorno's *Dialectic of Enlightenment* (1947), where liberal-democratic capitalism is depicted as a seamless web of reification, as implicitly totalitarian as its fascist and Stalinist opponents were openly, and the rise of instrumental reason is traced back to the first efforts of human beings to control nature. Reason is inextricably implicated in the domination of both nature and human beings. The task of critical theory (as the Frankfurt School tended to call their version of Marxism) is henceforth a negative one, endlessly to expose the unreconciled and unjust character of prevailing society, rather than to identify and promote tendencies leading to social transformation.

Marcuse managed to be part of this evolution, yet remain apart from it. On the one hand, *One-Dimensional Man* is in many ways a popularized and updated *Dialectic of Enlightenment*. Post-war capitalism, Marcuse argues, has overcome any tendency towards economic crisis. The attainment of abundance, however, leads not to liberation but to the generation of 'false needs', whose satisfaction leads to 'euphoria in happiness' and prevents individuals from making their decisions autonomously. The working class is in consequence unlikely to play the role assigned it by classical Marxism as the maker of socialist revolution, and has instead become part of the 'conservative social base' of capitalism. These changes are aspects of an emerging 'pattern of *one-dimensional behaviour* in which ideas, aspirations, and objectives that, by their content, transcend the established universe of discourse and action are either repelled or reduced to terms of this action' ([1964] 1968: 27). Critical theory is thereby forced merely to negate existing society. 'In the absence of demonstrable agents and agencies of social change, the critique is thus thrown back to a high level of abstraction' and 'it cannot be positive' ([1964] 1968: 11, 199).

None the less, as Jürgen HABERMAS observes, there is an 'affirmative feature of Herbert Marcuse's negative thinking' (Habermas 1988). This is perhaps most evident in Marcuse's most original book, *Eros and Civilization* (1955). He seeks to fuse Marx and FREUD, drawing especially on the latter's speculative metapsychological writings. Marcuse attempts to diminish the conservative force of Freud's claim that instinctual repression is a constant of human nature

dictated by the need for self-preservation. Instead, he argues that the 'performance principle' requiring the denial of sensual gratification is historically variable, changing according to the needs of different societies. Where class domination exists, surplus-repression arises – that is, repression that is required, not for self-preservation, but in the interests of the ruling class. Domination thereby roots itself deep within the unconscious. Consequently, 'from the slave revolts in the ancient world to the socialist revolution, the struggle of the oppressed has ended in establishing a new, "better" system of domination'. Nevertheless, 'the very progress of civilization under the performance principle has attained a level of productivity at which the social demands upon instinctual energy to be spent in alienated labour could be considerably reduced' ([1955] 1969: 75, 101). This offers the prospect of a social revolution which, by abolishing surplus-repression, would release considerable libidinal energies. Marcuse envisages a society in which the conflict between Freud's life and death instincts would be overcome, as they found common ground in an escape from suffering and repression, in a state of calm and repose which would represent a renunciation of what Marx called the realm of necessity, of material toil, a state of affairs in which, as Schiller had anticipated, work would be transformed into play, into 'a productivity that is sensuousness, play and song'.

3 Art and Being

Marcuse's philosophy of history is thus one in which 'the restless labour of the transcending subject terminates in the ultimate unity of subject and object: the idea of "being-in-and-for-itself", existing in its own fulfilment' ([1955] 1969: 88). The reconciling totality which Marcuse posits at the end of history is not, however, Lukács's identical subject–object. 'Being is experienced as gratification', Marcuse claims of the future society, 'so that the fulfilment of man is at the same time the fulfilment, without violence, of nature' ([1955] 1969: 122–3). The 'ultimate unity of subject and object' is thus one that harmonizes humankind with nature. Marcuse here remains faithful to the Heideggerian interpretation of Hegel which he developed in Freiburg at the end of the 1920s. In *Hegel's Ontology* and related writings he had argued that the most basic category of the Hegelian dialectic is that of Life, conceived as the 'unifying unity of subjectivity and objectivity as a "subjective substance"' ([1932] 1987: 155) – that is, nature must be thought of, not as an aggregate of static objects governed by mechanical laws, but as a single process of continual self-transformation which manages through all these changes, and of which consciousness is simply the most developed form.

Whatever we make of this interpretation of Hegel, which shows the influence of DILTHEY as well as Heidegger on the young Marcuse, its appeal to the idea of Life in order to conceptualize the unity of subject and object provides his later writings with their implicit structure and thus helps to explain why he remained, in Martin Jay's words, 'a prophet of identity and reconciliation' (1973). Marcuse believed that contemporary society offered, at its fault-lines, glimpses of 'the repressed harmony of sensuousness and reason'; the 'new sensibility' he discerned emerging in the counter-culture of the 1960s offered one such intimation, as did modern art. Marcuse was fond of quoting Stendhal's definition of beauty as 'the promise of happiness'. The radical minorities which had, in some way or other, come to see through the status quo (and, more important, to live beyond it) were, he believed, 'potential catalysts of rebellion within the majority'. Though such claims resonate with the (to most) hopelessly dated revolutionary hopes of the 1960s, many themes of Marcuse's philosophy – the totalizing power it accords to Life, for example, and the cognitive function assigned to art – recall rather German classical idealism from Schiller to Schelling. Perhaps he is best remembered as one of those (Bloch is another) who tried to continue this tradition in a Marxist idiom.

See also: FRANKFURT SCHOOL

List of works

Marcuse, H. (1932) *Hegels Ontologie und die Grundlegung einer Theorie der Geschichtlichkeit*, Leipzig and Frankfurt; trans. S. Benhabib, *Hegel's Ontology and the Theory of Historicity*, Cambridge, MA: MIT Press, 1987. (Marcuse's *Habilitationsschrift*, a reinterpretation of the Hegelian dialectic in the light of Dilthey's philosophy of Life and Heidegger's existentialist phenomenology.)

—— (1941) *Reason and Revolution*, London: Oxford University Press. (A powerful interpretation of the Hegelian tradition, culminating in Marx, in which this tradition is conceived as a 'negative philosophy', and counterposed to the positivist subordination of reason to 'the authority of established fact'.)

—— (1955) *Eros and Civilization*, New York: Beacon Press; repr. London: Sphere, 1969. (A highly original attempt to synthesize Marx and Freud by means of the conception of Life as the dynamic reconciliation of subject and object developed in Marcuse's early writings.)

—— (1958) *Soviet Marxism*, New York: Columbia University Press. (The most sustained effort within the Frankfurt School tradition to distinguish its version of Marxism from the official ideology of the Soviet Union.)

—— (1964) *One-Dimensional Man*, Boston: Beacon Press; repr. London: Sphere, 1968. (Marcuse's best-known work; a critique of contemporary Western society and thought which draws heavily on Horkheimer's and Adorno's *Dialectic of Enlightenment* and is notable for the vigour with which it pursues the natural sciences and anlytical philosophy as instances of one-dimensional 'positive thinking'.)

—— (1968) *Negations*, trans. J. Shapiro, London: Allen Lane. (A collection of essays that includes some of Marcuse's contributions to the *Zeitschrift für Sozialforschung* during the 1930s.)

—— (1969) *An Essay on Liberation*, London: Allen Lane. (Though written before the French upheaval of May-June 1968, this is perhaps Marcuse's most politically optimistic work, in which he defies the ban imposed by both orthodox and Frankfurt Marxism on 'utopian speculation'.)

—— (1972) *Studies in Critical Philosophy*, trans. J. de Bres, London: New Left Books. (Collection that includes an important early essay on Marx's *1844 Manuscripts*.)

—— (1978) *The Aesthetic Dimension*, London: Macmillan. (A late work representing a relatively extreme version of Marcuse's tendency to see art as an intimation of a reconciled human existence.)

References and further reading

* Adorno, T.W. and Horkheimer, M. (1947) *Dialectic of Enlightenment*, trans. J. Cumming, London: Allen Lane, and New York: Herder & Herder, 1972. (The Frankfurt School's most sustained critique of liberal-capitalist civilization, in which reason itself stands condemned for its role in establishing the domination of nature at the basis of social oppression.)

* Habermas, J. (1988) 'Psychic Thermidor and the Rebirth Rebellious Subjectivity', in R. Pippin et al., *Marcuse: Critical Theory and the Promise of Utopia*, South Hadley, MA: Bergin & Garvey, 3–12. (A sympathetic discussion of the 'affirmative' quality of Marcuse's thought by the philosopher generally thought of as the Frankfurt School's main heir.)

* Jay, M. (1973) *The Dialectical Imagination*, London: Heinemann. (A major intellectual history of the Frankfurt School.)

Katz, B. (1982) *Herbert Marcuse and the Art of*

Liberation, London: Verso. (Intellectual biography with a good bibliography.)

Kellner, D. (1984) *Herbert Marcuse and the Crisis of Marxism*, London: Macmillan. (Concerned, as the title suggests, with situating Marcuse within the Marxist tradition.)

Lukács, G. (1923) *History and Class Consciousness*, trans. R. Livingstone, London: Merlin, 1971. (The most important single work of twentieth-century Marxist philosophy; the English edition contains a highly self-critical preface written in 1967.)

MacIntyre, A. (1970) *Marcuse*, London: Fontana/ Collins. (A devastating critique concerned particularly – and somewhat ironically in the light of the author's later development – to demonstrate the defects in Marcuse's treatment of analytical philosophy and classical Marxism.)

Pippin, R., et al. (1988) *Marcuse: Critical Theory and the Promise of Utopia*, South Hadley, MA: Bergin & Garvey. (A valuable collection of essays that includes some of the best critical work on Marcuse, and an important interview in which he discusses his relationship with Heidegger.)

ALEX CALLINICOS

MARGINALITY

Traditional definitions of marginal persons include those who live in two worlds, but do not feel well integrated into either and those who live in societies which are in the process of being assimilated and incorporated into an emerging global society. The influence of Anglo-American and European cultures has brought this situation into existence. A broader, more contemporary understanding of marginality is the condition of feeling marginal in relation to various concepts of the centre. This state produces a stigmatized identity, which either aspires to inclusion or assimilation into the centre, or demands recognition of and respect for a separate but equal existence. This condition of marginality can be experienced in varying degrees by many kinds of people.

Often gender, sexual preference, age, ethnicity, geography and religion are factors which can influence perceptions of marginality. Those who perceive themselves, or who are perceived by others to be marginal are often female, dark-skinned, very young or elderly, poor, disabled, nonheterosexual, displaced, exiled, immigrant, rural, indigenous, 'foreign', outcast, persecuted, or otherwise 'different' from those who occupy positions of privilege in the centre, or the metropolis. Critics of the term 'marginality' believe it has become overused to
the point of losing descriptive precision because, they argue, almost everyone has experienced some form of marginality. In philosophy, however, the phenomenon of feeling, or being, perceived as peripheral, or on the margin, has generated critical perspectives which have enlightened discourse on social integration and stratification; personal suffering and economic, political, and cultural inequality. In addition, analyses of marginality have called into question notions of the 'universal' and the 'objective' set forth by many Western philosophers.

1   Forms of marginality
2   Marginality in philosophy
3   The value of marginality

1   Forms of marginality

People who live in two worlds, but do not feel well integrated into either, could include, for example, *Nuyoricans*. This group comprises people of Puerto Rican origin living in New York, who are often perceived as Puerto Ricans or, more generically, as Latinos or Hispanics by other New Yorkers. Nuyoricans are thought of as 'Americanized' by those who live in Puerto Rico and they are considered as traitors to 'real' Puerto Rican culture. The Nuyorican's existence is marginal on the US mainland as well as on the island of Puerto Rico.

Chicanos choose to identify themselves by a name other than Mexican-American to indicate that they are Mexicans with a nonAnglo image of themselves living in the USA. They are not Mexicans who would feel at home in Mexico, with which many of them are unfamiliar, yet neither do they feel assimilated or choose to identify with the mainstream Anglo-American culture they experience in Los Angeles and elsewhere.

Similarly, *black Latinos* often are categorized as, or feel pressurized into identifying with either African-Americans or Latinos, although they do live in both worlds. Immigrants and exiles in general may feel that they live a dual, conflicting existence, as they attempt to maintain familiar cultural traditions which may become increasingly distant while struggling to adapt to new environs and linguistic challenges which some fail to master to their satisfaction.

With the influence of Anglo-American and European cultures those who live in societies which are in the process of being assimilated and incorporated into an emerging global society include people in developing nations, like Africa, Asia and Latin America. Their awareness of dominant or metropolitan cultures is often reinforced by television and imported music. A proliferation of icons of North American popular culture can be found, for example, in the southern Mexican states of Oaxaca and Chiapas, where indigenous peoples have protested against their marginality relative to both Mexico City and the USA. Consciousness of marginality also influences debates in Latin America over which trade agreements would be most beneficial in bringing particular countries closer to the centres of power. A corollary response to the awareness of marginality and the process of assimilation is the rejection of incorporation into a mainstream. Instead, a defence of the interests and traditions of marginal groups and the right of these groups to coexist would be favoured, respecting pieties without adopting one another's values.

The broader condition of feeling marginal in relation to various concepts of the centre, thus possessing a stigmatized identity, is often linked to concepts of otherness and alienation. It should be noted, however, that while a marginal person may feel alienated, someone who feels alienated is not necessarily marginal. Marginal people are victims of a seemingly immutable, structural alterity. They feel or are made to feel voiceless rather than vocal, powerless rather than empowered, 'barbarous' rather than 'civilized' and unequal rather than equal. They may perceive themselves as subjects rather than as citizens as they often lack the tools, the means and the context to engage in transformational and participatory political processes (see CITIZENSHIP). Those whose marginality is not best captured by the earlier definitions of either living in but not belonging to two worlds, or living in an assimilating culture, fit into the alienated world of marginality, or subaltern otherness. Such marginal persons may be female, dark-skinned, very young or elderly, poor, disabled, lesbian, gay, bisexual, transsexual or transgendered, identified with religious or ethnic minorities, rural, or otherwise geographically or ideologically peripheral.

2 Marginality in philosophy

Philosophy produced by thinkers who feel themselves to be culturally or politically marginal is often different in significant ways from philosophy produced by those who perceive themselves as belonging to the 'centre'. This theme is present in the works of recent thinkers such as, James Baldwin, Edward Brathwaite, V.S. Naipaul, Octavio Paz, Adrienne Rich, Edward Saïd, Derck Walcott and Leopoldo Zea (see AFRICAN PHILOSOPHY, ANGLOPHONE; AFRICAN PHILOSOPHY, FRANCOPHONE; LIBERATION PHILOSOPHY; MEXICO, PHILOSOPHY IN; FEMINIST THOUGHT IN LATIN AMERICA).

There are in existence metropolitan philosophers, who may or may not be aware of their position of privilege, and there are those who have been 'expelled from the centre of the world and ... condemned to search for it through jungles and deserts or in underground mazes of the labyrinth' (1961: 209), as Octavio Paz has indicated. Aristotle maintained that the Greek man was a rational creature capable of governing those who are less rational, such as children, women and slaves. Such a stance testifies that marginality has been a time-honoured tradition throughout the history of Western philosophy. For Leopoldo Zea, marginality is a mechanism whereby one human can deny the other of humanity. One's humanity, in his view, becomes circumstantial, resting on accidents such as skin colour, gender, social class and level of education. Zea refers to the *occidentals*, as opposed to the *accidentals*; Frantz FANON uses the image of the 'wretched' (1961) and José Ortega y Gasset writes of the existentially 'shipwrecked'. The image offered by Mexican humanist Alfonso Reyes was that Mexican intellectuals would not be invited to the banquet table of Western civilization, although they had many contributions to offer.

3 The value of marginality

Argentine philosopher Arturo Andrés Roig believes that 'The truth is not found primarily in the totality, but in determinate forms of particularity with power to create and recreate totalities from a place outside the latter, as alterity' (1983: 113). Like Roig, most philosophers whose work arises out of marginality and marginalized peoples believe they are testifying that dominant philosophical canons are uninformed or underinformed by the experience of many who are socially and culturally removed from those metropolises in which mainstream philosophers live and think. Leopoldo Zea explains, 'The great Greek, medieval, modern, and contemporary philosophers never had to worry about being original or about their cultures being strange since both their cultures and the people who created these cultures were considered universal' (1971: 15). Zea maintains that the problem of philosophy in Latin America 'is the awareness that its existence is a marginal existence' (1971: 19).

However, being marginal is not necessarily a negative intellectual phenomenon. On the contrary, there is an ironic sense in which the philosophy of marginality is a gift from the centre to the margin. Marginality is a gift to philosophers who live and think on the margin in the sense that it affords them a certain latitude to make original contributions in areas that have been ignored through the undetected or unimagined provincialism of the mainstream. Marginality becomes a methodology which challenges how and by whom values are grounded to such an extent that marginal thinkers believe that their viewpoint offers a vantage point that better illuminates and more comprehensively grounds values.

Philosophy from the margin more easily lends itself to self-criticism, in opposition to philosophy from the centre which has no pressing need to criticize itself precisely because it represents the centre, or universal. Therefore, marginal philosophy can be more thought-provoking and compelling.

See also: ALTERITY AND IDENTITY, POSTMODERN THEORIES OF; CULTURAL IDENTITY

References and further reading

Baldwin, J. (1962) *The Fire Next Time*, New York: Dell. (Analysis of racism.)

* Fanon, F. (1961) *The Wretched of the Earth*, London: Penguin. (Analysis of colonialism.)

* Paz, O. (1961) *The Labyrinth of Solitude: Life and Thought in Mexico*, trans. L. Kemp, New York: Grove. (Discussion of solitude in Mexico.)

* Roig, A.A. (1983) *Teoría y crítica pensamiento latinamericano* (Theory and Criticism of Latin American Thought), Mexico: Fondo de Cultura Económica. (Essential book for specialists in Latin American thought.)

Stonequist, E.V. (1937) *The Marginal Man: A Study in Personality and Culture Conflict*, New York: Charles Scribner's Sons. (Discussion of marginality.)

Weinstein, M. and Weinstein D. (1981) 'The Problematic of Marginality in Mexican Philosophy', *Canadian Journal of Political and Social Theory* 4 (3). (Issues of marginality in Mexico are discussed.)

* Zea, L. (1971) *La esencia de lo americano* (The Essence of the American), Buenos Aires: Editorial Pleamar. (Discussion of certain characteristics of the inhabitants of the Americas.)

—— (1988) *Discurso desde la marginación y la barbarie* (Discourse of the Marginal and the Barbarous), Barcelona: Editorial Anthropos. (Analysis of marginality in relation to civilization and barbarism.)

—— (1992) *The Role of the Americas in History*, ed. A.A. Oliver, trans. S. Karsen, Savage, MD: Rowman & Littlefield. (Analysis of Latin American marginality.)

AMY A. OLIVER

MARITAIN, JACQUES (1882–1973)

Maritain was one of the most influential twentieth-century interpreters of the thought of Thomas Aquinas. His interests spanned many aspects of philosophy, including aesthetics, political theory, philosophy of science, metaphysics, education, liturgy and ecclesiology.

His acknowledged masterpiece is The Degrees of Knowledge *(1932). In this work, Maritain expands on Thomistic thought and seeks to explain the links between philosophy, science and religion as branches of wisdom. Rather than being a close study of Thomism, this work expands on Thomistic ideas and puts them into the context of the modern world. In natural science, for example, he distinguishes between empirical knowledge of nature and philosophy of nature; the latter consists in the knowledge of essence, while the former is concerned with the knowledge of form.*

In moral philosophy, Maritain expands on Aquinas, holding that no true conception of the human ultimate end is philosophically possible, and that moral philosophy therefore must be subordinated to moral theology. Later in his career, Maritain concentrated more strongly on theology, but throughout his life his Roman Catholic faith informed all of his works. He continues to be read widely today, with a worldwide reputation which is especially strong in France and North America.

1   Life
2   Thomism
3   Main arguments
4   Influence

1   Life

Jacques Maritain was one of the two or three most prominent Thomists during the long second phase of the revival of study of St Thomas Aquinas. It is difficult to think of an area of philosophy to which he did not devote himself. His first book appeared in 1906 and his last in the year he died. He lived through the period when Thomism was established throughout the Catholic world and survived into a post-conciliar period when that effort came under acute criticism.

Maritain was born in Paris in 1882. In 1900, while a student at the Sorbonne, he met Raissa Oumansov, a fellow-student; they were true soul mates, and were married in 1902. After their conversion to Catholicism, it was Raissa who first discovered St Thomas Aquinas. Their home in Versailles became a place where artists, authors, philosophers and theologians gathered. When they moved to Meudon in 1923, these meetings were formalized as the *Cercle d'Études Thomistes*. Maritain's *Prayer and Intelligence* (1922) sets forth the complementarity of the spiritual and intellectual lives.

Maritain taught first at the Lycée Stanislas, then at the Institut Catholique, but his thought and writings were not driven by academic duties. He first visited North America in 1933, and returned there in 1938. Étienne Gilson had hoped to enlist Maritain as a permanent associate at the Pontifical Institute of Mediaeval Studies in Toronto, but Maritain proved elusive. He became a frequent lecturer at Chicago and Notre Dame, and was with his wife in the United States when France fell in 1940; they remained until 1944, when Jacques was named French Ambassador to the Vatican. Raissa's two volumes of memoirs, *We Have Been Friends Together* and *Adventures in Grace*, acquainted a generation of Americans with their dramatic story, their friends, and the burgeoning Catholic culture of France.

Maritain served as the president of the French delegation to UNESCO during the drafting of the Universal Declaration on Human Rights, but resigned as ambassador to accept an appointment at Princeton in 1948. The Maritains returned to France in 1960, where the ailing Raissa died. Jacques settled in Toulouse, where he taught philosophy and theology to the Little Brothers of Jesus. In 1965, at the close of the Second Vatican Council, Paul VI presented Maritain with a message addressed to intellectuals. Maritain divided his time between Toulouse and Kolbsheim near Strasbourg. In 1970, this quintessential layman entered the religious life as a Little Brother of Jesus. He died in 1973 and is buried with Raissa at Kolbsheim.

2 Thomism

In *Aeterni Patris* (1879), Leo XIII called for a renewal of Christian philosophy, particularly that of St Thomas Aquinas, as a way of combating modern errors. The response to the encyclical occurred in stages, eventually fanning out across the globe. Journals were founded, new institutes and associations were formed, conferences were held, and there was a flood of interpretations and prolongations of the thought of Aquinas. At first a largely clerical phenomenon, the Thomistic revival became, with Maritain and Étienne Gilson, a lay effort which more effectively related traditional Catholic thought to the wider culture.

Maritain, like so many of his generation, came under the influence of Henri Bergson, whom he examined in comparison with Aquinas in his first book, *Bergsonian Philosophy* (1913). *Antimodern*

(1922) might suggest that Maritain saw Thomism simply as antithetical to contemporary thought, but that this was not his view is clear from *Angelic Doctor* (1929), as well as earlier works. However, the most comprehensive statement of his philosophical vision is given in *The Degrees of Knowledge* (1932).

The *Degrees* is Maritain's masterwork. He adopts Aquinas' distinction between philosophy and theology, whereby the latter is discourse whose principles are provided by divine revelation, and held by faith. One who does not hold the principles to be true will not hold as true the conclusions drawn from them. Theology, considered as a truth-seeking discipline, is thus an activity of believers. Philosophy, on the other hand, is discourse which proceeds from principles in the public domain, knowable by anyone; the philosopher must link his inferences to what everybody already knows.

This is obviously an Aristotelian view. Maritain sees Aquinas as an Aristotelian, and, accordingly, the Aristotelian division of philosophy into theoretical and speculative disciplines governs his thought. One of the interesting features of his work is the way he expands and reshapes that basic division to accommodate contemporary advances in thought.

Maritain's aim in the *Degrees* is to lay before us a vast and connected and hierarchical panorama so that we see our quest for knowledge as a graded ascent to wisdom *tout court*. He first discusses the relation between philosophy and experimental science, goes on to a plea for critical realism, discusses philosophical knowledge of sensible reality and then sets forth his metaphysics. The second part treats the relation between philosophy and mystical experience, and argues that the culmination of the human quest for truth is that wisdom which is a gift of the Holy Spirit. Like Aquinas, Maritain seeks a comprehensiveness which finds unity beyond necessary distinctions.

In 1931, thanks to a taunt by Émile Bréhier (in the *Revue de Métaphysique et de Morale*), a debate began on the nature of Christian philosophy. Was it possible for Christians to engage in philosophy or must their efforts be seen as the question-begging of believers? Maritain agreed that it would be nonsense to say that the Christian faith has no influence on the thinking of the believer. But the influence of faith has its analogue in the pre-philosophical assumptions of one ignorant of or hostile to the faith. Maritain distinguished between the act of philosophizing as a moral and human deed, and the product of such activity. With respect to the latter, believer and unbeliever, despite their differing existential starting points, must meet the same criteria for success. Maritain rejected the charge that Christian faith disqualifies one from philosophy; indeed, he considered it an aid and stimulus.

Few of Maritain's writings are exegetical, that is, close studies and interpretations of texts of Aquinas. Rather, having absorbed Aquinas, Maritain was interested in making him intelligible to modern philosophers, creating a new synthesis continuous with Aquinas' historical achievement. Étienne Gilson once wrote that he himself had spent his life seeking to know exactly what Aquinas meant, while Maritain was seeking to do in the present what Aquinas had done in the past.

3 Main arguments

Aesthetics. In 1920, Maritain published *Art and Scholasticism*, his second book. His wife was a poet, their friends were artists in various media – Rouault, Cocteau, Claudel, Péguy, Julien Green – and he felt a need to ask what the relation between art and philosophy is. The little book is a fascinating *mélange* of Aristotelian and Thomistic lore, but reveals as well Maritain's wide knowledge of literature and art. Many artists welcomed the Aristotelian truism that art aims at the perfection of the thing made, not of the maker. A salient mark of Maritain's aesthetics is his likening of poetic knowledge to the judgment of connaturality that Aquinas attributed to prudence. The Mellon Lectures, *Creative Intuition in Art and Poetry* (1953), bring to fruition Maritain's thoughts over many decades. They emphasize the knowledge which is prior to and may be expressed in artistic production.

Philosophy of science. For Aquinas, philosophy of nature establishes the possibility of a science beyond itself. If natural change ultimately requires an uncaused cause, and thus one outside the realm of things that come to be (natural things), a science which treats of all being and not just natural beings suggests itself. Change involves matter; the changeless lacks matter, so to be and to be material are not identical. The development of modern science called into question the validity of Aristotelian physics, and this led some Thomists to seek to bypass it and begin with metaphysics. Maritain developed a distinction between experimental or empiriological (Maritain's neologism) knowledge of nature and the philosophy of nature. The former, mathematical physics, falls short of knowledge of essence, the knowledge that characterizes philosophy of nature. This suggests that the matter/form analysis of sensible substance is ontological knowledge, profounder than the knowledge gained by the sciences. Developed in a number of books, Maritain's position on this matter is also the first discussion in *The Degrees of Knowledge*.

Metaphysics. While Maritain's position on metaphysics was initially similar to that of Aquinas, seeing the science of being as dependent for its very possibility on achievements in philosophy of nature, his approach changed, as is evident from *Existence and the Existent* (1947). There Maritain speaks of an intuition of being as the *sine qua non* of metaphysics. This intuition is not common to all, but is possessed only by a few. This development puts Maritain in the camp of those who feel that metaphysics can be undertaken without any prior science, philosophical or otherwise, of sensible reality. The 'intuition of being' seems to arise from the influence of existentialism. To some degree, it points to the need for a sense of wonder as the presupposition of philosophical questioning. Furthermore, it appears to be Maritain's response to the interpretation of Gilson, who saw Aquinas' use of *esse* as the key to his thought; the grasp of *esse* is part and parcel of the recognition that essence and existence are distinct, a recognition Gilson felt was missing from Aristotle.

Moral philosophy. It was in the area of moral philosophy that Maritain was most innovative. In Aquinas, we encounter the view that there are certain principles of action which are part of the natural repertoire of any human agent. Aristotle had articulated the ultimate end appropriate to the nature of the human agent, which end provides such limited happiness or fulfilment as is possible for humans. From the Christian point of view, Aristotle's sense of the inadequacy of human happiness is just what is to be expected, since humans are destined for a higher happiness after their earthly existence. Aquinas thus spoke of imperfect and perfect beatitude, with 'imperfect' representing Aristotle's own sense and not simply a Christian judgment. Maritain's view is markedly different: he holds that no true conception of the ultimate end for humans is philosophically possible. Moral philosophy 'adequately understood' must be subordinated to moral theology, that is, must accept as true a conception of an ultimate end beyond our natural powers to discover. Critics accused Maritain of smudging the distinction between philosophy and theology and he was soon caught up in elaborate defences of his position (in, for example, *Science and Wisdom* (1935)).

Political philosophy. From involvement with the right-wing Action Française, condemned by the Catholic Church in 1926, Maritain moved leftward to the position of *Integral Humanism* (1936). Visits to the USA altered his critique of capitalism (see, for example, *Reflections on America* (1957)). The fall of France, and its wartime occupation, deeply affected him, and he became a champion of democracy and human rights. The role he played in the Universal

Declaration on Human Rights of 1948 is evident in his Walgreen Lectures, which were published as *Man and the State* (1951). Here Maritain confronts the conflict between natural law and natural rights. He argues that the duties consequent on natural law and natural rights are two ends of the same thought.

A more timely problem arose from the fact that the signatories of the Universal Declaration held such radically different views of those rights. Maritain was incapable of a cynical explanation of this paradox, and he proposed a distinction between gnoseological and ontological natural law. Perhaps it would not simplify his point too much to say that the nature of the speakers and of the things spoken of in such situations provide an objective basis for agreement, whatever current misunderstandings obtain.

Theology. In the final phase of his career, Maritain's writings became overtly theological, doubtless because they were occasioned by teaching the Little Brothers of Jesus in Toulouse. He and Raissa had written *Liturgy and Contemplation* in 1959, and in *The Degrees of Knowledge* he had ventured into mystical theology. *On the Grace and Humanity of Jesus* (1967) and *On the Church of Christ* (1970) and much of the posthumously published *Approches sans entraves* (1973) are purely theological. Among the surprises to be found in these late writings is a questioning of the eternity of the punishment of the damned even though they are forever incapable of the beatific vision.

4 Influence

From the time of his conversion in 1906, Maritain regarded his Catholicism as the most essential thing in his life. The Christian vocation, the call to respond to grace and to the gifts of the Holy Spirit, was from the outset the frame within which his intellectual work was carried out. His understanding of the concept of Christian philosophy, as well as the constitution he wrote for the *Cercle d'Études Thomistes* (see his *Carnet de notes* (1965)), display his sense of the profound union of the intellectual and spiritual lives. Both Raissa and Jacques strove for holiness, and the testimony of friends suggests that their efforts were not unrewarded. They were instrumental in the return to the faith or conversion of many. The published correspondence between Maritain and Julien Green gives some flavour of what will be found in other, unpublished, letters.

Maritain's estimate of what was happening in the Church in the wake of Vatican II was not cheerful. *The Peasant of the Garonne* (1966) lamented the influence of Teilhard de Chardin and of phenomenology. He saw a resurgence of the modernism that had

been condemned by Pius X in 1907. Some dismissed Maritain as out of date and grumpy.

As it happens, his influence continues and, indeed, increases. The Jacques Maritain Center at the University of Notre Dame, Indiana, was founded in 1948, and soon such centres sprang up around the world. There are two international Maritain societies and many national societies. A fifteen-volume *Oeuvres complètes* was completed in 1994, and a twenty-volume English edition began to appear in 1995.

See also: THOMISM

List of works

Maritain, J. (1975, 1978) *Jacques Maritain Oeuvres*, ed. H. Bars, 2 vols. (By and large, these are selections rather than complete works; volume 1 covers the years 1912–39, volume 2 1940–63.)

—— (1982–94) *Oeuvres complètes*, ed. J.-M. Allion, M. Hany, D. Mougel, R. Mougel, M. Nurdin and H. Schmits, Fribourg: Éditions Universitaires, 15 vols. (The volumes are organized chronologically and cover the period 1906–60, including the writings of Raissa as well as Jacques. Each volume is well indexed, with bibliographical notes, and includes pieces from periodicals and prefaces to others' works, as well as some indication of the response to Maritain's work. The French text of this collection is definitive.)

—— (1995–) *Complete Works*, ed. R. McInerny, B. Doering and F. Crosson, Notre Dame, IN: University of Notre Dame Press. (With some exceptions, each volume contains a number of works. Volume 7, *The Degrees of Knowledge*, was one of those that appeared in 1995. The project should be completed by 2005.)

References and further reading

Bréhier, É. (1931) 'Y-a-t-il une philosophie chrétienne?' (Is There a Christian Philosophy?) *Revue de Métaphysique et de Morale*, April–June. (Started the debate on the nature of Christian philosophy described in §2.)

Doering, B.E. (1983) *Jacques Maritain and the French Catholic Intellectuals*, Notre Dame, IN: University of Notre Dame Press. (Places Maritain within the French intellectual scheme.)

Kernan, J. (1975) *Our Friend Jacques Maritain*, New York: Doubleday. (A charming personal memoir by an American friend of the Maritains.)

* Leo XIII (1879) *Aeterni Patris*, in J. Maritain, *Le Docteur angélique*, in *Oeuvres complètes*, vol. 4, Paris: Éditions Saint-Paul, 1983; trans. J.W. Evans

and P. O'Reilly, *St Thomas Aquinas*, New York: Meridian Books, 1958. (Includes a discussion of the encyclical, as well as its text.)

McInerny, R. (1988) *Art and Prudence: Studies in the Thought of Jacques Maritain*, Notre Dame, IN: University of Notre Dame Press. (A collection of essays written at various times, dealing chiefly with Maritain's aesthetic and moral positions.)

RALPH MCINERNY

MARIUS VICTORINUS
(*fl.* 4th century AD)

Gaius Marius Victorinus was a rhetorician active in Rome in the fourth century AD. Classically educated and with an interest in philosophy, he converted to Christianity late in life and transferred his philosophical interests to Christian works. Strongly influenced by Neoplatonism, particularly by the works of Plotinus and Porphyry, he sought to articulate Christian concepts such as the Trinity in Neoplatonic terms. His writings on the Trinity and the soul influenced Augustine and other patristic philosophers.

Born in Africa some time in the decade AD 281–91, Victorinus acquired a classical education, including considerable knowledge of philosophy and its history. He wrote commentaries on the works of Cicero, produced treatises on grammar and logic and translated Greek philosophical works into Latin. Associated with aristocratic and senatorial circles, his success as a rhetor is evinced by the commissioning of a statue in his honour in the Forum of Trajan during his lifetime. In these activities, Victorinus represents a well-established Roman cultural type: the successful rhetorician with a learned interest in philosophy. Yet Victorinus was in the cultural vanguard of his time in one critical respect, his conversion to orthodox Christianity. We learn from St Jerome that this occurred 'in extreme old age', perhaps in the mid 350s. His late career was as an author of Christian theology, generating a series of commentaries on the letters of St Paul (Ephesians, Galatians, Philippians), as well as treatises of intra-Christian polemics. It is from these later theological works, directed primarily against the Arian heresy, and his translation efforts that Victorinus' subsequent philosophical reputation is derived.

Victorinus' interest in the philosophy of his time went well beyond the norm for a learned rhetorician. He translated some of Aristotle's logical works into Latin, as well as a large number of treatises from the *Enneads* of PLOTINUS and possibly some works of PORPHYRY, including the *Isagōgē*. This effort suggests both technical knowledge of philosophy and serious commitment to a cultural programme. His goal appears to have been the dissemination into the Latin world of contemporary Neoplatonism, particularly that of the Plotinian school (see NEOPLATONISM). Here Victorinus was successful not only among pagan readers, but also among his subsequent co-religionists, the Christians. These translations were essential to the assimilation of Plotinian and Porphyrian thought by Latin Christian intellectuals in the late fourth century (see PATRISTIC PHILOSOPHY). This fact is famously attested in Augustine's conversion narrative, the *Confessiones*; here, in Books VII–VIII, he describes the intellectual effect of reading – in the mid-380s – 'some books of the Platonists' (*Confessiones* VIII. 9.13) translated by Victorinus. These Neoplatonic treatises were decisive in motivating Augustine's acceptance of Christian monotheism, as they must have been at an earlier time for Victorinus himself (see AUGUSTINE).

Of Victorinus' philosophical ideas, we have only an imperfect record. His goal was to articulate the Christian Trinity in Neoplatonic terms, and to do so in a fashion that secured the orthodox conception of the consubstantiality of the Father and the Son. This theological desideratum was the source of his philosophical originality. In order to secure their monotheism, Christian thinkers were inclined either (a) to describe the Father, Son and Holy Spirit as modes or names of a single God, or (b) to treat the Son and Spirit as ontological derivatives of a primordial Father (see TRINITY). The former, modalistic solution was articulated philosophically by Sabellius among others; the latter, subordinationistic approach was adopted by ORIGEN of Alexandria, the Christian student of Plotinus' teacher AMMONIUS, and more forcefully by his later followers, including Victorinus' Arian opponents. Victorinus appears to have sought a way through this scholastic dichotomy by resorting to the subtle hypostatic theories of the Plotinian–Porphyrian school.

His approach was to treat the divine Father as a first principle defined in a fashion similar to the Plotinian One. The Father was above all being, beyond both the material things of the physical world and the Platonic intelligibles. In Victorinus' view, God, as the primordial Father, was best understood as 'pre-being' (*proon*), an absolute and perfect source for all finite reality. Beyond specification or determinate description, the Father was therefore beyond knowledge and the capacity of human conceptualization. As such, the Father makes his presence known through his Word or Son, the first being. The Son is the initial determination of the unlimited Father, the perfect manifestation of his hidden divine source. As the visible aspect of God, the Son is the 'form of God', the divine principle that brings out the latent nature of the Father. The Son thus gives finite form to the indefinite or formless substance of God the Father.

What is especially interesting about this Neoplatonic treatment of these Christian notions is Victorinus' recognition of the non-subordinationistic possibilities of Plotinian theology. He insists that the Father, as the unbounded source of all reality, cannot be juxtaposed as a distinct entity, superior in its own nature to that of the Son. Rather, the Father is the ontological ground of the Son, and as such, cannot be viewed either as external to the Son or as another being superior to him. If the Father is 'pre-being', then he is directly present to his first definite manifestation, his Word. Ontological subordination would seem therefore to be a misreading of what is not a hierarchical relation between separate entities. In Victorinus' model, the omnipresence of the Plotinian One thus becomes the basis for securing the consubstantiality of Father and Son, the hallmark of Nicene orthodoxy.

Victorinus is also noteworthy for his treatment of the human soul. The soul is brought into being by the creative activity of the Word, and bears its image: its capacity for rational reflection in particular reflects the order and structure of the Word. Within the soul, Victorinus discerned a triad of aspects indicative of its source in the divine: being, life and intellect. While fallen, the human soul retains this divine image, and has the capacity to restore its likeness to the Logos by exercising its intelligence and sloughing off the effects of its descent into time and change. In emphasizing the triadic structure of the descended soul and its isomorphism with the divine Trinity, Victorinus anticipated Augustine's subsequent interest in Trinitarian models of the soul and so the Western Christian articulation of the relation of the human and the divine (see SOUL, NATURE AND IMMORTALITY OF THE).

See also: AUGUSTINE; ENCYCLOPEDISTS, MEDIEVAL; NEOPLATONISM; PLATONISM, MEDIEVAL; PATRISTIC PHILOSOPHY; PLOTINUS; SOUL, NATURE AND IMMORTALITY OF THE; TRINITY

List of works

Marius Victorinus, Gaius (after 355) *Marii Victorini Opera* (Works of Marius Victorinus), ed P. Henry, P. Hadot and F. Gori, Corpus Scriptorum Ecclesiasticorum Latinorum vol. 83, Vienna: Hoelder-Pichler-Tempsky, 1971–86. (Collected works of Victorinus.)

—— (after 355) *Ad Candidum* (To Candidus), ed. P. Henry and P. Hadot in *Traités théologiques sur la Trinité* I–II, Paris: Éditions du Cerf, Sources Chrétiennes, 1960, vols 68–9. (A theological reply to an extant letter from Candidus, an Arian Christian.)

—— (after 355) *Adversus Arium* (Against the Arians), ed. P. Henry and P. Hadot in Traités théologiques sur la Trinité I–II, Paris: Éditions du Cerf, Sources Chrétiennes, vols 68–9, 1960. (A major attack against Arianism in four books.)

—— (after 355) *In epistolam Pauli ad Ephesios* (On the Letter of Paul to the Ephesians), in J.P. Migne (ed.) *Patrologia Latina*, Paris, 1844, vol. 8, 1235–94. (Expository commentary on one of the Pauline epistles.)

—— (after 355) *In epistolam Pauli ad Galatas* (On the Letter of Paul to the Galatians), in J.P. Migne (ed.) *Patrologia Latina*, Paris, 1844, vol. 8, 1145–98. (Expository commentary on one of the Pauline epistles.)

—— (after 355) *In epistolam Pauli ad Philippenses* (On the Letter of Paul to the Philippians), in J.P. Migne (ed.) *Patrologia Latina*, Paris, 1844, vol. 8, 1197–1236. (Expository commentary on one of the Pauline epistles.)

References and further reading

Clark, M.T. (1976) 'Marius Victorinus Afer, Porphyry, and the History of Philosophy', in R. Baine Harris (ed.) *The Significance of Neoplatonism*, Norfolk, VA: Old Dominion University, 265–73. (A short study in the metaphysics of Plotinus, Porphyry and Marius Victorinus.)

—— (1981) 'The Neoplatonism of Marius Victorinus the Christian', in H.J. Blumenthal and R.A. Markus (eds) *Neoplatonism and Early Christian Thought*, London: Variorum, 153–9. (Victorinus and the concept of the divine One.)

—— (1982) 'A Neoplatonic Commentary on the Christian Trinity: Marius Victorinus', in D.J. O'Meara (ed.) *Neoplatonism and Christian Thought*, Albany, NY: State University of New York Press, 24–33. (An assessment of Victorinus' use of Neoplatonism in his theology.)

Cooper, S.A. (1995) *Metaphysics and Morals in Marius Victorinus' Commentary on the Letter to the Ephesians*, New York: P. Lang. (A study of Neoplatonism and Christian thought in the Ephesians commentary.)

Hadot, P. (1968) *Porphyre et Victorinus*, Paris: Études Augustiniennes, 2 vols. (A major study of Victorinus and Porphyry, including Greek and Latin texts.)

—— (1971) *Marius Victorinus: recherches dur sa vie et ses oeuvres* (Marius Victorinus: Research on His Life and Works), Paris: Études Augustiniennes. (A discussion of biographical evidence.)

Manchester, P. (1992) 'The Noetic Triad in Plotinus, Marius Victorinus, and Augustine', in R.T. Wallis and J. Bregman (eds) *Neoplatonism and Gnosticism*, Albany, NY: State University of New York Press, 207–22. (An examination of triadic schemes in the metaphysics of these figures.)

Markus, R.A. (1967) 'Marius Victorinus and Augustine', in A.H. Armstrong (ed.) *The Cambridge History of Later Greek and Early Medieval Philosophy*, Cambridge: Cambridge University Press, 329–40. (The best overview in English of Victorinus' thought.)

Steinmann, W. (1990) *Die Seelenmetaphysik des Marius Victorinus* (The Metaphysics of the Soul of Marius Victorinus), Hamburger Theologische Studien 2, Hamburg: Steinmann & Steinmann. (A detailed study of Victorinus' doctrines on the soul.)

JOHN PETER KENNEY

MARKET, ETHICS OF THE

Markets are systems of exchange in which people with money or commodities to sell voluntarily trade these for other items which they prefer to have. Most economic transactions in advanced societies are of this kind, and any attempt to replace markets wholesale with a different form of economic coordination seems destined to fail. But questions about the ethics of markets are still of considerable practical concern, for two reasons at least. First, we need to make collective decisions about the proper scope of markets: are there goods and services which in principle should not be distributed and exchanged through market mechanisms – medical care, for instance? Second, markets work within a framework of property rights which sets the terms on which people can exchange with one another, and this too is subject to collective decision: for instance, should a person's labour be regarded as a commodity like any other, to be bought and sold on whatever terms the parties can agree, or does labour carry special rights that set limits to these terms? Are employees morally entitled to a share of the profits of the companies they work in, to take a concrete issue?

To guide such decisions, we need to apply general ethical principles to market transactions. First, are markets justified on grounds of efficiency, as is often claimed? What criterion of efficiency is being used when such claims are made? Second, can we regard the outcome of market exchanges as just, or, at the other extreme, should we see them as necessarily exploitative? Third, do market exchanges necessarily alienate people from one another and destroy their sense of community? These are very different questions, but an overall assessment of market ethics needs to address each of them, and perhaps others besides.

1 Efficiency
2 Justice and exploitation
3 Alienation and community

1 Efficiency

Informally, we describe institutions as efficient when they satisfy people's desires or preferences to the greatest possible extent. In this informal sense, it is easy to understand the efficiency claims made on behalf of markets. Viewed narrowly as a system of commodity exchange, a market enables people to exchange items they desire less for items they desire more, whereas whenever such exchanges are prevented, some people will have less of what they want than they might otherwise have. Viewed more broadly, as a mechanism for producing goods and services as well as exchanging them, a market provides incentives for people to make goods and provide services that other people want to buy. It also, as Hayek (1967) in particular has argued, economizes on information: individual people can make rational decisions about what and how much to produce on the basis of limited information about the costs and prices of a small number of goods and services, whereas a non-market system of production (such as a centrally-planned economy) would require some agency to assimilate data and coordinate behaviour across the whole economy (see HAYEK, F.A. §2).

Economists have formalized the efficiency claim in the first theorem of welfare economics, which states that when a perfectly competitive market reaches equilibrium, this must be Pareto-optimal, meaning that no one's welfare can be further increased without reducing the welfare of someone else (see ECONOMICS AND ETHICS §4; PARETO PRINCIPLE).

The efficiency claim is, however, subject to some large qualifications (for a fuller discussion, see Buchanan 1985). Real markets usually fall far short of the idealized markets of economic theory. Competition is imperfect – for instance rigidities are introduced when people invest in machinery or skills which cannot be easily redeployed when demand changes; individuals have been shown not to behave as rational maximizers of their utility; and, perhaps most importantly, many economic transactions generate positive or negative externalities such as spill-over effects on third parties who have not consented to the exchange: Smith may open a new supermarket on the edge of town, and I and many others may voluntarily buy our groceries from him rather than from the corner store, but the effect is that the store has to close, imposing substantial costs on those who cannot easily travel to the supermarket; thus resulting in a negative externality. We cannot say therefore that real markets will be efficient, even by the Pareto criterion; there may be further resource transfers that such markets will not induce that would make everyone better off.

Next, Pareto optimality yields only a weak sense of efficiency. There are likely to be many resource allocations of which it is true that any reallocation will lower the welfare of at least one individual. The resource allocations generated by markets are characteristically quite unequal. By a stronger criterion of efficiency – for instance, a utilitarian criterion which tells us to aggregate welfare across individuals – efficiency would usually be increased by redistribution from the better off to the worse off, at least up to the point where incentives begin to be affected (see UTILITARIANISM).

Finally, markets are said to be efficient in so far as they satisfy individuals' felt desires, which are expressed in their market behaviour – for instance, in their choice of consumer goods. This argument depends on interpreting individuals' welfare subjectively, in terms of existing preferences (see WELFARE §1). If instead we were to measure welfare in terms of real interests or needs, then even the informal argument for market efficiency is put in question. Where markets meet desires that it is not genuinely to people's advantage to have satisfied, how can we advocate them on efficiency grounds?

In the light of these qualifications, the efficiency principle only provides a weak reason to favour markets; perhaps more importantly, it cannot adjudicate between economies in which almost everything is left to market mechanisms and economies where the state is more active in regulating the market and redistributing resources, such as social democracies (see SOCIAL DEMOCRACY).

2 Justice and exploitation

Whether market outcomes are considered just or unjust depends on the theory of justice being applied (see JUSTICE). At one extreme stands the view, associated particularly with Hayek, that the concept has no application to the results of a spontaneous process. Since no one intends to bring about the final outcome of a large set of market transactions, that outcome cannot be regarded either as just or as unjust. Against this, however, it has plausibly been argued that market outcomes are predictable, in their general shape if not their detail, and this is sufficient to bring the concept of social justice into play (Plant 1991).

Another view is that market transactions are always justice-preserving as long as they are fully voluntary – that is, neither side employs force or fraud to secure the transaction. This view appeals to a historical entitlement theory of justice of the kind favoured by Nozick and other libertarians (see LIBERTARIANISM; NOZICK, R. §2). However, it is vulnerable to the problem of externalities that we have already encountered: a voluntary exchange between A and B may alter, perhaps for the worse, the position of C. Thus it seems that we have to look beyond individual transactions to consider the overall distribution of resources that results from the operation of market mechanisms over time.

Experience tells us that this distribution is likely to be quite unequal. Many philosophers would argue that such inequality is just in so far as it reflects the different choices that individuals may make – the choice to work rather than play, or to save rather than consume, for instance. DWORKIN has developed a theory of this kind, where resources are initially to be divided equally among individuals, but where subsequent holdings may legitimately reflect such choices. On Dworkin's view, however, resource inequalities that stem from differences in native talent are unjust, and since much of the inequality in real-world markets appears to be of this kind, a just society would have to redistribute resources from the more talented to the less talented through a tax system.

This view can be challenged by invoking a stronger sense of desert, according to which people deserve the results of their productive efforts even when these depend on native abilities and dispositions that are not themselves deserved (see DESERT AND MERIT). Market outcomes could then be regarded as just in so far as they reflected the different productive achievements of individuals, as opposed to being the results of luck (Miller 1989). Such a justification will once again be vulnerable to the imperfections of real-world markets, where factors such as inherited advantage or monopoly power mean that many individuals will hold resources that by this criterion they do not deserve.

Philosophers in the socialist tradition have argued that many market transactions are exploitative. Notwithstanding their appearance of voluntariness, inequalities of resources or of bargaining power mean that one party is able to impose terms that make the exchange an unequal one. This applies particularly to labour contracts between workers and owners of capital. Marx developed the most celebrated theory of capitalist exploitation, arguing that an excess supply of labour would force workers to accept subsistence wages while their work created surplus value for their employers to appropriate (see MARX, K. §12). However, this theory relies on the one hand on a labour theory of value which now has few supporters, and on the other hand on a prediction about the future course of capitalism which has not been borne out.

More recent theories of economic exploitation have abandoned the labour theory of value, and have also attempted to widen the theory beyond the case of capital–labour exchanges. According to Roemer (1988), for instance, we can identify exploitation by asking whether there is a group of people who have to work for longer than is socially necessary to earn the bundle of goods they consume, and another group who need to work for less time. It emerges from these theories that although exploitation may emerge within markets, its source is always inequality in the assets or endowments that people bring to market exchanges. We can therefore enquire into the conditions under which markets can function without exploitation. This has led some political philosophers to develop theories of market socialism, examining the possibility of a market economy without private ownership of productive capital (Miller 1989; Schweickart 1993; Arnold 1994) (see SOCIALISM §6).

3 Alienation and community

Even if markets can be framed in such a way that they are reasonably just and non-exploitative, they may still be criticized on the grounds that they set participants against one another and prevent them from enjoying fraternal or communal relations. Although market behaviour need not be motivated by narrow self-interest, it is in standard cases 'non-tuistic' (to use Wicksteed's phrase), meaning that neither party to an exchange has any intrinsic concern for the welfare of the other. Each uses the other as an instrument for their own purposes, whatever these might be: when I buy oranges from the greengrocer, I have no interest in his wellbeing.

Marx once again gave fullest expression to this charge, when he described workers under capitalism as alienated, in part because they were prevented from enjoying those communal relations with their fellow workers which properly expressed their nature as human beings (see MARX, K. §4; ALIENATION §§3–5). But many others have attacked market

societies for fomenting individualism and competition at the expense of social solidarity and community (see COMMUNITY AND COMMUNITARIANISM §3).

In reply to this, defenders of the market point out that, where markets are working properly, self-interested (or non-tuistic) behaviour on the part of each individual may contribute to the welfare of everyone; as Adam SMITH famously argued, each is led by an 'invisible hand' to promote the interest of society more effectively than when they attempt to promote it directly (Smith 1776). Thus there is no conflict between producing or exchanging with a view to one's own advantage and contributing to the welfare of others.

This reply only partly answers the original charge, however, because the existence of a community depends not just on how people act but on their intentions. We cannot describe the relationships that exist between buyers and sellers in a market as inherently communal. Yet there is no reason why communal relations should not develop alongside those of market exchange, for instance in workplaces, local communities or political associations. A society might then have a communitarian character overall, even though its economy was predominantly market-based.

What seems certain is that a world in which people interacted with one another solely through market transactions would be not only morally barren, but probably unsustainable. The question that arises is how to prevent the market from encroaching upon spheres of social life that presently act as a counterbalance to it. Recently philosophers have begun to investigate the reasons why certain goods and certain human relationships need to be kept insulated from market mechanisms: for instance, why body parts should not be bought and sold, or why marriage should not be turned purely into a negotiated contract between husband and wife (Anderson 1993; Andre 1995; Walzer 1983). The reasons are quite varied, but one concerns the way exposure to market mechanisms may change the character of relationships for the worse, by, for instance, undermining trust: if I know that doctors stand to profit from the treatment they prescribe, will I have the same confidence in them as when they have no financial stake in the outcome?

A careful examination of the ethics of markets is likely to lead neither to an unqualified endorsement nor an unqualified rejection of market mechanisms. Instead it will encourage us to ask questions about the institutional framework of the market. How can we ensure that it remains competitive, and therefore efficient? Can we guarantee that each participant has access to sufficient resources that they will not be exploited? How do we prevent markets from encroaching into spheres of human life where they have no place?

References and further reading

Acton, H.B. (1993) *The Morals of Markets and Related Essays*, ed. D. Gordon and J. Shearmur, Indianapolis, IN: Liberty Press. (Rejects the claim that market exchange and competition must violate ethical principles.)

* Anderson, E. (1993) *Value in Ethics and Economics*, Cambridge, MA: Harvard University Press, ch. 7. (Explores the kinds of value that cannot be realized through market relationships.)

* Andre, J. (1995) 'Blocked Exchanges: A Taxonomy', in D. Miller and M. Walzer (eds) *Pluralism, Justice, and Equality*, Oxford: Clarendon Press. (Classifies grounds for holding that certain goods should not be privately owned or exchanged.)

* Arnold, N.S. (1994) *The Philosophy and Economics of Market Socialism*, New York: Oxford University Press. (A critique of market socialism, arguing that opportunities for exploitation are greater under such a system than under capitalism.)

* Buchanan, A. (1985) *Ethics, Efficiency, and the Market*, Oxford: Clarendon Press, ch. 2. (Perhaps the best general assessment of the ethical and efficiency arguments for and against the market.)

* Hayek, F.A. (1967) 'The Principles of a Liberal Social Order', in *Studies in Philosophy, Politics and Economics*, London: Routledge & Kegan Paul. (A summary version of Hayek's defence of the market, and his attack on ideas of social justice.)

* Miller, D. (1989) *Market, State, and Community: Theoretical Foundations of Market Socialism*, Oxford: Clarendon Press. (Principled defence of market socialism.)

* Plant, R. (1991) *Modern Political Thought*, Oxford: Blackwell, ch. 3. (Argues against Hayek's claim that ideas of distributive justice cannot be applied to markets.)

* Roemer, J. (1988) *Free to Lose: An Introduction to Marxist Economic Philosophy*, London: Radius. (Reworks and generalizes the Marxist theory of economic exploitation.)

* Schweickart, D. (1993) *Against Capitalism*, Cambridge: Cambridge University Press. (Ethical critique of capitalism, and defence of democratic market socialism.)

Sen, A. (1985) 'The Moral Standing of the Market', *Social Philosophy and Policy* 2 (2): 1–19. (Helpful brief survey of the ethical criteria by which markets can be assessed.)

* Smith, A. (1776) *An Inquiry into the Nature and Causes of The Wealth of Nations*, ed. R.H. Campbell, A.S. Skinner and W.B. Todd, Oxford: Clarendon Press, 1976, book IV, ch. 2. (Classic defence of market economy as contributing to social welfare.)

* Walzer, M. (1983) *Spheres of Justice*, Oxford: Martin Robertson. (Explores reasons why some goods should not be allocated by market mechanisms.)

DAVID MILLER

MARSILIUS OF INGHEN (1330–96)

The theological and philosophical works of Marsilius of Inghen are characterized by a logico-semantical approach in which he followed John Buridan, combined with an eclectic use of older theories, often dating from the thirteenth century. These were sometimes more Aristotelian and sometimes more Neoplatonist. The label 'Ockhamist', which is often applied to Marsilius, has therefore limited value. He was influential on Central European philosophy of later centuries, both through his own philosophy and by the way he stimulated reform of university programmes. In the sixteenth century there were still references to a 'Marsilian way' in logic and physics.

1 Logic
2 Theory of science
3 Natural philosophy

1 Logic

The semantic approach is pivotal in Marsilius' philosophy. In his theory on the properties of terms, *suppositio* is the acceptance of a term in a proposition for the thing(s) concerning which the term is verified by way of the copula of the proposition. For example, in the proposition 'a man is running', the term 'man' supposits for any man that exists, because concerning any of them it may be verified through the copula. The definition of supposition is in line with WILLIAM OF OCKHAM and, more strictly, with BURIDAN, but Marsilius' semantics has distinctive characteristics. Unlike Buridan, he accepts 'something imagined' as the significate of a fictional term such as *chimera*. Moreover, Marsilius does not adopt 'natural supposition', which in his view is a kind of atemporal signification, for example, of 'man' and 'animal' in 'man is an animal'. In his *Logic*, John Dorp (*fl.* 1400) follows Buridan in all respects except for the chapter on supposition, in which Marsilius is his model.

A commentary on Alexander of Villadei's *Doctrinale* is ascribed to Marsilius, probably correctly. In this work, he presents a 'conceptualistic grammar'; congruency in language is not relegated to the level of spoken thought (as it was by Ockham and Aurifaber), but is a property primarily of mental language. The result is that the grammar of mental language, on which spoken language is dependent, is a 'speculative science' (see LANGUAGE, MEDIEVAL THEORIES OF).

2 Theory of science

Both Marsilius and Buridan differ from Ockham in accepting a broader view of the formal object of a science. Whereas Ockham is more nominalistic (according to him the immediate formal object is a mental proposition), Buridan and Marsilius also accept a 'remote object' (the term) and a 'most remote object' (the thing) as significates. When trying to determine the formal object of theology, Marsilius agrees with Thomas AQUINAS that a science has one single formal object, which Marsilius defines for theology as 'God as goal of man'. This formal object is in fact a predicate, which supposits for God (Marsilius' semantic approach again), and to which all other objects are related. Any other science has a formal object analogous to theology, such as syllogism in the case of logic.

3 Natural philosophy

The concept of impetus received much attention in the history of medieval physics. According to Marsilius, a projectile when thrown moves forward not because it was pushed by the air (which in its turn was moved by the thrower), which is faster than the natural downward movement of the thing thrown (this was Aristotle's opinion). Instead, the action of the thrower gives the projectile a kind of property (the 'impetus') that causes the movement and diminishes on its own. Here Marsilius follows Buridan in certain respects, rather than Ockham.

In the medieval commentaries on Aristotle's *On the Heavens* the problem of the spot on the moon occupied a prominent place. Theories about the origin of the spot had to reckon with the generally accepted theory of the simple nature of the heavenly bodies. According to Marsilius and other fourteenth-century Parisian philosophers, the moon is one of the ethereal planets (it was not earthlike, as ALBERT THE GREAT thought). They denied that the moon's spot originated from outside (as Thomas Aquinas maintained). In a simple body like the moon, density and rarity follow primarily from the essence, Marsilius says, while the spot follows from it in a secondary sense, because the essence is dependent on the causality of the sun. In their different ways, these philosophers blurred the Aristotelian demarcation between heavenly bodies and the sublunary region (see NATURAL PHILOSOPHY, MEDIEVAL).

Marsilius also deals with two problems on the borderline between physics and theology. He holds that from the viewpoint of natural philosophy, there cannot be a plurality of worlds separate from each other. From the viewpoint of faith, however, God can create more worlds, in which natural kinds may differ from those in our world. Here Marsilius' view differs from that of most thirteenth-century philosophers. Marsilius believes that the world could not possibly be eternal, and in this he dissents from, for example Thomas Aquinas and Thomas of Strasbourg, who held that God's power to create an eternal world did not detract from his perfection and his own eternity (see ETERNITY OF THE WORLD, MEDIEVAL VIEWS OF).

See also: ARISTOTELIANISM, MEDIEVAL; BURIDAN, J. LOGIC, MEDIEVAL; NATURAL PHILOSOPHY, MEDIEVAL; WILLIAM OF OCKHAM

List of works

Marsilius of Inghen (1362–7) Treatises on the Properties of Terms, ed. and trans. E.P. Bos, *Treatises on the Properties of Terms: A First Critical Edition of the Suppositiones, Ampliationes, Appellationes, Restrictiones and Alienationes*, Dordrecht: Reidel, 1983. (See this work for Marsilius' views on semantics.)

—— (1362–77) *Abbreviationes super octo libros Physicorum Aristotelis* (Abbreviations on Aristotle's *Physics*), Venice: Octaviani Scoti Sociorum, 1521. (Includes Marsilius' impetus theory.)

—— (1362–77) *Quaestiones in De caelo* (Questions on Aristotle's *On the Heavens*), in MS Cuyk en St Agatha, Kruisherenklooster, C 12, f. 123ra–171rb. (See for the problem of the spot on the moon and the possibility of more worlds.)

—— (1392–4) *Quaestiones super quattuor libros Sententiarum* (Questions on the Four Books of Sentences), Strasbourg: Martin Flach, 1501; repr. Frankfurt: Martinus Flach, Jr, 1966. (A primary source for Marsilius' theory of science and his view of the eternity of the world.)

References and further reading

Braakhuis, H. and Hoenen, M. (eds) (1992) *Acts of*

the International Marsilius of Inghen Symposium, Nijmegen: Ingenium. (Recent articles on various aspects of Marsilius' philosophy.)

E.P. BOS

MARSILIUS OF PADUA (1275/80–1342/3)

Marsilius of Padua's Defensor pacis *(Defender of Peace), written in 1324, is the most revolutionary political treatise of the later Middle Ages. Discourse One of the* Defensor pacis *can plausibly be read as a complete theory of the secular state. In a much longer second discourse, Marsilius attacks papal and priestly political power, which, especially in the claims to 'fullness of power' (*plenitudo potestatis*) sometimes made for the papacy, he presents as a major threat to civic tranquillity. The distinctive features of Marsilian theory are (a) its emphasis on broad participation in the legislative process as a guarantee of sound law, and (b) its insistence that supreme coercive power in any community must be held by a single, secular, popularly authorized 'ruling part' (*pars principans*).

1 Life
2 The 'state' and its peace
3 Legislation and government
4 Religion

1 Life

Marsilius was born Marsilio dei Mainardini, son of a notary to the University of Padua. He lectured on natural philosophy and engaged in medical research and practice in Paris, where he was rector of the University in 1313. In 1326, when his authorship of the *Defensor pacis* (Defender of Peace) was discovered, he fled to the court of Ludwig of Bavaria, then at odds with the papacy over the need for papal approval of his election as emperor several years earlier. Marsilius defended Ludwig's authority as Roman emperor in the tract *De translatione imperii* (On the Transfer of the Empire), presumably written in 1326–7, through advice and action during Ludwig's Italian campaign of 1327–30, and in the *Defensor minor*, written by 1342. Marsilius was dead by April 1343.

2 The 'state' and its peace

The discussions of popular assemblies and civic affairs in Discourse One of the *Defensor pacis* are most easily understood in relation to the first of the two milieux in which Marsilius passed his political life, the northern Italian commune. From the beginning, however, Marsilius sought to construct a theory which could be used to resist papalist claims to power on any scale. Accordingly, the formal unit of his analysis is the *regnum*, which he defines, peculiarly, as 'something common to every species of temperate regime, whether in a single city or many' (*Defensor pacis* 1.2.2). The generic character of this definition, the dedication of the *Defensor pacis* to Ludwig of Bavaria, the Empire's history as a particular object of papal jurisdictional claims and the context of Marsilius' later life and writings give some support to an imperialist as well as a republican interpretation of his thought.

At any level, the aim of political association, according to Marsilius, is 'the sufficient life'. His exegesis of this Aristotelian concept is a comparatively modest one. Although he notes that those who live a civil life have leisure for the activities of the moral and intellectual virtues, the 'living well' of Aristotelian politics, Marsilius is less concerned than most medieval authors (for example, Thomas AQUINAS) with orienting politics toward the perfect natural or supernatural fulfilment of human nature. He is more concerned with the factors producing or impeding the peaceful resolution of disputes and the cooperative functioning of those parts of a community which are devoted to meeting basic earthly needs. Thus, while he follows ARISTOTLE (§27) in including the priesthood as one of the parts of a *regnum* (along with farmers, artisans, merchants and the like), he treats it as a part established and controlled by lay authority.

3 Legislation and government

The modest aim or final cause of Marsilian politics dictates an inclusive view of the parties qualified to participate as efficient causes in achieving that aim. To be sure, Marsilius is not a pure majoritarian. When he argues that the primary and proper efficient cause of the law is 'the people or the whole body of citizens, or the weightier part thereof', he immediately explains that by the 'weightier part' (*pars valentior*) he means to take into consideration both 'the quantity and the quality of the persons in that community over which the law is made' (*Defensor pacis* 1.12.3). Even with this qualification, however, Marsilius' conception of legislative authority is exceptionally populist for the period in which he wrote.

Marsilius follows Aristotle and medieval tradition in arguing that the rule of law is necessary for achieving civic justice, the common benefit and political stability. He departs from tradition (how sharply is controversial) in making coercive enforceability, rather than rational content, the essence of law. Hence, although the wisdom of experts may be called on to formulate proposed legislation, it is the people's consent that gives these proposals the force of law. Citizen participation in the legislative process is important for Marsilius even on the score of knowledge, for he holds that the people can discern what is for their mutual benefit and are thus able to assess and improve the counsels of the wise few.

Popular authorization is also required for the establishment (and, if necessary, correction) of a government to enforce the law. Although Marsilius argued for elective monarchy as generally the best form of government, he left the choice of administration by one, few or many rulers to the people. Whatever its internal makeup, however, it is vital that the supreme government of a city or larger community operate as a numerical unity in relation to local jurisdictions (if any) and in establishing and regulating the other parts of the state mentioned above. If there were a plurality of governments, not reduced or ordered under one as supreme, 'the judgement, command and execution of matters of benefit and justice would fail, and because men's injuries would therefore be unavenged the result would be fighting, separation, and finally the destruction of the city or regnum' (Defensor pacis 1.17.3). Marsilius compared the cooperative functioning of the various parts of a temperate political community to the functioning of a healthy, well-ordered animal, in which 'the primary principle which commands it and moves it from place to place is one' (Defensor pacis 1.17.8). It is by impeding the operation of government, the political primary moving principle, that papal and other ecclesiastical interventions in civic affairs are inimical to peace.

4 Religion

Marsilius' insistence that all coercive power be concentrated in a popularly controlled unitary secular government was rightly seen as an attack on the characteristic legal dualism of medieval society, in which church courts had jurisdiction over clerics in all matters and over lay people in some, while civil courts had jurisdiction over the laity in the matters that remained. In Discourse Two of the Defensor pacis, Marsilius defended his own position as the authentically Christian one. He argued that, in contrast with recent popes, Christ and the apostles were not a threat to secular peace. While teaching what must be believed and done to attain blessedness in the future life, they acknowledged the authority of emperors and other secular rulers in this life. In this part of his argument, Marsilius incorporated contemporary Franciscan contentions that poverty and lack of political power were appropriate for those who wished to follow Christ most closely. However, the leading Franciscan thinker of the day, WILLIAM OF OCKHAM, sharply criticized some of Marsilius' own theses (for example, that Peter had no authority over the other apostles and that final authority for determining Christian doctrine rests with a general council). Marsilius' views on the relations between clerical and lay authority were influential in the sixteenth century Protestant Reformation. His conception of popular participation as the source of all law and of all governmental authority has been seen as an anticipation of, if not a traceable influence on, ROUSSEAU.

See also: AQUINAS, T.; ARISTOTELIANISM, MEDIEVAL; JOHN OF JANDUN; NATURAL LAW; SOVEREIGNTY; WILLIAM OF OCKHAM

List of works

Marsilius of Padua (1324) Defensor pacis (Defender of Peace), ed. C.W. Previté-Orton, Cambridge: Cambridge University Press, 1928; trans. A. Gewirth, vol. 2 of Marsilius of Padua: The Defender of Peace, New York: Columbia University Press, 1956; repr. with new introduction in Cambridge Texts in the History of Political Thought, Cambridge: Cambridge University Press, 1996. (Marsilius' major contribution to contemporary political debate and to political philosophy.)

—— (1326-7?) De translatione imperii (On the Transfer of the Empire), ed. C. Jeudy and J. Quillet in Marsile de Padoue, Oeuvres Mineures, Paris: Editions de Centre National de la Recherche Scientifique, 1979; trans. C.J. Nederman, Marsiglio of Padua, Writings on the Empire, Cambridge Texts in the History of Political Thought, Cambridge: Cambridge University Press, 1993. (A discussion of transfers of imperial authority attacking the pope's power to make them.)

—— (by 1342) Defensor minor, ed. C. Jeudy and J. Quillet in Marsile de Padoue, Oeuvres Mineures, Paris: Éditions de Centre National de la Recherche Scientifique, 1979; trans. C.J. Nederman, Marsiglio of Padua, Writings on the Empire, Cambridge Texts in the History of Political Thought, Cambridge: Cambridge University Press, 1993. (Defensor minor is a summary of Defensor pacis, with a treatise on imperial jurisdiction in matrimonial cases.)

References and further reading

Gewirth, A. (1951) *Marsilius of Padua and Medieval Political Philosophy*, vol. 1 of *Marsilius of Padua: The Defender of Peace*, New York: Columbia University Press. (Unmatched in depth and analytic precision; the philosopher's best introduction to medieval political thought in general.)

Nederman, C.J. (1995) *Community and Consent: The Secular Political Theory of Marsiglio of Padua's Defensor Pacis*, Lanham, MD: Rowman and Littlefield. (Concise account of Discourse One, with the emphases indicated in the title. Bibliography, including references to selected studies in vols 5 and 6 (1979 and 1980) of *Medioevo: Rivista di Storia della Filosofia Medievale*, Padua: Editrice Antenore, which are entirely devoted to Marsilius.)

Quillet, J. (1970) *La Philosophie Politique de Marsile de Padoue*, Paris: Vrin. (Marsilius as primarily concerned with the Empire.)

A.S. McGRADE

MARSTON, ROGER
(*c.*1235–*c.*1303)

Roger Marston, an English Franciscan philosopher–theologian, was a pupil of John Pecham and a fellow student with Matthew of Aquasparta. Following closely in the footsteps of his master, Marston championed the views of Augustine in a conscious effort to counteract the growing fascination with Averroistic Aristotelianism. Of his works, three sets of Quaestiones disputatae *(Disputed Questions) and four sets of quodlibetal questions, the* Quodlibeta Quatuor *(Four Quodlibets), survive.*

Marston was born in England in the second quarter of the thirteenth century. As a Franciscan friar, he studied in Paris during the late 1260s and early 1270s, where he most likely heard the *collationes* of BONAVENTURE. He was a pupil of John PECHAM during the latter's Paris regency (1270–1) and a fellow student with MATTHEW OF AQUASPARTA. Upon returning to England and receiving the magisterium, he taught at Cambridge and Oxford between *circa* 1276 and 1284. He served as minister provincial of the English Franciscans from 1292 to 1298, when he was most instrumental in promoting the academic career of DUNS SCOTUS. He died around 1303 and was buried at Norwich. Of Marston's works, while his commentary on the *Sentences* of Peter LOMBARD appears to have been lost, three sets of *Quaestiones*

disputatae (Disputed Questions) – On Eternal Emanation, On the State of Fallen Nature and On the Soul – as well as four sets of quodlibetal questions, the *Quodlibeta Quatuor*, have survived.

Following closely in the footsteps of his master, John Pecham, Marston championed the views of Augustine in a conscious effort to counteract the growing Averroistic Aristotelianism (see AUGUSTINIANISM; AVERROISM). In response to the charge of arch-conservatism, he remarked that he did not cling to tradition out of mere habit but, after a reasonable scrutiny of the evidence, formed opinions that harmonized the writings of the saints with the wisdom of the philosophers. Marston must have felt his views vindicated by the 219 propositions condemned by Etienne Tempier in 1277, since he refers to these 'articles' occasionally in his *Quaestiones disputatae* (see ARISTOTELIANISM, MEDIEVAL).

Marston showed some interest in metaphysics, dismissing, for example, any real distinction between essence and existence. His concern with logic was predominantly with its application to other sciences. He was aware of the *ars obligatoria* (*Quodlibet* IV q.5: 375; *Quaestiones disputatae de anima* q.10: 453) (see LOGIC, MEDIEVAL). Apart from purely theological questions and matters of canon law, his philosophical thinking focused on epistemology, natural philosophy and psychology (as understood in medieval times).

Regarding epistemology, Marston maintained that the material elements of cognition – for example, grasping the terms of a proposition – come from sense knowledge or the imagination and reside in the intellectual memory. The formal elements, however – in other words, the infallible and immutable evidence for the truth – come from what Augustine called the 'eternal reasons' or divine illumination. Like Roger BACON, Marston claimed that this was the same as the agent intellect of ARISTOTLE and Averroes (see IBN RUSHD), although in opposition to Averroes, he claimed that there was no single agent intellect for all mankind, but that each individual had his own. Marston claimed that 'species' – for example, 'images' or 'idols' remaining after sensation or intellection – were necessary for knowledge. Like Pecham and unlike DUNS SCOTUS, Marston claims a direct intellectual knowledge of singulars.

In the realm of natural philosophy, Marston insists (contrary to AQUINAS) that matter has its own essence and positive nature apart from any form. Marston is likewise an indefatigable defender of the plurality of grades of the form theory (*Quodlibet* II q.22: 232–78), in opposition to the 'uniformism' of Aquinas and the 'dimorphism' of HENRY OF GHENT. The vegetative and sensitive functions (grades of the form) are not supplanted by the infusion of the rational soul, as Aquinas held, but they persist as grades of the rational soul considered as the form of the human being (see NATURAL PHILOSOPHY, MEDIEVAL).

Like his teacher Pecham, Marston advanced 'proofs' for the immortality of the soul. In much the same fashion as his protégé Duns Scotus, Roger strongly defended the freedom of the will to the degree that choice could be exercised not simply regarding means to the final end, but even with regard to man's final goal as well. In the footsteps of Bonaventure and Pecham, Marston rejected even the possibility of a created world eternally coexistent with the creator.

Roger Marston is noteworthy for the clarity and well-organized presentation of his views. He is likewise an invaluable witness to the doctrinal disputes prevalent at his time.

See also: AUGUSTINIANISM; DUNS SCOTUS, J.; MATTHEW OF AQUASPARTA; PECHAM, J.

List of works

Marston, R. (1276–84) *Quaestiones Disputatae* (Disputed Questions), Bibliotheca Franciscana Scholastica Medii Aevi VII, Quaracchi: Collegii S. Bonaventurae, 1932. (There are three sets of questions, on eternal emanation, on the state of fallen nature, and on the soul.)
—— (before 1303) *Quodlibeta quatuor* (Four Quodlibets), ed. G. Etzkorn and I. Brady, Bibliotheca Franciscana Scholastica Medii Aevi XXVI, 2nd edn, Grottaferrata: Colegii S. Bonaventurae, 1994. (Four sets of quodlibetal questions.)

References and further reading

Belmond, S. (1934) 'La theorie de la connaissance d'après Roger Marston' (The Theory of Knowledge According to Roger Marston), *La France Franciscaine* 17: 153–87. (Good introduction to Marston's theory of knowledge.)
Bonafede, G. (1939) 'Il problema del "lumen" in frate Ruggero di Marston' (The Problem of 'Light' According to Brother Roger Marston), *Rivista Rosminiana de Filosofia e di Cultura* 33: 16–30. (Marston on illumination.)
Cairola, J. (1951) 'L'opposizione a S.Tommaso nelle "Quaestiones disputatae" di Rugero Marston' (Opposition to St Thomas in the 'Disputed Questions' of Roger Marston), *Scholastica ratione historico-critica instauranda in Bibliotheca Pontificii Athenaei Antoniani VII*, Rome: Pontificium Athenaeum Antonianum, 447–60. (Marston's arguments against Aquinas.)
Daniels, A. (1911) 'Anselmzität bei dem Oxforder Franziskaner R. von Marston' (The Influence of St Anselm on the Oxford Franciscan R. Marston), *Theologische Quartelschrift* 93: 35–59. (A pioneering study on Anselm's influence.)
Etzkorn, G. (1962) 'The Grades of the Form according to Roger Marston, O.F.M.', *Franziskanische Studien* 44: 418–54.
Gilson, E. (1933) 'Roger Marston, un cas d'augustinisme avicennisant' (Roger Marston: A Case of Avicennizing Augustinianism), *Archives d'Histoire Doctrinale et Litteraire du Moyen Age* 8: 39–42. (An attempt to characterize historical influences on Marston.)
Glorieux, P. (1979) 'Marston (Roger) (d. 1303),' in *Catholicisme hier aujourd'hui demain VIII*, Paris: Letouzey et Ane, 724–5. (Short biography.)
Hissette, R. (1971) 'Les doctrines metaphysiques de Roger Marston' (The Metaphysical Doctrines of Roger Marston), unpublished dissertation, Louvain. (One of the few studies of Marston's metaphysics.)
—— (1972) 'Roger Marston, a-t-il professe l'hylemorphisme universel?' (Did Roger Marston Espouse Universal Hylomorphism?), *Recherches de Théologie Ancienne et Médiévale* 29: 205–23. (On Marston's metaphysics.)
—— (1980) 'Esse-essentia chez Roger Marston' (Existence and Essence According to Roger Marston), in *Sapientiae doctrina. Mélange de théologie et de litterature médiévales offerts à Dom Hildebrand Bascour, O.S.B.*, Louvain: Imprimerie Orientaliste, 110–8. (On Marston's views of essence and existence.)
Pelster, F. (1928) 'Roger Marston, O.F.M. (d. 1303), ein englischer Vertreter des Augustinismus' (Roger Marston, OFM (d. 1303), An English Champion of Augustinianism), *Scholastik* 3: 526–56. (An attempt to characterize Augustine's influence.)
Prezioso, F. (1950) 'L'attivita del soggetto pensante nella gnoseologia di Matteo d'Acquasparta e di Ruggiero Marston' (The Activity of the Thinking Subject in the Epistemology of Matthew of Aquasparta and Roger Marston), *Antonianum* 25: 259–326. (A good study of Marston's theory of knowledge.)

GIRARD J. ETZKORN

MARTIANUS CAPELLA

see ENCYCLOPEDISTS, MEDIEVAL

MARTINEAU, HARRIET (1802–76)

Harriet Martineau has been called the first woman sociologist and the first woman journalist in England, both better claims on the attention of posterity than her mostly derivative philosophical writings. Yet she is a revealing – and was in her own time widely influential – instance of the survival of eighteenth-century determinism and materialism. Although she eventually rejected the Unitarianism in which she had been brought up, the Necessarian philosophy she drew from it merged easily into her mature positivism. Her abridged translation (1853) of the Cours de philosophie positive *was the first introduction of this seminal work by Auguste Comte to English-speaking readers.*

Harriet Martineau was born in Norwich on 12 June 1802. As a child, she suffered ill health and more than the usual fears and loneliness; by the age of 20 she was almost totally deaf. Her excellent, if formally haphazard, early education was extended by carefully planned reading, with strong encouragement from a family solidly established among the liberal Unitarians in Norwich and elsewhere.

Devotional and religious themes marked her early writing – mostly in the Unitarian *Monthly Repository* – but she turned increasingly to philosophical issues. Entirely dependent on her pen after the death of her father, a textile manufacturer, in 1826, and the failure of the family firm three years later, in 1832 she launched *Illustrations of Political Economy*, a monthly series of 23 tales which caught, as she did so often, a new enthusiasm at its height, bringing her a celebrity she never lost. On completion of the tales, she spent the years 1834–6 in the USA. *Society in America* (1837), the first of two accounts of her travels, shows formidable powers of observation and synthesis and contains much original sociological comment, while in *How to Observe: Morals and Manners* (1838), she set out general principles for social analysis. *Deerbrook* (1839), her only large-scale novel, offered a characteristically sympathetic portrayal of middle-class life and enforced the subordination of passion to duty and service to others. Extraordinarily generous with her own modest income, she advocated many causes, among them anti-slavery, education, and the legal, political and economic liberation of women. Her radicalism

broadened as she grew older and the stringency of her early political economy lessened.

Stricken in 1840 by debilitating symptoms resulting from an ovarian cyst, she retreated to Tynemouth, where her writing continued apace and her thinking matured, with some oddly self-absorbed turns. In 1845, she pronounced herself cured by mesmerism and resumed an active life, eventually settling in the Lake District. An extended tour of the Near East, recorded in *Eastern Life, Present and Past* (1848), further distanced her from religion, and *Letters on the Laws of Man's Nature and Development*, written with Henry George Atkinson in 1851, proclaimed her loss of conventional belief. A brilliant, opinionated critic, a gifted contemporary historian and a keen observer of politics and international affairs, in 1852 she began to write regularly for the London *Daily News*, contributing more than 1,600 leading articles before her retirement in 1866. She died in Ambleside on 10 April 1876.

Harriet Martineau was no mere popularizer. Rather, insistent on candid 'publication of opinion' and determined to instruct the nation, she gathered together many of the major intellectual strands of her time, forcing them into broad public awareness at crucial moments.

Like most serious-minded English Unitarians of her generation, she was persuaded by Necessarianism, a deterministic philosophy derived from the psychological and religious speculations of David HARTLEY (§2), the systematizer of associationism, and transmitted through the scientist and theologian Joseph PRIESTLEY, from whom she also drew her materialism. Convinced that free will is an illusion, Necessarians distinguished their views from fatalism or Calvinist predestinarianism by insisting on the malleability of motives which, built up through association, inescapably determined all human actions. Education and personal influence could thus bring everyone to think rightly, to understand the laws of nature and even to attain perfection. This optimism and certainty survived her firm, unfairly scornful rejection of the Unitarianism that had engendered it.

Open to a wide range of current discussion, she added her own observations and experience, including mesmeric phenomena, to create a scientist synthesis in which Baconian faith in fact-based induction was conditioned by insistence on the importance of guiding, selective principle. As religion came to seem no more than a historically conditioned phenomenon, she turned to positivism, for which she had been prepared by the Saint-Simonian missionaries who came to London from France in the early 1830s. In 1853, she published an abridged translation of Auguste Comte's *Cours de philosophie positive*, its first introduction to the English-speaking world. Although she rejected social hierarchy, the subordination of women and the quasi-religious turn of Comte's later work, she found in the centrality he gave to laws of thought and to scientific views of society the final distillation of her Necessarianism (see COMTE, A.).

She had shared that early commitment with her younger brother James, a Unitarian minister who, from 1833, was in rebellion against Priestleyanism. Influenced by German theology and philosophy and by romanticism, he insisted that apprehension of religious truth was grounded in introspection rather than in revelation and evidences from nature. Their increasing alienation, culminating in his extremely hostile review of the Atkinson letters in the *Prospective Review*, made her a willing conspirator in the successful campaign in 1866 (led by the psychologist Alexander Bain) to deny him, as a minister, the chair of philosophy at the historically non-sectarian University College London, a post many thought a merited recognition of his periodical writings and his lectures at the Unitarian Manchester College. The lectures became books in the 1880s, too late to have the influence they might have commanded twenty years earlier.

The posthumous publication of her frank and judgmental autobiography inflicted considerable damage on her reputation, which, though she never lacked admirers, only began a real recovery in the 1960s, when historians, literary critics and feminists began to take proper measure of a career of astonishing energy and accomplishment.

See also: POSITIVISM IN THE SOCIAL SCIENCES §1

List of works

Martineau, H. (1829) 'Essays on the Art of Thinking', *Monthly Repository* 3: 521–6, 599–606, 707–12, 747–57, 817–22, reprinted in 1836 in H. Martineau, *Miscellanies*, Boston, MA, 2 vols. (Early summary of philosophical views.)
—— (1832–4) *Illustrations of Political Economy*, London: Charles Fox, 23 vols in 25. (Tales exemplifying economic principles.)
—— (1837) *Society in America*, London: Saunders & Otley, 2 vols. (Distinguished and original analysis.)
—— (1838) *How to Observe: Morals and Manners*, London: Charles Knight. (General principles of social analysis.)
—— (1839) *Deerbrook*, London: Moxon, 3 vols. (Overlong, didactic, but revealing novel.)
—— (1844) *Life in the Sickroom: Essays by an Invalid*, London: Moxon. (Self-conscious introspection suggestive of larger evolution of her thought.)

—— (1848) *Eastern Life: Present and Past*, London: Moxon, 3 vols. (Perceptive and revealing travel account of particular importance for evolving religious views.)
Martineau, H. and Atkinson, H.G. (1851) *Letters on the Laws of Man's Nature and Development*, London: Chapman. (Extravagant avowal of mesmerism and free thought.)
—— (1877) *Harriet Martineau's Autobiography, with Memorials by Maria Weston Chapman*, London: Smith, Elder, 3 vols. (Despite its idiosyncrasies, one of the great autobiographies of the century.)
—— (1983) *Harriet Martineau's Letters to Fanny Wedgwood*, ed. E.S. Arbuckle, Stanford, CA: Stanford University Press. (Extended series of charming, revealing letters.)
—— (1985) *Harriet Martineau on Women*, ed. G.G. Yates, New Brunswick, NJ: Rutgers University Press. (Illustrates and assesses Martineau's central, somewhat ambiguous place in feminist history.)
—— (1990) *Harriet Martineau: Selected Letters*, ed. V. Sanders, Oxford: Clarendon Press. (Representative sampling of a vast output by a brilliant correspondent.)
—— (1993) *Harriet Martineau and the Daily News*, ed. E.S. Arbuckle, New York: Garland. (Selection of leading articles.)

References and further reading

* Comte, A. (1853) *The Positive Philosophy of Auguste Comte, freely translated and condensed by Harriet Martineau*, London: Chapman, 2 vols. (Martineau's translation brought Comte's positivism to the English-speaking world.)
Hoecker-Drysdale, S. (1992) *Harriet Martineau: First Woman Sociologist*, London: Berg. (Brief, biographically structured, analysis of Martineau's sociology, with excellent bibliographies.)
Sanders, V. (1986) *Reason over Passion: Harriet Martineau and the Victorian Novel*, Hassocks: Harvester Press. (Extensive and balanced discussion of Martineau as a writer of fiction.)
Webb, R.K. (1960) *Harriet Martineau, a Radical Victorian*, London; Heinemann. (Primarily an intellectual biography, stressing Unitarian and Necessarian sources.)

R.K. WEBB

MARX, KARL (1818–83)

Karl Marx was the most important of all theorists of socialism. He was not a professional philosopher, although he completed a doctorate in philosophy. His life was devoted to radical political activity, journalism and theoretical studies in history and political economy.

Marx was drawn towards politics by Romantic literature, and his earliest writings embody a conception of reality as subject to turbulent change and of human beings as realizing themselves in the struggle for freedom. His identification with these elements in Hegel's thought (and his contempt for what he regarded as Hegel's apologetic attitude towards the Prussian state) brought Marx to associate himself with the Young Hegelians.

The Young Hegelians had come to believe that the implicit message of Hegel's philosophy was a radical one: that Reason could and should exist within the world, in contrast to Hegel's explicit claim that embodied Reason already did exist. Moreover, they also rejected Hegel's idea that religion and philosophy go hand in hand: that religion represents the truths of philosophy in immediate form. On the contrary, the Young Hegelians saw the central task of philosophy as the critique of religion – the struggle (as Marx himself was to put it in his doctoral dissertation) 'against the gods of heaven and of earth who do not recognize man's self-consciousness as the highest divinity'.

Marx came to be dissatisfied with the assumption that the critique of religion alone would be sufficient to produce human emancipation. He worked out the consequences of this change of view in the years 1843 to 1845, the most intellectually fertile period of his entire career. Hegel's philosophy, Marx now argued, embodied two main kinds of mistake. It incorporated, first, the illusion that reality as a whole is an expression of the Idea, the absolute rational order governing reality. Against this, Marx's position (and on this point he still agreed with the Young Hegelians) was that it is Man, not the Idea, who is the true subject. Second, he charged, Hegel believed that the political state – the organs of law and government – had priority in determining the character of a society as a whole. In fact, according to Marx, this is the reverse of the truth: political life and the ideas associated with it are themselves determined by the character of economic life.

Marx claimed that the 'species-being' of Man consists in labour, and that Man is 'alienated' to the extent that labour is performed according to a division of labour that is dictated by the market. It is only when labour recovers its collective character that men will recognize themselves as what they are – the true creators of history. At this point, the need to represent the essence of human beings in terms of their relation to

an alien being – be it the Christian God or Hegelian Geist – will no longer exist.

In the mature writings that followed his break with the Young Hegelians, Marx presented a would-be scientific theory of history as a progress through stages. At each stage, the form taken by a society is conditioned by the society's attained level of productivity and the requirements for its increase. In pre-socialist societies this entails the division of society into antagonistic classes. Classes are differentiated by what makes them able (or unable) to appropriate for themselves the surplus produced by social labour. In general, to the extent that a class can appropriate surplus without paying for it, it is said to be an 'exploiting' class; conversely, a class that produces more than it receives is said to be 'exploited'.

Although the exploiting classes have special access to the means of violence, exploitation is not generally a matter of the use of force. In capitalism, for example, exploitation flows from the way in which the means of production are owned privately and labour is bought and sold just like any other commodity. That such arrangements are accepted without the need for coercion reflects the fact that the ruling class exercises a special influence over ideas in society. It controls the ideology accepted by the members of society in general.

In Das Kapital *(Capital), the work to which he devoted the latter part of his life, Marx set out to identify the 'laws of motion' of capitalism. The capitalist system is presented there as a self-reproducing whole, governed by an underlying law, the 'law of value'. But this law and its consequences are not only not immediately apparent to the agents who participate in capitalism, indeed they are actually concealed from them. Thus capitalism is a 'deceptive object', one in which there is a discrepancy between its 'essence' and its 'appearance'.*

In Marx's view, it is inevitable that capitalism should give way to socialism. As capitalism develops, he believed, the increasingly 'socialized' character of the productive process will conflict more and more with the private ownership of the means of production. Thus the transition to collective ownership will be natural and inevitable. But Marx nowhere explained how this collective ownership and social control was to be exercised. Indeed, he had remarkably little to say about the nature of this society to the struggle to which he devoted his life.

The Critique of the Gotha Programme *envisaged two phases of communist society. In the first, production will be carried out on a non-exploitative basis: all who contribute to production will receive back the value of what they have contributed. But this, Marx recognized, is a form of 'equal right' that leaves the natural inequalities of human beings unchecked. It is a transitional phase, although inevitable. Beyond it there lies a society in which individuals are no longer 'slaves' to the division of labour, one in which labour has become 'not only a means of life but life's prime want'. Only then, Marx thought, 'can the narrow horizon of bourgeois right be crossed in its entirety and society inscribe on its banners: from each according to his ability, to each according to his needs!' This is the final vision of communism.*

1 **Life and works**
2 **Marx as a Young Hegelian**
3 **Philosophy and the critique of religion**
4 **Alienated labour**
5 **The critique of philosophy**
6 **The theory of ideology: (1) The reflective model**
7 **The theory of ideology: (2) The interests model**
8 **Historical materialism**
9 **Political economy**
10 **The fetishism of commodities**
11 **Morality**
12 **Socialism**

1 Life and works

Marx was born on 5 May, 1818, in Trier, a small, originally Roman city on the river Moselle. Many of Marx's ancestors were rabbis, but his father, Heinrich, a lawyer of liberal political views, converted from Judaism to Christianity and Marx was baptized with the rest of his family in 1824. At school, the young Marx excelled in literary subjects (a prescient schoolteacher comments, however, that his essays were 'marred by an exaggerated striving after unusual, picturesque expression'). In 1835, he entered the University of Bonn to study law. At the end of 1836, he transferred to Berlin and became a member of the Young Hegelian *Doktorklub*, a bohemian group whose leading figure was the theologian, Bruno BAUER. The views of the *Doktorklub* became increasingly radical (to some extent, it would seem, under Marx's influence) in the late 1830s.

Marx's father died in 1838 and in the next year – perhaps not coincidentally – Marx abandoned the law in favour of a doctorate in philosophy. His thesis, *Differenz der demokritischen und epikureischen Naturphilosophie* (Difference between the Democritean and Epicurean Philosophy of Nature) was accepted by the University of Jena in 1841. Marx had hoped to use it to gain an academic position, but, after Bruno Bauer's suspension from his post at the University of Bonn, it became apparent that such hopes would have to be abandoned in the current political climate.

Marx turned instead to journalism, involving himself with the newly-founded *Rheinische Zeitung*

and taking over the editorship in October 1842. However, the paper came increasingly into conflict with the Prussian government and was banned in March 1843. At this point, Marx decided to move abroad. In the summer he married Jenny von Westphalen (after an engagement of six years) and during a long honeymoon in Kreuznach worked on *Zur Kritik der Hegelschen Rechtsphilosophie* (Critique of Hegel's Philosophy of Right) and the essay 'Zur Judenfrage' ('On the Jewish Question') in which he started to formulate his disagreements with his fellow Young Hegelians. He and Jenny moved to Paris in October of that year. It was in 1844 that Marx met up again with Friedrich ENGELS (whom he had known slightly in Berlin) and the alliance was formed that was to last for the rest of Marx's life. Together Marx and Engels wrote *Die Heilige Familie* (The Holy Family) (1845a), a polemic against Bruno Bauer. More important, however, was the body of writing on economics and philosophy that Marx produced at this time, generally known as *The Paris Manuscripts* (1844).

Marx was expelled from France in 1845 and moved to Brussels. In the spring of 1845, he wrote for his own clarification a series of essays on Feuerbach. These 'Theses on Feuerbach' are one of the few mature statements we have of his views on questions of epistemology and ontology. In 1845–6 Marx and Engels wrote *Die deutsche Ideologie* (The German Ideology) which, although it too remained unpublished, contains an authoritative account of their theory of history and in particular of the place of ideas in society. Marx's developing economic views were given expression in a polemic against Proudhon, *La Misère de la Philosophie* (The Poverty of Philosophy), published in 1847.

Das Kommunistische Manifest (The Communist Manifesto), written by Marx and Engels as the manifesto of the Communist League in early 1848, is the classic presentation of the revolutionary implications of Marx's views on history, politics and economics. During the revolutionary upsurge of 1848 Marx returned to Germany, but with the defeat of the revolutionary movement he was forced to leave, first for Paris, and then, in August 1849, for London, where he would live in exile for the rest of his life.

The years of exile in Britain were difficult ones for Marx (and even more so for his loyal and devoted family). He was in constant financial difficulty and had to rely heavily on Engels and other friends and relations for support. His theoretical activities were chiefly directed to the study of political economy and the analysis of the capitalist system in particular. They culminated in the publication of the first volume of *Das Kapital* (Capital) in 1867. However, *Das Kapital* is the tip of a substantial iceberg of less important publications and unpublished writings. Among the former, the Preface to *Zur Kritik der politischen Ökonomie* (A Contribution to the Critique of Political Economy) published in 1859, contains the classic statement of Marx's materialist theory of history. The second and third volumes of *Das Kapital*, left unfinished at Marx's death, were edited and published posthumously by Engels. In addition, three volumes of *Theorien über den Mehrwert* (Theories of Surplus-Value), a series of critical discussions of other political economists, written in 1862–3, were published in the early twentieth century. An extensive and more or less complete work, the *Grundrisse der Kritik der politischen Ökonomie* (known both in English and in German as the *Grundrisse*) was written in 1857–8 but only published in 1939. The Introduction to the *Grundrisse* is the mature Marx's most extended discussion of the method of political economy. In addition, there exist numerous notebooks and preliminary drafts, many (if not, at the time of writing, all) of which have been published.

Political economy apart, Marx wrote three works on political events in France: *Die Klassenkämpfe in Frankreich* (Class Struggles in France) (1850), *Das achtzehnte Brumaire des Louis Bonaparte* (The Eighteenth Brumaire of Louis Bonaparte) (1852) and *The Civil War in France* (1871). Among his many polemical writings, the *Kritik des Gothaer Programms* (Critique of the Gotha Programme) (1875) is particularly important for the light it throws on Marx's conception of socialism and its relation to ideas of justice.

Marx was in very poor health for the last ten years of his life, which seems to have sapped his energies for large-scale theoretical work. However, his engagement with the practical details of revolutionary politics was unceasing. He died on 14 March 1883 and is buried in Highgate Cemetery, London.

2 Marx as a Young Hegelian

Marx is relevant to philosophy in three ways: (1) as a philosopher himself, (2) as a critic of philosophy, of its aspirations and self-understanding, and (3) by the philosophical implications of work that is, in Marx's own understanding of it, not philosophical at all. Broadly speaking, these three aspects correspond to the stages of Marx's own intellectual development. This and the following section are concerned with the first stage.

The Young Hegelians, with whom Marx was associated at the beginning of his career, did not set out to be critics of Hegel. That they rapidly became so has to do with the consequences they drew from certain tensions within Hegel's thought. Hegel's central claim is that both nature and society embody the rational order of *Geist* (Spirit). Nevertheless, the Young Hegelians believed, it did not follow that all societies express rationality to the fullest degree possible. This was the case in contemporary Germany. There was, in their view, a conflict between the essential rationality of *Geist* and the empirical institutions within which *Geist* had realized itself: Germany was 'behind the times' (see HEGEL, G.W.F. §§5–8; HEGELIANISM §§2–3).

A second source of tension lay in Hegel's attitude towards religion. Hegel had been prepared to concede a role to religion as the expression of the content of philosophy in immediate form. The Young Hegelians, however, argued that the relationship between the truths of philosophy and religious 'representation' was, in fact, antagonistic. In presenting reality not as the embodiment of reason but as the expression of the will of a personal god the Christian religion establishes a metaphysical dualism that is quite contrary to the secular 'this-worldliness' which (although Hegel himself might have been too cautious to spell it out fully) is the true significance of Hegel's philosophy.

This was the position endorsed by Marx at the time of his doctoral dissertation on Epicurus and Democritus. Its subject was taken from a period of Greek thought that displayed parallels with the Germany of Marx's own time. Just as the Young Hegelians faced the problem of how to continue philosophy after Hegel, so Epicurus wrote in the shadow of another great system, that of Aristotle. Epicurus is more successful than Democritus, Marx believes, in combining materialism with an account of human agency. Furthermore, Marx admires Epicurus for his explicit critique of religion, the chief task of philosophy, he asserts, in all ages.

In its destruction of the illusions of religion, the Young Hegelians believed that philosophy would provide both the necessary and the sufficient conditions for human emancipation and the achievement of a rational state. In the works that he wrote in Kreuznach in 1843 (the unpublished draft of the *Critique of Hegel's Philosophy of Right* and the essay 'On the Jewish Question') and shortly thereafter (the '*Critique of Hegel's Philosophy of Right*: Introduction') Marx called this position into question.

In the *Critique of Hegel's Philosophy of Right* Marx makes two main criticisms of Hegel. The first is that Hegel's real concern is to retrace in the political realm the outlines of his own metaphysics, rather than to develop an analysis of political institutions and structures in their own right. This gives his political philosophy an apologetic function, for it leads him to present the contradictions that he finds in reality as essentially reconciled in the supposedly higher unity of the 'Idea'. But they are not, says Marx. On the contrary, they are 'essential contradictions'.

Chief among such contradictions is that existing between the 'system of particular interest' (the family and civil society – that is, economic life) and the 'system of general interest', namely, the state. And this leads to Marx's second criticism. Hegel, Marx alleges, assumes that the state, because it is 'higher' from the point of view of Hegelian logic, can effectively reconcile the contradictions of economic life. In fact, in Marx's view, it is civil society that exists prior to the state. The state arises from the condition of civil society and is always subordinate to the form of the latter.

3 Philosophy and the critique of religion

Marx presents the implications of these criticisms for the critique of religion in the 'Critique of Hegel's Philosophy of Right: Introduction'. This short essay is a compressed masterpiece of vehement rhetoric, seething with antithesis and chiasmus. In Germany, Marx writes, 'the critique of religion is essentially completed'. Thus the problem is how to go beyond it. Marx's first step is to explain the significance of that critique, as he understands it.

The world of religion is a reflection of a particular form of society: 'This state, this society, produce religion, which is an inverted world consciousness, because they are an inverted world'. That is to say, only an inverted, secular world would produce religion as its offshoot. In religious belief, Man finds himself reflected in the 'fantastic reality of heaven', whilst he can find only 'the semblance of himself, only a nonhuman being' in this world. Religion thus provides a realm in which individuals can realize themselves, at least partially, given that full and adequate self-realization is not possible in the profane world. In this way, religion preserves the social order of which it is a by-product, both by deflecting attention from its defects and by providing a partial escape from it. In Marx's famous words, 'Religion is the sigh of the oppressed creature, the heart of a heartless world and the soul of soulless conditions. It is the opium of the people'.

Thus religion and the form of life associated with it are open to criticism at three points. (1) There is, first, the impoverished and distorted world of which religion is a by-product. (2) There is the way in which the image of reality produced by religion is falsely transfigured. (3) Finally, there is the failure by human beings to recognize the fact that religion has its origins in mundane reality.

It is this last element towards which the critique of religion is directed. Critique of religion connects religion back to its unacknowledged origins in social existence. Yet this is not enough. The critique of religion, inasmuch as it is a call to people to abandon their illusions, is also, according to Marx, 'the call to abandon a condition that requires illusions'. By itself the critique of religion cannot remove the distortion and impoverishment of the world from which religion arises. This is of course Marx's real project, for which the criticism of religion has merely prepared the ground.

Once the criticism of religion has done its work, philosophy must move on 'to unmask human self-alienation in its secular forms'. The critique of religion ends, Marx says, 'in the doctrine that man is the supreme being for man; thus it ends with the categorical imperative to overthrow all conditions in which man is a debased, enslaved, neglected, contemptible being' (1843a: 251).

Much of this analysis represents common ground between Marx and his Young Hegelian former associates. Marx concedes that philosophy has both a critical role to play in exposing the illusions of religion and an affirmative one in establishing an ideal of human fulfilment. Nevertheless, Marx takes the Young Hegelians to task for thinking that philosophy alone provides a sufficient condition for human emancipation. Philosophy, he maintains, must move beyond itself: 'criticism of the speculative philosophy of right does not remain within itself, but proceeds on to tasks for whose solution there is only one means – praxis'. For this, a material force – a 'class with radical chains' – is required, namely, the proletariat.

At this stage, then, Marx is critical not so much of the content of philosophy, but of what we might call the metaphilosophical belief associated with it: that it is possible (as he puts it in relation to the Young Hegelians) 'to realize philosophy without transcending it'. A truly successful critique of religion would require the transformation of the social conditions within which religion is generated and sustained.

4 Alienated labour

In Paris, Marx threw himself into the study of political economy. His objective was to amplify his critique of Hegel and the Young Hegelians with a more far-reaching account of the nature of 'civil society'. The Paris Manuscripts thus provide a unique link between Marx's economic theory and his philosophical view of human nature. The concept which brings the two together is that of alienation (Entfremdung) (see ALIENATION §§3–5). Although Marx had made little use of this term in his earlier writings, the structure of the concept is clearly

121

anticipated in his critique of religion. The fundamental idea is that an entity or agent gives rise to a product or expression that is distinct from but at the same time essential to itself. This secondary product comes to be cut off from its origin. In consequence, the agent suffers a loss of identity in some sense. Thus, for the agent to realize itself fully, it must remove the separation that has come between itself and its own product.

In the central discussion of the *Paris Manuscripts*, Marx sets out to apply the concept of alienation to the labour process. Alienation, Marx argues, is characteristic of a situation in which (1) labour is directed towards the production of commodities (that is, goods exchangeable in the market) and (2) labour itself is such a commodity. Marx divides the alienation involved in labour into three main forms.

(1) There is, first, the separation of the worker from the product of labour. It is in the nature of the labour process that it involves 'appropriating' the external world. But when labour is alienated, the sensible, external world becomes an object to which the worker is bound, something that is hostile to them, instead of being the means to their self-realization.

(2) At the same time, the labour process itself becomes alien to the worker. Because the imperatives according to which labour takes place come to the worker 'from outside' (that is, from the market, either directly or indirectly) labour is no longer an act of self-realization. It becomes, from the worker's point of view, 'an activity directed against himself, which is independent of him and does not belong to him'.

(3) Finally, Marx says, the consequence of these two forms of alienation is to alienate man from what he calls his 'species-being' (*Gattungswesen*). The latter concept (of which Marx made frequent use in 1843–4) is adapted from Ludwig Feuerbach. Man, says Marx, is a species-being 'because he looks upon himself as the present, living species, because he looks upon himself as a *universal* and therefore free being'.

An analogy that may help to clarify this apparently circular definition can be made with the family. In a limited sense, people can be part of a family without consciously behaving accordingly (at the limit, we can think of members of a family who do not even know that they are related). But in order to be a family in a fuller sense, people must relate to one another *as* a family, and at least a part of this is that they should be aware that they *are* a family. So it is with human species-being. While the fundamental phenomenon on which the family is based is a biological relation, in human species-being it is labour. Thus, as labour is alienated in other respects, so people become alienated from their species-being. The consequence is the alienation of members of the species from one another.

Each of these three points is, one might think, somewhat questionable. Surely, in any situation in which individuals do not produce entirely for themselves, it will be inevitable that the products of labour are 'separated' from the original producer. Likewise, the labour process cannot be something that is freely chosen by individuals as long as they are objectively constrained by the nature of the material world and the resources available to them in finding efficient means to given ends. Finally, it is not at all clear what is involved in human beings 're-appropriating' their 'species-being'.

One way of making the concept of alienated labour more precise is to ask what it might be for labour to be non-alienated. Marx addresses the issue at the end of a discussion of James Mill's *Elements of Political Economy*. 'Let us suppose', Marx begins, 'that we had produced as human beings'. In that case, he claims, each of us would have 'affirmed' both ourselves and our fellows in the process of production. In the first place, I, the producer, would have affirmed myself in my production. At the same time, I would be gratifying a human need – that of my neighbour, for whom I am in this case producing. Thus, in meeting your need, I would have mediated between you and the species: 'I would be acknowledged by you as the complement of your own being, as an essential part of yourself'. In this way, production and the meeting of needs involves a mutuality of self-realization and reciprocal recognition:

> In the individual expression of my own life I would have brought about the expression of your life, and so in my individual activity I would have directly *confirmed* and *realized* my authentic nature, my *human*, *communal* nature.

> (1844: 277–8)

These ideas help to explain Marx's antagonism towards what he would call 'bourgeois' political theory. In so far as traditional political philosophy takes as its fundamental question how to reconcile competing interests, its starting point is, from Marx's point of view, unacceptably individualistic. For what entitles us to assume that the interests of individuals are bound to be antagonistic? Rather than asking how to allocate rights and duties fairly when interests conflict, the task, Marx believes, is to move humanity towards a form of life in which conflicts of interest are no longer endemic.

5 The critique of philosophy

Although the *Paris Manuscripts* show Marx's increasing engagement with political economy, they do not represent an abandonment of his concern with philosophy. The attitude that Marx takes towards philosophy, however, now becomes more critical than it had been in his earlier, Young Hegelian period. In part, this can be traced to Ludwig Feuerbach, whom Marx quotes approvingly at several points (see FEUERBACH, L. §2). It was Feuerbach's great achievement, Marx writes, 'to have shown that philosophy is nothing more than religion brought into thought and developed in thought, and that it is equally to be condemned as another form and mode of existence of the alienation of human nature'. Thus Marx now regards philosophy as essentially continuous with religion, not a force directed against religion, as he had represented it at the time of his doctoral dissertation.

Marx makes a number of negative remarks regarding philosophy in general, but his more specific critical comments are directed towards Hegel. Like Feuerbach, he takes the view that Hegel has brought philosophy to a point of completion. The dynamic principle at the heart of Hegel's philosophy, according to Marx, is that of 'abstract mental labour'. Nevertheless, despite the genuinely critical elements contained within it, Hegel's philosophy is vitiated by its idealist assumptions. In the end, for Hegel, alienation is merely a matter of the separation of the products of thought from thought itself, something to be overcome by a philosophical reorientation of consciousness. To go beyond Hegel, it would be necessary to make the concept of real, concrete labour fundamental. But this, Marx suggests, leads beyond philosophy itself.

Marx pursues these ideas in the 'Theses on Feuerbach', written in the spring of 1845. Here he makes it explicit that his disagreement is not only with idealistic philosophies, such as Hegel's, but also with would-be materialist ones, Feuerbach's included. In incorporating within itself an idea of 'activity', idealism has important advantages over materialism. It is, Marx writes,

> the chief defect of all hitherto existing materialism (that of Feuerbach included) ... that the thing, reality, sensuousness, is conceived only in the form of the object or of contemplation, but not as sensuous human activity, praxis, not subjectively. Hence, in contradistinction to materialism, the *active* side was developed abstractly by idealism – which, of course, does not know real sensuous activity as such.
>
> (1845b: 421)

It should be noted that this passage is ambiguous. Is Marx envisaging a new kind of materialism (one that

would not have the defects of 'hitherto existing materialism') or is it a call to leave philosophy – both materialism and idealism – behind altogether? Interpreters of Marx who take the former view have ascribed an implicit philosophical position to him (often called 'dialectical materialism'). Nevertheless, the fact remains that Marx himself never developed such a position explicitly, and the conclusion of the 'Theses on Feuerbach' appears to lead away from philosophy entirely: 'The philosophers have only *interpreted* the world in various ways; the point is to *change* it.'

The German Ideology, which Marx and Engels wrote from September 1845 to the summer of 1846, continues this line of argument. As in so many of Marx's writings, the rhetorical trope from which the criticism starts is that of an inversion of an inversion. The Young Hegelians, Marx alleges, think of themselves as engaged in a struggle with the illusions that hold the Germans in their grip. But in fact they are in the grip of an illusion themselves: the illusion that ideas are an independent, determining force in political life. Feuerbach is not excepted from this criticism. Although he purports to demystify the realm of pure ideas, he still remains, according to Marx and Engels, 'in the realm of theory'. Feuerbach, they claim, 'never arrives at really existing, active men, but stops at the abstraction "man"'.

The alternative that Marx and Engels propose is, of course, also a theory, but it is a theory, they claim, of a quite different kind. 'In direct contrast to German philosophy, which descends from heaven to earth', their purpose is to present an account which will 'ascend from earth to heaven'. Instead of translating general ideas back into equally general anthropological categories, the aim is to give a specific account of their historical origins. In so doing, it undermines the presuppositions on which the philosophical enterprise rests and philosophy, as an independent branch of knowledge, loses its medium of existence:

> The philosophers would only have to dissolve their language into the ordinary language, from which it is abstracted, to recognize it as the distorted language of the actual world, and realize that neither thoughts nor language in themselves form a realm of their own, that they are only *manifestations* of actual life.
>
> (1845–6: 118)

6 The theory of ideology: (1) The reflection model

The German Ideology is filled with polemical assertions of the priority of material life over the world of religion, thought and speculation. But it sets out to do more than sloganize. Its aim is to develop the framework for a scientific explanation of how the material life conditions and determines thought and culture. By the time *The German Ideology* came to be written, the term 'ideology' had established itself in German as referring to systems of ideas detached from and out of proportion to empirical reality (Heinrich Heine, with whom Marx was on intimate terms in Paris, used it in that sense). In *The German Ideology* this is certainly part of the meaning of the term. But the concept also has a wider explanatory function (see IDEOLOGY).

Since the ancient world, political thinkers had been concerned with the role that 'false' or irrational forms of consciousness play in political life. To this extent, the Young Hegelian critique of religion represented the latest manifestation of a very long tradition. However, the originality of Marx's concept of ideology lies in the way that it brings the idea of false consciousness together with a distinctively modern conception of society.

At the end of the eighteenth and the beginning of the nineteenth century, a conception of society came to the fore in Germany and France, according to which societies, like organisms, have the power of maintaining and reproducing themselves through time. Marx was very much taken with this view, which he endorsed in the *Critique of Hegel's Philosophy of Right*. Chief among the conditions for a society to reproduce itself, according to Marx, are the ideas held by its members. Thus false consciousness, rather than being simply an accidental feature of human nature (albeit one with enormous political consequences) should be regarded as a phenomenon to be explained by the particular character of the society in which it is to be found.

If societies do not rest solely on coercion, then this is because those who are oppressed or exploited for some reason accept this. As Marx puts it bluntly: 'the ideas of the ruling class are in every epoch the ruling ideas'. But how does this come about? What sort of connection holds between the economic structures of a society and the ideas of its members? *The German Ideology* contains two analogies that might serve as mechanisms for the explanation of the connection between material life and ideas. The first is embodied in the following famous passage:

If in all ideology men and their circumstances appear upside-down as in a camera obscura, this phenomenon arises just as much from their historical life-process as the inversion of objects on the retina does from their physical life-process ... We set out from real, active men, and on the basis of their real life-process we demonstrate the development of the ideological reflexes and echoes of this life-process. The phantoms formed in the human brain are also, necessarily, sublimates of their material life-process, which is empirically verifiable and bound to material premises.

(1845–6: 47)

Let us call this the 'reflection model' of ideology. The idea is that ideology relates to material life as images do to reality in a camera obscura or on the retina of the human eye: items in reality are reproduced accurately, but in reverse.

Yet brief consideration of the analogy shows that, as it stands, it is completely inadequate. It is indeed true that the images on the human retina are 'upside-down'. But does this mean that human beings do not perceive the world about them accurately? Of course not. The fact is that, as far as human perception is concerned, 'upside-down' is the right way up for images to be on our retinas. And this points the way towards the problem with Marx's analogy. By describing *all* consciousness as reversed or inverted the contrast between 'true' and 'false' loses its sense.

A further objection arises later in the quoted passage in which Marx continues the reflection analogy when he speaks of the ideological 'reflexes and echoes' of real life-processes. Ideological ideas are, he goes on to say, 'phantoms' and 'sublimates'. These metaphors carry with them an important implication: ideological thought is the effect of real processes, but it is itself insubstantial, without material reality or causal power. If this is Marx's considered view, then it is clearly disastrous for the theory of ideology. For the point of the theory of ideology was to explain how it was that certain forms of thought served to sustain particular societies. Thus these forms of thought are, by assumption, not ineffective, but have very important causal effects: helping to maintain a particular social and economic order.

Finally, it is not obvious that ideology relates to material life as mind relates to matter. Is the implication that ideology is immaterial and material life non-intellectual? This plainly contradicts Marx's basic position. Not only would it be odd for an avowed materialist to suggest that ideas are something basically insubstantial, but, even more importantly, it conflicts with the idea that economic life, so far from being unconscious or unreflective, is the central part of man's cognitive engagement with external reality.

7   The theory of ideology: (2) The interests model

There is, however, another model at work in *The German Ideology*. While the reflection model draws on the parallel between the ideological process and a traditional, realist account of perception (the immaterial mind passively mirrors a mind-independent reality) what we may call the 'interests model' develops from a more instrumentalist approach to epistemology. That Marx was (at this time, at least) attracted to such views is apparent from the 'Theses on Feuerbach'. In the second thesis he writes, 'The dispute over the reality or non-reality of thinking that is isolated from practice is a purely *scholastic* question.' From this point of view, the most significant aspect of ideas is not their relationship to a mind-independent reality, but that they are the products of practical activity, and that this practical activity is itself guided by interests. The materialistic view of history that this leads to, Marx and Engels say: 'does not explain practice from the Idea, but explains the formation of ideas from material practice'.

The problem with the interests model does not lie in the view that ideas are the product of interests itself, which is, of course, very plausible (although it is more difficult to determine just what proportion of our ideas are products of interests in this way – surely not all of them – and to explain just how it is that interests should assert themselves in the process by which ideas are formed). The problem is that ideological ideas are not simply ideas formed in the pursuit of interests. They are, in fact, supposed to be ideas that go *against* the interests of a large number of those who hold them (and in this way further the interests of others). How do ideas of this kind come to be accepted?

Marx and Engels's answer starts from the following claim:

> The class which has the means of material production at its disposal, has control at the same time over the means of mental production, so that thereby, generally speaking, the ideas of those who lack the means of mental production are subject to it.
>
> (1845–6: 64)

But this is not a satisfactory solution. Marx and Engels seem to view those who live under the domination of the ruling class as passive victims, taking their ideas like obedient chicks from those who control the 'means of mental production', with no critical reflection as to whether the ideas are either true or in their own rational interests. Yet why should one suppose that the ruling class is capable of promoting its interests effectively and forms its ideas in response to those interests, while the dominated classes simply accept whatever is served up to them?

Marx and Engels do, however, attempt to make their claim more plausible in their discussion of the nature of mental production. It is, they write, the most significant development in the division of labour that mental and manual labour become separated:

> Division of labour only becomes truly such from the moment when a division of material and manual labour appears ... From this moment onwards consciousness *can* really flatter itself that it is something other than consciousness of existing practice, that it *really* represents something without representing something real; from now on consciousness is in a position to emancipate itself from the world and to proceed to the formation of 'pure' theory, theology, philosophy, ethics, etc.
>
> (1845–6: 51–2)

The separation between mental and manual labour, Marx and Engels maintain, does not really lead to the formation of autonomous ideas; the ideologists who produce ideas are still part of the ruling class whose interests their ideas represent. Nevertheless, it offers an explanation as to why such ideas should be accepted by those, the dominated classes, whose interests they oppose: they are accepted because they are apparently disinterested. The ideologist, on this view, is like a bribed referee: able to influence the outcome of a game all the more effectively for the fact that he is falsely believed to be impartial.

Are ideologists, then, engaged in deception? Do they know the partiality of their ideas but present them none the less as if they were neutral and disinterested? On the contrary. According to Marx and Engels, ideologists are sincere – and, because they sincerely believe in the independence and objective validity of their own ideas, they are able to persuade others to accept them as such all the more effectively. Herein, however, lies the problem. How are we to suppose it to be true that the ideologists should both be constrained so that they produce ideas in the interests of the ruling class of which they are, appearances to the contrary, a part, and that they (and those who accept the ideas from them) remain sincerely unaware of the nature of this connection? Why do they *think* that they are independent when in fact they are not? And, if they are not independent, how do the class interests they share with the rest of the ruling class assert themselves?

In any case, it is clear why Marx should now become so hostile to philosophy: like any supposedly 'pure' theory, philosophy represents a deceptive abstraction from the particular circumstances and material interests that it serves. This move to detach ideas that are the products of material interests from the interests that they represent is epitomized, for Marx and Engels, in Kant (the 'whitewashing spokesman' of the German bourgeoisie, as they call him). Kant, they write:

> made the materially motivated determinations of the will of the French bourgeois into *pure* self-determinations of 'free will', of the will in and for itself, of the human will, and so converted it into purely ideological determinations and moral postulates.
>
> (1845–6: 99)

For Marx and Engels, at this stage at least, 'moral postulates' are, by their very nature, ideological.

8   Historical materialism

'Where speculation ends – in real life – there real, positive science begins', according to Marx and Engels in *The German Ideology*. The science to which they are referring is the materialist theory of history, whose classic statement is given in the Preface to *Zur Kritik der politischen Ökonomie* (A Contribution to the Critique of Political Economy) (1859).

Taken most generally, the materialist theory of history asserts that the manner in which human beings produce the necessities of life determines the form of the societies in which they live. Every society other than the most primitive produces a 'surplus' beyond what it immediately consumes. The manner in which this surplus is 'appropriated' – taken from the direct producers and redistributed – determines the class structure of the society in question. If society is divided between direct producers and those who benefit from the former's 'unpaid surplus labour' (something that is true of all societies where a surplus exists, prior to the advent of socialism) the relationship between classes is antagonistic.

At any stage, the size of the surplus is an expression of the level of development of the 'productive forces' – the resources, physical and intellectual, upon which material production draws. Every society contains both an economic 'base', composed of 'relations of production' (the relations producers have to the means of production and to one another) and a legal and political 'superstructure', corresponding to the base. The relations of production favour the development of the productive forces up to a point. Beyond this they become, Marx says, 'fetters' upon the forces of production, and a conflict arises which leads eventually to the replacement of the existing relations of production with new and superior ones.

Presented in these terms, it is clear that the materialist theory of history is intended as an exercise in social science rather than philosophy. Thus it may seem surprising that it should have attracted such enduring attention on the part of philosophers.

However, scientific theories may be of concern to philosophers if their assumptions are novel, obscure or questionable, even if the intentions behind them are in no way philosophical (examples are Darwin, Freud and Newton). In the case of Marx's theory of history, it is not just the meaning of and evidence for the particular claims to be found in the theory that have been controversial. The more general issues of the form of explanation that Marx employs and the kind of entities such an explanation presupposes have been continuing matters of dispute.

Interpreters of Marx divide broadly into three groups on these questions. In the first are those for whom Marx's theory of history is intended to be scientific in the way that any other scientific theory is. With some qualifications, the majority of the earliest Marxists (for example, Engels himself, Kautsky and Plekhanov) fall into this group. On the other hand, those who believe that there is a contrast between Marx's conception of science and the natural sciences may be divided into those who see Marx's theory as a transformation of Hegel's theory of history and those for whom it is fundamentally anti-Hegelian. The most influential presentation of the former interpretation is to be found in Georg Lukács's *History and Class Consciousness* (1921), while the latter is particularly associated with the French philosopher, Louis Althusser (see ALTHUSSER, L. §§2–3; KAUTSKY, K.; LUKÁCS, G. §2; PLEKHANOV, G. §2).

In the late 1970s the first approach was revived in the English-speaking world by G.A. Cohen's seminal *Karl Marx's Theory of History: A Defence* (1978). According to Cohen, historical materialism can be presented in a way that contains nothing that should be unacceptable to anyone who accepts the legitimacy of Darwinian biology (see DARWIN, C.).

The two theories are, in Cohen's view, importantly parallel to one another, for both employ 'functional explanation' (see FUNCTIONAL EXPLANATION). When Marx says that the relations of production *correspond* to the forces of production, what he means, according to Cohen, is first that the relations are in some sense 'good for' the (development of the) forces and second that they obtain *because* they are good for the forces. (The same analysis, suitably adapted, applies to the correspondence between superstructure and base.) What is distinctive about Darwinian biology, however, is not just that it employs functional explanation, but that it provides a convincing account (what Cohen calls an 'elaborating explanation') of why its functional explanations are true: the process of natural selection. Does Marxism have an equivalent elaborating explanation?

All the indications are that it does not. In response to this, there have been two main lines of argument.

One is that the theory should have (but lacks) such an explanation and that it is the task of a sympathetic reconstruction of Marx to provide one. On the other hand, it is also possible to argue that the search for what Jon Elster has called 'micro-foundations' is misguided (1985). Thus the functional explanations that Marx invokes in the theory of history rest on the fact that there really are collective agents (classes, for example). On this 'collectivist' reading it is sufficient simply to appreciate the nature of collective agency to see why collective agents should feature in functional explanations: they have the power to act purposively to bring about their ends. No reductive 'elaborating explanation' is necessary.

To take this view is to align oneself with the second and third groups of Marx's interpreters and to affirm the fundamental gap between Marx's theory of history and the explanations of the natural sciences (where functional explanations are not simply left unelaborated). If so, the Marxist theory of history cannot draw on the general prestige of science for its justification.

9 Political economy

In contrast to his relatively brief and schematic statements concerning general history, Marx wrote very extensively about the economic system under which he himself lived. Das Kapital, which presents Marx's definitive analysis of capitalism, is a work of exceptional methodological complexity, as is already suggested by its sub-title, 'Critique of Political Economy'. The phrase is ambiguous. Is Marx's objective to criticize the bourgeois economy or bourgeois economics? In fact, Marx rejects this as a false antithesis: the subject matter of the book is both. Ten years before its publication, Marx described the work that was to become Das Kapital in a letter: 'The ... work in question is a *critique of the economic categories*, or, if you like, the system of bourgeois economy critically presented. It is a presentation [*Darstellung*] of the system and, simultaneously, a critique of it'.

The two aspects go together in Marx's view because economic categories are not simply the means employed by an observer to classify some inert mass of data. They are themselves a part of social reality, 'abstract forms' of the social relations of production.

Bourgeois economists, Marx alleges, characteristically fail to recognize that their categories are specific to capitalism, and so they treat the capitalist mode of production as one 'eternally fixed by nature for every state of society', Marx alleges. A 'critical presentation' of economics must counteract the false eternalization

of the economy that bourgeois economics carries within itself.

As it stands, this is a criticism of the limitations in the self-understanding of bourgeois economics rather than a challenge to its empirical content. Yet empirical explanation is a central part of Marx's project. 'It is', he writes in the Preface to *Das Kapital*, 'the ultimate aim of this work to lay bare the economic law of motion of modern society.' Has bourgeois economics failed to discover this law or has it simply not put its categories in historical context? At its strongest, Marx's case is that both criticisms are true and that the former failing is a result of the latter. The 'law of value' that Marx claims to have discovered could not, he says, have been discovered by economic science 'so long as it is stuck in its bourgeois skin'.

The connection that Marx sees between the categories of economic life and the categories of economic analysis is made more complicated by the structure that he ascribes to capitalism. Marx believes that an indispensable ingredient for understanding capitalism is the contrast between its 'essence' – its underlying determinants – and its 'appearance' – the way that it immediately strikes those who live in it. Corresponding to this distinction are two kinds of bourgeois economic thought: what Marx calls 'classical economy', on the one hand, and 'vulgar economy' on the other. Classical economy (the tradition whose greatest representatives were Ricardo and Adam SMITH) aims towards the essence of capitalism: it 'nearly touches the true relation of things', although it is not able to formulate that relation explicitly. According to Marx, it is the mark of the 'vulgar economy' of his own time, by contrast, that it 'feels particularly at home in the alienated outward appearances of economic relations'. Yet this means that it is fundamentally unscientific, for 'all science would be superfluous if the outward appearance and the essence of things coincided'. A truly scientific political economy must go beyond the immediately received categories of economic life. This is what Marx believes that he himself has achieved (and he considers himself for this reason to be the heir of the tradition of classical political economy).

In a letter to Engels, written at the time of the publication of the first volume of *Das Kapital*, Marx singles out what he calls the 'twofold character of labour' as the most important point in his book. Labour, Marx claims, is both the source of value and, at the same time, under capitalism, a commodity itself. Yet this commodity (labour-power, as Marx calls it) is a commodity of a special kind. Its value is not the same as the value of the commodities produced by the labour that is exercised on behalf of its purchaser, the capitalist. This discrepancy, in

Marx's view, explains the 'origin' of surplus-value – the fact that the capitalist appropriates the surplus-labour of the worker under the guise of a fair exchange. In discussing the manner in which, in capitalist society, labour is sold to capitalists as a commodity, in exchange for wages, Marx writes: 'Hence we may understand the decisive importance of the transformation of the value and price of labour-power into the form of wages, or into the value and price of labour itself. This phenomenal form, which makes the actual relation invisible, and, indeed, shows the direct opposite of that relation, forms the basis of all the juridical notions of both labourer and capitalist, of all the mystifications of the capitalist mode of production, of all its illusions as to liberty, of all the apologetic shifts of the vulgar economists'.

Thus we see Marx making three claims: (1) that we should see reality as layered, having a surface appearance governed by an underlying structure; (2) that to make such a distinction is characteristic of the scientific approach to reality in general; and (3) that the phenomenal form conceals the real relations (it 'makes the actual relation invisible and indeed shows the opposite of that relation').

However, claims (1) and (2) do not entail (3). According to claims (1) and (2) (in themselves extremely plausible) the way that we see the world is not, immediately, adequate for us to explain the way that the world is. But that does not make our immediate perception of the world false. It simply lacks a theory. Yet Marx's claim (3) is much stronger: reality presents itself in a way that deceives those who immediately perceive it. Marx's own statements to the contrary, it seems that this third claim is best understood not as a general consequence of the nature of scientific understanding but as a specific feature of capitalism. Capitalism mystifies those who live under it, Marx believes, because it is a 'deceptive object'. To penetrate its surface scientifically it is necessary to go beyond the limitations of bourgeois political economy.

10 The fetishism of commodities

The most detailed discussion that Marx provides of a case where the surface of capitalism presents itself as 'false' is to be found in 'The Fetishism of Commodities and the Secret Thereof', in *Das Kapital*. This discussion is a recognizable reworking of the central themes to be found in the treatment of alienated labour in the *Paris Manuscripts*.

In the eighteenth-century sense of the term, fetishists were those non-European peoples whose religion involved the worship of inanimate objects. Fetishism is a fallacy attributing to objects in the world some quality (power and personality) that they, in fact, lack. Marx's conception of commodity fetishism shares this structure, but differs in an important way. The fetishism of commodities is not a matter of subjective delusion or irrationality on the part of perceivers, but is somehow embedded in the reality that they face.

According to Marx, two separate facts or properties are distorted in the commodity-form. First, the 'social character' of human beings' labour appears (falsely) as 'objective characteristics of the products themselves', and second (in consequence of the first fact, as Marx asserts) the producers' own relationship to their 'collective labour' appears 'as a social relationship between objects, existing externally to the producers'.

The first issue concerns what the 'social character' that is apparently a property of the products themselves amounts to. Is it the sheer fact that the commodity *is* a commodity? This suggestion must be rejected, for the belief that the product is a commodity is in no way a false or deceptive one. Likewise, it cannot be something concealed from the producers that commodities *do* as a matter of fact exchange for one another in certain proportions: it is hard to see how anyone could live their lives within a market society without having an adequate understanding of facts of this kind (enough, at least, to be able to buy something to eat). The best interpretation of Marx's argument is that it is not such first-order facts about commodities but a second-order one that is the source of deception: it is not *that* commodities can be exchanged with one another in certain ratios but *the reason why* they exchange in the ratios that they do that is their hidden secret.

Marx's account of the illusion regarding the social character of the products of labour is complemented by the account he gives of the second element in commodity fetishism. Because commodity production takes place as a process by which the producers' activities are coordinated solely through the imperatives of a system of market exchanges, it follows, Marx says, that 'the social relations between their private acts of labour manifest themselves as what they are – that is, not as the immediate social relationships of persons in their labour but as material relationships between persons and social relationships between things'.

Implicitly, the market commensurates the labour of each individual with the labour of every other producer – individual labour has its value in relation to the way in which others perform the same labour. The socially useful character of the labour of the individual producers thus appears to them, according to Marx, 'only under those forms which are impressed upon that labour in everyday practice, in the exchange of products'.

Here again, Marx is indicating an illusion of the second rather than the first order. The individual producers are aware of the role of the market in determining the way in which they labour. In this they are quite correct. But they also believe (falsely) that it is the market that makes their labour useful (rather than recognizing it as a contingent fact about capitalist production that their socially useful labour takes on a market-determined form). Society generates such false beliefs spontaneously, Marx claims. The world of commodities 'veils rather than reveals', he says, the social character of private labour and of the relations between the individual producers.

That the true source of the value of commodities lies in the labour expended in their production is, Marx maintains, a matter of simple scientific truth. So, too, is the fact that the social character of private labour consists in the equalization of that labour under the auspices of the market. Nevertheless, fetishism is a matter of 'objective illusion' and knowledge of these truths does not dispel such false appearance. The discovery of the law of value 'by no means dissipates the objective illusion through which the social character of labour appears to be an objective character of the products themselves' any more than 'the discovery by science of the component gases of air' altered the atmosphere that people breathed.

The analogy that Marx chooses here is not a happy one. Admittedly, it is absurd to think that a scientist's discovery about an object should change the object itself. But that is not the issue. It is not a question of whether the atmosphere itself changes after the discovery of its component gases, but whether the way in which we think about it changes. It is only if we suppose that capitalism, unlike the atmosphere, is an object of a particular kind – a deceptive object – that it is possible to claim that it will continue to encourage such false beliefs in the face of contrary knowledge.

But it is not just that the individuals who live in a society based on commodity production are deceived by it regarding the way that it works. The way that it works is itself criticized by Marx. Above all, the 'social character of labour' is made private in actuality. This is not a misperception or false belief, but a contradiction: a discrepancy between what Marx takes to be the intrinsic nature of social labour and the way that it is in fact organized. Capitalism is not just deceptive, but also defective.

11 Morality

The question whether Marx's theory has a moral or ethical dimension is one of the most controversial of all issues surrounding the interpretation of his work, and the difficulty facing interpreters is easily seen. On the one hand, Marx has a number of uncompromisingly negative things to say about morality. Moreover, after 1845 at least, he affirms that his own theory is not a utopian or ethical one but 'real, positive science'. Yet, on the other hand, much of the language that he uses to describe capitalism is plainly condemnatory (for instance, that it is antagonistic, oppressive and exploitative). Does this not represent an inconsistency on Marx's part? Is he not moralizing and rejecting morality at the same time?

This section will present a line of interpretation according to which Marx is not inconsistent. The interpretation depends on a contrast between certain doctrines typical of moral philosophy (which, it will be argued, Marx rejects) and the rejection of ethical values as such (to which, it will be argued, he is not thereby committed). However, it should be noted that this interpretation is controversial and involves considerable reconstruction of the rather sparse evidence that we have of Marx's views.

It is helpful to start, as Marx himself did, with Hegel's critique of Kant. Both Marx and Hegel share the belief that morality, as embodied in Kant's moral philosophy, is, as they put it, 'abstract' (see HEGEL, G.W.F. §8). There appear to be three interconnected elements compressed into this criticism:

(1) First, morality is alleged to be abstract in the sense that it contains principles expressed in universal form (in Kant's case, the 'categorical imperative' to 'act only according to that maxim which you can, at the same time, will to be a universal law' (see KANTIAN ETHICS)). While such principles may function as a test upon proposed actions, they do not, the argument goes, determine the content of the action to be performed. Thus, the claims of moral philosophy to the contrary, specific content is surreptitiously imported into ethics from the existing institutions or codes of behaviour of the society in question.

(2) Second, morality is abstract to the extent that it takes the form of a mere injunction: an imperative that is addressed to people's 'moral reason', telling them to act in a certain way because that is 'good in itself'. Moral action is detached thereby from other forms of human action and, as a result, moral theory has nothing to say about the conditions under which the forms of behaviour that it commends will be realized in practice.

(3) Finally, morality may be said to be abstract in that it contains an unhistorical understanding of its own

status. It presents its principles as if they were the axioms of some timeless moral geometry. Yet, in fact, every system of morality is a way of seeing the world that arises in particular circumstances and responds to definite needs within those circumstances.

Although one or more of these features may be present in the forms of moral philosophy with which we are most familiar, it is not clear that they are a necessary feature of every view that one might call 'moral'. Not all ethical positions have to express themselves as systems of universal principles that we are enjoined to follow because they are good for their own sake. Admittedly, many philosophers would argue that to combine the value commitments characteristic of morality with the meta-level doctrine that such values are, in the end, expressions of interest (Marx's version of (3) above) inevitably undermines, as Nietzsche might have put it, the value of value itself. But it is at least arguable that the two standpoints are compatible. The path from sociological determinism to moral scepticism is not as steep, slippery and remorseless as it is sometimes claimed to be.

If this is conceded, we can draw a distinction between morality in two senses: morality as a quasi-Kantian system of principles (which Marx rejects) and morality as a set of values embodying a conception of what is good for human beings (which he can consistently accept). To present things in this way, however, may seem to give insufficient weight to the vehement hostility which Marx shows towards ideas of justice and rights, in particular. On the interpretation being proposed here, Marx's animus is best understood as aimed at what he sees as the assumptions behind such values, rather than at the fact of their being values as such.

Roughly speaking, we may think of rights as things that permit individuals to act in certain ways, in given circumstances, should they wish to do so, and to be able to claim correlative duties on the part of others. A duty, correspondingly, would require individuals to act in some way, whether they wished to or not. Justice (if we do not think of it simply as a matter of rights and duties) would consist of principles on which benefits and burdens are distributed in cases where interests conflict.

What these values have in common is that they provide a framework which regulates and limits the self-seeking behaviour of individuals. They are values that assume a conflict between (to put it in Kantian terms) 'duty' and 'inclination'. Just as Marx supposes that the categories of bourgeois economics eternalize the forms of bourgeois economic life, so, he believes, discussion of rights (which he denounces in the *Critique of the Gotha Programme* as 'ideological

nonsense') eternalizes a situation in which the good of each individual is independent and so can only be advanced at the expense of others. Right, moreover, can only apply a fixed and equal standard to unequal individuals, 'from outside'.

For the liberal, who is concerned to protect the individual's powers of self-direction against the intrusions of others, the attraction of the idea of rights is that it presupposes nothing about individuals' characters and personalities. For Marx, on the other hand, that is just its weakness: rights do nothing to transform human nature. Against this, it is clear that Marx, from the time of the *Paris Manuscripts*, sees social progress as characterized by a form of community in which (as he and Engels put it in the *Communist Manifesto*) 'the free development of each is the condition for the free development of all'. Marx's ethical ideal is one of solidarity in which all advance together.

Hence Marx's reluctance to use the language of justice to condemn capitalism becomes more intelligible. It is not that Marx thinks that exploitation, expropriation, oppression, slavery and misery (a few of the terms he applies to the capitalist system) are *just*. But he is reluctant to use language that would suggest that these are forms of injustice for which 'justice' (in the sense of giving 'each their due') is the final and sufficient remedy.

12 Socialism

It may seem odd, given that Marx devoted his life to the achievement of a socialist society, how brief and unspecific his accounts of it are. One explanation that is often advanced for this apparent neglect is the following. Marx believed, it is said, that thought is limited to its own time. Thus it would have been improper for him, living under capitalism, to try to anticipate the nature of the society that would replace it and to write (as he puts it in the Preface to the Second Edition of *Das Kapital*) 'recipes for the cookshops of the future'. While this may be part of the reason for Marx's reticence, it cannot alone suffice. For, even if we grant that Marx believed that each stage of society sets a boundary which thought cannot cross (and it is by no means beyond question that he did hold this view in such a strong form) he is also committed to the view that socialism is anticipated within capitalism.

In the Preface to *Zur Kritik der politischen Ökonomie* Marx makes the general claim that new forms of society are always prefigured within the old ones that they replace. 'Mankind', he writes, 'only sets itself such tasks as it is able to solve, since closer examination will always show that the problem itself arises only when the material conditions for its solution are already present or at least in the course of formation'.

Marx describes the process by which capitalism prepares the ground for socialism at the end of the first volume of *Das Kapital*. As the productive forces developed by capitalism grow, he claims, so too does the 'mass of misery, oppression, slavery, degradation, exploitation'. A stage is reached, however, at which the monopoly of capital becomes a 'fetter' on production and 'the centralization of the means of production and the socialization of labour at last reach a point where they become incompatible with their capitalist shell'. At this point, the shell 'bursts asunder', the 'death knell' sounds for capitalism and the 'expropriators are themselves expropriated'.

The first and most obvious difference between capitalism and socialism is that common ownership leads to a quite different pattern of distribution of the products of labour. No longer will the capitalist, in virtue of his ownership of the means of production, be able to exploit the individual producer. In the *Critique of the Gotha Programme* Marx distinguishes two stages of post-capitalist society. In the first, the direct producer receives back from society (after deductions for shared costs and social expenditure) 'what he has given to it as his individual quantum of labour'.

But this, Marx points out, is a principle of distribution that merely rectifies exploitation. It does not remedy the inequalities that arise from contingent differences in natural capacities between individual producers. Later, however, society will move beyond this, Marx claims, and 'the narrow horizon of bourgeois right' will be 'crossed in its entirety'. At this point, the principle upon which society will operate will be: 'From each according to his ability, to each according to his needs!' But socialism is distinguished by more than its principle of distribution. In particular, labour will be organized quite differently from the way that it is organized under capitalism.

One of Marx's few reasonably extensive accounts of the nature of the socialist organization of production is to be found in the section on the fetishism of commodities in *Das Kapital*, as part of a comparison between capitalist and other forms of production. Marx starts with Robinson Crusoe, whose productive activity he describes as 'simple and clear'. For Robinson, Marx says, the organization of production is a purely administrative operation: the end is known, as are the resources available and the techniques by which that end could be attained. Marx then moves from 'Robinson's island, bathed in light', via feudal and patriarchal forms of production, before alighting on: 'a community of free individuals, carrying on their labour with the means of production in common, in which the labour-power of all the different individuals is consciously applied as the combined labour-power of the community'.

Here, Marx says,

All the characteristics of Robinson's labour are ... repeated, but with this difference, that they are social, instead of individual ... The social relations of the individual producers to their labour and to the products of their labour remain here transparently simple, in production as well as in distribution. (1867 : 171–2)

The idea that labour could be 'consciously applied' in a complex modern society – resources and needs coordinated, efficient techniques adopted, innovation managed – with the same 'transparent simplicity' as an individual allocating his time to different tasks on a desert island is astonishingly implausible. And, even if it were not so, the question would still arise how that 'common and rational plan' (as Marx terms it elsewhere) would relate to the individuals whose task it was to carry it out. Would it not, from their point of view, be no less of an 'external' imperative to be followed than the dictates of the market that govern their labour under capitalism? Arguably, the idea that society under socialism would be spontaneously unified like one great, self-transparent super-individual represents an unacknowledged hangover in Marx's mature thought from Hegel's doctrine of *Geist*. However that may be, the presence of this doctrine goes a long way towards explaining why Marx had so little to say about the problems of socialist economic organization: he simply failed to see the difficulty. Few theoretical omissions, surely, have ever had more disastrous historical consequences.

See also: MARXISM, CHINESE; CIVIL SOCIETY; COMMUNISM; ECONOMICS, PHILOSOPHY OF §3; EXPLANATION IN HISTORY AND SOCIAL SCIENCE §§1–2; HISTORY, PHILOSOPHY OF; MARXISM, WESTERN; MARXIST PHILOSOPHY OF SCIENCE; MARXIST PHILOSOPHY, RUSSIAN AND SOVIET; MARXIST THOUGHT IN LATIN AMERICA; NEEDS AND INTERESTS; POLITICAL PHILOSOPHY, HISTORY OF; REVOLUTION; SOCIALISM

List of works

Marx, K. and Engels, F. (1975–) *Gesamtausgabe* (*MEGA*), Berlin: Dietz. (This outstanding edition of the collected works is often known as *MEGA* II. However, at the time of writing, *MEGA* II, like *MEGA* I, seems likely to remain uncompleted.)

—— (1961–83) *Werke* (*MEW*), Berlin: Dietz. (A very

adequate edition in German that contains all the works referred to in the text of the entry.)

—— (1975–) *Collected Works*, London: Lawrence & Wishart. (A complete edition in English. Marred, however, by patchy and dogmatic editorial work and poor translations. Other editions are generally to be preferred, if available.)

Marx, K. (1975–) *The Pelican Marx Library*, Harmondsworth: Penguin. (Not a complete edition, but a series that contains particularly good translations of *Das Kapital*, the *Grundrisse*, and the *Early Writings*, among others.)

—— (1841) *Differenz der demokritischen und epikureischen Naturphilosophie*, trans. *Difference between the Democritean and Epicurean Philosophy of Nature*, in *Collected Works*, London: Lawrence & Wishart, 1975–, vol. 1, 25–107. (Marx's doctoral dissertation.)

—— (1843a) *Zur Kritik der Hegelschen Rechtsphilosophie*, trans. R. Livingstone and G. Benton, *Critique of Hegel's Philosophy of Right*, in L. Colletti (ed.) *Early Writings*, Harmondsworth: Penguin, 1975, 57–198. (An extensive discussion of Hegel, abandoned by Marx.)

—— (1843b) 'Zur Judenfrage', trans. R. Livingston and G Benton, 'On the Jewish Question', in L. Coletti (ed.) *Early Writings*, Harmondsworth: Penguin, 1975, 211–42. (An important treatment of the idea of emancipation.)

—— (1844) *The Paris Manuscripts*, trans. R. Livingston and G. Benton in L. Coletti (ed.) *Early Writings*, Harmondsworth: Penguin, 1975, 279–400. (Contains Marx's ideas on alienation.)

Marx, K. and Engels, F. (1845a) *Die Heilige Familie*, trans. *The Holy Family*, in *Collected Works*, London: Lawrence & Wishart, 1975–, vol. 4, 15–211. (A polemic against Bruno Bauer and his associates.)

Marx, K. (1845b) 'Theses on Feuerbach', trans. R. Livingston and G. Benton in L. Coletti (ed.) *Early Writings*, Harmondsworth: Penguin, 1975, 421–3. (Brilliant aphorisms on philosophy.)

Marx, K. and Engels, F. (1845–6) *Die Deutsche Ideologie*, ed. C.J. Arthur, trans. *The German Ideology*, London: Lawrence & Wishart, 1970. (A well-produced version of this key work.)

Marx, K. (1847) *La Misère de la Philosophie*, trans. *The Poverty of Philosophy*, in *Collected Works*, London: Lawrence & Wishart, 1975–, vol. 6, 105–212. (Polemic against Proudhon.)

Marx, K. and Engels, F. (1848) *Das Kommunistische Manifest*, trans. *The Communist Manifesto*, in D. Fernbach (ed.) *The Revolutions of 1848*, Harmondsworth: Penguin, 1973, 62–98. (The classic statement of Marx's political and social programme.)

Marx, K. (1850) *Die Klassenkämpfe in Frankreich*, trans. *Class Struggles in France*, in D. Fernbach (ed.) *Surveys From Exile*, Harmondsworth: Penguin, 1973, 35–142. (Commentary on contemporary politics.)

—— (1852) *Das achtzehnte Brumaire des Louis Bonaparte*, trans. *The Eighteenth Brumaire of Louis Bonaparte*, in D. Fernbach (ed.) *Surveys From Exile*, Harmondsworth: Penguin, 1973, 143–249. (Commentary on contemporary politics.)

—— (1857–8) *Grundrisse der Kritik der politischen Ökonomie*, trans. M. Nicholas, *Grundrisse*, Harmondsworth: Penguin, 1973. (An abandoned draft on political economy – superseded by *Das Kapital*.)

—— (1859) *Zur Kritik der politischen Ökonomie*, trans. *A Contribution to the Critique of Political Economy*, in *The Pelican Marx Library*, Harmondsworth: Penguin. (Contains the classic statement of 'historical materialism'.)

—— (1862–3) *Theorien über den Mehrwert*, trans. E. Burns, *Theories of Surplus-Value*, London: Lawrence & Wishart, 1963, 3 vols. (Marx's studies on economic theory.)

—— (1867–) *Das Kapital*, trans. B. Foukes, *Capital*, Harmondsworth: Penguin, 1977. (Marx's mature masterpiece.)

—— (1871) *Der Französische Bürgerkrieg*, trans. *The Civil War in France*, in D. Fernbach (ed.) *The First International and After*, 1973, 187–268. (An important political text.)

—— (1875) *Kritik des Gothaer Programms*, trans. *The Critique of the Gotha Programme*, in D. Fernbach (ed.) *The First International and After*, 1973, 339–59. (Contains a rare, brief discussion of the nature of socialism.)

Marx, K. (1977) *Selected Writings*, ed. D. McLellan, Oxford: Oxford University Press. (At the time of writing, probably the best of the many good selections from Marx's work available.)

References and further reading

* Althusser, L. (1965) *For Marx*, Harmondsworth: Penguin. (The work that initiated the 'structuralist' or 'anti-humanist' interpretation of Marx.)

Callinicos, A. (1985) *Marxism and Philosophy*, Oxford: Oxford University Press. (A sympathetic defence.)

* Cohen, G.A. (1978) *Karl Marx's Theory of History: A Defence*, Oxford: Oxford University Press. (A masterpiece of sustained interpretative argument.)

* Elster, J. (1985) *Making Sense of Marx*, Cambridge: Cambridge University Press. (Less tightly focused than Cohen, but full of insight and perhaps less

one-sided. Contains a particularly good discussion of Marx's economics.)

Kolakowski, L. (1975) *Main Currents of Marxism*, Oxford: Oxford University Press, vol. 1. (A critical treatment, emphasizing the prophetic-metaphysical background to Marxism.)

* Lukács, G. (1921) *History and Class Consciousness*, London: Merlin, 1971. (First published in 1921, this is the book that initiated 'Hegelian' or 'humanist' Marxism.)

Popper, K. (1948) *The Open Society and its Enemies*, London: Routledge & Kegan Paul. (An influential critique of Marx's claims to 'science'.)

Roemer, J. (1982) *A General Theory of Exploitation and Class*, Cambridge, MA: Harvard University Press. (An ambitious reconstruction of Marxist economics.)

Rosen, M. (1996) *On Voluntary Servitude: False Consciousness and the Theory of Ideology*, Cambridge: Polity Press. (A critical account of the theory of ideology.)

Torrance, J. (1995) *Karl Marx's Theory of Ideas*, Cambridge: Cambridge University Press. (An extremely detailed account.)

Wood, A. (1981) *Karl Marx*, London: Routledge & Kegan Paul. (Places emphasis on the philosophical aspects of Marx's work. Contains an extended interpretation of Marx's view of morality quite different from the one advanced in this entry.)

MICHAEL ROSEN

MARXISM, CHINESE

Chinese Marxism is a mixture of elements from Confucianism, German Marxism, Soviet Leninism and China's own guerrilla experience. Because Mao Zedong (1893–1976) was in power longer than any other Chinese communist, the phrase 'Chinese Marxism' is commonly used to refer to Mao's own evolving mixture of ideas from these sources. However, the advocates of Chinese Marxism have come from many different factional backgrounds and have tended to emphasize different aspects in their own thinking. Even Maoism reflects many minds. For example, Mao's two most famous essays, 'Shijianlun' (On Practice) and 'Maodunlun' (On Contradiction) (1937) drew heavily from Ai Siqi, the author of the popular philosophical work Dazhong zhexue *(Philosophy for the Masses) (1934).*

The goals of the Chinese Marxists included the salvation of China from its foreign enemies and the strengthening of the country through modernization. Accordingly, they selected from other systematic theories those doctrines that appeared to facilitate those goals, and then paired these doctrines with others from theories that were sometimes incompatible. One should not, therefore, look for logical consistency in the relations between the ideas that the Chinese Marxists drew from these various sources.

The foundation of Chinese Marxism was undoubtedly Marx's materialist conception of history, and the concepts of class struggle and control of the forces of production shaped the thinking of many early Marxists. However, faced with the need to accelerate social change through class struggle rather than waiting for the full flowering of capitalism, Marxists such as Li Dazhao began focusing less on materialism or determinism and more on voluntarism. There also arose a doctrine, based on the ideas of Lenin and Trotsky, that right-minded people could 'telescope' the phases of the revolution and hasten the transition through the historical stages. This ultimately led to the doctrine of permanent revolution. First promulgated in China in the late 1920s, it reappeared in the 1950s. After Mao's death, the 'subjectivity' movement within Chinese Marxism sought to move the focus away from classes or groups and onto the individual subject as an active agent.

Throughout the evolution of Chinese Marxism, political struggles played a direct role in the formulation and discussion of philosophical positions. Mao's epistemological essay 'Shijianlun' clearly reflects the experience of leaders during the guerrilla period, and his theories of knowledge are analogous to the 'democracy' practised by the guerrilla leaders: the people were consulted for their knowledge and opinions, decisions were then made from the centre, and the resulting policies were taken back to the masses through teaching. In the same way, Mao believed, individuals perceive through their senses, form theories in their brains (the centre), and test the resulting theories in a manner analogous to teaching.

In China, right minds among the people were thought to arise through officials teaching the people. Here premodern Confucian legacy becomes important. It helps to explain the endurance of teaching as an official function in the Chinese Marxist discussion of democratic centralism. In Confucianism, the primary function of government was education, although it certainly had other tasks, such as the collection of taxes. All officials, including the emperor, had the task of transforming the character of the people. The education in which the state involved itself, through control of the curriculum and national examinations for the civil service, was moral education. The ultimate aim of state-controlled Confucian education was a one-minded, hierarchical society, meaning that people of all different strata would think the same on important matters.

Maoists also sought to create a one-minded people through officially controlled teaching.

If the focus of teaching is on right ideas, which are supposed to motivate people towards socialism, one such idea in later Maoist writing is egalitarianism of social status. This was challenged by others, notably Liu Shaoqi, and following Deng Xiaoping's assumption of power in 1978 it suffered a further blow with the switch in economic policy from central planning to market forces.

An example of the relevance of political struggle to the formulation of ideas was the heightening of the campaign against the philosophy called 'humanism', following a dispute in 1957 between Mao and President Liu Shaoqi. Liu made a speech in April of that year saying that capitalists had changed and so class struggle against them could be minimized; this was followed by a Maoist-inspired attack on humanism as a philosophy. The humanism that the Maoists attacked was a Confucian-inspired belief in a class-transcending humaneness or compassion for humankind or humaneness. In contrast, in the post-Mao years, the content of humanism has altered, and the term has come to refer to a doctrine inspired by both the early Marx and by the Western psychologist Maslow, namely that the goal of society is the individual's self-realization. This form of humanism is one of several competing positions that claim to carry on the Marxist tradition in new directions, and has been reinforced by one form of the subjectivity movement in the Deng Xiaoping era.

1   **Historical materialism**
2   **Permanent revolution**
3   **Democracy, centralism and epistemology**
4   **Distributional equality versus material incentives**
5   **Humanism and class struggle**
6   **Humanism and the end of alienation**
7   **Subjectivity**

1   Historical materialism

It was the German theories of MARX that furnished the vocabulary from which Chinese Marxists gradually developed their positions. The key expressions are the building blocks of Marx's 'materialist conception of history', found in the preface to his *A Contribution to the Critique of Political Economy* (1858). Here, Marx argues that human societies evolve progressively through historical stages and that there is an agent of change that propels them from one stage to another. This agent is the struggle between social classes ('relations of production') that have differing power ties to property, especially to property used in production. This class struggle begins when the existing class structure prevents further development of the technology used in making tools ('forces of production'). The combination of classes and tool technology constitutes the 'foundation' or base; everything significant that humans believe (their ideologies or 'consciousness') in the realms of legal, political, religious and aesthetic matters, plus the institutions that embody them, are the 'superstructures'. In this formulation, the materialist conception of history suggests that the base determines the superstructure. What we believe is determined by economic factors, the classes and tools.

The class that has the most advanced beliefs leads a society from one stage to the next. However, there is an inevitable sequence in this historical progression. There must first be economic development (in Marx's time, this meant the flowering of capitalism), then the acquisition of consciousness by the emerging social class that capitalism fetters (the proletariat), and only then can that progressive proletarian class carry out its struggle to move society forward.

The founders of the Chinese Communist Party included Li Dazhao (1888–1927) and Chen Duxiu (1879–1942). Li, once chief librarian at Beijing University, was later the first communist to join the Guomindang. Chen had been an editor of the influential journal *New Youth* and initially advocated guild socialism under the influence of John DEWEY. Li was at first only critically receptive to Marxism; although he accepted the need for class struggle, he viewed it as a sign of human evil. Marxism itself, he felt, lacked an ethical perspective. Good persons emerge as they learn mutual aid, a principle not stressed by Marx.

The early Chinese Marxists did ultimately retain the idea of a glorious future for China, a future guaranteed by the progressive view of history and embodied in historical materialism and the dynamics of class struggle. However, the sequence of the historical theory, the fact that a full flowering of capitalism was required before the agents of change could begin to guide the struggle to create a new society, caused problems. This process could take a long time in industrially backward China. During the years 1919 and 1920, many of the earliest Chinese Marxists, such as Li Dazhao, focused on economic determinism and were troubled by it. In an attempt to find a solution they turned to other theories, selecting those doctrines that appeared to facilitate their goals.

One such example of selective borrowing took from German Marxism. Li Dazhao and certain other Chinese Marxists played down base–superstructure determinism and the idea of the inevitable sequence of events (right ideas follow upon full economic development, and leadership of revolutionary struggle follows consciousness of those ideas) with which it was associated. They eliminated those parts that comprised the materialist conception of history, as well as the notion that historical stages are of long duration and that classes are to be defined solely in economic terms. Instead, they took the position that human consciousness or the minds of right-thinking, strong-willed persons can determine the future. This is voluntarism, the power of the conscious will (*voluntas*) to change the material world. In taking this position, Li and the others were influenced by non-Marxist intellectual currents in China, including even anarchism.

Although economic determinism in the Chinese Marxist theory of history faded, this did not mean the total disappearance of the economic variables in that determinism from the theories of the Marxist community. For example, enduring variables encompassed some economic determinants used in class analysis. These included differentiating urban factory proletarians from rural peasantry, and defining poor peasants in terms of amount of farm tools and animals owned. Another example is the explanation of historical stages in terms of the transition from one form of property ownership (bourgeois/capitalist) to another (socialist). Ideological disputes often centred on the nature of some of these economic variables, such as on the duration of stages. For example, Chen Duxiu initially opposed an alliance of the communists and the Guomindang in the 1920s, which was promoted by the USSR. He eventually accepted the alliance, while at the same time trying to preserve the independence of the communists, but he proclaimed that China would need a long capitalist/bourgeois stage before socialism could be achieved. During this period, Chen wanted the communists to focus on education in a multi-party state that protected civil rights. He regarded armed class uprisings at this stage as foolish.

Other factional disputes within the leadership centred on which economically-defined class was to play the dominant role in the revolution. As early as 1926, while the Communist International stressed organizing the urban proletariat, Mao saw the potential of peasant associations, believing that peasants could be successful agents of the communist revolution. In contrast, Li Lisan wanted the urban proletariat to control the rural communist councils. In 1931 came the end of the communist movement in the cities and the shift to rural areas. Mao's doctrine prevailed: the 'peasants' have proletarian ideas, and thus class definition came to be defined partly in economic terms and partly in terms of consciousness.

The voluntarist position that replaced economic determinism gradually became intertwined with another doctrine, that concerning the ability of right-minded people to telescope the process of transition through historical stages. This new doctrine drew elements from a thesis popularly associated with Trotsky, the theory of permanent revolution, from which Mao had nominally distanced himself. Trotsky in turn had borrowed most of the essentials of this theory from Marx and Lenin. This voluntaristic, unacknowledged theory of permanent revolution came to coexist with what was left of historical materialism in China after the unacceptable parts were eliminated. It is completely incompatible with the original German formulation of historical materialism and economic determinism that had so fascinated the first Chinese Marxists.

2 Permanent revolution

Impatient to move China into its safe and prosperous future, first Li Dazhao and then Mao Zedong adopted a stance that had been foreshadowed by Marx (in his 'Address of the Central Committee to the Communist League' in 1850), and then by Lenin (in 'Two Tactics of Social Democracy in the Democratic Revolution'). The voluntarist theories of Li and Mao changed the agent that precipitates class struggle in historical materialism. No longer was this agent the tension between tool technology and class structure; rather, it was the ideas in the minds either of a few elites who teach the masses (in the view of Mao), or of those elites aided by some positive ideas already in the minds of almost all Chinese people (in the view of Li). Armed with these ideas, elites can telescope the course of history, shortening the normal duration of a historical stage. They can do so by taking control of the historical period that really should be led by the capitalists. Although Mao and Liu Shaoqi did not start regularly using the term 'uninterrupted' (permanent) to describe revolution and society until the 1950s, Mao had accepted the principles of this doctrine of permanent revolution in the 1930s.

In this view, then, China does not need to wait for capitalism to flower before the right ideas enter the minds of its people; the elite can acquire the right ideas rapidly and proceed to lead the class struggle, take over leadership of the revolution and introduce socialism. This revolution is permanent in the sense that the attainment of one stage (bourgeois democracy) is not followed by a long period of peace and gradual growth into the next. Rather (and this was Lenin's contribution), the struggle that ushered in the new stage continues, as the few leaders with the right ideas take power away from those that would seem to be in charge (capitalists) and rapidly accelerate people into the new historical (socialist) phase.

Li Dazhao foreshadowed the doctrines of Mao

Zedong in important ways. First, he highlighted revolutionary consciousness as being able to arise independently of the existence of either a large capitalist or proletarian class. The correct ideas in the minds of even a small progressive class (the communists) could accelerate China's economic and social development. Second, he defined class partially in terms of the ideas in minds. Thus, as Maurice Meisner (1967) showed, it is permissible to speak of proletarian ('progressive') ideas in the minds of most Chinese people (who are peasants) as a result of their experience with foreign 'imperialists'. Third, in Li's view, China's revolution would be peasant-based rather than based on urban workers. China could change rapidly through class struggle. The agent that would initiate class struggle and modernize China was ideas in the minds of peasants or of most Chinese, a reversal of the sequence in historical materialism.

Mao differed from Li Dazhao in being China's quintessential Leninist. In his view, the right ideas are originally the exclusive preserve of a small elite within the Communist Party, rather than being more widely shared among the people. Mao also differed from Trotsky and other advocates of permanent revolution in identifying a democratic or bourgeois stage for China. This is an insignificant difference, however, because for Mao, such a stage (described in his 1940 essay 'Xin minzhu zhuyilun' (On New Democracy)) would last only a few years and would be controlled by the communists as much as possible. In fact, according to Mao, socialism was achieved and new democracy ended in 1955.

Not all of the early Chinese Marxists advocated the power of the mind to change objective conditions as strongly as did Li and Mao. This particular aspect of permanent revolution is less pronounced in, for example, the writings of Ai Siqi, the author of the popular philosophical work *Dazhong zhexue* (Philosophy for the Masses) and a resident ideologist in the Yenan guerrilla base.

3 Democracy, centralism and epistemology

The bridge between permanent revolution on the one hand, and democracy and epistemology as topics for study on the other hand, lies in the need for those who already have access to correct ideas to teach and thereby mobilize those who do not. Together, they initiate the struggle that modernizes China. Teaching is required by permanent revolution, a dictum reinforced by Confucian views on the role of rulers. The content of what is taught, or the epistemological element, derives in part from the Chinese Marxist understanding of democracy.

Ideas about democracy and epistemology in

Chinese Marxism owe as much to the guerrilla experience of the 1930s and 1940s as they do to Lenin's earlier insistence on the subordination of party debate to central leadership positions once decisions are made. In north China, the communists were dependent on local peasants for logistical support (avoiding long supply lines that could be cut) and for intelligence about the movements of Japanese and Guomindang troops. Being dependent, they had to maintain good relations with the local people. This is the origin of the communist custom of living with and consulting with the people about non-military and military matters.

Mao believed that the origin of knowledge lies in practice. Although he referred to production and science as forms of practice, uppermost in importance was the practical experience of conducting class struggle. Thus Mao regarded the knowledge of the Chinese people as developing in part during the guerrilla struggles with the Japanese and the Guomindang (in spite of the United Front with the latter, during which the communists and the Guomindang fought together against the Japanese). Democracy and centralism are forms of relationship between party officials and masses that generate knowledge in the course of the class struggle.

Mao understood the term 'democracy' to mean letting ordinary people speak out on topics about which they have some direct knowledge. They have useful concrete information that can help officials make good policies. Letting them speak out also helps to unify the party and the people; it promotes cohesiveness. Thus democracy is a useful tool for leaders to employ.

The expression 'mass line' arose during the guerrilla period to refer to the custom of consulting with local people or carrying out local investigations prior to expanding operations to a larger area, where that locally-derived information would be applicable. 'From the masses' is part of a slogan, and it refers to this grass roots consultation. Thus, for Chinese Marxists this aspect of the mass line practice embodied 'democracy'. Typical of the Maoist form of Chinese Marxism is the position that 'masses' refers primarily to the peasantry, a source of important raw data.

There is another aspect to the mass line, indicated by the rest of the slogan ('to the masses'), which refers to leadership, guidance or, especially, teaching by officials about policy for the local people. This takes place after prior consultation at headquarters, where the authority of centralism prevails.

In Maoist Marxism, the ideas of democracy and centralism are also intertwined with a theory of knowledge. In the stages of acquiring knowledge, an individual begins with perceptual or empirical knowledge gained through practical experience. Within the brain the individual then generalizes and formulates hypotheses or theories about such concrete data. The resulting rational knowledge is higher or more worthy than perceptual knowledge. Following this, individuals test their theories, observe and, if necessary, revise the theory. This process is discussed in Mao's essay 'Shijianlun'. Chinese Marxists extended the analogy of the individual's acquisition of knowledge to the mass line or to the leadership style required by democratic centralism. 'From the masses' consultation is analogous to sense perception by an individual; policy formulation at headquarters is analogous to theorizing in the brain; and testing/revising of theories is analogous to 'to the masses' teaching. Mao discusses this in several places, notably in 'Guanyu lingdao fangfa di rogan wenti' (Some Questions Concerning Methods of Leadership), written in 1943.

All of the above is compatible with the Leninist idea of elite officials knowing more than ordinary people. After all, they possess rational knowledge, which is higher than the perceptual knowledge of the masses. That possession justifies their privileges. The fusion of the mass line with a theory of knowledge also meets the demand of the doctrine of permanent revolution for the telescoping of progress through a historical stage. Leaders focus on transforming the minds or consciousness of the people as a way of rapidly modernizing the country socially and economically. Leaders are teachers who help transform the perceptual knowledge of the people into higher, rational knowledge. In consulting and then teaching, they satisfy the requirements of democracy and of centralism. Permanent revolution demands not only changing consciousness, it demands also the class struggle that follows in its wake. Other Marxists in China opposed the focus on struggle, advocating instead what they and their ideological opponents called 'humanism' (see §4).

After the communist victory in 1949 the consultative side of the mass line atrophied, but the leaders, members of the Communist Party, retained their instructional role. As during the imperial age, transforming the minds of the people remained a core function of officials. Among the many reasons why the consultative role evaporated was the increased difficulty of the task. Consulting in a small area such as the guerrilla bases was not difficult; consulting in a large country such as China was, especially when that country had no history of representative government. The difficult was ignored. Also, there were no built-in safeguards to the mass line consultation process; in gathering information, officials could easily filter out opinions or data they did not like. Finally, there was no institutionalized time period during which consultation had to be conducted.

As late as 1982, when China's leaders issued a constitution, there was still no procedure for representative government. The constitution document is not a contract between leaders and people involving the sharing of power; it does more to protect the state from individuals than to grant inalienable rights to participate in government to the people. Nor does the constitution treat the individual as the best judge of the individual's interests. Such an assumption is part of representative democracy and the obligation of leaders to consult with the people's representatives.

4 Distributional equality versus material incentives

The content of the right ideas that should motivate people from socialism forward are in part summed up in the terms 'class analysis' and 'class struggle'. However, there is another aspect, the priority of moral over material incentives. Like democracy, to which it is related, the principal Maoist thesis against significant wage differences took shape during the guerrilla period. Like democracy as mass line, its fate was affected by the switch from small societies in the guerrilla base areas during the 1930s and 1940s to its application to China in its entirety after 1949. The Maoist position was attacked intermittently by opponents during the next quarter-century, and finally evaporated after the death of Mao.

Marx himself had no special fondness for spreading wealth around equally, although popular writers often attribute such a concern to him. In *Critique of the Gotha Programme* (1875) he describes inequality of distribution as characterizing the first phase of communist society. Marx states that 'The right of the producers is proportional to the labour they supply'. The essential trait of communism is not distribution but the elimination of the division of labour. Mao himself criticized those absolute egalitarians who would object to officers riding on horses in periods of guerrilla warfare. Officers have responsibilities and needs that justify some unequal material privileges.

However, Mao idealized the roughly egalitarian society of Yenan and the other base areas during the anti-Japanese war. He wrote that they had a free supply system (take what you need) and minimal contention. After 1949, he stated, the introduction of a differential wage system along with status differences increased quarrelling. In his 'Reading notes on "The Soviet Union's Political Economy"', he wrote: 'Right up to the early stages of liberation, people on the whole lived an egalitarian life. They worked hard and fought bravely on the battlefront. They absolutely

137

did not rely on material incentive for encouragement, but on revolutionary spirit'. After 1949, wage differences did continue to exist, but the gap was modest.

There is always the assumption that people can be self-motivating in pursuit of communist goals, especially those whose minds have been transformed. For the Maoist, this obviates the need for material incentives. In Maoist theory, however, social arrangements must coexist with transformed minds in order for this nonreliance on material incentives to prevail. There must be at least the illusion of democratic decision making and equality of status. Here is one place where the topics of democracy and egalitarianism converge.

Critics of this position included economists and some supreme leaders (for example, President Liu Shaoqi in 1962), who questioned its impact on productivity. The argument was that people who have an 'iron rice bowl' (guaranteed wage) have no motive to work harder or to innovate. A free supply system would not work in a large country because it requires an abundance of wealth that can only come later in the development process. Inherent difficulties in the policy of opposing material incentives included the fact that it was incompatible with two values to which its advocates were also committed: social order and self-sufficiency. Social order requires a chain of command and differences between those who give and those who take orders. Efficiency in maintaining order dictates status distinctions between them, often manifest in their access to different styles of uniform, to houses and cars that have different monetary worth, and so forth. With regard to self-sufficiency, if officials ask regions to prize self-sufficiency, they are also telling poor regions to be satisfied with what they have and not ask for handouts from wealthier ones.

The major departure from the Maoist position came after Deng Xiaoping assumed power in 1978. Economic reformers argued that socialist goals could best be attained by rejecting central government planning in favour of market factors such as price and profit. This meant taking profit into account in organizing and running an enterprise, wide differences in wages, legal protection of contracts between economic entities and toleration of individual entrepreneurs. Given China's clan–village social structure, individual entrepreneurs could be either individual persons or villages taking the initiative in starting industries, using village-owned resources. The existing village elites (Communist Party officials) would see their incomes rise most rapidly, along with the incomes of managers working on contract to the village.

5 Humanism and class struggle

Within the ranks of Chinese Marxists, the most serious challenge to Maoism in the 1950s and 1960s came from critics characterized as 'humanists'. After Mao's death in 1976, those Marxists who criticized the Communist Party were also humanists. Some of them decried the alienation of people from leaders caused by the party's dictatorship. Others participated in the growth of a new movement, 'subjectivism', that centred on the autonomy of all individuals as possible and desirable.

'Humanism' stood for opposition to Maoism in the 1950s and 1960s because it was a broad term under which a variety of perspectives could unite. First and foremost, it symbolized repudiation of the Maoist position that class struggle is the principal agent of historical change and the agent that could propel China into the modern world. The doctrine of class struggle assumes that human society is divided into distinctly different classes, that analysis of humans in class terms is the only correct sociological methodology and that class hatred is an inevitable motive in that struggle. In an essay from 1942 entitled 'Zai Yenan wenyi zuotanhui shangdi jianghua' (Talks at the Yenan Forum on Art and Literature), Mao had taken two positions that authorize such conclusions. One is that there is no pan-human or universal human nature common to all people. There are only the differing natures of people of different classes; within a given class, natures are somewhat uniform. The other is that love or sympathy that transcends classes is impossible; there is only love for members of one's own class. Class antagonism is therefore inevitable.

Both these positions are totally alien to the dominant Confucian legacy regarding the nature of humans and the ethical position that should flow from that assumption about human nature (see CONFUCIAN PHILOSOPHY, CHINESE; XING). Together, these Confucian positions carry the label of 'humanism', although the term has several meanings in China. In attacking humanism, Maoists were simultaneously supporting class struggle and opposing the most powerful philosophical legacy of the past. This was the teachings of MENCIUS, who in the fourth century BC first formulated the concept of a universal human nature. The essential features of this universal nature are a mind that evaluates right and wrong, and a sentiment of compassion. Mencius based an ethical and political position on this psychological analysis, namely that each person has an obligation to implement these features. Acting on the sense of compassion, individuals should extend their affection beyond family members and those who suffer to encompass an increasingly large number of other persons. Class-transcending love and universal traits set Mencius in opposition to Mao. Thus, to attack humanism was to attack the old, or that part of the old that was the greatest ideological threat.

In modern China, three disciplines have inherited the traditional concern with the topic of human nature: literature, philosophy and psychology. During the 1950s and 1960s, each of these was affected by the conflict between class struggle and humanism. In literature, Ba Ren (a pseudonym of Wang Renshu, a literary editor, critic and diplomat) got into trouble in the 1960s for insisting on the right of authors to deal with things that all people universally share, namely the love of the fragrance of flowers and the song of birds, and the desire to eat and to be warm. The popular philosopher Feng Ding of Beijing University was attacked for claiming that there is a survival instinct common to all persons. Beginning in 1958, younger Chinese psychologists shifted away from an interest in neurologically-based character types to focus on the subjective class standpoint or thought that separates people into social groups.

These themes dominated intellectual activity, in so far as it existed during the Cultural Revolution, until Mao's death. They were reinforced by rivalry with the USSR. The Soviet leader Nikita Khrushchev had claimed that the Soviet Union had eliminated class antagonism and was thus a 'state of all the people'. This sounded to Maoists like an arrogant claim that the Soviet Union had leapt ahead of China into communism, and that Soviet leaders were practising class-transcending love where class divisions actually still existed. This Chinese critique appears in an influential essay published in 1963 by Chou Yang (1908–), a leader of the All-China Federation of Literary and Art Circles and a member of the Department of Philosophy and Social Science of the Chinese Academy of Sciences. In this case, international political disputes had spilled over into philosophical debates.

6 Humanism and the end of alienation

With the death of Mao, some prominent Chinese Marxists shifted their concerns away from opposing class struggle towards promoting the free development of the individual. They treated these goals as humanistic goals. However, they shifted the content of humanism away from its Confucian focus on humaneness, being interested instead in the development of other, different human traits. Influenced by the early writings of Marx, long popular in eastern Europe, they spoke of the individual's freedom as the absence of alienation and described it positively as the all-round development of the individual.

This was a monumental leap in China. Mao had manifested no interest in the individual at all, only in classes or groups. His idea of ending the division of labour and promoting all-round development was sending intellectuals to the farm and introducing peasants to schools. This was intended to end the mental–manual division of labour, an ideal with some Marxist justification. However, MARX in his early works had a richer vision, one symbolized in some famous words of *The German Ideology* (1846) that describe a person who can metaphorically 'hunt in the morning, fish in the afternoon, rear cattle in the evening, criticize after dinner', without ever being simply one-sided. This was also the Renaissance humanistic ideal of the fully-developed individual human.

The ideals of the early Marx are also remarkably convergent with the ideals of nineteenth-century British liberals. Indeed, John Stuart Mill was influenced by the same German Romantics that influenced Marx. For those Romantics, the heroes were the artists who put into canvas or into stone their own personalities; they realize themselves in their art (see GOETHE, J.W. VON; HÖLDERLIN, J.C.F.). These are also the heroes of Marx's *Economic and Philosophical Manuscripts* (1844). These manuscripts became popular with some Chinese Marxists because they directed attention away from class or group to individuals and their self-realization, thus providing the basis for an ethics in which individuals count for something. The *Manuscripts* do so by asserting that all people are born with basic needs (to realize themselves by means of variety in their lives and to be free agents in their productive work). However, most people are unable to satisfy those basic human needs. Marx described communism as humanism because in communism, all individuals are able to satisfy those needs and become fully human. To those Chinese Marxists who prized individual freedom, the contrast with the Maoist vision of communism could not have been more stark.

The most prominent of the advocates of this style of humanism after Mao's death was Wang Ruoshui, a former editor of the official newspaper *People's Daily* and one of the leading reform theorists. Wang accepted the premise (he never tried to prove it) that there are universal human needs, the most basic of which is for self-realization in an all-round, free manner. From this premise, he derived a standard to judge acts or policies. Good acts or policies foster the satisfaction of basic needs; bad ones cause individuals to feel alienated or separated from their natures. Wang used this standard to criticize the Communist

Party's dictatorship. In his view, in the 1980s the Party fostered alienation in the Chinese people; individuals had little control over their work and bureaucrats constantly intruded into their lives.

The counterattack on this brand of Chinese Marxist humanism was mounted by Hu Qiaomu, one-time secretary to Mao, author of a history of the Chinese Communist Party and, towards the end of his life, honorary president of the Academy of Social Sciences. With the help of ghostwriters from the Academy's Institute of Philosophy, Hu produced an article entitled 'Guanyu rendaozhuyi ho yihua wenti' (On Humanism and Alienation), which appeared in the journal *Hongai* (Red Flag) in 1984. Hu's thesis was that it is acceptable to incorporate humanism into Chinese Marxism when the term stands simply for routine ethical considerations, such as being kind to an elderly or sick person, but it is not permissible to treat it as a theory of history or as something generating a serious standard. This, he claimed, is what people like Wang Ruoshui had done, by describing humanity's gradual evolution from alienation to need-satisfaction over time and deriving from this process the top normative standard. This is to treat humanism as a theory of history, said Hu, which is wrong. It leads to the impermissible conclusion that the Chinese Communist Party causes alienation, which cannot exist in socialism. The only correct theory of history is historical materialism, with its claims about stages of history, and the standard that one can draw from historical materialism tells whether or not a given policy is right as a function of its appropriateness for a particular stage or moment in history. In Hu's analysis, the dictatorship of the party passes this test as it is appropriate for China's current stage.

7   Subjectivity

The other current away from Maoism that permeated Chinese Marxist philosophy, literary criticism and psychology was subjectivity. In some versions, it too made a place for the individual's worth. Especially in this regard, subjectivity represents a break during the Deng era from the Maoist social class-centred analysis of human beings. It focuses instead on individuals having unique identities. When it began in 1978, the subjectivity movement was a radical departure from the implications of the term 'materialism' in historical materialism. It rejected the idea of humans as puppets whose consciousness is entirely formed by their socio-economic environment; specifically, it was a departure from the Leninist theory of reflection (the inner or mental is simply a reflection of the outer or environmental) that had dominated

orthodox Leninist epistemology in China since 1949. Later, the subjectivity movement took two different directions.

Li Zehou, a Marxist philosopher from the Institute of Philosophy, took the lead among those who treated subjectivity as a new direction in epistemology. The objective world, they argued, is shaped by the subjective interests, interpretative paradigms or psychological memories unconsciously sedimented in human minds. The mind is active, not a passive reflector, and objectivity changes as subjects with different interests or (over time) differently sedimented memories come on the scene.

The other view of subjectivity flourished in literary and psychological circles. Here, subjectivity meant the ability and desirability of the individual acting autonomously. The literary critic Liu Zaifu of the Institute of Literature at the Academy of Social Sciences encouraged writers to portray in their works characters who act freely and are conscious of their autonomy. In psychology, this approach was seen as consistent with the worldwide movement away from Freudian psychological reductionism and behaviourism. The autonomous individual's inner needs and choices exist and count. These Marxists wished China to acquire the perspective of the European Enlightenment, wherein the beliefs of individuals do not need to be determined by gods, destiny or rulers. The individual can and should be in control. In working out these various positions on subjectivity, Chinese Marxists drew into their own heritage ideas from Immanuel KANT in the West and WANG YANGMING in China.

See also: See also: CONFUCIAN PHILOSOPHY, CHINESE; THEORIES OF HISTORY, CHINESE §5; LEGALIST PHILOSOPHY, CHINESE §2; MARX, K. §§4, 8–12; MARXISM, WESTERN; POLITICAL PHILOSOPHY, HISTORY OF

References and further reading

Ch'en, J. (1970) *Mao Papers*, London: Oxford University Press. (Writings from 1917 to 1969, along with an essay on Mao's literary style.)

Dirlik, A. (1989) *The Origins of Chinese Communism*, New York: Oxford University Press. (Ideology and organization in the early years, including the impact of such diverse strands as anarchism and guild socialism.)

* Lenin, V.I. (1888–1924) *Collected Works*, Moscow: Progress Publishers, 1990, 47 vols. (See for the essay 'Two Tactics of Social Democracy in the Democratic Revolution'.)

* Mao Zedong (1965) *Selected Works of Mao Tse-tung*,

Beijing: Foreign Languages Press, 5 vols. (The official collection of edited works attributed to Mao, including the essays cited in this entry.)

* —— (1968) *Four Essays in Philosophy*, Beijing: Foreign Languages Press. (Includes the two essays 'Shijianlun' (On Practice) and 'Maodunlun' (On Contradiction). These essays owe much to the thought of Ai Siqi.)

* —— (1974) 'Reading Notes on "The Soviet Union's Political Economy"', Joint Publications Research Service no. 61269-2, Washington, DC: US Government Printing Office. (This was not a public document in China; a copy was obtained and published by the US government.)

* Marx, K. (1843–83) *Collected Works*, London: Lawrence & Wishart, 1975. (A complete edition of Marx's works in English; see for the works cited in this entry.)

* Meisner, M. (1967) *Li Ta-chao and the Origins of Chinese Marxism*, Cambridge, MA: Harvard University Press. (On the reinterpretation of Marxism by one of the founders of the Chinese Communist party.)

Meissner, W. (1990) *Philosophy and Politics in China: The Controversy over Dialectical Materialism in the 1930s*, trans. R. Mann, Stanford, CA: Stanford University Press. (Discusses the meaning of 'philosophy' and 'science' in these years, with special attention to the essays 'On Practice' and 'On Contradiction'.)

Munro, D. (1978) *The Concept of Man in Contemporary China*, Ann Arbor, MI: University of Michigan Press. (The impact of Confucian and Soviet thought on the central theme of traditional Chinese philosophy in Chinese Marxism, and the resultant influence on education.)

Schram, S. (1963) *The Political Thought of Mao Tse-tung*, New York: Praeger. (Topically divided selections from Mao's writings, preceded by a lengthy interpretive introduction.)

—— (1974), *Chairman Mao Talks to the People: Talks and Letters 1956–1971*, New York: Pantheon. (Directives and statements that came to light in 'Red Guard' tabloids during the Cultural Revolution.)

Schwartz, B. (1958) *Chinese Communism and the Rise of Mao*, Cambridge MA: Harvard University Press. (The interaction of factional conflict and doctrine during the period 1918–33.)

DONALD J. MUNRO

MARXISM, WESTERN

Western Marxism is used here as an umbrella term for the various schools of Marxist thought that have flourished in Western Europe since Marx's death in 1883. It is sometimes used more narrowly to refer to those Marxist philosophers whose thinking was influenced by the Hegelian idea of dialectics and who focused their attention on the cultural as opposed to the economic aspects of capitalism. In the broader sense, Western Marxism does not denote any specific doctrine, but indicates a range of concerns that have exercised Marxist philosophers in advanced capitalist societies. These concerns primarily have been of three kinds: (1) epistemological – what would justify the claim that Marxist social theory and, in particular, the materialist conception of history are true?; (2) ethical – does the Marxist critique of capitalism require ethical foundations, and if so, where are these to be discovered; and (3) practical – if the economic collapse of capitalism can no longer be regarded as inevitable, who are the agents who can be expected to carry through a socialist transformation?

In relation to the first issue, the main debate has been between those who, following Engels, adhere to 'scientific socialism' (that is, the view that Marxism is a science in the same sense as the natural sciences), and those who claim that Marxist epistemology relies on a form of dialectics quite distinct from the methods of natural science. The most prominent exponent of this second view was the Hungarian philosopher Georg Lukács, who drew upon the dialectical method of Hegel, with class consciousness replacing Geist (Spirit) as the vehicle of dialectical reason. Thus, for Lukács the truth of historical materialism and the goodness of communism were both established dialectically, through the class consciousness of the revolutionary proletariat. Lukács' advocacy of dialectics was later taken up and developed by the philosophers of the Frankfurt School.

In relation to the second issue, early dissenters from the orthodox Marxism of Engels like Eduard Bernstein looked outside Marxism itself, and especially to the philosophy of Kant, for the ethical principles that would justify socialism. The position changed somewhat with the rediscovery of the young Marx's Paris Manuscripts (1844) from which later Marxists, and in particular those associated with the Frankfurt School, were able to extract a humanistic ethics centred on the notion of alienation.

In relation to the third issue, most Western Marxists continued to look to the proletariat as the agency of revolutionary change, often distinguishing, as did Lukács, between the true consciousness of that class and the false consciousness that reflected the distorting effects of bourgeois ideology. But in the case of the

Frankfurt Marxists, the critical theory that pointed the way to a liberated human future was detached from any specific agency and treated merely as critique. The most original contribution was made by the Italian Marxist Antonio Gramsci, who argued that the working class must use the power of its ideas to establish hegemony over the other classes in bourgeois society, who would then join the proletariat in overthrowing capitalism.

The disintegration of Western Marxism began in the 1960s when the French philosopher Louis Althusser attacked both the use of Hegelian dialectics by Marxists and the various forms of Marxist humanism. Althusser insisted that Marxism was a science which required no ethical foundations. His critique was informed by a conviction that human subjectivity, together with the philosophical problems generated by subject–object dualism, are illusions.

Althusserian Marxism became fashionable in English-speaking universities, but its cavalier and paradoxical style also led, by reaction, to the rise of analytic Marxism in the late 1970s. Analytic Marxists returned to interrogating Marx's texts in more conventional ways, using the methods of analytic philosophy and contemporary social science to reformulate them to withstand academic scrutiny by non-Marxists. A tendency rather than a movement, analytic Marxism perhaps marks the final stage of a process that began with Lukács, that of turning Marxism into a purely academic study remote from politics.

1 **Second International Marxism**
2 **Western Marxism**
3 **The disintegration of Western Marxism**

1 Second International Marxism

MARX died in 1883 leaving his philosophical position unclear to his followers. His early philosophical writings were largely unpublished and unknown. He called his approach 'materialist' but it was not certain what this indicated beyond opposition to idealist philosophy and to religion, and a theory of history giving explanatory primacy to the production and reproduction of material life. His place was taken by ENGELS (§3), whose influence, until his death in 1891, was crucial for the way this uncertainty was resolved by the next generation of Marxist theorists. Seldom philosophers, they were mostly politically engaged intellectuals involved in the rapidly growing working-class movements.

Engels considered Marx's economics a decisive scientific advance on classical political economy, and claimed that Marx did for history what Darwin had done for biological evolution. He believed these discoveries converged with those of natural science to demonstrate the truth of a dialectical and materialist ontology, and thought that epistemological and ethical questions could be resolved by scientific progress. Hence his description of Marxism as 'scientific socialism'.

Engels also tried to fill in the gaps in Marx's historical theory. He treated historical materialism as a causal theory, with causal interaction between 'base' and 'superstructure'. Development of the productive forces is determining only 'in the last instance'. He also added an 'ideological superstructure' to Marx's 'legal and political superstructure'. To keep scientific socialism from being ideological, he introduced the term 'false consciousness' (defined as a failure to see that the objective cause of supposed wants and ideals is class interest) and the notion that class interests, being the most powerful and uniform real motives, prevail in the long run by cancelling out short-term subjective motives. This was meant to explain why superstructures appear to be independent of, and neutral between, class interests when such is not the case, and why the scientific understanding of history differs from that of participants and chroniclers. But scientific socialism would enable the proletariat to pursue its class interest with the knowledge that its victory would then be inevitable, since it would coincide with the direction of material progress. Thus Engels pushed Marx's ideas rather naïvely towards a closed intellectual system.

Karl KAUTSKY, the leading theorist of Second International Marxism, interpreted Engels' philosophy in the light of the mixture of materialism, positivism and Darwinism popular among progressive German thinkers in the 1870s. Kautsky's outlook was highly determinist. He relied on the historical inevitability of capitalist crises and proletarian revolution for doctrinaire solutions to theoretical and political problems and failed to see that the inevitability of socialism supplied no moral argument for it. This determinism was allied to a cautious political strategy that welcomed trade unionism and parliamentarism as means of organizing the working class for the ultimate 'decisive hour', but denied that they could improve permanently the situation of the workers or prevent class polarization.

Kautsky's determinism was attacked by his revisionist colleague Eduard BERNSTEIN. Bernstein, whose empiricism and 'evolutionary socialism' were influenced by the English Fabians, aimed to purge Marxism of revolutionary doctrine, which he blamed on the influence of Hegelian dialectics. He advocated a reformist strategy to achieve socialism legally and democratically. Stretching Engels' conception of causal interaction between base and superstructure, he argued that social evolution would give morality an increasing influence over production. He justified his moral position in terms of ethical universalism, in a neo-Kantian manner, denying that a practical doctrine like socialism can be scientific.

Orthodox Marxism was also criticized by sympathetic neo-Kantian philosophers dissatisfied with Engels' outdated materialism. Ethical socialists of the Marburg School, arguing that ethics cannot be based on anthropology, held that the Kantian principle that every human being ought to be treated as an end and not as a means prohibits workers being treated as commodities. Karl Vorländer saw Marx's theory of history and Kant's ethics as mutually complementary: the irreducible value of each individual implies worldwide human solidarity and justifies the connection between proletarian revolution and human emancipation.

The Kantian revival made its greatest impact on the Austro-Marxist school. In the early nineteenth century the leading intellectuals of the Austrian Social Democratic Party, Max Adler, Otto Bauer, Rudolf Hilferding and Karl Renner, shared an empiricist conception of scientific socialism as a system of sociology. Hilferding applied this perspective to economics, Renner to law and Bauer to politics. They shared a neo-Kantian commitment to ethical universalism while Adler supplied the epistemological foundations. Adler claimed, against the prevailing mechanistic interpretation of Engels' causal theory, that since all social phenomena are mental, social causality can be studied empirically only if Marx's concept of 'socialized humanity' is treated as a transcendental category of knowledge which is given a priori. Other Austrian Marxists, influenced by the neo-positivism of Mach and the Vienna Circle, opposed this Kantian Marxism.

Divergences within Marxism reflected new intellectual currents, national diversity and the pull of competing working-class ideologies. Thus Bernstein's revisionism was influenced by liberal reformism and Luxemburg's radicalism by syndicalism (see LUXEMBURG, R.). Syndicalism, an anarchist brand of trade-union militancy that took shape in France, became a revolutionary alternative to Marxism before the First World War, finding a champion in the unorthodox Marxist Georges SOREL who anticipated some later tendencies in Western Marxism.

Sorel rejected the notion of scientific socialism, together with most other rationalist *motifs* in Marxism, regarding Marx instead as a moralist like himself. He read *Das Kapital* (1867–) as a description of the corrupting economic system responsible for the decadence of bourgeois society and looked to working-class morality for its redemption. Becoming disillusioned with revisionism, he turned to syndical-

ism and direct action. For Sorel, class war was the central reality, and Marxism a 'myth' whose function was not to predict or guide but to inspire the workers to revolutionary industrial militancy. United and purified by violence, they would acquire the heroic moral qualities needed to destroy capitalism and found a new society of producers.

Meanwhile, Italian Marxism had also received a less orthodox stamp from the work of Antonio LABRIOLA. An academic philosopher and anti-metaphysical Hegelian, Labriola's exposition of the materialist conception of history was opposed to inclusive, determinist and dogmatic interpretations, and his more open-minded approach, at once humanist and empirical, remained influential in Italy.

During this period the concept of ideology lost the negative connotation given to it by Marx and Engels as Marxists were forced to recognize the difference between science and morals. Bernstein argued that if all non scientific ideas are ideological, Marxism must be an ideology since it too is based on a moral ideal. Kautsky admitted the difference between scientific socialism and socialist ideals, but still distinguished the latter from 'bourgeois ideology' on the grounds that only these ideals now correspond with the needs of humanity. For Lenin, however, in exile in Switzerland, class struggle involved a straightforward conflict between bourgeois capitalist ideology and proletarian socialist ideology, whose outcome would be decided by history (see IDEOLOGY §1).

2 Western Marxism

Western Marxism in a narrower sense flourished between the Russian Revolution and the death of Stalin, an era of deepening division between Soviet communism and Western socialism. Its keynote was the claim that Marx was a dialectical philosopher in the Hegelian mould who had been misunderstood by Engels and Second International orthodoxy. It originated with Georg LUKÁCS and Karl Korsch, philosophers who wrote after participating in failed revolutions in Hungary and Germany. In *History and Class Consciousness* (1921) Lukács argued that for Marx, as for Hegel, human history was a dynamic totality, an unfolding of reason which must be understood dialectically, and that this understanding is part of the process by which the whole is transformed. Its truth is available only to the historical agent – the proletariat – which becomes identical with the whole through the revolutionary action of consciously and deliberately transforming it. The proletariat is thus doubly privileged by history; by freeing itself it emancipates mankind from exploitation and it resolves the antinomies of philosophy in a transparent unity of theory and practice.

Lukács criticized empiricists and revisionists for isolating social facts from the whole since they can be understood and changed only by a total social transformation. Against Kantian and positivist Marxists he argued that the dualism of 'is' and 'ought' expresses a social separation of contemplation from practice that is overcome in the historical process, and so can be transcended in a dialectical understanding of history. By denying the scientific claims that were important to Marx and Engels, Lukács made the validity of Marxism depend on his own historicist conception of truth. This minimized the difference between social science and ideology; both are expressions of the 'reified consciousness' of the bourgeoisie and reflect the reified social relations of the market to which economics gives an illusory objectivity. There are no 'laws of dialectic' which science proves, as Engels maintained, nor laws of history external to the consciousness of the proletariat. Historical materialism is a critical-revolutionary method, exemplified by Marx's critique of bourgeois political economy or Lukács' own critique of bourgeois philosophy.

But Lukács also warned that the workers, as the 'identical subject–object of history', could only escape reification and false consciousness if enlightened by Marxist leadership. He eventually interpreted this theory of class consciousness in Leninist terms, and reconciled himself to Stalinism as a lesser evil than capitalism. Thus his ideas had both a critical and an orthodox face, the latter increasingly predominant.

It was their critical aspect that inspired the 'critical theory' of the Frankfurt School. The Frankfurt Institute of Social Research was established in 1923. Its central figures, active in Germany or the USA for the next forty years, were Max HORKHEIMER, Theodor Wiesengrund ADORNO and Herbert MARCUSE. Primarily philosophers, scholars at the Institute none the less developed new Marxist approaches to economics, politics and literature. Erich Fromm, a founder of the culturalist school of psychoanalysis, was also a member (see FRANKFURT SCHOOL).

Frankfurt Marxists were radical in thinking modern civilization diseased beyond hope of reform. They believed in the possibility of a utopian future, but not in a proletarian revolution, and had no political programme. Since they shared Lukács' belief in the philosophical self-sufficiency of dialectics, their utopianism had to supply the dialectical premises, both epistemological and ethical, for their otherwise antifoundational critical stance. This was directed at both capitalism and Soviet state socialism, as well as at fascism, liberalism and all varieties of 'bourgeois'

philosophy, especially positivism and existentialism (see CRITICAL THEORY).

Treating Marxism as method rather than theory, they drew on psychoanalysis to explain the sources and mass appeal of authoritarianism and extended Max Weber's critique of bureaucracy. They emphasized the increasing integration of state and economy ('state capitalism') and the replacement of traditional ideology with standardized escapist products of the modern 'culture industry'. They carried to implausible extremes the idea that Enlightenment rationalism had culminated in the fetishization of science and technology, which eroded human values and led to a conservative, totalitarian manipulation of a dehumanized society in the name of 'instrumental reason'. This was contrasted, in Hegelian fashion, with dialectical reason, but Adorno's insistence on critical independence from all absolutes plunged his version of 'negative dialectic' into obscurity and irrationalism. Although Frankfurt Marxists were mostly pessimistic, Marcuse and Fromm criticized Freud's pessimism from the standpoint of Marx's theory of alienation and took a more optimistic view of the possibilities for human enjoyment, creativity and community, appealing to essentialist beliefs about human nature (see ALIENATION §§3–5).

These German developments were paralleled by the reflections of the Italian Communist Antonio GRAMSCI during his ten years in a fascist jail. Gramsci had imbibed a neo-idealist critique of positivism from CROCE (§4) and emphasized dialectical interaction between base and superstructure to a point where the concepts lost any precise meaning. Rejecting orthodox scientific socialism more radically than Labriola, and relying on Marx's *Theses on Feuerbach* (1845), he treated Marxism as a historicist philosophy of human praxis, in which thought is a socially conditioned activity and truth is relative to its historical function. Belief in historical laws, he argued, was merely a necessary illusion of the proletariat in its early struggles, an idea close to Sorel's view of Marxism as myth.

Gramsci's contribution to the study of ideology was his theory of hegemony. In addition to exercising domination through the coercive apparatus of the state, ruling classes seek hegemony (leadership) through control of the cultural institutions of 'civil society' – churches, schools, mass media and so on – and are stable only if they rule by consent. Since modern civil society is highly developed, the working class can introduce socialism only by achieving hegemony *before* seizing the state. Each class needs 'organic intellectuals' to articulate its values, but the weakness of the workers in this respect had left them 'passively consenting' to bourgeois values, although their actual behaviour showed this to be a type of false consciousness. Gramsci was a major source for the 'dominant ideology thesis' and has been criticized for exaggerating the role of ideas.

The strength of socialists and communists in France after 1945 encouraged fellow-travelling by *marxisant* philosophers. This coincided with a vogue for Hegel, the recent availability of Marx's *Paris Manuscripts*, and a new interest in existentialism and phenomenology. The hybrid Marxism of Jean-Paul SARTRE (§5), Maurice MERLEAU-PONTY and others was the result. For Sartre, Marxism meant historical materialism and class struggle, stripped of naturalistic justifications, and the philosophical task was to ground these existentially in individual praxis. He explained alienation by scarcity; subjective freedom is lost through the historical struggle to produce, resulting in the reified social objectivity of the 'practico-inert' – a view more Hegelian than Marxian. This condemns individuals to 'serial' consciousness from which they can be liberated only by the collective consciousness of the 'fused group'. Hence a Sorelian justification of violence for the sake of moral authenticity and, even more questionably, support for Stalinism as a radical denial of bourgeois objectivity (see VIOLENCE).

Like Sartre, Merleau-Ponty explicated Marx through Hegel's dialectic of master and slave. At first, like Lukács, he defended Soviet totalitarianism as a lesser evil, which might in time produce a society without wage slaves. But after Stalin's death he turned to social democracy and attacked Sartre's combination of existentialism and Bolshevism. French Marxists of this period affiliated to the Frankfurt School or Lukács rather than existentialism were Henri Lefebvre and Lucien Goldmann.

Leon Trotsky, exiled from Russia in 1919, became an involuntary contributor to Western Marxism. His political analyses were influential, although a book on Marxist ethics made little impact. Together with Western Marxism, Trotskyism contributed to the New Left movement, which arose in English-speaking democracies in reaction to the Cold War. Marcuse's *One-Dimensional Man* (1964) popularized a sub-Marxist analysis of late capitalism as a technocratic, consumerist totalitarianism. He endorsed militant students, racial minorities and Third World insurgents as the new agents of liberation. A side effect of the New Left was to promote research on subjects relevant to Marxism, and as Western Marxism penetrated east European universities it stimulated new critical studies there also.

3   The disintegration of Western Marxism

The French Communist philosopher Louis ALTHUSSER launched his structuralist alternative to dialectical Marxism in 1965 with the publication of his book, *Pour Marx*. It promised a scientific rehabilitation and modernization of Marx, drawing on a new theory of discontinuities in the history of science. Althusser claimed to detect an 'epistemological break' between the humanist and historicist ideology of Marx's youth, based on the 'problematic of the subject', and the science of his maturity, which described a 'history without subjects'. Psychoanalysis suggested a 'symptomatic reading' of *Das Kapital*, to extract the outlines of the new science, while structural linguistics provided a model for the resulting reinterpretation of historical materialism. This now became an ahistorical theory of 'structures in dominance', exercising a 'structural causality' whose effects are borne by human agents. In reality this was a kind of sociological functionalism. Gramsci's theory of hegemony was stretched to make ideology the universal social cement that reproduces social structures, even under communism, by giving individuals an illusion of free agency. The truth of these theories was treated in a question-begging manner, as an effect of theoretical structures that are scientific and not ideological. Althusser's approach, implausible as a reading of Marx, reflected a French philosophical interest in deconstruction of the subject which survived the eclipse of his school and the decline of French Marxism (see STRUCTURALISM).

Italian Marxism showed a parallel shift away from Hegelian Marxism, but in a different direction. Galvano della Volpe and Lucio Colletti reacted against the historicist aspects of Gramsci's Marxism in favour of more empiricist readings of Marx. This has led Colletti to reject dialectics and the theory of alienation and, finally, socialism – one example among many of 'post-Marxism'.

Elsewhere, Althusserian Marxism was bypassed by more eclectic theorists who maintained that a critique of modern society drawing on Marx's values could no longer be merely 'Marxist'. In Germany Jürgen HABERMAS transformed critical theory by supplementing Marx with theoretical perspectives drawn from sociology, linguistic philosophy and hermeneutics. He criticized Marx for viewing history and human emancipation reductively, in terms of labour, and claimed that interaction, involving communication and social norms, is an independent dimension of social life. A human interest in emancipation is the constitutive ground of the social sciences, whose method is critical because they are implicitly oriented to an 'ideal speech situation'. Their truth, like other human values, is a function of dialogue freed from ideological distortion by the equal participation of all. Habermas' critics, however, deny that he can demonstrate that free dialogue on equal terms presupposes consensus on values.

Analytic Marxism developed in English-speaking countries in the late 1970s and 1980s, partly as a reaction of academic socialists to Althusserian excesses. It is characterized more by respect for traditional canons of argumentation than by theoretical or political consensus. G.A. Cohen's cogent demonstration that Marx intended historical materialism to be a functional theory challenges both the causal (Engels) and dialectical (Lukács) interpretation. He defended Marx's functional explanations in a debate with Jon Elster, for whom functional statements are no more explanatory than dialectics. Elster's own contributions include a recasting of Marx's class theory in rational choice terms, and a psychological approach to the explanation of ideology. Other writers have sought to present Marx's epistemology as a form of scientific realism.

Analytic Marxists were responding in part to the resurgence of economic and political liberalism in the 1980s. This shows in their concern to make Marx's theory of exploitation independent of his discredited economics and, more generally, in a wish to reinstate individuals in Marx's thought – both methodologically, as providing microfoundations for historical explanations, and normatively, as intended beneficiaries of a communist utopia. Hence another debate, this time over whether Marx had, or ought to have had, a theory of justice, and whether it could be consistent with his theory of ideology. Radical critics see analytic Marxists as engaged in a bourgeois academic pastime. But they can also be seen as conservationists, preserving the valid residue of Marxism for a post-Marxian world.

See also: MARXIST PHILOSOPHY,CHINESE; MARXIST PHILOSOPHY, RUSSIAN AND SOVIET; MARXIST THOUGHT IN LATIN AMERICA

References and further reading

* Althusser, L. (1965) *Pour Marx*, Paris: Maspero; *For Marx*, trans. B. Brewster, London: Allen Lane, 1969. (Perverse, dogmatic, challenging and influential critique of Marxist humanism.)

Anderson, P. (1976) *Considerations on Western Marxism*, London: New Left Books. (Interesting critique by an independent-minded Marxist.)

Bottomore, T. and Goode, P. (1978) *Austro-Marxism*, Oxford: Clarendon Press. (Representative and still interesting selection, including Max Adler on causality and teleology.)

* Cohen, G.A. (1978) *Karl Marx's Theory of History: A Defence*, Oxford: Oxford University Press. (Convincing critical reconstruction of Marx's philosophy of history. A demanding text.)

Colletti, L. (1969) *Marxism and Hegel*, trans. L. Garner, London: Verso, 1979. (Wide-ranging and profound critique of the Hegelian heritage within Marxism.)

* Engels, F. (1878) *Anti-Dühring*, trans. E. Burns, *Herr Eugen Dühring's Revolution in Science*, Peking: Foreign Languages Press, 1976. (A polemic which provided the most systematic exposition of 'scientific socialism' as understood by Second International Marxists.)

—— (1888) *Ludwig Feuerbach and the End of Classical German Philosophy*, in K. Marx and F. Engels *Collected Works*, London: Lawrence & Wishart, 1975, ch. xxvi, 353–98. (Source of the orthodox view of how dialectical materialism superseded Hegelian idealism, and of Engels' theory of false consciousness.)

Elster, J. (1985) *Making Sense of Marx*, Cambridge: Cambridge University Press. (Brilliant and dramatic excision of dead wood by a leading analytic Marxist.)

Geras, N. (1985) 'The Controversy about Marx and Justice', *New Left Review* 150: 47–85; and A. Callinicos *Marxist Theory*, Oxford: Oxford University Press, 1989, ch. 7. (Comprehensive critical review of major controversy on Marx's ethics.)

Kolakowski, L. (1978) *Main Currents of Marxism*, vol. 2, *The Golden Age* and vol. 3, *The Breakdown*, trans. P.S. Falla, Oxford: Clarendon Press. (Magisterial and comprehensive critical account up to 1968; thinner on recent French and Italian Marxism.)

* Lukács, G. (1921) *History and Class Consciousness: Studies in Marxist Dialectics*, trans. R. Livingstone, London: Merlin, 1971. (Epoch-making essays, seminal for the Western Marxist revival of dialectic philosophy and for critical theory.)

* Marcuse, H. (1964) *One-Dimensional Man: Studies in the Ideology of Advanced Industrial Society*, Boston, MA: Beacon Press and London: Routledge. (Popularized Frankfurt Marxism, 1960s style.)

Marx, K. and Engels, F. (1934) *Selected Correspondence 1846–1895*, London: Lawrence & Wishart. (Of particular interest are the letters from Engels to Schmidt (27 October 1890) and Mehring (14 July 1893), which offer influential glosses on the interpetation of Marx's theory of history.)

Merquior, J.G. (1986) *Western Marxism*, London: Paladin. (Readable, sophisticated and engagingly judgmental account from Lukács and Gramsci to 'post-Marxism'; full bibliography.)

Volpe, G. della (1960) *Critique of Taste*, trans. M. Caesar, London and New York: Verso, 1991. (The author at his best, an original approach to Marxist aesthetics.)

JOHN TORRANCE

MARXIST PHILOSOPHY OF SCIENCE

Marx's approach to science is an intriguing combination of respect for the natural sciences and empirical inquiry, determination to go beyond the description of regularities among observable phenomena, and insistence on the inevitable impact of social circumstances on scientific inquiry. Marx thought that the human sciences and the natural sciences are governed by essentially the same methods, that natural-scientific theories give us enhanced insight into mind-independent reality, and that our most fundamental views are subject to revision through scientific inquiry. Yet Marx rejected the ideal of scientific method according to which rational scientific belief is tied to observational data through a canon of rules as general, timeless and complete as the rules of logical deduction. While traditional empiricists emphasize the economical description of empirical regularities which could, in principle, be used to predict the occurrence of observable phenomena, Marx emphasizes the description of underlying causal structures, employing concepts that are typically irreducible to the vocabulary of mere observation, and causal hypotheses that sometimes do not even sketch means of prediction. Similarly, though Marx shared the optimistic view that science gives rise to long-term improvement in our insight into underlying causes, he disagreed with many epistemic optimists in his insistence that scientific inquiry is inevitably and deeply affected by social interests and relations of social power.

Since Marx's general comments on scientific method are few and scattered, a 'Marxist philosophy of science' consists of the further development of this intriguing mixture.

1 **Explanation and theory in Marx**
2 **Holism**
3 **Materialism and dialectics**
4 **Objectivity and society**

1 Explanation and theory in Marx

MARX's social theorizing has been attacked as a muddled perversion of science, lacking adequate predictive power and insufficiently connected with empirical data. Consider Marx's materialist conception of history: any stable society's political and cultural institutions have their most important features because their having them serves to maintain the dominant relations of production (the relations of control that dominate material production); an internally-caused change in a society's dominant relations of production is due to processes within the mode of production (the relations of production, work relations and technology) which create desires and powers destroying the old system of relations of production. Marx was well aware that similar networks of relations of production have been stabilized by importantly different political and cultural institutions. He acknowledged that one process (for example, the formation of a proletariat under capitalism) may ultimately doom a social system while a similar process (for example, the formation of the Roman proletariat) has no transformative effect. In a poignant letter to Russian activists who sought his guidance, Marx denied that his general theory provides any 'master key' permitting one to distinguish transformative from non-transformative processes without knowing their outcomes. So all that is rational in his general theory of social change might seem to be trivial: a tautology, that basic change occurs when changes in the mode of production are powerful enough to produce them, together with a banality, that there are important changes within the mode of production in the period leading up to a fundamental change in society as a whole.

A Marxist philosophy of science counters with an alternative view of science. A theory provides a description (sometimes a vague one) of a repertoire of underlying mechanisms, and says that the instantiation of these mechanisms has a certain importance as the cause of certain phenomena. A theory is confirmed by showing that such reliance on its repertoire does a better job than reliance on rival theories of explaining phenomena that stand in need of explanation. Such an argument will partly consist of the explanation of particular phenomena, especially those that have posed long-standing problems for prior explanatory schemes. It will also depend on more general inferences, resting on shared background principles, as to the possible causes of the general kind of phenomenon in question – for example, Marx's arguments that stabilizing tendencies of cultural and political institutions will prevent basic change arising from parts of a social system that are outside the mode of production.

A theory that triumphs in this way need not be useful as a basis for prediction. Marx, of course, *was* committed to certain long-term predictions, but (in this controversial view of Marx which implies a distinctive philosophy of science) these predictions are based on his specific account of capitalism. For Marx, the essence of confirmation is the critical comparison of theories (as Althusser has emphasized), in which the empirical data to be explained are one crucial lever of comparison (which Althusser has been charged with neglecting).

The development of auxiliary hypotheses connecting the general mechanisms in the basic repertoire with relevant concrete phenomena may be an extremely demanding task. In remarks on his economics of capitalism which sometimes liken it to Daltonian chemistry, Marx emphasizes the distance between the processes of class struggle and technological change which he describes using the vocabulary of the labour theory of value, and the economic facts which the underlying processes help to explain, facts which are to be described in the vocabulary of commerce. Although he takes the former processes to be real and fundamental, he thinks they never produce their effects without the mediation of other, market-based processes, the topics of the second and third volumes of *Capital*. Nowak (1980) takes this process of abstraction from, followed by reconstruction of, concrete phenomena to be the essence of Marx's scientific method.

2 Holism

Marx has also frequently been charged with assuming an implausible dominance of social wholes over individual parts in which large-scale social processes have obscure powers to manipulate individual participants (see HOLISM AND INDIVIDUALISM IN HISTORY AND SOCIAL SCIENCE). Thus, the goals of Cromwell and his followers were mainly religious and political concerns, not concerns to end the feudal restriction of emergent capitalist forces of production. Yet Marx takes the English Revolution to inaugurate the transformation of England into a capitalist society, a transformation he explains as serving to overcome feudal barriers to expansive capitalist production.

Part of Marx's implicit answer to the charge of arcane manipulation is a distinction between explanatory adequacy and causal sufficiency. Marx's historical writings consist largely of the richly detailed description of networks of individualist causes, actions governed by the reasons and resources of individual participants. Yet he thinks such individua-

listic description lacks the depth needed to explain major social transformations: the transformation would have occurred anyway. Thus, if the political, religious and military events that led to the Commonwealth, the Stuart Restoration and the Glorious Revolution had not transpired, a modernizing, bureaucratic state, advancing the interests of enterprising gentry and manufacturers, would have arisen anyway, on account of prior trends within the mode of production.

Still, the social outcome will result from some network or other of individualist causes. How can large-scale functional characteristics such as the expansive needs of capitalist production regulate these individualist causes when the satisfaction of these functions is not a typical dominant reason for which participants act? Here, Marx is psychologically ingenious in a way that breaks down rigid separations of the structural from the individual. He thinks that the history of ideas (for example, the history of religious differences in seventeenth-century England) establishes the enormous importance of mechanisms moulding belief or desire that do not consist of the subject's reasons for belief or desire. For example, he emphasizes the tendency of beliefs and goals to adjust to material interests, even among those who would accurately deny that these interests are their reasons for believing and desiring as they do. In his favoured explanatory scheme, rational choices within the mode of production have unintended consequences, transforming the pattern of resources and material interests (most importantly, by creating an interest in the destruction of inhibiting social forms on the part of a newly powerful economic class); then, consequent adjustments of goals and beliefs give rise to new psychologies that are the vehicle of social change. Thus Marx's project of explaining large-scale phenomena is also the basis for a novel view of the mechanisms of change in individual participants.

3 Materialism and dialectics

Marx takes both the social and the natural sciences to vindicate a materialist, dialectical view of reality. In its broadest claim, Marx's materialism has it that everything that exists is made of matter and is governed by the causal powers that physics seeks to discover. However, his materialism is not reductive. Within the constraints that the laws of physics impose, other laws regulate phenomena, in ways that cannot be described in the vocabulary of physics (see DIALECTICAL MATERIALISM; REDUCTION, PROBLEMS OF; UNITY OF SCIENCE).

Marx's view of cognition is also materialist in that it gives priority to material interests and mind-independent causes. Cognition grows out of the effort to change reality in order to satisfy one's needs. Initially, our concepts mark as relevant the distinctions that are practically important to us. The frustration of our efforts and expectations, together with the social exchange of information which is our main resource for effective change, lead to the continual revision of beliefs and even of the concepts in which they are framed. Like those modern 'scientific realists' who emphasize the success of theory-dependent interventions, Marx took the question of whether the whole process of inquiry improves the truth of our beliefs to be settled by its contribution to our capacity to get our way with nature (see REALISM AND ANTIREALISM).

The dialectical side of Marx's outlook, which reconstructs Hegel's logic on a materialist basis, was presented much more systematically by his co-worker Engels. In this dynamic view, every part of total reality is at once an active source and a passive object of change and no part is completely distinguishable from the rest. It is of the nature of everything to change from internal causes, because what stabilizes anything is a temporary balance of polar opposites whose conflict dictates transformation and, eventually, self-destruction. (Two alleged examples are the antagonistic relation between the proletariat and the bourgeoisie that characterizes capitalism and the balance of attraction and repulsion in a physical object.) Engels also emphasizes the tendency, in appropriate circumstances, for quantitative changes to become qualitative (for example, when water becomes ice, or a rural English bourgeoisie emerged from the growing prosperity of the better-off Tudor farmers) and the prevalence of spiralling processes of change in which an initial transformation is followed by another that restores aspects of the first stage (the 'negation of the negation'.)

There is much banality and word-juggling in Engels' illustrations of these principles. But there is also much shrewdness and wide-ranging scientific erudition in his criticism of opposed 'mechanistic' approaches, which analyse systems as arrangements of passive, simple, unchanging elements.

4 Objectivity and society

If cultural institutions tend to serve the interests of economically dominant classes, then explanatory frameworks will often be favoured on account of processes with no tendency to produce truth. If cognition grows out of the effort to satisfy human needs in a largely purposeless world, then our ways of characterizing causes will probably always misrepresent nature's actual causal repertoire. Marx and Engels certainly take scientific inquiry to be subject to these limits. Thus, Marx associates the rise of a politically assertive working class in mid-nineteenth-century Britain with the retreat from hypotheses of conflicting class interests among established economic theorists, while Engels takes reluctance to countenance the evolution of species and celestial bodies to reflect commitment to the fixity of the social order. And both emphasize that any science is bound to misdescribe its subject matter in important ways.

However, mainstream Marxist thinking asserts that scientific inquiry has yielded rational truth claims of broader and broader scope. Outside of a few platitudes, the most that we can rationally claim is that a hypothesis is true within a certain limited sphere, or true enough for certain purposes, or capable of correctly resolving the current controversies with the most important bearing on scientific progress. But (as Lenin put it, in criticizing what would now be called 'social constructivist' philosophies of science) it is often rational to claim access to objective truths of this relative kind.

Scientific inquiry is, inevitably, social, and social processes are inevitably affected by social interests in ways of which the participants are not fully aware. Still, in Marx's view, the impact of social interests does not always distort truth or rationality. For example, he takes the process of increasingly collective resistance which gave rise to class-conscious workers' movements to be interest-driven *and* to have enhanced truth and rationality in theorizing allied with those movements. Nor is the pressure of social interests intellectually decisive, for him, all the time – as witness his respect for the achievements of the quite bourgeois economists of late eighteenth- and early nineteenth-century Britain.

Even if Marx's frequent attributions of religious, political and moral trends to truth-distorting social forces are not preliminaries to an anti-objectivist philosophy of science, they might be extended into the social history of philosophies of science and allied epistemologies themselves. For example, Lenin (1908) argues that the currency of Mach's radical empiricism is partly due to its appeal to those who seek to preserve room for escape into religious wishful thinking: if the most that theoretical science can do is to organize experience in satisfying ways, then religion does as well for the devout.

Lukacs' essay, 'Reification and the Consciousness of the Proletariat', is perhaps the most wide-ranging project of this kind. He traces the dilemmas of modern epistemology to the psychopathology of life in a market-dominated society. Routine dependence on labour-markets in which impersonal forces determine the monetary value of the use of one's labour-power leads people to separate their activities into an immediately experienced subjective sphere and an impersonal objective sphere and to question whether the subjective can reflect objective facts. Market-dominance also gives rise to a formal, calculative conception of rationality, on which people rely to re-establish objective validity. But this reliance only makes the problem more acute, since rationality based on formal principles gives no significance to the content of experience. LUKÁCS subsequently abandoned this approach, on the ground that it treated the real difference between the subjective and the objective as an artefact of ideology, but it has had an extensive influence on subsequent Continental criticisms of positivist philosophy of science, the main twentieth-century legacy of traditional empiricism.

Arguments that presuppose the truth of Marxist social theory have never been important in Anglo-American philosophy of science, and are now virtually extinct. But the larger attitudes toward science of Marx and his successors are very much alive in the search for a replacement for positivism that has dominated philosophy of science since the 1950s. For those who emphasize both the reality of theoretical posits and the need to connect them with observations, the inadequacy of canons of induction and the genuine limits of rational disagreement, the autonomy of large-scale structures and the importance of their micro-constitution, the objective validity of inquiry and its dominance by human interests, the Marxist tradition is as much a home as any and a richer source of inspiration than most.

See also: NEURATH, O.

References and further reading

Though none of these works employs extensive technical apparatus, those by Althusser and Lukács are notoriously obscure.

Althusser, L. and Etienne B. (1968) *Reading Capital*, trans. B. Brewster, London: New Left Books, 1970. (The first two parts, by Althusser, derive from Marx a conception of knowledge as internal to 'theoretical practice'.)

Cohen, G.A. (1978) *Karl Marx's Theory of History*, Princeton, NJ: Princeton University Press. (An argument for an interpretation of Marx's theory which would *not* require a distinctive philosophy of science sharply breaking with positivism.)

Engels, F. (1878) *Anti-Duehring*; trans. E. Burns, ed. C.P. Dutt, New York: International Publishers, 1939. (Influential discussions of dialectics and natural science, interspersed with polemics against the long-forgotten Dühring.)

—— (1934) *Dialectics of Nature*, trans. C. Dutt, Moscow: Progress Publishers. (Notebooks, 1873–86, in which Engels develops a dialectical interpretation of the achievements of natural science.)

* Lenin, V.I. (1908) *Materialism and Empirico-Criticism*, Moscow: Progress Publishers. (Criticisms of Russian followers of Mach, Duhem and other pioneers of modern philosophy of science, with plenty of tiresome invective but some shrewd and sensible thrusts.)

* Lukács, G. (1971) *History and Class Consciousness*, trans. R. Livingstone, Cambridge MA: MIT Press. (Includes 'Reification and the Consciousness of the Proletariat' 1922, and a 1967 preface in which Lukács criticizes his earlier views as insufficiently materialist.)

Marx, K. (1975) *Texts on Method*, trans. and ed. T. Carver, Oxford: Blackwell. (A useful pairing of Marx's two most extensive discussions of methodology, the Introduction (1857) to the *Grundrisse* and Notes (1879–80) on a textbook by Adolph Wagner. Marx's other, scattered comments on method and natural science are mostly in *Capital*, the *Grundrisse*, *The German Ideology*, the delphic 'Theses on Feuerbach' and his correspondence.)

Miller, R.W. (1984) *Analyzing Marx*, Princeton NJ: Princeton University Press. (Chapters 3–6 develop the interpretation of Marx's theories and methodology and their bearing on modern philosophy of science that was sketched in §§1–2 of this entry.)

* Nowak, L. (1980) *The Structure of Idealization*, Dordrecht: Reidel. (Derives from Marx's methods in *Capital* a conception of scientific reasoning as based on idealization.)

RICHARD W. MILLER

MARXIST PHILOSOPHY, RUSSIAN AND SOVIET

The history of Russian Marxism involves a dramatic interplay of philosophy and politics. Though Marx's ideas were taken up selectively by Russian populists in the 1870s, the first thoroughgoing Russian Marxist was G.V. Plekhanov, whose vision of philosophy became the orthodoxy among Russian communists. Inspired by Engels, Plekhanov argued that Marxist philosophy is a form of 'dialectical materialism' (Plekhanov's coinage). Following Hegel, Marxism focuses on phenomena in their interaction and development, which it explains by appeal to dialectical principles (for instance, the law of the transformation of quantity into quality). Unlike Hegel's idealism, however, Marxism explains all phenomena in material terms (for Marxists, the 'material' includes economic forces and relations). Dialectical materialism was argued to be the basis of Marx's vision of history according to which historical development is the outcome of changes in the force of production.

In 1903, Plekhanov's orthodoxy was challenged by a significant revisionist school: Russian empiriocriticism. Inspired by Mach's positivism, A.A. Bogdanov and others argued that reality is socially organized experience, a view they took to suit Marx's insistence that objects be understood in their relation to human activity. Empiriocriticism was associated with the Bolsheviks until 1909, when Lenin moved to condemn Bogdanov's position as a species of idealism repugnant to both Marxism and common sense. Lenin endorsed dialectical materialism, which thereafter was deemed the philosophical worldview of the Bolsheviks.

After the Revolution of 1917, Soviet philosophers were soon divided in a bitter controversy between 'mechanists' and 'dialecticians'. The former argued that philosophy must be subordinate to science. In contrast, the Hegelian 'dialecticians', led by A.M. Deborin, insisted that philosophy is needed to explain the very possibility of scientific knowledge. The debate was soon deadlocked, and in 1929 the dialecticians used their institutional might to condemn mechanism as a heresy. The following year, the dialecticians were themselves routed by a group of young activists sponsored by Communist Party. Denouncing Deborin and his followers as 'Menshevizing idealists', they proclaimed that Marxist philosophy had now entered its 'Leninist stage' and invoked Lenin's idea of the partiinost' ('partyness') of philosophy to license the criticism of theories on entirely political grounds. Philosophy became a weapon in the class war.

In 1938, Marxist-Leninist philosophy was simplistically codified in the fourth chapter of the Istoriia kommunisticheskoi partii sovetskogo soiuza (Bol'sheviki). Kraatkii kurs (History of the Communist Party of the Soviet Union (Bolsheviks). Short Course). The chapter, apparently written by Stalin himself, was declared the height of wisdom, and Soviet philosophers dared not transcend its limited horizons. The 'new philosophical leadership' devoted itself to glorifying the Party and its General Secretary. The ideological climate grew even worse in the post-war years when A.A. Zhdanov's campaign against 'cosmopolitanism' created a wave of Russian chauvinism in which scholars sympathetic to Western thought were persecuted. The Party also meddled in scientific, sponsoring T.D. Lysenko's bogus genetics, while encouraging criticism of quantum mechanics, relativity theory and cybernetics as inconsistent with dialectical materialism.

The Khrushchev 'thaw' brought a renaissance in Soviet Marxism, when a new generation of young philosophers began a critical re-reading of Marx's texts. Marx's so-called 'method of ascent from the abstract to the concrete' was developed, by E.V. Il'enkov and others, into an anti-empiricist epistemology. There were also important studies of consciousness and 'the ideal' by Il'enkov and M.K. Mamardashvili, the former propounding a vision of the social origins of the mind that recalls the cultural-historical psychology developed by L.S. Vygotskii in the 1930s.

However, the thaw was short-lived. The philosophical establishment, still populated by the Stalinist old guard, continued to exercise a stifling influence. Although the late 1960s and 1970s saw heartfelt debates in many areas, particularly about the biological basis of the mind and the nature of value (moral philosophy had been hitherto neglected), the energy of the early 1960s was lacking. Marxism-Leninism still dictated the terms of debate and knowledge of Western philosophers remained relatively limited.

In the mid-1980s, Gorbachev's reforms initiated significant changes. Marxism-Leninism was no longer a required subject in all institutions of higher education; indeed, the term was soon dropped altogether. Discussions of democracy and the rule of law were conducted in the journals, and writings by Western and Russian émigré philosophers were published. Influential philosophers such as I.T. Frolov, then editor of Pravda, called for a renewal of humanistic Marxism. The reforms, however, came too late. The numerous discussions of the fate of Marxism at this time reveal an intellectual culture in crisis. While many maintained that Marx's theories were not responsible for the failings of the USSR, others declared the bankruptcy of Marxist ideas and called for an end to the Russian Marxist tradition. Following the collapse of the Soviet Union in 1991, it seems their wish has been fulfilled.

1   The beginnings of Russian Marxism
2   Orthodoxy and revision before 1917
3   Controversies in the 1920s
4   The depths of the Stalin era
5   Renaissance after Stalin
6   *Perestroika* and dissolution

1   The beginnings of Russian Marxism

It is not surprising that Marxism captured the imagination of the radical Russian intelligentsia in the late nineteenth century. Questions of social justice, so pressing in Tsarist Russia, dominated philosophical debate. Marxism, a putatively scientific theory of history that promised humanity's self-realization through the liberation of the oppressed masses, appealed to Russian thinkers, preoccupied with human destiny and Russia's role within it, and anxious for a vision that would unite theory and practice. The story of the subsequent domination of Russian philosophy by Marxism is more remarkable, involving a dramatic interplay of philosophy and politics. On the one hand, the Bolshevik project was inspired and guided by a philosophical doctrine; on the other, it resulted in the almost total subordination of philosophical enquiry to political power.

Russian radicals in the 1870s were acutely aware that Marx's theories were written for the industrial nations of Western Europe, not a quasi-feudal autocracy like Russia with a largely peasant economy (*Capital* was published in a Russian translation in 1872). Thus Marxist ideas were at first adopted selectively. The Russian populists, whose leading thinkers were P.L. LAVROV (1823–1900) and N.K. MIKHAILOVSKII (1842–1904), invoked Marx's economic theory in their critique of the horrors of capitalism, but argued that Russia could avoid capitalism altogether by adopting directly a form of communism based on the peasant commune.

The populists differed on how this transformation was to be achieved. While some insisted the masses must engineer their own emancipation, others, like Pëtr Tkachëv (1844–86 NS), favoured a revolution led by a centralized party of conspirators. It was the adventurism of this latter group that pushed some in the populist movement towards a more comprehensive Marxism. Georgii Plekhanov (1856–1918) argued that the socioeconomic forces at work in Russia in fact conformed to Marx's theory of history: capitalism was indeed developing apace and could not be sidestepped. But the admission that capitalism was the unavoidable precondition of a socialist future raised a moral problem. How could revolutionaries endorse the coming of capitalism, when it would bring misery to the masses they sought to liberate? Plekhanov argued that it was futile to resist the inevitable on moral grounds. However, Marxists need not sit idly by; they must awaken the proletariat's self-consciousness. Plekhanov also maintained, percipiently, that the imposition of socialism would result in a 'patriarchal and authoritarian' communism, worse than enduring the evils of capitalism.

Plekhanov sought to justify his economic determinism by placing it in a broader materialist vision, and in *K voprosu o razvitii monisticheskogo vzgliada na istoriiu* (The Development of the Monist View of History) (1895) he articulates a conception of philosophy that came to dominate Russian Marxism. Inspired by ENGELS, Plekhanov argues that the history of philosophy is a battle between materialism and idealism. The former aspires to explain everything in material terms, the latter in terms of spirit or idea. (Like most Russian thinkers, Plekhanov is profoundly attracted to *monistic* positions; he simply dismisses dualism as unable to explain how its two explanatory principles – matter and spirit – are related (see DUALISM).) Endorsing materialism, Plekhanov praises the French thinkers of the eighteenth and nineteenth centuries, especially Helvétius, for holding that ideas are determined by the social environment. These thinkers, however, mistakenly portray human history as the outcome of ideas ('opinions govern the world') or a reflection of an unchanging human nature. Paradoxically, a more plausible materialism was made possible by Hegel's dialectical idealism. In contrast to static, metaphysical conceptions of reality, Hegel stressed that phenomena are interconnected and constantly changing. He saw that gradual, quantitative changes in phenomena eventually result in their abrupt qualitative transformations, that every phenomenon is eventually transformed into its opposite, and that contradiction is the motor of development. Hegel, however, also misunderstood history, representing it as a manifestation of the 'world spirit' (see HEGEL, G.W.F.). The genius of Marx and Engels was to invent a form of dialectical materialism (see DIALECTICAL MATERIALISM). Their view is materialist because it represents cultural, social, economic, legal, political and ideological relations (the superstructure) as ultimately determined by the level of development of material forces of production (the economic base). It is dialectical in its dynamic vision of history. Human beings, acting collectively and with the use of tools, are able to change their environment so radically that this in turn transforms their own nature. However, as the level of productive forces increases and human beings master the natural world, they become ever more enslaved to economic forces unleashed by their activity. Marx's theory of history reveals the true character of those forces and how they will be mastered with the emergence of communism. The proletarian revolution represents a transition from the realm of necessity to the realm of freedom. Human beings will no longer labour under alien powers, but will be able knowingly to conform their actions to the dictates of necessity.

2 Orthodoxy and revision before 1917

Though Plekhanov's dialectical materialism quickly became orthodoxy, it struck many as unsatisfactory, for his determinism seemed to preclude human agency and moral criticism. The school of legal Marxists, so called because its representatives published legally under their own names, responded to this failing. These thinkers, led by Pëtr Struve (1870–1944), endorsed Marx's economic theory as proof that Russian absolutism was doomed by the inevitable development of capitalism (which, in contrast to the populists, they saw as a progressive force). They argued, however, that Marxism could not inspire moral renewal unless supplemented with a broader philosophical and ethical perspective. To this end, the legal Marxists turned to Kant (anticipating Eduard BERNSTEIN). The resulting synthesis was fragile, and in 1900 most legal Marxists migrated from social democracy to form the basis of the liberal Constitutional Democratic Party. Struve, N.A. BERDIAEV (1874–1948), S.N. BULGAKOV (1871–1944) and S.L. FRANK (1877–1950) eventually embraced an idealism based on Russian religious thought, which they presented in the symposium *Vekhi* (Signposts) in 1909, provoking a scornful attack by Lenin (see SIGNPOSTS MOVEMENT).

Another significant revisionist view was the attempt, by A.A. BOGDANOV (1873–1928), A.V. Lunacharskii (1875–1933) and others, to reconcile Marxism with the empiriocriticism of Ernst MACH and Richard AVENARIUS. The Russian empiriocritics were drawn to Mach's positivist view of science, seeing it not as describing reality beyond appearance, but as providing progressively better ways of organizing experience. Scientific laws do not pick out real necessities in nature, but read order into the deliverances of the senses. The Russians supplemented Mach's neo-Darwinist epistemology with the view that reality is *socially* organized experience, taking this to fit Marx's view in the *Theses on Feuerbach* that objects should be conceived 'as sensuous human activity' (see RUSSIAN EMPIRIOCRITICISM).

Bogdanov's *Empiromonizm* (1905–6) maintains that the very dichotomy between materialism and idealism is confused. The mental–physical distinction does not pick out two kinds of entity or substance. It is rather a distinction drawn within experience. Some elements of experience are deemed 'mental' because they are given only to one subject; others are called 'physical' because given to many. Bogdanov argued that under communism, where disagreement and conflict are eradicated, people will share the same modes of organizing experience and the idea of individuals as separate mental worlds will break down. Other consequences of the theory were less extravagant. Bogdanov's interest in organization led him to develop tektology, a precursor of cybernetics and general systems theory.

In 1902, the Russian Social Democratic Party split into two factions. The Bolsheviks embraced the conception of the vanguard party set out in Lenin's *Chto delat'* (*What Is To Be Done?*) (1902), a centralized and disciplined organization of professional revolutionaries (reminiscent of Tkachëv's view). In contrast, the Mensheviks advocated a broad party embracing many kinds of proletarian support. This conflict reflected different conceptions of revolution. While the Bolsheviks saw revolution as something to be engineered, the Mensheviks awaited a spontaneous uprising precipitated by social forces beyond immediate control.

Although there were empiriocriticists in both factions, the philosophy was associated with Bolshevism, both because of Bogdanov's influence in the faction and because empiriocriticism's emphasis on activity suited the activism and voluntarism of Bolshevism. The association was an embarrassment to Lenin who distrusted empiriocriticism's eschewal of common-sense epistemology and its heady avant-gardism, manifested in Lunacharskii's attempt to supplement socialism with a secular religion celebrating humanity's powers of self-creation ('God-building'). In addition, the Mensheviks stressed that empiriocriticism was a Bolshevik philosophy in order to cast their opponents as revisionists and opportunists. In 1909, when Lenin no longer perceived an alliance with Bogdanov to be politically expedient, he broke a long-standing truce on philosophical matters and attacked empiriocriticism as a heresy. Thereafter, dialectical materialism was deemed the theoretical foundation of Bolshevism.

In *Materializm i empiriokrititsizm* (*Materialism and Empiriocriticism*) (1909), Lenin dismisses the idea that empiriocriticism transcends the dichotomy of materialism and idealism. On the contrary, it is a blatant form of idealism that represents matter as a construction of the mind. It therefore falls to the same arguments that defeated Berkeley and Hume. The new empiricism is motivated, Lenin argues, by the latest findings of physics, which suggest to the intellectually naïve that 'matter has disappeared' or that the laws of nature are human inventions. Such conclusions, Lenin maintains, are entirely wrongheaded. He defends a robust form of philosophical realism. The external world exists objectively prior to and independently of thinking subjects. We obtain knowledge through sense perception, on the basis of which we build theories of the world. Lenin wavers between direct and representative realism, suggesting sometimes that the mind is in immediate cognitive contact with reality and sometimes that perceptions and ideas are images or 'photographs' of objects. Either way, Lenin believes our conceptions may accurately represent reality. Objective truth is possible, though our theories are often only relatively, not absolutely, true. The criterion of truth is practice: a theory's truth explains why it is a reliable guide to practice.

Lenin denies that philosophy can dictate to science. Materialism establishes only that matter exists objectively, a view held by anyone who 'has not been an inmate of a lunatic asylum or a pupil of idealist philosophers'. Otherwise, it falls to science to establish what matter is like.

For the most part, Lenin's philosophy differs from Plekhanov's only on minor points (he rejects Plekhanov's view that sensations are 'signs' rather than depictions of objects) and in matters of emphasis (Lenin focuses on philosophy's relation to science rather than the philosophy of history). However, *Materialism and Empiriocriticism* reflects Lenin's Bolshevism in two respects. First, his obsession with objectivity fits his idea of the revolutionary vanguard armed with the truth that will lead the proletariat to victory. Second, his idea of the *partiinost'* ('partyness') of philosophy – the idea that philosophical positions are intrinsically related to class interests – politicizes all philosophical enquiry and suggests that philosophy is a weapon in the class war (see PARTIINOST').

The influence of *Materialism and Empiriocriticism* was enormous. Under Stalin, it was portrayed as a model of philosophical excellence and the foundation of a new, Leninist stage in Marxist thought (Lenin's debt to Plekhanov was forgotten). The concept of *partiinost'* was invoked to legitimize the criticism of philosophical theories on purely political grounds, and the coarse style of Lenin's writing, with its use of invective and abuse, became the official medium of philosophical discourse.

Materialism and Empiriocriticism was not Lenin's last word on philosophy. Between 1914 and 1916, he made a study of Hegel's philosophy. Lenin's notes, published 1929–30, show him arriving at a greater appreciation of the significance of dialectics. He declares that empiriocriticism was criticized more from the perspective of vulgar Feuerbachian materialism than Marxism, and suggests that the theorists of the 1910s (himself included) failed to understand Marx properly because of their ignorance of Hegel's *Science of Logic*. These and other aphorisms were later much quoted by Soviet philosophers endeavouring to elevate discussion beyond the crude materialism inspired by Lenin's early book.

3   Controversies in the 1920s

Although many areas of Soviet culture flourished after the Revolution, philosophy was beleaguered from the outset. First, the shortage of 'red specialists' meant that the 'philosophical leadership' charged with developing the Marxist ideas that had enabled and empowered the Revolution had to include non-Bolsheviks whom the Party viewed with suspicion. Moreover, when the first Soviet philosophy journal, *Pod znamenem marksizma* (Under the Banner of Marxism), was launched in 1922, it was attacked on the grounds that the very idea of Marxist philosophy was confused. S.K. Minin argued that since philosophy had only ever served to foster ideological myths in the service of the oppressing classes, it should simply be displaced by science. 'Science to the bridge, philosophy overboard!' was Minin's slogan.

This 'liquidationism' was quickly (and unfairly) dismissed as a species of philistine anti-intellectualism. However, the issue of philosophy's relation to science was soon the focus of a bitter controversy that divided the Soviet philosophical world: the debate between the 'mechanists' and the 'dialecticians' (or 'Deborinites').

The mechanists included scientists such as A.K. Timiriazev (1880–1955) and philosophers such as I.I. Skvortsov-Stepanov (1870–1928) and L.I. Aksel'rod (1868–1946). Bogdanov was associated with the movement, as was the Bolshevik luminary Nikolai Bukharin (1888–1938), whose *Teoriia istoricheskogo materializma* (*Historical Materialism*) had been published in 1921. Many mechanists were reductionists, who thought that science would eventually provide an exhaustive account of reality. But others, such as Aksel'rod, were drawn to mechanism by its defence of the autonomy of science. The mechanists argued that philosophy's role was to elucidate the concepts and laws employed by science, but not to interfere with scientific inquiry on a priori grounds.

The dialecticians included I.E. Sten (1899–1937), N.A. Karev (dates unknown), I.K. Luppol (1897–1943), V.F. Asmus (1894–1975) and the single most influential philosopher of the period, A.M. Deborin (1881–1963). Students of the history of philosophy, they saw their principal task as a materialist reworking of Hegelian dialectics. On this view, since the dialectical enterprise seeks to explain the very possibility of cognition, it cannot proceed by empirical generalization from scientific practice. Without philosophy, science cannot understand itself.

Between 1924 and 1929, the two schools fought in the literature and at gatherings in philosophical institutions. Despite the significance of the issues, neither side could move the other by argument and the debate degenerated into political wrangling. Eventually, the Deborinites used their greater institutional power to have their opponents condemned as revisionists.

The dialecticians' triumph was short-lived. In March 1930, a group of young activists at the Institute of Red Professors, led by M.B. Mitin

(1901–87), accused their Deborinite teachers of 'formalism' and idealism. Since the mechanists had been (implausibly) portrayed as ideologists of Bukharin's 'right deviationism', Mitin (yet more implausibly) argued that the dialecticians were allied with the Trotskyite 'left deviation'. The young radicals called for a 'battle on two fronts in philosophy', urging that Soviet philosophy had to be 'Bolshevized'. Despite spirited resistance, Deborin and his followers were crushed. In June 1930, *Pravda* published an article by Mitin, Ral'tsevich and Iudin complete with editorial endorsement. Dubbed 'Menshevizing idealists' (Stalin's term), the Deborinites were forced from power.

Fortunately these controversies are not all that occurred in Russian Marxist philosophy in the 1920s and early 1930s. Two thinkers on the fringes of the subject made significant and enduring contributions. The first was the psychologist L.S. VYGOTSKII (1896–1934), who sought a way between mechanistic, reductionist models of the mind and introspectionist accounts that put the mental beyond systematic analysis. Inspired by Marx, Vygotskii argued that the dominant 'reflexological', stimulus–response models were too unidirectional to account for the human mind. The 'higher mental functions' are *mediated* forms of psychological activity; human beings actively change their environment to create new stimuli that serve to control their behaviour. We fashion artefacts – tools and signs – for manipulating both the world and the behaviour the world calls from us. Vygotskii originally introduced the concept of mediation to supplement the stimulus–response model. However, he became fascinated with the concept of meaning, arguing that semiotic mediation creates not a new class of stimuli, but a completely transformed psychological relation to reality. Vygotskii argued that since the 'mediational means' are cultural creations, preserved in the interpretative practices of the community, mind itself is a cultural artefact. The child's mind develops not through merely natural evolution, but by the 'internalization' of social practices. Vygotskii's writings were blacklisted shortly after his death in 1934, but his legacy was preserved by his followers – including A.R. Luria (1902–77) and A.N. Leont'ev (1904–79) – in the 'cultural-historical' school of psychology.

Similar themes emerge in writings attributed to V.N. Voloshinov (*c.*1895–1936) (which may have been written by M.M. Bakhtin (1895–1975)). In *Marksizm i filosofiia iazyka* (*Marxism and the Philosophy of Language*) (1929), Voloshinov argues that the problematic relation between base and superstructure can be illuminated by a Marxist theory of language. This is because superstructural phenomena are ideological in

kind and ideology is a system of signs. Voloshinov rejects both psychologistic and abstract structuralist views of language, stressing that the linguistic sign exists in verbal utterance: meaning is inherently tied to use. This introduces a social dimension, since language is inherently dialogical. All utterance is explicitly or implicitly directed to another (or to oneself-as-another). This view has psychological consequences, for consciousness exists only in its material embodiment of signs, and signs exist only in dialogue in a socio-cultural setting. The mind is semiotically constructed in social space, and the structure of thought (inner speech) issues from the internalization of the forms of outer utterance. Voloshinov writes: 'Individual consciousness is not the architect of the ideological superstructure, but only a tenant lodging in the social edifice of ideological signs'.

Though suppressed in the USSR, Voloshinov's writings influenced Roman Jakobson and the Prague Linguistic Circle, and, like Vygotskii, his ideas have attracted a significant following in the West (see BAKHTIN, M.M. §§1–2).

4 The depths of the Stalin era

In the 1930s, all spheres of Soviet culture were brought to heel and made to glorify the Soviet Communist Party and the deeds of its General Secretary. The philosophers of the 'new philosophical leadership' eulogized Lenin's genius (how fortunate that Stalin was 'Lenin today'!) and spun a bizarre mythology about class enemies in philosophy, especially the Menshevizing idealists, now 'discovered' to be 'fascists' and 'terrorists'.

In 1938, the tenets of Marxism-Leninism were codified in the *Istoriia kommunisticheskoi partii sovetskogo soiuza (Bol'sheviki). Kratkii kurs* (*History of the Communist Party of the Soviet Union (Bolsheviks). Short Course*). The infamous fourth chapter, supposedly written by Stalin himself, presents the principles of dialectical materialism in schematic, canonical form, and offers strikingly simplistic examples of its application in historical materialism: that the base determines the superstructure follows from the primacy of the material over the ideal; class struggle reflects the dialectical law of 'the unity and struggle of opposites'; revolutions are instances of the transformation of the quantitative into the qualitative, and so on. (The law of the 'negation of the negation' was omitted, no doubt because it implies the mutability of all things, including Soviet communism.) Both the sense of history, and the thirst for argument, evident respectively in Plekhanov's and Lenin's writings, are conspicuously absent. In this primitive form, Marxist philosophy was propagated throughout the Soviet Union. Every literate person was compelled to assimilate the 'fourth chapter', and professional philosophers expounded it *ad infinitum*, unable to transcend its horizons for fear of challenging Stalin's authority.

Just as the Party put science in the service of industry, so the humanities were devoted to 'the engineering of the human soul', as Stalin described the role of Soviet literature. Philosophy was placed under the aegis of the Central Committee's Department of Propaganda and Agitation, directed between 1939 and 1947 by the philosopher G.F. Aleksandrov (1908–61). In this climate, many genuine philosophers turned to the history of philosophy, where they could still study the European tradition. However, before long this area was also the focus of political controversy. In the war years, when ideological constraints were otherwise somewhat relaxed, Soviet works which gave a sympathetic rendition of German classical philosophy were denounced. For this reason, in 1944 the third volume of a collective *History of Philosophy*, which included Aleksandrov himself among its editors, was targeted by the Central Committee, even though its authors had previously received the Stalin Prize.

The post-war years saw a remarkable clampdown throughout Soviet culture. This campaign, led by A.A. Zhdanov, combined fierce allegiance to Marxist-Leninist principles with a virulent form of Russian nationalism. The chauvinistic climate is well illustrated by another controversy surrounding Aleksandrov. In 1947, his textbook *Istoriia zapadnoevropeiskoi filosofii* (*A History of Western European Philosophy*) (1946) (which is entirely orthodox in spirit) was vilified as 'abstract', 'bookish', 'formal' and 'lacking *partiinost*' largely for its failure to emphasize the supremacy of Russian over Western philosophy. The philosophers who opposed this trend were eventually accused of 'cosmopolitanism', 'sycophancy before bourgeois philosophy' and 'kowtowing to the West'.

The Party also used philosophy to interfere in the natural sciences. In the late 1940s, theories in chemistry, cosmology and physics, especially relativity theory and quantum mechanics, were all criticized on ideological grounds when apparently in tension with dialectical materialism. And in the early 1950s, cybernetics was dismissed as a pseudo-science, since its global explanatory pretensions were at odds with Marxism. Chauvinism about Russian scientific achievements reached ridiculous heights, and the myth of a 'proletarian science' took hold. The most conspicuous example was the Party's long-standing support for T.D. Lysenko's Michurinist genetics, which defended the inheritance of acquired charac-

teristics (suggesting that the qualities of New Soviet Man could be genetically inherited by subsequent generations). These tragicomic episodes did incalculable damage to Soviet science.

5 Renaissance after Stalin

That any kind of philosophical culture survived the Stalin period is a remarkable fact. A significant number of philosophers perished in the purges, but a handful of participants in the debates of the 1920s survived and continued to teach. Although unable to publish much in this period, philosophers like Asmus, O.V. Trakhtenberg (1889–1959), P.S. Popov (1892–1964) and M.A. Dynnik (1896–1971) gave significant courses at Moscow University. B.M. Kedrov (1903–85) was also influential, despite being then estranged from the University for political reasons. In addition, several prominent psychologists, such as Luria, Leont'ev and S.L. Rubinshtein (1889–1960), who were members of the philosophy faculty at Moscow University, made a vital contribution to keeping philosophy alive. These older thinkers found a new generation of philosophers among students resuming their education after the Great Patriotic War. This generation, which includes E.V. IL'ENKOV (1924–79) and A.A. Zinov'ev (1922–) (who later emigrated, writing the dissident novels, *The Yawning Heights* and *The Radiant Future*), is sometimes called the 'iflitsy', after the unusually vibrant Moscow Institute of History, Philosophy and Literature (IFLI), where many of them had studied before the war. Despite the stifling atmosphere in most academic institutions, and the shortage of materials, the new generation was determined to renew Soviet philosophy by going 'back to Marx'. In the 1950s, their work focused on two principal areas. First, they explored the dialectical method, sketched by Marx in his 'Introduction to a Critique of Political Economy' and deployed in *Capital*. This produced scholarly readings of Marx's texts in which the 'method of ascent from the abstract to the concrete' was developed into a full-blown account of concept acquisition and theory construction, to be contrasted with empiricist views of scientific knowledge. Most significant is Il'enkov's *Dialektika abstraktnogo i konkretnogo v 'Kapitale' Marksa* (The Dialectics of the Abstract and the Concrete in Marx's 'Capital') (1960), but the writings of Zinov'ev, B.A. Grushin (1929–) and G.P. Shchedrovitskii (1929–93) (who formed the Moscow methodological circle) were also influential.

These methodological writings explore the preconditions of scientific understanding, not in abstract Kantian terms, but historically. This project naturally raised the question of the nature and origin of mind itself. How can a material world come to contain beings able to engage in the project of understanding themselves and their world? The question was answered by developing a philosophical anthropology centred on the concept of *activity*. In the 1960s, the Georgian philosopher Merab MAMARDASHVILI (1930–90), who worked in Moscow, produced an influential study of the concept of consciousness in Marx's thought, developing the concept of 'transmuted forms'. And Il'enkov developed his controversial account of 'the ideal', according to which humanity's active engagement with nature results in the objectification of non-material properties and relations in the natural world. We enculturate our material environment, and become conscious beings in so far as we appropriate social activities constitutive of humanity's spiritual culture. In this way, Il'enkov develops the Vygotskian idea that culture is a precondition of the existence of individual consciousness.

The work of this new generation, mostly published in the Khrushchev 'thaw', stimulated lively debate in many philosophical institutions, especially Moscow's Institute of Philosophy. At this time, a translation of Marx's *Paris Manuscripts* (prepared by Il'enkov among others) became available, provoking further interest in a critical, anthropocentric Marxist philosophy. However, many of the Stalinist old guard maintained their positions in the academy, and the Party continued to exercise control over philosophical discussion. Huge editions of one-dimensional Marxist-Leninist textbooks, such as the *Fundamentals of Marxist-Leninist Philosophy*, were used to disseminate the worldview of the Communist Party in all institutions of higher education. Contact with Western philosophers and their works was limited. Moreover, by the mid-1960s, the thaw began to ice over and the mood of creativity and optimism faded.

Although the next two decades lacked the inspiration of the early 1960s, there were many prominent controversies, often conducted on the pages of *Voprosy filosofii* (Questions of Philosophy), which had been the principal Russian philosophy journal since 1947. Some, such as the discussions of reflection theory and the laws of dialectics, were merely variations on themes of Marxist orthodoxy. Others, like the ongoing debates about the nature of Marxist philosophy and the relation between dialectical and formal logic, were more serious. There was a revival of interest in ethics, which had previously been ruled out by the orthodox view that morality was destined to 'wither away' under communism. Influential figures were O.G. Drobnitskii (1933–73), tragically killed in an air disaster, and Iu.N. Davydov (1929–). Knowl-

edge of contemporary Western philosophy became more widespread, due to the efforts of such thinkers as A.S. Bogomolov (1927–93) and A.F. Zotov (1931–), though works developing Soviet Marxism in critical dialogue with Western philosophy were few; the most successful was *Sub' 'ekt, ob' 'ekt, poznanie (Subject, Object, Cognition)* (1980) by V.A. Lektorskii (1932–), which ably contrasts an activity-centred epistemology with a variety of Western views.

One significant debate conducted in both academic and popular journals concerned the extent to which human psychological capacities are genetically determined. Many Soviet philosophers and psychologists, such as Il'enkov, Leont'ev, V.V. Davydov (1930–) and F.T. Mikhailov (1930–) argued that Marxism is committed to a conception of individuals as socially constituted beings, whose principal mode of psychological inheritance is cultural rather than biological. In contrast, their nativist opponents, who included scientists as well as such philosophers as D.I. Dubrovskii (1929–), argued that this view contradicted the physical basis of the mental. Though the theoretical value of these polemical exchanges is limited, the political dimensions of the debate are interesting. The nativists resented philosophical interference in what they took to be an empirical matter. In addition, they took their opponents' contructivism to be motivated by dreams of the creation of a 'New Soviet Man', and they turned to genetics to define a sphere where the individual was immune to social influence. The constructivists in turn saw nativism as reactionary, the result of a dehumanizing scientism, inspired by fascination with the so-called 'scientific-technological revolution'. Human beings are not just self-organizing machines to be manipulated by the state, however much they were made so by Stalinism, but beings infinitely capable of self-transcendence and renewal if society can only create the appropriate conditions.

6 *Perestroika* and dissolution

Soon after coming to power in 1985, Gorbachev instigated reforms designed to restructure the Soviet socioeconomic order (*perestroika*) and to encourage more critical debate and public accountability (*glasnost'*). To this end, he disavowed the Party's claim to privileged access to objective knowledge and, calling for greater democracy, urged an end to the 'bureaucratization' of Soviet life. Soviet philosophy underwent significant liberalization. Instruction in Marxism-Leninism became no longer mandatory in Soviet institutions of higher education; indeed, the term 'Marxism-Leninism' was soon abandoned. *Voprosy filosofii* published debates about democracy, the rule of law and civil society, discussions of the history of Soviet philosophy (never previously a possible subject of debate), articles by Western thinkers, and hitherto banned works by Russian philosophers, such as Berdiaev and V.S. Solov'ëv (1853–1900).

The ethos of 'official' Soviet philosophy under *perestroika* is illustrated by the writings of I.T. Frolov (1929–), then advisor to Gorbachev and editor-in-chief of *Pravda*. In his book *Man, Science, Humanism* (1986), Frolov speaks out against Soviet Prometheanism, arguing that although we look to science to improve the conditions of human life, we must recognize that scientific progress has brought dramatic threats to the future of humanity. A critical and humanistic Marxism strives to put science 'in the service of humanity'. Frolov stresses the 'open character' of Marxist theory, urging that its tenets are not absolute truths. He attacks the follies of proletarian science, suggests compromise solutions to entrenched Soviet controversies (for instance over the genetic basis of the mental), and urges dialogue with Western thinkers.

Though more liberal than previous party lines, Frolov's position retains the idea that all issues are best addressed from the perspective of an all-encompassing theory of humanity's place in nature, a theory whose fundamental tenets are beyond dispute. Frolov's writings represent a broadening of Soviet orthodoxy, but the spirit of radical criticism remains absent.

The theme of humanism was central to much philosophical discussion under *perestroika*. The concept of a person (*lichnost'*) as a centre of moral agency came to the centre of discussion, complementing debates about ethical responsibility and legal consciousness. This person-centred approach was reflected in a new official textbook, *Vvedenie v filosofiiu* (Introduction to Philosophy) (1990), focused on problems of human existence instead of the primacy of materialism and the laws of the dialectic. There was a renewed interest in the anthropocentric Marxism that flourished in the Khrushchev thaw, especially Il'enkov's philosophy, which, it was argued, anticipated many themes openly discussed under *glasnost'*.

The new climate precipitated a number of heartfelt public discussions on the question 'Is Marxism dead?' A number of significant philosophers, such as E.Iu. Solov'ëv (1934–), K.M. Kantor (1922–), V.M. Mezhuev (1934–) and V.I. Tolstykh (1929–) argued that Marx should not be quickly blamed for the failed Soviet experiment; Marxist thought deserves continued study like any other major philosophical system. In contrast, others, like A.S. Tsipko (1941–), poured

scorn on the pretensions of Marxist philosophy, stressing the emptiness of Marx's views and their inapplicability to contemporary reality. These discussions reveal an intellectual world in crisis, disoriented by the diminution of its central authorities.

With the collapse of the Soviet Union in 1991, Russia's commitment to Marxism was abandoned entirely. Although Marxist influences are often evident in their work, few Russian philosophers now see themselves as contributing to the Marxist tradition. The thirst for a grand explanatory perspective is no less intense, but Russian thinkers now seek one elsewhere, in the Russian religious philosophy suppressed by the Bolsheviks, or in Western ideas, such as Foucauldian postmodernism (taken up by V.A. Podoroga (1946–) and his associates). Where these developments will lead is an open question. It seems, however, that the history of Russian Marxism is over.

See also: Marxism, Chinese; Marxism, Western; Marxist philosophy of science §3; Marxist thought in Latin America

References and further reading

* Aleksandrov, G.F.; Bykhovskii, B.E.; Mitin, M.B. and Iudin, P.F. (eds) (1941–3) *Istoriia filosofii* (History of Philosophy), Moscow: Gospolitizdat, 3 vols. (A collective history of philosophy, written by B.E. Bykhovskii, V.F. Asmus and B.S. Chernyshev among others. Although the book had earlier won the Stalin prize, the third volume was denounced by the Central Committee for its sympathetic treatment of Western philosophy, and plans for a further three were abandoned.)

* —— (1946) *Istoriia zapadnoevropeiskoi filosofii*, Moscow; *A History of Western European Philosophy*, New York, 1949. (A typical textbook history of philosophy by a leading philosopher of the Stalin era. Despite its orthodoxy it was severely criticized in Zhdanov's campaign against 'cosmopolitanism' in 1947.)

Bakhurst, D. (1991) *Consciousness and Revolution in Soviet Philosophy: From the Bolsheviks to Evald Ilyenkov*, Cambridge: Cambridge University Press. (An account of the philosophical culture of the USSR focused on the work of E.V. Il'enkov.)

* Bogdanov, A.A. (1905–6) *Empiriomonizm*, Moscow: Dorovatorskii & Charushnikov (Delo), 3 vols. (Bogdanov's principal philosophical treatise; not translated into English.)

Bukharin, N.I. (1921) *Teoriia istoricheskogo materializma: populiarnyi uchebnik marksistkoi sotsiologii*, Moscow; 3rd edn trans. *Historical Materialism: A*

System of Sociology, New York: Russel & Russel Inc., 1925.

Davydov, Iu.N. (1982) *Ėtika liubvi i metafizika svoevoliia* (The Ethics of Love and the Metaphysics of Self-Will), Moscow: Molodaia gvardiia. (A significant and controversial study of moral philosophy in the existentialist tradition.)

Drobnitskii, O.G. (1974) *Poniatie morali* (The Concept of Morals), Moscow: Nauka. (The principal work of one of the most sophisticated moral philosophers of the Soviet period.)

* Frolov, I.T. (1986) *Man, Science, Humanism: A New Synthesis*, Moscow: Progress; repr. New York: Promethius Books, 1990. (A forthright statement of humanistic Marxism by an influential figure in the Soviet establishment under Gorbachev.)

* Guseinov, A.A., and Tolstykh, V.I. (eds) (1993) *Studies in East European Thought (Special Issue): Marxism and the Socialist Idea in Russia Today* 45, nos 1–2. (A transcription of the 'Is Marxism Dead?' debate at the Svobodnaia slovo (Free Word) club in Moscow in 1990.)

* Il'enkov, E.V. (1960) *Dialektika abstraktnogo i konkretnogo v 'Kapitale' Marksa*, Moscow: Academiia nauk; trans. S. Syrovatkin, *The Dialectics of the Abstract and the Concrete in Marx's 'Capital'*, Moscow: Progress, 1982. (An influential attempt to develop Marx's dialectical method into a comprehensive anti-empiricist theory of knowledge.)

—— (1974) *Dialekticheskaia logika*, Moscow: Politizdat; trans. H. Campbell-Creighton, *Dialectical Logic*, Moscow: Progress, 1977. (Il'enkov's materialist phenomenology of spirit, which includes, as ch. 8, his account of 'the ideal' so influential in the early 1960s.)

* *Istoriia kommunisticheskoi partii sovetskogo soiuza (Bol'sheviki). Kratkii kurs* (1938), Moscow: Gospolitizdat; *History of the Communist Party of the Soviet Union (Bolsheviks). Short Course*, Moscow: Foreign Language Publishing House, 1943. (The main ideological primer of the Stalin era.)

Kelly, A. (1981) 'Empiriocriticism: A Bolshevik Philosophy?', in *Cahiers du monde russe et soviétique* 22: 89–118. (An excellent study of Russian empiriocriticism and its political significance.)

Kolakowski, L. (1978) *Main Currents of Marxism*, trans P.S. Falla, Oxford: Oxford University Press, 3 vols. (A brilliant and comprehensive study of Marxist thought, containing, in vols 2 and 3, detailed discussion of Russian and Soviet Marxism.)

* Lektorskii, V.A. (1980) *Sub"ekt, ob"ekt, poznanie*, Moscow: Nauka; trans. S. Syrovatnik, *Subject, Object, Cognition*, Moscow: Progress, 1984. (An insightful discussion of Marxist epistemology in relation to prominent, contemporary Western theories.)

Lenin, V.I. (1895–1916) *Filosofskie tetradi*, in *Polnoe sobranie sochinenii*, Moscow: Gospolitizdat, 1958–69, 5th edn, vol. 29; trans. C. Dutt, *Philosophical Notebooks*, in *Collected Works*, vol. 38, Moscow: Progress and London: Lawrence & Wishart, 1968–9, 4th English edn. (A collection of notes on philosophical texts, the most significant being those taken in the 1910s on various writings of Hegel's.)

* —— (1902) *Chto delat'*, in *Polnoe sobranie sochinenii*, Moscow: Gospolitizdat, 1958–69, 5th edn, vol. 5; trans. J. Fineberg, *What Is To Be Done?*, in *Collected Works*, Moscow: Progress and London: Lawrence & Wishart, 4th English edn, vol. 5. (Lenin's classic statement of his vision of the revolutionary party and its tactics.)

* —— (1909) *Materializm i ėmpiriokrititsizm*, in *Polnoe sobranie sochinenii*, Moscow: Gospolitizdat, 1958–69, 5th edn, vol. 18; *Materialism and Empiriocriticism*, in *Collected Works*, Moscow: Progress and London: Lawrence & Wishart, 4th English edn, vol. 14. (Lenin's defence of dialectical materialism against positivism and other supposed idealist schools; established under Stalin as the central text in Soviet philosophy.)

* Mamardashvili, M.K. (1990) *Kak ia ponimaiu filosofiiu (How I Understand Philosophy)*, Moscow: Progress. (An interesting collection of writings and interviews, including Mamardashvili's 'The Analysis of Consciousness in Marx's Works' (the latter is translated in *Studies in Soviet Thought* 32: 101–20 (1986).)

Mikhailov, F.T. (1964) *Zagadka chelovecheskogo 'ia'*, Moscow: Politizdat, 2nd edn 1976; 2nd edn trans. R. Daglish, *The Riddle of the Self*, Moscow: Progress, 1980. (A lively and insightful presentation of a critical Marxist epistemology; conveys the spirit of the works of the Khrushchev thaw.)

O raznoglasii na filosofskom fronte (On a Disagreement on the Philosophical Front) (1930), *Vestnik kommunisticheskoi akademii*, vols 40–1 (12–165), vol. 42 (20–89). (A fascinating transcription of meetings at the Communist Academy where Deborin and his followers were denounced.)

* *Oznovy marksistko-leninskoi filosofii* (1959), Moscow: Politzdat; 5th edn (1980) trans. R. Daglish, *Fundamentals of Marxist-Leninist Philosophy*, Moscow: Progress, 1982. (The standard textbook of official philosophy in the post-Stalin era, written by a team of scholars, including A.S. Bogomolov and T.I. Oizerman, under the direction of F.V. Konstantinov.)

* Plekhanov, G.V. (1895) *K voprosu o razvitii monisti-cheskogo vzgliada na istoriiu*, St Petersburg: Skorokhodova; trans. A. Rothstein, *In Defence of Materialism: The Development of the Monist View of History*, London: Lawrence & Wishart, 1947. (The first comprehensive presentation of Marxist philosophy as dialectical materialism.)

Scanlan, J.P. (1985) *Marxism in the USSR: A Critical Survey of Current Soviet Thought*, Ithaca, NY: Cornell University Press. (A comprehensive survey of Soviet debates in all areas of philosophy in the post-Stalin era and before *perestroika*.)

Swiderski, E. (1993) 'The Crisis of Continuity in Post-Soviet Russian Philosophy', in B. Smith (ed.) *Philosophy and Political Change in Eastern Europe*, La Salle, IL: Monist Library of Philosophy. (A study of the climate in Russian philosophy immediately after the collapse of the USSR.)

* Voloshinov, V.N. (1929) *Marksizm i filosofiia iazyka*, Leningrad: Ranion, Nauchno-issledovatel'skii institut sravnitel'noi istorii literatur i iazykov zapada i vostoka; trans. L. Matejka and I.R. Titunik, *Marxism and the Philosophy of Language*, New York: Seminar Press, 1973. (The systematic attempt at a Marxist theory of language; possibly written by M.M. Bakhtin.)

* * *Vvedenie v filosofiiu (Introduction to Philosophy)* (1990), Moscow: Politizdat, 2 vols. (A textbook produced in the Gorbachev period by a large team of philosophers, including I.T. Frolov, V.A. Lektorskii and V.Zh. Helle; designed to replace traditional Marxist-Leninist views with a humanistic vision centred on 'the problem of man's place in the world'.)

Vygotskii, L.S. (1934) *Myshlenie i rech'*, Moscow: Gosudarstvennoe sotsial'no-ekonomicheskoe izdatel'stvo; abridged trans. E. Hanfmann and G. Vakar, *Thought and Language*, Cambridge, MA: MIT, 1962; 2nd edn trans. revised and edited by A. Kozulin, Cambridge, MA: MIT University Press, 1986. (Vygotskii's most mature statement of his philosophical psychology; blacklisted during the Stalin era, the text was highly influential in Russia and abroad.)

DAVID BAKHURST

MARXIST THOUGHT IN LATIN AMERICA

Marxism is a theory offering a critique of capitalist political economy. Marxism also views itself as an instrument or means of changing the world from a capitalist to a socialist (and/or communist), economic and political order. Given its interest in economic and political change, Marxism involves a philosophy of history which depicts the possibility of and conditions for change from a capitalist to a socialist order. Marxist intellectuals perform the dual task of analysing the failures or limitations of capitalist economic and political structures. The theory also proposes and evaluates socialist alternatives.

Latin American Marxism developed out of its own historical, economic, political and cultural conditions. Influenced by Lenin's analysis of imperialism as the highest stage of capitalism, it directed the critique of capitalist political economy towards the capitalist world market and its disadvantageous effects for the countries, particularly the impoverished classes and social sectors, of the Latin American and Caribbean regions. Latin American Marxism-Leninism argues, on political and economic grounds, that national liberation cannot be achieved without liberation from imperialism.

Marxists believe that although the protagonists of history's political projects are the workers (or if Leninist, the workers together with the peasants), in the end the interests of these groups represent the universal interests of humankind. Marxist political discourse often uses broader categories than those of 'workers' or 'peasants' to designate the agents of political emancipation, employing terms such as 'the people', 'the popular sectors' or 'the revolutionary masses'. In this way Marxism attempts to broaden its political base so as to make its goals more effective. The political discourse of the Cuban Revolution of 1959 and the Nicaraguan Sandinista Revolution of 1979 exemplify this practice.

There are and have been many differences among Marxists because of the different approaches to criticizing capitalism as well as the different conceptions held by those who profess a commitment to the ultimate Marxist goal of creating a nonexploitative socialist society. Representative issues in Latin American Marxism may be illustrated by focusing on three questions: the problem of orthodoxy, the socialist construction of a national identity and socialism's relation to ethics, religion and culture. In addressing these issues, this entry draws significantly from the work of Peruvian Marxist José Carlos Mariátegui, a prominent founder of Latin American Marxism.

1 The problem of orthodoxy
2 The construction of a national identity
3 Ethics, religion and culture

1 The problem of orthodoxy

The mechanisms for implementing Marxist orthodoxy were not clear when the ideology was first introduced and then began to take shape between the 1870s and 1920s. The newness of socialist and communist ideas led Marxists to view themselves as future-oriented and revolutionary thinkers. Among the best-known early Latin American Marxists were the Argentine Aníbal Ponce, the Peruvian José Carlos Mariátegui and the Cuban Julio Antonio Mella. Mella was a university student leader strongly influenced by the thought of the Cuban patriot José Martí. Ponce was involved in education and publishing, wrote on socialist humanism and from 1923–5 coedited, with the Argentine positivist philosopher José Ingenieros, the *Revista de Filosofía, cultura, ciencias, educación* (Journal of Philosophy, Culture, Science, Education) (1915–29). Ponce became sole editor after Ingenieros's death in 1925.

Mariátegui, a journalist and social critic, was acknowledged as the most influential of the early Latin American Marxist thinkers. Author of *Seven Interpretive Essays on Peruvian Reality* (1928) and editor of the journal *Amauta: Revista mensuel de doctrina, literatura, arte, polémica* (Amauta: Monthly Review of Doctrine, Literature, Art and Polemics) (1926–30), he developed a highly original position in Latin American Marxism by stressing the importance of ethnicity, or indigenous culture, in the construction of national identity. He did so by maintaining a flexible position with regard to the relationship of Marxism to the latest theoretical currents from Europe and the USA, namely Bergsonian philosophy, pragmatism and psychoanalysis (see BERGSON, H.-L.; PRAGMATISM). He also rejected the notion of an essential antagonism between Marxism and religious thought, thereby breaking with the orthodox Marxist view that a materialist philosophy of history necessarily presupposes a materialist metaphysics. Mariátegui expounded his original ideas as part of his commitment to both a Leninist Marxism and the project of building a socialist society in Peru. As founder of the Socialist Party of Peru, he was criticized during his short life for some of his views by the Communist International. The 'errors' in his ideas were especially criticized during the Stalinist era, until a resurgence of interest in his work took place in the 1960s and 1970s.

For the first generation of Marxists, orthodoxy was less of a problem than for succeeding generations, since their task was to forge the new political philosophy which was not without codification. Marxism's link between theory and practice inevitably has raised the problem of orthodoxy and heterodoxy. Marxism's role is explanatory and predictive as well as conceptual. It is a theory whose goal is to create a determinate set of political effects. Its difficult aim is to construct a society without class exploitation.

Of fundamental historical importance to Marxism have been the questions of the scientific correctness of the theory designed to change the world and the correct political orientation of the leaders charged with developing and applying the theory in historical conditions, subsequent to those experienced by Marx and Engels. Depending on one's critical approach, Marxist theory can range from a nonpolitical intellectual analysis and critique of various aspects of capitalism as they affect human life and society to a dogmatic exposition and defence of the main theses accepted collectively at Communist Party congresses.

Orthodoxy is a relative concept. A position is orthodox in relation to the dogmas, truths, or methods that are taken to be central to a particular doctrine or school of thought. A Marxist thinker may be a dissident with respect to one school of Marxism while representing an orthodox position in another. The degree to which a Marxist position is free from orthodoxy is determined by the extent of its ability to question the closest Marxist authority with which it is associated. Marxist politics tend to impose a collective discipline over an individual's analysis of social reality. In cases where Marxist philosophy is practised within a socialist state that permits only one political party, the collective constraints over individual thought can be highly exacting. Although not all Marxists defend a one-party political system, those who do assert that the defence of the emerging socialist state against imperialism must take the highest priority.

Traditionally, Marxism relies on the methodologies of dialectical and historical materialism. From Hegel's self-validating account of dialectical thinking, Marxists inherited the view that dialectics provide an insuperable scientific conception of reality (see HEGEL, G.W.F.). Using the logic of dialectical materialism, orthodox Marxism holds that reality is material and that it changes by oppositional as well as by qualitative movements governed by dialectical laws known to the human mind. Marxist orthodoxy gave the name of 'scientific socialism' to this perspective. Applying a dialectical and material concept of change to history, historical materialism posits that the development of history is caused by material (primarily economic) factors, that history progresses through stages and that the change from one historical stage to another takes place when internal contradictions lead the old economic structures to be phased out in favour of newer, stronger and more universal elements. Historical materialism postulates that at the point of qualitative change between capitalism and socialism there lies a social revolution that will dismantle the old class divisions within society and lead eventually to a classless society in which the exploitation of human beings by human beings ceases to exist.

As a political philosophy Marxism argued that such exploitation can only be overcome by a social and political revolution in which the working class plays the dominant and leading liberatory role. After Lenin, Marxism-Leninism broadened the class of revolutionary political subjects to include both workers and peasants, students and intellectuals, all of whom had the same revolutionary aspirations. The Italian Marxist Antonio GRAMSCI (1891–1937) called the revolutionary intellectuals who supported the social revolution 'organic intellectuals'. In Latin America this view influenced many leftist intellectuals to back popular revolutionary movements led by Marxist leaders, as in Cuba and Nicaragua. The Marxist-Leninist-Gramscian influence, augmented in the 1960s by the political impact of leaders such as Ernesto 'Ché' Guevara, distinguished a wide sector of Latin American Marxism from Western European critical Marxism, whose intellectual roots were closer to Hegel, Marx, phenomenology, existentialism and critical theory (see CRITICAL THEORY; EXISTENTIALISM; PHENOMENOLOGY IN LATIN AMERICA). In Western Marxism, the materialist view of the worker and peasant protagonists of history is downplayed while issues such as alienation, the individual and social justice and the combined effects of oppressive class, race, and gender relations in the critique of capitalist economics are foregrounded.

Despite the problem of orthodoxy which delimits the production of Marxist philosophy and social thought, as a critique of capitalism and capitalist social structures Marxism yields some important and original insights which are absent from bourgeois philosophy and ideology. Mariátegui's focus on the construction of an Indohispanic socialism in Peru is a case in point.

2 The construction of a national identity

In keeping with the theory of historical materialism, Mariátegui (1928) held that societies evolve according to the laws of their socioeconomic development and that historical progress involves the surpassing of feudalism by capitalism and of capitalism by socialism. Apart from this traditional framework of historical materialism, Mariátegui introduced a number of variants into his concept of socialism which, when considered together, lay the foundations for a specifically Latin American approach to socialist theory. Mariátegui questioned the linear concept of history as it applied to the narrative of the superiority of European culture over the indigenous cultures of the Americas. He took the Spanish conquest of the

Inca civilization to represent the defeat of a highly competent form of social organization by a less competent one. He claimed the conquest symbolized a rupture within the economic organization which grew out of the experiences of the earliest Peruvian people. These people combined a simple life with a highly sophisticated economic system which was based on hard work, discipline and the satisfaction of the people's material needs. By referring to the pre-Columbian Inca empire as a central, although defeated, player in the history of Peru, Mariátegui demonstrated that Peru's national identity should not be conceived without giving a prominent place to its indigenous people. As a Marxist his goal was to contribute to the formation of an Indohispanic socialism in Peru. This position involved, on the one hand, convincing non-Marxists that socialism was a superior system to capitalism in Peru, while on the other hand, convincing the white and mestizo minorities (including socialists) that the disenfranchised indigenous population of Peru was an essential and irreplaceable part of its national identity and character.

As a member of a generation of Latin Americans critical of positivist philosophy, Mariátegui combined a political interest in Marxism with other artistic and intellectual interests (see ANTI-POSITIVIST THOUGHT IN LATIN AMERICA; POSITIVIST THOUGHT IN LATIN AMERICA). He promoted the Peruvian pro-indigenous literary movement of *indigenismo* (indigenism) and the new thinking of the European avant-garde. He supported the merit of thinkers like Friedrich NIETZSCHE, Sigmund FREUD, James Joyce and Miguel DE UNAMUNO and linked aspects of their views and teachings to his socialist interpretation of human and social reality. Mariátegui's appreciation of the value of myth led him to the insight that the relationship between the Indian and the land could not be understood simply in materialist or strictly modern secular terms. It must include a full account of the Indian's deeply-rooted spiritual belief that life springs from the land and returns to the land. He perceived the indigenous peasants as socially oppressed both as a class and in terms of their racial and ethnic status. He argued for a notion of national identity that would allow the Indians to come to prominence. Mariátegui's analysis called for Marxist theory to be reformulated so that it would take into account both class and ethnicity, including the cultural aspects of ethnic beliefs.

3 Ethics, religion and culture

The concept of human nature articulated by Mariátegui included a blend of existential, pragmatist, and

Marxist influences (see EXISTENTIALISM; PRAGMA-TISM). It was best characterized by a rejection of Cartesian rationalism and positivism (see RATIONAL-ISM). He followed the Italian idealist philosopher Benedetto CROCE in holding that, without a set of moral principles, specifically a principle condemning human exploitation, Marx's critique of capitalist economy would not make sense (albeit that Marx was not interested in developing a moral philosophy). Influenced by the French labour theorist Georges SOREL, Mariátegui argued that socialism had an ethical function, which was to create a 'morality of producers' in the process of struggling against capitalism. Therefore, Mariátegui was interested in articulating a work ethic based on socialist principles which would raise the moral consciousness of workers as they aimed to transform the exploitative conditions of class society.

Mariátegui departed from a 'scientific' dialectical materialist account of social change by representing the proletariat, or working class, as an affirmative rather than a negative, social and political force. In his early writings Mariátegui argued that the characteristic gesture of the bourgeoisie was to negate, while that of the working class was to affirm. He counterposed bourgeois nihilism and decadence with working class optimism and confidence. In the Hegelian version of the dialectic, negation (rather than affirmation) was the process which moved history forward. This led Marxism to emphasize revolution as the negation of a previously established political order. However, in his account of Peruvian history, Mariátegui argued for socialism on positive grounds. Peruvian capitalism was described as weak and unable to undo the power of the rural conservative sectors, which retarded economic development. Socialism was depicted as the one solution that would incorporate the benefits of capitalism (creativity, discipline, productiveness) while accommodating the communitarian interests of the indigenous population.

In the light of Mariátegui's portrayal of the workers and indigenous peasants as positive social forces, it could be argued that his concept of ethics, with its connection to socialism, was as close to Nietzsche's idea of a superior morality as to Marx's concept of social revolution. Mariátegui saw the advent of socialism as resulting from its own vigorous and undisputed success, not as a result of a class war. The work ethic he advocated contained a forceful and explicit rejection of what Nietzsche called a 'slave morality', a moral system which was reactive rather than self-initiated in its positing of moral principles and/or practices (see NIETZSCHE, F. §8). Mariátegui also rejected the notion of a

teleological end-state after the achievement of which history would end and all oppression would cease. He declared that no revolution can foretell a subsequent revolution, despite the fact that seeds of political change may have been planted. Like William JAMES, Mariátegui attributed to human beings a basic 'will to believe'. However, he also held, after Sorel, that the object of the will to believe need not be a religion as traditionally understood: it could be a belief in social revolution. Such a belief, like religion, would satisfy the human hope for a better world. Mariátegui therefore subscribed to an open-ended concept of revolution, which favoured an adaptation of Marxist ideas to new historical circumstances, including new trends in theory beyond those with which Marx was acquainted, such as Hegelian philosophy.

Mariátegui's views have been of interest to religious leftists, particularly Christians, motivated by a belief in a just and nonexploitative society, such as those committed to a theology of liberation (see LIBERATION THEOLOGY). In the *Seven Interpretive Essays on Peruvian Reality* (1928) he claims that it is a fundamental error for Marxists to attack the clergy and the church as if these were the principal obstacles to socialist change when the real enemy is the socioeconomic structure of society. He argued that the will to believe is a basic factor of human existence and that historical materialism as a theory of historical development should not be confused with philosophical materialism as a comprehensive theory of all reality. This view, conjoined with the view that, according to myth Indians regard the land as their common mother, contributed to Mariátegui's most important theses that the exploitation of the Indians was due to the land tenure system of Peruvian society and that their liberation could only take place through a socialist structure respectful of the Indians' ancient relationship to the land and the inherited collective practices of working it. His position suggested that the acceptance of modern Western standards of development should be tempered by respect for the forms of communal organization and bonding which characterize the lives of Peruvians whose cultural legacy is of pre-Columbian (non-Western) indigenous origin.

Mariátegui united his defence of an Indohispanic Peruvian socialism with a strong Marxist anti-imperialist statement. He argued that as long as imperialism exists, a Latin American society cannot be nationalist unless it is socialist. The economic and political structure of imperialism prevents the full realization of nationality in countries whose economic development is locked into a weak and backward capitalist structure controlled by foreign economic

163

interests. He noted that imperialism implies racism in that the cultural values imposed by an imperialist north-over-south continental order were the values of a white bourgeois class, imported into the south by the white privileged classes of Latin America. The latter, he claimed, failed to question their own involvement in an exploitative and racist system. Mariátegui challenged capitalism in terms that emphasized class, race and a nation's dependent status on the world market without promoting divisiveness or separatism.

Although Latin America has produced some well-known Marxist academic philosophers, including the Heideggerian Marxist Carlos Astrada (1894–1970) and the Marxist aesthetician Adolfo Sánchez Vázquez (1915–), it is José Carlos Mariátegui, a self-educated working class mestizo intellectual, to whom most contemporary scholars turn when the subject of inquiry involves the articulation of a specifically regional, that is Latin American, Marxism.

See also: LIBERATION PHILOSOPHY; MARX, K.; MARXISM, CHINESE; MARXISM, WESTERN; MARXIST PHILOSOPHY, RUSSIAN AND SOVIET

References and further reading

* *Amauta: Revista mensuel de doctrina, literatura, arte, polémica* (Amauta: Monthly Review of Doctrine, Literature, Art and Polemics) (1926–30), Lima. (The term *Amauta* is Quechua for 'wise teacher'. Mariátegui's journal took the name to stress the Inca heritage of Peru and to give the term a new vanguardist meaning.)

Astrada, C. (1963) *Existencialismo y crisis de la filosofía* (Existentialism and the Crisis of Philosophy), Buenos Aires: Devenir. (An account of the status of Western philosophy at mid-century from an existential Marxist standpoint. Advanced reading knowledge of Spanish required.)

Bottomore, T. (ed.) (1983) *A Dictionary of Marxist Thought*, Cambridge, MA: Harvard University Press. (A helpful and substantive philosophical dictionary of Marxist authors and concepts, focusing primarily on Western Marxism.)

Fernández Retamar, R. (1989) *Caliban and Other Essays*, trans. E. Baker, Minneapolis, MN: University of Minnesota Press. (A Cuban theorist's influential interpretation of the figure of Caliban as a symbol of resistance against colonialism.)

Guadarrama González, P. (1994) *América Latina: Marxismo y Postmodernidad* (Latin America, Marxism and Postmodernity), Santa Clara, Cuba and Bogotá: Universidad de Las Villas and Uni-

versidad INCCA. (An orthodox Cuban Marxist's account of the 1990s crisis of Marxism. Reading knowledge of Spanish required.)

Hodges, D.C. (1986) *Intellectual Foundations of the Nicaraguan Revolution*, Austin, TX: University of Texas Press. (A study of the Sandinistas' complex intellectual history and its impact on the 1979 Nicaraguan revolution.)

Liss, S.B. (1984) *Marxist Thought in Latin America*, Berkeley and Los Angeles, CA: University of California Press. (An introductory historical overview of Marxist political thought, classified by countries, from the late nineteenth century up to the 1970s.)

Löwy, M. (ed.) (1982) *El Marxismo en América Latina*, Mexico City: Era, trans. M. Pearlman, *Marxism in Latin America From 1909 to the Present: An Anthology*, Atlantic Highlands, NJ: Humanities Press, 1990. (An informative anthology of Marxist political currents, selected according to political movements, parties, and tendencies, from 1909 to the 1970s. Reading knowledge of Spanish required.)

* Mariátegui, J.C. (1928) *Seven Interpretive Essays on Peruvian Reality*, trans. M. Urquidi, Austin, TX: University of Texas Press, 1971. (A clearly written classic in Latin American Marxism, best known for its original treatment of the Indian question. Its contents are the focus of a central portion of this entry.)

Sánchez Vázquez, A. (1965) *Las ideas estéticas de Marx*, Mexico City: Era, trans. M. Riofrancos, *Art and Society: Essays in Marxist Aesthetics*, New York: Monthly Review Press, 1974. (A contemporary account of the opposition between capitalism and artistic creation as developed by a prominent Spanish-born Marxist philosopher. Advanced reading knowledge of Spanish required.)

—— (1988–9) 'Marxism in Latin America', *The Philosophical Forum* 20 (1–2): 114–28. (A clear and accessible account of the historical and intellectual roots of Latin American Marxism.)

Santos Moray, M. (ed.) (1985) *Marxistas de América: Julio Antonio Mella, José Carlos Mariátegui, Aníbal Ponce, Juan Marinello*, Havana: Editorial Arte y Literatura. (A selection of Marxist classics focusing on accounts of culture and society. It includes a name index. Advanced reading knowledge of Spanish required.)

Schutte, O. (1993) *Cultural Identity and Social Liberation in Latin American Thought*, Albany, NY: State University of New York Press. (A study of representative intellectual and social movements for liberation from the 1920s to the 1980s, including an analysis of Mariátegui and the origins of Latin American Marxism. Contains an expanded account of some material covered in this entry.)

OFELIA SCHUTTE

MASARYK, TOMÁŠ GARRIGUE (1850–1937)

Masaryk was a philosopher, sociologist, politician and first president of the Czechoslovak Republic (1918–35). Initially he aimed to change the Habsburg monarchy into a democratic federal state, but during the First World War he began to favour the abolition of the monarchy and, with the help of the Allied powers and the Czechoslovakian foreign armed forces, won independence for his nation. Masaryk's philosophy of history posited democracy achieving victory over theocracy as a stage in world evolution. He regarded democracy as both a political system and a humanistic world outlook.

Tomáš Garrigue Masaryk was born into a poor family and gained access to higher education only with difficulty. After grammar school in Brno and Vienna he studied philosophy and classical philology at the University of Vienna where he became a student of Franz BRENTANO. Having achieved his Ph.D. in 1876, he studied in Leipzig where he met FECHNER and WUNDT and befriended the young HUSSERL. Masaryk's 1879 habilitation thesis at the University of Vienna was *Der Selbtstmord als sociale Massenerscheinung der modernen Civilisation* (Suicide and the meaning of civilization), which contained many ideas later developed and expanded in his philosophy. It concluded that suicide is a result of the prevalence of subjectivism, individualism and one-sided rationalism which had dismantled the Christian worldview. Masaryk sought the solution in an organic cultural synthesis, in education involving the unity of philosophy and science, theory and practice, in a new non-mythical religion, and in the reform of society according to sociological knowledge.

In 1882 Masaryk was appointed professor at the University of Prague. Here his focus went beyond academic activity, bringing supranational criteria to bear on provincial conditions and narrow national interests. Czech cultural life, until then looking exclusively to Germany, was becoming enriched with French and Anglo-American ideas, reflected in Masaryk's first philosophical work, *Základové konkrétné logiky* (Fundamentals of concrete logic) (1885). Although his most theoretical, this was a distinctly practical work, reflecting Masaryk's convic-

tion that theoretical knowledge must serve life and his aim to reform society. Following Comte he created a system from which it is possible to deduce a consistent philosophical and simultaneously scientific worldview, but he placed a greater stress on psychology and ethics and their social role (see COMTE, A.). He regarded metaphysics and theism as compatible with scientific knowledge.

Masaryk considered Czech politics of the time to be ineffectual, lacking both a theoretical basis and an ethical dimension. In *Česká otázka* (The Czech question) (1895) and other studies, he sought the *raison d'être* of the Czech nation and formulated a philosophy of Czech history. Its long humanitarian tradition based on religion he dated from the time of the Czech Reformation, continuing during the Czech National Revival at the beginning of the nineteenth century. This tradition, characterized by love of truth and genuine Christian life, was also democratic. Such humanitarian ideas parallel those of other progressive nations: consequently the Czech question represented the world question, and Masaryk believed its politics should be in harmony with this philosophy of history. His immediate target was the transformation of the Austrian multinational monarchy into a democratic federation, securing free evolution for all nations, and he actively pursued this idea until the outbreak of the First World War.

Masaryk's humanism centred around his interest in social problems, and he sympathized with many of the demands of the labour movement. He also concentrated on theory, balancing the philosophical and sociological perspectives of Marxism in *Otázka sociální* (The social question) (1898). He admired Marx's analysis of the importance of human labour, but rejected revolution as a solution to social conflict; rather, he emphasized reform in the spirit of humanism. His outlook is expressed by the aphorism 'Always for the worker, very often with socialism, rarely with Marxism' (Čapek 1938: 214).

Masaryk's interest in Russia culminated in his most extensive work *Rußland und Europa. Studien über die geistigen Strömungen in Rußland* (The Spirit of Russia) (1913). He analysed and critically evaluated the different trends in Russian thinking reflected in theoretical essays and literature. Dostoevskii's works, which he regarded as representing a new direction, challenge Masaryk's own conception of humanitarian philosophy.

The First World War proved a political turning point for Masaryk. He came to the conclusion that the Austrian monarchy could not be reformed by inner forces, as it directly represented a metaphysical evil which was partially to blame for the outbreak of war. For that reason Masaryk opted for an independent

Czech-Slovak state. Elected first president of the Czechoslovak Republic in 1918, he retired from academic life but did not ccasc to be interested in philosophy. He considered the Czech struggle to be part of a world revolution, a battle against theocracy which democracy can be expected to win, a viewpoint reflected in *Světová revoluce* (The Making of a State) (1924).

See also: CZECH REPUBLIC, PHILOSOPHY IN; SLOVAKIA, PHILOSOPHY IN; SUICIDE, ETHICS OF

List of works

Masaryk, T.G. (1879) *Der Selbtstmord als sociale Massenerscheinung der modernen Civilisation* (Suicide and the meaning of civilization), trans. W.B. Weist and R.G. Batson, intro. A. Giddens, Chicago, IL: University of Chicago Press, 1970. (Suicide assessed as a problem of modern mankind.)
—— (1885) *Základové konkrétné logiky* (Fundamentals of concrete logic), Prague: Bursík a Kahout. (Masaryk's theory of science and concept of philosophy, published in German as *Versuch einer concreten Logik* in 1887.)
—— (1895) *The meaning of Czech history*, trans. P. Kussi, ed. and intro. R. Wellek, Chapel Hill, NC: University of North Carolina Press, 1974. (Anthology of Masaryk's works including *The Czech Question, Palaky's Idea of the Czech Nation*, John Huss and Karel Havlíček.)
—— (1898) The Social question: philosophical and sociological foundations of Marxism, in *Masaryk on Marx; an abridged edition of T.G. Masaryk*, ed. and trans. E.V. Kohak, Lewisburg, PA: Bucknell University Press, 1972. (Anthology of Masaryk's work *The Social Question*.)
—— (1913) *The Spirit of Russia; studies in history, literature and philosophy*, trans. E. Paul and C. Paul; additional chapters and bibliographies J. Slavik, the former translated and the latter condensed and translated by W.R. Lee and Z. Lee (2nd, 3rd impressions), London: Allen & Unwin; New York: Macmillan, 1961. (This English translation includes the third, unpublished part of Masaryk's manuscript.)
—— (1920) *The New Europe (the Slav standpoint)*, ed. W. Preston and W.B. Weist, intro. O. Odlozilik, Lewisburg, PA: Bucknell University Press, 1972. (Project of the new political organization of European states after the First World War.)
—— (1924) *The Making of a state; memories and observations, 1914–1918*, ed. H. Wickham Steed, New York: F.A. Stokes Co., 1927. (Translation of *Světová*, reprinted by H Fertig in 1969.)

References and further reading

Beld, A. van den (1976) *Humanity: the political and social philosophy of Thomas G. Masaryk*, The Hague: Mouton. (Analysis of Masaryk's humanitarian philosophy).
Branch, M.A. (ed.) (1990) *T.G. Masaryk (1850–1937)*, London: Macmillan, 3 vols, vol. 1: 'Thinker and Politician', ed. S.B. Winters; vol. 2: 'Thinker and Critic', ed. R.B. Pynsent; vol. 3: 'Statesman and Cultural Force', ed. H. Hanak. (Critical assessments of Masaryk's achievements as philosopher, politician and publicist.)
* Čapek, K. (1938) *Masaryk on Thought and Life*, trans. M. Weatherall and R. Weatherall, London: Allen & Unwin; New York: Arno Press, 1971. (Interview with Masaryk.)
Kovtun, J.G. (1981) *Tomas G. Masaryk 1850–1937*, Washington, DC: Library of Congress. (A selected bibliography of reading materials in English.)
Novak, J. (ed.) (1988) *On Masaryk*, Amsterdam: Rodopi. (Collection of studies of Masaryk's philosophical and sociological views; texts in English and German.)
Skilling, H.G. (1994) *Against the Current. T.G. Masaryk 1882–1914*, London: Macmillan. (Masaryk's activity and his struggle in the Austrian monarchy until the First World War.)
Zeman, Zbynek A.B. (1976) *The Masaryks: the making of Czechoslovakia*, New York: Barnes & Noble. (Historical monograph about Masaryk's part in the foundation of Czechoslovakia.)
Zumr, J. and Binder, T. (eds) (1992) *T.G. Masaryk und die Brentano–Schule Praha/Graz*, Filosoficky ustav CSAV/Forschungstelle und Dokumentationszentrum für österreichische Philosophie. (Collection of studies directed to philosophy of science and religion and to Masaryk's place in history of philosophy – in English and German.)

Translated by G.R.F. Bursa
JOSEF ZUMR

MASHAM, DAMARIS (1658–1708)

Damaris Cudworth, who became Lady Masham on her marriage to Sir Francis Masham in 1685, was an English moral philosopher who published two short treatises on moral philosophy. These show that she became a disciple of John Locke, although her philosophical background was in Cambridge Platonism. She applied Lockean arguments to defend the education of women; her anti-idealism led her to oppose Male-branche and his English followers, John Norris and Mary Astell; and she also corresponded with Leibniz.

Lady Masham was one of the very first English women to publish philosophical writings. The daughter of Cambridge Platonist Ralph CUDWORTH, she was also a very close friend of John LOCKE, who spent his last years at her residence in Essex. Unlike most women of her time, Damaris Cudworth was able to develop her interest in philosophy thanks to the fortuitous circumstances first, of being born into an intellectual family and, second, of becoming the close acquaintance of the leading English philosopher of his generation. Little is known of her education beyond the fact that she learned French but not Latin, which suggests that she had no more than the grooming deemed fit for a lady. In 1685, shortly after Locke's departure for exile, she married Sir Francis Masham, an Essex squire with a family of nine children. She herself had one child.

There are three sources for documenting Lady Masham's activities as a philosopher: her correspondence with Locke, her two short books, and her letters to Leibniz. Her two books were published anonymously and her biography of Locke was printed in abridged form in Moreri's *Grand Dictionnaire Historique* (1728). It is clear from Lady Masham's early correspondence with Locke (dating from 1682) that her introduction to philosophy was through the writings of the Cambridge Platonists, Ralph Cudworth, Henry MORE and John Smith (see CAMBRIDGE PLATONISM). However, the letters also show that she was receptive to Locke's views, and her two books (published with the encouragement of Locke) show her assimilation of his philosophy. In these she draws on Locke in her opposition to the Malebranchian idealism of Mary ASTELL and John NORRIS, and in her arguments for the education of women. The same anti-idealist position informs her critique of LEIBNIZ. But her allegiance to Locke did not entail a repudiation of Cambridge Platonism in all respects: the Leibniz correspondence also includes a defence of her father against Pierre Bayle's imputation of covert atheism (see BAYLE, P.).

The connecting thread of Lady Masham's thought is religious and moral. Her published writings are broadly Lockean in epistemology. *A Discourse Concerning the Love of God* (1696) is a critique of the correspondence between John Norris and Mary Astell which had been published as *Letters Concerning the Love of God* (1695). Lady Masham objected that Norris' occasionalist account of human love of God denigrates created things and undermines the bonds of society. By contrast, Lady Masham argued,

humans come to know and to love God by observing the created world and comparing ideas 'received from *Sense* and *Reflection*'. She emphasizes practical morality, arguing that it is integral to religion. This position is developed in *Occasional Thoughts in Reference to a Vertuous or Christian Life* (1705) which contains an assessment of the role of reason in religious matters and, in particular, the relationship between religion and morality. Here she insists that civil and religious liberties are necessary for the exercise of virtue and that education is the key means to inculcate virtue. She displays an optimistic view of humankind as rational and social beings for whom the love of happiness is 'the earliest and strongest principle', happiness being the enjoyment of pleasure, and the pursuit of pleasure involving the regulatory exercise of reason which directs us to the greatest happiness. She is critical of Malebranche's pessimistic view of children as natural born sinners as a consequence of each child loving the body of its mother while in the womb. *Occasional Thoughts* concludes by arguing for the education of women on moral grounds: first, instruction of women by precept rather than reason produces the opposite of the desired result (superstition and immorality instead of right belief and virtue); second, since moral principles are best inculcated in childhood, women, as mothers, have an important role as teachers of their children.

In her letters to Leibniz, Lady Masham takes issue with him on a number of points, among them his concept of 'atomes de substance' – whether unextended substances exist and how free will can be maintained within pre-established harmony. Her most important point relates to her critique of Norris: namely that, if matter is denied a causal role in Leibniz's system, the organization of matter is rendered 'superfluous and lost labour'. Although Lady Masham helped to establish a place for women in philosophy, she accepted limitations on their philosophical activities: in *Occasional Thoughts* she notes that women should not spend their time in unnecessary speculations, but they should endeavour to improve their minds by more than merely doing their duty.

List of works

Note on correspondence: Lady Masham's correspondence has not been collected, apart from her letters to Leibniz which have been reproduced in *Die Philosophischen Schriften von Gottfried Wilhelm Leibniz* (ed. C.I. Gerhardt, Berlin: Weidmannsche Buchhandlung, 7 vols, 1875–90, vol. 3, 372) and to Locke in *The Correspondence of John Locke*, (ed. E.S. de Beer, 8 vols, Oxford: Clarendon Press, 1976–, vols. 2 and 3). Letters to Shaftesbury are in the London Public Records Office (PRO 30/24/20, fols. 266 7 and 273–4), while Amsterdam University Library has three letters to Philip van Limborch (MS M31c).

Masham, D. (1696) *A Discourse Concerning the Love of God*, London; French trans. *Discours sur l'Amour Divin*, Amsterdam, 1705. (A critique of *Letters Concerning the Love of God* (1695) by John Norris and Mary Astell.)

—— (1705) *Occasional Thoughts in Reference to a Vertuous or Christian Life*, London. (The second printing in 1747, *Thoughts on a Christian Life*, was misattributed to Locke.)

—— (1728) 'Locke, (Jean)', in L. Moreri, *Le Grand Dictionnaire Historique*, nouvelle edition, Paris, vol. 3. (This is a shortened version of a memoir of Locke, now in Amsterdam University Library (Remonstrants MSS J. 57a), which also forms the basis of *Eloge de feu Mr. Locke* by Jean Le Clerc in *Bibliotheque choisie*, vol. 6, 1705, 342–411.)

References and further reading

Ballard, G. (1752) *Memoirs of Several Ladies of Great Britain*, Oxford, 379–88; repr. Detroit, MI: Wayne State University Press, 1985. (General and uncritical on her philosophy.)

Hutton, S. (1993) 'Damaris Cudworth, Lady Masham: between Platonism and Enlightenment', *British Journal for the History of Philosophy* 1: 29–54. (A study of Masham's philosophy in relation to Locke and Cambridge Platonism.)

* Norris, J. and Astell M. (1695) *Letters Concerning the Love of God*, London. (Correspondence between John Norris and Mary Astell.)

Laslett, P. (1953) 'Masham of Oates', *History Today* 3: 535–43. (Biographical background.)

Simonutti, L. (1987) 'Damaris Cudworth Masham: una Lady della Repubblica delle Lettere', *Studi in Onore di Eugenio Garin* (Studies in honour of Eugenio Garin), Pisa: Scuola Normale Superiore, 141–65. (A study of Masham's philosophy.)

SARAH HUTTON

MASS TERMS

Mass terms are words and phrases such as 'water', 'wood' and 'white wallpaper'. They are contrasted with count terms such as 'woman', 'word' and 'wild wildebeest'. Intuitively, mass terms refer to 'stuff'; count terms refer to 'objects'. Mass terms allow for measurement ('three kilos of wood', 'much water'); count terms allow for counting, quantifying and individuating ('three women', 'each word', 'that wildebeest over there').

Philosophical problems associated with mass terms include (1) distinguishing mass from count terms, (2) describing the semantics of sentences employing mass terms, and (3) explicating the ontology presupposed by our use of mass versus count terms. Associated with these philosophical issues – especially the third – are the meta-philosophical issues concerning the extent to which any investigation into the linguistic practices of speakers of a language can be used as evidence for how those speakers view 'reality'.

1 Distinguishing mass and count terms
2 Semantics and ontology of mass terms

1 Distinguishing mass and count terms

The distinction between mass terms ('water', 'wood' and so on) and count terms ('woman', 'word' and so on) can be seen as syntactic, semantic or pragmatic. If the distinction is seen as syntactic, one might remark that mass terms occur with the quantifiers 'much' and 'little' and with the unstressed article 'some', that they are susceptible to measurement phrases such as 'litres of' and 'amount of', and that they do not exhibit a singular/plural distinction. Conversely, count expressions occur with the quantifiers 'each', 'every', 'many', 'several', 'few' and the stressed 'some', use the indefinite article 'a(n)', are susceptible to counting phrases such as 'five' and 'a score of', and exhibit a singular/plural dichotomy manifested in the count term itself and in agreement with the verb phrase.

If it is seen as semantic – a distinction between the different ways that mass and count terms refer – then one might remark that count expressions refer to discrete, well-delineated objects while mass terms refer without making it explicit how the referent is individuated (some have said that the referents of mass terms are continuous rather than discrete). This feature of mass reference gives rise to the 'cumulative reference test' (any sum of parts which are M is also M) and to the 'distributive [homogeneous] reference test' (any part of something which is M is also M).

If the mass/count distinction is seen as a pragmatic one, then one will look to how people use count terms to 'individuate' the world. This gives rise to such tests as whether there is a definite answer to the question 'How many X's are there in such-and-such place?'. In the philosophical literature (following Strawson 1959), terms which pass this counting test are often called 'sortal terms' – although they are equally often called count terms – and ones that fail the test are called mass terms. In this literature, with its emphasis on the pragmatic notions of 'identifying' and 'individuating', it is common to deny that such terms as 'thing', 'object' and so on are sortal (count), there being no definite answer to the question 'How many things are in the room?'. This is so despite the fact that such terms clearly satisfy the syntactic criteria.

All these tests – the syntactic, the semantic and the pragmatic ones – have been challenged. Writers have pointed out that mass terms such as 'wood' can also be used as count: 'a wood' might designate oak or spruce, for example. And 'wildebeest' can be used as a mass term: 'He's not really a vegetarian; he eats wildebeest'. Furthermore, a universal grinder would take an object that an alleged count term referred to – a chair, for example – and grind it up into a powder so that then there would be chair all over the floor. (This last sentence uses 'chair' in a mass manner, thereby showing that the language already has this usage of any count term in the background. And this usage exists despite the fact that we could also have said 'There is wood all over the floor'.)

The criteria just mentioned are usually seen as applying to entire noun phrases as well as to the simple nouns themselves. Furthermore, some writers attempt to apply the mass/count distinction to other syntactic categories, especially adjectives, verbs and adverbs. The application to verbs is especially interesting (see Mourelatos 1978).

2 Semantics and ontology of mass terms

The problem with giving a formal semantic analysis of mass terms arises because first-order predicate logic appears to assume that the entities in the domain of quantification are individuals, so it only makes sense to characterize them with count nouns. When we say, in the quantifier idiom, 'For all x, if x is F...', it is apparently assumed that the items in the domain have already been individuated. For if F were to be interpreted as 'snow', for example, what would be the values of x?

Famously, Quine (1960) held that mass terms are ambiguous: when in 'subject position' they are singular terms (names), but when in 'predicate position' they are general terms (predicates) which are 'true of each portion of the stuff in question, excluding only the parts too small to count'. As a name (when in subject position), Quine holds that a mass term 'differs none from such singular terms as "mama"..., unless the scattered stuff that it names be denied the status of a single sprawling object'.

This proposal has not satisfied various authors, who have objected to the nonuniform treatment and to various logical consequences of this approach. For

example, on Quine's analysis, 'Water is wet, and this puddle is water' does not imply 'This puddle is wet'; and 'Water is water' does not come out a logical truth. Writers after Quine have proposed many different approaches. Possibly the most popular alternatives involve mereology, according to which the main operator is 'is a part of'. Mass (and other) terms are taken to designate 'mereological wholes'. Some authors have grafted onto pure mereology a notion of 'having certain structural properties', so as to avoid the minimal parts problem alluded to in Quine. (The atoms, *inter alia*, which are part of water are 'too small' to count as water.) But these theories also have not satisfied all those involved in this area, usually because the treatment of certain logical inferences is thought incorrect: the formal semantic analyses do not mirror intuitive beliefs concerning logical consequence.

An alternative is to retain the idea that mass terms name some kind of object – a 'substance' – and to invoke a relational predicate such as 'is constituted of'. This presents a number of tricky issues and there are types of sentences for which such an analysis is not obviously suitable, but still various authors have adopted it. Besides the formal differences entailed by these two approaches (mereological calculus of individuals versus classical logic with a relational constant of constitution), there is an ontological difference, for mereological wholes are generally taken to be physical whereas substances or kinds are often viewed as abstract entities (see SUBSTANCE).

Another formal semantics of mass terms invokes sets as their denotation. Differences among theorists can then be seen as differences about what the sets contain. One question on which theorists differ is whether the sets contain only 'minimal entities' – the smallest items to which the mass term refers (flakes, maybe, for 'snow'; the items and size vary according to the mass term in question) – or whether it should contain 'ordinary objects' (flakes, drifts, snowmen, snowballs and so on; any object which can be said to be snow). The former proposal has not gained many adherents due to the difficulty of specifying a set of 'minimal entities' for such mass terms as 'garbage', 'speed' and 'information'. The latter proposal runs into difficulties in trying to account for the denotation of definite noun phrases (NPs) such as 'the snow on the table'. It is generally not true that there is exactly one snow-thing on the table. (There is one ball and also many flakes making it up, for example.) So the only reasonable proposal is for the NP to designate *all* the snow-things on the table. But then certain measurement sentences – for example, 'The snow on the table weighs one kilo' – come out wrong, since we will count the same snow-entities many times over.

Theories of mass terms show a fundamental division between those that are committed to abstract substances and those that are physicalistic in nature, invoking mereological wholes. On the physicalistic side are those theories which propose that the ontologically basic objects are the minimal entities, those which claim that the larger entities are 'constructions' out of these minimal entities, and those theories which propose that all these entities are equally basic. On the other side of the gulf are the various styles of substance theories, which usually invoke a lattice structure of kinds. Such ontological issues are discussed in Pelletier and Schubert (1989) and in Burkhardt and Smith (1991).

See also: LOGICAL AND MATHEMATICAL TERMS, GLOSSARY OF; MEREOLOGY

References and further reading

Bunt, H. (1985) *Mass Terms and Model-Theoretic Semantics*, Cambridge: Cambridge University Press. (This is the longest and possibly most thorough work on mass terms. It is aimed at a computer implementation of a natural language understanding system which will include mass terms. It invokes 'ensemble theory', which is a type of atomic mereology.)

* Burkhardt, H. and Smith, B. (1991) 'Mass Terms', in *Handbook of Metaphysics and Ontology*, Munich: Philosophia. (This entry goes into the metaphysical and ontological presuppositions of mass terms in more detail than is possible here. It includes some speculation about how the mass/count distinction might have arisen in natural language.)

Lønning, J.-T. (1987) 'Mass Terms and Quantification', *Linguistics and Philosophy* 10: 1–52. (An example of the direction that research into the mereological interpretation of mass terms has taken.)

* Mourelatos, A. (1978) 'Events, Processes, and States', *Linguistics and Philosophy* 2: 415–34. (Mourelatos draws explicit attention to the relationships that hold between certain types of verbs and verb phrases and the mass/count distinction.)

Pelletier, F.J. (ed.) (1979) *Mass Terms: Some Philosophical Problems*, Dordrecht: Reidel. (This anthology includes many of the classic articles on the topic of mass terms, especially in the philosophical tradition. It also includes a comprehensive bibliography up to 1978.)

* Pelletier, F.J. and Schubert, L.K. (1989) 'Mass Expressions', in D. Gabbay and F. Guenthner (eds) *Handbook of Philosophical Logic*, Dordrecht: Reidel, vol. 4, 327–407, esp. 391–4. (The most thorough summary of the work done on mass terms, both linguistic and philosophical. It also proposes two theories to account for the phenomena, and includes a comprehensive bibliography of work from 1978 to 1988, plus earlier work where relevant.)

* Quine, W.V. (1960) *Word and Object*, Cambridge, MA: MIT Press, 91–100. (Although this book has only a small section on mass terms, it formed the starting point of most future formal work on the topic. Quine proposed his 'dual analysis' here and asserted that mass terms come from an 'early, primitive stage in linguistic evolution'.)

Quirk, R., Greenbaum, S., Leech, G. and Svartvik, J. (1985) *A Comprehensive Grammar of Contemporary English*, London: Longman. (The most thorough descriptive account of the grammar of the English language, with a section about the mass/count distinction, especially as it is used in normal speech. It does not deal particularly with the formal semantics of the distinction.)

* Strawson, P.F. (1959) *Individuals: An Essay in Descriptive Metaphysics*, London: Methuen. (It is here that the distinction between 'feature-placing universal' and 'sortal universal' was drawn. Many writers wished to put mass terms in the former category, giving rise in the philosophical literature to the opposition 'mass/sortal'. Other writers thought of mass terms as a type of sortal term, while still others argued for a third category.)

JEFFRY PELLETIER

MASSILIANISM *see* PELAGIANISM

MATERIAL IMPLICATION, PARADOXES OF *see* INDICATIVE CONDITIONALS

MATERIALISM

Materialism is a set of related theories which hold that all entities and processes are composed of – or are reducible to – matter, material forces or physical processes. All events and facts are explainable, actually or in principle, in terms of body, material objects or dynamic material changes or movements. In general, the metaphysical theory of materialism entails the denial of the reality of spiritual beings, consciousness and mental or psychic states or processes, as ontologically distinct from, or independent of, material changes or processes. Since it denies the existence of spiritual beings or forces, materialism typically is allied with atheism or agnosticism.

The forms of materialism extend from the ancient Greek atomistic materialism through eighteenth- and nineteenth-century scientifically based theories, to recent sophisticated defences of various types of materialism.

1 Materialism
2 Ancient Greek atomism
3 Modern materialism
4 Recent materialism

1 Materialism

Materialism is the general theory that the ultimate constituents of reality are material or physical bodies, elements or processes. It is a form of monism in that it holds that everything in existence is reducible to what is material or physical in nature. It is opposed to dualistic theories which claim that body and mind are distinct, and directly antithetical to a philosophical idealism that denies the existence of matter. It is hostile to abstract objects, if these are viewed as more than just a manner of speaking (see ABSTRACT OBJECTS). An implication of materialism is that the diverse qualitative experiences we have are ultimately reducible to quantitative changes in objects or in our physiological functioning. All the properties of things, including persons, are reducible to properties of matter. Although the terms referring to psychic states such as intention, belief, desire and consciousness itself have a different sense and use than terms referring to material events, a consistent materialist would deny that mentalistic terms have reference to anything other than physical events or physiological changes in our brains. The enormous advances in the sciences have contributed storehouses of empirical data that are often used to support materialism. Many philosophers have been attracted to materialism both because of its reductive simplicity and its association with scientific knowledge.

2 Ancient Greek atomism

Although LEUCIPPUS is credited with inventing the atomic theory of matter in the fifth century BC, it was DEMOCRITUS (fourth century BC) who developed a systematic theory of atomistic materialism. This theory states that matter is composed of separate and minute elements that are 'uncuttable' (*atoma*), that these elements move in empty space or the

'void'. Atoms differ only in shape and volume, and all change occurs by the transfer through direct contact of movement from atoms in motion. These elementary entities are lacking in secondary qualities and are indestructible. Democritus held that things are hot or cold, sweet or bitter, or have different colours 'by convention'. In reality, 'there are atoms and the void'.

The essentials of early atomism were retained in Epicurus' physics, with the exception that Epicurus ascribed freedom to atoms in their movement through space. Epicurean materialism is lucidly expressed in the philosophic poem by LUCRETIUS, *De rerum natura* (On the Nature of Things), in the first century BC. This popularization of Epicurean thought did much to keep alive both atomistic materialism and what is already recognizable as a naturalistic understanding of humans and world (see EPICUREANISM).

3 Modern materialism

During the first half of the seventeenth century the atomistic materialism of the Greco-Roman period was revived in a paradoxical way by Pierre GASSENDI. He appreciated the scientific interpretation of nature and the methods of science but, at the same time, preserved the Christian idea of the immortality of the soul and conceived of God as the creator of the atoms. The English philosopher Thomas HOBBES presented a systematic theory of nature and human nature that was largely, though not completely, materialistic. Apart from attributing 'drive' or *conatus* to human action and sensation, Hobbes virtually banished the concept of 'incorporeal substance'. In theory and sentiment Hobbes was a materialist thinker, although not a consistent one. The early eighteenth century saw the publication of the first of many works that defended a materialistic and mechanistic interpretation of mankind's nature on the basis of physiological theory. In *L'Homme machine* (1748) Julien de LA METTRIE, a philosophical physician, described human beings as self-moving mechanisms and sought a neurological basis for mental activity. An advance on previous attempts to develop a systematic materialism is Paul H.D. d'Holbach's 1770 *Système de la nature* (*The System of Nature*). Here, a consistent naturalistic materialism is expounded in that cognitive and emotive states are reduced to internal material 'modifications of the brain'. Though not calling it such, d'Holbach presents a form of physiological determinism.

With the rapid growth of the sciences, the astronomical discoveries of COPERNICUS, the theories of GALILEO, and the systematic conception of nature in the physical theory of Isaac NEWTON, naturalistic

171

interpretations of a variety of phenomena became more and more prevalent. This scientifically founded picture of reality lent greater plausibility to the principles of materialistic theory. The astronomer and mathematician Pierre Laplace (1749–1827) produced a sophisticated astronomical theory which, he thought, illustrated that a supermind, knowing all the states and conditions of every existing entity, could predict the total state of the cosmos in the next moment. When Napoleon I was shown a copy of Laplace's work, he is supposed to have commented on the absence of any mention of God. Laplace replied, 'I have no need of that hypothesis'. Laplace's mechanistic materialism became, in the hands of many thinkers, the definitive explanatory principle of all events.

The formulation of the biological theory of evolution by means of natural selection by Charles DARWIN virtually eliminated teleological explanations of biological phenomena and thereby buttressed material and physical interpretations of organic development. With the advances in chemistry achieved by Lavoisier (1743–94) in France and John Dalton (1766–1844) in England, the reductive analysis of natural phenomena to chemical substances, elements and processes bolstered the empirical, naturalistic and materialistic interpretations of phenomena. During the nineteenth century many philosophical thinkers sought to build theories on the foundation of scientific facts, principles or laws. The historical materialism developed by Marx and Engels sought to formulate laws of social, economic and historical development, but did not defend metaphysical materialism (see DIALECTICAL MATERIALISM). The general appeal of materialism in the nineteenth century is shown by the popularity of the 1855 work by Ludwig BÜCHNER, *Kraft und Stoff* (Force and Matter), which passed through sixteen editions. Although philosophically crude, it is an accessible compendium of popular materialism. In 1852, Jacob Moleschott had defended the reduction of force to matter, the doctrine of the conservation of matter, and a species of objective relativism in *Der Kreislauf des Lebens* (The Cycle of Life). Following the ill-chosen analogy between the brain and thought and the digestive system in Jean Cabanis' *Rapports due physique et du moral de l'homme* (Relations of the Physical and the Mental in Man) (1802), Karl Vogt proclaimed that the brain 'secretes' thought the way the liver secretes bile. Despite such excursions into 'vulgar materialism', the nineteenth century became a period of intense debate for scientists and philosophers alike in regard to the limits of scientific knowledge and the epistemological problems of metaphysical materialism. This was fuelled by a

Neo-Kantian movement which, particularly in *Geschichte des Materialismus* (History of Materialism) (1865) by F.A. LANGE, held that materialism is a useful methodological principle in science, but questionable as a reductionist metaphysics. The concepts and postulates of science are theoretical entities or conventional notions formed by the mind. Their usefulness does not, according to Lange, warrant their role as bases for materialism.

4 Recent materialism

In the twentieth century, physicalism has emerged out of positivism. Physicalism restricts meaningful statements to physical bodies or processes that are verifiable or in principle verifiable. It is an empirical hypothesis that is subject to revision and, hence, lacks the dogmatic stance of classical materialism. Herbert Feigl defended physicalism in the USA and consistently held that mental states are brain states and that mental terms have the same referent as physical terms (Feigl 1958). The twentieth century has witnessed many materialist theories of the mental, and much debate surrounding them (see BEHAVIOURISM, ANALYTIC; FUNCTIONALISM; MATERIALISM IN THE PHILOSOPHY OF MIND; MIND, IDENTITY THEORY OF).

In the field of artificial intelligence, the mind is held to be analogous to computers in so far as it functions as an information-processing entity. Daniel DENNETT has, in a qualified way, argued that information-processing machines are valid models of the mind. In addition to the scientifically informed arguments for various forms of materialism, including nonreductive materialism, the twentieth-century conception of matter as composed of electrons, protons and other subatomic particles has spawned a rich speculative literature that effectively undermines previous forms of materialism. What the late US philosopher of science, Norwood HANSON, called the 'dematerialization' of matter, raises questions concerning what 'materialism' means in terms of the theories of microphysics. Many of the arguments that sustained earlier forms of materialism (including the assumption of causality as universal in nature) have been put in question. The confluence of contemporary theories about the structure and function of the mind and the nature of matter have introduced a complexity of detail and an array of paradoxical claims that make contemporary materialism a welter of intriguing, but conflicting and perplexing, theoretical elements.

See also: MATTER

References and further reading

Armstrong, D.M. (1968) *A Materialist Theory of the Mind*, London: Routledge & Kegan Paul. (Thorough analysis of mind and mental states in terms of central state physicalism.)

* Büchner, L. (1855) *Kraft und Stoff*, Frankfurt: Meidinger; trans. J.F. Collingwood as *Force and Matter*, London: Trübner, 1864. (Popular compendium of the bases of materialism; philosophically unsophisticated, but interesting.)

* Cabinis, J. (1802) *Rapports du physique et du morale de l'homme* (The relationship between the physical and moral aspects of man), Paris. (Cabinis is considered one of the earliest contributors to the science of psychophysics.)

Dennett, D.C. (1978) *Brainstorms: Philosophical Essays in Mind and Psychology*, London: Bradford Books. (Solid treatment of mind conceived of as an information-processing system.)

* Feigl, H. (1958) 'The "Mental" and the "Physical"', in *Minnesota Studies in the Philosophy of Science*, vol. 2, Minneapolis, MN: University of Minnesota Press. (Classic statement of physicalism.)

Gassendi, P. (1658) *Syntagma Philosophicum Epicurus*, The Hague. (Exposition and defence of Epicurus' philosophy, criticizing points that conflict with Catholic teachings.)

Hobbes, T. (1989) *Metaphysical Writings of Thomas Hobbes*, ed. M.W. Calkins, La Salle: Open Court. (Includes Hobbes' views on materialism.)

* Holbach, P.H.D. de (1770) *Système de la nature*, Amsterdam; trans. H.D. Robinson as *The System of Nature*, Boston, MA, 1868. (Excellent presentation of naturalistic materialism which includes interesting criticisms of freedom of the will.)

* La Mettrie, J.O. de (1748) *L'Homme Machine*, Leyden: Elie Luzac Fils; trans. as *Man a Machine*, La Salle, IL: Open Court, 1912. (A physician, La Mettrie presented one of the earliest theories of the physiological bases of a variety of psychic states or a strong version of physiological determinism.)

* Lange, F.A. (1865) *Geschichte des Materialismus*, Iserlohn: J. Baedeker; trans. E.C. Thomas as *The History of Materialism*, London: Routledge & Kegan Paul, 1925. (Thorough, detailed and insightful tracing of the development of materialism up to the 1870s, vitalized by Lange's penetrating insights and valuable commentary.)

Lucretius (1st century BC) *De rerum natura*; trans. W.H.D. Rouse, Cambridge, MA: Harvard University Press 1975. (Powerful philosophic poem which presents the philosophy of Epicurus in a generally accurate and appealing way.)

* Moleschott, J. (1852) *Der Kreislauf des Lebens* (The Cycle of Life), Mainz. (Study of the circular processes of life in nature with interesting observations on the relativity of perception among nonhuman beings and its application to human knowledge.)

Paulsen, F. (1892) *Einleitung in die Philosophie*, Berlin; trans. F. Thilly as *Introduction to Philosophy*, New York: Henry Holt & Co., 1895. (Lucid presentation of materialism as of the late nineteenth century, with Kantian-like critiques of its central claims.)

Smart, J.J.C. (1963) *Philosophy and Scientific Realism*, London: Routledge. (Clear, well-argued defence of a realist interpretation of the scientific world-picture primarily based on physics.)

GEORGE J. STACK

MATERIALISM, DIALECTICAL *see* DIALECTICAL MATERIALISM

MATERIALISM IN THE PHILOSOPHY OF MIND

Materialism – which, for almost all purposes, is the same as physicalism – is the theory that everything that exists is material. Natural science shows that most things are intelligible in material terms, but mind presents problems in at least two ways. The first is consciousness, as found in the 'raw feel' of subjective experience. The second is the intentionality of thought, which is the property of being about something beyond itself; 'aboutness' seems not to be a physical relation in the ordinary sense.

There have been three ways of approaching these problems. The hardest is eliminativism, according to which there are no 'raw feels', no intentionality and, in general, no mental states: the mind and all its furniture are part of an outdated science that we now see to be false. Next is reductionism, which seeks to give an account of our experience and of intentionality in terms which are acceptable to a physical science: this means, in practice, analysing the mind in terms of its role in producing behaviour. Finally, the materialist may accept the reality and irreducibility of mind, but claim that it depends on matter in such an intimate way – more intimate than mere causal dependence – that materialism is not threatened by the irreducibility of

173

mind. The first two approaches can be called 'hard materialism', the third 'soft materialism'.

The problem for eliminativism is that we find it difficult to credit that any belief that we think and feel is a theoretical speculation. Reductionism's main difficulty is that there seems to be more to consciousness than its contribution to behaviour: a robotic machine could behave as we do without thinking or feeling. The soft materialist has to explain supervenience in a way that makes the mind not epiphenomenal without falling into the problems of interactionism.

1 **From epiphenomenalism to functionalism**
2 **Functionalism and consciousness**
3 **Functionalism and matter**
4 **Alternatives to functionalism**
5 **Cognitive science and intentionality**
6 **Materialism and abstract objects**
7 **Materialism at the *fin de siècle***

1 From epiphenomenalism to functionalism

Would-be materialists in the latter part of the nineteenth century tended to be epiphenomenalists. They believed that the world was a physical machine, but felt obliged to concede that examination of its machinery, however minute, could never uncover nor explain consciousness. Consciousness was, therefore, an inexplicable left-over (see EPIPHENOMENALISM). Materialism in the twentieth century has largely been concerned to provide a more integrated form of physicalism. The attempt has taken 'hard' and 'soft' forms.

The source of all forms of contemporary hard materialism is behaviourism, which identifies mental states with facts about how people are disposed to respond to external stimuli (see BEHAVIOURISM, ANALYTIC). The essence of mind is not, therefore, something private to the subject, but something public and observable, a logical product of the relation of stimulus to response. Two fundamental problems plague behaviourism. A phenomenological objection is that we can supposedly tell just from being conscious that experience is more than a mere disposition to behave. A formal objection is that one cannot give necessary and sufficient conditions for being in a given mental state solely in terms of stimulus and response. Behaviourists treated the brain as a 'black box' about which the psychologist must not speculate, but the interdependence of our mental states so complicates the relation of stimulus to response that this relation can only be understood with the aid of a model of our inner workings.

The identity theory of mind, which emerged from Australia in the work of J.J.C. SMART (1959) and

D.M. ARMSTRONG (1968), was designed to cope with both problems (see MIND, IDENTITY THEORY OF). Armstrong accepted that mental states were dispositions, but identified these, not with abstract relations between stimulus and response, but with the states of the brain that tend to be caused by the appropriate stimulus and to cause the relevant behavioural response. This identifies experience with something occurrent and actual as well as with a disposition. Moreover, by identifying the mind with a complex internal neural structure, it allows mental states to be specified, *not* by any direct relation to stimulus and response but by a complex profile that relates them to stimulus, response *and* all the other mental states that might interact or interfere with their operation.

This theory was influenced by the development of computers and artificial intelligence (see ARTIFICIAL INTELLIGENCE). At first, identity theorists had tended to adopt *type identity*, according to which pain, or imagining the Eiffel Tower, would be identical with the same kind of brain state in every creature with these mental states. It was then argued both that such type identity was implausible and that it was not necessary: just as the same programme can be run on different hardware, the same network of causal relations that constitute the mind could be realized in differently built brains. This is the theory known as functionalism, according to which there is, at most, a token identity between brain and mental states; that is, each mental state is identical with some brain state or other (see FUNCTIONALISM). Some functionalists prefer to weaken the relation further by talking of the mind being *realized in* the brain rather than being identical to it.

2 Functionalism and consciousness

Functionalism is, therefore, either with or without token identity, that development from – or, perhaps, that developed form of – behaviourism, which is designed to give serious weight to inner processes. However, it faces many problems. It is questionable whether functionalism is phenomenologically any better than normal behaviourism. This doubt is expressed in a group of qualia problems, such as the 'inverted qualia' and 'absent qualia' problems. But the essence of 'qualia' worries seems to have become distilled in the 'knowledge argument' (see QUALIA). Take someone lacking a certain sensible capacity from birth – they are completely deaf, for example. Suppose, too, that they have learned all that a completed physical science could tell them about the physical processes and the functional organization of the hearing mechanism: call them 'the Deaf Scientist'. Third, suppose that they then gain their hearing. They would then gain some new knowledge, namely *what it is like to hear*, or *what sound is experientially like*. As they knew all the physical and functional information before, this kind of knowledge must concern something over and above the physical and functional; so the content of experience is something over and above the physical and functional.

Various strategies can be tried against this argument. First, one might argue that if the Deaf Scientist really did know all the physical and computational information about how hearing worked, they would know what sounds sound like. But this seems wrong, because a deaf person could not work this out from current science – more of the same physical and computational information (or the same in greater detail, which could be what a completed science gives), does not seem to be the right kind of thing to tell you what the actual experience of hearing is like. So, second, one might argue that what the formerly Deaf Scientist acquires when they find out what sound sounds like is not new knowledge, but a new way of getting a kind of knowledge they already possess; perception and science give you the same information, one directly through the senses, the other in a propositional form. So the difference is like that between getting the information that Tom is bald by seeing him and getting it by reading about him. But neither does this seem right, for though the Deaf Scientist does indeed acquire a new way of getting knowledge when they gain their hearing, they also gain knowledge of what it is like to hear. If this is not to be new knowledge, it would have to be just the same knowledge as they have as a scientist when they know about the relevant brain process, and this it does not seem to be.

At least it is clear that the knowledge they gain by hearing is not cast in the same neurological terms as the scientific information they already knew, so at least new concepts are involved. Does this imply that new information is acquired? It has been suggested that the necessity for different concepts need not mean that what is being presented are different properties of, or different facts about, the world. The same property or situation is presented in different ways, as when two concepts have the same property as reference while having different senses (for example, 'blue' and 'the colour of the sky' present the same feature of the world). But unless there is some reductive analysis of how the mental concepts capture the physical properties, such as the functionalist would provide, it is difficult to see why there should be need for new concepts to capture experience, unless it were that they captured different properties from those caught by the physical vocabulary.

Adopting a functionalist account of the mentalistic concepts that actual hearing calls into play is equivalent to admitting that the Deaf Scientist acquires only a kind of 'knowledge how' on coming to hear – that is, they come to be able to respond directly to sounds. This toughly neo-behaviourist view is sometimes seemingly alleviated by saying that what the Deaf Scientist comes to learn is how to imagine, or how to remember, the experience. This does not appear too harshly reductive, for what they come to be able to do does not appear to be mere behaviour. But that is only because we still need an account of the mentalistic notions of imaging, and of remembering what an experience was like: taking images (memory or otherwise) as basic is no different from taking 'raw feels' as basic. But if these notions are treated in functionalist terms, being finally explained in terms of an ability to say and outwardly do certain things, then the response has become totally reductive and will not convince anyone who thought there was a problem for the functionalist in the first place.

3   Functionalism and matter

It is a largely unexamined assumption of late twentieth-century materialists that the concept of matter, unlike that of mind, is unproblematic. Some philosophers, however, have followed Russell and argued that the conception of the physical world given to us by science is purely functional and formal; science, that is, tells us nothing about the intrinsic nature of anything, only about its behaviour and how to quantify it, and that this alone is an inadequate conception. Qualitative content is given to our conception of the world from the qualia presented in perception, and without that there would be no non-relational and non-formal content to our conception of the world. But functionalism denies that qualia are given in experience and presents the same kind of purely relational conception of experiential states as physical science does of the physical world. If functionalism is correct, we are stuck with a conception of the world which is entirely relational, with no intrinsic content to any of the relata. This may be an incoherent conception.

4   Alternatives to functionalism

One response to the problems faced by these reductive styles of materialism is to abandon the attempt to reduce mental properties and to admit a *dualism* of properties, while prescribing that the mental *supervenes* on the physical in such a tight way that the spirit of materialism is preserved (see SUPER-VENIENCE). This tightness would mean that the dependence was more than merely causal, without being analytic, in the way a reductive account would require.

The first problem this theory faces is to give a proper rationale for supervenience. The provision of a simple definition is easy: the mental supervenes on the physical if there cannot be a mental difference or change without a physical difference or change, and the 'cannot' depends on something stronger than a natural law. The problem comes in explaining what this stronger-than-natural necessity is, and why one should believe in it. No generally acceptable account of this seems to have been found. Furthermore, the question remains of whether the matter of the brain is influenced in its behaviour by the supervenient mind. If it is, then the physical system is being influenced by something not itself physical, and this is a species of interactionism. If it is not influenced, then the mind is an epiphenomenon. However, twentieth-century materialism had sought to avoid both interactionism of this kind and epiphenomenalism (see EPIPHENOMENALISM).

There is another and entirely opposite response to the difficulties of functionalism in accommodating the apparent data of thought and experience, and that is to deny that there are any such data. Various traditions came together to bear exotic fruit: the pragmatist doctrine that one should believe whatever is most convenient overall; the post-positivist tendency to deny the distinction between observation and theory; Wittgenstein's polemic against private data, produce the doctrine that nothing is so plainly revealed in everyday experience that it cannot be overridden by requirements of scientific elegance. Even the seemingly most obvious facts of experience are actually theoretical speculations and can be denied if science is thereby made easier (see ELIMINATIVISM; PRAGMATISM; PRIVATE LANGUAGE ARGUMENT).

Two conceptions of theory seem to be operating in such eliminativism, and they may not always be clearly distinguished. According to one, a theory is any generalization that can be used to provide explanations; according to the other, a theory is something not so blatantly obvious as to be free from revision. This latter, of course, goes naturally with the observation–theory distinction that the eliminativist rejects. But there are many explanatory principles that are totally beyond revision; for example, that wood generally floats, that pigs cannot fly and that cutting off someone's head kills them. Any higher-order theory that contradicted any of these would be false. Perhaps the use of the term 'folk psychology' to characterize our normal psychological generalizations makes them seem more like folklore – more like the belief that comfrey boiled in holy water relieves

rheumatism – than they are like the belief that pigs cannot fly. It seems plausible, however, that the law that we shout out because of pain, or eat because we feel hungry, belongs more with the pigs than the comfrey.

5 Cognitive science and intentionality

The development of Artificial Intelligence tended to switch philosophers' attention from sensation to cognition and, hence, to intentionality. The assumption has been that human behaviour is driven by computational activity in the brain. Two kinds of question have been raised. The first concerns the relation between this computation and the ordinary psychological explanations that we give of behaviour – rather coyly described as 'folk psychology' (see §4 above; FOLK PSYCHOLOGY; REDUCTIONISM IN THE PHILOSOPHY OF MIND). The other is more directly concerned with the problem intentionality poses for materialism. The language of a computer program works entirely as a formal syntax, and brain states, considered simply as biochemical, have no intrinsic meaning; how, then, does neural computation come to have semantic content? Everyone seems to agree that it must be in virtue of the functional relations inner representations have to their typical causes and their behavioural effects, possibly considered in relation to the wider environment and the evolutionary process that produced them (see FUNCTIONALISM §7). The details of this functional account are disputed, but the main problem is that it is entirely externalist (see CONTENT: WIDE AND NARROW). If one thinks of consciousness as something that goes on 'in the head', and that one's own consciousness of one's thoughts is consciousness of one's internal representations, and if those representations have meaning because of the *external* relations they stand in to the world outside the head, then it looks as if consciousness will not reveal to one the contents of any of one's thoughts, nor, indeed, of any kind of mental representation. For all purposes, we will be in the situation of Searle in his 'Chinese room', inspecting symbols we do not understand (see CHINESE ROOM ARGUMENT).

Tyler Burge (1988) has tried to answer this objection to externalism. He says that the holding of the external relations is an *enabling condition* for the representation to have meaning, but that knowing something – in this case the meaning – does not involve explicit knowledge of all the enabling conditions. So we can know the contents of our own thoughts although we do not know the relations that give them their content. The problem with this reply is that, although it is true that we do not, in general, need to know all the things that make something possible in order to know the thing itself, the external relations seem not to be just enabling conditions, but to constitute the content itself. Searle's thought experiment seems to show how ignorance of them actually constitutes ignorance of the meaning of the representations.

6 Materialism and abstract objects

Although materialists are mainly concerned with problems that flow from the philosophy of mind, abstract objects constitute a much less discussed but serious problem. If one believes that it is an irreducible fact that there are any or all of numbers, universals, properties, sets or propositions, then one believes there are things which are not material particulars. It might be that one did not mind adding such light baggage as abstract objects to one's otherwise materialist ontology; but if there are such things as universals and propositions, it looks as if they must enter intimately into our thinking, or, if numbers, into our counting. This would then create a problem for giving a materialist account of these activities, and so accepting abstract objects might have consequences for the philosophy of mind (see ABSTRACT OBJECTS).

7 Materialism at the *fin de siècle*

The materialist mood in the twentieth century has been poised between an almost triumphalist self-confidence and a more modest perplexity. The triumphalism is produced by the success of science, which makes materialism seem obviously true. In this mood, materialists are prepared to deny what seem to be the most obvious facts of mental life if their theory requires it. In a more sombre moment, however, some will confess that all attempts to tackle the problems have so far missed the mark. This more sober tendency became stronger in the 1980s and 1990s. *Nagel (1974)* had already declared that the mind–body problem could only be solved by a conceptual breakthrough we could not, as yet, imagine. *McGinn (1991)* pronounced the problem insoluble in principle because the mind cannot understand itself. *Galen Strawson (1994)* has denied that there is any conceptual connection between mind and behaviour. All these philosophers deem themselves to be materialists, of some not-yet-quite-articulable kind. The *Journal of Consciousness Studies* has been set up to 'take consciousness seriously' in a way it is said science has not so far done; but perhaps this underestimates the main reason why consciousness has been sidelined and treated harshly: namely because it seems so clearly impossible to say anything constructive about it within the materialist presuppositions of natural science.

References and further reading

* Armstrong, D.M. (1968) *A Materialist Theory of the Mind*, London: Routledge & Kegan Paul. (A classic – full of lucid philosophical argument.)
* Burge, T. (1988) 'Individualism and self-knowledge', *Journal of Philosophy* 85 (11): 649–63. (One of a series of pieces by Burge defending externalism. In this one he makes wide use of the notion of enabling conditions.)
Churchland, P.M. (1984) *Matter and Consciousness*, Cambridge, MA: MIT Press, 2nd edn. (An excellent general account of all the basic 'isms'.)
—— (1989) *A Neurocomputational Perspective*, Cambridge MA: MIT Press. (The most thorough-going and consistent eliminativist collection of papers.)
Dennett, D. (1990) *Consciousness Explained*, Harmondsworth: Penguin. (The opposite pole to Armstrong in philosophical style; an entertaining and provocative attempt to use science to bypass the philosophical problems.)
Foster, J. (1991) *The Immaterial Self*, London, Routledge. (A powerful attack on all forms of materialism.)
Hale, B. (1987) *Abstract Objects*, Oxford, Blackwell. (A defence of the irreducibility of abstract objects.)
Jackson, F. (1982) 'Epiphenomenal Qualia', *Philosophical Quarterly* 32 (127): 27–36. (The classic source for the 'knowledge argument'.)
Lockwood, M. (1989) *Mind, Brain and the Quantum*, Oxford, Blackwell. (Is worried by the purely relational scientific conception of matter and makes a serious attempt to rehabilitate Russellian neutral monism as a means to saving materialism. Excellent account of modern science.)
* McGinn, C. (1991) *The Problem of Consciousness*, Cambridge, MA and Oxford: Blackwell. (Chapter 1 contains the author's reason for thinking that the mind–body problem is insoluble. He argues, however, that this is not a disturbing conclusion.)
* Nagel, T. (1974) 'What is it like to be a bat?', *Philosophical Review* 83 (4): 435–50. (This article achieved great fame by elegantly reminding US philosophers that there was such a thing as subjectivity.)
Papineau, D. (1993) *Philosophical Naturalism*, Oxford: Blackwell. (This contains a well-worked-out version of the teleological-cum-evolutionary theory of representation.)
Robinson, H. (1982) *Matter and Sense*, Cambridge: Cambridge University Press. (A general critique of

materialism. Chapter 7 is concerned with problems in the concept of matter, especially the relational versions to which materialists seem forced.)

* Searle, J. (1980) 'Minds, brains and programs', *Behavioural and Brain Sciences* 3 (3): 417–24. (Contains the 'Chinese room' argument, followed by criticisms and a reply.)

—— (1992) *The Rediscovery of the Mind*, Cambridge, MA and London: MIT Press. (A lucid statement of the view that the emergence of mind is not a problem for materialism, because emergence occurs at all levels in nature.)

Shoemaker, S. (1984) *Identity, Cause and Mind*, Cambridge: Cambridge University Press. (Perhaps the most rigorous development of analytical functionalism. Chapters 10 and 11 defend the view that *all* properties are individuated causally.)

* Smart, J.J.C. (1959) 'Sensations and brain processes', *Philosophical Review* 68 (2): 141–56. (Important for popularizing the idea that awareness of one's own experience is grasping an inner state *topic neutrally*, under the aspect of its causal relations to a stimulus.)

Smith, A.D. (1993) 'Non-reductive physicalism?', in H. Robinson (ed.) *Objections to Physicalism*, Oxford: Clarendon Press, 225–50. (A clear discussion of the problems of supervenience and of the emergence of the kind favoured by Searle.)

* Strawson, G. (1994) *Mental Reality*, Cambridge, MA: MIT Press; London: Bradford Books. (An onslaught against any supposed conceptual connection between minds and behaviour.)

HOWARD ROBINSON

MATERIALISM, INDIAN SCHOOL OF

'Materialism' stands here for the Sanskrit term Lokāyata, the most common designation for the materialistic school of classical Indian philosophy. However, at the outset 'materialism' and 'Lokāyata' were not equivalent: early materialistic doctrines were not associated with Lokāyata, and early Lokāyata was neither materialistic nor even a philosophical school.

Classical Lokāyata stands apart from all other Indian philosophical traditions due to its denial of ethical and metaphysical doctrines such as karmic retribution, life after death, and liberation. Its ontology, tailored to support this challenge, allows only four material elements and their various combinations. Further support comes from Lokāyata epistemology: the validity of inference and Scriptures is denied and perception is held to be the only means of valid cognition. As offshoots, a fully fledged scepticism and a theory of limited validity of inference developed in response to criticism by other philosophers. Consistent with Lokāyata ontology and epistemology, its ethics centres on the criticism of all religious and moral ideals which presuppose invisible agents and an afterlife. Hostile sources depict its followers as promulgating unrestricted hedonism.

1 Sources
2 Lokāyata in early sources
3 Early materialists
4 The classical materialistic philosophy

1 Sources

With the single exception of Jayarāśi's *Tattvopaplavasiṃha*, no original Lokāyata works have survived. Our knowledge of Lokāyata is based mainly on fragments and references in often hostile and polemic Brahmanical, Buddhist and Jaina sources. Of the basic text of the materialistic Lokāyata, the *Bṛhaspatisūtra*, only a few fragments remain. Therefore doxographies are of particular importance for our impression of the philosophical system as a whole. Unfortunately, it is not certain to what extent these and other sources represent genuine Lokāyata doctrines. As it was the only philosophical school to deny rebirth and karmic retribution, it was criticized by all other schools. However, many of these refutations are perfunctory and do not add substantially to our knowledge.

2 Lokāyata in early sources

In the earliest references, found in the Buddhist Pāli canon (first committed to writing in the first century BC), Lokāyata designates a Brahmanical branch of learning concerned with the examination of fundamental statements about the nature of the world (equally called *lokāyata*). The *Saṃyuttanikāya* of the Pāli canon mentions four *lokāyatas*: (1) All exists; (2) All does not exist; (3) All is unity; (4) All is severalty. Such pairs of theses and antitheses were topics of public philosophical debate. A later Mahāyāna text, the *Laṅkāvatārasūtra*, mentions no fewer than thirty-one *lokāyatas* on topics such as the world, the soul, life after death, liberation (*mokṣa*), momentariness, space, the state between death and birth, and ignorance, desire and karma as causes of the world. Some of them are easily recognized as points of debate among various Hīnayāna Buddhist schools. A connection to materialism is not evident in these sources, nor in another early reference, in the *Arthaśāstra*, which subsumes Lokāyata under those branches of learning which proceed by or are concerned with reasoned investigation (see KAUṬILYA). By the second century BC there existed a Lokāyata commentary of unknown content by a certain Bhāguri.

3 Early materialists

The ascetic Ajita Keśakambala (Ajita Kesakambali) was a renowned teacher and contemporary of the Buddha, nicknamed after a blanket made of hair (keśakambala) which kept him hot in summer and cold in winter. He maintained that man consists of the four elements earth, water, fire and wind, and that after death his constituents return to the respective elementary mass: what is of earth goes to earth, what is of water to water, and so on; his senses join space. There is no afterlife. Thus sacrificial and moral works, good or bad, do not bear any fruit.

Materialism flourished also at kingly courts. Both the Jaina and Buddhist canons report the views and gruesome experiments of King Paesi (Pāyāsi), who argued that if the soul were different from the body and if a person's fate after death depended on deeds in this life, deceased relatives could be expected to come back from the other world to warn and admonish those left behind. He once had a thief condemned to death put into a hermetically sealed and guarded jar. The prisoner was found dead after a while and the escape of a soul was not observed. On another occasion, Paesi had an executed thief placed in a sealed jar. The jar was later found full of worms, although their souls could not have entered it. Weighing immediately before and after death and dissection of bodies did not yield evidence for the existence of a soul.

It is noteworthy that both the legendary founder of Lokāyata and the founder of a school of political science (arthaśāstra) bear the name Bṛhaspati. It is quite possible, though not yet provable, that Indian materialism developed in kingly and state administration circles as an alternative worldview counterbalancing that of the priestly class.

4 The classical materialistic philosophy

From at least as far back as the sixth century AD onwards, Lokāyata is referred to as a materialistic philosophical school. Its followers, the Lokāyatas or Lokāyatikas/Laukāyatikas, are also called Bārhaspatyas (followers of Bṛhaspati) and Cārvākas. These terms seem to apply only to the followers, not to the school itself. Some modern authors assume a subdivision into 'well-instructed' (suśikṣita) and 'cunning' (dhūrta) Cārvākas; however, both appellations refer mockingly to the Cārvāka philosopher

Udbhaṭa. The designation nāstika (nihilist, one who says '... does not exist') is also applied to the materialists. This broader term is used for those who deny life after death, the efficacy of sacrifices and moral deeds, and so on, as well as for those who do not accept the authority of the Veda. The latter usage includes not only materialists, but also Buddhists and Jainas.

Ontology. According to the Bṛhaspatisūtra, there are four 'great' elements, earth, water, fire and wind, although some Lokāyatikas accepted space/'ether' as a fifth element (see MATTER, INDIAN CONCEPTIONS OF §1). Certain Lokāyatikas may have admitted the existence of atoms; the majority, however, denied both atoms and space because they are not perceptible. The world in all its diversity is only the result of various combinations of the material elements. There is no determinative principle, such as God or karma, which is responsible for the properties of things. They are due to their own nature; no agent makes fire hot or water cool. Lokāyata causality operates with material causes only, and efficient causes are not recognized (see CAUSATION, INDIAN THEORIES OF §2).

The theory of elements formed the basis for various Lokāyata doctrines of the arising of consciousness. As stated by the Bṛhaspatisūtra, consciousness arises from the elements just as the power of intoxication arises from molasses and other substances when a fermenting agent is added. In other words, when certain material substances are mixed something new emerges, be it consciousness or the power of intoxication, that was not there before and could not be produced by these substances severally. The mixture conducive to the production of consciousness is obtained when the elements are transformed into the form of a body. Later Lokāyatikas, such as Kambalāśvatara, refined this theory by assuming further causal factors that support the body in the production of consciousness, notably the vital breaths and the senses. Strong criticism finally led some Lokāyatikas, probably including Udbhaṭa, to abandon the doctrine that consciousness arises from matter and to conceive it as a different entity. Consequently they admitted that consciousness arises only from consciousness and for the sake of, rather than from, the elements; this reverses the relationship between matter and consciousness as conceived in Sāṅkhya, according to which primordial matter evolves for the sake of consciousness (see SĀṄKHYA §§2, 6). However, these Lokāyatikas did not accept any doctrine of rebirth, but claimed that the consciousness of the new-born arises from that of the parents.

Lokāyata ontology seems to be largely subordinated to the school's ethical agenda. The main aim of all theories of elements and consciousness is to deny rebirth and thereby to destroy the cornerstone of Brahmanical, Buddhist and Jaina socio-religious and ethical ideals that presuppose karmic retribution over many lives (see KARMA AND REBIRTH, INDIAN CONCEPTIONS OF).

Epistemology. Indian epistemological doctrines centre on the pivotal concept of means of valid cognition (*pramāṇa*) (see EPISTEMOLOGY, INDIAN SCHOOLS OF §2; KNOWLEDGE, INDIAN VIEWS OF §§1–2). Lokāyata claims that there is only one means of valid cognition: sensory perception. Other means, such as inference and verbal testimony, especially Scriptures, are considered invalid. Undoubtedly their rejection has the purpose of refuting the foundation of social and ethical doctrines in any divine or supernatural power.

The inherent difficulties in this initial Lokāyata position were not immediately apparent. However, once epistemological issues became prominent in Indian philosophy (*circa* fifth century AD), the Lokāyatikas found themselves embarrassed over the justification of their single means of valid cognition. As all other means are denied, perception has to establish itself, which would involve a *petitio principii*, or not be established at all. Further, it became clear that the theory of four elements could not be established by perception alone; also, the denial of an eternal soul, karma and rebirth, or in fact any denial, cannot be arrived at without some form of reasoning.

At least four responses can be discerned to these challenges. Some Lokāyatikas retained the old doctrine, but developed new arguments against inference. By self-destructive logic they tried to prove that all inferences are invalid. For instance, what is the object of the paradigmatic inference from smoke to fire? If it is the universal 'fire-ness', the inference proves what is already proved, since the universal 'fire-ness' was already known before. If, on the other hand, a particular fire is to be proved, the inference fails because the required concomitance does not obtain between the universal 'smoke-ness' and a particular fire. Another response was to grant inference limited validity to avoid the difficulties of the initial position. A philosopher called Purandara claimed that the Cārvākas also admit inferences, but only those that are well known in everyday practice, such as the one from smoke to fire. Inferences meant to establish nonperceptible entities like God or a soul are rejected. To justify only limited use of inference, Purandara emphasized that inference is not an independent means, but depends on perception and therefore cannot transgress the scope of perception. A third response led to the acknowledgement of the indefensibility of perception and a coherent sceptical position. Jayarāśi, whose *Tattvopaplavasiṃha* is the only surviving Lokāyata text, preferred to give up perception rather than to admit the validity of inference. Epistemologically this position is irrefutable, but a high price has to be paid for it. If no means of valid cognition is accepted, the Lokāyata theories of elements and consciousness can no longer be maintained. Jayarāśi accepted this consequence and reinterpreted these doctrines of the *Bṛhaspatisūtra* as the opinions of an opponent that have to be rejected in the final analysis. As an anonymous fragment puts it, the sole purpose of the *sūtras* of Bṛhaspati is to question the opinions of others, and not to establish anything. As a fourth response, Udbhaṭa claimed that the number and characteristics of means of valid cognition cannot be determined. To substantiate his view he adduced examples of knowledge which cannot be derived from any of the recognized means of valid cognition.

Ethics. We are better informed about what Lokāyata condemns than what it prescribes. Many of the reported statements are directed against the efficacy of sacrifices. For instance, if the sacrificed animal goes to heaven, why does the sacrificer not put his own father in its place? The entire Vedic ritual is but a scheme of the Brahmans to make an easy living. Further statements on ethical issues are equally based on the denial of what is imperceptible, notably a transmigrating entity different from the body, an afterlife and the results of one's moral deeds. Thus, among the four 'aims of life' the Lokāyatikas admit only one: pleasure. Sometimes they also consider wealth, as a means to pleasure, to be a legitimate goal; however, the religious and soteriological aims, *dharma* and liberation (*mokṣa*), are always denied (see DUTY AND VIRTUE, INDIAN CONCEPTIONS OF §§1–3). No merit or demerit accrues from one's actions; there is neither heaven nor hell and death is the ultimate release. Accordingly, the Lokāyatikas are often described as hedonists. As long as one lives, they say, one should live happily. One should eat meat, drink spirits and indulge in sexual pleasures. That people have an unequal share of pleasure and pain is not due to any unseen force like karma, but to the different capacities of things caused by different combinations of the elements, just as bubbles on the ocean display a diversity of size, hue and duration.

References and further reading

Chattopadhyaya, D.P. in collaboration with Gangopadhyaya, M.K. (eds) (1990) *Cārvāka/Lokāyata*, New Delhi: Indian Council of Philosophical Research, in association with Ṛddhi-India, Calcutta.

(Although most of the materials published here have been published before, this convenient source book contains a good selection of translations concerning classical Indian materialism, as well as studies by modern scholars.)

Frauwallner, E. (1956) *Geschichte der indischen Philosophie* (History of Indian Philosophy), Reihe Wort und Antwort 6/II, Salzburg: Otto Müller Verlag, 295–309. (A clear and careful presentation of early materialism; contains a summary of the story of King Paesi.)

* Jayarāśi (*c* 800) *Tattvopaplavasiṃha*, first half trans. E. Franco, *Perception, Knowledge and Disbelief: A Study of Jayarāśi's Scepticism*, Wiesbaden: Franz Steiner, 1987; Delhi: Motilal Banarsidass, 2nd edn, 1994. (Contains parallel Sanskrit text and English translation of the first half of the *Tattvopaplavasiṃha* with copious notes.)

Jayatilleke, K.N. (1963) *Early Buddhist Theory of Knowledge*, London: George Allen & Unwin; repr. Delhi: Motilal Banarsidass, 1980. (Chapter 1 contains a good discussion of early Lokāyata, especially as referred to in the Pāli canon, but also in later texts such as the *Laṅkāvatārasūtra*. Sharp and justified criticism of previous scholarship, but uncritical acceptance of the interpretation of Lokāyata by late Pāli commentaries as 'the science of casuistry' (*vitaṇḍa-sattha*).)

MacQueen, G. (1988) *A Study of the Śrāmaṇyaphalasūtra*, Wiesbaden: Otto Harrassowitz. (Remarkable for its methodology, this study contains a convincing attempt to determine which heretical views belong to which heretical teachers, notably Ajita Keśakambala, on the basis of Pāli, Tibetan and Chinese versions.)

Namai, M. (1976) 'A Survey of Bārhaspatya Philosophy', *Indological Review* 2: 29–74; revised and enlarged in Chishō Namai, *Rinne no ronshō* (The Establishment of Rebirth), Osaka: Tōhō Shuppan, 1996, 561–5, 1–52. (Contains the best compilation to date of *Bṛhaspatisūtra* and other Lokāyata fragments. *Rinne no ronshō* includes further articles, mainly in Japanese, on the controversy between Buddhists and materialists about rebirth; Chishō is Professor Namai's monastic name.)

Purandara (*c.* 7th/8th century) *Paurandarasūtra*, trans. E. Franco, 'Paurandarasūtra', in M.A. Dhaky (ed.) *Pt Dalsukhbhai Malvania Felicitation Volume*, Aspects of Jainology 3, Varanasi: P.V. Research Institute, 1991, vol. 1: 154–63. (Only two fragments of this work of uncertain title survive. Franco's essay contains a new interpretation of them on the basis of Jaina sources. For a different interpretation, compare Solomon's study of Udbhaṭa.)

Solomon, E. (1977–8) 'Bhaṭṭa Udbhaṭa', *Annals of the Bhandarkar Oriental Research Institute*, 58–9: 985–92. (A reliable study of one of the most original Lokāyata philosophers.)

ELI FRANCO
KARIN PREISENDANZ

MATHEMATICS, FOUNDATIONS OF

Conceived of philosophically, the foundations of mathematics concern various metaphysical and epistemological problems raised by mathematical practice, its results and applications. Most of these problems are of ancient vintage; two, in particular, have been of perennial concern. These are its richness of content and its necessity. Important too, though not so prominent in the history of the subject, is the problem of application, or how to account for the fact that mathematics has given rise to such an extensive, important and varied body of applications in other disciplines.

The Greeks struggled with these questions. So, too, did various medieval and modern thinkers. The ideas of many of these continue to influence foundational thinking to the present day.

During the nineteenth and twentieth centuries, however, the most influential ideas have been those of Kant. In one way or another and to a greater or lesser extent, the main currents of foundational thinking during this period – the most active and fertile period in the entire history of the subject – are nearly all attempts to reconcile Kant's foundational ideas with various later developments in mathematics and logic.

These developments include, chiefly, the nineteenth-century discovery of non-Euclidean geometries, the vigorous development of mathematical logic, the development of rigorous axiomatizations of geometry, the arithmetization of analysis and the discovery (by Dedekind and Peano) of an axiomatization of arithmetic. The first is perhaps the most important. It led to widespread acceptance of the idea that space was not merely a Kantian 'form' of intuition, but had an independence from our intellect that made it different in kind from arithmetic. This asymmetry between geometry and arithmetic became a major premise of more than one of the main 'isms' of twentieth-century philosophy of mathematics. The intuitionists retained Kant's conception of arithmetic and took the same view of that part of geometry which could be reduced to arithmetic. The logicists maintained arithmetic to be 'analytic' but differed

181

over their view of geometry. Hilbert's formalist view endorsed a greater part of Kant's conception.

The second development carried logic to a point well beyond where it had been in Kant's day and suggested that his views on the nature of mathematics were in part due to the relatively impoverished state of his logic. The third indicated that geometry could be completely formalized and that intuition was therefore not needed for the sake of conducting inferences within proofs. The fourth and fifth, finally, provided for the codification of a large part of classical mathematics – namely analysis and its neighbours – within a single axiomatic system – namely (second-order) arithmetic. This confirmed the views of those (for example, the intuitionists and the logicists) who believed that arithmetic had a special centrality within human thinking. It also provided a clear reductive target for such later anti-Kantian enterprises as Russell's logicism.

The major movements in the philosophy of mathematics during this period all drew strength from post-Kantian developments in mathematics and logic. Each, however, also encountered serious difficulties soon after gaining initial momentum. Frege's logicism was defeated by Russell's paradox; Russell's logicism, in turn, made use of such questionable (from a logicist standpoint) items as the axioms of infinity and reduction. Both logicism and Hilbert's formalist programme came under heavy attack from Gödel's incompleteness theorems. And finally, intuitionism suffered from its inability to produce a body of mathematics comparable in richness to classical mathematics.

Despite the failure of these non-Kantian programmes, however, movement away from Kant continued in the mid- and late twentieth century. From the 1930s on this has been driven mainly by a revival of empiricist and naturalist ideas in philosophy, prominent in the writings of both the logical empiricists and the later influential work of Quine, Putnam and Benacerraf. This continues as perhaps the major force shaping work in the philosophy of mathematics.

1 Kant's views; reactions

The 'Problematik' that KANT established for the epistemology of pure mathematics focused on the reconciliation of two apparently incompatible features of pure mathematics: (1) the problem of necessity, or how to explain the apparent fact that mathematical statements (for example, statements such as that $1 + 1 = 2$ or that the sum of the interior angles of a Euclidean triangle is equal to two right angles) should appear to be not only true but necessarily true and independent of empirical evidence; and (2) the problem of cognitive richness, or how to account for the fact that pure mathematics should yield subjects as rich and deep in content and method, as robust in growth and as replete with surprising discoveries as the history of mathematics demonstrates.

In mathematics, Kant said, we find a 'great and established branch of knowledge' – a cognitive domain so 'wonderfully large' and with promise of such 'unlimited future extension' that it would appear to arise from sources other than those of pure unaided (human) reason (1783: §§6, 7). At the same time, it carries with it a certainty or necessity that is typical of judgments of pure reason. The problem, then, is to explain these apparently conflicting characteristics. Kant's explanation was that mathematical knowledge arises from certain standing conditions or 'forms' which shape our experience of space and time – forms which, though they are part of the innate cognitive apparatus that we bring to experience, none the less shape our experience in a way that goes beyond mere logical processing.

To elaborate this hypothesis, Kant sorted judgments/propositions in two different ways: first, according to whether they required appeal to sensory experience for their justification; and, second, according to whether their predicate concepts were 'contained in' their subject concepts. A judgment or proposition was 'a priori' if it could be justified without appeal to sensory content. If not, it was 'a posteriori'. It was 'analytic' if the very act of *thinking* the subject concept contained, as a constituent part, the *thinking* of the predicate concept. If not, it was either false or 'synthetic'. In synthetic a priori judgment – the type of judgment Kant regarded as characteristic of mathematics – the predicate concept was thought not through the mere *thinking* of the subject concept, but through its 'construction in intuition'. He took a similar view of mathematical inference, believing it to involve an intuition that goes beyond the mere logical connection of premises and conclusions (1781/1787: A713–19/B741–7).

Kant erected his mathematical epistemology upon these distinctions and, famously, maintained that mathematical judgment and inference is synthetic a priori in character. In this way, he intended to account for both the necessity and cognitive richness of mathematics, its necessity reflecting its a priority, its cognitive richness its syntheticity.

Kant applied this basic outlook to both arithmetic and geometry (and also to pure mechanics). He did not regard them as entirely identical, however, since he saw them as resting on different a priori intuitions.

Neither did he see them as possessing precisely the same universality (1781/1787: A163–5, 170–1, 717, 734/B204–6, 212, 745, 762). None the less, he regarded their similarities as more important than their differences and therefore took them to be of essentially the same epistemic type – namely, synthetic a priori. In the end, it was this inclusion of geometry and arithmetic within the same basic epistemic type rather than his more central claim concerning the *existence* of synthetic a priori knowledge that gave rise to the sternest challenges to his views.

In the decades following the publication of the first *Critique* (1781/1787), the principal source of concern regarding its views was the growing evidence for and eventual discovery of non-Euclidean geometries. This led many to question whether geometry and arithmetic are of the same basic epistemic character.

The serious possibility of non-Euclidean geometries went back to the work of Lambert and others in the eighteenth century. Building on this work, some – in particular, Gauss (1817, 1829) – stated their opposition to Kant's views even before the actual discovery of non-Euclidean geometries by Bolyai and Lobachevskii in the 1820s. Gauss' reasoning was essentially this: number seems to be purely a product of the intellect and, so, something of which we can have purely a priori knowledge. Space, on the other hand, seems to have a reality external to our minds that prohibits a purely a priori knowledge of it. Arithmetic and geometry are therefore not on an epistemological par with one another.

This reasoning became a potent force shaping nineteenth- and twentieth-century foundational thinking. Another such force was the dramatic development of logic and the axiomatic method in the mid- to late nineteenth century and early twentieth century. This included the introduction of algebraic methods by Boole and De Morgan, the improved treatment of relations by Peirce, Schröder and Peano, the replacement of the subject–predicate conception of propositional form with Frege's more fecund functional conception, and the advances in axiomatization and formalization brought about by the work of Frege, Pasch, Peano, Hilbert and (especially) Whitehead and Russell.

Certain developments in mathematics proper also exerted an influence. Chief among these were the arithmetization of analysis by Weierstrass, Dedekind and others, and the axiomatization of arithmetic by Peano and Dedekind. Of somewhat lesser importance, though still significant for their effects on Hilbert's thinking, were Einstein's relativistic ideas in physics.

2 Intuitionism

A variety of views concerning the asymmetry of geometry and arithmetic emerged in the late nineteenth and early twentieth centuries. That of the early intuitionists Brouwer and Weyl retained Kant's synthetic a priori conception of arithmetic.

They responded to the discovery of non-Euclidean geometries, however, by denying the a priori status of that part of geometry that could not be reduced to arithmetic by such means as Descartes' calculus of coordinates. They retained, none the less, a type of a priori intuition of time as the basis for arithmetical knowledge (see Brouwer 1913: 127–8). They also emphasized the synthetic character of arithmetical judgment and inference, and sharply distinguished them from logical judgment and inference.

Brouwer described his intuition of time as consciousness of change *per se* – the human subject's primordial inner awareness of the 'falling apart' of a life-moment into a part that is passing away and a part that is becoming. He believed that, via a process of abstraction, one could pass from this basal intuition of time to a concept of 'bare two-oneness', and from this concept to, first, the finite ordinals, then the transfinite ordinals and, finally, the linear continuum. In this way, parts of classical arithmetic, analysis and set theory could be recaptured intuitionistically. (See Brouwer 1907: 61, 97; 1913: 127, 131–2.)

Brouwer thus modified Kant's intuitional basis for mathematics. He also modified his conception of knowledge of existence. Kant believed that humans could obtain knowledge of existence only through sensible intuition. Only this, he believed, had the type of involuntariness and objectivity that assures us that belief in an object is not a mere compulsion or idiosyncrasy of our subjective selves. Like the post-Kantian romantic idealists, however, Brouwer (and Weyl, too) believed as well in knowledge of existence via a kind of 'intellectual intuition' – an intuition carried by a purely internal type of mental construction (1907: 96–7).

The early intuitionists (especially Brouwer and Poincaré) remained Kantian in their conception of mathematical reasoning and took it to be essentially different in character from 'discursive' or logical reasoning. Brouwer believed logical reasoning to mark not patterns in mathematical thinking itself but only patterns in its linguistic representation. It was therefore not indicative of the inferential structure of mathematical thinking itself and had no place within genuine mathematical reasoning *per se*. This was essentially the idea expressed in Brouwer's so-called 'First Act of Intuitionism' (1905: 2, 1981: 4–5).

Thus the early intuitionists (especially Brouwer and Weyl and, to some extent, Poincaré) discarded Kant's view of geometry, revised his conception of arithmetic and existence claims, and preserved his basic stance on the nature of mathematical reasoning and its relationship to logical reasoning. Later intuitionists (for example, Heyting and Dummett) did not keep to this plan. They rejected Brouwer's view of the divide between logical and mathematical reasoning and made a significant place for logic in their accounts of mathematical reasoning. Some of them (Dummett and his 'anti-realist' followers) even went so far as to make the question 'What is the logic of mathematical reasoning?' central to their philosophy of mathematics (see §5 below).

3 Logicism

The view of the logicist FREGE (and, to some extent, of Dedekind) accepted Kant's synthetic a priori conception of geometry but maintained arithmetic to be analytic. RUSSELL, another logicist, rejected Kant's views of both geometry and arithmetic (and also of pure mechanics) and maintained the analyticity of both. (See LOGICISM.)

Frege's logicism differed sharply from intuitionism. First, it differed in the place in mathematical reasoning it assigned to logic. Frege (1884: preface, III–IV) maintained that reasoning is essentially the same everywhere and that even an inference pattern such as that of mathematical induction, which appears to be peculiar to mathematics, is, at bottom, purely logical. Second, it differed in its conception of geometry. Like the early intuitionists, Frege regarded the discovery of non-Euclidean geometries as revealing an important asymmetry between arithmetic and geometry. Unlike them, however, he did not see this as grounds for rejecting Kant's synthetic a priori conception of geometry (1873: 3, 1884: §89), but rather as indicating a fundamental difference between geometry and arithmetic. Frege believed the fundamental concept of arithmetic – magnitude – to be both too pervasive and too abstract to be the product of Kantian intuition (1874: 50). It figured in *every* kind of thinking and so must, he reasoned, have a basis in thought deeper than that of intuition. It must have its basis in the very core of rational thought itself; the laws of logic.

The problem was to account for the cognitive richness of arithmetic on such a view. How could the 'great tree of the science of number' (1884: §16) have its roots in bare logical or analytical 'identities'? Frege responded by offering new accounts of both the objectivity and the informativeness of arithmetic. The former he attributed to its subject matter – the

so-called 'logical objects' (§§26, 27, 105). The latter he derived from a new theory of content which allowed concepts to contain (tacit) content that was not needed for their grasp. On this view, analytic judgments could have content that was not required for the mere understanding of the concepts contained in them. Consequently, they could yield more than knowledge of transparent logical identities (§§64–66, 70, 88, 91).

Unlike Kant, then, Frege maintained an important epistemic asymmetry between geometry and arithmetic – an asymmetry based upon his belief that arithmetic is more basic to human rational thought than is geometry. In addition, he departed from Kant in maintaining a realistic conception of arithmetic knowledge despite its analytic character. He saw it as being about a class of objects – so-called 'logical objects' – that are external but intimately related to the mind and therefore not the mere expression of standing traits of human cognition. The differences between arithmetical and geometric necessity were to be accounted for by separating the relationship the mind has to the objects of arithmetic from that which it has to the objects of geometry.

Russell's logicism differed from Frege's. Perhaps most importantly, Russell did not regard the existence of non-Euclidean geometries as evidence of an epistemological asymmetry between geometry and arithmetic. Rather, he saw the 'arithmetization' of geometry and other areas of mathematics as evidence of an epistemological symmetry between arithmetic and the rest of mathematics. Russell thus extended his logicism to the whole of mathematics. The basic components of his logicism were a general methodological ideal of pursuing each science to its greatest level of generality, and a conception of the greatest level of generality in mathematics as lying at that point where all its theorems are of the form 'p implies q', all their constants are logical constants and all their variables of unrestricted range. Theorems of this sort, Russell maintained, would rightly be regarded as logical truths.

Russell's logicism was thus motivated by a view of mathematics which saw it as the science of the most general formal truths; a science whose indefinables are those constants of rational thought (the so-called logical constants) that have the most ubiquitous application, and whose indemonstrables are those propositions that set out the basic properties of these indefinables (Russell 1903: 8). In his opinion, such a view provided the only precise description of what philosophers have had in mind when they have described mathematics as a necessary or a priori science.

Russell thus accounted for the necessity of mathematics by pointing to its logical character. He accounted for its richness principally by invoking a new definition of syntheticity that allowed all but the most trivial logical truths and inferences to be counted as informative or synthetic. Mathematical truths would thus be logical truths, but they would not, for all that, be analytic truths. Similarly for inferences. An inference would count as synthetic so long as its conclusion was a different proposition from its premises. Cognitive richness was conceived primarily as the production of new propositions from old, and, on Russell's conception (supposing the criterion of propositional identity to be sufficiently strict), even purely logical inference could produce a bounty of new knowledge from old.

Russell was thus able to account for both the necessity and the cognitive richness of mathematics while making mathematics part of logic. What had kept previous generations of thinkers and, in particular, Kant from recognizing the possibilities of such a view was the relatively impoverished state of logic before the end of the nineteenth century. The new logic, with its robust stock of new forms, its functional conception of the proposition and the ensuing fuller axiomatization of mathematics which it made possible, changed all this forever and provided for the final refutation of Kant. Such, at any rate, was Russell's position.

4 Hilbert's formalism

Hilbert accepted the synthetic a priori character of (much of) arithmetic and geometry, but rejected Kant's account of the supposed intuitions upon which they rest. Overall, Hilbert's position was more complicated in its relationship to Kant's epistemology than were those of the intuitionists and logicists. Like Russell, he rejected Kant's specifically mathematical epistemology – in particular, his conception of the nature and origins of its a priori character. Like Russell, too, he rejected the common post-Kantian belief in the epistemological asymmetry of arithmetic and geometry. Hilbert was, however, unique among those mentioned here in endorsing the framework of Kant's general critical epistemology and making it a central feature of his mathematical epistemology. Specifically, he adopted Kant's distinction between the faculty of the understanding and the faculty of reason as the guide for his pivotal distinction between the so-called 'real' and 'ideal' portions of classical mathematics (Hilbert 1926: 376–7, 392).

Hilbert took 'real' mathematics to be ultimately concerned with the shapes or forms (*Gestalten*) of concrete signs or figures, given in intuition and comprising a type of 'immediate experience prior to

all thought' (1926: 376–7, [1928] 1967: 464–5). Hilbert proposed this basic intuition of shape as a replacement for Kant's two a priori intuitions of space and time. Like Kant's a priori intuitions, however, Hilbert, too regarded his finitary intuition as an 'irremissible pre-condition' of all mathematical (indeed, all scientific) judgment and the ultimate source of all genuine a priori knowledge (1930: 383, 385).

The genuine judgments of real mathematics were the judgments of which our mathematical knowledge was constituted. The pseudo-judgments of ideal mathematics, on the other hand, functioned like Kant's ideas of reason. They neither described things present in the world nor constituted a foundation for our judgments concerning such things. Rather, they played a purely regulative role of guiding the efficient and orderly development of our real knowledge.

Hilbert did not, therefore, affirm the necessity of either arithmetic or geometry in any simple, straightforward way. Rather, he distinguished two types of necessity operating within both. One, pertaining to the judgments of real mathematics, consisted in the (presumed) fact that the apprehension of certain elementary spatial and combinatorial features of simple concrete objects is a precondition of all scientific thought. The other, pertaining to the ideal parts of mathematics, had a kind of psychological necessity, a necessity borne of the manner in which our minds inevitably or best regulate the development of our real knowledge.

This conception of the necessity of mathematics was different from both Kant's and the logicists' and intuitionists'. So, too, was Hilbert's view of the cognitive richness of mathematics, which he attributed both to the objective richness of the shapes and combinatorial features of concrete signs and to the richness of our imaginations in 'creating' complementary ideal objects.

In its overall structure, Hilbert's mathematical epistemology thus resembled Kant's *general* critical epistemology. This included his so-called 'consistency' requirement (that is, the requirement that ideal reasoning not prove anything contrary to that which may be established by real means), which resembled Kant's demand that the faculty of reason not produce any judgment of the understanding that could not in principle be obtained solely from the understanding (1781/1787: A328/B385).

5 Modifications

During the first four decades of the twentieth century, each of the post-Kantian programmes outlined above came under attack. Frege's logicism was challenged by Russell's paradox. Russell's logicism encountered difficulties concerning its use of certain existence axioms (namely his axioms of reducibility and infinity) which did not appear to be laws of *logic*. Both were challenged by Gödel's incompleteness theorems, as was Hilbert's formalist programme. Finally, the intuitionists were criticized both philosophically, where their idealism was called into question, and mathematically, where their ability to support a significant body of mathematics remained in doubt. Various modifications have been proposed.

Modifications of logicism. On the mathematical side, a chastened successor to logicism can perhaps be seen in the model-theoretic work of Abraham Robinson and his followers. They are interested in determining the mathematical content latent in purely 'logical' features of various mathematical structures or the extent to which genuinely mathematical problems concerning these structures can be solved by purely logical (that is, model-theoretic) means. They have been particularly successful in their treatment of various algebraic structures (see Macintyre 1977; Robinson 1979; Hodges 1993).

Philosophically, too, there have been attempts to renew logicism. It re-emerged in the 1930s and 1940s as the favoured philosophy of mathematics of the logical empiricists (see Carnap 1931; Hahn 1933). They did not, however, develop a logicism of their own in the way that Dedekind, Frege and Russell did, but, rather, simply appropriated the technical work of Russell and Whitehead (modulo the usual reservations concerning the axioms of infinity and reducibility) and attempted to embed it in an overall empiricist epistemology.

This empiricist turn was a novel development in the history of logicism and represented a serious departure from both the original logicism of LEIBNIZ (§10) and the more recent logicism of Frege (and Dedekind). It was less at odds with Russell's logicism which saw mathematics and the empirical sciences as both making use of an essentially inductive method (the so-called 'regressive' method – see Russell 1906, 1907).

Like all empiricists, the logical empiricists struggled with the Kantian problem of how to account for the apparent necessity of mathematics while at the same time being able to explain its cognitive richness. Their strategy was to empty mathematics of all non-analytic content while, at the same time, arguing that analytic truth and inference can be substantial and non-self-evident.

Their ideas came under heavy attack by W.V. QUINE, who challenged their pivotal distinction between analytic and synthetic truths (1951, 1954). He argued that the basic unit of knowledge – the basic item of our thought that is tested against experience – is science as a whole and that this depends upon empirical evidence for its justification. Mathematics and logic are used to relate empirical evidence to the rest of science and, so, are inextricably interwoven into the whole fabric of science. They are thus part of the total body of science that is tested against experience and there is no clean way of dividing between truths of meaning (analytic truths) and truths of fact (synthetic truths).

Within a relatively brief period of time, Quine's argument became a major influence in the philosophy of mathematics and the logicism of the logical empiricists was largely abandoned. Newer conceptions of logicism have, however, continued to appear from time to time. For example, Putnam (1967) addressed the difficult (for a logicist) question of existence claims, arguing that such statements are to be seen as asserting the possible (as opposed to the actual) existence of structures. They are therefore, at bottom, logical claims, and can be established by logical (or metalogical) means. Hodes (1984) takes a somewhat different approach, arguing that arithmetic claims can be translated into a second-order logic in which the second-order variables range over functions and concepts (as opposed to objects). In this way, commitment to sets and other specifically mathematical objects can be eliminated and, this done, arithmetic can be considered a part of logic.

Field (1980, 1984) also presents a kind of logicist view – namely, that mathematical knowledge is (at least largely) logical knowledge. Mathematical knowledge is defined as that knowledge which separates a person who knows a lot of mathematics from a person who knows only a little, and it is then argued that what separates these two kinds of knowers is mainly logical knowledge; that is, knowledge of what follows from what.

Modifications of Hilbert's programme. Hilbert's programme too has its latter-day adherents. For the most part, these have adopted one of two basic stances: that of extending the methods available for proving the consistency of classical ideal mathematics; or that of diminishing the scope and strength of classical ideal mathematics so that its consistency (or the consistency of important parts of it) can more nearly be proved by the kinds of elementary means that Hilbert originally envisaged.

Some in the first group (for example, Gentzen, Ackermann and Gödel) have argued that there are types of evidence that exceed finitary evidence in strength but which have the same basic epistemic virtues as it. Others (for example, Kreisel 1958; Feferman 1988; Sieg 1988) argue for a change in our conception of what a consistency proof ought to do. They maintain that its essential obligation is to realize an epistemic gain, and that finitary methods are not the only epistemically gainful methods for proving consistency.

Those in the second group – the so-called 'reverse mathematics' school of Friedman, Simpson and others – try to isolate the mathematical 'cores' of the various areas of classical mathematics and prove the consistency of these 'reduced' theories by finitary or related means. So far, significant success has been achieved along these lines. (See HILBERT'S PROGRAMME AND FORMALISM §4.)

Modifications of intuitionism. Regarding intuitionism, Heyting's work in the 1930s to formalize intuitionism and to identify its logic has led to a vigorous programme of logical and mathematical investigation (see Heyting 1956; Troelstra 1973, 1977; Beeson 1985 for descriptions of some of this work). In addition to Heyting and his students, Errett Bishop and his followers have extended a constructivist approach to areas of classical mathematics to which such an approach had previously not been extended (see Bridges 1987 for a survey).

On the more philosophical side, the most important development is the construction by Michael Dummett and his anti-realist followers of a defence of intuitionism based upon – in their view – the best answer to the question 'What is the logic of mathematics?'. Their answer is based upon what they take to be a proper theory of meaning – a theory which, following certain ideas set out by Wittgenstein in his *Philosophical Investigations,* equates the meaning of an expression with its canonical use in the practice to which it belongs. They then identify the canonical use of an expression in mathematics with the role it plays in the central activity of proof, and from this they infer an intuitionist treatment of the logical operators (Dummett 1973, 1977).

6 Later developments

Along with the modifications of the major post-Kantian viewpoints noted above, two other developments in the second half of the twentieth century are important to note. One of these is the shift towards empiricism that was brought about by Quine's (following Duhem's) merging of mathematics and the empirical sciences into a single justificatory unit governed by a basically inductive-empirical method. On this view, mathematics may on the whole be *less* susceptible to falsification by sensory evidence than is natural science, but this is a difference of degree, not kind.

This conception of mathematics dispenses with a 'datum' of mathematical epistemology that philosophers of mathematics from Kant on down had struggled to accommodate: namely, the presumed necessity of mathematics. It puts in its place a general empiricist epistemology in which all judgments – those of mathematics and logic as well as those of the natural sciences – are seen as evidentially connected to sensory phenomena and, so, subject to empirical revision.

To accommodate the lingering conviction that mathematics is independent of empirical evidence in a way that natural science is not, Quine introduced a pragmatic distinction between them. Rational belief-revision, he said, is governed by a pragmatic concern to maximize the overall predictive and explanatory power of one's total system of beliefs. Furthermore, predictive and explanatory power are generally aided by policies of revision which minimize, both in scope and severity, the changes that are made to a previously successful belief-system in response to recalcitrant experience.

Because of this, beliefs of mathematics and logic are typically less subject to empirical revision than beliefs of natural science and common sense since revising them generally (albeit, in Quine's view, not inevitably) does more damage to a belief-system than does revising its common sense and natural scientific beliefs. The necessity of mathematics is thus accommodated in Quine's epistemology by moving mathematics closer to the centre of a 'web' of human beliefs where beliefs are less susceptible to empirical revision than are the beliefs of natural science and common sense that lie closer to the edge of the web.

In Quine's view, merging mathematics and science into a single belief-system also induces a realist conception of mathematics. Mathematical sentences must be treated as true in order to play their role in this system, and the world is to be seen as being populated by those entities that are among the values of the variables of true sentences. Mathematical entities are thus real because mathematical sentences play an integral part in our best total theory of experience (see Quine 1948, 1951; Putnam 1971, 1975).

Quine's views have been challenged on various grounds. For example, Parsons (1980) argues that treating the elementary arithmetical parts of mathematics as being on an epistemological par with the hypotheses of theoretical physics fails to capture an epistemologically important distinction between the different kinds of evidentness displayed by the two. Even highly confirmed physical hypotheses such as 'The earth moves around the sun' are more 'derivative' (that is, roughly, more theory-laden) than is an elementary arithmetic proposition such as '$7 + 5 = 12$'. It is therefore not plausible to regard the two claims as based on essentially the same type of evidence.

Others have challenged different aspects of Quine's

position. Field (1980) and Maddy (1980), for example, both question his merging of mathematics and natural science, though in different ways. Field argues that natural science that utilizes mathematics is a conservative extension of it and, so, has no need of its entities. The mathematical part of natural science can thus, in an important sense, be separated from the rest of it. (See Shapiro (1983) for an apt criticism of Field's arguments.). Maddy investigates the possibility that our knowledge of at least certain mathematical objects might not be so diffuse and inextricable from the whole scheme of our natural scientific knowledge as Quine suggests. She argues that perceptual experience can be tied closely and specifically to certain mathematical objects (in particular, to certain sets) in a way that seems out of keeping with Quine's holism.

In addition to Quine, others have suggested different mergings of mathematics and natural sciences. Kitcher (1983), for instance, presents a generally empiricist epistemology for mathematics in which history and community are important epistemological forces. Gödel, on the other hand, argued that mathematics, like the natural sciences, makes use of what is essentially inductive justification ([1947] 1964: 477, 485) when it justifies higher-level mathematical hypotheses on the grounds of their explanatory or simplificatory effects on lower-level mathematical truths and on physics. He allowed, however, that only *some* of our mathematical knowledge arises from empirical sources and regarded as absurd the idea that all of it might do (1951: 311–12).

Another important influence on recent philosophy of mathematics is Benacerraf's 'Mathematical Truth' (1973), in which he argues that the philosophy of mathematics faces a general dilemma. It must give an account of both mathematical truth and mathematical knowledge. The former seems to demand abstract objects as the referents of singular terms in mathematical discourse. The latter, on the other hand, seems to demand that we avoid such referents. There are mathematical epistemologies (for example, various Platonist ones) that allow for a plausible account of the truth of mathematical sentences. Likewise, there are those (for example, various formalist ones) that allow for a plausible account of how we might come to *know* mathematical sentences. However, no known epistemology does both. Towards the end of the twentieth century a great deal of work has been devoted to resolving this dilemma. Field (1980, 1984), Hellman (1989) and Chihara (1990) attempt anti-Platonist resolutions. Maddy (1990), on the other hand, attempts a resolution at once Platonist and naturalistic. To date there is no general consensus on which approaches are the more plausible.

An earlier argument of Benacerraf's (see Benacerraf 1965, but also Dedekind 1888: §73; Hilbert 1900; Weyl 1949; Bernays 1950) was similarly influential in shaping later work. It is the chief inspiration of the position known as 'structuralism' – the view that mathematical objects are essentially positions in structures and have no important additional internal composition or nature (see Resnik 1981, 1982; Shapiro 1983). Apart from the desire for a descriptively more adequate account of mathematics, the chief motivation of structuralism is epistemological. Knowledge of the characteristics of individual abstract objects would seem to require naturalistically inexplicable powers of cognition. Knowledge of at least some structures, on the other hand, would appear to be explicable as the result of applying such classically empiricist means of cognition as abstraction to observable physical complexes. Structures identified via abstraction become part of the general framework of our thinking and can be extended and generalized in a variety of ways as the search for the simplest and most effective overall conceptual scheme is pursued.

Structuralism as a general philosophy of mathematics has been criticized by Parsons (1990) who argues that there are important mathematical objects for which structuralism is not an adequate account. These are the 'quasi-concrete' objects of mathematics – objects that are directly 'instantiated' or 'represented' by concrete objects (for example, geometric figures and symbols such as the so-called 'stroke numerals' of Hilbert's finitary arithmetic, where these are construed as types whose instances are written marks or symbols or uttered sounds). Such objects cannot be treated in a purely structuralist way because their 'representational' function cannot be reduced to the purely intrastructural relationships they bear to other objects within a given system. At the same time, however, they are among the most elementary and important mathematical entities there are.

See also: ANTIREALISM IN THE PHILOSOPHY OF MATHEMATICS; CONSTRUCTIVISM IN MATHEMATICS; DEDEKIND, J.W.R.; KRONECKER, L.; LOGICAL AND MATHEMATICAL TERMS, GLOSSARY OF; MODEL THEORY; PROOF THEORY; REALISM IN THE PHILOSOPHY OF MATHEMATICS

References and further reading

* Beeson, M.J. (1985) *Foundations of Constructive Mathematics*, Berlin: Springer. (Useful survey of recent logical and mathematical developments in constructive mathematics.)
* Benacerraf, P. (1965) 'What Numbers Could Not Be',

Philosophical Review 74: 47–73. (Structuralist argument that arithmetic is not a science concerning particular objects – the numbers – but rather a science elaborating the structure that all arithmetical progressions share in common. Dedekind argued for such a view a century earlier.)

* —— (1973) 'Mathematical Truth', *Journal of Philosophy* 70: 661–80; repr. in Benacerraf and Putnam (1964), 403–20. (Argues that existing philosophies of mathematics are subject to a dilemma – they cannot give a satisfactory account of both mathematical truth and mathematical knowledge.)

Benacerraf, P. and Putnam, H. (eds) (1964) *Philosophy of Mathematics: Selected Readings*, Cambridge: Cambridge University Press, 2nd edn, 1983. (Collection of influential papers in the philosophy of mathematics.)

* Bernays, P. (1950) 'Mathematische Existenz und Widerspruchsfreiheit', repr. in *Abhandlungen zur Philosophie der Mathematik*, Darmstadt: Wissenschaftliche Buchgesellschaft, 1976. (A kind of structuralist argument.)

* Bridges, D. (1987) *Varieties of Constructive Mathematics*, Cambridge: Cambridge University Press (Mathematical survey of recent developments in various constructivist approaches to mathematics. Requires some background and some knowledge of classical mathematics.)

* Brouwer, L.E.J. (1905) *Leven, Kunst, en Mystiek*, Delft; excerpts trans. 'Life, Art and Mysticism', in *Collected Works*, vol. 1, ed. A. Heyting, Amsterdam: North Holland, 1975; unabridged trans. W. van Stigt, *Notre Dame Journal of Formal Logic* 37 (3), 1996. (Early statement of various of Brouwer's philosophical views.)

* —— (1907) *Over de Grondslagen der Wiskunde*, Amsterdam and Leipzig; trans. 'On the Foundations of Mathematics', in *Collected Works*, vol. 1, ed. A. Heyting, Amsterdam: North Holland, 1975. (Brouwer's doctoral dissertation. First sustained presentation of his intuitionist philosophy.)

* —— (1913) 'Intuitionism and Formalism', *Bulletin of the American Mathematical Society* 20: 81–96; repr. in Benacerraf and Putnam (1964), 77–89. (Attempt by Brouwer to distinguish his intuitionist position from a position he labels 'formalism'. Includes an early statement of his antipathy to logical reasoning.)

* —— (1981) *Brouwer's Cambridge Lectures on Intuitionism*, ed. D. van Dalen, Cambridge: Cambridge University Press. (Late statement of Brouwer's intuitionist views, taken from lectures given 1946–51.)

* Carnap, R. (1931) 'Die logizistische Grundlegung der Mathematik', *Erkenntnis* 2: 91–105; trans. E.

Putnam and G. Massey, 'The Logicist Foundations of Mathematics', in Benacerraf and Putnam (1964), 41–52. (Statement of the type of logicist view that became popular among the logical empiricists of the 1930s and 1940s.)

* Chihara, C. (1990) *Constructibility and Mathematical Existence*, Oxford: Oxford University Press. (Argues that classical mathematics does not require commitment either to such linguistic objects as open sentences or to abstract objects (concepts) to which they might be taken to refer.)

* Dedekind, R. (1888) *Was sind und was sollen die Zahlen?*, Braunschweig: Vieweg; trans. W.W. Beman (1901), 'The Nature and Meaning of Numbers', in *Essays on the Theory of Numbers*, New York: Dover, 1963. (§73 includes an interesting statement of Dedekind's philosophical conception of the axiomatic method and its relationship to the older genetic method.)

* Dummett, M.A.E. (1973) 'The Philosophical Basis of Intuitionist Logic', in H.E. Rose and J.C. Shepherdson (eds) *Proceedings of the Logic Colloquium, Bristol, July 1973*, Amsterdam: North Holland, 1975, 5–40; repr. in *Truth and Other Enigmas*, London: Duckworth, 1978, 215–47; and in Benacerraf and Putnam (1964), 97–129. (Argues that an adequate account of the meanings of mathematical propositions reveals the logic of mathematics to be intuitionistic logic. The view of meaning proposed is like that of the later Wittgenstein in that it equates the meaning of a proposition with its canonical usage; takes the canonical usage of a sentence in mathematics to consist in the role it plays in giving proofs.)

* —— (1977) *Elements of Intuitionism*, Oxford: Clarendon Press, 1990. (Further development of the argument set out in Dummett (1973). Also gives a basic presentation of various notions of intuitionistic mathematics (for example, choice sequences and spreads) and intuitionistic logic and its metatheory.)

* Feferman, S. (1988) 'Hilbert's Program Relativized: Proof-Theoretical and Foundational Reductions', *Journal of Symbolic Logic* 53: 364–84. (Argues that finitary methods are not the only epistemically gainful methods for proving consistency and that significant partial realizations of Hilbert's programme can be realized by exploiting this fact.)

* Field, H. (1980) *Science Without Numbers*, Princeton, NJ: Princeton University Press. (Defence of the view that mathematical knowledge is, at least in large part, logical knowledge. Also argues, contra Quine and Putnam, that realism with respect to physics does not entail realism with respect to mathematics.)

* —— (1984) 'Is Mathematical Knowledge Just Logical Knowledge?', *Philosophical Review* 93: 509–52. (Argues that mathematical knowledge is predominantly logical in character.)

* Frege, G. (1873) 'Über eine geometrische Darstellung der imaginären Gebilde in der Ebene', doctoral dissertation, University of Göttingen; repr. in I. Angelleli (ed.) *Kleine Schriften*, Hildesheim, 1967; partial trans. in *Collected Papers on Mathematics, Logic and Philosophy*, ed. B. McGuinness, Oxford: Blackwell, 1984. (An attempt to vindicate the ultimately Kantian view that, at bottom, geometric laws – even those concerning imaginary points, lines, and so on – are all based on intuition, by showing how to replace imaginary items with real, intuitable items.)

* —— (1874) 'Rechnungsmethoden, die sich auf eine Erweiterung des Größenbegriffes gründen', *Habilitationsschrift*, University of Jena; trans. in *Collected Papers on Mathematics, Logic and Philosophy*, ed. B. McGuinness, Oxford: Blackwell, 1984. (Includes a statement of the basic precept of Frege's logicism; namely, that there can be no intuition of so pervasive and abstract a concept as that of magnitude or number.)

* —— (1884) *Die Grundlagen der Arithmetik: eine logisch-mathematische Untersuchung über den Begriff der Zahl*, Breslau: Koebner; trans. J.L. Austin, *The Foundations of Arithmetic: A Logico-Mathematical Enquiry into the Concept of Number*, Oxford: Blackwell, and Evanston, IL: Northwestern University Press, 2nd edn, 1980. (First full-length presentation of Frege's logicist view of arithmetic; focuses on its philosophical basis.)

* Gauss, K. (1817, 1829) letter to Olbers (1817), in *Briefwechsel mit H.W.M. Olbers*, Hildesheim: Olms, 1976; letter to Bessel (1929), in *Werke*, Leipzig: Teubner, 1863–1903, vol. 8, 200. (Includes statements of Gauss' view concerning the 'external' character of geometry versus the 'internal' character of arithmetic.)

* Gödel, K. (1947) 'What is Cantor's Continuum Problem?', *American Mathematical Monthly* 54: 515–25; revised version repr. in Benacerraf and Putnam (1964). (Basic expression of Gödel's realist and non-empiricist views of mathematics.)

* —— (1951) 'Some Basic Theorems on the Foundations of Mathematics and Their Implications', in *Collected Works*, vol. 3, ed. S. Feferman, J.W. Dawson Jr, W. Goldfarb, C.D. Parsons and R.M. Solovay, New York and Oxford: Oxford University Press, 1995. (Edited text of Gödel's 1951 Josiah Gibbs Lecture. Argues for a Platonist conception and against a conventionalist conception of mathematics. Also argues for a non-mechanist view of the human mind. Useful introductory essay by George Boolos.)

* Hahn, H. (1933) *Einheitswissenschaft*, vol. 2, *Logik, Mathematik und Naturerkennen*, ed. R. Carnap and H. Hahn; trans. 'Logic, Mathematics and Knowledge of Nature', in A. Ayer (ed.) *Logical Positivism*, New York: Free Press, 1959. (Influential statement of the type of logicist view of mathematics popular among the positivists.)

Heijenoort, J. van (ed.) (1967) *From Frege to Gödel: A Source Book in Mathematical Logic, 1879–1931*, Cambridge, MA: Harvard University Press. (Collection of basic papers in mathematical logic and the foundations of mathematics. Useful forewords and bibliography.)

* Hellman, G. (1989) *Mathematics Without Numbers*, Oxford: Oxford University Press. (Detailed development of a non-Platonist account of mathematics.)

* Heyting, A. (1956) *Intuitionism: An Introduction*, Amsterdam: North Holland; 3rd revised edn, 1971. (Introduction to philosophical considerations concerning intuitionism and a survey of intuitionist formalizations of logic and various parts of mathematics.)

* Hilbert, D. (1900) 'Mathematische Probleme. Vortrag, gehalten auf dem internationalen Mathematiker-Kongress zu Paris 1900', *Nachrichten von der königlichen Gesellschaft der Wissenschaften zu Göttingen, mathematisch-physikalische Klasse*: 253–97; trans. 'Mathematical Problems', *Bulletin of the American Mathematical Society* 8: 437–79, 1902. (Interesting remarks concerning the nature of mathematical truth and the axiomatic method.)

* —— (1926) 'Über das Unendliche', *Mathematische Annalen* 95: 161–90; trans. 'On the Infinite', in J. van Heijenoort (1967). (Mature statement of basic philosophical precepts of Hilbert's programme. Emphasizes the relationship with Kant's general critical epistemology.)

* —— (1928) 'Die Grundlagen der Mathematik', *Abhandlungen aus dem mathematischen Seminar der Hamburgischen Universität* 6: 65–85; trans. 'The Foundations of Mathematics', in J. van Heijenoort (1967). (Repeats some of the material covered in Hilbert (1926); also includes an important clarificatory remark concerning the character of Hilbert's 'formalism' (1967: 475).)

* —— (1930) 'Naturerkennen und Logik', *Die Naturwissenschaften* 18: 959–63; repr. in *Gesammelte Abhandlungen*, vol. 3, Berlin: Springer, 1935. (Perhaps the fullest statement of Hilbert's philosophical ideas; develops his view of the a priori and refines his 'formalism'.)

* Hodes, H. (1984) 'Logicism and the Ontological

Commitments of Arithmetic', *Journal of Philosophy* 81: 123–49. (Argues that arithmetical claims can be translated into a second-order logic in which the second-order variables range over functions and concepts.)

* Hodges, W. (1993) *Model Theory*, Cambridge: Cambridge University Press. (Thorough and up-to-date survey of model theory. Requires some background in logic.)

* Kant, I. (1781/1787) *Critique of Pure Reason*, trans. N. Kemp Smith, London: Macmillan, 1929. (Includes the classic statement of Kant's views in the philosophy of mathematics. The 'A' and 'B' prefixes to sources refer to pages of the 1781 and 1787 German editions respectively.)

* —— (1783) *Prolegomena to any Future Metaphysics that Shall Come Forth as Scientific*, trans. L. White Beck, Indianapolis, IN, and New York: Bobbs-Merrill, 1950. (Includes an abbreviated statement of the views on the nature of mathematics given in Kant (1781/1787).)

* Kitcher, P. (1983) *The Nature of Mathematical Knowledge*, Oxford: Oxford University Press. (Develops an empiricist conception of mathematics which emphasizes its similarities to natural science.)

* Kreisel, G. (1958) 'Hilbert's Programme', *Dialectica* 12: 346–72; revised version in Benacerraf and Putnam (1964). (Discussion of the possible significance of a Hilbert-type programme in light of Gödel's theorems and other more recent work in proof theory.)

* Macintyre, A. (1977) 'Model Completeness', in J. Barwise (ed.) *Handbook of Mathematical Logic*, Amsterdam: North Holland. (Survey of basic results and methods linking Robinson's notion of model completeness to various questions in algebra.)

* Maddy, P. (1980) 'Perception and Mathematical Intuition', *Philosophical Review* 84: 163–96. (Argues that we can perceive certain kinds of sets.)

* —— (1990) *Realism in Mathematics*, Oxford: Oxford University Press. (Attempt to show how realism in mathematics can be combined with a naturalistic mathematical epistemology.)

* Parsons, C. (1980) 'Mathematical Intuition', *Proceedings of the Aristotelian Society* 80: 145–68. (Criticism of Quine in which it is argued that the Quinean view cannot account for an important difference in the kind of evidentness displayed by elementary mathematical truths on the one hand, and hypotheses of theoretical physics on the other.)

* —— (1990) 'The Structuralist View of Mathematical Objects', *Synthese* 84: 303–46. (Argues that structuralism does not offer an adequate account of

certain very elementary mathematical objects, such as geometric figures.)

Poincaré, H. (1902) *La Science et l'hypothèse*, Paris: Flammarion; trans. in G.B. Halsted (ed.) *The Foundations of Science*, Lancaster, PA: The Science Press, 1946. (Chapter 1 presents Poincaré's basically Kantian conception of mathematical reasoning.)

—— (1905) *Le valeur de la science*, Paris: Flammarion; trans. *The Value of Science*, New York: Dover, 1958; and trans. in G.B. Halsted (ed.) *The Foundations of Science*, Lancaster, PA: The Science Press, 1946. (Part 1 presents Poincaré's basically intuitionist view of arithmetic, his so-called conventionalist view of geometry and his Kantian conception of mathematical inference or reasoning.)

—— (1908) *Science et méthode*, Paris: Flammarion; trans. in G.B. Halsted (ed.) *The Foundations of Science*, Lancaster, PA: The Science Press, 1946. (Book 2 gives a statement of Poincaré's view of logic and its place in mathematics.)

* Putnam, H. (1967) 'Mathematics Without Foundations', *Journal of Philosophy* 64: 5–22. (Argues that existence claims can be seen as asserting the possible (as opposed to the actual) existence of structures and, therefore, at bottom, can be treated as logical claims.)

* —— (1971) *Philosophy of Logic*, New York: Harper. (Presentation of a basically empiricist, pragmatist view of logic and mathematics.)

* —— (1975) 'What is Mathematical Truth?', in *Mathematics, Matter and Method: Philosophical Papers*, vol. 1, Cambridge: Cambridge University Press. (Defends a realist, though not immaterialist, view of mathematics. Once again stresses the basic motif that mathematics and the natural sciences are not qualitatively different.)

* Quine, W.V. (1948) 'On What There Is', *Review of Metaphysics* 2: 21–38. (Argument for mathematical realism.)

* —— (1951) 'Two Dogmas of Empiricism', repr. in *From a Logical Point of View*, Cambridge, MA: Harvard University Press, 1953; repr. New York: Harper & Row, 1963. (Influential attack on the analytic/synthetic distinction and empiricist reductionism of the logical empiricists.)

* —— (1954) 'Carnap and Logical Truth', repr. in Benacerraf and Putnam (1964). (Criticism of Carnap's conception of logical truth.)

* Resnik, M. (1981) 'Mathematics as a Science of Patterns: Ontology and Reference', *Noûs* 15: 529–50. (Formulates and defends a structuralist conception of meaning in mathematics.)

* —— (1982) 'Mathematics as a Science of Patterns: Epistemology', *Noûs* 16: 95–105. (Formulates a structuralist view of mathematical knowledge.)

* Robinson, A. (1979) *Selected Papers of Abraham Robinson*, vol. 1, *Model Theory and Algebra*, ed. H.J. Keisler *et al.*, Amsterdam: North Holland. (Collection of basic papers of the Robinson school applying model theory to algebra. See especially 'On the Application of Symbolic Logic to Algebra', the paper in which Robinson presented his ideas for applying logic to the resolution of problems in algebra.)

* Russell, B.A.W. (1903) *The Principles of Mathematics*, Cambridge: Cambridge University Press; 2nd edn, London: Allen & Unwin, 1937; repr. London: Routledge, 1992. (Russell's first full-length development of his logicist views.)

* —— (1906) 'Les paradoxes de la logique', *Revue de métaphysique et de morale* 14: 627–50; trans. 'On "Insolubilia" and their Solution by Symbolic Logic', in *Essays in Analysis*, ed. D. Lackey, London: Allen & Unwin, 1973. (Reply to Poincaré's views concerning the relationship between logic and mathematics. Also includes an early statement of the hypothetico-deductive conception of the justification of the basic laws of mathematics.)

* —— (1907) 'The Regressive Method of Discovering the Premises of Mathematics', in *Essays in Analysis*, ed. D. Lackey, London: Allen & Unwin, 1973. (Useful statement of the methodological view underlying Russell's logicism.)

* Shapiro, S. (1983) 'Mathematics and Reality', *Philosophy of Science* 50: 523–48. (Statement and defence of a structuralist view of mathematics.)

* Sieg, W. (1988) 'Hilbert's Program Sixty Years Later', *Journal of Symbolic Logic* 53: 338–48. (Discussion of the progress and changes in Hilbert's programme since its formulation in the 1920s.)

* Troelstra, A. (ed.) (1973) *Metamathematical Investigation of Intuitionistic Arithmetic and Analysis*, Lecture Notes in Mathematics, vol. 344, Berlin, Heidelberg and New York: Springer. (Metamathematical study of various intuitionist systems.)

* —— (1977) 'Proof Theory and Constructive Mathematics', in J. Barwise (ed.) *Handbook of Mathematical Logic*, Amsterdam: North Holland. (Survey of proof-theoretic work on intuitionist systems.)

* Weyl, H. (1927) 'Philosophie der Mathematik und Naturwissenschaft', in *Handbuch der Philosophie*, Munich: Oldenbourg; revised and expanded trans. *Philosophy of Mathematics and Natural Science*, Princeton, NJ: Princeton University Press, 1949. (Valuable collection of essays in the philosophy of mathematics by one of the twentieth century's preeminent scientific thinkers.)

Whitehead, A.N. and Russell, B.A.W. (1910) *Principia Mathematica*, vol. 1, Cambridge: Cambridge University Press, 2nd edn, 1925. (The classic symbolic formalization of logic and mathematics; a basis of much of the greatest work in mathematical logic and the foundations of mathematics in the twentieth century.)

MICHAEL DETLEFSEN

MATTER

Viewed as arising within the framework of a more general theory of substance, *philosophical treatments of matter have traditionally revolved around two issues: (1) The nature of matter: what are the distinguishing characteristics of matter or material substance(s) that define it and distinguish it from other substances, if any? (2) The problem of elements: do material things consist of elementary substances, or are there always further constituents? One possible view is that there is no fundamental level – that there are always further constituents, ingredients of ingredients. However, the view most often held by both philosophers and scientists has been that there are indeed fundamental elements out of which material things are made. Once this view is adopted, the question arises as to what they are and what properties distinguish them.*

These two issues were introduced, though only gradually, in ancient Greek philosophy. A significant turn came about in the seventeenth century, in which the work of Descartes and Newton led to a picture of matter as passive, inert and dead as opposed to minds and forces, both of which were conceived as being 'active'. Many philosophical problems and doctrines have been formulated in terms of this distinction. However, later developments in science, especially in the twentieth century, have brought about such profound changes that classical concepts of matter are no longer viable. These new developments profoundly alter the statements of philosophical doctrines and problems traditionally associated with matter.

1 Ancient and medieval conceptions of matter
2 Matter in early modern science and philosophy
3 Modern scientific views of matter and their philosophical relevance

1 Ancient and medieval conceptions of matter

In Aristotle's view, matter is not a substance or an element. His own term for matter was reserved for one aspect of individual substances – particular objects like Socrates – which he saw as having both 'matter' and 'form'. Matter has the potential to receive form; it is never found in the absence of form, being inseparable from it. Thus Aristotle's matter is a bare *capacity* to have properties; it itself does not have any. This is in contrast to the matter of the seventeenth-century philosophers and scientists, which did have essential properties. Thus, 'the problem of matter' as usually conceived in modern philosophy stems from the concept of substance, specifically from the version of that concept which asserts that there are elements. From the perspective of this later view, the problem of matter in Aristotle is the problem of whether individual substances have 'constituents of which they are made' – the problem of elements – and not the problem of the nature of the 'potential to receive form' (see ARISTOTLE §§13–14).

Aristotle attributed to his pre-Socratic predecessors the problem of the ultimate elements of which all things (material substances) consist. He thus saw the Milesian philosophers as maintaining that there is one material substance out of which all things are made – water for Thales, 'the Indefinite' for Anaximander, air for Anaximenes. Aristotle's interpretation of pre-Socratic philosophy is, however, questionable. According to some scholars, the Milesians (at least) were interested in the stuff *from which* things emerge, as things in nature grow from seeds or human beings 'come from' their parents, rather than, as Aristotle saw them, searching for the elementary constituents *of which* things are made. The shift of attention to the problem of elements was likely a gradual one, reaching relative maturity only with Empedocles, the atomists and Aristotle.

In Aristotle's interpretation, the Milesians were *monists*, believing that there is one material substance out of which all things are made. Monism was rejected following PARMENIDES, who maintained that if there is only one fundamental substance, change is impossible – a consequence his successors could not swallow. Parmenides argued that 'what is', or being, cannot have come into being, cannot change, cannot pass out of existence, is absolutely full (continuous, homogeneous, and as densely packed as possible), and is therefore 'one'. For example, it could only be separated by either nonbeing or being; but since nonbeing is nothing, it cannot separate anything; therefore between any parts of being there can only be more of the same, being. Similarly, if being changed, it could change only into being, that is, itself, since nonbeing is nothing. In order to account for the existence of change, post-Parmenidean philosophers turned to *pluralism*, the doctrine that there is more than one fundamental stuff (see REDUCTION, PROBLEMS OF). The atomists, Leucippus and Democritus, are clearest on this point. They admitted that ultimate

reality must have most of the characteristics attributed to it by Parmenides, changelessness and permanence in particular. But in order to admit the existence of change and motion, they argued that there are many ultimate Parmenidean realities – the atoms – and, further, that nonbeing has some minimal kind of existence. They identified nonbeing with empty space, through which the intrinsically unchangeable atoms could move and congregate to form the entities of our world (see ATOMISM, ANCIENT). Other pluralist philosophers responded to the Parmenidean arguments similarly, declaring ultimate reality to be intrinsically unchangeable, the objects of familiar experience not having ultimate existence. EMPEDOCLES held that the four elements of earth, air, fire and water, which alone were truly fundamental realities (neglecting for present purposes the agencies love and strife), had the Parmenidean character of being uncreated and indestructible. The entities we know correspond to Parmenidean nonbeing, formed by the intermingling of the four elements through their motions. ANAXAGORAS said that there are an infinite number of 'seeds', each of which contains a little of everything (flesh, gold, ...); larger bodies are formed when one of the infinite components of the seeds becomes dominant.

Plato, in the *Timaeus*, equated his equivalent of matter, the receptacle, with nonbeing, and also referred to it as space. Only the changeless forms truly exist, copies of them being embodied in the receptacle, which, like Aristotle's potentiality, is a mere capacity to receive form. As to the elements, the *Timaeus* presented a geometrical version of atomism in which the four elements, together with the universe, were identified with the five regular solids (see PLATO §16).

Aristotle adopted a version of Empedocles' four-element theory, but with three major changes. First, the elements, like other substances, have both matter, in the sense of potentiality, and form, specifically two of the fundamental forms which together constitute the essence of the particular element. Thus the element earth has the fundamental forms 'cold' and 'dry', water 'cold' and 'wet', air 'cold' and 'dry', and fire 'hot' and 'dry'. (Indeed, for Aristotle, each type of entity has a distinct 'essential form' which constitutes its essence, making it the kind of substance it is. Except for the interconvertible elements, different types or species are irreducibly distinct: there simply are different species.) Second, the elements are interconvertible (they were not for Empedocles) by change of form: one fundamental form can 'drive out' its opposite. For example, 'dry' can drive out and replace the 'wet' in water, converting water into air. Third, Aristotle connected the four-element theory with his view of the structure of the universe: the 'natural place' of the element earth is in the central core of the universe, that of water in a spherical layer above earth, of air and fire in layers successively above that.

The Stoics also adopted a version of the four-element theory, but emphasized a distinction, present in Aristotle but not generally emphasized by him, between *passive* and *active* elements. Earth and water are passive elements, unable to move or otherwise act unless acted upon. Air and fire are active elements, capable of self-motion. The analogies between life and the active elements were not missed by the Stoics; indeed, a mixture of the active elements, *pneuma*, was the principle of life and intelligence, and constituted the 'soul of the world' which held the universe together as a unified *cosmos*. Although the Stoics saw the active elements as otherwise on a par with the passive ones in being material, their doctrine presages the Cartesian–Leibnizian distinction of mind and matter (see STOICISM §3).

Aristotle rejected atomism on several grounds, including its dismissal of final causes in nature. Despite a revival of atomism by Lucretius, Aristotle's rejection of the doctrine persisted among his medieval followers. However, atomism was not completely absent in medieval philosophy, being explored particularly among Islamic thinkers who followed the discipline *kalam*. Early *kalam* thinkers developed an atomistic conception of the universe as being freely created by God, but their attempt to affirm God's omnipotence as a causal agent based on his ability to create and sustain matter were refuted by Islamic Aristotelians and later by AL-GHAZALI (see CAUSALITY AND NECESSITY IN ISLAMIC THOUGHT §3; ISLAMIC THEOLOGY).

The alchemists were responsible for most of the theoretical and experimental study of matter in the Middle Ages. Although their views were obscure, some were at least consistent with an Aristotelian viewpoint, seeing the purpose of alchemy as bringing the potential of matter to its fulfilment in the perfection of the higher metals and gems. Indeed, some of the alchemists seem to have believed that the formation of metals and gems in the earth was a natural process of growth and maturation, and that, through arcane knowledge, this process could be reproduced in the microcosmic laboratory. Thus they show the persistence of the ancient idea that things 'grow' in and from the ground (see ALCHEMY).

2 Matter in early modern science and philosophy

According to the conception of matter introduced in the Scientific Revolution of the seventeenth century, it is not the case that there are many distinct types of material substance, each with its own essential and irreducible nature; rather, there is only one universal type of matter, with universal essential properties or 'attributes'. All material bodies (and, for some, all entities whatever) are to be understood in terms of the motion of this fundamental matter. According to this view, introduced or at least popularized by Descartes and followed by Newton, matter is a *passive substance*, incapable of inducing its own action. All action of matter must be caused by an external agent. For Descartes, this external agent must be a *contact force*, and specifically an impact (collision); bodies will not move unless impacted (see DESCARTES, R. §11). In addition to impact forces, Isaac NEWTON allowed forces acting at a distance to affect matter. For Newton, matter consists of ultimate particles, atoms, which are discrete, localized, inert, 'solid, massy, hard, impenetrable, movable' and extended. (Note that the concept of inertness has shifted since Aristotle: whereas for him a body is inert if and only if it is at rest, for Descartes and Newton both rest and uniform rectilinear motion count as 'inertial', changeable only by the action of an external agent.) Passivity, inertness, deadness were now among the defining characteristics of material substance in addition to spatial extendedness, mobility and (Descartes excepted) impenetrability. Descartes distinguished such material substance sharply from *mind*, or *mental substance*, the latter being nonspatial and capable of initiating its own activity.

The basic difference between Descartes and Newton regarding matter was that Descartes conceived matter to be continuous and identified it with space, whereas Newton saw atoms as contingent occupants of space and consisting of physically (rather than logically) indivisible atoms occupying only a small proportion of the total space available in the universe. (In many places where he talks about the actual evolution of the universe and about particular physical problems, however, Descartes writes as though matter is a space-filling plenum rather than being identical with space.) Nevertheless, they agreed that it is of the nature of matter to persist in its inertial state of rest or uniform motion unless acted upon by an external force: that it is inert, dead, passive, blindly continuing in its present state, acting only when acted upon. Although Newton sometimes admitted action-at-a-distance (he also sometimes did not), he saw the power of attracting other bodies from a distance as contingently superimposed by God on matter, not part of the essential nature of matter, which was only passive. For most seventeenth-century thinkers, whether atomists or plenists, the basis of action in the universe was the impenetrability or hardness of matter, and action always took place by contact (see MECHANICS, CLASSICAL §4).

Leibniz criticized the Cartesian–Newtonian concept of matter on several grounds. He argued that the merely passive, whether space, time or matter, whether atomistic, plenum, purely space, cannot account for the unity of things, their individuation, change, resistance or impenetrability, or action. For example, the purely passive is incapable of explaining how one thing can affect another. Nor, since impenetrability is itself an activity of resistance, can the notion of a passive matter explain how objects can be affected by other objects. True substances – true fundamental realities – must be capable of action. Space, time and matter, being incapable of action, can only be 'well-founded phenomena', epiphenomena of non-material Active Forces or monads, which in their activity are more analogous to minds, capable of initiating their own activity, than to dead matter (see LEIBNIZ, G.W. §11).

The issues raised by the ancient Greeks concerning the nature of matter and change are still present in these disputes between Leibniz and his opponents. The Parmenidean view of ultimate reality as necessarily unchanging is echoed in early modern theories of matter: where matter, whether atomistic or a continuous and space-filling plenum, was conceived of as permanent, indestructible and incapable of action. This view was challenged by the doctrine that the fundamentally real is capable of activity, a view with roots in Anaximenes and Heraclitus, later maintained by the Stoics, and carried by Leibniz to the extreme of asserting that only the active could exist

3 Modern scientific views of matter and their philosophical relevance

In so far as the problem of matter is concerned with that of elementary constituents, an important development came in the history of chemistry. An empirically applicable concept of 'element' was utilized by Lavoisier: a material was to be treated as an element if: (a) with any of the means available to us, we cannot break it down into further constituents, (b) through such experiments, we always find members of the same class of substances as constituents, and (c) we find that other substances can be reconstructed by combinations of one or more of these ultimate breakdown products. Subsequent important steps in the history of chemistry revealed further evidence that there are a small number of such elements and that each element is fundamentally atomic. In the nineteenth century and culminating in the quantum-mechanical theory of the chemical bond, these developments led to a detailed theory of how atoms hold together in molecules and larger configurations (see CHEMISTRY, PHILOSOPHICAL ASPECTS OF §4). However, it is now understood that the means which Lavoisier and his nineteenth-century successors used to break down substances (for example, heat and electricity) are low-energy processes, to be distinguished as 'chemical' from the forces that hold atomic nuclei themselves together ('nuclear' forces). Thus chemical atoms are now understood to be composed of more fundamental particles, electrons, protons and neutrons, the latter two consisting of still more basic particles, quarks. Although there remain dissenters, the view of most present-day particle physicists is that quarks and leptons (a category which includes electrons) are truly fundamental, without further constituents.

Modern scientific studies of matter have introduced further departures from the Cartesian–Newtonian 'classical' conception which are of profound relevance to philosophical discussions. While the concept of the indestructibility and conservation of mass is central to classical theories of mechanics and chemistry, relativity theories recognize that mass varies with frame of reference, and with velocity as measured in that reference-frame, and, further, that mass is interconvertible with energy (see RELATIVITY THEORY, PHILOSOPHICAL SIGNIFICANCE OF). While Newton sharply distinguished forces from matter, in quantum mechanics forces are conveyed by transfer of a certain type of particles (the bosons) which has mass, like classical matter-particles. A second class of quantum-mechanical particles ('fermions') are intuitively closer analogues of classical matter in exhibiting impenetrability, but the correspondence is only rough. For example, fermions can also be exchanged in interactions, and they also exhibit wavelike (nonlocalized) behaviour. This latter feature is a consequence of deep features of quantum mechanics associated with the Heisenberg indeterminacy principles (see QUANTUM MECHANICS, INTERPRETATIONS OF). For example, while in classical mechanics a knowledge of the simultaneous precise positions and momenta of the particles in an isolated system allowed prediction of the state of that system at any other time, in quantum mechanics it is impossible to assign simultaneous precise positions and momenta to particles. While the vacuum, or empty space, of classical physics was truly empty 'nothingness', particles appear and disappear spontaneously (causelessly, in any classical sense) from the dynamic vacua of modern quantum field theories (see FIELD THEORY, QUANTUM §2). Those fields, while explanatory of immense bodies of scientific knowledge, are not classical entities with specific values of each of their assigned properties; the laws describing them are fundamentally probabilistic, treating them as superpositions of all quantum possibilities. Matter as conceived in modern physics is, in short, far different, and far more dynamic, than matter as conceived by Descartes and Newton. Finally, strong evidence indicates that there is far more matter in the universe than is detectable, at least by present instruments. Indeed, some observations and reasoning suggest that as much as 99 per cent of the matter in the universe may be of a kind different from the ordinary ('baryonic') matter we know (see COSMOLOGY §3).

Thus the concept of matter has been altered in such drastic ways that certain contemporary ideas correspond at best only roughly to classical scientific and philosophical counterparts. The sharp contrasts between inert, passive permanence and dynamic activity, ultimate constituency and change, matter and force, fail to appear in quantum-theoretical analogues of classical matter. Indeed, the merely approximate analogy of fermions and bosons to classical concepts of matter, the activity of the quantum vacuum, the character of quantum fields as superpositions of possibilities and many other features of the quantum world, together with the existence of dark matter, all conspire to dictate the reformulation of many traditional problems of philosophy, such as the free will problem, the doctrines of materialism and determinism, the distinction between actuality and possibility, and the topic of matter itself.

See also: MATTER, INDIAN CONCEPTIONS OF; SUBSTANCE; UNITY OF SCIENCE

References and further reading

Descartes, R. (1644) *Principia philosophiae* (Principles of Philosophy); ed. and trans. J. Cottingham, R. Stoothoff, D. Murdoch and A. Kenny, *The Philosophical Writings of Descartes*, vol. I, Cambridge: Cambridge University Press, 1984– 91. (The most mature statement of Descartes' views of matter, differing in important respects from those in his earlier works. The cited work contains excerpts.)

Guthrie, W.K.C. (1962–81) *A History of Greek Philosophy*, Cambridge: Cambridge University Press, 6 vols. (Excellent, clear studies of Greek philosophers, with abundant discussions of problems about matter.)

Jammer, M. (1961) *Concepts of Mass in Classical and Modern Physics*, New York: Dover. (Brief survey of the history of concepts of matter or mass, focusing primarily on scientific aspects. Somewhat technical.)

Koyré, A. (1965) *Newtonian Studies*, Chicago, IL: University of Chicago Press. (Classic treatment of seventeenth-century science, especially good on relations between thought of Descartes and Newton. Should be required reading for all interested in the historical topics relevant to the concept of matter.)

Krauss, L. (1989) *The Search for the Fifth Essence: The Search for Dark Matter in the Universe*, New York: Basic Books. (Popular survey of the 'dark matter' problem mentioned at the end of §3.)

Leibniz, G. (1969) *Philosophical Papers and Letters*, ed. L. Loemker, Dordrecht: Reidel. (Views on matter are scattered throughout; some especially significant discussions are found in 'On Nature Itself', 'Thoughts on the Principles of Descartes', 'The Confession of Nature against Atheists', and the correspondence with Clarke and with De Volder.)

McMullin, E. (ed.) (1963) *The Concept of Matter*, Notre Dame, IN: University of Notre Dame Press. (A collection of articles by historians and philosophers; most papers accessible to non-specialists.)

Newton, I. (1730) *Opticks or a Treatise of the Reflections, Refractions, Inflections and Colours of Light*; repr. New York: Dover, 1952. (The 'Queries' added to the end of this work give much insight into Newton's views on matter.)

* Plato (*c*.366–360 BC) *Timaeus*; ed. A. Rivaud, *Platon: Timée, Critias*, Budé series, Paris: Les Belles Lettres, 1925; trans. F.M. Cornford, *Plato's Cosmology*, London: Routledge & Kegan Paul, 1937; New York: Penguin, 1977. (Exposition of Plato's 'geometrical atomism'.)

Ross, D. (ed.) (1966) *Aristotle, Works*, vol. II, Oxford: Clarendon Press. (In addition to Aristotle's own views of matter, these writings contain criticisms of the views of his predecessors.)

Sambursky, S. (1956) *The Physical World of the Greeks*, London: Routledge & Kegan Paul. (Written by a physicist-historian, an excellent survey of Greek ideas about matter. Highly accessible.)

Shapere, D. (1991) 'The Universe of Modern Science and Its Philosophical Exploration', in E. Agazzi and A. Cordero (eds) *Philosophy and the Origin and Evolution of the Universe*, Dordrecht: Kluwer, 87–202. (Survey of ideas of contemporary physics and its relevance to philosophy.)

Toulmin, S.E. and Goodfield, J. (1962) *The Architecture of Matter*, New York: Harper & Row. (Very readable, clear presentation of the history of matter in philosophy and science.)

DUDLEY SHAPERE

MATTER, INDIAN CONCEPTIONS OF

During the long and complex history of Indian philosophy, a number of divergent conceptions of matter have been developed and explored. These conceptions diverge both with respect to the ontological analysis of matter, and with respect to its specific structural characteristics. In terms of ontological conceptions of matter, the rival positions of materialism, idealism and substance-pluralism are all advanced by competing schools of thought. For example, pure materialism is espoused by the Cārvāka school, while absolute idealism is defended by Advaita Vedānta, and varying forms of pluralism are advocated by the Sāṅkhya, Yoga, Nyāya and Vaiśeṣika schools.

Regarding the structural characteristics of matter, the most interesting conceptions are advanced by the pluralistic philosophies. In particular, the Vaiśeṣika and Nyāya schools recognize five physical substances, four of which are held to possess atomic structure. According to this conception, matter is composed of imperceptibly small units or paramāṇus, *which constitute the basic substrate in which perceptible qualities inhere. All macroscopic objects are transient composites of atoms, while the* paramāṇus *themselves are indivisible and indestructible. The atoms are held to be naturally at rest, and an external force is required to initiate motion.*

In contrast, the Sāṅkhya and Yoga traditions espouse a metaphysical dualism of the two basic categories of matter and consciousness, where the continuity and dynamic transformations of matter are emphasized. All of the diverse phenomena of the physical world result from modifications of a single underlying source known as pradhāna *or primal matter, which is said to be continuous, all pervading, indestructible and imperceptible.* Pradhāna *exists in a balanced and unmanifest state of* pralaya *until it is disturbed by the presence of consciousness. This disturbance leads to an imbalance between the internal constituents of* pradhāna, *and the resulting disequilibrium accounts for the evolutionary transformations of the physical world.*

1 **General survey**
2 **Vaiśeṣika atomism**
3 **Sāṅkhya dualism**

1 General survey

In the present context it is not possible to provide a comprehensive survey of Indian conceptions of matter, which have developed over several millennia among a number of divergent philosophical schools.

Thus the current section sketches some of the most prominent features of the intellectual landscape, and §§2–3 focus in more detail upon two particular theories concerning the structural characteristics of matter, selected on the basis of their conceptual importance and interest.

The metaphysical position of materialism is represented in Indian thought by the heterodox Cārvāka school, which upholds an ontology in which only the physical elements possess ultimate reality, and everything that exists is a composite of these elements formed through the operation of strictly natural processes. In common with ancient Greek theories, the Cārvāka school adopts the four elements of earth, water, fire and air – in distinction to most other schools of Indian philosophy, which accept *ākāśa* or 'ether' as a fifth material element. According to the Cārvākas, since only the material elements are real, matter is responsible for thought, and it is the material body which gives rise to consciousness. Therefore, dissolution of the body at death entails the cessation of associated mental activity (see MATERIALISM, INDIAN SCHOOL OF §4).

At the opposite end of the ontological spectrum, the idealist position that matter is ultimately 'unreal' was also advocated, most notably by the Advaita Vedānta school of Śaṅkara. According to this view, absolute consciousness (*cit*) is the fundamental reality, and all particular manifestations, including the material world, are at root illusory. *Māyā* is the principle which sustains the appearance of all relative phenomena, and thus matter is ultimately diagnosed as *māyā*, an illusory appearance entertained by consciousness.

However, while the positions of pure materialism and absolute idealism are both represented in the history of Indian thought, some form of metaphysical pluralism is embraced by the majority of schools. Amongst these, matter is conceived as ontologically independent of mind (and vice versa), and this conception naturally motivates a rigorous investigation of the structure of the independent material realm. The atomistic pluralism of the Nyāya and Vaiśeṣika schools will be examined in §2, and the dualism of Sāṅkhya-Yoga philosophy will be covered in §3. The heterodox Jaina tradition also embraced a form of atomism in many ways comparable to the Nyāya-Vaiśeṣika theory (see JAINA PHILOSOPHY §1).

The extended intellectual conflict between the Hindu and Buddhist camps served to stimulate the development and articulation of their respective positions, and the Hindu views discussed below implicitly assume the presence of Buddhist theory as a competing system. At the heart of Buddhist thought lies a vision of the world as a shifting and transitory array of particles, which lacks any underlying substrate to serve as the common thread holding the moments of existence together. According to the doctrine of momentariness (*kṣaṇikavāda*), the world is an evanescent flux which is not materially preserved from one moment to the next, but rather consists in a series of discrete 'instants' (*kṣaṇas*) of existence, followed by complete annihilation before the next instant begins. Material objects, which appear as unitary and enduring, are analysed as mere aggregates, and possess no reality beyond the sum of their elemental parts (*dhātus*). So material objects are conceived as ontologically fragmentary and temporally discontinuous; real existence at each moment is granted only to the basic elements. These elements form momentary compounds, which, when viewed over a series of such moments, give the appearance of integral and continuous objects, much as a series of discrete frames supplies an illusion of continuity in a motion picture (see BUDDHISM, ĀBHIDHARMIKA SCHOOLS OF §3; BUDDHIST PHILOSOPHY, INDIAN §5; MOMENTARINESS, BUDDHIST DOCTRINE OF).

2 Vaiśeṣika atomism

Kaṇāda, legendary author of the *Vaiśeṣikasūtra*, is regarded as the founder of the Vaiśeṣika school, one of the six *darśanas* of orthodox Hindu philosophy. The name derives from the term *viśeṣa*, meaning 'ultimate particular', and this indicates the distinctively metaphysical orientation of the school. The Nyāya *darśana* of Akṣapāda GAUTAMA is distinguished by its preoccupation with logic and epistemology, and forms the sister school to Vaiśeṣika. The atomistic theory discussed in this section is part of the shared Nyāya-Vaiśeṣika position, although it is primarily the contribution of the latter school (see NYĀYA-VAIŚEṢIKA).

In contrast to Buddhist philosophy, the Vaiśeṣika position is that all qualities must inhere in a substance; properties cannot exist without an underlying substrate (*āśraya*) to ground them. According to this pluralistic account, there are nine such substances: earth, water, fire, air, ether (*ākāśa*), time, space (*diś*), mind (*manas*) and spirit (*ātman*), of which the first five are considered material substances. Each substance forms the ground for a characteristic quality: earth has smell, water has taste, fire has colour, air has touch and ether supports sound. Each substance either has infinite dimension or else is atomic in structure, a structural distinction which cuts across the material/nonmaterial divide. Of the material substances, earth, water, fire and air are atomic, while ether is infinite; and of the nonphysical elements, mind is atomic, while time, space and *ātman* are infinite.

Thus Vaiśeṣika recognizes four kinds of material atom (*paramāṇu*). The various macroscopic objects of the natural world are analysed as composites formed from *paramāṇus* of these four kinds, where the qualities of all objects are due to the qualities of the atoms of which they are composed. *Paramāṇus* have a number of distinguishing characteristics: they are indivisible and without parts (that is, genuinely atomic), they are unalterable and eternal, they are imperceptible, and they in fact lack spatial extension altogether and are held to be infinitesimal. In this manner, all substances are fundamentally either infinite or infinitesimal in magnitude.

The different atoms of a particular substance are qualitatively indistinguishable, but are none the less distinct particulars (*viśeṣas*). And there is only a qualitative difference between the atoms of different substances. As stated above, each substance has its characteristic quality, but this quality is not manifested at the level of the single atom. Rather, two atoms must combine to form a dyad, and three dyads combine to form a triad, which is the smallest level at which qualities are manifest. A triad is said to be of the magnitude of a 'mote of dust in sunlight', and the experienced world of matter is built up from such triads.

In contrast to the doctrine of momentariness, atoms are held to be indestructible and hence must persist through time, as do the composite objects of which they form the parts. But the composite objects, though persistent over finite intervals, are themselves ultimately transient and will eventually decompose. Thus matter at the macroscopic level is unstable, and atoms in motion constantly combine, disperse and recombine in new patterns.

In addition to dissolution at the level of particular objects, there is also a cosmic cycle of dissolution, stasis and reactivation, which forms a recurrent theme in Indian philosophy. According to Vaiśeṣika thought, atoms are naturally passive, so the entire universe eventually runs down. During cosmic stasis (*pralaya*), atoms subsist at rest without producing any effects. Original movement is due to external impact or activation, so the material world is not a closed system. A new cycle of the universe is initiated when an outside and 'unseen' force (*adṛṣṭa*) supplies the impetus.

The need to appeal to an external and latently purposive source of activation is an explanatory defect in a theory of matter, and the Vedānta thinker Śaṅkara criticizes the Vaiśeṣika account in this regard. The infinitesimal status of atoms is also problematic, since it would seem to entail that no finite collection of atoms could possess spatial magnitude, yet a mere triad is said to have perceptible dimensions. Śaṅkara also criticizes the view that the atoms have no parts, since this seems to imply that they cannot structurally combine; if they combine as wholes, then they must collapse into each other and remain infinitesimal, and if they combine in parts then they are not indivisible.

A number of important differences distinguish Kaṇāda's view from the ancient Greek atomistic theories of DEMOCRITUS (§2) and Epicurus (see EPICUREANISM §3), indicating that the two conceptions are probably independent. The Greeks hold atoms to be spatially extended, while as mentioned above, Kaṇāda contends that they lack dimension and are hence comparable to points in mathematical space. Additionally, the Greeks hold atoms to differ only quantitatively and not qualitatively, so that qualitative differences reduce to quantitative ones (for example, the figure, size and weight of the different atoms). In contrast, Kaṇāda takes qualitative difference as fundamental, while quantitative differences are analysed as macro-level features. The Greeks also believe atoms to be naturally in motion, as opposed to the Vaiśeṣika account summarized above, in which atoms are naturally at rest. Finally, the Greek view would reduce mind to matter (as would the Cārvākas), but the Vaiśeṣikas take mind (manas) as an independent (but none the less atomic) substance (see ATOMISM, ANCIENT).

3 Sāṅkhya dualism

The Sāṅkhya darśana is one of the oldest philosophical traditions of India, and many of its ideas are traceable to the Ṛg Veda and early Upaniṣads. Its historical founder is Kapila, though the original Sāṅkhyasūtra he is said to have written during the sixth or seventh century BC is now lost, and the most important of the existing texts is the Sāṅkhyakārikā of Īśvarakṛṣṇa, from around the third century AD. The Sāṅkhya tradition has a great many points in common with the classical Yoga darśana expounded in Patañjali's Yogasūtra, and the conception of matter discussed in the present section is part of their shared philosophical framework (see SĀṄKHYA).

According to the Sāṅkhya-Yoga view, the varied phenomena of the material world are all manifestations of a single underlying source. The metaphysical principle underpinning all physical manifestation is pradhāna or primal matter, which can be thought of as a form of pure potentiality, the ultimate base supporting all modifications and transformations. Prakṛti is another term used synonymously with pradhāna to denote the metaphysical basis of matter. As such, prakṛti is the unmanifest (avyakta) and uncaused origin of the physical universe. Prakṛti is

said to be continuous, all-pervading and eternal. Although continuous, it is differentiated into three constituent powers or guṇas, and the interaction of the guṇas is responsible for the dynamics of manifestation and transformation. The three guṇas are sattva, rajas and tamas, which correspond roughly with 'transparency and form', 'energy and motion' and 'inertia and obstruction'. The guṇas are opposing and mutually unstable forces intrinsic to the nature of prakṛti, and they cannot be separated or merged. All three are present in all material phenomena, and the differences between diverse objects are ultimately traceable to the predominance or proportions of the different guṇas.

Prior to the phase of manifestation which results in matter, prakṛti exists in the equilibrium state of pralaya. This is not a passive state of rest as in Nyāya-Vaiśeṣika, but consists rather in the tension of opposing forces in perfect balance. When this balance is disturbed, the process of becoming is set in motion, and material manifestation is thus seen as a state of disequilibrium. Once out of balance, the 'mechanical' interplay of the guṇas results in the evolution of the universe; the destabilized triad of forces counterbalance and readjust in a shifting pattern of transmutation.

Pradhāna gives rise to the material elements, which are said to be atomic in structure. However, unlike the Nyāya-Vaiśeṣika theory, this atomism is a physical rather than a metaphysical thesis, since the atoms themselves are manifestations of a continuous substrate. Thus the atoms are not metaphysically discrete, and the five material elements still reduce to the three guṇas.

Material actuality emerges from the state of potentiality, and to that source it returns. There is no genuine creation or annihilation in the Sāṅkhya view, but rather a sort of metaphysical unfolding and consequent reabsorption into the realm of latent possibility. Like the Vaiśeṣika atoms, pradhāna itself is eternal and indestructible. Eventually the entire universe follows the same course as its individual members, and is reabsorbed into the state of potentiality; the equilibrium of pralaya is once again obtained, giving rise to the familiar cycle of cosmic emergence and dissolution.

Prakṛti is inherently unconscious, and is held to be incapable of producing consciousness as an effect; the evolution of matter is a 'blind' mechanical affair. According to the Sāṅkhya-Yoga view, subjective awareness belongs to a different ontological category altogether, the realm of puruṣa or pure sentience. Puruṣa forms the other metaphysical pole in the dualistic system, and is said to consist of undifferentiated consciousness which is immutable and inactive, formless and without parts. However, in sharp contrast to Cartesian dualism, Sāṅkhya theory holds that mental faculties and activities are at root material; the mind is a manifestation of *prakṛti* rather than *puruṣa*. Thought is characterized by form and motion, which are distinctive attributes of matter, while consciousness is formless and inactive. Hence the basic metaphysical schism between consciousness and matter then leads to an ancillary dualism between consciousness and mind.

Pure consciousness or *puruṣa* is passive and does not guide the evolution of matter, so it does not guide the progression of thought, which is a strictly material process. However, it is consciousness which triggers the disequilibrium leading from *pralaya* to manifestation. This is not an act of volition or agency on the part of *puruṣa*, but is said to be a mechanical force, like magnetic attraction, which results merely from the proximity of the two substances. So even though consciousness does not influence the specific development of matter, it supplies the initial disturbance that throws *prakṛti* into the disequilibrium of material processes.

Thus *puruṣa* plays a role similar to the Vaiśeṣika *adṛṣṭa* in triggering a cycle of material manifestation, though in the Vaiśeṣika account this is more a purposive or teleological event, while in Sāṅkhya thought it is involuntary. Also, in the Sāṅkhya picture, the energy which drives the evolution of matter does not derive from an external source, but rather is an expression of *prakṛti*'s inherent powers as they unconsciously unfold. But the Sāṅkhya-Yoga picture is still clouded with respect to the precise nature of the interaction between the two substances. The fact that *prakṛti* can be 'mechanically' influenced indicates that it is not a closed system, and the fact that *puruṣa* can affect *prakṛti*, even unintentionally, indicates that consciousness is not purely inactive.

After *pralaya* has been disrupted and the cycle of manifestation has commenced, the two substances must continue their 'interaction' to produce the phenomenon of conscious mental activity. Thought processes and mental events are conscious only to the extent that they receive external 'illumination' from *puruṣa*, and it is the *sattva* constituent of matter which is able to 'absorb' this conscious radiance. The *sattva guṇa* is held to be 'transparent', while consciousness is often compared to a ray of light. The component of the mind known as *buddhi* or pure intellect (which is in some ways comparable to the Greek *nous*) is believed to consist of a preponderance of the transparent *sattva guṇa*, and this enables the material thought process of *buddhi* to become illuminated by the external light of consciousness. However, pure consciousness is held to be entirely independent of the mental structures it illuminates, just as sunlight does not *choose* to pass through particular transparent objects which happen to lie in its path.

The translucent quality of *buddhi* distinguishes thought-stuff from the grosser material objects of thought and perception, which ordinarily contain a preponderance of the 'dark' or opaque *tamas guṇa*. Thus only the thought material of *buddhi* is capable of conscious illumination, rather than the entire material realm, since a preponderance of the *tamas guṇa* renders the external objects of the material realm opaque to the light of consciousness. This is why minds appear to be conscious while stones and tables do not; only the subtle stuff of the *buddhi* is a suitable medium for receiving sentience, and thus it is minds which are the apparent loci of awareness in the material world.

See also: ONTOLOGY IN INDIAN PHILOSOPHY

References and further reading

Dasgupta, S. (1922) *A History of Indian Philosophy*, Cambridge: Cambridge University Press, 5 vols. (A pioneering compendium of Indian philosophical thought.)

* Īśvarakṛṣṇa (3rd century AD) *Sāṅkhyakārikā*, in N. Sinha, *The Samkhya Philosophy*, New Delhi: Oriental Books Reprint Corporation, 1979. (Good general overview of the Sāṅkhya school.)

Misra, U. (1936) *The Conception of Matter According to Nyāya-Vaiśeṣika*, Allahabad: M.N. Pandey. (Exposition of the shared view of matter.)

* Patañjali (4th–2nd century BC) *Yogasūtra*, in H. Aranya, *Yoga Philosophy of Patañjali*, Albany, NY: State University of New York Press, 1983. (Excellent discussion of Yoga philosophy.)

Radhakrishnan, S. (1923) *Indian Philosophy*, London: Allen & Unwin, 2 vols. (A classic survey of Indian philosophy.)

Raju, P.T. (1985) *Structural Depths of Indian Thought*, Albany, NY: State University of New York Press. (Critical exposition of Indian philosophy with a useful glossary of Sanskrit terms.)

Schweizer, P. (1993) 'Mind/Consciousness Dualism in Saṅkhya-Yoga Philosophy', *Philosophy and Phenomenological Research* 53: 845–59. (Discusses Sāṅkhya dualism and compares it with issues in Western conceptions of mind and matter.)

PAUL SCHWEIZER

MATTHEW OF AQUASPARTA
(*c*.1238–1302)

Matthew walked in the footsteps of Bonaventure, which were widened by his first followers, Walter of Bruges, John Pecham and William of Mare. For them, the knowledge of God's existence is the first truth implanted in the human mind. God's existence cannot be proved a priori (from something prior to it), since it is the first truth. It is a truth that is immediately known, not in the sense that there is actual knowledge of God implanted in the mind at birth, but because any judgment we make presupposes that the mind has contact with the Truth that is the measure of all truth. Such a first Truth must exist.

Born in the Italian village of Aquasparta, near Todi, Matthew came from the distinguished Bentivenghi family. A Franciscan friar, who often provided a response from the school of BONAVENTURE to the philosophy of AQUINAS, he qualified as a *baccalareus biblicus* (lecturer on the Bible) at Paris in 1268 and *baccalareus Sententiarum* (lecturer on Lombard's *Sentences*) in 1273. He lectured at Bologna from 1273–7 and then became regent master at Paris from 1277–9, before being named lector at the Roman curia from 1279–87. He was elected General Minister of the Franciscans at Montpellier in 1287 and fulfilled this charge until 1289, even after being named a cardinal in 1288. He served the Holy See under Pope Boniface VIII until his death in 1302.

Following Anselm's path, Matthew argues: 'If the first and highest being is the first and highest being, it necessarily follows that the first and highest being exists, for what is first and highest is most actual and most perfect, and for this reason exists *in actu* (actually), since existence is of the very nature of a first and highest being. Indeed, existence is identical with such a being' (*Quaestiones disputatae de productione rerum et de providentia* (Disputed Questions on the Production of Things and on Providence) 11–12). Matthew, however, holds that it is also necessary to approach the question of God's existence from empirical grounds. Such an approach allows us to make more explicit the knowledge of God that is implied in any of our original judgments. He argues, first of all, from the imperfection and mutability of finite beings to the need for their perfect and immutable foundation, and then from the orderly way in which the world runs and the goals things naturally pursue, to a first efficient and final cause (*De productione rerum* 12–17).

As the first and highest being, God knows and loves in the highest degree. Infinitely fulfilled in his own perfection, 'the first being neither makes nor conserves anything unknowingly, nor irrationally, nor by chance, nor by the necessity of his nature, but knowingly and with foresight and in an orderly way' (*De productione rerum* 36). God, as first and highest being, does not need anything. If he created a universe, it could be only to share his supreme goodness. Out of this infinite goodness, Matthew argues, God created rational creatures capable of knowledge and love, and consequently capable of happiness, to manifest and share his boundless perfection (see CREATION AND CONSERVATION, RELIGIOUS DOCTRINE OF; GOD, CONCEPTS OF).

In treating of creation, Matthew enters into the debate raging in the 1270s between the Averroists contending that the eternity of the world could be rationally demonstrated and the theologians who denied the validity of their proofs (see AVERROISM). Aquinas, admitting the temporal character of creation as an article of faith, contended that reason could demonstrate neither the temporal nor the eternal nature of creation. Matthew attacked Aquinas' efforts to show that specific arguments against the eternity of the world are not demonstrations. For Matthew, an eternal world would imply the existence of an infinite number of souls, or revolutions of the sun, or generations. These arguments against an eternal creation are necessary reasons, and the attempts of Aquinas to rebut them are sophistical (see ETERNITY OF THE WORLD, MEDIEVAL VIEWS OF).

Matthew holds that the 'agent' and 'possible' intellects are cognitive faculties belonging to the soul itself. However, they need the assistance of divine illumination to arrive at perfect, evident and necessarily true cognition. In his commentary on Book I of the *Sentences* (d. 35, q. 8), following Guibert of Tournai, he portrays this illumination as a special created light given by God. In his later *Quaestiones disputatae de cognitione* (Disputed Questions on Knowledge), returning to Bonaventure's position, he argues that this light must be God himself. Special assistance is required because the spiritual nature of the soul prevents it from being affected by sensible objects. The agent intellect, then, assisted by divine illumination, forms intelligible species of sense objects and impresses them on the possible intellect. Objects and the intellect are partial causes of knowledge, but the intellect is the principal cause. In regard to certain and necessary knowledge, however, the intellect is a secondary efficient cause; the primary cause is the divine light. The soul has a direct knowledge of itself. Concepts of purely immaterial entities, such as God, angels, the good or first principles, are innate or impressed in the soul and are not abstracted from the outside world.

Matthew is very much influenced by Aristotle's

philosophy, especially as elaborated by AQUINAS. Even when he rejects Aquinas' positions, Matthew's arguments are not simply repetitions of those of Bonaventure and his early followers. They are serious attempts to overcome Aquinas' theses. For instance, when Aquinas holds that the will acts according to the directives it receives from reason or intellect, Matthew objects that, while needing enlightenment from the intellect, the will itself activates the intellect, giving it commands and stimulating it to action. The will is superior to the intellect, first because its perfection, charity, is superior to the intellect's perfection, faith; and secondly, because its object, goodness, is superior to the intellect's object, truth. Will, not reason, is also the centre of freedom. Reason is necessary to enable us to conceive the possible choices open to us, and to deliberate about them; but it is the will which produces free human action, since a person depends on will when deciding to accept or reject what reason proposes (see FREE WILL).

See also: ARISTOTELIANISM, MEDIEVAL; AUGUSTINIANISM; BONAVENTURE; GOD, CONCEPTS OF; ETERNITY OF THE WORLD, MEDIEVAL VIEWS OF; PECHAM, J.

List of works

Matthew of Aquasparta (*c.*1238–1302) *Quaestiones disputatae de aeternitate mundi* (Disputed Questions on the Eternity of the World), q. 9, utrum [mundus] potuit esse ab aeterno vel utrum Deus potuit ipsum ab aeterno producere, ed. E. Longpré, *Archives d'histoire doctrinale et littéraire du moyen-âge* 1, 1926: 293–308. (Edition of disputed questions.)

—— (*c.*1238–1302) *Quaestiones disputatae de anima VI* (Six Disputed Questions on the Soul), ed. A.-J. Gondras, *Archives d'histoire doctrinale et littéraire du moyen-âge* 32, 1957: 203–352. (Edition of disputed questions on the soul.)

—— (*c.*1238–1302) *Quaestiones disputatae de anima XIII* (Thirteen Disputed Questions on the Soul), ed. A.-J. Gondras, *Études de philosophie médiévale* 50, 1961. (Edition of disputed questions on the soul.)

—— (*c.*1238–1302) *Quaestiones disputatae de fide et de cognitione* (Disputed Questions on Faith and Knowledge), ed. Patres Franciscani, Bibliotheca Franciscana Scholastica Medii Aevi I, Quaracchi: Editiones Collegii Sancti Bonaventurae, 1957. (Edition of disputed questions.)

—— (*c.*1238–1302) *Quaestiones disputatae de incarnatione et de lapsu* (Disputed Questions on the Incarnation and the Fall), Bibliotheca Franciscana Scholastica Medii Aevi II, Quaracchi: Editiones Collegii Sancti Bonaventurae, 1957. (Edition of disputed questions.)

—— (*c.*1238–1302) *Quaestiones disputatae de gratia* (Disputed Questions on Grace), ed. V. Doucet, Bibliotheca Franciscana Scholastica Medii Aevi XI, Quaracchi: Editiones Collegii Sancti Bonaventurae, 1935. (Contains a detailed biography and examination of Matthew's extensive writings, approximately thirty volumes of 500 pages each.)

—— (*c.*1238–1302) *Quaestiones disputatae de productione rerum et de providentia* (Disputed Questions on the Production of Things and on Providence), ed. G. Gàl, Bibliotheca Franciscana Scholastica Medii Aevi XVII, Quaracchi: Editiones Collegii Sancti Bonaventurae, 1956. (Questions on metaphysics.)

—— (*c.*1238–1302) *Quaestiones disputatae de anima separata, de anima beata, de ieiunio et de legibus* (Disputed Questions on the Separated Soul, the Blessed Soul, Fasting, and Laws), Bibliotheca Franciscana Scholastica Medii Aevi XVIII, Quaracchi: Editiones Collegii Sancti Bonaventurae, 1959. (Edition of disputed questions.)

—— (*c.*1238–1302) *Quaestiones disputatae de Christo (Disputed Questions on Christ)*, ed. E. Hocedez, *Quaestio de unico esse in Christo*, Rome: Apud aedes Universitatis Gregorianae, 1933, 44–58. (Questions on the nature of Christ.)

—— (*c.*1238–1302) *Quaestiones disputatae de illuminatione* (Disputed Questions on Illumination), ed. Patres Franciscani, *De humanae cognitionis ratione*, Quaracchi: Editiones Collegii Sancti Bonaventurae, 87–177. (Matthew's views on illumination.)

—— (*c.*1238–1302) *Commentarium in I-IV Sententiarum (Commentary on the Four Books of Sentences)*. Lib. I, prol., q. 7, ed. L. Amorós, *Archives d'histoire doctrinale et litt,raire du Moyen Age* 9, 1934: 284–5; Lib. I, d. 2, qq. 1-2, ed. A. Daniels, *Quellenbeitr,ge und Untersuchungen zur Geschichte der Gottesbeweise im 13. Jahrhunderts*, Beiträge zur Geschichte der Philosophie und Theologie des Mittelalters 8, 1–2, Münster: Aschendorff, 1905, 51–63; Lib. II, d. 19, q. 1, ed. S. Vanni Rovighi, *L'immortalità dell'anima nei Maestri Francescani del secolo XIII*, Milan: Societa editrice 'Vita e pensiero', 1936, 255–72. (Book I includes Matthew's views on illumination.)

References and further reading

Beha, H.M. (1961) 'Matthew of Aquasparta's Theory of Cognition', *Franciscan Studies* 20: 161–204, 21: 383–465. (Describes Matthew's views on knowledge and its relation to illumination.)

Berubé, C. (1974) 'Henri de Gand et Mathieu d'Aquasparta interprètes de saint Bonaventure'

(Henry of Ghent and Matthew of Aquasparta: Interpreters of St Bonaventure), *Naturaleza y gracia* 21: 131–72. (Studies the development of different views of illumination.)

Bettoni, E. (1943) 'Rapporti dottrinali fra Matteo d'Aquasparta e Giovanni Duns Scoto' (Doctrinal Relations between Matthew of Aquasparta and John Duns Scotus), *Studi Francescani XV* (3rd series): 113–30. (Studies the influence on Scotus of Matthew's teaching on the object of the intellect.)

Dowd, J.D. (1974) 'Matthew of Aquasparta's De productione rerum and its Relation to St. Thomas Aquinas and St. Bonaventure', *Franciscan Studies* 34: 34–73. (Shows the influences of Aquinas and Bonaventure on Matthew.)

Emmen, A. (1959) 'Die Glückseligkeitslehre des Matthäus von Acquasparta' (The Teachings on Beatitude of Matthew of Aquasparta), *Wissenschaft und Weisheit* 22: 43–59, 101–18, 174–89. (Explains Matthew's teaching on beatitude.)

Hayes, Z. (1964) *The General Doctrine of Creation in the Thirteenth Century, with Special Emphasis on Matthew of Aquasparta*, Munich: Schöningh. (Matthew's creation doctrine in its context.)

Marrone, S.P. (1983) 'Matthew of Aquasparta, Henry of Ghent and Augustinian Epistemology After Bonaventure', *Franziskanische Studien* 65: 252–90. (Describes the influence of Bonaventure on later thinkers, including Matthew.)

Mazzarella, P. (1969) *La dottrina dell'anima e della conoscenza in Matteo d'Acquasparta (Matthew of Aquasparta's Teaching on the Soul and Knowledge)*, Collana di studi filosofici 17, Padua: Gregoriana. (Matthew's teaching concerning the soul and human knowledge.)

Payne, G.R. (1981) 'Cognitive Intuition of Singulars Revisited (Matthew of Aquasparta versus B.J. Lonergan)', *Franciscan Studies* 41: 346–84. (On Matthew's views on knowledge.)

Prezioso, F. (1950) 'L'attività del soggetto pensente nella gnoseologia di Matteo d'Acquasparta e di Ruggiero Marston' (The Activity of the Present Subject in the Epistemology of Matthew of Aquasparta and Roger Marston), *Antonianum* 25: 259–326. (Indicates the role of the knower as a cause of knowledge.)

Putallaz, F-X. (1991) *La connaissance de soi au XIIIe siècle. De Matthieu d'Aquasparta à Thierry de Freiberg* (Self-Knowledge in the Thirteenth Century: From Matthew of Aquasparta to Dietrich of Freiberg), Études de philosophie médiévale 67, Paris: Vrin. (Deals with self-knowledge in authors of the late thirteenth century.)

STEPHEN F. BROWN

MAUTHNER, FRITZ (1849–1923)

The work of Fritz Mauthner helps document the phenomenon of 'language crisis' or Sprachkrise in German-Austrian letters at the beginning of the twentieth century. In his Beiträge zu einer Kritik der Sprache (Contributions to a Critique of Language) (1901–2), Mauthner develops a theory of knowledge that draws on empiricism but also redefines certain basic concepts in terms of language. 'Language' refers to more than speech; it is the medium of all cognition and, as such, an instrument of knowledge. Mauthner's reformulation of epistemological questions in linguistic terms does more than replace one topic with another. When language becomes the focus of philosophical debate, the debate cannot help but involve a discussion of the nature and limits of the discussion itself. As epistemology or theory of knowledge gives way to critique of language, it spells the end of philosophy as a foundational discourse for the human sciences.

1 Language in thought and communication
2 Philosophy as critique of language
3 Reception and later works

1 Language in thought and communication

The philosophical tradition with which Mauthner aligns himself most consistently is that of empiricism (see EMPIRICISM). He acknowledges debts to KANT, LOCKE and HUME, and sees his work as the continuation or even completion of their inquiries into the possibility of knowledge. Mauthner also stresses his divergence from these three philosophers with his notion of the 'contingent senses' or *Zufallssinne*. He outlines a traditional-sounding sceptical thesis about the limits and accuracy of empirical knowledge, then gives the argument an evolutionistic turn. He holds that the senses are contingent on human needs and have undergone modifications over time corresponding to shifts in those needs. Therefore sense data reflect what is useful, and utility by no means implies accuracy. On the contrary, Mauthner presents the filtering, organizing activity of the senses as a process of distortion.

Out of his scepticism about knowledge through the *Zufallssinne* grows his thesis that language provides only *Zufallsbilder* ('contingent images') of the world. The process of concept formation that begins with sense information also marks the first instance of language. 'Language' is the very medium in which mental pictures of reality are created. According to Mauthner, language is synonymous with reason, cognition and the work of memory. By proclaiming that there is no such thing as 'pure reason' (*reine Vernunft*) but only 'linguistic reason' (*sprachliche Vernunft*), Mauthner echoes a criticism of Kantian epistemology voiced already by Hamann and Herder in the eighteenth century. In this connection he also introduces the term 'metaphor'. By describing the relation between mind and world as metaphorical, Mauthner underlines his point about the linguistic character of all knowledge, since 'metaphor' is a literary trope and an element of rhetoric. The term also serves as a reminder that knowledge is limited: it results from the transformation or translation of sensations into concepts, and something is always lost in translation.

Mauthner's scepticism about an individual's ability to achieve true knowledge also bears directly on his view of language as a means of communication. The notion of a gap between the sensible and intelligible is already introduced with the thesis of the *Zufallssinne*, and the gap widens twice: first, when sense data become schematized in language (here understood in the psychological sense), and again when translated into the language shared by members of a linguistic community. Spoken or written language in Mauthner's view thus stands at a double remove from reality. He contends that because no two people have the same perceptions or thoughts, what they express by means of their communal language is virtually worthless. While admitting that the 'misrepresentations' are adequate for the demands of daily life, Mauthner does not conclude that any other form of knowledge is unnecessary or impossible. He retains instead the premise that knowledge consists in accurate representations of reality, and predictably arrives at sceptical conclusions about the ability of language to provide such knowledge.

2 Philosophy as critique of language

At the beginning of *Beiträge zu einer Kritik der Sprache* (Contributions to a Critique of Language) (1901–2), Mauthner admits that language must play a double role: it is the vehicle of the critique, and also the object of study. But the full extent of the problem becomes clear only when he has developed the thesis about the inadequacy of language as an instrument of knowledge. This argument raises the question of whether it is possible to claim the inadequacy of language without at least implicitly granting the claim itself a special authoritative status. In other words, does Mauthner's critique itself reflect or bear out the claims about language that it makes? His scepticism would seem to point toward silence, yet Mauthner continues to write after finishing the

Kritik. Mysticism, too, receives considerable attention in his work, and suggests another possible outcome of language critique. Silence and mysticism, however, remain potential answers rather than actual responses, options that Mauthner discusses but does not choose. The reason lies in the fact that language also has a social dimension which even Mauthner, for all his emphasis on the individual, psychological aspect of language, cannot overlook. When writing about language as a form of communication, he dismisses it as the language of the 'herd', which he feels has nothing to do with the object of his critique. What complicates the situation is that he, too, remains subject to the social force of language. In short, while Mauthner decries the tyranny of language on the first page of his *Kritik*, he still cannot escape it, and he admits as much in several different but related ways.

Naming the individual as the locus of (epistemological) value is itself a gesture that reflects social or communal agreement. The implied community in this case consists of philosophers writing before and at the same time as Mauthner, who likewise concentrate on the individual subject when theorizing about knowledge. In this context he also retains traditional metaphors of vision and representation, and thereby signals once more that he is participating in an ongoing conversation. Perhaps the clearest indication of how the social character of language in effect wins out over the individual-oriented aspect lies in Mauthner's statements about the purpose of his critique. He observes that unless others read his work and adopt his ideas, the critique has absolutely no value, and in his eyes is not even 'real'. He emphasizes his dependence on a community with another metaphor: calling language both a 'social game' (*Gesellschaftsspiel*) and 'the social game of knowing', he characterizes his own efforts as an attempt to change the rules.

On occasion Mauthner seems to grant his own work a voice of authority in traditional Kantian fashion, but other passages reveal that he questions philosophy's ability to provide knowledge or access to truth. He declares for instance that although individual philosophers and philosophies (plural) exist, there is no such entity as 'philosophy' (singular). In his view, philosophy-as-language-critique is indeed the discipline that investigates the working assumptions of other disciplines, but because the inquiry is not written in any sort of metalanguage, philosophy no longer occupies the foundational position it once held. As critique of language it has irrevocably lost its authoritative voice.

3 Reception and later works

Several of Mauthner's later works move away from the emphasis on individual psychology that characterizes his critique. *Die Sprache* (Language) (1906), for example, addresses questions about language as a social phenomenon including attempts to develop an international language or Esperanto, and different forms of translation. Mauthner draws attention to the shift in focus when he notes that the concept of a *sensorium commune* has been borrowed from 'older' psychology and applied to language in a social context, where in his view it becomes more tangible and accessible than when used in reference to the individual mind.

In *Die Sprache* Mauthner mentions an ambitious, now abandoned plan to write an 'international' historical dictionary that would document processes of translation. The somewhat more modest project that takes its place is his *Wörterbuch der Philosophie* (Dictionary of Philosophy) (1910–1), subtitled 'New Contributions to a Critique of Language'. Beyond tracing semantic change in some two hundred philosophical terms, Mauthner hopes to persuade his readers that meanings are anything but stable and that, because there are no fixed referents in language, there is no true knowledge. Because his nominalism skews the perspective decidedly, the dictionary is not always entirely reliable as a reference work. None the less, individual articles contain a wealth of historical information, and also provide condensed versions of arguments advanced in the *Kritik*.

The other major work that Mauthner published during his lifetime was a four-volume history of atheism. Although quite different in style from his philosophical dictionary, this work reflects the same basic argument that linguistic meaning is determined by use, and therefore changes over time. In his autobiographical writings Mauthner admits that at the time he began speculating about the existence of God, he probably did not recognize any link between his religious doubts and his growing interest in language. But as an adult, and more specifically as the author of a work on atheism, he perceives and even insists on the connection. He describes the history as the 'history of a word, the negative word-history of the gradual devaluation of the word "God"' (*Der Atheismus und seine Geschichte im Abendlande*, 1920–3). He intends to prove that belief in 'God' as anything more than a word is a form of word superstition.

In addition to the dictionary and the work on atheism, Mauthner completed short monographs on Aristotle, Spinoza and Schopenhauer. He also wrote the first (and only) volume of his memoirs, and edited several volumes in the series *Bibliothek der Philosophen* (Library of Philosophers), which was discontinued at the beginning of the First World War. The volumes on which Mauthner worked were on Fritz Jacobi's *Spinozabüchlein*, Agrippa von Nettesheim and the nineteenth-century philosopher of language O.F. Gruppe.

During his lifetime Mauthner enjoyed wide recognition, albeit not as a philosopher. He worked as a professional journalist for over twenty years in Berlin and, prior to writing the *Kritik*, also published novels, novellas and essay volumes in addition to a popular collection of literary parodies. Mauthner's literary and journalistic writings led many academic philosophers to dismiss his language critique as the work of a dilettante, but his work was taken seriously by thinkers including Ernst MACH, Hans VAIHINGER and Martin BUBER. After his death, Mauthner's work came to attention only gradually, in part because his extreme scepticism was so incompatible with more dominant trends in philosophy such as phenomenology and logical positivism.

Mauthner has the dubious distinction of being mentioned by name in Ludwig Wittgenstein's *Tractatus Logico-Philosophicus* (1922: 4.31), where we read: 'All philosophy is a "critique of language". (Though not in Mauthner's sense.)'. Wittgenstein takes very different stances from Mauthner's on such issues as the possibility of scientific knowledge, and maintains that congruence actually does exist between reality and language (in the form of logical propositions). Despite this important basic difference, the *Tractatus* and Mauthner's *Kritik* both end with a turn toward mysticism. For Mauthner the premise that some unmediated and extralinguistic mode of experience exists leads to a mystical yearning for that kind of experience. Wittgenstein, after working through propositions about what is sayable, declares that some things still elude us, and that these things may ultimately be more important than any knowledge we do have.

How well Wittgenstein knew Mauthner's work is not clear, but there is general agreement that their affinities emerge more clearly if we look at Wittgenstein's later work, particularly *Philosophical Investigations* (1953), where the notions of language game and meaning as use recall Mauthner's positions. Wittgenstein's description of his project as a way of showing the fly the way out of the fly bottle also seems to echo Mauthner, who stresses the salutary effect of critique of language. His attacks on 'word fetishism' and his insistence on the impossibility of attaining knowledge earned him an early reputation as a nihilist, which he himself rejected. Critique of language unmasks and destroys idols in the name of liberation, he argues; it should not be feared as a threat but welcomed as a sorely needed form of philosophical therapy.

See also: WITTGENSTEIN, L.

List of works

Mauthner, F. (1901–2) *Beiträge zu einer Kritik der Sprache* (Contributions to a Critique of Language), Leipzig: Felix Meiner, 3rd edn, 3 vols. (Individual volumes on different topics: psychology of language, concepts in linguistics, grammar and logic.)

—— (1906) *Die Sprache* (Language), in M. Buber (ed.) *Die Gesellschaft*, vol. 9, Frankfurt am Main: Literarische Anstalt Rütten & Loening. (Short essayistic work with emphasis on social rather than psychological dimension of language.)

—— (1910–1) *Wörterbuch der Philosophie. Neue Beiträge zu einer Kritik der Sprache* (Dictionary of Philosophy: New Contributions to a Critique of Language), Leipzig: Felix Meiner, 2nd edn, 3 vols. (Historical dictionary of philosophical terms, informed by the notion that linguistic meaning is determined by use.)

—— (1920–3) *Der Atheismus und seine Geschichte im Abendlande*, repr. Frankfurt am Main: Eichborn, 1988, 4 vols. (Historical work tracing both the 'struggle for liberation from the belief in God' and the history of the word 'God'.)

—— (1986) *Fritz Mauthner. Sprache und Leben. Ausgewählte Texte aus dem philosophischen Werk*, ed. and intro. G. Weiler, Salzburg: Residenz. (Contains excerpts from *Kritik, Sprache, Wörterbuch* and *Atheismus*; also from *Totengespräche* (1906), *Der letzte Tod des Gautama Buddha* (1913), *Gespräche im Himmel und andere Ketzereien* (1914), *Erinnerungen* (1918), *Die Philosophie der Gegenwart in Selbstdarstellungen* (1924) and *Die drei Bilder der Welt* (1925).)

References and further reading

Arens, K.M. (1984) *Functionalism and Fin de siècle. Fritz Mauthner's Critique of Language*, Bern: Peter Lang. (Mauthner in relation to nineteenth-century linguistics and various scientific models.)

Bredeck, E. (1992) *Metaphors of Knowledge. Language and Thought in Mauthner's Critique*, Detroit, MI: Wayne State University Press. (Rhetorical analysis, with emphasis on links between Mauthner's thought and contemporary theory.)

Eschenbacher, W. (1977) *Fritz Mauthner und die deutsche Literatur um 1900*, Bern: Peter Lang. (Concentrates on literary-historical context.)

Kühn, J. (1975) *Gescheiterte Sprachkritik. Fritz Mauthners Leben und Werk*, Berlin: de Gruyter. (Contains useful bibliography of all Mauthner's writings including journalism, literary works and philosophical texts.)

Leinfellner, E. and Schleichert, H. (eds) (1995) *Fritz Mauthner. Das Werk eines kritischen Denkers*, Vienna: Böhlau. (Essay collection including photographs, chronology of Mauthner's life and up-to-date bibliography of secondary literature.)

Weiler, G. (1970) *Mauthner's Critique of Language*, Cambridge: Cambridge University Press. (Detailed discussion of philosophical issues, situates Mauthner in the history of philosophy.)

* Wittgenstein, L. (1922) *Tractatus Logico-Philosophicus*, trans. C.K. Ogden and F.P. Ramsey, London: Routledge; trans. D.F. Pears and B.F. McGuinness, London: Routledge, 1961. (Quoted in §3. The major work of Wittgenstein's early period and the only book published during his lifetime. The first English translation was revised and approved by Wittgenstein himself, though the later version is now standard.)

ELIZABETH BREDECK

MAXWELL, JAMES CLERK (1831–79)

For his two achievements of unifying electricity, magnetism and light, and of inventing statistical dynamics, Maxwell stands as the founding mind of modern theoretical physics. More than any other physicist's his also was a mind shaped and informed by a training in philosophy, even though, unlike Heinrich Hertz or Ernst Mach, for example, he never wrote a philosophical treatise. Therein lies the point, however. Mach's and Hertz's best discoveries seem remote from their metaphysics, Maxwell's are bound up with his. Particularly important philosophically are his interconnected uses of relation, analogy and classification. He is also responsible for introducing the word 'relativity' into physics, and for articulating the scientific problematic that led to Einstein's theory.

1 **Physics and metaphysics**
2 **The electromagnetic field**
3 **Gases, molecules, statistics**
4 **Relativity, reality, ether**

1 Physics and metaphysics

Born in Edinburgh, Maxwell spent three years at Edinburgh University and learned philosophy there from Sir William HAMILTON. Hamilton was a critical rather than systematic thinker, and was influenced by Kant. His greatest gift to Maxwell was a human one – contact with a searching and erudite mind. Most potent among specifics was his doctrine of the 'relativity' of human knowledge – a word he coined in opposition to the post-Kantian idealists Fichte, Schelling and Hegel. Contrasting knowledge with belief, Hamilton held that while we may believe in the absolute we know nothing absolutely. All knowledge involves relations, either our own to the object or of objects to each other.

Maxwell migrated to Cambridge in 1850. There he gained another, different Kantian guide, William WHEWELL. Whewell's focus was science. In 1830 his friend John Herschel had written a brilliant sketch of early nineteenth-century discovery framed to illustrate Baconian principles – the work from which John Stuart MILL borrowed the five methods of induction now called his (see SCIENCE, 19TH CENTURY PHILOSOPHY OF §4). Whewell demurred, holding that while each science starts with Baconian observation, sooner or later it undergoes transition to a higher Kantian state governed by certain 'appropriate ideas' having an inner authority of their own, independent of the experiments that suggested them. Take Newton's inverse-square law of gravitation. Why is this exact? Kant had guessed a connection with the tridimensionality of space, since the surface area of a sphere in three dimensions is $4\pi r^2$. Whewell gave other examples, arguing that one mark of 'appropriateness' is simplicity, or, as modern physicists say, 'beauty'.

First an artist, then a poet, then a geometer, all before he was fifteen, Maxwell was that paradox, a slowly maturing prodigy. Of his first nine publications other than poems, five treated geometry, two colour vision, one – half-experimental – physics. Not until after his graduation from Cambridge did he join physics to 'metaphysics [in] the rigid high style ... about ten times as far *above* Whewell as Mill is *below* him, or Comte or Macaulay *below* Mill, using above and below conventionally like up and down [trains] in Bradshaw['s railway timetable]' ([Letter to R.B. Litchfield 4 July 1856] Campbell and Garnett 1882: 261).

Maxwell's work is a barrage of classifications. Classification of dynamical quantities, of electrical ones, of transport processes, of colours, classification in thermodynamics, various mathematical classifications, classification by dimensional analysis, classifications of instruments, diagrams, experimental techniques, laboratory designs, modes of research, types of scientific paper, even (wittily) of scientific meetings – all occur. With this multiplicity, in but not limited to the classifications, are *dualities*: two ways of classifying dynamical topics, two of vectors, two of colours, two of physical quantities at large, a dual classification of electrical units, dualities in optics, thermodynamics, electromagnetism, two approaches to harmonic analysis, two to potential theory, a dual definition of electromotive force. In electromagnetism, these dualities and multiple classifications connect with Hamiltonian relativity, with Faraday's ideas, and with mathematical analogies by Maxwell's fellow Scot William Thomson (Lord Kelvin), as will now appear.

2 The electromagnetic field

Maxwell's theory united electricity, magnetism and light, it created radio, generated the relativity crisis, and set physics on a new path – field theory. Rich in discovery, new in form, startling in its picture of the electric current as an entity extending beyond the confines of the wire that guides it, this was more than a new theory. It was a new *kind* of theory.

According to Maxwell, two magnets (or charges or electric currents) do not act on each other directly. Each separately stores up energy in the surrounding space (the 'field') and the forces arise indirectly via the field. A natural question is whether this indirect transmission is instantaneous. To his astonishment Maxwell found that electrical signals propagate through space as waves with a velocity identical with that of light. Moreover, these waves *had to be* transverse. The problem of the longitudinal wave, the nightmare of mechanical ethers, had evaporated (see ELECTRODYNAMICS; FIELD THEORY, CLASSICAL).

Earlier workers had sought causes; Maxwell sought relations. Instead of *explaining* light or electromagnetism he established a relation between the two, and the central structure of his theory is neither a law nor a set of axioms but a system of relations among electric and magnetic quantities – Maxwell's equations. These he grouped in two ways. One, *electrical*, comprised the four equations we now call his; the other, *dynamical*, included also the 'Lorentz' force and the vector potential A. Compactness plus a belief that A is unphysical made his successors prefer the first. Maxwell saw further. He wrote in 1873: 'Our object at present is not to obtain compactness in the mathematical formulae but to express every relation of which we have any knowledge. To eliminate a quantity that expresses a useful idea would be rather a loss than a gain at this stage of our enquiry' (Maxwell 1873, vol. II: 234).

Electric currents produce not attractions, but *circular* magnetic forces. Why? Earlier opinion had been divided. To Ampère and Wilhelm Weber the effect was secondary, reducible to underlying attractive–repulsive forces, albeit forces entangling strange additional dependencies on angles (Ampère) or relative motions (Weber). To Faraday, the instinctive geometer mapping lines of force, such explanations seemed perverse, a reduction of the simple to the complex, especially when he found that even electrostatic forces act in curved lines. And so to Maxwell's first paper (1856).

Picture – the analogy is Thomson's – a fixed elastic solid in which is embedded a long straight wire. Pull the wire a distance i'. The solid will become cylindrically distorted, with displacements A' parallel to i' and consequent twistings B' about directions circling the wire. Different as they are physically, these quantities i', B', A' correspond geometrically to current i, magnetic force B and Maxwell's A in electromagnetism. Transcending geometry, Maxwell then made a spectacular discovery. Other electromagnetic phenomena also depend neatly on A. Here was a theory, dual to Weber's, advantageous precisely because it did not 'even in appearance, *account for* anything' (Maxwell 1890, vol. I: 207)

A second analogy, between lines of force and fluid motion, enabled Maxwell to mesh Faraday's curved lines of force with classical potential theory, and legitimize Kant's argument about the inverse-square law. Inverse-square forces entail a field satisfying a continuity equation. The law rests on experiment but any departure from it means large changes in theory – a different underlying geometry, say, as with gravity in Einstein's theory, or radically different field concepts as with nuclear forces.

Different equations, Maxwell's and Weber's, cover the same phenomena. Different phenomena, electric force and fluid motion, obey the same equations. Such dualities, with analogy, subvert conventional scientific explanation. Even more peculiar is the union, geometrical not physical, between Coulomb's and Faraday's theories, effected by an analogy unrelated physically to either. It is puzzles like these that destroy the well-known saying by Heinrich HERTZ, that 'Maxwell's theory is Maxwell's system of equations', and analogies merely 'gay garments' clothing 'the simple and homely figure' of nature (Hertz 1893: 21, 28). How strangely have Hertz's admirers failed to see his couturierial vision as itself an analogy, and a singularly inept one. For Maxwell's problem is just this – how to link fact, concept, and equation when each holds multiple meanings.

One duality that Maxwell, with magian prescience, illumined was between wave and particle theories of light. 'That theories so fundamentally opposed should have so large a field of truth common to both is a fact the philosophical importance of which we cannot fully appreciate until we have reached a scientific altitude from which the true relation between hypotheses so very different can be seen' (Maxwell 1890, vol. II: 228).

Was all theory analogy? Maxwell's in its dynamical form illustrates the complexities. It was in two senses hybrid. It inserted electrical energies into dynamical equations, and it contained some things literal, others analogical. Field energy was – energy. *Electrokinetic momentum*, Maxwell's new name for his old A, was an analogy.

That A resembles *momentum* for currents and *potential* for forces shows the subtlety of 'scientific metaphor'. Long neglected, the momentum analogy gained new life with quantum mechanics. In 1959, Y. Aharonov and D. Bohm proved, against eighty years of post-Maxwellian wisdom, that through it, A has direct physical meaning.

3 Gases, molecules, statistics

Maxwell did not introduce statistics into physics, or invent gas theory, or first fix molecular sizes. Yet he revolutionized all three, pondered metaphysical consequences and, long before Planck, quanta, and the 'ultraviolet catastrophe', saw here alongside triumph sudden scientific disaster.

It was Clausius who brought in statistics. Recognizing that the fast-moving molecules of gases must constantly collide, he defined in 1858 a characteristic mean *distance* between collisions, taking all molecules to have the same speed. Correcting this, Maxwell treated *speed* also statistically by computing a 'velocity distribution function'. Then came classification. Linking three disjoint phenomena, diffusion, viscosity, thermal conduction, to transport through the gas, respectively, of mass, momentum, and energy, he obtained, among much else, two separate, very good estimates of the free path in air ($\sim 6 \times 10^{-6}$cm), and the astonishing result that viscosity is over a wide range independent of pressure. Investigations of extreme technical sophistication followed, not least the great paper of 1867 on transport processes that electrified Boltzmann.

Are atoms real? If mass and diameter are primary qualities, yes – a reality suddenly unveiled in 1865 by J.J. Loschmidt from data on free paths and condensation-ratios. Here we must repudiate the myth that atomism had no physical basis prior to Einstein's and Perrin's work around 1905. The evidence was overwhelming. Maxwell's 1873 treatment (reprinted in 1890: 343–50) was the best, yielding estimates for molecular masses and dimensions, and Avogadro's number, remarkably near modern values.

Maxwell had found, and Boltzmann elaborated, a

most surprising statistical law, the equipartition theorem. It gave for specific heats of gases unequivocally wrong answers. Classical mechanics had failed. Reviewing and rejecting in 1875 all the supposed explanations, Maxwell could only urge that 'thoroughly conscious ignorance which is the prelude to every real advance in knowledge' (1877b).

Since 1925 many people have made quantum uncertainty the door to human free will. Randomness spells choice. Years earlier, Maxwell in an essay on 'Science and Free Will' (1873; Campbell and Garnett 1882: 434–44) explored similar thoughts as issues of analogy. There is science, there is life. Planetary orbits are exactly predictable; gas laws statistically so; other phenomena not at all because tiny changes in initial conditions produce through instability vastly different outcomes. That in essence is chaos theory (see CHAOS THEORY). Not every outcome is chaos, however. Human achievement lies in seizing such singular points, such 'tides in the affairs of men', and our deepest intuitions of free will connect with them. If that only advances us one step (elsewhere Maxwell said, 'states of the will only puzzle me' (1879; Campbell and Garnett 1882: 417)), it is a useful step.

Who but Maxwell would dare the inversion of basing physics on free will? Picking and choosing between fast and slow molecules, Maxwell's demon (in his *Theory of Heat* 1871) uses intelligence rather than work to transfer heat from cold to hot bodies, thereby defeating the second law of thermodynamics. Maxwell thus made entropy incomplete knowledge, refuting attempts by Clausius and Boltzmann to interpret it dynamically. Later (in 1877) Boltzmann derived a famous equation relating entropy to statistical disorder. In 1929 Leo Szilard sought exorcism through information theory, arguing that the demon's ordering of the world is outweighed by a quantum mechanical disordering within his own brain.

4 Relativity, reality, ether

Maxwell's philosophical position is best described as modified scientific realism (see SCIENTIFIC REALISM AND ANTIREALISM). Fundamental to it is Hamilton's distinction between knowledge and belief. Scientific knowledge is real but also limited, partly of the 'rigid high' kind, partly empirical, complicated by analogy, entangled in relations. A way through is classification, or rather multiplicity of classification. It is instructive to compare Maxwell's youthful essay 'Analogy' (1856; reprinted in Campbell and Garnett 1882: 235–44) with two later works, *Matter and Motion* (1877a) and the short 'Note on the Classification of the Physical Sciences' (1873; published

1884). By the 1870s he had defined a programme of dynamical reductionism which, except in its clarity and philosophical restraint, is strikingly modern. *Matter and Motion* is a masterpiece of natural philosophy, notable especially for introducing into physics the term *relativity* in a passage that combines strenuous scientific insight with a mystical awareness worthy of the fourteenth-century author of *The Cloud of Unknowing*.

Relativity now connotes Albert EINSTEIN. But the issues originated with Maxwell. He suggested the famous Michelson–Morley ether-drift experiment, and his equations necessitate the Lorentz transformation. About the ether Maxwell's problem was again knowledge versus belief. He accepted the ether; he did not finally describe it. His theory is a relational one. For him the ether had also another kind of relativity: it belonged to 'the science of 1876 (which may not agree with that of 1896)'. ([Letter to Bishop C.J. Ellicott, 22 November 1876] Campbell and Garnett 1882: 393) (see RELATIVITY THEORY, PHILOSOPHICAL SIGNIFICANCE OF).

List of works

Maxwell, J.C. (1871) *Theory of Heat*, London: Longmans & Co. (This textbook, which went through 11 editions, contains the first account of Maxwell's demon.)
—— (1873) *Treatise on Electricity and Magnetism*, Oxford: Clarendon Press, 2 vols. (The classic work.)
—— (1877a) *Matter and Motion*, London: Society for Propagation of Christian Knowledge. (Extremely illuminating both about Maxwell and about physics in the 1870s. Had a strong influence on Poincaré.)
—— (1877b) 'Review of "A Treatise in the Kinetic Theory of Gases" by Henry William Watson', *Nature* 18: 242–6. (Reprinted in Garber, Brush, and Everitt, 1995.)
—— (1881) *Elementary Treatise on Electricity*, Oxford: Clarendon Press. (Contains an interesting discussion of scientific analogy.)
—— (1884) 'Note on the Classification of the Physical Sciences', *Encyclopaedia Britannica*, vol. 19, 1–3. (Written in 1873.)
—— (1890) *The Scientific Papers of J. Clerk Maxwell*, Cambridge: Cambridge University Press, 2 vols. (Contains all but fifteen of Maxwell's published papers.)
—— (1990, 1995) *Scientific Letters and Papers of James Clerk Maxwell*, vol. 1, *1846–62*, vol. 2, *1862–73*, ed. P. Harman, Cambridge: Cambridge University Press. (Well-edited version of a large selection of Maxwell's previously unpublished writings.)

Garber, E., Brush, S.G. and Everitt, C.W.F. (eds) (1986) *Maxwell on Molecules and Gases*, Cambridge, MA: MIT Press. (See 1995.)
—— (eds) (1995) *Maxwell on Heat and Statistical Mechanics*, Bethlehem, PA: Lehigh University Press. (These two works contain all of Maxwell's published and known unpublished writings in this area, with fairly detailed commentary.)

References and further reading

Brush, S.G. (1972) *The Kind of Motion We Call Heat*, Amsterdam: North Holland. (Covers in technical detail the history of the kinetic theory of gases.)
Buchwald, J. (1985) *From Maxwell to Microphysics*, Chicago, IL: University of Chicago Press. (A thorough treatment of one group of Maxwell's followers. The treatment of the electric current is controversial.)
* Campbell, L. and Garnett, W. (1882) *Life of James Clerk Maxwell*, London: Macmillan. (In its account of Maxwell's first twenty-five years one of the most brilliant Victorian biographies. The later parts are less satisfactory.)
Everitt, C.W.F. (1975) *James Clerk Maxwell, Physicist and Natural Philosopher*, New York: Charles Scribner's Sons. (Brief technical account. Contains a detailed bibliography to 1975.)
Hendry, J.M. (1986) *James Clerk Maxwell and the Theory of the Electromagnetic Field*, Bristol: Adam Hilger. (A historical critical overview.)
* Hertz, H. (1893) *Electric Waves*, London: Macmillan. (Besides discussing the discovery of radiowaves contains an historically important review of Maxwell's electromagnetic theory.)
Hesse, M.B. (1961) *Forces and Fields*, London: Nelson. (A standard work.)
—— (1963) *Models and Analogies in Science*, London: Sheed & Ward. (A wide-ranging discussion of scientific analogy with references to Maxwell.)
Hunt, B.J. (1991) *The Maxwellians*, Ithaca, NY: Cornell University Press. (An account of three key Maxwellians: G.F. FitzGerald, Oliver Heaviside, Oliver Lodge.)
Siegel, D.M. (1991) *Innovation in Maxwell's Electromagnetic Theory: Molecular Vortices, Displacement Current and Light*, Cambridge: Cambridge University Press. (Masterly, if controversial, exposition of Maxwell's second paper on electromagnetism which revealed the connection with light.)
Whittaker, E.T. (1953) *History of the Theories of Aether and Relativity*, London: Nelson, 2 vols. (An indispensable source for nineteenth- and twentieth-
century physics at a high intellectual level. Regrettably, the chapter on Maxwell is weak.)

C.W.F. EVERITT

MEAD, GEORGE HERBERT (1863–1931)

Together with Charles Peirce, William James and John Dewey, George Herbert Mead is considered one of the classic representatives of American pragmatism. He is most famous for his ideas about the specificities of human communication and sociality and about the genesis of the 'self' in infantile development. By developing these ideas, Mead became one of the founders of social psychology and – mostly via his influence on the school of symbolic interactionism – one of the most influential figures in contemporary sociology. Compared to that enormous influence, other parts of his philosophical work are relatively neglected.

Mead was the son of a Protestant clergyman in Massachusetts. He spent the larger part of his childhood and youth at Oberlin College, Ohio, where his father was appointed professor and where he himself studied. After four years of bread-and-butter employment and intense intellectual struggle with the Darwinian revolution and Kant's moral philosophy, Mead entered graduate study at Harvard and continued at the Universities of Leipzig and Berlin, Germany, specializing in questions of psychology and philosophy. After teaching at the University of Michigan (1891–4), Mead was brought by Dewey to the newly founded University of Chicago where he taught until the end of his life in 1931. Publishing very little, but increasingly influential through his teaching and his life as an activist citizen during the Progressive Era, Mead's reputation has grown since his death. All his major works were published posthumously, based partly on student notes, partly on unfinished manuscripts from his remaining papers.

Mead's intellectual development and general outlook are quite similar to Dewey's: from neo-idealism to a pragmatism oriented to the emerging social-scientific disciplines and the debates about the fate of the democratic ideal in fully industrialized societies. Mead went beyond Dewey in his theory of the specificities of human communication and sociality. Human communication is, according to Mead, superior to animal forms of communication primarily because it operates through 'significant symbols': human beings are able to react to their own gestures and utterances in a way that is anticipatory and thus inwardly represents their fellow 'actors'' possible responses. This makes it possible for their own behaviour to be oriented towards the potential reactions of other actors. As these actors, too, are in possession of this ability, common collective action oriented towards a common binding pattern of mutual behaviour expectations becomes possible. This is for Mead the fundamental feature of all human sociality. 'Taking the role of the other' – one of Mead's famous expressions – is the anticipation of the other's behaviour in a specific situation of interaction.

The possibility of communication through the inner representation of the other's behaviour leads to the formation of different instances in the personality structure of the individual. This is due to the fact that individuals observe and estimate their own behaviour similarly to the way they see the behaviour of partners. The individuals are able to look at themselves from the perspective of the other. Alongside the dimension of impulses there is now an opportunity to evaluate those impulses, an instance which arises out of the expectations of the reactions caused by the manifestations of these impulses. In this context Mead speaks about 'I' and 'me'. The concept of the 'I' designates not only the principle of spontaneity and creativity, but also the endowment of the human being with impulses. 'Me' refers to my own mental presentation of the other's image of me, or, on a more primitive level, to my internalization of the other's expectations of me. The 'me' is both an instance of judgment for the structuring of spontaneous impulses and an element of my emerging self-image. As I face several different persons who have significance for me, I acquire several different 'me' images. These have to be synthesized to make a consistent self-image possible. A successful synthesis generates the 'self' as a unitary self-evaluation and as an orientation for action. Simultaneously, a personality structure develops which is stable and certain of its needs.

Mead's ideas about the development of the self can be found *in nuce* in his theory of children's play. Therein, he draws a line between 'play' and 'game'. 'Play' means the child's playful interaction with an imaginary partner in which the child mimes both parts of the interaction. Thereby the capacity for anticipation of behaviour is given practice: the other's behaviour is represented directly, for example, via imitation, and is complemented by the child's own behaviour. The child has reached this stage as soon as it is able to interact with different persons; that means, when the person with a cathectically high significance is no longer the solely important one. This stage of development is followed by the attainment of the ability to participate in 'games', that is, group

activities. In 'games' it becomes necessary that the behaviour of all partners – and not of one single partner – can be taken as the guideline for the child's action. The individual actor has to self orientate to a goal that is valid for all the actors concerned, and which Mead calls, trying to express its psychological bases, the 'generalized other'. In the case of games the generalized other's expectations of behaviour are the rules of the game; in general it means the norms and values of a group, differentiated in a specific way to take into account the specific positions in the group and specific situations. The orientation to a particular generalized other, however, reproduces on a new plane the same restriction which the orientation to a particular concrete other has. Thus follows the problem of an orientation to an ever more universal generalized other.

Mead further developed his ideas about human communication in the fields of general cognitive and moral development. The development of communicative abilities becomes a condition for cognitive progress inasmuch as it is the development of role-taking ability that allows the actors to assume a reflexive attitude towards themselves, and substantial cognitive achievements presuppose just such an attitude. Mead elaborates this idea in his late works, particularly with respect to the problem of the constitution of the permanent object. Its ethical implications are expounded at the individual level as universal role-taking ability and performance, and, at the societal level, in a concept of an ideal society with a universal capacity for communication. During the last decade of his life, Mead was particularly engaged in a dialogue with Dewey and Whitehead's new metaphysics and the role of sociality within it (see DEWEY, J. §3; WHITEHEAD, A.N. § 3).

See also: COMMUNICATION AND INTENTION; COMMUNICATIVE RATIONALITY; PRAGMATISM; PRAGMATISM IN ETHICS §4; SELF, INDIAN THEORIES OF; SUBJECT, POSTMODERN CRITIQUE OF THE; SOCIAL ACTION; SOCIAL NORMS; SYMBOLIC INTERACTIONISM

List of works

Mead, G.H. (1932) *The Philosophy of the Present*, ed. A. Murphy, La Salle, IL: Open Court. (Mead's philosophy of temporality.)

—— (1934) *Mind, Self, and Society*, ed. Ch. Morris, Chicago, IL: University of Chicago Press. (Mead's social psychology.)

—— (1936) *Movements of Thought in the Nineteenth Century*, ed. M.H. Moore, Chicago, IL: University of Chicago Press. (Mead's fragmentary intellectual history.)

MEANING AND COMMUNICATION

—— (1938) *The Philosophy of the Act*, ed. Ch. Morris, with J.M. Brewster, A.M. Dunham and D.L. Miller, Chicago, IL: University of Chicago Press. (Collection of manuscripts from Mead's remaining papers.)
—— (1964) *Selected Writings*, ed. A. Reck, Indianapolis, IN: Bobbs-Merrill. (Collection of some articles Mead published during his lifetime.)

References and further reading

Cook, G.A. (1993) *George Herbert Mead. The Making of a Social Pragmatist*, Urbana and Chicago, IL: University of Illinois Press. (Careful study of Mead's biography and intellectual development.)

Joas, H. (1985) *G.H. Mead. A Contemporary Reexamination of his Thought*, Cambridge, MA: MIT Press. (Comprehensive study of Mead's work, comparing it to Continental traditions in philosophy and social theory in general. The second edition of 1997 contains a new preface)

Miller, D.L. (1973) *G.H. Mead. Self, Language and the World*, Austin, TX: University of Texas Press. (Written by a student of Mead, this book gives a good overview of Mead's work and compares it to the tradition of analytic philosophy.)

HANS JOAS

MEANING *see* LANGUAGE, PHILOSOPHY OF; SEMANTICS

MEANING AND COMMUNICATION

The two fundamental facts about language are that we use it to mean things and we use it to communicate. So the philosophy of language tries to explain what it is for words and sentences to mean things and also what it is for us to communicate by using them. Although it cannot be accidental that meaning and communication go together, it is quite easy to see them as fundamentally distinct. Thus on some accounts the meaning of sentences is conceived in terms of a 'representative' power whereby they stand for either aspects of the world or ideas in the mind and their use in communication is derived from this property: language serves as a vehicle for meaning, itself thought of in independent terms. An alternative approach seeks to link the two more closely, seeing representation as

itself only possible through the use of terms of a common language, used in communication.

At its most primitive, communication may be simply akin to infection, as when one animal communicates fear or hostility to another. Simple signalling is also described as communication, as when bees communicate the direction and quantity of pollen to other bees, or when birds communicate territorial or sexual claims. Here the signaller issues a sign and the recipient modifies its behaviour upon perceiving it; the content of the signal is interpreted (by us) to be whatever goal seems to be served by issuing it: maximizing the success of the hive in obtaining honey, or keeping other birds out of a particular space, for example. Humans communicate in a similar sense, through the use of emotional and other signals, unconscious 'body language' or equally unconscious or semiconscious signs, which may include fashion statements or indications of status, for example. When we communicate successfully we share an understanding. Everything is open between us; nothing is concealed nor taken by one person in one way and another in a different way. With linguistic communication this common understanding can be put in terms of meaning: we each know what the other means. This implies that we understand not only the semantics of the utterance, but also the pragmatics: if the utterance states that something is the case then we know what this is, but we also know if the statement was meant ironically, or condescendingly, or with some other intent (see PRAGMATICS). It is plausible to think that the basic goal of speech is to achieve such communication, although there will be cases where we speak in order to conceal our thoughts, or to mislead the hearer. People fluent in the same language achieve open communication more or less effortlessly, at least where straightforward messages are concerned. But philosophers of language have not found this phenomenon easy to understand. Issues arising include: the place of intention in communication (see COMMUNICATION AND INTENTION); the place of linguistic convention in communication (see LANGUAGE, CONVENTIONALITY OF); the relationship between shared understanding and activities such as translation and interpretation (see RADICAL TRANSLATION AND RADICAL INTERPRETATION); the pervasive possibility of indeterminacy; and the nature of rules and the extent to which language is essentially social – and indeed the extent to which language is necessary to communication (see MEANING AND RULE-FOLLOWING). In the analytic tradition, major writings on this subject include works by Wittgenstein, Grice, Lewis, Bennett, Kripke, Searle

212

and Tuomela, while a more continental interest in the field is especially illustrated by Habermas (1984, 1987).

The classical tradition, including Aristotle, Hobbes and Locke, thinks of communication in terms of one party having an idea then using language as a medium for transmitting it to others. The meaning of the linguistic vehicle is then derived from the primitive representative powers of the idea. The analytic tradition has sought to bring our ability to represent things closer to our ability to express what we think linguistically, even to the point of reversing the dependency and making thought itself (or at least the kind of thought that could be expressed in language, unlike perhaps the thought of the graphic artist or the musician) dependent upon its linguistic expression. The question then becomes one of saying how language can generate 'intentionality', which is the power of being 'about' external and often absent situations which it represents truly or falsely (see INTENTIONALITY). If, for example, language is essentially a shared and social construction, and if it is necessary to thought, then we derive the result that a born Robinson Crusoe would not be capable of thought, at least until he acquired a social identity. The consequence seems uncomfortable, since it is easy to imagine such a Crusoe giving all sorts of signs of intelligent adaptation to his environment, and conceiving and executing complex plans. For some thinkers, such as John Searle (1983), this is because intentionality resides in our biological nature, in advance of and independent of language. For others, such as Jerry Fodor (1987), it is because we come equipped with an innate representative medium conceived on the model of a natural (social) language, but itself explaining the powers of natural languages: a 'language of thought' (see LANGUAGE OF THOUGHT).

Arguably too much of the theory of communication treats the process as one of interpretation or translation, in which the task of the hearer is to theorize about the thoughts intended by some act of communication of the speaker. This makes it seem as if each person is secure in their own 'ideolect', with it being relatively problematic whether the same ideolect is shared by others. This clearly distorts what it is to share a language, which surely entails finding ourselves (surprisingly literally) of one mind about meaning. We have a securely shared common understanding, in which I have no privileged access to my own meanings which is not communicable to others. Philosophers have therefore struggled against the vision of the infant, inducted into this shared language, as a kind of outsider or 'little linguist' busy theorizing (in what medium?) about the potential meanings of the utterances made by surrounding people. The proposed alternative derives from the *Verstehen* (literally 'to understand') tradition of humane sciences (see DILTHEY, W.), seeing the task of the infant not so much as one of theorizing as one of imitating and simulating the expressions of others. I achieve the openness of full communication with you, on such an account, when I know what it would be to make your words my own.

References and further reading

Bennett, J. (1976) *Linguistic Behaviour*, Cambridge: Cambridge University Press. (A lively development of Grice's work, especially valuable for its discussion of the relation between full intentionality and more primitive signalling systems.)

Blackburn, S. (1984) *Spreading the Word*, Oxford: Oxford University Press. (An attempt at an accessible discussion of most of the central issues, aimed at moderately advanced students.)

* Fodor, J.A. (1987) *Psychosemantics: The Problem of Meaning in the Philosophy of Mind*, Cambridge, MA: MIT Press. (The classic defence of the theory that meaning is the outcome of computational structures in the mind/brain.)

* Grice, H.P. (1957) 'Meaning', *Philosophical Review* 66; repr. in *Studies in the Way of Words*, Cambridge, MA, and London: Harvard University Press, 1989. (The seminal article in the field.)

* Habermas, J. (1984, 1987) *The Theory of Communicative Action*, trans. T. McCarthy, Boston, MA: Beacon Press, 2 vols. (An attempt to connect the social nature of language to the virtues of free democratic debate.)

Kripke, S.A. (1982) *Wittgenstein on Rules and Private Language*, Oxford: Blackwell. (A particularly accessible presentation of the thesis that meaning is essentially social.)

Lewis, D.K. (1969) *Convention: A Philosophical Study*, Cambridge, MA: Harvard University Press. (The classic modern analysis of the concept.)

Searle, J.R. (1969) *Speech Acts*, Cambridge: Cambridge University Press. (An accessible development of the work of J.L. Austin on the actions that generate meaning.)

* —— (1983) *Intentionality: An essay in the philosophy of mind*, Cambridge: Cambridge University Press. (Searle's work is perhaps the most impressive development of the notion of acts performed in speech, but also controversial through its firm belief that the intentional powers of language are derived from a prior biologically engendered capacity.)

Tuomela, R. (1984) *A Theory of Social Action*,

Dordrecht: Reidel. (An influential attempt to see collective action as arising from the individual intentions of the different parties.)

SIMON BLACKBURN

MEANING AND RULE-FOLLOWING

Wittgenstein's discussion of rules and rule-following, and the recent responses to it, have been widely regarded as providing the deepest and most challenging issues surrounding the notions of meaning, understanding and intention – central notions in the philosophy of language and mind. The fundamental issue is what it is for words to have meaning, and for speakers to use words in accordance with their meanings. In Philosophical Investigations *and* Remarks on the Foundations of Mathematics, *Wittgenstein explores the idea that what could give a word its meaning is a rule for its use, and that to be a competent speaker is to use words in accordance with these rules. His discussion of the nature of rules and rule-following has been highly influential, although there is no general agreement about his conclusions and final position. The view that there is no objectivity to an individual's attempt to follow a rule in isolation provides one strand of Wittgenstein's argument against the possibility of a private language.*

To some commentators, Wittgenstein's discussion only leads to the sceptical conclusion that there are no rules to be followed and so no facts about what words mean. Others have seen him as showing why certain models of what it takes for an individual to follow a rule are inadequate and must be replaced by an appeal to a communal linguistic practice.

1   **Meaning and rules**
2   **Rules and rule-followers**
3   **Kripke's Wittgenstein**
4   **Attempted solutions**
5   **McDowell's quietism**
6   **Wright's extension-determining approach**

1   Meaning and rules

Words are meaningful only if there is such a thing as using them correctly or incorrectly. To have determinate meanings they must have application in some situations and not others. Words that had application to just anything would be robbed of meaning and could not be distinguished from one another. But what gives a word meaning? And how does this determine what uses do and do not comply with it? Answers to these questions must be compatible with a credible epistemology of meaning: when we understand a word we must be able to use it in accordance with its meaning. If something were to settle the right or wrong use of a term, we must be able to take cognizance of this. The objectivity of meaning and linguistic judgment depends on this. We have to secure both of these simultaneously.

In his later writings, WITTGENSTEIN rejects the idea of meanings as mental or abstract entities to be associated with particular signs. Instead he takes the meaning of a sign, or word, to be its use in a language. However, in equating meaning with use he does not assume that every way of using a sign can contribute to its meaning. To have a meaning there must be some particular range of application that counts as using a word correctly. But what does the correct use of a word consist in? Wittgenstein explores the claim that a word is used correctly when it is used in accordance with a rule. If there are rules governing the use of words, then there are standards speakers have to meet to deploy words competently. Competence requires speakers to know what counts as applying the word correctly or incorrectly on any occasion. The appeal to rules is also thought to guarantee the range of things a word applies to: the rule can be thought of as settling the application of a term not only to cases considered so far, but also to hitherto undiscovered cases.

These features of rules bring out the normative element in meaning. Given that words have meanings there is something that counts as using them in accordance with these meanings: this is how words *should* be used. When meanings are given by rules of use, competent speakers are required to conform to these rules: a rule does not just describe the use we make of an expression, it says how we *ought* to use it.

To satisfy ourselves that there is some substance to the notion of meaning, we need to account for the nature of these rules and the requirements they impose on our correct use of words. We also need an account of how speakers succeed, if they do, in following these rules. The issues are connected. If no account can be given of what it takes to heed the requirements of a rule, it is hard to credit those rules with any normative force in determining the meanings of words in our language. On the other hand, the idea of us conforming our linguistic practice to the requirements of rules cannot be maintained if we can give no substance to the idea of there being rules to be followed in the first place.

2 Rules and rule-followers

Wittgenstein addresses the issue of what it is to follow one rule rather than another by considering the case of a learner asked to continue the arithmetical series: 2, 4, 6, 8 .... There are infinitely many options for them. They could go on by writing 10, 12, 14, or 10, 14, 18, and so on. All they are shown are finitely many cases and from there they must acquire the ability to continue the series the mathematician intended. To go on from any position to the next they need to know the rule for expanding the series. But how do they acquire that from their exposure to the examples? Wittgenstein reviews a number of models for such knowledge of rules, and rejects them as inadequate.

First, we might think of learners giving themselves an instruction (such as $n = x + 2$), which tells them what to do next. But no instruction is sufficient, since it can only be followed if the learners know what it means. If they know this, then we must ask in what their acting in accordance with the meanings or rules governing *that* instruction consists. Either we appeal to further instructions, thus setting up an infinite regress, or else we suppose they just know what the instruction means in which case we have no explanation of their understanding, and we are no further forward.

Perhaps a learner simply reacts to the presented cases in some way, and either does or does not satisfy the mathematician. But if this learner is simply caused to respond, we are unable to say what it is for them to go by the rule as opposed to merely reacting to instances of it. On a future occasion they could be caused to act in a way at odds with the intended series. Also, their reactions may be fortuitous: they may be fitting the rule but not following it, blind to what is required of them. Only if the learner and the mathematician follow the same rule is the possibility of coincidence neutralized.

The justification of each move, if there is one, will depend on the rule the learner is following. But which rule is this? There are infinitely many rules compatible with the learner's behaviour so far, and every move they subsequently make can be made to accord with some rule or other. So what reason is there to think, before the learner decides on their next move, that there is some particular rule they are following? Perhaps we do not consult anything to decide how we are using a sign (or expanding a series). Nevertheless, the temptation exists to say that there must be something that determines whether we are going right or wrong in what we decide to do.

We might then say the rule itself determines right and wrong moves, because it consists in the full expansion of the series with all the instances fixed. As Wittgenstein puts it, it is as if all the steps had already been taken. This is a picture of rules as rails stretching ahead of us to infinity, with the rules fixed in some abstract or Platonic realm: what is required of us in any given application of them would thus be constituted wholly independently of human propensities to judge. The difficulty with this picture is that it gives us no idea of how we recognize which standards to conform to. If rules were blankly external to the mind, there would be no way to discover what they require of us. However we used words, whether or not we coincided with these objective standards would be a matter settled independently of us. Such a conception makes it unclear how such rules or standards could inform our practices, and it is hard to see how we could attempt to conform to rules that fall outside our cognitive reach.

The Platonist's picture mislocates the normative dimension of speech. At best our judicious use of words would be a series of stabs in the dark with which we hoped to speak significantly by coinciding with the mind-independent meaning-facts. This picture may afford the idea of an objective standard for our linguistic judgments, but there would be no difference (from the point of view of the speaker) between observing this standard and following one's subjective inclination to use the words as one felt fit. Without speakers being apprised of the standards of use that regulate their linguistic practice, meaning-scepticism would arise, putting in doubt both the existence of Platonized rules and the possibility of a speaker using words in accordance with their meanings. It seems as if the trouble with Platonism is that it locates the meaning-determining rules wholly outside the mind of the speaker.

Wittgenstein next turns to the temptation to find some self-interpreting item in the mind which serves to stop the regress of interpretations, and by itself points to the correct application of a word. Wittgenstein tells us that when we review the instructions we might give ourselves for deploying a word, it is as if meaning was the last interpretation. The trouble now is that there are no candidates for this role. If we suppose that the meaning itself is an item in mind, or that we have an intuition of what is required of us on any occasion of use, we need to know how such things as items in consciousness could point to the conditions of application for a word. For if intuition leads us to apply the word in one way, it could just as easily mislead us: we are simply reacting in a way that feels right. No items whose properties we can scrutinize consciously seem to carry the right information about how we should use a word, or comply with a rule in unexamined cases. It is utterly mysterious how anything we consciously consult could do this. It might be said that knowledge of our intention in using the word will serve here, but this also proves unsatisfactory: we are trying to explain how we can have such an intention in the first place, and how we can tell whether or not we are conforming to it. The appeal to an inner item is thus no better than Platonism. Locating the item inside the mind has still not connected our use of a word to a norm we can appreciate and whose requirements we could take into account in our linguistic use.

We appear to have exhausted the options. Does this mean that when we judge how to use an expression there is nothing that counts as getting it right? To concede this would be to surrender the objectivity of linguistic judgments and settle for an absence of genuine constraints on how to use words. However we go on using a word in future, there would be nothing that counted as acting in accordance with the rules, since there would be nothing for the requirements of the rules to consist in. How could thinking about a rule show me what I was meant to do at this point? There may be a subjective impression of constraint, of going on in the right way. But is there anything this answers to? For any way I chose to use the word in a new case, can be made to conform to some rule or other. There are interpretations that can be made consistent with anything I do, as Wittgenstein tells us in *Philosophical Investigations*: 'any interpretation hangs in the air along with what it interprets, and cannot give it any support. Interpretations by themselves do not determine meanings' (1953: §198). If every way of employing a term can be made to conform to a rule, then 'whatever is going to seem right to me is right. And that only means that here we cannot talk about "right"' (1953: §258). Without a distinction between what 'seems right to me' and what *is* right in my use of language, there can be no objectivity to meaning.

This is the conclusion Saul KRIPKE sees Wittgenstein as reaching at §201 of *Philosophical Investigations*; a conclusion Kripke, in his influential reading of Wittgenstein, calls the sceptical paradox.

3 Kripke's Wittgenstein

As Kripke (1982) formulates it, the sceptical paradox arises for a subject who has already been using the symbol '+' satisfactorily to compute sums of numbers less than 57. Kripke's example supposes that they are then asked to add 68 and 57. They might answer '125', but what fact about them makes this the right answer? The challenge to the subject is to come up with a fact about previous mental, behavioural or physical history that constitutes meaning *plus* rather than the deviant operation *quus*: an operation which

shadows addition until we reach numbers greater than 57 at which point the answers are not the sum of those numbers, but always 5. If they meant *plus* by '+', then they are right; if previously they meant *quus*, then to answer correctly they should have answered '5'. They are only justified in answering '125' if there is a fact about what they mean by '+', a fact about which rule they have been following until now and continue to follow.

For Kripke this is not an epistemological problem about there being certain facts to which we cannot have access. He allows the sceptic to suppose that a subject has perfect recall and access to their past behaviour, conscious experiences, memories and so on, but points out that they are still unable to come up with any fact that constitutes their meaning *plus* rather than *quus*. The failure to do so leads Kripke's sceptic to conclude that there is no fact of the matter about a subject's meaning one thing rather than another. There are simply no facts of the matter concerning meaning. (Though Simon Blackburn (1992) argues that this claim cannot be made in the first person without it being self-defeating since the person must be able to distinguish *plus* from *quus* to appreciate the problem.) Although Kripke takes this damaging conclusion to be the upshot of Wittgenstein's rule-following considerations, he suggests that Wittgenstein tries to show that we can live with the consequences. (For Kripke's presentation of what he takes to be Wittgenstein's sceptical solution, see §4.)

Crispin Wright (1989a) and John McDowell (1984) both challenge Kripke's reading of Wittgenstein. They point out that Kripke's sceptic is forcing us to provide a reductionist answer to the question of what my meaning *plus* rather than *quus* consists in. To substantiate the claim to mean one thing rather than another, we are asked to come up with some fact other than that we mean *plus*, or had the intention to use the word as we previously did. McDowell suggests there is no way to avoid an appeal to the fact that we meant *plus* by our words all along, and he insists that we have to take this as a stopping place for explanation. No justification of this fact can be given: we simply have to remind ourselves of the meanings we know our words to have. This approach has come to be known as quietism (see §5). Wright thinks we have to appeal to speakers' previous intentions concerning their use of the word to settle questions of justification, but unlike McDowell he believes there is a constructive explanation of what it is to know one's intentions and conform to them (see §6).

Wittgenstein's remarks at §201 of the *Philosophical Investigations* certainly suggest a sceptical paradox which gives rise to the dilemma McDowell identifies: either we have an item to provide the interpretation and are saddled with Platonism or a regress of interpretations, or in using words as I do I simply act blindly and there is no fact of the matter about what I mean. According to McDowell, the paradox depends on an assumption to be discharged: namely that meaning something by a word must be a matter of attempting to give it an interpretation. In the second half of §201, Wittgenstein goes on to suggest that there must be a way of meaning something that is not a matter of interpretation. This recommends a different way of construing the presence of rules in linguistic behaviour. In following a rule, the individual does not search for an interpretation. He just acts without giving himself supporting reasons. But unlike Kripke's reading, this does not lead to the conclusion that there is no fact of the matter about what a speaker means. We are told at §289, that 'To use an expression without justification is not to use it without right.' What is needed is an alternative account of what it is to act in accordance with a rule and to use our words correctly.

This is where the appeal to the community comes in. Rather than train our sights on facts about an individual, following a rule is a matter of participating in a communal practice. This retains the idea that there must be something that counts as acting in accordance with a rule or going against it on any occasion, but now conceives of it as a matter of obeying a practice or going against it. The idea of rules as consisting in communal practices leaves room for a number of different treatments of the way an appeal to the community can help here. These are reviewed in §4 as attempted solutions to the sceptical paradox, after discussion of another popular response to Kripke: the dispositional response.

4 Attempted solutions

Dispositional response. The dispositionalist attempts to respond to Kripke's sceptic by insisting that while no occurrent facts about a speaker's behaviour or mental history determine what they meant by their words, their disposition to respond in particular ways to cases when confronted by them settles the matter. The dispositionalist is here relying on the fact that when a thinker is asked what '68 + 57' is, they will be disposed to reply '125'. However, the disposition of the subject can be tested in only finitely many cases, whereas addition is defined over an infinite range. Also, the subject may not have the disposition to respond in the case of very large sums where the computations are difficult, and they may be disposed to make mistakes. These cases could be dealt with by pointing to a different set of dispositions to work out the sum on paper and to check the results. However,

Kripke's main objection to the dispositionalist's solution is that it loses sight of the normative element of meaning. In each case, the dispositionalist tells us how we *would* respond but not how we *should* respond. If I am using a word in accordance with its meaning, there is a way in which I am obliged to use it if I want to apply it correctly. Kripke tells us that the dispositionalist simply equates correctness and performance.

Appeal to the community. One can perhaps resist the conclusion that there is no fact about what a speaker means by their words by bringing in a background of other users against which the use of a word can be measured. We could say that the speaker does attach a certain meaning to a word, if their use of it coincides with the way the majority of people in their linguistic community use it. This response parallels the dispositional response, except that it considers the dispositions of everyone in the linguistic community. The notion of correctness is established in this case not by appeal to a rule that the individual is following, but by appeal to a widespread pattern of use exemplified by fellow language-users. In so far as there is a fairly widespread and consistent pattern of use for a word, the individual will count as using a word correctly just in such cases as their use of the term coincides with this pattern. They need not know that it coincides, or even check that it does. On this view, a speaker's knowing what they mean will not be the effortless and direct matter it is for most people. For this speaker it will be a matter of determining their fit with the uses other people make of these words. We may submit to correction when a number of people point out how our use of a word diverges from theirs, but we can be offered no determinate advice on what is required of us in the future if we are to continue conforming to majority use. For at the community level, there is no fact of the matter about what we mean collectively or what rules we are following (see Wright 1980). The strategy establishes for each individual language-user a sense of their using words correctly or incorrectly, and to that extent determines some objectivity for their linguistic judgments, but the community itself does not go right or wrong, it simply goes. Such a strategy puts in doubt the existence of meaning for shared public languages. And as far as individuals are concerned, it does nothing to guide their use of language. They will merely coincide or fail to coincide with their fellow language-users.

Kripke's sceptical solution. Kripke's sceptical solution invokes a different appeal to the community. Unlike a straight solution this in effect concedes that there is no answer to the sceptical paradox, but attempts to show us that we can live with the consequences. Kripke maintains that although there are no meaning-facts to settle how my words *should* be used, I will go on using them like other people and be subject to correction by them. Claims about what my words mean will lack truth-conditions but, Kripke insists, they will have assertion-conditions: conditions under which people will be prepared to assert that someone is using a word in conformity with its meaning. There will be nothing about someone's use of a word to which this claim is answerable, but there will be uses we have for such statements that do not require their truth. There is no such thing as individuals taking themselves to mean something in isolation from the community, since there would be no background consensus to establish even assertion-conditions for claims about what they mean. The consensus depends on a community, so the appeal to the community rules out the possibility of someone using a private language.

The sceptical conclusion has been resisted by those who maintain that it is part of Wittgenstein's aim to defuse rather than accept the sceptical paradox. The paradox arises, it is claimed, because of a mistaken understanding of what is required to follow rules competently.

5 McDowell's quietism

As long as there is something that counts as obeying a practice or going against it on any occasion, there is such a thing as correctly following a rule. Rules will no longer be thought of a something I consult inwardly, or by reference to which I interpret what is required of me. Rather, they will simply be enshrined in our practices – the normative practices which inform our linguistic behaviour and impose constraints on the meaningful use of our terms. Individuals follow rules when they participate in communal practices. It has to be by reference to this notion of practice, that our judgments about how to use words come to have objectivity. So what is a practice and how does it provide for the idea of going right or wrong on any occasion?

The simple idea of *de facto* conformity with others cannot serve here. For according to that conception, being right in our use of a word is just a matter of whether we find ourselves in agreement with the majority, and this threatens to deprive the picture of its normative dimension (see §4). How can whether I am in step with my community determine how I should go on using and understanding a term? How can this show me how I ought to use language to be faithful to the meanings of my words?

What we need is to restore the idea of a community of speakers who operate according to the norms of meaning. John McDowell (1984) insists that such a picture is available to us when we observe Wittgenstein's warning not to try to dig below bedrock (the level, Wittgenstein says, at which justifications give out). We can dig down to the ground to find justifications but we will reach a level where no further explanation can be given by reference to what goes on at the level below. This is bedrock. McDowell characterizes bedrock for our linguistic practices as a level of activity at which norms are still in place, and where we must describe one another's linguistic behaviour in the meaningful terms available to us as speakers of the language in question. We will have to describe people's activities as 'saying that *such and such*' – where the words we use to describe what is said (*such and such*) are the very words used by the speaker. This kind of description will not be intelligible to those outside the practice.

This is a resolutely anti-reductionist approach to meaning and rule-following, and we are told that we can expect no explanations of meaningful speech and linguistic practice by reference to something else. We simply have to remind ourselves how familiar we are with the meanings of our words and what they require of us in so far as we participate in these normative practices. No explanation can be given of their significance, and none is called for. This position known is as quietism.

6 Wright's extension-determining approach

Crispin Wright (1989a) opposes both quietism and the sceptical paradox, believing that there is room to show what the rule-governed meaning-facts consist in. Wright accepts the challenge to show how it can be that the requirements of rules governing our words are not simply up to us, while it is also true that they are not constituted wholly independently of us. The aim is to avoid surrendering the objectivity of meaning while at the same time bringing it within epistemic reach.

Wright argues that what constitutes a correct application of a word, including its application to a new case, and how it was used previously, is not something that can be settled independently of human judgment. A contribution from us is required to settle the matter. Wright avoids a slide to subjectivism by claiming that our best opinions about what we previously meant or intended will settle the matter, and since not every opinion we form is best it is not true that whatever we judge to be right is right. Only those judgments we make in the most propitious conditions for judging go into determining the right use of a term. The key point is that our linguistic judgments under these conditions *determine* rather than *reflect* the correct application of our terms. These judgments about how to use words do not involve a tracking epistemology: we are not keeping up with Platonic standards or internalized instructions. According to Wright, if we can specify cognitively ideal circumstances for judging in a substantial and non-circular way, then there is nothing but our opinions in those circumstances to decide what we mean by these words. In this conception, meanings are like secondary qualities. Objections to this account question the plausibility of giving a non-circular specification of the ideal circumstances for judging meanings or conditions of application.

See also: PRIVATE STATES AND LANGUAGE; LANGUAGE, SOCIAL NATURE OF

References and further reading

* Blackburn, S. (1992) 'Theory, Observation and Drama', in *Mind and Language* 7: 187–203. (Aims to show how appeal to the first-person case can defeat Kripke's sceptic. Referred to in §3.)

Boghossian, P. (1989) 'The Rule-Following Considerations', *Mind* 98: 507–49. (A good summary of recent work on this topic taking up some issues not dealt with here. Contrasts with these discussions in trying to separate the issue of rule-following from the issue of the speaker's knowledge of the rules he is following.)

Budd, M. (1984) *Wittgenstein's Philosophy of Psychology*, London: Routledge. (Chapter 2 provides a clearly written and careful treatment of Wittgenstein's views on meaning and understanding.)

* Kripke, S.A. (1982) *Wittgenstein on Rules and Private Language*, Oxford: Blackwell. (Provides a lucid, highly accessible introduction to the problems. Referred to in §§3–4.)

* McDowell, J. (1984) 'Wittgenstein on Following a Rule', *Synthèse* 58: 325–63. (Thorough treatment of the issues discussed, including the position outlined in §§3 and 5. Also provides both an interpretation of Wittgenstein's thought and a critical discussion of Kripke and Wright.)

McGinn, C. (1984) *Wittgenstein on Meaning*, Oxford: Oxford University Press. (A clear and concise treatment of rule-following and the private language argument.)

* Wittgenstein, L. (1953) *Philosophical Investigations*, Oxford: Blackwell. (The principal source of the issues discussed here; see especially §§185–289, referred to in §§1–3. Notoriously subtle and elusive writings.)

* —— (1956) *Remarks on the Foundations of Mathematics*, Oxford: Blackwell. (Section 6 includes key passages on rule-following. Intriguing but not straightforward. Referred to in §2.)

* Wright, C. (1980) *Wittgenstein On the Foundation of Mathematics*, London: Duckworth. (See chapters 2 and 11 for Wright's early views on rule-following, mentioned in §4.)

* —— (1989a) 'Wittgenstein's Rule-following Considerations and the Central Project of Theoretical Linguistics', in A. George (ed.) *Reflections on Chomsky*, Oxford: Blackwell. (Difficult though rewarding reading, setting out the account described in §§3 and 6.)

—— (1989b) 'Critical Notice of *Wittgenstein on Meaning* by Colin McGinn', *Mind* 98: 289–305. (Section 3 contains a penetrating discussion of the principal themes and arguments from the key passages in Wittgenstein's *Philosophical Investigations* (1953) and *Remarks on the Foundations of Mathematics* (1956).)

BARRY C. SMITH

MEANING AND TRUTH

Analytic philosophy has seen a resurgent interest in the possibility of explaining linguistic meaning in terms of truth, which many philosophers have seen as considerably more tractable than meaning. The core suggestion is that the meaning of a declarative sentence may be given by specifying certain conditions under which it is true. Thus the declarative sentence 'Venus is red' is true just in case the condition that Venus is red obtains; and this is exactly what the sentence means.

As it stands, however, this suggestion provides us with no explanation of the meanings of the words and phrases that make up sentences, since in general they are not expressions that have truth-conditions. (There are no conditions under which the word 'Venus' is true.) Furthermore, it needs to be supplemented by some method of circumscribing the truth-conditions that embody the meanings of declarative sentences, since there are many conditions under which any given sentence is true: 'Venus is red' is true not merely when Venus is red, but also, for example, when Venus is red and 7 + 5 = 12; but it does not mean that Venus is red and 7 + 5 = 12.

Evidently the first problem can be solved only by finding other semantic properties which indicate the meanings of words and phrases. For example, it is sometimes thought that the meaning of a name can be specified by saying what it refers to; and that of a predicate by saying what it is true of. But notice that since the meaning of a declarative sentence can be grasped by first grasping the meanings of its basic components, meaning-indicating ascriptions of semantic properties to those components must entail a meaning-indicating statement of its truth-conditions. Semantic properties such as 'referring to' and 'being true of' satisfy this requirement, at least in the context of what is sometimes called a 'truth theory' for a language.

This still leaves the problem of how to circumscribe the right meaning-indicating statement of truth-conditions for declarative sentences. Indeed we now have a further problem. For if the meanings of the components of sentences are not stated directly, but merely in terms of what they refer to or are true of (say), then we must also find a way of determining which of the many ways of specifying what they refer to, or the conditions under which they are true of something, is meaning-indicating. These problems may arguably be solved by placing an appropriate truth theory for a language in a setting that allows us to appeal to the general psychology of its speakers.

Attempts to elucidate meaning in terms of truth-conditions induce a plethora of further problems. Many are a matter of detail, concerning the kinds of properties we should associate with particular idioms and constructions or, equivalently, how we are to produce truth theories for them. As a result of Tarski's work, we have a good idea how to do this for a wide range of categories of expressions. But there are many which, superficially at least, seem to resist straightforward incorporation into such a framework. More general difficulties concern whether truth should be central at all in the analysis or elucidation of meaning; two objections are especially prominent, one adverting to antirealist considerations, the other to the redundancy theory of truth.

1   The core suggestion and some problems
2   Truth theories
3   Providing correct meaning-specifications
4   Recalcitrant idioms and general difficulties

1   The core suggestion and some problems

Three of the most influential approaches to the understanding of linguistic meaning in contemporary analytic philosophy correspond to three different, though overlapping, roles of language: its role in communication; its role in reasoning; and its role in making statements. According to the first of these approaches, linguistic meaning should be analysed or elucidated in terms of the communication intentions of speakers (see COMMUNICATION AND INTENTION; MEANING AND COMMUNICATION). According to the second, it should be characterized in terms of the conceptual or inferential role of expressions of the language (see SEMANTICS, CONCEPTUAL ROLE). And the third, at least in the form in which it has been most fully articulated, requires meaning to be analysed or elucidated in terms of the truth-conditions of sentences whose characteristic role, at least in context, is to make statements. It is the third approach which is the subject of this entry.

The core suggestion (which we owe to Frege (1964)) is that the meaning of a declarative sentence is given by certain conditions under which it is true. Thus 'Venus is red' is true just in case Venus is red; and that Venus is red is precisely what the sentence means. However, this fact leaves us in the dark about the meanings of expressions which are not sentences. For example, none of the words that makes up the sentence 'Venus is red' is the kind of expression that can have truth-conditions. Furthermore, there are countless other conditions under which the sentence is true that do not reveal its meaning – that Venus is red and $7 + 5 = 12$, for example. So the core suggestion must be supplemented not only by some way of articulating word meaning, but also by a method of picking out those truth-conditions of declarative sentences that embody their meanings – a method which does not make reference to meaning itself. I shall call the problem of articulating word meaning 'Problem A', and the problem of picking out the right truth-conditions of sentences 'Problem B'.

Let us begin with Problem A. It is clear that to solve it we must find further semantic properties which can plausibly indicate the meanings of non-sentential expressions, just as particular truth-conditions are meant to indicate the meanings of declarative sentences. For example, it is plausible to claim that the meaning of a name can be specified by saying what it refers to, and that of a predicate by saying what it is true of: the meaning of the name 'Venus' may be specified by stating that its referent is Venus; and that of the predicate 'is red' by stating that it is true of something if and only if that thing is red.

However, two difficulties arise with this proposed solution to Problem A. The first – which I shall call D(i) – is an analogue of Problem B. This is that there are many ways of stating the referent of a name, and many ways of stating what predicates are true of, but not all of them are meaning-indicating. Thus, although we may say that the referent of 'Venus' is Venus, we may also say that it is Hesperus, or the thing that is both Venus and either green or not green; but only the first statement of its referent specifies its meaning. Equally, although we may say that 'is red' is true of something if and only if that thing is red, it is also true of something if and only if the thing is red and $2 + 2 = 4$, and so on; but again only the first biconditional specifies its meaning.

The second difficulty, D(ii), arises from the fact that anyone who understands the components of a given sentence is generally in a position to understand the sentence itself; no further information is needed. For example, if I understand both 'Venus' and 'is red', I can immediately go on to understand the sentence 'Venus is red'. Now this is tantamount to saying that the meanings of sentences are determined by the meanings of their components (see COMPOSITIONAL-ITY). Thus the meanings of 'Venus' and 'is red' determine that of 'Venus is red'. But if this is right, then any correct specifications of the meanings of a sentence's components should entail meaning-indicating statements of the truth-conditions of the sentence itself. In particular, the specifications of the meanings of 'Venus' and 'is red' should entail the meaning-indicating statement of the truth-conditions of 'Venus is red', namely that 'Venus is red' is true if and only if Venus is red. (If not, the putative meaning-specifications of 'Venus' and 'is red' must have left something out.) The problem, however, is that even in this simple case it is not immediately clear how to ensure this.

2 Truth theories

It is convenient to tackle difficulty D(i) after we have dealt with D(ii). We can then deal with D(i) along with Problem B (the corresponding difficulty for sentences). Turning to D(ii), then, how are we to ensure that correct meaning-specifications for a sentence's components entail a correct specification for the sentence itself? Here it is customary to appeal to what is often called a 'truth theory' for a language. For it is precisely by employing such a theory that statements of truth-conditions of sentences of a language can be deduced from statements about the semantic properties of their components (see TARSKI, A.).

What is a truth theory for a language? Ordinarily, it is taken to consist of three parts: syntactic, semantic and logical. The syntactic part comprises a set of clauses stating how sentences of the language are constructed out of the vocabulary of the language. These clauses allow us to construct a description of any sentence of the language which shows how it is composed out of its vocabulary. (Such descriptions are often called 'structural descriptions'.) For example, in a very simple subject–predicate language – call it L – whose vocabulary consists of the English names 'Venus' and 'Polaris' and the English predicates 'is red' and 'is bright', four sentences are constructible. Letting '$x^\wedge y$' mean the result of concatenating x with y, we may describe these sentences structurally as

follows: 'Venus' $^\wedge$ 'is red', 'Polaris' $^\wedge$ 'is red', 'Venus' $^\wedge$ 'is bright' and 'Polaris' $^\wedge$ 'is bright'. (This notation is rather clumsy, so, for ease of reading, I shall use quotation marks both in the ordinary way and to indicate structural descriptions.)

Next, the semantic part comprises a set of clauses specifying various semantic properties of the vocabulary of the language, together perhaps with a number of semantic properties of complex expressions articulated as a function of the semantic properties of their components. In tandem with the third part, which consists of a number of logical and set-theoretic principles, these clauses will determine the truth-conditions of sentences of the language. It is this last feature that allows us to see in principle how we might solve D(ii).

Consider the language L again. Our aim is to find semantic properties of its names and predicates which will determine the truth-conditions of sentences containing them. And if what we have said so far is right, this should involve a statement of what (according to the theory) the names refer to and the predicates are true of. Thus we might have

(1) The referent of 'Venus' = Venus;

(2) The referent of 'Polaris' = Polaris;

(3) 'is red' is true of something iff that thing is red;

(4) 'is bright' is true of something iff that thing is bright.

(Note that strictly speaking the semantic properties here should be relativized to L, for in other languages its names and predicates may refer to or be true of very different things. Suppressing the language parameter, however, makes the axioms more readable. The same is true of all semantic properties considered in this entry.)

At this point, of course, we still do not know how these clauses determine specific truth-conditions for sentences. But we may remedy this by adding the following general clause relating the truth of L-sentences to the semantic properties of their components:

(5) For all names γ and predicates F, 'γF' is true if and only if F is true of the referent of γ.

For assuming that the third, logical part of the truth theory includes elementary first-order logic, it is then a simple matter to deduce truth-conditions for the sentences. For instance, we may easily deduce that 'Venus is red' is true if and only if Venus is red. For (5) will entail that

'Venus is red' is true if and only if 'is red' is true of the referent of 'Venus';

(1) will entail that

> 'is red' is truc of the referent of 'Venus' if and only if 'is red' is true of Venus;

and (3) will entail that

> 'is red' is true of Venus if and only if Venus is red.

Similar reasoning will enable us to deduce that 'Polaris is red' is true if and only if Polaris is red, and so on for the other two.

We are thus able to deduce a statement of what are in fact meaning-indicating truth-conditions for each of the sentences of L on the basis of axioms which assign semantic properties to their components, along with a further axiom which characterizes their modes of combination. Of course, this only solves our difficulty for the very limited language L; but it does give a hint of how to solve it more generally.

3 Providing correct meaning-specifications

Let us turn now to Problem B – how to circumscribe in a non-circular manner those truth-conditions of declarative sentences which embody their meanings – together with D(i), the corresponding problem for sentence components. And let us begin by introducing a common abbreviation: let us call a biconditional of the form 'S is true iff p' a 'T-sentence'. Since T-sentences evidently express the truth-conditions of the declarative sentences mentioned on their left-hand sides, it follows that to deal with Problem B, we need a non-circular way of singling out those T-sentences which genuinely indicate the meanings of the declarative sentences from those which do not. One suggestion would be to require that for 'S is true iff p' to be a meaning-indicating T-sentence, 'p' must be a translation of S. But although this would certainly ensure that the T-sentence correctly indicated the meaning of the relevant sentence, it would not provide a non-circular elucidation of its meaning, since the notion of translation itself directly presupposes the notion of meaning: when A and B are distinct expressions, A is a translation of B if and only if A and B have the same meaning.

A second suggestion is to replace the notion of translation with more general anthropological considerations relating to interpretation. Speech and writing are activities which take place against a backdrop of broadly rational activity, and can be interpreted in the light of such activity with a view to making maximum sense of speakers' behaviour. Consequently, it should be possible in principle to determine whether speakers are saying, for example, that Venus is red when they utter a particular sentence S by assessing whether that would be the most sensible thing for them to be saying in the circumstances, and in the light of all their other behaviour. And if this is what they typically or characteristically say when they utter S, then (according to the second suggestion) we may identify this with the appropriate truth-condition for S.

This prompts the following thought: 'S is true iff p' is correctly meaning-indicating if, other things being equal, the supposition that speakers are saying that p in characteristic utterances of S makes maximum sense of their behaviour. But even this might be thought to invite a similar criticism to the one which undermined the first suggestion. For does not the use of speech acts such as saying just bring in meaning by the back door? It certainly seems to if saying that p is uttering something that means that p. But much depends on whether a deeper account of saying – and other speech acts – is possible (see RADICAL TRANSLATION AND RADICAL INTERPRETATION).

A third suggestion would be to fore go such use of speech acts in the characterization of meaning, and focus on speakers' knowledge of truth-conditions. It is clear that those who understand the sentence 'Venus is red' will know not merely that 'Venus is red' is true if and only if Venus is red, but that speakers are expected to know this. Moreover, it also seems clear that they will know that this is the strongest thing speakers are expected to know about the truth-conditions of 'Venus is red'. They will know, for example, that speakers are not expected to know that 'Venus is red' is true if and only if Venus is red and $7 + 5 = 12$. But this suggests the following proposal: that 'S is true iff p' is meaning-indicating if any speaker knows that S is true if and only if p, that speakers are expected to know this, and that this is the strongest thing speakers are expected to know about the truth-conditions of S. Our T-sentence which fails to specify the meaning of 'Venus is red' – 'Venus is red' is true if and only if Venus is red and $7 + 5 = 12$ – is then ruled out (see MEANING AND UNDERSTANDING).

Turning now to D(i), what of the components of sentences? How can we ensure that their meaning-specifications are correct? A thought that has occurred to several writers is to let whatever is the most satisfactory method of circumscribing the meaning-specifying truth-conditions of sentences do all the work: to say, for example, that the meaning of a non-sentential expression of a language can be specified by its clauses in any true truth theory that meets the above kinds of knowledge-expectation conditions for its sentences. For this to be adequate, however, every true truth theory for a language that meets those conditions would have to assign to those expressions the same or equivalent semantic properties. Unfortunately this not true.

To see this let us return to the truth theory of our language L. As we saw in §2, it is possible to use that truth theory to derive a T-sentence for each sentence of L; and each such T-sentence plainly satisfies the relevant knowledge-expectation conditions. What is more, its axioms plausibly specify the meanings of each of L's basic expressions. There are, however, other truth theories for L that meet the knowledge-expectation conditions for its sentences, but which do not specify the meanings of its basic expressions. For example, consider a truth theory for L which had the following axiom governing 'is red' instead of (3):

(6) 'is red' is true of something if and only if it is red and is either green or not green.

It would certainly be possible to derive all the correct meaning-indicating T-sentences for sentences of L on the basis of this axiom and the axioms governing the other basic expressions of the sentences. But (6) does not specify the meaning of 'is red' correctly.

It is true that we could rule out such cases by requiring that meaning-indicating T-sentences be proved in certain canonical ways – for instance, in the way we derived the T-sentence for 'Venus is red' in §2. For a proof that differed from that derivation only in using (6) instead of (3) would result in a T-sentence that did not satisfy the knowledge-expectation conditions, namely: 'Venus is red' is true if and only if Venus is red and is either green or not green. But this immediately raises the question why those ways should be thought of as canonical; and since the natural answer is that they ensure that the axioms governing the sentence's basic components specify their meanings correctly, it would seem that we must have some independent grip on what it is for those axioms to be so constrained as to have this property. The question is what provides us with that independent grip.

At this point, we may make a move analogous to the one made earlier in the case of sentences. There we noted that understanding the sentence 'Venus is red' involves knowing that it is true if and only if Venus is red, that speakers are expected to know this, and that this is the strongest thing speakers are expected to know about its truth-conditions. Similarly, we may say that understanding the predicate 'is red' involves knowing it is true of something if and only if that thing is red, that speakers are expected to know this, and that this is the strongest thing speakers are expected to know about the conditions under which it is true of something. (They will know, for example, that speakers will not be expected to know that it is true of something if and only if that thing is red and is

either green or not green.) Equally, understanding the name 'Venus' will consist in knowing that it refers to Venus, that speakers are expected to know this, and that this is the strongest thing speakers are expected to know about what it refers to. Notice again that this solves our difficulty only for the very limited language L; but we may expect it to be soluble quite generally by means of similar kinds of knowledge-expectation conditions relating to whatever clauses govern other expressions and their modes of combination.

It should be noted that these kinds of knowledge-expectation conditions appear to put a considerable burden on the ordinary speaker: can we really picture them as part of the stock of knowledge possessed by speakers of a natural language such as English? At this point, if we are not to jettison the present approach, there seem to be three strategies. One is to claim that the truth-theoretic clauses are correct, to deny that we have knowledge of them (in the ordinary sense), but to insist that we bear some kind of analogous cognitive relation to them (yet to be fully explicated). The second is again to claim that they are correct, but to try to justify the ascription of tacit knowledge of them in some way. And the third is to see the truth-theoretic clauses as stepping stones to more convincing clauses which we can uncontroversially accept that we know.

4 Recalcitrant idioms and general difficulties

We turn next to a number of problems for the truth-conditional approach to meaning. In the light of Tarski's work, it is now clear how to accommodate within a truth-theoretic framework declarative sentences made up of names, predicates, truth-functors and standard quantifiers. But natural language seems much richer than this. We here consider two idioms which cause problems for the framework, and which in their different ways may require it to be modified. Then we consider two more general difficulties. It should be noted that there are various further issues – such as how the truth-conditional approach melds with doctrines of logical form, transformational grammar or validity – which, for reasons of space, we cannot discuss here.

Until now we have simplified matters by restricting ourselves to languages whose only sentences are declarative. This restriction is convenient, since – ignoring context-sensitivity – it means that all the sentences in the relevant languages have truth-conditions; but it is not warranted by natural languages, which contain sentences of many different moods, including imperatives, interrogatives and optatives. Such sentences do not appear to be truth-evaluable – 'Open the door, Smith!' or 'Where's the butter?' do not look like the kinds of sentence that can be true or false. Yet if they lack truth-conditions, it seems puzzling how they can be accommodated within a truth-theoretic framework.

One response is to add a further component to the semantic theory – what is sometimes called a theory of 'force' (see PRAGMATICS §8). This states what kind of speech act a given sentence is conventionally or typically geared to express; and it transforms the sentence into a corresponding declarative sentence which can then serve as input to the truth theory. For example, the theory of force for English would tell us that 'Open the door, Smith!' is a command, and that its corresponding declarative sentence is 'Smith opens the door'.

A second response is to introduce a number of further semantic values analogous to truth for each of the new types of sentence: compliance, for instance, for imperatives and optatives. Such values could be integrated into appropriate truth theories by means of such axioms as: S! is complied with iff S is true, where S! is the imperative form of a declarative sentence S. And to ensure that we obtain meaning-indicating compliance conditions, we could again use knowledge-expectation conditions, similar to those proposed in the case of declarative sentences, but with compliance replacing truth. Note, however, that both responses have great difficulty accommodating a sentence such as 'Open the door, Smith, and I'll put the kettle on' which contains more than one mood. Associated with this sentence, there seems no single speech act, nor any straightforward value analogous to truth.

Next we come to sentences whose truth-conditions can vary from one context to another. Such sentences, which typically contain context-sensitive expressions such as personal pronouns, demonstratives, temporal and spatial indexicals, tense indicators and so on, evidently give rise to a problem for the programme of accounting for meaning in terms of truth-conditions. For although the truth-conditions of such sentences can vary from context to context, their meaning need not. The sentence 'I helped that man yesterday' means the same thing whoever utters it, whenever it is uttered and whoever the man is; but its truth-conditions will vary with the utterer, the time of utterance and the man indicated. Evidently, this is because in any ordinary way of taking the term 'meaning', the meanings of expressions such as 'I', 'yesterday' and so on are given by such general rules as that 'I' refers to the speaker, 'yesterday' refers to the day before the day of utterance and so on; but such meanings in themselves do not exhaust the contribution the expressions make to the truth-conditions of sentences containing them.

An amendment to the account is clearly needed. In particular, although we may take the truth-conditions of sentences to be identifiable with their meaning when they have context-free truth-conditions, we must identify those of context-sensitive sentences with a notion of content much stronger than ordinary meaning – roughly, with what the sentences express when the context has been fixed. This means that the semantic theory will in effect have to be divided into two parts: what supplies the context-free information relevant to truth-conditions; and what states the information about specific contexts that determines particular truth-conditions once the relevant context-free information has been supplied. The second part falls into the area of pragmatics (see PRAGMATICS; DEMONSTRATIVES AND INDEXICALS).

Is this adequate? We here restrict ourselves to noting one general difficulty with the proposal. It is likely that most context-free semantic axioms will involve relativized semantic predicates. The pronoun 'he', for instance, might be governed by an axiom such as:

(7) For all p, q, the referent of 'he' as uttered by p to indicate $q = q$.

However, it is hard to obtain content-specifying instances of this which satisfy the appropriate knowledge-expectation conditions involving reference (see §3). For suppose I am the speaker and the person I am indicating is Quine. Then to display the content of 'he' in my mouth, we need a metalinguistic expression synonymous with it – 'a', say. This would give us:

The referent of 'he' as uttered by me to indicate Quine $= a$.

But even if we had such an expression, we would still face the problem that not all English speakers, even those in my immediate linguistic circle, need know of the referent of 'he' in my mouth that it is a. Indeed, I may be the only person who knows this. In such extreme circumstances, we could restrict the class of speakers to me. But it would then have to be the case that the strongest thing I expect myself to know about its referent is that it is a. And unfortunately there is no reason to think that this is so.

Finally we turn to two general problems for the programme of elucidating meaning in terms of truth-conditions, both of which have considerable contemporary significance. The first, antirealist difficulty focuses on sentences whose truth-conditions we cannot decide. According to one model of understanding, we can acquire and manifest an understanding of a sentence only if we can recognize whatever meaning-indicating condition is associated with it as obtaining when it does obtain and as not obtaining when it does not. But for sentences whose truth-conditions we cannot decide, the supposition that truth-conditions are meaning-indicating conflicts with this requirement. So in the absence of another model, the attempt to elucidate meaning in terms of truth-conditions must be jettisoned (see INTUITIONISTIC LOGIC AND ANTIREALISM §6; REALISM AND ANTIREALISM §4).

The second difficulty concerns the definition of truth. It is clear that an extant notion of truth is needed to characterize meaning in the way we have been envisaging: we cannot use truth theories like the one described in §2 as analyses of truth, if only because they leave it unsaid how to apply the notion of truth to new languages. However, one of the most plausible independent accounts of truth, the 'redundancy theory' (see TRUTH, DEFLATIONARY THEORIES OF), is arguably incompatible with any attempt to characterize meaning in terms of truth. For on one natural construal, this theory requires that understanding what it is for 'Venus is red' (say) to be true is tantamount to understanding what it is to say that Venus is red by using the sentence 'Venus is red'. But to understand this, we already need to know the meaning of 'Venus is red'.

Both objections seem to require that we replace truth by some other notion in an elucidation of meaning. One that appeals to antirealists is that of warranted assertibility, since the conditions under which one would be warranted in asserting a sentence are arguably recognisable as obtaining when they obtain and as not obtaining when they do not. Other options would be to elucidate meaning in terms of communication intentions or conceptual role.

See also: DAVIDSON, D.; LOGICAL AND MATHEMATICAL TERMS, GLOSSARY OF

References and further reading

Davidson, D. (1984) *Inquiries into Truth and Interpretation*, Oxford: Oxford University Press. (These essays present the most influential contemporary defence of a truth-conditional account of meaning; see in particular Essays 2, 9 and 10. Essay 8 discusses the problem of non-declarative sentences; his own account is different from those noted in §4.)

Davies, M.K. (1981) *Meaning, Quantification, Necessity*, London: Routledge. (Includes truth theories for a range of English idioms; chapter 4 has a helpful discussion of tacit knowledge.)

Dummett, M.A.E. (1978) *Truth and Other Enigmas*, London: Duckworth. (Includes a number of seminal essays on antirealism; see in particular Essays 1, 12 and 21. Essay 1 and the Preface argue for the incompatibility of the redundancy theory of truth and the truth-conditions theory of meaning.)

Evans, G. and McDowell, J. (eds) (1976) *Truth and Meaning*, Oxford: Oxford University Press. (Includes an excellent introduction by the editors.)

* Frege, G. (1964) *The Basic Laws of Arithmetic*, trans. and ed. and with an intro. by M. Furth, Berkeley, CA: University of California Press. (This is a translation of parts of Frege's *Grundgesetze der Arithmetik*. The suggestion that the meaning of a declarative sentence may be given by the conditions under which it is true is to be found, wrapped up in Frege's own terminology, in §32.)

Higginbotham, J. (1991) 'Truth and Understanding', repr. in C. Peacocke (ed.) *Understanding and Sense*, Aldershot: Dartmouth, 1993, vol. 1. (Presents detailed elucidation of some of the material in §3; in particular suggests circumscribing truth-conditions and so on in terms of knowledge-expectation conditions.)

Larson, R. and Segal, G. (1995) *Knowledge of Meaning: An Introduction to Semantic Theory*, Cambridge, MA: MIT Press. (An excellent survey of truth theories for many English idioms; it also indicates how to integrate this material with current thinking in linguistics. The first three chapters include accounts of some of the basic ideas underlying the truth-conditional approach to meaning; chapter 13 discusses tacit knowledge.)

Lepore, E. (ed.) (1986) *Truth and Interpretation*, Oxford: Blackwell. (This volume includes important essays on and within the framework of truth-conditional theories of meaning. Particularly helpful are those by Higginbotham, Davidson and Dummett.)

McDowell, J. (1977) 'On the Sense and Reference of Proper Name', repr. in M. Platts (ed.) *Reference, Truth and Reality*, London: Routledge, 1980; and in C. Peacocke (ed.) *Understanding and Sense*, Aldershot: Dartmouth, 1993, vol. 1. (Suggests coupling a truth-conditional account with a theory of force in the way indicated briefly in §4. Also fills out material in §3.)

Peacocke, C. (ed.) (1993) *Understanding and Sense*, 2 vols, Aldershot: Dartmouth. (These volumes also include important essays on and within the framework of truth-conditional theories of meaning. In addition to those by Higginbotham and McDowell already recorded, the essays by Davidson on truth, by McDowell on antirealism and by Quine and Davies on tacit knowledge are notable.)

Platts, M. (ed.) (1980) *Reference, Truth and Reality*, London: Routledge. (Includes useful essays on Tarski's account of truth, by Field and McDowell.)

Wright, C. (1987) *Realism, Meaning and Truth*,

Oxford: Blackwell, 2nd edn, 1993. (Contains important essays on the antirealist critique of truth-conditional semantics. Introduction is particularly helpful.)

Yourgrau, P. (ed.) (1990) *Demonstratives*, Oxford: Oxford University Press. (A useful selection of essays on context-sensitivity.)

STEPHEN G. WILLIAMS

MEANING AND UNDERSTANDING

The existence of a close connection between the notions of meaning and understanding can hardly be denied. I may be said to understand you, on a given occasion of utterance, when I know what you then meant – or, at least, when I know the meaning of the words that you then uttered. An important and influential school of thought within the philosophy of language goes much further than these platitudes, however. Its members adhere to the view that questions about meaning are essentially questions about understanding: 'a model of meaning is a model of understanding'. Their approach contrasts with that of those who expect an account of meaning to elucidate the nature of understanding only indirectly – perhaps by explaining meaning in terms of truth, inference, synonymy or self-expression, and only then explaining understanding as the correct recovery of meaning.

1 **Dummett's account**
2 **Davidson's account**

1 Dummett's account

The text of this article sketches and constrasts the views of the school's two leading members: Dummett and Davidson. The dictum 'a model of meaning is a model of understanding' was formulated by Michael DUMMETT. He proceeds to gloss 'a model of understanding' as 'a representation of what it is that is known when an individual knows the meaning' of a possible object of understanding – as it might be, a word, a construction, or a whole language (1973: 217). To provide such a model is to spell out the kind of knowledge that constitutes, or at least sustains, various kinds of linguistic understanding. Dummett's view is that the central philosophical debates about the nature of meaning are properly understood to be debates about the character of such knowledge. Slogans such as 'The meaning of a sentence is the method of its verification' or 'The meaning of a sentence consists in its truth-conditions' mean (if they mean anything at all) that to *understand* a sentence is to know how it may be verified or to know under what conditions it is true. In emphasizing that the central philosophical questions about meaning are questions about understanding, Dummett was self-consciously departing from a prior tradition (of which the most celebrated manifestation is Quine's 'Two Dogmas of Empiricism'); this tradition took the central problem in the area to be that of spelling out the conditions for two expressions to mean the same thing (see esp. Dummett 1981: 74).

Although Dummett canvasses various accounts of knowledge of meaning, it is a presupposition of his discussion that the knowledge in question is propositional. To attempt to produce a model of understanding is to attempt to produce a *theory*, knowledge of which constitutes or sustains possession of a linguistic capacity. In saying so much, Dummett is not committed to denying that an understanding of a word or sentence is in the first instance a matter of knowing how to use it. However, he is committed to denying that this formulation provides a complete account of understanding, he argues that we need a more detailed specification of what such know-how consists in (1973: 222–3). Dummett is also clear that the propositional knowledge in question will in general be implicit. That is to say, it is knowledge that a subject may possess even though he is unable to express the proposition thereby known. From this observation, Dummett derives a consequence that crucially constrains the sort of knowledge which he thinks might constitute or sustain understanding. 'Implicit knowledge', he says, 'cannot meaningfully be ascribed to somebody unless it is possible to say in what the manifestation of that knowledge consists: there must be an observable difference between the behaviour and capacities of someone who is said to have that knowledge and someone who is said to lack it' (1973: 217). In particular, then, the propositional knowledge, implicit possession of which is said to underlie understanding, must be manifestable in behaviour.

The significance of this requirement emerges when we consider the two models of understanding that Dummett centrally considers. Both of these models take to be central the problem of characterizing our understanding of declarative sentences, and according to the first of them – which Dummett labels a 'realist' or 'truth-conditional' model – such understanding 'consists in our grasp of [the sentence's] truth-conditions, which determinately either obtain or fail to obtain, but which cannot be recognized by us in all cases as obtaining whenever they do' (1972: 23). Thus, our understanding of the sentence 'A city will never be built at the North Pole' is taken by the realist to consist in our knowing that it is true just on condition that a city will never be built at the North Pole, a condition that may obtain without our ever knowing so (Dummett 1959: 16–7). This, Dummett argues, is rendered problematical by the requirement of manifestability. 'It is quite obscure', he writes, 'in what the knowledge of the condition under which a sentence is true can consist, when that condition is not one which is always capable of being recognized as obtaining' (1973: 224). The crucial claim, in other words, is that there is something opaque about the attribution 'Tom knows that sentence S is true just on condition that a city will never be built at the North Pole'. Because the occasion may never arise on which somebody is granted the opportunity to give conclusive reasons for accepting the sentence as true or rejecting it as false, 'the knowledge which is being ascribed to one who is said to understand the sentence is knowledge which transcends the capacity to manifest that knowledge by the way the sentence is used'. Accordingly, the truth-conditional model of understanding cannot be one 'in which meaning is fully determined by use' (1973: 225).

Whether this really is a consequence of the truth-conditional model – and whether, if it is, it is sufficient to show that the realist model must be rejected – are questions that remain at the forefront of contemporary debate in the philosophy of language. As he made clear in 'Realism: A Valedictory Lecture' (1992), Dummett is not committed to particular answers. He has, however, articulated an alternative model of understanding which, whatever its other difficulties, is supposed to meet the requirement of manifestability. On this alternative 'antirealist' model, our understanding of a sentence will consist, not in knowing under what conditions it is true, but 'in knowing what recognizable circumstances determine it as true or as false' (1972: 23). Or, to deploy a formulation that Dummett treats as equivalent, it consists in knowing under what circumstances a sentence may be asserted. In addition to meeting the demand of manifestability, this model is supposed to have the merit of leading to a more plausible account of what learning a language involves:

> Thus we learn to assert 'P and Q' when we can assert P and can assert Q; to assert 'P or Q' when we can assert P or can assert Q.... We no longer explain the sense of a statement by stipulating its truth value in terms of the truth value of its constituents, but by stipulating when it may be asserted in terms of the conditions under which its constituents may be asserted.
>
> (1959: 17–18)

2 Davidson's account

It may seem as though Donald DAVIDSON is a clear example of a Dummettian realist – someone who takes our understanding of a declarative sentence to consist in knowing the conditions under which it is true. However, while Davidson certainly regards the notion of a truth-condition as central to an account of a subject's linguistic competence, there are nuances in his treatment of these matters that make such a characterization misleading. He begins a celebrated article thus:

> Kurt utters the words 'Es regnet' and under the right conditions we know that he has said that it is raining. Having identified his utterance as intentional and linguistic, we are able to go on to interpret his words: we can say what his words, on that occasion, meant. What could we know that would enable us to do this? How could we come to know it? The first of these questions is not the same as the question what we *do* know that enables us to interpret the words of others. For there may easily be something we could know and don't, knowledge of which would suffice for interpretation, while on the other hand it is not altogether obvious that there is anything we actually know which plays an essential role in interpretation.
>
> (1973: 125)

Davidson is surely right to draw attention to the difference between his central question about knowledge of meaning ('What could we know that would enable us to know what these words mean?') and Dummett's ('What *do* we know when we know what words mean?'). But it is disappointing that he does not give his grounds for doubting that 'there is anything we actually know which plays an essential role in interpretation'. For if there is such actual knowledge, then questions about its character must surely be deemed more urgent and important than the hypothetical question that Davidson chooses to address. We appear, in other words, to need a reason for taking as central the problem upon which he focuses.

Be that as it may, Davidson's own question is a clear one, and his writings contain two rather different answers to it. In his early papers (roughly speaking, those published before 1970, including the influential 'Truth and Meaning' of 1967), we are told that what would suffice for interpreting a speaker A at time t is knowledge of a truth theory that is interpretative for A at t. A truth theory, as Davidson conceives it, comprises statements (T-theorems) to the effect that a sentence is true (as potentially uttered by such-and-such a speaker at this or that time) just in case a certain condition is met. And such a theory will be interpretative, for a speaker at a time, if (intuitively) the condition that the theory associates with each sentence gives the meaning that it then has in that speaker's mouth. Plainly, this answer is of little interest without some independent specification of the condition for a theory to be interpretative (independent of the notion of meaning), which Davidson hopes to provide via the figure of the radical interpreter. Such an interpreter is an investigator who constructs a truth theory for a speaker (at a particular time) in accordance with certain general interpretative maxims or constraints, chief among which is the principle of charity (see Davidson 1973; Lewis 1974; CHARITY, PRINCIPLE OF §4; RADICAL TRANSLATION AND RADICAL INTERPRETATION §7–10). The idea, then, is that it is such maxims as these that give content to the requirement that a theory be interpretative, and thereby give content to the notion of meaning.

The model of understanding and meaning that results involves a substantial holism. The condition for a sentence S to mean that p as a speaker A uses it at time t, is that a truth theory that is interpretative for A at t (that is, a truth theory that optimally meets the constraints under which the radical interpreter operates) should contain among its T-theorems the result 'S is true (as potentially uttered by A at t) just in case p'. This makes it clear that the condition for a sentence to have a certain meaning involves reference, not just to the components of S, but to the totality of sentences that the relevant speaker is then disposed to utter (see Davidson 1976: 175). This holism does not alarm Davidson, but he has confessed to an important error in his earlier answer to his question. 'My mistake', he wrote in 1976, 'was to overlook the fact that someone might know a sufficiently unique theory [that is a theory that optimally satisfies such constraints as the principle of charity] without knowing that it was sufficiently unique' (1976: 173). He duly amends his account of what suffices for interpretation to correct this mistake: 'what somebody needs to know [in order to interpret speakers of a language L] is that some [sufficiently unique] T-theory for L states that... (and here the dots are to be replaced by a T-theory)' (1976: 174).

The occurrence in this formulation of the intentional and linguistic verb 'to state' may lead one to wonder whether the account is invoking a notion to which it is not entitled (compare Forster 1976). After all, if we are allowed to use a verb like 'state' in specifying the knowledge that would suffice for understanding, then why should we not bypass the complexities of truth theories completely, and say simply that what suffices for interpreting a speaker is knowing what he would be stating by affirming

declarative sentences, what he would be asking by uttering interrogative ones, and what he would be ordering by uttering imperative sentences? Davidson, however, has a convincing answer to this question. Although the use of the verb 'state' (or, as he eventually prefers, 'entail') 'brings in an appeal to a specifically linguistic notion', it is a notion that has been 'elicit[ed] by placing conditions on a theory of truth' (1976: 178). That is to say, its content must be understood in relation to the conditions for a truth theory to be interpretative.

All the same, one might wonder whether a more direct method of eliciting (or explaining) such a notion was not available. Instead of considering truth theories – and regarding the principle of charity and its ilk as providing conditions for a truth theory to be interpretative – why should we not consider theories entailing such claims as that:

By affirming S at t, A would state that p

and regard the relevant principles as conditions for such a theory to be *true*? Davidson's answer appears to be that certain logical difficulties arise in the latter case that are absent from the former. In an early paper, Davidson wrote that 'when we can regard the meaning of each sentence as a function of a finite number of features of the sentence, we have an insight not only into what there is to be learned; we also understand how an infinite aptitude can be encompassed by finite accomplishments' (1965: 8). The context makes it clear that the present occurrence of 'when' means 'when and only when' and the suggestion is that such insight will be gained only when we have an axiomatization – if not finite, then at least recursive – of the body of knowledge in question. Now Davidson also suggests that a theory whose theorems are in the form:

By affirming S at t, A would state that p

will resist axiomatization. 'It is reasonable to expect', he writes, 'that in wrestling with the logic of the apparently non-extensional "means that" [and, we might add, the equally non-extensional "would state that"] we will encounter problems as hard as, or perhaps identical with, the problems our theory is out to solve' (1967: 22).

But are such problems insuperable? Surely one can account for somebody's knowing that Kurt uses 'Es regnet und es schneit' to state that it is raining and snowing by reference to his knowing:

(1) that Kurt uses 'Es regnet' to state that it is raining
(2) that Kurt uses 'Es schneit' to state that it is snowing

and

(3) that $(p)(q)(S)(S')$ (If Kurt uses S to state that p, and uses S' to state that q, then he uses 'S und S'' to state that p and q)?

One source of concern about this last item of knowledge may be that the initial pair of quantifiers must be understood substitutionally (see QUANTIFIERS, SUBSTITUTIONAL AND OBJECTUAL), but it is noteworthy that on Davidson's preferred analysis of such constructions as 'states that', there is a far more acute problem. On his 'paratactic' analysis, what follows the word 'that' in an attribution such as 'Galileo stated that the earth moves' belongs in a semantically separate sentence from the properly attributive claim 'Galileo said that' (see DAVIDSON, D. §6; PROPOSITIONAL ATTITUDE STATEMENTS §3). Applied to (c), then, the substitutional quantifiers '(p)' and '(q)' would reach into a different sentence. Here, the 'direct' approach to theories of meaning seems to take us into uncharted logical waters. Unless Davidson's analysis of indirect discourse can be shown to be wrong, or unless some way can be discovered of charting these waters, we have a reason for answering his question in the way that he recommends.

See also: MEANING AND TRUTH; MEANING AND VERIFICATION

References and further reading

* Davidson, D. (1965) 'Theories of Meaning and Learnable Languages', in Y. Bar-Hillel (ed.) *Proceedings of the 1964 International Congress for Logic, Methodology, and Philosophy of Science*, Amsterdam: North Holland; repr. in D. Davidson, *Inquiries into Truth and Interpretation*, Oxford: Oxford University Press, 1984, 3–15. (Gives the rationale for requiring an interpretative truth theory to be finitely axiomatizable.)

* —— (1967) 'Truth and Meaning', *Synthèse* 17: 304–23; repr. in D. Davidson, *Inquiries into Truth and Interpretation*, Oxford: Oxford University Press, 1984, 17–36. (The classic statement of Davidson's earlier conception of a theory of meaning.)

* —— (1973) 'Radical Interpretation', *Dialectica* 27: 313–28; repr. in D. Davidson, *Inquiries into Truth and Interpretation*, Oxford: Oxford University Press, 1984, 125–39. (Elaborates Davidson's later conception of theories of meaning.)

* —— (1976) 'Reply to Foster', in G. Evans and J. McDowell (eds) *Truth and Meaning: Essays in Semantics*, Oxford: Oxford University Press, 33–41; repr. in D. Davidson, *Inquiries into Truth and Interpretation*, Oxford: Oxford University Press, 1984, 171–9. (Davidson compares his earlier and later views, explaining the reasons for the change.)

* Dummett, M.A.E. (1959) 'Truth', *Proceedings of the Aristotelian Society* 59: 141–62; repr. in M.A.E. Dummett, *Truth and Other Enigmas*, London: Duckworth, 1978, 1–19. (An early and influential presentation of the idea that to understand a sentence is to know under what conditions it could be asserted.)

* —— (1972) 'Postscript to Truth', in M.A.E. Dummett, *Truth and Other Enigmas*, London: Duckworth, 1978, 19–24. (Clarifies the thesis and argument of the previous article.)

* —— (1973) 'The Philosophical Basis of Intuitionistic Logic', in H.E. Rose and J.C. Shepherdson (eds) *Logic Colloquium '73*, Amsterdam: North Holland; repr. in M.A.E. Dummett, *Truth and Other Enigmas*, London: Duckworth, 1978, 215–47. (Contains Dummett's clearest and most influential formulation of the requirement that linguistic knowledge should be manifestable in use.)

—— (1981) *The Interpretation of Frege's Philosophy*, London: Duckworth. (The chapter entitled 'Synonymy' compares Dummett's way of formulating the questions that a theory of meaning ought to answer with previous conceptions, notably Quine's.)

* —— (1992) 'Realism: A Valedictory Lecture', Oxford: Oxford University Press. (Dummett's discussion of the state of the debate between truth-conditional theories of meaning and their rivals.)

Forster, J.A. (1976) 'Meaning and Truth Theory', in G. Evans and J. McDowell (eds) *Truth and Meaning: Essays in Semantics*, Oxford: Oxford University Press, 1–32. (An influential attack on Davidson's earlier and later theories.)

* Lewis, D.K. (1974) 'Radical Interpretation', *Synthèse* 27: 331–44. (Spells out explicitly the conditions under which the radical interpreter operates.)

Quine, W.V. (1951) 'Two Dogmas of Empiricism', *Philosophical Review* 60: 20–43. (Explains the problems attending the explication of 'synonymous'.)

Strawson, P.F. (1970) 'Meaning and Truth: an Inaugural Lecture', Oxford: Oxford University Press; repr. in P.F. Strawson, *Logico-Linguistic Papers*, London: Methuen, 1971, 170–89. (An influential attack upon the whole school of thought discussed here. Strawson argues that the enterprise of spelling out truth-conditions must be pursued within a theory that explains meaning as relating, in the first instance, to communicative intentions.)

IAN RUMFITT

MEANING AND VERIFICATION

The verifiability theory of meaning says that meaning is evidence. It is anticipated in, for example, Hume's empiricist doctrine of impressions and ideas, but it emerges into full notoriety in twentieth-century logical positivism. The positivists used the theory in a critique of metaphysics to show that the problems of philosophy, such as the problem of the external world and the problem of other minds, are not real problems at all but only pseudoproblems. Their publicists used the doctrine to argue that religion, ethics and fiction are meaningless, which is how verificationism became notorious among the general public.

Seminal criticism of verification from around 1950 argues that no division between sense and nonsense coincides tidily with a division between science and metaphysics, as the positivists had claimed. Quine later developed verificationism into a sort of semantic holism in which metaphysics is continuous with science. In contrast, Dummett argues from a reading of Wittgenstein's claim that meaning is use to a rejection of any sort of truth surpassing the possibility of knowledge, and thence to a defence of intuitionistic logic. But the claim that all truths can be known yields in an otherwise innocuous setting the preposterous consequence that all truths actually are known. There are ways to tinker with the setting so as to avoid this consequence, but it is best to conclude by reductio *that some truths cannot be known and that verificationism is false. That in turn seems to show that the prospects for an empiricist theory of meaning are dim, which might well shake a complacent confidence in meaning.*

1   Hume
2–3 Logical positivism
4   Objections to verificationism
5   Recent developments
6   Logical problems

1   Hume

Perception is the only channel to us from the world whose influx is generally accepted to justify our beliefs about the world. Beliefs figure as units of justification in this empiricist-sounding doctrine. Since justifying something is giving a reason for thinking it true, the units of justification should be the right size for being true or false. Word-sized bits, be they words themselves or their meanings or people's ideas of things, are too small, while paragraph-sized chunks are too big, but sentence-sized stretches are of just the right size and unity for having truth-values. It is natural to take the things believed and justified by experience to be sentence-sized or propositional.

But the unit of Hume's seminal empiricism seems smaller. He begins the *Treatise of Human Nature* (1739–40) with the doctrine that all ideas are derived from impressions. To the extent that Hume made a self-conscious distinction between words and sentences (on the language side), or between concepts and propositions (on the Platonic side), or between ideas and thoughts (on the psychological side), the ideas Hume had in mind seem smaller than sentence-sized. In that way, Hume's empiricism seems narrower than the doctrine with which we began.

Hume claimed ideas are derived from impressions by copying, the copies differing from their originals only in vivacity. Ideas and impressions were thus to be images, the ideas merely fainter reproductions of the impressions. Objections to taking abstract ideas as images predate Hume, but the doctrine at least places ideas in a familiar psychological category. Items in this category are accessible to inner sense or introspection if anything is, and thus are knowable by processes such as those of the five outer senses already empirically certified. Admittedly, images seem too particular to reflect the abstract nature of abstract ideas. But at least acquaintance with images could explain action. If we try to rethink ideas not as images but as capacities or dispositions, we seem left with bare possibilities or potentialities, ungrounded in actualities which could explain action. Faced with a choice between bad theory and none, we often seem to prefer the bad to none; at least bad theory may provide a (risky) basis for getting on, but none provides none. Thinking of ideas on the model of images does not go away.

The doctrine that ideas are images derived from sense impressions by copying can be put to work in two different ways. One might take it for granted that we do indeed have certain ideas we seem to have, and then cast about for impressions from which such ideas might be derived; such a cast might well hook surprisingly unfamiliar epistemic fish. Alternatively, one might start from a catalogue of familiar impressions, and then winnow out ideas that cannot be derived by copying any such impressions; such a purge might well leave a rather empirical residue.

Hume thought of himself as a sceptic. Causation and the self are two examples of this sceptical pattern in Hume. In the case of causation, he never seems to have said exactly which impressions are wanting. Kant writes that experience teaches us that a thing is so-and-so, but not that it cannot be otherwise (*Critique of Pure Reason*, 1787: B3). In Hume's terms, we have impressions only of actuality, never of necessity; we see red, but not having-to-be red. But then there is no impression of necessity from which to derive an idea of it, so there is no making sense of causation as necessitation. At most we experience regular succession (with temporal priority and spatial contiguity), so that is all there can be to our idea of causation. Thus Hume's scepticism about necessary connection in nature is linked to his doctrine of ideas. In the case of the self, HUME asserts quite explicitly that there simply is no such thing as an experience of oneself over and above the ideas and impressions revealed to introspection. So, he infers, there can be nothing to the self and our idea of it but the bundle of the contents of consciousness. This bundle theory of the self has always seemed one of the more shockingly sceptical parts of the *Treatise*.

2 Logical positivism

We have now seen how Hume can use his doctrine of impressions and ideas as a sceptical weapon. The Vienna Circle between the two world wars of the twentieth century claimed an intellectual lineage back to Hume, and it is the Circle to whom we credit (or on whom we blame) the verifiability theory of meaning (see VIENNA CIRCLE §3). It would be an anachronism to attribute to Hume our preoccupations with language, meaning and reference. But imagine a philosopher already so preoccupied reconsidering Hume's doctrine of impressions and ideas. Many find it difficult to become accustomed to a self-conscious distinction between the meaning of an expression and what a person means by that expression. Without such a distinction at one's fingertips, it is all too easy to slide between the meaning of an expression and the ideas expressed by people using that expression. If our philosopher also admires Hume's empiricism, they may incline towards the doctrine that these ideas must be derived from impressions. The core of empiricism is the view that sense experience is the basic sort of evidence we have for (that is, for verifying) our beliefs about the world. It is then not unnatural for this suspension – of meaning, ideas, impressions and verification – to precipitate out a verifiability theory of meaning, or at least the slogan that meaning is evidence.

The verifiability theory of meaning may not be present in the greatest works of Vienna positivism, such as Carnap's *Aufbau* or his *Logical Syntax of Language* (see CARNAP, R. §§1–3). But it does seem to animate his *Scheinprobleme in der Philosophie* (*Pseudoproblems in Philosophy*, 1967) and it is obvious in Ayer's *Language, Truth and Logic* (1936), an enormously noticed popularization of logical positivism (see AYER, A.J. §§2–3). In so far as the positivists had verificationism, they used it as a weapon of

criticism. Hume's scepticism can be taken as criticism of complacent confidence in causes and the self, but it would be a distortion to assimilate verificationist criticism without further ado to Hume's scepticism. On the contrary, Carnap's *Pseudoproblems* shows him using verificationism to criticize certain sceptical lines of thought, the problem of the external world and the problem of other minds.

Descartes (1641) denied the pretensions of sense experience to be utterly basic to knowledge and its justification. To that end, he asks how one knows one is not asleep and dreaming right now. Come to that, perhaps one has been asleep and dreaming all of one's life, and all one's experience, instead of reporting the world of matter it seems to present, is instead merely an interminable hallucination spun by oneself out of whole cloth. This difficulty is the problem of the external world (see DESCARTES, R. §9). Indeed, perhaps there is no matter at all, but only one's mind and the endless illusions one foists on oneself. Here we have two incompatible hypotheses. One says that there is the matter out there independent of us that there seems to be, subject to the laws of nature. The other says that there is no such matter, but only the hallucination of it one foists on oneself. It is crucial to Descartes' case that the sense experience forecast by these two hypotheses be indistinguishable. For we are to be sure that the matter hypothesis is true and the dreaming hypothesis is false, and since sense experience cannot separate the two, there must be some other way of knowing, perhaps even more basic than experience, since it is what entitles us to take our experience to support the matter hypothesis. Prominent along that way are the *Cogito* and the ontological proof of the existence of God. Many after Descartes are not persuaded that his way leads anywhere. So they are left without an answer to how they know they are not asleep and dreaming.

In the way one feels one's own headache and observes its location, extent and intensity, there is nothing remotely like feeling someone else's pain or apprehending another's experience. Still less can one see or hear or smell or touch or taste another's experience and come to know it in that way as they do. But then for an empiricist there arises the question of how one knows anyone else even *has* experience and feeling. Why could not all one's own experience not be just as it has been and yet all the other human bodies be mindless lumps (acting as if someone with thoughts and feelings and experiences were in there but really) driven only by blind chemical reactions? This is the problem of other minds, and does not seem to go back earlier than John Stuart Mill in the nineteenth century. Mill offered an argument from analogy to solve this problem. One knows first hand from one's own case that it is one's headache that makes one wince just so, and seeing a similar wince on another's face, one infers by analogy a similar cause, namely a headache, in that other. This argument from analogy proceeded from what must be a single case, namely, oneself alone, so can it justify much certainty? Beyond that, the argument seems not even to address the difficulty the problem of other minds may raise for empiricism, namely, how one could know things like another's pain which one simply could not experience.

3 Logical positivism (cont.)

One can make out connections between Hume's doctrine of ideas and the verifiability theory of meaning, but while Hume used his doctrine as a sceptical axe, the positivists used their story of meaning to undercut scepticism. The problems of the external world and of other minds came to figure centrally on the agenda of modern classical philosophy. Philosophical problems rarely if ever receive solutions consensually certified, so it is understandable (even if not quite right) that such problems apparently sit there forever unsolved. In that case, these problems can easily come to look like demonstrations that it is not known whether there is any matter out there and that it is not known whether there is anyone besides oneself. In that way the agenda of modern philosophy can seem to be a compendium of sceptical theses. But the verifiability theory of meaning was used to argue that these so-called problems are not problems deserving solutions, but pseudoproblems deserving only dissolution. If one asks of a bachelor whether his wife is English, both a yes and a no seem bad answers since both seem to confirm a mistake concealed in the question. This trite example is a very simple illustration of how a misconception can present itself as an insoluble problem. Some of what is or was modernist in philosophy was an idea of criticism not as demonstrating the opposite but rather as unmasking, and thus eliminating, fraudulent questions and problems.

How was this to work? Remember that Descartes designed the dreaming hypothesis with the intention that it and the matter hypothesis issue in exactly the same expectations for sense experience; everything would seem the same to one's senses no matter which of the two were true. So by design no sensory experience could settle the question of which is true; both hypotheses are equally well supported by all perceptual evidence. But on the verifiability theory, meaning is evidence. As the old slogan had it, a difference that makes no difference is no difference: claims that cannot be distinguished on the basis of

evidence must coincide. So since no sensory experience could discriminate between the matter and the dreaming hypotheses, and since empiricism is right, and sensory experience is the only evidence against which to judge claims about the world, then the two hypotheses have exactly the same evidence, and so, by verificationism, exactly the same meaning. Since they are synonymous, they are not incompatible at all, but as compatible as possible. Hence, there is no question at all of choosing between them, and so, since that question is what the problem of the external world was, there is no such problem. The problem has been dissolved.

In the case of the problem of other minds, it is granted that all we can observe of other people is their physical behaviour (and, for an audience some sixty or seventy years later, electrochemistry in their central nervous systems). The problem is whether they really have minds and thoughts, or are just mindless chemical machines. But it is granted that both these alternatives would issue in exactly the same observations of others, and, by empiricism, such observation exhausts the evidence for either. Hence, the alternatives do not differ in evidence and so do not differ at all. There is thus no choice between them, and so no problem of other minds.

Perhaps the truly devout will hang on to their faith no matter what. In that case it looks as though nothing could count against it. Equally, no experience really counts as evidence for faith. But if faith is free from sensory evidence, then, since by verificationism meaning *is* evidence, religion is meaningless. It was not an accident that believers found such irreligion (and affronts to ethics and poetry as well) in Ayer's potboiler, *Language, Truth and Logic*. (One thing that is distressing here is that some thought they could defend their faith only by showing it empirically verifiable rather than by rebutting verificationism. The devil has no right to pick the battlefield.)

4 Objections to verificationism

One sort of objection to verificationism begins with the observation that evidence for a present claim about ancient events will be contemporary with the claim rather than with the events. Then the claim about the past seems paradoxically to be about the present, and this paradox seems to be an objection to verificationism. But the objection seems to be founded in a confusion between the date of a report and the date, if any, mentioned by the report. It may be mysterious how words, simultaneous with their present meanings, can reach across time to refer to things past (see PROPER NAMES §4). But we have yet to be shown how, if present meaning is present evidence, that mystery is any deeper. Yet if present evidence must be present experience, and experience can only be experience of what is (pretty much) contemporary with it, then the objection may be more forceful. (The finiteness of the speed of light means we can see novae long past, but we cannot choose the temporal distance at which we see while we can choose that at which we refer.)

A monument in the criticism of verificationism is Carl G. Hempel's 'Problems and Changes in the Empiricist Criterion of Meaning' (1950). Let us ask in seeming innocence exactly what the verifiability theory of meaning is. It is natural to put the theory by saying that the meaning of a (declarative) sentence is the body of sensory experience that would conclusively establish the sentence; here verification is required to be knock-down. To this form of the theory, Hempel presents three objections. First, natural science, the positivists' paradigm of meaningfulness, is full of universal hypotheses, though, as the problem of induction shows, no genuinely possible body of evidence ever suffices to establish a universal claim conclusively. Second, suppose that S typifies what the positivists count as meaningful while N typifies what they count as meaningless nonsense. Note that the disjunction, S or N, follows from S; yet if a part is gibberish, one expects the whole to be so too – how can nonsense follow from sense? Third, let P be a feature one can observe an object to exhibit or to lack. One observation would suffice to establish conclusively that there is a thing with feature P. But then the sentence 'There is something with P' is meaningful, while its negation, being universal, is not, though it seems unbelievable that a sentence be meaningful, while its negation is not. These three arguments are not meant to be decisive. Instead they represent a turn in the dialectic both of Hempel's 1950 paper and of verificationism. But through the 1950s and into the 1960s, there was a rather general presumption that verificationism was dead, and that Hempel's paper was its headstone (see LOGICAL POSITIVISM §5).

5 Recent developments

But ideas are hardy. After Hume, the gap between experience and theory grows. Perhaps statements which are just about experience can be tested one by one against experience, but the more theoretical a statement, the less it can be so tested individually. Around 1900 Pierre Duhem argued that theoretical statements can be tested against observation only in relatively large, heterogeneous bodies (see Duhem 1906; DUHEM, P.M.M. §4). Half a century later, Quine (1961) inferred from verificationism that the smallest unit with meaning is the smallest unit to which empirical evidence attaches. By Duhem's thesis, such units of evidence are large and heterogeneous in the case of theoretical sentences (see QUINE, W.V. §3). But that is the more general case, and in it we cannot distinguish different meanings for different sentences; as it were, mostly there are no propositions. In particular, meanings for the mathematics used in theoretical science cannot be distinguished from meanings for the natural laws used there. Thus we lose all basis for saying such mathematics is true by virtue of its meaning (analytic), while those laws are not certified by their meanings alone. Quine thus uses one central tenet of positivism (verificationism) to undercut another (the analyticity of mathematics – see ANALYTICITY §3). This reopens a path to Platonic metaphysics in mathematics, a path positivism thought to block.

Quine develops verificationism towards a semantic holism rather alien from positivism (see HOLISM: MENTAL AND SEMANTIC). But from around 1970 Michael DUMMETT (1975), taking a cue from the later WITTGENSTEIN (§14), revives a verificationism more reminiscent of positivism. The later Wittgenstein sometimes seems to flirt with intuitionism in the philosophy of mathematics. The strictures intuitionism would impose on classical logic hardly seem obvious. But Dummett suggests that those strictures may fall out of a proper theory of meaning (see INTUITIONISTIC LOGIC AND ANTIREALISM §§4–6). Meaning, Wittgenstein said, is use, and use, Dummett says, is public; the upshot is what Dummett calls the extrusion of meaning (from, perhaps, the mind into, perhaps, public life). Sometimes he presents this extrusion as the proper response to two challenges, one of acquisition, another of manifestation. The point of the first is that no matter what ideas are innate, a child learning its mother tongue has only observations of which words those around it use in which circumstances on which to base its expressions of its ideas. Meaning must be publicly observable to be learned by speakers (see PRIVATE STATES AND LANGUAGE). These challenges are challenges to an account of meaning in terms of truth-conditions, an account of meaning that may have been present in Frege (1884) and that is explicit in Donald Davidson (1984). The idea here is that the meaning of a sentence is given by the conditions for its truth (see MEANING AND TRUTH §1). Taken standardly, there is no guarantee that we can tell of what is true that it is true; Dummett describes such truth as 'verification transcendent'. If the truth-conditions which constitute meaning transcend recognition, then it would seem there is no guarantee that meaning will be manifest enough to be acquired by native speakers. So, since meaning must be knowable for communication to be possible, verification-transcendent truth must be an illusion. But truth so conceived is crucial to the exposition of classical logic; when we say that a statement or its negation is always true, we mean to allow that neither need be known. If we treat from conditions of truth to those of assertibility, as Dummett thinks we must, the logic we get is, he argues, that of intuitionism.

6 Logical problems

It is a consequence of the rejection of verification-transcendent truth that all truths can be known. This may also be a consequence of verificationism itself: any truth is meaningful and so, by verificationism, has attached to it evidence that can be had, thus making the truth known. Dummett is quite clear about the commitment that all truths can be known. Here it seems important to separate possibility from knowledge. There is, presumably, a natural number n such that Caesar had exactly n hairs on his head at the instant Brutus's dagger first penetrated Caesar's body. To say that it can be known that Caesar then had n hairs may be true, while it is pretty clearly false that it is in fact known; the possibility of knowledge should allow for the fact of ignorance.

Take a system for the propositional calculus. Add to it a very weak modal logic in which necessary conditionals with necessary antecedents have necessary consequents (Gödel's axiom) and in which necessitations of theorems are also theorems; the latter is OK if all our axioms are necessary and all our other rules of inference preserve necessity. This weak modal logic is all we need about necessity and possibility on their own. As for knowledge, we make three postulates. A1 says that all truths can be known. This can be written 'If p then it is possible that ('$\Diamond$') it is known that p',

$$p \to \Diamond \mathrm{K}p.$$

A2 says that what is known is true. This can be written

$$\mathrm{K}p \to p.$$

A3 says that when a conjunction is known so are its conjuncts. This can be written

$$\mathrm{K}(p \,\&\, q) \to (\mathrm{K}p \,\&\, \mathrm{K}q).$$

A2 is part of all stories of knowledge, and as for A3, it is hard to see how an explicit conjunction could be known without being understood, and so its conjuncts known. Call the whole system F. In F, we can prove that all truths are known; this can be written

$$p \to \mathrm{K}p.$$

Here is how the proof goes. Suppose that p but that it is not known that p; suppose, in short, that $p \,\&\, {\sim}\mathrm{K}p$. By A1, $\Diamond \mathrm{K}(p \,\&\, {\sim}\mathrm{K}p)$. A3 says K distributes across conjunction, and weak though our modal logic is, it is strong enough to make the distribution inside the diamond. So $\Diamond(\mathrm{K}p \,\&\, \mathrm{K}({\sim}\mathrm{K}p))$. A2 says the outermost K of the second conjunct can be dropped, and weak though our modal logic is, it is strong enough to drop this K inside the diamond. So $\Diamond(\mathrm{K}p \,\&\, {\sim}\mathrm{K}p)$. This says an explicit contradiction could be true, a possibility refutable even in our weak modal logic. So our original supposition that $p \,\&\, {\sim}\mathrm{K}p$ has been reduced to absurdity, and thus we have shown that $p \to \mathrm{K}p$. (This argument has a curious provenance. It was published by Fitch in 1964, but Fitch attributes it to the anonymous referee of a paper he submitted, but did not publish, in 1945.)

General omniscience is utterly preposterous. If nothing else, it would collapse the distinction between knowledge and truth, leaving nothing to discover. If not all truths are known, then at least one of the postulates of F must be mistaken. Faulting the propositional calculus here seems excessive – like using cannon to hunt sparrows. If one is willing to countenance modality at all, then Gödel's axiom seems acceptable. Whether the rule of necessitation RN is acceptable depends on whether the axioms of F are necessary and the other rules preserve necessity. It is generally held by those who take necessity seriously that the laws of the propositional calculus are necessary and that, say, *modus ponens* preserves necessity. Gödel's axiom too is generally thought necessary by the friends of modality. That leaves only our axioms A1–A3 of knowledge. A2 says that only truths are known; this claim is generally held to be analytic and thus necessarily true. A3 says that the conjuncts of a known conjunction are known. This claim follows, for example, from the more general claim that the logical consequences of what is known are also known. The more general claim is usually rejected since, for example, one seems to be able to know the axioms of number theory but not to know all its theorems. Nevertheless, it is only A3 and not the more general claim that is at issue here. It is at least difficult to imagine how an explicit conjunction might be known, and hence understood, unless its conjuncts also were known. If so, A3 is necessarily true and, thus, true. That leaves only A1, the focus of our original interest. If A1 is not true, then neither is it necessarily true, in which case RN is not to be trusted in F. Quite independently of F, there is a suspicious hubris in A1. What would give sentient beings the arrogance to suppose themselves so smart as to be able to figure out everything? Perhaps good manners as well as good judgment urge the denial of A1.

Still, one might feel as if a trick were being played on one; can just this dinky little logic chopping really be all it takes to show there absolutely must be ignorance? This seems like too much out of too little to be believed. So one might think that maybe there is a blunder somewhere, and one thing in the argument that bothers some people is the way it nests K inside itself. So one might consider typing (assigning 'levels' or 'types' to) knowledge, rather as Russell (1908) typed classes, or Tarski (1933) levelled languages. It is by no means obvious how to distinguish types, but custom suggests treating them like numbers. Then we would have not a single K, but rather an infinity K_1, K_2 and so on *ad infinitum*. Aping Russell, our syntax might insist that K_n be applicable to a formula p only if, when there are operators K_m in p, n is the successor of the largest such m. A2 and A3 could be postulated for each such operator uniformly. The novelty would crop up in A1 to block the first step in the proof that $p \rightarrow K_n p$. Moreover, as Hans Kamp and Charles Parsons showed independently, the result is a consistent system in which $p \rightarrow K_n p$ fails.

This result depends on sealing off the positions in which types are mentioned from quantification. For otherwise we could re-introduce K so that Kp means that $(\exists n)K_n p$, and in this way recover the old proof that $p \rightarrow K p$. We are thus landed in an indefinitely extended realm of types (or levels or contexts) that we have to be able to distinguish and mention. Presumably we could introduce a predicate true of all and only the types. This makes it seem like mere artifice or arbitrary convention (like not using one's hands in soccer) not to allow quantification over types. We cannot even say that knowledge is always of some type. In other words, typing without quantification is more like hiding the paradox than solving it. There is nothing special here about knowledge, for types without quantification also seem equally unsatisfactory solutions to the set-theoretic and semantic paradoxes.

Typing is not the only way one might try to diagnose trickery in *F*. A more radical move would be to take our results about *F* as a refutation of A1, as a proof that not all truths can be known and so as a refutation of the verifiability theory of meaning. What might the falsity of verificationism tell us about meaning? Verificationism would fail if there were differences in meaning which no differences in evidence – and thus, granted empiricism, sensory evidence – answered. That would in turn happen were there two sentences that differed in meaning, which would be most convincing if they could or did differ in truth-value, but such that there would be no possible way to tell by looking, listening or otherwise observing, which is true. Here we have reached a description of Descartes' problem of the external world. The matter hypothesis says that there is matter, while the dreaming hypothesis does not. On the very face of it, the two hypotheses are incompatible, and so not synonymous. If a language is to be usable for communication among its speakers, then they must know what its expressions mean. In general, when two of its expressions seem non-synonymous to its speakers, they will be non-synonymous. The dreaming and matter hypotheses seem non-synonymous to us. So if the verifiability theory of meaning says they are synonymous, then so much the worse for verificationism. As a response to the problem of the external world, verificationism was whistling in the dark.

Differences in meaning are not guaranteed to be rooted in sensory differences. Put otherwise, in a more archaic vocabulary, ideas are not images; nor are they faint copies of impressions. This is hardly hot news, and yet it raises in an acute way a worry about whether an empirically acceptable account of what meaning is can be had. What kind of a thing is a meaning? How can that be a difficult question given that since you and I know a natural language, we are both familiar with lots of meanings?

See also: LOGICAL AND MATHEMATICAL TERMS, GLOSSARY OF

References and further reading

* Ayer, A.J. (1936) *Language, Truth and Logic*, London: Gollancz, 2nd edn, 1946. (Widely read and highly provocative. The second edition includes a famous introduction in which Ayer wrestles with objections to the verification principle.)
* Carnap, R. (1928) *Scheinprobleme in der Philosophie*, Berlin; trans. R.A. George, *Pseudoproblems in Philosophy*, with *The Logical Structure of the World*, Berkeley, CA: University of California Press, 1967. (Two seminal works by the leading member of the Vienna Circle.)
  Craig, E.J. (1982) 'Meaning, Use and Privacy', *Mind* 91: 541–64. (The first section of this paper is a critical discussion of Moritz Schlick's argument in favour of the verification principle.)
* Davidson, D. (1984) 'Truth and Meaning', in *Inquiries into Truth and Interpretation*, Oxford: Clarendon Press, 17–36. (A classic statement of the view that, taken properly, reference fixes sense.)
* Descartes, R. (1641) *Meditationes de prima philosophia*, trans., 'Meditations on First Philosophy', in *Descartes: Philosophical Writings*, trans. and ed. G.E.M. Anscombe and P.T. Geach, Indianapolis, IN: Bobbs-Merrill, 1971. (The book that started modern classical philosophy.)

* Duhem, P. (1906) *La Théorie physique, son objet et sa structure*, Paris: Chevalier et Rivière, 2nd edn, 1913; trans. P.P. Wiener, *The Aim and Structure of Physical Theory*, Princeton, NJ: Princeton University Press, 1992. (The source of the view that even all possible experience fails to settle all theoretical questions about the world.)

* Dummett, M. (1975) 'The Philosophical Basis of Intuitionistic Logic', *Studies in Logic and the Foundations of Mathematics* 80: 5–40; repr. in *Truth and Other Enigmas*, London: Duckworth, 1978. (An authoritative statement of Dummett's contemporary version of 'meaning-empiricism'. No easy read, but the most interesting defence of intuitionism in print.)

Edgington, D. (1985) 'The Paradox of Knowability', *Mind* 94: 557–68. (Discusses issues raised in §6 of this entry.)

* Fitch, F.B. (1964) 'A Logical Analysis of Some Value Concepts', *Journal of Symbolic Logic* 28: 135–42. (The first publication of the proof that if all truths can be known, then all truths are in fact known.)

* Frege, G. (1884) *Die Grundlagen der Arithmetik: eine logisch-mathematische Untersuchung über den Begriff der Zahl*, Breslau: Koebner; trans. J.L. Austin, *The Foundations of Arithmetic: A Logico-Mathematical Enquiry into the Concept of Number*, Oxford: Blackwell, 2nd edn, 1980, esp. Introduction. (Still the best single book in philosophy of mathematics ever written.)

* Hempel, C.G. (1950) 'Problems and Changes in the Empiricist Criterion of Meaning', *Revue internationale de philosophie* 4: 41–63; repr. in L. Linsky (ed.) *Semantics and the Philosophy of Language*, Urbana, IL: University of Illinois Press, 1952. (Highly influential critique of logical positivism.)

* Hume, D. (1739–40) *A Treatise of Human Nature*, ed. D.G.C. MacNabb, London: Fontana, 1962. (A masterpiece. See book 1 for Hume's sceptical account of meaning.)

* Kant, I. (1781/1787) *Critique of Pure Reason*, trans. N. Kemp Smith, London: Macmillan, 1963. (Another masterpiece. The second edition of 1787 contains the discussion outlined in §1.)

* Quine, W.V. (1961) 'Two Dogmas of Empiricism', in *From a Logical Point of View: Nine Logico-Philosophical Essays*, Cambridge, MA: Harvard University Press, 2nd edn, 1980. (Proposes a revamped meaning-empiricism of a holistic rather than molecular or atomistic sort.)

* Russell, B.A.W. (1908) 'Mathematical Logic as based on the Theory of Types', *American Journal of Mathematics* 30: 222–62; repr. in *Logic and Knowledge: Essays 1901–1950*, ed. R.C. Marsh, London: Routledge, 1992, 59–102. (Perhaps Russell's single best piece of work in logic.)

* Tarski, A. (1933) Pojęcie prawdy w językach nauk dedukcyjnych, Warsaw; trans. J.H. Woodger (1956), 'The Concept of Truth in Formalized Languages', in *Logic, Semantics, Metamathematics: Papers from 1923 to 1938*, Indianapolis, IN: Hackett Publishing Company, 2nd edn, 1983, 152–278. (The start of modern theories of truth.)

Williamson, T. (1982, 1987) 'Intuitionism Disproved?', *Analysis* 42: 203–8, 'On Knowledge and the Unknowable', *Analysis* 47: 154–8, and 'On the Paradox of Knowability', *Mind* 96: 256–61. (Articles which discuss logical issues of the kind described in §6 of this entry.)

W.D. HART

MEANING, EMOTIVE
see EMOTIVE MEANING

MEANING IN ISLAMIC PHILOSOPHY

The discussion of the notion of meaning in Islamic philosophy is heavily influenced by theological and legal debates about the interpretation of Islam, and about who has the right to pronounce on interpretation. The introduction of Greek philosophy into the Islamic world produced a new set of authorities on how to interpret texts, and this led to arguments over the potential benefits of the new approaches as compared with the traditional Islamic sciences. The discussion came to centre on the nature of ambiguity, equivocation and analogy, with different philosophers adopting diverse theories and thus attaining a variety of conclusions about how to interpret meaning. These variations have powerful implications for the understanding of their thought. Not only do the different approaches result in different conclusions, they also represent different approaches to the whole philosophical enterprise. The topic of meaning is not so much an aspect of Islamic philosophy as an interpretation of how to do Islamic philosophy itself. The main issues focus on identifying the people best qualified to interpret texts, valid interpretations of the texts, and the notion of meaning that should be employed in our understanding of the texts.

1   **Religious context**
2   **Language versus logic**

3 Ambiguity, equivocation and analogy
4 The main debate

1 Religious context

Since the Qur'an was transmitted in Arabic, an understanding of the nature of that language is a vital aspect to an understanding of the text itself. Those brought up within the traditions of jurisprudence, grammar and theology were of the opinion that they were the best positioned to pronounce on the meaning of the text (see ISLAMIC THEOLOGY §1). All scriptures require interpretation, and a wide diversity of views arose within the Islamic community over the correct reading of much of the Qur'an, with the creation of different schools of thought based upon political and religious divisions such as those between the Sunni and the Shi'i communities and between the Ash'arites and the Mu'tazilites (see ASH'ARIYYA AND MU'TAZILA §1). It was accepted quite early on that while some parts of the Qur'an are clear, others are less easy to grasp and so require more complex interpretations. Some passages are *zahir* (exoteric) while others are *batin* (esoteric), and naturally the commentators disagreed on occasion over which texts fell into which category and how the esoteric texts were to be read. In a religious text, of course, even the apparently plain and commonplace can be given a richer and deeper interpretation, and different interpreters produced different interpretations. None of these was arbitrary. All were based upon argument and a variety of Islamic sources, but this hermeneutic process was capable of arriving at a variety of conclusions.

2 Language versus logic

The arrival of Greek logic in the Islamic world caused great controversy in the fourth century AH/tenth century AD. It brought with it the view that logic is superior to language since the latter deals only with the contingent and conventional, while logic encompasses the necessary and the universal. Language deals only with *alfaz* (utterances), while logic gets to the heart of the matter by analysing *ma'ani* (concepts) themselves. This controversy was explored in the celebrated debate between the grammarian Abu Sa'id al-Sirafi and the logician Abu Bishr Matta in Baghdad in AH 320/AD 932. Matta argued that logic was more important than language since the meanings which are embedded in a particular language are analysable without reference to that particular language. Those meanings could exist in a whole variety of languages. Logic is the only rigorous tool for judging when language is used correctly or otherwise,

and the logician is the best qualified to adjudicate on such issues.

This was a very important debate, since if Matta were to carry the day it would imply that the traditional approach to Islamic texts rests on an error. Only logic, as understood by the Greeks and a non-Muslim such as Matta, is a sound vehicle for the understanding of texts. Al-Sirafi was clear on the significance of the debate, and he argued that it is impossible to separate language and logic in the way Matta wants. Although logic is useful at one level in dealing with concepts, it is far from comprehensive and is better suited to analysing the Greek language than the Arabic. Problems in understanding Arabic texts can only be answered by a good understanding of the Arabic language and the culture which surrounds it. Logic by itself is not sufficient (see LOGIC IN ISLAMIC PHILOSOPHY).

This sort of debate continued in the Islamic world for some time, albeit in a more sophisticated form. The debate is highly significant, since it is really about the appropriate notion of meaning to be employed. Must that notion of meaning be taken from the context in which the text to be analysed has itself originated, or can it come from elsewhere? How one answers this question has radical implications for the way in which Islamic philosophy is to be pursued, and the protagonists of the argument are well aware of this.

3 Ambiguity, equivocation and analogy

There are two main theories of meaning in Islamic philosophy, one broadly Neoplatonic and adopted by IBN SINA (Avicenna) and AL-GHAZALI, and one broadly Aristotelian and defended by IBN RUSHD (Averroes). On the former account, the definition of x does not include the existence of x, so that something else is required to move x from the realm of possibility to the realm of actuality if it is to be instantiated. For Ibn Sina the mover is another thing, ultimately God, which causally necessitates the change, while for al-Ghazali it is God who directly established quite arbitrary rules for the behaviour of contingent phenomena. This means that for al-Ghazali it is possible to think of something happening without its customary explanation, that is, without a natural explanation. God could always have brought it about that people on occasion write philosophy books without possessing a head, or that straw does not burn when in contact with fire.

Ibn Rushd operates with a different concept of meaning, in accordance with which the cause of an event is part of its definition or essence. If headless people were to start composing philosophical books we should need to construct an entirely novel conceptual scheme for such a possibility to make sense. Al-Ghazali, by contrast, argues that we can conceive of such changes to our conceptual scheme by using our imagination, and failure to approve the possibility of such changes is merely a result of intellectual laziness, not the flouting of necessity. It is possible, then, for God to do anything he wishes so long as it is logically possible. God can resurrect the dead, he can intervene in the natural world, he can be aware of events in the world, he can create that world at any time he wishes out of nothing. These are all actions which Ibn Rushd argued are not possible even for God, if what is meant when talking about such actions is similar to what we mean when we talk about what we do. Al-Ghazali suggests that any analysis of the properties of God which interprets them as equivocal, ambiguous or metaphorical is a subtle attack upon the notion of God in its religious sense. It involves pretending to make God part of one's metaphysics but changing the way in which one talks about him to such an extent that he no longer is equivalent to the God of Islam.

For Ibn Rushd, there are serious problems in talking about God using the same sort of language we use about ourselves. God cannot be defined in terms of a genus or species since he cannot consist of a plurality of qualities as we do. Rather, he is the exemplar of all things, and we must work towards a conception of him by thinking analogically about the things in the world of which we have experience. The way in which al-Ghazali talks about God seems to be in line with religion, but really it involves treating the deity as someone much like ourselves but more so, and as a plurality of predicates rather than a complete unity. Ibn Rushd goes along with Aristotle's argument that there can be no priority or posteriority within the same genus (see ARISTOTLE §§7–8), and so develops a theory of meaning which is based upon the *pros hen* notion of equivocation rather than the genus–species relation. We can use the same language about God as we use about ourselves, but we should realize that the latter type of use is derivative upon the former, since the latter concepts are aspects of the paradigm which is to be found when we talk about God. When we use the same concept to refer to God and to ourselves we are speaking not univocally but equivocally, acknowledging the very real difference which exists between the level of the human and the level of the divine.

4 The main debate

In al-Ghazali's concept of meaning, the appropriate people to interpret religious texts are those professionally involved in the religion, such as theologians,

jurisprudents and so on. They need to understand the religious context of the text and apply the terms univocally to God and to his creatures. The correct way to think analytically is to adopt the methodology of the thought-experiment, holding ideas together in the imagination to see if they can be combined without contradiction. If we can imagine dead people being resurrected and leaving their graves to continue a physical existence somewhere else, in hell or paradise, then there is nothing impossible about that idea and there is no need to suggest that it is a metaphorical or equivocal reference to something else. If the Qur'an refers to physical resurrection, and if we can think about physical resurrection without contradiction, then why not just accept that what is meant by physical resurrection is what we would normally understand by that miraculous event?

It follows from Ibn Rushd's approach that the best people to interpret difficult theological passages are not the theologians but the philosophers, since only the latter are skilled in understanding analytical and demonstrative thought. The philosopher can understand how a religious text may embody a whole range of meanings, some intended for a more sophisticated audience and some designed for a more naïve and practically-oriented audience. The latter might understand by physical resurrection that the consequences of what we do outlive us, and the moral status of what we do affects us in this life and others after we are dead. They might find this easier to understand if they can think of themselves, or something like themselves, surviving their death. The more sophisticated audience would understand by the religious text what the philosophers understand by it, what it really means. This sort of audience does not require the rhetorical and poetic language which is capable of moving the largest section of the community to action. Only philosophers are capable of resolving the meaning of a text once and for all. The other theoreticians who work within the Islamic sciences, such as theology and jurisprudence, will constantly disagree about the appropriate meaning, and as a result they will sow discord in the community. The role of the philosopher is to resolve the meaning of the text and then communicate that meaning to different kinds of audiences in different kinds of ways, each suited to the limitations of the audience to understand the real point of the text.

It can thus be seen that the issue of meaning in Islamic philosophy concerns not only the philosophy of language but also politics. It is linked to the question as to who is entitled to derive the meanings of a text and how that meaning may be communicated to others. Although the focus of discussion is generally on the relationship between ordinary language and language about God, it has far broader implications, and leads to a diversity of views on how to do philosophy itself.

See also: AESTHETICS IN ISLAMIC PHILOSOPHY; EPISTEMOLOGY IN ISLAMIC PHILOSOPHY; AL-GHAZALI; IBN RUSHD; IBN SINA; LOGIC IN ISLAMIC PHILOSOPHY; POLITICAL PHILOSOPHY IN CLASSICAL ISLAM

References and further reading

Abed, A. (1991) *Aristotelian Logic and the Arabic Language in Alfarabi*, Albany, NY: State University of New York Press. (A detailed and scholarly investigation of the concept of meaning and the logic versus language debate.)

Abed, S. (1996) 'Language', in S.H. Nasr and O. Leaman (eds) *History of Islamic Philosophy*, London: Routledge, ch. 52, 898–925. (Interesting and detailed account of the role that language plays in Islamic philosophy.)

Ibn Rushd (1179–80) *Fasl al-maqal* (Decisive Treatise), ed. and trans. G. Hourani, *Averroes on the Harmony of Religion and Philosophy*, London: Luzac, 1976. (An outstandingly clear exposition of the basic themes of Ibn Rushd on different kinds of meaning.)

—— (1180) *Tahafut al-tahafut* (The Incoherence of the Incoherence), trans. S. Van den Bergh, *Averroes' Tahafut al-tahafut*, London: Luzac, 1978. (A comprehensive comparison of the views of al-Ghazali and Ibn Rushd.)

Leaman, O. (1954–) '*Ma'na*', in *Encyclopedia of Islam*, Leiden: Brill, 347. (An account of the philosophical use of this Arabic term, equivalent in meaning to 'concept' or 'idea'.)

—— (1988) *Averroes and His Philosophy*, Oxford: Oxford University Press; 2nd edn, 1997. (A general account of the thought of Averroes (Ibn Rushd), with the emphasis upon his approach to language.)

—— (1997) 'Logic and Language in Islamic Philosophy', in B. Carr and I. Mahalingam (eds) *Companion Encyclopedia of Asian Philosophy*, London: Routledge, 950–64. (Summary of some of the major approaches to meaning in Islamic philosophy.)

Mahdi, M. (1970) 'Language and Logic in Classical Islam', in G.E. von Grunebaum (ed.) *Logic in Classical Islamic Culture*, Wiesbaden: Harrassowitz, 51–83. (The standard discussion of the battle between the logicians and the grammarians.)

OLIVER LEAMAN

MEANING, INDIAN THEORIES OF

The term artha *in Sanskrit is used for the notion of meaning, in the widest sense of the word 'meaning'; it can be the meaning of words, sentences and scriptures, as well as of nonlinguistic gestures and signs. Its meaning ranges from a real object in the external world referred to by a word to a mere concept of an object which may or may not correspond to anything in the external world. The differences regarding what 'meaning' is are argued out by the philosophical schools of Nyāya, Vaiśeṣika, Mīmāṃsā, Buddhism, Sanskrit grammar and Sanskrit poetics. Among these, Nyāya, Vaiśeṣika and Mīmāṃsā have realistic ontologies. Mīmāṃsā focuses mainly on interpreting the Vedic scriptures. Buddhist thinkers generally depict language as giving a false picture of reality. Sanskrit grammar is more interested in language than in ontology, while Sanskrit poetics focuses on the poetic dimensions of meaning.*

Generally, the notion of meaning is stratified into three or four types. First there is the primary meaning. If this is inappropriate in a given context, then one moves to a secondary meaning, an extension of the primary meaning. Beyond this is the suggested meaning, which may or may not be the same as the meaning intended by the speaker. Specific conditions under which these different varieties are understood are discussed by the schools.

The various Indian theories of meaning are closely related to the overall stances taken by the different schools. Among the factors which influence the notion of meaning are the ontological and epistemological views of a school, its views regarding the role of God and scripture, its focus on a certain type of discourse, and its ultimate purpose in theorizing.

1   *Artha* **in different Indian traditions**
2   **Varieties of meaning**
3   **Other dimensions of** *artha*
4   **Different views regarding sentence-meaning**
5   **Some important conceptions**
6   **Why the differences?**

1   *Artha* in different Indian traditions

The most common Sanskrit term for meaning is *artha*. In the Western literature on the notion of meaning in the Indian tradition, various terms, such as 'sense', 'reference', 'denotation', 'connotation', 'designatum' and 'intension', have been used to render the Sanskrit. However, these terms carry specific nuances of their own, and no single term adequately conveys the idea of *artha*. *Artha* basically refers to the object signified by a word. In numerous contexts, it stands for an object in the sense of an element of external reality. For instance, PATAÑJALI (second century BC) says that when a word is pronounced, an *artha*, 'object', is understood. So in the case of 'Bring a bull' and 'Eat yoghurt', it is the *artha* that is brought in and the *artha* that is eaten.

The logicians and ontologists belonging to the schools of Nyāya and Vaiśeṣika, and the later combined school of Nyāya-Vaiśeṣika, set up an ontology containing substances, qualities, actions, relations, generic and particular properties, and absences (see NYĀYA-VAIŚEṢIKA §§4–5). With this realistic ontology in mind, they argue that if the relation between a word and its *artha* were a natural ontological relation, there should be real experiences of burning and cutting in one's mouth after hearing words like *agni* ('fire') and *asi* ('sword'). Therefore this relation must be a conventional one (*saṃketa*), the convention being established by God as part of his initial acts of creation. The relationship between a word and the object it refers to is thought to be the desire of God that such-and-such a word should refer to such-and-such an object. It is through this established conventional relationship that a word reminds the listener of its meaning.

The school of Mīmāṃsā represents the tradition of the exegesis of the scriptural Vedic texts (see MĪMĀṂSĀ). However, in the course of discussing and perfecting principles of interpretation, this school developed a full-scale theory of ontology and an important theory of meaning. For the Mīmāṃsakas, the primary tenets are that the Vedic scriptural texts are eternal and uncreated, and that they are meaningful. In this orthodox system, which remarkably defends the scriptures but dispenses with the notion of God, the relationship between a word and its meaning is innate and eternal. Both Nyāya-Vaiśeṣikas and Mīmāṃsakas regard language as referring to external states of the world and not just to conceptual constructions.

While the various schools of Buddhism differ among themselves concerning the nature of the external world, they all seem to agree that language relates only to a level of conceptual constructions which have no direct relationship to the actual state of the world. The tradition represented by Theravāda and the Vaibhāṣikas argued that a word refers to a thing which, in reality, is nothing but a composite entity made up of components which are momentary and in a continual flux (see MOMENTARINESS, BUDDHIST DOCTRINE OF). The components, the momentary atomic elements (*dharma*), are presumed to be more real, but words do not refer to this level of

reality. Thus language gives us a less than true picture of what is out there. Other schools of Buddhism, such as Vijñānavāda, reduced everything to fleeting states of consciousness (*vijñāna*). From this point of view, the objects referred to by words are not even composites. They are more like fictions (*vikalpa*) or illusions (*māyā*) created by a magician. The Mādhyamika school of Buddhism focused on the essential emptiness (*śūnyatā*) of all objects which are subject to dependent origination (*pratītyasamutpāda*). This also leaves language far away from the level of reality, which in this case is the level of emptiness (see BUDDHIST CONCEPT OF EMPTINESS). Later Buddhist logicians, such as DIGNĀGA, developed a theory of word-meaning which we can call the 'exclusionary' theory of meaning (*apoha*). Briefly stated, if a word refers only to a conceptual construction, and not to a state of reality, then how are we to construe the conceptual construction? The *apoha* theory proposed by the Buddhist logicians says that external reality ultimately consists of momentary atomic elements which are so individualized and unique (*svalakṣaṇa*) that they are beyond perception and characterization. Our perceptions and conceptions involve generalization (*sāmānyalakṣaṇa*), and hence do not correspond to reality. A concept which corresponds to a given word must be finally construed as being nothing more than the exclusion of all other concepts. This theory ultimately says that all concepts are different from each other, and yet they cannot be defined by making a reference to any level of reality (see NOMINALISM, BUDDHIST DOCTRINE OF).

The tradition of the grammarians, beginning with BHARTṚHARI (fifth century), seems to have followed a middle path between the realistic theories of reference (*bāhyārthavāda*) developed by Nyāya-Vaiśeṣika and Mīmāṃsā on the one hand, and the notional/conceptual theories (*vikalpa*) of the Buddhists on the other. For them, the meaning of a word is closely related to the level of understanding. Whether or not things are real, we do have concepts. These concepts form the content of a person's cognitions derived from language. Without necessarily denying the external reality of objects in the world, the grammarians claimed that the meaning of a word is only a projection of intellect (*bauddhārtha*, *buddhipratibhāsa*). The examples they offer, such as *śaśaśṛṅga* ('horn of a rabbit') and *vandhyāsuta* ('son of a barren woman'), remain meaningful within this theory. The Sanskrit grammarians are thus not concerned with the truth-functional value of linguistic expressions. For them, the truth of an expression and its meaningfulness are not to be equated.

2 Varieties of meaning

By the middle of the second millennium AD, a certain uniformity came about in the technical terminology used by different schools. The prominent schools in this period were the new school of Nyāya – Navya-Nyāya – initiated by Gaṅgeśa, and the schools of Mīmāṃsā, Vedānta, and Sanskrit grammar. While all these schools engaged in pitched battles against each other, they seem to have accepted the terminological lead of the neo-logicians, the Navya-Naiyāyikas. Following the discussion of *artha* by the neo-logician GADĀDHARA, we can state the general framework of a semantic theory. Other schools accepted this general terminology, with some variations.

It may be said that the term *artha* stands for the object or content of a verbal cognition or a cognition which results from hearing a word (*śābdabodha-viṣaya*). Such a verbal cognition results from the cognition of a word (*śābdajñāna*) on the basis of an awareness of the signification function pertaining to that word (*padaniṣṭhavṛttijñāna*). Depending upon the kind of signification function (*vṛtti*) involved in the emergence of the verbal cognition, the meaning belongs to a distinct type. In general terms:

1 When a verbal cognition results from the primary signification function (*śakti/abhidhāvṛtti/mukhyavṛtti*) of a word, the object or content of that cognition is called primary meaning (*śakyārtha/vācyārtha/abhidheya*).
2 When a verbal cognition results from the secondary signification function (*lakṣaṇāvṛtti/guṇavṛtti*) of a word, the object or content of that cognition is called secondary meaning (*lakṣyārtha*).
3 When a verbal cognition results from the suggestive signification function (*vyañjanāvṛtti*) of a word, the object or content of that cognition is called suggested meaning (*vyaṅgyārtha/dhvanitārtha*).
4 When a verbal cognition results from the intentional signification function (*tātparyavṛtti*) of a word, the object or content of that cognition is called intended meaning (*tātparyārtha*).

Not all schools of Indian philosophy accept all of these different kinds of signification functions for words, and they hold substantially different views on the nature of words, meanings, and the relations between words and meanings. However, the above terminology holds true, in general, for most of the schools. Let us note some of the important differences. Mīmāṃsā claims that the sole primary meaning of the word 'bull' is the generic or class property (*jāti*) – 'bullness', say – and the individual object which possesses this generic property, namely a particular bull, is only secondarily and subsequently understood from the word 'bull'. The school called Kevalavyaktivāda, a segment of the Nyāya school, argues that a particular individual bull is the sole primary meaning of the word 'bull', while the generic property bullness is merely a secondary meaning. Nyāya generally argues that the primary meaning of a word is an individual object qualified by a generic property (*jātiviśiṣṭavyakti*), both being perceived simultaneously.

Sanskrit grammarians distinguish between various different kinds of meanings (*artha*). The term *artha* stands for an external object (*vastumātra*), as well as for the object that is intended to be signified by a word (*abhidheya*). The latter – that is, meaning in a linguistic sense – can be meaning in a technical context (*śāstrīya*), such as the meaning of an affix or a stem, or it can be meaning as understood by people in actual communication (*laukika*). Then there is a further distinction. Meaning may be something directly intended to be signified by an expression (*abhidheya*), or it can be something which is inevitably signified (*nāntarīyaka*) when something else is really the intended meaning. Everything that is understood from a word on the basis of some kind of signification function (*vṛtti*) is covered by the term *artha*. Different systems of Indian philosophy differ from each other over whether a given cognition is derived from a word on the basis of a signification function, through inference (*anumāna*), or through presumption (*arthā-patti*). If a particular item of information is deemed to have been derived through inference or presumption, it is not included in the notion of word-meaning.

3 Other dimensions of *artha*

The scope of *artha* is actually not limited in Sanskrit texts to what is usually understood as the domain of semantics in the Western literature. It covers elements such as gender (*liṅga*) and number (*saṃkhyā*), as well as such semantic/syntactic roles (*kāraka*) as 'agent-ness' (*kartṛtva*) and 'objectness' (*karmatva*). Tenses such as the present, past and future, and moods such as the imperative and optative are also traditionally included in the *arthas* signified by a verb root or an affix.

Another aspect of the concept of *artha* is revealed in the theory of *dyotyārtha*, 'co-signified' meaning. According to this theory, to put it in simple terms, particles such as *ca* ('and') do not have any lexical or primary meaning. They are said to help other words used in constructions with them to signify special aspects of their meaning. For instance, in the phrase 'John and Tom', the meaning of grouping is said to be not directly signified by the word 'and'. The theory of *dyotyārtha* argues that grouping is a specific meaning of the two words 'John' and 'Tom', but that these two words are unable to signify it if used by themselves. The word 'and' used along with them is said to work as a catalyst that enables them to signify this special meaning.

The problem of use and mention of words is also handled by Sanskrit grammarians by treating the word itself as a part of the meaning it signifies. This is a unique way of handling this problem.

4   Different views regarding sentence-meaning

Most schools of Indian philosophy have an atomistic view of meaning and the meaning-bearing linguistic unit. This means that a sentence is put together by combining words and words are put together by combining morphemic elements such as stems, roots and affixes. The same applies to meaning. The word-meaning may be viewed as a fusion of the meanings of stems, roots and affixes, and the meaning of a sentence may be viewed as a fusion of the meanings of its constituent words. Beyond this generality, different schools have specific proposals. The tradition of Prābhākara Mīmāṃsā proposes that the words of a sentence already convey contextualized/connected meanings (anvitābhidhāna) and that the sentence-meaning is not different from a simple addition of these inherently connected word-meanings. On the other hand, the Naiyāyikas and the Bhāṭṭa Mīmāṃsakas propose that the words of a sentence taken by themselves convey uncontextualized/unconnected meanings, and that these uncontextualized word-meanings are subsequently brought into a contextualized association with each other (abhihitānvaya). Therefore, sentence-meaning is different from word-meanings, and is communicated through the concatenation (saṃsarga) of words rather than by the words themselves. This is also the view of the early grammarians such as Patañjali and Kātyāyana.

For the later grammarian-philosopher Bhartṛhari, however, there are no divisions in speech acts and in communicated meanings. He says that only a person ignorant of the real nature of language believes the divisions of sentences into words, stems, roots and affixes to be real. Such divisions are useful fictions and have an explanatory value in grammatical theory, but have no reality in communication. In reality, there is no sequence in the cognitions of these different components. The sentence-meaning becomes an object or content of a single flash of cognition (pratibhā).

5   Some important conceptions

The terms śakyatāvacchedaka and pravṛttinimitta signify a property which determines the inclusion of a particular instance within the class of possible entities referred to by a word. It is a property whose possession by an entity is the necessary and sufficient condition for a given word to be used to refer to that entity. Thus the property of potness may be viewed as the śakyatāvacchedaka controlling the use of the word 'pot'.

Lakṣaṇāvṛtti (the 'secondary signification function') is invoked in situations where the primary meaning of an utterance does not appear to make sense in view of the intention behind the utterance, causing one to look for a secondary meaning. However, the secondary meaning is always something that is related to the primary meaning in some way. For example, the expression gaṅgāyāṃ ghoṣaḥ literally refers to a colony of cowherds on the river Ganges. Here it is argued that one obviously cannot have a colony of cowherds sitting on top of the Ganges. This would clearly go against the intention of the speaker. Thus there is both a difficulty in justifying the linkage of word-meanings (anvayānupapatti) and a difficulty in justifying the literal or primary meaning in relation to the intention of the speaker (tātparyānupapatti). These interpretive difficulties nudge one away from the primary meaning of the expression to a secondary meaning which is related to that primary meaning. Thus we understand the expression as referring to a colony of cowherds on the bank of the Ganges.

It is the third level of meaning, or vyañjanāvṛtti ('suggestive signification function'), which is analysed and elaborated by authors such as Ānandavardhana (ninth century) in the tradition of Sanskrit poetics. Consider the following instance of poetic suggestion. Her husband away on a long journey, a lovelorn young wife instructs a visiting young man: 'My dear guest, I sleep here and my nightblind mother-in-law sleeps over there. Please make sure you do not stumble at night.' The suggested meaning is an invitation to the young man to come and share her bed. Thus the poetic aspect of language goes well beyond the levels of lexical and metaphorical meanings, and heightens aesthetic pleasure through such suggestions.

6   Why the differences?

The nuances of these different theories are closely related to the markedly different interests of the schools within which they developed. Scholars of Sanskrit poetics were interested in the poetic dimensions of meaning. Grammarians were interested in language and cognition, but had little interest in ontology. For them, words and meanings had to be explained irrespective of one's metaphysical views. Nyāya-Vaiśeṣikas were primarily interested in logic, epistemology and ontology, and argued that a valid sentence was a true picture of a state of reality. The foremost goal of Mīmāṃsā was to interpret and defend the Vedic scriptures. Thus, for Mīmāṃsā, meaning had to be eternal, uncreated and unrelated to a person's intention, because its word *par excellence*, the Vedic scriptures, was eternal, uncreated and beyond any authorship, divine or human. The scriptural word was there to instruct people on how to perform proper ritual and moral duties. The Buddhists, on the other hand, aimed at weaning people away from all attachment to the world, and hence at showing the emptiness of everything, including language. They were more interested in demonstrating how language fails to portray reality, than in explaining how it works. The theories of meaning were thus a significant part of the total agenda of each school and need to be understood in their specific contexts.

See also: INTERPRETATION, INDIAN THEORIES OF; LANGUAGE, INDIAN THEORIES OF; LANGUAGE, PHILOSOPHY OF; MEANING IN ISLAMIC PHILOSOPHY

References and further reading

Biardeau, M. (1967) *Théorie de la connaissance et philosophie de la parole dans le brahmanisme classique* (Theory of the Understanding and Philosophy of the Word in Classical Brahmanism), Paris: Mouton. (A comprehensive discussion of theories of meaning and their evolution and interaction in the traditions of Sanskrit grammar, Mīmāṃsā and Nyāya-Vaiśeṣika; no English translation is available as yet.)

Deshpande, M.M. (1992) *The Meaning of Nouns: Semantic Theory in Classical and Medieval India*, Dordrecht: Kluwer Academic Publishers. (The bulk of the book is an annotated translation of a seventeenth-century Sanskrit text on the meaning of nouns. The introduction covers the history of a number of semantic theories in Sanskrit grammar and philosophy.)

Matilal, B.K. (1971) *Epistemology, Logic and Grammar in Indian Philosophical Analysis*, The Hague/Paris: Mouton. (Very readable general introduction to Indian approaches to meaning, logic and language.)

—— (1985) *Logic, Language and Reality: An Introduction to Indian Philosophical Studies*, Delhi: Motilal Banarsidass. (More extensive, but still very accessible, discussion of a wide range of issues in Indian philosophy of language.)

Raja, K. (1963) *Indian Theories of Meaning*, Adyar Library Series 91, Madras: Adyar Library and Research Centre. (A somewhat dated, but still very useful, account.)

MADHAV M. DESHPANDE

MEANING OF LIFE, see LIFE, MEANING OF

MEASUREMENT PROBLEM, QUANTUM see QUANTUM MEASUREMENT PROBLEM

MEASUREMENT, THEORY OF

A conceptual analysis of measurement can properly begin by formulating the two fundamental problems of any measurement procedure. The first problem is that of representation, justifying the assignment of numbers to objects or phenomena. We cannot literally take a number in our hands and 'apply' it to a physical object. What we can show is that the structure of a set of phenomena under certain empirical operations and relations is the same as the structure of some set of numbers under corresponding arithmetical operations and relations. Solution of the representation problem for a theory of measurement does not completely lay bare the structure of the theory, for there is often a formal difference between the kind of assignment of numbers arising from different procedures of measurement. This is the second fundamental problem, determining the scale type of a given procedure.

Counting is an example of an absolute scale. The number of members of a given collection of objects is determined uniquely. In contrast, the measurement of mass or weight is an example of a ratio scale. An empirical procedure for measuring mass does not determine the unit of mass. The measurement of temperature is an example of an interval scale. The empirical procedure of measuring temperature by use of a thermometer determines neither a unit nor an origin. In this sort of measurement the ratio of any two intervals is independent of the unit and zero point of measurement.

Still another type of scale is one which is arbitrary except for order. Moh's hardness scale, according to

243

which minerals are ranked in regard to hardness as determined by a scratch test, and the Beaufort wind scale, whereby the strength of a wind is classified as calm, light air, light breeze, and so on, are examples of ordinal scales.

A distinction is made between those scales of measurement which are fundamental and those which are derived. A derived scale presupposes and uses the numerical results of at least one other scale. In contrast, a fundamental scale does not depend on others.

Another common distinction is that between extensive and intensive quantities or scales. For extensive quantities like mass or distance an empirical operation of combination can be given which has the structural properties of the numerical operation of addition. Intensive quantities do not have such an operation; typical examples are temperature and cardinal utility.

A widespread complaint about this classical foundation of measurement is that it takes too little account of the analysis of variability in the quantity measured. One important source is systematic variability in the empirical properties of the object being measured. Another source lies not in the object but in the procedures of measurement being used. There are also random errors which can arise from variability in the object, the procedures or the conditions surrounding the observations.

1   **First fundamental problem: representation**
2   **Second fundamental problem: uniqueness**
3   **Classification of scales of measurement**
4   **Measurement and theory construction**
5   **Ordinal theory of measurement**
6   **Invariance and meaningfulness**
7   **Variability, thresholds and errors**

1   First fundamental problem: representation

Since the days of the Greek geometers, mathematicians, philosophers and empirical scientists have been discussing the nature of measurement. Eudoxus' development of the theory of proportion, which forms the substance of Book V of Euclid's *Elements*, is probably the first sustained analysis directly relevant to measurement. A systematic approach to the subject of measurement may well begin by formulating the two fundamental problems of any procedure of measurement. The first problem is to justify the assignment of numbers to objects or phenomena.

The early history of mathematics shows how difficult it was to divorce arithmetic from particular empirical structures. Thus the early Egyptians could not think of $2 + 3$, but only of 2 bushels of wheat plus 3 bushels of wheat. From a logical standpoint, there is

just one arithmetic of numbers, not an arithmetic for bushels of wheat, and a separate arithmetic for quarts of milk. The first problem for a theory of measurement is to show how this one arithmetic of numbers may be applied in a variety of empirical situations. This is done by showing that the relevant structure of the empirical situation investigated is isomorphic to an arithmetical structure. The purpose of the definitions of isomorphism given for each kind of measurement considered is to make the rough-and-ready intuitive idea of same structure precise. The great significance of finding such an isomorphism of structures is that we may then use all our familiar knowledge of computational methods, as applied to the arithmetical structure, to infer facts about the isomorphic empirical structure.

A procedure of measurement is needed in any area of science when we desire to pass from simple qualitative observations to the quantitative observations necessary for the precise prediction or control of phenomena. To justify this transition we need an algebra of empirically realizable operations and relations which can be shown to be isomorphic to an appropriately chosen numerical algebra. Satisfying this requirement is the fundamental problem of measurement representation.

2   Second fundamental problem: uniqueness

Solution of the representation problem for a theory of measurement is not enough. There is often a formal difference between the kind of assignment of numbers arising from different procedures of measurement. Consider the following three statements:

(1)   The number of people now in this room is seven.

(2)   Yesterday John weighed 150 lbs.

(3)   The maximum temperature tomorrow will be 89°F.

Here we may formally distinguish three kinds of measurement. Counting is an example of an 'absolute' scale. The number of members of a given collection of objects is determined uniquely. There is no arbitrary choice of a unit or zero available. In contrast, the measurement of mass or weight is an example of a 'ratio' scale. Empirical procedures for measuring mass do not determine the unit of mass. The choice of a unit is an empirically arbitrary decision, but the ratio of any two masses is independent of such choice. The measurement of distance is a second example of a ratio scale. The ratio of the distance between Palo Alto and San Francisco to the distance between Washington and New York is the same whether the measurement is made in miles or metres.

The measurement of temperature is an example of an interval scale. The empirical procedure of measuring temperature by use of a thermometer determines neither a unit nor an origin. In this sort of measurement the ratio of any two intervals is independent of the unit and zero point of measurement. Examples other than measurement of temperature are measurements of temporal dates, geographical longitude and cardinal utility.

In terms of the notion of absolute, ratio and interval scales we may formulate the second fundamental problem for a theory of measurement: determine the scale type of the measurements resulting from the procedure. (A detailed treatment of the theory of fundamental measurement from the standpoint of these two central problems is to be found in Krantz *et al.* the three-volume treatise *Foundations of Measurement*, 1971, 1989, 1990.)

3 Classification of scales of measurement

For the purpose of systematizing some of the discussion of the uniqueness problem in the previous section, we may define a scale as a class of measurement procedures having the same transformation properties. Examples of three different scales have already been mentioned, namely, counting as an absolute scale, measurement of mass as a ratio scale and measurement of temperature as an interval scale.

An 'ordinal' scale is one which is arbitrary except for order. A number is assigned to give a ranking. The social sciences extensively use such scales. Numbers are also sometimes used for naming or classification. The numerical assignment is completely arbitrary. The numbers on football players' shirts are examples of this sort of measurement. Such scales are usually called 'nominal' scales.

In the literature a distinction is often made between those scales of measurement which are fundamental and those which are 'derived'. A derived scale is one which in the procedure of measurement presupposes and uses the numerical results of at least one other scale. In contrast, a 'fundamental' scale does not depend on other scales. As might be expected, foundational investigations of measurement have been primarily concerned with fundamental scales, and such is the emphasis here (Krantz *et al.* 1971: ch. 10).

Another distinction common in the literature is that between extensive and intensive quantities or scales. For extensive quantities an empirical operation of combination can be given which has the structural properties of the numerical operation of addition. Intensive quantities are characterized by the absence of such an operation.

There is a fairly large literature on the problem of characterizing in what sense fundamental measurement of intensive quantities is possible. An early, significant example is the analysis of Nicole Oresme in the fourteenth century.

4 Measurement and theory construction

It has become a platitude of scientific method that measurement of some attribute is really only interesting if some theory about that attribute is available. It is common to criticize many psychometric scales in psychology on the ground that application of the scales leads nowhere. Put another way, the criticism is that measurement for measurement's sake is not very fruitful scientifically.

There are two other aspects of the relation between measurement and theory construction that are important and yet are somewhat neglected. The first is that a theory of measurement for some characteristic of empirical phenomena is itself a genuine scientific theory. Moreover, certain theories are practically coextensive with the theory of measurement of the quantities basic to the theory. For example, the heart of the theory of rational behaviour in situations of limited information is the measurement of subjective probability and utility (see DECISION AND GAME THEORY §2).

The second aspect is that the chief stumbling block to applying certain theories is a problem of measurement. A classical example in physics is the general theory of relativity. Of the three 'traditional' pieces of evidence for the general theory, namely, the advancement of the perihelion of Mercury, the deflection of light waves by the gravitational field of the sun, and the red shift of stellar spectra, only the first does not present really difficult measurement problems (see EINSTEIN, A. §3).

5 Ordinal theory of measurement

As a simple example of fundamental measurement, we may consider the ordinal theory of measurement. Models of this theory are customarily called weak orderings, defined as follows. Let A be a nonempty set and R a binary relation on this set. A pair (A, R) is a 'simple relation structure'. A simple relation structure (A, R) is a 'weak ordering' if and only if for every x, y and z in A (i) if xRy and yRx then xRz, and (ii) xRy or yRx.

The definition of isomorphism of simple relation structures illustrates nicely the general concept. A simple relation structure (A, R) is 'isomorphic' to a simple relation structure (A', R') if and only if there is a function f such that (i) the domain of f is A and the range of f is A', (ii) f is a one–one function, and (iii) if x and y are in A then xRy if and only if $f(x)R'f(y)$. To illustrate this definition of isomorphism let us consider the question: 'are any two finite weak orderings with the same number of elements isomorphic?' Intuitively it is clear that the answer is negative, because in one of the weak orderings all the objects can stand in the relation R to each other and not so in the other.

Homomorphism of models. In many cases a representation theorem in terms of isomorphism of models turns out to be less interesting than a representation theorem in terms of the weaker notion of homomorphism. Good examples are provided by theories of measurement. As already noted, when we consider general practices of measurement it is evident that in terms of the structural notion of isomorphism we would, roughly speaking, think of the isomorphism as being established between an empirical model of the theory of measurement and a numerical model. However, a slightly more detailed examination of the question indicates that difficulties about isomorphism quickly arise. In all too many cases of measurement, distinct empirical objects or phenomena are assigned the same number, and thus the one–one relationship required for isomorphism of models is destroyed. Fortunately, this weakening of the one–one requirement for isomorphism is the only respect in which we must change the general notion, in order to obtain an adequate account for theories of measurement of the relation between empirical and numerical models. The general notion of homomorphism is designed to accommodate exactly this situation. To obtain the formal definition of homomorphism for two simple relation structures as previously defined, we need only drop the requirement that the function establishing the isomorphism be one–one.

The concept of homomorphism is what we need to state a representation theorem for weak orders. First, a 'numerical' weak ordering is a weak ordering $(A, \leq)$ where A is a set of numbers. The selection of the numerical relation $\leq$ to represent the relation R in a weak ordering is arbitrary, in the sense that the numerical relation $\geq$ could just as well have been chosen. However, choice of one of the two relations $\leq$ or $\geq$ is the only intuitively sound possibility. The following theorem provides a homomorphic representation theorem for finite weak orderings, and thus makes the theory of finite weak orderings a theory of measurement:

(1) Every finite weak ordering is homomorphic to a numerical weak ordering.

(1) was restricted to finite weak orderings for good reason: it is false if this restriction is removed. In order to state the desired theorem for the infinite case one preliminary notion is needed. Let (A, R) be a simple relation structure, and let B be a subset of A. Define the strict ordering relation P in terms of R by the equivalence: xPy if and only if xRy and not yRx. Then we say that B is *R-order-dense* in A if and only if for every x and y in A and not in B such that xPy there is a z in B such that xRz and zRy. Note that the denumerable set of rational numbers is order-dense in the non-denumerable set of all real numbers with respect to the natural numerical ordering $\leq$. This relationship between the denumerable rational numbers and all real numbers is just the one that is necessary and sufficient for the existence of a homomorphism between an infinite and a numerical weak ordering.

(2) Let (A, R) be an infinite weak ordering. Then a necessary and sufficient condition that it be homomorphic to a numerical weak ordering is that there is a denumerable subset B of A such that (i) B is R-order-dense in A and (ii) no two elements of B stand in the relation E, for example, for any distinct x and y in B either not xRy or not yRx.

The proof is related to the classical ordinal characterization of the continuum by Cantor (1895) (see CONTINUUM HYPOTHESIS). The formulation and proof of (2) uses more mathematical apparatus than elementary logic. The restriction of the discussion of theoretical issues in the philosophy of science to the framework of first-order logic has too often meant a restriction of the extent to which the discussion could come into contact with other than highly simplified scientific theories especially constructed for the purpose at hand. An advantage of the set-theoretical formulation of theories such as theories of measurement is that standard mathematical methods are immediately available for both the formulation of the theory and the deductive analysis of the structure of its models (see THEORIES, SCIENTIFIC §3).

6 Invariance and meaningfulness

As already mentioned, the number assigned to measure mass is unique once a unit has been chosen. A more technical way of putting this is that the measurement of mass is unique up to a similarity transformation. A numerical function ϕ is a similarity transformation if there is a positive number α such that for every real number x, $\phi(x) = \alpha x$. In transforming from pounds to grams, for instance, the multiplicative factor α is 453.6. The measurement of temperature in °C or F has different characteristics. Here an origin as well as a unit is arbitrarily chosen.

Technically speaking, the measurement of temperature is unique up to a linear transformation. A numerical function ϕ is a 'linear' transformation if there are numbers α and β with $\alpha > 0$ such that for every number x, $\phi(x) = \alpha x + \beta$. In transforming from centigrade to Fahrenheit degrees of temperature, for instance, $\alpha = 9/5$ and $\beta = 32$.

Ordinal measurements are commonly said to be unique up to a monotone increasing transformation. A numerical function ϕ is a monotone increasing transformation if, for any two numbers x and y, if $x < y$, then $\phi(x) < \phi(y)$. Such transformations are also called 'order-preserving'.

An empirical hypothesis, or any statement in fact, which uses numerical quantities is empirically meaningful only if its truth value is invariant under the appropriate transformations of the numerical quantities involved. As an example, suppose a psychologist has an ordinal measure of IQ, and thinks that scores $S(a)$ on a certain new test T have ordinal significance in ranking the intellectual ability of people. Suppose further that the psychologist is able to obtain the ages $A(a)$ of the subjects. The question then is: should the following hypothesis be regarded as empirically meaningful? For any subjects a and b, if $S(a)/A(a) < S(b)/A(b)$, then $\mathrm{IQ}(a) < \mathrm{IQ}(b)$. From the standpoint of the invariance characterization of empirical meaning, the answer is negative. To see this, let $\mathrm{IQ}(a) \geq \mathrm{IQ}(b)$, let $A(a) = 7$, $A(b) = 12$, $S(a) = 3$, $S(b) = 7$. Make no transformations on the IQ data, and make no transformations on the age data. But let ϕ be a monotone-increasing transformation of the ordinal measurements $S(a)$ which carries 3 into 6 and 7 into 8. Then we have $3/7 < 7/12$, but $6/7 \geq 8/12$, and the truth value of the hypothesis is not invariant under ϕ.

The empirically significant thing about the transformation characteristic of a quantity is that it expresses in precise form how unique is the structural isomorphism between the empirical operations used to obtain a given measurement and the corresponding arithmetical operations or relations. If, for example, the empirical operation is simply that of ordering a set of objects according to some characteristic, then the corresponding arithmetical relation is that of less than (or greater than), and any two functions which map the objects into numbers in a manner preserving the empirical ordering are adequate. Only those arithmetical operations and relations which are invariant under monotone transformations have empirical significance in this situation.

We can easily state the uniqueness or invariance theorem corresponding to the representation theorem (1) for finite weak orders:

(3) Let (A, R) be a finite weak order. Then any two numerical weak orderings to which it is homomorphic are related by a monotone-increasing transformation.

Put in other language, the numerical representation of finite weak orders is unique up to an ordinal transformation. Invariance up to ordinal transformations is not a very strong property of a measurement, and it is for this reason that the hypothesis considered above turned out not to be meaningful, because it was not invariant under monotone transformations of the measurement data.

A measurement representation theorem should ordinarily be accompanied by a matching invariance theorem stating the degree to which a representation of a structure is unique. In the mathematically simple and direct cases of measurement it is usually easy to identify the invariant group of transformations. For more complicated structures, for example structures that satisfy the axioms of a scientific theory, it may be necessary to introduce more complicated apparatus, such as the Galilean or Lorentz transformations of physics, but the objective is the same, namely, to characterize meaningful concepts in terms of invariance.

One point needs emphasis. When the concepts are given in terms of the representation, for example a numerical representation in the case of measurement, or representation in terms of Cartesian coordinates in the case of geometry, a test for invariance is needed. When purely qualitative relations are given which are defined in terms of the qualitative primitives of a theory, for example those of measurement or geometry, then it follows at once that the defined relations are invariant and therefore meaningful. On the other hand, the great importance of the representations and the reduction in computations and notation they achieve, as well as understanding of structure, make it imperative that we have a clear understanding of invariance and meaningfulness for representations which may be, in appearance, rather far removed from the qualitative structures that constitute models of the theory (Krantz *et al.* 1990: ch. 22).

7 Variability, thresholds and errors

In the standard theory of fundamental measurement as discussed, qualitative axioms are formulated that lead to a numerical assignment unique up to some simple transformation. A widespread complaint about this classical foundation of measurement is that it takes too little account of the analysis of variability in the quantity measured. The sources of such variability can be of several different kinds. One important source is simply variability in the empirical properties of the object being measured. The height of a person for example varies on a diurnal basis and the variability of the weight of a person from day to day is a familiar fact of everyday experience. A quite different source of variability lies not in the object being measured but in the procedures of measurement being used. When the procedures being used lead to variability, these are ordinarily attributed to error. The study of error, especially in physical measurements goes back to the eighteenth century with fundamental work by Simpson, Lagrange, Laplace and, especially, Gauss. In the physical sciences the standard reporting of statistical errors in scientific publications began about the middle of the nineteenth century, especially in the publication of astronomical observations.

At least five kinds of error have been distinguished in astronomical observation, and they illustrate nicely the kind of analysis that can be made of errors in other empirical observations, even though changes in focus must be made when the empirical phenomena are quite different. For astronomers there are instrumental errors arising from imperfections in the production of the instruments of observation used such as telescopes and clocks. There are personal errors due to the response characteristics of the observer, for instance, coordinating a visual observation with the auditory beat of a clock, or with the nearly simultaneous visual observation of a clock, will lead to slightly different results for different observers. One example, Nevil Maskelyne, the fifth astronomer royal of Great Britain, discharged his assistant in 1796 because the assistant had observed the transits of stars and planets about a half-second later than Maskelyne himself. An objective of modern technology is to eliminate as much as possible such personal errors, but they certainly persist in many areas of empirical observation. Errors of the third kind are 'systematic' and are due to conditions that are themselves subject to observation and measurement. For example, steady winds in a given direction must be taken account of in many kinds of familiar procedures, such as a navigator setting a course of a ship or aeroplane. Fourth, there are 'random' errors which can arise from variability in the conditions surrounding the observations and are not necessarily due either to variations in the object being measured or in the procedures of measurement. Meteorological variations affecting astronomical observations are a good example. Of a different sort, and a fifth kind, are empirical errors of 'computation' once numerical observations have been recorded. It is important to emphasize that there is nothing fixed and a priori about the classification given here. Other classifica-

tions can be found in the literature, but there is a natural conceptual basis to support each of the types of error listed (Taylor 1982).

It is not possible here to examine in detail how the foundational investigations of measurement procedures have been able to deal with such problems of error. One point of interest has been the analysis of thresholds in psychological judgments. It is a familiar fact that if a person is asked to judge the weight of two objects that are very close together, psychological discrimination of a difference will not occur when the difference is sufficiently small. There is a large body of work and a large body of theory connected with such psychological thresholds (Krantz et al. 1989: ch. 16).

A central objective of foundational analysis in this area is to begin with qualitative axioms, but to expect the representation for a measurement property of an object to be in terms of a random variable with a given probability distribution rather than in terms of a fixed numerical assignment. Such assignment of random variables rather than numbers to objects is already an abstraction from the various kinds of measurement error distinguished above. Part of the reason for this is that the main objective of such analysis is to end up with probability distributions for the errors in the form of some standard probability distributions familiar in mathematical statistics and amenable to detailed statistical treatment.

The theory of measurement has been important in quantum mechanics, the most significant physical theory of the twentieth century, for two distinct but related conceptual reasons. One arises from the Heisenberg uncertainty principle which shows that it is not possible to measure simultaneously with arbitrary precision the position and momentum of particles such as electrons or protons. Closely connected with this is the second aspect of measurement in quantum mechanics, namely the recognition that there is a physical interaction between the measurement instrument and the measurement object, a subject not really developed at all in classical physics (von Neumann 1996; see QUANTUM MEASUREMENT PROBLEM).

In the social sciences and medicine a familiar kind of error is that which arises from finite sampling. If we wish to know something about the telephone habits, driving habits or reactions to a new medicine of a given population, we ordinarily do not plan to interview or test everyone in the population, but rather use a random sample to infer the distribution of habits or reactions in the entire population. The theory of such sampling is very much a twentieth-century subject (see STATISTICS AND SOCIAL SCIENCE §2).

References and further reading

* Cantor, G. (1895) 'Beiträge zur Begründung der transfiniten Mengenlehre', *Mathematische Annalen* 46: 481–512. (See §5.)

Clagett, M. (ed.) (1968) *Nicole Oresme and the Medieval Geometry of Qualities and Motions*, Madison, WI: University of Wisconsin Press. (Contains Oresme's *Tractatus de configurationibus qualitatum et motuum*, with an introduction, translation and commentary.)

Kisch, B. (1965) *Scales and Weights: A Historical Outline*, New Haven, CT: Yale University Press. (A detailed survey of the more practical aspects, with special emphasis on the history of the instruments used for scales and weights.)

* Krantz, D.H., Suppes, P., Luce, R.D. *et al.* (1971, 1989, 1990) *Foundations of Measurement*, vol. I, *Additive and Polynomial Representations*, vol. II, *Geometrical, Threshold, and Probabilistic Representations*, vol. III, *Representation, Axiomatization, and Invariance*, New York: Academic Press. (A comprehensive treatise in which the fundamental problems of measurement are given extensive treatment with many examples of representation and uniqueness theorems, and extensive references to the literature in many disciplines on the theory of measurement.)

* Neumann, J. von (1996) *Mathematical Foundations of Quantum Mechanics*, Princeton, NJ: Princeton University Press. (A classical treatise containing one of the most thorough and important discussions of the interaction between the measurement instrument and the measured object, with a particular reference to quantum mechanics but also applicable to measurement procedures generally.)

* Taylor, J.R. (1982) *An Introduction to Error Analysis*, Mill Valley, CA: University Science Books. (An excellent elementary text on uncertainties in physical measurement.)

PATRICK SUPPES

MECHANICS, ARISTOTELIAN

The central feature of Aristotle's mechanics is his discussion of local motion, a change of place, which he categorizes as either natural or violent. He further divides natural motion into celestial motion, which is uniform, circular and eternal, and terrestrial motion, which is rectilinear (straight up or down), and finite in both time and distance. All motions which are not natural are classified as violent.

For all motion Aristotle required a force in direct contact with the object being moved. We may represent the Aristotelian law of motion by the modern formula: Velocity = Force (motive power)/Resistance, or $V = kF/R$. In applying this law of motion to falling bodies, Aristotle associated the weight of the body with the force, and the resistance of the air (or other medium) with the resistance. Thus, Aristotle believed that heavy bodies fall faster than light ones.

The problem of what force is actually in contact with the body, and causes it to fall, posed a serious difficulty for Aristotle. Aristotle concluded that elements were created with a tendency to move to their natural place, barring any hindrance or interference. Projectile motion posed a similar problem for Aristotle. In the case of a thrown object, the force was provided by the hand of the thrower as long as the object was in contact with the hand. But one needed an explanation of why the object continued to move once it had left the thrower's hand. Aristotle concluded that the medium through which the projectile moved provided the force that kept it moving.

Aristotle also regarded both the existence of a void or any motion in it as impossible. A void contains nothing that could sustain the motion of a projectile once it left the projector. In addition, because a void can provide no resistance, the speed of an object in a void would be infinite.

1 Local motion
2 The causes of motion
3 The void

1 Local motion

This entry concentrates on Aristotle's discussion of motion and its causes as found in his work *Physics*. Aristotle's concept of motion includes not only local motion, a change of place, but any change from potential to actual being. This may include changes in shape, size, or properties of a body such as temperature or colour. The central feature of his mechanics is, however, his discussion of local motion. This includes the Aristotelian law of motion and the questions of falling bodies (and the related problem of the motion of the elements), projectile motion and the existence of a void.

Aristotle categorized local motion as either natural or violent. He further divided natural motion into celestial motion, which is uniform, circular and eternal, and terrestrial motion, which is rectilinear (straight up or down) and finite in both time and distance. The terrestrial motions are governed by the nature of the four elements which make up all substances: earth, air, fire and water, and by the idea of natural place. Earth, which is absolutely heavy, falls toward the centre of the universe (coincidently the centre of the earth), which is its natural place. Fire, which is absolutely light, rises to its natural place, a spherical shell inside the lunar sphere. Thus, the equilibrium distribution of an Aristotelian universe would be a spherical earth surrounded by concentric spherical shells of water, air and fire, surrounded by the heavens. Objects composed of a mixture of elements behave in the manner of their predominant element. All motions which are not natural are classified as violent; for example, projectile motion.

For both natural and violent motions Aristotle required a force in direct contact with the object being moved. This view that a force is necessary for motion to occur at all (everything that is moved is moved by something else) is quite different from the modern view (see MECHANICS, CLASSICAL). For living creatures the motive power required is provided by the soul. Celestial objects and planets are moved by celestial intelligences or spirits. Inanimate objects require a force in contact with the object itself and this posed a difficult problem in dealing with falling bodies, projectiles and with the motion of the elements themselves.

We may represent the Aristotelian law of motion by the modern formula:

$$\text{Velocity} = \text{Force (motive power)}/\text{Resistance} \quad \text{or}$$
$$V = kF/R.$$

Aristotle never stated his law of motion in this concise form, but rather discussed how either the distance travelled or the time of travel will change when either the force exerted on the object or the weight of the object changes. He discussed motion in this way because the concept of speed as the ratio of distance to time was not considered a proper ratio. One could have a proper ratio only of similar things such as the ratio of one distance to another distance, or of one time to another time.

If then: the mover A, has moved B, a distance C, in time D, then in the same time force A will move $\frac{1}{2}B$ twice the distance C, and in $\frac{1}{2}D$ it will move $\frac{1}{2}B$ the whole distance C: thus the rules of proportion will be observed. Again if a given force move a given weight a certain distance in a certain time and half the distance in half the time, half the motive power will move half the weight the same distance in the same time. Let E represent half the motive power A and Z half the weight B: then the ratio between the motive power

and the weight in the one case is similar and proportionate to the ratio in the other, so that each force will cause the same distance to be travelled in the same time (*Physics* VII 5).

It should also be emphasized that Aristotelian motion required the action of *both* the force and the resistance, discussed later.

Aristotle recognized that his law of motion did not have universal applicability. He knew that the application of a force might not result in any motion at all, even though his law of motion implies that it would, as would be the case with someone attempting to lift a very large weight. To solve the problem he added a subsidiary condition to the law that required the force to be greater than the resistance.

If, then, (a force) A move B a distance C in time D, it does not follow that E, being half of A, will in time D, or in any fraction of it, cause B to traverse a part of C, the ratio between which and the whole of C is proportionate to that between A and E (whatever fraction of A that E may be), in fact it might well be that it will produce no motion at all; otherwise one man might move a ship, since both the motive power of the ship-haulers and the distance that they all cause the ship to traverse are divisible into as many parts as there are men (*Physics* VII 5).

In applying this law of motion to falling bodies Aristotle associated the weight of the body with the force, and the resistance of the air (or other medium) with the resistance. Thus, he believed that heavy bodies fall faster than light ones. 'We see that bodies which have a greater impulse either of weight or of lightness, if they are alike in other respects, move faster over an equal space, and in the ratio which their magnitudes bear to each other' (*Physics* IV 8).

2 The causes of motion

The problem of what force is actually in contact with the body and causes it to fall posed a serious difficulty for Aristotle. This is closely connected to the question of the natural motion of elements. What force causes earth to fall to the centre of the universe and what force causes fire to rise? Aristotle's discussion of this question is quite complex and involves the change from potentiality to actuality, in this case from potential to actual motion (Lang 1992). Natural place is the actuality that moves the elements. Elements were created with a tendency to move to their natural place, barring any hindrance or interference.

The idea that natural place causes the motion is not an attraction to natural place (that is, up or down) or what we might call the force of gravity, even though Aristotle associated weight with the force that causes a body to fall, because either of these involves action at a distance and not a force in direct contact with the body. Whatever creates the body or element gives it an internal tendency for motion. Aristotle also knew that a falling body did not travel at constant speed, but that it did, in fact, accelerate. He did not offer any explanation of this acceleration, but the problem was considered by several of his later commentators.

Projectile motion posed a similar problem for Aristotle. In the case of a thrown object, the force was provided by the hand of the thrower as long as the object was in contact with the hand. But one needed an explanation of why the object continued to move once it had left the thrower's hand. Aristotle concluded that the medium through which the projectile moved provided the force that kept it moving. This occurred either by *antiperistasis* (replacement), in which the medium rushes around the body to prevent the formation of a void or vacuum and pushed the body from behind, or by the medium itself having acquired the power to be a mover from the original projector. (The theory of *antiperistasis* is more probably due to Plato and his followers than to Aristotle.)

The medium itself does not have to move, but rather possesses the power to move something else. This power is, however, imperfectly transmitted from one layer of the medium to the next and gradually dies away. Thus, as indicated above, the motion of the projectile seems to be complex, consisting of both its natural motion and the motion imposed on it. It is unclear what Aristotle believed the path of a projectile was. For example, in the case of a projectile thrown horizontally, did it first travel only horizontally, and then fall to its natural place, or did it exhibit both horizontal and vertical motions simultaneously, throughout its motion?

The resistance needed for motion is provided by the resistance, or friction, of the medium, but also seems to include the mass or weight of the projectile. The resistance of the medium is necessary to prevent the motion of the projectile from being infinite in both speed and extent, an impossibility for Aristotle, as discussed below. Aristotle's use of the medium to both sustain and resist motion seems paradoxical, and was commented on by several medieval critics.

3 The void

It is clear that Aristotle regarded both the existence of a void or any motion in it as impossible. First, a void contains nothing that could sustain the motion of a projectile once it left the projector. Second, because a void can provide no resistance, the speed of an object in a void would be infinite, or as Aristotle states, 'it

moves through the void with a speed beyond any ratio'. He further argues that although heavy bodies fall faster than do light ones in a medium, they would move at the same speed in a void, which he regarded as impossible.

In proposing a clear statement of the inertial principle, Aristotle also gave a proof of it by relating the persistence of motion, or inertial motion, to the homogeneity of space. However he turned the argument around and regards it rather as a proof of the impossibility of motion in a void. The inertial consequences of such motion would be (to Aristotle) the unacceptable result of motion that is infinite in extent.

Aristotle's physics forms the basis of subsequent medieval discussions of these questions. It is fair to say that medieval studies of motion consist of commentaries and criticisms of Aristotle's work.

See also: ARISTOTLE; ARISTOTELIANISM IN ISLAMIC PHILOSOPHY; ARISTOTELIANISM, MEDIEVAL; ARISTOTELIANISM, RENAISSANCE

References and further reading

* Aristotle (*c*.mid-4th century BC) *Physics* (Physica); trans. R.P. Hardie and R.K. Gaye, Oxford: Clarendon Press, 1930. (Main source text.)

Clagett, M. (1955) *Greek Science in Antiquity*, New York: Macmillan. (A useful account of Greek science.)

Cohen, M.R. and Drabkin, I.E. (1958) *A Source Book in Greek Science*, Cambridge, MA: Harvard University Press. (A good survey of Greek science, including quotations – in translation – from the original works.)

* Lang, H.S. (1992) *Aristotle's Physics and its Medieval Varieties*, Albany, NY: State University of New York Press. (A detailed discussion of Aristotle's physics as well as discussion from medieval commentators. Chapter 3 covers the change from potential to actuality mentioned in §2.)

ALLAN FRANKLIN

MECHANICS, CLASSICAL

Understood at its most general, 'classical mechanics' covers the approach to physical phenomena that dominated science from roughly the time of Galileo until the early decades of the twentieth century. The approach is usually characterized by the assumption that bodies carry an inherent mass and well-defined positions and velocities. Bodies subsist within a three-

dimensional absolute space and influence one another through reciprocal forces. These objects obey the three laws of motion articulated by Isaac Newton in 1686 in a deterministic *manner: once a mechanical system is assembled, its future behaviour is rigidly fixed. Such 'classical' assumptions were eventually rejected by Einstein's theory of relativity, where the assumption of a three-dimensional Euclidean space is abandoned, and by quantum mechanics, where determinism and well-defined positions and velocity are eschewed.*

Classical mechanics is frequently characterized as 'billiard ball mechanics' or 'the theory of mechanism' on the grounds that the science treats its materials in the manner of colliding particles, or clockwork. Such stereotypes should be approached with caution because the basic framework of classical mechanics has long been subject to divergent interpretations that unpack the content of Newton's 'three laws' in remarkably different ways. These differing interpretations provide incompatible catalogues of the basic objects that are supposed to comprise the 'classical world' – are they point masses, rigid bodies or flexible substances? Or, as many writers have suggested, should mechanics not be regarded as 'about' the world at all, but merely as a source of useful but fictitious idealizations of reality?

These foundational disagreements explain why classical mechanics has often found itself entangled in metaphysics. Much of modern philosophy of science is characterized by attitudes that were originally articulated during the nineteenth century's attempts to clarify the grounds of classical mechanics.

1   Newton's laws of motion, first law

Introductory textbooks usually sketch a simple, standardized approach to the content of classical mechanics, which, for reasons discussed in §4, may be called the *point mass interpretation*. Although this interpretation is often presented as 'the correct understanding of classical mechanics', few philosophers or physicists of the classical era would have accepted this reading as adequate. Its reading not only suffers empirical difficulties; it does not describe a universe that would have been pleasing to most practitioners. The point mass reading has gained its textbook centrality largely because alternative foundations for mechanics prove resistant to easy

articulation. Indeed, satisfactory alternatives were not fully developed until well into the twentieth century (largely by the engineering community, which requires a trustworthy classical basis for its endeavours). The mismatch between the conceptual simplicity of textbook orthodoxy and the expected characteristics of the subject is apt to cause students of philosophy much difficulty.

The essential content of classical doctrine is commonly held to reside in Isaac NEWTON's celebrated laws of motion. Unfortunately, these principles, in the form they were articulated by Newton, are subject to a surprising range of interpretations.

Electromagnetism is largely left out of account here. This is partly because 'classical' electromagnetism, as the subject is understood today, fits more neatly into a *relativistic* than a Newtonian framework. In the nineteenth century, light and other electromagnetic phenomena were regarded as vibrations within an 'ether' that was conceived as a material continuum in the manner of §6 (see FIELD THEORY, CLASSICAL).

In Thompson and Tait's (1879) translation of Newton (1726), Newton's laws are: first law: every body continues in its state of rest or of uniform motion in a straight line, except insofar as it may be compelled by force to change that state. Second law: change of motion is proportional to force applied, and takes place in the direction of the straight line in which the force acts. Third law: to every action there is always an equal and contrary reaction: or, the mutual actions of any two bodies are always equal and oppositely directed.

Newton borrowed the first law, also known as 'the principle of inertia', from Galileo and DESCARTES (although neither would have accepted the doctrine in its fullest generality) (see GALILEI, G.). According to it, the *natural motion* of a particle uninfluenced by external forces is always a straight line, whereas earlier scientists had often presumed such natural motions to be circular or directed towards a 'natural home' in the universe. 'Inertia' is the traditional term for the tendency of a body to retain its present state of motion; it is harder to stop a cannon ball than a baseball even if they are travelling at the same velocity. From a Newtonian point of view, 'inertia' is simply another name for 'mass', but it is common to speak of 'inertial *forces*' as well, a notion discussed in §3.

Henri Poincaré (1902) claimed that the first law (as well as much of the rest of the Newtonian framework) does not report genuine physical content, but instead represents a mere 'convention' (see POINCARÉ, J.H. §3). Newton presumed that a Euclidean space exists independently of matter and understood his first law as delineating how free matter will move upon this geometrical stage. Poincaré objected that we can have no knowledge of spatial structure independent of the behaviour of material objects found within it. The first law is not a straightforward 'fact', but merely articulates a *criterion* for erecting a geometry around material objects. No empirical facts can force a rejection of Newton's first law 'criterion' for the presence of 'straight lines', although, were the empirical facts otherwise, an alternative 'convention' might be favoured where the notions of geometry become coordinated to the movements of matter in a different fashion. This *conventionalism* has proved enormously influential within twentieth-century analytic philosophy and whether or not Poincaré's implied distinction between a 'convention' and a 'genuine fact of nature' can be sustained remains a controversial issue (see CONVENTIONALISM).

Newton has been widely criticized for assuming the existence of an enduring 'absolute space' in the first law, because (i) the notion sounds unduly 'metaphysical', (ii) its presence seems inherently unobservable, or (iii) the first law (on its strongest reading) forces a principle of *Galilean relativity*: no law of nature allows a determination of whether a set of objects lies at rest in absolute space or merely moves through it at a constant velocity (reference objects that move in either of these ways define *inertial frames*). One is therefore denied any means of relocating a point in absolute space after an interval of time passes (see SPACE §§2–3).

During the nineteenth century, followers of Kant saw Galilean relativity as evidence that absolute space does not represent a real condition found in nature, but merely reflects an organizational structure imposed upon reality by the human mind (Poincaré's conventionalism shares many affinities with such Neo-Kantian thinking) (see KANT, I. §5). But more sophisticated techniques articulated in the twentieth century (chiefly by Cartan) have suggested another resolution to the relativity problem: classical mechanics should follow Einstein's lead in rejecting the notion of an enduring *space* in favour of a blend of space and time (see SPACETIME). In Cartan's reformulation, the first law is interpreted as demanding a certain geometrical structure within the melded spacetime, avoiding the unobservable aspects of Newton's persisting space. Although this approach weakens Newton's geometrical assumptions somewhat, it agrees that spacetime possesses objective features independently of human decision or the placement of material objects within the spacetime.

Cartan also showed that gravitation could be 'geometrized away' within certain classical frameworks, in imitation of the techniques of general

relativity. It should be mentioned, however, that Galilean relativity was not universally accepted during the heyday of classical mechanics – various electrical effects once seemed as if they might provide criteria for detecting inertial movement within absolute space.

2 Newton's laws of motion, second law

Newton's second law is popularly known as '$F = ma$', where 'F' stands for 'force', 'm' for 'mass' and 'a' for 'acceleration'. The claim is that a particle will deviate from its inertial motion only insofar as a force is imposed from without, in which case the particle will accelerate to a degree conditioned by its mass. In a modern treatment (if uncomplicated by 'constraints'), '$F = ma$' provides the skeleton upon which the basic *equations of motion* for a collection of particles are constructed. The recipe is this:

(a) Delineate the particles whose interactions one wishes to study.
(b) Determine what kinds of specific force act between these (do they gravitationally attract one another?, do they display electrical attraction or repulsion?, and so on).
(c) For each particle a, decompose each of the forces that act upon a along a selected Cartesian axis – for example '$f_x^{a,e}$' might express the amount of electrical force that acts upon particle a along the x-axis.
(d) For each particle a and each Cartesian direction x, assemble all of the specific forces under (c) into a sum called the 'total force acting upon the particle acting in direction x'.
(e) Set this sum of forces equal to md^2x/dt^2 (that is, to what in the calculus is called 'the second derivative of a's location along the x-axis'). The upshot is a system of $3n$ second-order ordinary differential equations for a collection of n particles.

The list under (b) of specific force laws active within the system of particles are called the *constitutive principles* for the system at hand; crudely speaking, they delineate the basic manner in which forces bind the collection together. The equations of motion constructed by this recipe then fix (*modulo* occasional technicalities) how the system will behave at all future times once the positions and velocities of all particles are known at some specific time (such data represent the system's 'phase' or *initial condition*). That is, the equations of motion in classical physics *determine* the future states of the system as it evolves from its initial condition (usually past states are determined as well). The determinism of classical physics is a famous bugbear of ethical philosophy. Quantum mechanics no longer accepts determinism of the classical variety, but it is doubtful whether what it substitutes is preferable from an ethical point of view (see DETERMINISM AND INDETERMINISM; FREE WILL).

'Determinism' is not the same as 'predictability' in any reasonable sense. It has been realized for some time that most classical systems are so complicated that no computer could possibly track their behaviour accurately for more than a few seconds. Much of the recent fascination with so-called 'chaos' has evolved from the discovery of new ways to extract useful partial information from these otherwise unpredictable systems (see CHAOS THEORY).

The second law recipe has been described in some detail because Newton's less explicit formulation has proved a ripe source of philosophical confusion. Our 'recipe' approach becomes clearly established only within the investigations of Leonhard Euler in the eighteenth century. Expressing the principle as simply '$F = ma$' encourages the impression that the second law is merely a definition of 'force'. This objection overlooks the non-arbitrary decomposition into specific forces required in the recipe. Some writers have complained that Newton's laws are 'empty' because they describe systems either subject to one force (the second law) or no forces at all (the first law). But no real life system is like this. In the author's evaluation, this objection, and many others like it, fails to understand the Euler recipe correctly.

But if Newton's second law is understood in this Eulerian vein, physics should be greatly concerned to specify the complete set of specific force laws used in step (b). Newton's law of universal gravitation supplies an admirable example of the kind of law needed, but, beyond that paradigm, classical physicists were somewhat lackadaisical in their efforts to fill out the missing laws (they never agreed, for example, on the nature of the forces that glue matter together). Joseph Sneed (1979) none the less sees the demand for these as yet unarticulated force laws as a vital part of the *content* of classical physics – he hopes that Thomas Kuhn's celebrated notion of a 'scientific paradigm' can be clarified in this manner. In truth, the constraint tradition, described in §5, often herded the actual development of mechanics in directions other than the hypothesized search for specific force laws. As we shall see, the criticism of '$F = ma$' as an empty definition gains a greater cogency under the point of view of this school.

In general, many of the standard objections to Newton's laws originally grew out of substantial disputes over the fundamental trustworthiness of key mechanical propositions. As these origins were forgotten, the disputes became reinterpreted (particularly by the logical positivist school) as rather trivial squabbles over whether forces are 'observable' or not.

3   Newton's laws of motion, third law

The haziness of Newton's third law – 'action = reaction', as it is popularly known – is palpable in its very formulation. The textbooks often add three additional tenets to the claim: (a) All forces arise between pairs of particles. (b) Such forces are directed along the line between them (the forces are 'central'). (c) The strength of these forces depends only upon the spatial separation between the bodies and not, say, upon their relative velocities. One can then demand that if a exerts a specific force f upon b, then b will exert a reciprocating force upon a equal in magnitude to f, but reversed in direction. Although Newton's own law of gravitation suits these requirements, it is doubtful that he would have accepted the (a)–(c) supplements. Requirement (c) stands in apparent conflict with most frictional forces because their strength depends upon the rate that bodies slip past one another. Requirement (b) seems incompatible with *shearing forces*, which arise when, for example, one layer of water slips over another. Each layer exerts a retarding force upon the other, but these forces point along the layers' interface, not 'the line between them'.

The main motivation for including requirements (a)–(c) is that, on this approach, they are needed to prove fundamental tenets such as the conservation of energy. For example, (c) justifies the notion of 'potential energy'. Newton was unconcerned with these requirements because he had no notion that energy conservation holds. Indeed, he often understood the third law in a variant 'inertial force' manner.

Consider the sun and its planets. On the (a)–(c) interpretation, 'action = reaction' requires that each planet should exert a gravitational force upon the sun equal in strength to the solar gravitational pull that it feels. Since the sun is more massive than the planets, these planetary attractions will not accelerate it greatly. It does not lead to great mathematical error if the sun is treated as if it is the source of an *unreciprocated* force – that is, the solar attractions are described as dependent only upon the planet's position within an inertial frame. On the (a)–(c) reading, this treatment is only a useful fiction – the reciprocating pulls of the planets must dislodge the sun slightly from its assumed inertial motion. Disregarding the sun's minor wobblings allows the problem of planetary movements to be *effaced* from the complications of solar motion. When third law requirements can be overlooked in this manner, the force is called *external*; otherwise, they are dubbed *internal*.

However, a long tradition exists of regarding some external forces as nonapproximate in origin. How does a mechanical system balance such a force? Answer: it develops an 'inertial force of resistance' – its parts accelerate in such a manner that the sum over all particles of mass *times* acceleration exactly matches the external force. Most modern texts dismiss this approach to the third law as a mistake: no force should be regarded as truly external and inertial reactions do not qualify as forces at all. Indeed, the 'inertial force' reading seems merely to repeat the content of the second law over again.

The 'inertial force' understanding of the third law becomes more natural within the constraint-based approach of §5, where central forces drop from view. In the mechanics of continua (§6), the 'principle of material frame indifference' reveals some further affinities between inertial reactions and forces.

4 Point masses and idealization

Our discussion has involved much hazy talk of 'particles'; what kind of object is intended by this term? On the interpretation presented so far, a 'particle' needs to be a *point mass*: a movable point carrying a fixed mass (and possibly other quantities such as charge). Forces have been required to 'act along the line between particles'; this makes obvious sense only if 'particles' lie at uniquely defined points. Point masses must always remain separate, for the possibility of fusing would permit an infinite source of potential energy. On a point mass interpretation, all forces are of *action-at-a-distance* type, for they originate in one particle, yet act, across an intervening vacuum, somewhere else. *Contact forces*, where one body exerts a pressure immediately upon another through geometrical contact, are not tolerated on this approach to Newton's laws.

The point mass approach, standard in most modern textbooks, was first proposed by R.J. Boscovich in 1763. Boscovich's suggestion was rarely embraced during the heyday of classical mechanics. Most practitioners felt that their subject should deal directly with some variety of extended body, and not regard them merely as swarms of points. Newton, although often interested in arguing that objects in apparent contact were actually separated (see his discussion of 'Newton's rings'), also believed that atoms possessed hard cores of a certain size.

The point mass presentation of classical physics has gained great favour in modern textbooks partially because of a natural association between its mathematical structures and those of elementary quantum mechanics. 'Correspondence rules' exist to convert point mass equations to the partial differential equations of quantum theory. Under this transition, the quantum particles gain a surrogate for 'size' due to considerations peculiar to the newer theory, for instance, the exclusion principle. Many authors have been misled by such mathematical relationships into presuming that remarkable successes of classical physics in treating the large-scale phenomena of ordinary life can easily be explained by the way in which point mass theory 'reduced' to quantum theory. This impression is misleading, because the point mass interpretation at best provides an awkward basis for setting up the successful models of fluids and elastic bodies that are more adequately established following the programme of §6.

Sometimes it is clearly useful to treat extended bodies *as if* they were point particles. The *locus classicus* of this technique is Newton's observation that a rigid, perfectly spherical planet behaves gravitationally from its exterior as if it were a single point carrying the same mass. The orbit of a planet can then be calculated without worrying about its interior. Real planets, of course, are neither perfect globes nor rigid and the predictions of point mass celestial mechanics are slightly inaccurate as a result. None the less, this approximate effacement of the gross behaviour of the planets from their internal complications has inspired a popular 'as if' reading of Newton's laws: they delineate a range of *idealized models* that suit real life situations to a tolerable degree. When greater accuracy is desired, one shifts to modelling the planet as a large swarm of point masses. Each finer scale of idealized modelling provides predictions of increased accuracy, but we should never pretend that our constructions supply anything other than simplified portraits of reality (see IDEALIZATIONS; MODELS §3).

On this approach, it becomes difficult to see how Newton's laws could be shown *false*; at best, they might prove an *inconvenient* series of approximations to utilize. An important distinction should be drawn here: in *any* scientific theory, the successful treatment of everyday phenomena will require artificial simplification because the mathematics pertinent to a fully realistic approach is horrendously complex. But the 'idealization' thesis maintains that, quite apart from mathematical intractability, science must study simplified models because of an inherent lack of reality within the very fabric of physics. However, the 'lack of reality' in point masses may merely demonstrate that they do not provide the best foundation for a satisfactory classical mechanics.

5   Constraints and rigid bodies

A universe of point masses seems a far cry from standard stereotypes of classical mechanics: is not the subject supposed to treat the universe as a 'great clock'? Are not clocks composed of gears, rods and springs – extended bodies all? There is a variant tradition, stretching back to antiquity, that exploits the properties of *rigid bodies* in a direct geometrical way (gears and rods, but not springs, are rigid bodies). Typically, such bodies interact with another through contact along their boundaries: two gears intermesh; a bead slides along a wire; a wheel rolls along a plane. These linkages are specified by so-called *constraints*: equations that geometrically link the movements of distinct bodies. The presence of constraints clearly modifies Newtonian behaviour in various ways. For example, the bead will, if no external forces act against it, slide along the wire at a constant velocity forever (if the wire itself is not accelerated). Constraints alter Newton's law of inertia from 'travels with constant rectilinear velocity' to 'travels at an unchanging speed along the curvilinear constraint of the wire'. Principles of unhampered motion that are adapted to accommodate constraints are called *generalized laws of inertia*.

The existence of constraints, strictly speaking, is incompatible with the point mass reading. Let the bead slide past point p upon the wire. What *force* will the wire near p exert upon the bead as it slides past? 'Easy', the stock reply goes, 'compute the acceleration a needed to move the bead past p. Divide a by the mass of the bead to obtain the force exerted by the wire.' But let the bead slide past p with a greater velocity. The wire must generate a greater force to hold the bead in its rightful place at p. In short, the wire must be able to 'see' the bead's *velocity* before the force needed to maintain the constraint can be exerted. But the point mass understanding of the third law requires that forces be velocity independent; otherwise, conservation of energy might fail.

What should be done? Either constraints are regarded as convenient approximations to point mass reality or our fundamental principles must be modified to tolerate them. In most texts, constraints are introduced in so cavalier a fashion that the policy followed cannot be determined. On the first strategy, 'rigid bodies' are simply collections of particles welded together by very strong (but finite) forces. The masses within our wire must shift slightly when a faster bead passes, although these movements may be quite microscopic.

In 1788, however, J.L. Lagrange articulated a version of mechanics that incorporates genuine constraints and rigid bodies within its foundations.

He based his approach upon the law of virtual work (sometimes: virtual velocity) and d'Alembert's principle. The idea behind virtual work is illustrated nicely by the behaviour of a lever. Work can be done if weights are allowed to drop – falling water drives old-fashioned grist mills. String a series of masses along a lever arm; the rigidity of the arm links these weights together by a constraint. How must these weights be arranged if the lever is to stay in *equilibrium* (= at rest)? Answer: any work that might be gained if the weights on one side of the arm are allowed to *fall* must be expended to *raise* the weights strung along the other side. 'Virtual work' declares that equilibrium within any constrained set of mechanical parts will obtain just in case their hypothetical abilities to perform work cancel out in the manner described. Laws of this variety (which predate Lagrange) are called *variational principles* because a system's actual behaviour (equilibrium, in this case) is adduced from a comparison of hypothetical behaviour (that is, imaginary movements given to the weights). For systems not at rest, Lagrange appealed to d'Alembert's principle. This doctrine claims that if unbalanced external forces are applied to a mechanical system, it will display inertial reactions that exactly balance the external set. Recall (from §3) that an 'inertial reaction' is simply the acceleration of a body multiplied by its mass. D'Alembert's principle thus maintains that the system 'reacts' to external 'activity' by moving against the activity. We noted that Newton's third law is sometimes interpreted in this manner.

Classical mechanics is often presented using other forms of variational technique, for example, Hamilton's principle and other varieties of 'least action'. Although elementary textbooks often allege that such variants are equivalent to one another and to Newton's original set of laws, this is not true unless a number of background assumptions are made. Hamilton's treatment, especially, renders salient some important features of energy conserving systems, considered with respect to the so-called 'Hamiltonian flow within phase space'. But these matters must be left to standard texts.

Notice that, in dealing with the force upon the bead, we calculated in a direction reverse to what might seem the expected one. In celestial calculations, we compute the acceleration of the earth from a prior knowledge of the *forces* that apply to it. Newton's law of gravitation is the specific force law employed here. But in the bead case, we did not work with any specific force law; instead, the force was calculated merely from the *acceleration* that the wire requires of the bead. Forces induced by the satisfaction of constraints are traditionally called 'forces of reaction'.

Lagrange's approach tolerates both 'forces of reaction' and law specified forces, where the latter are of action-at-a-distance type. It had long been the hope of mechanics, in its 'clockwork' inspired moods, that action-at-a-distance effects might turn out to be the result of contact movements within a hidden medium linking the distant bodies. Descartes and Leibniz believed that the attraction of planets resulted from swimming in a common 'sea' that pushed them together. Appeal to action-at-a-distance forces was considered a retreat to the 'occult' qualities of medieval times. In the nineteenth century, J.C. MAXWELL suggested that electromagnetic effects might be communicated between distant bodies through a complicated set of intervening mechanical parts (see ELECTRODYNAMICS). Such proposals led H. HERTZ to reformulate mechanics based upon constraints alone (a wider range of these is needed than appear in standard Lagrangian practice). Hertz (1894) replaced Newton's laws by a simple principle of 'generalized inertia' and identified all forms of energy with actual energy of movement (kinetic energy). Most importantly, the notion of force is essentially discarded in Hertz's system, since only the derivative 'forces of reaction' are tolerated in his framework. Hertz's system provides the best realization of the philosophical dream of a truly machine-inspired mechanics. Interest in Hertz's project faded with the rise of quantum theory, but its distrust of the Newtonian notion of 'force' has proved longer lived. In the author's opinion, 'force' should occasion no unhappiness as long as mechanics remains faithful to a point mass interpretation; it is the frequent appeal to *post hoc* 'forces of reaction' that generates the uneasy sense that 'force' functions as an unnecessary ingredient within mechanics.

In any case, the notion that the universe could actually move as one great *machine* is less plausible than one might expect. Machines are designed (insofar as possible) so that their parts slip over each other without binding. If a collection of rigid parts is randomly assembled, without the guidance of a designer, they are likely to end in *overconstraint*: the expected conditions of sliding, rolling, and so on, among its parts cannot be satisfied all at once. To accommodate the overconstraint, some of the parts will need to distort or fracture, thus losing their postulated rigidity.

In other words, once the basic 'particles' of mechanics are granted any spatial extension at all, they are likely to lose their postulated rigidity at some time or another. How does this eventuality affect Lagrange's programme for the foundations of mechanics? A retreat to an 'idealization' defence is possible: mechanics tries to idealize real physical systems in terms of constrained rigid bodies, despite their lack of permanent reality. Some advantage over point mass idealization is gained, for a better set of modelling tools has been assembled. It would be preferable however, if an approach to mechanics could be found that accepts bodies which are capable of distortion at all levels of analysis. The materials in this reformulated mechanics should be truly flexible entities, such as springs and fluids, which can smoothly distort or flow when the right external pressures are exerted. Such objects are called 'material fields' or *classical continua*.

6 Continua

If one tries to describe continua directly, one quickly discovers that formulating plausible laws for genuinely flexible bodies introduces many conceptual problems. All of the problems of the 'infinitely divided' that have plagued philosophy and mathematics since the time of Zeno's paradoxes arise (see ZENO OF ELEA). Mechanics supplements these with some peculiar difficulties of its own.

For example, it seems natural to interpret the term 'particle' in Newton's laws as an 'infinitesimal portion of a continuous body'. If such a 'particle' belongs to a macroscopic body that stretches, must not that 'particle' enlarge infinitesimally under the stretching as well? But how can a point p sensibly expand to become a 'bigger point'? And what should '$F = ma$' require of p? If p enlarges under an applied force, should its 'mass' (or, more properly, its density) also alter? Traditional arguments concerning 'infinitesimals' were plagued by vagueness of this sort, as critics such as Bishop Berkeley swiftly observed (see BERKELEY, G. §§8, 11). Leibniz's celebrated philosophy of 'monads' represented, in part, a sophisticated attempt to surmount some of these problems by moving outside of the arena of space and time altogether (see LEIBNIZ, G.W. §4).

Although infinitesimal readings of Newton's second law are common in textbooks, the considered modern opinion holds that this is a mistake: '$F = ma$' should apply only to the *extended* parts of a continuous body. This shift in perspective introduces many unexpected conceptual subtleties. Suppose that A is a continuous body with external forces applied at various spots along its outer edge and within its interior. If A is a perfectly *rigid* substance, all of these forces can be added together as if they act at a common location. In a rigid body, a force applied at p can be shifted to any other position q and still pull A equally to the right. Applying a force at p rather than q affects only how A will *rotate*, not how it *translates*. Indeed, by defining the so-called 'moment' of A's array of forces (roughly, a measure of their 'off-centredness'), Euler showed how A's rotation could be calculated (the principle employed is called 'balance of angular momentum' or 'moment of momentum'). Euler's two principles – non-infinitesimal '$F = ma$' and 'moment of momentum' – completely settle how any rigid body will respond to applied forces.

But the success of these principles appears to trade upon A's postulated rigidity. If A is composed of flexible stuff, then how it reacts to a schedule of applied forces will clearly reflect the materials of which it is made – the same set of forces will move rubber and water in completely different fashions. To make further progress, we must consider the *contact forces* that arise upon the surfaces inside A that separate points p and q. Draw an imaginary boundary shell B around q that excludes p. An external force applied at p can transmit an indirect influence to q if it successively alters the conditions of the shells of matter that surround q. As the matter outside of B changes its state, a new set of forces will be applied against the *surface* of B *by direct contact*. These 'contact forces' will work their way successively through the shells surrounding q and eventually affect q itself. The mathematical characteristics of such 'contact forces' are rather different from those of the action-at-a-distance types considered previously.

In the 1820s, Cauchy showed how these two types of force could be harmonized in a fashion that supplies an adequate foundation for continuum mechanics. He first assumed that '$F = ma$' holds for (almost) every shell B enclosing q. 'F' represents the resultant of summing the contact forces around B, supplemented by whatever external forces operate within B's interior. '$F = ma$' then assigns an overall 'acceleration' to B. Unfortunately, these observations still allow individual *points* inside B to move in any of the variety of ways that are consistent with the *averaged* acceleration that noninfinitesimal '$F = ma$' assigns to B. But a framework of laws is not adequate to continua until the principles that govern *point* motion within a flexible body are articulated. At this juncture, Cauchy (1823) had the brilliant insight that, as the volume of B shrinks to 0, Euler's two principles ensure that a rather abstract assemblage of numbers, called the *stress tensor*, needs to be defined at each point q. Cauchy's 'stress' turns out to be the novel ingredient that renders the mechanics of continua quite distinct from the other formulations of classical physics we have considered. Popular books often encourage the impression that 'stress' is merely a synonym for 'force', but Cauchy's tensor actually supplies an abstract replacement for the naïve idea that a 'point' like q might possess an 'infinitesimal surface' upon which the surrounding materials can

tug and shear in different directions. In other words, 'stress' provides a subtle means of avoiding the paradoxical 'points with surfaces' that conceptually bedevilled earlier attempts to discuss continua.

With Cauchy's new notion in hand, the differences between water and rubber can be traced to the distinct manners in which states of stress affect stretching within the materials. The law of stretching for rubber – its so-called 'constitutive equation' – looks quite different from the law suitable for water. Such 'constitutive principles' together with Euler's two laws form the core of doctrine upon which continuum mechanics rests.

Cauchy's direct approach to continua usually provides a more reliable guide to the behaviour of real life materials than modelling them as arrays of classical points or rigid bodies. Some of the nineteenth-century hostility to 'molecules' stemmed from a recognition of this empirical superiority (the historical dispute over the so-called 'rariconstant' theory of elasticity was a case in point). But Cauchy's programme is complicated, and, without sufficient care, one can quickly return to conceptual absurdities such as 'points with infinitesimal surfaces'. Many modern texts treat continua as large swarms of point masses simply because this approach provides a 'quick and dirty' way of getting some key classical models up and running, without needing to worry about delicate foundational considerations. Handy appeals to the necessity of 'idealization' camouflage some otherwise awkward *non sequiturs*. But if one hopes to appreciate the conceptual issues with which a Leibniz would have struggled, the difficulties of continua need to be addressed more honestly.

In point of historical record, a variant programme for approaching continua based upon 'strain energy' rather than 'stress' was pursued in the late nineteenth century by the so-called 'energetic school'. See Harman (1982) for further details.

7 Retrospect

Which of these approaches to mechanics should the scientists of the nineteenth century have favoured? On the one hand, they had little doubt that the apparent continua of real life – strings, fluids, and so on – are lumpish in composition, possibly suggesting the suitability of rigid bodies as the basic objects of physics. But such molecules also seemed to be capable of vibration, indicating that the molecular 'lumps' might possibly act as flexible bodies at a microscopic level of analysis (the 'ether' that was thought to surround the molecules also acted like a continuum). Such uncertainties spawned lively arguments over the proper basis of classical mechanics, disputes that were never resolved simply because Nature decided to turn quantum mechanical at just the point where experiments might have settled matters.

Unfortunately, many popular accounts of the history of science and philosophy often forget these genuine conceptual worries and presume that 'classical mechanics' is correctly interpreted only from a point mass stance. The many philosophers and scientists who struggled to articulate variant conceptions are frequently dismissed as incompetents blind to the true mechanical light. But the deep philosophical heritage of classical mechanics is better appreciated if its basic internal tensions are more sympathetically understood.

See also: CONSERVATION PRINCIPLES; MECHANICS, ARISTOTELIAN

References and further reading

* Boscovich, R.J. (1763) *Theoria Philosophiae Naturalis*, Venice; trans. J.M. Child, *A Theory of Natural Philosophy*, Cambridge, MA: MIT Press, 1966. (First proposition of the point mass approach.)
* Cauchy, A.-L. (1823) 'Recherches sur l'équilibre et sur le mouvement intérieur des corps', *Bulletin des Sciences*, Paris. ('Contact forces' can be harmonized in a fashion that supplies an adequate foundation for continuum mechanics.)
Dijksterhuis, E.J. (1961) *The Mechanization of the World Picture*, Oxford: Oxford University Press. (Interesting discussion of Newton's understanding of his laws.)
Duhem, P. (1903) *L'évolution de la mécanique*, Paris: Joanin; German trans. P. Frank, *Die Wandlungen der Mechanik und der mechanischen Naturerklärung*, Leipzig: J.A. Barth, 1912; trans. M. Cole, *The Evolution of Mechanics, Monographs, and Textbooks on Mechanics of Solids and Fluids*, Alphen aan den Rijn, The Netherlands and Germantown, MD: Sijthoff & Noordhoff, 1980. (Important evaluation by a prominent scientist.)
Dugas, R. (1955) *A History of Mechanics*, London: Routledge & Kegan Paul. (Survey with many quotations from original sources.)
Friedman, M. (1972) *Foundations of Space-Time Theories: Relativistic Physics and Philosophy of Science*, Princeton, NJ: Princeton University Press. (Account of Cartan's work by a philosopher.)
* Harman, P.M. (1982) *Energy, Force, and Matter*, Cambridge: Cambridge University Press. (Readable survey of nineteenth-century developments including the 'energetics' school.)
* Hertz, H. (1894) *Die Principien der Mechanik*, Leipzig: J.A. Barth; also *Gesammelte Werke*, vol. 3, Leipzig: J.A. Barth, 1894; trans. D.E. Jones and J.T. Walley, *The Principles of Mechanics*, London: Macmillan, 1899; repr. New York: Dover, 1956. (The introduction is Hertz's main contribution to philosophy. Discussed in §5, the preface is wonderful.)
Mach, E. (1883) *Die Mechanik in ihrer Entwicklung historisch-critisch dargestellt*, Prague; trans. T. McCormack, 1893; *The Science of Mechanics*, La Salle, IL: Open Court, 1974. (A history of the evolution of science, including a comprehensive attempt to reconstruct classical mechanics on positivist lines. An influential critique.)
* Newton, I. (1726) *Isaac Newton's Philosophiae naturalis principia mathematica*; 3rd edn, with variant readings, A. Koyré and I.B. Cohen (eds) with assistance of A. Whitman, Cambridge, MA: Harvard University Press, 1972, 2 vols. (The classic, but hard to read.)
* Poincaré, H. (1902) *La Science et L'Hypothése*; repr. *Science and Hypothesis*, New York: Dover, 1952. (Parts II and III outline the 'conventionalism' discussed in §1.)
* Sneed, J. (1979) *The Logical Structure of Mathematical Physics*, Dordrecht: Reidel. (Mentioned in §2.)
* Thompson, W. and Tait, P.G. (1879) *A Treatise on Natural Philosophy*, Cambridge. (A classic of nineteenth-century thought; quoted in §1.)
Truesdell, C. (1968) *Essays in the History of Mechanics*, New York: Springer.
—— (1977) *A First Course in Rational Continuum Mechanics*, New York: Academic. (The many works by Truesdell supply the best guide to the continuum tradition of §6. The 'First Course' is advanced.)

MARK WILSON

MEDICAL EPISTEMOLOGY, HELLENISTIC *see* HELLENISTIC MEDICAL EPISTEMOLOGY

MEDICAL ETHICS

Medical ethics was once concerned with the professional obligations of physicians, spelled out in codes of conduct such as the ancient Hippocratic oath and elaborated by contemporary professional societies. Today this subject is a broad, loosely defined collection of issues of morality and justice in health, health care and related fields. The term 'bioethics' is often used interchangeably, though it is also used with its original broad meaning, which included issues in ecology.

The range of concerns grouped under 'medical ethics' begins with the relationship of doctor to patient, including such issues as consent to treatment, truth-telling, paternalism, confidentiality and the duty to treat. Particular moral uncertainty is engendered by contexts which demand divided allegiances of physicians, such as medical experimentation on human subjects, public health emergencies and for-profit medicine. Issues in medical ethics arise in every stage of life, from the fate of defective newborns to the withholding of life-sustaining therapies from the very old. Medical practices with patients who may not be competent to make their own medical decisions, including paediatrics and psychiatry, raise a distinctive set of ethical issues, as does medical genetics, which involves choices affecting family members, future individuals and offspring in utero. In recent years, medical ethics has broadened its focus beyond the individual physician or nurse to include the organization, operation and financing of the health care system as a whole, including difficult theoretical and practical uncertainties regarding the fair allocation of health care resources.

Medical ethics is at once a field of scholarship and a reform movement. The latter has campaigned in many countries on behalf of patients' rights, better care of the dying and freedom for women in reproductive decisions. As a field of scholarship, medical ethics addresses these and many other issues, but is not defined by positions taken on any of them. Though ethicists often favour an emphasis on informed consent, oppose paternalism, urge permission to end life-sustaining therapy (or choose suicide) and seek protection of human subjects of experimentation, a diversity of viewpoints finds expression in the medical ethics literature.

1   **Development of medical ethics**
2   **The doctor–patient relationship**
3   **Human experimentation**
4   **Ethical issues in psychiatry, paediatrics and geriatrics**
5   **Allocation of health care resources**
6   **Theory and methodology**

1   Development of medical ethics

Medical ethics, in the narrow sense of codes of professional conduct for physicians, has a history dating back to the Hippocratic oath of the fourth century BC (see HIPPOCRATIC MEDICINE). But medical ethics became a broad field of scholarship only after the Second World War. The terrible experiments carried out by Nazi scientists on nonconsenting human subjects were publicized and judged at the Nuremberg trials, alerting researchers and the public to the potential for abuse in clinical investigations. This lesson was learned anew in the two decades which followed as reports emerged in the United Kingdom and the United States of wrongs done to patients in the name of science, such as the injection of live cancer cells into unsuspecting patients, and the deliberate infection of institutionalized children with hepatitis. These and other abuses were detailed by the investigators in articles published in leading research journals.

Public attention was drawn to medical ethics, at least in the United States, by the moral dilemmas faced by the world's first kidney dialysis service, which had to choose which of many patients needing treatment would be permitted to live. The dialysis service, at Swedish Hospital in Seattle, created a committee in 1962 to ponder the patients' dossiers and to 'play God' in deciding who was most deserving (the winning candidates were often patients who most resembled the committee members). Even more widely discussed, a decade later, was the fate of Karen Quinlan, a young woman who had fallen into vegetative state. Her family sought permission from the courts to remove her from life-sustaining therapy, exercising a 'right to die'. A series of cases during this period involving the termination of treatment of defective newborns led not only to public debate but to stringent government guidelines for treatment, including, at one point, a national telephone number for reporting suspected doctors. Debates over doctors as agents of death intensified in many countries in the wake of increasingly liberal euthanasia policies in the Netherlands during the 1990s.

The public's fascination with medical ethics, which has increased year by year for over two decades, stems both from advances in medicine and from social changes which affect attitudes towards medical practice (see TECHNOLOGY AND ETHICS §3). Each new drug, device or technique, from the dialysis machine to genetically-engineered human growth hormone, necessitates a decision on its use. Media reports of these advances have come to include, as a matter of routine, some discussion of attendant ethical issues. A recent example is that of Dolly the sheep, cloned from a cell in another sheep's udder; global reportage of this case prompted ethical questions about the potential use of cloning techniques on humans. Just as important, however, have been issues arising from the reconsideration of traditional medical practices in light of changes in social attitudes. The turbulent 1960s, which gave rise to 'liberation' movements on behalf of many marginalized groups, led to a reconsideration of traditional physician authority, including prerogatives to withhold information and to decide the course of treatment. Thus a variety of traditional medical practices, ranging from choice of which women could be candidates for artificial insemination to the use of charity patients for medical experimentation, became targets of protest and subjects of debate.

The agenda for medical ethics has thus been determined by events outside the discipline itself rather than by its own path of intellectual progress. Anthologies and textbooks require frequent new editions, adding some topics and dropping others, tracking the course of new developments in medicine and the interests of the public. Medical ethics is thus a field of scholarship in public service. It is simultaneously a field of practice. Ethicists, those who are credited with expert knowledge of medical ethics, serve on the staffs of hospitals, in medical research institutes, and as staff members of public agencies (see MORAL EXPERTISE). A Society for Bioethics Consultation has functioned for many years in the United States, and ethics institutes in the Netherlands and elsewhere in Europe have been likewise composed of philosophers and others who provide ethical advice on a professional basis. National bioethics commissions in over twenty countries offer opinions on issues ranging from the definition of death to the rationing of health care resources (see DEATH §§1, 3). Medical ethics has become a global concern, and is debated in such bodies as UNESCO's International Bioethics Committee and the International Association of Bioethics, as well as regional groups in Europe, East Asia and South America.

Though the boundaries of the field of medical ethics are vague and shifting, a number of subjects form a recognizable core. Prominent among these are ethical issues arising in reproduction, genetics and death and dying (see GENETICS AND ETHICS; REPRODUCTION AND ETHICS; LIFE AND DEATH). Another central issue is the relationship between doctor and patient.

2 The doctor–patient relationship

In traditional medical ethics, the doctor held the reins of authority. The medical mission was to improve or protect the health of the patient. The doctor might accomplish this by giving patients the unvarnished truth, respecting their desire for confidentiality, and pointing out alternative courses of treatment. But if doctors judged these to stand in the way of health, their obligation might be to shade or withhold the truth, share information about patients with others, and manipulate patients into accepting their preferred mode of treatment.

Changes in social attitudes in English-speaking countries have brought demands for a relationship of doctor and patient based instead on respect for the patient's own wishes. This is understood to require the doctor to be entirely candid about the patient's condition, to disclose the full range of alternative therapies, with an account of their benefits and risks, and to share information about the patient with others only when given express permission by the patient.

Much of the early writing in medical ethics in the UK and US was devoted to supporting these new expectations, and self-determination has replaced paternalism as the organizing principle of medicine (see PATERNALISM). Traditionalist understandings of the doctor–patient relationship persist in other parts of the world, such as Asia and Latin America, where the Anglo-American insistence on self-determination in such matters as disclosure in the diagnosis of fatal illness is regarded as heartless and irresponsible, robbing the patient of hope.

In the older literature of medical ethics, which was chiefly concerned with the duties of the professional as such, rules on such unprofessional practices as fee-splitting, self-referral, and kickbacks played a prominent role in specifying the requirement of fidelity to the patient's interest (see PROFESSIONAL ETHICS). These issues were replaced at centre stage by the more dramatic questions of life and death which made medical ethics of great interest to the public. However, they have returned to prominence in recent years as innovations in health care financing have deliberately placed physicians, in some countries, in positions of potential conflict of interest in order to motivate them to limit the cost of care. In the United States, 'managed care' organizations often make the conflict explicit, withholding part of the doctor's pay if the latter has failed to be sufficiently frugal in ordering high-cost services for patients. Critics point to these arrangements as an abandonment of professionalism and a blow to patients' trust of doctors, while proponents point to the doctors' very professionalism as a safeguard against the temptation to exploit the patients' lack of medical knowledge when withholding needed care.

3 Human experimentation

Abuses of human subjects of medical experimentation, most notorious in Nazi medicine but now known to have been practised elsewhere, notably by Japanese physicians acting in occupied China, seem to have abated since the Second World War. Nevertheless, ethical dilemmas persist and have been a continuing concern of scholars and practitioners in medical ethics. The basic norms of humane research have been enforced in the UK and US for some decades and, as with clinical medicine, are founded on the two principles of physician concern for the patient and on patient self-determination, secured in large part through informed consent (see CONSENT). The former, however, is diluted inevitably by the physician-scientist's concern for future patients, who will receive no benefits unless the experiment is successful in scientific terms.

The potential conflict between the roles of therapist and scientist arises in many randomized clinical trials (RCTs), which is especially troublesome because the RCT has emerged as the gold standard of evidence of clinical efficacy. Patients recruited to RCTs are typically told that the investigators do not know which arm of the trial (for example, a drug or a placebo) is most beneficial. Even if this is true at the beginning of the study, however, RCTs typically enrol patients over a period of months or years, and later recruits may not be informed of trends in accumulating (if inconclusive) data which might lead a clinician to favour one treatment or the other rather than flipping a coin. The conflict in roles between healer and scientist remains.

4 Ethical issues in psychiatry, paediatrics and geriatrics

The currently favoured model of the doctor–patient relationship centres on the doctor's duties of care and advocacy for the patient and the patient's right of self-determination. The latter, however, assumes that patients are competent to make their own decisions. Physicians in psychiatry, paediatrics and geriatrics deal with patients whose decision-making capacities are sometimes lacking, and with others whose mental competence fluctuates over time.

No satisfactory substitute for full decision-making competence has yet been devised, but several strategies are used. For decisions at the end of life, particularly those which need to be made when they are debilitated by illness or are in vegetative state, some patients have executed 'living wills' setting out instructions for their care and have given trusted intimates 'durable power of attorney' to make decisions on their behalf. Unfortunately, these instruments have not proved effective: surveys have shown that physicians tend to overlook them and permit family members to override them. For mental patients, the so-called 'Ulysses Contract' (recalling the island of the Sirens) would permit the patient to waive, in advance, rights to refuse sedation and other treatment in the event of temporary loss of full competence, as in a manic episode. All these strategies

require an earlier period of mental competence in which the instruments are created, which makes them inapplicable to paediatric cases. In the latter, and often in psychiatric and geriatric cases as well, the physician must instead rely on others to decide on the patient's behalf or else rely on the decisions of a marginally competent patient. Since self-determination is valuable at least in part because of the protection it affords to the (competent) patient, this last strategy is sometimes self-defeating, though it may be the least unsatisfactory alternative.

5 Allocation of health care resources

The central ethical issues in allocation of health care resources – who should receive what kinds of care, and who should pay for it – are questions of distributive justice (see JUSTICE §2). Though the texts which sparked the revival of philosophical work in distributive justice, particularly Rawls' *A Theory of Justice* (1971), made little mention of health care, attempts to extend the philosophical work to the arena of health were not long in coming. These works addressed a series of questions of both philosophical interest and practical importance. Should health care be distributed in any distinctive way, different from other goods and services? Does it have any particular priority? Is there a floor or a limit on the share of social resources which should be devoted to health care? How equal should provision of health care be, and on what basis should scarce health care goods and services be allocated? What role should markets play in determining health care allocations, and what role democratic political choice?

In the United States, there is considerable debate among philosophers and the public alike on whether a society which fails to guarantee at least a basic level of health care benefits can be called just (in other industrialized countries, this is not questioned seriously). Even where basic health services are available to all, debate exists over the degree to which the remainder of health services ought to be delivered on an egalitarian footing, and over what kinds of allocations qualify as egalitarian.

Under the heading of 'prioritization', philosophers have addressed the issues involved in rationing decisions by government authorities, bedside clinicians, and private insurers alike. Ought the goal of rationing be to maximize health, understood as the greatest total number of years of life of all patients affected, discounted by remaining deficits in health? Or should the sickest patients, or those with the most urgent needs, be given priority? Should large gains in health take priority over smaller ones, even if the total gain in health, within a given budget, is achievable in a given instance by the aggregation of the smaller gains? Should the rationing agent consider the self-interest of each patient alone, or should the wishes of third parties (including family members, members of a risk pool, and, most generally, empathic fellow-citizens) also be taken into account?

Health policy has come to rely on the 'Quality-Adjusted Life Year' and other measures of the success of health care, but deep divisions over their implications persist in medical ethics. A commitment to maximizing QALYs, for example, tends (*ceteris paribus*) to choose the younger patient over the older, which strikes some theorists as proper but others as arbitrary or discriminatory.

Rationing decisions have been made in the past through a combination of means, including physician discretion, budget allocation and private purchasing in markets. The principles upon which allocation has been based have rarely been explicit. Though little consensus exists in medical ethics over the resolution of these controversies, the rising costs of health care prompt demands for allocation decisions which are principled, public and democratic. A very ambitious attempt to honour these demands, conducted by an agency of the state of Oregon, in the United States, has been scrutinized by health authorities around the globe, and several have initiated smaller-scale initiatives to the same end.

More broadly still, medical ethics has begun to address health related issues which transcend health care. Enduring differences in health status according to class and race, even in countries such as the UK which provide good health care to all citizens, prompt questions of social justice about other determinants of health. These inquiries are particularly important in consideration of medical ethics in developing countries (see DEVELOPMENT ETHICS).

6 Theory and methodology

With one foot in the academy and the other planted in the 'real worlds' of clinical medicine and health policy debate, medical ethics is, of necessity, an untidy discipline. The contexts in which ethicists perform their duties, be they an intensive care ward or a public agency, often preclude elaborate philosophical argumentation. Medical ethicists, moreover, are a varied lot. There is no credential nor any single disciplinary background: philosophers share the title with theologians, lawyers, physicians, social scientists and anyone else who claims it.

It is therefore not surprising that medical ethics lacks theories and a standard methodology. Though contributors to the subject may be informed by the traditions of moral thought, some writing, for example, as utilitarians, others as Kantians, and others as Roman Catholic moral theologians, there is no approach which any appreciable plurality share. The most widely-noted theoretical framework for medical ethics specifies a set of *prima facie* duties for health care professionals (Beauchamp and Childress 1979; Gillon and Lloyd 1994). These principles, however, must be weighted and applied in context by the decision-maker, and in the view of critics fall short of a comprehensive theory. In practice, ethicists approach a clinical case or a public policy issue more or less as anyone else would, except in being conversant with a literature which makes important distinctions, advances and criticizes leading lines of arguments, and dwells in rarefied abstraction. Ethicists begin with no standard set of assumptions, and do not necessarily converge in their conclusions.

What intellectual authority, then, does medical ethics bring to bear on ethical dilemmas in health care? Perhaps none; but this is not where its promise and its value lie in any case. Medical ethics is but one small part of the conversation of humankind, but it is, at its best, of particular interest. It is a formal and considered response to a remarkable challenge from within and without the profession of medicine to debate – publicly, impersonally and prospectively – whether medical practices are right and just. Its theoretical and methodological anarchy notwithstanding, this is an endeavour which can be commended to other arenas of public life.

See also: APPLIED ETHICS; BIOETHICS; BIOETHICS, JEWISH §2; MEDICINE, PHILOSOPHY OF; NURSING ETHICS

References and further reading

* Beauchamp, T. and Childress, J. (1979) *Principles of Biomedical Ethics*, Oxford: Oxford University Press; 4th edn, 1994. (Influential presentation of one theoretical approach in medical ethics.)

Bell, J.M. and Mendus, S. (1988) *Philosophy and Medical Welfare*, Cambridge: Cambridge University Press. (Papers on health care allocation, including the maximization of 'Quality-Adjusted Life Years'.)

Brock, D. (1993) *Life and Death*, Cambridge: Cambridge University Press. (Influential papers on clinical issues in medical ethics, and on health care delivery.)

Buchanan, A. and Brock, D. (1990) *Deciding for Others*, Cambridge: Cambridge University Press. (Theory of surrogate decision-making.)

Callahan, D. (1987, 1990) *Setting Limits* and *What Kind of Life?*, New York: Simon & Schuster; repr.

with reply to critics, Washington, DC: Georgetown University Press, 1995. (Widely-read discussions of allocation of resources.)

Daniels, N. (1985) *Just Health Care*, Cambridge: Cambridge University Press. (An account of justice in the allocation of health care resources.)

—— (1990) *Am I My Parents' Keeper?: An Essay on Justice Between the Young and the Old*, Oxford: Oxford University Press. (Allocation of health care resources across lifetimes.)

* Gillon, R. and Lloyd, A. (1994) *Principles of Health Care Ethics*, Chichester and New York: John Wiley & Sons. (A collection of papers on themes in medical ethics which apply Beauchamp and Childress' approach.)

Glover, J. (1977) *Causing Deaths and Saving Lives*, Harmondsworth: Penguin. (Broad, readable discussion of clinical issues in medical ethics.)

Kamm, F.M. (1993, 1996) *Mortality, Morality*, Oxford: Oxford University Press, 2 vols. (Closely argued, extended discussion of allocation of resources, euthanasia and other issues in medical ethics and beyond.)

Potter, V.R. (1971) *Bioethics, Bridge to the Future*, Englewood Cliffs, NJ: Prentice Hall. (Origin of term 'bioethics', broadly defined in ecological terms.)

* Rawls, J. (1971) *A Theory of Justice*, Cambridge, MA: Harvard University Press. (A work which stimulated recent debate on distributive justice.)

Reich, W. (ed.) (1994) *Encyclopedia of Bioethics*, New York: Macmillan. (Multi-volume, comprehensive set of discussions on major issues in medical ethics.)

Strosberg, M., Wiener, J.M., Baker, R. and Fein, A. (1992) *Rationing America's Medical Care: The Oregon Plan and Beyond*, Washington, DC: The Brookings Institution. (Essays on the Oregon rationing initiative.)

DANIEL WIKLER

MEDICINE, HIPPOCRATIC *see*
HIPPOCRATIC MEDICINE

MEDICINE, PHILOSOPHY OF

The philosophy of medicine can be generally defined as encompassing those issues in epistemology, axiology, logic, methodology and metaphysics generated by or related to medicine. Issues have frequently focused on the nature of the practice of medicine, on concepts of health and disease, and on understanding the kind of knowledge that physicians employ in diagnosing and treating patients.

The history of philosophical reflections concerning medicine reaches back to ancient Greece. Medical knowledge took a further step in the nineteenth century with the introduction of clinical pathological correlations, statistical methods, and systematic experimentation, out of which grew substantive literature exploring the character of medical reasoning and the framing of diagnoses. Debates also developed over contrasting physiological, ontological, nominalist and realist accounts of disease entities.

Contemporary philosophy of medicine has been concerned with the nature of medicine in an increasingly scientific context, a concern that has generated several models of medicine, including George Engel's biopsychosocial model, as well as analyses of the nature of the physician–patient interaction. The longstanding debate over the ontological status of health and disease has been recapitulated and extended by a number of authors, favouring an objective, statistically-based account, while others argue for an irreducible social and valuational element in these concepts. Several approaches to diagnostic logic, including Bayesian and computer-based analyses, have been developed, and sophisticated methods of determining disease causation and therapeutic efficacy, including analyses of the randomized clinical trial, have also been explored. Whether the philosophy of medicine is a distinct discipline or a branch of the philosophy of science has provoked vigorous arguments.

1 Definition and scope
2 History of the philosophy of medicine
3 Models of medicine
4 Concepts of health and disease
5 Logics of diagnosis, prognosis, and therapy evaluation
6 Relation of philosophy of medicine to philosophy of science

1 Definition and scope

The philosophy of medicine can be generally defined as encompassing those issues in epistemology, axiology, logic, methodology and metaphysics generated by or related to medicine. Though medical ethics is a component of the philosophy of medicine in its broadest conception, this article will not attempt to cover that discipline, except at a few critical points. Medicine is the art or science of restoring or preserving health, and may involve drugs, surgical operations, or other types of intervention. Though medicine has an extensive and continually increasing scientific basis, several physician-philosophers, including Otto Guttentag and Edmund Pellegrino, have seen the essence of medicine in its orientation to one distinct end – the affirmative response of the physician to a plea from the individual patient to help in restoring or preserving that patient's health. Issues in the philosophy of medicine have thus focused on the concept of health (and that of disease), and on understanding the kind of knowledge that physicians employ in diagnosing, treating and caring for patients. These issues have an extensive historical pedigree.

2 History of the philosophy of medicine

There is a rich, complex history of philosophical reflections concerning medicine reaching back to the beginnings of Greek philosophy (see HELLENISTIC MEDICAL EPISTEMOLOGY). These can retrospectively be recognized as part of the 'philosophy of medicine', though it was not until the nineteenth century that that expression (and 'medical logic') gained currency. By involving a significant self-critical appreciation of the difficulties in medical knowing, the philosophy of medicine contrasts with various speculative, non-empirical or only quasi-empirical, reflections on the etiology, pathogenesis and cure of disease that have been undertaken in all cultures. An explicit concern with the status of medical theories and medical claims is already present in the Hippocratic corpus (see HIPPOCRATIC MEDICINE). The *Precepts*, for example, offers an account of medical theory as a composite memory derived from sense perception; the author underscores the importance of relating medical theorizing to actual experience, thus reflecting a philosophy from the period.

From the time of the Hippocratic corpus into the nineteenth century, mainstream medicine offers an intertwining of speculative and empirical attempts to discover the true nature of disease and proper treatment, set against the background of occasional assessments of medical knowledge. Such intertwinings are found in the work of GALEN (129–c.210), who underscores the importance of observation and experiment. One finds them as well in René Descartes' attempts to determine the fundamental laws of metaphysics, physics and medicine, especially in the *Treatise on Man* (1662) (see DESCARTES, R. §2). The theoretical disputes of the seventeenth and eighteenth centuries between those using chemistry and those using mechanics, as the basis for theory and practice, were as much speculative as empirical, as were the debates about the nature of life and the status of medical systems. Often physicians who engaged in speculative, largely non-empirical, reflections on medicine, and also attempted to construct medical systems, had significant influence on the practice of medicine. On the other hand, one of the system builders, John Brown (1735–88), attracted the attention of contemporary philosophers such as Kant and Hegel.

In response to the uncritical incorporation of speculative reflections and theorizing into medical theory and practice, Thomas Sydenham (1624–89), the practice partner of John Locke (1632–1704), attempted to nurture a better appreciation of empirical observation in medicine. Inspired by the work of Sir Francis BACON, Sydenham engendered a cluster of substantial explorations of method in medicine. This literature developed Sydenham's concern not to allow theoretical presuppositions to distort clinical findings. It produced conceptually attentive assessments of medical nosologies and the status of medical knowledge. Among the contributors were Carl von LINNAEUS (1707–78) and François Boissier de Sauvages (1701–67). Reflections on the status of medical knowledge took a further step in the nineteenth century with the introduction of clinical pathological correlations, statistical methods, and systematic experimentation. One subsequent line of analysis came from medical scientists, who criticized previous medical knowledge and set out new claims regarding the status of disease entities. To this debate, François-Joseph-Victor Broussais (1772–1838) contributed a special meaning for the term ontological, using it to identify accounts that regarded diseases as in some sense abstract entities. The debates were complex and involved distinguished contributors, such as the cellular pathologist Rudolf Virchow (1821–1902). They encompassed analyses of etiological factors into necessary and sufficient causes. In these debates, distinctions were drawn between physiological and ontological accounts of disease, at times distinguishing physiological and anatomical explanations of disease, and at times nominalist and realist accounts of disease entities. This debate brought together long-standing concerns as to whether 'disease' identified a thing in the world (that is, a disease entity, an *ens morbi*), a recurring constellation of clinical findings, a set of causal factors, or was a term that conventionally identified particular findings.

The changes in medicine during the nineteenth century provoked further assessments of medical knowledge and method. Initially, this produced a mixture of the philosophy of medicine as a specialized speculative philosophy of nature and the philosophy of medicine as an assessment of scientific method in medicine. For example, Blane's *Medical Logick* (1819) incorporated both an enumeration of ten elementary principles of life, as well as a study of fallacies in medical reasoning (including Bartlett's *Philosophy of Medicine* (1844)). By mid-century, this literature

265

compassed a sophisticated appreciation of problems in medical investigation, observation and experiment, which placed concerns about medical knowledge in terms of problems of inductions. Out of this grew a substantive literature exploring the character of medical reasoning and the framing of diagnoses. This tradition of disciplined philosophical reflections concerning medicine and medical knowledge continued as interest in bioethics emerged (see BIOETHICS). This literature includes the contributions of Ludwik Fleck (1979), who in many respects anticipated the work of Thomas Kuhn in the 1960s. As the second half of this century began, the term 'philosophy of medicine' could identify a complex literature of philosophical reflections.

3 Models of medicine

Medicine has been most generally understood as helping the patient with the care of their health. This perspective makes intelligible why medicine was paradoxically characterized by the nineteenth-century pathologist Virchow as a 'social science', and also suggests why, in spite of the extraordinary advances in the application of reductionistic molecular biology in medicine, many endorse George Engel's 'biopsychosocial' model of medicine as a more appropriate vision of the discipline. This model is not antiscientific, but is viewed as a supplement to a narrower 'biomedical' model. The biopsychosocial model involves a recognition of complex causation, emphasizes that how a disease affects any one individual requires consideration of psychological, social and cultural factors, and stresses individual variability of a disease, which 'reflects as much... [psychological, social and cultural factors] as it does quantitative variations in the specific biochemical defect' (Engel 1977: 132). The centrality of the patient has also led the philosophy of medicine to examine the complexities of the physician–patient relationship, and has explored several different models of this interaction. Consensus, at least in the USA, has since 1970 tended away from a more traditional paternalistic approach to the patient and toward an account that emphasizes the moral importance of the autonomous and informed patient participating in shared decision making with the physician, tempered by the differing perspectives of each of the parties.

4 Concepts of health and disease

There appears to be a general consensus in philosophy of medicine that the debate over the concepts of health and disease has been the main contender for a 'defining problem' of the field of philosophy of

medicine. Reflections concerning concepts of disease, illness, malady and health have since the 1950s recapitulated traditional concerns regarding the status of disease entities. They have assessed the extent to which 'disease', 'illness', 'health', 'disability', and so on, identify states of affairs, reflect cultural values, or direct health care interventions. In 1954 Lester King noted how particular values mark states of health from states of disease. Debates concerning the value-laden and theory-laden character of disease and health concepts, as well as medical notions of normality and abnormality, have provoked attempts to justify culture-independent understandings through appeals to the ends of medicine, the essential functions of a being, the formal conditions of freedom or species-typical (statistically-based) levels of species-typical functions. Such approaches offer the promise of a straightforward critique of the use of medicine as a vehicle of political control, as well as a more unified account of disease and health for both humans and animals. Others have argued for the essentially culture- and value-laden character of concepts of health and disease, as well as the instrumental character of disease and illness, diagnosis, prognosis and treatment. In such accounts, concepts such as disease, illness and malady become warrants for medical interventions (Engelhardt 1996). Distinctions between mental and somatic diseases and illnesses have been developed and criticized, background concepts such as that of malady have been explored, and the role of diagnostic taxons in medical decision-making and artificial intelligence approaches to clinical problem solving and diagnosis have been studied, placing concerns with disease and health in terms of larger themes of medical explanation and reasoning. Recent advances in the molecular genetics of various diseases have occasioned several philosophical analyses of normality and genetic disease (Nordenfelt 1995).

5 Logics of diagnosis, prognosis, and therapy evaluation

Investigations into the logics of diagnosis and prognosis began in the 1950s, stimulated by the thesis of Paul Meehl (1954), that prognoses made by simple statistical models bettered prognoses made by clinicians. More explicit logical analyses of the diagnostic process developed in the 1960s and 1970s, employing both Bayesian inference and branching logics. The former approach was articulated and argued for by Ledley and Lusted in an influential article in 1959, and applied by other clinicians during the 1960s in a variety of medical specialties. The Bayesian approach uses Bayes' theorem to revise initial (or 'prior') probabilities in the light of the outcomes of further clinical tests (see INDUCTIVE INFERENCE §3; PROBABILITY, INTERPRETATIONS OF §5). The approach can outperform even experienced clinicians, if confined to narrow areas of inquiry, but requires exponentially growing amounts of data in broader or more complex domains. For many test results, this information is not available.

The branching logic approach is represented by a tree-like structure in which each branch point or node is a decision point for the physician, and can have two or more paths leading from it to additional decision nodes. This approach was defended by Alvan Feinstein in several articles in the 1970s, and applied in neurology by Kleinmuntz, and to the diagnosis of acid–base disorders by Bleich. Relics of this approach can still be seen in various diagnostic flow charts in textbooks of medicine. Branching trees can have 'chance' or probabilistic nodes inserted within them that can be subject to Bayesian inference. This type of structure, supplemented with quantitative measures of benefits and harms (utilities), constitutes the still vigorous subject of 'clinical decision analysis'. In spite of a large number of proponents still committed to the decision-theoretic approach, the need to adhere to a strict order of information presentation, and the lack of empirical information about certain key conditional probabilities, led other investigators of the diagnostic process, such as A. Gorry and J. Kassirer, to look toward the developing area of artificial intelligence for a more tractable approach.

Work in artificial intelligence in medicine (AIM) and philosophical commentary on it flourished during the late 1970s and 1980s, resulting in a number of accomplishments, including the INTERNIST-1 diagnostic program, later known as QMR (Quick Medical Record). The QMR program is now marketed for physicians, and used as a teaching tool. AIM research continues to be actively pursued under the more inclusive rubric of 'medical informatics', which has turned its attention beyond diagnostic reasoning to investigate the possibilities of a unified medical language and integrated medical information systems. In spite of the advances made in diagnostic, prognostic and therapeutic logics, there is at present no consensus that any one approach has fully captured the physician's reasoning process. Inquiry continues, and includes newer approaches such as connectionist systems, case-based reasoning and fuzzy logics.

Philosophical inquiry has also been directed at methods for determining the causes of disease and evaluating therapies. These issues are also addressed under the rubric of 'clinical epidemiology'. An analysis of how a specific agent can be identified as the 'cause' of a disease has its historical roots in Koch's postulates, which articulated a series of necessary and sufficient conditions for a disease's cause within the context of nineteenth-century bacteriology. Twentieth-century discoveries in microbiology have required the generalization of Koch's postulates, and the development of a more complex approach to the identification and confirmation of disease causation (Evans 1976). A protracted debate about the true cause of AIDS, begun by Duesberg in the late 1980s, has been conducted largely within the context of this inquiry. A related question involving causation, how to determine whether a medical intervention has had the effect of ameliorating or curing a disease, has generated an extensive literature (as well as numerous governmental regulations), most frequently in the area of new therapeutic drugs. Philosophers of medicine have participated, along with statisticians and clinicians, in analyses of various research designs, including the soundness, and the ethics, of what is generally acknowledged to be the 'gold standard' of efficacy determination: the randomized controlled clinical trial (Schaffner 1993) (see MEDICAL ETHICS §3; STATISTICS AND SOCIAL SCIENCE).

6 Relation of philosophy of medicine to philosophy of science

Since the inception of the current era of professional inquiry in the philosophy of medicine – inaugurated by the *Philosophy and Medicine Series* in 1975, *The Journal of Medicine and Philosophy* in 1976 and its sister publication *Theoretical Medicine* (née *Metamed*) in 1979 – an ongoing debate has occurred on whether the philosophy of medicine is a distinctive branch or field of philosophy, or whether it is reducible to or replaceable by some combination of philosophy of science (including the philosophy of biology), philosophy of mind and moral philosophy. Critics of the distinctiveness of the discipline, such as J. Shaffer and A. Caplan, have tended to the view that medicine is essentially the science of biology, and philosophy of medicine is (and should be best pursued as) philosophy of science. What is left out can be assigned to the realm of moral philosophy. Caplan elaborates (1992), arguing that philosophy of medicine is not at present a disciplinary 'field'. It is not a field because it is not integrated into its cognate areas of either philosophy or medicine, it has no set of core readings or 'canon', and it has no core problems (with the exception of the controversy about health and disease as reviewed) about which deep intellectual debates rage. Though Caplan does not deny the theoretical possibility of a philosophy of medicine – in fact, he suggests it should be a necessary foundation for bioethics, could have salutary consequences for philosophy of science, and could be important for medicine in its inquiries into clinical trials, computerized diagnosis and modern molecular genetics – he does not think such a discipline as yet exists.

Defenders of the distinctiveness of a discipline of philosophy of medicine, such as Pellegrino and Wulff, have argued that there are many and varied examples of the application of philosophical approaches and methods to medical topics, some of which would appear to fall into just those areas that Caplan urges be pursued. Sometimes these examples may be viewed as instances of philosophy *and* medicine or as philosophy *in* medicine, but these inquiries all share strong similarities with each other and buttress a more distinctive philosophy *of* medicine. The latter term Pellegrino (1976) prefers to reserve for a philosophical investigation of 'the clinical encounter with a human being experiencing health, illness, neurosis, or psychosis, in a setting which involves intervention into his existence'. Others may favour the broader definition of the term 'philosophy of medicine' used in the present article, which would include philosophical inquiries within medicine generally.

See also: BIOETHICS, JEWISH; QI

References and further reading

* Bartlett, E. (1844) *An Essay on the Philosophy of Medical Science*, Philadelphia, PA: Lea & Blanchard. (An exploration of medical knowledge medical causality, as well as contemporary theories of medicine, including nosologies; referred to in §2.)
* Blane, G. (1819) *Elements of Medical Logick or Philosophical Principles of the Practice of Physik*, London: Thomas & George Underwood. (An overview of the principles of life, as well as principles of reasoning and sources of error in medical reasoning; referred to in §2.)
* Broussais, F.-J.-V. (1821) *Examen des doctrines médicales et des systèmes de nosologie*, Paris: Méuignon-Marvis, 2 vols. (A contributor to the distinction between so-called physiological and ontological accounts of disease; referred to in §2.)
* Caplan, A. (1992) 'Does the Philosophy of Medicine Exist?', *Theoretical Medicine* 13: 67–77. (A critical reflection on the philosophy of medicine as a field; referred to in §6.)
* Descartes R. (*c.*1630–3) *Le Monde* (The World), excerpted in vol. 1 of *The Philosophical Writings of Descartes*, ed. and trans. J. Cottingham, R. Stoothoff, D. Murdoch and A. Kenny, Cambridge: Cambridge University Press, 1984–91. (Descartes'

first draft of a scientific system, including general physics, cosmology, terrestrial physics and human physiology. The *Treatise on Man* was first published in Latin translation in 1662, then in the French original in 1664.)
* Engel, G. (1977) 'The Need for a New Medical Model: A Challenge for Biomedicine', *Science* 196: 129–36. (The classic article developing the concept of the biopsychosocial model of medicine; referred to and quoted in §3.)
  Engelhardt, H.T., Jr and Erde, E. (1984) 'Philosophy of Medicine' in P.T. Durbin (ed.) *A Guide to the Culture of Science, Technology, and Medicine*, New York: Free Press, 364–461, 675–7. (The literature of the philosophy of medicine and bioethics is reviewed and an extensive bibliography provided; expansion of the material of §2.)
* Engelhardt, H.T., Jr (1996) *The Foundations of Bioethics*, New York: Oxford University Press, 2nd edn. (A systematic exploration of medical explanation and concepts of disease.)
* Evans, A.S. (1976) 'Causation and Disease: The Henle–Koch Postulates Revisited', *Yale Journal of Biology and Medicine* 49: 175–95. (The history and development of Koch's postulates; refered to in §5.)
* Fleck, L. (1979) *Genesis and Development of a Scientific Fact*, trans. F. Bradley and T.J. Trenn, Chicago, IL: University of Chicago Press. (A classic in the philosophy of medicine that originally appeared in German in 1935; referred to in §2.)
* *The Journal of Medicine and Philosophy* (1976–) Lisse: Swets & Zeitlinger. (Regularly has articles and issues directed to the philosophy of medicine.)
* King, L. (1978) *The Philosophy of Medicine: The Early Eighteenth Century*, Cambridge, MA: Harvard University Press. (An overview of the philosophy of medicine in the eighteenth century; material relevant to §§2 and 4.)
* Ledley, R.S. and Lusted, L.B. (1959) 'Reasoning Foundations of Medical Diagnosis', *Science* 130: 9–21. (A seminal article arguing for a Bayesian approach to modelling medical diagnosis; referred to in §5.)
* Linnaeus, C. von (1763) *Genera morborum, in auditorum usum*, Uppsala: Steinert. (An influential classification of disease offered by the great botanist; referred to in §2.)
  Meehl, P.E. (1954) *Clinical Versus Statistical Prediction; A Theoretical Analysis and a Review of the Evidence*, Minneapolis, MN: University of Minnesota Press. (Suggests statistical prediction is better than predictions made by clinicians; referred to in §5.)
  Nordenfelt, L. and Lindahl, B.I.B. (eds) (1984) *Health, Disease, and Causal Explanations in*

Medicine, Dordrecht: Reidel. (Articles and material relevant to §4 of this entry.)

* Nordenfelt, L. (1995) *On the Nature of Health*, Dordrecht: Kluwer. (An exploration of contemporary accounts of health and disease from the perspective of action theory.)

* Pellegrino, E. (1976) 'Philosophy of Medicine: Problematic and Potential', *The Journal of Medicine and Philosophy* 1: 5–31. (A seminal article that presents classical and contemporary themes in philosophy of medicine; referred to and quoted in §§1 and 6 of this entry.)

* Sauvages de la Croix, F.B. de (1763) *Nosologia methodica sistens morborum classes juxta Sydenhami mentem et botanicorum ordinem*, Amsterdam: Fratrum de Tournes, 5 vols. (A monumental attempt to provide a systematic nosology, compassing some 2,400 diseases; referred to in §2.)

Schaffner, K.F. (1981) 'Modeling Medical Diagnosis: Logical and Computer Approaches', *Synthèse* 47: 163–99. (A summary of contemporary approaches to the logic of diagnosis; contains references to the material of §5.)

—— (1992) 'Philosophy of Medicine', in M. Salmon *et al.* (eds), *Introduction to Philosophy of Science*, Englewood Cliffs, NJ: Prentice Hall, 310–45. (A development of the biopsychosocial model and its relation to reduction; expansion of the material of §§1 and 3.)

* —— (1993) 'Clinical Trials and Causation: Bayesian Perspectives', *Statistics in Medicine* 12: 1,477–94. (Addresses the concepts of causation found in clinical trials within the Bayesian framework; expansion of the material of §5.)

* Sydenham, T. (1848) *The Works of Thomas Sydenham, M.D.*, trans. R.G. Latham, London: Sydenham Society, 2 vols. (Explorations of medicine, medical theory and method; referred to in §2.)

* *Theoretical Medicine* (1979) Dordrecht: Kluwer. (Offers articles exploring issues in the philosophy of medicine and bioethics.)

Taylor, F.K. (1979) *The Concepts of Illness, Disease and Morbus*, Cambridge: Cambridge University Press. (A historical and philosophical overview of concepts of disease; articles and material relevant to §4.)

* Virchow, R. (1895) *Hundert Jahre allgemeiner Pathologie*, Berlin: Hirschwald. (A synthesis of medical explanation at the end of the nineteenth century by one of its most influential theoreticians; referred to in §2.)

KENNETH F. SCHAFFNER
H. TRISTRAM ENGELHARDT, JR

MEDIEVAL ARISTOTELIANISM

see ARISTOTELIANISM, MEDIEVAL

MEDIEVAL LOGIC *see* LOGIC, MEDIEVAL

MEDIEVAL PHILOSOPHY

Medieval philosophy is the philosophy of Western Europe from about AD 400–1400, roughly the period between the fall of Rome and the Renaissance. Medieval philosophers are the historical successors of the philosophers of antiquity, but they are in fact only tenuously connected with them. Until about 1125, medieval thinkers had access to only a few texts of ancient Greek philosophy (most importantly a portion of Aristotle's logic). This limitation accounts for the special attention medieval philosophers give to logic and philosophy of language. They gained some acquaintance with other Greek philosophical forms (particularly those of later Platonism) indirectly through the writings of Latin authors such as Augustine and Boethius. These Christian thinkers left an enduring legacy of Platonistic metaphysical and theological speculation. Beginning about 1125, the influx into Western Europe of the first Latin translations of the remaining works of Aristotle transformed medieval thought dramatically. The philosophical discussions and disputes of the thirteenth and fourteenth centuries record later medieval thinkers' sustained efforts to understand the new Aristotelian material and assimilate it into a unified philosophical system.

The most significant extra-philosophical influence on medieval philosophy throughout its thousand-year history is Christianity. Christian institutions sustain medieval intellectual life, and Christianity's texts and ideas provide rich subject matter for philosophical reflection. Although most of the greatest thinkers of the period were highly trained theologians, their work addresses perennial philosophical issues and takes a genuinely philosophical approach to understanding the world. Even their discussion of specifically theological issues is typically philosophical, permeated with philosophical ideas, rigorous argument and sophisticated logical and conceptual analysis. The enterprise of philosophical theology is one of medieval philosophy's greatest achievements.

The way in which medieval philosophy develops in

dialogue with the texts of ancient philosophy and the early Christian tradition (including patristic philosophy) is displayed in its two distinctive pedagogical and literary forms, the textual commentary and the disputation. In explicit commentaries on texts such as the works of Aristotle, Boethius' theological treatises and Peter Lombard's classic theological textbook, the *Sentences*, medieval thinkers wrestled anew with the traditions that had come down to them. By contrast, the disputation – the form of discourse characteristic of the university environment of the later Middle Ages – focuses not on particular texts but on specific philosophical or theological issues. It thereby allows medieval philosophers to gather together relevant passages and arguments scattered throughout the authoritative literature and to adjudicate their competing claims in a systematic way. These dialectical forms of thought and interchange encourage the development of powerful tools of interpretation, analysis and argument ideally suited to philosophical inquiry. It is the highly technical nature of these academic (or scholastic) modes of thought, however, that provoked the hostilities of the Renaissance humanists whose attacks brought the period of medieval philosophy to an end.

Historical and geographical boundaries

The terms 'medieval' and 'Middle Ages' derive from the Latin expression *medium aevum* (the middle age), coined by Renaissance humanists to refer to the period separating the golden age of classical Greece and Rome from what they saw as the rebirth of classical ideals in their own day. The humanists were writing from the perspective of the intellectual culture of Western Europe, and insofar as their conception of a middle age corresponds to an identifiable historical period, it corresponds to a period in the history of the Latin West. The historical boundaries of medieval intellectual culture in Western Europe are marked fairly clearly: on the one end by the disintegration of the cultural structures of Roman civilization (Alaric sacked Rome in AD 410), and on the other end by the dramatic cultural revolution perpetrated by the humanists themselves (in the late fourteenth and fifteenth centuries). There is some justification, therefore, for taking 'medieval philosophy' as designating primarily the philosophy of the Latin West from about AD 400–1400.

There were, of course, significant non-Latin philosophical developments in Europe and the Mediterranean world in this same period, in the Greek-speaking Byzantine empire, for example, and in Arabic-speaking Islamic and Jewish cultures in the Near East, northern Africa and Spain. None of these philosophical traditions, however, was radically cut off from the philosophical heritage of the ancient world in the way the Latin-speaking West was by the collapse of the Roman Empire. For that reason, those traditions are best treated separately from that of Western Europe. Accordingly, they are dealt with in this article only to the extent to which they influence developments in medieval philosophy in the Latin West.

(See BYZANTINE PHILOSOPHY; HELLENISTIC PHILOSOPHY; HUMANISM, RENAISSANCE; ISLAMIC PHILOSOPHY; JEWISH PHILOSOPHY; MEDIEVAL PHILOSOPHY, RUSSIAN; RENAISSANCE PHILOSOPHY.)

Beginnings

The general character of medieval philosophy in the West is determined to a significant extent by historical events associated with the collapse of Roman civilization. The overrunning of Western Europe by invading Goths, Huns and Vandals brought in its wake not only the military and political defeat of the Roman Empire but also the disintegration of the shared institutions and culture that had sustained philosophical activity in late antiquity. Boethius, a Roman patrician by birth and a high-ranking official in the Ostrogothic king's administration, is an eloquent witness to the general decline of intellectual vitality in his own day. He announces his intention to translate into Latin and write Latin commentaries on all the works of Plato and Aristotle, and he gives as his reason the fear that, lacking this sort of remedial aid, his own Latin-speaking and increasingly ill-trained contemporaries will soon lose access altogether to the philosophical legacy of ancient Greece. Boethius' assessment of the situation appears to have been particularly astute, for in fact in the six centuries following his death (until the mid-twelfth century), philosophers in the West depended almost entirely on Boethius himself for what little access they had to the primary texts of Greek philosophy. Moreover, since he had barely begun to carry out his plan when his execution for treason put an end to his work, Boethius' fears were substantially realized. Having translated only Aristotle's treatises on logic together with Porphyry's introduction to Aristotle's *Categories* (see ARISTOTLE; PORPHYRY) and having completed commentaries on only some of the texts he translated, Boethius left subsequent generations of medieval thinkers without direct knowledge of most of Aristotle's thought, including the natural philosophy, metaphysics and ethics, and with no texts of PLATO (though a small portion of the *Timaeus* had been translated and commented on by CALCIDIUS in the fourth century). Medieval philosophy was therefore significantly shaped by what was lost to it. It took root in an environment devoid of the social and educational structures of antiquity, lacking the Greek language and cut off from the rich resources of a large portion of classical thought. Not surprisingly, the gradual reclamation of ancient thought over the course of the Middle Ages had a significant impact on the development of the medieval philosophical tradition.

Medieval philosophy, however, was also shaped by what was left to it and, in particular, by two pieces of the cultural legacy of late antiquity that survived the collapse of Roman civilization. The first of these is the Latin language, which remained the exclusive language of intellectual discourse in Western Europe throughout the Middle Ages and into the Renaissance and Enlightenment. Latin provided medieval thinkers with access to some important ancient resources, including CICERO, SENECA, Macrobius, Calcidius, the Latin Church Fathers (see PATRISTIC PHILOSOPHY), Augustine and Boethius. These Latin sources gave early medieval thinkers a general, if not deep, acquaintance with classical ideas. Augustine is far and away the most significant of these Latin sources. His thought, and in particular his philosophical approach to Christianity and his Christianized Neoplatonist philosophical outlook, profoundly affect every period and virtually every area of medieval philosophy (see §5).

The second significant piece of late antiquity to survive into the Middle Ages is Christianity. Christianity had grown in importance in the late Roman Empire and, with the demise of the empire's social structures, the Church remained until the twelfth century virtually the only institution capable of supporting intellectual culture. It sustained formal education in schools associated with its monasteries, churches and cathedrals, and provided for the preservation of ancient texts, both sacred and secular, in its libraries and scriptoriums. Medieval philosophers received at least some of their formal training in ecclesiastical institutions and most were themselves officially attached to the Church in some way, as monks, friars, priests or clerks. In the later Middle Ages, the study of theology was open only to men who had acquired an arts degree, and the degree of Master of Theology constituted the highest level of academic achievement. Consequently, most of the great philosophical minds of the period would have thought of themselves primarily as theologians. Moreover, in addition to providing the institutional basis for medieval philosophy, Christianity was an important stimulus to philosophical activity. Its ideas and doctrines constituted a rich source of philosophical subject matter. Medieval philosophy, there-

fore, took root in an intellectual world sustained by the Church and permeated with Christianity's texts and ideas (see §5).

(See ARISTOTELIANISM, MEDIEVAL; AUGUSTINE; AUGUSTINIANISM; BOETHIUS, A.M.S.; CLEMENT OF ALEXANDRIA; LIBER DE CAUSIS; MARIUS VICTOR-INUS; NEMESIUS; ORIGEN; PATRISTIC PHILOSOPHY; PLATONISM, MEDIEVAL; PSEUDO-DIONYSIUS; STOICISM; TERTULLIAN, Q.S.F.; THEMISTIUS; TRANS-LATORS.)

Historical development

The full flowering of the philosophical tradition that grows from these beginnings occurs in the period from 1100 to 1400. Two developments are particularly important for understanding the rapid growth and flourishing of intellectual culture in these centuries. The first is the influx into the West of a large and previously unknown body of philosophical material newly translated into Latin from Greek and Arabic sources. The second is the emergence and growth of the great medieval universities.

Recovery of texts. Medieval philosophers before Peter Abelard had access to only a few texts of ancient Greek philosophy: those comprising 'the old logic' (Aristotle's *Categories* and *De interpretatione* and Porphyry's *Isagōgē*) and a small part of Plato's *Timaeus*. Abelard's generation witnessed with great enthusiasm the appearance in the Latin West of the remainder of Aristotle's logical works ('the new logic': the *Prior* and *Posterior Analytics*, the *Topics* and the *Sophistical Refutations*) (see LANGUAGE, MEDIEVAL THEORIES OF; LOGIC, MEDIEVAL). Over the next hundred years, most of Aristotle's natural philosophy (most importantly the *Physics* and *On the Soul*) and the *Metaphysics* and *Ethics* became available for the first time. Not all of these Aristotelian texts were greeted with the same enthusiasm, nor did medieval philosophers find them all equally congenial or accessible (even in Latin translation). However, it is impossible to overstate the impact that the full Aristotelian corpus eventually had on medieval philosophy. The new texts became the subject of increasingly sophisticated and penetrating scholarly commentary; they were incorporated into the heart of the university curriculum, and over time the ideas and doctrines medieval philosophers found in them were woven into the very fabric of medieval thought. Having never before encountered a philosophical system of such breadth and sophistication, philosophers in the thirteenth and fourteenth centuries understandably thought it appropriate to speak of Aristotle simply as 'the Philosopher'.

As medieval thinkers were rediscovering Aristotle

they were also acquiring for the first time in Latin translation the works of important Jewish philosophers such as Avencebrol (see IBN GABIROL) and MAIMONIDES, and Islamic philosophers such as Avicenna (see IBN SINA) and Averroes (see IBN RUSHD). Some of their works were commentaries on Aristotle (Averroes became known simply as 'the Commentator') whereas some (such as Avicenna's *Metaphysics* and *De anima*) were quasi-independent treatises presenting a Neoplatonized Aristotelianism (see ARISTOTELIANISM IN ISLAMIC PHILOSOPHY). Medieval philosophers of this period turned eagerly to these texts for help in understanding the new Aristotle, and they were significantly influenced by them. Averroes's interpretation of Aristotle's *On the Soul*, for example, sparked enormous controversy about the nature of intellect, and Avicenna's metaphysical views helped shape the famous later medieval debates about universals and about the nature of the distinction between essence and existence.

Rise of the universities. As abbot of the monastery at Bec in the 1080s, Anselm of Canterbury addressed his philosophical and theological writings to his monks. By contrast, the great philosophical minds of the next generations, thinkers such as Abelard, Gilbert of Poitiers and Thierry of Chartres, would spend significant parts of their careers in the schools at Paris and Chartres and address a good deal of their work to academic audiences. The growth of these schools and others like them at centres such as Oxford, Bologna and Salerno signals a steady and rapid increase in the vitality of intellectual life in Western Europe. By the middle of the thirteenth century, the universities at Paris and Oxford were the leading centres of European philosophical activity. Virtually all the great philosophers from 1250 to 1350, including Albert the Great, Thomas Aquinas, Bonaventure, John Duns Scotus and William of Ockham, studied and taught in the schools at one or both of these centres. It is partly for this reason that early modern philosophers (who were typically not associated with universities) refer to their medieval predecessors in general as 'the schoolmen'.

The migration of philosophical activity to the universities meant not only the centralization of this activity but also its transformation into an increasingly formal and technical academic enterprise. Philosophical education was gradually expanded and standardized, philosophers themselves became highly trained academic specialists and philosophical literature came to presuppose in its audience both familiarity with the standard texts and issues of the university curriculum and facility with the technical apparatus (particularly the technical logical tools) of the discipline. These features of later medieval philosophy make it genuinely scholastic, that is, a product of the academic environment of the schools.

The philosophical disciplines narrowly construed – logic, natural philosophy, metaphysics and ethics – occupied the centre of the curriculum leading to the basic university degrees, the degrees of Bachelor and Master of Arts. Most of the great philosophers of this period, however, went beyond the arts curriculum to pursue advanced work in theology. The requirements for the degree of Master of Theology included study of the Bible, the Church Fathers and (beginning perhaps in the 1220s) Peter Lombard's *Sentences* (which was complete by 1158). Designed specifically for pedagogical purposes, the *Sentences* is rich in quotation and paraphrase from authoritative theological sources, surveying respected opinion on issues central to the Christian understanding of the world. From about 1250, all candidates for the degree of Master of Theology were required to lecture and produce a commentary on Lombard's text. This requirement offered a formal occasion for scholars nearing their intellectual maturity to develop and present their own positions on a wide variety of philosophical and theological issues guided (often only quite loosely) by the structure of Lombard's presentation.

By virtue of its historical circumstances, medieval philosophical method had from its beginnings consisted largely in commentary on a well defined and fairly small body of authoritative texts and reflection on a canonical set of issues raised by them. Philosophers in the era of the universities took for granted a much larger and more varied intellectual inheritance, but their approach to philosophical issues remained conditioned by an established textual tradition, and they continued to articulate their philosophical views in explicit dialogue with it. Formal commentary on standard texts flourished both as a pedagogical tool and as a literary form. However, other philosophical forms, including the disputation – the most distinctive philosophical form of the thirteenth and fourteenth centuries – were essentially dialectical. In the university environment, the disputation became a technical tool ideally suited to the pressing task of gathering together, organizing and adjudicating the various claims of a complex tradition of texts and positions.

A disputation identifies a specific philosophical or theological issue for discussion and provides the structure for an informed and reasoned judgment about it. In its basic form, a disputation presents, in order: (1) a succinct statement of the issue to be addressed, typically in the form of a question admitting of a 'yes' or 'no' answer; (2) two sets of preliminary arguments, one supporting an affirmative and the other a negative answer to the question; (3) a resolution or determination of the question, in which the master sets out and defends his own position, typically by drawing relevant distinctions, explaining subtle or potentially confusing points, or elaborating the underlying theoretical basis for his answer; and (4) a set of replies specifically addressing the preliminary arguments in disagreement with the master's stated views. A disputation's two sets of preliminary arguments allow for the gathering together of the most important relevant passages and arguments scattered throughout the authoritative literature. With the arguments on both sides of the question in hand, the master is then ideally positioned to deal with both the conceptual issues raised by the question and the hermeneutical problems presented by the historical tradition. Academic philosophers held disputations in their classrooms and at large university convocations, and they used the form for the literary expression of their ideas. Aquinas' *Summa theologiae*, the individual articles of which are pedagogically simplified disputations, is perhaps the most familiar example of its systematic use as a literary device. The prevalence of the disputational form in later medieval philosophy accounts for its being thought of as embodying 'the scholastic method' (see LANGUAGE, MEDIEVAL THEORIES OF; LOGIC, MEDIEVAL).

(On the early Middle Ages (*circa* 600–1100), see CAROLINGIAN RENAISSANCE; DAMIAN, P.; ENCYCLO-PEDISTS, MEDIEVAL; ERIUGENA, J.N.; GERBERT OF AURILLAC; JOHN OF DAMASCUS.)

(On the twelfth-century philosophers, see ABE-LARD, P.; ANSELM OF CANTERBURY; BERNARD OF CLAIRVAUX; BERNARD OF TOURS; CHARTRES, SCHOOL OF; CLAREMBALD OF ARRAS; GERARD OF CREMONA; GILBERT OF POITIERS; HILDEGARD OF BINGEN; HUGH OF ST VICTOR; ISAAC OF STELLA; JOHN OF SALISBURY; LOMBARD, P.; RICHARD OF ST VICTOR; ROSCELIN OF COMPIÈGNE; THIERRY OF CHARTRES; WILLIAM OF CHAMPEAUX; WILLIAM OF CONCHES.)

(On the thirteenth-century philosophers, see ALBERT THE GREAT; ALEXANDER OF HALES; AQUI-NAS, T.; AVERROISM; BACON, R.; BOETHIUS OF DACIA; BONAVENTURE; DAVID OF DINANT; GROSSE-TESTE, R.; HENRY OF GHENT; JOACHIM OF FIORE; JOHN OF LA ROCHELLE; KILWARDBY, R.; NECKHAM, A.; OLIVI, P.J.; PECHAM, J.; PETER OF SPAIN; PHILIP THE CHANCELLOR; PSEUDO-GROSSETESTE; RICHARD RUFUS OF CORNWALL; SIGER OF BRABANT; THOMAS OF YORK; ULRICH OF STRASBOURG; WILLIAM OF AUVERGNE; WILLIAM OF AUXERRE; WILLIAM OF SHERWOOD.)

(On the fourteenth-century philosophers, see ALBERT OF SAXONY; ALIGHIERI, DANTE; AUREOL, P.; BRADWARDINE, T.; BRINKLEY, R.; BRITO, R.; BURIDAN, J.; BURLEY, W.; CHATTON, W.; CRA-THORN, W.; DIETRICH OF FREIBERG; DUNS SCOTUS, J.; DURANDUS OF ST POURÇAIN; FRANCIS OF MEYRONNES; GERARD OF ODO; GILES OF ROME; GODFREY OF FONTAINES; GREGORY OF RIMINI; HENRY OF HARCLAY; HERVAEUS NATALIS; HEYTES-BURY, W.; HOLCOT, R.; JAMES OF VITERBO; JOHN OF JANDUN; JOHN OF MIRECOURT; JOHN OF PARIS; KILVINGTON, R.; LLULL, R.; MARSILIUS OF INGHEN; MARSILIUS OF PADUA; MARSTON, R.; MATTHEW OF AQUASPARTA; MEISTER ECKHART; NICHOLAS OF AUTRECOURT; ORESME, N.; OXFORD CALCULATORS; PETER OF AUVERGNE; RICHARD OF MIDDLETON; SUSO, H.; TAULER, J.; VITAL DU FOUR; WILLIAM OF OCKHAM; WODEHAM, A.; WYCLIF, J.)

(On the fifteenth-century philosophers, see AILLY, PIERRE D'; DENYS THE CARTHUSIAN; GERSON, J.; HUS, J.; NICHOLAS OF CUSA; PAUL OF VENICE; THOMAS À KEMPIS.)

Doctrinal characteristics

At the most basic level, medieval philosophers share a common view of the world that underlies and supports the various specific developments that constitute medieval philosophy's rich detail.

Metaphysics. The common metaphysical ground of medieval philosophy holds that at the most general level reality can be divided into substances and accidents. Substances – Socrates and Browny the donkey are the stock examples – are independent existents and therefore ontologically fundamental. Corporeal substances (and perhaps also certain incorporeal substances) are constituted from matter and form (see SUBSTANCE). Matter, which in itself is utterly devoid of structure, is the substrate for form (see MATTER). Form provides a substance's structure or organization, thereby making a substance the kind of thing it is. Socrates's soul, for example, is the form that gives structure to Socrates's matter, constituting it as the living flesh and blood of a human body and making Socrates a particular human being. Accidents – Socrates's height, for example, or Browny's colour – are also a kind of form, but they take as their substrate not matter as such but a substance: Socrates or Browny. Accidents depend for their existence on substances and account for substances' ontologically derivative characteristics.

Medieval philosophers recognized matter and form, the fundamental constituents of corporeal substances, as fundamental explanatory principles. A thing's matter (or material cause) and its form (or formal cause) provide basic explanations of the thing's nature and behaviour. To these two principles they added two others, the agent (or efficient) cause and the end (or final cause). The agent cause is whatever initiates motion or change; the final cause is the goal or good toward which a particular activity, process, or change is directed.

Medieval philosophers disagreed about extensions and qualifications of this fundamental metaphysical view of the world. They debated, for example, whether incorporeal substances are like corporeal substances in being composed ultimately of matter and form, or whether they are subsistent immaterial forms. They also debated whether substances such as Socrates have just one substantial form (Socrates's rational soul) or many (one form constituting Socrates's body, another making him a living body with certain capacities for motion and cognition (an animal), and another making him a rational animal (a human being)). However, they never doubted the basic correctness of the metaphysical framework of substance and accidents, form and matter, nor are they in any doubt about whether the analytical tools that framework provides are applicable to philosophical problems generally.

(See Aristotelianism, medieval; Augustinianism; Eternity of the world, medieval views of; Platonism, medieval.)

Psychology and epistemology. Medieval philosophers understood the nature of human beings in terms of the metaphysics of form and matter, identifying the human rational soul, the seat of the capacities specific to human beings, with form. All medieval philosophers, therefore, held broadly dualist positions according to which the soul and body are fundamentally distinct. But only some were also substance dualists (or dualists in the Cartesian sense), holding in addition that the soul and body are themselves substances.

Medieval philosophers devote very little attention to what modern philosophers would recognize as the central questions of epistemology (see Epistemology, history of). Until very late in the period, they show little concern for sceptical worries and are not primarily interested in stating the necessary and sufficient conditions for the truth of the claim that some person knows a given proposition. For the most part they assume that we have knowledge of various sorts and focus instead on developing an account of the cognitive mechanisms by which we acquire it. They are especially interested in how we are able to acquire knowledge of universals and necessary truths – objects or truths that are immaterial, eternal and unchanging – given that the world around us is populated with particular material objects subject to change. The answers medieval philosophers give to this question vary considerably, ranging from Plato-

nistic accounts that appeal to our direct intellectual vision (with the aid of divine illumination) of independently existing immutable entities (such as ideas in the divine mind) to naturalistic accounts that appeal to cognitive capacities wholly contained in the human intellect itself that abstract universals from the data provided by sense perception (see Universals).

(See Aristotelianism, medieval; Augustinianism; Platonism, medieval)

Ethics. Medieval philosophers share a generically Greek framework of ethical theory, extended and modified to accommodate Christianity. Its main features include an objectivist theory of value, a eudaimonistic account of the human good and a focus on the virtues as central to moral evaluation (see Eudaimonia; Areté; Virtues and vices). According to the metaphysics of goodness inherited by medieval philosophers from Greek thought, there is a necessary connection between goodness and being. Things are good to the extent to which they have being. Evil or badness is not a positive ontological feature of things but a privation or lack of being in some relevant respect. The ultimate human good or goal of human existence is happiness or beatitude, the perfection of which most medieval philosophers identified as supernatural union with God after this life. The ultimate human good is attained both through the cultivation of the moral virtues and through divine grace in the form of supernaturally infused states and dispositions such as faith, hope and charity, the so-called theological virtues (see Theological virtues).

Within this framework, medieval philosophers debated whether human beatitude is essentially an affective state (a kind of love for God) or a cognitive state (a kind of knowledge or vision of God), and whether the virtues are strictly necessary for the attainment of beatitude. They also debated whether the rightness or wrongness of some actions depends solely on God's will. Contrary to caricatures of medieval ethics, no one unequivocally endorsed a divine command theory according to which the moral rightness (or wrongness) of *all* acts consists solely in their being approved (or disapproved) by God (see Voluntarism).

(See Aristotelianism, medieval; Augustinianism; Platonism, medieval.)

Logic and language. Medieval philosophers devote enormous attention – perhaps more attention than philosophers of any period in the history of philosophy apart from the twentieth century – to logic and philosophy of language. This phenomenon is explained primarily by the uniquely important role played by Aristotle's logic in the development of medieval thought. Until the early twelfth century, medieval philosophers' knowledge of Greek philosophy was restricted to a few texts of Aristotelian logic and, by default, those texts largely set the agenda for philosophical discussion. It is a passage from Porphyry's *Isagōgē*, for example, that enticed first Boethius and, following him, a long line of commentators to take up the philosophical problem of universals (see UNIVERSALS). The texts of the old logic, which remained a central part of the philosophy curriculum in the later Middle Ages, were eventually supplemented by the remaining treatises of Aristotle's logic, among which the *Topics* and the *Sophistical Refutations* In particular sparked intense interest in the forms of philosophical argument and the nature of meaning.

(See ARISTOTELIANISM, MEDIEVAL; LANGUAGE, MEDIEVAL THEORIES OF; LOGIC, MEDIEVAL.)

Natural philosophy. Medieval philosophers believed that a complete account of reality must include an account of the fundamental constituents and principles of the natural realm. Their earliest reflections on these matters were inspired primarily by two ancient accounts of the origins and nature of the universe, the biblical story of creation (in Genesis) and Plato's story of the Demiurge's fashioning of the world (in the *Timaeus*) (see PLATO). The confluence of these ancient sources produced a medieval tradition of speculative cosmological thought paradigmatically expressed in discussions of the six days of creation. This topic in particular gave medieval philosophers opportunity to reflect on the nature of the contents of the universe and the principles governing the created realm.

From the late twelfth century, medieval philosophy is profoundly affected by the new Aristotelian natural philosophy and the new scientific treatises by Islamic philosophers. Aristotle's *Physics* in particular received enormous attention, and medieval philosophers developed sophisticated tools of logical, conceptual and mathematical analysis to deal with problems raised by Aristotle's discussions of motion, change, continuity and infinity. Scientific treatises by Islamic thinkers such as Alkindi (see AL-KINDI), Alpetragius, Avicenna (see IBN SINA) and Alhasen provided the material and impetus for significant developments in astronomy, medicine, mathematics and optics.

(See ARISTOTELIANISM, MEDIEVAL; ETERNITY OF THE WORLD, MEDIEVAL VIEWS OF; LANGUAGE, MEDIEVAL THEORIES OF; NATURAL PHILOSOPHY, MEDIEVAL; OXFORD CALCULATORS; PLATONISM, MEDIEVAL.)

Philosophical theology

Christianity is not in itself a philosophical doctrine, but it profoundly influences the medieval philosophical world-view both from within philosophy and from outside it. On the one hand, Christian texts and doctrine provided rich subject matter for philosophical reflection, and the nature and central claims of Christianity forced medieval intellectuals to work out a comprehensive account of reality and to deal explicitly with deep issues about the aims and methods of the philosophical enterprise. In these ways, Christianity was taken up into philosophy, adding to its content and altering its structure and methods On the other hand, Christianity imposed external constraints on medieval philosophy. At various times these constraints took institutional form in the official proscription of texts, the condemnation of philosophical positions and the censure of individuals.

Augustine laid the foundation for medieval Christian philosophical theology in two respects. First, he provided a theoretical rationale both for Christian intellectuals engaging in philosophical activity generally and for their taking Christian doctrine in particular as a subject of philosophical investigation. According to Augustine, Christian belief is not opposed to philosophy's pursuit of truth but is an invaluable supplement and aid to philosophy. With revealed truth in hand, Christian philosophers are able to salvage what is true and useful in pagan philosophy while repudiating what is false. Moreover, Augustine argued that Christianity can be strengthened and enriched by philosophy. Christian philosophers should begin by believing (on the authority of the Bible and the church) what Christianity professes and seek (by the use of reason) to acquire understanding of what they initially believed on authority. In seeking understanding, philosophers rely on that aspect of themselves – namely, reason – in virtue of which they most resemble God; and in gaining understanding, they strengthen the basis for Christian belief. The Augustinian method of belief seeking understanding is taken for granted by the vast majority of philosophers in the Middle Ages.

Second, Augustine's writings provide a wealth of rich and compelling examples of philosophical reflection on topics ranging from the nature of evil and sin to the nature of the Trinity. Boethius stands with Augustine in this respect as an important model for later thinkers. He composed several short theological treatises that consciously attempt to bring the tools of Aristotelian logic to bear on issues associated with doctrines of the Christian creed. Inspired by the philosophical analysis and argumentation prominent in these writings, medieval philosophers enthusiastically took up, developed and extended the enterprise of philosophical theology.

With the emergence of academic structure in the new European schools and universities of the twelfth and thirteenth centuries, theology became the paramount academic discipline in a formal curriculum of higher education. However, the fact that great thinkers of the later Middle Ages typically studied philosophy as preparatory for the higher calling of theology should not be taken to imply that in becoming theologians they left philosophy behind. As a simple matter of fact, later medieval theologians continued throughout their careers to address fundamental philosophical issues in fundamentally philosophical ways. And it is clear why this should be so: those who took up the study of theology were among the most gifted and highly trained philosophical minds of their day, and they brought to theology acute philosophical sensitivities, interests and skills. Moreover, insofar as they viewed Christianity as offering the basic framework for a comprehensive account of the world, they were naturally attracted to the broadly philosophical task of building on that framework, understanding its ramifications and resolving its difficulties.

Despite the dominance of the Augustinian view of the relation between Christianity and philosophy, religiously motivated resistance to philosophy in general and to the use of philosophical methods for understanding Christianity in particular emerges in different forms throughout the Middle Ages. In the twelfth century, some influential clerics saw the flourishing study of logic at Paris as a dangerous influence on theology and used ecclesiastical means to attack Peter Abelard and Gilbert of Poitiers. In the thirteenth century the new Aristotelian natural philosophy prompted another period of sustained ecclesiastical reaction. In 1210 and 1215 ecclesiastical authorities proscribed the teaching of Aristotle's natural philosophy at Paris, and in 1277 the Bishop of Paris issued a condemnation of 219 articles covering a wide range of theological and philosophical topics. The condemnation seems largely to have been a reaction to the work of radical Averroistic interpreters of Aristotle. It is unclear how effective these actions were in suppressing the movements and doctrines they targeted.

(See Aristotelianism, medieval; Augustinianism; Averroism; Illumination; Natural theology.)

Scholarship in medieval philosophy

Contemporary study of medieval philosophy faces special obstacles. First, a large body of medieval philosophical and theological literature has survived in European libraries, but because many of these collections have not yet been fully catalogued, scholars do not yet have a complete picture of what primary source materials exist. Second, the primary sources themselves – in the form of handwritten texts and early printed editions – can typically be deciphered and read only by those with specialized paleographical skills. Only a very small portion of the known extant material has ever been published in modern editions of a sort that any reader of Latin could easily use. Third, an even smaller portion of the extant material has been translated into English (or any other modern language) or subjected to the sort of scholarly commentary and analysis that might open it up to a wider philosophical audience. For these reasons, scholarship in medieval philosophy is still in its early stages and remains a considerable distance from attaining the sort of authoritative and comprehensive view of its field now possessed by philosophical scholars of other historical periods with respect to their fields. For the foreseeable future, its progress will depend not only on the sort of philosophical and historical analysis constitutive of all scholarship in the history of philosophy but also on the sort of textual archeology necessary for recovering medieval philosophy's primary texts.

See also: Ancient philosophy; Islamic philosophy; Neoplatonism; Religion, philosophy of; Renaissance philosophy; Islamic philosophy: transmission into Western Europe

References and further reading

Armstrong, A.H. (ed.) (1967) *The Cambridge History of Later Greek and Early Medieval Philosophy*, Cambridge: Cambridge University Press. (A useful survey of medieval philosophy's historical antecedents, including the philosophical movements of late antiquity, and of the main figures of the medieval period through the beginning of the twelfth century.)

Dales, R. (1992) *The Intellectual Life of Western Europe in the Middle Ages*, Leiden: Brill. (A general historical introduction emphasizing philosophy and theology but giving some attention to broader intellectual culture, including literature and science.)

Dronke, P. (ed.) (1988) *A History of Twelfth-Century Western Philosophy*, Cambridge: Cambridge University Press. (A collection of sixteen articles exploring both the background to the philosophy of the twelfth century and its innovations and major figures; contains a good bibliography and useful bio-bibliographies of twelfth-century philosophers.)

Gilson, E. (1955) *History of Christian Philosophy in*

the Middle Ages, London: Sheed & Ward. (A classic one-volume compendium of medieval philosophy, outdated in some respects but still an enormously useful quick reference.)

Kretzmann, N., Kenny, A. and Pinborg, J. (eds) (1982) *The Cambridge History of Later Medieval Philosophy*, Cambridge: Cambridge University Press. (Forty-six articles providing a wide-ranging view of later medieval philosophy and significant recent developments in scholarship on the period; it gives special attention to the philosophy of the thirteenth and fourteenth centuries and to developments in logic and philosophy of language; contains a good bibliography and useful bio-bibliographies for later medieval philosophers.)

Marenbon, J. (1983) *Early Medieval Philosophy (480–1150): An Introduction*, London: Routledge, 2nd edn, 1988. (A readable and informative general introduction to the period.)

—— (1987) *Later Medieval Philosophy (1150–1350): An Introduction*, London: Routledge & Kegan Paul. (Part One provides a clear and succinct account of the pedagogical, institutional, and intellectual developments that shape later medieval philosophy; Part Two of the book is less successful.)

SCOTT MACDONALD
NORMAN KRETZMANN

MEDIEVAL PHILOSOPHY, RUSSIAN

The term 'philosophy' is itself highly problematic in the context of medieval Russia. Even in its most literal sense of love of learning, it was regarded with ambivalence, its devotees risking persecution. At the same time, Russia at any given point in the Middle Ages possessed what can best be described as a self-consciousness, a sense of its own destiny. Arising from the unusual circumstances of its Conversion in 988, this consciousness continues to draw heavily on Byzantium, with Russia at first in a dependent role but later, following Constantinople's fall, assuming that of the proud successor. The centrality of the Christian element to medieval Russian thought is underlined by the continuing significance both of the monastic movement and of its ancient cradle, Kiev, even as Moscow was being extolled as the Third Rome.

1   The pre-Mongol period
2   After the Mongol invasions

1   The pre-Mongol period

Access to literate culture having been gained relatively late and as part of the Conversion to Byzantine Christianity (988), those at the forefront of intellectual life in pre-Mongol Rus' were concerned primarily with formulaic imitation of Byzantium's Christian culture. This imitative trend, coupled with the emphasis on humility and rejection of worldly glory within Byzantine Christianity itself, resulted in 'philosophy' being used as a virtual synonym for, variously, the foreign, the dangerous and the heretical. While the Greek 'philosopher' who instructs Prince Vladimir, pre-Conversion, on Christian beliefs is presented by the Chronicle as essentially a positive figure, the charges of 'philosophy' levelled at metropolitan Klim Smoliatich in the mid-twelfth century carry clear condemnatory overtones. Similarly, though book learning directed to appropriate ends was regarded as a saintly virtue, parallel cases to that of Klim demonstrate that if taken to excess it was regarded with suspicion. The popularity enjoyed by the figure of the *iurodivyi*, or fool for Christ's sake, who deliberately practised folly in order to free himself from the world and its temptations, is testament to the honouring of humility above learning.

The ideology of rejection of worldly glory proved no barrier to princely propaganda programmes, which were able to base themselves on the new religion both concretely through sumptuous new churches – again copies of the Byzantine – and abstractly by presenting the prince as defender of the Truth, battling with God's enemies.

The spiritual life of the nation, meanwhile, was influenced perhaps above all by the monasteries, headed by the famous Caves Monastery in Kiev: these foundations held a near-monopoly on literacy, learning and contemplation. It was the monasteries with their scribes which acted as a filter for the Byzantine literary heritage, neatly discarding the secular almost in its entirety; and from the monasteries came forth writers, preachers and spiritual leaders. Resonant in their words from the start is a sense of the Rus', as God's chosen, prodigal people, having been called to Christianity at the eleventh hour: prominent examples are Ilarion's *Sermon on Law and Grace* (*c*.1049) and Nestor's *Life of Feodosii of the Caves* (*c*.1088). Feodosii in particular, being one of the earliest Russian saints, and peculiarly accessible in his humility, occupied a place of honour in the developing spiritual tradition.

2 After the Mongol invasions

The sense of Russia's special destiny remains constant through the medieval period. Under the Mongols, the Church as never before became the focus of national identity, and the monastic movement in particular gained unprecedented momentum, developing a number of peculiar tendencies which were to play an important part in the nation's consciousness. Of note were the trend towards withdrawal from the world for contemplative prayer, exemplified by Sergii of Radonezh (14th century), a close advisor to the prince; and the two linked ideologies of Hesychasm and Non-Possession, which developed from it a century later under Nil Sorskii. Opposed to the Non-Possessors was Iosif Volotskii, who defended the extensive estates which the Mongols' tolerant policies had permitted the monasteries. His theory of theocratic absolutism and of the divine origin of power helped him win the self-styled Tsar of all Rus', Ivan III, defeater of the Mongols, to his side.

The growing national consciousness was bolstered by the granting of autocephalous status to the Church (1448) and by the fall of Constantinople five years later. Where Russia had been effectively in the position of a cultural dependency, on the receiving end of a one-way flow of culture and religion, it now found itself the last repository of 'Orthodoxy'. Ivan demonstratively wed Sophia Paleologos, niece of the last Byzantine Emperor, thereby returning her to Orthodoxy from the Catholicism which, in a final indignity, the Emperor had accepted just before Constantinople fell. The ideology of 'Moscow the Third Rome' made its entrance: perceiving itself the sacred home of the Orthodox faith, the city assumed the trappings of the Byzantine court and Ivan took on the role of protector of the faith which had belonged to Byzantium's emperors. In a parallel move, the Bishop of Moscow was gradually raised to the status of patriarch.

Despite the glorification of Moscow, though, Kiev, both geographically and culturally closer to the West, remained an important centre of thought. In 1631 the Caves Monastery once more demonstrated its significance when Pëtr Mogila, its hegumen, founded what was to become the Academy of Kiev, offering for the first time in Russia schooling in the classics and Western scholastic theology and philosophy. The Academy in addition embarked on translations of philosophical and theological texts, thus making them available for the first time to the Russian readership. The foundation's significance was to continue far beyond the Middle Ages. Once the Ukraine came under full control of Moscow under Aleksei Mikhailovich, this trend spread into Russia, leading to the reform of the church books which brought about the schism in Russian Orthodoxy, as well as to the founding of a parallel Academy in Moscow and later in the other important Russian cities. Likewise, it was the Kiev Academy which was to exert a major influence over the ideas of the eighteenth-century Hryhorii SKOVORODA, who can perhaps be called the first Russian philosopher proper.

See also: BYZANTINE PHILOSOPHY; RUSSIAN PHILOSOPHY

References and further reading

Edie, J.M. *et al.* (eds) (1965) *Russian Philosophy*, vol. 1, Chicago: Quadrangle Books. (Short section on the beginnings of Russian philosophy.)

Fedotov, G.P. (1946, 1966) *The Russian Religious Mind*, Cambridge, MA: Harvard University Press, 2 vols. (Detailed exploration of the leading figures in medieval Russian Christianity, including Feodosii, Sergii and the fifteenth-century monastic polemicists.)

Fennell, J.L. (1995) *A History of the Russian Church to 1448*, London and New York: Longman. (Detailed account of the Church's influence on all aspects of life in early Rus'.)

Franklin, S. (1992) 'O "filosofii" i "filosofakh" v kievskoi Rusi' ('Philosophy' and 'philosophers' in Kievan Rus'), in *Byzantinoslavica* 53, 74–196. (Exploration of contemporary use of these terms, of the Byzantine precedent and of their appropriateness in the Kievan Russian context.)

Franklin, S. and J. Shepard (1996) *The Emergence of Rus 750–1200*, London and New York: Longman. (Useful chapters on ideology and imagery, both religious and political, during the early period.)

Ilarion (*c.*1049) *Sermon on Law and Grace*; trans. S. Franklin, in *Sermons and Rhetoric of Kievan Rus'*, Cambridge, MA: Harvard University Press, 1991. (Ilarion's eloquent analysis of Christianity and the significance of the conversion of Rus'.)

Nestor (*c.*1088) *Life of Feodosii of the Caves*; trans. P. Hollingsworth in *The Hagiography of Kievan Rus'*, Cambridge, MA: Harvard University Press, 1992. (One of the earliest *lives* to be produced in Rus', and which points to the existence of distinctive tendencies in Russian spirituality from the beginning.)

Zenkovsky, V.V. (1948–50) *Istoriia russkoi filosofii*, Paris: YMCA-Press, vol. 1, ch. 1; 2nd edn 1989; trans. G.L. Kline, *A History of Russian Philosophy*, London: Routledge & Kegan Paul and New York:

Columbia University Press, 1953, vol. 1, ch. 1. (Outlines the main trends in thought up to Peter the Great's time.)

CLAIRE FARRIMOND

MEDIEVAL SCIENCE *see*
NATURAL PHILOSOPHY, MEDIEVAL

MEGARIAN SCHOOL

The Megarians were a Greek 'Socratic' school of the fourth and early third centuries BC. After their founder Euclides, whose main doctrine was the unity of the good, the leading Megarian was Stilpo, best known for preaching the self-sufficiency of virtue. They propounded various puzzles and found objections to the possible–actual distinction, the copula and universals.

Euclides, an intimate associate of SOCRATES and author of Socratic dialogues, founded the Megarian (more correctly 'Megaric') school in his native Megara, a little west of Athens. His pupils included Eubulides of Miletus, who like his own pupil Alexinus of Elis was a noted propounder of paradoxes. It is not certain that these (or indeed *any* non-natives of Megara) were ever members of the Megarian school. And some other philosophical descendants of Euclides widely assumed to be Megarians, including the celebrated logician Diodorus Cronus from Iasos, in fact classified themselves as 'Dialecticians' (see DIALECTICAL SCHOOL). After Euclides, the most eminent Megarian was Stilpo of Megara, school head in the late fourth and early third centuries BC and a teacher of the founding Stoic ZENO OF CITIUM. Only scattered evidence of their work survives.

Doctrinally, the chief focus of the Megarians was ethical and metaphysical. Despite their interest in paradoxes, there is no evidence that they shared the Dialecticians' concern with logical theory. They were primarily Socratics, but with some debt to the Eleatic PARMENIDES too. Euclides held that 'the good is one thing, called by many names: sometimes wisdom, sometimes god, and at other times intellect etc.', and denied the existence of its supposed opposites (Diogenes Laertius II 106). This builds on Socrates' ethical doctrine of the unity of the virtues (see SOCRATES §5; STOICISM §16), to which the Megarians subscribed, but may also be influenced by Parmenides' metaphysical thesis that all names, even those supposedly opposite to each other, in reality refer to a single being (see PARMENIDES §7). The upshot seems to be a monism of value (possibly even entailing that the world is entirely good), but not the Eleatic metaphysics that some have attributed to the school.

That they were not considered Eleatic by their contemporaries is clear from Aristotle's treatment of their modal doctrine: only what is actual is possible, for example, only when he is building is a builder capable of building. Aristotle objects (*Metaphysics* IX 3) that this would eliminate all change – an Eleatic-sounding outcome which he implies they would not welcome.

Stilpo resembled the Cynics in his insistence on the autonomy of human good. Asked whether he had lost anything in the sack of Megara, he gave the famous reply that he had lost nothing that was his – meaning that moral and intellectual attainments are inalienable. He raised objections to the copula, dismissing all '*x* is *y*' statements as false identity-statements. An argument of his against Platonic Forms suggests a similar worry: you cannot say 'This is a vegetable', because vegetable (the universal) existed thousands of years ago, whereas this did not.

'Megarian questionings' acquired the reputation of sophistic arguments. Nevertheless, they may have included the important logical puzzles propounded by Eubulides, such as the sorites ('When does a collection of grains become a heap?'), the horned argument ('Have you lost your horns?'), the veiled argument ('You don't know the hooded man? He is your father. So you don't know your father.') and the liar paradox ('Is "I am lying" true or false?').

See also: SOCRATIC SCHOOLS

References and further reading

* Aristotle (c. mid 4th century BC) *Metaphysics* IX, in J. Barnes (trans. and ed.) *The Complete Works of Aristotle*, vol. 2, Princeton, NJ: Princeton University Press, 1984. (Chapters 3–4 include a critique of the Megarians on possibility.)
* Diogenes Laertius (c. early 3rd century AD) *Lives of the Philosophers*, trans. R.D. Hicks, *Diogenes Laertius Lives of Eminent Philosophers*, Loeb Classical Library, Cambridge, MA: Harvard University Press and London: Heinemann, 1925, 2 vols. (Book II 106–20 in volume 1 is a history of the Megarian school.)
Döring, K. (1972) *Die Megariker*, Amsterdam: Gruner. (Collection of testimonies with useful German commentary.)
Giannantoni, G. (1990) *Socratis et Socraticorum Reliquiae* (Fragments of Socrates and the

Socratics), Naples: Bibliopolis. (Volume 1 includes the fullest available collection of testimonies on the Megarians.)

Makin, S. (1996) 'Megarian Possibilities', *Philosophical Studies* 83: 253–76. (Brilliant defence of the Megarians' paradoxical identification of the possible with the actual.)

Zeller, E. (1869–82) *Die Philosophie der Griechen* (Greek Philosophy), Leipzig: Reisland, 3rd edn; the relevant part is available in English trans. by O.J. Reichel, *Socrates and the Socratic Schools*, Leipzig: Fues' Verlag (Reisland), 3rd edn, 1885. (Pages 250–80 of the translated version are sadly still the best general account of the Megarians available in English.)

DAVID SEDLEY

MEINECKE, FRIEDRICH (1862–1954)

Friedrich Meinecke was a German historian of moral and political ideas who addressed the problems of his age through critical study of the writings of past thinkers. He studied at the universities of Berlin and Bonn, before becoming a state archivist in Berlin for fourteen years. He went on to hold professorships at Strasbourg, Bonn and Berlin. He contributed to political thought through books on cosmopolitanism and nationalism, on the morality of states and on historicism. In these works he re-examined the European tradition of moral and political thought, attempting especially to find a middle way between the universalist and cosmopolitan ethic of the Enlightenment and the nineteenth-century belief in the particularity and historical uniqueness of national cultures. His life spanned the entire period from Bismarck to Hitler, and he sought to bring his deep historical learning to bear on the ethical dilemmas facing Germans during this time.

Friedrich Meinecke was the last great representative of the German Historical School, which began with Niebuhr and Savigny and enjoyed a prolonged flowering in such figures as Ranke, Mommsen, Treitschke, Sybel, Droysen and, in Meinecke's own day, Otto Hinze, Ernst TROELTSCH, Erich Marcks and Hans Delbrueck (and, although more loosely associated with it, Max WEBER). His more remote, but none the less omnipresent, intellectual ancestors were GOETHE, HERDER, and Wilhelm von HUMBOLDT. His awareness of a deep affinity with the great Swiss cultural historian, Jacob Burckhardt, whose profund-

ity of vision and melancholy pessimism contrasted with the more uncomplicated, optimistic outlook of Ranke and the Prussians, only grew with time. He virtually created the history of ideas in Germany as a separate, highly sophisticated and self-conscious discipline bestraddling both history and philosophy; and, although an individualist who respected individuals, displaying no apparent desire to be seen as the founder of a school (his desire for power in this as other matters was practically nonexistent), he nevertheless became the undisputed doyen of several generations of German historical scholars. His many US pupils, as well as the scholar refugees who fled the Third Reich, sowed the seeds of his historical approach in the USA. Never in the political limelight himself, Meinecke did informally advise politicians and public figures, particularly during the Weimar Republic, but his greatest contribution to political thought and practice is to be found in his three major works.

Weltbürgertum und Nationalstaat (Cosmopolitanism and the National State) (1907) was written in that period of liberal bourgeois optimism before the First World War which tended to see a harmony between intellect and power embodied in the state. To uncover the roots of the modern age was a central aim of German historians at this time: as Max Weber had discovered the source of the capitalist world in Calvinism, and Ernst Troeltsch had traced the links between modern culture and Protestantism, so Meinecke went in search of the origins of modern national consciousness. In a series of loosely connected individual studies, he submitted the views of the men and movements that influenced and finally brought about German unification to minute and sensitive analysis. From the cosmopolitan Enlightenment figure of Wilhelm von Humboldt, through early Romantics such as Novalis and Friedrich Schlegel, to the theorists of the state, Fichte and Adam Müller, and the practical reformers, vom Stein and Gneisenau, down to the later Hegel, Ranke and Bismarck, Meinecke sketched forth the gradual transition from German eighteenth-century cosmopolitanism to nineteenth-century nationalist particularism. Elements of the older, universal, humanistic outlook lingered on in the new ideology, but a novel world not wholly favourable to them had been born. Yet, at this stage Meinecke still hoped, rather idealistically, that the old values and the new could co-exist in harmony. Although, in the words of one sympathetic German critic, this book moves 'in the rarefied air of the highest intellectual regions', it is considered by many to be Meinecke's greatest work, and it had a permanent impact on subsequent German historiography.

Meinecke's second great work was *Die Idee der Staatsräson in der neueren Geschichte* (The Doctrine of Raison d'état in the Modern Age) (1925). Written in the aftermath of the First World War and the collapse of the Hohenzollern monarchy, this is a magisterial survey of the conflict between ethics and politics as exemplified by thinkers and men of action ranging from Machiavelli, Richelieu, and Montesquieu, to Frederick the Great, Hegel, Bismarck and Treitschke. Bringing immense insight and subtlety to the analysis of ideologies, Meinecke presents the history of political thought and action – in Germany at least – as a long chain of triumphs of the naked will to power in the service of the state over common morality, whether Christian or Kantian, and arrives at the bitter insight that, '[t]he state, so it seems, must violate the moral law' (1925 (1957)). The optimistic idealism of *Weltbürgertum und Nationalstaat* yields to a sombre, unsentimental recognition of the amorality and cynicism of governments. Nevertheless, Meinecke still insists that wielders of public power should act as guardians and promoters of a common ethical code, and that '[t]he state must become moral and strive for harmony with the universal moral law' (1925 (1957)). A view of history emerges which seeks to avoid the twin extremes, on the one hand, of the positivistic Enlightenment optimism of progress, Hegelian panlogism and Rankean faith in Providence, and, on the other hand, the yawning chasm of Schopenhauerian historical pessimism. The result is a clash between historical experience and the ethical imperative. Yet this tragic view does not exclude the possibility of genuine personal and historical greatness; rather, it requires it and makes it possible. For Meinecke the fact that historical man is constantly called upon to be a hero or an actor in a tragedy is what gives history its universal import and significance.

With the advent of national socialism, Meinecke was dismissed as 'an historical epigone' and divested of his chair and his editorship of *Historische Zeitschrift*. His last major work, *Die Entstehung des Historismus* (The Rise of Historicism) (1936), represents a vast stock-taking. Here Meinecke reaches out beyond the German cultural sphere to embrace Italian, French, and English figures in a grand survey of the emergence of modern historical consciousness itself. Examining such figures as Shaftesbury, Vico, Montesquieu, Herder and Goethe, he traces the profound shift from the static, rationalist, universalist presuppositions of the Renaissance, the Age of Reason, and the Enlightenment, themselves rooted in the much older tradition of Natural Law, to the new historicist, relativist insights into the nature of man and human history that mark our own era. The generalizing, typifying methodology which the older classical tradition shares with the sciences gives way increasingly to the genetic approach with its emphasis on origins, development, organic growth, and on the role of unique creative individuals and groups – nations, cultures, churches, peoples, races, and so on. He thus unearthed the roots of much that came later, including Ranke and the Historical School itself, Romanticism, and twentieth-century currents of relativism and irrationalism.

Die Entstehung des Historismus aimed above all to secure the autonomy of the historical realm and to protect it especially against 'scientistic' incursions, not least by figures such as Spengler with his crude and simplistic biological categories. History begins with creative human freedom 'where the spontaneous factor of human beings acting in the light of values intervenes decisively and thus creates something unique and singular' (1936 (1972)). Not only states and historical epochs are individualities on Meinecke's view, but also ideas and ideals. These are to be studied not only for their causal efficacy, but most of all for their intrinsic value and power to illuminate. They must be infused 'with as much life-blood' as the historian has to give them: 'The essence of history is not the political battle for power but the creation of lasting cultural values' (1936 (1972)).

In *Die Deutsche Katastrophe* (The German Catastrophe) (1946), Meinecke offers a brilliant and profound analysis of Germany's moral and political collapse. Among the ruins of the Bismarck–Hitler era, a path must be found back to the Age of Goethe. Meinecke's last book, *Schaffender Spiegel – Studien zur Deutschen Geschichtsschreibung und Geschichtsauffassung* (The Creative Mirror: Studies in German Historiography) (1948), contains studies on various aspects of 200 years of German historiography and is notable for his agonized reflections on the intractable problems of relativism thrown up by the historicist outlook he did so much to encourage.

Meinecke has often been accused of lacking sharp conceptual clarity and of ignoring material and economic factors in history. Particularly critical are Marxist historians. Yet none of this detracts from his unique achievement in unearthing the genesis and nature of the hitherto unexamined intellectual structures that underlie political thought and action in the modern world, and in describing them with a depth and breadth of minutely detailed learning, and a refined sense of nuance and atmosphere, probably unparalleled in his time or since.

See also: HISTORICISM

List of works

Meinecke, F. (1907) *Weltbürgertum und Nationalstaat* (Cosmopolitanism and the National State), trans. R.B. Kimber, Princeton, NJ: Princeton University Press, 1970.

—— (1925) *Die Idee der Staatsräson in der neueren Geschichte* (Machiavellism: The Doctrine of Raison d'État and its Place in Modern History), trans. D. Scott, London: Routledge & Kegan Paul, 1957.

—— (1936) *Die Enstehung des Historismus* (Historism: The Rise of a New Historical Outlook), trans. J.E. Anderson, London: Routledge & Kegan Paul, 1972. (Useful foreword by Isaiah Berlin and introduction by Carl Hinrichs.)

—— (1946) *Die Deutsche Katastrophe: Betrachtungen und Erinerungen* (The German Catastrophe: Reflections and Recollections), London: 1952.

—— (1948) *Schaffender Spiegel – Studien zur deutschen Geschichtsschreibung und Geschichtsauffassung* (The Creative Mirror: Studies in German Historiography), Stuttgart: Koehler.

References and further reading

Dehio, L. (1953) *Friedrich Meinecke: Der Historiker in der Krise* (Friedrich Meinecke: Historian in Crisis), Berlin: Dahlem.

Hofer, W. (1950) *Geschichtschreibung und Weltanschauung: Betrachtungen zum Werk Friedrich Meineckes* (Historiography and World-View: An Examination of the Work of Friedrich Meinecke), Munich: Oldenbourg.

ROGER HAUSHEER

MEINONG, ALEXIUS (1853–1920)

Meinong was an Austrian philosopher and psychologist who taught at the University of Graz. He contributed substantially to psychology, epistemology, value theory, ethics and probability theory, but is best known for his theory of objects, in which he advocates the radical view that there are objects which are wholly outside being, including impossible objects. Meinong influenced Russell and the American 'new realists'. Though widely rejected, his views have proved difficult to refute decisively and he has found sympathetic support from a number of logicians and philosophers.

1 Life, works and development
2 Intentionality and objects
3 Objects outside being
4 Incomplete objects and modality
5 Psychology and epistemology
6 Value theory and ethics
7 Philosophy as a discipline

1 Life, works and development

Alexius Meinong studied history at the University of Vienna, where he came under the influence of Franz BRENTANO, and turned to philosophy and psychology. His earliest works, the *Hume Studien* (Hume Studies) of 1877 and 1882, the first being his *Habilitationsschrift*, examined the nominalism of Locke and Hume and their theories of relations. Meinong thus grew up in the British philosophical tradition, rather than the German. After a short period as *Privatdozent* in Vienna, he moved in 1882 to Graz, where he remained until his death. In 1894 he established Austria's first psychology laboratory. A devoted teacher, he acquired talented students, including Ernst Mally, the psychologist Vittorio Benussi, and Stephan Witasek, whose early death Meinong described as the greatest blow of his life. Meinong's eyesight deteriorated early in life and he preferred to remain in Graz rather than accept a professorship in Vienna. Married and with a son, he was a competent violinist and composed *Lieder*.

Meinong's views developed slowly. Until the turn of the century his main work was in epistemology, psychology and the theory of value. Under the influence of Ehrenfels and TWARDOWSKI he turned to ontological concerns. *Über Annahmen* (On Assumptions) (1902, 2nd edn 1910) first introduced objectives, special objects of judgment, while the idea of a science of objects outside being occurs in the programmatic essay 'Über Gegenstandstheorie' ('On the Theory of Objects') (1904). These works attracted the notice of Bertrand RUSSELL, and a controversy developed over the question whether it was logically consistent to assume impossible objects. Meinong responded to Russell's criticisms with refinements, but did not relinquish his position. His ontological views reached their final form with the publication of *Über Möglichkeit und Wahrscheinlichkeit* (On Possibility and Probability) (1915) and *Über emotionale Präsentation* (On Emotional Presentation) (1917). Two volumes of collected essays were published during his lifetime, and an eight-volume *Gesamtausgabe* (Complete Edition) appeared from 1968 to 1978.

Meinong's style is clear but ponderous, and few of his many terminological coinages have passed into German philosophical currency. His views have been largely neglected in the German-speaking world, finding more resonance, both positive and critical, in English-language philosophy.

2 Intentionality and objects

Following Brentano, Meinong viewed the intentionality of the mental as its defining characteristic, but whereas Brentano originally regarded objects of consciousness as immanent, by 1890 Meinong was distinguishing an immanent from an external sense of 'object' (see INTENTIONALITY). Following Twardowski, Meinong then reserved the term 'object' (*Gegenstand*) for the external referent, denoting the immanent aspect by 'content' (*Inhalt*). He adopted Twardowski's view that all mental acts have objects, but that some such objects are nonexistent. This was the basis for the development of the theory of objects outside being. Meinong called the relation between object and subject 'presentation' (*Präsentation*).

Meinong's classification of mental acts also deviated from that of Brentano. He distinguished ideas (*Vorstellungen*), thoughts, feelings and desires. Whereas for Brentano all thoughts are judgments, Meinong added conjectures (*Vermutungen*) and assumptions (*Annahmen*), which may be playful or hypothetical: like judgments, they are positive or negative and may be true or false, but, like ideas, they do not involve intellectual commitment. This distinction between 'serious' and 'phantastic' acts was extended into the emotive and conative spheres. Each kind of act, whether serious or phantastic, came to have its own characteristic kind of object: ideas correspond to things (*Objekte*), for example, Graz, greenness; thoughts correspond to objectives (*Objektive*), for example, that Graz is in Styria; feelings or emotions correspond to dignitatives, such as the beauty of Graz; and desires correspond to desideratives, for instance, that Graz should have less traffic. Things and dignitatives are designatable by names whereas objectives and desideratives are designatable by clauses.

Meinong's rich ontology is thus the joint product of a unified conception of intentionality as presenting independent objects, and a rich taxonomy of the mental.

3 Objects outside being

Practical life enjoins attention to things around us, but in thought we range beyond what Meinong called the 'actual' or existent. Originally inclined to nominalism, Meinong progressively enlarged his ontology and came to decry the 'prejudice in favour of the actual'. Objectives, which resemble both 'states of affairs' and Russell's 'propositions', divide into those that are 'factual' or obtain, for example, that Graz is in Austria, and those that are 'unfactual' or do not obtain, for example, that Graz is in Slovenia. Meinong called 'true' only those factual objectives which someone grasps as factual. He regarded obtaining (*bestehen*) as a kind of timeless being: unfactual objectives are outside being (*außerseiend*). Similarly there exists no golden mountain, but the golden mountain is just as golden and mountainous as any existent: *what* and *how* a thing is is independent of *whether* it is. The converse does not hold: impossible objects, such as the round square, cannot exist.

Possible but non-actual objects had been accepted before, but Meinong's impossible objects were a largely new departure. Meinong recognized this and proposed a new, existentially uncommitted (*daseinfrei*) science, the theory of objects. It was impossible objects to which Russell took exception: his theory of descriptions aimed to dispense with all non-beings (see RUSSELL, B. §9). Russell claimed that Meinong's impossible objects offended against the law of contradiction. Meinong agreed but was unperturbed: his understanding of 'law of contradiction' derived from traditional logic, which said that a thing cannot both have and lack a certain property, whereas Russell meant that a proposition and its contradictory could both be inferred. Russell tried again: the *existent* round square is existent, round and square, and so it both exists and does not. Meinong replied that being existent is part of the existent round square's nature, whereas existing is not: being existent does not entail existing. Russell saw no difference and dropped the matter, satisfied he was right, but Meinong's view is in the tradition of Kant. Existence is not a (normal) property, though it has a 'watered-down' counterpart, being-existent. Meinong divided properties generally into two kinds, 'nuclear' ones which are part of the nature of a thing, and 'extra-nuclear' ones, such as existing, being simple or being complete, which are not.

Paradoxical objects such as Russell's set of all non-self-membered sets were harder to accommodate. Meinong called them 'defective objects', but could not decide whether they were just very deviant objects or whether there were none at all.

4 Incomplete objects and modality

'Incomplete' objects lack being for a different reason: they are undetermined one way or the other with respect to at least one property. The golden mountain, for instance, is undetermined with respect to its height. Meinong pressed incomplete objects into service as the senses of predicates and as epistemological intermediaries: in seeing a table I do not see all its characteristics, so the incomplete object corresponding to my perception is an 'auxiliary' object giving me access to the 'target' object, the table itself. An incomplete object with its suite of properties has a parasitic or 'implexive' being in the complete objects which have those properties.

In Meinong's theory of objective possibility and probability, incomplete objects are where possibility is 'at home'. Suppose I am about to throw a (fair) die. The actual throw will be a three, or not a three, but my thought that there is a one in six chance that I will throw a three has an objective foundation in that incomplete object, 'my next throw of the die'. This is subject of the objective 'that my next throw of the die will be a three', which is neither factual, nor unfactual, but 'subfactual'. It has a degree of factuality of 1/6, properly between 1 (factual) and 0 (unfactual). Meinong thus reconciled classical determinism with an objective foundation for probability statements, and showed the possibility of many-valued logic, which was later developed by Jan Łukasiewicz, who attended some of his lectures (see ŁUKASIEWICZ, J. §3).

Meinong considers necessity and impossibility to attach to objectives, not because of factuality or unfactuality in all possible worlds, but because their factuality and unfactuality are, he says, 'inhesive' to them. Notably, Meinong never considers God or any other supposedly necessary being.

5   Psychology and epistemology

Meinong carried out rudimentary classroom demonstrations in Vienna and Graz, and from this activity the Graz laboratory arose. His psychological studies were largely in the service of his epistemological interests, and his contributions were more empirical than those of Brentano. He examined among other things the psychology of abstraction, colour and Gestalt perception, phantasy, eye-movement, the feelings accompanying judgments, and sensory fatigue. His analysis of the role of indirect measurement in Weber's psychophysical law was noted by Russell. *On Assumptions* aimed originally at establishing the classificatory proposition that assumptions are different from both judgments and ideas; only in the course of writing did Meinong discover that he needed to consider objectives, the objects of judgment and assumption, for themselves. As object theory came to dominate Meinong's thinking, he left psychological experimentation to others and, like Husserl, rejected undue philosophical reliance on psychology, while allowing it an honourable role. The 1912 essay 'Für die Psychologie und gegen den Psychologismus in der allgemeinen Werttheorie' (For Psychology and Against Psychologism in General Value Theory) shows him striking this balance.

Meinong published several monographs and papers on epistemology, including studies on memory, conjectural conviction, the experiential basis of knowledge and an attempt to prove universal causality by inductive reasoning. The admission of conjectural conviction (*Vermutungsevidenz*), which, by contrast with Brentano's *Evidenz*, is fallible and may be inductively improved, is part of Meinong's general concern to describe those supposedly defective acts of mind often neglected by epistemologists. Our knowledge of the external world is for Meinong conjecturally, not apodictically certain. We have no reason to doubt it, but it is a posteriori and we might conceivably be mistaken. Meinong's work in epistemology has been less influential than in other areas, perhaps because he was never tempted by racy positions such as scepticism or idealism.

6   Value theory and ethics

In Vienna Meinong attended economics lectures by Carl Menger, and his own value theory attempts to extend the theory of value beyond economics, on the basis of our valuing experiences. Rejecting Brentano's assimilation of feeling to desire and will, he considered feeling or emotion to be the predominant source of value. Early lectures in Vienna, systematized in his *Psychologisch-ethische Untersuchungen zur Werth-Theorie* (Psychological-ethical Investigations in Value Theory) (1894) prompted his student Ehrenfels to counter with a subjectivistic desire-based theory, and in their constructive and friendly disagreement they conceded that value might attach *derivatively* to desires (Meinong) or feelings (Ehrenfels).

Meinong's views on value, like those on cognition, became progressively more objectivistic, and in his last works he staunchly upheld what he called 'impersonal' values, which we can recognize but do not create. Meinong's patient dissection of the principles governing values and valuation paved the way for Ernst Mally's first excursion into deontic logic.

7   Philosophy as a discipline

Meinong regarded philosophy as a congeries of disciplines rather than a single science, and his painstaking piecemeal method of philosophizing 'from below' contrasted with bolder systems and programmes. He described himself as an empirical thinker, but not an empiricist, and just this willingness to be led by the data was what recommended him to the young Russell. Nevertheless, his 'empirical thinking' led him to revolutionary conclusions, and towards the end of his life he can be seen connecting the pieces together. Meinong considered *On Emotional Presentation* to be his most important work, spanning psychology, epistemology, object theory and value theory in a single arch.

List of works

Meinong, A. (1968–78) *Alexius Meinong Gesamtausgabe* (Complete Edition), 7 vols, and *Ergänzungsband* (Supplementary Volume), Graz: Akademische Druck- und Verlagsanstalt. (Contains all the books and essays that Meinong published, together with his intellectual self-portrait (*Selbstdarstellung*) and major reviews. Volume 7 contains a comprehensive index. The supplementary volume contains a selection of posthumous material including lecture notes, notes on other philosophers' writings, and a lexicon of logic and epistemology.)

—— (1877) 'Hume-Studien I. Zur Geschichte und Kritik des modernen Nominalismus', *Sitzungsberichte der philosophisch-historischen Klasse der Kaiserlichen Akademie der Wissenschaften (Wien)* 87: 187–260; published separately, Vienna: Gerold; repr. in *Gesamtausgabe*, 1: 1–72; trans. K.F. Barber, in *Meinong's Hume Studies. Translation and Commentary*, Ann Arbor: University Microfilms, 1966, 98–192. (Distinguishes extreme (linguistic) from moderate (conceptualistic) nominalism and upholds the latter.)

—— (1882) 'Hume-Studien II. Zur Relationstheorie', *Sitzungsberichte der philosophisch-historischen Klasse der Kaiserlichen Akademie der Wissenschaften (Wien)* 101: 572–752; published separately, Vienna: Gerold; repr. in *Gesamtausgabe*, vol. 1; partially trans. K.F. Barber, in *Meinong's Hume Studies. Translation and Commentary*, Ann Arbor: University Microfilms, 1966, 194–229. (An early investigation of the ontology and epistemology of relations, with reference to Hume.)

—— (1894) *Psychologisch-ethische Untersuchungen zur Wert-theorie* (Psychological-ethical Investigations in Value Theory), Graz: Leuschner & Lubensky; repr. in *Gesamtausgabe*, vol. 3, 1–244. (An ethics and value theory based on feelings as the primary bearers of value.)

—— (1902) *Über Annahmen*, Leipzig: Barth, 2nd, revised edn, 1910; repr. in *Gesamtausgabe*, vol. 4; trans. and ed. J. Heanue, *On Assumptions*, Berkeley, CA: University of California Press, 1983. (The theory of assumptions and objectives. Probably Meinong's most influential work.)

—— (1904) 'Über Gegenstandstheorie', in A. Meinong (ed), *Untersuchungen zur Gegenstandstheorie*

und Psychologie, Leipzig: Barth, 1–50; trans. and ed. R.M. Chisholm, 'The Theory of Objects', in *Realism and the Background of Phenomenology*, Atascadero, CA: Ridgeview, 1982, 76–117. (The programme for the theory of objects. The whole 1904 collection, a showcase for the Graz School, was reviewed by Russell (1905).)

—— (1912) 'Für die Psychologie und gegen den Psychologismus in der allgemeinen Werttheorie' (For Psychology and Against Psychologism in General Value Theory), *Logos* 3: 1–14; repr. in *Gesamtausgabe*, vol. 3, 267–82. (While values are not all psychological or 'personal', psychology is of value to value theory.)

—— (1915) *Über Möglichkeit und Wahrscheinlichkeit. Beiträgezur Gegenstandstheorie und Erkenntnistheorie* (On Possibility and Probability), Leipzig: Barth; repr. in *Gesamtausgabe*, vol. 6. (Part 1 deals with 'objective' probability, understood in terms of incomplete objects and subfactual objectives. Part 2 concerns our subjective awareness of probability. Meinong's most mature object-theoretic work.)

—— (1917) 'Über emotionale Präsentation', *Sitzungsberichte der Akademie der Wissenschaften in Wien, philosophisch-historische Klasse* vol. 183 (appeared in 1924); also published separately, Vienna: Holder, 1917; repr. in *Gesamtausgabe*, vol. 3, 283–476; trans. and ed. M.-L. Schubert Kalsi, *On Emotional Presentation*, Evanston, IL: Northwestern University Press, 1972. (Emotions present independent value-bearers in much the same way as perception and thought present independent objects. Includes an inconclusive discussion of paradoxical ('defective') objects.)

—— (1921) 'A. Meinong [Selbstdarstellung]', Leipzig: Meiner, vol. 1, 91–150; 2nd edn, 1923, 101–60; repr. in *Gesamtausgabe*, vol. 7, 1–62; biography and section on theory of objects trans. R. Grossmann, in *Meinong*, London: Routledge & Kegan Paul, 224–36. (Short but revealing account by Meinong of his own life, works and views, written shortly before his death.)

—— (1965) *Philosophenbriefe. Aus der wissenschaftlichen Korrespondenz von Alexius Meinong* (Philosophical Correspondence), ed. R. Kindinger Graz: Akademische Druck- und Verlagsanstalt. (A selection of 43 letters to philosophers written between 1882 and 1920. Includes correspondence with Russell and Husserl.)

References and further reading

Barber, K.F. (1966) *Meinong's Hume Studies. Translation and Commentary*, Ph.D. dissertation, Uni-

versity of Iowa; Ann Arbor, MI: University
Microfilms. (A study of Meinong's earliest works.)

Findlay, J.N. (1963) *Meinong's Theory of Objects and
Values*, Oxford: Clarendon Press. (A marvel of
sympathetic exposition: Meinong's views in concise
form.)

Grossmann, R. (1974) *Meinong*, London: Routledge
& Kegan Paul. (Critically examines Meinong's
ontology and epistemology, emphasizing his development.)

Lambert, K. (1983) *Meinong and the Principle of
Independence*, Cambridge: Cambridge University
Press. (Examines, from the standpoint of modern
logic, the principle that how an object is is
independent of whether it is.)

Routley, R. (1980) *Exploring Meinong's Jungle and
Beyond*, Canberra: Australian National University.
(Compendious investigations of the theory of
objects (items) by an adherent more radical than
Meinong himself.)

Russell, B. (1904) 'Meinong's Theory of Complexes
and Assumptions', *Mind*, new series 13: 204–19,
336–54, 509–24; repr. in B. Russell *Essays in
Analysis*, ed. D. Lackey, London: Allen & Unwin,
1974, 21–76. (Russell's longest and most appreciative review of Meinong, notable in particular for its
praise of his method.)

* —— (1905) 'A. Meinong, *Untersuchungen zur Gegenstandstheorie und Psychologie*', *Mind* new series 14:
530–9; repr. in B. Russell *Essays in Analysis*, ed. D.
Lackey, London: Allen & Unwin, 1974, 77–88.
(This book review contains Russell's first sally
against Meinong's impossible objects.)

* —— (1907) 'A. Meinong, *Über die Stellung der
Gegenstandstheorie im System der Wissenschaften*',
Mind new series 16: 436–9; repr. in B. Russell
Essays in Analysis, ed. D. Lackey, London: Allen &
Unwin, 1974, 89–93. (Another book review, and
Russell's last word on impossible objects.)

PETER SIMONS

MEISTER ECKHART
(*c*.1260–1327/8)

*More than any other medieval thinker, Eckhart has
received widely divergent interpretations. The controversies stem from the fact that his writings fall into two
distinct groups, works written in the vernacular and
works written in Latin. The German writings, which
were intended for a wide audience, established Eckhart's
long-standing fame as a mystic. Another, more
academic Eckhart emerged when his Latin work was*
*rediscovered in 1886. The study of Eckhart's thought
today centres on the unity of the scholastic (Latin) and
the popular (German) work.*

Eckhart was born about 1260 at Hochheim, Germany, and died in 1327 (or early 1328), probably at
Avignon. After entering the Dominican Order, he
studied theology at the *studium generale* of the Order
in Cologne. In 1302–3 he was Master of Theology at
the University of Paris. In the next years he held
executive functions within his Order in Germany. A
token of the high esteem Eckhart enjoyed is that in
1311 he occupied the Dominican chair of theology at
Paris for a second time (an honour that also fell to
Thomas Aquinas). Thereafter he was the spiritual
master of religious communities and a teacher in
Cologne. In 1326 the archbishop of that city started
an inquiry into his doctrines on suspicion of heresy.
Eckhart appealed directly to the pope in Avignon, but
died before the conclusion of the trial. In the bull *In
agro dominico* of 27 March 27 1329, Pope John XXII
condemned twenty-eight propositions taken from his
works and sermons.

Eckhart's main Latin work is the *Opus tripartitum*.
As the title indicates, it was intended to consist of
three parts: the *Opus propositionum* (Work of Propositions) in which a thousand propositions were to be
explained; the *Opus quaestionum* (Work of Questions),
consisting of questions arranged according to the
order of Thomas Aquinas' *Summa theologiae*; and the
Opus expositionum (Book of Expositions), containing
commentaries on scripture and sermons. It is unknown whether Eckhart ever completed this grand
project. Only fragments of it have come down to us:
the General Prologue and the prologue to the *Opus
propositionum*, five questions disputed at Paris, and
several commentaries on scripture (Genesis, Exodus,
the Book of Wisdom and the Gospel according to
John) that were certainly intended to be part of the
Opus expositionum.

An important clue to Eckhart's self-understanding
is to be found in the prologue of his commentary on
the Gospel according to John. There he states that in
all his works his intention is to expound the doctrines
taught by the Christian faith by means of the natural
arguments (*rationes naturales*) of the philosophers.
This intention is clarified at the beginning of the
General Prologue of the *Opus tripartitum* by some
preliminary remarks, which Eckhart apparently considers basic to the interpretation of the whole work.
According to one of these remarks, the second and
third work of the work are so dependent on the *Opus
propositionum* that without it they are of little use. He
illustrates his method by stating the first proposition
('Being is God'), the first question ('Does God exist?')

and the first commentary on a text ('In the beginning God created heaven and earth'), and by showing how the proposition provides the answer to the question and elucidates the text. Eckhart's procedure implicitly criticizes the method of scholastic science. Aquinas' *Summa theologiae*, for instance, consists of thousands of concrete *quaestiones*, whose solution is founded on general principles, which are, however, not explained but presupposed (see AQUINAS, T.). In Eckhart's view, the scholastic method requires an axiomatic metaphysics.

A specification of this metaphysics is given in Eckhart's first remark in the General Prologue. The most general terms (*termini generales*), such as 'being', 'one', 'true' and 'good', should by no means be thought of as accidents. 'Being' and the terms convertible with it are not added to things as though posterior to them; on the contrary, they precede everything and are primary in things. The first four treatises of the *Opus propositionum* would deal with these most general terms, which are called *transcendentia* in the Middle Ages. They provide the philosophical foundation of the *Opus tripartitum*. Eckhart identifies the transcendentals with the divine; God alone is properly being, one, true and good. Every other thing is specified through its form to *this* or *that* being.

One of the problems in studying Eckhart is how the identification of God and *esse* in the *Opus tripartitum* can be reconciled with his criticism of ontotheology in the *Quaestiones Parisienses* (the questions disputed at Paris). In the latter, he argues that God is not being (*esse*), but understanding (*intelligere*). He observes ironically that the Evangelist John did not say 'In the beginning was being, and God was being', but 'In the beginning was the Word, and the Word was God'. Being belongs to the domain of the finite, the created.

Eckhart's German writings comprise numerous sermons and several spiritual treatises: *Reden der Unterweisung* (Talks of Instruction), *Vom edlen Menschen* (The Nobleman) and *Das Buch der göttlichen Tröstung* (The Book of Divine Consolation). In one of his sermons (53), Eckhart remarks that he usually preaches about just a few themes. His favourite theme is *Abgeschiedenheit* (detachment), and to it he devoted a separate treatise (*Vom Abgeschiedenheit*), which describes it as the highest virtue, higher even than love. The human person must empty itself and strip off the creaturely conditions of *this* or *that* being. It is by the virtue of detachment that a human being can be most closely united with God. The second theme is the birth of the Son or the Word in the soul. The unity of God the Father and God the Son is for Eckhart the model of the union of the soul with God (see Trinity). The third theme is the

'nobility' that God placed in the 'innermost' part of the soul. Eckhart calls it the 'spark of the soul', which consists in the intellect. 'If the soul were entirely of this nature, it would be wholly uncreated and uncreatable.' This proposition was one of those condemned in the trial of Eckhart, but in his apology he denied wiping out the boundaries between God and creature. He wrote that he had never taught that there is something in the soul which is uncreated, 'because then the soul would be composed of created and uncreated'. A human being is not pure intellect (see SOUL, NATURE AND IMMORTALITY OF THE).

See also: GOD, CONCEPTS OF; SUSO, H.; TAULER, J.

List of works

Meister Eckhart (*c.* 1260–1327/8) Works, *Die deutschen und lateinischen Werke*, herausgegeben im Auftrage der Deutschen Forschungsgemeinschaft, Stuttgart: Kohlhammer, 1936–. (The modern, almost completed, critical edition of Eckhart's works.)

—— (*c.* 1260–1327/8) *Opus tripartitum*. (Survives only in fragmentary form. The General Prologue, prologue to the *Opus propositionum* (Work of Propositions) and the five questions disputed at Paris are translated by A.A. Maurer in *Parisian Questions and Prologues: Master Eckhart*, Toronto, Ont.: Pontifical Institute of Medlaeval Studies. The prologue and chapter 1 of the commentary on the Gospel of St John, intended for the *Opus expositionum* (Work of Expositions) appear in J.M. Clark and J.V. Skinner, *Meister Eckhart, Selected Treatises and Sermons translated from Latin and German*, London: Faber & Faber, 1958.)

—— (*c.* 1260–1327/8) *Reden der Unterweisung* (Talks of Instruction), trans. in J.M. Clark and J.V. Skinner, *Meister Eckhart, Selected Treatises and Sermons translated from Latin and German*, London: Faber & Faber, 1958. (One of Eckhart's German spiritual treatises.)

—— (*c.* 1260–1327/8) *Vom edlen Menschen* (The Nobleman), trans. in J.M. Clark and J.V. Skinner, *Meister Eckhart, Selected Treatises and Sermons translated from Latin and German*, London: Faber & Faber, 1958. (One of Eckhart's German spiritual treatises.)

—— (*c.* 1260–1327/8) *Das Buch der göttlichen Tröstung* (The Book of Divine Consolation), trans. in J.M. Clark and J.V. Skinner, *Meister Eckhart, Selected Treatises and Sermons translated from Latin and German*, London: Faber & Faber, 1958. (One of Eckhart's German spiritual treatises.)

—— (*c.* 1260–1327/8) *Vom Abgeschiedenheit* (On Detachment), trans. in J.M. Clark and J.V. Skinner, *Meister Eckhart, Selected Treatises and Sermons translated from Latin and German*, London: Faber & Faber, 1958. (Eckhart here describes detachment as the highest virtue.)

References and further reading

Clark, J.M. (1957) *Meister Eckhart: An Introduction to the Study of his Works*, London: Nelson. (A good introduction.)

Goris, W. (1997) *Einheit als Prinzip und Ziel – Versuch über de Einheitsmetaphysik des 'Opus tripartitum' Meister Eckharts* (Unity as Principle and Objective – An Investigation of the Unity Metaphysics of Meister Eckhart's *Opus tripartitum*), Studien und Texte zu Geistesgeschichte des Mittelalters 59, Leiden: Brill. (Departing from the systematic perspective of the *Opus tripartitum*, this study gives a new orientation to the question of Meister Eckhart's philosophy.)

Largier, N. (1989) *Bibliographie zu Meister Eckhart* (Bibliography of Master Eckhart), Dokimion, vol. 9, Freiburg: Universitätsverlag. (An exhaustive survey of the literature on Eckhart.)

Mojsisch, B. (1983) *Meister Eckhart, Analogie, Univozität und Einheit* (Meister Eckhart: Analogy, Univocity and Unity), Hamburg: Meiner. (A good example of the philosophical approach to Eckhart. An English translation of this work is expected shortly.)

JAN A. AERTSEN

MELANCHTHON, PHILIPP (1497–1560)

Philipp Melanchthon was one of Luther's closest associates, helping to systematize Lutheran theology, and his Loci communes *(Commonplaces) (1521) was one of the most influential early works of Protestant theology. He was often a moderating influence in theological debates between Catholics and Protestants. Melanchthon was also involved in controversy over the relationship between human will and God's grace in the achievement of salvation. He was responsible for the reform of Protestant German education in the sixteenth century, through the large number of textbooks which he composed, and through his revisions of the statutes of universities (notably Wittenberg) and schools. As a scholar and reformer of education, he was a staunch follower of the humanism of Agricola and Erasmus, committed to teaching the best Latin authors and the Greek language. Many of his works are textbooks (often produced in different versions), frequently based on lecture notes, summarizing or commenting on classical authors or scripture. Although more important as a summarizer and popularizer than as a source of new ideas, Melanchthon nevertheless made important contributions to the development of logic, rhetoric, ethics and psychology, as well as to aspects of Reformation theology. In logic he contributed to the growth of interest in method. In ethics he established a place for classical moral teaching alongside but subordinate to the teaching of the Bible. His favourite philosopher was Aristotle, and he tended to pour scorn on rival ancient schools of philosophy. In psychology he favoured a simplified Aristotelianism, close to medieval faculty psychology, with strong emphasis on links with biology. He opposed scepticism wherever he encountered it.*

1 **Reformer of German education**
2 **Dialectic and rhetoric**
3 **Ethics**
4 **Psychology and physics**

1 Reformer of German education

Philipp Melanchthon, born Philipp Schwarzerd at Bretten, received a humanist elementary education, under the influence of his great-uncle, the famous Hebrew scholar and friend of Agricola, Johann Reuchlin. Starting out with Greek and a good knowledge of Latin literature, he was bored by the complex dialectical disputes of the traditional arts course at the University of Heidelberg, where he studied from 1509. His real education came, he said, at the University of Tübingen, where he studied from 1512. In the letter-preface to his *Opera omnia* (Complete Works) (1541) he mentions the importance of Oecolampadius' gift to him, in 1516, of a copy of the first edition of Rudolph Agricola's *De inventione dialectica* (On Dialectical Invention) (1479) (see AGRICOLA, R. §2). In 1518 he was called to the newly founded chair of Greek at Wittenberg, where he came strongly under Luther's influence, enrolling in the theology faculty in 1519. In 1521 he produced the *Loci communes* (Commonplaces), which attempts a systematic presentation of Protestant theology. Luther described it as 'a book which ought to be esteemed next to the Bible'. Melanchthon surprised his fellow humanists with the strength of his initial endorsement of Luther's views on the corruption of humanity, the enslavement of the will, and justification by faith alone (see LUTHER, M. §3). In the 1530 version of the *Loci communes* he modified these views somewhat, and in the 1543 version went even further, approaching

Erasmus' position on the freedom of the will, and the need for the will to cooperate with the Holy Spirit in order to obtain grace (see ERASMUS, D.).

He took part in several of the most famous debates of the early Reformation, including the Colloquy of Marburg (1529) and the Diet of Augsburg (1530). He was the main author of the Augsburg Confession, an authoritative statement of Lutheran doctrine, expressed in the most conciliatory language possible. Strict Lutherans sometimes regarded him as too willing to concede ground to Rome, particularly in the Leipzig Interim (December 1548), an attempt to make peace between Protestants and Catholics. In later life he gave most attention to writing textbooks, to the organization of church and schools, and to controversies with the Calvinists.

Melanchthon's most important contribution to Lutheran theology was his concept of forensic justification, which represents a development of Luther's ideas. According to Melanchthon, the sinful human being is declared to be righteous in God's heavenly court. This is an imputation by God rather than a change in the nature of the individual. This doctrine, which seems to be connected with Melanchthon's humanist interest in Roman legal practice, marks a strong distinction between the Protestant approach to justification and that of Augustine. However (as often in Melanchthon) this firm position is weakened by some of his other comments on the fourth article of the Augsburg Confession which state that a real change does take place.

Melanchthon soon came to dominate Wittenberg University. He was responsible for several reforms of the Wittenberg statutes, and for giving reformed or new statutes to other Protestant German universities (including Tübingen and Leipzig) and schools (for example in Eisleben, Magdeburg and Nuremberg). As an educational reformer his first commitment was to humanism and to the teaching of ancient languages, but he also placed a strong emphasis on mathematics and physics. Thus in his programme for the Wittenberg arts faculty in 1536, of ten lecturers there were one each for Hebrew, Greek, poetics, Latin grammar and literature, physics and moral philosophy, and two each for rhetoric with dialectic and mathematics. In 1546, the lecturers on poetics and moral philosophy, and one of the rhetoric/dialectic teachers made way for lecturers on physics with botany and two more teachers of Latin literature.

2 Dialectic and rhetoric

Between 1518 and 1547 Melanchthon wrote six books on rhetoric and dialectic. His *De rhetorica libri tres* (Three Books on Rhetoric) (1519) was mainly concerned with invention (the part of rhetoric concerned with generating the material of a composition). He insisted on the close connection between rhetoric and dialectic, as had Rudolph AGRICOLA. He next took the connection further by producing coordinated manuals of both subjects: *Compendiaria dialectices ratio* (Compendious Method of Dialectic) (1520) and *Institutiones rhetoricae* (Training in Rhetoric) (1521). In these books Melanchthon divided the two subjects in a more traditional way than Agricola had done or RAMUS was to do. Later in his career he wrote two further coordinated manuals, *Dialecticae libri quatuor* (Four Books of Dialectic) (1528) and *Elementa rhetorices* (Elements of Rhetoric) (1531). These were intended as introductions to Agricola and Aristotle, and presented each subject more fully than his earlier, more elementary textbooks. Finally in *Erotemata dialectices* (Questions on Dialectic) (1547) the dialectic was revised and enlarged to the point where it could be a self-sufficient course, replacing Aristotle altogether. These textbooks included many examples taken from classical literature and the Bible.

In rhetoric Melanchthon's principal innovations were the addition of a fourth genre of oratory (educational, in addition to judicial, deliberative and demonstrative), and the establishment of a simple type of invention for this genre and for 'simple' subjects. This consisted of a small group of questions for the speaker to consider: what is it? what are its parts? what are its causes? what are its effects? which things follow and which oppose? These questions were a selection from the topics, but they can also be seen as a development of the ideas on invention found in the *progymnasmata*, the exercises in short forms of composition which were often used in humanist grammar schools. In later versions he added to the traditional Ciceronian rhetoric syllabus sections on emotional manipulation (summarized from Aristotle), on amplification (based on Erasmus' *De copia*) and on the imitation of CICERO (§2), with particular attention to the theories of prose composition outlined in Cicero's *Orator*.

In dialectic Melanchthon gave particular attention to definition (under which he dealt with the predicables and the categories) and division. As in his rhetoric he introduced an additional but simpler form of invention for easy themes. In the earlier versions this consisted of four topics: definition, causes, parts and effects. By 1547 this became a list of ten questions and had been renamed the method. Method was a topic of considerable interest in the early sixteenth century, on the basis of remarks on the subject by PLATO (§§4–5) and GALEN (§4), and a reappraisal of Aristotle's *Posterior Analytics* (see ARISTOTLE §§4–6).

Melanchthon noticed the connection between method and invention, either through the topics or according to status theory (a technique for determining the key issue at stake in an argument and the best way to argue it) (see Cicero's *On Invention*). His ten questions (what does the word mean? does the thing exist? what is the thing? what are its parts? what is its species? what are its causes? what are its effects? which things are connected to it? what are its cognates? what are its opposites?) represent an amalgamation of the four kinds of question from the second book of Aristotle's *Posterior Analytics*, and a Ciceronian version of the topics. This left a slightly awkward question about the point of the full list of topics, which Melanchthon relegates to the end of his books on dialectic. In 1527 the topics were said to amplify the basic material. In 1547 Melanchthon explained that the method is applied to single words, with topical invention reserved for the proposition. Perhaps the four topics (1527) or the method (1547) were intended to help train beginners, while Melanchthon's basic respect for traditional materials encourages him to include the full list as well. Melanchthon's versions of the topics increase in size in the successive versions of the book. By 1547 they include not only a good deal of material from Agricola's version, but also rules that resemble Boethius' topical maxims (which Agricola rejected). This reflects Melanchthon's eclecticism and the tendency of his dialectic to become more inclusive. By 1547 such strictly scholastic ideas as the theory of supposition have found a place in his dialectic, alongside denunciations of the ancient sceptics and their modes of argument.

Throughout his career Melanchthon insisted on there being connections between rhetoric and dialectic, and on their practical value as guides to reading and composition. He taught manuals of rhetoric and dialectic alongside orations by Cicero or St Paul's letters, so that the precepts could be used to inform reading of the texts, while the texts could illustrate the practical value of the precepts. Melanchthon's published commentaries on Cicero and St Paul make considerable use of rhetoric and dialectic. His major commentary on Romans was entitled *Dispositio orationis in Epistola Pauli ad Romanos* (The Disposition of the Oration in St Paul's Epistle to the Romans) (1530) and devoted itself to the connections between the propositions in that work. In his commentary on Cicero's *Topics*, he analysed a passage from Psalm 1 to explore the similarity between the topics of invention and the figures of rhetoric. This idea goes further than Agricola's analysis of poetic effects in some of his topics entries.

Melanchthon's dialectic textbooks were very influential, going through more than ninety editions in the sixteenth century and becoming required reading in many Protestant German universities, while versions of his rhetoric were printed at least forty times. Many successful textbooks were also composed by his followers, including Thomas Wilson, whose *Arte of Rhetorique* and *Rule of Reason* were the most successful sixteenth-century textbooks of the two subjects in the English language.

3 Ethics

Melanchthon's principal work of moral philosophy was *Philosophiae moralis Epitome* (Epitome of Moral Philosophy) (1538), which he later revised as *Ethicae doctrinae elementorum libri duo* (Two Books of the Elements of the Teaching of Ethics) (1550). Melanchthon creates a space for moral philosophy by making a distinction between God's law and his gospel. Where the gospel is concerned with God's promise to humanity and the forgiveness of sins, the law tells people how they ought to behave in relation to God and other people. He wrote that: 'Moral philosophy is that part of the divine law which teaches about external actions' ([1497–1560] 1963: vol. 16, col. 21). As law, moral philosophy is reliable, but it treats only human external relations, not the relationship between God and the individual. By making clear the primacy of the gospel and allocating a distinct sphere of activity to moral philosophy, Melanchthon both legitimizes teaching the subject and tries to avoid arguments about contradictions between the Bible and philosophy. He produces quotations from scripture to support moral philosophy, and argues that it is useful as part of education, as the basis for human law, that it helps the theologian in interpreting scripture, and that it is a part of the knowledge which gives human beings pleasure.

Melanchthon's approach to moral philosophy is basically Aristotelian (see ARISTOTELIANISM, RENAISSANCE §7). Like Aristotle, he sets out by establishing the aim of humankind. In Christian terms this aim is to acknowledge God and take part in his glory. As a result of the Fall, Aristotle was unable to see this, but his idea that the purpose of human life is the exercise of virtue is assimilated by Melanchthon as the aim of external human behaviour. He is even able to accept Aristotle's analysis of virtue as a medium between vices, after a little discussion of the meaning of 'medium'. This contrasts with Luther's hostility to Aristotelian ethics, which he thought had corrupted Christian thought.

As part of his justification of moral philosophy Melanchthon touches on the issue of the freedom of the will. He explains that since philosophy is concerned with behaviour in civil life and not with spiritual issues, it must first be acknowledged that in everyday dealings with other people the will is free, both because scripture says so, and because otherwise there would be no need for laws. He goes on to argue that free will also plays a part in spiritual life, since although no man can feel true remorse or true faith without the help of the Holy Spirit, that help still partly depends on human will.

The list of virtues which Melanchthon discusses seems to have been influenced by Aristotle (for example he gives most space to justice, and he includes friendship), but the actual treatment combines Protestant concerns with the adaptation of Aristotle: there are discussions of the role of the prince in matters of religion, and the religious force of human laws. In contrast to his use of Aristotle, Melanchthon is generally hostile to other ancient schools of philosophy, rejecting the Epicurean position on pleasure and Stoic doctrines on fate and the need to rise above the emotions (see EPICUREANISM §10; STOICISM §§19–20). He also wrote commentaries on Aristotle's *Ethics* and Cicero's *On Duties* (*De officiis*).

4 Psychology and physics

Melanchthon's *Liber de anima* (Book on the Soul) (1540) was intended to be an elementary textbook. As such it was highly successful, going through forty editions and receiving eight commentaries in the sixteenth century. It explicitly avoids ancient and medieval controversies about the interpretation of Aristotle's text, preferring to give a simple exposition of faculty psychology (the theory by which the soul was considered to be divided into three aspects: vegetative, sentient and rational, each having its own range of distinct powers). Scripture takes precedence over philosophy, so for example Melanchthon took for granted the immortality of the individual soul rather than arguing through the implications of Averroes' interpretation of Aristotle and its associated controversies, which were still being argued over in sixteenth-century Italy. At the end of the book he turns away from the classical subject-matter of psychology with a more theological section upholding the freedom of the will (see ARISTOTELIANISM, RENAISSANCE §§4–5).

The discussion is conducted in a thoroughly humanist manner, with quotations in Greek, citation of literary texts, and a lengthy argument supporting Cicero's mistaken view (*Tusculan Disputations* I.x.22) that Aristotle's definition of the soul involved reference to *endelecheia* (continuance or eternity) rather than *entelecheia* (actuality) (see ARISTOTLE §17). Melanchthon adds to Aristotle's account of the

soul a lengthy discussion of anatomy and physiology (which refers to Vesalius' illustrations of dissections of the human body), a discussion of dreams, and an argument in favour of certainty and against scepticism. His major innovation was to avoid the controversy surrounding the 'possible' and 'agent' intellects by proposing a new, and far simpler, interpretation by which the agent intellect was the faculty of invention (in the rhetorical or dialectical sense) and the possible intellect the faculty of judgment (in the dialectical sense of checking the strength of arguments and putting them in set forms). This idea links his psychology with his dialectic. His work on physics, the *Initia doctrinae physicae* (Introduction to Physics) (1549) is a thoroughly Aristotelian manual, providing an elementary summary which follows the order of the *Physics*, but adding material from other parts of Aristotle's natural philosophy, and a long section on astronomy, according to the Ptolemaic model (see PTOLEMY).

See also: ARISTOTELIANISM, RENAISSANCE; HUMANISM, RENAISSANCE §§5–6; LOGIC, RENAISSANCE §§1, 7; LUTHER, M.

List of works

Melanchthon, P. (1497–1560) *Opera omnia* (Collected Works), in *Corpus Reformatorum*, Brunswick, 1834–60; repr. New York: Johnson, 1963, 28 vols. (The standard edition of Melanchthon's works. Most of the works mentioned in his biography can be found in this edition. For the others, see Mack 1993: 377.)

—— (1521) *Loci communes* (Commonplaces), trans. C.L. Hill, Boston, MA: Meador Publishing, 1944. (Useable modern English version of Melanchthon's most influential work.)

—— (1951–71) *Melanchthons Werke in Auswahl* (Selection from Melanchthon's Work), ed. R. Stupperich, Gütersloh: Gerd Mohn, 7 vols. (This selected edition includes Melanchthon's *Loci communes*, his commentary on Romans and part of the moral philosophy.)

—— (1988) *A Melanchthon Reader*, trans. R. Keen, New York: Peter Lang. (English translation of selected works.)

—— (1991–) *Melanchthons Briefwechsel. Kritische und kommentierte Gesamtausgabe* (Melanchthon's Correspondence: a Critical Edition with Commentary), ed. H. Scheible, Stuttgart: Frommann. (Excellent new edition of the correspondence.)

References and further reading

Archiv für Reformationsgeschichte, Literaturbericht (1972–), Gütersloh: Gerd Mohn. (Annual bibliography of reformation studies, including Melanchthon, with some annotation.)

* Cicero (c. 80 BC) *De inventione* (On Invention), trans. H. Hubbell, in Cambridge, MA: Loeb Classical Library, Harvard University Press, 1949. (Latin text and English translation of Cicero's handbook on rhetoric and informal argument, referred to in §2.)

* —— (late 45 BC) *Tusculanae disputationes* (Tusculan Disputations), trans. J.E. King, in Cambridge, MA: Loeb Classical Library, Harvard University Press, 1945; trans. A.E. Douglas, Warminster: Aris and Phillips, 1985, 1990. (The King translation gives the whole text in Latin and English, while Douglas provides Books I, II and V with notes. Referred to in §4.)

Green, L.C. and Froehlich, C.D. (eds) (1982) *Melanchthon in English: New Translations into English with a Registry of Previous Translations*, Sixteenth-Century Bibliography 22, St Louis, MO: Center for Reformation Research. (A bibliography of English translations.)

Hammer, W. (ed.) (1967–81) *Die Melanchthonforschung im Wandel der Jahrhunderte* (Melanchthon Research Across the Centuries), Gütersloh: Gerd Mohn, 3 vols. (Comprehensive bibliography of materials for the study of Melanchthon.)

Hartfelder, K. (1889) *Philipp Melanchthon als Praeceptor Germaniae* (Melanchthon as the Educator of Germany), Berlin: A. Hofmann; repr. Nieuwkoop: de Graaf, 1964. (Still the fundamental account of Melanchthon's activities as scholar and teacher.)

Keen, R. (1988) *A Checklist of Melanchthon Imprints through 1560*, Sixteenth-Century Bibliography 27, St Louis, MO: Center for Reformation Research. (Bibliography of early editions of Melanchthon's works.)

Mack, P. (1993) *Renaissance Argument*, Leiden: Brill, 320–33. (Agricola's influence on Melanchthon.)

Manschreck, C.L. (1958) *Melanchthon: The Quiet Reformer*, Nashville, TN: Abingdon. (Full-length study in English.)

Maurer, W. (1967–9) *Der junge Melanchthon zwischen Humanismus und Reformation* (The Young Melanchthon between Humanism and Reformation), Göttingen: Vandenhoeck & Ruprecht, 2 vols. (A good modern account of Melanchthon as a humanist.)

McGrath, A.E. (1986) *Iustitia Dei: A History of the Christian Doctrine of Justification*, Cambridge: Cambridge University Press, vol. 2, 23–32. (On Melanchthon's doctrine of forensic justification.)

Meerhoff, K. (1994) 'The Significance of Melanchthon's Rhetoric in the Renaissance', in P. Mack (ed.) *Renaissance Rhetoric*, London: Macmillan, 46–62. (Excellent account of the place of rhetoric in Melanchthon's teaching, with references to Meerhoff's other important studies.)

Petersen, P. (1921) *Geschichte der aristotelischen Philosophie im protestantischen Deutschland* (A History of Aristotelian Philosophy in Protestant Germany), Leipzig; repr. Stuttgart: Frommann, 1964. (Good account of Melanchthon's Aristotelianism.)

Risse, W. (1964) *Die Logik der Neuzeit: I, 1500–1640* (The Logic of the Modern Period), Stuttgart: Frommann. (A survey of sixteenth-century schools of logic.)

Spitz, L.W. (1963) *The Religious Renaissance of the German Humanists*, Cambridge, MA: Harvard University Press. (An old general account of Melanchthon in English.)

Vasoli, C. (1967) *La dialettica e la retorica dell'Umanesimo* (Humanist Dialectic and Rhetoric), Milan: Feltrinelli. (A good account of humanist rhetoric and dialectic, including a section on Melanchthon.)

Wiedenhofer, S. (1976) *Formalstrukturen humanistischer und reformatischer Theologie bei Philipp Melanchthon* (Formal Structures of Humanist and Reformation Theology...), Berne. (Links Melanchthon's humanism with his theology.)

PETER MACK

MELISSUS (mid or late 5th century BC)

Melissus was a Greek philosopher from the island of Samos. A second-generation representative of Eleatic metaphysics, he published one work, entitled On Nature *or* On That-Which-Is, *which has been partially reconstructed by editors. It defends a version of Parmenides' monism, but recast with terminology and arguments directly accessible to a readership schooled in the eastern Greek (Ionian) style of physical speculation, as distinct from Parmenides' western Greek background. Although it is uncertain how important Melissus was to his own contemporaries, his prosaic but clear presentation of Eleatic concepts was more widely adopted by later writers than the enigmatic pronouncements of Parmenides.*

Melissus argues that that-which-is is: (1) omnitemporal; (2) infinite in extent; (3) one; (4) homogeneous; (5) changeless, that is, without (a) reordering, (b) pain, (c) grief or (d) motion; (6) indivisible; and

(7) bodiless. Here (1) – 'it always was what it was, and always will be' – is a departure from Parmenides, who had outlawed past and future in favour of a static present. Likewise (2) contrasts with Parmenides' defence of spatially finite being. The remaining predicates are consonant with Parmenides, although (5)b–c suggest that the being Melissus has in mind is a living one, presumably a deity – an aspect not brought out by Parmenides. Melissus wrote 'If there were many things, they ought to be such as I say the One is' – a remark sometimes thought to have inspired his contemporaries the atomists.

1 **Life and work**
2 **Philosophical aims**
3 **Temporal and spatial infinity**
4 **Changeless unity**
5 **Attack on the senses**
6 **Influence**

1 Life and work

In his own day, Melissus may have won greater renown as an admiral than as a philosopher. The one firm date in his life is 441 BC, when he led the navy of his native Samos to victory over an Athenian fleet commanded by Pericles. Since his age at the time is unknown, the date of his book might be placed anywhere between 490 and 390 BC. One very suspect source makes his philosophy already known to the Athenian politician Themistocles, who died c.462 BC. But the Epicurean Colotes, in a work which after criticizing its principal target Democritus turned the attack onto a further eight philosophers in apparently chronological order, placed Melissus after Socrates, who was active c.440–399 BC, a clue which would bring his *floruit* well into the second half of the fifth century – late enough for him to have read Empedocles, Anaxagoras and perhaps even the atomists. The tradition that he studied under Parmenides is not particularly trustworthy, although it cannot be doubted that Parmenides was the dominant influence on his philosophy.

A number of verbatim fragments of his one book have been preserved by Simplicius. They can be pieced together with the help of Simplicius' ancillary paraphrase and another in the Peripatetic treatise *On Melissus, Xenophanes and Gorgias*.

2 Philosophical aims

Melissus' treatise is a methodical defence of Eleatic monism, written in unadorned Ionian prose. The conclusions are by and large Parmenidean, but the arguments are not. There is virtually no sign of

Parmenides' most characteristic argument against change – that it would entail not-being, an altogether inapplicable concept (see PARMENIDES §§2–4). Instead, Melissus relies on the barely controversial premise 'Nothing could ever come to be out of nothing' (fr. 1). Furthermore, whereas Parmenides had in the main inferred each predicate of that-which-is by an independent argument, nearly all Melissus' inferences form a single chain, with each predicate inferred directly from the previous one.

Melissus is not interested in Parmenides' highly refined mode of investigation through the logic of being. He writes as a physical thinker addressing a like-minded audience, and expounds the Eleatic One with arguments appropriate to Ionian cosmology. His title (probably authentic, despite some scholars' hesitation), *On Nature or On That-Which-Is* ['on nature' in Greek is *physis*], in effect announces that this is to be an Eleatic *physics*. His departures from Parmenides, in reverting to ordinary temporal language and in postulating a spatially infinite being, are more symptomatic of this project than of intellectual independence.

3 Temporal and spatial infinity

For the book's beginning we have a probably complete text. It opens as follows: 'It always was what it was, and always will be. For if it came to be, it is necessary that before it came to be there [or 'it'] was nothing. Well if there [or 'it'] was nothing, nothing could ever come to be out of nothing' (fr. 1). 'Since, then, it did not come to be, it both is and always was and always will be' (fr. 2, beginning).

Unlike Parmenides' highly paradoxical rejection of not-being, Melissus' opening move would be unsurprising to an audience familiar with earlier Ionian cosmologists in the tradition of ANAXIMANDER (§2), thinkers whose fundamental tenet had been the permanent existence of an underlying stuff. The commonly assumed causal (rather than ontological) principle 'Nothing could ever come to be out of nothing' was its basis. Equally unsurprising in an Ionian context (see Heraclitus, fr. 30) is Melissus' expression of this permanence in terms of omnitemporality, where Parmenides had chosen to collapse past and future into the present. It is probably misleading to call this a significant philosophical disagreement. Melissus is simply translating Parmenidean thought into the philosophical language which his audience speaks.

As in Parmenides, the rejection of past generation is not followed up with an explicit defence of future imperishability. This is assumed to follow by parity of reasoning. The ground this time would be that 'nothing could perish into nothing'.

In the following part of fragment 2 Melissus moves on from temporal to spatial infinity. (This clear division has been widely missed by scholars who have supposed that the new argument must start at the beginning of fragment 2.): 'And it has no [spatial] beginning or end, but is infinite. For if it had come to be it would have a [spatial] beginning (for it would have begun the process of coming-to-be at some time) and end (for it would have ended the process of coming-to-be at some time). But since it neither began nor ended [the process], and always was and always will be, it has no [spatial] beginning or end'.

The interpretation of this has been much debated. Critics from Aristotle on have detected the fallacious inference 'If *p*, *q*; but not-*p*; therefore not-*q*'. To see why this is unfair, it is crucial to appreciate that, where Parmenides' arguments had evidently addressed an audience accustomed to the concept of a finite universe (see PARMENIDES §3), Melissus assumes the opposite – that the universe will be infinite unless it can be shown to be otherwise. This is yet another sign of his audience's background in Ionian physics, where the infinity of the universe, prefigured as early as Anaximander, was by Melissus' day enshrined in Anaxagoras' cosmology and on its way to becoming central to atomism (see ANAXAGORAS §2; ATOMISM, ANCIENT.

Melissus' question is: what could have set bounds on that-which-is? If nothing, then it is infinite. Only one thing could have made it finite, and that is a process of generation. Since any generative process would have to be temporally bounded, it could only have produced a spatially finite being. You cannot *create* an infinitely large entity, any more than you can build an infinitely long road, given only that any such process must start at some time (and hence somewhere) and stop at some time (and hence somewhere). Since, therefore, it has already been demonstrated that that-which-is never came to be, there is nothing to limit it spatially, and it becomes infinite by default.

Having demonstrated first its temporal and then its spatial infinity, Melissus adds how the latter is both inferentially dependent on and parallel to the former: 'For what is not *all* would not be able to be *always*' (end of fr. 2). 'But just as it is always, so too it must also always be infinite in magnitude' (fr. 3). 'Nothing is either omnitemporal or infinite if it has a [spatial?] beginning and end' (fr. 4).

The first sentence is particularly obscure. Melissus is perhaps drawing once again on a common assumption of Ionian material monism, that only the underlying stuff of the universe, taken as a whole, is everlasting, while the individual portions of it which constitute animals etc. (*if* there are any, Melissus would add) are temporary. Therefore the entity which Melissus calls everlasting must be the whole of what there is. This, if not a sufficient condition of its being infinite, he clearly regards as a necessary condition.

4 Changeless unity

That-which-is is called 'the One' by Melissus, a new emphasis on unity only weakly prefigured in Parmenides. In fragment 6 Melissus formally infers its unity from its spatial infinity: 'For if there were two they would not be able to be infinite, but would have boundaries in relation to each other'. Oneness here appears to mean uniqueness, and unfortunately it is hard to find any reading of the preceding arguments for its infinity which does not already assume that there is just one of it. A further objection made by the Peripatetic Eudemus, that the inference depends on its being not merely infinite but infinite in all directions, is less worrying, since the argument for its infinity does indeed imply the latter.

The proof of the next attribute, 'alike', that is, homogeneous, survives only in a paraphrase: 'Being one, it is alike everywhere [or 'in every way']. For if it were unlike, there would be a plurality, and no longer one but many' (*On Melissus, Xenophanes and Gorgias* 974a12–14). Its homogeneity thus follows from its oneness. But whether the preceding arguments have shown it to be 'one' in the required sense (= 'partless' rather than 'unique'?) is debatable.

After a brief summary of the results so far (fr. 7.1), there follows a generic argument against change: 'And it could neither lose anything nor become larger nor be rearranged, nor does it suffer pain or grief. For if any of these happened to it, it would no longer be one. For if it changes, it is necessary that that-which-is is not alike, but that what previously was perishes while that-which-is-not comes to be. So if it were to become changed by a single hair in ten thousand years, it will all perish in the whole of time'.

Formally, this is meant to be an inference from the immediately preceding attribute 'alike', in conformity to Melissus' standard inference pattern (see §2). But this time the likeness has to be invariance over time, not space, and that has not been specifically defended. (The defence might be that variation over time would imply a plurality of temporal parts, bordering on each other and therefore failing to be omnitemporal.) We should perhaps think of the likeness–changelessness inference as dictated by formal considerations, and give primary weight to the more interesting final sentence. This implies a version of the Principle of Plenitude: given infinite time all possibilities are realized. *Any* piecemeal perishing, however nugatory, makes overall perishing a possibility, and therefore a certainty over an infinite timespan – contrary to the earlier demonstration of everlastingness.

Following the generic rejection of change, Melissus adds four arguments against four species of change: reordering, pain, grief and motion (frs 7.3–10). The first three largely reapply the generic objections, but with the added consideration that pain and grief, being weaknesses, are incompatible with everlastingness. Melissus' concern to deny human forms of suffering to his One has caused surprise. But it must be borne in mind that some Ionian thinkers had already endowed the unitary underlying substance with the characteristics of divinity (see ANAXIMANDER §2; ANAXIMENES §1). If, as suggested, Melissus is working within and correcting that tradition, a later report that he equated his One with God may be well founded.

The refutation of motion can be paraphrased as follows. Since void would be nothing, void clearly does not exist. Therefore that-which-is, lacking any admixture of void, cannot vary in density but is completely full. Therefore it cannot give way at any point. Therefore it cannot (internally) move (frs 7.7–10).

This rejection of void as 'nothing' is the nearest Melissus comes to accepting Parmenides' outlawing of not-being. But he also makes an important advance on Parmenides in rendering explicit the dependence of motion on void.

Two further inferences are recorded. Being motionless, it is indivisible, since division involves motion (fr. 10). And 'Being one, it must not have [a?] body. If it had bulk, it would have parts and no longer be one' (fr. 9). The latter is especially puzzling, since the One's incorporeality would seem to undermine the argument for its immobility on the grounds of 'fullness' (that is, solidity). It is likelier that Melissus would be denying that it has *a* body, one with organic parts, by way of objection to anthropomorphic conceptions of divinity. But it is doubtful whether the argument, at least as reported, can support this interpretation.

5 Attack on the senses

In fragment 8, apparently from a separate section of his book, Melissus follows the example set by Parmenides in turning his ontological conclusions against the senses. Since sense perception reports constant change, both between distinct stuffs and between pairs of opposite properties, it cannot be trusted. These many items, if real, would have to obey Melissus' strictures and be altogether changeless, each of them staying exactly as it seemed when first encountered. In short: 'If there were many things, they ought to be such as I say the One is'.

6 Influence

This last remark is often conjectured to have inspired early atomism, whose exponents LEUCIPPUS and DEMOCRITUS (§2) did indeed populate the universe with an infinite plurality of atoms, each internally changeless like a Melissan One. Likewise Melissus' insistence that void is a necessary condition of motion (see §4) may be seen as having helped prompt the atomists' rehabilitation of void.

However, the chronological relation of Leucippus to Melissus remains undetermined. The void–motion connection could as well be one that Melissus learnt from Leucippus as vice versa; and the atomists' introduction of an Eleatic plurality may have needed no impetus from Melissus, just their rehabilitation of Parmenidean not-being in the guise of void, which already implied the separation of Parmenidean being into a plurality of discrete parts. The seductive hypothesis of Melissan influence on the atomists must then remain unproven. Stronger evidence of his public recognition as a philosophical writer in his own day is the fact that his book *On Nature or On That-Which-Is* was evidently a primary target for Gorgias in his *On That-Which-Is-Not or On Nature*, a parody of Eleatic philosophy.

In subsequent generations Melissus never inspired the kind of reverence, or even respect, that Parmenides was accorded. But his generally clear formulations of Eleatic positions are much more widely reflected in later writers, especially Aristotle, than the high-flown obscurities of Parmenides. He can thus be regarded, if not as the driving intellect of Eleatic thought, at least as its leading public voice.

See also: MONISM

References and further reading

Barnes, J. (1979) *The Presocratic Philosophers*, London: Routledge & Kegan Paul. (Chapters 10, 11 and 14 include a subtle if sometimes over-generous appraisal of Melissus.)

—— (1987) *Early Greek Philosophy*, Harmondsworth: Penguin. (Chapter 10 is a translation of Melissus' fragments complete with the contexts in which they are preserved.)

Guthrie, W.K.C. (1962–78) *A History of Greek Philosophy*, Cambridge: Cambridge University Press, 6 vols. (Includes the most detailed and comprehensive English-language history of early

Greek thought; the treatment of Melissus in volume 2 pages 101–18 is very lucid.)

Anon. (date unknown) *On Melissus, Xenophones and Gorgias*, trans. W.S. Hett, in *Aristotle, Minor works*, Loeb Classical Library, Cambridge, MA: Harvard University Press and London: Heinemann, 1936. (Contains a summary of Melissus' argument.)

Kirk, G.S., Raven, J.E. and Schofield, M. (1983) *The Presocratic Philosophers*, Cambridge: Cambridge University Press, 2nd edn. (A valuable survey of Presocratic philosophy, including texts and translations; contains the best account of Melissus available in English.)

Melissus (mid or late 5th century BC) Fragments, in H. Diels and W. Kranz (eds) *Die Fragmente der Vorsokratiker* (Fragments of the Presocratics), Berlin: Weidemann, 6th edn, 1952, vol. 1, 258–76. (The standard collection of the ancient sources; includes Greek text of the fragments with translations in German.)

Reale, G. (1970) *Melisso. Testimonianze e frammenti*, Florence: La Nuova Italia. (The fullest and best guide to the ancient evidence and modern scholarship on Melissus.)

Stokes, M.C. (1971) *One and Many in Presocratic Philosophy*, Washington, DC: Center for Hellenic Studies. (Places Melissus' central theme in its historical context.)

DAVID SEDLEY

MEMORY

Memory is central to every way in which we deal with things. One might subsume memory under the category of intellect, since it is our capacity to retain what we sense, enjoy and suffer, and thus to become knowing in our perception and other activities. As intelligent retention, memory cannot be distinguished from our acquisition of skills, habits and customs – our capabilities both for prudence and for deliberate risk. As retention, memory is a vital condition of the formation of language.

Amnesia illustrates dramatically the difference between memory as retention of language and skills, and memory as the power to recollect and to recognize specific things. In amnesia we lose, not our general power of retention, but recall of facts – the prior events of our life, and our power to recognize people and places. Amnesiacs recognize kinds of things. They know it is a wristwatch they are wearing, while unable to recognize it as their own.

This recall of events and facts which enables us to recognize things as our own, is more than just the ability to give correctly an account of them. One might accurately describe some part of one's past inadvertently, or after hypnosis, or by relying on incidental information. Thus, present research on memory both as retention and as recall of specific episodes, attempts to characterize the connection which persists between experience and recall. Neurological or computer models of connectivity owe something to traditional notions of a memory trace, but emphasize also the re-tracing of original memories by later experience and by intervening episodes of recall.

1 **History of the interest in memory**
2 **Contemporary work: retention, imagery and feeling**
3 **Contemporary work: causal connections and traces**
4 **Contemporary work: challenges to fixed ideas of present and past**

1 History of the interest in memory

It is striking that in two standard compendia of Chinese and of Indian philosophy, there are no entries under memory, remembering, reminiscence or recall. Naturally, there are words used in those cultures which roughly match terms in European languages – any human being will speak of what they did at some time earlier; children begin to speak spontaneously of what they did the day before, and remark with delight or distress at things they have seen earlier. But memory as a philosophical preoccupation is specific to certain cultural periods; memory as our powers of retention is so central to intelligent activity as to be subsumed under intellect.

Within Western philosophy itself, there is no mention of memory in the pre-Socratic fragments. It seems that so long as the poetic history of Homer held sway, memory was not discussed by him or the philosophers. This was not for want of interest in the events of earlier times. Homer aptly and vividly evokes their reality. Then in Plato's Socratic dialogues, while Homeric poetry is attacked as endangering an interest in truth, concern with the past is displaced by a search into memory itself, and Plato's dialogues – his own artful contrivances – are presented as if recollections. Within this new myth of a historical anti-poetic Socrates we learn the philosophical values of truth as against poetry, and of strict recollection against mere fancy about the past.

Plato's Socrates argued initially that all knowledge is recollection. He denied that sensory experience (in the present) produces knowledge, and conjectured that recollection revived knowledge acquired in a life before birth (see PLATO §11). Thus not only the

Homeric tradition of finding significance in human affairs in a (partly legendary) past is rejected, but also the role of women, those responsible for the child gaining its foundational knowledge, is elided.

In Plato's later *Theaetetus* we find the image of memory as an imprint left in the soul by earlier experience, a trace of what has occurred. In place of Plato's allegory of knowledge as recollection of a state in which knowledge was gained without the impurities of sensory experience we find this more scientific speculation about possible mechanisms of memory, an idea taken up by his student and successor, Aristotle. About eight centuries later these connected concepts of memory and of the past were brought into crisis by the north African Augustine. The present hour consists not only of the present minute, but of past minutes and the minutes to come. In turn, the present minute consists not only of its present second, but of its past seconds and the seconds to come. Thus, successively, the present as an extended period disappears. It remains only as an extensionless cut between the periods of past and future. The picture of present memory as defining the reality of the past is erased (see AUGUSTINE §§5, 7).

In the seventeenth century Descartes excepted memory from his radical questioning of the senses, while his notion of instantaneous reasoning was to avoid the reliance of reason on memory in any case. That all understanding of the past rested on personal memory remained unquestioned by Locke and Hume, and yet all arguments for the validity of memory assumed what they tried to prove. While Locke took common sense as a sufficient reply, Hume drew radically sceptical conclusions. Kant tried to show that the forms of knowledge cast into doubt by Hume were conditions of any coherent experience. Memory, as retaining an awareness of what something is like over some finite period of time, for instance, is such a condition of intelligible experience.

This emphasis on the mind's contribution to the order of things led, however, to an idealism in which the mind knows, not the world itself, but its own forms of representation. Thus the sceptical empiricist tradition set in motion by Descartes, while shaken, was not overturned. The sceptical tradition was empiricist in locating the sources of knowledge within the elements of experience. The emphasis on this experience made it seem that experience itself rather than what we experienced was the primary object of knowledge. Towards the end of the nineteenth century Husserl, inspired by Frege, Brentano and Meinong, created a comprehensive alternative to empiricism – a phenomenology of experience as revealing, not itself but its objects. This phenomenology attempted an unprejudiced study of experience, including memory,

as ways in which we grasp the world itself (see PHENOMENOLOGY, EPISTEMIC ISSUES IN).

Husserl's enquiries led him finally to think of the human body itself, acting as part of a socially significant world, as the centre of conscious experience. Remembering is one of the activities by which we hold bodily sway in the world. This approach was developed by Heidegger, Sartre and Merleau-Ponty. Alternatives to mind-centred empiricism were also developed during much the same period within analytical philosophy by Wittgenstein, Ryle and J.L. Austin.

2 Contemporary work: retention, imagery and feeling

Retention and recollection. Those who suffer from amnesia, knowing neither who they are, nor any event of their previous lives, retain most of their know-how intact. An amnesiac victim might join in a philosophical discussion, only learning from the impression made on others that they must have practised philosophy during that lost section of their lives. No one is surprised that an amnesiac can speak their mother tongue, nor that they can walk, sing and bargain. Thus, memory as retention of skills is different from the recollection of events, neighbourhoods, smells and sounds.

Imagery. As practised by Wittgenstein, Ryle and J.L. Austin, philosophy broke away from an entrancement with memory as a present image within which one must discern pastness and valid indications of the past. Much of what we call remembering has little to do with the possession of imagery. And, though some events come back to us in flashes of imagery, more is required before one remembers anything coherently. On the other hand, aware of little but the buzz of our conversation we may be recalling things with great accuracy. Similarly, depending on no prior image of the tune, one may hum a melody heard at a concert the previous evening. The recall may leave us with images; images of the past need not have provided the recall. Unable to remember someone's expression, we might mimic it. A flash of an image *may* facilitate that mimesis but, equally, the effort of producing the facial expression may be what lets loose our imagery. Thus images, sometimes central to remembering, may be more product than cause of recall (see IMAGERY).

Feelings. Though displaced from the centre of our picture of memory, imagery remains strongly associated with our elemental feelings about this power to recall. Perhaps this is because of the importance to us of certain intimate forms of remembering, particularly reminiscing and reliving, which vitally involve either imagery or emotion. True, reliving the past in animated conversation may involve little imagery of it. Yet, in the absence of specific imagery, our feelings – some shadow or reanimation of how we felt at the time, are essential to our reliving the past rather than simply reporting it from memory. These feelings we have in reliving prior experiences themselves have something of the quality of images. So, while memory does not consist in a memory image, the existence of a complex interplay of image and affect in the processes of recall is important to the cluster of ideas brought together under memory.

The dead past. To undergo an experience of recall is to be subject to the return of the past – only a metaphor, yet irreplaceable in a philosophy of memory. (In French, the principal verbs of recall are *se souvenir* – to bring oneself under (the past), and *se rappeller* – to call (the past) back to oneself.) Yet, remembering as bringing back what happened, or as reliving the past, encounters an impasse – accounts of memory are haunted by the notion of the past as dead, as if requiring memory's miracle of resurrection. The desire to remember thus encounters the limits met by mourning – itself a principal paradigm and emblem for memory in general. As memory would revive the events known to be past, in mourning the impulse is to address, as if to recall, the one known to have died.

3 Contemporary work: causal connections and traces

The initial conceptual analysis of the language of memory concentrated on the everyday contexts in which we learn and use our language of memory, and centred on remembering as successful present performance. But the picture which emerged of remembering as simply getting it right about our own past is unsatisfactory. After all, we may describe events from early childhood, not from memory of them, but from having been told by others. Different aspects of our past, in contrast, may come to mind from our own recall. No one else might have been in a position to tell us of certain details which subsequent evidence corroborates. Hence, to remember something is not simply to represent it correctly later on. Nor can memory be defined by the idea of (Hume's) lively belief about one's past. Sometimes we are recalling something when engaged in what we think of as pure imagination. We might intend to write a fictional story, and others may point out that it matches, incident for incident, some episode of which, hitherto, no one had informed us.

Remembering cannot be defined, either, as the representation of one's past without the need for prompting. After all, quite without assistance, we might merely invent something which, coincidentally, did happen. Conversely, we may not remember something and then, upon being prompted, remember the event for ourselves. A reference to some connection between the past event and the present recall seems to be needed – someone suffering amnesia, but hypnotized to recount a traffic accident which, coincidentally, did happen to them is not thereby remembering it. If they now recount something, not in any way because it happened to them, but simply because of the hypnotist's suggestion, they are remembering only what the hypnotist told them.

This idea of a causal connection between the event and its subsequent recall involves its own difficulties, however. The hypnotist might think of the story only because they recall hearing about the accident from the subject before the subject suffered amnesia. So the subject's original experience of the accident plays a crucial causal role in the subject's now coming to recount the event. The causal connection requires more exact definition. The subject's original experience is causally relevant only for the hypnotist's suggesting the story to them subsequently. Assuming that the hypnosis does not actually revive the memory of the accident, it is causally irrelevant to the subject's accepting the story upon its being suggested to them by the hypnotist.

Alas, complication follows complication. It is easy to imagine that the trauma of the accident might have made the victim more highly suggestible to hypnotists' stories about accidents. So the subject's having been in the accident they subsequently describe might still be relevant to their acceptance of the hypnotist's suggestion, and not only relevant to the suggestion being made to them. It seems one must reinvoke the ancient idea of a memory trace which encodes the information the person gains from an experience. Only where there is an activation of such a trace is there the highly specific causal connection required for true remembering. Such an idea appeals both to common sense and to some contemporary scientific theories of how both general information and specific events might be stored – cortically, and also as conditioned reflexes, making possible muscle memory, as musicians and sports professionals speak of it.

This idea of memory is not universally accepted. Not enough is known about the physiological processes required for the memory of specific events, to say that we can insist upon the presence of such a strict trace. In reply, it will be insisted that while memory may be highly dispersed in alternative neural networks rather than encoded in specific brain cells, it is hard to imagine any alternative to a neural, or neuro-muscular process which would preserve the highly specific information about individual events which makes it possible for us to recall them with all the sensual and emotive feel which they commonly carry.

It has also been objected to such a causal analysis of remembering that memory is a power or disposition to recount things about one's past. Is it not absurd to suggest that some past event should continuously cause the continuation of such a power of recall? Is this not like saying that the capacity of one's living room curtains to keep their colour, day in, day out, is continually held in place by their originally having been dyed? In reply, a causal theorist will point out that it is not the power of recall which is continually upheld by an event in the past. What is required, more simply, is that the trace established by the event remembered should encode all the information genuinely recalled, and that if prompting is necessary (as normally it is), this prompting should activate that encoding trace.

4 Contemporary work: challenges to fixed ideas of present and past

These approaches, both through everyday concepts and by speculative scientific hypothesis, take for granted memory as reviving an already given past. The phenomenology of Sartre and Merleau-Ponty, too, takes the past as real in itself, not to be reduced in Augustinian fashion to the process of recollection. Nevertheless, their work emphasizes how much what we call past and present owe each other. The past does not so innocently create memories which then we deem to be valid. Perhaps half-consciously, we make nothing of aspects of our past in order to make something of other aspects. We might create a favourable past or, alternatively, one which embodies a harsh vision of our lives. What we remember is not entirely accidental. How we remember and what we recall partially constitutes our present and, conversely, what we countenance as part of our present bears on what we are prepared to recall.

The themes of memory are recalled in a classical enigma. When the present was present, it could not be remembered. Now it is past, its presence is only in recall. This presence in recall cannot be the presence it had when first it occurred. It is in this sense that remembering is, in Derrida's phrase, the raising up of 'a past that was never present'.

See also: MEMORY, EPISTEMOLOGY OF

References and further reading

Aristotle (384–322 BC) *On Memory*, in J. Barnes (ed.) *The Complete Works of Aristotle*, Princeton, NJ: Princeton University Press, 1984, 2 vols. (Thorough description of elementary forms of memory, and the development of the idea of a memory trace.)

Augustine (AD 400) *Confessions*, trans. H. Chadwick, Oxford: Oxford University Press, 1991, Book 10. (Vivid portrayal of puzzles about time and recollection, in the confessional mode. Clearly written, easy-to-medium difficulty.)

Derrida, J. (1986) *Memoires for Paul de Man*, New York: Columbia, lectures 1 and 2. (Lectures delivered on the death of Paul de Man. Evocative and moving study of images and concepts of memory, and the relation of mourning to memory.)

Deutscher, M. (1989) 'Remembering "Remembering"', in J. Heil (ed.) *Cause, Mind and Reality*, Dordrecht: Kluwer. (Analyses notions of representation, widens the range of forms of memory, contextualizes the idea of a memory trace.)

Hume, D. (1739) *A Treatise on Human Nature*, any edition, Part III, particularly sections 5 and 6, and Part IV. (Classic statement of the image theory of memory, and of attendant sceptical problems. Very clear, medium difficulty.)

Husserl, E. (1954) *Crisis of European Sciences and Transcendental Phenomenology*, trans. D. Carr, Evanston, IL: Northwestern University Press, 1970, Part II, sections 24–5 and Part III, sections 51–4. (Analyses the pitfalls in Hume's scepticism, the continuity of experience described in terms of detachment (transcendence) and of bodily involvement (sedimentation). Complex, difficult, rewarding.)

Krell, D. (1990) *Of Memory, Reminiscence and Writing*, Bloomington, IN: Indiana University Press. (Close, brilliant study of literary phenomenological, deconstructive and scientific sources of ideas of memory. Valuable bibliography.)

Locke, J. (1690) *Essay on Human Understanding*, Bk II, chs 10, 14, 27. (Ideas of memory as an idea or image, as a storehouse, as a condition for personal identity. Clear and thoughtful. Medium difficulty.)

Martin, C. and Deutscher, M. (1966) '"Remembering"', *Philosophical Review* LXXV 2: 161–96. (Describes wide variety of forms of memory, influential in re-establishing the idea of memory as including an information carrying trace, causally linking past with present.)

Merleau-Ponty, M. (1945) *Phenomenology of Perception*, trans. C. Smith, Routledge & Kegan Paul, 1962, Part I, section 6, Part III, section 2. (The body rather than the mind as centre of experience; analyses metaphors of the flow of time, and the intimate involvement of the present in describing the past. Medium difficulty, evocative, sometimes poetic prose.)

Plato (c.428–348 BC) *Phaedo*, trans. D. Gallop, Oxford

and New York: Oxford University Press, 1993. (The theory of knowledge as recollection. Easy to medium difficulty.)

* —— (*c.*428–348 BC) *Theaetetus*, trans. M.J. Levett, revised M. Burnyeat, Indianapolis, IN: Hackett Publishing Company, 1990. (Explanation and criticism of the idea of memory as a trace. Medium to difficult.)

Ryle, G. (1949) *The Concept of Mind*, London: Hutchinson, chs 6 and 8. (Explains the elusive character of the self, and of the present in terms of token reflexive expressions. Describes similarities between imagination and memory, and attacks the image theory of memory. Easy to medium difficulty.)

Squires, R. (1969) 'Memory Unchained', *Philosophical Review* LXXVIII: 178-96. (Witty attack on the idea of memory as involving a causal connection or trace.)

MAX DEUTSCHER

MEMORY, EPISTEMOLOGY OF

Memory appears to preserve knowledge, but there are epistemic questions about how this could be. Memory is fallible, and empirical research has identified various ways in which people systematically misremember. Even wholesale error seems possible: Russell (1927) proposed that it is logically possible for the world to have sprung into existence five minutes ago, complete with spurious ostensible memories of earlier times. In light of such possibilities, some sceptics argue that memory cannot yield knowledge.

Assuming that memory provides knowledge, there are serious epistemic issues about how it does this. For instance, does some introspectible quality of remembering provide distinctive evidence for what is remembered, or is it some other feature of memory that secures the epistemic justification needed for knowledge? How readily recollectible must a proposition be in order for it to be known while it is not being recalled? Does a full retention in memory of a previous basis for knowing something assure continuing knowledge of it? Does forgetting an original basis for knowing without replacing it imply a loss of knowledge?

1 **Memory and traditional epistemic issues**
2 **An epistemic problem specially involving memory retention**
3 **An epistemic problem specially involving memory loss**

1 Memory and traditional epistemic issues

Epistemic controversies about matters specific to memory are comparatively rare. There are two apparent reasons for this. One is that remembering is a source of reasons for belief with approximately the same problems and prospects as sensory perception (see PERCEPTION, EPISTEMIC ISSUES IN). The two processes share the salient features of being conscious, cognitive episodes that prompt new beliefs without apparent inference. Of the two, perception seems the more promising source of justification. This is principally because conscious sensory characteristics are clearly involved in ordinary sensory perception. They provide something that might confer justification on some resulting perceptual beliefs, though it is problematic how sensory characteristics could justify beliefs. In contrast to the perceptual case, no conscious qualities are clearly distinctive of recollective events. There may be less of a basis on which to explain how memory can furnish justification and knowledge. Thus, the outcome of investigations of the epistemic properties of perception is plausibly thought to carry over to the case of memory, with memory perhaps turning out to have weaker versions of the same epistemic capacities.

A second reason for the relative paucity of epistemic work on memory may be the prevalence in epistemology of disputes about scepticism. In virtually all sceptical controversies, remembering plays at most a derivative epistemic role. Memory on its own serves as a means of knowledge preservation, not knowledge acquisition. The fundamental sceptical issues concern whether justified belief or knowledge can be had in the first place. For instance, if some sceptical argument shows that we can have neither perceptual knowledge nor justified perceptual belief, then no important epistemic question about recalling perceptual beliefs seems to remain. If on the other hand scepticism about some such category of knowledge is refuted, then memory offers only the prospect of retention of knowledge in that category. This is not to say that knowledge retention is unimportant. Retaining nothing, we could know only the facts that we could learn entirely in a moment. But retention seems less epistemically fundamental than do capacities that arguably enable us to acquire new knowledge.

Some sceptical challenges have specifically addressed memory knowledge. The sceptical arguments have generally charged that something about the vulnerability of memory to error shows it not to be a source of reasons sufficiently strong to provide knowledge. But again, memory is not unique in the relevant epistemic respects. Assessments of analogous sceptical arguments concerning sensory perception carry over to this sort of attack on memory knowledge. The familiar mechanisms of deception such as ordinary sorts of error, the evil demon of Descartes and the illusory stimulations of electrodes, are capable of producing as pervasive and deceptive a replication of veridical experiences in the case of sensory experiences as in the case of ostensible memories. Anti-sceptical responses typically deny that such a deception is genuinely possible, or that its possibility shows that we lack knowledge (see SCEPTICISM). These denials have the same merits whether the argument is aimed at knowledge by perception or knowledge by recollection. Although memory knowledge is one of the most important applications of sceptical reasoning, memory does not raise any distinctive basic sceptical issues.

2 An epistemic problem specially involving memory retention

One epistemic problem of considerable interest does essentially involve the capacity of memory to preserve knowledge. Suppose that, at noon, Smith knows that Jones is smiling. Smith has reasons that are sufficient for him to know this, including clearly seeing Jones smile. At dusk Smith acquires compelling new evidence to the effect that Jones did not smile at noon, receiving sworn testimony from Robertson, a universally acknowledged pillar of integrity. In an honest error, Robertson sincerely and convincingly testifies that Jones has a double who stood in for Jones at noon. It seems plain that as a result of hearing this testimony Smith no longer knows that Jones smiled at noon. This can be puzzling. For one thing, at dusk Smith might perfectly recall his noontime reasons for believing that Jones smiled at noon. If those reasons were adequate for Smith to know this fact at noon, how can exactly the same reasons be inadequate later?

Also puzzling is the fact that at dusk Smith seems to possess a cogent argument for regarding Robinson's testimony as misleading. Prior to hearing the testimony, Smith unproblematically remembers and continues to know that Jones smiled at noon. This appears to enable Smith to know by inference that any evidence against Jones having smiled at noon is evidence against a truth, and hence misleading. But even if this inference is fresh in Smith's mind when he hears Robinson's testimony, at that point Smith would be unreasonable to regard Robertson's testimony as misleading. Yet why would this attitude be unreasonable, given the apparent cogency of Smith's argument for it?

Credible answers to these questions will not deny that we ever fully remember our previous reasons for holding some belief. A more promising approach is suggested by a careful look at the structure of epistemic support for a belief. We should observe that conspicuous positive evidence for a proposition cannot by itself justify believing the proposition. Epistemic justification is more holistic than that. In particular, at noon Smith's justified belief that Jones was then smiling was supported, not merely by Smith's seeing Jones smile, but also by perceptual indications and background information that argued that the situation was normal. These indications importantly include the lack of any clue of a deception. It is only this sort of comprehensive body of relevant considerations that can epistemically justify a belief. Anything less may fail to take account of pertinent information (see KNOWLEDGE, DEFEASIBILITY THEORY OF).

This structural feature of justification makes it clear that once Smith has new relevant evidence, even a perfect recollection of his previous evidence about Jones at noon does not guarantee that the belief that Jones smiled at noon continues to be justified. At dusk Smith becomes aware of a strong indication that he was deceived at noon. As a result, the new totality of his evidence does not justify the belief that Jones smiled at noon. Such changes in evidence show why retaining a previous basis for knowing does not entail continuing to know.

Similar considerations explain why Smith cannot reasonably regard Robinson's testimony as misleading once he hears it. Smith possesses a cogent argument that such evidence is misleading only when his evidence on balance supports that conclusion. Otherwise his evidence casts doubt on the conjunction of the argument's premises. Until Smith hears Robinson's testimony, what Smith retains from noon supports without challenge an argument for the conclusion that any evidence against Jones having smiled at noon is misleading. Once Smith hears Robinson's testimony however, any such argument is undercut. Smith's evidence may still include all that previously supported the conclusion. But now his evidence also includes his hearing of testimony which spoils that support. The premise asserting that Jones did smile at noon is essential to his justifiably inferring that contrary evidence is misleading. When Smith has heard the testimony, this premise ceases to be supported by the entirety of his pertinent considerations. Smith then has no cogent argument for regarding the testimony as misleading.

Epistemic justification for a belief at a time is constituted only by the totality of relevant considerations possessed at the time. Such a totality can mislead by a deceptive expansion. The justification needed for knowledge thus is holistic and transitory. These properties of justification serve to dispel the mystery of how someone might clearly remember his whole basis for knowing a proposition and for accurately classifying all evidence against it as misleading, and yet be straightaway misled by just such evidence and no longer know the proposition to be true.

3 An epistemic problem specially involving memory loss

Someone might come to know the date of the Battle of Waterloo by reading it in a clearly reliable text. Years later the person may continue to believe that the date is 1815, while entirely forgetting the source of this belief and without receiving any subsequent corroboration of that date. Does thus forgetting imply that the knowledge is lost? If so, then it seems that we cease to know most of what we recall, however securely we first came to believe it, since it is relatively rare for us to retain our original justification for beliefs not recently acquired. Yet if we do continue to know beliefs of forgotten justifying origins, then it seems that we must somehow manage to know them while lacking justification for them. Each of these alternatives is implausible.

An attractive response to this problem occupies a middle ground. It holds that some retained beliefs whose original justification has been forgotten and which are subject to no new doubts are still known, others not. The difference is made by the facts about how currently reasonable to the person is the proposition that continues to be believed. Retention of the original evidence is not required if one has indications that a reliable memory is operative in sustaining the belief. For instance, where the belief is accompanied by an impression of having some reputable source or other for it, and an impression of having often confirmed and seldom disconfirmed the beliefs that thus seem trustworthy, those impressions help to constitute a current justification for the belief. Where someone has nothing more on behalf of a belief than a sense that the proposition was assertively conveyed at some point, perhaps in fiction or even in a dream, the proposition will not be currently believed reasonably enough to be known.

This is an elaboration and application of the appealing view that a reliable memory is what preserves knowledge. The view tells us that we do not continue to know merely by having a recollective impression of a factual proposition that we once knew and to which we now have no substantial objection. Only those of our recollections that are evidently trustworthy can sustain our knowledge of such propositions.

See also: INNATE KNOWLEDGE; KNOWLEDGE, TACIT; MEMORY; REASONS FOR BELIEF; SCEPTICISM

References and further reading

Harman, G. (1986) *Change in View*, Cambridge, MA: MIT Press. (Chapter 4 presents a full exposition and suggests a different solution to the problem discussed in §3 above.)

Hume, D. (1739) *A Treatise of Human Nature*, ed. D.G.C. Macnabb, London: Collins, 1970. (Classic philosophical approach to the nature of memory is advocated in Book I.)

Ginet, C. (1980) 'Knowing less by knowing more', *Midwest Studies in Philosophy* 5: 51–60. (Presents a full exposition and suggests a different solution to the problem discussed in §2 above.)

Goldman, A. (1986) *Epistemology and Cognition*, Cambridge, MA: Harvard University Press. (Chapter 10 discusses the epistemic significance of some empirical work on the fallibility of memory.)

* Russell, B. (1927) *An Outline of Philosophy*, London: Allen & Unwin. (Source of the sceptical hypothesis that the world began five minutes ago, complete with ostensible memories.)

EARL CONEE

MENCIUS (4th century BC)

Mencius (Mengzi) was a Chinese Confucian philosopher, best known for his claim that human nature is good. He is probably the single most influential philosopher in the Chinese tradition, in that an interpretation of his thought became the basis of the civil service examinations in China in the fourteenth century and remained so for almost 600 years. The primary source for his thought is the collection of his sayings, debates and discussions known as the Mengzi.

Mencius (known in Chinese as Mengzi (Master Meng) or by his full name, Meng Ke) was born early in the fourth century BC in the state of Zou, now part of Shandong Province. Towards the end of that century he travelled from state to state, seeking a ruler who would put his philosophy into practice, and briefly served as a minister in the state of Qi. The collection of his sayings, debates and discussions is known simply as the *Mengzi*. It was compiled either by Mencius himself or by his disciples soon after his death.

Mencius saw his main intellectual task as defending the doctrines of Confucius against those of the egoist Yang Zhu and the universalistic consequentialist Mozi. In order to do this, he developed a novel and detailed theory of human nature which went beyond anything Confucius had said.

Mencius' claim that human nature is good has been given different interpretations (see XING). He clearly thought that humans innately have active but incipient tendencies toward virtue, which he describes, using an agricultural metaphor, as sprouts. Each sprout corresponds to one of his four cardinal virtues, and each virtue has an emotion or attitude that is characteristic of it: benevolence is characterized by compassion, righteousness by shame and disdain, wisdom by approval and disapproval, and ritual propriety by either respect or deference. In a famous example, Mencius says that our sprout of benevolence manifests itself in a spontaneous feeling of 'alarm and compassion' when we 'suddenly' see a child about to fall into a well (*Mengzi* 2A6). This same virtue shows itself in one's compassion for a suffering animal, one's service to and love of one's parents and the disinterested concern of virtuous rulers for their subjects.

Righteousness is similarly complicated, manifesting itself in such things as a beggar refusing to accept a handout given with contempt, a wife and concubine being ashamed of their husband's humiliation of himself to obtain luxuries, a chariot driver being ashamed to cheat in a ritual hunt, a person refusing to accept contemptuous forms of address, disdaining to serve base rulers, and obeying and respecting one's elder brother. One passage (*Mengzi* 5A9) suggests that a wise person is a good judge of the character of others, recognizes what is base and avoids it, is a prudent and perceptive judge of policy and a good administrator. Another passage (4A27) describes wisdom as understanding and being committed to benevolence and righteousness. Mencius does not clearly distinguish the virtue of ritual propriety, although it seems to be related to righteousness.

Neo-Confucian philosophers (see NEO-CONFUCIAN PHILOSOPHY) regarded the four sprouts as fully developed virtues whose operation was impeded (in the uncultivated individual) by selfish desires. However, it is more likely that Mencius thought the sprouts were only incipient virtues, which must be cultivated so that they develop into full virtues (see SELF-CULTIVATION IN CHINESE PHILOSOPHY). That is, we must 'extend' the reactions of the sprouts from the situations in which we already have them to relevantly similar situations in which we should, but do not yet, have them. Mencius seems to advocate several methods for achieving extension, including

'concentration', which probably includes the reflective and joyful exercise of the sprouts. He also taught his students through the study of poetry and 'case studies' of the actions of sages.

Mencius presents what is recognizable as a virtue ethic, but one that is importantly different in terms of its conception of flourishing, its cardinal virtues and its theory of ethical cultivation from classic Western examples such as those of ARISTOTLE and Thomas AQUINAS (see VIRTUE ETHICS). Like other virtue ethicists, Mencius regards ethics as objective, but eschews decision procedures based upon either rules or the weighing of utility and stresses the context-sensitivity of virtuous responses. As a Confucian, Mencius holds that virtuous individuals will have compassion for all humans, but he also thinks we have special obligations to, and should have greater concern for, those tied to us by particular bonds, including kinship. Mencius is also typically Confucian in his emphasis upon learning from tradition, and in his belief that the virtues first manifest themselves in the family.

In terms of style, Mencius prefers to focus on the specific and the concrete. For example, Mencius explores virtues and their semblances, not through a Socratic search for definitions but through contrasting concrete examples (for examples, *Mengzi* 2A2; 7B37). Furthermore, what he says is geared to the understanding and needs of his interlocutors on particular occasions. So, for instance, he may be oversimplifying his view of self-cultivation for his audience in *Mengzi* 6B2. However, careful study of the *Mengzi* suggests that underlying his concrete comments on specific occasions is a deep and systematic ethical view.

See also: CONFUCIAN PHILOSOPHY, CHINESE; NEO-CONFUCIAN PHILOSOPHY; VIRTUES AND VICES

List of works

Mencius (*c.*300 BC) *Mengzi*, trans. D.C. Lau, *Mencius*, New York: Penguin Books, 1970; trans. J. Legge, *The Works of Mencius*, New York: Dover Publications, 1970. (Lau is a good contemporary translation, with helpful appendices. Legge is a reprint of the 1895 translation, including the Chinese text and explanatory notes.)

References and further reading

Graham, A.C. (1990) 'The Background of the Mencian Theory of Human Nature', in A.C. Graham, *Studies in Chinese Philosophy and Philosophical Literature*, Albany, NY: State University of

New York Press, 7–66. (Detailed philological study of some key terms in early Chinese thought.)

Ivanhoe, P.J. (1990) *Ethics in the Confucian Tradition: The Thought of Mencius and Wang Yang-ming*, Atlanta, GA: Scholars Press. (A good general introduction to the thought of Mencius, emphasizing his differences from his later interpreters.)

Lau, D.C. (1970) 'On Mencius' Use of the Method of Analogy in Argument', *Mencius*, New York: Penguin Books: 235–63. (Explains some of the more puzzling passages in Book 6 of the *Mengzi*.)

Nivison, D.S. (1996) 'Motivation and Moral Action in Mencius' and 'Two Roots or One?', in B.W. Van Norden (ed.) *The Ways of Confucianism*, La Salle, IL: Open Court, 91–119 and 133–48. (Analyses of *Mengzi* 1A7 and 3A5, respectively.)

Shun, K.L. (1991) 'Mencius and the Mind-Inherence of Morality: Mencius' Rejection of Kao Tzu's Maxim in *Meng Tzu* 2A:2', *Journal of Chinese Philosophy* 18 (4): 371–86. (A careful analytic study.)

Van Norden, B.W. (1996) 'What Should Western Philosophy Learn from Chinese Philosophy?', in P.J. Ivanhoe (ed.) *Chinese Language, Thought and Culture: Nivison and His Critics*, La Salle, IL: Open Court. (Presents an overview of the literature on early Confucianism.)

Yearley, L.H. (1990) *Mencius and Aquinas: Theories of Virtue and Conceptions of Courage*, Albany, NY: State University of New York Press. (An excellent comparative study of Mencian and Thomistic treatments of the virtues.)

BRYAN W. VAN NORDEN

MENDELSSOHN, MOSES (1729–86)

A Jewish disciple of Leibniz and Wolff, Mendelssohn strove throughout his life to uphold and strengthen their rationalist metaphysics while sustaining his ancestral religion. His most important philosophic task, as he saw it, was to refine and render more persuasive the philosophical proofs for the existence of God, providence and immortality. His major divergence from Leibniz was in stressing that 'the best of all possible worlds', which God had created, was in fact more hospitable to human beings than Leibniz had supposed. Towards the end of his life, the irrationalism of Jacobi and the critical philosophy of Kant shook Mendelssohn's faith in the demonstrability of the fundamental metaphysical precepts, but not his confidence in their truth. They would have to be sustained by 'common sense', he reasoned, until future philosophers succeeded in restoring metaphysics to its former glory. While accepting Wolff's teleological understanding of human nature and natural law, Mendelssohn placed far greater value on human freedom and outlined a political philosophy that protected liberty of conscience. His philosophic defence of his own religion stressed that Judaism is not a 'revealed religion' demanding acceptance of particular dogmas but a 'revealed legislation' requiring the performance of particular actions. The object of this divine and still valid legislation, he suggested, was often to counteract forces that might otherwise subvert the natural religion entrusted to us by reason. To resolve the tension between his own political liberalism and the Bible's endorsement of religious coercion, Mendelssohn argued that contemporary Judaism, at any rate, no longer acknowledges any person's authority to compel others to perform religious acts.

1 Metaphysics/natural theology
2 Moral and political philosophy
3 Philosophy of Judaism

1 Metaphysics/natural theology

Affectionately called 'the German Socrates' by European admirers, and hailed by some of his Jewish disciples as a modern Maimonides, Moses Mendelssohn (born Dessau, died Berlin), despite his hunchback, cut a towering figure in his generation. Emerging from the ghetto with a solid command of traditional Jewish learning and a wide knowledge of medieval Jewish philosophy, he independently learned ancient and modern European languages, literature and philosophy. In an astonishingly short time he became an important cultural critic and went on to produce notable contributions to German philosophy, especially in metaphysics, ethics and political theory. Unlike SPINOZA, the only prior Jewish thinker of modern times to have had a major impact on European thought, Mendelssohn retained his affiliation with Judaism. He actively promoted and fostered modernization within the Jewish community and spoke out forcefully and effectively in governmental and intellectual fora for the bestowal of equal civil rights on Jews. Challenged by adversaries and well-intentioned 'friends' to explain his seemingly unjustifiable loyalty to an outmoded religion, Mendelssohn wrote some of the seminal works of modern Jewish philosophy.

Mendelssohn made almost no claim to originality in metaphysics. He described himself as little more than an exponent of the teachings of the Leibniz/Wolffian school, perhaps lending a more felicitous or up-to-date expression to the affirmations of God's existence and providence and human immortality that had been propounded by LEIBNIZ and WOLFF and their disciples. Here and there, however, he admitted modestly that he was providing a new version of an old argument or even saying something that had not been said before.

Mendelssohn made his reputation and set out his basic metaphysical stance in his *Abhandlung über die Evidenz in metaphysischen Wissenschaften* (Treatise on Evidence in Metaphysical Knowledge), an essay that took first prize in a competition sponsored by the Royal Academy in Berlin in 1763; Immanuel Kant received an honourable mention. The Academy's question was whether 'the truths of metaphysics in general, and the first principles of natural theology and morality in particular' can be shown to be as securely established as those of mathematics. Mendelssohn answered that such principles 'are capable of the same certainty' but are by no means as easily grasped. After discussing the obstacles to such comprehension, he went on to offer cosmological and ontological proofs for the existence of God. He sought to give the ontological argument an 'easier turn' by reversing its usual course and arguing first for the impossibility of God's nonexistence and then against the notion that the most perfect being would enjoy a merely possible existence.

Following Leibniz, Mendelssohn argued in a number of writings that the combination of divine goodness and greatness known as providence brings into being 'the best of all possible worlds'. He was certainly aware of the abundance of evil and injustice in the world. But he found that the good outweighed the evil, and indeed that the quantity of evil was less than Leibniz himself had supposed. For Mendelssohn joined with other, later representatives of the *Aufklärung* in rejecting the Christian dogma, accepted by Leibniz, that most human beings are destined for eternal damnation. This idea, so much at odds with Leibniz's recognition that the perfection and happiness of rational creatures are critical in God's design, was, he wrote, a notion of which 'neither our reason nor our religion knows anything' (see PROVIDENCE; EVIL, PROBLEM OF).

What reason teaches about the afterlife is, according to Mendelssohn, altogether consolatory. This view emerges most clearly in what was probably his most famous work, a philosophical dialogue entitled *Phädon, oder über die Unsterblichkeit der Seele* (Phaedo, or on the Immortality of the Soul) (1767). Borrowing from Plato the title and the setting, in Socrates' jail cell, Mendelssohn used the condemned philosopher as the mouthpiece for an argument he had admittedly derived from his own recent prede-cessors, including such Aufklärer as the natural theologian Hermann Samuel Reimarus and the liberal Protestant theologian Johann Joachim Spalding. 'Is it consistent', Mendelssohn's Socrates asks, 'with the Supreme Wisdom to produce a world in order to make the happiness of the creatures inhabiting it arise from the contemplation of its wonders and a moment later deprive them of the capacity for contemplation and happiness?' Pursuing the idea of divine goodness to its logical conclusion, Mendelssohn reasoned that the afterlife must be the arena in which the world's injustices are rectified and *all* rational creatures continue to progress towards ever higher perfection and happiness.

Going beyond his rhetorical question and other arguments of similar provenance, Mendelssohn proudly offered what he saw as an original argument for immortality, a 'proof from the harmony of our duties and rights': An individual who believed that death marked the end of his existence would find that his natural right to preserve his own life at all costs would conflict at times with the state's demand that he be prepared to lay down his life for the common good. But such a conflict can have no objective warrant. For in the mind of God, 'all the duties and rights of a moral entity are in the most perfect harmony'. Since the state's right to call for the supreme sacrifice is irrefutable, it is evident, Mendelssohn concludes, that the human soul does not die with the body.

In time Mendelssohn himself came to see weaknesses at many points in the philosophical structure he had upheld. Confronted, toward the end of his life, by the irrationalism of F.H. Jacobi and by the new critical philosophy of Immanuel KANT, whom he called the 'all-crusher', he felt compelled to acknowledge the insufficiency of rationalistic metaphysics. In his fullest exposition of the philosophy he had set forth, *Morgenstunden, oder Vorlesungen über das Dasein Gottes* (Morning Hours, or Lectures on the Existence of God) (1785), he sorrowfully ceased to reaffirm its irrefutable truth.

Yet, whatever speculative reason might seem to teach, he now argued, common sense still sufficed to orient people and guide them along the path to the most important truths. Just what Mendelssohn meant by common sense has been a subject of much dispute, both among his contemporaries such as Thomas Wizenmann and Kant himself and among modern scholars. But, however he conceived of this faculty, it is clear that he expected our reliance on it to be temporary. For, in the 'cyclical course of things', providence would cause new thinkers to arise who would restore metaphysics to its former glory.

2 Moral and political philosophy

Following Wolff, Mendelssohn affirmed that the fundamental moral imperative is a natural law obliging all rational beings to promote their own perfection and that of others. Unlike Wolff, he did not elaborate all the ramifications of this natural law. But he clearly saw perfection in much the same terms as Wolff, as an unending process of physical, moral and intellectual development, leading naturally to the increase of human happiness.

In sharp contrast to Wolff, Mendelssohn regarded liberty as an indispensable precondition of the pursuit of moral and intellectual perfection. Only a free person, he argued, can achieve moral perfection. For virtue is the result of struggle, self-overcoming and sacrifice, and these must be freely chosen. Intellectual perfection, too, can be attained only by one who is free to err. So, in place of Wolff's tutelary state, Mendelssohn developed a contractarian polity that left individuals largely free to define their own goals. Insisting above all on the inalienable liberty of conscience, he decried any state attempt to impose specific religious behaviour or to discriminate against members of a minority faith. While Mendelssohn's liberalism clearly flowed from his commitment to liberty itself, it was no doubt also informed by his concern for the situation of his fellow Jews, whom he ardently wished to see relieved of a degraded political and social status.

3 Philosophy of Judaism

Mendelssohn faced fewer difficulties in reconciling his Leibniz-Wolffian views with his Judaism than his mentors or their disciples had confronted in reconciling their philosophical views with Christianity. Because he saw little conflict between philosophy and Judaism and because his own position as the first Jew to be accepted by the intellectuals in a fundamentally intolerant society was precarious, he initially refrained from explaining to the general public his continued adherence to his ancestral religion. But he was by no means oblivious to the challenges that Enlightenment scepticism posed to all believers in revealed religions. Nor was he immune to attack. In response to repeated demands from critics that he account for his irrational adherence to Judaism, he wrote his celebrated treatise *Jerusalem* (1783). Subtitled *Über religiöse Macht und Judentum* (On Religious Power and Judaism), *Jerusalem* responds to August Friedrich Cranz's charge that the religious coercion of recalcitrant Jews countenanced in Judaism is blatantly incompatible with Mendelssohn's own political liberalism. In responding to this charge, Mendelssohn proceeded beyond the call of his immediate duty and outlined a general philosophy of Judaism.

Viewed against the backdrop of medieval Jewish philosophy, Mendelssohn's account contains both familiar and unfamiliar elements. Following in the footsteps of Saadiah Gaon, Judah Halevi and Maimonides (and seemingly ignoring the criticisms of Spinoza and various sceptics) he maintained that God's revelation at Sinai was an amply attested historical fact (see SAADIAH GAON; HALEVI, JUDAH; MAIMONIDES, M.). What God disclosed to the people of Israel, Mendelssohn held, was not a 'revealed religion' commanding the acceptance of particular dogmas but a 'revealed legislation' requiring the performance of particular actions. The Israelites at Sinai had already acquired, by unaided reason, a knowledge of the universal religion of humankind. What they learned from revelation was a set of God-given duties. Noting the broad range of these duties and the manifold aspects of life encompassed by them, Mendelssohn reflected at length on the so-called 'ceremonial law', problematized at least since the earliest days of the Christian critique of Judaism. This body of obligations, he reasoned, seems to be intended to combat idolatrous tendencies by ordaining actions that perpetually bring to mind the fundamental truths of natural religion. Observance of these divinely ordained regulations allowed Jews to maintain their grasp of true religion and so to serve as a salutary example to the other peoples of the earth (see HALAKHAH).

In keeping with the tenets of traditional Judaism, Mendelssohn insisted that the Bible's revealed legislation remained in force perpetually, subject only to such modifications as the changes of time and circumstance rendered advisable. But he parted company with tradition in arguing that the Roman destruction of the Temple in Jerusalem had transformed Jewish law from a corpus of communally enforceable obligations into a code which only the individual Jew had the right to impose on himself or herself. This unprecedented claim parried the charge of illiberalism. Whether it represents a reluctant and merely tactical concession to liberalism, as some have argued, or whether it reflects Mendelssohn's true convictions, as is more commonly believed, it was clearly the only means that Mendelssohn could find to render modern Judaism fully compatible with political liberalism.

See also: ENLIGHTENMENT, JEWISH; JEWISH PHILOSOPHY IN THE EARLY 19TH CENTURY; HALEVI, JUDAH; LEIBNIZ, G.W.; SAADIAH GAON; WOLFF, C.

List of works

Mendelssohn, M. (1929–30) *Moses Mendelssohn Gesammelte Schriften Jubiläumsausgabe*, Berlin: Akademie-Verlag. (The authoritative edition of Mendelssohn's collected works.)
—— (1997) *Philosophical Writings*, trans. and ed. D. Dahlstrom, Cambridge: Cambridge University Press. (Collection of Mendelssohn's early philosophical writings, including those on metaphysics, ethics and aesthetics.)
—— (1755) *Philosophische Gespräche* (Philosophical Speeches), Berlin. (In this work, Mendelssohn declares himself a disciple of the school of Leibniz and takes sides with Spinoza.)
—— (1755) *Briefe über die Empfindungen* (Letters on Feeling), Berlin. (Contains a philosophy of the beautiful and forms a chief basis of all philosophical-aesthetic criticism in Germany.)
—— (1763) *Abhandlung über die Evidenz in metaphysischen Wissenschaften* (Treatise on Evidence in Metaphysical Knowledge), Berlin: Mande und Spener, 1786. (Essay comparing the demonstrability of metaphysical propositions with that of mathematical ones.)
—— (1767) *Phädon, oder über die Unsterblichkeit der Seele* (Phaedo, or on the Immortality of the Soul), Vienna: C.F. Schade, 1812. (His chief philosophical work, dealing with the immortality of the soul, following Plato's dialogue of the same name.)
—— (1783) *Jerusalem, oder über religiöse Macht und Judentum* (Jerusalem, or on Religious Power and Judaism), trans. with notes by A. Arkush, *Jerusalem*, Hanover, NH: University Press of New England, 1983. (His epoch-making work calling for the emancipation of the Jews and setting out the conditions of religious freedom in a pluralistic state.)
—— (1785) *Morgenstunden, oder Vorlesungen über das Dasein Gottes* (Morning Hours, or Lectures on the Existence of God), Berlin: C. Voss, 1786. (Sets forth Mendelssohn's fundamental metaphysical beliefs and argues against pantheism.)

References and further reading

Altmann, A. (1969) *Moses Mendelssohns Frühschriften zur Metaphysik*, Tübingen: J.C.B. Mohr. (A detailed study of Mendelssohn's early writings on metaphysics.)
—— (1973) *Moses Mendelssohn: A Biographical Study*, Tuscaloosa, AL: University of Alabama Press. (A magisterial account of Mendelssohn's life and thought.)
Arkush, A. (1994) *Moses Mendelssohn and the Enlightenment*, Albany, NY: State University of New York Press. (Studies the relationship between Mendelssohn's general philosophy and his conception of Judaism.)

ALLAN ARKUSH

MENEDEMUS OF ERETRIA
see SOCRATIC SCHOOLS

MENG KI/MENGZI *see* MENCIUS

MENTAL CAUSATION

Both folk and scientific psychology assume that mental events and properties participate in causal relations. However, considerations involving the causal completeness of physics and the apparent non-reducibility of mental phenomena to physical phenomena have challenged these assumptions. In the case of mental events (such as someone's thinking about Vienna), one proposal has been simply to identify not 'types' (or classes) of mental events with types of physical events, but merely individual 'token' mental events with token physical ones, one by one (your and my thinking about Vienna may be 'realized' by different type physical states).

The role of mental properties (such as 'being about Vienna') in causation is more problematic. Properties are widely thought to have three features that seem to render them causally irrelevant: (1) they are 'multiply-realizable' (they can be realized in an indefinite variety of substances); (2) many of them seem not to supervene on neurophysiological properties (differences in mental properties do not always depend merely on differences in neurophysiological ones, but upon relations people bear to things outside their skin); and (3) many of them (for example, 'being painful') seem inherently 'subjective' in a way that no objective physical properties seem to be. All of these issues are complicated by the fact that there is no consensus concerning the nature of causal relevance for properties in general.

1 The problem
2 Cartesian dualism
3 Identity theories
4 Causal relevance

1 The problem

Mental causation is central both to our conception of ourselves as thinking and experiencing agents, and to some of the most promising theories of our behaviour. We ordinarily explain, for example, someone's drinking water by citing their thirst and their belief that water would quench it.

Despite the central place of mental causation in both folk and scientific psychology there is a long philosophical tradition that is sceptical about it. This scepticism is based on the apparent scientific intractability of intentionality and consciousness (see CONSCIOUSNESS; INTENTIONALITY). Intentionality is the property of mental states whereby they are 'about' things, and can be true or false. For example, the thought that the cat is crying is about the cat and represents it (truly or falsely) as crying. Consciousness involves further subjective and phenomenal properties, such as the taste of beer or the awfulness of pain. It has seemed to some philosophers that it is impossible to fit intentionality and consciousness within the causal order disclosed by physics and biology, and this has led some to the conclusion that there is no genuine mental causation.

2 Cartesian dualism

The *locus classicus* for the problems of mental causation is Cartesian philosophy. Descartes held that mental events and states are distinct from physical events and states: the latter involve changes in the properties (especially spatial properties) of extended bodies, while the former involve changes in the properties (especially properties involving thought) of non-extended mental substance (see DESCARTES, R. §8; DUALISM). He further held that these two kinds of events interact causally. In fact, Descartes thought that mental causes are required to explain linguistic and mathematical behaviour since they exhibit a kind of novelty that he believed could not be accounted for solely in terms of physical causes.

There are many difficulties with Descartes' position, but two are most relevant to our topic. One is that he provided no account of how mental–physical (or mental–mental) causation occurs. He hypothesized that the interaction between mental and bodily events takes place in the pineal gland. While this localizes mental–physical causation, it says nothing about why or how various types of mental states cause, or are caused by, various types of mental or physical states. These connections are posited as basic causal links. But it seems implausible that anything as complicated as mental events should be linked to physical events by basic causal relations.

The second problem is that, contrary to Descartes' view, it is now widely believed that every physical event can be accounted for solely in terms of antecedent physical events (up to whatever objective indeterminism obtains generally) (see MATERIALISM IN THE PHILOSOPHY OF MIND). So, for example, if Alma raises her hand, that movement can be accounted for causally, at least in principle, in terms of prior neurophysiological and other physical events. Alma's conscious decision to raise her hand, if distinct from these physical events, either casually over-determines the movement or is *epiphenomenal* with respect to it (see EPIPHENOMENALISM). But over-determination seems *ad hoc*, motivated only by a desire to provide some causal role for the mental. If overdetermination is rejected then, given the distinctness of mental and physical events, the only causal role available for the former is as the causes of non-physical, that is, other mental events. But even this seems implausible in view of the fact that at least some mental events can be causally accounted for in terms of prior physical events. Indeed, an empirically well-attested claim of modern science is the *causal completeness of physics*: every event, if it is caused at all, occurs by virtue of physical causes (see DETERMINISM AND INDETERMINISM). Consequently, the view that mental events are distinct from physical events plausibly leads to 'mental event epiphenomenalism', or the doctrine that mental events have no physical effects.

Mental event epiphenomenalism is radically at odds with our views about our mental lives. But, fortunately, the line of reasoning that leads to it can be resisted by rejecting the Cartesian view that mental events are distinct from physical events. Descartes' arguments for the distinctness are now generally thought to be weak. His view that mathematical and linguistic behaviour could not be accounted for in terms of antecedent physical events has been undermined by, for example, a computational theory of mind. His more philosophical arguments have not fared much better.

3 Identity theories

This leaves the way open for the position that every mental event *is* a physical event (see MIND, IDENTITY THEORY OF). The most prominent contemporary version of this view is the 'token identity theory', due to Donald Davidson (1984). DAVIDSON (§3) holds that every particular (or 'token' mental event is identical to some or other particular physical event, but that *classes* (or 'types') of mental events are not identical to natural classes of physical events (see TYPE/TOKEN DISTINCTION). For example, every particular event of someone's *wanting water* may be identical to some or other physical event, but the mental *type* event, *wanting water*, may not be identical to any (naturally definable) physical *type* event (see multiple realizability below).

In many people's minds, however, Davidson's view invites the suggestion that, although mental states and events are identical to physical ones, still mental *properties* are distinct from physical properties (see PROPERTY THEORY). Hence, while the token identity theory avoids mental event epiphenomenalism, it raises the problem of whether, and if so how, mental properties participate in casual relations. Consider a much-discussed example from Dretske (1988): when the soprano's singing causes the glass to break, it is the singing's having a certain *frequency*, not its having a certain *meaning* that is relevant to its having that effect. Given that all causation is physical causation, how could a mental property such as meaning become relevant?

This problem has two parts. One is to characterize the difference between a property's being causally relevant or irrelevant in a causal transaction. The other is to determine when, if ever, mental properties are causally relevant. This problem arises because, on the one hand, folk psychology and cognitive theories seem to assume that mental properties are sometimes causally relevant and, on the other hand, certain philosophical accounts of mental properties raise questions of whether they can be. The view that mental properties are not causally relevant is 'mental *property* epiphenomenalism'. If true, it would entail that, even if mental events are causes of behaviour, their mental properties are not causally relevant to it.

If mental properties were *identical* to the physical properties responsible for behaviour, then there would be no special problem of mental property causation, since it is generally thought that neurophysiological properties are the physical properties causally responsible for behaviour. But there are three reasons frequently cited for thinking that mental properties are not identical to neurophysiological ones: multiple realizability, externalism and subjectivity. The first two apply mainly to intentional mental properties and the third to consciousness.

Multiple realizability. To say that a property is 'multiply realizable' is to say that it can be exemplified in virtue of exemplifying different physical properties. Prime examples of such properties are *functional* properties, or properties an object or state has in virtue of its capacity to exemplify a certain pattern of causal relations. For example, a computer has the property of 'executing a print command' by virtue of running a certain program. Since very different physical objects can exemplify the same causal capacities, functional properties are multiply realizable, a fact reflected in the diversity of physical materials (radio tubes, silicon chips) out of which computers can be made.

It has become the received view in philosophy of mind that certain mental properties are functional properties (see FUNCTIONALISM). So, for example, to be a belief is to be a state that is generally caused by inferences from other beliefs and has the capacity to participate in further inferences that cause other beliefs, intentions and so forth. If mental properties are functional properties, then they are not *identical* to neurophysiological properties, though they are realized in us by neurophysiological properties. It may well be that properties other than neurophysiological ones can also realize mental properties. In any case, there seems to be a problem concerning how functional properties can be causally relevant to behaviour. The trouble is that neurophysiological properties are sufficient for causally accounting for behaviour. The functional mental properties they realize seem irrelevant to their capacity to produce behaviour.

Externalism. Externalism is the view that intentional mental properties are constituted, in part, by external relations between thinkers and items external to the thinker. Thought experiments due to PUTNAM (1975) and Burge (1979) have been taken to support externalism. For example, Putnam imagines two individuals, Oscar and twin-Oscar. They are neurophysiologically identical, but Oscar lives in an environment containing H_2O while twin-Oscar lives on another planet much like earth except that instead of H_2O it has a superficially indistinguishable substance XYZ. According to Putnam and most others who have thought about it, Oscar's expression 'water' refers to H_2O and not XYZ while twin-Oscar's expression 'water' refers to XYZ and not H_2O. The point carries over to their thoughts. Oscar's thought that he expresses by 'Here is some water' is true: he is in the presence of H_2O. It would be false should Oscar travel to twin earth and think the thought in the presence of XYZ (see CONTENT: WIDE AND NARROW; METHODOLOGICAL INDIVIDUALISM).

If externalism is true then intentional mental properties (like thinking 'Here is some water') are externally individuated since what thought a person has depends on features of their environment. Another way of putting this point is that intentional properties fail to *supervene* on neurophysiological properties (see SUPERVENIENCE OF THE MENTAL). This means that two individuals can be identical with respect to their neurophysiological properties while differing in their intentional properties. If neurophysiological properties are causally sufficient for behaviour then it is difficult to see how intentional mental properties can be causally relevant.

Subjectivity. Subjectivity involves the idea that experience is from a point of view. It has been argued that consciousness is essentially subjective and that this subjectivity cannot be accounted for in terms of physical (or any essentially objective) properties of any kind. One line of thought in support of this view is due to Nagel (1974) and Jackson (1986). According to them, it is possible to know all the physical and functional facts concerning the operation of human brains without, for example, knowing what it is like subjectively to experience vertigo. Assuming that knowing what it is like to experience vertigo is itself knowing a fact and that knowledge of a fact is not dependent on how the fact is described (both of which assumptions are questionable), it follows that the property of experiencing vertigo is not a neurophysiological or functional property. At best there are basic nomological connections between objective neurophysiological properties and subjective consciousness (see COLOUR AND QUALIA; QUALIA).

4 Causal relevance

If mental properties are not neurophysiological properties, then how can they be causally responsible for behaviour? One possibility is that they possess *emergent* causal powers. Mental property emergentism means that mental and *not* neural properties are responsible for grounding the causation of behaviour. However, this again violates the causal completeness of physics. So mental property emergentism is not a viable option.

Kim (1993) has argued that the causal completeness of physics *excludes* mental properties from causing behaviour. To suppose otherwise, he claims, is to suppose that behaviour is causally overdetermined by both neurophysiological and mental properties. More generally, Kim claims that the causal completeness of physical properties excludes properties not reducible to fundamental physical properties from possessing causal powers. Kim's conclusion contains both bad and good news for mental causation. On the one hand, it asserts that physical properties, and not mental properties, cause behaviour. On the other hand, mental properties are no worse off than other properties not reducible to fundamental physical properties. In particular they are no worse off, as far as Kim's argument is concerned, than neurophysiological properties since it is likely that these are not reducible to fundamental physical properties either.

A natural response to Kim's argument is to grant that non-reducible macro-properties do not possess causal powers in the way that fundamental physical properties do, but then to attempt to characterize a notion of causal relevance that permits macro-properties to be causally relevant. The motivation for this is the fact that we typically distinguish among an event those macroscopic properties which are, and those which are not, *relevant* to its having certain effects. For example, consider the event of Alma's sneezing and two of its properties – discharging a virus into the air and being loud. The first property but not the second is causally relevant to Bill contracting a cold, and so explains why. The second property but not the first is causally relevant to Hilary saying '*Gesundheit!*', and so explains why. The issue of mental property epiphenomenalism then is the question of whether mental properties are causally relevant to behaviour. If they are not, then it follows that mental properties do not causally explain behaviour; and this has significant consequences for our explanatory practices.

Whether or not mental properties are causally relevant to behaviour depends not only the nature of mental properties, but also on the account of causal relevance. Kim (1993) claims that all higher-level causation including mental causation rides piggyback on more basic causal relations. He calls such higher-level causation 'supervenient causation' (see SUPERVENIENCE). However, although higher-level causation may be supervenient causation, the relation is too weak to ground a robust notion of mental causation (Lepore and Loewer 1989). A further condition might be supplied by spelling out causal relevance in terms of counterfactuals (see COUNTERFACTUAL CONDITIONALS). An initial, although not completely satisfactory, proposal (Lepore and Loewer 1987; Horgan 1989) is that an instantiation of F is causally relevant to an instantiation of G if the counterfactual 'If F had not been instantiated then G would not have been instantiated' is true. Others appeal to the subsumption of events with their properties under general laws, which may be 'strict' (as in Davidson 1984) or looser, *ceteris paribus* ones (as in Fodor 1989). While deciding among these alternatives will make a difference to the question of mental causation, the question clearly depends upon issues independent of the decision.

See also: DETERMINISM AND INDETERMINISM; DUALISM; FREE WILL; SUPERVENIENCE OF THE MENTAL

References and further reading

Baker, L.R. (1993) 'Metaphysics and Mental Causation', in Heil and Mele (eds) *Mental Causation*,

Oxford: Oxford University Press. (Defends mental causal explanations and non-reductive physicalism.)

Block, N. (1990) 'Can the Mind Change the World?', in G. Boolos (ed.) *Meaning and Method*, London: Methuen. (Interesting discussion of the problems posed by functionalism for mental causation.)

* Burge, T. (1979) 'Individualism and the Mental', *Midwest Studies in Philosophy* 4: 73–121. (Another source, along with Putnam (1975), of thought experiments which are taken to support externalism.)

—— (1993) 'Mind–Body Causation and Explanation', in Heil and Mele (eds) *Mental Causation*, Oxford: Oxford University Press. (Defends folk-psychological causal explanations and argues that they are not incompatible with materialism properly understood.)

* Davidson, D. (1984) *Essays on Actions and Events*, Oxford: Oxford University Press. (Davidson's important papers on philosophy of mind in which he develops the position he calls 'anomalous monism'.)

* Dretske, F. (1988) *Explaining Behavior: Reasons in a World of Causes*, Cambridge, MA: MIT Press. (Develops his view that intentional mental properties are structuring causes.)

* Fodor, J. (1989) 'Making Mind Matter More', *Philosophical Topics* 17: 59–79. (Develops a nomological account of the causal relevance of properties and uses it to defend the causal relevance of intentional properties.)

* Horgan, T. (1989) 'Mental Quasation', *Philosophical Perspectives* 3: 47–76. (Develops a counterfactual account of the causal relevance of properties.)

* Jackson, F. (1986) 'What Mary Didn't Know', *Journal of Philosophy* 83: 291–5. (A famous argument for the view that subjective mental facts are not necessarily entailed by objective physical facts.)

* Kim, J. (1993) *Supervenience and Mind*, Cambridge: Cambridge University Press. (Important papers exploring the extent to which physicalism can be formulated in terms of supervenience and developing the idea of supervenient causation as a solution to the problem of mental causation.)

* Lepore, E. and Loewer, B. (1987) 'Mind Matters', *Journal of Philosophy* 84: 630–41. (This paper initiated much of the current discussion. It develops a counterfactual account of causal relevance and argues, contrary to the prevailing view, that Davidson's anomalous monism is compatible with the causal relevance of intentional mental properties.)

* —— (1989) 'More on Making Mind Matter', *Philosophical Topics* 17: 175–91. (Further development of a counterfactual account of causal relevance.)

Ludwig, K. (1994) 'Causal Relevance and Thought Content', *Philosophical Quarterly* 44: 334–53. (Argues that counterfactual and nomological accounts of causal relevance are inadequate.)

McLaughlin, B. (1989) 'Type Epiphenomenalism, Type Dualism and the Causal Priority of the Physical', *Philosophical Perspectives* 3: 109–35. (Develops a nomological account of causal relevance.)

* Nagel, T. (1974) 'What it's Like to be a Bat', in D. Rosenthal (ed.) *The Nature of Mind*, Oxford: Oxford University Press, 1991. (A famous argument for the view that subjective mental facts are not necessarily entailed by objective physical facts.)

* Putnam, H. (1975) 'The Meaning of "Meaning"', in *Philosophical Papers*, vol. 2, *Mind, Language, and Reality*, Cambridge: Cambridge University Press. (The classic statement of the 'twin earth' case and the intuitions behind 'externalist' accounts of intentional content.)

Sosa, E. (1984) 'Mind–Body Interaction and Supervenient Causation', *Midwest Studies in Philosophy* 9: 271–81. (Poses difficulties for accounts of mental causation.)

Yablo, S. (1992) 'Mental Causation', *Philosophical Review* 101: 245–80. (Develops a counterfactual analysis of causation and applies it to mental causation.)

BARRY LOEWER

MENTAL ILLNESS, CONCEPT OF

The mad were once thought to be wicked or possessed, whereas now they are generally thought to be sick, or mentally ill. Usually, this is regarded as a benign decision by a more enlightened age, but some see it as a double-edged sword – one that simultaneously relieved and robbed the mad of responsibility for their actions, eventually delivering more compassionate treatment, but also disguising value-laden judgments as objective science. The issue is made more difficult by the diversity of conditions classified as psychiatric disorders, and by the extent to which their causes are still ill understood. But the difficulty is also conceptual: what, after all, is physical illness? People usually agree that it involves abnormal body functioning, but how do we decide what is normal functioning? And even supposing that we know what we mean by a sick body, is there a parallel notion of a sick mind that is more than metaphor?

1   **Physical illness and normal functioning**
2   **Mental illness**
3   **Related ethical issues**

1   Physical illness and normal functioning

Somatic medicine is both applied biology and a social institution charged with curing and caring for people with complaints that have physiological causes. The ill-health concepts – illness, disease, injury, disability, and so on – reflect this dual nature.

On the one hand, it seems that some degree of biological functional impairment is a necessary condition for ill-health of any kind. That is why childbirth, teething and large noses can cause distress without counting as ill-health, for although they have physiological causes, they do not *per se* involve malfunctioning. On the other hand, the various ill-health concepts introduce additional social, ethical, or clinical considerations. For instance, injuries generally result from a visible collision with the environment, while diseases tend to be heritable or infectious and have less visible causes (for example, micro-organisms, viruses, genes). Furthermore, an illness is something a person has (your little finger can be injured or diseased, but not ill), and illness qualifies you for the sick role, which involves being excused from many normal duties and deserving of special care.

Due to the plethora of ill-health concepts, philosophers often use illness as a term of art – a catch-all that includes all states of ill-health. Neither in this sense, nor in its ordinary sense, is it controversial that it is, in part, a value-laden concept, or that it involves a core of biological dysfunction. The main controversy concerns the notion of dysfunction: is it also value-laden, or can a completely descriptive account of it be given?

Talk about biological functions is clearly normative in some sense. We ask of our bodily parts. Is it functioning properly? What is it supposed to do? Is it malfunctioning? But what is the basis of such norms?

Robert Cummins (1975) argues that functions have their most important explanatory role in biology in functional analysis – a recursive conceptual decomposition of a system and its activities into simpler and simpler subsystems and simpler and simpler tasks. Functions are causal contributions to some activity of a system that is explained by such an analysis, he says. The contribution a part makes is an objective feature of the system so described, but the activity we choose to explain depends on our interests, he adds: in physiology, we are interested in survival and reproduction and contributions to these (see FUNCTIONAL EXPLANATION).

Functional analysis is certainly important to biology, but many think that Cummins has not captured its normative dimension. There are numerous problems. For instance, we are most interested in how people die of cancer, but a tumour's causal contribution to death, although often complexly achieved and a candidate for a Cummins-style analysis, is not an instance of proper functioning.

Normativists claim that normal functioning is further value-laden: while we are deeply interested in both life and death, ease and pain, fertility and infertility, capacity and incapacity, we value the first of each pair, not the second, and that is why contributions to the one, and not the other, are cases of proper functioning, they say. In support, they emphasize the cultural relativity of disease classifications. (Engelhardt's history of masturbation in Western medicine is a good example, see Engelhardt and McCartney 1981). But this evidence is also compatible with the claim that doctors can make mistakes. If there are descriptive biological norms, it does not follow that doctors will never be biased, confused or even ignorant, when trying to apply them.

Naturalists claim that there is a purely descriptive notion of normal functioning. Christopher Boorse (1976) offered a theory somewhat like Cummins's, but the goals of survival and reproduction were, he argued, biologically given. As natural selection continually modifies a species-design in favour of an individual's survival and reproduction, these are the goals towards which organisms are goal-directed, he says. To abstract away from idiosyncratic deviations, Boorse suggested that the function of a trait is, roughly, its species-typical contribution to the individual's survival and reproduction, but *prima facie* this seems problematic, for deviations from proper functioning can be typical (for example, in epidemics or pandemics).

Aetiological theories (following Wright 1973) have become popular. According to these, the proper function of a trait is what it was selected for. On this kind of account, it is the function of the kangaroo's pouch to protect her young because that is what the pouches of ancestral kangaroos did that caused the underlying genotype to be selected.

Some are dissatisfied with both of these naturalist theories (see Bigelow and Pargetter 1987, but also Neander 1991) and offer still further suggestions for how biological norms should be understood.

A general feature of naturalist accounts is the claim that systems that have proper functions are the outcome of, or are subject to, selection. For biological functions, the relevant selection process is natural selection: a blind, impersonal and decidedly amoral force. If so, biological norms are not determined by what we value, nor by what God values, but rather by what matters for natural selection. There is no implication, therefore, that what is normal or natural is to that extent desirable. Our values need not be those of natural selection (hence contraception). Indeed, there is no deducing 'ought' from 'is' here, on either type of account. According to the normativist, judgments about normal functioning are value-laden anyway, and so judgments concerning them are as contentious as value-laden judgments generally are.

2 Mental illness

There is no doubt that mental illness can involve great distress and incapacity, or that it can be life-threatening. But does it involve dysfunction in the sense we have been discussing?

A partial answer is easy. Some psychiatric disorders are uncontroversially brain diseases that belong to medicine proper, for they clearly involve straightforward physiological dysfunction – the neurones having atrophied (as in Alzheimer's Disease) or some such thing. The controversial cases are those where, if there is any dysfunction characteristic of the purported disorder, it can only be described in psychological, not physiological, terms (that is, in terms of the conscious or unconscious beliefs and desires of the person). For instance, if a human being desires sex with a five-year-old child, we describe that desire as sick. But is this description merely metaphorical, or is there a genuinely medical judgment to be made here, as well as a moral one? (The causes of mental illness are often complex and multifarious, and there are many mixed cases between the two extremes just mentioned – the organic syndromes and the purely psychological disorders.)

Whether there can be specifically psychological dysfunction will depend partly on the nature of mind and partly on the nature of functions. For instance, if the best theory of functions gives a central place to functional analysis and to what a thing is selected for, it will depend on whether the mind lends itself to a functional analysis of the appropriate kind, and on whether (or to what extent) the mind is subject to selection.

Even if there is specifically psychological dysfunction, (somatic) medicine might still be irrelevant to its treatment, and so psychiatry might still need to be de-medicalized, as some people argue. These days, the mental illness debate is generally based on the assumption that the mind is the brain, and that mental processes are brain processes (see MIND, IDENTITY THEORY OF). But there is still much controversy regarding how talk of the one relates to talk of the other. Boorse (1987), for example, argues that psychology and biology are autonomous disciplines. Expertise in somatic medicine is therefore irrelevant to the treatment of psychological dysfunction, he argues, and there is no call for psychiatrists to have (somatic) medical training (although the latter is needed in a supporting role, for example, to first rule out the possibility of physiological causes.)

Others see psychology and biology as more intimately integrated. One popular, but highly controversial, approach to describing the mind is to try to characterize mental states and processes using a biological notion of a proper function (see SEMANTICS, TELEOLOGICAL). Many also believe that much of our psychology (learning processes, concepts and so on) is innate and part of our biological endowment (see NATIVISM), and hence presumably, but not inevitably, the result of natural selection.

These strands in contemporary philosophy of mind are the ones that promise to provide the most literal interpretation of mental illness, but until we have a more complete understanding of the theoretical details, as well as of the working of the mind, the implications for particular conditions currently classified as psychiatric disorders may well remain obscure.

3 Related ethical issues

Resistance to classifying mental problems as medical problems often centres around concern for the autonomy of, and respect for, persons.

Except in so far as we blame someone for becoming ill, we do not as a rule blame them for the symptoms of their illness (for example, we might blame someone for smoking and so for developing emphysema, but we do not otherwise blame them for coughing). This seems to imply that we are not held responsible for symptoms, and mental illness is often thought to excuse a person from responsibility. The other side of this double-edged sword is that the agency of those labelled mentally ill is assumed to be diminished, and their rights as persons (for example, to choose for themselves what is in their own best interest) may consequently be denied.

There are a number of reasons why the picture just described is too simple, however. For one thing, symptoms are not usually actions. But our behaviour could be an action that is caused by beliefs and desires, and it could also be a symptom, because the beliefs and desires themselves are caused in an abnormal way – they might be caused by depression due to hormonal imbalance, for example. It is unclear why those who act from beliefs and desires that are symptoms of either somatic or mental illness should be excused just because of this fact. If a paedophile's desire to have sex with children is no more compelling than the embezzler's desire for money, or the jealous husband's desire for revenge, paedophiles are equally responsible for their actions, some argue (see Feinberg 1981). On this view, mental illness provides no special ground for excuse. It excuses only if it causes the agent to be blamelessly ignorant or to suffer irresistible compulsion, which are sufficient excuses in their own right.

Similar care has to be taken with the difficult issue of the competence (and civil rights) of the mentally ill. Much mental illness is localized or episodic, and will often be irrelevant to the person's capacity to make reasonable decisions about, for example, voting in an election, deciding on treatment, or selling the family home. Hard issues arise, however, when a mentally ill person is judged to be generally incompetent. Should we give them similar rights to those we give to children, even if their condition is believed to be irreversible, for example?

See also: FOUCAULT, M. §2; MORAL AGENTS; RESPONSIBILITY

References and further reading

* Bigelow, J. and Pargetter, R. (1987) 'Functions', *Journal of Philosophy*, 84: 181–96. (Clear summary of objections to aetiological theories of functions. Offers alternative naturalist theory.)
* Boorse, C. (1976) 'What a Theory of Mental Health Should Be', *Journal for the Theory of Social Behaviour* 6: 61–84. (Introductory. Combines functionalist theory of mind with his causal contribution theory of functions.)
* Cummins, R. (1975) 'Functional Analysis', *Journal of Philosophy* 72: 741–65; repr. in E. Sober (ed.) *Conceptual Issues in Evolutionary Biology*, Cambridge, MA: Bradford MIT, 1994, 2nd edn, 49–69. (Medium difficulty. Describes functional analysis.)
* Engelhardt H.T. and McCartney J. (1981) 'Concepts of Health and Disease' in Caplan, A. (ed.) *Concepts of Health and Disease*, Reading, MA: Addison-Wesley. (Useful interdisciplinary collection on the history, analysis and social role of the concepts of health, illness and disease.)
* Feinberg, J. (1981) 'What Is So Special About Mental Illness?' *Reason and Responsibility: Readings in Some Basic Problems of Philosophy*, Belmont, CA: Wadsworth Publishing Company, 5th edn, 464–73. (Clear and simple introduction to ethical issues concerning mental illness, competence and responsibility.)
* Neander, K. (1991) 'Functions as Selected Effects', *Philosophy of Science* 58: 168–84. (Medium difficulty. Detailed defence of aetiological theories.)
Szasz, T. (1961) *The Myth of Mental Illness*, New York: Hoeber-Harper. (Best known and rather polemical work of the psychiatrist, Thomas Szasz. Argues that we should de-medicalize psychiatry.)
* Wright, L. (1973) 'Functions', *Philosophical Review* 82: 139–68; repr. in E. Sober (ed.) *Conceptual Issues in Evolutionary Biology*, Cambridge, MA: Bradford MIT, 1994, 2nd ed., 27–47. (Introduction to aetiological theories of functions.)

KAREN NEANDER

MENTAL STATES, ADVERBIAL THEORY OF

According to the adverbial theory, there are no mental objects of experience, no pains, itches, tickles, after-images, appearances. People certainly feel pains and have after-images; external objects certainly present appearances to people viewing them. But pains, after-images, and appearances are not real things. Statements which purport to be about such mental objects have a misleading grammatical form. In reality, such statements are about the ways in which people experience or sense or feel.

1 Motivation
2 Elaboration
3 Objections

1 Motivation

Suppose you are having a tooth drilled. Suddenly you feel intense pain. This is an objective fact about you, not dependent for its existence on anyone else seeing or thinking about your situation. But the pain you are feeling – that particular pain – is private to you. It is yours alone, and necessarily so. No one else could have that particular pain. Of course, conceivably somebody else could have a pain which felt just like your pain, but only you could have that very pain. What is true for this one pain is true for all mental objects of experience, for example after-images, appearances, itches, tickles. None of these items of experience can be shared. I can't have your images or feel your tickles. Physical objects, however, are not necessarily private in this way. Any physical object that is mine could be yours, my watch, for example, or even my heart (see PRIVACY).

There is another striking fact about mental objects of experience, or phenomenal objects, as they are often called. Any pain or itch or image is always *somebody's* pain or itch or image. Likewise, any appearance is always an appearance *to* someone or other. Each mental object of experience necessarily has *an* owner, unlike ordinary physical objects, for example, trees or tables or even legs. Legs can exist amputated, and trees and tables can belong to no one at all.

Any philosopher who wants to view the mind, and its contents, as natural physical phenomena faces a problem with respect to the necessary privacy and necessary ownership of phenomenal objects. The adverbial theorist solves this problem by arguing that while it is certainly true that people feel pains and itches, and have images, this way of talking is misleading. Really there are no such things as pains, itches, and images. The world itself contains no phenomenal objects. So, there is, in reality, nothing to have the physically problematic properties.

2 Elaboration

How can it be true that people feel pains, even though there really are no pains for them to feel? The answer, according to the adverbial theorist, is that our ordinary way of expressing ourselves here is deceptive. Grammatical form is sometimes misleading. Just as it can be true that the average family has 1.2 children even though there really are no families with a fraction of a child, so too you can feel an intense pain even though there really are no pains.

But what is it that we are asserting, then, when we say, in ordinary parlance, that someone *has* a blue after-image or a throbbing pain or a terrible itch? In the case of the claim that the average family has 1.2 children, the answer is reasonably obvious. We are talking about numbers, and what we are really asserting is that the number of children divided by the number of families equals the number '1.2'. In the case of phenomenal talk, however, if its grammatical form is indeed misleading, the answer is much less obvious. It is to be found, according to the adverbial theorist in our ordinary talk of other things – of smiles and limps, of voices and stutters.

Suppose we ask ourselves whether there really are, in the world, any such things as limps. If we reply 'Yes', then we seem to face some puzzling questions just like the ones raised for phenomenal objects. If Patrick has a pronounced limp, then can Paul have that very same limp (the token limp Patrick has, not one just like it but numerically different)? Can Patrick's limp exist without anyone at all having it?

One reasonable response to these puzzling questions is to deny that there really are such things as limps, to which people are related by the 'having' relation. On this view, when we say that Patrick has a pronounced limp, what we are really saying is that Patrick *limps* in a pronounced manner. Likewise for smiles, voices, and stutters. If Patrick also has a

charming smile, a loud voice, and a noticeable stutter, what is really the case is that he smiles charmingly, speaks loudly, and stutters noticeably. There are no smiles, voices, and stutters, conceived of as things people have.

Analogously, according to the adverbial theorist, there are no pains, itches, or visual images, conceived of as objects people have. Instead, to have a terrible itch is just to itch terribly; to have a throbbing pain is to hurt throbbingly or in a throbbing manner. Finally, to have a blue after-image is just to sense in a certain way, a way we may dub 'bluely'. Now the problem for physicalism supposedly disappears. There are no phenomenal *objects* as such, and so there is no question of trying to accommodate their necessary privacy and ownership in the physical world.

Unfortunately, life is not that easy. To begin with, talk of people sensing bluely or hurting throbbingly is hardly everyday. It cries out for further explanation. Secondly, if there are no phenomenal objects, then just what is it that makes phenomenal talk true? If, when I have a terrible itch, it is really true that I itch terribly, then what exactly is it about me which *makes* this true? Some account is needed here in order to show that the possession by me of a terrible itch has really been repudiated and not just hidden under a verbal smokescreen.

At this point, the adverbial theory of sensation or experience, splits into two. To understand these alternatives and their respective costs and benefits, it is necessary to make some brief general remarks about adverbs.

There are two major theories of adverbs in the philosophical literature: the predicate operator theory and the event predicate theory (see ADVERBS). According to the latter view, adverbs, or at least a very wide range of adverbs, are best understood as adjectives that are true of events. Consider, for example,

(1) Patrick is stuttering noticeably.

If we are to bring out what it is that makes (1) true, we should restate it, on the event predicate theory, as

(1a) There is an event of stuttering, which has Patrick as its subject, and that event is noticeable.

Similarly,

(2) Patrick is speaking loudly.

should be recast as

(2a) There is an event of speaking, which has Patrick as its subject, and that event is loud.

So, the adverbs 'noticeably' and 'loudly' are really functioning as adjectives or predicates that apply to events, in the one case, to a stuttering, and in the other, to a speaking. What must exist, then, for Patrick to stutter noticeably or speak loudly is a noticeable stuttering or a loud speaking, of which Patrick is the subject.

This view has a number of virtues, not the least of which is that it requires no alteration, or addition, to the materials available in first order quantificational logic, as far as the formal evaluation of arguments in which sentences like (1) and (2) occur (see PREDICATE CALCULUS). Secondly and relatedly, it provides us with a very simple explanation of why (1), for example, entails

(3) Patrick is stuttering.

(3) is reconstructed as:

(3a) There is an event of stuttering, of which Patrick is the subject.

and (3a) follows from (1) via elementary logical rules.

The alternative view takes adverbs to be operators which turn the predicates they modify into more complicated predicates. In (1), for example, 'noticeably' is held to operate on the predicate preceding it, namely 'stutters', and to convert that predicate into a syntactically more complicated predicate, namely 'stutters noticeably'. The idea is that adverbs stand for functions which map the properties expressed by the properties they modify onto other properties. On this view, what makes (1) true is not the fact that Patrick is the subject of an event (a noticeable stuttering) nor the fact that Patrick owns a special object (a noticeable stutter) but simply the fact that Patrick has a certain property, that of stuttering noticeably. So (1) really is a subject–predicate sentence, just as it appears to be. There is no hidden existential quantification, as there is the event predicate theory proposal.

This approach requires the admission that the resources of standard logic do not suffice to come to grips with arguments containing adverbs, together with an account of operator detachment which will validate inferences like the one from (1) to (3) above. So, it has significant costs. On the other hand, it allows us to take sentences like (1) and (2) entirely at face value. These sentences certainly look to be of the straightforward subject–predicate variety, and, by golly, so they are on the predicate operator proposal.

On the event version of the adverbial theory of sensation, statements putatively about phenomenal objects like pains and itches are really about events like hurtings and itchings. By contrast, on the predicate operator version of the adverbial theory, statements putatively about phenomenal objects are really about people or other sentient creatures and the phenomenal properties they instantiate, properties like itching terribly or hurting throbbingly.

3 Objections

These two developments of the adverbial theory face some serious difficulties. To begin with, the predicate operator theory is hard pressed to account for the truth of ordinary statements putatively about multiple phenomenal objects. For example, suppose that after staring at a bright light and turning away, I report the following:

(4) I have four pink after-images.

It is not a straightforward matter to provide a plausible account of what in the world makes this true, given only phenomenal properties that I possess. The problem becomes especially difficult once it is appreciated that glibly proposing

(4a) I sense four-pink-ly,

or some such contrived statement as the analysis, apparently fails to account for the fact that (4) entails, for example,

(5) I have at least three after-images.

It certainly *looks* here as if, given this entailment, (4) is true if, and only if, there are four pink after-images that I have. Another related difficulty arises in connection with the following two statements

(6) I have both a red, square after-image and a blue, round after-image.

and

(7) I have both a blue, square after-image and a red, round after-image.

These statements evidently are not equivalent: one can be true without the other. But if we analyse the former by

(6a) I sense redly and squarely and bluely and roundly.

and the latter by

(7a) I sense bluely and squarely and redly and roundly.

then the difference between (6) and (7) is lost. For the order of the conjuncts in a conjunction makes no difference to the conditions under which it is true.

These problems, it should be noted, are also challenging for the event version of the adverbial theory. In this case, however, there is a reasonably straightforward reply. Allow there to be as many different sensings as there *appear* to be after-images referred to in the original statements. Then (4) becomes

(4b) There are four pink sensings of which I am the subject.

Now the entailment to (5) is easy to explain. Likewise, there is no difficulty in distinguishing (6) and (7). In both cases, there are two sensings, but they have different properties.

But does it really make sense to talk of my undergoing four simultaneous sensings, each with the same property? Some philosophers have certainly thought not. And it must be admitted that it is not at all easy to find clearcut examples from ordinary life of cases where a single individual is the subject of multiple simultaneous events of exactly the same sort (and not involving any other objects). I can listen to you with my left ear and also simultaneously listen to you with my right, or I can inhale deeply through my left nostril and at the same time inhale deeply through my right, but in both of these cases other objects are also involved (namely ears and nostrils). I can simultaneously be the subject of a singing and a walking and a smiling, say, but apparently I cannot simultaneously be the subject of three singings or three walkings or three smilings.

So, the event version of the adverbial theory faces a serious challenge here, too. And there are other problems. What, for example, can it possibly mean to call an event 'pink' or 'square'?

The difficulties I have raised here have been addressed by adverbial theorists. And I think it is fair to say that there is no knockdown objection to the view. But whether it really provides us with the best response to the problems posed by the necessary privacy and ownership of phenomenal objects is a matter of considerable dispute.

Finally, although the adverbial theory is usually associated with sensory experience, it is occasionally generalized so as to apply to all mental states. Under this generalization, there are no beliefs or desires or fears that people *have*, any more than there are after-images or itches or pains. As before, there are again two possible ways of developing this proposal further, one of which countenances believings, desirings, and fearings, and the other of which restricts itself to the attribution of the appropriate psychological properties.

See also: PERCEPTION: PROPOSITIONAL ATTITUDES

References and further reading

Chisholm, R.M. (1957) *Perceiving*, London: Routledge & Kegan Paul. (Classic early presentation of the adverbial theory.)

Ducasse, C.J. (1942) 'Moore's Refutation of Idealism', in P.A. Schilpp (ed.) *Philosophy of G.E. Moore*, Chicago, IL: Northwestern University Press, 225–51. (Another good early statement of the view.)

Jackson, F. (1977) *Perception*, Cambridge: Cambridge University Press, 50–87. (Some incisive criticisms of the adverbial theory.)

Sellars, W. (1968) *Science and Metaphysics*, London: Routledge & Kegan Paul, 9–28. (Further development of the adverbial view.)

Tye, M. (1984) 'The Adverbial Approach to Visual Experience', *Philosophical Review* 93: 195–225. (Detailed formulation of the metaphysics and semantics of the position, and replies to objections.)

—— (1989) *The Metaphysics of Mind*, Cambridge: Cambridge University Press. (Extension of the adverbial theory to all mental states.)

MICHAEL TYE

MENTAL STATES, UNCONSCIOUS *see* UNCONSCIOUS MENTAL STATES

MENTION *see* USE/MENTION DISTINCTION AND QUOTATION

MERCY *see* FORGIVENESS AND MERCY; RECTIFICATION AND REMAINDERS (§3)

MEREOLOGY

Mereology is the theory of the part–whole relation and of derived operations such as the mereological sum. (The sum of several things is the smallest thing of which they are all parts.) It was introduced by Leśniewski to avoid Russell's paradox.

Unlike the set-membership relation, the part–whole relation is transitive. This makes mereology much weaker than set theory, but gives the advantage of ontological parsimony. For example, mereology does not posit the proliferation of entities found in set theory, such as $\emptyset, \{\emptyset\}, \{\{\emptyset\}\}, \ldots$.

Mereology has occasioned controversy: over whether many things really have a mereological sum if they are either scattered or, even worse, of different categories; over the uniqueness of sums; and over Lewis' claim that the non-empty subsets of a set are literally parts of it.

1   **Classical mereology**
2   **Mereology, set theory and atoms**

1   Classical mereology

Mereology is the theory of the part–whole relation. It was introduced by Leśniewski (1916) to avoid Russell's paradox (see PARADOXES OF SET AND PROPERTY). Taking the part–whole relation as primitive, we define a proper part as a part which is not identical to the whole. We define disjointness to mean having no part in common. Then, in addition to the transitivity of the part–whole relation, the following axiom schema, unique composition, characterizes classical mereology.

> If there is some F, there is precisely one thing (the sum or fusion of the Fs) of which every F is a part and which has no part disjoint from every F.

The supplementation principle now follows, namely that if a is a proper part of b, then b has some proper part disjoint from a. For otherwise both a and b are sums of all the parts of a, contradicting uniqueness. It also follows that there is a sum of everything, U; that any thing a which is not U has a complement, namely the sum of everything disjoint from a; and that any two overlapping things a and b have a product (or intersection), namely the sum of all things which are parts of both a and b. Apart from the absence of a null individual, mereology has, with these operations, the structure of a Boolean algebra (see BOOLEAN ALGEBRA §1).

Strictly speaking, what we take as the characteristic axiom schema will depend on the logic mereology is an extension of. In the above this is the predicate calculus with identity. Leonard and Goodman's formulation (the calculus of individuals) is an extension of (a fragment of) set theory. In that case, unique composition is the axiom that any non-empty set of individuals has a sum. Or suppose, like Lewis (1991), you are extending a logic which permits plural quantification. Then unique composition could be formulated as:

> For any things there is one thing which has those things as parts and which has no part disjoint from those things.

Yet again, in a finitist mereology the formulation would be:

> For any a and b there is a unique c of which a and b are parts and which has no part disjoint from a and b.

Classical mereology is, therefore, a family of theories, with unique composition adapted to the context.

Both the transitivity of the part–whole relation and unique composition have been rejected as counter-intuitive. Cruse (1979) gives an example, later discussed by Simons (1987: 107), which illustrates the supposedly counter-intuitive character of the transitivity of the part–whole relation: a handle is part of a door, a door is part of a house but, it might seem, the handle is not part of the house. This objection is based on a controversial interpretation of 'part' to mean 'significant part'.

Unique composition may be conveniently divided into the existence of sums and the uniqueness of these sums. Let us first consider uniqueness. The problem, as stated by Simons (1987:115–17), has to do with 'continuants', namely things which endure without having temporal parts. Continuants are themselves controversial, but let us suppose that cats are continuants. Now consider a whole cat, Tibbles, her tail, and the remainder of Tibbles, called Tib. If Tibbles loses her tail then, Simons argues, Tibbles and Tib will be non-identical things with precisely the same parts. They are non-identical because they are identical, respectively, to Tibbles and Tib prior to tail loss, which are obviously non-identical (in other words, Tibbles is still Tibbles with or without her tail). A similar problem can be stated in modal rather than temporal terms. While there may be several solutions, we might well restrict classical mereology to categories of items which are not continuants. In that case Simons' nonclassical mereology would be appropriate for continuants.

The existence of sums of disparate collections has seemed too strong to many. Here it is important to note that mereology is demonstrably consistent, so there is no analogue of Russell's paradox. The objection, therefore, is not formal. The worst case is the existence of sums of items from different categories, such as: a kettle, the process in the kettle in which water boils, the spatiotemporal region in which the process occurs, the property of being at 100°C, and the relation of contiguity. Even though all those items might be thought of in connection with the activity of boiling water, it seems queer to say there is something which is the sum of them.

Lewis has defended the existence of disparate sums on the grounds that describing the sum is doing nothing more than describing the parts, for there is no extra ingredient which somehow unifies the parts into a whole (1991: 79–81). He also points out that attempts to avoid the sum of a scattered collection of items of the same category will fail because in such cases queerness is a matter of degree. This leaves open, however, the possibility of restricting unique composition to sums of items all taken from the same category.

2 Mereology, set theory and atoms

An atom may be defined as something which has no *proper* part. We may ask whether there are any atoms and whether every thing is a sum of atoms. If the answer to the first question is negative then a mereology is called 'atomless'; if the answer to the second is positive then it is 'atomistic'. Now mereology does not have to be either atomistic or atomless – it might, for instance, be the case that every object has proper parts even though the space they occupy is a sum of points. It seems rather less plausible that any one category of thing (for example, physical objects) should have both atoms and atomless parts. Mereology restricted to a single category would seem, therefore, to be either atomistic or atomless. For example, mereology restricted to spatiotemporal regions is atomistic if all regions are sums of points, but atomless if points are idealized limiting cases of arbitrarily small regions (see Whitehead 1919; WHITEHEAD §2; see also Mortensen and Nerlich 1978; Clarke 1985).

Mereology is of theoretical interest partly because it has been used to provide either a replacement for, or a formulation of, the theory of sets. Because a sum of atoms has a unique decomposition into atoms, sums behave like sets of atoms. The chief difference between mereology and set theory is that two different sets of non-atoms, say, $\{a+b, c+d\}$ and $\{a+c, b+d\}$, can have the same sum, $a+b+c+d$. It was hoped that the resources of mereology would none the less be enough to replace sets in the foundations of mathematics. Thus Goodman and Quine (Goodman 1972: 173–98) showed how the ancestral (that is, a chain of instances) of a relation could be defined using the part–whole relation, avoiding set theory. They also showed how various statements such as 'There are exactly one-third as many Canadians as Mexicans' can be handled using mereology. Their approach ran into difficulties, however, with quantified numerical formulas, such as 'For all n, $n+n=2n$'.

Lewis, in his version of nominalistic set theory, adopted a rather different strategy, namely to imitate set theory using the resources of mereology (see Lewis 1991: 21–8). The chief difficulty seems to have been that without the resources of set theory the materials are lacking with which to construct enough pseudo-sets. Thus a sound Ockhamist reason for preferring mereology to set theory – its inability to generate

infinitely many things out of just one thing – restricts its use as a substitute.

Rather different is Lewis' later programme of treating the theory of sets and proper classes as itself an extension of mereology (1991). Excepting the special case of the empty set, we may treat subclasses as parts and thus treat set theory as the extension of mereology obtained by adjoining the singleton operator. This operator forms unit sets, which are always atoms, out of individuals. Lewis is in favour of treating it as primitive, but, relying on results by Burgess and Hazen, he also shows how we can develop an alternative, structuralist account, according to which there are many possible singleton operators, between which set theory does not choose.

See also: LOGICAL AND MATHEMATICAL TERMS, GLOSSARY OF; STRUCTURALISM

References and further reading

Burkhardt, H. (1990) 'Mereology in Leibniz's Logic and Philosophy', *Topoi* 9: 3–13. (Historical background.)
* Clarke, B.L. (1985) 'Individuals and Points', *Notre Dame Journal of Formal Logic* 26: 61–75. (Recent discussion of the mereology of space.)
* Cruse, D.A. (1979) 'On the Transitivity of the Part–Whole Relation', *Journal of Linguistics* 15: 29–38. (An examination of the linguistic evidence for the failure of transitivity. The author makes a useful distinction between parts and attachments.)
Eberle, R.A. (1970) *Nominalistic Systems*, Dordrecht: Reidel. (Includes simplifications to mereology based on the assumption of atomism.)
Goodman, N. (1956) 'A World of Individuals', in I. Bocheński, A. Church and N. Goodman, *The Problem of Universals*, Notre Dame, IN: University of Notre Dame Press; repr. in *Problems and Projects*, Indianapolis, IN: Bobbs-Merrill, 1972. (Along with the work of Leśniewski and Whitehead, this is one of the classics of mereology.)
* —— (1972) *Problems and Projects*, Indianapolis, IN: Bobbs-Merrill. (§4 includes two important and accessible papers: 'A World of Individuals' and, with Quine, 'Steps Toward a Constructive Nominalism'.)
Henry, D.P. (1991) *Medieval Mereology*, Amsterdam: Benjamin. (Historical background.)
Le Blanc, A. (1985) 'New Axioms for Mereology', *Notre Dame Journal of Formal Logic* 26: 437–43. (One of a series discussing the axiomatics of mereology.)
Lejewski, C. (1983) 'A Note on Leśniewski's Axiom System for the Mereological Notion of Ingredient

or Element', *Topoi* 2: 63–72. (A recent paper by a distinguished mereologist in the school of Leśniewski.)

* Leśniewski, S. (1916) 'Podstawy ogólnej teoryi mnogości I', *Prace Polskiego Koła Naukowe w Moskwie, Sekcya matematyczno-przyrodnicza* 2; trans. D.I. Barnett, 'Foundations of the General Theory of Sets I', in *Collected Works*, ed. S.J. Surma, J.T. Srzednicki and D.I. Barnett, Dordrecht: Kluwer, 1992, vol. 1, 129–73. (Classic paper on mereology. The word 'Sets' in the translation of the title is misleading. The paper is not about sets as we now understand them. Consult P. Simons' 'Discovering Leśniewski's Collected Works', *History of Philosophical Logic* 15: 227–35 (1994) for a useful list of typographical errors.)

* Lewis, D.K. (1991) *Parts of Classes*, Oxford: Blackwell. (A lucid presentation of set theory as an extension of mereology, using the minimum of technicality; also includes an excellent introduction to mereology (based on plural quantification), a defence of classical mereology, a discussion of nominalistic set theory and some important, though technical, appendices with J.P. Burgess and A.P. Hazen.)

* Mortensen, C. and Nerlich, G. (1978) 'Physical Topology', *Journal of Philosophical Logic* 7: 209–23. (Topology based on atomless mereology for space.)

* Simons, P. (1987) *Parts: A Study in Ontology*, Oxford: Clarendon Press. (A most comprehensive work discussing both the Leśniewski and the Leonard and Goodman formulations of mereology, providing some criticisms of classical mereology and developing a nonclassical theory. Of necessity, much of the discussion is technical. Includes an extensive bibliography.)

Smith, B. (ed.) (1982) *Parts and Moments: Studies in Logic and Formal Ontology*, Munich: Philosophia. (Includes an extensive bibliography.)

—— (1985) *Parts and Wholes*, vol. 3, Stockholm: Forskningsrådsnämnden. (Includes a further bibliography on mereology.)

Sobociński, B. (1934) 'O kolejnych uproszczeniach aksjomatyki "ontologii" prof. S. Leśniewskiego', in *Fragmenty Filozoficzne. Księga Pamiątkowa ku Uczczeniu Piętnastolecia Pracy Nauczycielskiej w Uniwersytecie Warszawskim Profesora Tadeusza Kotarbińskiego*, Warsaw: Nakładem Uczniów, 144–60; trans. 'Successive Simplifications of the Axiom-System of Leśniewski's Ontology', in S. McCall (ed.) *Polish Logic 1920–1939*, Oxford: Clarendon Press, 1967. (One of a series, mostly in the *Notre Dame Journal of Formal Logic*, by mereologists in the school of Leśniewski, in

which alternative axiomatics for mereology are discussed. For a survey, with references, see Simons (1987: ch. 2).)

Srzednicki, J.T.J., Rickey, V.F. and Czelakowski, J. (eds) (1984) *Leśniewski's Systems: Ontology and Mereology*, The Hague: Nijhoff. (Reprinted articles by mereologists in the tradition of Leśniewski, including Lejewski, Słupecki and Sobociński.)

* Whitehead, A.N. (1919) *An Enquiry concerning the Principles of Natural Knowledge*, Cambridge: Cambridge University Press. (Includes a formulation of mereology independent of, and almost as early as, Leśniewski's, with application to the theory of atomless spacetime.)

PETER FORREST

MERIT *see* DESERT AND MERIT

MERLEAU-PONTY, MAURICE (1908–61)

Merleau-Ponty belongs to the group of French philosophers who transformed French philosophy in the early post-war period by introducing the phenomenological methods of the German philosophers Husserl and Heidegger. His central concern was with 'the phenomenology of perception' (the title of his major book), and his originality lay in his account of the role of the bodily sense-organs in perception, which led him to develop a phenomenological treatment of the sub-personal perceptions that play a central role in bodily movements. This account of the sub-personal aspects of life enabled him to launch a famous critique of Sartre's conception of freedom, which he regarded as an illusion engendered by excessive attention to consciousness. None the less, he and Sartre cooperated for many years in French political affairs, until Merleau-Ponty became exasperated by the orthodox Marxism-Leninism of the French Communist Party in a way in which Sartre, who remained a fellow-traveller, did not. As well as several substantial political essays, Merleau-Ponty wrote widely on art, anthropology and, especially, language. He died leaving some important work incomplete.

Although his work is still esteemed within the French academic establishment, his influence in France has waned, because of a tendency there to study his German forebears almost to the exclusion of all else. But elsewhere, and most notably in the USA, Merleau-Ponty's work is widely studied, especially now that questions about the distinction between personal and sub-personal aspects of life have become so prominent.

1 Life

Merleau-Ponty studied philosophy at the École Normale Supérieure, graduating in 1930. As a student he was quickly drawn towards the works of the German phenomenologists, having attended Husserl's 1929 lectures in Paris (the 'Cartesian Meditations') and studied Heidegger's writings (see HUSSERL, E.; HEIDEGGER, M.). He wrote his first book, *The Structure of Behavior*, before serving briefly in the French Army in 1939–40. During the German Occupation he taught at the Lycée Carnot in Paris and wrote his major work, *The Phenomenology of Perception*, which was published in 1945. In the same year he took a position at the University of Lyon, before returning to Paris in 1950 as Professor of Psychology at the Sorbonne; in 1952 he moved to the prestigious Chair of Philosophy at the Collège de France, a position which he held until his early and unexpected death in 1961.

2 Mind and body

Much of Merleau-Ponty's first work, *The Structure of Behavior* (1942) is devoted to a detailed critical discussion of physiological psychology and the attempt to provide on its basis a reductive explanation of behaviour. In developing his argument Merleau-Ponty draws on Gestalt psychology and especially K. Goldstein's *The Organism* which emphasizes the holistic features of the life of organisms. Merleau-Ponty takes over Goldstein's holism and incorporates it into what he terms a 'dialectical' conception of the structures of behaviour, according to which as organisms evolve and become more sophisticated, higher 'forms' of behaviour develop which transform the life of the organism. So the new capacities characteristic of these higher forms are not simple additions to an otherwise unaltered neurophysiology; instead, through a process of 'dialectical' assimilation, these new capacities bring with them changes in the functioning of the underlying neurophysiology (see GESTALT PSYCHOLOGY).

Merleau-Ponty argues that this dialectical approach enables him to reject reductive theories without invoking the kind of vitalism espoused by BERGSON (see VITALISM). Equally, he argues, it provides a way of accommodating the phenomena of consciousness without dualist metaphysics: for, he writes, 'man is not a rational animal. The appearance of reason and mind does not leave intact a sphere of self-enclosed instincts in man' ([1942] 1963: 181). Thus there can be no partition of 'mind' from 'body' in human life: the mental is intrinsically bodily, a theme Merleau-Ponty illustrates through the role of the sense-organs in perception. Equally the body is intrinsically mental, in the sense that there can be no adequate understanding of human behaviour that does not conceptualize it as the behaviour of a normally rational agent. Merleau-Ponty's comment on Watson's behaviourism shows his aspirations clearly:

> what is healthy and profound in this intuition of behavior found itself compromised by an impoverished philosophy.... When Watson spoke of behavior he had in mind what others have called *existence*; but the new notion could receive its philosophical status only if causal or mechanical thinking were abandoned for dialectical thinking.
>
> (Merleau-Ponty [1942] 1963: 226)

3 *The Phenomenology of Perception*

Merleau-Ponty ends *The Structure of Behavior* with some enigmatic remarks to the effect that, just as there is no satisfactory causal account of perception, a realist account of the perceived world is equally unsatisfactory. With these remarks Merleau-Ponty points towards a main theme of his most important work, *The Phenomenology of Perception* (1945). An important difference, however, between the two books is that, as its title and preface ('What is Phenomenology?') indicates, the approach adopted in the second book is explicitly 'phenomenological'. The central theme of Merleau-Ponty's phenomenology is that a full understanding of the natural and social worlds which we inhabit inevitably leads back to aspects of our experience through which, in some sense, meaning is bestowed upon the objects of experience. Thus he sees the primary task of philosophy as one of quasi-Platonic *anamnesis* (see PLATO §§10–11), of re-awakening within us a recognition of these meaning-bestowing aspects of our own experience so that we can grasp how we are integrated into these worlds and how they, in their turn, are dependent upon us: philosophical reflection, he writes, 'steps back to watch the forms of transcendence fly up like sparks from a fire; it slackens the intentional threads which attach us to the world and thus brings them to our notice' ([1945] 1962: xiii). In developing this phenomenology Merleau-Ponty often expresses his debts to Husserl's late works, especially the unpublished papers which he had studied at Louvain. But how far, in fact, Merleau-Ponty is developing themes from Husserl's writings is disputable. He himself indicates his rejection of the transcendental subjectivism that is a prominent theme of most of Husserl's writings; similarly when he proclaims the impossibility of completing the phenomenological reduction and affirms the inseparability of essence and existence he is implying that Husserl's project of essentialist phenomenological analysis can never be accomplished. Thus it is arguable that Merleau-Ponty's conception of phenomenology is in fact closer to that characteristic of Heidegger's *Being and Time*, and one can certainly use Merleau-Ponty's detailed accounts of experience as a way of filling out Heidegger's all-too-abstract characterization of human life.

Merleau-Ponty's concentration upon perception rests on a thesis which is fundamental to his phenomenology, namely that perception is 'transcendental' in the sense that it cannot be adequately understood from within a fully objective, scientific conception of human life. In part this thesis just draws on the argument of *The Structure of Behavior*; but at a deeper level Merleau-Ponty argues that because perceptual experience is epistemologically fundamental it cannot be the case that perception itself is fully comprehended within the explanatory perspective of natural science, since this employs a conception of the world which draws on features that owe their significance to perceptual experience itself. Merleau-Ponty likes to adapt a phrase from the poet Paul Valéry to express this feature of perception: it is, he says, 'the flaw in this great diamond' since 'we can never fill up, in the picture of the world, that gap which we ourselves are' ([1945] 1962: 207). Merleau-Ponty's argument is, therefore, that the realist naturalizing project faces an inescapable blind-spot in connection with perception. Whether Merleau-Ponty is right about this remains disputable – his critics will maintain that, once we separate epistemological from metaphysical priorities, we can see that it is legitimate to regard our own experiences as facts caught up within, and dependent upon, the causal order of the natural world, even if we also acknowledge that our beliefs concerning this causal order rest upon perception.

This is the kind of issue which realists and idealists can debate endlessly, but whatever the outcome of that debate there can also be agreement that Merleau-Ponty's line of thought leads into one of the most innovative programmes of twentieth-century idealism. Central to this is his discussion of the status of the body. Merleau-Ponty once again uses Goldstein's work – in this case his studies of a patient (Schneider) who had suffered brain injuries during the First World War. But what is new in *The Phenomenology of Perception* is the use that Merleau-Ponty makes of his phenomenology in the characterization of Schneider's case and then, by an inversion, his use of Schneider's case to revise the phenomenological approach itself. Schneider's injuries, he argues, have brought with them the loss of the sub-personal perceptual fields, bodily spaces and tacit anticipations of possibilities that underpin ordinary human agency. So Schneider's disability is not merely neurophysiological; nor is it just a disorder of a consciousness detached from behaviour; instead it bears witness to the normal sub-personal union of mind and body through which a form of intentionality is expressed in unreflective but organized bodily movement. Once the further step is taken of recognizing that this is the basic form of intentionality, it follows that the phenomenological perspective itself needs to be relocated from the personal sphere of explicit thought to the sub-personal domain of bodily movement; thus, as Merleau-Ponty puts it, Schneider's case 'forces us to acknowledge an imposition of meaning which is not the work of a universal constituting consciousness' ([1945] 1962: 147) (see INTENTIONALITY).

Merleau-Ponty characterizes this revised phenomenological perspective as one in which the body is conceived as 'a natural self and, as it were, the subject of perception' ([1945] 1962: 206). Because of his transcendentalism concerning perception, the body thus conceived is not the body as characterized within the objective perspective of the natural sciences: 'what prevents it ever being an object ... is that it is that by which there are objects' ([1945] 1962: 92). His term for the body thus conceived is 'the phenomenal body' ([1945] 1962: 106) and he argues that by following the intentional threads which link the phenomenal body to the world we will be led to recognize the inadequacy of a purely objective conception of the world as a totality of objects, and to replace it with that of the 'phenomenal field', conceived as 'the horizon latent in all our experience and itself ever-present and anterior to every determining thought' ([1945] 1962: 92).

At this point the similarity with Kantian themes concerning space will be obvious (see KANT, I. §5), and Merleau-Ponty provides an extended account of the a priori status of the practical horizon which, he holds, enters into all our perceptual fields. But what is distinctive about Merleau-Ponty's account is its integration into a phenomenological psychology which preserves the basic metaphysics of transcendental idealism by making the body the transcendental subject. Arguably, however, in *The Phenomenology of Perception* Merleau-Ponty still replicates Husserl's problematic transcendental/empirical division of the self with his distinction between the 'phenomenal' and the 'objective' body. Hence it is notable that when he returns to the topic in his final work, *The Visible and the Invisible*, he attempts to go beyond this distinction by arguing that there is a yet more fundamental conception of the body – as 'flesh', which is a conception of the body that admits both an objective specification as 'a thing among things' and a phenomenal specification as 'what sees and touches' ([1964] 1968: 137). Indeed, despite the title of the book, it is significant that Merleau-Ponty here treats the sense of touch as phenomenologically fundamental and even, implausibly, construes sight as a species of touch (as 'a palpation with the look' ([1964] 1968: 134)); for touch has often been regarded as the sense which by manifesting the independent resistance of things reveals most clearly their objectivity. But because the book is incomplete it is not clear just how far this rebalancing of emphasis, to give equal weight to the 'objective' and the 'phenomenal' sides of life which are 'intertwined' in the human body, implies the need for a reworking of his whole phenomenology in a more objectivist direction. But it is clear, I think, that the position remains recognisably idealist in spirit, partly indeed through his explicit affirmation of the ideality of 'the flesh' ([1964] 1968: 152).

4   Consciousness and freedom

In the final chapters of *The Phenomenology of Perception* Merleau-Ponty uses his account of the sub-personal elements of life to elucidate the characteristic marks of personal life – self-consciousness and freedom. His discussion of these themes is, in part, an argument against their treatment by Sartre in *Being and Nothingness*, which was published two years earlier in 1943. Central to Sartre's account was the thesis that consciousness has a distinctive 'being' as 'being-for-itself' – that is, self-conscious – which is supposed to yield the conclusion that consciousness manifests an inescapable and absolute freedom (see SARTRE, J.-P. §3). As against Sartre, therefore, Merleau-Ponty argues that both self-consciousness and freedom are achievements that cannot be understood in isolation from the sub-personal aspects of life from which they are absent. They do not constitute an inescapable fate to which we are condemned; instead they are just the high points in the ebb and flow of our existence.

In the case of consciousness Merleau-Ponty argues that it is because 'all consciousness is, in some measure, perceptual' ([1945] 1962: 395), in the sense

that it draws upon our habitual sub-personal experience of the world, that self-consciousness is both capable of genuinely extending our knowledge and also vulnerable to error and illusion. A form of self-consciousness that was not thus vulnerable would be so totally detached from this tacit background that it would lack the concepts with which this background furnishes us and could, therefore, tell us nothing about ourselves. Similarly the exercise of genuine freedom presupposes a background engagement with the world that is not itself an exercise of freedom. If one seeks, as Sartre does, to find freedom in all acts of consciousness, one empties of any content the distinction between freedom and its absence by misconstruing the absence of a choice to act as a choice not to act. Instead, we need to acknowledge the impersonal significance of things which arises from our sub-personal needs, habits and constraints; only against this background can a 'strictly individual project' stand out briefly as an exercise of freedom before its significance too is compromised by its incorporation into the general run of events.

5   Language

For many years Merleau-Ponty aimed to extend his account of our perception of 'visible' objects to an account of speech about 'invisible' truths (hence the title of his last book). His most extended discussion occurs in *The Prose of the World*, which was written in 1950–2, though published only posthumously. The central claim he makes here is that speech has a transcendental role comparable to that of perception in the constitution of truth. We normally fail to notice this because just as naïve perception encourages the realist illusion of perfect objectivity, our normal uses of language to talk about things encourage a similar realist illusion of language as a transparent vehicle for ready-made meanings. Once, however, we re-awaken an awareness of the genuine phenomenon of 'speaking language' within which meanings are forged, it becomes apparent that the expression of truths is a cultural achievement that is only sustained through the use of a common language. Indeed the fact that language is essentially common enables it to play a role comparable to that of the body in relation to perception; it is, Merleau-Ponty says, a form of 'anonymous corporality' ([1969] 1974: 140), and as such it sustains our a priori involvement with others in much the way in which our physical corporality sustains our a priori involvement with the physical world in perception. So, in enabling us to share our lives with others, language equally enables us to live in a world of shared, and thus objective, truths.

6 Painting

Merleau-Ponty applied his phenomenology to a great variety of subjects, including issues in history, sociology and politics; but his discussions of painting are especially interesting.

The classical painting of the Renaissance, he argues, with its perspectival delineation of distinct objects, is an art that is informed by the goal of capturing what is seen as the appearance of objects in their own right, related to the eye only in ways legitimated by an objectivist conception of the world. Impressionists such as Cézanne, by contrast, 'did not want to separate the stable things which we see and the shifting way in which they appear; he wanted to depict matter as it takes on form' ([1948] 1964: 13). Thus painters such as Cézanne, to whom Merleau-Ponty returns frequently, aim to capture on canvas the true phenomenology of the visual field. In their paintings the elements of the scene depicted emerge only through the interplay of often indistinct colours and shapes, sometimes unfolding without a single perspective; and yet 'it is Cézanne's genius that when the overall composition of the picture is seen globally, perspectival distortions are no longer visible in their own right but rather contribute, as they do in natural vision, to the impression of an emerging order' ([1948] 1964: 14).

Similarly, one may say, it was Merleau-Ponty's genius to see that when classical phenomenology is combined with psychological insight, a new way of thinking about human life emerges, one that can throw light on modern painting as much as on old questions of metaphysics.

See also: IDEALISM; MARXISM, WESTERN §2; PHENOMENOLOGICAL MOVEMENT

List of works

There is a complete list of Merleau-Ponty's works, together with what was then a full list of secondary literature in: Lapointe, F. and Lapointe, C. (1976) *Maurice Merleau-Ponty and his Critics: An International Bibliography*, New York: Garland.

Merleau-Ponty, M. (1942) *La Structure de comportement*, Paris: Presses Universitaires de France; trans. A. Fisher, *The Structure of Behavior*, Boston, MA: Beacon Press, 1963. (Merleau-Ponty here develops his 'dialectical' approach to psychology.)

—— (1945) *Phénoménologie de la perception*, Paris: Gallimard; trans. C. Smith, *The Phenomenology of Perception*, London: Routledge, 1962. (Merleau-Ponty's major work, using psychology to reconstruct classical phenomenology.)

—— (1946) 'L'existentialisme chez Hegel' (Existentialism in Hegel), *Les Temps modernes* 1: 1311–19; repr. in M. Merleau-Ponty, *Sens et non-sens*, Paris: Nagel, 1948; trans. H.L. Dreyfus and P.A. Dreyfus, *Sense and Non-Sense*, Evanston, IL: Northwestern University Press, 1964, 63–70. (Discusses the existentialist themes in Hegel's thought.)

—— (1947) *Humanisme et terreur*, Paris: Gallimard; trans. J. O'Neill, *Humanism and Terror*, Boston: Beacon Press, 1969. (Merleau-Ponty's Marxist response to Koestler's *Darkness at Noon*; an unconvincing critique of liberal politics.)

—— (1948) *Sens et non-sens*, Paris: Gallimard; trans. H. and P. Dreyfus, *Sense and Non-Sense*, Evanston, IL: Northwestern University Press, 1964. (A collection of Merleau-Ponty's early essays, including some on literature and painting.)

—— (1955) *Les Aventures de la dialectique*, Paris: Gallimard; trans. J. Bien, *Adventures of the Dialectic*, London: Heinemann, 1974. (A collection of essays on Marxism, including Merleau-Ponty's critique of Sartre's 'ultra-bolshevism'.)

—— (1960) *Signes*, Paris: Gallimard; trans. R. McCleary, *Signs*, Evanston, IL: Northwestern University Press, 1964. (Merleau-Ponty's later essays, including some on language.)

—— (1964) *Le Visible et l'invisible*, ed. C. Lefort, Paris: Gallimard; trans. A. Lingis, *The Visible and the Invisible*, Evanston, IL: Northwestern University Press, 1968. (Merleau-Ponty's incomplete attempt to rework the central themes of his phenomenology.)

—— (1969) *La Prose du monde*, ed. C. Lefort, Paris: Gallimard; trans. J. O'Neill, *The Prose of the World*, London: Heinemann, 1974. (The text of a projected book on language, abandoned in 1952.)

References and further reading

Archard, D. (1980) *Marxism and Existentialism*, Belfast: Blackstaff Press. (A useful guide to the quarrel between Merleau-Ponty and Sartre.)

Edie, J. (1987) *Merleau-Ponty's Philosophy of Language: Structuralism and Dialectics*, Washington, DC: University Press of America. (An authoritative discussion by one of America's leading scholars.)

* Goldstein, K. (1934) *Der Aufbau der Organismus*, The Hague: Nijhoff; trans. *The Organism*, New York: American Book, 1938. (A classic work on the holistic aspect of the life of organisms, on which Merleau-Ponty relies in *The Structure of Behavior*.)

Hadreas, P. (1986) *In Place of the Flawed Diamond*, New York: Peter Lang. (A short but thoughtful Heideggerian account of Merleau-Ponty's work.)

* Husserl, E. (1931) *Méditations cartésiennes*, Paris:

Colin; trans. D. Cairns, Cartesian Meditations, The Hague: Nijhoff, 1960. (Husserl's Paris lectures, which Merleau-Ponty attended as a student in 1929.)

Madison, G. (1981) *The Phenomenology of Merleau-Ponty*, Athens, OH: Ohio University Press. (A general survey, especially useful in elucidating the significance of themes from Merleau-Ponty's later writings.)

Mallin, S. (1979) *Merleau-Ponty's Phenomenology*, New Haven, CT: Yale University Press. (An account which focuses on Merleau-Ponty as a phenomenologist.)

O'Neill, J. (1970) *Perception, Expression and History*, Evanston IL: Northwestern University Press; repr. as the introduction to J. O'Neil (ed.) *Phenomenology, Language and Sociology*, London: Heinemann, 1974, xi–lxii. (Although this latter volume is primarily a useful selection of Merleau-Ponty's essays, it contains O'Neill's important essay, which focuses on Merleau-Ponty's political writings, and a bibliography of works on Merleau-Ponty up to 1972.)

Olafson, F. (1967) 'A Central theme of Merleau-Ponty's Philosophy', in E. Lee and M. Mandelbaum (eds) *Phenomenology and Existentialism*, Baltimore, MD: Johns Hopkins University Press, 179–205. (An excellent introduction to Merleau-Ponty's philosophy of perception, by a scholar who also contributed an excellent article on Merleau-Ponty to Edwards' *Encyclopedia of Philosophy*.)

* Sartre, J.-P. (1943) *L'Être et le néant*, Paris: Gallimard; trans. H. Barnes, *Being and Nothingness*, New York: The Philosophical Library, 1956. (Sartre's classic work of existential phenomenology which Merleau-Ponty criticizes at the end of *The Phenomenology of Perception*.)

—— (1961) 'Merleau-Ponty vivant', *Les Temps modernes* 17 (184–5): 304–76; repr. in *Situations IV*, Paris: Gallimard, 1964; trans. B. Eisler, *Situations IV*, New York: Brazilier, 1965. (Sartre's moving and intelligent tribute to his old comrade; the whole issue of *Les Temps modernes* is taken up with tributes to Merleau-Ponty, from Lefort, Lacan and others. Curiously, Sartre's published text is an almost complete replacement of another, even better, text which is published in translation as 'Merleau-Ponty (I)', *Journal of the British Society for Phenomenology* 15 (2): 128–58.)

Waelhens, A. de (1969) *Une Philosophie de l'ambiguité* (revised edition), Louvain: Publications Universitaires de Louvain. (Still the best general account of Merleau-Ponty's work, especially good at situating it in relation to the work of other philosophers.)

THOMAS BALDWIN

MERSENNE, MARIN (1588–1648)

Marin Mersenne represents a new seventeenth-century perspective on natural knowledge. This perspective elevated the classical mathematical sciences over natural philosophy as the appropriate models of what can be known, of how it can be known and of the cognitive status of that knowledge. His early publications had the apologetic aim not only of combating various forms of heresy, but also of opposing philosophical scepticism, which was widely regarded in Catholic France of the early seventeenth century as undermining the certainty of religious dogma. To that end, Mersenne stressed the certainty of demonstrations in sciences such as optics, astronomy and mechanics, all of which stood as 'mathematical' sciences in the classifications of the sciences stemming from Aristotle. Mersenne's stress on the mathematical sciences contrasted them with natural philosophy in so far as the former concerned only the measurable external properties of things whereas the latter purported to discuss their inner natures, or essences. In accepting the considerable degree of uncertainty attending knowledge of essences, and juxtaposing it to the relative certainty of knowledge of appearances, Mersenne adopted a position (since called 'mitigated scepticism') that combated scepticism by lowering the stakes: in accepting that the essences of things cannot be known, he agreed with the sceptics; but in asserting that knowledge of appearances can, by contrast, be had with certainty, he rejected the apparent intellectual paralysis advocated by the sceptics. In furthering this programme, Mersenne embarked on a publication effort relating to the mathematical sciences, combined with a massive lifelong correspondence on largely philosophical as well as religious topics with a wide network of people throughout Europe.

1   Career and correspondence
2   Apologetics and anti-scepticism
3   Mathematics and music

1   Career and correspondence

Born in France at Oizé, Maine, Mersenne was educated at the Jesuit college of La Flèche soon after its foundation in 1604, where he was an older contemporary of Descartes. He left about 1609 to study theology in Paris at both the Sorbonne and the Collège de France. In 1611 he entered the austere Order of Minims, joining their Parisian convent off the Place Royale (now Place des Vosges) in 1619 where he lived for the rest of his life. His earliest publications date from 1623, and all have apologetic aims, culminating in *La verité des sciences* (1625). From 1626 onwards Mersenne's publications concentrated on the mathematical sciences, including the so-called 'mixed' mathematical sciences that concerned aspects of the physical world rather than simply pure quantity (whether discrete, as in arithmetic, or continuous, as in geometry). He is best known, perhaps, as Descartes' epistolary link to the learned world during the latter's residence in the Netherlands from 1629 until Mersenne's death; he assisted in the publication of Descartes' *Discourse on Method* (1637) and organized solicitation of the 'Objections' to the *Meditations* that appeared in 1641 (see DESCARTES, R. §I). In addition to Descartes, Mersenne corresponded with many other philosophers throughout Europe. He was the centre of an information network in which he acted as intelligencer and clearing-house, both communicating ideas and sometimes fomenting disputes. This tireless correspondence, amounting to seventeen volumes in its modern edition, has since earned him the label 'one-man scientific journal'.

The correspondence exemplifies aspects of Mersenne's wider religious and social concerns, in so far as it represents his increasing irenicism in the period following his early apologetic writings. Referred to late in his life as 'the Huguenot monk', Mersenne numbered Protestants as well as Catholics among his correspondents, and strove to overcome the doctrinal gaps between those camps. This generally took the form of gentle attempts at converting the Protestants to a moderate, reconciliatory form of Catholicism, and contrasts quite starkly with the ferocity of the assaults on heresy found in his early works. He never changed in his perception of the dangers of scepticism, however, and his so-called 'mitigated' scepticism amounted to a philosophical irenicism to match the religious. Mersenne's wide correspondence could itself proceed only within a broad discursive consensus, whether religious or philosophical.

Mersenne's engagement with the work of some of his illustrious philosophical contemporaries does not appear solely in relation to Descartes. During the 1630s, Mersenne publicized the work of GALILEO with two books, as well as in occasional discussions of Galileo's work in other publications and in correspondence. Mersenne travelled several times, to the Netherlands (meeting Isaac Beeckman there), provincial France and Italy. From the latter excursion he brought back news to France, in 1645, of the Torricellian barometric experiment, which led to the famous work of Blaise PASCAL on the weight of the air.

2 Apologetics and anti-scepticism

Mersenne's chief apologetic works contain a good deal of philosophical and mathematical content. They date from 1623, and include the recently rediscovered *L'Usage de la raison*, *Quaestiones celeberrimae in Genesim* and *Observationes et emendationes ad Francisci Georgii Venetii problemata* (generally bound together), *L'Impieté des deistes* (1624), and perhaps most significant, *La verité des sciences* (1625), a work that tackles the serious contemporary challenge of philosophical, particularly Pyrrhonian, scepticism with weapons drawn heavily from the mathematical sciences.

Quaestiones, his first major publication, is an uncompleted commentary on Genesis (a continuation exists in manuscript) containing lengthy digressions on such topics as astronomical systems and geometrical optics. Mersenne's ability to use such subject-matter for apologetic ends is typified by his use of optical theory to refute the naturalism of the sixteenth-century Paduan philosopher Pietro POMPONAZZI. Naturalism was a doctrine that regarded nature as a self-activating, self-motivating system that had no need of the supernatural to sustain it. It thus seemed to Mersenne, as to many others, to reduce or eliminate the natural world's dependence on God's superintendence. There was an element of circularity in Pomponazzi's position, in so far as what counted as 'natural' was practically defined as whatever occurred in the natural world; thus, by definition, whatever happens is natural rather than miraculous or supernatural. For Pomponazzi and later proponents of this position such as the magician Julius Caesar Vanini (executed for heresy in 1619), even the miracles described in the Bible had been events with natural explanations. Pomponazzi had tried to account in terms of optical illusion for an angelic visitation recorded in the Old Testament. Mersenne responded by using his own knowledge of geometrical optics: he expatiates at length in *Quaestiones* on optics, and especially on the properties of curved mirrors, to show that Pomponazzi's explanation could not possibly work.

Mersenne soon extended the significance for religious apologetics of the so-called 'mixed' mathematical sciences (such as optics, astronomy, mechanics and music theory, which made use of theorems from geometry and arithmetic). This arose from his explicit confrontation of Pyrrhonian scepticism, a form of ancient Greek scepticism that enjoyed a revival starting around the middle of the sixteenth century. The central texts were writings by SEXTUS EMPIRICUS (*c.*200 AD), including most famously his *Outlines of Pyrrhonism*. The Pyrrhonist maintained that no proposition could be held as absolutely certain – one could always find grounds, however outlandish, for doubt – and that, as a result, the wise man will always suspend judgment on all things, subscribing to no dogmatic beliefs, but simply conforming to prevailing norms. This position contrasts with so-called 'Academic' scepticism, also dating from antiquity, which recommended the exercise of probable judgment (see PYRRHONISM).

Pyrrhonism had become quite popular in some circles in France by the early seventeenth century, where it played a role in religious controversies. By the mid-1620s Mersenne had come to see it as just one example of a whole range of unorthodox philosophical positions that, like Pomponazzi's naturalism, threatened religious, and concomitantly social, stability. The most common tactic of its opponents in France at this time was to counter Pyrrhonian arguments piecemeal, precisely according to the form in which they were offered. Mersenne, by contrast, chose to attack Pyrrhonism by erecting an epistemological structure, with an associated natural philosophy, to act as a comprehensive bulwark; despite the later example of Descartes, reformulations of natural philosophy were not an inevitable tactic of opponents of Pyrrhonism in this period. A specific factor contributing to Mersenne's adoption of such an approach was his interest in natural philosophy and in the mathematical sciences.

For Mersenne, the problem with Pyrrhonism was not so much its use of sceptical arguments as the radical nature of the doubt that those arguments served to produce. Profound and generalized doubt came too close to promoting doubt in religion. Mersenne evidently thought that without the discipline of reason, heresy or unbelief would become too difficult to guard against. If scepticism were applied to sensitive areas like morality, it might not only promote immoral living, but also threaten social stability by questioning the principles on which social hierarchy was established. The difficulties therefore rested on the absoluteness of the challenge to certainty that Pyrrhonian scepticism posed. Mersenne responded by attempting to destroy the threat of total, universal doubt by establishing what might be called bridgeheads of certain knowledge, in the hope that these bridgeheads would prove sufficient to indicate a workable foundation for rational theology and rational, enforceable social order.

The main such bridgehead was that of the mathematical sciences. Mersenne had used the mathematical science of optics in *Quaestiones in Genesim* for apologetic purposes (to show the impossibility of naturalistic explanations of certain miracles), and its advantage there was one shared by all mathematical sciences: mathematics was conventionally treated as the exemplar of certain knowledge in contemporary school teachings, within a general context of a widespread moderate scepticism (greatly to be contrasted with the extremities of Pyrrhonism) promoted in the schools through the medium of humanist dialectic. This stressed the idea of probability rather than certainty in most practical affairs. Mersenne's Jesuit education had similarly emphasized the certainty of mathematics as a contrast to the merely probable knowledge available from qualitative Aristotelian physics. The author of the principal mathematical textbooks used in the Jesuit colleges, Christopher Clavius, tried to promote the status of the mathematical sciences in Jesuit pedagogy by exploiting the apparent contrast between the uncertainty of conclusions in natural philosophy and the certainty of those in mathematics, pointing out that a conclusion in dialectic 'is confirmed only probably', whereas a conclusion in mathematics is a matter of certain demonstration.

Mersenne's stance in *La verité des sciences* flows directly from this impact of humanist probabilism. One of the most characteristic aspects of his response to Pyrrhonian arguments regarding the uncertainty of most questions, and especially on the impossibility of achieving reliable knowledge of the essences of things, is that he generally *accepts* them. These were positions routinely accepted within early seventeenth-century scholastic natural philosophy. Mersenne departed from orthodoxy here only to the extent that his attempt to defeat Pyrrhonism required it. He did not absolutely reject any kind of knowledge that lacked absolute certainty; instead, he tended to discount it only because it did not serve his anti-Pyrrhonian argumentative strategy. He dismissed anything accepted as uncertain, so as to concentrate on the opportunities presented by what *was* certain; in practice, this tended to mean mathematics.

The certainty of mathematics would not in itself have been an adequate basis for an approach to *natural philosophy*. There were, in fact, three commonly-accepted sources of certainty recognized within mainstream humanist-influenced scholasticism by the early seventeenth century: mathematics, ordinary sense-perception and syllogistic logic. Although all three were themselves under fire from Pyrrhonist arguments, together they constituted the main ingredients of Mersenne's answer to Pyrrhonian scepticism. They worked together as interrelated elements of a form of natural philosophy that bypassed the essentialist claims of Aristotelianism. If accepted as reliable, ordinary sense-perception could serve to generate true statements whose consequences, through the application of syllogistic reasoning, might serve in turn to ground mathematical expressions of the appearances of things in the physical world. By a reversal of the process, mathematics then enables the determination of how sensory perceptions of appearances are affected by, or can be deliberately altered by, changes in circumstances or in the conditions of observation. Mersenne's proposal, therefore, is for a mathematical coordination of appearances, which can serve as an entirely satisfactory practical substitute for Aristotelian essentialist physics. Mersenne's prize examples of such a thing were, and remained, geometrical optics and music theory, although he also wrote on mechanics. The last took the form initially of quasi-Archimedean statics, although in the 1630s he took a considerable interest in Galileo's kinematics, an approach to change in the physical world that appealed greatly to Mersenne's project of modelling natural knowledge on the mathematical sciences.

An important aspect of Mersenne's approach is that of operationalism: being able to accomplish some practical task itself acts as a criterion of the possession of knowledge, much as we find in Francis Bacon (see BACON, F. §3). This in turn indicates a positive evaluation of practical utility as a proper goal of philosophical knowledge. Once again, the theme of the utility of applied mathematics is recurrent in late fifteenth- and sixteenth-century humanist encomiums to mathematics, and forms a significant part of Clavius' defence of mathematical studies.

Richard H. Popkin (1979) has described Mersenne's overall position, as originally laid out in *La verité des sciences*, as 'constructive' or (following Hume) 'mitigated' scepticism. In Mersenne's form, however, it is less a grounded philosophical argument than the outcome of a particular set of philosophical assumptions deployed in a specific polemical context. Mersenne opposes to Pyrrhonism the position of Ciceronian humanist probabilism as widely promulgated in the schools, including the greatly influential Jesuit colleges. He thus emphasizes the kinds of knowledge that this position typically allowed as certain. Since these did not include essentialism – knowledge of the inner natures of things – as sought by (among other systems) Aristotelian natural philosophy, Mersenne abandoned the latter, even while describing it as the 'most probable' such system. Since even a 'probable' essentialism was still open to the attacks of the Pyrrhonists precisely for not being certain (still the most important property of genuine knowledge, *scientia*), this left Mersenne upholding his favourite mathematical sciences as the models for a new natural philosophy.

Thus Mersenne should not be seen as substituting, like Descartes, a new philosophy in place of Aristot-

elianism, one that would be immune to the Pyrrhonist threat. Instead, he simply adapts most of the elements of his position from standard teachings, shifting the emphasis somewhat, in order to secure knowledge of nature (among other things) from Pyrrhonism. It would have been consistent with his arguments in *La verité* to have retained Aristotelian physics on a probabilistic basis. Indeed, his previous publications bear witness to just such a stance. But from *La verité* onwards, Mersenne effectively just ignores it in favour of mathematical sciences because physics implied knowledge of essences, and such knowledge was not certain – hence not an appropriate basis for a true science.

The philosophical inadequacy of Mersenne's response to Pyrrhonism is made clear by the lack of arguments provided in support of the central planks of his position. Pyrrhonism questioned the reliability of ordinary sense-perceptions; Mersenne merely asserts it, and claims that variations in appearance – such as the standard example of a stick appearing bent when half-immersed in water – could be understood and coordinated through a proper understanding of the contingencies surrounding them (in the case of the stick, a proper understanding of refraction). This response, of course, begs the question of how assertions about refraction itself are to be grounded. Similarly, there were standard Pyrrhonian arguments against the value of syllogistic inference, relying especially on the point that syllogisms are question-begging because the universals on the basis of which they establish their singular conclusions are themselves justified on the basis of just such singulars. Mersenne is content to respond by reasserting the certainty of syllogistic inference and recommending the logical works of Aristotle for further elucidation. In the case of mathematics, for which Pyrrhonists also had a battery of undermining arguments, Mersenne does try a little harder, in particular defending arithmetic and geometry against some specific criticisms found in Sextus Empiricus.

Mersenne's approach characterizes not just his lifelong opposition to extreme scepticism, but also his opposition to a variety of other deviant philosophies. That opposition had been manifested in previous writings (*Observationes*, directed especially against the recently executed magician Vanini, and the second volume of *L'Impieté des deistes*, which among other targets took on Giordano BRUNO). He was also to engage in polemics with Robert FLUDD slightly later in the 1620s. Although most of *La verité* takes the form of a dialogue between a 'Christian Philosopher' (evidently Mersenne's mouthpiece) and a 'Sceptic' (the latter routinely being deeply impressed by the former's display of mathematical truths), Book I, which contains most of the work's philosophical meat, presents a three-way discussion. The additional interlocutor is the 'Alchemist'. Mersenne's trick is to allow the Sceptic freely to demolish the foundations of the Alchemist's position (itself a variety of essentialism), and only when the Alchemist has been vanquished does the Christian Philosopher step in to show why the kind of knowledge that he prizes remains unthreatened by the criticisms directed at the Alchemist. Thus Mersenne's selective acceptance of certain sceptical arguments flows not simply from his inability to refute them, but also from his wish to use them for his own ends. Orthodoxy was, for Mersenne, threatened more by magical and alchemical philosophies than it would be by the bracketing-off of essentialist Aristotelianism.

3 Mathematics and music

In practice, Mersenne's work after 1625, both as a correspondent/intelligencer and as writer of books, focused on the promulgation of knowledge in the mathematical sciences and on the consideration of novelties in those fields. He is sometimes called a 'mechanist', a label reinforced by its use in the title of Robert Lenoble's classic study *Mersenne ou la naissance du mécanisme* (1943). The usual understanding of that term for seventeenth-century philosophy is not properly applicable, however. Lenoble's use of the term 'mechanism' equated it with instrumentalist, operational knowledge, whereas the usual meaning now among historians studying this period relates to specific *ontological* commitments, chief among them corpuscularianism or atomism. These stances, associated most closely with Descartes and GASSENDI respectively, are of course essentialist, in that they make commitments to views on the underlying natures of things. In Descartes' case the commitment, at this level of general matter-theory, was meant to be dogmatic rather than conjectural; in Gassendi's, it was explicitly hypothetical. But neither position seems to have appealed to Mersenne. His appreciation of sceptical views kept him from wholehearted acceptance of Cartesian mechanism, whereas his desire for certain knowledge made Gassendi's hypotheticalism unattractive. The model of the mixed mathematical sciences provided the perfect *via media*, since they neither committed to a particular ontological structure for the material world nor abandoned the goal of producing rigorous demonstrations of their conclusions.

His first publication specifically on the mathematical sciences was *Synopsis mathematica* (1626), a compendium of material on geometry, optics and also mechanics (a second edition appeared in 1644 under the title *Universae geometriae...synopsis*). In a similar vein he published *Les Mechaniques de Galilée* (1634e), a French paraphrase of an early Galilean work from the turn of the century on statics and simple machines, which had previously circulated only in manuscript; *Les Nouvelles pensées de Galilée* followed in 1638–9. The latter work presented paraphrased material from Galileo's 1638 *Discourses and Demonstrations Concerning Two New Sciences*, and provides further indication of the congeniality to Mersenne of Galileo's approach to issues of natural philosophy developed on the basis of 'mixed mathematics'.

Mersenne's first work devoted to music appeared in 1627, the *Traité de l'harmonie universelle*, on the heels of which he began composition of his great multi-volume *Harmonie universelle*, which finally appeared in 1636–7. These texts betray a further dimension of Mersenne's conception of mathematical knowledge and its relation to natural philosophy. He was much taken with Augustine's Neoplatonic emphasis on harmony as a foundational aspect of the created world's intelligibility. It is important to recall here that 'natural philosophy' in medieval and early-modern Latin culture was a branch of learning that treated the natural world as God's Creation. Music as a branch of mixed mathematics was concerned with ratios and proportions associated with certain privileged qualitative features of the world. It thus served to express the ineffable with mathematical precision. As a consequence, it was fit to act as the ideal basis for Mersenne's rather Augustinian conception of what he called 'universal harmony'. By seeing the constitution of the physical universe as being intelligible in the pre-established terms of musical ratios, Mersenne thought himself to have invested mathematical treatments of nature with genuinely natural-philosophical content. He attempted this extension by more than just drawing analogies or musical metaphors: he analysed the behaviour of balances in statics in terms of musical ratios, so as to represent their action as fulfilling precisely the same formal requirements as those of music, and completed the circle by representing musical consonances themselves as the product of the relative frequencies of series of air pulses. Indeed, in taking these latter as tantamount to sound itself, he went beyond the usual treatment, which usually only *correlated* sound with air disturbances, to *identify* sound with these mathematizable air pulses. He thus retained a kind of Platonic essentialism in his mathematical approach to physical phenomena.

See also: AUGUSTINE; AUGUSTINIANISM; NEOPLATONISM

List of works

Mersenne, M. (1623a) *L'Usage de la raison* (Use of reason), Paris. (Recently rediscovered work of apologetics.)

—— (1623b) *Quaestiones celeberrimae in Genesim*, Paris. (Uncompleted commentary on Genesis.)

—— (1623c) *Observationes et emendationes ad Francisci Georgii Venetii problemata*, Paris. (Bound together with *Quaestiones*; the two together are a major source on Mersenne's early views on magical and naturalistic systems.)

—— (1624) *L'Impieté des deistes* (The impiety of the deists), Paris, 2 vols; repr. vol. 1, Stuttgart-Bad Cannstatt: Friedrich Frommann, 1975. (Volume 2 has a lengthy critique of Giordano Bruno.)

—— (1625) *La verité des sciences (The truth of the sciences)*, Paris; repr. Stuttgart-Bad Cannstatt: Friedrich Frommann, 1969. (The classic statement of 'mitigated scepticism'.)

—— (1626) *Synopsis mathematica*, Paris; 2nd edn, 1644. (A compendium based on classical authors.)

—— (1627) *Traité de l'harmonie universelle* (Treatise on universal harmony), Paris. (On aspects of music theory.)

—— (1634a) *Traité des mouvemens* (Treatise on movement), Paris; repr. in *Corpus: Revue de philosophie* 2 (1986): 25–58. (On falling bodies.)

—— (1634b) *Questions inouyes*, Paris; repr. ed. A. Pessel, Paris: Fayard, 1985. (Mathematical and physical problems.)

—— (1634c) *Questions harmoniques*, Paris; repr. ed. A. Pessel, Paris: Fayard, 1985. (Musical matters, including a sceptical treatise by La Mothe Le Vayer.)

—— (1634d) *Questions theologiques*, Paris; repr. ed. A. Pessel, Paris: Fayard, 1985. (Similar to *Questions inouyes*.)

—— (1634e) *Les Mechaniques de Galilée*, Paris; repr. ed. A. Pessel, Paris: Fayard, 1985. (Paraphrase of a Galilean work on statics from the beginning of the century.)

—— (1634f) *Les Preludes de l'harmonie universelle* (Preludes of universal harmony), Paris; repr. ed. A. Pessel, Paris: Fayard, 1985. (Another discussion of various philosophical issues, with much musical content.)

—— (1636–7) *Harmonie universelle* (Universal harmony), Paris; repr. Paris: Centre Nationale de la Recherche Scientifique, 1963. (Mersenne's great treatise on music theory, musical instruments, and miscellaneous non-musical matters.)

—— (1638–9) *Les Nouvelles pensées de Galilée* (The new thoughts of Galilee), Paris. (Paraphrasing some material from Galileo's *Discorsi* of 1638.)

—— (1639) *L'Usage du quadran* (The use of the quadrant), Paris: Rocolet. (On a mathematical instrument.)

—— (1644a) *Cogitata physico-mathematica*, Paris. (Discusses a wide variety of mathematical subjects, including ballistics and mechanics as well as music.)

—— (1644b) *Universae geometriae, mixtaeque mathematicae synopsis*, Paris. (A new version of the *Synopsis* with optical treatises by Thomas Hobbes and Walter Warner.)

—— (1647) *Novarum observationum...tomus III*, Paris. (A continuation of *Cogitata*.)

—— (1648) *Harmonicorum libri XII*, Paris; repr. Geneva: Minkoff, 1972. (A short Latin condensation of material in *Harmonie universelle*, with some additions.)

—— (1651) *L'Optique et la catoptrique du Reverend Pere Mersenne Minime*, Paris. (A study on optics, published posthumously.)

—— (1932–88) *Correspondance du P. Marin Mersenne, religieux minime*, ed. C. de Waard, R. Pintard, B. Rochot, A. Beaulieu, Paris: Beauchesne, Presses Universitaires de France, Centre Nationale de la Recherche Scientifique, 17 vols. (The great modern edition; a goldmine on seventeenth-century philosophical networks.)

References and further reading

Costabel, P. (1993) 'Marin Mersenne', *Die Philosophie des 17. Jahrhunderts, Band 2: Frankreich und Niederlande*, ed. J.-P. Schobinger, Basel: Schwabe, 637–47, 700–2. (A useful overview in German with good bibliography.)

Coste, H. de (1649) *La vie du R. P. Marin Mersenne, théologien, philosophe et mathématicien, de l'ordre des Pères Minimes*, Paris; repr. in P.T. de Larroque, *Les correspondants de Peiresc* 2, Geneva: Slatkine, 1972, 436–97. (The chief near-contemporary biographical source.)

Crombie, A.C. (1974) 'Mersenne, Marin', *Dictionary of Scientific Biography*, vol. 9, ed. C.C. Gillispie, New York: Scribner's, 316–22. (A brief survey of Mersenne's career and publications.)

Dear, P. (1988) *Mersenne and the Learning of the Schools*, Ithaca, NY: Cornell University Press. (Stresses Mersenne's debt to scholastic, especially Jesuit, sources.)

Duncan, D.A. (1981) *The Tyranny of Opinions Undermined: Science, Pseudo-Science and Scepticism in the Musical Thought of Marin Mersenne*, Vanderbilt University Ph.D. dissertation. (A good treatment of Mersenne's musical work in its broader philosophical context.)

—— (1986–9) 'An International and Interdisciplinary

Bibliography of Marin Mersenne', *Bolletino di Storia della Filosofia dell'Università degli Studi di Lecce* 9: 201–42. (The fullest bibliography currently available.)

Études philosophiques (1994), 'Études sur Marin Mersenne', 1–170. (A miscellaneous collection from a recent French conference on Mersenne.)

Hine, W.L. (1984) 'Marin Mersenne: Renaissance Naturalism and Renaissance Magic', in B. Vickers (ed.) *Occult and Scientific Mentalities in the Renaissance*, Cambridge: Cambridge University Press, 165–76. (Discusses Mersenne's early attitudes towards magical philosophies.)

* Lenoble, R. (1943) *Mersenne ou la naissance du mécanisme*, Paris: Vrin, 1971. (The classic study, presenting Mersenne as something of a proto-positivist.)

* Popkin, R.H. (1979) *The History of Scepticism from Erasmus to Spinoza*, Berkeley, CA: University of California Press. (Contains the influential account of Mersenne's 'mitigated scepticism'.)

Quatrième centenaire de la naissance de Marin Mersenne, 1588–1988, *Actes du colloqué*, Le Mans: Faculté des Lettres, Univ. du Maine. (A recent miscellany of scholarly articles, largely historical rather than philosophical.)

Thuillier, R. (1709) *Diarium patrum, fratrum et sororum Ordinis Minimorum Provinciae Franciae*, Paris; repr. Geneva: Slatkine, 1972, vol. 2: 90–113. (Together with De Coste, the main early biographical account, in Latin.)

PETER DEAR

MESSER LEON, JUDAH
(*c*.1425–*c*.1495)

*Messer Leon was a philosopher, physician, jurist, communal leader, poet and orator. Ordained as a rabbi by 1450, Messer Leon was qualified to adjudicate legal cases among Jews and head an academy (*yeshivah*) for advanced studies in Jewish law. He also came close to embodying the Renaissance ideal of* uomo universale. *His learning was formally recognized in 1469, when Emperor Frederick III awarded him a doctorate in medicine and philosophy and granted him the unusual privilege of conferring doctoral degrees in those subjects on Jewish students.*

Messer Leon's contribution to Jewish philosophy was in the field of logic, the art considered by him to be the key to the proper harmonization of religion and philosophy. He regarded scholastic logic to be superior to Arabic logic and wrote supercommentaries on

Averroes' logical works as well as an encyclopedia of logic, Mikhlal Yofi *(Purest Beauty), in an attempt to shift Jewish philosophical education from the Judaeo-Arabic logical tradition to scholastic logic. Although his encyclopedia became a popular textbook, Messer Leon failed to mould the culture of Italian Jewry as he had intended. In particular, he could not curb the spread of Kabbalah, a tradition which he vehemently opposed because of its underlying Platonic metaphysics.*

Most importantly, Messer Leon composed the first manual of Hebrew rhetoric, entitled Nofet Tzufim *(The Book of the Honeycomb's Flow). Printed in 1476, this Jewish response to Latin humanism combines the Averroist-Aristotelianism tradition and the Ciceronian-Quintilian one. The appropriation of humanistic rhetoric was given a Jewish meaning when Messer Leon claimed that the Torah, rather than the writings of the pagan, classical orators, exemplified perfect speech because it was a revelation of perfect divine wisdom. By analysing Scripture from the perspective of classical rhetoric, Messer Leon legitimized the study of ancient pagan and Christian orators even as he argued for the supremacy of biblical rhetoric over all merely human eloquence.*

1 **Life and works**
2 **Philosophical standpoint**
3 **Rhetoric**
4 **Humanism and Kabbalah**

1 Life and works

Rabbi Judah ben Yehiel, called Messer Leon, wrote philosophic and scientific works in Hebrew to afford his *yeshivah* students university-level instruction, from which all but a tiny fraction of Jews were excluded. He lived in Ancona, Mantua, Padua, Bologna, Venice and Naples, always relocating his celebrated *yeshivah* wherever he went. Linked by kinship and business ties to Jewish banking families (the Da Pisas of Florence and the Norsas of Mantua) and honoured by titles and privileges in the Jewish and larger Italian community, Messer Leon without question enjoyed the highest social status held by a Jew in Renaissance Italy. He came to think of himself as the leader of Italian Jewry and issued decrees intended to shape Jewish religious practice, belief, and education. He even adopted the ancient title *Ro'sh Golah* (Head of the Diaspora). But his aristocratic pretensions were resented by other rabbis, and his attempts to lead all Italian Jews were hardly universally accepted. The time and place of his death are uncertain, but it is unlikely that he survived the conquest of Naples by the French armies of Charles VIII in 1494/5.

Deeply rooted in scholastic Aristotelianism and

staunchly loyal to Maimonides, the paramount figure in medieval Jewish Aristotelianism, Messer Leon saw philosophy as dedicated to the elucidation of authoritative texts. He was dedicated to logic and convinced that reasoning could resolve the apparent conflict between religion and philosophy. Trained by Christian logicians, he found scholastic logic superior to the Arabic logic taught by AL-FARABI and Averroes (see IBN RUSHD). Seeking to shift Jewish philosophical training to the Latin model, he wrote supercommentaries on Averroes' middle commentaries on the Organon, painstakingly collating their diverse textual traditions and harmonizing the Hebrew versions with the diverse Latin readings.

His 1454 compendium of Aristotelian logic, entitled *Mikhlal Yofi* (Purest Beauty), departed from medieval Arabic precedent by omitting the *Rhetoric* and *Poetics*, in effect emancipating these studies from their medieval status as mere arts of persuasion. *Mikhlal Yofi* excerpted several books of scholastic logic, notably the *Logica magna* of PAUL OF VENICE (*circa*1339/72–1429), which was also the primary source of Messer Leon's supercommentary on the *Posterior Analytics*. His supercommentary on Porphyry's *Isagōgē*, similarly, drew heavily on the *Super artem veterem expositio* of Walter BURLEY (*circa*1275–1345). The supercommentaries on *Categories*, *De interpretatione* and the *Prior Analytics*, all extant in manuscripts, again rely on scholastic sources. Usefully, Messer Leon wrote summaries (*sefeqot*) of the major philosophical questions debated in Italian universities.

His debt to scholastic authors led to charges by a philosophy instructor in his own *yeshivah*, now known only as David the Spaniard, that his writings were mere translations and that even his glosses bordered on plagiarism. The master publicly rebutted the accusations and dismissed his adversary as a exponent of the views of Jewish Averroists from Provence, chiefly, Levi ben Gershom (see GERSONIDES), whose apparent denial of God's knowledge of particulars seemed to undermine the idea of providence. Messer Leon tried to suppress Gersonides' recently printed commentary on the Pentateuch, but with little success. It was highly esteemed among native Italian Jews, and Gersonides' magnum opus, *Milhamot ha-Shem* (The Wars of the Lord), became a classic of Jewish philosophy among the educated.

2 Philosophical standpoint

The extant works and the letters of Messer Leon's son David (d. *circa* 1535), cite a number of philosophical and scientific works now lost: supercommentaries on Aristotle's *On the Soul*, *Metaphysics*, *Nicomachaean Ethics*, *Physics* and, possibly, the *Topics*. To prepare his students in medicine, he wrote a commentary on the first and second parts of Avicenna's *Canon*, and a short summary of essential medical information (*Yedi'ot ha-nehuzot le-Rofe'*). Despite his devotion to such studies, Messer Leon, like the medieval Jewish philosophers, did not view philosophy and its allied arts and sciences as ends in themselves, but saw them as preparation for higher study – of the divinely revealed religion. In keeping with his desire to articulate an official Jewish theology, he commented on the two most widely read texts of Jewish philosophy in fifteenth-century Italy: Maimonides' *Guide to the Perplexed* and Yeda'aya Bedersi's *Behinat 'Olam* (Examination of the Universe). The *Moreh Tzedeq* (Teacher of Righteousness), his commentary on the *Guide*, is now lost, but his commentary on *Behinat 'Olam* is extant in several manuscripts and awaits systematic study. A reading of it shows Messer Leon's kinship in approach to other Jewish Aristotelians of his time. Like Joseph Ibn Shem Tov (d. *circa* 1460), Abraham Bibago (d. *circa* 1489) and Abraham Shalom (d. *circa* 1492) in Spain, and Elijah DELMEDIGO (d.1493) in Crete and Italy, Messer Leon insisted on the rationality of a divinely revealed Judaism while recognizing the inherent limitations of natural human reason. Because philosophic understanding rests on sense perception, it is prone to errors, doubts, and uncertainties and cannot bring us to our ultimate goal, individual beatitude in the hereafter. It must be complemented by revealed truths beyond the ken of natural reason. But these suprarational truths cannot contradict the precepts of philosophy. A rational examination of Judaism, which Messer Leon apparently undertook in his now lost commentary on the Pentateuch, would show that the Torah of Moses is in full accord with the teachings of Aristotle, as properly understood.

3 Rhetoric

Messer Leon endorsed the Platonic elitism of the Maimonidean tradition: God's revelation is abstruse; ordinary people lack the intellectual perfection needed to grasp its truths directly. They must receive these through the veils of figurative language. But philosophical wisdom does grasp the inner meaning of the Torah, and this more penetrating understanding of the Torah's message and its tropes endows the philosopher with political authority – an authority that rests on exegesis, and so on the study of grammar and rhetoric.

Messer Leon's *Livenat ha-Sappir* (The Sapphire Stone) systematically applied the categories of European grammar to the Hebrew language. The work relied heavily on the writings of Abraham IBN EZRA (1089–1164). Distinctive in Messer Leon's approach was the influence of Renaissance humanism (see HUMANISM, RENAISSANCE). He saw grammar not merely as ancillary to logic but as praiseworthy in its own right. Its kinship with rhetoric made it an essential tool of cogent argument and elegant exposition and a *sine qua non* in exegesis.

In 1475, in Mantua, Messer Leon published a manual of Hebrew rhetoric entitled *Nofet Tzufim*, taking his title from the Psalms, where the image is applied to God's speech. Like his works on logic, this inventory of linguistic tropes combined Arabic and Latin traditions: the Averroist-Aristotelian tradition he knew through Todros Todrosi's Hebrew translation of Averroes' middle commentary on Aristotle's *Rhetoric*, and the Ciceronian-Quintilian tradition, which he knew chiefly through the pseudo-Aristotelian *Rhetorica ad Alexandrum*, Cicero's *De inventione*, the pseudo-Ciceronian *Rhetorica ad Herennium*, Quintilian's *Institutio oratoria*, and Marius Victorinus' commentary on Cicero's *De inventione*.

The first articulate Jewish response to the humanist cult of rhetoric and the concomitant revival of classical prose and poetry, *Nofet Tzufim* sparked a new appreciation for eloquence among Italian Jewish scholars. Siding with Ermolao Barbaro in his dispute with Giovanni PICO DELLA MIRANDOLA, Messer Leon prized eloquence as a complement to moral and intellectual perfection: a good orator must first be a good man and a good philosopher. In place of the 'golden age' Latin held up as a model by Renaissance writers, Messer Leon placed biblical Hebrew, the perfect exemplar of the Ciceronian ideal of a synthesis of wisdom with eloquence (see CICERO, M.T.). By analysing Scripture in this Ciceronian light, Messer Leon legitimized the study of ancient pagan and Christian orators even as he argued for the supremacy of biblical rhetoric over all merely human eloquence.

4 Humanism and Kabbalah

The Renaissance humanism he so admired presented Messer Leon with an acute political and intellectual problem. The humanists of the later fifteenth century, especially in the Platonic Academy of Florence, revived numerous non-Aristotelian cosmological constructs, including Platonic, Neoplatonic and Hermetic frameworks. Urging the unity of all truth, humanists like Marsilio FICINO and Pico della Mirandola sought an ancient syncretic wisdom in these religious and philosophic traditions. A vital part of the *prisca theologia* they sought was the Jewish esoteric and mystical tradition of Kabbalah (see KABBALAH). The humanists' deep respect for Kabbalah contrasted sharply with the disdain of medieval scholars towards rabbinic Judaism, but it was not devoid of missionarizing intent. For the syncretic tradition was seen as culminating in Christianity; and, among the many Jewish intellectuals drawn by the humanist revival of Platonism and fascination with Kabbalah, some became converts to Christianity.

Messer Leon attempted to stem the spread of Kabbalah in Italy, viewing the tradition as neither authentic nor authoritative *vis-à-vis* rabbinic Judaism. It was a mere medieval throwback, a human innovation closely akin to the inferior philosophy of Platonism, which compromised the absoluteness of God's unity and incorporeality. Distressed in particular by the Christian overtones of humanist interest in Kabbalah, Messer Leon forbade its study in his *yeshivah*, but he had little success in curbing its spread in Italy among Jews and non-Jews alike. His son David and two other students of Aristotelian philosophy, Yohanan ALEMANNO (d. after 1503/4) and Abraham de Balmes (d. 1523), cultivated the Kabbalah and sought to incorporate its doctrines into the framework of Jewish Aristotelianism.

Messer Leon played an essential role in keeping alive the traditions of medieval Aristotelian philosophy among Italian Jews in the later fifteenth century. Modelling the training in his *yeshivah* on the Italian university curriculum, he professionalized the study of philosophy among Italian Jews. His sensitivity to humanist ideals enabled him to create a cadre of Jewish scholars who could offer spiritual leadership and eloquent counsel to the Jewish community. But all his high-handed attempts to mould the culture of Italian Jewry failed. His own students did not accept his categorical preference for Aristotelian logic over Platonic metaphysics, and even his son did not follow him in rejecting Kabbalah. Sixteenth-century Italian Jewish scholars were increasingly influenced by Renaissance Platonism and Kabbalah, rather to the cost of Maimonidean rationalism, as the accepted theology of Judaism.

See also: ALEMANNO, Y.; ARISTOTELIANISM, MEDIEVAL; ARISTOTELIANISM, RENAISSANCE; HUMANISM, RENAISSANCE; PLATONISM, RENAISSANCE

List of works

Ben Yehiel, Judah (*c*.1449) *Perush al' Yeda'ya Berdesi's Behinat 'Olam* (Commentary on Yeda'ya Berdesi's *Examination of the Universe*), MS Florence: Biblioteca Medicea-Laurenziana Plut. 88.52/2; MS Vienna, 163. 8. (Berdesi's *Behinat 'Olam* was a very popular book among Jewish intellectuals in the first half of the fifteenth century. It articulated the worldview of medieval Jewish Neoplatonized Aristotelianism in a semi-poetic form. By writing a commentary on this text, Messer Leon intended to ground the accepted worldview in a more rigorous interpretation of Aristotelian philosophy.)

—— (1454) *Livenat ha-Sappir* (The Sapphire Stone), MS Oxford: Bodleian Library, 1491; MS London: British Museum, Add. 27. 094; MS Paris: Bibliothèque Nationale, Hebrew 1247; MS Parma: Biblioteca Palatina, 2477 (De Rossi 114); MS Cambridge: Trinity College, 88; MS Moscow: Guenzburg, 583 and 1386. (This text, which Abraham Mordecai Farissol copied for the Norsa family in Mantua between 1473 and 1475, was still used as a textbook for study of Hebrew grammar by Jewish scholars in Constantinople during the sixteenth century.)

—— (1454) *Mikhlal Yofi* (Purest Beauty), MS Leghorn (Livorno) 41; MS Rome: Biblioteca Casanatense, 162; MS Florence: Biblioteca Medicea-Laurenziana, 88.52, MS Paris: Bibliothèque Nationale, Hebrew 994 and 998; MS London: British Museum, Or. 5467 and Add. 27.087; MS Vienna, 162; MS Parma: Biblioteca Palatina, 2615 (De Rossi 1355); MS Cambridge: Trinity College, Hebrew Add. 398. (This textbook for the study of logic was very popular among Jewish students in the fifteenth and early sixteenth century, indicating the perpetuation of Aristotelian logic among the Jewish intellectuals.)

—— (*c.*1470) *Perush le-Mavo-ma'amarot-Melizah* (Supercommentary on *Isagōgē – Categories–De interpretatione*), ed. I. Husik, *Judah Messer Leon's Commentary on the Vetus Logica*, Leiden: Brill, 1906. (Husik's is a critical edition of a composite text. Husik used the manuscript which Abraham Mordecai Farissol prepared for the Norsa brothers in Mantua (MS Oxford: Bodleian 1392) and three other manuscripts listed in Bonfil's introduction.)

—— (1476) *Nofet Zufim* (The Book of the Honeycomb's Flow), ed. R. Bonfil, *Nofet Zufim on Hebrew Rhetoric*, Jerusalem: The Jewish National and University Library Press and Magnes Press, 1981; ed. and trans. I. Rabinowitz, *The Book of the Honeycomb's Flow: Sepher Nophet Suphim by Judah Messer Leon*, Ithaca, NY: Cornell University Press, 1983. (Written in Hebrew, Bonfil's excellent 'introduction' to his edition lists all the extant manuscripts of Messer Leon and situates Messer Leon in his socio-cultural context. Rabinowitz's superb critical edition and English translation has a detailed introduction, which lists most of the pertinent, albeit controversial, information about Messer Leon's life, as well as giving a partial list of

his works extant in manuscripts. Rabinowitz's elegant English translation and notes are especially valuable for situating this work in the context of Western rhetoric.)

References and further reading

Altmann, A. (1981) 'Ars Rhetorica as Reflected in Some Jewish Figures of the Italian Renaissance', in *Essays in Jewish Intellectual History*, Hanover, NH and London: University Press of New England, 97–118; repr. in B.D. Cooperman (ed.) *Jewish Thought in the Sixteenth Century*, Cambridge, MA: Harvard University Press, 1983, 1–22. (This scholarly masterpiece situates Messer Leon's rhetoric in the broader context of ancient, medieval and Renaissance approaches.)

Bonfil, R. (1992) 'The Book of the Honeycomb's Flow by Judah Messer Leon: The Rhetoric Dimension of Jewish Humanism in Fifteenth-Century Italy', in *The Frank Talmage Memorial Volume*, Haifa: Haifa University Press, vol. 2, 21–33. (A superb analysis of Messer Leon's rhetorical and philosophical activities. Indispensable for English readers without access to Bonfil's Hebrew essay.)

Carpi, D. (1972) 'R. Yehudah Messer Leon u-feulato ke-rofe' (R. Judah Messer Leon and His Activity as a Physician), *Michael* 1: 277–301; repr. in *Between Renaissance and Ghetto: Essays on the History of the Jewish in Italy in the 14th and 17th Centuries*, Tel Aviv: University Publishing Project, 1989; trans. D. Carpi, 'Notes on the Life of Rabbi Judah Messer Leon', in E. Toaff (ed.) *Studi sull'ebraismo italiano in memoria di Cecil Roth*, Rome: Barulli, 1975. (This ground-breaking essay established the salient facts of Messer Leon's life and medical work using newly discovered archival material.)

Ivry, A.L. (1983) 'Remnants of Jewish Averroism in the Renaissance', in B.D. Cooperman (ed.) *Jewish Thought in the Sixteenth Century*, Cambridge, MA: Harvard University Press, 243–65. (Surveys some of Messer Leon's younger contemporaries, focusing on Elijah del Medigo.)

Lesley, A.M. (1988) 'Jewish Adaptation of Humanist Concepts in Fifteenth- and Sixteenth-Century Italy', in M.C. Horowitz (ed.) *Renaissance Rereadings: Intertext and Context*, Urbana and Chicago, IL: University of Illinois Press, 51–65. (An important exposition of Jewish polemical adaptation of humanist educational ideals and aesthetic sensibilities.)

Melamed, A. (1978) 'Rhetorica u-Filosofia be-Sefer *Nofet Tzufim*' (Rhetoric and Philosophy in *Nofet Tzufim* by R. Judah Messer Leon), *Italia* 1: 7–38.

(Explores Messer Leon's views on the relationship between eloquence and wisdom and highlights the link between rhetoric and political theory in Jewish thought in Italy.)

Ruderman, D. (1981) *The World of a Renaissance Jew: The Life and Thought of Abraham ben Mordecai Farissol*, Cincinnati, OH: Hebrew Union College Press. (A detailed monograph about a student of Messer Leon's who popularized his works on logic among Italian Jews. A rich reconstruction of fifteenth-century Jewish culture in Italy.)

—— (1988) 'The Italian Renaissance and Jewish Thought', in A. Rabil, Jr (ed.) *Renaissance Humanism: Foundations and Forms*, Philadelphia, PA: University of Pennsylvania Press, vol. 1, 382–433. (Excellent overview, relates Messer Leon to the Aristotelian, Renaissance humanist, and Platonic traditions.)

Rosenberg, S. (1973) 'Logica ve-ontologiah ba-filosofia ha-hehudit ba-me'ah ha-arba esreh' (Logic and Ontology in Jewish Philosophy in the Fourteenth Century), unpublished Ph.D. dissertation, Jerusalem: Hebrew University. (Still the only survey of Jewish logic in the late Middle Ages; contains invaluable biographical and bibliographical information about Jewish logicians and the only analysis of general trends and themes in Jewish logic, including Messer Leon's attempt to shift Jewish logic from the Judaeo–Arabic to the Latin scholastic model.)

Tirosh-Rothschild, H. (1991) *Between Worlds: The Life and Thought of Rabbi David ben Judah Messer Leon*, Albany, NY: State University of New York Press. (A monograph on Judah Messer Leon's son, illustrating the shift from Aristotelian to Kabbalistic trends between 1450 and 1550. Chapter 1 summarizes the educational and political activities and reviews the recent scholarship.)

HAVA TIROSH-SAMUELSON

META-ETHICS *see* ANALYTIC

ETHICS

METAPHOR

A standard dictionary definition describes a metaphor as 'a figure of speech in which a word or phrase literally denoting one kind of object is used in place of another to suggest a likeness between them'. Although the theoretical adequacy of this definition may be questioned, it conveys the standard view that there is a difference between literal and nonliteral language; that figurative speech is nonliteral language and that a metaphor is an instance of figurative speech.

The three most influential treatments of metaphor are the comparison, interaction and speech act theories. According to the first, every metaphor involves a comparison; a specific version of this view is that every metaphor is an abbreviated simile. According to the second, every metaphor involves a semantic interaction between some object or concept that is literally denoted by some word, and some concept metaphorically predicated on that word. According to the third, it is not words or sentences that are metaphorical but their use in specific situations; thus, to understand how metaphors function, one must understand how people communicate with language.

1   **The comparison theory**
2   **The interaction theory**
3   **The speech act theory**

1   The comparison theory

The comparison theory asserts that every metaphor compares two things, one of which is designated by a word or phrase used literally and the other of which is designated by a word or phrase used metaphorically. The most interesting version of the comparison view of metaphor is the simile theory. According to its originator, Aristotle (*Rhetoric* III.4), a metaphor is an abbreviated simile: the sentence 'My lover is a red rose' is shorthand for 'My lover is like a red rose'. (The simile theory is also sometimes known as the abbreviation or substitution theory, because a metaphor is represented as being an abbreviation of or a substitution for a simile.) The merit of this view is its double simplicity. First, what looked like two things (metaphors and similes) are said to be one thing; second, the analysis that is given to similes is sometimes quite simple. A simile is true just in case there is some feature that each object has. The feature common to both constitutes the similarity.

One objection to this theory is that what has been represented as its first merit is in fact a misrepresentation. Metaphors and similes are different things because typically if a metaphor were literally asserted, the result would be a falsehood, while (virtually) all similes are true. For example, the metaphor 'My lover is a red rose' is literally false, while the simile 'My lover is like a red rose' is literally true. The pretence of saying something false is a crucial feature of how metaphors work. To hold that metaphorical sentences are in fact similes obscures this feature. This is not to deny that metaphors typically communicate a truth in some way; it is rather to hold that a metaphor communicates its truth in a different way to a simile.

Metaphors (unlike similes) do not state or express truths; they imply them. In order to speak truly, the words of a sentence must be conventionally or semantically appropriate to each other, but the words of a metaphor are not semantically appropriate in this sense. For example, in the metaphor 'Sally is a block of ice', 'Sally' and 'a block of ice' belong to categories so different that to juxtapose them results not merely in a falsehood but in an absurdity. Someone may reply that, since 'Sally is a block of ice' can be used metaphorically, 'Sally is not a block of ice' can also be used metaphorically; and since this latter metaphor results in a true assertion, its words cannot be semantically inappropriate to each other. The proper reply to this objection is to deny that 'Sally is not a block of ice' is a metaphor. (To assert it is to assert something that is obviously true, but that does not mean that the assertion is pointless any more than to assert that 'Business is business' need be pointless. To assert that 'Sally is not a block of ice' may imply that one rejects the metaphorical utterance of 'Sally is a block of ice'.) Sentences that may appear to be negations of metaphorical sentences, such as John Donne's memorable sentiment 'No man is an island', are simply instances of *meiosis* (intentionally saying something logically weaker than the speaker intends to convey, usually by using a negative). Philosophers who consider 'No man is an island' and 'Sally is not a block of ice' to be metaphors, are in effect conflating metaphor and meiosis. They make it difficult or impossible to distinguish something obviously, literally false ('Business is theft') from something obviously, literally true ('Business is business').

To deny an assertion is *ipso facto* to make an assertion; but to deny a metaphor is not to make a metaphor. Assertions are a type of speech act, performed through a literal use of words. But a metaphor is not a kind of speech act and relies on the literal use of words only in order to indicate that the speaker means to communicate something other than their literal meaning.

Another deficiency of the standard simile theory is that it does not account for the fact that some effort or mental computation is required in order to work out what a metaphor means, in contrast with a simile which usually means what it says. In order to meet this objection, a quasi-simile theory has been proposed. Suppose someone says 'My lover is a red rose'. To understand this metaphor, one considers the set of red roses plus the speaker's lover and then tries to work out which property or properties all the members of this set share; in other words, to say that one's lover is a red rose is to say that they are similar in some respects to red roses. The objection to this theory is the same as one raised to the original theory. As Davidson (1979: 36) points out, a metaphor only intimates what a simile declares.

2 The interaction theory

According to the interaction theory, a metaphor involves an interaction between a literal element in a sentence and a metaphorical element. So there are always two parts to a metaphor. Max Black (1962) calls the literal element the frame and the metaphorical element the focus. Searle (1979) has effectively refuted this version of the theory by pointing out that some metaphorical sentences do not contain any literal element which could plausibly serve the role of frame. For example, the sentence 'The bad news congealed into a block of ice' is a mixed metaphor, but it contains no word with a literal meaning that can serve as the frame. Another objection to the interaction theory is that the term 'interaction' is itself a metaphor. Since there is no literal interaction between words in a sentence or between concepts, the interaction theory never actually explains or describes how metaphors work. More recent treatments of the theory explain interaction as the placement of the object literally denoted within a conceptual system of commonplaces associated with the metaphorical term. Thus, to say 'Mary is a wolf' is to associate Mary and her attributes with the complex of properties associated with wolves: cunning, viciousness, unpredictability and so on. None the less 'interaction' seems to be the wrong word to convey this feature. Also, the interaction theory claims that the meaning of the words is affected by this interaction and that seems to be an inaccurate description of the phenomenon.

Donald Davidson has insisted that semantically metaphors mean what the words used to convey them literally mean and nothing more. His thesis constitutes a direct rejection of all views that hold that a distinction must be drawn at the level of words or sentences between two kinds of meaning: literal meaning and metaphorical meaning. While the literal meaning is usually taken as obvious, the metaphorical meaning is often said to be ineffable and ineffability is given as the reason why metaphors are used. Sceptics about ineffability would object to a kind of meaning that is inherently mysterious or unintelligible, even if individual speakers are unable to articulate what they mean. In any case, what is needed is an explanation of how metaphors are understood. Here, Davidson seems to be right when he says that understanding a metaphor is the same kind of activity as understanding any other linguistic utterance and all understanding requires an 'inventive construal' of what the literal meaning of the metaphorical utterance is and what the speaker believes about the world. Furthermore, this activity is 'little guided by rules'. Making a metaphor, like speaking generally, is a 'creative endeavour'.

3 The speech act theory

It is fair to demand that a theory of metaphor fit into some larger theory of language or communication. While the comparison and interaction theories do not meet this demand, the speech act theory does. H.P. Grice (1989) distinguished between 'utterance occasion meaning' (the meaning that an utterance has on some particular occasion of its use) and 'timeless utterance meaning' (the meaning an utterance has based upon its usual use and independent of any particular time). This latter form of meaning can be associated with literal or conventional meaning. In a metaphor, the speaker intends to have the audience work out the 'occasion' meaning of their utterance in part by understanding its 'timeless' meaning (see GRICE, H.P.).

How does this happen? Grice points out that normal conversation is directed by the cooperative principle: make your contribution to a conversation appropriate. This principle issues in various conversational maxims. For example, what a person says should be truthful and supported by evidence; it should be as informative as the audience needs it to be and not more so; and the information should be relevant to the topic of conversation. These maxims are related to the content of the message. There are also maxims concerning how the message is to be expressed: it should be clear, unambiguous, brief and orderly. Of course these maxims are not always fulfilled. Sometimes they go unfulfilled quietly and unostentatiously, such as when a person lies or makes an innocent mistake. Sometimes they are flouted, that is, openly and ostentatiously unfulfilled in order to achieve a certain effect. For example, one way to show disgust for or disappointment with someone is to say 'You're a fine friend'. In such instances of sarcasm or irony, the speaker flouts the maxim of truthfulness and thereby within the context of the conversation means exactly the opposite of what appears to be said. Other figures of speech can be explained in similar ways. Hyperbole is intentionally making an exaggerated statement in order to achieve a certain effect. Within the theory being sketched, hyperbole is also achieved by flouting the maxim of truthfulness: the speaker makes a statement that is logically stronger than the proposition they intend to communicate.

Within this theory, meiosis is achieved by flouting the maxim of quantity (which enjoins the speaker to make their statement logically as strong as possible); for example, by saying, 'John D. Rockefeller was not poor'. The audience, trying to make sense of the speaker's apparent nonfulfilment of the cooperative principle, infers that the speaker means something stronger than was said.

Metaphor fits into the same pattern of explanation although the calculation of what a metaphor means is more complicated. If someone says 'My lover is a red rose' in circumstances that are otherwise unexceptional, it is sensible for the audience to judge that the speaker is flouting the maxim of truthfulness. What then does the speaker mean? The audience's strategy in the case of metaphor, as in every other case of linguistic understanding, is to achieve a cognitive equilibrium by accepting those propositions that make the most sense of the situation. This involves making new beliefs fit in as smoothly as possible with existing beliefs and sometimes revising old beliefs as part of this process. Briefly, for the example above, it makes sense for the audience to believe that the speaker intends the audience to recognize that the speaker intends the audience to think of certain qualities of a rose – its beauty, value, delicacy, fragrance – and then attribute them to the lover. Such a search for cognitive equilibrium is close to what Davidson meant when he said that understanding language is 'a creative endeavour'.

See also: COMMUNICATION AND INTENTION; DAVIDSON, D.; SPEECH ACTS

References and further reading

* Aristotle (c.mid-4th century BC) *Rhetoric*, trans. G. Kennedy, *Aristotle on Rhetoric: A Theory of Civic Discourse*, New York: Oxford University Press, 1991, III 4. (The first statement of the simile theory.)
* Black, M. (1962) *Models and Metaphors*, Ithaca, NY: Cornell University Press. (Contains the most influential presentation of the interaction theory.)
* Davidson, D. (1979) 'What Metaphors Mean', in S. Sacks (ed.) *On Metaphor*, Chicago, IL: University of Chicago Press, 29–45. (Davidson emphasized that words themselves do not have a metaphorical meaning.)
  Goodman, N. (1968) *Languages of Art*, Indianapolis, IN: Bobbs-Merrill. (A sophisticated version of the interaction theory.)
* Grice, H.P. (1989) 'Logic and Conversation', in *Studies in the Way of Words*, Cambridge, MA: Harvard University Press, 22–40. (Contains Grice's

general theory of conversation, including a treatment of metaphor.)

Johnson, M. (1980) *Philosophical Perspectives on Metaphor*, Minneapolis, MN: University of Minnesota Press. (A collection of important articles on metaphor.)

Martinich, A.P. (1984) 'A Theory for Metaphor', *Journal of Literary Semantics* 13: 35–54; repr. in S. Davis (ed.) *Pragmatics*, Cambridge: Cambridge University Press, 1991, 507–18. (A speech act theory of metaphor with criticisms of Searle's version.)

Noppen, J.P. van (ed.) (1985, 1990) *Metaphor*, vol. 1, *A Bibliography of Post-1970 Publications*; vol. 2, *A Classified Bibliography of Publications*, Amsterdam: Benjamins. (Continues the bibliographical work begun by Shibles.)

Ortony, A. (ed.) (1979) *Metaphor and Thought*, Cambridge: Cambridge University Press; 2nd edn, 1994. (Contains important articles by philosophers, psychologists, linguists and literary theorists.)

* Searle, J. (1979) 'Metaphor', in A. Ortony (ed.) *Metaphor and Thought*, Cambridge: Cambridge University Press; 2nd edn, 1994. (A speech act theory of metaphor in an important volume that contains contributions by philosophers, psychologists, linguists and literary theorists.)

Shibles, W. (1971) *Metaphor: An Annotated Bibliography and History*, Whitewater, WI: Language Press. (The most complete bibliography on metaphor up to 1970.)

A.P. MARTINICH

METAPHYSICS

Metaphysics is a broad area of philosophy marked out by two types of inquiry. The first aims to be the most general investigation possible into the nature of reality: are there principles applying to everything that is real, to all that is? – if we abstract from the particular nature of existing things that which distinguishes them from each other, what can we know about them merely in virtue of the fact that they exist? The second type of inquiry seeks to uncover what is ultimately real, frequently offering answers in sharp contrast to our everyday experience of the world. Understood in terms of these two questions, metaphysics is very closely related to ontology, which is usually taken to involve both 'what is existence (being)?' and 'what (fundamentally distinct) types of thing exist?' (see ONTOLOGY).

The two questions are not the same, since someone quite unworried by the possibility that the world might really be otherwise than it appears (and therefore regarding the second investigation as a completely trivial one) might still be engaged by the question of whether there were any general truths applicable to all existing things. But although different, the questions are related: one might well expect a philosopher's answer to the first to provide at least the underpinnings of their answer to the second. Aristotle proposed the first of these investigations. He called it 'first philosophy', sometimes also 'the science of being' (more-or-less what 'ontology' means); but at some point in antiquity his writings on the topic came to be known as the 'metaphysics' – from the Greek for 'after natural things', that is, what comes after the study of nature. This is as much as we know of the origin of the word (see ARISTOTLE §§10 and following). It would, however, be quite wrong to think of metaphysics as a uniquely 'Western' phenomenon. Classical Indian philosophy, and especially Buddhism, is also a very rich source (see BUDDHIST PHILOSOPHY, INDIAN; HINDU PHILOSOPHY; JAINA PHILOSOPHY).

1 General metaphysics

Any attempt on either question will find itself using, and investigating, the concepts of being and existence (see BEING; EXISTENCE). It will then be natural to ask whether there are any further, more detailed classifications under which everything real falls, and a positive answer to this question brings us to a doctrine of categories (see CATEGORIES). The historical picture here is complex, however. The two main exponents of such a doctrine are Aristotle and Kant. In Aristotle's case it is unclear whether he saw it as a doctrine about things and their basic properties or about language and its basic predicates; whereas Kant quite explicitly used his categories as features of our way of thinking, and so applied them only to things as they appear to us, not as they really or ultimately are (see KANT, I.). Following on from Kant, Hegel consciously gave his categories both roles, and arranged his answer to the other metaphysical question (about the true underlying nature of reality) so as to make this possible (see HEGEL, G.W.F.).

An early, extremely influential view about reality seen in the most general light is that it consists of things and their properties – individual things, often called particulars, and properties, often called universals, that can belong to many such individuals (see PARTICULARS; UNIVERSALS). Very closely allied to this notion of an individual is the concept of substance, that in which properties 'inhere' (see SUBSTANCE). This line of thought (which incidentally had a biological version in the concepts of individual creatures and their species) gave rise to one of the most famous metaphysical controversies: whether universals are real entities or not (see SPECIES; NATURAL KINDS). In different ways, PLATO and Aristotle had each held the affirmative view; nominalism is the general term for the various versions of the negative position (see NOMINALISM).

The clash between realists and nominalists over universals can serve to illustrate a widespread feature of metaphysical debate. Whatever entities, forces and so on may be proposed, there will be a *prima facie* option between regarding them as real beings, genuine constituents of the world and, as it were, downgrading them to fictions or projections of our own ways of speaking and thinking (see OBJECTIVITY; PROJECTIVISM). This was, broadly speaking, how nominalists wished to treat universals; comparable debates exist concerning causality (see CAUSATION), moral value (see EMOTIVISM; MORAL REALISM; MORAL SCEPTICISM; VALUE, ONTOLOGICAL STATUS OF) and necessity and possibility (see NECESSARY TRUTH AND CONVENTION) – to name a few examples. Some have even proposed that the categories (see above) espoused in the Western tradition are reflections of the grammar of Indo-European languages, and have no further ontological status (see SAPIR-WHORF HYPOTHESIS).

Wittgenstein famously wrote that the world is the totality of facts, not of things, so bringing to prominence another concept of the greatest generality (see FACTS). Presumably he had it in mind that exactly the same things, differently related to each other, could form very different worlds; so that it is not things but the states of affairs or facts they enter into which determine how things are. The apparent obviousness of the formula 'if it is true that p then it is a fact that p', makes it seem that facts are in one way or another closely related to truth (see TRUTH, COHERENCE THEORY OF; TRUTH, CORRESPONDENCE THEORY OF) – although it should be said that not every philosophical view of the nature of truth is a metaphysical one, since some see it as just a linguistic device (see TRUTH, DEFLATIONARY THEORIES OF) and some as a reflection, not of how the world is, but of human needs and purposes (see TRUTH, PRAGMATIC THEORY OF; RELATIVISM).

Space and time, as well as being somewhat elusive in their own nature, are further obvious candidates for being features of everything that exists (see SPACE; TIME). But that is controversial, as the debate about the existence of abstract objects testifies (see ABSTRACT OBJECTS). We commonly speak, at least, as if we thought that numbers exist, but not as if we thought that they have any spatio-temporal properties (see REALISM IN THE PHILOSOPHY OF MATHEMATICS).

Kant regarded his things-in-themselves as neither spatial nor temporal; and some have urged us to think of God in the same way (see GOD, CONCEPTS OF). There are accounts of the mind which allow mental states to have temporal, but deny them spatial properties (see DUALISM).

Be all this as it may, even if not literally everything, then virtually everything of which we have experience is in time. Temporality is therefore one of the phenomena that should be the subject of any investigation which aspires to maximum generality. Hence, so is change (see CHANGE). And when we consider change, and ask the other typically metaphysical question about it ('what is really going on when something changes?') we find ourselves faced with two types of answer. One type would have it that a change is an alteration in the properties of some enduring thing (see CONTINUANTS). The other would deny any such entity, holding instead that what we really have is merely a sequence of states, a sequence which shows enough internal coherence to make upon us the impression of one continuing thing (see MOMENTARINESS, BUDDHIST DOCTRINE OF). The former will tend to promote 'thing' and 'substance' to the ranks of the most basic metaphysical categories; the latter will incline towards events and processes (see EVENTS; PROCESSES). It is here that questions about identity over time become acute, particularly in the special case of those continuants (or, perhaps, processes), which are persons (see IDENTITY; PERSONS; PERSONAL IDENTITY).

Two major historical tendencies in metaphysics have been idealism and materialism, the former presenting reality as ultimately mental or spiritual, the latter regarding it as wholly material (see BUDDHISM, YOGĀCĀRA SCHOOL OF; IDEALISM; MATERIALISM; MATERIALISM IN THE PHILOSOPHY OF MIND; MONISM, INDIAN; PHENOMENALISM). In proposing a single ultimate principle both are monistic (see MONISM). They have not had the field entirely to themselves. A minor competitor has been neutral monism, which takes mind and matter to be different manifestations of something in itself neither one nor the other (see NEUTRAL MONISM). More importantly, many metaphysical systems have been dualist, taking both to be fundamental, and neither to be a form of the other (see SĀṄKHYA). Both traditions are ancient. In modern times idealism received its most intensive treatment in the nineteenth century (see ABSOLUTE, THE; GERMAN IDEALISM); in the second half of the twentieth century, materialism has been in the ascendant. A doctrine is also found according to which all matter, without actually being mental in nature, has certain mental properties (see PANPSYCHISM).

2 Specific metaphysics

There is also metaphysics that arises in reference to particular subject matters, this being therefore metaphysical primarily with regard to the second question (what are things ultimately like? – or, what kinds of thing ultimately exist?) rather than the first. One of the most obvious cases, and historically the most prominent, is theology; we have already mentioned the philosophy of mind, the philosophy of mathematics and the theory of values. Less obviously, metaphysical issues also intrude on the philosophy of language and logic, as happens when it is suggested that any satisfactory theory of meaning will have to posit the existence of intensional entities, or that any meaningful language will have to mirror the structure of the world (see INTENSIONAL ENTITIES; LOGICAL ATOMISM). The political theorist or social scientist who holds that successful explanation in the social sphere must proceed from properties of societies not reducible to properties of the individuals who make them up (thereby making a society an entity that is in a sense more basic than its members) raises a metaphysical issue (see HOLISM AND INDIVIDUALISM IN HISTORY AND SOCIAL SCIENCE). Metaphysics, as demarcated by the second question, can pop up anywhere.

The relationship with metaphysics is, however, particularly close in the case of science and the philosophy of science. Aristotle seems to have understood his 'first philosophy' as continuous with what is now called his physics, and indeed it can be said that the more fundamental branches of natural science are a kind of metaphysics as it is characterized here. For they are typically concerned with the discovery of laws and entities that are completely general, in the sense that everything is composed of entities and obeys laws. The differences are primarily epistemological ones, the balance of a priori considerations and empirical detail used by scientists and philosophers in supporting their respective ontological claims. The *subject matter* of these claims can even sometimes coincide: during the 1980s the reality of possible worlds other than the actual one was maintained by a number of writers for a variety of reasons, some of them recognizably 'scientific', some recognizably 'philosophical' (see POSSIBLE WORLDS). And whereas we find everywhere in metaphysics a debate over whether claims should be given a realist or an antirealist interpretation, in the philosophy of science we find a parallel controversy over the status of the entities featuring in scientific theories (see REALISM AND ANTIREALISM; SCIENTIFIC REALISM AND ANTIREALISM).

It is true that there has been considerable reluct-ance to acknowledge any such continuity. A principal source of this reluctance has been logical positivism, with its division of propositions into those which are empirically verifiable and meaningful, and those which are not so verifiable and are either analytic or meaningless, followed up by its equation of science with the former and metaphysics with the latter (see DEMARCATION PROBLEM; LOGICAL POSITIVISM; MEANING AND VERIFICATION). When combined with the belief that analytic truths record nothing about the world, but only about linguistic convention, this yields a total rejection of all metaphysics – let alone of any continuity with science. But apart from the fact that this line of thought requires acceptance of the principle about meaninglessness, it also makes a dubious epistemological assumption: that what we call science never uses non-empirical arguments, and that what we regard as metaphysics never draws on empirical premises. Enemies of obscurantism need not commit themselves to any of this; they can recognize the continuity between science and metaphysics without robbing anyone of the vocabulary in which to be rude about the more extravagant, ill-evidenced, even barely meaningful forms which, in the view of some, metaphysics has sometimes taken.

Even the philosopher with a low opinion of the prospects for traditional metaphysics can believe that there is a general framework which we in fact use for thinking about reality, and can undertake to describe and explore it. This project, which can claim an illustrious ancestor in Kant, has in the twentieth century sometimes been called descriptive metaphysics, though what it inquires into are our most general patterns of thought, and the nature of things themselves only indirectly, if at all. Though quite compatible with a low estimate of traditional metaphysics as defined by our two primary questions, it does imply that there is a small but fairly stable core of human thought for it to investigate. Hence it collides with the view of those who deny that there is any such thing (see POSTMODERNISM).

See also: ARISTOTELIANISM IN ISLAMIC PHILOSOPHY; ARISTOTELIANISM IN THE 17TH CENTURY; ARISTOTELIANISM, MEDIEVAL; ARISTOTELIANISM, RENAISSANCE; BRAHMAN; BUDDHIST CONCEPT OF EMPTINESS; CAUSALITY AND NECESSITY IN ISLAMIC THOUGHT; CAUSATION, INDIAN THEORIES OF; CONTINGENCY; HEGELIANISM; INFINITY; MATERIALISM, INDIAN SCHOOL OF; MATTER, INDIAN CONCEPTIONS OF; NEGATIVE FACTS IN CLASSICAL INDIAN PHILOSOPHY; NEO-KANTIANISM; NEOPLATONISM; NEOPLATONISM IN ISLAMIC PHILOSOPHY; NOMINALISM, BUDDHIST DOCTRINE OF; ONTOLOGY IN INDIAN PHILOSOPHY; PLATONISM,

EARLY AND MIDDLE; PLATONISM IN ISLAMIC PHILOSOPHY; PLATONISM, MEDIEVAL; PLATONISM, RENAISSANCE; POTENTIALITY, INDIAN THEORIES OF; RELIGION, PHILOSOPHY OF; PROCESS PHILOSOPHY; SELF, INDIAN THEORIES OF; UNIVERSALS, INDIAN THEORIES OF

References and further reading

Kim, J. and Sosa, E. (eds) (1995) *A Companion to Metaphysics*, Oxford: Blackwell. (Encyclopedia-style volume with over 250 entries of varying length devoted to terms, theories, movements and individual philosophers. Some coverage of epistemological issues as well as metaphysics.)

EDWARD CRAIG

METHODOLOGICAL INDIVIDUALISM

Methodological individualism (MI) is the thesis that certain psychological properties are intrinsic properties, such as 'being made out of iron', rather than externally relational properties, such as 'being an aunt'. It has been challenged by influential 'anti-individualist' claims of, for example, Putnam and Burge, according to which the content of an individual's words or thoughts (beliefs, desires) is determined in part by facts about their social or physical environment. Putnam, for example, imagines a planet, 'twin earth', which is identical to the earth in 1750 (prior to modern chemistry) in all respects except that wherever earth had H_2O, twin earth had a different but superficially similar chemical, XYZ. Putnam argues that the English word 'water' in 1750 referred only to H_2O, while the twin word 'water' refers only to XYZ.

Historically, the term 'methodological individualism' has referred to the thesis that all social explanation must be ultimately expressible in terms of facts about individual human beings; not about economic classes, nations and so on. For a treatment of this subject, see EXPLANATION IN HISTORY AND SOCIAL SCIENCE §1.

1 Common arguments for MI
2 MI and the causal role of psychological properties
3 MI and the computational theory of vision

1 Common arguments for MI

Methodological individualism (MI) is a view about the representational contents of psychological states. There is a distinction between two kinds of such contents: narrow and wide (see CONTENT: WIDE AND NARROW). A content is 'wide' if its identity depends upon relations its thinkers bear to things outside their heads. Suppose, for example, that I am looking at a particular banana, *B*, and I think 'That banana is ripe'. My thought is then about that object, *B*. The thought is true if and only if *B* is ripe. In that sense, the content of the thought relates essentially to the banana itself. Had there been a different banana, *A*, my thought would have had a different content: it would have been true if and only if *A* had been ripe.

Content is 'narrow' if it is not relational, but is instead fully determined by intrinsic physical properties of individuals. Thus, any two individuals who were identical in all intrinsic physical respects would be identical in respect of all their narrow contents. Call such individuals 'twins'. Narrow content is content shared by twins (see IDENTITY OF INDISCERNIBLES §3). The above example of 'twin earth', due to PUTNAM (1975), challenges the view that the ordinary content we ascribe to people is narrow in this sense: the thought contents expressed by 'Water is wet' by the 1750 earthling and their twin-earthling would seem to be different, the first making a claim about H_2O, the second about XYZ.

MI is the view that, despite such twin cases, every psychological state has a narrow content, and that this content is, or should be, essential for psychological explanations. Thus, consider a pair of twins one of whom is thinking about banana *A* and the other about banana *B*. Each thinks 'That banana is ripe'. The methodological individualist will claim that the two thoughts have a content in common; a narrow content. They concede that the thoughts are about different external objects, but hold that the concepts involved – one twin's concept of *A* and the other's concept of *B* – are exactly the same. And this shared content, the one that includes exactly similar concepts, is crucial to psychological explanation. The same applies to Putnam's twins: their thoughts also have a shared narrow content.

Anti-individualists have presented three kinds of argument to show that contents attributed by both common sense and scientific psychological theory are wide rather than narrow. The first of these involves thought experiments, like Putnam's, in which one conceives of twins who inhabit environments that differ in crucial respects, and it is claimed that there is a strong intuition that the individuals' psychological states would have different contents. The second defends wide content on the basis of independently motivated theories of content, such as causal or teleofunctional theories (see SEMANTICS, TELEOLOGICAL; SEMANTICS, INFORMATIONAL). The third flow from studies of specific branches of scientific psychology.

Since the first two kinds of argument are treated in other entries, the present entry will discuss only the third, considering the question of whether contents attributed by scientific psychology are narrow or wide.

2 MI and the causal role of psychological properties

Jerry Fodor (1987) gives the following argument for MI.

(1) Psychological explanation is causal explanation. For example, we might cite someone's belief that water is good for plants as part of a causal explanation of why they filled a watering-can.

(2) A science that offers causal explanation individuates its subject matter with respect to causal powers. Specifically, it would not classify states as being of different kinds if they have the same causal powers.

(3) The causal powers of the psychological states of twins are the same. So, psychology would classify twins' psychological states as being of the same kind, hence as having the same content.

This argument may be questioned on various grounds (see, for example, Burge (1986); Fodor (1994), who has himself abandoned it). For example, the second premise is not obviously correct. The individuative practice of a science that offers causal explanations might be sensitive to various factors, not all of which are directly relevant to causal powers. For instance, a scientist might cite the action of the heart as part of a causal explanation of the workings of the cardiovascular system. However, the individuation conditions for hearts are not purely causal, but also involve historical, evolutionary considerations. Nevertheless, Fodor's argument has been influential, and methodological individualists may feel that there is something importantly right about it, even if it is not conclusive as it stands (see MENTAL CAUSATION §3).

3 MI and the computational theory of vision

One branch of psychology has been the focus of particular attention by philosophers discussing MI. This is the computational theory of vision, developed by David Marr (1982) and others (see VISION §4). The theory has received much attention because it is among the most developed areas of cognitive science. This makes it possible to look in detail at the actual practice and methodology of a psychological theory and give substance to the debates about the individuation of psychological states.

Tyler Burge (1982, 1986) argues that the theory has an anti-individualist methodology. He argues that the theory assumes that the human visual system has evolved to be successful on earth, and certain of the earthly environmental conditions that account for its success are relevant to the individuation of its representational states. Roughly, Burge's idea is that the content of certain representations is partly determined by what 'normally' cause them, where the 'normal' cause of a type of representation is the type of external condition that has caused it in the past, during the (phylogenetic) evolution of the system, under circumstances where it has been successful.

The argument proceeds by stating that one could envisage alternative possible circumstances in which intrinsically identical visual systems had evolved, but in which the 'normal' causes of some of the representations were different. In such a case, the representational contents, as attributed by the theory, would have been different from what they actually are. Hence MI is violated.

The situation Burge envisages can be schematically represented. On earth (E), the 'normal' cause of a particular physical type, T, of representation in the visual system is N. Thus Ts on E represent N. In a possible counterfactual circumstance, C, the prevailing conditions differ, but the visual system is intrinsically the same. In C, the 'normal' cause of T is W, where W is different from N. For example, N might be small, thin cracks and W might be small, thin shadows. When a visual system produces a representation of type T on E, it represents the presence of an N (its content being something like 'There is a small, thin crack'). When an intrinsically identical visual system in C produces a T, it represents the presence of a W (its content being something like 'There is a small, thin shadow').

Burge's argument is defended by a study of the theory of vision. However, it may be questioned on at least two grounds. First, it can be questioned whether the theory really accords such a crucial role to evolutionary considerations in its attributions of content. While it is true that Marr invokes evolutionary considerations at various points, it is far from clear that these considerations enter into the individuation of the contents of visual states in the decisive way that Burge claims (see Segal 1989). Second, even if the premises of the argument are granted, its validity can be questioned.

One way to question the validity of the argument involves considering in more detail the behaviour of twin subjects when they undergo a T. Let us consider two cases.

Case 1. Ns are circles and Ws are squares: these are the 'normal' causes of Ts on E and C, respectively. We can suppose that light bends in strange ways in *C*, so that squares there cause the same sorts of retinal images as circles do on E. Suppose we ask subjects who are undergoing a *T* to use their hands to trace in the air the shape they perceive. Since the subjects in the two environments are twins, they will make the same movements. If they trace a circle, this will indicate that *C* subjects are misperceiving squares as circles. *Mutatis mutandis* if they trace a square. Thus the twins would appear to be undergoing representations with the same content after all.

This first case brings out the point that vision must be successful in both environments, if Burge's argument is to work. The second case brings out a consequence of this point.

Case 2. Suppose that *W*s are thin shadows and *N*s are thin cracks. If the success constraint is to be met, then the subjects must not behave as if they are visually representing the items specifically as cracks or as shadows. If they did, then the behaviour in at least one environment would be inappropriate, and the constraint would be violated. If the constraint is to be met, the behaviour must be indiscriminately appropriate to either shadows or cracks. And this would suggest that the visual representations are not specific to either but represent the items in some more general way. They would represent them as a feature of surfaces that could be either a shadow or a crack: a thin, dark line perhaps.

The second case undermines the validity of Burge's argument, since it allows the premises to remain in place but negates the conclusion. If *T*s represent thin, dark lines in both environments, then it may remain true that the visual systems are successfully adapted and *T* type representations represent their 'normal' causes. For thin cracks and thin shadows are all instances of thin, dark lines. This point can be generalized to the schematic version of Burge's envisaged situation: *T*s do not represent *N*s or *W*s specifically as *N*s or as *W*s, but rather represent them by some more general content, *G*, where *G* includes both *N*s and *W*s. (The objection is given in Segal (1989), and related points are made by McGinn (1989) and Matthews (1988). For extensive discussion, see Egan (1991, 1992), Davies (1991), Wilson (1994) and Segal (1991).)

The debate between methodological individualists and their opponents remains unresolved. This is because the arguments are complete on neither side, both in the particular case of vision, which has been studied in detail, and in the more general, but more complex, case of psychology as a whole. Anti-individualists have tended to rest their positions on arguments the premises and validity of which may easily be doubted, or on general theories of content that are themselves highly controversial. On the other hand, no convincing considerations in favour of a generalized methodological individualism have yet been offered.

See also: CONTENT: WIDE AND NARROW; PUTNAM, H.; SEMANTICS, CONCEPTUAL ROLE; SEMANTICS, TELEOLOGICAL

References and further reading

Burge, T. (1979) 'Individualism and the Mental', in P. French, T. Uehling and H. Wettstein (eds) *Midwest Studies in Philosophy*, vol. 4, Minneapolis, MN: University of Minnesota Press. (The locus classicus of the argument that social factors are relevant to the individuation of the content of psychological states. The argument is spelt out in some detail and many objections are anticipated and responded to.)

* —— (1982) 'Other Bodies', in A. Woodfield (ed.) *Thought and Object: Essays on Intentionality*, Oxford, Clarendon Press. (Arguing that the content of non-singular concepts, such as concepts of water or arthritis, should not be thought of as analogous to indexical singular concepts, such as those expressed by 'now', 'here', 'this'.)

* —— (1986) 'Individualism and Psychology', *Philosophical Review* 95 (1): 3–46. (Arguing against the view that scientific psychology must be individualistic and for the view that the computational theory of vision is anti-individualistic.)

Crane, T. (1991) 'All the Difference in the World', *Philosophical Quarterly* 41 (162): 1–26. (A relatively accessible article challenging anti-individualist interpretations of twin earth experiments.)

Cummins, R. (1989) *Meaning and Mental Representation*, Cambridge, MA: MIT Press. (A general work on theories of contents from the perspective of philosophy of science, including a defence of individualism.)

* Davies, M. (1991) 'Individualism and Perceptual Content', *Mind* 100 (4): 461–84. (An article clarifying and defending Burge's argument (1986) that the computational theory of vision is anti-individualistic.)

* Egan, F. (1991) 'Must Psychology Be Individualistic?', *Philosophical Review* 100 (2): 179–203. (Criticizing Burge (1986) and arguing that the computational theory of vision is individualistic.)

* —— (1992) 'Individualism, Computationalism and Perceptual Content', *Mind* 101: 443–59. (Developing the individualism of Egan (1991).)

Field, H. (1978) 'Logic, Meaning and Conceptual Role', *Journal of Philosophy* 74: 379–409. (A relatively difficult article defending an individualist, functional role theory of psychological states.)

Fodor, J. (1981) 'Methodological Solipsism Considered as a Research Strategy in Cognitive Science', in *RePresentations*, Cambridge, MA: MIT Press. (An early defence of individualism based on a computational theory of cognition.)

* —— (1987) *Psychosemantics: The Problem of Meaning in the Philosophy of Mind*, Cambridge, MA: MIT Press. (A general work on content. Chapter 2 includes an extended defence of individualism.)

—— (1991) 'A Modal Argument for Narrow Content', *Journal of Philosophy* 78 (1): 5–26. (A relatively difficult article presenting an argument for narrow content based on certain modal considerations.)

* —— (1994) *The Elm and the Expert*, Cambridge, MA: MIT Press. (A short book in which Fodor withdraws from the individualism of his earlier work, and argues that a certain limited form of anti-individualism is true.)

Grimm, R. and Merrill, D. (eds) (1988) *Contents of Thought*, Tucson, AZ: University of Arizona Press. (Includes several useful articles, including Loar (1988) and Matthews (1988).)

Larson, R. and Segal, G. (1995) *Knowledge of Meaning: An Introduction to Semantic Theory*, Cambridge, MA: MIT Press. (A general introduction to formal semantic theory. Chapter 13 defends individualism with respect to the psychological states involved in understanding language.)

Loar, B. (1988) 'Social Content and Psychological Content', in R. Grimm and D. Merrill (eds) *Contents of Thought*, Tucson, AZ: University of Arizona Press. (An influential defence of individualism.)

* Marr, D. (1982) *Vision*, New York: Freeman Press. (An introduction to the computational theory of vision. Whether Marr's work is individualistic or not has been the focus of much debate.)

* Matthews, R.J. (1988) 'Comments on Burge, "Cartesian Error and the Objectivity of Perception"', in R. Grimm and D. Merrill (eds) *Contents of Thought*, Tucson, AZ: University of Arizona Press. (Discussing aspects of Burge's anti-individualism.)

* McGinn, C. (1989) *Mental Content*, Oxford: Blackwell. (A general work on mental content; includes a distinction between different kinds of anti-individualism, and a defence of individualism with respect to the content of perceptual states.)

Millikan, R.G. (1993) *White Queen Psychology and other Essays for Alice*, Cambridge, MA: MIT Press. (A collection of papers, many of which defend and elaborate an anti-individualistic, teleo-functional theory of content.)

Patterson, S. (1991) 'Individualism and Semantic Development', *Philosophy of Science* 58 (1): 15–35. (Arguing that a certain influential, psychological theory of concept acquisition is individualistic.)

* Putnam, H. (1975) 'The Meaning of "Meaning"', in K. Gunderson (ed.) *Minnesota Studies in the Philosophy of Science*, vol. 7, *Language, Mind and Knowledge*, Minneapolis, MN: University of Minnesota Press. (The original twin earth experiments.)

Searle, J. (1991) *Intentionality: An Essay in the Philosophy of Mind*, Cambridge: Cambridge University Press. (A general work in the philosophy of mind. Chapter 8 includes an extended defence of individualism.)

* Segal, G. (1989) 'Seeing What is Not There', *Philosophical Review* 98: 189–214. (Arguing, against Burge (1986), that the computational theory of vision is individualistic.)

* —— (1991) 'Defence of a Reasonable Individualism', *Mind* 100 (4): 485–93. (Elaborating and defending the claim that the contents of visual perception are narrow; argues against Davies (1991).)

* Wilson, R. (1994) 'Wide Computationalism', *Mind* 103: 351–72. (Arguing for anti-individualism with respect to a computational theory of cognition.)

Woodfield, A. (ed.) (1982) *Thought and Object: Essays on Intentionality*, Oxford: Clarendon Press. (A useful collection of relevant articles.)

GABRIEL SEGAL

MEXICO, PHILOSOPHY IN

Philosophy has been practised in Mexico for centuries, beginning with Nahuatl thought. Such thinking was rediscovered through laborious translation of surviving fragments of a document of exceptional value known as 'Coloquio de los Doce' (Debate of the Twelve) (1524). Since then, philosophy has come to enjoy a high degree of professionalization and a high quality of academic production. Generally, Mexican philosophical activity has evolved in accordance with world standards of rigour, information and quality of argumentation. In the twentieth century various philosophical groups have been created, namely the Ateneo de la Juventud, the contemporáneos and the Hyperion group.

Leopoldo Zea understood the essence of the Mexican and the Latin American as a historical being with a historically situated consciousness. Zea's history of ideas involved a philosophy of Latin American history which placed the being, destiny and meaning of the history of Mexico and Latin America in the context of the history of the world. The 1940s and 1950s were unusually productive to this end. In the 1970s small groupings of philosophers gathered to focus on problems, traditions, teaching figures, leaders and spheres of influence.

There has been considerable interest in political philosophy, philosophy of history, philosophy of science and ethics. Since the 1980s, works about the history of ideas in Mexico and the history of science and technology have proliferated.

1   Historical overview
2   The situation in the 1990s
3   Prospects

1   Historical overview

Before the arrival of the Europeans, a form of reflection was developed in Nahuatl society which was expressed aphoristically and poetically. Since the 1950s Nahuatl thought has been rediscovered through laborious translation of surviving fragments. A document of exceptional value is one known as 'Coloquio de los Doce' (Debate of the Twelve) (1524), a relatively brief fragment located in the Vatican archives. It records the encounter of cultures and the debate sustained by the first twelve Franciscan monk preachers who arrived in New Spain to preach the Gospel. The Franciscans met with native authorities and explained the New Testament to them. The natives believed that the questions were too complex and that they required the intervention of wise, erudite people. Their proposition of calling on their *tlamatinime* (wise persons or philosophers) was accepted by the monks. After listening attentively, the wise Nahuas claimed that the monks appreciated the information and greatly valued the sacrifices made by these foreigners in voyaging to transmit their truths, although the natives themselves had their own truths, which they also set forth. However, the Nahuas conceded that the monks were clearly in charge and could do whatever they wished with the Nahuas anyway. 'Coloquio de los Doce' (Debate of the Twelve) is important as testimony of a decisive encounter between the Western world and the so-called New World. Some of the most important topics of debate since the 1980s are addressed in a singularly ceremonial and dramatic manner: the experience of alterity, ethnocentrism, intercultural dialogue and the clash of argumentative styles. These documents reveal a rational, logical, rigorous, erudite and civilized mind on the part of the Nahuas.

After the arrival of the conquistadors from Spain in the sixteenth century a philosophy initially developed in Spain and a system of philosophical production and styles in accordance with the prevailing sociopolitical system was imposed over a period of three centuries (from the early sixteenth century to the mid-nineteenth century). Early on, the Spanish felt it important to establish a university system that would follow the model of the Universities of Salamanca and Alcalá de Henares. The University of Pontificia was founded in New Spain in 1553. The hegemonic philosophical thought in New Spain was fundamentally Scholastic. It was developed in the university, schools and seminaries and was primarily disseminated by the religious orders. Among the most important representatives is Fray Alonso de la Vera Cruz, the first to teach philosophy in the New World at the University of Pontificia in 1553.

Since the early years of the colonial period, two opposing types of reflection have been observed: colonialist and independent thought, the latter of which battles for freedom of thought and action. Sor Juana Inés de la Cruz and the Mexican Jesuits, who collaborated in the formation of a native conscience, were significant proponents of this second position (see FEMINIST THOUGHT IN LATIN AMERICA). At the end of the colonial period the same Scholastics continued to consolidate the thought of the Enlightenment, even when it seemed clear that the inspirational and legitimizing thought of independence was the so-called populist doctrine of Salamanca. The doctrine held that the people are the source of power and power should devolve to them when the King is not in a position to exercise authority, as was the case with Fernando VII.

The nineteenth century in Mexico has also been reexamined. It has been observed that thought under the rubric of liberalism is not homogeneous and requires multiple approaches. Diverse discourses have been placed in opposition to one another. Towards the end of the nineteenth century, positivism became predominant and remains one of the most debated philosophical movements in Mexican thought (see POSITIVIST THOUGHT IN LATIN AMERICA).

In the twentieth century a group of philosophers called the Ateneo de la Juventud quickly launched its anti-positivist spiritualist reaction during the Mexican revolution (1910–17) (see ANTI-POSITIVIST THOUGHT IN LATIN AMERICA). Subsequently, the Contemporáneos constituted another decisive group in the advance of Mexican thought. By the 1950s the Hyperion group had formulated a Mexican philosophy. José Vasconcelos and Antonio Caso of the Ateneo were influential in the world of philosophy, as were Samuel Ramos of the Contemporáneos and Leopoldo Zea, Luis Villoro, Emilio Uranga, Jorge Portilla and Joaquín Sánchez Macgregor of the Hyperion group.

A notable contribution to the development of modern Mexican thought was that by the exiles of the Spanish Republic who arrived in Mexico around 1939. José Gaos, Joaquín Xirau, Juan David García Bacca, José María Gallegos Rocafull, Eugenio Imaz, Eduardo Nicol and Wenceslao Roces remain exemplars of Mexican philosophical life in the late twentieth century. Philosophers of this time are disciples of this aforementioned group who were responsible for defining the philosophical task in Mexico. Each of them has reached international levels of excellence in debate, production, philosophical rigour, argumentation, technique and information.

2 The situation in the 1990s

The situation in the 1990s is not easy to delineate. It cannot be reduced to what has been produced since 1990, nor to what was produced after either the linguistic change, or the final works of the Hyperion group. Focusing on the second half of the twentieth century, it is possible to establish the state of debate and philosophical production in Mexico in the late 1990s.

The careful study of European thought, German in particular, resulted in the development of phenomenology and existentialism in Latin America. Both these schools of thought dominated the principal centre of reflection of the country in the 1950s, which was the department of philosophy and letters at the National Autonomous University of Mexico (UNAM) (see EXISTENTIALIST THOUGHT IN LATIN AMERICA; PHENOMENOLOGY IN LATIN AMERICA). José Gaos made the very first translation into Spanish of *Being and Time* (1943). In that environment, the efforts began of the Hyperion group, whose name was taken from J.C.F. HÖLDERLIN to signify the joining of heaven and earth. With the tools of phenomenology and existentialism, this group attempted to cast philosophical light on the essence of being Mexican. In an effort lasting around three years, they challenged the task of philosophy in Mexico and internationally, although they did not achieve their intended goals. Emilio Uranga (1952) published his classic analysis of the essence of the Mexican, but it was soon apparent that the achievements of this ontological route were meagre. However, a historicist trend developed and has been productive since the 1950s.

The thought of Leopoldo Zea understands the essence of the Mexican and the Latin American as a historical being with a historically situated consciousness. It is feasible to study the development of that historical consciousness expressed in the history of ideas in the region. From the beginning of that labour of reconstruction derive several modes of philosophizing. In the case of Zea, that history of ideas involved a philosophy of Latin American history which would place the being, destiny and meaning of the history of Mexico and Latin America in the context of the history of the world. The 1940s and 1950s were unusually productive to this end. In the 1970s philosophical positions were well defined, consolidated and manifested in compact groupings. Each one had its own problems, traditions, teaching figures, leaders and spheres of influence.

Leopoldo Zea led the group which focused on Latin America. He emphasized the study of the position of Latin America in the world situation and advanced the history of ideas in what José Martí called 'Our America'. The antecedents of these teachings, whose points of focus were Latin American identity incorporating a wide cultural focus, were Caso, Vasconcelos, Reyes, Henríquez Ureña, Ramos and Gaos (see CULTURAL IDENTITY).

Marxist reflections were headed by Eli de Gortari and Adolfo Sánchez Vázquez (see MARXIST THOUGHT IN LATIN AMERICA). De Gortari advanced the study of dialectical logic and the relations between philosophy and the hard sciences through his seminar on history and the philosophy of science. He also initiated the study of the history of science in Mexico. Sánchez Vázquez formulated a solid argumentation that understood Marxism principally as a philosophy of praxis and a tool for critical aesthetic reflection. Both philosophers employ up-to-date information and argumentative rigour and both have become engaged in the international Marxist debate with a critical, suggestive and stimulating slant. An explicit focus on both the Mexican and Latin American Marxist traditions would highlight the arguments of Lombardo Toledano and José Revueltas.

A third focus has been analytic thought characterized by the linguistic trend (see ANALYTICAL PHILOSOPHY IN LATIN AMERICA). Advanced by Luis Villoro, Fernando Salmerón and Alejandro Rossi, this group incorporated into academic debate the Anglo-Saxon tradition and the classic problems of philosophy of language, mind and science. Strongly professionalized, this group aspires radically to modify philosophical tradition in the region, incorporating modalities and styles of philosophical production in common with Anglo-Saxon countries. Their centre of study is the Institute of Philosophical Research at the National Autonomous University of Mexico. They do not refer to antecedents in the region and maintain a scientific conception of philosophy.

A fourth sector is metaphysical thought, which focuses on ancient philosophy in the tradition of

Eduardo Nicol and his principal disciple Juliana González. A preoccupation with the philological and an emphasis on genetic studies in an articulation of aesthetics, ethics and gnoseology mark their thought patterns.

This cartographic outline seemed immutable in those years. Nevertheless, by the end of the 1970s modification of the agenda in Mexico had begun. New generations developed new themes; the trauma of 1968 with its consequences on academic life, along with new social demands and changes in the world began to split this four-part schema, although derivations of their philosophies are still in evidence. The critical reception of, L.P. ALTHUSSER, political philosophy, epistemology, history, ethics and aesthetics were pushed to the foreground. During the 1980s decisive transformations were produced in contemporary Mexican life and changes at world level affected philosophical reflection which, with few exceptions, was maintained in cloistered areas from an endogenous academic viewpoint. Debates regarding structuralism, Marxism, semiotics and discourse theory; the production of knowledge, liberation, modernism; deconstruction and postmodernism tangentially traversed traditional boundaries which were previously impenetrable.

The philosophical positions developed throughout the 1970s and 1980s have not become outmoded, although they have crossfertilized to a degree and the forum for argumentation and frank debate has expanded. Philosophical activity has expanded outside of the institutions in which it was once confined, namely the department of philosophy and letters and the Institute of Philosophical Research at the UNAM. High-quality work has been carried out at the Autonomous Metropolitan University, especially the Iztapalapa and Xochimilco campuses, at the Jesuit Iberoamerican University, the Intercontinental University and the universities of Chihuahua, Toluca, Guadalajara, Xalapa and Ciudad Juárez.

The topics and areas of study have become richer and more varied. The history of ideas has been pursued with increased interest. There are as many works about Pre-Columbian thought in the Nahuatl field as in the Mayan, as well as in the area of recent indigenous thought, particularly that of the Huicholes. The colonial period is under exploration in an effort to refute its dismissal by positivist historiography. The development of philosophy in the nineteenth and twentieth centuries is under discussion. Monographic studies emphasize access to and retrieval of source material. All this historiographic work has brought advances in the debate over methodological and epistemological questions.

In the 1990s the precarious state of the history of science and technology in Mexico changed markedly. Rescue of sources, new methodological foci and the correlation of local with world history have facilitated work on the relationship between the history of science and ideas. In the area of the philosophy of science, work on the theory of argumentation, scientific language, models of justification and the links between hard sciences and social sciences have been produced. In political philosophy, work has been undertaken related to the idea of democracy, its processes of democratization, its manifestations of power, civil-state relations, mass communications and their prevalence in everyday life, national identity and ethnic and/or regional identities. Feminist thought has grown and developed widely in Mexico. Discussions about gender, ways of knowing and the role of women in the history of philosophy are of particular interest. Also, studies in the philosophy of law, human rights, minority rights and critical criminology have been produced. In the area of ethics, studies have come about stimulated by the deterioration of living conditions for the vast majority and the need to clarify the rules of social life. Debates regarding historical knowledge, historiographic methodology, the role and meaning of Mexico in the world, the discourses that make up the course of history, have arisen within the sphere of the philosophy of history. There has been an important effort to establish a hermeneutics of Mexican and Latin American culture which surpasses the traditional framework of philosophy of culture and incorporates the study of popular traditions.

Among the established philosophical journals in this area are *Cuadernos Americanos*, *Crítica*, *Dialéctica* and *Estudios*. The most active organizations in the promotion of philosophical activities have been the Asociación Filosófica de México (Mexican Philosophical Association), active for twenty-five years and counts among its members the most important and productive philosophers of the country, the Asociación Filosófica Feminista de México (Mexican Feminist Philosophical Association) and the Círculo Mexicano de Profesores de Filosofía (Mexican Circle of Professors of Philosophy).

There have also been numerous academic events in the Mexican philosophical agenda, such as the congresses of the Mexican Philosophical Association, the Mexican Circle of Professors of Philosophy, the Mexican Society for the History of Science and Technology and those dedicated to the study of philosophy in New Spain. The ninth Interamerican Congress of Philosophy took place in Guadalajara in 1985 and the first International Congress of Latin American Philosophy took place in Ciudad Juárez in 1991.

It is worthy of note that philosophy is still taught at the secondary level in Mexico. There is considerable interest in improving the quality of the teaching of philosophy to prepare students for life and future university studies.

3 Prospects

Despite the financial crisis and the budget restrictions that chronically affect Mexican academic institutions, the future of the philosophical agenda in Mexico is promising. Young people with excellent training are slowly becoming involved in philosophical production and other institutional frameworks are surfacing to support philosophy such as the professional associations. The growing social and cultural problems demand inclusion in the philosophical agenda. With a population subject to inhumane deficiencies and with the increase in poverty in real and absolute terms, philosophy is called upon to attempt adequate responses. Also, the process of democratization in the country is demanding philosophical contributions. Cultural creativity continues at its highest level and demands adequate aesthetic reflections which address the phenomenon. Globalization demands new conceptualizations which help address intellectual perplexity.

See also: ARGENTINA, PHILOSOPHY IN; BRAZIL, PHILOSOPHY IN; LATIN AMERICA, COLONIAL THOUGHT IN; LATIN AMERICA, PRE-COLUMBIAN AND INDIGENOUS THOUGHT IN

References and further reading

Bartra, R. (1987) *La jaula de la melancolías: identidad y metamorfosis del mexicano* (The Cage of Melancholy: Identity and Metamorphosis of the Mexican), Mexico: Grijalbo. (The changing situation of the Mexican is discussed.)

Cerutti Guldberg, H. (1986) *Hacia una metodología de la historia de las ideas (filosóficas) en América Latina* (Towards a Methodology of the History of (Philosophical) Ideas in Latin America), Guadalajara: University of Guadalajara. (A discussion of the methodological aspects of the history of philosophy in Mexico and proposals predicting the future of the philosophical task in the country.)

Escobar-Valenzuela, G. (1992) *Introducción al pensamiento filosófico en México* (Introduction to Philosophical Thought in Mexico), Mexico: Limusa. (A general study of philosophical thought in Mexico.)

* Léon de Portilla, M. (ed.) (1524) 'Coloquio de los Doce' (Debate of the Twelve), in *Coloquios y doctrina Cristiana* (Debates and Christian Doctrine), Mexico: National Autonomous University of Mexico and Fundación de Investigaciones Sociales, 1986. (An account of the twelve monks from San Francisco sent by Pope Adriano VI and the Emperor Carlos V to convert the Indians of New Spain. Includes the dialogues of Fray Bernardino de Sahagún and his collaborators Antonio Valeriano de Azcapotzalco, Alonso Vegerano de Cuahutitlán, Mart ín Jacobita and Andrés Leonardo de Tletelolco.)

Martí, O.R. (1989) 'Mexican Philosophy in the 1980s: Possibilities and Limits', in *Varios: Philosophy and Literature in Latin America. A Critical Assessment of the Current Situation*, Albany, NY: State University of New York Press, 36–63. (A good overview of Mexican philosophical production.)

Morales, C. (1990) 'La investigación filosófica en la UNAM' (Philosophical Investigation at the National Autonomous University of Mexico), in *Varios: Universidad Nacional y Cultura*, Mexico: National Autonomous University of Mexico and Porrúa, 155–78. (An examination of the development of philosophy at the most important university in Mexico after 1968: a key year in the political and intellectual life of the country.)

Osorio, I. (1989) *Conquistar el eco: la paradoja de la conciencia criolla* (Conquering the Echoes: the Paradox of the Creole Consciousness), Mexico: National Autonomous University of Mexico. (Unites important works about the development of philosophy in New Spain. Its bibliographical references and sources are especially useful.)

* Uranga, E. (1952) *Análisis del ser mexicano* (Analysis of Being Mexican), Mexico: Porrúa y Obregón. (A study of what it is to be a Mexican.)

Vargas-Lozano, G. (1980) 'Notas sobre la función actual de la filosof ía en México (la década de los setenta)' (Notes on the Current Trends of Philosophy in Mexico (in the 1970s)), in *Dialéctica* 9 (December): 81–108. (Still relevant, this study decribes the state of philosophy in Mexico in the 1970s.)

Villegas, A. (1993) *El pensamiento mexicano en el siglo XX* (Mexican Thought in the Twentieth Century), Mexico: Fondo de Cultura Económica. (A comprehensive view of the development of philosophy in Mexico in the twentieth century.)

HORACIO CERUTTI-GULDBERG

MEYERSON, ÉMILE (1859–1933)

Meyerson rejects the positivism of Comte and Mach, insisting that reason demands more of science than the identification of lawful regularities for the purpose of successful prediction. Reason demands an actual representation of reality based on genuine causal explanation, and causal explanation consists of demonstrating an underlying identity behind the apparent diversity of phenomena. If completely successful, however, such explanation would ultimately lead to the unchanging homogeneous and sterile universe of Parmenides. That it does not is due to what Meyerson calls 'irrationals': inexplicable elements in reality that can never be reduced to identity. Explanation, therefore, is never complete, and scientific laws are 'plausible' rather than universally and necessarily true.

Émile Meyerson was Polish by birth but French by choice. In 1882, after studies in Germany under the celebrated chemist R.W. Bunsen, he began his career in the inorganic chemistry laboratory at the Collège de France. Abandoning chemistry in 1889, he served as a foreign policy editor for the Havas News Agency, then turned to philanthropic work with Jewish emigrants to Palestine, eventually becoming director for Europe and Asia Minor of the Jewish Colonization Association.

Meyerson's erudition was legendary. Although he never held an academic post, he was enthusiastically accepted by the French intellectual community, and his office was a gathering point for eminent philosophers and scientists. When he wrote about the history of science, he had usually read the primary material in the original language. When he wrote about contemporary science, he had often discussed it personally with the scientists who created it.

Although often classified as an epistemologist and/or philosopher of science, Meyerson himself describes his work more broadly as 'philosophy of the intellect' (from 'Philosophie de la nature et philosophie de l'intellect' in 1936), which he differentiates both from logic, because he is concerned with how we actually think rather than how we ought to think, and from psychology, because he is concerned not with direct introspection, but with analysis of the products of thought in order to discover a posteriori the a priori component of our thought processes. On the basis of exhaustive concrete examples, especially from the history of science, but also from the history of philosophy and ordinary common sense reasoning, he identifies an a priori tendency in all reasoning to replace diversity in appearances with identity in reality.

To explain (*expliquer*) an event is to explicate (literally, to unfold) it from its cause to show that it already existed in the cause, and is in this sense identical with it (1921: 9) (see CAUSATION; EXPLANATION). In scientific reasoning, the example *par excellence* of this identity is conservation laws, which maintain that throughout changing appearances the underlying amount of mass, energy, inertia, and so on, remains constant, that is, identical (Zahar 1980) (see CONSERVATION PRINCIPLES). Such laws are both analytic and synthetic: analytic in so far as they exemplify the innate tendency to establish real identity behind apparent diversity, but synthetic in so far as what specifically is posited as identical, for example, momentum, is determined empirically. Meyerson classifies such laws as 'plausible' (1921: 410). This word is to be understood in a strong sense, for, because of their a priori basis, laws have an element of true necessity. But, because of their empirical content, this plausibility falls short of strict necessity.

Other scientific examples abound, such as the persistence of the same chemical elements in the raw material for a chemical reaction and its product, or the permanence of physical atoms throughout physical change, which allows us to explain the diversity of secondary qualities in terms of changes in position in homogeneous space of unchanging material particles. But the a priori tendency toward identity is not confined to formal science. Common sense also seeks to replace the diversity of experience with an underlying permanent reality. For example, we posit the existence of a real table that remains identical in spite of our changing, diverse sensations of the table, and we form the concept of table by ignoring the differences among individual tables and identifying a common (identical) essence.

The identification is never complete, however, whether in scientific or common sense reasoning; at some point we are inevitably confronted with brute diversity which cannot be reasoned away, that is, with one or more 'irrationals' (1908). Perceptual diversity remains even as we reduce the table to its defining geometrical elements, and salt clearly differs from sodium plus chlorine even after we have explained that it is simply sodium chloride. For Meyerson the example *par excellence* of such irrationals is the second law of thermodynamics, and Carnot has the place of honour in Meyerson's scientific pantheon. If there actually were a strict identity between cause and effect, then all physical processes would be reversible. But entropy necessarily increases; there are irreversible processes; identity of cause and effect is not complete (see THERMODYNAMICS). Quantum mechanics, with its indeterminacy principle, presents us with a startling new example of an intractable irrational in physical explanation (see HEISENBERG, W.; QUANTUM MECHANICS, INTERPRETATION OF §2), but classical mechanics provides examples as well. Even if the classical mechanist were to succeed in reducing all causal explanation to the physical impact of elementary particles, for example, the causal mechanism of the impact itself – how force or momentum is passed from one particle to another – would continue to defy analysis.

Although a scientific realist, Meyerson insists that his concern is not with metaphysics but only with the philosophy of the intellect. There must be a partial correspondence between our rational theories of reality and reality itself or the success of scientific inquiry could not be explained, but it is the a priori tendencies in our thought processes rather than the nature of physical reality in which he is interested. The correspondence between the structure of our thought and the structure of reality, though necessary, is not complete. Reality is also recalcitrant to our reasoning processes. We are inevitably confronted with irrationals, and there is no way of predicting when they will arise or in what form. We face an epistemological paradox (1921): reason demands identity, but even a Cartesian or Einsteinian world in which matter is reduced to the geometry of space fails to acheive complete identity; nothing less than the sterility of absolute Parmenidean homogeneity will do. Our reasoning is successful only in so far as it does establish identity, but its explanatory power depends also upon its ultimate failure. We succeed in explaining diversity by finding underlying identities while admitting that, nevertheless, there really is change and diversity, which, in the end, we cannot fully explain. Genuine explanation is possible only because the irrational cannot be completely eliminated.

List of works

Meyerson, É. (1908) *Identité et réalité*, Paris: Alcan; 5th edn, Paris: Vrin, 1951; trans. K. Loewenberg, *Identity and Reality*, New York: Macmillan, 1930. (Meyerson's classic, most concise statement of his thesis – the only book by which Meyerson was known to English readers for over fifty years.)

—— (1921) *De l'explication dans les sciences*, Paris: Payot, 2 vols; 2nd edn in 1 vol., 1927; trans. M.-A. and D.A. Sipfle, *Explanation in the Sciences*, Boston Studies in the Philosophy of Science, vol. 128, Dordrecht: Kluwer, 1991. (A more extensive argument for Meyerson's thesis, with a wealth of examples from current and past science and extensive treatment of Hegel's and Schelling's philosophies of nature.)

—— (1925) *La déduction relativiste*, Paris: Payot; trans. D.A. and M.-A. Sipfle, *The Relativistic Deduction*, Boston Studies in the Philosophy of Science, vol. 83, Dordrecht: Reidel, 1985. (Argues that Einsteinian relativity conforms to Meyerson's theory just as clearly as does classical physics – indeed that, given Meyerson's theory, a theory such as Einstein's is just what one would expect to emerge. A favourable review by Einstein and a fine introduction by Milič Čapek are included with the English translation.)

—— (1931) *Du Cheminement de la pensée* (The Ways of Thought), Paris: Alcan, 3 vols. (Two volumes of text and one of notes. A *tour de force* in which Meyerson extends his thesis to all realms of human thought, including common sense thought and prehistoric thought no less than logical, mathematical, and scientific thought.)

—— (1933) Reél et déterminisme dans la physique quantique (Reality and Determinism in Quantum Physics), *Actualités scientifiques et industrielles, vol. 68*, Paris: Hermann. (Argues for the need for a realistic, but not necessarily deterministic interpretation of quantum mechanics; preface by Louis de Broglie.)

—— (1936) *Essais* (Essays), Paris: Vrin. (A wide range of journal articles published throughout Meyerson's career and after his death. This volume includes some of Meyerson's most explicit and self-conscious attempts to explain his purpose and his methodology.)

References and further reading

Boas, G. (1930) *A Critical Analysis of the Philosophy of Émile Meyerson*, Baltimore, MD: Johns Hopkins University Press. (A critical exposition of Meyerson's first three books, written to call attention to a 'thinker, whose importance seemed underestimated in America'.)

Bulletin de la Société française de philosophie (April 1961) 55th year, no. 2. (Reports the 26 November 1960 meeting devoted to the centenary of Meyerson's birth (and of Gaston Milhaud's); contributions by André Lalande, Louis de Broglie, René Poirier, André Metz and Alexandre Koyré. Includes biographical details as well as philosophical appraisals.)

Kelly, T. (1937) *Explanation and Reality in the Philosophy of Émile Meyerson*, Princeton, NJ: Princeton University Press. (Argues that the divergence between explanation and reality is so great in Meyerson's earlier works that it should lead to scepticism, but that this problem is alleviated in *Du*

Cheminement de la pensée. Includes a comprehensive bibliography.)

Largeault, J. (1992) 'Émile Meyerson, philosophe oublié', *Revue philosophique de la France et de l'étranger* 182, 273–95. (A comprehensive exposition and appreciation of Meyerson's philosophy, looking back long after his influence had waned, nearly sixty years after his death.)

Loewenberg, J. (1932) 'Meyerson's Critique of Pure Reason', *Philosophical Review* 41, 351–67. (An insightful interpretation of Meyerson's position in Kantian terms. Meyerson expresses his approval in 'Philosophie de la nature et philosophie de l'intellect', *Essais*, 105n.)

* Zahar, E. (1980) 'Einstein, Meyerson and the Role of Mathematics in Physical Discovery', *British Journal of the Philosophy of Science* 31, 1–43. (§2 briefly explains Meyerson's principle of identity and its application to conservation laws, to the Cartesian reduction of matter to space, and to Einstein's special and general theories of relativity.)

DAVID A. SIPFLE

MI BSKYOD RDO RJE
(1507–54)

Mi bskyod rdo rje (Mikyö Dorje) was a Tibetan Buddhist of the Karma bKa'-brgyud (Gagyü) school. Particularly in his earlier thought, he defended the existence of a positive nondual Ultimate Reality (an Absolute) beyond all conceptuality but known in meditation, and apparently understood the purpose of Mādhyamika philosophy as solely the shattering of conceptualization and all philosophical positions as a preparation for this nonconceptual meditation. He was highly critical of Tsong kha pa (Dzongkaba, a notable philosopher of the rival dGe-lugs-pa (Gelukba) school), for being overly concerned with logical analysis of the foundations of everyday experience.

Mi bskyod rdo rje (Mikyö Dorje) was the Eighth Karma pa hierarch of the Karma bKa'-brgyud (Gagyü) school of Tibetan Buddhism. He was born in Damchu (East Tibet) and died of leprosy at Dakpo Shedrup Ling Monastery (East-Central Tibet). The bKa'-brgyud tradition inherited from its Indo-Tibetan yogic origins a dislike of philosophy and logic, which was seen as an over-concern with conceptuality. Emphasis was placed on direct experiential knowing, associated with a meditation system known as *mahāmudrā* ('the Great Seal'). *Mahāmudrā* is said to involve the immediate experience of one's own mind,

which is actually the primordial self-luminous empty mirror-like wisdom-Mind of Buddhahood. All things are the spontaneous unobstructed play of this fundamental Mind, which is held to be the primordial Reality beyond all conceptuality and linguistic distortion. The direction of bKa'-brgyud thought is primarily towards moulding a sufficient theoretical framework for this *mahāmudrā* meditation. Nevertheless, Mi bskyod rdo rje devoted impressive intellectual effort to establishing the philosophical position of his school, furnishing the Karma bKa'-brgyud tradition with its own commentaries on some of the principal works used in the Indo-Tibetan monastic curriculum.

At the time of his full ordination as a monk, Mi bskyod rdo rje was exhorted to promulgate 'the view of other-empty' (*gzhan stong*) (see TIBETAN PHILOSOPHY §1). This involves the existence of a true Ultimate Reality, empty of what is other than it in that it is essentially empty of whatever is non-Ultimate, but nevertheless an Absolute, an Ultimate Reality having itself all the intrinsic qualities of Buddhahood. This 'other-empty' position contrasts with a view held within Tibetan Buddhism notably by the dGe-lugs-pa (Geluk) tradition that all things without exception are empty of their own inherent existence (*rang stong*) and exist only relatively. There is no Ultimate Reality at all, as an actual Absolute. There is some suggestion that even at the early age of 23 Mi bskyod rdo rje wished to adopt an other-empty approach in a combative commentary he wrote on the Perfection of Wisdom (*Prajñāpāramitā*) scriptures. At about the same time he also wrote a short independent work on the other-empty perspective. In it he speaks of the other-empty view as that of the Great Madhyamaka. He traces it to Maitreya, Asaṅga and VASUBANDHU, but he wants to distinguish this Great Madhyamaka view from the 'Mind-only' (*cittamātra*) vision often associated with those figures, which for Mi bskyod rdo rje seeks to establish the flow of relative, tainted ('everyday') consciousness as the Reality (see BUDDHISM, YOGĀCĀRA SCHOOL OF §§1–4, 8). Mi bskyod rdo rje sees the Great Madhyamaka as also the final perspective of NĀGĀRJUNA. He is, however, very critical of certain 'pseudo-Mādhyamikas' (including apparently the renowned scholars Candrakīrti and Haribhadra) for whom there is no Ultimate Reality, and the ultimate truth is itself simply an emptiness of inherent existence (that is, the *rang stong* perspective). Such an emptiness is a mere negation, and could not be the Ultimate referred to in Mahāyāna Buddhist sources, an Ultimate which, as nonconceptual, is realized in direct yogic experience and is not accessible to the negations of logicians like Candrakīrti. The rival view that would make the ultimate *qua* Ultimate Reality nonexistent is a form of nihilism. By way of contrast with the Ultimate Reality, for Mi bskyod rdo rje in reality all conventional, relative, mistaken appearances simply do not exist, and are not known even by the Buddha's omniscience.

However, In Mi bskyod rdo rje's commentary on Candrakīrti's *Madhyamakāvatāra* (Supplement to the Middle Way), written many years later, he criticizes a number of important Tibetan figures associated with the other-empty tradition, and interprets Candrakīrti's text in a 'self-empty' (*rang stong*) manner. It has been suggested (Ruegg 1988) that this could be seen as Mi bskyod rdo rje's response to dGe-lugs criticisms. On the other hand, since he makes no mention in interpreting the *Madhyamakāvatāra* of any major other-emptiness lineage of interpretation, and given his criticisms of Candrakīrti in his previous work, it seems possible that Mi bskyod rdo rje wished to show that Candrakīrti (or conceptualized Madhyamaka) could only be interpreted in a self-empty and not an other-empty manner. In this commentary Mi bskyod rdo rje shows his impatience with those who see Candrakīrti as a system-builder. Candrakīrti's intention is simply absence of delusion, through demolishing all conceptual philosophical systems. We are left with nothing as far as conceptual philosophizing goes, and even terms like 'emptiness' are simply conceptual devices to be used pedogogically. Things having thus been cleared away, Mi bskyod rdo rje holds that we should now engage in direct yogic experience through *mahāmudrā*. Although even someone who follows Madhyamaka will continue with the pre-reflective activities of the 'person in the street', there can be no satisfactory systematically coherent and rational philosophical foundation for those activities. Mi bskyod rdo rje is particularly critical of TSONG KHA PA BLO BZANG GRAGS PA (Dzongkaba Losang dragba, 1357–1419) and the dGe-lugs tradition here. Tsong kha pa's view, as represented by Mi bskyod rdo rje, is that emptiness is the essence of things, *qua* their lack of their own inherent existence. Thus there is a level on which things are coherently founded, in order for them to be empty. Nevertheless *all* things are empty, including emptiness itself. So Tsong kha pa thinks that things can be rationally *shown* to have *an* existential status, although there is no Ultimate Reality at all. For Mi bskyod rdo rje, in the face of any critical analytic investigation nothing can be founded, and it is unseemly to be so concerned with founding the relative and mundane conventional. Also, he says, Tsong kha pa's emptiness is itself just a 'limited emptiness' (*itaretaraśūnyatā*), the relative, mundane emptiness that we see in the everyday context of two different things where '*x* is empty of *y*'. Tsong kha pa's emptiness could not be the Ultimate, the emptiness which could serve as a true basis for the path to liberation.

See also: BUDDHIST CONCEPT OF EMPTINESS; BUDDHISM, MĀDHYAMIKA: INDIA AND TIBET

List of works

Many of Mi bskyod rdo rje's writings are at present unavailable. The following unedited texts of philosophical interest have been published by the Tibetan refugee community. None has been translated.

Mi bskyod rdo rje (*c.*1530) *dBu ma gzhan stong smra ba'i srol legs par phye ba'i sgron me* (The Lamp Discriminating Properly the System of the 'Other-Empty' Mādhyamikas), Rumtek: probably Dharmachakra Centre, 1972. (An early work of Mi bskyod rdo rje on the 'other-empty' viewpoint.)

—— (1532–43) *Chos mngon pa'i mdzod kyi 'grel pa rgyas par spros pa grub bde'i dpyid 'jo* (A Spring-yield of Accomplishment and Happiness: The Commentary to the Abhidharmakośa Extensively Elaborated), New Delhi: T. Tsepal Taikhang, 1975, 2 vols. (Mi bskyod rdo rje's Commentary on Vasubandhu's *Abhidharmakośa*.)

—— (begun 1545) *dBu ma la 'jug pa'i rnam bshad dPal ldan dus gsum mkhyen pa'i zhal lung dvags brgyud grub pa'i shing rta* (A Chariot for the Accomplished of the Lineage of Dvags [the bKa'-brgyud], the Oral instructions of Glorious Dus-gsum-mkhyen-pa [the First Karma-pa]: A Commentary to the Madhyamakāvatāra), Rumtek: Dharmachakra Centre. (Mi bskyod rdo rje's Commentary on Candrakīrti's *Madhyamakāvatāra*.)

References and further reading

Broido, M. (1985) 'Padma dKar po on the two satyas', *Journal of the International Association of Buddhist Studies* 8 (2): 7–59. (Mi bskyod rdo rje discussed within the context of the dGe-lugs and bKa'-brgyud treatment of the two truths and Vajrayāna. Fairly technical.)

Douglas, N. and White, M. (1976) *Karmapa: The Black Hat Lama of Tibet*, London: Luzac. (Short biographies based on traditional sources.)

Richardson, H. (1958) 'The Karma-pa sect: A Historical Note', *Journal of the Royal Asiatic Society* 3–4: 139–64; documents in J.R.A.S. 1–2: 1–17, 1959. (Historical discussion of the Karma bKa'-brgyud school. A standard work.)

Ruegg, D.S. (1988) 'A Karma bKa' brgyud Work on

the Lineages and Traditions of the Indo-Tibetan dBu ma (Madhyamaka)', in G. Gnoli and L. Lanciotti (eds) *Orientalia Iosephi Tucci Memoriae Dictata*, Rome: Istituto Italiano per il Medio ed Estremo Oriente, 1249–80. (Through treating the list of lineages contained at the beginning of the *Madhyamakāvatāra* commentary, a leading authority pictures how Mi bskyod rdo rje saw Madhyamaka doctrine and his place within it. Fairly technical at times.)

Thinley, K. (1980) *The History of the Sixteen Karmapas of Tibet*, ed. D. Stott, Boulder, CO: Prajñā Press. (Short biographies based on traditional sources.)

Williams, P. (1983) 'A note on some aspects of Mi bskyod rdo rje's critique of dGe lugs pa Madhyamaka', *Journal of Indian Philosophy* 11: 125–45. (Mi bskyod rdo rje's criticisms of the dGelugs view of emptiness. Not particularly technical.)

PAUL WILLIAMS

MIDRASH

Midrash, a Hebrew word meaning 'investigation' or 'study', denotes both the method used by the Jewish rabbis of the second to sixth centuries AD to interpret the Bible and the extensive literature that resulted from the application of that method. In rabbinic parlance midrash, or the related term derash, can also designate a homiletic, non-literal way of reading the Bible. Midrash embodies a distinctive hermeneutic which at its most extreme treats the text of Scripture as a set of symbols or signs apparently to be manipulated by the interpreter at will. In recent years midrash has been compared to reader-response literary criticism. It has also been claimed that it represents a 'Judaic' as opposed to a 'Hellenic' mode of thinking which anticipates postmodernist hermeneutics.

1   Midrash as literature
2   The hermeneutic methods of midrash
3   Midrash as a 'Judaic' mode of thinking

1   Midrash as literature

The extensive midrashic literature falls into two broad types: exegetical midrashim, which comment more or less verse by verse on a biblical book (for example, *Bereshit Rabba* on Genesis), and homiletic midrashim which comment on the Scriptural readings for a series of festivals or special days of the liturgical year (for example, *Pesiqta de-Rav Kahana*). These texts are constructed out of small units of discourse which employ a limited number of highly patterned literary forms. These basic forms are organized into higher forms, larger units of discourse which make a single theological, homiletic, or legal point. The higher forms are then collected into documents or composite forms which usually have some sort of overarching programme. Thus the basic forms of a midrash (in the sense of a single exegetical operation), a *mashal* (parable) and a dictum may be combined into the higher form of a homily, and a number of homilies may in turn be combined into a composite form such the document known as *Pesiqta de-Rav Kahana*. The various documents are closely related to each other and share material. Later stages of the tradition often seem to be developing or reacting to earlier ones. The contents of the documents differ from manuscript to manuscript; and they are not authored texts in any strong sense of that term, but neither are they random collections. They are an evolving literary canon which holds the deposit of the teaching and preaching on the Bible in the rabbinic academies and the synagogues of Palestine in the second to sixth centuries AD.

2   The hermeneutic methods of midrash

In midrash, the Bible is seen as a unique text which originated in the mind of God. The contribution of its human authors is discounted. They wrote under the influence of a divine power ('the holy spirit') which neutralized their human failings and ensured that they transmitted accurately the divine message. The text is fixed, unalterable and authoritative for all time. It is completely consistent and can contain no errors of fact, nor any contradictions. When seeming contradictions appear they are harmonized. The possibility that earlier laws may have been abrogated by later laws is not admitted. All truth that is relevant to human knowledge and action is latent in Scripture and can be discovered therein if the text is investigated in the proper way. The potential of Scripture is maximized. Its text is polyvalent and can have a multiplicity of meanings. It is not seen as a problem if these contradict each other, provided they are properly derived, since it is assumed that the contradiction is resolved in the mind of God. The text of Scripture contains no redundancy. If the same statement is found in two places its meaning will be differentiated: for example, in one place it will be referred to the present age, in the other to 'the age to come' (that is, the Messianic age).

Seen from outside the tradition, the function of midrash is twofold: (a) to apply the fixed text of Scripture to changing historical circumstances; and (b) to validate post-biblical practices, institutions, ideas and laws from the Bible. From within the tradition this second function is rarely openly acknowledged. It is normally assumed that the exegete is drawing out meaning objectively contained within Scripture and not subjectively reading meaning into it. Various techniques are used to explicate or extract meaning from Scripture, some of them manipulative in the extreme. For example, in the device known as *gematria* meaning can be derived by computing the numerical value of the letters. Several lists of the hermeneutical rules (known as Middot) used in midrash are extant. But these listings by no means exhaust the techniques of midrash. Despite the appearances, midrash is a disciplined activity: there must be some objective 'peg' in the biblical text (for example, a lacuna in the narrative, or an unusual linguistic usage) on which to hang the interpretation.

The manipulative approach to the reading of Scripture created an obvious problem of authority, since it would also allow heretical (for example, Christian) views to be validated from Scripture. This problem was addressed in a number of ways. It was asserted that, whatever midrashic meanings were derived from Scripture, the text could never lose its simple or literal (*peshat*) sense. It was also claimed that the correct interpretation of Scripture could be given only by those who had studied in the rabbinic academies with approved teachers who stood in an unbroken tradition of teaching going back to Moses. The tradition of commentary was elevated to the status of Scripture. It was designated oral Torah in contrast to the written Torah (the Scriptures), and its origins were traced back to Sinai, the supreme moment of revelation when the written Torah was given to Israel.

3 Midrash as a 'Judaic' mode of thinking

The term 'midrash' has passed into contemporary academic discourse, because certain literary critics have suggested that midrash anticipates postmodernist ways of reading texts. They note with approval that midrash often behaves with remarkable freedom towards the text, offering a strong reading, which may at times stand the plain sense on its head. They compare the midrashic postulate that Scripture has a multiplicity of meanings to the postmodern claim that a text does not have a single absolute and objective sense, that its meaning varies from reader to reader and that no one reading can be privileged as more correct than another. Some go further and suggest that midrash embodies a distinctively 'Judaic' mode of thinking which is semiological, auditory and algebraic, in contrast to the ontological, visual and

geometrical 'Hellenic' mode of thinking that has dominated Western hermeneutics in modern times.

These claims are historically questionable. The methods of midrash may superficially resemble postmodern literary criticism, but there are important differences. The rabbis regard midrash as an activity that relates to one unique text alone, the Bible. They do not see it as a paradigm of how to read every text. Moreover, they believe that Scripture does have an objective and absolute meaning, although in its entirety this is known only to God. Their mode of interpretation is disciplined, not arbitrary. By the application of the correct procedures the duly accredited and responsible rabbinid exegetes could draw out hidden senses from Scripture, but these senses were all facets of a larger and deeper, *objective* truth. The rabbinic exegetes could no more exhaust the potential of the text than they could exhaustively know the mind of God. But the inexhaustibility of their readings was taken not as a badge of their own creativity but as the emblem of the richness of the text itself. The polarization of Judaic and Hellenic hermeneutics, moreover, ignores the fact that many of the midrashic techniques are found applied to the interpretation of texts in Greek late antiquity.

See also: Bible, Hebrew; Hermeneutics; Hermeneutics, biblical; Meaning in Islamic philosophy; Theology, Rabbinic

References and further reading

Alexander, P.S. (1990) 'Quid Athenis et Hierosolymis? Rabbinic Midrash and Hermeneutics in the Graeco-Roman world', in P.R. Davies and R.T. White (eds) *A Tribute to Geza Vermes*, Sheffield: Sheffield Academic Press, 101–24. (Criticizes Faur and Handelman below.)

* *Bereshit Rabba* (fifth century AD), trans. H. Freedman, in H. Freedman and M. Simon (eds) *Midrash Rabbah: Translated into English*, London: Soncino Press, 3rd edn, 1961, 2 vols. (Exegetical commentary on Genesis. The same edition has the full Pentateuch, translated by various hands.)

Boyarin, D. (1990) *Intertextuality and the Reading of Midrash*, Bloomington, IN: University of Indiana Press. (Considers midrash in relation to intertextuality.)

Faur, J. (1986) *Golden Doves with Silver Dots: Semiotics and Textuality in Rabbinic Tradition*, Bloomington, IN: Indiana University Press. (Examines the semiotics of midrash.)

Goldberg, A. (1985) 'Form-Analysis of Midrashic Literature as a Method of Description', *Journal of Jewish Studies* 36: 159–74. (Outlines a rigorous approach to the description of the literary structure of midrash.)

Handelman, S.A. (1982) *The Slayers of Moses: The Emergence of Rabbinic Interpretation in Modern Literary Theory*, New York: State University of New York Press. (Expands on the argument that midrash has passed into contemporary academic discourse and has anticipated postmodernist ways of reading texts.)

Neusner J. (1987) *What is Midrash?*, Philadelphia, PA: Fortress Press. (A readable non-technical introduction to midrash.)

* *Pesiqta de-Rav Kahana* (sixth century AD), trans. W.G. Braude and I.J. Kapstein, *Pesiqta de-Rab Kahana*, Philadelphia, PA: Jewish Publication Society of America, 1975. (Homiletic commentary.)

Samely, A. (1992) 'Scripture's Implicature: the Midrashic Assumptions of Relevance and Consistency', *Journal of Semitic Studies* 37: 167–205. (An important study of two of the fundamental axioms of midrash.)

Stemberger, G. (1996) *Introduction to Talmud and Midrash*, trans. M. Bockmuehl, Edinburgh: T. & T. Clark. (The standard introduction to the midrashic literature, with full bibliographies.)

Vermes, G. (1973) *Scripture and Tradition in Judaism: Haggadic Studies*, Leiden: Brill. (A pioneering study which adopts a thematic and tradition-historical approach to the analysis of midrash.)

PHILIP S. ALEXANDER

MIKHAILOVSKII, NIKOLAI KONSTANTINOVICH (1842–1904)

Along with Lavrov, N.K. Mikhailovskii, a non-academic social theorist and literary critic, was the most representative and influential thinker of Russian populism. His most distinctive contribution to populist ideology was his attempt to reconcile the 'principle of individuality', so dear to the Russian intelligentsia, with the old, communal 'principles of the people', represented by the non-Westernized Russian peasantry. Unlike Herzen and Lavrov, Mikhailovskii did not see the principle of individuality as a product of Western progress, that is to say, as something which should be introduced from outside to the archaic world of Russian village commune. He challenged the stereotype which associated individualism with the capitalist West; instead, he tried to prove that the principle of individuality was in fact fully compatible with old Russian communalism, and incompatible with Western-type modernization. He did so by a radical redefinition of the very concept of individuality. For him individuality was not the product of a process of 'individualization' in the sense of loosening the communal bonds, making people socially differentiated, functionally specialized and separated from each other. On the contrary, by individuality he meant the 'inner wholeness', that is to say, the non-alienated, many-sided and harmonious development of human beings. Following the romantic critics of modernity, he claimed that individuality, so conceived, was being destroyed by capitalist progress.

Mikhailovskii's notion of individuality was similar to the Slavophile ideal of 'integral personality'. Unlike Slavophilism, however, Mikhailovskii's 'sociological romanticism' was bound up with a secularist worldview and a semi-positivist position in philosophy. For this reason its affinity with Slavophile romantic anti-capitalism was relatively inconsequential and remained unnoticed.

1 **Anthropological relativism and ethical personalism**
2 **Theory of progress**
3 **The struggle for individuality**
4 **Mikhailovskii and Marxism**

1 Anthropological relativism and ethical personalism

Mikhailovskii admired the Russian word for truth – pravda – as designating not only theoretical truth but also truth as justice, truth of the moral consciousness. In his view the common root of the two sides of truth was provided by the principle of individuality, treating the concrete human individual as the measure of all things.

The application of this principle to epistemology led to a relativist, or 'subjectivist', theory of knowledge. Absolute truth, or truth in itself, cannot exist; there is only truth for man and, in addition, it is not the same for the entire human species. Concrete truth is always perspectivist; the so-called facts are not something objectively given, their perception and interpretation is preformed by the nature of our social bonds, the type of social cooperation and, last but not least, by the irreducible individual experience of each human being. Hence there is no escape from subjectivism in theoretical knowledge: 'truth is that which satisfies the mental cravings of man'.

However, this epistemological relativism was combined by Mikhailovskii with an unyielding ethicism, treating the human individual as the central and absolute value. For Mikhailovskii this axiological absolutism was simply the other side of his view that the individual was the only basis of truth. If this is so, he reasoned, human knowledge is always relative, but in the realm of values all humans should accept the principle of individuality as the absolute standard for truth as justice. The individual, he argued, is sacred and must never be sacrificed. The individual's need for wholeness was for him a universal phenomenon; therefore the wholeness of individual human beings was in his view the absolute criterion in axiology. Thus, his 'subjective sociology' was based on two tenets: extreme epistemological relativism, often taking the form of a sociological theory of knowledge, and ethical absolutism, elevating the value of the all-round human personality.

2 Theory of progress

The application of Mikhailovskii's axiology to social sciences led to a reversal of the liberal view of progress, as expressed, in particular, in Herbert Spencer's positivistic evolutionism (see SPENCER, H.).

In his treatise 'Chto takoe progress' (What is Progress?) (1869) Mikhailovskii accused Spencer of overlooking the fact that individual progress and social evolution (on the model of organic evolution) were mutually exclusive. Spencer defined progress in the organic world as transition from simplicity (homogeneity) to complexity (heterogeneity); in society the same organic evolution was being achieved through the development of the division of labour. The Russian thinker set against this theory a sociological conception which claimed that the development of the division of labour in society was essentially a retrogression, since it had been achieved at the expense of individuality, which had suffered fragmentation and disintegration. This was so because only in an undifferentiated, egalitarian society can human individuality be diversified, integral and well-rounded. True progress, Mikhailovskii concluded, 'is the gradual approach to the fullest possible and the most diversified division of labour among man's organs and the least possible division of labour among men'.

In his other works, especially in the series of articles 'Bor'ba za individualnost'' (The Struggle for Individuality) (1875–6), Mikhailovskii used this formula as an argument for a backward-looking peasant utopia, idealizing the natural economy of the Russian village commune. The Russian peasant, he argued, lived a life that was primitive but full; he was economically self-sufficient, and therefore independent, many-sided, making use of all his capacities, being a tiller and a fisherman, a shepherd and an artist in one person. The absence of complex cooperation made the Russian peasants mutually independent, while simple cooperation (that is, a cooperation in which people were involved as 'whole beings') united them in a moral solidarity based upon mutual sympathy and understanding. One should distinguish between *levels* and *types* of development. The peasant commune represented a lower level of development than the capitalist factory but was superior to it as a type of development; similarly, Western man belonged to a lower type of development than the Russian peasant, who had not yet lost his primitive 'wholeness'. Hence it was groundless to believe that capitalism had liberated the individual; on the contrary, it turned the individual into a 'mere organ' of the social organism, mercilessly sacrificing concrete living individuals to the idol of 'maximum production'.

3 The struggle for individuality

Despite his criticism of biological 'organicism' in sociology, Mikhailovskii yielded to it in his own theory of the 'struggle for individuality'. He attributed to complex societies a tendency to develop into a kind of superorganism whose human members would be reduced to the role of submissive organs. However, he challenged the Darwinian trust in the survival of the fittest with the pessimistic view that 'natural evolution' was accomplished at the cost of a constant lowering of quality and deserved therefore to be seen as a retrograde process.

Mikhailovskii's theory was founded on the proposition that there are different stages of individuality that struggle against each other and try to dominate each other. This proposition, derived from Haeckel's classification of biological organisms (see HAECKEL, E.H.), assumed the presence of an inevitable conflict between individual human beings and different supraindividual entities – such as factories (as units of complex cooperation), estates, nations, states and so on. All these *social* individualities could only develop at the expense of man's freedom and wholeness. Therefore, Mikhailovskii concluded, 'society is man's chief and worst enemy, an enemy against whom he must always be on guard'.

In his philosophy of history Mikhailovskii combined the theory of the struggle for individuality with Comte's conception of the phases of intellectual development (see COMTE, A.). He divided history into three great periods: the 'objectively anthropocentric' period, the 'eccentric' period, and the 'subjectively anthropocentric' period. The first period knew only simple cooperation and could therefore preserve the original fullness of human beings. The second one, bound up with the social division of labour, was the period of development through alienation, separating the faculties of the species, objectifying them and setting against each other. The third period, which was to be realized as a result of a socialist transformation, would overcome the extreme forms of dependence on the division of labour, liberate individuals from the rule of objectified economic mechanisms and enable them to cooperate with each other in a free, ethical community.

An interesting part of Mikhailovskii's social philosophy was his view on the question of gender. He thought that sexual differentiation of human beings had been greatly increased as a result of the extreme division of social roles and interpreted love as striving for reintegration through compensatory self-fulfilment in another being. It followed from this that in the homogeneously egalitarian society of the future the differences between sexes would be greatly reduced and the need for love much less important.

4 Mikhailovskii and Marxism

Among the authors who influenced Mikhailovskii's view on capitalism – the highest phase of the 'eccentric' period of history – the most important was MARX. As early as 1869, in his article 'Teoriia Darvina i obshchestvennaia nauka' (The Theory of Darwin and the Social Sciences), Mikhailovskii expressed solidarity with Marx's views on the negative effects of the division of labour; he referred also to Adam Smith and Ferguson but, as a rule, quoted them after Marx's *Capital*. He was profoundly impressed by Marx's account of capitalist development as necessarily involving the expropriation of the immediate producers. Like other populists, he concluded from this that his country should do its best to avoid the capitalist way. Moreover, the adaptation of Marxism to his own conception persuaded Mikhailovskii that modern socialism and 'medieval forms of production', as represented by the village commune, were but different levels of the same type and, hence, that the workers' cause in Russia was essentially a conservative cause. In his review of the Russian translation of *Capital* (1872) he supported this conclusion by wholeheartedly endorsing Marx's denunciations of the class nature of 'bourgeois democracy'.

A few years later, however, Mikhailovskii became aware that Marxism contained also the notion of 'objective laws of history' and, therefore, could be used as an argument for the necessity of capitalist development in Russia. In his article 'Karl Marks pered sudom g. Zhukovskogo' (Karl Marx Arraigned Before Mr Zhukovskii), published in *Otechestvennye zapiski* (Notes of the Fatherland), 1877, he reacted to this by formulating the dramatic dilemma of the Russian disciples of Marx, who as socialists saw capitalism as morally unacceptable but as historical determinists had to accept 'the capitalist phase', with all its painful consequences for the masses. Marx himself tried to dispute this diagnosis in his 'Pis'mo v redaktsiu Otechestvennikh zapisok' (Letter to the Editor of *Otechestvennye zapiski*) (written 1877, published 1886) but failed to convince his Russian followers. Both Georgii PLEKHANOV and Pëtr Struve, the leader of the so-called 'legal Marxists' of the 1890s, interpreted historical materialism as a rigidly deterministic theory, treating the capitalist development of backward countries as a historical inevitability. This caused Mikhailovskii to launch an energetic campaign against Marxism. He attacked Marxism as an 'inverted Hegelianism', trying to substitute the speculative concept of historical necessity for the empirical explanation of fact and thus justifying all the cruelties of history. Mikhailovskii's arguments exercised an influence on the 'legal Marxists', especially BERDIAEV, helping them to evolve in the direction of philosophical idealism.

See also: HERZEN, A.I.; LAVROV, P.L.; SLAVOPHILISM; POSITIVISM, RUSSIAN; POSITIVISM IN THE SOCIAL SCIENCES

List of works

Mikhailovskii, N.K. (1906–14) *Polnoe sobranie sochinenii* (Complete Works), St Petersburg: M.M. Stasiulevich, 4th edn, 10 vols.

Edie, J.M., Scanlan, J.P. and Zeldin, M.B. (1965) *Russian Philosophy*, vol. 2, Chicago, IL: Quadrangle Books. (See 170–98 for an English translation of fragments from Mikhailovskii's philosophical writings including his seminal essay 'What is Progress?')

References and further reading

Billington, J.H. (1958) *Mikhailovsky and Russian Populism*, Oxford: Clarendon Press. (The only comprehensive monograph on Mikhailovskii in English.)

Hecker, J.F. (1915) 'The Sociological System of Mikhailovsky', *Russian Sociology*, pt II, ch. 2, 120–55, New York: Columbia University Press. (A systematic presentation of Mikhailovskii's 'subjective sociology'.)

Walicki, A. (1969) *The Controversy Over Capitalism: Studies in the Social Philosophy of the Russian Populists*, Oxford: Clarendon Press. (Contains a comprehensive analysis of Mikhailovskii's social philosophy, with special emphasis on his relationship to Marxism.)

ANDRZEJ WALICKI

MIKI KIYOSHI (1897–1945)

A brilliant young philosopher and critic of his times, Miki Kiyoshi embodied in his life and thought Japan's tortured transition from Westernized modernity to world power. Associated with his teacher, Nishida Kitarō, he is generally regarded as representative of a Marxist turn on the Kyoto School.

As a young student, Miki chanced upon a copy of Nishida Kitarō's *Zen no kenkyū* (Study of the Good), which turned him to the study of philosophy (see NISHIDA KITARŌ). After studying under Nishida at Kyoto University, he spent two years in Germany, principally with HEIDEGGER, in whose person he came to understand the post-war angst of Europe in the 1920s. He felt drawn to the optimism of thinkers such as BERGSON and to the philosophical anthropology of DILTHEY and SIMMEL. In pursuit of his own position he moved to Paris for a year where he threw himself into the works of PASCAL, culminating in his maiden work, *Pasukaru ni okeru ningen no kenkyū* (Pascal's Anthropology), which appeared in 1925.

On returning from abroad in 1924, Miki felt himself out of tune with the 'logic of place' that was occupying Nishida's attention at the time. Eager to bring his humanistic interests in line with the questions of the historical world, he turned to Marxist thought. The following year he took a post as professor at Hōsei University, and began to publish essays on historical materialism. In 1928 he was arraigned in court on charges of making an illegal contribution to the Japan Communist Party and received a suspended two-year sentence. In his own defence he insisted that he had always taken a critical stance to Marxism, which in turn earned him the derision of the Marxist establishment.

Hardened in his resolve both to systematize his own philosophical humanism and to clarify his critique of the rising militant fascism of the time, Miki set to work on a major study, *Kōzōryoku no ronri* (The Logic of Structural Power). The serialized publication of the work (the final section of which was only published posthumously), coincided with the onset of the Sino-Japanese War. In 1938 Miki joined the controversial Shōwa Study Group where he was the chief architect of its idea of 'commonism' (*kyōdōshugi*) a curious blend of socialist, liberal, and quasi-fascist ideas which was offered as an alternative to the 'co-prosperity sphere' that the military regime was advancing as part of its 'new world order' in Asia. Miki was dismissed as a fool by leading right-wing ideologues and the study group was disbanded.

In 1943 Miki was sent as a war correspondent to the Philippines, an express punishment for his 'red'

tendencies. He returned at the end of the year, only to find that almost none of his writings would be accepted for publication. In June 1945 he was arrested on a charge of disrupting public order and the powers behind his detention saw to it that he was denied amnesty at the end of the war. He died in prison.

Miki's overriding concern with philosophy's 'duty to the times' (*jimu*) made for a certain choppiness in his thought. Had he lived to write in time of peace, there is every indication he would have brought the various threads together into a unified body of thought. In what we have of his work, perhaps the most central notion is what he calls *techné* (*gijutsu*), the transformation of reality that serves as the bridge between and final judge of all human logos and pathos. Without it, the angst of the age was apt to lead only to privatized despair and a flight from reality, a tendency he saw in Heidegger. In works like *Tetsugaku nyūmon* (Introduction to Philosophy) and *Gijitsu tetsugaku* (The Philosophy of Techné), Miki showed how industrial technology and its social problems belong to a wider phenomenon that begins in the natural world and rises all the way to intellectual disciplines and morality in 'the *techné* of the heart' in which existential anxieties are not only accepted but creatively reshaped.

See also: KYOTO SCHOOL

List of works

Very little has been written about Miki in English and his works have never been translated.

Miki Kiyoshi (1925) *Pasukaru ni okeru ningen no kenkyū* (Pascal's Anthropology), in *Miki Kiyoshi Zenshū* (The Complete Works of Miki Kiyoshi), Tokyo: Iwanami Shoten, vol. 1. (Miki's study of Pascal.)

—— (1937–43) *Kōzōryoku no ronri* (The Logic of Structural Power), in *Miki Kiyoshi Zenshū* (The Complete Works of Miki Kiyoshi), Tokyo: Iwanami Shoten vol. 8. (Miki's major philosophical work.)

—— (1940) *Tetsugaku nyūmon* (Introduction to Philosophy), in *Miki Kiyoshi Zenshū* (The Complete Works of Miki Kiyoshi), Tokyo: Iwanami Shoten, vol. 7. (Work which shows much of Miki's later thinking.)

—— (1941) *Gijitsu tetsugaku* (The Philosophy of Techné), in *Miki Kiyoshi Zenshū* (The Complete Works of Miki Kiyoshi), Tokyo: Iwanami Shoten, vol. 7. (Looks at how industrial technology is part of a wider social phenomenon.)

References and further reading

Akamatsu Tsunihiko (1994) *Miki Kiyoshi: Tetsuga-kuteki shisaku no kiseki* (Miki Kiyoshi: The Locus of Philosophical Speculation), Kyoto: Minerva. (Survey of Miki's thought.)

Karaki Junzō (1966) *Miki Kiyoshi*, Tokyo: Chikuma. (Biography of Miki Kiyoshi.)

Kawahara Hiroshi *et al.* (1978) *Kindai nihon no shisō* (Modern Japanese Thought), Tokyo: Yohikaku, 79–148. (A brief but clear résumé of Miki's major ideas.)

J.W. HEISIG

MIKYŌ DORJE *see* MI BSKYOD RDO RJE

MILESIANS *see* ANAXIMANDER; ANAXIMENES; THALES

MILL, HARRIET *see* TAYLOR, HARRIET

MILL, JAMES (1773–1836)

James Mill, who is today remembered mainly as Bentham's chief disciple and John Stuart Mill's father, was a British philosopher, political theorist, historian, psychologist, economist, educationist and journalist. He was also largely responsible for clarifying and system-atizing Bentham's utilitarianism, for introducing a distinction between 'lower', animal pleasures and 'higher', uniquely human ones, and for organizing the small but influential band of Bentham's followers that became known as the 'philosophic radicals'. In politics, he favoured representative democracy as the only practicable system of government capable of maximiz-ing individual and communal happiness.

A prolific author, Mill wrote five books and more than a thousand articles and reviews. The book for which he was best known during his lifetime was his three-volume *History of British India* (1818). His *Essays* (1825) on sundry subjects – including 'Gov-ernment' and 'Education' – was followed by his *Elements of Political Economy* (1826), his two-volume

Analysis of the Phenomena of the Human Mind (1829) and *A Fragment on Mackintosh* (1835).

Despite this diversity of topics, Mill's thinking is informed by a unified philosophical vision. In psychology he was an 'associationist' who held that our beliefs and behaviour are the product of pleasur-able and painful associations of ideas. In ethics he was a utilitarian who held that the proper aim of human actions and practices was the promotion of human happiness (see UTILITARIANISM). Unlike Jeremy Bentham (see BENTHAM, J. §2), however, who held that 'pushpin is as good as poetry' – that is, that a pleasure is a pleasure, whatever its source – Mill believed that happiness is not synonymous with pleasure, particularly of the 'lower' or 'animal' sort. Human happiness comes from developing and using uniquely human powers – reason, logic, the love of truth and beauty – to their fullest extent. Hence his interest in education, which leads people toward the right sorts of associations: to find truth pleasurable and error painful; to delight in doing right and experience pain in doing wrong; and so on.

These themes come together in Mill's political philosophy, which is summarized succinctly in his essay on 'Government'. Government, properly struc-tured, promotes the happiness of the whole community and its individual members. Humans not only natu-rally desire happiness; they seek to satisfy that desire by investing as little effort as possible in obtaining it. Labour is the means of obtaining happiness. Humans find labour painful; hence they will, if they can, live off the labour of others. But to the extent that some live off the labour of others, the latter's incentive to work is diminished, and the happiness and prosperity of the community is imperilled.

The point and purpose of government is to maximize the happiness of the whole community by minimizing the extent to which some members live off the labour of others. Mill maintains that this aim cannot be achieved in a monarchy, nor in an aristocracy, nor in a direct democracy (the last taking too much time away from labouring). The only system capable of maximizing individual and communal happiness is a representative democracy in which representatives are elected to serve short terms before returning to the ranks of the electorate. So structured, representative government gives representatives every incentive to serve the people instead of themselves.

During his lifetime James Mill was regarded as a radical in politics and philosophy. That his ideas now seem conventional or even conservative shows how the radicalism of one age can become the conserva-tism of another.

See also: MILL, J.S. §1

359

List of works

Mill, J. (1818) *History of British India*, ed., abridged and with intro. by W. Thomas, Chicago, IL: University of Chicago Press, 1975, 1 vol. (Written from a rather zealously reforming utilitarian perspective and highly critical of native Indian institutions.)

—— (1826) *Elements of Political Economy*, London, 3rd edn. (Mill's 'manual' or 'text-book' of Ricardian economics.)

—— (1829) *Analysis of the Phenomena of Human Mind*, London: Longman, Green, Reader & Dyer, 2 vols. (A classic 'associationist' account of mental phenomena.)

—— (1835) *A Fragment on Mackintosh*, London. (An acerbic attack on Sir James Mackintosh, a leading Whig apologist and critic of the Philosophical Radicals.)

—— (1992) *Political Writings*, ed. T. Ball, Cambridge: Cambridge University Press. (Includes Mill's essays on 'Government' and 'Education', T.B. Macaulay's famous attack on the former, and Mill's heretofore unknown reply.)

References and further reading

Bain, A. (1882) *James Mill: A Biography*, London: Longman Green; repr. New York, Augustus M. Kelly Publishers, 1966. (A useful, if somewhat dry, biography.)

Ball, T. (1994) *Reappraising Political Theory: Revisionist Studies in the History of Political Thought*, Oxford: Clarendon Press. (Chapters 6–8 reconsider aspects of James Mill's political philosophy.)

Plamenatz, J. (1958) *The English Utilitarians*, Oxford: Blackwell, 2nd edn. (A concise account and assessment of key themes and thinkers in the utilitarian tradition, including James Mill.)

Thomas, W.E.S. (1979) *The Philosophical Radicals*, Oxford: Clarendon Press. (An excellent history of Bentham and his sometimes-wayward followers, including James and John Stuart Mill.)

TERENCE BALL

MILL, JOHN STUART
(1806–73)

John Stuart Mill, Britain's major philosopher of the nineteenth century, gave formulations of his country's empiricist and liberal traditions of comparable importance to those of John Locke. He united enlightenment reason with the historical and psychological insights of romanticism. He held that all knowledge is based on experience, believed that our desires, purposes and beliefs are products of psychological laws of association, and accepted Bentham's standard of the greatest total happiness of all beings capable of happiness – the principle of 'utility'. This was Mill's enlightenment legacy; he infused it with high Romantic notions of culture and character.

In epistemology Mill's empiricism was very radical. He drew a distinction between 'verbal' and 'real' propositions similar to that which Kant made between analytic and synthetic judgments. However, unlike Kant, Mill held that not only pure mathematics but logic itself contains real propositions and inferences, and unlike Kant, he denied that any synthetic, or real, proposition is a priori. The sciences of logic and mathematics, according to Mill, propound the most general laws of nature and, like all other sciences, are in the last resort grounded inductively on experience.

We take principles of logic and mathematics to be a priori because we find it inconceivable that they should not be true. Mill acknowledged the facts which underlie our conviction, facts about unthinkability or imaginative unrepresentability, and he sought to explain these facts in associationist terms. He thought that we are justified in basing logical and mathematical claims on such facts about what is thinkable – but the justification is itself a posteriori.

What then is the nature and standing of induction? Mill held that the primitive form of induction is enumerative induction, simple generalization from experience. He did not address Hume's sceptical problem about enumerative induction. Generalization from experience is our primitive inferential practice and remains our practice when we become reflectively conscious of it – in Mill's view nothing more needs to be said or can be said. Instead he traced how enumerative induction is internally strengthened by its actual success in establishing regularities, and how it eventually gives rise to more searching methods of inductive inquiry, capable of detecting regularities where enumerative induction alone would not suffice. Thus whereas Hume raised sceptical questions about induction, Mill pushed through an empiricist analysis of deduction. He recognized as primitively legitimate only the disposition to rely on memory and the disposition to generalize from experience. The whole of science, he thought, is built from these.

In particular, he did not accept that the mere fact that a hypothesis accounts for data can ever provide a reason for thinking it true (as opposed to thinking it useful). It is always possible that a body of data may be explained equally well by more than one hypothesis. This view, that enumerative induction is the only authoritative source of general truths, was also important in his metaphysics. Accepting as he did that our knowledge of supposed objects external to consciousness consists only in the conscious states they excite in us, he concluded that external objects amount only to 'permanent possibilities of sensation'. The possibilities are 'permanent' in the sense that they can be relied on to obtain if an antecedent condition is realized. Mill was the founder of modern phenomenalism.

In ethics, Mill's governing conviction was that happiness is the sole ultimate human end. As in the case of induction, he appealed to reflective agreement, in this case of desires rather than reasoning dispositions. If happiness was not 'in theory and in practice, acknowledged to be an end, nothing could ever convince any person that it was so' (1861a: 234). But he acknowledged that we can will to do what we do not desire to do; we can act from duty, not desire. And he distinguished between desiring a thing as 'part' of our happiness and desiring it as a means to our happiness. The virtues can become a part of our happiness, and for Mill they ideally should be so. They have a natural base in our psychology on which moral education can be built. More generally, people can reach a deeper understanding of happiness through education and experience: some forms of happiness are inherently preferred as finer by those able to experience them fully.

Thus Mill enlarged but retained Bentham's view that the happiness of all, considered impartially, is the standard of conduct. His account of how this standard relates to the fabric of everyday norms was charged with the nineteenth century's historical sense, but also maintained links with Bentham. Justice is a class of exceptionally stringent obligations on society – it is the 'claim we have on our fellow-creatures to join in making safe for us the very groundwork of our existence' (1865b: 251). Because rights of justice protect this groundwork they take priority over the direct pursuit of general utility as well as over the private pursuit of personal ends.

Mill's doctrine of liberty dovetails with this account of justice. Here he appealed to rights founded on 'utility in the largest sense, grounded on the permanent interests of man as a progressive being' (1859: 224). The principle enunciated in his essay On Liberty (1859) safeguards people's freedom to pursue their own goals, so long as they do not infringe on the legitimate interests of others: power should not be exercised over people for their own good. Mill defended the principle on two grounds. It enables individuals to realize their potential in their own distinctive way, and, by liberating talents, creativity and energy, it institutes the social conditions for the moral development of culture and character.

1 Life

Mill was born in London on the 20 May 1806, the eldest son of a Scotsman, James MILL, and an English woman, Harriet Burrow. James educated his son himself – an education made famous by the account John Stuart gave of it in his Autobiography (1873). He taught John the classics, logic, political economy, jurisprudence and psychology – starting with Greek at the age of three. John was brought up in a circle of intellectual and political radicals, friends of his father, which included Jeremy BENTHAM and David Ricardo. In his twenties (not surprisingly, perhaps) he was afflicted by a deep depression from which he recovered partly through reading poetry. In those and subsequent years he also came to know some of the most interesting younger figures in English politics and culture. These included conservative critics of Benthamism, as well as radical adherents of it.

Mill followed his father into the East India Company, where he became an influential official, resigning only in 1858 when, following the Indian Mutiny, the Company was taken over by the Crown and the governance of India became the direct business of the British State. In 1851 he married Harriet TAYLOR, who in his own account greatly influenced his social philosophy. In the 1860s he was briefly a member of Parliament, and throughout his life was involved in many radical causes. Among them was his lifelong support for women's rights – see The Subjection of Women (1869).

Mill made his philosophical reputation with his System of Logic, published in 1843. The Principles of Political Economy (1848) was a synthesis of classical economics which defined liberal orthodoxy for at least a quarter of a century. His two best-known works of moral philosophy, On Liberty and Utilitarianism, appeared later – in 1859 and 1861. But he had been thinking about ethics and politics all his life, and it is his moral and political philosophy which is at present most widely read.

2 Language and logic

Nevertheless, Mill's epistemology and metaphysics remain as interesting and relevant as his better-known views in ethics and politics, and it is from these aspects of his philosophy that a general survey must start. In the *System of Logic* Mill distinguishes 'verbal' and 'real' propositions, and correspondingly, 'merely apparent' and 'real' inferences. An inference is merely apparent when no move to a new assertion has been made. For this to be so, the conclusion must literally have been asserted in the premises. In such a case, there can be no epistemological problem about justifying the apparent inference – there *is* nothing to justify. A verbal proposition can now be defined as a conditional proposition corresponding to a merely apparent inference. Propositions and inferences which are not verbal or merely apparent are real.

Mill argues that not only mathematics but logic itself contains real inferences. To demonstrate this he embarks on a semantic analysis of sentences and terms (he calls them 'propositions' and 'names'), of syllogistic logic and of the so-called 'Laws of Thought'. His analysis has imperfections and he does not unify it in a fully general account, but he supplies the foundations of such an account, and in doing so takes the empiricist epistemology of logic and mathematics to a new level.

The starting point is a distinction between the denotation and connotation of names. Names, which may be general or singular, denote things and connote attributes of things. A general name connotes attributes and denotes each object which has those attributes. Most singular names also connote attributes.

There is, however, an important class of singular names – proper names in the ordinary sense, such as 'Dartmouth' – which denote an object without connoting any property (see PROPER NAMES §§1, 6). Identity propositions which contain only non-connotative names, such as 'Tully is Cicero', are verbal, in Mill's view. They lack content in the sense that, according to Mill, the only information conveyed is about the names themselves: 'Tully' denotes the same object as 'Cicero' does. Mill's point is that there is no fact in the world to which 'Cicero is Tully' corresponds. But to class these propositions as verbal would require a change in the characterization of verbal propositions given above. Moreover, knowledge that Cicero is Tully is not a priori. We cannot know the proposition to be true just by reflecting on the meaning of the names – whereas Mill's overall intention is that the class of verbal propositions should be identical with the class of propositions which are innocuously a priori *because* they are empty of content. He does not comment on these difficulties.

The meaning of a declarative sentence – 'the import of a proposition' – is determined by the connotation, not the denotation, of its constituent names; the sole exception being connotationless proper names, where meaning is determined by denotation. (Again Mill does not explain how this thesis about the meaning of proper names is to be reconciled with the a posteriority of 'Cicero is Tully'.) Mill proceeds to show how the various syntactic forms identified by syllogistic theory yield conditions of truth for sentences of those forms, when the connotation of their constituent names is given.

Armed with this analysis he argues that logic contains real inferences and propositions. He assumes that to assert a conjunction, 'A and B', is simply to assert A and to assert B. He defines 'A or B' as 'If not A, then B, and if not B, then A'. 'If A then B' means, he thinks, 'The proposition B is a legitimate inference from the proposition A'. From these claims it follows that certain deductive inferences, for example, from a conjunction to one of its conjuncts, are merely apparent. But, Mill holds, the laws of contradiction and excluded middle are real – and therefore a posteriori – propositions. He takes it that 'not P' is equivalent in meaning to 'It is false that P'; if we further assume the equivalence in meaning of P and 'It is true that P', the principle of contradiction becomes, as he puts it, 'the same proposition cannot at the same time be false and true'. 'I cannot look upon this', he says, 'as a merely verbal proposition'. He makes analogous remarks about excluded middle, which turns – on these definitions – into the principle of bivalence: 'Either it is true that P or it is false that P'.

Mill adds an epistemological argument to this semantic analysis. If logic did not contain real inferences, all deductive reasoning would be a *petitio principii*, a begging of the question, and it could produce no new knowledge. Yet clearly it does produce new knowledge. So logic must contain real inferences.

Unfortunately, Mill mixes up this epistemological argument with an interesting but distinct objective. He wants to show that 'all inference is from particulars to particulars', in order to demystify the role that general propositions play in thought. He argues that in principle they add nothing to the force of an argument; particular conclusions could always be derived inductively direct from particular premises. Their value is psychological. They play the role of 'memoranda' or summary records of the inductive potential of all that we have observed, and they facilitate 'trains of reasoning' (for example, as in 'This

362

is A; All As are Bs; No Bs are Cs; so this is not C').
Psychologically they greatly increase our memory and
reasoning power, but epistemologically they are
dispensable.

This thesis is connected to Mill's rejection of
'intuitive' knowledge of general truths and to his
inductivism (see §5 below). But there is also a deeper
way in which a radical empiricist must hold that all
inference is from particulars to particulars. For
consider the inference from 'Everything is F' to 'a is
F'. Is it a real or merely apparent inference? It is
impossible to hold it real if one also wishes to argue
that real inferences are a posteriori. But the only way
in which Mill can treat it as verbal is to treat the
premise as a conjunction: 'a is F and b is F and...'. If
that approach is precluded, then all that remains is to
deny that 'Everything is F' is propositional – it must,
rather, express an inferential commitment. Both
approaches are very close to the surface in Mill's
discussion of the syllogism, though neither emerges
clearly.

3 Mathematics

The strategy which Mill applies to mathematics is
broadly similar to his approach to logic. If it was
merely verbal, mathematical reasoning would be a
petitio principii, but semantic analysis shows that it
contains real propositions.

Mill provides brief but insightful empiricist
sketches of geometry and arithmetic. The theorems
of geometry are deduced from premises which are real
propositions inductively established. (Deduction is
itself largely a process of real inference.) These
premises, where they are not straightforwardly true
of physical space, are true in the limit. Geometrical
objects – points, lines, planes – are ideal or 'fictional'
limits of ideally constructible material entities. Thus
the real empirical assertion underlying an axiom such
as 'Two straight lines cannot enclose a space' is
something like 'The more closely two lines approach
absolute breadthlessness and straightness, the smaller
the space they enclose'.

Applying his distinction between denotation and
connotation, Mill argues that arithmetical identities
such as 'Two plus one equals three' are real
propositions. Number terms denote 'aggregates' and
connote certain attributes of aggregates. (He does not
say that they denote those attributes of the aggregates,
though perhaps he should have done.) 'Aggregates'
are natural, not abstract, entities – 'collections' or
'agglomerations' individuated by a principle of
aggregation. This theory escapes some of the influential criticisms Frege later made of it, but its viability
none the less remains extremely doubtful. The

respects in which aggregates have to differ from sets
if they are to be credibly natural, and not abstract,
entities are precisely those in which they seem to fail
to produce a fully adequate ontology for arithmetic.
(One can, for example, number numbers, but can
there be aggregates of aggregates, or of attributes of
aggregates, if aggregates are natural entities?)

However this may be, Mill's philosophical programme is clear. Arithmetic, like logic and geometry,
is a natural science, concerning a category of the laws
of nature – those concerning aggregation. The
fundamental principles of arithmetic and geometry,
as well as of logic itself, are real. Mill provides the first
thoroughly empiricist analysis of meaning and of
deductive reasoning itself.

He distinguishes his view from three others –
'Conceptualism', 'Nominalism' and 'Realism'. 'Conceptualism' is his name for the view which takes the
objects studied by logic to be psychological states or
acts. It holds that names stand for 'ideas' which make
up judgments and that 'a proposition is the expression
of a relation between two ideas'. It confuses logic and
psychology by assimilating propositions to judgments
and attributes of objects to ideas. Against this
doctrine Mill insists that:

> All language recognizes a difference between
> doctrine or opinion, and the fact of entertaining
> the opinion; between assent, and what is assented
> to... Logic, according to the conception here
> formed of it, has no concern with the nature of
> the act of judging or believing; the consideration of
> that act, as a phenomenon of the mind, belongs to
> another science.
>
> (1843: 87)

The Nominalists – Mill cites Hobbes – hold that
logic and mathematics are entirely verbal. Mill takes
this position much more seriously than Conceptualism and seeks to refute it in detail. His main point is
that Nominalists are only able to maintain their view
because they fail to distinguish between the denotation and the connotation of names, 'seeking for their
meaning exclusively in what they denote' (1843: 91)
(see NOMINALISM §3).

Nominalists and Conceptualists hold that logic and
mathematics can be known non-empirically, while yet
retaining the view that no real proposition about the
world can be so known. Realists hold that logical and
mathematical knowledge is knowledge of universals
which exist in an abstract Platonic domain; the terms
that make up sentences being signs that stand for such
universals. Versions of this view were destined to stage
a major revival in philosophy, and semantic analysis
would be their main source, but it is the view Mill
takes least seriously.

In the contemporary use of the term, Mill is himself a nominalist – he rejects abstract entities (see ABSTRACT OBJECTS §4). However, just as severe difficulties lie in the way of treating the ontology of arithmetic in terms of aggregates rather than sets, so there are difficulties in treating the ontology of general semantics without appealing to universals and sets, as well as to natural properties and objects. We can have no clear view of how Mill would have responded to these difficulties had they been made evident to him. But we can be fairly sure that he would have sought to maintain his nominalism.

However, his main target is the doctrine that there are real a priori propositions (see A PRIORI). What, he asks, goes on in practice when we hold a real proposition to be true a priori? We find its negation inconceivable, or that it is derived, by principles whose unsoundness we find inconceivable, from premises whose negation we find inconceivable. Mill is not offering a definition of what is meant by such terms as 'a priori', or 'self-evident'; his point is that facts about what we find inconceivable are all that lends colour to the use of these terms.

They are facts about the limits, felt by us from the inside, on what we can imagine perceiving. Mill thought he could explain these facts about unthinkability, or imaginative unrepresentability, in associationist terms, and much of his work claims to do so. This associationist psychology is unlikely nowadays to convince, but that does not affect his essential point: the step from our inability to represent to ourselves the negation of a proposition, to acceptance of its truth, calls for justification. Moreover, the justification itself must be a priori if it is to show that the proposition is known a priori.

4 'Psychologism' and naturalism

Mill is often mistakenly accused of 'psychologism' in his treatment of logic – an accusation which seems to go back to HUSSERL (and one which Frege does not make). 'Psychologism' is the view that laws of logic are psychological laws concerning our mental processes; or that 'meanings' are mental entities, and that 'judgments' assert relationships among these entities. But Mill's view, as we have seen, is that logic and mathematics are the most general empirical sciences, governing *all* phenomena. He explicitly holds that the distinction between necessary and contingent truths, understood 'metaphysically', is empty. And he dismisses the Conceptualist claim that names refer to ideas and propositions express or assert a psychological relation between them.

What explains, then, the attribution of 'psychologism' to Mill? Husserl quotes a passage from *An Examination of Sir William Hamilton's Philosophy* (1865a), which has been cited many times since:

Logic is not the theory of Thought as Thought, but of valid Thought; not of thinking, but of correct thinking. *It is not a Science distinct from, and coordinate with Psychology. So far as it is a science at all, it is a part, or branch, of Psychology; differing from it, on the one hand as the part differs from the whole, and on the other, as an Art differs from a Science. Its theoretic grounds are wholly borrowed from Psychology, and include as much of that science as is required to justify the rules of the art.*

(1865a: 359; italics show portion quoted by Husserl)

To give this a psychologistic reading is to take it out of context. Mill means that the logician must formulate rules of reasoning in a manner which will be as helpful as possible to inquirers, and must draw on the psychology of thought to do so. It is in that sense that the art of the logician borrows from the science of the psychologist. How best to promote the art of clear thinking is a psychological question. None the less,

the laws, in the scientific sense of the term, of Thought as Thought – do not belong to Logic, but to Psychology: and it is only the *validity* of thought which Logic takes cognizance of.

(1865a: 359)

So it is wrong to accuse Mill of psychologism about logic. But there is a sense in which his view of our most basic forms of inductive reasoning is psychologistic, or naturalistic. For how does he respond to the Kantian claim that the very possibility of knowledge requires that there be a priori elements in our knowledge? Even if we accept his inductive account of logic and mathematics, must we not accept the principle of induction itself as a priori?

For Mill, the primitive form of reasoning – in both the epistemological and the aetiological sense – is enumerative induction, the disposition to infer that all As are B from the observation of a number of As which are all B. (Or to the conclusion that a given percentage of all As are B from the observation of that percentage of Bs among a number of As.) We spontaneously agree in reasoning that way, and in holding that way of reasoning to be sound. This method of reasoning, enumerative induction, is not a merely verbal principle. So it cannot on Mill's own account be a priori. Mill says that we learn 'the laws of our rational faculty, like those of every other natural agency', by 'seeing the agent at work'. We bring our most basic reasoning dispositions to self-consciousness by critical reflection on our actual practice. He is right to say that this reflective scrutiny of practice is, in a *certain* sense, an a posteriori process. It examines dispositions which we have before we examine them. Having examined our dispositions, we reach a reflective equilibrium in which we endorse some – and perhaps reject others. We endorse them as sound norms of reasoning. There is nothing more to be said: no further story, platonic or transcendental, to be told.

Unlike Hume, or even Reid, Mill shows no interest at all in scepticism. If one thinks that scepticism is both unanswerable and unserious this may be true philosophic wisdom. But to Mill's epistemological critics, whether they were realists or post-Kantian idealists, it seemed obvious that it was evasion, not wisdom. Naturalism could only seem to differ from scepticism by being uncritical, and in this we find the truth in the allegation that Mill's system of logic is 'psychologistic'; if it is sound criticism, it is sound criticism of all naturalistic epistemology.

5 Inductive science

Mill does not raise purely sceptical questions about simple generalization from experience; he none the less thinks it a highly fallible method. His aim is to show how reasoning methods can evolve from it which greatly reduce the fallibility of induction, even though they can never wholly eliminate it.

Humankind begins with 'spontaneous' and 'unscientific' inductions about particular unconnected natural phenomena or aspects of experience. As these generalizations accumulate and interweave, they justify the second-order inductive conclusion that *all* phenomena are subject to uniformity, and more specifically, that all have discoverable sufficient conditions. In this less vague form, the principle of general uniformity becomes, given Mill's analysis of causation, the Law of Universal Causation. It in turn provides (Mill believes) the grounding assumption for a new style of reasoning about nature – eliminative induction.

In this type of reasoning, the assumption that a type of phenomenon has uniform causes, together with a (revisable) assumption about what its possible causes are, initiates a comparative inquiry in which the actual cause is identified by elimination. Mill formulates the logic of this eliminative reasoning in his well-known 'Methods of Experimental Inquiry' (Chapter 7, Book 2 of *System of Logic*). (A full account is given in Mackie (1974).) His picture of the interplay between enumerative and eliminative reasoning, and of the way it entrenches, from within, our rational confidence in the inductive process, is elegant and penetrating.

The improved scientific induction which results

from this new style of reasoning spills back onto the principle of Universal Causation on which it rests, and raises its certainty to a new level. That in turn raises our confidence in the totality of particular enumerative inductions from which the principle is derived. So the amount of confidence with which one can rely on the 'inductive process' as a whole depends on the point which has been reached in its history – though the confidence to be attached to particular inductions always remains variable.

Mill's inductivism – his view that enumerative induction is the only ultimately authoritative method of inference to new truths – was rejected by William Whewell (see WHEWELL, W. §2), who argued that the really fundamental method in scientific inquiry was the Hypothetical Method, in which one argues to the truth of a hypothesis from the fact that it would explain observed phenomena (see INFERENCE TO THE BEST EXPLANATION). Mill had read Whewell's *History of the Inductive Sciences* (1837), and could hardly fail to be aware of the pervasiveness of hypotheses in the actual process of inquiry, or of their indispensability in supplying working assumptions – their 'heuristic' value, as Whewell called it. But what Mill could not accept was that the mere fact that a hypothesis accounted for the data in itself provided a reason for thinking it true.

Yet Whewell's appeal was to the actual practice of scientific reasoning, as observed in the history of science. An appeal of that kind was precisely what Mill, on his own principles, could not ignore. If the disposition to hypothesize is spontaneous, why should it not be recognized as a fundamental method of reasoning to truth, as enumerative induction is?

Mill's refusal to recognize it is not arbitrary. The essential point underlying it is a powerful one: it is the possibility that a body of data may be explained equally well by more than one hypothesis. Mill does not deny the increasingly deductive and mathematical organization of science – he emphasizes it. That is quite compatible with his inductivism, and indeed central to his account of the increasing reliability of the inductive process. He further agrees that a hypothesis can sometimes be shown, by eliminative methods of inductive reasoning which he accepts, to be the only one consistent with the facts. And he allows various other cases of apparently purely hypothetical reasoning which are, in his view, genuinely inductive.

When all such cases have been taken into account, we are left with pure cases of the Hypothetical Method, in which the causes postulated are not directly observable, and not simply because they are assumed to operate – in accordance with known laws, inductively established – in regions of time or space too distant to observe. What are we to say of such hypotheses? For example of the 'undulatory' theory of light? They cannot, Mill says, be accepted as inductively established truths, not even as probable ones.

> An hypothesis of this kind is not to be received as probably true because it accounts for all the known phenomena; since this is a condition sometimes fulfilled tolerably well by two conflicting hypotheses; while there are probably many others which are equally possible, but which from want of anything analogous in our experience, our minds are unfitted to conceive.
>
> (1843: 500)

Such a hypothesis can suggest fruitful analogies, Mill thinks, but cannot be regarded as yielding a new truth itself. The data do not determine a unique hypothesis: it is this possibility of underdetermination which stops him from accepting hypothetical reasoning as an independent method of achieving truth.

In seeing the difficulty Mill is certainly on solid ground. What he does not see, however, is how much must be torn from the fabric of our belief if inductivism is applied strictly. So it is an important question whether the difficulty can be resolved – and whether it can be resolved within a naturalistic framework which does not appeal to an underlying idealism, as Whewell did. If naturalism can endorse the hypothetical method, then among other things it can develop a more plausible empiricism about logic and mathematics than Mill's. But the ramifications of his inductivism are even wider, as becomes apparent from an examination of his general metaphysics.

6   Mind and matter

Mill sets out his metaphysical views in *An Examination of Sir William Hamilton's Philosophy*. HAMILTON was the last eminent representative of the Scottish Common Sense School, and a ferocious controversialist – in Mill's eyes a pillar of the right-thinking establishment, ripe for demolition. The result is that Mill's discussion of general metaphysical issues is cast in a highly polemical form which leaves important issues shrouded in obscurity. He does however give himself space to develop his view of our knowledge of the external world.

He begins with a doctrine which he rightly takes to be generally accepted (in his time) on all sides: 'that all the attributes which we ascribe to objects, consist in their having the power of exciting one or another variety of sensation in our minds; that an object is to us nothing else than that which affects our senses in a certain manner' (1865a: 6). This is 'the doctrine of the Relativity of Knowledge to the knowing mind'. It makes epistemology, in Mill's words, the 'Interpretation of Consciousness'. He proceeds to analyse what we mean when we say that objects are external to us:

> We mean, that there is concerned in our perceptions something which exists when we are not thinking of it; which existed before we had ever thought of it, and would exist if we were annihilated; and further, that there exist things which we never saw, touched or otherwise perceived, and things which have never been perceived by man. This idea of something which is distinguished from our fleeting impressions by what, in Kantian language, is called Perdurability; something which is fixed and the same, while our impressions vary; something which exists whether we are aware of it or not, constitutes altogether our idea of external substance. Whoever can assign an origin to this complex conception, has accounted for what we mean by the belief in matter.
>
> (1865a: 178–9)

To assign this origin Mill postulates that

> we are capable of forming the conception of Possible sensations; sensations which we are not feeling at the present moment, but which we might feel, and should feel if certain conditions were present.
>
> (1865a: 177)

> These possibilities, which are conditional certainties, need a special name to distinguish them from mere vague possibilities, which experience gives no warrant for reckoning upon. Now, as soon as a distinguishing name is given, though it be only to the same thing regarded in a different aspect, one of the most familiar experiences of our mental nature teaches us, that the different name comes to be considered as the name of a different thing.
>
> (1865a: 179–80)

Physical objects are 'Permanent Possibilities of Sensation' (There is a change in the 'permanent' possibilities of sensation whenever there is change in the world. Mill also uses other terms, such as 'certified' or 'guaranteed'.) We often find that whenever a given cluster of certified possibilities of sensation obtains, then a certain other cluster follows. 'Hence our ideas of causation, power, activity... become connected, not with sensations, but with groups of possibilities of sensation' (1865a: 181) (see PHENOMENALISM §1).

However, even if our notion of matter as the external cause of sensations can be explained on psychological principles, it is still possible to hold that good grounds can be given for thinking the notion to have instances. There might be a legitimate inference from the existence of the permanent possibilities and their correlations to the existence of an external cause of our sensations. It is at just this point that Mill's inductivism plays a part. The inference would be a case of hypothetical reasoning, to an explanation of experience which transcended all possible data of experience; and that is precisely what Mill rejects: 'I assume only the tendency, but not the legitimacy of the tendency, to extend all the laws of our own experience to a sphere beyond our experience' (1865a: 187).

If matter is the permanent possibility of sensation what is mind? Can it also be resolved into 'a series of feelings, with a background of possibilities of feeling'? Mill finds in this view a serious difficulty: to remember or expect a state of consciousness is not simply to believe that it has existed or will exist; it is to believe that *I myself* have experienced or will experience that state of consciousness.

If, therefore, we speak of the Mind as a series of feelings, we are obliged to complete the statement by calling it a series of feelings which is aware of itself as past and future; and we are reduced to the alternative of believing that the Mind, or Ego, is something different from any series of feelings, or possibilities of them, or of accepting the paradox, that something which *ex hypothesi* is but a series of feelings, can be aware of itself as a series.

(1865a: 194)

Thus although Mill is unwilling to accept 'the common theory of Mind, as a so-called substance', the self-consciousness involved in memory and expectation drives him to 'ascribe a reality to the Ego – to my own Mind – different from that real existence as a Permanent Possibility, which is the only reality I acknowledge in Matter' (1865a: 208).

This ontology, Mill thinks, is consistent with common sense realism about the world. Phenomenalism – the conception of matter as possibility of experience – allegedly leaves common sense and science untouched. In particular, mind and experience is still properly seen as a part of the natural order.

Yet if phenomenalism is right, only the experiences are real. Mill thinks we are led to that conclusion by the very standards of reasoning recognized in a naturalistic 'science of science', or 'system of logic'. If he is right, then the naturalistic vision of the world which sees minds as part of a larger causal order is self-undermining. For if we are led to the conclusion that only states of consciousness are real by *an application of naturalism's own standards*, then that conclusion has to be understood on the same level as

the naturalistic affirmation that states of consciousness are themselves part of a larger causal order external to them – and therefore as inconsistent with it. Causal relations cannot exist between fictional entities which are mere markers for possibilities of sensation.

This is the fault-line in Mill's epistemology and metaphysics. Either naturalism undermines itself, or there is something wrong with Mill's inductivist analysis of our natural norms of reasoning, or with his endorsement of the doctrine of the Relativity of Knowledge, or with both. It is not obvious that Mill's most fundamental tenet – his naturalistic view of the mind – can be safeguarded by rejecting inductivism and endorsing the hypothetical method. There is still something implausible about hypothesizing the world as an explanation of pure experience. Mill himself explicitly acknowledged that memory, as well as induction, has epistemic authority. Had he analysed the significance of such an acknowledgment more thoroughly, he might have noted a parallel: on the one hand a primitive epistemic norm which warrants assertions about the past based on present memory-experiences; on the other, primitive epistemic norms which warrant assertions about the physical world based on perceptual experience. But perhaps that would have taken him too far in the direction of Reid's principles of common sense.

7 Freedom and the moral sciences

The sixth and last book of the *System of Logic* is a classical statement of methodology in the 'moral' sciences (that is, the human sciences). Its strength derives partly from the fact that Mill was a philosopher who also practised the whole range of these sciences as they then stood. He was mainly known as a political economist, but had strong interests in psychology and in the nascent science of sociology. He thought as an economist as well as a philosopher about socialism, taxation and systems of property, and he thought in sociological terms about such topics as democracy and the role of moral and intellectual elites. He also took an interest in a variety of psychological topics, including desire, pleasure and will, and the origins of conscience and justice.

The phenomena of mind and society are, in Mill's view, causal processes. If mind and society are part of the causal order, and causation is regular succession, then the general model of explanation he has proposed, according to which explanation subsumes facts under laws linking them to their causal antecedents, will apply, he thinks, to the moral sciences. It may be hard for moral science to live up to it, in view of the complexity of its data, but the model stands as an ideal. Important issues remain about the character of and relationships between the various moral sciences, and Mill treats these issues in detail. But he does not think that the very idea of a moral science raises new metaphysical or epistemological problems (see EXPLANATION IN HISTORY AND SOCIAL SCIENCE §3).

Psychological concepts are intentional and, correspondingly, the moral sciences are interpretative. Can laws of individual behaviour be formulated, as Mill assumed, in this interpretative vocabulary? His analysis of the moral sciences takes their fundamental laws to lie in the domain of psychology. He was familiar with a different view, that of Auguste COMTE, who held that the fundamental and irreducible moral science was sociology (a term coined by Comte). There was no deeper moral science, no science of psychology; the next level below sociology was the physical science of biology. Mill rejected that view, but enthusiastically shared Comte's vision of a historical sociology. Psychology may be the irreducible theoretical basis of the moral sciences; historical sociology is to be, as far as Mill was concerned, their prime exhibit.

Associationism and a Comtean historical sociology are thus the driving ideas in Mill's logic of the moral sciences. They interlock. Associationism fortifies his belief in the mutability of human nature: different social and historical formations can build radically different patterns of association. The bridge between historical sociology and the invariant laws of associationist psychology can be provided, Mill thinks, by an innovation of his own: a science he calls 'Ethology', which will study the different forms of human character in different social formations. He intended to write a treatise on the subject; significantly, he failed.

How, on this naturalistic view of mind and society, can human beings be free? The question mattered deeply to Mill. The conclusion others drew from the doctrine of determinism, namely, that we have (in Mill's phrase) no 'power of *self*-formation', and hence are not really responsible for our character or our actions, would have destroyed his moral vision. Self-formation is the fulcrum of his ideal of life, and 'moral freedom', the ability to bring one's desires under the control of a steady rational purpose, is a condition of self-formation, of having a character in the full sense (see FREE WILL §§3–4).

Thus Mill had to show how causally conditioned natural objects can also be morally free agents. The sketch of a solution in the *System of Logic* (Book 6, chapter 2), which Mill thought the best chapter in the book, is brief but penetrating. (There is a longer discussion in *An Examination of Sir William Hamil-*

ton's Philosophy, chapter 26.) One of its leading features is a distinction between resistible and irresistible causes; 'in common use', only causes which are 'irresistible', whose operation is 'supposed too powerful to be counteracted at all', are called necessary:

> There are physical sequences which we call necessary, as death for want of food or air; there are others which, though as much cases of causation as the former, are not said to be necessary, as death from poison, which an antidote, or the use of the stomach-pump, will sometimes avert ... human actions are in this last predicament: they are never (except in some cases of mania) ruled by any one motive with such absolute sway, that there is no room for the influence of another.
> (1843: 839)

An action caused by an irresistible motive (a 'mania') is plainly not free. This is certainly very pertinent. Yet something is added when we move from the idea of motives being resistible by other motives to the idea of moral freedom, the idea that *I* have the power to resist motives. It is the ability to recognize and respond to reasons. I act freely if I could have resisted the motive on which I in fact acted, had there been good reason to do so. A motive impairs my moral freedom if it cannot be defeated by a cogent reason for not acting on it. Mill fails to bring this connection between freedom and reason into clear view, but he relies on it in his ethical writings. He takes it that I am more or less free overall, according to the degree to which I can bring my motives under scrutiny and act on the result of that scrutiny. So I can *make* myself more free, by shaping desires or at least cultivating the strength of will to overcome them.

> A person feels morally free who feels that his habits or his temptations are not his masters, but he theirs: who even in yielding to them knows that he could resist ... we must feel that our wish, if not strong enough to alter our character, is strong enough to conquer our character when the two are brought into conflict in any particular case of conduct. And hence it is said with truth, that none but a person of confirmed virtue is completely free.
> (1843: 841)

The identification of moral freedom with confirmed virtue, and (less explicitly) of confirmed virtue with steady responsiveness to reasons, is present in Mill as in Kant (see KANT, I. §11). But Mill does not address crucial questions such as what is it to grasp a reason, or how reason can be efficacious. To vindicate the coherence of his view one would have to show how to answer such questions in a way which is compatible with naturalism. The problem remains central in contemporary philosophy – certainly Mill himself never took full stock of it.

8 Happiness, desire and will

Mill's single ultimate standard of theoretical reason is enumerative induction. His single ultimate standard of practical reason is the principle of utility; its standard is the good of all. But what is the good? According to Mill, it is happiness, understood as 'pleasure, and freedom from pain' (1861a: 210) (see HAPPINESS). His case rests on the following principle of method:

> The sole evidence it is possible to produce that anything is desirable, is that people do actually desire it. If the end which the utilitarian doctrine proposes to itself were not, in theory and in practice, acknowledged to be an end, nothing could ever convince any person that it was so.
>
> (1861a: 234)

Mill is not claiming that the conclusion that happiness is desirable follows deductively from the premise that people in general desire it. He gives some ground for that misinterpretation when he compares the move from 'desired' to 'desirable' to those from 'seen' and 'heard' to 'visible' and 'audible'. Nevertheless, his procedure is simply an appeal to reflective practice, just as in the case of enumerative induction – where again the 'sole evidence' that enumerative induction is an ultimate norm of reasoning is that we acknowledge it as such 'in theory and in practice'.

However, a question which is appropriate by Mill's own principle of method is whether reflective practice shows that happiness is the *only* thing we desire. Do not human beings, in theory and in practice, desire things other than happiness? Mill anticipates this question and responds to it at length. He claims that when we want a particular object for its own sake and with no further end in view (let us say, when we have an underived desire for it), then we desire it because we think of it as enjoyable: 'to desire anything, except in proportion as the idea of it is pleasant, is a physical and metaphysical impossibility' (1861a: 238). But this does not mean that we desire all objects as *means* to our pleasure. The desire for an object is genuinely a desire for that *object*; it is not the desire for pleasure as such. Mill's way of marking this is to say that the object is desired as a 'part' or an 'ingredient' of happiness, not as a means to it. His rejection of psychological egoism was one of the points on which he took himself to be at odds with Bentham (see BENTHAM, J. §3). When a person does something because they think it will be pleasant – for example a

generous person who gives a present – it does not follow that they are acting selfishly (see EGOISM AND ALTRUISM). Generous people take pleasure in the prospect of giving, not in the prospect of getting pleasure; their desire to give is not derived from the desire to get pleasure. Giving is a part of their happiness, not a means to it.

Thus Mill's case for the claim that happiness is the sole human end, put more carefully, is this: 'Whatever is desired otherwise than as a means to some end beyond itself, and ultimately to happiness, is desired as itself a part of happiness, and is not desired for itself until has become so' (1861a: 237). Nothing here assumed Hume's view that every action must ultimately flow from an underived desire. That is a quite separate issue, and Mill's view of it is closer to that of Kant or Reid than to that of Hume. He insists 'positively and emphatically'

> that the will is a different thing from desire; that a person of confirmed virtue, or any other person whose purposes are fixed, carries out his purposes without any thought of the pleasure he has in contemplating them, or expects to derive from their fulfilment.
>
> (1861a: 238)

This distinction between purpose and desire is central to Mill's conception of the will. When we develop purposes we can will against mere likings or aversions: 'In the case of an habitual purpose, instead of willing the thing because we desire it, we often desire it only because we will it' (1861a: 238). Every action is caused by a motive, but not every motive is a liking or aversion:

> When the will is said to be determined by motives, a motive does not mean always, or solely, the anticipation of a pleasure or of a pain...A habit of willing is commonly called a purpose; and among the causes of our volitions, and of the actions which flow from them, must be reckoned not only likings and aversions, but also purposes.
>
> (1843: 842)

The formation of purposes from desires is the evolution of will; it is also the development of character. Mill quotes Novalis: 'a character is a completely fashioned will' (1843: 843). Not that this reflects the whole of his view of character; character for him requires the cultivation of feeling as well as the cultivation of will: 'A person whose desires and impulses are his own – are the expression of his own nature, as it has been developed and modified by his own culture – is said to have a character' (1859: 264). Developed spontaneity of feeling is part of fully-perfected character, but certainly moral freedom is too – 'none but a person of confirmed virtue is completely free'. As noted in §7 above, Mill does not address the crucial question of what it is for a purpose to be informed by reason. Still, the distinction between purpose and desire does allow him to recognize conscientious action, action which flows not from any inclination but solely from a habit of willing; he asserts the possibility and value of a 'confirmed will to do right' (1861a: 238), distinct from motives of anticipated pleasure and pain. That 'virtuous will', however, is not for him an intrinsic good, as it is for Kant. It is

> a means to good, not intrinsically a good; and does not contradict the doctrine that nothing is good to human beings but in so far as it is either itself pleasurable, or a means of attaining pleasure or averting pain.
>
> (1861a: 239)

9 Qualities of pleasure

Happiness – pleasure and the absence of pain – is the sole final end of life. But Mill's idea of it is altogether more romantic and liberal than that of earlier utilitarians. He takes into account the fact that a variety of notions – for example, purity, elevation, depth, refinement and sublimity, and their opposites – enter into our assessments of pleasure. We do not assess pleasures along a single dimension. In his general ethical and political writing, Mill freely draws on that extensive and flexible language. He sees the need to recognize it also in utilitarian theory, but here he does so rather more mechanically by distinguishing 'quality' and 'quantity' of pleasure. From the first publication of *Utilitarianism*, at least three sorts of question have been asked about this famous distinction. The first is whether it is reconcilable with hedonism. The second is epistemological: is there a cogent way of establishing that some pleasures are superior in 'quality'? The third question, perhaps the most challenging, though less often discussed, is how the distinction fits into the framework of utilitarianism.

As to the first question: there is indeed, as Mill says, no reason in logic why more than one characteristic of pleasures should not be relevant to estimating their value – though if we call those characteristics 'quantity' and 'quality', we need to maintain a careful distinction between the quantity and quality of a pleasure on the one hand and its degree of value on the other. All that hedonism requires is that the only things that make a pleasure valuable are its characteristics as a *pleasure* (see HEDONISM).

Nevertheless, an impression lingers that Mill's discussion appeals to intuitions which are not hedonistic. For example:

> Few human creatures would consent to be changed into any of the lower animals, for a promise of the fullest allowance of a beast's pleasures; no intelligent human being would consent to be a fool, no instructed person would be an ignoramus, no person of feeling and conscience would be selfish and base, even though they should be persuaded that the fool, the dunce, or the rascal is better satisfied with his lot than they are with theirs.
>
> (1861a: 211)

He also notes that a 'being of higher faculties requires more to make him happy, is capable probably of more acute suffering, and is certainly accessible to it at more points, than one of an inferior type' (1861a: 212). So a being of higher faculties may be faced with a choice: on the one hand a life of acute suffering, with no access to any of the higher pleasures which its faculties make it capable of appreciating, on the other, a cure (for example, an operation) which relieves its suffering but leaves it only with the pleasures available to a fool or a dunce. Is Mill saying that in *all* such cases the life of suffering should be preferred? He does not say so explicitly and if he does adhere to hedonism he should not. For cases are surely possible in which life after the cure offers a stream of pleasures more valuable overall, taking quality as well as quantity into account, than the life of suffering in which one retains one's higher faculties but is bereft of higher pleasures.

What of the epistemological question? Mill compares assessments of the comparative quality of pleasures to assessments of their comparative quantity: both are determined by 'the feelings and judgments of the experienced' (1861a: 213). But a judgment that the pleasure derived from film A is of a higher kind than that derived from watching film B is clearly, as Mill conceives it, an evaluative judgment. The proper comparison would have been with the evaluative judgment that pleasure as such is desirable. And Mill could have said that with this judgment, as with basic evaluative judgments in general, the only criterion is reflective practice – self-examination and discussion. In such discussion, some people emerge as better judges than others – this is not a circularity but an inherent feature of normative judgment.

Yet now the third question becomes pressing: how are such judgments of the quality of pleasures to be registered in the utilitarian calculus? In requiring utilitarianism to take them into account Mill makes a move of political as well as ethical significance. For what rank do we give to these pleasures in our social ordering – the rank which highly developed human natures attach to them or that which lower human natures attach to them? Mill's answer is unambiguous: it is the verdict of 'competent judges' which stands.

Suppose that beings of highly developed faculties place the pleasures of scientific discovery or artistic creation so much higher than those of material well-being that (above a certain modicum of physical comfort and security) any amount of the former, however small, is ranked by them above any amount of the latter, however large. Suppose, however, that beings of considerably less developed faculties would not share this assessment. And now suppose that the question is put to Mill, how much of the lower pleasure of the less developed being may be sacrificed to maintain the more highly developed being's higher pleasure? Mill's view is that the more highly developed being delivers the correct assessment of the relative value of the higher and lower pleasures. But, by hypothesis, it would be prepared to sacrifice any amount of the lower pleasure, down to a modicum of physical comfort and security, for the smallest amount of the higher. Must the same hold for the interpersonal case? Must it be correct for the utilitarian to sacrifice any amount of the lower pleasures of lower beings, down to a level at which they are provided with the modicum of comfort and security, in order to secure some higher pleasure for a higher being? Mill provides no answer.

10 The utility principle

Though Mill deepened the utilitarian understanding of pleasure, desire, character and will, he never adequately re-examined the principle of utility itself. When he states the utilitarian doctrine before considering what kind of proof can be given of it, he states it thus: 'Happiness is desirable, and the only thing desirable, as an end, all other things being only desirable as means to that end' (1861a: 210). In effect, he takes his task to be that of demonstrating the truth of hedonism. All he has to say about the move from hedonism to the utility principle is that if 'each person's happiness is a good to that person' then 'the general happiness' must be 'a good to the aggregate of all persons'. In a letter in which he explains this unclear remark, he says: 'I merely meant in this particular sentence to argue that since A's happiness is a good, B's a good, C's a good, etc, the sum of all these goods must be a good' (1972: 1414). This contains two inexplicit assumptions. The more obvious point is that an egoist may accept that Mill has shown that 'each person's happiness is a good to that person', but deny that he has shown that

happiness is a good tout *court*. The egoist denies that Mill has shown that *everyone* has reason to promote the happiness of anyone. That requires a separate postulate, as Henry Sidgwick pointed out.

The second inexplicit assumption is more subtle. At the end of the last chapter of *Utilitarianism*, 'On the Connexion between Justice and Utility', Mill does explain that he takes 'perfect impartiality between persons' to be part of the very meaning of the Greatest Happiness Principle:

That principle is a mere form of words without rational signification, unless one person's happiness, supposed equal in degree (with the proper allowance made for kind), is counted for exactly as much as another's. Those conditions being supplied, Bentham's dictum, 'everybody to count for one, nobody for more than one', might be written under the principle of utility as an explanatory commentary.

(1861a: 257)

So here Mill supplies the required postulate of impartiality. However, the concept of impartiality does not, on its own, yield utilitarianism's aggregative principle of distribution. Maximizing the *sum* of individuals' happiness, if it makes sense to talk in this way at all, is one way of being impartial: no individual's happiness is given greater weight than any other's in the procedure which determines the value of a state of affairs as a function of the happiness of individuals in that state of affairs. In this sense the procedure implements the principle, 'Everybody to count for one, nobody for more than one'; but so does maximizing the average of all individuals' unweighted happiness. Here too all individuals count for one and no more than one. In fact a wide variety of non-equivalent distributive principles is impartial in this way. The most one could get from combining a postulate of impartiality with hedonism is that ethical value is a positive impartial function of individual happiness and of nothing else. In a footnote to the paragraph Mill glosses the requirement of perfect impartiality as follows: 'equal amounts of happiness are equally desirable, whether felt by the same or by different persons'. That does yield aggregative or average utilitarianism, but it follows neither from the thesis that happiness is the only thing desirable to human beings, nor from the formal notion of impartiality (see IMPARTIALITY §2).

11 Morality and justice

When we turn to Mill's conception of the relationship between the utility principle and the fabric of principles which regulate everyday social life, we find him again at his most impressive. He stresses that a utilitarian standard of value cannot itself tell what practical rules, aims or ideals we should live by. In his autobiography he dates this conviction to the period of his mental crisis. He now 'gave its proper place, among the prime necessities of human well-being, to the internal culture of the individual' (1873: 145–7). The prime task for human beings was to attend to that internal culture – to develop whatever was best in themselves. The indirect role in which he now cast the utility principle became a fundamental structural feature of his moral and political philosophy. For example, he accuses Auguste Comte of committing:

the error which is often, but falsely, charged against the whole class of utilitarian moralists; he required that the test of conduct should also be the exclusive motive of it . . . M. Comte is a morality-intoxicated man. Every question with him is one of morality, and no motive but that of morality is permitted.

(1865b: 335–6)

Mill gives a succinct statement of his own doctrine at the end of the *System of Logic*. As always, he affirms 'that the promotion of happiness is the ultimate principle of Teleology'. But, he continues,

I do not mean to suggest that the promotion of happiness should be itself the end of all actions, or even of all rules of action. It is the justification, and ought to be the controller, of all ends, but is not itself the sole end . . . I fully admit that . . . the cultivation of an ideal nobleness of will and conduct, should be to individual human beings an end, for which the specific pursuit either of their own happiness or of that of others (except so far as included in that idea) should, in any case of conflict, give way. But I hold that the very question, what constitutes this elevation of character, is itself to be decided by a reference to happiness as the standard.

(1843: 952)

The happiness of all is 'the test of all rules of conduct' – and not only rules of conduct but also of cultivation of feelings. How is the test applied? Here Mill learned more from COLERIDGE (§2) than from Bentham; that is, from historical criticism directed at the abstract social visionaries of the enlightenment. They did not see that moral sentiments can only grow in a stable tradition and social setting. They did not grasp the conditions necessary for such a tradition and setting – education of personal impulses to a restraining discipline, shared allegiance to some enduring and unquestioned values, 'a strong and active principle of cohesion' among 'members of the same community or state'. Hence

They threw away the shell without preserving the kernel; and attempting to new-model society without the binding forces which hold society together, met with such success as might have been anticipated.

(1840: 138)

This feeling for the historicity of social formations and genealogies of morals gives Mill's ethical vision a penetration which is absent from Bentham (and also from the excessively abstract discussions of utilitarianism in twentieth-century philosophy). On the other hand the analysis of morality, rights and justice which Mill fits into this ethical vision owes much to Bentham.

Mill examines the concept of justice in chapter 5 of *Utilitarianism*. Having observed that the idea of something which one may be constrained or compelled to do, on pain of penalty, is central to the idea of an obligation of justice, he notes that it nevertheless 'contains, as yet, nothing to distinguish that obligation from moral obligation in general':

The idea of penal sanction, which is the essence of law, enters not only into the conception of injustice, but into that of any kind of wrong. We do not call anything wrong, unless we mean to imply that a person ought to be punished in some way or other for doing it; if not by law, by the opinion of his fellow creatures; if not by opinion, by the reproaches of his own conscience.

(1865b: 246)

This is a normative, not a positive, account of morality: the morally wrong is that which *ought* to be punished, by law, social opinion or conscience. It would be a circular account if the 'ought' in question were itself a moral 'ought'. But the utility principle is the ultimate principle of 'Teleology'. Teleology is the 'Doctrine of Ends'; 'borrowing the language of the German metaphysicians', Mill also describes it as 'the principles of Practical Reason' (1843: 949–50). So the 'ought' is the 'ought' of Practical Reason – which, making appropriate use of 'laws of nature', produces the 'Art of Life'. Morality itself is only one department of this art. Moral concepts and judgments issue from the moral sentiments, the sentiments involved in guilt and blame; but are corrigible by a rational doctrine of ends. And that doctrine, in Mill's view, is the utility principle.

From this account of morality Mill moves to an account of rights and justice. A person has a moral right to a thing if there is a moral obligation on society to protect them in their possession of that thing. Obligations of justice are distinguished from moral obligations in general by the existence of corresponding rights:

> Justice implies something which it is not only right to do, and wrong not to do, but which some individual person can claim from us as his moral right... Whenever there is a right, the case is one of justice.
>
> (1865b: 247)

Upholding rights is one of society's vital tasks. For on it depends our security – which is 'to every one's feelings the most vital of interests':

> This most indispensable of all necessaries, after physical nutriment, cannot be had, unless the machinery for providing it is kept unintermittedly in active play. Our notion, therefore, of the claim we have on our fellow-creatures to join in making safe for us the very groundwork of our existence, gathers feelings around it so much more intense than those concerned in any of the more common cases of utility, that the difference in degree (as is often the case in psychology) becomes a real difference in kind.
>
> (1865b: 251)

In this way the claim of justice comes to be felt as a claim of a higher kind than any claim of utility. Justice, Mill concludes,

> is a name for certain classes of moral rules, which concern the essentials of human well-being more nearly, and are therefore of more absolute obligation, than any other rules for the guidance of life.
>
> (1865b: 255)

Mill spells out in detail what these moral rules should be in his writings on various social questions. In *Utilitarianism*, he is concerned with the more abstract task of showing how justice-rights take priority over the direct pursuit of general utility by individuals or the state, just as they take priority over the private pursuit of personal ends. His position is thus more complex than that of philosophers in a Kantian tradition who assume, in John Rawls' phrase, that the right (or just) is prior to the good. For Mill, good is philosophically prior to right – but politically and socially right constrains the pursuit of good (see JUSTICE §3).

12 Liberty and democracy

The most celebrated part of Mill's social philosophy, his essay *On Liberty*, must be read in terms of this conception of the right and the good. Mill is not a social contract or 'natural rights' liberal. He appeals instead to 'utility in the largest sense, grounded on the permanent interests of man as a progressive being' (1859: 224). He has in mind the higher human nature, capable of development by self-culture, which he believes to be present in every human being. Self-culture opens access to higher forms of human happiness, but it has to be *self*-culture, first because human potentialities are diverse and best known to each human being itself, and second because only when human beings work to their own plans of life do they develop moral freedom, itself indispensable to a higher human nature.

Given the importance free self-culture thus assumes in Mill's idea of human good, and the account of rights which has just been considered, it will follow that individual liberty must be a politically fundamental right. For self-development is one of 'the essentials of human well-being'. Thus Mill is led to the famous principle enunciated in *On Liberty*:

> the only purpose for which power can be rightfully exercised over any member of a civilized community, against his will, is to prevent harm to others. His own good, either physical or moral, is not a sufficient warrant. He cannot rightfully be compelled to do or forbear because it will be better for him to do so, because it will make him happier, because, in the opinion of others, to do so would be wise, or even right.
>
> (1859: 223–4)

A society which respects this principle enables individuals to realize their potential in their own way. It liberates a mature diversity of interest and feeling, and it nurtures the moral freedom of reason and will. Throwing open the gates to talent, creativity and dynamism, it produces the social conditions of moral and intellectual progress. This Millian argument remains the strongest defence of any liberalism founded on teleological ethics. It is a resource upon which teleological liberals will always be able to draw, whether or not they accept Mill's hedonistic conception of the human good or his aggregative conception of the good of all.

However, it is also connected with Mill's ambivalence about democracy. Like many other nineteenth-century thinkers, liberal as well as conservative, Mill felt a deep strain of anxiety about democratic institutions and the democratic spirit (see DEMOCRACY §2). Certainly he applauded the end of the *ancien régime* and sympathized with the moral ends of the French Revolution – liberty, equality, fraternity – but he learned from it, as had the continental liberals, to fear an enemy on the left, as well as an authoritarian enemy on the right. In its revolutionary form the enemy on the left threatened Jacobin terror, or the disasters which attend any attempt to achieve moral ideals by restarting history at year zero. Its settled form, on the other hand, could be observed in the 'democratic republic' of America: a continuous and unremitting pressure towards conforming mediocrity.

The Romantic-Hellenic ideal of human life both inspired Mill's democratic ideals and fuelled his fears about realized democracy. It was an ideal he shared with left Hegelians like Marx, who experienced less difficulty in combining it with democratic egalitarianism. Mill too had a long-term vision in which the emancipation and education of the working class could bring free self-culture to all human beings. He was able to believe, on the basis of his associationist psychology, that all human beings have an equal potential to develop their higher faculties. This warded off the possibility that utilitarianism might recommend an extremely inegalitarian pursuit of higher forms of well-being as the equilibrium state of a fully-developed human society.

Thus Mill remained more of a democrat than other liberals of the nineteenth century, such as de TOCQUEVILLE or Burckhardt, but like them he saw how moral and cultural excellence and freedom of spirit could be endangered by mass democracy. Like them, his attitude to the immediate prospect of democratic politics was decidedly mixed. What he wanted was a democratic society of freely developed human beings; he did not think it a proximate or certain prospect, and he thought that bad forms of democracy could themselves pose a threat to it by drifting into 'collective despotism' – a danger to which America had already succumbed.

His advice for warding off this threat was not less democracy but more liberty:

> If the American form of democracy overtakes us first, the majority will no more relax their despotism than a single despot would. But our only chance is to come forward as Liberals, carrying out the Democratic idea, not as Conservatives, resisting it.
>
> (1972: 672)

This was the importance of the essay on Liberty, and particularly of the defence of liberty of thought and discussion contained therein. Nor were freedom of speech and liberty of the individual the only instruments by which Mill hoped to steer away from bad forms of democracy towards good. Some of his recommendations – plural voting, a public ballot, a franchise restricted by educational qualification – may now seem misguided or even quaint. Others, including proportional representation of minorities and, not least, his life-long advocacy of equal rights for women, make him seem ahead of his time. At any

rate, in political philosophy from Plato's *Republic* to the present day, Mill's discussion of democracy has few rivals – for its open-mindedness, its historical and psychological awareness, and its underlying ethical power.

See also: CAUSATION §3; CONSEQUENTIALISM; ECONOMICS, PHILOSOPHY OF §3; EMPIRICISM; FEMINISM §3; FREEDOM AND LIBERTY; GOOD, THEORIES OF THE; INDUCTION, EPISTEMIC ISSUES IN; INDUCTIVE INFERENCE; LIBERALISM; NISHI AMANE; UTILITARIANISM

List of works

Mill, J.S. (1991) *Collected Works of John Stuart Mill*, ed. J.M. Robson, London: Routledge and Toronto, Ont.: University of Toronto Press. (The standard edition of Mill's writings, in thirty-three volumes. The introductions are invariably worth reading. Volume and page numbers given below refer to this edition.)

—— (1838) *Bentham*, in *Collected Works of John Stuart Mill*, London: Routledge, vol. 10, 75–115, 1991. (Mill's radical assessment of Bentham, usually read in conjunction with the essay on Coleridge.)

—— (1840) *Coleridge*, in *Collected Works of John Stuart Mill*, London: Routledge, vol. 10, 117–63, 1991. (These two essays most accessibly illustrate how Mill wove together Enlightenment and Romanticism.)

—— (1843) *System of Logic: Ratiocinative and Inductive*, in *Collected Works of John Stuart Mill*, London: Routledge, vols 7 and 8, 1991. (The nineteenth century's most penetrating exposition of a naturalistic philosophy of logic and science, including social science. The pagination of volumes 7 and 8 is consecutive; volume 8 begins at page 639.)

—— (1848) *Principles of Political Economy*, in *Collected Works of John Stuart Mill*, London: Routledge, vols 2 and 3, 1991. (A synthesis of classical economics, this work also contains much interesting social philosophy.)

—— (1859) *On Liberty*, in *Collected Works of John Stuart Mill*, London: Routledge, vol. 18, 213–310, 1991. (One of liberalism's canonical texts.)

—— (1861a) *Utilitarianism*, in *Collected Works of John Stuart Mill*, London: Routledge, vol. 10, 203–59, 1991. (A central text of moral philosophy – its extraordinary succinctness means that much in it remains to be fully charted and quarried.)

—— (1861b) *Considerations on Representative Government*, in *Collected Works of John Stuart Mill*,

London: Routledge, vol. 29, 371–577, 1991. (One-man report on the prospects of democracy.)

—— (1865a) *An Examination of Sir William Hamilton's Philosophy*, in *Collected Works of John Stuart Mill*, London: Routledge, vol. 9, 1991. (Mill's main treatment of metaphysical issues, including the nature of mind and matter, free will, logic and thought.)

—— (1865b) *Auguste Comte and Positivism*, in *Collected Works of John Stuart Mill*, London: Routledge, vol. 10, 261–368, 1991. (An assessment, from Mill's later years, of a philosopher who greatly influenced him in his youth.)

—— (1869) *The Subjection of Women*, in *Collected Works of John Stuart Mill*, London: Routledge, vol. 21, 259–340, 1991. (Manifesto of nineteenth-century liberal feminism.)

—— (1873) *Autobiography*, in *Collected Works of John Stuart Mill*, London: Routledge, vol. 1, 1–290, 1991. (Famous account of Mill's early education, 'mental crisis', and subsequent intellectual and moral projects.)

—— (1874) *Three Essays on Religion*, in *Collected Works of John Stuart Mill*, London: Routledge, vol. 10, 369–489, 1991. (Posthumously published articles, in which Mill argues that religious hope is legitimate, whereas religious belief is not.)

—— (1879) *Chapters on Socialism*, in *Collected Works of John Stuart Mill*, London: Routledge, vol. 5, 703–53, 1991. (Posthumously published assessment of socialism which complements the *Principles of Political Economy* and *On Liberty*.)

—— (1972) *Later Letters*, in *Collected Works of John Stuart Mill*, London: Routledge, vols 14–17, 1991. (Mill's extensive correspondence after 1848, published in four volumes.)

References and further reading

Berger, F.R. (1984) *Happiness, Justice and Freedom: The Moral and Political Philosophy of John Stuart Mill*, London: University of California Press. (The most comprehensive study of Mill's moral and political philosophy; full of information.)

Crisp, R. (1997) *Mill on Utilitarianism*, London: Routledge. (The most up-to-date study of *Utilitarianism*.)

Gray, J. (1996) *Mill on Liberty: a Defence*, London: Routledge, 2nd edn. (Relates Mill's approach to liberty to his indirect utilitarianism.)

Kahan, A.S. (1992) *Aristocratic Liberalism. The Social and Political Thought of Jacob Burckhardt, John Stuart Mill, and Alexis de Tocqueville*, Oxford: Oxford University Press. (Informative comparative study of the political thought of these three thinkers.)

Lyons, D. (1994) *Rights, Welfare, and Mill's Moral Theory*, Oxford: Oxford University Press. (Important essays on the interpretation of Mill's ethical theory.)

* Mackie, J.L. (1974) *The Cement of the Universe*, Oxford: Oxford University Press. (Analyses causation in the spirit of Mill's treatment in the *System of Logic*; the appendix comprehensively surveys and revises his 'Methods of Empirical Inquiry'.)

Ryan, A. (1974) *J.S. Mill*, London: Routledge & Kegan Paul. (Useful survey, not just of Mill's philosophy but of his thought as a whole.)

Scarre, G. (1989) *Logic and Reality in the Philosophy of John Stuart Mill*, Dordrecht: Kluwer. (Study of Mill's metaphysics and philosophy of science.)

Skorupski, J. (1989) *John Stuart Mill*, London: Routledge. (Comprehensive account of Mill's philosophy.)

—— (ed.) (forthcoming) *The Cambridge Companion to Mill*, Cambridge: Cambridge University Press. (Articles covering various aspects of Mill's philosophy.)

Ten, C.L. (1980) *Mill on Liberty*, Oxford: Oxford University Press. (The most useful student guide to *On Liberty*.)

* Whewell, W. (1837) *History of the Inductive Sciences, from the Earliest to the Present Time*, London: J.W. Parker, 3 vols. (Major historical survey, used by Mill.)

Wilson, F. (1990) *Psychological Analysis and the Philosophy of John Stuart Mill*, Toronto, Ont.: University of Toronto Press. (Mill and the history of psychology.)

JOHN SKORUPSKI

MILLAR, JOHN (1735–1801)

John Millar elevated law teaching from mere instruction in technicalities to the level of a genuinely liberal subject, largely by using his teaching to educate students in the science of legislation. A pupil and disciple of Adam Smith, Millar, through his teaching and writing, established his reputation as a key figure in the Scottish Enlightenment movement.

Millar was born on 22 June 1735, a son of the manse of Kirk o'Shotts in Lanarkshire, just as the first signs of 'the great awakening' in Scotland were materializing. He entered Glasgow University in 1746, leaving in 1752 to pursue a legal career. In 1761, at the age of

26, Millar was elected to the Regius Chair of Civil Law in Glasgow and there he taught until his death in 1801.

He was not a prolific writer. There are only two works which can definitively be attributed to him. The first, *The Origin of the Distinction of Ranks* (1771), is the book on which his reputation primarily rests. In *Ranks* Millar broke away from a traditional cyclical view of progress in which the conduct of politics was rooted in a dialectic between virtue and corruption, and presented the development of civil society as a process of unilinear advance. Millar's account constitutes a succinct statement of historical materialism: there are four stages – hunting, pasture, agriculture and commerce – through which societies pass and each form of economic organization gives rise to 'correspondent habits, dispositions and ways of thinking'. Millar argued that this was a natural progression – from ignorance to knowledge, from rude to civilized manners – and, though the general method was not novel, he seems to have been the first to have indicated the causes of growth through each of the sequential phases.

The other book, *An Historical View of the English Government* (1787), is a constitutional history from Saxon times to the Stuarts. Millar here utilizes the method employed in *Ranks*, mainly to challenge the vulgar Whiggism of writers such as William BLACK-STONE who tended to view English constitutional history in terms of a gradual restoration of the ancient Anglo-Saxon constitution which had been undermined by the Normans. Millar, presenting a 'scientific Whig' account, argued that the 'low ranks' secured their liberty not by appeals to a romantic idea of the ancient constitution and not by pieces of paper but by industry and material progress. The origin of liberty in Britain is modern, not ancient; it was a seventeenth-century endeavour culminating in 1688.

Millar's general theoretical approach was historical and sociological rather than conceptual. He rejected any idea that law is determined by higher norms of divine origin or theories of law rooted in social contract. In this sense, he adopted a modern, sociological view that any theory of law must be rooted in a theory of society. Assessments of Millar's originality vary, but it is undoubtedly the case that he made a significant contribution to a remarkable period of, not only Scottish, but European intellectual history.

See also: ENLIGHTENMENT, SCOTTISH; JURISPRUDENCE, HISTORICAL §1; LAW, PHILOSOPHY OF; SMITH, A. §4; SOCIAL THEORY AND LAW

List of works

Millar, J. (1771) *The Origin of the Distinction of Ranks: or An Inquiry into the Circumstances which give rise to Influence and Authority, in the Different Members of Society*, Edinburgh: William Blackwood; 4th edn, London: Longman, 1806; repr. London: Thoemmes Press, 1990. (The 1990 edition is prefixed by the 1806 John Craig account of the life and writings of John Millar.)

—— (1787) *An Historical View of the English Government from the Settlement of the Saxons in Britain to the Revolution in 1688*, Edinburgh: William Blackwood; 3rd edn, 4 vols, London: Longman, 1803. (Constitutional history from Saxon times to the Stuarts.)

Anon. (1796) *Letters of Crito*, Edinburgh: William Blackwood. (Collection of newspaper articles; almost certainly the work of Millar.)

Anon. (1796) *Letters of Sidney*, Edinburgh: William Blackwood. (Occasionally ascribed to Millar but more likely to be the work of John Craig, his nephew and early biographer.)

References and further reading

Forbes, D. (1953–4) 'Scientific Whiggism: Adam Smith and John Millar', *Cambridge Journal* 7: 643–70. (Millar as scientific Whig.)

Haakonssen, K. (1985) 'John Millar and the Science of a Legislator', *Juridical Review* 30: 41–68. (On Millar's theory of law, government and property.)

Ignatieff, M. (1983) 'John Millar and Individualism', in I. Hont and M. Ignatieff (eds), *Wealth and Virtue: The Shaping of Political Economy in the Scottish Enlightenment*, Cambridge: Cambridge University Press. (On Millar caught between the languages of civic humanism and political economy.)

Lehmann, W.C. (1960) *John Millar of Glasgow*, Cambridge: Cambridge University Press. (The standard biography.)

MARTIN LOUGHLIN

MĪMĀṂSĀ

The school of Mīmāṃsā or Pūrva Mīmāṃsā was one of the six systems of classical Hindu philosophy. It grew out of the Indian science of exegesis and was primarily concerned with defending the way of life defined by the ancient scripture of Hinduism, the Veda. Its most

important exponents, *Śabarasvāmin, Prabhākara and Kumārila, lived in the sixth and seventh centuries* AD. *It was realist and empiricist in orientation. Its central doctrine was that the Veda is the sole means of knowledge of* dharma *or righteousness, because it is eternal. All cognition, it held, is valid unless its cause is defective. The Veda being without any fallible author, human or divine, the cognitions to which it gives rise must be true. The Veda must be authorless because there is no recollection of an author or any other evidence of its having been composed; we only observe that it has been handed down from generation to generation. Mīmāṃsā thinkers also defended various metaphysical ideas implied by the Veda – in particular, the reality of the physical world and the immortality of the soul. However, they denied the existence of God as creator of the world and author of scripture. The eternality of the Veda implies the eternality of language in general. Words and the letters that constitute them are eternal and ubiquitous; it is only their particular manifestations, caused by articulations of the vocal organs, that are restricted to certain times and places. The meanings of words, being universals, are eternal as well. Finally, the relation between word and meaning is also eternal. Every word has an inherent capacity to indicate its meaning. Words could not be expressive of certain meanings as a result of artificial conventions.*

The basic orientation of Mīmāṃsā was pragmatic and anti-mystical. It believed that happiness and salvation result just from carrying out the prescriptions of the Veda, not from the practice of yoga or insight into the One. It criticized particularly sharply other scriptural traditions (Buddhism and Jainism) that claimed to have originated from omniscient preceptors.

1   **History**
2   **Knowledge and reality**
3   **Language and scripture**

1   History

Mīmāṃsā, one of the six systems (*darśanas*) of Hindu philosophy, was not originally a system of philosophy at all but an auxiliary of Vedic study (see HINDU PHILOSOPHY §§6–7). Mīmāṃsā literally means 'investigation' or 'analysis'; it refers specifically to the analytic discussion of Vedic ritual. (The Veda is the most ancient scripture of the Hindus.) The *Mīmāṃsāsūtra*, the earliest treatise of the school, which is attributed to Jaimini and dated around the second century BC, is a compendium of debates about how rituals should be carried out; it resolves the debates by carefully analysing the language of the scriptural passages in which the rituals are enjoined. Thus, the school of Mīmāṃsā was first and foremost

concerned with exegesis. It developed a system of rules of interpretation that were widely employed elsewhere in Indian philosophical and scientific literature; they were especially used in interpreting and expounding the Dharmaśāstras, works relating to Hindu ethics and law.

At an early stage, Mīmāṃsā took on the broader role of defending Hindu *dharma* as a whole. *Dharma* means what one ought to do and avoid doing, the proper way to conduct oneself in this world and to attain salvation in the next. It includes not just the carrying out of certain rituals but also the observance of the minute details of everyday custom and etiquette. The Brahmanical or priestly conception of *dharma*, which was central to the culture that called itself 'Aryan' in ancient India and which became the core of classical Hinduism, was attacked by various heterodox movements, especially Buddhism and Jainism, from around the fifth century BC. Mīmāṃsā undertook to defend the Brahmanical system by attempting to demonstrate, in particular, the sole authority of the Veda with regard to matters of religion and ethics, and the falsehood of other scriptures. This apologetic enterprise led into the consideration of various philosophical issues, including metaphysical doctrines implied by the Veda and epistemological and linguistic doctrines upon which the claim of the authority of the Veda was based.

As in the case of the other Hindu philosophical systems, Mīmāṃsā was expounded chiefly in commentaries and subcommentaries on a foundational *sūtra* text (a treatise in the form of short statements or aphorisms), namely the *Mīmāṃsāsūtra*. The *Mīmāṃsāsūtra* originally contained material relating both to the interpretation of the ritual portions of the Veda and to the mystical-philosophical texts known as the Upaniṣads. The *sūtras* relating to the latter, however, were at an early date separated off and, known as the Vedānta or *Brahmasūtra*, became the focus of a distinct tradition of philosophical reflection, namely Vedānta. The oldest existing commentary on the Pūrva or 'prior' *Mīmāṃsāsūtra* – the *sūtras* concerned with ritual – is that of Śabarasvāmin, the *Śābarabhāṣya*, dated around the sixth century AD. Other, older commentaries, such as that of Upavarṣa, have not been preserved. Two principal subschools of Mīmāṃsā thought, the Bhāṭṭa and the Prābhākara, are based on subcommentaries on the *Śābarabhāṣya* by Kumārila (also known as Kumārilabhaṭṭa) and Prabhākara respectively. A trio of commentaries by Kumārila, the *Ślokavārttika*, *Tantravārttika* and *Tuptīkā*, have been preserved; Prabhākara's commentary is titled the *Bṛhatī*. Both authors may be assigned to the seventh century. Another great figure of the early period was Maṇḍanamiśra, who was sympathetic to the views of Kumārila but also composed works on Advaita Vedānta. Other important figures of the Bhāṭṭa school were Umbekabhaṭṭa (eighth century), Pārthasārathimiśra (tenth century), Sucaritamiśra (tenth century), Someśvarabhaṭṭa (twelfth century) and Khaṇḍadeva (seventeenth century). The principal exponent of the Prābhākara school after Prabhākara himself was Śālikanāthamiśra (ninth century). A third school of Mīmāmsā, which, unlike the other two, accepted the existence of God – the so-called Seśvara Mīmāmsā – was established by Murārimiśra in about the eleventh century. The following exposition is based primarily on the teachings of the more influential Bhāṭṭa school, although occasional references will be made to distinctive Prābhākara positions.

2 Knowledge and reality

The Mīmāmsā claim of the sole authority of the Veda with regard to *dharma* is based on two highly controversial doctrines: the eternality of the Veda and the intrinsic validity of cognitions. According to Mīmāmsā, any error in cognition derives from defects in the causes of the cognition. A conch shell, which is in fact white, appears yellow to someone whose eye is affected by jaundice; a notion derived from verbal testimony can be false if the witness is dishonest or incompetent. On the other hand, a cognition whose causes are not defective will necessarily be true. Thus, cognitions arising from the Veda must be true, because the Veda is eternal – it was never composed by anyone but has just been handed down from time immemorial, from generation to generation – hence they cannot have a defective cause. They are not in any way contingent on the knowledge and honesty of a fallible author.

Kumārila developed the theory of 'intrinsic validity' (*svataḥ prāmāṇya*) as a general epistemological theory. *All* cognitions, he argued, present themselves initially as true; they arise together with a sense of conviction that matters really are as they indicate. Cognitions are deemed false only when they are directly overturned by other cognitions or undermined by the discovery that their causes are defective. Cognitions of Vedic injunctions, indeed, are never effectively contradicted by other means of knowledge such as perception, inference or testimony, and, as stated, there can be no suspicion that their source is defective, for the Veda is eternal. Prabhākara held not just that all cognitions initially *appear* true but that all cognitions, strictly speaking, *are* true; there is no such thing as error. Every cognition apprehends something real. It is only our judgments, which combine cognitions together, that are mistaken. If I think

'This conch shell is yellow', I am not in fact misperceiving anything. I correctly perceive the conch as 'this', and I correctly perceive the yellow colour, which is due to the jaundice afflicting my eye. It is only the attribution of the yellow to the conch instead of my eye that is wrong. The theory of intrinsic validity evoked a violent reaction from other Hindu, Buddhist and Jaina philosophers, who argued that a cognition can be considered valid only when it is confirmed by another cognition, in particular, a cognition of the 'causal efficacy' (*arthakriyā*) of the object (see EPISTEMOLOGY, INDIAN SCHOOLS OF §3).

The Mīmāmsā theory of intrinsic validity was conducive to the adoption of realist positions on a variety of metaphysical issues. Kumārila, along with most other Hindu thinkers, rejected the idealism of the Yogācāra school of Buddhism (see BUDDHISM, YOGĀCĀRA SCHOOL OF §§2–4). His principal argument for realism was simply that the perception of the world as comprising externally existing, physical objects must be considered valid unless and until it is contradicted by other perceptions, in the way dreaming is contradicted by waking consciousness. He also charged that the Buddhist view of experience as comprising self-luminous moments of consciousness – that is, cognitions that reveal, not external objects, but their own inherent forms – violates the principle that the same thing cannot function as both agent and object in the same act (in this case, an act of cognition). More crucially, Kumārila held that we are not aware of cognitions (*jñāna*) at all in experience; we do not, at the time we perceive an object, also perceive a cognition. Our awareness, rather, is completely absorbed in being aware of the object. Hence, there is no basis for suggesting that object and cognition are the same thing, for they never occur together. Kumārila, then, was a direct realist. He believed that we only infer the existence of a cognition (*jñāna*) as the cause of the fact that we have become aware of an external object.

The Prābhākara school, on the other hand, held, like the Buddhists, that consciousness (*samvitti*) is self-luminous; it simultaneously reveals the object, itself, and the knower. Yet it reveals itself always as the conscious principle, never as the object, hence, contrary to the Buddhist teaching, experience itself shows us that object and consciousness are distinct. At the same time, 'cognition' (*jñāna*), in the sense of the act of mind which produces consciousness, is only inferred.

Not only does perception reveal an external world, it reveals its nature. The cognitions we have of objects as endowed with certain properties and being of certain types – as a white man, a walking cow, and so on – are true unless and until overturned by other cognitions. Moreover, such cognitions are perceptual and can be referred to as 'conceptualized perceptions' (*savikalpaka pratyakṣa*); they are caused by the contact of our sense organs with objects, though they are preceded by a moment of nonconceptualized perception (*nirvikalpaka pratyakṣa*) in which the various features of the object are not identified as particular *types* of features or named. Buddhist philosophers, on the other hand, held that conceptualized cognition is not perceptual but mainly involves an act of the imagination by which mentally constructed properties are projected onto things; it is a kind of illusion. Kumārila argued – once again appealing to the principle of intrinsic validity – that the enduring validity of most of our cognitions of objects as qualified by qualities, actions, universals, and so on suggests that in general they are not errors; if they were, they would always be overturned. The specific Buddhist charge that a conceptualized cognition involves the superimposition of a mere *word* upon the object is rejected on the grounds that in fact we first see what a thing is before we apply a word to it. The world is perceived as it is prior to language, and we speak about it in a certain way because of the way we perceive it.

The above teaching implies an acceptance of the reality of universals. Mīmāṃsā philosophers were at the forefront of the debate with the Buddhists over universals. While the Buddhists were nominalists, Hindu and Jaina philosophers held that universals must be posited to account for common notions and common terms, that is, the fact that we cognize various things as being of the same type and refer to them by the same word. Kumārila in particular developed trenchant criticisms of the Buddhist theory that common concepts are just mentally constructed 'exclusion classes', the so-called *apoha-vāda* (see UNIVERSALS, INDIAN THEORIES OF §2). The Bhāṭṭa view of universals was somewhat different from that of other realist schools, however, in that it considered universal and particular to be different aspects of one thing and not entirely distinct; the same thing is universal from one angle, particular from another. (It developed a similar view of nonbeing, *abhāva*: a thing is both what it is and what it is not. When we judge that a pot is *not* a cloth, we are apprehending a real, negative aspect of the pot. This tendency of Bhāṭṭa thought is believed by some to reflect the influence of Jainism.) Kumārila criticized the Nyāya-Vaiśeṣika notion that universal and particular are externally related to each other by virtue of 'inherence' (*samavāya*) (see NYĀYA-VAIŚEṢIKA §5). The Prābhākara school, meanwhile, adopted the more conventional stance that universals are distinct from the individuals in which they inhere, but it worked out a more felicitous theory of inherence.

Mīmāṃsā philosophers – again in concert with other Hindu thinkers and against the Buddhists – defended the existence of the soul. An immortal soul is clearly implied by Vedic injunctions of certain sacrifices for the attainment of heaven. Kumārila argued that the existence of an unchanging self is established by the fact that I recognize *myself* as the subject of remembered experiences, hence I must have existed continuously from the past to the present. He also held the self to be essentially self-conscious, the Prābhākara, on the other hand, held that the self becomes manifest only in empirical consciousness and has no consciousness of its own.

Although an apologist for Vedic tradition, the Mīmāṃsaka (Mīmāṃsā philosopher) rejected a supreme being as creator of the universe and author of the Veda. This accords with his staunch empiricism and his belief that the positing of any author of scripture, even a divine one, tends to call it into question. Kumārila extensively refuted the Nyāya arguments for the existence of God as creator. What could his purpose have been in creating the universe? Not the fulfilment of the past karma of living beings, because living beings did not then exist; not 'sport' or amusement, for that would imply some lack in God. Yet if he did it without desire or purpose, he could not be considered intelligent, for no intelligent person acts without a purpose. And so on. Kumārila even rejected the Hindu mythological idea of a periodic creation and destruction of the universe, asserting that we have no evidence that the world has ever been different from how it is now. References to gods in the Veda are not to be taken literally but just as eulogies that serve to recommend certain sacrifices. Heaven is just a region, whose location is indefinite, where one experiences 'pure happiness'. The soteriological goal of *mokṣa*, liberation from the cycle of rebirth, is negatively conceived, not as an experience of transcendental bliss but as the cessation of all association with a body due to the exhaustion of karma (see KARMA AND REBIRTH, INDIAN CONCEPTIONS OF §§1–4). Thus, Mīmāṃsā is decidedly rationalistic in its interpretation of Vedic religion. The religious life, for Mīmāṃsā, consists not in the practice of yoga or the attainment of insight into the oneness of everything, but in the scrupulous observance of *dharma* as laid down in Vedic prohibitions and commandments.

3 Language and scripture

Mīmāṃsā insisted on the eternality of the Veda on the grounds that its composition has not been observed, nor is there any memory of its having been composed by anyone in the past. Rather, we observe simply that it has been transmitted from generation to generation. What sense, however, can there be in suggesting that there could be a discourse that was never composed by anyone? Language surely always expresses the thoughts of intelligent beings, and depends on the articulation, by living speakers and writers, of symbols that are conventionally linked with certain meanings. Precisely such a view of language is what Mīmāṃsā rejected; in its place, it defended the eternality (*nityatva*) of language in general.

Individual words themselves must be eternal, for we routinely recognize a word we use as 'the same word' we used before. We never utter new words but only the same ones over and over. Nor should it be thought that a word is perishable because it consists of momentarily heard sounds. Rather, articulated sounds (*dhvani*) serve only to evoke an awareness in the hearer of the eternal, ubiquitous word; they are not identical with the word itself. In particular, they are not its letters (*varṇa*) – Kumārila insisted, against the grammarian BHARTṚHARI, that a word, though eternal, is not an indivisible entity (*sphoṭa*) but comprises a sequence of letters – for letters, too, are omnipresent and eternal. We also recognize a particular letter as 'the same letter' as before. It is cognized at a particular time and place due to an alteration in the ear brought about by a disturbance of the air caused by the vocal organs (see LANGUAGE, INDIAN THEORIES OF §3). The meanings of words are also eternal, according to Mīmāṃsā, for they are universals.

But surely the conventions by which words are assigned certain meanings were fixed by intelligent beings at a certain time, in which case the Veda could not be altogether eternal? The Mīmāṃsaka denied even this; rather, he held that a word does not refer to its meaning by virtue of a convention but rather by an inherent capacity (*śakti*). Kumārila, in particular, argued that the connection of word and meaning cannot be a human construct. A uniform convention devised by humans could only be based on some underlying natural relationship, while diverse conventions observed by different users would render communication impossible. That uniform conventions were established by God at the beginning of time is precluded by doubts about the existence of God. Moreover, it would seem that the devising of conventions by anyone already presupposes the existence of language. Finally, in contrast to the custom with other conventional practices in ancient India, we do not recall the authors of particular conventions when we employ words. (The Mīmāṃsā school holds that in the performance of rituals, for example, we do always recall their authors.) All we observe, in fact, is that we learn what words mean from our elders, who in turn learned the meanings from their elders, and so on; we never observe anyone originally establishing the meanings of common words such as 'cow'. The Mīmāṃsaka, of course, was cognizant of the fact that other cultures used different words for things, but he insisted that only Aryas speaking proper Sanskrit used the *correct* words! Others use words that do not really mean what they think they mean and whose expressiveness derives only from similarity to Sanskrit words. The fact that there is a natural connection between word and meaning does not entail that everyone must automatically know what a word means, either. Although the connection is natural, it still must be learned.

Nor, finally, is the meaning of a particular utterance dependent on the intention of the utterer. Mīmāṃsā rejected the view, propounded by both Buddhist philosophers and the Hindu Vaiśeṣika school, that verbal testimony is a form of inference, in the sense that we infer facts about the world from what a person says via the belief that what is said expresses the state of mind of the speaker. By contrast, Mīmāṃsā held that language of itself says things. We can, for example, understand what a sentence means without knowing who uttered it or whether that person is reliable or not. A speaker selects a certain pattern of words to express a thought just because those *words* already express a certain state of affairs. Bhāṭṭa and Prābhākara philosophers differed, however, on the matter of how the eternal meanings of individual words combine to form sentence meanings. The Bhāṭṭa view (the so-called *abhihitānvayavāda*) was that individual words first indicate their 'own meanings', which in turn combine into the sentence meaning; the Prābhākara view (the *anvitābhidhānavāda*) was that a word originally indicates a meaning that is modified by the other words with which it stands in syntactic relation in the sentence. The latter theory implies that a word never means exactly the same thing in any two sentences.

Part and parcel of the Mīmāṃsā defence of the authority of the Veda was the effort to debunk other scriptures. The Buddhists and Jainas grounded the authority of their scriptures on the claim that they contained the utterances of omniscient beings – the Buddha and Mahāvīra respectively. Kumārila, in particular, ridiculed the idea of omniscience. We do not know of any omniscient people now, so on what basis should we believe that there were omniscient people in the past? Indeed, we observe that some people are smarter and more talented than others, but that hardly justifies believing in the existence of people who literally knew everything! Moreover, the statements of the Buddha and Mahāvīra, each claimed by his tradition to be omniscient, contradict each other. Given also the observation that humans for the most part say what is false, and that, especially when it comes to religion, charlatans abound, it is altogether safer to rely on a tradition that does not make outrageous claims about the omniscience of its founder, or, for that matter, appeal to any fallible human author at all. Indeed, humans cannot know what *dharma* is through their own faculties. For *dharma* is 'that which is conducive to the good', that is, the happiness of humans, and humans are incapable of knowing through their own faculties which actions yield happiness after death. For that reason, *dharma* is not to be based on rationally conceived, universal ethical principles such as non-violence or 'benefiting others'. *Dharma* is just what the Veda tells us to do.

See also: DUTY AND VIRTUE, INDIAN CONCEPTIONS OF; INTERPRETATION, INDIAN THEORIES OF §4; MEANING, INDIAN THEORIES OF

References and further reading

Bhatt, G.P. (1962) *Epistemology of the Bhāṭṭa School of Pūrva Mīmāṃsā*, Benares: Chowkhamba Sanskrit Series. (A detailed treatment of Bhāṭṭa views.)

Dwivedi, R.C. (ed.) (1994) *Studies in Mīmāṃsā*, Delhi: Motilal Banarsidass. (A collection of articles by contemporary scholars.)

Jha, G. (1942) *Pūrva Mīmāṃsā in its Sources*, Benares: Benares Hindu University. (A standard, if outdated, survey and comparison of Bhāṭṭa and Prābhākara doctrines.)

* Kumārila (7th century) *Ślokavārttika*, trans. G. Jha, Delhi: Sri Satguru Publications, 1983. (Translation of Kumārila's *magnum opus*.)

* Prabhākara (7th century) *Bṛhatī*, ed. A. Chinnasvami Sastri, Chowkhamba Sanskrit Series 69, Benares: Chowkhamba Sanskrit Series, 1929–33. (The subcommentary on the *Śābarabhāṣya* that became the foundation of the Prābhākara school of Mīmāṃsā.)

* Śabarasvāmin (6th century) *Śābarabhāṣya*, trans. G. Jha, Gaekwad's Oriental Series 66, 70, 73, Baroda: Oriental Institute, 1933–6. (Translation of the *Mīmāṃsāsūtra*, together with Śabarasvāmin's commentary.)

JOHN A. TABER

MIMĒSIS

A crucial term in the literary theories of Plato and Aristotle, mimēsis *describes the relation between the words of a literary work and the actions and events they recount. In Plato, the term usually means 'imitation' and suggests that poetry is derived from and inferior to reality; in Aristotle, it loses this pejorative connotation and tends to mean simply 'representation' and to indicate that the world presented in a poem is much like, but not identical with, our own.*

A relation of *mimēsis* to authoritative figures from the past – heroes, fathers, philosophers, authors – was deeply ingrained in ancient Greek and Roman culture, and laid the groundwork for the post-classical notions of the pedagogical value of antiquity as a whole that shaped the classical tradition. *Mimēsis* is usually translated 'imitation', but in fact its central meaning is closer to 'actualization': objects, events, or actions which, because they are divine, past or canonical, belong to a more valuable domain of reality than our quotidian lives but are therefore in some way remote from us, enjoin upon us the obligation to restore their actuality; this is achieved by establishing a privileged sector within our present concerns in which we can (re-)enact them, thereby illuminating our banal world with some of their splendour while rescuing them from the perils of abstraction and irrelevance. Hence the term *mimēsis* is intrinsically ambivalent and, depending upon the circumstances, can emphasize either the actualization's inferiority compared to its model or the relative superiority it acquires by its temporary participation in the model's prestige.

This cultural complex provides the context for Plato's introduction of *mimēsis* as a concept of philosophical aesthetics and literary theory. Three different levels of generalization can be distinguished in Plato's usage of the term in the *Republic* (see PLATO §14). First, discussing poetry's content in Book II, he applies the term broadly to the relation of signification between utterances and the entities to which they refer. Then, moving on to poetry's form in Book III, he exploits the fact that in Greek tragedy ordinary human actors played the roles of legendary heroes and gods to invent the novel, highly specific application of *mimēsis* as a technical term to that whole literary genre, drama, in which authors never speak in their own voice, in contrast to the narrative, in which they always so speak, and to mixed forms. Finally, once he has established the tripartition of the soul in Book IV and the way in which lower levels of reality imitate higher ones (the divided line and the analogy of the cave in Books VI and VII) he can return in Book X more fundamentally and drastically to his critique of non-philosophical *mimēsis*; now all poetry, including non-dramatic forms, is deceptively mimetic, in the sense that it is at three removes from true reality. Unless a defender can be found to plead its case in prose, it must be exiled from Plato's ideal city.

In his *Poetics*, Aristotle accepts Plato's challenge (see ARISTOTLE §29). Against *Republic* III he generalizes *mimēsis* beyond the criterion of the dramatic genre and against *Republic* X he empties it of any hint of inferiority with regard to an independent reality: instead, now all imaginative literature, including Plato's dialogues, is mimetic, in the sense that it describes not what really happened but the sort of thing that could happen. Aristotle's *Poetics* is a theory of the poet's making (*poiēsis*) of a representation (*mimēsis*) of characters' actions (*praxis*): in a tragedy, their *praxis* will turn out badly; in a good tragedy, the poet's *poiēsis* will turn out well. If the tragedian directly made actions, people would really commit and suffer outrages and we would be appalled; instead, by making a *mimēsis* of actions, the tragedian can represent them for our considered pleasure. *Mimēsis* is no longer the unique province of the deceived and deceiving artist, but instead an anthropological universal that distinguishes us from most other animals (as in fact imitation does) and provides specifically cognitive pleasures to all humans: we enjoy recognizing what we already knew and saying that 'this man' (whom we see before us) is 'that man' (of whom we had always heard).

Greek aesthetics never comes closer to the modern concept of fictionality than it does in Aristotle's universally generalizing, thoroughly non-derogatory use of the term *mimēsis*. Yet Aristotle, who never analyses the term, remains committed to the view that the world portrayed by poetry is not a fictional world, but a recognizable version of our own real one: poetry does not show us what actually happens or happened, but it does show us the kinds of things that could have happened and might happen. *Mimēsis* prevents the poet's *poiēsis* from making a real *praxis*; but the possibilities it describes are real, not fictional, ones. That is precisely why Aristotle can insist upon a limited cognitive component in aesthetic pleasure.

See also: AESTHETICS; KATHARSIS; TRAGEDY

References and further reading

* Aristotle (c. mid 4th century BC) *Poetics*, trans. S. Halliwell, Loeb Classical Library, Cambridge, MA: Harvard University Press and London: Heinemann, 1995. (Greek text with an English prose translation on facing pages.)

Belfiore, E.S. (1992) *Tragic Pleasures: Aristotle on Plot and Emotion*, Princeton, NJ: Princeton University Press, esp. 45–70. (Argues for the cognitive and anthropological importance of *mimēsis* in Aristotle.)

Else, G.F. (1957) *Aristotle's Poetics: The Argument*, Cambridge, MA: Harvard University Press. (A provocative and original critique of widely shared views.)

—— (1986) *Plato and Aristotle on Poetry*, ed. P. Burian, Chapel Hill, NC, and London: University of North Carolina Press. (A more generally accessible presentation of some of the arguments in Else (1957).)

Golden, L. (1992) *Aristotle on Tragic and Comic Mimēsis*, Atlanta, GA: Scholars Press. (An eloquent defence of a more cognitive view of *mimēsis* than the one presented here.)

Halliwell, S. (1986) *Aristotle's Poetics*, London: Duckworth. (A general introduction to the treatise with a full treatment of *mimēsis*, pp. 109–37.)

Lucas, D.W. (ed.) (1968) *Aristotle: Poetics*, Oxford: Clarendon Press, 258–72. (The standard English commentary, with a good discussion of *mimēsis*.)

* Plato (c. 370s BC) *Republic*, trans. G.M.A. Grube, Indianapolis, IN: Hackett, 1974. (See Books II–III, X for Plato's treatment of mimēsis.)

Rorty, A.O. (ed.) (1992) *Essays on Aristotle's Poetics*, Princeton, NJ: Princeton University Press. (A stimulating collection of recent articles on *mimēsis* and many related issues; good bibliography.)

GLENN W. MOST

MIND, BUNDLE THEORY OF

This theory owes its name to Hume, who described the self or person (which he assumed to be the mind) as 'nothing but a bundle or collection of different perceptions, which succeed each other with an inconceivable rapidity, and are in a perpetual flux and movement' (A Treatise of Human Nature I, IV, §VI). The theory begins by denying Descartes's Second Meditation view that experiences belong to an immaterial soul; its distinguishing feature is its attempt to account for the unity of a single mind by employing only relations among the experiences themselves rather than their attribution to an independently persisting subject. The usual objection to the bundle theory is that no relations adequate to the task can be found. But empirical work suggests that the task itself may be illusory.

Many bundle theorists follow Hume in taking their topic to be personal identity. But the theory can be disentangled from this additional burden.

1   **Origins and nature of the theory**
2   **Objections and replies**

1   Origins and nature of the theory

Hume's bundle theory originated in his response to what he took to be a natural illusion about personal identity:

> [S]ome philosophers... imagine we are every moment intimately conscious of what we call our SELF; that we feel its existence and its continuance in existence; and are certain, beyond the evidence of a demonstration, both of its perfect identity and simplicity.
>
> (*A Treatise of Human Nature* I, IV, §VI)

He thought that if that were so, the self would be an item within one's experience. But the self is not such an item: rather, it is that to which our experiences are ascribed. Neither can the existence of the self be inferred from, or found in any other way in, experience. If I introspect, all I find are thoughts, sensations, emotions, not the thing which has them.

This Cartesian self, then, is a myth. But how did the myth arise? Hume's own answer was that relations of resemblance and causation among one's different experiences lead one to suppose, mistakenly, that there is some real underlying unity. (A rough analogy would be getting the impression, in darkness, of a single light's travelling, by seeing adjacent lamps successively illuminated, each going on as its neighbour is extinguished.) This should not be interpreted as his offering some set of conditions for the truth of statements of the form '*x* is the same person as *y*'. Hume regarded it as his job not to give an account of personal identity, but merely to explain how we come to have the notion at all. But subsequent philosophers have conceived the bundle theory as just such an account.

One thing Hume's explanation of the origin of the notion of personal identity lacked was an answer to this question: given that there *are* bundles which constitute particular minds, what is it that ties a particular set of experiences into *that* bundle? Something must do so, because according to Hume, one gets one's false ideas about real identity by being presented with a limited set of experiences *already bundled* (not with all the experiences that there are, for most belong to other people). A Cartesian ego would do the job; but that is already condemned. And it would anyway not do a further job: lying as it does beyond the reach of experience, it would not on its own give one the notion of one's own self. Kant noticed this difficulty (*Critique of Pure Reason*, A103–10), and is sometimes read (for example by Strawson 1966: 163) as suggesting that a necessary element of the linking principle was the possibility of regarding one's experiences as *of* objects independent of those experiences, objects which provide the possibility of experiences which are not one's own (see KANT, I. §6). Be this as it may, bundle theorists have always been exercised by the need to provide suitable unifying links among experiences. Such links have to be capable of accounting for the unity of a single person, both at one time (synchronic unity) and across time (diachronic unity).

Hume's assumption of the identity of self and mind exacerbates his problem. For it multiplies the demands that a bundle theory has to meet. And defenders of the bundle theory have usually been those who have *argued* for this identity, so that they regard themselves as facing the task described of supplying links among experiences adequate to account for both the synchronic and diachronic unity of a person. But it is in principle possible for a bundle theorist of mind to hold, for example, a body-based account of personal identity (see PERSONAL IDENTITY). Certain natural objections to the theory would then immediately collapse. One such is this: it seems obviously true that I might have had a quite different set of experiences from the set I have had. But if I just *am* a set of experiences, this 'obvious truth' must in fact be false.

Treating the bundle theory, then, as purely a theory of the nature of mind, what sort of theory is it? Initially, little more than a denial of the necessity of an immaterial owner of experiences, the bundle theory is almost defined by its claiming there to be no item in the category of mental substance to which experiences must be attributed. But it is also committed to the denial of the necessity for a material owner. The theory's most natural form would thus be something like Russell's post-1919 neutral monism (see RUSSELL, B.A.W. §13; NEUTRAL MONISM). But it is compatible with versions of dualism and physicalism that do not have the strong ownership commitments just described. In this sense the bundle theory is only a partial account of the nature of mind.

2   Objections and replies

A common objection is that experiences are identity-dependent on their owners, that the only way in which a particular experience can be identified is as an experience of some person, and that the bundle theory is committed to denying this. But a bundle theorist could without inconsistency admit the claim of identity-dependence, and still ask for proof that the necessary owner must be something other than the rest of the bundle; only this further step would actually refute the theory.

Another, related, objection is that the theory has the supposedly absurd implication that experiences can exist in isolation from each other, for a bundle consists of things that can exist outside the bundle, and can in principle fall apart. If they cannot so exist, then Hume's atomist version of the theory, where the experiences are mutually independent, would be false. But a non-atomist version of the theory, where the experiences are inextricably interlinked, such as one might find in William James's neutral monism, could survive this objection (see JAMES, W. §2).

More difficult is the problem of unity – finding suitable candidates for the cross-experiential links. Hume's suggestions, resemblance and causation, seem more suited to solving the problem of diachronic rather than synchronic unity. But, jointly or severally, these are neither necessary nor sufficient for either. There is more resemblance among different people's experiences of one thing than among one person's experiences of different things; and experiences in one mind may have no causal relations between them (for example I hear the doorbell while watching television), whereas experiences in two minds might be cause and effect (for example if telepathy is possible).

Another possibility is that certain experiences embrace others. Synchronic unity would have to be guaranteed by something like a second-order awareness of co-presentation of several first-order experiences. But it is hard to see that such second-order awareness is always present, while its mere possibility seems itself to require explanation in terms of a single mind. (A possible response to this criticism would be that there is no such requirement, that we have reached bedrock.) Further, it would still leave the problem of diachronic unity, which needs another kind of embracing, for example memory's spanning a sequence of experiences. This, on the face of it, would imply that an experience I do not remember belonged to a different mind. Again, the appeal to possibility seems no help.

Some bundle theorists have postulated diachronic links of a more sophisticated kind: if there is enough psychological connectedness over time, then there is a single mind. Connectedness is exemplified by recall of a previous experience, by the carrying out of a prior intention, or by the persistence of personality traits. It is a matter of degree, and hence can approach zero over the career of a single mind. It thus needs supplementation with psychological continuity, which is the holding of overlapping chains of a high degree of connectedness. But even together these links would allow a single mind to divide, with each successor having an equal claim to be the original, yet their diversity defeating that claim via the logic of identity. (If $b \neq c$, then it cannot be true both that $a = c$ and $a = b$.)

It is not clear what we should infer from this. One possibility is that the connectedness/continuity account is wrong. Another is that we should allow identity to admit degrees, and rewrite its logic. But one might conclude that these constant difficulties in finding links that guarantee both synchronic and diachronic identity of the mind may show merely that the theory's implication that the unity of mind is an illusion needs to be taken seriously.

From this perspective, better arguments for a bundle theory may lie less in a priori considerations than in empirical work by psychologists and brain scientists, which reveals striking breakdowns in mental unity (see SPLIT BRAINS). This suggests to some that the mind may best be viewed in terms not of linked experiences, but of hierarchies, systems and modules of monitoring and control of experience and activity, with all the unity there is being provided contingently by its embodiment in a normally functioning single organism. The bundle theory's natural home may thus turn out to be with functionalist accounts of mind.

See also: CONSCIOUSNESS §1; DUALISM; MODULARITY OF MIND; PERSONS; STRAWSON P.F. §§6–7

References and further reading

Brennan, A. (1989–90) 'Fragmented Selves and the Problem of Ownership', *Proceedings of the Aristotelian Society* LXXXX: 143–58. (Argues that the theory's failure to provide tight conditions for synchronic and diachronic unity of the self is a reason for accepting rather than rejecting it. Contains many useful references to other discussions.)

—— (1994) 'The Disunity of the Self', in J.J. MacIntosh and H. Meynell (eds) *Faith, Scepticism and Personal Identity: Essays in honour of T.M. Penelhum*, Calgary, Alta.: University of Calgary Press. (A defence of the theory against some standard objections; expands some points made very briefly in §2 above.)

Canfield, J. (1990) *The Looking-Glass Self: An Examination of Self-Awareness*, New York: Praeger. (Presents a no-self account of the person, connecting it with the philosophy of Wittgenstein and with Buddhism. Written for the general reader.)

Carruthers, P. (1986) *Introducing Persons*, London: Routledge, ch. 2. (Accessible to beginners without being simplistic; criticizes the bundle theory without treating it as a theory of personal identity.)

* Descartes, R. (1641) *Meditations on First Philosophy*, trans. J. Cottingham, R. Stoothoff and D. Murdoch, in *The Philosophical Writings of René Descartes*, Cambridge: Cambridge University Press, 1984. (Classic statement and defence of dualism.)

Giles, J. (1993) 'The No-Self Theory: Hume, Buddhism, and Personal Identity', *Philosophy East and West*, 43 (2): 175–200. (A careful account and defence of Hume. Argues a case like Brennan's, and claims that Buddhist thinkers held a similar view. Contains useful references to Buddhist literature on the topic.)

* Hume, D. (1739–40) *A Treatise of Human Nature*, ed. L.A. Selby-Bigge, Oxford: Clarendon Press, 1978, I, IV, VI. (The seminal statement of the theory.)

Kant, I. (1787) *Critique of Pure Reason*, trans. N. Kemp Smith, London: Macmillan, 1933. (An influential but obscure treatment of the unity of the mind's experience.)

Lowe, E.J. (1991) 'Real Selves: Persons as a Substantial Kind', in D. Cockburn (ed.) *Human Beings*, Cambridge: Cambridge University Press. (Attacks the bundle theory on grounds of necessity of ownership. Clear and vigorous, but not for beginners.)

Parfit, D. (1984) *Reasons and Persons*, Oxford: Clarendon Press, chaps 10 and 11. (An influential version of the bundle theory as an account of synchronic unity and personal survival, embedded in a wider discussion of personal identity, rationality and ethics. A major work which has provoked much controversy.)

Quinton, A. (1962) 'The Soul', *Journal of Philosophy* 59 (15), repr. in J. Perry (ed.), *Personal Identity*, London: University of California Press, 1975. (Defends a version of the theory in a materialist context. Clearly written.)

Strawson, P.F. (1959) *Individuals: An Essay in Descriptive Metaphysics*, London: Methuen, ch. 3. (The most definitive statement of the necessity-of-ownership objection to the bundle or 'no-owner-ship' theory. Difficult but rewarding.)

—— (1966) *The Bounds of Sense*, London: Methuen. (A widely used but somewhat idiosyncratic essay on Kant's *Critique of Pure Reason*.)

Stroud, B. (1977) *Hume*, London: Routledge & Kegan Paul, ch. 6. (A very good, but intricate, account of Hume's treatment of personal identity. Accessible to undergraduates, but not to complete beginners.)

STEWART CANDLISH

MIND, CHILD'S THEORY OF

Knowledge of other minds poses a variety of unusual problems due to the peculiarly private nature of mental states. Some current views, impressed by the contrast between the apparently direct access we have to our own mental states and the inaccessibility of others' mental states, argue that we understand the mental states of others by imagining that they are our own by 'simulation'. Other current views propose that we infer both our own mental states and the mental states of others by employing a set of conjectures arrived at through general inductive reasoning over experience: a 'folk psychology' or 'theory of mind'.

Experimental studies, by contrast, suggest that we possess an 'instinct' for comprehending the informational mental states of other minds. Children develop mental state concepts uniformly and rapidly in the preschool period when general reasoning powers are limited. For example, children can reason effectively about other people's beliefs before they can reliably calculate that 2 plus 2 equals 4. In the empirical study of the 'theory of mind' instinct there have been three major discoveries so far: first, that normally developing 2-year-olds are able to recognize the informational state of pretending; second, that normally developing children can, by the age of 4 years, solve a variety of false belief problems; and lastly, that this instinct is specifically impaired in children with the neurodevelopmental disorder known as 'autism'.

1 False belief understanding
2 The significance of pretending
3 Why do normal 3-year-olds and autistic children fail false belief tasks?
4 Alternative theories of 'theory of mind' development

1 False belief understanding

The study of false belief has come to dominate much of the investigation of the child's theory of mind. Interest in false belief arose initially out of an article published by Premack and Woodruff (1978) on whether or not chimpanzees have a 'theory of mind'. The findings strongly suggested that chimpanzees have some awareness of an agent's goal because they made inferences concerning the use of objects as tools.

In so far as understanding the use of tools in relation to an agent's goals is part of 'theory of mind', chimpanzees demonstrated a version of theory of mind. In a commentary on Premack and Woodruff's paper, Dennett (1978) has suggested that a stronger test of an animal's understanding of mental states would involve an understanding of false belief. In understanding false belief, the animal has to understand a belief that is not its own and therefore that does not simply reflect reality as the animal construes it. Such tests with chimpanzees have returned essentially negative results (see Premack 1988; ANIMAL LANGUAGE AND THOUGHT). However, the idea was taken up by Wimmer and Perner who developed scenarios for testing not chimpanzees, but human children.

In the first of these, Wimmer and Perner (1983) showed that 6-year-old children could predict an agent's behaviour from a false belief attributed by the children to the agent. Wimmer and Perner's original task was somewhat more complex than necessary. When Baron-Cohen, Leslie and Frith (1985) simplified the task, they found that the vast majority of normally developing 4-year-old children could successfully calculate Sally's belief in the following scenario. Sally puts her candy in a cupboard and goes out to play. Anne comes in, finds the candy and moves it to a nearby drawer. Now Sally comes back for her candy. Where does Sally think her candy is? Where will she look for it? Eighty-five per cent of 4-year-olds were able to attribute a false belief to Sally and thus to predict her erroneous behaviour. Children younger than 4, however, tend to predict Sally's behaviour from the candy's current position, as if Sally would know this.

Likewise, 4- but not 3-year-olds succeed in the following scenario from Perner, Leekam and Wimmer (1987). The child is shown a *Smarties* box and asked what it contains. '*Smarties*' [candy] is the invariable reply. The child is then shown that, actually, the box contains only a pencil. Disappointment. The pencil is placed back in the box and the lid closed again. The child is reminded that a friend is outside waiting to come in. Then the test question is asked, 'What will your friend say (/think) is in the box when we first show it to him/her? Again most 4-year-olds correctly predict '*Smarties*', while most 3-year-olds expect the friend to say, 'A pencil'.

The second key finding is that children suffering from the neurodevelopmental disorder known as 'childhood autism' have a focused and specific impairment in the capacity to recognize and reason about mental states. Autism is a life-long disorder resulting from complex biological causes (Frith 1989), characterized by social and communicative impair-

ments beyond that expected on the basis of whatever degree of mental retardation may also be present (Wing and Gould 1979).

Baron-Cohen, Leslie and Frith (1985) presented three groups of children with the Sally/Anne scenario outlined above. One group consisted of normal 4-year-olds, one of Down's syndrome children and one of (older) autistic children. It was deliberately arranged that the autistic group had a mental age considerably higher than that of the Down's group. Furthermore, their IQs were in the borderline to normal range (mean 82), while the Down's children averaged an IQ of 64, in the moderately retarded range. The results of this study showed that, while around 85 per cent of both the normal and Down's groups correctly predicted Sally's false belief, only 20 per cent of the autistic group did so, despite their intellectual and age advantage. Any difficulty the autistic children might have with this task, therefore, cannot be attributed to general intellectual level.

In a follow-up study, Baron-Cohen, Leslie and Frith (1986) compared, across these same three groups, the children's ability to understand different types of events. They used a 'picture sequencing' task. Some picture sequences depicted physical-causal events, and some sequences depicted events which could only be appreciated if one took into account the (false) beliefs of the protagonists. The pictures in each sequence were jumbled and the children were asked to order each sequence so that the story 'made sense'. The results were again quite striking. The autistic children showed a specific difficulty. They performed well on the physical-causal stories but slumped to chance performance on the false belief stories. The younger normal children scored almost 100 per cent on these last stories, while the more retarded Down's group still out-performed the autistic group. Finally, analysis of the children's verbal descriptions of the stories showed that the autistic children produced much more physical-causal language but much less mental state language than the other two groups. Leslie and Frith (1988) subsequently showed that high-ability autistic children had difficulty understanding true-but-incomplete beliefs as well as false beliefs. Perner *et al.* (1989) showed that autistic children failed the *Smarties* task.

The findings of the above initial sets of studies on both normal and autistic children have subsequently been confirmed and extended in a large number of studies (see, for example, Baron-Cohen, Tager-Flusberg and Cohen 1993). Together, they raise the following question. How can the young brain attend to mental states when they cannot be seen, nor heard, nor felt? Leslie (1994) argues that this is the fundamental question to ask, because the child has to be able to attend to mental states before they can learn anything about them. The only plausible answer so far has been to suggest that children are equipped with a specialized cognitive mechanism that appears early in development when encyclopedic knowledge and general reasoning abilities are still severely limited. The pattern of development seen in childhood autism can then be understood as reflecting, at least in part, early biological damage to this specialized mechanism, damage which spares general intelligence (see MODULARITY OF MIND).

2 The significance of pretending

There is a certain form of false belief which is understood much earlier even than 4 years. This is 'make-believe' or pretending. Two-year-olds have no trouble recognizing when someone playfully pretends; when someone acts as if they believed an imaginary situation were real. Two-year-olds can readily figure out the specific content of the pretence (Leslie 1994). Likely as not, the 2-year-old will join in the game and proceed to contribute their own appropriate counterfactual inferences. This ability, which first emerges between 18 and 24 months, has been analysed by means of a cognitive model, the so-called 'metarepresentational theory of pretence', which identifies the main properties of the internal representations required by this ability (see Leslie 1987; AESTHETIC ATTITUDE). These representations turn out to express the key information required to represent propositional attitudes. This led to the suggestion that these representational mechanisms form the specific innate basis of the child's capacity to acquire and elaborate a 'theory of mind'. Autistic children are impaired in their capacity to pretend and, for example, do not spontaneously pretend play. Indeed, this was a key consideration that led to the studies of belief understanding in autism outlined above.

One key feature of the capacity for pretence is that as soon as a child becomes capable of pretending in isolation, by themselves, they also become capable of understanding pretence-in-others (Leslie 1987, 1994). Thus, there is a 'developmental yoking' between being able oneself to pretend that a banana is a telephone and being able to understand that someone else is pretending that a banana is a telephone. This is strikingly different from the case of belief. Most psychologists agree that infants a few months olds can have beliefs, for example, that there is an object behind a screen. But no one thinks that these young infants simultaneously have the capacity to understand that someone else can have that same belief: there is no yoking between the capacity to have beliefs

and the capacity to understand beliefs-in-others (see BELIEF; PROPOSITIONAL ATTITUDES).

The metarepresentational theory of pretence referred to earlier explains the above pattern in the following way. Let us say, for expository purposes, that to have a belief is to stand in a certain kind of functional or processing relation to an internal representation (see LANGUAGE OF THOUGHT). Let us call this functional relation the 'belief box'. If a given representation r is placed in the belief box, then the organism comes to believe that r. In a similar vein, we might talk of a 'desire box', such that if r is placed in the desire box, then the organism comes to desire that r. In this vein, the metarepresentational theory of pretence says that there is no such thing as a 'pretend box'. Instead, in pretending, a representation 'I pretend that r' or a representation 'Mother pretends that r' is placed in the belief box and results, respectively, in solitary pretence or in understanding pretence-in-others. What determines the developmental emergence of pretending, then, is not the appearance of a 'pretend box', a new functional relation, but the appearance of new representations of the form 'X pretends that r', that is, the appearance of metarepresentations. The understanding of belief-in-others likewise depends upon the emergence of metarepresentations of the form 'X believes that r' and is delayed relative to the appearance of the 'belief box' at least as long as pretending is.

3 Why do normal 3-year-olds and autistic children fail false belief tasks?

How long after understanding pretence-in-others do children understand belief-in-others? So far what we have said suggests something of the order of two years. However, this may be an over-estimate. The 'standard' tasks used to assess false belief understanding seem to impose general problem-solving demands that 3-year-old children find hard to meet. These performance demands may be masking their underlying competence. Psychologists have been developing versions of the false belief tasks that make reduced demands and 3-year-olds do better on these simplified tasks.

For example, Wellman (1990) found that 3-year-olds could pass a version of the Sally/Anne task in which the position of the target object was not known but simply guessed. Wherever the child guessed, the experimenter said that Sally thought it was some other place. When asked to predict Sally's search behaviour, then, the child has to predict on the basis of Sally's different belief. Under these circumstances most 3-year-olds succeed. Apparently, the child's efforts to represent Sally's belief are not swamped by current reality if reality is only guessed at and not known for sure (see also Zaitchik 1991). In the *Smarties* task, certain memory cues built into the procedure seem to facilitate false belief success in 3-year-olds (Mitchell and Lacohe 1991). Roth and Leslie (1991) showed that normal 3-year-old children, while failing standard false belief tasks, may nevertheless attribute propositional attitudes to participants in a conversation. Roth and Leslie's autistic subjects, however, failed to perform even at the 3-year-olds' level.

If 3-year-olds fail standard false belief tests because of performance limitations, might not the same be true for autistic children? It is nigh impossible to think up, let alone rule out, every potential general processing resource that might be required by these tasks and be impaired in autism. Many such accounts are possible: working memory, language ability, visual imagery ability, abstract reasoning, executive functioning, a cooperative attitude, and so on. Fortunately, such explanations can be ruled out by the following results. Zaitchik (1990) devised a task that closely parallels the standard false belief tasks but instead of an agent forming a belief that subsequently goes out of date, the task involves a camera taking a Polaroid photograph that subsequently goes out of date. So the camera takes a photograph of the candy in the cupboard. The photograph is placed faced down on the table without the child seeing it (after all, the child does not get to see Sally's belief either). Now the candy is moved from the cupboard to the drawer. The usual 'control' questions are asked: 'Where was the candy when I took a photograph of it?' and 'Where is the candy now?'. As usual, the child must get these questions right if they are to be tested further. The child is asked, 'In the photograph, where is the candy?'.

Results with normal children show that, typically, 3-year-olds fail both the out-of-date photograph and belief tasks, while most 4-year-olds pass both. However, if a normal child passes only one of these tasks, there is a reliable tendency for them to pass the false belief rather than the out-of-date photograph task. Leslie and Thaiss (1992) showed that autistic children show near ceiling performance on out-of-date photographs while being severely impaired on the similar out-of-date belief task. (Incidentally, this effect is not restricted to cameras and photographs; it works just as well with maps and drawings.) This is impressive evidence for the domain specificity of autistic impairment. It also contradicts the perhaps natural assumption that understanding mental states and understanding representations should simply be different facets of the same psychological mechanism (see, for example, Fodor 1992).

4 Alternative theories of 'theory of mind' development

Other current positions in the literature view the development of 'theory of mind' knowledge as the discovery by young children of a succession of 'theories' much as scientists have created and abandoned successive theories of the natural world (for example, Gopnik 1993; Perner 1991; Wellman 1990; see FOLK PSYCHOLOGY). However, the obvious differences between the historical achievements of talented individuals and the rapid, early and uniform acquisitions of ordinary preschool children imply in the latter case a process more akin to the unfolding of an albeit 'articulated' instinct than to the scientific process. Yet another recent position wants to deny the existence of theory-like knowledge or inference over data structures by substituting the notion that we 'simulate' the mental states of others (Harris 1992; Goldman 1992). Simulation theory proposes that we understand other people's actions by modelling their circumstances and predicting their actions by means of the very mechanisms that generate our own actions. We are said to run our action-planning system 'off-line', supplying it with 'pretend' inputs, to 'simulate' the other person's mental life by, as it were, placing our self 'in the other person's shoes'.

However, there are a number of quite different processes that could be called 'simulation' and their contributions to 'theory of mind' abilities will each have to be determined empirically (see Nichols *et al.* 1996). It may well turn out that 'simulation' is one of the abilities associated with deploying folk psychological knowledge. However, Leslie and German (1995) have pointed out a number of problems for the radical claim that the existence of simulation abilities means there is no need for 'theory of mind' (meta) representations.

Neither of these current alternative views has addressed the fundamental problem of 'theory of mind' development, namely, how is it possible for the young brain to attend to mental states in the first place? The metarepresentational theory was designed for this problem. The theory proposes that the young brain attends to an agent's behaviour and infers an underlying causal state of the agent having the properties specified by the metarepresentation. The metarepresentation is computed by a specialized, probably modular, innate mechanism. This mechanism allows the young brain to attend to and learn about invisible mental states and promotes the early and rapid development of 'theory of mind'. When early occurring biological damage prevents the normal expression of this mechanism in the developing brain, the result is the core symptoms of autism.

See also: COGNITION, INFANT; MODULARITY OF MIND; NATIVISM; OTHER MINDS

References and further reading

* Baron-Cohen, S., Leslie, A.M. and Frith, U. (1985) 'Does the Autistic Child Have a "Theory of Mind"?', *Cognition* 21: 37–46. (This paper tested the first prediction of the 'metarepresentational' theory and reported the discovery of the 'theory of mind' impairment in autism.)

* Baron-Cohen, S., Leslie, A.M. and Frith, U. (1986) 'Mechanical, Behavioural and Intentional Understanding of Picture Stories in Autistic Children', *British Journal of Developmental Psychology* 4: 113–25. (A follow-up to the 1985 paper by the same authors, shows children with autism performing well on a test of understanding stories with mechanical or behavioural themes but poorly on stories with mental state themes.)

* Baron-Cohen, S., Tager-Flusberg, H. and Cohen, D. (eds) (1993) *Understanding Other Minds: Perspectives from Autism*, Oxford: Oxford University Press. (A very useful recent collection of articles on the 'theory of mind' impairment in autism.)

* Dennett, D.C. (1978) 'Beliefs about Beliefs', *Behavioral and Brain Sciences* 1: 568–70. (This short commentary on Premack and Woodruff (1978) helped shape subsequent psychological research.)

* Fodor, J.A. (1992) 'A Theory of the Child's Theory of Mind', *Cognition* 44: 283–96. (Fodor argues that 3-year-olds' failure on the false belief problem is the result of a performance limitation.)

* Frith, U. (1989) *Autism: Explaining the Enigma*, Oxford: Blackwell. (An outstandingly interesting and readable account of the nature of autistic disorder.)

* Goldman, A. (1992) 'In Defense of the Simulation Theory', *Mind and Language* 7: 104–19. (A leading philosophical proponent argues for 'theory of mind' as simulation.)

* Gopnik, A. (1993) 'How We Know our Minds: The Illusion of First-Person Knowledge of Intentionality', *Behavioral and Brain Sciences* 16: 1–14. (Argues for the 'theory-theory' and for the claim that we do not have privileged access to our own mental states.)

* Harris, P.L. (1992) 'From Simulation to Folk Psychology: The Case for Development', *Mind and Language* 7: 120–44. (A leading psychological proponent argues for 'theory of mind' as simulation.)

* Leslie, A.M. (1987) 'Pretense and Representation: The Origins of "Theory of Mind"', *Psychological Review* 94: 412–26. (First major statement of the metarepresentational theory of normal and abnormal development.)

* —— (1994) 'Pretending and Believing: Issues in the Theory of ToMM', *Cognition* 50: 211–38. (Updated statement of the metarepresentational theory.)

* Leslie, A.M. and Frith, U. (1988) 'Autistic Children's Understanding of Seeing, Knowing and Believing', *British Journal of Developmental Psychology* 6: 315–24. (Autistic children understand basic conditions for seeing and not-seeing, but are impaired on understanding knowing and not-knowing, and on understanding falsely believing.)

* Leslie, A.M. and German, T.P. (1995) 'Knowledge and Ability in "Theory of Mind": One-Eyed Overview of a Debate', in M. Davies and T. Stone (eds) *Mental Simulation: Philosophical and Psychological Essays*, Oxford: Blackwell, 123–50. (Critique of the radical simulation account of theory of mind.)

* Leslie, A.M. and Thaiss, L. (1992) 'Domain Specificity in Conceptual Development: Neuropsychological Evidence from Autism', *Cognition* 43: 225–51. (Reports key findings on 'theory of mind' impairment in autism and refutes the 'representational theory-theory'.)

* Mitchell, P. and Lacohe, H. (1991) 'Children's Early Understanding of False Belief', *Cognition* 39: 107–27. (A simple manipulation produces substantially better performance on a standard false belief test in normally developing 3-year-olds.)

* Nichols, S., Stich, S., Leslie, A.M. and Klein, D. (1996) 'Varieties of Off-Line Simulation', in P. Carruthers and P.K. Smith (eds) *Theories of Theories of Mind*, Cambridge: Cambridge University Press. (Critical assessment of the simulation theory in the light of available evidence.)

* Perner, J. (1991) *Understanding the Representational Mind*, Cambridge, MA: MIT Press. (Major statement of the 'theory-theory' that preschool children have to discover that mental states are really mental representations.)

* Perner, J., Frith, U., Leslie, A.M. and Leekam, S.R. (1989) 'Exploration of the Autistic Child's Theory of Mind: Knowledge, Belief and Communication', *Child Development* 60: 689–700. (The *Smarties* task produces excellent performance in specific-language-impaired children but poor performance in verbal-ability-matched autistic children.)

* Perner, J., Leekam, S.R. and Wimmer, H. (1987) 'Three-Year-Olds' Difficulty with False Belief: The Case for a Conceptual Deficit', *British Journal of Developmental Psychology* 5: 125–37. (The *Smarties* task.)

* Premack, D. (1988) '"Does the Chimpanzee Have a Theory of Mind?" Revisited', in R.W. Byrne and A.

Whiten (eds) *Machiavellian Intelligence: Social Expertise and the Evolution of Intellect in Monkeys, Apes, and Humans*, Oxford: Clarendon Press. (Premack returns to chimpanzee's theory of mind and notes some limitations.)

* Premack, D. and Woodruff, G. (1978) 'Does the Chimpanzee Have a Theory of Mind?', *Behavioral and Brain Sciences* 4: 515–26. (This paper coined the term 'theory of mind' and spurred the interest of psychologists.)

* Roth, D. and Leslie, A.M. (1991) 'The Recognition of Attitude Conveyed by Utterance: A Study of Pre-school and Autistic Children', *British Journal of Developmental Psychology* 9: 315–30; repr. in G.E. Butterworth, P.L. Harris, A.M. Leslie and H.M. Wellman (eds) *Perspectives on the Child's Theory of Mind*, Oxford: Oxford University Press, 315–30. (Autistic children perform less well even than 3-year-olds, who are more willing, under some circumstances, to attribute false beliefs than are 5-year-olds.)

* Wellman, H.M. (1990) *The Child's Theory of Mind*, Cambridge, MA: MIT Press. (Major statement by a leading theory-theorist argues for early emergence of a concept of desire and for an early 'copy theory' of belief.)

* Wimmer, H. and Perner, J. (1983) 'Beliefs about Beliefs: Representation and Constraining Function of Wrong Beliefs in Young Children's Understanding of Deception', *Cognition* 13: 103–28. (Seminal paper which developed the false belief task.)

* Wing, L. and Gould, J. (1979) 'Severe Impairments of Social Interaction and Associated Abnormalities in Children: Epidemiology and Classification', *Journal of Autism and Developmental Disorders* 9: 11–29. (A classic paper establishing the general nature of social impairment in autism.)

* Zaitchik, D. (1990) 'When Representations Conflict with Reality: The Preschooler's Problem with False Beliefs and "False" Photographs', *Cognition* 35: 41–68. (Elegant experimental study comparing young children's performance on the false belief task with a highly similar 'false photograph' task, with some unexpected results.)

* —— (1991) 'Is Only Seeing Really Believing?: Sources of True Belief in the False Belief Task', *Cognitive Development* 6: 91–103. (Experimental study showing that 3-year-old children find the attribution of false belief to someone else easier if they are not completely confident in their own belief.)

ALAN M. LESLIE

MIND, COMPUTATIONAL THEORIES OF

The computational theory of mind (CTM) is the theory that the mind can be understood as a computer or, roughly, as the 'software program' of the brain. It is the most influential form of 'functionalism', according to which what distinguishes a mind is not what it is made of, nor a person's behavioural dispositions, but the way in which the brain is organized. CTM underlies some of the most important research in current cognitive science, for example, theories of artificial intelligence, perception, decision making and linguistics.

CTM involves a number of important ideas. (1) Computations can be defined over syntactically specifiable symbols (that is, symbols specified by rules governing their combination) possessing semantic properties (or 'meaning'). For example, addition can be captured by rules defined over decimal numerals (symbols) that name *the numbers. (2) Computations can be analysed into 'algorithms', or simple step-by-step procedures, each of which could be carried out by a machine. (3) Computation can be generalized to include not only arithmetic, but deductive logic and other forms of reasoning, including induction, abduction and decision making. (4) Computations capture relatively autonomous levels of ordinary psychological explanation different from neurophysiology and descriptions of behaviour.*

1   **Syntax, semantics and algorithms**
2   **Primitive processors**
3   **Syntactic engines**
4   **Other forms of reason**
5   **Gödel's incompleteness theorem**
6   **Different modes of computation**
7   **Different explanatory levels**

1   Syntax, semantics and algorithms

Crucial to understanding computational theories of mind (CTM) is the distinction between the syntax and the semantics of a symbol system. *How* symbols may be combined comprises the syntax of a system and what the symbols *mean* or *name* comprises its semantics. For example, consider three different notational systems for numbers: decimal numerals ('1', '2', '3',...), Roman numerals ('I', 'II', 'III',...) and binary numerals ('1', '10', '11',...). These different types of *numerals* name the same *numbers* ('5' names the same number as 'V' and '101') but the rules for combining the numerals in calculations are very different. In other words, these systems each have a different syntax, but (approximately) the same semantics.

When children learn arithmetic, they learn reliable rules, or 'algorithms', for computing *syntactically* with numerals (symbols) in ways that mirror their *semantics* (in particular, the arithmetical relations among the corresponding numbers). Children doing calculations with decimal numerals should get the same answers as a computer working in binary, but the algorithms each uses look very different.

An algorithm is a 'mechanical' step-by-step procedure operating on syntactically well defined symbols in a way that captures relations among the things the symbols represent. Alan TURING developed a general account of algorithms, conceiving what are called 'Turing machines', perfectly mechanical computing devices that arrive at a determinate answer or 'output' to a question, given certain data or 'input' (see TURING MACHINES). According to the influential 'Church–Turing thesis' Turing machines can systematically compute anything that is intuitively 'computable' (see CHURCH'S THESIS). This idea is the inspiration for much of the modern computer industry. CTM extends it to psychology: the suggestion is that all intelligent processes can be systematically decomposed into algorithms consisting of steps that can be executed by primitive processors of a machine.

2 Primitive processors

The specific architecture of a Turing machine involves a 'tape' consisting of an infinite number of individual cells and a 'scanner', whose primitive processes consist in registering whether it is scanning a '1' or a '0', and then moving left and right from cell to cell (see TURING MACHINES). This is only one among many possible computational architectures. What is essential to a computer is merely that the primitive processes be realizable by some physical means or other. To make computational theories of mind (CTM) remotely plausible as an account of the *human* mind, we will think here in terms of the kinds of electrical devices that seem at least to be available in the human nervous system (but are also exploited in commercial computers).

A good example of a primitive processor is a 'gate'. An 'and'-gate is a device that accepts two inputs and emits a single output. If both inputs are '1's (that is, sum to 2), the output is a '1'; otherwise, the output is a '0'. An 'exclusive-or' (either but not both) gate is a 'difference detector': it emits a '0' if its inputs are the same and it emits a '1' if its inputs are different (or sum exactly to 1).

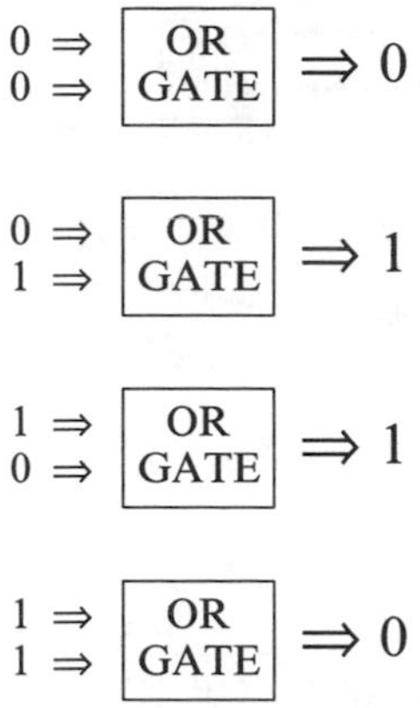

$$0 \Rightarrow \boxed{\begin{array}{c}\text{OR}\\\text{GATE}\end{array}} \Rightarrow 0 \qquad 0 \Rightarrow \boxed{\begin{array}{c}\text{AND}\\\text{GATE}\end{array}} \Rightarrow 0$$

$$0 \Rightarrow \boxed{\begin{array}{c}\text{OR}\\\text{GATE}\end{array}} \Rightarrow 1 \qquad 0 \Rightarrow \boxed{\begin{array}{c}\text{AND}\\\text{GATE}\end{array}} \Rightarrow 0$$

$$1 \Rightarrow \boxed{\begin{array}{c}\text{OR}\\\text{GATE}\end{array}} \Rightarrow 1 \qquad 1 \Rightarrow \boxed{\begin{array}{c}\text{AND}\\\text{GATE}\end{array}} \Rightarrow 0$$

$$1 \Rightarrow \boxed{\begin{array}{c}\text{OR}\\\text{GATE}\end{array}} \Rightarrow 0 \qquad 1 \Rightarrow \boxed{\begin{array}{c}\text{AND}\\\text{GATE}\end{array}} \Rightarrow 1$$

Figure 1a. Firing pattern of an "exclusive-or"-gate

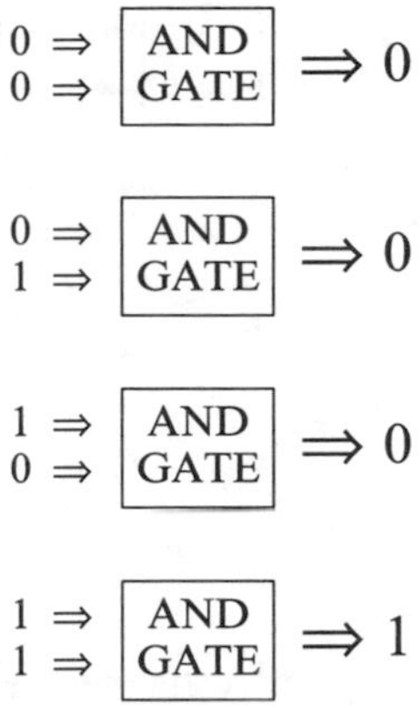

Figure 1b. Firing pattern of an "and"-gate

This talk of '1' and '0' is a way of thinking about the 'bi-stable' states of computer representers: they are almost always in one or the other of two states; the in-between states are not exploited computationally.

Using these gates, one could construct a binary 'adder' that operated according to the following rules of binary addition:

$$0 + 0 = 0$$
$$1 + 0 = 1$$
$$0 + 1 = 1$$
$$1 + 1 = 10$$

The two digits to be added are connected both to an 'and'-gate and to an 'exclusive-or'-gate as illustrated. Consider figure 2a first. The digits to be added are '1' and '0', and they are placed in the input register (the top pair of boxes). The 'exclusive-or'-gate sees different things, and so outputs a '1' to the right-most box of the answer register (the bottom pair of boxes). The 'and'-gate outputs a '0' except when it sees two '1's, so it now outputs a '0'. In this way, the circuit computes '1 + 0 = 1'. For this problem, as for '0 + 1 = 1' and '0 + 0 = 0', the 'exclusive-or'-gate does all the real work. The role of the 'and'-gate in this circuit is 'carrying', which is illustrated in figure 2b. The digits to be added, '1' and '1', are again placed in the top register. Now, both inputs to the 'and'-gate are '1's, so the 'and'-gate outputs a '1' to the left-most box of the answer (bottom) register. The 'exclusive-or'-gate puts a '0' in the right-most box, and so we have the correct answer, '10'.

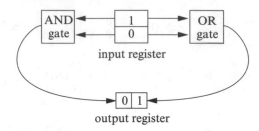

Figure 2a. Adder computing 1 + 0 = 1

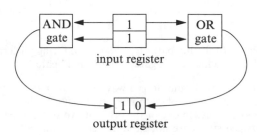

Figure 2b. Adder computing 1 + 1 = 10

3 Syntactic engines

The key idea behind the adder is that of a mirroring, or an isomorphism, between syntactic relations among numerals and their semantics, namely the relations among the numbers the numerals represent (see §1 above). This idea need not be confined to arithmetic. In their development of modern 'formal' logic, Frege and Russell showed how deductive logic can be formalized: that is to say, it can be characterized in terms of syntax, and this syntax can be characterized in terms of the physical *form* of sentences that receive a systematic semantic interpretation. In particular, it can be shown that a certain set of syntactically and formally specifiable rules is adequate to capture a significant class of deductively valid arguments (see FORMAL LANGUAGES AND SYSTEMS).

Ordinarily, sentences in logic are manipulated by people consciously following explicit rules, such as *modus ponens*, that are defined over their syntactic form, and it is often feared that CTM is committed to 'homunculi' in the brain executing the rules. However, the rules could also be obeyed by a Turing machine or, alternatively, a machine constructed along the lines of our simple adder: for example, whenever the machine detected sentences of the form 'P' and '$P \Rightarrow Q$' as input, it could print 'Q' as output, thereby

obeying *modus ponens*. In general, Turing showed that there could be a sequence of physical processes that realized any finite piece of deductive reasoning simply as a consequence of its physical organization. Consequently, one's reasoning could be in accordance with the rules of logic, not by virtue of someone representing and following them, but as a result of the causal organization of the brain. This is what is meant by the expression a 'syntactic engine driving a semantic one' (see Fodor 1975, 1980; Newall 1980). As Dennett (1975) put it, intelligent processes are broken down into separate processes so stupid that a mere machine could execute them.

Note that, although the machine's operations can be defined without mentioning the meaning of symbols, this does not entail that the symbols are meaningless, any more than the fact that bachelors are defined without reference to hair entails that bachelors are bald. Indeed, computations are standardly defined over symbols that are presumed to have some meaning or other (a point often missed by critics of CTM such as Searle (1984: 33); see CHINESE ROOM ARGUMENT).

How do symbols in computers acquire meaning? In the case of most artificial computers, their semantics are pretty much whatever their designers say they are. However, this might not always be so: philosophers have proposed a wide variety of conditions, involving both the internal states of a system, and their (for example, causal and co-variant) relations to external phenomena, that arguably would provide natural conditions for the states of a machine – or of an evolved animal like ourselves – having specific meanings (see SEMANTICS, INFORMATIONAL; SEMANTICS, TELEOLOGICAL; SEMANTICS, CONCEPTUAL ROLE). These theories could provide semantic interpretations for the syntactic states postulated by CTM.

4 Other forms of reason

Deductive arguments were the inspiration, and remain the clearest success, for CTM. Similar hopes are entertained by many philosophers and cognitive scientists for a logic of induction, abduction, practical reason and decision making (see INDUCTIVE INFERENCE; INFERENCE TO THE BEST EXPLANATION; RATIONALITY, PRACTICAL). The following affords an extremely simple example of what they have in mind.

Imagine that a computer is provided with programs that perform operations on sentences in a formal language like that of modern symbolic logic, and that it is supplied with certain hypotheses, say, about circles and squares, to which it assigns certain initial probabilities. A video camera presents it with some inputs that directly cause it to access those hypotheses, deducing from each of them, one by one, the consequences regarding the character of the input that would be expected if the hypothesis were true. These consequences are compared in each case with the actual input that is received, and that hypothesis is 'accepted' which satisfies some threshold value of a function of the initial probabilities and the highest degree of fit between its consequences and that input.

Imagine also that the machine is capable of performing certain basic actions: for example, whenever certain sentences (for example, 'Move right!') are in certain 'command' registers, then its 'arms' (say) are caused to move in a corresponding way. And suppose that the sentences that end up in these command addresses are the result of a program that spells out familiar decision-theoretic reasoning ('If more squares are wanted, and the probability of getting some by moving right is greater than by moving left, then move right') that are applied to an arbitrary set of basic preferences that are wired into the machine (say, that it prefers to replicate squares and obliterate circles).

If the machine now operated according to these programs, its actions would seem to be explainable along familiar mentalistic lines. Although reasoning in most animals is massively more complex than this, these programs would seem to capture what is essential to such processes as perception, hypothesis testing, belief, desire and decision making. That, at any rate, is the claim of CTM.

5 Gödel's incompleteness theorem

It is often thought that Gödel's famous 'incompleteness' theorem, which proved that no formal system can prove all the truths of arithmetic (see GÖDEL'S THEOREMS §§3–4), showed that the human mind cannot be a computer, and that CTM must therefore be false (see Lucas 1961; Penrose 1989). After all, Gödel appreciated the truth of the very sentences he is supposed to have proved to be unprovable!

There are a great many problems in this reasoning (for a start, CTM is not committed to all reasoning being deductive), but perhaps the most basic one arises from not appreciating the essentially disjunctive character of Gödel's theorem: what he proved was that *either* a formal system of arithmetic was inconsistent *or* it was incomplete. If people managed to do something that counted as proving the relevant undecidable sentence for their own system of arithmetic, they would do this at the expense of no longer being consistent: a contradiction could now be derived from their axioms. But this would not be a particularly remarkable fact: they would not explode

or die. They would simply be disposed to believe a contradiction (a disposition many of us possess already). It is true that there are things no machine can do, namely, prove all the truths of arithmetic without contradicting itself; but it has yet to be established that any human being can do them either (see Putnam 1960; Lewis 1969, 1979).

6 Different modes of computation

There are many different ways in which computations can be carried out. Along lines closest to the original computers described here, there are the 'classical', 'symbolic' approaches that typically involve a 'language of thought' that is encoded and manipulated in the hardware of the computer (see Fodor 1975; Newall 1980; LANGUAGE OF THOUGHT). But more recently there have emerged 'non-symbolic', 'connectionist' approaches that eschew sentence-like structures, and exploit networks of interconnected cells subject to varying degrees of excitation (see, for example, Churchland and Sejnowski 1992; CONNECTIONISM). However, the two approaches need not be exclusive: through ingenious encoding, connectionist programs can be (and standardly are) run on computers constructed along classical lines, and vice versa. This is why one cannot tell simply by looking at the physical architecture of the brain whether the mind 'really' has a classical or connectionist 'cognitive architecture'.

7 Different explanatory levels

This last point highlights an issue central to computational approaches to the mind: that there may be many different explanatory levels for describing the brain (see EXPLANATION). Note, for example, that what is essential to the success of the computations of even our little adder (see §§2–3 above) does not depend upon the gates being realized electronically. An indefinite variety of devices (composed of pipes of water, or of mice in traps) could obey the same rules. Two primitive processors (such as gates) count as computationally equivalent if they have the same input–output function, that is, the same actual and potential behaviour, even if one works hydraulically and the other electrically. So CTM describes the organization of the brain at a level that abstracts from most of its biology.

This is not to say that the computer model is incompatible with a biological approach. Sometimes important information about how a computer works could be gained by examining its circuits. As Lycan (1981) emphasizes, there may well be indefinitely many different levels of description and explanation of a system's processes, within both CTM and biology itself.

CTM is thus a paradigm of a functionalist approach to the mind, whereby mental states are individuated by their role in an organization (see FUNCTIONALISM). Unlike dualism and physicalistic reductionism, it is not committed to any particular claims about the substance out of which minds might be composed. But, unlike behaviourism, CTM is not entirely indifferent to what goes on inside the head.

In particular, although computational equivalence of primitive processors is defined in terms of their input and output, the equivalence of *non*-primitive devices is not. Consider two multipliers that work via different programs. Both accept inputs and emit outputs only in decimal notation. One of them converts inputs to binary, does the computation in binary, and then converts back to decimal. The other does the computation directly in decimal. These are not computationally equivalent multipliers despite their identical input–output functions. Thus, not only might creatures made of different stuff have the same mental lives, but behaviourally indistinguishable creatures might have very different ones.

See also: ARTIFICIAL INTELLIGENCE; CHINESE ROOM ARGUMENT; COGNITIVE ARCHITECTURE; VISION

References and further reading

Bechtel, W. and Abrahamsen, A. (1991) *Connectionism and the Mind*, Oxford: Blackwell. (The most comprehensive philosophical discussion of the connectionist approach to cognition.)

Block, N. (1990) 'The Computer Model of the Mind', in D. Osherson and E. Smith (eds) *An Invitation to Cognitive Science*, vol. 3, *Thinking*, Cambridge, MA: MIT Press. (A fuller exposition of CTM.)

* Churchland, P.S. and Sejnowski, T.J. (1992) *The Computational Brain*, Cambridge, MA: MIT Press/Bradford Books. (An excellent introduction to the study of neural computation using artificial neural networks.)

* Dennett, D. (1975) 'Why the Law of Effect Will Not Go Away', in *Brainstorms*, Cambridge, MA: MIT Press. (Discussion of how computational processes do not presuppose intelligence to execute them.)

* Fodor, J. (1975) *The Language of Thought*, New York: Crowell. (Influential exposition and defence by a philosopher of the hypothesis that thought consists in computations over syntactically specified, semantically valuable representations encoded in the brain.)

* —— (1980) 'Methodological Solipsism Considered as a Research Strategy in Cognitive Psychology',
Behavioral and Brain Sciences 3: 417–24. (Argues that psychology need only concern itself with internal computations over formally specified representations, independent of their external interpretation.)

* Lewis, D. (1969) 'Lucas against Mechanism', *Philosophy* 44: 231–3. (A reply to Lucas' argument against CTM.)

* —— (1979) 'Lucas Against Mechanism II', *Canadian Journal of Philosophy* 9 (3): 373–5. (A further reply to Lucas.)

* Lucas, J. (1961) 'Minds, Machines and Gödel', *Philosophy* 36: 112–27. (One of the original efforts to argue against CTM on the basis of Gödel's theorem.)

* Lycan, W. (1981) 'Form, Function and Feel', *Journal of Philosophy* 78: 24–50. (Useful discussion of how 'multi-realizability' recurs at innumerable levels of scientific explanation.)

* Newall, A. (1980) 'Physical Symbol Systems', *Cognitive Science* 4 (2): 135–83. (Discussion by a leading computer scientist of the hypothesis that thought consists of computations defined over syntactic objects.)

* Penrose, R. (1989) *The Emperor's New Mind: Concerning Computers, Minds, and the Laws of Physics*, New York: Oxford University Press. (A recent attack on CTM, based in part on Gödel's theorem.)

* Putnam, H. (1960) 'Minds and Machines', in *Philosophical Papers*, vol. 2, *Mind, Language and Reality*, Cambridge: Cambridge University Press, 1975. (An early, influential statement of CTM.)

Rey, G. (1997) *Contemporary Philosophy of Mind: A Contentiously Classical Approach*, Oxford: Blackwell. (An exposition and defence of CTM as an approach to philosophy of mind quite generally.)

* Searle, J. (1984) *Minds, Brains and Science*, Cambridge, MA: Harvard University Press. (Discussion of the 'Chinese room' objection to CTM.)

NED BLOCK
GEORGES REY

MIND, IDENTITY THEORY OF

We know that the brain is intimately connected with mental activity. Indeed, doctors now define death in terms of the cessation of the relevant brain activity. The identity theory of mind holds that the intimate connection is identity: the mind is the brain, or, more precisely, mental states are states of the brain. The theory goes directly against a long tradition according to which mental and material belong to quite distinct ontological categories – the mental being essentially conscious, the material essentially unconscious. This tradition has been bedevilled by the problem of how essentially immaterial states could be caused by the material world, as would happen when we see a tree, and how they could cause material states, as would happen when we decide to make an omelette.

A great merit of the identity theory is that it avoids this problem: interaction between mental and material becomes simply interaction between one subset of material states, namely certain states of a sophisticated central nervous system, and other material states. The theory also brings the mind within the scope of modern science. More and more phenomena are turning out to be explicable in the physical terms of modern science: phenomena once explained in terms of spells, possession by devils, Thor's thunderbolts, and so on, are now explained in more mundane, physical terms. If the identity theory is right, the same goes for the mind. Neuroscience will in time reveal the secrets of the mind in the same general way that the theory of electricity reveals the secrets of lightning. This possibility has received enormous support from advances in computing. We now have at least the glimmerings of an idea of how a purely material or physical system could do some of the things minds can do.

Nevertheless, there are many questions to be asked of the identity theory. How could states that seem so different turn out to be one and the same? Would neurophysiologists actually see my thoughts and feelings if they looked at my brain? When we report on our mental states what are we reporting on – our brains?

1 **Origin of the identity theory**
2 **Early objections**
3 **Qualia**
4 **Functionalism and the identity theory**

1 Origin of the identity theory

The identity theory of mind holds that each and every mental state is identical with some state in the brain. My desire for coffee, my feeling happy, and my believing that the dog is about to bite are all states of my brain. The view is not that mental states and brain states are correlated but that they are literally one and the same. Despite its name, the identity theory of mind is strictly speaking not a view about the mind as such, but about mental phenomena. However, most protagonists of the identity theory, and most contemporary philosophers of mind if it comes to that, hold some version of the view that the mind is a construction out of its states in somewhat the way that an army is a construction out of its soldiers.

The identity theory of mind arose out of dissatis-

faction with dualism, and with behaviourism as an attempt to avoid dualism. According to dualism, mental states are quite distinct from any material states, including brain states (see DUALISM). The most famous challenge to dualism is to give a satisfactory account of the causal interactions between mental states and material states, and most especially to give a satisfactory account of causation from mental states to bodily occurrences. We believe that sometimes my desire for ice cream causes my arm to move in such a way that an ice cream is in my mouth, that my pangs of hunger cause me to tighten my belt, and so on. But how do states allegedly 'outside' the material world cause material goings on like arm movements? How do they do this in such a way as to avoid violating the various conservation laws in physics? And how do they do this in such a way as not to conflict with what the physical sciences, and especially neuroscience, tell us about how bodily movements are caused?

The last question is particularly pressing. The success of the physical sciences in explaining phenomena in their own, physical, terms has been striking. We now know that lightning is not caused by Thor's actions, that epilepsy is not caused by demonic possession, and that plants do not grow because they contain a vital essence but because their cells divide (see VITALISM). It is hard to believe that bodily behaviour is unique in resisting in-principle explanation in purely physical terms. The dualist can respond to this challenge by denying the common-sense view that mental states sometimes cause bodily behaviour, a position known as epiphenomenalism. This position holds that although physical states on occasion cause mental states, mental states themselves never cause anything, being mere epiphenomena of the brain states that, along with the appropriate material surroundings, are the true causes of the behaviour we associate with mental states. Apart from flying in the face of common-sense, this position makes it hard to see why the mind evolved (see EPIPHENOMENALISM).

Behaviourism treats mental states in terms of behaviour and dispositions to behaviour. Its inspiration comes from facts such as these: that those creatures we credit with mental states are precisely those manifesting sophisticated behaviour and possessing sophisticated behavioural capacities; that psychology became a serious science when psychologists started to investigate the mind via the investigation of behavioural capacities; and that there are conceptual links between mental states and behaviour – it is, for instance, part of the concept of an intention that having an intention goes along with behaving in a way that tends to fulfil it, and it is part of the concept of intelligence that the intelligent are better problem solvers than the unintelligent (see BEHAVIOURISM, ANALYTIC).

Behaviourists delight in pointing out that it is hard to see how dualists could explain the last two points. Why should investigation of an immaterial realm be especially aided by looking at behaviour? How could the way things are in some immaterial realm be *conceptually* linked to brute behavioural facts? However, for our purposes here the crucial point is that behaviourists, like dualists, have trouble over the causation of behaviour.

The common-sense position is that mental states are causally responsible for behaviour – the itch causes the scratching – and responsible for behavioural dispositions and capacities – people's intelligence is responsible for their capacity to solve hard problems. But then mental states are not the same as behaviour and behavioural dispositions and capacities, being rather their underlying causes. And so they are, says the identity theorist. Mental states are those brain states that all the scientific evidence points to as being causally responsible for the behaviour, and behavioural dispositions and capacities, distinctive of those creatures we credit with a mental life.

2 Early objections

Here are some of the many objections that greeted the identity theory when it became well known through, especially, Smart (1959).

It was objected that the ancients knew about mental states while knowing next to nothing about the brain. How could this be if mental states are identical with brain states? However, as identity theorists observed, science has established many identities that were unknown to the ancients. They did not know that lightning is identical with an electrical discharge, temperature in gases is mean molecular kinetic energy, and water is H_2O. The identity of mental states with brain states is, identity theorists urged, of a piece with scientific identities in general. We learned, for example, that temperature is mean molecular kinetic energy by discovering that it is mean molecular kinetic energy that is responsible for the phenomena we associate with temperature. In the same general way, identity theorists claim, we have discovered that mental states are brain states by discovering that brain states are responsible for the behavioural phenomena that we associate with mental states, and we will discover which particular brain states are which particular mental states by discovering which particular brain states are responsible for the behavioural phenomena associated with those mental states.

Identity theorists also noted that water, lightning, and temperature do not present themselves to us *as* H_2O, electrical discharge, and mean molecular kinetic energy, respectively; so it cannot be an objection to their theory that mental states do not present themselves *as* brain states.

Many objected that the identity theory violates Leibniz's Law that if x = y, then x and y share all properties (see IDENTITY), on the ground that mental states and brain states differ in their properties. An after-image is, say, yellow and in front of my face, but my brain states are not yellow, and are inside my head; again, an itch is, say, in the middle of my back, but my brain is not in the middle of my back. They also pointed out that brain states are at a certain temperature but that it is surely absurd to hold that my belief that the Earth is not flat is at a certain temperature.

Identity theorists replied by arguing that our talk about mental states is, from a logical point of view, misleading. We talk as if mental states involved relations to mental objects. We say, for example, 'I have a headache', and this apparently has the same logical structure as 'I have a car': in both cases we seem to be asserting a relation between a person, me, and an object – a headache in one case, a car in the other. However, as identity theorists noted, cars are very different from headaches: cars can exist without their owners (if I die suddenly, my car will go on existing), but headaches cannot exist independently of being experienced (if I die, any headache of mine necessarily dies with me). Headaches, and mental states in general, are necessarily someone's. In consequence, they argued, we should think of headaches in the way we think of limps: limps are not things we have when we limp. When I say that I have a limp, I am simply saying that I limp; similarly, to say that I have a headache is to say that my head aches. Attributing properties to aches and limps is really attributing properties to ach*ings* and limp*ings*. To have a bad limp is to limp badly, and to have a winning smile is to smile winningly; likewise, to have a bad headache is to have a head that aches badly (see MENTAL STATES, ADVERBIAL THEORY OF). Strictly speaking, there are no mental objects, and so, in particular, no after-images to be yellow and in front of faces, and no itches to be in backs; there are experiences of having after-images and of having one's back itching. These experiences are not yellow, not in front of us or in our backs, and so the fact that brain states are not yellow, not in front of us and not in our backs is no objection to the identity theorist's claim that these experiences are identical with brain states.

The discussion of belief followed a different course. There is an important distinction between my believing something, my state of belief, and what I believe. My believing that there is a tiger before me is, most likely, caused by seeing a tiger and is a state of mine, whereas what I believe – that there is a tiger before me, the *proposition* believed, as it is often put (see PROPOSITIONAL ATTITUDES) – is not caused by my seeing the tiger and is not a state of mine. Again, there is my belief that the Earth is not flat, thought of as a state of mine that causes me, say, to reassure a traveller that they do not have to worry about falling off the edge, and there is the proposition that the Earth is not flat, which is *what* I accept. Now, the identity theory is not a view about the objects of belief, the propositions; it restricts itself to claiming that the state of believing is a state of the brain. And, identity theorists argued, although it would be absurd to hold that the objects of belief are at a certain temperature, it is not absurd to hold that the believings are.

Finally, some philosophers objected that the behaviour associated with having a mind, and in particular, that associated with intelligence, rationality and free action, displays a flexibility and sophistication incompatible with a purely material etiology. There are complex issues here, but we can note two serious problems for this objection. First, computers have enlarged our conception of the behavioural flexibility and sophistication compatible with a purely material etiology; and, second, it is hard to see how having an *immaterial* etiology would make any difference to the conceptual issues at stake (and, of course, quantum mechanics has broken the tie between having a material etiology and being determined).

3   Qualia

There was, however, one early objection to the identity theory that proved harder to dismiss. It concerns a perennial problem in the philosophy of mind: the nature of conscious experience and the sensuous side of psychology. But first, some stage setting.

The identity theory of mind is typically seen as part of the programme of giving a purely naturalistic or physicalistic view of the mind (see MATERIALISM IN THE PHILOSOPHY OF MIND). It is not a species of dual attribute theory of mind, according to which, although mental states are brain states they are brain states with special, non-physical properties, properties quite distinct from the kinds of properties neuroscience in particular, and the physical sciences in general, might attribute to them. The problem with dual attribute theories is that the question of how, in the light of what science is teaching us about the

physical nature of the causation of behaviour, these non-physical properties could be causally relevant to behaviour seems just as pressing as the question, raised earlier, of how non-physical states could be causally relevant to behaviour. In consequence, most identity theorists see their theory as a purely naturalistic account of the mind: the denial of 'spooky' properties or attributes is as much part of the theory as the denial of 'spooky' entities or states.

The perennial objection is that the identity theory, when seen, as it should be, as part of a purely naturalistic view of the mind, leaves out the nature of conscious mental experience, the phenomenal side of psychology. We distinguish those mental states that are not associated with a characteristic 'feel' from those that are. Paradigmatic examples are belief, on the non-sensuous side, and bodily sensations and sensory perceptions, on the sensuous side. My belief that the world is round does not have a characteristic conscious feel available to introspective awareness; my itch and my sensing of a red sunset do. But, runs the objection, no amount of neurophysiological information about our brains tells us what it is like to itch, see a sunset, or smell a rose. Protagonists of this objection often use the term 'qualia' ('quale' is the singular) for the special properties that they insist that the identity theory leaves out of account. Typically, they hold that these qualia are epiphenomenal features. They avoid the implausibility of denying that pains and sensings of red *per se* are causally inefficacious but acknowledge that they have to allow that the *distinctive feel* of pains and sensings of red is causally irrelevant (see QUALIA).

4   Functionalism and the identity theory

When identity theorists first discussed the qualia objection they urged that when we itch, smell a rose, and quite generally when we are in a mental state, we are not introspectively aware of the intrinsic nature of the mental state. For they granted, as we noted earlier, that mental states do not present themselves to us as states of the brain. The identity theorists held that what happens when we introspect is that we are aware of highly relational properties of our mental states, properties like being like what goes on in me when a pin is stuck in me (in the case of pain), being like what goes on in me when I see blood and geranium petals (in the case of sensing red), and being of a kind apt for the production of scratching behaviour (in the case of itches). In bringing relational properties into the picture, the early identity theorists can be seen as precursors of functionalist theories of mind. For functionalism is a theory according to which what makes something the mental state it is is a highly relational feature of it, that feature known as its functional role.

According to functionalism, we can think of mental states as causal intermediaries between inputs from the environment, outputs in the form of behavioural responses, and other mental states. Pain, for instance, is an internal state that is typically caused by bodily damage, and typically causes the desire that it itself cease along with behavioural responses that tend to minimize the damage. The perception that there is coffee in front of me is an internal state typically caused by coffee in front of me, which in turn causes belief that there is coffee in front of me, and this belief, when combined with desire for coffee, typically causes movement towards the coffee. Mental states are, that is, specified in terms of their place in a huge network of interlocking states (of which we have just described a tiny fragment) (see FUNCTIONALISM). Our concern here is with the implications of this general approach for the identity theory.

Functionalism can be, and often is, regarded as entirely consonant with the identity theory, being indeed a good way of arguing for it; or functionalism can be, and often is, regarded as a major objection to the identity theory. It all depends on the kind of identity theory.

If mental states are defined by their place in a network, then the question of what some given mental state *is* comes down to the question of what state occupies the relevant place in the network. An analogy: money can be defined in terms of a characteristic functional role, a role we are all only too familiar with through our knowledge of what you can do if you have money, and cannot do if you do not have money. In consequence, the question of what money is is the question of what plays, or occupies, the money-functional role, be it paper notes, coins, cowrie shells, or whatever. But, identity theorists observe, by far the most plausible candidates for what play the functional roles associated with mental states are various states of the brain. Thus, functionalism gives us a simple argument for the identity theory of the following structure: pain = what plays the pain-role; what plays the pain-role = a state of the brain (say, C-fibres firing); therefore, pain = C-fibres firing. And likewise for all the mental states. Identity theorists who see the identity theory as a natural offshoot of functionalism, often refer to the identity theory as 'central state materialism'.

Approaching the identity theory through functionalism commits identity theorists to an anti-essentialist theory of mind. For the brain state that occupies the pain-role and so is, according to them, pain, might not have done so, and so might not have been pain.

And the same goes for all mental states. Early expositions of the identity theory made this point by insisting that the identity of pain with, say, C-fibres firing was a *contingent* identity, and drew an analogy in this regard with the scientific identities we mentioned before. However, at least some of these identities are arguably necessarily true. It is arguable that water is necessarily H_2O. Certainly, we had to discover the identity of water and H_2O by empirical investigation, which makes it an a posteriori matter, but what we discovered was an essential feature of water. However, the identity theory must hold that the identities it posits are contingent. They are like the identity of the President of the United States in 1997 with Bill Clinton, which is contingent because that which occupies the role definitive of being President in 1997 is a contingent matter. (Dole was swimming against an economic tide, not a logical one.)

Although functionalism is a good way of arguing for the identity theory, it is a major objection to one kind of identity theory. We noted that identity theorists appeal to scientific identities in explaining and introducing their theory. These identities concern kinds or *types*. When scientists tell us that lightning is an electrical discharge, they are not merely telling us that the instance or *token* of lightning we saw last night is an instance or token of an electrical discharge; they are telling us, in addition, about what kind of happening lightning in general is. Again, the claim that temperature is mean molecular kinetic energy is a claim about kinds or types; it tells us what the property of temperature (in gases, anyway) is – namely, mean molecular kinetic energy. This suggests that we should think of the (mind-brain) identity theory as a type-type identity theory. Moreover, the theorists' favourite illustration – 'Pain = C-fibres firing' – is a type-type identity statement.

The problem is that different types of state might occupy the pain-role in different creatures. Perhaps it is C-fibres firing in humans but D-fibres firing in dolphins. But dolphins with their D-fibres firing would then be just as much in pain as we are when our C-fibres are firing. It is the role occupied, not the occupier, that matters for being in pain according to functionalism. And the point is independently plausible. We feel sorry for dolphins that exhibit all the signs of pain despite not knowing in any detail how intrinsically alike our and their brains are. But the identity theorist cannot allow both that pain = C-fibres firing, and that pain = D-fibres firing. That would, by the transitivity of identity, lead to the false contention that C-fibres firing = D-fibres firing.

Two responses are possible. Identity theorists can retreat to a token-token identity theory. Each and every token or instance of mental state M is some token brain state, but mental types are not brain types, being instead functional types. Alternatively, they can allow that the identities between mental types and brain types may need to be restricted. Think again of the example of money. Although different types of things are money in different societies, we can make true identity claims about the types of things that are money in the different societies. For instance, money in our society = notes and coins produced by the mint, whereas money in early Polynesian society = cowrie shells (or whatever). Similarly, although temperature in gases = mean molecular kinetic energy, in substances of which the molecules do not move freely it is something else. In the same way, if indeed it is C-fibres in us but D-fibres in dolphins that play the pain-role, then identity theorists must restrict themselves to 'Pain in humans = C-fibres firing' and 'Pain in dolphins = D-fibres firing'. The question of what humans in pain and dolphins in pain have in common would remain, of course, for they would not *ex hypothesi* share the same kind of brain state. And the identity theorists' answer must be that what they would have in common would be that each has a state inside them playing the pain-role, although not the same state.

See also: REDUCTIONISM IN THE PHILOSOPHY OF MIND

References and further reading

Armstrong, D. M. (1968) *A Materialist Theory of the Mind*, London: Routledge & Kegan Paul. (Classic presentation of the 'central state' version of the identity theory, combined with detailed discussions of alternative theories and analyses of various key mental concepts.)

Borst, C. V. (ed.) (1970) *The Mind/Brain Identity Theory*, London: Macmillan. (Useful collection of articles for and against the identity theory.)

Jackson, F., Pargetter, R. and Prior, E. (1982) 'Functionalism and Type-Type Identity Theories', *Philosophical Studies* 42: 209–25. (Detailed discussion of the choice between type-type and token-token identity theories from a functionalist perspective.)

Lewis, D. (1972) 'Psychophysical and Theoretical Identifications', *Australasian Journal of Philosophy* 50: 249–58. (Presents the identity theory in the context of a general and powerful treatment of theoretical identification in general.)

Rosenthal, D.M. (ed.) (1991) *The Nature of Mind*, London: Oxford University Press. (Large collection of important articles and extracts from books covering the philosophy of mind in general. Contains a comprehensive bibliography.)

* Smart, J.J.C. (1959) 'Sensations and Brain Processes', *Philosophical Review* LXVIII: 141–56. (Classic early statement of the identity theory.)

FRANK JACKSON

MIND, INDIAN PHILOSOPHY OF

Despite the enormous complexity of the Indian philosophical tradition, all the different schools developed within a common worldview mapped out by the three ideas of saṃsāra, karma *and* mokṣa *(or* nirvāṇa *in the case of Buddhism). This soteriological context, which informs much of Indian philosophy, is of particular importance for the philosophy of mind, giving it a distinctive character unparalleled in the Western tradition. Speculations about the nature of mind originated in Upaniṣadic teachings that salvific knowledge comes from looking inwards. We see in the earlier Upaniṣads (from about the eighth to the fifth centuries* BC*) a careful classification of normal states of consciousness, but eventually liberation from the cycle of rebirth and suffering was framed in terms of the individual's ability to manipulate and ultimately transcend such states through the pursuit of a set of ascetic practices known as yoga. These ascetic practices led to a liberating state of consciousness which the Upaniṣads equated with the realization of a transcendental Self known as the* ātman. *With the development of Buddhist thought in India (from the fifth century* BC*), the philosophical tradition became divided. Generally, Buddhist schools of thought were united in their opposition to the existence of the* ātman, *whereas the so-called orthodox Hindu schools continued to favour the Upaniṣadic position. The practical quest for liberation from suffering remained central, however, to the entire philosophical tradition as the Upaniṣads gave way to a more systematic philosophizing. Subsequently, Buddhists and non-Buddhists alike continued to accept the results of meditative practice as being a legitimate concern for philosophical speculation. A dialectical relationship between theory and practice meant that philosophical disagreements created not just differences in the interpretation of meditative experiences, but also shaped such practices themselves in different ways. The apparent empirical vein of the Upaniṣads was also continued in all schools of thought, leading to richer and more detailed phenomenological classifications of experience. This* *rich ontological landscape is what gives Indian philosophy of mind its distinctive character.*

1   Philosophy of mind in the Upaniṣads

The Upaniṣads viewed the human individual as a composite of psychological and physical elements. Upaniṣadic thinkers set themselves the task of sifting through this psychophysical complexity in the belief that the solution to human suffering lay in some aspect of human existence itself. The urgency and practical nature of this project yielded a rich variety of classificatory schemes as one solution was discarded in favour of another. The Bṛhadāraṇyaka Upaniṣad, for example, distinguishes three generically different types of consciousness in the experiential life of all individuals. The first of these, the waking state, is characterized by pain and pleasure and its content is determined by the external world. It provides the raw materials for the second state, that of dreaming. Dreaming, however, differs from wakefulness, for in dreams we assume a greater power to construct our own worlds. Yet dreaming still subjects us to pain and pleasure and is viewed as a transition to the third state, that of deep sleep. This third state is characterized by serenity and lack of desire, and, being without content, is also a state in which the distinction between subject and object disappears. This Upaniṣadic classification of experience is thus both descriptive and hierarchical, ranking the three states of consciousness against the requirements of what a liberatory state should be. This tripartite division of everyday experience remained common currency in subsequent philosophy of mind but it was discarded as a solution to the problem of endless rebirth into a world of suffering. The Māṇḍūkya Upaniṣad thus extends the threefold classification to a fourfold classification of experience with the addition of a fourth, liberatory, state of consciousness (*turīya*). This fourth state is a specialized state of consciousness which lies beyond the everyday experience of the individual and is attainable only on the basis of yogic techniques developed for that purpose.

Parallel to the phenomenological analysis, the Upaniṣads also analysed the individual in terms of constituent elements. Many such schemes are to be found in the Upaniṣads, but perhaps the most important for later thought is that presented in the Kaṭha Upaniṣad. This uses an image of a horse-drawn chariot to present the human individual as a composite of different elements in a hierarchical relationship to each other. The horses are likened to the senses (*indriya*), the reins to the mind (*manas*), the charioteer to the intellect (*buddhi*), the chariot to the body (*śarīra*), and the passenger riding in the chariot is the Self (*ātman*). Just as a charioteer needs to gain control of his horses using the reins, so too an individual aspiring to liberation must gain control of the senses using the mental disciplines of *yoga*.

Whether it be in positing a fourth state of consciousness, or in viewing the *ātman* as a passenger in the chariot rather than as the charioteer, it is clear that Upaniṣadic thinkers sought to separate the agent of normal phenomenal experience from the transcendental *ātman*. Indeed, the very failure to distinguish between these two selves is at the root of human suffering, and liberation from rebirth demands that the individual ultimately negate and transcend empirical individuality.

Upaniṣadic thought is thus of necessity dualist in nature. If liberation is to enable the individual to transcend the spatiotemporal world, then there must be some aspect of the individual's existence which lies beyond such a world. On the other hand, if liberation is to be attainable, then it must be amenable to individual experience. There is a tension here between the need to keep these two domains apart and the need to bring them together at some point. It was left to later schools of thought to wrestle in a more systematic way with the consequences of this Upaniṣadic worldview. For example, because of its immutability, the *ātman* is not subject to rebirth. This demands an explanation of the precise mechanism of rebirth. What is it that gets reborn? It also makes the very notion of liberation itself fraught with difficulty. Liberation cannot simply be a liberation of the *ātman* because of course the *ātman* must already lie beyond the spatiotemporal world. Who then is liberated and how? The Sāṅkhya-Yoga and Advaita Vedānta schools gave particular attention to solving the problems of their Upaniṣadic legacy and, in doing so, needed to address the question of the relationship between the *ātman* and the empirical individual (see SĀṄKHYA §§2–3, 6; VEDĀNTA §§1–3).

The dualism of Upaniṣadic thought is distinct from the dualism between the mind and the body in Western philosophy. In Cartesian dualism, the two domains that are sharply distinguished are the mental and the physical. While Indian philosophers certainly recognized such a distinction, they were more impressed by what the mental and the physical had in common, namely that they were both thought to be causally conditioned, with cause preceding effect in a regular, predictable way. Indeed, it was the regular, predictable nature of the mind that enabled spiritual practitioners to manipulate it to their desired goal of quiescence, once the causal mechanisms were understood. Later schools of thought, therefore, developed a rich understanding of the empirical workings of the mind. This is seen in the more complex classificatory schemes that Indian philosophers developed. In the later Yoga school, for example, the fourth state of consciousness described in the Māṇḍūkya Upaniṣad becomes a complex of eight different types of meditative experience. The sharpest distinction arising from Upaniṣadic thought occurs in the opposition of the ātman to both the mental and the physical, inasmuch as the latter are firmly located in the empirical world.

A second important difference between the Cartesian model of the mind and that developed by orthodox Indian philosophers is the distinction the latter make between the ātman and the 'I' given in ordinary experience. As one of the psychophysical elements of the individual, the 'I' is just another temporary causally conditioned aspect of the individual with no ultimate value. Again, it was left to later systems of thought to work out the exact nature of the relationship between the ātman and the empirical sense of individuality. In Upaniṣadic and subsequent philosophy of mind, there is no transcendental ego in the Cartesian sense, only a transcendental impersonal Self.

2 Philosophy of mind in early Buddhism

Buddhism inherited and propagated the Upaniṣadic view of the human individual as a composite of psychological and physical elements, and the scholasticism of early Buddhist thought presents us with a huge variety of such classifications. Buddhism, however, abandoned the Upaniṣadic idea of an enduring Self. Indeed, the very purpose of Buddhist classifications was meant to reveal the absence of any such entity. In an early post-canonical Buddhist text, the *Milindapañha* (Questions of Milinda), the monk Nāgasena prompts King Milinda towards the correct view. Milinda is led, through a series of questions, to realize that the term 'chariot' designates nothing more than a pole, axle, set of wheels, chariot body, bannerstaff, goad and pair of reins. Similarly, the term 'Nāgasena' is but a way of designating a collection of ever-changing physical and psychological elements. The passenger who rides in the chariot of the Kaṭha Upaniṣad is here conspicuous by his absence. There is no permanent substratum underlying our existence.

A personal proper name thus refers to a stream of causally connected elements. As Buddhist thought developed, philosophers of all schools presented increasingly detailed and distinctive descriptions and classifications of these elements. Prevalent in these schemas is a broad distinction between those elements that are mental and those that are physical. This is seen in the distinction made in the early Buddhist texts between name (*nāma*) and form (*rūpa*), and also in the widely influential classification of the elements into five categories (*skandha*). This latter classification, which purported to be an exhaustive description of the elements, divided them into five different types: physical form (*rūpa*), sensation (*vedanā*), conceptualization (*saṃjñā*), dispositions (*saṃskāra*) and consciousness (*vijñāna*). Four of the five categories relate to different types of mental events, indicating the importance of the latter, even though Buddhist philosophers from the different schools understood these categories somewhat differently.

It is important to understand exactly what Buddhists wished to deny with their 'no-self' theory (*anātma-vāda*) and this cannot be done without developing an adequate understanding of the complexity of Buddhist practice and the functions of different types of Buddhist texts. The no-self theory did not prohibit our usual ways of talking about the self in literature of a narrative and ethical nature. Where the theory is important is in the more technical, philosophical literature, where any talk of a permanent Self is prohibited by Buddhist ontology (see BUDDHIST PHILOSOPHY, INDIAN §5; BUDDHIST CONCEPT OF EMPTINESS §1). In the great systematic treatises of Buddhism, such as the fifth-century Vaibhāṣika text, the *Abhidharmakośa* (Treasury of Metaphysics), we see the attempt to construct a comprehensive Buddhist ontology in which the objects of conventional discourse will disappear. VASUBANDHU, its author, construes ultimate reality in terms of seventy-five different types of unique, self-sufficient, momentary particulars known as *dharmas* (see BUDDHISM, ĀBHIDHARMIKA SCHOOLS OF).

The no-self theory was also important in terms of its influence on meditational practice, since theory and practice were not seen as two separate activities. The Buddhist doctrine itself was an important focus for one type of meditational practice, in which the aim was to augment a mere intellectual understanding of the doctrine with an actual change in the cognitive and perceptual apparatus of the practitioner by internalizing the doctrinal categories of thought. For example, the *dharma* analysis of the Vaibhāṣika system, as well as being an intellectual enterprise, was also linked to meditational practices aimed at deconstructing the categories of everyday experience. The Buddhist rejection of the ātman also meant that Buddhism did not equate meditational states of consciousness with the realization of a liberatory Self.

Although valuable, meditational states were still causally conditioned, and hence temporary, states of existence. As such, they could not be the final solution to the problem of suffering.

Despite their differences, it should be remembered that Buddhism and Upaniṣadic thought were both responses to a common problem, the suffering of the individual caught up in an endless round of rebirth. Buddhism rejected the idea of an enduring Self largely on the grounds that, as an idea, it was unhelpful in freeing the individual from suffering. Both traditions viewed empirical individuality as problematic. Buddhist philosophers did not frame the no-self theory as a challenge to the idea of rebirth. Rather, they themselves were challenged to address the intellectual problems that arose once these two ideas were brought together. If the theory could not be reconciled with the belief in rebirth, then so much the worse for the no-self theory. As with Upaniṣadic thought, it was left for later systematic philosophy to address some of these questions.

3 Personal identity in Indian philosophy of mind

In the Western analytic tradition, personal identity and the mind–body problem have been central and related questions in the philosophy of mind. In the context of Indian philosophy of mind, parallel questions do arise, but in such a different context that the cross-cultural philosopher cannot make any simple comparisons. Personal identity is largely problematic in Indian philosophy because of the mistaken value individuals attach to it. For both Buddhist and non-Buddhist alike, any account of personal identity must at the same time reveal its lack of absolute value for that individual. This point is especially important for the correct interpretation of karma and rebirth doctrines, which should not necessarily be interpreted as doctrines requiring the personal survival of bodily death. Buddhist philosophers, for example, did have a problem reconciling their no-self view with the belief that actions performed in one life can have repercussions in another, but it was largely a problem of explaining how the past can be causally efficacious in the present. This was not so much a problem of making sense of the notion of moral responsibility in the absence of either bodily or memory continuity, but, rather, was a mechanistic problem of bringing a cause and its temporally distant effect together. This became a particularly intractable problem given the Buddhist metaphysics of constant change and the Buddhist view of consciousness as being intentional in nature. Together these two ideas could lead to the view that an individual is but a flux of events conditioned only by the present. The 'warehouse consciousness' (*ālaya-vijñāna*) posited by the Yogācāra school of Buddhism was one attempt to solve this problem. Although momentary in nature, the warehouse consciousness was nonintentional and thus provided a locus for 'karmic seeds' until they were ripe for maturation (see BUDDHISM, YOGĀCĀRA SCHOOL OF §§6–8).

Some Western philosophers have believed that a sense of self is given directly as a separate content of our experience. The word for 'I' in Indian philosophy is *ahaṃkāra*, meaning literally 'I-maker'. This indicates a view common to both Buddhist and non-Buddhist philosophers, that the 'I' is made on the basis of something else. Indian philosophers of mind were interested in discovering how experience gives rise to this sense of 'I'. The word *ahaṃkāra* also indicates the view that it is through our constant utterances of 'I' or 'this is mine' that we solidify our sense of empirical individuality. Thus even where non-Buddhist philosophers – for example, in the Advaita Vedānta school – used arguments strikingly similar to the *cogito ergo sum* argument of Descartes, indicating that the self really is a genuine datum of experience, they would want to add that the self given by such an argument is the self of waking consciousness, and hence a necessarily limited self in relation to the *ātman*. Philosophers of the Advaita Vedānta school were concerned to develop an understanding of the relationship between the *ātman* and the self as given in the schema of three generically different kinds of consciousness inherited from the Upaniṣads (waking, dreaming, deep sleep). Some philosophers of the Advaita Vedānta school viewed the empirical self as a distorted reflection of the *ātman*, while others viewed it as the result of limitations being placed upon the *ātman*. Ignorance (*avidyā*) is in each case responsible for the misperception (see MONISM, INDIAN §§1–2).

Buddhist philosophers were resolute in their resistance to converting the sense of 'I' given in empirical experience into any kind of theoretical or absolute reality. Consciousness is a changing, conditioned phenomenon and there is no self beyond any given moment of conscious experience. Thus, for example, the *dharma* theory of the Vaibhāṣika tradition was also a meditational technique enabling practitioners to view their experience in impersonal rather than subjective terms.

4 The mental and the physical in Indian philosophy of mind

While Indian philosophers certainly recognized the distinction between the mental and the physical, both phenomenologically and often ontologically, this difference did not become of such overriding importance as it did in Western philosophy of mind. Rather, the different schools of thought focused on the complex task of mapping out the network of causes underlying the occurrence of any individual mental event, which could be the product of a complex which might include both mental and physical causes. Perceptual events, for example, were generally viewed as the result of a causal interaction involving both mental and physical causes. Six sense organs were acknowledged by Indian philosophers, those of vision, hearing, smell, taste, touch and the mind. The mind (*manas*) was classified along with other sense organs and was responsible for inner cognition, as well as being able to coordinate the other sense organs (see SENSE PERCEPTION, INDIAN VIEWS OF §§1–2). Where the schools differed in their understanding of perception, it was largely on account of differences in their wider metaphysical beliefs concerning the status of physical objects and the existence of an external world. There would be no uniform response from Indian philosophers to the Lockean proposition that it is impossible to perceive without perceiving that one perceives. This was a point of considerable contention between the different schools. It was agreed, however, that waking consciousness was intentional in nature: being awake meant being awake to something. Despite the many differences between the schools and the complexity of the tradition, Indian philosophers were united in their characterization of consciousness as a complex continuum of causally conditioned mental events fuelled by the inherent restlessness of the human condition. Their need to understand the principles governing this continuum lay at the heart of Indian philosophy of mind.

See also: AWARENESS IN INDIAN THOUGHT; KARMA AND REBIRTH, INDIAN CONCEPTIONS OF; MATTER, INDIAN CONCEPTIONS OF §3; SELF, INDIAN THEORIES OF; XIN (HEART-AND-MIND)

References and further reading

Biardeau, M. (1965) 'Ahaṃkāra in the Upaniṣads', *Contributions to Indian Sociology* 8. (A discussion of the important distinction between the Self (*ātman*) and the ego principle (*ahaṃkāra*) in the Upaniṣads.)

Collins, S. (1982) *Selfless Persons*, Cambridge: Cambridge University Press. (Describes in rich detail the Buddhist notion of a person in the light of its no-self theory.)

Deutsch, E. (1969) *Advaita Vedānta: A Philosophical Reconstruction*, Honolulu, HI: University of Hawaii Press. (A good philosophical account of this important orthodox school of Indian philosophy, with a chapter on the place of the Self in the overall system.)

Griffiths, P. (1986) *On Being Mindless: Buddhist Meditation And The Mind–Body Problem*, La Salle, IL: Open Court. (In discussing the problems raised by a particular type of Buddhist meditative experience, the attainment of cessation, Griffiths also succeeds in giving a comprehensive account of Buddhist theories of the mind.)

Matilal, B.K. (1986) *Perception: An Essay on Classical Indian Theories of Knowledge*, Oxford: Clarendon Press. (A comprehensive account of theories of perception and consciousness in relation to the epistemological theories of the different schools of Indian philosophy.)

* *Milindapañha* (*c.*150 BC), trans. I.B. Horner, *Milinda's Questions*, Sacred Books of the Buddhists 22–3, London: Pali Text Society. (A good translation of an important early Theravāda text.)

* Vasubandhu (5th century) *Abhidharmakośa*, ed. D. Śāstri, *Abhidharmakośa and Bhāṣya of Acārya Vasubandhu with Sphuṭārthā Commentary of Acārya Yaśomitra*, Bauddha Bharati Series 5–8, Varanasi: Bauddha Bharati, 1970–3; repr. 1981, 2 vols. (A small portion of the *Abhidharmakośabhāṣya* is translated as Appendix B in Griffiths 1986.)

JOY LAINE

MIND, MATERIALISM IN THE PHILOSOPHY OF

see MATERIALISM IN THE PHILOSOPHY OF MIND

MIND, MODULARITY OF

see MODULARITY OF MIND

MIND, PHILOSOPHY OF

'Philosophy of mind', and 'philosophy of psychology' are two terms for the same general area of philosophical inquiry: the nature of mental phenomena and their connection with behaviour and, in more recent discussions, the brain.

Much work in this area reflects a revolution in psychology that began mid-century. Before then, largely in reaction to traditional claims about the mind being non-physical (see DUALISM; DESCARTES), many thought that a scientific psychology should avoid talk of 'private' mental states. Investigation of such states had seemed to be based on unreliable introspection (see INTROSPECTION, PSYCHOLOGY OF), not subject to independent checking (see PRIVATE LANGUAGE ARGUMENT), and to invite dubious ideas of telepathy (see PARAPSYCHOLOGY). Consequently, psychologists like B.F. SKINNER and J. B. Watson, and philosophers like W.V. QUINE and GILBERT RYLE argued that scientific psychology should confine itself to studying publicly observable relations between stimuli and responses (see BEHAVIOURISM, METHODOLOGICAL AND SCIENTIFIC; BEHAVIOURISM, ANALYTIC).

However, in the late 1950s, several developments began to change all this: (i) The experiments behaviourists themselves ran on animals tended to refute behaviouristic hypotheses, suggesting that the behaviour of even rats had to be understood in terms of mental states (see LEARNING; ANIMAL LANGUAGE AND THOUGHT). (ii) The linguist NOAM CHOMSKY drew attention to the surprising complexity of the natural languages that children effortlessly learn, and proposed ways of explaining this complexity in terms of largely unconscious mental phenomena. (iii) The revolutionary work of ALAN TURING (see TURING MACHINES) led to the development of the modern digital computer. This seemed to offer the prospect of creating ARTIFICIAL INTELLIGENCE, and also of providing empirically testable models of intelligent processes in both humans and animals. (iv) Philosophers came to appreciate the virtues of realism, as opposed to instrumentalism, about theoretical entities in general.

1 Functionalism and the computational theory of mind

These developments led to the emergence in the 1970s of the loose federation of disciplines called 'cognitive science', which brought together research from, for example, psychology, linguistics, computer science, neuroscience and a number of sub-areas of philosophy, such as logic, the philosophy of language, and action theory. In philosophy of mind, these developments led to FUNCTIONALISM, according to which mental states are to be characterized in terms of relations they bear among themselves and to inputs and outputs, for example, mediating perception and action in the way that belief and desire characteristically seem to do. The traditional problem of OTHER MINDS then became an exercise in inferring from behaviour to the nature of internal causal intermediaries.

This focus on functional organization brought with it the possibility of multiple realizations: if all that is essential to mental states are the roles they play in a system, then, in principle, mental states, and so minds, could be composed of (or 'realized' by) different substances: some minds might be carbon-based like ours, some might be computer 'brains' in robots of the future, and some might be silicon-based, as in some science fiction stories about 'Martians'. These differences might also cause the minds to be organized in different ways at different levels, an idea that has encouraged the co-existence of the many different disciplines of cognitive science, each studying the mind at often different levels of explanation.

Functionalism has played an important role in debates over the metaphysics of mind. Some see it as a way of avoiding DUALISM and arguing for a version of materialism known as the identity theory of mind (see MIND, IDENTITY THEORY OF). They argue that if mental states play distinctive functional roles, to identify mental states we simply need to find the states that play those roles, which are, almost certainly, various states of the brain. Here we must distinguish identifying mental state tokens with brain state tokens, from identifying mental types with brain types (see TYPE/TOKEN DISTINCTION). Many argue that multiple realizability shows it would be a mistake to identify any particular kind or type of mental phenomenon with a specific type of physical phenomenon (for example, depression with the depletion of norepinepherine in a certain area of the brain). For if depression is a multiply realized functional state, then it will not be identical with any particular type of physical phenomenon: different instances, or tokens, of depression might be identical with tokens of ever different types of physical phenomena (norepinephrine deletion in humans, too little silicon activation in a Martian). Indeed, a functionalist could allow (although few take this seriously) that there might be ghosts who realize the right functional organization in some special dualistic substance. However, some identity theorists insist that at least some mental state types – they often focus on states like pain and the taste of pineapple, states with QUALIA (see also the discussion below) – ought to be identified with particular brain state types, in somewhat the way that lightning is identified with electrical discharge, or water with H_2O. They typically think of these identifications as necessary a posteriori.

An important example of a functionalist theory, one that has come to dominate much research in cognitive science, is the computational theory of mind (see MIND, COMPUTATIONAL THEORY OF), according to which mental states are either identified with, or closely linked to, the computational states of a computer. There have been three main versions of this theory, corresponding to three main proposals about the mind's COGNITIVE ARCHITECTURE. According to the 'classical' theory, particularly associated with JERRY FODOR, the computations take place over representations that possess the kind of logical, syntactic structure captured in standard logical form: representations in a so-called LANGUAGE OF THOUGHT, encoded in our brains. A second proposal, sometimes inspired by F. P. RAMSEY's view that beliefs are maps by which we steer (see BELIEF), emphasizes the possible role in reasoning of maps and mental IMAGERY. A third, recently much-discussed proposal is CONNECTIONISM, which denies that there are any structured representations at all: the mind/brain consists rather of a vast network of nodes whose different and variable excitation levels explain intelligent LEARNING. This approach has aroused interest especially among those wary of positing much 'hidden' mental structure not evident in ordinary behaviour (see LUDWIG WITTGENSTEIN §3 and DANIEL DENNETT).

The areas that lend themselves most naturally to a computational theory are those associated with logic, common sense and practical reasoning, and natural language syntax (see COMMON-SENSE REASONING, THEORIES OF; RATIONALITY, PRACTICAL; SYNTAX); and research on these topics in psychology and ARTIFICIAL INTELLIGENCE has become deeply intertwined with philosophy (see RATIONALITY OF BELIEF; SEMANTICS; LANGUAGE, PHILOSOPHY OF).

A particularly fruitful application of computational theories has been to VISION. Early work in GESTALT PSYCHOLOGY uncovered a number of striking perceptual illusions that demonstrated ways in which the mind structures perceptual experience, and the pioneering work of the psychologist, David Marr, suggested that we might capture these structuring effects computationally. The idea that perception was highly cognitive, along with the functionalist picture that specifies a mental state by its place in a network, led many to holistic conceptions of mind and meaning, according to which parts of a person's thought and experience cannot be understood apart from the person's entire cognitive system (see HOLISM: MENTAL AND SEMANTIC; SEMANTICS, CONCEPTUAL ROLE).

However, this view has been challenged recently by work of JERRY FODOR. He has argued that perceptual systems are 'modules', whose processing is 'informationally encapsulated' and hence isolatable from the effects of the states of the central cognitive system (see MODULARITY OF MIND). He has also proposed accounts of meaning that treat it as a local (or 'atomistic') property to be understood in terms of certain kinds of causal dependence between states of the brain and the world (see SEMANTICS, INFORMATIONAL). Others have argued further that PERCEPTION, although contentful, is also importantly non-conceptual, as when one sees a square shape as a diamond but is unable to say wherein the essential difference between a square and a diamond shape consists (see CONTENT, NON-CONCEPTUAL).

2 Mind and meaning

As these last issues indicate, any theory of the mind must face the hard topic of meaning (see SEMANTICS). In the philosophies of mind and psychology, the issue is not primarily the meanings of expressions in natural language, but of how a state of the mind or brain can have meaning or content: what is it to believe, for example, that snow is white or hope that you will win. These latter states are examples of PROPOSITIONAL ATTITUDES: attitudes towards propositions such as that snow is white, or that you will win, that form the 'content' of the state of belief or hope. They raise the general issue of INTENTIONALITY, or how a mental state can be about things (for example, snow) and properties (for example, white), and, particularly, 'about' things that do not exist or will not happen, as when someone believes in Santa Claus or hopes in vain for victory.

There have been three main proposals about mental content. A state might possess a specific content: (i) by virtue of the role it plays in reasoning (see SEMANTICS: CONCEPTUAL ROLE); (ii) by virtue of certain causal and lawful relations the state bears to phenomena in the world (see SEMANTICS: INFORMATIONAL; FUNCTIONALISM); or (iii) by virtue of the function it plays in the evolution and biology of the organism (see SEMANTICS: TELEOLOGICAL; FUNCTIONAL EXPLANATION). Related to these proposals are traditional philosophical interests in CONCEPTS, although this latter topic raises complicating metaphysical concerns with UNIVERSALS, and epistemological concerns with A PRIORI knowledge.

Special problems are raised by indexical content, or the content of thoughts involving concepts expressed by, for example, 'I myself', 'here', 'now', 'this', and 'that' (see CONTENT, INDEXICAL; DEMONSTRATIVES AND INDEXICALS; PROPOSITIONAL ATTITUDES §3). Does the thought that it is hot here, had in Maryland, have the same content as the thought that it is hot here, had in Canberra? The conditions under which such thoughts are true obviously depends upon the external context – for example, the time and place – of the thinking.

This dependence on external context is thought by many to be a pervasive feature of content. Drawing on recent work on reference (see REFERENCE; PROPER

NAMES), Hilary PUTNAM and Tyler Burge have argued that what people think, believe and so on depends not only on how they are, but also upon features of their physical and social environment. This raises the important question of whether an organism's psychology can be understood in isolation from the external world it inhabits. Defenders of methodological individualism insist that it can be (see METHODOLOGICAL, INDIVIDUALISM); Putnam, Burge and their supporters that it can't. Some theorists respond to the debate by distinguishing between wide and narrow content: narrow content is what 'from the skin in' identical individuals would share across different environments, whereas wide content might vary from one environment to the next (see CONTENT: WIDE AND NARROW). These theorists then give distinctive roles to the two notions in theoretical psychology, although this is a matter of great controversy.

3 Alternatives to functionalism

Not everyone endorses functional and computational theories of mind. Some, influenced by RYLE and the later WITTGENSTEIN, think that such concern with literally inner processes of the brain betrays a fundamental misunderstanding of mental talk, which, they argue, rests largely on outward CRITERIA. Others think that computational processes lack the means of capturing the basic properties of CONSCIOUSNESS and INTENTIONALITY that are essential to most mental phenomena. JOHN SEARLE, in particular, regards his CHINESE ROOM ARGUMENT as a devastating objection to computational approaches. He thinks that mental phenomena should be understood not functionally, but directly in biological or physical terms.

The hardest challenge for functionalism is posed by QUALIA – the properties that distinguish pain, the look of red, the taste of pineapple, and so on, on the one hand, from mental states like belief and understanding on the other. (See also BODILY SENSATIONS; SENSE-DATA; PERCEPTION). Some argue that unnecessary problems are produced in this area by an excessive reification of inner experience, and recommend instead an adverbial theory of mental states (see MENTAL STATES, ADVERBIAL THEORY OF). However, some problems persist, and can be made vivid by considering the possibility of 'inverted qualia'. It seems that two people might have colour experiences that are the complements of one another (red for green, yellow for blue, etc.), even though their behaviour and functional organization are identical. This issue is explored in COLOUR AND QUALIA and leads inevitably to the hard problems of CONSCIOUSNESS: What is it? What things have it? How do we tell? What causal role, if any, does it play the world?

There is also an issue for functionalists over MENTAL CAUSATION. A principal reason why DUALISM has few adherents today is the problem of explaining how non-physical or non-natural phenomena can causally affect a physical world. And although some dualists retreat to EPIPHENOMENALISM, the view that mental phenomena are caused by, but do not themselves cause any physical phenomena, this is widely seen as implausible. However, functionalists also have a problem. Even though they can and do insist that functional states are realized physically, arguably the functional states *per se* do no causing; what does the causing would seem to be the underlying physical properties of the physical realization. So, although functionalists avoid giving causal roles to the 'non-natural', it seems they must allow that mental properties *per se* do no causing.

Although the view that the mind is a natural phenomenon is now widely accepted (principally because of the causal problem for dualism), what this implies is highly contentious. Some hold that it simply means that mental phenomena supervene on physical nature in the sense that there can be no mental difference without a physical difference (see SUPERVENIENCE OF THE MENTAL). DONALD DAVIDSON thinks this can be true without there being any strict laws connecting the physical and the mental (see ANOMALOUS MONISM). Others insist that a naturalist about the mind must reduce the mental to the physical in somewhat the way thermodynamics has been reduced to statistical mechanics, so delivering neat lawful biconditionals linking the mental and the physical (see REDUCTIONISM IN THE PHILOSOPHY OF MIND).

Much in this discussion turns on the status of FOLK PSYCHOLOGY, the theory of mind allegedly implicit in ordinary (folk) thought and talk about the mind. On one view, mental states are simply the states that fill the roles of this implicit theory, and the reduction consists in finding which internal physical states fill the roles and are, thereby, to be identified with the relevant mental states. However, defenders of ELIMINATIVISM, noting that any theory – especially a folk one – can turn out false, argue that we should take seriously the possibility that the mental states postulated by folk psychology do not exist, much as it turned out that there are no witches or phlogiston.

4 Issues in empirical psychology

Empirical psychology has figured in philosophy not only because its foundations have been discussed in the above ways, but also because some of its specific findings have been relevant to traditional philosophical claims. Thus, experiments on SPLIT BRAINS have undermined traditional conceptions of PERSONAL IDENTITY (see also MIND, BUNDLE THEORY OF), and research on the reliability of people's self-attribution of psychological states has cast doubts on introspection as a source of specially privileged knowledge about the mind. The work of FREUD on psychopathology (see MENTAL ILLNESS, CONCEPT OF; PSYCHOANALYSIS, POST-FREUDIAN; PSYCHOANALYSIS, METHODOLOGICAL ISSUES IN) and of CHOMSKY in linguistics, suggests that the states of most explanatory interest are not introspectively accessible (see KNOWLEDGE, TACIT; UNCONSCIOUS MENTAL STATES). Chomsky's ideas also seem to revive RATIONALISM's postulation of innate knowledge that was long thought to have been discredited by EMPIRICISM (see also NATIVISM; INNATE KNOWLEDGE; LANGUAGE, INNATENESS OF). And they have stimulated research beyond knowledge of grammar, into infant cognition (see COGNITION, INFANT) generally (some of which treats the MOLYNEUX PROBLEM of whether newly sighted people would be able to recognize shapes that they had previously only touched). Other questions about the basic categories in which people understand the world have benefited from work on how these categories are understood and evolve in childhood (see PIAGET, J; COGNITIVE DEVELOPMENT; MORAL DEVELOPMENT). A particularly important issue for the philosophy of mind concerns the origin of our mental concepts, a topic of lively current research (see MIND, CHILD'S THEORY OF) that affects our understanding of FOLK PSYCHOLOGY.

5 Philosophy of action

Whether or not it is ultimately vindicated by empirical research, folk psychology is a rich fund of distinctions that are important in human life. The examination of them has tended to focus on issues in the explanation of ACTION, and, in a related vein, on psychological issues relevant to ethics (see MORAL PSYCHOLOGY).

The traditional view of action, most famously advocated by DAVID HUME, is that an action needs both a desire and a belief. The desire provides the goal, and the belief the means of putatively achieving it (see also REASONS AND CAUSES; DESIRE; BELIEF). But what then is the role, if any, of INTENTION? Are intentions nothing more than some complex of belief and desire? And how, if at all, do we find a place in the Humean picture for the will? Is it something that can somehow act independently of beliefs and desires, or is it some kind of manifestation of them, some kind of 'all things considered' judgment that takes a person from dithering to action? (See WILL, THE.) Notoriously difficult questions in this regard concern whether there actually is anything as FREE WILL,

and how it is possible for a person to act against their better judgement, as they seem to do in cases of AKRASIA, or 'weakness of will'.

Beliefs and desires seem intimately connected with many other mental states. Belief about the past is of the essence of MEMORY. PERCEPTION delivers belief about how things are around one, and DREAMING seems to be the having of experiences during sleep akin to (rather fragmented) perceptions in the way they tend to make you believe that certain things are happening. Even emotions (see EMOTIONS, NATURE OF) and BODILY SENSATIONS seem to have belief and desire components: anger involves both a belief that one has been wronged and a desire to do something about it, and pain involves the belief that something is amiss and the desire that it stop. Much contemporary philosophy of mind and action is concerned with teasing out the relationship between beliefs and desires and various other mental states, although approaches in cognitive science often focus upon more computationally active states, such as: noticing, deciding, and 'on line' processes of reasoning.

See also: AKAN PHILOSOPHICAL PSYCHOLOGY; AWARENESS IN INDIAN THOUGHT; EMOTIONS, NATURE OF; IMAGINATION; JUNG, C.G.; MATERIALISM IN THE PHILOSOPHY OF MIND; MIND, INDIAN PHILOSOPHY OF; NEUTRAL MONISM; NOUS; PLEASURE; PSYCHOLOGY, THEORIES OF; SECONDARY QUALITIES; SELF-DECEPTION; VYGOTSKII, L.S.

References and further reading

Braddon-Mitchell, D. and Jackson, F. (1997) Philosophy of Mind and Cognition, Oxford: Blackwell. (Discusses most of the live positions in the philosophy of mind; sympathetic to analytical functionalism.)

Guttenplan, S. (ed.) (1994) A Companion to the Philosophy of Mind, Oxford: Blackwell. (Collection of substantial essays by some the best-known figures in the philosophy of mind.)

Rey, G. (1997) Contemporary Philosophy of Mind, Oxford: Blackwell. (Discusses most of the live positions in the philosophy of mind; sympathetic to the representational theory of mind.)

Smith, P. and Jones, O.R. (1986) The Philosophy of Mind, Cambridge: Cambridge University Press. (An excellent, elementary introduction to philosophy of mind and action, from the standpoint more of traditional philosophy than of cognitive science.)

FRANK JACKSON
GEORGES REY

MINDS, OTHER *see* OTHER MINDS

MIR DAMAD, MUHAMMAD BAQIR (d. 1631)

Mir Damad is primarily a gnostic philosopher, arguing that the activity of the mind makes possible the experience of spiritual visions, while visionary experience gives rise to rational thought. He brings together a variety of different traditions in Islamic philosophy, incorporating both the sort of philosophy advocated by Aristotle and its later development by the Neoplatonists, and combining them with the mystical views of Islamic thinkers. The principles of his thought are the backbone of the celebrated 'School of Isfahan', which developed this rich mixture of philosophical traditions even further. His approach to the analysis of being was a considerable extension to previous views on this subject, and enabled him to make important contributions to the notion of time. Mir Damad's philosophical style is characterized by a treatment of abstract concepts behind which lies the living experience of the mystic.

1 Life and philosophy of being
2 Philosophy of time
3 Philosophical style

1 Life and philosophy of being

Mir Burhan al-Din Muhammad Baqir Damad, whose poetic *nom de plume* was 'Ishraq' and who was also referred to as 'the Third Master' (after ARISTOTLE and AL-FARABI) was born into a distinguished religious family. Another honorific title by which Mir Damad has been known is Sayyid al-Afadil, 'Prince of the Most Learned'.

Mir Damad was born in Astarabad but grew up in Mashhad, the religious capital of Shi'i Persia. He received his early education there, and studied Ibn Sina's texts closely (see IBN SINA). Prior to coming to Isfahan during the reign of Shah 'Abbas, he also spent some time in Qazvin and Kashan. In Isfahan, Mir Damad continued his education, paying equal attention to rational and transmitted sciences. He died in AH 1041/AD 1631 when he fell ill on his way to Karbala, in the entourage of Shah Safi. He was buried in Najaf.

As is evident from his contemporary sources, Mir Damad was recognized simultaneously as a jurist, a mystic and a philosopher – a rare but not altogether impossible combination in Muslim intellectual his-

tory. His writings reflect his comprehensive and encyclopedic interests. He wrote on philosophy and theology, prophetic and Imami traditions, Shi'i law, Qur'anic commentary, ethics and mysticism as well as on logic. Mir Damad's ascetic exercises have been noted particularly by some of his biographers (see the introduction to the 1977 edition of *Kitab al-qabasat* (Book of Embers), page xxviii). These exercises are combined, if his biographers' sometimes hyperbolic tone is to be believed, with a precocious attention to philosophy.

Despite his prominent status as both a mystic and a jurist, an uneasy combination made possible by certain specific features of the School of Isfahan, it was principally as a philosopher that Mir Damad recognized, praised and distinguished himself, as in his many self-praising poems, for example:

> I conquered the lands of knowledge,
> I lent old wisdom to my youth.
> So that I made the earth with my *al-Qabasat*
> The envy of the heavenly abodes

(Hadi 1984: 134)

Al-Qabasat is Mir Damad's most significant philosophical work, containing the essence of his philosophy. *Al-Qabasat* consists of ten *qabas* ('a spark of fire') and three conclusions. Its central question is the creation of the world and the possibility of its extension from God. The first *qabas* discusses the variety of created beings and the divisions of existence. In the second he argues for a trilateral typology of essential primary notions and the primacy of essence. The duality of perspectives through which essence is subdivided and an argument to that effect through pre-eternal principles constitutes the third *qabas*. In the fourth, Mir Damad provides Qur'anic evidence, as well as references from the Prophetic and Imami traditions, to support his preceding arguments. The fifth *qabas* is devoted to a discussion of the primary dispositions through an understanding of natural existence. The connection (*ittisal'*) between 'time' and 'motion' is the subject of the sixth, where Mir Damad also argues for a 'natural order' in time. Here too he argues for the finality of numeral order and against the infinity of numbers in time-bound events (*al-hawadith al-zamaniyya*). He then devotes the seventh *qabas* to a refutation of opposing views. In the eighth, he verifies the divine authority in the establishment of such orders and the role of reason in ascertaining this truth. The ninth proves the archetypal substance of intellect (*al-jawahar al-'aqliyya*); in this chapter also, Mir Damad argues for the existence of an order in existence, a cycle of beginning and return. Finally, in the tenth *qabas*, he discusses the matter of divine ordination (*al-qada' wa al-qadar*), the necessity of supplication, the promise of God's reward, and the final return of all things to his judgment.

In *al-Qabasat*, Mir Damad engages in the age-old debate over the priority of 'essence' (*mahiyya*) versus that of 'existence' (*wujud*). He ultimately decides on the priority of essence, a position that would later be fundamentally disputed by his distinguished pupil MULLA SADRA. *Al-Qabasat* has remained a central text of Islamic philosophy since its first appearance. A number of philosophers of later generations have written commentaries about it, including Mulla Shamṣa Giṭlani and Aqa Jani Mazandarani (Ashtiyani 1972). Mir Damad wrote *al-Qabasat* in response to one of his students, who had asked him to write a treatise proving that the Creator of creation and being is unique in his pre-eternality, pre-eternal in his continuity, continuous in his everlastingness, and everlasting in his post-eternality. In this text, therefore, he set himself to prove that all existent beings, from archetypal models to material manifestations, are 'contingent upon nothingness' (*masbuqun bi'l-'adam*), 'inclined towards creation' (*tarifan bi'l-huduth*), 'pending on annihilation' (*marhunun bi'l-halak*), and 'subject to cancellation' (*mamnuwwun bi'l-butlan*) (*Kitab al-qabasat*: 1). The question of the pre-eternity (*qidam*) or createdness (*huduth*) of the world is one of the oldest and most enduring questions of Islamic philosophy, deeply rooted in the early Mu'tazilite codification of Islamic theology (Watt 1962: 58–71; Fakhry 1983: 67–8; Leaman 1985: 11–12, 132–4). Mir Damad reminds his readers that even IBN SINA considered the debate on this question to be 'dialectical' (*jadali*) rather than based on 'proof' (*burhan*).

For Mir Damad, being is circulated through a cycle of emanation from the divine presence to the physical world and then a return to it. In a progression of distancing emanations, the material world gradually emanates from the divine presence. From the Light of Lights (*nur al-'anwar*) first emanate the archetypal lights ('*anwar qahira*), of which the Universal Intellect ('*aql-i kull*) is the first component. From this stage emanate the 'heavenly souls' (*nufus-i falakhyya*), the 'ruling lights' ('*anwar-i mudabbira*), of which the 'universal souls' (*nafs-i kull*) is the primary member. The 'natural souls' (*nufus-i muntabi'a*) were subsequently created by the 'universal soul'. The archetypes of the heavens, planets, elements, compounds and the four natures were thus created. The final stage of this ontological emanation of being is the creation of matter from these archetypal origins. There is then a reverse order through which matter is sublimated back to light. Through this order, absolute or irreducible body (*jism-i mutlaq*) is advanced to the mineral stage of compound compositions. The minerals are then sublimated to the vegetative stage and then upward to the animal. Man is the highest stage of this upward mobility before the absolute matter rejoins the Light of Lights.

'Creation' (*ibda'*) is the 'bringing into being' of something from absolute-nothing. That which is 'evident' (*ma'lum*), if left to its own 'essence' (*dhat*), would not be. It is only by virtue of something outside it (in other words, its cause) that it is or, more accurately, is brought into being. Things in their own essence have an essential, not a temporal, primacy over things that are located outside of them, such as their cause for becoming evident and manifest. Thus the secondariness of the caused over the primacy of its cause is an essential, not a temporal, secondariness. From this it follows that unless the relation between the cause and the caused is a temporal one, not every caused is created in time, that is, not every *ma'lul* (caused) is a *muhaddath* (created-in-time). Only that caused is created-in-time which is contingent upon time (*zaman*), motion (*haraka*), and change (*taghayyur*) (*Kitab al-qabasat*: 3). That created-being which is not subsequent to time is either subsequent to absolute nothingness, whose creation is called *ibda'* (or 'brought into beginning'), or subsequent to not-absolute-nothingness, in which case its creation is called *ihdath* (or 'brought into being in time'). If the created being is subsequent to time, it can have only one possibility, which is its being-in-time subsequent to its being-in-nothingness (*Kitab al-qabasat*: 3–4) (see CAUSALITY AND NECESSITY IN ISLAMIC THOUGHT).

2 Philosophy of time

There is also a hierarchical conception of time that Mir Damad begins to develop, mostly from arguments used by IBN SINA, Nasir-i Khusrow and Khwajah Nasir AL-TUSI. First there is time (*zaman*), superior and more expansive than which is the atemporal (*dahr*) and ultimately the everlasting (*sarmad*). This hierarchy of timespan is also to be understood in terms of relationship. *Sarmad* postulates the relation of the permanent to the permanent; *dahr*, the relation of the permanent to the changing; and *zaman*, a relation of the changing to the changing. From this trilateral conception of time, Mir Damad reaches for his unique understanding of creation. Both *huduth* (creation) and *qidam* (pre-eternity) are of three kinds; *dhati* (essential), *dahri* (atemporal), and *zamani* (temporal). Essential pre-eternality (the counterpart of the essential createdness) is that whose being and actuality is not subsequential to its not-being (*laysiyya*) and/or nothingness (*'adam*). Atemporal pre-eternality (the counterpart of the atemporal createdness) is that whose being and actuality are not subsequential to its absolute nothingness in the span of the atemporal. On the contrary, from pre-eternity it is in-being. Finally, temporal pre-eternity (the counterpart of temporal createdness) is that temporal thing whose being is not specific to a time and whose already-being (*husul*) is constantly present in the course of all time, and of whose being has no temporal beginning.

As a believing Muslim, Mir Damad must accept the createdness of being. Neither essential createdness (*al-huduth al-dhati*) nor temporal createdness (*al-huduth al-zamani*) is subject to disagreement among philosophers because they are self-evident. It is only over the question of atemporal createdness (*al-huduth al-dahri*) that disagreement arises. God's creation of the universe, Mir Damad concludes, is of the *ibda'* (brought into beginning) and *sun'* (brought into createdness) kind as it pertains to atemporal created-ness and of the *ihdath* (brought into being in time) and *takwin* (brought into existence) kind as it pertains to temporal createdness.

Mir Damad proceeds to distinguish between three kinds of 'worlds'. First is the Everlasting World (*al-'alam al-sarmadi*), which is the space for Divine Presence, his essence and attributes; second is the Atemporal World (*al-'alam al-dahri*), which is the space for the pure archetypes (*al-mujarradat*); and third is the Temporal World (*al-'alam al-zamani*), which is the space for daily events, created beings and generation and corruption. There is a hierarchical relationship among these three worlds: the Ever-lasting World encompasses the Atemporal and the Temporal. The Temporal World is the weakest and least enduring of the three.

As temporal events are contingent upon time – that is, there are times when they are not and then they are 'produced', or brought into being, in time – the same contingency governs the hierarchical order of *sarmad* (everlasting), *dahr* (atemporality) and *zaman* (temporality). Every inferior stage, such as *zaman*, is in actual state of non-being to its superior state, in this case *dahr*. The real existence of the superior stage is identical to the actual non-being of the inferior stage. Reversing the order, the accidental defectiveness of the inferior stage – *zaman* to *dahr*, or *dahr* to *sarmad* – is not present in the superior stage. In other words, the in-itself existence of the superior stage is the *ipso facto* non-existence of the inferior stage in-itself. Mir Damad then concludes that the contingent non-being of the world of the archetypals of the *dahri* stage in the stage of *sarmadi* existence is a real and self-evident non-being. Thus all created beings and their arche-typals are consequent to real and self-evident non-

being. Their creation is an atemporal (*dahri*) creation and not, as theologians maintain, a temporal (*zamani*) creation. From this it follows that beyond their essential creation (*al-huduth al-dhati*), all temporal events are contingent upon and consequent to three real modes of non-existence: temporal, atemporal and everlasting. All the archetypal beings in the stage of temporal being are also contingent upon and consequent to one kind of non-being, namely the everlasting; and, of course, the everlasting world is not contingent upon or consequential to anything.

What Mir Damad achieves through this systematic separation of a trilateral stipulation of existence is the effective isolation of God at the top of the hierarchy, where he can initiate and sustain the world and yet not be subsequent to temporal corruption, to which all visible creations must yield. Moreover, the necessary contingency of an agent of creation, which is evidently active in the *zamani* and *dahri* stages of existence, is not necessary in the superior stage of *sarmadi*. As one commentator rightly observes, 'by devising the concept of *huduth-i dahri* (atemporal creation), he has succeeded in establishing a compro-mise between the theologian and the philosopher, in other words, between the religious law and reason' (Musawi Bihbahani in introduction to 1977 edition of *Kitab al-qabasat*: lxix).

3 Philosophical style

Mir Damad's philosophical discourse is indexical and suggestive, symbolic and referential. He relies heavily on a thorough knowledge of previous Islamic philo-sophy, and has a particular penchant for obscure Arabic words. The legendary difficulty of his philo-sophical prose should be understood as a response to the anti-philosophical climate of the period promoted by the politically powerful nomocentric jurists. Perhaps the greatest philosopher of this period, Mulla Sadra, was forced to leave the capital city of Isfahan at the instigation of the high clerical establishment precisely because of the articulate clarity of his writing. A story in *Qisas al-'ulama* is illustrative: Mulla Sadra saw Mir Damad in a dream and asked why people condemned him as a blasphemer when he had just repeated what Mir Damad had already said. 'The reason is', Mir Damad answered, 'that I wrote about philosophical matters in such a way that the religious authorities (*'ulama*) could not understand them, and that nobody other than philosophers would comprehend them. But you have vulgarized the philosophical issues and expounded them in such a way that a teacher at an elementary religious school can understand them. That is why they have called you a blasphemer and not me' (Tunikabuni 1985: 334–5).

See also: BEING; COSMOLOGY; GOD, CONCEPTS OF; ILLUMINATIONIST PHILOSOPHY; MULLA SADRA; MYSTICAL PHILOSOPHY IN ISLAM; SOUL IN ISLAMIC PHILOSOPHY; TIME

List of works

Mir Damad (before 1631) *Kitab al-qabasat* (Book of Embers), ed. M. Mohaghegh, T. Izutsu, M. Bihbahani and I. Dibaji, Tehran: McGill University, Institute of Islamic Studies, Tehran Branch, 1977. (Important edition of Mir Damad's work, together with extensive commentaries by some of the main authorities and a valuable introduction by the translators.)

References and further reading

* Ashtiyani, S. (1972) *Muntakhabati az athar-i hukama-yi ilahi-yi Iran: az 'asr-i Mir Damad va Mir Findiriski ta zaman-i hadir* (Selection from Iranian Metaphysical Thinkers: Mir Damad, Mir Findiriski and Their Contemporaries), Tehran and Paris: Département d'Iranologie de l'Institut Franco-Iranien de Recherche. (Accounts of some of the commentaries on *al-Qabasat*.)
Corbin, H. (1972) *En Islam iranien: Aspects Spirituels et Philosophique* (Iranian Islam: Spiritual and Philosophical Aspects), Paris: Gallimard, 4 vols. (Detailed acocunt of some of the main Persian thinkers, including Mir Damad.)
Dabashi, H. (1996) 'Mir Damad and the Founding of the School of Isfahan', in S.H. Nasr and O. Leaman (eds) *History of Islamic Philosophy*, London: Routledge, ch. 34, 597–634. (An authoritative and detailed discussion of this crucial period of Persian thought.)
* Fakhry, M. (1983) *A History of Islamic Philosophy*, New York: Columbia University Press. (A standard work on this subject.)
* Hadi, A. (1984) *Sharh-i hal-i Mir Damad va Mir Findiriski* (Commentary on the Thought of Mir Damad and Mir Findiriski), Isfahan: Maytham Tamar Publications. (Many interesting details of Mir Damad's life and contemporaries.)
* Leaman, O. (1985) *An Introduction to Medieval Islamic Philosophy*, Cambridge: Cambridge University Press. (Account of some of the main philosophical and theological debates.)
Mulla Sadra, S. (*c.*1628) *al-Shawahid al-rububiyya* (Divine Testimonies), ed. S. Ashtiyani, Mashhad: Mashhad University Press, 1967. (Discussions by Mir Damad's most famous pupil which show the differences in their views, with annotations and introduction by the editor.)
Nasr, S.H. (1966) 'The School of Isfahan', in M.M. Sharif (ed.) *A History of Muslim Philosophy*, Wiesbaden: Otto Harrassowitz, vol. 2: 904–32. (General account of the intellectual period by the leading expert.)
—— (1978) *Sadr al-Din Shirazi and His Transcendent Theosophy*, Tehran: Imperial Iranian Academy of Philosophy. (Clear account of the thought of this period.)
Savory, R. (1980) *Iran: Under the Safavids*, Cambridge: Cambridge University Press. (The historical context of Mir Damad's life and works.)
* Tunikabuni, M.M. (1985) *Qisas al-'ulama'* (Stories of the Scholars), Tehran: Intisharat-'illmiyyah Islamiyyah. (Amusing and intriguing accounts of stories about thinkers including Mir Damad.)
* Watt, W.M. (1962) *Islamic Philosophy and Theology*, Edinburgh: Edinburgh University Press. (Concise guide to the general set of questions which formed Mir Damad's intellectual background.)

HAMID DABASHI

MIRACLES

Does God at times miraculously intervene in earthly affairs? That is, do some events occur because God has entered our space-time continuum and directly modified or circumvented the relevant natural laws? Few philosophers today deny that this is possible. But many question whether we could ever justifiably maintain that such intervention has taken place.

According to some philosophers, it is not even necessary to grant that the types of events believers label miracles – for instance, healings or resurrections – actually occur as reported. Since the evidence supporting the occurrence of such events is the personal testimony of a few, possibly biased, individuals, while the basis for doubt is the massive amount of objective research upon which the relevant laws are based, it is always justifiable, according to this view, to conclude that such reports are erroneous. Others contend, however, that the presence of some forms of evidence – for instance, independent confirmation from reputable sources – could make it most reasonable in some cases to acknowledge that even the most unexpected of events had actually occurred.

Some philosophers also deny that we could ever justifiably conclude that an event could not have been produced by natural causes alone. Since we will never be in a position to identify all that nature can produce, they declare, it will always be most reasonable for the scientist facing a currently unexplainable counterin-

411

stance to a natural law to continue to look for a natural explanation. Many believers, however, are quite willing to grant that nature could in principle produce any event, since what they wish to maintain is only that nature does not do so in the case of miraculous interventions.

Finally, while many philosophers acknowledge that belief in direct divine intervention may at times be justifiable for those who already believe that God exists, some also argue that no single event or series of events could ever compel all thoughtful individuals to acknowledge the existence of a perfectly good supernatural causal agent, given all we experience – for instance, the tremendous amount of horrific evil in our world. Many believers, though, are also willing to grant this point.

1   **Definition**
2   **The possibility of miracles**
3   **The credibility of personal testimony**
4   **Miracles as events unexplainable by natural causes**
5   **Miracles as acts of God**

1   Definition

The term 'miracle' is sometimes used in ordinary discussions to refer to the occurrence of any unexpected event – from the sudden discovery of a lost possession to the unanticipated passing of an exam. Within philosophical circles, however, 'miracle' is almost always discussed in its more restricted sense: as a designation for an unusual event that is the result of direct divine circumvention or modification of the natural order.

Philosophers, as well as religious believers, differ on the exact nature of the conceptual relationship between miraculous divine interventions and the natural order. For those who understand miracles to be violations of natural laws, a miracle is not simply an event that nature *did* not alone produce. It is an event that nature *could* not have produced on its own – an event that will always be incompatible with the relevant natural laws (see LAWS, NATURAL). For example, as proponents of the violation model understand it, to maintain that someone has miraculously been healed, it is not sufficient to maintain simply that God was directly involved. It is also necessary to maintain that the state of affairs in question could not have occurred naturally (that no totally natural explanation could be forthcoming).

Other philosophers, and many believers, however, deny that a miraculous divine intervention must be defined as an event for which no plausible natural explanation is, or could be, available. It is sufficient, they believe, to maintain that God was directly involved. For example, to maintain that someone's

cancer has miraculously entered remission, it is not necessary to hold that nature alone could not have brought it about (to maintain that it could not have happened naturally). It is sufficient to maintain that nature alone did not do so in this case.

2   The possibility of miracles

Some philosophers (for example, McKinnon 1967) have claimed that the concept of a miracle, if defined as a violation of a natural law, is incoherent. Natural laws, they point out, are really only generalized descriptions of what does in fact happen. That is, these laws summarize for us the actual course of events. Accordingly, to claim that an occurrence is a violation of a natural law is to claim that the event in question is a suspension of the actual course of events and this is, of course, impossible. Events may well occur, they acknowledge, that seem at present to be incompatible with how we believe things normally happen. But a true counterinstance to what we now believe to be a natural law only shows the law to be inadequate. Since natural laws, by definition, only summarize what actually occurs, we must always be willing in principle to expand our laws to accommodate any occurrence, no matter how unusual. We can never have both the exception and the rule.

Others, however, take this line of reasoning to be based on a confusion. To maintain that a natural law accurately describes the natural order, they point out, is to say only that it correctly identifies that which will occur under a specific set of natural conditions. But to maintain that an event is a miraculous counterinstance to a natural law is not to maintain that some event has occurred under the exact set of natural conditions covered by this law and nothing more. To say that water has miraculously turned into wine, for example, is not to say that water has turned into wine only under the exact set of natural conditions under which the relevant laws tell us this will not occur. It is to maintain that an additional non-natural causal factor, namely direct divine activity, was also present in this case. Accordingly, these philosophers contend, unless it is assumed that supernatural activity is impossible, it cannot be assumed that a miraculous counterinstance to a natural law – a counterinstance produced in part by divine circumvention or modification of the natural order – is conceptually impossible. That is, unless it is assumed that supernatural intervention is impossible, we can have both the exception and the rule.

Of course, many individuals do in fact deny the existence of any type of supernatural being. And even some who affirm the existence of such a being – for example, process theists (see PROCESS THEISM) – deny that this being can unilaterally intervene in earthly affairs in the sense necessary to produce miraculous events. However, few philosophers today maintain that the existence of a supernatural being, or the ability of such a being (if it exists) to intervene, can be demonstrated to be impossible. That is, while most philosophers agree that the existence of a super-natural being who intervenes in earthly affairs can justifiably be denied, most also agree that it is possible to maintain justifiably that such a being does exist. Consequently, few deny that miracles, even if defined as violations of natural laws, could occur. Since the time of David HUME (§2), however, philosophers have continued to debate vigorously a number of questions related to our ability to *identify* miraculous events.

3 The credibility of personal testimony

One such question is whether we need even acknowl-edge that alleged counterinstances to well-confirmed natural laws actually occur. Most philosophers agree that reports of repeatable counterinstances – counter-instances that can in principle be produced by anyone under a specified set of natural conditions – cannot justifiably be dismissed. But there are a number of philosophers (most notably Flew 1961) who believe that if the events in question are nonrepeatable – if they cannot be reproduced under specifiable natural conditions – the situation is quite different. It is clearly possible, they acknowledge, that nonrepeatable counterinstances to well-confirmed natural laws have occurred (or will occur). They acknowledge, for instance, that nonrepeatable counterinstances to our current laws describing the properties of water or human tissue may have occurred (or might occur). However, the evidence supporting the adequacy of laws of this type, they point out, is very strong. These laws not only can be, but are, tested and reconfirmed daily by people with no vested interest in the outcome. On the other hand, they are quick to add, reports of presently nonrepeatable counterinstances to such laws – a claim, for instance, that water has turned into wine or that someone has been raised from the dead – will be supported at best only by the personal testimony of a few people who may well have a vested interest in the outcome. Consequently, as long as alleged counterinstances remain nonrepeatable, we can never possess better reasons for believing that the events in question have actually occurred as reported than for believing that they have not. And therefore, following the Humean maxim that the wise person proportions belief to the evidence, these philosophers conclude that it is always justifiable to deny the accuracy of such reports.

However, there are those (for instance, Swinburne 1967) who believe that this conclusion is much too strong. They acknowledge that reports of seemingly nonrepeatable counterinstances to well-established laws must be approached with appropriate scepticism, since deception or misperception is always possible. But from their perspective it is unreasonable to assume that the evidence supporting even the most highly confirmed laws would *always* furnish a sufficient basis for dismissing reports of counter-instances to them.

First and foremost, they argue that to make this assumption fails to take into account the *prima facie* reliability of our visual belief-forming faculties. We all rely on these faculties daily and, in general, they serve us quite well. In fact, the general reliability of such faculties must be presupposed by those formulating our natural laws. Thus, in cases where we had no reason to doubt the reliability of these belief-forming faculties – for instance, if we were to observe a seeming counterinstance ourselves or if it were directly observed by a friend whose character and objectivity were beyond question – it is not clear, they maintain, that it would always be justifiable to decide in favour of the natural laws in question, even if they were very well established.

Moreover, these philosophers add, we might in some cases have compelling physical traces to con-sider. In the case of an alleged healing that runs counter to well-established laws, for instance, we might have more than personal testimony. We might have objective data – photographs or videotapes or X-rays or medical records – that would stand as strong evidence for the occurrence of the event in question, evidence so convincing that it would be unreasonable to reject it. Thus they conclude that decisions concerning the accuracy of reports of alleged counter-instances – even if the events in question are nonrepeatable – must be made on a case-by-case basis.

4 Miracles as events unexplainable by natural causes

Even if some occurrences can justifiably be labelled counterinstances to our current laws, could we ever be in a position to maintain justifiably that any such event is permanently unexplainable scientifically? That is, could we ever be in a position to maintain that an acknowledged counterinstance is a state of affairs that nature could never produce on its own?

In addressing this question, it is important to clarify a potential ambiguity that has been glossed over so far in this entry. By definition, no specific state of affairs produced even in part by direct supernatural activity (by direct circumvention or modification of the natural cause/effect patterns) could ever be given a totally natural explanation. Accordingly, if we were ever in a position to maintain justifiably that some event was actually a direct act of God, we would automatically be in a position to maintain justifiably that this specific occurrence was, itself, permanently unexplainable scientifically.

As currently understood by most philosophers, however, the primary purpose of natural science is not to determine what nature has in fact produced. The main objective of science, rather, is to determine what nature is capable of producing – what can occur under solely natural conditions. For instance, the primary purpose of natural science is not to determine whether natural factors alone actually did cause any specific person's cancer to enter remission. The primary purpose of science is to determine whether natural factors alone could have done so.

Hence, when philosophers ask whether we could ever be in a position to maintain justifiably that an event is permanently unexplainable scientifically, they are not asking whether we could ever be in a position to maintain justifiably that a specific state of affairs *was* not produced by nature alone. They are asking, rather, whether we could ever be in a position to maintain justifiably that a specific event *could* not have been produced by nature alone.

In considering this question, it should first be noted that no philosopher believes that we as human beings are in a position to state with absolute certainty what nature could or could not produce on its own. All acknowledge that the scientific enterprise is continually discovering new, often startling and unexpected, information about the causal relationships that obtain in our universe. And all freely admit that the annals of science record numerous instances in which supposed counterinstances to natural laws were later demonstrated to be consistent with such laws or revisions of them.

However, as some philosophers (such as Swinburne 1967 and Holland 1965) see it, some of our natural laws are so highly confirmed that any modification we might suggest to accommodate counterinstances would be clumsy and so *ad hoc* that it would upset the whole structure of science. For example, from their perspective, to attempt to modify our current laws relating to the properties of water to allow for the possibility that water could turn into wine naturally, or to attempt to modify our current laws relating to the properties of nonliving human tissue to allow for the possibility that a dead body could be resuscitated naturally, would make these laws of little practical value. Consequently, if we were in a position to maintain justifiably that a counterinstance to a law of this type had actually occurred, we would be required, for the sake of the scientific enterprise, to maintain that this event was permanently unexplainable by

natural causes – that this event could never have been produced by nature on its own.

Critics (for instance, Basinger and Basinger 1986) consider this line of reasoning to contain a false dilemma. If faced with an acknowledged counterinstance to a natural law, even one that was very highly confirmed, we would not, they contend, be required at that moment either to modify the law to accommodate the occurrence or to affirm the adequacy of the law and declare the event permanently unexplainable by natural causes. Rather, since only naturally repeatable counterinstances falsify natural laws, the appropriate initial response to the occurrence of any seeming counterinstance to any law, no matter how highly confirmed, would be to acknowledge both the law and the counterinstance while further research was undertaken.

Moreover, these critics argue that such research could never make it most reasonable to conclude that something beyond the ability of nature to produce had actually occurred. If it were discovered that the seeming counterinstance was naturally repeatable – if it were found that the event in question could be produced with regularity under some set of purely natural conditions – a revision of the relevant laws would indeed be necessary. But then this event would no longer be naturally unexplainable. On the other hand, if natural repeatability could not be achieved, the appropriate response, they contend, would still not be to maintain that this occurrence was permanently unexplainable. Since nonrepeatable counterinstances do not present us with competing hypotheses to the relevant law(s), the appropriate response, rather, would be to label the counterinstance an anomaly while continuing to accept the functional adequacy of the law(s) in question.

Even if this line of reasoning is correct, however, nothing of significance follows for those who maintain only that a miracle is an event that would not have occurred at the exact time and in the exact manner it did if God had not somehow directly circumvented or modified the natural order in the specific case in question. Only those who believe that a miracle must be a violation of a natural law – who believe that a miracle must be an event that nature could not have produced – are affected.

5 Miracles as acts of God

Regardless of the perceived relationship between miracles and nature, however, questions concerning our ability (or inability) to identify events as direct acts of God remain important. For many philosophers, the most significant question of this sort continues to be whether there are imaginable conditions under which all rational individuals would be forced to acknowledge that God has directly intervened. And although most philosophers believe the answer to be no, some (for example, Larmer 1988) believe an affirmative response is required. They acknowledge that with respect to many states of affairs which believers do in fact maintain have been brought about by God – for example, many alleged cases of divine healings – it is possible for a rational person to grant that the event has occurred as reported and yet justifiably deny that it was the result of direct divine intervention. But let us assume that someone who has been dead for twenty-four hours is raised from the dead when divine intervention is requested. Or let us assume that the missing fingers of a leper instantaneously reappear following a prayer for healing. In such cases, they argue, there would be very strong evidence supporting supernatural causation and no evidence supporting purely natural causation. In fact, the evidence would be so strong that to continue to hold out indefinitely for a totally natural explanation in such contexts would be unjustified in that this would simply demonstrate an unreasonable a priori naturalistic bias.

In response, critics (for example, Basinger and Basinger 1986) do not deny that there might be conceivable cases which, if considered in isolation, would appear to make divine intervention a very plausible causal hypothesis. However, to acknowledge that God exists and has beneficially intervened in some specific case(s), they point out, is also to acknowledge that God's existence is compatible with all we experience – for example, that it is compatible with the tremendous amount of horrific human pain and suffering that appears to fall disproportionately on the innocent and disadvantaged. And even if it is possible to claim justifiably that God's existence is compatible with all we experience, it cannot be argued successfully that everyone must agree. Disbelief in God also remains a justifiable response (see EVIL, PROBLEM OF §6). Consequently, these critics conclude, the belief that there exists a solely natural cause for any specific occurrence always remains a justifiable option, regardless of the extent to which it may appear that divine intervention was involved.

For many philosophers, though, the crucial question is not whether there are imaginable conditions under which all rational individuals would be compelled to acknowledge divine intervention but rather whether there are conditions under which those who already believe in God would be justified in doing so. Even if it is true that the occurrence of no single event (or set of events) can justifiably compel belief in divine intervention, it is also true (so philosophers such as Wainwright 1988 and Abraham

1985 contend) that the occurrence of no event (or set of events) – for instance, no amount of evil – can rule out justified belief in God's existence as a supernatural causal agent in our world. And given this fact, it is argued, as long as believers themselves possess good theistic reasons for assuming that God has directly intervened in a given case – for instance, because the occurrence appears clearly to fit an accepted pattern of divine action – they are justified in making this assumption.

It must be added, however, that even if this is correct, an important inverse relationship between miracles and evil remains. For instance, to respond to evil by claiming that God cannot both grant humans significant freedom and yet beneficially intervene on a consistent basis is, at the same time, to cite a reason why miracles should not be expected with frequency. And to respond to evil by claiming that 'God's ways are above our ways' places the believer in a less secure position to say when and where miraculous intervention has occurred.

See also: DEISM §§1–2; NAHMANIDES, M. §2; OCCASIONALISM; RELIGION AND SCIENCE; REVELATION §§1–2

References and further reading

* Abraham, W.J. (1985) *An Introduction to the Philosophy of Religion*, Englewood Cliffs, NJ: Prentice Hall, ch. 13. (A very accessible response to the Humean arguments against miracles.)
* Basinger, D. and Basinger, R. (1986) *Philosophy and Miracle: The Contemporary Debate*, Lewiston, NY: Edwin Mellen Press. (An accessible summary and assessment of contemporary thought on all aspects of the issue.)
* Flew, A. (1961) *Hume's Philosophy of Belief*, New York: Humanities Press. (A strengthened contemporary restatement of Hume's critique.)
* Holland, R.F. (1965) 'The Miraculous', *American Philosophical Quarterly* 2 (1): 43–51. (An influential defence of our ability, in principle, to identify the miraculous.)
Houston, J. (1994) *Reported Miracles: A Critique of Hume*, Cambridge: Cambridge University Press. (A thoughtful assessment of Hume's position.)
Hume, D. (1777) 'On Miracles', in *Enquiries Concerning the Human Understanding and Concerning the Principles of Morals*, ed. L.A. Selby-Bigge, Oxford: Clarendon Press, 2nd edn, 1972. (The classic critique of miracles, used by almost all as a starting point in the discussion.)
* Larmer, R.A.H. (1988) *Water into Wine*, Kingston,

Ont.: McGill–Queen's University Press. (A thoughtful defence of belief in the miraculous.)

—— (ed.) (1996) *Questions of Miracle*, Kingston, Ont.: McGill–Queen's University Press. (An accessible collection of articles on many key issues.)

* McKinnon, A. (1967) '"Miracle" and "Paradox"', *American Philosophical Quarterly* 4 (3): 308–14. (An influential challenge to the coherence of the concept of miracle.)

* Swinburne, R. (1967) *The Concept of Miracle*, London: Macmillan. (A short, accessible response to Humean criticism.)

—— (ed.) (1989) *Miracles*, New York: Macmillan. (A balanced collection of essays on all aspects of the issue.)

* Wainwright, W.J. (1988) *Philosophy of Religion*, Belmont, CA: Wadsworth, ch. 2. (A brief, objective discussion of the basic issues.)

DAVID BASINGER

MKHAS GRUB DGE LEGS DPAL BZANG PO (1385–1438)

mKhas grub dge legs dpal bzang po (Kaydrup gelek belsangbo) was one of the early masters of the dGa'-ldan-pa (Gandenba) or dGe-lugs-pa (Gelukba) school of Tibetan Buddhism. His importance derives primarily from his close association with the founder of that school, Tsong kha pa (Dzongkaba, 1357–1419), whose religious and philosophical tradition he was instrumental in preserving and transmitting. A prolific writer, whose interests ranged across the entire spectrum of Buddhist doctrine, from the exoteric (Sūtra) to the esoteric (Tantra), his work is highly regarded for its ability to encapsulate lucidly entire fields of knowledge (for example, Tantra, the Mādhyamika doctrine of emptiness, and the pramāṇa *tradition of logic and epistemology).*

mKhas grub dge legs dpal bzang po (Kaydrup gelek belsangbo; often called mKhas grub rje) was born in Western Tibet in 1385. Like his younger brother, Ba so Chos kyi rgyal mtshan (Baso chogyi gyeltsen, 1402–73), another important figure in the early dGe-lugs-pa school, he became a novice monk at an early age and studied under some of the most distinguished masters of the Sa-skya-pa school, including the great Red mda' ba gZhon nu blo gros (Rendawa Shönnu lodrö, 1349–1412), one of Tsong kha pa's own teachers, from whom mKhas grub rje received full ordination at the age of twenty (see TSONG KHA PA BLO BZANG GRAGS PA). As was the custom, he made the rounds of the great Tibetan monastic universities of his day, pitting his knowledge of the Buddhist doctrinal tradition against that of his peers and establishing a reputation as a great debater. Especially important in this regard was his encounter (at a mere sixteen years of age) with the renowned Bo dong Phyogs las rnam rgyal (Bodong choklay namgyel, 1375–1450), in debate with whom he is said to have defended, with great flair, the views of SA SKYA PAṆḌITA (Sagya paṇḍita, 1182–1251).

In 1407, on Red mda' ba's advice, mKhas grub rje went to central Tibet in search of Tsong kha pa (Dzongkaba). An instant rapport was established between the two when they met. In the dGe-lugs-pa tradition to this day, mKhas grub rje is known as the closest of Tsong kha pa's spiritual sons. From the time of his meeting with Tsong kha pa, mKhas grub rje began to apply himself earnestly to the study of the latter's teachings, receiving instruction as well from Tsong kha pa's more senior student and direct heir, RGYAL TSHAB DAR MA RIN CHEN (Gyeltsap darma rinchen, 1364–1432). He succeeded rGyal tshab rje as the heir to the lineage of Tsong kha pa, becoming the third holder of the throne of dGa'-ldan monastery, a position that he held until his death in 1438. mKhas grub rje's philosophical and religious views are preserved in the eleven volumes of his collected works (gSungs 'bum).

Most of mKhas grub rje's philosophical and religious writings have yet to be analysed by Western scholars. From the work done to date, however, we know that, following Tsong kha pa, the following themes were central to his philosophical systematization of Buddhist doctrine: (1) that the public study of the great textual tradition of India, and not the private oral instruction lineages prevalent in Tibet, should form the basis for Buddhist study and practice; (2) the importance of ethics, as epitomized in the monastic way of life, as the basis for Buddhist practice; (3) the importance of self-generation, that is, the visualization of oneself in the form of a deity, as a defining characteristic of Buddhist Tantra; (4) the fact that the emptiness that is the object of meditation in both the Sūtra (that is, the Madhyamaka) and Tantra (for example, in the Kālacakra) traditions is identical; (5) that even though the analytical understanding of emptiness must be transformed, through the practice of meditation, into direct yogic experience, the object of both the analytical and yogic insights – the emptiness itself – is the same, so that emptiness as the object of analytical/conceptual thought is not a lower or corrupt form of emptiness (as maintained by some of Tsong kha pa's opponents) but is instead, like the object of the more sublime yogic consciousness, the full-blown reality of things, the ultimate truth that is the true mode of existence of persons and phenomena; (6) that the methods of logic and epistemology as systematized in the Prāmāṇika tradition of India are indispensable to the spiritual path, and, especially, to the initial understanding of emptiness; (7) that the highest expression of the Madhyamaka theory of emptiness, that of Candrakīrti's *Prāsaṅgika, is compatible with the overall thrust of the Indian logical/epistemological (*pramāṇa*) tradition, and, especially, that the principle of contradiction is valid even in the Madhyamaka system, so that the understanding of emptiness does not require a deviant logic which repudiates that principle; (8) that since conventional reality is the basis for the acquisition of the merit essential to spiritual progress, emptiness is not a repudiation of the existence of things, but only the negation of a specific false quality attributed to things by the ignorance innate in all sentient beings; and (9) that systems of meditation that repudiate analysis and conceptualization represent quietist/nihilist corruptions of the Buddha's teachings.

It is important to note that much of mKhas grub rje's philosophical work is at least partially polemical in tone. This derives on the one hand from a personal predilection for a combative style of argumentation acquired and refined on the debating grounds of Tibet's great monasteries. On the other hand, his polemical style is a direct outcome of the task he set himself, namely, that of clearly demarcating, systematizing and defending the doctrines of his master, Tsong kha pa.

See also: Buddhist concept of emptiness; Mādhyamika: India and Tibet; Tibetan philosophy

List of works

mKhas grub dge legs dpal bzang po (1385–1438) *gSungs 'bum* (Collected Works), ed. Lhasa Zhol, Dharamsala: Shes rig par khang, 1981; ed. sKra shis lhun po, New Delhi: Ngawang Gelek Demo, 1983. (Two different editions of the eleven volumes of mKhas grub rje's collected works in the original Tibetan.)

—— (1385–1438) *sTong thun chen mo* (The Great Digest on Emptiness), trans. J.I. Cabezón, *A Dose of Emptiness: An Annotated Translation of the sTong thun chen mo of mKhas grub dge legs dpal bzang*, Albany, NY: State University of New York Press, 1992. (Translation of mKhas grub rje's great Madhyamaka classic, containing an introduction to his philosophy, a brief biography based on five Tibetan sources and oral traditions of the dGe-lugs-

pa school, and a bibliographical survey of literature on him.)

—— (1385–1438) *rGyud sde spyi rnam (General Exposition of the Division of the Tantra)*, trans. F.D. Lessing and A. Wayman, *Mkhas grub rje's Fundamentals of the Buddhist Tantras*, The Hague: Mouton, 1968. (A critical edition and translation, with an introduction.)

References and further reading

Hopkins, J. (1983) *Meditation on Emptiness*, London: Wisdom Publications. (A general introduction to the dGe-lugs-pa interpretation of Madhyamaka.)

Kuijp, L.W.J. van de (1985, 1986) 'Studies in the Life and Thought of Mkhas grub rje', part 1, 'mKhas grub rje's Epistemological Oeuvre and his Philological Remarks on Dignāga's Pramāṇasamuccaya I' in *Berliner Indologische Studien*, (1985) 75–105; part 4, 'mKhas-grub-rje on Regionalisms and Dialects' in *Berliner Indologische Studien*, (1986) 23–49. (Very little secondary literature is devoted to mKhas grub rje. Of what is available, these two articles are the most interesting and accurate.)

Ruegg, D.S. (1981) *The Literature of the Madhyamaka School of Philosophy in India*, Wiesbaden: Otto Harrassowitz. (Contains some useful material on Tibet.)

Snellgrove, D. (1987) *Indo-Tibetan Buddhism*, 2 vols, Boston: Shambhala. (A useful scholarly overview, especially with regard to Tantric Buddhism.)

Williams, P. (1989) *Mahāyā Buddhism: The Doctrinal Foundation*, London and New York: Routledge. (A general overview, containing some useful material on Tibetan Buddhism.)

JOSÉ IGNACIO CABEZÓN

MO TI/MO TZU *see* Mozi; Mohist philosophy

MODAL LOGIC

Modal logic, narrowly conceived, is the study of principles of reasoning involving necessity and possibility. More broadly, it encompasses a number of structurally similar inferential systems. In this sense, deontic logic (which concerns obligation, permission and related notions) and epistemic logic (which concerns knowledge and related notions) are branches of modal logic. Still more broadly, modal logic is the study of the class of all possible formal systems of this nature.

It is customary to take the language of modal logic to be that obtained by adding one-place operators '□' for necessity and '◇' for possibility to the language of classical propositional or predicate logic. Necessity and possibility are interdefinable in the presence of negation:

$$\Box A \leftrightarrow \neg \Diamond \neg A \text{ and}$$

$$\Diamond A \leftrightarrow \neg \Box \neg A$$

hold. A modal logic is a set of formulas of this language that contains these biconditionals and meets three additional conditions: it contains all instances of theorems of classical logic; it is closed under modus ponens *(that is, if it contains A and A → B it also contains B); and it is closed under substitution (that is, if it contains A then it contains any substitution instance of A; any result of uniformly substituting formulas for sentence letters in A). To obtain a logic that adequately characterizes metaphysical necessity and possibility requires certain additional axiom and rule schemas:*

$$K \quad \Box(A \rightarrow B) \rightarrow (\Box A \rightarrow \Box B)$$

$$T \quad \Box A \rightarrow A$$

$$5 \quad \Diamond A \rightarrow \Box \Diamond A$$

Necessitation   A/□A.

By adding these and one of the □–◇ biconditionals to a standard axiomatization of classical propositional logic one obtains an axiomatization of the most important modal logic, S5, so named because it is the logic generated by the fifth of the systems in Lewis and Langford's Symbolic Logic *(1932). S5 can be characterized more directly by possible-worlds models. Each such model specifies a set of possible worlds and assigns truth-values to atomic sentences relative to these worlds. Truth-values of classical compounds at a world w depend in the usual way on truth-values of their components. □A is true at w if A is true at all worlds of the model; ◇A, if A is true at some world of the model. S5 comprises the formulas true at all worlds in all such models. Many modal logics weaker than S5 can be characterized by models which specify, besides a set of possible worlds, a relation of 'accessibility' or relative possibility on this set. □A is true at a world w if A is true at all worlds accessible from w, that is, at all worlds that would be possible if w were actual. Of the schemas listed above, only K is true in all these models, but each of the others is true when accessibility meets an appropriate constraint.*

The addition of modal operators to predicate logic poses additional conceptual and mathematical difficul-

ties. On one conception a model for quantified modal logic specifies, besides a set of worlds, the set D_w of individuals that exist in w, for each world w. For example, $\exists x \Box A$ is true at w if there is some element of D_w that satisfies A in every possible world. If A is satisfied only by existent individuals in any given world $\exists x \Box A$ thus implies that there are necessary individuals; individuals that exist in every accessible possible world. If A is satisfied by non-existents there can be models and assignments that satisfy A, but not $\exists x A$. Consequently, on this conception modal predicate logic is not an extension of its classical counterpart.

The modern development of modal logic has been criticized on several grounds, and some philosophers have expressed scepticism about the intelligibility of the notion of necessity that it is supposed to describe.

1   **History**
2   **Propositional S5**
3   **Philosophical questions about S5**
4   **Quantified S5**
5   **Weaker systems**
6   **General results**

1   History

Modal logic in the narrow sense was a topic of considerable interest to ancient and medieval philosophers. It occupied two chapters of Aristotle's *De Interpretatione*, and a substantial part of the *Prior Analytics*. Discussion of argument forms involving necessity and possibility that included, and sometimes transcended, commentary on Aristotle's was standard fare in Hellenistic and medieval treatises on logic (see LOGIC, MEDIEVAL). From our vantage point the ancient and medieval discussion can be interpreted as including distinctions among various kinds of possibility and necessity and investigations of the logical relations among them, as well as logical investigations of the interactions between modalities and negation, modalities and conditionals or consequence, and modalities and quantifier expressions. Aristotle determines in *De Interpretatione*, for example, that 'It may be' and 'It cannot be' are contradictories, as are 'It may not be' and 'It cannot not be' (see LOGIC, ANCIENT). Furthermore, 'from the proposition "It may be" it follows that it is not impossible' and in one sense 'the proposition "It may be" follows from the proposition "It is necessary that it should be"'. In another sense (which we might gloss as 'It is merely possible that'), 'It may be' is logically incompatible with 'It is necessary that it should be'.

Besides these purely modal principles, Aristotle and his commentators were concerned with arguments that we might think of as mixing time and modality. A notorious example is the fallacious 'sea battle' argument for determinism that he tries to debunk in *De Interpretatione* (see ARISTOTLE §20). In addition to the admixture of temporal considerations, one should observe that the notion of necessity involved in these discussions is not likely to be the same as the one whose logical behaviour was summarized above. Aristotle himself catalogues four senses of the word 'necessary' in *Metaphysics* (V 5), and makes other distinctions elsewhere.

Although necessity and possibility have never ceased to play an important role in philosophical discourse, their logical properties were largely neglected in modern philosophy until the beginning of the twentieth century. The contemporary revival was sparked by C.I. Lewis' critique of Whitehead and Russell's *Principia Mathematica*. The logical system elaborated in *Principia* contained as theorems the formulas $p \supset (q \supset p)$ and $\sim p \supset (p \supset q)$, which Whitehead and Russell understood as asserting the apparently paradoxical propositions that if a sentence is true it is implied by any sentence and if a sentence is false it implies any sentence. Lewis maintained that these propositions, while unavoidable and unobjectionable with respect to Russell and Whitehead's understanding of implication, were false with respect to a more natural 'strict' sense of implication (see RELEVANCE LOGIC AND ENTAILMENT §§1–2).

Lewis embarked on a project of determining the appropriate axioms of strict implication with which to supplement this system. In *Principia* the 'material' implication $p \supset q$ is considered true unless p is true and q false. In Lewis' systems, the strict implication $p \Rightarrow q$ is considered true only if it is *impossible* that p is true and q false. Thus Lewis' strict implication can be defined from Russell and Whitehead's conjunction and negation signs and a new connective, '$\Diamond$', of possibility.

$$p \Rightarrow q = \sim\Diamond(p \,\&\, \sim q)$$

Conversely, possibility can be defined from strict implication.

$$\Diamond p = \sim(p \Rightarrow \sim p)$$

Hence Lewis' project of finding the correct logical principles for his notion of strict implication is tantamount to that of finding the correct logical principles for possibility or, equivalently, those for necessity.

Lewis and Langford's *Symbolic Logic* (1932) describes five different axiom systems as candidates for the logic of strict implication. Much effort was expended in the first half of the century investigating these systems and variations of them. Even showing that all five are distinct (in the sense that they produce

different classes of theorems) required considerable ingenuity. Fifteen years after the publication of *Symbolic Logic*, Carnap (1947) gave a non-axiomatic characterization of 'logical' necessity. ⌜Necessarily A⌝ is true, according to Carnap, if A is 'L-true', that is, if A is true in all state descriptions. (A 'state description' is a kind of canonical inventory of the primitive relations that hold and fail to hold of each sequence of individuals.) Thus Carnap can be seen as making precise the old idea that necessity is truth in all possible worlds. This idea is usually associated with Leibniz, but it is traced to Descartes by Curley (1984) and to Duns Scotus by Knuuttila (1982).

The logic determined by Carnap's interpretation turned out to be S5, the fifth of the Lewis and Langford systems. In the late 1950s and early 1960s, several authors proposed interpretations that refined and generalized Carnap's idea by introducing something like the accessibility relation described above (see Kanger 1957; Montague 1960; Hintikka 1963; Kripke 1963). 'Kripke models', which are essentially the models described above, are the neatest formulation of this idea. Kripke and a continuing line of successors have shown that a great variety of modal systems can be characterized by models of this kind. This enormously simplified the kinds of investigations of axiomatic systems mentioned above and opened new lines of research.

Kripke models were particularly fruitful in the study of modal logic in the broader sense. It had long been noted that the pairs 'It will always/sometimes be the case that', 'it is obligatory/permitted that' and 'it is known/consistent with knowledge that' exhibit logical behaviour similar to that of 'necessarily/possibly'. The success of Kripke's treatment of necessity encouraged analogous treatments of these other notions.

GA (⌜It will always be the case that A⌝) is true at time t if A is true at all times after t.

FA (⌜It will sometimes be the case that A⌝) is true at t if A is true at some times after t.

OA (⌜It is obligatory that A⌝) is true at world w if A is true at all worlds at which the obligations of w are discharged.

PA (⌜It is permitted that A⌝) is true at w if A is true at some such worlds.

KA (⌜It is known that A⌝) is true at world w if A is true in all worlds consistent with what is known at w.

The resulting systems are labelled 'tense logic', 'deontic logic' and 'epistemic logic' to distinguish them from the original 'alethic' modal systems for necessity. In the last two areas this account probably takes the analogy with necessity too far, but it still serves as a useful point of departure (see DEONTIC LOGIC; EPISTEMIC LOGIC).

Among other broadly modal systems that have received attention recently are the 'dynamic logics' or 'logics of computation' for reasoning about computer programs. Here worlds become computation states, which can be thought of as specifications of all the program variables at a particular time, and relative possibility becomes program accessibility, which holds between two states if a program can start in the first and terminate in the second. Such logics may be useful in verifying, without interminable testing, that a large program is 'correct', that is, that it does what it is supposed to do (see DYNAMIC LOGICS).

The development of accessibility semantics led naturally to general questions about the classes of systems that can be characterized by various versions of it. Some of these are discussed below. Before the development of the accessibility interpretation, questions about the scope of axiomatic systems were often answered by devising suitable algebraic interpretations, and algebraic methods remain important tools for studying more general questions. Possible worlds semantics, however, seems less *ad hoc* than the algebraic methods. It is not clear whether they provide an analysis of necessity and possibility, or whether the notions that they incorporate, possible world and accessibility, are themselves to be analysed in terms of necessity and possibility. Either way, there is a close fit between the meanings of modal terms and their possible-worlds interpretations. The notion of possible world has proved useful in philosophical discussions on topics other than necessity and possibility: supervenience, causality, and the nature of propositions, properties and relations, to mention a few examples. The general utility of possible worlds has, in turn, inspired modal languages more expressive than the standard 'box and diamond' variety.

2 Propositional S5

As suggested above, S5 is the set of formulas provable from the axioms of classical propositional logic (PL) together with the axiom schemas *K*, *T*, *5* and $\Diamond A \leftrightarrow \neg \Box \neg A$ (henceforth Df$\Diamond$) and the rules *modus ponens* (MP) and necessitation (Nec). It is important to understand that Nec states that $\Box A$ is a theorem if *A* is, and not that $\Box A$ is true if *A* is. Given *T* and the replacement of equivalents, the latter condition would make $\Box A$ and *A* freely interchangeable, rendering modal logic pointless.

To identify a modal system in this way with its theorems and to refer to such systems as modal logics is to follow standard, though misleading, practices.

One would expect a 'logic' to indicate which conclusions follow logically from which premises, and perhaps the deductions by which they so follow. Furthermore, although S5 and other modal systems are intended to represent formal truths, that is, sentences true in virtue of form, it is not clear that they are intended to represent *logical* truths, that is, sentences true in virtue of logical form, for it is not clear that necessity is a logical constant (see LOGICAL FORM; LOGICAL CONSTANTS). The first of these concerns can be somewhat reduced by stipulating that *A* follows from a set of formulas with respect to a logic *L* if, and only if, *L* contains a conditional whose antecedent is a conjunction of those formulas and whose consequent is *A*.

A model (for S5) is a pair (W, V) where *W* is a non-empty set (the possible worlds) and *V* is a function (the valuation function) that assigns a truth-value (T or F) to each sentence letter and each possible world $w \in W$. If $M = (W, V)$ is a model and $w \in W$, the notion '*A* is true at *w* in *M*' (written $(M, w) \models A$) is defined inductively, the key clauses being:

$(M, w) \models \Box B$ if, for all $v \in W$, $(M, v) \models B$; and

$(M, w) \models \Diamond B$ if, for some $v \in W$ $(M, v) \models B$.

A formula is true in *M* if it is true at all possible worlds in *M*, and it is valid if it is true in all S5-models.

The 'soundness theorem' for S5 says that the semantics respects the logic in the sense that every formula in the logic is valid. The 'completeness theorem' states that every valid formula is in the logic. To say that S5 is both sound and complete with respect to the interpretation given is to say that validity and theoremhood coincide. Soundness is proved by an easy inductive argument appealing to the axiomatization: each axiom is observed to be valid and the two rules are shown to preserve validity. Completeness requires more ingenuity. A common approach is to adapt Henkin's proof of the completeness of classical logic. (For details see Lemmon (1966) or Chellas (1980).) One can get an idea of the value of an interpretation and completeness theorem by trying, with and without them, to demonstrate that $\Box p \rightarrow \Box \Box p$ is a theorem of S5.

In S5, all 'nesting' or 'iteration' of modality can be eliminated. For example, if a formula has the form $M_1 \ldots M_n A$ where each M_i is $\Box$, $\Diamond$ or negation, an equivalent formula can be obtained by deleting all the $\Box$'s and $\Diamond$'s except the innermost. Taking a modality to be a string of $\Box$'s, $\Diamond$'s and $\neg$'s, it follows that there are only six non-equivalent modalities in S5: the empty string, $\neg$, $\Box$, $\Diamond$, $\neg\Box$ and $\neg\Diamond$, corresponding to simple truth, falsity, necessity, possibility, non-necessity and impossibility.

One important schema of classical propositional logic that is not provable in S5 is extensionality:

$(\text{Ext})(A \leftrightarrow A') \rightarrow (B \leftrightarrow B')$, where B' is the result of replacing an occurrence of the subformula A in B by A'.

For example, if p and q are both true at world w but only q is true at world v, then

$$(p \leftrightarrow q) \rightarrow (\Box p \leftrightarrow \Box q)$$

is false at w. By completeness it follows that

$$(p \leftrightarrow q) \rightarrow (\Box p \leftrightarrow \Box q)$$

is not a theorem of S5. Ext says that replacement of one subformula by another of the same truth-value will not affect the truth-value of the whole. Its failure is often viewed as characteristic of modal systems in general. Note, however, that provably equivalent formulas can be substituted for each other.

S5 is a relatively strong modal system. Its only extensions are the trivial logic, containing all instances of $\Box A \leftrightarrow A$ and, for every natural number n, the 'n-possibility logic', containing all instances of

$$(\Diamond A_1 \wedge \ldots \wedge \Diamond A_{n+1}) \rightarrow \text{Dis},$$

where Dis is the disjunction of all formulas $\Diamond(A_i \wedge A_j)$ such that $i < j \leqslant n+1$ (n-possibility logic is complete with respect to the class of all models with at most n possible worlds.)

The formulas of (propositional) S5 correspond to formulas of classical monadic predicate logic in one variable. For example, $\Diamond(p_1 \wedge \Box p_2)$ corresponds to $\exists x(P_1 x \wedge \forall x P_2 x)$. Since decision procedures for monadic predicate logic are known, this correspondence allows one to determine effectively whether a formula is in S5 by testing the corresponding monadic formula for validity. A more direct proof of decidability rests on the result that S5 has the 'finite model' property: every non-theorem is false in some model with finitely many worlds. To test whether A is in S5, one checks first whether A is provable in one step or falsifiable in a one-world model, then whether it is provable in two steps or falsifiable in a two-world model, and so on. Each step can be completed in finite time. By the finite model property, there is some step n at which the process yields the desired answer.

3 Philosophical questions about S5

The most important philosophical question about S5 is whether it captures the inferences and truths it was intended to. This may depend, of course, on the kind of necessity that '$\Box$' is supposed to represent. On the usual view this is broadly logical or metaphysical necessity. Truths necessary in this sense include those true in virtue of logical form (the logical truths), those true in virtue of meaning (the analytic truths) and a more problematic category of those true in virtue of the basic nature of things. The last category has been said to contain truths of mathematics, the proposition that water is H_2O, and the proposition that Queen Elizabeth came from the egg and sperm that she did (see ESSENTIALISM). All these examples are controversial, but those who argue whether particular propositions are metaphysically necessary may nevertheless share a common conception of what it is to be metaphysically necessary. Furthermore, examples of propositions that lack metaphysical necessity seem uncontroversial: 'Napoleon invaded Russia', 'Asbestos is carcinogenic', 'Paris is the capital of France'.

The question of whether S5 (or any other system) is the right 'logic' for metaphysical necessity can be divided into two parts, corresponding to the two parts of the completeness theorem. Say that S5 is 'correct' if every theorem represents a formal truth about metaphysical necessity. Say that it is 'adequate' if every formal truth (with 'and', 'not', 'or' and 'if' as well as 'necessarily' and 'possibly') is represented by a theorem. Correctness and adequacy, then, are philosophical counterparts of soundness and completeness.

Correctness can be established by an argument similar to that for soundness: first show that the axioms represent formal truths and then that the rules transform formulas representing formal truths into formulas representing formal truths. Instances of axiom schema T, for example, clearly represent formal truths. ('If necessarily $87 + 25 = 112$ then $87 + 25 = 112$' is true in virtue of its form.) The difficult cases are axiom schema 5 and the rule Nec. For the former case we need to establish that sentences of the form ⌐If possibly S then necessarily possibly S⌐ are true in virtue of their form. One argument is as follows. To say possibly S is to say that ⌐Not S⌐ does not follow logically or analytically from a description of the natures of things or from logical truths or analytic truths, that is, that S is logically and analytically consistent with the basic natures of things. But a proposition that something is consistent with logical laws, meanings and basic natures in this way is true or false in virtue of those logical laws, meanings and basic natures. So ⌐Possibly S⌐, if true, is necessarily true. And since this argument does not appeal to S, the conditional is true in virtue of its form. An argument for the rule Nec might go as follows. Once it is established that all the axioms represent formal truths and that MP preserves formal truth, we know that everything proved without Nec represents a formal truth. Since formal truths are either logical or analytic, they are necessarily true. Since the argument that any of these sentences S is necessary relies only on the form of S, necessarily S is true in virtue of its form. This establishes that the first application of Nec results in formulas that represent formal truths. But if a sentence S proved with one application of Nec is shown to be a formal, and hence necessary, truth by an argument that appeals only to S's form, then ⌜Necessarily S⌝ must be true in virtue of its form. In this way, the argument can be extended to any subsequent application of Nec.

Adequacy might be established indirectly. Suppose that S5 were not adequate for metaphysical necessity. Then there would be some formal truth S, with 'necessarily', 'possibly', 'and' and so on, represented by a formula A that is not a theorem of S5. We should, then, be able to 'improve' the adequacy of S5 by adding A as an axiom. Furthermore, all the substitution instances of A will represent sentences with the form of S, which, if S is a formal truth, will also be formal truths. So we should be able to add all the substitution instances of A as well, obtaining an extension of S5. But, as was noted above, the extensions of S5 must contain either $\Box A \leftrightarrow A$ or, for some n, $(\Diamond A_1 \land \ldots \land \Diamond A_{n+1}) \to$ Dis. All these are incorrect for metaphysical necessity.

4   Quantified S5

Consider a language obtained by adding '$\Box$' and '$\Diamond$' and a special predicate E of existence to a version of predicate logic with predicates $P_1, P_2, \ldots$, individual constants, $t_1, t_2, \ldots$, and the identity sign, '='. A model is a triple (W, D, V) where W is a non-empty set (the possible worlds), D is a function that assigns to each $w \in W$ a set D_w (the domain of w) and V is a function that assigns to each constant t a member of the union $\cup D$ of the sets D_w (the possible object 'denoted' by t_i) and to each world and n-place predicate an n-ary relation on $\cup D$. A definition of truth at a world is obtained from the previous one by replacing the base clause and adding clauses for '$\forall$', '$\exists$', '=' and E. The quantifier clauses state that, for example, $\forall x Px$ is true at w if, for every d in D_w, Pt is true at w when t denotes d, and that $\exists x Px$ is true at w if, for some d in D_w, Pt is true at w when t denotes d. $s = t$ is true at w if s and t denote the same possible objects. Es is true at w if $V(s) \in D_w$.

This interpretation reflects several choices. First, constants are 'objectual', that is, V assigns a possible object directly to each constant. $\Box Pcd$ is true at w if the possible objects $V(c)$ and $V(d)$ are related, at every world w, by $V(P, w)$. Thus $\Box Pcd$ expresses a *de re* necessity: it asserts that particular objects, independently of their descriptions, are necessarily related.

This treatment of constants makes the schemas

$$(c = d) \to \Box(c = d) \quad \text{('necessary identity') and}$$
$$\neg(c = d) \to \Box \neg(c = d) \quad \text{('necessary difference')}$$

valid. Kripke has influentially argued that this is appropriate if c and d represent proper names of natural language, but generally inappropriate if they represent definite descriptions (see PROPER NAMES). The alternative to treating constants objectually is to allow their denotations to vary from world to world. An (individual) concept is a function from worlds to individuals. For example, the concept 'first person to reach the South Pole' might assign Amundsen to this world, Scott to the possible world in which Scott wins his race with Amundsen, and nothing to possible worlds in which the Pole is never (or always) occupied by people. We can regard a constant with a non-objectual interpretation as denoting a concept rather than an individual. On this 'conceptual' interpretation, necessary identity and necessary difference are not valid. Quantification may be treated conceptually as well: $\forall x A$ is declared true at w if every individual concept assigns to w an object to which A applies at w. In that case, quantified necessary identity and difference formulas,

$$\forall x \forall y (x = y \to \Box x = y) \text{ and}$$
$$\forall x \forall y (\neg(x = y) \to \Box \neg(x = y)),$$

lose their validity as well. The quantification described above, by contrast, is objectual.

Second, quantification is 'actualist'. The truth of $\forall x Px$ at w requires only that the objects in D_w have the appropriate property. It follows that the Barcan formula

$$\forall x \Box Px \to \Box \forall x Px$$

and its converse

$$\Box \forall x Px \to \forall x \Box Px$$

are both invalid. Suppose, for example, that for some world w, P is a predicate that holds everywhere of just the objects that exist in w, and that D_u contains something not in D_w. Then at w, 'Everything is necessarily P' is true while 'Necessarily, everything is P' is false. Conversely, suppose that, at every world w, P holds of just the objects that exist at w, and that D_v contains something not in D_u. Then at v 'Necessarily everything is P' is true, while 'Everything is necessarily P' is false. More generally, $\forall x \Box \forall y \Box A$, $\Box \forall x \forall y \Box A$, $\Box \forall x \Box \forall y A$, and $\Box \forall x \Box \forall y \Box A$ are logically distinct.

If quantification is 'possibilist', that is, if $\forall x A$ means that A is true of all objects in $\cup D$, then these formulas are all equivalent and the Barcan formula and its converse are valid. The distinction between actualist and possibilist quantification is significant only because the models defined above have domains that vary from world to world. If one stipulates 'constant domains', that is, that $D_u = D_v$ for all worlds u and v, then the possible objects are just the actual ones, and the distinction collapses. Barcan and its converse are again valid.

Third, predicates can be truthfully applied to constants denoting non-actual objects. Since quantification is actualist, this implies that the classical theorems $Pc \to \exists x Px$ and $\forall x Px \to Pc$ are not valid. These principles can be retained by insisting that the application of predicates to constants denoting non-actuals is always false (defining models so that $V(P_i, w)$ is a relation on D_w). But to do so would be to adopt a kind of atomism according to which the properties and relations expressed by atomic formulas with free variables had a special status. Furthermore, although it would save the particular classical theorems above, some of their substitution instances, such as $\neg Ex \to \exists x \neg Ex$, would still fail. Another alternative is to stipulate that formulas in which predicates are applied to constants denoting non-existents lack truth-value. If validity is taken as 'false in no model', both the formulas and their instances are saved. On the other hand, that approach would seem to make $\Box Ec$ valid (if necessity is 'nowhere false') or to make $\Box(Fc \vee \neg Fc)$ invalid (if necessity is 'everywhere true').

Finally, domains are permitted to be empty. This implies that

$$\Diamond \exists x(Fx \vee \neg Fx), \Box \exists x(Fx \vee \neg Fx) \text{ and } \exists x(Fx \vee \neg Fx)$$

are all invalid. If one regards the first as expressing a formal truth, one can require that some world have non-empty domain; if the second, that all worlds do. If one regards the third as expressing a formal truth one can require that each model specify – in addition to the possible worlds, domains, and valuation – a particular possible world (the actual) that has a non-empty domain. Truth in a model is then redefined as truth at the actual world of the model.

5 Weaker systems

A Kripke model is a triple (W, R, V), where W and V are as in §2, and R (accessibility) is a binary relation on W. Truth at a world is defined as before except for the '$\Box$' and '$\Diamond$' clauses:

$(M, w) \models \Box A$ if, for all $v \in W$ such that wRv,
$\quad (M, v) \models A$

$(M, w) \models \Diamond A$ if, for some $v \in W$ such that wRv,
$\quad (M, v) \models A$

Truth in a model and validity are defined as before. The formulas valid in this sense comprise the logic K. K can be axiomatized by the schemas PL, K and Df$\Diamond$ and the rules MP and Nec. Since it lacks the schema $\Box A \to A$, K is not adequate for necessity under any construal. It occupies an important position in modal logic in the broader sense, however, because many well-known modal systems are simple extensions of it. The systems in the leftmost column of the table, for example, are obtained by adding the schemas in the middle column to PL, K and Df$\Diamond$ and the rules MP and Nec.

The schema D (see the table) is formally true when '$\Box$' and '$\Diamond$' are read 'it is obligatory that' and 'it is permitted that', and the system D is known as the standard deontic logic. T was one of the earliest modal logics to be characterized precisely (see Feys 1937, 1938) and it seems to be the weakest logic in which '$\Box$' can plausibly be regarded as representing a reading of 'it is necessary that'. If, as some have suggested, the remaining S5 axioms are not correct for physical necessity, T would be a plausible

System	Characteristic axioms	Conditions on R
D	$D: \Box A \to \Diamond A$	seriality: $\forall x \exists y Rxy$
T	T	reflexivity: $\forall x Rxx$
S4	T $4: \Box A \to \Box\Box A$	reflexivity transitivity: $\forall x \forall y \forall z(Rxy \,\&\, Ryz \to Rxz)$
S4.3	$T, 4$ $H: \Diamond A \,\&\, \Diamond B \to \Diamond(A \wedge \Diamond B) \vee \Diamond(\Diamond A \wedge B) \vee \Diamond(A \wedge B)$	reflexivity, transitivity connectedness: $\forall x \forall y(Rxy \vee Ryx)$
GL	$W: \Box(\Box A \to A) \to \Box A$	transitivity no infinite chains: $\quad Rx_1x_2 \,\&\, Rx_2x_3 \,\&\, \ldots \to \exists i(x_i = x_{i+1})$

candidate for the logic of that notion. S4 was the fourth of the Lewis systems. Gödel (1933) gave it a characterization like the one above and showed it to be intertranslatable with intuitionistic propositional logic. S4.3 (so named, in part, because it is intermediate in strength between S4 and S5) is correct and adequate for a reading of '□' as 'it is and always will be the case that' if time is assumed to be linear (see TENSE AND TEMPORAL LOGIC). If sentence letters represent statements about numbers and '□' is interpreted as 'provable in arithmetic' then the system GL contains exactly the formulas that are themselves provable in arithmetic (where a statement about provability is 'provable' if its Gödel number is the number of a theorem of arithmetic – see GÖDEL'S THEOREMS). By adding all instances of $\Box A \rightarrow A$ to the theorems of GL (without allowing any new applications of the rule Nec) one obtains the system GLS, which may be regarded as the logic of arithmetic provability. Whereas GL comprises the arithmetically provable formulas about provability, GLS comprises the truths about provability (see PROVABILITY LOGIC).

Each of these logics can also be characterized semantically, just as we have done with K. A 'D-model' is a Kripke model whose accessibility relation is 'serial', that is, every world is related to some world or other, and models appropriate for each of the other systems can be similarly defined by the conditions in the table. In each case, soundness and completeness results like those for S5 sketched above can be given.

Not all broadly 'modal' systems can plausibly be interpreted by Kripke models. Suppose $\Box A$ is read 'usually A'. There is no relation on times such that 'usually A' is true now if A is true at all related times. Rather, the truth of 'usually A' depends on the number, and perhaps the distribution, of all the times at which A is true. This suggests a more general kind of modal semantics, one formulation of which is the 'neighbourhood semantics'. A 'neighbourhood model' is a triple (W, R, V), where W and V are as before, and R is a relation between worlds and sets of worlds (the 'neighbourhoods' of those worlds, although there is no requirement that the neighbourhood of a world contain the world itself, or even that it be non-empty). The definition of truth at a world is as before except that $\Box A$ is true at w just in case w is related to the 'truth-set' of A, that is, the set of worlds at which A is true; and $\Diamond A$ is true at w if w is unrelated to the 'falsity-set' of A.

The modal system determined by the set of all such models is the system E, axiomatized by the schemas PL and Df◇ and rules MP and 'equivalents' (RE): 'If $A \leftrightarrow B$ is provable, so is $\Box A \leftrightarrow \Box B$'. Like K, E provides a convenient base from which a variety of systems of interest can be constructed, rather than a

characterization of the formal truths for some particular reading of '□'. This idea can be carried even further. Operator logic (OL) is the system in the language with '□' that is axiomatized just by PL (see Kuhn 1981). The modal operators of S5, K, E and OL can be regarded as being successively more schematic and having successively less content, the theorems of OL being the modal sentences that are true in virtue of their logical form, and the stronger modal systems being theories of operators based on that logic.

6 General results

Much of the contemporary study of modal logic is directed, not towards investigating any particular one of the systems described above in more detail, but towards a general understanding of classes of such systems. The modal logics, as defined above, form a lattice structure. A Kripke model $M = (W, R, V)$ can be viewed as the addition of a valuation V to the 'Kripke frame' (W, R). M is then said to be 'based on' (W, R). Similarly, the neighbourhood model (W, N, V) is based on the neighbourhood frame (W, N). A formula is valid in a frame if it is true in all models based on the frame, and it is valid in a class of frames if it is valid in all frames of the class. A 'frame for L' is a frame in which all the theorems of L are valid. The set of formulas valid in a class of frames is a logic, the logic determined by that class. A logic is sound for a class of frames if every formula in the logic is valid in the class; it is sufficient for the class if every formula valid in the class is a member of the logic; it is complete (for the class) if it is sound and sufficient.

The logic determined by a class of frames is, by definition, complete for that class. It might also be complete for other classes. K, for example, is determined by (and therefore complete for) the irreflexive Kripke frames as well as all Kripke frames. Fine (1974) and Thomason (1974) independently showed that there are finitely axiomatizable extensions of K that are not determined by any class of Kripke frames. Such logics are incomplete: formulas true in every frame that verifies the axioms are unprovable. It is now known that the incompleteness phenomenon is widespread. For every extension L of the logic T there are uncountably many incomplete logics whose frames are exactly the frames for L. (This result holds for both Kripke frames and neighbourhood frames; see Benton 1985.) The incomplete logics that have been exhibited in the literature are generally complex and *ad hoc*, but one simple example is obtained from GL by replacing the first conditional of the schema W by a biconditional. In the other direction, results of Bull (1966) and Fine (1971) imply that every extension of S4.3 that admits the necessitation rule is complete and decidable.

Much work has also been done on the correspondences between modal and classical formulas. The schema T corresponds to the classical formula $\forall x R x x$ in the sense that the frames for the former are just the first-order models for the latter. Most modal schemas that have arisen naturally in philosophical discussion correspond similarly to first-order formulas. The schemas in the second column of the table, for example, correspond to formulas in the third column. The McKinsey schema, $\square \lozenge A \rightarrow \lozenge \square A$, on the other hand, corresponds to no first-order formula (see van Benthem 1975; Goldblatt 1975), and no modal schema corresponds to irreflexivity: $\forall x \neg R x x$. (The latter fact follows from the remark above that K itself is complete for the irreflexive frames.)

The general study of modal logic encompasses a variety of other topics, including: model theory (transformations of frames and models may preserve truth-values of classes of formulas); boundary investigations (some logics have properties that all their extensions lack); expressive power (some classes of modal connectives can be defined from a few representatives); and connections with non-modal logics (such as that between S4 and intuitionistic logic). The completeness and correspondence investigations discussed above, however, have formed the core of contemporary investigations.

See also: LOGICAL AND MATHEMATICAL TERMS, GLOSSARY OF; MODAL LOGIC, PHILOSOPHICAL ISSUES IN

References and further reading

* Aristotle (c.mid 4th century BC) *De Interpretatione, Prior Analytics* and *Metaphysics*, trans. and ed. J. Barnes, in *The Revised Oxford Translation*, vols 1 and 2, Princeton, NJ: Princeton University Press, 1984. (Referred to in §1.)
* Benthem, J.F. van (1975) 'Some Connections Between Modal and Elementary Logic', in S. Kanger (ed.) *Proceedings of the Third Scandinavian Logic Symposium*, Amsterdam: North Holland. (Referred to in §6.)
* Benton, R. (1985) 'General Modal Incompleteness and Finite Axiomatizability', Ph.D. dissertation, University of Michigan. (Referred to in §6.)
  Boolos, G. (1993) *The Logic of Provability*, Cambridge: Cambridge University Press. (Thorough and readable exploration of the arithmetic provability interpretation of $\square$ discussed in §5.)
* Bull, R.A. (1966) 'That all Normal Extensions of S4.3 Have the Finite Model Property', *Zeitschrift für*

Mathematische Logik und Grundlagen der Mathematik 12: 341–44. (Referred to in §6.)
* Carnap, R. (1947) *Meaning and Necessity: A Study in Semantics and Modal Logic*, Chicago, IL: University of Chicago Press; 2nd, enlarged edn, 1956. (Referred to in §1.)
* Chellas, B.F. (1980) *Modal Logic: An Introduction*, Cambridge: Cambridge University Press. (Referred to in §2. Careful and clear introductory text on propositional modal logic, emphasizing completeness and decidability.)
* Curley, E.M. (1984) 'Descartes on the Creation of the Eternal Truths', *Philosophical Review* 93: 569–97. (Referred to in §1.)
* Feys, R. (1937, 1938) 'Les logiques nouvelles des modalités', *Revue Néoscholastique de Philosophie* 40: 517–53, 41: 217–52. (Referred to in §5.)
* Fine, K. (1971) 'The Logics Containing S4.3', *Zeitschrift für Mathematische Logik und Grundlagen der Mathematik* 17: 371–6. (Referred to in §6.)
* —— (1974) 'An Incomplete Logic Containing S4', *Theoria* 40: 23–9. (Referred to in §6.)
  Fine, K. and Kuhn, S. (forthcoming) *Modal Logic.* (Text and survey that is attentive to philosophical concerns, including the issues of correctness and adequacy discussed in §3.)
  Gabbay, D. and Guenthner, F. (eds) (1984) *Handbook of Philosophical Logic*, vol. 2, *Extensions of Classical Logic*, Dordrecht: Kluwer. (The articles by Bull and Segerberg, van Benthem, Garson and Cocchiarella constitute an advanced survey of central topics. The volume also contains excellent articles on modality and time by R. Thomason, modality and self-reference by Smorynski, and others on topics somewhat more peripheral to the present one.)
* Gödel, K. (1933) 'Eine Interpretation des intuitionistischen Aussagenkalküls', *Ergebnisse eines Mathematischen Kolloquiums* 4: 39–40; trans. 'An Interpretation of the Intuitionistic Propositional Calculus', in *Collected Works*, ed. S. Feferman, J.W. Dawson, W. Goldfarb, C.D. Parsons and R.M. Solovay, Oxford and New York: Oxford University Press, 1995, vol. 3, 296–302. (Referred to in §5.)
* Goldblatt, R. (1975) 'First-order Definability in Modal Logic', *Journal of Symbolic Logic* 40: 35–40. (Referred to in §6.)
* Hintikka, J. (1963) 'The Modes of Modality', *Acta Philosophica Fennica* 16: 65–81; repr. in *Models for Modalities*, Dordrecht: Kluwer, 1969. (Referred to in §1.)
  Hughes, G.E. and Cresswell, M.J. (1968) *An Introduction to Modal Logic*, London: Routledge; revised edn, *A New Introduction to Modal Logic*, London:

Routledge, 1996. (The classic modern textbook; still useful.)

—— (1984) *Companion to Modal Logic*, London: Routledge. (A sequel to the previous book that incorporates subsequent developments in the field, including an incompleteness result.)

* Kanger, S. (1957) *Provability in Logic*, Stockholm: Almqvist & Wicksell. (Referred to in §1.)

* Knuuttila, S. (1982) 'Modal Logic', in N. Kretzmann, A. Kenny and J. Pinborg (eds) *Cambridge History of Later Medieval Philosophy*, Cambridge: Cambridge University Press. (Referred to in §1. Brief survey of some medieval thought on modality, including that of Boethius, Scotus and Buridan.)

—— (1993) *Modalities in Medieval Philosophy*, London and New York: Routledge. (More comprehensive survey than Knuuttila (1982), with an extensive bibliography.)

* Kripke, S.A. (1963) 'Semantical Analysis of Modal Logic I: Normal Modal Propositional Calculi', *Zeitschrift für Mathematische Logik und Grundlagen der Mathematik* 9: 67–96. (Referred to in §1.)

* Kuhn, S. (1981) 'Constants, Logical Symbols and Operator Logic', *Journal of Philosophy* 78: 487–99. (Referred to in §5.)

* Lemmon, E.J. (1966) *An Introduction to Modal Logic*, ed. K. Segerberg, Oxford: Blackwell, 1977. (Referred to in §1. Draft of initial chapters of a planned collaboration with D. Scott. In fewer than 100 pages, it includes a historical survey and many applications of the Henkin completeness method.)

* Lewis, C.I. and Langford, C.H. (1932) *Symbolic Logic*, New York: Century. (Appendix II, which was written by Lewis, lays out the axiom systems S1–S5 for strict implication that are mentioned in §1.)

Mints, G. (1992) *A Short Introduction to Modal Logic*, Stanford, CA: Center for the Study of Language and Information, Stanford University. (A concise treatment of the systems S5, S4 and T that emphasizes refutation procedures inspired by Gentzen's sequent calculi, rather than the axiomatic characterizations presented here.)

* Montague, R. (1960) 'Logical Necessity, Physical Necessity, Ethics and Quantifiers', *Inquiry* 4: 259–69; repr. in *Formal Philosophy*, New Haven, CT: Yale University Press, 1974. (Referred to in §1.)

* Thomason, S.K. (1974) 'An Incompleteness Theorem in Modal Logic', *Theoria* 40: 30–4. (Referred to in §6.)

STEVEN T. KUHN

MODAL LOGIC, PHILOSOPHICAL ISSUES IN

In reasoning we often use words such as 'necessarily', 'possibly', 'can', 'could', 'must' and so on. For example, if we know that an argument is valid, then we know that it is necessarily *true that if the premises are true, then the conclusion is true. Modal logic starts with such modal words and the inferences involving them. The exploration of these inferences has led to a variety of formal systems, and their interpretation is now most often built on the concept of a possible world.*

Standard non-modal logic shows us how to understand logical words such as 'not', 'and' and 'or', which are truth-functional. The modal concepts are not truth-functional: knowing that p is true (and what 'necessarily' means) does not automatically enable one to determine whether 'Necessarily p' is true. ('It is necessary that all people have been people' is true, but 'It is necessary that no English monarch was born in Montana' is false, even though the simpler constituents – 'All people have been people' and 'No English monarch was born in Montana'– are both true.)

The study of modal logic has helped in the understanding of many other contexts for sentences that are not truth-functional, such as 'ought' ('It ought to be the case that p') and 'believes' ('Alice believes that p'); and also in the consideration of the interaction between quantifiers and non-truth-functional contexts. In fact, much work in modern semantics has benefited from the extension of modal semantics introduced by Richard Montague in beginning the development of a systematic semantics for natural language.

The framework of possible worlds developed for modal logic has been fruitful in the analysis of many concepts. For example, by introducing the concept of relative possibility, Kripke showed how to model a variety of modal systems: a proposition is necessarily true at a possible world w if and only if it is true at every world that is possible relative to w. To achieve a better analysis of statements of ability, Mark Brown adapted the framework by modelling actions with sets of possible outcomes. John has the ability to hit the bull's-eye reliably if there is some action of John's such that every possible outcome of that action includes John's hitting the bull's-eye.

Modal logic and its semantics also raise many puzzles. What makes a modal claim true? How do we tell what is possible and what is necessary? Are there any possible things that do not exist (and what could that mean anyway)? Does the use of modal logic involve a commitment to essentialism? How can an individual exist in many different possible worlds?

1   What makes a modal claim true?

Alice ate vegetable soup today. What makes that true? Alice's activities and their relationship to vegetable soup. Alice *could have* eaten cream of tomato soup. What makes that true? This is less clear. No activity of Alice's seems to make this statement about possibilities true.

If we ask what makes something possible, the context of the question sometimes sets a standard: it was possible for Alice to have eaten cream of tomato soup because it was on the menu, there was plenty of it available, there was nothing barring her from ordering it and nothing standing in the way of the waiter's bringing it to her. Yet it seems that there is a more absolute sense of possibility, according to which it was at least logically possible for Alice to have eaten cream of rutabaga soup (even if no one had ever made such a thing), because no logical or conceptual barrier prevents its existence or her eating it.

In contrast, Alice could not eat cream of tomato soup without eating it, and she could not have vegetable soup that involved no vegetables at any stage of its preparation. For logical or conceptual reasons, these are not activities open to Alice. Not every description picks out something that is possible.

Once we get a view of this broader notion of possibility, it seems that possibility can get a negative characterization. A description of an event or state of affairs describes something possible if no logical or conceptual consideration rules out what it describes. It is possible if it is not impossible; and the impossible is whatever is ruled out by logical or conceptual considerations. If a proposition is necessary, then its negation is impossible. The proposition

> If Alice eats tomato soup, then Alice eats tomato soup

is necessary; and so a negation of that, a proposition equivalent to

> Alice eats tomato soup without eating tomato soup,

is impossible. It is necessary that

> All vegetable soup involves vegetables in its preparation;

so it is impossible that

> Something is vegetable soup and does not involve vegetables in its preparation.

Understanding what is impossible will follow upon an understanding of what is necessary.

All of this suggests that we can understand what makes something possible if we can get a general understanding of what makes something a necessary truth. An event or state of affairs p is not possible if and only if p is impossible; p is impossible if and only if the negation of p, $\sim p$, is necessary. Ordinarily the box symbol is used before a sentence to stand for necessity ('$\Box p$' stands for 'It is necessary that p') and the diamond is used to stand for possibility ('$\Diamond p$' stands for 'It is possible that p'), and we have just taken note of these related equivalences:

$$\Diamond p \text{ iff } \sim\!\Box\!\sim\! p.$$
$$\sim\!\Diamond p \text{ iff } \Box\!\sim\! p.$$

Because of these logical relationships between possibility and necessity, we can understand what makes something possible by developing an understanding of what makes something necessary. A state of affairs is possible if and only if its negation is not necessary. So what makes something a necessary truth? Our examples so far have consisted of logical and conceptual truths, but it seems that the category of necessary truths is broader. My pet cat could not exist without being an animal; it is necessary that if she exists, then she is an animal. I could not have existed if a certain sperm and ovum had never existed; it is necessary that if I exist, then those cells existed. No right hand can precisely fill the space taken up by any left hand; it is necessary that if a space S is filled by a left hand, then S cannot be precisely filled by any right hand. Logic and definitions do not seem to suffice as the source of the necessity of these truths.

In exploring logical relationships, logicians have introduced the concept of a possible world. This has been of enormous benefit in understanding logical relationships among modal claims. A statement is a necessary truth if and only if it is true at every possible world; a statement is possibly true if and only if it is true at at least one possible world. Thus our symbols can be connected with a systematic semantics for modal language in which possible worlds are reference points:

> Any sentence of the form '$\Box p$' is true iff p is true at every possible world.

> Any sentence of the form '$\Diamond p$' is true iff p is true at at least one possible world.

Kripke's elaboration of this, employing the notion of relative possibility, has been very important in exploring a range of modal systems that give a range of different results concerning the logical relationships among modal sentences (see KRIPKE, S.A.; MODAL LOGIC). With further elaboration, introducing a 'closeness' relation, this framework has been extended (see Lewis 1973, Stalnaker 1968) to provide a better semantics for counterfactuals: roughly, a counterfactual 'If it were the case that *p*, then it would be the case that *q*' is true at *w* if and only if *q* is true at all of the closest worlds to *w* in which *p* is true.

Such systematizations seem to give us an account of the necessity and possibility of propositions that can help us to see more clearly what is and what is not possible. This account, however, is not an ultimate answer to the question of what makes something possible, because there is no independent account of what a possible world is. We are left with the question of what makes it the case that Alice's eating rutabaga soup is included in some possible worlds, whereas my cat's being a plant is not. At a possible world, every necessary truth must be true, every state of affairs which obtains must be possible, and the possible world must meet some maximality condition (for example, that every proposition or its negation must be true at that world) – but then judging what is included in a possible world takes us back to the question of judging what is possible. So we have a circle of concepts. The exploration of such a circle of concepts can be very enlightening concerning their logical relationships, and it can help us to make more consistent judgments about the application of the concepts, but it cannot give an independent answer to the question of what makes a modal statement true (see POSSIBLE WORLDS; SEMANTICS, POSSIBLE WORLDS).

Thus we are led to a root philosophical problem about modality, the problem of giving a general account of what makes modal claims and related claims true – or, which amounts to the same problem, the problem of saying in general what makes a set of propositions true of a possible world (or what makes a set of states of affairs constitute a possible world). Any answer that is non-modal seems inadequate, and any answer that is modal merely enlarges the circle. Perhaps the kind of understanding that we get by enlarging the circle and exploring the relationships among modal concepts is the best we can hope for (see Blackburn 1993).

2 The merely possible

Even when we work within the circle of modal concepts, attempting to get a coherent, systematic semantics for modal claims, we come upon many puzzles. Understanding the relationship between the actual and the possible is at the root of much of the difficulty.

It seems clear that there could have been more carrier pigeons. If people had not shot so many of them, they would be flying now, perhaps in flocks so large that they would darken the skies. In saying this – in using the word 'they' to refer to some carrier pigeons that *would be* flying now – I seem to be referring to carrier pigeons that do not exist. Are there carrier pigeons that do not exist, that is, some nonexistent, merely possible carrier pigeons? We should hope not. Yet in a systematic treatment of modality, it is difficult to avoid the problem of requiring the existence of merely possible objects, and various strategies have been employed to deal with this problem. (Not everyone regards a commitment to nonexistent objects as a problem; see MEINONG, A.)

One strategy is to note a distinction between existence and actuality. Some things – possibilia – exist without being actual, and the merely possible carrier pigeons are among them. In fact, it might be said that if possible worlds exist without being actual, why should we regard it as a new problem to accept the existence of the things that make up those worlds, such as possible carrier pigeons? If the possible worlds exist, it seems that the things in them should exist as well. The use of modal language commits us to both possible worlds and possibilia, according to this view.

The view that there are some merely possible objects, just as there are merely possible worlds, seems grounded in a puzzle, however, and we can separate that view from the thesis that other possible worlds exist. A distinction between existence and actuality makes sense for possible worlds, on most conceptions, because a possible world is really an abstract representation; a way things might be, rather than a way in which they are. (The conception for which David LEWIS argues is an important exception to this; see Lewis 1986.) Thus we can say that there are worlds very much like this one except that Quine becomes a full-time geographer and never becomes a philosopher. There are such ways for things to be, but they are not actualized: things are not that way. This distinction between existing and being actualized holds among worlds as it does for stories or dreams, because a world is a way things might be; a maximal state of affairs or a maximally consistent set of propositions. This distinction does not carry over to individuals such as Quine and carrier pigeons. If nonactual carrier pigeons are carrier pigeons, then they are not the sort of thing that can exist without being actualized. This is the puzzle of possibilia, because we cannot see how any carrier pigeon can exist without being actual (in the way that a story can exist without being actual), and the idea that possible worlds and possible objects are on an existential par seems unacceptable. Possibilia cannot simply ride in on the coat tails of possible worlds.

One way out of this is to interpret the semantics as being about something more abstract than individuals – concepts or individual essences (see Plantinga 1974, for example). Instead of using the ordinary concept of satisfaction in the semantics, we can use a concept 'satisfaction*', saying that an individual essence e satisfies* 'x is a geographer' at a world w if and only if e is an essence of something that would be a geographer if that world, w, were actual. These individual essences can then be things that exist even when they are not actualized and that are actualized by the same individual at every world at which they are actualized. The individual essences of many carrier pigeons exist without being actualized. That is why it is true that other carrier pigeons could have existed.

On this view, individual essences rather than individuals are components of propositions. This allows the propositions to exist even when the individuals do not exist. This conflicts with David Kaplan's view that a typical singular proposition is contingently existent, existing only in those possible worlds in which the individual that it is about exists (see Kaplan 1989; DEMONSTRATIVES AND INDEX-ICALS §2). But it need not conflict with his more central views: that singular propositions do not contain concepts that can be used to pick out the individual the proposition is about; and that the propositional component is determined by the individual rather than the other way around. This would only mean that possible worlds in which an individual does not exist provide no resources for singling out that individual's essence. Nothing in this approach conflicts with that.

The approach in terms of essences leaves puzzles, too. What are these things? How many of them are there? These questions are not easy to answer, and so we are left with some discomfort in understanding modal claims no matter how we try to deal with the problem of possibilia.

3 Quantification, modality and essentialism

Many of those who have considered the concept of necessity have regarded it as a logical concept, applying to sentences in virtue of their form. An idea like one of the following would be typical.

A sentence of the form '$\Box p$' is true iff p is a logical truth.

A sentence of the form '$\Box p$' is true iff p is analytic.

W.V. QUINE has expressed grave misgivings about this at two levels. First, he questions the intelligibility of the notion of analyticity, and at times seems even to question the concept of logical truth. Thus he will reject any notion of necessity construed in this way. Quine's misgivings about logical truth and analyticity are explored elsewhere (see ANALYTICITY).

Quine (1961, 1966) has a further objection to the intermingling of quantifiers and modalities. Even if one grants a concept of analyticity or logical truth to serve as the basis for the concept of necessity, there are two problems for quantified modal logic: the problem of quantifying into modal contexts; and the related problem of intersubstituting coreferential names.

We can see the problem of quantifying in more easily if we consider first the problem of quantifying into truth-functional contexts. This is a real problem, because we ordinarily give an account of truth-functional connectives in terms of the truth-values of the constituents. Thus 'Fa & Ga' is true if and only if 'Fa' is true and 'Ga' is true. However, if we quantify, writing '$(\exists x)(Fx$ & $Gx)$', then '&' no longer connects two sentences that have a definite truth-value. Some new interpretation for '&' must be found, so that we can understand how the semantic value of the unit 'Fx & Gx' is determined.

Tarski (1933) found a systematic way to do this. Even though 'Fx' has no truth-value, it has a truth-value *relative to an assignment of an individual i to 'x'*. 'Fx & Gx' is true relative to an assignment if and only if 'Fx' is true relative to that assignment and 'Gx' is true relative to that assignment. We can also say that an assignment or an individual satisfies the open sentence 'Fx & Gx' if and only if it satisfies 'Fx' and satisfies 'Gx'. This solves the problem of quantifying into truth-functional contexts (see TARSKI'S DEFINITION OF TRUTH).

To interpret '$\exists x \Box Fx$' we need to know when an individual i satisfies '$\Box Fx$'. It is not so immediately evident how to account for this, especially if you think that the necessity of 'Fa' comes from features of 'Fa' (for example, an analytic association of 'a' with 'Fx') rather than from features of the individual i that 'a' denotes. An individual can be singled out by many different conditions, and perhaps some of those are analytically associated with 'Fx' though others are not. For example, the condition '$x = 3^3$' has '$x > 7$' as a necessary consequence (that is, it is a necessary truth that whatever satisfies one satisfies the other); but 'x numbers the planets' does not have this necessary consequence. The condition '$x > 7$' is necessarily connected with some ways of specifying nine but not with others. We can ask whether nine is necessarily greater than seven, but Quine finds no grounds for answering this question one way rather than another, because he believes that all necessity must be grounded in analytic consequence relationships and he finds no basis for favouring one specification of nine over the other. By this standard, either answer to the question of whether nine is necessarily greater than seven seems equally justified. Beginning with an account of necessity in terms of analyticity or logical truth should lead one to Quine's suspicions about quantification into this context.

The attempt to explain satisfaction of a modal condition in terms of analytic consequence seems doomed. But how else? Saying directly that some properties are necessary and others are not repels Quine. Quine sees such distinctions as an objectionable essentialism (see ESSENTIALISM), and accordingly he dismisses quantified modal logic.

Kripke provides an alternative account of what it is for an individual to satisfy '$\Box Fx$'. The account, in terms of possible worlds, has puzzled Quine; and puzzlement about existence of an individual in different possible worlds is closely related to Quine's puzzlement about essentialism. For existence in multiple possible worlds to have significance, it seems that there must be something that makes it possible for an individual to exist with some sets of properties and not others – some are essential and some are not. We must distinguish between properties that an individual has: for example, my cat satisfies 'x is an animal' and also 'x has eaten chicken livers', but she has the first property (being a cat) essentially and the second (having eaten chicken livers) only contingently. Kripke provides at least the formal framework for an account (1963), and in later work (1972) does much to defend the substantive metaphysics that goes with it.

Terence Parsons (1969) has pointed out that we can make at least one kind of distinction between essential and non-essential properties in a way that even Quine should not object to. Properties expressed by sentences of the form 'If Fx, then Fx' will be essential to everything. Such essential properties seem unproblematic. We encounter problematic essentialism only if we find two individuals that differ in their essential properties. This point is limited in its scope, however. Within any fixed model verifying the assumption that all individuals have the same essential properties, any sentence with quantifying in is true in all of the same worlds as some sentence that lacks quantifying in. The resources that troubled Quine – quantification into modal contexts – seem to serve no expressive purpose (see McKay 1975 and Fine 1978b).

4   Counterparts

Although Barney is eating a sandwich for lunch, he could have had a salad instead. Most modal theorists take that claim to involve the existence of a certain non-actual but possible situation: the possibility that Barney eats a salad for lunch.

David Lewis (1968) thinks that no such possible situation exists. Barney could have eaten a salad, but that really means that there is a possible world very much like this one in which the person most like Barney eats a salad. A non-actual world will never include Barney; it may, however, include a counterpart of Barney, an individual that is more like him than is any other in that world. The fact that one of his counterparts eats a salad makes it true that Barney could eat a salad, according to Lewis.

This approach has seemed unintuitive and ill-motivated to many (Plantinga (1974) and Kripke (1972), for example). When considering what is possible for Barney, it seems natural to suppose that we are considering possibilities that involve Barney rather than someone else. In addition, it seems that in another possible world Barney could have been very different from the way he is while someone else was more like our actual Barney. As arguments against counterpart theory, however, such intuitive considerations are inconclusive. They might be answered by denials (citing a conflict of intuitions) or, for the last objection, by clarifications of the theory that elaborate the relevant similarity notion.

Formal considerations are also significant, however. The identity relation is transitive, but there is no reason to think that the counterpart relation is transitive, and this will produce different valid formulas. In the modal systems S4 and S5 (see MODAL LOGIC), for example, the following is ordinarily valid:

$$\forall x(\Diamond\Diamond Fx \to \Diamond Fx).$$

But as long as the counterpart relation is not transitive, we could not expect that to be valid, even in S5. (An individual i might have a counterpart that has a counterpart that satisfies 'Fx' even though no counterpart of i satisfies 'Fx'.) Whether this difference would be an advantage or a drawback would need further consideration.

One technical feature is directly related to some of the intuitive considerations against counterpart theory. Lewis allows that an individual in one world might have two counterparts within a single world. If that is the case, then some laws involving identity will fail. Ordinarily, the principle of necessary identity is valid:

$$\Box\forall x\forall y(x = y \to \Box x = y).$$

And there seems to be a good argument for this, based

on two other fundamental principles, the necessity of self-identity and Leibniz's Law (see IDENTITY):

$$\Box \forall x \Box x = x$$
$$\forall x \forall y (x = y \rightarrow (\phi x \leftrightarrow \phi y))$$

One substitution instance of Leibniz's Law is this:

$$\forall x \forall y (x = y \rightarrow (\Box x = x \leftrightarrow \Box x = y)).$$

Given the assumption of the necessity of self-identity, the principle of necessary identity then follows. To defend counterpart theory, one must locate a fault with the necessity of self-identity or with this application of Leibniz's Law, or one must add features to the counterpart theory that will validate the principle of necessary identity (see Forbes 1985).

5 The logic of ability

Having surveyed some of the difficulties in interpreting modal logic, we now return to an illustration of the use of the possible worlds framework to shed light on inferences that are important for philosophy.

Although 'might' and 'can' are often thought of as possibility operators, they are clearly different. 'John might hit the target' and 'John can [is able to] hit the target' are very different, and Mark Brown's semantics for a logic of ability extends the possible worlds resources to make it clear what the difference is (1988).

Suppose that John is throwing darts, but does not reliably hit the target. Is John *able* to hit the target? He might hit it, but he does not have an ability that enables him to hit it reliably. In ordinary discussion, 'John is able to hit the target' is perhaps ambiguous. It could represent 'He might hit it', but is more likely to mean 'He has the ability to hit it reliably'. This suggests that there are two possibility operators, and these are distinguishable in Brown's system.

We can also give a more formal motivation for such a system. When we consider the context 'He has the ability to . . . reliably', we find that it does not obey the following law K◇ of the most fundamental normal modal system K:

$$\Diamond (p \vee q) \rightarrow (\Diamond p \vee \Diamond q).$$

If John has the ability to hit the target reliably, then he is able to bring it about that he hits either the right half or the left half. It need not be true that he has the ability to hit the right half reliably, and it need not be true that he has the ability to hit the left half reliably. So K◇ does not seem true, if '◇' is to represent an ability operator.

Also, in almost all standard modal systems (all that include T), we have this principle: $p \rightarrow \Diamond p$. But

suppose that John will, by luck, hit the target. It does not follow that he has the ability to do that reliably. So T◇ is not true, if '◇' is to represent an ability operator.

Brown introduces a family of new modal operators that we can add to the standard ones. We will use these symbols: ◇, ◈, ⊡ and ⊟. The semantics is based on a binary relation S, relating worlds in W to sets of worlds (that is, $S \subseteq (W \times \wp(W))$). We can define the new modal operators as follows (where we use 'K' as a variable for sets of possible worlds):

◇p is true at w iff $\exists K$ such that wSK and $\forall w'$ such that $w' \in K$, p is true at w'. (Informally: John is able to bring it about that p reliably. John can perform some action such that p is sure to be true if that action is performed.)

◈p is true at w iff $\exists K$ such that wSK and $\exists w'$ such that $w' \in K$, p is true at w'. (John might bring it about that p. Some action that John can perform allows for the possibility of p.)

⊡p is true at w iff $\forall K$ such that wSK, $\exists w'$ such that $w' \in K$, p is true at w'. (No matter what John does, p might be true.)

⊟p is true at w iff $\forall K$ such that wSK, $\forall w'$ such that $w' \in K$, p is true at w'. (No matter what John does, p will be true.)

Given this understanding of these operators, it is natural to make at least the following assumptions about the relation S, validating the formulas ◇$p \rightarrow$ ◈p and $p \rightarrow$ ◈p:

$\forall w \forall K$ such that wSK, $K \neq \emptyset$. (Validates D◇: ◇$p \rightarrow$ ◈p)

(Nothing John can do annihilates all possibilities. Everything John can do has some possible outcomes.)

$\forall w \exists K$ such that wSK and $w \in K$. (Validates T◇: $p \rightarrow$ ◈p)

(The actual world is a possible outcome of at least one of John's actions.)

Focus first on ◇, the modal operator representing ability. If we think of an action as being represented by a set of possible outcomes, then we can consider each set K of possible worlds such that wSK to correspond to the outcomes of some action that the agent under consideration might take. Each such set K would be a set of possible worlds that might be actual if the agent performed some particular action. So if the agent can hit the dartboard, but has no control over where, then a set of possible worlds that vary in where the agent hits the dartboard would be a set K such that wSK, and it could correspond to the action of throwing a dart. To say that ◇A is to say that there is some action (that is, some set K of outcomes; that is, some set K such that wSK) that guarantees A (that is, A is true throughout K). To say that the agent can hit the dartboard is to say that there is some such action (that is, some set K such that wSK, and throughout K the agent hits the dartboard).

The word 'could' is associated with possibility and ability. Three of our new modal operators involve possibility, and we can give an example that is three ways ambiguous:

He could win the lottery.

This could mean that he bought a ticket, and so nothing he can do would guarantee to make him a non-winner, that is, ⊠A. This could mean that he can buy a ticket, and then he might win, that is, ◇A. Or this could mean that he has special powers such that if he exercised them he would win, that is, ◇A. (The King could win the lottery (if he wanted to), but he hates to interfere in the peasants' fun.)

Thus we have a resource for disambiguation and for the exploration of logical relationships that are central to some philosophical work in ethics and metaphysics. Even though we have seen how many puzzles arise in the acceptance of the possible worlds framework, we should not lose sight of the many reasons we have to value it.

See also: LOGICAL AND MATHEMATICAL TERMS, GLOSSARY OF; MODAL OPERATORS; MONTAGUE, R.M.

References and further reading

* Blackburn, S. (1993) 'Morals and Modals', in *Essays in Quasi-Realism*, Oxford: Oxford University Press. (Discusses the problem of §1: what makes modal claims true.)
* Brown, M. (1988) 'On the Logic of Ability', *Journal of Philosophical Logic* 17: 1–26. (An extension of standard modal logic to accommodate statements of ability, such as 'John can [is reliably able to] hit the target', and related concepts. Discussed in §5.)
Fine, K. (1978a) 'Model Theory for Modal Logic. Part I: The De Re/De Dicto Distinction', *Journal of Philosophical Logic* 7: 125–56. (Relates technical results to some philosophical considerations.)
* —— (1978b) 'Model Theory for Modal Logic. Part II: The Elimination of the *De Re*', *Journal of Philosophical Logic* 7: 277–306. (Technical results and philosophical issues related to those discussed in §3.)
—— (1981) 'Model Theory for Modal Logic. Part III: Existence and Predication', *Journal of Philosophical Logic* 10: 293–307. (Technical results and philosophical issues related to a version of actualism, a

view that ascribes a special status to actual or existent objects. Related to issues discussed in §2.)
* Forbes, G. (1985) *The Metaphysics of Modality*, Oxford: Oxford University Press. (A discussion of metaphysical issues associated with modal logic.)
* Kaplan, D. (1989) 'Demonstratives', in *Themes from Kaplan*, ed. J. Almog, J. Perry and H.K. Wettstein, Oxford: Oxford University Press. (A classic discussion of demonstrative reference, with a semantics that builds on possible worlds models. Makes clear the distinction between necessity and analyticity mentioned in connection with §3.)
* Kripke, S.A. (1963) 'Semantical Considerations on Modal Logic', *Acta Philosophica Fennica* 16: 83–94; repr. in L. Linsky (ed.) *Reference and Modality*, Oxford: Oxford University Press, 1971. (This presents the semantic framework for modal logic.)
* —— (1972) 'Naming and Necessity', in D. Davidson and G. Harman (eds) *Semantics of Natural Language*, Dordrecht: Reidel, 252–355. (This important article illuminates the concept of metaphysical necessity and identifies important principles of identity. There is material relevant to every section of this entry.)
* Lewis, D.K. (1968) 'Counterpart Theory and Quantified Modal Logic', *Journal of Philosophy* 65: 113–26. (Presents and defends counterpart theory. See §4.)
* —— (1973) *Counterfactuals*, Cambridge, MA: Harvard University Press. (In discussion of the main topic, conditionals, there is a valuable development of the possible worlds framework. There is also some general discussion of the nature of possible worlds and of counterpart relations.)
* —— (1986) *On the Plurality of Worlds*, Oxford: Blackwell. (Further development of Lewis' view of possible worlds, with some important challenges to other views of modality.)
Linsky, L. (ed.) (1971) *Reference and Modality*, Oxford: Oxford University Press. (A collection of important articles on the topics of §§2, 3.)
* McKay, T. (1975) 'Essentialism in Quantified Modal Logic', *Journal of Philosophical Logic* 4: 423–38. (Results mentioned in §3, concerning Quine's linking of modal logic and essentialism.)
Montague, R. (1974) *Formal Philosophy*, New Haven, CT: Yale University Press. (In these papers, Montague developed the semantic framework of possible worlds in beginning to give a more general semantics for natural language.)
* Parsons, T. (1969) 'Essentialism and Quantified Modal Logic', *Philosophical Review* 78: 35–52; repr. in L. Linsky (ed.) *Reference and Modality*, Oxford: Oxford University Press, 1971, 73–87.

(Anti-essentialist models introduced as part of a response to Quine. See §3.)

* Plantinga, A. (1974) *The Nature of Necessity*, Oxford: Oxford University Press. (An excellent introduction to topics in the metaphysics of modality. Relevant to §§1–4 of this entry.)

* Quine, W.V. (1961) 'Reference and Modality', in *From a Logical Point of View: Nine Logico-Philosophical Essays*, Cambridge, MA: Harvard University Press, 2nd edn, 1980; repr. in L. Linsky (ed.) *Reference and Modality*, Oxford: Oxford University Press, 1971. (Misgivings about the interaction of modality with reference and quantification. Discussed in §3.)

* —— (1966) 'Three Grades of Modal Involvement', in *The Ways of Paradox*, New York: Random House. (Misgivings about the interaction of modal sentence operators with reference and quantification. Discussed in §3.)

* Stalnaker, R. (1968) 'A Theory of Conditionals', in N. Rescher (ed.) *Studies in Logical Theory*, Oxford: Blackwell. (A very readable presentation of a theory of conditionals that builds on the semantic framework of possible worlds.)

* Tarski, A. (1933) *Pojęcie prawdy w językach nauk dedukcyjnych*, Warsaw; trans. J.H. Woodger (1956) 'On the Concept of Truth in Formalized Languages', in *Logic, Semantics, Metamathematics*, ed. J. Corcoran, Indianapolis, IN: Hackett Publishing Company, 2nd edn, 1983, 152–278. (The semantics for quantification for non-modal logic. See §3.)

THOMAS J. McKAY

MODAL OPERATORS

Modal logic is principally concerned with the alethic modalities of necessity and possibility, although this branch of logic is applied to a wide range of linguistic and conceptual phenomena, including natural language semantics, proof theory, theoretical computer science and the formal characterization of knowledge and belief. This wide range of application stems from the basic form of modal assertions, such as 'it is necessarily the case that φ', where an entire statement φ is embedded within a context possessing rich logical structure.

When constructing a formal representation of these embedding contexts, there are several choices concerning their specific symbolic form. The most standard approach symbolizes modal contexts as operators, which combine directly with formulas of the object language to yield new formulas. The primary alternative to this approach is to treat modal contexts as *predicates, which attach not to formulas directly, but to names of formulas, and thereby attribute a metalinguistic property to a syntactic object. A variation on the operator approach, which assumes the interpretive framework of possible worlds semantics, is to treat modal contexts as quantifications over possible worlds. Finally, a variation on the predicate approach is to analyse modal contexts as predicates of propositions rather than as predicates of syntactic objects.*

1 **Monadic connectives**
2 **Sorted quantifiers**
3 **Predicates of expressions**
4 **Predicates of propositions**

1 Monadic connectives

On the most standard approach, the modal operators '□' for necessity and '◇' for possibility are introduced as new logical constants (although only one need be taken as primitive). These modal operators are syncategorematic expressions, since they are not assigned an explicit reference, rather their semantic import is carried in a recursive clause of the formal definition of truth. In terms of the syntactic formation rules, the modal operators behave as monadic connectives, structurally comparable to negation in classical logic. The modal assertion 'it is necessarily the case that φ' will have the symbolic form '□φ', where the necessity connective 'operates' on the formula φ to yield the new formula '□φ'. However, unlike the negation connective, the modal operators are not truth functional: it is not possible to determine the truth-value of a modal statement simply on the basis of the truth-value of the formula it embeds. In this sense, introduction of the modal operators constitutes a significant departure from the pure extensionality of classical logic, and this has led to criticism of their legitimacy, most notably from W.V. QUINE.

Quine has argued that non-extensional contexts are logically permissible only if construed as 'referentially opaque', that is, the constituent symbols within these contexts are treated as occurring non-referentially. Quotation is a paradigmatic case of such a context since, for example, in the true statement '"John walks" is a short sentence', the occurrence of the string 'John' does not refer to anyone (see USE/MENTION DISTINCTION AND QUOTATION). Quine (1953) argues that since modal contexts are non-extensional, they are properly viewed as quotational, wherein the embedded sentence φ is mentioned rather than used (this theme will be continued in §3; see PROPOSITIONAL ATTITUDES §2). However, treatment of modal contexts as operators suggests that the logical structure of the embedded formula is semantically relevant, even though it occurs within a non-extensional context. Indeed, since '□' operates at the same linguistic level as the formula ϕ, it follows that the semantic value of ϕ should directly contribute to the compositional value of '□ϕ'. Thus the '□' operator must utilize information not contained in the extension of the embedded expression.

2 Sorted quantifiers

According to possible worlds semantics for modal operators, introduced by Saul KRIPKE (1959), the non-extensional value of modal statements is determined by appeal to the extension of the embedded expression in alternative possible worlds (see SEMANTICS, POSSIBLE WORLDS). The sentence '□ϕ' is evaluated as true at a given world just in case ϕ is true in all worlds possible relative to the given world, while the sentence '◇ϕ' is true just in case there is at least one possible world in which ϕ is true. So in this standard semantic framework, the truth definition for modal statements is specified in the metalanguage by quantifying over the set of possible worlds; the truth of an assertion of necessity is expressed in terms of a universal quantification, while an assertion of possibility is evaluated as an existential quantification. Somewhat more formally, a Kripke model M comes equipped with a set W of worlds (or points or indices) and a binary relation R on W such that a world $w' \in W$ is possible relative to a world $w \in W$ just in case wRw'. In the simplest case, where R is universal (that is, every world in W is possible relative to itself and every other), reference to R can be dropped. Then '□ϕ' is true in w just in case ϕ is true in all worlds $w' \in W$, and '◇ϕ' is true in w just in case there is at least one $w' \in W$ in which ϕ is true.

It is therefore possible to recast the logical form of modal statements as quantifiers rather than operators, where the structure of the truth definition is explicitly manifested in the structure of the object-language formula. In the general case, this will require the use of many-sorted quantificational logic, where the domain of discourse is divided into distinct subdomains, and typographically different variables are used to quantify over these respective subsets. In the modal case, the set W of possible worlds will form one such subdomain, and a distinct type of intensional variable will range over this set. Thus where the extension of an expression ψ varies according to the index of evaluation, this same 'intensional' effect can be mirrored by adding a variable to yield the expression $\psi(i)$, where i ranges over possible worlds. The interpretation function will assign to ψ a value which gives the standard type of extension when applied to worlds as arguments. To translate operator modality into the quantifier formulation, a straightforward mapping is defined where $(\psi)^* = \psi(i)$ for nonlogical constants ψ, where logical form is preserved for the extensional connectives and where $(\square\phi)^* = \forall i(\phi)^*$ and $(\Diamond\phi)^* = \exists i(\phi)^*$. In this manner, the necessity operator is explicitly recast as a universal quantifier, and possibility is represented as an existential quantifier. The quantifier approach is perhaps most attractive as an alternative to intensional type theory (see MONTAGUE, R.M.), where the different sorts of variables correspond to distinct logical types.

3 Predicates of expressions

While the quantifier interpretation is a natural variation on the use of operators (given the framework of possible worlds semantics), the predicate approach to modality constitutes a more divergent analysis. Under this development, modal contexts are symbolized by a monadic predicate, say N, which is categorematic and receives a normal first-order extension (that is, a set of objects). But admissible extensions of N must satisfy the constraints imposed by its intended meaning as a modal device, and in this sense N is comparable to the binary predicate symbol '=' normally used to designate the identity relation.

On the predicate approach to modality, syntactic expressions are themselves named by singular terms, and the necessity predicate N attaches to such terms to yield new atomic formulas. Quotation is often adopted as a convenient method for constructing terms that name expressions. Thus if $\ulcorner\phi\urcorner$ is the official quotation term denoting the object-language formula ϕ, then the assertion that ϕ is necessary will have the form $N(\ulcorner\phi\urcorner)$. In this manner, modal formulas are viewed as attributing a metalinguistic property to a linguistic expression treated as an object of discourse. The two most natural properties to attribute in this context are that the object-language formula is valid with respect to some class of models, or that it is provable in some formal system. On this latter reading, the predicate approach is quite suitable for applications to proof theory (see GÖDEL'S THEOREMS §6) and for applications to the symbol-processing accounts of epistemic contexts common in artificial intelligence.

On the predicate analysis, the named formula is mentioned rather than used, and this is amenable to the Carnap–Quine position that the logic of modalities should be expressed in an extensional metalanguage (see Carnap 1937), and that the attempt to express modality in an intensional object language rests on a confusion between use and mention. It is also compatible with Quine's view (see §1) that modal contexts are referentially opaque. The fact that the modal predicate attaches to a term denoting a formula indicates that there are no free variables inside a modal context, and this would prohibit the articulation of quantified modal logic. Therefore, Quine has argued that the only legitimate development of 'intensional' logic is comprised by that fragment which can be rendered in terms of the extensional clarity of a metalinguistic predicate.

However, Montague (1963) has subsequently demonstrated that for any language endowed with the 'self-referential' capacities of elementary number theory, the addition of even very weak modal assumptions leads to inconsistency under the predicate approach. In systems that extend the theory Q of Robinson arithmetic, Gödel's diagonal lemma establishes that for any open formula $\beta(x)$ with one free variable, there exists a closed formula θ such that $\vdash \theta \leftrightarrow \beta([\theta])$, where $[\theta]$ is the Gödel numeral code for θ. If necessity is formalized as a predicate $N(x)$ within such a system, then the diagonal lemma establishes that there will be a sentence μ such that $\vdash \mu \leftrightarrow \neg N([\mu])$, where μ 'says of itself' that it is not necessary. μ is the modal analogue of the celebrated Gödel sentence that asserts its own unprovability, and of the liar sentence that underpins Tarski's theorem on the undefinability of truth (see SEMANTIC PARADOXES AND THEORIES OF TRUTH). And in a manner analogous to the Gödel–Tarski results, μ can be used to deduce a contradiction, given fairly minimal principles governing the logic of N.

In light of these negative results, the predicate view of modality must be approached with some care. A crucial point is that not all the formulas in which N occurs will correspond to statements that can be articulated using the resources of the operator. In particular, there is no operator counterpart to the 'self-referential' sentence μ, since the '$\square$' connective must apply to formulas rather than to their names. And if radically new formulas such as μ are allowed to instantiate the relevant modal schemata, then new axioms are added to the modal system, and this in turn yields an unwanted increase in deductive power. Thus it is possible to avoid inconsistency by inverting the Quinean perspective and defining the predicate system so that it precisely mirrors the expressive-deductive power of the operator.

4 Predicates of propositions

In addition to treating them as predicates of syntactic objects, it is also possible to formalize modal contexts as predicates of semantic objects. In systems of higher-order intensional logic such as Montague's

system IL, semantic value is divided along Fregean lines into both an extensional and an intensional component (see SENSE AND REFERENCE). Montague's scheme utilizes Carnap's insight that the intensional component of semantic value can be modelled as a function from possible worlds to extensions. The intension of a sentence is a proposition, while its extension is a truth-value, and hence a proposition is modelled as a (characteristic function of a) set of possible worlds, namely that set of worlds in which the sentence is true. The object language is equipped with an intensional operator '^' which, when attached to an expression, yields a term that denotes the intension of the expression. So the term $\hat{\phi}$ denotes the proposition expressed by ϕ, which is the set of possible worlds in which ϕ is true. Necessity can then be rendered as a higher-order predicate Nec, which applies to sets of worlds and is meant to assert that the set in question is identical to the set of all worlds in the model. In this framework, the statement that ϕ is necessary will then have the form $Nec(\hat{\phi})$, which asserts that the set of worlds constituting the intension of ϕ is identical to the set of all worlds in the model, and this is equivalent to the standard operator interpretation that ϕ is true in all possible worlds.

See also: LOGICAL AND MATHEMATICAL TERMS, GLOSSARY OF; MODAL LOGIC; MODAL LOGIC, PHILOSOPHICAL ISSUES IN; POSSIBLE WORLDS §2

References and further reading

* Carnap, R. (1937) *The Logical Syntax of Language*, London: Routledge & Kegan Paul. (Expounds the view that modality should be expressed in an extensional metalanguage.)

Dowty, P., Wall, R. and Peters, S. (1981) *Introduction to Montague Semantics*, Dordrecht: Reidel. (Provides an introduction to Montague's system of intensional type theory.)

Gallin, D. (1975) *Intensional and Higher-Order Modal Logic*, Amsterdam: North Holland. (Gives a treatment of modal operators as quantifiers within the framework of type theory.)

* Kripke, S.A. (1959) 'A Completeness Theorem in Modal Logic', *Journal of Symbolic Logic* 24: 1–15. (Introduces possible worlds semantics for modal logic.)

* Montague, R. (1963) 'Syntactical Treatments of Modality, with Corollaries on Reflexion Principles and Finite Axiomatizability', in R. Thomason (ed.) *Formal Philosophy*, New Haven, CT: Yale University Press, 1974. (Presents inconsistency proofs for predicate version of modal logic.)

* Quine, W.V. (1953) 'Three Grades of Modal Involvement', in *The Ways of Paradox and Other Essays*, Cambridge, MA: Harvard University Press, 1966. (Advocates the view that modal contexts are quotational.)

Schweizer, P. (1992) 'A Syntactical Approach to Modality', *Journal of Philosophical Logic* 21: 1–31. (Addresses Montague's argument that the predicate approach to modality is inconsistent.)

Skyrms, B. (1978) 'An Immaculate Conception of Modality', *Journal of Philosophy* 75: 77–96. (Addresses Montague's argument that the predicate approach to modality is inconsistent.)

PAUL SCHWEIZER

MODEL THEORY

Model theory studies the relations between sentences of a formal language and the interpretations (or 'structures') which make these sentences true or false. It offers precise definitions of truth, logical truth and consequence, meanings and modalities. These definitions and their consequences have revolutionized the teaching of elementary logic.

Model theory also forms a branch of mathematics concerned with the ways in which mathematical structures can be classified. This technical work has led to philosophically interesting results in at least two areas: it has thrown light on the nature of the set-theoretic universe, and in nonstandard analysis it has suggested new forms of argument (where we prove something different from what we intended, but then use a general model-theoretic argument to change the result into what we wanted).

The word 'model' has many other uses. For example, model theory is not about scientific theories as models of the world. It is also a controversial question – not considered here – how model theory is connected with the 'mental models' which appear in the psychology of reasoning.

1 Basic ideas

In 1954 Alfred Tarski announced that a new branch of metamathematics had come into being. He called it 'model theory'; it studied 'mutual relations between sentences of formalized theories and mathematical [structures] in which these sentences hold'. Model theory quickly became an active area of research on the boundary between logic and other branches of mathematics (see §5 below). The name 'model theory' is sometimes applied more broadly, particularly by philosophers, to include any inquiry which uses formal languages, structures and a truth definition. For example, a model-theoretic approach to English semantics is one which treats English as a formal language and attaches meanings to English phrases in terms of possible worlds, regarding these worlds as mathematical structures.

When Tarski spoke of a 'sentence of a formalized theory', he meant what logicians have also called a 'sentence schema', that is, a string of meaningful words and meaningless symbols (sometimes called schematic variables), which becomes a meaningful sentence when the symbols are given meanings. For example, the string

(1)   Everything which is a P is a Q.

is a sentence schema. If we interpret 'P' as meaning 'cow' and 'Q' as meaning 'quadruped', then the schema comes to mean the same as the sentence 'Every cow is a quadruped'. In model theory we always assume that the word 'everything' needs interpretation too; the interpretation will say what set of things counts as everything, and any set may be allowed. For example, if we take 'everything' to range over the set of objects in China, then the original string comes to mean 'Every object in China which is a cow is a quadruped'.

A 'mathematical structure' is a way of interpreting the symbols in a schema. It consists of a set of objects which is the range of quantifier words such as 'everything' and 'there exists'; and a family of sets, relations, functions and so on which express the meanings of the schematic variables. The set of objects is called the 'domain' or 'universe' of the structure, and its members are called the 'elements' of the structure. For example, the structure which gives our interpretation of (1) has the set of objects in China for its domain; it attaches the set of cows in China to the symbol 'P' and the set of quadrupeds in China to the symbol 'Q'. (More formally, we can regard a structure M as an ordered pair $\langle \text{dom}(M), Y \rangle$ where $\text{dom}(M)$ is the domain of M and Y is a function which takes each interpreted symbol s to its interpretation $Y(s)$, also written s^M. Many mathematical objects can also be thought of as structures in this sense; thus a group G is a pair $\langle X, Y \rangle$ where X is the set of elements of G and Y is a function taking the group product symbol '·' to the group multiplication '$\cdot^G$'.)

In our schema (1), the meaningful expressions are those written in English. Model theorists often use logical symbols for the meaningful words. For example, 'and' is often written '&' or '∧'; for 'it is not true that' one writes '∼' or '¬'; one writes '(x)' or '$\forall x$' to mean 'for every element x'. When this is done, a sentence schema is the same thing as a sentence of formal logic with uninterpreted non-logical symbols (see PREDICATE CALCULUS).

2 Truth and satisfaction

The central device of model theory is the truth relation, written '⊨'. (Pronunciations vary, but 'double turnstile' is safe, using 'turnstile' for '⊢'.) Suppose ϕ is a sentence schema and M is a structure which interprets ϕ. Interpreted, ϕ says something which is either true or false. If it is true, we say that ϕ is true in M, or that M is a model of ϕ; in symbols, $M \models \phi$. Tarski showed how one can give a precise mathematical definition of the relation '⊨'. His definition is correct in the sense that it agrees with our intuitive notions about when an interpretation M makes a formula ϕ into a true sentence. (See TARSKI'S DEFINITION OF TRUTH for the context of Tarski's definition. See also SEMANTICS, GAME-THEORETIC for an interesting variant.)

In defining '⊨', Tarski assumed that each structure M is a set-theoretic object and that the schemas ϕ are sentences of a conventional formal logic. Also M must interpret every non-logical symbol in ϕ. It is usual to ensure this by stating Tarski's definition relative to a set S of non-logical symbols; we assume that M interprets just these symbols, and that ϕ uses no non-logical symbols besides those in S. This set S is then called the 'signature' (or similarity type) of M and ϕ.

In fact Tarski defined a slightly more complicated relation, namely satisfaction. Suppose M is a structure, $a_1, \ldots, a_n$ are elements of M and $\phi(x_1, \ldots, x_n)$ is a formula with free variables $x_1, \ldots, x_n$. We write $M \models \phi[a_1, \ldots, a_n]$ (pronounced 'a_1 to a_n satisfy ϕ in M') to mean that when M is used to interpret the symbols of ϕ apart from the free variables, and x_i is read as the name of the element a_i for $1 \leqslant i \leqslant n$, then ϕ becomes a true sentence. The truth relation is the special case where $n = 0$. (The set of all n-tuples $(a_1, \ldots, a_n)$ such that $M \models \phi[a_1, \ldots, a_n]$ holds is called the relation (or set) defined in M by ϕ.)

Tarski's definition of satisfaction has several clauses, depending on the form of the formula ϕ.

For example, if ϕ is of the form $\psi \wedge \chi$ then $M \models \phi[a_1, \ldots, a_n]$ holds if and only if $M \models \psi[a_1, \ldots a_n]$ and $M \models \chi[a_1, \ldots, a_n]$ both hold. If ϕ is of the form $\forall x_2 \psi(x_1, x_2)$, then $M \models \phi[a_1]$ holds if and only if for every element b of M, $M \models \psi[a_1, b]$ holds. These and similar clauses allow us to break ϕ down into its smallest component formulas, known as atomic formulas. For atomic formulas, Tarski's definition refers directly to the interpretations of symbols given by the structure M.

By applying Tarski's definition, we can reduce the statement that $M \models \phi[a_1, \ldots, a_n]$ to a purely set-theoretic statement. To illustrate this, let $\phi(x)$ be the first-order formula '$\forall y(y = c \wedge Py \rightarrow y = x)$', and let M be a structure with a set P^M to interpret the symbol 'P' and an element c^M to interpret the constant c. Suppose b is an element of M. Then according to Tarski's definition of satisfaction (with a very small simplification),

(2) $\quad M \models \phi[b]$

holds if and only if

(3) $\quad \{c^M\} \cap P^M \subseteq \{b\}$.

(Intuitively, every member of the set P^M which is equal to c^M is equal to b. The schema ϕ defines in M the set $\{c^M\}$ if c^M is in P^M, and the set of all elements of M otherwise.)

3 Classes defined by axioms

Model theory grew out of a development in mathematics. Around the turn of the twentieth century it was becoming common to define classes of structures in terms of the axioms which are true in them; such classes are said to be axiomatically defined. The classes of groups, rings and Boolean algebras are three examples (see BOOLEAN ALGEBRA). Certain questions arise naturally in this context. Let us note three. First, what can we tell about an axiomatically defined class by looking at the syntactic form of its axioms? Second, given an axiomatically defined class, when is one of the symbols redundant in the sense that its meaning in any structure in the class is determined by the meanings of the other symbols? Third, given a set of axioms T, one of which is ϕ, when is ϕ redundant in the sense that the class axiomatically defined by T would not be altered if we left out ϕ? These are all typical questions of model theory.

By a theory we mean a set of sentences of a formal language. We say that a structure M is a model of the theory T if M is a model of every sentence in T. So the class of all models of T is the axiomatically defined class whose set of axioms is T. First-order model theory, which is by far the largest part of the subject, studies the case where T is a set of first-order sentences. Many interesting mathematical classes of structures – including groups, rings and Boolean algebras – are defined by first-order axioms.

Here are two sample theorems of first-order model theory, which illustrate the first and second questions above. We shall turn to the third question in the next section.

Two structures are said to be 'elementarily equivalent' if they are models of exactly the same first-order sentences. Our first theorem states that if M is a structure with infinitely many elements and λ is an infinite cardinal, then we can cut down M (if it has more than λ elements) or add new elements (if it has fewer) so as to form a structure N which is elementarily equivalent to M and has exactly λ elements. This theorem is known as the downward Löwenheim–Skolem theorem (when elements are removed) or the upward Löwenheim–Skolem theorem (when elements are added). The upward and downward theorems together are equivalent to the axiom of choice, which is an indication that in general it is impossible to give an explicit description of N. The upward theorem follows from the compactness theorem of §4.

If T is a first-order theory, and a symbol R of the signature of T is redundant in the sense described at the start of this section, then we say that R is implicitly definable relative to T. Our second theorem states that if R is implicitly definable relative to T, then it is explicitly definable in the sense that there is some first-order sentence which is true in all models of T and which says, 'R means such-and-such'. (See BETH'S THEOREM AND CRAIG'S THEOREM for further details.) In practice this theorem is generally used backwards: we are given that R is not explicitly definable relative to T, and we use the theorem to find two models of T which agree in the interpretations of all symbols except R.

4 Semantic and syntactic consequence in first-order logic

The question of redundant axioms goes back several hundred years. Already in the thirteenth century Persian geometers were trying to show Euclid's parallel postulate to be redundant in his axioms for geometry. In fact it is not, and proofs of this fact by Beltrami and others in the late nineteenth century gave a boost to the development of model theory. Beltrami introduced the word 'interpretation' in 1868.

Some notation will help. If T is a theory and ϕ a sentence, we write

(4) $T \models \phi$

to mean that every model of T is also a model of ϕ. (4) is sometimes read 'ϕ is a semantic consequence of T'. (This double use of '$\models$' is unfortunate, but the usage has become firmly entrenched. In (4) there is a theory to the left of '$\models$', not a structure as in (2).) So ϕ is redundant in the theory consisting of T and ϕ, if and only if $T \models \phi$.

The central theorem here is Gödel's completeness theorem, proved in his doctoral dissertation of 1929 and published in 1930. It states that if T and ϕ are first-order, then (4) holds if and only if ϕ is deducible from T in a standard proof calculus for first-order logic. We write $T \vdash \phi$ when this condition holds; so Gödel's theorem says that the structural relation '$\models$' (in the sense of (4)) is equivalent to the purely syntactic relation '$\vdash$'. Like all later logicians, Gödel proved his theorem by assuming that ϕ is not deducible from T and constructing a model of T in which ϕ is false. Later logicians have usually built the model out of the expressions of the first-order language; Gödel, perhaps influenced by Hilbert's constructions of counterexamples in geometry, used numbers as the elements of the model and showed that appropriate relations could be found to interpret the symbols of the language. (See GÖDEL'S THEOREMS. Gödel proved his theorem for one particular proof calculus and a countable signature, but both these restrictions are unnecessary.)

Of the many applications of Gödel's completeness theorem, two are worth noting here. First, when T is the empty theory in (4), we leave it out and write simply '$\models \phi$'; and likewise with '$\vdash$'. Compare the forms of the following two statements.

(5) $\vdash \phi$, that is, there is a proof of ϕ.

(6) $\models \phi$, that is, there is not a model of $\neg\phi$.

By Gödel's theorem, (5) and (6) are equivalent, both saying that ϕ is a theorem (or valid sentence) of first-order logic. The difference between the forms of (5) and (6) is very convenient. If ϕ is a theorem, according to (5) we can show it by giving a proof of ϕ. If ϕ is not a theorem, then by (6) we can show it by giving a structure in which ϕ is not true. Either way, we know what we have to produce in order to establish the fact. (A strengthening of the completeness theorem, proved independently by Hasenjäger and Kleene in 1952, allows us to do better. If ϕ is a first-order sentence but not a theorem, then there is a model of $\neg\phi$ which consists of the natural numbers together with some arithmetically definable sets, relations and functions. So in the second case we can specify the model by giving some arithmetical formulas.)

Now that we know Gödel's theorem, we can try to prove a first-order sentence ϕ by showing that its negation $\neg\phi$ has no model. This idea leads quickly to tableau proofs (see NATURAL DEDUCTION, TABLEAU AND SEQUENT SYSTEMS §4). Of course the tableau method itself is a purely syntactic calculus. But it can be motivated very directly in terms of the model-theoretic relation (4); with a good class of students one can explain the principle and leave it as a homework exercise to work out the rules.

Second, suppose T is a first-order theory and every finite subset of T has a model. Then there is no finite subset T' of T such that every model of T' is a model of the contradictory statement '$\neg\forall x\, x = x$' (since no structure is a model of this statement). So by Gödel's theorem, T has no finite subset from which we can formally prove '$\neg\forall x\, x = x$'. But then we cannot prove '$\neg\forall x\, x = x$' from T at all, since any formal proof would use only a finite part of T. Hence by Gödel's theorem again, it is not true that every model of T is a model of the contradiction; in other words, T has a model. By this roundabout route we have deduced the 'compactness theorem': if every finite subset of a first-order theory has a model, then the whole theory has a model. This is the single most important theorem of model theory. All the applications in the next section use it.

5 First order model theory: four applications

This section relates some of the mathematical successes of first-order model theory. It can be skipped without breaking continuity.

First, suppose T is a first-order theory, and for every natural number n there is a model M_n of T in which there are at least n elements which satisfy the formula Px. For each n we can write a first-order sentence which says, 'There are at least n elements x such that Px'; let U be the set of these sentences for all n. Our assumption about T implies that if we take just finitely many sentences from U, then there is some model of T in which all these sentences are true. Then the compactness theorem tells us that there is a model of T in which all the sentences are true, so that infinitely many elements satisfy Px. This argument has many applications. It shows, for example, that if T has arbitrarily large finite models then T has an infinite model. It also shows that there is a structure N which is elementarily equivalent to the field R of real numbers (and in fact contains it), but which has infinitesimal elements; these are elements greater than 0 but less than 1, $\frac{1}{2}$, $\frac{1}{3}$ and so on. Since N contains infinitesimals, we can do calculus in N in the way that Leibniz intended, calculating $\mathrm{d}y/\mathrm{d}x$ as a ratio of two infinitesimal

numbers $\mathrm{d}y$ and $\mathrm{d}x$ (this is a slight oversimplification). Suppose that we can use infinitesimals to prove that a certain first-order sentence ϕ is true in N. Then ϕ must be true in R too, since R and N are elementarily equivalent. This ingenious way of doing calculus has sprouted into a new branch of mathematics (see ANALYSIS, NONSTANDARD).

In 1982 Shelah gave a very different application of model theory. Confining himself to structures of countable signature, he looked at elementary equivalence classes, that is, classes that consist of a structure and every other structure elementarily equivalent to it. Two structures are said to be isomorphic if one is an exact copy of the other. (Formally, M is isomorphic to N if there is a bijection from the domain of M to that of N, which takes the interpretation s^M of each symbol s of the signature to the interpretation s^N.) Shelah proved that a dichotomy holds: each elementary equivalence class is either very good or very bad. 'Very good' means that we can classify all the structures in the class, up to isomorphism, by means of a few numerical invariants (such as dimension in the case of vector spaces). 'Very bad' means that we can construct two structures in the class which are not isomorphic but are extremely hard to distinguish from each other. Shelah sees this work as a step towards bringing the more chaotic areas of mathematics under control.

In 1992 Hrushovski and Zil'ber proved a theorem which says that algebraically closed fields can be recognized through certain model-theoretic properties of their Zariski topologies. Hrushovski then used this result to prove an open case of the geometric Mordell–Lang conjecture (an important conjecture in diophantine geometry). Zil'ber had long been convinced that there must be some kind of characterization of algebraically closed fields in terms of their model-theoretic properties, partly because these fields are such fundamental objects in mathematics. It was also partly because Macintyre had already shown that if M is an infinite field, then M is algebraically closed if and only if the set T of all first-order sentences true in M is λ-categorical for every uncountable cardinal λ – that is, that any two models of T with exactly λ elements must be isomorphic. (A theory is said to be categorical if all its models are isomorphic. By the upward Löwenheim–Skolem theorem, if a first-order theory has a model with infinitely many elements, then it cannot be categorical, though it may be λ-categorical for some cardinal λ.)

Finally, one achievement of the twentieth century has been to base all mathematics on axiomatic set theory. A theorem is reckoned to be proved if we know in principle how to write it as a formal deduction from the axioms of ZF (Zermelo–Fraenkel set theory). Unfortunately ZF seems to leave unanswered many natural questions about sets and infinite cardinals. Since the 1960s, set theorists have studied these questions by examining models of the ZF axioms. For example, in 1963 Paul Cohen showed that the axiom of choice is not deducible from the other axioms of ZF, by constructing models of these other axioms in which the axiom of choice is false. Model theorists have devised several techniques for constructing interesting models of a given theory, and two of these techniques have led to other advances in set theory. Ultraproducts, which are good for constructing 'fat' models in which there are as many types of element as possible, are an essential tool for studying the colossal (but possibly non-existent) cardinals that set theorists call large cardinals. The technique of indiscernibles, which constructs 'thin' models with as few types of element as possible, is used to show the enormous differences between Gödel's constructible universe and a universe of sets which contains very large cardinals. (See SET THEORY.)

6 Limitations of first-order model theory in mathematics

First-order logic has a delicate balance of expressiveness: it can say things about a fixed number of elements at a time, but it is very bad at expressing statements which involve infinitely many, or arbitrarily large finite numbers of, elements. For example, it is easy but boring to write down a first-order sentence which says, 'The number of elements x such that Px is exactly 10,556,001'. By contrast there is no first-order sentence that says, 'There are infinitesimals'. (The definition of infinitesimals involves the infinitely many elements $1, \frac{1}{2}, \frac{1}{3}$ and so on.) Also we saw that no first-order sentence expresses 'There are just finitely many x such that Px'. Even if we restrict attention to finite structures, there is no first-order sentence which is true in just those structures for which the set of elements satisfying the formula 'Px' has an even number of elements.

We have other formal languages in which these things can be expressed. For example, there are languages, known as 'infinitary' languages, in which we can form infinite conjunctions 'S_1 and S_2 and S_3 and ...'. The statement that an even number of things satisfy 'Px' can be written as an infinite conjunction 'There is not exactly one thing x such that Px, and there are not exactly three things x such that Px, and there are not exactly five things...'. Infinitary languages can say more than first-order languages; but by the same token it is harder to construct models of theories in infinitary languages, and this makes them less useful for applying model-theoretic arguments in mathematics (see INFINITARY LOGICS). The study of different kinds of formal languages and their expressive power is called 'generalized model theory' (see the encyclopedic volume of Barwise and Feferman 1985).

In 1969 Lindström proved some theorems which compare first-order languages with other languages that have greater expressive power. For each signature S there is a first-order language $L(S)$; it consists of just those formulas which can be built up from the symbols in S using the first-order logical expressions. Suppose that we add some new expressions, for example, quantifiers which express that an even number of things have this or that property. Then each signature S will give rise to a richer language $L'(S)$. One of Lindström's results is that if the upward and downward Löwenheim–Skolem theorems (quoted in §3 above) hold for 'elementary equivalence' in the sense of the languages $L'(S)$ instead of $L(S)$, then for every sentence of $L'(S)$ there is already a sentence of $L(S)$ which has exactly the same models. Roughly speaking, any logic which is at least as strong as first-order logic, but not strong enough to distinguish one infinite cardinal from another, must be first-order logic. Lindström's theorems show that the choice of first-order languages as the main languages of model theory was not just a happy accident. But they also raise the question of whether there might be purposes for which first-order languages are not the best choice. We may find such purposes outside mathematics.

7 Truth and possible worlds

The interest of model theory for philosophers rests mainly on two items: Tarski's truth definition and Tarski's characterization of logical deduction. Let us begin with the truth definition. (One philosophical text published in 1992 even defines model theory as the programme of giving a truth definition for quantified predicate logic!)

In model-theoretic versions of Tarski's truth definition we define a relation '$\models$' between structures and sentences; '$M \models \phi$' says that the sentence ϕ is true in the structure M. But a typical sentence of English, for example,

(7) Pollution is not the sole cause of the rise in asthma.

can be assessed as true or false; no structure is involved.

Some writers contrast absolute truth with model-theoretic truth; the latter is relative to a structure, the former is not. This is a misleading contrast. Truth means the same in model theory as it means anywhere else – the difference lies in the sentences whose truth is being assessed. A typical sentence of a formal language of logic is a schema with schematic variables in it; by itself it does not make a statement. A structure is needed to give meanings to the variables. By contrast, the sentence (7) has no variables, so it needs no structure.

There are some analogues of schematic variables in natural languages. The closest analogues are indexical expressions such as 'I', 'he', these' and 'now' (see DEMONSTRATIVES AND INDEXICALS). To assess the truth of the sentence

(8)   He took those.

we need to know who he is and what those are. An answer of the form 'If he is Christopher Naples and those are my football boots, then (8) is true' has almost exactly the same content as the statement that the schema 'X took Y' is true in a certain structure.

Nor does (8) determine the time and place referred to. Maybe the sentence was false yesterday but will be true tomorrow. When we assess its truth, we normally take the default time and place – namely here and now; but any account of the truth or otherwise of (8) needs to make some assumption at least about the time. (Strictly there may also be a question about domains of quantification: in (7) what range of possible causes are we considering?)

Some philosophers go further: we need to know whether (8) is taken to be about this world or some other possible world. Even further: there are sentences such as

(9)   It is possible that it will rain tomorrow.

whose truth now in this world may depend on what is true in other possible worlds. (Is there a possible continuation of this world in which it will rain tomorrow?)

None of these relativities depends on model theory. But model theory offers a format for handling them. Sentence (8) is true in the structure where the possible world is this one, the time and place are as follows, he is so-and-so and those are such-and-such. Over-simplifying a little, sentence (9) is true in possible world i if and only if there is a world j which is possible relative to i, such that 'It will rain tomorrow' is true in j. Montague (a student of Tarski) offered a truth definition for substantial fragments of English, using devices of exactly these kinds (see MONTAGUE, R.M.). Similar ideas appear in the semantics of many languages used in philosophy and artificial intelligence; see, for example, MODAL LOGIC; TENSE AND TEMPORAL LOGIC; INTENSIONAL LOGICS. (See also SEMANTICS, POSSIBLE WORLDS.)

There may be ontological problems about what a possible world is, but model theory neither adds to nor subtracts from these problems. Most of the structures that one meets in model theory are set-theoretic objects which have nothing to do with possible worlds.

8   Logical truth and consequence

As we saw in the previous section, model theory provides a setting for studying how the truth of a statement is affected if we alter some features of the statement. One traditional way of defining and classifying necessary truths is by noting that they stay true under various kinds of alteration. For example, a necessary truth stays true if we change the possible world; an eternal truth stays true if we change the time; a logical truth stays true if we systematically reinterpret all the words in it except the logical ones. Classifications along these lines are sometimes described as model-theoretic.

In 1936 Tarski offered just such a definition of logical consequence. On his account, a sentence S is a logical consequence of sentences T if one cannot reinterpret the non-logical words in S and T so as to make S false and all the sentences of T true. He was deliberately vague about which words are logical; he suggested that different choices might lead to different notions of consequence (such as analytic consequence). (See CONSEQUENCE, CONCEPTIONS OF §5.)

Tarski's definition makes no mention of structures, since he applied it directly to meaningful sentences. To adapt it to a model-theoretic style, we first have to consider formal languages L whose symbols are all either logical expressions or schematic variables. Then, as in §4, if U is a theory and ϕ a sentence in such a language L, we write '$U \models \phi$' to mean that every model of U is a model of ϕ. Finally, we say that S is a logical consequence of T if and only if there are a theory U and a sentence ϕ in some such language L such that $U \models \phi$ and T, S is a substitution instance of U, ϕ. (We say that a sentence S is a 'substitution instance' of a schema ϕ if S comes from ϕ by replacing each schematic variable by a meaningful expression – the same expression at all occurrences of the variable; and likewise for a theory.)

9   Model theory in computer science

Computers are good at handling formulas; they are not so good at set theory. So when model theory appears in computer science, it usually has a super-visory role, for example, to describe what computers or robots are supposed to be doing, or how a computer language is intended to work, or what kind of information a database is capable of retrieving.

There is virtually no place in computer science where the class of all models of a theory has any importance at all; in fact it is hard to see how large uncountable structures could possibly be relevant to computing. But sometimes (a) one is interested in the finite models of some theory. For example, these can represent the possible states of a database, or the possible states of a machine during a computation. Sometimes (b) the relevant models are those in which every element is named by a term; these appear as datatypes, or as representations of the behaviour of a machine through time. Another important case is (c) where one is only interested in a single structure, and the question is which sets and relations can be defined in this structure. The model-theoretic semantics of PROLOG is a case in point: the structure in question is the term algebra, and the relations are defined by PROLOG programs. Computer science is open-ended and fast developing, so that other uses of model theory are very likely to appear.

In the 1980s some theoretical computer scientists started to voice a damaging criticism of first-order model theory. The model-theoretic questions which arise naturally in computer science are to do with defining classes of finite structures, or single structures, or relations within a given structure. The classes are defined in terms of the behaviour of a machine or program. For model theory one needs logical languages in which these same classes can be defined. In practice, first-order languages usually turn out to be grossly unsuitable.

For example, if M is a finite structure representing the information in a database, and the relations of M include a set P and a binary relation R, then it is easy to compute whether the number of elements in P is even, or whether it is possible to get from one given element a to another element b by a chain: $aRc_1R\ldots Rc_nRb$. But neither of these questions can be phrased as a first-order sentence. Or, again, the relations defined by a PROLOG program are rarely definable by first-order formulas; this is because the program can perform recursion, so that the relations are built up inductively.

On the other hand, the properties of first-order logic that Lindström pointed to (see §6), such as the Löwenheim–Skolem theorems, are largely irrelevant for computer science.

No definitive replacement for first-order logic has appeared, but computer scientists have begun to develop some very interesting new languages, for example, languages in which one can express the transitive closure of relations. There is also a thriving branch of model theory devoted to finite structures.

Here the interesting classes of structure are, for example, the class of structures which give the answer 'yes' to a certain database query, or the class of those structures which can be picked out by an algorithm in a certain complexity class. (See COMPLEXITY, COMPUTATIONAL; QUANTIFIERS, GENERALIZED.)

See also: LOGICAL AND MATHEMATICLA TERMS

References and further reading

* Barwise, J. and Feferman, S. (eds) (1985) *Model-Theoretic Logics*, New York: Springer. (A mathematical survey of various logics, unfortunately before there was much model-theoretic work on logics for computer science.)

Doets, K. (1996) *Basic Model Theory*, Stanford, CA: CSLI Publications. (A good introduction for readers who know some logic but are not mathematicians.)

Ebbinghaus, H.-D., Flum, J. and Thomas, W. (1984) *Mathematical Logic*, Berlin and New York: Springer, 2nd edn, 1994. (A readable general introduction to mathematical logic which emphasizes model theory; includes proofs of Lindström's theorems.)

Hintikka, J. (1988) 'On the Development of the Model-Theoretical Tradition in Logical Theory', *Synthese* 77: 1–16. (A philosophical discussion of model theory by a model theorist.)

Hodges, W. (1986) 'Truth in a Structure', *Proceedings of the Aristotelian Society* 86: 135–51. (Another philosophical discussion of model theory by a model theorist.)

—— (1993) *Model Theory*, Cambridge: Cambridge University Press. (A general mathematical text of model theory.)

* Tarski, A. (1954) 'Contributions to the Theory of Models I', *Indagationes Mathematicae* 16: 572–81. (The paper which first named model theory.)

—— (1956) *Logic, Semantics, Metamathematics: Papers from 1923 to 1938*, trans. J.H. Woodger, Oxford: Clarendon Press; ed. J. Corcoran, Indianapolis, IN: Hackett Publishing Company, 2nd edn, 1983. (Includes important papers on the conceptual background of model theory, in particular, 'The Concept of Truth in Formalized Languages' (1933), 'On the Concept of Logical Consequence' (1936) and 'On Definable Sets of Real Numbers' (1931).)

WILFRID HODGES

MODELS

Of the many kinds of things that serve as 'models', all function fundamentally as representations of what we wish to understand or to be or to do. Model aeroplanes and other scale models share selected structural properties with their originals, while differing in other properties, such as construction materials and size. Analogue models, which resemble their originals in some aspect of structure or internal relations, are important in the sciences, because they can facilitate inferences about complicated or obscure natural systems. A collection of billiard balls in random motion is an analogue model of an ideal gas; the interactions and motions of the billiard balls are taken to represent – to be analogous to – the interactions and motions of molecules in the gas.

In mathematical logic, a model is a structure – an arrangement of objects – which represents a theory expressed as a set of sentences. The various terms of the sentences of the theory are mapped onto objects and their relations in the structure; a model is a structure that makes all of the sentences in the theory true. This specialized notion of model has been adopted by philosophers of science; on a 'structuralist' or 'semantic' conception, scientific theories are understood as structures which are used to represent real systems in nature. Philosophical debates have arisen regarding the precise extent of the resemblances between scientific models and the natural systems they represent.

1   **Types of model**
2   **Models in metamathematics**
3   **Models in science**
4   **Models in philosophy of science**

1   Types of model

Generally, we use models as representations of various things, including desires, hopes and actions, as well as objects and systems in the real world. Not only do many distinct types of thing serve as models, but they also relate in a variety of ways to the world and to us. Fundamentally, to be a model is to serve in a triadic relation: *a person* takes *something* as a model of *something else* (Wartofsky 1979).

One very general meaning of 'model' is as an ideal or paradigm case or exemplar, for example a 'model student', curious and energetic. Here, models serve as ideals towards which people are encouraged to adapt themselves (see EXAMPLES IN ETHICS).

Scale models, for example, model aeroplanes and other miniaturized representations, are objects whose properties and relative proportions resemble their originals. Only some properties, however, are the same

in the model and the original; usually the construction materials differ, and the functions of the model and the original differ. Still, scale models exhibit the basic relations which enable one thing to stand in for another; in Charles S. PEIRCE's terminology, the model is an *icon* which represents the original. Icons are different from symbols in their relationship to the things represented: symbols are tied to their originals purely by convention, and any thing can serve as a symbol for any other thing; icons, in contrast, bear some resemblance or similarity to the things that they represent to us. That is, there must be something about the icon itself which is similar or analogous to the object or system of which it is a model. Thus, scale models are a simple kind of iconic model.

Analogue models are usually more abstract than scale models, and resemble their originals primarily in some aspect of structure or internal relations, rather than in materials or appearance. A collection of billiard balls in random motion is an analogue model of an ideal gas in virtue of certain internal relations and interactions among the billiard balls, and not because any thing in the substance or appearance of gas molecules is *like* billiard balls.

Mathematical models are even more abstract than analogue models, in that the objects and their interrelations in the model are all mathematical entities. In the sciences, mathematical models are used to represent a wide variety of real objects and situations.

Finally, there are metamathematical models, which are technical entities used to understand formal systems, such as mathematical systems themselves.

2   Models in metamathematics

In metamathematics (or 'metalogic', the study of the features of formal systems), a 'model' is a structure that makes all of the sentences in a theory true, where a 'theory' is a set of sentences in a language, the various terms of which are mapped onto objects in the system and their relations. Even in metamathematics, though, 'model' is used in several ways: most generally, a model is a special kind of interpretation, where an interpretation of a theory consists in both the assignment or mapping of terms in the theory to objects, and to a structure, which consists of objects and their relations to one another. More specifically, an interpretation of a language specifies: (1) a domain (universe of discourse), for example, the range of any variables that occur in any sentence in the language; (2) a designation (denotation, bearer, reference) for each name in the language; (3) a function f, which assigns a value in the domain for any sequence of arguments in the domain, for each function symbol in the language; (4) a truth-value for each sentence letter in the language; and (5) a characteristic function for each predicate letter (Boolos and Jeffrey [1974] 1980). In these cases, models are defined as those interpretations under which all the sentences in the theory are true.

Alternatively, models are simply the structures themselves under a specified mapping assignment (where the mapping assignment is taken to be external to the model; Robinson 1965; Tarski 1941). Models can be any kind of structure; in metalogic, models are usually expressed in terms of set theory, but technically any group of objects and their relations could serve as the model for a theory, provided that it displayed the right structure.

For example, take as a theory the sentences: 'object A is touching object B'; 'object C is touching object B'; and 'object C is not touching object A' (where A, B and C are terms in the theory, and 'is touching' is a relation between two or more of the terms). We can easily construct or imagine a structure which 'satisfies' or makes true all of these sentences in the little theory: it could consist of three objects in a row, 1, 2, 3, each one touching only the next. Notice that they could be any kind of object, including cats, jars of jam, and so on, or some mixture of these. The *mapping assignment* for the theory might map A onto 1, B onto 2 and C onto 3. (Equally, it could map A onto 3, B onto 2, and C onto 1.) On the usual logical definition, then, the objects 1, 2, 3 constitute one model of the theory, because a 'model' is a structure which can be interpreted so as to make all the sentences in a specific theory true (see MODEL THEORY).

3 Models in science

Several uses of 'model' are standard in the sciences. In each case, models are substitute systems used to investigate and understand the real systems they model. In biology, certain organisms are selected as 'models' on the basis of ease of investigation and manipulation; they are investigated intensively, in the hope that the results generalize to other organisms. In biomedical research, for instance, mice are often used as models or stand-ins for studies of drug effects in human beings.

One of the most basic uses of models in physics involves mechanical models of natural processes. Thus, billiard balls in random motion are taken as a model for a gas. This modelling relation does not imply that billiard balls are like gas particles in all respects, simply that gas molecules are analogous to billiard balls. Under the model, some properties of billiard balls ought to be ascribed to gas molecules, that is, motion and impact (the 'positive analogy', in

Mary Hesse's terms), while other properties of billiard balls ought not be ascribed to molecules, such as colour and hardness (the 'negative analogy'). There is also the 'neutral analogy', used when we do not know whether the properties are shared; according to Hesse, these properties are what allow us to make new predictions (Hesse 1966: 9). Max Black argued that 'use of a particular model may... help us to notice what otherwise would be overlooked, to shift the relative emphasis attached to details – in short, to *see new connections*' (Black 1962: 237). N.R. CAMPBELL (1920) claimed that during the development of the kinetic theory of gases, this mechanical billiard ball model of the theory played an essential part in its extension, and thus, that the availability of a working model of a theory is essential to successful theorizing in the sciences. Pierre DUHEM, in contrast, argued that such use of models in science was preliminary, optional, and potentially misleading, and that proper scientific theories were expressed abstractly and systematically (Duhem 1914).

Many of the philosophical and scientific discussions about the roles of models in science seem to have mixed together several distinct issues. All participants in these debates agree that there must be some analogy between a model used in the sciences (whether mechanical or not) and the phenomena it is being used to explain. One primary concern was how realistically and completely a model – especially a mechanical model – is supposed to represent the aspect of reality under investigation. Hence, Peter Achinstein (1968) suggests a hierarchy of models based on their ontological commitments: at one end, we have models which are simply supposed to provide possible mechanisms for how natural systems might be operating, while at the other end, we have concrete claims that the real world is thoroughly like the entities and dynamics in the model. In the latter case, the choice of model amounts to a metaphysical commitment regarding the contents of the universe – which things and relations really exist. A great deal of discussion has thus centred around which of these attitudes – from purely instrumental to strongly ontological – scientists and philosophers should take to the models they use.

The degree to which a model is taken as exactly and adequately representing reality is one of the most significant ways that claims about models in science can differ. What is frequently called an 'instrumental' use of models amounts to treating the models as calculating devices; slightly more committed, ontologically, are idealized models, which can be seen as either false-but-handy simplifications of processes in the natural system being discussed, or as approximately true representations of some of the forces operating in the natural system (see IDEALI-ZATIONS).

One link between the metamathematical and scientific uses of models lies in the notion of interpretation. In the sciences, models are sometimes used as tools for making sense of theories which are not otherwise immediately comprehensible; a model can thus help the community of scientists articulate and pursue scientific theories. The wave and particle interpretations of light and of quantum mechanics are well-known examples; both the wave and particle models offer ways to understand the theoretical (and well-confirmed) equations, but they present different and incompatible features (see QUANTUM MECHANICS, INTERPRETATIONS OF).

Finally, models are generally acknowledged to be psychologically valuable to scientists; they serve the heuristic functions of helping scientists envisage very complex systems, and they help simplify inferences about those systems. Even models that are known to be misrepresentations of the real world may sometimes possess these virtues (Wimsatt 1987).

4 Models in philosophy of science

While discussion of the above uses of models in the sciences occupied philosophers of science for many decades, one of their basic assumptions was that models are essentially different from scientific theories. This distinction has come under scrutiny since the 1950s, and much work in recent philosophy of science going under the name of 'structuralist' or 'semantic' approaches has centred on analysing scientific theories in terms of metamathematical models.

For the middle third of the twentieth century, the reigning logical positivist approaches to science understood scientific theories as 'sets of deductively connected sentences in a formal language' combined with rules for interpreting some of the terms of that language. In contrast to this linguistic view of theories, some philosophers advocated viewing theories as structures, 'which are propounded as standing in some representational relationship to actual and physically possible phenomena' (Suppe 1979: 320). More specifically, scientific theories are understood as presenting models in the metamathematical sense, that is, arrangements of objects and their relations. These structures function as iconic models for the scientists using them: they characterize, in idealized circumstances, the systems that they represent.

Take evolutionary population genetics as an example. Population geneticists tend to present their theories in the form of mathematical models. This means that, given the mathematical models, it is possible to examine the structures that instantiate that theory. Under this 'semantic approach' to theories, the focus is on the structures themselves, rather than on an attempt to reconstruct, in some theoretical language, the sentences of the theory, as demanded by the axiomatic and positivist approaches to theory structure. (It remains a matter of debate whether there is an important difference between viewing a theory as a set of sentences and viewing it as a set of models. Some philosophers have suggested that the difference is merely pragmatic or heuristic: scientists sometimes find it more natural to regard a theory one way rather than another, but the two views are in principle intertranslatable. See Schaffner 1993: 99–125.)

This use of metamathematical models is an extension from their use in interpreting formal systems. When models serve as icons, some aspects of the model's entities and their interrelations are taken to be similar to the phenomena in the natural world that are being investigated. In metamathematics, the more precise notion of isomorphism is central to evaluating the similarity of models. Two models are isomorphic if it is possible to make a one-to-one mapping from each element in one model to an element in the other model, and to make a one-to-one mapping from each relation among elements in one model to a relation among corresponding elements in the other model. While the notion of similarity between model and nature may be intuitive, precision demands that the natural system be represented, abstracted or measured in some fashion, if evaluations of isomorphism between the theoretical model and nature itself are to be attempted. Typically, measurements or data from the natural system are arranged into a 'data model', which provides the basic entities and relations to which the theoretical models are compared (Suppes 1962).

Many questions can be raised about the relations between scientific theories – when understood as models – and the real world. For instance, it is possible that there are relations or entities that appear in the models that have no correspondence in the real world. Alternatively, there may be mechanisms represented in the model which are hypothesized to represent the way the natural world really works; the model might then be interpreted as an approximation or idealization of the real world systems, including mechanisms that we cannot observe directly. Debates among philosophers about 'scientific realism' and 'antirealism' have centred on the issues of what sorts of inference are necessary, or are justified, by the successful application of a scientific model to the real world (Churchland and Hooker 1985; van Fraassen 1980; Giere 1988; Suppe 1989).

See also: SCIENTIFIC METHOD; SCIENTIFIC REALISM AND ANTIREALISM; THEORIES, SCIENTIFIC

References and further reading

* Achinstein, P. (1968) *Concepts of Science*, Baltimore, MD: Johns Hopkins University Press. (Referred to in §3. Careful analysis of various conceptions of models and their uses in the sciences.)
* Black, M. (1962) *Models and Metaphors: Studies in Language and Philosophy*, Ithaca, NY: Cornell University Press. (Referred to in §3. Insightful discussion of philosophical understanding of models and the uses of models in scientific thought; not very technical.)
* Boolos, G. and Jeffrey, R.C. (1972) *Computability and Logic*, New York: Cambridge University Press; 2nd edn 1980. (Second edition referred to in §2. Standard text for metalogic. Requires familiarity with predicate logic.)
  Burks, A.W. (1949) 'Icon, Index, and Symbol', *Philosophical and Phenomenological Research* 9: 673–89. (Review of Peirce's semiotics, good explication of the concept of 'icon' proposed by Peirce.)
* Campbell, N.R. (1920) *Physics, the Elements*, Cambridge, Cambridge University Press; repr. as *Foundations of Science*, New York: Dover, 1957. (Referred to in §3. Controversial early advocacy of the centrality of models in scientific research.)
  Carnap, R. (1942) *Introduction to Semantics*, Cambridge, MA: Harvard University Press. (Provides more background and discussion than many other basic texts. Useful introductory chapters and examples of metamathematical models.)
* Churchland, P.M. and Hooker, C.W. (1985) *The Image of Science*, Chicago, IL: University of Chicago Press. (Referred to in §4. Useful collection of essays addressing the interpretation of models in science.)
* Duhem, P. (1914) *The Aim and Structure of Physical Theory*; trans. P.P. Wiener, Princeton, NJ: Princeton University Press, 1954, 2nd edn. (Referred to in §3. Influential criticism of the role of mechanical models in physics.)
* Fraassen, B.C. van (1980) *The Scientific Image*, Oxford: Clarendon Press. (Referred to in §4. Influential discussion of models in science. Defence of empiricist interpretation of scientific theories.)
* Giere, R. (1988) *Explaining Science: A Cognitive Approach*, Chicago, IL: University of Chicago Press. (Referred to in §4. Accessible discussion and applications of the semantic conception of scientific theories. Excellent introductory chapters.)
* Hesse, M.B. (1966) *Models and Analogies in Science*, Notre Dame, IN: University of Notre Dame Press.

(Referred to in §3. Original and influential discussion of the scientific and logical uses of models.)
* Peirce, C.S. (1934) *Collected Papers of Charles Sanders Peirce*, vol. II, Cambridge, MA: Harvard University Press. (Original, foundational work on semiotics, icons, symbols; fairly challenging.)
* Robinson, A. (1965) *Introduction to Model Theory and to the Metamathematics of Algebra*, Amsterdam: North Holland. (Referred to in §2. Authoritative text, primarily technical.)
* Schaffner, K.F. (1993) *Discovery and Explanation in Biology and Medicine*, Chicago, IL: University of Chicago Press. (Referred to in §4. Discusses the semantic view and alludes to the debate about differences between the semantic and syntactic views.)
  Suppe, F. (1977) *The Structure of Scientific Theories*, Urbana, IL: University of Illinois Press, 2nd edn. (Excellent review of scientific and philosophical discussions concerning models. Comparison of logical positivist and semantic conceptions of theory structure. Outstanding bibliography.)
* —— (1979) 'Theory Structure', *Current Research in Philosophy of Science*, East Lansing, MI: Philosophy of Science Association. (Quoted in §4; useful brief review of some central issues in philosophy of science.)
* —— (1989) *The Semantic Conception of Theories and Scientific Realism*, Urbana, IL: University of Illinois Press. (Referred to in §4. Best source for history and context of treatments of models in philosophy of science. Careful discussion of issues regarding how extensively scientific theories represent the natural world.)
* Suppes, P. (1962) 'Models of Data', in E. Nagel, P. Suppes and A. Tarski (eds) *Logic, Methodology, and Philosophy of Science: Proceedings of the 1960 International Congress*, Stanford, CA: Stanford University Press. (Referred to in §4. Sophisticated but accessible analysis of the extraction and organization of quantitative evidence from nature, and of its role in theory testing.)
  —— (1967) 'What is a Scientific Theory?', in S. Morgenbesser (ed.) *Philosophy of Science Today*, New York: Basic Books. (Influential defence of the use of metamathematical models in philosophy of science. Clear and accessible.)
* Tarski, A. (1941) *Introduction to Logic and to the Methodology of the Deductive Sciences*, New York: Oxford University Press; 2nd edn, 1946. (Referred to in §2. Presentations of formal logic and models by one of the developers of metamathematics.)
* Wartofsky, M. (1979) *Models: Representation and the Scientific Understanding*, Dordrecht: Reidel. (Referred to in §1. Original essays discussing the

metaphysical, epistemological and social significance of various types of model. Excellent and
readable.)

* Wimsatt, W. (1987) 'False Models as Means to Truer
Theories', in N. Nitecki and A. Hoffman (eds)
Neutral Models in Biology, London: Oxford University Press. (Referred to in §3. Insightful discussion of a variety of attitudes towards models in the
sciences.)

ELISABETH A. LLOYD

MODERNISM

*As a period in cultural history, modernism usually
denotes advanced or avant-garde European and American art and thought, though it has also been used to
describe more general social conditions and attitudes.
Most historians of literature and the plastic arts – the
fields in which the term has most play – date it from the
late 1880s to the Second World War. Modernism is
thus distinguished from the 'modern' of 'modern
history' (understood as anything since medieval history), 'modern life' (popular contemporary attitudes
and difficulties), and other broad uses of the term
'modern'. In fact, recognition of the ism in modernism is
a key to understanding it – intense self-awareness being
an essential characteristic or value, allied to modernism's complex engagement with avant-garde status.
Other values that consistently underpin modernism
include a propensity to create 'culture shock' by
abandoning traditional conventions of social behaviour,
aesthetic representation, and scientific verification; the
celebration of elitist or revolutionary aesthetic and
ethical departures; and in general the derogation of the
premise of a coherent, empirically accessible external
reality (such as Nature or Providence) and the
substitution of humanly devised structures or systems
which are self-consciously arbitrary and transitory.*

1   **Epistemic trauma**
2   **Reality and observation**
3   **Major manifestations**
4   **Towards postmodernism**

1   Epistemic trauma

In religious history, the term modernism still refers
narrowly to the late nineteenth- and early twentieth-
century movement within Roman Catholicism, and
also to analogous developments in Protestantism and
reformed Judaism. It constituted an attempt to bring
nineteenth-century critical methods, especially those
of pragmatism, to bear on subjects formerly regarded
as beyond their influence, including the interpretation
and application of sacred texts and other doctrines
(see PRAGMATISM). It was condemned as a heresy in
1907 by Pope Pius X. This religious movement shares
some of the values of the period in cultural history
now commonly referred to as modernism, but
remains quite distinct from it.

Given the historical intensity and complexity of the
period, it is helpful to abstract several general values
that characterize most manifestations of modernism.
Such values are not specifically substantive or
thematic, but dynamic and structural. They are the
dominant qualities that sustain and distinguish the
most advanced intellectual activity from the 1880s to
the Second World War.

The most readily apparent of these values is that of
epistemic trauma. This formulation signifies a kind of
primary or initial difficulty, strangeness or opacity in
modernist works; a violation of common sense, of
laboriously achieved intuitions of reality; and an
immediate, counter-intuitive refusal to provide the
reassuring conclusiveness of the positivist realism that
preceded modernism. This traumatic otherness stems
in part from a conscious refusal by modernist artists
and other thinkers to give their audiences the kind of
spatial and temporal orientation that art and literature had been providing since the Renaissance and
that had reached a high finish in the mid-nineteenth
century, when novelists took pains to provide their
'dear Reader' with temporal and spatial coordinates
and when the subject matter of most paintings was
generally accessible. In a surprising and historically
sudden contrast to this traditional solicitude, the
cutting-edge artistic culture of modernism – and
much contemporary social and scientific thinking –
offered this quality of trauma everywhere. In the
painting of Picasso and Braque, in the music of
Stravinsky and Schoenberg, in the fiction of Kafka
and Faulkner, in the poetry of Yeats and Eliot, the
immediate difficulty, the epistemic trauma, is a given
of the modernist aesthetic.

The *kind* of difficulty we find in modernist artistic
culture resembles the kind of difficulty contempora-
neous advances in mathematics and the natural
sciences presented to the scientific establishment. In
both spheres, the difficulty arises not so much from
developments and complications of traditional techniques (what might be called *baroque* difficulty), but
more often from what is left out. Relativity Theory
(viewed as a vehicle for cultural values, like works of
art and literature) provides a notorious example. For
many physicists, the initial difficulty of the Special
Theory lay in the fact that Einstein found the
nineteenth-century hypothesis of an ether 'super-

fluous', thus radically pruning physics of a laborious but comfortably familiar hypothesis. In all manifestations of the modernist breakthrough, thinking people missed those qualities or techniques on which they had customarily relied for meaning, such as single-point perspective in painting, tonality in music, neutral and uniform time in narrative, and unvarying temporal and spatial reference frames in physics.

Out of this fundamental value of epistemic trauma a number of cognate characteristics emerged. Modernism quickly developed an affinity to what seemed (when viewed from the tradition of realism) an addiction to gratuitous *difficulty* and *distortion*, either for their own sakes or for the sake of being avant-garde. In fact, discussions of modernism regularly equate it with the avant-garde; and while this equation ignores functional distinctions between the two terms, modernism's commitment to being at the cutting edge, to being shocking and difficult, quickly became a major value. In early modernism, when Cézanne began to depart from single-point perspective in the interest of greater truth to our visual experience of Nature, when Henry James began to introduce ambiguities of motive intolerable to the realist tradition, or when Max Planck introduced energy quanta, the apparent distortions and difficulties, the elitist value of being avant-garde, was not a principal motive or effect. But in a very short period, by the time Picasso had re-represented the human figure in *Les Demoiselles d'Avignon* and Kafka had transformed his protagonist into an insect in *The Metamorphosis* and Einstein had employed obscure mathematics to model a finite but unbounded universe in his General Theory, the antagonistic relation of modernism to popular culture was irreversible: it gradually led to the almost complete bifurcation of serious and popular culture. 'Modern [that is, modernist] art', wrote Ortega y Gasset in 1925 (1968: 5), 'will always have the masses against it. It is essentially unpopular; moreover, it is anti-popular' (see ORTEGA Y GASSET, J.).

2 Reality and observation

One of the most prominent and lasting achievements of modernism in all its manifestations is the devaluation of the premise that we occupy an 'objective' reality, accessible to but independent of human perception. In traditional realism, artists and critics, social thinkers and scientists were thought to make direct statements about this reality, whether it be natural, social or psychological. Modernism essentially turns away from this realist enterprise and towards discussion and analysis of human measurement or observation.

This rich and profound departure is difficult to describe in brief, but an example from modernist physics helps to illustrate it. In the natural sciences, the great model of an objective, constant, external universe was based on Newtonian mechanics. Einstein undermined this coherent and rational structure by redirecting attention from the nature of reality to the nature of measurement, from what was taken to be our direct contact with nature to our observation of it. In his 1905 paper on Special Relativity, Einstein did not ask what time *is*: he asked how we *measure* it. He asked what we *mean* by the time of an event. In Relativity Theory, a measurement is neither a subjective impression (a unique event in a single mind that cannot be fully communicated) nor a constant, necessary description of an independent external object or event. Instead, it may be seen as a kind of middle ground – literally a mediation – between the observer and the observed phenomenon. And this middle ground is the characteristic epistemological location of modernism: its focus is on neither subject nor object but on the act of human observation of a reality presumed but not proved to be external to the observer.

In modernist painting we can see other manifestations of this shift in value. Cubism – with its subject-matter of bottles, tables, shreds of newspaper, musical instruments – clearly deflects our interest from the subject to its representation. In this process it derogates the specific importance of the historically or religiously or sentimentally significant subject (Christ on the Cross, the *Mona Lisa*, *The Rape of the Sabines*) to the problematics of representation, the aesthetics of composition, the formal language. What is significant about Picasso's *Portrait of Ambroise Vollard*, for example, is not the subject (Vollard's distinctive physical features, his support of modernist art, his aesthetic intuition) but how Picasso *presents* Ambroise Vollard. Just as Relativity Theory focused attention away from the nature of reality towards the nature of measurement and observation, so Cubism focused attention away from what was being represented towards how it was being represented.

Similar illustrations of this shift can be found in most movements of modernist art and literature, as well as in modernist developments in philosophy (see PHENOMENOLOGICAL MOVEMENT). But what is of greatest significance here is the liberating nature of this change in values. The practitioners of modernism felt themselves no longer locked into the limiting dichotomies of object and representation, world and observer. They began to move from one side to the other, to explore without interruption the unceasing interaction between the object and its space, or the event and its temporality. The old categories lost their integrity and the artist and subject, or observer and object, came to inhabit a middle ground of observation itself. In this sense of liberation, the modernist model for reality becomes the *field* (as in scientific field models), where observers are also participants (as in cubist painting or quantum theory), where readers help to create the text (as in Kafka's *The Castle* or Faulkner's *Absalom, Absalom!*), or in the many other modernist constructions in which all constituents are interdependent and in which all participate and interrelate without privilege.

3 Major manifestations

The major literary and artistic movements most often cited as major manifestations of modernism include Post-Impressionism, Fauvism, Cubism, Expressionism, Futurism, Symbolism, Imagism, Vorticism, Dadaism and Surrealism. But such a list will be regarded as necessarily incomplete, and by definition it omits many modernist developments in architecture, philosophy, social science, psychology and the natural sciences – all areas sustained by and manifesting the values discussed above. But a catalogue of movements has the advantage of demonstrating one more value of modernism, that of *reflexivity*: the characteristic of self-awareness and of conscious programmatic direction. We have been regarding modernism as a historical period in high culture and therefore as what Astradur Eysteinsson (1990) calls a 'cultural force', but to the extent that each of the movements contained in modernism was aware of its newness and its cohesiveness (that is, of being avant-garde) it can be viewed as an 'aesthetic project', the self-conscious endeavour of a group of innovators to further certain values and achieve recognition.

4 Towards postmodernism

Cultural historians and theorists of modernism tend to view what is now called postmodernism in one of two general ways: as part of the original revolutionary gesture in which postmodernism constitutes a late and distinguishable development; or as a new ethos and a new aesthetic (new collection of 'values'). Preference for one view or the other depends largely on the size of one's historical canvas, but in either case such discussion proves helpful in defining modernism itself. This is because we can see changes in or departures from the values that constituted modernism, and these changes help to establish their original identities.

In the place of epistemic trauma, postmodernism affirms a denial of prescriptive norms and derogates the *value* of the normative. Where modernism wrestled with the difficulties caused by the absence of universal temporal, spatial, and ethical coordinates, postmodernism adopts without struggle the surreal, bizarre, and meta-natural. Where modernism negotiated the difficult transition from examination of reality to examination of observation, postmodernism accepts the premise that all values are 'constructions' on the model of language – local, contained, self-referential. Where modernism sought depth and abstraction, postmodernism turns toward surface and particularity. For what was in modernism a dominant value of 'order', postmodernism substitutes 'design' and 'pattern'. Finally, the reflexivity of modernism, its self-awareness, becomes in postmodernism a more radical and complete self-referentiality moving toward visions of total (and so completely free) self-containment (see POSTMODERNISM).

See also: ART, ABSTRACT; RELATIVITY THEORY, PHILOSOPHICAL SIGNIFICANCE OF

References and further reading

Bradbury, M. and McFarlane J. (eds) (1976) *Modernism: 1890–1930*, London: Penguin. (Excellent historical essays.)

Ermarth, E.D. (1992) *Sequel to History: Postmodernism and the Crisis of Representational Time*, Princeton, NJ: Princeton University Press. (So far the most accurate and theoretically complete study of postmodernism.)

* Eysteinsson, A. (1990) *The Concept of Modernism*, Ithaca, NY and London: Cornell University Press. (A full account of critical usage.)

Kern, S.J. (1983) *The Culture of Time and Space: 1880–1918*, Cambridge, MA: Harvard University Press. (Unruly but indispensable and comprehensive cultural history of modernist technology and culture.)

Ortega y Gasset, J. (1923) *The Modern Theme*, New York: W.W. Norton, 1933. (Ortega's assessment of his contemporary culture which remains valuable, despite being partial and opinionated.)

* —— (1925) *The Dehumanization of Art and Other Writings on Art and Culture*, Princeton, NJ: Princeton University Press, 1968. (A major statement on the subject of modernism that has itself become an important modernist document.)

Vargish, T. and Mook, D. (1998, forthcoming) *Inside Modernism: Relativity Theory, Cubism, Narrative*. (An analytic description of modernism through the identification of values common to physics, painting, and narrative.)

THOMAS VARGISH

MODI *see* MOZI

MODULARITY OF MIND

A common view in recent philosophy of science is that there is no principled distinction between theoretical and observational claims, since perception itself is thoroughly contaminated by the beliefs and expectations of the observer. However, recent psychological and neurological evidence casts doubt on this latter claim and suggests, instead, that perceptual processing is to a significant extent 'cognitively impenetrable': it takes place in informationally encapsulated 'modules' that cannot be rationally influenced by beliefs or other 'central' cognitive states, or even other portions of the perceptual system.

1 Claims and distinctions
2 Evidence

1 Claims and distinctions

It might appear that what we see depends heavily on what we expect and what we know about the situation at hand. That is how magicians manage to deceive us, and how we sometimes deceive ourselves into hearing and seeing what we have reason to believe is there, missing, for example, typographical errors that we recognize only when they are explicitly brought to our attention. This idea has also been supported by hundreds of experiments carried out in the 1950s, and has been the basis for a widespread view in psychology associated with Jerome Bruner (1957) and referred to as the 'New Look in Perception'. It has also been very influential among philosophers of science such as HANSON (1958) and KUHN (1962), who have taken for granted that how we perceive the world is thoroughly conditioned by our prior expectations and beliefs (see OBSERVATION §§3–4; PERCEPTION).

In recent years, however, doubt has been cast on the premise that such processes as visual perception, face recognition, language comprehension are equally 'cognitively penetrable'. The issue is whether the flow of information among cognitive functions is governed by fixed architectural principles, or whether failures to access relevant information in the course of perceptual processing, though widespread, are adventitious (see COGNITIVE ARCHITECTURE). Despite the widespread acceptance of the idea that perception is contaminated by cognition, a careful examination of the psychological evidence actually favours the view that perception operates autonomously from the system of beliefs and inferences. Jerry Fodor (1983) has argued that certain cognitive capacities seem to be 'modular' or 'informationally encapsulated'. He focuses particularly on what he calls 'input systems', which include cognitive systems for perception and language (see FODOR, J.A.).

To make Fodor's views clear, however, we need to make some critical distinctions.

(1) The distinction between 'what we see' and what we come to believe about what we are looking at.

(2) The distinction between perceptual and post-perceptual effects such as those that depend on the exigencies of memory and decision processes, including the decision to make a particular response. (Sometimes post-perceptual effects can be mathematically factored out using a signal-detection method that allows one to separate 'detection' from 'response selection' effects – the latter of which clearly depend on beliefs and utilities; see Samuel (1981).)

(3) The distinction between *extra*-modular *cognitive* penetration of perception, and other top-down but *intra*-modular effects. It is clear that how certain local features are perceived may depend on more global aspects of percepts – for example, how a phoneme is perceived may depend on word-level acoustical perception – but these generally are not effects of cognition but of broader aspects of perception. There are plenty of examples in vision where how a local feature is perceived depends on how the larger scene is perceived, but where the latter itself is insensitive to more general beliefs and inferences.

2 Evidence

Perhaps the most striking evidence for modularity of perception is the imperviousness of various illusions to knowledge: even when you have every reason to believe that something you are seeing is an illusion, you cannot make the illusory percept disappear. Moreover, perception appears to have a logic all its own: if you see some part of a pattern in a certain way you will automatically tend to see other parts of the pattern in a compatible way. For example, if you see the reversing Necker cube (see GESTALT PSYCHOLOGY §2) in one orientation you will see each of its edges in the appropriate relative location, and will even see the apparently-further face as bigger.

There is a great deal of evidence for the existence of pre-recognition stages in perception that are clearly immune to cognitive influences. (Stich (1978) calls the output of such stages, characterized by their lack of 'inferential promiscuity', 'sub-doxastic states'.) In addition there appear to be even finer submodules within the visual system. For example, there is considerable independence of the colour perception system, the motion detection system, and the form recognition system. Stereo depth and motion-induced depth perception (so-called kinetic depth effect) do not require prior recognition of form. Examples of this sort are commonplace, and all point to there being architectural constraints on communication among parts of the visual system and between the visual system and the rest of cognition. In the face of this kind of evidence it appears that at least the principle of modularity is well established, even when the exact locus of the modules and the type and extent of encapsulation may be open to debate.

Related evidence is also provided by various pathologies of perception. In these cases of dysfunction (due to brain damage or illness) patients frequently show signs of dissociation of functions, providing clear evidence that a certain function, which is absent in particular patients, is not required in order to accomplish some other function, which remains intact in those patients. For example, colour-blindness can occur without form-blindness.

Although functional decomposition is commonplace, it is the special case of the dissociation of much of perception from the rest of the cognitive system that is of particular importance to philosophy. What such cognitive impenetrability suggests is that there is reason to distinguish between *data*-driven and *theory*-driven aspects of perception. And if that is the case, then the observation/theory distinction may have some empirical support after all, and one of the arguments for epistemological holism may also be undermined. (See the exchange between Fodor (1984, 1988) and Churchland (1988) for discussion of this issue.)

See also: COGNITIVE ARCHITECTURE; PERCEPTION, EPISTEMIC ISSUES IN; PERCEPTION; VISION

References and further reading

* Bruner, J. (1957) 'On Perceptual Readiness', *Psychological Review* 64: 123–52. (Early defence of the claim that observation was thoroughly penetrated by theory.)
* Churchland, P. (1988) 'Perceptual Plasticity and Theoretical Neutrality: A Reply to Jerry Fodor', *Philosophy of Science* 55: 167–87. (Reply to Fodor 1984.)
* Fodor, J. (1983) *The Modularity of Mind: An Essay on Faculty Psychology*, Cambridge, MA: MIT Press. (The main statement of the modularity thesis.)
* —— (1984) 'Observation Reconsidered', *Philosophy of Science* 51: 23–43. (Fodor's effort to use his claims about modularity to resuscitate the observation/theoretic distinction in the philosophy of science.)
* —— (1985) 'Précis of *Modularity of Mind*', *Behavioral and Brain Sciences* 8: 1–42. (Short version of Fodor (1983), with commentaries by many philosophers and psychologists and replies by the author.)
* —— (1988) 'A Reply to Churchland's "Perceptual Plasticity and Theoretical Neutrality"', *Philosophy of Science* 55: 188–98. (Reply to Churchland's 1988 reply to Fodor 1984.)
Garfield. J. (ed.) (1987) *Modularity in Knowledge Representation and Natural Language Understanding*, Cambridge, MA.: MIT Press. (A diverse collection of essays by philosophers and psychologists on the issue of modularity.)
* Hanson, N. (1958) *Patterns of Discovery*, Chicago, IL: University of Chicago Press. (Early philosophical effort to show how observation was inseparable from theory.)
* Kuhn, T. (1962) *The Structure of Scientific Revolutions*, Chicago, IL: University of Chicago Press. (Highly influential attack on the suggestion that there was any theory-neutral observations that could provide a neutral basis for comparing theories.)
* Samuel, A. (1981) 'Phoneme Restoration: Insights from a New Methodology', *Journal of Experimental Psychology: General* 110 (4): 474–94. (Subtle discussion of how to distinguish experimentally between 'signal detection' and 'response selection'.)
* Stich, S. (1978) 'Beliefs and Sub-Doxastic States', *Philosophy of Science* 45: 499–518. (Introduces the idea of isolated belief-like states that are relatively independent of the rest of one's belief system, as in the case of the kind of 'knowledge' of grammar that Chomsky attributes to normal language speakers.)

ZENON W. PYLYSHYN

MOHIST PHILOSOPHY

Mohist philosophy describes the broad-ranging philosophical tradition initiated by Mo Ti or Mozi (Master Mo) in the fifth century BC. Mozi was probably of quite humble origins, perhaps a member of the craft or artisan class. Early in life, he may have studied with followers of Confucius. However, he went on to become the first serious critic of Confucianism.

Mozi's philosophy was part of an organized utopian movement whose members engaged in direct social action. He was a charismatic leader who inspired his followers to dedicate themselves to his unique view of social justice. This required them to lead austere and demanding lives, as he called upon them to participate in such activities as the military defence of states unjustly attacked.

Mozi is arguably the first true philosopher of China. He was the first to develop systematic analyses and criticisms of his opponents and present carefully argued positions of his own. This led him and his later followers to develop an interest in and study of the forms and methods of philosophical argumentation, which contributed significantly to the development of early Chinese philosophy.

Mozi saw ideological differences and the factionalism they spawned as the primary source of human suffering, and he hotly criticized the familially-based ethical and political system of Confucius for its inherent partiality. In its place he advocated three basic goods: the wealth, order and the population of the state. Against the Confucians, he argued for jian'ai (impartial care). Jian'ai is often translated as 'universal love', but this is misleading. Mozi saw the central ethical problem as an excess of partiality, not a lack of compassion; he was interested not in cultivating emotions or attitudes, but in shaping behaviour. He showed remarkably little interest in moral psychology and embraced an extremely thin picture of human nature, which led him away from the widely observed Chinese concern with self-cultivation. His general lack of appreciation for psychological goods and the need to control desires and shape dispositions and attitudes also led him to reject the characteristic Confucian concern with culture and ritual.

Mozi believed human beings possess an extremely plastic and malleable nature, and he advocated a strong form of voluntarism. For several different reasons, he believed that people could be induced to take up almost any form of behaviour. First, he shared a common early Chinese belief in a psychological tendency to respond in kind to the treatment one receives. He further believed that, in order to win the favour of their rulers, many people are inclined to act as their rulers desire. Those who do not respond to either of these influences can be motivated and controlled by a system of strict rewards and punishments, enforced by the state and guaranteed by the support of Heaven, ghosts and spirits. Most important of all, Mozi believed that rational arguments provide extremely strong if not compelling motivation to act: presented with a superior argument, thinking people act accordingly.

The social and political movements of the later Mohists lasted until the beginning of the Han Dynasty (206 BC). They continued Mozi's early interests and developed sophisticated systems of logical analysis, mathematics, optics, physics, defensive warfare technology and strategy and a formal ethic based upon calculations of benefit and harm. All the philosophical concerns of the later Mohists can be found in the early strata of the Mozi, and seem to reflect the teachings of the tradition's founder.

1 Nature of the work

The present text of the Mozi consists of fifteen books unevenly divided into seventy-one chapters, eighteen of which are now lost (for a complete list, see the table of contents of Y.P. Mei's translation (1929)) (see Mozi). Contemporary scholars tend to divide the book into five parts: the Epitomes (chapters 1–7), Essays (8–39, seven of which are lost), Logical Chapters (40–5), Dialogues (46–50) and Military Chapters (51–71, nine of which are lost). The Epitomes are clearly of later origin and, in several cases, of questionable provenance. The Essays are the core of the text and offer a complete and consistent account of Mohist philosophy. Depending on one's view, they present either ten or eleven different themes: 'elevating the worthy', 'identifying with one's superior', 'impartial care', 'against aggressive warfare', 'economy in expenditures', 'economy in funerals', 'heaven's intention', 'explaining ghosts', 'against music', 'against fate' and 'against Confucians'. For both textual and philosophical reasons, the last does not seem to fit with this group and will not be considered here as part of the Essays' corpus.

Originally there were three separate versions of each of the remaining ten themes, which are thought to represent three different sects of later Mohism. The existence of three later Mohist sects is attested to in collateral sources, though we know very little about their distinctive natures or their relationship to these chapters. Graham (1985) argued for a rearrangement of the chapters, which he believed revealed distinct doctrinal differences, but his analysis remains controversial and the philosophical differences he identified are not significant. The repetitive and unadorned style of these triadic chapters has led several scholars to speculate that they may be different versions of recorded sermons or lectures, or part of an original oral tradition. In any event, they present the central doctrines of early Mohist philosophy and may even be an accurate record of the teachings of Mozi himself. Later Mohists tend to write in a similarly unembellished fashion but ostensibly for a definite purpose: they sought to eliminate all stylistic flourish, believing it could only obscure the weakness or interfere with the strength of an argument.

The Dialogues seem to be of slightly later date and, like the *Analects* of Confucius (see CONFUCIUS), record conversations between Mozi and various disciples and opponents and stories about his exploits and travels. The Logical Chapters and Military Chapters both appear to be of considerably later date, and develop in systematic fashion Mozi's early concern with the forms of argumentation and the practical aspects of defensive warfare.

2 Central philosophical doctrines

Like XUNZI (and also like Thomas HOBBES), Mozi described a state of nature which is an unfulfilling war of all against all. However, he did not see this state as the result of our having shared and unruly desires which lead us into competition and conflict over scarce goods. For Mozi, human beings are led to fight with one another because they hold individual and irreconcilable notions of what is *yi* (right). The fundamental problem is a fragmentation of values. Hence the most pressing task is to get people to agree on a single notion of what is right. Mozi believed that the right consists in maximizing the collective well-being of the group: those who support and work for this unified goal put the common good ahead of their personal well-being and hence are, by definition, the most 'worthy' people for public office. Thus they deserve to be promoted to positions of authority in the state and deferred to by those they supervise. Mozi argues for these ideas in the first two groups of synoptic chapters: 'Elevating the Worthy' and 'Identifying with One's Superior'.

Mozi believed that the control and redirection of human desires was not a problematic task, nor did he believe one needed to develop virtuous attitudes and dispositions in order to behave ethically. Since he saw no need to develop or shape the self through ritual practice, introspection or insight, he was not, like most early Chinese philosophers, a self-cultivationist (see SELF-CULTIVATION IN CHINESE PHILOSOPHY). Nevertheless, he was not a Hobbesian-style contractarian either. He believed that people could be influenced to adopt a non-competitive mode of behaviour through a variety of means. Hence, in theory at least, he avoided the difficulties associated with problems like the prisoner's dilemma (see RATIONAL CHOICE THEORY §3).

Mozi relied upon four basic techniques to influence people's behaviour. First, he appealed to a rather mechanistic version of the generally accepted early Chinese belief that people are inclined to respond in kind to the treatment they receive. Second, he believed that many would act as their ruler desired, simply to curry favour. Third, he advocated a system of well-defined rewards and punishments designed to move people away from certain types of behaviour and toward others. Consistent with his moral psychology, his list of rewards and punishments contained only material goods, with the single exception of 'honour' or 'prestige'. In this respect he anticipated later Legalist philosophers such as HAN FEIZI, who like him were not self-cultivationists and who relied upon the power of the state to shape behaviour through a publicly-proclaimed system of rewards and punishments (see LEGALIST PHILOSOPHY, CHINESE). However, Mozi differed from these later thinkers in believing that his system of rewards and punishments had Heaven's active and direct support (see TIAN). In the seventh group of synoptic chapters, 'Heaven's Intention', he claimed that Heaven directly intervenes in human affairs to reward and punish, and in the eighth group, 'Explaining Ghosts', he argued that ghosts and spirits act as Heaven's agents to ensure that justice is upheld.

Mozi's fourth basic approach to influencing people's behaviour entailed an extreme form of voluntarism. He believed that most, or at least many, people could simply take up a form of behaviour and would do so if they were given good reasons for adopting it. Mozi argued that anyone who truly understood that a given form of behaviour does indeed maximize the common good (as he understood it) would immediately act accordingly. This belief in the inexorable power of argument is of a piece with his sparse moral psychology and belief in the plasticity of human nature, and helps to explain his active and persistent interest in the forms and method of philosophical debate.

3 Central philosophical doctrines (cont.)

The most important philosophical position Mozi sought to establish is *jian'ai* (impartial care). He argues for this view in the third group of synoptic chapters, which take this theme as their title. Impartial care is the key to Mozi's philosophical system and the basis for many of his other teachings. He believed it is the only way to correct the destructive tendency to form factions and show preference to oneself, one's family and one's group. The unity that results when everyone adopts a policy of impartial care optimizes the wealth, population and order of the state.

Mozi often asserts or assumes that maximizing these collective goods will result in maximizing individual good. At times he does argue for this connection: for example, he argues that a truly filial man will embrace impartial care as the best way to serve his parents, wife and children. Like CONFUCIUS,

Mozi develops his ethical philosophy from the perspective of groups rather than individuals. Here, their major difference is that for Confucius the family is primary while for Mozi the collective or state is most important. Impartial care does not entail egalitarianism. Mozi saw *jian'ai* as perfectly compatible with a strict social hierarchy and an absolute monarchy. Like almost every early Chinese philosopher, he appealed to a past golden age when his own proposed policy had been actually practiced. Such an appeal was thought to show first, that his theory was feasible, and second, that the practice of this theory was the reason for the success of earlier society (see HISTORY, CHINESE THEORIES OF).

Mozi further believed that Heaven itself practised impartial care, and desired human beings to do the same. He argued for this view in the seventh group of synoptic chapters, 'Heaven's Intention'. In early China, it was widely held that if one could discern and follow Heaven's plan, one would be in accord with a pattern inherent in the universe itself, which would normally lead to ease in action and to success. Mozi accepted this general idea and insisted that following Heaven's plan would guarantee reward. As he argued in the tenth group of synoptic chapters, 'Against Fate', to believe anything less was to succumb to a pernicious form of fatalism. Since Heaven practises impartial care and is omniscient and all-powerful, good people will always be rewarded for their good deeds and bad people will always suffer punishment. Since the ideal state is modelled on the pattern of Heaven, rewards and punishments will be the strict policy of any just ruler.

Another important and related Mohist assumption is that the good is always useful, in the sense of directly producing material benefit for the world. One can see this throughout Mozi's philosophical teachings. Impartial care is good and directly benefits the world. A belief in 'fate' is bad and entails the negative consequences of complacency and defeatism. This linkage of the good with the useful occasionally led Mozi to conflate the notions of the 'good' and the 'true'. For example, as part of the justification for his claim that ghosts and spirits exist, Mozi argues that believing in their existence is useful: it influences people to be ethical. It is tempting to claim that Mozi is merely relying on a 'useful fiction' in order to achieve a greater good, but such an interpretation must ignore or explain away considerable textual evidence supporting his belief in ghosts and spirits, in particular the entire eighth group of synoptic chapters. Such a view must also ignore or explain away Mozi's belief that Heaven guarantees that there is absolute justice in the world. Finally, such an interpretation must ignore the fact that Mozi did not

support this claim with an appeal to its utility alone. In fact, he employed three basic tests for any doctrine.

In the last group of synoptic chapters, 'Against Fate', Mozi presents the three tests that any theory should pass. It is significant that the word translated here as 'test' is literally a gnomen, an astronomical instrument used to determine the direction of the rising and setting sun. Thus Mozi's three tests allow one to orient oneself to the way things are in the world: 'We must set up a standard of judgement, for to try to speak without a standard of judgement is like trying to establish the direction of sunrise and sunset with a revolving potter's wheel...' (*Mozi* 35, in Watson 1963: 117–8). These three tests are precedent, evidence and utility.

The first test is an appeal to the policies and beliefs of idealized past sages. While the Mohists recognized the need for technological innovation, they share the common Chinese belief that the important theoretical discoveries regarding self and society were all known to a select group of past sages (see CHINESE CLASSICS). The Mohists tended to appeal to the earlier sage-king Yu rather than to the favourite Confucian exemplar, the Duke of Zhou, but they often appealed to the same individuals as the Confucians did, ascribing to them different beliefs and practices. Any proffered theory ought to find precedent in the practices and beliefs of these former sages. Such precedent establishes both its feasibility and efficacy. The second test is an appeal to commonly held beliefs and practices, something like an appeal to 'common sense'. Any theory that is not supported by evidence derived from the 'eyes and ears' of the people is not to be accepted. Finally, the third test concerns measuring the consequences the theory has for the common good: the aggregate wealth, order and population of the state. As Graham has pointed out (1989: 37–8), the theories presented in the ten synoptic chapters themselves are all supported by these three tests. However, for most, only the first and third tests are applied. The second test is only employed to establish Mozi's claims regarding the existence of ghosts and spirits and the non-existence of destiny.

Mozi did not rank the three tests in any way. While it is true that he often pointed to the purported good consequences of his proposals, this may have been motivated more by rhetorical than logical considerations. It seems most reasonable to believe that for Mozi and his followers the truth of their theories was strongly over-determined: it could never be the case that the precedents of the sages or the common-sense views of the people could conflict with optimizing the collective good.

The three tests can be seen as related to another

principle which Mozi developed and employed both to criticize his opponents and to establish his own case, namely, consistency. For example, in condemning aggressive wars Mozi argued that someone who steals one peach or kills one person is recognized as guilty, but those who steal and slaughter whole states are not (this argument was later parodied in the *Zhuangzi*). Here the call to consistency is combined with an appeal to common sense. In another chapter from the same group, Mozi argues that while aggressive warfare has worked for a few states, it comes only at the expense of many others. To claim that, as a principle, aggressive war is right '... is rather like the case of a doctor who administers medicine to over ten thousand patients but succeeds in curing only four' (*Mozi* 19, in Watson 1963: 59). Here the principle of consistency is combined with an appeal to the common good.

4 Central philosophical doctrines (cont.)

The remaining four groups of synoptic chapters, 'Against Aggressive War', 'Economy in Expenditures', 'Economy in Funerals' and 'Against Music', are all reactive policies. The first is directed against the general practice of rulers in his time, and the last three are specifically aimed at his Confucian competitors. While motivated as criticisms, these chapters are perfectly consistent with and representative of Mohist philosophy as a whole. All are justified by appeals to the three tests of a doctrine as well as Mozi's principle of consistency. Moreover, they all reveal his characteristic lack of appreciation for the value of psychological goods.

For example, in 'Against Aggressive War', Mozi deploys his full array of arguments: aggressive war fails all three tests and the asymmetry between the condemnation of killing one person and the celebration of killing whole populations violates his principle of consistency. As Lowe (1992: 18) has noted, Mohists were not really pacifists although they are often described as such. Mozi and his followers had a just-war theory and participated in what they regarded as ethically warranted warfare, but, as these chapters reveal, they were adamantly opposed to wars of expansion. What is striking in Mozi's searing and well-argued condemnation of aggressive war is the complete absence of descriptions of the horror of war. All Mozi seems to see is the unprofitability of war. His overriding concern with li ('benefit' or 'profit') led him to ignore a broad range of psychological goods and harms (see WAR AND PEACE, PHILOSOPHY OF §1).

This absence of any consideration of psychological consequences is manifested throughout the remaining three groups of synoptic chapters, in which Mozi argues against the elaborate cultural embellishments, funeral practices and court music advocated by Confucians. While a reasonable case could be made against extravagance in any of these pursuits, Mozi does not acknowledge the possibility that such activities, properly moderated, might possess some value. He not only rejects the idea of their inherent value, he does not even consider that they might be instrumentally valuable in the task of shaping human behaviour.

Mozi's complete rejection of psychological goods shows that it is inaccurate to describe him as a utilitarian, at least in the classical sense (see UTILITARIANISM). He is not working to optimize aggregate pleasure and pain. In the absence of this classical utilitarian concern, it is at first glance difficult to see what justification or motivation Mozi can provide to support his ethical theory: in particular his call for impartial care. However, there is a clear foundation for his ethical vision: his belief that it accords with or, more accurately, mirrors what Heaven intends (Lowe 1992: 132).

Mozi often appeals to a kind of divine sanction as justification for his ethical views, but it is important to understand that his notion of Heaven is not strongly theistic. While Heaven has intentions, these are a set of natural patterns or forces in the world, not acts of will originating from an independent agent standing outside the world and sustaining it. Heaven did not create the world and, while Heaven provides a model for human activity by showing impartial care for all, it is always reactive in showing its support or displeasure. Heaven is not a personal God who loves individuals, but a force which ensures that certain actions are met with appropriate reactions.

The relationship between human beings and Heaven is quite revealing and representative of Mozi's general orientation. The first point to note is that a person's attitude toward Heaven is not devotional: there is little or no emotion – never mind passion – involved. The intercourse between people and Heaven is a simple form of behaviour, a kind of transaction. There is nothing mysterious or awe-inspiring about Mozi's Heaven. As long as people act in accordance with the Heavenly pattern of impartial care, they can be assured that they will receive Heaven's support. If they deviate from this plan, they act against Heaven and will not escape its punishment.

Confucius believed that Heaven was on the side of good people and that acting in accordance with Heaven's will was the only way to realize certain personal and social goods. However, he also believed that no one was guaranteed Heaven's support. Heaven sometimes acts in ways that were inscrutable to human beings and this should not affect the way one behaves. He also believed that good people tend to have a strong influence on others that elicits from them reciprocal acts of goodness, and that this is the only legitimate way to influence others to be good; but again, one could never be guaranteed that such reciprocity is forthcoming. In either case, there was something fundamentally wrong with attempting to manipulate Heaven or humans by consciously working these natural tendencies to personal advantage. Even self-consciously pursuing virtue ran the risk of tainting one's character with thoughts of self-aggrandizement and pride (see CONFUCIAN PHILOSOPHY, CHINESE).

Mozi's philosophy opposed almost all of these fundamental tenets of Confucius' thought. He believed that if there were not a direct and immediate guarantee of reward or punishment, the idea that Heaven supported ethical conduct was empty. If Heaven proved to be unknowable or unreliable, people would lose all faith in affecting their future improvement and would resign themselves to whatever they perceived as their fate. In a similar way, Mozi believed that people could be motivated to 'care' for others only by embracing a wholly impersonal system of the equitable distribution of material goods which guaranteed them treatment in kind. Mozi and his followers could never see virtue as, in any way, its own reward (see VIRTUE ETHICS).

5 Later Mohist philosophy

The later Mohists developed and extended the philosophical interests of their tradition's founder. Some of their most important advances came in what might be described as the science of argumentation (see LOGIC IN CHINA). They laid out definitions of necessary and sufficient conditions, inference and a priori, developed a version of the law of excluded middle, and analyzed and discussed such notions as universals and particulars. However, the way they approached these issues was distinctive and in some cases significantly different from the way early Greek thinkers worked (see ZENO OF ELEA). The Mohists were more empirical than abstract in their approach. They were trying to sort out certain problems; their work bore a greater resemblance to careful accounting, taxonomy or cartography than theoretical mathematics. It is significant, as Graham (1989: 60) has pointed out, that although the later Mohists took geometry as paradigmatic of clear and exact thinking, they never developed a discipline of geometric proof. They were content simply to illustrate that certain relationships and regularities obtained by appeal to geometric paradigms.

Owing at least in part to the nature of the classical Chinese language, where many logically significant distinctions within sentences such as number and tense are unmarked, the later Mohists did not develop formal logic. Like most Chinese philosophers, they began with *ming* (names) and sought to map these onto the things and events in the world in a clear and consistent fashion. Working in this way, they built up terms and strings of names to form sentences which would then either be 'so' (*ran*) or 'not so' (*buran*) of a given case. They noticed and sought to make clear that semantic differences – particularly those arising from the idiomatic meanings of compound terms – generate considerable problems when one attempts to draw parallels and analogies between sentences and arrange them into classes.

One well-known example is the later Mohist treatment of the parallel sentences: 'Robbers are people' and 'Killing robbers is not killing people'. While the second sentence simply appears false in English, this is because it has been rendered literally, thereby obscuring the semantic ambiguity of key terms. In Chinese, *shadao* (killing robbers) has the sense of 'executing robbers', while *sharen* (killing people) has the sense of 'murder'. Thus the immediate sense of the sentence is something like, 'Executing robbers is not murdering people'. Many related cases were also studied, such as the sentences, 'Increasing the number of robbers is not increasing the number of people' and 'Caring for robbers is not caring for people'.

The later Mohist approach to these problems is largely an attempt to define criteria for class membership. On the primary level of things, they sought to establish definite and distinct *lei* ('categories' or 'classes') based on observable similarities and differences. They were not seeking Platonic essences nor even the generic definitions of ARISTOTLE; they were thoroughgoing and somewhat naïve nominalists (see NOMINALISM). Nevertheless, since they insisted on a strict accounting of what does and does not merit inclusion in a given category, they avoided many problems that have bedevilled Western philosophy concerning the notion of what is 'true', while still having a workable and functionally equivalent concept. They used a similar approach on the level of sentences, which they viewed as strings of names.

In order to argue for the similarity of separate cases, the later Mohists also developed the notion of 'inference' (*tui*). Again, Graham (1989: 150) is highly instructive in noting that the later Mohist notion of inference differs from induction, whereby one moves from the known to the unknown. Rather, it is used to argue for the *actual* similarity between cases. At their most abstract, the later Mohists employed an established category as a kind of template to assess the status of some actual thing or situation, to see whether or not it warrants inclusion within a given set. As is clear from the examples involving 'people' and 'robbers' presented above, class membership can be critically important (see CATEGORIES).

Mohist ideas regarding 'categories' and 'inference' had a profound effect on early Chinese philosophy. For example, they were adopted and played a major role in the thought of MENCIUS. As well as using Mohist logical terms of art, Mencius adapted them, in some cases enlarging their sense, to make specific points critical to his philosophical position. For example, he argued that the sage is the same in kind (*lei*) as other human beings (*Mengzi* 2A2, 6A7). He further argued that in order to 'fill out the category' of human being, one must 'infer' (*tui*) or 'draw the analogy' between paradigmatic cases of moral action and relevantly similar ones (*Mengzi* 1A7, 2A9). In a justly famous passage (*Mengzi* 1B8) strongly reminiscent of the Mohist examples presented above, Mencius argues that past sages who rebelled against and killed their evil rulers did not perpetrate the crime of regicide, since these rulers were not 'kings' but rather 'mutilators' and 'outcasts'.

In the later Mohist material, there is a discussion of the relationship between benefit and harm and liking and disliking that appears to present a genuinely utilitarian ethic. However, closer inspection reveals that what is of value are not raw states of pleasure or pain nor even more lofty feelings of altruism or compassion. What is 'liked' or 'disliked' is determined a priori by 'the sage', who enjoys what produces the greatest collective good for the state. What is new is the explicit use of a functionally defined ideal observer, the sage. Earlier Mohists appealed to the authority of sages, but their appeal was always to actual past sages.

This was not the only change that later Mohists made in their ethical theory. In *Mengzi* 3A5, we find the Mohist Yi Zhi proposing a modified form of voluntarism (Nivison 1980). The debate begins with Mencius criticizing Yi Zhi for advocating frugal burials while at the same time providing lavishly for the burial of his own parents (essentially accusing Yi Zhi of failing to meet his own Mohist criterion of consistency). Yi Zhi replies first by quoting a classical passage (thus invoking the third 'test' and employing an appeal the Confucians themselves should accept), which he presents as supporting the Mohist teaching of 'impartial care'. He then argues that while such care is the ideal and ultimate end, it naturally begins in the home. We start by caring for our parents and then, by applying the teachings of Mozi, we are to universalize this feeling until we care equally for all. Thus Yi Zhi softens the strong voluntarism of early

Mohism and attempts to ground it in a Mencian-style appeal to innate moral inclinations.

Although they shared many important assumptions and concerns with other early Chinese thinkers, the later Mohists were remarkably different in their approach. They did not seek for wisdom guided by the contemplation and synthetic grasp of historical paradigms, nor did they turn to intuitions about or reflections upon human nature. They trusted in careful observations and precise analyses with the aim of attaining a comprehensive and systematic understanding. The later Mohists were highly successful for several centuries but then, for reasons that remain obscure, their movement died out rather suddenly around the beginning of the Han Dynasty (206 BC). Nevertheless, they live on in at least one sense, in the profound and pervasive effect they have had on the Chinese philosophical tradition.

See also: CHINESE CLASSICS; CHINESE PHILOSOPHY; CONFUCIAN PHILOSOPHY, CHINESE; DAOIST PHILOSOPHY; LAW AND RITUAL IN CHINESE PHILOSOPHY; LEGALIST PHILOSOPHY, CHINESE; LOGIC IN CHINA; MOZI

Reference and further reading

Graham, A.C. (1978) *Later Mohist Logic, Ethics and Science*, Hong Kong: The Chinese University Press, and London: School of Oriental and Asian Studies. (A remarkable reconstruction and analysis of the later Mohist sections of the *Mozi* which concern the systematic study of argumentation, ethics and science.)

* —— (1985) *Divisions in Early Mohism Reflected in the Core Chapters of Mo-tzu*, Singapore: National University of Singapore, Institute of East Asian Philosophies. (An intriguing though not altogether persuasive study which argues that the synoptic chapters can be rearranged to reveal three schools of later Mohist thought, each with a distinct political agenda and philosophical position.)

* —— (1989) *Disputers of the Tao: Philosophical Argument in Ancient China*, La Salle, IL: Open Court Press. (Contains an insightful study of the Mohist movement within the context of early Chinese thought.)

* Lowe, S. (1992) *Mo Tzu's Religious Blueprint for a Chinese Utopia*, Lewiston, NY: Mellen Press. (A general study of early Mohist thought. Offers brief though incisive criticisms of most of the contemporary scholarship available in English.)

* Mozi (c.470–c.391 BC) *Mozi*, trans. Mei Yi-pao, *The Ethical and Political Works of Mo Tzu*, London: Arthur Probsthain, 1929; trans. B. Watson, *Mo*

Tzu: Basic Writings, New York: Columbia University Press, 1963. (Mei is the most complete translation of Mozi's works available in English. Watson is the most readable, selective English translation of the *Mozi*; it contains all of the synoptic chapters plus the two 'Against Confucians' chapters.)

Needham, J. (ed.) (1956) *Science and Civilisation in China*, vol. 2, repr. Taipei: Caves Books Ltd, 1985: 165–203. (A study of Mohist thought from the perspective of its contributions to science and logic.)

* Nivison, D.S. (1980) 'Two Roots or One?', *Proceedings and Addresses of the American Philosophical Association* 53 (6): 739–61. (A philosophically sophisticated discussion of the ethical thought and theory of moral action of the later Mohist, Yi Zhi.)

Schwartz, B.I. (1985) *The World of Thought in Ancient China*, Cambridge, MA: The Belknap Press, 1985. (An incisive account of the Mohists from a socio-logical-historical perspective.)

PHILIP J. IVANHOE

MOKSHA *see* KARMA AND REBIRTH, INDIAN CONCEPTIONS OF

MOLECULAR BIOLOGY

Molecular biology is the study of the structure, function and kinetics of biologically important molecules. Historically, molecular biology has often been identified with molecular genetics. Similarly, the chief philosophical concern with molecular biology has been the possibility of the reduction of classical genetics to molecular genetics. The nature and boundaries of molecular biology, however, are themselves disputed. To some, molecular biology seems to be a morass of molecular details without any overarching theory. To others molecular biology is an integrated interlevel theory. How philosophical issues, such as reduction, are addressed can depend importantly on how molecular biology is initially characterized.

1 **Molecularizing biology**
2 **Interlevel theories**
3 **Practices**

1 Molecularizing biology

Although molecular biology can be broadly defined as the study of the structure, function and kinetics of biologically important molecules, the origins of molecular biology are usually traced back to two specific research traditions: the informational school and the structural school. This historical approach has been strongly disputed. Nevertheless, it provides a starting place for historical analysis.

The informational school is identified with the study of bacterial viruses (bacteriophage or phage) begun in the late 1930s by Max Delbruck, Salvador Luria and Alfred Hershey. The phage group, as they would come to be known, took as its goal the elucidation of the physical basis of heredity through careful experimental study of virus self-replication within bacterial hosts. The problem of replication was itself a means of investigating how molecules could store and transmit genetic information. Chromosomes were the accepted material basis of heredity and were known to be mixtures of nucleic acids and proteins. Proteins, by virtue of their known linear arrangement of specific units, were thought to be better candidates for information storage and transfer than were nucleic acids. This emphasis on proteins was overthrown by Alfred Hershey and Martha Chase's experiments published in 1952 demonstrating that deoxyribonucleic acid (DNA) alone was injected into host bacteria. With the use of their Waring blender, Hershey and Chase had ingeniously shown that DNA, not protein, was responsible for virus replication.

At roughly the same time that the informational school was starting out in the 1930s, the structural school began extending traditions in structural chemistry to the study of biological molecules. In the USA, Linus Pauling used his expertise as a structural chemist to explain the helical structure of polypeptides essential to important biological proteins such as hemoglobin and myoglobin. In England, W.T. Astbury and J.D. Bernal began using X-ray crystallography to study the internal structure of proteins. This programme was expanded as the Cavendish Laboratory at Cambridge and King's College in London began X-ray diffraction studies of biological molecules.

These two schools of thought came together in the 1950s with the collaboration of James Watson and Francis Crick. Watson's knowledge of phage genetics and Crick's knowledge of X-ray crystallography both contributed to their now famous discovery of the double helical structure of DNA in 1953. The two-stranded model of DNA with its complementary base pairs explained the structural features of the DNA molecule and suggested how DNA could both store and transfer information.

The neat division of the origins of molecular biology into these two schools has been disputed on historical as well as historiographical grounds. The structural and informational schools were introduced as historical categories in the 1960s as biologists struggled to define molecular biology. Gunther Stent, a member of the phage group, strongly identified the phage group with the origins of molecular biology. John Kendrew, who won the Nobel Prize in 1962 for determining the structure of myoglobin, had a completely different experience of the emergence of molecular biology. Kendrew introduced the idea that there were two schools. Gunter Stent agreed and extended Kendrew's analysis in his reply. At the time Kendrew and Stent were writing, the emphasis in molecular biology was on integration of structure and function in biological molecules à la Watson and Crick. In effect Kendrew and Stent projected the reality of 1960s molecular biology into the past and in doing so created a history that legitimated present practice (Abir-Am 1985).

The structural and informational schools do not encompass the origins or the present state of molecular biology. It is not even clear to what extent the loose association of individuals doing structural work on biological molecules can be considered a school. The origins of molecular biology as well as its current practice represent a much more diverse array of traditions.

Molecular biology, as it was first defined by the National Science Foundation in 1954, covered a wide variety of biological phenomena, such as the:

> identification and structure of particulate matter such as mitochondria, chloroplasts, chromosomes, viruses, enzyme structure and kinetics – chemistry of coenzymes, electrochemical phenomena, membranes and fibers, solid and liquid state phenomena, reactions of proteins – long range forces, mathematical approaches to biological problems
> (quoted in Zallen 1993: 81).

Clearly, molecular biology could be seen as drawing on long-standing traditions in biochemistry, cell biology and bioenergetics, as well as those in phage research and structural chemistry. The history of molecular biology may be dominated by the history of molecular genetics, but the practice of molecular biology is and has been much more diverse.

2 Interlevel theories

As philosophers tried to come to grips with molecular biology and particularly the question of the reduction of classical genetics to molecular genetics, they were faced with the problem of how to characterize the structure of molecular biology (see GENETICS §4). While some thought of molecular biology as a scientific theory, characterized as a set of general laws or a set of axioms, others began to conceive of molecular biology in terms of interlevel theories and practices. These different approaches to theory structure can have important consequences for other philosophical issues, such as reduction.

Kenneth Schaffner has argued that most biomedical theories, including molecular biological theories, should be thought of as a series of overlapping interlevel temporal models (Schaffner 1993a, 1993b). This proposed analysis treats theories as families of models, as polytypic aggregates with some specified core characteristics. The entities represented by these models are usually undergoing some process and so are temporal. The theory is an interlevel theory because the entities represented by the theory can be grouped according to level of aggregation. Entities at one level of aggregation may share parts with entities at lower levels, but the defining properties of the entity at the higher level require organizing principles not found at the lower level.

It is often assumed that the successful reduction of a higher level theory to a lower level theory will result in the replacement of the higher level theory by the lower level theory. This strict reduction–replacement approach requires that the lower level theory use only lower level terms and entities. Schaffner's interlevel theories require that this strict model of reduction–replacement be relaxed to allow partial or patchy reductions as a result of more complex connections between parts of different interlevel theories. With the complex interlevel processes considered in molecular biological theories, one should not expect complete unilevel reduction of a higher level theory to a lower level biochemical theory, which itself is often an interlevel theory. Molecular biological explanations, according to this view, are facilitated by partial reductions and causal generalizations regarding the temporal sequence of events represented by the relevant model (Schaffner 1993b).

3 Practices

Schaffner's appreciation of the complexity of molecular biology is shared by Sylvia Culp and Philip Kitcher's analysis of molecular biology in terms of practices. A practice consists of a language used by the scientific community of interest, the set of statements that community accepts, the set of questions they take to be important, the patterns of reasoning they use to answer those questions, the methodological directives or standards they use to evaluate solutions and experiments, and a set of experimental techniques (Culp and Kitcher 1989). Using this account of practices, Culp and Kitcher argue that the contemporary practice of molecular biology can be understood in terms of a hierarchy of questions concerning why some biologically important process occurs, and how accepted statements and experimental techniques contribute to the solution of that problem. The interlevel complexity described by Schaffner is captured in Culp and Kitcher's practices by the hierarchy of questions. In the case of cell biology, for instance, Culp and Kitcher start out with the fundamental question of 'how do organisms move?'. This question is then followed by the supposition that 'motion requires contraction and extension of muscles' and the related question of 'how do muscles contract?'. This question is then followed by the supposition that 'muscle cells contain actin and myosin' and the related question of 'how do actin and myosin contribute to the contraction of a cell?' (Culp and Kitcher 1989). This nested set of questions leads to a nested set of explanations. Cellular theories of motion do not reduce to molecular biology within this hierarchy; instead the explanations of the action of myosin and actin extend the cellular explanatory scheme. An explanatory scheme is a schematic argument with specific filling instructions.

What makes explanatory extension different from strict reduction–replacement is that it allows different parts of an explanatory scheme to be extended in different directions by different theories. Molecular biology does not provide the only route for explanatory extension and it is not the case that all explanatory extensions will ultimately end with molecular biology (Kitcher 1984). Schaffner's complex reduction–replacement model with its partially overlapping interlevel theories also allows theories and explanations to be elaborated in a number of ways, and agrees with much of Kitcher's explanatory extension approach, although Schaffner and Kitcher and Culp continue to disagree on how to characterize theories in molecular biology (Schaffner 1993a).

One further aspect of Culp and Kitcher's characterization of molecular biology deserves comment: namely, their emphasis on experiment. One of the most striking features of molecular biology is the prominence of experimental techniques (see EXPERIMENT). A vital aspect of the structure of molecular biology is the presence and exportation of sets of techniques to address a vast array of different biological problems. While philosophers of science have been traditionally concerned with theories, the ongoing study of sciences like molecular biology is fuelling the growing concern with experimentation, so

much so that it now seems difficult to characterize molecular biology without discussing the central role of experimental techniques, such as X-ray diffraction, electrophoresis, or polymerase chain reactions (Zallen 1993).

See also: REDUCTION, PROBLEMS OF; THEORIES, SCIENTIFIC

References and further reading

* Abir-Am, P. (1985) 'Themes, Genres, and Orders of Legitimation in the Consolidation of New Scientific Disciplines: Deconstructing the Historiography of Molecular Biology', *History of Science* 23: 73–117. (Historiographical analysis of four major traditions in the history of molecular biology, including the history of the informational and structural schools.)

Cairns, J., Stent, G. and Watson, J. (eds) (1992) *Phage and the Origins of Molecular Biology*, Cold Spring Harbor, NY: Cold Spring Harbor Laboratory Press. (Volume of papers in honour of Max Delbruck. The expanded edition includes Kendrew and Stent's papers contesting the informational and structural schools.)

* Culp, S. and Kitcher, P. (1989) 'Theory Structure and Theory Change in Contemporary Molecular Biology', *British Journal of the Philosophy of Science* 40: 459–83. (An analysis of structure and change in molecular biology based on a case study of the discovery on enzymatic RNA.)

Judson, H.F. (1979) *The Eighth Day of Creation: Makers of the Revolution in Biology*, New York: Simon & Schuster. (A detailed history of molecular biology notable for its attention to the individual contributions and accomplishments of a diverse array of scientists.)

* Kitcher, P. (1984) '1953 and All That: A Tale of Two Sciences', *Philosophical Review* 93: 335–73. (An antireductionist argument based on intertheoretic relationships and the concept of explanatory extension.)

Olby, R. (1974) *The Path to the Double Helix*, Seattle, WA: University of Washington Press. (A detailed reconstruction of the historical precursors to Watson and Crick's discovery of the structure of DNA. It further develops the idea of the structural and informational schools.)

* Schaffner, K. (1993a) *Discovery and Explanation in Biology and Medicine*, Chicago, IL: University of Chicago Press. (A broad survey and analysis of a number of important issues such as reduction, theory testing and explanation.)

* —— (1993b) 'Theory Structure, Reduction, and

Disciplinary Integration in Biology', *Biology and Philosophy* 8: 319–47. (An analysis of theory structure in terms of integrated interlevel theories that allow for partial reduction and integration.)

* Zallen, D. (1993) 'Redrawing the Boundaries of Molecular Biology: The Case of Photosynthesis', *Journal of the History of Biology* 26: 65–87. (A convincing argument for the reconception of molecular biology as a more diverse and complex field based on a case study of the history of bioenergetic research on the process of photosynthesis.)

MICHAEL R. DIETRICH

MOLINA, LUIS DE (1535–1600)

A leading figure in sixteenth-century Iberian scholasticism, Molina was one of the most controversial thinkers in the history of Catholic thought. In keeping with the strongly libertarian account of human free choice that marked the early Jesuit theologians, Molina held that God's causal influence on free human acts does not by its intrinsic nature uniquely determine what those acts will be or whether they will be good or evil. Because of this, Molina asserted against his Dominican rivals that God's comprehensive providential plan for the created world and infallible foreknowledge of future contingents do not derive just from the combination of his antecedent 'natural' knowledge of metaphysically necessary truths and his 'free' knowledge of the causal influence – both natural (general concurrence) and supernatural (grace) – by which he wills to cooperate with free human acts. Rather, in addition to God's natural knowledge, Molina posited a distinct kind of antecedent divine knowledge, dubbed 'middle knowledge', by which God knows pre-volitionally, that is, prior to any free decree of his own will regarding contingent beings, how any possible rational creature would in fact freely choose to act in any possible circumstances in which it had the power to act freely. And on this basis Molina proceeded to forge his controversial reconciliation of free choice with the Catholic doctrines of grace, divine foreknowledge, providence and predestination.

In addition to his work in dogmatic theology, Molina was also an accomplished moral and political philosopher who wrote extensive and empirically well-informed tracts on political authority, slavery, war and economics.

1   Life and writings
2   Grace and freedom
3   Providence and middle knowledge
4   Political philosophy

1   Life and writings

Luis de Molina was a leading figure in the remarkable sixteenth-century revival of scholasticism on the Iberian peninsula that also produced the likes of Pedro da FONSECA, Domingo de SOTO, Domingo BÁÑEZ and Francisco SUÁREZ. After entering the Jesuit noviciate in 1553, Molina studied philosophy and theology for ten years at Coimbra and Évora in Portugal, and then taught at these same colleges until retiring in 1583 to devote himself to writing. He spent the next sixteen years in Évora, Lisbon and Cuenca, before being summoned just before his death to teach moral theology in Madrid.

The most famous and controversial of Molina's three published works was the *Liberi arbitrii cum gratiae donis, divina praescientia, providentia, praedestinatione et reprobatione concordia* (A Reconciliation of Free Choice with the Gifts of Grace, Divine Foreknowledge, Providence, Predestination and Reprobation) (first published in 1588). Popularly known simply as the *Concordia*, this work was in large part extracted from the *Commentaria in primam divi Thomae partem* (Commentaries on the First Part of Aquinas' *Summa theologiae*), subsequently published at Cuenca in 1592. Molina also wrote a five-volume work on political philosophy, *De Justitia et Jure* (On Justice and Law), the first complete edition of which appeared only posthumously. Although there are also modern editions of a few unpublished pieces, most of Molina's shorter tracts and commentaries survive only in manuscript.

The publication of the first edition of the *Concordia* ignited a fierce controversy about grace and human freedom that had already been smouldering for two decades between the youthful Society of Jesus (founded in 1540) and its theological opponents. At Louvain, the Jesuit Leonard Lessius had been assailed by the followers of Michael Baius for harbouring views on grace and freedom allegedly contrary to those of St Augustine. In Spain and Portugal, the Jesuits were accused of doctrinal novelty by theologians of the more established religious orders, especially the Dominicans, led by the redoubtable Báñez.

When the dispute began to jeopardize civil as well as ecclesiastical harmony, political and religious leaders in Iberia implored the Vatican to intervene. In 1597 Pope Clement VIII established the *Congregatio de Auxiliis* (Commission on Grace) in Rome, thus initiating a ten-year period of intense investigation – including eighty-five hearings and forty-seven debates – that rendered the *Concordia* one of the most carefully scrutinized books in Western intellectual history. At first, things did not go well for the Jesuits; Molina died in Madrid amid rumours that he was being burned in effigy in Rome. However, due to the efforts of Cardinals Robert Bellarmine and Jacques du Perron, Molina's views emerged unscathed in the end. In 1607 Pope Paul V issued a decree allowing both parties to defend their own positions but enjoining them not to call one another's views heretical.

2 Grace and freedom

Both sides of the dispute over grace and freedom agree that in addition to creating and conserving contingent beings, God acts as an immediate efficient cause of all the effects produced by created or secondary causes, including acts of free choice (see GRACE; FREE WILL).

First, God acts as an immediate 'general' or 'universal' cause of all the natural effects produced through the powers rooted in the essences of natural substances. This immediate causal contribution is called God's general concurrence (*concursus generalis*) because even though in any given case the effect proceeds as a whole from both God and the relevant secondary causes, the fact that the effect is of one species rather than another is primarily traceable not to God's concurrence but to the natures and causal contributions of the created agents, which for this reason are called 'particular causes'. So, for instance, when a gas flame makes a pot of water boil, the fact that the effect is the boiling of water rather than, say, the blossoming of a flower is traceable primarily not to God's causal contribution, but rather to the specific natures and causal contributions of the secondary causes (gas, water, and so on). Likewise, any defectiveness in the effect is traced back causally to a defect or impediment within the order of secondary causes rather than to God's causal contribution, which is always, within its own order, causally sufficient (in the sense of 'enough') for its intended effect, even when that effect is not produced. When the intended effect is produced, God's concurrence is said to be 'efficacious' with respect to it; when it is not produced, God's concurrence is said to be 'merely sufficient' with respect to it. If a defective effect is instead produced, its defectiveness is something that God merely permits rather than intends.

This account applies straightforwardly to morally good and evil acts emanating from the power of free choice that rational creatures are endowed with by nature. No such act can occur without God's general concurrence, and in causally contributing to it God intends that the act be morally upright rather than sinful. None the less, because of defects in the free agents with whom God cooperates, his general concurrence is often merely sufficient – and thus inefficacious – with respect to the morally good act he intends. So even though God must concur causally in order for even a sinful act to be elicited, none the less, the act's defectiveness is traced back to the free created agent rather than to God, who permits the defect without intending it (see SIN). By contrast, when a morally good act is freely elicited, God's concurrence is efficacious with respect to it.

Second, God also cooperates with free human acts by means of the particular causal influence of supernatural grace, merited for the human race by the salvific death and resurrection of Jesus Christ. By this grace, God empowers and prompts human beings to elicit free acts of will that are supernaturally salvific, and he cooperates as a simultaneous cause in the very effecting of these acts. By eliciting such free acts of faith, hope, charity and the other infused virtues, human agents are able to attain and foster that intimate friendship with God which in its fullness constitutes their highest fulfilment as rational beings. Still, in so far as grace operates prior to the consent of human free choice, it can be freely resisted; and when it is resisted, it is said to be inefficacious, or merely sufficient, with respect to the salvific act God intends (see SALVATION §4).

All this is accepted by both Molina and his Báñezian opponents (see BÁÑEZ, D.). Their dispute has to do with the 'intrinsic' character of God's simultaneous causal cooperation with free human acts. Regarding the natural order, Báñezians insist that there is an intrinsic ontological difference between efficacious and merely sufficient concurrence, so that of itself efficacious concurrence necessarily attains its intended effect, whereas of itself merely sufficient concurrence necessarily fails to attain its intended effect. So God grants intrinsically efficacious concurrence when and only when the human agent freely elicits the morally good act that God intends; and God grants intrinsically merely sufficient concurrence when and only when the human agent freely fails to elicit the morally good act that God intends. An immediate consequence is that God infallibly foreknows whether or not a human agent will freely elicit a morally good act at a given time, simply by virtue of knowing whether or not he himself will grant intrinsically efficacious concurrence with respect to that act.

The Báñezians hold a parallel position concerning the grace by which God operates to elicit supernaturally salvific acts. God grants intrinsically efficacious grace when and only when the human agent elicits the supernaturally salvific act God intends; and God grants intrinsically merely sufficient grace when and only when the human agent resists and thus fails to elicit the supernaturally salvific act that God intends.

Molina argues that this doctrine is incompatible with human freedom and falls into the strict determinism advocated by the Lutherans and Calvinists. For even though the Báñezians, like Molina, insist that a free act of will cannot result by natural necessity from antecedently acting causes, they none the less assert that an act of will can be free even if God has predetermined to cooperate with it contemporaneously by a concurrence or grace that is intrinsically efficacious (or inefficacious). This Molina denies: 'That agent is called free who, with all the prerequisites for acting having been posited, is able to act and able not to act, or is able to do one thing in such a way that he is also able to do some contrary thing' (*Concordia*: 14). Numbered among these prerequisites is God's fixed intention to confer his general concurrence and grace. So if God has decided to confer only intrinsically efficacious (or intrinsically inefficacious) grace or concurrence in a given situation, the created agent's freedom is destroyed.

Molina's alternative thesis is that God's grace and general concurrence are intrinsically neither efficacious nor inefficacious. Rather, they are intrinsically 'neutral' and are rendered efficacious or inefficacious 'extrinsically' by the human agent's free consent or lack thereof. Báñezians retort that this position savours of Pelagianism and violates the Catholic doctrine that God is the primary source of morally good and supernaturally salvific acts (see PELAGIANISM).

3 Providence and middle knowledge

Molina's views about grace and freedom seem at first glance to jeopardize the Catholic tenets that God is perfectly provident and has infallible and comprehensive knowledge of future contingents.

According to the traditional doctrine of divine providence (see PROVIDENCE §1), God freely and knowingly plans, orders and provides for all the effects that constitute the created universe with its entire history, and he executes his chosen plan by playing an active causal role that ensures its exact realization (see PROVIDENCE). Since God is the perfect craftsman, not even trivial details escape his providential decrees. Whatever occurs is specifically decreed by God; more precisely, each effect produced in the created universe is either specifically and knowingly intended by him or, in concession to the defectiveness of creatures, specifically and knowingly

permitted by him. Divine providence thus has both a cognitive and a volitional aspect. By his pre-volitional knowledge God infallibly knows which effects would result, directly or indirectly, from any causal contribution he might choose to make to the created sphere. By his free will God chooses one from among the infinity of total sequences of created effects that are within his power to bring about and, concomitantly, wills to make a causal contribution that he knows with certainty will result in his chosen plan's being effected down to the last detail (see OMNIPOTENCE; OMNISCIENCE).

This much is accepted by both Molina and the Báñezians. They further agree that it is because he is perfectly provident that God has comprehensive foreknowledge of what will occur in the created world. That is, God's speculative post-volitional knowledge of the created world – his so-called 'free knowledge' or 'knowledge of vision' – derives wholly from his pre-volitional knowledge and his knowledge of what he himself has willed to do. Unlike human knowers, God need not be acted upon by outside causes in order for his cognitive potentialities to be fully actualized; he does not have to, as it were, look outside himself in order to find out what his creative act has wrought. Rather, he knows 'in himself' what will happen precisely because he knows just what causal role he has freely chosen to play within the created order and just what will result given this causal contribution. In short, no contingent truth grasped by the knowledge of vision can be true prior to God's specifically intending or permitting it to be true or to his specifically willing to make the appropriate causal contribution towards its truth.

Molina's problem can now be stated succinctly. As noted above, he affirms against the Báñezians that God's cooperating grace and general concurrence are intrinsically neither efficacious nor inefficacious. So if God has only his antecedent 'natural knowledge' of metaphysically necessary truths plus knowledge of his own total causal contribution to the created world, he cannot specifically provide for or know any actual or 'absolute' future contingents. His natural knowledge tells him only what each free secondary cause would be able to do, not what it would in fact do, in any possible situation in which it could act; and if his grace and general concurrence are intrinsically neutral, then his own causal contribution to the contingent effects of secondary causes cannot uniquely determine what those effects will be. How, then, can God be perfectly provident and have comprehensive knowledge of future contingents?

Molina replies that since there is genuine freedom and indeterminism in the created world, God can be perfectly provident in the way demanded by orthodoxy only if his pre-volitional knowledge includes comprehensive knowledge of which effects would in fact result from causal chains involving free or indeterministic created causes. That is, God must have infallible and comprehensive pre-volitional knowledge of 'conditional future contingents' or *futuribilia* – metaphysically contingent propositions specifying how any possible indeterministic created cause would in fact act in any set of circumstances it might find itself in. Since this knowledge is of metaphysically contingent truths, it is not part of God's natural knowledge; since it is pre-volitional, it is not part of God's free knowledge. It stands 'midway' between natural knowledge and free knowledge – hence its title, 'middle knowledge' (*scientia media*).

According to Molina, then, the basis for God's providence and his foreknowledge of absolute future contingents is threefold: (1) his pre-volitional natural knowledge of metaphysically necessary truths, (2) his pre-volitional middle knowledge of *futuribilia*, and (3) his post-volitional knowledge of the total causal contribution he himself wills to make to the created world. By (1) he knows which spatio-temporal arrangements of secondary causes are possible and which contingent effects might possibly emanate from any such arrangement. By (2) he knows which contingent effects would in fact emanate from any such arrangement. By (3) he knows which secondary causes he wills to create and precisely how he wills to cooperate with them via his intrinsically neutral cooperating grace and general concurrence. So given God's pre-volitional natural knowledge and middle knowledge, he is able to choose a comprehensive providential plan; and given further his post-volitional knowledge of what his own causal contribution to the created world will be, he has free knowledge of all absolute future contingents.

The Báñezians counter by denying that any metaphysically contingent propositions, including any *futuribilia*, can be true prior to God's freely making them true by his predetermining decree. This dissatisfaction with middle knowledge provides another reason for Báñezians to reject Molina's strongly libertarian account of freedom, which engendered the need for middle knowledge in the first place. (Interestingly, by way of contrast, the main opponents of middle knowledge in twentieth-century analytic philosophy of religion retain Molina's account of freedom and reject instead the traditional doctrines of divine providence and foreknowledge.)

4 Political philosophy

Molina holds a 'translation' account of political authority (see POLITICAL PHILOSOPHY, HISTORY OF). Unlike the ecclesiastical authority of the pope, which is bestowed immediately by God on the person designated by the ecclesiastical community, the governing authority of the political ruler is bestowed immediately by a community which has established itself as a commonwealth and in which political authority resides by natural law. Hence, unlike the ecclesiastical community, the political commonwealth not only designates its rulers but also legitimately limits the power it transfers to them and restricts their use of that power. Because of this, the individual members of the commonwealth can, under certain extreme circumstances, legitimately resist and defend themselves against tyrannical rulers.

Molina also addresses at length a wide variety of moral questions regarding war, slavery and economic matters such as taxation, free markets, monetary policy and price regulation. Given his historical circumstances, Molina's ruminations about slavery are especially interesting. Like his Aristotelian predecessors, he believes that slavery is morally justifiable under certain limited circumstances. For example, those lawfully condemned to death may legitimately have their death sentences commuted to perpetual servitude; enemy populations conquered in a just war may legitimately be enslaved in restitution for damages to the victors; and free and willing adults may legitimately sell themselves into slavery. None the less, Molina's many conversations in Lisbon with the captains of slave ships led him to conclude that the African slave trade as it was actually being carried out by the Portuguese was 'unjust and wicked' and that those who engaged in it, both sellers and buyers, were almost surely 'in a state of eternal damnation' (see SLAVERY).

See also: BÁÑEZ, D.; FREEDOM, DIVINE; GOD, CONCEPTS OF; GRACE; MOLINISM; OMNISCIENCE; PREDESTINATION; SUÁREZ, F. §1

List of works

Molina, L. de (1592) *Commentaria in primam divi Thomae partem* (Commentaries on the First Part of Aquinas' *Summa theologiae*), Cuenca. (Provided the basis for Molina's more famous work, the *Concordia*.)

—— (1588) *Liberi arbitrii cum gratiae donis, divina praescientia, providentia, praedestinatione et reprobatione concordia* (A Reconciliation of Free Choice with the Gifts of Grace, Divine Foreknowledge, Providence, Predestination and Reprobation), Lisbon, 1st edn; 2nd edn, Antwerp; ed. J. Rabeneck, Oña and Madrid: Collegium Maximum, 1953;

trans. A.J. Freddoso, *On Divine Foreknowledge: Part IV of the 'Concordia'*, Ithaca, NY: Cornell University Press, 1988. (Translation of and introduction to Molina's theory of middle knowledge, including references to twentieth-century discussions.)

—— (1614) *De Justitia et Jure* (On Justice and Law), Venice. (The first complete edition of this work appeared posthumously in 1614.)

—— (1935) *'Neue Molinaschriften'* (New Writings by Molina), ed. F. Stegmüller, *Beiträge zur Geschichte der Philosophie und Theologie des Mittelalters*, vol. 32, Münster: Aschendorff. (A collection of unpublished treatises and letters.)

References and further reading

Adams, R.M. (1977) 'Middle Knowledge and the Problem of Evil', *American Philosophical Quarterly* 14: 109–17. (Introduced the debate over middle knowledge into twentieth-century analytic philosophy of religion.)

Brodrick, J. (1928) *The Life and Work of Blessed Robert Francis Cardinal Bellarmine, S.J.*, vol. 2, New York: Kenedy. (Chapter 19 contains an extensive historical account of the sixteenth-century dispute over grace and freedom.)

Costello, F. (1974) *The Political Philosophy of Luis de Molina, S.J.*, Spokane, WA: Gonzaga. (Helpful and clear introduction to Molina's political thought.)

Flint, T. (1988) 'Two Accounts of Providence', in T. Morris (ed.) *Divine and Human Action*, Ithaca, NY: Cornell University Press, 147–81. (Clear exposition by a Molinist of some key differences between Molinists and Thomists.)

Garrigou-Lagrange, R. (1943) *The One God*, St Louis, MO: Herder. (Contains a trenchant neo-Thomist critique of Molinism.)

Hasker, W. (1989) *God, Time, and Knowledge*, Ithaca, NY: Cornell University Press. (Contains the best critique of middle knowledge in analytic philosophy of religion.)

Pegis, A. (1939) 'Molina and Human Liberty', in G. Smith (ed.) *Jesuit Thinkers of the Renaissance*, Milwaukee, WI: Marquette, 75–131. (Comparison of Molina with Aquinas.)

ALFRED J. FREDDOSO

MOLINISM

Molinism, named after Luis de Molina, is a theological system for reconciling human freedom with God's grace and providence. Presupposing a strongly libertarian account of freedom, Molinists assert against their rivals that the grace whereby God cooperates with supernaturally salvific acts is not intrinsically efficacious. To preserve divine providence and foreknowledge, they then posit 'middle knowledge', through which God knows, prior to his own free decrees, how any possible rational agent would freely act in any possible situation. Beyond this, they differ among themselves regarding the ground for middle knowledge and the doctrines of efficacious grace and predestination.

Molinism is an influential system within Catholic theology for reconciling human free choice with God's grace, providence, foreknowledge and predestination. Originating within the Society of Jesus (the Jesuits) in the late sixteenth and early seventeenth centuries, it encountered stiff opposition from Báñezian Thomists (see BÁÑEZ, D.) and from the self-styled Augustinian disciples of Michael Baius and Cornelius Jansen.

Molinism's three distinguishing marks are a strongly libertarian account of human freedom (see FREEDOM AND LIBERTY §1); the consequent conviction that the grace whereby God cooperates with supernaturally salvific free acts is not intrinsically efficacious (see GRACE); and the postulation of divine middle knowledge (*scientia media*), by which God knows, before any of his free decrees regarding creatures, how any possible rational being would freely act in any possible situation (see MOLINA, L. DE §§2–3; OMNISCIENCE).

Beyond this, Molinists disagree about three important issues. The first is the question of how God knows the 'conditional future contingents' or *futuribilia* that constitute the objects of middle knowledge. Molinists cannot accept the Báñezian claim that God knows *futuribilia* by virtue of his freely decreeing their truth, since according to Molinism *futuribilia* have their truth prior to any free divine decree. Nor can Molinists claim that God knows *futuribilia* simply by virtue of comprehending all possible creatures, if 'comprehending' a creature means just understanding all the metaphysical possibilities involving it. For such comprehension is insufficient for knowing how a possible creature would freely act – as opposed to how it could act – in any possible situation.

Molina himself claims that because God's cognitive power infinitely surpasses the natures of creatures, God is able to know those natures 'in a more eminent way than that in which they are knowable in themselves' (*Concordia*: 343). So God not only comprehends possible creatures but also 'supercomprehends' them, as later Molinists put it, and in this way knows *futuribilia* involving them. One

465

corollary, explicitly defended by Molina, is that God does not know *futuribilia* concerning his own free decrees, since his cognitive power does not infinitely surpass his own nature.

Other Molinists retort that no amount of insight into the natures of possible creatures can yield infallible knowledge of *futuribilia*, since such natures are exhausted by their metaphysical possibilities and do not include *futuribilia*. Instead, God has direct knowledge of *futuribilia*, unmediated by his knowledge of natures, and this is simply because the *futuribilia* are true and hence intelligible to an infinite intellect. From this viewpoint there is no reason why God should not know *futuribilia* concerning his own free decrees – a result Molina takes to be incompatible with God's freedom.

The second dispute concerns the reason for the efficaciousness of the grace whereby God cooperates with supernaturally salvific acts of free choice. Suppose that in circumstances C, influenced by grace G, Peter freely elicits salvific act A. All Molinists agree that God places Peter in C with G knowing full well that Peter will freely elicit A; and they also agree that G is not intrinsically efficacious and hence does not causally predetermine A. However, there is strong disagreement about whether or not it is Peter's free consent alone that 'extrinsically' renders G efficacious in C with respect to A.

One possibility is that God first resolves absolutely that Peter should freely elicit A in C and then, as it were, consults his middle knowledge to see just which particular graces would, if bestowed on Peter in C, obtain his free consent and thus issue in A. It follows that, given his antecedent resolution, God would have conferred some grace other than G if he had known by his middle knowledge that G would turn out to be 'merely sufficient' with respect to A, that is, that Peter would not freely consent to G in C. So G is rendered efficacious not only by Peter's free consent but also, and indeed more importantly, by God's antecedent predetermination to confer a 'congruous' grace that will guarantee Peter's acting well in C. This model, which brings Molinism more into line with Báñezianism, is known as Congruism and was worked out in detail by Robert Bellarmine and Francisco SUÁREZ (§1). In 1613 Congruism was mandated for all Jesuit theologians by the Father General Claude Aquiviva.

Another possible model, which seems to be Molina's own, is that God simply wills to put Peter into C with G, knowing that Peter will freely elicit A but not having absolutely resolved beforehand that Peter should freely elicit A. This model does not entail that if God had known that Peter would act badly in C with G, he would have conferred some grace other

than G in order to guarantee A. Accordingly, it is Peter's free consent alone that renders G efficacious.

An analogous dispute arises over predestination, where the question concerns not one or another of Peter's acts, but his eternal salvation. Some Molinists, including Bellarmine and Suárez, agree with the Báñezians that God antecedently elects certain people to eternal glory and only then consults his middle knowledge to discover which graces will guarantee their salvation. Thus, in Peter's case, God would have chosen different graces if those he actually chose had been foreknown to be merely sufficient and not efficacious for Peter's salvation. Other Molinists, including Molina himself, vigorously reject any such antecedent absolute election of Peter to salvation. They insist instead that God simply chooses to create a world in which he infallibly foresees Peter's good use of the supernatural graces afforded him, and only then does he accept Peter among the elect in light of his free consent to those graces.

See also: BÁÑEZ, D.; FREEDOM, DIVINE; MOLINA, L. DE; PREDESTINATION; PROVIDENCE; SUÁREZ, F. §1

References and further reading

Bellarmine, R. (1873) *Opera Omnia* (Complete Works), vol. 5, ed. J. Fèvre, Paris: Louis Vivès. (Contains the tract *De Gratia et Libero Arbitrio*, one of the main sources for Congruism.)

Garrigou-Lagrange, R. (1952) *Grace*, St Louis, MO: Herder. (Chapters 7 and 8 contain a Báñezian assessment of the Molinist and Congruist accounts of efficacious grace.)

* Molina, L. (1953) *Liberi arbitrii cum gratiae donis, divina praescientia, providentia, praedestinatione et reprobatione concordia* (A Reconciliation of Free Choice with the Gifts of Grace, Divine Foreknowledge, Providence, Predestination and Reprobation), ed. J. Rabeneck, Oña and Madrid: Collegium Maximum; trans. A.J. Freddoso, *On Divine Foreknowledge: Part IV of the 'Concordia'*, Ithaca, NY: Cornell University Press, 1988. (Translation of, and introduction to, Molina's theory of middle knowledge.)

Pohle, J. (1947) *Grace: Actual and Habitual*, ed. A. Preuss, St Louis, MO: Herder. (Gives a weaker characterization of Congruism than that laid out above in order to classify Molina himself as a Congruist.)

Suárez, F. (1963) *Opera Omnia* (Complete Works), vols 7–11, ed. C. Berton, Brussels: Culture et Civilisation, 1963. (Suárez's voluminous treatise

De Gratia, containing the most sophisticated explication and defence of Congruism.)

ALFRED J. FREDDOSO

MOLYNEUX PROBLEM

The origin of what is known as the Molyneux problem lies in the following question posed by William Molyneux to John Locke: if a man born blind, and able to distinguish by touch between a cube and a globe, were made to see, could he now tell by sight which was the cube and which the globe, before he touched them? The problem raises fundamental issues in epistemology and the philosophy of mind, and was widely discussed after Locke included it in the second edition of his Essay concerning Human Understanding.

1 **The origin of the problem**
2 **Philosophical responses**

1 The origin of the problem

William Molyneux (1656–98) was a leading Irish scientist whose wife became blind shortly after marriage. His consequent interest in vision gave rise to *Dioptrica Nova* (New optics) (1692), a treatise on optics which also touches on the psychology of vision. The main problems for seventeenth-century theories of vision arose from the apparent conflict between physical theories about light and the phenomenology of perception. For example, optics demonstrates the inversion of the retinal image, but we perceive the object the right way up. Moreover, the retinal image is flat, but we perceive distance and depth. In response to these problems, DESCARTES postulated an innate judgment by which the soul corrects the inverted retinal image, and he ascribed the perception of distance partly to 'natural geometry'. We unconsciously calculate the distance of objects from the angles of the incoming light rays and the distance between our eyes.

Molyneux's treatment of the perception of distance or depth falls into two parts. Perception of the distance of far-off objects, he agrees, involves an act of judgment: 'For Distance of itself, is not to be perceived, for 'tis a Line (or a Length) presented to the Eye with its End towards us, which must therefore be only a Point, and that is Invisible' (Molyneux 1692: 113). But perception of near-distance is assigned, somewhat vaguely, to unconscious natural capacities. Near objects are perceived 'by the turn of the eyes, or by the angle of the optic axes' explanations going

back, via Descartes and Kepler, to medieval theories of perception.

While writing *Dioptrica Nova* Molyneux read the French abstract, published in 1688, of Locke's *Essay concerning Human Understanding*, and sent the author the following problem:

A Man, being born blind, and having a Globe and a Cube, nigh of the same bigness, committed into his Hands, and being taught or Told, which is Called the Globe, and which the Cube, so as easily to distinguish them by his Touch or Feeling; Then both being taken from Him, and Laid on a Table, let us suppose his Sight Restored to Him; Whether he Could, by his sight, and before he touch them, know which is the Globe and which the Cube? Or Whether he could know by his sight, before he stretched out his Hand, whether he Could not Reach them, tho they were Removed 20 or 1000 feet from him.

(Letter to Locke, 7 July 1688)

Despite receiving no reply, Molyneux dedicated his book to the 'incomparable Mr. Locke' and sent him a copy. In the ensuing correspondence Molyneux again posed the problem. This time Locke judged it an 'ingenious problem', including it in the second edition of his *Essay* (1694).

2 Philosophical responses

Philosophers' answers to Molyneux's problem and their conception of its significance reflect their general epistemology. Both Locke's empiricism and his requirement that any idea is such as the subject perceives it to be rule out the possibility of the sort of innately guided, unconscious reasoning postulated by Descartes. The perception of distance is therefore an acquired ability and the answer to Molyneux's question is negative. This reply may seem inconsistent with Locke's doctrine that ideas of primary qualities, such as shape or motion, resemble their causes: visual and tactual ideas of such qualities have common causes, which implies that they resemble each other. However, Locke saw Molyneux's problem simply as showing that 'the Ideas we receive by sensation are often in grown People alter'd by the Judgement, without our taking notice of it' (1689: ch. II, §8). The ideas we receive by sight are allegedly only two-dimensional patterns of light and colour. In order to be able to recognize a three-dimensional shape or body in these patterns, we need to know how to correlate them with information provided by touch. The visual idea is like a word which induces in a hearer the associated idea, but is itself hardly noticed (see LOCKE, J. §§2, 4).

Leibniz (1765) accepted that the connection between the visual and the tactual sensations is not innate. However, if the blind person has been given the information that a cube and a globe lie in front of him, they can work out which is which from the geometric features the visual and the tactual ideas share. In the cube there are eight points distinguished from all the others, whereas in the globe there are none. This shows, Leibniz concludes, how important it is to distinguish sensory images from 'exact ideas constituted by definitions' (see LEIBNIZ, G.W. §8). Another of Locke's contemporaries, Edward Synge (1695), insisted on a somewhat similar distinction between image and sensation on the one hand, and idea and perception on the other. He argued that, although the images acquired by sight and touch are different, the ideas are identical. In recognizing a cube by sight and by touch only one conceptual ability is involved.

Berkeley took a contrary view, rejecting Locke's account of primary qualities and arguing that ideas of sight and touch are radically heterogeneous, connected only by contingent correlations known through sense experience. His reasons for endorsing the negative answer to the problem, and for his enthusiastic development of the analogy with language, are thus far more radical than Locke's (see BERKELEY, G. §4)

The Molyneux problem was widely discussed in the eighteenth and nineteenth centuries (indeed Ernst CASSIRER has claimed that it was the fundamental question for both continental and Anglo-saxon epistemology and psychology in the eighteenth century). Among the contributors were CONDILLAC and DIDEROT whose *Lettre sur les aveugles* (Letter on the blind) contains a fascinating description of the difference between the 'life-world' of the blind and that of the sighted. Various attempts have been made to answer the question empirically, the first being 'Cheselden's case', named after the surgeon who, in 1728, reported an operation performed on a boy with congenital cataract. Since it took some time for the boy to perceive and recognize objects by sight, Cheselden's case was supposed to confirm the negative reply. Yet even Leibniz had foreseen that the subject might be 'dazzled and confused by the strangeness'. In any case, since blindness is a symptom resulting from different diseases of the eyes and along the optical tract, it is difficult to assess what bearing empirical data have on the Molyneux problem.

On any interpretation, the Molyneux problem raises the issue of the relation between the perceptual representation of space attributable to the blind and that made available by sight. Berkeley's radical assertion of heterogeneity assigned primary spatial experience to touch, treating visual ideas as mere signs of impending or available tactual ideas. Conversely, it might be questioned whether the blind possess genuine spatial concepts, on the grounds that they only have successions of tactual experiences. Possession of spatial concepts, however, involves thought of distinct objects existing not in succession but simultaneously. Yet both these views ignore the fact that there is only one behavioural space for a subject to move around in. Simply to act, a subject – whether blind or sighted – must have experience of egocentric space involving an ability to locate what is perceived, however perceived, in relation to their body. If that is correct, the chief question remaining is how readily a blind subject, made to see, is able to generalize spatial concepts to visual experiences.

References and further reading

Ayers, M.R. (1991) *Locke*, London: Routledge, 2 vols; repr. as *Locke. Epistemology and Ontology*, 1993. (Locke's response to the Molyneux problem is discussed in the context of an extensive examination of Locke's notion of an idea.)

Berkeley, G. (1709) 'An Essay towards a New Theory of Vision', in *Philosophical Works*, intro. and notes M.R. Ayers, London, J.M. Dent & Sons Ltd, Everyman's Library, 1989: 3–59. (Berkeley's first work in which he expounds his theory of vision, which is the foundation for the idealist philosophy he developed in his later works. In this work he discusses and refers to Molyneux's *Dioptrica Nova*.)

Brandt Bolton, M. (1994) 'The Real Molyneux Question and the Basis of Locke's Answer', in G.A.J. Rogers (ed.) *Locke's Philosophy: Content and Context*, Oxford: Oxford University Press, 75–99. (Establishes the importance of situating the Molyneux problem within the context of seventeenth-century theories of vision.)

Degenaar, M. (1996) *The Problem of Molyneux*, Dordrecht: Reidel. (A discussion of eighteenth- and nineteenth-century – and more recent – responses to the Molyneux problem, with emphasis on empirical attempts to settle the question; extensive bibliography.)

* Diderot, D. (1749) *Lettre sur les aveugles*; trans. as *The Letter on the Blind for the Benefit of Those Who See*, Albuquerque, NM: American Classical Collection Press, 1983. (A fascinating work arguing that being blind affects not only a person's sight but also their metaphysical, religious and moral convictions.)

Evans, G. (1985) 'Molyneux's Question', in *Collected Papers*, Oxford: Oxford University Press, 364–99. (Argues convincingly that the heart of the Molyneux problem is whether the spatial concepts possessed by the blind are identical to those possessed by the sighted.)

* Leibniz, G. W. (1765) *New Essays on Human Understanding*, trans. and ed. P. Remnant and J. Bennett, Cambridge: Cambridge University Press, 1981. (A commentary on Locke's *Essay*, unpublished in Leibniz's lifetime, which contains an excellent treatment of the Molyneux problem on pages 136–8).

* Locke, J. (1688) 'Essai philosophique concernant l'Entendement où l'on montre quelle est l'étendue des connaissances certaines, et la manière dont nous y parvenons', *Bibliothèque Universelle et Historique*, January–March: 49–142, Amsterdam, ed. J. Le Clerc. (Locke's first major publication in the journal of his Swiss friend Jean Le Clerc, whom he met in The Netherlands. It is a substantial abridgement of his as yet unpublished *Essay concerning Human Understanding* and often referred to with the term Abrégé, because it was later republished separately and translated into English in 1692 as an extract of a book entitled *A Philosophical Essay upon Human Understanding*.)

* —— (1689) *Essay concerning Human Understanding*, ed. P.H. Nidditch, Oxford: Clarendon Press, 1985. (Locke's magnum opus, breathtaking in its scope and depth, still worth consulting on every topic it discusses. The second edition appeared in 1694.)

Molyneux, W. (1688) Letter to Locke of 7 July 1688, in E.S. de Beer (ed.) *The Correspondence of John Locke*, Oxford: Clarendon Press, 1978, vol. 3, 482, letter no. 1064.

* —— (1692) *Dioptrica Nova*, London: Benjamin Tooke. (A treatise in the tradition of similar works by Kepler and Descartes, which is mainly devoted to the physical aspects of optics, containing also several remarks on the psychology of vision.)

* Synge, E. (1695) *The Correspondence of John Locke*, vol. 5, ed. E.S. de Beer, Oxford: Oxford University Press, 1974. (Letter 1984 (pages 494–6) from Molyneux to Locke, quotes in full the interesting letter by Synge – later Archbishop of Tuam – which anticipates several later objections to Locke's reply.)

MENNO LIEVERS

MOMENTARINESS, BUDDHIST DOCTRINE OF

*The object of the Buddhist doctrine of momentariness is not the nature of time, but existence within time. Rather than atomizing time into moments, it atomizes phenomena temporally by dissecting them into a succession of discrete momentary entities. Its fundamental proposition is that everything passes out of existence as soon as it has originated and in this sense is momentary. As an entity vanishes, it gives rise to a new entity of almost the same nature which originates immediately afterwards. Thus, there is an uninterrupted flow of causally connected momentary entities of nearly the same nature, the so-called continuum (*santāna*). These entities succeed each other so fast that the process cannot be discerned by ordinary perception. Because earlier and later entities within one continuum are almost exactly alike, we come to conceive of something as a temporally extended entity even though the fact that it is in truth nothing but a series of causally connected momentary entities. According to this doctrine, the world (including the sentient beings inhabiting it) is at every moment distinct from the world in the previous or next moment. It is, however, linked to the past and future by the law of causality in so far as a phenomenon usually engenders a phenomenon of its kind when it perishes, so that the world originating in the next moment reflects the world in the preceding moment.*

At the root of Buddhism lies the (never questioned) conviction that everything that has originated is bound to perish and is therefore, with the exception of factors conducive to enlightenment, ultimately a source of frustration. There is no surviving textual material that documents how this law of impermanence came to be radicalized in terms of momentariness. It seems that by the fourth century the doctrine of momentariness had already assumed its final form. Characteristically, the debate became more and more dominated by epistemological questions, while the metaphysical aspect faded into the background.

1 Exposition
2 Relevance
3 Development
4 Doctrinal background
5 Proofs

1 Exposition

The doctrine of momentariness entails that entities are too shortlived to undergo change. Thus, if an entity has always engendered a new entity of exactly the same kind and with exactly the same properties, the worlds arising at every moment anew would be identical, so that there could be no evolution. This, however, is not the case because the process of reproduction of a given entity may be manipulated by outside factors in such a way that the newly created entity differs qualitatively from the preceding entity. If exposed to fire, for instance, a wood entity does not give rise to an identical wood entity when it perishes, but to a wood entity which bears the mark of impairment by fire and so is slightly charred. (According to later parlance, the wood as the main cause forms, together with the fire as a subsidiary cause, a causal complex which produces the slightly charred wood entity.) Thus, change is not constituted by the transmutation of persisting entities, but by the qualitative difference between earlier and later entities within a series.

Not only the transformation of series but also their cessation (that is, what is ordinarily conceived of as the utter annihilation of temporally extended objects), is caused by an external agent, which affects the process of reproduction of the object exposed to it in such a way that this process comes to a complete standstill. Hence, in the case of murder, the victim dies because the murderer affects the final moment of the breath of life (*prāṇa*), that is, the vital principle accounting for the body's animation, in such a way that it fails to reproduce itself. Since the final moment (like all preceding ones) passes out of existence automatically, murder is, microscopically speaking, not destruction but the interception of the process of reproduction. In this way the teaching that all entities pass out of existence spontaneously without depending for this upon any external cause is reconciled with the observation on a macroscopic level that wood is burnt by fire, or that one dies when knifed by a murderer.

Independently of the doctrine of momentariness, the Buddhists, like many other Indian schools, also dissected everything spatially into atoms (see MATTER, INDIAN CONCEPTIONS OF). Thus, in the final analysis, the world is made up of momentary atoms, which by their spatial arrangement and by their concatenation with earlier and later atoms of the same kind, give rise to the illusion of persisting compact things. This analysis of existence can be illustrated by referring, anachronistically, to cinematography. Just as the rapid projection of distinct pictures evokes the illusion of continuous action on the screen, so the fast succession of distinct momentary entities gives rise to the erroneous impression that the world around us (and we ourselves) exist continuously without undergoing destruction and being recreated every moment. Similarly, as the change of events on the screen is caused by the qualitative difference between earlier and later pictures on the film reel, so the change in the world is brought about by the qualitative difference between earlier and later entities. Moreover, as people vanish from the screen because they are not featured in the subsequent frame, so things cease to exist because they stop reproducing themselves. Finally, just as each projected picture only consists of differently shaded points, which by their specific arrangement give rise to the perception of composite shapes, so the world around us consists of nothing but distinct atoms which are arranged in such a way that they convey the impression of compact bodies.

2 Relevance

The Buddhist doctrine of momentariness does not challenge our experiences of macroscopic events as such, but only our interpretation of these events on a microscopic level. The claim that macroscopic objects are constituted by a succession of distinct momentary units only affects the intuitive conception of these objects as self-identical units (think of the notion of an uninterrupted line in contrast to one made up of distinct but contiguous points), but it does not affect the question of how these macroscopic objects behave, whatever their analysis on a microscopic level.

The doctrine of momentariness was not viewed as a purely metaphysical theory without practical relevance. On the contrary, the contemplation of the constant rise and fall of phenomena was employed to induce a particularly poignant experience of their impermanence, thus revealing the unsatisfactory nature of all existence. Moreover, in a Mahāyāna context this contemplation served as a tool for undermining (but not negating) the substantial existence of phenomena. However, since only advanced yogins seem to have been able to perceive momentariness directly, the soteriological significance of this doctrine remains very limited. This explains why it only played a marginal role in the wider context of Buddhist spirituality.

3 Development

The doctrine of momentariness is postcanonic and may have originated in the first century. It is for the first time presupposed in the *Vibhāṣa* (both in the Chinese translation by Xuanzang (Hsüan-tsang) and by Buddhavarman) of the Sarvāstivādins, one of the major Hīnayāna schools of Buddhism. In this scholastic compendium, the better part of which was probably compiled in the second century, the momentariness of all phenomena is not treated as a topic in its own right, but is frequently taken for granted when dealing with other issues.

Doxographical reports and other evidence confirm the impression that it was in the milieu of the Sarvāstivādins that all phenomena, more precisely all conditioned entities (*saṃskṛta, saṃskāra*), came to be looked upon as momentary. (The Sarvāstivādins treated space and two forms of suppression of certain factors as unconditioned entities (*asaṃskṛta*) which have never been created and, hence, are not subject to the law of impermanence, hence the specification at this point that momentariness only applies to conditioned entities and not to all phenomena.) Although the Sarvāstivādins reduced the duration of all phenomena to a moment, they still conceived of their existence much in the same way as they had done before the introduction of the doctrine, insisting that even within one moment they first originate, then persist and decay and finally perish. This treatment violated the common conception of the moment (*kṣaṇa*) as the shortest conceivable unit of time and consequently was rejected by the Dārṣṭāntikas and Sautrāntikas, who are closely related to the Sarvāstivādins and may have evolved from them. These two schools argued that contradictory events cannot take place within one moment. From this they concluded that all things perish as soon as they have originated. Since destruction was conceived of as the spontaneous cessation of existence and not as a time-consuming process, the existence of entities was reduced to mere acts of origination, flashes into existence.

With this radicalization of the instantaneous nature of existence, the doctrine of momentariness assumed its final form. Such a form was adopted by the Yogācāras, one of the two main Indian schools of Mahāyāna Buddhism, and came to be known by other Buddhists and non-Buddhists. The Yogācāras with a Mahāyāna orientation, however, only accepted the doctrine of momentariness as valid on the level of relative truth. In so far as the doctrine affirms the existence of discrete entities (although they are reduced to mere point instants), it is characteristic of the realism of Hīnayāna Buddhism and at odds with their Mahāyāna stance that all phenomenal entities are ultimately, on the level of highest truth, unreal (see BUDDHISM, YOGĀCĀRA SCHOOL OF).

4 Doctrinal background

The surviving sources do not record how the doctrine of momentariness originated. Hence the reconstruction of this process has to be hypothetical. The anti-substantialist tendency characteristic of Buddhism negates that entities have a substantial core beyond the sum of their properties and thus equates the properties with the entities themselves. Hence, phenomena in Buddhism are called *dharmas*, a term with a wide range of meanings which is used in this context because it may stand for 'property' and 'quality'. Since change was viewed as the replacement of one quality for another, the identification of property and entity led to the position that any qualitative change

implies numeric difference, that is, the substitution of one entity for another. When Buddhists applied this understanding of change to their analysis of ageing they were bold enough to conclude that the ageing body must at every moment vanish to be replaced by a new, slightly modified body. As all things were conceived of as constantly changing, momentariness had to be attributed in this way not only to bodily matter but also to all other things. The conviction that everything is always changing (in as much as it is always subject to ageing) had resulted from the contemplation of the law of impermanence.

The discovery of the doctrine of momentariness in this way was possible because at a much earlier stage the momentariness of all mental entities had already been established in an apparently analogous way. This way was the denial of a permanent Self, a cardinal tenet of scholastic Buddhism which led to the conception of the mind as a flow of mental events conceived of as entities in their own right (see BUDDHIST CONCEPT OF EMPTINESS). Their momentariness was probably deduced from the speed with which mental events normally follow each other. The establishment of the doctrine of momentariness may have benefited from the testimony of yogins who are reported to have access to the direct experience of the incessant rise and fall of phenomena at every moment.

5 Proofs

Such a doctrine, fundamentally at odds with the appearance of the world, met great opposition. Initially, it was rejected by large sections of the Buddhist community, notably the Vātsīputrīyas and related schools. Later, when it had gained ground among Buddhists, it was fervently opposed by the Brahmanical schools as it contradicted their postulation of eternal entities of one sort or another (souls, atoms, primary matter, a supreme deity). This rejection made it necessary to defend the doctrine by argumentation.

The oldest transmitted proofs of momentariness are recorded in early Yogācāra sources. They are still primarily directed against other Buddhists and derive the momentariness of all phenomena in three different ways. First, it is presupposed that the mind is momentary – this stance is also shared by Buddhist opponents who do not accept the momentariness of matter – and on this basis it is concluded that matter, too, has to be momentary. This conclusion is based on the demonstration that mind and matter can only depend upon each other and interact as they do because they have the same duration. Second, by referring to ageing and similar processes it is proved that everything changes all the time and thus undergoes origination and destruction at every moment. This argument rests on the presupposition that any form of transformation implies the substitution of one entity for another. This proof from change reflects the presumable doctrinal background underlying the formation of the doctrine of momentariness. Third, it is argued that everything has to perish as soon as it has originated because, otherwise it would persist eternally. This would be at odds with the law of impermanence. The argument rests on the presupposition that destruction cannot be brought about from without and that it is impossible for an entity to perish on its own account after it has persisted as this would require a change of nature. The latter presupposition reflects the view that self-identical entities cannot change.

VASUBANDHU (fourth–fifth century) marks the gradual transition between the earlier phase when the debate was still confined to Buddhism and the later phase when it was carried out between Buddhists and non-Buddhists. Vasubandhu only adopted the third type of proof, deducing momentariness from the spontaneity of destruction. He developed this idea further with the argument that destruction cannot be caused since, as mere nonexistence, it does not qualify as an effect. Up to the time of DHARMAKĪRTI (c. 600–60) and to a lesser extent thereafter, this proof of momentariness, the so-called inference from perishability (vināśitvānumāna), dominated the controversy.

With Dharmakīrti, the doctrine entered a new phase. He developed a new type of proof, the so-called inference from existence (sattvānumāna), that derives the momentariness of all entities (without presupposing their impermanence) directly from the fact that they exist. On the basis of the premise that existence entails causal efficiency, Dharmakīrti demonstrates that all existing things have to be momentary as it is impossible for nonmomentary entities to function as efficient causes. This impossibility derives from the idea that, if the entities already produce their effect in the first moment, they also have to produce it again and again at all subsequent moments of their existence. This is an absurd position as their nature then does not differ from their nature in the first moment; nor can they discharge their causal efficiency gradually. If they were not able to produce their effect completely from the beginning, neither should they be able to do so later as this would entail a change of nature. This argument is also based on the premise that one and the same entity cannot change its properties.

The inference from existence became more prominent than the inference from perishability, although it never superseded it completely. Its prominence can be explained partly by the logical peculiarity of this proof which gave rise to an epistemological debate about the correct form of a valid syllogism. Since momentariness is to be proved for everything, all entities are the subject of inference (pakṣa). Thus, the inference from existence fails to fulfil two of the three classical conditions (trairūpya) for a valid syllogism, namely a positive and negative exemplification of the logical nexus (vyāpti) between the reason (to be existent) and the argued property (to be momentary) outside the subject (see INFERENCE, INDIAN THEORIES OF).

Among other responses, this problem led to the modification of the conditions of a syllogism in such a way that those vyāptis also became accepted as valid where the logical relation between reason and argued property is not induced from other cases. This solution was already developed by Dharmakīrti himself, however, it was neglected until the time of Ratnākaraśānti (eleventh century). He argued that in those syllogisms where the proving property is intrinsic to the subject (svabhāvahetu), the logical nexus is to be established by demonstrating that the proving property cannot inhere in a locus that is lacking the argued property.

Frequently, as a corollary of these proofs of momentariness, the Brahmanical arguments against this doctrine are refuted. The most prominent argument – that the recognition of phenomena disproves their contended momentariness – is invalidated by the contention that recognition is a mixture of perception and memory and does not therefore qualify as a valid means of knowledge (pramāṇa). The related argument, that the mind cannot be a mere stream of momentary mental entities because memory and the discernment of causal relationships presuppose an enduring subject, is rejected. It is so on the grounds that the knowledge of the past is, by the principle of causal concatenation, passed on from one mental entity to the next. Thus, it is transmitted down to the present moment in a way which we may compare to the transmission of historic data from generation to generation.

Over the centuries the debate on the doctrine of momentariness developed to such an extent that Ratnakīrti (eleventh century) felt the need to deal with the inference from perishability, the inference from existence and the refutation of the proof of duration each in a separate treatise.

See also: BUDDHISM, ĀBHIDHARMIKA SCHOOLS OF; BUDDHIST PHILOSOPHY, INDIAN; MUJŌ; POTENTIALITY, INDIAN THEORIES OF

References and further reading

The pertinent textual material has to be accessed in the following studies where it is presented in reliable translations (in English, French, or German) which can also be consulted by readers without Indological training.

Mimaki, K. (1976) *La Refutation bouddhique de la Permanence des Choses (sthirasiddhidūṣaṇa) et la Preuve de la Momentanéité des choses (kṣaṇaṅgasiddhi)* (The Buddhist Refutation of the Permanence of Things and the Proof of the Momentariness of Things), Paris: Publications de l'institut de civilisation indienne, fasc. 41. (Deals with later proofs of the doctrine of momentariness.)

Oetke, C. (1993) 'Bemerkungen zur buddhistischen Doktrin der Momentanheit des Seienden. Dharma-kīrtis Sattvānumāna' (Remarks on the Buddhist Doctrine of Momentariness. Dharmakīrti's Sattvā-numāna (Inference from Existence)), *Wiener Studien zur Tibetologie und Buddhismuskunde 29*, Vienna: Arbeitskreis für Tibetsich und Buddhistische Studien Universität Wien. (Employs contemporary analytical logic for the analysis of the *Sattvānumāna*.)

Rospatt, A. von (1995) 'The Buddhist Doctrine of Momentariness: A Survey of the Origins and Early Phase of this Doctrine up to Vasubandhu', *Alt- und Neu-indische Studien 47*, Stuttgart: Steiner. (Deals with the early phase of the doctrine of momentariness and analyses it doctrinal background on the basis of earlier proofs of momentariness; presents the most complete collection of primary sources (all translated into English) available on the subject matter.)

Steinkellner, E. (1968/9) 'Die Entwicklung des Kṣaṇikatvānumāna bei Dharmakīrti' (The Development of the Kṣaṇikatvānumāna (Proof of Momentariness) by Dharmakīrti), *Wiener Zeitschrift für die Kunde Südasiens 12–13*: 361–77. (Traces the development of the *Sattvānumāna* by Dharmakīrti.)

ALEXANDER VON ROSPATT

MONBODDO, LORD (JAMES BURNETT) (1714–99)

In speculating that orang-utans' vocal organs must have been designed for speech, Monboddo was convinced that these creatures were primitive humans who had not yet entered society. His chief contribution to the history of linguistics and anthropology turns upon two propositions: that language is not natural to man, and that close physical resemblance between species is evidence of biological relation.

By training as a jurist and through his writings as a linguist and anthropologist, Monboddo was one of the most learned figures in eighteenth-century Scotland. Appointed a law lord or judge on the Scottish Court of Session in 1767 (from which his title derives), he drew lifelong inspiration from the classicism of Thomas Blackwell, whose writings on Homer and Augustus had helped to convince him of the decline of modern man and the decadence of modern forms of speech by contrast with the heroism of the ancient Greeks and Romans and the poetic resonance of their languages. More hostile to the empiricist tendencies of contemporary British philosophy than any other predominantly secular writer of the Scottish Enlightenment, he sought to rescue the glorious achievements of ancient science, ethics and rhetoric in reformulating an essentially Aristotelian interpretation of the human faculties, published in six volumes from 1779 to 1799, entitled *Antient Methaphysics* (see ENLIGHTENMENT, SCOTTISH).

A similar enthusiasm for classicism over modernity is manifest in Monboddo's more influential work of roughly the same period, *Of the Origin and Progress of Language*, also published in six volumes between 1773 and 1792. In addition to commenting on the splendours of ancient Latin and Greek, this text discusses the nomenclature of a variety of exotic languages, including Huron, Carib, Eskimo and Tahitian, which Monboddo had learned through dictionaries and travellers' reports. His attempt to trace the natural history of languages as an expression of both the universal capacities of the human mind and the specific genealogies of diverse cultures drew Monboddo in the direction of the nascent sciences of etymology and historical linguistics along lines developed by Sir William Jones (1746–89), with whom he corresponded. But he was even more drawn to the anthropological linguistics sketched in the *Discours sur l'inégalité* (Discourse on the Origin of Inequality) (1755) of Jean-Jacques ROUSSEAU, from which Monboddo adopted and developed two main propositions: first, that language must be cultivated and mastered in society and hence is not natural to man; and, second, that the 'orang-utan' (in the Enlightenment a generic term for all the great apes) is human, since the inarticulacy of this creature so similar to a human being is attributable to its not yet having had the opportunity to enter society and therein to exercise its larynx, pharynx and other organs of speech. Monboddo imagined that analogous physical traits characteristically signify homologous functions, so that unless Nature had been so uneconomical as to engage in redundant design, the apparently human vocal organs with which orang-utans are endowed must have been intended for speech. It is a wonder that some of our forebears invented language at all, he claimed, since language does not spring spontaneously from our lips as does sight from our eyes or hearing from our ears. In time, and with proper tuition, he concluded, as some primatological researchers still do today, orang-utans would bridge the putative gulf created by language between human nature in society and the conduct of apes outside it (see ANIMAL LANGUAGE AND THOUGHT).

See also: HUMAN NATURE, SCIENCE OF IN THE EIGHTEENTH CENTURY

List of works

Monboddo (1773–92) *Of the Origin and Progress of Language*, Edinburgh: Balfour.
—— (1779–99) *Antient Metaphysics*, Edinburgh: Balfour.

References and further reading

Cloyd. E.L. (1972) *James Burnett: Lord Monboddo*, Oxford: Clarendon. (A concise intellectual biography.)
Sherwin, O. (1958) 'A man with a tail – Lord Monboddo', *Journal of the History of Medicine*, 23: 435–67. (A bibliographically detailed study of Monboddo's primatological anthropology.)
Wokler, R. (1988) 'Apes and races in the Scottish Enlightenment: Monboddo and Kames on the nature of man', in P. Jones (ed.), *Philosophy and science in the Scottish Enlightenment*, Edinburgh: John Donald. (A comparison of two conjectural histories of anthropology.)

ROBERT WOKLER

MONISM

'Monism' is a very broad term, applicable to any doctrine which maintains either that there is ultimately only one thing, or only one kind of thing; it has also been used of the view that there is only one set of true beliefs. In these senses it is opposed to the equally broad term 'pluralism'. But it is also often contrasted with 'dualism', since so much philosophical debate has focused on the question whether there are two different kinds of thing, mind and matter, or only one.

The ending '-ism' suggests a particular theory or school; but in the case of 'monism' this is somewhat misleading. Less misleading is to think of certain philosophies as monistic in respect of some central doctrine, realizing that which doctrine this is may differ widely from case to case. This approach gives the flexibility to see that a philosophy which is from one perspective a variety of monism may well be, in respect of some other central doctrine, not monistic at all. For instance, Spinoza took the view that there was and could be only one substance (see SUBSTANCE). But he also held that this substance had infinitely many attributes, of which all but two (the mental and the physical) are unknown to us. There is nothing wrong with calling Spinoza a monist – provided it is said with an eye to a particular feature of his system.

With that warning in mind, we can say that the most common use of 'monism' is to describe philosophies which maintain that there is, ultimately, only one thing, and that 'the Many' are aspects of it or, to a more radical way of thinking, simply an illusion resulting from our mis-perception of the One. What they are not, for an ontological monist, is a collection of independent existences. Bertrand Russell once wrote that Hegel thought reality was like a tin of treacle, whereas he (Russell) thought it was like a heap of shot – the metaphor is even better if we keep the treacle in mind and forget the tin.

A spectacular early example of monism is found in the thought of Parmenides, who obscurely argued that reality could consist only of one thing, changeless and undifferentiated, and that the appearance of plurality was illusory (see PARMENIDES §7). In later antiquity, PLOTINUS influentially declared that everything emanated from another such changeless and undifferentiated entity, 'the One'. In the nineteenth century the view (associated in particular with F.H. Bradley) became widespread that relations between distinct entities cannot ultimately be real: for if two such entities are related by some relation *R*, there would be need of further relations to relate the relation *R* to each of them, and so on into infinite regress. Therefore there can only really be one thing, for if there were more they would have to be in some way related to each other. A similar argument occurs in Indian thought (see MONISM, INDIAN §3). Those who are sceptical will suspect that it rests on the tacit and dubious assumption that a real relation would have to be a kind of thing, like the things it relates.

A very different group of doctrines is also often called 'monism': those doctrines which assert, not that there is only one thing, but that there is ultimately only *one kind* of thing, one basic stuff of which the many kinds we observe are variant forms. Tradition unreliably has it that THALES, the earliest Greek philosopher of whom we have record, taught that this basic substance was water; a little later ANAXIMENES held a similar view, but chose air as his elemental stuff. They were therefore monists in this second sense, as is anyone who believes that the variety of the world is really nothing more than different arrangements of atoms which are themselves identical (see ATOMISM, ANCIENT).

One version of the 'one stuff or more?' debate has been especially prominent in modern philosophy: are there two kinds of substance – matter and mind – or only one, and, if so, which? Here the question is not 'are there one or more?' but 'are there one *or two*?', and when philosophers speak of monism as the alternative to dualism (without saying one or two *what?*) it is nearly always this issue that they are referring to. (A quite different use of the term 'dualism' is used in religious thought to refer to the view that the world is the work of two powers, one good and one bad – see MANICHEISM §§1, 4.) In modern times, Descartes is the classic exponent of mind–body dualism, though hardly its inventor – he was only giving precision and proof to the very old idea that as well as matter there are spirits or souls, and that the latter are very different in kind from the former. Ranged on the other side are various styles of monist. There is idealist monism, typified by Berkeley, which holds that there are only minds or spirits, and that material bodies are nothing but a way of speaking about mental states (see PHENOMENALISM); there is material monism, steadily more popular with the rise of the natural sciences, which views everything as material, and reduces the supposedly mental to facts about matter (see MATERIALISM IN THE PHILOSOPHY OF MIND). And there is a doctrine associated in particular with the names of Mach, James and Russell, which sees the mental and the physical as different aspects of a single basic stuff that in itself is neither mental or physical (see NEUTRAL MONISM).

Because of its very general meaning, 'monism' lends itself to a wide variety of uses easily understood from their context. Thus one may see 'value-monism' – meaning an ethical system which recognizes only one thing as having value in itself, for example happiness (see UTILITARIANISM). And one may speak of monism about truth, meaning that there is one unique set of truths – in opposition to pluralism, relativism and perspectivalism, according to which conflicting or incommensurable views may be equally true.

See also: PLURALISM

References and further reading

Bradley, F.H. (1897) *Appearance and Reality*, London: Allen & Unwin, 2nd edn, Appendix II. (A *locus classicus* for the argument to monism from the unreality of relations.)

Gallop, D. (1984) *Parmenides of Elea*, Toronto, Ont.: Toronto University Press. (Text and translation of the *c.*150 extant lines by Parmenides.)

James, W. (1909) *A Pluralistic Universe*, London: Longman, Green & Co. (Chapter 2, 'Monistic idealism', is a lively polemic against nineteenth century monists. Accessible.)

Moore, G.E. (1922) 'External and Internal Relations', in *Philosophical Studies*, London: Routledge & Kegan Paul, 276–309. (Moore resists the view – dear to the 'tin of treacle' type of monist – that nothing can be the thing it is without standing in all the relations to other things it actually does stand in.)

Plotinus (*c.*250–70) *Enneads*, trans. S. MacKenna, London: Penguin, 1991. (See in particular Enneads IV–VI; for readers in a hurry, VI.9: 535–49. Difficult reading.)

Spinoza, B. (1677) *Ethics*, in *The Collected Works of Spinoza*, trans. and ed. E. Curley, Princeton, NJ: Princeton University Press, 1985. (Part I, 'Of God', contains Spinoza's proof that there is only one substance.)

EDWARD CRAIG

MONISM, INDIAN

The prominent classical and modern Indian philosophy known as Advaita Vedānta, which insists on the single reality of Brahman (the Absolute), is often identified as Indian monism. But the monism of Advaita is only a portion, albeit central, of the Advaita view. Furthermore, a monism in theology (Brahman as God) is important to almost all expressions, classical and modern, of Indian theism.

The monism of Advaita is principally psychological. Nondual awareness is considered the true self; that is to say, in the self's native state, the object of awareness and awareness itself are identical. This kind of awareness is claimed to be presupposed by all dualistic consciousness. Moreover, it is said that only self-aware self-awareness itself cannot be revealed by experience to be illusory. And according to Advaita, a supreme mystical experience, popularly called liberation, does in fact, when it occurs, reveal self-awareness to be the sole reality. A dialectical Advaita adds the further contention that it is impossible to define and explain coherently diverse appearances. This contention is cashed out by long and intricate attacks on the pluralistic ontologies of rival schools, particularly Nyāya-Vaiśeṣika.

The monism of Indian theism centres on the reality of God, who is constrained by metaphysical law to create out of the single spiritual substance that God is. The world is commonly said to be God's body. Various ramifications of God's being in some way everything can be discerned in Indian theology.

1 **The Advaita view of self**
2 **Sublatability**
3 **Dialectical Advaita**
4 **Theological monism**

1 The Advaita view of self

Advaita Vedānta is a scripturally derived philosophy centred on the proposition, first found in early Upaniṣads (800–300 BC), that Brahman – the Absolute, the supreme reality – and the self (*ātman*) are identical. The identity is understood as an objectless consciousness, as awareness nondualistically self-aware. Arguments in support of the view that nondual awareness is the sole reality are developed by classical and modern Advaitins, from Gauḍapāda (*c.*600 AD) and Śaṅkara (*c.*700 AD), in hundreds of texts. Some of these are suggested in Upaniṣads.

Scripture – that is, Upaniṣadic passages – is the principal reason cited why, in the first place, awareness aware of nothing but itself should be considered a reality. A supreme mystical experience, deemed the goal of life, is said to be just such a state, and scripture is interpreted as teaching this. But that so-and-so reports such mystical experience is not cited, at least not commonly, in support of the view that such self-awareness occurs. Scripture is the testimony of the occurrence.

That nondual awareness is the only possible *self*-awareness is defended by a *reductio* argument. If a further awareness C_2, having C_1 as content, is required for self-awareness, then since there would be no awareness of C_2 without awareness C_3, *ad infinitum*, there could be no self-awareness, that is, unless the self is to be understood as limited to past awareness only. For self-awareness to be an immediate awareness, self-awareness has to be nondual. It is a further question how self-aware awareness accounts for our everyday sense of self and our commitment to the reality of self, a question of psychology that in particular a few late classical Advaitins struggle with. It is problematic, for example, how our native self-awareness, aware only of itself, accounts for our everyday sense of ourselves as a body. Moreover, self-

awareness, as understood by Advaita, is said to be presupposed by all consciousness, but the precise connection – other than as an ongoing possibility of meditative self-absorption – is not clearly worked out. Nevertheless, the argument that self-awareness would be impossible without nondual awareness is forceful, it is said, for all who admit self-awareness, and forceful, so it is presumed by many Advaitin advocates, independently of the question of the precise nature of the tie to the everyday sense of self.

In support of awareness as self-illumining, the great Advaitin ŚAṄKARA (often taken to be the very founder of Advaita) argues that no one says 'I am not.' This Advaita argument for self-illumination is often compared to Descartes' *Cogito*. As self-illumining, awareness blocks doubt: the doubt never occurs, 'Am I aware or not?' In this way an appeal is made to what is sometimes called pragmatic contradiction: there would be contradiction between essence and content were someone to have an awareness verbalizable as 'I am not aware.' (Compare a speaker saying 'I am not speaking.')

From self-illumination it is argued that an epistemic principle known as self-certification (*svaprāmāṇya*) is right concerning all questions about awareness, since only an awareness itself has, so to say, access to itself. Awareness itself is the only consideration relevant to any question about awareness itself, its existence or its nature. Self-certification is thus grounded in self-illumination. And self-certification is key to further Advaita arguments.

2 Sublatability

The most commonly voiced argument in defence of the Advaita view of self-awareness as the single reality centres on a presumed sublatability of all indications of awareness other than self-awareness itself. Perceptual illusion shows that there is no worldly content of an experience that could not prove unreal. In contrast, (again) no one says, or could say (in good faith), 'I am not.' The self, unlike objects presented perceptually, all of which might not be, cannot, if presented, possibly not be. Self cannot be sublated. Perceptual illusion shows that anything else can be. The appearances of a rope as a snake, of mother-of-pearl as silver, and so on, show that the worldly content of experiences is not to be trusted. Only self-experience is sure (see ERROR AND ILLUSION, INDIAN CONCEPTIONS OF §1).

Thus awareness self-certifyingly illumines self-awareness but not anything else. External objects are not self-certifyingly illumined because any presentation of an external object is sublatable, whereas the self-illumination of awareness itself is nonsublatable.

All awareness may be *prima facie* self-certifying, but only self-awareness is *ultima facie* self-certifying, for all content other than self-illumination is sublatable, negatable experientially.

Advaitins move from these Cartesian-like considerations to embrace a very strong criterion for ontic commitment. An absolute nonsublatability is the mark, they say, of the real, or existent, *sat*. That which is not sublatable by any manner or means is to be accepted as real. Only self-awareness meets the criterion. Self-awareness is the single reality.

There is another argument centring on a sublatability of a different sort, not the experiential sublatability of presentations other than self, but a propositional defeasibility. Brahman, the Absolute, with which in the Upaniṣads the self is declared to be identical, is presented in the Upaniṣads as also including everything (*sarvam idaṃ brahma*, 'All this is Brahman'). The scripturally conveyed cognition of Brahman is not the same as self-awareness aware only of itself, for the scripturally conveyed cognition of Brahman is verbal, conveyed linguistically. It is only self-awareness that cannot possibly be sublated experientially and thus it is only that awareness that indicates reality in the truest sense of the word. But (unfortunately) we do not live our lives in such a state of self-absorption. Within the sphere of everyday life, we adopt a modified self-certificationalism: A cognition is to be accepted as true unless defeated by countervailing considerations. That is to say, innocence, or an assumed warrantedness, is the epistemic default. Now this holds concerning the scripturally conveyed monistic cognition 'Brahman' (Brahman is everything). But also, Advaitins argue, Brahman cognition is in principle indefeasible, for two reasons. First, it is the proper province of scripture, and of scripture only, to tell us things of this order, as the sun (says Śaṅkara, who is echoed in dozens of texts) is the proper illuminer of colour. Second, a proper challenger to Brahman cognition would similarly have to be about everything. But if a cognition were truly about everything (including itself) it would be identical with Brahman cognition. Thus there can be no challenger of Brahman cognition other than Brahman cognition itself, which is no challenger. Brahman cognition is both *prima facie* warranted (innocence is the justificational default) and *ultima facie* warranted, in that it cannot be challenged.

The monism of an all-inclusive Brahman as declared in the Upaniṣads is not the heart of the Advaita position, which is instead the psychological monism of self-awareness. But the two are related, as we can see by looking at another argument, namely that the *summum bonum*, popularly termed 'liberation' and by philosophers 'knowledge (or mystical experience) of Brahman' (*brahma-vidyā*), does in fact, when it occurs, reveal self-awareness to be the sole reality. The fundamental reason why scripture teaches that Brahman is everything is to provide a meditational support helpful in achieving the supreme good. There may seem to be some truth in the idealist view that Brahman is the ground and support of everything – indeed its material reality, as the material reality of a gold bracelet is just the gold – in that every appearance appears just to the self. However, there is no more truth in this view than in the theistic position that God is the creator and sustainer of things, a teaching also helpful for some. Scripture's purport is thoroughly soteriological; that is to say, it aims at bringing us to the realization of self-illumining self-awareness. Scripturally conveyed cognitions are sublated, like every cognition other than self-awareness itself, in the supreme experience. But the monism of an all-inclusive Brahman declared by scripture is, within the sphere of spiritual ignorance (*avidyā*), a most helpful teaching for transcending spiritual ignorance – as well as one that is indefeasible by everyday experience and knowledge. (Advaita's exegetical strategy is similar, as suggested, with regard to Upaniṣadic teachings about God.)

There are more or less obvious problems with these arguments, problems that classical and modern opponents of Advaita have identified. We shall mention just a few. First, it is not clear that self-illumining self-awareness is nonsublatable experientially, particularly as Advaitins understand (experiential) sublation – that is, on analogy with an experiential correction of a perceptual illusion. A nonveridical perception of a snake is sublated and corrected by a veridical perception of a rope. For Advaitins, it seems to be the posteriority of the correcting perception that is key. Why then could not a fuller experience of self as embodied, or being in the world, follow a meditational experience of self-absorption? Second, Brahman is declared in the Upaniṣads to be bliss, among other attributions, not only self-awareness. Could there not be, then, a distinct challenger to the scriptural teaching about Brahman which was similarly about everything: for example, 'All-inclusive Brahman is not bliss?' And finally, there are Buddhists and others who say that the supreme mystical experience does not reveal a self, but, for example, a no-self. Whom should we believe?

3 Dialectical Advaita

Although Śaṅkara and other early Advaitin philosophers concern themselves principally with the logic of illusion along with exegetical questions, they also launch dialectical attacks against rival schools, and specifically against the category of external relationality crucial to all realist and pluralist ontology. In the twelfth century, an Advaitin named Śrīharṣa ingeniously expands the earlier polemics, aiming in particular at the realist system known as Nyāya-Vaiśeṣika and purporting to dismantle it plank by plank. Śrīharṣa takes more seriously the all-inclusiveness and simplicity of Brahman presumed to be taught by scripture, and believes that the reality of Brahman means that it is impossible to define and explain coherently apparent diversities. He cashes out this commitment with an onslaught upon Nyāya's pluralist ontology, an onslaught in which attacks on relations figure prominently (see NYĀYA-VAIŚEṢIKA §§4–5). Later Advaitins (including modern philosophers) rework some of his arguments to explode other views.

If there are two things *a* and *b* related by the relation *R* – thus *aRb* – in virtue of what is *R* related to *a*, and likewise to *b*? A second relation and a third, *ad infinitum*, would seem to be required. Śrīharṣa employs this logic (in the West sometimes called the Bradley problem (see BRADLEY, F.H. §5)) in a variety of contexts, for example, regarding the relation between a property-bearer and a property:

> If the property is unrelated to the property-bearer, there is an obvious problem; [if, on the other hand, it is related] there will be an endless number of relations and thus infinite regress. Or if at the beginning or the end the relation is admitted to be of the very nature of one of the terms [property or property-bearer], then since even the other term of the relation would enter into the very nature of that [the combined relatee-relator], nothing but nondistinctness would result.
>
> (*Khaṇḍanakhaṇḍakhādya*, 107)

Three options are sketched: (1) a property, such as blue, is unrelated to its bearer, such as a pot; (2) if there is a relation that relates them, such as inherence, then there have to be further relations to relate the inherence to each of the terms, the blue and the pot, *ad infinitum* (*aRb*, *aR'R*, *aR''R'R*, *ad infinitum*, likewise with the second term); unless (3) it is the very nature of one of the terms to link with the other: such linkage would amount to nondistinctness. The third seems the only viable option. Nondistinctness, however, is at odds with Nyāya pluralism, and thus the argument (along with others), Śrīharṣa concludes, shows that there is no coherent Nyāya challenger to the monism of Brahman taught by the Upaniṣads.

In sum, distinct things have to be in relation, but relations are impossible. Thus by presupposing fundamentally distinct things, pluralists run into a host of difficulties, as indicated by this demonstration

of incoherence (and others). GAṄGEŚA (*fl. c.*1325), a later logician of the Nyāya school, responds that it is an error to treat a relator as the same type of thing as its relatees, and it is this mistake that engenders the appearance of vicious regress. Of course, Advaitin followers of Śrīharṣa find further problems with the response, and the controversy, one of the finest preserved in Sanskrit, continues for several more centuries.

4 Theological monism

The cornerstone of the monism of Indian theism is found in an Upaniṣadic story of a father teaching his son about Brahman:

> Just being, my son, was this [universe] in the beginning, one alone, without a second. There are, to be sure, some that say, "Just non-being was this [universe] in the beginning, one alone, without a second. From that non-being, being arose." But how, my son, could it be so?... How from non-being could being arise? On the contrary, just being, my son, was this [universe] in the beginning, one alone, without a second.
>
> (Chāndogya Upaniṣad 6.2.1–2)

Here we find an early expression (700 BC?) of the metaphysical law *ex nihilo nihil fit*, 'nothing from nothing'. The Upaniṣads weave several fanciful stories about how the One becomes many, stories that are interpreted by later theologians as underscoring emanationism. God looses forth (*sṛjate*) gods, Vedas and Upaniṣads, humans, animals, plants, rocks and dust out of God's own substance. The universe is God's body.

Indian theists commit themselves to a thoroughgoing reality of a plurality of things; spiritual monism none the less provides an absolute boundary, or a resource, for their theorizing (except with the Dvaita, 'Dualist', Vedānta school). For example, evil, a challenge to any view that would uphold the goodness of a Creator (see EVIL, PROBLEM OF), has a different look within a theological monism as opposed to a theism that has God separate from the world, creating *ex nihilo*. God, being everything, shares in everyone's suffering; evil looks more like masochism than a matter of God's harming others. Moreover, God's being everything is thought to guarantee a universal harmony. It is impossible for society, for example, to disintegrate into chaos. If there were such a threat, God would appear (would be forced to appear) in a special manifestation, *avatāra*, to assure a return to harmony. This is a principal message of the *Bhagavad Gītā* (Song of God) and other theistic texts.

Finally, the monistic dimension of Indian theism

spawns, in contrast with the illusionism of Advaita Vedānta and much Buddhism as well, a distinct attitude towards the body and physical things. Nature is enchanted, the body a mystic instrument. To be sure, asceticism, much admired in classical Indian society in accord with Advaita and Buddhist teachings, colours the religious practices of Indian theism. But worship and other practices reflecting belief in a divine immanence tend to prevail.

See also: AWARENESS IN INDIAN THOUGHT §3; BRAHMAN; GOD, INDIAN CONCEPTIONS OF; MONISM; SELF, INDIAN THEORIES OF; VEDĀNTA

References and further reading

Aurobindo, Sri (1914–20) *The Life Divine*, Pondicherry: Sri Aurobindo Ashram Trust, revised edn, 1943–4, 2 vols. (Aurobindo is a modern Indian theist who expresses the logic of theological monism particularly well.)

* *Bhagavad Gītā* (200 BC–AD 200, disputed), trans. F. Edgerton, Harvard Oriental Series 38–9, Cambridge, MA: Harvard University Press, 1944, paperback repr. 1972. (Though Edgerton's interpretive essay – orginally volume 39 in the HOS – too much reflects outworn assumptions of nineteenth-century indologists, his translation is excellent, faithful and elegant. There are, however, dozens of acceptable translations into English and other modern languages.)

Dasgupta, S. (1922–55) *A History of Indian Philosophy*, Cambridge: Cambridge University Press, 5 vols. (Volume 4 has a section on the late classical debate between dialectical Advaita and the Dualist school of Vedānta, whose pluralist ontology has much in common with Nyāya.)

Phillips, S.H. (1995) *Classical Indian Metaphysics: Refutations of Realism and the Emergence of 'New Logic'*, La Salle, IL: Open Court. (Focuses on dialectical Advaita and responses provoked.)

Potter, K.H. (ed.) (1981) *Encyclopedia of Indian Philosophies*, vol. 3, *Advaita Vedānta*, Princeton, NJ: Princeton University Press. (Contains an excellent introduction to Advaita philosophy as well as summaries of works in the early Advaita school.)

* Śrīharṣa (12th century) *Khaṇḍanakhaṇḍakhādya*, ed. N. Jha, Kashi Sanskrit Series 197, Varanasi: Chowkhamba, 1970. (The title translates as 'Delectable Refutations'; this is *the* classic of dialectical Advaita Vedānta.)

Thibaut, G. (trans.) (1890) *The Vedānta Sūtras of Bādarāyaṇa, with the Commentary by Śaṃkara*, New York: Dover. (An excellent, highly readable translation of Śaṅkara's principal philosophical work.)

* *Upaniṣads* (800–300 BC), trans. P. Olivelle, *Upaniṣads*, Oxford: Oxford University Press, 1996. (A new translation that may well be the best; readable and accurate. The translations in the present entry are by Stephen Phillips.)

STEPHEN H. PHILLIPS

MONOTHEISM

Judaism, Christianity and Islam are usually cited as the major monotheistic religions. These are religions which acknowledge only a single god, and which construe that god as transcendent – that is, as a being who is distinct from the ordinary world and superior to it. They also construe this god as a person or as very much like a person. The polytheistic religions agree with monotheism, for the most part, in construing the gods in personalistic terms, but they acknowledge a plurality of gods. Pantheists, on the other hand, usually accept the singularity of the deity, but reject the transcendence, identifying the deity more closely with the ordinary universe, perhaps as a certain aspect of the universe or as the totality of the universe considered in a certain way. They also are likely to reject the personalistic idea of the deity.

This entry will discuss some philosophical aspects of the contrast between monotheism and polytheism. There are different ways of understanding 'acknowledge' in the characterization of monotheism given above. One may believe that there exists only one god. Or one may believe that more than one god exists, but worship only one, or hold that it is wrong to worship more than one. A closely related issue concerns the concept of deity that is employed in such beliefs and claims. The 'high' Anselmian conception of Christianity's god – a being than whom no greater can be conceived – is only one account. Perhaps of most philosophical interest is the problem as to whether logical argument can demonstrate polytheism to be false and establish the truth of the Anselmian account.

1   **Types of monotheism**
2   **Concepts of deity**
3   **Rationales for monotheism**

1   Types of monotheism

Monotheism contrasts on one side with atheism and on the other with polytheism. Philosophers, initially at least, may take monotheism to be a doctrine to the effect that there exists exactly one god, no more and no less. Atheism, then, would be the doctrine that there exist no gods at all, and polytheism would be the claim that there are several gods (see ATHEISM §1). A monotheist would be a person who accepts the monotheistic doctrine, and similarly for atheists and polytheists.

All three of these 'isms', however, are ambiguous in an important way. Consider another contrasting pair of notions, which mark an important distinction among various social systems – monogamy and polygamy. Hardly anyone would take seriously the suggestion that we should construe a monogamist as a man who believes that there is only one wife, or that we should take monogamy to be the doctrine that one and only one wife exists. It would be much more plausible to construe monogamy simply as a practice – that of having only one wife – and a monogamist would then be a man who had only one wife. Polygamy, of course, would then be the contrasting practice of having more than one wife. And some people might want to add a somewhat more theoretical and doctrinal element to these conceptions, perhaps saying that monogamy includes a normative claim, the claim that it is not proper for a man to have more than one wife; polygamy would then involve the contrasting normative claim.

In an analogous way, there is a religiously important sense of monotheism in which it consists simply in having only one god – that is, in committing oneself to, worshipping, obeying, and so on, only one god. There is a second sense in which monotheism is the doctrine that there is something improper and illegitimate in worshipping more than one god (and perhaps also that there is something improper about not worshipping any god). And then there is a third sense, that in which monotheism is the doctrine that there exists one and only one god. These will be referred to in this entry as, respectively, *cultic monotheism*, *normative monotheism* and *descriptive monotheism*.

It is useful to keep these distinctions in mind when considering classical texts dealing with this general idea. Pre-Christian Judaism, for example, is often cited as an early example of monotheism, and indeed as the precursor of monotheistic Christianity. But consider a classic monotheistic Hebraic text, the first of the Ten Commandments: 'Then God spoke all these words: I am the LORD your God, who brought you out of the land of Egypt, out of the house of slavery; you shall have no other gods before me' (Exodus 20: 1–3). Pretty clearly, cultic monotheism is here being enjoined on Israel. They are to 'have' no other gods than the LORD (Yahweh). And perhaps the fact that this commandment is attributed to God

himself may suggest that there is also a normative element in this monotheism. (Even so, this text would not support the view that it is improper for anyone to have more than one god, or one of those other gods. This command is explicitly addressed to Israel.) But the text seems to have no suggestion in it at all of descriptive monotheism. In fact, it may well be construed as positively envisaging the possibility of the existence of other gods.

Cultic and normative monotheism are logically compatible with descriptive polytheism, and apparently they are religiously compatible with it also. There have been, and probably still are, religions whose adherents clearly recognize the existence of gods to whom they themselves give no allegiance. An interesting and explicit biblical example comes from the monarchic period of Israel's history. In that story, some Aramean army officers undertake to explain to their king why they were defeated by the Israelites. 'Their gods are gods of the hills,' they say, 'and so they were stronger than we.' And they propose a different strategy for the next encounter: 'Let us fight against them in the plain, and surely we shall be stronger than they' (I Kings 20: 17–25). The Arameans of this story express no doubt about the existence of the Israelite gods – in fact, they attribute their own defeat to the power of those foreign gods in the hill country of northern Israel. But they themselves have no allegiance to those gods. They do not profess to worship them or to serve them. In fact, they are plotting to defeat them at the next opportunity, by fighting on the plains where their own gods are at home. These Arameans were descriptive polytheists with respect to the Israelite gods, and probably they were both cultic and descriptive polytheists with regard to another set of gods, their own.

2 Concepts of deity

If the story of the Arameans seems strange and awkward, this reflects the fact that the word 'god' (and 'God') involves an ambiguity similar to the one we have been considering. There is a sense of this word, fairly common now, in which it has a cultic element built into it. In this sense, to use the word 'god' to describe or identify some being is *ipso facto* to profess a certain attitude – worship, obedience, reverence, and the like – towards that being. Sometimes this cultic element is made explicit in something like a definition. Perhaps the best-known modern definition of this sort is that attributed to Paul TILLICH (§3), that God is the object of ultimate concern. A person who accepted that account would speak paradoxically, to say the least, if they were to say 'Of course God exists, but he is of no concern to me.' Some students of early Buddhism, however, think that just this combination may well have been the view of Gautama the Buddha (see BUDDHA). They suspect that Gautama held that (perhaps only probably) there are gods, but that they have no concern with human life and so we need not concern ourselves with them. A similar view is sometimes attributed to Epicurus (see EPICUREANISM §9).

This raises a question about the concept of a god. Monotheism, polytheism and atheism differ with respect to the number of gods, but all are equally in need of some elucidation of the concept of a god. Anyone who professes one of these 'isms' seems to need some idea of the nature of a god. What sort of thing is it of which only one, or more than one, or none at all is supposed to be worshipped? What sort of thing is it of which there is just one, or more than one, or none at all? Throughout the Christian period, Western philosophical theology has gone very strongly to extremely 'high' conceptions of the deity. Perhaps the best-known formulation of a high conception is that of ANSELM OF CANTERBURY (§4), who understood God to be a being than whom no greater can be conceived (*Proslogion*, ch. 2). Whether this conception guarantees descriptive monotheism will be considered in §3 (see GOD, CONCEPTS OF §§3–6).

For the moment, however, it is useful to recognize that there have surely been religions, and perhaps there still are some, that do not construe their gods in this high way. The Arameans referred to earlier certainly cannot have had anything remotely like Anselm's idea in mind when they spoke about gods, either their own or those of the Israelites. For they construed those gods as beings whose power would probably run out forty miles from home, in the transition from the hill country to the Syrian plains. The gods of pre-Christian Greek and Roman popular religion also do not seem to make a plausible fit with anything like the Anselmian notion. And so on. Is there any other notion of a god, something radically non-Anselmian, which would be applicable to a wide range of actual religions? Some philosophers think so. Richard Swinburne, for example, says 'I understand by a god a non-embodied rational agent of great power' (1970: 6). Probably the gods as the Arameans construed them, along with the gods of ancient Greece and Rome, and many others, would fit this definition fairly well. And so, for that matter, would God as he is construed in Christian theology. The Anselmian concept might be a more adequate account of the Christian deity, and perhaps a more interesting and provocative account. But God, as he is described by orthodox Christian theologians, would also satisfy Swinburne's definition. He too is a non-embodied rational agent of great power.

With reference to Swinburne's definition, then, the Arameans of the biblical story were probably doubly polytheistic in the descriptivist sense, believing in the existence of several gods to whom they owed allegiance and also in the existence of several to whom they did not owe allegiance. The ancient Greeks and Romans were apparently also descriptive (and cultic) polytheists. Perhaps more interestingly, most Christians are descriptive polytheists in Swinburne's sense of 'god' because angels (and devils also) fit his definition perfectly well. But of course Christians are not, on that account at least, cultic polytheists. For though they often profess to believe in the existence of angels and devils, they do not characteristically profess to worship these beings.

Many Christians, of course, will feel uncomfortable with Swinburne's definition, and would not like to be identified as polytheists. This perhaps reflects the strongly cultic connotations which the word 'god' now has, especially when it is capitalized. These Christians, quite properly, do not want to be taken for worshippers of angels, or even for people who think that it might be appropriate to worship an angel. But they are, for the most part, content to be known as people who believe in the existence of angels. And being a descriptive polytheist, in Swinburne's sense of 'god', need not involve anything more than that.

3 Rationales for monotheism

The most common sort of rationale given for cultic monotheism is strongly religious in character. So in the Hebraic account, for example, God is said to have rescued the people of Israel from their bondage in Egypt, exercising his power on their behalf. He then makes a covenant with them, and one element of this covenant is that they will have no other god. The idea of this covenant is deeply embedded in the self-identification of this people. People who accept that self-identification as their own thereby accept a commitment to that deity. That god, and no other, will be their god.

Sometimes the commitment is made on a more personal level. The biblical story of Ruth, for example, is the story of a young widow who decides to leave her home in Moab and to move to Israel with her mother-in-law. Declaring her decision, Ruth says to Naomi, 'your people shall be my people, and your God my God' (Ruth 1: 16). She has made her decision to take up a new life in a new place and a new community, and part of that decision involves making a commitment to a new god and abandoning whatever commitment she may have had to the gods of Moab. She may have been a cultic polytheist in Moab, but now, she resolves, she will commit herself to the one god whom Naomi worships.

Rationales for descriptive monotheism often have a more philosophical flavour, appealing to more general principles, such as logic. They may thus be of more general philosophical interest. Especially for attempts to establish descriptive monotheism, it is crucial to fix somehow on the relevant concept of deity. And it is important also to remember that descriptive monotheism has a contrast on each side of it – atheism and polytheism. Establishing monotheism must involve ruling out both of these alternatives.

Perhaps it seems easiest to attack descriptive polytheism first. The most attractive strategy for this project is analytic or definitional. One looks for a concept of deity which is such that it would be logically impossible for more than one actual existent to satisfy it. Of course, Swinburne's concept will not be satisfactory for this purpose. There is nothing in it which rules out the possibility that several beings could satisfy it. But maybe there is some 'higher' concept which guarantees singularity.

Christian theologians have often included the attribute of omnipotence in their idea of God, and this may seem to provide a convenient connection with singularity (see OMNIPOTENCE §1). Initially at least, it is plausible to think that there could not possibly be two omnipotent beings. Which one would prevail, after all, if they came to blows? A little more formally, it might be thought that an omnipotent being ought to be able to overcome any external obstacle and also to thwart any external initiative. So, if there were two distinct omnipotent beings, A and B, then A should be able to overcome B, and B should also be able to resist A and thwart him. But that combination seems logically incoherent; if so, then it may constitute a *reductio ad absurdum* disproof of the suggestion that there could be two distinct omnipotent beings.

The concept of omnipotence, however, is itself surprisingly difficult to clarify, and that in turn generates a difficulty for this line of argument. At least since the time of Thomas Aquinas, most Christian theologians have construed omnipotence in such a way that it does not involve the power to do logically impossible tasks. Given this understanding of omnipotence, it is hard to see how to carry out the *reductio* successfully. Assume (for the *reductio*) that both A and B exist and are omnipotent. Perhaps it can then be assumed that the omnipotence of A should enable him to overcome any resistance offered by B. Well and good. But, on this understanding of omnipotence, the failure of B to resist A successfully does not count against B's omnipotence. For, on this reading, thwarting A is a logically impossible task.

After all, A is omnipotent; he cannot be resisted. And the impossibility of the task removes it from the sphere of omnipotence. Therefore, the fact that B cannot succeed in the logically impossible project of resisting A does not represent a failure of omnipotence in B. There is no contradiction in the admission that B, though omnipotent, cannot thwart A. And so the *reductio* fails.

Suppose we reject the 'majority' view of omnipotence associated with Aquinas and opt instead for the minority view. On this view, omnipotence enables its possessor to do even those things which are logically impossible. Given this reading of omnipotence, B is not excused from the task of thwarting A merely because that task is impossible. But now the *reductio* runs into difficulty at a different point. For now we can say that A, being omnipotent, will certainly succeed in his project, and B, also omnipotent, will surely be able to thwart A. Of course, that seems thoroughly incoherent, the description of a logically impossible state of affairs. It entails that A both succeeds and fails to succeed, and also that B both succeeds and fails. But given the minority understanding of omnipotence, what would be the significance of discovering this logical incoherence or impossibility? After all, on the minority view, impossible things fall within the power of omnipotence. If A and B are omnipotent in the minority sense, then they may well be able to bring about this logically impossible state of affairs. Here too the attempt to construct the desired *reductio* seems to fail. As far as these arguments go, then, we are left with the possibility that there might indeed be two omnipotent beings.

On neither of these views of omnipotence, therefore, is it clear that we can rule out descriptive polytheism simply by including omnipotence in our concept of a god. We might, of course, try some other attribute which theologians generally include in a high conception of the deity. But in fact there would seem to be an easier way to succeed along these lines. We can simply attach an explicit singularity requirement, perhaps by adding the phrase 'the one and only', to some already formulated specification of a concept of deity. We can, for example, start with Anselm's account, and generate from it the revised formula 'the one and only being than whom no greater can be conceived'. Let us call this the 'singularity' concept of deity. If we adopt the singularity concept, then at least one half of the descriptive monotheist position is guaranteed. There is not, and there cannot be, more than one actually existent being who satisfies this description. Furthermore, we can say that if there is exactly one existing being who satisfies Anselm's original concept, then that same being also satisfies the singularity version. And if nothing satisfies Anselm's concept, then nothing satisfies the singularity version either.

This strategy, however, also costs something. It provides a comparatively easy way to rule out descriptive polytheism (for the chosen concept of deity, of course), but it makes it harder to rule out atheism. In the example just given, for example, we can notice that if two (or more) existent beings satisfy Anselm's concept, then nothing at all satisfies the singularity concept. For in that case there would be no being who was the one and only being than whom no greater can be conceived. There would instead be several beings who were tied for the position of maximal conceivable greatness. But, of course, none of these beings would satisfy the singularity requirement.

Anselm, of course, argued that there is an existent being who satisfies his concept – that is, that there actually is a being than whom no greater can be conceived. And there have been some impressive and provocative recent reformulations of the Anselmian line of argument (for example, Plantinga 1974). But neither Anselm nor his recent followers clearly address the question of whether there may be more than one being than whom no greater can be conceived. We might say, therefore, that if their arguments are successful they may refute 'Anselmian atheism' and establish Anselmian theism, where Anselmian atheism and theism are defined by reference to Anselm's concept of God. But there is also 'singularity atheism', which consists of the claim that nothing satisfies the singularity concept. The arguments of Anselm and his followers do not seem to refute singularity atheism. Consequently, they do not establish descriptive monotheism according to either the Anselmian or the singularity concept of deity.

There are, of course, other lines of argument that might be explored. We might specify, for example, that we think of God as the creator of the world, and then go on to argue that the universe exhibits so much unity that it is plausible to attribute it to a single creator. That strikes some philosophers as rather attractive. But David HUME (§6) suggested that it is just as plausible to think that the universe was created by a committee (1779: part V). So this line of argument is not convincing to everyone. In fact, it is likely that no sort of philosophical argument for descriptive monotheism will be universally attractive. If we are concerned about descriptive monotheism at all, it might be just as well to rely here too on distinctively religious considerations, perhaps indeed on some appeal to divine revelation (see REVELATION §§1–2).

See also: GOD, ARGUMENTS FOR THE EXISTENCE OF; PANTHEISM; RELIGIOUS PLURALISM; TRINITY §§1–2

References and further reading

* Anselm (1077–8) *Proslogion*, trans. J. Hopkins, *A New Interpretive Translation of St Anselm's Monologion and Proslogion*, Minneapolis, MN: Arthur J. Banning Press, 1986. (This short book contains the most widely known formulation of the ontological argument for the existence of God, as well as a very influential formulation of the concept of God.)
Aquinas, T. (1266–73) *Summa theologica*, trans. Fathers of the English Dominican Province (1911), Westminster, MD: Christian Classics, 1981, 5 vols. (A concise discussion and defence of descriptive monotheism by one of the greatest philosopher-theologians of the medieval period; see particularly Ia, q.11, a.3.)
* Hume, D. (1779) *Dialogues Concerning Natural Religion*, ed. N.K. Smith, Indianapolis, IN: Bobbs-Merrill, 1947. (This is an extensive discussion and critique of arguments which purport to prove the existence of God on the basis of the order and design in the world.)
* Plantinga, A. (1974) *The Nature of Necessity*, Oxford: Clarendon Press. (Much of this book consists of rather technical discussions of modal logic, but the chapter on the ontological argument (196–221) contains one of the most influential modern versions of that argument. It requires careful reading, but it is understandable without much background in modal logic.)
* Swinburne, R. (1970) *The Concept of Miracle*, London: Macmillan. (This is mainly a discussion of the possibility of miracles, but it includes an interesting and provocative specification of the concept of a god.)

GEORGE I. MAVRODES

MONTAGUE, RICHARD MERETT (1930–71)

Richard Montague was a logician, philosopher and mathematician. His mathematical contributions include work in Boolean algebra, model theory, proof theory, recursion theory, axiomatic set theory and higher-order logic. He developed a modal logic in which necessity appears as a predicate of sentences, showing how analogues of the semantic paradoxes relate to this notion. Analogously, he (with David Kaplan) argued that a special case of the surprise examination paradox can also be seen as an epistemic version of semantic paradox. He made important contributions to the problem of formulating the notion of a 'deterministic' theory in science.

Much of Montague's work in philosophical logic consisted in bringing the resources of possible worlds semantics to bear on metaphysical and logical problems. He pioneered the idea of generalizing possible worlds semantics to include tense logic and the logic of demonstratives, in which an expression is evaluated for truth not just at a possible world, but at an index consisting of a world, a time, a location, an addressee, and so on. He called this general framework 'pragmatics'. Constraining the indices in various ways yields traditional logics: limiting them to times alone yields traditional tense logic, limiting them to possible worlds alone yields traditional modal logic, and taking them without limitation yields a general kind of logic in which one may capture the interrelations, for example, of tense, modality and demonstratives. As part of this enterprise he studied different ways of formulating nonextensional notions, examining the connections between languages in which modal notions are captured by modal operators and languages in which these same notions are captured by explicit characterization of propositions. In the former, the sentence 'Necessarily, snow is white' has the form '$\square$(Snow is white)'; in the latter it has the form '$\exists p(p =$ that-snow-is-white & p is necessary)'.

Montague espoused the metaphysical reduction of problematic philosophical entities to constructions out of the metaphysical ingredients needed for possible worlds semantics. He assumes that properties are functions that map worlds to sets of entities, mapping each world to the set of entities that have the property in that world. He suggests that pains may be reduced to relations between persons and moments of time, that events may be reduced to properties of moments (or intervals) of time, and so forth. These reductions are to be justified by their logical fruit; for example, we can analyse 'an event of Caesar's running happened at t' as 'the property of being a time at which Caesar runs is possessed by t'. He extends this idea to mass terms – holding, for example, that 'water' denotes the property of being a body of water.

Montague's most influential work lies in the semantics of natural language. In 'Universal Grammar' (1970), he formulated a quite abstract, general framework for semantics, and in 'English as a Formal Language' (1970) and 'The Proper Treatment of Quantification in Ordinary English' (1973), he gave particular semantical systems that represent fragments of English.

'Proper Treatment of Quantification' contains the suggestion, contra Russell, that denoting phrases do have meanings of their own, but that they stand not for individuals but for intensions of sets of properties of individuals. An intension of this sort is a function that picks out from each possible world a set of properties, not necessarily the same set in every world. For example, 'no giraffe' stands for the function that maps each world to the set that contains each property of individuals that is not possessed by any giraffe in that world; then, 'No giraffe runs' is true in a world w just if the property of running is in the set to which that function maps w.

He used this idea to address the 'opaque' readings of transitive verbs, such as 'seek', which may take as objects terms which do not have an actual referent. Simplifying somewhat, the denotation of 'seek' (on this reading) is a relation between individuals (the seekers) and intensions of sets of properties, the sorts of intensions that will be denoted by a direct object of the verb 'seek'. With no additional constraints, this permits 'seek a unicorn' to be true of individuals who 'seek unicorns' without there actually being any unicorns; the seekers of unicorns in a world w are those individuals who are appropriately related (in w) to the intension that in every possible world picks out the set of properties possessed by some unicorn in that world. (The appropriate relation is not further defined; it is to be given by our understanding of the meaning of 'seek'.) An ordinary nonopaque verb has the same kind of logical form, but special principles (called 'meaning postulates') reinstate traditional inferences for them. For example, let *find** be the denotation of 'find', so that *find** is a relation between individuals (the finders) and intensions of sets of properties. Then a meaning postulate for the verb 'find' would be:

There is an ordinary relation, *find*, between individuals such that necessarily *find** relates (in world w) an individual i to an intension P of a set of properties just if the property of being a thing such that i *finds* it is a member of the set that P picks out in world w.

It is a consequence of this postulate that if you find a unicorn, then there is a unicorn that you find, but this consequence will not follow without the meaning postulate. Since there is no similar meaning postulate for 'seek', you may seek a unicorn without there being a unicorn that you seek.

These essays, particularly 'Proper Treatment of Quantification', led to a tradition dubbed 'Montague Grammar', in which one studies natural language by giving a rigorous semantics for a formal system that resembles a fragment of a natural language; much fruitful work has been pursued within this tradition, often based on some version of the 'pragmatic' model theory discussed above. This has been an influential element in the development of semantical work by theoretical linguists, as well as the popularity among philosophers and linguists of appealing to possible worlds in informal semantical accounts.

See also: INTENSIONAL LOGICS; MODAL LOGIC; MODAL LOGIC, PHILOSOPHICAL ISSUES IN; MODAL OPERATORS; POSSIBLE WORLDS; SEMANTICS, POSSIBLE WORLDS

List of works

Montague, R.M. (1974) *Formal Philosophy: Selected Papers of Richard Montague*, ed. R.H. Thomason, New Haven, CT, and London: Yale University Press. (Contains most of Montague's influential writings in philosophy and semantics. Formidable reading for the layman.)

—— (1970) 'Universal Grammar', *Theoria* 36: 373–98. (Formulates a quite abstract, general framework for semantics.)

—— (1970) 'English as a Formal Language', in R. Thomason (ed.) *Formal Philosophy: Selected Papers of Richard Montague*, New Haven, CT, and London: Yale University Press, 188–221. (Develops a formal semantics for significant fragments of a natural language.)

—— (1973) 'The Proper Treatment of Quantification in Ordinary English', in R. Thomason (ed.) *Formal Philosophy: Selected Papers of Richard Montague*, New Haven, CT, and London: Yale University Press, 1974, 247–70. (Also known as 'PTQ'. Develops a formal semantics for significant fragments of a natural language.)

Hintikka, J., Moravcsik, J. and Suppes, P. (eds) (1973) *Approaches to Natural Language*, Dordrecht: Reidel. (Contains Montague's only work on mass terms as well as comments by others on the proper treatment of quantification.)

References and further reading

Partee, B. (1989) *Possible Worlds in Model-Theoretic Semantics: A Linguistic Perspective*, in S. Allen (ed.) *Possible Worlds in Humanities, Arts, and Sciences: Nobel Symposium 65*, Berlin and New York: de Gruyter. (Sketches the fruit of Montague's ideas in linguistic semantics and contains useful references.)

TERENCE PARSONS

MONTAIGNE, MICHEL EYQUEM DE (1533–92)

Montaigne was a sixteenth-century French philosopher and essayist, who became known as the French Socrates. During the religious wars between the Catholics and the Protestants in France, he was a friend and adviser to leaders of both sides, including the Protestant leader Henri de Navarre, who converted to Catholicism and became King Henri IV. Montaigne counselled general toleration for all believers, a view promulgated by the new king in the Edict of Nantes (1598). His main literary work was in the form of essais *(a word originally meaning 'attempts'), or discussions of various subjects. In these he developed various themes from the sceptical and Stoic literature of antiquity, and in his unique digressive way presented the first full statement in modern times of Pyrrhonian scepticism and cultural relativism. In particular, he presented and modernized the ancient sceptical arguments about the unreliability of information gained by the senses or by reason, about the inability of human beings to find a satisfactory criterion of knowledge, and about the relativity of moral opinions. His advocacy of complete scepticism and relativism was coupled with an appeal to accept religion on the basis of faith alone. His writings became extremely popular, and the English translation by John Florio, first published in 1603, was probably known to Shakespeare and Francis Bacon. Montaigne, whose essays provided the basic vocabulary for modern philosophy written in vernacular languages, was one of the most influential thinkers of the Renaissance, and his works are regarded as classics of literature and philosophy.*

1 Life
2 Scepticism and fideism
3 Philosophical scepticism
4 Influence

1 Life

Michel Eyquem de Montaigne was born into a very well-to-do family. His father, Pierre Eyquem, was a Catholic merchant and his mother, Antoinette de Louppes, came from an important Jewish family which had fled to southern France from Spain towards the end of the fifteenth century. Montaigne studied at the Collège de Guyenne in Bordeaux, an elite institution that had been recently set up by Portuguese New Christian refugees (that is, Jewish converts to Christianity) to educate the new middle-class students in the city. (Montaigne's distant cousin, Francisco SANCHES, the physician and sceptical philosopher, attended the same school, but not at the same time.) The teaching staff included the Scottish poet and theological leader, George Buchanan, and some of the leading Portuguese humanistic scholars of the period who had studied at the University of Paris. After being educated at the Collège, Montaigne may also have studied briefly at the University of Toulouse (where Sanches became a famous professor). Montaigne studied law, and became a magistrate and a counsellor to the *parlement* of Bordeaux. After a lengthy retreat from public life, followed by a period of travel to Switzerland, Germany and Italy, described in his *Journal de Voyage*, he was Mayor of Bordeaux from 1581–5. During the religious wars which divided France for a good part of the sixteenth century, Montaigne was a friend of many of the leading personalities of the Reformation and the Counter-Reformation in France, including Henri de Navarre, the Protestant leader who became the Catholic King Henri IV.

Montaigne's first work was a letter portraying the death in 1563 of his very close friend, Etienne la Boétie, who had written against slavery and for toleration, views Montaigne continued advocating after his friend's death. In 1569 he published a translation of the *Theologia Naturalis sive Liber Creaturarum* (Natural Theology or Book of Creatures), a treatise by the Spanish theologian Raymond Sebond (Ramon Sibiuda, d. 1436), who had taught at the University of Toulouse, and who claimed that almost all of the Christian dogmas could be proved by rational means. Montaigne's father, who thought highly of the work, had requested that his son undertake this task. It was during his period of retreat from public life (1571–80) that Montaigne began writing on a variety of subjects. He presented his ideas in the form of *Essais*, and he was one of the first persons to introduce this literary style of expression. He was also one of the very first thinkers to write on philosophical subjects in French rather than in Latin, the standard language for philosophy and theology for centuries. In so doing, Montaigne had to create a philosophical vocabulary in French. His essays are usually very digressive, starting with a quotation, or a thought, and rambling on in different directions to related subjects. The first version of his *Essais* was published in 1580, and he added to and revised them in later editions. The final and most complete edition appeared posthumously in 1595.

2 Scepticism and fideism

Montaigne's philosophy has to be gleaned from various of the essays, for he was not a systematic thinker who presented his views in didactic form. His

longest essay by far, the 'Apology for Raymond Sebond' of which large parts were written 1575–6, is the most extended treatment of his philosophy. It was composed shortly after Montaigne had read the works of the ancient Greek sceptic, SEXTUS EMPIRICUS, whose writings had been published in Latin in 1562 and 1569. At the same time he was undergoing a personal sceptical crisis, in which he found that everything he had previously believed was in doubt. Montaigne carved mottoes from Sextus' text in the rafter beams of his study, so that if he was attacked by any dogmatic thoughts, he could lean back and regain his sceptical outlook by looking at the ceiling.

The 'Apology' begins by saying that many readers, especially women, had asked Montaigne to explain and defend Sebond's views in the face of criticisms levelled against them. Montaigne then offered as the defence of Sebond that one cannot expect his reasons to be convincing when nobody else's reasons are defensible, and when nobody is able to achieve certainty through reasoning. In order to show this, Montaigne then proceeded to develop in a gradual manner the many kinds of problem that make people doubt the reliability of human reason. He pointed out that human beings believe that they are able to understand the cosmos without the aid of Divine Light, and that they alone of the creatures on the planet can comprehend the world which they think was made for their own benefit. But if human beings are compared with the animals, it is obvious that they have no special faculties that are lacking among the animals. The vaunted rationality of the human being is just a form of animal behaviour. To show this, Montaigne cited materials from Sextus Empiricus, including the story (attributed to Chrysippus) of the dog who is supposed to have worked out a disjunctive syllogism. Montaigne further contended that even religion appears in animals as well as people, citing evidence that elephants seem to pray.

The comparison of animal abilities to those of humans presumably creates doubt about human intellectual pretensions. Montaigne contrasted the glories of the animal kingdom with the vain, stupid, immoral activities of human beings. Our so-called knowledge has not helped us to create a better world or to solve our problems. In spite of all our learning we are ruled by bodily demands and passions. What we consider our wisdom is just presumption which achieves nothing for us. 'The plague of man is the opinion of knowledge. That is why ignorance is so recommended by our religion as a quality suitable to belief and obedience' ([1563–92] 1957: 360). Wisdom has never actually helped anyone. On the other hand, the recently discovered natives of Brazil, the noble savages, manage to live in admirable simplicity, uneducated, with neither laws nor kings nor religion. Each society's laws are just the product of customs, with no genuine basis in reason. People are Christians in France and Muslims in Turkey by the accident of where they were born. So, according to Montaigne, one should take seriously the Christian message that we should cultivate complete ignorance and believe by faith alone. 'The participation that we have in the knowledge of truth, whatever it may be, has not been acquired by our own powers. God has taught us ... his admirable secrets. Our faith is not of our acquiring, it is a pure present of another's liberality' ([1563–92] 1957: 369). Montaigne then quoted St Paul (I Corinthians 1) to the effect that God 'will destroy the wisdom of the wise, and bring to nothing the understanding of the prudent', and will save those who believe 'by the foolishness of preaching'.

After this introduction to scepticism and advocacy of complete fideism, Montaigne turned to the arguments from Sextus Empiricus about Pyrrhonian scepticism, and explained their value for religion. The Pyrrhonists, he insisted, are not negative dogmatists like the Academic sceptics. The Pyrrhonists suspend judgment about all propositions or assertions, even the one that says all is subject to doubt. They oppose all knowledge claims, and if their opposition has merit, it shows the ignorance of the opponent. Alternatively, if it has no merit, then it shows the ignorance of the Pyrrhonists. In either case, human ignorance must be acknowledged. Once the state of complete doubt is reached, these sceptics then live according to nature and custom. This state is the finest human achievement, and is the one that is most compatible with religion, for the human being becomes 'a blank tablet prepared to take from the finger of God such forms as he shall be pleased to engrave on it' ([1563–92] 1957: 375) (see PYRRHONISM).

These ancient sceptics had not only reached the summit of human wisdom, they also unknowingly provided a defence for Catholicism against the Reformation. If a person has no positive views, they cannot have wrong views. The sceptics, accepting the laws and customs of their society, would naturally accept Catholicism (as the customary religion of sixteenth-century France), and would have no reason for changing their faith. Moreover, the complete sceptic is in the perfect state to receive whatever revelation God cares to give.

3 Philosophical scepticism

Montaigne contrasted his monumental picture of Pyrrhonism with the deplorable history of dogmatic philosophers whose endless disputes and heterodox views exhibit nothing but human stupidity and credulity. In the best tradition of Renaissance humanists, Montaigne cited the vast range of opinions of ancient thinkers from Greece and Rome that had recently been discovered (see HUMANISM, RENAISSANCE §1). In view of the enormous diversity of points of view, can one really determine what to believe or to accept as true? In all fields of inquiry the dogmatists have finally had to confess their ignorance, and their inability to come to definitive and unquestionable conclusions. Indeed, even the Pyrrhonists have fallen into the trap of asserting that they doubt, when what they need is a negative non-assertive language. It is better to question, and ask 'What do I know?' ('Que sçay-je?'), a phrase that Montaigne adopted as his motto (see SCEPTICISM, RENAISSANCE §5).

After surveying all kinds of philosophy, from ancient times to the present, Montaigne concluded that 'philosophy is but sophisticated poetry' ([1563–92] 1957: 401). He also used the information presented by explorers ancient and modern concerning the great variety of customs and behaviour in different parts of the planet in order to raise the question of whether there was any way of determining right or true standards, or whether one had to recognize that customs and behaviour just are relative to the cultures in which they occur.

Science fared no better than philosophy and morality. What thinkers have been offering through their theories are just human inventions, and philosophers never find out what actually happens in nature. What occurs is that some traditional opinions have been taken as authoritative, indubitable principles. Questioners are told that one cannot dispute with people who deny first principles, but, Montaigne observed, 'there cannot be first principles for men, unless the Divinity has revealed them; all the rest – beginning, middle, and end – is nothing but dreams and smoke' ([1563–92] 1957: 404). Even the new scientists of the Renaissance such as COPERNICUS or PARACELSUS are just offering personal opinions that will probably be replaced by other people's opinions at some future time.

Having built up a general sense of why one should be a sceptic, Montaigne finally turned to the fundamental philosophical reasons for accepting the Pyrrhonian view that all is in doubt. These concern the unreliability of information gained by the senses or by reason, and the inability of human beings to find a satisfactory criterion of knowledge. Montaigne argued that if the dogmatists claim that human reason can know and understand things, they should show how in fact this occurs. If the claim is that sense experience provides this knowledge and understanding, the dogmatists should make clear what it is that we actually experience and whether we do in fact experience the very things that we think we experience. In fact, the senses are clearly subject to illusion, and we ourselves are constantly changing as our physical and emotional conditions alter. Once it becomes clear that the senses are full of uncertainty, the dogmatists will appeal to reason, but 'no reason can be established without another reason'. The dogmatists will have to provide a criterion of right reasoning, and a criterion of the criterion, and so on *ad infinitum*.

Montaigne suggested that people should suspend judgment on all matters, and then wait until God reveals principles to them. Until then, he said, one should just follow customs, traditions and social rules undogmatically, and one should be tolerant of other people's views. Religious beliefs should be based solely on faith rather than on dubious evidence (see FAITH §§4–5).

4 Influence

Montaigne's rambling presentation of Pyrrhonian scepticism quickly became the best known and most influential statement of this view. Francis BACON, DESCARTES, and PASCAL, among other readers, were greatly influenced by him. His pleasant literary presentation of the sceptical attitude as well as the arguments behind it effectively provided many with a basis for rejecting the entire intellectual world of the time. He also provided reasons for accepting the status quo: his advocacy of accepting customary views because there was no adequate reason to change them became a defence of Catholicism against the Reformation during the seventeenth century in France. Leading churchmen, such as Bishop Jean-Pierre Camus, the secretary of St François de Sales, and Father François Veron, the official defender of the faith under Louis XIV, employed sceptical arguments as 'a machine of war' to defeat the intellectual claims of the Calvinists. On the other hand, Montaigne's leading disciples, Pierre CHARRON, Marie de Gournay, and François de La Mothe Le Vayer, are usually treated as being *libertins érudits*, possible secret non-believers in any form of Christianity, whose scepticism prefigured that of the Enlightenment, and who were really trying to undermine religion.

The question of what Montaigne himself actually believed has been debated for the last four centuries with some interpreters insisting that he was trying to undermine all belief, including any religious belief, and other readers insisting that he was a genuine Christian believer who was offering a sceptical defence of Catholicism in the age of the Counter-Reformation.

he lived, and we have conflicting testimonies from his friends and from early readers. We know that Montaigne came from a family whose views encompassed the main religious beliefs of the time. His mother was half Jewish, and it has been suggested by Donald Frame that his tolerant, cosmopolitan, humanistic attitude may in part have been derived from his Jewish heritage (Frame 1965: 28). His father was a Catholic, and he had Protestant siblings. He was related to leading Calvinists in Belgium as well as to some important Catholics in France. He reported in his *Journal de Voyage* that when he visited Rome the Catholic censors seemed quite pleased when they read the manuscript of the first draft of the *Essais*. At the time they actually invited the author to stay in Rome and to 'assist the Church with [his] eloquence'. (The *Essais* were put on the Index late in the seventeenth century, principally because of Montaigne's suggestion that elephants engage in prayer.) Montaigne turned down the invitation, preferring retirement at his chateau near Bordeaux where he could gently muse about the human comedy, and discuss it in his many essays. He said at one point that in the essays 'I paint myself'.

What kind of a self was thereby indicated? Commentators have offered all sorts of readings. Without going into details about these many kinds of interpretations, it can be said that the sceptical fideism that is offered in the 'Apology for Raymond Sebond' is compatible with both a religious and an irreligious evaluation of the author's intentions, as either defending or undermining Christian belief. Essentially Montaigne's avowed fideism rests upon a *non sequitur*, namely that since all is in doubt, we should therefore accept Christianity on faith alone. This has been said by extremely religious persons like Pascal and Kierkegaard. And it has been said, presumably ironically, by agnostic or irreligious thinkers like Hume. In evaluating people who make this fideistic assertion we usually appeal to other information about their character and their activities in order to ascertain whether or not they are being sincere. Montaigne does not appear to have been particularly devout or fervent in his religious life, and his own acceptance of Catholicism seems tepid. He was generally interested in the variety of religious experience, ancient and modern, but he appears to have been indifferent to the major spiritual tendencies of his day, and was much more concerned with creating a peaceful social world in which all people could believe and practice what they wished. He was active in trying to bring about toleration of different religious practices and views, and he opposed and ridiculed different kinds of religious fanaticism and superstition. Pascal, who was very much influenced by reading Montaigne's *Essais*, considered him a sceptical non-believer who exhibited the misery of man without God. However, Montaigne himself said that to philosophize is to learn to die, and his sceptical outlook may have prepared him to live undogmatically in a troubled world, and to accept whatever might come afterwards.

See also: HUMANISM, RENAISSANCE; POLITICAL PHILOSOPHY, HISTORY OF §7; SCEPTICISM, RENAISSANCE

List of works

Montaigne, M. de (1563–92) *Oeuvres complètes* (Complete Works), ed. A. Thibaudet and M. Rat, Paris: Bibliothèque de la Pléiade, 1962. (Standard edition of Montaigne in French.)
—— (1563–92) *The Complete Works of Montaigne*, trans. D.M. Frame, Stanford: Stanford University Press, 1957. (Includes Montaigne's letters, as well as the *Essais* and *Journal de Voyage*; contains an annotated bibliography and fine introduction.)

References and further reading

Boase, A.M. (1935) *The Fortunes of Montaigne: A History of the Essays in France, 1580–1669*, London: Methuen. (A study of the impact and influence of Montaigne's writings.)
Brush, C.B. (1966) *Montaigne and Bayle. Variations on the Theme of Skepticism*, The Hague: Martinus Nijhoff. (A study and comparison of two important sceptics.)
Busson, H. (1957) *Le rationalisme dans la littérature française de la Renaissance (1533–1601)* (Rationalism in French Literature of the Renaissance), Paris: Vrin. (An interpretation of Montaigne as a freethinker, and a participant in rationalist irreligious currents.)
Dréano, M. (1936) *La pensée religieuse de Montaigne* (Montaigne's Religious Thought), Paris: Beauchesne; revised edn, *La religion de Montaigne*, Paris: Nizet, 1969. (Portrays Montaigne as a sincerely religious thinker.)
Frame, D.M. (1955) *Montaigne's Discovery of Man. The Humanization of a Humanist*, New York: Columbia University Press. (A study of the development of Montaigne's thought.)
* —— (1965) *Montaigne: A Biography*, New York: Harcourt Brace. (Biography by leading Montaigne scholar.)
Hallie, P.C. (1966) *The Scar of Montaigne, an Essay in Personal Philosophy*, Middleton, CT: Wesleyan University Press. (Important interpretation of Montaigne's philosophy.)
Laursen, J.C. (1992) *The Politics of Skepticism in the Ancients, Montaigne, Hume and Kant*, Leiden, New York and Cologne: Brill. (Tries to connect Montaigne's scepticism with his political actions.)
Malvezin, T. (1875) *Michel de Montaigne, son origine, sa famille* (His Origins and his Family), Bordeaux: Lefebvre. (Deals with Montaigne's family background and his milieu.)
Popkin, R.H. (1979) *The History of Scepticism from Erasmus to Spinoza*, Berkeley, CA: University of California Press. (Places Montaigne in the course of Renaissance scepticism.)
Schiffman, Z.S. (1984) 'Montaigne and the Rise of Skepticism in Early Modern Europe: A Reappraisal', *Journal of the History of Ideas* 45: 499–516. (Attempts to trace Montaigne's scepticism to his early education before he came in contact with Pyrrhonian scepticism.)
Shaefer, D.L. (1990) *The Political Philosophy of Montaigne*, Ithaca, NY, and London: Cornell University Press. (Argues that Montaigne is best understood from the perspective of political philosophy and that he anticipates classical political liberalism.)
Villey, P. (1908) *Les sources et l'évolution des Essais de Montaigne* (The Sources and Development of Montaigne's *Essais*), Paris: Hachette. (The basic study of the sources used by Montaigne, showing how they were employed in the development of the *Essais*.)

RICHARD H. POPKIN

MONTESQUIEU, CHARLES LOUIS DE SECONDAT (1689–1755)

Montesquieu, one of the greatest figures of the Enlightenment, was famous in his own century both in France and in foreign lands, from Russia to the American colonies. Later generations of French philo-philosophes took for granted his concern to reform the criminal laws, to replace the Inquisition with a reign of tolerance, and to repudiate the vicious conquests of the Spaniards in the Americas. They also accepted his finding that Protestant, commercial, and constitutionalist England and Holland represented all the best possibilities of Europe; whereas Catholic, economically backward, and politically absolutist Portugal and Spain represented the worst of the Western world and constituted a warning to the French.

Although the findings and specific reforms proposed by Montesquieu were repeated by many another figure of the French Enlightenment, his work in certain respects remained unique in the circles of the most advanced thinkers. In his efforts to think systematically about politics and to do so by employing the comparative method, he stands virtually alone in his age. Other thinkers sharing his commitments resorted to the universalizing language of natural rights when they ventured into the realm of political philosophy. Or, like Voltaire, they tied their thoughts about politics to a succession of specific issues, each essay bearing so indelibly the imprint of specific time and place that there was no room for theory in their writings. Finally, as is true of Diderot or D'Alembert, many of the philosophes *were slow to recognize what Montesquieu knew from the outset, that if Enlightenment does not extend to politics it is futile.*

Steeped in Montaigne's scepticism, Montesquieu found that in the absence of absolutes there were good reasons to appreciate the 'more than/less than' and 'better than/worse than' judgments of comparative analysis. In his notebooks he commented that the flaw of most philosophers had been to ignore that the terms beautiful, good, noble, grand, and perfect are 'relative to the beings who use them'. Only one absolute existed for Montesquieu and that was the evil of despotism, which must be avoided at all costs.

Montesquieu wrote three great works, each teaching lessons about despotism and freedom, The Persian Letters *(1721), the* Considerations of the Grandeur of the Romans and the Cause of Their Decline *(1734), and* The Spirit of the Laws *(1748).*

1 *The Persian Letters*
2 **The** *Romans*
3 *The Spirit of the Laws*
4 **Legacy and reputation**

1 *The Persian Letters*

A year before his death Montesquieu wrote a new preface to *The Persian Letters* (first published in 1721). Looking back, he recommended that the letters be read not individually but in their interconnections, since they are held together by a 'chain'. The letters form 'a kind of novel'; they tell a story and that story is the meaning of the book. Hence he repeatedly refused requests to add new letters, because more letters would signify less meaning.

As the story begins we learn that Usbek, a Persian, is travelling in the West with his countrymen Rica and Rhedi. The letters we read are exchanges among these tourists or between them and the persons they have left behind; many of the letters are the correspondence of Usbek with his wives or with the eunuchs who govern the household in his name during his absence. Between the first letter and the last, some nine years pass, during which the Persians learn much about Europe. The more they understand a foreign culture, the more they gain insight into their own as well. One cannot imagine a more entertaining or convincing argument for the comparative method than that which Montesquieu sets forth by example in *The Persian Letters*.

As Montesquieu indicated in 1754, his strategy was to portray the 'genesis and development' of the ideas of the Persians. Initially the Oriental visitors comprehend little of what they observe, so their earliest commentaries afford Montesquieu ample opportunity to satirize Western ways, as when Rica naïvely writes that the Pope is a magician who has the king believing that three are one and that bread is not bread, wine not wine. Eventually the Persians become so familiar with Western mores, customs, science and philosophy that the 'otherness' of Europe fades into their pasts. At the same time, however, their native Persia seems ever more foreign and even hideous from the standpoint of their transformed beliefs. When he first stepped foot on European soil in Italy Usbek sensed, 'even in the most insignificant of details, something that I feel and cannot express'. Later he and his comrades come to realize that it is freedom they have encountered in their new environment, and that for them to utter the word 'freedom' in reference to the West is inevitably to speak of 'despotism' when designating their own country.

Virtually alone in his circle, Montesquieu recognized that to hold enlightened beliefs is not necessarily to be a tolerant person. Who could be more of a *philosophe* than Usbek, author of the most intellectually sophisticated of the Persian letters? And who could have better intentions than this same Usbek who dared to carry truth to the court of the Persian king, in consequence of which his days would have been numbered had he not found an excuse to visit foreign countries? Yet Usbek, after writing a series of letters diagnosing the malady of Oriental despotism, turns around and demands that his eunuchs initiate a reign of terror against his wives.

Jealousy is Usbek's undoing, a jealousy that must not be mistaken for the reverse side of love, because, as Usbek admits in an unguarded moment, he is incapable of loving his wives. In Persia women are the property of men; and although a man may fear losing his woman, exactly as he is disturbed by the loss of any of his prized possessions, it is impossible for him to love a creature who by the very nature of the mores and laws is not fully a human being. Near the end of the novel Usbek, provoked to hear of growing disorder in his seraglio, decides to return to Persia in order to reclaim his possessions, and in the meantime he deputizes the chief eunuch to rule his wives by fear and terror.

Far from an island of peace and contentment, the Persian family is a replication in miniature of the most insidious characteristics of the surrounding society and polity. Where Oriental despotism reigns, the family, too, is despotic. It is the curse of arbitrary power that it infects all human relationships, affairs of the heart no less than affairs of state.

Self-deception is a recurring theme in the novel. Usbek has come to know Oriental despotism for what it is, but he lacks the strength to apply the lessons he has learned to his personal relations. The wives are even more determined to avoid the truth. Slaves by the laws of their country, they prefer to regard themselves as enslaved by their love of Usbek. Only the eunuchs stand outside the web of self-deception; they, in order to feel less diminished by castration, dominate the women by self-consciously manipulating oppressive Persian notions of virtue.

The story ends with the suicide of Roxane, the one woman who mattered to Usbek. By holding herself aloof and refusing to be treated as property, she aroused Usbek's ardour. During his absence Roxane avenges herself by taking a lover and dies by her own hand rather than submit to Usbek's despotic rule. Her act proves a truth Usbek himself had enunciated, that under despotism everyone loses, the despot as well as his long-suffering subjects. It was Usbek who proclaimed that systematic injustice is self-destructive, little realizing that he would one day demonstrate his point at his own expense.

2 The *Romans*

Montesquieu's monograph on the Romans, *Considerations of the Grandeur of the Romans and the Cause of Their Decline* (1734), usually figures in modern scholarship as a warming up exercise for the causal reasoning found in his magnum opus, *The Spirit of the Laws* (1748). Such an interpretation is not incorrect but it is wanting in so far as it permits his third book to define the meaning of his second, as if his *Considerations on the Romans* had no significance in its own right. One might do better to see his second major publication as a variation on the theme of his first book. Previously he had argued that because of its internal injustice Oriental despotism is inherently self-destructive. Now he adds that the ancient Roman republic, though sometimes reasonably just internally, destroyed itself through the unrelenting external injustice of its foreign policy.

Montesquieu's Romans knew 'not even the justice of brigands'. After inflicting military defeat upon a prince, they exacted excessive war reparations that left him with no choice but to collect exorbitant taxes – 'a new kind of tyranny that forced the prince to oppress his subjects and lose their love'. Similarly, the Romans destroyed Carthage, 'saying they had promised to save the people but not the city itself'. Whenever possible the Romans fostered factional strife so as to weaken and eventually conquer foreign cities. 'If princes of the same blood were disputing the crown, the Romans sometimes declared them both kings. If one of them was under age, they decided in his favour'. A city that lost its battle with Rome inevitably found itself compelled to fight with Rome to subdue another people, after which the Romans stripped their erstwhile allies of their remaining freedoms. These practices of the Romans were 'in no way just particular actions occurring by chance; these were ever-constant principles'.

If nothing could sound more Machiavellian than Montesquieu's Romans, that is because his account of ancient history is taken directly from the great Florentine's *Discourses on Livy* (see MACHIAVELLI, N.). Why not follow the lead of Machiavelli in turning the Roman senators into the most Machiavellian of ruling classes if to do so is the best way to discredit power-politics? Each Roman conquest, Montesquieu insisted, brought Rome that much closer to the day when the republic would perish, and Rome would begin to terrorize itself in much the same manner as it had long terrorized other city-states.

The more Rome expanded, the less it could sustain the integrity of its republican way of life. Civic mindedness yielded to civic neglect; private pursuits replaced public concerns. Frugality gave way to luxury and ostentation when returning soldiers carried plunder and foreign mores back to Rome. Removed from Rome for ever longer campaigns, soldiers no longer identified with their city but rather with their commander who offered them riches in return for their assistance in elevating him to political power.

Faced with evidence that the ruthlessness of the senators had added the name of Rome itself to the list of republics undone by Roman imperialism, Machiavelli hastened to place the blame on *fortuna*, which eventually undoes even the best laid plans. Montesquieu countered by denying that chance had anything to do with the demise of the republic. What was at work, he insisted, was nothing less than the operation of causal necessity. Any republic which grows beyond a certain point necessarily undermines its civic culture. Since the republic had to perish, it was only a question of how, and by whom, it was to be overthrown.

> It is not chance that rules the world... There are general causes, moral and physical, which act in every [regime], elevating it, maintaining it, or hurling it to the ground.
>
> (*Considerations on the Romans*, chaps 11, 18)

Montesquieu's objective in the *Considerations* was to set forth a causal argument that eliminated not just *fortuna* from historical explanation but Providence as well. Bishop Bossuet had preceded Montesquieu both in accepting Machiavelli's reading of Roman history and also in drawing the conclusion that the Roman republic destroyed itself by the systematic injustice of its foreign policy. Dedicated to vindicating the Christian view of history, Bossuet in the *Discourse on Universal History* (1681) deliberately set out to expunge pagan *fortuna* from the historical record. To that end he announced that 'the true science of history' was one in which the investigator identified the underlying causes which account for the revolutions of empires. Those causes turn out to be much the same as the ones cited later by Montesquieu, especially the decline of civic life and the demise of the large, frugal, agrarian middle class which, as Aristotle noted, was the backbone of a popular republic.

When Montesquieu approached Roman history he found that Bossuet had prepared the way for his *Considerations*. Specifically, the good bishop had driven *fortuna* off the historical stage and effectively pleaded the case for causal reasoning. All Montesquieu had to do to arrive at a historical science fit for the Enlightenment was to bracket off Providence as an unnecessary hypothesis, and with that act he had moved to a stage of thought which was both post-pagan and post-Christian.

3   The Spirit of the Laws

The centrepiece of Montesquieu's most comprehensive and systematic treatise is its typology of socio-political forms. Monarchy in politics is matched in society by an ethos revolving around the 'principle' of aristocratic honour; Oriental despotism is characterized by the principle of fear; and the ancient republic was enlivened by civic virtue.

By 'monarchy' Montesquieu understands feudal government in its final incarnation during the Old Regime. Absolute in theory, the power of the king is thwarted in fact by 'intermediary bodies' – the first and second estates (clerics and nobles) and the *parlements*, which were judicial institutions, not legislative bodies. Corporate and hierarchical, the social order is so thoroughly under the sway of the privileged estates that the members of the middle class, far from challenging the aristocrats, want nothing more than to amass enough wealth to buy a noble title and to pay someone – as did Molière's bourgeois gentleman – to teach them how to put on aristocratic airs.

VOLTAIRE believed that *The Spirit of the Laws* was in reality nothing more than an apology for the privileged classes to which Montesquieu, a noble and former member of the Bordeaux *parlement*, belonged. The ancient republic was something lost and gone forever, and Oriental despotism was not only the worst of all possible worlds but a constant reminder that to remove the intermediary bodies from a monarchy is to invite disaster. Hence, Voltaire concluded, Montesquieu was a formidable apologist for all the abuses of the Old Regime. If Montesquieu championed the English example, Voltaire assumed the hidden agenda was to suggest that power be taken away from the French monarch and turned over to nobles seated in a legislature.

Modern historians, Marxists and all those who wish for a ready-made link between social and intellectual history, have repeated Voltaire's charges. It is therefore crucial to note that other *philosophes* refused to follow Voltaire's lead, and to ask why. The best place to begin our reexamination of *The Spirit of the Laws* is with the recognition that, in its pages, England figures not only as the most free country in the world but also as the only monarchy that no longer possesses intermediary bodies, whereas Spain is portrayed both as the nation in which the intermediary bodies could not be more powerful and as a country plagued by a peculiarly Western variety of despotism.

'Abolish the privileges of the lords, the clergy, and cities in a monarchy', wrote Montesquieu, 'and you will soon have a popular state, or else a despotic government'. Although in despotism Montesquieu found nothing but evil, he did have considerable sympathy for the popular state that had emerged from the ashes of a feudal past. 'The English, to favour their liberty, have abolished all the intermediate powers of which their monarchy was composed.' During the upheavals of the seventeenth century, the remnants of feudalism perished in England, with the consequence that in Montesquieu's day the English had a monarch but no Old Regime. England was the first new nation.

Call England a monarchy and Montesquieu will not object, for such it once was and such it still is on the surface. But on a closer look England is much better described as a 'republic hiding under the form of a monarchy'. Unlike the republics of antiquity, but like Holland across the Channel, England is a commercial republic. Politically, however, there is a significant difference between Holland and England: the Dutch live in a confederate republic, the English in a centralized republic.

As a result of purging the feudal 'intermediary bodies' England is, at one and the same time, the most free country and the one in which freedom is in greatest danger of declining into its opposite. No sooner has Montesquieu applauded English liberty than he issues a stern warning: the English 'have a great deal of reason to be jealous of this liberty; were they ever to be so unhappy as to lose it, they would be one of the most servile nations upon earth'. Under the conditions of a post-feudal world, where power is centralized as never before, only a 'system' of liberty will suffice, a constitutional structure wherein there is a sharp separation of legislative, executive and judicial functions. In the famous Book XI, chapter 6, Montesquieu outlines his proposal for a system of freedom and deems it especially appropriate for the British; in Book XIX, chapter 27, he makes it clear that the spoils system (of Robert Walpole) is what actually exists in England.

Whatever his misgivings about England and Holland, Montesquieu was convinced that they were not only the most free but also the most powerful nations. Each age, he remarked in his notebooks, has its spirit, and the spirit of the modern age is that of commerce. Conquests weaken the conqueror, trade strengthens the most economically progressive nations. Both Holland and England are small; neither has much of a standing army; and yet these two commercial nations may well be the most formidable powers of Europe.

Altogether different is the situation of once proud Spain. Fields lie uncultivated, trade is nonexistent, and the Spaniards sit by idly while 'the rest of the European nations carry on in their very sight all the commerce of their monarchy'. It is the very power of the 'intermediary bodies', the nobility and the clergy, that accounts for the increasing powerlessness of the nation which in early modern history had been the leading country in Europe. The Church does nothing with its ever growing holdings of land, nor do the nobles produce anything since the aristocratic code of honour forbids titled persons to engage in commercial activity.

Enrichment through plunder, conquest, and murder is 'honourable'; indeed, it is holy as well when combined with forcible baptism. Thus the Church blessed the bloody conquests of greedy and cruel Spanish nobles in the Americas, as did the state which, following a mercantilist policy, was only too happy with the mounds of gold the conquistadores

shipped back to the old world. Which is to say, the Spaniards mistook a symbol of wealth for wealth itself. As the quantity of gold in the king's coffers piled up, the value of gold declined: 'Spain behaved like the foolish king who desired that everything he touched might be converted into gold, and who was obliged to beg of the gods to put an end to his misery' (*The Spirit of the Laws*, XXI, ch. 22). Well in advance of Adam SMITH, Montesquieu declared that the wealth of nations depended on the production of goods and services.

A regressive economy was one consequence of the influence of Spain's powerful intermediary bodies; the Inquisition was another. That the French government might well follow Spain in permitting the Catholic Church to dictate oppressive public policies, even at the cost of undermining the power of the state, was indicated, Montesquieu believed, by the Revocation of the Edict of Nantes (1685). The Huguenots sent into exile by Louis XIV were the most able economic producers in France; in eliminating them Louis inflicted serious damage on the economic resources without which there can be little political power. Let the heirs of Cardinal Richelieu talk as much as they wish about reason of state; policy will never be reasonable when the king's confessor advocates the destructive measures dictated by the fanatical politics of divine right.

From his earliest writings to his last, Montesquieu was constantly attentive to Spain, the country which was a living example of what form despotism was likely to assume in the Western setting. In the Orient it is the absence of intermediary bodies that makes despotism so devastating. In the Western world it is the very triumph of those same bodies that fosters a less overt and less total despotism but a despotism nonetheless.

When Montesquieu looked to Spain and England he saw countries which, like France, had evolved from the embryo of a feudal past. Both those countries were further down the road of historical development than his native land. Would France duplicate the Spanish example, as Montesquieu feared? Or would it break with its feudal past, as had England? The best possibility, to Montesquieu's mind, was for France to chart its own course, one that would be constitutionalist, assuredly, but more politically decentralized than the British government. How to accomplish this task of reconstruction, he was the first to admit, was far from obvious. Surely the Catholic Church would not readily relinquish its stranglehold in France, nor would the nobility readily learn how to succeed economically or how to share political power. Historical and comparative analysis tell us what our problem is; they provide no easy solutions.

4 Legacy and reputation

The *philosophes* regarded Montesquieu, quite rightly, as an eloquent and penetrating spokesman for the outlook of the Enlightenment. For DIDEROT and D'ALEMBERT, editors of the *Encyclopédie* (1751–72), it was a great victory for the party of humanity that the illustrious Montesquieu agreed to submit an article on taste to their undertaking in collective and committed publication. Yet most of the *philosophes*, despite their admiration of *The Spirit of the Laws*, denied that climate, a physical rather than a 'moral' cause, played the dominant role in the non-Western world that Montesquieu attributed to it. Frequently, too, the *philosophes* displayed some impatience that Montesquieu spent so much time discussing what is, when they were more interested in what ought to be.

In the nineteenth century HEGEL, who acknowledged his intellectual debts, praised Montesquieu as superior to other writers of his age in taking an historical approach to his subject matter and in 'always treating the part in its relation to the whole'. Among noteworthy French authors Benjamin Constant's writings make incessant use of insights and formulations gleaned from Montesquieu; this includes Constant's frequently cited *Liberty of the Ancients Compared with that of the Moderns* (1819). Not only did Constant agree with Montesquieu in championing modern notions of freedom as privacy, but the two writers were alike again in their estimation that the freedom to pursue our individual desires will never be safe if we completely abandon the public and civic conceptions of liberty which prevailed in antiquity.

Finally, TOCQUEVILLE must be mentioned. His entire manner of conducting comparative analysis is reminiscent of *The Spirit of the Laws* (1835), and the specific objective of *Democracy in America* (1840), to fathom the political, economic, social, and cultural possibilities of a post-feudal republic, is already present a century earlier in Montesquieu's examination of England.

There are signs that the scholarship of our age is finally removing the onus with which Voltaire burdened Montesquieu's reputation. No longer is it common to see Montesquieu diminished to the lowly stature of an apologist for the privileged orders of his day. Unquestionably, he now figures as a far more profound thinker than Voltaire, and has begun to compete with Diderot and Rousseau for the title of the greatest French thinker of his time. Despite the historical specificity of his method, Montesquieu continues to speak to all persons who adhere to the ideals and aspirations of the Enlightenment.

See also: HISTORY, PHILOSOPHY OF

List of works

Montesquieu, C. Baron de (1951) *Oeuvres complètes*, ed. Caillois, R. Paris: Pléiade, 2 vols. (Contains the major works.)

—— (1721) *Lettres persanes*, trans. J.R. Loy, *The Persian Letters*, New York: Meridian Books, 1961. (Includes an introductory essay by Loy.)

—— (1734) *Considérations sur les causes de la grandeur des Romains et de leur décadence*, trans. D. Lowenthal, *Considerations on the Grandeur of the Romans and the Cause of Their Decline*, Ithaca, NY: Cornell University Press, 1965. (The only English translation.)

—— (1748) *L'Esprit des lois*, trans. A. Cohler *et al.*, *The Spirit of the Laws*, Cambridge: Cambridge University Press, 1989.

References and further reading

Althusser, L. (1959) *Montesquieu, la politique et l'histoire* (Montesquieu, Politician and Historian), Paris: Presses Universitaires de France. (A Marxist account making Montesquieu the spokesman for a social class.)

Hulliung, M. (1976) *Montesquieu and the Old Regime*, Berkeley, CA: University of California Press. (A refutation of the efforts of Voltaire and his descendants to reduce Montesquieu to his social class.)

Shackleton, R. (1961) *Montesquieu: a Critical Biography*, Oxford: Oxford University Press. (The standard biography.)

Shklar, J. (1987) *Montesquieu*, Oxford: Oxford University Press. (The best brief overview.)

Starobinski, J. (1953) *Montesquieu par lui-même* (Montesquieu by Himself), Paris: Editions du Seuil. (Autobiographical jottings and commentary.)

MARK HULLIUNG

MOORE, GEORGE EDWARD (1873–1958)

G.E. Moore was one of the most influential British philosophers of the twentieth century. His early writings are renowned for his rejection of idealist metaphysics and his insistence upon the irreducibility of ethical values, and his later work is equally famous for his defence of common sense and his conception of philosophical analysis. He spent most of his career in Cambridge, where he was a friend and colleague of Russell, Ramsey and Wittgenstein.

The best-known thesis of Moore's early treatise on ethics, Principia Ethica *(1903), is that there is a fallacy – the 'naturalistic fallacy' – in almost all previous ethical theories. The fallacy is supposed to arise from any attempt to provide a definition of ethical values. The validity of Moore's arguments is much disputed, but many philosophers still hold that Moore was right to reject the possibility of a reductive definition of ethical values. The book is also renowned for Moore's affirmation of the pre-eminence of the values of Art and Love.*

Moore's later writings concern the nature of the external world and the extent of our knowledge of it. In opposition to idealist doubts about its reality and sceptical doubts concerning our knowledge of it, Moore defends 'common sense' by emphasizing the depth of our commitment to our familiar beliefs and criticizing the arguments of those who question them. But although he insists upon the truth of our familiar beliefs, he is remarkably open-minded concerning their 'analysis', which is intended to clarify the facts in which their truth consists.

1   **Ethics**
2   **The rejection of idealism**
3   **A defence of common sense**
4   **Philosophical analysis**

1   Ethics

Moore studied philosophy at Cambridge University in the 1890s. At this time the idealist philosophy of F.H. BRADLEY was the dominant influence within British universities, and, under the influence of J.M.E. MCTAGGART, Moore became a disciple of Bradley. After graduating in 1896, however, Moore began to turn against the idealist tradition in philosophy. His first writings concern the foundations of ethics, and in the course of a critical study of Kant's ethical theory Moore argued that the idealist programme was deeply flawed: it was, he thought, a mistake to suppose that the fundamental principles of ethics require justification by reference to the will, reason or any similar criteria (see KANT, I. §9; KANTIAN ETHICS §1). For they concern a domain of values which is as objective as any physical fact, though Moore held that ethical values are not themselves physical or 'natural' facts; in his view the fundamental truths of ethics are abstract necessary truths concerning the intrinsic value of different types of state of affairs. He famously propounded this position in *Principia Ethica* (1903), where he argued that there is a fallacy, the 'naturalistic fallacy', in all theories which offer naturalistic accounts of ethical values and that much the same fallacy afflicts idealist theories of value.

Moore assumed that such accounts always involve a definition, or analysis, of ethical value, so the thesis he sought to establish was that goodness, which he believed to be the fundamental ethical value, is indefinable. His main argument was that any supposed definition of goodness (for instance, as that which we desire to desire) can be seen to be incorrect when we recognize that it incorporates a substantial ethical thesis (for example, that whatever one desires to desire is *ipso facto* good). For, Moore maintained, if the original definition had been correct, then there should seem to us to be no more of an 'open question' concerning its truth than there is concerning the result of applying the definition to itself, that is, concerning the thesis that whatever we desire to desire we desire to desire.

As Moore's many critics have observed, this argument is problematic. It is not clear that definitions need to be obviously self-applicable in the way that Moore seems to assume (a point he later acknowledged in his discussions of the 'paradox of analysis'). His conclusion is also vulnerable to revisionists who offer an alternative, perhaps naturalistic, set of ethical concepts. These critics will argue that even if Moore is correct concerning the indefinablity of our concept of goodness, then so much the worse for our concept; we would do better to abandon it in favour of something less metaphysically demanding. Hence Moore's thesis can really only be made secure when it is embedded in a broader metaphysics which elucidates the nature of ethical concepts and explains thereby why they are indefinable. Moore himself offers a Platonist metaphysics of goodness as a simple, non-natural property whose a priori relationships to the natural properties of things we are able to discern through reflective ethical intuitions. Not surprisingly, few of his successors were able to accept this. As a result many of those who accepted his thesis that ethical concepts are indefinable held that the distinctive feature of ethical statements arises, not from any special ethical facts they purport to describe, but from the special role of these statements as expressions of emotion, or as recommendations and prescriptions (see EMOTIVISM; HARE, R.M. §1; PRESCRIPTIVISM).

This linguistic version of Moore's thesis is no longer popular because it does not appear to do justice to the content of ethical judgments. The reaction against it has not, however, led to a return to Moore's abstract conception of ethical values; instead it is Moore's anti-naturalist argument that is questioned, in particular his assumption that ethical naturalists have to offer a reductive definition of ethical value (see NATURALISM IN ETHICS §1). In this case, however, Moore might respond that his thesis (implicit in *Principia Ethica*, explicit in later writings) that the ethical value of a state of affairs supervenes upon its natural properties shows that this naturalist position cannot be correct (see SUPERVENIENCE §1). For if ethical values are just simple natural properties, it is quite unclear why they should supervene on other natural properties. The ethical naturalist might well reply *ad hominem* that supervenience looks just as much a problem for Moore's conception of ethical value as a simple non-natural property. More deeply, however, the naturalist may want to claim that ethical values have an explanatory role within human psychology through their involvement in reasons for action which explains both their supervenience and their irreducibility. So at this point the debate about ethical naturalism connects with other debates about reductionism and naturalism in the philosophy of mind (see REDUC-TIONISM IN THE PHILOSOPHY OF MIND).

Although Moore's ethical theory is now primarily studied because of his critique of naturalism, at least two other aspects of it merit attention – his ideal utilitarianism and his emphasis on the value of art and love (see UTILITARIANISM). Moore's ideal utilitarianism owes much to another of his teachers, Henry SIDGWICK, who had argued that utilitarianism, which he endorsed, involves two distinct doctrines: (1) the right action is that which makes the world as good as possible; (2) pleasure is the ultimate good. Moore agreed with Sidgwick on the first point (which is constitutive of ideal utilitarianism) but rejected the second, arguing that once we recognize that pleasure occurs within 'organic wholes' which include an affective response to perceived or anticipated states of affairs we can understand how there are evil as well as good pleasures (see HEDONISM §1). None the less, Moore's own supreme goods, art and love, are themselves pleasures, so it is basically a refined hedonism that Moore himself commends; and it was certainly as such that his position was understood by his friends within the Bloomsbury Group (such as J.M. KEYNES, Lytton Strachey and Leonard Woolf). Admittedly, in *Principia Ethica* itself Moore maintained that certain states of affairs not involving human consciousness possess intrinsic value; but in subsequent writings he affirmed the thesis, which became characteristic of the Bloomsbury Group, that it is only certain pleasant states of consciousness which have positive intrinsic value.

2 The rejection of idealism

Moore's criticisms of idealist ethical theory are accompanied by similar criticisms of idealist metaphysics (see IDEALISM). Moore directs his criticisms at three different idealist positions: he argues (1) that

Berkeley's thesis that *esse* is *percipi* confuses the 'object' of perception with its 'content' (see BERKE-LEY, G. §3); (2) that Kant's 'Copernican Revolution' wrongly treats a priori truths as if they were dependent upon the nature of human reason; and (3) that Bradley's 'Absolute Idealism' rests upon the assumption that all relations are internal, which itself only reflects confusions concerning identity and difference. For Moore these last two points connect closely with the distinction in whose terms the first is couched – that between the 'content' and 'object' of thought. His rejection of Kantian and Bradleian idealism is founded upon the thesis that the objects of thought are 'propositions', possible states of affairs which, in the case of a true proposition, actually obtain. The existence and truth of such propositions is altogether independent of our thought or knowledge of them; so there is no internal relation between the truth of a proposition and anyone's grasp of it, even in the case of a priori propositions.

Moore's initial reaction against idealist metaphysics led him to an extreme realist position concerning the existence of propositions and sensory objects, on the basis of which he held that traditional sceptical arguments could be easily rejected. But in his 1910–11 lectures *Some Main Problems of Philosophy* (1953) he recognized that matters cannot be quite so simple. He here abandons belief in the existence of propositions because he is no longer able to accept the existence of false ones (which, on his view, would be non-actual states of affairs). He also abandons his previous naïve realism concerning sensory objects, and takes the view that the objects of sense experience, which he here calls 'sense-data' (thereby introducing the term into the philosophy of perception), are non-physical representations of the physical world. And, having accepted this last point, he acknowledges that it is a good deal more difficult to find the fault in traditional sceptical arguments than he had previously supposed.

It is in discussion of these issues that Moore begins to develop two new methods of argument which combine to give his later writings their distinctive style – the appeal to common sense and the use of philosophical analysis.

3 A defence of common sense

Moore's appeal to common sense is not a dogmatic affirmation of the truth of the 'common-sense view of the world' in the face of critical or sceptical arguments to the contrary. Instead it belongs within a higher-order scepticism concerning the epistemic status of philosophical arguments themselves. Moore's claim is that the general principles upon which critical and sceptical philosophies rely are answerable to our everyday employment of the concepts they involve in our 'common-sense' judgments concerning particular matters of fact. Hence, Moore argues, critical and sceptical philosophers undermine the reasons for accepting the general principles on which they base their arguments. We are more certain that we know such things as that 'this is a pencil' than we can be of the premises of any sceptical argument which disputes such knowledge.

Moore's critics urge that this is too simple; after all, most sceptical arguments begin by exploiting entirely familiar grounds for doubt. And the status of 'common sense' is not itself unchallengeable; Moore, an agnostic, would not have welcomed an attempt to defend religious knowledge by an appeal to 'common-sense' religious convictions; but then he would have had to explain why common-sense beliefs about the physical world have an epistemic authority that simple religious convictions lack. In fact towards the end of his life Moore himself came to feel that more needed to be said in order to deal properly with sceptical arguments. Although in his famous lecture 'A Proof of an External World' (1939) he argued that, contrary to the claims of idealists, one could prove the existence of an external world by demonstrating the existence of one's hands, in his comments on this lecture Moore denied that one could prove in a similar way that one possessed *knowledge* of the existence of an external world. To do this one had to be able to refute sceptical arguments, and this could not be done by simply waving one's hands at them. Moore himself attempted this task of refutation in two of his very last papers, but in fact by the end of the second one he seems almost ready to concede defeat, while equally maintaining that scepticism about the external world is literally incredible.

4 Philosophical analysis

As Moore's 'A Defence of Common Sense' (1925) shows well, his appeal to common sense is typically combined with an emphasis on philosophical analysis. The background to Moore's conception of analysis lies in his early conception of a proposition as both the object of thought and a possible state of affairs. Thus conceived propositions are complex structures of objects and properties, and an analysis of their structure as objects of thought is equally a metaphysical account of the structure of reality. But Moore's conception of the role of analysis was greatly enhanced by his appreciation of Russell's work in logical theory, especially the theory of logical fictions (see RUSSELL, B.A.W. §9). One issue to which Moore applied this theory was that of propositions themselves. For although he regularly represented himself

as concerned with the analysis of propositions, he did not think that his talk of propositions had to be taken as carrying with it a commitment to the existence of propositions, as genuine entities to which reference is made in the analysis of propositional attitude idioms. But whether his treatment of this issue was altogether consistent can reasonably be doubted (see PROPOSITIONAL ATTITUDES).

The context beyond all others to which Moore applied his conception of analysis was that of perception: he maintained that although there is no doubt concerning our *knowledge* of such propositions as 'This is a hand', their *analysis* is deeply puzzling. For Moore their analysis led directly into the philosophy of perception since he took it that the demonstrative 'This' refers here to a sense-datum, whose relationship to one's hand requires clarification through further analysis. Moore took it that there were three alternative positions here: (1) a direct realist position, according to which the sense-datum is part of the hand (for instance, part of its surface); (2) an indirect realist position, according to which the sense-datum is a non-physical representation of one's hand; (3) a phenomenalist position, according to which all talk of one's hand turns out, when fully analysed, to involve no more than descriptions of actual and possible sense-data (see PERCEPTION §2). Moore moved through different versions of these positions at different stages of his career without ever finding one that commanded his wholehearted assent, though in later writings he seems to have favoured the phenomenalist alternative. Moore's indecision is perhaps best regarded as a *reductio ad absurdum* of his initial assumption that demonstratives always refer to a sense-datum. For even though this assumption is intended to be compatible with direct realism, the fact that Moore assumes that there cannot be a failure of reference, even when there is no appropriate physical object to be demonstrated, shows that his conception of a sense-datum is that of an object of experience whose existence is independent of the physical world.

Moore was always emphatic that he did not think that all the problems of philosophy could be resolved by means of philosophical analysis. He resisted the conception of logical analysis propounded by WITTGENSTEIN in his *Tractatus Logico-Philosophicus* (1921) (even though he regarded the book, to which he gave the name by which it is now known, as a work of genius); and he was equally suspicious of Wittgenstein's later attempts to show that philosophical problems arise from a misunderstanding of our language. Yet there is no doubt that analysis did play a central role in Moore's philosophical thought: again and again in his writings, he approaches a question by offering an analysis of the propositions which enter into his initial formulation of it. One can best appreciate the role of such analyses by reflecting upon the fact that Moore was inclined to favour a phenomenalist analysis of propositions such as 'This is a hand' at the very time at which he was propounding his anti-idealist proof of an external world by demonstrating the existence of his hands to his audience. For this shows that Moore's appeal to common sense was more limited than is sometimes appreciated. According to Moore, we can employ this appeal to assure ourselves of the truth of such propositions as 'This is a hand'; but such an appeal tells us little about what their truth consists in. For this, we require an analysis of these propositions, and this can be as radically unfamiliar as one likes, as long as the truth values of our common-sense judgments are respected. Thus the apparent conservatism of Moore's defence of common sense is somewhat deceptive. To put the matter in Fregean terms, common sense constrains us to respect the reference of our ordinary judgments, but it does not thereby reveal their sense, whose elucidation rests instead upon the outcome of philosophical analysis.

For this reason, Moore is rightly regarded as a paradigm 'analytic philosopher'. Indeed his early writings played a crucial part in the development of analytic philosophy, since they implied that the analysis of the logical structure of propositions could be of direct metaphysical significance. But because Moore never subscribed to the broad metaphysical doctrines of logical atomism and logical positivism, his conception of philosophical analysis remained somewhat pragmatic, piecemeal and idiosyncratic. None the less, particularly because of his emphasis upon common sense, his work constitutes one of the essential elements within that broad conception of philosophy which we think of as 'analytic philosophy'.

See also: ANALYTICAL PHILOSOPHY §§1–2

List of works

Moore, G.E. (1899) 'The Nature of Judgment', *Mind* new series 8: 176–93. (The paper which signals Moore's youthful rejection of idealism.)
—— (1903) *Principia Ethica*, Cambridge: Cambridge University Press; revised edn, ed. T. Baldwin, 1993. (Moore's classic work of ethical theory, largely concentrating on the issue of the 'naturalistic fallacy'.)
—— (1912) *Ethics*, London: Williams & Norgate. (Moore's attempt at an elementary exposition of ethical theory, interesting in parts but rather pedestrian in style.)
—— (1922) *Philosophical Studies*, London: Routledge. (A collection of Moore's important papers from the period 1903–19.)
—— (1925) 'A Defence of Common Sense', in *Contemporary British Philosophy*, 2nd series, ed. J.H. Muirhead, London: Allen & Unwin; repr. in Moore (1959) and Moore (1993). (Moore's classic formulation of his complex attitude to 'common sense'.)
—— (1939) 'Proof of an External World', *Proceedings of the British Academy*, 25: 275–300; repr. in Moore (1959) and Moore (1993). (Moore's famous 'proof', which consisted in holding up his hands and declaring 'Here is one hand and here is another'.)
—— (1953) *Some Main Problems of Philosophy*, London: Allen & Unwin. (The text of lectures given in 1910–11 which sets the agenda for Moore's later thoughts.)
—— (1959) *Philosophical Papers*, London: Allen & Unwin. (A collection of Moore's important papers from the period 1923–55)
—— (1966) *Lectures on Philosophy*, ed. C. Lewy, London: Allen & Unwin. (A selection of Moore's lecture notes for the period 1929–34.)
—— (1986) *G.E. Moore: The Early Essays*, ed. T. Regan, Philadelphia, PA: Temple University Press. (Contains most of Moore's papers from the period 1897–1904.)
—— (1993) *Selected Writings*, ed. T. Baldwin, London: Routledge. (A collection of Moore's important papers and some further selections.)

References and further reading

Ambrose, A. and Lazerowitz, M. (eds) (1970) *G.E. Moore: Essays in Retrospect*, London: Allen & Unwin. (Contains useful critical essays on Moore's work.)
Baldwin, T.R. (1990) *G.E. Moore*, London: Routledge. (The only critical study of all of Moore's work.)
Keynes, J.M. (1949) 'My Early Beliefs', in *Two Memoirs*, London: Hart-Davis; also in J.M. Keynes, *Collected Writings X*, London: Macmillan, 1972. (Provides a classic account of the influence of *Principia Ethica* on the Bloomsbury Group.)
Levy, P. (1979) *Moore: G.E. Moore and the Cambridge Apostles*, London: Weidenfeld & Nicolson. (Describes Moore's friendships with the Bloomsbury Group.)
Regan, T. (1986) *Bloomsbury's Prophet*, Philadelphia, PA: Temple University Press. (Discusses Moore's early writings.)

Schilpp, P.A. (ed.) (1942) *The Philosophy of G.E. Moore*, Evanston, IL: Northwestern University Press; 3rd edn, La Salle, IL: Open Court, 1968. (Rather old-fashioned, but contains some classic papers by Bowsma, Ducasse and Frankena, together with Moore's autobiography and his reply to his critics.)

Stroud, B.A. (1984) *The Significance of Philosophical Scepticism*, Oxford: Clarendon Press. (Chapters 3 and 4 provide a sympathetic discussion of Moore's epistemology; but see chapter 9 of Baldwin (1990) for criticism of Stroud.)

Sylvester, R.P. (1990) *The Moral Philosophy of G.E. Moore*, ed. R. Perkins and R. Sleeper, Philadelphia, PA: Temple University Press. (A scholarly discussion of Moore's treatment of ethical values.)

THOMAS BALDWIN

MORAL AGENTS

Moral agents are those agents expected to meet the demands of morality. Not all agents are moral agents. Young children and animals, being capable of performing actions, may be agents in the way that stones, plants and cars are not. But though they are agents they are not automatically considered moral agents. For a moral agent must also be capable of conforming to at least some of the demands of morality.

This requirement can be interpreted in different ways. On the weakest interpretation it will suffice if the agent has the capacity to conform to some of the external requirements of morality. So if certain agents can obey moral laws such as 'Murder is wrong' or 'Stealing is wrong', then they are moral agents, even if they respond only to prudential reasons such as fear of punishment and even if they are incapable of acting for the sake of moral considerations. According to the strong version, the Kantian version, it is also essential that the agents should have the capacity to rise above their feelings and passions and act for the sake of the moral law. There is also a position in between which claims that it will suffice if the agent can perform the relevant act out of altruistic impulses. Other suggested conditions of moral agency are that agents should have: an enduring self with free will and an inner life; understanding of the relevant facts as well as moral understanding; and moral sentiments, such as capacity for remorse and concern for others.

Philosophers often disagree about which of these and other conditions are vital; the term moral agency is used with different degrees of stringency depending upon what one regards as its qualifying conditions. The

Kantian sense is the most stringent. Since there are different senses of moral agency, answers to questions like 'Are collectives moral agents?' depend upon which sense is being used. From the Kantian standpoint, agents such as psychopaths, rational egoists, collectives and robots are at best only quasi-moral, for they do not fulfil some of the essential conditions of moral agency.

1 **Agents versus recipients**
2 **Understanding**
3 **The inner life and the Kantian view**
4 **Collectives and moral agency**

1 Agents versus recipients

Moral agents should be distinguished from moral recipients (see MORAL STANDING). Moral agents are those who are morally accountable for at least some of their conduct. They are subject to moral duties and obligations, and, therefore, to moral praise and blame. Moral recipients are those who are owed moral consideration for their own sakes (see RESPECT FOR PERSONS). On certain views moral agents and moral recipients are coextensive. Thus according to Kantians persons are the only moral agents and the only moral recipients (see Kant 1785). We should not be cruel to animals, not because animals are owed anything for their own sakes, but because cruelty to animals may indirectly harm persons who are the only ends in themselves (see ANIMALS AND ETHICS). According to utilitarians all sentient beings are owed consideration to the extent that they have feelings; so on this view there are moral recipients who are not moral agents – for instance, animals, or at least their feelings. Can there be moral agents who are not moral recipients? It would seem not, unless perhaps one uses moral agency in a weak sense which includes among moral agents nonsentient entities such as robots and corporations.

2 Understanding

The view that moral agents must have the capacity to conform to some of the external demands of morality is consistent with the view that there are parts of morality that they cannot conform to. Thus kleptomaniacs do not have the capacity to conform to certain moral requirements about not stealing, but it does not follow that they are not moral agents or that they should not be held morally responsible for murders that they might commit (see RESPONSIBILITY). Moral agents must be morally responsible for some of their conduct, not necessarily for all. What, then, are the conditions of moral agency?

One essential condition is that the agent must have

the relevant understanding (or capacity for understanding) of what the external requirements of morality are (see MORAL KNOWLEDGE §1). Thus in the case of murder one must understand that murder is wrong and that a particular act is an instance of murder. Exactly how much understanding is required is not easy to specify. There are plenty of borderline cases, but there are clear cases on both sides of the line. A baby does not have the relevant understanding of any of the requirements of morality, while an average adult citizen does at least sometimes. Of course even average citizens are very ignorant in many matters, but that at most is relevant to assessing their responsibility in these matters; it does not prevent them being moral agents.

Some existentialist philosophers insist that moral agency requires the ability to create and choose one's own values, unconstrained by objective or rational considerations (see EXISTENTIALIST ETHICS). It is objected that such creation involves a capricious freedom, since the agents have no guide as to how they should choose their values. Charles Taylor (1982) attempts to overcome this problem by suggesting that moral agency requires that one should have the capacity to choose one's values, after reflection, in accordance with one's deepest and most authentic nature (see TAYLOR, C. §§4–5). Does this requirement provide the necessary guidance for the agent? Critics would point out that this just shifts the problem. In what sense are we responsible for our deepest nature?

It seems that moral accountability requires that the agents should have an objective basis for choosing their moral values. They could then be held morally accountable to the extent that they have the capacity to find out what the relevant moral requirements are and, to the extent that they have the capacity, to conform to such requirements in the relevant ways. People who cannot reason properly (such as the severely mentally ill) or those who lack certain volitional abilities lack the capacity to conform to the relevant moral requirements.

In order to be morally accountable, an agent does not always have to know or even have the correct opinion about what the moral requirements are. The capacity for finding out such things can be enough. For instance, some Nazis who persecuted Jews may have thought sincerely that they were doing the right thing; but if they could and should have known better then they can be censured for moral negligence. Had they thought things through, which they could and should have done, they would have realized how wrong such acts were. Or so it is believed by those of us who want to hold them morally responsible.

To have the capacity to find out that something is

morally wrong does not necessarily involve having the capacity to know why. It is plausible to distinguish having right opinions on moral matters from knowledge of them. The person who has knowledge in moral matters not only has the right opinions but also has them for the right reasons. Even after a study of moral philosophy many people do not know why things like stealing and murder are morally wrong; they do not understand the grounds for such judgments. True, theories have been advanced to answer such problems, but there is no general agreement on correct answers. An ideal moral agent, who exists only in the imagination of philosophers, might have knowledge of all moral matters, but ordinary moral agents have only opinions (for example, that stealing is wrong) and the capacity to find out such opinions in areas where they are held morally responsible.

According to some philosophers it is not enough to have the intellectual ability to tell right from wrong. There are psychopaths who are quite intelligent in general, and can even talk intelligently about morality. They might be able to tell us what things are wrong and even why, but they lack moral sentiments, such as remorse and consideration for others, and are unable to act for the sake of moral considerations. Many would say that they are not moral agents, and therefore not subject to moral condemnation, nor to punishment in so far as punishment presupposes moral condemnation. Bradley (1894) thought that psychopathic killers are not moral agents and so we cannot morally condemn them or punish them in the way we punish moral agents, but we have the right to use social surgery, even to kill them if that is necessary for social welfare, somewhat as we have a right to kill dangerous animals; considerations of justice do not apply to those who are not moral agents. Bradley forgot that considerations of humanity may still apply to them.

Bradley's view has been endorsed by Jeffrie Murphy (1972) but with two important qualifications. First, he points out that there is the danger of abuse in such a system. If we were permitted to go in for social surgery against nonmoral agents, moral agents might sometimes be wrongly diagnosed as nonmoral agents. Second, many people become psychopaths because of bad social conditions, and not of their own free will. Murphy rejects Aristotle's view that psychopathic wickedness is like a disease that people are responsible for acquiring by their voluntary conduct. He argues that psychopaths are those whose potential moral agency has been destroyed by society, and that they should therefore not be treated too harshly.

John Rawls (1971) maintains that only those who can give justice are owed justice (see RAWLS, J.). And he stresses the importance for moral personality of acting from the sense of justice. On this view those who cannot act from a sense of justice would not be moral agents and so would not be owed duties of justice. But there is a weaker thesis according to which it will suffice to be owed justice if people can give justice even if they are not motivated by the sense of justice. In the case of potential criminals, even if they are incapable of acting out of a sense of justice, or for the sake of moral considerations, we can apply considerations of justice to them and respect their rights if they respect the rights of others, even if their reasons for doing so are egoistic.

Indeed some Hobbesian philosophers contend that rational egoists can set up a just society, without the aid of a moral sense or a sense of justice (see CONTRACTARIANISM §§2–3). Similarly, one could operate with a sense of moral agency, according to which agents have a capacity to conform to some of the external requirements of morality, but may lack the capacity to act for the sake of the moral law. They could sustain something like a morality. From a pragmatic point of view it would not matter too much why people conformed to moral requirements as long as they continued to do so. Jeremy Bentham (1817) thought that human beings were primarily egoistic, and that basic human nature was unalterable. He suggested that the setting up of the right institutions, such as representative democracy, and sanctions, such as punishment, would lead all members of the public, including the rulers, to see that contributing to the common good would be in their own best interests; thus rulers who acted against the public interest would be unlikely to be re-elected (see BENTHAM, J.). But would such rational egoists be moral agents? This is partly a verbal matter. They would satisfy the requirement that people should have the capacity to conform to some of the external requirements of morality, but they would not meet the Kantian requirement about being able to act for the sake of moral considerations.

3 The inner life and the Kantian view

The substantial question is whether the Kantian requirement is legitimate. Different moral theories give different answers to this question. Critics of the Kantian view might ask: if members of your family rescue you from a burning house, would you not think better of them if they did this out of affection for you rather than out of a sense of duty? Kantians would reply that if they did it out of affection, this would not at that time involve an exercise of their moral agency. This is consistent with the view that there may have been some exercise of moral agency in the past if the agent cultivated the right feelings and dispositions out of a sense of duty. Some people through good luck have better feelings and dispositions than others. Their qualities may even be wonderful, but do they deserve *moral* credit? Wittgenstein thought that G.E. Moore's lack of vanity and his innocence generally might be loveable but Moore did not deserve any moral credit, for he was not 'talking of the innocence a man has fought for, but of an innocence which comes from a natural absence of a temptation' (see Malcolm 1966: 80). But what of the family members who fight against a selfish temptation to run away from the burning house where you are, and overcome it not out of a sense of duty but because of their love for you?

Persons who, through no fault of their own, have temptations to commit serious crimes are at a serious disadvantage compared to those of us who are lucky and do not have these temptations (see MORAL LUCK). The former may deserve moral credit for conquering their temptations and for attempting to cultivate the right dispositions. Moral agency in one important sense of the term is to be contrasted with what happens as a result of luck. The conduct of individual agents is produced by a combination of factors: heredity, environment and free will. On the Kantian view, since personal choice is the only contribution to conduct made by agents themselves, it is only for this last factor that they are to be held morally accountable (see FREE WILL).

The Kantian view of moral agency presupposes an enduring self that has the power of acting freely in a strong libertarian (or nondeterministic) sense. The enduring self on this view is different from an enduring character. The self is that which has the character and is autonomous in the sense that it has the power after reflection to change or not to change the character to some degree (see AUTONOMY, ETHICAL). It is only to the extent that it has this power that it is held morally accountable for actions that issue from it or its character. If there is no enduring self, if the later self is a different self from the earlier one, then the later self cannot be morally accountable for the acts of its predecessor any more than a child can be for the deeds of its parents. Critics point out that the free will and the enduring self that are presupposed are incoherent. Either the character is determined by various factors that are ultimately outside the agent's control or, if there is a break in the causal chain, then the act is a chance or random event and so again there can be no freedom.

Kantians reply that this objection loses force once we acknowledge the existence of the inner standpoint of the moral agent. C.A. Campbell (1957) has pointed out that from the internal standpoint we can make sense of a free act that is neither determined by factors outside our control nor a random event. Campbell appeals to our phenomenological experience of moral effort in the face of moral temptation, in which we can make sense of the creative agency of the self, when the self has the power to go beyond its formed character. On this view what is really admirable about moral agents is that they can obey the moral law, rising above their feelings and passions by efforts of will made for the sake of the moral law. So the existence of the inner life is considered, at any rate on the Kantian view, to be another essential requirement of moral agency. It is this requirement that is not met by robots, corporations, states and other groups. Even if they instantiate rational systems or functional systems such that it makes sense to attribute actions (in a functionalist sense) to them, they do not have an irreducible inner phenomenology (see FUNCTIONALISM). Thus a corporation or a state is not joyous and does not suffer (in the phenomenological sense) except in the sense that is reducible to the suffering and joys of its members. To say this is consistent with the view that such entities are extremely important in the influence they have over their members and that their behaviour and the laws governing them are not reducible to the behaviour and the laws governing the behaviour of their members.

William James (1907) pointed out that what gives significance to human life is that we can set ourselves ideals or goals and then pursue them with zest, overcoming obstacles in the way (see JAMES, W. §3). If there were no struggle in human endeavour there would be nothing heroic about us. When we admire individuals for their struggle against temptation, or against disease, or their heroic attempt at conquering mountains or solving mathematical problems, we are appealing to an inner life. If a computer solves a mathematical problem, however ingenious its solution, there is nothing heroic about it.

It might be objected that one can understand the duty versus temptations battle without appealing to an inner life; one may give a dispositional analysis of temptation as well as of overcoming it. But Kantians would reply that we can only make sense of moral effort and free will if we assume an internal point of view. If we look at things from a purely objective point of view neither the presence of determinism nor its absence can make sense of our free will and of our moral agency.

4 Collectives and moral agency

There is sometimes disagreement about whether such categories as the insane, children, robots and collec-

tives are moral agents. This disagreement can partly reflect different standards of moral agency being used. It can also be due to different views about the facts. Thus some of us may deny that robots are moral agents on the ground that they lack an inner life. Others may disagree with us on the grounds that an inner life is not essential to moral agency; and some may argue that even though an inner life is essential, robots of the sophisticated variety might be constructed in the future who have inner lives in the sense that human beings do.

People often wonder whether collectives such as nations, states and corporations are moral agents. On the assumption that they lack an irreducible inner life or that they lack a permanent or enduring self, they will not fulfil an essential condition for moral agency in the Kantian sense. But if we use moral agency in a weaker sense, then they too could be moral agents. Kantians would say that they are at best quasi-moral agents, but critics of the Kantian approach would complain that the Kantian view is too stringent; it has presuppositions that are unverifiable and controversial. Some of these critics prefer a practical solution where terms like free will and moral agency are used in a weaker sense.

On a Humean view people can be given moral praise if they meet the external requirement of morality by promoting social welfare, provided their conduct reflects their character (see HUME, D. §4). Similarly, they can be apportioned moral blame and punished if they produce social misery, provided their conduct stems from their character (rather than by accident). No permanent or enduring self in any deep sense is required. What is required is that the individual being blamed has the same character traits (in the relevant respects) as the one who committed the act. We are free to the extent that our conduct reflects our character. Deep problems like whether we are responsible for acquiring our characters are bypassed on this view. It implies that collectives too could be moral agents in the way that individual persons are.

Indeed Hume explicitly compared the person's self to a republic or a commonwealth. So the argument that groups are less eligible for moral agency than individual human beings collapses on this view. Individual human beings can have character traits that persist; but so can groups. And though groups do not have an irreducible inner life, neither do individual human beings on the Humean view, according to which the ultimate constituents are the items of experience. The person does not persist over time in any deeper sense than groups do. The person's relation to the individual items of experience is like the relation of the republic to individual members who compose it (see MIND, BUNDLE THEORY OF). So on this view an individual can be morally accountable in much the same sense as collectives; this is one of the corollaries of his view that Hume did not notice.

Much communal violence presupposes ideas of collective moral agency. For instance, during the partition of India, when some Muslims in one part of the country persecuted Hindus, another group of Hindus would take retributive actions against some other Muslims in another part of India. The Hindus would often justify such conduct on the grounds that the people they attacked shared common characteristics with their coreligionists who committed the evil deeds elsewhere. The Muslims would use a similar justification against the Hindus and the vicious circle would continue. Jonathan Edwards (1758) thought that human beings are now morally accountable for the sins of Adam, for they belong to the same collective, humanity, and share the same fallen nature as Adam (see EDWARDS, J.). On the Kantian view (as well as on some other individualist views) this is not enough. Persons now are separate moral agents and have a separate centre of consciousness from Adam, even if they have similar character traits; the self is different from and transcends the character. Such requirements are often violated by those who mete out retribution at a collective level.

But we do seem to make moral demands upon collectives. Thus one might say that the IMF (International Monetary Fund) ought to provide more facilities for the poorer countries. And it has been claimed that some of these demands are not reducible to demands upon individuals. If this claim is correct, it would follow that at least a part of our moral language is addressed to those who are moral agents in the weak sense but not in the Kantian sense. This can also be seen in the case of young children, with whom we sometimes use moral language before they have become moral agents in the full Kantian sense. Indeed it is partly by participating in such use of language that children gradually acquire moral sentiments.

The Kantian sense of moral agency is presupposed only by parts of our moral system, especially that part which is concerned with apportioning moral desert from the point of view of cosmic fairness. If certain wrongdoers are not Kantian moral agents, the view that they deserve to suffer for their conduct is undermined. We do say to a child of two that it ought not to kill. We may even punish the child for its wrongs if that does some good; but we do not think that if it did not suffer for its wrongs in this life, it would be fair if there were another world, a hell, where it would be made to suffer, in the way that it would be fair if Stalin (assuming that he was a Kantian moral agent) were made to suffer in hell. As for the IMF, even God would not be able to send it to hell or make sense of its deserving to suffer (in the irreducible phenomenological sense) as a collective.

See also: ACTION; DESERT AND MERIT; KANTIAN ETHICS; MORAL JUSTIFICATION; MORAL MOTIVATION; MORALITY AND IDENTITY; PRAISE AND BLAME

References and further reading

Although they involve intricate argument, none of these items is particularly technical. All except the Kant are fairly easy to follow.

* Bentham, J. (1817) *Plan for Parliamentary Reform*, in J. Bowring (ed.) *The Works of Jeremy Bentham*, vol. 3, Edinburgh, 1843. (Proposes that the setting up of the right institutions, such as representative democracy, and sanctions, such as punishment, would lead all members of the public, including the rulers, to see that contributing to the common good would be in their own best interests, and therefore that rulers who acted against the public interest would be unlikely to be re-elected.)
* Bradley, F.H. (1894) 'Some Remarks on Punishment', *International Journal of Ethics*; repr. in *Collected Essays*, Oxford: Oxford University Press, 1935, vol. I, essay 7. (Advocates Darwinism and social surgery against nonmoral agents.)
—— (1927) *Ethical Studies*, Oxford: Oxford University Press, 1927, ch. 1. (Outlines some of the conditions of moral responsibility.)
* Campbell, C.A. (1957) *Selfhood and Godhead*, London: Allen & Unwin, 376–85. (A Kantian defence of free will and moral agency.)
* Edwards, J. (1758) 'Original Sin', in C.A. Holbrook (ed.) *Works of Jonathan Edwards*, New Haven, CT: Yale University Press, 1970, part IV, ch. 3. (Argues in favour of collective moral accountability.)
Haksar, V. (1964) 'Aristotle and the Punishment of Psychopaths', *Philosophy* 39: 323–40; repr. in J. Walsh, and H. Shapiro (eds) *Aristotle's Ethics*, Belmont, CA: Wadsworth, 1967, 80–101. (Discusses whether psychopaths are morally accountable for their actions and examines Aristotle's views on moral agency.)
—— (1991) *Indivisible Selves and Moral Practice*, Edinburgh: Edinburgh University Press, chaps 2 (section 2), 9 and 10. (Examines the analogy between individuals and collectives.)
* James, W. (1907) *Talks to Teachers on Psychology and to Students on Some of Life's Ideals*, London:

Longman's Green and Co., 265–301. (Discussion of what makes life significant.)

* Kant, I. (1785) *Grundlegung zur Metaphysik der Sitten*, trans. with notes by H.J. Paton, *Groundwork of the Metaphysics of Morals* (originally *The Moral Law*), London: Hutchinson, 1948; repr. New York: Harper & Row, 1964. (Advocates 'strong' interpretation of conditions required for moral agency.)

* Malcolm, N. (1966) *L. Wittgenstein, A Memoir*, Oxford: Oxford University Press. (Includes Wittgenstein's views on G.E. Moore's 'innocence'.)

* Murphy, J. (1972) 'Moral Death: A Kantian Essay on Psychopathy', *Ethics* 91: 284–98. (Discussion of psychopathy from a Kantian standpoint.)

* Rawls, J. (1971) *A Theory of Justice*, Cambridge, MA: Harvard University Press, ch. 8. (Expounds the view that a moral personality must have the capacity to act from a sense of justice.)

* Taylor, C. (1976) 'Responsibility for Self', in A. Rorty (ed.) *The Identities of Persons*, Berkeley, CA: University of California Press, 281–99; repr. in G. Watson (ed.) *Free Will*, Oxford: Oxford University Press, 1982, 111–26. (Suggests moral agency consists in the capacity to choose one's values in accordance with one's authentic nature.)

VINIT HAKSAR

MORAL DEVELOPMENT

The concept of moral development has its roots in Plato's metaphor of ascent from the dark recesses of the cave to the initially blinding sight of the form of the good. Influenced by the developmental theories of Jean Piaget, Lawrence Kohlberg proposed a sequence of stages beginning with two stages of egoism, followed by stages of conventionalism, contractarianism, consequentialism, and finally a Kantianism emphasizing the role of universalizable laws. Recent empirical work has not, however, corroborated moral stage theory. There seems not to be a unified mode of thought that applies to all and only moral problems.

In the 1920s, Jean PIAGET articulated the idea that cognitive development in a number of domains (regarding, for example, substance, space, time) involved the development of progressively more adequate ways of thinking about each domain. Children's thinking could be classified according to Piaget in terms of unified modes of thought at each of four stages, in terms of what he called a 'genetic epistemology'. Like the Platonic picture of ascent (see PLATO §14), stage progression involved progress towards seeing the nature of things more and more clearly.

In 1932 Piaget published *The Moral Judgment of the Child*, a book he called a 'preliminary piece of work', in which he presented two discoveries of note. First, young children, but not older children, judge the goodness or badness of actions more on outcomes than on motives: accidentally breaking a lamp is worse than intentionally breaking a less expensive object. Second, children initially think of prescriptive rules as unchangeable, and as originating outside human convention and social life; only later do they come to see rules as conventions designed for profitable human interaction and as adjustable accordingly. But, by the time a child is 10 or 11, rules are seen as emanating from humans engaged in complex social interactions, trying to harmonize interaction and avoid conflict. The rules are not so much forced upon us from the outside as are chosen by reasonable persons trying to engage in productive interaction. Adopting Kantian terminology, Piaget referred to this shift in the moral understanding of the child as a progression from a stage of 'heteronomy' to the stage of 'autonomy'.

Beginning in the 1950s, Kohlberg (1981, 1984) pursued Piaget's Kantian assumptions, claiming that individuals at the highest stage of moral development respond to moral problems 'in moral words such as duty or morally right and use them in a way implying universality, ideals, and impersonality'. In Kohlberg's hands, Piaget's two stages yielded to a six-stage scheme:

(1) egoism: right is what is rewarded and what is wrong is what is punished;

(2) instrumentalism: right is what serves one's needs and satisfies fair agreements;

(3) conventionalism: right is what conforms to age, gender, occupational and social role conventions;

(4) social contract: right is conceived in terms of the conventions of the society as a whole, especially the legal conventions;

(5) consequentialism: right is what promotes the general welfare even if this might involve breaking the law, for example, laws that discriminate on the basis of race or gender;

(6) Kant's 'categorical imperative': right is acting in accordance with rules that you would be willing to recognize as universal laws.

The descriptive sequence of moral stages follows a universal and irreversible sequence, and although not everyone reaches the highest stage of moral development, those who do will see the highest stage they reach as more adequate than the previous stages they occupied. Thus, a stage (5) consequentialist who is exposed to stage (6) Kantianism will judge it an improvement.

The empirical sequence of the stages, and the normative preferences of those occupying the stages, were thought by Kohlberg to increase the plausibility of the claim that the stages of moral development were in fact increasingly more adequate from a moral point of view. Although Kohlberg did not test the relationship between moral judgment and moral action, he explicitly assumed that there was a significant correlation between the two.

At the present time, moral stage theory is in a state of considerable disarray. Starting in the late 1970s, Carol Gilligan (1982) argued that Kohlberg's longitudinal study, based as it was on an all-male sample, was not listening to the ways women speak, and thus think, about moral problems. She claimed that males deliberate from a perspective that weights heavily respect for impersonal rules and rights, whereas females are more likely to find the particular needs of others salient and to respond to moral problems out of direct care, concern and feeling for the other. Although Kohlberg claimed in only one co-authored paper to have found small gender differences between males and females, and generally concurred with finding of colleagues that there were none using his way of testing, Gilligan's critique opened the possibility of gender bias. Kohlberg was eventually forced to acknowledge that his was a theory of 'justice reasoning', but not of moral reasoning more generally (see FEMINIST ETHICS §1).

Gilligan's theory did not emerge unscathed, however, since subsequent analyses of male and female moral reasoning using a wide variety of testing procedures and types of problems show that the only significant gender difference has to do with the moral problems males and females think they face, but not with how they reason about different kinds of moral problems (Walker 1984).

Another problem for stage theory is the evidence of moral regression: people who at one time exhibit stage (6) Kantian reasoning may later endorse more conventionalist views. During the 1980s Kohlberg and his colleagues revised their scoring manual to eliminate regressors. However, in doing this they also unfortunately eliminated any confirmed cases of stage (6) justice reasoning.

Although the idea of moral development is still alive, the prospects of a unified moral stage theory seems dim. Moral philosophers and moral psychologists increasingly agree that the domain of morality contains heterogeneous types of moral problems and responsiveness to different types of problems may well require different special-purpose competencies, or 'virtues', not some general 'moral faculty'.

See also: COGNITIVE DEVELOPMENT; FEMINIST ETHICS; JUSTICE; KARMA AND REBIRTH, INDIAN CONCEPTIONS OF; MORAL EDUCATION

References and further reading

Flanagan, O. (1991) *Varieties of Moral Personality*, Cambridge, MA: Harvard University Press. (An argument for a psychologically realistic ethics containing a critical assessment of moral stage theories, the debate about morality and gender, as well as discussions of several alternative approaches to the study of moral psychology.)

* Gilligan, C. (1982) *In a Different Voice*, Cambridge, MA: Harvard University Press. (A challenge to Kohlberg's theory on the grounds that it privileges a conception of morality that is gender-biased.)

Kagan, J. and Lamb, S. (eds) (1987) *The Emergence of Morality in Young Children*, Chicago, IL: University of Chicago Press. (A collection of mostly empirical papers offering an alternative to moral stage theory in which temperament, moral emotions and the like are highlighted.)

Kittay, E. and Meyers, D. (eds) (1987) *Women and Moral Theory*, Totowa, NJ: Rowman & Littlefield. (An interesting collection of papers, mostly by philosophers, on the topic of gender differences in morality.)

* Kohlberg, L. (1981, 1984) *Essays on Moral Development*, New York: Harper & Row, 2 vols. (All of Kohlberg's most important papers covering the empirical evidence for moral stages and his various defences of the philosophical conclusion that the highest stage is the most adequate from the moral point of view.)

* Piaget, J. (1932) *The Moral Judgment of the Child*, New York: Free Press. (A study of how children conceive of prescriptive rules, truth-telling and the relative importance of motives and intentions versus consequences.)

* Walker, L. (1984) 'Sex Differences in the Development of Moral Reasoning: A Critical Review', *Child Development* 57: 677–91. (A meta-analysis of all the research on gender differences in moral reasoning with the finding that there are none, except in the types of problems males and females think they characteristically face.)

OWEN FLANAGAN

MORAL DILEMMAS *see* MORAL PLURALISM (§5)

MORAL EDUCATION

This entry looks at three contemporary approaches to moral learning and education, all of which have roots in the history of philosophy. The first holds that just as children grow, or develop, in a physical sense, so they also develop in their moral dispositions or judgments. A central issue here is whether the concept of development is applicable outside its biological home.

The second sees moral learning not as a natural process, but as a deliberate induction into socially approved norms or values. On one version of this view, it is not enough to bring children to follow the rules enshrined in conventional moral codes as they need to learn to sift these in the light of higher-order rational principles. Problems arise here both about moral motivation and about whether morality is wholly to do with rules and principles. For other theorists moral education is more a matter of shaping children's nature-given desires and emotions into settled dispositions or virtues on Aristotelian lines. While the 'rational principle' view focuses on the morally autonomous individual, this view has its roots in communal moral traditions.

Despite Plato's belief that only knowledge is teachable, and therefore that it is doubtful whether moral goodness can be taught at all, the third view of moral learning maintains that it must include the acquisition of relevant knowledge and understanding, and cover the formation of dispositions. All this bears on how moral education should feature in schools – on the role of school ethos, learning by example, and the contribution of the whole curriculum.

1 Moral development
2 Moral education: the place of rules and principles
3 Moral education: the place of virtues and community
4 Procedures of moral education

1 Moral development

Let us start with a biological approach to moral growth in children. On this view morality develops in us from within, given appropriate external circumstances, from innate seed through to maturity. Rousseau's *Émile* (1762) has been a key text here for modern developmentalists, although few have followed his specific suggestion that the moral sentiments appear only with adolescence (see ROUSSEAU, J.-J. §4). Jean PIAGET charted the development of moral judgment (as distinct from moral behaviour) in children, identifying three main stages through which they pass: from a pre-moral lack of awareness of moral rules, via a perception of them as sacrosanct, to

a more reflective understanding of their point in fostering cooperation and mutual flourishing. Subsequent psychological investigations by Lawrence Kohlberg (1981) of children's moral judgments, as revealed in their responses to stories involving moral dilemmas, told a broadly similar story (see MORAL DEVELOPMENT).

Developmentalist accounts have appealed to that brand of 'child-centred' educator wary of attempts to mould or indoctrinate children into socially approved codes and attitudes and eager to leave as much as possible to children's own resources. They have not been without their critics. Carol Gilligan (1982) has drawn attention to the fact that Kohlberg's subjects were all boys; when girls' judgments were studied, their responses showed less evidence of detached appeal to principles and more of a caring response to particular individuals' needs and desires. While Gilligan's work has been important in psychology in pointing to gender differences in moral learning, it also raises the philosophical questions of what is meant by 'moral maturity' and how this is to be identified (see FEMINIST ETHICS §1). The claim that the morally highest state is consciously to be guided by abstract principles might be accepted by philosophers of a Kantian persuasion, but others might disagree (see UNIVERSALISM IN ETHICS §3).

On one view, the notion of moral development, if taken strictly, is incoherent. This view sees moral learning as a matter of being shaped in certain desired directions by one's parents, teachers and perhaps social influences more generally. It rejects the atomic individualism implicit in the developmental model, where social phenomena are at best environmental influences nurturing moral growth rather than intrinsic features of human personhood (see HUMAN NATURE §2).

2 Moral education: the place of rules and principles

An uncomplicated notion of moral education favoured by some governments, religious bodies and no-nonsense members of the public identifies it as bringing children's behaviour into line with moral rules to do with such things as telling the truth, refraining from physical harm, and keeping one's promises. In especially uncomplicated versions, these rules are 'moral absolutes', allowing of no exceptions.

Many philosophers have argued that moral education must go further than mere rule-following. For one thing, the view of what is morally wrong – that masturbation is sinful, for instance – might itself be baseless. Moral education must help young people critically to assess the acceptability of these and other rules, otherwise it may degenerate into indoctrination.

Moral autonomy is the central aim: indeed, as long as pupils are 'blind' rule-followers, they cannot strictly be said to be acting morally at all, but at best sub-morally (see AUTONOMY, ETHICAL; MORAL AGENTS). This position is clearly akin to Piaget's and Kohlberg's, except that acting according to moral principles is not the end point of a developmental process, but the product of conscious social direction. As to how the moral principles should be characterized, philosophers of education have held different views. While some have been attracted by utilitarianism, others have been more Kantian (see UTILITARIANISM; KANTIAN ETHICS). The latter group include the early R.M. Hare (1952), despite his un-Kantian insistence on individual 'decisions of principle', and Peters (1981), who would replace Kant's monistic emphasis on the categorical imperative with a broader array of 'transcendentally deduced' ultimate principles, such as impartiality, benevolence, truth-telling and liberty.

Critics of this general approach have pointed to weaknesses in its central demand that moral beliefs be based on higher-order principles. Given the disagreements just mentioned about their content and capability of rational justification, what happens if the learners, encouraged to find an incontrovertible, rational basis for their moral beliefs, fail to find one? Moral autonomists are only a hair's-breadth away from moral sceptics: if there is, after all, no good reason for being moral, why strive to be so (see MORAL SCEPTICISM; MORAL JUSTIFICATION §3)?

The question is as old as Plato, whose rationalist approach to moral education has contemporary echoes in the view under discussion. Plato's *Republic* is partly an answer to Thrasymachus' question at the outset asking why it is in his interests to be just. The account of the education of the guardians later in the work shows them learning to base their conduct not on taken-for-granted orthodoxy, but on the sure foundations of knowledge of the Good. Whether Plato's arguments here and elsewhere in the *Republic* succeed in answering Thrasymachus is disputable, as is also his assumption that if the guardians attain a proper knowledge of the Good, this is enough to guarantee their acting well (see PLATO §14). Contemporary rationalists tend to rate moral knowledge a necessary, rather than a sufficient, condition of moral learning, for in addition children have to acquire appropriate dispositions to bring their behaviour into line with what they know to be right (see MORAL KNOWLEDGE §§1–2; MORAL MOTIVATION §§1–2). Like Plato, however, their whole account is vulnerable if its foundations prove shaky.

This approach to moral education has also come under fire for the narrowness of its conception of morality. In concentrating so heavily on the rules and principles that one morally ought to follow, it does less than justice to other features of the ethical life, especially the virtues (see VIRTUES AND VICES §§1–3). True, it puts weight on intellectual virtues like clarity and independence of thought, as these will be necessary when one makes the abstraction to moral principles; true, too, that the names of proposed principles, like benevolence or impartiality, are also names of moral virtues; and that the great weight put on getting learners to see what they morally ought to do and act accordingly may be said to imply a master virtue of moral conscientiousness. But what can the theory say about children's learning to be courageous, kind, self-controlled, moderate in their bodily appetites, friendly, generous, cooperative, confident, or equipped with a proper measure of self-esteem? Even where benevolence comes into the rationalist account, as in Peters, it presupposes learners who finally come to act benevolently because this is what they morally ought to do, and not out of some more spontaneous fellow-feeling for the other. We come back to Gilligan's difficulty with Kohlberg, as well as, more broadly, to the question of the relative roles of reason and emotion in moral motivation (see MORALITY AND EMOTIONS).

3 Moral education: the place of virtues and community

Children need to learn how to regulate their feelings of anger when frustrated, as well as their bodily appetites for food, drink and in due course sex. Contemporary approaches to moral education influenced by Aristotle (for example, Carr 1991) start, as his does in *Nicomachean Ethics*, with biological features of human nature such as emotions and physical desires like these and see the educator's task as helping to shape them in desirable directions (see ARISTOTLE §22). Acquiring the virtue of self-control, for instance, is a matter of learning such things as when to feel anger or express it in appropriate behaviour, to what degree, on what occasions, and towards which people (see SELF-CONTROL).

Similar points could be made about the bodily appetites in relation to the virtue of moderation, fear in relation to courage, our inbuilt reactions to others as social animals in relation to virtues like friendliness or generosity. In each case children need habituation in responses fitting the particular occasion. These cannot be subsumed under rules as they require flexible and intelligent adjustment to circumstances (see VIRTUE ETHICS).

On such an account, moral education starts by getting children to behave in the way which a virtue would require in different particular situations. At first, they can have little or no understanding of why they have to do this, but they gradually learn to make the flexible responses just mentioned and thereby come to see what they feel and do under the aspect of, say, the courageous or the considerate, rather than, more primitively, as eliciting pleasure or preventing pain. Rationality is already at work in the shape of the practical *nous* which generates the flexible responses. It comes in, too, at a deeper level as children begin to grasp how self-control, generosity and the other virtues fit together in a wider picture of their wellbeing, Aristotle's *eudaimonia* (see EUDAIMONIA). For Aristotle, indeed, practical wisdom is the master virtue, embedded in the other virtues, but also helping us, against a larger canvas, to lead a flourishing life overall. It presupposes a theoretical understanding of whatever material is necessary for our appropriate responses. One contemporary illustration: in coming to terms with their sexual desires and knowing what to do when, young people these days have to have some knowledge of biological functions, contraception, AIDS, and their own and others' psychology.

On this view rationality has to do not with subsumption of actions under rules and rules under principles, but with relating particular responses to more global pictures of one's wellbeing (see VIRTUE ETHICS §6). The latter, in Aristotle, is inextricable from the flourishing of wider groups. While the rationalist account of moral education focuses on individuals and what they morally ought to do, the Aristotelian starting point is the ethical life of a political community (see COMMUNITY AND COMMUNITARIANISM). Learners learn the subtleties of what to do and feel within not fully articulated traditions of response embedded in their family and broader communal life (see FAMILY, ETHICS AND THE §6). In addition, the virtues they acquire – courage, temperance, justice and others – are necessary not only for their own flourishing, but also for that of those around them.

There are differences of opinion about how far this Aristotelian approach is applicable to moral education not only in the Greek city state, but also in societies of scores or hundreds of millions of people like the political units in which we live today. Has the tradition of virtues-education been eroded irreparably except within favoured religious and other communities not destroyed by the ravages of modernism, as Alasdair MACINTYRE has suggested?

Two other issues remain. First, could virtues-education be the whole of moral education? Should it be combined with elements of a rules-and-principles approach? And are there actions which do not feature in children's moral upbringing as such, but belong beyond the pale, in the realm of the unthinkable – perhaps things like murder, physical harm, or theft? Second, should children be brought up, as in the Aristotelian tradition, to see their own flourishing as inextricable from that of others? Or is 'morality' to be kept apart from 'prudence' (see PRUDENCE)? If the former, is there still any place for moral education as a distinguishable part of education?

What seems clear is that there is a great diversity of ethical values jostling for a place in children's upbringing – Aristotelian virtues, utilitarian considerations, Kantian values of impartiality, autonomy and respect for persons, role-obligations, beyond-the-pale prohibitions, commitments to one's personal projects, and more besides. If these, or most of these, are to be included, are children to be taught to arrange them, in the rationalist mode, in some kind of systematic hierarchy of importance? Or are they to be encouraged, more after the Aristotelian pattern, to resolve conflicts intelligently within and between irreducible values in the light of specific circumstances (see EXAMPLES IN ETHICS §2)?

4 Procedures of moral education

Plato first raised the question in the *Protagoras* whether morality – including the virtues of good citizenship – can be taught. Socrates doubted this on the grounds that there are no specialist teachers in this area as there are in, say, architecture or naval design (see SOCRATES §2). Socrates was assuming that teaching is a matter of transmitting knowledge. On this assumption, there is indeed a problem – despite Plato's later position in the *Republic*, described above – since the acquisition of knowledge, either propositional knowledge or skills, is no proof against wickedness. Children need to become good, not merely to know about the good. Hence the vital importance of cultivating desirable dispositions in them – which may count as teaching morality on a broader definition of 'teaching' than Socrates'. As a part of this enterprise the narrower kind of teaching of empirical knowledge is important, too, as the example of sex education shows, but only as an adjutant to the dispositions. Some moral educators would also put weight on giving children – perhaps even younger children – a more philosophical understanding of the nature of moral issues; but not all would agree with this.

As to how the dispositions and their attendant knowledge – of whatever sort – are best acquired, answers will differ according to the emphasis one puts on a communal starting point for morality and to one's views on the separability of morality from personal wellbeing. Most writers on the topic stress learning by example. As for school learning in particular, some would start with the educative ethos of the whole institution, others with classroom activities. For some, like Dewey (1909) for instance, moral education is not a separate subject, but should pervade every aspect of the life of the school community, while for others it is closely allied to religious education. For an Aristotelian the teaching of literature could be especially important in revealing conflicts of ethical value and subtleties of judgment (see EXAMPLES IN ETHICS §3).

See also: EDUCATION, PHILOSOPHY OF; EDUCATION, HISTORY OF PHILOSOPHY OF; LEARNING

References and further reading

* Aristotle (*c.* mid 4th century BC) *Nicomachean Ethics*, trans. with notes by T. Irwin, Indianapolis, IN: Hackett Publishing Company, 1985. (Book II discusses the moral virtues in general; later books look at particular virtues.)
* Carr, D. (1991) *Educating the Virtues*, London: Routledge. (A contemporary Aristotelian account of moral education, including discussions of opposing viewpoints.)
* Dewey, J. (1909) *Moral Principles in Education*, Carbondale and Edwardsville, IL: Southern Illinois University Press, 1975. (A spirited short account, in the Aristotelian tradition, of the school's contribution to moral education.)
* Gilligan, C. (1982) *In a Different Voice: Psychological Theory and Women's Development*, Cambridge, MA: Harvard University Press, chaps 1 and 2. (These chapters of this psychological study of the distinctive nature of women's moral development discuss Kohlberg's theory.)
* Hare, R.M. (1952) *The Language of Morals*, Oxford: Oxford University Press, ch. 4. (Raises questions about moral learning and teaching.)
* Kohlberg, L. (1981) *Essays on Moral Development*, New York: Harper & Row, 2 vols. (Volume I is on the philosophy of moral development, volume II on its psychology.)
* Peters, R.S. (1981) *Moral Development and Moral Education*, London: Allen & Unwin. (A collection of Peters' essays, including discussions of Piaget and Kohlberg.)
* Plato (*c.*386–380 BC) *Protagoras*, trans. W.K.C. Guthrie, in E. Hamilton and H. Cairns (eds) *Plato, The Collected Dialogues including Letters*, Oxford: Oxford University Press, 1975. (A spirited Socratic dialogue on the theme of whether virtue can be taught.)
* —— (*c.*380–367 BC) *Republic*, trans. P. Shorey, in E. Hamilton and H. Cairns (eds) *Plato, The Collected*

Dialogues including Letters, Oxford: Oxford University Press, 1975. (The first treatise on education firmly based on a philosophical system.)
* Rousseau, J.-J. (1762) *Émile: ou, de l'éducation*, trans. A. Bloom, *Emile: or, On Education*, Harmondsworth: Penguin, 1991. (An account of an ideal education in accordance with nature.)
White, J. (1990) *Education and the Good Life*, London: Kogan Page. (Explores issues raised in §3 and §4 in the context of a discussion of the aims of education as a whole.)

JOHN WHITE

MORAL EXPERTISE

Moral experts are best defined as those who have studied moral questions carefully, know the main theories developed in response to such questions, and (where possible) know and are able to offer arguments that would convince reasonable people.

In scientific and technical areas, one important feature of a successful answer is that it works, in the sense that it makes accurate predictions. We can say that successful answers to moral questions take the form of arguments which, if examined carefully, would persuade reasonable people and lead to convergence in their moral views.

The moral responsibility of individuals for themselves does not preclude the role of moral advisor. Many self-pronounced moral experts might be interfering, condescending and hypocritical, but such characteristics need not accompany moral expertise. Probably no one could claim a high degree of expertise in all areas of ethics.

1   Attempts at a definition
2   Moral expertise and scientific expertise
3   Some concerns about moral expertise

1   Attempts at a definition

Moral expertise certainly involves more than merely knowing what moral views are prevalent within a profession or a society (see MORALITY AND ETHICS §2). There are people who study different professions' 'codes of ethical practice' (see PROFESSIONAL ETHICS). There are social scientists who study and know a lot about the moral views prevalent in one or more societies. Are such people moral experts? Only the most extreme form of moral relativist will think that these people must be moral experts. The crucial question here is whether to know what a given group's moral views are is necessarily to know what actions or practices would really be morally right. Extreme moral relativism seems implausible. The moral views prevalent in some groups certainly seem morally worse than those prevalent in other groups (see MORAL RELATIVISM). Moral expertise presumably involves some ability to sort the better from the worse moral views.

We might go further and say that, if there is a distinction between better and worse moral views, then the people with the best moral views could qualify as moral experts. However, if what makes certain people moral experts is that their moral views are best, then in order to determine who the moral experts are we would first have to determine which moral views are best. Yet once we find out for ourselves which moral views are best, why do we need the notion of moral experts? If we make having the best moral views the criterion for moral expertise, it is unclear what role moral expertise has left to play.

We could try the view that experts are those who have studied the relevant questions and problems and who know the competing theories about them and whatever evidence there is. We do not have to know which controversial view in physics is right to know who the experts in physics are. Likewise, we might think of experts in some area of morality (such as business ethics or medical ethics) as those who have studied the area's moral problems, considered the opposing moral arguments, and even tested their own arguments and principles on informed audiences. The experts are sometimes proved wrong about what the correct view is, but they are the ones to whom we would reasonably go for help.

2   Moral expertise and scientific expertise

The comparison between morality and science immediately raises the question of whether a difference between them makes the idea of expertise appropriate in science but not in morality. There is broad agreement that one important feature of successful answers to scientific questions is that they make predictions that turn out to be correct. In applied sciences like medicine and mechanics, a successful answer is the one that cures the patient or makes the machine do what we want. We can then say that an expert in such fields is someone who regularly returns answers that are successful in that they achieve some agreed upon aim. So the question will be whether in ethics there is an agreed upon aim that would specify what would count as successful answers to moral questions.

Some would say that the agreed upon aim is to find ways of living and behaving that reasonable people would accept as justified. Just as an expert in medicine might be expected to give advice which, if followed, would maximize our chances of a long life, a moral expert might be expected to provide arguments which, if examined carefully, would persuade reasonable people and produce convergence in their moral views.

The criterion of success in moral arguments cannot be mere success in convincing people (after all, sophistry can be good at convincing people). Rather, the arguments must be ones whose careful examination would resolve moral disagreements. What counts as careful examination? Certainly, the arguments must be ones that would stand up to logical scrutiny. They must also be arguments whose premises and conclusions would still seem compelling after people with powerful imaginations teased out all the implications.

We should not go so far as to claim that no one can have moral expertise unless they can present moral arguments that will persuade everyone who is reasonable and considers the arguments carefully. In other disciplines, there can be expertise without convergence of opinion, so why not in ethics? But where there are arguments whose careful consideration would persuade every reasonable person, then those who can mount these arguments have greater moral expertise in this respect than those who cannot.

The stress on good arguments in ethics suggests another difference from science, especially from applied natural science. With scientific questions, we sometimes might merely want the answer that works and not really be interested in the background theories and evidence that support the answer. In ethics, however, asking for the answer to a moral question without wanting to know the reasoning behind it looks like an attempt to duck responsibility.

3   Some concerns about moral expertise

What is the point of looking for moral experts if each of us must take responsibility for the morality of our own actions and way of life? That we must take responsibility for the morality of our own actions and way of life does not preclude a role for moral advisors. Indeed, when we face difficult moral decisions, consulting judicious advisors might often be the responsible thing to do.

Nevertheless, in mainstream Western culture to call someone a moral expert would seem ironic. It would typically be thought to suggest that the person is judgmental, interfering, condescending, self-important, hypocritical and perhaps close-minded about morality. Self-righteousness is almost never attractive. But moral expertise does not inevitably lead to an unpleasant personality. On the contrary, honesty will require those with moral expertise to acknowledge their own moral mistakes and fallibility.

It will also require them to acknowledge their limitations. Few could plausibly claim a high degree of moral expertise in all of many different areas. Think how much time and energy it would take to study in depth (even just most of) the problems and theories in the ethics of medicine, business, law and government, not to mention military ethics, ethics in international affairs, academic ethics, and the ethics of personal relationships. Although there may be some features common to problems in all these areas, there are also morally relevant differences between them. So expertise in one such area does not carry over into expertise in another. Part of having an expertise can be knowing its limits.

See also: APPLIED ETHICS; MORAL KNOWLEDGE; THEORY AND PRACTICE

References and further reading

Maclean, A. (1993) *The Elimination of Morality: Reflections on Utilitarianism and Bioethics*, London: Routledge. (Contends that modern, mainly utilitarian, philosophers have been wrong to claim that they are uniquely qualified to teach moral expertise. Maclean holds that philosophy does not settle moral questions, and that philosophers do not possess special moral expertise and so cannot teach such expertise to others.)

Plato (*c.*395–387 BC) *Gorgias*, trans. W.D. Woodhead, in E. Hamilton and H. Cairns (eds) *The Collected Dialogues*, Princeton, NJ: Princeton University Press, 1961. (Classic discussion of the relationship between possessing virtue and teaching it.)

—— (*c.*386–380 BC) *Meno*, trans. W.K.C. Guthrie, in E. Hamilton and H. Cairns (eds) *The Collected Dialogues*, Princeton, NJ: Princeton University Press, 1961. (Investigation of the teachability of virtue.)

—— (*c.*386–380 BC) *Protagoras*, trans. W.K.C. Guthrie, in E. Hamilton and H. Cairns (eds) *The Collected Dialogues*, Princeton, NJ: Princeton University Press, 1961. (Another dialogue focusing on the relationship between possessing virtue and teaching it.)

Williams, B. (1995) 'Truth in Ethics', *Ratio* 8 (2): 227–42; repr. in B. Hooker (ed.) *Truth in Ethics*, Oxford: Blackwell, 1996. (Rejects the idea that having a certain kind of degree (for example, in medical ethics) qualifies someone for deciding certain moral matters. But Williams goes on to explain how there is a place for the idea of a helpful advisor on whether a particular 'thick ethical

concept' (such as 'treacherous', 'kind', 'honest') applies in a given case.)

BRAD HOOKER

MORAL JUDGMENT

The term 'moral judgment' can refer to four distinguishable things. First, the activity of thinking about whether a given object of moral assessment (be it an action, person, institution or state of affairs) has a particular moral attribute, either general (such as rightness or badness) or specific (insensitivity, integrity). Second, the state that can result from this activity: the state of judging that the object has the attribute. Third, the content of that state: what is judged by us, rather than our judging it. And fourth, the term can be read as commendatory, referring to a moral virtue that we might also call 'moral discernment' or 'moral wisdom'. There are three principal questions regarding moral judgment. The first asks what kind of state the state of moral judgment is, and in particular whether this state is to be characterized, either wholly or in part, as a state of belief. The second is concerned with the activity of moral judgment, investigating especially the role within this activity that is played by the application of rules. The third examines the conditions under which a person is justified in making a moral judgment with a given content.

1 **Cognitivism versus noncognitivism**
2 **Moral rules and deliberation**
3 **Moral rules and justification**
4 **The virtue of moral judgment and moral epistemology**

1 Cognitivism versus noncognitivism

When I think that something has a certain moral attribute (that an action is wrong, say), the state I am in seems to have features both of cognitive (belief-based) and noncognitive states (see ANALYTIC ETHICS §1). First, my moral attributions aspire to objective truth – to being true independently of my attitude towards them. For my moral attitudes can take the form 'This action is wrong, and would have been wrong even if I had approved of it', committing me to moral facts of the matter that I can be right or wrong about (see MORAL REALISM §1). And a state that aims to be true to independently obtaining facts must be thought of as a belief, it seems (see BELIEF). However, attributing a moral or any other evaluative feature to something seems to go beyond being in a merely cognitive state: it seems to involve orienting myself towards or away from the object of the attribution. In particular, it is often maintained that there is a certain sort of 'internal connection' between the state of moral judgment and the judge's motivation: it is part of the concept of judging something to be wrong that if I judge that it is wrong to perform this action in these circumstances, then (provided I am not weak-willed, and other things equal) I am motivated to avoid it in these circumstances (see MORAL MOTIVATION §§1–2).

Thus cognitivism about the state of moral judgment – the view that it consists essentially in a belief – seems to be supported by its objectivity-presupposing character, while noncognitivism (the denial of cognitivism) seems to be supported by the internal connection to motivation. The problem is not simply resolved by characterizing moral judgment as a compound state, comprising both a belief and a noncognitive companion state. For this would seem to require as an isolable component a pure belief that the action is wrong, and the possibility of such a belief is precisely what is at issue.

Beyond this, four main options present themselves. Each side of the dispute can either deny the claim being adduced in support of the other, or accept the claim while denying the relationship of support. Thus, first, a cognitivist might deny the internal connection, insisting that to the (unsurprisingly widespread) extent that moral judges tend to care about morality, this is only contingently true. A second, less plausible view is a noncognitivism that simply denies that moral judgments presuppose objectivity. Perhaps, as emotivism suggests, objectivity-presupposing moral judgments ought to be rejected and replaced with something else (see EMOTIVISM); it seems hard to deny that moral judgment as it actually exists does have this objectivity-presupposing character. This leaves two possibilities, each of which attempts to allow for both the objectivity-presupposing nature of moral judgment and its internal connection to motivation. According to the cognitivist internalism of John McDowell (1979), moral judgments are indeed beliefs, but beliefs of a special kind, in being internally connected to the believer's motivational states. And according to the noncognitivist objectivism of Simon Blackburn (1984) and Allan Gibbard (1990), the objectivity-presupposing character of moral judgments can be explained without construing them as beliefs. The central thought here is that the attitude expressed by 'This action is wrong, and would have been wrong even if I had approved of it' can be explained as a noncognitive attitude that ranges across counterfactual as well as actual possibilities – as an attitude of approval of the action not only in the

world as it is, but in the world as it would have been if I had happened to approve of the action but the world were otherwise unchanged.

It remains unclear, however, whether noncognitivism can supply a satisfactory treatment of the full range of semantic features of moral judgment-contents, and in particular, of unendorsed occurrences of moral terms, such as the first occurrence of 'wrong' in 'If blasphemy is very seriously wrong, then it is wrong to associate with blasphemers' (see ANALYTIC ETHICS §2). If not, we should be cognitivists about our actual states of moral judgment. Whether sense can be made of the objective moral facts seemingly presupposed by moral judgment is a further question – the question of moral realism (see MORAL REALISM).

2 Moral rules and deliberation

What is the role of rule-application in good deliberation about the moral attributes of things? A widespread view is this: good moral thinking identifies correct moral principles under which the moral judge then subsumes particular instances to produce a moral verdict about them (see LOGIC OF ETHICAL DISCOURSE §6; UNIVERSALISM IN ETHICS §3).

On this view, though, not much actual moral deliberation can qualify as good. Few moral judges are equipped with an exhaustive set of exceptionless moral principles by reference to which all their moral judgments are made. Most of the time, when we deliberate about whether a case instantiates a moral concept, we are engaged in an activity of moral discernment or judgment that is not simply a matter of applying a fully determinative, independently articulable rule to the case. Moreover, there seem to be good reasons not to conceive of moral deliberation as consisting ideally in the application of an exhaustive set of exceptionless moral rules. This view confronts a dilemma. Either our set of principles would be small and readily comprehensible – perhaps consisting of a single member, as in direct utilitarianism (see UTILITARIANISM) – but would need to be framed in such general terms as to make their application to even the simplest cases a difficult matter to determine; or they would be framed in terms specific enough to make the assessment of their application to particular circumstances straightforward, but would thereby need to be so numerous and highly qualified as to be unusable.

This does not yet show that good deliberation cannot consist solely in the application of rules, however. On R.M. Hare's consequentialist view (1981), the response to this problem should be to equip ourselves with a set of familiar moral rules of thumb (for instance, 'Promise-breaking is wrong, other things being equal'), together with a meta-rule that in cases where these rules conflict we should apply a fundamental principle of direct consequentialism (see CONSEQUENTIALISM; HARE, R.M.). Alternatively, Barbara Herman's Kantian theory (1985) tells us to equip ourselves with an equally familiar set of rules of moral salience – rules identifying certain features of the maxims on which actions are performed as those showing that the actions bear the burden of moral justification – together with a meta-rule that, when an action has a morally salient feature, its permissibility is to be judged in terms of the fundamental categorical imperative principle (see KANTIAN ETHICS).

3 Moral rules and justification

The views just described allow that it is proper for much of our deliberation to proceed by appealing to merely *prima facie* rules – rules specifying defeasible reasons (reasons capable of being outweighed) for making a moral attribution – but they supplement them with more fundamental, fully determinative rules governing judgment in cases where the *prima facie* rules conflict. But why should we seek rules of the fully determinative kind? The natural answer is this: good moral deliberation issues in judgments that are justified; if an all-things-considered judgment I make, in a case where my *prima facie* rules conflict, is to be justified, it cannot be arbitrary; and a judgment of mine can only be non-arbitrary if it instantiates a fully determinative rule.

When it is said that judgments are only justified by the existence of rules, two things might be intended:

(a) What makes it right to apply this concept to this object is a rule for doing so.
(b) What warrants me in judging that this concept applies to this object is a rule for doing so.

Claim (a), we might say, concerns the 'constitutive justification' of a judgment-content, whereas (b) concerns the epistemic justification of a state of judging (see JUSTIFICATION, EPISTEMIC).

Claim (a) pictures constitutive justification as consisting in the subsuming of instances under rules. This picture has been attacked, on the ground that it betrays a fallacy about rule-following (see WITTGENSTEIN, L.J.J. §10; MEANING AND RULE-FOLLOWING). Our ability to discern whether a given case falls under a rule cannot consist in our grasp of an independent meta-rule, on pain of regress. This applies to the rule 'Identify instances falling under concept *c*' as much as to any other. Proceeding correctly in the application of a concept cannot require sensitivity to an independently articulable rule which one's practice of applying the concept follows. If so, then this leaves open the possibility that there are no such further rules that justify our practice of moral concept-application. The onus is on a proponent of such rules to produce compelling examples that do square with our practice; the criticism is that they have failed to do so.

According to opponents of (a), then, there is no obstacle to the claim of 'moral pluralists' that the only defensible moral rules are *prima facie* ones (see MORAL PLURALISM). A further claim is that there are not even rules of this limited kind. This is held by moral 'particularists', who claim that there are no properties that always count as reasons for the same moral attribution. Often, the fact that an action of mine will harm someone is a reason for the wrongness of the action; but sometimes (for instance, if I am rightly administering a just punishment), it will count morally as a reason for its rightness (see LOGIC OF ETHICAL DISCOURSE §6). If so, we need to exercise a form of moral judgment that goes beyond the application of rules not only in order to determine how moral reasons relate to each other, but to determine when a consideration counts as a moral reason (see VIRTUE ETHICS §6)

4 The virtue of moral judgment and moral epistemology

If claim (a), with its subsumptive picture of constitutive moral justification, ought to be rejected, then so should (b), concerning epistemic justification. If there need be no independently articulable rule for a correct moral attribution, then there need be no such rule for my being warranted in judging that the attribution is correct. This still leaves it open to claim a relation of mutual epistemic support between my judgments concerning *prima facie* moral principles and my judgments concerning the existence of moral reasons on particular occasions, given a coherence conception of epistemic justification (see KNOWLEDGE AND JUSTIFICATION, COHERENCE THEORY OF). However, concerning the justification of my judging that, all things considered, a particular object has a given moral attribute, it seems that we must say simply that this is justified provided it is the attribution that would be made by a person with the virtue of moral judgment or discernment.

How can one ever be warranted in believing this? If the correctness of a moral judgment depends on its endorsement by an agent with a virtue the conditions for the possession of which are not independently specifiable, then it seems that any claims to epistemic justification will amount to dubious claims of self-evidence (see INTUITIONISM IN ETHICS). To progress beyond this, we should need to be able to cite the convergence in judgment of those whom we have independent reason to identify as good moral judges (see MORAL EXPERTISE).

See also: EPISTEMOLOGY AND ETHICS; FEMINIST ETHICS; MORAL JUSTIFICATION; MORAL KNOWLEDGE; OBJECTIVITY

References and further reading

* Blackburn, S. (1984) 'Evaluations, Projections, and Quasi-Realism', in *Spreading the Word*, Oxford: Clarendon Press, 181–223. (A prominent defence of noncognitivism against the objection that it cannot accommodate the objectivity-presupposing character of moral judgment.)

Dancy, J. (1993) *Moral Reasons*, Oxford: Blackwell, chaps 4–6. (A defence of particularism about moral reasons.)

Gaut, B. (1993) 'Moral Pluralism', *Philosophical Papers* 22: 17–40. (A defence of moral pluralism.)

* Gibbard, A. (1990) *Wise Choices, Apt Feelings*, Oxford: Clarendon Press. (Another prominent defence of noncognitivism.)

* Hare, R.M. (1981) *Moral Thinking*, Oxford: Clarendon Press. (A utilitarian account of moral judgment as exhausted by rule-application.)

* Herman, B. (1985) 'The Practice of Moral Judgment', *Journal of Philosophy* 82: 414–36. (A Kantian account of moral judgment as exhausted by rule-application.)

Larmore, C. (1981) 'Moral Judgment', *Review of Metaphysics* 35: 275–96. (Argues that moral deliberation is not rule-governed.)

* McDowell, J. (1979) 'Virtue and Reason', *The Monist* 63: 331–50. (A defence of cognitivism and the need for the virtue of moral judgment for the possession of moral knowledge.)

—— (1981) 'Non-Cognitivism and Rule-Following', in S.H. Holtzman and C.M. Leich (eds) *Wittgenstein: To Follow a Rule*, London: Routledge & Kegan Paul, 141–62. (An attack on the subsumptive conception of justification which seeks to support moral cognitivism.)

GARRETT CULLITY

MORAL JUSTIFICATION

Questions of justification arise in moral philosophy in at least three ways. The first concerns the way in which particular moral claims, such as claims about right and wrong, can be shown to be correct. Virtually every moral theory offers its own account of moral justification in this sense, and these accounts naturally differ from each other. A second question is about the justification of morality as a whole – about how to answer the question, 'Why be moral?' Philosophers have disagreed about this, and about whether an answer is even possible. Finally, some philosophers have claimed that justification of our actions to others is a central aim of moral thinking. They maintain that this aim provides answers to the other two questions of justification by explaining the reasons we have to be moral and the particular form that justification takes within moral argument.

1 Three questions of justification
2 Justification within morality
3 Justification of morality
4 Justification as an aim of morality

1 Three questions of justification

Questions of justification arise in moral philosophy in at least three different ways. First, it is generally taken as a central task of moral philosophy to clarify the structure of first-order moral thinking. A theory should, for example, explain 'what makes acts right'(see MORALITY AND ETHICS §1). Is the status of an action as morally right or wrong determined by its actual or expected consequences, by its conformity to certain rules or standards, or in some other way (see CONSEQUENTIALISM; DEONTOLOGICAL ETHICS)? Any theory that answers these questions provides us with an account of moral justification, that is to say, of justification *within* morality.

A second task of moral philosophy is to explain why we should care about morality and give its requirements priority over other considerations. This can be seen as a matter of providing a justification of morality.

Third, some philosophers have argued that it is a central aim of morality (or of some part of it, such as principles of justice) to provide a basis for justifying our actions or our institutions to one another, and that this aim provides a basis for understanding the importance of morality and for determining its content. According to these writers, justification is an aim of morality.

2 Justification within morality

Every moral theory offers its own account of moral justification. There is, however, a more general methodological question that transcends particular accounts of 'what makes acts right', namely the question of how the claim of any such account to be the correct account of moral justification can itself be justified.

One answer to this general methodological question has been formulated by Rawls (1971) as the method of 'reflective equilibrium' (see RAWLS, J.). According to this method, one begins by identifying one's 'considered moral judgments', those judgments in which one has the highest degree of initial confidence. These may be judgments of any degree of abstraction: judgments about the rightness or wrongness of particular actions, about the correctness of general moral principles, or about the moral relevance of various considerations. One then tries to find the set of principles (the account of the particular area of morality in question) that best fits with these judgments. This fit will almost certainly be imperfect, so one then proceeds to consider whether and how to modify the principles one has formulated to yield a better fit with one's considered judgments, and whether and how to modify these judgments in the light of the principles at which one has arrived. This process of revision leads to a new set of principles, and hence to a new stage of adjustments of principles and judgments. The process continues until 'equilibrium' between principles and judgments is reached; the principles one has formulated at that stage are to be taken as justified as an account of the area of morality in question.

This account of how moral principles are to be justified has been attacked, chiefly on the ground that it gives too much authority to the considered judgments with which the process begins. This is sometimes put in the form of a charge that it is circular to base an argument for a particular form of moral justification on some of the very beliefs that are to be justified. It is also objected that two people, using this same method, might arrive at quite different principles, because they began with a high degree of confidence in different sets of judgments. In reply, it can be said that the charge of circularity is misplaced, since the aim of the process is not to supply a needed justification for every moral belief we have, but rather to come up with the best general account of the subject matter. How else could we arrive at justified conclusions about a subject except by relying, at the outset, on those beliefs about that subject that seem to us most likely to be true? Moreover, in the search for reflective equilibrium no particular judgment is assumed, irrevocably, to be correct. Any reasons we might have for mistrusting particular beliefs are taken account of in the process as described, either as possible reasons for denying them the status of considered judgments to begin with or as reasons for abandoning them later when their incompatibility with the best account of our other beliefs comes to light.

3 Justification of morality

Turning now to the question of justifying morality itself, circularity looms when the bases of a proposed justification seem themselves to be moral in character. One cannot answer the question 'Why care about right and wrong?' by saying that it would be morally deficient not to. There is a dilemma here, however, since a justification for morality that appeals ultimately to values that are clearly not moral (such as those of self-interest) does not seem to give the right kind of explanation of morality's importance. It does not seem that virtuous people care about what is morally right because doing so is conducive to their self-interest.

Prichard (1917) concluded from this dilemma that moral philosophy, or at least that part of it that seeks to provide a justification of morality, 'rests on a mistake' (see PRICHARD, II.A. §2). A less pessimistic conclusion would be that an adequate justification, or explanation, of the authority of moral requirements must appeal ultimately to considerations which are evidently relevant to morality yet have a significance which is not wholly dependent on it. The appeal of utilitarianism for some people, and the conviction of others that morality must have a basis in religion, can be explained in part by the fact that the ideas of the greatest happiness of the greatest number and of divine will appear, to members of these groups, to be the only plausible solutions to this problem. That is to say, these reasons have seemed to represent values both relevant to morality and able to supply it with the proper authority, but not (so it is claimed) dependent on it. One question is whether there are other kinds of reasons that have this status.

The task of finding such reasons is made more difficult by morality's claim to unconditional authority, and to priority over all other values. A justification for such authority seems to require starting points that are peculiarly inescapable, and it may seem that reasons grounded in what is merely one value among others could not meet this test. Accordingly, many have attempted to justify morality by showing that it is entailed, or presupposed, by something to which everyone is committed. So, for example, Kant (1785) argued that we must take ourselves to be bound by morality in so far as we regard ourselves as rational agents, and Habermas (1990) has maintained that moral requirements are entailed by the idea of communication with others (see HABERMAS, J. §3; KANT, I. §9).

4 Justification as an aim of morality

Moral and political theories that may be broadly classed as 'contractualist' emphasize justification as an aim of morality (see CONTRACTARIANISM §9). They argue, for example, that our thinking about right and wrong is guided by the idea of what could be justified to others on grounds they could not reasonably reject (Scanlon 1982), or that principles of justice are to be defended on the ground of their suitability to serve as public standards for the assessment of claims against the basic institutions of a society (Rawls 1993).

These ideas are related to questions of justification of the two kinds already discussed. First, it can be claimed that the aim of justifiability to others determines the content of justification within morality. Rawls, for example, concludes from the thesis just mentioned about the aim of justice that principles of justice and the basic institutions of a society must be justifiable on a basis that is independent of controversial world views and conceptions of the good life. Second, it can be argued that the value of being able to justify one's actions to others has the right combination of connection with morality and independence of it to serve as an explanation of the significance that morality has for us. These claims are, however, controversial. Against them it can be maintained that the idea of justifiability to others lacks sufficient importance to account for the authority of morality and that some deeper standard of right and wrong must be presupposed as a standard of justifiability.

See also: EPISTEMIC RELATIVISM §2; FALLIBILISM; MORAL JUDGMENT; MORAL MOTIVATION §§4–7; MORAL SCEPTICISM

References and further reading

Brandt, R. (1979) *A Theory of the Good and the Right*, New York: Oxford University Press, esp. ch. 1. (Criticizes the method of reflective equilibrium and defends an alternative view of justification, appealing to ideas of rationality and to empirical psychology.)

Brink, D. (1989) *Moral Realism and the Foundations of Ethics*, Cambridge: Cambridge University Press, esp. ch. 5. (Critical discussion of issues concerning moral justification, defending a method like that of reflective equilibrium.)

Daniels, N. (1979) 'Wide Reflective Equilibrium and Theory Acceptance in Ethics', *Journal of Philosophy* 76: 256–82. (Reformulation and defence of Rawls' notion of reflective equilibrium.)

* Habermas, J. (1990) 'Discourse Ethics: Notes on a Program on Philosophical Justification', in *Moral Consciousness and Communicative Action*, trans. C. Lenhardt and S. Nicholson, Cambridge, MA: MIT Press, 1990, 43–115; repr. in S. Benhabib and F. Dallmayr (eds) *The Communicative Ethics Controversy*, Cambridge, MA: MIT Press, 1990, 60–110. (Argues that moral requirements are entailed by the idea of communication with others.)

Hare, R.M. (1973) 'Critical Study: Rawls' Theory of Justice', in two parts, *Philosophical Quarterly* 23: 144–55, 241–52; repr. in N. Daniels (ed.) *Reading Rawls*, Oxford: Blackwell, 1975. (Attacks the methods of justification employed in Rawls' *A Theory of Justice*.)

* Kant, I. (1785) *Grundlegung zur Metaphysik der Sitten*, trans. with notes by H.J. Paton, *Groundwork of the Metaphysics of Morals* (originally *The Moral Law*), London: Hutchinson, 1948; repr. New York: Harper & Row, 1964. (Classic attempt to base morality on rationality.)

* Prichard, H.A. (1917) 'Does Moral Philosophy Rest on a Mistake?', *Mind* 21 (81): 21–37; repr. in *Moral Obligation, Essays And Lectures*, ed. and with a note by W.D. Ross, Oxford: Clarendon Press, 1949. (Argues that it is a mistake to attempt to justify morality by offering an answer to the question, 'Why be moral?')

* Rawls, J. (1971) *A Theory of Justice*, Cambridge, MA: Harvard University Press, section 9. (Describes the method of reflective equilibrium, and defends principles of justice by arguing that they would be agreed to in a suitably defined 'original position'.)

* —— (1993) *Political Liberalism*, New York: Columbia University Press, esp. lectures IV, VI. (Defends a view of how basic institutions and claims of justice should be justified in a pluralistic society.)

* Scanlon, T.M. (1982) 'Contractualism and Utilitarianism', in A. Sen and B. Williams (eds) *Utilitarianism and Beyond*, Cambridge: Cambridge University Press, 103–28. (Argues that justifiability to others is the guiding aim of our ideas of right and wrong.)

T.M. SCANLON

MORAL KNOWLEDGE

One possesses moral knowledge when, but only when, one's moral opinions are true and held justifiably. Whether anyone actually has moral knowledge is open to serious doubt, both because moral opinions are so hard to justify and because there is reason to think moral opinions are expressions not of belief (which might be evaluated as true or false) but of taste or preference. A successful defence of the view that people do have moral knowledge requires assuaging these doubts. Attempts in this direction standardly emphasize the respects in which our moral opinions, and the evidence we have for them, are analogous to the opinions and evidence we have concerning nonmoral matters, such as logic, mathematics, science, psychology and history. In the process they attempt to show that we do have good reason to think some of our moral opinions are true.

1   Confidence and evidence
2   Noncognitivism
3   Scepticism

1   Confidence and evidence

People frequently, and quite casually, assume they have moral knowledge, in so far as they stand ready to act on the moral views they embrace. Yet people are circumspect when it comes to claiming moral knowledge, largely because so much of morality is controversial, but also because it is disturbingly difficult to defend in detail any particular moral view. Indeed, the confidence people have in their own moral convictions, although not easily shaken, often looks poorly backed by anything reasonably thought of as evidence or argument.

This apparent mismatch between confidence and evidence is largely explainable by noting that morality requires knowing how – how to act, react and feel – and not knowing that – that injustice is wrong, courage is laudable, kindness a virtue. One might well have the requisite abilities and skills without being able to articulate, let alone offer evidence for, one's moral views. Appreciating the practical dimension of morality is crucial to understanding its intimate connection with action. At the same time, it suggests that a proper account of morality must avoid an excessively intellectualized picture of the capacities it requires.

Still, on most accounts, people count as having moral knowledge, as opposed to moral virtue, only if (a) their moral beliefs are true and (b) those beliefs are justified. Thought of in this way, moral knowledge is an intellectual accomplishment. Against this background, arguments for thinking no one has moral knowledge commonly take one of two forms. Some hold that moral convictions are not properly seen as beliefs at all, which would mean we cannot satisfy (a). Others grant that people do have moral beliefs, but hold that such beliefs are all unjustified, which would

mean we do not satisfy (b). A defence of moral knowledge must meet both threats (see MORAL SCEPTICISM §3).

2   Noncognitivism

The first threat, posed by noncognitivists, usually travels with a positive account of moral convictions, according to which moral judgments reflect the preferences, or desires, of those who make them, but do not express beliefs. Noncognitivism finds support from the fact that moral opinions seem not to be empirically verifiable. As Hume put the point (1739/40), there appears to be no way to derive an 'ought' from an 'is', no way to establish a moral conclusion by appeal only to empirical premises (see HUME, D. §4.8; LOGIC OF ETHICAL DISCOURSE). G.E. Moore (1903) pressed this observation against all attempts to define moral claims in empirical terms, using what has come to be called the 'open question' argument (see MOORE, G.E. §1). He maintained that all definitions of a moral term (say, 'good') using nonmoral terms (say, 'pleasure') are undermined by the fact that it always makes sense, in a way that it would not if the terms had the same meaning, to ask whether something describable by the empirical terms was describable using the moral term. It makes sense, for instance, to ask whether something pleasant is good in a way that it does not make sense to ask whether something pleasant is pleasant. Moore himself concluded that moral claims describe non-empirical, *sui generis* facts (see INTUITIONISM IN ETHICS). Noncognitivists, in contrast, have held that if a claim is not empirically verifiable, it does not describe anything whatsoever. They conclude that the open question argument shows that moral claims, precisely because they cannot be defined in empirical terms, have no (descriptive) meaning and so cannot express beliefs (see ANALYTIC ETHICS).

Noncognitivists frequently come to the same conclusion via another route by appealing to the apparently intimate connection between thinking that some action is morally required or good and being motivated (at least to some degree) to perform it. This connection is easily explained, the noncognitivists note, once we see moral 'beliefs' not as genuine beliefs but instead as motivational states akin to desires or preferences (see MORAL MOTIVATION §§1–2).

Whichever way one comes to the conclusion that moral claims do not express beliefs, the implications for moral knowledge are the same. For if a person's moral view fails to express a belief then that view, however salutary, cannot rightly be dignified as knowledge.

Against this threat, many cognitivists argue that, on a suitably sophisticated understanding of empirical verification, moral claims actually are verifiable. And they maintain that the open question argument establishes at most that moral claims are not synonymous with empirical claims, not that they are empirically unverifiable. Others, though, grant that moral claims are not empirically verifiable, but argue against empirical verifiability as a proper criterion for meaningfulness. As for the connection between moral conviction and motivation, cognitivists either deny that the connection is as intimate as the noncognitivists suppose, or argue that the intimate connection can be just as well explained without abandoning the view that moral convictions are expressions of belief. However these particular responses play out, cognitivists regularly stress the extent to which moral convictions resemble beliefs. We see them as answerable to evidence and argument, talk of them as true or false, and distinguish between those who know right from wrong and those who do not. All of this suggests that adopting a moral conviction is a matter of forming a belief about how things are morally.

3   Scepticism

The second threat to moral knowledge, posed by sceptics, leaves unchallenged the contention that we have moral beliefs. Instead, it attacks our right to see these beliefs as justified. We may believe that deliberate cruelty is wrong, and that slavery is unjust, but (the sceptic maintains) we have, at bottom, no good reason for thinking such beliefs are true.

The sceptical challenge, to the extent it raises a special problem for *moral* knowledge, depends on drawing a contrast between moral and nonmoral beliefs that shows the former to be especially suspect. Three considerations are standardly marshalled in support of such an unflattering contrast.

The first is that even a cursory glance across cultures, or back through history, reveals an astonishing diversity of moral views (see MORAL RELATIVISM). That people so frequently come to such different, and incompatible, opinions makes the thought that they form their opinions in response to evidence or argument radically implausible. At the same time, the diversity exhibits a telling pattern. It looks as if the opinions people hold by and large reflect either their own interests or the interests of the powerful. This recommends seeing the moral views people embrace as mere rationalizations or as reflections of systems of social control and regulation (see IDEOLOGY). Either way, moral beliefs emerge as views we have no reason to think true – even when the views happen to be advantageous.

The second consideration picks up on Hume's point that there is an unbridgeable gap between 'is' and 'ought' and highlights the way in which, in defending one moral belief against others, we seem inevitably to appeal to other moral commitments that are equally contentious. In arguing with particular people we sometimes find common ground and can proceed, using our shared assumptions, to resolve a debate. The resolution is available, however, only because we share some moral view with them that others could reasonably challenge. To meet such a challenge, rather than ignore it or oppose it with force, we will (again inevitably) need to appeal to some other moral view in order to defend the one in question. Yet we will then just be pushing the issue back, finding ourselves appealing to another assumption which is itself either unsupported or supported by an undefended moral assumption. Thus the is/ought gap appears to entail that the only defence one might offer of one's moral beliefs is one that illegitimately presupposes others. So again our moral beliefs emerge as views we have no reason to think true – even when we can appeal to some in defending others.

The third consideration focuses on what the world would have to be like in order for our moral beliefs to be true and justified. Moral facts putatively stand as authoritative guides to action. Yet it is hard to make sense of this authority at all, and harder still to reconcile such authority with a plausible view of the natural world. Moreover, if there are moral facts, they are presumably connected in some way to various nonmoral facts. After all, we often appeal to nonmoral facts to explain moral ones, saying for instance that some action is good because it causes pleasure. But the connection between these nonmoral facts and the moral facts looks to be utterly mysterious. Perhaps most troubling of all, there seems to be no good way to explain how we discover these peculiar facts and their connection to the more mundane facts upon which they supposedly depend. These difficulties all provide reason to think the world is not the way it would have to be in order for our beliefs to be true and justified (see MORAL REALISM §6; NATURALISM IN ETHICS). This time our moral beliefs emerge not only as views we have no reason to think true, but as views we have positive grounds for rejecting as false.

Against the sceptics, those who hold that moral beliefs are sometimes justified standardly note, to start, that moral disagreement is not as widespread as the sceptics suggest nor noticeably more common than disagreements concerning empirical matters. At least when it comes to fundamental moral principles (concerning, say, the value of life, the importance of honesty, the nobility of courage) there is actually a striking consensus. Disagreements at a less fundamental level are, of course, common. Yet these disagreements frequently turn on differences of opinion concerning plain matters of fact. When they do not, the arguments we offer on behalf of a particular moral view will, as the sceptic says, inevitably implicate further moral assumptions. However, in this respect, moral arguments resemble nonmoral arguments in that the latter too must always be advanced against a background provided by additional (in these cases, nonmoral) assumptions. Indeed, whether the disagreements are moral or not, almost any argument one side offers will appeal to considerations the other side might intelligibly call into question. Thus, it seems, neither of the first two considerations advanced by sceptics stands as an especially strong argument for thinking our moral beliefs suffer by contrast with other sorts of beliefs we readily acknowledge as (sometimes) justified.

In response to the third consideration, many argue that neither moral facts nor our epistemic access to them are as mysterious as sceptics maintain. To a large extent, the suggestion that moral facts, and so our access to them, would have to be mysterious rests on rejecting the view that such facts are reducible to, or constituted by, natural facts. Yet the standard arguments against naturalism, which appeal to the open question argument and the is/ought gap, lose much of their force in light of recent developments in semantics and metaphysics. Such developments suggest, first, that the open question argument mistakenly assumes that moral and nonmoral terms can refer to the same property only if they are synonymous and, second, that our inability to infer moral conclusions from nonmoral premises is no more significant than our similar inability to infer biological or psychological conclusions from nonbiological or nonpsychological premises. If naturalism concerning moral facts is defensible, then our epistemic access to moral facts is no more puzzling than is our access to nonmoral facts, even if it is sometimes more tenuous.

Whether or not naturalism is, in the end, defensible, many argue that we have strong evidence for some of our moral views anyway. They make their case by emphasizing the significant respects in which the evidence we have for our moral views is analogous to the evidence we can marshal for certain nonmoral views. Moral sense theorists, for instance, see some moral beliefs as analogous to perceptual judgments and suggest these justify our other moral views in much the way perception provides support for our scientific theories (see MORAL SENSE THEORIES). Alternatively, intuitionists and rationalists maintain

that we come to know certain moral truths – truths that can then provide evidence for others – in just the way we come to know certain fundamental truths of mathematics or logic, by relying on reason and reflection. These particular proposals usually play out against the assumption that justification is possible at all only if at least some fundamental beliefs can serve to justify others without themselves needing support. But even those who reject this foundationalist view, and embrace instead a coherentist conception of justification, argue that moral beliefs, no less than various nonmoral beliefs, are justified to the extent that they stand in relations of mutual support (see KNOWLEDGE AND JUSTIFICATION, COHERENCE THEORY OF; FOUNDATIONALISM). The common thread in all these suggestions is the persistent pressure to recognize that our grounds for accepting particular moral views are not significantly different in kind from the grounds we have for other views that are standardly thought to be unproblematic. And the suggestion is that experience, reason and reflection, which are the main tools we have for learning about the world, may help us as well in coming to a justified view of morality.

See also: COMMON-SENSE ETHICS; EMOTIVISM; JUSTIFICATION, EPISTEMIC; KNOWLEDGE, CONCEPT OF; MORAL EXPERTISE; MORAL JUDGMENT; PRESCRIPTIVISM

References and further reading

Ayer, A.J. (1936) *Language, Truth and Logic*, London: Gollancz; 2nd edn, 1946. (Classic appeal to verifiability considerations in defence of noncognitivism.)

Brink, D. (1989) *Moral Realism and the Foundations of Ethics*, Cambridge: Cambridge University Press. (Offers a defence of cognitivism combined with a coherentist epistemology.)

Daniels, N. (1979) 'Wide Reflective Equilibrium and Theory Acceptance in Ethics', *Journal of Philosophy* 76: 256–82. (Articulates method of 'reflective equilibrium' with special attention to its epistemological implications.)

Ewing, A.C (1947) *Ethics*, London: Macmillan. (Defends a fallibilist version of intuitionism.)

Harman, G. (1977) *The Nature of Morality*, New York: Oxford University Press. (Mobilizes forcefully the worry that moral beliefs might be unjustified because they do not figure in the best explanations of our experiences.)

Hudson, W.D. (1969) (ed.) *The Is/Ought Question*, London: Macmillan. (Collection of papers exploring the plausibility and significance of the gap between 'is' and 'ought'.)

* Hume, D. (1739/40) *A Treatise of Human Nature*, ed. L.A. Selby-Bigge, revised by P.H. Nidditch, Oxford: Clarendon Press, 2nd edn, 1978. (Seminal expression of arguments often taken to support either moral scepticism or noncognitivism, but also (on some interpretations) a defence of moral sense theory.)

Kant, I. (1785) *Grundlegung zur Metaphysik der Sitten*, trans. with notes by H.J. Paton, *Groundwork of the Metaphysics of Morals* (originally *The Moral Law*), London: Hutchinson, 1948; repr. New York: Harper & Row, 1964. (Classic articulation of the view that morality can be grounded in rationality.)

Mackie, J.L. (1977) *Ethics: Inventing Right and Wrong*, Harmondsworth: Penguin. (Defends moral scepticism by appeal to the ontological and epistemological difficulties that attend a belief in moral facts.)

* Moore, G.E. (1903) *Principia Ethica*, Cambridge: Cambridge University Press. (Classic defence of intuitionism that has shaped most of twentieth-century meta-ethics.)

Ross, W.D. (1930) *The Right and the Good*, Oxford: Oxford University Press. (Important extension and elaboration of intuitionism.)

Sayre-McCord, G. (ed.) (1988) *Essays on Moral Realism*, Ithaca, NY: Cornell University Press. (Collection of papers devoted to issues related to noncognitivism and scepticism.)

Sinnott-Armstrong, W. and Timmons, M. (eds) (1996) *Moral Knowledge?*, New York: Oxford University Press. (Collection of contemporary papers on moral knowledge.)

Stevenson, C.L. (1937) 'The Emotive Meaning of Ethical Terms', *Mind* 46: 14–31. (Influential defence of noncognitivism that highlights the pragmatic role of moral language.)

GEOFFREY SAYRE-McCORD

MORAL LUCK

The term 'moral luck' was introduced by Bernard Williams in 1976 to convey the idea that moral status is, to a large extent, a matter of luck. For example, that Bob grows up to be vicious and Tom to be virtuous depends very much on their different family conditions and educational background. Following Williams, Thomas Nagel widened the scope of moral luck. The position taken by both stands in stark contrast to the widely-held view, influenced by Kant, that one is morally accountable only for what is under one's control, so that moral accountability is not a matter of luck. This idea is so deeply entrenched in our modern concept of morality that rejecting it would call for a rethinking and reformulation of the most basic notions of morality. Some have argued that the paradox of moral luck provides a strong reason to abandon traditional moral theories, and lends support to virtue ethics.

1 Domains of moral luck
2 Arguments for and against moral luck
3 Theoretical implications

1 Domains of moral luck

Bernard Williams introduced the term 'moral luck' in 1976, to convey the idea that moral status is largely a matter of luck. Williams' main interest lies in how luck may influence agents' reflective assessment of their actions, that is, in their ability to justify rationally their decisions and actions to themselves. He uses the example of Gauguin, who abandoned his family to pursue his artistic aspirations in Tahiti. In Williams' view, whether Gauguin's choice can be justified depends on the success of his venture, a success not entirely under his control and, thus, in part, a matter of luck. Two obstacles block the agent's capacity to guarantee retroactive justification in such decisions. First, at the time of the decision-making the agent can never know how things will turn out. Second, in projects like that of Gauguin's, the project often changes the very character and attitudes of the agent. The Gauguin at the time of the decision has no way of knowing whether Gauguin after the decision will approve retroactively of the project (see WILLIAMS, B.A.O. §2)

While Williams is concerned mainly with luck from the 'subjective' point of view, namely, with how agents relate to the justification of their own actions, Thomas Nagel seeks to show the influence of luck from a more 'objective' point of view. According to Nagel (1976), luck affects morality in four ways. The first is 'constitutive luck', luck in the kind of person one is, which depends, at least partially, on factors beyond one's control (such as heredity and environment). The second is 'circumstantial luck', luck in the kind of problems and situations one faces. Nagel offers the example of some young Germans who were morally lucky to have left Germany in the early 1930s. Had they stayed, they would have been faced with a terrible moral test which many of them would probably have failed. Thus, according to Nagel, whether or not a person became a Nazi murderer was, to a significant extent, a matter of circumstantial luck.

The other two ways luck is believed to influence morality have to do with the causes and effects of actions. One is concerned with the way antecedent circumstances determine the acts of the will itself (see WILL, THE). If determinism is true, then our very choices are beyond our control, and thus a matter of (good or bad) luck (see FREE WILL). The other and last kind of luck, sometimes referred to as 'resultant luck', is luck in the outcome of one's actions and projects. This includes cases of decisions made with uncertainty, as when a political leader decides to go to war knowing full well at the time of the decision that if the venture fails, the decision can never be justified retroactively; and cases of negligence, such as that of two reckless drivers, one of whom is lucky, not causing any injury, the other being unlucky, hitting a child crossing the road. The independence of these different kinds of luck from one another makes life difficult for critics of moral luck. To sustain the alleged immunity of morality to luck, they have to show that each and all of them have no effect of morality.

Attempts to apply the contemporary debate on moral luck to ancient philosophy focus on another aspect of luck, namely, its relation to wellbeing. Some ancient schools, especially those of the Cynics and Stoics, argued that immunity to luck is a necessary condition for wellbeing, while others, notably Aristotle, emphasized the essential vulnerability of human happiness (eudaimonia) (see CYNICS; STOICISM, ARISTOTLE §21; EUDAIMONIA). According to Martha Nussbaum (1986), their different attitudes towards the role of luck mark an important difference between Aristotle and Plato (see PLATO).

2 Arguments for and against moral luck

To resolve the paradox of moral luck, some have criticized the vivid examples presented by Williams and Nagel. With regard to the lucky and unlucky drivers, for example, it has been argued that our different ways of relating to them are not to be explained by reference to the drivers' ultimately different moral status – they were equally reckless – but to our epistemic shortcomings. In most cases, we know about other people's personalities and intentions only through their actual behaviour. Hence, contra Williams and Nagel, luck does not affect one's real desert, but only our knowledge of it.

Proponents of moral luck have argued that any attempt to detach ourselves from the unintentional and unforeseen aspects of our actions would make it impossible for us to retain our identity and character as agents. Since every aspect of our moral life results from factors which are beyond our control, there seems to be nothing left for us to be responsible for and the area of genuine agency, the traditional locus of moral judgments, shrinks to an extensionless point. Such a detachment also carries with it unwanted normative implications. If responsibility were to be limited strictly to what is under our control, we would be able to walk away from the sick, the old, and the otherwise helpless, provided their helplessness was not an intended result of any agent's actions. A world without moral luck, that is, a world where the boundaries of our responsibilities are determined by what is under our control, would thus be – on this argument – a place in which most of us would not want to live (see RESPONSIBILITY §§2–3; DESERT AND MERIT §§2–3).

3 Theoretical implications

Acceptance of the existence of moral luck has significant implications for ethical theory. Williams and others have argued that the paradox of moral luck provides us with a powerful reason to abandon the ethics of duty and to adopt some kind of virtue ethics (see VIRTUE ETHICS). Virtue ethics is expected to escape the problem of moral luck by focusing on good and bad traits of character, instead of on notions of moral responsibility and blame. While we refrain from attributing responsibility and blame in cases where luck is involved in the action under question, we do not change our judgment of character if having a certain character is a matter of luck.

Allowing luck to encroach into the realm of morality means assigning less importance to the category of the voluntary, as the boundaries of our responsibility and obligations would on this view extend beyond the limits of our voluntary actions. If moral luck exists, we might be accountable for results we could not control, and we might be responsible for other people even if we never voluntarily committed ourselves to them. Since reference to the voluntary versus the nonvoluntary seems to be embodied in the very notion of the 'moral', acceptance of moral luck would imply abandoning, or assigning much less significance to, the common distinction between the moral and the nonmoral. Such a move is indeed made by most proponents of moral luck.

See also: PRAISE AND BLAME

References and further reading

Kenny, A. (1993) 'Aristotle on Moral Luck', in R.W. Sharples (ed.) *Modern Thinkers and Ancient Thinkers*, London: University College London.

(An attempt to relate the modern debate on moral luck to its ancient and medieval antecedents.)

* Nagel, T. (1976) 'Moral Luck', *Proceedings of the Aristotelian Society*, supplementary vol. 50: 137–51. (Responds to Williams' essay of the same title (published in the same issue of this journal), disagreeing on some points but accepting and further expanding the notion of the vulnerability of morality to luck.)

* Nussbaum, M. (1986) *The Fragility of Goodness: Luck and Ethics in Greek Tragedy and Philosophy*, New York: Cambridge University Press. (Discusses attitudes to luck in ancient literature and philosophy, especially in the work of Plato and Aristotle.)

Statman, D. (1991) 'Moral and Epistemic Luck', *Ratio* 4: 146–56. (Explores the relation between the problem of moral luck and that of epistemic luck.)

* —— (ed.) (1993) *Moral Luck*, Albany, NY: State University of New York Press. (Includes the articles of Williams and Nagel, as well as most of the important discussions of the topic, a postscript of Williams to his 1976 paper, and a comprehensive introduction by the editor.)

* Williams, B. (1976) 'Moral Luck', *Proceedings of the Aristotelian Society*, supplementary vol. 50: 115–36; repr. in *Moral Luck: Philosophical Papers 1973–80*, Cambridge: Cambridge University Press, 1981, 20–39. (Introduces the term 'moral luck' and explains the central role played by luck in morality, especially in retroactive justification.)

DANIEL STATMAN

MORAL MOTIVATION

Questions about the possibility and nature of moral motivation occupy a central place in the history of ethics. Philosophers disagree, however, about the role that motivational investigations should play within the larger subject of ethical theory. These disagreements surface in the dispute about whether moral thought is necessarily motivating – 'internalists' affirming that it is, 'externalists' denying this.

The disagreement between externalists and internalists reflects a basic difference in how the subject matter of ethics is conceived: externalism goes with the view that ethics is primarily about the truth of theories, construed as sets of propositions, while internalists see morality as a set of principles meant to guide the practical deliberations of individual agents. Internalists interpret questions of objectivity in ethics as questions of practical reason, about the authority of moral principles to regulate our activities. Here controversy has centred on whether the authority of practical principles for a given agent must be grounded in that agent's antecedent desires, or whether, instead, practical reason can give rise to new motivations.

There are also important questions about the content of moral motivations. A moral theory should help us to make sense of the fact that people are often moved to do the right thing, by identifying a basic motive to moral behaviour that is both widespread and intelligible, as a serious source of reasons. Philosophers have accounted for moral motivation in terms of self-interest, sympathy, and a higher-order concern to act in accordance with moral principles. But each of these approaches faces difficult challenges. Can egoistic accounts capture the distinctive character of moral motivation? Can impartial sympathy be integrated within a realistic system of human ends? Can we make sense of responsiveness to moral principle, as a natural human incentive?

1 **Internalism and externalism**
2 **Implications**
3 **Reason and desire**
4 **Explanation and justification**
5 **Egoism and self-interest**
6 **Altruism and sympathy**
7 **Principle-dependent motives**

1 Internalism and externalism

Internalism states that moral considerations are necessarily motivating for those who grasp them. The most common version of this position is the claim that sincere acceptance of a moral judgment implies that the person who accepts it has some motive – not necessarily overriding – for compliance with the judgment. Externalists deny this, insisting that one might sincerely accept a moral judgment without any corresponding motivation. On this view, psychological questions about human motivation are completely distinct from issues about the truth of moral judgments or the nature and constitution of moral facts (see MORAL JUDGMENT §1; MORAL REALISM §1).

The categories 'internalism' and 'externalism' were introduced only in the middle of the twentieth century. It is often unclear how exactly these categories are to be understood, inviting confusion about their precise extension. (Which moral judgments are supposed to be motivationally effective? How are we to understand the notion of a motive that is present, but not necessarily overriding?) So it is often hard to classify moral philosophers as internalists or externalists as such.

Nevertheless, David Hume is presumably giving

voice to an internalist point of view when he makes central to his theory the idea that 'morals excite passions, and produce or prevent actions' (1739/40: 457). In characteristic internalist fashion, Hume interprets this idea as placing the important constraint on an account of moral distinctions that it must explain how grasping moral distinctions could immediately give rise to passions and actions, in the way it seems to do. By contrast, the hermetic distinction drawn by John Stuart Mill (1861), between the proof of the principle of utility and the sanctions for compliance with it, suggests an externalist position. On this position, it would be possible to accept a moral principle without having any tendency to act in accordance with it; the question of the truth of a moral principle is thus taken to be completely distinct from the psychological issue of whether and how the principle can be rendered effective in people's motivations (see HUME, D. §4.8; MILL, J.S. §§7–8).

2 Implications

The issue of moral motivation is a crux in discussions about the nature and status of moral judgments and moral values. Noncognitivists, who hold that moral judgments express emotions or preferences rather than report genuine truths, often start out by affirming that moral judgment is directly motivating, a version of internalism (see MORAL JUDGMENT §1; EMOTIVISM) Underlying the position that only noncognitivism can explain this fact is the assumption that the cognitive states through which we grasp judgments capable of genuine truth are motivationally inert.

In a more metaphysical vein, irrealists or error theorists, who deny the reality of moral values in the world, similarly argue from internalist assumptions. Real moral values would have to have the distinctive property of affecting the will directly. But, it is argued, items with this property would be mysterious–utterly unlike the other kinds of things with which we are familiar in the world–and so we should be reluctant to include them in the inventory of reality (see MORAL REALISM §7).

Philosophers who wish to resist these conclusions may either accept internalism, and try to show that cognitivist or realist views can account for the motivational effects of ethical reflection, or reject internalism (see MORAL REALISM §§4–5). Those who pursue the second option need not deny that people are often motivated to do what they judge to be morally right or good. Like Mill, however, they insist that motivations of this kind are not necessarily built into moral reflection; rather it is the task of moral education to supply them.

The interest of this dispute lies in its connection

with fundamentally divergent ways of thinking about moral objectivity and the subject matter of ethics. Externalism goes naturally with the view that moral philosophy is essentially about moral theories, construed as sets of propositions setting out what it is morally right or good to do. On this conception, questions of objectivity in ethics turn primarily on the truth of the propositions that make up competing moral theories. But whether a given proposition is true or false seems independent of the psychological question of whether and how people may be moved to act in accordance with it. Taking this approach seriously, we may be led to the conclusion that the true moral theory should be esoteric, so that the theory itself provides good reasons for discouraging people from accepting it, a conclusion countenanced by Sidgwick and other utilitarians (see SIDGWICK, H. §2).

Internalist approaches, by contrast, conceive of moral philosophy as dealing with common principles for public moral discourse and practical deliberation. On this view, the issue of objectivity in ethics is conceived primarily as an issue of practical reason, about the title of moral principles to regulate our activities. Moral reflection is accordingly thought of as a form of practical deliberation, yielding verdicts about what is to be done, and questions about the truth of moral propositions assume a subsidiary role. If we conceive of the subject in this way, then some form of internalism will seem inevitable, since it is the distinguishing mark of practical deliberation that it affects the will directly. Furthermore, it will hardly make sense to suppose that the criteria of right defined by the correct moral theory should be esoteric, since the kind of objectivity aimed at primarily in ethical theory is precisely an objectivity within practical reason (see PRACTICAL REASON AND ETHICS).

3 Reason and desire

Within the internalist camp, there are striking disagreements about the degree to which the motivational consequences of practical reason effectively constrain our philosophical options. On one side are the Humeans, who hold that practical reasoning must always be grounded in the noncognitive psychological states of individual agents – what Bernard Williams calls their 'subjective motivational sets' (1980) (see WILLIAMS, B.A.O. §3). Combined with internalism, this view has the consequence that moral principles are hostage to antecedent, empirical facts about the motivational sets of the agents to whom the principles apply. This conclusion in turn exerts some pressure in the direction of relativism, since motives to comply with moral principles may, as a matter of empirical fact, fail to show up in the subjective sets of all agents (see MORAL RELATIVISM).

On the other side, Kantians deny that empirical facts about people's subjective motivational sets place substantive restrictions on the content or normative force of moral principles. They point out that any theory of practical reason must allow for the phenomenon of motivational irrationality (see AKRASIA). Thus I may fail to take steps that I know to be necessary if I am to attain some end that I hold dear. The principle that I ought to pursue those means that are necessary for realizing my ends does not entail that I will necessarily be motivated accordingly, but only that I will be motivated accordingly in so far as I am rational. This has been pointed out by Christine Korsgaard (1986). If she is right, then it cannot be inferred from the fact that a given agent lacks an empirical motive for compliance with a candidate principle that the principle is not binding on the agent, since it is possible that the agent is irrational. To decide whether that is the case, however, we will need to determine – in a way that is not circumscribed by antecedent facts about people's motives – the content of principles of practical reason.

A central question in this dispute concerns the role of desires in the explanation of motivation. Humean resistance to the idea of practical principles that are not grounded in people's subjective sets stems from the idea that motivation is essentially a noncognitive orientation to the world. Kantians – most notably including Thomas Nagel (1970) – have granted that motivation always involves a state of desire, but suggested that reasoning in accordance with practical principles may give rise to new desires, so that the validity of such principles for a given agent need not be constrained by the items already contained in that agent's subjective motivational set (see NAGEL, T. §5).

4 Explanation and justification

However this dispute is resolved, it cannot be denied that the disposition to respond to moral principles is reliably awakened and strengthened in the normal course of human psychological development. Furthermore, moral reasons often weigh heavily with people in their practical deliberations, leading them to take remarkable steps to avoid doing what would be wrong. It seems a reasonable constraint on moral theories that they should help us to make sense of these facts. A theory on which it appeared utterly mysterious that people naturally respond to moral considerations and take them seriously in their deliberations would be to that extent implausible.

What is needed is an account of the content of our moral incentives. Moral theories typically identify some common pattern of motivation, such as sympathy or self-interest, and try to show how motivations of that type might lead people to comply with principles of right, as the theory characterizes them. In practice, human motives are heterogeneous, complex and fluid; why should we suppose that there is any general account to be had of our responsiveness to moral considerations? This supposition is linked to two controversial normative assumptions. First, there is the assumption that moral considerations hang together in such a way that a uniform account can be provided of what makes actions morally wrong (in terms, for instance, of the effects of the actions on general utility, or the failure of universalizability). Philosophers who accept this assumption naturally expect to find a complementary general pattern of moral motivation, while those who deny it – some virtue theorists, perhaps – will be more sceptical.

Second, it is commonly assumed that modern morality aspires to a kind of objectivity within practical reason, providing public principles that make claims on virtually all agents. Here controversy centres not so much on whether morality represents itself as authoritative in this way, as on its title to such authority. How this controversy is resolved will depend in part on whether we can identify incentives to moral behaviour that are both widespread in human nature and intelligible as serious sources of reasons, for the availability of such common motivational structures would seem a necessary condition for the objective authority of morality.

It would not, however, be sufficient. If Nietzsche and Freud are right, for instance, then there are common motivational structures at the root of moral responsiveness, involving internal mechanisms for enforcing compliance with moral norms that draw on the redirection of aggressive impulses back against the self (see NIETZSCHE, F. §§8–9; FREUD, S. §8). These accounts suggest a ready explanation of the urgency with which moral demands are invested in the deliberations of many agents; indeed, they have the further advantage of being able to explain the characteristic pathologies of the moral life, such as moralistic forms of extreme self-denial. But the explanations provided by these accounts seem to undermine rather than to vindicate the authority of morality, suggesting that the common patterns of moral motivation are essentially harmful for the individuals subject to them.

This shows that the authority of morality will depend not just on the availability of a common incentive to moral behaviour, but on the content of the common incentive that is identified. An account of moral motivation congenial to morality's normative ambitions would, at a minimum, identify a motive to moral behaviour that can be cultivated without necessarily causing dire psychological harm to the individual who has the motive. Beyond this, an effective moral motive should be capable of being integrated within an agent's overall system of ends, so as to produce a stable and self-reinforcing personality.

5 Egoism and self-interest

Very few philosophers accept egoism, construed as the psychological thesis that our motives are uniformly self-interested. This bald thesis flies in the face of the many occasions on which people act without any apparent concern for their own interests, however broadly conceived. Even when our motives are self-interested, the specification of our interests would seem to presuppose some core of nonegoistic concerns, a point well made by Joseph Butler (1726) (see BUTLER, J. §3; EGOISM AND ALTRUISM §3).

Still, self-interest is an undeniably widespread and powerful pattern of motivation, and this makes it an obvious candidate in terms of which to reconstruct moral concern. Thus, suppose that compliance with moral principles could be shown to conduce to the long-term interest of each individual. We would then have a ready explanation to hand of the ease with which moral incentives emerge in the course of psychological development, and of the urgency with which moral considerations present themselves in practical deliberation: these phenomena would reflect the natural concern of humans for their own well-being, and the equally natural use of practical reason in the service of this concern. This explanation would in turn support rather than undermine the authority of morality. Those who make morality regulative of their activities would thereby achieve integration and stability of personality in an exemplary degree, since morality, far from being inimical to our other interests, would represent the condition for their effective pursuit.

This broadly Hobbesian strategy for understanding morality rests on the idea that each of us benefits enormously from the availability of certain public goods – such as peace, security, and trustworthiness – that can be secured only through general compliance with moral norms (see PRUDENCE §3; HOBBES, T. §5). Discussions of the strategy have become highly sophisticated, drawing on advances in the theory of rational choice (see RATIONAL CHOICE THEORY). But the increasing sophistication of its formulation cannot compensate for the inadequacy of the strategy as an account of moral motivation. The strategy might show that something like moral norms make claims on all of us. But to the extent that our incentive to comply with these norms is self-interest, the norms themselves seem to lose their distinctively moral character, for it is part of our understanding of moral requirements that they are to be followed even when it is inexpedient for us to do so. The problem is made vivid by the figure of the prospective 'free rider', who asks why they should comply with social norms when sufficiently many other people follow them to secure the public goods of cooperation. However this question may be answered, the very fact that it needs to be asked shows that the prospective free rider is not an ordinary moral agent at all.

6 Altruism and sympathy

A genuinely moral agent – as opposed to an egoist – is altruistic, in the sense of having some immediate concern for the interests of others. Furthermore, the capacity for sympathetic identification seems natural to human beings; it is the rare person who is not directly moved by exposure to human suffering, and this tendency to sympathetic response can be nurtured through moral education. For these reasons, many have followed Hume and Schopenhauer (1840) in taking sympathy to be the paradigmatic moral motivation (see HUME, D. §4; SCHOPENHAUER, A. §6; MORAL SENTIMENTS §1).

If sympathy is to play this role, however, then it will need to be corrected and refined. Actual sympathy is notoriously partial and erratic, directed (for instance) at those individuals with whom one has some personal connection, whereas morality seems to demand impartiality of response. Thus, whether morality requires that I help a given person should not depend just on whether I happen to know them, but also (for instance) on the comparative urgency of the claims of others. The standard way to deal with this problem is to subject the mechanism of sympathetic identification to the discipline of impartial reflection. One is to adopt the perspective of an informed spectator, abstracting from one's knowledge of one's own position in the world, and treating each person's welfare as equally important; the morally right action is what sympathy, refined by this procedure of reflection, would then lead one to approve of. Though liable to many different interpretations, this general approach to moral motivation has been associated traditionally with utilitarianism (see IMPARTIALITY §§1–2; UTILITARIANISM).

The utilitarian approach yields an impersonal conception of ethical impartiality, on which moral requirements take an agent-neutral rather than agent-relative form. Consider the familiar moral prohibition on murder. This is ordinarily understood as an agent-relative requirement, proscribing my killing another person even if by doing so I could prevent a number of other murders. But a prohibition of this kind would not survive utilitarian impartial reflection. Once we abstract from our knowledge of our local position in the world, it is no longer possible to sustain a proprietary concern for the character of our own actions. When sympathy is subjected to a filter of impersonal reflection, it can only endorse requirements that are agent-neutral in form, and hence capable of being accepted and acted on by any other agent as well (an injunction to prevent murder, say, instead of the conventional agent-relative prohibition on killing people oneself). In this way, the impersonal interpretation of impartiality defines a standpoint that is available to be occupied by any moral agent.

Questions arise, however, about the authority and motivational effectiveness of the claims made from this point of view. To take the latter first, it is supposed to be an advantage of the utilitarian approach that it accounts for moral motivation in terms of the familiar operations of sympathy. But there is a vast difference between the immediate, impulsive sympathy that develops naturally in human beings and the impersonal concern to maximize the good. The utilitarian claims that sympathy is transformed into a responsiveness to agent-neutral reasons as a result of moral reflection, but one may wonder whether sympathy, thus transformed, remains a natural pattern of motivation.

As for authority, the question is whether impersonal sympathy can be integrated into a person's system of ends. It gives us a standing first-order aim – the maximization of the good – which is set over against our other first-order aims, and likely to conflict fundamentally with them (given the demands that the maximization of the good notoriously imposes on individuals). The result is that we must either radically curtail the pursuit of our ordinary interests for the sake of morality, or resign ourselves to living in a way that is not morally justifiable. Utilitarians reply that morality is a hard thing, and that we should not expect to be able to accommodate its demands within the contours of ordinary bourgeois life. But the difficulty of integrating impersonal sympathy within a normal system of human ends is likely to raise a doubt about the authority of a morality construed in these terms: by what right does it demand this degree of sacrifice of us?

7   Principle-dependent motives

Kantian approaches typically trace moral concern to a higher-order motive, such as the concern to act only in ways that are permitted by moral principles (see KANTIAN ETHICS). Motives of this type will some-times give an agent first-order ends, namely when moral principles require a certain course of action (keeping a promise, say). But when moral principles do not impose requirements in this way it will be open to agents to pursue their first-order ends while at the same time completely satisfying their higher-order moral concern. Morality regulates our first-order pursuits, but because the moral motive does not automatically supply a standing first-order end it is not inevitably in conflict with those pursuits, and so the possibility of integrating moral concern within a realistic system of human ends is left open.

Whether this possibility is realized will depend on the content of moral principles. If those principles instructed us always to maximize the good, then they would in effect determine a standing first-order end. In that case the higher-order concern to act in ways that are permitted by moral principles might be as difficult to integrate with our other ends as impersonal sympathy would be. But Kantians reject such maximizing interpretations of morality, taking moral requirements to derive from reflection on the universalizability of our aims, and contending that these universality procedures yield specific agent-relative obligations that function as limiting conditions on our activities (see UNIVERSALISM, ETHICAL §5).

The idea that morality supplies a higher-order motive invites the charge that it is self-indulgent, reflecting a fastidious concern for one's own virtue rather than a direct responsiveness to the needs of others. Further, the involvement of moral principles in Kantian moral motivation seems to deny moral worth to spontaneous and heartfelt actions, and threatens to erect an alienating screen of reflection between moral agents and their projects. A more fundamental question is whether the motive of duty can be rendered intelligible, as a natural human incentive. Why should the concern to act in ways that are universalizable emerge so readily in moral development, and present itself to us as a serious source of reasons?

To this, Kant (1785) replies that the motive of duty is constitutively rational, and that acting on it enables us to realize the supreme good of autonomy (see KANT, I. §9). Somewhat less ambitiously, T.M. Scanlon (1982) observes that people commonly want to be able to justify their conduct to others on grounds that could not reasonably be rejected, arguing that moral principles tell us what we have to do to satisfy this familiar desire. Either of these strategies might derive support from the readiness with which people respond to 'golden rule' arguments, in which we invite them to consider what it would be like to change positions with those who would be affected by their actions (see UNIVERSAL-

ISM, ETHICAL §4). This phenomenon suggests that the concern to act in ways that are universalizable may be a powerful and *sui generis* pattern of human motivation.

See also: MORAL JUSTIFICATION §3; MORAL MOTIVATION

References and further reading

Baier, A.C. (1987) 'Hume, the Women's Moral Theorist?', in E. Kittay and D. Meyers (eds) *Women and Moral Theory*, Lanham, MD: Rowman and Littlefield, 37–55; repr. in *Moral Prejudices: Essays on Ethics*, Cambridge, MA: Harvard University Press, 1994, 51–75. (Offers an account of reflective sympathy interestingly different from the standard utilitarian interpretation discussed in the text.)

* Butler, J. (1726) *Fifteen Sermons Preached at the Rolls Chapel*, Sermons I, II, III, XI, XII; repr. in S. Darwall (ed.) *Five Sermons Preached at the Rolls Chapel and A Dissertation Upon the Nature of Virtue*, Indianapolis, IN: Hackett Publishing Company, 1983, Sermon XI.

Foot, P. (1985) 'Utilitarianism and the Virtues', *Mind* 94: 196–209; repr. in S. Scheffler (ed.) *Consequentialism and its Critics*, Oxford: Oxford University Press, 1988, 224–42. (Suggests that benevolence and sympathy have a place within the moral life, as one of the virtues, but that they are distorted when made the global basis of moral motivation.)

Freeman, S. (1991) 'Contractualism, Moral Motivation, and Practical Reason', *Journal of Philosophy* 88: 281–303. (Sophisticated contractualist account of moral motives as highest-order desires that are principle-dependent, and based in practical reason.)

Herman, B. (1981) 'On the Value of Acting from the Motive of Duty', *Philosophical Review* 90: 359–82; revised version repr. in *The Practice of Moral Judgment*, Cambridge, MA: Harvard University Press, 1993, 1–22. (Argues that the Kantian motive of duty functions as a higher-order limiting condition, leaving scope for action on other first-order ends.)

—— (1983) 'Integrity and Impartiality', *Monist* 66: 233–50; revised version published as 'Rules, Motives, and Helping Actions', *Philosophical Studies* 45 (1984): 369–77; revised version repr. in *The Practice of Moral Judgment*, Cambridge, MA: Harvard University Press, 1993, 23–44. (Defends Kantian morality against the charge that the commitment to moral principle would alienate us from our projects and emotional attachments.)

* Hume, D. (1739/40) *A Treatise of Human Nature*, ed. L.A. Selby-Bigge, revised by P.H. Nidditch, Oxford: Clarendon Press, 2nd edn, 1978. (Book III emphasizes the motivational consequences of moral thought, and develops an account of moral motivation in terms of sympathy; book II, part 3 argues that practical reason has its roots in our desires.)

* Kant, I. (1785) *Grundlegung zur Metaphysik der Sitten*, trans. L.W. Beck, *Foundations of the Metaphysics of Morals*, Indianapolis, IN: Bobbs-Merrill, 2nd edn, 1995, section 2. (Argues that the motive of duty is constitutively rational, and that acting on it enables us to realize the supreme good of autonomy.)

* Korsgaard, C. (1986) 'Skepticism about Practical Reason', *Journal of Philosophy* 83 (1): 5–25. (Important discussion of internalism; denies that the motivational dimension of practical reason places constraints on the content of practical principles.)

* Mill, J.S. (1861) *Utilitarianism*, ed. G. Sher, Indianapolis, IN: Hackett Publishing Company, 1979. (Distinguishes between the question of the truth of a moral principle and the question of the sanction or motive for compliance with it.)

* Nagel, T. (1970) *The Possibility of Altruism*, repr. Princeton, NJ: Princeton University Press, 1978. (Challenging and suggestive argument that practical reason can give rise to new motivations, and that altruism is based in reflection from an impersonal point of view.)

—— (1986) *The View from Nowhere*, New York: Oxford University Press. (Chaps 8 and 9 discuss the prospects for objectivity in practical reason, and the differences between agent-centred and agent-neutral requirements, while ch. 10 deals with the prospects for reconciling moral concern with one's personal ends; helpful bibliography.)

* Scanlon, T.M. (1982) 'Contractualism and Utilitarianism', in A. Sen and B. Williams (eds) *Utilitarianism and Beyond*, Cambridge: Cambridge University Press, 103–28. (Interprets moral motivation in terms of the desire to be able to justify one's conduct to others on grounds they could not reject; includes a good general discussion of the demands made by moral motivation on moral theory.)

Scheffler, S. (1992) *Human Morality*, New York: Oxford University Press. (Subtle and wide-ranging discussion of naturalistic approaches to moral motivation and their implications for the content and authority of moral demands; contains extensive bibliographic references.)

* Schopenhauer, A. (1840) *Über die Grundlage der Moral*, trans. E.F.J. Payne, *On the Basis of Morality*, Providence, RI and Oxford: Berhahn

Books, 1995, sections 16, 22. (Suggests that sympathy is the paradigmatic moral motivation.)

Smith, M. (1994) *The Moral Problem*, Oxford: Blackwell. (Sophisticated discussion of internalism and how it functions in theoretical and metaphysical debates in ethics; helpful bibliography.)

Williams, B. (1976) 'Persons, Character and Morality', in A.O. Rorty (ed.) *The Identities of Persons*, Berkeley, CA: University of California Press, 197–216; repr. in *Moral Luck: Philosophical Papers 1973–80*, Cambridge: Cambridge University Press, 1981, 1–19. (Influential argument that Kantian impartial motivations cannot be made regulative of one's projects without alienating one unacceptably from them.)

* —— (1980) 'Internal and External Reasons', in R. Harrison (ed.) *Rational Action*, Cambridge: Cambridge University Press; repr. in *Moral Luck: Philosophical Papers 1973–80*, Cambridge: Cambridge University Press, 1981, 101–13. (Contends that practical reasons must be grounded in an agent's 'subjective motivational set'.)

R. JAY WALLACE

MORAL PARTICULARISM

Moral particularism is a broad set of views which play down the role of general moral principles in moral philosophy and practice. Particularists stress the role of examples in moral education and of moral sensitivity or judgment in moral decision-making, as well as criticizing moral theories which advocate or rest upon general principles. It has not yet been demonstrated that particularism constitutes an importantly controversial position in moral philosophy.

Moral particularism is the view that general moral principles play less of a role in moral thought than has often been claimed. In its most extreme form, particularism states that there are no genuine moral principles, and that therefore moral agents who attempt to guide their action by reference to moral principles, and philosophers who attempt to construct moral theories based on principles, are seriously mistaken (see MORAL REALISM §5; SITUATION ETHICS).

Many particularists are influenced by the view of WITTGENSTEIN that one acquires a concept not by being taught some universal rule for its application, but through introduction into a human practice and a way of seeing things (see WITTGENSTEINIAN ETHICS §3). The particularist view of moral education will stress the importance of examples and actual experience of individual moral cases rather than the learning of universal moral rules under which particular cases can be subsumed (see EXAMPLES IN ETHICS §2; MORAL EDUCATION §3).

A link is often drawn between moral particularism and so-called 'antitheory' in ethics. Antitheorists suggest that ethical theorists are in error in postulating principles according to which actions are right to the extent that they are in accord with these principles. Utilitarianism, for example, claims that acts are right to the extent that they maximize utility (see UTILITARIANISM). A further link is often alleged between particularism, anti-theory and virtue ethics (see VIRTUE ETHICS). But this link may rest on a confusion between particularism about moral theory and particularism about moral agency. Virtue ethics has its own principle: right actions are those that the virtuous person would do. The virtuous person will indeed not in practice proceed by attempting to apply this principle directly. Here, however, virtue ethics and utilitarianism are in agreement, since most utilitarians have claimed that moral agents should not attempt to apply utilitarianism in practice.

Moral particularism can also emerge out of the theory of reasons for action. On the view of Dancy (1993), reasons are not universalizable across cases, so that what counts as a reason in one case need not be assumed to function as a reason in the same way in other cases (see LOGIC OF ETHICAL DISCOURSE §7). My enjoying giving you a present counts in favour of my action; but my enjoying torturing you counts against. Against this, it can be suggested that reasons are universalizable at a higher level (*innocent* pleasure, perhaps, always counts as a reason), and that to deny this is to embrace a form of irrationalism.

According to less extreme particularists, principles can play some role in theory and in practice (see CASUISTRY). On one view, they serve as useful generalizations, but there is always a need for judgment in particular cases (see MORAL JUDGMENT §2; THEORY AND PRACTICE §2). ARISTOTLE is best seen as such a particularist. Once again, it is not clear that, for example, utilitarians or Kantians would wish to deny such a role for judgment (see KANTIAN ETHICS; UNIVERSALISM IN ETHICS §3).

See also: AESTHETICS AND ETHICS

References and further reading

* Aristotle (*c.* mid 4th century BC) *Nicomachean Ethics*, trans. with notes by T. Irwin, Indianapolis, IN: Hackett Publishing Company, 1985, book 6.

(Contains an account of moral judgment or 'practical wisdom'.)

* Dancy, J. (1993) *Moral Reasons*, Oxford: Blackwell. (Central outline and defence of modern particularism. Difficult.)

McDowell, J. (1979) 'Virtue and reason', *Monist* 62: 331–50. (Defence of a form of particularist virtue ethics involving both Aristotle and Wittgenstein. Difficult.)

Ross, W.D. (1930) *The Right and the Good*, Oxford: Clarendon Press, chaps 1–2. (Has been influential on the development of modern particularism.)

ROGER CRISP

MORAL PHILOSOPHY

see ETHICS

MORAL PLURALISM

Moral pluralism is the view that moral values, norms, ideals, duties and virtues are irreducibly diverse: morality serves many purposes relating to a wide range of human interests, and it is therefore unlikely that a theory unified around a single moral consideration will account for all the resulting values. Unlike relativism, however, moral pluralism holds that there are rational constraints on what can count as a moral value. One possible, though not necessary, implication of moral pluralism is the existence of real moral dilemmas. Some philosophers have deemed these to be inconceivable; in fact, however, they do not constitute a serious threat to practical reason. Another possible implication of moral pluralism is the existence within a society of radically different but equally permissible moralities. This poses a challenge for political philosophy, and might justify a liberal view that particular conceptions of the good life ought not to be invoked in the formulation of public policy.

1 **Moral pluralism and moral theory**
2 **Relativism and moral dilemmas**
3 **Moral pluralism and political philosophy**

1 Moral pluralism and moral theory

Moral pluralism is the view that moral values, ideals, duties and virtues cannot be reduced to any one foundational consideration, but that they are rather irreducibly diverse. As such, moral pluralism is a metaphysical thesis, in that it tells us what moral

considerations there are. Pluralist moral philosophers disagree as to exactly what the plural sources of moral value are. For example, Sir David Ross (1930) distinguished six species of duty, including duties of fidelity and reparation, of gratitude, of justice, of beneficence, of self-improvement and of non-maleficence; and Thomas Nagel (1979) has claimed that the conflicts among diverse moral principles are due to there being five distinct sources of value – special allegiances, universal rights, utility, perfectionist ends of self-development, and individual projects (see NAGEL, T. §5) Despite the differences between these accounts of the sources of moral value, the resolution of which constitutes a challenge for substantive moral theory, these thinkers can be seen as united in the view that morality has developed to protect and promote basic interests related to human wellbeing and flourishing, but that since there is no unique form that human wellbeing must take, there can consequently not be a theory of morality unified around one supreme value (see HAPPINESS §3; WELFARE).

This is not to say that the truth of moral pluralism disqualifies any attempt at formulating a moral theory (see MORALITY AND ETHICS §§1–2). Among the many moral values which human beings pursue, there are undoubtedly some that can be grouped together and accounted for in terms of some more general value relevant to the particular set of human interests with which they are all in one way or another concerned. Moral pluralism implies simply that none of these values could plausibly claim hegemony over the entire set of moral considerations.

Historically, moral pluralism has been linked with controversial positions in moral epistemology and the ontology of value, according to which moral facts are real and non-natural, and are given as self-evident to a distinct human faculty of moral intuition (see MORAL REALISM; INTUITIONISM IN ETHICS). It is in fact compatible with a wide range of philosophical positions on these issues, including anti-realism and naturalism.

Some philosophers have argued that the diversity of our moral concepts is a distinctive feature of modernity. Alasdair MACINTYRE, for example, has claimed that the plurality of conflicting considerations which make up the moral lexicon of the modern agent is a sign of cultural decay. Modern morality is for MacIntyre a congeries of concepts which have been inherited by modern agents from past forms of life, but which have been torn from the coherent concrete human practices within which they originated, and in the context of which alone they have any real meaning. Moral pluralism is therefore in his view a symptom of our moral discomfiture.

Moral pluralism has also been challenged by

defenders of classical single-principle moral theories. Yet there have also been signs of theoretical rapprochements. Indeed, many modern consequentialists are abandoning the simple view of human wellbeing embodied in classical utilitarianism in favour of more multifaceted accounts (see CONSEQUENTIALISM). And many deontologists can be read as formulating rational priority rules ranking deontological constraints over other types of moral considerations, rather than as banishing the latter completely from the realm of the moral (see DEONTOLOGICAL ETHICS).

2 Relativism and moral dilemmas

It is important to distinguish moral pluralism from a thesis with which it has too often been confused, namely that of moral relativism. A relativist claims that the truth of moral judgments is relative to the conventions of the social group (or even to the individual whim) of the person issuing the judgment, and that these conventions or whims are not themselves subject to any further criterion of adequacy. There are therefore according to relativists no rational constraints on what can count as a moral value, and it is therefore senseless in their view to speak of the truth, falsity or justification of moral judgments (see MORAL RELATIVISM). Moral pluralism in contrast holds that while the variety of moral principles applying to human beings is irreducible, it is not infinite. Rather, there are constraints on what can count as a moral value (and there is therefore sense in speaking of moral truth and falsity). These constraints might, for example, have to do with the (inherently diverse but not infinite) forms which human wellbeing and flourishing can take.

Moral pluralism is therefore compatible with the existence of rational constraints upon moral thought.- But the fact that a number of statements to do with moral value might all be true while apparently recommending incompatible actions, and that real, as opposed to merely apparent, moral dilemmas emerge as a real possibility, has been thought by some philosophers to disqualify it as a theory of value by making it sin against basic axioms of deontic logic. These include the principle that 'ought implies can' and the principle of agglomeration, which states that if I ought to do A and I ought to do B, then I ought to do A and B. This troubling apparent consequence of moral pluralism must, however, be qualified by a number of observations. First, as Michael Stocker has observed (1990), the premise that statements about moral value are always act evaluations is an unvindicated assumption of much modern moral theory, yet moral pluralism only leads to moral dilemmas if this assumption is granted. There might

be a number of true moral descriptions of a situation, emphasizing different moral considerations present in it. Any one of these might well on its own give rise to an 'ought' statement, but given the presence of other moral considerations it may give rise only to what Ross has called a *prima facie* obligation. As the latter are not directly action-guiding, they need not conform to the strictures of deontic logic. Second, certain axioms of deontic logic might actually embody controversial first-order moral propositions. The fact that they conflict with the hypothesis of moral dilemmas does not therefore automatically place the burden of proof upon defenders of the latter. Third, the reality of moral dilemmas need not, as philosophers such as Bernard Williams (1965) have suggested, put paid to all attempts to rationally order our, at times conflicting, moral values. There are reasons supporting both sides of a moral dilemma, and the presence of a moral dilemma, rather than signalling the necessary end of moral inquiry, can point to the need to undertake inquiry into these reasons in a more fine-grained manner. Moral pluralism involves the denial of the existence of a supreme value from which all others might be derived; it does not entail incommensurability, the view that moral considerations cannot be compared and ranked. Thus, for example, there may be rational priority rules allowing us to order the claims of different moral values.

3 Moral pluralism and political philosophy

The plurality of moral values can manifest itself in a number of different ways. Most relevantly from the point of view of political philosophy, it can involve the existence within a society of a number of equally acceptable moral forms of life. This form of social pluralism poses a set of challenges for political philosophers, suggesting that there may be no simple way of adjudicating conflicts between adherents of equally admirable moral forms of life, or of engaging in the interpersonal welfare comparisons often seen as necessary for the formulation of theories of distributive justice. Moral pluralism has been seen by many philosophers, including John Rawls (1971), Thomas Nagel and Charles Larmore (1987), as calling for the liberal doctrine of state neutrality, the view that particular conceptions of the good ought not to be invoked in the formulation of public policy.

See also: AXIOLOGY; DUTY; IDEALS; PLURALISM; RELIGIOUS PLURALISM; VALUES; VIRTUES AND VICES

References and further reading

Berlin, I. (1969) *Four Essays on Liberty*, Oxford:

Oxford University Press. (The classic twentieth-century statement of moral pluralism.)

* Larmore, C. (1987) *Patterns of Moral Compexity*, Cambridge: Cambridge University Press. (Argues that a purely political conception of liberalism flows from the plurality of moral forms of life in a society.)

* MacIntyre, A. (1984) *After Virtue*, Notre Dame, IN: Notre Dame University Press, 2nd edn. (Argues that moral pluralism and conflict result from moral concepts no longer being embedded in concrete social forms.)

* Nagel, T. (1977) 'The Fragmentation of Value', in H.T. Englehardt, Jr, and D. Callahan (eds) *Knowledge, Value and Belief*, Hastings-on-Hudson, NY: Institute of Society, Ethics and the Life Sciences; repr. in *Moral Questions*, Cambridge: Cambridge University Press, 1979. (A clear statement of the different sources of moral value.)

* Rawls, J. (1971) *A Theory of Justice*, Cambridge, MA: Harvard University Press, 34–40. (A standard modern argument against a form of moral pluralism identified as 'intuitionism'.)

* Ross, W.D. (1930) *The Right and the Good*, Oxford: Oxford University Press, 21. (The classic statement of an intuitionist moral pluralism.)

* Stocker, M. (1990) *Plural and Conflicting Values*, Oxford: Oxford University Press. (Argues that value pluralism does not threaten the possibility of sound practical reason.)

* Williams, B. (1965) 'Ethical Consistency', *Proceedings of the Aristotelian Society*, supplementary vol. 39; repr. in *Problems of the Self: Philosophical Papers 1956–72*, Cambridge: Cambridge University Press, 1973. (Raises problems for moral reasoning caused by the plurality of values.)

DANIEL M. WEINSTOCK

MORAL PSYCHOLOGY

Moral psychology as a discipline is centrally concerned with psychological issues that arise in connection with the moral evaluation of actions. It deals with the psychological presuppositions of valid morality, that is, with assumptions it seems necessary for us to make in order for there to be such a thing as objective or binding moral requirements: for example, if we lack free will or are all incapable of unselfishness, then it is not clear how morality can really apply to human beings. Moral psychology also deals with what one might call the psychological accompaniments of actual right, or wrong, action, for example, with questions about the nature and possibility of moral weakness or self-deception, and with questions about the kinds of motives that ought to motivate moral agents. Moreover, in the approach to ethics known as 'virtue ethics' questions about right and wrong action merge with questions about the motives, dispositions, and abilities of moral agents, and moral psychology plays a more central role than it does in other forms of ethical theory.

1   Psychology and the possibility of morality
2   Psychology and moral judgment

1   Psychology and the possibility of morality

We can divide the main traditional concerns of moral psychology as a distinctive philosophical discipline into questions about the psychological assumptions necessary to the validity of morality, or moral rules, in general, and questions about the psychological concomitants or underpinnings of particular actions evaluated either as good/right or as bad/wrong. The question of whether human beings have free will or freedom of choice (see FREE WILL) naturally falls within the first of these areas. If human beings lack free will, then, it has over the millennia typically (though not universally) been assumed, they cannot be held responsible for their actions and cannot be bound by moral obligations any more than are animals or small children. Thus those who have systematically elaborated one or another view of moral right and wrong have usually thought it necessary to defend, or at least explicitly assume, the existence of human free will, or freedom of choice.

In the first instance this standardly involves saying something about free agency in relation to universal causal/nomic determinism. If the world is universally governed by causal or physical laws, then it is unclear how anyone could possibly have behaved otherwise than they in fact did, and so have been responsible for what they did. So defenders of (objective) morality typically feel called upon either to argue that human beings are in important ways not subject to iron-clad causal determination, or else to show that causal determinism does not in fact deprive us of free will (see, for example, Watson 1982; DETERMINISM AND INDETERMINISM).

Another metaphysical or quasi-metaphysical issue that looms large in moral psychology concerns the human capacity for morality. Most moral codes and moral philosophies require, for example, that people occasionally put aside self-interest in the name of honour, fairness, decency, compassion, loyalty or the general good. But if one believes in psychological egoism, one will hold that people lack the capacity for these forms of self-sacrifice, and it then becomes problematic whether human beings really have the obligations that various non-egoistic moral views/ theories claim that they do (see EGOISM AND ALTRUISM).

But even if one rejects both psychological and ethical egoism (for example, Butler 1950), there are moral-psychological issues about how much morality can fairly be demanded of people. These issues arise especially in connection with utilitarianism (see UTILITARIANISM) and Kantianism (see KANTIAN ETHICS). Utilitarianism is usually stated in a 'max-imizing' form that treats it as a necessary and sufficient condition of right action that one do the best/most one circumstantially can to advance the happiness of humankind (or sentient beings). But such a doctrine seems to entail that if one is in a position to relieve the suffering, hunger or disease of others, one is morally obliged to do so, even if that means giving up one's own life plans and most of what one really cares about in life. The traditional utilitarian moral standard is thus very demanding, and some philosophers have questioned whether morality can properly, or, one might say, fairly, require so much of people (see, for example, Stocker 1976; Swanton 1993). In particular, it may be wondered whether most people have the capacity to live up to such a stringent morality as is presented by maximizing utilitarianism.

Certain doctrines of Kantian ethics can likewise be seen as going against the grain of human nature or capacities, not by demanding too much of a sacrifice of self-interest, but by laying down rather stringent or narrow psychological conditions for the moral admirability of actions. According to Kant, if one helps someone in need or in trouble out of fellow-feeling or friendship, one's act lacks all moral worth, because it was not performed out of a sense of duty and respect for the moral law. And many ethical thinkers have either implicitly or explicitly held such a view of moral virtue to be too narrow and out of keeping with realistic human psychology, and have argued that certain primary, immediate or natural motives such as compassion or friendly feeling not only have moral worth, but can often be even more praiseworthy than a cool appeal to duty or to something as abstract as the moral law (see, for example, Martineau 1891; Stocker 1976). But Kantians question the durability and reliability of mere feeling or emotion, and there remains considerable debate in this area (Blum 1980).

2 Psychology and moral judgment

Another topic that has recently occupied moral psychologists and ethicists is the relevance of so-called 'moral emotions' to moral judgments. Some philosophers have considered the validity of one or another moral theory to depend, in part, on whether people tend to feel guilty for violating its dictates (see, for example, Williams 1981). But others have held that there are situations where guilt is inevitable, but that that fact constitutes no sort of evidence of wrong-doing. Indeed, it is sometimes argued that the question of whether guilt for some action is *appropriate* or *justified* is separate from the issue of whether that action was actually wrong (Greenspan 1988). (Is it, for example, appropriate to feel guilty about injuries one caused in a traffic accident that was someone else's fault entirely?) Other philosophers, however, seek to connect the moral emotions with morality by arguing that the seeming *ineradicability* of our emotions of anger and resentment provides some sort of underpinning for human judgments about justice and injustice, praiseworthiness and blame-worthiness (see Strawson in Watson 1982; MORALITY AND EMOTIONS; MORAL SENTIMENTS).

In addition, moral psychologists concern them-selves with various forms of situational moral failure, such as self-deception and weakness of will (see SELF-DECEPTION; AKRASIA). The very existence of these phenomena is often questioned on grounds of their paradoxical character. If one is motivated to deceive oneself about some difficult matter (for example, the needs of one's children), how can one possibly succeed unless one knows what it is one has to deceive oneself about – in which case, in what way is one actually deceived? Similarly, if moral weakness, or weakness of will more generally, means allowing anger or passion to lead one to act against one's better judgment, is it not natural to reconfigure our understanding of what is happening so as to suppose that the reasons for anger or passion warp one's sense of what really is best (for one) – in which case, in what way has one actually acted against one's (however momentary) better judgment?

Both weakness of will and self-deception are, therefore, inherently problematic, and moral psychol-ogy has sought ways of either making sense of these moral phenomena or showing them definitively to be incoherent and consequently impossible (see, for example, Pears 1984). Either 'solution' has bearing on the moral assessment of actions (and desires). If self-deception is possible, what sort of blame attaches to it when it leads to bad consequences (for example, neglect of children)? Should it be counted as a deliberate, intentional act; or it is more like negli-gence, or heedlessness? But if self-deception is not possible, then what masquerades as such may be more like intentional wrongdoing, and perhaps even more blameworthy, than it initially appears (see SELF-

DECEPTION, ETHICS OF). Then too, if weakness of will is not possible, many cases we are inclined (at most) partially to excuse on grounds of weakness may be cases in which the agent is actually compelled, psychologically, to act wrongly – or else perhaps momentarily ignorant of the difference between right and wrong. Such conclusions are bound to affect the character and/or severity of the blame or punishment directed at those who initially seemed to be acting weakly.

Another set of issues in moral psychology arises within the tradition of moral theory known as virtue ethics, which treats issues of moral psychology as essential to our understanding of right and wrong action (see VIRTUE ETHICS). Thus, rather than basing morality on moral rules or on the production of 'good consequences', Aristotelian virtue ethics denies the possibility of universal moral rules and thinks of the virtuous individual as someone who intuitively perceives what is right or noble in various situations and, fairly effortlessly, acts accordingly. To that extent, the Aristotelian tradition in virtue ethics approaches the idea of moral rightness in some measure indirectly, by focusing on the character, habits and abilities of the virtuous individual who tracks rightness in thought and actions (see FEMINIST ETHICS).

In addition, there is a more radical tradition of virtue ethics in which the moral evaluation of actions and moral rules is directly derived from characterizations of good and bad motivation and how these may be expressed or realized in someone's actions. Perhaps the best-known historical example of such an approach can be found in Plato's *Republic* (Book IV), where it is said that good actions are those that enhance or support the health and harmony of the soul (see PLATO §14).

A more recent and 'purer' example (because it does not mention anything like the Form of the Good) can be found in James Martineau's *Types of Ethical Theory* (1885, 1891). Martineau ranks all human motives on an absolute scale – for example, compassion is placed above ambition, the latter above sexual desire, and the latter, in turn, above vindictiveness – and claims that right action is action that comes from the higher or highest motive operating in any given situation of moral choice. This then allows moral rules of thumb to be derived from generalizations about which motives are likely to operate in various morally familiar situations.

These varying virtue-ethical approaches put moral psychology at the very centre of ethics. However, for the foreseeable future, the chief role of moral psychology will probably be as a discipline ancillary to, rather than as the main focus of, moral theory.

References and further reading

Baron, M. (1984) 'The Alleged Moral Repugnance of Acting from Duty', *Journal of Philosophy* 81: 197–219. (A critical examination of views about the moral worth of various kinds of motivation.)

* Blum, L. (1980) *Friendship, Altruism and Morality*, London: Routledge. (An extended critique of Kantian ideas about the moral significance of the emotions.)

Broadie, S. (1991) *Ethics with Aristotle*, New York: Oxford University Press. (A thoroughgoing examination of Aristotle's ethics.)

* Butler, J. (1950) *Fifteen Sermons Preached at the Rolls Chapel*, New York: Bobbs-Merrill. (A classic refutation of the arguments for psychological egoism.)

Garcia, J. (1993) 'The New Critique of Anti-Consequentialist Moral Theory', *Philosophical Studies* 71: 1–32. (An account of virtue ethics that bases morality in motives, rather than consequences.)

* Greenspan, P. (1988) *Emotions and Reasons: An Inquiry into Emotional Justification*, New York: Routledge. (A full-scale examination of the rational status of emotions.)

Hursthouse, R. (1991) 'Virtue Theory and Abortion', *Philosophy and Public Affairs* 20: 223–46. (A defence of neo-Aristotelian virtue ethics.)

Kagan, S. (1989) *The Limits of Morality*, Oxford: Oxford University Press. (A defence of utilitarianism generally and against the charge that it is 'too demanding'.)

* Martineau, J. (1885, 1891) *Types of Ethical Theory*, Oxford: Clarendon Press, 2 vols. (The classic defence of motive-based morality.)

* Pears, D. (1984) *Motivated Irrationality*, Oxford: Oxford University Press. (An extended analysis of weakness of will and other forms of irrationality.)

Slote, M. (1993) 'Virtue Ethics and Democratic Values', *Journal of Social Philosophy* 24: 5–37. (A defence of current-day political ideals in virtue-ethical terms.)

* Stocker, M. (1976) 'The Schizophrenia of Modern Ethical Theories', *Journal of Philosophy* 73: 453–66. (A critique of moral theories that make happiness difficult or that treat conscientiousness as the morally best of motives.)

* Swanton, C. (1993) 'Satisficing and Virtue', *Journal of Philosophy* 90: 33–48. (A critique of the 'over-demandingness' of Aristotelian virtue ethics and various theories of practical reason.)

* Watson, G. (ed.) (1982) *Free Will*, Oxford: Oxford University Press. (An anthology of recent articles on free will and moral responsibility.)

* Williams, B. (1981) *Moral Luck*, Cambridge: Cambridge University Press. (A collection of essays that, among other things, questions the realism of much recent ethical theory.)

MICHAEL SLOTE

MORAL REALISM

Moral realism is the view that there are facts of the matter about which actions are right and which wrong, and about which things are good and which bad. But behind this bald statement lies a wealth of complexity. If one is a full-blown moral realist, one probably accepts the following three claims.

First, moral facts are somehow special and different from other sorts of fact. Realists differ, however, about whether the sort of specialness required is compatible with taking some natural facts to be moral facts. Take, for instance, the natural fact that if we do this action, we will have given someone the help they need. Could this be a moral fact – the same fact as the fact that we ought to do the action? Or must we think of such a natural fact as the natural 'ground' for the (quite different) moral fact that we should do it, that is, as the fact in the world that makes it true that we should act this way?

Second, realists hold that moral facts are independent of any beliefs or thoughts we might have about them. What is right is not determined by what I or anybody else thinks is right. It is not even determined by what we all think is right, even if we could be got to agree. We cannot make actions right by agreeing that they are, any more than we can make bombs safe by agreeing that they are.

Third, it is possible for us to make mistakes about what is right and what is wrong. No matter how carefully and honestly we think about what to do, there is still no guarantee that we will come up with the right answer. So what people conscientiously decide they should do may not be the same as what they should do.

1 **Realism, objectivism, cognitivism**
2 **Arguments for realism, and an outline of its history**
3 **American moral realism**
4 **British moral realism**
5 **Realism and minimalism**
6 **Arguments against realism**

1 Realism, objectivism, cognitivism

These three terms are hard to keep separate, but it is worth the effort. Cognitivism is the claim that moral attitudes are cognitive states rather than noncognitive ones. The distinction between cognitive and noncognitive states is not clear; the best way of drawing it is by appeal to the distinction between two 'directions of fit'. Beliefs, which are the paradigm examples of a cognitive state, have one direction of fit; desires, which are the paradigm examples of a noncognitive state, have the other. A belief, that is, has to fit the world; the world is given, as it were, and it is the belief's job to fit that world, to get it right. A desire is not like that; the desire's job, if anything, is to get the world to fit it, to make things be the way it wants them to be. Crucially, a desire is not at fault if things are not as it wants them to be; a belief is at fault if things are not as it takes them to be. The question whether moral attitudes are cognitive states or noncognitive ones is the question whether they have the direction of fit of a belief, or that of a desire. They could, of course, be complex states with a mixture of both; but noncognitivism is the view that moral attitudes have either wholly or partly the direction of fit of a desire. This is normally expressed more briefly as the view that moral attitudes either are or at least contain desires; to think an action right is a sort of 'pro-attitude', and pro-attitudes are wantings (see BELIEF; DESIRE; MORAL JUDGMENT §1).

Realists, believing that there are distinct moral facts, are likely to be cognitivists, since the appropriate attitude to a fact is belief rather than desire. It is for this reason that the opposition to realism is normally called 'noncognitivism'. Realists, holding there to be moral facts, maintain for that reason that moral attitudes are beliefs; noncognitivists, holding that moral attitudes either are or include desires, claim for that reason that there are no facts to be the objects of those attitudes.

Objectivism is harder to distinguish from realism, since the two are very closely linked. Objectivity is something to do with independence from us. Realism, as characterized above, combines three theses: a distinctness thesis, a metaphysical thesis and an epistemological thesis. The metaphysical thesis is the claim that moral facts are objective. If moral facts are independent in some way, what exactly is it that they are independent of? To say 'independent of us' is little help at best, and straightforwardly wrong at worst. Moral facts concern agents and actions, which are human matters, and so they are not completely independent of us; if we were different, different actions would be wrong. The phrasing used above, 'independent of any beliefs and thoughts we might have about them', attempts to be more precise, at the cost of excluding too much. Is the limitation involved in 'about them' justified? If not, what other limitation would be better? This matter is very difficult to resolve (see VALUES; OBJECTIVITY).

Realism, on this showing, is a complex of claims. The distinctness claim carves out a distinctive subject matter for ethics. The independence claim tells us something about the sort of fact that ethics is concerned with. The epistemological claim tells us that we have a less than perfectly secure grip on those facts. Moral realists have, however, generally been willing to say that we are capable of moral knowledge, even if we do not achieve it very often. They would all agree that are we capable of justified moral beliefs (if they are cognitivists).

Readers should be aware that the characterization of moral realism is a matter of hot debate. In particular, as well as the sort of account offered in the present entry, there is a form of realism that, taking its start from the claim that there are facts of the matter in ethics, and so moral truths, holds that there must therefore be 'truth-makers' – things that make the truths true. In the moral case, what makes moral truths true must be the possession of moral properties by suitable agents and actions. Realism, so understood, is the commitment to moral properties and relations as no less 'real' than other properties. It is possible, however, to combine these two strands of realist thinking without strain.

2 Arguments for realism, and an outline of its history

Corresponding to the three elements of realism, there are three things commonly urged by realists in favour of their position. In different ways, they all suggest that we should take seriously the way things initially appear to us. Realists try to hold that things are as they appear, despite noncognitivist arguments that they cannot possibly be. This is sometimes called 'the appeal to phenomenology'.

First, realists claim that moral thought appears to have its own subject matter, distinct from science and all natural inquiry. Second, they argue that moral judgment appears to be an attempt to determine a matter of fact that is independent of any beliefs we might have about it; the fact is one thing, and what we think about it another. Third, realists hold that moral judgment presents itself to the judger as risky and fallible. When facing a difficult choice, especially, we have a sense of thin ice; we know that, with the best will in the world, the view we come to may be wrong. Only the second two of these three claims may properly be termed 'phenomenological'.

Most moral theorists have been realists, from Plato and Aristotle through Price and Hutcheson to Sidgwick and Mill, and then, in the twentieth century, to Moore and the intuitionist tradition (see INTUI-TIONISM IN ETHICS). It is the opposition to realism that needs to be documented. Here the patron saint of noncognitivism is Hume, whose work flowered, though altered in many respects, in the noncognitivist tradition of Stevenson, Ayer and Hare (see EMOTI-VISM). Leading contemporary noncognitivists are Blackburn and Gibbard.

Advances in the philosophy of language, philosophy of mind and philosophy of science in the 1960s and 1970s persuaded many that the noncognitivist arguments against realism, which had dominated the intellectual scene since 1930, were less powerful than they had appeared (see ANALYTIC ETHICS §2). Two quite distinct forms of moral realism emerged, American and British. (This means only that most proponents of the first form are American, and most proponents of the second are British.) In the next two sections, the differences between these two positions will be charted in three areas: metaphysics, epistemology and theory of motivation.

3 American moral realism

Metaphysics. American moral realists are naturalists: they suppose that moral facts are either natural facts or configurations of natural facts (see NATURALISM IN ETHICS §1). As suggested in the initial summary, it is possible that the fact that if I do this I will have helped someone and harmed nobody else just is the fact that I ought to do this action. Perhaps, however, the moral fact is more complex than this natural fact (and than any other single natural fact), without this meaning that it is not some combination of natural facts. If so, those natural facts will have to be combined in the right sort of way – in the sort of way that they are here – if they are together to make the moral fact that I ought to do this action. Then the moral fact will be identical with this configuration of natural facts.

This form of naturalism in ethics is often, though not always, accompanied by some form of conse-quentialism. A certain sort of natural fact is a moral fact because there is a relation between that fact and certain consequences (see CONSEQUENTIALISM). Naturalism in ethics is now a live option again because of a growing sense that G.E. Moore's 'open question' argument is flawed (see MOORE, G.E. §1).

Epistemology. American moral realists, seeing moral facts as natural facts, suppose that they are knowable in whatever ways natural facts can be known, including science. To identify those facts as moral facts, we will need to combine the best scientific theory with the best moral theory.

Theory of motivation. How is it possible to reconcile the claim that moral facts are natural facts with the widespread sense that moral facts have an intrinsic authority – that they make demands on us to which we should respond, whatever our personal choices and preferences? This 'intrinsic authority' is hard to understand in any detail. Perhaps the best attempt is Kant's distinction between categorical and hypothetical imperatives (see KANT §1; KANTIAN ETHICS). Moral imperatives such as, 'Help those less fortunate than you', are categorical, in the sense that one cannot escape their relevance to oneself by saying, 'I just don't care very much about that sort of thing'. By contrast, a hypothetical imperative such as, 'Use fresh eggs to make an omelette', has no grip on those who just do not care about how their omelettes taste.

However we understand it, the idea of the authority of moral facts does not sit easily with ethical naturalism. Natural facts, however configured, do not seem able to have any such authority over the will (see MORAL MOTIVATION §§1–2). American realists generally respond to this by doubting the claim that any fact could have that sort of authority. The world, whether in its moral or its more obviously natural clothes, is one whose grip on us depends on our bringing to it a sort of moral concern (which will have been the product either of evolution or of education). If we lack that concern, we will be unmotivated by moral distinctions, even though we will be still perfectly capable of discovering which actions are right and which are wrong. To know the right is one thing, and to bend one's will to it another. Moral judgment is cognitive; it is the discovery of facts. But facts are motivationally inert; whether one is motivated by them depends not so much on them as on what one cares about. So moral imperatives are hypothetical, despite appearances.

In these thoughts, American realists adopt what is sometimes called a 'Humean' theory of motivation. Neither belief nor desire alone can lead to action; only a combination of the two can do that. (For an action we need two mental states, one with each direction of fit.) Moral facts are the objects of belief. No such belief can motivate alone; for there to be an action, the agent must have some desire or preference as well as the belief. Moral facts cannot motivate in their own right, therefore; their ability to make a difference to how we act depends upon the independent contribution of a desire. This being so, they cannot have such a thing as an intrinsic authority over us; for whether they can make a difference to how we act depends on something over which they have no control (see PRACTICAL REASON AND ETHICS §2).

4 British moral realism

The British variety of moral realism denies everything that the American variety claims.

Metaphysics. British moral realism is non-naturalist: moral facts are not natural facts, nor are they are natural configurations of natural facts. They may be non-natural configurations of natural facts, but that is another matter. Natural facts are relevant to moral ones, of course, since they are the reasons why actions are right or wrong. It follows from this that any two situations that are naturally indistinguishable must be morally indistinguishable (see SUPERVENIENCE). But this sort of supervenience is a far cry from any identity between the natural and the moral.

In terms of the characterization of moral realism given earlier, the British thus attribute far greater distinctness to moral facts, considering them to be metaphysically distinct from natural ones. The Americans have a harder task in showing what is distinctive about the moral, though not an impossible one. They can say, for instance, that moral facts are distinguished by their subject matter, or by the sort of configuration of natural facts that they are.

Epistemology. If moral facts are not natural facts, the normal methods of finding out how things are will not suffice for the discovery of the moral. Admittedly, British realists have been prone to talk of seeing that an action is right. But it appears that they mean by this neither that rightness is visible, nor that there is a moral sense in addition to the normal five senses. Talk of seeing that the action is right is intended to echo Aristotle's remark that right and wrong are not matters of rules so much as of the nature of the case before us, and that to discern what is right we have to concentrate on the details of the present situation (see VIRTUE ETHICS §6). They deny, therefore, that moral judgment is a matter of subsumption, of bringing the present case under some moral rule. Moral judgment is the application of concepts, but those concepts are not rules. Indeed, it is characteristic of British realists to be sceptical about the very possibility of moral rules or principles. For them, moral judgment is a matter of recognizing the reasons for action as they present themselves in the present case, and responding to them as such (see UNIVERSALISM IN ETHICS §3; LOGIC OF ETHICAL DISCOURSE §7). This sort of recognition is not perceptual, but it is cognitive and practical at once – for what one is recognizing is a reason for action, that is, a normative state of the world.

Theory of motivation. American realists are 'externalists' about moral judgment. They hold that the ability of a moral judgment to motivate, that is, to make a difference to how one acts, is dependent on the presence of a quite different mental state, namely some sort of desire. British moral realists are generally 'internalists', holding that a moral judgment motivates in its own right, and does not get its ability to affect action from a desire that is present at the same time (see MORAL MOTIVATION §1). To make this out, they have to reject the standard Humean picture of motivation, though they do not agree among themselves about quite how to do this. Wiggins (1987) and McDowell (1978) hold that action does require a combination of belief and desire, but that in the moral case it is belief that leads and desire that follows. Dancy (1993) suggests that it is belief alone that motivates, since mere recognition of relevant reasons should be enough for action; he sees desire as a state of being motivated (by the reasons), not as what motivates. Either way, the suggestion that there are genuinely normative and non-natural facts is combined with the claim that recognition of these facts motivates in its own right, in a way that is not dependent on the presence of an independent desire.

This raises problems. The first is that Humeanism is more or less received wisdom; so the British are fighting an uphill battle in rejecting it. The second is that it is very hard to make sense of the idea of a state of the world, or fact, that stands in some intrinsic relation to the will. It is normal to think that facts are motivationally inert; to recognize them is one thing, and to bend the will to them another. The British hold that the response to the fact, which we call recognition, is itself motivational. The preferred way of doing this is by appeal to the 'dispositional conception of value' (see McDowell 1985). This conception is inspired by a supposedly similar dispositional conception of colour: a red object is one that is disposed to cause in us a characteristic sort of experience (see COLOUR, THEORIES OF §2). Similarly, a valuable object is conceived as one which is disposed to elicit a certain response from us, an inclination of the will. As such, it is not totally independent of us, since it consists (at least partly) in a certain relation to us; and this means that it is not fully objective, if objectivity is to be understood in terms of independence from us. But it is still objective in a weak sense, since value can still be conceived as there for us to recognize and there whether we recognize it or not (see VALUE, ONTOLOGICAL STATUS OF).

There are two difficulties with this appeal to dispositions. The first is that the analogy with colours is hotly disputed. The second is that, in order to keep values in the world, their objectivity has had to be diminished. For some, this weaker conception of objectivity is hardly to be distinguished from subjectivity.

5 Realism and minimalism

In this entry, realism has been seen as a combination of three distinct theses. But there is an alternative account of what realism is that sees it as nothing more than a claim about truth. The realist, on this account, holds that moral statements are capable of truth, and indeed that some are true. If we say this, we can still distinguish between realism and objectivism in ethics. Realism is the claim that moral judgments are sometimes true; objectivism is the claim that the sort of truth they have is objective truth.

We can distinguish two sorts of opposition to this form of realism. The first accepts that moral statements are capable of truth, but holds that all are false (see MORAL SCEPTICISM §3); the second holds that truth is not the appropriate form of success for a moral judgment, and that we would do better to think of them as sincere or insincere, or as more or less well connected with other judgments, or as ones that we ourselves would agree with. One should not try to combine these two sorts of opposition.

Crispin Wright (1992) has suggested that, if this is what is at issue between realism and noncognitivism, the matter will be quickly resolved in favour of realism. In his view, the mere fact that moral discourse is assertive, and that moral utterances are governed by norms of warranted assertibility, is enough to establish that we make no mistake in calling some true and others false. The question should not be, then, whether moral judgments are capable of truth, since everyone really admits that they are. Instead, the debate about realism should focus on other questions. According to Wright, among these questions are:

(1) Is it a priori that differences of moral opinion can only be explained in terms of divergent input, unsuitable conditions or malfunction (such as prejudice and dogma)?

(2) Do the supposed moral facts serve to explain anything at all? Suppose that they explain (some of) our moral beliefs. Do they explain anything else in a way that is not mediated by our beliefs? That is to say, do moral facts directly explain anything about how the world goes?

Wright suggests that we only get a 'full-blooded' moral realism if our answer to these questions is 'yes'. There will, therefore, be degrees of realism, and in a way the question is not whether we should be realists, but what sort of realists we should be. How far should our realism go?

6 Arguments against realism

Since realism comes in different forms, arguments against it are more likely to attack some particular form than to attack realism as such. The main difficulties for the American and the British realist schools have already been mentioned. In both cases they were metaphysical. The Americans have difficulty in keeping moral facts both natural and moral. The British have difficulty in explaining how the world can be other than 'motivationally inert'.

The two general challenges to realism that are most often mentioned are those made by John Mackie and Gilbert Harman. Harman (1977) asks what, if anything, is explained by moral facts that cannot be equally well explained by moral beliefs. If moral belief alone is enough for all such explanations, why suppose that the facts exist in addition to the beliefs? The facts appear to be explanatorily redundant. We might suggest that at least the facts explain the beliefs, but Harman replies that the beliefs can be equally well explained in other ways, for example, by appeal to upbringing and education. This leaves the facts explaining nothing; they are mere metaphysical danglers, hanging in the air and not related to anything else at all. We are better off without such things. (This is different from Wright's view above, because Wright allows that moral facts could explain moral beliefs; he only asks whether they could explain anything else 'directly'.)

Mackie (1977) suggests that values, if they existed, would be very peculiar things, unlike anything else in the universe; so queer are they that, if they existed, we would need a special faculty of moral perception or intuition to perceive them. Their queerness lies in the idea that an objective value would necessarily be pursued by anyone who recognized it, because such values have 'to-be-pursuedness' built into them. Even if such things are possible, which nobody influenced by Hume would allow, something of that sort is of a different order from anything else with which we are acquainted.

Mackie also asks about the supposed relation between moral facts and natural facts. We ordinarily say, for instance, that an action was wrong because it was cruel. But 'just what *in the world* is signified by this "because"?' (1977: 41; original emphasis). Not only is there the wrongness and the cruelty, but also a totally mysterious 'consequential link' between the two.

These arguments of Mackie's are answered in different ways by the different varieties of realism. The Americans deny the possibility of 'to-be-pursuedness'; the British admit it, but try to explain it by appeal to the dispositional theory of value. As for the mysterious 'consequential link', both sides would, in their different ways, try to say that the wrongness is somehow 'constituted' by the cruelty.

See also: LOGIC OF ETHICAL DISCOURSE; MORAL JUSTIFICATION; MORAL KNOWLEDGE; MORAL RELATIVISM; PROJECTIVISM; REALISM AND ANTI-REALISM

References and further reading

Brink, D. (1989) *Moral Realism and the Foundations of Ethics*, Cambridge: Cambridge University Press. (The only book-length presentation of American realism.)

* Dancy, J. (1993) *Moral Reasons*, Oxford: Blackwell. (A recent full-scale expression of British realism.)

Darwall, S., Gibbard, A. and Railton, P. (1992) 'Towards *Fin de Siècle* Ethics', *Philosophical Review* 101 (1): 115–89. (An advanced survey of late twentieth-century ethics.)

* Harman, G. (1977) *The Nature of Morality*, New York: Oxford University Press, ch. 1. (An influential introductory text.)

Little, M. (1995) 'Recent Work in Moral Realism', *Philosophical Books* 35 (3): 145–53; 35 (4): 225–33. (A two-part comparison of British and American realism.)

* Mackie, J. (1977) *Ethics: Inventing Right and Wrong*, Harmondsworth: Penguin, ch.1. (A very influential introductory text, which starts by attempting to undermine realism.)

* McDowell, J. (1978) 'Are Moral Requirements Hypothetical Imperatives?', *Proceedings of the Aristotelian Society* supplementary vol. 52: 13–29. (Gives reasons for rejecting a Humean conception of moral motivation.)

* —— (1979) 'Virtue and Reason', *The Monist* 62: 331–50. (Attacks 'subsumptive' accounts of moral rationality, in favour of 'perceptual' ones.)

* —— (1985) 'Values and Secondary Qualities', in T. Honderich (ed.) *Morality and Objectivity*, London: Routledge, 110–29. (Gives a dispositional account of normativity in the world, appealing to the analogy with secondary qualities.)

Pettit, P. (1992) 'Realism', in J. Dancy and E. Sosa (eds) *A Companion to Epistemology*, Oxford: Blackwell, 420–4. (An accessible account of what it is to be a realist in any area, which sees realism as a complex combination of claims; the present entry is much influenced by Pettit's account.)

* Wiggins, D. (1987) 'Truth, Invention and the Meaning of Life', in *Needs, Values, Truth: Essays in the Philosophy of Value*, Oxford: Blackwell. (This and

the other papers in the work represent the ethical thought of another leading British realist.)

* Wright, C. (1992) *Truth and Objectivity*, Cambridge, MA: Harvard University Press. (Sets out Wright's sophisticated conception of how the debate between realists and their opponents should be conducted, in a way that focuses on, but is not at all restricted to, *moral* realism.)

JONATHAN DANCY

MORAL RELATIVISM

Often the subject of heated debate, moral relativism is a cluster of doctrines concerning diversity of moral judgment across time, societies and individuals. Descriptive relativism is the doctrine that extensive diversity exists and that it concerns values and principles central to moralities. Meta-ethical relativism is the doctrine that there is no single true or most justified morality. Normative relativism is the doctrine that it is morally wrong to pass judgment on or to interfere with the moral practices of others who have adopted moralities different from one's own. Much debate about relativism revolves around the questions of whether descriptive relativism accurately portrays moral diversity and whether actual diversity supports meta-ethical and normative relativism. Some critics also fear that relativism can slide into nihilism.

1   Descriptive relativism
2   Meta-ethical relativism
3   Normative relativism
4   Relativism and moral confidence

1   Descriptive relativism

From the beginnings of the Western tradition philosophers have debated the nature and implications of moral diversity. Differences in customs and values the Greeks encountered through trade, travel and war motivated the argument attributed to the sophist Protagoras in Plato's *Theaetetus*: that human custom determines what is fine and ugly, just and unjust (see PROTAGORAS). Anthropologists in the twentieth century, such as Ruth Benedict (1934), have emphasized the fundamental differences between the moralities of small-scale traditional societies and the modern West. For example, many traditional societies are focused on community-centred values that require the promotion and sustenance of a common life of relationships, in contrast to both the deontological morality of individual rights and the morality of

utilitarianism that are the most prominent within modern Western moral philosophy. Within this philosophy itself moral diversity is represented by the debates between utilitarians and deontologists, and more recently criticism of both camps by defenders of virtue theory and communitarianism (see DEONTOLOGICAL ETHICS; UTILITARIANISM; VIRTUE ETHICS; COMMUNITY AND COMMUNITARIANISM). Such differences have motivated the doctrine of *descriptive relativism*: that there exists extensive diversity of moral judgment across time, societies and individuals, and that it concerns central moral values and principles.

Critics of descriptive relativism argue that it fails to account for important moral similarities across cultures such as prohibitions against killing innocents and provisions for educating and socializing the young. A relativist response given by Michael Walzer (1987) is to argue that shared norms must be described in an extremely general way and that once one examines the concrete forms they take in different societies, one sees significant variety, for example, in which persons count as 'innocent'. The descriptive relativist might go so far as to assert that no significant similarities exist, but an alternative position is that broad similarities exist that are compatible with significant differences among the moralities human beings have held.

Critics of descriptive relativism also argue that many moral beliefs presuppose religious and metaphysical beliefs, and that these beliefs, rather than any difference in fundamental values, give rise to much moral diversity (see RELIGION AND MORALITY §3). Also, differences in moral belief across different societies may not arise from differences in fundamental values but from the need to implement the same values in different ways given the varying conditions obtaining in these societies. One relativist reply is that while such explanations apply to some moral disagreements, they cannot apply to many others, such as disagreements over the rightness of eating animals or the moral status of the foetus or the rightness of sacrificing an innocent person for the sake of a hundred more.

2   Meta-ethical relativism

The most heated debate about relativism revolves around the question of whether descriptive relativism supports *meta-ethical relativism*: that there is no single true or most justified morality. There is no direct path from descriptive to meta-ethical relativism; the most plausible argument for meta-ethical relativism is that it is part of a larger theory of morality that best explains actual moral diversity.

539

Critics of meta-ethical relativism point out that moral disagreement is consistent with the possibility that some moral judgments are truer or more justified than others, just as disagreement among scientists does not imply that truth is relative in science. Some relativists are unimpressed by the analogy with science, holding that disagreements about the structure of the world can be sufficiently radical to undermine the assumption that there is an absolute truth to be found. This defence of meta-ethical relativism amounts to founding it upon a comprehensive *epistemological relativism* that expresses scepticism about the meaningfulness of talking about truth defined independently of the theories and justificatory practices of particular communities of discourse (see EPISTEMIC RELATIVISM).

An alternative relativist response is to take a nonrelativist stance towards science and to drive a wedge between scientific and moral discourse. Defenders of such a *morality-specific meta-ethical relativism* argue that scientific disagreements can be explained in ways that are consistent with there being a nonrelative truth about the structure of the physical world while moral disagreements cannot be treated analogously. For example, much scientific disagreement may be traced to insufficient or ambiguous evidence or distortions of judgment stemming from personal interests. Relativists have argued that such explanations will not work for moral disagreements such as the ones mentioned above concerning the eating of animals, abortion, and the sacrifice of an innocent to save more lives.

In offering alternative explanations of moral disagreement, morality-specific relativists tend to adopt a 'naturalistic' approach to morality in the sense that they privilege a scientific view of the world and fit their conceptions of morality and moral disagreement within that view. They deny that moral values and principles constitute an irreducible part of the fabric of the world and argue that morality is best explained on the theory that it arises at least in part from custom and convention. On Wong's view (1984), for example, a good part of morality arises out of the need to structure and regulate social cooperation and to resolve conflicts of interest. Meta-ethical relativism is true because there is no single valid way to structure social cooperation.

Morality-specific relativism divides into *cognitive* and *non-cognitive* versions (see MORAL JUDGMENT §1). On C.L. Stevenson's emotivist view (1944), for example, moral discourse merely expresses emotion and influences the attitudes and conduct of others (see EMOTIVISM). Cognitive relativists, such as Mackie, Harman, Foot and Wong, interpret moral judgments as expressing belief, on the grounds that moral judgments are often argued or judged true or false on the basis of reasons. Within cognitive relativism, there are those who believe that there is no single true morality because more than one morality is true, and those who believe that there is no single true morality because all are false. J.L. Mackie (1977) represents the latter camp, on the ground that while morality actually arises out of custom and convention, the meanings of moral terms presuppose a mistaken reference to *sui generis* properties that provide everyone with a reason for acting according to morality (see VALUE, ONTOLOGICAL STATUS OF). Other cognitive relativists see no need to construe moral terms as containing a reference to nonexistent properties and instead tie their cognitive content to certain standards and rules.

According to such a standards relativism, moral language is used to judge and to prescribe in accordance with a set of standards and rules. Different sets of standards and rules get encoded into the meaning of ethical terms such as 'good', 'right' and 'ought' over time, and into individuals, groups, or societies in such a way that two apparently conflicting moral beliefs can both be true. Though under a relativist analysis the beliefs express no conflicting claims about what is true, they do conflict as prescriptions as to what is to be done or as to what kinds of things are to be pursued. The disagreement is purely pragmatic in nature, though parties to the disagreement may not be aware of this if they erroneously assume they share the relevant standards.

Another crucial question for the standards relativist concerns *whose* standards and rules apply when someone makes a moral judgment. Suppose that Jones makes a moral judgment about what Smith ought to do, but that the standards Jones applies to guide his own conduct are not the same as the standards Smith uses to guide hers. One possibility is that Jones uses Smith's standards to judge what she ought to do. Another possibility offered by Harman in some of his writing about relativism is that one must judge others by standards one shares with them. His theory is that morality consists of implicit agreements for the structuring of social cooperation. Moral judgments implying that the subjects have a reason to do what is prescribed make sense only as prescriptions based on what the speakers and subjects (and the intended audience of the judgments) have agreed to do. Other standards relativists observe that people use their own standards in judging the conduct of others, whether or not they believe these others to share their standards.

There are *radical* and *moderate* versions of meta-ethical relativism. Radical relativists hold that any morality is as true or as justified as any other.

Moderate relativists, such as Foot (1978), Walzer and Wong (1984), deny that there is any single true morality but also hold that some moralities are truer or more justified than others. On Wong's view, for instance, certain determinate features of human nature and similarities in the circumstances and requirements of social cooperation combine to produce universal constraints on what an adequate morality must be like. It may be argued, for example, that a common feature of adequate moralities is the specification of duties to care and educate the young, a necessity given the prolonged state of dependency of human offspring and the fact that they require a good deal of teaching to play their roles in social cooperation. It may also be a common feature of adequate moralities to require of the young reciprocal duties to honour and respect those who bring them up, and this may arise partly from role that such reciprocity plays in ensuring that those who are charged with caring for the young have sufficient motivation to do so. Such common features are compatible with the recognition that adequate moralities could vary significantly in their conceptions of what values that cooperation should most realize. Some moralities could place the most emphasis on community-centred values that require the promotion and sustenance of a common life of relationships, others could emphasize individual rights, and still others could emphasize the promotion of utility.

3 Normative relativism

Does meta-ethical relativism have substantive implications for action? *Normative relativism* – the doctrine that it is morally wrong to pass judgment on or to interfere with the moral practices of others who have adopted moralities different from one's own – is often defended by anthropologists, perhaps in reaction to those Western conceptions of the inferiority of other cultures that played a role in colonialism. It also has application to disagreements within a society such as that concerning the morality of abortion, where the positions of the disputing parties seem ultimately to be based on fundamentally different conceptions of personhood.

As in the case of descriptive and meta-ethical relativism, however, there is no direct path from metaphysical to normative relativism. One could hold consistently that there is no single true morality while judging and interfering with others on the basis of one's own morality. Wong has proposed a version of normative relativism consistent with the point that nothing normative follows straightforwardly from meta-ethical relativism. Meta-ethical relativism needs to be supplemented with a liberal contractualist ethic

to imply an ethic of nonintervention. A liberal contractualist ethic requires that moral principles be justifiable to the individuals governed by these principles. If no single morality is most justified for everyone, *liberal normative relativism* may require one not to interfere with those who have a different morality, though the requirement of noninterference may not be absolute when it comes into conflict with other moral requirements such as prohibitions against torture or the killing of innocents (see LIBERALISM).

4 Relativism and moral confidence

A reason why relativism has been feared is the thought that it could easily slide into moral nihilism. Could one continue living according to one's moral values, which sometimes require significant personal sacrifice, if one can no longer believe that they are truer or more justified than other values that require incompatible actions? One relativist response is that one may reasonably question the importance of certain features of one's morality upon adopting a view of their conventional origin. Consider that duties to give aid to others are commonly regarded as less stringent than duties not to harm them. Gilbert Harman (1975) has proposed that this difference results from the superior bargaining position of those with greater material means in the implicit agreement giving rise to morality. Those with lesser material means may reasonably question this feature of morality, if they are persuaded of Harman's explanation. Notice, however, that it is not merely the supposition that this feature arose from convention that may undermine one's confidence in it. With regard to other features of one's morality, one may adopt a relativist view of them and continue to prize them simply because they are as good as any other and because they help to constitute a way of life that is one's own.

Admittedly, people who condemn torture and unremitting cruelty as an offence against the moral fabric of the world may possess a certitude not available to relativists and may find it easier to make the personal sacrifices morality requires. Moral certitude has its own liabilities, however, and has itself contributed to the unremitting cruelty that human beings have inflicted upon each other.

See also: MORALITY AND ETHICS; RELATIVISM; SOCIAL RELATIVISM

References and further reading

* Benedict, R. (1934) *Patterns of Culture*, New York: Penguin. (Argues that different cultures are orga-

nized around different and incommensurable values.)

* Foot, P. (1978) *Moral Relativism (The Lindley Lectures)*, Lawrence, KS: University of Kansas Press. (Defends a form of moderate relativism.)

* Harman, G. (1975) 'Moral Relativism Defended', *Philosophical Review* 84: 3–22. (Argues that morality is founded on implicit agreement and that moral 'ought to do' judgments presuppose that speaker, subject and intended audience share the relevant moral standards.)

Harman, G. and Thomson, J. (1996) *Moral Relativism and Moral Objectivity*, Cambridge, MA: Blackwell. (Most comprehensive statement of Harman's relativism. Modifies some earlier positions taken.)

MacIntyre, A. (1988) *Whose Justice? Which Rationality?*, Notre Dame, IN: University of Notre Dame Press. (Accepts a strong version of descriptive relativism in which different moral traditions contain incommensurable values and standards of rational justification, but argues against meta-ethical relativism on the grounds that traditions may be compared with respect to their ability to resolve internal problems and to explain why other traditions have failed to solve their own problems.)

* Mackie, J.L. (1977) *Ethics: Inventing Right and Wrong*, Harmondsworth: Penguin. (Defends a sceptical form of relativism under which moral judgments lack the objectivity they purport to have. Hence no standard moral judgments are true.)

Nagel, T. (1986) *The View from Nowhere*, New York: Oxford University Press. (Criticism of arguments for meta-ethical relativism from moral diversity.)

* Plato (c.380–367 BC) *Theaetetus*, in *The Collected Dialogues of Plato*, ed. E. Hamilton and H. Cairns, Princeton, NJ: Princeton University Press, 1961. (Statement of a conventionalist and relativist view of morality attributed to Protagoras.)

* Stevenson, C.L. (1944) *Ethics and Language*, New Haven, CT: Yale University Press. (Defends a noncognitivist theory of moral judgment.)

* Walzer, M. (1987) *Interpretation and Social Criticism*, Cambridge, MA: Harvard University Press. (Defence of moderate meta-ethical relativism based on the theory that the meaning of general values is given through specific practices.)

* Wong, D. (1984) *Moral Relativity*, Berkeley, CA: University of California Press. (A defence of moderate relativism based on a naturalistic approach. Some chapters presuppose contemporary philosophy of language that some may regard as technical.)

—— (1991) 'Three Kinds of Incommensurability', in M. Krausz (ed.) *Relativism: Interpretation and Confrontation*, Notre Dame, IN: University of Notre Dame Press. (Discusses ways in which value differences between cultures may result in different criteria for the rationality of belief about the world.)

—— (1996) 'Pluralistic Relativism', *Midwest Studies in Philosophy* 20: 378–400. (More discussion about the constraints that all adequate moralities would have to meet.)

DAVID B. WONG

MORAL SCEPTICISM

Scepticism in general is the view that we can have little or no knowledge; thus moral scepticism is the view that we can have little or no moral knowledge. Some moral sceptics argue that we cannot have moral knowledge because we cannot get the evidence necessary to justify any moral judgments. More radical moral sceptics argue that we cannot have moral knowledge because in morality there are no truths to be known. These radical sceptics argue either that moral judgments are all false because they erroneously presuppose the real existence of 'objective values', or that moral judgments aim to express feelings or influence behaviour instead of stating truths. Critics of moral scepticism, in turn, argue that in at least some cases moral judgments aim to state truths, some of these judgments are in fact true, and we have enough evidence to say that we know these moral truths.

1 Types of moral scepticism
2 The problem of justification
3 The problem of truth
4 Responses to moral scepticism

1 Types of moral scepticism

Moral scepticism is the view that we can have little or no knowledge about ethics, about right and wrong, good and bad, virtue and vice (see MORAL KNOWLEDGE §3). It is one of a cluster of views that would challenge or limit traditional philosophical accounts of ethics. Moral relativism claims that moral truth is relative to cultural convention or personal commitment (see MORAL RELATIVISM); moral subjectivism claims that moral truth is determined by the preferences, feelings, and other subjective states of persons; moral egoism is the claim that it is always obligatory to advance one's own interests (see EGOISM AND ALTRUISM). These positions are motivated by some of the same problems about morality that motivate moral scepticism, but they are not properly speaking sceptical positions, since they are all consistent with the claim that we have extensive knowledge of right and wrong, good and bad, virtue and vice.

Theoretically, at least, sceptics about morality can be divided into global sceptics and specifically moral sceptics. That is, some philosophers are sceptical about morality because they are sceptical about everything, claiming that no one has knowledge of morals because no one has knowledge about anything (see SCEPTICISM). Other philosophers claim that we can and do have knowledge of many things, but not of morality in particular. Global scepticism is not of interest here, and in any event has been comparatively rare in the history of philosophy. Specifically moral scepticism has been more common, mainly because of the intractability of some moral disagreements, the difficulty in providing any plausible account of how we could be causally related to the objects of moral knowledge, and the perception that morality suffers badly when compared with natural science, widely accepted as the paradigm of knowledge. Moral sceptics can be divided into total moral sceptics, who claim that we can have no moral knowledge, and partial moral sceptics who claim that we can have knowledge of some aspects of ethics, but not of others (for example, of good and bad, but not of right and wrong).

Moral sceptics may differ in their accounts of why we fail to have moral knowledge, and these differences can be explained in terms of the traditional analysis of knowledge (see KNOWLEDGE, CONCEPT OF). Traditionally, a judgment has been counted knowledge only when it is both true and justified. Thus, moral sceptics generally argue that in ethics (or some aspect of ethics) one or the other of these conditions is unsatisfiable. Some find fault with the justification of moral judgments; others find fault with their truth.

2   The problem of justification

The first sort of moral sceptic holds that we lack moral knowledge because we lack adequate justification for the moral judgments in question. This inadequacy may be characterized in terms of one of the following: (1) A slim evidential basis for moral judgments, comprising, for instance, only empirical and logico-mathematical truths. (2) Limited kinds of inference admitted in moral reasoning, such as deduction and induction. (3) A strong characterization of moral judgments such that if there were any true moral judgments, they would have to be universal, necessary, and action-guiding. (4) Doctrines such as the 'is/ought gap', according to which no good inferences are possible, from the slim evidential basis to strongly characterized moral conclusions, via the limited kinds of inference admitted (see LOGIC OF ETHICAL DISCOURSE).

In antiquity, doubts about the adequacy of justification led some to total moral scepticism. Pyrrhonists such as Sextus and Philo argued that one and the same thing appears good to one set of people and bad to another, due to differences in their customs, laws, mythical beliefs, and so on (see PHILO OF LARISSA; PYRRHONISM; SEXTUS EMPIRICUS). These appearances are the only justification we have for the moral value of the things in question, but since a thing cannot be both good and bad simultaneously, and since we have no reason to trust one set of appearances over another, no moral judgment has more rational support than its contradictory, and the appropriate attitude toward all moral matters is suspension of belief.

In modern philosophy, doubts about justification have led some to partial moral scepticism. G.E. Moore, for example, held in *Principia Ethica* (1903) that we could have knowledge of the good, and that right actions were by definition those that produced the most good, but that we could not know which actions were right, because we could not know enough about their causal consequences in the distant future (see MOORE, G.E. §1). Similarly, it has been argued by W.D. Ross (1930) that we could know the general principles of *prima facie* duty, but we could rarely, if ever, know in particular circumstances which action was our actual duty, because of the moral complexity of every particular set of circumstances (see ROSS, W.D.). In both cases, these philosophers hold that we lack moral knowledge simply because we lack the factual or moral information needed to justify the moral judgments in question.

3   The problem of truth

The second, and more radical, sort of total moral sceptic holds that we lack moral knowledge because in matters of morality there are no truths to be known. Some, often called 'noncognitivists', argue that moral judgments have no truth-value, because they do not express cognitively meaningful propositions (see ANALYTIC ETHICS; MORAL JUDGMENT §1). Others, often called 'error theorists', hold that moral judgments have a truth-value, but are in fact all false. Noncognitivism and error theory are often classified as 'anti-realist' theories of ethics, since they reject the realist's claim that some moral judgments are literally true, independently of anyone's beliefs or attitudes about them. It should be noted, however, that they are not the only possible anti-realist positions in ethics, and that anti-realism in ethics need not entail scepticism in ethics.

Noncognitivism was perhaps first suggested by David Hume, who argued that morality was the object of feeling not of reason, and that 'when you pronounce any action or character to be vicious, you mean nothing, but that from the constitution of your nature you have a feeling or sentiment of blame from the contemplation of it' (1739/40: 469) (see HUME, D. §4). Following Hume, early emotivists such as A.J. Ayer (1936) argued that moral judgments such as 'Stealing is wrong' cannot be literally true or false, since they express emotions, as in 'Stealing! Boo!', instead of cognitively meaningful propositions (see AYER, A.J. §5; EMOTIVISM). Later emotivists, such as C.L. Stevenson (1944), argued that moral judgments serve to express the speaker's attitudes and evoke similar attitudes in the hearer, and prescriptivists such as the early R.M. Hare (1952) argued that they are prescriptions, rather than statements of fact (see STEVENSON, C.L.; HARE, R.M. §1; PRESCRIPTIVISM).

Error theory is the claim that all moral judgments are false, because they aim to state facts about good and bad or right and wrong, but that these facts do not obtain because the objective value entities they presuppose do not exist. J.L. Mackie (1977) argues against objective moral values on the grounds that, if they were to exist, they would be utterly unlike any other sort of entity with which we are familiar. Similarly, Gilbert Harman (1977) argues against objective moral facts and properties on the grounds that they play no role in the best explanation of any observations (see NATURALISM IN ETHICS §3; MORAL REALISM).

4 Responses to moral scepticism

Thinking moral scepticism an encouragement to immorality, and an outrageous denial of obvious human experience, numerous philosophers have defended moral knowledge from sceptical criticisms of both types. Defences of the justification of moral judgments can be classified as responses to the four factors outlined in §2.

(1) Some have argued for an expansion of the evidential basis so as to include, for instance, moral intuitions or theological information. (Proponents of the method of 'reflective equilibrium' in ethics claim that moral intuitions should be admitted as the data for moral theorizing just as perceptual judgments are admitted as the data for scientific theorizing – see MORAL JUSTIFICATION §2.) (2) Some have argued for a richer view of the kinds of inference admissible in moral reasoning. (Stephen Toulmin (1970) has argued that the standards of reasoning appropriate for ethics

and other areas of everyday life are different from those of the natural sciences.) (3) Others have tried to lessen the distance between premises and conclusion by reducing the content of the moral judgments in need of justification. (A utilitarian might try to meet Moore's scepticism about right action by redefining 'right' in terms of 'maximal expected utility' instead of 'maximal utility' (see RATIONALITY, PRACTICAL).) (4) Still others, including many in the Aristotelian tradition, have argued against doctrines such as the 'is/ought gap', by providing examples of valid 'is-to-ought' inferences, or denying the sharp distinction between empirical and moral judgments which such doctrines appear to presuppose (see LOGIC OF ETHICAL DISCOURSE §3).

Similarly, defences of the truth of moral judgments can be classified as responses either to noncognitivism or to error theory. Critics of noncognitivism emphasize the similarity between moral judgments and other types of fact-stating judgment, minimize the tension between the fact-stating and action-guiding functions of moral judgments, or highlight the inadequacies of particular emotivist accounts. (Moral philosophers such as Peter Geach (1972) have criticized noncognitivism as unable to account for the meaning of judgments in unasserted contexts such as the antecedents of material conditionals.) Certain philosophers who are widely thought of as noncognitivist, such as R.M. Hare, have worked to reconcile prescriptivism or emotivism with the possibility of true, hence knowable, moral judgments. In his essay 'Objective Prescriptions' (1993), Hare argues that any moral judgment that fully satisfies the requirements implicit in the logical meaning of moral words, and takes into account all the relevant empirical information, may be called 'true', even though prescriptions are not ordinarily thought of as 'stating facts'. Realist critics of error theories, such as David Brink, Geoffrey Sayre-McCord, and Nicholas Sturgeon, play down the differences between moral facts and properties on the one hand, and physical facts and properties on the other, arguing that the former have a legitimate role in the best explanation of moral and other phenomena. Other critics, such as Ronald Dworkin, Thomas Nagel and John McDowell, reject explanatory potency as an appropriate criterion for existence of values. Still others, such as Crispin Wright, argue for minimalist or coherentist accounts of truth in ethics, which allow moral judgments to be true (hence in principle knowable) despite their failure according to more robust correspondence theories of truth (see MORAL REALISM §6).

See also: MORAL EXPERTISE; MORAL JUSTIFICATION; VALUE, ONTOLOGICAL STATUS OF

References and further reading

Annas, J. and Barnes, J. (1985) *The Modes of Scepticism*, Cambridge: Cambridge University Press, esp. 151–71. (Contains excerpts of the Pyrrhonist sceptical arguments and useful commentary.)

* Ayer, A.J. (1936) 'Critique of Ethics and Theology', in *Language, Truth and Logic*, London: Gollancz; 2nd edn, 1946; 2nd edn repr. in G. Sayre-McCord (ed.) *Essays on Moral Realism*, Ithaca, NY: Cornell University Press, 1988, ch. 1. (Probably the most accessible introduction to noncognitivism in ethics.)

* Geach, P. (1972) 'Assertion', in *Logic Matters*, Oxford: Blackwell. (A difficult but influential criticism of noncognitivism.)

* Hare, R.M. (1952) *The Language of Morals*, Oxford: Oxford University Press. (The original, and most influential, presentation of universal prescriptivism.)

* —— (1993) 'Objective Prescriptions', in A.P. Griffiths (ed.) *Ethics*, Cambridge: Cambridge University Press, 1–17. (A moderately accessible attempt to reconcile the prescriptivity and objectivity of moral judgments.)

* Harman, G. (1977) *The Nature of Morality*, New York: Oxford University Press. (An accessible introduction to ethics, containing an influential 'explanatory' criticism of moral knowledge.)

* Hume, D. (1739/40) *A Treatise of Human Nature*, ed. L.A. Selby-Bigge, revised by P.H. Nidditch, Oxford: Clarendon Press, 2nd edn, 1978, esp. 455–76. (A classic source of sceptical arguments, both in general and with regard to ethics.)

* Mackie, J.L. (1977) *Ethics: Inventing Right and Wrong*, Harmondsworth: Penguin, esp. 1–49. (The original, and most influential, source of error theory in ethics.)

* Moore, G.E. (1903) *Principia Ethica*, Cambridge: Cambridge University Press, esp. ch. 5. (An influential presentation of intuitionism about value, including partial moral scepticism about obligation.)

* Ross, W.D. (1930) *The Right and the Good*, Oxford: Oxford University Press, esp. ch. 2. (A classic exposition of pluralist intuitionism about obligation, combined with partial moral scepticism.)

Sinnott-Armstrong, W. and Timmons, M. (eds) (1996) *Moral Knowledge? New Essays in Moral Epistemology*, Oxford: Oxford University Press. (A collection of moderately difficult but important essays on moral knowledge and moral scepticism, with a useful annotated bibliography.)

* Stevenson, C.L. (1944) *Ethics and Language*, New Haven, CT: Yale University Press. (An early but sophisticated version of noncognitivism.)

* Toulmin, S.E. (1970) *Reason in Ethics*, Cambridge: Cambridge University Press, esp. part III. (The original, and most accessible, presentation of the 'good reasons' approach in ethics.)

MARK T. NELSON

MORAL SENSE THEORIES

In Leviathan (1651), Thomas Hobbes argued that since good and evil are naturally relative to each individual's private appetites, and man's nature is predominantly selfish, then morality must be grounded in human conventions. His views provoked strong reactions among British moral philosophers in the seventeenth and eighteenth centuries. Moral sense theories comprise one set of responses. A moral sense theory gives a central role to the affections and sentiments in moral perception, in the appraisal of conduct and character, and in deliberation and motivation. Shaftesbury and Francis Hutcheson argued that we have a unique faculty of moral perception, the moral sense. David Hume and Adam Smith held that we cultivate a moral sensibility when we appropriately regulate our sympathy by an experience-informed reason and reflection.

1 The moral sense
2 Regulated sympathy

1 The moral sense

Moral sense theory originated in the work of Shaftesbury (1711), as he drew on aspects of the seventeenth-century English rationalist tradition that dealt with the emphasis HOBBES had placed on self-interest (see SHAFTESBURY; RATIONALISM). Hobbes (1651) had argued that natural circumstances lead each man to favour his own interests at the expense of more socially-directed affections, and when men enter into the social compact and obey the dictates of morality they do so primarily from self-interested motives (see CONTRACTARIANISM §2). Following the Cambridge Platonist Henry MORE, Shaftesbury conceived of the moral sense as a part of intellect. According to More (1667), our 'boniform faculty' distinguishes goodness, discovering in it a 'sweetness and flavour' that in turn induces us to act virtuously. In his *Inquiry Concerning Virtue and Merit* (1711), Shaftesbury combines the notion of an intellectually grounded taste with Locke's notion of reflection, and argues that our moral sense directs reflexive sentiments of praise or censure to the form of virtue or vice in our affections and resolutions, the psychological springs of conduct (see LOCKE, J. §3; VIRTUES AND VICES §2–5). Certain 'pre-conceptions' in the mind guarantee a correct correspondence between the pleasure of moral admiration and virtuous affections. The virtuous agent is one who achieves a balance of the self-interested and social affections. Shaftesbury's argument concerning how we achieve this balance links obligation with self-interest, and is intended to show both that Hobbes was wrong about the weakness of our other-regarding motives, and that self-love obliges us to virtue. The moral sentiments are disinterested evaluations of virtuous and vicious affections. Our moral admiration of our social affections nevertheless enriches the latter, rendering them 'master-pleasures' that govern all our other motives. Moreover, since such pleasures in turn yield the highest 'self-enjoyment', virtuous action undertaken from other-regarding motives provides agents with the chief means for promoting their own interest.

In his *Inquiry into the Original of Our Ideas of Beauty and Virtue* (1725), Francis HUTCHESON defended Shaftesbury's views against the criticisms of MANDEVILLE. Hutcheson followed his predecessor in stressing the instinctively reflexive character of our moral sentiments. In employing an empiricist framework and analogizing the moral sense to our physical senses, however, he severed the intimate connection forged by Shaftesbury between the moral sense and intellect. With Locke, he asserted that reason could not be the source of any new ideas, including our moral perceptions (see LOCKE, J. §2; MORAL KNOWLEDGE §3). Approbation and blame consist in perceptions of pleasure and pain, and these simple ideas are the immediate and necessary responses of our moral sense to an agent's benevolent or unkind affections. We rely on reason to draw inferences about an agent's character and to inform us of the tendencies of the actions and affections that we evaluate morally, but it cannot by itself determine our moral response.

To counter the claim advanced by rationalists such as CLARKE and WOLLASTON that our rational apprehension of goodness obliges us to virtuous conduct, Hutcheson constructed new arguments concerning reason's limits in *Illustrations on the Moral Sense* (1728). He drew a distinction between reasons for approving or blaming and reasons for acting, while showing that both presuppose our affective nature. In his account of justifying reasons, he acknowledged that we need to justify our particular moral evaluations of actions and characters. Justifying reasons establish the grounds for our approval or disapproval by stating truths about the tendencies of

particular actions and motives. Since our approval of benevolence (which Hutcheson regarded as the sole virtue) is uniquely determined by the moral sense, not by the truth of a justifying reason, the justificatory function of such reasons presupposes the moral sense. Exciting reasons are truths concerning the motives of agents, and therefore presuppose affections. Since we may present a justifying reason for approving some action in the distant past that cannot possibly motivate us, or have exciting reasons for acting in ways that we neither approve nor blame, our reasons for evaluating and our reasons for acting are distinct from one another.

Hutcheson rejected the view of Hobbes and some of the natural lawyers that moral obligation needed the backing of sanctions (see NATURAL LAW). He also minimized Shaftesbury's emphasis on the connection between obligation and interest, since it made self-love, not itself a virtuous motive, the sole obligation to virtue. He conceded that there is an interested sense of obligation that concerns the happiness of the agent and presupposes self-love. But he redefined moral obligation to mean the determination of the agent disinterestedly to approve and perform virtuous actions. The unease agents feel if they omit a required benevolent action makes them conscious of their failure with respect to their obligation, without invoking either sanctions or advantage to themselves.

2 Regulated sympathy

In *A Treatise of Human Nature* (1739/40), Hume borrowed Shaftesbury's and Hutcheson's arguments concerning our natural sociality, added to Hutcheson's arguments about the limits of reason, and revised his doctrine of moral obligation (see HUME, D. §§3–4). Both Hume and Adam SMITH agreed that our moral sentiments distinguish between virtue and vice, and take as their objects the characters of agents. Aware of rationalist criticisms of the notion of an original moral sense, they appealed instead to the principle of sympathy, regarding it as the foundation for a moral sensibility that is essentially social in character, and requires cultivation through education and experience.

In an important concession to Hobbes, Hume argued that prior to establishing conventions of justice, value responses are relative to each individual in part because of the natural limitations of our social affections and sympathy. In order to resolve the conflicts stemming from each individual's partiality, a more reflective form of interest naturally obliges us to establish rules of justice. Our extended sympathy with all who participate in the convention makes us feel uneasy when others disapprove of our breaking the rules, and this gives rise to our sense of moral obligation. As in Hutcheson's account, moral obligation is connected with our moral sentiments, and does not depend on sanctions. The extensive sympathy underpinning our moral sensibility enables us to adopt general perspectives from which we correct our individual biases and form shared sentiments of praise and blame. Although this more cultivated moral sensibility depends on human conventions, Hume argued that it results from the natural and necessary 'progress of the sentiments'.

Hume distinguished between artificial virtues whose motives arise only when certain conventions are in place, and natural virtues that presuppose natural affections. He also emphasized the importance to us of self-regarding virtues, and argued that we cannot draw a fine line between our approval of virtue and our approval of agents' talents or natural beauty. He agreed with Shaftesbury and Hutcheson that our interested contemplation of the pleasures yielded by moral approval gives us a reason to endorse having a virtuous character. But he also urged that his version of our moral sensibility gains an advantage for virtue because it accommodates our disinterested approval of the experience-informed reason and sympathy that lead us to correct and improve our moral sentiments.

In *The Theory of Moral Sentiments* (1759), Smith refined Hume's account of sympathy, distinguishing between judgments of propriety and judgments of merit. The former arise when impartial spectators sympathize with the agent's motive and approve of its propriety, the latter when they sympathize with both the agent's proper motive and the gratitude elicited by the recipient of the virtuous action. Smith used the distinction to argue for a greater variety of moral sentiments. Hume and Smith argued that our shared moral sensibility enables us to see our conduct and character mirrored in one another's sentiments. But Smith was less sceptical than Hume about the influence of moral judgment on deliberation. When we become the impartial spectator of our own character, we develop a conscience. We can rely on the internal promptings of conscience to guide our own conduct (see CONSCIENCE).

Towards the end of the eighteenth century, Reid's connection between moral choice and free will, and the emphasis on the consequences of action for social reform in the utilitarianism of James Mill and Bentham, displaced the moral sense theorists' concentration on our internal sentiments (see REID, T.; UTILITARIANISM).

See also: CAMBRIDGE PLATONISM §4; COMMON-SENSE ETHICS; MORAL MOTIVATION

References and further reading

Cragg, G.R. (ed.) (1968) *The Cambridge Platonists*, Oxford: Oxford University Press. (Contains More's *Enchiridion ethicum*, and other rationalist responses to Hobbes.)

Darwall, S. (1995) *The British Moralists and the Internal 'Ought': 1640–1740*, Cambridge: Cambridge University Press. (Discusses developments of the notion of obligation, and relates the British moralist tradition to contemporary ethics.)

* Hobbes, T. (1651) *Leviathan*, in W. Molesworth (ed.) *The Collected Works of Thomas Hobbes*, vol. 3, London: Routledge/Thoemmes Press, 1994. (Ground-breaking work sparking debate about the reality of morality and the source of obligation.)

Hope, V.M. (1989) *Virtue by Consensus*, Oxford: Clarendon Press. (Discusses the moral sense and sympathy in Hutcheson, Hume and Smith.)

* Hume, D. (1739/40) *A Treatise of Human Nature*, ed. L.A. Selby-Bigge, revised by P.H. Nidditch, Oxford: Clarendon Press, 2nd edn, 1978, book III. (Presents Hume's account of our sense of morality.)

—— (1748, 1751) *Enquiries Concerning Human Understanding and Concerning the Principles of Morals*, ed. L.A. Selby-Bigge, revised by P.H. Nidditch, Oxford: Clarendon Press, 3rd edn, 1975. (A more concise and philosophically sophisticated account of morality than that given in the *Treatise*.)

* Hutcheson, F. (1725) *An Inquiry Into the Original of Our Ideas of Beauty and Virtue*, in *Collected Works of Francis Hutcheson*, vol. 7, Hildesheim: Olms, 1969. (An account of various internal senses, including the aesthetic and the moral sense.)

* —— (1728) *Illustrations Upon the Moral Sense*, ed. B. Peach, Cambridge, MA: Harvard University Press, 1971. (Especially good for Hutcheson's criticism of the rationalist tradition.)

* More, H. (1667) *Enchiridion ethicum* (An Account of Virtue), trans. as *An account of virtue: or, Dr. Henry More's abridgement of morals, put into English*, London, 1690; repr. in G.R. Cragg (ed.) *The Cambridge Platonists*, Oxford: Oxford University Press, 1968.

Raphael, D.D. (1947) *The Moral Sense*, Oxford: Oxford University Press. (Good introductory work. Contains chapters on Hutcheson, Hume and Reid.)

—— (ed.) (1969) *British Moralists: 1650–1800*, Oxford: Clarendon Press, 2 vols, 1969; repr., Indianapolis, IN: Hackett Publishing Company, 2 vols, 1991. (Excellent selections from the major works.)

Schneewind, J.B. (ed.) (1990) *Moral Philosophy from Montaigne to Kant*, Cambridge: Cambridge University Press, 2 vols. (Useful compilation that places the work of British moralists in a broader European context. Excellent bibliography.)

* Shaftesbury, A.A.C. (1711) *Inquiry Concerning Virtue and Merit*, in *Characteristics of Men, Manners, Opinions, and Times*, ed. D. Walford, Manchester: Manchester University Press, 1977. (Contains Shaftesbury's major ethical writings.)

* Smith, A. (1759) *The Theory of Moral Sentiments*, ed. D.D. Raphael and A.L. Mackie, Oxford: Clarendon Press, 1976. (An edited reprint of the 6th edn of the work, published in 1790, this is Smith's major contribution to ethics. In part VII, Smith contrasts contemporary views of virtue with those of the ancients, and criticizes the rationalist, selfish and moral sense schools of moral thought.)

JACQUELINE A. TAYLOR

MORAL SENTIMENTS

Moral sentiments are those feelings or emotions central to moral agency. Aristotle treated sentiments as nonrational conditions, capable of being moulded into virtues through habituation. The moral sense theorists of the Enlightenment took sentiments to provide the psychological basis for our common moral life. Kantian approaches deny the primacy of sentiments in moral personality, and treat moral sentiments as conditioned by our rational grasp of moral principles.

A central issue is whether moral sentiments incorporate moral beliefs. Accounts which affirm a connection with moral beliefs point to the complex intentionality (object-directedness) of such states as resentment or indignation. Against this, some observe that moral emotions may be felt inappropriately.

Of special interest are the sentiments of guilt and shame. These seem to reflect different orientations towards moral norms, and questions arise about the degree to which these different orientations are culturally local, and whether either orientation is superior to the other.

1   **Historical perspectives**
2   **Sentiment and moral belief**
3   **Guilt and shame**

1   Historical perspectives

Sentiments have played various roles in ethical theory. On Aristotle's view, set out in *Nicomachean Ethics*, moral virtue is essentially a condition of the sentiments. It is a state of character, involving a disposition to feel the emotions connected with pleasure and pain in ways appropriate to one's circumstances. Moral virtue is distinguished from other states of character by the fact that the virtuous person's sentiments are responsive to practical reason, which determines what it is right to do or to feel in any given situation. One acquires this state of character through habituation, which refines one's susceptibility to pleasure through repeated performance of virtuous actions, and indirectly affects one's ability to deliberate effectively about the true goods of human life (see ARISTOTLE §23). This complex view of moral sentiments treats them as parts of the nonrational soul, which nevertheless both influence and are influenced by one's capacities for practical reflection; it was opposed in the ancient period by the Stoics, who interpreted sentiments essentially as rational judgments (see STOICISM §19).

A different approach was taken by the sentimentalist theorists of the eighteenth century. Setting themselves against the apparent scepticism and egoism of Thomas Hobbes, these philosophers grounded our autonomous moral faculties not in reason but in the moral sense. The moral sense was interpreted as an innate susceptibility to feel sentiments of approval when confronted with morally virtuous character traits, under conditions of suitably impartial reflection. Virtuous traits were understood primarily in terms of benevolence (or other traits, such as justice, which are useful on the whole); and later proponents of the approach took the moral sense that approves of those traits to rest on a mechanism of sympathetic identification with others (see MORAL SENSE THEORIES).

This conception is like Aristotle's in treating moral sentiments as nonrational phenomena – moral approval cannot incorporate moral judgments, because such judgments would presuppose a rational grasp of moral distinctions of the sort the sentimentalists denied. In this respect, the sentimentalists were very much the precursors of modern noncognitivists, who hold, for instance, that moral judgments serve to express emotions of approval or disapproval (see EMOTIVISM; ANALYTIC ETHICS §1). In contrast with Aristotle, however, the sentimentalists treated the susceptibility to moral sentiments as an innate part of our common human nature, the emergence of which does not require elaborate habituation; this befits the role of the emotions in moral sense theory, as providing a common psychological basis for moral life (see MORALITY AND EMOTIONS §1).

Kant and his followers ground our common moral capacities in reason rather than the emotions. This approach is popularly thought to be hostile to the idea that sentiments contribute positively to the moral life – Kant himself, for instance, notoriously claimed that actions motivated by sentiment have no moral worth (see KANTIAN ETHICS). But the denial that moral sentiments play a foundational role in moral thought and motivation does not mean that they have no contribution to make.

Outlined in his *Critik der practischen Vernunft* (*Critique of Practical Reason*) (1788), Kant's account of the sentiment of respect for the moral law suggests that distinctively moral emotions are structured by our independent rational grasp of moral principles: this approach can be extended to such emotions as indignation, resentment and guilt, which are usually responses to the violation of moral principles. The susceptibility to such moral sentiments shows that one has internalized moral principles, and it is an important task of moral theory to consider whether the principles it proposes can be so internalized that a society organized around them will be a stable and self-sustaining one.

2 Sentiment and moral belief

A leading issue is whether the moral sentiments incorporate moral beliefs. Philosophers who deny this (such as the sentimentalists, and modern noncognitivists) tend to emphasize the passivity of the moral sentiments, and interpret questions of emotional justification primarily in strategic terms ('Is it good for the agent to be subject to sentiments of this type?'). Kantians and others who take moral sentiments to rest on moral beliefs see greater scope for active control of the moral sentiments, through exercise of our rational capacities for moral judgment; and they treat moral sentiments as open to nonstrategic forms of assessment ('Is a particular moral sentiment really appropriate to its object?').

This difference in approach is difficult to resolve in the abstract: moral sentiments are of many different kinds, ranging from pleasure or approval to such highly structured emotions as pride or regret, and there is no reason to expect any single account to apply to all of them. It is more fruitful to explore the difference with reference to a restricted class of moral sentiments.

Resentment, for instance, is characteristically a reaction to a moral offence, and this aspect of the emotion is naturally accounted for by supposing the emotion to rest on the moral belief that one has been treated wrongly. This moral belief gives the emotion a propositional object, and opens it to assessment in nonstrategic terms ('Was the action I resent really wrong?'). Those who favour this approach can readily explain the difference between resentment and closely related sentiments, such as indignation or disdain, in terms of the moral beliefs that the different emotions incorporate. Opponents point out that resentment is often felt irrationally, on occasions when one does not really take oneself to have been morally wronged. This phenomenon seems hard to reconcile with the claim that episodes of resentment necessarily incorporate a moral belief.

An alternative approach treats resentment and other moral sentiments as refinements of underlying biological syndromes, to be identified not by the moral beliefs they incorporate but by their characteristic causes and behavioural effects. By depriving moral sentiments of their propositional objects, however, this approach seems to deny something essential to states of resentment, namely that they involve a distinctive way of thinking of the person one resents, different from the way one conceives the targets of indignation or anger (which may have similar causes and behavioural effects).

3 Guilt and shame

A different set of questions concerns the degree to which moral sentiments are culturally conditioned (see MORAL RELATIVISM). Many theories hold that a susceptibility to distinctively moral sentiments such as sympathy or even resentment is built into human nature, providing a common basis for moral discourse and response. But other sentiments have seemed more parochial. Guilt, for instance, is sometimes conceived of as a sentiment available only within cultures whose ethical systems are organized around the notions of law, obligation and individual freedom. In other cultures, where ethical precepts are taken to describe a public ideal of honourable behaviour, shame is the characteristic emotional sanction.

Early statements of the contrast between guilt and shame cultures took the latter to be the more primitive, lacking the resources for fully internalizing moral demands. This 'progressivism' has been reversed in more recent treatments of the distinction, which have seen in shame a moral sentiment that lacks the objectionable aspects of guilt – the metaphysical assumption of absolute freedom before the law, and the pointless cruelty that seems to characterize the bad conscience.

This contrast may be sustained even by those who remain agnostic on the question of whether there are any pure shame cultures. Shame and guilt seem to reflect two different orientations towards moral norms: the personality in which guilt predominates sees them as harsh and punitive requirements, while those in whom shame is the dominant moral sentiment view moral norms as articulations of an ideal way of life, a set of excellences which they aspire to exemplify. (This opposition is sometimes expressed in psychoanalytic literature in terms of a contrast between the super-ego and the ego-ideal; scc FREUD, S. §§8–9.) Important questions here are whether we can really do without the guilt-orientation to moral norms, and whether it is as metaphysically and morally suspect as its critics have alleged.

See also: CONSCIENCE; MORAL JUDGMENT; MORAL KNOWLEDGE; MORAL MOTIVATION; RECTIFICATION AND REMAINDERS

References and further reading

* Aristotle (*c.* mid 4th century BC) *Nicomachean Ethics*, trans. W.D. Ross, revised by J.L. Ackrill and J.O. Urmson, Oxford: Oxford University Press, 1980, books II–V. (Discusses the role of sentiments in moral virtue, or excellence of character.)

Baier, A.C. (1993) 'Moralism and Cruelty: Reflections on Hume and Kant', *Ethics* 103: 436–57; repr. in *Moral Prejudices: Essays on Ethics*, Cambridge, MA: Harvard University Press, 1994, 268–93. (Attacks guilt-based moralities as cruel, by comparison with moralities oriented around shame, and associates the two with the theories of Kant and Hume respectively.)

Gibbard, A. (1990) *Wise Choices, Apt Feelings: A Theory of Normative Judgment*, Cambridge, MA: Harvard University Press. (Argues that moral sentiments do not rest on moral judgments, and that moral norms are norms for the appropriateness of moral sentiments.)

Hume, D. (1751) *An Enquiry Concerning the Principles of Morals*, ed. J.B. Schneewind, Indianapolis, IN: Hackett Publishing Company, 1983. (Characteristic and accessible statement of the moral sense theory.)

* Kant, I. (1788) *Critik der practischen Vernunft*, ed. and trans. L.W. Beck, *Critique of Practical Reason*, New York: Macmillan, 3rd edn, 1993, part 1, book I, ch. 3. (Discusses respect for the law as a sentiment conditioned distinctively by the rational grasp of moral principles.)

Rawls, J. (1971) *A Theory of Justice*, Cambridge, MA: Harvard University Press, part III. (Contains an important discussion of the nature and genesis of moral sentiments, and considers the prospects for internalizing competing principles of justice in the sentiments of individual agents.)

Strawson, P.F. (1962) 'Freedom and Resentment', *Proceedings of the British Academy* 48: 1–25; repr. in G. Watson (ed.) *Free Will*, Oxford: Oxford University Press, 1982. (Influential defence of the view that our moral relations are thoroughly structured by our susceptibility to moral sentiments, drawing implications for the issue of freedom of will.)

Taylor, G. (1985) *Pride, Shame, and Guilt: Emotions of Self-Assessment*, Oxford: Clarendon Press. (Subtle discussion of the sentiments mentioned in the title, emphasizing their cognitive dimensions.)

Wallace, R.J. (1994) *Responsibility and the Moral Sentiments*, Cambridge, MA: Harvard University Press. (Offers an interpretation of guilt, resentment and indignation, and traces the role of these moral sentiments in our practice of holding people morally responsible.)

Williams, B. (1993) *Shame and Necessity*, Berkeley, CA: University of California Press. (Argues that the shame morality depicted in ancient Greek literature is far more sophisticated than its critics have grasped.)

R. JAY WALLACE

MORAL STANDING

Towards whom is it appropriate to direct fundamental moral consideration? This is the question of moral standing. Many different answers have been offered: all and only those creatures that are themselves capable of extending moral concern and consideration; all humans, whether capable of functioning as moral agents or not; humans plus certain other 'higher' animals (such as gorillas, chimpanzees and porpoises) that can think, reason and be self-aware; creatures capable of feeling sensations such as pain, no matter how otherwise rudimentary their psychological existence; living beings, whether sentient or not; 'holistic' entities such as political states, cultural traditions, biological species, natural ecosystems.

The moral standing issue has great significance both practically and theoretically. Earnestly reconsidering who, or what, counts morally could change what we eat, how we clothe ourselves, the extent to which we spread out over the land. Even those who believe that only humans count morally must still address the theoretically challenging question of what it is about humans that warrants such exclusive concern.

To try to resolve this difficult issue, philosophers have pursued several different strategies. Some work from plausible convictions about particular cases (such as '"Normal" healthy adult humans have moral standing, if anyone does') and then, subject to the demand for principled consistency, try to extrapolate to a more general account of what confers moral standing. Others try to articulate a broad view of the general nature of moral consciousness (as involving, for example, the disposition to empathize with others or promote their good) and work back from that to an account of the most basic conditions of the possibility of being conscientiously considered (for instance, having feelings with which others can empathize or a good which they can take into account).

1 The nature of moral standing
2 Positions on moral standing
3 Theoretical and practical import
4 How to decide moral standing: possibilities and pitfalls

1 The nature of moral standing

Philosophers often grapple with two major issues. Which considerations would guide and shape a morally decent life, and of whom is morally decent living required? But there is a third very large philosophical concern about the nature of morality: towards whom is it appropriate to direct fundamental moral consideration? This is the issue of basic moral standing: which entities matter morally, not merely for the sake of others, but in their own right?

Essentially the same issue has been formulated in a variety of different vocabularies. What does it take to be a 'moral patient' (as opposed to a 'moral agent')? Who or what is 'morally considerable'? Who can be regarded properly as an 'object' of moral concern (as distinct from the active 'subject' who entertains the concern)? But there are also less appropriate ways to pose the question. Thus it is sometimes rendered as 'Who or what deserves moral consideration?', or 'Who is entitled to such consideration?'. These formulations unduly narrow the scope of the question: being deserving and having a right are only two of the grounds on which beings who matter morally can be taken into consideration for their own sake (see DESERT AND MERIT; RIGHTS).

The use of the expression 'moral standing' is modelled on, but in some measure also diverges from, the notion of standing as employed in the context of the law. To have legal standing is to be legally authorized to raise, or have raised on one's behalf, a complaint in court. Thus it is possible to have standing (a) with respect to some legal matters, but not others; and (b) within certain judicial venues only. The notion of moral standing parallels such possibilities: (a) a creature capable of suffering but incapable of thinking and communicating might have a morally significant claim on others not to be treated cruelly but no meaningful claim to 'freedom of thought and speech'; (b) the prospect of being pressed into service as a beast of burden could give an animal moral

standing in the 'court' of humanity's conscience; attacks by nonhuman predators in the wild might not. Despite these parallels, moral and legal standing are not equivalent. There can be moral standing without the corresponding legal standing (consider, for example, the emotional support that close friends can rightly expect but not legally compel); and legal standing without fundamental moral standing (consider the fiction of business corporations as legal 'persons').

2 Positions on moral standing

Who, then, has basic moral standing? Many different answers have been offered. At one end of the spectrum is 'all and only those creatures that are themselves capable of extending moral concern and consideration'. But common sense rejects this answer as too restrictive in scope. Young children are thought to fall within the domain of direct moral concern even before they are able to be morally considerate themselves; perhaps their standing derives from the fact that they are in the process of developing the ability to take others into moral consideration. But the same answer will not do with respect to humans who are profoundly, and permanently, retarded or demented; nor for animals who have desires and feelings, but are not capable of moral understanding and motivation.

At the other extreme, the answer 'everything has moral standing' raises at least two difficulties. (1) The greater the number and variety of entities that are to be regarded as having standing, the greater is the potential for serious conflicts of putatively legitimate need and interest. The task of resolving such conflicts justly becomes immensely, perhaps hopelessly, complicated. (2) If even insensate and inanimate entities are to be counted as falling within the domain of basic moral consideration, it remains to be explained what the nature and basis of that consideration could be. Just what ought to be done for the sake of a rock or a mud-hole?

Between these extremes several other answers have been proposed: for example, any creature capable of experiencing sensations such as pain; beings who, though not rational, are more than merely sentient, that is, who have enough psychological structure and complexity to count as ongoing 'subjects of a life' or as havers (however nonreflectively) of reasons; all living beings, whether sentient or not; biological species and/or natural ecosystems; societies, political states, cultures and traditions.

Thus, in trying to clarify who or what has moral standing, we will be prompted to investigate other difficult issues: What is it to be a moral agent – is it to be the conscious and self-conscious subject of a life, or to have reasons? What is involved in being sentient and how is sentience different from mere reactivity? What is it to be alive? How is biological life relevantly different from homeostatic mechanism? What is a species, an ecosystem? What differentiates one species from another, one ecosystem from another?

For each putatively relevant criterion (such as rationality, self-awareness, conscience, sentience and life), there are difficult questions as to which beings actually satisfy it: Who or what has the capacity for self-awareness and rational reflection – do porpoises and chimpanzees? Who or what is sentient – are clams and oysters? Could plants, slow-responding though they may be, be said to experience anything? Who or what is alive? Do viruses count? Are ecosystems living (super-) organisms too? Shall we say that the earth, or at least the outer crust and atmosphere known as the biosphere, is a living being ('Gaia') in its own right?

Perhaps there is some wisdom in more than one such view. As there are several different dimensions of moral concern, so it might be the case that different kinds of entities warrant different kinds of concern. This possibility is illustrated by Hume's claim (1751) that while humans must treat animals kindly, they are not required to treat animals in accordance with rules of justice (which for Hume have to do primarily with property and contract) (see HUME, D. §5; JUSTICE). Whatever we may think of the specifics of Hume's position, the general insight behind it seems plausible. How a morally virtuous human agent ought to treat beings of another kind depends on the nature and capacities of the being in question: towards a sentient creature lacking the capacity to form expectations and harbour hopes, there is a duty to refrain from cruel treatment but no duty to keep 'promises'; towards a living being incapable of experiencing pain and suffering, there is no duty to refrain from cruel and inhumane treatment, but there may yet be a duty to preserve its life, or the possibility of reproducing its kind.

Thus moral standing need not be all or nothing. Unfortunately, deciding on which entities are to be included within the domain of basic moral consideration does not by itself decide the question of how to resolve conflicts of legitimate need and interest. To help meet this problem, some philosophers argue that in the event of conflict moral priority ought to be given to beings with self-consciousness or with the capacity to reason or to creatures of the same species (or culture or community) as oneself. Other thinkers urge a more egalitarian approach.

3 Theoretical and practical import

The question of moral standing should have profound theoretical significance. Even ethicists who prefer to limit their focus to the domain of humankind must come to terms with the question: what is it about fellow humans that warrants such (exclusive) concern or consideration? Is it because they are capable of having experiences, feelings, hopes, desires? Then it would seem to follow that at least some nonhuman beings ought to be taken into consideration as well. Or is it a matter of 'species-solidarity' – the mere fact that we humans are all members of the same biological species? From this it follows that intelligent beings visiting from another planet would be entitled to conquer and enslave us, or at least to be completely indifferent to how their actions affected us, because we and they are not all members of the same biological species. It seems more plausible to suggest that as thinking, feeling beings, humans do matter morally and hence that it would be unreasonable of other-worldly but morally responsible agents, even those of a different biological species, not to extend to us at least a measure of respect and consideration.

At the same time, the moral standing issue also holds more than purely theoretical interest. Agriculture, urban development, biomedical research, energy technology – these are some of the respects in which human practice could be altered profoundly by earnest reconsideration of who or what has basic moral standing (see AGRICULTURAL ETHICS; BIOETHICS; TECHNOLOGY AND ETHICS). Even within the human sphere, there are difficult cases to address: future generations (see FUTURE GENERATIONS, OBLIGATIONS TO); the deceased; people suffering from earthquake, famine or persecution, who live in distant places (see HELP AND BENEFICENCE); pre-natal human organisms (see REPRODUCTION AND ETHICS); human beings who are profoundly retarded or demented; and human organisms in a persistent vegetative state (see LIFE AND DEATH §3).

Of course, even if plants, animals, endangered species and ecosystems turned out not to have basic moral standing, many of the same restrictions on human conduct could conceivably be generated by purely 'anthropocentric' considerations, such as the concern not to undermine environmental conditions crucial to human survival; the desirability of keeping open the range and variety of humanly valued (emotional, aesthetic and even scientific) experiences; and the importance of reinforcing inhibitions and compunctions (against such factors as cruelty and wastefulness) that humans sorely need to cultivate in their dealings with one another.

Arguments such as these make the moral status of

nonhuman entities contingent upon putative facts (psychological and ecological) of human life. Animal liberationists, reverence-for-life theorists, and 'deep ecology' advocates typically seek to ground the moral significance of nonhuman entities in properties wholly intrinsic to the entities themselves (see ANIMALS AND ETHICS; ENVIRONMENTAL ETHICS). They dismiss human-regarding defences of respect for nonhuman nature as too limited, uncertain and shallow. Despite the large theoretical gulf that separates the two opposing schools of thought, the extent to which they might nevertheless converge in their specific policy prescriptions remains an open, and largely empirical, question.

4 How to decide moral standing: possibilities and pitfalls

How, then, can we make progress towards resolving this profoundly difficult issue? Philosophers often start with intuitively plausible convictions about particular cases (such as '"Normal" healthy adult humans have moral standing, if anyone does') and then try to extrapolate, subject to the demand for principled consistency, to a more general account of what confers moral standing. Working from the other direction, philosophers sometimes try to trace out the implications of a well-established normative theory. Taking a utilitarian perspective, for example, one might reason that what confers moral standing is the capacity to experience pleasure and pain, or to form preferences whose satisfaction or frustration could be said to matter to oneself (see UTILITARIANISM). From a Kantian perspective, it might be argued that the only beings who ought to be taken into respectful consideration for their own sake are those who are (actually or potentially) capable of reasoning about what to do and of regulating their conduct accordingly (see KANTIAN ETHICS). Somewhere in between, there is the possibility of working back from such 'mid-level' common-sense considerations as kindness, fidelity and fairness, to the conditions of the possibility of being thus considered. For example, if there is a duty not to be cruel, then it applies to all and only those creatures who can suffer; if there is a duty to be honest, then creatures who have the capacity to form beliefs and expectations ought not to be deceived and defrauded. A fourth possibility is to articulate a broader, more procedural account of what is involved in being morally thoughtful. For example, moral consciousness seems to involve a willingness (1) to empathize with others, to try to imagine what it is like to be in their position; (2) to take their good or wellbeing into account; and (3) to deal with them in ways that can be justified to them. From these

observations it seems to follow that nothing can be treated with morally thoughtful consideration unless there is something it feels like to be that being, a perspective of its own with which to empathize; or unless it has a good or wellbeing that can be taken into benevolent consideration; or unless it has a mind or will that can be respectfully consulted and addressed.

Such approaches are not without their pitfalls. Relying on (1) the paradigm of humanness, we might well be accused of being anthropocentric, extending moral concern only to those beings that resemble ourselves to a degree sufficient to inspire our parochial interest and concern. Relying on (2) a familiar theoretical approach or on (3) everyday mid-level moral considerations, we run the risk of working from a perspective that is already tailored to an overly narrow conception of the domain of proper moral consideration. But charges of self-bias, anthropocentrism, speciesism and the like cannot be pressed indefinitely without losing some of their force. For suppose it were suggested that a grain of sand has moral standing and that to deny this is only to betray an unduly biased perspective. To respond to this challenge one could reasonably raise any or all of the following questions. What is the perspective of the grain of sand and what would it be like to empathize with it? In what does its good or wellbeing consist? What could count as respectfully consulting or addressing its will, or as justifying oneself to it?

See also: RESPECT FOR PERSONS

References and further reading

Aquinas, T. (*c*.1259–65) *Summa contra gentiles* (Synopsis [of Christian Doctrine] Directed Against Unbelievers), trans. V.J. Bourke, Notre Dame, IN: University of Notre Dame Press, 1975, III.2, c.12. (Argues that we must refrain from cruelty to nonrational animals lest we become cruel to one another.)

Aristotle (*c*. mid 4th century BC) *Politics*, trans. T.J. Saunders, Oxford: Clarendon Press, 1995, I 5, 8. (Contends that plants 'exist for the sake of' animals and 'animals for the sake of man'.)

Bentham, J. (1789) *An Introduction to the Principles of Morals and Legislation*, ed. J.H. Burns and H.L.A. Hart, revised F. Rosen, Oxford: Clarendon Press, 1996, ch. 17, section 1. (Classic utilitarian account which insists that moral concern not be limited to rational beings but extended to any creature capable of suffering.)

Callicot, J.B. (1989) *In Defense of the Land Ethic: Essays in Environmental Philosophy*, Albany, NY:

State University of New York Press. (Appeals to human sentiments (but not to human self-interest) to explain why species and ecosystems should matter to us in their own right.)

Coady, C.A.J. (1992) 'Defending Human Chauvinism', in C. Mills (ed.) *Values in Public Policy*, Fort Worth, TX: Harcourt Brace. (An entertainingly pointed reply to those who deny that human beings should have moral priority.)

Feinberg, J. (1974) 'The Rights of Animals and Unborn Generations', in W.T. Blackstone (ed.) *Philosophy and Environmental Crisis*, Athens, GA: University of Georgia Press, 43–68; repr. in *Rights, Justice, and the Bounds of Liberty*, Princeton, NJ: Princeton University Press, 1980. (Modern classic arguing that to have moral rights a being must have, or be capable of having, interests and that to have interests it must be capable of having conscious experiences, desires and beliefs.)

—— (1978) 'Human Duties and Animal Rights', in R.K. Morris and M.W. Fox (eds) *The Fifth Day: Animal Rights and Human Ethics*, Washington, DC: Acropolis Books, 45–69; repr. in *Rights, Justice, and the Bounds of Liberty*, Princeton, NJ: Princeton University Press, 1980. (Like the earlier work, this piece focuses on what qualifies a being as having moral rights.)

Goodpaster, K. (1978) 'On Being Morally Considerable', *Journal of Philosophy* 75 (6): 308–25. (Careful defence of the claim that living beings, whether sentient or not, have genuine interests that ought to be taken into basic moral consideration.)

Hume, D. (1751) *Enquiry Concerning the Principles of Morals*, ed. L.A. Selby-Bigge and P.H. Nidditch, Oxford: Clarendon Press, 1978, section 3, part I. (Maintains that while humans must be kind to animals, animals are not within the protective scope of justice.)

Johnson, E. (1983) 'Life, Death and Animals', in H.B. Miller and W.H. Williams (eds) *Ethics and Animals*, Clifton, NJ: Humana Press, 23–33. (Critique of key arguments for attributing moral priority to humans or any other beings capable of forming second-order preferences.)

Kant, I. (1797) *Metaphysische Anfangsgründe der Tugendlehre*, trans. M.J. Gregor, *The Doctrine of Virtue*, New York: Harper & Row, 1964. (Argues that duties regarding nonhuman animals and inanimate nature are grounded in a duty to oneself, namely, to cultivate and improve one's own moral character.)

Korsgaard, C.M. (1996) *Sources of Normativity*, Cambridge: Cambridge University Press, lecture IV. (Makes a Neo-Kantian case for our having

duties to, not merely regarding, nonhuman animals.)

Leopold, A. (1949) 'The Land Ethic' and 'On a Monument to the Pigeon', in *A Sand County Almanac with Other Essays on Conservation*, Oxford: Oxford University Press; repr. New York: Sierra Club/Ballantine, 1970. (Suggests that we must respect the way in which various forms of life are interconnected ecologically, and argues that if humans have a claim to superiority it is because of their seemingly unique capacity to care about the extinction of other species.)

Lovelock, J.E. (1979) *Gaia*, New York: Oxford University Press. (Makes a case for regarding the biosphere itself as a living organism.)

Naess, A. (1974) *Økologi, samfunn og livsstil. Utkast til en økosofi*, Oslo: Universitetsforlaget; trans. D. Rothenberg, *Ecology, Community and Lifestyle: Outline of an Ecosophy*, Cambridge: Cambridge University Press, 1989. (The classic statement of 'deep ecology' – a nonanthropocentrically based respect for ecosystems.)

O'Neill, O. (1996) *Towards Justice and Virtue: A Constructive Account of Practical Reasoning*, Cambridge: Cambridge University Press. (Suggests how, instead of trying to discover comprehensive and definitive criteria, we might 'construct' a solution to the problem of moral standing that is adequate for practical purposes.)

Regan, T. (1983) *The Case for Animal Rights*, Berkeley, CA: University of California Press. (A defence of why we must treat adult mammals as ends-in-themselves.)

Rolston, H. (1988) *Environmental Ethics: Duties to and Values in the Natural World*, Philadelphia, PA: Temple University Press. (Argues on nonanthropocenctric grounds for the significance of whole species and ecosystems.)

Scanlon, T.M. (1982) 'Contractualism and Utilitarianism', in A. Sen and B. Williams (eds) *Beyond Utilitarianism*, Cambridge: Cambridge University Press. (Includes an explanation of how a contractarian approach can still account for the moral standing of nonhuman animals and other beings who would not be able to make or keep agreements.)

Singer, P. (1993) *Practical Ethics*, Cambridge: Cambridge University Press, 2nd edn, chaps 3, 5, 6, 10. (Clear discussions of the pros and cons of attributing moral standing to animals, plants, species, ecosystems and, within the human sphere, foetuses, future generations and impoverished persons in other societies.)

Stone, C. (1972) *Should Trees Have Standing?*, Los Altos, CA: William Kaufmann. (A defence of the claim that living beings have a good of their own that we can discern and ought to promote.)

Taylor, P.W. (1986) *Respect for Nature: A Theory of Environmental Ethics*, Princeton, NJ: Princeton University Press. (Holds that each living being ought to be taken into respectful consideration; offers some guidelines for resolving conflicts of need and interest that are likely to arise.)

ARTHUR KUFLIK

MORALISTES

The moralistes constitute a tradition of secular French writing about human nature and political and social behaviour principally in the context of the court and the salon. Their non-systematic observations about mankind are couched in literary forms, such as the maxim and the pen-portrait, appropriate to the social context from which they emerged. The four principal moralistes of the ancien régime *were La Rochefoucauld, La Bruyère, Vauvenargues and Chamfort. La Rochefoucauld's* Maximes *(1665) constitute a sharp attack on the neo-Stoic moral optimism of the first half of the seventeenth century, and determine self-love to be the mainspring of all human behaviour. La Bruyère's* Caractères *(1688) is a more diverse work in both form and content: it contains a satire of the follies and vices of his age, as well as vivid pen-portraits. There are implicit contradictions in the moral norms governing this often indignant denunciation of men and society. Vauvenargues, writing some fifty years later, expresses more confidence in human nature, rehabilitating the passions and arguing for the moral value of self-love of a certain kind. This optimism is not shared by Chamfort, whose* Maximes et pensées *(1795) reverts to the cynical tone of his seventeenth-century predecessors in the genre. These writers do not attempt to systematize their thoughts, and they choose to express themselves in urbane and witty ways rather than in sober prose, but they carry out the Cartesian programme of employing 'common sense' and native intellectual powers to the end of uncovering aspects of human nature and behaviour accessible to observant people free from moral or religious preconceptions.*

1   'Moralistes'

The term 'moraliste', which first became current in its modern sense in the mid-eighteenth century, designates thinkers (usually not professional philosophers) who study humanity in a non-systematic, secular way, examining personal, social and political conduct with clear-sightedness and objectivity. In some accounts, this predominantly French tradition is said to stretch from MONTAIGNE in the late sixteenth century to Paul Valéry in the twentieth; but it is more usual to see the heyday of the moralistes as the *ancien régime*, and especially the latter half of the seventeenth century. The practice of setting down dispassionate observations about human motives and behaviour in non-specialized terminology has very diverse roots, among which are: the educational exercise of keeping commonplace-books, in which students recorded pithy sentences from their reading; the practice of dialectical reasoning, which included the collection of points or *loci* to support a given conclusion; the existence of popular collections of proverbs, adages, and apophthegms; the habit of extracting realistic political doctrine in the form of precepts from historical writing and debunking the claims of Stoic virtue, whose most notorious practitioner was Machiavelli (see STOICISM); the development of manuals of civility and books of advice to courtiers based not on the morality of behaviour but its practical benefit to the individual and to society as a whole; the cult of witty conversation at court and in the salons; and finally, the invitation of DESCARTES to all people to examine their own thoughts with the free use of their innate powers of reasoning.

The mode of writing most associated with the moralistes is the maxim, although they also express themselves in short moral reflections and essays. The maxim can be distinguished from the proverb and apophthegm by its greater abstraction and elegance of form although, like the proverb, its author is not identified and it is given no specific context in time or place. It very often embodies a paradox, either of the kind which refutes a commonly received opinion about human nature and institutions (women are said to be better than men, for example, and tyranny than monarchy), or it is a paradox of a linguistic or terminological kind which breaches the rule of non-contradiction (such as the claim that it is foolish to be wise). In either form it is designed to surprise readers, by revealing to them some hitherto unnoted aspect of human society or by unmasking one of the ways in which human beings are dupes of their own nature. The more discursive literary forms adopted by moralistes do not necessarily have all these features, but there is the same combination of neutral, dispassionate, anonymous, general presentation with an implied social context of witty, secular, non-pedantic, urbane conversation. The four principal moralistes are usually said to be La Rochefoucauld, La Bruyère, Vauvenargues and Chamfort: all were either members of the highest level of French salon and court society, or its clients.

2 La Rochefoucauld

François, duc de La Rochefoucauld (1613–80) was born into the highest aristocracy. After a career in the army, followed by hectic involvement in domestic political intriguing, he suffered a short period of banishment from Paris and the court before returning to both in the 1650s. His *Réflexions ou sentences et maximes morales* (Reflections or moral aphorisms and maxims) had its first authorized edition in 1665, having been produced in consultation, if not colla-boration, with Jacques Esprit and Mme de Sablé: its fifth, much emended, edition appeared in 1678. The preface to the second edition of the work makes explicit its secular nature, but the Augustinian (or Jansenist) tone and vocabulary of much of the work are manifest. The preface also invites the reader to engage in a search for coherence which the form of the maxim frustrates, through its use of qualifying adverbs (often, usually, rarely, sometimes, mostly), its ambiguous syntax and inconsistent or vague use of terms, and its changes in tone, which varies from the cynical to the urbane; but a certain number of conclusions can be drawn from this deliberately disordered collection of discrete aphorisms. It is uniformly anti-Stoic: the heroic ethic which had dominated French literary and moral writing in the first half of the seventeenth century is systematically debunked. Human claims to know themselves through the exercise of reason, human contempt for death and for fortune in all its guises, human mastery over the will and passions, human love of virtue for its own sake, are all shown to be illusory or false; the subjection to their *amour-propre*, to their physiologi-cal nature and to the demands made upon them by the social environment in which they live are amply demonstrated. Much of this material is specific to the cultural context from which it emanates, being the product of a clear-sighted member of a disillusioned generation of aristocratic adventurers living in a society which placed great value on wit and urbanity. Its presentation in the form of aphorisms lends it however that air of universality which is traditionally associated with the classical age in France.

3 La Bruyère

Jean de la Bruyère (1645–96) was a member of the bourgeoisie and a client of the high nobility and of the theologician Jacques-Bénigne Bossuet, whose reli-gious and political views he shared. He published his *Caractères ou les moeurs de ce siècle* (The characters or mores of our age) in 1688, on the coat-tails of a translation of *Characters* by THEO-PHRASTUS; a ninth, much augmented edition ap-peared in 1696, by which time an unofficial key to the pseudonymous society portraits it contained had been published. The fifteen, rather disparate sections of the work consist of a mixture of short moral essays, maxims and pen-portraits; they were said by La Bruyère to culminate in the last section which purports to be a refutation of free-thinking, although it is difficult to substantiate, from internal evidence, the claim that such a refutation is the main point of the work.

La Bruyère's work differs from La Rochefoucauld's in its broader consideration of society and its preoccupation with writers and literary criticism. There are many apparent inconsistencies in the work: it claims not only to inculcate moral lessons, but also characterizes men as incorrigible; it favours the recognition of personal merit and social mobility in one section, only to denounce violently the social ascension of bourgeois financiers and the abandon-ment of the old feudal order in another; it strongly defends the use of the classics as aesthetic yardsticks at one point, only to engage in 'modern' techniques of literary composition at another. The work may best be viewed as a satire, in which La Bruyère deploys a wide range of rhetorical voices and devices, some-times presenting himself as a detached, impartial observer, sometimes as a professional writer, some-times as a representative of the bourgeoisie, some-times as La Bruyère the oppressed client of the aristocracy; in this way he sets out to elicit a wide range of responses in his readers, ranging from indignation at the manifest injustices of society to detached amusement at its less harmful follies. Except in the rather unsatisfactory last section in which he sets out to prove the existence of God, he chooses to depict vice and folly rather than to enunciate the (often contradictory) moral norms which their denunciation implies. In his pen-portraits, which show him to be a very talented observer and painter of his age, he succeeds in using concrete details to flesh out the sometimes schematic moral character being described. He was one of the great stylists of his day, and a writer committed to promoting the cause of art and artists, but never at the expense of his satirical purposes.

4 Vauvenargues

Luc de Clapiers, marquis de Vauvenargues (1715–47) was, like La Rochefoucauld, a member of the aristocracy who did not receive a formal education but, unlike La Rochefoucauld, he played no part in the court or the salons of Paris; he served for a time as an army officer, before premature retirement and death from ill-health. His *Introduction à la connaissance de l'esprit humain, suivie de réflexions et maximes* (Introduction to the knowledge of the human mind, followed by reflections and maxims) (1746) did not receive the same attention as the works of La Rochefoucauld and La Bruyère when they were published. In three books he deals with the mind, the passions, and the vices and virtues; his maxims were written very much with La Rochefoucauld and PASCAL in mind, but where his predecessors had stressed human's enslavement to passions and the impotence of reason, Vauvenargues claims for humankind a degree of moral autonomy and a capacity for virtue. Passions are not to be seen in exclusively negative terms, but rather as the mainspring of moral thought and action; they are the very sources of intellectual activity, not forces which pervert it. Before ROUSSEAU, he made the distinction between *amour-propre* (self-love) and *amour de nous-mêmes* (love of self), seeing the latter sort of love as compatible with virtue. This anti-Jansenist stance, which Vauvenargues shares with VOLTAIRE and which he derives to some degree from SPINOZA, is accompanied by a tolerant Deism, making Vauvenargues representative of his age, and suggesting parallels with the aphoristic productions of Voltaire himself (in his *Dictionnaire philosophique* (Philosophical dictionary) of 1764) and of DIDEROT (in the more contentious *Pensées philosophiques* (Philosophical thoughts) of 1746).

5 Chamfort

Nicolas-Sébastien Roch (1741–94), alias de Chamfort, has more in common with La Bruyère, being like him a client of aristocratic society and a reputed wit. A fervent supporter of the French Revolution, he none the less became suspect under the Terror, attempted to take his own life, and died shortly thereafter. His *Maximes et pensées, caractères et anecdotes* (Maxims and thoughts, characters and anecdotes) – also published with the ironic title *Produits de la civilisation perfectionnée* (The products of perfected civilisation) – first appeared posthumously in 1795. They claim to steer a middle course between the pessimistic depiction of human nature found in such thinkers as La Rochefoucauld and the optimism of idealist philosophers such as SHAFTESBURY, but the often cynical or pungent tone suggests more affinity with the former. Chamfort expresses great admiration for English philosophy, and especially BACON; he recommends a radical inductive approach to social and political philosophy as well as to science, but most of his observations are directed at the corrupt aristocratic society of the last years of the *ancien régime*, and suggest an attitude of resignation rather than revolution, taking particular delight in representing social and political life through the metaphor of the theatre.

6 Conclusion

These moralistes embody a philosophical approach in so far as they set out to liberate themselves from preconceptions and observe humankind in its social and political context impartially; but what they have to say and the forms through which they express themselves are closely linked to their envisaged readership. Even the maxim form, which appears to state abstract, general truths outside any social context, is impregnated with the intention to shock, unsettle and surprise. It is therefore reasonable to claim that moralists reflect the thinking of their day in moral matters, but much less plausible to characterize them as independent thinkers making significant contributions to the history of moral thought.

See also: CYNICS

References and further reading

Arnaud, C. (1988) *Chamfort: une biographie*, Paris: Laffont; trans. D. Dusinberre as *Chamfort: a biography*, Chicago, IL and London: Chicago University Press, 1992. (A recent biobibliography.)

* La Bruyère, J. de (1688) *Caractères ou les moeurs de ce siècle* (The characters or mores of our age), ed. R. Garapon as *Caractères*, Paris: Garnier, 1962; trans. J. Stewart as *Characters*, Harmondsworth: Penguin, 1970. (A good scholarly edition.)

* Chamfort, de (Nicolas-Sébastien Roch) (1795) *Maximes et pensées, caractères et anecdotes* (Maxims and thoughts, characters and anecdotes), Paris: Gallimard, 1982; trans. E.P. Mathers as *Maxims and Considerations*, Waltham St Lawrence: Golden Cockerel Press, 1926, 2 vols. (Plain-text edition.)

* Clapiers, L. de, marquis de Vauvenargues (1746) *Introduction à la connaissance de l'esprit humain, suivie de réflexions et maximes* (Introduction to the knowledge of the human mind, followed by reflections and maxims); repr. as *Réflexions et maximes*, Paris: Gallimard, 1971; trans. F.G.

Stevens as *The reflections and maxims*, London: Humphrey Milford, 1940. (Plain-text edition.)

Delft, L. van (1971) *La Bruyère moraliste: quatre études sur les Caractères* (La Bruyère as moralist: four studies on the Characters), Geneva: Droz. (A mainly literary analysis of the Caractères.)

Fine, P.M. (1974) *Vauvenargues and La Rochefoucauld*, Manchester: Manchester University Press. (A study in influence.)

Mourgues, O. de (1984) *Two French moralists*, Cambridge: Cambridge University Press. (The best available introduction to La Rochefoucauld and La Bruyère, aimed at an undergraduate readership.)

* La Rochefoucauld, F., duc de (1665) *Réflexions ou sentences et maximes morales* (Reflections or moral aphorisms and maxims), ed. J. Truchet as *Maximes*, Paris: Garnier, 1967; trans. L.W. Tancock as *Maxims*, Harmondsworth: Penguin, 1959. (The best available scholarly edition.)

IAN MacLEAN

MORALITY AND ART *see* ART AND MORALITY

MORALITY AND EMOTIONS

Emotions such as anger, fear, grief, envy, compassion, love and jealousy have a close connection to morality. Philosophers have generally agreed that they can pose problems for morality in a variety of ways: by impeding judgment, by making attention uneven and partial, by making the person unstable and excessively needy, by suggesting immoral projects and goals.

The place of emotions in moral theories depends on whether they are conceived of merely as impulses without thought or intentional content, or as having some sort of cognitive content. Plato argued that emotions form a part of the soul separate from thought and evaluation, and moved, in the course of his writings, from a sceptical view of their contribution to morality to a more positive appraisal. Aristotle connected emotions closely with judgment and belief, and held that they can be cultivated through moral education to be important components of a virtuous character. The Stoics identified emotions with judgments ascribing a very high value to uncontrolled external things and persons, arguing that all such judgments are false and should be removed. Their cognitive analysis of emotion stands independent of this radical normative thesis, and

has been adopted by many philosophers who do not accept it.

Modern theories of emotion can be seen as a series of responses and counter-responses to the Stoic challenge. Descartes, Spinoza, Kant and Nietzsche all accepted many of the Stoics' normative arguments in favour of diminishing the role played by emotions in morality; they differed, however, in the accounts of emotion they proposed. Focusing on compassion or sympathy, Hutcheson, Hume, Rousseau, Adam Smith and Schopenhauer all defended the role of some emotions in morality, returning to a normative position closer to Aristotle's (though not always with a similarly cognitive analysis).

Contemporary views of emotion have been preoccupied with the criticism of reductive accounts that derive from behaviourist psychology. By now, it is once again generally acknowledged that emotions are intelligent parts of the personality that can inform and illuminate as well as motivate. Philosophers' views have been enriched by advances in cognitive psychology, psychoanalysis and anthropology. Feminist accounts of emotion differ sharply, some insisting that we should validate emotions as important parts of moral character, others that emotions shaped by unjust conditions are unreliable guides.

1 Morality and conceptions of emotion
2 Emotions and character-based theories
3 Ancient Graeco-Roman theories of emotion: Plato, Aristotle, Stoics
4 Modern supporters of the Stoic normative thesis
5 Modern anti-Stoics: the defence of sympathy
6 Contemporary views: influences from psychology and anthropology
7 Feminist accounts of morality and emotion

1 Morality and conceptions of emotion

Emotions are usually considered to be distinct both from bodily appetites, such as hunger and thirst, and from objectless moods, such as irritation and endogenous depression (see EMOTIONS, NATURE OF). Major members of the class have traditionally been love, anger, grief, fear, envy, jealousy, guilt and pity (compassion) (see LOVE; MORAL SENTIMENTS; RECTIFICATION AND REMAINDERS). Some philosophers have adopted an account of these experiences that makes them rather close to appetites after all: emotions are surges of affect or energy in the personality, unreasoning movements that push people into acting without being very much connected to their thoughts about the world. This view is frequently connected to the idea that emotions derive from an animal part of our nature, often by thinkers who do not have a high regard for animal intelligence.

Seen this way, emotions figure in morality only as forces that either advance or impede the purposes of moral judgment or will. They can be trained and to some extent conditioned, but in a relatively mechanical manner. Thus they will never be what makes a virtuous character virtuous, though a virtuous person can take pride in having exercised an appropriate degree of discipline over them (see SELF-CONTROL; VIRTUES AND VICES §3).

Other philosophical theories about emotions hold that they involve interpretation and belief. An emotion such as grief is not simply a mindless surge of painful affect: it involves a way of seeing an object, an appraisal of that object as important, and the belief that the object is lost. Fear involves the belief that bad events are impending, and that one is not fully in control of warding them off. Such theories hold that changes in the relevant beliefs entail changes in emotion: one who learns that danger is not really at hand will cease to fear. When we scrutinize the beliefs involved in the emotions, it emerges that they are of two sorts: beliefs about what is happening in the world (Is the person really dead? Is the enemy really at hand?) and evaluative beliefs (Is the person really worth getting upset about? Is the danger serious?). Many of the evaluative beliefs derive from social teaching, some of it moral in nature. We learn what insults are worth getting upset about, what losses are serious, what damages are to be avoided.

Seen this way, emotions become intelligent parts of the moral personality, which can be cultivated through a process of moral education (see MORAL EDUCATION §3). Such a process will aim at producing adults who not only control their anger and fear, but experience anger and fear appropriately, towards the appropriate objects at the appropriate time in the appropriate degree. Merely self-controlled persons look to these theorists like those whose moral development is incomplete or imperfect. If we find them hating foreigners, but controlling their behaviour towards them, we will judge that there is some further moral work they should be doing before they can claim to be fully virtuous.

2 Emotions and character-based theories

All moral theories have some occasion to talk about emotions, but some focus on their cultivation more than others. Theories that focus on the calculation of utility will see emotions as forces that either promote or eclipse such calculations and the appropriate acts (see UTILITARIANISM). Theories that focus on duty can have a substantial place for an account of emotion, since emotions will be seen as motives that either promote or impede action in accordance with duty (see DEONTOLOGICAL ETHICS; DUTY). But if the account of duty is not supplemented with an account of virtue, it will not be clear how these motives should be integrated into the personality. Kant's theory of virtue (1797) shows us that a duty-based view need not neglect emotions as elements in virtue (see KANT, I. §10; EMOTIONS, PHILOSOPHY OF §3). Since this theory has a noncognitive conception of emotion, and also a rather negative view of the contributions made by emotion, it gives emotions a rather restricted role; but there is nothing to prevent a virtue-theory such as Kant's from giving more positive attention to the cultivation of emotion.

Theories of character based on Aristotle and other Greek thinkers, however, have been Western philosophy's most substantial sources for thought about the proper cultivation of emotion within morality (see EMOTIONS, PHILOSOPHY OF §2). Aristotle's norm of a reasonable person is one whose character is infused completely by the correct reasons for action, which have shaped all their motives and attitudes. Because he aims to describe the cultivation of a whole person and way of life, rather than simply to prescribe a list of duties, he has ample scope for discussing emotional self-shaping.

3 Ancient Graeco-Roman theories of emotion: Plato, Aristotle, Stoics

Plato argues in the *Republic* that the soul contains three distinct parts: the calculative part, the appetitive part, and the 'spirited' part (see PLATO §14). This last part seems to be where Plato locates emotions such as anger, grief and fear. Although his account is cryptic, he suggests that the emotions differ from appetites in their responsiveness to changes in belief, and also in the fact that they are less brutish and more discriminating. But he refuses to construe them as belonging to the 'part' that performs evaluative reasoning. In normative terms, the *Republic* argues that all pity, fear and grief should be prevented from developing by a process of moral education that teaches young people that there is nothing for a good person to fear or grieve over; anger is apparently allowed to remain, but is channelled for military purposes. In the *Phaedrus*, Plato's account of the emotional 'part' seems more positive: focusing on emotions of reverence and awe, he shows how this element in the personality makes a crucial contribution to virtue and understanding.

For Aristotle, emotions are combinations of a feeling of pleasure or pain with a belief (or perhaps a more rudimentary cognitive attitude, a seeing *x* as *y*).

Fear, for example, combines painful feeling with the thought that there are bad events impending. The combination is not casual: the pain is pain *at the thought of* that impending danger. Therefore, changes in belief will change emotions. (Aristotle makes these arguments in *Rhetoric*, showing how an orator can manipulate the passions of the audience.) In normative terms, Aristotle argues that the virtuous person is one who has attained balance and appropriateness in emotion as well as action. A person who completely lacked anger at an insult to loved ones, for example, would be culpably deficient; but excessive anger is strongly criticized, and the condition to aim for is 'mildness of temper' (see ARISTOTLE §§22–4).

Epicurus and his school (including the Roman poet Lucretius) presented impressive accounts of several emotions, in particular the fear of death (see EPICUREANISM §13). They argued that this fear poisons individuals' lives and causes social distress. Since they agreed with Aristotle about its cognitive basis, they argued that it could be completely removed by teaching people that death is not a bad thing for the person who has died.

The Greek and Roman Stoics were the great passion theorists of antiquity. They produced impressive analyses and taxonomies of the passions, arguing powerfully in favour of the view that they are essentially evaluative judgments that ascribe to things or persons outside our control great importance for our flourishing (see STOICISM §19). This analysis is continuous with Aristotle's, but it goes a step further, denying that there is any bodily feeling over and above the cognition that is essential to the identity of a particular emotion. This apparently counter-intuitive view is rendered plausible by extensive consideration of the power of thought to transform the personality.

One might accept this analysis of emotion and still hold, with Aristotle, that many of the judgments involved in emotions are true and appropriate: when one's child dies, for example, it is right to think that something of enormous importance has been lost. The Stoics, however, held that all the judgments involved in all the passions are false, because all ascribe too much importance to external things and persons, making people dependent on the world for their happiness. To this argument they added several others: emotions weaken the personality, robbing it of force and integrity; they make one prone to excessive and violent acts; and, finally, they are not necessary to motivate good acts, which can be chosen out of duty alone.

Their conclusion is thus that the emotions should be extirpated from human life. Moved especially by the damage done by anger in social life, and convinced that there is no getting rid of anger without getting rid of the attachments to externals that are also involved in love and grief and fear, they came to the radical conclusion that we can stop cruelty and violence only by cultivating utter detachment from everything that used to matter to us. They then strove valiantly to show that we can motivate an active concern for humanity without relying on emotion. Removing emotions is not expected to be like removing false beliefs about more trivial matters: because the evaluations involved are transmitted early through social and parental teaching, they have become deeply habitual, and can be changed, if at all, only through a lifetime of patient effort. Their hope was that as this effort is exercised with greater success, the personality as a whole would become enlightened.

Because their analyses are so compelling and humanly rich, and because they focus with convincing examples on the depredations of emotion in politics, writers such as SENECA and MARCUS AURELIUS continue to make this radical thesis compelling.

4 Modern supporters of the Stoic normative thesis

The Stoics set the agenda for early modern moral theories of emotion. Most thinkers, though not all, accept some version of the cognitive Stoic analysis of passion; they then differ sharply over the normative thesis. Descartes (1649) modified the Stoic analysis to fit into his divided account of mind and body, but his definitions of the passions are related closely to those of the Stoics; his normative judgments, while not quite as severe, are similar (see DESCARTES, R. §10).

Spinoza accepted the Stoic analysis and the radical normative thesis, holding, with Seneca, that philosophical therapy can free us from bondage to our emotions (see SPINOZA, B. DE §9). He gave the normative programme new urgency by insisting that all strong attachments are essentially ambivalent: we love an external person or thing because we find that it assists our efforts to flourish. But anything that can assist us, so long as it is separate from us, can also frustrate us; so all love is mixed with hate. Like the Stoics, Spinoza held that there is a type of joy that is not an emotion in the sense that it is not based on a overvaluation of the significance of externals; it is the contemplative joy with which one regards the deterministic system of the universe as a whole. Like the Stoics, Spinoza identified that order with god; thus the good state is designated the 'intellectual love of god'.

Kant did not accept the Stoic analysis of the passions. Oddly enough, he presented no arguments against it, and no substantial analysis of his own; but he plainly conceived of passions as pre-rational, impulsive and undiscriminating. Thus, the only role he saw passions playing in virtue was a rather mechanical one, as forces that either aid or impede duty. In general, he thought they impede it, and he therefore conceived of virtue as a kind of strength of will, in which the will maintains its control over the potentially disrupting passions.

Kant was well aware of the Stoic normative view. To a great extent he shared it, praising the Stoics for cultivating detachment from passion, and for promoting active beneficence rather than relying on compassionate emotion. But he showed considerable ambivalence, and was unwilling to dismiss compassionate emotion utterly. He understood that it may be difficult to motivate beneficence without this emotion, that motives of duty by themselves may not suffice. He therefore urged people to seek out experiences in which they will naturally be moved to compassion, so that their beneficence will have the strength of passion behind it.

A surprising ally of the Kantian position was Nietzsche (1881), who objected to pity as an emotion that insults the dignity of the suffering person by implying that this is a person who really needs the things of this world. Equipped with a rather romantic picture of strength and self-sufficiency, Nietzsche believed that the truly strong can rise above life's ills through will, and therefore do not need compassion, grief or fear. Citing the Stoics, Spinoza and Kant as his predecessors, Nietzsche denounced the Christian/democratic tradition of praising compassion as a basic social motive.

5 Modern anti-Stoics: the defence of sympathy

Opposition to the Stoic normative thesis began in the ancient world, with Augustine, who insisted that the goal of self-sufficiency was an inappropriate one for a Christian to pursue. Characterizing the ideal Stoic wise man as obtuse in his detachment from longing and pain, he concluded: 'The fact that something is tough does not make it right; and the fact that something is inert does not make it healthy.' Subsequent Christian views have agreed in characterizing moral error as due to wrongly placed love, and in making love itself an essential ingredient of the cure. Dante's *Divina Commedia* (*The Divine Comedy*) (1313–21) famously ends with the visionary experience of a harmony of emotion and will. Because emotional error is understood (in an anti-Stoic fashion) to be rooted in the body itself and its sexuality, it is expected that this perfected state will arrive only in paradise, after the purifications of purgatory. Most important Christian thinkers make pity or compassion central parts of Christian life,

arguing that these emotions are appropriate expressions of and responses to our vulnerable and imperfect earthly condition.

The eighteenth century saw the flowering of a number of distinct approaches to the sympathetic emotions. Although Christian views did not cease to exert an influence, the notion of original evil was contested increasingly in favour of a view of natural goodness in which basic emotional equipment played a salient role. Hutcheson and Hume made the capacity for sympathy a basic part of human nature (see HUTCHESON, F. §2; HUME, D. §3). Hume (1739/40) made many valuable observations about the role of sympathy in motivating moral conduct (see MORAL MOTIVATION §6). But his conviction that desires and passions are basically noncognitive, and that reasoning is capable only of devising means to ends set by desire, led him to short-change many aspects of the passions that even his own concrete analyses at times acknowledge. Although he connected passions with a characteristic object, he seems not to have treated the connection as essential to the identity of the passion: a passion is simply a particular type of impression caused by the object. Hume's enormous influence has led to the sharp split between passion and cognition that characterizes much modern Anglo-American thought (see EMOTIONS, PHILOSOPHY OF §§3–4).

Rousseau gave the emotion of *pitié*, compassion, a central role in social morality (see ROUSSEAU, J.-J. §4). Describing the education of young Émile (1762), he shows that the experience of being astonished and pained at the pain of another is an essential foundation for all society. Compassion leads us to recognize the vulnerability that all humans share, and to appreciate the pain that disasters of various types cause others. Thus, the emotion leads us to be sceptical of distinctions that situate some people as high above others, their fortunes as vastly more secure. Rousseau evidently thought that emotions, involving complex imagining and thought, convey moral information that it would be difficult to obtain in any other way. Accepting a version of the Stoic idea of original human innocence, he seems to have held that excesses in self-love derive from experience of unequal social conditions.

Adam Smith's *The Theory of Moral Sentiments* (1759) provides one of the modern tradition's most detailed analyses of the moral contributions of emotion. Heavily indebted to the Stoics, Smith develops a richly detailed account of the cognitive content of passions such as anger and sympathy. He differs with the Stoics on the normative question, taking up a more Aristotelian view about attachments to family and loved ones. His device of the 'judicious spectator', modelled on Stoic conceptions of self-scrutiny and conscience, gives the moral agent a way of estimating the point of propriety in passion: we are to ask what a concerned spectator, not personally involved, would feel at the events, and this will help us identify bias and irrationality deriving from our own personal immersion. Despite his positive view of sympathy and other emotions, Smith thought them inconstant and unreliable as guides to social choice, since he observed that we are most easily moved by events closest to ourselves: an earthquake in China means less to a person than an injury to his own finger (see SMITH, A. §§2–3).

Another philosopher who defended the fundamental role of compassion in morality was Schopenhauer (1840). Criticizing Kant, he argued that all genuinely moral action must be grounded in other-directed emotion (see SCHOPENHAUER, A. §6). Imagining compassion as involving a mysterious union of the self with the other, he leaves the reader unclear as to precisely why it is not, therefore, a form of self-concern. Schopenhauer's account had, nevertheless, tremendous influence in a culture dissatisfied with duty-based views.

6 Contemporary views: influences from psychology and anthropology

The middle of the twentieth century saw the rise of noncognitive views of emotion in both behaviourist psychology and in Freudian psychoanalysis (see BEHAVIOURISM, METHODOLOGICAL AND SCIENTIFIC; FREUD, S.; PSYCHOANALYSIS, POST-FREUDIAN). Philosophers such as Anthony Kenny, Robert Solomon, Robert Gordon, William Lyons, Ronald de Sousa and Michael Stocker have by now demonstrated the poverty of such accounts and our need for some type of cognitive view (see EMOTIONS, NATURE OF §2). (Kenny also in the process offered cogent criticisms of Hume's elusive and influential account.)

During this period, cognitive psychology was itself evolving. By now, psychologists no longer expect to be able to give purely behavioural accounts of emotion in terms of stimulus and response, and most of the dominant accounts hold that emotions are a form of intelligent interpretation in which an animal takes in news of how things are in the world with respect to its most important goals and projects. Richard Lazarus (1991) has argued that emotion's evolutionary contribution is best explained this way: emotions give animals information that is essential to survival. Psychologists generally agree that we have reason to credit many animals at least with the capacity for complex appraisals suited to this account of emotion. Their work has enriched the philosophical debate.

At the same time, anthropologists have produced fascinating accounts of the role played by social norms in shaping the emotion-categories of different societies. These accounts raise questions about the extent to which an emotional repertoire is malleable; at least with respect to specific sub-types and internal demarcations within categories, there appears to be considerable cross-cultural variation in emotion-types, and also, presumably, at least some variation in emotional experience (see MORAL SENTIMENTS §3; MORALITY AND ETHICS §4).

This returns us to the moral problem with which the Stoics grapple: for if we see that emotions are learned with the learning of social norms, and we are convinced that our society is not perfect, then it might be unwise to trust the emotions too much as guides to conduct. One society described by anthropologist Jean Briggs (1971), the Utku Eskimos, actually embodies a relatively successful Stoic programme for the elimination of anger, thus prompting us to ask how we should think about our own goals and moral projects.

7 Feminist accounts of morality and emotion

Women have frequently been devalued on the grounds of being emotional and making decisions by consulting emotion. This has led many feminist thinkers to defend the contribution that emotions might play in moral reasoning, arguing that it is the (male) denigration of emotion that is mistaken. Philosophers such as Annette Baier, Lawrence Blum, Sara Ruddick, Virginia Held and Nel Noddings have defended a normative ethical view in which care for others plays a central role, and have seen this as a way of promoting feminist goals (see FEMINIST ETHICS).

On the other hand, feminists who consider the social origins of the appraisals involved in emotion have reasons for doubt. If women have a great propensity to care for others, is this always a good thing? Is it not the case that men have standardly urged women to see themselves as care-givers, rather than as sources of worth and agency in their own right? J.S. Mill (1869) argued that even women's desire to please men has a social origin and is a legacy of women's subordination. This line of argument has been continued recently in the work of Catharine MacKinnon (1989), who argues that women's emotions and desires are in significant ways created by inequality and injustice, and that we should therefore be highly sceptical of the claim that women's instincts of care are always trustworthy and morally valuable.

It is not necessary to choose between these extremes. We can hold that many emotions are valuable parts of the moral life without giving implicit trust to any that have been shaped in imperfect and unjust social conditions – judging, with Aristotle and Adam Smith, that emotions can be good guides as elements in a life organized and examined by critical reflection.

See also: EMOTIVISM; FAMILY, ETHICS AND THE

References and further reading

Aristotle (*c.* mid 4th century BC) *Nicomachean Ethics*, trans. with notes by T. Irwin, Indianapolis, IN: Hackett Publishing Company, 1985, books II–IV. (On the role of passions in virtue.)

* —— (*c.* mid 4th century BC) *Rhetoric*, trans. G. Kennedy, *Aristotle on Rhetoric: A Theory of Civic Discourse*, New York: Oxford University Press. (Illustrates Aristotle's view that, since emotions are combinations of a feeling of pleasure or pain with a belief, changes in belief will change emotions.)

Baier, A.C. (1994) *Moral Prejudices: Essays on Ethics*, Cambridge, MA: Harvard University Press. (Discusses the role of care in moral theory.)

Blum, L. (1980) *Friendship, Altruism, and Morality*, London: Routledge. (Defends the role of compassion in moral judgment.)

* Briggs, J. (1971) *Never in Anger*, Cambridge, MA: Harvard University Press. (Anthropological study of a society that removes anger.)

* Dante A. (1313–21) *Divina Commedia*, trans. J. Ciardi, *The Divine Comedy*, New York: E.P. Dutton, 3 vols, 1989. (Highly influential medieval Christian account of love, which ends with the visionary experience of a harmony of emotion and will.)

* Descartes, R. (1649) *Les passions de l'âme*, trans. *The Passions of the Soul*, in *The Philosophical Writings of Descartes*, ed. and trans. J. Cottingham, R. Stoothoff, D. Murdoch and A. Kenny, Cambridge: Cambridge University Press, vol. 1, 1984. (Analysis of passions in accordance with mind–body dualism.)

De Sousa, R. (1987) *The Rationality of Emotion*, Cambridge, MA: MIT Press. (Excellent account of the cognitive content of emotions and its evolutionary role.)

Gordon, R. (1987) *The Structure of Emotions*, Cambridge: Cambridge University Press. (Valuable philosophical analysis of emotion/cognition relationship.)

Held, V. (1993) *Feminist Morality: Transforming Culture, Society, and Politics*, Chicago, IL: University of Chicago Press. (Care ethics and social justice.)

—— (ed.) (1995) *Justice and Care: Essential Readings in Feminist Ethics*, Boulder, CO: Westview Press. (Collection of different feminist viewpoints on care ethics.)

* Hume, D. (1739/40) *A Treatise of Human Nature*, ed. L.A. Selby-Bigge, revised by P.H. Nidditch, Oxford: Clarendon Press, 2nd edn, 1978. (Influential account of the relationship between emotion and action.)

* Kant, I. (1797) *Metaphysische Anfangsgründe der Tugendlehre*, trans. J.W. Ellington, *Metaphysical Principles of Virtue*, Indianapolis, IN: Hackett Publishing Company, 1964; repr. in *Immanuel Kant: Ethical Philosophy*, Indianapolis, IN: Hackett Publishing Company, 1983. (Discussion of role of emotions in virtue; critique of pity as moral emotion.)

Kenny, A. (1963) *Action, Emotion and Will*, London: Routledge. (Influential and devastating critique of behaviourist and Humean conceptions of desire.)

Klein, M. (1921–45) *Love, Guilt, and Reparation and Other Works, 1921–45*, London: Tavistock, 1985. (Central psychoanalytic account of emotion and morality.)

* Lazarus, R. (1991) *Emotion and Adaptation*, Oxford: Clarendon Press. (Critique of behaviourism and account of the field's return to cognitive conceptions of emotion by leading cognitive psychologist.)

Long, A.A. and Sedley, D.N. (1987) *The Hellenistic Philosophers*, Cambridge: Cambridge University Press, 2 vols. (Basic sources for Hellenistic views of morality and emotion, with fine commentaries.)

Lutz, C. (1988) *Unnatural Emotions: Everyday Sentiments on a Micronesian Atoll*, Chicago, IL: University of Chicago Press. (Valuable anthropological study of role of social norms in emotion.)

Lyons, W. (1980) *Emotion*, Cambridge: Cambridge University Press. (Well-argued defence of a cognitive-Aristotelian account.)

* MacKinnon, C. (1989) *Feminism Unmodified*, Cambridge, MA: Harvard University Press. (Argues that women's subordination to men has shaped their emotions and desires.)

* Mill, J.S. (1869) *The Subjection of Women*, in J. Gray (ed.) *On Liberty and Other Essays*, Oxford: Oxford University Press, 1991. (Argues that women's emotions are shaped by unjust social conditions.)

* Nietzsche, F. (1881) *Morgenröte*, trans. R. Hollingdale as *Daybreak*, ed. M. Clark and B. Leiter, Cambridge: Cambridge University Press, 1997. (The central locus for Nietzsche's attacks on pity.)

Noddings, N. (1984) *Caring: A Feminine Approach to Ethics and Moral Education*, Stanford, CA: Stanford University Press. (Argues that women's experience of maternal care should be the basis for ethics; opposes abstract principles.)

Nussbaum, M. (1994) *The Therapy of Desire: Theory and Practice in Hellenistic Ethics*, Princeton, NJ: Princeton University Press. (Discussion of ancient Graeco-Roman views of passion and morality.)

Oatley, K. (1992) *Best-Laid Schemes: The Psychology of Emotions*, Cambridge: Cambridge University Press. (Valuable account by a cognitive psychologist.)

Plato (*c*.386–380 BC) *Symposium*, trans. A. Nehamas and P. Woodruff, Indianapolis, IN: Hackett Publishing Company, 1989. (Describes the ascent of love to contemplation of the immortal form of beauty.)

* —— (*c*.380–367 BC) *Republic*, trans. G.M. Grube, Indianapolis, IN: Hackett Publishing Company, 1992, book IV. (Account of the structure of the soul and the role of the passions in virtue.)

* —— (*c*.366–360 BC) *Phaedrus*, trans. A. Nehamas and P. Woodruff, Indianapolis, IN: Hackett Publishing Company, 1995. (Illustrates how emotions play a positive role in connecting the person to beauty and truth.)

* Rousseau, J.-J. (1762) *Émile: ou, de l'éducation*, trans. A. Bloom, *Emile: or, On Education*, Harmondsworth: Penguin, 1991, book IV. (Contains a fundamental account of compassion's role in social morality.)

* Ruddick, S. (1989) *Maternal Thinking: Toward a Politics of Peace*, Boston, MA: Beacon Press. (Balanced account of the moral importance of maternal care.)

* Schopenhauer, A. (1840) *Über die Grundlage der Moral*, trans. E.F.J. Payne, *On the Basis of Morality*, Providence, RI and Oxford: Berhahn Books, 1995. (Argues that all proper moral action must be grounded in other-directed emotion.)

* Seneca, L.A. (before AD 52) *On Anger*, in J.M. Cooper and J. Procopé (eds) *Seneca: Moral and Political Essays*, Cambridge: Cambridge University Press, 1995. (Influential account of the removal of anger as social goal.)

Sherman, N. (1989) *The Fabric of Character: Aristotle's Theory of Virtue*, Oxford: Clarendon Press. (Excellent account of role of emotion in virtue.)

* Smith, A. (1759) *The Theory of Moral Sentiments*, ed. D.D. Raphael and A.L. Macfie, Oxford: Clarendon Press, 1976. (Rich account of balance in passion, and of role of sympathy in morality.)

Solomon, R. (1976) *The Passions: Emotions and the Meaning of Life*, Indianapolis, IN: Hackett Publishing Company; repr. 1993. (Influential philosophical account of emotion.)

Spinoza, B. (1677) *Ethica Ordine Geometrico Demonstrata* (Ethics Demonstrated in a Geometrical Manner), trans. E. Curley, *Ethics*, Harmondsworth: Penguin, 1996. (Analyses our 'bondage' to passions as cause of strife, urges a therapeutic programme to remove passions.)

Stocker, M. (1996) *Valuing Emotions*, Cambridge: Cambridge University Press. (Valuable analysis of evaluative dimensions of emotion.)

MARTHA C. NUSSBAUM

MORALITY AND ETHICS

Morality is a distinct sphere within the domain of normative thinking about action and feeling; the whole domain, however, is the subject of ethics.

How should the moral sphere be characterized? The three most influential suggestions are that morality should be characterized by its function, by the supremacy of the moral, or by the distinctive moral sentiments. It is plausible that moral codes have a social function, such as that of maintaining beneficial cooperation; but it does not seem an a priori truth. In contrast, it may be true a priori that moral obligations are supreme – accepting an obligation as moral is accepting that it should be carried out whatever else may be said against doing so. But even if this is a priori, it does not provide a criterion for demarcating the moral. A better characterization takes an obligation to be moral if and only if certain sentiments, those invoked in blame, are justified towards an agent who fails to comply with it.

This provides a criterion for demarcating the moral, but only if the sentiments can be identified. The sentiment at the core of blame is sometimes held to be a species of anger – indignation, for example. However it seems that one may feel the sentiment involved in guilt or blame without feeling indignation. A view deriving from Hegel's conception of wrongdoing may be more accurate. Whereas indignation disposes to aggressive restorative action, the sentiment of blame itself disposes to withdrawal of recognition, expulsion from the community. Punishment can then be seen, with Hegel, as a route whereby recognition is restored.

Criticisms of morality are broadly of two kinds, though they often overlap: that moral valuation rests on incoherent presuppositions, and that morality is a dysfunctional system. The leading source of the first kind of criticism (and one source of the second) is Nietzsche; in contemporary philosophy related ideas are developed by Bernard Williams. One of Williams' criticisms centres on something which does indeed seem to be presupposed by moral valuation, at any rate in modern moral thought: that moral obligations exist independently of one's desires and projects yet of *themselves give one a reason to act. Other doubts about the coherence of the moral focus on a conception which, again, may be distinctively modern – being associated particularly with some forms of Protestant Christianity and with Kant; the conception takes it that all are equally autonomous and that the only true worth is moral worth. Criticisms of this conception occur (in different ways) in Nietzsche's treatment of modern morality and in Hegel's treatment of what he calls Moralität.*

The idea that morality is dysfunctional, that blame and guilt deny life or impose pain without securing compensating gains, has considerable influence in contemporary culture (as does the idea that they are compromised by the interests of those who can shape them). Such criticism must come from a conception of ethical value, and assume that there is an alternative to morality. Unless one believes in the possibility of a communal life unmediated by any disciplinary forces at all, the assumption being made must be that there could be a discipline which was better, ethically speaking, than the discipline of guilt and blame.

1 Morality, practical deliberation and ethics
2 Characterizing the 'moral'
3 Blame
4 Do all societies have morality?
5 Criticisms of morality

1 Morality, practical deliberation and ethics

Morality is but a part of the whole domain of normative thinking about action and feeling. Many questions about what one should do or what kind of activity or character one should admire are not ordinarily held to be moral questions. Furthermore, it may be asked whether one should do what one has a moral obligation to do, or why one should do it. The question is not empty: those who ask it are not asking whether or why they should do what they should do, or have a moral obligation to do what they have a moral obligation to do. They are deploying two distinct concepts.

It is possible to go further and be sceptical about the very tenability of the notion of moral obligation, without denying that there are reasons for acting (see MORAL SCEPTICISM). In a well-known passage, Nietzsche denies that any moral judgment is true. He denies morality, he says, as he denies alchemy. But he adds:

> It goes without saying that I do not deny – unless I am a fool – that many actions called immoral ought to be avoided and resisted, or that many called moral ought to be done and encouraged –

but I think that the one should be encouraged and the other avoided *for other reasons than hitherto*. We have *to learn to think differently* – in order at last, perhaps very late on, to attain even more: *to feel differently*.

> (1881: §103; original emphasis)
> (see NIETZSCHE, F. §§8–9)

We may use the term 'ethics' broadly to cover the normative theory of conduct, of what reasons there are for doing this rather than that. Through its concern with reasons for action, ethics will also be concerned with ideas about ends and character-ideals in so far as these bear on action (see IDEALS). And by that route it also becomes concerned with questions about what there is reason to feel, and how reasons to feel connect with reasons to act. Inevitably, then, it shades into aesthetic questions; but not all questions of value dealt with in aesthetics fall within its scope. The dominant concern of ethics is conduct, right action – right feeling comes in in so far as it bears on right action rather than as a fully general subject of study in its own right. In this broad sense Nietzsche's repudiation of morality and insistence that we have to learn 'to feel differently' remains an ethical teaching.

2 Characterizing the 'moral'

How then is morality to be characterized? A number of suggestions have been put forward.

(1) By its *function*. Morality is that set of convictions whose function is to promote human flourishing, to enable us to live together on terms of mutually beneficial cooperation – or whatever one's doctrine as to its function may be. (2) By its *supremacy* in relation to other deliberative conclusions. Morality is a subsystem of deliberation about what one ought to do, whose conclusions in principle override all others. To take an obligation as a moral obligation is to take it that one should fulfil it whatever else can be said against doing so. (3) By the distinctive *sentiment* which is involved in moral valuations (see MORAL SENTIMENTS). On this view, a precept is moral if particular sentiments are appropriate towards those who do not comply with it – the sentiments involved in guilt and blame (see PRAISE AND BLAME; RECTIFICATION AND REMAINDERS §4).

According to (1), then, the morality of a society will consist in those of its generally acknowledged rules or convictions which can be characterized as functioning in it to produce a certain outcome. If this is taken as a definition, 'morality' is a functional term, like 'tuner'. A tuner in a sound system is by definition the device in the system whose function is to enable a user to select and receive radio signals. It is not obvious, however, that there is any function which morality by definition has. Certainly it is plausible that the existence of commonly acknowledged moral convictions has the effect of facilitating, for example, beneficial cooperation. But to say that that is their function, as against their consequence, is to say something stronger: roughly, that that is what they are there for. This is a substantial thesis. It may be true, for instance, in virtue of natural selection, or God's design (EVOLUTION AND ETHICS; RELIGION AND MORALITY §3). Even if moral convictions do have a particular function, though, it is still not obvious that that is what it is, by definition, for them to be *moral* convictions.

(2) holds that the criterion of morality is the supremacy of moral obligations. In a positive sense the morality of a person or society is that which they take to be supreme; in a normative sense morality is that which is supreme. In the normative sense, then, accepting that an obligation to do X is a moral obligation is accepting that the obligation is of such a kind that one should do X whatever else can be said against doing X.

But what kind of obligation is that? In one sense any deliberative conclusion about what I should do, all things considered, is supreme: if my conclusion is correct then I should do that thing, whatever it is, despite everything which can in fact be said against it. However the idea of supremacy is that the total set of considerations, moral and nonmoral, cannot outweigh the moral ones alone. This may be true, and indeed true a priori. But it cannot serve as a definition because it already presupposes a distinction between moral reasons and reasons other than moral ones.

Consider (3). Hume said:

> When you pronounce any action or character to be vicious, you mean nothing, but that from the constitution of your nature you have a feeling or sentiment of blame from the contemplation of it.
>
> (1739/40: 469)

He appears to define moral censure in terms of the feeling or sentiment of blame – but too simply. Suppose I pronounce something to be vicious without having any feeling or sentiment of blame towards it. It does not follow that my pronouncement is false. The question of its viciousness turns rather on whether it is appropriate or reasonable to blame it. So a better analysis would make the normative element explicit: when you pronounce any action to be vicious you are claiming that the feeling or sentiment of blame is an appropriate response to its agent. This explicitly normative line was taken by J.S. Mill (1861); he implied that believing oneself the object of justified blame is already a form of punishment. This 'idea of penal sanction' enters into the notion of moral wrongness: an action is morally wrong if it is appropriate to respond to it with the penal emotions involved in blame (see MILL, J.S. §11).

3 Blame

Blame is an act which stands to a specific feeling, the blame-feeling or sentiment of disapproval, as the act of apology stands to feeling sorry, the sentiment of regret. In each case the action is a judgment that a certain feeling is appropriate towards an action. This is a narrow notion of blame, blame as censure. It is not the wider notion in which we can blame the cheap pen for the ink blot or the weather for the traffic delays. For we are not then saying that a particular penal sentiment is appropriate towards them, but only that they were the relevant cause of a bad outcome (see PRAISE AND BLAME §1). Note also that since blame is an action, not a feeling, there may be situations in which it is unreasonable to blame explicitly, or blame at all, even though it is reasonable to feel the sentiment which is invoked in blame. If someone is in an emotionally distressed state it may be wrong to burden them with blame even if they are indeed blameworthy. And it might be expedient to put aside guilt feelings, refrain from self-blame, when time is short and there are things to be done, even though the feeling is reasonable. So defining the morally wrong as the blameworthy – understood as that towards which it is reasonable to have the blame-feeling – leaves open the possibility that one should not blame an action even though it is morally wrong.

If the morally wrong is characterized as the blameworthy it becomes possible to characterize the other moral concepts by reference to the sentiment of blame. The morally right is that which it is morally wrong not to do. 'X is morally obligatory' will hold just if non-performance of X is blameworthy. We admire people for going beyond the call of duty even though we do not blame them for not doing so: admiration of such actions is moral admiration if we admire them for the reasons that impelled them and those reasons are moral reasons (see SUPEREROGATION). And we can say that they are moral reasons – as against, say, prudential or aesthetic reasons – when their absence from a person's mind beyond a certain point becomes blameworthy. The virtues involve sensitivity to various types of reason for acting which we recognize as moral reasons; they are also traits of character which we could be blamed for not attempting to attain or lose, when it is possible for us to do something to attain or lose them (see VIRTUES AND VICES §§2–3). This sets them apart from admirable qualities in general.

The last point is controversial. Hume (1748, 1751) treated the distinction between virtues and talents, vices and defects, as 'merely verbal', and understood blame in a correspondingly wide sense, as referring to any disvaluing emotion. He took himself in this respect to be following the ancients. Aristotle, for example, argued that we disapprove of those who become ugly through 'want of exercise and care' (*Nicomachean Ethics* 1114a23–25). (He is translated as saying that we 'blame' or 'censure' them, but these words may be too narrow for the kind of disapproval, thinking less of, that he has in mind.) But he added that we do not disapprove of those who are naturally ugly – maintaining a link between disapproval and the voluntary even if he does not distinguish moral defects from disapprovable defects in general (see ARISTOTLE §20). Now, however, we do make the distinction and it plays a role in our feelings. We would blame a person who is wantonly ugly only in contexts which generated an obligation to look after one's looks (they accepted a job as a model and bankrupted the company). Otherwise their ugliness, whether it be natural or wanton, may provoke derision or disesteem and disapproval if it is wanton, though it still remains their business. Thus we make a three-way distinction between moral blame, more general forms of disapproval which link with the voluntary, and disvaluing emotion as such. If Aristotle seems to conflate the first two elements in the distinction, Hume seems to conflate all three.

On the other hand Mill's notion that moral disapproval is penal picks out the relevant difference. But even if we accept that there is a distinctively penal sentiment of blame it does not follow that the morally wrong can be defined in terms of it as that towards which it is a justified response. This could not, in the first place, be a definition if it proposed that the morally wrong is that which there is a moral obligation to blame. We have distinguished, however, between the act of blame and the sentiment of blame itself; to judge that the sentiment is justified is to make a judgment about what one ought to feel in the sense of what feeling is reasonable. That need not be, arguably cannot be, a moral 'ought'.

A more serious objection arises from the intentional content of the blame-feeling. Is not the blame-feeling directed properly only at that which is believed to be morally wrong? This circularity is harder to set aside; it may force the conclusion that 'morally' in 'morally wrong' is a semantically primitive modifier (see Skorupski 1993). But even so the thesis that an action is morally wrong if and only if the sentiment of blame towards its agent is justified (or some refinement of that thesis) may be a conceptual truth which supplies a criterion for demarcating the moral system

of evaluations in a society from others, by reference to the distinctive sentiment involved in guilt and blame – so long as we can get some independent grip on that sentiment.

Characterizing morality in this way is consistent with holding that it has a function. Our spontaneous responses as to what is reasonably blamed serve to maintain beneficial social cooperation; it is not implausible that they persist in their character and content because they do that. What of the supremacy of morality? Is the claim that moral obligations are overriding consistent with characterizing the moral in terms of sentiments of blame? Suppose it would be blameworthy not do X. Does it follow that one should do X, whatever can be said against doing it? At least this much seems true: if there is no reason why a person should not do X where 'reason' is being used in the general deliberative way – then there is no reason to blame that person for doing X. This is a point about the intentional content of the blame sentiment, like the point that if something is in no way dangerous there is no reason to fear it. If it is correct, and if an action is morally wrong just if it is reasonable to blame a person who does it, then it follows from the fact that it is morally wrong that there is reason not to do it, without need of any extra premise. We might call this the thesis that morality is constraining. To say that morality is supreme is stronger. It requires something like this: if doing X is, all things considered, optimal (there is nothing there is more reason to do) then there is no reason to blame a person for doing X. If that is intrinsic to the intentional content of the blame sentiment, then so is the supremacy of morality.

4 Do all societies have morality?

All sustainable societies have spontaneous disciplinary systems maintaining solidarity and prohibition – in the sense that they flow from spontaneously shared favourable and hostile attitudes to actions and are not codified systems of law enforced by instituted penalties. Artificial disciplines psychologically presuppose them and could not sustainably replace them, not just because (outside utopia) the enforcement costs would be too great.

But need these spontaneous disciplines be based on the emotions involved in guilt and blame? Here questions on the borders of philosophy and anthropology arise. Among them are: How do guilt and blame relate to or depend on religious emotions of transgression and expiation or redemption, or to emotions mobilized by the ideas of purity and pollution? And how are they related to shame and disdain? A distinction has been proposed between shame cultures and guilt cultures; spontaneous discipline is realized in the former through the experience of shame rather than of guilt (Benedict 1947). E.R. Dodds (1951) suggested that the development from Homeric to classical Greece was a development from shame to guilt culture; the Christian West is often thought of as *par excellence* a guilt culture (see MORAL SENTIMENTS §3).

In attempting to pin down a sentiment one looks to its intentional content and the action to which it disposes. Some have suggested that the core of blame is a species of anger – indignation or resentment. Resentment, however, is specifically occasioned by what is taken as injury to oneself. Indignation, it is true, is more general: it is occasioned by what is taken to be wrongdoing whether or not it involves injury to oneself. Yet it seems mistaken to make it the emotional core of blame, even though wrongdoing is its object. Rather, indignation is what people of spirit feel on witnessing a religious or moral violation. It impels them to right the wrong done, aggressing if necessary against the violator. The blame-feeling as such does not dispose to aggressive restorative action: it resembles, in extreme cases, a kind of horror akin to the reaction to pollution and disposes to withdrawal of recognition, casting out of the community (see RECOGNITION). It further disposes to punishment; but punishment is not the expression of anger. When it is not a simple deterrent discipline it is an atonement – a regaining of recognition. Or rather, punishment as such is never just deterrence. The concept is not applicable to the entirely wild, though it can apply in some degree to animals which are incorporated into the social order. The blameworthy but unpunished agent is in a liminal state between community and wilderness. Hegel held punishment to be the right of the wrongdoer; his view is understandable when punishment is seen as the mechanism for regaining recognition. Expulsion is the first moment of blame, redemption and return the second and third. The punishment must be accepted: guilt – self-blame – is a withdrawal of recognition from oneself and a movement to redeeming self-punishment.

This human pattern which lies at the core of blame can plausibly be held to exist in all cultures. But that does not mean that institutional and ideological structures which mobilize and channel it do so in the same way or degree. For example many societies connect transgression to impurity or pollution, and associate with them rituals of cleansing such as the scapegoat carrying its burden of evil into the wilderness (see ATONEMENT). (The impure can have unexpected connections with the sacred: the impure transgresses law, the sacred is above it.) Christianity's heaven and hell take integration into the community or expulsion from it to their furthest limit; this life becomes a liminal phase preceding final integration or expulsion. But we should not infer too easily that the very notions of wrongdoing and punishment depend on such religious or magical extensions. They remain the root notion of criminal as against civil law, for example, even when law is shorn of magic and religion.

How then do guilt and blame contrast with shame and disdain? Central to those latter feelings is the notion of personal standing, status or rank. The behaviour to which disdain disposes is not exclusion from the community but demotion within it, not withdrawal of recognition as such but loss of status. Shame, disdain directed towards oneself, is the experience of loss of standing in one's own eyes. With loss of standing there is no analogue to the recognized antidote, so to speak, provided for exclusion by atonement. Presumably that is because standing requires qualities that may be non-voluntary whereas membership only requires compliance (see HONOUR). Blame relates to the quality of the will, something redeemable of whose redemption one can give a sign; whereas disdain need not. A shameful defect is not necessarily, or even typically, a defect of will and it may not be possible to remedy it by effort.

The responses of exclusion and demotion are elemental, but develop and shade into each other in many ways. A contrast between 'blame cultures' and 'shame cultures' may be too simple to capture the diversity and continuity among cultures that is actually found. Yet it is plausible that modern Western culture stands out by the marked reliance it places on the discipline of guilt and blame and the way it isolates or 'purifies' that discipline, shearing it of any magico-religious setting, distinguishing it from customary law, and disentangling it from systems of shame and disdain, which it radically downgrades (the most recent step in this process has been the removal of shame from the sexual domain). Theologically, this tendency was led by Protestant Christianity; philosophically, it is epitomized in the abstract, though not the practical, ethics of KANT. One can seek to explain it in various ways: by the internal dynamics of the West's Judaeo-Christian legacy, or as part of the transition from aristocratic values to modern bourgeois notions of individual responsibility, or simply by the general modern tendency to differentiate social functions (see RESPONSIBILITY). These questions belong to the humanities as a whole. But there is also a question of ethical assessment which must be of special interest to moral philosophy. Granting that the modern West is singular in the degree to which, and the way in which, it isolates and relies on guilt and blame, is this reliance wise? Or does it throw up illusions and downgrade valuable ideals? Does morality as we have come to understand it – 'modern morality' – play an indefensible role in our ethical thought? It was Nietzsche's achievement to put these questions firmly on the agenda. In recent moral philosophy they have been pursued by Bernard Williams (1985, 1993).

5 Criticisms of morality

Criticisms of morality – or of 'modern morality' – fall into two kinds, claiming respectively that it is incoherent and that it is dysfunctional.

The object of the blame-feeling seems to be, as one may call it, transgression. Transgression is avoidable wrongdoing. It is recognizable as such by a responsible agent; responsibility is the capacity to respond to it as 'constraining' in the sense explained in §2 – to acknowledge that there is reason to avoid it as such. Moreover transgressive wrongness is a wrongness independent of the agent's desires and projects. Bernard Williams criticizes this idea of wrongdoing on the ground that there are no 'external reasons' – nothing which one has reason to avoid as such, irrespective of one's desires or projects. If transgression is indeed the intentional object of the blame-feeling, his criticism undermines the coherence of blame: it would follow that nothing is blameworthy, in the way that if nothing is dangerous it follows there is nothing to fear. Williams (1985, 1995), however, holds this notion of wrongdoing, and the corresponding notion of responsibility, to be a fiction peculiar to what he calls 'the morality system' – in present terms, modern morality (see WILLIAMS, B.A.O. §§2–3).

Whether there are 'external reasons' is a controversial issue in epistemology and the philosophy of mind (see MORAL MOTIVATION). Williams' rejection of external reasons stems from a neo-Humean view of those issues which has been widely influential but is also widely rejected. However there is a distinct criticism, of modern morality at least, also sketched by Williams. Modern morality seems to hold that those who are bound by the moral law at all are bound by it equally. Is this inherent in the blame-feeling as such? Certainly the blame-feeling presupposes no doctrine of degrees of rank, or of ideals of life underpinning such degrees – disdain in contrast works with a notion of what can be expected from the superior and the inferior. But modern morality seems markedly to strengthen this feature of the blame-feeling. Kant (1785) stressed that the moral law must be accessible to any autonomous being and it is part of his metaphysics of the person that everyone has an equal potential for rational autonomy (see AUTONOMY, ETHICAL). More generally, the problem of 'free will' is typically presented in modern moral philosophy as an all or nothing affair: either all lack free will and thus responsibility (because of the truth of determinism, for example) or all are equally free; either way there are no degrees of moral agency (see FREE WILL). A connected and very powerful modern thought is that no system of valuation has the existential finality of the moral. Its extreme formulation is Kant's thesis that the only real human worth is moral worth; it fits onto the thesis that all are equally capable of acknowledging and acting on the moral law. Taken together the two theses imply that differences of human worth stem exclusively from what is equally within all human agents' control. One may call the idea that this must be so the egalitarianism of pure desert, or of pure autonomy.

The right response to it may be that moral agency does come in degrees and that there are admirable or contemptible forms of agency other than the moral. This may be incompatible with the egalitarianism of pure autonomy but is it incompatible with morality as such? Ordinary moral thought is quite willing to allow that there can be diminished responsibility and that it implies diminished blame. It also allows that natural virtues may be differentially distributed and it does not extirpate systems of valuation other than the moral. Perhaps the egalitarianism of pure autonomy or desert arises from the profoundly Christian, or more narrowly, Protestant character of modern ethical thought and not from moral valuation, grounded in the sentiment of blame, as such.

These lines of response take account of Nietzsche's criticism of Christianity and modern morality (see §1) but seek to disentangle it from his rejection of moral valuation itself. Another influential critique, which focuses on somewhat related aspects of modern morality, is found in Hegel's *Philosophy of Right* (1821). Here too a contrast between Hellenic and modern ethical conceptions plays a vital role. Hegel divides the ethical sphere, which he thinks of as the sphere of freedom, into three aspects or phases – 'abstract right', *Moralität* and *Sittlichkeit* (see HEGEL, G.W.F. §8). Abstract right treats of the external, juridical regulation of persons conceived of as property owners and the rights implied thereby. The latter two terms are usually translated as 'morality' and 'ethics' or 'ethical life', but in the present context those translations are misleading, for both terms denote aspects or kinds of morality. *Moralität* develops the subjective side of moral agency. Hegel takes as its characteristic form the Kantian notion of a self-legislating subject evolving, entirely from its own reflection, the content of the moral law. He sees this, in particular its idea that true moral agency arises from rational insight into universal law, as a moment in the development of modern freedom from primitive *Sittlichkeit*, or communal moral order. But he also holds that it is doomed to emptiness by its own purism. Taken as rejection of the very possibility of abstract ethical theory, as it sometimes is, Hegel's criticism would be vitiated by its excessive focus on the specifically Kantian treatment of the issue. But if it is seen as a criticism of the ahistorical and asocial distortions which modern morality's egalitarianism imposes it is on target. It is a critique of the one-sided subjectivity or individualism of certain modern conceptions of moral valuation – but Hegel also thinks that this one-sidedness is bound to be overcome. In modern *Sittlichkeit*, the objective ethical life to which Hegel thinks modernity eventually tends, moral valuation is relocated in institutions whose rationality enables one to achieve freedom by taking up a social role.

Rejecting some of the distinctive components in the ideology of modern morality, then, is not necessarily rejecting morality as such. But it may still be asked whether it is a good thing to entrench the emotions of guilt and blame into a social discipline. The question must come from some conception of ethical value, and it must assume that there is an alternative. To think morality is dysfunctional one must have an ethical end in mind which is not itself moral. For example, a utilitarian might claim that the blame-sentiment should be downgraded as dysfunctional, perhaps after some level of social development has been reached (see Utilitarianism). Blame and guilt are after all hostile feelings which cause pain. Yet is there any conception of ethical value which does not make the idea that we would be better off without the social authority those feelings presently carry utopian? Can human beings reach a level of rationality or goodness at which the need for any discipline, spontaneous or artificial, drops away? If not, the choice lies between spontaneous systems and costly and repressive artificial ones, and then within the spontaneous, between the system of guilt and blame and other systems such as that of shame and disdain. A society which shifted emphasis towards the latter would also have to shift – how far is hard to tell – from modern individualism and egalitarian respect.

See also: Duty; Moral agents; Moral judgment; Moral realism; Universalism in ethics

References and further reading

* Aristotle (*c.* mid 4th century BC) *Nicomachean Ethics*, trans. W.D. Ross, Oxford: Oxford University Press, 1954, book III. (Discusses the conditions of responsibility.)

* Benedict, R. (1947) *The Chrysanthemum and the Sword: Patterns of Japanese Culture*, London: Secker & Warburg. (Perceptive comments on guilt and shame in Japan and the West.)

* Dodds, E.R. (1951) *The Greeks and the Irrational*, London, Berkeley and Los Angeles, CA: University of California Press. (Influential discussion of ethical concepts in Homeric and classical Greece.)

Gibbard, A. (1990) *Wise Choices, Apt Feelings*, Oxford: Clarendon Press. (Includes extended discussion of the moral sentiments.)

Hare, R.M. (1963) *Freedom and Reason*, Oxford: Clarendon Press. (Principles are moral if they are universal, prescriptive and supreme ('overriding').)

* Hegel, G.W.F. (1821) *Naturrecht und Staatswissenschaft im Grundrisse. Grundlinien der Philosophie des Rechts* (Natural Law and Politics in Outline. The Principles of the Philosophy of Right), trans. H.B. Nisbet and ed. A. Wood, *Elements of the Philosophy of Right*, Cambridge: Cambridge University Press, 1991, §§82–104. (Discussion of punishment, which deals with Wrong (*Das Unrecht*), a concept whose development, according to Hegel, marks the transition from 'abstract right' to *Moralität*.)

* Hume, D. (1739/40) *A Treatise of Human Nature*, ed. L.A. Selby-Bigge, revised by P.H. Nidditch, Oxford: Clarendon Press, 2nd edn, 1978. (Book 3, part I, sections 1 and 2 give Hume's view of the connection between moral valuation and the sentiments. For his view of reasons for action, see book 2, part II, section 3.)

* —— (1748, 1751) 'Of some verbal Disputes', in *Enquiries Concerning Human Understanding and Concerning the Principles of Morals*, ed. L.A. Selby-Bigge, revised by P.H. Nidditch, Oxford: Clarendon Press, 3rd edn, 1975, appendix IV. (Dismisses the distinction between moral virtues and other good qualities as merely verbal.)

* Kant, I. (1785) *Grundlegung zur Metaphysik der Sitten*, trans. L.W. Beck, *Foundations of the Metaphysics of Morals*, Upper Saddle River, NJ: Prentice Hall, 2nd edn, 1995, ch. 1. (Emphasizes that the moral is available to the common understanding of all.)

Mackie, J.L. (1977) 'The object of morality', in *Ethics: Inventing Right and Wrong*, Harmondsworth: Penguin, ch. 5. (A clear statement of the functional view of morality.)

* Mill, J.S. (1861) *Utilitarianism*, in J. Robson (ed.) *The Collected Works of John Stuart Mill*, vol. 10, London and Toronto: Routledge and University of Toronto Press, 1969, 203–59. (Mill's characterization of morality comes as part of his account of justice.)

* Nietzsche, F. (1881) *Morgenröte*, trans. R. Hollingdale with an introduction by Michael Tanner, *Daybreak, Thoughts on the Prejudices of Morality*, Cambridge: Cambridge University Press, 1982. (This work, with the following two, gives a comprehensive picture of Nietzsche's critique of morality.)

—— (1886) *Jenseits von Gut und Böse*, trans. R.J. Hollingdale with an introduction by Michael Tanner, *Beyond Good and Evil: Prelude to a Philosophy of the Future*, Harmondsworth: Penguin, 1990. (Contrasts modern morality, conceived as incipiently nihilistic, with Nietzsche's conception of what is noble.)

—— (1887) *Zur Genealogie der Moral*, trans. with an introduction and notes by D. Smith, *On the Genealogy of Morals: A Polemic by Way of Clarification and Supplement to my Last Book, Beyond Good and Evil*, Oxford: Oxford University Press, 1996. (Three essays dealing with the origins of moral concepts, the nature of guilt, and the meaning of asceticism.)

* Skorupski, J. (1993) 'The definition of morality', in A. Phillips (ed.) *Ethics*, Cambridge: Cambridge University Press, 121–44. (Argues that morality can be characterized – though not defined – in terms of blame, and discusses the nature of blame.)

Taylor, G. (1985) *Pride, Shame and Guilt: Emotions of Self-Assessment*, Oxford: Clarendon Press. (Detailed discussion of these related emotions.)

Wallace, G. and Walker, A.D.M. (eds) (1970) *The Definition of Morality*, London: Methuen. (Articles covering a variety of approaches to the definitional problem.)

* Williams, B. (1985) 'Morality the Peculiar Institution', in *Ethics and the Limits of Philosophy*, Cambridge, MA: Harvard University Press and London: Fontana, ch. 10. (The fullest statement of his critique of morality.)

* —— (1989) 'Internal Reasons and the Obscurity of Blame', *Logos* 10: 1–12; repr. in *'Making Sense of Humanity' and Other Philosophical Papers 1982–1993*, Cambridge: Cambridge University Press, 1995. (Describes a 'proleptic' mechanism of blame by which he explains the categoricity and apparent unavoidability of moral requirements.)

* —— (1993) *Shame and Necessity*, Berkeley, CA: University of California Press. (A discussion of Greek and modern ethical thought. Endnote 1 concerns 'Mechanisms of shame and guilt'.)

JOHN SKORUPSKI

MORALITY AND IDENTITY

Philosophers have drawn connections between morality and identity in two ways. First, some have argued that metaphysical theories about personal identity – theories about what makes one the same person over time – have important consequences for what ought to matter to a rational agent. Second, others have argued that understanding the concrete identities of persons – the social contexts and personal commitments that give life substance and meaning – is essential if moral philosophy is to address real human concerns.

How are metaphysical questions about personal identity supposed to bear on morality? The thought is that what unifies a series of experiences into a single life illuminates what we are, and what we are helps determine how we ought to live. More broadly, it is natural to seek coherence in our metaphysical and our moral views about persons. This pursuit of a comprehensive account has its dangers; perhaps we will tailor a metaphysical view to fit our moral prejudices, or distort moral philosophy and judgment to fit a false metaphysics. But the pursuit has its attractions too; perhaps we will come to understand what we are, and how we ought to live, in a single package.

Philosophers who attend to concrete rather than metaphysical identity characterize persons as committed by social and historical circumstances to a particular range and ordering of values, and as committed by proximity and affection to a particular circle of other persons. These concrete and individual characteristics at least constrain what morality can reasonably demand. But this interpretation suggests that morality stands back from the rich texture of each life, and moderates its demands to accommodate that life. Some philosophers think of morality instead as part of the texture, as intimately connected to, rather than constrained by, concrete identity.

1 **Some historical background about personal identity**
2 **Parfit's metaphysical and moral revisionism**
3 **Criticisms of Parfit**
4 **Concrete identity**

1 Some historical background about personal identity

Does anything about a person survive bodily death? This is a natural way for metaphysical questions about identity to acquire practical and moral urgency (see PERSONAL IDENTITY). For example, Plato argued for the existence of an immortal soul, and used this metaphysical view to buttress his moral claims (see PLATO §13). Thus, it is always wrong to harm others because doing so also harms your soul, the most enduring and valuable part of yourself. Theologians too have an abiding interest in such issues. For whether persons survive in resurrected bodies or as permanently disembodied souls, they must survive in *some* form to receive God's justice, or God's mercy. The thought of such justice and mercy plays an important moral role for many religious believers (see SOUL, NATURE AND IMMORTALITY OF THE).

In his paper, 'Of Identity and Diversity' (1694), John Locke focuses not on what might survive bodily death, but on what accounts for identity over time during our earthly lives (see LOCKE, J. §9). Locke invites us to imagine these possibilities: two sets of character traits and memories (or, for brevity's sake, two psychologies) alternate in possession of a single body; a single psychology is transferred from one body to another; a single soul is associated with two different psychologies; a single psychology has 'underlying' it not a single soul, but rather a rapid succession of souls. Locke argues that our best responses to these imagined cases indicate that neither sameness of body nor sameness of soul is necessary or sufficient for identity. Instead, the right kind of psychological continuity determines personal identity over time.

Locke's positive theory of personal identity has been dubbed the memory theory: at time t_2, I am identical with a person at some earlier time t_1 if and only if I can remember the t_1 experiences *as my own*. This theory gives rise to numerous problems; Locke himself broaches some of them. For instance, Locke admits that, were he to lose irretrievably the memories of certain experiences, he would no longer be the same person that had those experiences. But he tries to soften this odd-sounding claim. He says that he would be the same biological being ('man') in spite of his forgetting; but he would not be the same *person*, because a person is an amalgam of the actions for which that person can take responsibility, and one cannot take responsibility for what one cannot remember. So Locke's sense of the moral role of the concept of the person shapes his metaphysical account of personal identity.

Such manoeuvres did little, however, to forestall criticism of the memory theory. Some criticisms focused simply on identity: Thomas Reid, for instance, elaborated variations on the theme that forgetfulness does not destroy identity (see REID, T. §9). But some criticisms were moral: Joseph Butler argued that the memory theory provides such a loose sort of identity that it renders our ordinary self-concern mysterious (see BUTLER, J. §6). The deeper aim of such critics was to restore the soul to its rightful identity-producing role. But they failed to counter Locke's arguments against the soul's having such a role.

David Hume, in his *Treatise of Human Nature* (1739/40), extended Locke's criticisms of the enduring-soul theory of personal identity by arguing that the concept of the soul has no empirical content. He also revised Locke's positive account of identity by supplementing memory with causation. It is appropriate to speak of a previous experience as my experience, Hume says, even if I cannot remember it, if it played some suitable role in causing other experiences of mine. Hume further claims that all experiences or perceptions are, strictly speaking, 'loose and separate', so that the idea of personal identity over time is a fiction, even if an indispensable fiction (see MIND, BUNDLE THEORY OF). But Hume draws no moral conclusions from this extreme or sceptical view. Instead he draws moral conclusions from his attack on the soul, supporting his opposition to religious values ('monkish virtues') by denying the favourite religious account of personal identity.

2 Parfit's metaphysical and moral revisionism

In *Reasons and Persons* (1984), Derek Parfit revives and extends Lockean and Humean themes. Parfit argues that ordinary beliefs about personal identity are mistaken, and that correct beliefs about identity might engender altruism and support consequentialism (which says that an action is right if it promotes the best outcome overall, impersonally considered) (see CONSEQUENTIALISM; EGOISM AND ALTRUISM).

Parfit first describes ordinary belief. We do not believe that the changing surface facts about us account for personal identity over time. Instead, some unchanging 'further fact' constitutes personal identity. When this further fact has received any explication, it has been understood as the Christian soul or the Cartesian ego.

However, Parfit says, there is no good reason to believe in any such further fact. To bear out this and other claims, Parfit produces thought experiments along Lockean lines, but fleshed out with science-fiction details; for instance, he imagines cases of teletransportation and of brain fission. The former procedure involves destroying a body at one place and simultaneously creating a precisely similar new body, realizing a precisely similar psychology, at another place; the latter procedure involves splitting the brain in two and transplanting each half into a new body. Examining our best responses to such cases shows us that we ought to be *reductionists* about personal identity, and that the right kind of reductionism is *psychological* (see PERSONAL IDENTITY §3). Personal identity over time is constituted by the holding of certain psychological relations (which Parfit labels

'Relation R'), whether the physical cause of these relations is the stuff of science fiction, or is familiar and normal. (The normal cause of Relation R is the spatiotemporal continuity of the body, including the brain, that realizes the related psychologies). There is, though, this proviso: however extensive the psychological relations that hold between A at t1 and B at t2, A and B are not the same person if there exists at t2 another person, C, whose psychological relations to A are equally extensive. In Parfit's terminology, identity requires that there be *no branching*.

Parfit claims that, from his general account of the metaphysics of identity, it follows that identity (1) is not all-or-nothing and (2) is not 'what matters' (what is most valuable to a rational agent). These conclusions challenge ordinary practical reasoning, which gives pride of place to the determinate and meaningful self.

(1) Identity (hence survival) is a matter of degree, rather than all-or-nothing, for psychological relations that are themselves a matter of degree constitute identity. We can imagine cases where many identity-producing psychological relations hold, but many do not, so that we are *unsure* whether these are cases of identity and survival; our uncertainty shows that in such borderline cases there is no fact of the matter about whether the later person is identical to the earlier person. But even in mundane cases, the unity of a person's past, present, and future 'selves' is a matter of degree, constituted by Relation R. And Relation R holds not just *within* persons, but also *across* persons; for two people can share many values and projects and character traits. So the same relation that imperfectly unifies the self also connects us with other people.

(2) In branching cases, the kind of psychological relation that obtains in unproblematic instances of identity obtains twice. But this very surplus rules out identity-claims; for we should not say that two numerically distinct persons are *both* identical to some earlier person, and we have no grounds for preferring one identity-candidate to the other. Now Parfit believes that few people would say that a branching case is as bad as ordinary death; and most people would say that such a case is about as good as ordinary survival. (The imagined future contains two agents who share your values, and will pursue your projects as you would have.) Thus branching cases contain what matters in ordinary survival, without containing identity. Parfit concludes that, even in ordinary cases, what matters in survival is not identity, but the obtaining of the right psychological relation with some future person.

What, then, is Parfit's desired practical and moral upshot? He hopes that the reductionist will have more

reason to be *impartial* and *impersonal* than the non-reductionist does (see IMPARTIALITY). For reductionism lessens the gap between persons. It shows that my relation to other people is more like my relation to my own past and future than non-reductionist common sense allows. So reductionism undermines the belief that it is most rational for me to pursue my own long-term self-interest; and believing reductionism might cause me to promote my values and projects (part of the content of Relation R) without special regard for the particular people involved. Thus reductionism might move us towards greater *altruism*; and, because this altruism focuses not on other enduring individuals but on impersonally promoting certain values and projects, reductionism might move us closer to *consequentialism*.

However, Parfit qualifies these conclusions, in two ways. First, he admits that a rational person could believe that only a further fact could be what matters, so that reductionism would show that nothing matters. Parfit believes this 'extreme view' is rationally indefeasible, but also not rationally compelling. That is, Parfit believes his own optimistic view about what matters in the absence of a 'further fact' is as rational as the extreme view is. Second, Parfit hopes not that people will become selfless, only that they will become somewhat less self-interested, when they learn the reductionist truth about personal identity. He suggests that there are evolutionary reasons for thinking in terms of identity, and for acting in self-interested ways (see EVOLUTION AND ETHICS §2). But, where hope for psychological revolution might be naïve, hope for psychological reform might be well-grounded. Parfit hopes for reform, in the direction of consequentialism, once people become reductionists about personal identity.

3 Criticisms of Parfit

We now consider four main criticisms of Parfit.

(1) The most straightforward and ambitious criticism says that personal identity *does* consist in the holding of some 'further fact' (the existence of an unchanging soul). Making out this criticism involves showing that the scientific picture of human beings is irremediably incomplete, or at least that Parfit offers no good reason for thinking otherwise. Assessing this ambitious criticism is beyond this entry's scope; but it is worth noting that the criticism attacks Parfit at his strong point, and where he can find many allies.

(2) A subtler criticism of Parfit's metaphysics agrees that some form of reductionism is correct, but disagrees with his permissive attitude towards the cause of Relation R and with his exclusively psychological reductionism. The critics (including

Peter Unger (1990)) argue that Parfit underestimates the importance of the normal cause of Relation R, namely the physical continuity of a living body. The most plausible reductionism refers to both psychological relations and physical continuity. This partly-physical reductionism captures our deepest notions about what makes for the same person over time in our usual circumstances; the appeal of disembodied Cartesian egos or of Parfitian teletransported psychologies is shallow, compared to the appeal of an embodied this-worldly self. Partly-physical reductionism also does *not* commit us to substantially revising our deepest values. Instead, it helps explain why we value whole persons and maintain clear distinctions between persons, rather than valuing isolated psychological characteristics and blurring the distinctions between persons.

(3) Parfit believes that it is possible and desirable to become less committed to particular persons (oneself included) and more committed to general features of people (character traits, patterns of concern). But perhaps it is a practical necessity that we conceive and order our commitments in terms of whole and enduring persons – enduring, that is, at least over the course of a lifetime. Or perhaps, though we *might* come to think of the human world as a collection of psychological characteristics variously related, this new way of thinking would impoverish our lives. For instance, it might might make it hard for us to conceive of love or friendship.

(4) Parfit argues that ordinary normative practices are founded on false metaphysics, and that coming to believe the true metaphysics gives us opportunity and incentive to revise our practices. But perhaps our practices are founded not on any metaphysical view about persons, but on our circumstances and needs. Perhaps ordinary non-reductionist metaphysics is just window-dressing.

To each of these last three criticisms, Parfit's best response might be a partial accommodation. He has been willing to entertain the possibility that the best reductionist account of personal identity refers to the normal cause of Relation R. He admits that there are limits to our ability to excise identity from practical reasoning, and that even a partial excision must be judged by its consequences. Finally, it would indeed be unreasonable to claim that *all* our ordinary practices are *entirely* shaped by false metaphysical views; but it is possible, perhaps likely, that *some* practices are *partly* shaped in this way. (But which practices depend on false metaphysics? To what extent? Can we revise the practices to fit the true metaphysics? Is this revision morally desirable?)

4   Concrete identity

Advocates of 'concrete identity', the second broad approach to connecting issues of morality and identity, side with Parfit's critics. Parfit's view is, according to concrete identity theorists, one manifestation of a widespread mistaken approach to ethics – an approach that abstracts away from the richness of actual psychology and social and historical context, thus losing sight of real human lives. Kantians appeal to a general and formal feature of persons, their rational agency, in constructing moral theories and testing moral injunctions (see KANTIAN ETHICS). Consequentialists see persons simply as causes of good and bad consequences, or the locations where those consequences are embodied. Such artificially restricted views of the person distort one's view of morality, the concrete-identity theorists argue; to see morality clearly, we must see people whole.

Starting from this complaint about abstraction, philosophers have pursued two paths: the first psychological, the second social and historical. Bernard Williams has put the psychological case forcefully, arguing that abstract moral theories miss or dismiss important moral phenomena, and fundamental facts about human motivation (see WILLIAMS, B.A.O. §2). Effective reasons for action are deeply personal; how can the stripped-down agents of Kantianism and consequentialism have reasons to act at all? It is absurd to require that agents abandon the commitments that give their lives shape and meaning, in order, for example, to produce the best consequences overall. Close personal attachments have independent moral value; it is impertinent, perhaps monstrous, to demand that we justify our special attachments in light of abstract moral principles (see FRIENDSHIP; LOVE §1). In short, moral insight into a person, and effective moral appeals to that person, had better be based on actual features of *that* person's rich psychology, rather than on abstract general features of the person or of moral agency.

Charles Taylor (1989) makes the case for a social and historical approach to concrete identity (see TAYLOR, C. §§4–5). Taylor does furnish a general theory of sorts about identity: each person shapes an identity through self-interpretative activity, activity that employs the interconnected resources of community, language, and a conception of the good life. This theory connects morality and identity by connecting the questions 'What do I value?' and 'Who am I?'; it also directs our attention towards social and historical particulars. So Taylor's method for investigating our moral situation is to see how the modern identity, that is the modern range of conceptions of the good life, has been shaped and enriched over a long history.

The method is not to pare down the concept of identity to its essentials, but to build it up in all its complexity.

It would be folly to deny that concrete identity theorists point at important phenomena. Moral philosophers of all bents should strive at least to show that their theories are consistent with the concrete aspects of identity and of moral life; even better, moral philosophers might strive to connect the abstract and the concrete. But concrete identity theorists often aim at more than providing a salutary reminder to other moral philosophers. They suggest that abstract moral theorizing distorts our lives beyond recognition, that there is no use for the sort of abstraction that whittles people down to a few essential characteristics. In response to these ambitious criticisms, traditional moral philosophers can claim that to abstract away from psychology and culture and history, for special purposes and for the sake of clarification, is not to deny the existence or importance of the things we abstract away from. Understanding our moral lives might require that our attention move back and forth between general features of persons, and persons in their particularity.

This survey has examined two ways in which questions of identity matter to moral philosophers, and two approaches to moral philosophy. Ranged on one side are philosophers who focus on general and trans-historical aspects of being a person or a moral agent. On the other side are philosophers who focus on human beings and societies in their particularity, and who eschew abstraction (or practise a different kind of abstraction, rooted in psychological and historical rather than metaphysical facts). In spite of the apparent conflict between the abstract and the concrete, it is unclear whether these two approaches to thinking about morality and identity are mutually exclusive, or complementary.

See also: IDEALS; MORAL AGENTS; SELF-REALIZATION; SELF-RESPECT

References and further reading

Flanagan, O. and Rorty, A.O. (eds) (1990) *Identity, Character, and Morality: Essays in Moral Psychology*, Cambridge, MA: MIT Press. (The essays in this volume discuss many of the issues grouped under the label 'concrete identity'; the volume includes an extensive bibliography.)

* Hume, D. (1739/40) 'Of the Immateriality of the Soul' and 'Of Personal Identity', in *A Treatise of Human Nature*, ed. L.A. Selby-Bigge, revised by P.H. Nidditch, Oxford: Clarendon Press, 2nd edn,

1978, book 1, part IV, sections 5–6. (In three essays, Hume attacks the belief in a substantial or enduring self.)

Johnston, M. (1992) 'Reasons and Reductionism', *Philosophical Review* 101 (3): 589–618. (A thorough and forceful criticism of Parfit's attempt to draw moral conclusions from his metaphysical account.)

Kymlicka, W. (1991) *Liberalism, Community, and Culture*, Oxford: Oxford University Press. (Discusses and responds to criticisms of liberal political philosophy for neglecting concrete identity and community.)

* Locke, J. (1694) 'Of Identity and Diversity', in *An Essay Concerning Human Understanding*, extended 2nd edn, ed. P.H. Nidditch, Oxford: Oxford University Press, 1975, book II, ch. 27. (In this paper Locke proposes and defends the memory theory of personal identity.)

* Parfit, D. (1984) *Reasons and Persons*, New York: Oxford University Press, part III. (Elaborates a reductionist view of personal identity, and argues that adopting this view might bring about morally desirable consequences. Parfit's work has been the most influential recent discussion of the metaphysics of personal identity, and of the connections between metaphysical identity and morality.)

Perry, J. (ed.) (1975) *Personal Identity*, Berkeley, CA: University of California Press. (Includes the passages from Locke, Butler, Hume, and Reid, referred to in §1; modern revisions and criticisms of Locke's memory theory; an article by Parfit anticipating the themes of *Reasons and Persons*; and an article by Bernard Williams, 'The Self and the Future', suggesting that a bodily criterion of identity retains a strong hold on our imaginations even when it conflicts with a psychological criterion. The collection is an excellent introduction to the issues discussed in §§1–3.)

Rorty, A.O. (ed.) (1976) *The Identities of Persons*, Berkeley, CA: University of California Press. (See especially Perry, 'The Importance of Being Identical', for reflections on Parfitian topics, and Williams, 'Persons, Character, and Morality', for a seminal discussion of concrete identity.)

* Taylor, C. (1989) *Sources of the Self*, Cambridge, MA: Harvard University Press. (A wide-ranging, detailed, yet accessible book, narrating the historical growth of the modern concrete identity.)

* Unger, P. (1990) *Identity, Consciousness, and Value*, New York: Oxford University Press. (A sustained and detailed criticism of Parfit, which argues that our deepest intuitions favour a physical standard of personal identity. This volume contains a useful bibliography about metaphysical identity.)

Wolf, S. (1986) 'Self-Interest and Interest in Selves',

Ethics 96 (4): 704–20. (Argues that Parfit's desired moral reforms may not be possible, probably would not be desirable, and in any event have to be evaluated by normative rather than metaphysical standards.)

IRA SINGER

MORALITY AND LAW *see* LAW AND MORALITY

MORALITY AND RELIGION
see RELIGION AND MORALITY

MORE, HENRY (1614–87)

The English philosopher Henry More was one of the leaders of the movement known as Cambridge Platonism. Like his Cambridge colleague Ralph Cudworth, More elaborated a constructive metaphysics which, although deeply informed by the new philosophy and science of the seventeenth century, recovered what More saw as an ancient truth or 'cabbala'. The articulation of this truth was an exercise of reason, guided by innate notions or inherent, God-given cognitive propensities. More's ultimate aim as a philosopher was religious or ethical. His 'one main Design', he explained, was 'The knowledge of God, and therein of true Happiness', so far as *Reason* can cut her way through those darknesses and difficulties she is encumbered with in this life' (1662: iv). Among the central themes of the ancient truth More rediscovered and defended were the existence of a God whose leading attributes are wisdom and goodness; the immateriality and immortality of the human soul (the hope of immortality being, as More explained in the Preface to his poem Psychathanasia (1642), 'the very nerves and sinews' of religion); a dualism of active spirit and passive matter that differed significantly from the dualism of Descartes, despite More's early enthusiasm for (and continuing engagement with) Cartesianism; the animation of matter by an immaterial but unthinking spirit of nature; and the existence of an infinite, substantial space, really distinct from matter, in which God is everywhere present and everywhere potentially active.

?More's appeals to experiment in defence of the spirit of nature provoked criticism from Robert Boyle. His doctrine of infinite, substantial space was (in the opinion of some historians) an important influence on

Isaac Newton. Space seems, on More's portrayal, to be something divine; this troubled George Berkeley, who thought that by assigning space the 'incommunicable' or unshareable attributes of God, More in the end encouraged the atheism he worked so hard to defeat.

More is usually represented as a rationalist in religion: 'I conceive', he once wrote, 'Christian Religion rational throughout' (1662: iv). It is important to distinguish, however, between More's appeal to reason as a writer defending Christianity, and his appraisal of reason's role in an ordinary Christian life. More was conscious of living in 'a Searching, Inquisitive, Rational and Philosophical Age', and he saw it as his duty to serve God by 'gaining or retaining the more Rational and Philosophical' of his contemporaries in the Christian faith (1664: 482). Rational and philosophical genius was not, however, required of every Christian: although More's accounts of faith vary somewhat from work to work, they typically call not for a rational assessment of argument and evidence, but for moral purity, and for a belief in (and devotion to) a relatively short list of 'essentials'. More sought a statement of these essentials that would reach across Protestant sectarian divides. He also defended a liberty of conscience or religion that was, he said, the natural right of every nation and every person. It was, however, a liberty that could be forfeited, and More thought it had *been* forfeited by some (atheists, for example, and at least some Catholics and Muslims) who might be found claiming its protection.

1   **Life and works**
2   **Theory of knowledge**
3   **The possibility and existence of spirit**
4   **More and Descartes**
5   **The spirit of nature and the nature of space**
6   **Religion**

1   Life and works

More gives an absorbing account of his early life in the general preface to his *Opera omnia* (1675–9). He was born in Grantham, England, to parents who were 'earnest Followers of *Calvin*'. He himself could never 'swallow down that hard Doctrine concerning *Fate*' because it seemed so at odds with God's justice. As a student at Eton and at Christ's College, Cambridge (where he arrived in 1631), More was possessed by an 'insatiable Desire and Thirst... after the *Knowledge* of things'. At first he took this to be a love of knowledge simply for its own sake, but when he discovered that even the most eager study of philosophy did not quench it, he determined that it was, at bottom, really a form of self-love. He resolved to extinguish or annihilate his own 'proper *will*' and seek 'full union' with the will of God, and was rewarded with the intellectual satisfaction he had earlier failed to find – a 'greater *Assurance*', he said, 'than ever I could have expected'. More became a fellow of Christ's College in 1641, and was ordained in the Church of England in the same year. His career as a writer can be divided into three broad periods, marked not by shifts in doctrine but by changes in the shape and scope of his literary projects.

In the 1640s More published a series of philosophical poems defending the Neoplatonic Christianity he embraced when he came to Cambridge – influenced not only by his study of Plato, but by Renaissance Neoplatonists such as FICINO and POMPANAZZI (see NEOPLATONISM). These poems argue for the soul's immortality, for its pre-existence and for its consciousness after death. Memories ('the bundle of the souls duration') preserve the soul's identity after it parts from its earthly vehicle. Memories also account, at least in part, for one soul's distinctness from others. It was in the middle of this period, around 1645, that More first read Descartes. In *Democritus platonissans* (1646: [iii]), a poem defending the infinity of worlds on new-scientific and Platonic principles, More describes Descartes as a '*sublime and subtill Mechanick*'. '*Though he seem to mince it,*' More continues, Descartes '*must hold infinitude of worlds, or... one infinite one*', because his 'indefinite' extension is simply infinite extension under another name. This is one of several criticisms More developed in letters he exchanged with Descartes in 1648–9. More's side of the correspondence is deeply respectful – almost reverential – but his disagreements with Descartes were fundamental, and as his awareness of their implications grew, More's attitude towards Descartes and Cartesianism became increasingly hostile.

In the 1650s More translated the philosophy of his poems into prose. Works published in this second period include *An antidote against atheisme* (1653a), *Enthusiasmus triumphatus* (Enthusiasm Defeated) (1656), and *The immortality of the soul* (1659). The period culminated in 1662 with the appearance of *A collection of several philosophical writings of Dr. Henry More*. This incorporated the three earlier prose works (the books for which More is now best known), the *Conjectura cabbalistica* (1653b), and More's correspondence with Descartes.

From 1662 until his death, More completed three main projects in philosophy: Latin summaries of his views on ethics (*Enchiridion ethicum* (Handbook of Ethics) 1667) and metaphysics (*Enchiridion metaphysicum* (Handbook of Metaphysics) 1671); the first volume of *Divine dialogues* (1668), the most accessible presentation of his proofs of God's existence, his account of the natural world, and his theodicy; and the translation of his English philosophical works into Latin (in volume 2 of his *Opera omnia*). These were labours of codification more than of inquiry; as Ward suggests in an unpublished manuscript, in this third period More turned towards theology, proving the 'Truth and Nature of *reveald Religion* as before of *natural*' (Gabbey 1982: 222). More's theological works of philosophical interest include *An explanation of the grand mystery of godliness* (1660), *A modest enquiry into the mystery of iniquity* (1664), and the second volume of *Divine dialogues* (1668).

More remained a fellow of Christ's until his death. He consistently refused to consider larger and more prestigious responsibilities such as the mastership of his college (a position filled by CUDWORTH) and the provostship of Trinity College Dublin. More's second home, where he often rushed as soon as term time ended, was Ragley, north of Oxford, the estate of his friend Anne CONWAY. More's correspondence with Conway, published in *The Conway Letters*, is an intimate record of a philosophical friendship. When More, consoling Conway on the death of her two-year-old son from smallpox, tells her that 'there is nothing tragicall to those that are truly good' (1930: 169), his theodicy is tested more severely than it ever could be tested in a treatise.

2 Theory of knowledge

More recognized three sources of knowledge: common notions (which he defined as 'whatever is *Noematically* true, that is to say, true at first sight to all men in their wits, upon a clear perception of the Terms'); external sense (including memory, its 'faithfull Register'); and the 'undeniable deductions' of reason ([1659] 1925: 61). More portrays these sources as clear and compelling and he often claims to demonstrate his main conclusions. But he does not expect his arguments to convince a complete sceptic. 'Perfect *Scepticisme*', he wrote, 'is a disease incurable, and a thing rather to be pitied or laughed at, [than] seriously opposed' ([1659] 1925: 59). When he promises to demonstrate that there is a God, he explains, he does not mean that the reader 'shall be forced to confesse that it is utterly unpossible that it should be otherwise'. It is possible, after all, that '*Mathematical evidence* it self may be but a constant undiscoverable Delusion'. But More's arguments 'shall be such as shall deserve *full assent*, and win *full assent* from any unprejudic'd mind' ([1653a] 1925: 4–5).

More sometimes presents arguments in geometric form, drawing attention to their dependence on an ordered list of 'axioms'. Many of these axioms are laid down as noematic truths but, as More makes clear in several places, his axioms are sometimes merely probable. Some of his axioms are rules for the guidance of inquiry: a crucial axiom in the *Immortality*, for example, declares that whatever is clear from common notions, external sense or rational deduction must *'be held undoubtedly true'* when none of the three sources speaks against it ([1659] 1925: 61). In an *Apology* attached to the *Mystery of iniquity* (1664), More lays down several rules for the conduct of a public intellectual concerned to preserve the peace and authority of the established church. A theorem, he cautions, should be embraced 'no farther then as Rational'; we should be 'wary' in asserting its 'absolute reality and truth' (1664: 488).

Though any truth must be clear of contradiction, we can know that something is the case without being able to explain it. *'Our Senses'*, for example, 'do assure us of such things that no faculty can conceive how they are such as *our Senses* warrant them to be' (1664: 454). This principle plays an important role in More's defence of the possibility of spirit and the authority of revelation.

Although he admits that thinking is first occasioned by external objects, More thinks it is vital to distinguish between the 'extrinsecall Occasions' of our ideas and their 'adequate or principal Causes'. There are *'Innate Notions and Ideas'* in the mind; the soul is no *tabula rasa* or blank slate. Innate ideas do not '[flare] to the *Animadversive Faculty*, like so many *torches* or *Starres*'. There is, instead, 'an active sagacity in the Soul, or quick recollection, as it were, whereby some small businesses being hinted unto her, she runs out presently into a more clear and large conception' ([1653a] 1925: 14). Damaris Cudworth (later MASHAM) quoted these words of More in a letter to Locke. She followed More in suggesting that even though there are no actual representations in the mind innately, the mind has a native power to form conceptions that reach beyond the experience that prompts them. More himself illustrated this dispositional interpretation of innate ideas by comparing the soul to a sleeping musician who can finish a tune after a friend hums the opening notes.

Geometrical ideas are among those that cannot be explained by experience alone; no object of experience approaches the accuracy of our idea of a circle or triangle. Relative notions provide further instances. Cut off half of a pound of lead, More points out, and another pound, at first its equal, becomes its double, without any change in its corporeal makeup. Equal and unequal, he concludes, are not physical affections of matter, from which it follows that they cannot enter the mind through the corporeal organs of sense.

Besides single ideas, there are innate complex ideas (including whole truths or 'common notions'). The idea of God is More's leading example, and in the *Antidote*, its innateness plays what seems to be a crucial role in his primary argument for God's existence. Yet in the *Appendix* added to the second edition of the *Antidote* in 1655, More claims that it is 'all one' to his argument whether the idea of God is innate or not. He does go on to insist, however, that the idea is not 'a crafty Figment of *Politicians*'. It does seem important to More, then, as it had been to Descartes, that the idea of God should not be arbitrary or factitious. But More offers no clear test of factitiousness. To the objection that existence can be derived from the idea of a being which is absolutely evil, he is content to reply that we 'can easily discover the difference betwixt such arbitrarious and forced Figments and fancies' as this, and the 'naturall and consistent *Ideas* of our own Mind' ([1653a] 1662: 156).

3 The possibility and existence of spirit

The greatest obstacle to the belief in immortality, More believed, was 'that confident opinion in some' – he was thinking above all of HOBBES – that 'the very notion of *a Spirit*' is 'a piece of Non-sense and perfect Incongruity in the conception thereof' ([1659] 1925: 65). In the *Immortality*, More set out to free both spirit in general and the several kinds of spirit from 'the imputation of either obscurity or inconsistency' ([1659] 1925: 96).

More defined body as a substance impenetrable and *discerpible* (that is, separable into parts), and spirit as a substance penetrable and *indiscerpible* (not separable into parts). His main argument on behalf of spirit is that every term in its definition is as 'intelligible and congruous' as its counterpart in the definition of body. The 'precise Notion' of substance (elsewhere defined as any being subsisting by itself) appears in both. 'And it is as easy to understand what *Penetrable* is as *Impenetrable*', he writes, 'and what *Indiscerpible* as *Discerpible*' ([1659] 1925: 66). If the positive denominations were all on the side of body, it could be said that the intelligibility of spirit, being derived by negation, was second-rate. But each of More's definitions, as he points out, is partly negative and partly positive.

More's definition of body is in fact misleading because, according to the *Immortality*, the smallest bodies – atoms or *'minima corporalia'* – are indiscerpible. As the young Isaac Newton wrote in his notebooks, 'that matter may be so small as to be indiscerpible the excellent Dr More in his book of the soul's immortality has proved beyond all controversy' (Newton 1644–5: 341). More's indiscerpible atoms resist separation into parts, as Newton realized, only because they are so tiny. Despite their small size they remain, in More's view, 'purely' or 'mathematically' divisible; it is simply that no force in nature has the power to break them apart. 'It is of the very Essence of *Matter* to be *divisible*', More wrote, 'but it is not at all included in the essence thereof to be *discerpible*' ([1659] 1925: 77).

Perhaps the most perplexing feature of spirit as More understood it was *extension*: not the extension distinctive of matter, which involves a juxtaposition of parts, but 'a certain *Amplitude of Presence*' that enables the human soul, for example, to be 'at every part [of the body] at once' ([1653a] 1662: 172). Spirit, More reasoned, has the power to move matter, and it must be present wherever that power is exerted. But if the extension of spirit reaches as far as its power, why is spirit not discerpible? In reply More offers an analogy: a 'luminous orb' diffused in all directions from a single and inexhaustible point of light. The spreading light can of course be blocked or contracted by an opaque body, but according, for example, to the Aristotelians (whose hypothesis can be accepted for the sake of unfolding the analogy), it is impossible for the rays to be 'clipt off, or cut from this *lucid point*, and be kept apart by themselves' ([1659] 1925: 71). In a similar way, More proposes, a spirit's 'Centre of Life' gives rise to a 'Secondary Substance' spread around it. The inmost point is an 'emanative cause' of the surrounding extension, one that 'merely by Being, no other activity or causality interposed', produces an effect ([1659] 1925: 74). The effect must therefore be instantaneous. Because the centre of life is an *absolutely* indivisible point, it is, in the end, less perplexing than an atom of matter, whose indiscerpibility coexists uneasily with its (absolute) divisibility.

If spirit is extended, extension cannot be the mark of material substance, as Descartes (for example) proposed. And if God's power is unlimited, God must be extended throughout space. In a letter to More in April 1649, Descartes distinguished between the extension of a substance and the extension of its power. God, he granted, is everywhere, but only in virtue of his power. More replied that the power of God is a mode of God, and because a mode cannot occur apart from the substance it modifies, it is necessary that God is everywhere, a point he repeated years later in the *Enchiridion metaphysicum*.

More defended the intelligibility of both God and finite spirits. He defines a finite spirit, for example, as 'a substance Indiscerpible, that can move it self, that can penetrate, contract, and dilate it self, and can also penetrate, move, and alter the Matter'. More supported the various characteristics in this definition by comparing them to the equally perplexing characteristics of matter. Those who deny spirit, for example,

are in no position to quarrel with spirit's ability to move itself, because they themselves take matter to be self-moving (since it obviously moves, and there is, on their view, nothing but matter to get things going in the first place). In the end, we may not understand how spirit moves matter and unites with it. But it is no easier to understand how matter moves matter and how it holds itself together.

More defines God as a being fully and absolutely perfect ([1653a, 1659] 1925: 10, 68). Because necessary existence is among the attributes entailed by full perfection, it follows that God exists. More supports this version of the ontological argument (derived from Descartes) with a second: any being we can contemplate, God included, is either contingent, impossible or necessary. But God is neither contingent (contingency being 'incompatible to an *Idea of a Being absolutely Perfect*') nor impossible (the idea of God 'being compiled of no Notions but such as are *possible* according to the Light of Nature') ([1653a] 1925: 22). Hence God exists, a conclusion confirmed by the natural remorse of conscience, our sense of hope and our feelings of religious veneration. More also employed versions of the cosmological argument and the argument from design: 'No *Matter* whatsoever of its own Nature has any active Principle of *Motion*' ([1659] 1925: 102). Motion is 'superadded' to matter by God, who then conserves it. A 'blind *impetus*' could never produce the admirable order we observe in nature and in ourselves.

There are four main categories of finite or created spirits: seminal forms, the souls of brutes, human souls, and the spirits actuating angels. A seminal form is 'a created Spirit organizing duly-prepared Matter into life and vegetation proper to this or the other kind of Plant' ([1659] 1925: 83). An animal soul is the source of both vegetation and sensation. More's argument for the existence of an incorporeal human soul turns on our awareness of faculties and operations 'utterly incompatible to *Matter* considered *at large* without any *particular* organization' and beyond the capacity of matter (or the 'tumbling of atoms') however organized. These faculties include sense, reason, and liberty, which More defines as the power, notwithstanding external assaults, to cleave to virtue. (Our liberty is known by '*Internal Sense*'. In both the *Immortality* and the *Enchiridion ethicum*, More argues at length against Hobbesian determinism.) The soul is also responsible for the frame of the human body and its vital powers. The human soul as More understands it is therefore not just a mind (as it was for Descartes), but an agent of bodily development and maintenance. More must therefore repudiate Descartes' main argument for dualism. He faults Descartes for inferring a 'real precision' (or real distinction) from a precision in thought. Our vital powers can be conceived apart from our power to reflect and reason, but it does not follow that we have two souls.

More viewed apparitions ('speakings, knockings, opening of doors when they were fast shut, sudden lights' – [1659] 1925: 105) and the efficacy of witchcraft as further proofs of spirit. He contributed reports of apparitions to the 1681 edition of Joseph Glanvill's *Saducismus Triumphatus*. 'Those that lay out... well-attested Stories of Witches and Apparitions', More wrote in a letter included in the volume, '*do real service to true Religion and sound Philosophy*' (Glanvill 1681: 26). The phenomena reported, though not miraculous, cannot be accounted for mechanically (see GLANVILL, J.).

4   More and Descartes

More's initial enthusiasm for Descartes had moderated by the late 1650s, but even as late as 1662 he was able to describe the books in his *Collection* as combining Platonism and Cartesianism. The *Divine dialogues* marks a clear break. The book was published without More's name, but his earlier books are cited in the dialogues themselves and in a prefatory letter from 'the Publisher' – a letter actually written by More. The letter takes note of the author's '*over-plain and open opposing that so-much-admired...Descartes*' (1668: [x]). Some earlier writers admit that there may be '*some few effects*' in nature that are '*purely Mechanicall*'. (Here the publisher refers to the author of the *Epistola ad V.C.* (1662) – the More of the late 1650s.) But the present book, the publisher vows, shows abundantly that '*there is no purely-Mechanicall Phenomenon in the whole Universe*' (1668: [xii]). In the ensuing dialogues, Descartes' views are represented by the character Cupuphon, a 'zealous, but Airie-minded, *Platonist* and *Cartesian*, or *Mechanist*'. Cartesian views are shown to be incompatible with scripture and serviceable to religion only in so far as they display (against their intention) the limits of mechanism. The publisher does credit Descartes with discovering the 'most credible Material Causes' of phenomena; More never abandoned the Cartesian view that matter is of one uniform or 'homogeneal' nature, and that change in body is, in itself, nothing but local motion. But the explanatory *causes* of bodily change – the causes that prompt and guide it – were another matter. More had many other quarrels with Descartes; in the fiercely critical *Enchiridion metaphysicum*, for example, he scornfully crowns Descartes prince of the 'nullibilists', a party of philosophers who endanger religion by asserting that spirit is nowhere (see DESCARTES, R. §8).

5   The spirit of nature and the nature of space

Changes in body that cannot be 'resolved into mere Mechanical powers' are, according to More, the work of the spirit of nature, the 'Vicarious power of God upon... matter' ([1659] 1925: 169; 1662: 13). It is an immaterial substance without sense or thought, pervading the 'whole matter' of the universe. It accounts for departures from the laws of mechanism but also, as a 'natural Transcript' of those laws (1662: xvi), for matter's submission to them. Among the phenomena that argue powerfully for the spirit of nature are sympathetic pains, assuagements and cures. But even the falling of a stone or bullet is a sign of its influence because, given only the laws of mechanism, a stone or bullet should recede from the earth instead of falling towards it.

In the *Enchiridion metaphysicum* More presented some of Robert Boyle's hydrostatic experiments as evidence of the spirit of nature. Boyle, in his *Hydrostatical discourse* (1672), defended a mechanistic interpretation of his results. There Boyle stopped with the claim that More's 'hylarchical' principle is unnecessary, but in his *Inquiry into the vulgarly received notion of nature* (1686) he made broader criticisms (without naming More). Some of Boyle's points were elaborated by Robert Hooke (1677), who asked, in effect, by what laws More's spirit operates, since it is surely true, even on More's view, that it does not simply do what it pleases (see BOYLE, R.).

More's primary argument in defence of immaterial substance in the *Enchiridion metaphysicum* was simply that there is an infinite, substantial space or 'immobile extension' really distinct from matter. He proceeded to assign to it many of the names or attributes traditionally reserved for God: infinite, incomprehensible, uncreated, absolutely independent. Infinite space is, he concluded, a 'rough representation of the divine essence'. Other remarks strongly suggest that it *is* God, or at least an aspect of God. More did caution that the attributes on his list pertain not to God's 'life and operation' but only to God's presence. He promised to take up the connection between the divine life and the divine presence in a sequel to the *Enchiridion* (which was published as 'Part One'), but a second part never appeared. The influence of More's divinized space on the absolute space of Newton is still a matter of debate.

6   Religion

The main theme of More's writing on religion, aimed against atheists on one side and 'enthusiasts' on the other, was the 'Reasonableness' of Christianity. *Enthusiasmus triumphatus* (1656) was a satire on the vice of enthusiasm, which More defined as the 'misconceit of being inspired', or 'moved in an extraordinary manner by the power or spirit of God to act, speak, or think what is holy, just, and true' (1656: 2). Enthusiasm is caused, More argued, by an imagination overpowered by melancholy; its remedy consists in temperance, humility and reason.

The *Mystery of godliness* (1660) was More's major work in defence of the Christian religion. 'A *Mystery*', he explains in the Preface, 'is a piece of Divine knowledge *measurably Abstruse*, whereby it becomes *more Venerable*, but yet *Intelligible* that it may be *Communicable*, and *True* and *Certain* that it may win *firm Assent*, and lastly *very Useful* and *Effectual* for the *perfecting* of the Souls of men, and restoring them to that *Happiness* which they anciently had faln from' (1660: 2). His aim is to represent the fundamentals of Christianity – the faith, plainly propounded in scripture, which is all that is required for salvation. He therefore says little about forms of worship and nothing about church government, but he ends the book with a plea for liberty of conscience. Toleration should be extended to all who believe in God and in punishment and reward in a life to come, provided their beliefs do not call for violations of moral law or disloyalty to their rightful rulers.

See also: CAMBRIDGE PLATONISM

List of Works

More, H. (1925) *Philosophical writings of Henry More*, ed. F. Mackinnon, The Wellesley Semi-Centennial Series, New York: Oxford University Press; repr. New York: AMS Press, 1969. (Remains the best anthology of More's philosophical writings. Selections from the *Antidote* and the *Immortality*, together with the final chapters of the *Enchiridion Metaphysicum* as they appeared in the *Saducismus Triumphatus*. Mackinnon's 'Outline Summary of More's Philosophical Theory' on pages 159–71 will be especially useful to anyone reading More for the first time.)

—— (1642) *Psychodia platonica; or, a platonicall song of the soul, consisting of foure severall poems; viz., Psychozoia, Psychathanasia, Antipsychopannychia, Antimonopsychia*, Cambridge: R. Daniel. (Verse-arguments for the soul's immortality and pre-existence, its consciousness after death, and its distinctness from other souls.)

—— (1646) *Democritus platonissans; or, an essay upon the infinity of worlds out of Platonick principles*, Cambridge; repr. Los Angeles, CA: William Andrews Clark Memory Library, University of California, 1968. (Philosophical poem defending the infinity of worlds.)

—— (1653a) *An antidote against atheisme, or an appeal to the natural faculties of the mind of man, whether there be not a God*, London; 2nd edn, with appendix, London, 1655, repr. Bristol: Thoemmes Press, 1997. (Arguments, a priori and empirical, for '*a Being absolutely Perfect*'.)

—— (1653b) *Conjectura cabbalistica*, London; repr. Bristol: Thoemmes Press, 1997. (An attempt to lay bare the hidden meanings – scientific, metaphysical, and moral – in the first three chapters of *Genesis*.)

—— (1656) *Enthusiasmus triumphatus: or, a discourse of the nature, causes, kinds, and cure, of enthusiasme; written by Philophilus Parresiastes*, London and Cambridge; repr. Los Angeles, CA: Clark Memorial Library, University of California, 1996; repr. Bristol: Thoemmes Press, 1997. (The cause and cure of enthusiasm, or 'misconceit of being *inspired*', in religion and philosophy.)

—— (1659) *The immortality of the soul, so farre forth as it is demonstrable from the knowledge of nature and the light of reason*, London and Cambridge; repr. Bristol: Thoemmes Press, 1997; modern edn, ed. A. Jacob, *Henry More. The immortality of the soul*, Dordrecht: Martinus Nijhoff, 1987. (Defends the possibility of spirit and the existence and immortality of an immaterial human soul.)

—— (1660) *An explanation of the grand mystery of godliness; or, a true and faithful representation of the everlasting gospel of our Lord and Saviour Jesus Christ*, London and Cambridge; repr. Bristol: Thoemmes Press, 1997. (More's main defence of the Christian religion.)

—— (1662) *A collection of several philosophical writings of Dr. Henry More*, London and Cambridge; repr. New York: Garland, 1978. (Contains the *Antidote* and its *Appendix*, *Enthusiasmus triumphatus*, the *Immortality* (with some additions), More's correspondence with Descartes (introduced by an exchange of letters between More and Claude Clerselier), and the *Epistola ad V.C.*, an appraisal of Cartesianism written around 1658 and first published here.)

—— (1664) *A modest enquiry into the mystery of iniquity, the first part, containing a careful and impartial delineation of the true idea of antichristianism*, London and Cambridge. (An attack on the idolatry of Catholics.)

—— (1667) *Enchiridion ethicum* (Handbook of ethics), London and Cambridge; trans. as *An account of virtue: or, Dr. Henry More's abridgement of morals, put into English*, London, 1690: repr. New York: The Facsimile Text Society, 1930; repr. Bristol: Thoemmes Press, 1997. (More's only book devoted to ethics. He defines virtue as an intellectual power by which the soul overrules '*Right Reason*', an innate copy of an eternal and immutable morality. The soul is also equipped with a '*Boniform Faculty*', enabling it to 'relish' what is best.)

—— (1668) *Divine dialogues.... Collected and compiled by the care and industry of Franciscus Palaeopolitanus*, London, 2 vols. (Volume 1 contains More's most accessible presentation of his proofs of God's existence. Volume 2, which is more theological, contains *A brief discourse of the true grounds of the certainty of faith in points of religion*, where the certainty of faith is said to presuppose certainty of sense and certainty of reason.)

—— (1671) *Enchiridion metaphysicum;.... Pars prima: de existentia & natura rerum incorporearum in genere* (Handbook of metaphysics;.... Part one: concerning the existence and nature of incorporeal things in general), London and Cambridge; repr. Bristol: Thoemmes Press, 1997; modern translation, ed. A. Jacob, *Henry More's Manual of Metaphysics. A Translation of the Enchiridium Metaphysicum with an introduction and notes*, Hildesheim: Georg Olms, 1995, 2 vols. (Latin summary of More's metaphysics.)

—— (1675–9) *Opera omnia* (Complete works), London, 3 vols; repr. vols 2 and 3, Hildesheim: Georg Olms, 1966. (Volume 1 is theological, volumes 2 and 3 philosophical. More's autobiography appears in the *Praefatio generalissima*, volume 2.)

—— (1930) *The Conway Letters: The Correspondence of Anne, Viscountess Conway, Henry More, and their Friends, 1642–1684*, ed. M.H. Nicolson, revised edn, ed. S. Hutton, Oxford: Clarendon Press, 1992. (Contains More's correspondence with Conway, with connecting commentary by Nicolson. Hutton adds several letters of philosophical importance, as well as an introduction that is, in part, a brief survey of recent work on More.)

References and further reading

* Boyle, R. (1772) *The Works of the Honourable Robert Boyle*, London: J. & F. Rivington, 6 vols. (*An hydrostatical discourse, occasioned by the objections of the learned Dr. Henry More* appears in volume 3, pages 596–628. *A free inquiry into the vulgarly received notion of nature* appears in volume 5, pages 158–254, where the spirit of nature seems to be under attack on, for example, page 191.)

Burtt, E.A. (1954) *The Metaphysical Foundations of Modern Physical Science*, Garden City, NY: Doubleday. (Chapter 5 contains a highly readable account of More's views on the extension of spirit, the spirit of nature, and absolute space. More's influence on Newton is discussed in chapter 7.)

Colie, R. (1957) *Light and Enlightenment*, Cambridge: Cambridge University Press. (More's relation to Spinoza and Spinozism is discussed in chapters 5 and 6.)

Copenhaver, B.P. (1980) 'Jewish Theologies of Space in the Scientific Revolution: Henry More, Joseph Raphson, Isaac Newton and their Predecessors', *Annals of Science* 37: 489–548. (A richly documented account of More's sources and his influence.)

Coudert, A. (1975) 'A Cambridge Platonist's Cabalist Nightmare', *Journal of the History of Ideas* 36: 633–52. (On More and Conway, their friend Francis Mercury van Helmont, and the cabala. More's eventual disenchantment with cabalism is discussed on pages 645–52.)

Descartes, R. (1991) *The Philosophical Writings of Descartes*, vol. 3, ed. J. Cottingham, R. Stoothoff, D. Murdoch and A. Kenny, Cambridge: Cambridge University Press. (Contains English translations from Descartes' letters to More.)

* Glanvill, J. (1681) *Saducismus triumphatus: or, full and plain evidence concerning witches and apparitions*, 2nd edn. (Contains several contributions by More, including the two final chapters of *Enchiridion metaphysicum*, translated into English.)

* Gabbey, A. (1982) '*Philosophia Cartesiana Triumphata: Henry More (1646–71)*', in T.M. Lennon, J.M. Nicholas and J.W. Davis (eds) *Problems of Cartesianism*, Kingston and Montreal, Que.: McGill-Queen's University Press, 171–250. (The leading account of More's engagement with Descartes.)

Greene, R.A. (1962) 'Henry More and Robert Boyle on the Spirit of Nature', *Journal of the History of Ideas* 23: 451–74. (Traces the rise and fall of the experimental defence of the spirit of nature.)

Hall, A.R. (1990) *Henry More: Magic, Religion and Experiment*, Oxford: Blackwell. (The most thorough study of More's relation to the science of his day.)

* Hooke, R. (1677) *Lampas: or, descriptions of the some mechanical improvements of lamps and waterpoises*, in R.T. Gunther (ed.) *Early Science in Oxford*, vol. 8, Oxford: R.T. Gunther, 1931. (Hooke criticizes More's *Enchiridion Metaphysicum* on pages 182–96.)

Hutton, S. (ed.) (1990) *Henry More: Tercentenary Studies*, Dordrecht: Kluwer. (The single most useful secondary source on More. Among the most valuable contributions are Crocker's 'Henry More: A Biographical Essay' and 'A Bibliography of Henry More', Gabbey's 'Henry More and the Limits of Mechanism', Henry's 'Henry More versus

Robert Boyle: The Spirit of Nature and the Nature of Providence', and Coudert's 'Henry More and Witchcraft'.)

Koyré, A. (1957) *From the Closed World to the Infinite Universe*, Baltimore, MD: Johns Hopkins University Press. (An especially influential study. More is discussed in chapters 5 and 6; his relation to Newton is touched on in chapters 7 and 8.)

Lichtenstein, A. (1962) *Henry More: The Rational Theology of a Cambridge Platonist*, Cambridge: Harvard University Press. (A study of tensions in More's theology.)

* Newton, I. (1664–5) *Certain Philosophical Questions: Newton's Trinity Notebook*, ed. J.E. McGuire and M. Tamny, Cambridge: Cambridge University Press, 1983. (Newton refers to More on pages 341 and 393.)

Norris, J. (1688) *The theory and regulation of love*, Oxford. (Includes *Letters philosophical and moral between the author and Dr. Henry More*.)

* Ward, R. (1710) *The life of the learned and pious Dr. Henry More*, London, 1710; modern edn ed. M.F. Howard, London: Theosophical Society, 1911; repr. Bristol: Thoemmes Press, 1997. (Includes long passages, translated from the original Latin into English, from More's account of his early life in the general preface to his *Opera Omnia*.)

KENNETH P. WINKLER

MOSCOW-TARTU SCHOOL

*The Moscow-Tartu School of semiotics (theory of signs) was formed when a diverse group of scholars joined informally from the 1950s to 1980s to provide alternatives to the regnant Soviet approaches to language, literature and culture. Their work develops the linguistics of Saussure, elaborated by Trubetzkoi and Hjelmslev, with its central notions of sign as union of signifier and signified, its distinction between language as system (*langue*) and language as utterance (*parole*), and its analysis in terms of the significant differences between paired equivalent elements in a system (that is, meaning is a matter not of individual elements, but of the relationship between comparable elements). In its early stages members of the Moscow-Tartu School did intricate analyses of lyric poetry and of highly conventional prose works (such as detective stories) using statistical and linguistic methods. They subsequently came to treat art works and other cultural artefacts as the products of 'secondary modelling systems', that is, as elements arranged according to rules that could be seen as language-like and hence accessible to analysis by the procedures of structuralist linguistics. The group shared an interest in Western and pre-Stalinist Russian literary theory – especially in the Russian formalists – and in contemporary linguistics, semiotics and cybernetics. In a time of pervasive intellectual stagnation this loose confederation sought to formulate objective and exact methods for literary scholarship, to republish works of Russian theory that had been repressed from the 1930s to 1950s, and to bring scholarship in the humanities into line with developments in other scholarly fields. During the 1970s prominent members of the group, such as Iu. M. Lotman and B.A. Uspenskii, turned from more theoretical and formalized work to historical studies of culture as a system of semiotic systems.*

1 History: the Soviet context and the rise of semiotics
2 Doctrine: general topics and the work of Uspenskii and Lotman

1 History: the Soviet context and the rise of semiotics

It is difficult to comprehend the extent to which the policies of the Stalin era hindered the unfolding of academic life. A vigilant censorship, the prescriptions of party congresses, and academic hierarchies established not by intellectual distinction but by survival skills, all combined to discourage critical thinking. Literary scholarship, which had rejected the formalists' attempts to examine literature as a process with its own dynamics and evolution (see RUSSIAN LITERARY FORMALISM), became particularly vulnerable to the demands of the political apparatus. By an irony of cultural history Soviet literary criticism had followed the pattern of innovation and mechanization outlined by the formalist theory of literary evolution: the innovatory and socially committed literary criticism of the nineteenth-century Russian intelligentsia, with its utilitarian view of literature and its understanding of art as a reflection of reality, had become institutionalized and stultifying, a barrier to re-examining the considerable role of literature in Russian society. Yet some disciplines, because of their remoteness, abstractness (linguistics) or technological promise (cybernetics, machine translation) were relatively exempt from the blatant ideologization of academic life. It was to these disciplines that a number of young linguists and 'philologists' (scholars trained in literature, historical linguistics and the history of ideas) turned for support in renewing the humanities. Their fascination with the 'exact methods' and 'objective scholarship' that these disciplines offered ultimately must be understood in the context of the impasse that scholarship had reached.

One of the group's most erudite members, the

linguist V.V. Ivanov, would in 1976 trace the rise of Soviet semiotics to the research and theories of Russian and foreign linguists and anthropologists. He specifically identified the psychologist Vygotskii, the cinematographer Eisenstein, the information theorists A.N. Kolmogorov and Claude Shannon (see INFORMATION THEORY), the phenomenologist G.G. SHPET, the philologist M.M. BAKHTIN and his colleague V.N. Voloshinov, for their work in reconstructing ancient cultures, in developing theories of the sign and in studying the structures and levels of art. The group's acquisition of these interests was achieved through conferences, informal gatherings and harsh debates between 'physicists' and 'lyricists' in scholarly and popular periodicals.

During the 1950s structuralist analysis slowly began to develop in the Soviet Union, enabled in part by Stalin's 1950 articles on linguistics, which in effect freed the discipline from Marxism's base—superstructure model, licensing the study of grammar and internal laws of language development. Two conferences brought the movement into focus and lent it its particular Soviet concern with cybernetics and information theory: a conference in Gorky (1961) 'On the Application of Mathematical Methods to the Study of the Languages of Artistic Literature' and a symposium in Moscow (1962) 'On the Structural Study of Sign Systems'. The first conference centred around the interest of Academician Kolmogorov in poetry's special potential for conveying information, but already the papers showed the group's wide range of interests and approaches: I.I. Revzin used Noam Chomsky's *Syntactic Structures* (1957) to speculate on the generative structures of literary texts, Ivanov surveyed the achievements of Western structuralism, and A.K. Zholkovskii constructed a genealogy from the works of the Russian Formalists and Sergei Eisenstein. He and Iu.K. Shcheglov would subsequently develop their own 'generative poetics', a pragmatic one which focused on the effects generated by the poetic text. The Moscow Symposium, organized by Ivanov, included many of the same participants, but had a more semiotic and less cybernetic focus. Danish semiotic theory ('glossematics') (see STRUCTURALISM IN LINGUISTICS §3) offered the promise of interaction between mathematics and semiotics and the possibility of joining the human sciences in a common and exact methodology. A group of papers on art as a semiotic system served as a beginning of the movement beyond verbal texts; papers on etiquette, games, and fortune-telling began the group's investigations of behaviour and popular culture.

The Tartu presence in the Moscow-Tartu School began with Iu.M. Lotman's 1963 essay 'On the Delimitation of the Concept of Structure in Linguistics and Literary Scholarship' and his Lektsii po struktural'noi poètike (Lectures on Structural Poetics), which appeared in the first issue of an important new series, *Trudy po znakovym sistemam* (Works on Sign Systems)(1964). As Uspenskii notes in his account of the School's beginnings, Tartu University brought a different scholarly culture to the movement: more oriented towards canonical literature and the history of ideas, less concerned with linguistics and with popular genres. Tartu University also brought the legacy (however constrained by Soviet reality) of having been the Russian Empire's most European university, with a tradition of academic autonomy that the other Russian universities had not always enjoyed.

The high point of the Moscow-Tartu School's activity was its five summer schools (1964–74), held at Kääriku in rural Estonia and in Tartu itself. Described by their participants as 'carnivalesque', 'utopian' and 'hermetically sealed', they centred around lively discussions rather than formal presentations, and their proceedings give brief lists of theses rather than lengthy formal papers. The summer schools brought together the Moscow semioticians and the philology faculty from Tartu, occasional guests (such as Jakobson in 1966), and a number of younger scholars who would continue to develop the school's themes and concepts after it ceased to exist.

The publications of the Moscow-Tartu School, *Trudy po znakovym sistemam* and other periodicals from Tartu, appeared in shoddy editions whose print runs could not come close to meeting the domestic and international demand for them. Their opponents in Soviet academic life published in much more widely circulated publications and levelled a consistent series of charges against the semioticians, as Peter Seyffert has noted: that semiotics was mere fashion, formalism couched in incomprehensible shibboleths; that its claim to universal applicability could not be sustained; and that 'mathematical methods' and 'exact science' were promises often unrealized and unrealizable. Certainly the School's focus on the sign and on language opposed the entrenched Russian view of art as 'thinking in images', and certainly its view of culture as a semiotic mechanism rather than a reflection of the means of production, challenged the dogma of Soviet Marxism.

For a variety of internal and external reasons, the Moscow-Tartu School had ceased to function by the mid-1970s. Growing government opposition to intellectual unorthodoxy met with opposition from the Tartu faculty, especially over the invasion of Czechoslovakia in 1968. A number of members of the School emigrated from the Soviet Union and made successful careers in the West. The growing interest of members of the School in questions of culture, which began with studies of typology and increasingly branched out into highly specific research with little attention to theory, led to methodological diffuseness. Nevertheless, the publications of the Moscow-Tartu School continued to appear in periodicals and, increasingly, in book form. By the 1990s Lotman was starring in a highly regarded television series on Russian culture. By another irony of cultural history the Moscow-Tartu School, condemned for neglecting traditional Russian views on literature and society, had become the principal interpreter of both, and of their interrelations for the new Russian Republic. After Lotman died in 1993, this canonization was completed by generous obituaries in the Russian press and by the republication of his semiotic studies.

2 Doctrine: general topics and the work of Uspenskii and Lotman

Because so many of the School's works were experimental and because their work was so far-ranging, it can be difficult to generalize about their activity. During the two decades of their most intense activity the School tried out many variants of semiotic analysis, moving from an early interest in mathematical modelling, cybernetics and information theory to work more akin to cultural history and cultural anthropology, two disciplines which were virtually non-existent in the Soviet Union. Nevertheless, a common feature was their use of linguistic models. This was also the case with American, Danish, French and Italian structuralism, but the use of linguistic models stands out even more sharply in the Soviet context because the regnant approach to literature focused on 'images', not 'signs', and on social determinism rather than on self-regulating sign systems. Against this background the Moscow-Tartu School could be seen as a movement, even though its members were drawing upon a number of different linguistic and semiotic theories: C.S. Peirce's theory of the sign, Saussure's understanding of semiotic systems, Danish glossematics, Trubetzkoi's phonemics, Jakobson's poetry of grammar and Chomsky's transformational grammar, to name the most important (see CHOMSKY, N. §1; PEIRCE, C.S. §8; SAUSSURE, F. DE §2; STRUCTURALISM IN LINGUISTICS §§2–3; SYNTAX §3). Yet members of the School tended not to pursue linguistic models as exhaustive sets of discovery procedures, as did Jakobson in his studies in the 'poetry of grammar': they moved from the mechanisms of meaning-production towards interpretation and beyond the study of closed systems towards contextual studies. As the group moved beyond language to other semiotic systems – 'secondary modelling systems', as Uspenskii termed them – the ties to linguistic theory could become tenuous. Nevertheless, even in these later essays one detects an enduring fascination with language, language use (pragmatics), and analytic operations learned from formal linguistics (such as analysis in terms of binary opposition). The problems that the group addressed tended to follow logically from this fundamental appeal to linguistic models: how does poetry convey information with its formal resources, how does poetry use the resources of language to model reality and the artist's worldview, how may other cultural spheres (including social behaviour) can be analysed using the model of linguistic analysis, what is the text that is available for semiotic analysis, how do different cultures in different historical periods use signs differently, what is the impact of such secondary modelling systems (such as literature, art, or the theatre) upon human cognition and behaviour? The logic of their methodology did not, however, lead them into exploring deeply such subjects as 'the death of the author' (who would become a 'guest of the text' for such French semioticians as Roland Barthes) or the theory of tropes. Unlike Western structuralists and post-structuralists, the Moscow-Tartu group tended to view the text as a unity, however multilayered and however rich its resources for generating interpretations. Language retained for them its ability to represent reality, complexities of coding notwithstanding, and the human subject was inevitably seen as the constitutor, or at least the user, of codes, more than constituted by them. In this the Moscow-Tartu semioticians, especially those who worked on such canonical figures as Pushkin and Gogol', contributed a semiotic version to the traditional Russian heroic portrayal of authors and to the traditional Russian veneration of high cultural texts.

Members of the School did innovatory work on many subjects: on various aspects of semiotic theory and on text theory, on mythology and the reconstruction of ancient symbol systems (Ivanov, V.N. Toporov, E.M. Meletinskii, D.M. Segal), on musical semiotics (B.M. Gasparov) and on lyric poetry (Zholkovskii, Revzin, Ivanov). Borrowing a favourite technique from the School's analytic procedures, description by analysis of pairs of equivalent elements in a system, one may treat the group's concerns by focusing on the work of two leading members, one from each centre: Iu.M. Lotman, by training as a literary scholar and intellectual historian (he had studied in Leningrad with surviving formalists) and B.A. Uspenskii, by training as a linguist and Slavic philologist (he had studied briefly in Denmark). Lotman's primary research area was Russian literature and culture of the 1780s to 1830s; Uspenskii's was the Russian language of the late medieval period and of the eighteenth century, although each ranged far afield in search of telling instances and challenging sign systems. By the late 1960s, however, each had moved towards the interests of the other, towards the investigations of ideology and point of view that marked Lotman's early work, towards studies of multiple linguistic codes that had interested Uspenskii, and some of their best work was collaborative.

Lotman's changing interests may be seen in four studies of Pushkin's novel in verse, *Evgenii Onegin*. The first (1960) analysed the construction of character in the novel; this piece is richly contextual, relating character development to contemporary trends in Russian thought, but treating the novel as an 'organic whole'. In 1966 he took a radically different approach in a paper on the artistic structure of *Evgenii Onegin*: here the operative concepts are modelling, a hierarchy of relationships, multiple points of view, system and anti-system, relationships, binary oppositions, and the inevitability of multiple interpretations given the text's multiplication of segments through the organization of its complex stanzas. Interpretation and the reader's role in the literary process become prominent, although they are governed by the internal relationships of the text. Lotman published a separate monograph on the novel in 1975. Here he achieves a synthesis of his work in intellectual history, his semiotic analysis of paired opposition, and his Bakhtin-inspired study of multiple points of view as embodied in multiple discourses. He continues to study relations between the literary text and what lies outside it and the text's potential impact on a reader. In 1980 Lotman's commentaries to the novel treated culture in an anthropological sense, as the rituals, customs and conventions of Pushkin's Russia. But analysis by binary opposition – gentry/folk, Russian/European – remains an operative principle.

Uspenskii's work follows a similar trajectory, moving from the analysis of point of view towards studies of Russian culture in a broad, anthropological sense. His *O semiotike ikony* (Semiotics of the Russian Icon) (1971) subjects the 'language' of icons to linguistic analysis (syntactic, semantic, pragmatic), paying particular attention to the 'internal perspective' of medieval icons, according to which painter and viewer establish their point of view within the painting, not outside it. *Poetika kompozitsii* (A Poetics of Composition) (1970) had treated point of view more generally, and, although terms are not always defined with desirable precision, the book suggests an innovatory alternative to plot-based narratology, namely, the analysis with respect to four levels of point of view (ideological, phraseological, spatial and temporal, psychological).

For Lotman, as for Uspenskii, the text is both a sign (in the secondary modelling system) and a sequence of signs in verbal language. Both continued to focus their attention on problems of communication and point of view. Lotman's *Struktura khudozhestvennogo teksta* (Structure of the Artistic Text) (1970) and *Analyz poeticheskogo teksta* (Analysis of the Poetic Text) (1972) share some of the same problems of definition and focus that appeared in Uspenskii's *A Poetics of Composition*. But Lotman, the literary scholar, pays more attention to linguistic analysis and to information theory (the latter generally used metaphorically) than the linguist Uspenskii. While problems of integration in moving from level to level and in moving from analysis to interpretation are not solved theoretically, these books offer many suggestive ideas and fragments of literary analysis. Lotman's treatment of 'event' in the first book as 'the shifting of a character across the borders of a semantic field', as a transgression, or as the violation of an expectation, has been widely influential in studies of narrative.

From these large synthetic works on artistic texts, Lotman and Uspenskii moved to speculative discussions on an even higher level of synthesis, the typology of culture. In their 1971 essay, 'On the Semiotic Mechanism of Culture', culture becomes a system of sign production marked off from non-culture, a system of constraints and prescriptions. Here they differentiate cultures by modes of sign production and, predictably, Lotman and Uspenskii identify two opposed types of culture: cultures oriented towards expression (which view themselves in terms of an aggregate of texts) and cultures oriented towards content (which see themselves as a system of rules). In a more specific and controversial essay, 'Binary Models in the Dynamics of Russian Culture' (1977), they treat Russian culture as marked by a binary opposition between the 'sacred' and 'profane', an opposition which dictates diametrically opposed modes of behaviour. The same terms, for instance new/old, can in different periods occupy different positions in this hierarchy. Lotman and Uspenskii oppose this binary structure to a European ternary one, in which a neutral middle sphere allows for new systems to develop gradually, not catastrophically.

Subsequent research by Lotman and Uspenskii in the concrete phenomena in Russian cultural history address topics of moral and political significance: lying, theatricality, obscenity, religious dissent, pretenders to the throne and the use of multiple languages. Lotman's penultimate book, *Kul'tura i vzryv* (Culture and Explosion) (1992), published just after the fall of the Soviet Union, returns to speculative semiotic-based historiography to re-examine the relationship of culture to what is outside it and to explore Russia's new possibility of entering the 'European ternary system', with its concomitant development by gradual change as opposed to change by violent overthrow. Lotman's last book, his *Besedy o russkoi kul'ture* (Conversations About Russian Culture) (1994), returns to the turn of the nineteenth century to give a thick description of the daily life and traditions of the Russian gentry – its rituals, fashions and social patterns and the meaning that these had for those who practised them. The principled theoretical argumentation of these books, and their rigorous wide-ranging research and openness to experiment, encompass the main achievement of the Moscow-Tartu School.

See also: SEMIOTICS; STRUCTURALISM IN LINGUISTICS

List of works

Baran, H. (ed.) (1976) *Semiotics and Structuralism: Readings from the Soviet Union*, White Plains: IASP. (Well-introduced selection of papers on culture, mythology and literature.)

Lotman, Iu.M. (1960) 'K èvoliutsii postroeniia kharakterov v romane "Evgenii Onegin"' (On the Evolution of the Construction of Characters in the Novel *Eugene Onegin*), in *Pushkin: Issledovaniia i materialy*, vol. 3, Moscow-Leningrad: Nauka, 131–73. (An excellent example of Lotman's early work in intellectual history.)

—— (1964) *Lektsii po struktural'noi poètike* (Lectures on Structural Poetics), in *Trudy po znakovym sistemam* (Works on Sign Systems), vol. 1, Tartu: Uchënye zapiski Tartuskogo Gos. Universiteta, No. 160. (Introduction to the structure of verse.)

—— (1966) 'Khudozhestvennaia struktura "Evgenii Onegin"' (The Artistic Structure of 'Eugene Onegin') in *Uchënye zapiski Tartuskogo Gos. Universiteta* 184: 5–32. (An important early example of Lotman's structuralist analysis.)

—— (1970) *Struktura khudozhestvennogo teksta*, Moscow; trans. G. Lenhoff and R. Vroon, *The Structure of the Artistic Text*, Ann Arbor, MI: Michigan Slavic Contributions, 1977. (The most complete discussion of structuralist poetics, together with topics relevant to prose, such as plot and character; difficult to read.)

—— (1972) *Analyz poeticheskogo teksta*, Leningrad; trans. D.B. Johnson, *Analysis of the Poetic Text*, Ann Arbor, MI: Ardis, 1976. (Further development of the theory of verse together with close analyses of a dozen lyric poems.)

—— (1973) *Semiotika kino i problemy kinoèstetiki*, trans. M.E. Suino, *Semiotics of Cinema*, Ann Arbor, MI: Michigan Slavic Contributions, 1976. (A brief, accessible outline of selected topics in a grammar of cinematography.)

—— (1975) *Roman v stikhakh Pushkina 'Evgenii Onegin'* (Pushkin's Novel in Verse 'Eugene Onegin'), Tartu. (An example of Lotman's structuralist analysis, more extensive and less technical than the 1966 article on *Eugene Onegin*.)

—— (1980) *Roman A.S. Pushkina 'Evgenii Onegin': Kommentarii* (A.S. Pushkin's Novel 'Eugene Onegin': Commentaries), Leningrad. (Semiotic analysis, tending towards cultural anthropology; very accessible.)

—— (1990) *Universe of the Mind: A Semiotic Theory of Culture*, trans. A. Shukman, Bloomington, IN: Indiana University Press. (A well-integrated collection of papers on text, rhetoric, space and culture.)

—— (1992) *Kul'tura i vzryv* (Culture and Explosion), Moscow: Gnosis. (A semiotic approach to culture and historical transformation.)

—— (1992–3) *Izbrannye stat'i* (Selected Articles), Tallinn: Aleksandra, 3 vols. (Prepared by Lotman himself, includes essays on semiotics, cultural history and literature.)

—— (1994) *Besedy o russkoi kul'ture: Byt i traditsii russkogo dvorianstva (XVIII-nachalo XIX veka)* (Conversations About Russian Culture: Everday life and traditions of the Russian gentry (18th to early 19th century)), St Petersburg: Iskusstvo. (Popular, easily accessible discussions of such topics as duels, cardplaying, balls and gender relations.)

Lucid, D.P. (1977) *Soviet Semiotics: An Anthology*, Baltimore, MD: Johns Hopkins University Press. (Papers on general concepts, modelling systems, communication, art and culture.)

Matejka, L. *et al.*, (eds) (1977) *Readings in Soviet Semiotics (Russian Texts)*, Ann Arbor, MI: Michigan Slavic Publications. (Excellent selection, especially of the School's early papers.)

Nakhimovsky, A.D. and A.S. (eds) (1985) *The Semiotics of Russian Cultural History: Essays by Iurii M. Lotman, Lidiia Ia. Ginzburg, Boris A. Uspenskii*, Ithaca, NY: Cornell University Press. (Well-chosen papers on cultural typology and history.)

Paperno, I. (1988) *Chernyshevsky and the Age of Realism: A Study in the Semiotics of Behavior*, Stanford, CA: Stanford University Press. (Highly accessible and intelligent development of the School's ideas on text, behaviour, modelling and culture.)

Shukman, A. (ed.) (1978) *Soviet Semiotics and Criticism: An Anthology*, special issue of *New Literary History* 9 (3). (Includes 'On the Semiotic Mechanism of Culture' and well-chosen studies in the semiotics of literature.)

—— (ed.) (1984) *The Semiotics of Russian Culture*, Ann Arbor, MI: Michigan Slavic Contributions. (Comprehensive set of papers on topics in cultural history.)

Tsiv'ian, T.V. (1987) *Issledovaniia po strukture teksta* (Studies in the Structure of the Text), Moscow: Nauka. (Important papers by V.V. Ivanov and others on the theory, linguistics and analysis of texts.)

Uspenskii, B.A. (1970) *Poetika kompozitsii*, Moscow; trans. V. Zavarin and S. Wittig, *A Poetics of Composition*, Berkeley, CA: University of California, 1973. (An original approach to artworks in terms of point of view.)

—— (1971) *O semiotike ikony* (The Semiotics of the Russian Icon), Tartu; ed. S. Rudy, Lisse: Peter de Ridder, 1976. (An important application of semiotics to a non-verbal art form.)

—— (1994a) *Izbrannye trudy* (Selected Works), Moscow: Gnosis, 2 vols. (Selected papers on semiotics and cultural history.)

—— (1994b) *Kratkii ocherk istorii russkogo literaturnogo iazyka (XI–XIX vv.)* (A Brief Outline of the History of the Russian Literary Language (eleventh–nineteenth centuries)), Moscow: Gnosis. (Important, controversial papers on diglossia and bilingualism.)

References and further reading

* Gasparov, B. (1985) 'Introduction', in A.D. and A.S. Nakhimovsky (eds) *The Semiotics of Russian Cultural History: Essays by Iurii M. Lotman, Lidiia Ia. Ginzburg, Boris A. Uspenskii*, Ithaca, NY: Cornell University Press. (An elegant, insightful account of the School's history and work on culture.)

* Ivanov, V.V. (1976) *Ocherki po istorii semiotiki v SSSR* (Outlines of the History of Semiotics in the USSR), Moscow: Nauka. (An important attempt to draw a genealogy for the School.)

* Koshelev, A.D. (1994) *Iu. M. Lotman i Tartusko-moskovskaia semioticheskaia shkola* (Iu.M. Lotman and the Tartu-Moscow School of Semiotics), Moscow: Gnosis. (Includes memoirs by members of the School, and a bibliography of Tartu works on semiotics, 1964–92.)

* Seyffert, P. (1985) *Soviet Literary Structuralism. Background. Debate. Issues*, Columbus, OH:

Slavica. (An invaluable, exhaustive discussion of the Soviet debates about semiotics up to 1971.)

* Shukman, A. (1977) *Literature and Semiotics: A Study of the Writings of Yu. M. Lotman*, Amsterdam: North Holland. (The most comprehensive and intelligent survey of Lotman's work, together with useful lists of papers from the Gorky conference, the 1962 symposium, and the first four summer schools.)

WILLIAM MILLS TODD III

MOSES BEN MAIMON
see MAIMONIDES, MOSES

MOSES BEN NAHMAN
see NAHMANIDES, MOSES

MOSES IBN EZRA *See* IBN EZRA, MOSES BEN JACOB

MOSES MAIMONIDES
see MAIMONIDES, MOSES

MOTIVATION, MORAL
see MORAL MOTIVATION

MOTOORI NORINAGA (1730–1801)

Motoori Norinaga was a pivotal figure in Japan's 'Native Studies' or 'National Learning' (kokugaku) movement. An accomplished philologist, he helped decipher the idiosyncratic eighth-century orthography of the Japanese chronicle of history and myth, the Kojiki (Records of Ancient Matters). This was part of his broader scholarly project of defining the nature of the ancient Japanese sensitivity or 'heart-and-mind' (kokoro). In so doing, he articulated an influential religious philosophy of Shintō and an axiology of traditional Japanese values, which he considered as primarily emotivist and aesthetic.

The eldest son in a merchant family, Motoori

relinquished his business interests to concentrate on scholarly pursuits. In order to support himself he also practised traditional, Chinese-based medicine. Motoori's driving passion, however, was the study of ancient Japanese culture. Although his times were dominated by a fascination with Chinese thought, Motoori gravitated towards the 'Native Studies' movement and its appreciation of, and romanticized return to, the values of pre-Sinified Japanese culture (see JAPANESE PHILOSOPHY §7). In this regard he felt himself to be the disciple of Kamo no Mabuchi (1697 1769), even though he had only once met the latter in person.

Motoori was also a devout follower of Shintō, believing his own birth to have been the answer to his parents' prayer to the gods. The early Native Studies scholars such as Kamo no Mabuchi had often specialized in the historical philology necessary for studying Japan's most ancient texts, primarily literary or poetic. Because of his religious interests, however, Motoori applied his philological expertise to interpreting the *Kojiki* (Records of Ancient Matters), a text written in an experimental, short-lived orthography that had been virtually unintelligible for a millennium. Motoori believed the *Kojiki* contained the actual accounts of creation. For four decades, therefore, he analysed the text line by line, translating it into language intelligible to the ordinary reader of his own day.

The connection between Motoori's religious and aesthetic theories lay in his understanding of *kokoro* and its relation to both language and reality (see KOKORO). Motoori argued that the ancient Japanese believed in the self-expressive character of things. In human beings, the *kokoro* is the responsive centre of both emotions and intellect. According to his interpretation of the classical Japanese world view, however, things and words also have *kokoro*. Having a 'genuine *kokoro*', the person is touched by the '*kokoro* of things', thus activating the spiritual and poetic 'power of words' (*kotodama*). If the audience lets themselves be touched by those words with a pure heart, they encounter the *kokoro* of the original expressive event. In short, language is ideally not simply a human product, but the outgrowth of a special resonance among the involved persons, things and words.

This view of ideal expression was intimately related to Motoori's reverence for the *Kojiki*. He believed the tradition that the *Kojiki* was a literal transcription of the ancient Japanese oral tradition, which itself supposedly went back to the original words spoken at the time of creation and arising out of the *kokoro* of that moment. Therefore, if his philological studies could recapture those words, Motoori believed he

could, in effect, ritually participate in the re-enactment of creation.

Of course, such a cosmogony necessarily privileged ancient Japan, its language, its gods and the role of its emperor as the intermediary between the gods and humanity. If those claims about origins seemed incredible, Motoori argued, that very incredible appearance only made their truth more likely. The more rationalistic accounts of China (or the West) were suspect precisely because they better met human standards of reasoning; generations of narrators could have corrupted the miraculous facts to make them more acceptable to human reason. Motoori argued that the sacred should inspire awe rather than rational appreciation. Because the *Kojiki* had been written in an orthography that had quickly become unintelligible to the ancients, its account preserved the irrational character of the miracle of creation (see CREATION AND CONSERVATION, RELIGIOUS DOCTRINE OF).

Although Motoori himself might not have been an ultranationalist, his account of Japan in world history lent itself to such a world view. Shortly after his death, the Native Studies movement took a more ethnocentric and nationalistic turn. In that way, Motoori's Shinto philosophy became intertwined with both national and international political agenda.

In his theory of poetics, Motoori focused on the role of aesthetic community, the culture that both articulates and serves as audience for literary expression (see AESTHETICS, JAPANESE). In this respect, he regarded the culture of the Heian court (794–1185) to be the zenith of aesthetic culture. According to Motoori, the genuine *kokoro* of the ancient period was best expressed when there were elaborate rules and a common aesthetic regimen governing the interaction of writer and audience. Such a context, he believed, could generate a heightened sensitivity, subtlety and elegance.

In conclusion, through his philological studies, his formulation of Shintō thought and his detailed theory of poetics, Motoori articulated many principles that continue to be influential in Japanese attempts at cultural or ethnic self-understanding.

See also: AESTHETICS, JAPANESE; JAPANESE PHILOSOPHY; KOKORO; SHINTŌ

List of works

Motoori Norinaga (1747–1801) *Motoori Norinaga zenshū* (Complete Works of Motoori Norinaga), ed. Ōkubo Tadashi and Susumu Ōno, Tokyo: Chikuma Shobō, 1968–93, 23 vols. (The standard edition of the original works.)
—— (1771) *Naobi no mitama* (The Way of the Gods),

trans. Nishimura Sey, 'The Way of the Gods: Motoori Norinaga's *Naobi no mitama*', *Monumenta Nipponica* 42, 1991: 21–41. (An essay section of Motoori's commentary on the *Kojiki*, outlining his understanding of the Shintō worldview.)

—— (1781) *Tamakushige* (The Jeweled Comb-Box), trans. J.S. Brownless, 'The Jeweled Comb-Box: Motoori Norinaga's *Tamakushige*', *Monumenta Nipponica* 43, 1988: 35–61. (Translation of Motoori's response to a neo-Confucian critique of Native Studies.)

—— (1798) *Uiyamabumi* (First Steps into the Mountains), trans. Nishimura Sey, 'First Steps into the Mountains: Motoori Norinaga's *Uiyamabumi*', *Monumenta Nipponica* 42, 1987: 449–93. (Translation of Motoori's classic essay about the methodology of Native Studies.)

References and further reading

Harootunian, H.D. (1988) *Things Seen and Unseen: Discourse and Ideology in Tokugawa Nativism*, Chicago, IL: University of Chicago Press. (Provocative Marxian critique of the Native Studies movement from the standpoint of political ideology.)

Maruyama Masao (1952) *Nihon seiji shisō shi kenkyū*, trans. Mikiso Hane, *Studies in the Intellectual History of Tokugawa Japan*, Tokyo: University of Tokyo Press, 1974. (A classic study of the relation between Tokugawa thought and politics with sections I: 4 and II: 5 especially addressing Motoori's thought.)

Matsumoto Shigeru (1970) *Motoori Norinaga 1730–1801*, Cambridge, MA: Harvard University Press. (Helpful intellectual biography examining the connections between Motoori's life and thought.)

Nosco, P. (1990) *Remembering Paradise: Nativism and Nostalgia in Eighteenth-Century Japan*, Harvard–Yenching Institute Monograph Series 31, Cambridge, MA: Harvard University Press. (Good study of the romantic qualities in the Native Studies scholars' treatment of literature and history.)

Yoshikawa Kōjirō (1975) *Jinsai Sorai Norinaga*, trans. Y. Kikuchi, *Jinsai Sorai Norinaga: Three Classical Philologists of Mid-Tokugawa Japan*, Tokyo: The Tōhō Gakkai (The Institute of Eastern Culture), 1983. (The essay on Motoori is an excellent overview of his thought with a special emphasis on his theory of language.)

THOMAS P. KASULIS

MOZI (5th century BC)

Mozi was the first philosopher to question the ideas of Confucius. Scholarly debate centres around the issue of whether Mozi was a 'weak' or a 'strong' utilitarian, an 'act' or 'rule utilitarian', and whether he was a 'language utilitarian' or rather placed the religious authority of a personalized Heaven at the centre of his system. He is noteworthy for being the first thinker to develop a tripartite methodology for verifying claims to knowledge and for attacking the Confucian emphasis on ritual and the centrality of the family as the basis for social and political action.

Little is known about the life of Mozi (otherwise known as Modi or Zi Mozi (the Master Mozi)) except what is recorded in later, apocryphal stories, and scholars are even unsure what his name 'Mo' means or designates. Although he is credited in the 'Treatise on Bibliography' in the *Hanshu* (History of the Former Han Dynasty) with being a member of the aristocratic elite of *daifu* rank in the state of Song, some argue that 'Mo', literally 'black ink', refers to the fact that he was a carpenter of low social status; others claim that he was at some time a convict and branded on the face.

Mozi elaborated ten theses in opposition to Confucian doctrine, now found in the book *Mozi*, which contains all that is left of writings from the Mohist tradition. These theses are 'elevating the worthy', 'conforming with superiors', 'universal love' (also interpreted as 'concern for everyone' and 'impartial love'), 'rejecting aggression', 'thrift in use', 'thrift in funerals', 'heaven's will' (or intent), 'elucidating ghosts', 'rejecting music' and 'rejecting destiny'.

Mozi gathered numerous disciples, founding a sect organized on military lines with a single designated leader who had the powers of life and death over his followers. The Mohists specialized in defensive warfare and hired themselves out as experts to rulers of cities under attack. Towards the end of the Warring States period the Mohists may have divided into three separate groups, each of which criticized the others as being heretical; yet all were deeply involved in defending their master's original vision from attack by contemporary philosophers, producing a second major stage of philosophical theorizing.

Severely damaged, Mohist writings were almost totally ignored throughout Chinese history until restored by the Qing scholar and official Bi Yuan (1730–97). Since then, the greatest effort has gone into rediscovering and interpreting later Mohist thought, with its forays into disciplines now identifiable as logic, ethics and science, especially geometry, optics, mechanics and economics. This later Mohist corpus, written in three stages – 'Expounding the Canons', the 'Canons' and 'Explanations', and 'Names and Objects' – developed a rigorously logical, rational and systematic discourse for determining the three sources and four kinds of knowledge, eliminating the grounding of the philosophy in the divine.

See also: CHINESE PHILOSOPHY; CONFUCIAN PHILOSOPHY, CHINESE; LOGIC IN CHINA; MOHIST PHILOSOPHY

List of works

Mozi (5th century BC) *Mozi*, ed. and trans. Mei Yi-Pao, *The Ethical and Political Works of Motse*, London: Arthur Probsthain, 1929; trans. A. Forke, *Me Ti: des Sozialethikers und seiner Schuler philosophische Werke* (Mo Di: Philosophical Works of Social and Ethical Thinkers and of the Mohist School), Berlin: Kommissionsverlag der Vereinigung Wissenschaftlicher Verleger, 1922; ed. and trans. B. Watson, *Mo Tzu: Basic Writings*, New York: Columbia University Press, 1963. (Forke is the first translation of the *Mozi* into a Western language, with a detailed introduction and explanatory and textual comments, that attempts, prematurely, to indentify an 'Ur-text'. Watson is a more up-to-date English translation.)

References and further reading

Graham, A.C. (1978) *Later Mohist Logic, Ethics and Science*, Hong Kong: The Chinese University Press, and London: School of Oriental and African Studies. (A highly technical reconstruction, translation and analysis of the later Mohist corpus, including a valuable analysis of the linguistic features of Mohist writings.)

—— (1985) *Divisions in Early Mohism Reflected in the Core Chapters of Mo-tzu*, Singapore: National University of Singapore, Institute of East Asian Philosophies. (A preliminary attempt to identify three different schools of Mohism on the basis of a technical linguistic analysis of the triads of chapters expounding the ten theses of the *Mozi*.)

Lowe, S. (1992) *Mo Tzu's Religious Blueprint for a Chinese Utopia: The Will and the Way*, Lampeter: The Edwin Mellen Press. (Analysis of the essay and dialogue sections of *Mozi* from a religious perspective that argues that Mohist religion is a coherent, practical system, based on the Will of Heaven, for transforming society and establishing an ideal state.)

Needham, J. and Yates, R.D.S. (1994) *Science and Civilisation in China*, vol. 5, *Chemistry and Chemical Technology*, Part VI, 'Military Technology: Missiles and Sieges', Cambridge: Cambridge University Press. (Extensive analysis and discussion of Mohist defensive tactics in historical and cross-cultural perspective.)

Sun Yirang (ed.) (1936) *Mozi xiangu* (Casual commentaries on *Mozi*), Shanghai: Shangwu yinshuguan. (The most detailed and valuable edition and commentaries on the *Mozi* by a Chinese scholar.)

Yates, R.D.S. (1980) 'The City under Siege: Technology and Organization as Seen in the Reconstructed Text of the Military Chapters of Mo Tzu', unpublished Ph.D. dissertation, Harvard University. (A technical reconstruction, with introduction, and translation of chapters 14–15 of the *Mozi* on defensive warfare.)

Yan Lingfeng (1975) *Wuqiubeijai Mozi jicheng* (Collected Editions of *Mozi* from the Studio that does not Seek for Completion), Taibei: Chengwen chubanshe, 46 vols. (Collection of the most important editions of and commentaries on the *Mozi* from pre-twentieth and twentieth century sources.)

ROBIN D.S. YATES

MUHAMMAD 'ABDUH
see 'ABDUH, MUHAMMAD

MUHAMMAD IQBAL *see* IQBAL, MUHAMMAD

MUJŌ

A Japanese word originating in Buddhism, mujō *means impermanence, transience or mutability. It characterizes all phenomena of experience, but is especially significant for human endeavours to achieve happiness. In the Buddhist analysis of existence, all things arise and perish through dependent origination; they are impermanent, without substance and continually subject to change. This presents human beings with an imperative existential problem, for they ignore or fail to realize the pervasiveness of impermanence. Endeavouring to secure lasting satisfaction, they cling to what is transient and mutable. The result is suffering, the unsatisfactory nature of ordinary – unenlightened – human existence.*

The problem of impermanence is fundamental to Buddhism from its inception, but interpretations of the concept varied with the evolution of other doctrines, most notably the Mahāyāna notion of emptiness. The indigenous Japanese sensitivity to the transience of life and nature interacted with Buddhism to articulate, often in aesthetic terms, not only the threats but also the contributions of impermanence to meaningful human existence. The most thorough examination of mujō is offered by the Zen Buddhist Dōgen, who in his exposition of the radical temporality of existence as being-time identifies the full realization of impermanence with Buddha-nature or enlightenment.

1 The problem of impermanence
2 Background developments in Buddhism
3 Japanese affirmation of impermanence
4 Dōgen

1 The problem of impermanence

Mujō is the Japanese word for the Buddhist concept of impermanence (the corresponding Sanskrit term is *anitya*). The traditional Buddhist statement of impermanence is 'all conditioned things are impermanent', meaning that they arise, pass away and are subject to change (see MOMENTARINESS, BUDDHIST DOCTRINE OF). *Mujō* may thus be translated as 'transience' or 'mutability'. The two Chinese characters making up the word literally mean 'without constancy', which further indicates the possible irregularity of change and implies a spatial sense of instability. *Mujō* can also mean evanescence; things may be so fleeting as to have only a tenuous, dreamlike existence.

Originally, the concept of impermanence was descriptive of all experienced phenomena. In the early Buddhist formulation of the fundamental doctrine of dependent origination (*pratītyasamupāda*), all things arise and cease dependent upon causes or conditions. All existence is thus impermanent and nonsubstantial. Importantly, a person has no permanent self but is only a stream of changing interdependent factors. These claims are made on the basis of a close inspection of experience, including meditative states.

The primary implication of impermanence – the problem it presents – is that ordinary ways of seeking satisfaction or meaning in human life are ultimately unsatisfactory and induce suffering (*duḥkha*). That is, human beings mistakenly formulate the concept of a permanent self and seek lasting and secure satisfaction through it and its attachment to things, all of which – self, satisfactions, attachments and things – are actually transient and mutable, hence undepend-

able. The continual pursuit of these dependent and undependable satisfactions is *saṃsāra*; in contrast, *nirvāna* is nondependent or unconditioned (see NIRVĀNA).

The cause of suffering, however, is not impermanence *per se* but ignorance of 'things as they are', for example in their conditional arising and impermanence, and the disposition to seek satisfaction through attachments or dependencies. Since the causes of suffering arise conditionally, they too are impermanent and removable. Their elimination, however, requires a thorough transformation of one's whole person. A key factor in this is the existential awareness of impermanence, for as it deepens so too does the realization of the futility of attachments and the motivation for release from them (see SUFFERING, BUDDHIST VIEWS OF ORIGINATION OF).

2 Background developments in Buddhism

To enhance awareness of impermanence, the scholastic Buddhism that evolved in the centuries following the Buddha's death (*circa* 483 BC) postulated a theory of moments as part of an analysis of things into their ultimate, atomistic constituents (*dharma*). The Sautrāntika, for example, dissolved the apparent temporal durations of ordinary experience into a succession of discrete, virtually durationless moments, resulting in such a discontinuous conception of change that it raised serious problems in accounting for dependent origination. The Sarvāstivāda theory, on the other hand, attempted to account for continuity by arguing – surprisingly for Buddhists – that all *dharmas* are unchanging real existents at all times and change is mere appearance. Other disputes arose over theories that tried to mitigate the problem of impermanence by introducing a permanent self, principle, or transcendent form of the Buddha. Since impermanence was associated with *saṃsāra*, *nirvāna* was often viewed as permanent.

Mahāyāna Buddhism sought to avoid such controversies by reformulating the nonsubstantiality originally implied by impermanence and dependent arising through the more spatially derived notion of emptiness (*śūnyatā*) (see BUDDHIST CONCEPT OF EMPTINESS). This occurred especially in the Perfection of Wisdom literature (*circa* 100 BC–AD 500) and the works of Nāgārjuna (*circa* AD 150–250). Emptiness means lack of any independent self-nature or defining essence. Everything exists only in relative interdependence, and linguistic distinctions cannot be assumed to designate independently real or substantially existing referents. This empties all ontological categories of any claims to ultimacy, and thus of anything to which one could form attachments.

The emptiness of all conceptual designations means that impermanence and permanence are relatively dependent and neither can be taken as describing the true nature of things. The *Heart Sutra* (*circa* AD 350), for example, states this in the language of nonduality as all *dharmas* marked with emptiness are equally not produced and not destroyed. The distinctions between past, present and future are likewise relatively dependent and not absolute. Dependent origination itself is consequently not conceived in temporal terms of arising and passing away but rather as relative interdependence, or emptiness. Nāgārjuna argues that arising, abiding and perishing are like an illusion or dream. While the language of impermanence may have practical usage at the conventional level, it is not descriptively true, as was posited in early Buddhism, of things as they are.

The lack of defining essence or self-nature in temporal concepts led to relational theories of time in China such as the Tiantai notion of 'three thousand worlds in one instant of thought' and the Huayan conception of 'ten ages'. The ten ages are the present, past and future to each of the three time periods of past, present and future, together with their inclusion in one instant. That is, each moment is interdependently related to a vast field of time, and all time originates interdependently with each moment. The interplay of relations within this temporal field, which seem modelled on spatial relationships, are elaborately explained to show how each time is what it is in relation to all other times, and yet is just itself right now. In Huayan terms, the times interpenetrate each other but do not obstruct each other (see BUDDHIST PHILOSOPHY, CHINESE).

The actual aim of such metaphysical theories is to return one to spontaneous and harmonious participation in the immediate dynamics of experience, free from delusory mediation, by substantializing concepts and dispositional striving. Impermanence is still conjoined with dissatisfaction and suffering if one holds to a linear conception of time as sequential arising and passing away, but this is only a partial understanding which is to be supplanted by a holistic, relational view of time in light of emptiness.

3 Japanese affirmation of impermanence

The Japanese have often viewed impermanence not only as a problem but also as a fundamental condition contributing to the realization of meaningful human existence. There is a long-standing tradition that emphasizes a deep emotional response to transience and often sees evanescence as heightening the appreciation of beauty.

Affective responses of sorrow or longing can affirm the value and meaningfulness of that which is lost or longed for and, through revealing the shared nature and fate of all things in their transience, allow identification with them. This affective affirmation is enhanced by focusing on the most poignantly beautiful aspects of natural change, typically on such things as autumn leaves, spring blossoms or morning dew, which are beautiful in and through their transience. Evanescence further accentuates this beauty through such qualities as temporal rarity, purity or dreamlike delicacy (see AESTHETICS, JAPANESE).

The aesthetic appreciation of transience stands in complex relation to the primary thrust of Buddhism, for while both see the affective response to impermanence as sorrow, the former treats emotion as revelatory of dimensions of value, whereas the latter views emotion as leading to attachment and enmeshment in delusion. This tension was creatively explored in classical and medieval literature where impermanence was a major theme, and where the modes of temporality could be investigated and expressed through literary form as well as content.

As Japanese responses to transience became more fully informed by Buddhist conceptions in the twelfth to sixteenth centuries, the view of change widened to include such grim aspects as social upheaval and natural catastrophe. An austere aesthetic of impermanence evolved that admired first the muted and then the cold, desolate beauty associated with the elemental reduction of things through attrition and loss. This aesthetic contributed to theoretical developments in Nō drama, the tea ceremony and linked poetry. The reduction of life to its most extreme conditions reveals the latent, regenerative power of nature and balances perishing and dissolution against arising and creativity. Neither side can exist without the other. In this delicate balance the inconstancy, incompleteness and nonsubstantiality associated with transience become conditions and means for creatively engaging and affirming an impermanent world. As affective responses shade more fully into the Buddhist view, they move from attachment to compassion.

4 Dōgen

The Japanese Zen master Dōgen gives impermanence special prominence by identifying *mujō* (impermanence) with Buddha-nature and offering a descriptive exposition of the radical temporality of existence in terms of being-time. In Dōgen's view, 'The expounding, practising and realizing (enlightening) of impermanence by the impermanent themselves all must be

593

impermanent'. That is, the problem of impermanence is resolved through deepening one's realization of impermanence, which occurs most fundamentally through the practice of Zen meditation.

The identification of impermanence with Buddha-nature means that there are not separate realms where one achieves enlightenment (the realization of Buddha-nature) by escaping or transcending impermanence. Furthermore, Buddha-nature is not to be construed as an essence or attribute which one has or acquires. Rather, it is the occurrence of things as they are, free from the imposition of delusory notions of fixed essences and attachments. As identified with impermanence, it is ongoing, continually occurring and being relinquished in each situation. Experientially, the event of Buddha-nature has an original wholeness and fullness which we reflectively objectify and divide through such distinctions as self and world, being and time, now and then.

Dōgen clarifies the temporality of *mujō* in terms of being-time, stating that 'time, just as it is, is being, and being is all time'. Time and being are inseparable; there is only temporal existence. This reaffirms the nonsubstantiality, or emptiness, of all things through their temporality. Things are better understood as events taking place as constituents of the interrelational temporal–spatial field of an occasion.

Dōgen offers two primary characterizations of the temporality of being-time: right now (*nikon*) and seriatim passage (*keireki*). The former is the immediate presence of events as they are within the temporal occasion, seen in discontinuity with the before and after of other times. It has a dimension of constancy as it is 'always' right now, but it is not like a point on a line or a container within which things occur. Such views, according to Dōgen, are inadequate to lived experience and contribute to the separation of time from being, and from oneself, which results in the problem of impermanence.

Each present occasion can also be viewed in its timefulness, that is, in its continuity with other times, their relations contributing to what it is as in the Huayan view. Seriatim passage indicates this continuity or interdependency with the extended field of other times. Dōgen depicts these interrelations as multidirectional, but unlike Huayan, he presents his views through descriptions of the temporality of experience rather than through metaphysical speculation.

Principally through renewed interest in Dōgen by twentieth-century Japanese philosophers, most notably of the Kyoto school (see KYOTO SCHOOL), the concept of *mujō* has begun to enter comparative discussions with Western views of temporality and time.

See also: BUDDHIST CONCEPT OF EMPTINESS; BUDDHIST PHILOSOPHY, CHINESE; BUDDHIST PHILOSOPHY, JAPANESE; DŌGEN; MOMENTARINESS, BUDDHIST DOCTRINE OF

References and further reading

Abe Masao (1971) 'Dōgen on Buddha Nature', repr. in Masao Abe, *Zen and Western Thought*, ed. W.R. LaFleur, Honolulu, HI: University of Hawaii Press, 1985, 25–68. (General introduction to Dōgen, with discussion of identification of impermanence and Buddha-nature.)

Conze, E. (1958) *Buddhist Wisdom Books*, repr. New York: Harper, 1962. (Includes translation and commentary on the *Heart Sutra*.)

Dōgen (1240) *Shōbōgenzō*, trans. N. Waddell, 'Being Time, Dōgen's *Shōbōgenzō Uji*', *The Eastern Buddhist* new series 12 (1) 1979: 114–29. (Reliable translation of a demanding text.)

—— (1241) 'Dōgen's *Shōbōgenzō Buddha-nature*', part 2 trans. N. Waddell and Masao Abe, *The Eastern Buddhist* new series 9 (1) 1976: 87–105. (Identifies impermanence and Buddha-nature. Japanese text of both fasciles available in *Dōgen* I, ed. T. Terada and Y. Mizuno, *Nihon shisō taikei* vol. 12, Tokyo: Iwananami Shoten, 1970.)

Fung Yu-lan (1953) *A History of Chinese Philosophy*, trans. D. Bodde, Princeton, NJ: Princeton University Press, vol. 2, 354–5, 370–4. (A standard history, giving the Huayan view of time.)

Inada, K. (1970) *Nāgārjuna: A Translation of his Mulamadhyamakakarika*, Tokyo: Hokuseido Press. (See especially chapters 7 and 19.)

Kalupahana, D.J. (1992) *A History of Buddhist Philosophy: Continuities and Discontinuities*, Honolulu, HI: University of Hawaii Press. (An introductory history; useful on early and scholastic Buddhist interpretations of impermanence.)

Karaki, J. (1965) *Mujō* (Impermanence), Tokyo: Chikuma Shobo. (A history of impermanence in Japanese thought and literature, with special attention to Dōgen. Part 1, section 6 on the aesthetics of impermanence is translated and adapted in 'Wafting Petals and Windblown Leaves: Impermanence in the Aesthetics of Shinkei, Sōgi and Bashō', trans. A. Birnbaum, *Chanoyu Quarterly* 37 (1980): 7–27.)

LaFleur, W.R. (1983) *The Karma of Words: Buddhism and the Literary Arts in Medieval Japan*, Berkeley, CA: University of California Press. (Includes treatment of impermanence by selected literary figures.)

Nishitani Kenji (1982) *Religion and Nothingness*, trans. J. Van Bragt, Berkeley, CA: University of California Press. (A Kyoto school philosopher who discusses impermanence together with time and emptiness.)

Stambaugh, J. (1990) *Impermanence is Buddha-nature: Dōgen's Understanding of Temporality*, Honolulu, HI: University of Hawaii Press. (Interprets and compares Dōgen with Western philosophers.)

MONTE S. HULL

MULLA SADRA (SADR AL-DIN MUHAMMAD AL-SHIRAZI) (1571/2–1640)

Sadr al-Din al-Shirazi (Mulla Sadra) is perhaps the single most important and influential philosopher in the Muslim world in the last four hundred years. The author of over forty works, he was the culminating figure of the major revival of philosophy in Iran in the sixteenth and seventeenth centuries. Devoting himself almost exclusively to metaphysics, he constructed a critical philosophy which brought together Peripatetic, Illuminationist and gnostic philosophy along with Shi'ite theology within the compass of what he termed a 'metaphilosophy', the source of which lay in the Islamic revelation and the mystical experience of reality as existence.

Mulla Sadra's metaphilosophy was based on existence as the sole constituent of reality, and rejected any role for quiddities or essences in the external world. Existence was for him at once a single unity and an internally articulated dynamic process, the unique source of both unity and diversity. From this fundamental starting point, Mulla Sadra was able to find original solutions to many of the logical, metaphysical and theological difficulties which he had inherited from his predecessors. His major philosophical work is the Asfar (The Four Journeys), *which runs to nine volumes in the present printed edition and is a complete presentation of his philosophical ideas.*

1 **The primacy of existence**
2 **The systematic ambiguity of existence**
3 **Substantial motion**
4 **Epistemology**
5 **Methodology**

1 The primacy of existence

Sadr al-Din Muhammad ibn Ibrahim ibn Yahya al-Qawami al-Shirazi, known variously as Mulla Sadra, Sadr al-Muta'allihin, or simply Akhund, was born in Shiraz in central Iran in AH 979–80/AD 1571–2. He

studied in Isfahan with, among others, MIR DAMAD and Shaykh Baha' al-Din al-'Amili, Shaykh-e Baha'i, before retiring for a number of years of spiritual solitude and discipline in the village of Kahak, near Qum. Here he completed the first part of his major work, the *Asfar* (The Four Journeys). He was then invited by Allah-wirdi Khan, the governor of Fars province, to return to Shiraz, where he taught for the remainder of his life. He died in Basra in AH 1050/AD 1640 while on his seventh pilgrimage on foot to Mecca.

Safavid Iran witnessed a noteworthy revival of philosophical learning, and Mulla Sadra was this revival's most important figure. The Peripatetic (*mashsha'i*) philosophy of IBN SINA had been elaborated and invigorated at the beginning of the Mongol period by Nasir al-Din AL TUSI, and there existed a number of important contributors to this school in the century before Mulla Sadra. Illuminationist (*ishraqi*) philosophy, originated by Shihab al-Din AL-SUHRAWARDI, had also been a major current (see ILLUMINATIONIST PHILOSOPHY). The speculative mysticism of the Sufism of IBN AL-'ARABI had also taken firm root in the period leading up to the tenth century AH (sixteenth century AD), while theology (*kalam*), particularly Shi'ite theology, had increasingly come to be expressed in philosophical terminology, a process which was initiated in large part by al-Tusi (see MYSTICAL PHILOSOPHY IN ISLAM; ISLAMIC THEOLOGY). Several philosophers had combined various strands from this philosophical heritage in their writings, but it was Mulla Sadra who achieved a true fusion of all four, forming what he called 'metaphilosophy' (*al-hikma al-muta'aliya*), a term he incorporated into the title of his magnum opus, *al-Hikma al-muta'aliya fi'l-asfar al-'aqliyya al-arba'a* (The Transcendent Wisdom Concerning the Four Intellectual Journeys), known simply as the *Asfar*.

Mulla Sadra made the primacy of existence (*asalat al-wujud*) the cornerstone of his philosophy. ARISTOTLE (§§11–12) had pointed out that existence was the most universal of predicates and therefore could not be included as one of the categories, and AL-FARABI added to this that it was possible to know an essence without first knowing whether it existed or not, existence thus being neither a constitutive element of an essence nor a necessary attribute, and that therefore it must be an accident. But it was IBN SINA who later became the source for the controversy as to how the accidentality of existence was to be conceived. He had held that in the existence–quiddity (*wujud–mahiyya*) or existence–essence relationship, existence was an accident of quiddity. IBN RUSHD had criticized this view as entailing a regress, for if the existence of a thing depended on the addition of an accident to it, then the same principle would have to apply to existence itself. This was merely an argument against the existence–quiddity dichotomy, but AL-SUHRAWARDI had added to this another argument, asserting that if existence were an attribute of quiddity, quiddity itself would have to exist before attracting this attribute in order to be thus qualified. From this, al-Suhrawardi deduced the more radical conclusion that existence is merely a mental concept with no corresponding reality, and that it is quiddity which constitutes reality.

It was this view, that of the primacy of quiddity (*asalat al-mahiyya*), which held sway in philosophical writing in Iran up to Mulla Sadra's time. Indeed, Mir Damad, Mulla Sadra's teacher, held this view. However, Mulla Sadra himself took the opposite view, that it is existence that constitutes reality and that it is quiddities which are the mental constructs. By taking the position of the primacy of existence, Mulla Sadra was able to answer the objections of Ibn Rushd and the Illuminationists by pointing out that existence is accidental to quiddity in the mind in so far as it is not a part of its essence. When it is a case of attributing existentiality to existence, however, what is being discussed is an essential attribute; and so at this point the regress stopped, for the source of an essential attribute is the essence itself.

2   The systematic ambiguity of existence

A concomitant of Mulla Sadra's theory that reality and existence are identical is that existence is one but graded in intensity; to this he gave the name *tashkik al-wujud*, which has been usefully translated as the 'systematic ambiguity' of existence. AL-SUHRAWARDI, in contrast to the peripatetics, had asserted that quiddities were capable of a range of intensities; for example, when a colour, such as blue, intensifies it is not a new species of 'blueness' which replaces the old one, but is rather the same 'blue' intensified. Mulla Sadra adopted this theory but replaced quiddity with existence, which was for him the only reality. This enabled him to say that it is the same existence which occurs in all things, but that existential instances differ in terms of 'priority and posteriority, perfection and imperfection, strength and weakness' (making reality similar to al-Suhrawardi's Light). He was thus able to explain that it was existence and existence alone which had the property of combining 'unity in multiplicity, and multiplicity in unity'.

Reality is therefore pure existence, but an existence which manifests itself in different modes, and it is these modes which present themselves in the mind as quiddities. Even the term 'in the mind', however, is merely an expression denoting a particular mode of

being, that of mental existence (*al-wujud al-dhihni*), albeit an extremely attenuated mode. Everything is thus comprehended by existence, even 'nothingness', which must on being conceived assume the most meagre portion of existence in order to become a mental existent. When reality (or rather a mode of existence) presents itself to the mind, the mind abstracts a quiddity from it – being unable, except in exceptional circumstances, to grasp existence intuitively – and in the mind the quiddity becomes, as it were, the reality and existence the accident. However, this 'existence' which the mind predicates of the quiddity is itself merely a notion or concept, one of the secondary intelligibles. It is this which is the most universal and most self-evident concept to which the Aristotelians referred, and which al-Suhrawardi regarded as univocal. But in reality there are not two 'things', existence and quiddity, only existence – not the concept, but the reality – and so 'existence' cannot be regarded as a real attribute of quiddity; for if this were possible quiddity would have to be regarded as already existent, as al-Suhrawardi had objected.

3   Substantial motion

Another of the key properties of existence for Mulla Sadra is its transubstantiality, effected through what he termed motion in substance (*al-haraka fi'l-jawhar*) or substantial motion (*al-haraka al-jawhariyya*). The peripatetics had held that substance only changes suddenly, from one substance to another or from one instant to another, in generation and corruption (and therefore only in the sublunar world), and that gradual motion is confined to the accidents (quantity, quality, place). They also held that the continuity of movement is something only in the mind, which strings together a potentially infinite series of infinitesimal changes – rather in the fashion of a film – to produce the illusion of movement, although time as an extension is a true part of our experience. What gives rise to movement is an unchanging substrate, part of the essence of which is that it is at an indefinite point in space at some instant in time; in other words, movement is potential in it and is that through which it becomes actual. Mulla Sadra completely rejected this, on the grounds that the reality of this substance, its being, must itself be in motion, for the net result of the peripatetic view is merely a static conglomeration of spatio-temporal events. The movement from potentiality to actuality of a thing is in fact the abstract notion in the mind, while material being itself is in a constant state of flux perpetually undergoing substantial change. Moreover, this substantial change is a property not only of sublunary elemental beings (those composed of earth, water, air and fire) but of celestial beings as well. Mulla Sadra likened the difference between these two understandings of movement to the difference between the abstracted, derivative notion of existence and the existence which is reality itself.

Existence in Mulla Sadra's philosophical system, as has been seen, is characterized by systematic ambiguity (*tashkik*), being given its systematic character by substantial motion, which is always in one direction towards perfection. In other words, existence can be conceived of as a continual unfolding of existence, which is thus a single whole with a constantly evolving internal dynamic. What gives things their identities are the imagined essences which we abstract from the modes of existence, while the reality is ever-changing; it is only when crucial points are reached that we perceive this change and new essences are formed in our minds, although change has been continually going on. Time is the measure of this process of renewal, and is not an independent entity such that events take place within it, but rather is a dimension exactly like the three spatial dimensions: the physical world is a spatio-temporal continuum.

All of this permits Mulla Sadra to give an original solution to the problem which has continually pitted philosophers against theologians in Islam, that of the eternity of the world. In his system, the world is eternal as a continual process of the unfolding of existence, but since existence is in a constant state of flux due to its continuous substantial change, every new manifestation of existence in the world emerges in time. The world – that is, every spatio-temporal event from the highest heaven downwards – is thus temporally originated, although as a whole the world is also eternal in the sense that it has no beginning or end, since time is not something existing independently within which the world in turn exists (see ETERNITY).

4 Epistemology

Mulla Sadra's radical ontology also enabled him to offer original contributions to epistemology, combining aspects of Ibn Sina's theory of knowledge (in which the Active Intellect, while remaining utterly transcendent, actualizes the human mind by instilling it with intellectual forms in accordance with its state of preparation to receive these forms) with the theory of self-knowledge through knowledge by presence developed by al-Suhrawardi. Mulla Sadra's epistemology is based on the identity of the intellect and the intelligible, and on the identity of knowledge and existence. His theory of substantial motion, in which existence is a dynamic process constantly moving towards greater intensity and perfection, had allowed

him to explain that new forms, or modes, of existence do not replace prior forms but on the contrary subsume them. Knowledge, being identical with existence, replicates this process, and by acquiring successive intelligible forms – which are in reality modes of being and not essential forms, and are thus successive intensifications of existence – gradually moves the human intellect towards identity with the Active Intellect. The intellect thus becomes identified with the intelligibles which inform it.

Furthermore, for Mulla Sadra actual intelligibles are self-intelligent and self-intellected, since an actual intelligible cannot be deemed to have ceased to be intelligible once it is considered outside its relation to intellect. As the human intellect acquires more intelligibles, it gradually moves upwards in terms of the intensification and perfection of existence, losing its dependence on quiddities, until it becomes one with the Active Intellect and enters the realm of pure existence. Humans can, of course, normally only attain at best a partial identification with the Active Intellect as long as they remain with their physical bodies; only in the case of prophets can there be complete identification, allowing them to have direct access to knowledge for themselves without the need for instruction. Indeed, only very few human minds attain identification with the Active Intellect even after death.

5 Methodology

Even this brief account of Mulla Sadra's main doctrines will have given some idea of the role that is played in his philosophy by the experience of the reality which it describes. Indeed he conceived of *hikma* (wisdom) as 'coming to know the essence of beings as they really are' or as 'a man's becoming an intellectual world corresponding to the objective world'. Philosophy and mysticism, *hikma* and Sufism, are for him two aspects of the same thing. To engage in philosophy without experiencing the truth of its content confines the philosopher to a world of essences and concepts, while mystical experience without the intellectual discipline of philosophy can lead only to an ineffable state of ecstasy. When the two go hand in hand, the mystical experience of reality becomes the intellectual content of philosophy.

The four journeys, the major sections into which the *Asfar* is divided, parallel a fourfold division of the Sufi journey. The first, the journey of creation or the creature (*khalq*) to the Truth (*al-haqq*), is the most philosophical; here Mulla Sadra lays out the basis of his ontology, and mirrors the stage in the Sufi's path where he seeks to control his lower *nafs* under the supervision of his *shaykh*. In the second journey, in the Truth with the Truth, the stage at which the Sufi begins to attract the divine manifestations, Mulla Sadra deals with the simple substances, the intelligences, the souls and their bodies, including therefore his discussion of the natural sciences. In the third journey, from the Truth to creation with the Truth, the Sufi experiences annihilation in the Godhead, and Mulla Sadra deals with theodicy; the fourth stage, the journey with the Truth in creation, where he gives a full and systematic account of the development of the human soul, its origin, becoming and end, is where the Sufi experiences persistence in annihilation, absorbed in the beauty of oneness and the manifestations of multiplicity.

Mulla Sadra had described his blinding spiritual realization of the primacy of existence as a kind of 'conversion':

> In the earlier days I used to be a passionate defender of the thesis that the quiddities are the primary constituents of reality and existence is conceptual, until my Lord gave me spiritual guidance and let me see His demonstration. All of a sudden my spiritual eyes were opened and I saw with utmost clarity that the truth was just the contrary of what the philosophers in general had held.... As a result [I now hold that] the existences (*wujudat*) are primary realities, while the quiddities are the 'permanent archetypes' (*a'yan thabita*) that have never smelt the fragrance of existence.
>
> (*Asfar*, vol. 1, introduction)

Therefore it is not surprising that Mulla Sadra is greatly indebted to Ibn al-'Arabi in many aspects of his philosophy. Ibn Sina provides the ground on which his metaphilosophy is constructed and is, as it were, the lens through which he views Peripatetic philosophy. However, his work is also full of citations from the Presocratics (particularly PYTHAGORAS), PLATO, ARISTOTLE, the Neoplatonists (see NEO-PLATONISM IN ISLAMIC PHILOSOPHY) and the Stoics (taken naturally from Arabic sources), and he also refers to the works of AL-FARABI, and Abu'l Hasan AL-'AMIRI, who had prefigured Mulla Sadra's theory of the unity of intellect and intelligible. This philosophical heritage is then given shape through the illuminationism of AL-SUHRAWARDI, whose universe of static grades of light he transformed into a dynamic unity by substituting the primacy of existence for the latter's primacy of quiddity. It is in this shaping that the influence of Ibn al-'Arabi, whom Mulla Sadra quotes and comments on in hundreds of instances, can be most keenly felt. Not only is that apparent in Mulla Sadra's total dismissal of any role for quiddity in the nature of reality, but in the

importance which both he and Ibn al-'Arabi gave to the imaginal world (*'alam al-mithal, 'alam al-khayal*).

In Ibn Sina's psychology, the imaginal faculty (*al-quwwa al-khayaliyya*) is the site for the manipulation of images abstracted from material objects and retained in the *sensus communis*. The imaginal world had first been formally proposed by al-Suhrawardi as an intermediate realm between that of material bodies and that of intellectual entities, which is independent of matter and thus survives the body after death. Ibn al-'Arabi had emphasized the creative aspects of this power to originate by mere volition imaginal forms which are every bit as real as, if not more real than, perceptibles but which subsist in no place. For Mulla Sadra, this world is a level of immaterial existence with which it is possible for the human soul (and indeed certain higher forms of the animal soul) to be in contact, although not all the images formed by the human soul are necessarily veridical and therefore part of the imaginal world. For Mulla Sadra, as also for Ibn al-'Arabi, the imaginal world is the key to understanding the nature of bodily resurrection and the afterlife, which exists as an immaterial world which is nevertheless real (perhaps one might say more real than the physical world), in which the body survives as an imaginal form after death.

Philosophy has always had a tense relationship with theology in Islam, especially with the latter's discourse of faith (*iman*) and orthodoxy. In consequence, philosophy has often been seen, usually by non-philosophers, as a school with its own doctrines. This is despite the assertions of philosophers themselves that what they were engaged in was a practice without end (for, as Ibn Sina had declared that what is known to humankind is limited and could only possibly be fulfilled when the association of the soul with the body is severed through death), part of the discipline of which consisted in avoiding *taqlid*, an uncritical adherence to sects (see ISLAM, CONCEPT OF PHILOSOPHY IN). It is the notable feature of Mulla Sadra's methodology that he constantly sought to transcend the particularities of any system – Platonic, Aristotelian, Neoplatonic, mystical or theological – by striving to create through his metaphilosophy an instrument with which the soundness of all philosophical arguments might be tested. It is a measure of his success that he has remained to the present day the most influential of the 'modern' philosophers in the Islamic world.

See also: EXISTENCE; IBN AL-'ARABI; IBN SINA; ILLUMINATIONIST PHILOSOPHY; ISLAMIC PHILOSOPHY, MODERN; METAPHYSICS; MIR DAMAD; AL-SABZAWARI

List of works

Mulla Sadra [Sadr al-Din al-Shirazi] (c.1628) *al-Hikma al-muta'aliya fi-'l-asfar al-'aqliyya al-arba'a* (The Transcendent Wisdom Concerning the Four Intellectual Journeys), ed. R. Lutfi *et al.*, Tehran and Qum: Shirkat Dar al-Ma'arif al-Islamiyyah, 1958–69?, 9 vols; vol. 1, 2nd printing, with introduction by M.R. al-Muzaffar, Qum: Shirkat Dar al-Ma'arif al-Islamiyyah, 1967. (This is Mulla Sadra's major work, often known simply as *Asfar* (The Four Journeys). The full edition includes partial glosses by 'Ali al-Nuri, Hadi al-Sabzawari, 'Ali al-Mudarras al-Zanuzi, Isma'il al-Khwaju'i al-Isfahani, Muhammad al-Zanjani and Muhammad Husayn al-Tabataba'i.)

—— (c.1628) *Kitab al-masha'ir* (The Book of Metaphysical Penetrations), ed., trans. and intro. by H. Corbin, *Le livre des pénétrations métaphysiques*, Paris: Départment d'Iranologie de l'Institut Franco-Iranien de Recherche, and Tehran: Librairie d'Amerique et d'Orient Adrien-Maisonneuve, Bibliothèque Iranienne vol. 10, 1964; French portion re-edited Lagrasse: Verdier, 1988; ed. and trans. P. Morewedge, *The Metaphysics of Mulla Sadra*, New York: Society for the Study of Islamic Philosophy and Science, 1992. (Corbin is a synopsis of Mulla Sadra's ontology, with a useful bibliography of Mulla Sadra's writings and introduction by Corbin. Morewedge provides a parallel Arabic English edition; the translation is based on Corbin's edition of the text.)

—— (c.1628) *al-Hikma al-'arshiyya* (The Wisdom of the Throne), ed. with Persian paraphrase by G.R. Ahani, Isfahan, 1962; trans. and intro. J.W. Morris, *The Wisdom of the Throne: An Introduction to the Philosophy of Mulla Sadra*, Princeton, NJ: Princeton University Press, 1982. (A useful summary of Mulla Sadra's views on theology and eschatology; the introduction to the English translation provides an informative general introduction to Mulla Sadra work.)

References and further reading

Izutsu Toshihiko (1971) *The Concept and Reality of Existence*, Studies in the Humanities and Social Relations 13, Tokyo: Keio Institute of Cultural and Linguistic Studies. (Although concerned primarily with the philosophical ideas of Mulla Sadra's principal nineteenth century follower, Mulla Hadi al-Sabzawari, this work contains an extremely valuable exposition of the history of the existence–essence controversy in metaphysics, and deals with Mulla Sadra's views in many places.)

Nasr, S.H. (1978) *Sadr al-Din Shirazi and His Transcendent Theosophy: Background, Life and Works*, Tehran: Imperial Academy of Philosophy. (The first part of a planned, but so far uncompleted, two-volume work, the second volume of which is intended to deal with Mulla Sadra's philosophical ideas; contains the best bibliography of Mulla Sadra's works.)

—— (1996) 'Mulla Sadra: His Teachings', in S.H. Nasr and O. Leaman (eds) *History of Islamic Philosophy*, London: Routledge, 643–52. (Short summary of Mulla Sadra's thought.)

Rahman, F. (1975) *The Philosophy of Mulla Sadr (Sadr al-Din al-Shirazi)*, Albany, NY: State University of New York Press. (To date, the only full-scale study of Mulla Sadra's philosophy in English.)

Ziai, H. (1996) 'Mulla Sadra: His Life and Works', in S.H. Nasr and O. Leaman (eds) *History of Islamic Philosophy*, London: Routledge, 635–42. (Biographical essay discussing Mulla Sadra's influence and works.)

JOHN COOPER

MULTICULTURALISM

Multicultural political philosophy explores ways of accommodating cultural diversity fairly. Public policies often have different consequences for members of different cultural groups. For example, given the importance of language to culture, and the role of the modern state in so many aspects of life, the choice of official languages will affect different people very differently. Similar issues arise concerning the cultural content of education and the criminal law, and the choice of public holidays. To avoid policies that create unfair burdens, multicultural theory turns to abstract inquiries about such things as the relation between culture and individual welleing, or the relation between a person's culture and the appropriate standards for judging them. Multiculturalism raises related questions for democratic theory also. Culture may be important to deciding on appropriate units of democratic rule and to the design of special mechanisms for representing minorities within such units. Each of these questions is made more difficult in the context of cultures that reject the demands of liberty or equality. The challenge for philosophers is to develop a principled way of thinking about these issues.

1 Multiculturalism and political thought
2 Liberal theories of cultural membership
3 The politics of identity

1 Multiculturalism and political thought

Political philosophers from Plato to Mill largely managed to ignore the question of culture. The societies in which they wrote enabled them in large part to take it for granted that the appropriate unit about which to ask questions concerning justice or democracy was a society that shared a culture. As a result, problems of justice or democracy were seen as superimposed on a homogeneous community. Although Mill saw nation states as inevitable, he believed that members of smaller cultural groups would readily give up their inherited culture to join other, stronger nations.

Demographic and political changes throughout the twentieth century have made traditional assumptions about the relations between culture and politics largely irrelevant to public life. Almost all of the world's countries now have substantial minorities from more than one culture. As a result, the ideals of political philosophers, whether concerning democracy, justice or membership, must be redeemed in settings very different to those for which they were first proposed.

Different states are multicultural in different ways. Belgium, Switzerland and Canada are federations of different language groups. Australia, Canada and the USA have substantial aboriginal populations. And most developed countries have large but geographically dispersed immigrant populations. Geographical concentration makes federalism and secession viable options for dealing with cultural difference. In its absence, what is needed is some way of building a political culture that does not exclude those who are different.

2 Liberal theories of cultural membership

Theories of cultural rights divide on a number of questions. While not all cultures are individualistic, most prominent views about multiculturalism share a root commitment to the view that culture matters because of its role in individual people's lives. They differ, however, in their detailed accounts of how and why it matters. Three accounts are prominent. First, some have suggested that culture is largely incidental to political life. While this cosmopolitan view does not deny that people have strong cultural attachments, it supposes that the state has no business taking up any sort of stance in relation to them. Instead the state should treat culture in the way many states treat religion, as a private matter on which the state is officially neutral (see NEUTRALITY, POLITICAL). Ideally people will be able to help themselves to the resources and possibilities of all of the world's

cultures. Second, some have assigned each person's own culture an important role, either as an important aspect of identity or as a precondition of that person's ability to develop autonomously. On this view, the demands of justice are the same across cultures, but among those demands is the protection of the cultural conditions essential to individuality. Third, some have claimed that politics is an essential form of cultural expression, and that institutions should be designed to allow cultures to express themselves politically.

Cosmopolitanism is in many ways an attractive ideal, but there is some reason to doubt that it provides a realistic model for organizing political life. Most of the world's people have neither the resources nor the opportunities to move readily between cultures. Perhaps as important, few have any real inclination to do so. In the light of these circumstances and the central role of the modern state in coordinating economic and other activities, states have no real alternative to adopting policies with significant cultural consequences. Official languages must be chosen and the legal framework within which people go about their affairs defined. Any response to these issues will make it easier for some cultural groups and more difficult for others. While advocates of cosmopolitanism might doubt the long-term significance of such effects, important questions of fairness arise concerning the effects of any such choices.

Multicultural liberals make fairness the starting point for their accounts of cultural policies. They insist that accommodating cultural difference is fundamentally different from discredited policies of segregation that sought to exclude minorities. For example, Will Kymlicka (1995) argues that aboriginal peoples should be given extra resources and political protection in order to enable them to maintain their cultural context. Because that context provides the background against which they are able to become autonomous, the state has a special responsibility to make sure that it is secure. Otherwise they would be unfairly deprived of something others receive free. The only way to protect that interest is to allow them to exclude outsiders from their society. In the same way, boundaries between states should be drawn in such a way as to enable as many people as possible to find themselves with a secure culture (see NATION AND NATIONALISM) Within self-governing areas, immigrants may be chosen with an eye to the society's cultural stability. Others have made parallel arguments emphasizing the extent to which cultural identification provides a secure anchor in a changing world.

Still, any way of drawing boundaries will leave some people as members of dispersed minorities.

Kymlicka advocates integrative policies for such groups so that maintaining some of their traditional practices does not pose a barrier to successful participation in the larger society in which they find themselves. Examples of such policies include allowing religious groups special exemptions from common pause days (when most businesses tend to be closed) or providing heritage language classes for the children of immigrants. In the UK, some have advocated extending anti-blasphemy laws to non-Christian religions. On similar grounds, many liberals advocate an inclusive educational curriculum. Such policies are sometimes said to offer advantages for members of the dominant culture as well as for minorities. In the longer term, they may well lead to the disappearance of many aspects of the cultures they aim to protect. As a result, the ultimate consequence of multicultural liberalism may well be the development of a cosmopolitan culture, in which cultural difference has a status little different from that of religion. While such a loss of diversity may be regarded as unfortunate, multicultural liberals defend their policies in terms of the interests of the current generation, and so have no commitment to diversity as such.

For multicultural liberals, cultural rights are always understood as rights that individuals have to certain cultural conditions. They are not rights that cultures have over their members. Those who wish to reject their inherited culture are always entitled to do so, however difficult they may find it. As a result, multicultural liberals insist that illiberal cultural practices are outside the bounds of toleration. While there are sometimes pragmatic and humanitarian grounds for limiting the use of force to eradicate such practices, communities that coerce dissident members are not entitled to support in so doing. Thus, everything from arranged marriages to coerced participation in religious rituals is outside the range of special protection or even toleration, however important they may be to the survival of the cultural context. Rights of exit are important for the same reasons (see LIBERALISM §3; TOLERATION §2).

Differing conceptions of property rights also complicate liberal attempts to protect minority cultures. Many aboriginal cultures (and some religious groups) have traditionally held land in common. If members wish to leave to join the surrounding society, they cannot take their share of the land with them without endangering the material basis of the culture. In such cases, there may be no way of protecting culture without sacrificing individual liberty.

3 The politics of identity

Advocates of identity politics insist that various forms of membership are far more important than cosmopolitans or multicultural liberals suppose them to be. It is sometimes suggested that cultures, as such, are worthy of respect, and that, as such, they require some form of political expression. So put, such a position is attributed more often to opponents than advocated seriously. But something like it marks a fundamental divide in thought about multicultural politics. For liberals, politics should aim to be fair, and so must be fair in its treatment of cultural difference. For others, politics aims to be expressive, and the suggestion that political institutions could ever avoid being carriers of a particular culture is at best naïve.

Expressivist views of politics and culture lead to a variety of policy suggestions. Many of these aim at ensuring long-term cultural survival, while others are supposed to ensure special political representation for groups whose views have been neglected in the past. The differences between these and the policies advocated by multicultural liberals are sometimes unclear. However, the bases for the claims are very different. In particular, where multicultural liberals insist on treating cultural membership as voluntary and so protect rights of exit, advocates of identity politics sometimes suggest the state has a special responsibility to protect found identities, or at least to tolerate groups that seek to do so. In this they come close to the philosophical position of communitarians, and adapt their political views to accommodate the fact of diversity (see COMMUNITY AND COMMUNITARIANISM §10).

Identity politics derives some of its appeal from the fact that many of the groups in whose name it is put forward have been treated badly by liberal societies. Perhaps its most important shortcoming is its inability to articulate a philosophical basis that does not apply equally well to cultural practices that have in the past been oppressive, especially to women. This problem is particularly pronounced when it is allied to a commitment to cultural survival as a fundamental political goal. Many of the most important aspects of human self-definition, from religious dissent through choice of sexual orientation, are called into question by the idea that cultural groups have some sort of claim over their members.

Recent developments in world politics have led some to scepticism about the prospects for multicultural societies and to arguments that liberal societies can only survive in the context of a shared culture. Only with a shared culture, it is suggested, will people be able to live together in peace and harmony, and only with a shared culture will there be enough social solidarity to call forth the sacrifices necessary to sustain fair terms of social cooperation. At present, such pessimism seems premature. The psychology of sacrifice is at best very poorly understood. While goodwill and the absence of grudges are surely needed for peaceful coexistence, and familiarity doubtless facilitates cooperation, the relation of these to culture in any more robust sense is unclear. A shared culture bears no clear relation to the more everyday demands of justice. (Were the relationship direct, it is probable that culturally homogeneous countries would have achieved a higher level of justice.) Justice needs a model of citizenship and a civic culture. One possible form such a culture can take is a multicultural world in which people learn to appreciate difference and to respect each other. Such a civic culture is perhaps the best hope for a world made up of multicultural societies.

See also: CITIZENSHIP (§3); CULTURE

References and further reading

All of these works are written in nontechnical language, accessible to those with little or no background in political philosophy. Because of the explosion of interest in the topic, many new books and special issues of journals continue to appear.

Gutmann, A. (1993) 'The Challenge of Multiculturalism in Political Ethics', *Philosophy and Public Affairs* 22 (3): 171–206. (An examination of different proposals for dealing with culturally plural societies.)

Kukathas, C. (1992) 'Are There Any Cultural Rights?', *Political Theory* 20 (1): 105–39. (A critique of Kymlicka, advocating toleration of illiberal communities.)

* Kymlicka, W. (1995) *Multicultural Citizenship*, Oxford: Clarendon Press. (A defence of liberal approaches to cultural difference.)

Multiculturalism (1992), special issue of *University of Michigan Journal of Law Reform* 25 (3). (A wide variety of legal and philosophical perspectives on multiculturalism.)

Parekh, B. (1986) 'The Concept of Multicultural Education', in S. Mogdil, G. Verma, K. Mallick and C. Mogdil (eds) *Multicultural Education: The Interminable Debate*, London: Falmer Press, 19–32. (A defence of multicultural education for both minority and non-minority students.)

—— (1990) 'The Rushdie Affair', *Political Studies* 38 (4): 695–709. (A discussion of the political debates raised by the attempt to ban Salman Rushdie's *The Satanic Verses* as blasphemous.)

Rorty, A.O. (1992) 'The Hidden Politics of Cultural Identification', *Political Theory* 22 (1): 152–66. (An examination of the ambiguities in the notion of cultural membership.)

Taylor, C. (1994) *Multiculturalism: Examining the Politics of Recognition*, ed. A. Gutmann, Princeton, NJ: Princeton University Press. (A leading essay by Taylor offers cultural survival as a rationale for state policies towards culture. Responses to Taylor's essay, by Kwame Anthony Appiah, Jürgen Habermas, Stephen Rockefeller, Michael Walzer and Susan Wolf cover most of the theories and issues described in this article.)

Waldron, J. (1992) 'Minority Cultures and the Cosmopolitan Alternative', *University of Michigan Journal of Law Reform* 25 (3): 751–93. (A defence of the cosmopolitan approach described in §2.)

Young, I.M. (1990) *Justice and the Politics of Difference*, Princeton, NJ: Princeton University Press. (A defence of differentiated citizenship.)

ARTHUR RIPSTEIN

MULTIPLE-CONCLUSION LOGIC

Ordinary arguments can have any number of premises but only one conclusion. Multiple-conclusion logic also allows for any number of conclusions in an argument, regarding them as setting out the field of possibilities among which the truth must lie if the premises are true. Such an argument counts as valid if it is impossible for all the premises to be true and all the conclusions false. Anything that can be said about premises can now be said, mutatis mutandis, *about conclusions, and much of the interest of the subject comes from exploiting this duality. Putting conclusions on a par with premises reflects the idea that truth and falsity, and likewise acceptance and rejection, are polar notions standing on a par with one another.*

1 Multiple-conclusion arguments
2 Motivation and applications

1 Multiple-conclusion arguments

Multiple conclusions can best be understood by analogy with multiple premises. Premises function collectively: a number of premises taken together have a strength which far exceeds the sum of their separate strengths. The very existence of deductive logic turns on this fact, which is not undermined by the fact that a finite number of premises are always equivalent to a single one, namely their conjunction. For this equivalence itself relies on the working of the rule 'From A and B infer $A \& B$', understood as involving two separate premises (not one conjunctive one), so it does nothing to establish the redundancy of arguments with more than one premise.

Multiple conclusions also function collectively: a set of conclusions will typically be deducible although no single conclusion is deducible. They are best thought of disjunctively, as setting out the field within which the truth must lie on the assumption that the premises are all true. Just as enlarging a set of premises strengthens them (makes more things follow from them), so enlarging a set of conclusions weakens them (makes them follow from more things): as the field containing the truth becomes larger it becomes less informative. Of course, a finite number of conclusions are equivalent to a single one, namely their disjunction, but this no more makes multiple conclusions redundant than the analogous fact about conjunction makes multiple premises redundant.

The definition of logical consequence or implication is now that a set of premises implies a set of conclusions if it is impossible for all the premises to be true and all the conclusions false. The transitivity of implication is a key property of it, which in conventional single-conclusion logic takes the form of the 'cut' principle; that if a set of premises Γ implies a conclusion A, and if Γ, A imply B, then Γ implies B. The corresponding multiple-conclusion principle takes this novel form: if Γ, Θ_1 implies Θ_2, Δ for every partition of the set Θ into two disjoint parts Θ_1 and Θ_2, then Γ implies Δ.

Logicians often depict arguments by diagrams in which a horizontal line indicates that the sentence immediately below is inferred from those immediately above, so that the diagram branches upwards from one conclusion. Multiple-conclusion arguments can be represented in a similar fashion, except that now the graph can branch downwards as well as upwards. So (1) shows one variety of 'proof by cases', where one starts with a premise of the form 'A or B' and presents the alternatives as distinct cases as a preliminary to establishing the conclusion by separate, parallel arguments for case A and case B.

$$(1) \quad \frac{A \vee B}{A \quad B} \qquad (2) \quad \frac{\dfrac{A \vee B}{A \quad B}}{A \& B}$$

$$\vdots \quad \vdots$$

$$C \quad C$$

(1) is untypically simple, for in general the combination of upward and downward branching means that branches which have split may subsequently rejoin, creating circuits. Moreover, it turns out that it is essential to allow for circuits (or some equivalent sophistication) if one is to obtain an adequate variety of arguments. But some circuits are vicious, (2), for example. Much of the mathematical development of the subject has therefore been concerned with finding criteria for a diagram to have a valid pattern, in the sense that any argument which has the same bare layout (that is, abstracting altogether from the sentences involved and paying attention only to the way the steps are arranged relative to one another) is bound to be valid provided its component steps are individually valid. This is a good example of a new concept which, because patterns of single-conclusion argument are so rudimentary by comparison, is scarcely appreciable within the conventional framework.

2 Motivation and applications

Multiple-conclusion logic commends itself to the attention of the philosophical logician because putting conclusions on a par with premises is a natural corollary of acknowledging that truth and falsity are polar notions which stand on a par with one another, and likewise acceptance and rejection. Deduction is no longer tilted towards acceptance alone: an argument regarded as going from premises Γ to conclusions Δ with an eye to acceptance can equally be regarded as going from Δ to Γ with an eye to rejection. The connection can be stated in suitably symmetrical terms, namely that if the argument is valid it is irrational to accept all of Γ and reject all of Δ.

For the mathematical logician the removal of the asymmetry embodied in single-conclusion logic means that some anomalies disappear, and distinctions and results which needed qualification become unconditional. Recall, for example, the conventional way of developing a system of logic. First the semantics is set out, then implication is defined in semantic terms and finally, where possible, it is axiomatized, that is, shown to be equivalent to formal deducibility according to some system of rules of inference. This exposes a deficiency. Evidently the notion of implication can be used to say things about the assignments of truth-values determined by the semantics – for example, that none of them makes certain premises true and a certain conclusion false. But the information that can be conveyed in this way is only a fraction of the whole. For example, there is no way of saying in terms of implication alone whether the set of all sentences is satisfiable or not. And even if all the notions with which logicians work – logical truth, implication, satisfiability and so on – are taken together, the situation is similar. What we would surely like, but do not have, is a logical notion or notions capable of saying all there is to say about the semantics at the level appropriate to sentences.

In a similar vein, Carnap (1943) pointed out that, although one may manage to axiomatize a logic initially given semantically, one can never work back and retrieve the semantics from the axiomatization. For example, any axiomatization which is sound and complete for classical propositional logic will equally be sound and complete with respect to a nonstandard semantics in which, in addition to the classically possible assignments of truth-values, every sentence (and its negation) is simultaneously satisfiable. In short, there is no way, in purely formal deductive terms, of expressing the fact that '$\sim$' signifies negation. The situation is akin to the non-categoricity of theories, whereby a first-order theory of real numbers will also have a nonstandard interpretation in a merely countable domain (see LÖWENHEIM–SKOLEM THEOREMS AND NONSTANDARD MODELS). Those who are rightly concerned about the implications of that notorious result might do well to reflect that things are no better for negation.

Multiple-conclusion logic remedies both deficiencies. Implication is now an adequate vehicle for saying all there is to say about any semantics at the level of sentences, for every fact of the form 'It is (is not) possible for these sentences Γ to be true and those ones Δ false' is expressible by the statement that Γ does not (does) imply Δ. And by using multiple-conclusion rules one can obtain axiomatizations from which the intended semantics can be uniquely reconstructed. For example, one can work back from the rules 'From A, $\sim A$ infer' and 'Infer A, $\sim A$' to the classical truth table for '$\sim$'.

Multiple-conclusion rules of inference can also provide an elegant alternative to the often complicated rules involving assumptions and their discharge, which characterize natural deduction systems. (1) above illustrates the idea by using a multiple-conclusion rule in place of the natural-deduction rule of $\vee$-elimination. A profound application of this idea can be found in Gentzen's work on 'sequents' if one interprets his sequents metalogically as statements about multiple-conclusion implication, though this was not how Gentzen himself regarded them (see NATURAL DEDUCTION, TABLEAU AND SEQUENT SYSTEMS).

See also: LOGICAL AND MATHEMATICAL TERMS, GLOSSARY OF

References and further reading

* Carnap, R. (1943) *Formalization of Logic*, Cambridge,

MA: Harvard University Press. (The first explicit appearance of the subject.)

Kneale, W.C. (1956) 'The Province of Logic', in H.D. Lewis (ed.) *Contemporary British Philosophy*, 3rd series, London: Allen & Unwin; abridged in W. Kneale and M. Kneale, *The Development of Logic*, Oxford: Clarendon Press, 1962, ch. 9, §3. (Another pioneering piece, with a very readable introduction.)

Shoesmith, D.J. and Smiley, T.J. (1978) *Multiple-Conclusion Logic*, Cambridge: Cambridge University Press. (A systematic treatise, including a discussion of the history of the subject.)

TIMOTHY SMILEY

AL-MUQAMMAS, DAUD
(*fl.* 9th century)

*Daud ibn Marwan, called al-Muqammas, is the first Jewish thinker known to have written in Arabic and one of the earliest Arabic speaking theologians whose work is extant. He also wrote on logic, Biblical exegesis, doxography and polemical matters. His pioneering efforts toward a systematic Jewish philosophy show the influence both of Muslim theology (*kalam*) and the Aristotelian philosophy taught in the Syriac Christian academies.*

The main sources for al-Muqammas' biography are the tenth century Karaite author al-Qirqisani and al-Muqammas' own works. He was called al-Raqqi, suggesting that he came from the city of Raqqa, located in what is today northern Syria; he was also called ha-Bavli, 'the Mesopotamian'. The sobriquet 'al-Muqammas' ('he who wears a *qamis*', the latter referring to a shirt or shift) reflects his position at the crossroads between the early Arabicized Jewish commmunity and the Syriac-speaking Christian community; an Arabic life of St Anthony applies this term to an Arab or one who dressed like an Arab. By his own testimony, he took part in a theological debate with a Muslim in Damascus. At one point he converted to Christianity and studied philosophy for many years in Nisibis with one Nana (probably Nonnus of Nisibis, d. *circa* 860), but his anti-Christian polemics show that he returned to Judaism, and all his extant works were written after that point. Although he was claimed by later Karaite authors there is no independent evidence to date that he was a Karaite (see KARAISM).

Al-Muqammas' writings reflect the intellectual curiosity that may have been a factor in his conversion and reconversion. In a *summa* entitled *'Ishrun maqala*

(Twenty Chapters), almost sixteen chapters of which are extant, al-Muqammas sought answers to basic philosophical questions about knowledge, the world, God, humanity, and revelation. His questions were about the existence and character (the what, how and why of each of his subjects). In dealing with these matters, he was prepared to weigh the merits of rival religious traditions. After a short introduction to Aristotelian logic, the *'Ishrun maqala* follows the pattern well known to us in works of *kalam*, arguing each of its points against the background of a refutation of rival opinions. Thus al-Muqammas accompanies his arguments for *ex nihilo* creation with polemics against sceptics and materialists. His proofs of God's existence and unity include lengthy polemics against dualism, Christianity, and anthropomorphism. The same polemical or apologetic posture is adopted in the discussions of free will, prophecy (and the veracity of the Mosaic revelation) and accountability in the hereafter. The final chapters, which discussed other religions, are lost. Although clearly meant to vindicate Judaism, the work notably lacks quotations in Hebrew and other features that might have limited its audience to a Jewish readership. The Christian influence is highly visible throughout, not least in the extended polemics against Christianity.

Al-Muqammas' anti-Christian polemics also include a short, aggressive work entitled *al-Masa'il al-khamsin radd 'ala al-nasara min tariq al-qiyas* (Fifty Questions for the Logical Refutation of Christianity), fragments of which were found in the Cairo Geniza, and a lost longer work, the *Kitab al-dara'a* (Book of Urging on to Attack), which apparently discussed the history of Christianity. Al-Muqammas translated from Syriac and adapted to Judaism commentaries on Genesis and Ecclesiastes. A surviving fragment of the commentary on Genesis reveals that this earliest example of Judaeo-Arabic exegesis follows the rationalistic hermeneutical method of the Syriac Christian exegetes. Al-Muqammas also wrote a commentary on Aristotle's *Categories* and a refutation of Indian religions, both known to us only by title.

Al-Muqammas' writings preserve an early stage of Judaeo-Arabic philosophy, which in turn reflects the early stages of Islamic philosophy and theology. Thus we see the formulaic and apologetic character of *kalam* (see ISLAMIC THEOLOGY) alongside the fusion of Neoplatonic and Aristotelian ideas characteristic of *falsafa* (see ARISTOTELIANISM IN ISLAMIC PHILOSOPHY; NEOPLATONISM IN ISLAMIC PHILOSOPHY). The boundaries between these disciplines were then much less pronounced than the later became, but the hybridization may also reflect al-Muqammas' unique position rather than the state of the disciplines in his time. As a Jewish author

uncommitted to Muslim or Christian traditions, he could freely borrow from both. As one of the first Jews to write in Arabic, he was not constrained by set patterns of borrowing.

Al-Muqammas' polemics against predestination and anthropormorphism have close Islamic parallels, especially in Mu'tazilite writings (see ASH'ARIYYA AND MU'TAZILA). In discussions of physical theory, however, the Christian influence is more pronounced. Thus, in a manner that was typically Christian but was later widespread among Jewish thinkers, he defines 'substance' and 'accident', as 'that which exists in itself' and 'that which exists in another'. These definitions echo the Aristotelian approach and break sharply with the atomism of the occasionalist Muslim *mutakallimun* (theologians or dialecticians, practitioners of *kalam*) (see EPISTEMOLOGY IN ISLAMIC PHILOSOPHY); but al-Muqammas does not develop a systematic Aristotelian cosmology, and he hardly ever uses the concepts of matter and form.

Often, al-Muqammas fuses Muslim and Christian ideas. For example, in subordinating God's attributes to his absolute unity, he uses formulae found in later *kalam* works ('God lives with a life that is identical with Him', or 'God lives but not by life'). To elucidate these statements, however, he uses similes found in Christological treatises as illustrations of trinitarianism.

Al-Muqammas' originality is hard to gauge. A certain stiffness in his style may be the price he paid for venturing into new areas. Today his ideas and expositions look familiar or trite, but it is easy to forget that their familiarity to us comes from later authors. Al-Muqammas' openness to neighbouring cultures and his ability to adapt their materials are clearly the basis of his most original contributions to Jewish philosophy.

His influence is most noticeable in the works of al-Qirqisani and the later Karaites. In Rabbanite circles he is overshadowed by the towering figure of SAADIAH GAON, but he is cited by Rabbanite authors including Bahya IBN PAQUDA, Moses IBN EZRA, Judah ben Barzillai and Yedaya Ha-Penini, in a tradition extending down to the fourteenth century. That his work was apparently never translated *in toto* into Hebrew both expresses and contributes to the loss of his influence among later thinkers.

See also: ISLAMIC THEOLOGY; ISLAM, CONCEPT OF PHILOSOPHY IN

List of works

al-Muqammas, Daud (9th century) *'Ishrun maqala* (Twenty Chapters), ed. S. Stroumsa, *Dawud Ibn*

Marwan al-Muqammis's Twenty Chapters ['Ishrun Maqala], Leiden: Brill, 1989. (An edition and annotated English translation of al-Muqammas' Summa.)

References and further reading

Vajda, G. (1959) 'À propos de la perpétuité de la rétribution d'outre-tombe en théologie musulmanne' (On the Eternal Retribution in the Hereafter in Islamic Theology), *Studia Islamica* 11: 29–38. (A paraphrase and analysis of the sixteenth chapter of al-Muqammas' *'Ishrun maqala*.)

—— (1967a) 'Le problème de l'unité de Dieu d'après Dawud ibn Marwan al-Muqammis' (The Problem of the Unity of God According to Daud ibn Marwan al-Muqammas), in A. Altmann (ed.) *Jewish Medieval and Renaissance Studies*, Cambridge, MA: Harvard University Press, 49–73. (A paraphrase and analysis of the eighth chapter of al-Muqammas' *'Ishrun maqala*.)

—— (1967b) 'La prophétologie de Dawud ibn Marwan al-Raqqi al-Muqammis' (The Prophetology of Daud ibn Marwan al-Raqqi al-Muqammas), *Journal Asiatique* 265: 227–35. (A paraphrase and analysis of the fourteenth chapter of al-Muqammas' *'Ishrun maqala*.)

—— (1974) 'Le pari de Pascal dans un texte judéo-arabe du IXe siécle' (Pascal's Wager in a Judaeo-Arabic text from the Ninth Century), in *Mélanges d'histoire des religions offerts à Henri-Charles Puech*, Paris: PUF, 569–71. (A translation and analysis of a surviving fragment from the twentieth chapter of al-Muqammas' *'Ishrun maqala*.)

Stroumsa, S. (1991) 'The Impact of Syriac Tradition on Early Judaeo-Arabic Bible Exegesis', *Aram* 3: 83–96. (On al-Muqammas' exegetical work.)

SARAH STROUMSA

MUSIC, AESTHETICS OF

The aesthetics of music comprises philosophical reflection on the origin, nature, power, purpose, creation, performance, reception, meaning and value of music. Some of its problems are general problems of aesthetics posed in a musical context; for example, what is the ontological status of the work of art in music, or what are the grounds of value judgments in music? Other problems are more or less peculiar to music, lacking a clear parallel in other arts; for example, what is the nature of the motion perceived in music, or how can the marriage of music and words best be understood?

Attempts to define the concept of music generally begin with the fact that music involves sound, but also posit such things as cultural tradition, the fulfilment of a composer's aims or the expression of emotions as essential features of music. Perhaps any plausible concept, though, has to involve the making of sounds by people for aesthetic appreciation, broadly conceived. In deciding what is meant by a musical work, further considerations come into play, such as might lead to the identification of it with a sound structure as defined by a given composer in a particular musico-historical context.

In what sense can a piece of music be said to have meaning? Some hold it has meaning only internally – in its structure as an arrangement of melodies, harmonies, rhythms and timbres, for instance – while others have claimed that its meaning lies in the communication of things not essentially musical – such as emotions, attitudes or the deeper nature of the world. The most popular of these beliefs is that music expresses emotion. This is not to say, however, that the emotion expressed in a work is necessarily experienced by those involved in its composition or performance: composers can create peaceful or furious music without themselves being in those states, and the same goes for the performance of such music by performers. Also, the emotions evoked in listeners seem of a different nature from those directly experienced: negative emotions expressed in music do not preclude the audience's appreciation, and in fact commonly facilitate it. Ultimately, a work's expressiveness should be seen as something directly related to the experience of listening to that work. Music is often said to have value primarily in so far as it is beautiful, its beauty being whatever affords pleasure to the listener. But the quality of a work's expressiveness, its depth, richness and subtlety, for example, also seems to form an important part of any value judgment we make about the work.

1 The concept of music
2 The ontology of music
3 Musical performance
4 Musical form and musical perception
5 Musical understanding
6 Musical meaning: general
7 Musical meaning: expression
8 Musical meaning: representation
9 Musical meaning: other aspects
10 The value of music

1 The concept of music

A fundamental question in the aesthetics of music is 'What is music?', understood as a request for a definition or delineation of the general concept of music. Theorists have adopted a number of different approaches to the question, often depending on their further purposes in asking it. Perhaps the only thing that all theorists agree on is that music is necessarily sound.

The most conservative approach seeks to define music in terms of the standard features of most music, to wit, melody, harmony, rhythm, metre, instruments, voices and tone production; but in addition to being inadequate to a number of modes of contemporary composition – serialism, minimalism, *musique concrète*, computer music, aleatory music – it ignores many practices remote from us in space or time that we acknowledge as musical. A more liberal approach to defining music – a structuralist one – issues in the formula of music as 'organized sound'; though music so conceived need not exhibit the standard features of music noted above, for on this conception something is music in virtue of its intrinsic properties alone. On another approach, which may be termed 'experiential' (or 'phenomenological'), music is any sounds that are heard as music, it then being incumbent on the theorist to say what makes such hearing musical; salient implications of this approach are, first, that natural and accidental sounds may be music, and second, that the status of an item as music is relative to the listener and the occasion of listening.

Attempts have been made to define music as a type of sound-involving activity distinguished by certain cultural or sociological traits, for example, a particular cultural function, such as the accompaniment of ritual or the enhancement of group memory, or particular social relationships, such as apprenticeship. Alternatively, music may be defined in an essentially historical manner as those sound-involving items, activities and practices that have evolved, historically and reflexively, from certain earlier such items, activities and practices, and so on, it being incumbent on the theorist to indicate some non-question-begging way of picking out the musical strand of human history from all others (for instance, the linguistic one) that are sound-involving.

Finally, one may attempt to characterize music intentionally, from the producer's point of view, by appeal to distinctive aims or purposes on the part of makers of sound. One approach of long standing conceives music as sounds made in order to express, evoke or elicit emotions or feelings. Another conceives it as sound used as a vehicle of communicable but non-linguistic thought. But the most common approach of this kind proposes simply that music is sounds made or arranged for aesthetic appreciation.

If one is concerned to define music as an art, to preserve a measure of objectivity for the status of music, and yet to avoid making music's import

necessarily either emotional or intellectual, one could do worse than to accept this last suggestion. However, in order comfortably to cover a wide range of cross-cultural phenomena easily recognized by us as music, but in which we would be hard put to discern a norm of aesthetic appreciation in operation, a more inclusive notion of the aim with which sounds are made must be invoked. The following suggests itself: music is sounds humanly made or arranged for the purpose of enriching experience via active engagement (such as through performing, listening, dancing), with the sounds regarded primarily as sounds. Such a definition looks to be adequate to cover virtually everything intelligibly accounted music.

The proposal accommodates even John Cage's notorious *4' 33"*, an ostensibly soundless musical composition. Designating a period of silence is (though a limiting case) an organization of sounds in a given span of time, presumably done here with a view to heightening consciousness. In addition, as the composer clearly envisaged, even a span of time specified as one to be left silent by the performer is inevitably filled with sounds of various sorts originating from the environment in which the piece is performed.

2 The ontology of music

The central question of the ontology of music, in musical domains where the notion of a work – a repeatable and non-occasion-bound musical entity – has purchase, is that of what manner of thing a musical work precisely is.

It is clear that the standard musical work of the Western tradition is not any physical object or event whatsoever. In particular, it is not identical with any performance of it. It is equally not to be identified with any score of it, whether original manuscript or mass-produced copy, for such things are evidently seen and not heard. Furthermore, a musical work generally predates any of its performances, and can survive the destruction of all of its scores. Yet scores and performances remain of great importance: musical works in this tradition are largely defined by the former and experienced through the latter.

If a work of music is not a physical entity, what is it? There are four views on this question with some currency, three of which hold that a musical work is some variety of abstract entity. The first is that a musical work is a set or class of performances. The second is that it is a universal or pure type, such as a sound structure or pattern. The third is that it is a mental rather than an abstract entity, something existing properly in the minds of composers as well as perhaps of their interpreters and audiences. And the fourth is that a musical work is a qualified or contextualized type, akin to other products of culture in being creatable and bound to specific persons, times and places of origin. Finally, it is also possible to take an eliminativist view of musical works, denying that there really are any such things, and recognizing only scores, performances, intentions and associated practices.

Eliminativism aside, of the four views indicated above there are arguably conclusive objections to all but the last. Focusing on the second view, the idea that a musical work is simply a sound structure (or tonal-instrumental structure) confronts grave problems. One is that such a thing does not admit of being created; the total musical structure ultimately settled on by the composer, the upshot of various acts of choosing and arranging tones and instrumentations, already exists as an abstract object within the musical system in which composition takes place, and so cannot be brought into being by the composer. But a more important problem is that, conceived as simply a sound structure, a musical work cannot support the complex of aesthetic and artistic predications justifiably made of it. Two musical works, composed within the same musical system, may be identical in musical structure and yet differ in the aesthetic or artistic features that are ascribed to them, for example, brashness, wittiness or originality. This is due to the different contexts in which they were composed, and the different contexts of correct performance, audition, and understanding that this entrains. Only a view such as the fourth noted above, that individuates musical works more finely – for example, as composer-initiated types whose identity is bound up with person, time and place – can be adequate to musical works as they figure in our experience and description of them. The act of composing a standard musical work is thus one of the composer indicating, in a specific musico-historical context, a musical structure, so creating the work which is precisely the structure-as-indicated-by-the-composer-in-that-context (see ART WORKS, ONTOLOGY OF §§2–3).

3 Musical performance

A number of questions about the performance of music have received attention. Foremost is 'What is it to perform?' or 'What criteria must be satisfied if a performance can be said to have taken place?' One issue is whether performing requires a pre-existing work, or whether improvising is not also a kind of performing. Another issue is what sort of intentions a performer must have in order for their actions to count as a performance of such-and-such a work, what sorts of means must be employed, and what

success conditions *vis-à-vis* a target audience might also need to be satisfied. The question of what it is to perform a work at all shades readily into the question of what it is to perform a work correctly and of what it is to perform it well. Issues such as these about the nature of musical performance and issues concerning the ontology of music are closely interrelated.

Much discussed is the matter of historical authenticity in performance – both what is required in order to achieve it, and why, or even whether, achieving it is desirable. Writers have variously emphasized the specific sound of original performance, the means of sound production employed, the manner of playing then current, or the physical venue and social circumstances of such performance. Alternatively, authority may be claimed to rest with the composer's intentions, though this also raises problems: there are officially declared intentions, represented by scores, and privately held intentions; low-order intentions, merely implementational in nature, and high-order intentions, definitive of aesthetic goals; and intentions regarding what is essential for proper performance, in contrast to intentions in regard to achieving optimal performance.

The nature of the interpretation involved in performing has been queried, and compared and contrasted with critical interpretation. The status of musical performance as an art of its own has been explored, as have analogies between performing and other actions, for example, those of quoting, displaying, translating or enacting. The phenomenon of virtuosity has attracted attention, as attaching not only to performances but to works themselves. Finally, issues regarding the recording of music and its effect on the performance and the reception of music are beginning to be widely addressed (see ART, PERFORMING).

4 Musical form and musical perception

Questions about the basic form of music and the nature of the perception involved in grasping music at ground level are closely intertwined. For the basic form of music is arguably that in virtue of which it is heard as music, or that which is necessarily tracked in the course of perceiving the music.

Though all agree that music is sound which is organized and apprehended in time and thus that the form of music must be both audible and temporal, there is disagreement on many further points. Some hold the fundamental form of music to be local, and to reside in moment-to-moment connections between small-scale parts, while others hold global form, governing large-scale and temporally distant sections of a piece, to be equally basic. Some regard musical form as *sui generis*, involving irreducible and specifically musical qualities, while others take notions, particularly spatial ones, rooted in other domains – such as balance, proportion, symmetry and overall shape – to apply directly to musical form.

Debate also flourishes concerning the nature of the fundamental musical perception by which musical form is grasped. Some philosophers think registration of even the most basic musical features, such as tones, rhythms, motifs and chords, or at least the experience of musical connectedness and movement requires either a special mode of perception, or the metaphorical projection of concepts not literally applicable to sequences of sound, or the exercise of a species of imagination; others hold such posits to be unnecessary, claiming that ordinary perception is adequate to the phenomena at hand. A compromise position about musical movement may be this: even if such movement fails to result from either metaphorical projection or aural imagining, music is *heard as* moving, most notably in its melodic rise and fall, harmonic progression and rhythmic propulsion, despite failing to contain anything that literally moves in the way it is heard as moving.

Currently there is much empirical work on the cognitive psychology of music worthy of the attention of philosophers, concerning principles of grouping, the grasp of melodic contour, the mechanisms of memory and attention, and the limits of sensitivity to key relationships. Also of interest is the role of unconscious processing in the perception of music, including assignment by a musical processor of syntactic or semantic structure to music as it is heard.

5 Musical understanding

What does the listener's understanding of music consist in? It is arguably a species of knowing-how, or experiential knowing, as opposed to knowing-that, or propositional knowing. Reflection suggests that understanding music is basically a matter of hearing the music in a certain way, of registering or responding to certain aspects of the music. The understanding of music, in other words, is continuous with perception of music; it is not a matter of technical analysis, causal explanation or discursive construal, but of a certain sort of listening experience (see ART, UNDERSTANDING OF §5).

This is not to deny that there are kinds and levels of musical understanding, some of which may essentially involve propositional knowledge, that understanding at any level may be shallow or deep, and that different sorts of music may call for different kinds of understanding. But the ability to describe music in articulate terms is not a *sine qua non* of core musical

understanding, even if ability to describe music is requisite for the kind or level of musical understanding appropriate to a teacher or critic.

Still, there is a question of the extent to which the listener's understanding of music is informed by concepts of various sorts, in what manner and with what degree of recoverability by the subject. There is also the issue of how similar the understanding of music is to the understanding of language, and of how the understanding of music relates to the appreciation and evaluation of it.

6 Musical meaning: general

It is common to divide views on the meaning or significance of music into two sorts, autonomist and heteronomist. The autonomist position is that music has no meaning, or else that it means only itself (thus yielding what is sometimes called 'intra-musical' meaning). The heteronomist position is that music has some sort of meaning that is other than the music itself (sometimes denominated 'extra-musical' meaning).

It is difficult to find thinkers whose views wholly exemplify either position. Perhaps Hanslick, who regarded music as essentially just a glorious succession of tones, and who held music incapable of conveying anything more than the dynamic qualities exhibited indifferently by phenomena of various sorts, is closest to a complete autonomist; Schopenhauer, who regarded music as an image of the inner nature of the world and held it to signify the infinite varieties of willing or striving, is perhaps closest to a complete heteronomist (see HANSLICK, E.; SCHOPENHAUER, A. §5). Gurney's view, contrary to common belief, is as much heteronomist as autonomist, though he regards music's expression of mental states as detachable from, and less important than, its purely musical beauty or impressiveness (see GURNEY, E. §2). Langer's view is substantially heteronomist, postulating that music is symbolic of emotional life, though Langer denies that such symbolism carries as far as individual emotions. The view of Leonard Meyer is substantially autonomist, in that it accords pride of place to embodied meaning, consisting roughly in the implications that musical events have for other musical events in a musical fabric; yet room is also made for designative meaning of an emotional sort, explained as a by-product of the play of expectations involved in sensing the implications for continuation that a musical composition at every point presents (Meyer 1956, 1967).

It seems reasonable to take musical meaning and understanding to be correlative concepts, so that the meaning of a stretch of music would comprise whatever is understood in understanding it. Viewed from that perspective, the question of whether music has any meaning beyond itself becomes that of whether in understanding music we need register or respond to anything more than purely musical events and relationships. The answer to this would seem clearly to be yes; though order and connectedness in purely musical dimensions is the basis of musical discourse, it does not exhaust it, and a comprehending experience of that discourse accordingly goes beyond a grasp of musical relationships *per se*.

7 Musical meaning: expression

The sort of extra-musical meaning in music that has seemed to most observers to be of greatest importance is expressive meaning, that is, the expression by music of psychological states. The states music has been held to be capable of expressing include emotions, feelings, moods, attitudes and traits of personality.

Philosophical explication of the concept of musical expressiveness must not be conflated with investigation of the grounds or causes of such expressiveness. The identification of factors involved in making music expressive – tempo, timbre, major or minor mode, or similarities between music and vocal utterance, for example – is one thing, and the logical analysis of what musical expressiveness consists in quite another.

The expressiveness of music, though evidently related to the literal expression of psychological states by persons through behaviour, countenance and demeanour, must yet be clearly distinguished from it. Taking emotions as the paradigm states involved, the expression of emotion by a person is a dated occurrence, involving outward manifestations that warrant a reasonable inference to the person's being in the given emotional state, and requires that the person actually feel the emotion being expressed. When, however, a musical passage is expressive of an emotion, the emotion is not an occurrent one, and any inference to emotion felt on the part of the composer would be unwarranted, and probably mistaken; nor is a musical passage literally a behavioural manifestation of any sort. Musical expressiveness, in short, is a property of music, not of individuals who happen to be connected to the music.

The logical distinctness of musical expressiveness and personal expression still allows for a remarkably persistent hypothesis, sometimes called the 'Expression Theory' of music, to the effect that the emotion a piece of music is expressive of is always as a matter of fact one that was experienced by the composer, and that the expressiveness of music is always in effect the expression of the composer's own emotion, imparted to the music in the act of composing. But apart from its romantic appeal, the hypothesis has little to recommend it. The composing of music is typically too indirect, intellectually mediated, temporally extended and discontinuous for such a generalization to hold, even roughly. A composer in a sanguine frame of mind can very well write sanguinary music, or the reverse, with this being as comprehensible as the only somewhat more frequent match of music and mood mistakenly posited as universal by the Expression Theory. And talented composers can craft music expressive of a number of emotional states without themselves being in any of them at the time.

The emotional expressiveness of music must also be distinguished from its power to arouse or evoke corresponding feelings in listeners. There are numerous reasons for this, but two of the more important seem to be these. First, the expressiveness of music presents itself as a manifest property of it, or at any rate, something about how it is readily heard, rather than as an inferred power to raise affect in us. And second, the affects that music does produce in us while listening will often differ, in degree, kind and polarity, from those which it is expressive of; if they did not, it would be puzzling both that music expressive of negative emotion was as popular as it was, and that the aesthetic appreciation of expressive music of any sort, which calls for a certain amount of clear-headed attention, was possible at all.

As for what emotional expressiveness in music might consist in, a number of ideas are currently under consideration. They include music's having a sound resembling the behavioural expression of an emotion; music's metaphorically exemplifying some emotion; music's sounding the way some emotion feels; music's presenting the appearances of an emotion; music's corresponding to an emotional state or being seen as suitable to its expression; music's being imagined to be the gestures of an individual experiencing emotion; and music's being hearable as, or as if it were, the personal expression of an emotion. In any event, it seems clear that the expressiveness of a musical passage should be conceived as something not detachable from, or experienceable apart from, the passage that possesses it.

Some theorists who fully acknowledge the expressive dimension of music balk at describing this as a species of musical meaning. Music's expressiveness would only be a form of meaning, they maintain, if in addition to possessing and exhibiting expressive qualities music also referred to, denoted or was otherwise about the emotions or other states corresponding to such qualities. But the issue can be mooted by simply speaking of music's expressive content, rather than meaning (see Artistic Expression; Emotion in response to art §§4, 6).

8 Musical meaning: representation

Musical representation means the depiction by music of concrete persons, things or events. This is least problematic for sounds, or objects with characteristic sounds, that music can obviously imitate or approximate. But the scope of musical representation plausibly extends beyond this to concrete phenomena that can be heard in music, or that a passage of music might be heard as, which hearing may obtain in the absence of notable sonic resemblance between music and the phenomenon in question, but in virtue instead of certain structural parallels or isomorphisms between them.

There is an important distinction between musical depictions that attuned listeners recognize as such unaided, and those that are only so recognized upon provision of a verbal cue or label, but there seems little reason to identify that with the distinction between representational and nonrepresentational music *per se*. The issue has also been raised of whether musical representation requires the composer's intention to represent the putative subject, and whether this intention must be signalled by a composer-given title, or otherwise publically recorded.

Some have questioned whether even the most explicitly programmatic music is ever truly representational, on the grounds that representation requires more than securing perceptual reference to some object or event, representation being held to require also a characterization of what is referred to or the attribution of predicates to it, which music is claimed powerless to accomplish. But it is not clear either that such a demand is warranted, or, if it is, that music cannot meet it.

Philosophers have also been concerned to assess the importance of such musical representation as there is. It has been asked whether, when a piece of music is representational, its representational aspect must be grasped if the piece is to be understood, whether such music is not sometimes equally enjoyable if its representational aspect is ignored, and whether the representational and expressive properties of music are not often interdependent – in which event, assuming expressive properties are always of artistic moment, the appreciative relevance of the representational aspect of music in such cases would be assured.

9 Musical meaning: other aspects

The expression of mental states and the representa-

tion of concrete objects and events by no means exhausts the modes of meaning music has been held to possess. Additional meanings that have been ascribed to music fall mostly into one of two broad categories, metaphysical and sociocultural.

Metaphysical meanings include suggestions of a fairly moderate sort, such as that music symbolizes, in addition to or in lieu of individual psychological states, the sphere of feeling generally (Langer 1942), or that music exemplifies general patterns of continuation, growth or development in the natural world (Beardsley 1981), or that music is capable of modelling states of mind in which truths of human existence stand revealed (Sullivan 1927). Metaphysical meanings of a more radical sort have also been posited: Schopenhauer, for example, thought of music as a direct image of the cosmic will, and Nietzsche viewed music as divulging the pain and suffering at the root of earthly existence.

Cultural meanings are implicated in suggestions to the effect that music possesses ideological content, reflecting or endorsing existing political arrangements or social structures, or moral content, personifying and displaying virtues of character, or that it embodies a society's attitudes towards sex, reason or religion. Unlike the expressive and representational meanings considered above, meanings of this sort, where justifiably ascribed, may be carried by whole genres of music, or by acts or contexts of presentation, rather than by specific works.

Supporters of broader meanings for music must indicate criteria for the possession of such meanings by music, mechanisms by which music may conceivably effect them, and reasons for holding them to be intersubjectively valid. The more extrinsic the kind of meaning proposed as attaching to music, the more difficult it will be to hold both that the understanding of music requires grasp of such meanings, and that such understanding will be primarily experiential in nature.

10 The value of music

The value of individual pieces of music must be distinguished from the value to a culture of music as a whole – though the latter will likely depend, in various ways, on the former. The artistic value of an individual piece of music may plausibly be identified, in the main, with the intrinsic value of correct experience of it.

Chief among the artistic values of music is presumably beauty – what Gurney labelled simply 'musical impressiveness', and what Hanslick regarded as inherent in 'tonally moving forms'. Musical beauty, it might be said, is that in virtue of which music is inherently pleasurable to follow, apprehend or contemplate. It is a point of contention whether such beauty is susceptible to explanation in terms of principles, if any, governing the emergence of beauty in other spheres, or is rather uniquely musical (see BEAUTY).

The other obvious artistic value of music derives from its expressiveness or extra-musical dimension generally. Music seems more valuable the more expressive it is, or the more richly, finely or profoundly it embodies whatever content it possesses beyond the purely musical.

Broadly speaking, views on the value of music divide into views that locate such value primarily in music's presentation of an autonomous world of sound, one whose forms and qualities can be appreciated without reference to those of life, and whose virtue consists in removing one satisfyingly from ordinary human affairs, and views that locate such value primarily in music's reflection of the real world, whose virtue is the effecting of a deeper or more intense immersion in the world, revealing or clarifying aspects of life that ordinarily remain obscure or only dimly grasped.

See also: OPERA, AESTHETICS OF

References and further reading

Adorno, T. (1938) 'On the Fetish Character in Music and the Regression in Listening', in A. Arato and E. Gebhardt (eds), *The Essential Frankfurt School Reader*, New York: Continuum, 1982. (Condemns 'easy listening' music and habits, partly for socio-political reasons.)

Alperson, P. (1984) 'On Musical Improvisation', *Journal of Aesthetics and Art Criticism* 43: 17–30. (Identifies the distinguishing features of improvised music.)

—— (ed.) (1987) *What is Music?*, New York: Haven; reprinted University Park, PA, Penn State Press, 1994. (A collection of essays, mostly by philosophers, with substantial introductions and bibliographies.)

* Beardsley, M. (1981) 'Understanding Music', in K. Price (ed.), *On Criticizing Music*, Baltimore, MD: Johns Hopkins University Press. (Distinguishes different types of understanding and explores the possibilities for semantic understanding of music in accord with Goodman's notion of artistic exemplification.)

Budd, M. (1985) *Music and the Emotions*, London: Routledge. (A masterly critical survey of influential theories of musical expression and evocation.)

—— (1985) 'Understanding Music', *Proceedings of the Aristotelian Society Supplement* 59: 233–48. (Explores dimensions of musical understanding, and criticizes Scruton (1983).)

—— (1995) *Values of Art*, London: Allen Lane, The Penguin Press. (Advances in its last chapter an important positive account of the relationship of music and emotion.)

Callen, D. (1982) 'The Sentiment in Musical Sensibility', *Journal of Aesthetics and Art Criticism* 40: 381–93. (Analyses musical expressiveness as representation of fictive acts of emotional expression.)

Cavell, S. (1969) 'Music Discomposed', in *Must We Mean What We Say?*, New York: Charles Scribner's Sons. (Charges that certain modern modes of music-making are artistically fraudulent.)

Clifton, T. (1983) *Music as Heard*, New Haven, CT: Yale University Press. (An approach to musical comprehension from a phenomenological perspective, drawing mainly on the ideas of Husserl.)

Cone, E. (1974) *The Composer's Voice*, Berkeley, CA: University of California Press. (Develops a thesis about musical communication in terms of the composers' musical personae, in both song and instrumental music.)

—— (1989) *Music: A View from Delft*, Chicago, IL: University of Chicago Press. (A collection of essays by the prominent music theorist, half of which have a philosophical dimension.)

Cook, N. (1990) *Music, Imagination and Culture*, Oxford: Oxford University Press. (A stimulating and provocative look at music from the point of view of both composer and listener, and a defence of the primacy of the latter.)

Cooke, D. (1959) *The Language of Music*, Oxford: Oxford University Press. (Proposes that music is indeed the language of the emotions and seeks through a wide range of examples to locate the individual units of emotive meaning in music; responds to Hindemith (1952).)

Dahlhaus, C. (1981) *Esthetics of Music*, trans. W. Austin, Cambridge: Cambridge University Press. (A historically informed survey of the subject by the leading German musicologist-historian.)

Davies, S. (1987) 'Authenticity in Musical Performance', *British Journal of Aesthetics* 27: 39–50. (Locates authenticity of performance in fidelity to the composer's publically expressed and correctly understood intentions.)

—— (1991) 'The Ontology of Musical Works and the Authenticity of Their Performance', *Nous* 25: 21–41. (A sensitive discussion of the interrelationship of these issues, with significant attention to non-Western musical traditions.)

—— (1994) *Musical Meaning and Expression*, Ithaca,

NY: Cornell University Press. (A comprehensive and painstaking survey of its topics, covering some of the same ground as Budd (1985), but with a focus on work of the past twenty years.)

DeBellis, M. (1995) *Music and Conceptualization*, Cambridge: Cambridge University Press. (Explores the nature of expert and nonexpert hearing of music, and the role and degree of conceptualization in each; draws on work in cognitive psychology.)

Dipert, R. (1980) 'The Composer's Intentions: An Examination of Their Relevance for Performance', *Musical Quarterly* 66: 205–18. (Argues for the importance of distinguishing low-, middle- and high-level intentions on a composer's part.)

Elliott, R.K. (1966) 'Aesthetic Theory and the Experience of Art', *Proceedings of the Aristotelian Society* 67: 111–26. (Illuminatingly contrasts the experience of music 'from within' with the experience of music 'from without'.)

Evans, M. (1990) *Listening to Music*, London: Macmillan. (A recent discussion of some problems of musical meaning and comprehension, informed by the philosophy of Wittgenstein.)

Fisher, J. (1991) 'Discovery, Creation, and Musical Works', *Journal of Aesthetics and Art Criticism* 49: 129–36. (Argues cogently for a creationist view of musical composition.)

Godlovitch, S. (1988) 'Authentic Performance', *The Monist* 71: 258–77. (Canvasses a large number of defences of authenticity in musical performance.)

Goehr, L. (1992) *The Imaginary Museum of Musical Works*, Oxford: Oxford University Press. (Surveys with dissatisfaction current accounts of the nature of a musical work, proposes instead adoption of a historical-cultural method, and suggests that the full-blown notion of a musical work may not predate 1800.)

Goldman, A. (1992) 'The Value of Music', *Journal of Aesthetics and Art Criticism* 50: 35–44. (Suggests that the central value of music is its presenting us with another world, removed from that of everyday life.)

—— (1995) 'Emotions in Music: A Postscript', *Journal of Aesthetics and Art Criticism* 53: 59–69. (Assesses the debate between Kivy and Radford on musical arousal of emotion.)

Goodman, N. (1968) *Languages of Art*, New York: Bobbs-Merrill. (A seminal treatise in contemporary aesthetics, containing influential proposals regarding the relationship of works and performances and the nature of musical expression.)

Gurney, E. (1880) *The Power of Sound*, New York: Basic Books, 1966. (His major work, an important contribution to aesthetics of music in the nineteenth century.)

Hanslick, E. (1891) *Vom Musikalisch-Schönen*, trans. G. Payzant, *On the Musically Beautiful*, Indianapolis, IN: Hackett Publishing Company, 1986. (The classic statement of formalism about music.)

Higgins, K. (1991) *The Music of Our Lives*, Philadelphia, PA: Temple University Press. (Charges that contemporary philosophy of music largely ignores certain dimensions of musical experience, and argues in particular for the ethical role and significance of music.)

Hindemith, P. (1952) *A Composer's World*, Cambridge, MA: Harvard University Press. (A searching, if one-sidedly formalistic, examination of some fundamental issues of musical aesthetics.)

Ingarden, R. (1957) *The Work of Music and the Problem of Its Identity*, trans. A. Czerniawski, Berkeley, CA: University of California Press, 1986. (Advances a view of the musical work as an intentional object, one culturally shaped and sustained, created in time and subject to dissolution.)

Kivy, P. (1984) *Sound and Semblance*, Princeton, NJ: Princeton University Press. (A careful study of the basis of musical representation, and the different species thereof.)

—— (1989) *Sound Sentiment*, Philadelphia, PA: Temple University Press. (A partly historical and widely influential account of the nature and causes of musical expressiveness, with supplementary essays defending the author's thoroughgoing cognitivism about music. Includes *The Corded Shell*, Princeton University Press, 1980.)

—— (1990) *Music Alone*, Ithaca, NY: Cornell University Press. (An account of the experience of 'music alone', focusing on the role of explicit, articulable cognitions in the understanding of music.)

—— (1995) *Authenticities*, Ithaca, NY: Cornell University Press. (A philosophical analysis of the whys and wherefores of the currently ascendant norm of 'authentic performance'.)

Krausz, M. (ed.) (1993) *The Interpretation of Music*, Oxford: Oxford University Press. (A collection of new essays by nineteen philosophers.)

* Langer, S. (1942) *Philosophy in a New Key*, Cambridge, MA: Harvard University Press. (Advances the view of music as a presentational, rather than discursive symbol, and claims that what it symbolizes, though non-specifically, is the human life of feeling.)

Levinson, J. (1990) *Music, Art, and Metaphysics*, Ithaca, NY: Cornell University Press. (Contains six essays devoted to philosophy of music, covering the definition, ontology, meaning, performance and appreciation of music.)

—— (1997) *Music in the Moment*, Ithaca, NY: Cornell University Press. (Contains four essays devoted to philosophy of music, including ones on song, musical literacy, musical expressiveness and musical interpretation.)

—— (1997) *Music in the Moment*, Ithaca, NY: Cornell University Press. (An account, inspired by Edmund Gurney, of what the listener's core understanding of music consists in.)

Lippman, E. (1994) *A History of Western Musical Aesthetics*, Lincoln, NB: University of Nebraska Press. (The latest historical survey of the subject, beginning with ancient thought, but covering writers as recent as Leonard Meyer and Roger Scruton.)

McClary, S. (1991) *Feminine Endings: Music, Gender, and Sexuality*, Minneapolis, MN: University of Minnesota Press. (A feminist reinterpretation of the tradition of Western tonal music, raising many philosophical questions about the basis and grounds of musical meaning.)

Mark, T. (1980) 'On Works of Virtuosity', *Journal of Philosophy* 77: 28–45. (Proposes that the distinctive mark of works of musical virtuosity is a kind of musical reflexiveness or self-reference.)

Maus, F. (1988) 'Music as Drama', *Music Theory Spectrum* 10: 54–73. (Proposes that musical discourse be conceived as essentially dramatic, as an arena in which musical characters perform acts of various sorts.)

* Meyer, L. (1956) *Emotion and Meaning in Music*, Chicago, IL: University of Chicago Press. (The first of Meyer's books, setting out his view in psychologistic terms, in which the notion of expectation figures prominently.)

* —— (1967) *Music, the Arts, and Ideas*, Chicago, IL: University of Chicago Press. (Ranges beyond music as such to other arts, and reframes some of Meyer's key ideas in terms of information theory.)

Newcomb, A. (1984) 'Sound and Feeling', *Critical Inquiry* 10: 614–43. (A critical discussion of Kivy (1984).)

Nietzsche, F. (1872) *The Birth of Tragedy*, trans. W. Kauffmann, New York: Vintage Books, 1967. (Discusses the conflict of the Apollonian and the Dionysian at the heart of Greek tragedy, and the relation of this to 'the spirit of music'.)

Radford, C. (1989) 'Emotions and Music: A Reply to the Cognitivists', *Journal of Aesthetics and Art Criticism* 47: 69–76. (Replies to Kivy (1989), and argues for the power of music to induce simple emotions and moods in listeners.)

Raffman, D. (1993) *Language, Music and Mind*, Cambridge, MA: MIT Press. (Argues for three sorts of ineffability in connection with music, the most important being carried by uncategorizable nuances of sound as produced in concrete performance.)

Rantala, V., Rowell, L. and Tarasti, E. (eds) (1988) *Essays on the Philosophy of Music*, Helsinki: Acta Philosophica Fennica. (A collection of twenty essays, representing a variety of approaches: analytic, semiotic, historical and phenomenological.)

Ridley, A. (1995) *Music, Value and the Passions*, Ithaca, NY: Cornell University Press. (An impressive recent contribution, defending an emotionalism about music that mediates between cognitivist and arousalist approaches.)

Robinson, J. (1994) 'The Expression and Arousal of Emotion in Music', *Journal of Aesthetics and Art Criticism* 52: 13–22. (Emphasizes the importance of music's capacity to affect the feelings directly, in cognitively unmediated ways.)

—— (ed.) (1997) *Music and Meaning*, Ithaca, NY: Cornell University Press. (A collection of ten recent essays by philosophers and theorists of music.)

Rowell, L. (1983) *Thinking About Music*, Amherst, MA: University of Massachusetts Press. (An introduction to the philosophy of music with an ethnographic flavour.)

Schoenberg, A. (1950) *Style and Idea*, New York: Philosophical Library. (Definitive statements by the founder of 12-tone music.)

Schopenhauer, A. (1819, 1844) *Die Welt als Wille und Vorstellung*, trans. E.F.J. Payne, *The World as Will and Representation*, New York: Dover Publications, 1966, 2 vols. (Contains a powerful brief for the metaphysical significance of musical process.)

Scruton, R. (1976) 'Representation in Music', *Philosophy* 51: 273–87. (Argues that music is incapable of representation in a robust sense.)

—— (1983) 'Understanding Music', in *The Aesthetic Understanding*, London: Methuen. (Argues that musical understanding is a species of intentional understanding, and that musical features are strictly distinct from sonic ones.)

—— (1987) 'Analytical Philosophy and the Meaning of Music', *Journal of Aesthetics and Art Criticism* 46: 169–76. (Argues for a conception of musical meaning as inseparable from the experience of music.)

Serafine, M. (1987) *Music as Cognition*, New York: Columbia University Press. (A cognitive psychologist's view of music.)

Sessions, R. (1950) *The Musical Experience of Composer, Performer, Listener*, Princeton, NJ: Princeton University Press. (Offers exactly what its title suggests, and is illuminating in regard to each of its topics.)

Sloboda, J. (1985) *The Musical Mind: The Cognitive*

Psychology of Music, Oxford: Oxford University Press. (A valuable recent survey.)

Sparshott, F. (1994) 'Music and Feeling', *Journal of Aesthetics and Art Criticism* 52: 23–35. (Sensitive to the many senses of 'feeling' invoked in claims about musical expression and evocation.)

Stravinsky, I. (1956) *Poetics of Music*, New York: Vintage Books. (Reflects an extreme formalism about music, arguably inconsistent with the composer's own practice.)

* Sullivan, J.W.N. (1927) *Beethoven: His Spiritual Development*, London: Jonathan Cape. (Suggests that some music, such as the last compositions of Beethoven, embodies and communicates to a listener spiritually and cognitively valuable states of mind.)

Tanner, M. (1985) 'Understanding Music', *Proceedings of the Aristotelian Society Supplement* 59: 215–32. (Emphasizes a hierarchy of levels of understanding music, with higher levels presupposing lower ones if they are to have any point.)

Thom, P. (1993) *For an Audience: A Philosophy of the Performing Arts*, Philadelphia, PA: Temple University Press. (Advances a naturalistic understanding of works in the performing arts.)

Tormey, A. (1971) *The Concept of Expression*, Princeton, NJ: Princeton University Press. (A seminal philosophical analysis, containing a devastating attack on the Expression Theory of music.)

—— (1974) 'Indeterminacy and Identity in Art', *The Monist* 58: 203–15. (Explores the sort of ontology of music suggested by, or appropriate to, certain modes of avant-garde composition.)

Walton, K. (1996) *Looking, Listening, Imagining*, Oxford: Oxford University Press. (A collection of essays by a leading aesthetician, some of which bring the author's doctrine of make-believe to bear on issues about musical understanding and content.)

Wolterstorff, N. (1980) *Works and Worlds of Art*, Oxford: Oxford University Press. (Contains important proposals regarding the ontology and composition of music.)

Zuckerkandl, V. (1956) *Sound and Symbol: Music and the External World*, Princeton, NJ: Princeton University Press. (A wide-ranging examination of the phenomenon of music, focusing on the paradox of tonal motion and the experience of musical time.)

JERROLD LEVINSON

MUSLIM ETHICS *see* ETHICS IN ISLAMIC PHILOSOPHY

MUSLIM PHILOSOPHY
see ISLAM, CONCEPT OF PHILOSOPHY IN; ISLAMIC PHILOSOPHY

MUSLIM THEOLOGY
see ISLAMIC THEOLOGY

MUSONIUS RUFUS
(1st century AD)

Gaius Musonius Rufus was a Stoic philosopher who taught in Rome. Active on the margins of political life, he was twice exiled and recalled. His surviving work focuses on practical ethics. Besides his distinctive views on marriage, sexual morality and women's education, Musonius is important for his influence on Epictetus.

Born before AD 30 in Etruria, Musonius was a member of the wealthy equestrian class, not the senatorial aristocracy. He taught in Greek, and his influence in Neronian and Flavian Rome was considerable. After being exiled by Nero for his links to Stoic senators, his fame grew and followers joined him on the island of Gyara. Recalled to Rome at Nero's death, he resumed lecturing and successfully prosecuted the persecutor of a Stoic senator. He was later exiled and recalled again under the Flavian emperors. By the time of his death, probably before AD 100, he had become a symbol of the philosophical life for the Roman aristocracy.

Although Musonius wrote nothing, accounts of many of his lectures were taken down and published after his death. Extracts from twenty-one survive in a late anthology; these and some short quotations and anecdotes are all that remain today. His thought is rooted in the Socratic tradition. Happiness (see EUDAIMONIA) is the ultimate goal; the human species is defined by its natural rationality and desire for the good. The virtues (see ARETĒ) include justice, courage, wisdom and self-control (*sōphrosynē*), though emphasis is given to self-control, especially in matters of sex, food and personal adornment. Virtues are understood partly in terms of the traditional craft analogy. Training (*askēsis*) and endurance are emphasized; practical application overshadows theory.

As a Stoic, Musonius held that human nature is essentially rational and that our function is to act in accordance with reason and the providential plan for the world laid down by the gods (see STOICISM).

Human reasoning is to be used to support and complement our nature, never to transcend it or transform it. Since women have the same nature as men, they need and deserve the same education. Although their social roles differ, men and women have equal need of philosophy to guide their lives; similarly kings should practise philosophy, though the manual work of farming is held to be the ideal activity for a philosopher.

Musonius advanced the distinctive view that the natural function of sexual activity is only to produce offspring; hence all other sexual relations, heterosexual or homosexual, are improper and reveal a lack of self-control. Even in marriage, sex for pleasure alone is wrong. The goal of marriage is the rearing of many children (abortion and exposure of infants being contrary to nature) and the cultivation of companionship between spouses, which is both a symbol of and the foundation for social relations generally. Though we may suspect the influence of Roman social values on this teaching, Musonius supports his position with arguments based on natural teleology. His central theme is the importance of self-control in the service of a rationally articulated understanding of human nature.

References and further reading

Arnold, E.V. (1911) *Roman Stoicism*, Cambridge: Cambridge University Press. (Standard work, somewhat dated but still useful.)

Laurenti, R. (1989) 'Musonio, maestro di Epitteto' (Musonius, Master of Epictetus), in W. Haase (ed.) *Aufstieg und Niedergang der römischen Welt*, Berlin and New York: de Gruyter, II 36 3: 2,105–46. (Good survey of Musonius' views with emphasis on his relationship to Epictetus.)

Musonius Rufus (1st century AD) Surviving Writings in O. Hense, *C. Musonius Rufus Reliquiae*, Leipzig: Teubner, 1905; C.E. Lutz, 'Musonius Rufus "The Roman Socrates"', *Yale Classical Studies* 10: 3–147, 1947; A. Jagu, *Musonius Rufus. Entretiens et fragments. Introduction, traduction et commentaire*, Hildesheim and New York: Olms, 1979; I. Andorlini and R. Laurenti, *Corpus dei papiri filosofici Greci e Latini*, Florence: Olschki, 1992, vol. 1, 480–92. (Hense is the standard critical text; Lutz includes the text and a complete English translation of the discourses preserved by Stobaeus, with useful introduction; Jagu offers French translation and commentary; Andorlini and Laurenti edit further fragments found on papyrus.)

Van Geytenbeek, A.C. (1963) *Musonius Rufus and the Greek Diatribe*, Assen: Van Gorcum. (A useful treatment of his life, intellectual affiliations and distinctive views.)

BRAD INWOOD

MU'TAZILA *see* ASH'ARIYYA AND MU'TAZILA

MYSTICAL PHILOSOPHY IN ISLAM

Mystical philosophy has an intimate connection with the mainstream of Islamic philosophy. It consists of several main strands, ranging from Isma'ili thought to the metaphysics of al-Ghazali and Ibn al-'Arabi, and with a continuing powerful presence in the contemporary Islamic world. Although mystical thinkers were aware that they were advocating an approach to thinking and knowledge which differed from much of the Peripatetic tradition, they constructed a systematic approach which was often continuous with that tradition. On the whole they emphasized the role of intellectual intuition in our approach to understanding reality, and sought to show how such an understanding might be put on a solid conceptual basis. The ideas that they created were designed to throw light on the nature of the inner sense of Islam.

1 **Mystical philosophy as Islamic philosophy**
2 **Isma'ili and Hermetic philosophy**
3 **Illuminationist philosophy**
4 **Philosophy in the Maghrib and Spain**
5 **Illuminationist thought in the East**
6 **Sufism and the Akbarian tradition**

1 Mystical philosophy as Islamic philosophy

It is important at the outset to ask what is meant by mystical philosophy in the context of the Islamic philosophical tradition. The term in Arabic closest to the phrase 'mystical philosophy' would perhaps be *al-hikmat al-dhawqiyya*, literally 'tasted philosophy or wisdom', which etymologically corresponds exactly to sapience from the Latin root *sapere*, meaning to taste. As understood in English, however, the term 'mystical philosophy' would include other types of thought in the Islamic context, although *al-hikmat al-dhawqiyya* was at its heart. *Al-hikmat al-dhawqiyya* is usually contrasted with discursive philosophy, or *al-hikmat al-bahthiyya*. Mystical philosophy in Islam would have to include all intellectual perspectives, which consider not only reason but also the heart-intellect, in fact primarily the latter as the main instrument for the gaining of knowledge. If this definition is accepted, then most schools of Islamic philosophy had a mystical element, for there was rarely a rationalistic philosophy developed in Islam which remained impervious to the distinction between reason and the intellect (as *nous* or *intellectus*) and the primacy of the latter while rejecting altogether the role of the heart-intellect in gaining knowledge.

This entry concentrates on those schools which not only include but emphasize *noesis* and the role of the heart-intellect or illumination in the attainment of knowledge. We shall therefore leave aside the Peripatetic school, despite the mystical elements in certain works of AL-FARABI, the 'oriental philosophy' of IBN SINA (Nasr 1996b) and the doctrine of the intellect adopted by the Muslim Peripatetics (*mashsha'un*) in general. Instead, the discussion will concentrate primarily upon the Isma'ili philosophy so closely connected with Hermetic, Pythagorean and Neoplatonic teachings, the school of Illumination (*ishraq*) of al-Suhrawardi and his followers, certain strands of Islamic philosophy in Spain and later Islamic philosophy in Persia and India. However, it would also have to include the doctrinal formulations of Sufism and its metaphysics from al-Ghazali and Ibn al-'Arabi to the present.

2 Isma'ili and Hermetic philosophy

Isma'ili philosophy was among the earliest to be formulated in Islam going back to the *Umm al-kitab* (The Mother of Books) composed in the second century AH (eighth century AD). It expanded in the fourth century AH (tenth century AD) with Abu Hatim al-Razi and Hamid al-Din Kirmani and culminated with Nasir-i Khusraw (Corbin 1993, 1994). By nature this whole philosophical tradition was esoteric in character and identified philosophy itself with the inner, esoteric and therefore mystical dimension of religion. It was concerned with the hermeneutic interpretation (*ta'wil*) of sacred scripture and saw authentic philosophy as a wisdom which issues from the instructions of the Imam (who is identified on a certain level with the heart-intellect), the figure who is able to actualize the potentialities of the human intellect and enable it to gain divine knowledge. The cosmology, psychology and eschatology of Isma'ilism are inextricably connected with its Imamology and the role of the Imam in initiation into the divine mysteries. All the different schools of Isma'ili philosophy, therefore, must be considered as mystical philosophy despite notable distinctions between

them, especially, following the downfall of the Fatimids, between the interpretations of those who followed the Yemeni school of Isma'ilism and those who accepted Hasan al-Sabbah and 'The Resurrection of Alamut' in the seventh century AH (thirteenth century AD).

Two of the notable philosophical elements associated with Shi'ism in general and Isma'ilism in particular during the early centuries of Islamic history are Hermetism and Pythagoreanism, the presence of which is already evident in that vast corpus of writings associated with Jabir ibn Hayyan, who was at once alchemist and philosopher. The philosophical dimension of the Jabirian corpus is certainly of a mystical nature, having incorporated much of Hermeticism into itself, as are later works of Islamic alchemy which in fact acted as channels for the transmission of Hermetic philosophy to the medieval West. When one thinks of the central role of Hermeticism in Western mystical philosophy, one must not forget the immediate Islamic origin of such fundamental texts as the *Emerald Tablet* and the *Turba Philosophorum*, and therefore the significance of such works as texts of Islamic mystical philosophy. Obviously, therefore, one could not speak of Islamic mystical philosophy without mentioning at least the Hermetical texts integrated into Islamic thought by alchemists as well as philosophers and Sufis, and also Hermetic texts written by Muslim authors themselves. It should be recalled in this context in fact that the philosopher Ibn Sina had knowledge of certain Hermetic texts such as *Poimandres* and the Sufi Ibn al-'Arabi displays vast knowledge of Hermeticism in his *al-Futuhat al-makkiyya* (The Meccan Illuminations) and many other works (Sezgin 1971).

As for Pythagoreanism, although elements of it are seen in the Jabirian corpus, it was primarily in the *Rasa'il* (Epistles) of the Ikhwan al-Safa' in the fourth century AH (tenth century AD), who came from a Shi'ite background and whose work was wholly adopted by later Isma'ilism, that one sees the full development of an Islamic Pythagoreanism based upon the symbolic and mystical understanding of numbers and geometric forms (Netton 1982) (see IKHWAN AL-SAFA'). What is called Pythagorean number mysticism in the West had a full development in the Islamic world, and was in fact more easily integrated into the general Islamic intellectual framework than into that of Western Christianity (see PYTHAGOREANISM).

3 Illuminationist philosophy

Perhaps the most enduring and influential school of mystical philosophy in Islam came into being in the sixth century AH (twelfth century AD) with Shihab al-Din AL-SUHRAWARDI, who founded the school of *ishraq* or Illumination. Al-Suhrawardi's basic premise was that knowledge is available to man not through ratiocination alone but also, and above all, through illumination resulting from the purification of one's inner being. He founded a school of philosophy which some have called theosophy in its original sense, that is, mystical philosophy through and through but without being against logic or the use of reason. In fact, al-Suhrawardi criticized Aristotle and the Muslim Peripatetics on logical grounds before setting about expounding the doctrine of *ishraq*. This doctrine is based not on the refutation of logic, but of transcending its categories through an illuminationist knowledge based on immediacy and presence, or what al-Suhrawardi himself called 'knowledge by presence' (*al-'ilm al-huduri*), in contrast to conceptual knowledge (*al-'ilm al-husuli*) which is our ordinary method of knowing based on concepts (Ha'iri Yazdi 1992).

In his masterpiece *Hikmat al-ishraq* (The Philosophy of Illumination), translated by the foremost Western student of al-Suhrawardi, Henry Corbin, as *Le Livre de la Sagesse Orientale* (The Book of Oriental Wisdom), the Master of Illumination presents an exposition of a form of mystical philosophy which has had a following up to the present day. Based upon the primacy of illumination by the angelic lights as the primary means of attaining authentic knowledge, the school of *ishraq* in fact was instrumental in bestowing a mystical character upon nearly all later Islamic philosophy, which drew even closer to Islamic esotericism or Sufism than in the earlier centuries of Islamic history without ever ceasing to be philosophy. Although the wedding between philosophy and mysticism in Islam is due most of all to the gnostic and sapiential nature of Islamic spirituality itself, on the formal level it is most of all the school of Illumination or *ishraq* which was instrumental in actualizing this wedding, as eight centuries of later Islamic philosophy bears witness (see ILLUMINATION-IST PHILOSOPHY).

4   Philosophy in the Maghrib and Spain

The rise of intellectual activity in the Maghrib and, especially, Andalusia was associated from the beginning with an intellectual form of Sufism in which IBN MASARRA was to play a central role. Most of the later Islamic philosophers of this region possessed a mystical dimension, including even the Peripatetics IBN BAJJA and IBN TUFAYL. The former's *Tadbir al-mutawahhid* (Regimen of the Solitary), far from being a political treatise, deals in reality with man's inner being. Ibn Tufayl's *Hayy ibn Yaqzan* (Living Son of the Awake), interpreted by many in the West in naturalistic and rationalistic terms, is a symbolic account of the wedding between the partial and universal intellect within the human being, a wedding which results consequently in the confirmation of revelation that is also received through the archangel of revelation, who is none other than the objective embodiment of the universal intellect. Moreover, this mystical tendency is to be seen in its fullness in less well-known figures such as Ibn al-Sid of Badajoz who, like the Ikhwan al-Safa', was devoted to mathematical mysticism, and especially the Sufi IBN SAB'IN, the last of the Andalusian philosophers of the seventh century AH (thirteenth century AD), who developed one of the most extreme forms of mystical philosophy in Islam based upon the doctrine of the transcendent unity of being (*wahdat al-wujud*) (Taftazani and Leaman 1996). Andalusia was also the home of the greatest expositor of Sufi metaphysics, Ibn al-'Arabi (see §6).

5   Illuminationist thought in the East

In eastern lands of the Islamic world and especially Persia, which was the main theatre for the flourishing of Islamic philosophy from the seventh century AH (thirteenth century AD) onward, primarily mystical philosophy was dominant during later centuries despite the revival of the discursive philosophy of the *mashsha'i*s, such as Ibn Sina, by Khwajah Nasir al-Din AL-TUSI and others. It was in the East in the seventh and eighth centuries AH (thirteenth and fourteenth centuries AD) that the doctrines of *ishraq* with its emphasis on inner vision and illumination were revived by al-Suhrawardi's major commentators, Shams al-Din al-Shahrazuri and Qutb al-Din al-Shirazi, who was also a master of Ibn Sinan philosophy. The next three centuries saw mystical ideas and doctrines become ever more combined with the philosophical theses of the earlier schools, and figures such as Ibn Turkah Isfahani sought consciously to combine the teachings of Ibn Sina, al-Suhrawardi and Ibn al-'Arabi.

This tendency culminated in the tenth century AH (sixteenth century AD) with the establishment of the School of Isfahan by MIR DAMAD and the foremost metaphysician of later Islamic thought, MULLA SADRA, in whom the blending of ratiocination, inner illumination and revelation became complete (Corbin 1972). In this school the most rigorous logical discourse is combined with illumination and direct experience of ultimate reality, as seen so amply in Mulla Sadra's masterpiece *al-Asfar al-arba'ah* (The Four Journeys). This later Islamic philosophy is certainly mystical philosophy, relying as it does on 'experiential' knowledge and direct vision of ultimate reality and the angelic worlds, a vision that is associated with the eye of the heart (*'ayn al-qalb* or *chism-i dil*). However, it is also a philosophy in which the categories of logic are themselves seen as ladders for ascent to the world of numinous reality in accordance with the Islamic perspective, in which what would be called Islamic mysticism from a Christian perspective is of a gnostic (*'irfani*) and sapiental nature, Islamic mysticism being essentially a path of knowledge of which love is the consort, rather than a way of love exclusive of knowledge.

In any case it was this type of philosophy, associated especially with the name of Mulla Sadra, that has dominated the philosophical scene in Persia during the past few centuries and produced major figures such as Hajji Mulla Hadi AL-SABZAWARI and Mulla 'Ali Zunuzi in the thirteenth century AH (nineteenth century AD), both of whom were philosophers as well as mystics. It is also this type of philosophy that continues to this day and has in fact been revived during the past few decades. Nearly all philosophers in Persia associated with the school of Mulla Sadra, which is also known as *al-hikmat al-muta'aliya* (literally the 'transcendent theosophy'), have been and remain at once philosophers and mystics.

In India likewise, Islamic philosophy began to spread only after al-Suhrawardi and during the past seven centuries most Islamic philosophers in that land have been also what in the West would be called mystics. It is not accidental that the school of Mulla Sadra spread rapidly after him in India and has had expositors there to this day. Perhaps the most famous of Muslim intellectual figures in India, Shah Waliullah of Delhi, exemplifies this reality (see SHAH WALI ALLAH). He was a philosopher and Sufi as well as a theologian, and his many writings attest to the blending of philosophy and mysticism. It can in fact be said that Islamic philosophy in India is essentially mystical philosophy, despite the attention paid by the Islamic philosophers there to logic and in some cases to natural philosophy and medicine.

6 Sufism and the Akbarian tradition

No treatment of mystical philosophy in Islam would be complete without a discussion of doctrinal Sufism and Sufi metaphysics, although technically speaking in Islamic civilization a clear distinction has always been made between philosophy (*al-falsafa* or *al-hikma*) and Sufi metaphysics and gnosis (*al-ma'rifah*, *'irfan*). However, as the term 'mystical philosophy' is understood in English, it would certainly include Sufi

metaphysical and cosmological doctrines which were not explicitly formulated until the sixth and seventh centuries AH (twelfth and thirteenth centuries AD) although their roots are to be found in the Qur'an and hadith and the sayings and writings of the early Sufis. The first Sufi authors who turned to an explicit formulation of Sufi metaphysical doctrines were Abu Hamid Muhammad AL-GHAZALI in his later esoteric treatise such as *Mishkat al-anwar* (The Niche of Lights) and *al-Risalat al-laduniyya* (Treatise on Divine Knowledge), and 'Ayn al-Qudat Hamadani who followed a generation after him.

The writings of these great masters were, however, a prelude for the vast expositions of the master of Islamic gnosis Muhyi al-Din IBN AL-'ARABI, perhaps the most influential Islamic intellectual figure of the past seven hundred years. Not only did he profoundly influence many currents of Sufism and establish an 'Akbarian tradition' identified with such later masters as Sadr al-Din Qunawi, 'Abd al-Rahman Jami and, in the last century, Amir 'Abd al-Qadir and Shaykh Ahmad al-'Alawi. He and his school also influenced formal philosophy to such an extent that a figure such as Mulla Sadra would not be conceivable without him. The Ibn al-'Arabian doctrines of the transcendent unity of being, the universal man, the imaginal world and eschatological realities are not only esoteric and mystical doctrines of the greatest significance in themselves for the understanding of the inner teachings of Islam, but are also sources of philosophical meditation for generations of Islamic philosophers to the present day, who have cultivated diverse and rich schools of mystical philosophy during the past eight centuries and brought into being currents of philosophical thought that are still alive in the Islamic world. One need only think of such fourteenth century AH (twentieth century AD) figures as 'Alalamah Tabatab'i in Persia and 'Abd al-Halim Mahmud in Egypt to realize the significance of the wedding between philosophy and mysticism in the Islamic intellectual tradition, not only over the ages, but as part of the contemporary Islamic intellectual scene (see ISLAMIC PHILOSOPHY, MODERN).

See also: GNOSTICISM; IBN AL-'ARABI; ILLUMINATIONIST PHILOSOPHY; MYSTICISM, HISTORY OF; MYSTICISM, NATURE AND ASSESSMENT OF; AL-SUHRAWARDI

References and further reading

Chittick, W. (1989) *The Sufi Path of Knowledge*, Albany, NY: State University of New York Press. (The standard account of the nature of mystical knowledge.)

—— (1994) *Imaginal Worlds: Ibn al-'Arabi and the Problem of Religious Diversity*, Albany, NY: State University of New York Press. (An analysis of the concept of the *mundus imaginalis*.)

Chodkiewicz, M. (1993) *Seal of the Saints – Prophethood and Sainthood in the Doctrine of Ibn 'Arabi*, trans. L. Sherrard, Cambridge: Islamic Texts Society. (Close account of the key concepts of prophecy and sainthood.)

* Corbin, H. (1972) *En Islam iranien* (On Persian Islam) Paris: Gallimard. (The most important collection of sources of Persian philosophy.)

—— (1980) *Avicenna and the Visionary Recital*, trans. W. Trask, Houston, TX: Spring Publications. (Ibn Sina's account of mystical perception.)

* —— (1993) *The History of Islamic Philosophy*, in collaboration with S.H. Nasr and O. Yahya, trans. P. Sherrard, London: Kegan Paul International. (The first history to lay proper emphasis on Persian philosophy.)

* —— (1994) *Trilogie ismaélienne* (Isma'ili Trilogy), Paris: Verdier. (Discussion of some of the most important Isma'ili texts.)

Cruz Hernández, M. (1981) *Historia del pensamiento en el mundo islámico* (History of Thought in the Islamic World), Madrid: Alianza Editorial. (Excellent general account of Islamic philosophy.)

* Ha'iri Yazdi, M. (1992) *The Principles of Epistemology in Islamic Philosophy – Knowledge by Presence*, Albany, NY: State University of New York Press. (The best account of *'ilm al-huduri*, knowledge by presence.)

Knysh, A. (1993) 'The Diffusion of Ibn 'Arabi's Doctrine', in S. Hirtenstein and M. Tiernan (eds) *Muhyiddin ibn 'Arabi – A Commemorative Volume*, Shaftesbury: Element, 307–27. (Discussion of the influence of Ibn al-'Arabi.)

Nanji, A. (1996) 'Isma'ili Philosophy', in S.H. Nasr and O. Leaman (eds) *History of Islamic Philosophy*, London: Routledge, ch. 9, 144–54. (Examination of Isma'ili philosophy including the influence of Neoplatonism.)

Nasr, S.H. (1975) *Three Muslim Sages*, New York: Delmar. (Excellent introductions to Ibn Sina, al-Suhrawardi and Ibn al-'Arabi.)

—— (1978) *Islamic Life and Thought*, Albany, NY: State University of New York Press. (General introduction to the role of mysticism in Islamic culture.)

—— (1996a) 'Ibn Sina's Oriental Philosophy', in S.H. Nasr and O. Leaman (eds) *History of Islamic Philosophy*, London: Routledge, 247–51. (Argument for the existence and importance of the 'oriental philosophy'.)

* —— (1996b) *The Islamic Intellectual Tradition in Persia*, Richmond: Curzon Press. (Deals with the Persian contribution to philosophy and mysticism.)

* Netton, I. (1982) *Muslim Neoplatonists: An Introduction to the Thought of the Brethren of Purity*, London: Allen & Unwin. (The standard account of the Ikhwan al-Safa'.)

* Sezgin, F. (1971) *Geschichte des arabischen Schrifttums* (History of Arabic Literature), vol. 4, Leiden: Brill. (Sources on Hermetism in Islamic literature.)

* al-Suhrawardi (1154–91) *Hikmat al-ishraq* (The Philosophy of Illumination), trans H. Corbin, *Le livre de la sagesse orientale*, Paris: Verdier, 1986. (Very important illuminationist text.)

* Taftazani, A. and Leaman, O. (1996) 'Ibn Sab'in', in S.H. Nasr and O. Leaman (eds) *History of Islamic Philosophy*, London: Routledge, 346–9. (Discussion of the significance of the thought of Ibn Sab'in.)

Ziai, H. (1990) *Knowledge and Illumination*, Atlanta, GA: Scholars Press. (Very clear account of the links between illuminationist philosophy and epistemology.)

SEYYED HOSSEIN NASR

MYSTICISM, HISTORY OF

Contemporary authors generally associate mysticism with a form of consciousness involving an apparent encounter or union with an ultimate order of reality, however this is understood. Mysticism in this sense, it is argued, can be found in virtually all cultures and religious traditions, and is perhaps as old as humanity itself. None the less, there is no agreement on the identifying characteristics of mystical states; the term 'mysticism' and its cognates have undergone long evolution and been used in a bewildering variety of ways.

Such ongoing disputes about the nature and significance of mysticism only underscore both the challenge and the importance of studying its history. On the one hand, without consensus on a definition, scholars disagree on which texts and figures merit inclusion in a historical survey of mysticism. On the other hand, arguments about whether mystical experiences are 'everywhere the same' can hardly be settled apart from attention to the historical evidence.

1 **Methodological issues**
2 **Mysticism of ancient and indigenous communities**
3 **Indian mysticism**
4 **Mysticism in China and Japan**
5 **Jewish mysticism**
6 **Christian mysticism**
7 **Islamic mysticism**

1 Methodological issues

Increasingly, scholars debate not only the data but also the proper methodology for studying mysticism's history. Lack of consensus on a definition of mysticism gives rise to corresponding disagreements over who and what to classify as truly mystical, a problem compounded by the modern tendency to identify mysticism exclusively with certain subjective experiences involving 'pure undifferentiated consciousness' or 'union'. We have no direct access, after all, to the states of consciousness of past mystics, but only to the texts and other artefacts they have left behind, from which it is generally difficult to extract clear 'phenomenological' descriptions of the sort modern commentators seek.

Another problem is that if, according to some definitions, mysticism is a fundamental mode of human consciousness present in every era, or even a tacit dimension of all human experience, a comprehensive history of mysticism would have to include all human history and experience, something obviously impossible. Still, we may suppose that for every mystic recognized today, hundreds more have left behind no traces (for example, because they lived in pre-literate communities, or their works were lost, or they felt no urge to record their experiences). Thus any account of the history of mysticism has an essentially modest scope, since it illuminates only a small portion of the totality of human mystical experience, most of which will remain forever inaccessible. At the same time, however, modern scholarship is opening up a wealth of new material that has been forgotten or under-utilized in the tradition. Feminists, for example, are retrieving the testimony of women mystics, noting what is distinctive about their experience. Such research continues to enlarge and modify our understanding of mysticism's history.

The present entry briefly traces several strands of mysticism according to the religious traditions out of which they emerged. No claim is made that this is the best or most complete approach; mystical experiences may occur to people of no formal religious affiliation. Nevertheless, even the most unorthodox of the great mystics generally have their roots in a specific religious tradition, and cannot be adequately understood apart from it.

2 Mysticism of ancient and indigenous communities

So-called 'extrovertive' or 'nature' mysticism, involving an experience of a sacred unity in and with all things, is a relatively common human phenomenon, even where evidence for other forms of mystical experience is wanting (an example here is the alleged 'mystical' quality of many prehistoric cave paintings or ancient carvings). The spiritualities of many archaic cultures and indigenous peoples involve the celebration (and sometimes restoration) of a communal and individual sense of 'oneness' with the whole created order.

Eliade (1964) and others discern a mystical element in shamanism, and in the 'spirit possession' of African mediums. Native American peoples of the Central Plains region retain the tradition of the 'vision quest', in which seekers undertake an ascetic discipline to encounter their 'spirit guide'. Though the results of these practices may not be an experience of 'undifferentiated unity', the processes involved and the ecstatic states attained bear certain affinities to the mystical disciplines of more familiar traditions.

3 Indian mysticism

Among the earliest recorded manifestations of mysticism are those from the Indian subcontinent. Even before the second millennium BC, the pre-Aryan civilization apparently practised a form of yoga. The polytheistic religion of the invading Aryans centred on ritual sacrifice, but gradually evolved in a mystical direction as its practitioners reflected upon the inner significance of the sacrifices, and Brahman (originally identified with the sacred power contained in the rites) came increasingly to be understood as a universal principle or power underlying all reality.

Out of this context, and over many centuries, emerged the Vedas, a fluid canon of sacred writings accepted as revelation (śruti) by orthodox Hindus; among these the Upaniṣads propose a path of mystical insight allowing liberation (mokṣa or mukti) from the vicissitudes of human existence. The Upaniṣads are concerned with the relationship between Brahman (the Supreme Soul or Absolute) and ātman (the eternal inner soul or self), a relationship summarized in the classic formulation tat tvam asi, 'thou art that'; in other words, the eternal self, realized through meditation and asceticism, is ultimately one with the Absolute (see BRAHMAN).

The Upaniṣads themselves, however, incorporate a variety of tendencies from the preceding traditions. The Śvetāśvatara Upaniṣad, for example, contains an unusually strong theistic strain, and speaks of the path to union with the Supreme Self through devotion (bhakti); other Upaniṣads seem to support a strict identity between ātman and Brahman. The Māṇḍūkya Upaniṣad, often cited in Western philosophical discussions of mystical experience, speaks of a state of consciousness beyond dreamless sleep: 'unperceived, unrelated, incomprehensible, uninferable, unthinkable, and indescribable', 'all peace, all bliss, and nondual', 'this is *ātman*, and this has to be realized' (Māṇḍūkya Upaniṣad, 7).

Other movements emerging between 800 and 500 BC developed approaches to mysticism that were atheistic or agnostic in their implications. Like the Sāṅkhya philosophy associated with classical yoga, Jainism maintains the ultimate status not of a single divine monad but of an infinity of individual souls; the goal of the mystical journey is to isolate this self-monad from its immersion in materiality. Early Buddhism, by contrast, developed the doctrine of 'no self' (*anatta*) and impermanence (*anicca*), analysing persons as a series of transitory states and denying the existence of any underlying eternal self. According to Buddhist tradition, Prince Gautama Siddhartha (born perhaps in the latter half of the sixth century BC) left home and family to seek the cause of human suffering and the way to liberation from it. After years of harsh asceticism and searching, he discovered the Middle Path (between sensuality and excessive austerity) and, while meditating beneath a *bo* (or *bodhi*) tree, attained *nirvāṇa*, that is, supreme peace and enlightenment (*bodhi*) – hence the title 'Buddha' ('Enlightened One'). The BUDDHA taught his disciples that by following the Noble Eightfold Path and attaining *nirvāṇa*, the cycle of rebirth, the illusion of selfhood, and the suffering caused by ignorance and craving can be overcome. In succeeding centuries, as it flourished and spread to other parts of Asia, Buddhism underwent extensive scholastic systematization (for example, in the dialectical method developed by Nāgārjuna in the second century) and evolved into several schools, most notably Theravāda (probably closer to the Buddha's original doctrine and found today in Sri Lanka, Myanmar and southeast Asia) and Mahāyāna (in China, Japan and Korea).

Crucial to the development of later Indian mysticism is the *Bhagavad Gītā*, a famous mystical poem (in the form of a dialogue between Lord Arjuna and Krishna) which presents three paths to salvation – the way of knowledge, the way of works, and the way of devotion (*bhakti*) or loving adoration – and which (on some interpretations) seems to give a higher place to *bhakti* than to contemplative yoga. Since Krishna is a manifestation of Vishnu, the poem clearly contains a theistic element, but there are monistic strains as well.

Such diverse tendencies eventually gave rise in the medieval period to three main schools of Vedānta (the 'end' or systematic explanation of the Veda) (see VEDĀNTA). ŚAṄKARA gave the Upanishadic formula 'thou art that' its most radical nondualistic (*advaita*) interpretation, insisting on a strict numerical identity between the soul and Brahman; though allowing for worship and devotion on the level of appearances, he believed these to be transcended in union. Against this view, the eleventh-century thinker RĀMĀNUJA developed a position of 'qualified nondualism'; he recognized an impersonal mysticism of undifferentiated unity, but ranked it inferior to loving communion with a personal God. Two centuries later, MADHVA propounded a dualistic (*dvaita*) system of thought. He argued for a radical pluralism among God (*īśvara*), individual souls and non-intelligent substances, and maintained that it is God who decides the destinies of all finite selves.

More recently, AUROBINDO GHOSE has attempted to combine elements of traditional Hindu theology with an evolutionary mysticism. But perhaps the best-known modern representative of Vedāntic spirituality is Ramakrishna (1834–86), whose life and message of universalism were popularized in the West by Swami Vivekananda (1862–1902), organizer of the Ramakrishna Mission, which combined Advaita philosophy with a deep concern for social issues (see RAMAKRISHNA MOVEMENT).

4 Mysticism in China and Japan

Despite its influence on later Hinduism, Buddhism largely died out within India itself after the revival of Vedantism. Elsewhere in Asia, however, Buddhism continued to spread and evolve as it encountered other traditions.

With its focus on harmonious relations between the 'superior individual' and a well-ordered society, early Confucianism appears as a form of ethical humanism, though a mystical element emerges more clearly in the *Book of Mencius* and in later neo-Confucianism, under Daoist influence (see CHINESE PHILOSOPHY §§4–5). By contrast, the *Daodejing* (ascribed to Laozi, considered the founder of Daoism) has a more mystical tone. Here the Dao or Way is regarded as both the natural order of the universe, and a life lived in harmony with that order. Laozi advises the sage to act spontaneously and effortlessly, through non-action (*wuwei*). The *Daodejing* is relatively silent on mystical disciplines or states of consciousness, which are treated in more detail in the later *Book of Zhuangzi* (see DAODEJING).

Daoism exerted a powerful influence on *Chan* (Japanese *Zen*) Buddhism, a school of Mahāyāna Buddhism developed in China and Japan (see JAPANESE PHILOSOPHY §5). Here there is a strong emphasis on sudden illumination (*satori*), often after prolonged sitting meditation (*zazen*), concentrating under the direction of a master (*roshi*) on an assigned *koan* (a paradoxical question or answer designed to stop ordinary conceptual thinking). The two principle surviving Zen schools are Rinzai and Sōtō, brought to

Japan by Eisai (1141–1215) and DŌGEN respectively. Dōgen and the Sōtō school emphasize the centrality of the Zen meditation practice itself, not as a means to an end, but as the realization of one's own already present Buddha-nature. By contrast, *roshis* of the Rinzai school have traditionally used *koans* and even startling and eccentric behaviour (slaps, sudden gestures, and so on) to evoke in their pupils a condition of great doubt and mental tension leading to the sudden breakthrough of *satori*. Revitalized in the eighteenth century by Hakuin (1685–1768), who systematized the use of *koans* and left detailed descriptions of his own mystical experiences, Rinzai has become the best-known branch of Zen in the West, largely through the efforts of D.T. Suzuki (1870–1966).

5 Jewish mysticism

Though the Hebrew Scriptures describe many encounters with the God of Israel (for example, Moses before the burning bush, Elijah at Horeb, Isaiah's Temple vision), encounters often treated as paradigmatic in later Jewish and Christian mystical texts, many modern scholars prefer to classify these as numinous states, since they seem to involve the overwhelming sense of a sacred presence external to the subject, rather than an absorption into the divine. In the post-exilic period, Jewish spirituality became increasingly eschatological, even apocalyptic, giving rise in the first century BC to *merkavah* (chariot) mysticism, involving Gnostic-influenced mystical speculations on Ezekiel's vision of the throne-chariot (Ezekiel 1), and the possibility of ascending through various spheres to the divine throne. Though *merkavah* mysticism declined in the Middle Ages, it left its imprint on the more popular movement of medieval Hasidism, which through prayer and religious practices cultivated intense awareness of the omnipresent creator (see HASIDISM).

The first-century philosopher PHILO OF ALEXANDRIA (§§1, 4), so deeply influenced by Greek thought, is usually ranked among the Hellenistic philosophers rather than within the main currents of Jewish spirituality. Nevertheless, he encourages pursuit of the direct vision of God, and develops a highly allegorical method for discerning mystical meanings in scriptural texts.

The Jewish spiritual movement known as Kabbalah found classic expression in the *Zohar* (Splendour), a massive and esoteric work claiming great antiquity but more probably dating from the thirteenth century. According to its complex speculations, echoing Gnostic and Neoplatonic themes, God is conceived as the Eyn Sof (Infinite), without qualities, but

emanating ten ideal qualities, or Sefirot, the lowest of which includes the created order. Creation occurs within God, through a divinely initiated self-differentiation, and each soul contains some of the Sefirot. But since Adam's Fall, the *Shekinah*, or divine presence, has been exiled from the Eyn Sof, and so the goal of the devout is to become aware of the divine presence within and thus help reunite the *Shekinah* with the Eyn Sof, restoring the cosmic order. Isaac Luria (1534–72), a major figure of this mystical school, conceived Adam as a cosmic figure (Adam Kadmon) whose Fall brought about the shattering of the ideal universe into the present material world, with the divine light broken up into the many sparks of individual souls; through prayer and concentrated devotion (*kevannah*) human beings could take an active role in the ultimate reintegration (*tikkun*) of all things (see KABBALAH).

More popular than speculative, modern Hasidism originated in the eighteenth century with Israel Baal Shem Tov (1700–60) and his successor Baer of Meseritz (1710–72). This mystical and devotional movement emphasizes especially the role of the Tzaddik, or perfectly righteous person, who alone can guide others effectively in their spiritual journey. Hasidism remains a strong force within contemporary Judaism.

6 Christian mysticism

Christianity rests upon Jesus of Nazareth, and his consciousness of a deep continual communion with the God of Israel, whom he boldly addresses as 'Abba' ('dear Father'). This so-called 'Abba-experience' has been compared with the experiences of mystics, though Jesus himself (according to the evidence of the Gospels) seems to have claimed an utterly unique and unprecedented intimacy with the divine (Christian dogma identifies him as the sole incarnation of the Second Person of the Trinity) (see INCARNATION AND CHRISTOLOGY §1).

Strikingly, though states arguably 'mystical' in the contemporary sense are reported among Jesus' first followers, the word *mystikos* itself appears nowhere in the New Testament; on the other hand, 'mystery' (*mysterion*) figures prominently in the Pauline letters. Past historians of religion detected here the influence of ancient mystery cults, and claimed that Christian mysticism was largely imported. Louis Bouyer (1990) and others have argued, however, that while the secrecy of the mystery religions pertained only to their rituals, St Paul uses 'mystery' in a different sense, Semitic in origin, to refer to God's hidden plan for the salvation of the world, now revealed in Christ.

None the less, Hellenistic influences on the

subsequent evolution of Christian spirituality and mystical theology are undeniable, beginning with ancient Alexandria, where Plotinus (founder of Neoplatonism) and Origen (Christianity's first great theologian) shared the same teacher, Ammonius Saccas. The views of PLOTINUS (§§3, 6) on the immanent presence within the intelligible and material order of the divine One from which they have emerged, and his goal of a mystical return to the One through asceticism and contemplation, struck a responsive chord with Augustine and many others. ORIGEN (§2) was especially concerned with discovering the 'mystical sense' of Scripture, by which he understood the hidden presence of Christ within the biblical text. Later Christian authors of the first four centuries extended the scope of *mystikos* to Christ's hidden presence in the sacraments, particularly the Eucharist.

With the conversion of Constantine, the early Christian ideal of martyrdom was recast in terms of austere self-sacrifice; the Desert Fathers and Mothers, as well as the major figures of the monastic movement, such as Anthony the Great (c.251–356), Pachomius (c.290–346), Basil the Great (c.330–79), John Cassian (c.360–435) and Benedict (480–543), provided guidance for a life dedicated to prayer, asceticism and the search for God.

In terms showing thorough familiarity with Neoplatonic thought, the mystical implications of God's incomprehensibility were explored by Gregory of Nyssa (c.335–95), and even more thoroughly by the (apparently) late-fifth-century Syrian monk now known as PSEUDO-DIONYSIUS, so called because his writings purported to be from the Dionysius converted by Paul in Athens (Acts 17: 34). The presumed apostolic pedigree gave the Dionysian texts enormous authority throughout the Middle Ages and into modern times. In *The Mystical Theology*, this author proposes a *via negativa* or 'apophatic' ascent into the 'dazzling darkness' of the 'superessential' divinity by successively rejecting the applicability of all predication to it; elsewhere he outlines a corresponding *via affirmativa* or 'kataphatic' approach, attempting to explain in what sense God may be called perfect, good, omnipotent, and so on.

Later mystics of the Eastern Church, such as John of Damascus (c.674–749) and especially Simeon the New Theologian (949–1022), stressed the role of the divine Light in the divinization of the human person, restoring the divine image obscured by Adam's Fall. Simeon in turn influenced the development of hesychasm (from *hesychia*, 'quietness'), involving the constant repetition of the mantra-like Jesus Prayer ('Lord Jesus Christ, Son of God, have mercy on me, a sinner') in pursuit of the vision of divine Light.

Hesychasm was successfully defended by Gregory Palamas (c.1296–1359), who identified the divinizing Light with the uncreated 'energies' of God.

In the vastly influential works of AUGUSTINE (§11) comes a shift towards a more psychological approach to mystical themes. Augustine traces the image of the Trinity in the faculties of the soul (intellect, memory and will), and shows interest in the differences between various types of visionary and ecstatic phenomena. The Christocentric love-mysticism of the Cistercian Bernard of Clairvaux (1090–1153) characterizes loving union with the Incarnate Word in affective rather than metaphysical terms, not as a 'union of essences' but a 'concurrence of wills', leading none the less to an experience of apparent absorption in God. Meanwhile, the mysticism of the renowned Benedictine abbess HILDEGARD OF BINGEN (1098–1179), as well as the Cistercian nuns Mechthild of Magdeburg (c.1210–80), Gertrude the Great (c.1256–1302) and Mechthild of Hackeborn (1240–98), involved numerous visionary experiences and revelatory messages. Francis of Assisi (d. 1226) and his Franciscan followers (for example, Clare of Assisi, Jacopone da Todi, Angela of Foligno, and Bonaventure) ushered in a new era of intense devotion to the humanity of Christ, with a correspondingly higher appreciation of the created order in its own right as intrinsically worthy of holy human love because the object of God's love. Mystical themes were sometimes clothed in narrative form in the popular (if often fanciful) medieval *vitae* of Christian saints. Jacobus de Voragine's *Legenda aurea* (Golden Legend), one of the most famous books of the Middle Ages, recounts the life of the noble and learned Catherine of Alexandria, regarded as patroness of scholars and philosophers because she was allegedly martyred in the early fourth century after converting the family of Maxentius and defeating by her wise argumentation fifty philosophical opponents handpicked by the Emperor. Despite the lack of any early evidence that she ever existed, medieval accounts of her mystical marriage to Christ helped popularize her cult.

The most significant figure among Rheno-Flemish mystics of the thirteenth and fourteenth centuries is the brilliant Dominican theologian and preacher MEISTER ECKHART, whose more startling and paradoxical expressions in vernacular sermons brought accusations of heresy. His mystical writings are still subject to the most divergent interpretations, and parallels with Hindu and Buddhist mysticism are often noted. For Eckhart, only God truly is, since being in the strictest sense is God alone. Human creatures possess existence only 'in and through God', who is immanent in the soul's uncreated apex or ground, which is eternally one with the divine. The mystical goal is therefore to divest oneself of everything, so that God may bring the Word to birth within the soul. Eckhart likewise speaks of a Godhead beyond God, a completely unknowable and indescribable 'Ground' beyond the distinction into a Trinity of Divine Persons. Despite the official condemnations, Eckhart's influence continued in John Tauler (c.1300–61), Henry Suso (c.1295–1366), and the Friends of God movement, whose teachings were crystallized in the anonymous mystical classic, the *Theologica Germanica*.

For Jan van Ruysbroeck (John Ruusbroec, 1293–1381), the empty desert of the Godhead itself has a Trinitarian orientation, and mystics who attain union with this nameless unity are not static, but move out with the Father into the world created in the divine image. Catherine of Siena (1347–80) provides an impressive example of the apostolic force of Christian love mysticism, since her 'mystical marriage with Christ' bore fruit in a remarkable involvement with contemporary social needs, as did the mystical experiences of Catherine of Genoa (1447–1510). The fourteenth-century English mystics – among them Richard Rolle (c.1300–49), Walter Hilton (d. 1395), Julian of Norwich (c.1342–after 1413) and the author of *The Cloud of Unknowing* – offer an appealing and approachable spirituality which has found a wide audience in our own times.

The famed *Spiritual Exercises* of St Ignatius of Loyola (c.1491–1556) appear at first glance to have little mystical about them, but are designed to lead to a direct encounter with God. The Spanish Carmelites Teresa of Avila (1515–81) and John of the Cross (1545–91) were declared Doctors of the Church for their spiritual teaching. John is best known for his classic analysis, in *The Dark Night of the Soul* and other works, of the passive purifications endured in the search for God, though his descriptions of the joys of mystical union are even more eloquent. In various writings Teresa sought to identify, through their spiritual and psychological effects, the various stages and pitfalls in the spiritual quest; her masterpiece, *The Interior Castle*, describes the process as a journey inwards through seven progressively more interior dwelling places, leading finally to a permanent union with the Triune God already present in the soul's centre.

Francis de Sales (1567–1622), a key figure in the seventeenth-century French school of spirituality, described how a 'devout life' could be lived in any state, without requiring withdrawal from the world. Pierre de Bérulle (1575–1629) offered a theocentric and Christocentric spirituality, directed towards conformity with the 'states' or inner dispositions of the Incarnate Word. Madame Jeanne Guyon (1648–1717) advocated quiet prayer to the exclusion of all other methods, while her disciple and director, François Fénelon (1651–1715), defended a mysticism of 'pure love' of God, free of all self-interest, even in one's own salvation; critics charged that such teachings opened the door to complete moral and religious indifferentism. Within Catholic circles, the condemnation of quietism created a distrust of mystical spirituality that persisted into the twentieth century, while evoking an interest in the suspect doctrines and authors among many Protestants.

Ironically, despite its emphasis on the experience of personal salvation, the Protestant tradition has often regarded mysticism (especially in its Roman Catholic expressions) with mistrust, as a form of 'works righteousness', or a misguided attempt to bypass the mediatorial role of Jesus. Nevertheless, Protestantism has had its own mystics, such as Jakob Boehme (1575–1624), George Fox (1624–91), William Law (1686–1761) and John Woolman (1720–72), and certain Protestant movements, such as Quakerism and pietism, have a decidedly mystical flavour.

7 Islamic mysticism

Scholars who distinguish sharply between mystical and prophetic experiences do not usually classify the prophet Muhammad as a mystic, although his experiences and certain texts in the Qur'an have lent themselves to later mystical interpretations. But Islamic mysticism seems to have first emerged on a broader scale as part of a reaction against the worldliness of the expanding Muslim empire, stressing deep personal devotion and an ascetic lifestyle in the quest for inner illumination and loving communion with God. The term 'Sufism', by which Islamic mysticism is generally known, may itself have been inspired by this lifestyle, since *suf* refers to the undyed wool worn as a sign of simplicity.

Rabi'ah (d. 801) 'is generally regarded as the person who introduced the element of selfless love into the austere teachings of the early ascetics and gave Sufism the hue of true mysticism' (Schimmel 1975: 38). Subsequent Sufi mysticism is love mysticism, and uses much of the same love imagery found in the Christian mystical tradition. The search for *marifa* (direct knowledge of God), however, sometimes led to seemingly unorthodox results. Abu Yazid (d. 875) introduced the notion of *fana*, the passing away of the empirical self, a crucial and sometimes controversial theme in later Sufi mysticism; his famous words 'Glory to me, how great is my majesty!' seemed to make a blasphemous claim to divinity. Al-Hallaj (854–922) was in fact put to death for blasphemy, after seeming to assert identity with God. AL-GHAZALI (§4) was able to reconcile Sufism with orthodoxy by explaining the mystics' sense of identity with God as a kind of passing illusion brought on by the intensity of the experience.

The pantheistic Sufism of IBN AL-'ARABI (§5), though unorthodox, exerted a strong influence on the mystical poet Rumi (1207–73), who founded the Mevlevi *darwish* order, whose members engage in ritual swirling movements to induce states of intense religious devotion (the so-called 'dervish dances'). After a long decline, Sufism has enjoyed a resurgence in the West in recent years (see MYSTICAL PHILOSOPHY IN ISLAM).

See also: BONAVENTURE; HASIDISM; MYSTICISM, NATURE OF; PANTHEISM; RELIGIOUS EXPERIENCE; RELIGIOUS PLURALISM

References and further reading

Most of the Western mystical authors and works mentioned in this entry (including the *Mystical Theology* of Pseudo-Dionysus, the *Zohar*, the Ignatian *Spiritual Exercises*, and St Teresa's *Interior Castle*) can be found in 'Classics of Western Spirituality', an ongoing series from Paulist Press. Readers are also recommended to refer to Crossroad's *World Spirituality: An Encyclopedic History of the Religious Quest*, a 25-volume series on all the major traditions of spirituality, including their mystical elements.

* *Bhagavad Gītā* (200 BC–AD 200, disputed), trans. D. White, *The Bhagavad Gītā*, American University Studies, Series 7, Theology and Religion, vol. 39, New York: Peter Lang, 1989, 1993. (Also includes a commentary on the text.)
Bouyer, L. (1980) 'Mysticism: An Essay on the History of the Word', in R. Woods (ed.) *Understanding Mysticism*, Garden City, NY: Image Books. (Outlines evolution of the term 'mystical' from Greek origins through patristic era. Translation of 1952 article from *La Vie Spirituelle*.)
* —— (1990) *The Christian Mystery: From Pagan Myth to Christian Mysticism*, Edinburgh: T. & T. Clark. (Reviews the development of Christian mysticism, arguing against its origin in mystery religions.)
Bouyer, L. *et al.* (1969) *A History of Christian Spirituality*, New York: Seabury, 3 vols. (A classic survey of Christian spirituality.)
* *Daodejing* (c.350–250 BC), trans. D.C. Lau, *Tao Te Ching*, Baltimore, MD: Penguin, 1963. (This popular work is traditionally – although now controversially – ascribed to the sage Laozi.)
Dasgupta, S. (1927) *Hindu Mysticism*, New York:

Unger. (Dated but useful overview of the subject, first presented as six lectures at Northwestern University.)
Dumoulin, H. (1988–90) *Zen Buddhism: A History*, New York: Macmillan, 2 vols. (Widely regarded as the standard work on the history of Zen, now greatly amplified and updated.)
Dupré, L. (1987) 'Mysticism', in M. Eliade (ed.) *The Encyclopedia of Religion*, New York: Macmillan. (Useful survey of the nature and history of mysticism, organized according to its own distinctive typology.)
* Eliade, M. (1964) *Shamanism*, London: Routledge. (Shows links between elements of shamanism and mysticism.)
Freemantle, A. (1964) *The Protestant Mystics*, New York: New American Library. (A study of an important and neglected topic, but includes figures not ordinarily considered 'mystical'.)
Lewis, I.M. (1971) *Ecstatic Religion*, Baltimore, MD: Penguin. (A noted social anthropologist describes 'mystical' aspects of African spirit possession.)
Lossky, V. (1957) *The Mystical Theology of the Eastern Church*, Cambridge and London: James Clarke & Co. (Classic study of Orthodox mysticism.)
Merlan, P. (1969) *Monopsychism, Mysticism, Meta-consciousness: Problems of the Soul in the Neoaristotelian and Neoplatonic Tradition*, The Hague: Martinus Nijhoff. (Technical but rewarding discussion of the often overlooked or misinterpreted tradition of 'rationalistic mysticism' in the West.)
Parrinder, G. (1976) *Mysticism in the World's Religions*, New York: Oxford University Press. (Problematic in some of its positions, but contains useful material.)
* Schimmel, A. (1975) *Mystical Dimensions of Islam*, Chapel Hill, NC: University of North Carolina Press. (Standard work on Sufi mysticism.)
Scholem, G.G. (1946) *Major Trends in Jewish Mysticism*, New York: Schocken. (Classic study of Jewish mystical traditions, but interprets 'mystical' more broadly than many other authors.)
Smart, N. (1967) 'Mysticism, History of', in P. Edwards (ed.) *Encyclopedia of Philosophy*, New York: Macmillan. (Excellent brief survey, somewhat coloured by Smart's own views on the 'common core' of mystical experience.)
Smith, M. (1976) *Way of the Mystics: The Early Christian Mystics and the Rise of the Sufis*, London: Sheldon Press. (Popular work on the connections between Christian and Islamic mysticism.)
Spencer, S. (1963) *Mysticism in World Religions*, Baltimore, MD: Penguin. (A good introduction to the major mystical traditions.)
* *Upaniṣads* (800–300 BC), trans. P. Olivelle, *Upaniṣads*,

Oxford: Oxford University Press, 1996. (A readable and accurate translation.)

Various authors (1933–95) *Dictionnaire de spiritualité*, Paris: Beauchesne, 21 vols. (Massive dictionary of major figures and themes in Christian spirituality.)

* Voragine, Jacobus de (13th century) *Legenda aurea*, trans. W.G. Ryan, *The Golden Legend: Readings on the Saints*, Princeton, NJ: Princeton University Press, 1993. (One of the most popular and influential books of the Middle Ages.)

Wiseman, J.A. (1993) 'Mysticism', in M. Downey (ed.) *The New Dictionary of Catholic Spirituality*, Collegeville, MN. Liturgical Press. (Brief survey with theological reflections upon the history of mysticism.)

—— (1970) *Concordant Discord*, Oxford: Clarendon. (The author's Gifford Lectures contain further discussion of issues raised in the previous work.)

STEVEN PAYNE

MYSTICISM, JEWISH

see KABBALAII

MYSTICISM, NATURE OF

Mysticism continues to elude easy definition, and its nature and significance remain the subject of intense debate. The terms 'mystic', 'mystical' and 'mysticism' have been used in an astonishing variety of ways by different authors in different eras.

Nevertheless, modern philosophical discussions have tended to focus on so-called 'mystical experiences', understood as certain states or modes of awareness, allegedly found within (and even outside) virtually all faith-traditions, and variously characterized as 'consciousness without content', 'the experience of absolute oneness', 'union with the transcendent', 'immediate consciousness of the presence of God', and so on. Philosophers are particularly interested in whether such experiences constitute a 'way of knowing', and whether they provide any support for either traditional religious beliefs or unusual metaphysical claims made by certain mystics (for example, that time is illusory). Some authors argue affirmatively, on the basis of an alleged 'universal consensus among mystics', for example, or the parallels between mystical consciousness and other modes of experience accepted as cognitive. Others, however, challenge these views, noting that mystics often appear to disagree precisely along the lines of their prior religious convictions, that mystical aware-ness seems capable of explanation in terms of natural causes, that mystical claims (like claims about one's private feelings) do not admit of ordinary testing, or that the alleged 'ineffability' of mystical states frustrates any attempt at rational analysis.

These concerns, then, tend to shape the kinds of questions typically addressed in contemporary philosophical discussions of mysticism, such as: What is mysticism? What are the identifying characteristics of mystical experience? Is mysticism 'everywhere the same', and if so, in what sense? Are there different types of mystical experience? What is the relationship between mystical awareness and its interpretation? Are mystical experiences a 'way of knowing'? Do they involve some form of union or contact with God? Are mystical experiences 'ineffable' or 'nonlogical', and in what sense? Can drugs or other natural stimuli induce mystical experiences, and would that affect their cognitive value?

Finally, in light of the increasingly technical nature of much of the philosophical debate, in which the primary mystical sources themselves often play a relatively minor role (except as mined for brief 'proof texts'), there have been calls for renewed attention to the larger historical, cultural and religious contexts from which mysticism and mystical literature emerge, and within which they must be interpreted.

1 Background
2 Defining mysticism
3 Mystical experience and its interpretation
4 Mysticism and God
5 Other questions

1 Background

Like 'mystery' (Greek *mysterion*), the adjective 'mystical' (Greek *mystikos*) is derived from the Greek verb *myein* ('to close', especially the eyes and lips), suggesting something secret or concealed. The term was used by Christian authors of the patristic era to refer to the 'mystical sense' of Scripture, the hidden presence of Christ in the biblical text and, by extension, in the sacraments, especially the Eucharist. Only in the late medieval and modern periods did the use of the term begin to shift to reflect a growing interest in the 'private' experiences of those alleged to have encountered the divine. The noun 'mysticism', as Michel de Certeau (1992) has shown, is itself a seventeenth-century French creation (*la mystique*), marking a turn 'away from the liturgical and scriptural context of patristic and medieval Christianity to a situation in which private illumination and unusual psychosomatic experiences became the criteria' (McGinn 1991: 312).

The academic study of mysticism developed in the late nineteenth century, with William James' classic *The Varieties of Religious Experience* (1902) offering one of the most influential early contributions to the field (which also included important works by William Ralph Inge, Friedrich von Hügel, Joseph Maréchal, Rudolf Otto, Evelyn Underhill and others). James devotes considerable attention to mysticism, offers numerous examples of mystical reports, and identifies 'four marks which, when an experience has them, may justify us in calling it mystical': ineffability, noetic quality, transiency and passivity. Of these, the 'noetic quality', or the recipient's impression that these are 'states of knowledge', is particularly important, and James argues that 'mystical states, when well developed, usually are, and have the right to be, absolutely authoritative over the individuals to whom they come', though not to those who stand outside the experience (James [1902] 1936: 414) (see JAMES, W. §4).

Comparativist R.C. Zaehner's famous work *Mysticism: Sacred and Profane* (1961) draws upon cross-cultural differences in the descriptions of various mystical states to support a typology of three fundamentally distinct kinds of mysticism: panenhenic (associated with 'nature mysticism'), monistic (or 'soul' mysticism) and theistic (allegedly the highest form). Despite his greater familiarity with the primary texts, Zaehner's typology has often been criticized as a form of special pleading on theism's behalf, and for improbably lumping together, under the heading of 'soul mysticism', traditions with such radically divergent views on the soul as Sāṅkhya-Yoga, Advaita Vedānta and Buddhist mysticism.

More influential in shaping contemporary Anglo-American philosophical discussions of mysticism has been Walter T. Stace's *Mysticism and Philosophy* (1960a). Stace first identifies two main types of mystical consciousness: 'extrovertive', involving an apprehension of the oneness of all things, and 'introvertive', involving 'Unitary Consciousness, from which all the multiplicity of sensuous or conceptual or other empirical content has been excluded, so that there remains only a void and empty unity'. He goes on to argue, however, that these states are related as 'two species of one genus', and share a 'universal core' of common characteristics, including 'the apprehension of an ultimate nonsensuous unity in all things' (though realized differently in extrovertive and introvertive states), blessedness, paradoxicality, alleged ineffability, and a sense of objectivity (Stace 1960a: 110, 131–2; 1960b: 14). Most importantly and controversially, Stace explains apparent conflicts among mystical reports from different religious traditions as the result of later interpretations superimposed on what are essentially the same experiences. He is particularly critical of Zaehner for failing to grasp the implications of the experience/interpretation distinction, and for simply concluding that Christian and Indian mysticism are different 'from the mere fact that the *beliefs* which Christian mystics based upon their experiences are different from the *beliefs* which the Indians based on theirs' (Stace 1960a: 35–6).

Stace's own views on the relation between experience and interpretation have since been strongly criticized, especially by some of the authors represented in Steven Katz's anthologies *Mysticism and Philosophical Analysis* (1978) and *Mysticism and Religious Traditions* (1983), who insist that the mystics' religious backgrounds and prior beliefs play a much greater role in actually shaping the specific character of the experience. More recently, the contributors to Robert Forman's collection *The Problem of Pure Consciousness* (1990) have criticized in turn this 'constructivist' position, defending the possibility of 'pure consciousness events' experientially indistinguishable across different religious traditions. Meanwhile, Peter Moore (Katz 1978), Nelson Pike (1992) and others have pointed out that many mystics themselves describe not a single mystical state, but successive degrees of mystical union, and that the ordered pattern of these distinct stages may itself have epistemic significance. At the same time, Bernard McGinn (1991) has argued that 'presence' is a far more useful category for the understanding of certain mystical traditions than that of 'union', despite the latter's prominence in philosophical analyses (though it is not yet clear whether McGinn is simply replacing what is arguably too narrow a category with one too broad).

2 Defining mysticism

What, then, is mysticism, and what are the identifying characteristics of mystical states? Following the lead of certain mystics themselves, modern commentators often sharply distinguish mystical awareness from sensory experience, discursive thought, the ordinary reflective exercise of mental imagery and concepts, and such extraordinary phenomena as visions, voices and levitations. More controversially, some authors (for example, Ninian Smart 1965) also exclude numinous and prophetic experiences from the 'mystical' category, though in fact all of these experiences are hard to disentangle in the lives and testimony of actual mystics. Many would agree with James that mystical experiences seem to their recipients to be states of knowledge or insight, to possess what is variously called a 'noetic quality', a 'sense of objectivity or reality', or a 'perception-like' character. Most importantly, it is often claimed (though seldom in terms equally acceptable to all religious traditions) that those undergoing mystical experiences feel themselves to have attained some supreme goal, and to be in the presence of, or in union with, the Absolute, the Transcendent, the One.

However, as the brief overview in §1 suggests, a deeper philosophical consensus on mysticism's scope and nature seems unlikely at this point, at least in part because the terminology and focus of the discussion have changed so dramatically over time, and attempts at more precise definitions now appear almost unavoidably tendentious; philosophers are naturally disinclined to count as truly 'mystical' anything which does not seem to fit their particular theories. Indeed, some (for example, in Katz 1983) have argued that the whole modern preoccupation with identifying the internal features of these relatively rare and unusual states of consciousness has tended to impede a more comprehensive philosophical understanding of mysticism in all its dimensions and manifestations.

3 Mystical experience and its interpretation

Is mysticism 'everywhere the same'? This apparently simple question provokes endless philosophical debate, not only because of disagreements about the nature of mysticism, but also in part because of a lack of clarity about the kind of sameness or difference at issue. Presumably any two experiences are the same at least to the extent that they are both experiences, and different at least to the extent that they are distinguishable as two. Presumably even otherwise indistinguishable states of 'pure consciousness' or 'undifferentiated unity' may differ in intensity, duration, clarity, time of occurrence, and so on.

But what primarily interests philosophers, it seems, is whether mystical states are sufficiently alike across different periods and cultures to offer some *prima facie* support for belief in their cognitive value (or, correspondingly, to undermine any one tradition's claim to be the sole possessor of authentic mysticism). The underlying assumption here is that, other things being equal, the greater the consensus, the stronger the case in mysticism's favour (just as we tend to give greater credence to reports of unusual sightings when there is multiple attestation from independent sources). Of course, this assumption can be challenged; there are certainly cases of mass delusion. None the less, even many otherwise sceptical authors, as well as those inclined to make exclusivist claims for particular mystical traditions, have found the apparent cross-cultural similarities striking, and something that requires explanation.

Yet first impressions can deceive. As James admits, when we examine the broader field of mystical reports more closely, 'we find that the supposed unanimity largely disappears... [Mysticism] is dualistic in Sankhya, and monistic in Vedanta philosophy' ([1902] 1936: 416). Christian mystical literature speaks of union with God; Theravāda Buddhism does not. In short, mystics of different backgrounds describe their experiences in radically different ways.

To maintain the 'common core' hypothesis in the face of conflicting descriptions, authors typically distinguish the mystical experience as such from its interpretation. Ninian Smart, for example, argues that 'phenomenologically, mysticism is everywhere the same', but that 'different flavours accrue to the experiences of mystics because of their ways of life and modes of auto-interpretation' (Smart 1965: 87). Stace, as noted above, maintains that all authentic introvertive mystical states are in fact experiences of 'pure undifferentiated unity', but that 'the same mystical experience may be interpreted by a Christian in terms of Christian beliefs and by a Buddhist in terms of Buddhistic beliefs' (1960b: 10). Thus 'union with God', according to Stace, 'is not an uninterpreted description of any human being's experience', but 'a theistic interpretation of the undifferentiated unity' (Stace 1960a: 103-4).

Interestingly, Stace's approach is sometimes turned on its head in popular writings on mysticism, by authors who seem to imply that all mystics in fact experience union with God, but that some interpret this union in non-theistic terms. Most proponents of the 'common core' hypothesis, however, seem to favour 'undifferentiated unity' or 'pure consciousness without content' as the essential feature of all introvertive mystical states.

Stace in turn has been roundly criticized for his naïve approach to the experience/interpretation distinction. Peter Moore notes that, besides the 'raw experience' (that is, 'features of experience unaffected by the mystic's prior beliefs, expectations, or intentions'), the interpretive element found in mystical reports may be not only retrospective (as in Stace's view) but also reflexive ('spontaneously formulated either during the experience itself or immediately afterwards') or incorporated ('caused or conditioned by a mystic's prior beliefs, expectations and intentions') (Katz 1978: 108-9). Steven Katz goes further, insisting that 'there are NO pure (i.e., unmediated) experiences'. Rather, 'the experience itself as well as the form in which it is reported is shaped by concepts which the mystic brings' to the experience, so that Hindus have Hindu mystical experiences, Jews have quite distinct Jewish mystical experiences, and so on (Katz 1978: 26). As critics have pointed out, Katz seems to assume rather than prove the 'constructed' character of all experience, and makes his case more by way of persuasive examples than conclusive demonstration. Pressed to its limits, his radically pluralist, contextual and constructivist approach would seem to have the counterintuitive consequence of making all mystical states (and indeed all experiences) unique and incommensurable.

In response, Forman and others have argued that so-called 'pure consciousness events', involving 'a wakeful though contentless (non-intentional) consciousness', can and do occur, and that such mystical states cannot be adequately accounted for on the 'constructivist' model, since they contain no inner content to be 'constructed' in the requisite way. Moreover, in so far as such experiences occur across different traditions and cultures, they would seem to provide a clear instance of what Katz claims is impossible: a type of mystical consciousness virtually the same everywhere. Whether Forman has identified a convincing counterexample to the 'constructivist' position, or whether 'pure consciousness events' are what most classic mystical texts are actually describing, is still under debate.

Other authors, without adopting Katz's radical pluralism, nevertheless sort out mystical states into a smaller number of basic types. Here, too, the question arises of which differences in the way such states are described correspond to important differences among the experiences themselves. Many surveys of mysticism divide their material according to the major religious traditions, although ordinarily for expository reasons alone. Zaehner, as we have seen, sharply distinguishes theistic 'love' mysticism from the monistic or 'soul' mysticism found in certain Asian religions. Neo-Thomist Jacques Maritain (1944) likewise sharply differentiates 'supernatural mystical experience, by means of affective connaturality with the deity', from the purely natural mysticism of Hindu yogis, involving 'an intellectual (negative) experience of the substantial esse of the soul'. Critics charge that such distinctions are dictated as much by Maritain's and Zaehner's theological presuppositions as by careful attention to the mystical reports themselves. Yet while acknowledging such criticisms, Wainwright and others have defended the legitimacy in principle of a typological approach, and pointed the way towards a more sophisticated typology of mystical states.

Such ongoing disputes have spawned a vast and often highly technical literature on the relationship between experience and its interpretation, with important implications not simply for the understanding of mysticism but for epistemology in general. These discussions underscore the complexity of the hermeneutical task in interpreting mystical reports, and the necessity of focusing not just on isolated psychological states, but on the larger historical and cultural context in which they occur.

4 Mysticism and God

Although at times the 'consensus of the mystics' has been invoked on behalf of monism, idealism and other less well-known metaphysical doctrines, Anglo-American philosophers have tended to approach mysticism primarily in terms of what it might contribute to questions about the nature and existence of God. Authors debate whether mystical states in particular, and religious experiences in general, should be considered cognitive, and whether they provide any support for theistic belief. Most often, therefore, mysticism is discussed in conjunction with the so-called 'argument from religious experience', as a possible source of premises upon which one could base an inference (causal, explanatory or otherwise) to the existence of God (see RELIGIOUS EXPERIENCE §2). Alston and others take a different approach, arguing that putative mystical perceptions of God are part of a justified belief-forming practice, in which 'people sometimes do perceive God and thereby acquire justified beliefs about God' (Alston 1991: 3), in much the same way that we acquire justified beliefs about external objects by directly perceiving them, and not just by an inference from internal sensory impressions.

Such an approach presumes, of course, that at least some mystical experiences have an intentional structure, and that it makes sense to talk of 'theistic mystical experiences'. This assumption may be challenged. Forman's 'pure consciousness events', for example, are characterized as 'contentless' and 'non-intentional'. Stace's states of 'pure undifferentiated unity' are similarly described. If one holds, with Stace, that all introvertive mystical consciousness is of this nature, then it is difficult to see how such experiences could be phenomenally 'of' anything. Pike has argued that even an experience of undifferentiated unity might count as 'phenomenologically theistic' if this 'climax moment of the paradigm union experience is preceded by specifically theistic experience having dualistic structure' (Pike 1992: 164). That is, just as we might correctly describe our experience of 'stun-stars and fading consciousness' as 'the experience of being hit by a baseball' if in fact we had observed the course of ball before impact, so too an undifferentiated unity might be correctly described as (apparent) union with God if it comes as the culmination of a sequence of states in which the subject–object distinction seems gradually to disappear as God and the soul draw closer.

None the less, some philosophers apparently want

to claim something stronger: that the climactic experiences described by mystics such as Ruusbroec and St Teresa are not merely states of undifferentiated unity having a 'theistic' phenomenological ancestry, but are themselves 'perception-like', involving a nonsensuous (putative) presentation of God to the mystic. The cognitive value of such experiences can then be defended by invoking some variant of what Richard Swinburne calls the 'principle of credulity', that 'in the absence of special considerations what one seems to perceive is probably so', and 'how things seem to be is good grounds for a belief about how things are' (Swinburne 1979: 254).

But are there in fact 'special considerations' that might limit the application of this principle? Antony Flew (1966), Ronald Hepburn (1967a), C.B. Martin (1959) (most famously) and others have argued that religious experiences (and thus, by implication, mystical states) do not qualify as a 'way of knowing' at least in part because they do not meet certain standards of testability that experiences must satisfy if they are to count as cognitive. If someone reports seeing a skunk in the basement, for example, I know how to confirm or disconfirm this (by looking, smelling, setting a trap, and so on), but 'when someone claims to have direct awareness of God, to encounter, see, or intuit the divine, we are not able to suggest a test performance of an even remotely analogous kind' (Hepburn 1967a: 166).

Alston (1991), Wainwright (1981) and others have responded that, in fact, religious communities use many checks and testing procedures for evaluating the authenticity of alleged mystical perceptions of God, such as: the consequences of the experience for the mystic and for others, the orthodoxy of the claims based on the experience, the similarity to paradigmatic mystical states, the judgment of qualified religious authorities, and so on. Critics reply that such tests are inadequate, especially since a sceptic can admit that a mystical state satisfies them all while denying that it constitutes an experience of God. To this, however, the usual counter-response is that standards of testability must be appropriate to the nature of what is allegedly perceived; it is not clear that different or more stringent checking procedures can reasonably be demanded for alleged perceptions of an immaterial, all-good, all-powerful personal God free to decide the occasion and recipient of divine self-manifestations.

Again, one crucial test for evaluating most perceptual claims is whether they agree with those of other qualified observers. Ordinarily, the testimony of virtually all normal observers asked to verify the same putative sensory perception (for example, of a skunk in the basement) would be more or less unanimous. By contrast, critics charge, mystics disagree even among themselves, and theistic mystical experiences seem to occur only to those who already believe in God, monistic experiences to those from monistic traditions, and so on. This suggests that mystical 'perceptions' of God are shaped more by the mystic's prior beliefs and expectations than by anything independent. One possible response is to challenge the extent of the disagreements among mystics of different backgrounds, or the conformity to the recipient's prior beliefs. Mystics seem to recognize each other across denominational boundaries, and most speak of the novelty and wonder of mystical union; in many cases, recipients have no particular religious affiliation or prior faith. The underlying issue here may be whether the actual distribution and frequency of theistic experiences across cultures is what we might antecedently anticipate if in fact God exists and is perceived in these states, or whether we would otherwise expect such experiences to be more common; philosophers argue somewhat inconclusively over God's possible reasons for more or less self-disclosure.

Another 'special consideration' often mentioned is that the occurrence of mystical states seems capable of other explanations (physiological, psychological, psychoanalytical, and so on). Some authors have claimed that mystical experiences can be experimentally evoked through sensory deprivation, 'deautomatization' (a term coined by A.J. Diekman to describe the undoing of habitual patterns of perception by techniques such as staring steadily at an object or image; see Diekman in Woods 1980), taking hallucinogens, and so on; there is, in fact, an extensive literature on the question of drugs and mysticism. One may argue that 'instant chemical mysticism' is somehow too cheaply bought, and dispute whether the states thus produced actually correspond with what the mystics describe. But the mere fact that physiological and psychological processes may be involved in a mystical experience hardly discredits it, since such processes are involved in ordinary perception as well, and one can always argue that drugs simply open the doors of mystical perception rather than entirely creating the mystical experience. Of course, in most perceptual theories, putative perceptions must have the right kind of causal connection with what is allegedly perceived, but given the 'primary causality' traditionally attributed to God, any experience will be grounded in God's causal activity, whatever the 'secondary causes' involved. To be sure, a putative mystical experience after taking drugs may be discredited, but on other grounds (for example, its bad effects).

In short, one important line of defence of the

cognitive value of mysticism, and of the practice of forming beliefs based on theistic mystical experiences, appeals to the analogy between mystical experience and other modes of experience accepted as cognitive (especially sensory experience). How plausible one finds this appeal will depend on how much significance one attaches to the various points of similarity and difference. Critics remain unconvinced, arguing that the dissimilarities outweigh the similarities.

5 Other questions

Mystics' comments about the strangeness of their experiences or their difficulties in describing them have sometimes provoked elaborate philosophical analyses of the 'ineffability' and 'paradoxicality' of mystical states. Yet few mystics actually claim that their experiences are radically 'ineffable' or 'paradoxical' in the self-defeating sense so easily refuted in philosophical discussions. Perhaps these discussions are most useful as reminders of the complex and creative use of language in mystical literature: sometimes descriptive, sometimes prescriptive, often evocative (the frequent recourse to poetry and symbolism is notable).

Again, while some authors assert that mystics experience union with the Supreme Good and the source of all morality, others claim that mystics pass beyond all oppositions, including the distinction between good and evil. Not surprisingly, therefore, philosophers have shown some interest in the relationship between mysticism and ethics.

Certain neo-scholastics (Jacques Maritain, Réginald Garrigou-Lagrange) and 'transcendental Thomists' (Karl Rahner, Bernard Lonergan), as well as authors from other traditions (process thought, for example), have developed their own distinctive approaches to the understanding of mysticism, relatively neglected by contemporary analytic philosophers perhaps because couched in unfamiliar categories and terminology. More generally, the 'turn to the subject' in modern theology and efforts (since Schleiermacher) to ground theological claims in religious experience raise important philosophical issues as well. A particularly delicate question is to determine how mystical and religious experience might provide more than mere reinforcement of what is already believed, without adding to or subtracting from the original revelation.

Finally, despite analytic philosophy's tendency to focus on mystical states of awareness, it should not be thought that this is all mysticism has to offer philosophy. Historically, philosophers have often been influenced by their reading of mystics (for example, Schelling by Boehme, Schopenhauer by the Upaniṣads, Heidegger by Eckhart) in much more complex ways. Mysticism, understood broadly, may have contributions to make in many areas, such as the philosophical understanding of the self and personal identity, for example, or aesthetic theory. Most importantly, contemporary philosophers need to recall that, for all their interest in the internal characteristics of mystical consciousness, they generally have no direct access to mystical states, but only to mystical texts, composed in a particular genre, for a particular audience, in a particular cultural and historical setting, and so on. Without greater attention to the special hermeneutics of mystical texts, contemporary philosophers will continue to run the risk of analysing with ever greater sophistication a 'mysticism' that exists nowhere in reality, and seems far removed from the actual experience and testimony of actual mystics.

See also: GOD, ARGUMENTS FOR THE EXISTENCE OF; MYSTICISM, HISTORY OF; OTTO, R.; PANTHEISM; RELIGION AND EPISTEMOLOGY; RELIGIOUS EXPERIENCE; RELIGIOUS PLURALISM

References and further reading

* Alston, W.P. (1991) *Perceiving God: The Epistemology of Religious Experience*, Ithaca, NY: Cornell University Press. (Sustained defence of the contribution of religious experience to the grounds for belief in God. Contains valuable discussion of many epistemological issues and the possibility of 'mystical perceptions of God'.)

* Certeau, M. de (1992) *The Mystic Fable*, vol. 1: *The Sixteenth and Seventeenth Centuries*, Chicago, IL: University of Chicago Press. (Difficult but rewarding discussion of the term 'la mystique' and the fundamental change it represents in the Western approach to the sacred. Incorporates semiotics, linguistics and psychoanalytic theory.)

Davis, C.F. (1989) *The Evidential Force of Religious Experience*, Oxford: Clarendon. (Treats mysticism in the context of religious experience, as part of a cumulative case for theism. Discusses many issues raised in this article.)

* Flew, A. (1966) *God and Philosophy*, New York: Delta Books. (Chapter 6 is a sustained attack on arguments from religious experience, raising the issues of testability and agreement.)

* Forman, R.K.C. (ed.) (1990) *The Problem of Pure Consciousness: Mysticism and Philosophy*, New York: Oxford University Press. (The contributors criticize Katz's 'constructivism' and argue for new models of mystical experience. Authors defend the

possibility and actual occurrence of 'pure consciousness events'.)

Gale, R.M. (1991) *On the Nature and Existence of God*, New York: Cambridge University Press. (Chapter 8 challenges religious experience arguments, with a long critique of Alston and Wainwright on the analogy between religious and sensory experience.)

* Hepburn, R.W. (1967a) 'Religious Experience, Argument for the Existence of God', in P. Edwards (ed.) *Encyclopedia of Philosophy*, New York: Macmillan, vol. 7. (Deals with issues of testability, agreement, natural explanations, and so on.)

—— (1967b) 'Mysticism, Nature and Assessment of', in P. Edwards (ed.) *Encyclopedia of Philosophy*, New York: Macmillan, vol. 5. (Discusses conflicts of interpretation, mystical paradoxes, and so on. Sympathetic towards mysticism as a valuable human phenomenon, but agnostic concerning its religious implications.)

Hügel, F. von (1908) *The Mystical Element of Religion as Studied in Saint Catherine of Genoa and her Friends*, London: James Clarke & J.M. Dent, 2 vols, 1961. (Unusual mixture of biography, theology and philosophy. Difficult and not entirely successful, but rewarding.)

Inge, W.R. (1899) *Christian Mysticism*, London: Methuen. (Classic early survey with famous appendix listing twenty-six definitions of 'mysticism' and 'mystical theology'. Marred by the author's biases.)

* James, W. (1902) *The Varieties of Religious Experience: A Study in Human Nature*, New York: Modern Library, 1936. (Lectures 16 and 17 treat the characteristics and significance of mystical states, with a wealth of examples. Enormously influential.)

* Katz, S.T. (ed.) (1978) *Mysticism and Philosophical Analysis*, New York: Oxford University Press. (Important articles by Katz, Peter Moore and others criticizing the view that mysticism is 'everywhere the same', and stressing the role of mystics' beliefs and expectations in shaping the very quality of their experience.)

* —— (ed.) (1983) *Mysticism and Religious Traditions*, New York: Oxford University Press. (Contributors further explore themes from the preceding anthology, arguing that mysticism can only be understood in the context of the particular religious and cultural traditions within which it occurs.)

Maréchal, J. (1926, 1937) *Studies in the Psychology of the Mystics*, trans. A. Thorold, Albany, NY: Magi Books, 1964. (Difficult but rewarding analysis of epistemological preconditions for mystical intuition of God, by a precursor of transcendental Thomism.

This is a partial translation of the two-volume French edition.)

* Maritain, J. (1944) 'The Natural Mystical Experience and the Void', in *Redeeming the Time*, London: Geoffrey Bles Centenary Press. (Goes beyond the following work in allowing the possibility of natural mystical experiences, associated primarily with certain Asian religions.)

—— (1959) *Distinguish to Unite, or The Degrees of Knowledge*, trans. G.B. Phelan, New York, Scribner, 4th edn. (Magisterial study by a pre-eminent Neo-Thomist which presents mystical knowledge as the summit and goal of all knowing.)

* Martin, C.B. (1959) *Religious Belief*, Ithaca, NY: Cornell University Press. (Chapter 5, 'Seeing God', is an influential and often reprinted critique of religious experience as a 'way of knowing', on the grounds that appropriate tests are lacking. An earlier version appeared in *Mind* in 1952.)

* McGinn, B. (1991) *The Presence of God, A History of Western Christian Mysticism*, vol. 1: *The Foundations of Mysticism: Origins to the Fifth Century*, New York: Crossroad. (The first in a projected four-volume history, this contains a long and valuable appendix on theological, philosophical, comparativist and psychological approaches to mysticism.)

Otto, R. (1958) *The Idea of the Holy*, New York: Oxford University Press. (Classic attempt to root religion in a prerational feeling of the 'numinous'. Includes a discussion of mysticism.)

—— (1970) *Mysticism East and West*, New York: Macmillan. (Problematic but important comparison of Śankara and Eckhart.)

* Pike, N. (1992) *Mystic Union: An Essay in the Phenomenology of Mysticism*, Ithaca, NY: Cornell University Press. ('Phenomenography' of successive states of infused contemplation as described by Christian mystics, and analysis of their philosophical implications.)

Proudfoot, W. (1985) *Religious Experience*, Berkeley, CA: University of California Press. (Chapter 4 argues controversially that 'ineffability' and 'noetic quality' are not simply qualities of the mystic experience, but 'conceptual constraints on what experiences are identified as mystical'.)

Rahner, K. (1983) *The Practice of Faith: A Handbook of Contemporary Spirituality*, New York: Crossroad. (Sections 13 and 14 briefly outline some of Rahner's views on mystical theology and 'everyday mysticism'.)

* Smart, N. (1965) 'Interpretation and Mystical Experience', *Religious Studies* 1: 75–87. (An attempt to define the scope of mysticism.)

* Stace, W.T. (1960a) *Mysticism and Philosophy*, Lon-

don: Macmillan. (This classic defence of the 'common core' hypothesis and other controversial claims has set the agenda for most subsequent philosophical discussions.)

* —— (1960b) *The Teachings of the Mystics*, New York: New American Library. (Companion anthology to the preceding work.)

* Swinburne, R. (1979) *The Existence of God*, Oxford: Clarendon Press. (Chapter 13 invokes the 'principle of credulity' in defending the argument from religious experience.)

Underhill, E. (1965) *Mysticism: A Study in the Nature and Development of Man's Spiritual Consciousness*, Cleveland, OH, and New York: World, 12th edn. (Classic popular introduction to mysticism and the stages of the mystical journey, focusing primarily on Christian mystics.)

Wainwright, W. J. (1978) *Philosophy of Religion: An Annotated Bibliography of Twentieth Century Writings in English*, New York: Garland. (Pages 367–438 offer concise and perceptive evaluations of over 200 works on mysticism and religious experience.)

* —— (1981) *Mysticism: A Study of its Nature, Cognitive Value and Moral Implications*, Madison, WI: University of Wisconsin Press. (Dense, masterly discussion of many issues raised in the present entry.)

* Woods, R. (ed.) (1980) *Understanding Mysticism*, Garden City, NY: Doubleday. (Perhaps the best and most comprehensive anthology of notable articles on the nature of mysticism, its various forms in world religions, and its scientific, philosophical and theological appraisal.)

Yandell, K.E. (1993) *The Epistemology of Religious Experience*, New York: Cambridge University Press. (General defence of evidential force of religious experience, with discussion of ineffability and other topics.)

* Zaehner, R.C. (1961) *Mysticism: Sacred and Profane: An Inquiry into Some Varieties of Preternatural Experience*, New York: Oxford University Press. (Influential study, sharply distinguishing three fundamental types of mysticism: panenhenic, monistic and theistic.)

STEVEN PAYNE

N

NÆSS, ARNE (1912–)

As professor of philosophy in Oslo between 1939 and 1970, Arne Næss contributed to a strengthening of the position of philosophy in Norwegian academic life. During the German occupation (1940–5) he played an active part in the resistance movement. In the 1940s and 1950s he was the inspiration for and centre of a group of students of philosophy and social science, the 'Oslo School', whose members became influential in the later development of these fields. His philosophical thinking passed through an early 'scientistic' period of radical empiricism to 'possibilist' and pluralist views, and an undogmatic scepticism. After resigning his professorship in 1970, he became the protagonist of a version of ecological philosophy, 'deep ecology'. He has always been an admirer of Spinoza and has also sought inspiration in Spinozism for his ecological philosophy.

Although the Norwegian philosopher Arne Næss had contact with the Vienna Circle of logical positivists in 1934–6, his early views were more influenced by pragmatism than by positivism (see LOGICAL POSITIVISM; PRAGMATISM). He did not accept that empirical methods have no place in philosophy, and he had reservations about the logical positivists' use of a priori formal-logical methods. But he shared their high esteem of science and the idea of making philosophy more scientific, and he supported the international movement for unified science.

In his first major work, *Erkenntnis und wissenschaftliches Verhalten* (Cognition and Scientific Behaviour, written in Vienna 1934–5), Næss sketched a programme for an empirical science of science, attacking 'subjective models' in traditional accounts of cognition and research. During his first years as professor of philosophy in Oslo he developed a programme of empirically based foundation research involving criticism of unclear use of language. He provided the groundwork for a scientific semantics by introducing a conceptual framework which made semantic hypotheses testable by empirical investigations of actual usage. Næss' empirical semantics became a common methodological basis for a circle of students from different fields who attached themselves to his programme of foundation research – the 'Oslo School'. In this milieu, key formulations in the history of philosophical ideas were regarded not as expressions of definite doctrines but as highly ambiguous formulations which might be interpreted in an indefinite number of directions, and which could be made more precise.

Næss was inclined to consider the difference between normative and descriptive statements as one of degree rather than a clear dichotomy. He rejected the view that moral philosophy must be meta-ethics, a science *about* norms and their function and not a doctrine *in* morals. He envisaged a value-theoretical foundation research that sought justifications for norms, compared norm systems and sharpened normative formulations. Such a view was the basis for his later investigations of norm systems such as Gandhi's ethics of non-violence (see GANDHI, M.K.).

Næss employed concepts and methods of empirical semantics on politically controversial subjects, in several investigations of uses of the term 'democracy', for example, in studies supported by UNESCO (see DEMOCRACY); he also undertook empirical studies of philosophically relevant terms.

In the early 1950s Næss moved away from the semantically and empirically oriented platform of the Oslo School. He continued his Spinoza studies, but also started work on a comprehensive history of philosophy, making extensive use of his semantic methods on philosophical texts. He also began to reflect critically on empiricism as a fundamental position. In a series of lectures in 1953 (see Næss 1959) he discussed the presuppositions of empiricism, and considered standpoints resulting from negating or abolishing one or more such premises (see EMPIRICISM). He sketched a series of different views, from 'narrow scientism' via 'empiricism without dogmas' and 'probabilism' to extremely wide 'possibilism'. His work in the history of philosophy changed his conception of philosophy, and inspired him to a pluralistic doctrine of philosophical systems and 'total views', which was connected with his possibilism. He espoused a thesis of 'incommensurability' of total systems (see INCOMMENSURABILITY).

In *Scepticism* (1968) Næss discussed Pyrrhonism, which he considered the most radical and important form of scepticism, taking his point of departure from SEXTUS EMPIRICUS (see PYRRHONISM). Næss' own position was a kind of spectator standpoint, he was a 'sympathetic metasceptic' trying to present the sceptic in as favourable and coherent a light as possible. But the sceptical attitude obviously appealed to Næss and was in harmony with deep tendencies in himself: the need for distanced, theoretical non-attachment, except in questions in which he was emotionally strongly engaged.

A tension between engagement and distance seems to mark his development. After theoretical work in philosophy of science in the 1930s, Næss played an active part in the resistance movement during the war, at considerable personal risk. After technical work in empirical semantics, logic and the philosophy of language, studies of Spinoza and the history of philosophy, and investigations of norm systems in the 1950s and 1960s, he became strongly interested in ecological philosophy from about 1970. He took part in nonviolent action for the preservation of nature, and he became known among environmentalists all over the world as a protagonist of 'deep ecology'.

In his famous 1973 paper, 'The Shallow and the Deep, Long-Range Ecology Movement', Næss distinguished between a shallow and a more 'revolutionary' deep ecology movement. The purpose of the former is to fight against pollution and resource depletion; its central objective is to promote the health and affluence of people in the developed countries. In contrast, the deep ecology movement rejects the distinction between humans and environment, emphasizing their intrinsic relationship and total-field image. Further, the deep ecology movement stresses biospherical egalitarianism in principle, promoting a deep-seated respect for ways and forms of life; it emphasizes principles of diversity and symbiosis, repudiates class differences, favours complexity over complication, local autonomy and decentralization against centralization – and fights against pollution and resource depletion, but without losing sight of the other points. In the theoretical foundation for deep ecology, Næss integrates elements of his earlier philosophical achievements and adds new points. In 'The World of Concrete Contents' (1985) he suggests that the difference between environment conservers and developers is one of ontology rather than ethics. Clarification of differences in ontology may contribute significantly to the clarification of different policies and their ethical basis. As an ontological basis for deep ecology, Næss explores a kind of neutral monism identifying the world (reality) with the set of 'concrete contents' in the form of Gestalts, as against abstract structures such as those developed in scientific theories. This 'Gestalt ontology' is contrasted with an ontology distinguishing things in themselves with 'objective' primary qualities and relations from 'subjective' secondary and tertiary qualities (see PRIMARY–SECONDARY DISTINCTION). *In* the concrete contents there are no subject–object, primary–secondary or fact–value distinctions (see FACT/VALUE DISTINCTION).

See also: ECOLOGICAL PHILOSOPHY; SCANDINAVIA, PHILOSOPHY IN §5

List of works

Næss, A. (1936) *Erkenntnis und wissenschaftliches Verhalten* (Cognition and Scientific Behaviour), Oslo: Det Norske Videnskapsakademi i Oslo. Skrifter. II. Hist.-filos.kl. (1936: 1) . (Outlines and discusses a radical programme for an 'objectivist' science of science to replace traditional 'subjectivist' philosophical disciplines, for example, epistemology and theory of meaning. Næss' project in this work is a parallel to, and anticipates, later eliminativist projects of replacing 'folk psychology' by non-mentalist terminology and theory. The programme is reconsidered and moderated in (1965a) below.)

—— (1938) *'Truth' as conceived by those who are not Professional Philosophers*, Oslo: Det Norske Videnskapsakademi i Oslo. Skrifter. II. Hist.-filos.kl. (1938: 4). (Report on empirical investigations of what non-philosophers understand by 'truth'. The study revealed that all the main philosophical 'theories of truth' were represented in non-technical versions among 'ordinary people'. In Næss' opinion, his study showed that philosophers' claims about what 'the ordinary man' means or does not mean by truth were unfounded and irresponsible.)

—— (1947) *Endel elementære logiske emner* (Some elementary logical topics), Oslo; trans. A. Hannay as *Communication and Argument. Elements of Applied Semantics*, Oslo: Scandinavian University Books, 1966. (Elementary introduction to applied semantics – ambiguity, interpretation, precisation (disambiguation), definition, misunderstandings in communication – argumentation and debating.)

—— (1953a) *Interpretation and Preciseness. A Contribution to the Theory of Communication*, Oslo: Det Norske Videnskapsakademi i Oslo. Skrifter II. Hist.filos.kl. (1953: 4). (A technical treatment of the same topics as in his 1947 work. Here, Næss endeavours to provide the conceptual and methodological foundation for an empirical semantics.)

—— (1953b) *Filosofiens historie. En innføring i filosofiske problemer* (The History of Philosophy. An Introduction to Philosophical Problems), Filosofiske Problemer 16, Oslo: Akademisk forlag. (A not-entirely-elementary history of philosophy.)

—— (1956) *Democracy, Ideology and Objectivity. Studies in the Semantic and Cognitive Analysis of Ideological Controversy*, with J.A. Christophersen and K. Kvalø, Oslo: Oslo University Press. (Report on empirical studies of east–west ideological conflicts.)

—— (1959) 'Refleksjoner om helhetssyn, sannhet og kunnskap' (Reflections on Total Views, Truth and Knowledge), *Festskrift til A.H. Winsnes på syttifemårsdagen*, Oslo, 285–308. (A first publication of ideas originally discussed in lectures in Oslo in 1953 – ideas further developed in various later publications on possibilism and pluralism.)

—— (1960) *Gandhi og atomalderen*, Oslo: Universitetsforlaget; trans. A. Hannay as *Gandhi and the Nuclear Age*, Totowa, NJ: Bedminster Press, 1965. (A discussion of the relevance of Gandhi's principles of non-violence in the nuclear age.)

—— (1963) *Logikk og metodelære. En innføring*; trans. A. Hannay as *Introduction to Logic and Scientific Method*, Paterson, NJ, 1968. (An elementary introduction to logic and scientific method.)

—— (1964) 'Pluralistic Theorizing in Physics and Philosophy', *Danish Yearbook in Philosophy*, 1, Copenhagen, 101–11. (Development on Næss (1959) above.)

—— (1964–5) 'Reflections about Total Views', *Philosophy and Phenomenological Research* 25: 16–29. (Development on Næss (1959) above.)

—— (1965a) 'Science as Behaviour: Prospects and Limitations of a Behavioural Metascience', in B.B. Wolman (ed.) *Scientific Psychology. Principles and Approaches*, New York, 50–67. (Development on Næss (1936) above.)

—— (1965b) *Moderne filosofer*, Stockholm: Almqvist & Wiksell; trans. A. Hannay as *Four Modern Philosophers: Carnap, Wittgenstein, Heidegger, Sartre*, Chicago, IL: The University of Chicago Press, 1969. (Elementary introductions to the philosophies of Carnap, Wittgenstein, Heidegger and Sartre.)

—— (1966) 'Psychological and Social Aspects of Pyrrhonian Scepticism', *Inquiry* 9: 301–21. (Outline of a non-dogmatic form of scepticism ascribed to Pyrrho; discussion of possible beneficial effects of this kind of non-dogmatic attitude.)

—— (1968) *Scepticism*, London: International Library of Philosophy and Scientific Method. (A thorough discussion of non-dogmatic, Pyrrhonian scepticism, the kind claimed by Næss to be generally overlooked in modern critiques of scepticism.)

—— (1969) *Hvilken verden er den virkelige?* (Which World is the Real One?), Oslo: Universitetsforlaget. (Discussion of total views and problems involved in describing, comparing and evaluating near-total views.)

—— (1972a) *Freedom, Emotion and Self-Subsistence. The Structure of a Central Part of Spinoza's 'Ethics'*, Oslo: Oslo University Press, 1975. (A somewhat technical discussion of a part of Spinoza's *Ethics*.)

—— (1972b) *The Possibilist and Pluralist Aspects of the Scientific Enterprise*, Oslo: Oslo University Press. (Development on Næss (1959) above.)

—— (1973) 'The Shallow and the Deep, Long-Range Ecology Movement' *Inquiry* 16: 95–100. (A famous early expression of Næss' ideas of 'deep ecology'.)

—— (1974) *Økologi, samfunn og livsstil. Utkast til en økosofi*, Oslo: Universitetsforlaget; trans. D. Rothenberg as *Ecology, Community and Lifestyle: Outline of an Ecosophy*, Cambridge: Cambridge University Press, 1989. (A more comprehensive discussion of the philosophy of 'deep ecology'.)

—— (1974) *Gandhi and Group Conflict. An Exploration of Satyagraha – Theoretical Background*, Oslo: Oslo University Press. (A more thorough discussion of the same themes as developed in Næss (1960) above.)

—— (1975) *Freedom, Emotion and Self-Subsistence. The Structure of a Central Part of Spinoza's 'Ethics'*, Oslo: Oslo University Press. (A further discussion of Spinoza's *Ethics*.)

—— (1979) 'Towards a Philosophy of Wide Cognitivism' in *Theory of Knowledge and Science Policy*, Ghent.

—— (1985) 'The World of Concrete Contents', *Inquiry* 28: 417–28. (An outline of an ontology of 'neutral monism' as a foundation for 'deep ecology'.)

—— (1986) 'The Deep Ecology Movement: Some Philosophical Aspects', *Philosophical Inquiry* 8; repr. in G. Sessions (ed.) *Deep Ecology for the Twenty-First Century*, Boston, MA: Shambhala, 1995. (Further development of themes discussed in (1973) and (1974a) above.)

—— (1995a) 'Deepness of Questions and the Deep Ecology Movement', in G. Sessions (ed.) *Deep Ecology for the Twenty-First Century*, Boston, MA: Shambhala. (Further development of themes discussed in (1973) and (1974a) above.)

—— (1995b) 'Self-Realization: An Ecological Approach to Being in the World', in G. Sessions (ed.) *Deep Ecology for the Twenty-First Century*, Boston, MA: Shambhala. (Further development of themes discussed in (1973) and (1974a) above.)

References and further reading

Glasser, H. (1995) 'Deep Ecology Clarified: A Few Fallacies and Misconceptions', *The Trumpeter Journal of Ecosophy* 12: 138–42.

Gullvåg, I. and Wetlesen, J. (eds) (1982) *In Sceptical Wonder. Inquiries into the Philosophy of Arne Naess on the Occasion of his 70th Birthday*, Oslo:

Universitetsforlaget and Columbia University Press.

Light, A. and Rothenberg, D. (eds) (1996) 'Arne Naess's Environmental Thought', special issue of *Inquiry* 39. (Essays on Næss' thought, published in honour of his eighty-fifth birthday.)

Reed, P. and Rothenberg, D. (eds) (1993) *Wisdom in the Open Air; the Norwegian Roots of Deep Ecology*, Minneapolis, MN: University of Minnesota Press. (Traces the Norwegian roots of 'deep ecology', with contributions from many prominent Norwegian thinkers, including Næss.)

INGEMUND GULLVÅG

NĀGĀRJUNA (*c.* AD 150–200)

Nāgārjuna was the first Buddhist philosopher to articulate and seek to defend the claim that all things are empty, that is, devoid of their own essential nature. A native of South India, as the founder of the Madhyamaka school of Mahāyāna Buddhism he exerted a profound influence on the further development of Buddhist thought in South and East Asia. When he claimed that all things are empty, he denied that anything exists solely in virtue of its own inherent nature. If, as all Buddhists hold, existents only arise in dependence on other existents, then nothing may be said to have a determinate nature apart from its relations to other things. Yet prior developments in Buddhist philosophy had presumably shown that anything lacking an independent nature is a conceptual fiction and not ultimately real. Thus if all things are empty, nothing is ultimately real. Still Nāgārjuna claimed not to be a nihilist. Emptiness is rather the defeat of all metaphysical theories, all attempts at grasping the ultimate nature of reality – including nihilism. Insight into emptiness is said to free us from our tendency conceptually to construct an ultimate truth, a tendency that bolsters our sense of self. Thus realization of emptiness is, Nāgārjuna held, required in order to attain full liberation from the suffering caused by clinging.

1 Historical context
2 Arguments for emptiness
3 Interpretations of Nāgārjuna

1 Historical context

Nāgārjuna was the first philosopher systematically to develop the assertion made in the *Prajñāpāramitā* (Perfection of Wisdom) literature of early Mahāyāna Buddhism that all things are empty (*śūnya*). His principal work, *Mūlamadhyamakakārikā* (Fundamental Treatise on the Middle Path) serves as the foundational text of Madhyamaka, one of the two chief philosophical schools of Mahāyāna. Another surviving text, *Vigrahavyāvartanī* (Refuting the Opponents), replies to various objections to the doctrine of emptiness. Modern scholars are divided over the authorship of several other works traditionally attributed to Nāgārjuna.

Nāgārjuna's claim that all things are empty, that is, devoid of 'own essential nature' (*svabhāva*), is in part a response to earlier developments in Buddhist philosophy. Early Buddhists held a reductionist view of persons, according to which the continued existence of a person just consists in the occurrence of a causal continuum of impersonal, impermanent, physical and psychological elements. In the Abhidharma or scholastic phase of Buddhism, this reductionist tendency was developed into a thoroughgoing denial of all partite entities as mere conceptual fictions, things that are commonly thought to exist only because of our use of such convenient designations as 'forest', 'chariot', and 'person'. Yet our use of such convenient designations does have utility, and this fact requires explanation. Thus it was thought that while the chariot is ultimately unreal, there must be some set of ultimately real impartite entities, the behaviour of which explains our use of 'chariot'. Such an ultimately real entity is a *dharma*, defined as that which bears its own essential nature. This definition was arrived at by way of the fact that the essential properties of a complex entity are all borrowed from its parts: that a chariot serves as a mode of transportation is to be explained in terms of facts about its parts and their relations. Since such explanation must terminate in entities that are ultimately real, these must be conceived of as bearing their own essential nature. Thus when Nāgārjuna states that all things are empty, he is denying that there are any ultimately real entities.

2 Arguments for emptiness

Nāgārjuna's basic strategy in arguing for the emptiness of all existents is to seek to show that the assumption that real entities bear their own essential nature leads to absurdities: implications that either contradict the official position of some Abhidharma theory, or else fly in the face of common sense. The argument of *Mūlamadhyamakakārikā* 3 is an instance of the first sort of *reductio*. It was a received view among Ābhidharmikas that there are six sense faculties (the sixth being a kind of inner sense), each with its own distinct class of sense-object (see BUDDHISM, ĀBHIDHARMIKA SCHOOLS OF §§3–4).

Since consciousness was claimed to arise in dependence on contact between sense-faculty and sense-object, this doctrine could be used to demonstrate the radical impermanence of consciousness (and thus to support the view that there is no self). But Nāgārjuna points out that if, for example, the faculty of vision is thought to be a *dharma*, then it must bear its own essential nature of seeing. Yet vision cannot see itself, as no (impartite) entity may operate on itself. Vision manifests its essential nature of seeing only in the presence of a visible sense-object and light. Thus vision may not be said to bear its own essential nature of seeing; rather, it borrows its essential nature from the conditions on which seeing depends. Vision is not, then, an ultimately real entity, but merely a conceptual fiction. And if consciousness does arise, it can only do so in dependence on causes and conditions that are themselves ultimately real. Thus the Ābhidharmika may not claim that consciousness arises in dependence on vision, or any of the other sense faculties either.

The view that ultimately real existents bear their own essential nature also contradicts common sense, for example, the fact that existing things undergo alteration. For if all existents are indeed impermanent, then alteration must ultimately require that things lose their essential nature, which is incoherent. If being young is the essential nature of the youth, and being old the essential nature of the aged, who is it that undergoes ageing (*Mūlamadhyamakakārikā* 13.5)? Indeed, it would appear that if what makes an entity ultimately real is that it bears its own essential nature, then the ultimately real could never be created or destroyed. For creation involves the acquisition of essential nature from the causes and conditions responsible for creation, which would make essential nature 'borrowed' and not 'its own'. And since destruction involves loss of essential nature, there can be no ultimately real subject of destruction.

An additional though related problem with the notion of a *dharma* concerns the relation between essential nature and the bearer or substrate of essential nature (*Mūlamadhyamakakārikā* 5). If it is the function of essential nature to characterize the bearer, then presumably the bearer must itself be an existent. But if the bearer is itself of some determinate nature, then the function of essential nature becomes redundant. Yet it seems incoherent to suppose that the bearer is in itself utterly devoid of any nature; we only seem able to imagine such a thing because we tacitly supply the bearer with the nature of being devoid of determinate nature. Finally, it would be wrong to suppose that a *dharma* consists only of essential nature without underlying bearer, since then

we should be unable to distinguish between distinct instances of a given *dharma*.

Through arguments such as these, Nāgārjuna seeks to show that all things are empty, that is, that it is not the case that there are ultimately real entities. This is not, however, nihilism, for neither is it the case that ultimately there is nonexistence. Nāgārjuna claims that in order to grasp the concept of the nonexistent, we must understand the notion of the existent. What we have presumably discovered through the investigation of the concept of a *dharma* is that the notion of the ultimately existent is incoherent. It follows, then, that we cannot give coherent content to the nihilist's claim that reality is ultimately devoid of existents. To say that all things are empty is not to propound a metaphysical thesis, is not to seek to characterize the ultimate nature of reality, but rather to reject the very idea. Nāgārjuna calls those for whom emptiness is itself a metaphysical thesis 'incurable' (*Mūlamadhyamakakārikā* 13.8). Emptiness is not itself a property of ultimately real things; emptiness is just a conceptual fiction, it too is empty.

To this it was objected (*Vigrahavyāvartanī* 5–6) that Nāgārjuna cannot consistently seek to demonstrate that all things are empty, since such demonstration would require that there ultimately exist valid means of knowledge, as well as objects on which these means or instruments operate. Any 'proof' of emptiness would then be fallacious, in that it would presuppose the existence of ultimately real entities. To this objection Nāgārjuna replies (*Vigrahavyāvartanī* 30–51) by first denying that he seeks to prove a thesis. He then argues that there can ultimately be no such things as valid means of knowledge: any attempt to demonstrate that a given procedure is a means of knowledge will either be a mere dogmatic assertion, or else be subject to either circularity or infinite regress. Thus all supposed means of knowledge are likewise empty: none has the nature of a valid means of knowledge independently of other existents.

3 Interpretations of Nāgārjuna

Nāgārjuna's response to the above objection, to the effect that his position is self-stultifying, is ambiguous. He might be taken as claiming that it is futile to assert any thesis concerning the ultimate nature of reality because its true nature is only obscured through such conceptual constructions as the so-called means of knowledge. In this case he does recognize such a thing as the ultimate nature of reality, though perhaps as apprehended only through some non-discursive means such as mystical intuition. Alternatively, he might be understood as a kind of global anti-realist, claiming that since a cognitive procedure could count as a valid means of knowledge only in the context of certain concrete human institutions and practices, the very idea of 'the ultimate nature of reality' is incoherent, since it requires that we be able to give content to the notion of how things are independently of any human institutions and practices.

Nāgārjuna's claim that emptiness is itself empty results in a paradox: the ultimate truth is that there is no ultimate truth. This and related paradoxes came to play a central role in Mahāyāna Buddhist practice. The two different ways of understanding Nāgārjuna are reflected in two different ways of understanding such paradoxes. One way is to see them as pointing beyond our conventional discursive practices to a reality that cannot be grasped conceptually. But on the global anti-realist reading, such paradoxes are instead meant to force us to abandon the quest for ultimate truth by getting us to see the very idea of ultimate truth as the final obstacle to attaining enlightenment. On this interpretation, the ultimate truth is that there is only conventional truth, a set of discursive practices that originate in dependence on contingent human needs and interests.

Nāgārjuna suggests the first interpretation when he speaks of ultimate reality as 'at peace, not populated with conceptual fictions, devoid of construction, not having many meanings' (*Mūlamadhyamakakārikā* 18.9). But it is the second interpretation that is supported when he goes on to equate such soteriologically privileged terms as *nirvāṇa*, the Buddha and liberation with the ostensibly opposed mundane concepts of, respectively, cyclic rebirth, the unenlightened and bondage. These equations – made on the grounds that both members of each pair are equally empty – suggest that enlightenment through realization of emptiness should not be construed as insight into a reality somehow purified of all conceptual contamination. To realize emptiness is just to see that our practices do not require grounding in things that bear their own essential nature.

One final piece of evidence derives from the frequency with which Nāgārjuna appears to violate either non-contradiction or excluded middle, as in his claim that an existing substance such as earth or space is not existent, not nonexistent, not both, and not neither (*Mūlamadhyamakakārikā* V.6–7). This sort of statement has sometimes been taken to show that Nāgārjuna rejects logic altogether in his account of reality. The Buddha, however, used a similar locution to emphasize the point that the subject of some predication fails to refer: just as we would not ask concerning a fire that has gone out in what direction it has gone, so we cannot say of, for example, the enlightened person that they are reborn, not reborn, both, or neither – since ultimately there are no persons. Thus those who favour reading Nāgārjuna as a global anti-realist would claim that when he says reals neither arise nor fail to arise nor both nor neither, he is best seen as simply denying that coherent sense can be made of the notion of how things ultimately are.

See also: BUDDHISM, MĀDHYAMIKA: INDIA AND TIBET §1; BUDDHIST CONCEPT OF EMPTINESS; BUDDHIST PHILOSOPHY, INDIAN; KNOWLEDGE, INDIAN VIEWS OF §4; SENGZHAO

List of works

Nāgārjuna (*c.* AD 150–200) *Mūlamadhyamakakārikā* (Fundamental Treatise on the Middle Path), ed. P.L.Vaidya, under the title *Madhyamakaśāstra (Mūlamadhyamakakārikā)*, India: Mithila Institute, 1960; trans. J.L. Garfield, *The Fundamental Wisdom of the Middle Way: Nāgārjuna's Mūlamadhyamakakārikā*, New York: Oxford University Press , 1995. (Contains the chief arguments for the doctrine of emptiness; *Madhyamakaśāstra* is an alternative title. Garfield supplies a commentary in addition to his translation, which is based largely on the Tibetan text.)

—— (*c.* AD 150–200) *Vigrahavyāvartanī* (Refuting the Opponents), ed. and trans. K. Bhattacharya, *The Dialectical Method of Nāgārjuna*, Delhi: Motilal Banarsidass, 1978. (Contains replies to a variety of objections, including the charge that Nāgārjuna's position is self-stultifying.)

References and further reading

Lindtner, C. (1982) *Nagarjuniana: Studies in the Writings and Philosophy of Nāgārjuna*, Copenhagen: Akademisk Forlag. (Contains translations of a number of works traditionally attributed to Nāgārjuna but concerning which there is no modern scholarly consensus.)

Murti, T.R.V. (1955) *The Central Philosophy of Buddhism*, London: Allen & Unwin. (A classic statement of the thesis that Nāgārjuna holds ultimate reality to be ineffable.)

Ruegg, D.S. (1977) 'The Uses of the Four Positions of the Catuṣkoṭi and the Problem of the Description of Reality in Mahāyāna Buddhism', *Journal of Indian Philosophy* 5: 1–71. (Contains a careful discussion of Nāgārjuna's treatment of non-contradiction and excluded middle.)

Siderits, M. (1980) 'The Madhyamaka Critique of Epistemology I', *Journal of Indian Philosophy* 8: 307–35. (Discusses the debate between Nāgārjuna and classical Indian realists over the possibility of a theory of knowledge.)

Streng, F.J. (1967) *Emptiness: A Study in Religious Meaning*, Nashville, TN: Abingdon. (Clear presentation of the anti-realist interpretation of Nāgārjuna.)

Tuck, A.P. (1990) *Comparative Philosophy and the Philosophy of Scholarship: On the Western Interpretation of Nāgārjuna*, New York: Oxford University Press. (Discusses the variety of interpretive approaches to Nāgārjuna taken by modern scholars.)

Wood, T. (1994) *Nāgārjunian Disputations: A Philosophical Journey Through an Indian Looking Glass*, Monographs of the Society for Asian and Comparative Philosophy 11, Honolulu, HI: University of Hawaii Press. (Defends a nihilist interpretation of Nāgārjuna's doctrine of emptiness.)

MARK SIDERITS

NAGEL, ERNEST (1901–85)

Ernest Nagel was arguably the pre-eminent American philosopher of science from the mid 1930s to the 1960s. He taught at Columbia University for virtually his entire career. Although he shared with Bertrand Russell and with members of the Vienna Circle a respect for and sensitivity to developments in mathematics and the natural sciences, he endorsed a strand in the thought of Charles S. Peirce and John Dewey that Nagel himself called 'contextual naturalism'. Among the main features of contextual naturalism is its distrust of reductionist claims that are not the outcomes of scientific inquiries.

Nagel's contextual naturalism infused his influential, detailed and informed essays on probability, explanation in the natural and social sciences, measurement, history of mathematics, and the philosophy of law. It is reflected, for example, in his trenchant critiques of Russell's reconstruction of the external world and Russell's epistemology as well as cognate views endorsed at one time or another by members of the Vienna Circle.

1   Life
2   Philosophy of science
3   Observation and theory
4   Explanation
5   Probability, confirmation and induction
6   Other topics

1   Life

Ernest Nagel was born on 16 November 1901 in Novomesto, Slovakia. He came to New York City in 1911. Educated in the New York City school system, he received a BS degree from The College of the City of New York in 1923. While teaching mathematics in the New York City public schools, he received an MA from Columbia University in 1925 and a Ph.D. in 1931 for a dissertation on the logic of measurement. After spending one year as an instructor at The College of the City of New York in 1930–1, he moved to Columbia University in 1931. He became a full professor in 1945, was appointed to the John Dewey professorship in 1955 and to a University professorship from 1967 until he retired in 1970. He served as an editor of *The Journal of Philosophy, Philosophy of Science* and *The Journal of Symbolic Logic*. He died on 20 September 1985.

2   Philosophy of science

According to Nagel, science, understood as an 'institutionalized art of inquiry' has contributed to the articulation and realization of 'aspirations generally associated with the idea of a liberal civilization' (1961: vii). As a consequence, the relatively recent identification of philosophy of science as a special branch of study should not let us forget that topics covered under this rubric 'are continuous with those that have been pursued for centuries under such traditional divisions of philosophy as "logic", "theory of knowledge", "metaphysics" and "moral and social philosophy"'. Nagel wrote interestingly on all of these subjects; but his most extensive and best-known contributions are focused on topics in what he called 'the logic of science'. As with the later PEIRCE and with DEWEY, Nagel understood logic to cover methodological issues as well as formal syntactic and semantic questions. He thought the logic of science could be divided conveniently into three parts: (a) the nature of scientific explanations, including not only their formal characterization but also the relations of the different types of explanation to one another, their functions in inquiry and how they contribute to systematizing knowledge; (b) the structure of scientific concepts, including their linkages to observational data, conditions of meaningfulness and explication via methods of definition and measurement; (c) evaluation of claims to knowledge, including the structure of probable inference, criteria for weighing evidence and the validation of inductive arguments. Nagel's best-known and most extensive publications have focused on topics related to explanation, probability and probable reasoning, but his many articles cover aspects of all three parts of this classification (see SCIENTIFIC METHOD).

3 Observation and theory

In 'Verifiability, Truth and Verification' of 1934 (Nagel 1956: ch. 7) and his critique of RUSSELL's phenomenalism in the 1940s, Nagel insisted that the reports articulating the observed results of experiment and controlled observation used in scientific inquiry assume background information. In this sense, they are 'theory laden'. However, in *The Structure of Science* (1961) and in his comments on M. Hesse and P. Feyerabend in the late 1960s and early 1970s, Nagel denied that understanding reports of outcomes of tests of a hypothesis need or should ever presuppose the hypothesis under test. Laws that are explained by a given theory are experimental in that context when their terms may be interpreted observationally and can be confirmed or disconfirmed without presupposing the theory. Universal generalizations within a theory that cannot meet these context-relativized requirements for being experimental utilize concepts whose 'structural' features are characterized by the basic principles of the theory (that Nagel thought could be formally presented as a 'calculus' at least in principle). How such structural features are characterized is first elaborated in two papers Nagel wrote in the 1930s, on the emergence of the notion of pure geometry as distinct from a theory of spatial relations and pure mathematics as distinct from a science of quantity. Nagel sought to bypass the conflict between his two teachers, the realist M.R. Cohen and the instrumentalist J. Dewey, by arguing that realist and instrumentalist understandings of scientific theories and theoretical entities do not reflect a substantive disagreement (see SCIENTIFIC REALISM AND ANTI-REALISM; OBSERVATION; LAWS, NATURAL).

4 Explanation

Nagel claimed that the 'distinctive aim' of scientific inquiry is 'to provide systematic and responsibly supported explanations'. Because explanation is a distinctive aim of inquiry, Nagel recognized that a clarification of the common features of scientific explanations is also a clarification of common features of the aims of scientific inquiries. Consequently, an account of scientific explanation is inevitably going to require an examination of pragmatic aspects of scientific explanation. For example, Nagel insisted that deductive explanations of laws require that the law to be explained be less general than the explaining laws in a manner that required reference to the intended domains of application of the laws whose levels of generality are being compared.

In addition to deductive explanation, Nagel wrote on probabilistic, functional and statistical explanation. According to his classic discussion of goal-directed systems and functional explanation in biology and the social sciences, the claim that a system S is goal directed with respect to goal G is explained by showing it to be a logical consequence of a set of explanatory premises including causal laws that show how goal state G is realized relative to a variety of antecedent conditions. Ascribing a function F to the system S presupposes that S is goal directed to some goal and that F contributes to the realization of that goal. Nagel applied his account of functional explanation both to biology and to anthropology and sociology where he undertook a critical examination of the notions of functional explanation promoted by Malinowski and Radcliffe-Browne (see FUNCTIONAL-ISM IN SOCIAL SCIENCE).

Nagel's relativization of the deterministic or non-deterministic character of theories to how states of systems characterized by such theories and their laws are specified allowed him to claim that theories such as classical statistical mechanics may be viewed as deterministic when the states of aggregates are represented statistically and as indeterministic when the states are represented as mechanical states (see DETERMINISM AND INDETERMINISM). The contextual naturalism infusing his informed discussion of reduction of one theory to another is manifested by the remark: 'if and when the detailed physical, chemical and physiological conditions for the occurrence of headaches are ascertained, headaches will not thereby be shown to be illusory' (1961: 366) (see EXPLANATION; REDUCTION, PROBLEMS OF).

5 Probability, confirmation and induction

Nagel's classic monograph *Principles of the Theory of Probability* (1939) is a philosophical survey of issues pertaining to applications of the calculus of probability as these issues were seen in the 1940s and 1950s. Nagel tended to favour the limit of relative frequency interpretation of VENN and Von Mises as a way of understanding applications of the calculus of probability within scientific theories. Although he was sympathetic to efforts to clarify conceptions of weight of evidence and evidential support, he was a trenchant critic of the efforts of KEYNES, CARNAP and REICH-ENBACH to use various interpretations of the calculus of probability to develop notions of degree of confirmation and evidential support. In this connection, the methodological parts of Nagel's collaboration with M.R. Cohen, *An Introduction to Logic and*

Scientific Method, should also be mentioned (see PROBABILITY, INTERPRETATIONS OF).

6 Other topics

Nagel wrote extensively on the methodology of the social sciences as well as the natural sciences. He was concerned to defend the autonomy of the aims of scientific inquiry from those who insisted that science was laden with moral, political or social agenda. He was a sceptical critic of psychoanalytic theory, and had interesting things to say about philosophy of law.

Nagel shared with many members of the VIENNA CIRCLE the notion that extending the methods of inquiry used in the natural and social sciences to social and political problems would promote an approach to such problems free of the totalitarian tendencies so prevalent in Europe during much of his career. However, his association with the logical empiricists did not reflect a sympathy with the their positivist tendencies. He was, as he put it, a contextualist naturalist throughout.

See also: LOGICAL POSITIVISM; NATURALIZED PHILOSOPHY OF SCIENCE

List of works

Cohen, M.R. and Nagel, E. (1934) *An Introduction to Logic and Scientific Method*, London: Routledge & Kegan Paul. (Widely used textbook for two decades, which pioneered in presenting elementary introductions to topics in propositional logic. The discussion of the distinction between deductive and inductive reasoning, Mill's methods and elementary topics in statistics continue to have interest.)

Nagel, E. (1939) *Principles of the Theory of Probability*, International Encyclopedia of Unified Science, vol. 1, number 6, Chicago, IL: University of Chicago Press. (A survey of a variety of interpretations of the calculus of probability focused primarily on controversies concerning the domain of application of frequency interpretations.)

—— (1954) *Sovereign Reason*, Glencoe, IL: Free Press. (A selection of essays and reviews including critical discussions of Peirce, Dewey, Whitehead, Russell, Eddington, and a sustained critique of Reichenbach's views on probability that retains its relevance.)

—— (1956), *Logic without Metaphysics*, Glencoe, IL: Free Press. (A selection of essays and reviews including the well-known 'Logic without Ontology' and 'A Formalization of Functionalism' together with essays – especially chapters 7, 8 and 9 – that should afford a more accurate picture of Nagel's

relations to analytic philosophy and the logical empiricists than has been offered in recent commentaries on his work.)

Nagel, E. and Newman, J.R. (1960) *Gödel's Proof*, New York: New York University Press. (An effort at providing a popular presentation of Gödel's incompleteness theorem.)

Nagel, E. (1961) *The Structure of Science: Problems in the Logic of Scientific Explanation*, New York: Harcourt Brace. (Presents Nagel's classification of types of explanation in science and discussions of them, his conception of theories and their cognitive status, determinism, reduction, teleological, functional and statistical explanation in biology and social science, subjectivity and value in social inquiry, methodological individualism and a chapter on the 'logic' of historical inquiry.)

—— (1979) *Teleology Revisited and Other Essays in the Philosophy and History of Science*, New York: Columbia University Press. (Contains two classic essays on the history of mathematics, Nagel's John Dewey Lectures of 1977, a critique of Carnap's theory of inductive logic and several other essays including a discussion of Popper and Feyerabend.)

References and further reading

Morgenbesser, S., Suppes, P. and White, M. (eds) (1969) *Science and Method: Essays in Honor of Ernest Nagel*, New York: St Martin's Press. (Contains a full bibliography.)

Reck, A.J. (1968) *The New American Philosophers: An Exploration of Thought Since World War II*, Baton Rouge, LA: Louisiana State University Press; repr. New York: Dell, 1970.

ISAAC LEVI

NAGEL, THOMAS (1937–)

The comprehensiveness of Thomas Nagel's approach to philosophy sets him apart among late-twentieth-century analytic philosophers. Nagel develops a compelling analysis of the fundamental philosophical problems, showing how they result from our capacity to take up increasingly objective viewpoints that detach us from our individual subjective viewpoints as well as from the viewpoints of our community, nation and species. Our essentially dual nature, which allows us to occupy objective as well as subjective viewpoints, poses unsolvable problems for us because subjective and objective viewpoints reveal conflicting facts and values. Our ability to undertake increasingly detached view-

points from which objective facts come into view indicates that we are contained in a world that transcends our minds; similarly, our ability to examine our values and reasons from a detached or impartial objective viewpoint implies that moral values are real in the sense that they transcend our personal motives and inclinations. Yet Nagel also holds that our capacity for objective thought is limited by the fact that we cannot detach ourselves completely from our own natures in our attempts either to know our world or to act morally. Subjective facts are equally a part of reality and our moral outlook is essentially the outlook of individual agents with personal and communal ties. Consequently, Nagel argues against any form of reductionism which holds that only objective facts and values are real or which attempts to explain subjective facts and values in terms of objective ones.

1   Life

Thomas Nagel was born in 1937 in Belgrade, Yugoslavia, becoming a naturalized US citizen in 1944. He was educated at Cornell University, Oxford University and Harvard University. His career began at the University of California, Berkeley, where he spent three years before moving to Princeton University in 1966 and then to New York University in 1980.

Nagel stands out among his contemporaries for the breadth of his work, which encompasses metaphysics, epistemology and moral philosophy, and for his development of a comprehensive realistic approach. He is also distinguished by the nontechnical nature of his argumentation, which is accessible to non-professionals.

2   Metaphysics

Nagel's realism is complex in that it advances one intuitive idea at the core of the realist outlook, the idea of a world that contains and radically transcends us, at the cost of the intuitive and equally core idea of a single objective reality. For Nagel, the 'pure idea of realism' is the idea 'that there is a world in which we are contained' (1986: 70). He understands the idea of containment in terms of mind-independence. Thus, the world is independent of us not only causally, but also epistemically: the way things are might comple-

tely transcend our ability to know them, even to think about them. His development of this idea in terms of the distinction between subjective and objective standpoints entails that there is no single way that things are in themselves. If, as Nagel holds, reality includes all the myriad subjective viewpoints and the subjective facts they make available, then there is no one way that things are. It is not possible to give a single account from the completely detached or objective view, because such an account would fail to include subjective facts (that are only available from irreducibly distinctive subjective viewpoints).

Hence Nagel's approach is not only anti-verificationist and anti-idealist in its commitment to the intuitive idea of a mind-independent world. His realism is also anti-reductionist, because of its denial of the idea of a single objective reality. As both reductionism and idealism are prevailing tendencies in contemporary philosophy, Nagel's views on many issues challenge the prevailing positions. On the one hand, Nagel objects that many contemporary approaches, such as that of the later WITTGENSTEIN, are essentially idealist in that they involve 'a broadly epistemological test of reality'. On the other hand, as we will see, Nagel opposes a variety of reductionist accounts by arguing that the phenomena at issue are subjective facts or values that cannot be described or explained from a more objective standpoint in terms of objective facts or values. Nagel's anti-reductionist arguments thus depend on whether he is right that the recalcitrant phenomena are essentially subjective (see REALISM AND ANTIREALISM).

3   Theory of knowledge

Nagel's realist construal of the distinction between subjective and objective viewpoints affirms a traditional understanding of the problem posed for theories of knowledge that does not allow for revisionist resolution. The problem, according to Nagel, is that while knowledge needs to be objective and so requires that we undertake increasingly objective standpoints, we can only do so to a limited extent, since any outlook that we can occupy will be to some extent subjectively bounded.

Since we cannot attain the completely detached viewpoint from which we could examine our own attempts at understanding the world, Nagel affirms the possibility of sceptical doubt, opposing the anti-sceptical trend which holds that sceptical worries are unwarranted or even incoherent because they impose a theoretical demand for justification of our system of beliefs as a whole from an unobtainable, completely objective standpoint. Moreover, since Nagel urges that knowledge should be of what is correct, even if it is inaccessible to us, he opposes reductive theories which attempt to meet scepticism by reducing the aim or scope of knowledge to concern the way the world appears from the limited objective viewpoints that we can undertake rather than the way it really is. Though he believes that the possibility of limited objectivity is associated with the possibility of scepticism, Nagel endorses a heroic approach to knowledge, like that of Descartes, which acknowledges that we cannot detach from our perceptual and cognitive faculties completely, but attempts to use a priori argumentation to form a conception of our situation as knowers none the less (see DESCARTES, R. §3; SCEPTICISM).

4 Theory of mind

Commitment to the irreducibility of subjective facts leads Nagel to argue that the mind–body problem could only be solved, if at all, by a complete and as yet unimaginable revision of our conception of the basic constituents of the universe. Nagel explains that the relation of the mind and the body seems problematic if, as a result of the success of physical science, one holds a physical conception of objective reality, and espouses a reductionist programme according to which all phenomena must be explainable reductively in terms of physical objective facts. In opposition, he argues that the qualitative nature of conscious experience is a subjective feature of reality available only from a first person subjective viewpoint. Hence, though the qualitative aspects of conscious experiences are part of reality, they cannot be explained in terms of objective facts in general or physical objective facts in particular.

The precise force of Nagel's denial of the possibility of psychophysical reduction is important. He is not denying that we are physiological organisms or that the central nervous system (in vertebrates) and its physical states is necessary for subjective mental states. He is not denying that conscious organisms are made up of the same ultimate constituents that constitute all the physical phenomena in the universe. Rather, Nagel is proposing that our conception of the ultimate constituents as physical is too narrow for explaining that some combinations of those constituents have conscious experience. He is arguing for a dual-aspect approach, according to which the ultimate constituents are dual in nature – both physical and mental– in the sense that they can be combined to form physical things which have physical properties and conscious organisms which have the subjective properties of conscious experience (see CONSCIOUSNESS §2; QUALIA).

5 Moral philosophy

Nagel uses the distinction between subjective and objective viewpoints to articulate a non-metaphysical understanding of moral realism, to explain the bifurcation in moral philosophy between consequentialist and deontological approaches and to argue against consequentialism, even while showing that the tension between more and less impartial moral outlooks often cannot be reconciled (see CONSEQUENTIALISM; DEONTOLOGICAL ETHICS). Nagel's discussion of these issues illuminates the differences between the role of the objective standpoint in moral as opposed to factual or empirical thought.

According to Nagel, 'the view that values are real is not the view that they are real occult entities or properties, but that they are real values: that our claims about value and about what people have reason to do may be true or false independently of our beliefs and inclinations' (1986: 144). To be ethical is to examine one's reasons for acting from more than one's own particular perspective. Hence, unlike factual understanding, moral understanding 'is not a question of bringing the mind into correspondence with an external reality which acts causally on it, but of reordering the mind itself in accordance with the demands of its own external view of itself' (1986: 148). Consequently, while the truth about the empirical world may completely transcend our theoretical reason, the truth about how we should act could not completely transcend our practical reason. Hence, unlike metaphysical versions of moral realism, Nagel's normative realism is not associated with the possibility of moral scepticism according to which the objective viewpoint shows that there are no values, only facts about people's inclinations and motives.

Since consequentialism has been understood as advocating an impartial point of view, that of an impartial spectator, Nagel's discussion of moral theory in terms of the possibility of undertaking an impartial or objective viewpoint is not entirely new. However, Nagel gives a more complete and nuanced treatment of both deontological and consequentialist approaches by distinguishing between agent-relative and agent-neutral reasons in terms of two correlative distinctions that are also generated by our dual viewpoints: the distinction between what we do and what happens and between choosing actions as opposed to choosing states of the world. Reasons that are relative to the agent are 'specified by universal principles which nevertheless refer ineliminably to features or circumstances of the agent for whom they are reasons'. Reasons that are neutral with respect to the agent 'depend on what everyone ought to value, independently of its relation to himself' (1991: 40). As agents, we act on agent-relative reasons because even though actions affect what happens in the world, in the first instance one's choice is necessarily between one's own actions. However, each of us also has an objective self which views the world in detachment from one's particular perspective. Consequently, the objective self chooses between different possible states of the world and its choice is based on agent-neutral reasons. So, moral conflict is due to the fact that 'every choice is two choices', every choice is at once a choice between actions and between states of the world. Moral conflict arises when the agent's choice concerning what to *do* conflicts with the objective self's choice concerning what should *happen*.

Nagel thus explains that consequentialism gives primacy to the agent-neutral values on the basis of which the objective self chooses between world-states. In contrast, deontological theories give primacy to certain agent-relative reasons which restrict agents from acting in certain ways. His own position is both complex and modest. It does not allow for a general championing of one kind of reason over another. Against consequentialism, Nagel argues that not all values are agent-neutral. But he also voices some uncertainty about whether there really are agent-relative reasons. However, while he does not argue for their existence directly, he explains them, especially the most problematic deontological ones, in lucid and compelling terms. The modesty of Nagel's position lies in his conviction that we are far from a developed moral outlook. In contrast to his view that subjective and objective facts are irreconcilable, Nagel believes that it is possible, in principle, to develop our agent-relative values to be more consonant with agent-neutral values. However, as we will see in Nagel's discussion of political theory, he finds little hope that the actual conditions of human life will allow us to school our moral outlook (see MORAL REALISM).

6 Political philosophy

While political theory is typically understood as dealing with the relationship of the individual and society, Nagel holds that it deals with the relation of each individual to themselves, since each one of us occupies both a particular individual viewpoint and the detached standpoint of the collectivity. So the problem of designing morally justified social institutions that would reconcile the conflicts between the individual and society is the problem of designing social institutions that would allow each of us to reconcile those two standpoints within ourselves.

Nagel argues that a justified political system would be a unanimously supported, strongly egalitarian one, because in taking on a more objective standpoint, we see that everyone is equal not only in the sense that no person's life matters any more than any other's, but in the sense that it is more important to improve the lives of the worse off than to add to the advantages of the better off. The conflict between this impersonal, strongly egalitarian dictate and our personal motivation to lead our own lives could be resolved by general principles that can be universalized in a Kantian manner: principles that each of us can will to be universal laws. That is, we need to find our way to wanting 'to live by principles that anyone can accept' (1991: 48).

Nagel holds that we need political institutions to help integrate and develop our dual motivations. He suggests that the 'general form' of a solution is 'a moral division of labour between individuals and institutions'. According to such a division, the social institutions in which we participate would allow us to act on our impartial, egalitarian motives. This would allow us to act on our personal motives outside of our social roles. However, Nagel argues pessimistically against the possibility of developing such institutions given the initial duality of motives. In sum, since he is drawn to a strongly egalitarian social ideal, to whose recognition the duality of standpoints is necessary, but to whose realization the duality of standpoints seems to present great obstacles, Nagel does not see how to embody that ideal in a morally and psychologically viable system (see EQUALITY).

See also: REDUCTION, PROBLEMS OF §2

List of works

Nagel, T. (1970) *The Possibility of Altruism*, Oxford: Clarendon Press. (Incorporates material from Nagel's B.Phil. and Ph.D. theses. Focuses on the motivational basis for morality, arguing that altruism is a basic rational requirement on moral action. This first work gives a stronger role to the objective standpoint and its deliverances than does Nagel's subsequent work in moral philosophy.)

——(1979) *Mortal Questions*, Cambridge: Cambridge University Press. (Essays on a wide variety of topics that were published between 1969 and 1979, including the highly influential 'Moral Luck' and 'What is it like to be a bat?'. Several essays deal with issues of public policy and are motivated by events and policies associated with the Vietnam War.)

Nagel, T., Cohen, M. and Scanlon T. (eds) (1980) *Marx, Justice and History*, Princeton, NJ: Princeton University Press. (Essays by a variety of authors in

Philosophy and Public Affairs from 1972 to 1979 that bring together contemporary analytic moral philosophy and Marxist social theory.)

Nagel, T. (1986) *The View From Nowhere*, Oxford: Oxford University Press. (Presents Nagel's systematic and comprehensive treatment of the fundamental philosophical issues in terms of the essential duality between objective and subjective points of view and the distinctive facts and values that they make available.)

—— (1987) *What Does It All Mean?*, Oxford: Oxford University Press. (A concise and 'direct' or non-historical introduction to nine basic philosophical problems.)

——(1991) *Equality and Partiality*, Oxford: Oxford University Press. (Incorporates Nagel's 1990 John Locke Lectures. A detailed development of Nagel's proposal that the central problem of political theory– that of reconciling the conflicts between the individual and society – is posed by the division between these standpoints within each individual and needs to be addressed accordingly.)

—— (1995) *Other Minds: Critical Essays, 1969–1994*, Oxford: Oxford University Press. (These essays focus on the views of particular philosophers in the philosophy of mind and in ethics and political theory. In the philosophy of mind, Nagel addresses the views of Freud, Wittgenstein, Chomsky, Fodor and Dennett among others. In ethics and political theory, Nagel treats the views of philosophers such as Rawls, Nozick, MacIntyre and Williams as well as Schelling and Kolakowski. The book opens with a fascinating intellectual autobiography entitled 'Introduction: The Philosophical Culture'.)

References and further reading

Darwall, S. (1987) 'The View From Nowhere', *Ethics* 98: 137–57. (Focuses on Nagel's normative realism, §5 of this entry. Criticizes the account of agent-relative reasons while arguing that Nagel's views on autonomy provide the resources for a successful account.)

McGinn, C. (1987) 'The View From Nowhere', *Mind* 96: 263–72. (Focuses primarily on Nagel's discussion of the mind–body problem, §4 of this entry.)

Peacocke, C. (1989) 'No Resting Place: A Critical Notice of The View From Nowhere by Thomas Nagel', *Philosophical Review* 98: 65–82. (Focuses on Nagel's account of conscious states and his normative realism, §§4 and 5 of this entry.)

Raz, J. (1990) 'Facing Diversity: The Case of Epistemic Abstinence', *Philosophy and Public Affairs* 19: 3–46. (Criticizes John Rawls' as well as Nagel's attempt to accommodate the diversity of views in pluralistic societies with the notion that justified political arrangements and actions require individual consent, §6 of this entry.)

SONIA SEDIVY

NAHMANIDES, MOSES (1194–1270)

One of the most influential medieval Jewish thinkers to engage with the philosophical tradition, Nahmanides was also a leading Talmudist, biblical exegete, and a founding figure of the Jewish mystical tradition (Kabbalah) that emerged in thirteenth-century Spain. Generally critical of Aristotle, he was deeply influenced by predecessors such as Moses Maimonides. As the leading rabbi in Catalonia, Nahmanides played a central role in the 'Maimonidean controversy' of 1232–3, a dispute that raged over the permissibility of philosophical study. He was also at the centre of the 'Barcelona disputation' of 1263, conducted with the apostate Pablo Christiani over the issue of philosophically motivated allegories.

Unlike his Provençal contemporaries, Nahmanides wrote neither free-standing philosophical treatises nor commentaries on Graeco-Arabic philosophical texts. Instead, he developed his original metaphysical views in sermons and his highly influential biblical commentaries treating such topics as miracles, providence and idolatry. The commentaries proved especially influential through their thematic treatments of philosophical questions raised by the biblical text and for their suggestive expositions of mystical and theosophical ideas.

1 Relation to the philosophical tradition
2 Metaphysics: miracles and divine providence
3 Hermeneutics and explanation of the divine commandments

1 Relation to the philosophical tradition

Moses Nahmanides, Rabbi Moses ben Nahman, known in Hebrew texts by the acronym 'Ramban' and in Christian literature as Bonastrug de Porta was born in Gerona, Catalonia, and died at Acre in Palestine. He became the leading Catalonian thinker in the intellectually tumultuous period following the publication of Maimonides' *Guide to the Perplexed*, whose Hebrew translation in 1204 by Samuel ibn Tibbon brought about the first major encounter of Jewish thinkers in Christian Spain and Provence with Graeco-Arabic and specifically Aristotelian philosophy. Although standardly portrayed as a conservative defender of rabbinic traditions, Nahmanides showed a nuanced ambivalence towards rationalism in general (which had a long indigenous Andalusian tradition) and the thought of Aristotle and Maimonides in particular. In the 'Maimonidean controversy' of 1232–3 Nahmanides joined ranks with the anti-rationalist camp to forbid unrestricted public study of philosophy, but he also vigorously defended Maimonides and attempted to prevent the banning of the *Guide* and Maimonides' philosophical oopening sections of his fourteen-volume code of Jewish law, the *Mishneh Torah*. Comparable dualities run throughout his thought. He repeatedly criticized Aristotle for his empiricism and doctrine of the world's eternity and reproved Maimonides for his challenges to rabbinic theological traditions. But his own doctrines are constructively influenced by the philosophy of the *Guide*. His decision to present his ideas primarily in commentaries on Scripture is exemplary of his outlook: philosophical reasoning may be essential to the strengthening of belief but it must remain subservient to divine revelation and the revealed tradition. Nahmanides repeatedly emphasizes the importance of rational understanding. In *Sha'ar ha-Gemul* (The Gate of the Reward), he recalls the words of Saadiah Gaon, in *Kitab al-mukhtar fi'l-amanat wa'l-'i'tiqadat* (The Book of Critically Chosen Beliefs and Opinions), attacking those who spurn philosophical reflection as 'fools who despise wisdom' (see *Kitvei ha-Ramban* II: 21).

Nahmanides' cautiously critical stance towards philosophy stands out in his influential views on midrash *aggadah*, the immense literature of non-legal (non-*halakhic*) rabbinic exegesis, homilies and imaginative writing (see MIDRASH), whose interpretation and authority were centrally at issue in both the Maimonidean controversy and the 'Barcelona disputation' of 1263. In the latter event, Nahmanides was summoned to engage in a public argument with the apostate Pablo Christiani. Maimonists viewed the rabbinic midrash (and the non-legal sections of the Hebrew Bible) as philosophical allegories, contemplation of whose truths was the highest form of worship. Anti-Maimonists insisted on the primacy of practice, the life of the divine commandments or *mitzvot*. Rejecting philosophically motivated allegories as a potential source of antinomianism, grounded in a suspected substitution of contemplation for religious observance, they urged that midrash *aggadah* be accepted virtually at face value, even when its mythic and supernatural claims violated reason. In the Barcelona disputation, Christiani put *aggadic* and scriptural materials to allegorical use in behalf of Christianity, rendering the allegorical method all the

more suspect. Nahmanides' position in both confrontations was novel. His rationalist sensibilities forbade him to interpret all *aggadah* literally. Following his Andalusian predecessor Abraham IBN EZRA, he subjected *aggadah* to the same interpretive standards of philology, grammar and reason that he applied to biblical interpretation itself. But he undercut the antinomian potential of philosophical allegorization and the evangelical impact of Christian misappropriations by denying that midrash *aggadah* is authoritative. Relying on some imaginative philology, he argued that *aggadah* is merely homiletic – or, even less, 'things one man tells another'. It is never authoritative in belief or practice, as are *halakhic* texts. This conservative and anti-Maimonidean approach deeply influenced later Jewish dogmatics and polemics by restoring action rather than belief as the essence of Judaism. The immediate consequences for Nahmanides were not, however, favourable. While the disputation was a theological victory for him, his Dominican opponents responded by charging him with abusing Christianity and he was forced to flee to Palestine.

Nahmanides' turn to mystical theosophy reflects his opposition to the Maimonists' assumption that the deepest truths of the Law are somehow coextensive with the received tradition of Aristotelian physics and metaphysics. Nahmanides presents Kabbalah as an indigenous Jewish alternative to Graeco-Arabic philosophy, a *prisca philosophia* (archaic or antidiluvean philosophy) based on a revealed (and hitherto oral) tradition rather than reason, and a fixed canon of theosophic exegeses of biblical verses and commandments (see KABBALAH). Thus, in place of Maimonides' account of evil in terms of matter, he proposes a theodicy based on transmigration; instead of Maimonides' anthropological-historical account of the Temple sacrifices, he turns to the theory of divine emanations (Sefirot).

2 Metaphysics: miracles and divine providence

Perhaps the most original and philosophically interesting of Nahmanides' doctrines is his theory of revealed and hidden miracles (see MIRACLES). Revealed miracles such as the splitting of the sea in Exodus 14 violate the observed regularities of nature and cannot be explained by natural causes but must be attributed to divine intervention. Nahmanides believed that the Bible provides reliable evidence of such manifest miracles. Typically witnessed by the entire community, they provide empirical verification for the three fundamental principles of Judaism: *ex nihilo* creation, divine knowledge, and providence. Such empirical appeals, rather than rational demonstrations, are Nahmanides' primary epistemic grounds for faith. In the case of creation, for example, he argues against Aristotelian eternalism, suggesting that if the world were eternal, nature as it is would be necessary and God would be unable to shorten the wing of a fly if he wished. But this consequence is baldly disconfirmed by the experience of revealed miracles in which God has violated presumed necessities of nature. Eternalism, then, is refuted and, Nahmanides concludes, the world must have been created *ex nihilo*. To be sure, this conclusion does not follow. As Maimonides (from whom Nahmanides drew this argument) observed, the existence of miracles does not exclude a third alternative, the Platonic theory of *formatio mundi*, creation from eternal matter. Indeed, from other statements, in which Nahmanides claims that what was created *ex nihilo* was matter, or potentiality, without form, it is not clear how well he understood Aristotelian metaphysics or its differences from Platonic or Platonizing doctrines. However, his argument for creation *ex nihilo*, which appeals to miracles as empirical data, is still of interest. After repeatedly describing Aristotle as an empiricist who believed only in what our senses perceive, Nahmanides tries to turn empiricism against Aristotle, arguing, in effect, that one cannot be both an empiricist and an eternalist.

Nahmanides' doctrine of hidden miracles underlies his theory of providence — specifically, of divine rewards and punishments (see PROVIDENCE). Such miracles violate no observed regularities and may even have obvious explanations in terms of intermediate natural causes. The same events, however, can be explained by attributing them to God, who brings them about as rewards or punishments of the absolutely righteous and wicked. Such direct attributions, Nahmanides argues, are simpler and more sensible than the naturalistic alternatives: while caused by God under conditions we may never know in full, hidden miracles follow in law-like patterns as consequences of human actions; and because they occur only in response to the acts of absolutely righteous and wicked persons, not the ordinary individuals who fall between these two extremes, Nahmanides can uphold a nature whose laws govern these ordinary people. So despite some strong rhetoric in which he appears to deny the existence of nature *tout court*, Nahmanides does not seem to be an occasionalist. Rather, his doctrine seems to expand upon Maimonides' theory of 'natural' providence, whereby all species (and ordinary individuals as their members) are endowed with natures to provide for their wellbeing, and certain perfected individuals can transcend the vicissitudes of nature, achieving an additional kind of individual providence. The main

differences from Maimonides here turn on the nature of that individual perfection and on the role of miracles. For Maimonides, individual providence is consequent on intellectual development: only those who become 'acquired intellects' rise (in that measure) above matter and the conditions of natural evil. Miracles have no place in this process. Nahmanides, by contrast, makes individual reward and punishment consequent on moral character and religious practice. He offers no metaphysical explanation of its operations but makes miracles its unseen vehicles. He takes over the structure of Maimonides' account but substitutes more traditional rabbinic categories for Aristotelian ones.

Paralleling the individual providence that attends the actions of the absolutely righteous and wicked, Nahmanides affirms a special providence over the nation and land of Israel. This special providence is described by Nahmanides in relation to his views on astrology and astral determinism, theories shared by many of his Andalusian predecessors and contemporaries, with the notable exception of Maimonides. On Nahmanides' theory, there exist real forces associated with the constellations created by God to govern the nations. There is also a hierarchy of angels and demons. The people and land of Israel, however, remain directly under the dominion of God. It is forbidden as idolatry for Jews to worship any other power, not because such powers do not exist but because no other power is the rightful Lord of Israel. Similarly with the complex hierarchy of powers, Kabbalistic Sefirot, *within* the deity. It is a kind of idolatry to worship any of these emanations apart from the deity as a whole. Such worship is tantamount to denying God's unity.

3 Hermeneutics and explanation of the divine commandments

Nahmanides pursues three distinct levels of biblical exegesis with exceptionally systematic care. He typically offers (1) a literal interpretation (*peshat*) according to the philologically determined senses of words, syntax, historical context and narrative structure; (2) an interpretation containing moral or political wisdom (*hokhmah*); and (3) a riddle-like secret theosophic interpretation (*sod*), which he calls 'the way of truth'. At this third level, he was the first to incorporate Kabbalistic mysteries, even if only allusively, in an exoteric commentary. Some of his most original and enduring exegetical contributions, however, work at the first two levels. He was the first, and perhaps the only, medieval Jewish exegete to offer typological interpretations like those found in Christian exegesis. In reaction to Maimonides' radical devaluation of literal meanings, he also did much to restore the status of *peshat* and to enrich its traditional scope, making it more thematic and conceptual, and at times even subsuming the philosophical and mystical exegeses of the text.

Like Maimonides, Nahmanides was a vigorous advocate of inquiry into the reasons for the *mitzvot*, although he often disagreed with the explanations of the *Guide to the Perplexed*. Applying his exegetical method, he argued that, besides their moral, political and commemorative purposes, the commandments have an inner theurgic function in serving divine needs. Here, as in his exegesis, his multi-levelled explanations, ranging from the popular to the esoteric, and his brilliance as a stylist made Nahmanides an exceptionally influential writer.

See also: BIBLE, HEBREW; KABBALAH; MAIMONIDES, M.; MIDRASH; PROVIDENCE

List of works

Nahmanides, Moses (1194–1270) Works, ed. C.B. Chavel, *Kitvei Ha-Ramban* (Writings and Discourses of Nahmanides), Jerusalem: Mosad Ha-Rav Kook, 1963, 2 vols; trans. C.B. Chavel, New York: Shilo, 1978. (A collection of Nahmanides' speculative writings, including his sermons, a record of the 'Barcelona disputation', and a commentary on the Book of Job, as well as some misattributed works. The translation is not always sensitive to philosophical usage.)

—— (1194–1270) *Perush Ha-Ramban 'al ha-Torah* (Commentary on the Torah), ed. C.B. Chavel, Jerusalem: Mosad ha-Rav Kook, 1959–63, 2 vols; trans. C.B. Chavel, *Commentary on the Torah*, New York: Shilo, 1976. (Nahmanides' highlty influential commentary on the Torah.)

References and further reading

Berger, D. (1983) 'Miracles and the Natural Order in Nahmanides', in I. Twersky (ed.) *Rabbi Moses Nahmanides (Ramban): Explorations in His Religious and Literary Virtuosity*, Cambridge, MA: Harvard University Press. (An excellent analysis of Hahmanides' theory of revealed miracles, his theory of providence, and conception of nature.)

Funkenstein, A. (1982) 'Nahmanides' Symbolical Reading of History', in J. Dan and F. Talmage (eds) *Studies in Jewish Mysticism*, Cambridge, MA: Association for Jewish Studies. (An insightful study of Nahmanides' use of typological interpretation.)

Idel, M. (1983) 'We Have No Kabbalistic Tradition on This', in I. Twersky (ed.) *Rabbi Moses Nahmanides*

(Ramban): Explorations in His Religious and Literary Virtuosity, Cambridge, MA: Harvard University Press. (A careful discussion of Nahmanides on the relations of mysticism and philosophy.)

Maimonides, Moses (*c.*1185) *Mishneh Torah* (The Law in Review), Books I and II trans. M. Hyamson, *The Book of Knowledge and the Book of Adoration*, Jerusalem: Feldheim, 1974; Books III–XIV trans. as *The Code of Maimonides*, Yale Judaica Series, New Haven, CT: Yale University Press, 1949–72. (Maimonides' highly influential fourteen-volume codification of rabbinic law, which ranges from beliefs through ritual and civil law to the Temple cult and laws of war and political governance.)

* —— (*c.*1190) *Dalalat al-Ha'irin* (*Moreh Nevukhim*, Guide to the Perplexed), ed. S. Munk, *Le Guide des Égarés*, Arabic text, critically edited, with annotated French translation, Paris, 1856–66, 3 vols; repr. Osnabrück: Zeller, 1964; trans. S. Pines, with an introductory essay by L. Strauss, *The Guide of the Perplexed*, Chicago, IL: University of Chicago Press, 1969. (Maimonides' major philosophical work, which served as the starting-point for all subsequent medieval Jewish philosophical thought.)

Novak, D. (1992) *The Theology of Nahmanides Systematically Presented*, Atlanta, GA: Scholars Press. (Exposition of Nahmanides' thought on the soul, commandments, miracles, eschatology, and other topics, with key texts culled from his works and organized thematically.)

* Saadiah Gaon (early 10th century) *Kitab al-mukhtar fi 'l-amanat wa 'l-'i'tiqadat* (The Book of Critically Chosen Beliefs and Opinions), trans. J. Kafih, *Sefer ha-Nivar ba-Emunot uva-De'ot*, Jerusalem: Sura, 1970; trans. S. Rosenblatt, *The Book of Beliefs and Opinions*, New Haven, CT: Yale University Press, 1948. (The passage to which Nahmanides refers can be found on p. 13 of the Rosenblatt translation. This is the first systematic work of Jewish rational theology; it shows the influence of Islamic *kalam*.)

Septimus, B. (1983) '"Open Rebuke and Concealed Love": Nahmanides and the Andalusian Tradition', in I. Twersky (ed.) *Rabbi Moses Nahmanides (Ramban): Explorations in His Religious and Literary Virtuosity*, Cambridge, MA: Harvard University Press. (A fine historical essay on Nahmanides' place in Spanish Jewish thought, with special attention to his rationalism, literary style and role in the 'Maimonidean controversy'.)

Stern, J. (1995) 'Nahmanides' Conception of Ta'amei Mitzvot and its Maimonidean Background', in D. Frank (ed.) *Community and Covenant: New Essays in Jewish Political and Legal Philosophy*, Albany, NY: State University of New York Press. (On the relation of Nahmanides to Maimonides, with special attention to their accounts of the reasons for the commandments.)

Wolfson, E.R. (1989) 'By Way of Truth: Aspects of Nahmanides' Kabbalistic Hermeneutic', *AJS Review* 14: 103–78. (An important analysis of Nahmanides' exegetical method.)

JOSEF STERN

NAMES *see* PROPER NAMES

NANCY, JEAN-LUC (1940–)

Jean-Luc Nancy has disclosed significant political and social dimensions to the general project of deconstructing Western philosophy. Existence does not precede essence, according to Nancy; existence is without essence, and it is therefore impossible both to represent existence and to exist alone. Being is always 'being in common'. The task of philosophy consists in rethinking the commonality of being without relying on any prior conception of identity, unity or wholeness. 'Being in common' means that nothing – no substance, no identifiable trait– is held in common. The absence of a common substance or spiritual identity does not then generate a command to make up for this lack by means of socially useful work. As the exposure of each singularity to its ungrounded commonality, 'being in common' is the always surprising 'fact' upon which all of Nancy's investigations into philosophy, literature, psychoanalysis and political phenomena are oriented.

As a professor of philosophy at the University of Human Sciences in Strasbourg, Jean-Luc Nancy remains on the periphery of contemporary academic philosophy in France. The proximity of Strasbourg to Germany is reflected in many aspects of his work. Not only has Nancy translated seminal texts of German philosophy and literary theory, his writings constantly engage those post-Kantian German thinkers – Hegel, Marx, Nietzsche, Freud, Heidegger – who declare, each in his own way, that philosophy has come to an end. Both his critical commentaries on philosophical texts and his attempts to rethink the terms in which political and social philosophy are cast take their point of departure from what Heidegger called 'the end of philosophy'. This phrase means, for Nancy, that the resources of representation have been exhausted: philosophy can no longer claim to bring the essence of a phenomenon into view on the basis of

a unified subject of any sort. Since philosophy has come to an end, and since it cannot be simply overcome, there is no choice but to repeat the history of philosophy. There are two ways to undertake this repetition: either ignore the end of philosophy and proceed to rework previous philosophical positions, or expose philosophy to its end and thus develop a 'finite' thought of community, sharing, meaning, freedom – to name a few of the topics Nancy has explored in detail. By re-examining these topics from the perspective of what Jacques Derrida has called the 'closure of metaphysics', Nancy has made a significant contribution to the general project of deconstructing the history of Western metaphysics.

Nancy's readings of philosophical texts closely match those of DERRIDA. What distinguishes his writings from other versions of 'deconstruction' (see DECONSTRUCTION) is his decision to rethink certain topics often associated with existentialism (see EXISTENTIALISM). By reconsidering such topics as existence, abandonment, embodiment, freedom, community and communism on the basis of a more rigorous reading of Hegel and Heidegger than any of the existentialists could claim, Nancy has been able to disclose significant political and social dimensions to the project of deconstruction. His attempts to rethink these terms are all oriented on one 'fact': existence is without essence. Nancy does not proclaim, as does Sartre, that 'existence precedes essence' but that existence precedes, exceeds and succeeds itself, for existence is sheer non-coincidence with itself. From its inception, philosophy has interpreted the 'fact' that existence precedes itself by representing it in terms of a subject that underlies and is thus prior to its various attributes and accidents. Even when the subject is viewed as an ideal or as an incomplete project, the basic structure of 'infinite' and thus 'onto-theological' thought remains intact: the subject grounds itself in its prior or future essence. The 'finite thought' Nancy proposes never proceeds beyond the 'fact' that existence is without essence and without ground. Forever receding from representation, existence consists in an exposure to the groundlessness of being.

One of the most innovative aspects of Nancy's work is the way in which it brings the existential analysis of *Being and Time* into conjunction with Heidegger's late reflections on *Ereignis* ('event of appropriation') (see HEIDEGGER, M. §5). Nancy presents being (*être*) not as the essence of things or the ground of phenomena but as a 'free' and 'generous' event: being takes place as existence. Since existence cannot support itself, it can never be alone or on its own. 'Being in common' thus defines 'finite' existence. No one participates in any*thing* when existence takes part in, or 'shares' being. Existence can even be understood as co-exposure to the absence of anything held in common as long as this absence is not then represented as something communal or 'socially useful' work could seek to repair. If 'being in common', which Nancy associates with 'the political' as opposed to 'politics', is represented in terms of a programme for securing what society lacks, it – and therefore the 'political' – are destroyed. Drawing on Kant's thesis of radical evil, Nancy presents the destruction of 'being in common' in *L'Expérience de la liberté* (1988b) (*The Experience of Freedom*, 1993) as 'wickedness'.

Many of Nancy's later writings explore the bodily character of 'being in common'. Thought itself is presented as bodily: to think (*penser*) is not simply to weigh (*peser*) various options but to be weighed down. The kind of thinking that takes its point of departure from the 'fact' that existence cannot be represented is indistinguishable from touching, for, according to Nancy, to touch and to be touched are two modes of being at the limit of representation. Nancy thus counters the Kantian conception of thought as spontaneity with a 'passive' thinking whose 'passion' consists in an exposure to an always antecedent sense. *Sens* ('sense', 'meaning'), according to Nancy, precedes and exceeds all signification; it cannot be grasped, granted, discovered or produced. As long as the body is the locus of sense, it cannot be securely located, only absolved, shared, and parcelled out: 'There is no whole, no totality of the body – but its absolute separation and sharing out. There is no such thing as *the* body. There is no body' (1993b: 207). All of Nancy's explorations of the political and social dimensions of deconstruction assign themselves the same task as his writings on 'the body': they gesture toward what allows for and what destroys 'being in common'.

See also: DECONSTRUCTION; HEIDEGGER, M.; LACOUE-LABARTHE, P.

List of works

Nancy, J.-L. and Lacoue-Labarthe, P. (1972) *Le Titre de la lettre*, Paris: Éditions Galilée; trans. D. Pettigrew and F. Raffoul, *The Title of the Letter: A Reading of Lacan*, Albany, NY: State University of New York Press, 1992. (One of the best and most difficult analyses of Lacan's thought, that shows its relation to Heidegger's conception of truth as the interplay of concealment and unconcealment.)

Nancy, J.-L. (1973) *La Remarque spéculative: un bon mot de Hegel* (The Speculative Remark: A Hegelian Witticism), Paris: Éditions Galilée. (An analysis of the relation between certain 'speculative' terms in Hegel's work – especially *Aufhebung* – and his explorations of certain excessive explosions of 'wit' and 'frivolity'.)

—— (1976) *Le Discours de la syncope* (The Discourse of Syncopation), vol. 1, *Logodaedalus*, Paris: Aubier-Flammarion. (A reading of Kant oriented towards the 'syncopation', or the punctuating rhythm, which makes it possible for consciousness to identify itself as itself but which cannot be understood either as a form or a content of consciousness.)

Nancy, J.-L. and Lacoue-Labarthe, P. (1978) *L'Absolu littéraire: théorie de la littérature du romanticisme allemand*, Paris: Éditions du Seuil; trans. P. Barnard and C. Lester, *The Literary Absolute: The Theory of Literature in German Romanticism*, Albany, NY: State University of New York Press, 1987. (A wide-ranging presentation of early German romanticism's conception of the relation between literature and philosophy. The French edition includes extensive translations of German texts.)

Nancy, J.-L. (1979) *Ego Sum*, Paris: Flammarion; 'Dum scribo' trans. I. Macleod, *Oxford Literary Review* 3 (2), 1978; 'Larvatus pro Deo' trans. D. Brewer, *Glyph* 2, 1977; 'Mundus est fabula', trans D. Brewer, *Modern Language Notes* 93, 1978. (A reading of Descartes oriented towards those 'autobiographical' moments in Cartesian texts where the indexical 'ego' marks a dislocation and interruption of 'the ego', that is, the thinking subject.)

—— (1982) *Le Partage des voix*, Paris: Éditions Galilée; 'Sharing Voices', trans. G. Ormiston in *Transforming the Hermeneutic Context: From Nietzsche to Nancy*, ed. G. Ormiston and A. Schrift. Albany, NY: State University of New York Press, 1990. (An incisive reading of Plato's *Ion* that develops out of a reading of Heidegger's brief remarks on the use of the word *hermeneus* in this dialogue.)

—— (1983) *L'Impératif catégorique* (The Categorical Imperative), Paris: Flammarion; '"Our Probity!" On Truth in the Moral Sense in Nietzsche', trans. P. Conner, in *Looking after Nietzsche*, ed. L. Rickets, Albany, NY: State University of New York Press. (A collection of essays, the first of which is an extensive examination of Kant's 'fact of reason'. Other essays analyse moments in the repercussion of Kant's moral theory in Nietzsche, Heidegger and Derrida.)

—— (1986a) *L'Oubli de la philosophie* (The Forgetting of Philosophy), Paris: Éditions Galilée. (A sustained critique of contemporary philosophical trends that call for a 'return to the subject'. These calls are shown to arise from a desire to evade an exposure to 'sense' by securing an order of 'signification'.)

—— (1986b) *La Communauté désoeuvrée*, Paris: Christian Bourgois; trans. P. Connor, L. Garbus, M. Holland and S. Sawhney, *The Inoperative Community*, ed. C. Fynsk. Minneapolis, MN: University of Minnesota Press, 1991. (An analysis of what happens to the thought and practice of community once it is no longer understood in terms of a common identity or common substance. A community thus understood does not belong to the order of representation and it cannot be a community for which anyone works. It consists of those who are co-exposed to their own lack of identity and substantiality.)

—— (1988a) 'L'Offrande sublime', in *Du Sublime*, ed. J.-L. Nancy. Paris: Belin; trans. J. Librett, 'The Sublime Offering', in *Of the Sublime: Presentation in Question*, Albany, NY: State University of New York Press, 1993. (An innovative reading of Kant's Analytic of the Sublime in the *Critique of Judgment*.)

—— (1988b) *L'Expérience de la liberté*, Paris: Éditions Galilée; trans. B. McDonald, intro. P. Fenves, *The Experience of Freedom*, Stanford, CA: Stanford University Press, 1993. (One of the landmarks of contemporary continental philosophy. Drawing on Heidegger's shift from a discourse of freedom in his early work to a thought of an open – or free – spatiality in his later thought, the book explores in an interconnected series of essays the modern project of grounding philosophical thought and political practice on the idea of freedom.)

—— (1990) *Une Pensée finie* (A Finite Thought), Paris: Éditions Galilée. (A collection of essays on philosophy and literature, many of which are translated in *The Birth to Presence*, 1993.)

Nancy, J.-L. (1991a) *Le Poids d'une pensée* (The Weight of a Thought), Québec-Grenoble: Presses Universitaires de Grenoble; 'Les Iris', trans. M. Syrotinski, *Yale French Studies* 81, 1992. (A collection of essays, most of which are concerned with contemporary artists and artistic practices.)

—— (1991b) 'Of Being in Common', trans. J. Creech in Miami Theory Collective (eds) *Community at Loose Ends*, Minneapolis, MN: University of Minnesota Press. (A succinct exposition of the thought and practice of community once it is freed from the categories of identity, substantiality and work.)

Nancy, J.-L. and Baily, J.-C. (1991) *La Comparution (politique à venir)*, Paris: Christian Bourgois; 'La Comparution/The Compearance: From the Existence of "Communism" to the Community of "Existence"', trans. T. Strong, *Political Theory* 20 (3), 1992. (An analysis of what happens to 'communism' now that the project of maintaining a 'real, existing socialism' has collapsed. The book is an exploration of the political dimensions of 'being-in-common'.)

Nancy, J.-L. and Lacoue-Labarthe, P. (1991) *Le Mythe nazi*, La Tour d'Aigue: L'Aube; trans. B. Holmes, 'The Nazi Myth', *Critical Inquiry* 16 (2), 1990. (An analysis of Nazi ideology from the perspective of modern German philosophy and intellectual history.)

Nancy, J.-L. (1992) *Corpus*, Paris: Métailié. (An extensive analysis of embodiment, corporeality, incarnation, and the dislocated body as the site of a 'sense' that forever evades all philosophical and scientific attempts to make it into a place of 'signification'.)

—— (1993a) *Le Sens du monde*, Paris: Éditions Galilée; trans. J. Librett, *The Sense of the World*, Minneapolis, MN: University of Minnesota Press, 1996. (A series of short chapters in which the thought of a single 'fact' is pursued in a variety of ways: there is no sense of the world as long as 'sense' is understood as 'meaning', but the world itself is 'sense' if this word is understood as the limit of 'signification'.)

—— (1993b) *Birth to Presence*, trans. B. Holmes, T. Harrison, C. Laennec, M. Syrotinski, M. Caws, P. Caws *et al.*, Stanford, CA: Stanford University Press. (A wide range of essays, including an exemplary analysis of 'decision' in Heidegger's *Being and Time*, the place of the monarch in Hegel's *Philosophy of Right*, and an explication of what Nancy calls 'exscription': the inscription of an ineluctable exteriority in literary texts.)

—— (1994) *Les Muses* (The Muses), Paris: Éditions Galilée; trans. P. Kamuf, *The Muses*, Stanford, CA: Stanford University Press, 1966. (A collection of essays on art and art theory that begins with the question: 'Where are there several arts and not simply one?')

References and further reading

Blanchot, M. (1988) *The Unavowable Community*, trans. P. Joris, Barrytown, NY: Station Hill Press. (A response to Nancy's earliest essays on the 'inoperative community' by one of France's most influential writers and critics.)

Kamuf, P. (1993) *Paragraph: On the Works of Jean-Luc Nancy*, Edinburgh: Edinburgh University Press. (A volume of essays devoted to analysing the work of Nancy, with difficult but rewarding contributions from Derrida, Hamacher, Garciá-Düttmann, and others; the only extensive bibliography of Nancy's writings.)

Miami Theory Collective (eds) (1991) *Community at*

Loose Ends, Minneapolis, MN: University of Minnesota Press. (Several essays discuss Nancy's 'Of Being in Common' and consider the consequences of his thought for contemporary political and social philosophy.)

Sparks, S., Sheppard, S. and Thomas, C. (1997) *The Philosophy of Jean-Luc Nancy*, London: Routledge. (A collection of essays that analyses Nancy's work, assesses and develops certain lines of his thought.)

PETER FENVES

NARRATIVE

Narrative, in its broadest sense, is the means by which a story is told, whether fictional or not, and regardless of medium. Novels, plays, films, historical texts, diaries and newspaper articles focus, in their different ways, on particular events and their temporal and causal relations; they are all narratives in the above sense. Accounts of mathematical, physical, economic or legal principles are not. A narrower sense of narrative requires the presence of a narrator mediating between audience and action, and contrasts with imitative discourse wherein the action is presented directly, as in drama. The boundary between narration narrowly construed and imitation is disputed, some writers arguing that apparently imitative forms are covertly narrated.

Attempts have been made to characterize fictional narratives in linguistic terms; another view is that fictions are things which have certain (intended or actual) effects on the audience. Theorists of narrative have mostly concentrated on narratives of the fictional kind and have developed a complex taxonomy of the various narrative devices, some of which are discussed in more detail below. Recently, pressure has been placed on the distinction between historical and fictional narrative by those who believe that history is nothing distinct from the various and conflicting narrative versions we have. It has also been argued that value accrues to an agent's life and acts when those acts conform to a conception of that life as exemplifying narrative.

1 **Narrative and fiction**
2 **Narrative theory**
3 **Narrative and antirealism**
4 **Narrative and value**

1 Narrative and fiction

On one view, narratives are identifiable as fictional by their use of distinctively fictional language. But while devices like free indirect discourse (for example, 'She was damned if she would go') may be peculiar to fiction, there are fictions which do not employ them and which are linguistically indistinguishable from nonfiction. Nor can fictionality be explained in terms of lack of reference or truth, since fictions often concern real people and events, while much nonfiction is false. An alternative view is that fictional narratives function in a certain way. On one version of this theory, the reader is intended to *imagine* the occurrence of the events described in the narrative, rather than to treat those descriptions as assertions judgeable by standards of evidence and truth. This suggestion will be employed in the next section.

2 Narrative theory

Work on the theory of narrative has largely concentrated on fictional narratives; the results so far constitute a suggestive taxonomy rather than a systematic theory. An important distinction should be made between the story presented and the discourse that presents it. For example, *anachrony* occurs when the temporal order of events as they happen in the story is not reflected in the discourse; we hear first of A and then of B, though B occurred before A. Again, it may be a feature of the discourse that the story is told by a certain narrator, or from the point of view of a certain character; these are not features of the story itself unless it is part of the story (or, as I shall say, it is fictional) that someone with knowledge of these events performs an act of telling.

Narration and point of view are themselves distinct concepts; the narrator may tell the story from the point of view of a character, with shifts in point of view without change of narrator. The narrative is said to be 'focalized' through a character when the narrator presents the story as it is experienced by that character. It is sometimes said that the story is focalized through the narrator when there is no character through whom it is focalized. This is confusing, because the narrator's act of telling is not in general an act of experiencing the events of the story. Other unhelpful extensions of focalization have been made; it has been said that when character A hears character B speak of character C, C is focalized at the third degree. But C's relation to B and to A in this case is not at all like the relation of a character to the narrator who narrates from that character's perspective (Chatman 1986). Focalization needs a treatment of greater care and parsimony than it has yet received.

The narrator is often said to be distinct from the author. (Until now, I have been using 'narrator' in a sense which does not distinguish them.) The narrator is a construct of the work itself, and either within the world of the story tells us what they know or believe to be true (or, as in an unreliable narrative, tries to mislead us about what has happened), or, alternatively, from outside that world, tells us a fictional story. Watson is the internal or 'intradiegetic' narrator of the Sherlock Holmes stories, while the narrator of *Tom Jones* is external or 'extradiegetic'. The author is also distinguished from the implied author, who is an imagined creature constructed by the reader as the personality who seems to have written this work; the implied author of *Anna Karenina* might be more tolerant, generous and understanding than the real Tolstoy apparently was.

Could the implied author take on the role otherwise assigned to the extradiegetic narrator? Advocates of the extradiegetic narrator point to works in which the narrator's outlook is one the reader seems to be expected to reject; it is natural to say that there is in such cases a tension between narrator and implied author and consequently that we must conceptualize the work by invoking two distinct personalities. But cases of this kind can be handled without appeal to the extradiegetic narrator, by assuming that the implied author is speaking ironically; it is the implied author who speaks, but what is said is intended by that same speaker to be ridiculed or rejected. We can, therefore, dispense with the idea of an extradiegetic narrator in favour of the implied author. Intradiegetic narrators, on the other hand, are certainly present in some fictions; Watson, in the Holmes stories, is one. In other cases no narrator within the story is evident. Theorists have sometimes postulated hidden narrators, intra- or extradiegetic, for such works on the grounds that the events of the story must be told to us by someone (Chatman 1990: 133). Since the argument just given abolishes the extradiegetic narrator, let us concentrate on the claim that every fictional narrative requires an intradiegetic narrator, even where no such narrator is apparent in the text. In assessing this postulate, it is important to distinguish between what is true and what is fictional. It is true of all stories that they are told by someone, namely the author. The author's act of telling is an invitation to us to imagine various things, and these things jointly constitute what is fictional in the story. Among the things we may be asked to imagine is that someone with knowledge of the events of the story is telling them to us as fact; in that case we have a fictional story with an intradiegetic narrator. On the other hand, we may be invited to imagine merely that the events of the story occurred and that no one in particular is telling them to us. Once we distinguish really telling a fictional

story (something the author does) from fictionally telling a true story (something an intradiegetic narrator does) we see that while every fictional story is told as fiction, not every such story is fictionally told as fact. If the reasoning of this paragraph is correct, no works have extradiegetic narrators, only some have intradiegetic ones, and consequently some narratives have no narrator.

In dispensing with a narrator we need not reject the idea that a narrative needs to be understood as the product of an intending agent. But some writers in the structuralist tradition have claimed to identify a kind of writing that lacks the devices which signal the presence of a writer or speaker, such as indexicals or the past tense. They say that narrative in this sense is objective (or purports to be), and the events of the story 'speak themselves' (Benvenista 1966). This is a mistake. Even writing that contains no verbal indicators of agency presupposes the existence of one who speaks or writes, for something counts as language – and not as meaningless marks or sounds, – only if it was produced by an agent intending to conform their sound/mark production to the conventions of a language.

3 Narrative and antirealism

Antirealists (see REALISM AND ANTIREALISM §2) reject the idea that there is a determinate reality, largely independent of human activity and conception, to which our cognitive powers give us only limited access. They claim that the world is indeterminate in those regions inaccessible to our investigations or – in a more extreme version – multiple and conflicting in a way that mirrors our own multiple and conflicting conceptions of the world. Some antirealists have supposed that science, biography and history are species of fiction, giving rise to narratives unconstrained by correspondence with reality.

One version of this argument holds that historical narrative imposes on a series of events features that the series does not intrinsically possess, by means of selectivity, teleology and closure. Narrative selects among events, highlighting some and placing others in the background; but the events themselves do not stand in relations of salience and no event is intrinsically more important than any other. Narrative is teleological in so far as the reason for including events in a narrative is their contribution to outcomes distant from those events and identifiable, once again, only in terms of interests that are variable across cultures, times and individuals. Narrative imposes closure on events by claiming to identify a natural stopping place for the narrative; in fact there are no natural stopping places intrinsic to the events themselves, but only relative to the events as they are ordered and selected by interest. Let us call such features 'plot-like', so as to remind us of the antirealist's presumption that they are features which push historical writing into the realm of the fictional.

One realist response would be to argue that plot-like features, while not intrinsic to the historical events themselves, are none the less real, relational features of those events, much as colours are said to be real, relational properties of things, since the colour of a thing depends on the kind of visual experience it causes us to have. And just as an account of the colours of things can be thought of as reporting matters of fact, so the attribution of plot-like features to events and their relations in an historical narrative counts as (potentially) fact-stating. On this view, narratives which seem to disagree in their attributions of plot-like features may genuinely contradict one another, and only one narrative can be right. But another possibility for the realist is that the appearance of disagreement is the result of the failure of the plot-like features to be properly relativized. Such a conflict would dissipate if what is said to be significant according to one narrative and insignificant according to another is intended to be understood as significant from one point of view according to the first narrative, and insignificant from another point of view according to the second.

A more moderate realist response admits that plot-like features are not genuinely features of the historical events themselves. It insists, however, that there is another set of features (hereafter 'truth-making' features), which are genuine features of the events themselves, and that historical narratives can be thought of as correct if and only if they attribute these features correctly. Correctness of a narrative in this sense is independent of its plot-like aspects, in that narratives will only count as rivals when they differ over attributions of truth-making features. When they differ over the attribution of plot-like features, they merely count as alternatives. Thus two correct but different narratives would be like two photographs of the same scene taken from different angles. Each photograph/narrative is correct as far as it goes, though one might be more comprehensively correct than the other. Perspective-related differences between the pictures that affect the apparent spatial relations of objects will not count as disagreements between them. Likewise, differences between the narratives in respect of plot-like features will not count as genuine contradictions.

4 Narrative and value

It has been argued that our lives constitute narratives,

and that this gives them value. It is difficult to decide what literal truth there is in this idea. How could a life *be* a narrative, rather than simply contain the material for a narrative? If narrative is what someone, perhaps the agent, tells of that life, in what sense does the value of the narrative constitute the value of the life? We know from literature that there can be valuable narratives of bad or otherwise valueless lives. Perhaps a life can be a narrative in this sense: the agent's actions are determined by the agent's conception of past and present actions and future goals as part of a coherent narrative; the agent's life would then be lived 'as narrative'. We can only guess how many lives are in this sense narrative, and in what proportions value is distributed between lives lived as narrative and lives not: of the former many would be reduced in value to the extent that the subject's narrativization of their actions and goals was the result of misunderstanding or self-delusion. Another suggested association between narrative and value is that our present and future actions can affect the value of past actions, for instance in cases where a bad act is to some extent redeemed by its role in the actor's subsequent change of heart. To make a thesis about narrative of this it is not, however, sufficient to say that later acts can affect the value of earlier ones, for that could be true even when the change of heart is related to any story-telling on the subject's part or on anyone else's part. It must be claimed in addition either that (1) value is transmitted from later acts to earlier ones *only* when the later act is the outcome of the agent's conceiving the past act within a narrative framework, or, more modestly, that (2) while value can accrue to the past act without any such narrativizing taking place, additional value accrues when the later act *is* the outcome of such narrativizing.

See also: BARTHES, R.; HISTORY, PHILOSOPHY OF; NIETZSCHE, F.; STRUCTURALISM IN LITERARY THEORY

References and further reading

Barthes, R. (1966) 'Introduction à l'analyse structurale des récits' *Communications* 8; trans. S. Heath, 'Introduction to the Structural Analysis of Narrative', in *Image, Music, Text*, New York: Wang & Hill, 1977; London, Fontana, 1977. (An influential version of the structuralist approach to narrative.)

* Benvenista, E. (1966, 1974) *Problèmes de linguistique générale*, Paris: Gallimard, 2 vols; vol. 1 trans. M.E. Meek, *Problems in General Linguistics*, Coral Gables, FL: University of Miami Press, 1971. (A source for the idea of narrative without utterance.)

Booth, W.C. (1983) *The Rhetoric of Fiction*, Harmondsworth: Penguin, 2nd edn. (A classic study of the forms of narrative, with emphasis on the idea of the implied author. Excellent bibliography.)

Carroll, N. (1990) 'Interpretation, History and Narrative', *The Monist* 73: 134–66. (A careful exposition and criticism of some antirealist views about historical narrative.)

* Chatman, S. (1986) 'Characters and Narrators', *Poetics Today* 7: 189–204. (Criticizes some extensions of the notion of focalization.)

Currie, G. (1993) 'Interpretation and Objectivity', *Mind* 102: 413–28. (Argues that there is a degree of relativism inherent in the attempt to interpret narratives.)

—— (1994) 'Unreliability Refigured: Narrative in Literature and Film', *Journal of Aesthetics and Art Criticism* 53: 19–29. (Critical of standard assumptions of narrative theory concerning the role of the implied author and of the narrator.)

Genette, G. (1972) 'Discours du récit', in *Figures III*, Paris: Editions du Seuil; trans. J.E. Lewin (1980) *Narrative Discourse*, Ithaca, NY: Cornell University Press. (A classic development of narrative theory through close readings of Proust.)

MacIntyre, A. (1985) *After Virtue*, London: Duckworth, 2nd edn. (Argues for 'a concept of a self whose unity resides in the unity of a narrative'.)

Nehamas, A. (1985) *Nietzsche: Life as Literature*, Cambridge, MA: Harvard University Press (An interpretation and defence of Nietzsche assimilation of 'the ideal person to the ideal literary character and the ideal life to the ideal story'.)

Savile, A. (1996) 'Instrumentalism and the Interpretation of Narrative', *Mind* 105: 553–76. (Argues for the objectivity of narrative interpretation.)

White, H. (1987) *The Content of Form*, Baltimore, MD, and London: Johns Hopkins University Press. (The work of an influential historical antirealist.)

GREGORY CURRIE

NATION AND NATIONALISM

No one observing political events in the world today could deny the continuing potency of nationalism. Many of the most intractable conflicts arise when one national community tries to break away from another, or when two such communities lay claim to the same piece of territory. Yet to outsiders the basis for such conflicts often seems mysterious. People are prepared to fight and die for their nation, yet what exactly is this 'nation' that commands such loyalty? Why should it matter so much that a person is governed by leaders drawn from one community rather than from another?

Philosophers are often inclined to dismiss nationalism as having no rational basis, but as resting merely on tribal instincts and brute emotions. Such a response overlooks the different forms that nationalism has taken: in particular, the contrast between authoritarian nationalism, which allows national cultures to be imposed by force and which may justify acts of aggression against neighbouring peoples, and liberal nationalism, which upholds the rights of individuals to form political communities with those with whom they feel identified and to protect their common culture. We need to examine carefully the arguments that have been advanced by nationalist thinkers in order to decide which form of nationalism, if any, is rationally defensible.

1 **What is a nation?**
2 **The evolution of nationalism**
3 **Problems of nationality**

1 What is a nation?

Defining 'nation' has proved a difficult task for political philosophers. In common speech 'nation' is often used loosely to mean 'state', as it does in phrases such as 'United Nations'. But this loose usage is not helpful in political philosophy, one of the central questions of which is whether there are indeed such things as nations, and if there are, whether nations have a valid claim to be self-governing – or to put it more crudely, whether each nation is entitled to have its own independent state. When questions such as these are asked, 'nation' must refer to something that exists apart from and prior to the political institutions of the state.

A nation, we may say, is a community of people who recognize that they are distinct from other communities and wish to control their own affairs. But a community of this sort is clearly very different from the small face-to-face communities that may first spring to mind when the idea of community is invoked (see COMMUNITY AND COMMUNITARIANISM §1). Since I shall never know more than a tiny fraction of my fellow countrymen personally, how can I say that we form a community? What is the source of unity that holds nations together?

Broadly speaking, two answers have been given to this question. On one side stand those who take a subjective view, claiming that nations are essentially voluntary associations of people held together simply by the continuing will of their members. We form a nation because we want to be politically associated. The reasons behind this desire are irrelevant: all that finally matters is that each of us wants to associate with this group of people rather than that. On the other side we find those who maintain that nations are marked out by certain objective characteristics that their members share – by racial descent, by language, by religion, by common traits of character, and so forth. On this view it makes sense to speak of dormant nations whose members have in common whatever is taken to be the essential defining characteristic of nationality, but who as yet display no consciousness of nationhood or desire to form a political community.

Neither of these answers seems adequate as it stands. Objective accounts of nationhood fall down when we take the proposed characteristics one by one and see that none is adequate to distinguish all those communities that we recognize to be separate nations (Renan 1939). If we take the objective view and focus on a feature such as language, we find on the one hand that there can be distinct nations with a shared language – the English-speaking countries for instance – while on the other hand there can be bi- or tri-lingual nations such as Belgium or Switzerland. The subjective account avoids this pitfall, but this does not clear up the mystery of why people should care so much who they associate with politically. A more adequate answer must combine elements of both viewpoints. A nation exists when its members recognize one another as belonging to the same community and as bearing special obligations to one another, but this is by virtue of characteristics that they believe they share: typically, a common history, attachment to a geographical place and a public culture that differentiates them from their neighbours.

Because nations are communities on a large scale, they are inevitably 'imagined communities', in Benedict Anderson's evocative phrase, meaning that they depend for their existence on collective acts of imagining which take place through media of communication such as books, newspapers and television (Anderson 1990). It is from these media that we acquire our understanding of what it means to belong to this particular nation. Does this imply that national communities are after all spurious? This by no means follows, although it may justify a degree of scepticism about the received content of national identities. First, such identities usually incorporate a certain proportion of historical myth, in the sense that past events are interpreted in such a way as to highlight their continuity with events in the present. Although we actually know very little about our thirteenth-century ancestors, for example, we are invited to see their heroic struggles against their neighbours as the precursors of our own. Second, nations tend to exaggerate their own homogeneity,

supposing that every member conforms more or less precisely to the cultural stereotype that forms part of the national identity. Third, national identities are to some degree able to be manipulated by powerful groups, especially political leaders, whose command of the media enables them to refashion the content of the imagining to suit their purposes. No political leader can invent a nation where one does not exist; but it may be possible to persuade a nation that its legitimate territorial boundaries stretch more widely than it had hitherto imagined, or that a particular subcommunity – an ethnic group for instance – that has long lived happily as part of the nation does not after all belong there. The practical consequences of such refashioning may be very serious, as experiences of the twentieth century readily illustrate.

For reasons such as these, most philosophers have been ambivalent both about the validity and about the practical relevance of national identities.

2 The evolution of nationalism

Nationalism is primarily a phenomenon of nineteenth- and twentieth-century political thought. Its constituent ideas, however, stretch back much further in time. Among the Jews of the Old Testament and among the ancient Greeks we find the sense of belonging to a distinct people marked off from the rest of the world by special characteristics – an embryonic sense of national superiority (Kohn 1944, ch. 1). In the classical period, moreover, patriotism was regarded as a leading virtue. Patriotism is not the same as nationalism: it means a love of one's native country and a willingness to sacrifice oneself to defend it, but it need not invoke the idea of a self-conscious nation discussed in §1, nor need it imply that the country in question should enjoy political self-determination. Like nationalism, however, patriotism involves the idea that one owes special obligations to one's compatriots, that one should be willing to protect and defend them at the expense of outsiders – an ethical stance that many philosophers have found difficult to accept.

Nationalism proper began to emerge in the second half of the eighteenth century, when to the ideas of distinct nationhood and patriotic loyalties were added the idea that nations are the source of legitimate political authority. There is a close link here between nationalism and the doctrine of popular sovereignty, which replaced the older belief that political authority flowed downwards from the king or the emperor (Kamenka 1976). ROUSSEAU (§3) provides a striking illustration of this link, holding on the one hand that the general will of the people was the only legitimate source of legislative authority, and on the other that every citizen must be taught to love their native country before all else: 'That love makes up his entire existence: he has eyes only for the fatherland, lives only for his fatherland; . . . the moment he has no fatherland, he is no more' (Rousseau 1770–1: 19).

In these words, Rousseau anticipates the more extreme forms of nineteenth-century nationalism. The contribution of the early nineteenth century was the Romantic belief that each nation formed an organic unity, with its own soul and its own special destiny. Of particular importance was HERDER (§§2, 6), whose expressive theory of language underpinned his idea that each nation was the bearer of a unique culture, immersion in which was the only path to human self-fulfilment. Herder's nationalism was primarily cultural rather than political; he wanted to see each national culture thriving in peaceful coexistence with its neighbours, and he had no sympathy with the aggressive militarism of the Prussian state. None the less he continued to link nationality and popular self-government: 'The roses for the wreath of each nation's liberty must be picked with its own hands, and must grow happily out of its own wants, joys, and love' (Kohn 1944: 431). This message found a ready response among those cultural minorities of Europe struggling for political independence from long-established empires.

Cultural nationalism and political self-assertion coalesced in the later thought of FICHTE (§7). Fichte combined three doctrines: the idea that nations were organic wholes, each with its own language and culture; that each person owed supreme loyalty to their own nation that indeed freedom consisted of identifying oneself with the higher cause represented by the nation; and that each nation had its own peculiar mission. Fichte also attenuated the link between nationalism and popular self-government: national leaders might be justified in using coercive methods of education in order to create strong and united peoples. Here we see the foreshadowing of an authoritarian form of nationalism which is willing to override liberties domestically in the name of national unity, and which may justify acts of aggression against neighbouring states in the name of national destiny.

The same period also witnessed the growth of a liberal form of nationalism, according to which the cause of national independence and the cause of political liberty go hand in hand. This was the view of Mazzini, the father of Italian nationalism, and it was echoed by J.S. MILL, who in *Considerations on Representative Government* (1861) emphasized the role played by national sympathies in checking the power of government and making free institutions workable. Liberal nationalism treats all nations as having equally good claims to self-determination, resists ideas of 'national destiny' and argues that national cultures will flourish best when freedom of expression and other liberties are secure.

The subsequent history of nationalism can be seen as a struggle between authoritarian and liberal forms of nationalism. The latter can be seen at work in the doctrine of national self-determination promulgated by Woodrow Wilson at the end of the Second World War and embodied in the League of Nations; the former found its final expression in the fascist movements of the inter-war years (see FASCISM). Thus nationalism continues to present us with two very different faces. On the one hand it stands for a people's right to protect and develop their inherited cultures and to be politically independent in association with those they regard as their compatriots. On the other hand it stands for forcible indoctrination in the national culture and the promotion of national interests abroad at the expense of other peoples. Once again we see why philosophers have very often reacted ambivalently to nationalist ideas.

3 Problems of nationality

Nationalist ideas raise a number of important questions in ethics and political philosophy. This section addresses three. Do we owe special obligations to our compatriots? How can the idea of national self-determination be justified? How should we resolve disputes about borders, and in particular secessionist demands by national minorities?

The first question arises because the claim, common to all forms of nationalism, that we owe special loyalties to our compatriots, seems to collide directly with the idea that morality requires us to show an equal regard for every human being, without making distinctions. Most moral philosophers, especially utilitarians and Kantians, embrace the idea of 'equal regard', which may be labelled ethical universalism. We should weigh the interests of all human beings equally, or show each person equal respect regardless of their particular relationship to us. This points to a form of cosmopolitanism (see INTERNATIONAL RELATIONS, PHILOSOPHY OF §4). But many of these philosophers, recognizing how demanding and how far removed from ordinary moral ideas strict universalism is, have also tried to make room for particular loyalties, including national loyalties. They argue, for instance, that duties that are universal in scope may be discharged most effectively if each us takes responsibility for the welfare of a small number of others. Or they argue that members of particular communities may be regarded as contractually obliged to give one another special assistance, the justification for such contracts (or quasi-contracts) again being universal in form.

The weakness of these arguments is that they have difficulty showing why nations should be singled out as the groups to which special obligations are owed. If I am a utilitarian, for instance, why should I acknowledge a special responsibility to contribute to the welfare of the poorer members of my own national community when there are people much worse off in other countries? Even if my sympathies are presently biased towards those closest to me, do I not have a duty to correct this bias for the sake of maximizing overall utility? It seems that if we are to recognize national obligations, we have to abandon universalism as a complete picture of ethics and allow particular obligations to enter at ground level, so to speak. We need a picture which allows us to connect questions about personal identity – who we are, where we belong – with questions about our responsibilities to others (MacIntyre 1984).

Turning next to national self-determination, critics of nationalism such as Kedourie (1966) have argued that nationalist appeals to a national or popular will are fundamentally misguided, and that our concern should be with the quality of government – whether it observes the rule of law and protects our rights, for instance – rather than with its source. If we are governed well by outsiders, we have no justified grounds for complaint. This challenge forces us to look more closely at the reasons for favouring self-determination, of which there are several.

One such reason has to do with our interest in protecting and fostering the common culture that provides us with the resources for a meaningful life. This is especially the case when the culture in question is the culture of what Margalit and Raz (1990) have called an 'encompassing group'. The best guarantee that such cultures will not be destroyed or forcibly altered is to be governed by representatives who also participate in the national culture. Given the pressures currently exerted on national cultures by worldwide commercial forces, this argument has obvious force.

A second reason concerns the part played by nationality in fostering trust between the members of a political community. Where a shared national identity creates mutual trust, it becomes easier to agree on particular disputed issues – each side having more incentive to reach a compromise – and there is also a better chance of winning support for policies that aid one section of the community at the expense of others. Of course this argument can be turned on its head by those who favour a state with minimal responsibilities: if your aim is to disable the state from doing very much, you should prefer it to be multi-national in character, so that each community will try to block policies that favour the others (this argument was advanced by Lord Acton (1907)). But those for whom social justice is an important value, and those who place a premium on achieving political agreement by democratic means, will favour political communities that are held together by national solidarity.

Finally we come to the problems posed for nationalist doctrines by disputed boundaries and demands for secession. If the peoples of the world were neatly divided into separate nations living on well-defined territories, the principle of national self-determination would be easy to apply. But in reality populations are very often interspersed in such a way that any territorial division will leave many people living under national governments with which they do not identify; and national identities, too, may be somewhat ambivalent. What are we to say about groups such as the Basques, the Québecois and the Scots, who appear to identify in part with larger nations but also have distinct identities of their own that they want to express politically?

Problems such as these have led many liberals to conclude that appeals to nationality cannot settle the question of where the borders of states should be drawn. We must be guided by other values: we should decide borders on the basis of individual consent, allowing any subcommunity to secede from the state by majority vote as long as it extends the same right to its own minority groups (Beran 1984); or we should permit secession when the seceding group can show that it is the victim of serious injustice or that it is threatened with cultural extinction (Buchanan 1981).

These responses may underestimate the versatility of nationalist principles, however. The solution prescribed by these principles will vary depending on the facts of each particular case. Where a state currently houses two or more distinct and well-defined national communities, the case for a peaceful divorce will be very strong. Where a small minority lacks a territorial base and is dispersed throughout a larger national community, the best solution may be to open up the existing national identity to that minority by removing or playing down divisive elements – for instance, by diminishing the role played by religion – so that in the longer term it will be able to integrate without annihilating its own culture. Where we find subcommunities nesting inside larger communities, as in the examples given above, national self-determination suggests devolving power to these subcommunities so that they are able to protect and express their own culture, without breaking up the state as such, since this continues to give expression to their wider identities and loyalties.

There will none the less be tragic cases in which no

redrawing of borders or restructuring of political authority is able to give divided communities adequate protection and self-determination. Conflicts such as that created by the partition of Bosnia cannot be resolved by appeals to these principles. Such cases remind us that nationalism cannot by itself be a complete political philosophy. At the very least we need to add to it principles such as human rights, which set limits to what may be done to communities and individuals in the name of the nation.

See also: JUSTICE, INTERNATIONAL; STATE, THE; ZIONISM

References and further reading

* Acton, Lord (1907) 'Nationality', in J.N. Figgis (ed.) *The History of Freedom and Other Essays*, London: Macmillan. (A defence of multinational states from a liberal perspective.)

* Anderson, B. (1990) *Imagined Communities*, London: Verso, revised edn. (Wide-ranging study of national identities, emphasizing the part played by mass media in their creation and dissemination.)

Beitz, C. (1983) 'Cosmopolitan Ideals and National Sentiment', *Journal of Philosophy*, 80 (10): 591–600. (Careful exploration of the question whether universalist reasons can be given for acknowledging special obligations to compatriots.)

* Beran, H. (1984) 'A Liberal Theory of Secession', *Political Studies* 32 (1): 21–31. (Appeals to the principle of consent to defend a universal right of secession.)

Berlin, I. (1981) 'Nationalism: Past Neglect and Present Power', in H. Hardy (ed.) *Against the Current*, Oxford: Oxford University Press. (An interpretation of nineteenth-century nationalism, and an attempt to explain the continuing appeal of nationalist ideas.)

* Buchanan, A. (1981) *Secession*, Boulder, CO: Westview Press. (Comprehensive critical assessment of liberal arguments for and against secession.)

Fichte, J.G. (1922) *Addresses to the German Nation*, Chicago, IL: Open Court. (The main statement of Fichte's German nationalism and appeal for a national scheme of education.)

Gellner, E. (1983) *Nations and Nationalism*, Oxford: Blackwell. (An interpretation of the rise of nationalism, hinging upon the need for a common high culture in modern industrial societies.)

Greenfeld, L. (1992) *Nationalism: Five Roads to Modernity*, Cambridge, MA: Harvard University Press. (A comparative study of the evolution of nationalist ideas in Britain, France, Germany, Russia and the USA.)

Herder, J.G. (1969) *Herder on Social and Political Culture*, ed. F.M. Barnard, Cambridge: Cambridge University Press. (An anthology of texts covering Herder's explanation of the cultural diversity of humankind and his exploration of the links between national cultures and political communities.)

* Kamenka, E. (1976) 'Political Nationalism – The Evolution of the Idea', in *Nationalism: The Nature and Evolution of an Idea*, London: Edward Arnold. (Explores the origins of nationalism, stressing its connection with the idea of popular sovereignty.)

* Kedourie, E. (1966) *Nationalism*, London: Hutchinson. (Critical study of nationalism by a classical liberal.)

* Kohn, H. (1944) *The Idea of Nationalism*, New York: Macmillan. (A classic study of the development of nationalist ideas, beginning with ancient Israel.)

* MacIntyre, A. (1984) 'Is Patriotism a Virtue?', in R. Beiner (ed.) *Theorising Citizenship*, New York: State University of New York Press, 1995. (Critique of contemporary ethical theories in terms of their incapacity to understand patriotism as a virtue.)

* Margalit, A. and Raz, J. (1990) 'National Self-determination', *Journal of Philosophy* 87 (9): 439–61. (Argues for a right to self-determination to protect the interests that people have as members of 'encompassing groups'.)

* Mill, J.S. (1861) *Considerations on Representative Government*, London: Dent, 1971. (Chapter 16 contains Mill's argument that for representative government to work successfully, state boundaries should coincide, if possible, with national boundaries.)

Miller, D. (1995) *On Nationality*, Oxford: Clarendon Press. (Sympathetic discussion of nationalist ideas, exploring in greater depth the issues addressed in this entry.)

Nathanson, S. (1993) *Patriotism, Morality and Peace*, Lanham, MD: Rowman & Littlefield. (An attempt to separate defensible 'moderate' patriotism from indefensible 'extreme' patriotism.)

* Renan, E. (1939) 'What is a Nation?', in A. Zimmern (ed.) *Modern Political Doctrines*, London: Oxford University Press. (Much-cited essay, critical of objective definitions of nationality.)

* Rousseau, J.-J. (1770–1) *The Government of Poland*, trans. W. Kendall, Indianapolis, IN: Bobbs-Merrill, 1972. (Rousseau's most explicit account of how and why citizens must be imbued with national loyalty.)

Scruton, R. (1990) 'In Defence of the Nation', in *The Philosopher on Dover Beach*, Manchester: Carcanet. (A conservative defence of the nation as an object of loyalty.)

Tamir, Y. (1993) *Liberal Nationalism*, Princeton, NJ: Princeton University Press. (An attempt to show that liberalism and nationalism can be reconciled with one another.)

Walzer, M. (1990) 'Nation and Universe', in G.B. Petersen (ed.) *The Tanner Lectures on Human Values*, Salt Lake City, UT: University of Utah Press, vol. 11. (Separates forms of nationalism which proclaim the superiority of a particular culture from those that extend the same recognition to all.)

DAVID MILLER

NATIVE AMERICAN PHILOSOPHY

Native American philosophies are multiple and multiply different, though with some palpable commonalities. Cosmologically, Native American thought posits phased differentiations of form from a primordial void. Form is fundamentally animate, and widespread metaphysical premises indicate a pervasive animism. The relationship between language and reality is grounded in the semiotic manipulation of animate forces. Encompassing force – like Siouan wakan *or Iroquoian* orenda *– is the originating source of human ontology and subjectivity, which are strongly characterized by ideas of consciousness and will. Mind is critically informed by transcendental experience (dreams, visions and so on) as well as by reason. Ethically, the harnessing of individual energies to specified social goals is discursively and dramatically prominent especially in ritual performance. Ethical principles are extended to non-human 'persons' (particularly animals and deific forms) who operate within the human moral compass. Native American reason emphasizes analogy (especially in Lévi-Strauss' interpretations) and aetiology, and there is a central concern with formal composition and decomposition. The latter is strongly evident in the ubiquitous philosopher-figure 'Trickster' – a subversive transgressor of constituted order.*

1 **Background**
2 **Cosmology, metaphysics and ontology**
3 **Being and mind**
4 **Ethics**
5 **Epistemology and reason**

1 Background

Prior to 1492 Native North America included ten to fifteen million people, speaking 250 distinct languages (none written), belonging to more than twenty largely unrelated language families. There were upwards of 300 separate 'cultures' – that is, forms of life constitutively differentiated according to language, livelihood, social form and belief. Larger groupings into 'culture areas', united by geographic proximity, subsistence practices and customs, minimally include (with examples of named peoples in parentheses): Northeast Woodlands (Mohawk, Seneca, Pequot, Delaware), Southeast (Cherokee, Creek, Choctaw, Chickasaw), Plains (Lakota, Cheyenne, Comanche, Kiowa), Southwest (Hopi, Zuni, Navajo, Pima-Papago), Great Basin (Paiute, Shoshone, Washo, Ute), Plateau (Nez Perce, Klamath, Yakima, Kutenai), California (Yurok, Pomo, Yokuts, Maidu) Northwest Coast (Tlingit, Kwakiutl, Tsimshian, Nootka), Sub-Arctic (Koyukon, Beaver, Cree, Montagnais-Naskapi), and Arctic (numerous Eskimo/Inuit groups and Aleut).

While philosophical forms cannot be read from economic adaptation, certain limitations are imposed by population size and density, and ensuing social contexts. State-level societies, for example, seem prerequisite for higher mathematics and, correlatively, symbolic logic. Some North American number and calendrical systems were quite complex: the Pomo, who participated in a wide-ranging shell-disc currency, had a counting capacity up to 40,000; likewise, prehistoric Anasazi astronomical observations were notably fine-grained. But both mathematical and astronomical differentiation were significantly greater in the Classic Maya state, with its interlinked day- and year-counts, observatories and writing-system.

Each culture-area is characterized by ecosystems allowing particular modes of adaptation. Maize-beans-squash agriculture, the foundation of stratified states in Mesoamerica, occurred in the Northeast, Southeast and small areas of the Plains and Southwest; in these regions status differences distinguished ritual priest-leaders as the intellectual specialists. Elsewhere, dependence on hunting (Plains, Plateau, Sub-Arctic and Arctic), and wild plant collection (Great Basin, California and parts of the Southwest) are associated with smaller populations and more egalitarian societies; here, individual shamans ('medicine-men') are the philosophical experts. Interestingly, the fishing societies of the Northwest Coast produced fairly dense hierarchical communities that marked the metaphysical qualities of high-ranking individuals with titles, crests, masks and other insignia, all subject to contestation in elaborate ceremony (the 'potlatch').

Sociocultural diversity is accompanied by extensive historical differences. Archaeological remains attest to states in the Southeast – the 'Mississippian' – and the Southwest – 'Anasazi' and 'Hohokam'. These civilizations collapsed before 1492, though elements of the former persisted into the seventeenth century (especially with the Natchez), and elements of the latter are still found in Pueblo and Pima-Papago societies. European contact was devastating. Population declined massively (up to ninety per cent) from introduced diseases and genocidal wars. Today many languages are dead and numerous systems of thought are irretrievable. Yet in some areas indigenous culture remains strong; many Hopis and Navajos, for example, still speak their own languages, and some cultural forms are largely unaltered from pre-European times.

The corollary of a traumatic history is the erasure of records. There was little genuine interest in Native thought, peremptorily dismissed as 'savage' or 'primitive'. The meditations of Montaigne, Locke or Rousseau on Native social and natural philosophy were largely oppositive projections of European conceptions onto people who typified the 'state of nature' – ornamented with frequently misconceived observations by explorers or missionaries (Lafitau's *Moeurs des sauvages amériquains* (1724) is a partial early exception). Since the languages were oral, philosophical thought often did not survive unless translated and transcribed by chroniclers literate in a European language. Most early intellectually-oriented inquisitors were missionaries, whose epistemological intents were not neutral. Recorded occasions of genuine philosophical dialogue are sparse (those of turn-of-the-century physician James R. Walker with George Sword and other Lakota shamans are noteworthy). Even with sincere interest, interlocutors have typically had an insufficient grasp of notoriously complex linguistic forms for effective understanding. One of the few academic philosophers to undertake field research likens his dialogue with an elderly monolingual Navajo, translated by younger bilinguals, to 'trying to talk to Plato with an Attican peasant as interpreter!' (Ladd 1957: 201). In sum, the difficulties of knowing much genuine Native American philosophy are manifold, owing to its multiplicity and diversity, as well as to problems of translatability, both linguistic and social, compounded by historical circumstances.

2   Cosmology, metaphysics and ontology

For many Native American philosophies, a pervasive animism – denoted by Siouan *wakan*, Iroquoian *orenda*, Algonquian *manitou*, and Kwakiutl *nawalak* – is fundamental. This widespread idea posits, in all things and processes, an inherent vital force which has compulsive effects on events and conditions, may become attached to or the possession of individual 'persons' (not only human), and was the originating source of all phenomena. Iroquoian *orenda*, for example, is a:

> hypothetic principle ... conceived to be immaterial, occult, impersonal, mysterious in mode of action, limited in function and efficiency, and not at all omnipotent, local and not omnipresent, and ever embodied or immanent in some object, although it was believed that it could be transferred, attracted, acquired, increased, suppressed, or enthralled by the orenda of occult, ritualistic formulas endowed with more potency.
>
> (Hewitt 1906. 147)

Likewise, Siouan *wakan* is 'the animating force of the universe, the common denominator of its oneness' (DeMallie 1987: 28); the totality of life-forces are *wakan tanka* ('the great *wakan*', popularly translated 'Great Spirit'). Conceptually, wakan is typically characterized by its impenetrability, and in use has radiating synecdochic and metaphoric referents. But its multiplex significations are formally divided by shamans into sixteen hierarchical (four times four) aspects (see Figure 1). Each of these has particular powers of creation and transformation in the founding of the universe and its continual unfolding in human experience and practice.

Here the abstraction of universal power converges with the constitution of human subjectivity. The Sioux person is animated at birth by three *wakan* elements given by *skan* ('Energy'): 'consciousness or will' (*sicun*, a guardian against evil); a ghost 'which comes from the stars'; and 'a spirit, evidently an immaterial but immortal reflection of the body'. 'After the death, the guardian escorts the spirit to the spirit world beyond the Milky Way; the guardian and the ghost return to the places from which *skan* originally got them' (DeMallie and Lavenda 1977: 157). These elements of ontogeny and ontology depict a human essence and matter particulate to universal totality. Simultaneously, a sense of phylogeny is central.

Narratives of origin vary, but many identify consecutive phases (for Zuni there are four, for Hopi three, for Tewa two). The natural and cultural world is progressively differentiated out of formlessness through active intervention by mystical forces (for Navajo these include coloured mists, swallows, and insects). At intermediate junctures, transformer-heroes appear in various guises, like Changing Woman and the monster-slayers, her twin sons by the Sun, for the Navajo and Apache. Gradually transformers produce sufficient order for humanoid forms, which evolve from primitivity to modernity (for example, Brightman 1990).

The Tewa (Pueblo) world was formed and ordered

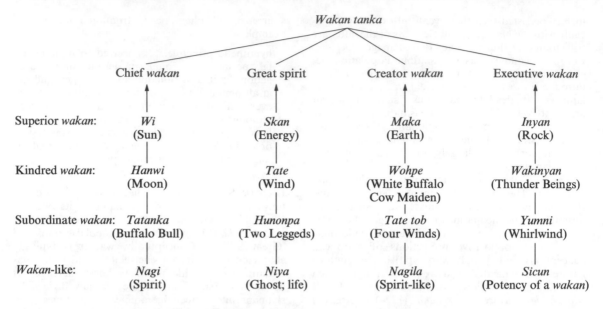

Figure 1. Tobtob kin, the four times four. (DeMallie and Lavenda 1977)

after the emergence of proto-humans from a primordial lake (Ortiz 1969). Various culture-heroes (including Mountain Lion the Hunt Chief, Summer Chief, Winter Chief, and six pairs of varicoloured sibling deities of the directions) were sent up by the originating Mothers, 'Blue-Corn Woman near to summer', and 'White Corn Woman near to ice'. They harden the ground and order time, space, topography, seasonality, biology and social mores. The constructed world is bounded at its corners by four sacred mountains (with 'earth-navels' on the peaks); towards the centre these are successively linked to four flat-topped hills, four shrines at the village-margins, and finally four dance plazas in each Tewa village. The world ordering affects all aspects of Tewa existence and is dramatically reiterated in ritual; the culture heroes are impersonated, and all ritual trajectories – in speech, song, dance-movements and so on – insistently re-mark the tetradic structures, both temporally and spatially. In short, origin-narratives both explain the world and set the terms for human action within it.

Hopi metaphysics and ontology, evidenced in linguistic forms, emphasizes 'events', or 'eventings', that are objectively 'expressed mainly as outlines, colours, movements, and other perceptive reports', in contrast with the static substances, masses and entities foremost in European languages (Whorf 1956: 147). According to Whorf:

Every language contains terms that have come to crystallize in themselves the basic postulates of an unformulated philosophy... Such are our words 'reality, substance, matter, cause,' and ... 'space, time, past, present, future.' Such a term in Hopi is the word most often translated 'hope' – *tunatya* – 'it is in the action of hoping, it hopes, it is hoped for, it thinks or is thought of with hope,' etc.... The verb *tunatya* contains in its idea of hope something of our words 'thought,' 'desire,' and 'cause,' which sometimes must be used to translate it. The word is really a term which crystallizes the Hopi philosophy of the universe in respect to its grand dualism of objective and subjective: it is the Hopi term for SUBJECTIVE. It refers to the state of the subjective, unmanifest, vital and causal aspect of the Cosmos, and the fermenting activity toward fruition and manifestation with which it seethes – an action of HOPING; i.e. mental-causal activity, which is forever pressing upon and into the manifested realm.

(Whorf 1956: 61–2)

The difficulties of translating Native philosophies are partly descriptive. With some adjustments, Whorf's rendering of Hopi metaphysics calls to mind Heidegger's theory of being, particularly of existence as an emergence-into-presence (see HEIDEGGER, M.).

Despite valuable criticism (for example, Malotki 1982), much of Whorf's analysis holds true. In Whiteley's (1988) research, one Hopi philosopher, Yoywayma, emphasized a triadic principle of idea, intention, and action – *tunatya, pasiwni, okiw antani.* In combination with *natwani*, an exteriorization of self, this triad suggests that – as for Husserl – intentionality and its worldly engagement is the defining feature of a conscious self (see INTENTIONALITY). *Tunatya*, explained with a characteristic horticultural metaphor, refers to a 'seed of thought' – the germ of an idea, we might say – that occurs in one's consciousness. *Pasiwni*, planning, means bringing together and setting into motion all the necessary technical and symbolic resources to germinate the seed and bring it to fructifying life. *Okiw antani*, 'let it be this way,' refers to proper mental attitude and is also a prayer that sanctifies the intention to control deific forces.

Pueblo thought discloses a common metaphysics (the 'Pueblo' Indians include the Hopi, Zuni, Tewa, Tiwa, Towa and Keres, all with entirely different languages but other cultural similarities):

> The general Pueblo conception of causality is that everything – animate and inanimate – counts and everything has its place in the cosmos. All things are thought to have two aspects, essence and matter. Thus everything in the cosmos is believed to be knowable and, being knowable, controllable. Effective control comes only from letter-perfect attention to detail and correct performance, thus the Pueblo emphasis on formulas, ritual, and repetition revealed in ritual drama. Among human beings, the primary causal factors are mental and psychological states; if these are harmonious, the supernaturals will dispense what is asked and expected of them. If they are not, untoward consequences will follow just as quickly, because within this relentlessly interconnected universal whole the part can affect the whole, just as like can come from like. Men, animals, plants and spirits are intertransposable in a seemingly unbroken chain of being.
>
> (Ortiz 1972: 143)

In Navajo metaphysics, causality and consciousness are linked through speech. Speech, especially in ritual, has causal power, simultaneously *doing* what it says: 'Ritual language does not describe how things are, it determines how they will be. Ritual language ... disperses evil, reverses disorder, neutralizes pain, over-comes fear, eliminates illness, relieves anxiety, and restores order, health, and well-being'. Ritual speech derives from foundational knowledge of which reality itself is composed. In Navajo creation narratives:

> language is the means by which form is projected onto substance.... The symbol was not created as a means of representing reality; on the contrary, reality was created or transformed as a manifestation of symbolic form. *In the Navajo view of the world, language is not a mirror of reality; reality is a mirror of language.*
>
> (Witherspoon 1977: 34, emphasis in original)

3 Being and mind

The (Iroquoian) Huron believed in a soul both 'divisible and physical' with terms for the divisible parts. One part, *,aata*, is equated with the body, and with the body's life-force, but also with aspects of 'the self', particularly in moral interrelationship with other selves, in emotions and in personality. It also operates conjunctively, in an overall conception that is fundamentally dualistic:

> One major Huron conception of the soul, that of the perceptive or sensitive-animating one, is linked and is comprised of the emotive soul, *eiachia* or heart..., the general body-soul, *,aata*, and the general life-soul, *onnhek8i*. The second Huron conception, the rational or intellectual free soul, combined the intellectual soul, *,andi,onra* (mind), and the free soul, *oki*.
>
> (Pomedli 1991: 60)

The intellectual soul is the means of thought. In European philosophy, thinking is generally depicted as a process in which mind absorbs sensory impressions from external reality and then deliberates internally with the abstracted residue:

> Hurons, however, emphasize a more extrinsic method of thinking. For them, the mind, in the process of thinking, transports itself or is transported into the object or event in question.... Instead of the mind using its power to assimilate, it rather has the power to move into an object, enrich it, name it, make it meaningful, and empower it. The object or event remains out there, nevertheless, but is now changed and made similar to the mind because of the free-moving thinking process.... While for Europeans thinking involves the conscious and deliberative, that is, discursive activities, for Hurons it focuses on the imaginative and intuitive, that is, excursive activities.
>
> (Pomedli 1991: 65–8)

In conscious thought and in dreams there is an internal dialogue – an 'immanent intersubjectivity' – among Huron soul forms. A conception of multiple, particularly dual, souls (where one – the free soul or psyche – is detachable from the animate body) is widespread throughout North America.

Li'maqsti, 'mind', among the Nuu-cha-nulth (or

Nootka) of the Northwest Coast, is conceptualized as a column of ten connected spiritual homunculi resident in the spinal cord. *Li'maqsti* incorporates 'reason' and 'will' and serves as a sort of transducer between sensation, mentation and action, between 'internal and external states'. The realization of action from intention involves a colloquy:

> Each of the [ten connected] persons is an individual...and each is capable of autonomous thought. A man acts, in effect, by majority rule. If the ten persons are in complete agreement he knows just what to do; if they are in balanced disagreement, then he is incapable of acting at all.
> (Golla 1988: 4)

Concepts of mind emerge also in the widely remarked Native attention to dreams. Iroquois dream theory is 'basically psychoanalytic':

> They recognized conscious and unconscious parts of the mind.... [They made] the distinction between the manifest and the latent content of dreams and employed what sounds like the technique of free association to uncover the latent meaning. And they considered that the best method for the relief of psychic and psychosomatic distresses was to give the repressed desire satisfaction, either directly or symbolically.
> (Wallace 1969: 63)

Dream theories vary, but there are numerous echoes of Iroquois views (for example, Lincoln 1935), especially with regard to dreams as guides for conscious action. For the sub-Arctic Cree:

> Dream images may be understood as prophetic, as literal or symbolically disguised representations of future states of affairs. Memories of the dream are then retained by the waking self, providing foreknowledge of future occurrences....
>
> [But] Crees say that dream events may *determine* the occurrence of like events – their worldly simulacra – that have not yet happened but that will transpire in waking life only as a result of their having initially been dreamed. The dreamer... [further] conceives him or herself as capable of influencing worldly outcomes by choosing certain courses of action in the anticipatory dream.
> (Brightman 1993: 97–9)

In other sub-Arctic hunting societies, dreams may link a hunter's psyche with that of an individual prey animal, or with a master-soul of the species, who guides the hunter to a waking bodily form as part of a reciprocal life-death compact between human beings and game animals from originary times. But in all cases, interpretive criticism and failure are centrally acknowledged, belying an inference of naive mysticism.

In some cultures, a *totem* (an Ojibwa word from the Great Lakes – far from the misnamed 'totem poles' of the Northwest Coast), or guardian-spirit, watches over a person's life. It may be appointed at birth or acquired in a 'vision-quest', especially at puberty. The widespread vision-quest, for both sexes, is a socially sanctioned will-to-power, involving fasts on mountain tops or other secluded spots deemed powerful, where through privation the individual seeks a transcendent vision, which, though more intense, is like ordinary dreaming in its informing of conscious action. If successful, a spirit-animal or deity representative appears, and conveys a personal power that may subsequently be invoked at will.

4 Ethics

Major visions were used to guide community actions and were ritually enacted in collective performance. The mutual dependence of self and society is also strikingly illustrated in the Plains Sun Dance. Individual men may elect to undergo extreme physical pain by piercing muscles with rawhide thongs attached to a pole representing the *axis mundi*, and pulling away until the flesh is broken or they lose consciousness – an act of self-sacrifice for the spiritual benefit of the whole community.

The individuated yet relational self is often associated with concrete ethical manifestations in objective reality. For the Hopi, ethical values prescribe modesty, self-effacement, interpersonal and environmental responsibility, industry, courtesy, circumspection, and humility. *Natwani*, the exterior reflection of one's performance, may refer to crops, children or other fruits of personal effort; if these turn out well, they accrue to the individual's virtue as '*hopi*' (an ethical term in itself, encapsulating the values mentioned). Ethically composed and judged selves in intersubjective relationship engender and reproduce moral community. After detailed field study, philosopher Richard Brandt (1954: 72) concluded that, 'it is doubtful whether there is any evidence for ethical attitudes or remorse in Western society which cannot be matched among the Hopi'.

Ladd (1957: 212–13) interprets Navajo ethics as 'rational' (especially in terms of moral justification for action), 'prudential' (particularly regarding the individual's welfare), 'egoistic' (promoting individual satisfaction), and 'utilitarian' (aimed at happiness for all) (see EGOISM AND ALTRUISM; UTILITARIANISM). The central goal is *Sạah Naagháii Bik'eh Hózhǫ* which refers, *inter alia*, to the continuous reproduction of beauty, health, long-life and happiness for self and community (Witherspoon 1977: 13–46).

In many Native societies, high value is placed on both individual autonomy and harmonious cooperation. Coercion is rare and social adherence depends on individual assent. Conformism is perhaps most strongly emphasized in Pueblo values, although the standard Hopi phrase '*pi um 'i*" ('it is up to you'), stresses individual choice. Individual autonomy is especially strong in northern hunting societies, but here too is accompanied by a powerful sense of mutual reliance. While there are exceptions (as in the institution of partial slavery in Northwest Coast societies), this conjoint ethos of individual autonomy and interpersonal responsibility is so widespread it represents a deep-seated moral choice in the Native American *conscience collective*, and an implicit rejection of the Enlightenment social contract, conceived as the surrender of 'natural rights' to a sovereign, from which much contemporary Western social and political philosophy stems.

Ethical principles are also extended to non-human 'persons', particularly game-animals. According to Penobscot (Eastern Algonquians):

The animals know beforehand when they are to be slain, when their spirits have been overcome by the hunter's personal power or magic. They exact also a certain respect, which is shown to them in different ways, through generally by the proper treatment of their remains after they have been killed for their flesh or skins. If this respect is not accorded to them, the animals refuse to be killed or their souls may not be reborn.

(Speck 1935: 32–3)

How, though, do these beliefs differ from mere anthropomorphism? Rock Crees 'ascribe animateness, self-awareness, intelligence, and sometimes covert humanoid characteristics to many non-human beings and objects'. But they simultaneously depend on a detailed pragmatic knowledge that emphasizes human-animal differences that are 'constitutive of and endlessly objectified in the human practice of killing and eating animals' (Brightman 1993: 77, 179). The dualism of ethical consubstantiation and pragmatic differentiation reflects the central metaphysical dichotomy between 'matter and essence' noted above for Pueblo world-view. It is the essential forms of nature that are included within the ethical sphere of 'persons'; the material forms are objects of pragmatic interaction.

5 Epistemology and reason

Native knowledge systems are grounded in the metaphysical and ontological principles so far described. In Hopi, knowledge as an abstraction is denoted by *navoti*, the closest equivalent to 'philosophy', but also implying such European paradigms as *scientia*, theology, epistemology, psychology, hermeneutics and with a determinist cast in which events are fore-ordained (with a causal nexus in mystical forces). What is known through *navoti* may, by the same token, be acted upon. *Navoti*, especially in ritual use, is, like Navajo speech, causative: a *pouvoir/savoir* addressed to supernatural causes attributed with conscious animate force.

Many Native American societies denominate social units by natural species and elements: the Hopi have more than thirty matrilineal clans, including Bear, Spider, Greasewood, Badger, Butterfly, Sun, Parrot and Eagle. Lévi-Strauss has produced a penetrating analysis of this 'totemic logic', which, he argues, is fundamentally relational:

The homology they [totemic institutions] evoke is not between social groups and natural species but between the differences which manifest themselves on the level of groups on the one hand and on that of species on the other. They are thus based on the postulate of a homology between *two systems of differences*, one of which occurs in nature and the other in culture.

(Lévi-Strauss 1966: 115)

Natural classes are thus 'good to think', that is, as metaphorical vehicles for conceptual differentiation – behaviourally, epistemologically and socially. The inferred mode of thought is fundamentally analogical, operating with a 'system of concepts embedded in images' that serve to build 'mental structures that facilitate an understanding of the world in as much as they resemble it' (Lévi-Strauss 1966: 264, 263).

Lévi-Strauss extrapolates Native American systems of thought from mythological narratives (especially), social forms, arts and architecture. In myth, embedded codes of meaning operate both episodically ('syntagmatically') and thematically ('paradigmatically'). The narratives unfold via a series of binary oppositions ranged along multiple intersecting planes, including geography, economy, sociology and cosmology – 'each one of these levels together with the symbolism proper to it, being seen as a transformation of an underlying logical structure common to all of them' (Lévi-Strauss 1968: 1). The oppositions derive from contradictory principles in social experience. Myths, then, seek to 'resolve' paradoxes and contradictions, which are in fact irresolvable, by correlating oppositions from the different planes and postulating syntheses. In a Tsimshian (Northwest Coast) story, for example, Asdiwal, a supernatural transformer-hero, is the figure of attempted synthesis between (*inter alia*): endogamy versus exogamy, famine versus plenty, salmon versus candlefish, mountain-hunting versus sea-hunting, female versus male, movement versus immobility, patrilocal residence versus matrilineal descent, downstream versus upstream, mother versus daughter, and heaven versus earth. The mythic interplay of these oppositions configures the attempt epistemologically to overcome their individual contradictions. This 'fundamental notion of dualism in a perpetual state of disequilibrium' Lévi-Strauss sees as pervading Native American systems of thought:

> In Amerindian thought a sort of philosophical bias seems to make it necessary for things in any sector of the cosmos or society to not remain in their initial state and for an unstable dualism to always yield another unstable dualism, regardless of the level on which it might be apprehended.
>
> (Lévi-Strauss 1995: 231)

Lévi-Strauss' position is persuasive. Dual forms of social and conceptual organization are common, from the Red-White social binaries of the Creek confederacy to paired masks of the Kwakiutl and Salish, the Winter-Summer Tewa moieties, diametric town-plans of the Winnebago and oppositive species in Keresan emergence myths. Ortiz (1969) confirms a pervasive dualism in Tewa culture, but challenges its supposed insolubility. Tewa social oppositions are resolved cyclically through temporal alternations where one or the other of the Summer-Winter pair has successive executive authority. Herein lies an indication of the limits of Lévi-Strauss' interpretation of Native thought, removed as it is from first-hand empirical inquiry.

The Hegelian and Kantian foundations of Lévi-Strauss' approach are clear: the former in his dialectical reason and the latter with his tacit reliance on a transcendental subject. Both principles are, then, inferred as key components of Native American thought *sui generis*. But if a major logical process in Native thought systems is autogenously dialectical, this operates largely without the conscious intervention of any Native thinker: Lévi-Strauss (1970) holds that mythological thematic operators (oppositions, or figures like Asdiwal himself) *think themselves* out through individual minds and tellings rather than vice versa.

While of great heuristic value, Lévi-Strauss' semiotic reductions result in an abstract logical and aesthetic formalism, where the endless interplay of binary oppositions becomes a hall of mirrors (see LÉVI-STRAUSS, C.). In use in Native discourse, species names and denotations are both literal and often multiply symbolic. A re-analysis of Hidatsa names with Frege's notions of sense and reference opens out the understanding of Native signification considerably further (Barnes 1980). Similarly, for the Hopi, who continue to gather fledgling eagles each May, species meanings are more than mere logical abstractions. Eagles are 'persons' from a Hopi point of view and reincarnate clan ancestors. Eagles are, then, good to think, but they are also sentient spirits who are good to be with and who mediate prayers to deity, in a cosmos saturated with sentient subjects rather than rote mechanistic forms.

Particularly for shamans, narratives of personal relationship with animals and elements are frequent. Eskimo shamans, for example, were thought capable of detaching part of their selves from their bodies and visiting the under-sea homes of deities. Some shamanic initiations among Tikigaq Eskimos involve metamorphosis into animal forms, like whales . Yet indigenous scepticism of both particular claims and general principles is clearly apparent (Lowenstein 1992: 91, 78–84). A well-known example of scepticism involves a Kwakiutl man, Quesalid, who doubts shamanic claims. He proceeds, as an empirical test, to apprentice himself, and goes about exposing the fraud of others. But he also becomes a highly successful curer himself. Quesalid's apprenticeship does not entail a transition to uncritical belief, but rather a comprehension of the social and psychological contexts in which shamanic techniques productively operate.

If in origin narratives a central concern is ordering by categorial differentiation, and if ritual's key intent is to exert control over a deterministic world, these are always accompanied by a simultaneous indeterminacy principle. In myths, this is instantiated by Trickster, and in rituals, by formal clowning and games. Trickster resists structure, is instinctual and without ethics or conscience. He/she/it is (willy-nilly) a major creative force in some instances, in others ancillary to more prominent creators. But everywhere, Trickster – embodied as Coyote, Hare or Raven, or a bodiless figure of metamorphosis – represents the chance element, the subversion and transgression of order, and, through selfish desire, vanity, lust, greed and gluttony, is both inverse ethical exemplar and an avenue of comic release and communal therapy. Trickster is a protohuman cheerleader for flawed humanity, who mocks the claims to righteousness of gods or pious humans. But Trickster is, reflexively, a satire of creatural vanity, displaying an ironic, ambivalent sense of the human condition marked by a continual failure to live up to ideals, and he/she/it ostensibly defines the provisionality of all established forms:

The symbol which Trickster embodies is not a static one. It contains within itself the promise of differentiation, the promise of god and man.... He represents not only the undifferentiated and distant past, but likewise the undifferentiated present within every individual. This constitutes his universal and persistent attraction. And so he became and remained everything to every man – god, animal, human being, hero, buffoon, he who was before good and evil, denier, affirmer, destroyer and creator. If we laugh at him, he grins at us. What happens to him happens to us.

(Radin 1956: 168–9)

In Winnebago narratives, *wadjunkaga*, 'the tricky one', passes through a series of episodes in a developmental cycle; along the way, his left and right hands fight and cause serious injury to each other, he wounds his own (personified) anus for failing to guard a brace of ducks, eats his own intestines, punishes a chipmunk with his penis that gets chewed off in return, changes sex to marry a chief's son, claims to be a war chief but systematically violates all the taboos, and so on. The cycle depicts a journey from a formless, childlike id ruled by immediate sensory and intellectual gratification, in which everything is misconceived – biology, cosmology, social roles, sexuality, mortality and morality – towards biological, social, and psychological definition. In a conscious mythological world where other creatures comment adversely on his exploits, Trickster the protohuman blunders about, asocial and isolated, largely unconscious of the effects of his actions. Logically and cosmologically, trickster is antithesis, subversion, imbalance.

Mixed-blood Anishinabe philosopher Gerald Vizenor extends Trickster into his own work, showing further how it operates as a sign. He writes both *of* and *as* Trickster against the reification of social-scientific analysis:

Tricksters, the wild ironies of survivance, transformation, natural reason, and liberation in stories, are marooned as obscure moral simulations in translations.... *The trickster is a language game*, a counter causal liberation of the mind.

Trickster is androgynous, a comic healer and liberator in literature: the whole figuration that ties the unconscious to social experience. The trickster sign is communal, an erotic shimmer in oral traditions; the narrative voices are *holotropes* [total figures] in a discourse.

(Vizenor 1994: 76–7, 89, first emphasis added)

Trickster frees from structure, a semiotic sign forever darting in and out of established meaning and reference (including its own), and a Native counterpart to postmodernism's free play of signification and subversion of master-narratives (see POSTMODERNISM).

Hopi clowns play out the same philosophical drama in a two-day ceremony. To begin with, clowns, *tsutskut* ('the pointed ones', after a feature of their costume, but also 'those who are making a point' – the double meaning also works in Hopi) specifically symbolize undifferentiated consciousness, humanity in a childlike state innocent of understanding, virtue or evil. During a line-dance performance by kachinas (masked representations of spirits, which here embody pure essences of the differentiated cosmos) unmasked clowns appear in counterpoint, lampooning everything sacred or normative in Hopi values, and following Trickster's trajectory of semi-successful category learning by the end of the ceremony. At a critical moment, under threat of death by moralizing warrior kachinas, they agree to try order, and to demonstrate this they imitate the kachinas in the line-dance. After a few tries, however, they fall apart, hopelessly incapable.

Several key themes of Native American philosophy are conjoined in this performance. When they first appear in the plaza, clowns are the children of the Sun arriving in a formless void (initially they do not notice the kachinas) where they start iconically building the world and their place within it, though with frequent reversals of contemporary significations. Their transgressions are comically played out for the Hopi audience, which then reflexively inspects the world's categories and codes, re-notes their arbitrariness and provisionality, delights in the cathartic subversion of the intending human self, its acts and foibles, and is reminded of the virtue and vitality of created natural and social order. This play of order and disorder dialectically deconstructs the human condition – cosmologically, metaphysically, ontologically, biologically, ethically and epistemologically. Trickster, in a word, is the philosopher.

See also: LATIN AMERICA, PHILOSOPHY IN

References and further reading

* Barnes, R.H. (1980) 'Hidatsa Personal Names: an Interpretation', Plains *Anthropologist* 25 (90): 311–31. (Philosophically sophisticated, cogent analysis of Hidatsa naming and subjectivity, employing Frege's conception of sense and reference.)

Basso, K.H. (1996) *Wisdom Sits in Places: Landscape and Language among the Western Apache*, Albuquerque, NM: University of New Mexico Press. (Deeply insightful analysis of Apache discursive use of place-names as metonyms of moral narratives; shows how the intersubjectively cognized landscape may serve as a philosophical text in oral societies, suggesting that argument is not limited to the subjective authority of interior memory; assesses some Apache concepts of mind versus brain.)

* Brandt, R.B. (1954) *Hopi Ethics: a Theoretical Analysis*, Chicago, IL: University of Chicago Press. (A thorough field study in the 1940s by an academic philosopher interviewing numerous Hopis.)

* Brightman, R.A. (1990) 'Primitivism in Missinippi Cree Historical Consciousness', *Man* (n.s.) 25: 399–418. (Insightful, approachable reflection on Cree evolutionary epistemology.)

* —— (1993) *Grateful Prey: Rock Cree Human-Animal Relationships*, Berkeley, CA: University of California Press. (An exemplary ethnographic inquiry into Cree natural philosophy, ethics and metaphysics.)

* DeMallie, R.J. (1987) 'Lakota Belief and Ritual in the Nineteenth Century', in R.J. DeMallie and D.R. Parks (eds) *Sioux Indian Religion: Tradition and Innovation*, Norman, OK: University of Oklahoma Press. (Fine synthetic analysis of Lakota metaphysics and ontology within a religious frame of reference.)

* DeMallie, R.J. and Lavenda, R.H. (1977) '*Wakan*: Plains Siouan Concepts of Power', in R.D. Fogelson and R.N. Adams (eds) *The Anthropology of Power: Ethnographic Studies from Asia, Oceania and the New World*, New York: Academic. (Lucid discussion of the concept of pervasive animate force suffusing the cosmos in Sioux thought.)

* Golla, S. (1988) 'Persons, Names and Selves among Traditional Nuu-chah-nulth', paper presented to the symposium 'Persons and Selves in Pueblo and Northwest Coast Societies: Marcel Mauss Reconsidered', American Anthropological Association Annual Meetings, Phoenix, AZ. (Penetrating, user-friendly analysis of Nuu-chah-nulth concepts of mind, subjectivity and action.)

* Hewitt, J.N.B. (1906) 'Orenda', in F.W. Hodge (ed.) 'Handbook of American Indians', *Bureau of American Ethnology Bulletin* 30 (II): 147–8. (A still-valuable summary of Iroquois metaphysical thought; the author, an anthropologist, was Tuscarora (Iroquois).)

* Ladd, J. (1957) *The Structure of a Moral Code: A Philosophical Analysis of Ethical Discourse applied to the Ethics of the Navaho Indians*, Cambridge, MA: Harvard University Press. (A philosophically detailed and informed attempt at intercultural interpretation of ethics; Ladd is criticized by Navajo specialists for his reliance on a single informant, yet the inferences are often sophisti-

cated and ring true, although perhaps excessively dependent on a Western analytical model.)

* Lafitau, J.F. (1724) *Moeurs des sauvages amériquains comparées aux moeurs des premiers temps*, Paris, 4 vols; trans. and ed. W.N. Fenton and E. Moore as *Customs of the American Indians compared with the customs of primitive times*, Toronto, Ont.: Champlain Society, 1974–7. (One of the earliest serious attempts at ethnographic description of ethics and beliefs, based on the long-term work of the Jesuit missions among Huron and Iroquois – see Thwaites (below).)

* Lévi-Strauss, C. (1966) *The Savage Mind*, Chicago, IL: University of Chicago Press. (Arguably the twentieth-century's most brilliant attempt to engage intellectually with the epistemology and ontology of non-Western cultures, with some particular emphasis on thought in the indigenous Americas. Occasionally intractable, Lévi-Strauss is consistently provocative, philosophically speaking, and simultaneously keeps faith with some basic premises of Amerindian conception.)

* —— (1968) 'The Story of Asdiwal', trans. N. Mann, in E.R. Leach (ed.) *The Structural study of Myth and Totemism*, London: Tavistock. (Perhaps the most cogent single demonstration by Lévi-Strauss of the multiple planes on which Native American mythological dialectics operate.)

* —— (1970) *The Raw and the Cooked: Introduction to a Science of Mythology*, London: Jonathan Cape. (First of the four-volume magnum opus *Mythologiques* (the others are *From Honey to Ashes*, *The Origin of Table Manners*, and *The Naked Man*), analysing the mythology of the Americas.)

* —— (1995) *The Story of Lynx*, trans. C. Tihanyi, Chicago, IL: University of Chicago Press. (An analysis of Native American thought via myths from the Plateau and Northwest Coast.)

* Lincoln, J.S. (1935) *The Dream in Primitive Cultures*, London: Cresset. (Though limited interpretatively by its time, contains substantive discussion of psychology and philosophy of dreams, with detailed cases from Native North America.)

* Lowenstein, T. (1992) *The Things That Were Said of Them: Shaman Stories and Oral Histories of the Tikigaq People told by Asatchaq*, trans. Tukummiq and T. Lowenstein, Berkeley, CA: University of California Press. (A sensitive approach to Eskimo thought through oral literature.)

* Malotki, E. (1982) *Hopi Time: a Linguistic Analysis of the Temporal Concepts in the Hopi Language*, The Hague: De Gruyter & Mouton. (A detailed linguistic analysis that effectively dislodges Whorf's view of timelessness in Hopi linguistic forms.)

McNeley, J.K. (1981) *Holy Wind in Navajo*

Philosophy, Tucson, AZ: University of Arizona Press. (Focuses on *nil'chi*, 'wind', 'air', or 'atmosphere', the Navajo version of pervasive animate force.)

* Neihardt J.G. (1932) *Black Elk Speaks: Being the Life Story of a Holy Man of the Oglala Sioux*, New York: William Morrow. (A now controversial, but widely popular, account of a Lakota shaman's life and thought, which remains valuable for its insights into Sioux metaphysics; the controversy derives from the extent of editorial intervention that, *inter alia*, neglects Black Elk's active Catholicism by the time his autobiography was dictated.)

* Ortiz, A. (1969) *The Tewa World: Space, Time, Being and Becoming in a Pueblo Society*, Chicago, IL: University of Chicago Press. (A superb, detailed analysis of Tewa cosmology and metaphysics by an anthropologist from San Juan (a Tewa) Pueblo.)

* —— (1972) 'Ritual Drama and the Pueblo World View' in A. Ortiz (ed.) *New Perspectives on the Pueblos*, Albuquerque, NM: University of New Mexico Press. (A development of the above, focused on Pueblo ritual.)

* Pomedli, M.M. (1991) *Ethnophilosophical and Ethnolinguistic Perspectives on the Huron Indian Soul*, Lewiston, NY: Edwin Mellen. (One of the best analyses of seventeenth and eighteenth century Jesuit records from the Huron missions – see Thwaites below.)

* Radin, P. (1945) *The Road of Life and Death: a Ritual Drama of the American Indians*, Bollingen Series V, New York: Pantheon. (A thorough, albeit authorially idiosyncratic, account of a key Winnebago ritual, The Medicine Rite, with useful inferences particularly regarding metaphysics and eschatology.)

* —— (1956) *The Trickster: A Study in American Indian Mythology*, New York: Philosophical Library. (The classic account of the Winnebago Trickster narrative cycle, with comparisons to other Native American Trickster myths, and both philosophically and psychologically inflected interpretations; C.G. Jung offers his usual archetypalist view.)

* Ridington, R. (1988) *Trail to Heaven: Knowledge and Narrative in a Northern Native Community*, Iowa City, IA: University of Iowa Press. (An insightful examination of Beaver mystical and pragmatic thought.)

* Speck, F. (1935) 'Penobscot Tales and Religious Beliefs', *Journal of American Folklore* 48: 1–107. (Nice illustration of Native American moral extensions to animate environmental forms.)

Sturtevant, W. (ed.) (1979–) *Handbook of North American Indians*, Washington, DC: Smithsonian Institution Press, 20 vols. (This emerging twenty-volume work is the principal source to begin all inquiries into Native American culture, history, and thought.)

* Tanner, A. (1979) *Bringing Home Animals: Religious Ideology and Mode of Production of the Mistassini Cree Hunters*, New York: St Martin's Press. (A particularly fine-grained and thoughtful explication of Cree thought.)

Tedlock, B. (1992) *The Beautiful and the Dangerous: Encounters with the Zuni Indians*, New York: Viking. (A personalized account of the author's long-term ethnographic work at Zuni Pueblo: contains nuanced interpretations of Zuni aesthetics, and natural and social philosophy.)

Tedlock, B. and Tedlock, D. (eds) (1975) *Teachings from the American Earth: Indian Religion and Philosophy*, New York: Liveright. (A useful collection of interpretations, with discussions of several philosophical perspectives.)

Tedlock, D. (1983) *The Spoken Word and the Work of Interpretation*, Philadelphia, PA: University of Pennsylvania Press. (Contains several searching analyses (including the preceding item) of complexities of translation, particularly from oral languages to written, with a major focus on Zuni.)

Thwaites, R.G. (ed.) (1896–1901) *The Jesuit Relations and Allied Documents, Travels and Explorations of the Jesuit Missionaries in New France, 1610–1791*, Cleveland, OH: Burrows Brothers, 73 vols. (The source for early European interpretation of Iroquolan philosophy, from accounts of the missions.)

* Vizenor, G. (1994) *Manifest Manners: Postindian Warriors of Survivance*, Hanover, NH: Wesleyan University Press. (A literary and philosophical critique of representations of Native identity and experience, including further reflections on Trickster. Vizenor, a mixed-blood Anishinabe, is one of the most philosophically engaged contemporary Native scholars, and his writings, often Trickster-esque, offer subtle insights into Native thought, informed by poststructuralist theory.)

* Walens, S. (1981) *Feasting with Cannibals: an Essay on Kwakiutl Cosmology*, Princeton, NJ: Princeton University Press. (A searching examination of Kwakiutl metaphor and metaphysics, based on the ethnography of Franz Boas.)

* Walker, J.R. (1896–1914a) *Lakota Belief and Ritual*, ed. R.J. DeMallie and E.A. Jahner, Lincoln, NB: University of Nebraska Press, 1980. (Walker's field notes of interviews with Lakota intellectuals, collected while he was Agency physician at the Pine Ridge Reservation.)

—— (1896–1914b) *Lakota Myth*, ed. E.A. Jahner, Lincoln, NB: University of Nebraska Press, 1983.

(More of Walker's field notes of interviews with Lakota intellectuals)

* Wallace, A.F.C. (1969) *The Death and Rebirth of the Seneca*, New York: Random House. (A historically focused interpretation of Seneca (Iroquois) religious revitalization, with a psychologically informed analysis of Seneca thought.)

* Whiteley, P.M. (1988) *Deliberate Acts: Changing Hopi Culture through the Oraibi Split*, Tucson, AZ: University of Arizona Press. (Extends some of the author's observations on Hopi intentionality and philosophy of action in social and historical context.)

—— (1992) 'Burning Culture: Auto-da-fe at Oraibl', *History and Anthropology* 6: 46–85. (Examines intentionality and action in a Hopi historical event, drawing especially on the formulations of Donald Davidson and Richard Wollheim.)

* Whorf, B.L. (1956) *Language, Thought and Reality*, ed. J.B. Carroll, Cambridge, MA: MIT Press. (Selected writings of Benjamin Lee Whorf who, with Edward Sapir, is the key figure in linguistic relativism, which suggests that differences in thought are systemically conditioned by language differences, resulting in incommensurable phenomenologies: this anthology contains Whorf's central arguments, with specific foci on Hopi language and thought.)

* Witherspoon, G. (1977) *Language and Art in the Navajo Universe*, Ann Arbor, MI: University of Michigan Press. (A linguistically and culturally well-informed philosophical analysis of Navajo metaphysics and epistemology.)

PETER M. WHITELEY

NATIVISM

Traditional empiricism claims that the mind is initially equipped only with the capacity for experience and the mechanisms that make it possible for us to learn from experience. Nativists have argued that this is not enough, and that our innate endowment must be far richer, including information, ideas, beliefs, perhaps even knowledge.

Empiricism held the advantage until recently, partly because of a misidentification of nativism with rationalism. Rationalists such as Descartes and Leibniz thought nativism would explain how a priori knowledge of necessary truths is possible. However, the fact that something is innate does not establish that it is true, let alone that it is necessary or a priori.

More recently, nativism has been reanimated by Chomsky's claims that children must have innate language-specific information that mediates acquisition of their native tongue. He argues that, given standard empiricist learning procedures, the linguistic data available to a child underdetermines the grammar on which they converge at a very young age, with relatively little effort or instruction.

The successes in linguistics have led to fruitful research on nativism in other domains of human knowledge: for example, arithmetic, the nature of physical objects, features of persons, and possession of concepts generally.

1 **Nativism and empiricism**
2 **Linguistic nativism**
3 **Nativism in philosophy and empirical science**

1 Nativism and empiricism

The fact that we human beings understand the world to the extent that we do depends on two factors: our inherent nature as thinkers, and the specific course of our experience. One of the great oppositions in the history of philosophy has centred on the relative contributions of each of these factors. Empiricists hold that experience provides all the raw materials out of which knowledge and understanding is fashioned: the mind is often compared to a *tabula rasa* (blank slate) initially equipped only with the capacity for experience and the ability to build upon and learn from past experience. Nativists have argued that this is not enough, and that our innate endowment is richer than the empiricist allows (see EMPIRICISM).

Although nativists agree that empiricism is mistaken, they differ widely over the sorts of things that are innate – for example, ideas, principles, knowledge, dispositions, biases, representations, concepts, strategies, theories – as well as about the domains in which innateness must be invoked: Leibniz argued for it primarily for logic and mathematics; Plato for all *genuine* knowledge (see INNATE KNOWLEDGE). The matter is further complicated by the fact that empiricists themselves must inevitably incorporate some nativist elements in their own theorizing. At the very least, the ability to experience the world and the basic machinery that makes building on such experience possible must be innate and not learned. But empiricists typically argue that such commitments are innocuous, not specific to any domain, and (especially in recent empiricism) do not involve the elaborate mental machinery that nativists standardly posit.

Perhaps what unifies all nativist positions is a

reliance on what Noam Chomsky has called the 'poverty of the stimulus' argument scheme. Nativists point to some discrepancy between our experience (the stimulus) and the knowledge (or ideas, concepts, principles, and so on) that we eventually come to have, and argue that this discrepancy cannot be made up by invoking the sorts of simple learning mechanisms posited by empiricists – association and conditioning, for example. It follows that we must be contributing something substantial 'from our side' in the construction of knowledge, and this is what is innate.

The earliest nativist argument is in Plato's *Meno*, where Socrates' questioning enables Meno's uneducated slave to discover 'for himself' a theorem of geometry (*Meno* 80a–86c). Socrates argues that his questions have 'reminded' the slave of what he knew innately. Indeed, for SOCRATES, all knowledge (properly construed) is acquired by recollecting what is innate in the soul from an earlier existence (the doctrine of anamnesis – see PLATO §11). In the *Phaedo* (73c–78b) is a related argument: Socrates claims that the notion of equality involved in perceiving a pair of sticks as equal could not have its source in experience and therefore must be innate.

A similar pattern of argument pervades seventeenth-century rationalist defences of innateness. Descartes and Leibniz argue that our knowledge of the necessary truths of mathematics seems to be justifiable a priori, or 'independently of experience': mathematicians do not need to perform experiments to test whether $2 + 2 = 4$. They thought that nativism would explain how such knowledge was possible (see RATIONALISM).

However, this is a dubious explanatory strategy. Nativism is a claim about the *origins* of knowledge; *rationalism* is a claim about its *justification*. The fact that something is innate does not establish that it is true, let alone that it is necessary or a priori: someone might be born believing that space is Euclidean or that smiling faces are to be trusted, neither of which is even true.

Empiricists attacked nativism in two ways. One approach challenged the legitimacy of nativism as a plank in a theory of knowledge. LOCKE, for instance, argued that nativism reduces either to the nonsensical view that we are, in an everyday sense of the term, literally born knowing things, or to the trivially true and empty view that we have an innate capacity to think and to discover truths. Of course, he then needed an account of how knowledge was possible. He and later empiricists offered what may be termed 'adequacy of the stimulus' counter-arguments (see BEHAVIOURISM, METHODOLOGICAL AND SCIENTIFIC; HUME, D.; LOGICAL POSITIVISM; QUINE, W.V.). They

constructed theories of the mechanisms of inductive inference, of concept formation and so on, and applied them to specific cases (for example, our idea of infinity, our knowledge of general causal laws) to argue that such mechanisms can indeed generate our knowledge given the raw materials of experience. This philosophical effort was in the twentieth century reinforced by the concurrent growth of an independent science of associationist–behaviourist psychology, as well as, more recently, connectionist models of cognitive processing, all based on empiricist principles (see CONNECTIONISM).

2 Linguistic nativism

The dominant philosophical view for most of the twentieth century was that the empiricists had won. But all this changed in the 1960s, due in large measure to Noam Chomsky's arguments that empirical research in linguistics vindicated the rationalist innateness doctrine (as well as its attendant mentalism) over its empiricist counterpart (see CHOMSKY, N.; LANGUAGE, INNATENESS OF).

Chomsky's ground-breaking work has been largely responsible for the development of linguistics as a deeply theoretical empirical science. He argued that language users have an internal representation of a set of rules that relate utterances to meaning and thereby enable them to understand and produce sentences of their language. These rules constitute the grammar of the particular language in question, and determine which patterns constitute well-formed sentences of the language and which do not. The central finding of modern linguistics is that the grammatical rules that govern natural languages are surprisingly complex and non-obvious: they cannot be known by mere casual reflection on one's own linguistic practice, and bear only a remote connection to the traditional schoolbook grammars. Indeed, their specification seems to require a very sophisticated technical apparatus, and what they allow and disallow cannot be accounted for in terms of any generic requirements on communication (see SYNTAX).

Furthermore, if we compare the linguistic data available to the child to the grammar of the specific language the child comes to master, we see that the data severely underdetermines the grammatical rules. There are many alternative rules that could claim as strong inductive support from the child's data as the rules children actually master. Nevertheless, all normal children who learn a language arrive at the same set of rules at a very young age, with relatively little effort, and with little (if any) relevant explicit instruction. Despite disagreement within linguistics about how to specify the particulars of this picture, the preponderant view of the evidence as it now stands is that such a nativist approach is unavoidable.

Philosophers committed to empiricism have responded to Chomsky's linguistic nativism in a variety of ways. Some claim that knowing a language is not a matter of knowing *that*, but rather knowing *how*: one can know how to walk without knowing the specific physical principles that govern walking. Empiricists can then freely grant that there is innate know-how without having to claim there are any innate ideas. Some, echoing Locke, have challenged innate 'Universal Grammar' because of the remoteness of such rules from consciousness (see CONSCIOUSNESS §7; KNOWLEDGE, TACIT; UNCONSCIOUS MENTAL STATES).

Still others have claimed that the most that Chomsky-style nativist arguments show is that speakers of a language have various innate *beliefs*, but no *knowledge*; for, after all, the neonate's beliefs are not *justified* (see KNOWLEDGE, CONCEPT OF). Finally, Hilary Putnam has argued that Chomsky's conclusions are premature because we still have a poor understanding of the general inductive principles that make learning from experience possible (see INDUCTIVE INFERENCE). Until and unless we understand how induction works, we will be in no position to argue that it cannot account for the acquisition of a grammar. Notice, however, that at the very least, this argument concedes the force of the nativist evidence and admits that the long-dominant empiricist paradigm remains underdeveloped.

A more forceful but speculative nativist line of response would challenge the whole notion of general inductive principles. The idea would be that, for any domain of knowledge, we either have special-purpose innate structures that mediate its acquisition, or else we adapt one of the special-purpose structures already in place and refit it for a new domain (for example, applying innate combat strategies to chess). Such a hypothesis does posit some sort of general purpose 'refitting' function, but it clearly has a central nativist core.

3 Nativism in philosophy and empirical science

The success of the Chomskian paradigm in linguistics has strongly influenced research in cognitive development, and there are a number of empirical research programmes aimed at showing that, contrary to the empiricist and Piagetian paradigms, different domains of human knowledge rest on domain-specific innate bases (see COGNITIVE DEVELOPMENT; COGNITION, INFANT; MIND, CHILD'S THEORY OF; PIAGET, J.).

For example, recent findings suggest that 5-month-olds already have some expectations about the results of simple arithmetic operations, manifesting surprise (measured in looking time) at scenes displaying one object where two were to be expected, as a result of either addition or subtraction of objects by hands disappearing behind screens (Wynn 1992). Similar work suggests that the infant's notion of what constitutes a single physical object and certain elementary physical principles may be innately understood (Kelman and Spelke 1983; Baillargeon 1987). There seem to be innate ideas about specific kinds of objects: newborn babies (even less than 10 minutes old!) will look longer at a schematic of a normal human face than at a face with scrambled features (see Morton and Johnson 1991).

Of course, showing that a concept is already present in a 6- or even a 4-month-old does not show that it is innate (although it is hard to extend such scepticism to an infant only 10 minutes old). But as the evidence mounts for earlier and earlier concepts and knowledge, the burden of argument shifts to the anti-nativist camps (which generally predict later onset).

An important philosophical development associated with the Chomskian revolution is Jerry Fodor's radical concept-nativism, which also has roots in Plato and Descartes. FODOR (1981) argues that no empiricist theory of concept learning is viable; all our concepts (to a first approximation) are therefore innate. He points out that empiricist theories implicitly assume that that there is a set of unlearned primitive concepts, typically sensory ones such as hard or red, and propose 'reducing' all other concepts to these (see CONCEPTS §6). However, he argues, such 'reductionist' efforts have been notorious failures, as leading empiricists including Quine (1953) and Putnam (1965) have conceded. Moreover, recent experimental studies indicate that what the empiricist would take to be complex concepts are not represented in the mind as complex mental representations. So, Fodor concludes, these too must be primitive, and therefore innate. Needless to say, these arguments have stirred substantial controversy, both about the resources of reduction, and the interpretation of these latter experimental studies.

In place of the empiricist picture of concepts learned from experience, Fodor offers a triggering model that is familiar in cognitive ethology. Ethologists have discovered that for some bird species, the young bird has only to hear some song or other for it to begin singing its species-characteristic song (see LEARNING §2). This is plainly not a matter of learning from experience; experience is more of a release or trigger. Fodor's suggestion is that concepts – like some birds' song – are innate but dormant, waiting patiently for the right experience to trigger them and bring them into cognitive play. This would doubtless be music to Socrates' ears.

See also: COGNITIVE DEVELOPMENT; INNATE KNOWLEDGE; MIND, CHILD'S THEORY OF

References and further reading

* Baillargeon, R. (1987) 'Object Permanence in 3- and 4-Month-Old Infants', *Developmental Psychology* 23: 655–64. (Study of infants' expectations about enduring physical objects.)

Carruthers, P. (1992) *Human Knowledge and Human Nature*, Oxford: Oxford University Press. (An interesting attempt to divorce nativism from classical rationalism and join it to classical empiricism.)

Chomsky, N. (1965) *Aspects of the Theory of Syntax*, Cambridge, MA: MIT Press. (Chapter 1 lays out a blueprint for linguistics that puts the question of language acquisition – and therefore of nativism – at the heart of the enterprise.)

—— (1988) *Language and Problems of Knowledge*, Cambridge, MA: MIT Press. (One of many recent expositions and defences of nativism that are accessible to the non-specialist – see especially chapters 1, 2, 5.)

Descartes, R. (1641) *Meditations on First Philosophy*, in *The Philosophical Writings of Descartes*, trans. and ed. J. Cottingham, R. Stoothoff, D. Murdoch and A. Kenny, Cambridge: Cambridge University Press, 1984–91, 3 vols. (Descartes' nativistic proof of the existence of God is in Meditation III.)

Edgley, R. (1970) 'Innate Ideas', in *Knowledge and Necessity*, Royal Institute of Philosophy Lectures, vol. 3, London: Macmillan. (Includes an important discussion of the interplay of nativism, empiricism and realism touched on at the end of §2.)

* Fodor, J. (1981) 'The Present Status of the Innateness Controversy', in *Representations*, Cambridge, MA: MIT Press. (A tour-de-force defence of a very radical form of concept nativism.)

Hook, S. (ed.) (1969) *Language and Philosophy: A Symposium*, New York: New York University Press. (Includes a number of philosophical responses – mostly negative – to Chomsky's nativism and mentalism, along with Chomsky's replies. See especially papers by Chomsky, Quine, Schwartz, Nagel, Harman and Goodman.)

* Kelman, P.J. and Spelke, E.S. (1983) 'Perception of Partially Occluded Objects in Infancy', *Cognitive Psychology* 15: 483–524. (Study of the conditions under which infants take what is given in a visual array to constitute a single object.)

Leibniz, G.W. (1704) *New Essays on Human Understanding*, trans. and ed. P. Remnant and J. Bennett, Cambridge: Cambridge University Press, 1981. (A paragraph-by-paragraph rationalist response to Locke's empiricist *Essay* (1689). The preface and first chapters are especially important.)

Locke, J. (1689) *An Essay concerning Human Understanding*, ed. P.H. Nidditch, Oxford: Oxford University Press, 1975. (Chapter 1 includes a blistering anti-nativist polemic. It has never been clear precisely whom Locke was attacking, but its effect was to make nativism a virtual dead letter for 250 years.)

* Morton, J. and Johnson, M.H. (1991) 'CONSPEC and CONLEARN: A Two-Process Theory of Infant Face Recognition', *Psychological Review* 98: 164–81. (Evidence that newborn infants have a specialized system for face recognition.)

Piattelli-Palmarini, M. (ed.) (1980) *Language and Learning*, Cambridge, MA: Harvard University Press. (Papers from a conference bringing together Piaget and Chomsky and hoping to find common ground. The conference was not successful in its stated purpose, but Chomsky and Fodor set out the nativist position(s) and the book closes with a spirited debate between these two and Hilary Putnam.)

Pinker, S. (1994) *The Language Instinct*, New York: William Morrow. (An extremely readable account of the state of the art in our understanding of language; defends the nativist view.)

* Putnam, H. (1965) 'The Analytic and the Synthetic', in *Collected Papers*, Cambridge: Cambridge University Press, vol. 2. (With Quine (1953), a classic discussion of the empiricist effort to reduce all concepts to sensory ones.)

* Quine, W.V. (1953) 'Two Dogmas of Empiricism', in *From a Logical Point of View*, New York: Harper & Row. (The seminal paper attacking the empiricist conception of meaning. Although Quine does not react to the difficulty by embracing nativism – he defends empiricism in a different way – Fodor draws his conclusions in part from this attack.)

Samet, J. (forthcoming) *Nativism*, Cambridge, MA: MIT Press. (An extended study covering all of the material in this entry (and more) in depth.)

Scott, D. (1996) *Recollection and Experience: Plato's Theory of Learning and its Successors*, Cambridge: Cambridge University Press. (Discussion of the historical nativist–empiricist debate, with special attention to the ancient world.)

Starkey, P., Spelke, E.S. and Gelman, R. (1990) 'Numerical Abstraction by Human Infants', *Cognition* 36: 97–127. (Presents evidence that infants respond differentially to visual arrays with different numerosities.)

Stich, S. (ed.) (1975) *Innate Ideas*, Berkeley, CA:

California University Press. (A very useful but out-of-print collection of historical texts and contemporary discussions of innateness, with an excellent introduction by Stich. A number of papers address the relevance of linguistics to the debate.)

* Wynn, K. (1992) 'Addition and Subtraction by Human Infants', *Nature* 358: 749–50. (Presents evidence that infants have some sort of grasp of elementary arithmetical operations.)

JERRY SAMET

NATORP, PAUL *see* NEO-KANTIANISM

NATURAL DEDUCTION, TABLEAU AND SEQUENT SYSTEMS

Different presentations of the principles of logic reflect different approaches to the subject itself. The three kinds of system discussed here treat as fundamental not logical truth, but consequence, the relation holding between the premises and conclusion of a valid argument. They are, however, inspired by different conceptions of this relation. Natural deduction rules are intended to formalize the way in which mathematicians actually reason in their proofs. Tableau systems reflect the semantic conception of consequence; their rules may be interpreted as the systematic search for a counterexample to an argument. Finally, sequent calculi were developed for the sake of their metamathematical properties.

All three systems employ rules rather than axioms. Each logical constant is governed by a pair of rules which do not involve the other constants and are, in some sense, inverse. Take the implication operator '→', for example. In natural deduction, there is an introduction rule for '→' which gives a sufficient condition for inferring an implication, and an elimination rule which gives the strongest conclusion that can be inferred from a premise having the form of an implication. Tableau systems contain a rule which gives a sufficient condition for an implication to be true, and another which gives a sufficient condition for it to be false. A sequent is an array $\Gamma \vdash \Delta$, where Γ and Δ are lists (or sets) of formulas. Sequent calculi have rules for introducing implication on the left of the '$\vdash$' symbol and on the right.

The construction of derivations or tableaus in these systems is often more concise and intuitive than in an axiomatic one, and versions of all three have found their way into introductory logic texts. Furthermore, every natural deduction or sequent derivation can be made more direct by transforming it into a 'normal form'. In the case of the sequent calculus, this result is known as the cut-elimination theorem. It has been applied extensively in metamathematics, most famously to obtain consistency proofs. The semantic inspiration for the rules of tableau construction suggests a very perspicuous proof of classical completeness, one which can also be adapted to the sequent calculus. The introduction and elimination rules of natural deduction are intuitionistically valid and have suggested an alternative semantics based on a conception of meaning as use. The idea is that the meaning of each logical constant is exhausted by its inferential behaviour and can therefore be characterized by its introduction and elimination rules.

Although the discussion below focuses on intuitionistic and classical first-order logic, various other logics have also been formulated as sequent, natural deduction and even tableau systems: modal logics, for example, relevance logic, infinitary and higher-order logics. There is a gain in understanding the role of the logical constants which comes from formulating introduction and elimination (or left and right) rules for them. Some authors have even suggested that one must be able to do so for an operator to count as logical.

1 **Natural deduction**
2 **The sequent calculus**
3 **Comparing sequents and natural deduction**
4 **Tableau systems**

1 Natural deduction

Systems of natural deduction were first devised in the late 1920s by Gerhard GENTZEN (1935), a student of Hilbert's, and, independently, by Stanislaw Jaśkowski. Their derivations formalize proofs from assumptions and are most conveniently represented as tree-like structures with the conclusion at the root and an assumption at the top of each branch. Assumptions may be discharged by the application of a rule in the course of the derivation, and the conclusion will depend only on the undischarged assumptions. Here is one formulation of the introduction and elimination rules for the usual logical operators:

(1) $\dfrac{A \quad B}{A \wedge B}$ (2) (a) $\dfrac{A \wedge B}{A}$

(b) $\dfrac{A \wedge B}{B}$

(3) (a) $\dfrac{A}{A \vee B}$ (4) $\dfrac{A \vee B \quad \overset{[A]}{C} \quad \overset{[B]}{C}}{C}$

(b) $\dfrac{B}{A \vee B}$

(5) $\dfrac{\overset{[A]}{B}}{A \rightarrow B}$ (6) $\dfrac{A \quad A \rightarrow B}{B}$

(7) $\dfrac{\overset{[A]}{\bot}}{\neg A}$ (8) $\dfrac{A \quad \neg A}{\bot}$

(9) $\dfrac{A(a)}{\forall x A(x)}$ (10) $\dfrac{\forall x A(x)}{A(a)}$

(11) $\dfrac{A(a)}{\exists x A(x)}$ (12) $\dfrac{\exists x A(x) \quad \overset{[A(a)]}{C}}{C}$

Rule (3a), for example, adds a new root to the tree, transforming a derivation of A from unspecified assumptions into a derivation of $A \vee B$ from those same assumptions. Introductions are written on the left, eliminations on the right. '$\bot$' is a constant for falsity. A formula enclosed in square brackets indicates that assumptions of this form in the derivation of the premise displayed below it may be discharged by the inference in question.

In rules (9) and (12), a cannot occur in $A(x)$ and is called the 'proper parameter' of the inference; it must satisfy the following restrictions. In (9), a cannot occur in any assumption on which the premise depends; in (12), a cannot appear in C nor in any assumption upon which the premise C depends except for those of the form $A(a)$. Because they allow the discharge of assumptions, it is better to view applications of the rules $\rightarrow$-introduction and $\vee$- and $\exists$-elimination as operating on whole derivations rather than simply on their conclusions. A similar remark can be made about $\forall$-introduction because it requires that the derivation of $A(a)$ in its premise satisfy an extra condition. This system of introductions and eliminations constitutes minimal logic. A system equivalent to Heyting's axiomatization of intuitionistic logic is obtained by adding a rule which allows any formula to be inferred from a falsehood.

$$\dfrac{\bot}{A}$$

Classical logic can be obtained by adding to the intuitionistic system as axioms all instances $A \vee \neg A$ of the law of the excluded middle, or a rule such as the following.

$$\dfrac{\neg \neg A}{A}$$

The major premise of an elimination is the formula whose principal operator is displayed in the statement of the rule. A 'maximum formula occurrence' in a derivation is both the conclusion of an introduction and the major premise of an elimination. It constitutes a needless detour and can be removed. This can be illustrated in the case of implication by the following pair of derivations (where Π_1 and Π_2 are derivations of A and B, respectively):

$$\begin{array}{ccc} & \overset{[A]}{\underset{\Pi_2}{}} & \\ \underset{\Pi_1}{} & B & \Pi_1 \\ \dfrac{A \quad A \rightarrow B}{B} & & \dfrac{A}{\underset{\Pi_2}{}} \\ & & B \end{array}$$

The one on the right is obtained from Π_2 by replacing each occurrence of the assumption A discharged by the application of $\rightarrow$-introduction by a copy of the derivation Π_1 of A. If no assumption is discharged, the derivation on the left is just replaced by Π_2. In either case, the result is a more direct derivation of the same conclusion from the same or fewer assumptions. A transformation of this kind is called a 'reduction' step, and similar reductions can be defined for the other operators. The special form of the elimination rules for '$\vee$' and '$\exists$' give rise to what are called 'maximum segments'. These consist of consecutive occurrences of the same formula such that the first is the conclusion of an introduction, the last is the major premise of an elimination and all except the first are conclusions of an application of $\vee$- or $\exists$-elimination. To remove such segments it is necessary to permute applications of $\vee$- and $\exists$-elimination with other inferences.

A derivation is said to be 'normal' if it contains no maximum formula occurrence or segment. Gentzen's normal form theorem states that for every derivation in the intuitionistic system, there is a normal one of the same conclusion from the same or fewer assumptions. It is proved by prescribing a method for systematically removing all detours from a derivation, and thus a stronger result is established – sometimes called the 'normalization theorem' – namely, that every derivation Π can be *reduced* to one in normal form. The reduction steps can be so chosen that every sufficiently long sequence of them beginning with Π terminates in a unique normal derivation. This is called the strong normalization theorem. Roughly speaking, a normal derivation is constructed by first breaking up its assumptions using eliminations and then building up its conclusion using introductions. That is why every formula appearing in the derivation will be a subformula of an assumption or the conclusion. All three forms of the theorem have been exploited to yield various proof-theoretic results for formalized mathematical theories. In addition, the significance of the normalization procedure itself has been studied in a more general context. It has been argued that the steps required to reduce a derivation to normal form do not change its meaning. In consequence, derivations which reduce to the same normal form have the same meaning or express the same proof. More controversially, the converse has also been claimed to hold.

2   The sequent calculus

The theorems discussed at the end of the previous section do not extend straightforwardly from the intuitionistic to the classical version of natural deduction. By exploiting the definability of disjunction and existential quantification in classical logic, however, they can be shown to hold for a system of natural deduction adequate for classical logic. A rather more sophisticated argument is required to establish them for a classical natural deduction calculus in which all the usual logical constants are taken as primitive. Gentzen, however, did not extend his theorem to the classical system described above. He chose rather to reformulate it as a calculus of sequents. It is a trivial matter to rewrite the introductions and eliminations as sequent rules by placing the assumptions on which a formula depends on the left-hand side of the sequent. The rules for '→', for example, will look as follows.

$$\frac{A,\Gamma \vdash B}{\Gamma \vdash A \to B} \qquad \frac{\Gamma \vdash A \to B \quad \Delta \vdash A}{\Gamma,\Delta \vdash B}$$

Although assumptions have been eliminated in favour of axioms of the form $A \vdash A$, nothing else of significance has been changed. In fact, the resulting calculus is just a notational variant of natural deduction. Gentzen's idea was to rewrite only the introduction rules in this way, and to replace the eliminations by new rules for introducing a formula on the left side of a sequent. These left rules are displayed below. (a cannot occur anywhere in the conclusion of the last rule.)

$$\frac{A,\Gamma \vdash C}{A \wedge B,\Gamma \vdash C} \qquad \frac{B,\Gamma \vdash C}{A \wedge B,\Gamma \vdash C}$$

$$\frac{A,\Gamma \vdash C \quad B,\Gamma \vdash C}{A \vee B,\Gamma \vdash C}$$

$$\frac{\Gamma \vdash A \quad B,\Delta \vdash C}{A \to B,\Gamma,\Delta \vdash C}$$

$$\frac{\Gamma \vdash A}{\neg A,\Gamma \vdash}$$

$$\frac{A(a),\Gamma \vdash C}{\forall x A(x),\Gamma \vdash C}$$

$$\frac{A(a),\Gamma \vdash C}{\exists x A(x),\Gamma \vdash C}$$

The rules may be read in different ways. Their connection with natural deduction is best brought out by interpreting the symbol '⊢' as derivability. Then the last of them, for example, asserts that a derivation of C from $A(a),\Gamma$ can be transformed into one of C from $\exists x A(x),\Gamma$ (subject to the restriction on a).

In addition, Gentzen introduced some structural rules: 'interchange' for permuting formulas on a list, 'contraction' for amalgamating two occurrences of the same formula, and 'thinning' or 'weakening' for adding formulas to a list. Because an empty list on the right of a sequent can be interpreted as falsity, there is no longer any need for the constant '⊥'. Furthermore, the intuitionistic negation rule can now be derived because thinning on the right justifies the inference from $\Gamma \vdash$ to $\Gamma \vdash A$. In the presence of the structural rules, it does not matter whether the left rule for '∨' is formulated as above or as follows.

$$\frac{A,\Gamma \vdash C \quad B,\Delta \vdash C}{A \vee B,\Gamma,\Delta \vdash C}$$

And likewise for the other two premise rules, both left and right. Recently J.-Y. Girard, in his work on linear logic (see Girard 1995), has embarked upon a searching investigation of the proof-theoretic significance of the structural rules, and of the consequences of omitting or weakening them in various ways. In their absence, he distinguishes two versions of disjunction, for example: an additive and a multiplicative one according to which formulation of its left rule is adopted.

3   Comparing sequents and natural deduction

It is easy to translate a derivation of the sequent $\Gamma \vdash A$ into a derivation in natural deduction of A from assumptions included in the list Γ – into a normal one, in fact. Call this derivation its $\mathcal{N}$ translation. Applications of right rules translate directly into introductions. The situation with left rules is only slightly more complicated. Consider conjunction, for example, and suppose that Π is the $\mathcal{N}$ translation of a derivation of $A, \Gamma \vdash C$, then the required derivation of C from assumptions in $A \wedge B, \Gamma$ is obtained by substituting copies of the two-line derivation

(†)
$$\frac{A \wedge B}{A}$$

for the appropriate occurrences of the assumption A in Π.

Converting natural deduction derivations into sequent ones is less straightforward. Introductions correspond as before to applications of a right rule. To translate eliminations, however, we need not only the corresponding left rule, but also a rule called 'cut'.

$$\frac{\Gamma \vdash A \quad A, \Delta \vdash C}{\Gamma, \Delta \vdash C}$$

With the addition of this rule every sequent derivation will still have an $\mathcal{N}$ translation, although we can no longer be sure that it will be normal. The $\mathcal{N}$ translation of a derivation which ends with the cut displayed above is obtained by substituting copies of the $\mathcal{N}$ translation of the derivation of its left premise for the appropriate occurrences of the assumption A in the $\mathcal{N}$ translation of the derivation of its right one.

To see why cut is needed for translating the elimination rules, consider again the case of conjunction and suppose that we have already succeeded in translating a derivation Π of $A \wedge B$ from assumptions Γ into a derivation δ of the sequent $\Gamma \vdash A \wedge B$. Then what needs to be shown is that δ can be converted into a derivation of $\Gamma \vdash A$. This is accomplished by a cut applied to the conclusions of δ and a derivation whose $\mathcal{N}$ translation is (†) above, as shown in the following figure.

$$\frac{\delta \qquad A \vdash A}{\dfrac{\Gamma \vdash A \wedge B \quad A \wedge B \vdash A}{\Gamma \vdash A}}$$

This translation exploits the fact that the result of applying $\wedge$-elimination to Π is the same as substituting Π for the assumption $A \wedge B$ in the derivation (†) above. The other elimination rules are handled similarly.

Clearly, every formula appearing in the premise(s) of a left or right rule is a subformula of a formula appearing in its conclusion, and the same holds for the structural rules. Consequently, any derivation constructed only by the use of these rules will be such that it contains only subformulas of formulas occurring in its final sequent. Gentzen's normal form theorem in this context takes the form of a cut-elimination theorem, and he was able to prove that

every derivation can be transformed into a cut-free derivation of the same sequent. His proof, although similar in kind to the one for natural deduction, does involve additional complications. Furthermore, cut-free forms are not in general unique. It would appear therefore that little advantage has been gained by passing from natural deduction to a sequent calculus, especially since sequent derivations are for the most part less intuitive.

In favour of sequent derivations is the fact that the absence of assumptions makes them easier to work with from a metamathematical standpoint. To verify the correctness of a sequent derivation it is enough to check it locally, that is, to look at each sequent and its immediate successors individually. There are no global conditions on the derivation that need to be satisfied (as, for example, that a certain parameter cannot appear in any assumption). This also makes coding derivations by means of Gödel numbers much easier. A more significant advantage, however, concerns the relationship between the calculus described above and classical logic. Gentzen observed that, by the simple expedient of allowing a list containing more than one formula to appear on the right-hand side of a sequent, he could obtain a system adequate for classical logic. The classical versions of the right and left rules for '$\rightarrow$', for example, read as follows.

$$\frac{A, \Gamma \vdash \Delta, B}{\Gamma \vdash \Delta, A \rightarrow B} \qquad \frac{\Gamma \vdash \Delta, A \quad B, \Psi \vdash \Phi}{A \rightarrow B, \Gamma, \Psi \vdash \Delta, \Phi}$$

All the remaining rules, including cut, are similarly generalized; no new rules need to be added. To see that the resulting calculus is adequate for classical logic, note that the sequent $\vdash A \vee \neg A$ is now easily derivable. Applying $\neg$-right to $A \vdash A$ yields $\vdash A, \neg A$, from which the desired sequent follows by two applications of $\vee$-right and a couple of structural inferences. It is possible therefore to give a single proof of the cut-elimination theorem for both classical and intuitionistic systems. The proof for the classical system involves no new ideas, and it specializes immediately to a proof for the intuitionistic one. One need simply observe that each reduction prescribed in the proof yields an intuitionistic derivation when applied to one.

Gentzen's theorem has been fruitfully applied to yield a variety of results in proof theory. The Craig interpolation theorem, for example, follows from it easily, as do various decidability results. Gentzen himself utilized the method of cut elimination to prove the consistency of formal number theory, that is, of a system obtained by augmenting the sequent calculus with appropriate arithmetical principles. (In fact, his original proof was for a theory based on natural deduction, but he subsequently rewrote it for the sequent calculus.) His methods have since been adapted and extended, in many different ways and to a variety of different situations. A version of the cut-elimination theorem for second-order logic, for example, has yielded a consistency proof for analysis, formalized as a theory of second-order arithmetic (see PROOF THEORY §4). The information provided by results such as these depends upon the methods required to establish them, and their significance is understood differently in different foundational traditions. Nevertheless, there is no doubt that the methods pioneered by Gentzen have been one of the mainstays of proof theory in the tradition of Hilbert, as it has developed in the wake of Gödel's theorems.

Although cut-free derivations are in some sense simpler and more direct than their counterparts containing cuts, the elimination procedure described by Gentzen increases the length of a derivation each time a cut is removed from it. Furthermore, this turns out to be an essential feature of any cut-elimination procedure. The same holds true for the elimination of maximum formula occurrences from natural deduction derivations and, as one might expect, the efficiency of the tableau method described below is correspondingly increased when an analogue to the cut rule is added to the system. This simple fact has given rise to a great deal of research on the complexity of derivations, and very refined bounds on the length of cut-free ones have been established for a variety of systems and theories. The subject of complexity has attracted particular attention from researchers interested in implementing automated reasoning systems (see COMPLEXITY, COMPUTATIONAL).

4   Tableau systems

The discussion of the previous sections was based on an interpretation of the sequent calculus as characterizing the relation of derivability under assumptions in natural deduction. With the passage from intuitionistic to classical sequents, this interpretation is no longer possible. The classical rules are easily seen to be correct under a semantic interpretation, however, according to which $\Gamma \vdash \Delta$ is taken to mean that for every model of Γ there is at least one formula in Δ that is true in it. If the rules are read backwards, from conclusion to premise(s), they represent steps in the search for a counterexample to $\Gamma \vdash \Delta$, a model in which all the formulas in Γ are true, while all those in Δ are false. To find a counterexample to $\Gamma \vdash \Delta, A \wedge B$, for example, we may search in one of two directions, either for a counterexample to $\Gamma \vdash \Delta, A$ or for one to $\Gamma \vdash \Delta, B$. The first person to exploit this feature of the rules seems to have been E.W. Beth. It underlies the tableau system for classical logic which he formulated

in the mid-fifties (see his later work of 1964 for details). However, the general idea of a no-counter-example treatment of logic is also to be found in the works of other logicians of the period, including J. Hintikka, S. Kanger and K. Schütte.

A semantic tableau for the sequent $\Gamma \vdash \Delta$ begins as a figure consisting of two columns, with the formulas in Γ listed at the head of the left one and the formulas in Δ at the head of the right. The rules extend the tableau by operating on individual formulas in these lists. A left rule operates on A in Γ and allows us to enter into the tableau subformulas of A in such a way that the truth of the left entries together with the falsity of the right ones together constitute a sufficient condition for A to be true. Similarly, a right rule operates on A in Δ and allows us to enter subformulas whose truth and falsity are sufficient for A to be false. As before, there are pairs of rules for each of the logical constants, and some of these rules require the tableau to split into a pair of subtableaus, each with its own left and right column. Since all the classical connectives and quantifiers are definable in terms of '¬', '→' and '∃', it will be sufficient to list tableau rules for just these three operators:

If $\neg A$ appears in the left column, write A in the right one.

If $\neg A$ appears in the right column, write A in the left one.

If $A \rightarrow B$ appears in the left column, split the tableau into two subtableaus, write B in the left column of one subtableau and A in the right column of the other.

If $A \rightarrow B$ appears in the right column, write B below it and A in the left column.

If $\exists x A(x)$ appears in the left column, write $A(a)$ in the left column, where a is a new parameter.

If $\exists x A(x)$ appears in the right column, write $A(a)$ in the right column, where a is any parameter that has already been introduced into the tableau (or a new one if none has been introduced).

The left rule for '→', for example, reflects the fact that in classical logic there are two ways to verify an implication: its antecedent may be false or its consequent true. The right rule reflects the fact that there is only one way to refute one: its antecedent must be true and its consequent false. In all cases except the last, the formula to which the rule has been applied is cancelled to indicate that the rule cannot be applied to it again. In the case of right '∃', the possibility of applying the rule with respect to a different parameter is left open. A subtableau is closed if there is at least one formula which occurs in both its left and right column. A tableau is closed if all its subtableaus are closed. $\Gamma \vdash \Delta$ is derivable if it has a closed tableau. Finally, a tableau has been terminated if it is not closed, but no further rules are applicable to any of its subtableaus.

By way of example, the following closed tableau establishes the validity of the sequent

$$\neg \exists x \neg (A(x) \to B) \vdash \exists x A(x) \to B.$$

$\neg \exists x \neg (A(x) \to B)$	$\exists x A(x) \to B$
$\exists x A(x)$	B
$A(a)$	
	$\exists x \neg (A(x) \to B)$
	$\neg (A(a) \to B)$
$A(a) \to B$	
^{1} $\quad$ ^{2} B	^{1} $A(a)$ $\quad$ ^{2}

Each line is obtained from a previous one by applying one of the rules for tableau construction. Notice that the initial tableau splits into two subtableaus after line six. (The first and third cells of line seven are the left and right columns of one, the second and fourth of the other.) Both subtableaus are closed, the one because $A(a)$ appears on the left in line three and on the right in line seven, and the other because B appears on the right in line two and on the left in line seven.

The rules for tableau construction are really nothing other than upside-down versions of the classical sequent rules. Indeed, one need do little more than invert a closed tableau to convert it into a cut-free derivation in the sequent calculus. There is no need to augment the tableau rules by a rule analogous to cut because their deductive adequacy can be demonstrated directly without reference to the derivations of any other system. The rules may be applied to a sequent in any order (although it is convenient to postpone applying right '∃' for as long as possible) and three possibilities can arise:

(1) The tableau closes after a finite number of steps, in which case the disjunction of the formulas in Δ is a classical consequence of the formulas in Γ.

(2) The tableau is terminated after a finite number of steps. This will be because every uncancelled formula (other than existential ones to which right '∃' is no longer applicable) is atomic. It is then easy to construct a model in which each atomic formula appearing on the left of an open subtableau is true and each one appearing on the right is false. Such a model turns out to be a counterexample to the original sequent in the

sense that all the formulas in Γ are true in it while those in Δ are false.

(3) The tableau is never terminated. This possibility arises because right '∃' may be applied repeatedly to a formula as needed. Nevertheless, as Beth showed, we can prove generally that a counterexample can also be constructed from any such infinite tableau.

The upshot is that the rules of tableau construction provide a complete proof procedure for classical logic. Despite their semantic motivation, it should be emphasized that these are purely syntactic rules – and hence that there is a cut-free derivation of every derivable sequent in the sequent calculus as well. This semantic approach to the cut-elimination theorem is less elementary than Gentzen's original proof. More significantly, however, the connection between a derivation and its cut-free form is lost.

Because tableaus may split into subtableaus, the method is cumbersome to use. A considerable simplification was effected by Raymond Smullyan, who introduced the idea of 'signed' formulas. Given $\Gamma \vdash \Delta$, the formulas in Γ receive the sign T and those in Δ the sign F. A tableau now begins with a single list of signed formulas, and left and right rules are reformulated as rules for formulas with the signs T and F respectively. The result is a single tree, rather than a series of tableaus, which branches instead of splitting. A closed branch will contain an occurrence of some formula A with the sign T and another occurrence with the sign F, and a tree is closed when every branch is closed. (Alternatively, one can dispense with signs and form a single list from the formulas in Γ together with the negations of those in Δ.) It is in this form, rather than the original one, that the tableau method has found its way into the literature. An analogous modification of the sequent calculus was introduced by Kurt Schütte. Here the effect is to make derivations less intuitive, although the calculus is more concise and better suited for some applications.

Just as natural deduction seems to be a more appropriate system for intuitionistic logic, so tableaus seem better adapted to express classical consequence. Nevertheless, as Beth showed, they can be modified to yield a proof procedure for intuitionistic logic. Subsequently, tableau techniques were extended to modal systems, by Kripke among others, and what are now called Kripke models have their origin in constructions deriving from these.

See also: LOGICAL AND MATHEMATICAL TERMS, GLOSSARY OF

References and further reading

* Beth, E.W. (1964) *The Foundations of Mathematics*, Amsterdam: North Holland; New York: Harper & Row, 2nd edn, 1966. (§§67–70, 144–5 include accounts of tableaus for classical and intuitionistic logic, respectively; one of the few places where tableaus are presented in their original two-column form.)

Boolos, G. (1984) 'Don't Eliminate Cut', *Journal of Philosophical Logic* 13: 373–8. (Includes a striking illustration of just how much shorter than its cut-free counterpart a derivation with cut can be.)

Došen, K. (1993) 'A Historical Introduction to Substructural Logics', in K. Došen and P. Schroeder-Heister (eds) *Substructural Logics*, Oxford: Clarendon Press, 1–30. (A brief and readable survey of the motivations for and effects of restricting structural rules in sequent calculi, with a useful bibliography.)

Fitting, M. (1983) *Proof Methods for Modal and Intuitionistic Logics*, Dordrecht: Reidel. (A thorough and self-contained presentation of natural deduction, sequent and tableau methods for a variety of logics, including classical.)

* Gentzen, G. (1935) 'Untersuchungen über das logische Schließen', *Mathematische Zeitschrift* 39: 176– 210, 405–565; repr. Darmstadt: Wissenschaftliche Buchgesellschaft, 1969; trans. in *The Collected Papers of Gerhard Gentzen*, ed. M.E. Szabo, Amsterdam and London: North Holland, 1969, 68–131. (Gentzen's original, and very readable, account of sequent and natural deduction systems for classical and intuitionistic logic.)

* Girard, J.-Y. (1995) 'Linear Logic: Its Syntax and Semantics', in J.-Y. Girard, Y. Lafont and L. Regnier (eds) *Advances in Linear Logic*, Cambridge: Cambridge University Press, 1–42. (An introductory, albeit challenging, account of linear logic by its originator.)

Kleene, S.C. (1967) *Mathematical Logic*, New York: Wiley. (Chapter 4 describes a very direct proof of the completeness of the classical cut-free sequent rules.)

Prawitz, D. (1965) *Natural Deduction: A Proof-Theoretical Study*, Uppsala: Almqvist & Wiksell. (A thorough but elementary presentation of natural deduction and the normalization theorem.)

—— (1971) 'Ideas and Results in Proof Theory', in J.E. Fenstad (ed.) *Proceedings of the Second Scandinavian Logic Symposium*, Amsterdam: North Holland, 235–307. (A survey of some proof-theoretic applications of natural deduction.)

Schwichtenberg, H. (1977) 'Proof Theory: Some Applications of Cut-Elimination', in J. Barwise (ed.) *Handbook of Mathematical Logic*, Amsterdam: North Holland, 867–95. (A survey of some proof-theoretic applications of the sequent calculus; requires more background than the previous item.)

Stålmarck, G. (1991) 'Normalization Theorems for Full First Order Classical Natural Deduction', *Journal of Symbolic Logic* 56 (1): 129–49. (This article is rather technical.)

Sundholm, G. (1983) 'Systems of Deduction', in D. Gabbay and F. Guenthner (eds) *Handbook of Philosophical Logic*, Dordrecht: Reidel, vol. 1, 133–88. (A more detailed survey of the systems discussed in this article, with a useful bibliography; recommended as the next thing to read.)

—— (1986) 'Proof Theory and Meaning', in D. Gabbay and F. Guenthner (eds) *Handbook of Philosophical Logic*, Dordrecht: Reidel, vol. 3, 471–506. (Another well-written survey article; explains how natural deduction and related systems may contribute to a theory of meaning which does not depend on the notion of truth.)

A.M. UNGAR

NATURAL KINDS

Objects belonging to a natural kind form a group of objects which have some theoretically important property in common. For example, rabbits form a natural kind, all samples of gold form another, and so on. Natural kinds are contrasted with arbitrary groups of objects such as the contents of dustbins, or collections of jewels. The latter have no theoretically important property in common: they have no unifying feature. Natural kinds provide a system for classifying objects. Scientists can then use this system to predict and explain the behaviour of those objects. For these reasons, the topic of natural kinds is of special interest to metaphysics and to the philosophy of science.

1   The notion of natural kinds
2   Two major questions
3   Essentialism
4   Conventionalism

1   The notion of natural kinds

Objects belonging to a natural kind form a group of objects which have some theoretically important property, or properties, in common. Standard examples of natural kinds include biological species such as rabbits, oaks and whales, chemical elements and compounds such as oxygen, carbon and aluminium, and stuffs such as salt, wool and heat. An object's membership of a given natural kind bears upon how that object will behave, the properties it can or cannot acquire, and the types of interaction in which it can figure. Natural kinds thereby provide a scheme of classification for science to chart (see TAXONOMY). Scientists can use such a system to predict, explain and (perhaps) control the behaviour of those objects. Knowledge of natural kinds can also provide a basis for inductive and counterfactual scientific reasoning: knowledge about how past members of a natural kind behaved may warrant beliefs about how present or future members of that kind will behave, as well as how hypothetical members of that kind would behave.

Closely related is the question regarding which predicates are 'projectible': the question of which predicates are admissible in inductive reasoning. Predicates such as 'is a rabbit' and 'is an oak' are admissible, but not every predicate is. The predicate 'is a roak', which is hereby defined as being true of an object if and only if it is a rabbit or an oak, seems inadmissible. The notion of a natural kind may help in explicating this distinction between projectible and non-projectible predicates (see GOODMAN, N. §3).

Again, a theory's terms are apparently open to deviant interpretations. A theory containing (say) the predicate 'is a rabbit' is standardly interpreted as meaning rabbit, but this predicate can be deviantly interpreted as meaning (say) rabbit or oak. To meet this problem, we might invoke the principle that among meaning assignments we should prefer those in which the assigned meaning concerns natural kinds, rather than non-natural ones.

2 Two major questions

The topic of natural kinds raises two major related questions. There is a metaphysical question: what is a natural kind? Natural kinds are standardly distinguished from arbitrary groups of objects, such as what you had for breakfast. They are also standardly distinguished from so-called artefact kinds such as books, tables or cars. A full account of the metaphysics of natural kinds should clarify these distinctions and explain the rationale behind them. Furthermore, it should explain the sense in which different members of a natural kind have a property in common. On one possible account, different members of a natural kind share a universal: they have a property which is literally identical between them (see UNIVERSALS). But on a rival account, different members of a kind have a property in common only in the sense that each member bears a certain similarity relation to every other member of the kind.

There is also an epistemological question: how do we tell what natural kinds there are? Every object has many properties, yet we think that only some properties determine natural kinds. But what reasons guide our thinking that certain properties rather than others determine natural kinds? Furthermore, our beliefs about what natural kinds there are, and which objects belong to them, may be inaccurate to some degree. These beliefs may only approximately describe what natural kinds there are, and what their members are. But then how are we to establish how accurate these beliefs are?

Such metaphysical and epistemological questions are also of interest outside philosophy. For instance, it is a live issue among biologists whether species are natural kinds, and there is a further issue of whether it is morphological, reproductive or phylogenetic factors which determine a creature's membership of a given species (see SPECIES).

3 Essentialism

Locke (1689) and, following him, Kripke (1972) and Putnam (1975), each offer an account of how our understanding of a given natural kind can develop over time. At an initial stage, speakers classify certain objects as members of the same natural kind because they perceive those objects to have certain properties in common. Such common properties form the 'nominal essence' (Locke) or 'stereotype' (Putnam) associated with that kind. The speakers, however, further believe that these objects are members of the same natural kind if and only if they have some underlying, though perhaps currently unknown, common property. This is the 'real essence' of that kind. In the case of chemical elements, it will perhaps be some microstructural property. In the case of organisms, it will perhaps be some genetic structure. Moreover, given how laws of nature relate a kind's real essence to its nominal essence, an object's real essence explains why that object has the nominal essence that it does. It then falls to empirical science to discover the real essences of objects.

In sum, an object's nominal essence serves as a heuristic, a guide for thinking whether that object is a member of a certain natural kind. But whether in fact that object is a member of the kind in question is determined by whether it has the appropriate real essence. For instance, various objects may once have been classified as members of the natural kind lemon because of their yellow appearance, tart taste, thick skin and oval shape. These properties form the kind's nominal essence. However, scientific inquiry may subsequently reveal the real essence of lemons – a common genetic structure, let us suppose. Since something is a lemon if and only if it has this genetic structure, we may revise to some degree our original classification of which objects are lemons. On this view, fruit which are superficially similar to lemons but which have a different genetic structure, are not lemons. In contrast, unripe, mouldy, or squashed fruit with the same genetic structure as lemons are lemons, even though superficially they do not appear to be so.

Kripke and Putnam further argue that it is (metaphysically) necessary that something is a member of a given kind if and only if it has a certain real essence. Hence if the real essence of, for example, gold is a certain atomic number, then, necessarily, something is gold if and only if it has that atomic number. Kripke and Putnam conclude that there are certain *de re* necessities which can be discovered only empirically (see DE RE/DE DICTO; ESSENTIALISM). Other philosophers have since argued that essentialism about natural kinds entails that the laws of nature which govern kinds are also *de re* necessary.

4 Conventionalism

Kripke and Putnam assume that what natural kinds there are, and which objects are members of those kinds, are matters which obtain independently of our attempts at classification. Conventionalism about natural kinds denies this assumption. It says that our classification of objects into natural kinds does not reflect any pre-existing divisions in nature. Instead, it is based on human convenience, and its goal is the prediction and control of observable events, not the discovery of underlying essences.

Locke ultimately took this view. Frequently, he is interpreted as taking it for an epistemological reason, namely that real essences, if there are any, would be unobservable and so unknowable. More recently, Bas van Fraassen (1980) has taken a similar view, but for a different reason, believing that science need be concerned only with observable entities, and so not with real essences. Hence the latter are redundant: they are 'metaphysical baggage'. The dispute between realists and conventionalists about natural kinds is then located within the more general dispute between scientific realism (which claims that science describes an unobservable world) and constructive empiricism (which is agnostic about whether science does this). A further reason for scepticism about essentialism about natural kinds, and one which Locke and van Fraassen share, is a suspicion of what *de re* or metaphysical necessity is supposed to be. The suspicion is that the thesis that there are necessities in nature is obscure, and that instead the only source of necessity lies in human conventions. Accordingly, the thesis that objects have real essences in virtue of which they are

members of certain natural kinds is held to be infected with this obscurity.

See also: MASS TERMS; REFERENCE §§3–4

References and further reading

Ayers, M. (1981) 'Locke versus Aristotle on Natural Kinds', *Journal of Philosophy* 78 (5): 247–72. (Careful and thorough discussion of Locke's views on the topic.)

* Fraassen, B. van (1980) *The Scientific Image*, Oxford: Clarendon Press. (Chapters 1–3 present van Fraassen's brand of empiricism.)

Goodman, N. (1954) *Fact, Fiction, and Forecast*, Cambridge, MA: Harvard University Press. (See chapters 2 and 3 for the problem of projectibility and one possible solution.)

Kornblith, H. (1992) *Inductive Inference and its Natural Ground*, Cambridge, MA: MIT Press. (Part I presents a response to Locke's views. Part II is an extended discussion of the epistemological issues concerning natural kinds.)

* Kripke, S. (1972) 'Naming and Necessity', in D. Davidson and G. Harman (eds) *Semantics of Natural Language*, Dordrecht: Reidel, 253–355; repr. Cambridge, MA: Harvard University Press and Oxford University Press, 1980. (Kripke's views on natural kinds and natural-kind terms are developed from his more general views about how names refer. Lecture III presents his views on natural kinds, but begins with a helpful summary of the conclusions reached in the preceding lectures.)

* Locke, J. (1689) *An Essay Concerning Human Understanding*, Oxford: Oxford University Press, 1975. (Locke's views on natural kinds are found particularly in book 2 chapter 27, and in book 3 chapters 3 and 6.)

* Putnam, H. (1975) *Mind, Language, and Reality: Philosophical Papers volume II*, Cambridge: Cambridge University Press. (Chapters 8, and 10–12 are relevant and best read in that order.)

Riggs, P. (ed.) (1996) *Natural Kinds, Laws of Nature, and Scientific Methodology*, Dordrecht: Kluwer Academic Press. (Collection of papers including sophisticated defences of essentialism about both natural kinds and laws of nature.)

Schwartz, S.P. (ed.) (1977) *Naming, Necessity, and Natural Kinds*, London and Ithaca, NY: Cornell University Press. (Collection which reprints important papers by Kripke, Putnam, and others. It also contains a helpful introduction and a comprehensive bibliography.)

Wilkerson, T.E. (1995) *Natural Kinds*, Aldershot:

Avebury Press. (Lucid defence of essentialism about both natural kinds and laws of nature.)

Wolfram, S. (1989) *Philosophical Logic: An Introduction*, London and New York: Routledge. (Chapter 7 §1 is extremely clear and a good place to start. The end of the chapter lists further reading.)

CHRIS DALY

NATURAL LAW

When made within the discourse of ethics, political theory, or legal theory or philosophy of law, the claim that there is a natural law is an offer to explain and defend certain claims often made, in different terms, in the discourse of moral argument, politics or law. In pretheoretical moral discourse, certain choices, actions or dispositions may be asserted to be 'inhuman', 'unnaturally cruel', 'perverse' or 'morally unreasonable'. In pretheoretical political discourse, certain proposals, policies or conduct may be described as violations of 'human rights'. In international law and jurisprudence, certain actions may be described as 'crimes against humanity' and citizens may claim immunity from legal liability or obligations by appealing to a 'higher law'. A natural law theory offers to explain why claims of this sort can be rationally warranted and true. It offers to do so by locating such claims in the context of a general theory of good and evil in human life so far as human life is shaped by deliberation and choice. Such a general theory can also be called a general theory of right and wrong in human choices and actions. It will contain both (1) normative propositions identifying types of choice, action or disposition as right or wrong, permissible, obligatory and so on, and (2) nonnormative propositions about the objectivity and epistemological warrant of the normative propositions.

1 **Why called natural? Why called law?**
2 **Critique of scepticism and dogmatism**
3 **Cognitivism and natural law theories**
4 **Derivation of positive law**
5 **Inviolable human rights**

1 Why called natural? Why called law?

Theorists who describe their theory of good and evil, right and wrong, as a 'natural law theory' are not committed to asserting that the normative propositions which they defend are 'derived from nature' or 'read off' or 'inspected in the nature of things'. Still less are natural law theorists committed to claiming that the normative propositions they defend stand in

some definite relationship to, or are warranted by, the 'laws of nature' in the sense of the regularities observed, and explanatory factors adduced, by the 'natural sciences'. Nor is the typical natural law theory (classical, medieval or contemporary) concerned with any alleged 'state of nature', in the sense of some golden age or state of affairs prior to human wrongdoing or to the formation of human societies or of states or political communities (see Laws, NATURAL).

As for the term 'law', as understood in the phrase 'natural law', it does not connote that the relevant principles and norms have their directive force precisely as the imperatives or dictates of a superior will. Even when a natural law theorist argues (as most do) that the ultimate explanation of those principles and norms (as of all other realities) is a transcendent, creative, divine source of existence, meaning and value, the theorist usually will maintain also that moral precepts divinely commanded are commanded because fitting and obligatory, not fitting or obligatory because commanded (or that the source of their obligation is rather divine wisdom than divine will). Rather, the term 'law' in the phrase 'natural law' refers to standards of right choosing, standards which are normative, that is rationally directive and 'obligatory', because they are true and choice otherwise than in accordance with them is unreasonable.

The term 'natural' in this context signifies any one or more of the following: that the relevant standards are not 'positive', that is, are directive prior to any positing by individual decision or group choice or convention; that the relevant standards are 'higher' than positive laws, conventions and practices, that is, provide the premises for critical evaluation and endorsement or justified rejection of or disobedience to such laws, conventions or practices; that the relevant standards conform to the most demanding requirements of critical reason and are objective, in the sense that a person who fails to accept them as standards for judgment is in error; that adherence to the relevant standards tends systematically to promote human flourishing, the fulfilment of human individuals and communities.

2 Critique of scepticism and dogmatism

Historically, natural law theories have been articulated as part or product of a philosophical critique of ethical scepticisms (see SCEPTICISM), and have included in their critique a differentiation of the rationally grounded norms of natural law from moral dogmatism or conventionalism. In contemporary thought, scepticism about natural law (and about all moral theories claiming to be objective or true) is very often based upon a logically illicit and rationally unwarranted inference from certain propositions about what 'is' the case to certain propositions about what is good or obligatory. This particular form of invalid reasoning was assiduously employed in the ancient manuals of scepticism (notably by Sextus Empiricus, *c.* AD 200), and reintroduced into European discourse in the sixteenth century. Sextus Empiricus uses the term 'dogmatism' to insinuate that all non-sceptical ethical theories, such as natural law theory, are uncritical; but this charge is not well grounded, and the term is used here to refer to moral positions held without openness to critical questions.

Examples of the invalid reasoning commonly encountered include:

X is not universally regarded as good/obligatory; therefore X is not good/obligatory.

In modern thought X is widely regarded as not good/obligatory; therefore X is not good/obligatory.

In contemporary society X is widely regarded as good/obligatory; therefore X is good/obligatory.

I have a sentiment of approval of X; therefore X is good (or worthwhile...or obligatory...), at least for me.

I have opted for or decided upon or am committed to the practical principle that X ought to be done; therefore X ought to be done, at least by me.

As this list of *non sequiturs* suggests, there is a link between ethical scepticism (at least in its popular forms) and ethical conventionalism. There are many natural law theories, on the other hand, which are not guilty of these or other fallacies, fallacies that consist in concluding to a normative judgment from premises which include no normative proposition.

David Hume (1740) suggests that 'every system of morality' prior to his critique illogically purports to infer ought or ought not from is or is not (see HUME, D.). The suggestion is ungrounded, though the illicit inference may perhaps be detected in certain eighteenth-century rationalists (especially Samuel Clarke) whom Hume seems to have had prominently in mind when writing this part of his *Treatise*. In so far as Hume's predominant view concerning the nature and basis of moral judgments was that they are judgments about what characteristics and actions arouse approval or disapproval, Hume was himself plainly guilty of this kind of illegitimate inference. The same cannot be said of Plato, Aristotle and Aquinas, for example.

Max WEBER is often, and with some plausibility, said to have introduced the modern form of the 'fact/value distinction' and denial of the 'objectivity of value judgments'. Weber's primary argument for this denial seems to have been simply that people, or educated people, in fact disagree with each other about values. This argument has no more validity than the popular arguments listed above; the fact of disagreement no more disproves a proposition than the fact of agreement proves it. Weber had three other lines of argument. The first was a Neo-Kantian argument that all judgments must rest upon presuppositions, and that selection among competing presuppositions must be non-rational. This argument is self-refuting in its general form, and there is no way to limit it (as Weber sought to do) to judgments of value. Weber's next argument pointed, like Sartre after him, to certain supposed political and/or ethical dilemmas before which reason is supposed to fall silent. In fact, however, such 'dilemmas' are no more than a stimulus to a more nuanced and resourceful practical reasoning, which may identify more than one option as morally acceptable in the situation. Weber's final argument alleged that there are distinct and incommensurable 'spheres' of practical judgment, such as the political, the erotic and the ethical, each with its own ultimate values between which reason cannot adjudicate because reason operates only within spheres. This final claim is never defended by Weber, and is contradicted by his own acknowledgement that the spheres interpenetrate one another.

Perhaps the most fruitful critique of ethical scepticism is one which takes its cue from Aristotle's critique of general scepticism (*Metaphysics* IV). If sceptics are willing to affirm their position as rationally warranted they can be shown to be denying (1) something given, instantiated, in the activity of rationally considering and proposing their or any other position, and/or (2) some proposition to which their assertion of their position rationally commits them. In the case in hand, the relevant givens include the rationality norms which guide the rational inquiries of those who choose to follow them and to resist temptations to reach conclusions by subrational processes; and the propositions to which an argued assertion commits the person asserting it include the proposition that knowledge of truth (at least the truth of such propositions as the one asserted) is a good worth pursuing and instantiating in that argument and assertion, a good worthwhile for its own sake as well as for any instrumental advantage it might yield.

3   Cognitivism and natural law theories

Not every non-sceptical ethics is appropriately called a natural law theory. Natural law theories are distinguished from the broader set of cognitivist or objectivist ethical theories in four main ways.

First, they are differentiated from any ethics in a Kantian mould by their willingness to identify certain basic human goods, such as knowledge, life and health, and friendship, as the core of substantive first principles of practical reasoning (see KANTIAN ETHICS). Taken together, these basic human goods give shape and content to a conception of human flourishing and thus, too, to a conception of human nature. For an axiom of Aristotle's method, deployed more generally by Aquinas, shows that while nature is metaphysically (ontologically) fundamental, knowledge of a thing's nature is epistemically derivative: an animate thing's nature is understood by understanding its capacities, its capacities by understanding its activities, and its activities by understanding the objects of those activities. In the case of the human being the 'objects' which must be understood before one can understand and know human nature are the basic goods which are the objects of one's will, that is, one's basic reasons for acting, that give reason for everything which one can intelligently take an interest in choosing.

Second, natural law theories are distinguished from any theory which asserts that moral truths are known essentially by discrete 'intuitions' (see INTUITIONISM IN ETHICS §3). Rather, these theories argue that specific moral judgments concerning obligation or right are applications or specifications of higher principles. The first principles of the 'system' are known by insight without deduction via any middle term (they are *per se nota*: Aquinas, *Summa theologiae* IaIIae.94. 2). But the insights whose content is the self-evident principles of practical knowledge are not intuitions – insights without data. Rather they are insights whose data are, in the first place, natural and sensory appetites and emotional responses. These data are subsequently enriched by theoretical knowledge or true opinion about possibilities (for example, about what threatens and enhances health, or about what knowledge is available), and by experience of disharmony (frustrated intentions). It should be added that the classical natural law theorists would reject Jacques Maritain's theory that the knowledge of first practical principles is 'connatural' or 'by affinity or congeniality' or 'through inclination' rather than conceptual. There is compelling reason not to accept Maritain's claim that Aquinas must have been referring to such 'knowledge' when saying (in the passage cited above) that 'reason naturally understands as good all the objects of man's inclinations'. For Aquinas all knowledge is conceptual (*De veritate* 4.2.5), and the understanding of basic human goods is quite ordinary, unmysterious, *conceptual* understanding (Grisez 1965), albeit practical, that is, directive or prescriptive ('is-to-be-done-and-pursued'), rather than theoretical or descriptive ('is'). The first principles of natural law are not inclinations, but fundamental human goods understood as reasons for action.

Third, natural law theories are distinguished from any fundamentally aggregative conception of the right and the just. For viable natural law theories postulate no one end to which all human actions might be effective means, no one value in terms of which one might commensurate alternative options as simply better or worse, and no one principle which, without further specification in other principles and norms, should guide deliberation and choice. Rather they claim to identify a number of basic human goods, none of which is simply a means to or simply a part of any other such basic good. A number of principles are also identified to guide ('morally') the choices necessitated by the variety of basic goods and reasons for action and the multiple ways of instantiating these goods and acting on these reasons for action by intelligent and creative choice (as well as by misguided choices whose primary motivation is not reasons but emotion).

Fourth, natural law theories typically differ from other ethical theories by offering to clarify not only the normative disciplines and bodies of discourse, but also the methods of the descriptive and explanatory social theories (political theory or political science, economics, legal theory and so on). How best can human societies and their formative concepts be understood, without illusions, but in a general way (as in a project such as Aristotle's *Politics* or Max Weber's *Wirtschaft und Gesellschaft* (Economy and Society))? Could such projects be 'value-free'? Or must even descriptive-explanatory theorists, in selecting concepts, rely upon some definite conceptions of what is important in human existence? Must they not use such conceptions as criteria for selecting topics for study, and concepts for describing those topics? Must they not also employ such criteria in judging some types and instantiations of human institutions or practices to be the 'central cases' of such institutions or practices, and also in judging some uses of terms such as 'law' or 'constitution' or 'authority' to be, for critical descriptive theory, the 'focal' uses and senses of those terms? And must not such conceptions and criteria of importance be the subject, not of selection by 'demonic' personal preference (Weber) or silent conformism to academic fashion or political *parti pris*, but rather of an open, public, critical justification? Natural law theories of the classical type, such as those of Aristotle and Aquinas, claim to offer such a justification (see Finnis 1980).

4 Derivation of positive law

The history of moral and political philosophy, and of natural law theory, is much affected by the lacunae in Aquinas' work. He was the thinker who most clearly articulated and developed the elements of practical philosophy in Aristotle (and thus, in a sense, in Plato), so as to represent them as propositions of or about natural law. Yet he failed to give a clear, full, careful and consistent statement of the first principles of practical reason, and a satisfying set of illustrations of the way in which first practical principles (such as 'human life is a good to be advanced and respected') or first moral principles (such as the 'golden rule') are given specificity in less fundamental principles and norms. This failure contributed significantly to the spread of voluntarist and fideistic currents which virtually overwhelmed the tradition of natural law theory as a living school of thought.

Aquinas was the first philosophical thinker to exploit the concept of 'positive law' which emerges in mid twelfth-century theological and juristic speculation. He gave an original and helpful sketch, scarcely surpassed even today, of the differing types of relationship between the high-level principles of natural law and (1) the more specified principles which can be attained by practical reasoning about the implications of those principles in recurrent types of human predicament and opportunity; and (2) norms, rules, precepts and juridical institutions which cannot be said to be required as the conclusion of any course of practical reasoning, yet which are in some other way rationally connected to, or derived from, principles of the first two sorts, and are authoritative for upright judges and good citizens if and when chosen and promulgated ('posited') by an appropriate authority. Laws, rights and institutions derived in the second way are 'positive', yet have much the same moral force in conscience as the higher-level principles of natural law, provided that their positing was by a person or body constitutionally authorized to make such decisions and making them without serious disregard either for other relevant moral principles and rights or for the 'common' (as opposed to partisan) good of all the members of the community subject to their authority.

This second mode of derivation was called by Aquinas *determinatio*, which might be translated 'concretization'. It is best understood by a comparison such as he offered by way of explanation. From his commission ('build a maternity hospital for our town') an architect can deduce various specifications (the building must be more than one metre in height, and must include doors, means of warming the spaces in winter, and so on). But no amount of attention to the commission (the 'principle' of his work) and to the circumstances (including the 'nature of things') will yield a single, rationally required answer to the unavoidable questions. Should the doors be 2.1 or 2.2 metres high? Of this metal or that? Questions of this kind must be answered by decisions (*determinationes*) which are rationally under-determined, yet intelligibly related to (and in this weak sense 'derived from') the master principle (the commission taken with its more or less necessary implications).

In this account the sheer positivity of much of a country's legal system is fully acknowledged. But at the same time the moral significance of the law's directives and institutions is affirmed and explained. The affirmation is conditional. If the relationship of 'derivation', albeit nondeductive and 'free', is broken by *ultra vires* (lack of authority) or unjust discrimination or violation of inviolable rights, the positive law's proper moral authority is eliminated. From the point of view of the conscientious judge, citizen or indeed legislator, this lack of the proper ('normal') moral authority was marked by the sayings found in Plato, Cicero, Aquinas and most of the philosophical, theological and juridical tradition down to the nineteenth century: an unjust law, albeit valid by the legal system's own criteria of validity (and in this sense properly described as a law), is not really a law, or is not a law *simpliciter*, that is, without qualification. It can have some collateral obligatoriness, in that it may be unfair to others to disobey it publicly (for example, because doing so would encourage others to disobey other laws without good reason). This classical thesis, *lex iniusta non est lex* (an unjust law is not a law), properly interpreted, is fully compatible with the jurist's or historian's wish to employ an amoral criterion of 'legal validity' or historical cognizability (see AQUINAS, T. §13).

5 Inviolable human rights

The collapse of Christianity and other religious cultures, as the matrix for contemporary legal and political orders, has posed a challenge to those who wish to affirm that there is a natural law. In general, the challenge is to show that, even without the support of a religiously warranted ethic (revealed divine law) having an identical or overlapping content, there are philosophically sound reasons to affirm the truth of non-posited principles or norms which, although not claiming to be authoritative because posited, are sufficiently definite to exclude gross 'crimes against humanity' (Nuremberg, 1945; chattel slavery; non-voluntary euthanasia; and so forth) and to underpin the main institutions of civilized societies (family, property, religious liberty and so forth).

In particular, the challenge is to show that aggregative conceptions of moral and political reasoning, such as classical or contemporary utilitarianism or consequentialism or 'economic analysis of law', are unsound (see UTILITARIANISM §5; CONSEQUENTIALISM §2; LAW, ECONOMIC APPROACH TO §3).

Contemporary work in natural law theory therefore includes extensive attempts to criticize aggregative ethics, by showing that their conceptions of value overlook some or all of the basic human goods, and/or that their master principle of maximizing value overlooks the incommensurability not only of one basic human good relative to other such goods, but also of particular instantiations of even one and the same good in alternative options for morally significant choice. The supposition of those undertaking these critiques is that, if they are successful, the way will be open to identifying a richer set of moral principles guiding choice. A working postulate has been that any principle which has been the organizing or dominant principle of an entire philosophical ethic (for example, Kantian universalizability, Epictetan detachment, the principle of commitment expounded by Royce and Marcel) has some place in a developed natural law theory.

But theoretical reflection has yielded a more systematic and unifying 'master principle of morality'. This principle is reached by way of the consideration that, so far as it is in one's power, one should allow nothing but the principles corresponding to the basic human goods to shape one's practical thinking. Aquinas' first practical principle, 'Good is to be done and pursued and evil avoided', taken as it stands, requires only that one not act pointlessly, that is without reason; it requires only that one take at least one of the principles corresponding to a basic human good and follow through to the point at which one somehow instantiates that good through action. The first moral principle makes the stronger demand, not merely that one be reasonable enough to avoid pointlessness, but that one be entirely reasonable in one's practical thinking, choice and action. It can be formulated: in voluntarily acting for human goods and avoiding what is opposed to them, one ought to choose and otherwise will those and only those possibilities whose willing is compatible with a will towards integral human fulfilment (that is, the fulfilment of all human persons and communities).

Integral human fulfilment, so defined, is not a goal towards which actions could be organized as means. But it is not empty of critical force, in identifying choices motivated by emotion fettering and deflecting reason. Unfairness, acting contrary to the golden rule (a principle superior in determinacy to Kant's substitute, universalizability (see KANTIAN ETHICS §4)), is one sort of willing that is incompatible with openness to integral human fulfilment. A choice to destroy some instantiation of basic human good out of hatred is another. A choice precisely to destroy or damage some instantiation of a basic human good as a means to some other end is yet another, which comes into view as a demand of reason once the critique of aggregative theories has demonstrated the rational incommensurabilities overlooked by those who think that the goods promised by the end 'outweigh' the destruction or damage to human personal goods which is intended in a choice of this type.

This third moral principle corresponds not only to the traditional 'the end does not justify these means' but also to the Kantian 'treat humanity always as an end and never as a means only' – though 'humanity' is to be understood without Kant's dualistic restriction of it to the rational faculties as such. It is a principle specified (made more specific) in the form of the traditional moral norms against murder and fraud. As such it is the backbone, so to speak, of traditional and modern legal systems. Articulated from the viewpoint of the beneficiaries of its moral protection, it is specified in those human rights which are not only fundamental but also, properly speaking, inalienable. It is the resultant of the classical principle that reason neither need nor should be the slave of the passions, together with both a precise understanding of free choice (enabling a firm and definite distinction between what is chosen and what is only accepted as a side-effect), and an understanding, developed in dialectic with Enlightenment and post-Enlightenment aggregative ethics, of the incommensurabilities of the goods, persons and probabilities at stake in alternative options for choice. In these and related ways one can think that natural law theory of the classic type is capable of philosophically warranted development (see RIGHTS §3).

See also: GROTIUS, H.; LAW, PHILOSOPHY OF; LEGAL IDEALISM; LEGAL POSITIVISM

References and further reading

* Aquinas, T. (1256–9) *De veritate*, *Opera omnia*, vol. 22, Rome: Commissio Leonina, 1970–4; trans. R.W. Mulligan *et al.*, Chicago: Regnery, 1952–4. (In which Aquinas argues that all knowledge is conceptual.)

* —— (1266–73) *Summa theologiae* (Synopsis of Theology), Milan: Edizioni Paoline, 1988; trans. T. Gilby, London: Eyre and Spottiswoode and New York: McGraw Hill, 60 vols, 1963–73. (Aquinas' greatest and most characteristic work.)

* Aristotle (c.384–322BC) *Metaphysics* (*Metaphysica*), W.D. Ross (ed.), 2 vols, Oxford: Oxford University Press, 1924; Books IV–VI, trans. C.A. Kirwan, Oxford: Oxford University Press, 1971. (Include's Aristotle's critique of general scepticism.)

* Finnis, J. (1980) *Natural Law and Natural Rights*, Oxford: Clarendon Press. (A wide-ranging and fundamental treatment with some, but not exclusive, emphasis on legal philosophical issues; suitable, though difficult, for a first approach to the subject.)

—— (ed.) (1991) *Natural Law*, vols 1 and 2, Aldershot: Dartmouth Press; New York: New York University Press. (An extensive collection of previously published essays by various Anglo-American authors stating the case for and against natural law theory, and including several debates; gives a broad coverage of recent discussions.)

* Grisez, G. (1965) 'The First Principle of Practical Reason: A Commentary on the *Summa theologiae*, 1–2, Question 94, Article 2', *Natural Law Forum* 10: 168–201. (Also in Finnis 1991, vol. 1. A classic article reinterpreting Aquinas and launching what might be called 'new classical natural law theory'; a seminal essay.)

* —— (1978) 'Against Consequentialism', *American Journal of Jurisprudence* 23: 21–72. (Also in Finnis 1991, vol. 2. A wide-ranging critique of utilitarianism, consequentialist, proportionalist, and other aggregative ethical methods.)

Grisez , G., Boyle, J. and Finnis, J. (1987) 'Practical Principles, Moral Truth, and Ultimate Ends', *American Journal of Jurisprudence* 32: 99–151. (Also in Finnis 1991, vol. 1. A restatement and defence of new classical natural law theory against mainly conservative philosophical critics.)

* Hume, D. (1740) *A Treatise of Human Nature*, 2nd edn, ed. L.A. Selby-Bigge and P.H. Nidditch, Oxford: Oxford University Press, 1978. (Book III contains the classic dismissal of natural law theory for alleged derivation of 'ought' from 'is', and for treating reason as a fundamental ground of action.)

Rommen, H. (1947) *The Natural Law: A Study in Legal and Social History and Philosophy*, St Louis, MO, and London: Herder Book Company. (A full and careful statement of implications and applications of natural law theory in politics and economics as seen from a mid twentieth-century Catholic perspective.)

JOHN FINNIS

NATURAL LAWS *see* LAWS, NATURAL

NATURAL PHILOSOPHY, MEDIEVAL

Medieval Latin natural philosophy falls into two main periods, before the rise of the universities (mainly in the twelfth century, when works were produced in connection with aristocratic patrons, monastic institutions or cathedral schools) and after their rise. In the earlier period, the dominant Greek influence is that part of Plato's Timaeus *which had been translated into Latin and commented on by Calcidius. In the university period, the central works are those of Aristotle, often together with commentaries by Averroes.*

Before the twelfth century, there was very little that could be described as natural philosophy. Such work as existed fell mainly into the genres of natural history (encyclopedic works using Pliny and the like as sources), didactic works (perhaps following a question and answer format on the model of Seneca's Natural Questions*) or biblical commentary (especially commentaries on the Hexaemeron, or six days of creation). In the twelfth century, however, there are a number of original texts that may be considered as natural philosophy; examples include William of Conches'* Philosophia mundi *(Philosophy of the World), Bernard Sylvester's* Cosmographia *or Hildegard of Bingen's* Scivias *(Know the Ways). Greek natural philosophy also reached the Latin West through its influence on medical works and on art, for example on drawings of the cosmos, heaven, angels and hell.*

The high and late Middle Ages (thirteenth and fourteenth centuries) was perhaps the preeminent period in all of history for natural philosophy. Natural philosophy was an official area of study in the arts faculties of medieval universities, alongside and distinct from the seven liberal arts (the trivium – grammar, rhetoric and logic – and the quadrivium – arithmetic, geometry, astronomy and music), moral philosophy or ethics, and first philosophy or metaphysics. As a subject of the arts faculty, natural philosophy was also defined as distinct from the subjects studied in the graduate faculties of theology, medicine and law.

The most common approach to natural philosophy in the thirteenth and fourteenth centuries was to comment on, or to dispute questions arising from, the natural works of Aristotle, especially his Physics, On the Heavens, On Generation and Corruption, Meteorology *and* On the Soul, *as well as his various works in biological areas and the so-called Parva Naturalia, a* group of short works on psychological topics. Medieval investigations of the cosmos that were largely mathematical – for example, most of astronomy – were considered in the Middle Ages to belong not to natural philosophy but to the quadrivium or perhaps to the so-called 'middle sciences' (such as optics, statics or the newly developed 'science of motion'). What little medieval experimental science there may have been (for instance that appearing in Peter Peregrinus' De magnete (On the Magnet), in Frederick II's De arte venandi cum avibus (On the Art of Hunting with Birds) and perhaps in some works on alchemy) seems not to have been done within the university setting. In the fourteenth century the new methods of medieval logic (supposition theory, propositional analysis or exposition, rules for solving sophismata and so on) are prominently used in natural philosophy.

Thirteenth- and fourteenth-century natural philosophy began with the general assumption of the Aristotelian world view, but later medieval natural philosophers did not hold to the Aristotelian view rigidly or dogmatically. In some cases, Christian faith seemed to contradict or to add to Aristotle's ideas, and natural philosophers tried to resolve these contradictions or to make the appropriate additions, as in the case of heaven and hell and angels. A number of difficulties, inconsistencies and sticking points in Aristotle were special subjects for discussion and received new resolutions as time went on.

Within the medieval university, natural philosophy was considered to be a part of general education, but it was also thought to be useful as a tool for theology and medicine. In northern universities such as Paris and Oxford, some of the most fundamental original work in natural philosophy was done in connection with the investigation of theological problems, for which natural philosophy, together with the other disciplines of the arts faculty, served as important aids. In Italian universities, where faculties of theology were less prominent or non-existent, natural philosophy was similarly tied to the resolution of medical questions.

European libraries contain many manuscript commentaries on Aristotelian works that still await modern analysis. The medieval university system did not as a rule identify, encourage or reward originality or uniqueness. Many natural philosophers claimed to be explaining Aristotle's meaning, even when they were introducing a novel interpretation of or variation on his ideas. When they made use of the ideas of earlier commentators, they rarely mentioned them by name. What we now know about medieval natural philosophy is not a mirror reflection of what happened in the thirteenth and fourteenth centuries, because modern scholars have chosen to study those subjects and individuals relevant to their own present situations:

Dominicans have emphasized the history of Dominican natural philosophy in such thinkers as Albert the Great and Thomas Aquinas, Franciscans have studied Franciscans such as John Duns Scotus and William of Ockham, historians of science have studied those individuals who had something to say about the subjects of modern science such as bodies, forces, velocities and resistances, logicians have studied logic, and so on. Because natural philosophy as such is not the focus of attention of many modern philosophers or other scholars, much medieval natural philosophy remains unread, sometimes in large-scale and handsomely produced commentaries on Aristotle's works, sometimes in hastily scribbled student notebooks.

1   Natural philosophy before and outside universities
2–5   Natural philosophy in the medieval university
6   The Aristotelian cosmos
7   Self-consciousness of philosophers and the philosophic life
8–9   Medieval variations on Aristotelian natural philosophy

1   Natural philosophy before and outside universities

From the beginning of the Middle Ages until the rise of the universities, relatively few people had time or opportunity for natural philosophy. At the beginning of the Middle Ages, Boethius set out to translate the works of Plato and Aristotle from Greek to Latin, and also proposed to write textbooks in Latin on the seven liberal arts. Before his imprisonment for treason in mid-career, he had succeeded in translating some of Aristotle's logical works and in editing textbooks of arithmetic, geometry and music. While in prison awaiting execution, he completed the classic De consolatione philosophiae (The Consolation of Philosophy), in which he reflects on the pleasures of philosophy. Unfortunately, Boethius' early death prevented him from translating all of Aristotle's works or any of Plato's, and he did not translate any of Aristotle's natural philosophy.

Earlier, the Neoplatonist CALCIDIUS had translated part of Plato's Timaeus into Latin. In this dialogue, Plato told a myth about the origins and nature of the cosmos and transmitted a number of Greek ideas (for example, that there are four elements, earth, water, air and fire, which can be transformed into each other). Because Aristotle's physical works were not available in Latin until the twelfth century, Calcidius' version of Timaeus was heavily used by early medieval thinkers as their source of knowledge about natural philosophy.

From 500–1000 AD, most of those who had the training and opportunity to study natural philosophy were connected with the church, as monks, priests, bishops or nuns. A century after Boethius, the bishop Isidore of Seville wrote his encyclopedic work *De rerum natura* (On the Nature of Things), and a work of the same name was produced a further century later by the Venerable Bede in Northumbria. Both men were attempting to improve the low state of knowledge by condensing and transmitting the natural knowledge found, for example, in Pliny's *Natural History*, an encyclopedic compilation dating from the first century AD (see ENCYCLOPEDISTS). By the year 800, Charlemagne had established his court school under the direction of Alcuin of York, where the latter supervised the copying of manuscripts and oversaw the correction of existing copies of the Latin Bible. Among the Carolingians, Hrabanus Maurus again wrote the encyclopedic work *De rerum natura* (On the Nature of Things) as part of his programme for reforming the education of the clergy. Although Isidore of Seville, the Venerable Bede and Alcuin were among the best-educated people of their times, the intellectual communities in which they worked were small and isolated, consisting of monasteries and a few court-based schools (see CAROLINGIAN RENAISSANCE).

By the turn of the tenth century, however, perhaps partly as a result of the efforts of Charlemagne and Alcuin, the situation was changing. John Scottus ERIUGENA, recruited from the British Isles into the Frankish court of Charlemagne's grandson, was able to make use of sources written in Greek. Through Eriugena, many of the ideas of the Neoplatonists, particularly those of the mysterious PSEUDO-DIONYSIUS the Areopagite, were imported into the West in Latin translation. Through Eriugena's translation of Pseudo-Dionysius' *De coelesti hierarchia* (On Celestial Hierarchy), the West inherited its elaborate notion of nine orders of angels (angels, archangels and principalities, dominions, powers and authorities, and cherubim, seraphim and thrones). Though some of Eriugena's work was condemned as heretical in the thirteenth century, and although Pseudo-Dionysius was later shown not to have been Paul's Athenian disciple as had been thought (but rather someone living after the time of Proclus), nevertheless an elaborate taxonomy of angels was accepted as an intrinsic part of the cosmos throughout the later Middle Ages. Angels were considered no less real by medieval scholars than neutrinos or quarks are to educated people of the late twentieth century, despite their invisibility to the ordinary eye.

By the year 1000, GERBERT OF AURILLAC, tutor to the Holy Roman Emperor Otto III, had already travelled to Spain to bring Islamic knowledge to the rest of Europe. Gerbert was perhaps the first person

to be able to operate on an intellectual level comparable to that of Boethius, at least as regards the seven liberal arts (especially the trivium). It was at about this time that something that might be called natural philosophy began to appear in the schools established in cathedrals in urban centers such as Chartres, Paris and Laon. Such natural philosophy might take the form of a creation myth, such as Bernard Sylvester's *Cosmographia*, a work that combined ideas of Genesis with ideas of Plato's *Timaeus* to describe the origin and organization of first the macrocosm (natural world) and then of the microcosm (the human being) (see BERNARD OF TOURS). Some twelfth-century authors, for example WILLIAM OF CONCHES, attempted to give an explicitly natural explanation of the cosmos, albeit within an assumed Christian context. The general world picture that these Platonistic Christian authors passed on to the natural philosophers of later centuries was one in which God first establishes and then maintains order in the cosmos, so that there is a natural design which natural philosophers may study using purely human, rational and empirical means.

Before the rise of the universities in the twelfth century, then, there was a well-established intellectual culture in the Latin West, largely dependent on clergymen but extending also to a few nuns and a few of the aristocratic laity of both sexes. Apart from the subjects of elementary education, manuscripts might concern religious topics, medicine (including compilations about medical plants), animal lore (bestiaries), basic astronomy for calendrical purposes (*computus*), or astrology and meteorology. Clerical readers might make use of animal lore in preparing sermons, taking examples of courage from lions or of compassion from pelicans and the like.

In the twelfth century, the available writings on nature were suddenly vastly increased by a spate of translations from Arabic to Latin, either of Greek works that had previously been translated into Arabic, or of original Arabic works (see TRANSLATORS; ISLAMIC PHILOSOPHY: TRANSMISSION INTO WESTERN EUROPE). Thus in the late twelfth and early thirteenth centuries, as the universities were beginning to develop, philosophers suddenly had access to the natural philosophical works of Aristotle, which had previously been unavailable in Latin. Although the works of Aristotle were over fifteen hundred years old by the year 1200, they represented a level of natural philosophical sophistication well above what had been available in the earlier Middle Ages. They were therefore highly attractive to the clerical scholars who read them despite the fact that they contained ideas at least superficially contradicting Christianity, such as Aristotle's purported proof that the universe must always have existed. Initially, popes and bishops tried to forbid the reading or teaching of Aristotle's natural works, but by the mid-thirteenth century these works became the basic teaching texts at the University of Paris and other universities. In the later thirteenth century, ALBERT THE GREAT, Thomas AQUINAS, Robert GROSSETESTE and Roger BACON were among the first Latin commentators to lecture to university audiences Aristotle's *Physics*, *On the Heavens* and other natural works. In doing this, they often made use of translations of the Arabic commentaries of Averroes (see IBN RUSHD), composed in Muslim Spain in the previous century. They also used Latin translations of the works of other Islamic and Jewish authors such as AL-KINDI, AL-FARABI, Avicenna (see IBN SINA) and MAIMONIDES.

Finally, there was the study of subjects such as astrology and alchemy, which were at least peripherally related to natural philosophy but were not part of official university curricula. Both these disciplines made considerable use of Aristotelian ideas of the cosmos, celestial influences on earth, the elements, chemical change and so forth. The situation is confused by the fact that there are works on astrology, alchemy and even magic attributed to prominent university scholars such as Albert the Great and Thomas Aquinas. These works, if authentic, cast considerable light on the natural philosophical views of their authors, even if they are not by the individuals to whom they are ascribed, these works can tell us much about the general ambience of medieval natural philosophy, and particularly about the perceived connection between the heavens and the earth.

2 Natural philosophy in medieval universities: sources

In the thirteenth and fourteenth centuries, natural philosophy was done most directly in the form of disputing questions arising from Aristotle's natural works. Although, as has been stated, a distinction was maintained in the medieval university between the discipline of natural philosophy on the one hand and the disciplines of the liberal arts and higher faculties of theology and medicine on the other, nevertheless some natural philosophy, including some of the most advanced and innovative work, was also done under the umbrellas of theology (especially in northern universities) or medicine (especially in southern universities).

The primary sources upon which thirteenth- and fourteenth-century natural philosophers drew were the natural works of ARISTOTLE and later commentaries on these works. Aristotle himself often dis-

cussed the views of his predecessors, and his medieval commentators followed him in this practice. Thus a medieval commentator might contrast Aristotle's views with those of the Presocratics – including THALES, ANAXIMANDER, ANAXIMENES, HERACLITUS, PYTHAGORAS, PARMENIDES, ZENO OF ELEA, ANAXAGORAS, EMPEDOCLES, LEUCIPPUS and DEMOCRITUS – or he might compare Aristotle's ideas to those of PLATO. Additional sources of ideas included medical works, such as those of Hippocrates (see HIPPOCRATIC MEDICINE) and GALEN among the Greeks as well as various medieval medical authors. Medieval natural philosophers also knew something about the ideas of the Stoics (see STOICISM), the Epicureans (see EPICUREANISM), the Neoplatonists, including SIMPLICIUS and PHILOPONUS (see NEOPLATONISM), and Roman and medieval Latin authors from Pliny and SENECA to CALCIDIUS, Macrobius, Martianus Capella, BOETHIUS, Isidore, Alcuin, John Scottus ERIUGENA, GERBERT OF AURILLAC and various others (see ENCYCLOPEDISTS). Among Islamic authors the most influential were AL-KINDI, Avicenna (see IBN SINA) and Alhazen as well as Averroes (see IBN RUSHD) and his many Islamic predecessors whom Averroes discussed in his commentaries on Aristotle, such as Avempace (see IBN BAJJA). A few Jewish authors, such as MAIMONIDES, were also used.

Although they were not likely to cite them in purely philosophical work, medieval commentators on Aristotle's natural philosophy also knew earlier, specifically Christian writings such as the various works of AUGUSTINE and other church fathers, including commentaries on Genesis and discussions of predestination, the nature of the soul, the sacraments and so on (see PATRISTIC PHILOSOPHY). As medieval theology developed, it not infrequently led to partly philosophical speculations which, in turn, had an influence on natural philosophy. Theological discussions of God's power, eternity, infinity, the Eucharist, the soul and the angels produced results that subsequently fed into the further development of natural philosophy. Thus for example, the idea that in the Eucharist the qualities of the bread and wine are present without inhering in any substance led to the conclusion that it was not self-contradictory that there might be accidental forms that existed independently.

3 Natural philosophy in medieval universities: goals

The purpose of natural philosophy as taught in medieval universities was to understand nature: that is, the created world, or cosmos, and everything contained in it. As indicated above, the materials used by university scholars for their study of the cosmos were the writings of their predecessors, pre-eminently the works of Greek philosophers (especially Aristotle and Plato and their followers), but also Muslim and Jewish philosophers insofar as their works had been translated into Latin, and earlier writers in Latin. It was quite unusual for medieval natural philosophers to draw new empirical information into their work except by reference to common knowledge and daily experience.

Theology, however, did provide what were considered new facts to be taken into account by natural philosophers insofar as they took theology to be a science comprised of truths about the world. For example, theology taught that angels were real created beings; consequently, medieval natural philosophers took angels into account in forming general metaphysical or natural philosophical theories. If angels were thought to be both indivisible and moveable, then natural philosophers might question Aristotle's argument that it is impossible for an indivisible to move.

Natural philosophy, along with the liberal arts, was thus a 'handmaiden' or service discipline to theology, but it would be a mistake to confuse the situation in medieval universities with that found among some fundamentalists today. By and large, intellectual integrity and exactness were hallmarks of medieval university scholars including the members of the theology faculties, who were nothing if not rational. Going as far back as Augustine (and to Philo Judaeus before him), Christian scholars had come to the conclusion that if Christians were not well-educated they could not win the respect of non-Christians in their societies, who were often, as in the case of the Greeks, highly educated themselves. Moreover, Christian scholars wanted to learn the truth about the world in its natural as well as its divine aspects, and they did not expect that true philosophy would contradict true religion. They had not yet imagined a 'warfare' of Christianity and science, such as later occurred between the Copernican view of the universe and the Catholic church in the case of Galileo, or between Darwinian evolution and creationism. Medieval scholars understood that God gave human beings reliable minds and sense organs so that humans could learn about the cosmos, as well as about God's plan for it.

The goal of medieval natural philosophy was therefore to discover the truth about the world for its own sake. Medieval natural philosophy differed from modern science not in being tied to religious dogma and authority, but rather in the fact that it was *not* tied to technological application or economic spin-off. Modern scientific critics sometimes discredit medieval natural philosophy on the grounds that it was not sufficiently experimental or mathematical, and seems to have spun fantastical theories solely on the basis of cloistered speculation. Medieval natural philosophers might defend themselves against this criticism on the ground that their job was to teach future priests, ecclesiastical or secular administrators, lawyers and physicians for whom scholastic methods were well suited. Had they been asked to teach future engineers, their approach might certainly have taken more mathematical and empirical directions. To ask whether medieval natural philosophers should have had a technological goal is beyond the scope of this article: the relevant point here is that the goal of medieval natural philosophy was knowledge of the world for its own sake and as a sturdy and flexible tool for use in the higher faculties, not for use in technology (the modern Western assumption that rapid technological progress is possible and good is the exception rather than the rule within world history).

4 Natural philosophy in medieval universities: practitioners

Because natural philosophy was mainly a university subject, and because medieval students and faculty were considered to be clergymen of a sort, the practitioners of medieval natural philosophy were almost always celibate men. Rarely and marginally, a work with natural philosophical content was written by a medieval woman, usually a nun – HILDEGARD OF BINGEN, for instance, who was the author of books of visions including visions of the cosmos – or by a non-clerical man – for example, the Emperor Frederick II, who was the author of a work on falconry including natural philosophical content.

Modern scholars, writing from Marxist, feminist or third world points of view, have faulted medieval natural philosophy (and medieval scholasticism in general) for its narrowness, arguing that because its study was limited to celibate white Christian men, it represented the interests and biases of only a very small segment of society. Certainly this narrowness may explain why the study of natural philosophy was devoted to a certain kind of knowledge, with no concern for the material well-being of society as a whole. Then as now, however, some authors were motivated by narrow self-interest while others had a more generous point of view. Because the medieval church was a powerful social institution that placed a high value on intellectual inquiry and supported scholars, many highly intelligent men were attracted into the universities and were given the institutional support to devote their entire attention to intellectual matters.

5 Natural philosophy in medieval universities: literary genres

The forms in which medieval natural philosophy was written were mainly determined by the teaching practices of medieval universities. This teaching fell into two main types, the lecture and the disputation. Lectures in natural philosophy most frequently involved the reading (*lectio*) of one of the books of Aristotle, either 'cursorily,' simply reading the book rather quickly, or in the more formal 'ordinary' fashion, with pauses in which the lecturer explained the structure of the text, emphasized Aristotle's main points or conclusions, cleared up special difficulties and so on. In a disputation, on the other hand, not only the lecturer but several disputants, often including advanced students, took part. Some disputations were tied to the texts covered in the lectures and concerned questions that arose from the text. One or more individuals (the 'opponent') would raise problems about the question, and one or more individuals (the 'respondent') would reply. After this had gone on for some time, the master overseeing the disputation would give what he considered to be the correct answer to the question (the 'determination'), organizing logically the main points that had been made in the disputation, reinforcing the arguments that supported his view and responding to arguments for alternative positions. More rarely there were disputations on more general themes, not closely tied to any one text. One type of disputation detached from texts was the disputation on sophismata (*de sophismatibus*), in which students tried to untangle the possible truth-values of seemingly paradoxical statements, some of which concerned natural subjects such as heating and cooling or the traversal of distances. Contrary to stereotypes deriving from the trial of Galileo in the seventeenth century, medieval university disputants pursued their inquiries with relentless logic and were not constantly looking over their shoulders lest the expression of heretical views might lead to their condemnation. In fact, medieval university disputants were often themselves the authorities whose job it was to determine what was true and what was not.

These oral lectures and disputations sometimes led to written accounts, and masters of arts also occasionally wrote expositions of texts or determinations of questions in advance of lecturing or instead of taking part in oral disputations. There are also marginal glosses and brief expositions on the manuscripts of Aristotle's natural philosophical works, which formed a large percentage of the medieval natural philosophical textbooks; an example is Robert Grosseteste's notes or commentary on Aristotle's

Physics. Some scholars, such as Albert the Great, wrote paraphrases of the Aristotelian texts, perhaps to make the meaning clearer. (The Latin translations of Aristotle, either directly from the Greek or indirectly through an intermediate Arabic translation, were often difficult to understand simply because of the wording.) More important in terms of the specifically medieval contribution to natural philosophy were compilations of 'questions' on the Aristotelian texts. Written in the standard 'scholastic' form, these 'questions' began with a question related to the text and then gave arguments for and against a number of possible answers to the question, before going on to the author's preferred answer. Almost always one finds the question and then one or more 'principal arguments' that are opposed to the position that the author will ultimately adopt. Then there are brief arguments for the other side (*in oppositum* or *sed contra*), followed by the 'determination.' This determination may begin with clarifications or definitions, then give the preferred answer, put forth objections to this answer and answer the objections. Finally, there are responses to the principal arguments put forth at the start.

In sum, medieval natural philosophy was predominantly studied in medieval universities, based on texts of Aristotle together with a series of later commentaries on the latter's works. Medieval philosophy began by assuming the truth of the general view of the cosmos advocated by Aristotle, but over time natural philosophers modified this view in many respects, although without overturning it. When the natural works of Aristotle first became available in Latin in the early thirteenth century, they were rejected, most notably at Paris, because of their conflicts with Christianity. Before long, however, Aristotle's natural works became widely-used textbooks, and their incompatibilities with Christianity provided the grist for repeated disputations and efforts to discover where the truth lay. By the end of the Middle Ages, a few scholastics composed their own treatises on natural philosophical topics (for example John Dumbleton's *Summa logicae et philosophiae naturalis* (Summa of Logic and Natural Philosophy), but these almost always dealt with Aristotelian themes (see LOGIC, MEDIEVAL).

6 The Aristotelian cosmos

Medieval natural philosophy was therefore predominantly a series of more or less far-reaching variations on the theme of Aristotelian natural philosophy. Basing themselves on ARISTOTLE, with a lesser reliance on PLATO, medieval natural philosophers assumed that the natural world or cosmos is finite and spherical, with a spherical earth at the centre surrounded by spherical shells of water, air and fire (with some mixing, especially at the boundaries, such as the surface of the earth). The moon and all the rest of the heavenly bodies are contained in spherical shells of a fifth element called aether, turning in uniform circular motion about the centre of the cosmos, at which the earth is located. Technical astronomy, in order to account exactly for apparent motions of the planets, sun and moon, modified this idea by allowing additional aether spheres that rotated about centres other than the center of the cosmos. Such additional spheres were called eccentrics and epicycles.

For Aristotle, the cosmos ended with the outermost aether sphere (*primum mobile*), which contained the stars and rotated at a rate of approximately once per day, carrying all the other heavenly bodies with it. Outside the *primum mobile* was nothing, not even empty space. Medieval theologians and authors such as DANTE in his *Divine Comedy* reconciled this Aristotelian picture with Biblical accounts of heaven and hell by placing hell in the center of the earth and by adding a last, unmoved sphere, the empyrean heaven containing the souls of the blessed, outside the *primum mobile*, and fourteenth-century theologians also supposed that God was outside the cosmos. Medieval technical astronomers also sometimes added an extra empty sphere to account for the precession of the equinoxes, the apparent motion relative to the stars of the points at which the sun crosses the celestial equator. The *primum mobile* could then be thought to be an empty sphere rotating approximately once a day, inside of which would be the sphere of the fixed stars, carried around by the *primum mobile* outside it but with its own proper rotation in the opposite direction about a different axis, with a period of about 26,000 years.

Following Plato and Aristotle, medieval natural philosophers assumed that everything in the cosmos (or everything except the movers of the heavenly spheres) is composed fundamentally of prime matter, which has no characteristics of its own, and forms, which give characteristics to matter. The technical term for an individual thing existing in the cosmos was 'substance'; for example, a human being is a substance, a tree is a substance, a stone is a substance and so on. Each substance has a substantial form that makes it what it is or gives it its so-called 'essential' characteristics. For example, the substantial form of human beings makes them rational animals: anything that is not rational or not an animal is not human. Each substance also has many so-called 'accidental' forms such as colours or temperatures. These accidental forms happen to characterize a substance, but are not essential to it, as it is not essential for a human being to have blue eyes or even five fingers on each hand.

Following the ideas of Aristotle's *Physics*, medieval natural philosophers also took it for granted that all or most things in the cosmos move, understanding by the term 'motion' not only local motion but also alteration (or change of quality) and augmentation and diminution (or change of size). The task of the natural philosopher was to explain or give the causes why the bodies in the cosmos move or change as observed. Thus medieval natural philosophy tried to answer such questions as, why do the sun, moon and stars move through the sky as they appear to move? Do animals move themselves, or is there an external cause of their motion; for instance, the food they see in front of them? How are metals formed? How do animals reproduce? How does nutrition occur?

The sorts of causes that natural philosophers looked for were usually forms, either substantial forms or accidental forms. In the terrestrial realm, from the centre of the earth up to the sphere of the moon, there were four elements – earth, water, air and fire – and many compound bodies formed by the interaction of these elements, including minerals, plants, animals and humans. Each of the terrestrial elements was thought to have two basic qualities: earth is cold and dry, water is cold and wet, air is hot and wet, fire is hot and dry. If one asked, 'Why does water evaporate and become steam or air?' the answer might be that fire, which is hot, heats the water so that its coldness is changed to warmth, with the result that the cold and wet water becomes hot and wet air. When they considered that an element such as water has a substantial form that makes it water as well as basic qualities that make it cold and wet, then natural philosophers might debate whether it is the heat of the fire or the substantial form of the fire that heats the water. Assuming further that the first result of heating water is hot water, natural philosophers might try to understand more exactly when and how the hot water changes its substantial form to become air. The usual answer was that the substantial form does not change until the very end of the process (when, in our terms, evaporation occurs): a less common answer was that, in reality, water and air have the same substantial form, differing only in their accidental qualities.

When the elements interacted to form minerals, plants or animals, questions about changes of substantial form became more serious. Gold, for instance, was assumed to have a substantial form that made it gold as well as being generated by a combination of earth, water, air and fire or by interactions of hot, cold, wet and dry. One not uncommon Platonic or Neoplatonic model was that the terrestrial elements interacted up to a certain point and then influences from the celestial realm, the planets and stars, led to the introduction of the substantial form into the prepared matter. For those thinking in a specifically Christian context, the idea was that God sometimes chooses to act using the heavenly bodies as instruments. In the case of humans, the rational soul might be supposed to be introduced into the embryo in this way, leading to 'quickening' and noticeable motion within the womb. This would be the point in time at which the embryo became a human being. This whole scheme provided a rationale for astrology, the study of the configurations of the heavenly bodies to predict a person's nature and likely fortune, since the exact configuration of the heavens at the time of the introduction of the rational soul would likely affect its nature at least accidentally.

In considering the whole realm of compound bodies on the surface of the earth, medieval natural philosophers followed Aristotle and Greek medical theorists in assuming that there are levels of souls or faculties active in living things, where a 'soul' is understood as a source of motion or activity in the substance or thing (see HIPPOCRATIC MEDICINE). Plants have a 'nutritive soul' that explains their growth and reproduction; animals have a 'sensitive soul' that explains their motion and sensation as well as their growth and reproduction; and humans then have a 'rational soul' that explains their ability to think as well as all of the lower functions. It was a matter of disagreement whether each living thing has only one substantial form, which is the source of all its motions or actions, or whether the higher living things have forms that make them bodies and also souls. In more physiological or medical contexts, philosophers also made use of the concept of 'spirit' (*pneuma*), with the idea that the soul, conceived as pure form, uses spirit, conceived as the thinnest possible gas-like stuff, to move the body, whether in nutrition, sensation or local motion.

In the inanimate realm (things without souls of any sort), forms were also used to explain the natural motions of the elements and compound bodies. The elements earth and water were understood to be heavy, that is, to have a form called 'gravity' which leads them to move downward whenever this is not prevented or whenever they are not as close as possible to the centre of the cosmos. Likewise air and fire were supposed to be characterized by lightness or 'levity' as a form, leading them to move upward whenever they are below their natural places and not hindered from moving higher. Thus it might be an internal characteristic (form) of a heavy or light body that explained its downward or upward natural motion, toward or away from the centre of the

cosmos. The cause of gravity was not 'attraction' between bodies across empty space, as it would later be understood following Newtonian physics. For an Aristotelian, there is no empty space, and, even if there were, there could be no action at a distance without any intermediary. From the Aristotelian point of view, the only cases of apparent action at a distance between inanimate bodies were the attraction of magnets for iron and electrostatic attraction or repulsion, as between amber and chaff. Even these phenomena were explained without supposing action at a distance between inanimate bodies; instead, bodies were supposed to multiply forms of a sort (so-called 'species') into the medium surrounding them and up to the other bodies on which they might act.

Occasions on which elements, or compounds in which given elements were predominant, did not move in their natural directions (heavy bodies downward and light bodies upward) were also explained by medieval natural philosophers along Aristotelian lines, arguing that there must be an external force causing these elements or compounds to move in an unnatural direction and that this external force must be in contact with them. This idea followed obviously from everyday experience: loaded carts, for instance, do not move along the road unless some person or animal is in contact with them and pulls or pushes them. In the later books of the *Physics*, Aristotle had broadened this common conception to argue that everything that is moved is moved by something else (*omne quod movetur ab alio movetur*). In an apparent inconsistency with what he said elsewhere about souls being sources of motion in substances that have them, Aristotle argued in the *Physics* that living things and even elements in their natural motions have outside movers. Medieval Christian Aristotelians sometimes resolved this apparent inconsistency by concluding that only human beings, because of their free will, can act independently of outside forces.

In the celestial realm, it was supposed to be natural for aether to move in a circle around the centre of the universe. Apparently there was nothing to resist this motion since, according to Aristotle, it had been going on forever with no change of velocity whatsoever. An ox pulling a cart becomes fatigued because of the resistance to its pulling and, after a time, slows down. The celestial movers, however, must experience nothing similar since their motion continues unretarded for time without end. Because what happens on earth and what happens in the heavens are quite different, the explanation for the motion of the heavenly spheres is different from the explanation of terrestrial motion. To make a rough comparison, the movers of the heavens were supposed to move the celestial spheres in the way that hay causes a horse to move toward it, that is, by arousing in the moved body the desire to move. Unlike hay, however, the movers of the heavenly spheres were supposed to be immaterial, as Aristotle had argued they must be if they are to remain unmoved themselves; they must be so-called 'intelligences' or 'separated substances' (separated, that is, from matter). In more thoroughly Christianized versions of these theories, the celestial intelligences were sometimes identified as angels. In a view that was condemned by the Bishop of Paris in 1277, the celestial spheres were supposed to have their own souls, united to their matter, by which they perceived the separated substances and were therefore motivated to rotate. While this view of souls of the spheres helped to complete the analogy between the cause of their rotation and the cause of the motion of animate beings such as animals and humans, it was opposed to the Christian conception of the cosmos; if it were true, it would seem to imply that the celestial spheres were the most perfect beings in the cosmos, more perfect than humans because their matter was more perfect, although they were alike in having rational souls.

However, if in the Aristotelian cosmos the heavens were thought to be very different from the terrestrial realm below the sphere of the moon, the two realms were not disconnected. Influences from the heavens upon the earth were supposed to occur constantly, through the agency of light or other similar forms. In the Aristotelian explanation of light, a light source (*lux*) does not send out particles or anything else material; rather, the light source affects the medium immediately surrounding it, producing in it an illumination (*lumen*), which in turn causes the next part of the medium to light up, and so on. Thus no matter is moved in the spreading of light, but rather a form reproduces itself in decreasing degrees in successive contiguous parts of a transparent medium. In this model of light, other forms (for example, the form that causes magnetism) might be thought to reproduce themselves in contiguous bodies. This process, called by the generic name 'the multiplication of species', occurred constantly throughout the cosmos. In this usage, the word 'species' referred to forms that copy the form that causes them while not being entirely identical or not having identical power, like images in a mirror (*speculum*). From the time of the Greeks, optics, or the geometrical study of the ways in which light propagates itself, had been highly developed, including studies of reflection, refraction and the decrease in intensity with distance. In the later Middle Ages, the model of optics was widely presupposed in the understanding of how other forms, such as heat and cold, might act on neighbouring bodies. Some alchemists believed that

the substantial form of gold might under proper circumstances multiply itself in a similar way, transforming other metals into gold. Pharmacists likewise assumed that drugs act on the body not through the material of the drug incorporating itself into the human body (as happens with food), but through the substantial and accidental forms of drugs heating, cooling, moistening or drying the tissues with which they came into contact, or by the drug multiplying some other 'species' or effect of a specific form into parts of the body.

The medieval Aristotelian cosmos, then, was almost the opposite of the universe of the ancient atomists (see ATOMISM, ANCIENT). Whereas for the atomists the universe is infinite, for Aristotelians it is finite. Whereas for the atomists the universe is made up of particles alike in their matter separated by empty space, for Aristotelians bodies differ from each other intrinsically by their substantial and accidental forms, not only by their size, position and motion; moreover, empty space is impossible. The atomists further theorized that fundamental particles have a size but cannot be cut into pieces ('atom' means uncuttable in Greek), while for the Aristotelians there is no limit to divisibility; no matter how finely something has been divided, it can still be divided further. This was expressed by saying that matter is potentially but not actually infinitely divisible; in other words there is no limit to the number of times one can divide a body into smaller and smaller pieces (this is the potential infinity), but one could not actually finish dividing the body infinitely many times (to finish an infinite process was considered to be a self-contradiction).

7 Self-consciousness of philosophers and the philosophic life

This, then, was the basic view of the cosmos accepted by medieval natural philosophers. From about the middle of the thirteenth century, when Aristotle's books were adopted as the textbooks for natural philosophy, philosophers began to clarify and suggest modifications in the received Aristotelian view. Sometimes obscure even in Greek, these texts had become far more difficult in the process of translation, especially when there had been an Arabic intermediary between the Greek and Latin; the differing vocabularies and grammatical structures of Arabic and Greek required many modifications in order to translate as literally as possible from Greek to Arabic, and with similar problems again occurring during the later translation from Arabic to Latin.

The difficulty of the Aristotelian texts was further compounded when one asked whether or how they fit with Christian faith. What should a person teaching natural philosophy do with the texts in which Aristotle ostensibly proves that the world has always existed, when Genesis says it was created? There were also the commentaries of Averroes who, although he was a monotheist, could not be expected to adhere to specifically Christian beliefs (see IBN RUSHD). Commentators on Aristotle often held degrees in arts but not in theology (though they might simultaneously be students in a faculty of theology). Lecturers on philosophy were not authorized to discuss specifically theological points in the classes of the arts faculty, but they were taken as authoritative on purely natural issues.

In these circumstances, BOETHIUS OF DACIA at the University of Paris argued that a philosopher should always resolve every philosophical difficulty solely from the point of view of philosophy. In his view, this was a matter of disciplinary integrity. Aristotle had said in the first book of the *Physics* that a geometer need not argue with someone who denies his principles or axioms; if a person denies one of the axioms of geometry, it will be impossible to prove something to him using those axioms or anything better known than the axioms. So too, Aristotle said, a physicist need not argue with someone such as PARMENIDES, who denies that motion occurs. That all or some things move, Aristotle argued, is the most obvious fact of physics, so that if a person denies that things move, it will be impossible to find a more obviously true principle on which to build a physical proof that motion occurs. In a similar way, each discipline has fundamental principles that are not proved but are taken as obvious for the purposes of that discipline, and on the basis of these principles, the practitioners of that discipline reason to conclusions. When people are practising a given discipline, they can and should assume that its principles are true.

Arguing on this basis, Boethius of Dacia claimed the right to conclude, when he was working in natural philosophy, that the world had no beginning because, rationally speaking and accepting the principles of Aristotelian natural philosophy, Aristotle proves that the world, if it exists at all, must be eternal or perpetual: something does not come from nothing; something is not caused by nothing and so on (see ETERNITY OF THE WORLD, MEDIEVAL VIEWS OF). On the other hand, as a Christian, Boethius of Dacia believed that the world was created by God as told in the book of Genesis; but, in his opinion, this did not affect the cogency of Aristotle's philosophical argument for the eternity of the world. When Boethius was speaking as a natural philosopher, he was speaking not as a Christian but as someone who accepted the principles of natural philosophy.

In the furore that these views caused among Boethius of Dacia's contemporaries, some thought that he could not and should not assert, even when doing natural philosophy, something that contradicted Christian faith and that he should be disciplined for teaching such a heresy. In reply, Boethius tried to explain why he should be able to assert without blame, when acting as a philosopher, conclusions contradicting Christian beliefs that he himself shared. In the excitement of defending his position, Boethius added to his armament many claims about the joys of the philosophical life, such as that no one lives a higher or happier human life than the philosopher.

In opposition to Boethius of Dacia, Thomas AQUINAS developed a position allowing for a synthesis or merging of philosophical and Christian views. Arguing that Boethius' position amounted to claiming that there can be two truths that contradict each other, the truth of philosophy and the truth of Christianity, Aquinas emphasized that there is only one truth and that true philosophy cannot contradict true Christianity. In the view of knowledge proposed by Aquinas, the truths of philosophy and the truths of faith are partially overlapping and partially separate. There are some things we know only by reason, some things we know only by faith and some things we know both by reason and by faith. That there are four terrestrial elements, for instance, we know only by natural philosophy and experience of the physical world, and that God is a trinity of Father, Son and Holy Ghost, we know only by faith; but that God exists, as the creator, mover and highest good of the universe, we know both by reason and by faith. Thus Aquinas proposed several cosmological and teleological arguments, generally founded on natural philosophy, which he claimed prove rationally the existence of God (see GOD, ARGUMENTS FOR THE EXISTENCE OF).

With regard to Aristotle's supposed proof of the eternity of the world, Aquinas adopted the strategy of Maimonides' *Guide to the Perplexed*, arguing that Aristotle's proof is not demonstrative. Though Aristotle may have thought he had proved that the world is eternal, the argument could be refuted on rational grounds by pointing out that creation is after all supposed to be a supernatural rather than natural act. But, neither can it be proved philosophically that the world was created a finite time in the past. Thus for Aquinas the question of the eternity or newness of the world is philosophically neutral or undecided. Since philosophy leaves the question open, Aquinas could determine on the basis of faith that the world is created, with no inconsistency with natural philosophy.

Thus Aquinas, like Boethius of Dacia, argued that philosophy has an important role to play for the Christian as well as for the non-Christian. By dint of long study, Aquinas became one of the most knowledgeable and skillful Aristotelian philosophers of his day. On the basis of his synthesis of Aristotelianism and Christianity, other thinkers, prominently Dante in his *Divine Comedy*, developed a view of the cosmos that included both Aristotelian and Christian elements.

However, Aquinas' proposal of a Christian-Aristotelian synthesis did not convince everyone, nor did it survive for long unmodified after his death. In the 1270s, the Bishop of Paris issued two condemnations which included theses put forth by Aquinas as well as by Boethius of Dacia (see ARISTOTELIANISM, MEDIEVAL). In the later of these condemnations, a primary target was those natural philosophers who claimed that even God could not do what was impossible according to Aristotelian physics. If Aristotle proved that a vacuum cannot exist, so said these natural philosophers, then even God cannot make a vacuum. To the contrary, implied the condemnation of 1277, God is not limited by what is possible or impossible according to Aristotelian natural philosophy.

In arguing that the world cannot have had a beginning in time, Aristotle had adopted what has been called the statistical interpretation of modality or of possibility and necessity. On this interpretation, what is impossible never happens, what is necessary is always the case, and what is contingent or possible is sometimes the case and sometimes not. This implies that what is possible must sooner or later occur. As Maimonides reported in his *Guide to the Perplexed*, the *mutakallimun*, in defence of monotheistic religion, had adopted a different conception of possibility, making the possible not what sometimes happens, but what can be imagined without contradiction (see MAIMONIDES).

In the Latin West, John DUNS SCOTUS was the first to make use of the concept of 'logical possibility' (*possibilitas logica*), saying that what is contingent is not what is neither necessary nor impossible, but rather such that its opposite could have happened at the very same time that it did. Something is possible if it is not self-contradictory, whether or not it ever exists in reality. Following along these lines, fourteenth-century natural philosophers and theologians often discussed counterfactual cases according to imagination (*secundum imaginationem*). Even if there are no vacuums in the cosmos, they asked, what would happen if God made a vacuum and if a projectile were placed within it: would it move infinitely fast, with a finite velocity, or not at all? Or what would happen if God rotated the cosmos as a whole? Since there would then be no fixed point of reference, how could the rotation of the cosmos be distinguished from rest? In such discussions *secundum imaginationem*, natural philosophers often made a distinction between God's absolute power (*potentia Dei absoluta*) and God's ordained power (*potentia Dei ordinata*). God's ordained power referred to the ways in which God has chosen to create and sustain the universe, as pictured in twelfth-century cosmogonies making use of Plato's *Timaeus*, with its image of the Demiurge or Craftsman who forms an orderly cosmos out of a pre-existing chaos. God's absolute power, on the other hand, covered everything that God might have chosen or done, even though God has not so chosen in fact. God chose to make a single cosmos with the earth in the centre, but God could have made more than one cosmos. Although there are no vacua in the universe, if God had wanted to create vacua, God could have done so.

In this distinction between God's absolute and ordained powers, natural philosophy was understood to focus on the world as it has been formed by God's ordained power. On the other hand, arguments *secundum imaginationem* or *de potentia Dei absoluta* might be used to help clarify what things are and are not distinct, or independent of each other. So, WILLIAM OF OCKHAM might argue, if motion or quantity are really distinct things, then God can create motion without any moving body, or quantity without anything that is extended or quantified. If God cannot cause motion to exist without a mobile (the very concept being self-contradictory), so Ockham might argue, it follows that the word 'motion' does not refer to anything other than substances or qualities. In this way, arguments *secundum imaginationem* involving God's absolute power were used to support nominalism or a minimalist ontology without necessarily implying that God actually puts his absolute power into effect as imagined.

Thus in the late medieval understanding, God establishes but is not limited by the laws of nature. The only things that God could not do are those whose existence would be a self-contradiction. God could not make a square circle, because a square circle is logically impossible. God can and does, however, create accidents that do not inhere in any substance: this is physically impossible, but not logically or supernaturally impossible. Although naturally there are never accidental forms where there is no substance, such as whiteness where there is nothing to be white, in the Eucharist God miraculously causes the accidental forms of the bread and wine to persist without inhering in any substance (the substances of bread and wine having become the body and blood of Christ, without Christ's body and blood having taken on the accidental forms of bread and wine).

The significance of all this for the status of natural philosophy was that nearly everyone in the later medieval university accepted a view that had elements of the views of both Boethius of Dacia and Thomas Aquinas. Aristotelian natural philosophy was understood to describe the cosmos as established by God's ordained power. One could understand that within the cosmos as it currently exists, creation is impossible, and so Aristotle's argument for the eternity of the world is valid given the laws of nature as they are currently established. On the other hand, the creation of the world as recounted in Genesis could be understood as an event that occurred not within the laws of nature as currently constituted, but rather supernaturally as the effect of God's absolute power, the occasion upon which God's ordering of the world was established. Likewise, miracles could be understood as departures from the laws of nature; which departures, as such, did not show that these laws of nature do not exist. God is the first cause of everything that happens, but, except for creation and miracles, events also have secondary causes that act instrumentally according to the patterns described by Aristotelian natural philosophy.

Thus later medieval natural philosophers found a *modus vivendi* in which they were free to follow the dictates of reason and observation in further developing their natural philosophy. They developed a number of methods and theories that were impressively successful, so that fourteenth-century theologians often adopted the methods of the faculty of arts for their own purposes. At the same time, later medieval theology not infrequently posed new concerns which natural philosophers subsequently took into account. If, according to the theologians, God could create a vacuum *de potentia absoluta*, then natural philosophers considered what implications the existence of a vacuum might have for the basic laws and concepts of Aristotelian natural philosophy. If in the Eucharist there are qualities not inhering in any substance, then natural philosophers took this possibility into account. If, according to faith, God sends messages to earth using angels, then natural philosophers assumed that angels or separate substances were included among the types of entities that exist and whose properties may be discussed by natural philosophy (in fact, they supposed, the Aristotelian prime movers of the heavenly spheres are angels, even if Aristotle does not call them by this name).

Although in this way there was general agreement among the scholastics about how natural philosophy should operate, the results were by no means monolithic. If all agreed that, on the whole, the cosmos consists of substances made up of matter and form, they did not all agree what should be said, for instance, about the matter of the heavens as opposed to that of the sublunar elements. On each of the many problems that could be raised concerning Aristotelian physics, alternative solutions were proposed. University officials did not require natural philosophers to adhere to a single party line. The Dominicans might favour a position different from that of the Franciscans, and students and masters not belonging to any of the mendicant orders might hold still other positions.

8 Medieval variations on Aristotelian natural philosophy: new methods

Students in the faculty of arts in medieval universities perhaps spent more time studying logic than any other discipline, and it was from logic that later medieval natural philosophy adopted many of its most widely successful and transforming methods (see LANGUAGE, MEDIEVAL THEORIES OF; LOGIC, MEDIEVAL). Because modern science uses mathematics rather than logic as its predominant tool (leaving aside experiment and data collection), historians of science have rarely recognized or understood how logic could play such an important and transformative role in medieval natural philosophy.

Put simply, medieval grammar, logic, natural philosophy and metaphysics together developed scholastic Latin to the point where it could map or model the world as exactly as mathematics does in modern science, albeit without the flexibility to describe very great complexity. This was especially the case for those logicians who took a nominalist or Ockhamist point of view, asserting that of the Aristotelian categories, only substance and quality refer to things existing outside the mind (see NOMINALISM). The basic idea was that words in propositions stand for objects in the physical world, while the syntax of the proposition indicates exactly the relationships between those objects represented in the proposition's assertion. Thus in one view, in the proposition, 'All humans are featherless,' the word 'humans' stands for all and only existing humans, the word 'featherless' stands for all and only existing featherless things, and the syntax of the sentence asserts the claim that every one of the things for which the word 'humans' stands falls also within the group of things for which the word 'featherless' stands.

This general strategy, known as the theory of the 'supposition' of terms in propositions, was then elaborated to apply to the exact interpretation of the propositions of natural philosophy. Many words, the so-called 'categorematic terms,' were supposed to stand for entities falling within the ten Aristotelian categories, especially for substances and qualities in the outside world or for concepts in the mind. Other words important to natural philosophy were explained to be 'syncategorematic terms' or logical operators, words that do not themselves stand for objects in the external world but rather affect the way that other terms appearing after them in the same proposition stand for things in the world. A given syncategorematic term was then associated with a paired 'exposition', in which a single proposition was shown to be expoundable into two or more propositions, the terms of each of which stood for things in the external world in a more standard way than did the terms of the original proposition.

Thus in the proposition, 'Socrates begins to be white', the term 'begins' was explained to be the sort of term that requires exposition, and the proposition was said to mean either (1) Socrates is not now white and immediately after this he will be white, or (2) Socrates is now white and immediately before this he was not white. Then, depending on the characteristics of the predicate term 'white', the natural philosopher/ logician could determine which of the two expositions was the correct one. So-called 'permanent' characteristics, like whiteness, were said to have a first instant of being, but no last instant of non-being at their start, while so-called 'successive' characteristics, like running, were said to have a last instant of non-being at their start, but no first instant of being.

Natural philosophy, then, was understood to be exact talk about the things in the external world and their motions and changes, and the propositions of natural philosophy were formulated and interpreted to make this exact description possible. In the case of the nominalists (WILLIAM OF OCKHAM, John BURIDAN, ALBERT OF SAXONY and others), this was associated with a great clarity about and minimization of the number of types of things that were supposed to exist in the cosmos. Following Aristotle's *Categories*, the world was supposed to be filled with individual substances, each of which could be qualified by various accidental forms. All the categories except substance and quality (and possibly also quantity) were supposed to involve only manners of speaking or modes of existence of the primary substances and qualities, not additional entities in the universe; thus time, place, relation, position and the rest were not separate things in the universe that natural philosophy had to deal with. All propositions that referred to time, for instance, could be expounded into propositions involving only substances and qualities and perhaps quantities. Aristotle had defined time as 'the number of motion'. Scholastic natural philosophers following Aristotle could say

that, since this is what the word 'time' means, time exists only if there is a body in motion and a mind observing that motion and measuring it or assigning a number to it. (In this view, numbers also are not independently existing things in the universe, but require a mind counting substances.) Understanding that this is what time is could serve in part to solve the problem of whether the cosmos had a beginning in time. The cosmos has existed for all time, it might be said, because when there was no cosmos but only God in existence, there was no motion and hence no time. Time begins when God creates the moving cosmos, and it exists fully only if there is a mind numbering that motion (see COSMOLOGY; TIME).

A similar precision concerning the supposition of terms in propositions might be used to help solve problems of the possibility that there is a vacuum or empty space outside the cosmos, because 'space' in Aristotelian physics is an apparently significant term that in fact does not and cannot stand for anything to which its definition applies. 'Space', as used by the atomists, is supposed to be an extension in which there is nothing, but according to the medieval understanding of Aristotle, extensions can only be extensions of things; of substances or, in the special case of the Eucharist, of qualities. If it was supposed that God, according to God's absolute power, could create an empty space, that it was not a contradiction in terms, then it was typically concluded that, even so, there would be no extension there, or only an imaginary extension, because only bodies are extended. Even if God was supposed to be in infinite empty space outside the cosmos (as Thomas BRAD-WARDINE and Nicole ORESME both suggested), this did not necessarily imply that there would be extension there because God was understood to be wholly present at every point, not extended with one part in one place and another part in another. Just as God's existence 'before' the creation of the cosmos did not mean that there was time before creation, so God's existence 'outside' the cosmos did not mean that there was real space or extension there.

If the most widespread methodological innovation of medieval natural philosophy was the application of the precision of supposition theory, natural philosophers did also make progress in the application of mathematics. In an influential application, Thomas Bradwardine, writing at Oxford in 1328, found a new way to apply the Euclidean theory of ratios as it had been applied to the understanding of musical harmony, to describe the ratios of forces, resistances and velocities in motions. This innovation was so pleasingly apt, appearing very simple yet overcoming important drawbacks of the more authentically Aristotelian view, that it was adopted by nearly everyone.

Paired with this innovation in the understanding of the relation of motion to its causes came progress in the exact mathematical description of motion in terms of its effects in the traversal of space, heating, change of size and so on. Corresponding to distances traversed in space, the concepts of 'latitude' and 'degree' were developed to measure intensive changes or the so-called intension and remission of forms. In later decades, the disputations on sophismata that had previously been used at Oxford to demonstrate students' abilities to apply the rules of logic were expanded to involve the new uses of mathematics as well as logic or, more rarely, grammatical theory. From this came the work of authors such as Richard KILVINGTON, William HEYTESBURY, Richard Swineshead and the other Oxford Calculators (see OXFORD CALCULATORS). Absolutely typical of later medieval natural philosophy and theology was the widespread use of what have been called 'analytical languages' or 'conceptual algorithms', that is, standard patterns of analysis repeatedly used to solve almost any problem. These 'analytical languages' included the Bradwardinian theory of the ratios of velocities in motions, the analysis of first and last instants, and analysis in terms of maxima and minima.

In their commentaries on Aristotle's *Posterior Analytics*, medieval natural philosophers were clear that the starting point for natural philosophy is experience. One starts from observation and works back to find the causes of the effects observed, demonstrating that (*quia*) the causes exist. Natural philosophy as a demonstrative science was supposed to be complete when the philosopher could start from the causes and demonstrate why (*propter quid*) the effects as originally observed occur. However, if medieval natural philosophers believed in empiricism, they did not believe it was their role to actually conduct observations, let alone experiments. In practice, what medieval natural philosophers did was to try to perfect Aristotelian natural philosophy, making the meaning of its propositions more exact through logic and arguing the merits of various interpretations and modifications of Aristotle through formal public disputations.

9 Medieval variations on Aristotelian natural philosophy: traditions and research programmes

Our current knowledge of medieval natural philosophy has been built up in the twentieth century, for the most part through the combined efforts of historians of science, theology and philosophy. In the last twenty years, important work relevant to the history of medieval natural philosophy has also been done by historians of logic. From the perspective of the history of science, the original motivation, following the groundbreaking work of Pierre Duhem (1985), was to show how the roots of many of the ideas of early modern science could be found in the Middle Ages. For example, the medieval idea of impetus was seen as leading to the early modern idea of inertia, fourteenth-century analyses of uniformly accelerated motion were seen to foreshadow Galileo's analysis of balls rolling down inclined planes (see GALILEI, GALILEO), and medieval ideas of God's omnipresence were seen to have contributed to Newton's conception of absolute space (see NEWTON, I.).

In contrast to historians of science, some historians of theology have taken an interest in the history of medieval natural philosophy insofar as it interacted with theology, contributing, for example, to the medieval Christian–Aristotelian synthesis and to the subsequent threat to this synthesis posed by the Copernican thesis that the earth rotates and orbits the sun (see ARISTOTELIANISM, MEDIEVAL; COPERNICUS, N.). In telling the story of medieval natural philosophy, some historians have taken Aquinas' Christian–Aristotelian synthesis as the high-water mark of medieval Christian philosophy, portraying the nominalist path as a falling away from or dissolution of this synthesis. On the other hand, some historians of the Reformation have taken WILLIAM OF OCKHAM as the hero of medieval natural philosophy, and have portrayed his nominalism or preference for a minimalist ontology as a fortunate paring away of the overdevelopment of previous scholastic thought. The theological position known as 'voluntarism' has been seen as equally salutary. While Aquinas thought he could reason how the cosmos must be on the grounds that God, as the highest good and all powerful, must have done things in the best possible way, the voluntarists argued that God had a choice, that there were many more things God could have done by his absolute power than he chose to do by his ordained power. If, according to the voluntarists, humans cannot reason what God must have done, they must instead observe the world as it actually is to determine how God in fact chose to create it. Thus, it is suggested, voluntarism in theology led to empiricism in science, and Ockham led to Copernicus and Galileo.

By the sixteenth century, natural philosophers often described their predecessors as followers of the realist way (*via realium*) or followers of the nominalist way (*via nominalium*), but thirteenth- and fourteenth-century natural philosophers less commonly labelled themselves according to philosophical schools. On the other hand, the Dominican and Franciscan orders ran their own houses of study, and a Dominican or a

Franciscan friar would likely have studied a somewhat different curriculum before appearing on the scene at Oxford, Cambridge or Paris. Early on, the Dominicans adopted Thomas Aquinas as their intellectual model and so upheld the theory of the unity of the substantial form, that each substance is composed of a substantial form inhering directly in prime matter and that there are no intermediary forms, such as Averroes' 'indeterminate dimensions' (*dimensiones interminatae*) preparing the matter to receive a substantial form.

Some recent historians question the validity or usefulness of categorizing medieval thinkers as nominalists, terminists or Ockhamists. They have also claimed for earlier and less well-known thinkers many of the ideas previously associated particularly with Ockham, and have questioned whether nominalism was as important in the fourteenth century as earlier historians believed. Similarly, some recent historians have questioned the usefulness of the term 'Averroist,' previously applied to medieval natural philosophers to signify either philosophers who followed Averroes' opinion on certain questions – for instance, the question of the nature of the human soul – or philosophers such as Boethius of Dacia who chose to emphasize a purely natural or secular approach without obvious Christian modifications (see AVERROISM). The usefulness of labels such as 'nominalist' or 'Averroist' varies depending on where one's attention is directed, whether to issues of logic, psychology or theology.

The organization of medieval natural philosophy into schools and trends is also made more complicated by the fact that it was not common for medieval philosophers to claim originality. Someone such as Roger BACON, who was quick to criticize his contemporaries for what he considered their ineptness, was the exception rather than the rule. Not only did scholastics generally not claim originality, but there were a number of scholastic practices that tended to further obscure their differences. To begin with, the same tools of logic and mathematics – the same analytical languages – could be used by individuals of very different theological persuasions. In commenting on Aristotle, many authors claimed that they were only describing and not advocating the opinions of Aristotle and Averroes. They said that they had recited the arguments for a particular point of view for the sake of (their own or the students') exercise, and not because they necessarily held them to be persuasive, and they often argued that more than one position on a given issue might be 'probable'; that is, one could develop a respectable argument on either side of a disgreement, and no one could demonstrate that one and only one solution was correct. Some texts existed as handbooks to prepare students for obligatory disputations, so they include the source arguments for alternative positions that a student might try to defend.

Sometimes church leaders advocated a sort of decorum so that clergymen would not be seen by the laity to disagree, but this did not apply in general to discussion of natural philosophy within the university because it could be assumed that these would not spill over into public consciousness. Within the university, then, scholars did disagree over natural philosophy issues, but this might not attract much attention unless the given issue had repercussions for theology and individual thinkers were much more likely to fall into camps over differences of opinion in theology than in natural philosophy.

In sum, because natural philosophy was rarely a life or death matter in the medieval university and because the answers to many questions really did remain open, many individual natural philosophers could present views that were somewhat tentative or that evolved over time. On the other hand, if a modern historian follows the discussion of a particular point over time, there is often a definite trend and progress in the solutions given, with some previous difficulties resolved to general agreement. Some of the most prominent commentaries on Aristotle have been studied, but many anonymous or poorly labelled commentaries on Aristotle's natural works still lie unstudied in manuscript form. Historical conceptions of the trends in medieval natural philosophy are likely to continue to evolve. John DUNS SCOTUS seems to have been a pivotal thinker for many natural philosophical topics, even though his influence was exerted through commentaries on Peter Lombard's *Sentences* rather than through commentaries on Aristotle. Walter BURLEY has been labelled an Averroist and a realist in contrast to Ockham's nominalism, but Burley's position remains unclear, perhaps because there is no modern group such as the Dominicans or Franciscans that takes him as a special ancestor. Depending upon the perspectives of modern historians, new images of medieval natural philosophy can be expected to emerge in the future.

See also: ALBERT THE GREAT; ALCHEMY; AQUINAS, T.; ARISTOTELIANISM, MEDIEVAL; AVERROISM; BACON, R.; BRADWARDINE, T.; COPERNICUS, N.; COSMOLOGY; GALILEI, GALILEO; ETERNITY OF THE WORLD, MEDIEVAL VIEW OF; LANGUAGE, MEDIEVAL THEORIES OF; LOGIC, MEDIEVAL; MECHANICS, ARISTOTELIAN; MEDIEVAL PHILOSOPHY; NECKHAM, A.; ORESME, N.; OXFORD CALCULATORS; RELIGION

AND SCIENCE; SCIENCE IN ISLAMIC PHILOSOPHY; SCIENTIFIC METHOD

References and further reading

Representative primary sources in translation

Aquinas, Thomas (1257–9) *Expositio super librum Boethii De trinitate* (Commentary on Boethius' *De trinitate*), trans A. Maurer, *Faith, Reason and Theology: Questions I-IV of his Commentary on the De Trinitate of Boethius*, Toronto, Ont.: Pontifical Institute of Mediaeval Studies, 1987. (A central medieval expression of the organization of the sciences.)

—— (1266–73) *Summa theologiae*, vol. 10, *Cosmogony*, ed. and trans. W.A. Wallace, New York: McGraw-Hill, 1967. (An example of how medieval natural philosophy appears in a theological context.)

—— (1271) *De aeternitate mundi* (On the Eternity of the World), trans. C. Vollert, L. H. Kendzierski and P.M. Byrne, Milwaukee, WI: Marquette University Press, 1964. (The eternity of the world was perhaps the most debated question of thirteenth century natural philosophy in conjunction with theology; this was Aquinas' contribution.)

Bacon, R. (before 1292) *De multiplicatione specierum* (On the Multiplication of Species), ed. and trans. D. Lindberg in *Roger Bacon's Philosophy of Nature*, Oxford: Clarendon Press, 1983. (The multiplication of species, or action of a body on its surroundings, was a key concept in medieval natural philosophy.)

Bernard of Tours (*c.* 1174) *Cosmographia*, trans W. Wetherbee, *The Cosmographia of Bernardus Sylvestris*, New York: Columbia University Press, 1973. (A good example of twelfth-century natural philosophy in the form of mythography, as associated with the cathedral of Chartres.)

Boethius of Dacia (*c.* 1275) *De summo bono* (On the Supreme Good), trans. J.F. Wippel, *On the Supreme Good, On the Eternity of the World, On Dreams*, Toronto, Ont.: Pontifical Institute of Mediaeval Studies, 1987. (Expresses Boethius of Dacia's high regard for the philosophic life.)

—— (*c.* 1275) *De aeternitate mundi* (On the Eternity of the World), trans. J.F. Wippel, *On the Supreme Good, On the Eternity of the World, On Dreams*, Toronto, Ont.: Pontifical Institute of Medieval Studies, 1987. (Boethius' views on creation.)

Bonaventure (1250–73) *De aeternitate mundi* (On the Eternity of the World), trans. C. Vollert, L. H. Kendzierski and P.M. Byrne, Milwaukee, WI: Marquette University Press, 1964. (Bonaventure's contribution to the debate on the eternity of the world.)

Maimonides, Moses (*c.* 1190) *Dalalat al-Ha'irin* (*Moreh Nevukhim*, Guide to the Perplexed), trans. S. Pines, Chicago, IL: University of Chicago Press, 1963. (Good example of the sorts of ideas from Islam and Judaism available in Latin from the mid-thirteenth century, *c.* 1230–5.)

Oresme, Nicole (1377) *Le livre du ciel et du monde* (The Book of the Heaven and Earth), ed. A.D. Menut and A.J. Denomy, trans. A.D. Menut, Madison, WI: University of Wisconsin Press, 1968. (Oresme's translation into French and commentary on Aristotle's *On the Heavens*; shows both what fourteenth-century Aristotelian commentaries were like and how a commentary on Aristotle might be modified for a lay audience.)

—— (*c.* 1351–55?) *Tractatus de configurationibus qualitatum et motuum* (Treatise on Configurations of Qualities and Motions), ed. and trans. M. Clagett, *Nicole Oresme and the Medieval Geometry of Qualities and Motions*, Madison, WI: University of Wisconsin Press, 1968. (Represents the peak of fourteenth-century development of a science combining natural philosophy and quantification.)

Siger of Brabant (*c.* 1272) *De aeternitate mundi* (On the Eternity of the World), trans. C. Vollert, L. H. Kendzierski and P.M. Byrne, Milwaukee, WI: Marquette University Press, 1964. (Siger's contribution to the debate on the eternity of the world.)

Secondary sources

Cadden, J. (1995) 'Science and Rhetoric in the Middle Ages: The Natural Philosophy of William of Conches', *Journal of the History of Ideas* 56: 1–24. (How twelfth-century natural philosophy reflects the audience addressed.)

Caroti, S. and Souffrin, P. (1997) *La nouvelle physique du xiv^e siecle* (The New Physics of the Fourteenth Century), Biblioteca di Nuncius, Studi e Testi XXIV, Florence: Olschki. (Eleven articles related to such topics as natural philosophy and sophismata in the thirteenth century, the debate over Ockham's physical theories at Paris, God's absolute power, reaction and so on.)

Chenu, M.-D. (1968) *Nature, Man and Society in the Twelfth Century*, ed. and trans. J. Taylor and L.K. Little, Chicago, IL: University of Chicago Press. (Classic expression of twelfth-century world view.)

Clagett, M. (1979) *Studies in Medieval Physics and Mathematics*, London: Variorum. (Key studies of medieval natural philosophy from the point of view of the history of science.)

Courtenay, W. (1984) *Covenant and Causality in Medieval Thought*, London: Variorum. (Theological trends with an impact on natural philosophy.)

Crombie, A.C. (1953) *Robert Grosseteste and the Origins of Experimental Thought*, Oxford: Clarendon Press. (Classic statement of the argument that medieval thinkers developed an empirical epistemology.)

Davidson, H. (1987) *Proofs for Eternity, Creation and the Existence of God in Medieval Islamic and Jewish Philosophy*, Oxford: Oxford University Press. (A superb survey of Islamic and Jewish sources for the subjects listed.)

Dronke, P. (ed.) (1988) *A History of Twelfth-Century Western Philosophy*, Cambridge: Cambridge University Press. (Essential compendium for the twelfth century.)

* Duhem, P. (1913–59) *Medieval Cosmology: Theories of Infinity, Place, Time, Void and the Plurality of Worlds*, ed. and trans. R. Ariew, Chicago: University of Chicago Press, 1985. (Translation of selections from Duhem's *Système du monde*, Paris, 10 vols. A groundbreaking work for twentieth century interest in medieval cosmology.)

Flint, V.I.J. (1991) *The Rise of Magic in Early Medieval Europe*, Princeton, NJ: Princeton University Press. (An essential reminder that the context of medieval natural philosophy was shaped in part by belief in magic.)

Funkenstein, A. (1986) *Theology and the Scientific Imagination from the Middle Ages to the Seventeenth Century*, Princeton, NJ: Princeton University Press. (A stimulating series of insights into the ways in which ideas of medieval and early modern theology and science may have been connected with one another.)

Goddu, A. (1984) *The Physics of William of Ockham*, Leiden: Brill. (An assessment of the role of Ockham in medieval natural philosophy.)

Grant, E. (1981a) *Much Ado About Nothing: Theories of Space and Vacuum from the Middle Ages to the Scientific Revolution*, Cambridge: Cambridge University Press. (A survey in depth of medieval ideas of place and space.)

—— (1981b) *Studies in Medieval Science and Natural Philosophy*, London: Variorum. (Collected articles especially relevant to cosmology, the impact of the condemnations of 1277, the roles of John Buridan and Nicole Oresme in fourteenth century natural philosophy, and the longevity of the Aristotelian world view.)

—— (1994) *Planets, Stars and Orbs: The Medieval Cosmos 1200–1687*, Cambridge: Cambridge University Press. (See especially the catalogue of scholastic questions asked about the cosmos from 1200 to 1687 and its analysis.)

—— (1996) *The Foundations of Modern Science in the Middle Ages, their Religious, Institutional and Intellectual Contexts*, Cambridge: Cambridge University Press. (Argues that the translations from Greek and Arabic, the development of the universities and the activities of theologian–natural philosophers prepared the way for modern science.)

Kretzmann, N., Kenny, A. and Pinborg, J. (eds) (1982) *The Cambridge History of Later Medieval Philosophy*, Cambridge: Cambridge University Press. (In addition to chapters by Weisheipl, Grant, Sylla and Murdoch on natural philosophy, provides essential background in logic, metaphysics, epistemology and other philosophical subjects essential to natural philosophy.)

Maier, A. (1982) *On the Threshold of Exact Science: Selected Writings of Anneliese Maier on Late Medieval Natural Philosophy*, trans. S.D. Sargent, Philadelphia, PA: University of Pennsylvania Press. (A small selection from Maier's fundamental studies of late medieval natural philosophy published in German, 1952–77. Maier's work is still the most important single authority on medieval natural philosophy.)

Molland, A.G. (1995) *Mathematics and the Medieval Ancestry of Physics*, Aldershot and Brookfield, VT: Variorum. (Collected articles especially on the relation of mathematics to natural philosophy.)

Moody, E. (1975) *Studies in Medieval Philosophy, Science and Logic: Collected Papers 1933–1969*, Berkeley, CA: University of California Press. (Represents pioneering work on medieval natural philosophy.)

Murdoch, J.E. (1969) 'Mathesis in Philosophiam Scholasticam Introducta. The Rise and Development of the Application of Mathematics in Fourteenth Century Philosophy and Theology', in *Actes du Quatrième Congrès International de Philosophie Médiévale*, Montreal, Que.: Institut d'Études Médiévales, 215–54. (How medieval natural philosophers introduced quantification into their work.)

—— (1975) 'From Social into Intellectual Factors: An Aspect of the Unitary Character of Medieval Learning', in J.E. Murdoch and E.D. Sylla (eds) *The Cultural Context of Medieval Learning*, Dordrecht: Reidel, 271–339. (Describes in some detail the conceptual algorithms or analytical languages used throughout much of fourteenth-century philosophy and theology and connecting philosophy to theology through common methods.)

North, J. (1984) 'Natural Philosophy in Late Medieval Oxford', in J.I. Catto and R. Evans (eds) *The History of the University of Oxford*, Oxford: Oxford

University Press, vol. 2, 65–174. (Provides North's angle on late medieval natural philosophy and the mixed sciences in general, given the difficulty of distinguishing what belonged to Oxford and what to other centres of intellectual activity. See also North's article 'Astronomy and Mathematics' and other articles on theology and logic in the same volume.)

Pederson, O. (1953) 'The Development of Natural Philosophy, 1250–1350', *Classica et Medievalia* 14: 86–155. (An early attempt at synthesis.)

Schmitt, C. (1984) *The Aristotelian Tradition and Renaissance Universities*, London: Variorum. (Aristotelian natural philosophy in its Renaissance manifestations.)

Sorabji, R. (1983) *Time, Creation and the Continuum: Theories in Antiquity and the Early Middle Ages*, Ithaca, NY: Cornell University Press. (Wide-ranging discussion of the essential late Hellenistic background to medieval natural philosophy.)

Sylla, E.D. (1993) 'Aristotelian Commentaries and Scientific Change: The Parisian Nominalists on the Cause of the Natural Motion of Inanimate Bodies', *Vivarium* 31: 37–83. (A case study of how commenting on Aristotle worked as a form of scientific – or natural philosophical – practice.)

Tachau, K. (1988) *Vision and Certitude in the Age of Ockham: Optics, Epistemology and the Foundations of Semantics, 1250–1345*, Leiden: Brill. (Argues for the centrality of the optical metaphor in medieval theories of knowledge.)

Weisheipl, J.A. (ed.) (1980) *Albertus Magnus and the Sciences: Commemorative Essays, 1980*, Toronto, Ont.: Pontifical Institute of Mediaeval Studies. (Albert the Great is essential to understanding the nature of Aristotelian natural philosophy in the thirteenth century.)

Wilson, C. (1956) *William Heytesbury: Medieval Logic and the Rise of Mathematical Physics*, Madison, WI: The University of Wisconsin Press. (Demonstrates the interaction of logic and sophismata with medieval natural philosophy.)

Wolfson, H.A. (1929) *Crescas' Critique of Aristotle: Problems of Aristotle's 'Physics' in Jewish and Arabic Philosophy*, Cambridge, MA: Harvard University Press. (Classic study by a renowned scholar of a fifteenth-century Hebrew commentary on Aristotelian physics, useful as a comparison to Latin sources.)

EDITH DUDLEY SYLLA

NATURAL THEOLOGY

Natural theology aims at establishing truths or acquiring knowledge about God (or divine matters generally) using only our natural cognitive resources. The phrase 'our natural cognitive resources' identifies both the methods and data for natural theology: it relies on standard techniques of reasoning and facts or truths in principle available to all human beings just in virtue of their possessing reason and sense perception. As traditionally conceived, natural theology begins by establishing the existence of God, and then proceeds by establishing truths about God's nature (for example, that God is eternal, immutable and omniscient) and about God's relation to the world.

A precise characterization of natural theology depends on further specification of its methods and data. One strict conception of natural theology – the traditional conception sometimes associated with Thomas Aquinas – allows only certain kinds of deductive argument, the starting points of which are propositions that are either self-evident or evident to sense perception. A broader conception might allow not just deductive but also inductive inference and admit as starting points propositions that fall short of being wholly evident.

Natural theology contrasts with investigations into divine matters that rely at least in part on data not naturally available to us as human beings. This sort of enterprise might be characterized as revelation-based theology, in so far as the supernatural element on which it relies is something supernaturally revealed to us by God. Revelation-based theology can make use of what is ascertainable by us only because of special divine aid. Dogmatic and biblical theology would be enterprises of this sort.

Critics of natural theology fall generally into three groups. The first group, the majority, argue that some or all of the particular arguments of natural theology are, as a matter of fact, unsuccessful. Critics in the second group argue that, in principle, natural theology cannot succeed, either because of essential limitations on human knowledge that make it impossible for us to attain knowledge of God or because religious language is such as to make an investigation into its truth inappropriate. The third group of critics holds that natural theology is in some way irrelevant or inimical to true religion. They argue in various ways that the objectifying, abstract and impersonal methods of natural theology cannot capture what is fundamentally important about the divine and our relation to it.

1   A strict conception of natural theology
2   A broader conception of natural theology
3   Reason, revelation and faith

1   A strict conception of natural theology

An influential traditional understanding of natural theology is based on a model of theoretical inquiry derived from Aristotle's account of demonstrative science (see ARISTOTLE §6). The model of demonstrative science describes the logical structure of the truths comprising a given area of theoretical inquiry and the corresponding epistemic structure of the beliefs one has when one has attained theoretical knowledge of that area. On this model, theoretical knowledge is constituted by two sorts of truths: those that are basic or fundamental and those that are dependent on them. Truths of the first sort are facts whose nature is such that they are open to our immediate cognitive gaze. Our knowledge of them consists in our having direct access to or awareness of them, and so they can be thought of as *evident*. They are self-evident if they are accessible to us in virtue of being immediately present to our strictly intellective capacities, or evident to sense perception if they are accessible in virtue of being immediately present to our sensory capacities. When we are directly aware of evident truths in either of these ways, we are epistemically justified in holding them just in virtue of our immediate grasp of their truth. Truths of this sort are epistemically privileged in the sense that one's epistemic justification for holding them is independent of one's justification for any other truths one might happen to hold. They can suitably ground other sorts of knowledge because they require no epistemic ground beyond themselves.

The second sort of truths constitutive of theoretical knowledge in demonstrative science are those derivable from the basic truths by means of demonstrative proofs or deductively valid arguments. These truths are accessible to us by virtue of our capacity for discursive reasoning. In so far as they are known as conclusions of demonstrative proofs they are epistemically dependent, mediated by our awareness of the truth of the relevant premises and the validity of the relevant inferences. We are inferentially justified in holding these truths by virtue of our having derived them in appropriate ways from truths we are independently and non-inferentially justified in holding.

Conceiving of natural theology as a kind of demonstrative science allows us to characterize it precisely: it consists of truths about God which are either (1) self-evident or evident to sense perception, or (2) derived by deductively valid proofs the (ultimate) premises of which are self-evident or evident to sense perception. Thomas AQUINAS (§14) is perhaps the most famous Christian theologian to develop Aristotle's account of demonstrative science and adapt it to theological inquiry. His famous proofs for the existence of God (the so-called five ways) and his arguments establishing such truths as that God is one, immutable and eternal – his proofs for what he sometimes calls the preambles of faith – are paradigms of natural theology understood as an Aristotelian demonstrative science (he himself prefers to call this enterprise divine science). Aquinas' influential articulation and development of this model of natural theology in the opening sections of his two great theological works, *Summa theologiae* and *Summa contra gentiles*, have made this a dominant conception of that enterprise.

Because its method – deductive argument – is clear and subject to precise and well-understood standards, intellectual inquiry that conforms to the model of demonstrative science is open to the sort of rigorous assessment and evaluation crucial to theoretical objectivity. Moreover, when successful, demonstrative science offers for its results the strongest sort of certification possible. By deriving its conclusions from evident truths by means of necessarily truth-preserving forms of reasoning, a demonstrative science guarantees their truth; we can be certain of them and can claim to have conclusively established them. But these virtues are purchased at a price: a demonstrative science's criteria for admissible data and methods are very strict. Indeed, few philosophers today are sanguine about the prospects of satisfying them outside the realms of logic and mathematics.

2   A broader conception of natural theology

Philosophers have always recognized the importance of arguments that fall short of the paradigm of demonstrative proof – that is, arguments that carry epistemic weight but in some way fall short of being utterly truth-guaranteeing. Following a long tradition, we might call arguments of this sort dialectical arguments. The criteria for good or acceptable dialectical arguments will be more generous than those definitive of demonstrative science. On the one hand, dialectic allows as data propositions that we have some appropriate degree of epistemic justification in believing, though they need not be evident either to reason or sense perception. On the other hand, dialectic admits the use of methods of reasoning other than deduction. It allows inductive reasoning broadly conceived – enumerative induction, probabilistic reasoning, argument from analogy, inference to the best explanation and so on. These requirements on the data and methods of dialectic mean that dialectical reasoning might fall short of demonstrative proof in any of three ways: by having evident premises but lacking a deductive argument form; by having a deductive argument form but lacking evident premises; or by lacking both evident premises and a deductive argument form. Of course these specifications of the data and methods of dialectic are imprecise, and philosophers might well disagree about what propositions are admissible as data (that is, have an appropriate degree of justification) and whether certain particular inductive arguments are strong or weak.

Our engaging in inquiry using only methods and data satisfying the criteria of dialectical reasoning requires us to use nothing beyond our natural cognitive resources. Hence, we ought to acknowledge a corresponding natural theology – dialectical natural theology – that consists in philosophical investigation, of the sort allowed by dialectic, into divine matters. We might call the genus of which strict, demonstrative natural theology and dialectical natural theology are species *broad* natural theology. The practitioner of broad natural theology will attempt to establish truths or acquire knowledge about God using deductive or non-deductive arguments the premises of which are evident or justified to some appropriate degree.

Two important contemporary projects in the philosophy of religion demonstrate some of the different ways natural theology might extend beyond the limits of the strict conception. In *The Existence of God* (1979), Richard Swinburne develops inductive versions of the traditional proofs for God's existence and treats theism as a theoretical hypothesis that claims to offer the best explanation for certain phenomena in the world. Swinburne shares with the strict natural theologian the aim of providing good arguments for the truth of certain theological propositions, in particular that the theistic God exists. But he rejects strict natural theology's requirement that limits the natural theologian to arguments satisfying the strict criteria of demonstrative proof, relying instead on techniques and standards derived from recent developments in the philosophy of science and the logic of probability.

By contrast, philosophers such as Alvin Plantinga and Nicholas Wolterstorff have objected to what they see as the epistemological assumptions underlying both strict natural theology and the work of many practitioners of broad natural theology. Reformed epistemology, as they call it, challenges the view that establishing or defending the rationality of belief in God requires the development of arguments, whether strictly or broadly conceived, for certain theological propositions. They claim that it can be rational to believe in God even if one has *no* evidence for God's existence (see Plantinga and Wolterstorff 1983). Despite this seemingly bold denial of the need for evidence of the sort natural theology might provide, Reformed epistemology does not reject traditional natural theology's general aim of securing appropriate epistemic grounding for certain theological propositions; it rejects only its understanding of what can constitute appropriate grounding. Reformed epistemology allows that belief in God can be properly basic, that is, that the belief that God exists (and other religious beliefs) might appropriately be included among the starting points or data of natural theology. It is therefore a particular kind of defence of the epistemic rationality of our belief in God, and so a kind of broad natural theology (see RELIGION AND EPISTEMOLOGY §§1–3.)

Broad natural theology is not a new phenomenon. It has a long history and includes among its practitioners some of the best-known representatives of strict natural theology. Aquinas, for example, recognizes that some theological truths can be established by means of what he calls merely probable, persuasive or dialectical arguments. John LOCKE (§7), too, allows that reasoning about theological matters that depends solely on our natural faculties can depend on probabilities as well as on necessary reasoning.

3 Reason, revelation and faith

A strict conception of natural theology provides grounds for a clear distinction between natural and revelation-based theology. This is because revelation-based theology, in so far as it is based on divine revelation, is ultimately based on someone's testimony (God's, a divinely authorized agent's or that of historical witnesses to revelatory events). But no proposition whose epistemic grounding essentially involves testimony is either evident or strictly demonstrable. Hence, parts of revelation that are accessible only because they have been revealed are inaccessible to the strict natural theologian and belong exclusively to the domain of revelation-based theology. (The Christian doctrines of the Trinity and the Incarnation have been taken to be paradigm examples.)

AUGUSTINE (§11) and the long line of thinkers who have followed him in defining faith as belief based on authority have held that the contents of revelation are appropriate matters for faith and that the truths accessible only by revelation and not also by strict natural theology are strictly matters of faith and cannot be objects of theoretical knowledge or understanding. They have held, however, that natural theology can provide us with theoretical knowledge or understanding of some matters that can be held by faith. When we acquire a rational proof for a proposition previously held on testimony or come to see the theoretical explanation of it, our faith (with respect to that proposition) is thereby replaced with or converted to knowledge or understanding. Hence, to the extent that natural theology is successful we will have knowledge or understanding, but in so far as we must rely on revelation and testimony for truths about God we will have only faith (see FAITH §4).

If we adopt a broader conception of natural theology, however, we lose the basis for a clear distinction between faith and knowledge or understanding. This is because, unlike demonstrative science, some forms of dialectical inquiry can make use of arguments that appeal to legitimate authority. Augustine points out that virtually everything we believe about the past, other parts of the world, and other people's thoughts and attitudes is based on someone's testimony. Since we typically suppose that we have good reasons for believing things of this sort (because we typically suppose we have good reason to accept the testimony on which those beliefs are based), it follows that propositions whose epistemic grounding essentially involves testimony may not be in principle inaccessible to the natural theologian who uses dialectic. Broad natural theologians might find themselves in a position to establish, solely on the basis of our natural cognitive resources (broadly construed), the legitimate authority of some body of revelation (for example, the historical reliability of the biblical accounts of extraordinary manifestations of divine activity). In that case, the truth of any proposition contained in that body of revelation, including those that must remain for the strict natural theologian strictly matters of faith, might be accessible to the broad natural theologian.

It might turn out, then, that with respect to their contents, there is no distinction between broad natural theology and revelation-based theology. That is to say, it might be that there is no territory open to the practitioner of revelation-based theology that is not in principle also open to the practitioner of broad natural theology. Even so, we might still distinguish between the two enterprises on epistemological grounds. Practitioners of broad natural theology will accept a proposition only in so far as they take it to be an acceptable datum for natural theology or grounded by a suitable argument in it. By contrast, practitioners of revelation-based theology can accept a proposition simply because they believe it to be revealed, regardless of whether that belief or the proposition itself is adequately grounded for them.

4 Critiques of natural theology

Most philosophical attacks on natural theology are directed at particular arguments in natural theology – at one or another of the proofs for God's existence, for example. Objections to Anselm's ontological argument date back to Anselm's contemporary, the eleventh-century monk Gaunilo (see ANSELM OF CANTERBURY §4). René Descartes' proofs for God's existence found a contemporary critic in Thomas HOBBES (§3) (see DESCARTES, R. §6). David HUME (§6) offered a sustained critique of the argument from design popular among Enlightenment thinkers and developed his empiricist principles into an attack on the possibility of miracles and the evidential value of appeals to their alleged occurrence. The Humean project has been elaborated and extended in the twentieth century by the influential work of J.L. Mackie (1982).

Other critics have objected not only to the particular arguments of natural theology but also to the enterprise itself. Immanuel KANT (§8) argued that human knowledge is attainable only within the realm of possible human experience, and he concluded that since God is an object outside that realm, human knowledge cannot extend to divine matters. Hence, in so far as natural theology aims at attaining knowledge of the divine, it must fail. This rejection of natural theology, however, might be taken as relevant only to a certain kind of strict natural theology. In fact if Kant's own 'practical' arguments for the existence of God and the immortality of the soul can be understood as providing some epistemic justification for their conclusions (though not justification sufficient to give us knowledge strictly speaking), then they might be understood as arguments in dialectical (or broad) natural theology.

Some twentieth-century philosophers, following contemporary accounts of the nature of language, have developed analyses of religious discourse that undermine natural theology. Developing one strain of empiricism, A.J. AYER (§2) and R. Braithwaite, for example, have defended non-cognitivist views of religious language. According to Ayer (1946), to say that God exists is to make a metaphysical utterance that is empirically unverifiable and so neither true nor false. Religious discourse, in so far as it purports to describe a transcendent reality, is therefore literally meaningless. Working in the same tradition, Braithwaite (1955) has argued that although religious beliefs are neither true nor false, they are expressive of a practical commitment to a certain religious way of life. On views of this sort, there are no propositions about God for natural theology to establish (see RELIGIOUS LANGUAGE §3).

Following Wittgensteinian insights into the nature of language, philosophers such as Norman Malcolm (1977) have argued that religious discourse constitutes a particular language game. As with any language game, there can be no question about the truth, justifiability or legitimacy of the game itself. Questions about the truth or falsity of the beliefs that constitute a language game can be asked only from within the game itself. On this view, a natural theology that aims at providing ultimate grounding for religious beliefs is fundamentally misconceived.

Some critics have had religious grounds for scepticism about the very enterprise of natural theology. Søren KIERKEGAARD (§§4–5), for example, claimed that objective reflection on the truth of divine matters of the sort that is essential to natural theology necessarily fails to attain religious truth. According to Kierkegaard, the highest truth attainable by an existing individual is an infinite subjective passion that is itself paradoxical from the objective point of view. Natural theology will be not just useless but inimical to the attainment of religious truth. Developing both Kantian and Kierkegaardian objections, theologians such as Karl BARTH (§§2–4) have claimed that the Christian God is wholly other and, as such, knowable only in virtue of God's own self-revelation. Barth (1960) concluded that any enterprise that relies solely on natural human resources cannot arrive at knowledge of God.

5 Natural atheology and apologetics

Natural theology is typically thought of as aiming at a positive result – that is, at proving that God exists, establishing that theism is true, or justifying religious belief in general or particular religious beliefs. Arguments in natural theology that are unsuccessful fail to achieve these positive results. But the truth about God (or divine matters generally) might be negative, that is, it might be that there is no God, that theism is false and so forth. So we might think of arguments that have these negative results as also being part of natural theology. Alternatively, we might think of them as part of a distinct enterprise, natural *atheology*, that aims at establishing the falsity of theism or of certain sorts of religious belief.

Natural atheology has had two prominent strands. One strand argues that the concept of God is in some way incoherent or internally inconsistent. Some philosophers have supposed that the concepts of certain attributes commonly thought to be essential to God are incoherent, and that therefore no being possessing such attributes can exist. The well-known paradoxes of omnipotence – for example, that an omnipotent being must be able to create a stone too big for an omnipotent being to lift – purport to show that no being could be omnipotent (see OMNIPOTENCE §2). Others have maintained that certain of the divine attributes are incompatible with one another. It has been argued, for example, that no being could be both omniscient and immutable, since an omniscient being's knowledge must be constantly changing as facts about the world change (see IMMUTABILITY §3).

The other main strand of natural atheology argues that the existence of God or the truth of some set of religious beliefs is incompatible with things we know about the world. By far the most famous atheological argument, the argument from evil, attempts to show that the existence of an omnipotent, omniscient, perfectly good God is incompatible with the existence of evil, or that the kinds and amount of evil we find in our world in some way make improbable the existence of the theistic God or render the theistic hypothesis less probable than some rival hypothesis (see EVIL, PROBLEM OF).

Defending theism against atheological attack has been the traditional role of apologetics. Defence might consist merely in showing that atheological arguments do not succeed in establishing their negative conclusions, or it might involve the more ambitious project of showing how the difficulties alleged against theism can be accommodated and explained by theism. The latter, more ambitious sort of defence against the argument from evil is theodicy – the attempt to justify God's goodness by identifying the morally sufficient reason that justifies God in causing or permitting the evil that in fact exists. Apologetics generally and theodicy in particular can be thought of as parts of natural theology.

6 Clarificatory and philosophical theology

Natural theology, whether strictly or broadly conceived, is justificatory in nature; that is, it is concerned with establishing the truth of certain theological propositions using standard techniques of reasoning starting from propositions that have some appropriate degree of epistemic justification. Many sorts of philosophical reflection, however, are primarily clarificatory rather than justificatory in nature. Philosophical reflection on and explication of the nature and content of a particular theory typically involves the analysis of the concepts central to that theory, the examination of the theory's coherence and internal consistency, and the assessment of the theory's relations to other theories and beliefs. These kinds of analytic and systematic tasks can be and often are carried out apart from questions about the theory's truth or our justification in accepting it; indeed the successful completion of some of these clarificatory tasks is in some ways a prerequisite for assessing the truth of a theory. We can therefore identify an enterprise whose aim is the philosophical clarification and explication of theories about divine matters or the particular beliefs that comprise such theories. We might call this enterprise *clarificatory* theology.

Clarificatory theology is like natural theology with respect to its methods: it uses standard techniques of reasoning (where those include tasks such as definition and conceptual analysis as well as techniques for constructing and evaluating arguments). But it is unlike natural theology in placing no epistemic restrictions on the sorts of propositions or theories that it can take as its starting points. Clarificatory theology might, for example, take the Christian notion of atonement as a datum and engage in philosophical clarification and explication of that notion without requiring that we justifiably believe or know that God exists, that an atonement has in fact occurred or anything of the sort.

If we think of the justification and clarification of religious beliefs and theories as two ways in which our natural cognitive resources can be brought to bear on divine matters, then we can take natural theology and clarificatory theology to be species of a single genus that we might call *philosophical* theology. Philosophical theology is the enterprise that attempts to understand divine matters using the techniques and methods of human reason, particularly as those have been developed within philosophy.

See also: AGNOSTICISM; ATHEISM; GOD, ARGUMENTS FOR THE EXISTENCE OF; GOD, CONCEPTS OF §§2–6; RELIGION, HISTORY OF PHILOSOPHY OF; REVELATION §§1–2

References and further reading

Anselm of Canterbury (1077–8) *Proslogion*, in *Anselm of Canterbury*, ed. and trans. J. Hopkins and H. Richardson, London: SCM Press, 1974, vol. 1. (Contains Anselm's famous presentation of the ontological argument; Gaunilo's reply *On Behalf of the Fool* is included in this volume, as is Anselm's *Monologion*, which contains his development of the concept of God.)

Aquinas, T. (1257–9) *Faith, Reason and Theology* (qq. I–IV of the commentary on Boethius' *De trinitate*), trans. A. Maurer, Toronto, Ont.: Pontifical Institute of Mediaeval Studies. (Aquinas' systematic reflections on the nature and methods of intellectual investigation of divine matters.)

* —— (1259–65) *Summa contra gentiles* I, trans. A.C. Pegis, Notre Dame, IN: University of Notre Dame Press, 1975. (A classic reflection on and defence of natural theology.)

* —— (1266–73) *Summa theologica* I, trans. Fathers of the English Dominican Province, Westminster, MD: Christian Classics, 1981. (Aquinas' most mature attempt at natural theology; contains the famous five ways.)

Augustine (392) *On the Usefulness of Believing*, trans. J.H.S. Burleigh, *Augustine: Earlier Writings*, Philadelphia, PA: Westminster Press, 1953, 291–323. (An argument for the epistemological and practical justification for believing certain propositions when one lacks conclusive proof.)

* Ayer, A.J. (1946) *Language, Truth and Logic*, London: Victor Gollancz. (Ayer's famous statement of the verificationist principle of meaning and his application of it to metaphysical, ethical and religious language.)

* Barth, K. (1960) *Anselm: Fides quaerens intellectum*, trans. I.W. Robertson, Richmond, VA: John Knox Press. (A manifesto for Barth's theological position, but controversial as an interpretation of Anselm.)

* Braithwaite, R. (1955) *An Empiricist's View of the Nature of Religious Belief*, Cambridge: Cambridge University Press. (A fully developed account of a non-cognitivist theory of religious language.)

Descartes, R. (1641) *Meditations on First Philosophy*, ed. G.E.M. Anscombe and P. Geach, *Philosophical Writings*, Indianapolis, IN: Bobbs-Merrill, 1971. (Descartes' proofs can be found in the third and fifth of his *Meditations*. Hobbes' objections are published together with the *Meditations*.)

Hume, D. (1748) *Enquiry concerning Human Understanding*, ed. C.W. Hendel, Indianapolis, IN: Bobbs-Merrill, 1955, section X. (Hume's famous discussion of miracles.)

—— (1779) *Dialogues concerning Natural Religion*, ed. R. Popkin, Indianapolis, IN: Hackett Publishing Company, 1980. (An engaging dialogue focusing on the argument from design.)

Kant, I. (1781/7) *Critique of Pure Reason*, trans. N.K. Smith, London and Basingstoke: Macmillan, 1978, esp. A567/B595–A642/B670. (Kant's general critique of natural theology and his objections to the proofs for God's existence.)

—— (1788) *Critique of Practical Reason*, trans. L.W. Beck, Indianapolis, IN: Bobbs-Merrill, 1978. (Contains Kant's 'practical' arguments for the existence of God and the immortality of the soul.)

Kierkegaard, S. (1846) *Concluding Unscientific Postscript*, trans. D. Swenson and W. Lowrie, Princeton, NJ: Princeton University Press, 1941, esp. 177–88. (Kierkegaard's most detailed defence of the subjectivity of religious truth.)

Kretzmann, N. (1997) *The Metaphysics of Theism: Aquinas' Natural Theology in Summa contra gentiles I*, Oxford: Oxford University Press. (An excellent philosophical assessment of Aquinas' natural theology as presented in *Summa contra gentiles*, book 1.)

Locke, J. (1689) *An Essay Concerning Human Understanding*, ed. P. Nidditch, Oxford: Clarendon Press, book IV, ch. 18. (His position as outlined in §2.)

* Mackie, J.L. (1982) *The Miracle of Theism: Arguments for and against the Existence of God*, Oxford: Clarendon Press. (A lucid, critical discussion of the main arguments for the existence of God.)

* Malcolm, N. (1977) 'The Groundlessness of Belief', in S. Brown (ed.) *Reason and Religion*, Ithaca, NY: Cornell University Press, 143–57. (An analysis of the nature of religious belief relying on the Wittgensteinian notion of a language game.)

Morris, T. (1987) *Anselmian Explorations: Essays in Philosophical Theology*, Notre Dame, IN: University of Notre Dame Press. (A collection of essays developing perfect-being natural theology from an Anselmian perspective.)

Plantinga, A. (1991) 'The Prospects for Natural Theology', in J. Tomberlin (ed.) *Philosophical Perspectives 5: Philosophy of Religion*, Atascadero, CA: Ridgeview Publishing. (Plantinga's assessment of the project of natural theology in light of his religious epistemology.)

* Plantinga, A. and Wolterstorff, N. (eds) (1983) *Faith and Rationality: Reason and Belief in God*, Notre Dame, IN: University of Notre Dame Press. (A seminal collection of essays presenting the foundations of the anti-evidentialist movement in religious epistemology.)

* Swinburne, R. (1979) *The Existence of God*, Oxford: Clarendon Press. (Defence of inductive versions of many of the major arguments for theism within the context of a cumulative-case argument that, given our total evidence, theism is more probable than not.)

Webb, C.C.J. (1915) *Studies in the History of Natural Theology*, Oxford: Clarendon Press. (An older but illuminating general study of different historical approaches to natural theology.)

SCOTT MACDONALD

NATURALISM IN ETHICS

Ethical naturalism is the project of fitting an account of ethics into a naturalistic worldview. It includes nihilistic theories, which see no place for real values and no successful role for ethical thought in a purely natural world. The term 'naturalism' is often used more narrowly, however, to refer to cognitivist naturalism, which holds that ethical facts are simply natural facts and that ethical thought succeeds in discovering them.

G.E. Moore (1903), attacked cognitivist naturalism as mistaken in principle, for committing what he called the 'naturalistic fallacy'. He thought a simple test showed that ethical facts could not be natural facts (the 'fallacy' lay in believing they could be), and he took it to follow that ethical knowledge would have to rest on nonsensory intuition. Later writers have added other arguments for the same conclusions. Moore himself was in no sense a naturalist, since he thought that ethics could be given a 'non-natural' basis. Many who elaborated his criticisms of cognitivist naturalism, however, have done so on behalf of generic ethical naturalism, and so have defended either ethical nihilism or else some more modest constructive position, usually a version of noncognitivism. Noncognitivists concede to nihilists that nature contains no real values, but deny that it was ever the function of ethical thought to discover such things. They thus leave ethical thought room for success at some other task, such as providing the agent with direction for action.

Defenders of cognitivist naturalism deny that there is a 'naturalistic fallacy' or that ethical knowledge need rest on intuition; and they have accused Moore and his successors of relying on dubious assumptions in metaphysics, epistemology, the philosophy of language and the philosophy of mind. Thus many difficult philosophical issues have been implicated in the debate.

1 Naturalism versus other issues
2 Vindicating and debunking
3 Metaphysics
4 Epistemology

1 Naturalism versus other issues

The focus in contemporary debates about ethical naturalism is on the relation of ethics to a naturalistic worldview, one that takes the emerging scientific picture of the world as approximately accurate and that rejects belief in the supernatural. Ethical nihilists deny that real values can fit into such a picture. Cognitivist naturalists reply that they can, and that we can learn about them by methods similar to those by which we learn of other natural facts. Noncognitivists disagree with cognitivists on both counts; they distinguish themselves from nihilists, however, by insisting that the primary function of ethical thought is not to discover ethical truths but rather to direct action, a task at which it may succeed (see ANALYTIC ETHICS; MORAL REALISM).

These debates need to be distinguished from others

with which they are sometimes confused. The ancient Sophists initiated a discussion, for example, about whether morality exists by nature or by convention (see SOPHISTS; NATURE AND CONVENTION). Although answers to this somewhat ill-defined question may bear on contemporary issues about ethical naturalism, the relation is not simple. That morality requires 'following nature' is sometimes a version of cognitivist naturalism, but sometimes not (as when 'following nature' is explained in theological terms). Many versions of cognitivist naturalism take no stand on this thesis, moreover, and others, such as versions of social relativism, appear to come down on the 'convention' side of the older debate (see SOCIAL RELATIVISM).

Questions about naturalism should also be distinguished from more general issues about 'facts and values' (see FACT/VALUE DISTINCTION). One question is whether there are ethical facts. Cognitivist naturalists answer yes, but so did Moore and so do theological moralists. Noncognitivists such as R.M. Hare (1952), to be sure, reject cognitivist naturalism because they think values could not be facts of any sort, even if there were (or are) supernatural facts; and in this they can claim inspiration from Moore (1903), who introduced his peculiar category of the 'nonnatural' to accommodate ethical facts precisely because he thought such facts could be neither natural nor 'metaphysical' (his term for the supernatural) (see MOORE, G.E. §1). But others who applaud Moore's arguments against cognitivist naturalism, such as J.L. Mackie (1977), think there would be no bar to taking certain supernatural facts (for example, about Plato's forms), if there were such facts, to be ethical facts.

So there seems no thesis about whether there are, or could be, ethical facts, which uniquely distinguishes either generic ethical naturalists, cognitivist naturalists or their critics. Another question is whether, from premises entirely about nonethical facts, there are reasonable inferences to any ethical conclusions (see LOGIC OF ETHICAL DISCOURSE §§2–4). Here all critics of cognitivist naturalism answer no. (The doctrine they thereby affirm is called the autonomy of ethics.) Many writers, again beginning with Moore, and including some defenders of cognitivist naturalism, have thought the latter doctrine committed to answering yes. Indeed, in the third quarter of the twentieth century, this question was often understood to be the central issue between cognitivist naturalists and their critics. For reasons which shall be noted, however, many cognitivist naturalists after that time have seen no need to deny the autonomy of ethics. Thus, on this issue, there is agreement among critics of cognitivist naturalism but none among its defenders.

2 Vindicating and debunking

We have distinguished ethical naturalism in the generic sense from significant subcategories: nihilist, cognitivist, noncognitivist. Within these latter two categories we can note one other important distinction. All versions of cognitivist naturalism will allow for discovering that some ethical statements are true, but they may nevertheless differ greatly on how important a 'success' they thereby make possible for ethical thought. For some of these views – for example, the suggestion that judgments of right and wrong merely report local social conventions – seem intended to represent ethical considerations as far less important and less worthy of respect than they have seemed; whereas others, such as ideal contractarian or Aristotelian views, seem designed not to debunk but instead to vindicate the practical importance conventionally ascribed to ethics. Positions at the debunking end of this scale thus join with nihilism in deflating the importance of ethical thought, though on the basis of a thesis about what makes ethical beliefs true rather than on the grounds that they are never true.

A similar distinction can be drawn within noncognitivism. Any noncognitivist theory will specify some role, such as guiding conduct, at which ethical discourse may succeed. But early versions, such as A.J. Ayer's (1936), did not suggest that this would be success at anything rational or likely to command respect (see EMOTIVISM). Later versions, however, such as those of Simon Blackburn (1993) or Allan Gibbard (1990), disown carefully any intention of representing ethical thought as defective or 'second-rate'. Crucial to their case is the claim that, even on a noncognitivist understanding, ethical thought can systematically mimic most of the features – such as answerability to evidence and to requirements of consistency – that make it appear to aim at discovering ethical truths. This defence suggests a way, however, in which even the most vindicatory version of noncognitivism is likely to seem at a disadvantage when compared with a comparably motivated cognitivist naturalism, if the latter is truly available. For why settle for mimicry if one could have the real thing? The answer, according to these noncognitivists, is that the real thing is not available; and their reasons are mostly familiar from the tradition noted above, of thinking cognitivist naturalism vulnerable to objections of principle. So we need to turn to those objections.

3 Metaphysics

These arguments may for convenience be divided into

the metaphysical and the epistemological, although the best-known of them, the 'open question' argument, through which Moore tried to expose the fallacy in all 'naturalistic ethics', draws a metaphysical conclusion from partly epistemic premises. Moore assumed, in what is arguably already an oversimplification, that any version of cognitivist naturalism would rest on a reductive property-identification such as 'goodness = pleasure'. Further, he thought (1) that any such identification could be true only if the expressions flanking the identity-sign are synonyms for a speaker who understands them both, and (2) that the terms could be shown not to be synonyms by the mere fact that such a speaker could conceivably doubt the identity-statement: by the fact, in other words, that it remains in this minimal sense an 'open question' whether the identification is correct. Thus, from the mere fact that doubt about this sample doctrine is conceivable, Moore took it to follow that it is false. Even on these assumptions, it is unclear why he was confident that every version of cognitivist naturalism would fail his test; but his assumptions have in any case met severe criticism. Assumption (2) has been attacked as too stringent a test for synonymy, assumption (1) questioned on the deeper ground that synonymy seems in any case not required for the truth of identifications of this form, as illustrated by such significant discoveries as that water is H_2O or that heat is molecular motion.

Critics of cognitivist naturalism have asked in reply how good a model these scientific identifications could provide for any proposed in ethics. Certainly, there could be little resemblance if Gilbert Harman (1977) were right that ethical notions never seem useful in explaining any natural facts or events. For these scientific identifications are accepted partly because of an approximate match between, for example, the effects common sense explains by reference to heat and the ones attributed to molecular motion. But cognitivist naturalists have replied to Harman that the explanatory use of ethical notions is endemic to ordinary thought. Social justice has long been conceived as a condition that, without undue deception or coercion, will stabilize a society and permit it to flourish; moral decency is taken to be a trait that keeps some people from doing things that come easily to others.

Another cluster of objections concerns the reason-giving and motivating roles of moral facts. Some critics deny that natural facts could possess the rational authority for action expected of ethical facts. Others, especially noncognitivists, deny that natural facts could motivate as ethical facts would have to do when recognized (see MORAL MOTIVATION). To both challenges cognitivist naturalists typically offer a two-part response. First, any vindicatory version will attempt to show about at least some ethical values why, on a full understanding, they would command a strong allegiance from most reflective agents. Anyone who knows or assumes that such an account is available would tend to be motivated by ethical considerations, moreover.

Second, even naturalists who hope to vindicate much of ethics in this way will oppose attempts to dismiss debunking accounts prematurely and for the wrong reason. Conventional thought may accord ethical considerations rational authority, but as with many conventional beliefs about ethics it remains to be seen how well this assumption will withstand critical challenge. Plato has Thrasymachus in the *Republic* say that justice is nothing but the interest of the ruler; on a plausible reading, Karl Marx holds (to oversimplify considerably) that it is nothing but the interest of a ruling class (see Wood 1981). These are both on their face naturalistic but deliberately debunking accounts. It strikes cognitivist naturalists as too easy a victory over such disturbing suggestions to hold that they can be rejected a priori simply because they threaten the conventional assumption that justice merits respect. Critics sometimes maintain that at least the most general ethical categories (the good, the right) must be immune from such debunking challenges, but cognitivist naturalists argue that the history of ethical debate suggests otherwise. If they are right, then they can point to agents, those advancing the debunking positions, who are recognized as joining issue with more conventional views, but for whom these ethical considerations are not motivating.

4 Epistemology

Moore thought that ethical knowledge would have to rest on ethical intuition, a source unlikely to be welcomed by an ethical naturalist (see INTUITIONISM IN ETHICS). But there is a simple argument for Moore's view from two premises that have been widely accepted by philosophers. One is that ethics is autonomous, that there is no reasonable inference to any ethical conclusion from entirely nonethical premises (see AUTONOMY, ETHICAL §5). The other is a traditional and very influential doctrine about knowledge called foundationalism (see FOUNDATION-ALISM). According to foundationalism, everything we know to be true must either be based on a reasonable inference from other things we know, or else must be known directly, without inference; and all knowledge of the first sort must ultimately rest entirely on a foundation provided by the other, noninferential kind. Together these doctrines entail that if we have any ethical knowledge at all, some of it must be noninferential (or, in equivalent traditional terminology, intuitive). For if we have any ethical knowledge by inference, that knowledge must (by foundationalism) be obtainable by a reasonable inference from things we know without inference; and (by the autonomy of ethics) the premises of that inference must be partly ethical.

For much of the twentieth century, most cognitivist naturalists, when faced with this argument, agreed with their critics that they would have to deny the autonomy of ethics. But that doctrine has continued to seem more plausible than the arguments often proposed in its defence. Prominent defences of it have appealed to the controversial theses already mentioned, deriving it, for example, from the principle (itself not obvious) that action-guiding conclusions cannot be inferred from premises that severally lack this property. The resilience of the doctrine is arguably due less to such defences than to its being an instance of what has come to be recognized as a more general phenomenon: that when evidence from one area is brought to bear on a second, it typically has to be applied in light of assumptions one already has about the second area. Thus, to take an important example, it was a fond hope of empiricist philosophy of science to display standard scientific reasoning as proceeding from a foundation of empirical observation, guided only by methodological principles that are entirely neutral on scientific issues; but there has come to be near-consensus that this cannot be done. Scientific reasoning instead adjusts information about empirical evidence along with a diverse body of theory already tentatively in place, in the direction of a better overall fit. The process is quite similar to what John Rawls (1971) has called the search for a 'reflective equilibrium' among our views at different levels of generality, although Rawls described the procedure only for ethics (see MORAL JUSTIFICATION §2).

One moral drawn from these considerations by many philosophers is that foundationalism is mistaken. Although there is controversy over what account of knowledge to substitute, moreover, the reasonable alternatives have in common that, even when conjoined with the autonomy of ethics, they do not require that ethical knowledge rest on intuition. One suggestion, for example, is that scientific reasoning can lead to knowledge because the process of progressive readjustment described above is generally reliable, in that it tends over time to eliminate error and bring the body of scientific beliefs closer to the truth; and that scientific reasoning has had this feature partly because enough of the theoretical beliefs from which it begins have been at least approximately true. Some cognitivist naturalists have

defended a similar thesis about ethical reasoning; and their position no more requires noninferential knowledge of goods or duties than the comparable thesis about science requires intuitions of quarks or electrons.

Each of these objections to cognitivist naturalism can be further elaborated, as can the replies. If a fallacy is a mistake easily agreed upon once it is pointed out, there is no naturalistic fallacy. There remains, however, a complex debate about whether any form of cognitivist naturalism can prove satisfactory, a debate that quickly takes one into all the major areas of philosophy.

See also: MORAL JUDGMENT; MORAL KNOWLEDGE; VALUE, ONTOLOGICAL STATUS OF

References and further reading

Many of these readings are demanding but, except as noted, are not especially technical.

* Ayer, A.J. (1936) *Language, Truth and Logic*, London: Gollancz; 2nd edn, 1946, ch. 6. (Presents one of the earliest explicit versions of noncognitivism.)

* Blackburn, S. (1993) *Essays in Quasi-Realism*, New York: Oxford University Press, essays 6–11. (Defends a version of noncognitivism, here called 'projectivism', and of 'quasi-realism', the thesis that this understanding will largely vindicate rather than debunk ethical thought.)

* Boyd, R. (1988) 'How to be a Moral Realist', in G. Sayre-McCord (ed.) *Essays on Moral Realism*, Ithaca, NY: Cornell University Press, 181–228. (A defence of cognitivist ethical naturalism, especially important on the comparison of ethical to scientific epistemology; the volume includes an extensive bibliography, much of it relevant to debates about ethical naturalism.)

Foot, P. (1978) *Virtues and Vices*, Berkeley, CA: University of California Press. (Essays by a prominent defender of cognitivist naturalism. Chaps 7–9 question the autonomy of ethics, 10–13 its rational authority.)

* Gibbard, A. (1990) *Wise Choices, Apt Feelings*, Cambridge, MA: Harvard University Press. (Perhaps the most carefully worked out version of noncognitivism, which extends that doctrine beyond ethics to cover judgments of rationality; a sympathy for 'Moore-like' dismissals of cognitivist naturalism is conjoined with the reflection that the author's disagreement with that position may in the end be empirical. Pages 150–250 explore the extent to which, on the account presented, normative judgment 'mimics the search for truth' (218).)

* Hare, R.M. (1952) *The Language of Morals*, Oxford: Clarendon Press. (A highly influential presentation of noncognitivism, which attempts to derive the autonomy of ethics from the distinctively action-guiding character of ethical language. Like most writers influenced by Moore, Hare uses the term 'naturalism' for what this entry calls cognitivist naturalism.)

* Harman, G. (1977) *The Nature of Morality*, New York: Oxford University Press, chaps 1–2. (Presents the argument that supposed moral facts seem irrelevant to naturalistic explanation, without committing himself to this conclusion.)

* Mackie, J.L. (1977) *Ethics: Inventing Right and Wrong*, Harmondsworth: Penguin, ch. 1. (Makes a vigorous naturalistic argument for ethical nihilism.)

* Moore, G.E. (1903) *Principia Ethica*, Cambridge: Cambridge University Press, sections 1–17. (Dense, technical and, by Moore's later admission, sometimes confused, this passage presents the 'open question' argument and claims to refute cognitivist naturalism, called by Moore 'naturalistic ethics'.)

* Plato (*c*.380–367 BC) *Republic*, trans. G. Grube, revised by C. Reeve, Indianapolis, IN: Hackett Publishing Company, 1992, book I. (Presents a classic debate about the nature and value of justice.)

Railton, P. (1992) 'Some Questions about the Justification of Morality', in J.E. Tomberlin (ed.) *Ethics, Philosophical Perspectives* 6, Atascadero, CA: Ridgeview Publishing Co., 27–53. (A subtle discussion of how vindicatory a naturalistic theory of ethics can be, and should be required to be.)

* Rawls, J. (1971) *A Theory of Justice*, Cambridge, MA: Belknap Press, ch. 1, section 9. (Describes the process of seeking a 'reflective equilibrium' among one's ethical and other beliefs. This is accepted as an approximately accurate account of thoughtful reasoning in ethics by many who then disagree about the philosophical implications.)

Sturgeon, N.L. (1985) 'Moral Explanations', in D. Copp and D. Zimmerman (eds) *Reason, Truth and Morality*, Totowa, NJ: Rowman and Allenheld, 49–78. (A defence of ethical naturalism, with special reference to the explanatory relevance of ethical facts.)

* Wood, A.W. (1981) *Karl Marx*, London: Routledge & Kegan Paul, chaps 9, 10. (Defends a careful version of an interpretation according to which Marx holds (to put it much less carefully) that justice is nothing but the interest of a ruling class.)

NICHOLAS L. STURGEON

NATURALISM IN SOCIAL SCIENCE

Naturalism is a term used in several ways. The more specific meanings of 'naturalism' in the philosophy of social sciences rest on the great popular authority acquired by modern scientific methods and forms of explanation in the wake of the seventeenth-century scientific revolution. For many of the thinkers of the European Enlightenment and their nineteenth-century followers the success of science in uncovering the laws governing the natural world was used as an argument for the extension of its methods into the study of morality, society, government and human mental life. Not only would this bring the benefit of consensus in these contested areas, but also it would provide a sound basis for ameliorative social reform. Among the most influential advocates of naturalism, in this sense, was the early nineteenth-century French philosopher Auguste Comte.

The authority of the new mechanical science, even as an account of non-human nature, continued to be resisted by romantic philosophers. However, the more limited task of resisting the scientific 'invasion' of human self-understanding was taken up by the Neo-Kantian philosophers of the latter part of the nineteenth century, in Germany. Followers and associates of this tradition (such as Windelband, Rickert, Dilthey and others) insist that there is a radical gulf between scientific knowledge of nature, and the forms of understanding which are possible in the sphere of humanly created meanings and cultures. This view is argued for in several different ways. Sometimes a contrast is made between the regularities captured in laws of nature, on the one hand, and social rules, on the other. Sometimes human consciousness and self-understanding is opposed to the non-conscious 'behaviour' of non-human beings and objects, so that studying society is more like reading a book or having a conversation than it is like studying a chemical reaction.

1 Varieties of naturalism
2 Methodological naturalism
3 Ontological naturalism
4 Non-reductionist naturalisms

1 Varieties of naturalism

A 'naturalistic' approach to the social sciences may express a view about the nature and limits of our knowledge of the different subject matters, or about the appropriateness of certain methods of inquiry, or about the essential sameness of the subject matters of natural and social sciences. So, we may usefully distinguish epistemological naturalism, methodological naturalism and ontological naturalism. Also, in the case of ontological naturalism, it is important to distinguish between, on the one hand, 'reductionist' versions, and, on the other, 'non-reductionist' versions, such as 'emergent powers' or 'dialectical' naturalisms.

In most of the literature of the philosophy of social science, naturalism is taken to be primarily an epistemological doctrine, and, frequently, to be more or less identical with 'positivism' (see POSITIVISM IN THE SOCIAL SCIENCES §1). Epistemological naturalism is the thesis that the social life of humans is knowable in just the same sense, and will take the same form, as knowledge of the natural world. So, the natural sciences – physics, chemistry and biology – are taken as paradigmatic for social scientific knowledge. Historically, the most influential accounts of the natural sciences have been empiricist ones, according to which scientific knowledge is characterized by its openness to empirical testing (generally by the use of experimental method), the law-like character of its general statements, the symmetry of explanation and prediction, and the clear distinction between value-judgements and factual statements. The nineteenth-century French sociologist, Auguste COMTE is generally credited as the founding figure of a positivist movement, devoted to extending scientific knowledge, on this model, to the spheres of psychology and human social life. The positivists and their latter-day followers have also been committed to a view of the social sciences as technically applicable knowledge, in much the same way as knowledge in the physical sciences has enabled a degree of control and regulation of natural phenomena.

Critics of positivism have most commonly been adherents of epistemological or ontological anti-naturalism. However, the proliferation of non-empiricist accounts of the natural sciences, especially, in the Anglophone world, since the work of Thomas S. Kuhn (see KUHN, T.S.) has opened up the possibility of versions of epistemological naturalism that reject positivism. 'Conventionalist' accounts of empirical testing serve to undermine the fact/value distinction as a distinguishing mark of science, while, various realist approaches to the nature of the natural sciences put the emphasis on the role of analogy and metaphor in the discovery of mind-independent causal mechanisms and structures in nature.

These non-empiricist accounts of natural scientific knowledge open up a complex range of possible forms that might be taken by the social sciences within the general terms of non-empiricist epistemological naturalism. The work of Rom Harré and his associates in the field of social psychology, and of Roy Bhaskar in developing a 'critical realist' reconstruction of historical materialism are two notable developments along these lines (see CRITICAL REALISM).

2 Methodological naturalism

Methodological naturalism may be defined as the commitment to applying natural science methodology for purposes of developing the social sciences. Again, methodological naturalism is most commonly associated with the positivist tradition. The central priority for such an approach is to render social processes and relations measurable and so mathematically analysable. It is widely accepted that the direct use of experimental methods is rarely possible in the social sciences – either for ethical or legal reasons, or because of the impossibility of controlling extraneous variables. So, methodological naturalists tend to opt for two main substitutes. One of these, typical of historical sociology, is the comparative method. Societies that differ in only a small number of significant features are compared with respect to some historical outcome (for example, the emergence of dictatorships or democracy) whose causes are sought. Alternatively, analysis may be carried out on large-scale data-sets to discover statistical associations (for example, between social class and morbidity or mortality) which may allow of causal inferences. Many of these techniques are common to both social and (some) natural sciences (such as epidemiology and population biology). Émile Durkheim's *Suicide* (1897) is a classic text for methodological naturalism in sociology (see DURKHEIM, É. §3).

Opponents of methodological naturalism commonly argue that the relation, in the social sciences, between researcher and subject matter is quite different from that which obtains in the natural sciences. Participants in human social life do so on the basis of their own understandings of what they are doing. The forms of understanding developed by social scientists are, therefore, secondary, 'understandings of understandings'. Social scientific understanding, on this view, is more like textual interpretation or, perhaps, dialogue, than it is like the external relation between the natural scientists and the physical structures and processes they study. The hermeneutic tradition that flourished in Germany in the late nineteenth century, and which returned to the philosophy of Immanuel Kant for ways to resist positivist 'invasion' of the humanities, has been the most powerful source of opposition to methodological naturalism. The British philosopher, Peter Winch, in his influential *The Idea of a Social Science* (1958), deployed his reading of the later work of Wittgenstein to reach very similar conclusions. The subsequent 'linguistic turn' in the social sciences, and the associated introduction of literary modes of social analysis under the banner of 'postmodernism' have served to put the proponents of methodological naturalism very much on the defensive.

Again, however, it may be argued that an identification of 'methodological naturalism' with comparative method and statistical analysis as experiment substitutes, relies on a narrow and distorted view of the range of methods of investigation used by natural scientists themselves. There are, for example, many parallels between the fieldwork methods of animal ethologists and the 'qualitative' research of social scientific ethnographers.

3   Ontological naturalism

However, the more fundamental objections to both epistemological and methodological naturalism tend to turn on matters of ontology. For anti-naturalists, humans, their symbolic creations, their social relations and institutional forms, are radically different in kind from the order of nature. In their different forms, anti-naturalisms may emphasize free choice and spontaneity (ruling out deterministic laws and scientific prediction), self-definition (cognitive authority of participants, not observers), rule-following (as against causal determination), or the creation of meaning (requiring interpretation, as distinct from explanation) as the key ontological feature that defeats the naturalist project. Sometimes the case for human-social ontological uniqueness is made by way of a dualistic opposition between physical mechanisms or processes, and those of the human social world, or, alternatively, some version of human/animal dualism may be relied upon.

The case for a dualistic opposition between humans and animals (what has come to be called, by its opponents, 'human exemptionalism') may rest on a range of supposedly unique features of human individuals, or of the species as a whole. The attributes of self-consciousness, language-use, and moral agency are most commonly emphasized, but especially in traditions of thought influenced by Marx and Hegel, such distinctive properties of human groups as social production (rather than mere collection), tool-use, and historicity may be emphasized.

Against this, ontological naturalists have available two broad strategies. One is to focus on those aspects of their lives which humans have in common with (other) animal species. The other is to rely on modern research in the life sciences that seems increasingly to have 'closed the gap' in just those areas of human 'uniqueness' which the anti-naturalists prize. The Darwinian revolution established the phylogenetic kinship between humans and other animal species, and set the scene for later approaches to the study of animal behaviour in the field, and of the ecology of the human species itself. Tool-use and the learning of elements of human sign-language among chimps, as well as widespread evidence of high levels of social cooperation, emotional complexity and a rich psychic life in other animal species are now difficult to deny.

Proponents of naturalism sometimes accuse anti-naturalists of an arrogant 'species-chauvinism', and point to the inability of 'human-exemptionalist' explanatory strategies to deal with the material dimensions of human ecological destruction. Advocates of ontological naturalism also point out how the reduction of human social life to 'text', which is implicit in the 'linguistic turn', obscures or renders marginal the material dimensions of human deprivation, oppression, and unnecessary suffering that has been at the heart of much critical social science.

But the anti-naturalists can, with some force, point out that, in its various forms, ontological naturalism in the social sciences has itself served oppressive interests. The Malthusian 'law of population', social Darwinism, Nazi racial science, and, in our own day, sociobiology have all been used as means of oppression. Naturalisms of various kinds have also been widely used to represent as 'natural' and therefore unalterable all manner of unjust and exploitative institutions.

4   Non-reductionist naturalisms

It may be that no single solution may be found to the dilemmas and tensions posed by this confrontation between naturalisms and their opponents. It is certain that there are no easy or simple ways forward. However, from the side of ontological naturalism a number of intellectual strategies are available which show some promise of answering the main objections made by anti-naturalists. It is quite possible, for example, within a broadly naturalistic framework, to acknowledge the specificity of the human species without denying our kinship with other species. Indeed, human powers of symbolic communication, autonomous agency and capacity for history can themselves be seen not as *sui generis*, but as consequences of our biological peculiarities – 'premature' birth, prolonged infantile dependency, bipedalism, highly developed central nervous system, and so on.

The social world humans create as their 'second nature' may also be understood as irreducibly heterogeneous in its make-up – some of it is, literally, text, while much more of it is text-like. Humans live all their social relations through some form of symbolic understanding, so that a hermeneutic aspect, or moment, is necessary to all social science. However, to suppose that human social life is composed wholly of understandings, as if there were nothing beyond discourse which these 'understandings' are understandings (or misunderstandings) of, would be to commit a linguistic reduction as difficult to defend as its polar opposite naturalistic reductionism.

For an advocate of naturalism to go this far in the direction of the anti-naturalist case would require a complex and open-textured ontology, incompatible with the forms of reductionist naturalism widely criticized by the linguistic and hermeneutic traditions. In other words, to be defensible against the main anti-naturalist critique, naturalism would need to avoid the 'reductionist' project of representing the subject matter of the social sciences as the direct or unmediated effect of the operation of laws and mechanisms proper to the natural sciences.

A non-reductionist naturalism, making use of the ideas of a hierarchy of more or less autonomous levels of organization of matter, each with its own, qualitatively new, 'emergent' powers or properties has been one fruitful way of sustaining the main insights of a naturalistic approach, without falling foul of what is valid in the anti-naturalistic critique.

Such hierarchical, 'emergent powers' ontologies enable their advocates to recognize in the various subject matters of the different natural and social sciences, more or less discrete and autonomous object-domains, while at the same time making no concessions to spiritualistic, vitalist, or supernatural beliefs. 'Emergent powers', or 'dialectical' naturalisms remain committed to the doctrines that the beings making up the object-domains of the various sciences are all ultimately composed of the same basic 'stuff', and that at whatever level of organization they exist, they behave consistently with the laws governing the lower levels of organization.

On this view, social (economic, political, and so on) structures and practices are held to exist independently of our (social scientific) knowledge of them, and as objects of study in their own right, with their own distinctive sets of properties, powers, tendencies, and so on. Nevertheless, and this is the hallmark of a naturalistic approach, these structures and practices, with their distinctive properties, powers and tendencies exist only in virtue of their status as more or less enduring forms of organization of the lower-level entities (people, buildings, tools, animals and plants), and so on down the hierarchy of organization.

Clearly, ideas such as 'emergent powers' enable people who want to work within a naturalistic framework to take account of the very powerful arguments used by anti-naturalists against reducive

forms of naturalism (such as sociobiology and Malthusianism). To some extent this may lead to a convergence of views between non-reductive naturalisms and the less extreme forms of anti-naturalism. However, in research-practice in the social sciences, this difference of view tends to take the shape of a division of labour between different topics and sub-disciplines. So, for example, cultural anthropology and sociology of culture have tended to be dominated by anti-naturalistic approaches, while studies of social 'systems', power-structures, social class and stratification and so on, have more commonly been governed by epistemological and methodological, if not ontological naturalism.

See also: DILTHEY, W.

References and further reading

Andreski, S. (ed.) (1974) *The Essential Comte*, London: Croom Helm. (Translation of part of Comte's classic *Course in Positive Philosophy*, which outlines the case for a naturalistic social science.)

Benton, E. (1991) 'Biology and Social Science', *Sociology* 25 (1): 1–29. (Argues that sociologists should take account of biological insights, but can do so without becoming committed to naturalistic reductionism.)

Bhaskar, R. (1979) *The Possibility of Naturalism*, Hemel Hempstead: Harvester, 1989. (Argues for an epistemological naturalism that recognizes both methodological and ontological peculiarities of the human sciences.)

Catton, W.R. and Dunlap, R.E. (1978) 'Environmental Sociology: a New Paradigm', *American Sociologist* 13: 41–9. (Introduces the term 'human exemptionalism' to characterize anti-naturalistic sociology, and proposes an environmentally oriented sociology as an alternative to it.)

Dilthey, W. (1883) *Introduction to the Human Sciences*, trans. R.J. Betanzos, Hemel Hempstead: Harvester, 1988. (Another classic statement of an anti-naturalistic foundation for the social sciences.)

* Durkheim, É. (1897) *Suicide: A Study in Sociology*, trans. J.A. Spaulding and G. Simpson, Glencoe, IL: Free Press, 1953. (A methodological classic, which uses official statistics to establish the role of social facts in the explanation of suicide rates.)

Kuhn, T.S. (1970) *The Structure of Scientific Revolutions*, Chicago, IL: University of Chicago Press. (Major work, that did more than any other English-language work to undermine the authority of empiricist and 'positivist' views of the nature of scientific knowledge.)

Rose, S. (ed.) (1982) *Towards a Liberatory Biology*,

London: Allison and Busby. (An influential collection of articles devoted to developing non-reductionist or 'dialectical' versions of biology.)

Rose, S., Kamin, L.J. and Lewontin, R.C. (1982) *Not in Our Genes*, Harmondsworth: Penguin. (Wide-ranging critique of naturalistic reductionism and attempt to develop an alternative naturalistic approach.)

Wilson, B. (ed.) (1970) *Rationality*, Oxford: Blackwell. (A classic collection of papers devoted to issues posed by anti-naturalist arguments, centring on the possibility of cross-cultural criteria of rationality, and the intelligibility of 'alien' cultures.)

* Winch, P. (1958) *The Idea of a Social Science*, London: Routledge & Kegan Paul. (Another classic anti-naturalist work, which makes use of the later philosophy of Wittengenstein.)

TED BENTON

NATURALISTIC FALLACY

see MOORE, GEORGE EDWARD;
NATURALISM IN ETHICS

NATURALIZED EPISTEMOLOGY

The term 'naturalized epistemology' was coined by W.V. Quine to refer to an approach to epistemology which he introduced in his 1969 essay 'Epistemology Naturalized'. Many of the moves that are distinctive of naturalized epistemology were made by David Hume, but Quine's essay fixes the sense of the term as it is used today.

Naturalized epistemology has critical as well as constructive thrusts. In a critical spirit, 'naturalists' (theorists who identify with the label 'naturalized epistemology') abandon several assumptions that are part of the tradition. They reject Descartes' vision of epistemology as the attempt to convert our beliefs into an edifice resting on a foundation about which we have complete certainty. Descartes is wrong to equate knowledge with certainty, and wrong to think that knowledge is available through a priori theorizing, through reasoning which makes no use of experience. Nor should epistemology continue as David Hume's attempt to rest knowledge on an introspective study of the mind's contents. Moreover, the global sceptic's claim that there is no way to justify all our views at once, should either be conceded or ignored.

On the constructive side, naturalists suggest that in investigating knowledge we rely on the apparatus, techniques and assumptions of natural science. Accordingly, naturalized epistemology will be a scientific (and hence neither indefeasible nor a priori) explanation of how it is that some beliefs come to be knowledge. Issues of scepticism will be addressed only when they come up in the course of a scientific investigation.

Quine's seminal essay lays out the core of naturalized epistemology, but subsequent naturalists disagree on the appropriate responses to several issues, among them the following: First, may theories be tested on the basis of (independently plausible) theory-neutral observation, or are observations simply more theory? Second, after being naturalized, does epistemology survive as an autonomous discipline? Quine argues that epistemology should become a subfield of natural science, presumably a part of psychology, so that there is no separate field left specifically to philosophers. But can all our questions about knowledge be answered by natural scientists? Third, the claim that epistemology explains how knowledge comes to be suggests that epistemology will merely describe the origins of beliefs we take to be known; but what is the relationship between such descriptive issues and normative issues such as that of how we ought to arrive at our views? Fourth, to what extent is the new approach to epistemology susceptible to sceptical concerns such as those that so plagued traditional epistemologists, and how effective a response can be made to those concerns?

1 **Hume's anticipation of naturalized epistemology**
2 **Internalism versus externalism**
3 **The role of observation**
4 **The autonomy of epistemology**
5 **The role of normative issues**
6 **The significance of scepticism**

1 Hume's anticipation of naturalized epistemology

The naturalizing movement in epistemology is the continuation of Hume's rebellion against Descartes' view about knowledge. Like Descartes, Hume wanted to conduct an investigation of the mind and its operations, including 'the operations we perform in our reasonings'. But five features of Hume's approach place him far closer to contemporary naturalism than to Cartesianism.

First, while Descartes wished to leave no room for doubt, Hume explicitly took for granted the trustworthiness of the very faculties whose operations he wanted to investigate. Later naturalists (theorists who identify with the label 'naturalized epistemology') make a parallel move: they trust the techniques and assumptions of science even while investigating how (scientific) knowledge is possible. Hume assumed that our mental faculties are trustworthy because it would be pointless to attempt to test their accuracy; after all, any test required their use. In fact, it was *because* Hume supposed that the mental faculties generated knowledge (or at least rational belief) that he thought the clarification of their workings would shed light on the normative question of what an epistemic agent ought to believe. His project still had a critical edge, for when Hume found any belief that could not be satisfactorily accounted for in terms of standard human faculties, he recommended throwing it out as baseless.

Second, like later naturalists, Hume modelled his epistemology after the emerging natural sciences, where empirical confirmation served as the basis for claims. He thought that knowledge encompasses everything we can discover using all our mental faculties, including experience and what we can discover by applying our mental faculties to themselves.

Third, like contemporary naturalists, Hume was prepared to say that some knowledge is the product of purely causal mechanisms rather than reason (or reasoning), since through introspection Hume thought he could detect a causal mechanism at work. The mechanism he detected itself produces knowledge of causal relations, on the basis of which we believe in matters of fact, which are facts that hold contingently and whose negations indicate real possibilities (see HUME, D. §2; CAUSATION §1). Custom, prompted by experience, is the mechanism through which we form our suppositions concerning causal relations. Hume does not recommend doubt about the products of custom. After all, the mind is functioning in a healthy, normal way when it is under the influence of custom, and reasoning can begin only after custom does its work. We should begin to question our beliefs only when we find that they are arrived at while the mind is not functioning in the normal way science describes.

Fourth, like many contemporary naturalists, Hume explains some of the mechanisms responsible for knowledge (such as custom) in terms of survival value. The linking of causes to effects is so important to human survival that it would have been a mistake for 'nature' to entrust it to our reason 'which is...extremely liable to error'. Better to entrust it to 'some instinct or mechanical tendency, which may be infallible in its operations, may discover itself at the first appearance of life and thought, and may be independent of all the laboured deductions of the understanding' (Hume [1748/51] 1975: 55). Years later, W.V. QUINE and other naturalists will speak in the same vein. Quine (1974: 20) explains induction in terms of natural selection, and disavows any claim to

have justified induction. 'In the matter of justifying induction we are back with Hume, where we doubtless belong'.

Fifth, Hume is with contemporary naturalists in their reactions to scepticism. As he had to, since he put his trust in his faculties, Hume rejected Descartes' idea that to know that our beliefs are true is to be in a position to place all our beliefs beyond doubt at once. Hume saw that it is not even possible to *justify* all our views at once. No more than Descartes could Hume use his faculties to assess his epistemic prospects without first assuming that they were reliable. In the last section of the *Enquiry Concerning Human Understanding* (1748/51), Hume mentions scepticism and simply acknowledges that truly global doubts would be 'entirely incurable'.

2 Internalism versus externalism

Like Hume, contemporary naturalists are empiricists. For example, in 'Epistemology Naturalized' Quine explicitly affirms a version of Humean empiricism:

> It was sad for epistemologists, Hume and others, to have to acquiesce in the impossibility of strictly deriving the science of the external world from sensory evidence. Two cardinal tenets of empiricism remained unassailable, however, and so remain to this day. One is that whatever evidence there is for science is sensory evidence. The other...is that all inculcation of meanings of words must rest ultimately on sensory evidence.
> (Quine 1969: 75)

But contemporary naturalists do not have in mind the introspective sort of empiricism advocated by Hume but, rather, intersubjective empiricism. Instead of simply taking our mental faculties and the data of introspection for granted and accounting for knowledge from that perspective, Quine and other naturalists suggest that we take a more full-bodied version of scientific practice for granted, and account for knowledge from *that* perspective. The empiricist science on which naturalists rely is conducted in the public domain. Scientists use microscopes and other instruments to extend their senses, and the observations upon which they rely are not data of introspection but rather observations that are at least in principle publicly confirmable (see EMPIRICISM; INTROSPECTION).

Naturalists think that the stimulation of sensory receptors helps to determine whether or not people know the truth of beliefs that are causally linked to those stimulations. Yet the stimulations themselves are usually not noticed by the people in whom they occur. Naturalists are *externalists*, defined by Laurence BonJour (1985), following D.M. Armstrong (1973), as theorists according to whom facts that are external to an agent's conception of the situation can serve to justify that agent's beliefs in a way that is sufficient for knowledge (see INTERNALISM AND EXTERNALISM IN EPISTEMOLOGY). *Internalists*, by contrast, would insist that all knowledge is based on justifications that are in some sense in the cognitive possession of the knower. A related view is that epistemology, or knowledge about knowledge, is based on such justifications. Consider the following arguments for these internalist positions.

First, as BonJour emphasizes, justifications that are in no way possessed by an agent are completely arbitrary (unsupported), at least so far as the agent can tell from the agent's own point of view, and accepting arbitrary beliefs is a bad idea from the standpoint of getting to the truth, which is the goal of the epistemic agent. Yet externalists claim that it is possible for agents to acquire knowledge through sources about which those agents believe little or nothing. Their sources might be a causal chain, a reliable belief-formation process, an information channel, or all three (see KNOWLEDGE, CAUSAL THEORY OF; INFORMATION THEORY AND EPISTEMOLOGY; RELIABILISM). Internalists disagree, since it is epistemically irresponsible to believe something through some avenue without checking out the truth-conductivity credentials of that avenue.

The main problem with this first line of thought is that the internalists' assumptions seem to lead immediately to sceptical results. For internalists want an avenue to the truth but they want to accept nothing except what is justifiable, and nothing as justification except what is available to them 'from the inside'. That means they need an avenue to the truth that can be defended as such on the basis of what is available 'from the inside', a task that appears to be impossible. No empirical premise will serve in the defence since empirical premises will either be accepted without justification (arbitrarily) or justified on the basis of some other empirical premise, thus initiating a regress.

A second line of argument gives up on the attempt to show that all knowledge conforms to internalist assumptions, but purports to show that epistemology fits the internalist view: since logic is a priori accessible if any body of knowledge is, the thought that there is an inductive as well as a deductive logic may lead theorists to suggest that knowledge is the product of reasoning that conforms to valid deductive and inductive forms of argument. Some of the assumptions that are fed into the arguments might not conform to internalist assumptions, but the reasoning does. So we can understand epistemology to be an a priori study of the argument forms to which reasoning ought ideally to conform.

One problem here is that, unlike deductive logic, inductive logic is not the study of argument forms. Ultimately inductive logicians invoke appeals to the way the world is, appeals which internalists want to avoid. Except in trivial cases, that one statement makes another probable is a claim about the world, not about the forms of those statements. More seriously, in the phrase 'reasoning that conforms to valid argument forms' there is a conflation of argument with reasoning. As Gilbert Harman (1986) and others have emphasized, these are quite distinct things. The study of arguments and argument forms is logic; the study of reasoned belief revision is the study of the belief-management practices governing those revisions. Principles of belief management would tell us when epistemic agents should retain their beliefs and when and how they should revise them. The inference rules of logic do not tell us when revision is appropriate. Inference rules can tell us many things; for example, suppose that we believe the premises of an argument – inference rules can tell us that the premises of that argument entail its conclusion. But that is not the same thing as a recommendation that (say) we affirm the conclusion. In fact, belief-management principles might tell us that we ought to drop one of the premises rather than accept the conclusion.

Once we distinguish between logic and belief management, like Harman we may become quite sceptical about the existence of anything like an inductive logic. An inductive logic would be a logic that resembles deductive logic except that the conclusions of 'valid' inductive arguments are merely made probable by their premises, not entailed by them. That such a logic exists is not entailed by the existence of inductive reasoning, and the fact that so little progress has been made towards developing an inductive logic might lead us to suspect that there is no such subject to be investigated (see INDUCTIVE INFERENCE). Moreover, if inductive logic does not exist, good inductive reasoning cannot be simply reasoning that conforms to inductive logic. (Some have held that probability theory provides the basis of inductive logic – see PROBABILITY THEORY AND EPISTEMOLOGY.)

So the epistemic activity of inductive reasoning might not be illuminated by advances in 'inductive logic'. A related point is that much epistemic activity probably does not involve beliefs or any other proposition-related states at all. As Paul Churchland (1979: 128) has argued, a great deal of information is processed by infants, and their prelinguistic behaviour does not invite ascriptions of propositional attitudes to them. 'Rational...intellectual development in an infant cannot be...usefully represented by a sequence of sets of sentences suitably related'. Information processing in infants, as well as the processing by virtue of which sensory stimulations are assimilated by adult brains prior to the formation of beliefs, would presumably be articulated by principles of which epistemic agents themselves are entirely unaware and to which they could not purposely conform even if they wanted to. Churchland takes such facts to suggest that any account of knowledge in terms of 'sentences suitably related' is bound to be superficial; a proper theory would deal in more primitive parameters that apply to pre-linguistic processing, and would account for the way epistemic agents deal with beliefs as a derivative case.

In sum, critics of naturalized epistemology who say that knowledge or epistemology is based on justifications in the cognitive possession of knowers face some severe difficulties.

3   The role of observation

Naturalists disagree on many points, among them the role of observation in knowledge, the degree to which natural science is separable from epistemology, the role of normativity in epistemology, and the significance of scepticism (these latter three points are discussed in subsequent sections). One view about the role of observation in knowledge, that of Quine, is that ultimately the 'evidence for' or 'test of' our theory of the world is the prediction of the stimulations of exteroceptors. The components of our view that are most directly tested by these stimulations are observation sentences such as 'It is raining' or 'There is a rabbit'. These are directly tested by stimulations because what each *means* is a set of stimulations that prompts assent to and a set that prompts dissent from the sentence. The test of our theory of the world is therefore its ability to predict the observation sentences that verbalize our stimulations (see QUINE, W.V. §2).

But many naturalists reject Quine's version of the empiricist claim that our theory rests on observation. One concern is that it is unclear how sensory stimulations can serve as *evidence* for a theory. It is relatively clear how a sentence can serve as evidence for a theory, so that we can see how observation sentences test theories, but stimulations are not sentences nor, for all we can see, any sort of propositional attitude. Moreover, the relationship between our stimulations and our assenting to observation sentences is causal, not evidential.

Another problem concerns the distinction between observation sentences (which are purported to have a special plausibility due to their intimacy with experience, so that they may serve to test theories) and the sentences in which theory is couched. Several philosophers (for example, N.R. Hanson 1968 and Paul Feyerabend 1986) have argued that there is no theory–observation distinction. There is no such thing as observation sentences whose meanings are determined by stimulations or the like. 'Observation' statements are just theoretical claims themselves, though ones we are accustomed to. So it will not do to say that our theory of the world rests on or is tested by non-theoretical observation statements. It is theory all the way down (see OBSERVATION §§3–4).

4   The autonomy of epistemology

All naturalists reject the Cartesian view that epistemology is entirely separable from and prior to other disciplines such as the sciences. But just how much autonomy epistemology retains is controversial. The most extreme view is that of Quine, who suggests that epistemology has no autonomy at all. Once we drop the idea that 'the epistemologist's goal is validation of the grounds of empirical science' we can and should, he says, 'surrender the epistemological burden to psychology'. We are to construe epistemology as the attempt to 'understand the link between observation and science', and consider ourselves 'well advised to use any available information, including that provided by the very science whose link with observation we are seeking to understand' (Quine 1969: 75–6). Hence epistemology collapses without residue into sciences such as biology and psychology. Its work is turned over to evolutionary epistemologists such as Campbell (1974) and genetic epistemologists such as Jean PIAGET who attempt to explain the development of knowledge, the former explicitly in terms of the biological theory of evolution. But exactly how the sciences will distribute the work of studying knowledge is unclear. The scientific fields that study knowledge are somewhat fledgling and are not clearly differentiated. Nor is it clear how these fields are related to the sociology or sociobiology of knowledge, fields which also can be construed as part of naturalized epistemology (see SOCIOLOGY OF KNOWLEDGE).

Some philosophers sympathetic to the naturalizing movement reject the claim that all legitimate epistemic issues can be investigated scientifically: (1) Alvin Goldman (1986) says that while epistemology and natural science are relevant to and continuous with each other, the former is not contained entirely in the latter. For example, the philosophy of logic is a branch of epistemology, but Goldman doubts that logic can be investigated scientifically. (2) Another argument is that epistemology progresses in part by studying the basic epistemic concepts, such as 'justification', 'rationality', 'warrant', 'certainty', 'knowledge' and so on. Such study is the basis for claims about what constitutes knowledge, yet philosophers, not scientists, undertake it. (3) Moreover, Goldman and many others would say, one task of epistemology is to settle normative questions such as that of how we ought to arrive at our conclusions, but science is unequipped to handle normative issues. It seems limited to telling us how we *do* arrive at our conclusions. Accordingly, epistemology might survive as an autonomous discipline in so far as it continues to deal with deductive logic and the normative issues involved in knowledge.

Quine would reject each of these attempts to preserve an autonomous form of epistemology. To deny the first two, he would use arguments developed in 'Two Dogmas of Empiricism' (1953). (For a discussion of his approach to the third, see §5 below.) (1) That even claims of logic must face the tribunal of experience is suggested by the Quine-Duhem thesis: all statements face the 'tribunal of sense experience not individually but only as a corporate body' (Quine: 1953: 41). Hence 'no statement is immune to revision. Revision even of the logical law of the excluded middle has been proposed as a means of simplifying quantum mechanics' (Quine: 1953: 43) (see QUINE, W.V. §3). (2) Progress in epistemology based on the analysis of terms is made very difficult, but is not ruled out, by Quine's holism – his claim that the meanings of particular statements and *a fortiori* terms overlap with the meanings of other statements, so that describing the meaning of a particular term requires describing its role in a complex of theory (see ATOMISM, ANCIENT; HOLISM: MENTAL AND SEMANTIC). Moreover, analysis merely clarifies the epistemic concepts we have been employing. It does not rule out the possibility that we ought to employ different concepts, such as ones suggested by an empirical study of the brain's workings.

5 The role of normative issues

Epistemology's *descriptive* task is to identify how people actually arrive at beliefs. But what people actually do is not necessarily what they ought to do. Epistemology's *normative* task is to identify how people ought (rationally) to arrive at their beliefs, and this seems to go well beyond the descriptive task (see NORMATIVE EPISTEMOLOGY). Not all naturalists hope that they can do away with traditional epistemology entirely and replace it with natural science. But those with this hope have trouble finding a place in their project for the normative task of epistemology, since

science seems incapable of prescription. Radical naturalists could argue that the normative issue is not worth pursuing, so that reducing epistemology to its descriptive task leaves out nothing worth doing. But this is an implausible option on its face. However, their only other choice is daunting: they must argue that science can tell us how we ought to arrive at our beliefs.

Naturalists who want to argue that science can answer the normative question have two options. In the spirit of Hume they can assume that the way we arrive at our beliefs *is* (more or less) the way we ought to. (But is this assumption a scientific or an epistemological claim?) Epistemology's descriptive task is clearly within the province of science; if we completed the normative by completing the descriptive task, then science could handle both sides of traditional epistemology. Unfortunately, the claim that we ought to maintain our existing belief-management practices more or less as they are faces difficulties. The main problem lies in the data that psychologists have already gathered. These data show that normal human cognitive processes are shot through with faulty logic, bad probabilistic inferences and wishful thinking (Nisbett and Ross 1980; Taylor 1989). Beliefs with such origins do not count as knowledge.

Perhaps radical naturalists need not assume that people ought to maintain their actual belief-management practices, however. Instead, they could try arguing that discoverable facts about things other than our actual belief-management practices will allow us to accomplish epistemology's normative task (but will they be able to make these discoveries without relying on the belief-management practices they question?). For example, scientists might be able to determine that all (rational?) human beings have a common epistemic goal, whether it is reaching the truth or predicting the future course of sensory stimulation or whatever. If so, then, as Quine (1992) has pointed out, epistemology's normative task could be performed by engineers. Engineers could work out the best ways available to people (given our limited faculties and resources) for reaching their epistemic goal. We could say that these efficient methods are the ones people ought to adopt, even at the expense of fairly radical changes in their actual practices. Normative epistemology becomes part of engineering science, not a branch of epistemology that is outside of science.

But while engineers investigate efficient ways to do such things as to transport or kill people, they do not investigate the issue 'Ought we to transport or kill people?' Only after it is established that it is important to achieve some goal does engineering come into play.

The issue of what epistemic agents ought to aim at is not an engineering issue. It remains a philosophical issue which cannot be absorbed into science.

The problem would be rather trivial if scientists discovered that there is a single, unvarying goal (or prioritized set of goals) which everyone wants to reach by managing their beliefs as they do, and which does not look silly on its face. Even if the goal is 'wired in', we would worry about committing a 'naturalistic fallacy' and say 'The fact that something is everyone's goal does not entail that it ought to be'. Even the fact that a goal is forced on everyone does not show that we have grounds for pursuing it. Still, the temptation to take this goal as the one we ought to pursue would probably be overwhelming. However, it is by no means obvious that such a single, unvarying goal exists. In different cultures at the same time, and in the same culture at different times, people might be aiming to accomplish a variety of things by believing what they do, and the (conscious and unconscious) belief-management principles they employ might also differ widely. Given the possibility of significant diversity, epistemologists need some way to decide which competing goals and sets of belief-management principles are right for cognitive agents. Perhaps the diversity would be reduced if we focused on the goals of scientists during those times when they are being scientific. But even if it were so reduced, we would need some way of arguing that the goals of the scientists are the ones which epistemic agents ought to pursue. Several ways to handle such normative issues are open to radical naturalists.

First, they could say that belief-management principles should be evaluated from the point of view of natural selection, so that the greater the survival value of these principles, the better the principles. Once this (epistemological?) claim is made, then science can take over, by describing the belief-generating mechanisms of human beings (and other animals?) and explaining how they have the survival value they do. (But how will naturalists absorb the growing data that suggest that wishful thinking, a paradigm case of irrationality, is adaptive?)

Second, naturalists could exploit the elastic boundaries of science in order to call conceptual analysis science. Then they could use conceptual analysis to defend some view about what epistemic agents' goals or evaluative concepts are, and make the (epistemological?) claim that belief-management principles should be evaluated from the standpoint of those goals or concepts. Supposing, as several epistemologists have, that conceptual analysis reveals truth or predictive power to be the goal of epistemic agents, then (theoretical) scientists can go on to clarify the extent to which people naturally achieve the epistemic aim. And engineering will be useful in that it might help people to find better ways to achieve the epistemic goal.

Third, Stephen Stich (1988) suggests a pragmatic approach to normative issues. First he criticizes the strategy of using conceptual analysis to discover the goals and concepts of epistemic agents. The goals and evaluative epistemic concepts that are part of ordinary language are as likely as belief-management principles themselves to vary from culture to culture (see COGNITIVE PLURALISM). So it is arbitrary to rely on them when we select management principles. 'In the absence of any reason to think that the locally prevailing notions of epistemic evaluation are superior to the alternatives, why should we care one whit whether the cognitive processes we use are sanctioned by those evaluative concepts?' (Stich 1988: 406). Then Stich points out that there are many common values, such as happiness or reproductive success, that are not epistemic values but can be considered relevant to our cognitive lives. Stich suggests a pragmatic approach: he makes the (epistemological? ethical?) claim that we should evaluate belief-management principles from the standpoint of these non-epistemic values. Here again theoretical science will help us to evaluate our actual belief-forming mechanisms and engineering will help us to improve upon them.

6 The significance of scepticism

Like Hume, contemporary naturalists view epistemology as the attempt to clarify how the apparatus people use in investigating the world works when used in applications for which, we assume, it is reliable, and to identify what ought and ought not count as knowledge by identifying what sorts of beliefs are endorsed by the proper use of that apparatus. Contemporaries depart from him chiefly in thinking that more must be taken for granted than the reliability of mental faculties. Recent naturalists help themselves to the whole of natural science, which can be thought of as the combination of our mental faculties with techniques and devices that extend them.

Accordingly, there is a compelling case for saying that naturalists cannot hope to put global scepticism to rest. Global scepticism says that our belief schemes (including science) are irrational because: (1) ultimately our beliefs are based on arbitrary assumptions, claims that, even upon some reflection, we cannot link to a consideration that suggests it is true; and (2) it is irrational to make arbitrary assumptions (see SCEPTICISM §5). To argue that scientific apparatus is reliable after having simply assumed that it is would be circular, so naturalists seem committed to granting

(1). Perhaps this is why naturalists rarely confront global scepticism.

Attempts, none the less, have been made. One approach involves *coherentism*, which is the claim that beliefs may derive justification by cohering one with another (see KNOWLEDGE AND JUSTIFICATION, COHERENCE THEORY OF). If coherentism were correct, then since it sanctions some circular justifications, naturalists could use it against (1), and argue that all our beliefs can be justified at once. Another common approach is to turn the tables on the global sceptic and point out that, like everyone else who investigates knowledge, sceptics, too, must take for granted the reliability of their investigative apparatus. As an attack on (1) this table-turning would not work. Sceptics can retort: 'Yes, all of us are in the same boat: there are assumptions we simply take for granted'. But it might well prove useful as part of an attack on (2).

It is important to notice that the global sceptic needs both (1) and (2). Once we do, we can see that even if naturalists cannot defeat (1), they can still respond to scepticism if they defeat (2). Naturalists could accept the sceptic's discovery that ultimately our views are, perforce, arbitrary, and insist that it is sometimes all right, it is sometimes rational, to believe things we simply take for granted (Luper-Foy 1990).

See also: KNOWLEDGE, CONCEPT OF; NATURALIZED PHILOSOPHY OF SCIENCE; SOCIAL EPISTEMOLOGY

References and further reading

* Armstrong, D.M. (1973) *Belief, Truth and Knowledge*, Cambridge: Cambridge University Press. (Referred to in §2 above. A difficult, technically sophisticated but groundbreaking defence of an externalist theory of knowledge.)
* BonJour, L. (1985) *The Structure of Empirical Knowledge*, Cambridge, MA: Harvard University Press. (Discussed above in §2. Important and highly accessible defence of an internalist approach to the theory of knowledge.)
* Campbell, D.T. (1974) 'Evolutionary Epistemology', in P.A. Schilpp (ed.) *The Philosophy of Karl Popper*, bk 1, La Salle, IL: Open Court. (Referred to in §4 above. Helpful account of the field of evolutionary epistemology.)
* Churchland, P. (1979) *Scientific Realism and the Plasticity of Mind*, Cambridge: Cambridge University Press. (Discussed in §2 above. Reasonably accessible and influential attack on the idea that knowledge is 'sentences suitably related'.)
* Feyerabend, P.K. (1986) *Realism, Rationalism and Scientific Method: Philosophical Papers Volume 1*, Cambridge: Cambridge University Press. (Discussed in §3 above. Demanding essays in the philosophy of science.)
* Goldman, A. (1986) *Epistemology and Cognition*, Cambridge, MA: Harvard University Press. (Discussed above in §4. Reasonably accessible and influential defence of a moderately naturalized epistemology.)
* Hanson, N.R. (1968) *Patterns of Discovery: An Enquiry into the Conceptual Foundations of Science*, New York: Cambridge University Press. (Discussed in §3. Accessible introduction to the philosophy of science.)
* Harman, G. (1986) *Change in View: Principles of Reasoning*, Cambridge, MA: MIT Press. (Discussed in §2 above. Highly accessible defence of a moderately accessible naturalized epistemology.)
* Hume, D. (1748/51) *Enquiries Concerning Human Understanding and Concerning the Principles of Morals*, ed. L.A. Selby-Bigge, revised P.H. Niddich, Oxford: Clarendon Press, 3rd edn, 1975. (Referred to in §2 above. Accessible and extremely influential.)
Kitchener, R.F. (1986) *Piaget's Theory of Knowledge: Genetic Epistemology and Scientific Reason*, New Haven, CT: Yale University Press. (Exhaustive discussion of genetic epistemology.)
Kornblith, H. (ed.) (1985) *Naturalizing Epistemology*, Cambridge, MA: MIT Press. (Contains an introductory essay which defends the idea that the distinctive feature of naturalized epistemology is its position on the relationship between the normative question of how we ought we to arrive at our beliefs, and the descriptive issue of how we do we arrive at our beliefs. Also contains leading naturalist essays and an exhaustive bibliography up to 1984. Most of the material is accessible to non-specialists.)
—— (1993) *Inductive Inference and its Natural Ground: An Essay in Naturalistic Epistemology*, Cambridge, MA: MIT Press. (Accessible and lucid explanation of inductive inference from the perspective of naturalistic epistemology.)
* Luper-Foy, S. (1990) 'Arbitrary Reasons', in *Doubting*, Dordrecht: Kluwer. (Referred to above in §6. Argues that it is rational to accept arbitrary beliefs.)
* Nisbett, R. and Ross, L. (1980) *Human Inference: Strategies and Shortcomings of Social Judgment*, Englewood Cliffs, NJ: Prentice Hall. (Referred to in §5 above. Accessible survey of literature on irrationality.)
* Quine, W.V. (1953) 'Two Dogmas of Empiricism', in *From a Logical Point of View*, New York: Harper Torchbooks. (Referred to in §4 above. Spells out

much of the theory that suggested naturalized epistemology. Most of it is accessible.)

* —— (1969) 'Epistemology Naturalized', in *Ontological Relativity & Other Essays*, New York: Columbia University Press. (Referred to in §§2 and 4. The definitive essay of naturalized epistemology. Accessible.)

* —— (1974) *The Roots of Reference*, La Salle, IL: Open Court. (Referred to above in §1. Discusses induction and hints at an externalist refutation of scepticism. Accessible.)

* —— (1992) *Pursuit of Truth*, Cambridge, MA: Harvard University Press. (Referred to in §5 above. Section 8 of this book elaborates (in the minimalist fashion typical of Quine) on the role of normativity in naturalized epistemology.)

* Stich, S. (1988) 'Reflective Equilibrium, Analytic Epistemology and the Problem of Cognitive Diversity', *Synthese* 74 (3): 391–415. (Discussed above in §5. Defends a pragmatic approach to belief management. Accessible.)

* Taylor, S. (1989) *Positive Illusions: Creative Self-Deception and the Healthy Mind*, New York: Basic Books. (Referred to in §5 above. Very accessible argument for the claim that self-deception is adaptive.)

STEVEN LUPER

NATURALIZED PHILOSOPHY OF SCIENCE

Naturalized philosophy of science is part of a general programme of naturalism in philosophy. Naturalists reject all forms of supernaturalism, holding that reality, including human life and culture, is exhausted by what exists in the causal order of nature. Naturalists also reject any claims to a priori knowledge, including that of principles of inference, holding instead that all knowledge derives from human interactions with the natural world. Philosophically, naturalists identify most closely with empiricism or pragmatism. David Hume was a naturalist. So was John Dewey. The logical empiricists were naturalists regarding fundamental ontological categories such as space, time and causality, but non-naturalists about scientific inference, which they came to regard as a branch of logic. Most naturalists now dismiss searches for 'philosophical foundations' of the special sciences, treating the basic principles of any science as part of scientific theory itself.

The main objection to naturalism has been at the level of general methodological principles, particularly those regarding scientific inference. Here non-natural-

ists object that, being limited to 'describing' how science is in fact practised, naturalists cannot provide norms for legitimate scientific inferences. And providing such norms is held to be one of the main goals of the philosophy of science. Naturalists reply that the only norms required for science are those connecting specific means with the assumed goals of research. These connections can be established only through further scientific research. And the choice of goals is, for naturalists, not a scientific question but a matter of practical choice guided by an empirical understanding of what can in fact be achieved.

Among naturalists, the main differences concern the relative importance of various aspects of the practice of science. These aspects exist at different levels: neurological, biological, psychological, personal, computational, methodological, social and cultural. Each of these levels has its champions among contemporary naturalists, some insisting that everything ultimately be reduced to their favourite level. Perhaps the wisest approach is to allow that influences at all levels are operative in any scientific context, while admitting that some influences may be more important than others in particular cases, depending on what one seeks to understand. There may be no simple, one-level, naturalistic theory of science.

1   **Naturalism and the philosophy of science**
2   **The problem of epistemic norms**
3   **The bases for naturalization**

1   Naturalism and the philosophy of science

Philosophical naturalism is the view that an adequate philosophical account of the natural world, including humans, can be given solely in terms of objects and processes occurring in the natural causal order. No appeal to anything supernatural or transcendent is required. Materialism and other forms of reductionism imply naturalism, but naturalists need not be reductive materialists. Thus a naturalist might deny the reducibility of psychology to biology so long as psychology itself functions as a natural science in its methods and forms of explanation (see REDUCTION, PROBLEMS OF; UNITY OF SCIENCE).

Naturalism is not new. David Hume was clearly a naturalist in holding that the operations of the mind could be understood solely in terms of natural processes such as perception, memory and the association of ideas. His goal has been rightly characterized as that of becoming the Newton of the mind. J.S. Mill continued the naturalist tradition in Britain. Descartes, on the other hand, counts as a non-naturalist because his theory of knowledge required an immaterial soul with special powers for ascertaining truths involving clear and distinct ideas. Kant was a more sophisticated non-naturalist. For Kant the operations of individual minds take place in the causal order of appearances. But all perception and judgment is constrained by categories that are discoverable only by the special philosophical method of transcendental deduction. In the mid-nineteenth century, other German scientist-philosophers, such as Hermann HELMHOLTZ attempted to naturalize Kant's categories, particularly those pertaining to spatial perception, through physiological and psychological investigations.

The late nineteenth-century debate in Germany between naturalists and non-naturalists was echoed in the USA where philosophers also attempted to assimilate the findings of the sciences, particularly psychology. John DEWEY exemplified this debate within his own philosophical development. Beginning as a Hegelian who saw psychology as applying only to individuals while philosophy uncovered the universal laws of rational thought, Dewey ended up a pragmatic naturalist who looked to science for all knowledge of the world and to philosophy primarily for investigation into the social values that should direct the employment of scientific knowledge for human betterment.

The non-naturalist cause found a major champion in Gottlob Frege who, beginning in the 1880s, insisted on a sharp distinction between patterns of inference actually employed by individuals and objectively valid arguments. The former may be studied as part of empirical psychology; the later are the province of logic, an a priori discipline which is part of philosophy (see FREGE, G. §4). Frege's views were incorporated into the programme of scientific philosophy promoted by the Vienna Circle led by Moritz Schlick and Rudolf Carnap, and by the Berlin Society for Scientific Philosophy led by Hans Reichenbach (see VIENNA CIRCLE §3). The major thrust of scientific philosophy was the naturalization of metaphysics, that is, the replacement of Neo-Kantian philosophical metaphysics with a scientific metaphysics. In particular, the fundamental properties of space, time and causality, they argued, cannot be learned through any sort of purely philosophical inquiry, but only through the study of the appropriate scientific theories, particularly relativity theory and the quantum theory (see GENERAL RELATIVITY, PHILOSOPHICAL RESPONSES TO §3). The task left to philosophy was the logical analysis of scientific theories, a purely a priori undertaking. Eventually included in this analysis was the *epistemological* relationship between statements of evidence and statements of theory. Following Frege, this came to be regarded as the logical study of inductively valid or rationally justified inference, independent of any inferences actual scientists might in fact make (see INDUCTIVE INFERENCE).

In the face of German National Socialism, most of the scientific philosophers left the German-speaking world and the vast majority, including Carnap and Reichenbach, ended up in the USA. Their incorporation into the American philosophical world was fostered primarily by pragmatist philosophers. By the mid-1950s, what in Germany had been a radically anti-establishment scientific philosophy had become in North America the established philosophy of science. Ironically, pragmatism and its associated naturalism were eclipsed by a rival empiricist programme incorporating a militantly non-naturalistic view of scientific method (see PRAGMATISM; LOGICAL POSITIVISM §§3-4).

The revival of naturalism owes much to the works of Kuhn and Quine during the 1960s. In *The Structure of Scientific Revolutions* Kuhn attempted to explain the historical development of science in terms borrowed from fields such as linguistics, psychology, and sociology – a thoroughly naturalistic project. (see KUHN, T.S. §2). Quine, by contrast, argued for a naturalized epistemology by demonstrating the impossibility of carrying out any programme of reducing all knowledge to sense impressions, a programme that had come to be synonymous with a Fregean approach to epistemology (see QUINE, W.V. §2; NATURALIZED EPISTEMOLOGY) Unfortunately, the empirical resources available in the 1960s, gestalt psychology, behaviourism and structural-functional sociology of science, were not sufficient to develop the naturalistic programmes of either Kuhn or Quine. Since the mid 1970s, however, developments in the cognitive sciences and constructivist sociology of science have provided far richer resources (see CONSTRUCTIVISM). By the mid-1980s, a naturalized philosophy of science had become once again a viable option.

2 The problem of epistemic norms

The most persistent objections to the re-emergence of naturalism in the philosophy of science involve the status of epistemic norms, or principles of rational inference. The problem may be stated as follows: a naturalistic philosophy of science, it is said, can at most provide *descriptions* of actual scientific practice. But science requires *normative principles* which distinguish those claims legitimately warranted by available evidence from those not so warranted. So no naturalized philosophy of science can be a complete philosophy of science. A more pointed way of framing the same sort of objection is this: a naturalized philosophy of science appeals to established theories of various sciences. But one of the conclusions of any philosophy of science should be an account of what makes some theories warranted and others not. So a naturalized philosophy of science either begs a central question or remains viciously circular.

Naturalists respond to the more pointed objection by questioning the presupposition that it is possible to justify any principles of scientific inference a priori. Here naturalists can point to nearly 300 years of attempts by empiricist philosophers to find an adequate justification of induction that does not beg the question (see INDUCTION, EPISTEMIC ISSUES). Such considerations, of course, do not constitute an a priori proof that no such justification will ever be forthcoming. But where, the naturalist asks, might such a justification be found? In logic, in intuition, or in an a priori theory of human judgment? These have all been tried without acknowledged success. Where could we turn next? The naturalist concludes that there most likely is no place beyond the province of science that could provide such a justification. The supposition that there must be some such place looks to be the product of an unwarranted yearning for some sort of absolute foundation for scientific claims.

Positively, naturalists recommend a non-foundational, pragmatic approach to epistemology. Individually and collectively we can do no better than begin where we are, with the theories and methods we have inherited, historically contingent though these may be. Any theory or method may be questioned, though not without a specific reason, and not all at once. The general goal is not to ground what we think we know, but to improve upon it. As for all-encompassing sceptical worries, naturalists take comfort in evolutionary biology. We as a species would not be here if our evolved sensory and motor skills were not good enough to secure the necessities of life and procreation. This reflection begs the question against a radical sceptic of course, and does little to explain how we achieved our current advanced state of scientific knowledge, including that of evolutionary biology. But it provides a naturalistic starting point.

As for the general problem of epistemic norms, naturalists insist that categorical principles of rational inference are not to be had. But that still leaves conditionally normative principles of the form: if you wish to accomplish goal G, try method M. The warrant for such principles consists in finding empirical evidence that doing M in fact promotes achievement of G. In this sense, all knowledge has potential normative implications, for example, as nuclear physics had implications for how to go about building a powerful bomb.

Contemporary naturalists disagree about the kind of principle to be sought, and the kind of evidence relevant to normative claims. Some, for example Larry Laudan, look for general methodological rules such as: successful prediction of novel facts provides stronger evidence for a theory than does explanation of previously known facts. And the relevant evidence is said to be found in historical instances in which theories which generated successful predictions turned out to be better than others which did not. Other naturalists doubt the usefulness of rules at this level of generality either for the practice of science or for explaining how science works. And they doubt that the historical record can in fact furnish the required evidence. Rather, it is argued, we need a deeper theory of how scientists do science and of the methods they employ. Such a theory could help us explain why some scientists were successful and others not. It could even provide some general normative guidance for scientists themselves, or for those who determine priorities for funding scientific research. And it could explain the circumstances in which more general rules, like that regarding the value of successful predictions, may be operative. The evidence for such a theory of science would have to go beyond mere correlation between supposed applications of a rule and the end results. It would be more like evidence which supports any general theory in such areas as biology, statistics, the cognitive sciences or sociology. Here it is important that statistics and experimental design be seen as themselves scientific theories relating experimental designs, experimental results, and correct decisions among alternative hypotheses.

Finally there is the question of the general epistemic goals of science. Naturalists reject attempts to determine a priori what the epistemic goals of science should be. They doubt there are any justifiable principles on which to base such attempts. Rather, we can investigate only what epistemic goals have in fact been pursued by various scientists and, perhaps, the empirical consequences of pursuing various goals. One need not presume that all scientists everywhere have pursued the same epistemic goals, or even that their professed goals are the same as their actual goals. Naturalists thus reject general philosophical arguments for or against 'realism' or for or against 'empiricism' (see SCIENTIFIC REALISM AND ANTIREALISM §3). The historical record shows that scientists have pursued both sorts of goal, sometimes successfully and sometimes not.

3 The bases for naturalization

Naturalists differ among themselves mainly on the sorts of scientific knowledge they deem most relevant to a naturalistic understanding of science. Individual naturalists typically stress one type of knowledge over all others, and the types of knowledge tend to represent different levels of organization. Paul Churchland, for example, attempts to understand scientific explanation and theorizing at the neuro-computational level. Paul Thagard argues that conceptual revolutions can be explained by relationships of explanatory coherence among statements that can be modelled in a quasi-connectionist computer program. Many naturalists, following in the footsteps of DARWIN himself, appeal to evolutionary biology, though in different ways (see EVOLUTION, THEORY OF). Michael Ruse thinks that evolution yielded general methodological rules we follow intuitively and discover by reflecting on our practice. David Hull (1988) argues for strict isomorphisms among organic evolution, the evolution of scientific communities, and the evolution of scientific concepts. Others, including Stephen Toulmin, Donald Campbell and Abner Shimony make less strict use of evolutionary ideas in their philosophies of science. Still other naturalists, such as Nancy Nersessian, focus on concepts and results developed in cognitive psychology. Some would add here a theory of human judgment and experimental design. Finally, others, such as Steve Fuller, find the most explanatory power at the level of social interaction and communication. What is an aspiring naturalist to conclude?

The wise course is to recognize that there can be no such thing as a homogeneous theory of science. Science is far too complex a phenomenon for that. Rather, we must settle for a diverse set of models in terms of which we can understand how science works in specific instances. These models will be inspired by models first developed in a wide variety of sciences. The best to be hoped for is that the various models employed are complementary. Where applications overlap, the results should at least be compatible. But we must also realize that there is a limit to theoretical naturalistic explanations of science. Some features of various sciences will have no deeper explanation than the existence of various historical contingencies in their origin and development. As a human activity, even as an activity expressly designed to produce faithful representations of nature, science will always contain elements of historical contingency.

References and further reading

Giere, R.N. (1988) *Explaining Science: A Cognitive Approach*, Chicago, IL: University of Chicago Press. (A comprehensive naturalistic theory of science emphasizing contributions from the cognitive sciences.)

—— (ed.) (1992) *Cognitive Models of Science*, Minnesota Studies in the Philosophy of Science, vol. 15, Minneapolis, MN: University of Minnesota Press. (Includes original essays by leading cognitive naturalists mentioned in §3, including Churchland, Fuller, Nersessian and Thagard.)

Hatfield, G. (1989) *The Natural and the Normative: Theories of Perception from Kant to Helmholtz*, Cambridge, MA: MIT Press. (A masterly though demanding history of naturalism in German philosophy.)

* Hull, D. (1988) *Science as a Process: An Evolutionary Account of the Social and Conceptual Development of Science*, Chicago, IL: University of Chicago Press. (A detailed elaboration of an evolutionary model of science. See §3.)

Kitcher, P. (1992) 'The Naturalists Return', *Philosophical Review* 101: 53–114. (A survey of contemporary philosophical naturalism emphasizing the influence of Frege.)

Kornblith, H. (ed.) (1985) *Naturalizing Epistemology*, Cambridge, MA: MIT Press. (Includes classic papers by Campbell (§3) and Quine (§1).)

Laudan, L. (1987) 'Progress of Rationality? The Prospects for Normative Naturalism', *American Philosophical Quarterly* 24: 19–31. (Laudan's answer to the problem of epistemic norms in a naturalistic philosophy of science, §2.)

Laudan, L. *et al.* (1986) 'Scientific Change: Philosophical Models and Historical Research', *Synthèse* 69: 141–223. (Sets out Laudan's programme for the empirical study of scientific change §2.)

Ruse, M. (1986) *Taking Darwin Seriously*, Dordrecht: Reidel. (Contains an evolutionary account of science grounded in sociobiology, §3.)

Wilson, D.J. (1990) *Science, Community, and the Transformation of American Philosophy, 1860–1930*, Chicago, IL: University of Chicago Press. (A historian's view of naturalism in American philosophy before the logical empiricists.)

RONALD N. GIERE

NATURE, AESTHETIC APPRECIATION OF

In the Western world, aesthetic appreciation of nature and its philosophical investigation came to fruition in the eighteenth century. During that time, aestheticians made nature the ideal object of aesthetic experience and analysed that experience in terms of disinterestedness, thereby laying the groundwork for understanding the appreciation of nature in terms of the sublime and the picturesque. This philosophical tradition reached its zenith with Kant, while popular aesthetic appreciation of nature continued primarily in terms of the picturesque.

In the late twentieth century, renewed interest in the aesthetics of nature has produced various positions designed to avoid assimilating appreciation of nature with traditional models for aesthetic appreciation of art. Three are especially noteworthy. The first holds that the appreciation of nature is not in fact aesthetic; the second rejects the traditional analysis of aesthetic experience as disinterested, arguing instead that the aesthetic appreciation of nature involves engagement with nature; the third attempts to maintain the traditional analysis, while distinguishing aesthetic appreciation of nature by dependence on scientific knowledge.

These positions have a number of ramifications. In freeing aesthetic appreciation of nature from artistic models, they pave the way for a general environmental aesthetics comparable to other areas of philosophy, such as environmental ethics. Moreover, the significance given to scientific knowledge in the third position both explains the aesthetic appreciation associated with environmentalism and provides aesthetic appreciation of nature with a degree of objectivity that may make aesthetic considerations more effectual in environmental assessment.

1 **History**
2 **Background to the present**
3 **Positions and problems**
4 **Ramifications**

1 History

Although a tradition of viewing art as the mirror of nature has existed since antiquity, the idea of aesthetically appreciating nature itself is sometimes traced to Petrarch's novel passion for climbing mountains, simply in order to enjoy the prospect. Yet from the dawn of the Renaissance to the present, the development of aesthetic appreciation of nature has been uneven and episodic. Initially such appreciation, together with its philosophical investigation, was hamstrung by a religious tradition that saw mountains as despised heaps of wreckage left behind by the flood, wilderness regions as fearful places for punishment and repentance, and all of nature's workings as a poor substitute for the perfect harmony lost in humanity's fall. It took the rise of a secular science and an equally secular art to free nature from such associations and open it up for aesthetic appreciation. Thus, in the Western world, the evolution of aesthetic appreciation of nature has been intertwined with the objectification of nature achieved by science and the subjectification of it completed by art.

Early in the eighteenth century, British aestheticians initiated a tradition that gave theoretical expression to the connection between aesthetic appreciation of nature and scientific objectivity. Empiricist thinkers, such as Joseph Addison and Francis Hutcheson, took nature rather than art as the ideal object of aesthetic experience and developed the notion of disinterestedness as the mark of such experience. In the course of the century, this notion was elaborated so as to exclude from aesthetic experience an ever-increasing number of associations and conceptualizations. Thus, the objects of appreciation favoured by the tradition – British landscapes – were eventually severed not only from religious associations, but from an appreciator's personal, moral and economic interests. The upshot was a mode of aesthetic appreciation that looked upon the natural world with an eye not unlike the distancing, objectifying eye of science. In this way, the tradition laid the groundwork for the idea of the sublime, by which even the most threatening of nature's manifestations, such as mountains and wilderness, could be distanced and appreciated rather than simply feared and despised (see SUBLIME, THE §§2–3).

However, if disinterestedness laid the groundwork for the sublime, it also cleared the ground for another, quite different idea: the picturesque. This idea secured the connection between aesthetic appreciation of nature and the subjective renderings of nature in art. The term literally means 'picture-like' and indicates a mode of appreciation in which the natural world is divided into scenes, each aiming in subject matter or in composition at an ideal dictated by art, and especially by poetry and landscape painting. Thus, while disinterestedness and the sublime stripped and objectified nature, the picturesque dressed it in a new set of subjective and romantic images: a rugged cliff with a ruined castle, a deep valley with an arched bridge. Like disinterestedness, the picturesque had its roots in the theories of early eighteenth-century aestheticians, such as Addison, who thought 'works of nature' more appealing the more they resembled art. The trend of the picturesque culminated later in the century, when, popularized primarily by William Gilpin and Uvedale Price, it became the aesthetic ideal of English tourists as they pursued picturesque scenery in the Lake District and the Scottish Highlands. Indeed, the picturesque remains the preferred mode of aesthetic appreciation for the form of tourism that sees the natural world in the light of travel brochures, calendar photos and picture postcards.

While the picturesque lingered on as a popular appreciative mode, theoretical study of the aesthetics of nature, after flowering in the eighteenth century, went into decline. Many of the main ideas, such as disinterestedness and the centrality of nature rather than art, reached their climax with Kant (SUBLIME, THE §3), and in his third critique these ideas received such exhaustive treatment that a kind of closure was achieved. In the new world order initiated by Hegel, art was a means to the Absolute, and it, rather than nature, was destined to became the favoured subject of philosophical aesthetics.

2 Background to the present

However, as theoretical study of the aesthetics of nature declined, a new view of nature was initiated that eventually gave rise to a different kind of aesthetic appreciation. This mode of appreciation was rooted in the nature writings of Henry David THOREAU and reinforced by George Perkins Marsh's recognition that humanity is the major cause of the destruction of nature's beauty. It achieved its classic realization at the end of the nineteenth century in the work of the American naturalist John Muir. Muir saw all nature and especially wild nature as aesthetically beautiful and found ugliness only where nature was subject to human intrusion. These ideas strongly influenced the North American wilderness preservation movement and continue to shape the aesthetic appreciation of nature associated with contemporary environmentalism. This kind of appreciation may be called positive aesthetics and, in so far as it eschews humanity's marks on the landscape, contrasts sharply with picturesque appreciation, with its delight in the signs of human presence. It became and remains the rival of the picturesque as the popular mode of aesthetic appreciation of nature, although popular appreciation is typically an uneasy balance of the two.

In spite of these developments in popular appreciation of nature, however, philosophical aesthetics, with few exceptions, ignored nature during the nineteenth and much of the twentieth centuries. Friedrich SCHELLING and a few thinkers of the Romantic movement dealt with it to some extent, and George Santayana and John Dewey both discussed it. But, by and large, aesthetics was dominated by an interest in art. By the mid-twentieth century, philosophical aesthetics in the analytic tradition was virtually equated with philosophy of art. Moreover, when aesthetic appreciation of nature was mentioned, it was treated, by comparison with that of art, as a messy, subjective business of little philosophical significance. In this context Ronald Hepburn's work in the 1960s had special importance. Hepburn argued that aesthetic appreciation of nature was as significant and as rich as that of art, and that it could be, though not a carbon copy of appreciation of art, similar to that of art – shallow or deep, appropriate or not. It required serious philosophical study.

3 Positions and problems

In the latter part of the twentieth century, renewed interest in the aesthetics of nature has generated a number of different positions on aesthetic appreciation of nature. Many of them share the view that such appreciation cannot simply be assimilated with standard accounts of aesthetic appreciation of art. In this they affirm Hepburn's insight that the appreciation of nature, although comparable to that of art, does not mimic it. The rejection of some of the traditional modes of aesthetic appreciation is implied. For example, it is argued that appropriate appreciation of nature cannot involve viewing natural objects in the same way that we frequently view traditional art objects such as works of sculpture – that is, as passive objects of contemplation divorced from both their and our spatial and temporal contexts. By contrast, natural objects belong in an environment that not only surrounds and engages them, but surrounds and engages the appreciator. Thus, the physical or contemplative removal of natural objects or ourselves from their environments results in inappropriate appreciation. Likewise, it is held that viewing nature as we might view a landscape painting, that is, as a static scene that we behold from a predetermined distance, is equally inappropriate in that it misleadingly reduces nature to a series of two-dimensional scenic views.

Given the rejection of traditional modes of aesthetic appreciation of nature, an alternative approach becomes necessary. The most radical of such alternatives elevates the neglect of nature by analytic aesthetics to a philosophical position, denying either implicitly or explicitly the possibility of aesthetic appreciation of nature. When explicitly developed, this position leaves traditional modes of appreciation intact for art, but concerning nature argues as follows: aesthetic appreciation necessarily involves aesthetic judgment, which entails judging the object of appreciation as the achievement of a designing intellect. However, since nature is not the product of a designing intellect, appreciation of it is not aesthetic. In the past, the appreciation of nature was deemed aesthetic only because of the assumption that nature is the handiwork of a designing creator; this assumption is either false, or at least inadequate for grounding an aesthetic of nature. This position is problematic, however, since it runs against both the orthodox view that everything is open to aesthetic appreciation and the common-sense idea that at least some natural objects, such as certain landscapes and sunsets, constitute paradigm objects of aesthetic appreciation.

A second alternative rejects traditional modes of aesthetic appreciation not only for nature but for art as well. This position argues that the disinterestedness tradition involves a mistaken analysis of the aesthetic and that this is most evident in the field of aesthetic appreciation of nature. In such appreciation the quality of disinterestedness, with its isolating, distancing and objectifying gaze, is out of place, for it is the means by which both natural objects and appreciators are wrongly abstracted from the environments in which they properly belong and in which appropriate appreciation is achieved. Thus, this position replaces disinterestedness with engagement, distance with immersion, and objectivity with subjectivity, and calls for a new aesthetic of engagement. Such an aesthetic, it is argued, yields a mode of appreciation not only more appropriate for nature, but also for most works of art, at least for those of the twentieth century. However, this second position is also problematic. First, since disinterestedness constitutes the favoured analysis of the aesthetic, its rejection may constitute a rejection of the aesthetic itself, reducing this second alternative to a version of the first. Second, this position seemingly embraces an unacceptable degree of subjectivity in aesthetic appreciation of both nature and art.

A third position attempts to maintain much of the traditional analysis of the aesthetic, while yet accommodating features unique to nature. The motivation for this alternative is not only to find a mode of aesthetic appreciation especially appropriate for nature, but also to avoid excessive subjectivity. This position notes that in aesthetic appreciation of art both appropriateness of appreciative mode and objectivity are achieved by tying appreciation to understanding in terms of art-historical and art-critical knowledge. It thus adopts a parallel approach for aesthetic appreciation of nature. However, although the appropriate knowledge for art is derived from art history and art criticism, nature is not art and such knowledge is not relevant to nature's appreciation. For nature, it is argued, the relevant knowledge is that which provides our understanding of the natural world, that is, the knowledge given by the natural sciences. For example, just as art-historical knowledge of mid-twentieth century schools of painting endows appreciation of an abstract expressionist work with appropriateness and objectivity, so knowledge of geology, biology and ecology similarly endows appreciation of an alpine meadow. In this way, aesthetic appreciation of nature is once again linked to the objectifying eye of science.

Like the other two alternatives, however, this third alternative faces some philosophical difficulties. One is that a scientific approach may not yield real aesthetic appreciation. However, unlike the second alternative, the third position does not reject traditional resources, such as disinterestedness, as constitutuents of aesthetic appreciation. Thus, a science-based mode of appreciation can be sufficiently disinterested to be truly aesthetic. Indeed, the problem may be the opposite one, that such a mode of appreciation, given its essential dependence on science, is too distancing, too objectifying. It thus runs the risk of wrongly abstracting natural objects from their environment and in this way making appropriate appreciation impossible. In reply it is argued that since aesthetic appreciation necessarily involves distancing and thus some degree of abstraction, the issue is not whether to abstract. Rather it is how to supplement the required abstraction so as to achieve rich and appropriate appreciation. The problem with traditional approaches is not that they involve abstraction, but that, having abstracted nature, they reconstitute it by means of artistic models, such as the picturesque, and not in terms of relevant knowledge, such as science provides. Moreover, science is not, or at least is no longer, the severely abstracting endeavour it is popularly taken to be. Modern natural science, as exemplified by ecology, increasingly views nature in holistic terms.

4 Ramifications

These approaches to the aesthetics of nature have a number of ramifications. One is that, concerning popular appreciation of nature, they seemingly support positive aesthetics as opposed to the picturesque. Appreciating nature in terms of artistic models, such as the picturesque, is rejected by all these approaches, and the scientific approach in particular accords well with the positive aesthetic model. When nature is aesthetically appreciated in virtue of natural science, positive aesthetic appreciation seems singularly appropriate, for, on the one hand, humanity's marks on the landscape appear especially out of place, while, on the other, wild, pristine nature becomes an aesthetic ideal. Moreover, as the natural sciences increasingly find, or at least appear to find, unity, order and harmony in nature, nature itself, when appreciated in the light of such knowledge, increasingly appears more profoundly beautiful. Science replaces the once despised wreckage of God's deluge with inspiring manifestations of orderly geological forces; and the harmony lost in humanity's fall is superseded by a perfect harmony of science's own making.

Two other ramifications concern aesthetics and philosophy more generally. First, all three positions (and particularly the scientific approach), in rejecting artistic models for appreciation of nature and in replacing them with a dependence on knowledge of the object of appreciation, provide a blueprint for aesthetic appreciation in other non-art cases. It is made evident that in aesthetic appreciation of, for example, toys, furniture, people, cornfields, pets, neighbourhoods, shoes and shopping malls, what is appropriate is not an imposition of various artistic models, but rather a dependence on knowledge that is pertinent to the nature of the object of appreciation. This suggests a general and universal aesthetics, which may be termed environmental aesthetics, distinct from traditional aesthetics, which is too easily equated with philosophy of art. Second, there is an alignment of this universal aesthetics with other areas of philosophy in which there is a rejection of archaic, inappropriate models and a new-found dependence on knowledge relevant to the particular objects in question. For example, environmental aesthetics parallels environmental ethics in its rejection of anthropocentric models for the moral assessment of the natural world, replacing them with models based on science, most notably ecology (see ENVIRONMENTAL ETHICS).

Lastly, if approaches such as the scientific one described above endow aesthetic appreciation of nature with a degree of objectivity, they might have some practical relevance in a world increasingly engaged in landscape and environmental assessment. Individuals making such assessments are often reluctant to acknowledge the importance of aesthetic considerations, regarding them at worst as totally subjective or based at best on culturally relative artistic modes of appreciation. A scientific approach suggests the need to re-evaluate such opinions.

See also: AESTHETIC ATTITUDE §§1–3; HEGEL, G.W.F. §8

References and further reading

* Berleant, A. (1992) *The Aesthetics of Environment*, Philadelphia, PA: Temple University Press. (An elaboration of the second position mentioned in §3 of this entry.)
Berleant, A. and Carlson, A. (eds) (1998) Special Issue on Environmental Aesthetics, *Journal of Aesthetics and Art Criticism* 56. (A special issue of the journal, with a number of essays on the aesthetics of nature.)
* Carlson, A. (1979) 'Appreciation and the Natural Environment', *Journal of Aesthetics and Art Criticism* 37: 267–76. (A sketch of the third position mentioned in §3 of this entry.)
—— (1981) 'Nature, Aesthetic Judgment and Objectivity', *Journal of Aesthetics and Art Criticism* 40: 15–27. (A discussion of the possibility of objectivity in aesthetic appreciation of nature.)
—— (1984) 'Nature and Positive Aesthetics', *Environmental Ethics* 6: 5–34. (A discussion of the positive aesthetics mode of nature appreciation and its relationship to science.)
Elliot, R. (1982) 'Faking Nature', *Inquiry* 25: 81–93. (An example of the first position mentioned in §3 of this entry.)
* Hepburn, R.W. (1966) 'Contemporary Aesthetics and the Neglect of Natural Beauty', *British Analytical Philosophy*, ed. B. Williams and A. Montefiore, London: Routledge & Kegan Paul, 285–310. (Hepburn's classic discussion mentioned in §2 of this entry.)
Kemal, S. and Gaskell, I. (eds) (1993) *Landscape, Natural Beauty and the Arts*, Cambridge: Cambridge University Press. (A useful collection of essays by a number of the main contributors to this area of research.)
Sepänmaa, Y. (1993) *The Beauty of Environment*, Denton: Environmental Ethics Books, 2nd edn. (A discussion of a number of key issues in the field, together with a useful bibliography.)

ALLEN CARLSON

NATURE AND CONVENTION

The nature–convention distinction opposes instinctual or 'spontaneous' modes of comportment (those which follow from 'human nature') to those which are socially instituted or culturally prescribed. Its philosophic interest resides in its use to justify or contest specific forms of human behaviour and social organization. Since the 'conventional' is opposed to the 'natural' as that which is in principle transformable, the adherents of a particular order in human affairs have standardly sought to prove its 'naturality', while its critics have sought to expose its merely 'conventional' status. Relatedly, 'conventions' may be associated with what is distinctive to 'human', as opposed to 'bestial' nature, or denounced for their role in repressing our more 'natural' impulses.

The nature–convention antithesis is one of a number of cognate dualisms (nature–culture; natural–artificial; animal–human) through which Western thought conceptualizes what is distinctive to the 'being' of humanity, and demarcates between that which is independent of and pre-given to human activity and that which is humanly achieved or contrived. Though many would dispute whether any clear-cut division can be drawn between the 'human' and the 'animal', the very posing of the question of our affinity with or distinction from other creatures is reliant on a prior appreciation of those features which are specific to humans. One of the most notable of these is that human beings establish 'conventions': customs, rules, or norms of behaviour which are socially instituted as opposed to naturally dictated. The establishment of conventions is thus intimately bound up with those capacities for moral thought and action which mark us off from other animals. To follow (or contest) a convention presupposes an ability to understand prescription, and to act otherwise than in obedience to the dictate of instinct.

The nature–convention opposition has its origins in Greek antiquity, in the fifth century BC, where the distinction between *physis* and *nomos* becomes the site of a dispute about the cultural relativity of political and moral values (see PLATO; SOPHISTS) which has remained a central concern of philosophy ever since. Thus it is by reference to the multiplicity of human conventions, that relativists have often challenged claims about the existence of a common 'human nature' or universally applicable morality (see RELATIVISM §1).

Conventions may be very culturally specific, transient, and readily transformed codes of conduct, or more perduring customs or institutional forms which are none the less particular to given societies. In some instances the conventional prescriptions or prohibitions may be trans-cultural and deeply entrenched (as in the case of the law against incest, which Claude Lévi-Strauss presents as marking the arrival of the 'cultural'), while remaining in principle revisable as norms of conduct precisely in virtue of their being humanly ordained.

It is the double association of the conventional both with what is 'right' for human beings and with what is transformable, and of the 'natural' both with the 'bestial' and with what is deemed immutable, which accounts for the complex ideological disputes that attach to the distinction. The rules that human beings set themselves (against murder, or incest, for example) have very frequently been viewed as preserving them from the degeneracy or 'wickedness' of nature's ways (a position argued very forcibly by John Stuart Mill in his essay 'Nature' (1874)). But in the Rousseauan or Romantic conception, nature is viewed as a source of goodness or authenticity, and hence invoked as a model from which humanity should take its cue. These differing perspectives, however, may both seek confirmation in terms that tend to blur or confound the nature–convention

distinction: those forms of behaviour which distinguish us from the beast being endorsed as qualities of human nature (and hence denied the status of 'mere' convention); and those which nature inspires being pitted against those supposedly natural rules of conduct which it is claimed are more properly to be viewed as repressive convention.

The philosophic interest of the nature–convention distinction lies therefore in the normative disputes that are conducted in its terms: that which is socially instituted is at once both defended by its adherents as part of the order of nature, and thus untransformable, and exposed by its critics as conventional and hence mutable. Relations of class, and discriminations on grounds of gender, race and sexuality, for example, have all been said to be natural by those seeking to sustain their social hierarchies, and denounced as illegitimate and oppressive norms by those seeking to overthrow them. Within this challenge, however, to the naturalization of what is socially instituted, we may distinguish between those who would contest what is said to be natural in the name of the more authentic naturality of what they seek to institute; and those (like Michel Foucault) who would insist upon the always normative and constantly revisable quality of what is said to be natural to human societies at any point in time. For example, one may contest existing social relations, institutions and sexual 'norms' in terms of their 'alienation' from or 'repression' of nature, or dispute the very existence of natural, as opposed to socially 'constructed' or inculcated needs and desires. It is arguable, however, that without recourse to an idea of nature there can be no coherent or self-consistent critique of custom or convention.

See also: CONVENTIONALISM; CULTURE; NATURALISM IN SOCIAL SCIENCE

References and further reading

Horigan, S. (1988) *Nature and Culture in Western Discourses*, London: Routledge. (A critical survey of the ways in which the nature–culture divide has been conceptualized in anthropology.)

Lovejoy, A.O. (1948) 'Nature as Aesthetic Norm', in *Essays in the History of Ideas*, Baltimore, MD: Johns Hopkins University Press. (Briefly lists and comments on the inflections acquired by the term 'nature' when used in reference to human conduct.)

* Mill, J.S. (1874) 'Nature', in *Three Essays on Religion*, London: Longman. (Usefully distinguishes between non-normative and normative uses of the term, and illustrates the tensions to which the latter are subject.)

Nussbaum, M.C. (1986) *The Fragility of Goodness:*

Luck and Ethics in Greek Tragedy and Philosophy, Cambridge: Cambridge University Press. (For many insights on classical Greek thought concerning the distinction. See especially pp. 397–421.)

Soper, K. (1995) *What is Nature? Culture, Politics and the Non-human*, Oxford: Blackwell. (Discusses the contested nature of 'nature' in contemporary theory and social movement politics.)

Taylor, C. (1989) *Sources of the Self*, Cambridge: Cambridge University Press, part IV, pp. 305–68. (Illuminating discussion of Enlightenment, Rousseauan and Romantic conceptions of 'nature' and its role as guide to human conduct.)

KATE SOPER

'NATURE, PHILOSOPHY OF'

see NATURPHILOSOPHIE

NATURPHILOSOPHIE

Naturphilosophie *refers to the philosophy of nature prevalent especially in German philosophy, science and literary movements from around 1790 to about 1830. It pleaded for an organic and dynamic worldview as an alternative to the atomist and mechanist outlook of modern science. Against the Cartesian dualism of matter and mind which had given way to the mechanist materialism of the French Encyclopedists, Spinoza's dual aspect theory of mind and matter as two modes of a single substance was favoured. The sources of this heterogeneous movement lie in the philosophy of German idealism as well as in late classicism and Romanticism. The leading figure, Schelling, assimilated and stimulated the major trends and ideas through his work.*

After the death of Hegel (1831) and of Goethe (1832), Naturphilosophie *quickly disappeared from the mainstream. Yet it survived in various different forms, especially as an undercurrent of German culture and science, until the twentieth century.*

1   **Kant and Fichte**
2   **Schelling and the** *Naturphilosophen*
3   **Major doctrines of** *Naturphilosophie*

1   Kant and Fichte

The leading role among the various trends in *Naturphilosophie* was played by Schelling's philosophy of nature. To understand it, it is necessary to examine also the philosophy of Kant and subsequently that of Fichte.

Kant had a threefold influence on the movement of *Naturphilosophie*: through his *Metaphysische Anfangsgründe der Naturwissenschaft* (Metaphysical Foundations of Natural Science) (1786) where he took forces as the defining properties of matter; through his third critique, the *Kritik der Urteilskraft* (Critique of Judgment) (1790), where he treated the concept of purpose in nature, and finally in providing a frame for these ideas through the transcendental idealism of his first critique, the *Kritik der reinen Vernunft* (Critique of Pure Reason) (1781/87).

In his *Metaphysical Foundations* Kant tried to clarify the concept of matter as it has to be presupposed by all possible scientific investigation. In contesting Newton's views, he saw matter as constituted by the opposing forces of attraction and repulsion. Matter fills space by its repulsive force. The resulting dispersion is counteracted and limited by an attractive force. Thus Kant arrives at a dynamic view of matter which takes active opposing forces as fundamental and which avoids the conception of the atom and of empty space. His theory advanced a dynamic view of nature ('dynamism') as a research programme in physics, and made similar conceptions of the sciences appear in a new light (for example, positive and negative forces in magnetism and electricity).

In the *Critique of Judgment*, Kant tried to come to terms with the teleological structure of nature. Organisms as products of nature cannot be completely explained in the causal way in which one would explain a mechanical system. For in organisms not only do the parts determine the whole, but the purpose guiding the organism as a whole also determines its parts. In understanding organism and nature as a whole we have thus to grasp it as fulfilling a purpose, to see it as a self-organizing system which has the cause and effect of its action in itself (Kant 1790: §64). However, since we can talk of purposes only in relation to free action and since nature is not an intelligent being we can ascribe purposes to nature only in a metaphorical, regulative sense, *as if* it were a free acting creature with its own purposes. Our grasp of organic nature is therefore inherently subjective and can never reach the objective validity of explanations by mechanical causality. Later *Naturphilosophen* attempted to overcome this Kantian limitation and to furnish nature with an objective, purposive structure which is constitutive of it, and thus to see nature as an autonomous and even indeterministic system.

In the *Critique of Pure Reason*, Kant had claimed that experience is not passively received by our mind but is determined and even produced by categories intrinsic to our own understanding. The unity of our self-consciousness, the synthetic apperception, as the 'highest point' of philosophy is responsible for our sense impressions being synthesized into genuine knowledge. Thus every philosophy has to start with an inquiry into the transcendental conditions of the mind itself which make knowledge possible.

Before he became acquainted with Kant's writings, Johann Gottlieb Fichte believed determinism to be unavoidable. His view changed dramatically, however, when he realized that Kant's transcendental idealism can be radicalized so as to make room for absolute human freedom. Nature is a system of necessity only because it is conceived by us that way. In Kant, the unity of self-consciousness was only the *formal* condition of our knowledge; some material must be given to our senses which ultimately stems from the thing-in-itself. For Kant, the process of being affected by objects does not depend on the self. Fichte, however, came to reject the idea of the thing-in-itself and claimed that the unity of self-consciousness is also the *material* condition of our knowledge. The self with its capacity for synthesizing knowledge is not reacting to something given, it is autonomously producing its reality, including itself. Knowledge of objects is derived from an initial act of self-positing; objects are the result of a law-governed production of the ego. The 'I', the self, is in this case not to be thought of as the consciousness of an individual person, but as a general structure independent of individual realization.

2   Schelling and the *Naturphilosophen*

Schelling originally started in complete harmony with Fichte's viewpoint, but later gradually shifted away from it. Whereas Fichte stressed the certainty of which the I disposes in positing itself, Schelling tried to uncover the origin of the I, the kind of being from which it stems. '*I am*! My I comprises a being which precedes all thinking and conceiving' (Schelling [1795] 1856–61, vol. 1: 167). This being is now seen as more comprehensive than the ego: namely nature. The I is not its own product, as Fichte would have it, but the I and the material objects are produced by nature as a ground deeper than the I. 'Nature's reality stems from herself – she is her own product – a whole which is organized out of itself and organized by itself' (Schelling [1799] 1856–61, vol. 3: 17). With this move, Schelling could ascribe to nature the structure which Fichte had claimed for the I. Schelling also thought that this would make it possible to overcome the limitations which Kant thought were necessary in our grasp of nature. Nature can now be seen as a reality which is a self-determining system for which

purpose is a constitutive idea and not a regulative one as Kant had it.

From 1797 to 1806 Schelling made various attempts to formulate his philosophy of nature. This necessarily brought him into conflict with Fichte's soulless mechanical conception of nature. For Fichte nature was just the 'system of necessity', the inanimate realm of the 'not-I' or 'non-ego', posited by the I itself. Schelling, however, envisaged nature as a vital process from whose activity the consciousness of the ego and the mind emerges. Whereas Fichte asked how the self gets at nature, Schelling had the problem of how nature finally arrives at the I.

At the beginning of his development away from Fichte, Schelling envisaged *Naturphilosophie* as being of equal status with transcendental philosophy; from 1801 onwards, however, *Naturphilosophie* became primary for Schelling and independent from it. He claimed that we cannot grasp nature by merely investigating her products as they present themselves to our experience. This would be to see nature merely as an inanimate object, as *natura naturata*. Nature as 'productivity', or 'absolute activity', in its 'infinite becoming' requires studying her as *natura naturans*, as a subject, a productive process which eventually gives rise to mind and crystallizes in its products (Schelling [1799] 1856–61, vol. 3: 284). This view eventually flowed into a critique of Newtonian mechanical physics taken as the paradigm of modern science. Mechanism starts from material bodies which are supposed to have the property of attracting and/or repulsing each other. Yet, in order to conceive nature as an entity that is able to produce the self and the objects in like manner, it is necessary to give attraction and repulsion a more basic status and to take them as defining properties from which material objects and also consciousness are derived. Schelling did not attack the experimental and empirical side of science but its premature objectivism which leaves out the subjective element in nature and its developmental aspect.

In carrying out his programme Schelling was influenced by the experimental physicist and founder of electrochemistry, Johann Wilhelm Ritter (1776–1810), and influenced him in turn. Ritter pleaded for a strong connection of galvanism and chemistry and saw the living organism as a system of nested galvanic chains. When he found that the galvanic process is not necessarily bound to organic material, he considered galvanic action to be the key to the activity of the whole universe.

HEGEL was the other post-Kantian idealist who occupied himself with *Naturphilosophie*. He was decisively stimulated by Schelling before he came to work out a fundamentally different system. For

Hegel, nature as the realm of the idea in its otherness is not to be grasped as an evolutionary process but as a conceptual development of the idea on the way to self-knowledge.

3 Major doctrines of *Naturphilosophie*

Schelling's *Naturphilosophie* set the tone for many similar undertakings. Although these attempts sometimes differ very much in detail from each other, we can distinguish several recurrent tenets. First, and foremost, there is the view of the 'unity of mind and matter'. Schelling and many *Naturphilosophen* argued that nature is animated, that there is an original unity or 'identity' of nature and mind which allows us to infer nature's laws from the laws of the mind and vice versa: 'The system of nature is at the same time the system of our mind' and 'Nature must be visible spirit, and mind invisible nature' (Schelling [1797] 1856–61, vol. 2: 39, 56). This view was primarily directed against both Cartesian dualism and eighteenth-century materialism. It had a great impact on the Romantic movement, both in literature and science. Hans Christian Ørsted, for example, who discovered electromagnetism in 1820, claimed that all objects are materialized ideas. And according to the biologist Lorenz OKEN, it was the task of *Naturphilosophie* 'to show that the laws of the mind are not different from the laws of nature but that both represent each other. Philosophy of nature and philosophy of mind range, therefore, parallel to each other' (Oken 1843: §13). Later, one of the sharpest critics of *Naturphilosophie*, Hermann von HELM-HOLTZ saw the principal error of this movement precisely in the mingling of the necessary laws of nature with the spontaneous activity of mind. A last remnant of the identity view of nature and mind can be found in the dual aspect view of mind and body as it was embraced by a large number of physiologists, psychologists and many philosophers up to and including Rudolf Carnap's *Der Logische Aufbau der Welt* (The Logical Construction of the World) (1928).

A second doctrine is the prevalence of the organism as an explanatory model. For Schelling (as for Kant), mechanical explanations of nature have to be supplemented by organic ones. It is not possible, Schelling claimed, for the universe to be simply a causal mechanism as its organic structure is logically prior to its mechanical one. 'One and the same principle' is at work in both organic and inorganic nature which binds all of it 'into a general organism' (Schelling [1798] 1856–61, vol. 2: 350). Organisms are causally self-contained, they are their own cause and effect and they are self-movable, whereas causal mechanisms can only be moved from the outside

and are therefore essentially passive. Carl Friedrich Kielmeyer, who decisively influenced Schelling in his organic thought, explained the organism in terms of three organic forces: irritability, reproduction and sensibility (Kielmeyer 1793). Irritability is organic activity or movement, sensibility is organic receptivity or sensation, and reproduction refers to the metabolism, to growth and procreation.

A third related doctrine of *Naturphilosophie* is the unity of nature and its forces, and thereby also of science. There was a strong tendency to exhibit nature in all its different aspects as a development from a small number of fundamental forces. Ørsted, whose dissertation had examined Kant's *Metaphysical Foundations of Natural Science*, had claimed that there is a 'unity of all the forces' of heat, chemistry, electricity and magnetism and that 'the former physical results [*Kenntnisse*] thus combine into a physics of one piece' (Ørsted 1803: 209). Similar claims have been made by scientists such as Faraday, Mohr, Grove, J. R. Mayer and others, which eventually led to the establishment of the energy conservation principle. The inorganic as well as the organic realms were seen as directed by the same principles, so that there is no essential difference between them. This does not mean that nature reduces to mechanism, but that the inorganic world has to be conceived as the product of an inherent organic natural process. *Naturphilosophie* developed the tendency to impose the organic categories found in the study of nature even on culture, society and the state. In this sense, it also helped to prepare the ground both for the later materialist and naturalist movement as well as for organic conceptions of the state and society.

In viewing nature as a unity, the movement of *Naturphilosophie* was also influenced by Goethe's search for an underlying idea of the organic and inorganic realms of nature. In morphology, he argued that all plants are modifications of one primordial plant, the *Urpflanze*, and that all plant organs were variations of a single fundamental organ, the leaf (see GOETHE, J.W. VON §3).

Another doctrine of *Naturphilosophie* concerns the developmental aspect of nature. Instead of viewing nature and its parts in static terms, *Naturphilosophie* tried to conceive of it as the outcome of an evolutionary graduated succession. Very often this process was seen as being initiated and maintained by a polar antagonism of forces. Models for conceiving this process were either taken by way of analogical reasoning from some philosophical source (Kant's *Metaphysical Foundations*, Fichte's idea of the self determining itself by positing the I and the not-I at the same time) or some scientific theory of the time (magnetism, galvanism, electricity, chemistry, physiology). Other sources included Goethe and HERDER who also held influential theories of development. In all this, the concept of polarity played a prominent role and was seen as the continuous principle for every development and activity. Oken, for example, viewed living organisms as governed by two opposing processes: an individualizing one which increases the organism's vitality, and a universalizing one that leads to death and is a drive to the absolute (see ABSOLUTE, THE).

See also: ROMANTICISM, GERMAN §6; GERMAN IDEALISM

References and further reading

Amrine, F. (ed.) (1986) *Goethe and the Sciences: A Reappraisal*, Dordrecht: Kluwer. (Goethe in the history of science and his relevance to philosophical treatment of nature today. Annotated bibliography.)

Bonsiepen, W. (1997) *Die Begründung einer Naturphilosophie bei Kant, Schelling, Fries und Hegel. Mathematische versus spekulative Naturphilosophie* (Foundations of the philosophy of nature in Kant, Schelling, Fries and Hegel: mathematical versus speculative philosophy of nature), Frankfurt: Klostermann. (Detailed and thorough account of German idealism's different philosophies of nature and of the opposing mathematical philosophy of nature of J.F. Fries and his school. Much philosophical and historical context.)

Böhme, G. (ed.) (1989) *Klassiker der Naturphilosophie. Von den Vorsokratikern bis zur Kopenhagener Schule* (Classics of the philosophy of nature: from the Presocratics to the Copenhagen School), Munich: Beck. (Essays on the leading philosophers of nature and philosophical cosmologists, from the Presocratics to Einstein and the Copenhagen interpretation of quantum mechanics. Includes entries on Kant, Goethe, Schelling, and Hegel.)

Caneva, K.L. (1997) 'Physics and *Naturphilosophie*: A Reconnaissance', *History of Science* 35: 35–107. (Critical and thorough review of claims for the influence of *Naturphilosophie* on early nineteenth-century physics. Valuable and extensive bibliography.)

* Carnap, R. (1928) *Der logische Aufbau der Welt*, Berlin-Schlachtensee: Weltkreis-Verlag; trans. R. George as *The Logical Structure of the World*, Berkeley, CA: University of California Press, 1967. (Attempt to carry out the programme of early Logical Empiricism to reduce all concepts to elementary experiences. Gives a solution to the mind–body problem in terms of a double-aspect

theory that is reminiscent of the Spinozism of *Naturphilosophie*.)

Cohen, R.S. and Wartofsky, M.W. (eds) (1984) *Hegel and the Sciences*, Dordrecht: Reidel. (Essays on Hegel's philosophy of nature, its relation to logic and on his treatment of various sciences.)

Cunningham, A. and Jardine, N. (eds) (1990) *Romanticism and the Sciences*, Cambridge: Cambridge University Press. (Essays on Romanticism in general and on its relation to the sciences of the organic and inorganic, as well as on Romantic literature and the sciences.)

Engelhardt, D. von (1978) 'Bibliographie der Sekundärliteratur zur romantischen Naturforschung und Medizin 1950–1975' (Bibliography of secondary literature on Romantic science and medicine, 1950–1975), in R. Brinkmann (ed.) *Romantik in Deutschland. Ein interdisziplinäres Symposion* (Romanticism in Germany: An interdisciplinary symposium), Stuttgart: Metzler, 307–30. (Comprehensive bibliography for the given period. The volume contains other relevant material.)

—— (1988) 'Romanticism in Germany', in R. Porter and M. Teich (eds) *Romanticism in National Context*, Cambridge: Cambridge University Press, 109–33. (Places *Naturphilosophie* in the wider context of the German Romantic movement.)

Engelhardt, D. von and Musto, R. (eds) (1993) *Annali. Sezione Germanica* NS 3: 1–3. (A collection of nineteen essays, in Italian, on a wide range of topics concerning science and philosophy in the age of Romanticism; the collection has no special title.)

Esposito, J.L. (1977) *Schelling's Idealism and Philosophy of Nature*, Lewisburg, PA and London: Associated University Presses. (Short account of Schelling's philosophy of nature. Useful chapter on Schelling's contemporary critics and on his influence on nineteenth-century America)

Fichte, J.G. (1794) *Grundlage der gesammten Wissenschaftslehre*, Jena/ Leipzig: Gabler; repr. in *Sämmtliche Werke*, ed. I.H. Fichte, Berlin: Veit, 1845–6, vol. 1, 83–328; trans. P. Heath and J. Lachs as *The Science of Knowledge*, Cambridge: Cambridge University Press, 1982. (Theoretical foundation of Fichte's philosophical system.)

Fischer, K. (1902) *Schelling's Leben, Werke und Lehre* (Schelling's life, work, and doctrine), Heidelberg: Winter, 3rd edn. (Elaborate and vivid account of Schelling's life and work. Sometimes dated but still valuable, with a wealth of information.)

Frank, M. (1985) *Eine Einführung in Schellings Philosophie* (An introduction to Schelling's philosophy), Frankfurt: Suhrkamp. (Short but useful introduction to Schelling's work which puts stress on his *Naturphilosophie*.)

Giovanni, G. di (1979) 'Kant's Metaphysics of Nature and Schelling's *Ideas for a Philosophy of Nature*', *Journal of the History of Philosophy* 17: 197–215. (Argues for the closeness of Schelling's *Ideen* to Kant.)

Gloy, K. and Burger, P. (eds) (1993) *Die Naturphilosophie im Deutschen Idealismus* (The philosophy of nature in German idealism), Stuttgart: Frommann-Holzboog. (Collection of essays on German idealism's concept of nature: on Kant, Fichte, Schelling, Hegel and the Romantics.)

Gode-von Aesch, A. (1941) *Natural Science in German Romanticism* New York: Columbia University Press; repr. New York: AMS Press, 1966. (Deals with science and literature as two intertwined aspects of the German Romantic movement.)

Gower, B. (1973) 'Speculation in Physics: The History and Practice of *Naturphilosophie*', *Studies in History and Philosophy of Science* 3 (4): 301–56. (Authoritative and influential survey which includes treatment of Ritter and Ørsted.)

Hasler, L. (ed.) (1981) *Schelling. Seine Bedeutung für eine Philosophie der Natur und der Geschichte* (Schelling: his significance for a philosophy of nature and history), Stuttgart: Frommann-Holzboog. (Includes essays on Schelling's relation to the sciences of his day and on his philosophy of history.)

Heckmann, R., Krings, H. and Meyer, R.W. (eds) (1985) *Natur und Subjektivität. Zur Auseinandersetzung mit der Naturphilosophie des jungen Schelling* (Nature and subjectivity: a discussion of the young Schelling's Naturphilosophie), Stuttgart: Frommann-Holzboog. (Essays on the place of Schelling's *Naturphilosophie* in German idealism, its reception by its contemporaries and an assessment from a present-day point of view.)

Hegel, G.W.F. (1817) 'Naturphilosophie', part 2 of *Enzyklopädie der philosophischen Wissenschaften im Grundrisse*, Heidelberg: Oßwald; 2nd edn repr. in *Gesammelte Werke*, Hamburg: Meiner, 1989, vol. 19, 183–283; trans. M.J. Petry as *Hegel's Philosophy of Nature*, London: Allen & Unwin, 1970, 3 vols. (Hegel's major work on his own specific version of *Naturphilosophie*.)

Helmholtz, H. (1855) *Ueber das Sehen des Menschen* (On human vision), Leipzig: Voss; repr. in *Vorträge und Reden*, 5th edn, 2 vols, Braunschweig: Vieweg, 1903, vol. 1: 85–117. (One of the first documents of rising Neo-Kantianism. Kant's epistemology, interpreted in terms of sensory physiology, is proposed as a remedy for the extravagances of *Naturphilosophie*.)

Heuser-Keßler, M.-L. (1986) *Die Produktivität der Natur. Schellings Naturphilosophie und das neue Paradigma der Selbstorganisation in den Naturwissenschaften* (Nature's productivity: Schelling's philosophy of nature and the paradigm of self-organization in the natural sciences), Berlin: Duncker & Humblot. (Account of Schelling's conception of (especially organic) nature and its autogeneric ordering processes. Schelling's work is related to conceptions of self-organization in present-day science, in the work of I. Prigogine and H. Haken.)

Heuser-Keßler, M.-L. and Jacobs, W.G. (eds) (1994) *Schelling und die Selbstorganisation. Neue Forschungsperspektiven* (Schelling and self-organization: new research perspectives), *Selbstorganisation*, vol. 5, Berlin: Duncker & Humblot. (Deals with Schelling's concept of self-organization, its contemporary and present-day reception.)

Horstmann, R.-P. and Petry, M.J. (eds) (1986) *Hegels Philosophie der Natur. Beziehungen zwischen empirischer und spekulativer Naturerkenntnis* (Hegel's philosophy of nature: relations of empirical and speculative natural science), Stuttgart: Klett-Cotta. (Essays on Hegel's *Naturphilosophie*.)

* Kant, I. (1781/1787) *Kritik der reinen Vernunft*, Riga: Hartknoch; trans. N.K. Smith as *The Critique of Pure Reason*, New York: St Martin's Press, London: Macmillan, 1964. (Explanation and justification of the a priori forms of reason that constitute the basis of any theoretical knowledge. Kant's doctrine of the spontaneity of the subject and the autonomy of reason was especially relevant for *Naturphilosophie*.)

* —— (1786) *Metaphysische Anfangsgründe der Naturwissenschaft*, Riga: Hartknoch; trans. J. Ellington as *Metaphysical Foundations of Natural Science*, Indianapolis, IN: Bobbs-Merrill, 1970. (In his metaphysics of nature, Kant formulates the principles that specify the transition from the critique of pure reason to actual empirical science. His dynamic definition of matter from attractive and repulsive forces was important for *Naturphilosophie*.)

* —— (1790) *Kritik der Urteilskraft*, Berlin: Lagarde; trans. J.C. Meredith as *Kant's Critique of Judgement*, Oxford: Clarendon Press, 1952. (In a way, the cornerstone of Kant's philosophy. Tries to show that the realms of nature and freedom, of causality and teleology are compatible. The second part, 'Critique of teleological reason', became especially relevant for *Naturphilosophie*.)

Kanz, K.T. (ed.) (1994) *Philosophie des Organischen in der Goethezeit. Studien zu Werk und Wirkung des Naturforschers Carl Friedrich Kielmeyer (1765–1844)* (Philosophy of the organic during the time of Goethe: studies in the work and influence of the naturalist Carl Friedrich Kielmeyer), Stuttgart: Steiner. (Essays on Kielmeyer's vision of the organism and biology in general, its context and influence.)

* Kielmeyer, C.F. (1793) *Ueber die Verhältnisse der organischen Kräfte unter einander in der Reihe der verschiedenen Organisationen, die Geseze und Folgen dieser Verhältnisse* (On the relation of the organic forces to each other in the series of the different organisms, the laws and the successions of this relation), Stuttgart and Tübingen: Heerbrand; repr., intro. K.T. Kanz, Marburg: Basilisken-Presse, 1993. (Living systems fulfil three main functions: sensation, motion and self-preservation. Organic forms differ from each other by the different amount in which these functions are fulfilled. A concise statement of the problem situation at the end of the eighteenth century.)

Knittermeyer, H. (1928) *Schelling und die romantische Schule* (Schelling and the Romantic movement), Munich: Ernst Reinhardt. (Lengthy account of Schelling's *Naturphilosophie* and of the ideas of many of his followers, especially from philosophy.)

Kuhn, Th.S. (1959) 'Energy Conservation as an Example of Simultaneous Discovery', in M. Clagett (ed.) *Critical Problems in the History of Science*, Madison, WI: University of Wisconsin Press, 321–56; repr. in *The Essential Tension. Selected Studies in Scientific Tradition and Change*, Chicago, IL: University of Chicago Press, 1977, 66–104. (In this influential piece, Kuhn shows how *Naturphilosophie* served as a philosophical background for the simultaneous discovery of energy conservation by many different scientists. Compare the comments by Caneva 1997.)

Mutschler, H.-D. (1990) *Spekulative und empirische Physik. Aktualität und Grenzen der Naturphilosophie Schellings* (Speculative and empirical physics: actuality and limits of Schelling's Naturphilosophie), Stuttgart: Kohlhammer. (A critique of Schelling's *Naturphilosophie* from a present-day point of view.)

* Oken, L. (1843) *Lehrbuch der Naturphilosophie*, Zurich: Schultheß, 3rd. edn; repr. Hildesheim: Olms, 1991; trans. A. Tulk as *Elements of Physiophilosophy*, London: Ray Society, 1847. (Exposition of a *naturphilosophisches* system of the life sciences; a mixture of an unscrupulous usage of polarity principles and of an effusive naturalism.)

* Ørsted, H.Ch. (1803) *Materialien zu einer Chemie des Neunzehenten Jahrhunderts* (Materials for a chemistry of the nineteenth century), Erstes Stück, Regensburg: Montag & Weiß; repr. in *Naturvidenskabelige Skrifter*, ed. K. Meyer, Copenhagen: Høst 1920, vol. 1, 133–210. (Enthusiastic exposition of the chemical system of J.J. Winterl, which claimed the principles of electricity as fundamental for acids, bases, heat, light and magnetism.)

* —— (1849) *Aanden i naturen*; trans. K.L. Kannegiesser as *Der Geist in der Natur*, Leipzig: Lorck, 1850; trans. L. Horner and J.B. Horner as *The Soul in Nature*, London: Bohn, 1852, repr. London: Dawsons of Pall Mall, 1966. (Series of articles exhibiting physical nature as permeated and dominated by the mind.)

Petry, M.J. (ed.) (1987) *Hegel und die Naturwissenschaften* (Hegel and the natural sciences), Stuttgart: Klett-Cotta. (Collection of essays expounding Hegel's relation to the sciences.)

Poggi, S. (1996) 'La "Naturphilosophie" dell'idealismo e del romanticismo: lo stato della ricerca', (The *Naturphilosophie* of idealism and of Romanticism: The state of research), *Rivista di Filosofia* 87 (1): 111–28. (Concise overview of contemporary research on Naturphilosophie.)

Poggi, S. and Bossi, M. (eds) (1994) *Romanticism in Science: Science in Europe, 1790–1840*, Dordrecht: Kluwer. (Essays on Romanticism and *Naturphilosophie* in biology, chemistry, psychology, philosophy and mathematics.)

Sandkühler, H.J. (ed.) (1984) *Natur und geschichtlicher Prozeß. Studien zur Naturphilosophie F.W.J. Schellings* (Nature and historical development: studies in Schelling's Naturphilosophie), Frankfurt: Suhrkamp. (Collection of essays on Schelling's *Naturphilosophie* and its relation to history.)

* Schelling, F.W.J. (1795) *Vom Ich als Princip der Philosophie oder über das Unbedingte im menschlichen Wißen*, Tübingen: Herrbrandt; repr. in *Sämmtliche Werke*, ed. K.F.A. Schelling, Stuttgart, 1856–61, vol. 1, 149–244; trans. F. Marti as *The Unconditional in Human Knowledge: Four Early Essays 1794–6*, Lewisburg, PA: Bucknell University Press, 1980. (On the absolute ego as the foundation of philosophy. A confrontation of Fichte's philosophy with that of Spinoza.)

* —— (1797) *Ideen zu einer Philosophie der Natur als Einleitung in das System dieser Wissenschaft*, Leipzig: Breitkopf & Härtel; repr. in *Sämmtliche Werke*, ed. K.F.A. Schelling, Stuttgart 1856–61, vol. 2, 1–343; trans. E.E. Harris and P. Heath, intro. R. Stern, *Ideas for a Philosophy of Nature as Introduction to the Study of that Science*, Cambridge: Cambridge University Press, 1988. (Schelling's major work on *Naturphilosophie* aiming to overcome the split of mind and nature, of subject and object. Follows Kant in constructing matter from expansive and contractive forces.)

* —— (1798) *Von der Weltseele, eine Hypothese der höheren Physik zur Erklärung des allgemeinen*

Organismus (On the world-soul: a hypothesis of higher physics in order to explain the general organism), Hamburg: Perthes; repr. in *Sämmtliche Werke*, ed. K.F.A. Schelling, Stuttgart 1856–61, vol. 2, 345–583. (Explanation of organic nature in terms of a general dualism of opposing forces.)

* —— (1799) *Erster Entwurf eines Systems der Naturphilosophie* (Outline of a system of the philosophy of nature), Jena/Leipzig: Gabler; repr. in *Sämmtliche Werke*, ed. K.F.A. Schelling, Stuttgart 1856–61, vol. 3, 1–268. (Elaboration of a developmental theory of life as proposed in the *Weltseele*. Influenced by Kielmeyer and Herder.)

—— (1994) *Ergänzungsband zu Werke Band 5 bis 9. Wissenschaftshistorischer Bericht zu Schellings Naturphilosophischen Schriften 1797–1800* (Supplementary volume of vols 5 to 9 of the works: The scientific background of Schelling's works on Naturphilosophie 1797–1800), Stuttgart: Frommann-Holzboog. (Supplement to the critical edition of the Bavarian academy of the sciences (1976–) ed. H.M. Baumgartner *et al.* Essays on chemistry, magnetism, electricity, galvanism and physiology in Schelling's day aiming to recover the contemporary scientific context of Schelling's *Naturphilosophie*.)

Schmied-Kowarzik, W. (1993) 'Selbst und Existenz. Grundanliegen und Herausforderung der Naturphilosophie Schellings' (Self and existence: the challenge of Schelling's Naturphilosophie), in H.M. Baumgartner und W.G. Jacobs (eds) *Philosophie der Subjektivität? Zur Bestimmung des neuzeitlichen Philosophierens* (Philosophy of subjectivity? On the characteristics of modern philosophy), Stuttgart: Frommann-Holzboog, vol. 1, 111–30. (Thoughtful defence of Schelling's approach and an appreciation of its relation to modern science.)

Snelders, H.A.M. (1970) 'Romanticism and Naturphilosophie and the Inorganic Natural Sciences 1797–1840: An Introductory Survey', *Studies in Romanticism* 9 (3): 193–215. (A clear presentation of the influence of Romantic thinking and *Naturphilosophie* on the inorganic sciences in Germany. Claims that the influence was positive and fruitful.)

—— (1994) *Wetenschap en intuitie: Het Duitse romantisch-speculatief natuuronderzoek rond 1800* (Science and intuition: German Romantic and speculative natural science around 1800), Baarn: Ambo. (Balanced and authoritative account of the impact of *Naturphilosophie* on science and vice versa from about 1790 to 1830. Includes vivid and expressive accounts of central and marginal figures of the time. Helpful annotated bibliography.)

Strack, F. (1994) *Evolution des Geistes: Jena um 1800. Natur und Kunst, Philosophie und Wissenschaft im Spannungsfeld der Geschichte* (Evolution of the spirit: Jena around 1800. Nature and art, philosophy and science under the tension of history), Stuttgart: Klett-Cotta. (Essays on the most brilliant period of the University of Jena as the origin of the German Romantic movement in philosophy, art, literature and the sciences. Includes essays on philosophical ideas about nature in Goethe, Hölderlin, Novalis, Schelling and Ritter.)

Wilson, A.D. (1997) 'Die romantischen Naturphilosophen' (The romantic Naturphilosophen), in K. von Meyenn, *Die grossen Physiker. Erster Band: Von Aristoteles bis Kelvin* (Great Physicists. Vol. 1: From Aristotle to Kelvin), Munich: Beck, 319–35. (The role of Naturphilosophie in the physics of Ritter, Ørsted and Faraday.)

MICHAEL HEIDELBERGER

NAVYA-NYĀYA *see* NYĀYA-VAIŚEṢIKA

NECESSARY BEING

Many think that God is perfect, or free from defect, and that being able not to exist is a defect. These infer that God is not able not to exist – that is, that God exists necessarily. Some add that what makes God perfect also makes him exist necessarily, and so trace his necessity to his immateriality (Aristotle), eternity (Plotinus) or simplicity (Aquinas). Others trace God's necessity to his relation to creatures (Ibn Sina, Anselm). Spinoza and Leibniz held that what makes God necessary explains his very existence.

Many have thought that if God exists necessarily, there is a sound ontological argument for God's existence, or that if there is a sound ontological argument for God's existence, God exists necessarily. But both claims are false. Some have used philosophical views of the nature of necessity – for example, that all necessity is conventional, a matter of how we choose to use words – to challenge God's necessary existence. But the theories which best support these challenges have fallen from favour, and in fact, even if one accepts the theories, the challenges fail.

1 Contingent and necessary existence
2 The evolution of divine necessity
3 Divine necessity and the ontological argument
4 Objections to divine necessity

1 Contingent and necessary existence

Our lives depend on many things. Had our parents not had us, we would not exist. Were there not enough food, or had we the bad luck to be there when a bomb goes off, we would not continue to exist. Our lives are thus contingent on parents, food and other things. To be contingent in this way is to be vulnerable. Such vulnerability seems a defect. So if we think God perfect, we will deny that God exists contingently.

If God exists and does not exist contingently, then:

(GN)   God exists necessarily.

Thus (GN) emerges when we think about God's perfection. (GN) asserts that God exists, could not have failed to exist and cannot fail to exist. Equivalently, (GN) asserts that God exists and would always exist, no matter what. One can read (GN) as:

(GN1) the proposition 'God exists' is necessarily true,

or

(GN2) there necessarily is some individual or other who is God,

or

(GN3) whoever is God exists necessarily,

or

(GN4) the individual who is God exists necessarily.

If

(GN5) whoever is God is necessarily God

is false, (GN1) and (GN2) are equivalent, but logically independent of (GN3) and (GN4), and (GN3) entails (GN4), but (GN4) does not entail (GN3). If (GN5) is true, (GN1)–(GN4) are equivalent.

(GN) uses the concept of necessity. So as philosophers' grasp of necessity changed, what they meant by (GN) changed. But the impulse to ascribe maximal perfection to God always pushed towards claiming for God's existence the strongest sort of necessity a philosopher's modal theory would allow. Sometimes stronger doctrines of divine necessity subsume weaker ones; for instance, a God necessary in Leibniz's sense is also necessary in Aristotle's.

2 The evolution of divine necessity

ARISTOTLE (§16) held that God exists throughout infinite time (*Metaphysics* XII, 7), and that:

(1)   if something exists throughout infinite time, it exists necessarily (*Generation and Corruption* II, 11).

Aristotle rests (1) on a claim that any *x* is possibly *F* only if something is able to make it *F*, and a principle of plenitude, that any genuine ability (at least of certain sorts) sooner or later is used (*On the Heavens* I, 11). Thus for Aristotle, if a thing can cease to exist, it sooner or later does so. So if something exists throughout infinite time, it must be unable to cease to exist. A thing which exists and cannot not exist exists necessarily. Aristotle thinks that God's immateriality explains his necessity (*Metaphysics* XII, 6): things can cease to exist only if made of matter, for a thing *A* ceases to exist only if the matter making up *A* loses the constituting ('substantial') form whose presence in that matter makes *A* exist.

PLOTINUS (§3) asserts (GN) of *Nous*, a being like Aristotle's God (*Enneads* VI). *Nous* is atemporal due to its fullness and perfection of being (*Enneads* III). So *Nous* has no potentialities, since potentialities for Plotinus as for Aristotle are abilities to *become* different and so require time to be actualized (*Enneads* II). If *Nous* has no potentialities, it has no potentiality not to exist, and so exists necessarily.

IBN SINA (§5), by contrast, held that (GN) 'means that God is a being without a cause, and…is the cause of other than himself' (*al-Risalat al-'arshiya*, 1951: 32). Other Muslim and Jewish philosophers added that God needs no cause or cannot be caused to exist. So read, (GN) does not entail that God or God's nature explains God's existence, or that anything explains God's existence, or therefore that there is an explanation for the fact that there is something rather than nothing at all.

This remains true even for AQUINAS (§11), who held that 'God exists' is 'self-evident in itself' (*Summa theologiae* Ia, 2, 1), a status which entails broadly logical necessity. For that 'God exists' is self-evident in itself entails only that its truth would be self-evident to one who perceived God's nature, not that the perceiver would see why it is true or that God's nature would explain that truth. For Aquinas, 'God exists' is 'self-evident in itself' due to the doctrine of divine simplicity (see SIMPLICITY, DIVINE §§1–2). Given God's simplicity, God, his nature and his existence are identical (*Summa theologiae* Ia, 3, 3 and 4). If:

(2)   God = God's existence,

Aquinas reasons, the subject and predicate of 'God exists' have the same reference. Thus 'God exists' is in effect an identity-claim, 'self-evident in itself' as all identities are: 'the reason for the necessity of God's existence is that His essence is His existence' (*Quaestiones disputatae de veritate*, 3, 1, *ad*. 7).

Thus Aquinas in effect traces God's necessity of existence to the necessity of identity. The necessity of identity is logical: statements of the form '$A = A$' instance the logical law of identity $(\forall x)(x = x)$, and so their contradictories are inconsistent with theorems of logic. Therefore even if Aquinas did not have this concept of necessity or mean to ascribe it to God, there is a sense in which, for Aquinas, God's existence is logically necessary. It may be that this holds for divine simplicity's many earlier medieval friends as well. Note that in Thomas' hands, (GN) does not *explain* God's existence. Divine simplicity makes (GN) true by entailing (2). But (2) *presupposes* that God exists. (If there is no Sherlock Holmes, 'Holmes = Holmes' is not true.) So divine simplicity and (GN) cannot explain God's existence.

Anselm's treatment of (GN) begins from the claim that God's will is the source of all necessity (*Cur Deus homo* II, 18). If it is, God's will makes God's existence necessary. How can it do so? To Anselm, 'necessarily, God is F' really says that nothing distinct from God can make it the case that God is not F (*Cur Deus homo* II, 18). If so, to Anselm, (GN) means 'nothing distinct from God can make it the case that God does not exist'. God makes this claim true if he creates only creatures who lack the requisite power, or if he does not create. For Anselm, what is so by necessity, properly speaking, is so because of compulsion, external constraint or some genuine inability (*Cur Deus homo* II, 5). So for Anselm, (GN) is an indirect way to say that God's power to exist cannot be overcome. For Aquinas, (GN) rests on something about God's own makeup. For Anselm, (GN) is true due to God's relations to creatures. For neither does (GN) explain God's existing (see ANSELM OF CANTERBURY §§2–4, 8).

DUNS SCOTUS (§§7–11) popularized the view that a state of affairs is possible just in case it does not entail a contradiction, and is necessary just in case its negation entails a contradiction (*Commentaria oxoniensa* I, 36). This view evolved into our current concept of broadly logical necessity. So like many writers after Scotus, Descartes took (GN) to assert God's broadly logical necessity. Descartes held both the doctrine of divine simplicity and a theory of God's responsibility for modal facts which may have been more radical than Anselm's (see Plantinga 1980). So for Descartes, (GN) is overdetermined. As Descartes held that God causes the truth of logically necessary ('eternal') truths, being logically necessary did not for him entail being uncreated or wholly independent. Thus the meaning Descartes gave (GN) was wholly discrete from the meaning it had for such medievals as Ibn Sina.

In other Continental rationalists, (GN) also took on a new import. SPINOZA (§§2–3) held that each existing thing's existence must be explained (*Ethics* I,

8, n.2). In the case of God, who is necessarily uncaused, only his intrinsic nature can provide this explanation. So Spinoza infers that God's nature entails and explains his existence (*Ethics* I, 11). Spinoza adds that 'existence... insofar as it is conceived to follow necessarily from the definition alone of the [existing thing]... is conceived as an eternal truth' (*Ethics* I, df.8). Spinoza's eternal truths, like Descartes', are broadly logically necessary. So for Spinoza, something exists necessarily only if and because its nature entails and explains its existence, and (GN) asserts or entails that such an explanation exists. LEIBNIZ (§§3, 7) holds a principle of sufficient reason even stronger than Spinoza's (1717: 16), and reasons much as Spinoza does (1697: 85–6). Neither Leibniz nor Spinoza held to divine simplicity as Aquinas and other medievals understood it. Leibniz held the eternal truths to depend on God's intellect (*Theodicy*, 184), and so also divorced necessity and independence.

3 Divine necessity and the ontological argument

Some writers (for example, Penelhum 1971: 183–4) nearly equate (GN) with the claim that there is a sound ontological argument for God's existence (see GOD, ARGUMENTS FOR THE EXISTENCE OF §§2–3). In this they follow Spinoza: 'God is substance, which necessarily exists, i.e. to whose nature it pertains to exist, or (what is the same) from whose definition it follows that He exists' (*Ethics* I, 19).

But there could be a sound ontological argument even if (GN) were false. Some such arguments (including Anselm's in *Proslogion* 2) end in contingent propositions asserting God's existence. An ontological argument is an a priori existence-proof. Descartes' *Cogito* may try to prove a priori that a contingent being exists. If the *Cogito* does, it is not therefore absurd. In Kaplan-style indexical logics, 'I exist' is both contingent and an analytic or logical truth; there are also such truths in systems of modal logic employing actuality-operators (see Zalta 1988). One can hold both that it is provable a priori or even broadly logically necessary that a certain property is exemplified (as when mathematicians prove that there exist numbers with certain properties) and that the item having that property exists contingently (as on the theory that numbers are sets of sets of concrete things).

Conversely, even if (GN) is true, there might be no sound ontological argument: if (as Gödel reminds us) not every necessary truth is provable, perhaps 'God exists' is not. Some who take it that (GN) is true only if there is a sound ontological argument for God's existence assume that if 'God exists' is necessary,

'God does not exist' is or entails a contradiction. But this is debatable. Arguably, both

(IO) there can be an immovable object, and

(IF) there can be an irresistible force

are necessarily true if true at all. At most one is true: if nothing can resist a certain force, the supposed immovable object cannot, and so is not after all immovable. But neither (IO) nor (IF) seems to entail a contradiction.

4   Objections to divine necessity

Some philosophers (for example, Findlay 1955) argue that:

(3) All necessary truths are true by convention.
(4) If (GN) is true, 'God exists' is necessarily true.
(5) So if (GN) is true, 'God exists' is true by convention.
(6) Merely conventional truths do not assert real facts.
(7) So if (GN) is true, 'God exists' asserts no real fact.

Findlay thinks (GN) a conceptual truth. So having argued for (7), he infers that 'God exists' asserts no real fact – that is, that God does not really exist. Theists might instead take (3)–(7) as a *reductio* of (GN). But (3) no longer seems patently true. Further, even if conventionalism is true, (5) is not. On conventionalism, if (GN) is true, our ways of using words determine the modality of 'God exists' and so determine whether (GN) is true. It doesn't follow that our usage determines whether God *exists*. Perhaps we have the power Anselm thought God has, to make God's existence necessary but not to make God exist.

If 'God exists' is necessary but conventionally so, (GN) entails 'God exists' without explaining or grounding it. If this is the case, one has to ask why our conventions have the good luck to affirm as necessary what really does exist. But such questions are not unanswerable. (For instance, if there is a God, he might want us to believe (GN), and might design us to do so.) If (GN) is conventionally true, (GN) is not a good reason to affirm that God exists; until we find on other grounds that God exists, we have no guarantee that we do not have the wrong convention. But this does not even entail giving up all forms of ontological argument, so it has little significance.

Some philosophers (for example, Edwards 1976) argue that:

(8)   if (GN) is true, 'God exists' is analytic, or true due to its meaning.
(9)   If 'God exists' is analytic, it is true because its

subject-concept (God) contains its predicate-concept (existence).
(10) So if 'God exists' is analytic, existence is a predicate.
(11) Existence is not a predicate (as Kant argued).
(12) So (GN) is false.

(8)–(11) may even imply that (GN) is conceptually incoherent, since it assigns 'exists' to the wrong semantic category. Edwards rests (8) on the theory that broadly logical necessity is analyticity. But this theory is now widely rejected. Rather, a proposition is broadly logically necessary if and only if true in all broadly logically possible worlds. Some such propositions seem not to be analytic – for example , that everything green has some spatial property (Adams 1987: 45–6). Some might argue, following Anselm, that 'God exists' is true in all possible worlds because whatever 'possible worlds' are, they depend on God for their existence (see Morris and Menzel 1986).

A different sort of objection to (GN) arises because (GN) implies that 'something exists' is necessarily true. We seem able to conceive (in some sense) there being nothing at all. Being able to conceive (in some sense) that this is true is defeasible evidence that it is possible. If possibly there is nothing, 'something exists' is not necessarily true. Still, there are many sorts of conceivability. They do not all have equal weight as evidence for possibility. Adams (1971: 285–6) suggests that conceiving that *P* is greater evidence that *P* is possible the closer it is to imagining the actual experiences one would have were *P* true. One cannot do this for 'nothing exists', for if nothing existed, there would be no experiences, or minds to have them.

See also: GOD, CONCEPTS OF; NATURAL THEOLOGY

References and further reading

* Adams, R.M. (1971) 'Has It Been Proven That All Real Existence is Contingent?', *American Philosophical Quarterly* 8 (3): 284–91. (Clear reply to challenges from Findlay, Edwards and others.)
* —— (1987) 'Divine Necessity', in T. Morris (ed.) *The Concept of God*, New York: Oxford University Press, 41–53. (A rich, important defence, rigorous but not technical.)
* Anselm (1077–8) *Proslogion*, trans. J. Hopkins and H. Richardson, in J. Hopkins and H. Richardson (eds and trans), *Anselm of Canterbury*, Toronto, Ont.: Edwin Mellen Press, 1974, vol. 1. (*Locus classicus* of perfect-being theology.)
* —— (completed 1098) *Cur Deus homo*, in F.S. Schmitt (ed.) *S. Anselmi opera omnia*, Edinburgh: Nelson,

1946, vol. 2. (Important text for Anselm's theory of modality.)

* Aquinas, T. (1256–9) *Quaestiones disputatae de veritate*, in *Quaestiones disputatae*, Rome: Taurini, 1927, vol. 3. (Questions 1–3 reveal much of Aquinas' metaphysics of modality.)

* —— (1266–73) *Summa theologiae*, New York: Benziger Brothers, 1948. (Question 2 treats the modal and epistemic status of the proposition 'God exists'.)

* Aristotle (mid 4th century BC) *On the Heavens* (*De caelo*), trans. J. Stocks, in R. McKeon (ed.) *The Basic Works of Aristotle*, New York: Random House, 1941. (His view of the physical world; ties everlasting and necessary existence.)

* —— (mid 4th century BC) *Generation and Corruption* (*De generatione et corruptione*), trans. H.H. Joachim, in R. McKeon (ed.) *The Basic Works of Aristotle*, New York: Random House, 1941. (Analysis of coming and ceasing to exist; ties everlasting and necessary existence.)

* —— (mid 4th century BC) *Metaphysics*, trans. W.D. Ross, in R. McKeon (ed.) *The Basic Works of Aristotle*, New York: Random House, 1941. (Book 12 treats God's existence and nature, and ties immateriality and necessity.)

Curley, E.M. (1984) 'Descartes on the Creation of the Eternal Truths', *Philosophical Review* 93 (4): 569–97. (Fine, careful reading of Descartes.)

* Duns Scotus, J. (c.1300–7) *Commentaria oxoniensa*, Florence: Quaracchi, 1912, vol. 1. (Distinctions 2, 36, 39 and 43 are good sources for Scotus' views of modality and God's necessity.)

* Edwards, P. (1976) 'The Cosmological Argument' in P. Angeles (ed.) *Critiques of God*, Buffalo, NY: Prometheus, 43–58. (Interesting critique of attempted proofs of God's existence.)

* Findlay, J.N. (1955) 'Can God's Existence Be Disproved?' in A. Flew and A. MacIntyre (eds) *New Essays in Philosophical Theology*, New York: Macmillan, 47–56. (Classic argument that God must be, yet cannot be, 'logically' necessary.)

* Ibn Sina (Avicenna) (early 11th century) *al-Risalat al-'arshiya*, in A. Arberry (trans.) *Avicenna on Theology*, Westport, CT: Hyperion, 1951. (Treats many issues in philosophical theology.)

Knuuttila, S. (1993) *Modalities in Medieval Philosophy*, New York: Routledge. (Goldmine of information on evolving concepts of necessity. At times technical.)

* Leibniz, G.W. (1697) 'On the Ultimate Origination of the Universe', in P. Schrecker and A. Schrecker (trans.) *Leibniz: Monadology and Other Philosophical Essays*, Indianapolis, IN: Bobbs-Merrill, 1965. (His cosmological argument for God's existence.)

* —— (1710) *Theodicy*, trans. D. Allen, Indianapolis, IN: Bobbs-Merrill, 1966. (Important discussion of God's nature and goodness.)

* Leibniz, G.W. and Clarke, S. (1717) *The Leibniz–Clarke Correspondence*, ed. H.G. Alexander, Manchester: University of Manchester Press, 1956. (Rich exchange on space, time and God, dense but not technical.)

* Morris, T. and Menzel, C. (1986) 'Absolute Creation', *American Philosophical Quarterly* 23 (4): 353–62. (Proposes that God is the source of all necessity.)

Plantinga, A. (1974) *The Nature of Necessity*, New York: Oxford University Press. (Classic account of broadly logical necessity, with application to God and the ontological argument. Exact and exacting.)

* —— (1980) *Does God Have a Nature?*, Milwaukee, WI: Marquette University Press. (Full, careful treatment of God's relation to necessity. Includes interesting exegesis of Descartes, with references to important literature.)

* Penelhum, T. (1971) 'Divine Necessity' in B. Mitchell (ed.) *The Philosophy of Religion*, New York: Oxford University Press, 179–90. (Highly critical.)

* Plotinus (c.250–66) *Enneads* II, III, VI, trans. A.H. Armstrong, Cambridge, MA: Loeb Classical Library, Harvard University Press, 1979, 1980, 1988. (Neoplatonist metaphysics, discusses modal matters intermittently. Not technical but sometimes obscure.)

* Spinoza, B. (1676) *Ethics*, in E. Curley (trans.) *The Collected Works of Spinoza*, Princeton, NJ: Princeton University Press, 1985. (Book I is the main source for his view of God. Sometimes obscure.)

* Zalta, E. (1988) 'Logical And Analytic Truths That Are Not Necessary', *Journal of Philosophy* 85 (2): 57–74. (Somewhat technical argument for contingent analytic truths.)

BRIAN LEFTOW

NECESSARY TRUTH AND CONVENTION

Necessary truths have always seemed problematic, particularly to empiricists and other naturalistically-minded philosophers. Our knowledge here is a priori – grounded in appeals to what we can imagine or conceive (or can prove on that basis) – which seems hard to reconcile with such truths being factual, short of appealing to some peculiar faculty of a priori intuition. And what mysterious extra feature do necessary truths possess which makes their falsity impossible? Conventionalism about necessity claims that necessary truths obtain by virtue of rules of language, such as that 'vixen' means the same as 'female fox'. Because such rules govern our descriptions of all cases – including counterfactual or imagined ones – they generate necessary truths ('All vixens are foxes'), and our a priori knowledge is just knowledge of word meaning. Opponents of conventionalism argue that conventions cannot ground necessary truths, particularly in logic, and have also challenged the notion of analyticity (truth by virtue of meaning). More recent claims that some necessary truths are a posteriori have also fuelled opposition to conventionalism.

1   **The linguistic theory of necessity**
2   **Necessity a posteriori**

1   The linguistic theory of necessity

Many of the clearest necessary truths – such as 'Squares are rectangles' – seem simply to reflect the meaning of the words involved: we need not postulate some metaphysical essence of squareness which the necessity of 'Squares are rectangles' reflects. Thus, the position common to conventionalists is that necessary truths are explained by conventional rules of language, rather than a mind-independent modal structure of the world. For this reason, the general conventionalist position has often been called the linguistic theory of necessity (or, of the a priori). This was the dominant view about necessity from the 1930s–50s, particularly under the influence of logical positivism (see LOGICAL POSITIVISM). Drawing largely upon claims they found in Wittgenstein's *Tractatus* (see below), the positivists rejected Kant's claim that there are synthetic a priori truths, trumpeting the slogan 'The a priori is analytic' (see ANALYTICITY). What exactly analyticity was – beyond, in some way, truth by virtue of the meanings of words – was not entirely clear, which gave rise to different versions of the linguistic theory. But for most, conventionalism itself was beyond doubt and, apart from the few explicitly engaged in trying to spell out just how conventions explained necessity, most writers used different ways of articulating the view ('All necessary truths are tautologies', 'Necessity simply reflects linguistic rules') interchangeably simply to invoke the linguistic theory.

An early expression of conventionalism is found in Locke's proposal that all essences are merely nominal – they simply reflect the meaning of the subject term, as in 'Gold is a metal'. In this, Locke meant to contradict the then-received view that essences are determined by a mind-independent sorting of things. Similarly, he says essences 'are made by the mind' (1689: III.vi.26), and since 'kinds' – or in Locke's

terms, 'sorts' – are the kinds they are because of their essences, Locke says the sorts themselves are 'the Workmanship of the Understanding' (1689: III.vi.12) (see LOCKE, J. §4). This well exemplifies the metaphysically deflationary thrust of conventionalism.

While there are various conventionalist views, they agree negatively both in their suspicion of appeals to imagination and conceivability as sources of factual knowledge, and in their finding the notion of necessary facts – and a distinction between essential and accidental properties – rather mysterious (see ESSENTIALISM). On the positive side, they agree in seeing appeals to imagination and conceivability as appeals to what we would *say* in various imagined situations, which they see as a way to find out what rules of language we are implicitly employing.

The version of conventionalism presented in Wittgenstein's *Tractatus* focuses on the notion of 'tautology', that is, truth-functional compound statements, such as 'If it is raining, then it is raining', which are true for all assignments of truth-values to the propositions from which they are built (1922: 4.46). Wittgenstein argues that tautologies say nothing about the world; rather, the symbols, given their meanings, themselves determine the truth of such statements (1922: 4.461–4661, 5.142). He claims that all truths of logic are tautologies (1922: 6.1–112) and seems to hold this for all a priori truths (for example, 1922: 5.134, 5.634). There are necessary truths which are not truths of logic, such as 'All bachelors are unmarried'. However, since 'bachelor' means 'unmarried man', the statement, when analysed, says, 'All unmarried men are unmarried', the form of which is 'Whatever is F and G is F', which is a tautology. One problem this version of conventionalism faced was accounting for necessary truths such as 'Nothing can be simultaneously both red and green all over' – for it is hard to see how to assign meanings to 'red' and 'green' whereby this can be reduced to a tautology.

Other conventionalists have concentrated more on the general idea that truths such as 'All squares are rectangles' express rules of language. Their 'truth by convention' could perhaps serve as a model for all necessary truths. One version of this idea was that 'Necessarily, all squares are rectangles' simply means 'It is a rule of language that "square" applies to something only if "rectangle" also applies'; A.J. Ayer wrote that necessary propositions 'simply record our determination to use words in a certain fashion' (1936: 84). This view was regularly criticized for identifying necessary a priori truths with contingent empirical statements about a language or its speakers. A subtler variant was that one should not really speak of necessary truths at all – what look to be assertions are really, covertly, prescriptions ('Do not apply "square" to anything you would not apply "rectangle" to') or perhaps decisions of some sort. One problem here is that necessary statements can stand in logical relations, can figure essentially in truth-functional compounds, and so on, which seems to require that they have truth-values, unlike prescriptions. The most common version of this view is simply that the rule determines the truth of the sentence; given the rule, nothing can count as a square but not a rectangle. This view does not require that all rules have the form of definitions which allow us, via substitution, to reduce all necessary truths to syntactical tautologies; a rule prohibiting the simultaneous use of 'red all over' and 'green all over' to an object need not be rooted in a full, necessary-and-sufficient-conditions style definition of some constituent term (see Carnap 1952).

While many attacks on conventionalism only properly address particular versions, certain problems challenge any sweeping conventionalism. By the late 1950s, not only was conventionalism no longer dogma but, to many, seemed simply mistaken. One central problem concerns the fact that whether some convention obtains is always a contingent matter – but how can something which is contingent make anything necessary? For instance, even conventionalists (generally) acknowledge that different conventions would not affect the necessity of: if if *p* then *q*, and *p*, then *q*. But if different conventions would not change what is necessary, how can the conventions be responsible? Different conventions can change which proposition is expressed – but not the necessity of the proposition actually expressed. Another general problem concerns the idea that logical truths obtain by convention. The conventionalist wants to say that, given certain rules, it follows that certain statements are true (and necessary). But 'follows' is an expression of necessitation. Quine (1966) and others argue that in order to derive the truths of logic from conventions, one must apply logical rules – one must presuppose logic in order to derive logic. Additionally, attacks on the analytic/synthetic distinction, particularly vivid in arguments put forward by Putnam (1975) that apparently analytic truths are actually revisable empirical claims ('Cats are animals'), cast further doubt on the analytic explanation of necessity. If there are no analytic truths, they cannot explain necessity (see ANALYTICITY).

2 Necessity a posteriori

In *Naming and Necessity* (1980), Saul KRIPKE argued that the supposition that all necessary truths are a priori is mistaken. His examples included empirical identity statements, such as 'Hesperus is Phosphorus', statements of material origin, such as 'This lectern was originally made of (a particular piece of) wood' and statements of kind essence and identity, such as 'Gold has atomic number 79'. Since these are not a priori, they cannot simply be true by convention, and if conventionalism was already on the wane, Kripke's examples, and similar ones from PUTNAM (1975), seemed to kill it decisively. Because these truths are not logically necessary, but are still necessary absolutely, they are sometimes called 'metaphysically necessary'.

However, it has been noted that even if these necessary truths are not true by convention, they may still owe their necessity to convention (see Coppock 1984, Sidelle 1989). The arguments for proposed necessary a posteriori truths each involve commitment to some general principle, for instance, that if a material object originates in bit of matter *M*, then it essentially originates in *M*. These principles – in so far as the arguments for the necessities are plausible – are plausibly a priori, for the arguments rest on the familiar appeals to what we can imagine, or would be willing to say. The conventionalist proposal, then, is that these general principles are analytic, and that while these conventions do not determine which non-modal statements are true (what bit of matter something did originate in), they are responsible for these truths being necessary (the principle determines that nothing with a different origin can count as this object). So conventionalism does not require that all necessary truths are *true* by convention, but only that this is why they are necessary.

See also: CONVENTIONALISM; ESSENTIALISM; LANGUAGE, CONVENTIONALITY OF; LOGICAL AND MATHEMATICAL TERMS, GLOSSARY OF

References and further reading

* Ayer, A.J. (1936) *Language, Truth and Logic*, London: Gollancz; repr., New York: Dover, 2nd edn, 1946, 16–18 and ch. 4. (Influential and often cited presentation of conventionalism about necessity (and a priori truth); seen by many as claiming that necessary truths say that there is a convention.)
* Carnap, R. (1952) 'Meaning Postulates', *Philosophical Studies* 3: 65–73. (Introduces a device for trying to account for non-tautological necessary truths.)
* Coppock, P. (1984) 'Review of N. Salmon, *Reference and Essence*', *Journal of Philosophy* 81: 261–70. (Sketches a conventionalist account of necessary a posteriori truths.)
Ewing, A.C. (1940) 'The Linguistic Theory of A Priori Propositions', *Proceedings of the Aristotelian Society*: 207–44. (Classic criticism of conventionalism.)

Kneale, W. (1946) 'Truths of Logic', *Proceedings of the Aristotelian Society*: 207–34. (Argues against a conventionalist view of logic.)

* Kripke, S.A. (1980) *Naming and Necessity*, Cambridge, MA: Harvard University Press. (Argues for the conceptual separation of necessity and a prioricity, and for necessary a posteriori truths.)

* Locke, J. (1689) *An Essay concerning Human Understanding*, ed. P.H. Nidditch, Oxford: Clarendon Press, 1979. (Referred to in §1. Locke's discussion of substance in III.vii classically expounds his conventionalism about essence and kinds.)

Pap, A. (1958) *Semantics and Necessary Truth*, New Haven, CT: Yale University Press, esp. ch. 7. (An extended argument against conventionalist views of necessity.)

* Putnam, H. (1975) *Philosophical Papers II: Mind, Language and Reality*, Cambridge: Cambridge University Press, 1979. ('Is Semantics Possible?' (referred to in §1) argues against the traditional view of meaning upon which analyticity rests; development of Quine 1953. 'The Meaning of "Meaning"' (referred to in §2) argues for necessary a posteriori status for certain claims about natural kinds, such as 'Tigers are mammals' and 'Water is H_2O'.)

Quine, W.V. (1953) 'Two Dogmas of Empiricism', in *From a Logical Point of View: Nine Logico-Philosophical Essays*, Cambridge, MA: Harvard University Press, 2nd edn, 1980. (Most often cited argument against the analytic-synthetic distinction, and so against truth by convention.)

* —— (1966) 'Truth By Convention', in *The Ways of Paradox and Other Essays*, Cambridge, MA: Harvard University Press. (Referred to in §1. A classic argument against accounting for truth by convention alone.)

Schlick, F.A.M. (1931) 'Gibt es ein materiales Apriori?', trans. 'Is There a Factual A Priori?', in H. Feigl and W.S. Sellars (eds) *Readings in Philosophical Analysis*, New York: Ridgeview, 1982. (Highly representative example of assertion that necessity and a prioricity can only derive from linguistic convention.)

* Sidelle, A. (1989) *Necessity, Essence and Individuation: A Defense of Conventionalism*, Ithaca, NY: Cornell University Press. (Referred to in §2. Defends a conventionalist account of necessary a posteriori truths.)

* Wittgenstein, L.J.J. (1922) *Tractatus Logico-Philosophicus*, trans. C.K. Ogden and F.P. Ramsey, London: Routledge; trans. D.F. Pears and B.F. McGuinness, London: Routledge, 1961. (Highly influential source of the view that all necessary truths are tautologies and that tautologies say nothing about the world.)

ALAN SIDELLE

NECKAM, ALEXANDER

see NECKHAM, ALEXANDER

NECKHAM, ALEXANDER (1157–1217)

Alexander Neckham is one of the leading thinkers in the English appropriation of the new science made available during the twelfth century. His best known writings, especially De naturis rerum *(On the Natures of Things), show a prodigious acquaintance with natural history. Neckham was most concerned, however, that the study of the natural world be made to serve the purposes of theology. He thus strove not only to draw moral lessons from nature, but to apply to theological method the doctrines of the new logic, especially Aristotle's* Topics. *While Neckham cannot be said to have mastered the texts that were flooding into the Latin West, he certainly did realize the challenges and the possibilities that they offered to inherited theologies.*

Alexander Neckham (also Neckam or Nequam) displays in his writings that zeal for new learning that characterizes the 'renaissance' of the twelfth century in Latin-speaking schools of western Europe. Neckham lived out his life in these schools. He studied and then taught in Paris from about 1175 to 1182, where his subjects were the liberal arts and theology, with some law and more medicine. Neckham remarks that he was a student of the school on the Petit-Pont, and his writings reflect the doctrines of the school's most famous master, Adam of Petit-Pont. From Paris, Neckham returned to England to teach in the grammar schools of Dunstable and St Albans. Not long after 1190 he was in the schools at Oxford, which were just then beginning to reorganize themselves in ways that would make them into a university. There are many references in Neckham's writing to Scholastic techniques, such as the exercise of the *disputatio* or disputed question, and there survives a set of theological questions that he determined. The appropriation of newer techniques was also perfectly compatible with the cultivation of older ones. Neckham established himself at Oxford as an important preacher and as the author of a commentary on the

Athanasian creed. About 1200, he withdrew to the monastery of Augustinian canons in Cirencester, where he was elected abbot in 1213. Neckham's most extended and important works were written at the monastery. He died there, as abbot, in 1217.

Neckham is best known to historians of philosophy as a student of natural philosophy. Part of this reputation is due to his being the recipient of lavish praise in a contemporary treatise, Alfred of Shareshill's *De motu cordis* (On the Motion of the Heart). Alfred wrote the treatise at Neckham's prompting while the latter was still at Oxford. However, Neckham's reputation as a student of natural philosophy is due more substantially to several of his own works, especially *De naturis rerum* (On the Natures of Things) and *De laudibus divinae sapientiae* (Praise of Divine Wisdom).

De naturis rerum takes the form of an immense prologue to a commentary on Ecclesiastes. The relation of 'prologue' and body is not entirely clear, especially since *De naturis rerum* itself begins as a commentary on the account of creation in Genesis. Whatever Alexander's exact motive, the work quickly enough becomes something like an encyclopedia of moralized natural philosophy. It is loosely organized around the four elements of ancient physics – fire, air, water, earth – but the range of erudition is enormous. In 272 chapters over two books, Neckham rehearses most of the natural history known to him, from problems in astronomy, through the hydrodynamics of fountains and the properties of precious stones, to the behaviour of animals, wild and domestic. Although much of the material is taken from ancient sources, such as Pliny, Neckham frequently adds information or anecdote of his own. More importantly, he regularly reads the facts he recites so as to yield a moral lesson. Indeed, the whole of *De naturis rerum* ends with a sustained attack on human vices, thus making a bridge to the reading of Ecclesiastes.

Neckham returned to these topics in a metrical compendium, his *De laudibus divinae sapientiae*. It too is ordered around the four elements, but ranges widely. In it the reader finds Neckham reciting catalogues of the stars and of Europe's main rivers, as well as descriptions of jewels, herbs and trees and the liberal arts. Still not satisfied with his comprehensiveness, Neckham returned to natural history again in a *Suppletio defectuum* (Remedy of Defects) appended to *De laudibus*, where he offers new descriptions of animals and their habits.

The ordering of natural knowledge to theology, always a concern, seems to have occupied Neckham increasingly. He tries to show the right ordering of them in his last great work, the *Speculum speculationum* (Mirror of Speculations). The work is announced

and begun as a refutation of the heresies of the Cathars. It is in fact, and from the beginning, organized roughly along the lines of Peter Lombard's *Sentences* (see LOMBARD, P.). It expands on the topics of the *Sentences*, increasing the number of arguments and the length of their analysis. Neckham does much, for example, to bring in the still relatively little known works of ANSELM OF CANTERBURY. Of course, some of his erudition is drawn from theological *florilegia*, anthologies of excerpts drawn from the Christian Bible, the Church Fathers or medieval theologians of the Latin tradition. Neckham also knows and uses the Platonic and Neoplatonic texts popular among philosophical writers earlier in the century: Plato's *Timaeus* with Calcidius's commentary, BOETHIUS with his medieval commentators, and at least some of THIERRY OF CHARTRES, WILLIAM OF CONCHES and Bernard Silvestris (see BERNARD OF TOURS; PLATONISM, MEDIEVAL).

What is more striking, because it is much newer, is Neckham's appropriation for theology of the 'new logic' and newly translated works by Aristotle (see ARISTOTELIANISM, MEDIEVAL). Certainly Neckham knew the logical works well. In constructing his dialectical theology, he makes much use of Aristotle's *Topics*, so becoming one of the first theologians to capitalize on this recently rediscovered text. His relation to other Aristotelian works is more difficult to discern. Neckham refers by name to *On the Soul*, *Metaphysics* and *Nicomachean Ethics*, and he quotes without reference from *On the Heaven and the Earth*. Such early access to these works suggests that Neckham may have brought them back with him from the continent. Equally striking is an implicit citation of Avicenna's *On the Soul*, one of the new wave of Arabic works just finding their way into Latin and into the northern schools. To say that Neckham mentions or sometimes uses these texts is not to say that he has mastered them. On the contrary, he stands at the beginning of what will be a very long effort to read and then to understand the texts that were pouring into Latin so rapidly from both Greek and Arabic (see TRANSLATORS).

See also: CHARTRES, SCHOOL OF; NATURAL PHILOSOPHY, MEDIEVAL

List of works

Neckham, Alexander (before 1182?) *De nominibus utensilium* (On the Names of Utensils), ed. A. Scheler, 'Trois traités de lexicographie latine du XIIe et due XIIIe siècle', *Jahrbuch für romanische und englische Literatur* 7, 1866: 58–74, 155–73. (An elementary survey of technical terms from arts and crafts as encountered in ordinary use; modelled after a work by Adam Parvipontanus.)

—— (before 1182?) *Corrogationes Promethei* (Collections of Prometheus, that is, of one who teaches rudimentary arts), excerpts ed. P. Meyer, 'Notice sur les Corrogationes Promethei d'Alexandre Neckham', *Notices et extraits des Manuscrits de la Bibliothèque Nationale* 35 (2), 1896: 641–2. (An introduction to grammatical theory, based on teaching in the Paris schools; incomplete.)

—— (1194–1204) *De naturis rerum* (On the Natures of Things), ed. T. Wright, Rolls Series, London: Longman, Green, Longman, Roberts and Green, 1863; Books 3–4 never printed. (A comprehensive survey of knowledge about the natural world; the work is the first two parts of a five-part commentary on Ecclesiastes, the remainder of which has never been printed.)

—— (c.1213) *De laudibus divinae sapientiae* (Praise of Divine Wisdom), ed. T. Wright, Rolls Series, London: Longman, Green, Longman, Roberts and Green, 1863. (A metrical rehearsal of the order of nature.)

—— (1216–7) *Suppletio defectuum* (Remedy of Defects), excerpts ed. H. Walther, 'Zu den kleineren Gedichten des Alexander Neckham', *Mittellateinisches Jahrbuch* 2, 1965: 111–21. (A correction and supplement to the *De naturis rerum*; incomplete.)

—— (1201?–17) *Speculum speculationum* (Mirror of Speculations), ed. R.M. Thomson, Oxford: Oxford University Press, 1988. (Treatment of all the major topics in Christian theology, with dialectical analysis and ample use of the pertinent authoritative texts; incomplete.)

References and further reading

Alfred of Shareshill [Sareshel] (*c.*1195) *De motu cordis* (On the Motion of the Heart), ed. C. Baeumker, Beiträge zur Geschichte der Philosophie und Theologie des Mittelalters 23.1–2, Munich: Aschendorff, 1923. (This edition is neither complete nor critical.)

Hunt, R.W. (1984) *The Schools and the Cloister: The Life and Writings of Alexander Nequam*, ed. and revised M.T. Gibson, Oxford: Clarendon Press. (Revised from a doctoral dissertation completed in 1936.)

MARK D. JORDAN

NÉDELLEC, HERVÉ
see HERVAEUS NATALIS

NEEDS AND INTERESTS

To have an interest in something is to have a stake in how that thing goes. Needs can be thought of as interests instrumental to a specified purpose, as an artist will need paint, or as general essential interests, like the needs associated with physical survival. Both needs and interests can be contrasted with wants, in being more objectively assessable. A concrete specification of needs and interests is better done by means of a list than by a criterion stipulated in terms of goods that would be chosen in a hypothetical situation. The concept of need can be used to justify a claim to economic resources, even though it only states a minimal demand. However, when total resources will not meet all needs, it is necessary to work with the principle of the equal consideration of interests rather than that of needs, as in the case where health care needs may outstrip available resources. The concept of interests can be misused in defence of authoritarian political systems, but does not have to be used in this way. Although citizens may have an interest in performing their duty, it is likely that there will always be a continuing conflict between duty and interests in politics.

1   The concepts of needs and interests
2   Needs, interests and economic distribution
3   Interests in politics
4   Interests and moral powers

1   The concepts of needs and interests

As concepts, needs and interests are closely related, although not identical. If I say that I need to go to the dentist, I will normally be taken to imply that dental treatment would be in my interest. However, not everything in a person's interest is a need. For example, securing tax allowances may be in the interests of the rich, but it is not something that they need.

It would be difficult to imagine political, legal, moral and practical discussion without the concept of interests. Political parties advance certain interests, legal institutions arbitrate between interests, moral systems restrain the scope of self-interest and practical reason considers how actions will promote interests. Indeed, on one theory of action, agents are moved only by their own interests.

It is possible to distinguish between something

being in someone's interest and someone taking an interest in something. I may take an interest in something purely for the sake of curiosity, for example the performance of my local sports team, without my interests being affected by that performance, as they would be if I had a financial stake in their results. However, there are many aspects of life where the two notions coalesce. For example, parents will have an interest in their child's career success if that affects their own household income, but typically they will also take an interest in it, in the sense of being personally concerned.

What then are interests? In a well-known definition John Locke (1689: 15) defined interests as 'life, liberty, health, and indolency of body; and the possession of outward things, such as money, lands, houses, furniture and the like'. This definition takes the form of a list of things that are thought to be the generalized means, in the form of personal conditions and external possessions, to some supposed human good. Feinberg (1984) has expressed the matter by saying that to have an interest in something is to have a stake in it, and to have a stake in X is to stand to lose or gain depending on what happens to X.

Needs may be regarded as a subset of interests, namely those interests that are in some sense essential or necessary to one's affairs. As necessary conditions, needs can be stipulated in a weak or strong sense. In the weak sense, they are simply the conditions required to achieve any goal or general aim. In this sense, an artist will need paints and brushes in order to work. In such cases the claims of need depend upon an evaluation of the end state to which the need is instrumental.

In the strong sense, needs are the conditions required to achieve some basic goal like survival. In this case needs designate those items necessary to having any purposes at all, or to avoid serious harm. These may thus be called vital interests, their claims being correspondingly higher than instrumental needs.

Both needs and interests may be contrasted with wants. I may not want to go to the dentist, but I may need to, because my health will suffer if I do not. One way of putting this point is to note a logical difference in the inferences that can be drawn from sentences concerned with wants and those concerned with needs. Wants are always characterized from the point of view of those with the wants, and in consequences their full implications may remain obscure to their possessor. For example, I may want to take the fastest train to my destination, but not know that I want to take the 1300, because I do not know that it is the fastest. Thus, one cannot validly infer from my wanting X that I want Y, which is identical with X,

unless I am also known to identify X and Y. By contrast, if I need X it can be validly inferred that I need Y identical to X, independently of my own state of mind.

A similar point holds in respect of interests. There is therefore an objectivity about needs and interests that there is not about wants. The contrast is not absolute, and the concept of interest can sometimes come close to a more subjectivist notion of welfare or want-satisfaction, since how people conceptualize their interest or balance conflicting interests can vary (see WELFARE §1). So, we cannot say that the religious who pursue their spiritual development at the cost of poverty are acting against their own interests. But that is partly because people can have an interest in the conditions of their own personal development, and this can clash with material interests.

Since interests need to be balanced in this way, can we state a general criterion for identifying how this would be done? One suggestion is to identify interests thus balanced with the informed hypothetical choices that agents might make. On this account, the balance of interests represented by policy X is more in my overall interests than that produced by policy Y, were I to prefer the results of X to those of Y when I experience them both. However, unless the hypothetical choice occurs, it would seem that the only way we could know what choices someone would make is to have a sense of what their interests already involve, so that the prediction of choice is grounded in our understanding of needs and interests and not vice versa. In this sense, interests are logically prior to choice.

2 Needs, interests and economic distribution

The concept of need is frequently linked to questions of economic justice. For example, modern health and welfare services are often said to be based on the principle of meeting need irrespective of the ability to pay. But can the principle of need be used in this way to underscore a claim for resources?

Of the two meanings of need that we have so far distinguished, it is clear that the sense relevant is the strong one stated in terms of means to basic goals like survival. Distribution according to need thus means no more than that people should be assured of the means of subsistence and survival.

It may be urged that as a principle of distribution the appeal to needs is too undemanding, since the means of survival are widely available in modern societies, and therefore economic justice should be concerned with broader claims of justice, for example that there should be an equal consideration of interests above the minimum needed for mere survival (see JUSTICE).

However, the proposal to dispense with a principle of need in economic matters has to be treated with some caution. The notion of survival is not itself clear-cut, and it can include the means to secure self-respect in society. Adam Smith (1776) pointed out that, although Romans did without a linen shirt, even the poorest labourer in Smith's day would be ashamed to appear in public without one. Thus, what is necessary to survival has a cultural, as well as a material, component which varies from society to society, so that needs will expand over time as an economy grows.

Moreover, in the context of claims for the international redistribution of resources, the appeal of the principle of need is strong, since on a global scale not all are assured of the means of survival even in the physical sense. In this context, a basic-needs strategy of economic development would entail some significant redistribution, and the principle would be neither empty nor without force (see JUSTICE, INTERNATIONAL).

Yet the principle of the equal consideration of interests may come to supplant the needs principle in some circumstances. For example, distribution of care according to need has been a traditional principle in medicine. Yet modern technology makes it possible to meet an increasing range of medical needs, but only at impossibly high cost. Where resources are inadequate to meet the sum of needs, certain needs will have to remain unmet, and an alternative principle found for rationing resources, for example that all are entitled to an equal consideration of their health interests.

3 Interests in politics

The concept of interests in politics has historically been associated with the democratic idea that government should act in the interests of the governed, rather than acting, say, for an abstract ideal like national glory or spiritual purity. However, the appeal to interests can also be ambiguous in democratic terms, since a government may well appeal to the idea of interests as a way of ignoring popular sentiment and opinion. Exploiting the logical space opened up by the distinction between wants on the one side and needs or interests on the other, a government might claim to know what is in the interest of people better than the people itself. A strong notion of interests might therefore seem to lend itself to a paternalist or authoritarian notion of government.

The danger of paternalist or authoritarian government arising from this substitution of elite judgement for the opinion of the people has been widely feared. However, it is difficult to dispense with the idea that there may be some occasions when governments should act according to the interests of citizens rather than being responsive merely to expressed wants. For example, when people underinsure themselves against age dependency or ill health, the government might properly compel individuals to act in their own long-term interests by instituting compulsory pension and health insurance schemes. Indeed, even the most liberal government will not allow individuals to sell themselves into slavery (see PATERNALISM).

We can distinguish between people wanting a policy and people wanting the results of a policy. One way in which it is possible to guard against the paternalist or authoritarian tendencies implicit in the idea that governments should act in the interests of the people is to say that these interests should be related to the policy results that people were seeking. Thus, if citizens value economic security, requiring compulsory savings to achieve this may well be justified as it would not be justified to impose puritan policies restricting individual liberty of action when spiritual purity was desired only by a few.

4 Interests and moral powers

So far we have considered interests as personal conditions and external possessions determining how individuals fare. But Rawls (1993) has proposed the concept of 'higher-order interests' (see RAWLS, J. §1). Citizens with a conception of their own good and a sense of justice also have these higher-order interests in the development and exercise of these two powers. On this conception, then, instead of thinking of interests as the basis of claims on resources, we are to think of them as motivations to cooperative social action, making it in the interests of citizens to observe principles of justice.

To extend the notion of interest in this way has certain advantages, not least in understanding how citizens might have an interest in acting justly. Conflicts between the duties of justice and acting on one's own self-interest would, in effect, become conflicts within one's own sense of self-interest. To adopt this construction would have the disadvantage, however, of running contrary to the common observation that acting justly may often involve acting against one's self-interest. Moreover, as a statement of philosophical psychology, it is hard to see how it is empirically supported.

Yet, even if interests are often opposed to duty, individuals can think of their interests as being wider than simply their own personal concerns and can identify with the interests of their community. In this sense, the idea of moral powers may point to a socializing of interests that is essential to any workable conception of justice.

References and further reading

Barry, B. (1965) *Political Argument*, London: Routledge & Kegan Paul; repr. Berkeley, CA: University of California Press. (Has an excellent chapter on the concept of interest.)

Braybrooke, D. (1987) *Meeting Needs*, Princeton, NJ: Princeton University Press. (A sophisticated discussion of the concept.)

Doyal, L. and Gough, I. (1991) *A Theory of Human Need*, Basingstoke: Macmillan. (Usefully brings together philosophical and social science analyses of needs.)

* Feinberg, J. (1984) *Harm to Others*, vol. 1 of *The Moral Limits of the Criminal Law*, New York and Oxford: Oxford University Press. (Chapter 1 discusses interests in the context of discussing harm as a set-back to interests.)

—— (1986) *Harm to Self*, vol. 3 of *The Moral Limits of the Criminal Law*, New York and Oxford: Oxford University Press. (Discusses the conditions under which paternalist legislation in people's own interests may be permissible.)

* Locke, J. (1689) *A Letter Concerning Toleration*, ed. M. Montuori, The Hague: Martinus Nijhoff, 1963. (Contains a definition of civil interests.)

Miller, D. (1976) *Social Justice*, Oxford: Clarendon Press. (Discusses need in the context of theories of social justice.)

Plant, R. (1991) *Modern Political Thought*, Oxford: Blackwell. (Has a good discussion of various approaches to the concept of needs.)

* Rawls, J. (1993) *Political Liberalism*, New York: Columbia University Press. (Lecture II uses the concept of higher-order interests and Lecture V sets out the view of primary goods as citizen's needs.)

* Smith, A. (1776) *An Inquiry into the Nature and Causes of the Wealth of Nations*, Oxford: Clarendon Press, 1979. (Book V, chapter 2, has the definition of necessaries.)

Thomson, G. (1987) *Needs*, London and New York: Routledge & Kegan Paul. (A good philosophical discussion of the concept of needs, defending a strong account of needs as the basis of justified claims.)

ALBERT WEALE

NEGATIVE FACTS IN CLASSICAL INDIAN PHILOSOPHY

Like their European counterparts, the philosophers of classical India were interested in the problem of negative facts. A negative fact may be thought of, at the outset at least, as a state of affairs that corresponds to a negative statement, such as 'Mr Smith is not in this room.' The question that perplexed the philosophers of India was: How does someone, say Ms Jones, know that Mr Smith is not in the room? There are essentially four possible metaphysical positions to account for what it is that Ms Jones knows when, after entering a room, she comes to know that her friend is not present there. Each of the positions has been adopted and defended by certain classical Indian philosophers. On the one hand, some take the absence of the friend from the room as a brute, negative fact. Of these, some hold knowledge of this fact to be perceptual, while others hold it to be inferential. On the other hand, some hold that the absence of the friend from the room has no real ontic status at all, and believe that what there really is in the situation is just the sum of all the things present in the office. These latter philosophers hold that knowledge of one's friend's absence is just knowledge of what is present, though some believe the knowledge results from perception, while others believe it to result from inference. These four positions were maintained by, respectively, the Nyaya philosopher Jayanta, the Mīmāṃsā philosophers Kumārila Bhaṭṭa and Prabhākara, and the Buddhist Dharmakīrti.

1   **Introduction to the problem**
2   **The view of Dharmakīrti**
3   **The view of Kumārila Bhaṭṭa's followers**
4   **The view of Prabhākara**
5   **The view of Jayanta**

1   Introduction to the problem

Negative facts have perplexed Western philosophers ever since the time of Plato. But the philosophers of Europe and America have not been the only philosophers to have been perplexed by them; classical Indian philosophers too have pondered their nature. The problem, as raised by classical Indian philosophers, is easy enough to state. Suppose that someone, say Ms Jones, enters a room and her friend, Mr Smith, is not there. How does Ms Jones know that Mr Smith is not there? One obvious answer, tendered by the classical Indian philosopher Kumārila Bhaṭṭa, is that Ms Jones fails to perceive Mr Smith (*Ślokavārttika* 9.11). While this answer has the ring of common sense, there are reasons to baulk at accepting it. To begin with, perception and inference are, in one sense, faculties or cognitive capabilities, whereas nonapprehension (*anupalabdhi*), the act of failing to perceive something, is not. There is, however, a more important reason to abandon the view that nonapprehension of something is a means of knowledge of its absence – something may be present yet not be perceived. Suppose that when Ms Jones enters a room, it is night, the lights are out, and the room is completely dark. Under these conditions, she would fail to see Mr Smith, even though he might very well be present.

Four main responses to the problem of negative facts can be discerned in classical Indian thought: that they are correctly analysed as straightforward positive facts known through inference; that there are real negative facts but that they can only be known through inference; that negative knowledge comes directly from perception of positive presences; and that we directly perceive real negative facts. Below, arguments for and against these positions are stated, although no attempt is made to track down their metaphysical origins and the related arguments. Rather, the exposition is confined to the authors whose treatments of the issue are the earliest ones which are both complete and sustained. They are those of Dharmakīrti (*c.*600–60), a Buddhist; of the followers of Kumārila Bhaṭṭa (*c.*620–80), an adherent of Mīmāṃsā; of Prabhākara (*c.*650–720), another adherent of Mīmāṃsā; and of Jayanta (*fl.* 890), an adherent of Nyāya.

2 The view of Dharmakīrti

The first classical Indian philosopher known to have understood and addressed the problem which confronts the view of Kumārila Bhaṭṭa was his older contemporary, Dharmakīrti. According to Dharmakīrti, both in his *Nyāyabindu* (Drop of Logic; 2.12–) and his *Pramāṇavārttika* (Commentary on Valid Cognition; 3.3–6 and commentary), one knows something when one correctly reports, having entered a room under the right conditions, that one's friend is absent from it; but what one knows is not a negative fact and is not known by perception. Rather, what one knows is a simple (positive) fact and it is known by inference.

A form of inference which comes to mind here is one advocated by Raphael Demos (1917) in an article in which he criticized Bertrand Russell's espousal of the existence of negative facts in his *The Philosophy of Logical Atomism*. Demos suggested that knowledge of absences is based on the relation of inconsistency between, on the one hand, the simple (positive) fact

one observes upon, say, entering a room, and, on the other hand, the state of affairs of one's friend's presence.

To be sure, Dharmakīrti holds that the relation of inconsistency plays a role in many inferences which warrant one's claim to know some allegedly negative facts. For example, he holds that from the presence of heat one can infer an absence of cold, since heat and cold are inconsistent (with respect to the same locus). But it is not his view that inference based on the relation of inconsistency plays a role in the case where Ms Jones enters a room and comes to know that her friend is not there. In such a case, Dharmakīrti maintains, Ms Jones reasons as follows: the causal conditions of perception known are such that, if her friend were present in the room, she would see him; she does not see him; therefore, he is not present. The inference is counterfactual (see Gillon 1986 for further discussion).

Does Dharmakīrti's counterfactual inference obviate the need to invoke the existence of absences? It seems not. Suppose, for example, one knows that one's friend is absent from a room. This can be symbolized as $\neg p$. According to Dharmakīrti, one knows this because one has inferred it from two premises which one already knew: first, the counterfactual conditional that if one's friend were present in the room, then one would know that the friend were present there; and second, the fact that one does not know that the friend is present in the room. These facts can be symbolized as $p \rightarrow Kp$ and $\neg Kp$ (where 'K' denotes the epistemic operator corresponding to the English 'a knows that' and '$\rightarrow$' denotes the connective for counterfactual conditionals). But this gives rise to a dilemma: how does one know that one does not know that one's friend is present in the room? In other words, how does one know that $\neg Kp$? On the one hand, if Dharmakīrti holds that one perceives that one does not know that one's friend is present in the room, that is to say, that one perceives that $\neg Kp$, then Dharmakīrti accepts thereby not only the existence of negative facts, in this case, negative mental facts, but also their perceptibility, both of which he wants to deny. On the other hand, if Dharmakīrti holds that one infers that one does not know that one's friend is present in the room, that is to say, that one infers that $\neg Kp$, then there must be an inference to ground that claim, just as there is an inference to ground the initial claim that one's friend is not present in the room, that is, $\neg p$. An infinite regress of inferences becomes inescapable, despite Dharmakīrti's protestations to the contrary (see *Pramāṇavārttika* 3.3 and commentary).

3 The view of Kumārila Bhaṭṭa's followers

A different position regarding negative facts and knowledge of them is the one adopted by the followers of Kumārila Bhaṭṭa. Though they maintained, unlike Dharmakīrti, that there are negative facts, they none the less seem to have adopted his view that knowledge in such cases is derived only from counterfactual inferences. These philosophers, unlike Dharmakīrti, but like most other classical Indian philosophers, considered counterfactual reasoning (*tarka*) neither as a form of inference (*anumāna*) nor, in general, as a standard means of knowledge (*pramāṇa*). The case of counterfactual reasoning yielding knowledge of negative facts was set aside by them as a means of knowledge unto itself, called 'nonapprehension' (*anupalabdhi*). Their view, of course, suffers from the very same dilemma just raised with respect to Dharmakīrti's view, namely the dilemma of having either to concede the perception of some negative facts or to accept, for any negative fact said to be known, an infinite regress of inferences of negative facts.

4 The view of Prabhākara

A younger contemporary of Kumārila Bhaṭṭa, Prabhākara, who shared many of his philosophical assumptions, adopted the view that what one knows when, upon entering a room, one comes to know that one's friend is absent from the room is some visually perceived, positive fact, that is, some presence. But what would be the plausible candidate for such a presence? Well, suppose Ms Jones' friend, Mr Smith, usually sits in some chair in the room. According to Prabhākara, the pertinent presence would be the presence of the chair Mr Smith usually sits in. What else could there be to the absence of Mr Smith from his chair than the presence of the chair he usually sits in? After all, as Gerd Buchdahl (1961: 176–7) has observed in considering this problem in the Western philosophical tradition, one needs to draw only one picture to draw a picture either of the chair Mr Smith usually sits in or of the same chair without him in it. Yet Prabhākara's metaphysical opponents were sceptical of the validity of this retort: they pointed out that if Mr Smith's absence were identical with the presence of the chair he usually sits in, then any time Ms Jones perceives the chair, including the times when Mr Smith is in it, she should know that Mr Smith is absent. This, according to the opponents, is patently absurd.

Prabhākara apparently sought to extricate himself from this objection by denying that the presence of Mr Smith in the chair he usually sits in is the same as the presence of his chair without him in it: in the former case there are two presences, that of Mr Smith and that of the chair he usually sits in; but in the latter there is only one, namely that of the chair Mr Smith usually sits in. Opponents suspected that this distinction cannot be made without directly or indirectly relying on an assumption of the existence of absences; for, as they pointed out, to distinguish the presence of one's friend in his chair from the presence of only his chair requires the use of such expressions as 'only' (*eva*) or 'merely' (*mātra*), which are implicitly negative expressions, since to say that there is only one presence is to say that there is at least one presence and there is no more than one presence.

Prabhākara faced another objection. How could he account for the fact that, when one sees simply one's friend's chair, what one comes to know is the friend's absence and not one of the infinity of other absences which are also then present? One reply is to maintain that there is a difference between what one sees and what one remarks upon, and that this difference obtains equally in cases of perception of what are unquestionably presences as well as in cases of perception of what are allegedly absences. For the very same reason that when one looks at a desk and remarks that there is a pad of paper on it, but fails to remark that there is a pencil on it, one remarks on Mr Smith's absence from a chair he usually sits in, but one does not remark on the absence of, say, an elephant from it.

5 The view of Jayanta

An alternative to Prabhākara's position is one advocated by Jayanta. He agrees with Prabhākara that perception is the relevant means for Ms Jones to know that Mr Smith is absent from a room, but disagrees with him that all that is relevant to Ms Jones' knowledge of Mr Smith's absence is her perception of some presence. Rather, Jayanta holds that absences are brute facts unto themselves and that Mr Smith's absence in the case described is known through perception. Like others of the same school (Nyāya), he thought of perception as a causal process, the linchpin of which is contact between the object of perception and the appropriate sense organ. Thus, for example, in the tactile perception of the pencil in one's hand, the key causal link is the contact of the organ, the skin, with the pencil. This view of perception, however, raised an immediate problem: if contact between an object of perception and the appropriate sense organ is the key link in the causal process of perception, how can there be perception of absences, for surely it is absurd to think of any sense organ as coming into contact with an absence?

Jayanta's response to this objection was to revise the definition of sense perception: he restricted the above definition to the perception of positive facts and provided a special clause to account for perception of negative facts. According to Jayanta, this move was not *ad hoc*; and at least within his overall metaphysical framework there are independent grounds for its adoption, for he believed that, though universals do not come into contact with the sense organs, they none the less can be perceived. In general, something is perceived just in case it is a physical thing suited to a sense organ and in contact with it, or it is a universal inhering in a physical thing and both the universal and the physical thing are suited to the sense organ, or it is an absence related to a place and both the absence and the place are suited to the sense organ.

See also: KNOWLEDGE, INDIAN VIEWS OF; MĪMĀṂSĀ §§1–2; NYĀYA-VAIŚEṢIKA §6

References and further reading

* Buchdahl, G. (1961) 'The Problem of Negation', *Philosophy and Phenomenological Research* 22: 167–78. (A clear and simple presentation of the problem of knowledge of negative facts within the Western philosophical tradition.)

Datta, D.M. (1932) *Six Ways of Knowing: A Critical Study of the Vedānta Theory of Knowledge*, Calcutta: Calcutta University Press, 2nd rev. edn, 1960. (Book 3, chapter 4 provides a comprehensive modern survey of absences and their knowability.)

* Demos, R. (1917) 'A Discussion of a Certain Type of Negative Proposition', *Mind* 26: 188–196. (A historically important article on negative facts, not recommended to the philosophical neophyte.)

* Dharmakīrti (*c.*600–60) *Pramāṇavārttika*, ed. R. Gnoli, *The Pramāṇavārttikam of Dharmakīrti: The First Chapter with the Autocommentary*, Serie Orientale Roma 23, Rome: Istituto Italiano per il Medio e Estremo Oriente, 1960; partly trans. R.P. Hayes and B.S. Gillon, 'Introduction to Dharmakīrti's Theory of Inference as Presented in *Pramāṇavārttika Svopajñavṛtti* 1–10', *Journal of Indian Philosophy* 19: 1–73. (A very difficult and important work on logic and metaphysics in the Indian philosophical tradition. The Gnoli edition provides critical notes as well as the Sanskrit text.)

* —— (*c.*600–60) *Nyāyabindu*, ed. D. Malvania, *Paṇḍita Durveka Miśra's Dharmottarapradīpa, Being a Sub-commentary on Dharmottara's Nyāyabinduṭīkā, a Commentary on Dharmakīrti's Nyāyabindu*, Tibetan Sanskrit Works Series 2, Patna: Kashiprasad Jayaswal Research Institute, 1955; 2nd edn, 1971; trans. T. Stcherbatsky, in *Buddhist Logic*, vol. 2, New York: Dover Publications, 1962. (A clear but all too concise compendium of its author's views on logic and metaphysics.)

* Gillon, B.S. (1986) 'Dharmakīrti and his Theory of Inference', in B.K. Matilal and R.D. Evans (eds) *Buddhist Logic and Epistemology*, Dordrecht: Reidel, 77–87. (A self-contained explanation of how Dharmakīrti treats knowledge of absences as a form of inference.)

—— (1997) 'Negative Facts and Knowledge of Negative Facts', in P. Bilmoria and J.N. Mohanty (eds) *Relativism, Suffering, and Beyond: Essays in Memory of Bimal K. Matilal*, Delhi: Oxford University Press, 1969, 128–49. (A contemporary philosophical treatment of the issue, which takes into account both Western and Indian views.)

Jayanta (*c.*890) *Nyāyamañjarī*, ed. K.S. Varadacharya, *Nyāyamañjarī of Jayanta Bhaṭṭa with Ṭippaṇi – Nyāyasaurabha by the Editor*, Mysore: The Oriental Research Institute, University of Mysore, 1969, 2 vols; trans. J.V. Bhattacharya, *Nyāya-Mañjarī: The Compendium of Indian Speculative Logic*, New Delhi: Motilal Banarsidass, 1978, 102–32. (This work provides a clear and comprehensive overview of the issues of classical Indian philosophy. The last fifth of the first āhnika (pages 102–33 of the English translation, 130–67 of the Sanskrit edition) provides a useful summary of views on the knowledge of absences.)

* Kumārila Bhaṭṭa (*c.*620–80) *Ślokavārttika*, ed. G.Ś. Musalgaonkar, *Mīmāṃsā Darśana Ślokavārttika of Kumārilabhaṭṭa with Śābarabhāṣya, the Commentary Nyāyaratnakara and Notes*, New Delhi: Bharatiya Vidya Prakashan, 1979, 2 vols; trans. G. Jhā, *Śloka-vārttika: Translated from the Original Sanskrit with Extracts from the Commentaries of Sucarita Miśra (The Kāśikā) and Pārthasārathi Miśra (Nyāyaratnākara)*, Bibliotheca Indica 146, Calcutta: Asiatic Society of Bengal, 1907; repr. New Delhi: Sri Satguru Publications, 1983. (This work is the fundamental text of the school of Mīmāṃsā founded by Kumārila Bhaṭṭa.)

* Russell, B. (1918) *The Philosophy of Logical Atomism*, ed. D. Pears, La Salle, IL: Open Court, 1985. (This important philosophical work contains a passage which is a rejoinder to Demos' proposed treatment of negative facts.)

Stcherbatsky, T. (1930) *Buddhist Logic*, Bibiotheca Buddhica 26, Leningrad: The Academy of Sciences of the USSR, 2 vols; repr. New York: Dover Publications, 1962. (This important yet tendentious and often unclear introduction to Buddhist logic contains a usable translation of Dharmakīrti's *Nyāyabindu*.)

BRENDAN S. GILLON

NEGATIVE THEOLOGY

The term 'negative theology' refers to theologies which regard negative statements as primary in expressing our knowledge of God, contrasted with 'positive theologies' giving primary emphasis to positive statements. The distinction was developed within Muslim, Jewish and Christian theism. If the negative way (via negativa) is taken to its limits, two questions arise: first, whether one may speak of God equally well in impersonal as in personal terms (blurring the distinction between theism and, say, the philosophical Hinduism of Śaṅkara); and second, whether it leads ultimately to rejecting any ultimate being or subject at all (blurring the distinction between theism and, say, the atheism of Mahāyāna Buddhism). However, within their original theistic context, positive and negative statements about God are interdependent, the second indispensably qualifying the first, the negative statements taken alone useless.

Negative qualifications on positive statements attributing so-called 'perfections' to God – for example, existence, life, goodness, knowledge, love or active power ('strength') – are obviously necessary if God is unimaginable. If his presence is always of his whole being and life all at once, in each place in space and time, he must be non-spatial and non-temporal in being and nature, and clearly he must be unimaginable. However, his supposed 'simplicity' and 'infinity' imply that he is much more radically outside the reach of understanding or 'comprehension', imposing the negative way at a deeper level than mere unimaginability. This unimaginability and incomprehensibility are key to theistic accounts of prayer and the mystical life.

1 **The negative way in older Christian tradition**
2 **Negative theology in Thomas Aquinas**
3 **Later developments**
4 **The negative way and arguments about meaningfulness**

1 The negative way in older Christian tradition

Within Christian theology, the negative way (called 'apophatic' from Greek) has two very different roles. First, if God is unimaginable and incomprehensible, this negative way is integral to any right understanding within theology as a 'theoretical' ('speculative') study considering models and using discourse and argument to assist understanding of God and his plan for creation (so far as this understanding is linguistically expressible). Second, the negative way is essential to the use of the intellect as directed practically towards union with God, that is, to the theology of spirituality and what Lossky (1957) calls 'mystical' theology. However, such theology seems to depend on positive statements about God, first for its context – some particular teaching and liturgy – enabling the mind to be directed in attention and love towards God and no other, and second for its verbal expression. This being directed towards God is typified when the mind is moved towards a loving, non-conceptual knowledge of God, setting aside images and concepts; this is illustrated in the mystical writings of Gregory of Nyssa and the poetry and commentaries of John of the Cross, their teaching being 'practical' in the sense explained by Jacques Maritain (1959). This love, whether realized in mystical prayer or as the unseen root of more active forms of life and prayer, is essentially directed to God, one who is holy or 'wholly other' (Otto 1917), not to any finite object of which we might form an image, or grasp or comprehend in nature.

The pre-Christian idea of a name as a means of control over what is named, bringing it within reach of human science and manipulation, is echoed in the negative emphasis both in the Old Testament and the Greek Fathers, who said that God 'has no name', or is 'ineffable'. This negative perspective was reinforced by Exodus 33: 18–23, which represents Moses as unable to see God's face, but only his back, and is echoed in the Gospels: 'no man has seen God at any time' (John 1: 18). Basil speaks of God as descending to us in his operations and John of Damascus suggests three possible etymologies deriving the word *theos* (God) from an operation. From these suggestions and the fifth-century writings of PSEUDO-DIONYSIUS, later Eastern tradition developed the idea that we never say anything positive of God's 'essence' (God as he is in himself), but only about his 'uncreated energies' – a development especially marked in Gregory Palamas and Eastern councils in 1351 and 1357. Latin tradition never accepted any distinction between God's essence and uncreated energies, but insisted that when we refer to God's existence, life, goodness, greatness, love, strength and suchlike, we refer to God's essence, that is, to God as he is in himself ('*substantialiter*' in Aquinas); however, it still maintained a parallel negative bent, which is highlighted in the Fourth Lateran Council's statement in 1215 that 'between Creator and creature no similarity can be expressed without including a greater dissimilarity' (Tanner 1990: 232).

759

2 Negative theology in Thomas Aquinas

The classic Western solution of the problem was presented by Thomas Aquinas (*Summa theologiae* Ia, qq.1–13). He explains that we speak of things according to the way in which we know them (q.13, a.1), and speak of God as 'we know him from created things as their cause (*principium*), by way of excellence and by negation (*remotio*)'. In this traditional phraseology, he was not referring to three distinct kinds of statement about God, but to how we are to understand positive statements attributing 'perfections' to God, for example, existence, life, goodness, knowledge, love and active power. In each case, God as cause or principle of creatures possessed the perfection beforehand in a more eminent way, and not in any of the finite ways in which the perfection concerned is exemplified in creatures (see GOD, CONCEPTS OF §§1–6).

Any such approach, allowing certain terms to be applied both to God and to creatures, but in different ways, absolutely involves some flexibility in our use of these terms – Aquinas saw this flexibility in the possibility of middle ways between terms being used 'equivocally' and being used 'univocally' (in identical senses in different cases). 'Analogy' was his blanket term covering all such middle ways.

For Aquinas, the words we use to signify things belonging to the essence of a particular sort of creature express things stateable in its definition, whereas what they signify in God's case cannot be contained in a definition. A definition makes the thing defined the object of human comprehension in some particular science. In Aquinas' conception, no kind of theology can yield comprehension (meaning master grasp, rather than loose understanding), and there is no science of God in the sense applicable to other sciences. Theology proper can only arise because by revelation God gives us some participation in his own knowledge of himself and of the way to him, participation in a style appropriate to human nature, and therefore using human language and concepts, including metaphors (*Summa theologiae* Ia, q.1). Aquinas has no conception of any self-contained natural theology, but only of a general metaphysics reaching some theological conclusions which, despite their limited character, give metaphysics some fuller integration (see AQUINAS, T. §§9, 14).

In Aquinas' view, we can know the relevant statements about God to be true, some through philosophical reflection, and these and others through revelation, but we cannot comprehend God or the way he exists, lives, knows, loves and is good, or his mode of relation or action towards creatures, and so we have no comprehension or imagination of what

makes these statements true. Terms for such 'perfections' apply truly to God in their proper or literal sense – it would, for example, be absurd to suppose that the cause of other things existing existed in a less real or proper sense than its effects. None of these most general positive terms has one definition even with regard to all creatures, each being used of different kinds of creature according to different definitions, or – in modern parlance – according to different criteria. Each such term is used of different types of thing 'analogically'. Although we learn to use them of creatures first, as applying in this or that way or respect, they apply unrestrictedly only to God. With regard to God, they have no 'scientific' definition. (The special term 'God' applies only to God and presents different but related problems: 'God' is the name of a nature, grammatically parallel to terms such as 'angel', 'animal', 'human being' and 'horse', and is not a formal or category term such as 'substance' or 'quality'; but still neither 'God' nor any other term applying to God alone has any real definition.)

For Aquinas as for Leibniz, without some positive predicates there would be no subject, and he rejects the more extreme negative way of Maimonides, for whom affirmative statements had only a negative content. Aquinas argues that this would not explain why we prefer some affirmative statements to others, would imply that God existed, was good, and so on, only in a secondary sense, and would be contrary to the intention of those speaking about God. Maimonides may have thought that our statements lock onto God as their object only because they are given direction by an adherence to God's law inspired from the heart. Aquinas would have replied that the love of heart or will, as distinct from sensory love, presupposes some knowledge by intellect, a reply also telling against more recent noncognitive approaches (see Mitchell 1971).

The completeness of Aquinas' embracing of the negative way appears in his exposition of God's simplicity (*Summa theologiae* Ia, q.3), where he successively announces different facets of the unlikeness between God and creatures immediately after proving God's existence (see SIMPLICITY, DIVINE §§1–2). This unlikeness is above all plain in God's different way of possessing existence; God alone possesses it intrinsically, is able to communicate it (*Summa theologiae* q.45, a.5; q.104, a.1), contains only active rather than passive potentiality, and is the ultimate cause of the being and continuance of anything with any real kind of contingency. Aquinas views God's act of existing (identical with his acts of living, knowing and loving) as identical with what he is (his *essentia*, his stuff, being or nature).

This last embodies Aquinas' rejection of self-causation, but its key importance is in marking the misleadingness of the ordinary structures of human language when applied to God. The subject/predicate structure of our statements does not make them false with regard to God, but makes them misleading. True, God exists, lives and loves, but our linguistic way of speaking ('by composition and division') suggests distinctions between the subject and the attribute predicated which are not real in the case of God. A term's 'way of signifying' (*modus significandi*) differs according to whether it signifies concretely ('God' or *Deus*, 'wise' or 'is wise') or abstractly ('deity', 'wisdom'), although the thing signified (*res significata*) is the same. Although we can make true statements about God, our language-formed way of thinking is in this way radically inappropriate, suggesting (for example) that God is one among many others who live, are good, know, act and exist. On the contrary, he cannot be grouped with them in the same genus – even the widest – as if the terms concerned might apply in the same sense or way. Rather, God not only exemplifies these attributes more perfectly, but also is his own life, goodness, and so on, and is the archetype (cause and *principium*) of life, goodness, and so on, in others – and this eminence implies the denial of every finite mode of possession of these attributes. Such is Aquinas' conception. At the same time, he always assumes the concreteness of God, the three divine persons being three primary substances in Aristotle's sense, rejecting the idea that God might be Existence, Life and Love in the Platonic sense of abstracted common properties shared by things which exist, live or love.

3 Later developments

The importance of the negative way appears in its contrast with rival, more positive theologies. Duns Scotus insisted that the terms for the divine perfections are used in the same sense of God and of creatures (univocally, not merely analogously), a view extended in Descartes' conception that we have a clear and distinct idea of infinity as attributed to God, as well as of these perfections. More recently, an empiricist natural theology has tended to model accounts of the relation between God and the world on a dualist conception of the relation between mind and body, and to rely on arguments for God from design (thinking of God's motivations in a parallel way to human ones) more than on cosmological arguments. This seemingly more common-sense approach rejects traditional ideas of God's simplicity, non-temporal nature and foreknowledge, and conceives his eternity only as an everlasting existence in

parallel with creation, and therefore as compatible with a changing or developing God, as in process theology (see PROCESS THEISM §§1–3). Such empiricism tends to conceive infinity in terms of magnitude, rather than in terms of the negation of all finite properties and finite modes of realization of 'perfections' (see Mitchell 1971, papers 1–3).

This 'common-sense' theology thinks of our capacity to speak of God as based on a supposed likeness of God to creatures, supposing the terms we use to apply literally only to creatures and to God in a derived or secondary sense. Yet this might seem absurd or even blasphemous in the case of the so-called 'perfections' – as if God could exist in a less real sense than his creatures, live, know, understand, love, be good or have active or causal power in a less full sense than creatures. In the older view the terms applied unrestrictedly to God, but only in some limited ('finite') respect to creatures.

These tendencies encourage an idolatry of creature-likeness in place of the Platonic idolatry that makes God an abstract entity; both these were rejected by Aquinas, and both invited Pascal's reaction, that the God of Abraham, Isaac and Jacob is not the god of the philosophers. Since 1700, the antipathy of theologians and spiritual men and women towards philosophical theology has steadily intensified. This reaction, rejecting Hegel's idea that God's nature and purposes can be read from history, reached its extremes in Kierkegaard and Karl Barth.

4 The negative way and arguments about meaningfulness

Does the negative way destroy the possibility of religious language's having any cognitive meaning? In the classic picture, since we know various positive statements about God to be true, and thence also know them to be meaningful (in the strong sense of being coherent enough to be capable of truth), some content remains, and not mere nonsense, even after all our negative qualifications. What we say, whether from revelation or tradition or from these assisted by philosophy, constitutes a pointer, and, in a structure of related statements, embodies some beginnings of thought or understanding, albeit not comprehension. It may contain paradox, defeating the imagination, but not intrinsic self-contradiction. Atheism and agnosticism, however, transform this situation: if we do not know that what is said is true, we have no way of knowing that any cognitive content at all remains behind after so many negative qualifications together with the adverbs 'infinitely' or 'unsurpassably'. The idea of the infinite as a degree of intensive magnitude is unhelpful, since the atheist or agnostic has been given no reason why there should be any maximum in modes of existence, life, goodness, knowledge, love or causal power. There is then no ground for supposing these statements meaningful in any fuller sense than science-fiction stories or fairy tales – indeed they lack even the benefit of the imaginability that gives these stories their power.

This problem, of whether religious language has any cognitive meaning, is not just insoluble for the atheist and agnostic, but for any philosophy of religion which makes it a point of method always to consider questions about the meaning of types of statement (in this case, about God) in advance of considering their truth – as if to agree a neutral ground specific to the philosophy of religion from which to debate with agnostics or atheists. The supposed problem of meaningfulness is only solvable if knowledge of the truth of at least some of a class of statements is prior to knowledge of meaningfulness – for example, because given by revelation (the only solution admitted in Karl Barth's theology), by philosophy (questions of the meaningfulness of the terms we use being resolved in general philosophy, before we turn to using the same terms with regard to God) or somehow by 'experience'. Always some have assumed truth on the basis of faith, independently of and prior to considering how meaningfulness arises, and this has allowed a negative theology grounded in faith to be endemic, sometimes in distinguished figures scarcely noticed by later tradition, such as Nicholas of Cusa.

Older Jewish, Christian and Muslim traditions are strongly set against appeals to 'experience' as the key to knowledge of truth and meaningfulness. In this life, we know God by faith, not by sight; inner or outer experience can always be supposed in retrospect or by another person to have a different explanation from that which the experiencer thought certain at the time, and therefore cannot be the basis of the certainty of faith. If we follow the phenomenologists and Wittgenstein, no two 'religious experiences' described in quite different terms with different kinds of object or relations to different systems of motivation could be the same. The writings of R.C. Zaehner are typical of many suggesting just such differences (see Zaehner 1958). But with the increase of emphasis on 'experience' in religion over the nineteenth and twentieth centuries (see PHENOMENOLOGY OF RELIGION §§1–2), and the decrease in the value put on teaching, ritual and reasoning in this sphere, the negative way has eased the way towards supposing that all the main world religions are set on the same objects and values, whether the 'ultimate' is described in impersonal or personal terms.

See also: MYSTICISM, HISTORY OF §6; PATRISTIC PHILOSOPHY §2; RELIGION AND EPISTEMOLOGY; RELIGIOUS LANGUAGE; RELIGIOUS PLURALISM

References and further reading

* Aquinas, T. (1266–73) *Summa theologiae*, London: Blackfriars, 1961–70, Ia, qq.1–13, 44–5, 104. (Q.3 presents the basis of the negative way in Aquinas, which is illustrated in qq.7–12, and is the key to his understanding of analogy in q.13; the utter difference of God's way of possessing being is best explained in q.45, a.5 and q.104, a.1. Q.4 and q.13 explain how a statement's positive and non-metaphorical character can remain despite negative qualification, and q.1 explains the role of metaphor.)

Dupré, L. (ed.) (1990) *Nicholas of Cusa, American Catholic Philosophical Quarterly* 64 (1), Washington, DC: Catholic University of America. (Useful introductory scatter of papers.)

John of the Cross (1966) *Collected Works*, ed. K. Cavanaugh and O. Rodriguez, London: Nelson; trans. A. Peers, *Complete Works*, London: Burns & Oates, 1934. (The poems themselves, reminiscent of the Scriptural 'Song of Songs', show how deeply the negative way is set within the context of a personal love-relationship.)

* Lossky, V. (1957) *Mystical Theology of the Eastern Church*, London: James Clarke. (See especially pages 8–11 and chapters 2 and 4 for a common Eastern Orthodox perspective.)

* Maritain, J. (1959) *The Degrees of Knowledge*, London: Geoffrey Bles. (Part II, especially chapters 8–9, focuses on the epistemological situation of John of the Cross' mystical writings.)

* Mitchell, B. (ed.) (1971) *The Philosophy of Religion*, Oxford: Oxford University Press. (On the meaning of religious assertions: papers 1 (parts A and C), 2 and 3 present or discuss some modern cognitive approaches; papers 1 (part B), 4 and 7 present some modern noncognitive ones.)

* Otto, R. (1917) *The Idea of the Holy*, trans. J.W. Harvey, London: Oxford University Press, 1923. (Philosophically expressive of the idea that emotions have to have an object.)

* Tanner, N.P. (ed.) (1990) *Decrees of the Ecumenical Councils*, vol. 1, London: Sheed & Ward, and Washington, DC: Georgetown University Press. (This standard, widely available work provides both original text and translation.)

* Zaehner, R.C. (1958) *At Sundry Times*, London: Faber & Faber; Westport, CT: Greenwood, 1971. (Detailed contrasting of the differences in object of different types of mysticism; see also his *Mysticism:*

Sacred and Profane, London: Oxford University Press, 1957.)

DAVID BRAINE

NÉGRITUDE *see* AFRICAN PHILOSOPHY, ANGLOPHONE; AFRICAN PHILOSOPHY, FRANCOPHONE

NEMESIUS (*fl. c.*390–400 AD)

Nemesius' treatise De natura hominis *(On the Nature of Man) is the first work by a Christian thinker dedicated to articulating a comprehensive philosophical anthropology. Like many of his pagan and Christian contemporaries, Nemesius employs Platonic, Aristotelian and Stoic ethical psychologies in developing his views, but he also provides remarkably detailed accounts of the physiological structure and function of the sense-faculties based on extensive medical knowledge.*

Information on the life of Nemesius is limited. He probably became bishop of Emesa in Syria during the last decade of the fourth century AD, and his philosophical treatise *De natura hominis* (On the Nature of Man), written in Greek, dates from this same period. As late as the Middle Ages this work was attributed to Gregory of Nyssa, his better known contemporary, though seventh-century writers such as Maximus Confessor recognized Nemesius as the author. Such confusion was common in a literary tradition which stipulated an impersonal style of writing, often accompanied by an injunction to avoid originality.

Nemesius received an excellent liberal Greek education, which was broadened to include extensive knowledge of the medical tradition stemming from Hippocrates and GALEN and deep familiarity with the spiritual metaphysics of late antique Neoplatonism (see HIPPOCRATIC MEDICINE; NEOPLATONISM). Scientific knowledge about the human body and its physiological functions is harmonized with the Platonic doctrine of the soul; Aristotle's theory of free choice (see ARISTOTLE) is reconciled with Christian providence. Nemesius relies heavily on the voluminous writings of Galen on anatomy and physiology. His treatise is a rich source of information on a wide variety of topics and on lost works by Galen and by other Christian authors, such as the *Commen-*

tary on Genesis of ORIGEN. The localizations of the sense and cognitive faculties in various parts of the brain were transmitted to ALBERT THE GREAT and Thomas Aquinas in the thirteenth century by Latin translations of *De natura hominis*.

Despite the rich philosophical and scientific content of the work, its focus is religious and spiritual. It is clearly a piece of Christian apologetic addressed to Hellenic intellectuals not yet committed to Christianity. Nemesius' informative, multi-layered doxography, with its extensive medical knowledge of the body, made for an anthropology sophisticated enough for educated Hellenes yet also consonant with Christian doctrines. This interest in the concrete is reflected in his theological adherence to the school of Antioch, which stressed the historical character of the Gospel and the humanity of Christ.

The long and important first three chapters of the treatise aim at harmonizing Platonic and Aristotelian psychology and Platonic and Stoic metaphysics. On the latter topic, Nemesius endorses the Platonic/ Neoplatonic hierarchy and continuity of being, but stresses the continuity from one level to the next, from inanimate entities through animals to human beings and beyond to the intelligible world. He objects to the radically transcendent character of Neoplatonism because it leaves discontinuous gaps in the structure of reality. This more vitalistic and less hierarchical metaphysic has been traced by some to the influence of the first-century BC Platonizing Stoic Posidonius of Apamea, parts of whose largely lost works may have been preserved in Origen's lost *Commentary on Genesis*. At the centre of the picture, Nemesius situates human nature as the link between the spiritual realm and the physical universe.

In the important second chapter on the soul, Nemesius begins with an extensive doxographical survey of psychological theories from the Presocratics through Aristotle, the Stoics, Epicureans, Neoplatonists, various Christian authors and the Manicheans (see PRESOCRATIC PHILOSOPHY; STOICISM; EPICUREANISM; MANICHEISM). Adopting Plato's view that the soul is an independent substance, he rejects Aristotle's claim that the soul is a part of the composite human being. For Nemesius, then, the soul is a self-moving, incorporeal and immortal principle which employs the body as its instrument; it is not the body's perfection or entelechy, as Aristotle held. Chapter 3 of *De natura hominis* tackles a basic problem: if soul and body comprise some sort of unity, how can the soul be immortal? Nemesius relies on Neoplatonists who argued that in its essence the soul is an immutable substance which, when united with a body, suffers no change or alteration. He illustrates the relation between soul and body by comparison with Christological doctrine: the being of the Logos is not diminished when united with human nature (see SOUL, NATURE AND IMMORTALITY OF THE).

Subsequent chapters take up the location of various faculties in bodily structures and their physiological description. Chapters 6–11 respectively cover imagination, sight, touch (which is defined as the 'consciousness of feeling due to nerves proceeding from the brain and spreading into every part of the body'), taste, hearing and smell, which are located in the frontal lobes of the brain; intellect is located in the middle of the brain (Chapter 12), and memory in the back lobes (Chapter 13). A distinctive feature of the localization of the sense-faculties in parts of the brain is the citation of empirical evidence (for example, brain lesions) derived from Galen. Chapter 13 also reveals Nemesius' commitment to the Neoplatonic doctrine of the pre-existence of the soul in which souls recollect things they learned in the intelligible world before taking birth in bodies.

Various models of parts of the soul are reviewed in chapter 15. His analysis of the passions and pleasures in Chapters 16–18 relies on Epicurus' distinction among natural, necessary and non-necessary desires which is grafted on to the Platonic tripartite model of the soul, consisting of rational, emotional and appetitive parts. Discussion of the nutritive, generative and life-sustaining faculties or capacities in Chapters 23–8 closely follows Galen. Chapters 29–34 develop a largely Aristotelian theory of action which adroitly employs Aristotle's accounts of the voluntary, involuntary, deliberation and choice. In the ensuing Chapters 35–40, Nemesius relies on the power of human deliberative rationality to ground his attack on fatalism and his argument in favour of the freedom of the will (see FREE WILL). Some have seen in this account of freedom and rationality evidence of Pelagian optimism about human nature (see PELAGIANISM). Nemesius insists, however, that free choice is a divine gift and that it is exercised exclusively within the orbit of God's providence (Chapters 42–4).

See also: NEOPLATONISM; PATRISTIC PHILOSOPHY; PLATONISM, MEDIEVAL; SOUL, NATURE AND IMMORTALITY OF THE

List of works

Nemesius (*c.*390–400) *De natura hominis* (On the Nature of Man), ed. M. Morani, Leipzig: Teubner, 1987; trans. W. Telfer in *Cyril of Jerusalem and Nemesius of Emesa*, Library of Christian Classics vol. 4, London: SCM Press, 1955. (This is the

standard critical edition of the Greek text of *De natura hominis*.)

References and further reading

Jaeger, W. (1914) *Nemesios von Emesa*, Berlin: Weidmann. (Comprehensive treatment of the Greek philosophical influences on Nemesius.)
Telfer, W. (1955) *Cyril of Jerusalem and Nemesius of Emesa*, Library of Christian Classics vol. 4, London: SCM Press, 203–455. (Useful introduction and valuable chapter-by-chapter commentary accompanying the translation.)

JOHN BUSSANICH

NEO-CONFUCIAN PHILOSOPHY

Chinese neo-Confucian philosophy, or 'neo-Confucianism', is a term which refers to a wide variety of substantially different Chinese thinkers from the Song dynasty (960–1279) through the Qing dynasty (1644–1911). In at least one respect the term is misleading, for unlike Neoplatonists, most neo-Confucians saw themselves as reviving, not revising, the earlier Confucian tradition. What united all these thinkers was a common allegiance to Confucius and his thought. Many of the central debates within the tradition concern the issue of who could claim to be Confucius' legitimate heir.

Despite their shared dedication to Confucius' legacy, a number of the central beliefs of neo-Confucians were unknown to Confucius and his early followers and appear to be at odds with early Confucian views. Many of these beliefs were part of a novel, elaborate and comprehensive metaphysical scheme linking human beings (as microcosm) to the universe (as macrocosm). Such cosmological theories provided a new ground for Confucian ethical claims and strengthened a tendency towards the mystical identification of the self with the universe. These changes also helped to transform the earlier Confucian concern with self-cultivation and steady moral improvement to a more dramatic quest for spiritual enlightenment, replete with a distinctly Confucian style of meditation.

One widely accepted account of the rise of neo-Confucianism sees it as a reaction on the part of Confucian scholars to the perceived dominance of Buddhist thought. On this view, Confucians had become complacent in the period between the end of the Han dynasty, in the early third century AD, to the beginnings of the neo-Confucian movement late in the ninth century. Fearing that their way of life was in peril, these later Confucians resolved to overcome their Buddhist competitors and revive their tradition. Purportedly, these later Confucians realized that in order to accomplish these goals they would need to develop and deploy an account of the Confucian tradition that could compete with and overcome the complex metaphysical schemes the Buddhists had used to argue against them. For these strategic reasons, early neo-Confucians focused their attention on texts like the Mengzi (Mencius), Daxue (Great Learning) and Zhongyong (Doctrine of the Mean) and began to evolve a version of Confucianism that was supported by the kind of comprehensive and complex metaphysical system described above.

A different account of the rise of neo-Confucianism can be given, however, in which the selection of certain texts and the development of new styles and practices of reasoning are not seen as self-conscious strategic borrowings from Buddhism and Daoism. Rather, these characteristic features of neo-Confucianism are consequences of the profound and pervasive effect that Buddhist and Daoist thought had exerted for centuries upon Chinese intellectuals. There was no organized or distinct group of thinkers who identified and thought of themselves as Confucians in the centuries immediately prior to the neo-Confucian revival. Rather, Chinese intellectuals had come to accept a wide range of philosophical ideas and spiritual practices as part and parcel of literati culture. When certain of these broadly read and eclectically trained individuals began looking back to the writings of early Confucian figures, they did so through the categories and with the concerns and approaches of their age. Their angle of vision had changed, and as a result they saw these earlier sources differently. This new orientation led them to elevate certain texts to canonical status; in some cases, these were texts that were unknown to the sages they claimed to follow. Moreover, these later Confucians developed particular aspects of the classical writings in ways that would have been unrecognizable to the founding figures of the tradition they so adamantly defended.

The great impetus for the revival of Confucianism came with a series of social and political crises that came to a head roughly in the middle of the eighth century. Under the dual pressures of internal rebellion and economic distress and external attack on a number of different fronts, Chinese intellectuals began to question their fundamental beliefs and practices. Rather than calling for reform or progress, such reflection led them back to their roots. Increasingly, they came to believe that the primary source of their troubles was that they had lost their Way. Like the foreign enemies who plagued them from without, they were being undermined by a foreign force from within:

the non-Chinese religion of Buddhism and its spiritual cousin Daoism. These had led them to abandon the true source of their strength and former glory: the culture of classical China. Their course was clear. They must retrieve and revive the classical culture that was their very essence. In so doing they would replay the roles their most revered sages, Confucius and Mencius, had played in their own degenerate ages. This call to defend and promote 'this culture' served as the rallying point for the neo-Confucian movement.

Towards the end of the neo-Confucian period, Chinese Confucians themselves began to recognize the degree to which earlier neo-Confucians had incorporated beliefs and styles of reasoning that were alien to Confucius' way of thinking, specifically ideas drawn from Buddhism and Daoism, into the tradition. A number of these Qing dynasty thinkers saw their task primarily in terms of purging the tradition of these foreign elements in an effort to reconstitute a purer form of Confucius' original vision.

1   **Historical background**
2   **Central concepts and terms**
3–6 **The Song dynasty (960–1279)**
7   **The Yuan dynasty (1280–1368)**
8–9 **The Ming dynasty (1368–1644)**
10–11 **The Qing dynasty (1644–1911)**
12   **Conclusion**

1 Historical background

During the 'Northern and Southern Dynasties' (AD 317–588), China experienced a prolonged period of instability and upheaval. Buddhism, which had arrived in China as early as the first century AD, became the dominant religious and intellectual force in the country (see BUDDHIST PHILOSOPHY, CHINESE). Daoism also flourished and became a powerful and elaborate institutional religion (see DAOIST PHILOSOPHY). Under the short-lived Sui dynasty (589–618), Buddhism was adopted and promoted as the state ideology, and it continued to flourish and develop in the succeeding Tang dynasty (618–905). This period witnessed prolific growth in Buddhist philosophical ideas and systems of thought, several of which were to have a profound effect on neo-Confucian philosophy. Daoism also continued to exert a strong and pervasive influence throughout Chinese society. The Tang imperial family claimed one of the mythical founders of Daoism, Laozi, as an ancestor and actively supported and practiced Daoism.

These three traditions, Confucianism, Daoism and Buddhism, did not always coexist peacefully. There were a number of Buddhist persecutions instigated by Confucian and Daoist elements within the imperial court. The worst of these occurred during the Tang dynasty, from 841–5, when a Daoist emperor launched a severe and wide-ranging persecution of Buddhism. To a large extent, this reaction against Buddhism was brought on by the decline of Chinese political and economic fortunes in the closing years of the Tang. This anti-Buddhist sentiment was to play a major role in the resurgence of Confucianism.

The founding of the Sui dynasty had marked the revival of a centralized Chinese state. With it came bureaucratic institutions and practices, among them the civil service examinations, modelled on paradigms drawn from the earlier Han dynasty (206 BC–AD 220). The Sui rulers turned to these neglected Confucian institutions and practices as the most effective available means of organizing and governing their state. However, there was little concomitant interest in the philosophical ideas behind these institutions and practices. Buddhism and Daoism continued to be the primary interests of intellectuals during the Sui dynasty and throughout most of the Tang dynasty.

In the middle of the Tang period, the Chinese empire began to experience intense economic and political strain. Because of rapid population growth, increased fluidity between socio-economic classes, the monetary drain of large, tax-exempt monastic estates, rising military expenditures and a lack of leadership by the imperial court, the tax system began to break down. In addition to these economic woes, in 751 the Chinese state suffered defeat in two important military campaigns, against a Thai army in the south and an Arab army in the west. These military debacles precipitated a disastrous internal rebellion by a young general named An Lushan in 755. After this, the Tang court was never again fully in control of China.

Not long after these events, HAN YU began what was to become the Confucian revival. His blistering criticisms of Buddhism as a socially parasitic and quintessentially anti-Chinese religion are among the earliest and most powerful statements of sentiments that were coming to the surface during the later Tang dynasty, feelings fuelled by the indignation and frustration arising from the economic and political difficulties described above. Han Yu's condemnation of Buddhism as a foreign system of thought which had invaded China and weakened it – laying the ground for the foreign invaders who were now plaguing Chinese territory – provided a focus and point of departure for what was to come.

Han Yu argued that the Chinese needed to rid themselves of this foreign influence and return to their true roots. These ran back to Confucius and the idealized past culture which he preserved and advocated. Daoism and Buddhism were both accused of being 'other-worldly' and incapable of providing guidance in the all too real world of domestic and foreign challenges. Han Yu himself was not philosophically inclined. His great talent was literature, and his belief in the need to revive ancient literary style expresses both his own predilection and the degree to which he saw ideas in terms of the specific cultural practices of an idealized past. Nevertheless, he provided the founding vision and voice for the Confucian revival.

2 Central concepts and terms

Traditional accounts of the rise of neo-Confucianism agree in describing it as a reaction against Buddhism and Daoism. However, most overlook the economic and political events which precipitated this reaction. Moreover, they contend that the central texts and ideas which neo-Confucians embraced were consciously chosen for their efficacy in the fight against Buddhist and Daoist thought. According to such accounts, texts such as the *Mengzi* (Mencius), *Daxue* (Great Learning) and *Zhongyong* (Doctrine of the Mean) were chosen because these were the best sources from which to draw in defending Confucianism (see DAXUE; MENCIUS; ZHONGYONG). The present account differs from this view in seeing the choice of texts and ideas as a consequence of the pervasive and profound influence exerted by Buddhism and Daoism throughout the Chinese intellectual world of this period. When Confucians of the Song dynasty looked back to the early sources of their tradition, they saw them through many layers of Buddhist and Daoist influence. This altered their perception of what was most central to the tradition as well as their understanding of traditional philosophical concepts. In order to understand neo-Confucianism, it is important to realize how some of these ideas evolved.

Through its interaction with indigenous Chinese thought, particularly Daoism, Buddhism changed dramatically and developed distinctively Chinese forms. The early Buddhist belief that all imperfect aspects of reality are ultimately unreal became transformed into the idea that our less savoury aspects are not really part of our nature. According to this view, our fundamental nature is equally the nature of all things, part of a transpersonal *foxing* (Buddha-nature) which is reflected in each and every thing in the world. Once one realizes that one is part of all reality, one no longer will feel the inevitable anxiety and fear of the eventual loss of one's self at death; instead one comes to see the common belief in an enduring and separate self as the source of all suffering. A person with this 'right' view of things manifests universal compassion towards all sentient beings, as manifestations of Buddha-nature (see BUDDHIST PHILOSOPHY, CHINESE).

Since the beginning of their tradition, Confucians had offered competing theories about the true character of human nature (see XING). It was therefore natural that the notion of Buddha-nature had a profound influence on neo-Confucian views. Neo-Confucians began to talk about *benxing* (original nature) and *qizhi zhixing* (material nature), the former perfect and complete, the latter flawed and needing refinement. These terms are not found in pre-Buddhist Chinese philosophy. Within this conceptual scheme, Mencius' claim about the original goodness of human nature came to be understood as referring to the original, perfect and pure state of human nature rather than to certain of its nascent tendencies (see MENCIUS).

In order to appreciate fully this new view of human nature, we need to understand two additional neo-Confucian terms of art: *li* and *qi*. *Li* ('pattern' or 'principle') appears in early Daoist texts and means the underlying pattern running throughout the world. Different things, including human beings, possess their own individual structures or 'patterns' and contribute to a larger, grand 'pattern' or scheme (see LI). Under the influence of Buddhist philosophy, particularly the notion of Buddha nature as described above, this concept changed dramatically. The underlying pattern of the universe came to be seen as completely present in every mote of dust, with each aspect of reality reflecting all others.

However, neo-Confucians believed that any given thing only manifests certain particular *li* and this is what makes a thing the thing it is. Only certain *li* are manifested because of the effect of *qi* (ether). *Qi* is what makes up the world. It is a kind of lively – not inert – matter which exists in various grades of purity. As a function of its purity, the *qi* of different things obscures, to varying degrees, the *li* that are within them, only allowing some to shine through. So while all things equally possess all the *li*, their different endowments of *qi* make them different. Human beings are unique in that they alone have the ability to become aware of the *li* within them by refining their *qi* to the highly tenuous state which allows all the *li* within to shine forth. Other creatures are stuck at different levels of 'clarity'; the *qi* of inanimate things is so 'dense' that they lack consciousness (see QI). Neo-Confucians tended to equate *li* with the 'original nature' of human beings and contrasted this with the idea of 'material nature', which is *li* embedded in *qi*. The task of moral self-cultivation was to refine one's *qi* and move from relative ignorance to complete and comprehensive knowledge (see SELF-CULTIVATION IN CHINESE PHILOSOPHY).

3 The Song dynasty (960–1279)

These terms of art and the basic concepts were developed and made systematic during the Song. In particular, the speculative metaphysics that came to serve as the foundation for neo-Confucian philosophy was forged during the early part of the dynasty. These early Song thinkers did not always share the social, political and ethical concerns of later neo-Confucians.

SHAO YONG was one of the first early Song figures associated with the rise of neo-Confucianism in the eleventh century. His major interest was explaining the cosmology of the *Yijing* (Book of Changes) (see YIJING). Shao is distinctive for linking his cosmological speculations to an elaborate system of numerology. In this regard, his thought is not unlike that of the Pythagoreans (see PYTHAGOREANISM) or LEIBNIZ, who was familiar with some of his ideas.

Shao assumed that there was a discernable correlation between the hexagrams of the *Yijing* and the structure and function of the universe. Hence, anyone with a proper understanding of the text could not only understand but foretell events in the world. He wove his philosophical system around a passage from the *Xicizhuan* (Commentary on the Appended Phrases, also known as the *Dazhuan* (Great Commentary)) of the *Yijing*, which he believed described this relationship: 'And so within the Changes is the *taiji* [Supreme Ultimate]. It produces the two Principles [symbolized by *yin* and *yang*]. The two Principles produce the four Forms. The four Forms produce the eight Trigrams' (*Xicizhuan* A11). Shao read this passage in terms of numerology, relying upon the notion of *shen* (spirituality). *Shen* is an active and impersonal conscious power which both animates things in the world and allows one to understand them. It is able to act immediately at a distance, and as understanding can instantly 'penetrate' throughout the universe. Shao believed that *shen* produces numbers, corresponding to the initial distinction of *yin* and *yang* (see YIN–YANG), and that from number the 'images' of things (the four Forms) arise. These then generate the actual things and events in the world. Human beings have *shen* as part of their nature; they can therefore tap into its activity and understand its movement by grasping the underlying numbers which give rise to all things.

Following this scheme, Shao saw the world in terms of sets of four (corresponding to the four Forms): there were four earthly substances (water, fire, earth, stone), four living things (animals, birds, grasses and trees) and so on. In addition to these fundamental classes of things, Shao used this scheme to describe four phases of history, which recur in unending cycles of fixed numerical length. He showed little interest in many of the basic issues that later came to characterize neo-Confucianism, and was not regarded by Zhu Xi (see §6) as part of the orthodox Confucian revival. Shao was neither anti-Buddhist nor anti-Daoist; he was not a moralist, a political or social reformer or a self-cultivationist. His most important work, the *Huangji jingshi* (Supreme Principles Governing the World), concerns as its title suggests the underlying patterns and principles of the universe. It is primarily a work of cosmology.

4   The Song dynasty (960–1279) (cont.)

ZHOU DUNYI shared Shao Yong's interest in the cosmology of the *Yijing*. However, he did not share Shao's numerological theories, and his cosmological system placed human beings more clearly at the centre of the universe. He served briefly (1046–7) as a teacher of CHENG HAO and CHENG YI (see §5). His two most important works, the *Taiji tushuo* (Diagram Explaining the Supreme Ultimate) and the *Tongshu* (Comprehending the Book of Changes) were instrumental in the development of neo-Confucian metaphysics. Zhu Xi regarded him as the founding figure of the neo-Confucian revival.

In the *Taiji tushuo*, Zhou presents a chart with accompanying commentary explaining how the Supreme Ultimate (*taiji*) contains within itself the two modes of stillness and activity. These give rise to *yin* and *yang* respectively. These produce the *wuxing* (five elements), which in turn generate the two fundamental principles: the heavenly principle, *qian*, and the earthly principle, *kun*. These then produce all the things in the world. Human beings are unique among creatures in that they receive the most pure forms of the five elements and thus are able to play a critical role in both understanding and guiding the course of the universe.

An important feature of Zhou Dunyi's thought concerns the relationship between the unity of the *taiji* and the variety of things in the world. According to Zhou, the *taiji* produces the two fundamental *qi* 'ethers', *yin* and *yang*. As things take shape, they move through a progression of increasing distinctiveness; and yet, while they become separate individual things, all partake of the original unity of *taiji*. Zhou makes this idea explicit in his *Tongshu*, where he talks about how the myriad things are really one and the one is present in each of the myriad things. We can see the ethical implications of this idea in a well-known anecdote about Zhou. He refused to cut the grass in front of his window, saying that he thought of the grass as he thought of himself. The idea that the universe is coextensive with oneself and that its comprehensive unity (*taiji*) is present in each and

every aspect of it, becomes a cornerstone of neo-Confucian thought.

A source of considerable controversy among the neo-Confucians who followed Zhou was his equation of the Supreme Ultimate with *wuji*, the 'infinite' or 'ultimate of non-being'. Both these readings of *wuji* present problems. The first seems to be a tautology; the second seems perilously close to the Daoist claim that existence comes from non-existence, a claim most neo-Confucians would emphatically deny. However, *wuji* can be understood as describing the tenuous state of the universe prior to there being any discrete things present. Zhou would then be saying that this original undifferentiated state is the origin of all things.

Another point of controversy concerns Zhou's claim that one should make *jing* (stillness) one's guiding principle. The idea is that one should cultivate one's mind in order to attain the lucid and tenuous state of the *taiji* itself. The mind then can sympathetically detect the subtle, emerging form and direction of things, and one can act to maintain a state of universal harmony and balance. Cheng Yi, and later Zhu Xi, took exception to this aspect of Zhou's thought and sought to replace his emphasis on 'stillness' with an emphasis on another notion, represented by a different word (also pronounced *jing*) meaning 'reverential attention' (see §§5, 6).

Traditionally, ZHANG ZAI is the second great figure of neo-Confucianism. He was the uncle and teacher of Cheng Hao and Cheng Yi. His most important works include the *Zhengmeng* (Correcting Delusions) and the *Ximing* (Western Inscription). The latter was originally part of the former work, but was inscribed on the west wall of Zhang's study and came to be regarded as a free standing text.

Zhang's thought was based on his interpretation of the *Yijing* and the *Zhongyong*. While he owed much to Zhou Dunyi and Shao Yong, he did not employ the charts that were central to their method of explication, nor did he show any interest in numerology. Zhang's interest in metaphysics was primarily as a guide to morals. He simplified earlier metaphysical theories, arguing that the *taiji* was simply undifferentiated *qi* (ether) which arises from an inchoate, primordial state called *taixu* (the supremely tenuous). The nature of human beings and all things contains all that is in the *taiji* and the human mind can attain knowledge of these things; the self and the universe are fundamentally one. However, in order for people to realize this unity they must attain a state of lucidity, purity and tenuousness, like that of the *taixu* itself, through a process of self-cultivation.

The driving thrust of Zhang's philosophy is this imperative to realize the fundamental unity of human beings with the rest of the universe. Zhang Zai described this goal as the task of forming one body with all things. Perhaps it would be more accurate to say the goal is realizing (both in the sense of grasping it intellectually and manifesting it personally) the underlying unity between the self and the universe. This idea is expressed beautifully in the opening section of his famous *Ximing*:

> Heaven is my father, earth my mother; even an insignificant creature such as I finds an intimate place between them. And so, all that fills the universe I take as my body and what gives it direction I take as my nature. All people are my brothers and sisters, all creatures my companions.
>
> (*Ximing*)

5 The Song dynasty (960–1279) (cont.)

CHENG HAO and CHENG YI were brothers responsible for the mature statement of neo-Confucianism. They elevated the notion of *li* ('pattern' or 'principle') to a pre-eminent position and identified the 'pattern' within things and events with *tianli* (heavenly principle), the pattern of the entire universe. Here we see an explicit statement of the idea (discussed in §2 above) of the universe being present in each of its parts. Cheng Yi is credited with the famous dictum: '*Li* is one but its manifestations are many.' The Chengs also explicitly equate this universal pattern or principle with *xing* (nature) and *xin* (mind) (see XING; XIN (HEART-AND-MIND)).

The Chengs do not talk about the notion of *taiji* and show little concern with how the universe evolved. Their metaphysical scheme consists of two fundamental notions: *li* (pattern) and *qi* (ether) (see LI; QI). They are dualists but of a special kind. While they believe the universe is composed of these two constituents, they insist that *li* cannot be found apart from *qi*, and qi without li would lack any shape or meaning. In a sense, the distinction between them is logical and not actual. For both brothers, the mind is *li*, and we come to understand the things of the world when we match up the *li* in our minds with the *li* of individual things and events (thus explaining the notorious problem of how we can recognize something as right). Most people are born with impure endowments of *qi* which prevents the *li* of their minds from properly matching up with things. Moral self-cultivation is the process of refining one's *qi* to remove the impediments to the *li* within. The ultimate result is complete and perfect knowledge of both self and the world.

The brothers differ most in their views concerning how to carry out this process of self-cultivation. Cheng Hao was the more mystical of the two and

emphasized the power of moral intuition (in the sense of a feeling rather than an insight). He believed in a universal, creative spirit of life, *ren* (benevolence), which permeates all things just as *qi* permeates one's body. Playing on the multiple senses of the word *ren*, he likened an 'unfeeling' (that is, non-benevolent) person to one with an 'unfeeling' (paralyzed) limb. Neither realizes the unifying 'oneness' of themselves (in the case of the former, this involves failing to feel that he is 'one body' with all things). For Cheng Hao, the task is to locate and pay attention to this inner feeling and allow it to guide one throughout one's life.

Cheng Yi presented a more developed and detailed philosophical system. His method of self-cultivation urges one to awaken the *li* within the mind by perceiving the *li* within the world. One could do this by carefully attending to one's daily affairs, but since the classic texts of Confucianism present these 'patterns' in their clearest and most accessible form, the primary source for such understanding was study of the classics. In either case, as one came to understand a given *li* one was to *tui* ('extend' or 'infer') its interconnection with other *li* until one achieved a complete and comprehensive understanding of them all. This process must be carried out with an attitude of *jing* (reverential attention) in order to insure that one's knowledge is affectively appropriate as well as cognitively accurate. Such knowledge is *zhenzhi* (real knowledge) as opposed to *changzhi* (ordinary knowledge) (see KNOWLEDGE, CONCEPT OF). Cheng Yi illustrates this distinction with an allegory about people who 'know' (that is, they have heard) that tigers are dangerous versus one who 'knows' because he has been mauled.

Both brothers employ a scheme of learning sketched in another text that was to become central to neo-Confucianism, the *Daxue* (Great Learning). One was to *zhizhi* (extend knowledge) by *gewu* (investigating things). For Cheng Hao, this involved a regimen of introspection and internal self scrutiny with the aim of correcting any errant thoughts. For Cheng Yi, the process was more externally directed: one came to understand the world by a careful inspection of paradigmatic cases in the classics and practical problem solving in one's own life (see MORAL EDUCATION; MORAL DEVELOPMENT; SELF-CULTIVATION IN CHINESE PHILOSOPHY).

6 The Song dynasty (960–1279) (cont.)

ZHU XI is rightfully regarded as the greatest neo-Confucian synthesizer. While he drew a great deal of his thought from Cheng Yi (see §5), he gave it novel form and introduced significant innovations of his own design. The system of thought that emerged quickly became one of the two primary 'schools' of neo-Confucianism: Cheng–Zhu Learning or *lixue*, the 'Learning of Principle'.

Zhu reintroduced Zhou Dunyi's term *taiji* (see §4) and explained that it is the sum of all the *li* in the universe. It exists before the universe comes into being and is reflected in every aspect of reality. He illustrated this latter point with the metaphor of the moon being reflected in countless bodies of water. Zhu was a stronger dualist than Cheng Yi, insisting that *li* existed before the universe did and would remain even if it were destroyed. However, at times he presents this as merely a notional, not real, possibility. For all practical purposes, one can never find *li* and *qi* apart from one another. This question generated a long and acrimonious debate among later neo-Confucians in China and Korea.

Zhu also emphasized a distinction between *daoxin* (the mind of the Way) and *renxin* (the human mind). The former was pure *li* and hence perfect; the latter was *li* embedded in *qi* and hence necessarily obscured and prone to error. The concept of *daoxin* was in a certain sense a limiting notion. Zhu did believe that people could attain this level of refinement (and become a sage), but even the minds of sages are a mixture of *li* and *qi* (albeit an extremely refined and limpid *qi*), and so they are still susceptible to error should they grow complacent. Given this view, even the sage must engage in a life of constant moral scrutiny.

Among Zhu Xi's many innovations was his grouping together of four texts, the *Analects*, *Mencius*, *Zhongyong* and *Daxue*, as a set called the 'Four Books'. This set soon became the core of neo-Confucian learning. Zhu's text and commentaries to the Four Books served as the basis for public education and the civil service examinations from 1313 until 1905. Zhu also helped to shape the Chinese education system by working to establish *shuyuan* (academies), Confucian institutions modelled on Buddhist monastic schools. These served a critical role in the neo-Confucian tradition until they were absorbed into a system of state schools during the Qing dynasty.

Zhu Xi also established the notion of *daotong*, the 'transmission of the Way', as a central neo-Confucian concern. It was he who argued that the orthodox understanding of Confucius' teaching had been lost after Mencius and only recently retrieved by Zhou Dunyi, then handed down through Zhang Zai, the Cheng brothers and (by implication) to Zhu himself. Zhu's influence on later Confucian thinking and Chinese society cannot be overstated. His view of the later tradition and its place in the larger context of Chinese history still greatly influences contemporary scholarship on Chinese philosophy throughout the world.

LU XIANGSHAN represented what became the main alternative 'school' within neo-Confucianism known as *xinxue*, the 'learning of the mind'. It was later associated with the thought of Wang Yangming (see §9) and so also came to be called 'Lu–Wang Learning'. Lu's metaphysical disagreements with Zhu Xi are slight but significant. They mainly concern the issue of the nature of the mind: Zhu held that the mind was *li* embedded in *qi*, whereas Lu insisted that the mind is *li*. In a related disagreement, Lu rejected Zhu's distinction between the 'mind of the Way' and the 'human mind', arguing that there is only one mind and that it is principle. These doctrinal differences reflect deep and important disagreements about the character of human nature and the proper method of moral self-cultivation. Lu believed that our true mind is an innate moral mind which we can access and bring to bear in all our thoughts and action. The deluded mind exists only because of a kind of self-deception regarding our true nature.

Lu saw Zhu Xi's strong dichotomy between *li* and *qi* as establishing a corresponding dichotomy between moral knowledge and human desire. Lu thought that if one embraced this dichotomy, one would come to see self-cultivation in terms of the suppression of one's emotions and the accumulation of disconnected empirical facts about the world instead of the discovery and cultivation of one's innate moral feelings. One would then come to confuse broad learning with moral wisdom. The effort to acquire such learning would lead one into competition with others, which would only further obscure one's innate moral feeling of benevolence for all. The knowledge being talked about here was primarily knowledge of classical texts, the kind of knowledge that was the primary prerequisite for success in the civil service exams; and so, another danger associated with Zhu's method was the confusion of the quest for moral wisdom with the search for worldly success.

In contrast to Zhu, Lu argued that the human mind (in particular, our moral sense) was both necessary and sufficient for self-cultivation. Without it, one would fail to develop the affective dimension of 'real knowledge'. If one could only keep one's innate moral sense before one, it would guide one to identify and remove and selfish desires obscuring the *li* of the mind. Lu's difference with Zhu can be seen in his attitude towards the classics. Lu was not opposed to study of the classics *per se*, but he thought that a deep and personal understanding of some small part of them was preferable to the comprehensive knowledge Zhu Xi recommended. In particular, Lu advocated coming to a personal understanding, a kind of *verstehen*, of the mind of the sages as revealed in the classics. His position follows easily from his belief in a transpersonal 'mind' shared by all people and is neatly summed up in his well-known maxim regarding study of the classics: 'If only one understands what is fundamental, the six classics are all one's footnotes' (see CHINESE CLASSICS; XIN (HEART-AND-MIND); SELF-CULTIVATION IN CHINESE PHILOSOPHY).

The differences between Lu and Zhu were made clear in two debates between them, held at Goose Lake Monastery in 1175. In these debates, the intimate relationship between their metaphysical differences and their views on moral self-cultivation are evident. Lu accused Zhu Xi of ignoring the task of *zundexing* (honoring the virtuous nature) at the expense of *dao wenxue* (pursuing inquiry and study). In effect, he was accusing Zhu of forsaking what was commonly regarded as the most fundamental tenant of Confucianism: the innate goodness of human nature. In reply, Zhu accused Lu of mistaking his own subjective view of things as universal truth. In essence, this was to accuse Lu of the ultimate neo-Confucian error: selfishness.

7 The Yuan dynasty (1280–1368)

The Yuan dynasty marked the beginning of nearly one hundred years of Mongol rule over China. During this period, elite Chinese culture gave way to the nomadic, tribal customs of the conquering Mongols. In addition, the Chinese were exposed to a variety of other, equally alien cultural influences that came in the wake of far-ranging Mongol conquests. At the same time, Chinese influences were carried along in the flow of Mongol victories and spread to other lands.

While Mongol influence was strong at the court and higher echelons of Chinese society, it often coexisted peacefully with indigenous Chinese beliefs and practices and probably had little influence on the lives of the vast majority of Chinese. On the one hand, this was the result of the Mongol practice of general non-intervention in local customs and practices, due in part to their inability to manage their immense realm on a local level and in part to their tendency to tolerate diversity as long as it posed no threat. On the other hand, this policy was simply a function of the substantial numerical superiority of the Chinese. Like earlier conquerors of China, the Mongols realized that existing Confucian institutions were indispensable for ruling their newly-gained empire. These institutions helped preserve much of neo-Confucian thought and even contributed to its acceptance as the orthodox state ideology and its spread to foreign lands.

Cheng–Zhu Learning did particularly well during this period and in 1313 was officially adopted as the state orthodoxy. The reason for the triumph of this 'school' of neo-Confucianism and the decline of the teachings of Lu Xiangshan had a good deal to do with the relative superiority of Zhu Xi's system as a basis for the civil service examinations. It was much more detailed, systematic and accessible. Zhu had composed extensive, meticulous and persuasive commentaries on all of the Chinese classics. He had provided a handy summary of Confucian learning in the form of the text of and accompanying commentaries on the Four Books, and he had also produced numerous anthologies and primers of Confucian learning. One of these, the *Xiaoxue* (Elementary Learning), intended for the moral education of the young, found wide appeal among the Mongols themselves.

Zhu Xi's thought provided a well-defined system that was basically quite conservative in nature, well-suited to the role of a bureaucratic ideology under occupation. This is not intended to slight the genuinely moral aspects of almost all of Zhu Xi's writings; had his philosophy not provided concerned Chinese intellectuals with a powerful moral calling, it would undoubtedly not have succeeded as well as it did throughout the Yuan dynasty and on into our own time. Its great power lay precisely in its ability to channel moral and patriotic feelings in constructive directions under a variety of circumstances. Given the situation at the time, Zhu's philosophy provided a way for the Chinese to continue their own culture and to a significant degree Sinicize the conquering Mongols. However, Zhu Xi's philosophy is not easy to see as a revolutionary creed, and during the Yuan dynasty we see little if any of the philosophical creativity and debate that marked the preceding dynasty and the one to follow.

8 The Ming dynasty (1368–1644)

The Ming period marked a revival and development of Lu Xiangshan's challenge to the Cheng–Zhu orthodoxy. One of the earliest figures in this movement was Chen Xianzhang, also known as Chen Baisha (1428–1500). Chen argued that the strong dualism of the Cheng–Zhu school did not reflect the central neo-Confucian belief in the inherent unity between human beings and the universe. In particular, the strong distinction between *li* and *qi* tended to value speculative theory and the intellect at the expense of practical concerns and the emotions. This resulted in a general distrust of feeling and intuition and a gross overemphasis on the intellect and study of the classics as the proper methods of moral self-cultivation.

Chen argued for the inherent unity of human beings and the universe. He also promoted the idea that human beings spontaneously move in harmony with the natural realm and fail to do so only when they impose their own selfish ideas upon the world. In this latter view in particular, as well as in several other aspects of Chen's thought, one can see the influence of the early Daoist philosopher ZHUANGZI.

Chen's criticism of the Cheng–Zhu school's over-reliance on intellect and study and his belief in the reliability of spontaneous intuitions to guide human action shifted the focus of moral self-cultivation away from study of the classics and speculative philosophy and towardss reflection and self-scrutiny. One could describe this as a shift towards 'subjectivity', but only with the qualification that he believed the intuitions of properly cultivated individuals would agree in every significant respect. He was not advocating individual expression in the modern Western sense of expressing one's unique individuality; he was encouraging the discovery and personal expression of a shared, transpersonal mind. Any strong sense that one's actions were uniquely one's own was a sign of selfishness – not of the moral mind. Chen's views greatly diminished the prestige of the classics as the ultimate source of moral knowledge. In his view, individuals possessed a moral sense that was at least equal in value as a moral guide.

A related feature of Chen's views is his belief that moral judgments are highly context-sensitive. The difficult situations one encounters in life are so complex, nuanced and specific that no appeal to rules or precedents could ever provide adequate guidance. Fortunately, each person possesses an inherent moral guide which one can make contact with and engage through a process of reflection and inner self-scrutiny. This aspect of Chen's thought further eroded the status of the classics and with it the plausibility of the Cheng–Zhu school's entire approach to moral self-cultivation.

9 The Ming dynasty (1368–1644) (cont.)

Many of these ideas were taken up and developed into a powerful challenge to the Cheng–Zhu school by the most important Ming thinker, WANG YANGMING. Like Chen, Wang emphasized that the goal of moral self-cultivation was to realize that one was 'one body' with all things. Also like Chen, he believed in an innate faculty of moral intuition and the critical need to rely upon this faculty in making moral judgments. And like both Lu Xiangshan and Chen, Wang believed that the mind itself is *li* (principle) (see LI). However, Wang developed these ideas in novel ways and combined them with others of his own design to produce a much more sophisticated and powerful philosophical system than either of these earlier thinkers.

Wang borrowed a term of art from Mencius in order to describe our innate and infallible moral sense: *liangzhi* (pure knowing). *Liangzhi* is an ever-present faculty that will spontaneously guide us in making proper moral judgments if only we can succeed in eliminating the selfish desires which normally obstruct it. We eliminate these by bringing them to complete awareness, where they are consumed by the light of *liangzhi*. The task is to maintain a constant state of internal scrutiny, monitoring our nascent thoughts to ferret out and eliminate any existing or emerging selfish thoughts.

Given this picture, Wang took issue with Zhu Xi's teachings on moral self-cultivation (see §6). Zhu believed that the major focus of one's effort should lie in coming to understand *li* by engaging in *gewu*, the 'investigation of things' (in other words, investigating the principles in the classics and in the world). Wang first objected to Zhu Xi's emendation and rearrangement of the text of the *Daxue* in support of this view, and advocated the original form of this classic. According to Wang, the original text shows that *gewu* is not a preliminary step in a process of acquiring knowledge of *li*; rather, it refers to the act of preserving the inherent integrity of the mind by 'correcting one's thoughts'. The task of moral self-cultivation thus does not rely upon the acquisition of knowledge through empirical inquiry, but rather the restoration and preservation of the mind through the elimination of incorrect (that is, selfish) thoughts (see SELF-CULTIVATION IN CHINESE PHILOSOPHY).

According to Zhu Xi's interpretation of the text, one is to first cultivate one's virtue in order to care for all people. Wang insisted that these are simply different aspects of the same event. One cannot cultivate oneself *without* caring for others, and properly caring for others *is* cultivating oneself. Zhu Xi's view created a false division between the moral mind and the universe; Wang insisted that they were one. Zhu Xi's view also created a division between moral knowledge and action which Wang insisted was both wrong and pernicious. Wang's response to Zhu on this issue resulted in his most well-known teaching: the unity of knowledge and action.

Wang relied upon the distinction, first developed by Cheng Yi, between 'real knowledge' and 'ordinary knowledge' to argue that anyone who really knew any moral truth must necessarily act upon it. Such action was a necessary constituent of real knowledge. One actually had to engage in filial activity in order to know what filial piety really is, and all those who possessed such knowledge would spontaneously act in accordance with their knowledge when faced with an appropriate situation. People who claim to know filial piety but do not act filially simply do not really know.

Wang saw his approach as addressing the most severe consequence of the Cheng–Zhu view. Wang believed that Zhu Xi's approach led people to regard moral self-cultivation as one thing and the affairs of their lives as another. Wang saw Zhu as counselling people to study the classics and calm themselves through quiet sitting in order to improve themselves morally, and then go out and face the world. Wang insisted that this could never work. First, like Lu and Chen before him, he insisted that the moral problems we face are extremely context-sensitive; no appeal to precedents or rules of conduct can provide us with the guidance we need. As Wang was fond of pointing out, the sages had no such precedents when they acted.

Wang's deeper objection concerned the efficacy of Zhu Xi's method of self-cultivation. Wang did not believe that studying moral theory or contemplating moral paradigms contributed to one's moral development. Such pursuits often had the exact opposite result, for they easily became sources of additional selfish thoughts. In order to improve oneself morally, one needed to work on the actual moral problems of one's own life. Only these engaged one both cognitively and affectively, and only solving such 'real' problems would result in moral improvement.

This antinomian aspect of Wang's thought opened up moral self-cultivation to a much wider range of people, for one no longer needed to be a highly-educated intellectual to grasp the true meaning of the classics (in fact, such an approach would actually lead one farther from self-cultivation). It also gave to his thought an existential flavour; one was made profoundly aware of the weight of one's individual responsibility for one's own moral well-being. The anxiety of such an awareness may even have been critical to gaining true moral understanding. However, Wang's 'existentialism' differs in significant ways from most of its Western advocates. Unlike KIERKEGAARD, Wang held 'God' to be within each individual and reflected in every feature of the universe; unlike SARTRE, existence for Wang does not precede essence for they are one and the same: the mind *is* principle. Properly cultivated individuals faced with similar situations would render similar judgments.

The idea that the mind itself is *li* led Wang to one of his most controversial teachings, known as the Four Sentence Teaching. In his *Chuanxilu* (Instructions for Practical Living), he said, 'There is neither good nor bad in the mind itself. Good and bad are the activity of thoughts. To know good and bad is pure knowing.

To do good and eliminate bad is *gewu* [correcting one's thoughts]'. The first sentence of this teaching seems to contradict not only the central neo-Confucian belief in the innate goodness of the mind, but also Wang's own claims about *liangzhi*. Perhaps Wang is saying that in itself the mind, being the sum of all the principles in the world, is simply how things are in their natural state. In such a state the predicates good and bad are simply inappropriate; they apply only in cases where there is an agent striving either to do good or bad actions. But the mind in itself has no intentions; it just is as it is. Similarly, the people who attain the highest state of moral self-cultivation are not aware that they are doing good. Those who have such thoughts are still striving for goodness and run the risk of becoming 'obscured' by selfish attachment to their own moral progress. The actions of sages, on the other hand, simply happen *through* them. Thus while the actions that result from the fully cultivated mind (that is, the mind itself) will all be good when seen from the perspective of those who observe them, the mind itself is neither good nor bad. Even to say that what the mind does is good is to view its actions from the perspective of the unenlightened. While this view of things profoundly diminishes a person's sense of individual agency, it also lends to their actions a remarkable feeling of necessity.

In the closing years of the Ming dynasty, Wang's ideas – in particular the Four Sentence Teaching – were interpreted by several of his later followers as warranting idiosyncratic judgments of right and wrong. Several of these followers became quite controversial, and a few even died in prison. Later neo-Confucians were to blame these individuals and, by implication, Wang himself for the eventual downfall of the dynasty. While such claims are clearly absurd, they do reveal the perception among the educated elite that the more radical of Wang's later followers showed a degree of independence that many found uncomfortable if not dangerous. These thinkers threatened the order and hierarchy characteristic of Confucian society and advocated such 'radical' ideas as the intellectual and moral equality of women. With the fall of the Ming, these ideas and the intellectual tendencies that gave rise to them came to a halt in a general and dramatic reaction against what was viewed as the Song–Ming drift into radical subjectivism. In its place emerged a movement that again called for a return to 'true' Confucianism based upon a solid 'objective' approach to the classics.

10 The Qing dynasty (1644–1911)

When the Manchus conquered China and established the Qing Dynasty, Chinese intellectuals once more found themselves facing the problem of how to explain the failure of the Confucian Way. Again, their answer was that the Way had been misunderstood and poorly practised. So began a prolonged and wide-ranging attack on the whole of the neo-Confucian tradition, from the Song through the Ming. One of the first and most important figures in this new movement was WANG FUZHI.

Wang attacked both the Cheng–Zhu and Lu–Wang schools. Most of his objections turn on his rejection of their basic metaphysical schemes. He insisted that there was no *li* ('pattern' or 'principle') apart from *qi* (ether). *Li* is simply the 'pattern' of 'actual things and events'. Wang rejected the notion that there exists something called the *taiji* or anything like it which is the sum of all *li* and the related claim that all things somehow reflect all the *li* in the world. This of course meant that he also rejected the Lu–Wang school's equation of principle and mind. He believed that both schools tended to reify *li*, turning people's attention away from the actual things and events in the world and towards the search for some fanciful, ultimate *li*. He further believed that this 'other-worldly' speculation was a direct consequence of Daoist and Buddhist corruption of Confucianism and the primary cause of the defeat of the Chinese at the hands of the Manchus.

Wang's views had further quite profound implications. For example, while he admitted that the actual things and events in the world tended to fall into natural types and patterns and are related through an ongoing process of evolution, his strong denial of any ahistorical universal 'principles' and his belief in the steady historical improvement of social institutions and practices led him to advocate quite radical notions of social reform.

The next important figure in the Qing dynasty is Yan Yuan. Like Wang Fuzhi, he rejected both of the Song–Ming Schools. One of his main arguments against the Song Confucians rests upon his claim that they mistook the meaning of the word *wen* (culture), interpreting it instead as 'writing'. The Chinese graph he is referring to appears throughout the classics and can have either of these meanings, but Yan argued that Confucius' primary interest was 'culture'. Song neo-Confucians mistakenly believed that they were following Confucius when they engaged in the extensive writing of commentaries and explanatory essays on the classics. Yan responded by saying that Confucius only engaged in these activities when it became evident that no ruler in his time would employ him and put the Way into practice. He turned to the task of preserving the *dao* only when faced with this intractable fate; and he did so after having mastered the *dao* through years of diligent practice.

Yan advocated a return to the institutions and practices of the sages, and on this issue he differed dramatically from Wang Fuzhi and shows important similarities to XUNZI. One should practise the six arts which Confucius had taught: ceremony, music, archery, charioteering, reading and mathematics. Such concrete practice would lead one to sagehood. For Yan, *gewu* was neither the discovery of some underlying 'principle' (Zhu Xi) nor the rectification of one's 'thoughts' (Wang Yangming). It was the task of mastering the skills and abilities of the sages. For Yan, sages were individuals of sound mind, spirit and body: men of action. Yan harshly criticized the Confucians of his day for being effeminate and ineffective intellectuals, and he saw their personal moral failure manifested in the defeat of the Chinese state. Like many Confucians, Yan believed that those who were really following the Way could not but create a flourishing, peaceful and strong society. At times he almost seems to be arguing for a kind of pragmatism. However, what appears as a 'pragmatic' appeal is the widely held Confucian belief in the efficacy of the Way. In the face of defeat at the hands of the Manchus, Yan's natural response was that his predecessors had lost the true Way.

11 The Qing dynasty (1644–1911) (cont.)

The greatest philosopher of the Qing dynasty was DAI ZHEN. Dai had a lifelong dedication to philosophy, but until recently was not appreciated for his philosophical contributions. He was however a highly respected mathematician, geographer, astronomer and philologist. This is largely a result of the particular *Zeitgeist* of the Qing, which had a profound appreciation of 'hard sciences' such as textual study and little tolerance for speculative philosophy. Ahead of his time, Dai denied this distinction.

One can gain a significant insight into Dai's views by studying the form of his two major philosophical works: the *Yuanshan* (On the Good) and the *Mengzi ziyi shuzheng* (The Meaning of Terms in the Mencius Explained and Verified). Both of these are works of philosophical philology, commentaries on the meaning of key philosophical terms taken from the Confucian classics, which argue against common interpretations and provide both argument and philological evidence for a new view. Since Dai believed that the classics were the key to understanding the *dao*, his philosophical method necessarily contained a strong philological component. For one cannot understand the classics without understanding the words of these texts, and only sound philological method allows one to do this. On the other hand, Dai insisted that philological inquiry only had value when employed in the service of philosophy, for all inquiry should be directed towards an understanding of the *dao*.

His philological method reflects or perhaps more accurately prefigures his philosophical views. Dai believed one clearly cannot rely upon raw intuition in deciding the meaning of a term; one must resort to careful study of its uses throughout the classics. As one refines one's initial theory in the light of different cases, one moves closer to the correct meaning, the one that accounts for all the cases. This approach is clearly manifested in the two works cited above, where he provides extensive evidence to argue against both the Cheng–Zhu and Lu–Wang interpretations of the key terms of Confucian philosophy. Dai convincingly demonstrates how the interpretations of both schools are not attested in the classical sources and further argues for their Daoist and Buddhist origins. Both the Cheng–Zhu and Lu–Wang schools were overly subjective in the sense that they read into the classical texts their own personal views. This is one example of a general type of error that was the focus of much of Dai's attention.

For Dai, the most common error people make is to mistake their private 'opinions' (*yijian*) as 'unchanging standards' (*buyi zhize*). This applies to determining the meaning of a philosophical term as well as to making an ethical judgment; for Dai, these were but two sides of a very thin coin. In the case of ethical standards, one moved from 'opinion' to 'unchanging standard' by applying the Confucian Golden Rule: not doing to others what one would not want done to oneself (see CONFUCIUS). This mirrors the logic of moving from one's initial impression of what a term means to the correct interpretation: both involve a progression from personal opinion to a comprehensive or universal view. In the specific case of ethical judgments, Dai believed that this movement led one from what is 'spontaneous' (*ziran*) to what is 'necessary' (*biran*). That is, one begins with one's spontaneous reaction to a situation and, through an appeal to the Golden Rule, tests this reaction to see if it passes muster as a universal standard. If it does then the reaction is certified as 'correct', something that one 'necessarily' must do. If it fails this test, it is revealed as merely one's own selfish 'opinion' (see CONFUCIAN PHILOSOPHY, CHINESE).

Dai offered a remarkably novel and powerful interpretation of the Confucian vision. He is rare if not unique among Confucians for his strongly rational and intellectualist approach towards moral self-cultivation. Yet, while he provided compelling criticisms of the Daoist and Buddhist elements within earlier neo-Confucian thought, he himself was not

without such influences. Unlike early Confucians who believed that one needed to acquire or at least extend and expand one's moral sensibility, Dai seems to have held that one already possesses the ability to make proper moral judgments. The problem for him is not that we lack the proper sense, but rather that we also have many improper reactions that must be identified and eliminated.

It is tempting to see Dai as one step away from a kind of Kantian view of ethics with his appeal to a type of universalizability criterion (see KANT, I.), but this would be to misrepresent Dai's thought. For one thing, he believed in an inextricable link between philosophy and philology: one could not find ethical truth apart from understanding of the classics. Dai did not see the Confucian Golden Rule (itself an idea derived from the classics) as free-standing; it did not generate all and only correct ethical judgments. It was a winnowing process to determine which among our spontaneous reactions were in fact in accord with the *dao*. These reactions were feelings about the rightness or wrongness of a given act, and if they were found to be genuine 'necessary' moral feelings, then this recognition produced a profound feeling of joy within the individual. Dai was very much a Confucian defending his tradition.

12 Conclusion

This survey of neo-Confucian thinkers is necessarily selective in terms of the figures covered. It also is confined to what might be called pre-modern philosophers. In the closing period of the Qing dynasty several extremely interesting and innovative thinkers such as Kang Youwei, Tan Sitong and, in the twentieth century, Feng Yulan produced new versions of Confucian philosophy which incorporated and synthesized their understanding of Western philosophy, religion and science. These new forms of Confucian thought continue to be developed in contemporary times, but as they represent a new and distinct stage in the Confucian tradition, they warrant a separate and detailed study in their own right.

See also: CHENG HAO; CHENG YI; CHINESE CLASSICS; BUDDHIST PHILOSOPHY, CHINESE; CONFUCIAN PHILOSOPHY, CHINESE; CHINESE PHILOSOPHY; HISTORY, CHINESE THEORIES OF; DAI ZHEN; DAOIST PHILOSOPHY; KNOWLEDGE, CONCEPT OF; LI; LU XIANGSHAN; MENCIUS; MORAL EDUCATION; MORAL DEVELOPMENT; QI; SELF-CULTIVATION IN CHINESE PHILOSOPHY; SHAO YONG; WANG FUZHI; WANG YANGMING; XUNZI; ZHANG ZAI; ZHOU DUNYI; ZHU XI

References and further reading

Birdwhistell, A.D. (1989) *Transition to Neo-Confucianism*, Stanford, CA: Stanford University Press. (An intellectual historical account of Shao Yong and his thought with philosophical sensibility.)

Black, A.H. (1989) *Man and Nature in the Philosophical Thought of Wang Fu-chih*, Seattle, WA: University of Washington Press. (An intellectual historical account of Wang Fuzhi and his thought.)

Chan Wing-tsit (1963) *A Source Book in Chinese Philosophy*, Princeton, NJ: Princeton University Press. (Selective translations and brief introductions of most of the major neo-Confucian thinkers.)

—— (trans.) (1963) *Instructions for Practical Living and Other Neo-Confucian Writings by Wang Yang-ming*, New York: Columbia University Press. (A translation of Wang's most important works.)

—— (ed.) (1986) *Chu Hsi and Neo-Confucianism*, Honolulu, HI: University of Hawaii Press. (An anthology of essays on Zhu Xi and his thought. Note in particular Graham's contribution.)

Elman, B. (1984) *From Philosophy to Philology*, Cambridge, MA: Harvard University Press. (An insightful historical account of the cultural and institutional context of Qing Dynasty Confucians.)

Ewell, J.W., Jr (1990) 'Reinventing the Way: Dai Zhen's Evidential Commentary on the Meanings of Terms in Mencius (1777)', Ph.D. dissertation, University of California at Berkeley. (The best translation of Dai Zhen's most important work; includes a long introduction.)

Gardner, D.K. (1990) *Learning to be a Sage: Selections from the Conversations of Master Chu, Arranged Topically*, Berkeley, CA: University of California Press. (Translation with commentary of selections from Zhu Xi's works.)

Graham, A.C. (1992) *Two Chinese Philosophers*, La Salle, IL: Open Court. (The best study available on the Cheng brothers, containing many translated passages. Philosophically astute though it does not demonstrate a full appreciation of the role played by Buddhist and Daoist philosophy).

Huang Siu-chi (1977) *Lu Hsiang-shan: A Twelfth Century Chinese Idealist Philosopher*, Westport, CT: Hyperion Press. (A brief and quite dated study of Lu Xiangshan's thought. Still useful.)

Ivanhoe, P.J. (1990) *Ethics in the Confucian Tradition: The Thought of Mencius and Wang Yang-ming*, Atlanta, GA: Scholars Press. (A comparative study that seeks to provide a philosophical introduction to the thought of both Mencius and Wang which illustrates the contrasts as well as the continuities between them.)

—— (1993) *Confucian Moral Self-cultivation*, Frankfurt: Peter Lang. (A study of the origin and development of this characteristically Chinese philosophical concern in the Confucian tradition. Chapters 4–6 are devoted to Zhu Xi, Wang Yangming and Dai Zhen.)

Kasoff, I.E. (1984) *The Thought of Chang Tsai (1020–1077)*, Cambridge: Cambridge University Press. (A sinological study of Zhang Zai.)

Metzger, T.A. (1977) *Escape From Predicament*, New York: Columbia University Press. (An insightful study of neo-Confucianism. One of the few works that shows the proper appreciation of their metaphysical commitments and the relationship of these to their ethical views.)

Nivison, D.S. (1973) 'Moral Decision in Wang Yang-ming: The Problem of Chinese "existentialism"' *Philosophy East and West* 23: 121–38. (A very helpful study demonstrating that there are at best thin similarities between Wang and Western existentialists.)

Tu Weiming (1976) *Neo-Confucian Thought in Action: Wang Yang-Ming's Youth (1472–1509)*, Berkeley, CA: University of California Press. (A detailed historical study of Wang Yangming's early life and his struggle to attain sagehood.)

PHILIP J. IVANHOE

NEO-KANTIANISM

In contrast to earlier research, which chose to distinguish up to seven schools of thought within the field of Neo-Kantianism, more recent scholarship takes two basic movements as its starting point: the Marburg School and the Southwest German School, which are based respectively on systematically oriented works on Kant published during the 1870s and 1880s by Hermann Cohen and Wilhelm Windelband.

Cohen held that Kant's concern in all three Critiques was to reveal those a priori moments which above all give rise to the domains of scientific experience, morality and aesthetics. Windelband on the other hand held that Kant's achievement lay in the attempt to create a critical science of norms which, instead of giving a genetic explanation of the norms of logic, morality and aesthetics, aimed instead to elucidate their validity. In both approaches, an initial phase during which Kant's doctrines were appropriated subsequently developed into the production of systems. Thus Cohen published a 'System of Philosophy' during the early years of the twentieth century, which consisted of the Logik der reinen Erkenntnis (Logic of Pure Knowl-

edge) (1902), the Ethik des reinen Willens *(Ethics of Pure Will) (1904) and the* Ästhetik des reinen Gefühls *(Aesthetics of Pure Feeling) (1912) and which radicalized the operative approach of his work on Kant. Later, Cohen conceived a* Religion der Vernunft aus den Quellen des Judentums *(Religion of Reason from the Sources of Judaism) (1919). Windelband, on the other hand, who made a name for himself primarily in the sphere of the history of philosophy, understood philosophy to be essentially concerned with value, anchored in transcendental consciousness. He emphatically linked the classical division of philosophy into logic, ethics and aesthetics to the values of Truth, Goodness and Beauty and also tried to situate the philosophy of religion in this context.*

Apart from Cohen, the Marburg School is represented by Paul Natorp and Ernst Cassirer, whose early works followed Cohen's philosophical views (compare Natorp's interpretation of the Platonic doctrine of ideas and Cassirer's history of the problem of knowledge), but whose later works modified his approach. Nevertheless, their extensions and developments can also be explained within the framework of the original Marburg doctrines. The ontological turn which Natorp undertook in his later years can be seen as a radicalization of Cohen's principle of origin, which Natorp believed could not be expressed in terms of pure intellectual positing, and the operative moment introduced by Cohen lives on as a theory of creative formation in Cassirer's theory of symbolic forms.

In addition to Windelband, the Southwest German school of Neo-Kantianism is represented by Heinrich Rickert, Emil Lask, Jonas Cohn and Bruno Bauch. Windelband instigated the systematic approach of the Southwest School, but it was left to Rickert to develop it fully. Unlike Windelband, who traced the difference between history and science back to the difference between the idiographic and the nomothetic methods, Rickert distinguished between the individualizing concepts of history and the generalizing concepts of science. During his middle period he turned his attention to the problem of articulating a system of values. In his later works, Rickert also turned towards ontology, a development which should not necessarily be interpreted as a break with the constitutional theories of his early years. In concrete terms, building on his earlier theories concerning the constitutive role of concepts in experience, Rickert henceforth distinguishes not only the realm of scientific and cultural objects and the sphere of values, but also the further ontological domains of the world of the free subject and the metaphysical world, which is the object of faith and which can only be comprehended by thinking in symbols.

Lask's theoretical philosophy was characterized by a turn to objectivism. In contrast to the classical Neo-Kantian conception of knowledge, according to which everything given is determined by the forms of cognition, Lask sees matter as that element which determines meaning. Accordingly, at the centre of his theory of knowledge is not the subject's activity in constituting the object, but the subject's openness to the object. In the final stage of his philosophy, however, he once more attributed to the subject an autonomous role in the actualization of knowledge. Cohn contributed to Southwest German Neo-Kantianism not only his Allgemeine ästhetik *(General Theory of Aesthetics) (1901), but also works on the philosophy of culture and education as well as on the systematic articulation of values and the problem of reality. During the 1920s Cohn moved towards dialectics. In contrast to Hegel, however, he understood this to mean critical dialectics inasmuch as it does not aim to sublate or overcome opposition, but merely sets itself the unending task of attempting to resolve irreconcilable contradictions.*

Finally, Bauch can be regarded as the most essentially synthetic thinker of the Southwest German Neo-Kantian school. He tried to demonstrate the inseparable connectedness of individual problems which had generally been treated separately. Apart from his great Kantian monographs, these ideas are also put forward in his systematic works on the questions of theoretical and practical philosophy, such as his study Wahrheit, Wert und Wirklichkeit *(Truth, Value and Reality) (1923) and his* Grundzüge der Ethik *(Fundamentals of Ethics) (1935).*

Despite the one-sidedness of its reception of Kant's doctrines, Neo-Kantianism was important for the momentum it gave to research into Kantian philosophy during the twentieth century. Its systematic achievement lies in its development of the normative concept of validity and its programmatic outline for a philosophy of culture.

1   **Delimitations and affiliations**
2   **The origins of Neo-Kantianism**
3-5 **The Marburg School: Cohen, Natorp and Cassirer**
6-8 **The Southwest German School: Windelband, Rickert, Lask, Cohn and Bauch**
9   **The significance of Neo-Kantianism**

1   Delimitations and affiliations

The term 'Neo-Kantianism' arose in the 1870s and owes its origins to the need to characterize that overall reassessment of the theories of Immanuel KANT which was then taking place in various different forms. The terminological problem concerns how broadly or narrowly the expression should be applied. Earlier research tended to work with definitions which encompassed ever-increasing circles. Thus T.K. Oesterreich claimed to distinguish seven different approaches to Neo-Kantianism: a physiological approach (of Hermann von HELMHOLTZ and Friedrich Albert LANGE), a metaphysical approach (of Otto Liebmann and Johannes Volkelt), a realistic approach (of Alois Riehl), a logicist approach (of Hermann COHEN, Paul Natorp and Ernst CASSIRER), an approach based on a theory of values (of Wilhelm Windelband and Heinrich Rickert), a relativist approach (of Georg SIMMEL) and a psychological approach (of Leonhard Nelson). This classification is problematic for a number of reasons. Not only is it doubtful whether Simmel and Nelson should be included among the Neo-Kantians in the first place; it is also questionable whether the specific attitudes of Lange's particular understanding of Kant justifies his inclusion among the supporters of the physiological approach. Furthermore, it is unfortunate that, in the chronological list of the individual approaches, the metaphysical approach of Liebmann is listed before the logicist Neo-Kantians, for Liebmann's turn towards a metaphysical approach came after the beginning of the Marburg School, which based its theories on a logicist approach. Finally, this list gives no mention of the representatives of the philological approach to the doctrines of Kant. More recent research has moved away from comprehensive definitions of this nature and now distinguishes between the Marburg School and the Southwest German School of Neo-Kantianism, and a Kantian movement which extends beyond these limitations. The latter movement did not remain confined to Germany but could also be found in other European countries such as France (in the philosophy of Charles RENOUVIER) or Italy (with Carlo Cantoni), where it demonstrated its debt to Kant in a variety of ways.

Even if we accept that Neo-Kantianism is restricted to these two main schools, we must ask which writers should be ascribed to which school. To all intents and purposes, the Marburg School is limited to Cohen and Natorp and the Southwest German School to Windelband, Rickert and Emil Lask. However, should one include among the Neo-Kantians Cassirer in his middle and later periods along with Jonas Cohn and Bruno Bauch, though they are both writers whose important works were mostly published after the First World War? There is no consensus among Neo-Kantian scholars on this point. Some writers operate with a very narrow definition of Neo-Kantianism, while others apply the term in a much wider sense. The representatives of the first position argue that the First World War marked the end of the Neo-Kantian movement. Therefore they take all publications which appeared after the end of the First World War and illustrated a Neo-Kantian approach as in one way or another influenced by Neo-Kantian thought. The scholars who adopt a wider definition of Neo-Kantianism distinguish on the other hand between first- and second-generation Neo-Kantianism and assume in this context that Neo-Kantianism did not simply come to an end after the First World War. The first approach is supported by the fact that the First World War did also represent the end of an era in the philosophical world. After 1918 other philosophical trends gained ground and forced Neo-Kantianism out of the dominant position which it had enjoyed since the late nineteenth and early twentieth century, at least in Germany. Significant factors in this respect are the phenomenology of Edmund HUSSERL, who demonstrated the validity of transcendental thought in a different way from the Neo-Kantians; a logical positivism which challenged Neo-Kantianism on its own ground, in other words, epistemology and theory of science; attempts at a metaphysical interpretation of Kant which then developed; and cultural-critical philosophies of life which dominated public discussion. At the same time, a number of movements set themselves apart from the main trend. Nikolai Hartmann distanced himself from his Neo-Kantian origins in his attempt to re-establish an ontology, as did Martin HEIDEGGER in his attempt to find a solution to the question of being. Richard Kroner, a pupil of Rickert, consciously made the transition to Neo-Hegelianism (see HEGELIANISM §6). However, if one considers not only the changed background conditions but also the internal theoretical development within both schools, it will become clear that the second position also has good arguments to support it. For it cannot be maintained that the followers of the Neo-Kantian school failed to react to the changes in philosophical climate as a whole. This is shown not only in the later works of Natorp and Rickert: the philosophical thought of Cassirer, Bauch and Cohn must also be interpreted in the light of this approach. It is clear that these developments in the growth of the theory are just as much a part of the history of Neo-Kantianism as the phase of theoretical systems produced before the First World War. For this reason, this extended definition of Neo-Kantianism will be taken as the starting point for the following discussion.

Cohen, Natorp and Cassirer, on the one hand, and Windelband, Rickert, Lask, Bauch and Cohn, on the other, are merely the most important representatives of Neo-Kantianism. Apart from them, a large number of other philosophers can be included among the followers of both main trends, or at least associated with them. Earlier research assumed a close-knit school containing the various proponents of these doctrines; more recent approaches, however, have been more cautious in this respect. As far as Marburg Neo-Kantianism is concerned, it is possible to distinguish between a group of scholars closely associated with Cohen, including – apart from Natorp and Cassirer – Karl Vorländer and Albert Görland, and a wider circle of disciples among whom were Hartmann and Heinz Heimsoeth. None the less, Natorp's attitude to a term like 'The Marburg School' was decidedly ambivalent. Although he accepted this definition for the purposes of academic debate, he wanted it to be understood merely as a term of collaborative association.

The relationships within the Southwest German School of Neo-Kantianism are similar. The labelling of Windelband and Rickert as the two leaders of the school is problematic inasmuch as Windelband had only sketched his systematic position, whereas Rickert must be credited with the true development of the Southwest German system. A circle of disciples also grew up around the latter in Heidelberg, among whom were Eugen Herrigel and Hermann Glockner. Furthermore, as in the case of Marburg Neo-Kantianism, a whole series of writers, such as Georg LUKÁCS and Max WEBER, found important inspiration in the philosophy of Southwest German Neo-Kantianism. There are also links with the work of Gottlob FREGE. Finally, of considerable significance for the spread of Southwest German Neo-Kantianism was the fact that the periodical *Logos* provided a publication outlet from 1910.

For an understanding of Neo-Kantianism it is important to recall that the discussion of specifically Neo-Kantian ideas also continued outside the framework of the Marburg and Southwest German approaches. Richl's pupil Richard Hönigswald adopted, on the one hand, a critical approach to the Neo-Kantian logic of scientific method, because in his eyes the latter was based upon an undifferentiated concept of experience and pursued a different path from the Neo-Kantian approach to subjectivity by projecting a theory of the concrete subject within the context of his philosophical psychology. On the other hand, he continued to endorse the Neo-Kantian concept of normative validity, even though he attempted to develop this concept further in terms of a novel theory concerning the differentiation of spheres of validity.

Hönigswald, moreover, like his Jewish colleagues Cohn and Cassirer, was deprived of his professorial chair and had to emigrate after Hitler's rise to power. The expulsion of the leading representatives of Neo-Kantianism from German universities was mainly responsible for bringing to a halt philosophical research into the problems posed within the Neo-Kantian doctrines, and the Second World War exacerbated this situation. In the post-war development of German philosophy only a few philosophers, such as Wolfgang Cramer, Hans Wagner and Rudolf Zocher, chose to continue in this theoretical tradition.

2 The origins of Neo-Kantianism

In earlier research the overriding tendency was to trace Neo-Kantianism back to certain founding figures. Thus, for example, the role of inaugurator of the Neo-Kantian movement was attributed to Liebmann. This view was based mainly on his early work *Kant und die Epigonen* (Kant and the Epigones) (1865), in which he had accused all branches of post-Kantian philosophy of working with a variously interpreted notion of the thing-in-itself. In the true Kantian view this was a false approach, and in each case he concluded his criticism of the schools of idealism (Fichte, Schelling, Hegel), realism (Herbart), empiricism (Fries) and transcendentalism (Schopenhauer) with a demand that scholars should return to Kant. In the same way, Helmholtz and Lange were credited with having founded the Neo-Kantian movement, since they both based their doctrines on the Kantian a priori, which they admittedly (mis)interpreted in terms of innate species-specific capacities (*Gattungsorganisation*), turning their backs on the simplistic objectivism popular during the 1850s in the context of the debate concerning materialism. Finally, Eduard Zeller was also frequently associated with the origins of Neo-Kantianism. In his lecture *Über die Bedeutung und Aufgabe der Erkenntnistheorie* (On the Meaning and Purpose of the Theory of Knowledge) (1877) he was the first philosopher to win academic acceptance for epistemology or the theory of knowledge, which played a central role within the framework of the Neo-Kantian system.

Modern research sees the birth of Neo-Kantianism as being more clearly determined by certain developments which were characteristic of the philosophy of the post-Hegelian period. In the first instance a central role was played by a departure from pure thought and from the systematic philosophy (*Systemphilosophie*) of the idealist tradition, as exemplified in the works of Friedrich SCHLEIERMACHER or Adolf Trendelenburg. The latter are important for the development of Neo-Kantianism, first because the concept of theory of science is articulated as early as the second edition of Trendelenburg's *Logische Untersuchungen* (Logical Investigations) (1840), and second because with his *Dialektik* (Lectures on Dialectics) (1839) Schleiermacher can be regarded as the originator of the theory of knowledge. Further-more, the thesis that German philosophy from Fichte to Hegel pursued a mistaken course which could only be corrected by establishing a direct link with the Kantian tradition was not first formulated by Liebmann, but can be found in the earlier doctrines of Christian Weisse and Friedrich Beneke. A third problem area in post-Hegelian philosophy is the relationship between philosophy and the individual sciences. The attempts by Helmholtz and Lange to provide Kant's theory of knowledge with a sensory-physiological basis against the background of re-instating cooperation between philosophy and science was just one way of overcoming the problem. There was also the opposite tendency, which aimed at rejecting the inclusion of individual and special scientific knowledge in an attempt to maintain the autonomy of philosophy. This attitude can be found in the works of Kuno Fischer, Liebmann's teacher, who propagated a neo-idealistic interpretation of Kant in the manner of Fichte and played an important role in the foundation of Southwest German Neo-Kantianism. Fourth, in addition to the critical approach to the idealist point of view there was also the tendency to insist on the necessity for a critique of knowledge in the hope that it would finally provide a means of settling disputes about funda-mental questions of worldview or '*Weltanschauung*'. Such a tendency is to be found not only in the works of Zeller and Lange, but also in the those of J.B. Meyer, a hitherto largely unknown philosopher in the field of Neo-Kantian research. In his essay *Über Sinn und Wert des Kritizismus* (On the Meaning of Criticism) (1857), Meyer emphasizes that the relation-ship between body and soul belongs, like all meta-physical questions, to those problems which transcend the horizon of our possible knowledge, and that the significance of '*kritizistischen Kant*' ('Kant the Criti-cist') lay in the way in which he had demonstrated this fact. Similarly, in his programmatic deliberations concerning the theory of knowledge, Zeller repudiated the exploitation of specific, scientific knowledge for the purpose of establishing a worldview, just as Lange was eventually concerned to refuse universal claims based on such a worldview, of whatever kind they were.

Therefore, even if the extensive pre-history of the Kantian movement is taken into account, there can be no doubt that its real breakthrough occurred during the 1870s and 1880s. In 1871 Cohen published his work *Kants Theorie der Erfahrung* (Kant's Theory of Experience), which set out to establish Kant's doc-trine of the a priori. Cohen's central thesis is that only those things can be seen to be objective which are produced a priori by subjectivity. Thus he under-stands Kant's *Critique of Pure Reason* to be a theory of experience in which Kant's aim was to reveal those a priori moments which make scientific experience possible. In the same vein he maintains that in ethics and aesthetics Kant was also concerned with the revelation of those a priori elements which in the first instance generate the sphere of morality and art. This concept of generation thus provided the basis for a new form of systematic appropriation of Kant which was significantly different from the subjective-idealis-tic Kant interpretation of Kuno Fischer or Lange's naturalistic interpretation. Cohen considers both interpretations inadequate because neither manages to provide a stable basis for the sphere of the ideal. In the case of Lange in particular, Cohen criticized the fact that, although he attempted in his *Geschichte des Materialismus* (History of Materialism) to save ethics in opposition to the mechanistic-deterministic world-view, he nevertheless failed to justify the idealist point of view in a scientific manner. Cohen believed that he had found the means of achieving this in his concept of generation. In his view, modern natural science is the best evidence for the fact that reality as objective has been created by us, since we are only capable of knowing that which we have put into things.

This realist attitude was given a different emphasis in the Kantian research of Friedrich Paulsen and Alois Riehl. Paulsen's *Versuch einer Entwicklungs-geschichte der Kantischen Erkenntnistheorie* (Attempt at a History of the Development of Kant's Theory of Knowledge) (1875) aims, as the title indicates, at a historical and systematic reconstruction and not, like Cohen's work, at a new and improved presentation of Kant's doctrine of the a priori. Thus Paulsen's goal was not a productive assimilation of Kantian thought against a background of the specifically nineteenth-century conflict between idealism and materialism, but an attempt to understand the philosophy of Kant from its historical context, against a background of the contrast between rationalism and empiricism during the eighteenth century. Riehl's three-volume work *Der philosophische Kritizismus und seine Be-deutung für die positive Wissenschaft* (Philosophical Criticism and its Significance for Positive Science) (1876–7) aimed to place Kant within a tradition of critical thought which began with John Locke. In his view, Kant's critical position tends towards a 'Phe-nomenalism of Intuitions' which is at the same time a 'Realism of Things'. Riehl regarded the epistemolo-gical scepticism represented by David Hume as the precursor of such a position, since it can be seen as a means of securing a positive content for thought. Thus, in his presentation of Kant, Riehl undertakes an attempt to bridge the gap between Kantianism and positivism. This approach can also be seen in his history of philosophy, which assumes as its basic concept a parallelism between scientific and philosophical history. Benno Erdmann completes the spectrum of Kant interpretations during this period. His works use a purely historical approach to reconstruction and rejected all attempts to update Kantian thought.

Finally, during this period Windelband founded the Kantian approach of the Southwest German School, and this represents a second type of systematic Kantian assimilation beside that of Cohen. Mindful of the overwhelming significance of Kant for all subsequent philosophical endeavours, Windelband investigates the nature of the critical method put forward by Kant. According to him, what is essential in this respect is the contrast with every type of genetic method. Unlike the genetic method, it is not a question of explaining how certain norms in the realm of logic, ethics and aesthetics were established. Instead, Windelband's critical method questions the correctness of the norms that have come into existence in these areas. In other words, its aim is the clarification of the question of justification. Windelband is convinced that Kant and his three Critiques made a significant contribution to the critical science of norms. Thus philosophy, if it wishes to counter the relativism which inevitably results from a consistent application of the genetic method, is obliged to return to Kant. At the same time, however, Windelband emphasizes that such a 'return' to Kant cannot involve simply a revival of the historically conditioned form of his philosophy, but remains a task for all contemporary engagement with the philosopher from Königsberg: to understand Kant means to go beyond him.

3 The Marburg School: Cohen

Cohen's three-part philosophical system serves as a paradigm for the development of the Marburg School system. It consists of the *Logik der reinen Erkenntnis* (Logic of Pure Knowledge) (1902), the *Ethik des reinen Willens* (Ethics of Pure Will) (1904) and the *Ästhetik des reinen Gefühls* (Aesthetics of Pure Feeling) (1912) and attempts to demonstrate in a consistent manner the point of view of pure generation, that is, creation which does not make appeal to any particular preconceptions.

This is particularly clear in the *Logik*, which forms the first part of his system. Cohen differs markedly from Kant in refusing to preface his logic with a doctrine of sensibility. Indeed, his attempt at logic can be characterized by the claim, 'We take thought as our starting point. Thought cannot have any origin outside itself.' According to the 'Logic of Origin' as

conceived by Cohen, therefore, thought is grounded solely in itself and is thus a hypothesis in the original Greek sense. The denial of the Kantian theorem of the dual origin of knowledge (intuition and thought) results in the abandonment not only of the transcendental aesthetic as a doctrine of the principles of sensibility, but also of the transcendental deduction (see KANT, I. §§5–6). What remains of Kant's approach is no more than the programme of a transcendental method for the foundation of science, which is obliged to take the existence of science as its starting point. In his doctrine of judgment Cohen differentiates between judgments involving the laws of thought (Origin, Identity, Contradiction), of mathematics (Reality, Plurality, Totality), of mathematical natural science (Substance, Law and Concept) and of method (Possibility, Reality, Necessity). In his doctrine of categories, he starts from the necessary incompleteness and essential extendibility of the system of categories, since he is convinced that new scientific problems will also make new categories necessary.

Cohen sees ethics, which he seeks to base on the fact that a science of right exists, as a doctrine of humanity. The ideal collective subject which ethics deals with is humankind as a whole. It is important that this term is not taken to mean the human species in a biological sense, but rather an ethical expression encompassing humans as moral individuals. Such an interpretation of the concepts of universality also permits a new definition of the concept for the individual as the idea of the human being in every person. However, the medium which allows us to establish a correlation between these two concepts is the state. For within the state the common will can be realized through the harmony achieved between the actions of the individual and the actions of everyone else. The model of the state which Cohen takes as the basis for his discussion has a cooperative constitution. The essential characteristic of cooperatives is that the common will is legally capable of action. This distinguishes it from communities which only recognize the ruling will of the individual. Against this background Cohen developed the concept of an ethical socialism which aims at overcoming the existing 'state dominated by the estates and the ruling classes' (Cohen 1904: 582), without deteriorating, like the materialist historical perspective, into economic determinism.

In *Ästhetik*, Cohen modifies his system, no longer linking aesthetics back to the fact of an existing science of art, but rather attempting to deduce the a priori law-like character of pure feeling directly from works of art. In doing so he specifically defines pure feeling itself as the feeling of love towards human nature. This is the presupposition not only of the creation of art but also of its reception. With regard to the objectivity of aesthetic experience, Cohen emphasizes that although there are no further objects as such apart from nature and morality, it is possible for the aesthetic orientation of consciousness to shape and transform these spheres of objectivity and thus 'bring forth beauty as a new object' (Cohen 1899: 100).

It is a feature of Cohen's development that during his later years he devoted much of his attention to questions concerning the philosophy of religion. Although during his Marburg years he had argued for the incorporation of religion into ethics, he later recognized that religion also makes a special contribution to the problem of culture. In his essay *Der Begriff der Religion im System der Philosophie* (The Concept of Religion in the Philosophical System) (1915) he attempts to determine this contribution on the basis of the three systematic disciplines of logic, ethics and aesthetics. If logic is concerned with the being of nature, then religion is concerned with the unique being of God, and if the God of ethics stands for the endless continuation of the moral tasks of the human race, then the God of religion must ensure that the moral striving of the individual does not ultimately come to nothing. If aesthetic love is related to humankind as a type, then religious love embraces the human being as individual. Irrespective of this special contribution to culture in its entirety which is accomplished by religion, the latter is not regarded as being independent of culture, but rather as possessing a special character within the framework of culture as a whole. The quest for a non-reductionist understanding of religion is also one of the dominant themes in Cohen's posthumous work *Religion der Vernunft aus den Quellen des Judentums* (*Religion of Reason out of the Sources of Judaism*) (1919). It cannot be said, however, that Cohen achieved a position of ultimate clarity with regard to religion. Evidence for this can be found, for example, in the interpretative dispute concerning an idealistic or dialogical interpretation of the term 'correlation', which plays a central role in Cohen's later philosophy of religion. Is Cohen envisaging simply a relationship between two concepts which are mutually required (in much the same way as the concept of the sinful individual necessarily calls for the concept of God, who forgives sins), or does he have in mind a real contrast of two partners as is suggested by the definition of prayer as 'dialogue with God'? Furthermore, there is a tension in Cohen's posthumous work between the ethically orientated interpretation of the religious statements which he attempts to provide and the simultaneous reversion to statements reflecting a metaphysical doctrine of divinity. On the one hand he

states that the doctrine of divine attributes should not be interpreted in terms of ontological statements about God, but rather in terms of statements which make clear how human behaviour should be governed. On the other hand, Cohen characterizes God as the one and only unique Being as opposed to all Becoming, as the Infinite as opposed to all spatial limitations, as the source of all movement, and as the Eternal in contrast to all Change. Cohen was unable to carry out his plans for a fourth work to complete his 'System of Philosophy', a psychology conceived on a science of the unity of cultural consciousness.

4 The Marburg School: Natorp

Natorp was able to present his thoughts in a clearer and more comprehensible form than Cohen, and hence he was largely responsible for the spread of the doctrines of the Marburg School of Neo-Kantianism. Unlike Cohen, he is not famous for a comprehensive range of studies on Kant. None the less, he also made a name for himself by virtue of his works on the history of philosophy. Of greatest relevance in this context is his controversial and subsequently modified interpretation of Plato, in which he understood the Platonic 'idea' as a hypothesis from the perspective of the modern concept of the laws of nature.

In his systematic thought, Natorp at first operated systematically within the terms laid down by Cohen. None the less, even in *Kant und die Marburger Schule* (Kant and the Marburg School) (1912a) he emphasized that philosophy did not merely refer back to scientific facts (natural sciences and humanities) but was also related fundamentally to morality, art and religion. Its subject is therefore 'the entire creative work of culture', which is expressed in the 'theoretical-scientific description of phenomenal appearance' as well as in the 'practical formation of social orders', 'in artistic creativity' and 'in the inmost forms...of religious life'.

In his *Allgemeine Psychologie nach kritischer Methode* (General Psychology According to the Critical Method) (1912b) Natorp goes further than Cohen in setting a subjective foundation for knowledge alongside the objective one. He is guided by the following consideration: in every phenomenal appearance we can differentiate between a relationship to the object and a relationship to our consciousness. The former is the subject matter of the theory of knowledge which establishes the laws of cognitive objectification; the latter is the subject matter of psychology, which proceeds back to the objective phenomenon of knowledge from the already accomplished objectifications, since the 'immediacy of consciousness' does not permit any immediate psychological comprehension.

In his doctrine of knowledge, Natorp attempts to interpret Cohen's concept of origin in the context of Kant's synthetic unity. According to this theory, that which characterizes the thinking process is the basic structure of the relation between the one and the many. In this fundamental relation there are two tendencies: a differentiating tendency, which aims at quantity, and a unifying tendency, which aims at quality. Quantity results when the manifold as such is emphasized in the fundamental relation; quality results, on the other hand, when thought is directed towards the unity of the manifold. The relation arises with the establishment of interdependency between the unities, which are determined in a quantitative-qualitative manner, whereby the modality determines the contribution of each level of the 'thought-functions' constituting the object to the knowledge of that object. In contrast to Cohen, Natorp does not base this system of fundamental logical functions on a system of sciences, although he asserts that the systematic logical structure it contains will prove its validity in the fact that the basic scientific facts can be connected with the logical ones. In fact, Natorp starts out from a reciprocal interrelationship between science and the logic of knowing. While the latter tends towards the centre, in other words towards the basic law of synthetic unity, the former tends towards the periphery, that is, the manifold diversity of the particular instances of knowledge. The difference between this and Cohen's position also becomes clear since, for Natorp, the reason belonging to science proves itself in the foundation of the objective sciences from the perspective of synthetic unity, while for Cohen reason proves itself in demonstrating the origin of all knowledge out of pure thought.

Natorp's social educational theories, which he developed after becoming professor of philosophy and education in Marburg, were very influential. The subtitle of *Sozialpädagogik* (1899), his major work on the subject, is *Theorie der Willenserziehung auf der Grundlage der Gemeinschaft* (Theory of the Formation of Will on the Basis of the Community): it makes clear that Natorp sees the formation of will as the most important aspect of education, particularly inasmuch as the former is determined by life within the community and has an effect on the community. In the development of will Natorp distinguishes three stages of activity: instinct, will and the rational will. Whereas instinct is wholly governed by the sensory object, will on the other hand provides for the possibility of choice in this respect. True moral orientation, however, occurs only in the case of the rational will. Although a restructuring of society in accordance with the principles of ethical socialism implies changes within its economic and political institutions, Natorp none the less sees the real motor for change in the sphere of social education, since only education can bring about a change of consciousness.

At the heart of Natorp's later philosophy stands his attempt at a new definition of the doctrine of categories, whose goal is a unified foundation of every kind of positing of an object ('*Gegenstandssetzung*'). Natorp starts concretely with a closed system of basic categories – modality, relation and individuation – which are to serve as the basis for the construction of an open system of categories. By adopting this distinction between categories and basic categories he attempts to do justice both to Kant's assumption of a comprehensible number of basic concepts of understanding and to the fact that the process of investigation means that a number of categories cannot be determined in advance. Natorp's system of basic categories is also built up in a different way from Kant's, inasmuch as he begins here with the categories of modality (Possibility, Necessity and Reality) and places the categories of Quantity, Quality and the intuitive forms of Space and Time in the third group of categories. The second group of categories (Substance, Causation and Interaction) corresponds on the other hand with the original Kantian architectonic which Natorp had mainly used as a starting point in his early attempt at a system of categories, *Die logischen Grundlagen der exakten Wissenschaften* (The Logical Foundations of the Concrete Sciences) (1910). The order of categories within the individual groups occurs in each case according to the scheme: universality, particularization, individuality. This structure applies not only to the theoretical sphere but also to the practical and what Natorp calls the 'poetic' (that is, productive) spheres. Natorp's later philosophy is characterized by the insight that the process of categorization assumes the acceptance of the as yet totally undetermined original fact of 'it is' and ends with the determination of the individual as the concrete objective existent. This ontological modification of Natorp's late philosophy need not necessarily be interpreted – as it frequently is – as a break with the Marburg theoretical outlook; it can also be seen in terms of a radicalization of the original Marburg theory.

5   The Marburg School: Cassirer

Like Cohen and Natorp, Cassirer, who was Cohen's principal disciple, made a name for himself initially in the history of philosophy. After his doctoral thesis under Cohen on *Leibniz' System in seinen wissenschaftlichen Grundlagen* (Leibniz's System in its Scientific Foundations) (1902), he enjoyed immediate success with the first two volumes of his four-volume *Geschichte des Erkenntnisproblems* (History of the Problem of Knowledge) (1906–20). In it he demonstrated in particular the emergence of a new definition of knowledge during the Renaissance which reached its climax in the philosophy of Kant. Thus Cassirer attempted to make plausible Cohen's claim concerning the harmony of his basic ideas with the historical development of scientific and philosophical thought.

Cassirer also turned his attention to the theory of the exact sciences, publishing his *Substanzbegriff und Funktionsbegriff* (The Concept of Substance and the Concept of Function) (1910) at the same time as Natorp's investigation *Die Logischen Grundlagen der exakten Wissenschaften*. Here, Cassirer makes it plain that any attempt to represent the whole of knowledge ends in certain ultimate form-concepts which express the various possible ways in which contents can be related to one another. In this respect, what we call the object of knowledge is dissolved in a network of relations. What applies to the concept of the object in general is also relevant for the concept of the objects with which the individual sciences operate. They too do not represent an absolute beyond the logical forms of knowledge, but that which is to be expressed through them is nothing but a functional relation within these forms. In concrete terms, Cassirer sees in the serial ordering which manifests itself in the relations of space and time, of size and number and of dynamic interaction and interrelationship of events, the moment in the process of knowledge which determines its real empirical content. The logical determination of the object of knowledge thus leads ultimately to an original relation which can be understood in various ways: as a relation of form and matter, of the universal and particular, and of being or normative validity. What is important is that this relation between reciprocally determining elements remains irreducible. Taken as a whole, what distinguishes Cassirer's concept of knowledge is the insight that concepts are intellectual constructs which cannot be understood as an imitation of the objective given but as 'symbols for relations and functional connections within the real'.

A third major theme in Cassirer's philosophical work is the philosophy of culture. His *Philosophie der symbolischen Formen* (*The Philosophy of Symbolic Forms*) (1923–9) is relevant in this respect. Cassirer understands by the term 'knowledge' not only that mathematical-scientific form of knowledge which remained paradigmatic for the Marburg School, but rather 'any intellectual activity in which we construct a world for ourselves with a characteristic form, order and particular character' (1956: 208). The concept of symbolic form implies on the one hand a formal function, for it is essential that 'an intellectual meaning is attached to a concrete sensory sign and internally allocated to this sign' (1956: 175). On the other hand, Cassirer also marks out in this manner as characteristic areas of such formation, such concrete areas of culture as language, myth, art and science. Although the symbolic activity linked to signs is that activity which runs through all productive achievements of consciousness as a unifying theme, further differentiations with regard to the basic functions of the symbolic form will result. Here Cassirer distinguishes between the function of expression, the function of presentation and the function of meaning. The almost physical function of expression is particularly relevant in the case of myth, the distancing presentation function is the preserve of language, and the function of meaning is found in particular in the world of science. The systematic implications of Cassirer's theory of symbolic forms are further developed in his final works, *An Essay on Man* (1944) and *The Myth of the State* (1946), produced after his emigration to America.

Like the later works of Natorp, the works of Cassirer's middle and later periods raise the question of whether they should really belong to the Marburg School of Neo-Kantianism. This is a subject of lively debate even today. It is certainly the case that Cassirer's middle and late works transformed Cohen's approach, which revolved around the problem of knowledge and science. Similarly, it cannot be maintained that Cassirer in his later development actually abandoned his Neo-Kantian beginnings, for even in his conception of a philosophy of symbolic forms he retains the typical emphasis upon the generative-theoretical approach characteristic of the Marburg School.

6 The Southwest German School: Windelband

Although the real development of the Southwest German system was the work of Rickert, and Windelband merely sketched his systematic approach in a collection of essays with the descriptive title *Präludien* (Preludes) (1884) as well as in his *Einleitung in die Philosophie* (Introduction to Philosophy) (1914), the importance of Windelband as an initiator is not to be underestimated. Windelband understands philosophy as a whole to be concerned with values. He rejects a purely objectivist conception of value and attempts instead to solve the problem of the objectivity of values in a transcendental manner by having recourse to an archetypal consciousness (*Normalbewußtsein*) which is able to make value judgments, and for which the Kantian 'Pure Consciousness' (*Bewußtsein überhaupt*) serves as a foil. He traces the traditional division of philosophy into the disciplines of logic, ethics and aesthetics back to the way in which these disciplines are orientated to the values of Truth, Goodness and Beauty. Like Cohen, Windelband also attributes a special role to religion. According to him, the sphere of human value judgments is exhausted by these logical, ethical and aesthetic values. Religion, whose proper concern is with the sacred, does not represent a separate cultural domain. Correspondingly, the sacred does not represent a specific class of values with universal validity alongside truth, goodness and beauty; it embodies all these values inasmuch as they are all related to a supersensible reality.

Like the philosophers of the Marburg School, Windelband also sees the significance of Kant in his re-establishment of the relationship between science and philosophy. At the same time he criticizes Kant – and this distinguishes him from the Marburg School – for his bias in favour of the mathematically orientated natural sciences. In the face of the triumphant emergence of the historical sciences throughout the nineteenth century he sees this as an anachronism. Therefore his efforts are directed towards bringing out their special structure in contrast to the natural sciences. In his speech as Rector of Strasbourg University he defined his approach: the natural sciences operate with universal, apodeictic judgments. They aim at universal statements, which explains their interest in a reality which always remains constant. Their approach is nomothetic, because their aim is to reveal relationships between laws. The price paid for this method is a tendency to abstraction. The historical sciences mitigate this by means of singular, assertive judgments. They are directed towards the particular, which explains their interest in what reveals itself as a unique, intrinsically determined content of reality. Their approach is idiographic, because what they aim to make visible are concrete configurations. For this reason their procedure depends upon intuitive self-presentation.

The main emphasis of Windelband's publications lay in the sphere of the history of philosophy. He was the author of, among other works, a two-volume *Geschichte der neueren Philosophie* (History of Modern Philosophy) (1878–80) and a *Lehrbuch der Geschichte der Philosophie* (Textbook of the History of Philosophy) (1892), which was continued by Heimsoeth and is still reprinted regularly today. In Windelband's view, the history of philosophy has a threefold task. It should:

1 Establish precisely what can be ascertained concerning the living conditions, the intellectual development and the doctrines of the individual philosophers from the existing sources;

2 Reconstruct from this information the genetic process in such a way that in the case of each philosopher it is possible to understand the relationship of his teachings to those of his predecessor, to the general ideas current at the time, to his individual character, culture and education;

3 To judge from an observation of the whole what value can be ascribed to the teachings which have been discovered and whose origins have been explained in the light of the history of philosophy in its totality.

(Windelband 1902: 13)

7 The Southwest German School: Rickert and Lask

As far as Rickert's philosophical development is concerned, his main interest originally lay in questions related to the theory of knowledge and methodology. In his habilitation essay, *Der Gegenstand der Erkenntnis* (The Object of Knowledge) (1921), he criticizes the customary definition of knowledge, which is based on the opposition between real being and a consciousness which groups such being as it is reflected in our representations. He puts forward instead a new concept of knowledge. His starting point for this is a reflection on the primary aim of knowledge, namely the striving after truth. Truth, for Rickert as for Aristotle, lies not in representation but in judgment. However, even if we have to relinquish the concept of a world that is independent of our representations, if judgment as the locus of truth is to be ascribed a central role in the process of knowledge, this approach will allow us to demonstrate a world that is independent of the judging subject, because every judgment is based on the recognition of an 'ought'. Although this 'ought' represents a transcendental order as far as knowledge is concerned, it is not a matter of the order of a transcendent reality, for what we are able to discover is no more than the correct order belonging to the content of awareness, that is to say 'the relationships of representations to each other, which ought to exist and which must therefore be affirmed'.

In his scientific methodology Rickert does not distinguish as Windelband does between nomothetic and idiographic methods, but rather between generalizing and individualizing concept formation. Even if all terms are general inasmuch as they bind general elements together to form conceptual unities, these unities are of a universal nature in the sphere of the sciences, but individual in the sphere of history. For Rickert, the formation of such individual conceptual unities can be explained by their relationship to universal values. This permits a selection to be made from the immeasurable variety of individual given facts within the world of experience. However, the historian's value-orientated procedure should not be understood as representing a subjective valuation of historical events. It is not the historian's job to pronounce on the worth or lack of worth of a particular event such as the French Revolution, but rather to enquire as to the significance of such an event for the history of Europe as a whole. Admittedly, that such historical concept-formation is not arbitrary naturally presupposes the existence of certain generally recognized cultural values. This conclusion, which Rickert recognized was hardly self-evident in his own period, was none the less essential for his argument. His methodological reflections thus culminate in an objective doctrine of value which claims that values enjoy the ontological mode of 'validity' as distinct from the ontological mode of 'existence'.

In his middle period, Rickert drafted a *System der Philosophie* (Philosophical System), which, however, remained a fragment. In it he conceives of philosophy as articulating a worldview intended to illuminate the meaning of life for us. This, however, involves actually bringing to consciousness the values which make life meaningful. Rickert therefore projects a system of values which he conceives of as an open system. His goal is not 'a complete grasp and enumeration of all valid values', but merely 'a complete formal classification of various types of value' (Oakes 1990: 134). Specifically, this means that he distinguishes between a sphere of contemplative, non-social and substantive values on the one side and a sphere of active, social and personal values on the other.

The attempt to engage with ontological questions is characteristic of Rickert's later phase of thought, yet this need not be interpreted as a break with his original theoretical approach to the problem of transcendental constitution. Indeed, it could be seen as an attempt to pursue this line of thought more deeply. Relevant to Rickert's later philosophy are his *Thesen zum System der Philosophie* (Theses on the Philosophical System) (1932). Here he made it clear that the task of the individual sciences is to comprehend the world of the senses 'either in a universalizing manner (as nature, in so far as it is governed by a system of laws) or in an individualizing manner (as the history of "culture")' (Rickert 1932: 99). On the other hand, he sees a system of values as necessary in order to articulate the intelligible world, because 'meaning and significance can only be properly and rigorously explained by recourse to concepts of value' (1932: 99). Admittedly this 'dualist idea of the world' (*Weltdualismus*) immediately prompts the question of whether there might be an encompassing unity which could bind the two worlds of being and value together. Rickert recognizes this unity of reality and value primarily in the sphere of the non-objectifiable being of human subjects and distinguishes therefore, in addition to the world of experience of sensible and intelligible subjects, a third 'pro-physical' type of worldly being. Of course, the question of the unity of the world is not adequately resolved by this concept. It is impossible to avoid the question concerning a 'transcendent' unity of the world in which value and reality are even more closely connected than in the pro-physical sphere. While in the latter value and reality are only connected through the free acts of the subjects, and otherwise remain separate from one another, here the problem concerns the possibility of an original unity of reality and value in the supersensuous ground of the world. Rickert leaves us in no doubt that this metaphysical transcendence can only be grasped with the aid of symbolic thought, which interprets material taken from this world as a simile or an image for the beyond.

Lask wrote his doctoral thesis under Rickert on *Fichtes Idealismus und die Geschichte* (Fichte's Idealism and History) (1923–4) and then completed his postdoctoral teaching qualification under Windelband with a study of the philosophy of law. This is an important work for the philosophical system of the Southwest German School because in it Lask understood law as an independent sphere of validity and developed at the same time a methodology of the science of law. However, questions of theoretical philosophy stand at the centre of Lask's philosophical works. For him, everything that can be conceived is divided between the categories of existence and validity. Correspondingly it is necessary to distinguish between knowledge of being and knowledge of validity. Form bears validity, while material being, on the other hand, is utterly foreign to form and therefore does not enjoy the status of validity. The sphere of the sensuously given is then revealed as a realm which lacks this status. For what is sensuously given cannot be deduced by means of logical processes, but can only be acknowledged in its factuality.

It is a characteristic of Lask's understanding of the doctrine of form and material being that a particular form of validity no longer bears a direct relationship to the material, but rather corresponds to a specific material to which it clings (as it were). For Lask, therefore, material being functions as an element which determines meaning. By virtue of this theory of the differentiation of meaning, an independence is attributed to the material of knowledge which stands in direct opposition to the classical Neo-Kantian concept of knowledge, according to which the entirety of the given is determined by the forms of cognition. Correspondingly, at the centre of Lask's conception of the subject we find, not the constitutive activity of the subject with respect to objects, but rather the subject given over to the object. For the relationship of form to the material, which the subject is required to comprehend, precedes all subjectivity. Lask's objectivistic tendency can also be clearly seen in the fact that for him validity is in the first instance free of a relationship to the subject. This relationship only arises when validity is experienced by the subject as an 'ought'. Inasmuch as the subject experiences validity in the shape of a demand, then the conflict of values also comes into play. This occurs because the activity demanded of the subject as regards the recognition of the 'ought' can either succeed or fail. If it succeeds, then the truth attained through this activity appears as a positive value; if it fails, as a negative value. The actual relationship to the validity-content occurs as the judging act which connects subject and predicate and simultaneously contains the affirmation and denial of this connection. It is now important for Lask that the truth lies outside the judgment in the configuration of matter and form. The judgment can correspond to this structure or contradict it. Therefore we can only speak of the judgment's appropriateness to truth or untruth, but not of its truth or falsity as such.

During the final phase of his philosophical development Lask abandons such pure objectivism. Knowledge as a subjective act is once again seen as an independent problem area of philosophy, although Lask was not prepared to take back any part of his claim concerning the significance of the objectively true with regard to the process of knowing.

8   The Southwest German School: Cohn and Bauch

Cohn's turn towards dialectics is important for his philosophical development. Cohn defines as 'dialectical' all knowledge which 'uses the appearance, the resolution and the reappearance of contradiction as a means of acquiring knowledge'. In contrast to Hegel, Cohn supports a 'critical' dialectic in that he does not presuppose the dogma of the complete transparency of the world to reason. His dialectic is only a 'thinking towards the absolute', but not the kind of thought which could expound the absolute speculatively.

This conception of thought is also evident in Cohn's treatment of the problem of reality. First he distinguishes between three 'forms of reality': (1) the immediate experience of reality, which in his view is the beginning and the point of departure for all other conceptions of reality and thus also the basis for the process of objectivization, (2) the so-called existing

factual reality, which represents a first stage in the process of objectivization, because here 'the non-sensational aspects of immediate experience' are excluded, and finally (3) physical reality, which as the final stage of the process of objectivization embodies a 'reality of maximum objectivity' (Flach and Holzhey 1980: 59). But what about the unity of reality in the face of these diverging conceptions of reality? According to Cohn, although this unity is the ultimate aim of human knowledge, it remains unrealizable. It therefore remains an idea in the Kantian sense: it retains the character of a task which is as essential to knowledge as it is unachievable. Thus Cohn's posthumously published work, which is focused upon the implications of the theory of knowledge for the concrete sciences, is entitled *Wirklichkeit als Aufgabe* (Reality as Task) (1955).

Cohn is not merely interested in questions of theoretical philosophy, as is shown by his major investigation, *Voraussetzungen und Ziele des Erkennens* (Presuppositions and Goals of Knowledge) (1908). Because in general he understands philosophy as a discipline concerned with questions of value, in addition to the realm of logical value he also investigates the realm of aesthetic values; his *Allgemeine Ästhetik* (General Aesthetics) (1901) presents the 'only major work on aesthetics in the Southwest German School' (Holzhey 1992: 45). Questions concerning the systematization of values are the subject of a major work entitled *Wertwissenschaft* (Science of Values) (1932), in which he rejects the thought of a closed value system and interprets the relationship of values to each other in terms of a 'teleological completion' (*teleologische Ergänzung*).

In connection with the problem of values, Cohn also turned his attention to the philosophy of culture, and on the eve of the First World War he published a paper entitled *Der Sinn der gegenwärtigen Kultur* (The Meaning of Contemporary Culture) (1914). This takes as a starting point the theory that while culture does indeed arise from aspects of human behaviour based on values, it is not created by man's conscious purposive behaviour, because the individual always already finds himself in a specific configuration of cultural life, 'from which he draws substantial content and value' (Cohn 1923: 14), and which he can, of course, seek to transform. With regard to the development of culture in general this produces the following schema: all culture is in the first instance 'bound', that is to say the individual lives totally within the forms which he takes over as being both necessary and self-evident. His consciousness is directed towards interpreting, maintaining and actualizing these forms. In this process his intelligence is strengthened and comes to regard the status quo critically. This means that human beings are presented with new possibilities for shaping their environment, albeit at the price of spiritual homelessness. Against this background, Cohn interprets the present as a time in which the liberated spirit strives to find a new form of fulfilment in life after recognizing this homelessness.

For Cohn, the practical discipline corresponding to the philosophy of culture is pedagogy or theory of education. For this reason he also attempted to establish a philosophical basis for this discipline and saw his treatise *Der Geist der Erziehung* (The Spirit of Education) (1919) as supplementing his study on the meaning of contemporary culture. In his view, the central task of education is the conscious 'development and perpetuation of culture' (*Fortbildung der Kultur*). Education must both encourage the autonomy of the pupil and at the same time ensure their membership of a historical cultural community. This dialectic of liberation and integration is essential to the process of education.

Cohn's importance lies in his development of the initial theories of the Southwest German Neo-Kantianism in the direction of a critical dialectics. Bauch, on the other hand, can be considered as the synthesizer of Southwest German Neo-Kantianism. His major monograph on Kant set out to understand the individual problems of Kant interpretation from the standpoint of the 'Kantian spirit in its entirety'. His systematic works all have a similar aim, suggested by the title of his main philosophical work *Wahrheit, Wert und Wirklichkeit* (Truth, Value and Reality) (1923): he tries to combine various approaches to problems which are generally tackled separately.

On the problem of knowledge, Bauch claims that we must assume a correlation between knowledge of the object and the object of knowledge. Knowledge and object do not simply coincide, but neither can they be completely separated from each other. However, this presupposes that they are both subject to the same conditions. Bauch finds these shared conditions in truth. He analyses individually the structural forms of truth in judgment, category and concept. In the case of judgment he distinguishes between the actual judgment as a 'connection of representations' (*Beziehung der Vorstellungen*), and the logical judgment as an 'objective relationship of validity' (*objektive Geltungsrelation*). The factual judgment can succeed or fail, in other words it is either valid or invalid. It is only valid when it connects up with the validity relation given in the logical judgment. For this, however, it is necessary that it subordinate itself to the latter's validity or, in Bauch's words, that it 'recognizes it'. On the category, Bauch agrees with Kant that 'the category determines

the judgment ... because the judgment is inseparable in its logical significance from the function of unity which the category represents'. Since the category only makes possible a one-sided determination of the object, if we are to arrive at a complete determination then we must appeal to the concept which, in contrast to the category, refers to the object as concretely given in intuitive isolation. However, the concept may not be considered in isolation, but must be seen as part of a network of concepts. Bauch names this network 'idea'.

From the concept of 'idea' Bauch makes the transition to the concept of the 'world', which for him is nothing more than the appearance of the idea. In this context the concept of system also becomes comprehensible together with the concept of the world. If the idea can be thought of as a system of mutually conditioning concepts, then the world can be seen as a 'system or relation of conditional things'. In the final analysis, the world cannot be conceived of without an 'I', a subject which conceives of the world as having arisen from the idea.

In his practical philosophy Bauch assumes that we encounter the ethical principle *qua* value principle in three forms: (1) as a demand on the will which addresses itself to the will of every rational creature, (2) as a demand for action in the light of the fact that there are certain duties which are only meaningful if specific possibilities of acting exist (consider the Hippocratic oath taken by doctors) and (3) as an essential demand, by which he means the obligation of the individual person to realize their specific essential being. Depending on whether the values as tasks and demands apply to the community as a whole or to individual members of the community, Bauch distinguishes between communal and personal values, which can no more be thought of isolated from one another than can the terms 'personality' or 'community'. On the totality of values, Bauch leaves us in no doubt that values form an 'interconnected sphere' and do not exist alone in isolation from each other. Of course this interconnection does not entail enclosure and rigidity. Just as in the development process of knowledge new categories can be created, so the discovery of new values cannot be excluded.

9   The significance of Neo-Kantianism

Neo-Kantianism has often been dismissed as sterile academic philosophy, but this fails to do justice to its real significance. Despite the one-sidedness of its approach, the Neo-Kantian attitude to Kant profoundly influenced the twentieth-century study of Kant's works. From the perspective of systematic philosophy, the significance of Neo-Kantianism lies first in its development of the concept of 'validity' and second in its projected philosophy of culture.

On the first point, the essence of Neo-Kantian thought lies in the strict division it makes between the realm of objects to be grounded and the principles of validity which essentially perform this grounding. According to Neo-Kantianism these principles must show themselves to possess an entirely different character.

If we understand what is principally grounded as the 'world', then the transcendental subject which grounds it principally is 'extramundane'. The consequence of this conception is that all empirical features of the subject must be ascribed to the principal grounded domain, and further that all ontology which regards being as an immediate object of access in itself must be declared obsolete. It was essential to question the radical feasability of the development and transformation of Neo-Kantianism in terms of both the subject and ontology. In the long term, therefore, the issues of the subject and of an ontological presupposition of any kind were equally impossible to ignore.

The significance of the second contribution of Neo-Kantianism, the projected philosophy of culture, lies first in its attempted philosophical reflection on the existence and nature of science. The Marburg School placed its emphasis here on the so-called exact sciences, while the Southwest German School concentrated more on the so-called human sciences. It would be a mistake, however, to reduce the Neo-Kantian philosophy of culture to a specific kind of philosophical theory of value, for Neo-Kantianism devoted itself also to questions of practical philosophy, philosophy of art and philosophy of religion. It is disputed just how far Neo-Kantianism succeeded in its philosophy of culture in gaining a perspective on the political and social reality of its time. It is unquestionable, however, that Neo-Kantianism attempted to advance in this direction, as can clearly be seen, for example, in Cohen's concept of an ethical socialism, Natorp's pedagogy, Cassirer's engagement with the myths of the twentieth century and Cohn's philosophy of culture. Aside from the question of whether these attempts succeeded, however, it cannot be ignored that the school of Neo-Kantianism also included representatives of a regressive and nostalgic conservatism, such as Bruno Bauch, who in their later works openly defended a populist-naturalist position.

Despite the undeniable limitations of the Neo-Kantian systematic approach and the historical distance between Neo-Kantian and contemporary thinkers, the concern and themes of the Neo-Kantian philosophers have lost none of their relevance. For now, as then, the issue at stake is the defence of the autonomy of the subject. Since this was seen to be in danger, the Neo-Kantians of both the Marburg and the Southwest German schools insisted on the generative moment inherent in the scientific and cultural form of objectivization, or on an evaluative element which necessarily comes into play with such objectivization. If philosophy today does not wish to capitulate to the current trend towards the repudiation of the subject, then it must follow the strategy already preached by the Neo-Kantians, namely to return to Kantian insights and develop Kant's thought further in a systematic manner.

See also: COHEN, H.; NISHIDA KITARŌ; NEO-KANTIANISM, RUSSIAN

References and further reading

Primary literature

Bauch, B. (1917) *Immanuel Kant*, Leipzig: Goschen. (General interpretation of Kantian thought from the perspective of the Southwest German School of Neo-Kantianism.)

* —— (1923) *Wahrheit, Wert und Wirklichkeit* (Truth, Value and Reality), Leipzig: Meiner. (Deals with the problems of systematically linking theories of truth, reality and ethics.)

—— (1926) *Die Idee* (The Idea), Leipzig: Reinecke. (Presentation of the Idea as a unity of logical functioning.)

—— (1931) *Selbstdarstellung* (Self-Portrayal), in H. Schwarz (ed.) *Deutsche systematische Philosophie nach ihren Gestaltern* (German Systematic Philosophy According to its Creators), Berlin: Junker & Dünnhaupt, vol. 1, 237–9. (A philosophical autobiography leading up to the 1930s.)

* —— (1935) *Grundzüge der Ethik* (Fundamentals of Ethics), Stuttgart: Kohlhammer. (An outline of the ethics of value-formation.)

* Cassirer, E. (1902) *Leibniz' System in seinen wissenschaftlichen Grundlagen* (Leibniz's System in its Scientific Foundations), Marburg: N.G. Elwertsche Verlagsbuchhandlung. (An epistemological interpretation of Leibniz's thought.)

* —— (1906–20) *Das Erkenntnisproblem in der Philosophie und Wissenschaft der neuen Zeit* (The Problem of Knowledge in the Philosophy and Science of the Modern Age), Berlin: Bruno Cassirer, 4 vols. (A history of epistemology from a scientific-historical perspective.)

* —— (1910) *Substanzbegriff und Funktionsbegriff* (The Concept of Substance and the Concept of Function), Berlin: Bruno Cassirer. (Describes the

transition from the concept of substance to that of function characteristic of modern thought.)

* —— (1923–9) *Philosophie der symbolischen Formen*, Darmstadt, 3 vols, 2nd edn, 1977–85; trans. R. Manheim, *The Philosophy of Symbolic Forms*, New Haven, CT: Yale University Press, 1955. (Outline of a comprehensive cultural philosophy based on his theory of symbolism.)

* —— (1944) *An Essay on Man*, New Haven, CT, and London: Yale University Press. (Outline of a philosophical anthropology.)

* —— (1946) *The Myth of the State*, New Haven, CT: Yale University Press. (Outline of a social philosophy.)

* —— (1956) *Wesen und Wirkung des Symbolbegriffs* (The Nature and Influence of the Concept of Symbol), Darmstadt: Wissenschaftliche Buchgesellschaft. (A collection of important essays on Cassirer's understanding of 'symbol'.)

* Cohen, H. (1871) *Kants Theorie der Erfahrung* (Kant's Theory of Experience), Berlin: Dümmler, 2nd edn, 1885. (Reconstruction of Kant's first critique.)

—— (1877) *Kants Begründung der Ethik* (Kant's Foundation of Ethics), Berlin: Dümmler. (Reconstruction of Kant's second critique.)

—— (1899) *Kants Begründung der Ästhetik* (Kant's Foundation of Aesthetics), Berlin: Dümmler. (Reconstruction of Kant's third critique.)

* —— (1902) *Logik der reinen Erkenntnis* (Logic of Pure Knowledge), Berlin: Bruno Cassirer. (Reconstruction of the foundation of a theory of knowledge.)

* —— (1904) *Ethik des reinen Willens* (Ethics of Pure Will), Berlin: Bruno Cassirer. (Theory of the foundations of ethics.)

* —— (1912) *Ästhetik des reinen Gefühls* (Aesthetics of Pure Feeling), Berlin: Bruno Cassirer, 2 vols. (Theory of the foundations of ethics.)

* —— (1915) *Der Begriff der Religion im System der Philosophie* (The Concept of Religion in the Philosophical System), Gießen: Töpelmann. (Interpretation of the relationship between religious thinking and Neo-Kantian system concepts.)

* —— (1919) *Religion der Vernunft aus den Quellen des Judentums*, Frankfurt am Main: J. Kaufmann; trans. S. Kaplan, *Religion of Reason out of the Sources of Judaism*, New York: Ungar, 1972. (An attempt to synthesize Neo-Kantian systems and Jewish religious thought.)

* Cohn J. (1901) *Allgemeine Ästhetik* (Universal Aesthetics), Leipzig: Engelmann. (Outline of a theory of aesthetics based on moral philosophy.)

* —— (1908) *Voraussetzungen und Ziele des Erkennens* (The Presuppositions and Ends of Knowledge), Leipzig: Engelmann. (Outline of a morally oriented theory of knowledge.)

* —— (1914) *Der Sinn der gegenwärtigen Kultur* (The Meaning of Contemporary Culture), Leipzig: Meiner. (An interpretation of the cultural situation on the eve of the First World War.)

* —— (1919) *Geist der Erziehung. Pädagogik auf philosophischer Grundlage* (The Spirit of Education: Pedagogy on a Philosophical Basis), Leipzig: Teubner. (Outlines an educational philosophy based on moral philosophy.)

* —— (1923) *Selbstdarstellung* (Self-Presentation), in R. Schmidt (ed.) *Die deutsche Philosophie der Gegenwart in Selbstdarstellungen* (Self-Presentation of Contemporary German Philosophy), Leipzig: Meiner, vol. 2, 61–81. (Autobiographical account of Cohn's philosophy until the 1920s.)

—— (1926a) 'Erlebnis, Wirklichkeit, Unwirkliches' (Experience, Reality and the Unreal), *Logos* 15: 194–215. (An essay on the problems of understanding the concept of reality.)

—— (1926b) *Befreien und Binden, Zeitfragen der Erziehung überzeitlich betrachtet* (Liberation and Commitment, Contemporary Questions of Education from a Super-temporal Perspective), Leipzig: Quelle & Meyer. (Collection of essays on educational philosophy.)

—— (1932) *Wertwissenschaft* (Science of Value), Stuttgart: Frommann. (Outline of a systematic moral philosophy.)

* —— (1955) *Wirklichkeit als Aufgabe* (Reality as Task), Stuttgart: Kohlhammer. (Outline of a science of reality.)

* Lange, F.A. (1866) *Geschichte des Materialismus und Kritik seiner Bedeutung in der Gegenwart*, Iserlohn: J. Baedeker; 2nd edn, Iserlohn and Leipzig, J. Baedeker, 1873–5, 2 vols; trans. E.C. Thomas, *History of Materialism*, Boston, MA, Osgood, 1877, 3 vols. (A detailed study of the history of materialism from the ancient Greeks to the 1870s including material on contemporary developments in physics, biology and social theory, and their impact on a Neo-Kantian thought.)

* Lask, E. (1923–4) *Gesammelte Schriften* (Collected Writings), Tübingen: J.C.B. Mohr, 3 vols. (Includes posthumous writings. *Fichtes Idealismus und die Geschichte* (Fichte's Idealism and History), Lask's doctoral thesis referred to in §4, can be found in volume 1, pages 1–273.)

* Liebmann, O. (1865) *Kant und die Epigonen* (Kant and the Epigones), Stuttgart: Carl Schober. (A critique of post-Kantian philosophy and its un-Kantian orientation towards the thing-in-itself.)

* Meyer, J.B. (1857) *Über Sinn und Wert des Kritizismus* (On the Meaning and Value of Critical Philosophy). (Pleads for a self-limitation of philosophy regarding ideological questions.)

Natorp, P. (1884) *Forschungen zur Geschichte des Erkenntnisproblems im Altertum* (Investigations into the History of the Problem of Knowledge in Antiquity), Berlin: Hertz. (An investigation into classical epistemology.)

—— (1899) *Sozialpädagogik* (Social Pedagogy), Stuttgart: Frommann. (Outline of a concept of social pedagogy.)

—— (1902) *Platons Ideenlehre* (Plato's Doctrine of Ideas), Leipzig: Meiner; 2nd edn, 1922. (Epistemological interpretation of Platonic idealism.)

* —— (1910) *Die logischen Grundlagen der exakten Wissenschaften* (The Logical Foundations of the Exact Sciences), Leipzig; Berlin: Teubner. (A study of the foundational problems in the exact sciences.)

—— (1911) *Die Philosophie, ihr Problem und ihre Probleme* (Philosophy, Its Problem and Its Problems), Göttingen: Vandenhoek & Ruprecht. (General overview of philosophy from a Marburg Neo-Kantian perspective.)

* —— (1912a) *Kant und die Marburger Schule*, Berlin: Reuther & Reichard. (Presents the Marburg School's interpretation of Kant.)

* —— (1912b) *Allgemeine Psychologie nach kritischer Methode* (General Psychology According to the Critical Method), Tübingen: J.C.B. Mohr. (Outlines a philosophical psychology.)

—— (1925) *Vorlesungen über praktische Philosophie* (Lectures in Practical Philosophy), Erlangen: Verlag der philosophischen Akademie. (Foundations for a practical philosophy.)

—— (1958) *Philosophische Systematik* (The Systematic Structure of Philosophy), Hamburg: Meiner. (Outlines a theory of categories.)

Paulsen, F. (1875) *Versuch einer Entwicklungsgeschichte der Kantischen Erkenntnistheorie* (Contribution Towards a History of the Development of Kant's Theory of Knowledge), Leipzig: Fues's Verlag (R. Riesland). (Reconstructs the genesis of Kantian epistemology.)

* Rickert, H. (1921) *Der Gegenstand der Erkenntnis* (The Object of Knowledge), Tübingen: J.C.B. Mohr, 5th edn, improved. (Outline of the general foundation of the theory of knowledge.)

—— (1896–1902) *Die Grenzen der naturwissenschaftlichen Begriffsbildung* (The Limits of Scientific Concept Formation), Tübingen: J.C. Mohr, 2 vols. (The classic work of the Southwest German School of Neo-Kantianism on the logic of a historical science.)

—— (1915) *Kulturwissenschaft und Naturwissenschaft*, Tübingen: J.C.B. Mohr, 3rd edn; trans. G. Reisman, *Science and History*, Princeton, NJ: Van Nostrand. (Presents the dualistic epistemology characteristic of the Southwest German School of Neo-Kantianism.)

—— (1920) *Die Philosophie des Lebens* (The Philosophy of Life), Tübingen: J.C.B. Mohr. (Discussion of the philosophy of life.)

—— (1921) *System der Philosophie* (System of Philosophy), Tübingen: J.C.B. Mohr, vol. 1. (Develops a philosophical system, which remained unfinished.)

—— (1930) *Die Logik des Prädikats und das Problem der Ontologie* (Predicate Logic and the Problem of Ontology), Heidelberg: Winters Universitätsbuchhandlung. (Develops a liguistic-philosophical approach to ontology.)

* —— (1932) *Thesen zum System der Philosophie* (Theses on the Systematic Philosophy), *Logos* 4: 97–102. (Sketches a general outline of philosophy.)

—— (1934) *Grundprobleme der Philosophie, Methodologie, Ontologie, Anthropologie* (Fundamental Problems of Philosophy, Methodology, Ontology, Anthropology), Tübingen: J.C.B. Mohr. (Essential philosophical problems from a methodological, ontological and anthropological point of view.)

* Riehl, A. (1876–7) *Der philosophische Kritizismus und seine Bedeutung für die positive Wissenschaft* (Philosophy of Criticism and its Significance for Positive Science), Leipzig: Engelmann Verlag, 3 vols. (Develops of a realistic interpretation of Kant.)

* Schleiermacher, F.D.E. (1839) *Dialektik* (Dialectic), ed. Jonas, Berlin: G. Reimer. (The first post-Kantian attempt to construct a theory of knowledge based on pure thought as well as on sensory perception.)

* Trendelenburg, A. (1840) *Logische Untersuchungen* (Logical Investigations), Leipzig: Hirzel Verlag, 1870, 2 vols. (Develops a non-speculative logic oriented towards the particular sciences.)

* Windelband, W. (1878–80) *Geschichte der neueren Philosophie in ihrem Zusammenhange mit der allgemeinen Kultur und den Wissenschaften* (History of Modern Philosophy in its Relation to General Culture and the Sciences), Leipzig: Breitkopf & Haertel, 2 vols. (A history of philosophy from the Italian Renaissance to the psychologism of Fries and Beneke.)

* —— (1884) *Präludien* (Preludes), Tübingen: J.C.B. Mohr, 2 vols. (A collection of essays on philosophical-historical and systematic questions.)

* —— (1902) *Lehrbuch der Geschichte der Philosophie* (Textbook of the History of Philosophy), Tübingen: J.C.B. Mohr, 17th edn, 1994. (Reviews problems in the history of philosophy.)

* —— (1914) *Einleitung in die Philosophie* (Introduction

to Philosophy), Tübingen: J.C.B. Mohr. (Systematic introduction to moral philosophy.)

* Zeller, E. (1877) *Über Bedeutung und Aufgabe der Erkenntnistheorie* (On the Significance and Task of the Theory of Knowledge), in *Vorträge und Abhandlungen* (Addresses and Essays), Leipzig: Fues's Verlag (R. Reisland), 479–96. (Presents a theory of knowledge as a formal basis for the whole of philosophy.)

Secondary literature

Brelage, M. (1965) *Studien zur Transzendentalphilosophie* (Studies on Transcendental Philosophy), Berlin: de Gruyter. (Places Neo-Kantianism in the context of the problem of 'Transcendental Philosophy and concrete Subjectivity'.)

* Flach, W. and Holzhey, H. (1980) *Erkenntnistheorie und Logik im Neukantianismus* (Theory of Knowledge and Logic in Neo-Kantianism), Hildesheim: Olms. (Contains, apart from a collection of important source texts, an introduction to the theoretical philosophy of Neo-Kantianism.)

* Holzhey, H. (1992) *Der Neukantianismus*, in A. Hügli and P. Lübke (eds) *Philosophie im 20. Jahrhundert* (Philosophy in the Twentieth Century), Hamburg: Rowohlt-Verlag, vol. 1, 19–51.

Holzhey, H. and Orth, E.-W. (1994) *Neukantianismus. Perspektiven und Probleme. Eine Zwischenbilanz der jüngsten Neukantianismusforschung* (Neo-Kantianism: Perspectives and Problems; An Assessment of Contemporary Research into Neo-Kantianism), Hildesheim: Königshausen & Neumann. (Attempt at a summary of recent international research into Neo-Kantianism.)

Köhnke, K.C. (1986) *Entstehung und Aufstieg des Neukantianismus* (The Development and Rise of Neo-Kantianism), Frankfurt am Main: Suhrkamp. (Comprehensive investigation into the beginnings of Neo-Kantianism.)

* Oakes, G. (1990) *Die Grenzen der kulturwissenschaftlichen Begriffsbildung* (The Limits of the Formation of Expression in the History of Culture), Frankfurt am Main: Suhrkamp. (Discusses the relationship of Rickert's philosophy to Weber's methodology.)

Oelkers, J., Schulz, W.K. and Tenorth, H.-E. (1989) *Neukantianismus. Kulturtheorie, Pädagogik und Philosophie* (Neo-Kantianism: Theory of Culture, Pedagogy and Philosophy), Weinheim: Deutscher Studien Verlag. (Contains contributions to an appreciation of Neo-Kantian educational theory.)

Ollig, H.-L. (1987) *Materialien zur Neukantianismus-Diskussion* (Material on the Discussion of Neo-Kantianism), Darmstadt: Wissenschaftliche Buchgesellschaft. (Collection of important essays on research into Neo-Kantianism.)

Willey, T. (1987) *Back to Kant. The Revival of Kantianism in German Social and Historical Thought 1860–1914*, Detroit, MI: Wayne State University Press. (Casts light on the return to Kant in its contemporary context.)

Translated from the German by Jane Michael and Nicholas Walker

HANS-LUDWIG OLLIG

NEO-KANTIANISM, RUSSIAN

A rather amorphous movement, Russian Neo-Kantianism, in the first decades of the twentieth century, found its most visible and enduring representatives in A. Vvedenskii and his student/disciple I. Lapshin, both of St Petersburg University, who together took a distinct stance within the movement as a whole. Both were chiefly concerned with epistemological issues although their respective publications revealed a much wider field of interests. Both maintained an allegiance to the spirit of Kantian philosophy while devoting little attention to the intricacies of the three Kantian Critiques. In addition, at Moscow University G. Chelpanov adhered to the ideality of the Kantian categories although he upheld an ultimate realism. In the social sciences P. Novgorodtsev and B. Kistiakovskii defended positions revealing a significant debt to the Baden School of German Neo-Kantianism, and as such they were deeply involved in methodological investigations. Several others (N. Berdiaev, P. Struve, G. Shpet) within Russia also briefly espoused a Neo-Kantianism after abandoning Marxism and before moving on to a usually more idealistic stance. Still another, younger group a decade later, centred chiefly around the journal Logos, maintained an idiosyncratic, though not fully articulated, amalgam of Kantian and Hegelian doctrines. The Bolshevik Revolution led to a decimation of what remained of the movement within Russia and a dispersal of its members, who became increasingly isolated from current philosophical trends and issues.

1 Overview of the movement

Russian Neo-Kantianism was neither a unified nor a fully self-conscious movement. Largely as the result of being sent to Germany for further graduate study many young Russian-born scholars returned to their homeland imbued with the dominant trend of their host institution. Like their German counterparts (see NEO-KANTIANISM) the Russians themselves often shared little more than a conviction that genuine philosophy must begin, though not necessarily end, with KANT. Also similarly to their German counterparts, the Russian Neo-Kantians were not above quarrelling. Yet with their attention fixed on the scene abroad, particularly in Germany, and with their individual, narrow concerns they usually ignored one another, never developing anything similar to the trenchant mutual critiques we find in the competing German Neo-Kantian schools. Although several Russians showed an impulse to systematization, none, with the possible exception of their last representative (Veideman), ever produced a unified work systematically addressing all major philosophical issues. Nor did the Russian Neo-Kantians pen methodic commentaries on any of the three Kantian 'Critiques' despite one notable excursus into Kant-philology by their leading representative. Partly because they were few in number, but probably more importantly because of the sheer political difficulty of establishing a periodical during the Tsarist era, the Neo-Kantians in Russia had no journal of their own, let alone one for each separate group as in Germany. Even the Russian edition of *Logos*, which was securely in the hands of a young generation of Neo-Kantians, proclaimed itself open to all philosophical directions. The events of 1917 did much to hasten the demise of Neo-Kantianism, although by then its younger members were rapidly moving towards a neo-Hegelian stance.

2 Epistemological Neo-Kantianism

Some scholars trace the beginnings of Russian Neo-Kantianism as far back as the early writings of Pëtr LAVROV in the 1860s and Vladimir Lesevich in the 1870s. Nevertheless the first explicit stirrings date from the following decade. Although, unlike the Germans, the Russian Neo-Kantians in general paid little attention to the natural sciences, the initiator, leader and philosophically most influential member of the movement Aleksandr Vvedenskii (1856–1925) started his career with a lengthy master's thesis – he never attained a doctorate – on the concept of matter. In it he upheld the basic thrust of Kant's dynamic model of elementary physical processes against the backdrop of contemporary theories. In his mature years he came to call his own stance 'logicism', which he conceived as a logical proof of the impossibility of metaphysical knowledge and, not immodestly, as the distinctive Russian contribution to philosophy on a par with British empiricism, French positivism and German Kantianism in their opposition to such knowledge. Logicism, in Vvedenskii's eyes, presupposed no theory of a priori judgment or conclusions about the nature of space and time. Yet he believed it possible to demonstrate, without the elaborate reasoning and considerations found in Kant's *Critique of Pure Reason* (see KANT, I, §§4–8), that the objects studied by the natural sciences are mere representations of 'true being', the thing-in-itself, which as such remains totally transcendent.

As all metaphysical hypotheses are irrefutable some can be incorporated into a worldview, though purely on the basis of faith. There is, however, another group of 'views' that consists neither of metaphysical hypotheses, since the views make no reference to transcendent objects, nor of knowledge claims, since they concern activity in the immanent world. This group is that of our moral tenets. We must integrate into our worldview only those metaphysical hypotheses that are demanded by our moral tenets, only those that we must hold to be true if we are to believe in the 'absolute obligatory nature of moral duty'. Among these hypotheses, or postulates of practical reason, are those discussed by Kant (see KANT, I, §§9–11), but in addition there is one he largely failed to elaborate, namely the existence of mental activity similar to my own in the other.

The Cartesian thesis of the privacy of the mental, that there are no objective criteria by which I know that the other has thoughts and feelings like mine, is one Vvedenskii continued to defend throughout his long professional career at St Petersburg University. The argument from analogy can be of use only in explaining how I extend my conviction in the existence of the other's mental activity to a number of others but not how I come to my initial recognition (see OTHER MINDS). Just as we speak of a moral sense in referring to the recognition of moral obligation, so too can we speak of a metaphysical sense in referring to my acknowledgement of the other's mental processes. Furthermore, since moral obligation is contingent on the existence of at least one other animate being, I am as certain of the existence of mental activity in the other as I am of the obligatory nature of my duties. In fact, the metaphysical and the moral sense are the same; the former is merely what Vvedenskii called 'the cognitive aspect' of the latter. In his later years Vvedenskii spoke less of a metaphysical sense and more of accepting the other's mental activity as a 'working hypothesis' that proved 'convenient' in the construction of a scientific psychology.

Not surprisingly, then, Vvedenskii held that psychology as a science yielding knowledge relies necessarily and fundamentally on personal self-observation. Nevertheless he allotted a role, albeit on a secondary level, in a properly conceived psychology to experiment and what he termed 'collective or comparative self-observation', the accumulation and comparison of introspective observational data by a number of individuals.

Despite Vvedenskii's wish to found a distinct school of thought his only disciple was Ivan Lapshin (1870–1952), who also taught at St Petersburg University prior to his expulsion from the Soviet Union in 1922. Extending Kant's original transcendentalism, Lapshin held that even formal logic is grounded in an a priori categorical synthesis. Consequently, anyone who rejects Kantian (or, rather, Neo-Kantian) epistemology has no basis for using the laws of logic. As those laws cannot justifiably be applied in contexts beyond possible experience metaphysics lies beyond the pale of science. Such is the purest expression of 'critical idealism'. Disagreeing with Kant, Lapshin maintained that space and time were essentially not pure intuitions but categories of cognition along with causality, substantiality and so on. Intuited parts of space are merely conceptual 'illustrations' of space. As a category space is intimately involved in all judgments including analytical ones such as the law of non-contradiction.

Like Vvedenskii, Lapshin devoted considerable attention to the problem of 'the other'. He too claimed that my experience of an immediate givenness of another's intimate self is illusory. For the most part we analogically infer the other's mental states from observed bodily movements or positions. Even whether all other rational beings think in accordance with the same laws of logic must be answered agnostically. We are forced to turn to faith. Yet faith can be either immanent or transcendent. A transcendent faith in the other's self, in other words, that the other has mental states exactly as I do and that they are the 'essence' of the empirical being before me, is both unnecessary and philosophically unjustified, since it treats the other's self as a thing-in-itself. On the other hand, immanent faith means we have supreme confidence in the empirical reality, the 'objective significance', of positing mental states within the other's empirically observed body.

3 Epistemological Neo-Kantianism (cont.)

While not a disciple of Vvedenskii, Georgii Chelpa-nov (1863–1936), a professor first at Kiev and then at Moscow University, is almost invariably classed as a Neo-Kantian, although even this is not incontestable. As active in psychology as philosophy he upheld Wundt's programme in experimental psychology (see WUNDT, W.) and defended psychophysical parallelism throughout his career. Vvedenskii himself sharply rebuked Chelpanov for his reliance on J.S. Mill's ideas in an elementary logic textbook. Yet Chelpanov, unlike many others, sought to retain a role for the thing-in-itself, viewing it as a transcendent something that 'evokes', along with the forms of consciousness, a particular representation of an object. Likewise, something analogous to our representation of space 'evokes' in us that representation. Explicitly in opposition to those who evaded the issue of how to account for a particular representation and called such a position 'transcendental idealism', Chelpanov termed his stance 'critical realism' or 'ideal-realism'.

While uninterested in the problem of other minds Chelpanov sought to defend the Kantian apriority of space in the light of non-Euclidean geometry by arguing that our particular spatial relations and therefore a particular set of geometrical axioms are formed under the influence of experience. Nevertheless as idealizations the axioms of Euclidean geometry are produced in and by consciousness. Another set of spatial relations will produce another set of axioms. The concept of space simpliciter, however, is a priori in the sense that it is a condition of perception in general. Every space is characterized by its exteriority, and the particular dimensionality of a space is derived from the establishing of a relation between points.

We should also mention Chaim Flekser (pseudonym Akim Volynskii) (1863–1926), a prominent literary critic and editor for a time of the important journal *Severnyi vestnik*. Despite his support for an idiosyncratic, but undeveloped, mysticism Volynskii in an early and lengthy article in that journal held that Kant had conclusively resolved the problems concerning cognition. Kant's practical philosophy, on the other hand, being based on a 'practical faith', he held to be imbued with the purest dogmatism.

4 Neo-Kantianism in the social sciences

Pavel Novgorodtsev (1866–1924) took an active role in politics in addition to his duties as professor of jurisprudence at Moscow University. He came under the influence of the Baden and Marburg schools (see NEO-KANTIANISM §§3–8) during a lengthy stay in Western Europe, particularly in Freiburg. Although endorsing Kant's epistemology Novgorodtsev's interests lay mainly in practical philosophy. Whereas

Kant's morality is centred around the notion of duty (see KANTIAN ETHICS), Novgorodtsev sought to reconstruct it around that of the unique, harmonious person understood as the sole norm. He seeks to retain the rigour of Kant's ethical doctrine while recognizing the force of Hegel's criticism of its formalism by allowing, especially in his early writings, for natural law with a changing content. All practical actions are necessarily limited and incomplete and must be evaluated with their finitude in mind. Nevertheless, laws themselves must be framed keeping in mind the moral foundation of law, the indisputable authority of moral consciousness. In his later writings as the First World War approached Novgorodtsev retreated from his Neo-Kantian programme to a somewhat more traditional conception of natural law.

Bogdan Kistiakovskii (1868–1920) studied for a time under Simmel in Berlin and completed his doctoral studies under Windelband in Strasbourg. After returning to Russia he taught at several institutions including for a short time Moscow University. Kistiakovskii termed his stance, basically a defence of Windelband's, 'scientifico-philosophical idealism'. He held that just as the basic category in the natural sciences is natural necessity, so in the various disciplines of 'scientific philosophy' it is found in a consciousness of what should be. Broadly speaking, logic determines what is valuable in a cognitive relation, whereas ethics is concerned with the valuable in practical activity. The normative character of logic is Kant's greatest discovery in the *Critique of Pure Reason*. Epistemology is concerned not with the very existence of scientific knowledge as a given fact but with the means by which humanity obtains such truths, and with the justification of science.

Nevertheless, Kistiakovskii's chief interest was not logic but philosophy of the social sciences, where he stood close to the position of Rickert and Weber in Germany. For the social sciences to be legitimate, separate branches of inquiry we must understand how concepts are formed in them. Kistiakovskii denied that categories applicable in the natural sciences can be immediately applied in the social sciences unaltered. Absolute necessity, for example, in the natural sciences is something sought, whereas in the social sciences the search for necessity is but one viewpoint.

Also among those influenced by the Baden school was the historian Aleksandr Lappo-Danilevskii (1863–1919), who taught at St Petersburg University. Although chiefly noted for his concrete historical studies he accorded a singular role to epistemology in the elaboration of principles and methods without which scientific advancement is inconceivable. While sharing the Baden view that the natural sciences are nomothetic and the social sciences primarily but not exclusively idiographic, he also saw a difference in their goal. The natural scientist sought to explain nature whereas the social scientist strives for understanding of a phenomenon.

The most partisan Russian disciple of the Marburg School, particularly in the philosophy of the social sciences, was Vasilii Savalskii (1873–1915). In his chief work from 1908 he engaged in polemics against Kistiakovskii and Novgorodtsev while expounding the position of Hermann COHEN in ethics and jurisprudence.

5 Transitional Neo-Kantians

Several notable Russian intellectuals early in their respective careers abandoned Marxism and briefly adopted a Neo-Kantian position before moving on to another, usually more idealistic philosophy. Perhaps best known among these was Nikolai BERDIAEV (1874–1948). Although acknowledging the primacy of practical reason in one of his earliest publications from 1900, he nevertheless saw this as a psychological truth. Berdiaev held Kant's atemporal postulates of practical reason to be 'temporary postulates of people of a specific socio-psychological formation'. At a different time other interests could predominate leading to a different set of postulates. However, Berdiaev came to the view that there were unalterable moral values which, while atemporal, were in the course of history expounded by different classes. Along these lines he attempted to combine Kantian idealism with a lingering sympathy for Marxian sociology.

Pëtr Struve (1870–1944), a dynamic personality in Russian politics as well as intellectual history, came to Neo-Kantianism largely out of dissatisfaction with the account of freedom and necessity in Marxian philosophy of history. During his Neo-Kantian phase he retained a belief in the validity of a thorough-going determinism for the phenomenal realm while asserting that freedom, conceived as indeterminism, was a 'reality' in the activity of the human individual.

In his first published article from 1907 on Hume and Kant, Gustav SHPET (1879–1937) sided with the Baden-school outlook that while the validity of the law of causality was undemonstrable, we must believe in it for the sake of cognition. Within a few years, however, he abandoned Neo-Kantianism altogether, drawing close to Husserlian phenomenology.

6 The journal *Logos*

A Russian edition of the international journal *Logos* began in 1910 under the responsible editorship of Sergei HESSEN (1887–1950) and Fëdor Stepun

(1884–1965). In 1911 Boris Iakovenko (1884–1948) was added. Hessen studied in Heidelberg and Freiburg with among others Windelband and Rickert, under whom he wrote a notable dissertation. After returning to Russia he taught in St Petersburg and Tomsk. Subsequently after the Bolshevik Revolution he taught in Prague and Warsaw. Although later in emigration he wrote on pedagogy and philosophy of law his early writings reveal a strong debt to the Baden School. He argued that in the natural sciences to subsume a particular natural event under a general law, thereby illuminating it in a causal sequence, is to understand it. The individual or historical event too is marked with necessity even though the degree of generality appears markedly different in historical and scientific explanations. To understand an event in history is to understand it in its concreteness, its individuality but also its necessity no less than in the natural sciences.

Stepun studied in Heidelberg under Windelband under whom he wrote a slim dissertation on Solov'ëv. Shortly after the Revolution he briefly served as cultural director at a state theatre in Moscow. Later he taught sociology at Dresden University and from 1946 in Munich. His early affiliation with Neo-Kantianism consists chiefly in his view that philosophy must examine all cultural fields, distinguishing in them a 'transcendental-formal element' from that which is merely contingent. This formal element is a manifestation of the absolute and as such is what gives cultural 'creations' their universality and necessity. Unfortunately Stepun failed to develop these thoughts more precisely or fully.

After 1917 Iakovenko first lived in Italy and then Berlin and Prague. Despite his many writings he devoted little attention to enunciating his own position either in detail or rigorously. In short he held to an absolute monism but proclaimed transcendental philosophy to be the intellectual path to the Absolute. In it philosophy has attained a self-consciousness. The next and last step for philosophy is to return to the original unity revealed in mythology. When philosophy has come full circle it will then be critical and rational.

7 The last Russian Neo-Kantians

Vasilii Sezeman (1884–1963) was born in Finland and studied in St Petersburg. After graduation from the university there he went abroad to Marburg and Berlin for further study. Returning to Russia he taught during the First World War in Petrograd and later in Saratov. In the early 1920s he lived briefly in Berlin and then in Lithuania, where he taught philosophy at the Universities of Kaunas and Vilnius. During this later period his major writings were composed in German, although a few years prior to his death he published a Lithuanian translation of Aristotle's *De Anima*. Particularly interested in bestowing a transcendental significance on the concept of evolution without falling into psychologism, Sezeman held that knowledge at any particular time is incapable of seizing the transcendent object. Absolute knowledge remains the ideal, but it itself is inseparable from the path leading to the latter. Each stage in the advance of knowledge functions as a constitutive element in this ideal. As truth is a regulative idea there are no absolute, self-evident truths; all propositions are subject to evolution including the categories or seemingly ultimate elements of knowledge. Sezeman thus rejects interpreting the thing-in-itself as some causative transcendent reality and views it instead as an ideal, self-contained system.

Aleksandr Veideman (1879–?) published in Latvia in 1927 the only attempt at a systematization in Russian Neo-Kantianism which nevertheless stands as the 'swan song' of the movement. Situating himself between Kant and Hegel, Veideman faulted the former for limiting himself to the possibility of mathematical and scientific knowledge, not knowledge in general. Had Kant done so he would have affirmed that all being is created by thought dialectically. As thought here is conceived to be a logical not individual process, solipsism is averted. The impetus for creative cognition receives its answer in ethical striving. Aesthetics represents the field wherein the finite is raised to an ideal.

As in the parallel German movement concern with the historical Kant was greatest during the early years of the respective protagonists and gradually diminished. In some cases this was simply a matter of an evolving thought-process, whereas in others external events surely played a decisive role. Vvedenskii distanced himself from the intricacies of Kant's 'First Critique', seeking an independent and 'easier proof of philosophical Criticism'. Chelpanov, witnessing the consolidation of Marxism in Russia in the 1920s, sought above all to defend moderation and the toleration of competing viewpoints in philosophy. To this end he emphasized his own hostility and that of Marx to transcendent metaphysical explanation. Lapshin, increasingly isolated in Prague, turned ever more towards studies of Russian culture. As the years turned into decades Sezeman, perhaps alone among the Neo-Kantians in the Russian diaspora, continued working without thematic abatement on problems traditionally conceived as philosophical, keeping abreast of the latest developments.

List of works

Berdiaev, N. (1900) 'F.A. Lange i kriticheskaia filosofiia' (F.A. Lange and Critical Philosophy), in *Mir bozhii* (1900) July: 224–54. (Reveals a side to his thought far different from his later 'existentialist' turn.)

Chelpanov, G. (1896–1904) *Problema vospriiatiia prostranstva v sviazi s ucheniem ob apriornosti i vrozhdënnosti* (The Problem of the Perception of Space in Connection with Theories of Apriority and Innateness), Kiev: Kushnerov, 2 vols. (Of his numerous works his most scholarly.)

—— (1905) *Vvedenie v filosofiiu* (Introduction to Philosophy), 6th edn, Moscow: V.V. Dumnov, 1916. (Admirably clear and simple prose.)

Hessen, S. (1909) *Individuelle Kausalität. Studien zum transzendentalen Empirismus* (Individual Causality. Studies in Transcendental Empiricism), Berlin: Reuther & Reichard. (A treatment of an issue central to the Baden School of Neo-Kantianism.)

Kistiakovskii, B. (1899) *Gesellschaft und Einzelwesen. Eine methodologische Untersuchung* (Society and the Individual. A Methodological Investigation), Berlin: Verlag Otto Liebmann. (A Neo-Kantian examination of the foundations of sociology that paralleled much of Weber's methodological work.)

—— (1916) *Sotsial'nye nauki i pravo* (Social Sciences and the Law), Moscow. (A general theory of law from the standpoint of sociology.)

Lappo-Danilevskii, A. (1910–13) *Metodologiia istorii* (The Methodology of History), St Petersburg, 2 vols. (A monumental study by a distinguished historian.)

Lapshin, I. (1906) *Zakony myshleniia i formy poznaniia* (Laws of Thinking and Forms of Cognition), St Petersburg. (Despite its frequent departure from academic style this is his basic work.)

—— (1924) 'Oproverzhenie solipsizma' (A Refutation of Solipsism), repr. in *Filosofskie nauki* (1992) 3: 18–45. (A valiant though vain attempt to overcome the limitations of his own essentially methodological solipsistic stance.)

Novgorodtsev, P. (1901) *Kant i Gegel' v ikh ucheniiakh o prave i gosudarstve* (Kant and Hegel on Law and the State), Moscow: Moscow University. (Far more than simply an examination of Kant and Hegel.)

—— (1909) *Krizis sovremennogo pravosoznaniia* (The Crisis of Contemporary Legal Consciousness), Moscow: Moscow University. (The major statement of his fully developed position.)

Savalskii, V. (1908) *Osnovy filosofii prava v nauchnom idealizme* (Foundations of the Philosophy of Law in Scientific Idealism), Moscow: Moscow University. (Highly polemical.)

Sezeman, V. (1911) 'Ratsional'noe i irratsional'noe v sisteme filosofii' (The Rational and the Irrational in a Philosophical System), in *Logos* 2: 93–122. (An early generally mediocre essay.)

Shpet, G. (1907) *Problema prichinnosti u Iuma i Kanta,* (The Problem of Causality in Hume and Kant), Kiev: St Vladimir University. (Unfortunately Shpet states his own position only at the very end.)

Veideman, A. (1927) *Myshlenie i bytie* (Thinking and Being), Riga. (An almost unknown, albeit sketchy, amalgam of Neo-Kantianism with elements of Hegelianism.)

Volynskii, A. (1889) 'Kriticheskie i dogmaticheskie elementy v filosofii Kanta' (Critical and Dogmatic Elements in Kant's Philosophy), in *Severnyi vestnik,* (1889) 7: 67–87; 9: 61–83; 10: 89–109; 11: 51–72; 12: 55–78. (Surprising support for Kant from an unexpected corner.)

Vvedenskii, A. (1901) *Filosofskie ocherki* (Philosophical Essays), 2nd edn, Prague, 1924. (Contains a number of valuable pieces illuminating his general philosophical outlook.)

—— (1909) *Logika, kak chast' teorii poznaniia* (Logic as a Part of a Theory of Cognition), 3rd edn, St Petersburg: Stasjulevich, 1917. (His basic text on epistemology.)

References and further reading

Putnam, G. (1977) *Russian Alternatives to Marxism,* Knoxville, TN: University of Tennessee Press. (Useful and very readable discussion of Novgorodtsev.)

Vucinich, A. (1976) *Social Thought in Tsarist Russia,* Chicago, IL: University of Chicago Press, 106–52. (Incisive and highly informative particularly on Kistiakovskii.)

Walicki, A. (1987) *Legal Philosophies of Russian Liberalism,* Oxford: Clarendon Press, 291–465. (Exciting and learned discussion of Novgorodtsev, Kistiakovskii and Hessen.)

Zenkovsky, V.V. (1948–50) *Istoriia russkoi filosofii,* vol. 2, Paris: YMCA-Press; 2nd edn 1989; trans. G.L. Kline, *A History of Russian Philosophy,* London: Routledge & Kegan Paul and New York: Columbia University Press, 1953, vol. 667–705. (Despite its age this remains the best secondary source.)

THOMAS NEMETH

NEOPLATONISM

Neoplatonism was the final flowering of ancient Greek thought, from the third to the sixth or seventh century AD. Building on eight centuries of unbroken philosophical debate, it addressed questions such as: What is the true self? What is consciousness and how does it relate to reality? Can intuition be reconciled with reason? What are the first causes of reality? How did the universe come into being? How can an efficient cause retain its identity and yet be distributed among its effects? Why does the soul become embodied? What is the good life?

There were several flavours of Neoplatonism, reflecting the concerns and backgrounds of its practitioners, who ranged from Plotinus and his circle of freelance thinkers to the heads of the university schools of the Roman Empire, Proclus, Ammonius and Damascius. In the later, more analysed form, we see a rich scheme of multi-layered metaphysics, epistemology and ethics, but also literary theory, mathematics, physics and other subjects, all integrated in one curriculum. Neoplatonism was not just a philosophy but the higher education system of its age.

The Neoplatonism that came to dominate the ancient world from the fourth century was an inseparable mixture of inspired thought and scholastic order. To this may be traced some of its internal conceptual conflicts: for example, the free individual soul versus the ranks of being, personal experience versus demonstrative knowledge. To this may also be traced its appeal to polar audiences: mystics and mathematizing scientists, romantics and rationalists.

To the Neoplatonist, knowledge consists of degrees of completion. Take the example of tutor and student. Both study the same things, but the tutor has a wider and more intimate knowledge. The tutor opens the student's mind to the breadth and intricacies of the study-matter, and corrects the student's deliberations. So it is with the Neoplatonic levels of knowledge. Every level has access to the entire spectrum of what there is to know, but each with its appropriate adverbial modifier. At the 'lower' level an individual comprehends things 'particularly' and is concerned with the 'images' or presentations of mind and sense-impressions of the qualities of physical things. At the 'higher' level, an individual apprehends things 'wholly', as universal statements (often called 'laws' and 'canons'). The concern is with propositions about what is true or false, self-grounded and logically necessary. Thus the higher level corrects and supplies the 'criterion' for the lower level.

Knowledge, however, is not an end in itself, but a means to salvation. Increasing awareness puts us in touch with the levels of reality of which we ourselves are

part. The ultimate reality is none other than the fundamental unity out of which all came into being: God. In this union we recover our true good.

As the summation of ancient Greek philosophy, Neoplatonism was transmitted to Byzantium, Islam and western Europe. It was the prime intellectual force behind the protagonists of the Italian Renaissance, and its influence was felt until the nineteenth century.

1   Who, what, when?
2   The curriculum of knowledge and virtue
3   Epistemology, metaphysics and the daring soul
4   Philosophy of science
5   Influence

1   Who, what, when?

The modern label 'Neoplatonism' conveniently describes the philosophy of late antiquity, and at once misrepresents it. It was neither 'new', a departure from Plato, nor simply a 'Platonism' (see PLATO; PLATONISM, EARLY AND MIDDLE). The more we learn of the philosophers from the first century BC to the second century AD, such as Cicero, the Middle Platonists and Neo-Pythagoreans, the more we discern a continuous line of thought (see CICERO; NEO-PYTHAGOREANISM). How far back it stretches is still intriguing and controversial, since several leading scholars have indicated independently a proximity in thought between Neoplatonism and the late Plato and his immediate successors in the Old Academy (see SPEUSIPPUS; XENOCRATES). The Neoplatonists were known in their time as 'Platonists'; those at Athens regarded themselves the true successors to Plato, and called their school the 'Academy'. But these ancient labels mislead as much as the modern, and to understand the sources of Neoplatonism we have to look also to the Stoics and the commentators on Aristotle (see STOICISM; ARISTOTLE COMMENTATORS). Plato's and Aristotle's schools disappeared as institutions in the first century BC. Freelance philosophers took up their different causes. In the second century AD the Roman emperor-philosopher MARCUS AURELIUS (§1) established chairs of philosophy at Athens (apparently bearing the title 'successor') in Platonism, Aristotelianism, Stoicism and Epicureanism. Alexander of Aphrodisias, in his endeavour to unify the Aristotelian corpus, identified the active intellect (*nous*) with god and with its intelligible object, unintentionally easing the absorption of Aristotle in mild Platonism. By the beginning of the third century imperial funding for the chairs had vanished, and by the end of that century only Platonists survived. Some, who were more inclined to scholasticism, flourished at the prestigious teaching centres of the late Roman Empire, Athens and Alexandria. Others, particularly those of the Neo-Pythagorean tendency, such as NUMENIUS, flourished at other centres, notably Apamea (Syria). Both sorts took up relevant ideas from past Greek philosophies, including Aristotelian theories of logic and mind, and rejected those they considered fruitless (Epicureanism) or wrong (for example, the dualism of the Platonist PLUTARCH OF CHAERONEA §3).

This is the philosophy that PLOTINUS, PORPHYRY and IAMBLICHUS turned into a fresh, highly integrated school of thought, now called, for lack of a better term, Neoplatonism. Each of the three founders contributed something different, often in reaction to their teacher. Plotinus abandoned scholastics in favour of a Pythagorizing Platonist, Ammonius Saccas, at Alexandria. Later, he set up his own circle of followers in Rome, which was to prove highly influential. Porphyry first studied under the leading scholastic at Athens (Longinus) but then studied under Plotinus. Only five years later he abandoned Plotinus and pursued his explicit 'harmonization' of Aristotle with Plato. Iamblichus taught philosophy at Apamea. He had read Porphyry and may have been his student, but disagreed with him over the approach to the divine. One of Iamblichus' disciples, Aedesius, founded a celebrated school at Pergamum, and proselytized the emperor Julian. By the fifth century the Iamblichean version had spread to the main teaching establishments at Athens (see DAMASCIUS; PROCLUS; SIMPLICIUS) and Alexandria (see AMMONIUS, SON OF HERMEAS; PHILOPONUS), as well as Gaza (which was Christian).

Neoplatonists saw their metaphysics in all forms of expression, provided they could find the appropriate level of interpretation. Language is the mediator of concepts and realities, and so even literary works (for example, those by Homer and Hesiod) allude to metaphysical truths. Similarly, revelatory proverbs, the Orphics and the Chaldaean Oracles, point to truths that transcend ordinary description (see ORPHISM; CHALDAEAN ORACLES). The Neoplatonists did not admit irrationalism, however, remaining within the Greek rationalist manner of explanation.

Their writings are mostly commentaries on classical greats, Plato and Aristotle – although there are notable exceptions, including the *Enneads* of Plotinus, Porphyry's *On Abstinence from Animal Food*, Iamblichus' *On the Mysteries*, Proclus' treatises *On Providence, On Fate, On Evil* and *Platonic Theology* and Damascius' treatise *Problems and Solutions on First Principles*. As a textual form, the commentary is no evidence of lack of originality: it was the conventional form of scholarly writing of the middle and late imperial period, and was useful for teaching.

Good interpretative works contained critical appraisals and innovative theories using the set text as a frame for the commentator's own reflections. That two Athenian heads of school (Proclus and Damascius) wrote most of the commentaries on Plato, while the Alexandrians concentrated on Aristotle, was not due to an ideological split, but to avoidance of duplication. The Alexandrian professors were envious of the rich endowments given to the Athenians and the Athenians looked with disdain on the money-making compromises of the Alexandrians, but the two schools enjoyed close bonds, and students from the one regularly travelled to take positions at the other (for example, Hierocles, Hermeias, Ammonius, Damascius and Simplicius).

On the Latin side, Plotinus' and Porphyry's works were translated by the pagan Macrobius and the Christian convert Marius Victorinus. The latter transformed Neoplatonism to a form suited to Roman Christianity and influenced Augustine and Boethius (see MARIUS VICTORINUS; AUGUSTINE ; BOETHIUS, A.M.S.).

On the Greek side, Neoplatonists supported Hellenism as a civilizing culture and as a universal, pagan religion, at a time of Christian emperors. The school at Athens ended with the emperor Justinian's imperial ban on pagan public teaching in 529. There was an unsuccessful sojourn to Persia, but it is still a mystery what finally happened to the last Athenian scholarchs, Damascius, and especially Simplicius, who flourished after the ban. At Alexandria, Neoplatonic teaching continued with the pagan Olympiodorus, and then with Christians (Elias and David). In the seventh century, Alexandrian teaching transferred to the Byzantine capital, when Stephanus was invited to teach at the university of Constantinople (see BYZANTINE PHILOSOPHY §§2,3).

2 The curriculum of knowledge and virtue

The Neoplatonic curriculum was established by Iamblichus, and maintained with minor changes by Athenians and Alexandrians over three centuries until the end of independent Neoplatonist schools (whence it was transmitted to Byzantium). It consisted of thematic topics tuned to educational 'scopes'. Beginning with Aristotle's logic (first through Porphyry's *Introduction*) and practical ethics, it progressed to physics, the mathematical sciences, Aristotle's metaphysics, and twelve of Plato's dialogues culminating with the *Timaeus* and *Parmenides*. After approximately six years of university education, the student graduated as a philosopher and a virtuous person.

From Socrates and Aristotle, Neoplatonists accepted that *aretē* (virtue) can be taught (see ARETĒ):

however, this is not to say that teachers impart goodness to students, but that they make the students fully aware of their true nature. Each grade of the curriculum was meant to stimulate the appropriate virtue. According to the Platonic *Alcibiades I*, *psychē* (soul/life/mind) is the human essence (see PSYCHĒ). Educating the person means educating the soul as to its true origins and place in the scheme of things. Thus, education and ethics are grounded in epistemology and metaphysics. Concentrating on the essence of things involves a certain detachment from incidentals, the temporal, physical events. The soul must be 'unaffected' (*apathēs*) by externals. Eventually a sense of completion and full awareness bring about the state of wellbeing (*eudaimonia*) that is the goal of human life (EUDAIMONIA). Ultimately this is nothing else than 'becoming similar to God'.

As there are many degrees of awareness, so there are many levels of virtue. The physical (*physikai*) virtues relate to a well-maintained body: for example, genetic characteristics, beauty, state of health, stamina. Ethical (*ēthikai*) virtues relate to the sense of justice, courage, temperance and truth (the four Platonic cardinal virtues) and, generally to the temperament of the individual, including, it seems, the quality of memory. Social (*politikai*) virtues measure regard for one's fellow human beings, participation in politics and affairs at large: for example, standing up for human welfare and dignity against state officialdom (compare Aristotle's definition of the human being as social animal). The three types outlined above belong to the 'lower' level because they refer to passing matters, not to the atemporal essence of life. The first of the 'higher' virtues are the purifying (*kathartikai*) virtues. The detachment of the soul can be assisted through a simple lifestyle consisting of abstinence and vegetarianism (Porphyry was the first to write on its philosophy), fasting and praying. Erotic love was not shunned, and most of the Neoplatonist scholarchs enjoyed fertile marriages. The aim was to redirect desire towards the eternal. Next are the intellectual (*theōrētikai*) virtues: learning about names (*onomata*) as signifying concepts (*noēmata*) of real objects (*pragmata*), both natural and divine. Iamblichus added also a sixth type, the theurgic virtue. What exactly he meant is still controversial, but it included initiation in magic, prediction of natural disasters, out-of-body visions and, in general, acting like god while being a mortal. The leap to the transcendent absolute was theurgy's highest aim. Finally, there was the 'paradigmatic' virtue, which in earlier Neoplatonism denoted the exemplary state of divine union but in later Neoplatonism was reserved solely for divine beings.

3 Epistemology, metaphysics and the daring soul

Pure sense-perception ranks low in the scale of certainty, because its information is incidental and transient. Mind arrives at an opinion or judgment (*doxa*) by assimilating sense-impressions into images (*phantasiai*) and comparing them with preconceived patterns of thought, which are intelligible and can be articulated, thus forming the mind's internal objects. Certain, scientific knowledge (*epistēmē*) is the result of reasoning. This is the mental discourse (*dianoia*) in which mind weighs concepts, some abstracted from physical properties, others found inherent in formal relations (for example, mathematics) or in the method of pure reasoning. Above discursive reasoning Neoplatonists placed 'intellection' (*noēsis*), which is contemplation. They saw it as pure thinking (*nous*) in the sense of grasping unmediated truths as a 'simultaneous whole'. For Plotinus this meant that the knower identifies with what is to be known. Others asserted that the two coincide (Proclus, *Platonic Theology* I, ch. 21, 97.22–98.5) so that we can still articulate propositions: perfect identity comes at a higher level. Grasping the ultimate truth, which has no differentiation, entails a complete unity, an 'illumination'. Plotinus described it as mental rapture, but Iamblichean Neoplatonists deduced that it is fully supra-intellectual, brought about by 'faith' (*pistis*).

We assimilate knowledge with our *psychē* (soul, or the personal mind). It is what makes us alive and thinking. Not localized in a part of body or anywhere in the cosmos, it is as individual as the body it animates. *Psychē* exercises diverse activities, non-rational, vital, intellectual and spiritual. It can combine divine, intellectual inspiration and sensory perceptions into one mental object. Plotinus made *psychē* very flexible. The rest kept it between intellect and body, and sometimes distinguished its non-rational 'nature' (*physis*).

Education, knowledge, science, ethics and psychology are thus grounded in metaphysics: the kind of existence that substantiates them. Degrees of learning, awareness or 'consciousness' and virtue, reflect degrees of being. Humans, plants, gods and every existent thing are made up of a 'bundle' of the appropriate layers of being. In the basic scheme these are: physicality, soul, intellect, the One. Intellect (*nous*) is the objective, self-absorbed intelligence that creates by imposing 'form'. On a universal scale it is the Creator. The unqualified One is the supreme principle of all that exists in some sense: that is, the ultimate God. In itself it is beyond the system, transcending determination. Later Neoplatonists distinguished aspects within soul and intelligence. In this way, they arrived at a richer scheme: pure body, physicality, rational soul, intellect, life-principle (process), substantive essence (object-pattern) and the One. They also distinguished class properties as 'wholes' and 'parts'. For example, the complete soul is an unanalysed whole, but its 'parts' are the souls resident in individual living beings. This distinction helped specify 'unity' (*henas*) as the 'root' of the characteristic identity of a being, whether universal or particular. In later Neoplatonism (notably in Proclus) this is the spark of divinity.

The grades of being can be imagined as spheres of increasing comprehensiveness. Bodily existence is perfected by soul, this by the objective intellect, and so on. The One embraces everything. Conversely, there is a cascade of causation, from the One to the 'many'. Neoplatonists were still faced with problems: How can diversity emerge from undifferentiated unity? Why should a perfect state give rise to others? In response they proposed that such causation is not voluntary but a necessary consequence of perfection, which has no external limits (so divine action is not a mystery, unlike in the revealed religions). Existence 'unfolds'. This dispersion is like a light 'emanating' from its source and diffusing into space, or as a 'procession' of numbers from one to two, three, four.... Things (and levels) lose their foremost identity by gaining separate existence. They preserve the character that determines them by an act of 'returning'. However, Neoplatonists were not satisfied with the One being both the original cause of intelligible reality and transcending it, and to the end argued over solutions (as indeed cosmologists and theologians do to this day).

The problem also appeared at the level of soul. Why does *psyche* leave its own proper level of being and 'descend' to a mortal body? Ontology requires an organizing principle to preserve the ever-disintegrating body. But something complete in itself cannot want something like the material body. Soul's self-consciousness gives a sense of 'dare' (*tolma*) that enables its departure and blind fall. Later Neoplatonists pointed out that perfect souls (for example, the moving and organizing principle of the cosmos) do not suffer such a fate. The 'particular' souls are not completely aware what they are, and so leave their own order: either to 'fall' to body, or to 'ascend' towards the One. In this way the daring soul acquires a wide but personal experience.

4 Philosophy of science

The Neoplatonists taught the mathematical quadrivium of arithmetic, geometry, astronomy and harmonics, and the physics of Aristotle and Plato: Plato's *Timaeus* belonged to the highest section of the curriculum. In the sixth century we also see Galen's medicine appearing at the Alexandrian school, and we have a certain Stephanus of Athens writing as a philosopher-physician.

The programme of mathematization can be traced to Iamblichus' reform (with the influence of Neo-Pythagoreans), although Pythagorizing mathematics is found in Plato himself. Part of the enterprise was the mathematization of physics and matter. Proclus and Simplicius declared that 'quantity' is more fundamental than 'quality'. Iamblichus and later Neoplatonists were excited about mathematics because mathematical knowledge alone proceeds by the 'solidity of scientific demonstration' (Elias, *On Porphyry's Introduction* 28.24–9). Religious speculation and the physicist's empiricism do not, and therefore need mathematics to support them. Mathematics thus became a pillar of Neoplatonic metaphysics and epistemology. Proclus pointed out that mathematical proofs rely on indemonstrable axioms, and so philosophy has to turn to a higher science – Platonic dialectic.

In ancient philosophy the concept of time related to change, movement and the psychological experience of events. Place was associated with the container where change happens and so with theories of matter. Neoplatonists stayed true to the Platonic outline, that time is the 'moving image of eternity', but in fleshing it out they arrived at startling conclusions. For Plotinus, time is the product of psychological movement. It is the life of the soul as it moves from one activity to another 'restlessly'. Since soul is not confined to individuals but is what gives life and movement to the universe, there is a cosmic time. By this account, eternity is the timelessness 'of that quiet life... which belongs to that which exists and is in being, all together and full, completely without extension or interval' (*Enneads* III.7.3). The later Neoplatonists rejected Plotinus and followed Iamblichus in giving time its own reality. In this way they finally broke with Greek tradition. The time of ordinary experience is not true time but the 'flowing' appearance of it. Even the cosmic clocks, the stars and planets and the revolution of the universe as a whole, do not reveal what time is. Like the 'centre of a rotating wheel' (Proclus, *Commentary on Plato's Timaeus* 3.27), primary time is singular and motionless, and abides before creation. Damascius took Neoplatonic innovation further by proposing that ordinary time flows not by atomic instants but as a series of 'strides' or 'leaps' (each of which is a temporal part).

Neoplatonists rejected Aristotle's view of place as a boundary. In developing instead Plato's 'receptacle' of creation, they arrived at the full identification of place

NEOPLATONISM

with three-dimensional space (see SPACE). Proclus equated space with massless body, and contemplated universal space as the absolute frame of cosmic motion. Others saw space as incorporeal. For the Christian Neoplatonist Philoponus, pure space is more fundamental than matter, and is a void. Iamblichus elevated place to the realm of Forms, and made space the instrument by which the world-soul binds things in their proper positions. For Damascius place really was the power that keeps the members of the universe in their arrangement. Simplicius returned to space as extension, and distinguished relative from absolute space, the latter being indistinguishable from essence. In examining the relationship of 'when' and 'where', he concluded that the two are 'siblings', thereby anticipating the modern equal ranking of time and space.

5 Influence

Neoplatonists were influential through their philosophy, through their preservation of ancient Greek thought (for example, Simplicius is one of our two major sources for the Presocratics), and in their capacity as the educators of late antiquity. Their curriculum passed to the Byzantines, and a Latin fifth-century Neoplatonist, Martianus Capella, devised an influential allegory on the seven liberal arts. Indeed, it is hard to find thinkers of the early medieval period who were not influenced by Neoplatonism. In eleventh-century Byzantium we still find scholars arguing for (Psellus) or against ancient Neoplatonists, and so to the end in the fifteenth century (Plethon).

Theologians found it appealing that rational argument can sustain religion and a life of selfless goodness. However, several philosophical conclusions – for example, that God the transcendent is distinct from the Creator, involuntary divine action, the perpetuity of the physical world, the unimportance of accidental events (incarnation) – conflicted with religions based on the Bible. Moreover, the Neoplatonists tended to defend the Hellenic religion: Porphyry wrote an extensive scholarly refutation of Christianity. As a result Neoplatonist influence often went uncredited. A striking example of this was, the late fifth century theologian who wrote under the name 'Dionysius the Areopagite' (see PSEUDO-DIONYSIUS §9). He produced an entire Christian theology, 'hierarchy', by adapting the Athenian multi-layered system. Between the seventh and ninth centuries this was taken up by leading theologians of the Greek East and the Latin West. It is even claimed that a prototypical Gothic cathedral, St Denis, was built on Pseudo-Dionysian/Neoplatonic

principles. Another example was a collection of works attributed to Aristotle but compiled from Plotinus and Proclus. They first occur in Arabic. Later they were translated into Latin. Both the Pseudo-Dionysian and pseudo-Aristotelian corpora were correctly identified by Aquinas.

Muslims came into contact with Neoplatonism with their first conquests of Syria and Egypt (seventh century). In the next three centuries they translated and paraphrased most of the Greek texts they found. With the Muslim expansion into Spain, the Arabic books became a source of Greek ideas for western Europeans. Some Neoplatonic texts still survive only in Arabic. Neoplatonism influenced Islamic philosophy and religion (Ismailism) (see IBN SINA; NEOPLATONISM IN ISLAMIC PHILOSOPHY).

Jewish thinkers had already participated in Platonism with PHILO OF ALEXANDRIA. Much later, living in the Muslim dominion, the eleventh century thinkers Gabirol (see IBN GABIROL) and GERSONIDES developed Plotinian themes on intelligible matter and the active intellect. In the twelfth century, Neoplatonism was influencing the emerging Kabbalah in the south of France (see KABBALAH). Next we find it in Renaissance Kabbalism (see BRUNO, G.; PICO DELLA MIRANDOLA, G.), and finally in the famous Dutch Jew, SPINOZA.

Western Europe first inherited Plotinian-Porphyrian Neoplatonism through Augustine and Boethius, and later received Byzantine Neoplatonism. They influenced both mystics and logicians, for example, DUNS SCOTUS, ANSELM OF CANTERBURY, ABELARD, ERIUGENA, ALBERT THE GREAT, GROSSETESTE and Thomas AQUINAS. The Renaissance marked the recovery of Greek texts in the original, and a new wave of influence began (see PLATONISM, RENAISSANCE). Proclus had been recognized since Aquinas' time; now Plotinus (and Plato) became finally known. The Byzantine Neoplatonist Plethon was invited by the Medici to set up the Platonic Academy of Florence, where Ficino and Pico della Mirandola taught. Their impact extended to European art, literature and landscape theory. The Hellenic rationalism of Neoplatonism appealed to the Humanists, particularly the idea that individuals possess their own means for salvation. This was also the message of Christian mystics such as Eckehart: even theologians such as NICHOLAS OF CUSA upheld it. The late Neoplatonists' love for mathematics appealed to scientists who disliked medieval explanations by qualities. In art, the Neoplatonic light metaphysics and theories on mathematics and representation proved fruitful in the invention of perspective.

When Plato was separated from Platonists, (Neo)-platonic influence declined. Notable exceptions were the Cambridge Platonists (see CAMBRIDGE PLATO-NISM) and the Idealists – both the British (see BERKELEY, G.; BRADLEY, F.H.) and, especially, the Continental (see BERGSON, H.-L.; SCHELLING, F.W.J. VON; HEGEL, G.W.F.). In science, Schelling and Hegel contributed to *Naturphilosophie*, which saw the forces of nature (magnetism, electricity, gravity) as the unfolding of one unified force (see NATURPHILOSO-PHIE). In literature, the English Romantics (Blake, Shelley) were influenced through Thomas Taylor. Coleridge was interested both in *Naturphilosophie* and, preoccupied with the origin of inspiration, in Schelling's investigations into the 'unconscious'.

See also: HYPATIA; KABBALAH; NUMENIUS; RENAISSANCE PHILOSOPHY

References and further reading

Anon., (6th–7th century AD) *Prolegomena to Platonic Philosophy*, ed. L.G. Westerink, Amsterdam: North-Holland, 1962; *Prolégomènes à la philosophie de Platon*, eds L.G. Westerink, J. Trouillard and A. Segonds, Paris: Les Belles Lettres, 1990. (1962 is parrallel Greek text and English translation of a late Alexandrian work on the Neoplatonic curriculum. 1990 is a new edition of the Greek text with a parrallel French translation and extensive annotation.)

Armstrong, A.H. (ed.) (1970) *Cambridge History of Later Greek and Early Medieval Philosophy*, Cambridge: Cambridge University Press. (Excellent introduction, with chapters on links with Plato, on Alexander of Aphrodisias and on Christian thinkers.)

Blumenthal, H.J. (1996) *Aristotle and Neoplatonism in Late Antiquity: Interpretations of the 'De Anima'*, Ithaca, NY: Cornell University Press. (Key study on the assimilation of Aristotle in Neoplatonic psychology and metaphysics, and its influence.)

Bowersock, G.W. (1990) *Hellenism in Late Antiquity*, Ann Arbor, MI: University of Michigan Press. (Concise examination of the historical, religious and social context.)

Gersh, S. (1978) *From Iamblichus to Eriugena*, Leiden: Brill. (Detailed account of Neoplatonic metaphysics and the transition to medieval theology, including pseudo-Dionysius; major themes are illustrated with diagrams.)

—— (1986) *Middle Platonism and Neoplatonism: The Latin Tradition*, Notre Dame, IN: University of Notre Dame Press. (Two source volumes for Latin Platonism from Cicero to medieval period; volume two covers Neoplatonism.)

—— (ed.) (1992) *Platonism in Late Antiquity*. Notre Dame, IN: University of Notre Dame Press. (Articles mainly on metaphysics and religion.)

Haas, F.A. (1997) *John Philoponus' New Definition of Prime Matter: Aspects of its Background in Neoplatonism and the Ancient Commentary Tradition*, Leiden and New York: Brill. (New account of the theories of matter and space in the context of Neoplatonic thought.)

Lamberton, R. (1986) *Homer the Theologian: Neoplatonist Allegorical Reading and the Growth of the Epic Tradition*, Berkeley and Los Angeles, CA: University of California Press. (On the Neoplatonic theory of literary interpretation.)

Lindberg, D.C. (1986) 'The Genesis of Kepler's Theory of Light: Light Metaphysics from Plotinus to Kepler', *Osiris* 2: 5–42. (Definitive study on the influence of Neoplatonic light metaphysics in medieval and early modern science.)

Lloyd, A.C. (1990) *The Anatomy of Neoplatonism*, Oxford: Clarendon Press. (The best analytical account of Neoplatonic logic and metaphysics; for the advanced philosophy reader.)

O'Meara, D.J. (1982) *Pythagoras Revived: Mathematics and Philosophy in Late Antiquity*, Oxford: Clarendon Press. (Key study on later Neoplatonic metaphysics and theory of knowledge.)

Saffrey, H.D. (1990) *Recherches sur le néoplatonisme aprés Plotin* (Studies of Neoplatonism After Plotinus), Paris: Vrin. (Collected articles about Porphyry, Iamblichus and Proclus, on theological themes, by a leading scholar in the field.)

Siorvanes, L. (1996) *Proclus: Neoplatonic Philosophy and Science*, Edinburgh and New Haven, CT: Edinburgh and Yale University Presses. (Covers Neoplatonism to Philoponus and Simplicius, suitable for newcomers.)

Steel, C. (1978) *The Changing Self: A Study on the Soul in Later Neoplatonism: Iamblichus, Damascius, Simplicius*. Brussels: Royal Academy. (Seminal study of late Neoplatonic psychology.)

Wallis, R.T. (1972) *Neoplatonism*, London: Duckworth. (Compact but thorough account suitable for a newcomer to the subject.)

Westerink, L.G. (1964) 'Philosophy and Medicine in Late Antiquity', *Janus* 51: 169–77. (On medical interests, primarily at the late Alexandrian school.)

LUCAS SIORVANES

NEOPLATONISM IN ISLAMIC PHILOSOPHY

Islamic Neoplatonism developed in a milieu already saturated with the thought of Plotinus and Aristotle. The former studied in Alexandria, and the Alexandrine philosophical syllabus included such figures as Porphyry of Tyre and Proclus. Associated with these scholars were two major channels of Islamic Neoplatonism, the so-called Theology of Aristotle *and the* Liber de Causis *(Book of Causes). Other cities beloved of the philosophers at the time of the rise of Islam in the first century AH (seventh century AD) included Gondeshapur and Harran.*

Islamic Neoplatonism stressed one aspect of the Qur'anic God, the transcendent, and ignored another, the creative. For the Neoplatonists, all things emanated from the deity. Islamic philosophers were imbued to a greater or lesser degree with either Aristotelianism or Neoplatonism or, as was often the case, with both. Al-Kindi, the father of Islamic philosophy, has a Neoplatonic aspect, but the doctrine reaches its intellectual fruition in the complex emanationist hierarchies developed by al-Farabi and Ibn Sina. Their views are later developed (or metamorphosed) by later thinkers into an emanative hierarchy of lights, as with Shihab al-Din al-Suhrawardi, or the doctrine of the Unity of Being espoused by Ibn al-'Arabi. While al-Ghazali and Ibn Rushd both vigorously opposed Neoplatonic views, the latter attacked the former for his general opposition to the philosophers.

Neoplatonism itself had a major impact on that sectarian grouping of Muslims known as the Isma'ilis, and became the substratum for its theology. Historically, Neoplatonism in Islam achieved its climax with the Fatimid Isma'ili conquest of Egypt towards the end of the fourth century AH (tenth century AD). While Neoplatonism later declined in philosophical importance in the face of rampant Aristotelianism and Hanbalism, it may be said to have bequeathed an important religious, historical and cultural legacy to the Islamic world, which in the Isma'ili movement endures to this day.

1   **Milieu and sources**
2   **The God of Islamic Neoplatonism**
3   **Reaction and counter-reaction**
4   **The influence and legacy of Islamic Neoplatonism**

1   Milieu and sources

Islamic Neoplatonism developed in a milieu which was familiar with the doctrines and teachings of PLOTINUS. The city of Alexandria, into which the Arab armies of Islam marched in AD 642, had down the centuries been home to many philosophies and philosophers: Plotinus himself, the founding father of Neoplatonism, studied in Alexandria for eleven years under the scholar Ammonius Hierocles. The Alexandrian philosophical syllabus was imbued with Neoplatonism and coated with Aristotelianism. The works of important Neoplatonists such as PORPHYRY and PROCLUS were studied there. Two works, whose exact authorship is unclear but which became associated with Porphyry and Proclus respectively, were the famous *Theology of Aristotle* and the work which became Latinized as the *Liber de causis* (see LIBER DE CAUSIS). Both these works, regardless of their actual authorship, were major channels of Islamic Neoplatonism. The *Theology of Aristotle*, despite its name, had nothing to do with Aristotle but summarized, with some additions, Books IV–VI of Plotinus' *Enneads*. The *Liber de causis* (Book of Causes) had its basis in the *Elements of Theology* by Proclus. The Neoplatonic themes in both the *Theologia* and the *Liber* are not difficult to identify, ranging from the key doctrine of emanation through references to the hypostases such as the Universal Intellect and Universal Soul (*Theology of Aristotle*) or the Procline hypostases of the One, Existence, Intellect and Soul (*Liber de causis*), to the sublime attributes of the One (see NEOPLATONISM).

However, Alexandria was not the only major city in the Middle East to foster the rise of Neoplatonism before the rise of Islam. Another was Gondeshapur, a great centre of Greek Byzantine learning, especially in the fields of philosophy and medicine, where Aramaic rather than Persian appears to have been the dominant language. This city, built by Shapur I in the mid-third century AD, acted as a magnet to many Middle Eastern intellectuals in both the pre-Islamic and Islamic periods. The great father of the Arabic translation movement, Hunayn ibn Ishaq, studied there; earlier, Nestorian scholars had fled to that city after the Council of Ephesus in AD 431. These scholars knew the work of Aristotle, but they had also studied Porphyry and so were familiar with the teachings of Neoplatonism. The closeness of Gondeshapur to what became Baghdad meant that the former city was able to infiltrate the latter, when it became an Islamic seat, with a variety of Greek elements.

Then there was Harran in northern Syria, a city which was home to the star-loving Sabaeans, a pagan sect whose transcendent theology was imbued with Neoplatonic elements. In the third century AH (ninth century AD) Harran was visited by refugee scholars from the schools of Alexandria; in the following century these scholars moved from Harran to Baghdad, bringing to that last city elements, both

Aristotelian and Neoplatonic, from the rich philosophical heritage of both Alexandria and Harran. Of course, cities such as Alexandria, Gondeshapur and Harran were not the only sources of Neoplatonic thought, but their examples serve to illustrate the ease with which the expanding Arab-Islamic Empire came into contact with Greek thought, especially in its Aristotelian and Neoplatonic incarnations. And it was between the latter that the pendulum of Islamic philosophy frequently swung in the writings of the individual Islamic philosophers, when they were not actually mixing the two in a glorious intellectual syncretism as happened with the thought of the Ikhwan al-Safa' (see IKHWAN AL-SAFA').

2 The God of Islamic Neoplatonism

The description of God in the Qur'an is by and large fairly clear, though it did give rise to complexities of interpretation in Islamic theology centring on such matters as anthropomorphism, God's omnipotence and man's free will, and the attributes of God. The Qur'anic God, however, is both transcendent and immanent. There is none like him but he is also closer to man than man's jugular vein. He intervenes in human history to reveal himself to man, for example in the revelations of the Qur'an, and sends angels to fight for his prophet Muhammad, as at the Battle of Badr in AD 624. Here he is often like the God beloved of today's process theologians (see PROCESS THEISM). Above all, however, the Qur'anic God is one who creates *ex nihilo*. There is no concept of Neoplatonic emanation in the Qur'an. In contrast, for Aristotle, God is the Unmoved First Mover. The emphasis in Aristotelian theology is much more on God's movement rather than on his creation, which is limited in any case to his production of form in prime matter which has existed eternally. With the Neoplatonists, the emphasis moves from the concept of creation to that of eternal emanation: God or the One or the Good – however he is to be characterized – does not create *ex nihilo* but 'engages' in eternal emanation of all that is below him.

Thus in the Middle East at the time of the rise and spread of Islam there were at least three different 'theologies' vying for space, emphasising different qualities of their deity. There is the Qur'anic God as creator *ex nihilo*; there is the Aristotelian God as first Mover; and there is the Neoplatonic God as eternal emanator. The debate which was engendered about the relationship between God and the rest of observable and intangible reality and phenomena became a fundamental characteristic of the writings of the Islamic philosophers. The Qur'anic God was linked to his creation by the sheer power of creativity,

the Aristotelian God was linked – much less feelingly – with that which moved, while the Neoplatonic God bridged, or attempted to bridge, the huge gulf between transcendence and corporeal reality by the device of emanation. A brief survey of the thought of some individual Islamic philosophers will serve to illustrate how the debate featured in their writings, and thus in the general development of Islamic philosophy.

Abu Yusuf ibn Ishaq AL-KINDI is universally acknowledged by scholars of Islamic philosophy as the 'Father of Islamic Philosophy'. Al-Kindi's God has four faces or aspects. Doctrinally, he is classically rooted in and derived from the Qur'an, and bears such epithets as 'creator' and 'active'. God has an essential unity which does not derive from anything else. He also has Aristotelian aspects – he is, for example, unmoved – but of course al-Kindi's deity is much more than a mere Mover. God's attributes are also discussed by al-Kindi in Mu'tazilite terms and al-Kindi espouses a Mu'tazilite antipathy towards anthropomorphism (see ASH'ARIYYA AND MU'TAZILA §4). Finally, we can detect a Neoplatonic influence on al-Kindi's thought. He was the first major Islamic philosopher to reflect significant aspects of the Neoplatonic tradition, and is a bridge to the thought of philosophers such as al-Farabi and Ibn Sina.

It is with these latter two philosophers that Islamic Neoplatonism reaches its apotheosis, where such fundamental Neoplatonic concepts as hierarchy and emanation are fully developed and integrated into a metaphysics of being. AL FARABI is rightly regarded as the father and founder of Islamic Neoplatonism, while IBN SINA, though less original, is often considered to be Islam's greatest Neoplatonic philosopher. While the deity that he portrays certainly has other aspects, it is the Neoplatonic aspects which draw our attention. Like al-Farabi, Ibn Sina has a complex scheme of emanation with ten intellects emanating from the Necessary Being. Again as with al-Farabi, emanation constitutes a bridge between the unknowable God of Neoplatonism and earthbound humanity. However, the theological terminology deployed in Ibn Sina's thought is perhaps less negative than that of al-Farabi; this is particularly true of the mystical dimension of Ibn Sina's thinking.

Neoplatonism in Islam may be said to have reached its furthest limits of development in the thought of Isma'ili theologians such as Hamid al-Din al-Kirmani on the one hand, and that of Shihab al-Din Yahya AL-SUHRAWARDI and Muhyi al-Din IBN AL-'ARABI on the other. Al-Kirmani espouses a Farabian elaboration of God and ten intellects in his Neoplatonic emanationist hierarchy. Al-Suhrawardi, 'the Master of Illumination' (*shaykh al-ishraq*), as he became known, established an extraordinary complex Neoplatonic hierarchy of lights in which the divine and quasi-divine are seen all in terms of light. God is the Light of Lights (*nur al-anwar*), and from him emanates the First Light from which emanates the Second Light and so on; but bound into the whole system is a complex three-tier system of Angelic Lights. Because of the doctrine of emanation, the lights (or intellects) have an ontological or noetic precedence, the one over the other, but not a temporal precedence. By contrast, Ibn al-'Arabi employs Neoplatonic terminology to bolster his doctrine of the Unity of Being (*wahdat al-wujud*). The circularity of his thought, however, precludes the elaboration of a classical system of emanation following Plotinian, or even Farabian, lines. It may be argued that the terms 'theophanies' or 'manifestations' (*tajalliyat*) of the divinity, rather than 'emanations', are a more accurate rendering of his thought.

3 Reaction and counter-reaction

The reaction and counter-reaction to the infiltration of Neoplatonism into Islamic thought and philosophy may usefully be studied in the writings of the great Abu Hamid al-Ghazali, Sunni theologian and mystic, on the one hand and those of Islam's most notable Aristotelian, Abu'l Walid Muhammad ibn Rushd, also known as Averroes, on the other. In his *Tahafut al-falasifa* (Incoherence of the Philosophers), AL-GHAZALI (§3) attacked both the Neoplatonists and Aristotle. He rebutted, for example, the idea that the world was eternal, and tried to show mathematically that the thesis of the Neoplatonists was illogical. He believed that the Neoplatonists had failed to prove that God was One, and attacked their beliefs about a variety of other fundamental and crucial points such as divine knowledge and the question of the immutability of God. The two principal philosophers whose views al-Ghazali attacked were al-Farabi and Ibn Sina. As al-Ghazali himself put it:

> However, the most faithful – as Aristotle's translators – and the most original – as his commentators – among the philosophizing Muslims are al-Farabi Abu Nasr, and Ibn Sina. Therefore, we will confine our attention to what these two have taken to be the authentic expression of the views of their misleaders.... Therefore, let it be known that we propose to concentrate on the refutation of philosophical thought as it emerges from the writings of these two persons.
>
> (Tahafut al-falasifa: 5)

In all, al-Ghazali itemized twenty particular problems 'in whose discussion in this book we will expose the contradiction involved in the philosopher's theories'.

If al-Ghazali represents Islamic theology's most biting attack on philosophy and severest reaction to Neoplatonism in Islam, IBN RUSHD represents the counter-reaction. This is not to say that the latter wholeheartedly espoused the views of the Neoplatonists: indeed, very far from it. In his *Tahafut al-tahafut* (Incoherence of the Incoherence), referring to the incoherence of al-Ghazali's *Tahafut al-falasifa*, Ibn Rushd wrote a work which Fakhry has described as 'the product of Ibn Rushd's maturest thought [which] constitutes a systematic rebuttal of al-Ghazali's critique of Greco-Arab philosophy' (Fakhry 1983: 276). Al-Ghazali is accused of misunderstanding, and it is clear that Ibn Rushd is concerned to defend the merits of philosophy as a mode of non-heretical thought while at the same time not accepting the theses of the Neoplatonist philosophers. Despite his intention in the *Tahafut al-tahafut* of defending the philosophical targets of al-Ghazali's wrath, Ibn Rushd, as Bello points out, 'more often than not ... does not, in fact, defend al-Farabi and Ibn Sina .... Instead, he shows to what extent they have departed from the authentic Aristotelian philosophical doctrines, and sometimes joins his voice with that of Ghazali in convicting them of heresy' (Bello 1989: 15). Thus Ibn Rushd, despite his defence of philosophy and philosophers, is more than happy to declare open war on Neoplatonism.

4 The influence and legacy of Islamic Neoplatonism

While it is certainly untrue to say that Islamic philosophy came to a sudden end with the death of Ibn Rushd, we can say that his death in AH 595/AD 1198 marks the approaching end of the great debates about Neoplatonism in Islamic thought. By then the kind of peripateticism espoused by Ibn Rushd may be said to have at least revived, if not definitely triumphed over, other forms of philosophy. The death of Ibn al-'Arabi in AH 638/AD 1240 marks that triumph, for the latter's doctrine of *wahdat al-wujud* was perpetuated by only a few faithful disciples. Furthermore, other movements had arisen in competition with Neoplatonism and Aristotelianism, such as the literalism of the Spanish Muslim IBN HAZM, and the Hanbalism of IBN TAYMIYYA. Neoplatonism as a radical system of philosophical thought with a controversial theological agenda was enshrined in the writings of such thinkers as the IKHWAN AL-SAFA', but generally speaking its greatest surviving influence was, and is, on the theology of the Isma'ili sect in Islam, one of the three great divisions of Shi'ism. This sect achieved its political apotheosis with the coming to power of the Fatimid Isma'ili dynasty in North Africa and Egypt in the fourth and fifth centuries AH (tenth and eleventh centuries AD). The Mosque-University of al-Azhar was a beacon of Isma'ili (and thus Neoplatonic) thought before the Ayyubids took possession of Egypt and returned it to the Sunni fold. Today, Neoplatonism in Islam survives principally as the philosophical substratum which underpins the theology of the Isma'ilis, a group which, though itself split over issues of leadership, nonetheless holds many theological and philosophical points in common.

If we examine the impact of Neoplatonism on Islamic thought generally, it is clear that this philosophy served to emphasize that transcendent aspect of God which is to be found clearly in the Qur'an, sometimes at the expense of the immanent. The impact of Neoplatonism on the course of Islamic history itself has been considerable in some regions. Among many examples we may note that the Fatimid dynasty came to power in Egypt and ruled there from AH 297–567 (AD 969–1171); the Isma'ili Assassins flourished at the Castle of Alamut from AH 483–654 (AD 1090–1256); and a Nizari Isma'ili imamate later moved from Persia to India. Theologically then, it is clear that a body of doctrines, so many of which seemed at odds with mainstream Islamic teaching, served at times to highlight the Qur'anic emphasis on transcendence and was actually absorbed by one, albeit heterodox, sect to become the foundation for that sect; while historically, Neoplatonism from its mainly theoretical Middle Eastern origins in Alexandria, Harran, Gondeshapur and elsewhere became sufficiently powerful to 'hijack' an entire dynasty, the Fatimid.

We may extrapolate from all this, then, the paradigm of an 'alien' cult which becomes 'Middle-Easternized' and 'Islamicized' and which acts on occasion as theological stimulus, irritant, gadfly or foundation, and in so doing ultimately inserts itself from a variety of perspectives into the broad and multivalent fabric of Islam. Alternatively, we may choose to examine the phenomenon of Neoplatonism rather more closely, assess its emphasis on order, structure, emanation, hierarchy, transcendence, intellect and soul, and extrapolate a rather different paradigm, perhaps more akin to that preferred by the Isma'ilis. According to this view, Neoplatonism would not be regarded as a foreign or invasive growth within the body politic of Islam but rather as something which, despite its emphasis on emanation rather than *creatio ex nihilo* and other real differences from mainstream Islamic theology, addressed an aspect or aspects of Islam which had been neglected or overlaid by other matters in the development of that faith. It is useful perhaps to ponder Lenn and Madeleine Goodman's observation: 'Emanation was perfected by the neo-Platonists, quite consciously as an alternative to

creation because the learned neo-Platonic philosophers did not choose to redescend into the anthropomorphic cosmogenies from which Aristotle had rescued them with great difficulty only a few centuries earlier' (Goodman and Goodman 1983: 31).

See also: ARISTOTELIANISM IN ISLAMIC PHILOSOPHY; al-FARABI; al-GHAZALI; GREEK PHILOSOPHY: IMPACT ON ISLAMIC PHILOSOPHY; IBN RUSHD; IBN SINA; ILLUMINATIONIST PHILOSOPHY; NEOPLATONISM

References and further reading

* Bello, I.A. (1989) *The Medieval Islamic Controversy Between Philosophy and Orthodoxy*, Islamic Philosophy and Theology Texts and Studies vol. III, Leiden: Brill. (Deals with the conflict between al-Ghazali and Ibn Rushd with special reference to *ijma'* and *ta'wil*.)
* Fakhry, M. (1983) *A History of Islamic Philosophy*, 2nd edn, London: Longmans; New York: Columbia University Press. (A superb introduction to the whole field.)
* al-Ghazali (1058–1111) *Tahafut al-falasifa* (Incoherence of the Philosophers), English trans. S.A. Kamali, Lahore: Pakistan Philosophical Congress, 1963. (A translation of al-Ghazali's attack on the philosophers.)
* Goodman, L.E. and Goodman, M.J. (1983) 'Creation and Evolution: Another Round in an Ancient Struggle', *Zygon* 18 (1): 3–43. (A fascinating and thought-provoking article.)
Henry, P. and Schwyzer, H.R. (eds) (1959) *Plotini Opera*, vol. 2, Paris: Desclée de Brouwer; Brussels: L'Édition Universelle. (Contains G. Lewis' English translation of the *Theology of Aristotle*.)
* Ibn Rushd (c.1180) *Tahafut al-tahafut* (Incoherence of the Incoherence), trans. and intro. S. Van Den Bergh, *Averroes' Tahafut al-Tahafut (The Incoherence of the Incoherence)*, 'E.J.W. Gibb Memorial' new series XIX, London: Luzac, 1978. (Ibn Rushd's famous response to al-Ghazali.)
Leaman, O. (1988) *Averroes and his Philosophy*, Oxford: Clarendon Press; 2nd edn, Richmond: Curzon, 1997. (An introduction to the philosophy of Ibn Rushd arranged according to metaphysics, practical philosophy, and reason, religion and language.)
Nanji, A. (1996) 'Isma'ili Philosophy', in S.H. Nasr and O. Leaman (eds) *History of Islamic Philosophy*, London: Routledge, ch. 9, 144–54. (Examination of Isma'ili philosophy including the influence of Neoplatonism.)
Netton, I.R. (1989) *Allah Transcendent: Studies in the*

Structure and Semiotics of Islamic Philosophy, Theology and Cosmology, London and New York: Routledge. (Contains major chapters on al-Farabi and Ibn Sina.)

Shayegan, Y. (1996) 'The Transmission of Greek Philosophy into the Islamic World', in S.H. Nasr and O. Leaman (eds) *History of Islamic Philosophy*, London: Routledge, ch. 6, 98–104. (Detailed account of how the transmission took place, paying particular attention to the Persian background.)

IAN RICHARD NETTON

NEO-PYTHAGOREANISM

Neo-Pythagoreanism is a term used by modern scholars to refer to the revival of Pythagorean philosophy and way of life in the first century BC. It coincides with the redevelopment of Platonic thought known as Middle Platonism. Neo-Pythagoreans elaborated a mathematical metaphysics in which the highest level of being was occupied by a transcendent principle, equated with 'the One' or 'the Monad' and regarded as the source of all reality. Neo-Pythagorean anthropology reaffirmed the ancient Pythagorean belief in the immortality of the soul. Although Neo-Pythagoreanism is often indistinguishable from Middle Platonism, it is characterized by a tendency to see Pythagoras as the father of all true philosophers, including Plato. In the third century AD Neo-Pythagoreanism was absorbed into Neoplatonism.

As the name implies, Neo-Pythagoreanism is a renewal of Pythagoreanism (see PYTHAGOREANISM). Since the reanimators were philosophers of a Platonic stamp, it is particularly the kind of Pythagoreanism found in Plato and the early Academy that came to be renewed and developed further. Plato incorporated Pythagorean number theory in the *Timaeus* (see PLATO §16) to provide a mathematical structure for the universe. In the so-called 'Unwritten Doctrines' he posited two first principles, the One (or Monad) and the Indefinite Dyad, essentially developments of the Pythagorean primal opposites, Limited and Unlimited (see PHILOLAUS §2; PLATO §5; PLATONISM, EARLY AND MIDDLE §2–4; PYTHAGOREANISM §2). The One, identified with the Good, is the determining principle, which acts upon the Dyad (the Two), the passive principle. Their interaction generates numbers that are equated with the Platonic Forms (the Form-numbers), of which the physical world is but a reflection. The One and the Dyad were taken over, with certain modifications, by Plato's immediate successors, SPEUSIPPUS (§2) and XENOCRATES (§2).

In the subsequent history of Platonism, until the first century BC, Pythagorean metaphysical speculation went into abeyance, notably during the sceptical phase of the Academy when all forms of dogmatism, which would include the positing of mathematicals as the eternal and invariable archetypes of reality, were rejected (see ACADEMY; ARCESILAUS §2).

Although the Hellenistic age marks a fallow time for the serious pursuit of Pythagoreanism, it was a period remarkably productive of Pythagorean texts, known as pseudepigrapha. Their authors either preferred to remain anonymous or purported to be older Pythagoreans. Some of these compositions are religious-didactic, some philosophical but with little original inspiration. None the less, their concern to show that the teachings of Plato and Aristotle were of ancient Pythagorean provenance found great resonance with Neo-Pythagoreans, and several pseudepigrapha were considered authoritative texts.

Pythagorean philosophy resurfaced in earnest in the early first century BC after ANTIOCHUS issued his call 'to follow the ancients'. In the course of a renewed interest in the original works of Plato, the *Timaeus* gained particular prominence, a dialogue that now came to be seen virtually as a Pythagorean tract. A notable commentator on the *Timaeus* was Eudorus of Alexandria. His first principles are Monad and Dyad, but above these he posits a supreme One, also called the Supreme God. 'Becoming like God' was the goal of life. While Eudorus is a Platonist, he presents his doctrines as 'Pythagorean' and thus counts as an important witness to the 'Pythagoreanizing' current in Platonism (see PLATONISM, EARLY AND MIDDLE §§4,8–9).

The first *bona fide* Neo-Pythagorean was Moderatus of Gades. In his *Pythagorean Lectures* he establishes a system of three Ones: a One beyond being, a One in the realm of the Ideas that acts as a divine craftsman (Demiurge) upon the Dyad, bringing matter into existence, and a One that participates in the first two and permeates the world (the World-Soul). Moderatus' triad foreshadows the three *hypostases* – One, Intellect, Soul – of NEOPLATONISM (§3).

Nicomachus of Gerasa has a similar triad. His first God, the Monad, appears, however, to be identified with the Demiurge, who in combination with the Dyad produces the Logos – or the Forms, equated in accentuated Pythagorean-Platonic fashion with mathematicals (see LOGOS §1). Much of Nicomachus' philosophy must be extracted from his *Theological Arithmetic*, a work in which he identifies the traditional Hellenic gods with numbers. This number-mysticism excited the interest of later Neoplatonists, especially Iamblichus.

With NUMENIUS of Apamea (Syria) we reach the

zenith of Neo-Pythagorean thought. While a Platonist from our viewpoint, Numenius put Pythagoras, Socrates and Plato on an equal footing and was generally regarded as a Pythagorean in antiquity. He also proclaimed three gods, but in his attempts to separate the Monad, the absolute Good, from all association with creative activity and matter (the Dyad for Numenius is co-eternal with the Monad and embodies an evil principle), his philosophy assumes a starkly dualistic character, reminiscent of ancient Pythagoreanism.

In addition to metaphysics, Neo-Pythagorean philosophers reaffirmed the immortality of the soul and transmigration (see PYTHAGOREANISM §3). There are also indications that, along with the renewal of Pythagorean philosophy, came a revival of the Pythagorean lifestyle with its emphasis on spiritual and bodily purity. This is evidenced especially in Roman Pythagoreanism. Cicero credits one Nigidius Figulus with renewing an extinct Pythagoreanism. Although we know nothing of the speculative thought of Figulus, Cicero's testimony accords well with the general picture of a Pythagorean reawakening in the first century BC, which in the Roman world undoubtedly took a very practical form. In the next century, under the emperor Augustus, a circle of Pythagorean philosophers formed around Quintus Sextius, the 'Sextii', whose ethical precepts had considerable impact on SENECA (§1). The emperor Tiberius employed a Pythagorean court-philosopher named Thrasyllus.

After flourishing in the hands of Numenius, Neo-Pythagoreanism came to an end with the waning of the second century AD. But with Middle Platonism, with which it had always gone hand in hand, it lived on as major force in Neoplatonism. PLOTINUS, PORPHYRY, IAMBLICHUS, PROCLUS, to name just the most famous Neoplatonists, not only wrote on Pythagorean themes (we owe two of our extant biographies of Pythagoras to Porphyry and Iamblichus) but also were indelibly marked by the philosophy that bore the name of Pythagoras.

See also: ORPHISM; PLATONISM, EARLY AND MIDDLE §1

References and further reading

Armstrong, A.H. (ed.) (1970) *The Cambridge History of Later Greek and Early Medieval Philosophy*, Cambridge: Cambridge University Press. (In chapter 5 Merlan briefly discusses the Pythagorean pseudepigrapha and several Neo-Pythagoreans, among them Moderatus, Nicomachus and Numenius; for a more comprehensive treatment of these authors see Dillon (1977).)

Dillon, J.M. (1977) *The Middle Platonists: A Study of Platonism*, 80 BC to AD 220, London: Duckworth. (Chapter 1 includes valuable pointers to Pythagorean currents in Plato, Speusippus and Xenocrates; chapter 7 covers the individual Neo-Pythagoreans against the background of Middle Platonic thought.)

Guthrie, K.S. (1987) *The Pythagorean Sourcebook and Library*, Grand Rapids, MI: Phanes Press. (Contains English translations of many of the pseudo-Pythagorean texts, including those that were highly influential on Neo-Pythagoreanism, such as the fragments of pseudo-Philolaus and pseudo-Archytas, *On the Nature of the Universe* by Ocellus Lucanus, *On the World and the Soul* by Timaeus of Locri, and the *Golden Verses of Pythagoras*.)

Kingsley, P. (1995) *Ancient Philosophy, Mystery, and Magic: Empedocles and Pythagorean Tradition*, Oxford: Oxford University Press. (In chapter 20 Kingsley examines the later history of Pythagoreanism, arguing that Neo-Pythagoreanism was not so much a revival as a continuation of early Pythagorean traditions that were kept alive in small circles of practising Pythagoreans.)

O'Meara, D.J. (1989) *Pythagoras Revived: Mathematics and Philosophy in Late Antiquity*, Oxford: Oxford University Press. (A short introduction to Neo-Pythagoreanism is followed by an account of the Neoplatonic adaptation of Pythagorean philosophy, particularly the mathematization of reality, by Iamblichus, Hierocles, Syrianus and Proclus.)

Reale, G. (1990) *A History of Ancient Philosophy IV: The Schools of the Imperial Age*, trans. J.R. Catan, Albany, NY: State University of New York Press. (Pages 237–72 discuss the revival of Pythagoreanism, stressing the incorporeal and transcendental aspects of Neo-Pythagoreanism.)

Thesleff, H. (1961) *An Introduction to the Pythagorean Writings of the Hellenistic Period*, Åbo Finland: Åbo Akademi. (A scholarly account of the Pythagorean pseudepigrapha and their sources. Although the dating of these texts is a subject of controversy, Thesleff's discussion of the genre remains useful.)

HERMANN S. SCHIBLI

NEUMANN, FRANZ
see FRANKFURT SCHOOL

NEUMANN, JOHN VON (1903–57)

Von Neumann was one of the great mathematical minds of the twentieth century. His work has affected philosophy on several fronts, including logic and the philosophy of science. He also had great influence upon developments in the philosophy of mind: the computer model of mind employed during the middle-to-late twentieth century was explicitly based upon the von Neumann computer architecture. Although late twentieth-century philosophy of mind has largely rejected the von Neumann machine as a model of brain activity, his pioneering work in cellular automata has provided a basis for subsequent development in 'distributed' or 'connectionist' computer architectures.

John von Neumann was described by mathematician Jacob Bronowski as 'the cleverest man I ever knew, without exception. And he was a genius, in the sense that a genius is a man who has *two* great ideas'. But von Neumann was even cleverer than that, doing foundational work in logic and set theory, quantum mechanics, computer design and the theory of computation, and game theory, to mention only those contributions of immediate interest to philosophers. In pure mathematics, von Neumann also produced important work in measure theory and the spectral theory of operators in Hilbert space, as well as introducing the theory of 'rings of operators' (now known as von Neumann algebras). In applied mathematics, he did groundbreaking work in numerical analysis in connection with fluid dynamics, the theory of turbulence and the physics of shock waves.

Born in Budapest, Hungary, von Neumann was educated at the Lutheran *Gymnasium* and was then tutored privately in mathematics when his extraordinary abilities became apparent. Though enrolled at the University of Budapest, von Neumann appeared there only to take exams, instead spending his time in Germany and Switzerland studying physics and chemistry and visiting David Hilbert in Göttingen to discuss mathematics. He took a chemical engineering degree at the Federal Institute of Technology in Zürich in 1925 and a doctorate in mathematics at Budapest in 1926 (his dissertation concerned the axiomatization of set theory). He was named *Privatdozent* at the University of Berlin (1927–9), and then at Hamburg (1929–30). In 1930–1 he became a visiting lecturer at Princeton University in New Jersey, and subsequently professor of mathematics there until he joined the Institute for Advanced Study (also at Princeton) in 1933, becoming its youngest permanent member. During the Second World War, von Neumann participated in various war-related scientific enterprises for the USA, in particular the atomic bomb project at Los Alamos. In 1954 von Neumann was appointed to the USA's Atomic Energy Commission. He died of bone cancer in Washington, DC in 1957.

Among von Neumann's accomplishments in set theory (see SET THEORY) are his elegant treatment of ordinal numbers (in which each ordinal number is the set of all smaller ordinal numbers), the first rigorous treatment of definition by transfinite induction, and an axiomatization of set theory more technically intricate than that of Ernst Zermelo and Abraham Fraenkel. This axiomatization and its successors have turned out to be useful in mathematical research. With respect to mathematical logic, von Neumann participated in Hilbert's programme in metamathematics, publishing proofs of consistency for parts of arithmetic until Kurt Gödel's 1931 results made such activity moot (see GÖDEL'S THEOREMS).

In quantum theory, von Neumann provided the first rigorous axiomatization of quantum mechanics, contributed to measure theory and proved an ergodic theorem for quantum systems. His *Mathematische Grundlagen der Quantenmechanik* (*Mathematical Foundations of Quantum Mechanics*, 1932) gives his argument that no introduction of 'hidden parameters' can eliminate the statistical character of statements of quantum theory unless the theory itself is fundamentally changed (see QUANTUM MECHANICS, INTERPRETATION OF).

Von Neumann introduced the theory of games in a 1928 paper, providing a mathematical description of games and strategy and stating and proving the minimax theorem (see DECISION AND GAME THEORY). (Game theory is also known as 'decision theory' because a game in von Neumann's sense includes bluffing and, in selecting a move, taking into account what you think your opponent thinks you are going to do.) His later collaboration with Oskar Morgenstern (1944) extended game theory to mathematical economics.

Computer design and theory of computation are the areas of von Neumann's work which have had the most widespread influence among philosophers. Von Neumann's computer design was influential for two main reasons: the machine architecture appears 'brain-like' at an abstract level (or so many philosophers thought); and the design could be implemented using high-speed components available at the time (resulting in an actual computer which could perform impressive computations).

A von Neumann machine consists of three primary components (a 'central control unit', a 'central arithmetic unit' and a finite uniform 'memory') and input and output 'organs'. (The analogy with the human body is discussed in von Neumann's 'First Draft of a Report on the EDVAC' (1945).) The central control unit interprets instructions while the central arithmetic unit executes operations on data contained in the memory; a crucial feature of a von Neumann machine is that the instructions are also stored in the uniform memory. Thus the functional status of the contents of any particular memory location is indeterminate: if it is executed, it is an instruction; if it is operated upon, it is data. A von Neumann machine exploits this indeterminacy: the machine can modify its own program during execution. This feature both allows the high-speed implementation of basic programming constructs and explains why the von Neumann architecture was regarded as 'brain-like'.

Subsequent developments in artificial intelligence and neuroscience, however, have led to the rejection of the von Neumann machine as a model of brain activity. Basic cognitive processes (for example, pattern recognition) are computation-intensive, and neurons are too slow (and too unreliable) to complete them accurately in real time given a von Neumann computer organization. If the brain is a digital computer, it must have a non-von Neumann architecture.

Interestingly, in the 1940s von Neumann was already working on developing a general theory of natural and artificial automata; his particular areas of concern were self-reproducing automata and the synthesis of reliable systems from unreliable components. His early work on McCulloch–Pitts 'neural networks' (see McCulloch and Pitts 1943) made von Neumann himself a pioneer in non-von Neumann computer architectures.

See also: LOGICAL AND MATHEMATICAL TERMS, GLOSSARY OF

List of works

Neumann, J. von (1961–3) *The Collected Works of John von Neumann*, ed. A.H. Taub, Oxford and New York: Pergamon Press, 6 vols. (Organized chronologically by topic, with an exhaustive bibliography. Of particular interest to philosophers: papers on logic, set theory and quantum mechanics in volume 1; computer design and automata theory in volume 5; and game theory in volume 6.)

—— (1986) *Papers of John von Neumann on Computing and Computer Theory*, ed. W. Aspray and A. Burks, The Charles Babbage Institute Reprint Series for the History of Computing, vol. 12, Cambridge, MA: MIT Press. (The best introductory

source for von Neumann's writings on computing; includes relevant papers from the *Collected Works*, including the 1945 and 1946 papers on von Neumann architecture, some papers not in that collection, and the first part of von Neumann (1966), with useful introductions by A. Burks. Includes a bibliography of von Neumann's publications in all subjects, and a convenient bibliography of computer research contemporary with von Neumann and building on his work.)

—— (1928) 'Zur Theorie der Gesellschaftsspiele', *Mathematische Annalen* 100: 295–320; trans. S. Bargmann, 'On the Theory of Games and Strategy', in *Contributions to the Theory of Games*, vol. 4, Princeton, NJ: Princeton University Press, 1959, 13–42. (The paper in which von Neumann invented game theory; includes the first statement and proof of the minimax theorem.)

—— (1932) *Mathematische Grundlagen der Quantenmechanik*, Berlin: Springer; trans. R. Beyer, *Mathematical Foundations of Quantum Mechanics*, Princeton, NJ: Princeton University Press, 1955; repr. in the Princeton Landmarks in Mathematics and Physics series, Princeton, NJ: Princeton University Press, 1983. (Von Neumann's axiomatization of quantum mechanics and his development of a mathematical theory of measurement in quantum mechanics; includes his argument that if the basic structure of quantum theory is to remain unchanged, the statistical nature of statements of the theory cannot be eliminated by the introduction of 'hidden parameters'.)

Neumann, J. von and Morgenstern, O. (1944) *Theory of Games and Economic Behavior*, Princeton, NJ: Princeton University Press. (The foundational work in mathematical economics. Chapter 1, which explains the basis for the extension of game theory to economics, is accessible to a general audience, but the remainder very quickly becomes technically intricate.)

Neumann, J. von (1945) 'First Draft of a Report on the EDVAC' (for the US Army Ordnance Department/University of Pennsylvania), repr. in *Papers of John von Neumann on Computing and Computer Theory*, ed. W. Aspray and A. Burks, Cambridge, MA: MIT Press, 1986; corrected version, *IEEE Annals of the History of Computing* 15 (4): 27–75, 1993. (This paper specifies the first logical design of an electronic computer whose program could be both stored and modified electronically. It incorporated, without credit, work by J.P. Eckert, Jr and J. Mauchly, which led to a dispute over who really originated the 'von Neumann' architecture. See Goldstine (1972) and especially Williams (1985) for accounts of the controversy. For justification of the corrections in the 1993 version, see Godfrey and Hendry (1993).)

Neumann, J. von, Burks, A. and Goldstine, H. (1946) 'Preliminary Discussion of the Logical Design of an Electronic Computing Instrument' (US Army Ordnance Department/Institute for Advanced Study, Princeton, NJ), repr. in *The Collected Works of John von Neumann*, ed. A.H. Taub, Oxford and New York: Pergamon Press, 1963, vol. 5, 34–79; and in *Papers of John von Neumann on Computing and Computer Theory*, ed. W. Aspray and A. Burks, Cambridge, MA: MIT Press, 1986, 97–142. (This paper completes the description of what became known as the 'von Neumann architecture' by incorporating a random access memory along with the stored program concept articulated in von Neumann (1945).)

Neumann, J. von (1950) *Functional Operators*, vol. 1, *Measures and Integrals* (Annals of Mathematics Studies 21), vol. 2, *The Geometry of Orthogonal Spaces* (Annals of Mathematics Studies 22), Princeton, NJ: Princeton University Press. (Notes compiled from lectures on measure theory given at the Institute for Advanced Study at Princeton in 1934.)

—— (1951) 'The General and Logical Theory of Automata', in L. Jeffress (ed.) *Cerebral Mechanisms in Behavior: The Hixon Symposium*, New York: Wiley, 1–31; repr. in *The Collected Works of John von Neumann*, ed. A.H. Taub, Oxford and New York: Pergamon Press, 1963, vol. 5, 288–328; and in *Papers of John von Neumann on Computing and Computer Theory*, ed. W. Aspray and A. Burks, Cambridge, MA: MIT Press, 1986, 391–431. (A slightly revised version of a paper delivered at the Hixon Symposium (1948) reflecting on the influence of McCulloch and Pitts (1943) on the design of digital computers, and speculating on the direction von Neumann would later take in his work on self-reproducing automata; accessible to a general audience and a nice introduction to his work in this area.)

—— (1958) *The Computer and the Brain*, New Haven, CT: Yale University Press. (The text of the 1956 Mrs Hepsa Ely Silliman memorial lectures, which von Neumann was too ill to deliver at Yale University; accessible to a general audience.)

—— (1960) *Continuous Geometry*, Princeton, NJ: Princeton University Press. (Notes from lectures given at Princeton 1935–7 on a topic von Neumann invented in 1935 by considering geometric interpretations of von Neumann algebras.)

—— (1966) *Theory of Self-Reproducing Automata*, ed. A. Burks, Urbana, IL: University of Illinois Press. (Based on lectures given at the University of Illinois in 1949.)

References and further reading

Arbib, M. (1964) *Brains, Machines, and Mathematics*, New York: McGraw-Hill; 2nd revised edn, New York: Springer, 1987. (An introduction to the theory of automata and computation, including discussion of von Neumann machines, self-reproducing automata and neural nets. The second edition includes material on connectionism.)

Aspray, W. (1990) *John von Neumann and the Origins of Modern Computing*, Cambridge, MA: MIT Press. (A detailed intellectual biography of von Neumann, concentrating on his contributions to the theory of computation, computer design and scientific computer applications. Provides accurate glosses of the technical work for a general audience.)

Brink, J. and Haden, C. (eds) (1989) *The Computer and the Brain: An International Symposium in Commemoration of John von Neumann (1903–1957)*, special issue of *Annals of the History of Computing* 11 (3). (Selected and revised essays from a 1987 symposium of biologists, computer scientists, electrical engineers, historians, linguists, philosophers, physicists and psychologists. Topics include aspects of von Neumann's life, his correspondence with Hungarian physicist Rudolph Ortvay (in which von Neumann worked out some of his ideas in automata theory), his contribution to computing and the effect of his influence on subsequent developments in the field.)

Glimm, J., Impagliazzo, J. and Singer, I. (eds) (1990) *The Legacy of John von Neumann*, Proceedings of Symposia in Pure Mathematics, vol. 50, Providence, RI: American Mathematical Society. (Twenty-two articles examining the mathematical ideas of von Neumann and tracing their subsequent development and evolution; includes a short note on von Neumann's philosophical development by his brother. A useful successor to Oxtoby, Pettis and Price (1958).)

Godfrey, M. and Hendry, D. (1993) 'The Computer as Von Neumann Planned It', *IEEE Annals of the History of Computing* 15 (1): 11–21. (Discusses the motivation for the logical architecture and design in the 'First Draft of a Report on the EDVAC' (1945) and contrasts the machine described with the EDVAC actually constructed. Argues for some corrections to von Neumann's original first draft and points out errors which have crept into subsequent reprints.)

Goldstine, H. (1972) *The Computer from Pascal to von Neumann*, Princeton, NJ: Princeton University Press. (A thorough history of digital computing with particular attention paid to the circumstances surrounding von Neumann's 1945 and 1946 papers.)

Heims, S. (1980) *John von Neumann and Norbert Weiner: From Mathematics to the Technologies of Life and Death*, Cambridge, MA: MIT Press. (Part biography and part exploration of the connections between science, technology and politics; provides a nontechnical discussion of von Neumann's work in historical context. Of particular biographical interest is chapter 14, which presents a non-hagiographic portrait of von Neumann.)

* McCulloch, W. and Pitts, W. (1943) 'A Logical Calculus of the Ideas Immanent in Nervous Activity', *Bulletin of Mathematical Biophysics* 5: 115–33; repr. in M. Boden (ed.) *The Philosophy of Artificial Intelligence*, New York: Oxford University Press, 1990, 22–39. (The original paper describing how computations could be performed by networks of threshold logic units (artificial neurons). Accessible to those familiar with logical formalisms; a more gentle (though still rigorous) introduction is Arbib (1964).)

Oxtoby, J., Pettis, B. and Price, G. (eds) (1958) *John von Neumann, 1903–1957*, special issue of the *Bulletin of the American Mathematical Society* 64 (3, part 2). (Includes Ulam (1958) and seven articles which provide good introductions to particular aspects of von Neumann's mathematical work, including quantum theory, game theory and automata theory; most trace developments arising from von Neumann's work and each has a selected bibliography.)

Poundstone, W. (1992) *Prisoner's Dilemma: John von Neumann, Game Theory, and the Puzzle of the Bomb*, New York: Doubleday. (A partly biographical essay which presents the theory of games for a general audience; includes a bibliography.)

Ulam, S. (1958) 'John von Neumann, 1903–1957', *John von Neumann, 1903–1957*, special issue of the *Bulletin of the American Mathematical Society* 64 (3, part 2): 1–49. (A good introductory survey of von Neumann's mathematical work, particularly useful as Ulam explains and assesses von Neumann's contributions while giving specific pointers to his published work; also includes a brief biography and a bibliography of von Neumann's publications.)

Williams, M. (1985) *A History of Computing Technology*, Englewood Cliffs, NJ: Prentice-Hall. (A reliable and very accessible introduction to computing devices, with particular attention paid to mechanical details; includes a balanced account of the attribution controversy over the von Neumann architecture.)

BRIAN ROSMAITA

NEURATH, OTTO (1882–1945)

An Austrian socialist philosopher, economist, sociologist and historian, Neurath was a charismatic orator and an energetic cultural activist. Deeply concerned with education as a tool for social progress and cooperation, he founded museums and created the Isotype language for visual education. During the Bavarian Revolution he headed a plan for the centralized socialization of the Bavarian economy. A determined supporter of the scientific attitude and opponent of metaphysics (which he believed to have pernicious political and social consequences), he was a founder member of the Vienna Circle and a heterodox proponent of logical empiricism. He spearheaded the Unity of Science Movement that launched the project of an encyclopedia of unified science.

1 Life
2 Science and society: empiricism in the social sciences (1910–31)
3 Scientific language and scientific method: the Vienna Circle and Neurath's logical empiricism (1931–5)
4 Unity of science and the encyclopedia-model (1934–45)

1 Life

Otto Neurath was born on 10 December 1882, in Vienna, son of Gertrud Kaempfert and Wilhelm Neurath, social reformer and political economist. He received a doctoral degree in Berlin in the history of economics in 1906. A study of the Balkans led to his theory of war economy as a natural (non-monetary) economy upon which he based his programme for full socialization. In 1919 the short-lived Bavarian socialist government appointed him head of the Central Planning Office. From 1920 to 1934 Neurath participated actively in the direction of Viennese socialist politics, especially in housing and adult education. He founded the Social and Economic Museum of Vienna, which created the 'Vienna method' of picture statistics and the Isotype language ('International System of Typographic Picture Education'); the Verein Ernst Mach, which, with the publication of an intellectual manifesto in 1929, became the public face of the Vienna Circle; the International Foundation for Visual Education at the Hague; and the International Unity of Science Movement. The latter, inspired by the ideas of the French Encyclopedists, launched the project of an Encyclopedia for Unified Science. Together with the pictorial languages, this scientific encyclopedia would promote social solidarity and progress at an international level. Neurath fled from the Nazis, first to The Hague, then in 1940 to England, where after nine months of internment he resumed activities related to the Isotype method and the unity of science. He died in Oxford on 22 December 1945.

2 Science and society: empiricism in the social sciences (1910–31)

Neurath championed 'the scientific attitude'. He denied any value to philosophy over and above the pursuit of work on science, within science and for science. His views on the language, method and unification of science were led throughout by his interest in the social life of individuals and their well-being. This concern is reflected in his engagement both in political life and in social science. For Neurath, to theorize about society is inseparable from theorizing for and within society (see MARXIST PHILOSOPHY OF SCIENCE). Science is in every sense a social and historical enterprise. It is about social objectives as well as objects, about social realizations as well as reality.

Neurath drew upon the spirit – if not the letter – of two major turn-of-the-century thinkers: Ernst MACH and Karl MARX. Mach introduced a radical anti-metaphysical approach into the analysis of science which Neurath embraced, in part because he believed that metaphysical obscurantism underwrote social institutions that attacked enlightenment values such as equality, freedom and progress. Neurath's aim was to apply the empirical attitude throughout the social sciences. He attacked the distinction drawn by Dilthey, Rickert and Weber between the natural and the social sciences, which rested on non-empirical practice (like the 'empathic' method). A purely empiricist language would represent one big step towards unified science. Methodologically, the job of the social sciences, like the natural sciences, would be to establish correlations – statistical when possible – and to deduce predictions about the future.

Neurath saw in Marx a model of social science without metaphysics and also of unification – of sociology, economics and politics. Marx inspired in him the belief in the social and historical contingency of language and concepts, including those of science ('there is no *tabula rasa*'), and the enlightenment idea that the scientific attitude possesses a practical and socially redemptive (revolutionary) value: the social scientist is also a social engineer. This influence is reflected in Neurath's work in natural economy and his activities as social planner. During the 1910s he articulated, following ideas of Popper-Lynkeus (see Wachtel 1955), an 'ecological' economic programme based on central planning and non-monetary struc-

ture. The goal was not the increase of wealth, but the allocation of exhaustible resources and goods in a way that increased the standards of living of individuals; the method, an empirical calculus of needs and satisfaction that introduced 'qualitative exactness' in place of the quantitative monetary calculations and a central organization in place of a market and monetary unit. The centralized programme required, Neurath realized, a practical, cooperative unification of the sciences: unity at the point of action.

Neurath's ideas also reflect the influence of Henri POINCARÉ and P.M.M. DUHEM (see CONVENTIONALISM). A multiplicity of theories can accord equally well with the same data. Science is methodologically open-ended. For Neurath the objective was not to determine which theory is true but which theory, or combination, should be used for a given purpose. This decision is pragmatic: the social scientist is to examine all possible theories and predictions that fit the data, in order, like the engineer, to design (social) machines that have never yet been built.

Neurath rejected all pictures of 'ideal' science as gross metaphysics. His attention to the inextricable link between science and society had several consequences: the amount of knowledge available can never be exhaustive; the uncertainty involved in justifying decision-making 'scientifically' can only be honestly and rationally eliminated through extra-empirical 'auxiliary' motives (to deny this limitation in the power of scientific justification amounts to 'pseudorationalism'); the empirical language of science cannot be a precise and atomic Machian one, on pain of losing descriptive, predictive and explanatory power; the introduction of vague, ambiguous terms into the 'physicalist' language is inevitable; abstract analysis prompts the adoption of a multiplicity of conventional idealized concepts – social factors or indicators – which are value-laden and historically contingent.

3 Scientific language and scientific method: the Vienna Circle and Neurath's logical empiricism (1931–5)

Neurath's later views on the language and method of science represented his simultaneous response to problems in the social sciences and to problems addressed by the Vienna Circle between 1928 and 1934, and by Karl POPPER (see VIENNA CIRCLE §§2–3). A primary aim of the Vienna Circle was to account for the objectivity of scientific knowledge claims without resort to metaphysics. The method was to investigate the logical and linguistic frameworks of scientific knowledge (the linguistic turn). The 'orthodox' position was that revisable theoretical scientific statements stand in appropriate logical relations to unrevisable elementary observation statements (the data), called 'protocol statements'.

Neurath took the objectivity of scientific knowledge to be provided by the public and social nature of its representations and rules for acceptance. By 1931 his proposed scientific language was 'radical physicalism': scientific statements must speak of material things (not necessarily from the domain of physics) in space and time. Objectivity and the avoidance of metaphysics require that sentences be compared only with sentences, not with 'reality' ('it is impossible to step outside language'). Protocol statements preserve strict 'linguistic empiricism' by avoiding both reference to 'reality' (contra SCHLICK and Popper) and to subjective (phenomenalistic) experience (contra CARNAP and Schlick). They are not items of personal experience but public reports of scientific observations, like a laboratory notebook. They are thus syntactically complex and 'rich in theory', not atomic and purely observational, unavoidably incorporating into science complex and vague cluster-concepts from natural language that lack the 'ideal' precision of theoretical terms. This makes scientific language a historically provided 'jargon'.

Neurath rejected both Carnap's methods of verification and Popper's method of falsification (see SCIENTIFIC METHOD). With Duhem he believed first that not one but only groups of hypotheses can be confronted with empirical data, hence leaving undetermined how to assign praise or blame within the group (Duhem–Quine problem), and second, that any number of such groups can always fit the same data (see QUINE, W.V.; UNDERDETERMINATION §3). Moreover, protocol statements are revisable (see FALLIBILISM). In case of conflict between the prediction of theory and a protocol statement, either the theory or the protocol can be rejected (the Neurath principle). Finally, in many cases the presence of imprecise terms will leave the protocol statements in an indeterminate logical relation to the theoretical ones, thus rendering both verification and falsification logically inconclusive. Neurath concluded that the belief in a general unambiguous scientific method is a 'pseudorational' ideal and that all theory choice is ultimately pragmatic. His views are illustrated with his image of the ship: 'We are like sailors who have to rebuild their ship on the open sea, without ever being able to dismantle it in dry-dock and reconstruct it from its best components' (1983: 92).

4 Unity of science and the encyclopedia-model (1934–45)

The ship metaphor also illustrates Neurath's idea of the unification of the sciences as a historical and communal enterprise. In 1934 he articulated the ideas on the unity of science that had been developing in his works since 1910 (see UNITY OF SCIENCE). He opposed the myth of the 'system-model': a unique, axiomatic, deductively closed and complete hierarchy of sciences. Instead he proposed the more realistic 'encyclopaedia-model': the coherent totality of the accepted scientific statements at a given time, in flux, incomplete, not void of imprecise statements and logical gaps, unified linguistically by the physicalist 'jargon', and methodologically by the general use of certain techniques (statistics, probabilities and so on) and the empiricist spirit; on the whole, in Neurath's terms, like a 'mosaic', an 'aggregation' of the sciences, or an interdisciplinary 'orchestration' of the scientists' efforts.

See also: HOLISM AND INDIVIDUALISM IN HISTORY AND SOCIAL SCIENCE; NATURALISM IN SOCIAL SCIENCE; VIENNA CIRCLE §4

List of works

Neurath, O. (1981) *Gesammelte philosophische und methodologische Schriften* (Collected Philosophical and Methodological Writings), ed. R. Haller and H. Rutte, Vienna: Holder-Pichler-Tempsky. (This work does not include Neurath's economic writings, which are currently being edited by R. Haller, his numerous political writings nor those on the Isotype language.)

—— (1939) *Modern Man in the Making*, New York: Knopf. (Popular socio-historical-cum-philosophical account of the rise of modernity, with ISOTYPE illustrations.)

—— (1944) *Foundations of the Social Sciences*, International Encyclopaedia of Unified Science vol. 2, no. 1, Chicago, IL: University of Chicago Press. (An account of the place of the social sciences in his controversial 'encyclopedic' conception of unified science.)

—— (1973) *Empiricism and Sociology*, ed. R.S. Cohen and M. Neurath, Dordrecht: Reidel. (A collection of memoirs of Neurath and a selection from his philosophical, scientific, pedagogic and economic writings; includes Vienna Circle manifesto and Anti-Spengler.)

—— (1983) *Philosophical Papers 1913–1946*, ed. R.S. Cohen and M. Neurath, Dordrecht: Reidel. (Selection of philosophical writings, predominantly from Neurath's Vienna Circle period.)

—— (1991) *Gesammelte bildpädagogische Schriften*, ed. R. Haller and R. Kinross, Vienna: Hölder-

Pichler-Tempsky. (Collected writings on picture statistics and visual education, 1925–45.)

—— (forthcoming) *Gesammelte ökonomische Schriften*, ed. R. Haller, Vienna: Hölder-Pichler-Tempsky. (Collected economic writings, 1904–45.)

—— (forthcoming) *Selected Economic Writings*, ed. R.S. Cohen and T.E. Uebel, Dordrecht: Kluwer. (Selections from Neurath's economic writings, 1909–45.)

References and further reading

Cartwright, N., Cat J., Fleck, K. and Uebel, T. (1995) *Between Science and Politics: The Philosophy of Otto Neurath*, Cambridge: Cambridge University Press. (A study of the joint development of Neurath's social science, his political activities and his philosophical point of view.)

Nemeth, E. and Stadler, F. (eds) (1996) *Otto Neurath: Encyclopedia and Utopia*, Dordrecht: Kluwer. (This volume contains recent works reassessing Neurath's views on philosophy, the social sciences and education.)

Uebel, T.E. (ed.) (1991) *Rediscovering the Forgotten Vienna Circle*, Dordrecht: Kluwer. (A collection and translation of recent German and Austrian scholarship.)

—— (1992) *Overcoming Logical Positivism from Within*, Amsterdam: Rodopoi. (A critical philosophical history and investigation of Vienna Circle views.)

Wachtel, H.I. (1955) *Security for All and Free Enterprise: A Summary of the Social Philosophy of Josef Popper-Lynkeus*, New York: Philosophical Library. (An account of Popper-Lynkeus's life and work, based on his *Die allgemeine Nährpflicht als Lösung der socialen Frage* (1912).)

Zolo, D. (1989) *Reflexive Epistemology: The Philosophical Legacy of Otto Neurath*, Dordrecht: Kluwer. (A philosophical and historical account focusing on Neurath's views about knowledge and method.)

JORDI CAT
NANCY CARTWRIGHT

NEUTRAL MONISM

Neutral monism is a theory of the relation of mind and matter. It holds that both are complex constructions out of more primitive elements that are 'neutral' in the sense that they are neither mental nor material. Mind and matter, therefore, do not differ in the intrinsic nature of their constituents but in the manner in which the constituents are organized. The theory is monist only in claiming that all the basic elements of the world are of the same fundamental type (in contrast to mind–body dualism); it is, however, pluralist in that it admits a plurality of such elements (in contrast to metaphysical monism).

Historically, neutral monism had its origins in Ernst Mach's sensationalism (see MACH, E.). According to Mach (1885), the relative permanence of both bodies and the ego are due to their being composed of large numbers of elements not many of which are replaced at any one time. He called these elements 'sensations', though the phenomenalist suggestions carried by this term are misleading, for Mach's sensations are neither mental nor physical.

Mach directly influenced both William James and Bertrand Russell, the philosophers most widely regarded as neutral monists. James' early psychological work, notably his *Principles of Psychology* (1890), was explicitly dualist, although his neutral monism began to appear soon afterwards – for example, in his account of colour perception in *Psychology. A Briefer Course* (1892: 332) – and some commentators have suggested the dualism of the *Principles* was merely methodological. James' monism emerges clearly in 'The Knowing of Things Together' (1895), where he claimed (rather loosely) that the object known and the mind that knows it were 'only two names that are given to the one experience, when, taken in a larger world of which it forms a part, its connections are traced in different directions' (1895: 379). For the next couple of years, in classes and notebooks, James developed these ideas into the view, very similar to Mach's, that there was no 'pure ego' and no material substance, only experience. This, however, remained unpublished until, in 1904–5, he wrote most of the essays which were posthumously collected in *Essays in Radical Empiricism* (1912), and which contains his fullest statement of the theory (see JAMES, W. §6).

It seems to have been Russell who coined the term 'neutral monism' in the course of criticizing the theory in 1913. (James always referred to it as 'radical empiricism', though he had applied the term 'neutral' to experiences in notes written in the 1880s.) Russell did not embrace neutral monism until 1919. In doing so he was influenced to lay aside his earlier objections partly by Hume's arguments for the unintrospectibility of the self (which also impressed James), but most importantly by Wittgenstein's (1921) treatment of belief, which 'shows... that there is no such thing as the soul' (see WITTGENSTEIN, L. §§3–5). James' treatment of belief had been a particular target of Russell's earlier criticism and

Russell's first work as a neutral monist was an account of belief (Russell 1919; 1925).

Russell treated the theory more broadly in *The Analysis of Mind* (1921), where he attempted to show how both the mind and material objects could be constructed out of elements he called 'events', the differences between mind and matter arising from the irreducibly different types of causal law each obeyed (see RUSSELL §13). As parts of material objects, events were related by physical causal relations expressed ultimately by differential equations; as parts of the mind they were related by 'mnemic' causal laws, in which a past state of the mind is among the proximate causes of its current state. Although Russell changed details in subsequent works, he never abandoned this general picture (Russell 1956).

In developing his theory, Russell was influenced by recent advances in physics (especially as interpreted by the subjectivist philosophy of A.S. Eddington) and by behaviourism. He said that modern physics had shown matter to be less material than formerly supposed, while modern psychology had shown mind to be less mental. He thought of neutral monism as the natural outcome of these two developments. Despite the evident influence of behaviourism, he rejected the behaviourist attempt to reduce mental phenomena to physical ones. Indeed, Russell insists that mental states, despite their status as logical constructions, are causally efficacious. This has led Baldwin (1995) to suggest that Russell's neutral monism is best seen as an early form of functionalism.

Historically, however, the most obvious heir of neutral monism was the brain–mind identity theory. Here, neurophysiology takes the place of behaviourist psychology and the account is (typically) given a more materialist slant than the neutral monists would have accepted. None the less, many neutral monist ideas reappear in the identity theory, as identity theorists have acknowledged (Feigl 1967).

See also: BEHAVIOURISM, ANALYTIC; FUNCTIONALISM; MIND, IDENTITY THEORY OF; MONISM

References and further reading

Ayer, A.J. (1968) *The Origins of Pragmatism: Studies in the Philosophy of Charles Sanders Peirce and William James*, San Francisco, CA: Freeman, Cooper. (Pages 224–336 provide a readable and comprehensive survey of James' neutral monism.)

—— (1971) *Russell and Moore. The Analytical Heritage*, London: Macmillan. (Chapter 5 contains a good, brief account of Russell's neutral monism.)

* Baldwin, T. (1995) 'Introduction', in B. Russell *The Analysis of Mind*, London: Routledge. (A very useful, brief survey of *The Analysis of Mind*, linking Russell's ideas to current work.)

* Feigl, H. (1967) *The 'Mental' and the 'Physical'. The Essay and a Postscript*, Minneapolis, MN: University of Minnesota Press. (A nearly comprehensive survey of the literature on the brain–mind identity theory to 1967, which recognizes Russell as a precursor – but, surprisingly, not James.)

* James, W. (1890) *The Principles of Psychology*, New York: Dover, 1950, 2 vols. (James' pre-neutral monist psychology.)

* —— (1892) *Psychology. A Briefer Course*, ed. F.H. Burkhardt and I.K. Skrupskelis, Cambridge, MA: Harvard University Press, 1984. (Contains James' first hints of neutral monism.)

* —— (1895) 'The Knowing of Things Together', in *Essays in Philosophy*, ed. F.H. Burkhardt and I.K. Skrupskelis, Cambridge, MA: Harvard University Press, 1978, 71–89. (James' address to the American Psychological Association; it contains the first full statement of his neutral monism.)

* —— (1912) *Essays in Radical Empiricism*, ed. F.H. Burkhardt and I.K. Skrupskelis, Cambridge, MA: Harvard University Press, 1976. (The *locus classicus* for James' neutral monism. Two essays, 'Does "Consciousness" Exist?' and 'A World of Pure Experience' are particularly important.)

* Mach, E. (1885) *The Analysis of Sensations and the Relation of the Physical to the Psychical*, 5th edn, 1906, trans. C.M. Williams and S. Waterlow, New York: Dover, 1959. (The first appearance of neutral monism.)

Perry, R.B. (1938) *In The Spirit of William James*, New Haven, CT: Yale University Press. (Contains a sympathetic account of James' position by a friend, follower and fellow neutral monist.)

* Russell, B. (1913) *Theory of Knowledge. The 1913 Manuscript*, ed. E.R. Eames and K. Blackwell in *The Collected Papers of Bertrand Russell*, vol. 7, London: Allen & Unwin, 1983. (Chapter 2 contains Russell's criticisms of neutral monism.)

* —— (1919) 'On Propositions: What They Are and How They Mean', *Aristotelian Society* supplementary vol. 2: 1–43; reprinted in *The Collected Papers of Bertrand Russell*, vol. 8, ed. J.G. Slater, London: Allen & Unwin, 1986, 278–306. (Russell's first published neutral monist work, concerned especially with the analysis of belief and other 'propositional' attitudes.)

* —— (1921) *The Analysis of Mind*, London: Routledge, 1995. (Russell's first full statement of his neutral monism.)

* —— (1925) 'Truth Functions and Others', Appendix C in B. Russell and A.N. Whitehead *Principia*

Mathematica, 2nd edn, 1925–7, 3 vols, Cambridge: Cambridge University Press, 659–66. (Russell's most detailed attempt at a neutral monist analysis of belief.)

* —— (1956) 'Mind and Matter' in *Portraits from Memory and Other Essays*, London: Allen & Unwin, 1956, 140–60. (Russell's last statement of his neutral monism.)

Sainsbury, R.M. (1979) *Russell*, London: Routledge. (Pages 261–8 give a good critical survey of Russell's early objections to neutral monism and his subsequent response to them.)

Wild, John (1969) *The Radical Empiricism of William James*, New York: Doubleday. (A good introductory account that emphasizes the affinities of James' radical empiricism with phenomenology.)

* Wittgenstein, L. (1921) *Tractatus Logico-Philosophicus*, trans. D.F. Pears and B.F. McGuinness, London: Routledge & Kegan Paul, 1966. (Propositions 5.541–5.5421 give the main reasons that led Russell to embrace neutral monism.)

NICHOLAS GRIFFIN

NEUTRALITY, POLITICAL

The principle of political neutrality, which requires the state to remain neutral on disputed questions about the good, is an extension of traditional liberal principles of toleration and religious disestablishment. However, since neutrality is itself a contested concept, the principle remains indeterminate: is it, for example, a requirement of neutral reasons for legislation (or neutral legislative intentions) or is it a more exacting requirement of equal impact in so far as legislative consequences are concerned? The answer must surely reflect the deeper values that are used to justify the neutrality principle. This raises further problems, however. If the principle is based upon certain value commitments – such as the importance of equality or individual autonomy – then it cannot require us to be neutral about all values. It requires some sort of distinction between principles of right (of which neutrality is one) and conceptions of the good (among which neutrality is required). Critics believe that liberal principles of right are symptomatic of a deeper liberal bias in favour of individuality as a way of life. Perhaps liberals should embrace this point, and accept that the neutrality they advocate is quite superficial compared to the depth of their own value commitments.

1   The neutrality principle
2   Defending political neutrality
3   Intentions, reasons or consequences?
4   The distinction between the right and the good

1   The neutrality principle

In recent political philosophy, the idea of neutrality has been used by Bruce Ackerman, Ronald Dworkin, John Rawls and others to express a liberal position concerning the possibility of bias or commitment on the part of the state in ethical and religious controversies. The citizens of modern pluralist societies disagree on almost everything, but particularly on issues of faith, philosophy and value. The principle of political neutrality requires the state to stay out of all such controversies, and to refrain from throwing the weight of its authority – or worse still, the coercive power at its command – behind any particular view about what makes life worth living.

2   Defending political neutrality

Neutrality may be understood as a reformulation and extension of the traditional principles of religious toleration and disestablishment. Liberal philosophy has always involved an affirmation of political secularism and a rejection of the idea of a confessional state. Political neutrality extends that to encompass the rejection not just of religious establishment, but of ethical perfectionism also (see PERFECTIONISM; TOLERATION).

The extension is motivated in part by a sense that people's individual ethical values play much the same role in their lives as their religious convictions. To impose a religious orthodoxy is to strike at the heart of a person's freedom, for it threatens to displace the criteria which they regard as most important in organizing and disciplining their life. For many people, however, this central role is played not by religious beliefs but by ethical convictions. The broader doctrine of neutrality therefore requires the state to stand back and let people live their individual lives on whatever terms they choose, whether or not those terms have the aura of sanctity associated with religion.

Neutrality can also be defended by arguing that the means which the state characteristically uses to achieve its goals – namely, force and the threat of legal sanctions – are inappropriate for promoting religious or ethical objectives. Proponents of religious toleration such as John Locke believed that a faith imposed coercively from the outside was as good as no faith at all – 'I cannot be saved by a religion that I distrust, and by a worship I abhor' (1689: 32) – and the development in the nineteenth and twentieth centuries of the idea of ethical individuality led to a similar conclusion about values generally. As Ronald Dworkin put it: 'No life is a good one lived against the grain of conviction. It does not help someone else's life but spoils it to force values upon him he cannot accept but can only bow before out of fear or prudence' (1993: 168).

Alternatively, neutrality may be defended on pragmatic or consequentialist grounds. It has not been our experience that those who wield governmental power are endowed with profound ethical insight. In the real world, non-neutral government may well lead to the inculcation and enforcement of superficial or inappropriate ethical standards. More affirmatively, defenders of neutrality may appeal to the case made by J.S. Mill in the second chapter of *On Liberty* (1859), where he argued that the existence of a diverse array of ethics and lifestyles, competing with one another in the marketplace of ideas, is the best way of arriving at the truth, if there is any truth, about the good for human beings. Non-neutral action on the part of the government amounts to loading the dice in favour of one view or set of views in a way that is likely to distort the market-like processes whereby truths and half-truths are winnowed out from error.

3   Intentions, reasons or consequences?

The justification of the neutrality principle is crucial for our understanding of what, exactly, it requires. Does neutrality simply mean *not taking sides*, or does it mean *going out of one's way to ensure that one does not have an unequal impact*, in the struggle or controversy in which one is supposed to be neutral? Is the liberal state supposed to be neutral in virtue of its intentions or neutral in virtue of the consequences of its laws and policies?

A number of writers – for example, Alan Montefiore (1975) and Joseph Raz (1986) – have interpreted liberal neutrality as concerning primarily the consequences of legislative action. For example, the legislator must take care that the laws do not increase the chances of a hedonistic lifestyle flourishing at the expense of adherence to traditional Christian values. It must enhance or retard the prospects of these lifestyles to the same degree. But this conception gives rise to a number of difficulties. It involves the postulation of some baseline, relative to which differential effects of state action may be measured. And in practical terms it is a very difficult requirement to live up to, because it is so hard to predict what the effect of a law is going to be on lifestyles and mores. If that is how neutrality were to be understood, we should have grave doubts about whether it was ever reasonable to require legislators to be neutral.

Instead of neutrality of impact, the liberal may be talking about neutrality of intention – that is, neutrality in relation to the motives and reasons that the legislator uses to justify the laws. On this account, the fact that a law against Sunday trading would accord with the requirements of a Sabbatarian faith is not a good reason for having such a law; but the fact that it is necessary to prevent shop employees from being overworked may be. The latter reason can be a good reason, and the legislation neutral on that account, even though the law undoubtedly benefits Sabbatarianism over other sects.

This interpretation also faces difficulties however. It is often hard to determine the real intentions behind what lawyers would call a 'facially neutral' statute; a law banning animal sacrifice might be promulgated in the name of public health, but what if some of the lawmakers voted in favour of it because of their antipathy to an animal sacrifice cult? It may be wiser to reformulate neutrality of intention in terms of a principle governing what counts as a good reason for a law or policy. Such a principle would not condemn a piece of legislation if there were in fact neutral reasons in favour of it, whether or not those reasons actually figured in the conscious intentions of the lawmakers.

Which of these conceptions – neutral impact or neutral reasons – should the modern liberal adopt? This must depend on the grounds upon which neutrality is ultimately valued. For example, the Lockean argument about the impossibility of coercing religious faith may yield or justify one conception of neutrality – neutrality of reasons – since it is only the use of coercion to *achieve* religious objectives that is said to be self-defeating. The 'marketplace-of-ideas' argument, on the other hand, may be more congenial to consequentialist concerns. If ethical diversity is valued as a medium in which truth can emerge and progress be made, then we ought to be careful that our political action (whatever its intentions) does not accidentally diminish the diversity of lifestyles.

Something similar applies to the question of non-coercive state action. Is the state required to be neutral in everything it does, or only in its use of force? In England, there is an established state Church, but nowadays no one is obliged to belong to it. Does this violate the neutrality constraint? What about the official institution of (heterosexual) marriage? What about government subsidies to the arts? These policies and institutions do not compel any citizen to do anything in particular, but arguably they still represent the state taking sides in ethical and religious disputes. Can the liberal principle be violated then in this purely symbolic way? It is impossible to find answers to these questions by considering the word 'neutrality' (or, for that matter, the word 'coercion'). The answers must be dictated by the deeper concerns that lie behind our choice of this particular terminology in which to phrase liberal commitments.

4 The distinction between the right and the good

The move from religious toleration to a broader neutrality about values generally poses one other difficulty for liberal political theory. Liberals believe that governments are set up to do justice, to respect rights, to promote the general welfare and to protect freedom. Thus they cannot hold that the state should be neutral in relation to *all* moral values. After all, neutrality is itself a value: it is a normative position, a doctrine about what legislators and state officials ought to do. Liberals favour neutrality, in Ronald Dworkin's words, 'not because there is no right and wrong in political morality, but because that is what is right' (1978: 142).

It follows that a principle of political neutrality has to be able to justify certain discriminations among values or principles. We have to be able to distinguish value controversies in which the liberal legislator is required to get involved (such as controversies about justice), from those value controversies in which they are required by the principle not to get involved (such as controversies about lifestyle, sin or salvation). The distinction is sometimes characterized in terms of the difference between 'the right' and 'the good' (see RIGHT AND GOOD). Neutrality itself and the principles associated with it, such as justice, freedom and individual rights, are principles of political right: their point is to define a framework within which individuals ought to be able to pursue any conception of the good they please. The conception they choose must of course fit within the framework of right, for the framework exists in order to ensure that each person's pursuit of the good (as they see it) is compatible with everyone else's pursuit of the good (as they see it). In this sense, the right is said to be prior to the good, even though the right exists in order to accommodate the good.

But the distinction between the right and the good has itself been subject to heavy criticism, most notably by Michael Sandel (1982), Charles Taylor (1985) and other communitarian writers (see COMMUNITY AND COMMUNITARIANISM §2). They doubt whether any sensible system of right can be defined without reference to a determinate conception of human good: how, for example, can we define a set of rights to cope with the fact of our mutual vulnerability, without some detailed account of what counts as harm and thus some correlative account of interests,

needs, health and a person's good? They also note that many people's conceptions of the good life already involve a view of the good society and they may therefore already implicate principles of right: think of an Englishman yearning for a life of traditional service in the established Church, or an Algerian who believes that the practice of his religion is impossible except under a system of Islamic law. Since the liberal doctrine directly challenges these aspirations, it is evidently *not* neutral between all conceptions of human fulfilment, but only (or at most) between those that fit a certain individualistic pattern.

This is not a surprising result. Even the old principle of toleration never claimed to be neutral between all religions: it condemned human sacrifice, the torture of heretics and compulsory tithing, even though these were – strictly speaking – religious practices. It was neutral only between non-coercive faiths. The liberal proponent of political neutrality rejects (and refuses to accommodate) communitarian conceptions of the good for similar reasons.

Still, the critics are right to insist that the liberal framework of right itself embodies certain assumptions about the good. Liberals believe that the shaping of human lives by the individuals who are living them is a good thing, and so they adopt principles of right (including the principle of neutrality) which seek to minimize the coercive impact of other people's views on that process. It is true that some individuals choose to shape their lives (or would like to shape their lives) in accordance with a communitarian conception. But that choice amounts in part to a proposal to govern or interfere with others' shaping of their lives, and this the liberal cannot tolerate. In other words, far from the liberal being required to be neutral between communitarian and non-communitarian conceptions of the good, the liberal's adoption of the neutrality principle is an expression of opposition to the very idea of a communitarian conception of the good.

See also: LIBERALISM

References and further reading

Ackerman, B. (1980) *Social Justice in the Liberal State*, New Haven, CT: Yale University Press. (An argument that liberal justification consists in dialogue constrained by a principle of neutrality concerning conceptions of the good.)

Barry, B. (1965) *Political Argument*, London: Routledge & Kegan Paul, 75–9. (The argument, alluded to in §3 of this entry, that political neutrality is impossible, on the assumption that it means neutrality of impact.)

* Dworkin, R. (1978) 'Liberalism', in S. Hampshire

(ed.) *Public and Private Morality*, Cambridge: Cambridge University Press. (An argument that the basic liberal commitment to equality is best understood in terms of a principle of political neutrality.)

* —— (1993) *Life's Dominion: An Argument about Abortion, Euthanasia and Individual Freedom*, New York: Alfred A. Knopf. (Arguing for an extension of the principles of religious toleration and disestablishment to cover secular views about the value of life.)

Goodin, R. and Reeve, A. (eds) (1989) *Liberal Neutrality*, London: Routledge. (A collection of original essays on the subject of neutrality, applied to various institutions of liberal society, such as the law, the market and the university.)

Larmore, C. (1987) *Patterns of Moral Complexity*, Cambridge: Cambridge University Press, esp. 40–68. (A strong defence of the neutrality principle, purportedly on grounds that are themselves also neutral.)

* Locke, J. (1689) *A Letter Concerning Toleration*, ed. J. Horton and S. Mendus, London: Routledge, 1991 (The classic defence of religious toleration on the grounds of the inefficacy of coercion to produce sincere belief, referred to in §§2 and 3 of this entry.)

* Mill, J.S. (1859) *On Liberty*, ed. C.V. Shields, Indianapolis, IN. Bobbs-Merrill, 1956. (A defence of individuality on the basis of the likelihood that truth will emerge from the free interplay of rival lifestyles and conceptions of the good.)

* Montefiore, A. (ed.) (1975) *Neutrality and Impartiality*, Cambridge: Cambridge University Press. (A discussion of the neutrality of the modern university.)

Nagel, T. (1973) 'Rawls on Justice', *Philosophical Review* 82: 220–34. (A version of the argument, alluded to in §4 of this entry, that liberal theories of justice are decidedly non-neutral between individualistic and communitarian conceptions of the good life.)

Rawls, J. (1971) *A Theory of Justice*, Oxford: Oxford University Press. (A liberal discussion of social justice, emphasizing the distinction between the right and the good, discussed in §4 of this entry.)

—— (1993) *Political Liberalism*, New York: Columbia University Press. (An argument to the effect that liberal principles must not rest on controversial philosophical principles, but must command overlapping support among a wide variety of ethical and philosophical conceptions in a modern pluralist society.)

* Raz, J. (1986) *The Morality of Freedom*, Oxford: Clarendon Press, esp. 107–162 and 369–430. (A critique of political neutrality and an argument that the value of individual autonomy commits liberals to ethical perfectionism.)

* Sandel, M. (1982) *Liberalism and the Limits of Justice*, Cambridge: Cambridge University Press. (A communitarian critique of the liberal distinction between the right and the good.)

* Taylor, C. (1985) *Philosophy and the Human Sciences: Philosophical Papers 2*, Cambridge: Cambridge University Press, esp. 187–247. (The argument, mentioned in §4 of this entry, to the effect that liberal principles are incoherent unless underpinned by a distinctive conception of human flourishing.)

Waldron, J. (1989) 'Legislation and Moral Neutrality', in R. Goodin and A. Reeves (eds) *Liberal Neutrality*, London: Routledge. (A defence of the neutrality principle; along the lines of this entry.)

JEREMY WALDRON

NEWMAN, JOHN HENRY (1801–90)

John Henry Newman was the principal architect of the Catholic revival (the Oxford or Tractarian movement) within the Church of England in the 1830s, and went on to become probably the most seminal of modern Roman Catholic thinkers. Although primarily a theologian, Newman regarded his defence of religious belief in terms of a philosophical justification of non demonstrable certainty as his most important life work.

Newman was born in London, the elder son of a banker. Elected a fellow of Oriel College, Oxford, in 1822, he became vicar of the university church of St Mary the Virgin in 1828. The five sermons he preached there between 1839 and 1841 on the relation of faith to reason, published in *Sermons, chiefly on the Theory of Religious Belief, preached before the University of Oxford* (1843), are a brilliantly original challenge to the received Lockean understanding of rationality. His defence of the reasonableness of religious belief, which he completed in *An Essay in Aid of a Grammar of Assent* (1870), involves an epistemology which gives both works a wider philosophical significance.

Newman's reception into the Roman Catholic Church in 1845 was followed by the publication of the *Essay on The Development of Christian Doctrine*, his most famous theological work which itself presupposes the anti-Enlightenment theory of knowledge he had sketched in the *Sermons*. Founding President of the new Catholic University of Ireland from 1851 to 1858, Newman's *The Idea of a University* (1873) propounds a philosophy of education concerned with the development of the whole mind rather than only those faculties of utilitarian value. Created a cardinal in 1879, he died in Birmingham in 1890 at the Oratory he had founded there.

The target of the *Sermons* is essentially the restriction of reason to Cartesian rationalism and Lockean empiricism, that is, the assumption that knowledge must either be deduced from logical, a priori truths or derived a posteriori from sense experience by induction. Newman argues that religious faith is only a particular instance of the many perfectly reasonable convictions which we reach in a variety of areas. This kind of reasoning depends not so much on specific arguments and evidence as on pre-existing assumptions and expectations. Someone may legitimately reason in this informal sense without necessarily being able to provide any analysis of their reasoning or even produce their reasons. Thus people may argue badly and yet reason perfectly well. In some kinds of reasoning, and especially in matters of religious belief, the moral factor is especially important because it largely determines the relevant underlying assumptions that in turn form the actual reasons for believing something to be true. Newman thought that the philosopher and the factory worker who are believers share the same 'antecedent probabilities', which in turn rest on the same 'first principles'. The fact that people may not be able to state clearly what they believe and why is because of the distinction between what Newman calls 'explicit' and 'implicit' reasoning. Nor is there one single model of informal reasoning, since there are as many different types of reasoning as there are subjects on which to reason.

If religious belief involves the same kind of informal reasoning that we unhesitatingly employ in other intellectual matters, still the question remains whether certainty is possible and how it differs from the objective certainties of logically necessary propositions and empirically verifiable factual statements. The *Essay in Aid of a Grammar of Assent* is Newman's final attempt to answer the problem. He begins by distinguishing between the assent one makes to a proposition and the conclusion one draws from an inference: assenting and inferring are thus two distinct kinds of activity, however close they may sometimes seem to be. Assent may be 'notional' or 'real', depending on whether the apprehension of a proposition is notional or real. Newman's usage is confusing because, though 'notional' seems to mean what is abstract or general and 'real' what is concrete and individual, nevertheless the distinction is not in fact between sense perceptions and mental abstractions

but between experiential and non-experiential knowledge. For one can give a real assent to an apparently abstract idea if that idea becomes a real 'thing' in the imagination (an 'image'), because one then grasps the force of the idea in an experiential and personal way. Indeed, a mental act may bring before the mind a more vivid image than a sensible object. Thus Newman's argument from conscience for the existence of God is that the intimations of conscience are the echoes of a magisterial voice suggestive of a God of whom we gain a real image from and in these dictates of conscience.

Given that assent is not simply the conclusion to an inference (from which it is distinct), then it does not follow, as Locke claimed, that the only certainty is logical certainty. Propositions that are true by definition normally command assent, but even here assent may be withheld until the conclusion is accepted. Where formal logical inference is impossible, Newman argues that it is the cumulation of probabilities which leads to certainty (see BUTLER, J.). But assent to the truth of nonlogical propositions involves personal judgment as the mind evaluates both the strength of the individual probabilities and their combined strength. This judgment, which is akin to Aristotle's *phronesis*, Newman calls the 'illative sense', and it operates more or less implicitly and instinctively, without formal verbal analysis.

In his sensitivity to the actuality and complexity of human rationality and its linguistic expression, Newman clearly anticipates the central concerns of the later Wittgenstein. The other factor which has given his epistemology a new significance is his refusal to take the path of Schleiermacher in conceding to science all factual knowledge and claiming for religious utterances merely emotional, imaginative and existential significance; he has found unexpected support from modern philosophers of science who, while accepting the validity of scientific method, nevertheless recognize that the truth claims of science are not as self-evident and unproblematic as used to be assumed.

See also: RELIGION AND EPISTEMOLOGY

List of works

Newman, J.H. (1843) *Sermons, Chiefly on the Theory of Religious Belief Preached before the University of Oxford*, London and Oxford: Rivington & Parker; repr. (1872) with a new preface and notes and an additional sermon as *Fifteen Sermons preached before the University of Oxford, between A.D. 1826 and 1843*, London: Rivingtons, in the collected uniform edition of Newman's works in 36 vols,

1868–81, all the volumes of which from 1886 were published by Longmans, Green & Co. of London. (All these editions are out of print, but there have been modern paperback reprints.)

—— (1870) *An Essay in Aid of a Grammar of Assent*, London: Burns, Oates. (In the uniform edition cited above. There is a modern critical edition by I.T. Ker, Oxford: Clarendon Press, 1985, as well as various paperback reprints.)

—— (1969–70) *The Philosophical Notebook of John Henry Newman*, ed. E.J. Sillem, Louvain: Nauwelaerts, 2 vols. (The first volume, a somewhat wooden and wordy introduction to Newman's philosophy, includes a survey of the background influences. Although the notebook is fragmentary and was never intended for publication, it contains some penetrating and suggestive observations that are sometimes uncannily similar to the gnomic utterances of Wittgenstein, who appreciated Newman's originality.)

—— (1976) *The Theological Papers of John Henry Newman on Faith and Certainty*, ed. H.M. de Achaval, S.J. and J.D. Holmes, Oxford: Clarendon Press. (Exploratory papers on faith and certainty in preparation for the *Grammar of Assent*.)

References and further reading

Ferreira, M.J. (1980) *Doubt and Religious Commitment: The Role of the Will in Newman's Thought*, Oxford: Clarendon Press. (The best full-length book on certain aspects of Newman's philosophy. Readable but philosophically demanding.)

Hick, J. (1967) *Faith and Knowledge*, Ithaca, NY: Cornell University Press, 69–91. (Straightforward introduction to Newman's main ideas.)

Kenny, A. (1990) 'Newman as a Philosopher of Religion', in *Newman: A Man for our Time*, ed. D. Brown, London: SPCK, 98–122. (Useful exposition of Newman's ideas in their context.)

Ker, I.T. (1985) Introduction to *An Essay in Aid of a Grammar of Assent*, Oxford: Clarendon Press. (Includes survey and discussion of secondary literature.)

—— (1990) *The Achievement of John Henry Newman*, Notre Dame, IN: University of Notre Dame Press; London: Collins, ch. 2. (Succinct introduction to Newman's philosophy.)

Mitchell, B. (1990) 'Newman as a Philosopher', in *Newman after a Hundred Years*, ed. I. Ker and A.G. Hill, Oxford: Clarendon Press, 223–46. (An extremely readable and important account of Newman's philosophical significance.)

Owen, H.P. (1969) *The Christian Knowledge of God*, London: Athlone Press. (Contains stimulating critical discussions of Newman's ideas of the illative sense, probability and assent. Highly readable.)

Price, H.H. (1969) *Belief*, London: Allen & Unwin; New York: Humanities Press, 130–56, 315–48. (Two lucid, vigorous chapters devoted to Newman's theory of assent.)

IAN KER

NEWTON, ISAAC (1642–1727)

Newton is best known for having invented the calculus and formulated the theory of universal gravity – the latter in his Principia, *the single most important work in the transformation of natural philosophy into modern physical science. Yet he also made major discoveries in optics, and put no less effort into alchemy and theology than into mathematics and physics.*

Throughout his career, Newton maintained a sharp distinction between conjectural hypotheses and experimentally established results. This distinction was central to his claim that the method by which conclusions about forces were inferred from phenomena in the Principia *made it 'possible to argue more securely concerning the physical species, physical causes, and physical proportions of these forces'. The law of universal gravity that he argued for in this way nevertheless provoked strong opposition, especially from such leading figures on the Continent as Huygens and Leibniz: they protested that Newton was invoking an occult power of action-at-a-distance insofar as he was offering no contact mechanism by means of which forces of gravity could act. This opposition led him to a tighter, more emphatic presentation of his methodology in the second edition of the* Principia, *published twenty-six years after the first. The opposition to the theory of gravity faded during the fifty to seventy-five years after his death as it fulfilled its promise on such issues as the non-spherical shape of the earth, the precession of the equinoxes, comet trajectories (including the return of 'Halley's Comet' in 1758), the vagaries of lunar motion and other deviations from Keplerian motion. During this period the point mass mechanics of the* Principia *was extended to rigid bodies and fluids by such figures as Euler, forming what we know as 'Newtonian' mechanics.*

1 Life
2 Experimental philosophy in the light and colours debate
3 Space, time and the laws of motion
4 Inferences from phenomena and rules of natural philosophy

5 Gravity as a universal force of interaction
6 Mathematics
7 Studies in alchemy and theology

1 Life

Isaac Newton entered Trinity College Cambridge in 1661, and began investigations of mathematics in 1664. These investigations culminated two years later in the binomial theorem and the fundamentals of the calculus. During the so-called *annus mirabilis* of 1666, while the university was closed because of the plague, and in the years immediately following, he extended his mathematical work; he also conducted optical experiments and worked on several basic problems in mechanics, including impact and circular motion. He became Lucasian Professor of Mathematics at Cambridge in 1669.

Although some of Newton's mathematical manuscripts were in circulation, yielding him some renown, his only notable publications before the *Principia* were a series of communications in the *Philosophical Transactions* of the Royal Society from 1672 to 1676 on his experiments on light and colours and the reflecting telescope. The debate which this work provoked led Newton to begin articulating what he called his 'experimental philosophy', which focused on *establishing* propositions by means of experiment.

In an exchange of letters in late 1679, Robert Hooke, himself an eminent scientist, asked Newton to use his mathematical methods to determine the trajectory of a body under a combination of inertial motion and an inverse-square force directed towards a central point – that is, the force Newton later named 'centripetal'. But the intense effort that culminated in the publication of the *Principia* (1687) did not begin until 1684, after a visit from young Edmond Halley, who later became Astronomer Royal.

Newton spent most of the years after 1689 in London. He was elected to represent Cambridge University in Parliament in 1689 and again in 1701, the year in which he resigned his professorship. He became Warden of the Mint in 1696, and Master of it in 1699. In 1703 he became President of the Royal Society, a post he held until he died. He was knighted in 1705.

During his London years Newton engaged in an acrimonious dispute with Leibniz over who had priority for inventing the calculus. One element fuelling this dispute was Newton's failure to publish his work, save for a three-page summary of a handful of results in Book II of the *Principia*. His first formal publications on the calculus appeared in 1704, when two earlier manuscripts were included as supplements

in the first edition of the *Opticks*. (A Latin edition of the *Opticks* appeared two years later.)

Newton gave some thought to a restructured edition of the *Principia* in the early 1690s. But the second edition was not published until 1713, after four years of effort under the constructively critical eye of its editor, Roger Cotes. A third edition followed in 1726. These editions sharpened the contrast between his approach and that of Leibniz and the Cartesians. The second English edition of the *Opticks* (1717/18) included Queries that summarized his conjectures on atomism. These Queries end with a concise statement of his method for establishing scientific knowledge on the basis of experiment and induction; so too does his final riposte in the priority dispute with Leibniz, his anonymous 'An Account of the Book Entitled *Commercium epistolicum*'.

2 Experimental philosophy in the light and colours debate

Newton's 1672 paper on light and colours reported only a small fraction of the optical experiments he had conducted. The debate it initiated concerned what the reported experiments had established. According to Newton, these experiments had conclusively shown that the oblong shape of the image cast by sunlight that has passed through a round hole and has then been refracted by a prism is caused by sunlight's consisting of rays that are refracted in different degrees by the prism. (The correspondence between these different refrangibilities and different colours led Newton to invent the first reflecting telescope, which eliminates the problems of chromatic aberration that had marred the refractive telescopes of the era.)

Hooke, interpreting Newton as claiming that the experiments established a corpuscular theory of light, insisted that a wave theory could account for the results just as well. Newton responded that the hypothesis that light is a body was put forward only as a conjecture suggested by the experiments, and not as part of what he claimed to have been established by them. He granted that Hooke's wave hypothesis could explain the conclusion the experiments had established; but this conclusion spoke of light only abstractly as 'rays' propagating in straight lines from luminous bodies, with no commitment to any specific 'mechanical' hypothesis.

His Dutch contemporary, Christiaan Huygens argued that Newton had failed to show the nature and difference of colours because he had offered no 'hypothesis by motion' to explain them. Newton responded that he 'never intended to shew, wherein consists the nature and difference of colours, but only to shew that *de facto* they are original and immutable qualities of the rays which exhibit them' (1958: 144).

Newton's contemporaries had trouble understanding his attempt to construe light rays abstractly in a way that would allow experiments to decide claims about them – this, independently of any mechanical account of light. In his replies, Newton outlined how, according to his experimental philosophy, diligently establishing properties of things by experiment takes precedence over framing hypotheses to explain them. Yet he also made clear that the propositions he regarded as conclusively established by experiment were nevertheless subject to correction based on detailed criticism of the experimental reasoning that had established them or on further experimental results challenging them (see OPTICS §§1–2).

3 Space, time and the laws of motion

Two aspects of the *Principia* provoked philosophical controversy in the decades following its publication: first, the appeal to absolute space and motion, and second, the insistence on establishing properties of gravity, especially its universality, without appeal to any mechanical hypothesis that could begin to explain how gravity is produced.

The *Principia* opens with two short sections, 'Definitions' and 'Axioms, or Laws of Motion', that have drawn philosophical fire ever since. The distinctions between absolute and relative time, space and motion are drawn in the first of these, following his introduction of the concept of mass and definitions pertaining to quantity of motion and force. For Newton, the distinction between absolute (or true) and relative (or apparent) motion is primary, and the parallel distinctions concerning space and time serve mostly to support this one (see MECHANICS, CLASSICAL; SPACE §§2–3). Newton was acutely aware of the empirical difficulties raised by such distinctions:

It is certainly very difficult to find out the true motions of individual bodies and actually to differentiate them from the apparent motions, because the parts of that immovable space in which the bodies truly move make no impression on the senses. Nevertheless, the case is not utterly hopeless. For it is possible to draw evidence partly from apparent motions, which are differences between the true motions, and partly from the forces that are the causes and effects of the true motions .... But in what follows, a fuller explanation will be given of how to determine true motions from their causes, effects, and apparent differences, and, conversely, how to determine from motions,

whether true or apparent, their causes and effects. For this was the purpose for which I composed the following treatise.

(Newton 1687: Scholium to Definitions)

The reference here is to the laws of motion and their corollaries, which immediately follow this last remark, as well as to the ninety-eight demonstrated Propositions of Book I and the fifty-three of Book II.

Like Descartes, Newton appealed to forces to distinguish true from apparent motions. And, again like Descartes, the true motion of greatest importance to him in the sequel is curvilinear motion, most notably the true motion of the planets that would distinguish between their equivalent relative motions in the Copernican and Tychonic systems. Unlike Descartes, however, Newton refused to offer hypotheses concerning the forces in question (see DESCARTES, R. §11). He required that the forces be inferred from phenomena with the help of the mathematical principles of Books I and II, many of which licence inferences from observed motions to measures of force. Inconsistencies among the inferred quantities of force or the motions subsequently inferred from them would indicate a failure to be dealing with true motions. But this is an empirical question, to be decided by carrying out the investigation of motions under forces to its fullest extent, insisting on no less than complete agreement between observed and calculated motions. Thus, the successes, and also the limitations, of the appeal to absolute space, time and motion were, for Newton, empirical issues that the long-term development of an exact science of motion would decide, and not something he thought was open to a priori resolution.

4 Inferences from phenomena and rules of natural philosophy

The Propositions of Books I and II are powerful resources for establishing conclusions about forces from phenomena of motion. For example, according to Propositions 1 and 2, Kepler's area rule holds if and only if the force acting on the moving body is centripetal. A corollary adds that the areal velocity is increasing when the force is off-centre in the direction of motion and decreasing when it is in the opposite direction. *The variation of the areal velocity is thus a measure of the direction of the force.* Similar systematic dependencies are involved in the inferences from Kepler's 3:2 power rule and the absence of discernible orbital precession to the inverse-square variation of celestial centripetal forces (see KEPLER, J.).

Rules of reasoning, which in the second and third editions are singled out at the beginning of Book III under the title *Regulae philosophandi*, strengthen the inferences that can be drawn from phenomena by licensing inductive generalizations (see SCIENTIFIC METHOD §2). The first two rules, for example, underlie the inference that the force holding the moon in orbit is terrestrial gravity – this, on the basis of the inverse-square relation between the centripetal acceleration of the moon and the acceleration of gravity at the earth's surface. The third rule, appearing for the first time in the second edition, supports the inference that all bodies gravitate towards each planet with weights proportional to their masses – this, on the basis of pendulum experiments and the common acceleration of Jupiter and its satellites toward the sun.

The fourth rule authorizes the practice of treating propositions that are supported properly by reasoning from phenomena as 'either exactly or very nearly true notwithstanding any contrary hypotheses, until yet other phenomena make such propositions either more exact or liable to exceptions'. It was added in the third edition to justify treating universal gravity as an established scientific fact in the face of complaints that it was unintelligible without an explanation of how it results from mechanical action by contact. This rule, and the related discussion of hypotheses at the end of the General Scholium added in the second edition, distinguish Newton's experimental philosophy most sharply from the mechanical philosophy of his critics.

5 Gravity as a universal force of interaction

The systematic dependencies by means of which Keplerian phenomena become measures of celestial forces are one-body idealizations. Universal gravity entails interactions among bodies, producing perturbations that require corrections to the Keplerian phenomena. The *Principia* includes a successful treatment of two-body interactions and some promising, though limited, results on three-body effects in lunar motion. But the full significance of the inferences that could be drawn from universal gravity did not become clear until Clairaut's analysis of the precession of the lunar orbit in 1749, and Laplace's determination in 1785 of the roughly 880-year 'Great Inequality' in the motions of Jupiter and Saturn.

Such successful treatments of perturbations do more than provide corrections to Keplerian phenomena. They also show that Newtonian measurements of inverse-square centripetal forces continue to hold to high approximation in the presence of perturbations. Interactions with other bodies account for the precessions of all the planets except Mercury. Even in the case of Mercury, the famous 43 seconds-of-arc-per-century residual in its precession yields

-2.000000157 as the measure of the exponent, instead of the exact -2 measured for the other planets. That such a small discrepancy came to be a problem at all testifies to the extraordinary level to which Newton's theory of gravity demonstrates an ideal of empirical success.

6 Mathematics

Newton engaged in extensive mathematical research throughout much of the period from 1664 until he left for London in 1696, and even after that he produced new results on some problems. Besides the many lines along which he developed and applied the calculus, he made substantial discoveries in algebra and in pure as well as analytic geometry. The mathematics of the *Principia* is itself a new form of synthetic geometry, incorporating limits. (Contrary to the still-persisting myth, there is no evidence that Newton first derived his results on celestial orbits within the symbolic calculus and then recast them in geometric form.)

Newton's invention of the calculus grew out of his attempts to solve several distinct problems, often employing novel extension of the ideas and methods of others. For example, his initial algorithms for derivatives of algebraic curves combined Cartesian techniques with the idea of an indefinitely small, vanishing increment. He exploited a method of indivisibles that John Wallis had used in obtaining integrals of algebraic curves; but he reconceptualized the method to represent an integral that grows as the curve extends incrementally, and then joined this with the binomial series to yield integrals via infinite series of a much wider range of curves. Geometrical representations of these results revealed the inverse relation between integration and differentiation. Then, adapting his Lucasian predecessor Isaac Barrow's idea to treat curves as arising from the motion of a point, Newton recast the results on derivatives, replacing indefinitely small increments with his 'fluxions'. The first full tract on fluxions, 'To Resolve Problems by Motion', is dated 1666, but the first manuscript to circulate was *De analysi per aequationes infinitas* of 1669.

Mathematicians in England used Newtonian methods and notation into the nineteenth century. But the Leibnizian tradition had gained so much momentum by the time Newton's works appeared that the calculus, as we know it, stems far more from that tradition. Ironically, it was such figures as the Bernoullis and Euler (belonging to the Leibnizian tradition) who recast the *Principia* into the language of the calculus.

7 Studies in alchemy and theology

Newton's unpublished manuscripts contain voluminous studies on alchemy, theology, prophecy and Biblical chronology. His alchemical work led to a number of elaborate chemical experiments carried out from the mid-1670s until 1693. His notes from these efforts display his great skill as an experimenter, but they appear to include nothing that would have altered the course of chemistry had they become public at the time (see ALCHEMY).

He first became preoccupied with theology in the early 1670s, probably in response to the requirement that he accept ordination to retain his Trinity fellowship. (He was granted a dispensation in 1675.) By 1673 he had rejected the doctrine of the Trinity and concluded that Christianity had become a false religion through a corruption of the Scriptures in the fourth and fifth centuries. He returned to these studies in subsequent decades, especially in the last years of his life. During his lifetime, however, he conveyed his radical views to only a few. They became widely known only when *Observations upon the Prophecies* was published in 1733.

Recent investigations of the alchemical and theological writings suggest that Newton's hope in natural philosophy was to look through nature to see God, that it was to be part of a larger investigation that would give meaning to life. His engagement with these larger issues may have helped him to free himself from the narrower restraints of the mechanical philosophy.

See also: COSMOLOGY §2; FIELD THEORY, CLASSICAL; RELATIVITY THEORY, PHILOSOPHICAL SIGNIFICANCE OF; SPACE §2; THEORIES, SCIENTIFIC

List of works

Newton, I. (1687) *Philosophiae naturalis principia mathematica*, London: Joseph Streater (for the Royal Society); 2nd edn, Cambridge, 1713; 3rd edn, London: Guil. & Joh. Innys (for the Royal Society), 1726. (Newton's monumental contribution, forever transforming science.)
—— (1715) 'An Account of the Book Entitled *Commercium epistolicum*', *Philosophical Transactions* 29 (342): 173–224. (Newton's anonymous review of the Royal Society's findings in the dispute over whether he or Leibniz had priority for inventing the calculus. Reprinted in Hall 1980.)
—— (1730) *Opticks or a Treatise of the Reflections, Refractions, Inflections and Colours of Light*, 4th edn; New York: Dover, 1952. (Based on the fourth edition of 1730. Newton's other major contribution to science.)
—— (1733) *Observations upon the Prophecies of Daniel, and the Apocalypse of St John*, London; repr. W. Whitla, *Sir Isaac Newton's Daniel and the Apocalypse with an Introductory Study... of Unbelief, of Miracles and Prophecy*, London: John Murray, 1922. (Published posthumously, Newton's most influential work in theology.)
—— (1958) *Isaac Newton's Papers and Letters on Natural Philosophy and Related Documents*, ed. I.B. Cohen, assisted by R.E. Schofield, Cambridge, MA: Harvard University Press. (Contains the publications in the dispute on light and colours as they appeared in the *Philosophical Transactions* of the Royal Society. Second revised edition 1978.)
—— (1959–77) *The Correspondence of Isaac Newton*, eds H.W. Turnbull, A. Scott, A.R. Hall and L. Tilling, Cambridge: Cambridge University Press, 7 vols. (Newton's correspondence from 1661 to 1727, including correspondence by others and related papers.)
—— (1962) *Unpublished Scientific Papers of Isaac Newton*, eds A.R. Hall and M.B. Hall, Cambridge: Cambridge University Press; repr. 2nd edn, 1978. (Contains several early papers in mechanics as well as the first full tract on the calculus, 'To Resolve Problems by Motion'.)
—— (1965) *The Background to Newton's Principia: A Study of Newton's Dynamical Researches in the Years 1664–84*, ed. J.W. Herivel, Oxford: Clarendon Press. (Contains most early papers and fragments leading to the *Principia*, with commentary and analysis.)
—— (1967–81) *The Mathematical Papers of Isaac Newton*, ed. D.T. Whiteside, Cambridge: Cambridge University Press, 8 vols. (Newton's mathematical manuscripts from 1664 to 1722, authoritatively annotated in invaluable detail.)
—— (1972) *Isaac Newton's Philosophiae naturalis principia mathematica* (from the 3rd edn of 1726) with variant readings, eds A. Koyré and I.B. Cohen, with assistance of A. Whitman, Cambridge, MA: Harvard University Press, 2 vols. (Includes not only all variants from the first two editions, but also those from Newton's manuscripts and annotated copies.)
—— (1983) *Certain Philosophical Questions: Newton's Trinity Notebook*, eds J.E. McGuire and M. Tamny, Cambridge: Cambridge University Press. (Newton's notebook from his early years at Cambridge, displaying his scientific style before it had matured.)
—— (1984) *The Optical Papers of Isaac Newton*, vol. 1, ed. A.E. Shapiro, Cambridge: Cambridge University Press. (The first volume of Newton's extensive unpublished writings on optics, detailing his numerous experiments.)

—— (1995) *Newton – A Norton Critical Edition*, eds I.B. Cohen and R.S. Westfall, New York: W.W. Norton. (A selection of Newton's writings from all areas of his work, with commentaries that extend across four centuries.)

—— (1997) *Isaac Newton's Mathematical Principles of Natural Philosophy*, trans. I.B. Cohen and A. Whitman, Los Angeles: University of California Press. (The first entirely new English translation of Newton's *Principia* since Andrew Motte's of 1729.)

References and further reading

Bricker P. and Hughes R.I.G. (eds) (1990) *Philosophical Perspectives on Newtonian Science*, Cambridge, MA: MIT Press. (Among the many excellent collections inspired by the 300th anniversary of the first edition of the *Principia*, this one is especially focused on philosophy.)

Cohen, I.B. (1974) 'Isaac Newton', in Ch. Gillispie (ed.) *Dictionary of Scientific Biography*, New York: Charles Scribner's Sons, vol. 10, 42–103. (A comparatively brief, but authoratitive survey of Newton's life and work.)

—— (1980) *The Newtonian Revolution*, Cambridge: Cambridge University Press. (An analysis of Newton's style in science, as exemplified in the *Principia*.)

Dobbs, B.J.T. (1990) 'Newton as Alchemist and Theologian', in N.J.W. Thrower (ed.) *Standing on the Shoulders of Giants: A Longer View of Newton and Halley*, Berkeley, CA: University of California Press. (An extensive discussion of the topics of §7.)

Earman, J. (1989) *World Enough and Space-Time: Absolute versus Relational Theories of Space and Time*, Cambridge, MA: MIT Press. (This together with Stein's paper in Palter 1971 is good background for §3.)

Gjertsen, D. (1986) *The Newton Handbook*, London: Routledge & Kegan Paul. (Contains a complete listing of Newton's works and an extensive bibliography of secondary sources.)

Hall, A.R. (1980) *Philosophers at War: The Quarrel Between Newton and Leibniz*, Cambridge: Cambridge University Press. (The history of the priority dispute over the calculus; includes Newton 1715.)

—— (1992) *Isaac Newton: Adventurer in Thought*, Oxford: Oxford University Press. (The best concise biography of Newton.)

Harper, W.L. (1997) 'Isaac Newton on Empirical Success and Scientific Method', in J. Earman and J. Norton (eds) *The Cosmos of Science*, Pittsburgh, PA: University of Pittsburgh Press. (This paper gives further development of material in §§3–5.)

Harper, W.L. and Smith, G.E. (1995) 'Newton's New Way of Inquiry', in J. Leplin (ed.) *The Creation of Ideas in Physics: Studies for a Methodology of Theory Construction*, Dordrecht: Kluwer. (This paper expands on material in §§2, 4–5.)

Harrison, J. (1978) *The Library of Isaac Newton*, Cambridge: Cambridge University Press. (A listing of the books in Newton's personal library.)

Koyré, A. (1968) *Newtonian Studies*, Chicago, IL: University of Chicago Press. (Classic material especially for §§3, 4.)

Palter, R. (ed.) (1971) *The Annus Mirabilis of Sir Isaac Newton 1666–1966*, Cambridge, MA: MIT Press. (This classic collection contains papers still relevant to most sections.)

Stein, H. (1991) 'From the Phenomena of Motions to the Forces of Nature: Hypothesis or Deduction?', in A. Fine, M. Forbes and L. Wessels (eds) *PSA 1990*, East Lansing, MI: Philosophy of Science Association, vol. 2, 209–22. (Relevant to material in §§4–5.)

Theerman, P. and Seeff A.F. (eds) (1993) *Action and Reaction*, Newark, DE: University of Delaware Press. (Includes papers relevent to §7 as well as to most other sections.)

Westfall, R.S. (1980) *Never at Rest: A Biography of Isaac Newton*, Cambridge: Cambridge University Press. (The most thorough intellectual biography of Newton, also available abridged as *The Life of Isaac Newton*, 1993.)

Whiteside, D.T. (1991) 'The prehistory of the *Principia* from 1664–1686', in *Notes and Records, The Royal Society of London* 45: 11–61. (A review of the steps from Newton's earliest investigations of motion to the first edition of the *Principia*.)

Wilson, C. (1989) 'The Newtonian Achievement in Astronomy', in R. Taton and C. Wilson (eds) *Planetary Astronomy from the Renaissance to the Rise of Astrophysics*, Cambridge: Cambridge University Press. (A critical summary of the contributions Newton's *Principia* made to planetary astronomy.)

WILLIAM L. HARPER
GEORGE E. SMITH

NICHIREN (1222–82)

Fiery prophet, religious reformer, founder of a major religious movement, brilliant preacher and erudite writer, Nichiren is one of Japan's most controversial religious figures. His thought derived from the Tendai tradition, from which he inherited both his veneration of the Lotus Sutra *and the idea of an eternal Buddha woven into the stuff of all reality.*

Born on the southeastern seacoast of Japan, the son of a fisherman, Nichiren entered a local Buddhist monastery at eleven and was ordained four years later with the monastic name Rencho. He subsequently studied Pure Land and Zen in Kamakura, and Shingon on Mount Kōya. In 1253 he returned to his home temple, changed his name to Nichiren (Sun Lotus), and announced that he would devote his life to ridding Buddhism of the heresy and corruption that had overtaken it. Like many in the Kamakura period, he believed that Buddhism was entering the age of *mappō* (latter days of the Dharma, a period of ten thousand years beginning with the third millennium after the death of the Buddha), which only a faith of the utmost purity could hope to survive.

For Nichiren, the loadstone of that purity was the *Lotus Sutra*, the chanting of whose name (*Namu-myōhō-rengekyō*) and living out of whose teachings alone would insure salvation. Proclaiming himself the embodiment of the original *bodhisattva*, Jōgyō, who had first received that scripture from the Buddha himself, Nichiren took on himself the mission of saving the soul of Japan.

Traditionally Buddhism recognized two means of spreading the Dharma: accommodation (*shōju*) and confrontation (*shakabuku*). In the age of *mappō*, only the latter would do, and Nichiren set out to demonstrate this. He rejected Zen meditation, Pure Land *nenbutsu*, Shingon rituals, and Ritsu (*vinaya*) discipline as diabolical. So sweeping were his condemnations that some contemporary scholars have even questioned whether the sects that venerate him as founder deserve to be called Buddhist at all. Loyalty to the *Lotus Sutra* took precedence over everything else in his life and provoked one conflict after another with civil and religious authorities.

As Nichiren saw it, belief in 'provisional' Buddhas, central to the first half of the *Lotus Sutra*, ended up in superstition for the ordinary faithful and abstract debate for the scholars. Only single-minded faith in the reality of the one, absolute Buddha, central in the second half of the *sūtra*, could awaken the world from its dark ignorance, and only the recitation of the sacred name of the *sūtra* could bridge the gap between the two. Further, since he was persuaded that Japan was destined to replace India as the centre from which Buddhism would spread to the rest of the world, he insisted that the scripture be read not only with the lips but with the whole body: that is, that it lead to the transformation of society. Perhaps the most systematic statement of Nichiren's thought appears in a work entitled *Kanjin honzon shō* (A Clear Mind on Supreme Reality) and in the graphic portrayal of his *Great Mandala*, both completed in exile in the year 1273.

See also: BUDDHIST PHILOSOPHY, JAPANESE

List of works

Nichiren (1273) *Kanjin honzon shō* (A Clear Mind on Supreme Reality), ed. P.B. Yampolsky and B. Watson in *Selected Writings of Nichiren*, New York: Columbia University Press, 1990. (This edition is part of a reliable and easily accessible selection of Nichiren's writings.)

References and further reading

Anesaki Masaharu (1966) *Nichiren: The Buddhist Prophet*, Gloucester, MA: Peter Smith. (The classic source in English for the life and thought of Nichiren, written in easy prose for the non-specialist.)

Matsunaga, A. and Matsunaga, D. (1988) *Foundation of Japanese Buddhism*, Tokyo: Buddhist Books International, vol. 2, 137–81. (Includes a reliable and objective account of Nichiren's major teachings.)

J.W. HEISIG

NICHOLAS OF AUTRECOURT (*c*.1300–69)

Unlike most of his late medieval contemporaries, Nicholas of Autrecourt did not subscribe to Aristotelianism. Instead, he radically challenged the foundations of Aristotle's metaphysics and epistemology by asking two questions: first, how are we supposed to explain the basic constituents of the world, given that the Aristotelian categories are mere theoretical constructions and not immediately perceivable? Second, what can we know with absolute certitude, given that sense perception – the starting point in Aristotelian epistemology – is fallible and unreliable? Focusing on these two questions, Nicholas elaborated an atomistic metaphysics and defended an epistemology that emphasizes knowledge of a logical principle (the principle of non-contradiction), dismissing all knowledge based on inductive reasoning as uncertain.

1 Life and works
2 Epistemology
3 Metaphysics
4 Semantics

1 Life and works

Nicholas of Autrecourt (also Autricuria or Ultricuria), a scholastic theologian and philosopher, was born around 1300 in the diocese of Verdun. He studied at the University of Paris around 1330 and lectured there on Peter Lombard's *Sentences*. In 1340 he was summoned to Avignon to answer charges of heresy. His trial was interrupted by the death of Pope Benedict XII but was resumed under Pope Clement VI, by Cardinal William Curti. In 1346, the papal jury concluded that Nicholas was unworthy to continue his academic career. He was forced to recant many of his philosophical and theological theses and was expelled from the university. In 1347 his works were publicly burned. His appointment as deacon at the cathedral of Metz in 1350 may be seen as an indication that he was no longer considered a heretic. He probably died in Metz in 1369.

Only a small portion of Nicholas' works has been transmitted. Extant works include two complete letters addressed to the Franciscan Bernard of Arezzo, mostly dealing with epistemological problems, along with fragments of seven other letters to Bernard; a letter written to a certain Giles, also concerned with epistemological issues; the treatise *Exigit ordo executionis* (The Universal Treatise), surviving in a single incomplete manuscript, which is inspired by a decisive anti-Aristotelianism and focuses on metaphysics and natural philosophy; and a short theological question. In addition, the condemned articles contain important information about some of Nicholas' semantic theses.

2 Epistemology

Nicholas' main goal was to defend the possibility of evident, certain knowledge against Bernard of Arezzo's sceptical challenges. According to Bernard, one can never infer '*x* exists' from '*x* is perceived and thought of', because one may have a mere thought object that is not immediately caused by or founded upon a real, actually existing object. For instance, one may think about Caesar although Caesar is not actually existing and may never have existed, or one may have a perception of whiteness although there is no white thing in reality.

In order to reject Bernard's conclusion that no certain knowledge is possible, Nicholas maintained that there is one kind of absolutely certain knowledge (apart from the certitude of faith): knowledge of the principle of non-contradiction (de Rijk 1994: 58). This is the first principle in a negative sense because nothing is prior to it, and the first principle in a positive sense because all other certain knowledge is reducible to it. One can have certain knowledge of an implication (*consequentia*), Nicholas claimed, only if the consequent is identical with or part of the antecedent. Otherwise it would not be evident that the antecedent is inconsistent with the denial of the consequent. For instance, one can have certain knowledge of 'If the house exists, then the wall exists' only if the wall is a part of the house: otherwise it would not be evident that 'If the house exists, then one of its parts does not exist' violates the principle of non-contradiction. Nicholas held that we have to confine ourselves to this basic knowledge if we aim at certitude. From the fact that one thing is known to exist, the existence or non-existence of another thing can never be known with absolute certitude. Nor can one have any certain knowledge based on inductive reasoning: 'In the past, my hand was warmed when I put it toward the fire; therefore it will be warmed now if I put it toward the fire' cannot be known with certitude. My present action is not identical with or part of my past action, and no violation of the principle of non-contradiction results if I say 'Although in the past my hand was warmed when I put it toward the fire, it will not be warmed now when I put it toward the fire'.

It is clear that Nicholas' strict limitation to knowledge of the first principle involves a radical critique of theories of causality and of induction. Strictly speaking, one can never know that a certain effect *e* is brought about by a cause *c*, and one can never predict that *e* will be brought about if *c*, not hindered by any impediment, will be active. All one can do is have a sense perception of *c* and *e*, and then evaluate whether or not the two contradict each other. Because of this radical claim, Nicholas has been labelled 'a medieval Hume' by some modern commentators (Rashdall 1906–7). Yet it is important to see that Nicholas had no sceptical intentions. In pointing out that absolutely evident, though narrowly limited knowledge is possible, he in fact aimed to refute scepticism.

3 Metaphysics

Humans would live better lives, Nicholas polemically claimed, if only they would abandon their studies of Aristotle (de Rijk 1994: 154–5). Aristotle and his successors posited many entities that are mere theoretical constructions and cannot be known with certitude. All we can immediately experience are (1) the objects of our five exterior senses, and (2) our own acts. It is not evident on the basis of (1) that there are entities belonging to the Aristotelian categories (substances, qualities and so on); all we can say is that we have sense experience of constantly changing objects. Nor is it evident on the basis of (2) that there is a soul with three powers. We are only entitled to say that we are aware of inner acts having certain functions (thinking, willing and so on). We have no justification for introducing any concrete or abstract entities beyond the objects of our external or internal experience.

Nicholas also harshly attacked the Aristotelian thesis that there is generation and corruption of things. We do not know with certitude that substances or qualities come into and go out of existence; all we know is that things we perceive appear to change. This appearance can be explained in terms of an atomistic theory, wherein the world consists of eternally existing particles which constantly change their constellation; when things appear to change, or to come into or go out of existence, there is nothing but aggregation and separation of the atomic particles (see ATOMISM, ANCIENT).

In this manner, Nicholas broke radically from the then prevailing Aristotelian metaphysics. He used atomism as a decisive tool in his natural philosophy, in particular in his theory of the continuum. Contrary to many Aristotelians, he held that a continuum is not composed of infinitely divisible parts, but that it has atomic particles as its ultimate constituents. Although radical, however, this thesis was not completely new; indivisibilism can be traced back to several early fourteenth-century authors including HENRY OF HARCLAY, Walter CHATTON and GERARD OF ODO.

4 Semantics

No work documenting Nicholas' semantics has been transmitted, but some of his most controversial theses can be reconstructed on the basis of the condemned articles. Article 1.1 states: 'I have said and written that this sentence "Man is an animal" is not necessary according to faith, not paying attention for the moment to the necessary linkage between the foresaid terms' (de Rijk 1994: 146). This article is clearly connected with a famous late medieval sophism that raises the problem of whether the truth of a sentence requires the actual existence of the things referred to by the terms of the sentence. Some authors (for example, Roger BACON and BOETHIUS OF DACIA) gave an affirmative answer: if no man exists, they claimed, the term 'man' has no reference, and if there is no referent, the sentence is false. Therefore the sentence is not necessarily true. Others (such as SIGER OF BRABANT and Robert GROSSETESTE) held that the terms in this sentence refer not to individual men and animals but to the eternally existing species and genus; therefore 'man' always has a referent, even if no man actually exists, and the sentence is necessarily

true. Nicholas obviously chose the former explanation, but this was taken to be heretical (and indeed had already been condemned at Oxford in 1277). Contrary to Christian doctrine, the sentence 'Christ is a man' is not necessarily true if one claims that terms exclusively refer to actually existing things. During the three days in the tomb Christ was not an actually existing man; therefore the term 'man' did not have a reference during this period and the sentence was temporarily false.

Another important semantic issue is raised in Article 16.4: '[I have said] that what is signifiable in a complex way (*complexe significabile*) through the sentence "God and creature are distinct" is nothing (*nihil*)' (de Rijk 1994: 160). This article raises the question of whether the entire sentence signifies an entity that is not reducible to any other entity. Does 'God and creature are distinct' signify the state of affairs that God and creature are distinct, something reducible neither to the extramental things (that is, God, creature and their relation) nor to the concepts of these things? Nicholas clearly gave a negative answer. A state of affairs is nothing: there is no third entity in addition to extramental and mental entities. Thus, Nicholas did not deny the existence of God and creature, as his judges may have thought; rather, he rejected the claim (supported by GREGORY OF RIMINI and other Parisian authors) that a state of affairs is a peculiar kind of thing.

The semantic theses show clearly that Nicholas tackled some of the most prominent problems of his time. Although a radical critic of the dominant Aristotelianism and excluded from the intellectual centre, Nicholas was not simply an academic outsider. Most of his criticisms are developed within the framework of prevailing philosophical doctrines, and attack either the framework itself (especially in epistemology and metaphysics) or some widely accepted theses within it.

See also: ARISTOTELIANISM, MEDIEVAL; EPISTEMOLOGY, HISTORY OF; LANGUAGE, MEDIEVAL THEORIES OF; NATURAL PHILOSOPHY, MEDIEVAL

List of works

Nicholas of Autrecourt (c.1300–69) *Exigit ordo executionis* (The Universal Treatise), ed. J.-R. O'Donnell in 'Nicholas of Autrecourt', *Mediaeval Studies* 1, 1939: 179–280; trans. L. Kennedy, R. Arnold and A. Millward, *The Universal Treatise of Nicholas of Autrecourt*, Milwaukee, WI: Marquette University Press, 1971. (This edition is taken from the single incomplete manuscript which has survived.)

—— (c. 1300–69) Letters, ed. L.M. de Rijk, *Nicholas of Autrecourt: His Correspondence with Master Giles and Bernard of Arezzo*, Leiden: Brill, 1994. (Critical edition with English translation and extensive commentary.)

References and further reading

* de Rijk, L.M. (ed.) (1994) *Nicholas of Autrecourt: His Correspondence with Master Giles and Bernard of Arezzo*, Leiden: Brill. (Critical edition of Nicholas' letters with English translation, accompanied by an extensive commentary.)

Imbach, R. and Perler, D. (1988) *Nicolaus von Autrecourt: Briefe* (Nicholas of Autrecourt: Letters), Hamburg: Meiner. (Contains a reprint of the condemned articles as well as an edition of Nicholas' letters.)

Lappe, J. (1908) *Nicolaus von Autrecourt, sein Leben, seine Philosophie, seine Schriften* (Nicholas of Autrecourt, His Life, Philosophy and Writings), Beiträge zur Geschichte der Philosophie des Mittelalters 6.2, Münster: Aschendorff. (First edition of all the letters and condemned articles, and also a pioneering study of Nicholas' life and intellectual context.)

* Rashdall, H. (1906–7) 'Nicholas de Ultricuria, a Medieval Hume', *Proceedings of the Aristotelian Society* 7: 1–27. (Pioneer study of Nicholas' alleged scepticism.)

Scott, T.K. (1971) 'Nicholas of Autrecourt, Buridan, and Ockhamism', *Journal of the History of Philosophy* 9: 15–41. (Discussion of Nicholas' epistemology in the light of the Ockhamist and Anti-Ockhamist movements in Paris.)

Tachau, K.H. (1988) *Vision and Certitude in the Age of Ockham: Optics, Epistemology and the Foundations of Semantics 1250–1345*, Leiden: Brill. (Chapters 11–12 focus on Nicholas' condemnation in the context of the 1340s and shed new light on the anti-sceptical strategy.)

Thijssen, J.M.M.H. (1990) 'The "Semantic Articles" of Autrecourt's Condemnation', *Archives d'histoire doctrinale et littéraire du moyen-âge* 65: 155–75. (Detailed analysis of most semantic articles; interesting comparisons with fourteeth-century debates.)

Weinberg, J. (1948) *Nicholas of Autrecourt*, Princeton, NJ: Princeton University Press. (Most comprehensive, still important study that takes into account both Nicholas' epistemology and his metaphysics.)

DOMINIK PERLER

NICHOLAS OF CUSA (1401–64)

Also called Nicolaus Cusanus, this German cardinal takes his distinguishing name from the city of his birth, Kues (or Cusa, in Latin), on the Moselle river between Koblenz and Trier. Nicholas was influenced by Albert the Great, Thomas Aquinas, Bonaventure, Ramon Llull, Ricoldo of Montecroce, Master Eckhart, Jean Gerson and Heimericus de Campo, as well as by more distant figures such as Plato, Aristotle, Proclus, Pseudo-Dionysius and John Scottus Eriugena. His eclectic system of thought pointed in the direction of a transition between the Middle Ages and the Renaissance. In his own day as in ours, Nicholas was most widely known for his early work De docta ignorantia *(On Learned Ignorance). In it, he gives expression to his view that the human mind needs to discover its necessary ignorance of what the Divine Being is like, an ignorance that results from the infinite ontological and cognitive disproportion between Infinity itself (that is, God) and the finite human or angelic knower. Correlated with the doctrine of* docta ignorantia *is that of* coincidentia oppositorum in deo, *the coincidence of opposites in God. All things coincide in God in the sense that God, as undifferentiated being, is beyond all opposition, beyond all determination as* this *rather than* that.

Nicholas is also known for his rudimentary cosmological speculation, his prefiguring of certain metaphysical and epistemological themes found later in Leibniz, Kant and Hegel, his ecclesiological teachings regarding the controversy over papal versus conciliar authority, his advocacy of a religious ecumenism of sorts, his interest in purely mathematical topics and his influence on the theologian Paul Tillich in the twentieth century. A striking tribute to Nicholas' memory still stands today: the hospice for elderly, indigent men that he caused to be erected at Kues between 1452 and 1458 and that he both endowed financially and invested with his personal library. This small but splendid library, unravaged by the intervening wars and consisting of some three hundred volumes, includes manuscripts written in Nicholas' own hand.

1 Biography

Of Nicholas' early life, little is known. He was one of four children born to Johan Krebs and Katharina Roemer Krebs. Still unconfirmed is the speculation that his father, a successful ferryman and hauler of merchandise up and down the Moselle, sent him to Deventer in Holland for part of his primary education. As for higher learning, Nicholas studied the liberal arts at the University of Heidelberg during 1416–7. Subsequently, he transferred to the University of Padua, where he came under the influence of the Italian humanists and acquired familiarity with the latest physical and mathematical theories. At Padua he studied principally canon law, receiving his *doctor decretorum* in 1423. In the spring of 1425 he continued his study of canon law at the University of Cologne where, apparently, he also gave lectures and where Heimericus de Campo introduced him to the ideas of Ramon LLULL and PSEUDO-DIONYSIUS. In 1425 and 1426 he held benefices from the archbishopric of Trier, and by 1427 he was secretary to the archbishop himself, Otto von Ziegenhain. In 1428 and again in 1435 he was offered a chair in canon law at the University of Louvain, but on both occasions he declined, preferring to continue with his canonical and administrative work on behalf of the archdiocese and – at the Council of Basel – with his work as a member of the Council's committee on matters of faith.

During his 'Basel period' (1432–8, not all of which time he was in Basel) he wrote, among other things, *De communione sub utraque specie* (On Communion Using Both the Bread and the Wine), against the Hussites, in 1433; *De concordantia catholica* (The Catholic Concordance) in 1433 and *De auctoritate praesidendi in concilio generali* (On Presidential Authority in a General Council) in 1434, both of which concern the demarcation of papal authority; and *De reparatione kalendarii* (On Amending the Calendar) in 1436, a proposal for revising the Julian calendar. At Basel he met John of Torquemada, whose treatise against the Muslims, *Tractatus contra principales errores perfidi Machometi* (Tractate Against the Principal Errors of the Infidel Muhammad) (1459), was to influence his own *Cribratio Alkorani* (A Scrutiny of the Qur'an) in 1461. Also affecting his response to the incursion of Islam into the West were his first-hand experiences of Islam in 1437, while present in Constantinople for two months (24 September–27 November). The delegation to which he belonged had been sent by the minority party of the Council of Basel to encourage both the Byzantine emperor and the Greek patriarch to reunite with the Roman patriarchate. It was on his return voyage from Constantinople, while still at sea, that Nicholas came to embrace the notion of learned ignorance.

Sometime between 1436 and 1440, Nicholas was ordained a priest. On 20 December 1448 he was named cardinal, and to him was assigned, on 3 January 1449, the titular church of St Peter ad Vincula in Rome. Some fifteen months thereafter (23 March 1450) he was designated bishop of Brixen in Tirol, where later his attempts to introduce monastic and diocesan reforms engendered enmity with Archduke Sigismund, whose threats forced him twice to flee to Rome. His death came on 11 August 1464 in Todi, Italy, as he was travelling from Rome to Ancona.

2 Two basic themes

The themes of *docta ignorantia* and *coincidentia oppositorum* were misunderstood by Nicholas' contemporary and adversary John Wenck of Herrenberg, who in *De ignota litteratura* (On Unknown Learning) inveighed against Nicholas' treatise *De docta ignorantia*. In a response, *Apologia doctae ignorantiae* (A Defence of Learned Ignorance), Nicholas made clear that the doctrine of learned ignorance is not intended to deny knowledge of the existence of God but only to deny all knowledge of God's nature (except on the part of God himself). All our discourse about God is metaphorical; moreover, when we are conceiving positively of God, we are obliged to conceive of him in accordance with those metaphors that signify the highest perfections. The doctrine of *docta ignorantia* goes on to teach that the quiddities of created objects are unknowable by us precisely; that is, they are unknowable exactly as they are in themselves. Yet, although the objects are unknowable exactly *in themselves*, the *objects themselves* are not unknowable. Rather, they are apprehensible by us *in coniectura*, Nicholas' expression for what is knowable only imperfectly and perspectivally. The doctrine of learned ignorance constitutes a radical break with the scholastic affirmation of a real, but remote, resemblance between God and his creation. The late scholastic WILLIAM OF OCKHAM had repudiated the validity of all alleged analogical knowledge of God's nature, though he nonetheless maintained that the predicate 'being' is used univocally in discourse about divine being and created being. By contrast, Nicholas regards even 'being' as an equivocal and metaphorical predicate when used of God.

The doctrine of *coincidentia* does not mean, as in John Wenck's construal of it, that the universe coincides with God, nor does it serve to contravene the Aristotelian principle of non-contradiction within the legitimate domain of that principle's application – that is, its application to the realm of finite affairs. All things are present in God ontologically prior to their creation, as illustrated by an effect's being present in the priority of its cause. But just as, in its cause, an effect is the cause, so in God all things are God rather than being their differentiated, finite selves. Nicholas nowhere teaches, unqualifiedly, that all things are God; indeed, he expressly rejects pantheism and its variants. Though he speaks of God as not *other* than (*non aliud a*) the universe, he does not mean that God is identical with (*non aliud quam*) the universe, but rather that God transcends the domain of comparison with all finite objects.

3 Ontology

Nicholas' ontology has been interpreted along two very different lines. According to one line of interpretation, Nicholas regards finite objects as having no respective positive essence of their own, for God himself is the self-identical essence of each finite thing. Accordingly, the relative identity of each thing is said to consist only in its difference from all other finite things, all such differences being accidental and all relations between these things being internal relations. Thus in this view, propounded in Europe by Heinrich Rombach (1965) and in North America by Thomas P. McTighe (1964), created things are not substances and do not differ from one another substantially. According to the second, more generally accepted line of interpretation – one taking its lead from Nicholas' *Apologia* – some created things are substances, and these do have positive essences of their own. In accordance with their respective essences, finite things differ essentially from one another. God is the Essence of these things in that he is the Essence of the respective essences of these things, even as he is *being* itself (*entitas*), which sustains in existence whatever is *a* being (*ens*). This distinction between *being* and *beings* Nicholas draws from MEISTER ECKHART; and it is one of the distinctions that influence both Paul TILLICH and Martin HEIDEGGER.

In *De filiatione Dei* (On Being a Son of God) 3, Nicholas' likening of all created beings to mirrors that mutually reflect one another prefigures Leibniz's systematic use of a similar theme (see LEIBNIZ, G.W.). Also parallel with tenets in Leibniz are the assertions (1) that each kind of thing – though not each individual within that kind – is as perfect as that kind of thing can be and (2) that physical objects (which, for Leibniz, are 'well-founded appearances') are, in principle, infinitely divisible. Nicholas' various utterances regarding *nihil* (not-being) in relation to

esse (being) have struck some interpreters as inchoately Hegelian, in a dialectical sense (see HEGELIANISM). Others have seen Nicholas not as working with logico-ontological categories but as being a metaphysical nominalist. In the last analysis, his theory of universals (if not his theory of transcendentals) must be reckoned to be a moderate realism that is cognate with that of ARISTOTLE and AQUINAS.

4 Cosmology

At times Nicholas denies that the universe is finite and also denies that it is infinite; at other times he asserts that it is both finite and infinite. It is not finite, he tells us, in that it is not physically limited by anything outside its dimensions; on the other hand, it is finite in that it has a definite measure, known to God alone. In other words, the universe is finite but unbounded; yet, Nicholas terms it *privatively* infinite, in contradistinction to God, who is *negatively* infinite, since he is not even conceivably limited.

Because there is no perfect precision in the world, explains Nicholas, the universe's circumference is not perfectly spherical, nor is the earth a perfect sphere. Consequently, neither the universe nor the earth has an exact physical centre and, thus, the earth is not the fixed centre of the universe. Indeed, the earth is not stationary but, like all stars and planets, has a circular movement of its own, though this movement is undetectable by us, its inhabitants. Likewise, the earth appears to us to be at the centre of the universe, and we infer that the 'fixed' stars are at the outer circumference. However, these stars also have inhabitants, who will judge themselves to be at the centre and the earth to be on the periphery. Furthermore, both the earth and the moon, as also the other heavenly bodies, emit a light and a heat of their own, even though both the earth and its moon also reflect the sun's light and heat. Nicholas' cosmological claims do not anticipate those of COPERNICUS, but they do deviate in important respects from those of Aristotle and Ptolemy.

5 Epistemology

In *De visione Dei* (The Vision of God) 24, Nicholas states that 'there cannot be in the intellect anything which is such that it was not first in the senses', thus rejecting the notion of innate concepts. Yet, in *Idiota de mente* (The Layman on the Mind) and elsewhere, he allows that the mind, through construction, can make concepts of things (such as a spoon) whose forms are not found in nature. Moreover, the mind has an innate power of judgment (*vis iudiciaria*) by which to weigh the strength of rational considerations and through which it is familiar, a priori, with basic moral principles (*Compendium* 10). Although human beings cannot know the exact quiddity of any given thing, they do nevertheless perceive the things themselves, through the medium of sensory images and conceptual forms. In places, Nicholas emphasizes (1) sensory and conceptual perspectivity, (2) the role of reason (*ratio*) as synthesizer and (3) the conditioning operations of the intellect (*intellectus*). (One must be careful, however, not to exaggerate his dim prefiguring of KANT.) Mathematical knowledge he regards as a priori and certain, because mathematical entities are conceptual entities elicited from, and known in a precise way by, our reason (*De possest* (On Actualized-possibility) 43–4). In *Idiota de mente* 6 he seems to endorse the doctrine that these conceptual numbers are 'images', as it were, of God's thought. The mathematical puzzle with which he is principally preoccupied is that of how to square the circle: in other words, how in a finite number of steps to construct, using only an unmarked straight-edge and a drawing compass, a square whose area is equivalent to that of a given circle.

6 Christology

Nicholas' Christology is orthodox, inasmuch as he considers Jesus to be the incarnate second member of the Trinity, uniting in his divine person his divine nature with a human nature. In accordance with the divine nature, Jesus is the Absolute Maximum; in accordance with his human nature, he is the contracted maximum individual. The Absolute Maximum is Infinity itself and is such that nothing greater than it can be conceived; the contracted maximum is an individual creature that is of maximum perfection within its kind. (By 'contracted', Nicholas means restricted, differentiated or delimited, so as to be *this* thing and not *that* thing.) Thus Jesus' human nature is the perfection of the possibility of human nature. Furthermore, since human nature, which consists of a body and a rational soul, is a middle nature – a nature in between the higher intelligible natures (namely, angels) and the lower corporeal natures (namely, brute animals and non-animate things) – Jesus' perfect human nature is 'the fullness of all the perfections of each and every thing'. Thus, reminiscent of Eriugena's *De divisione naturae*, the perfect world that went forth from God in creation is reunited to God through the subsumption of Christ's human nature in his divine nature.

7 Ecclesiology

In *De concordantia catholica*, Nicholas seeks to demarcate the respective authority of a universal council and of the pope. A universal council (in contrast to a patriarchal council) is one to which bishops and select ecclesiastics from all five patriarchates have been called – a call issued usually by a patriarch or a patriarchal council, or an agent of either. A universal council may depose a heretical pope. A decision (on matters of faith) reached with a high degree of agreement by a universal council is more trustworthy than would be a decision on such matters by the pope alone. Yet, on matters of faith, the pope's consent as well as the council's is required for declaring a decision infallible. Nicholas speaks of degrees of infallibility, and he relates these to degrees of consensus: the greater the consensus within a universal council and beween this council and the pope, the greater the infallibility of the decision reached. Nicholas later was to abandon his claim that the authority of a universal council in which there is substantial agreement is superior to the pope's authority.

8 Ecumenism

The dialogue *De pace fidei* (On Peaceful Unity of Faith) serves to challenge the various leaders of the different religions to adopt *religio una in rituum varietate*, a common religion that admits of diverse rites. The spirit of this 'ecumenism' is reinforced in *Cribratio Alkorani*, where Nicholas seeks to find common ground between Christianity and Islam. Yet Nicholas' is not a genuine ecumenism, for he aims to show how other religions can be led to discern the truth of the doctrines essential to Christianity while retaining many of their own diverse rituals and liturgies. Through his programme of learned ignorance, he envisions the possibility of worshipping a God who, as infinite, is neither trine nor one in any sense in which trineness and oneness are positively conceivable by us. By thus adapting Eckhart's distinction between God and Godhead, Nicholas can regard the doctrine of the Trinity as no longer a stumbling block to Jews and Muslims.

9 Conclusion

Nicholas' system of thought is often misapprehended, sometimes in a way that detracts from his real genius, sometimes in a way that is all too flattering of his intellectual accomplishments. A proper grasp of his ideas will locate him, no doubt, somewhere between the invective of John Wenck, who condemns him as a corrupter of Aristotelianism, and the praise of Heinrich Rombach, who sees him as a new Aristotle for the modern period, as someone whose anti-substantive, functionalist ontology is as revolutionary as was Aristotle's introduction of hylomorphism in the first place.

See also: COSMOLOGY; INCARNATION AND CHRISTOLOGY; ONTOLOGY; TILLICH, P.

List of works

Major Latin editions

Nicholas of Cusa (1433–64) Collected Works, Strasbourg: Martin Flach, 1488. (Based upon codices Latini Cusani 218 and 219. Newly reprinted as *Werke*, ed. Paul Wilpert, Berlin: Walter de Gruyter, 1967, 2 vols.)

—— (1433–64) Collected Works, Paris: Jacques Le Fèvre d'Etaples, 1514; repr. Frankfurt: Minerva, 1962. (Adds to the Strasbourg edition *De concordantia catholica, De deo abscondito, Coniectura de ultimis diebus*, certain mathematical *opuscula* and excerpts from the *Sermones*. Contains many editorial emendations. The later Basel edition of 1565 follows the wording of the Paris edition but adds several mathematical works; like previous editions, it lacks *De li non aliud*.)

—— (1433–64) Collected Works, Heidelberg Academy of Letters edition, Leipzig/Hamburg: Meiner, 1932–. (Series remains in progress. The most reliable of the editions.)

—— (1445–59) Mathematical Writings, trans. J. Hofmann, *Die mathematischen Schriften*, Hamburg: Meiner, 2nd edn, 1979. (A German translation of the mathematical works, together with an introduction, extensive notes and important manuscript information.)

Individual works

—— (1433) *Opusculum contra Bohemorum errorem: De usu communionis* (A Short Work Against the Error of the Hussites: On the Celebration of Communion), in the Paris edition of Collected Works, vol. II, 2, ff. 5^r–13^v. (This is a single work, though the Paris edition divides it into two works.)

—— (1433) *De maioritate auctoritatis sacrorum conciliorum supra auctoritatem papae* (On the Superiority of the Authority of the Sacred Councils to the Authority of the Pope), text ed. E. Meuthen, printed in Abhandlungen der Heidelberger Akademie der Wissenschaften, Philosophisch-historische Klasse, 1977, Abhandlung 3. (One of Nicholas' early works, on papal authority.)

—— (1433) *De concordantia catholica* (The Catholic Concordance), trans. P. Sigmund, Cambridge:

Cambridge University Press, 1991. (On the demarcation of papal authority.)

—— (1433) *Libellus inquisitionis veri et boni* (A Short Book Investigating the True and the Good). (No longer extant.)

—— (1433 or 1434) *De modo vero habilitandi ingenium ad discursum in dubiis* (On the Correct Manner of Training the Mind for Reasoning about Doubtful Matters). (No longer extant.)

—— (1434) *De auctoritate praesidendi in concilio generali* (On Presidential Authority in a General Council), trans. H.L. Bond *et al.*, *Church History* 59, 1990: 19–34. (On the demarcation of papal authority.)

—— (1436) *De reparatione kalendarii* (On Amending the Calendar), text ed. V. Stegemann, in *Die Kalenderverbesserung. De correctione kalendarii*, Schriften des Nikolaus von Cues, Heidelberg: Kerle, 1955. (Nicholas' proposals for reforming the calendar.)

—— (1440) *De docta ignorantia* (On Learned Ignorance), trans. J. Hopkins, *Nicholas of Cusa on Learned Ignorance*, Minneapolis, MN: Banning, 1985. (Nicholas' best-knwon work, setting out his doctrine of 'learned ignorance'.)

—— (1441–2) *De coniecturis* (On Surmises), trans. W.F. Wertz, *Toward a New Council of Florence*, Washington, DC: Schiller Institute, 1993. (Recent translation.)

—— (1444 or earlier) *De Deo abscondito* (On the Hidden God), trans. J. Hopkins, *A Miscellany on Nicholas of Cusa*, Minneapolis, MN: Banning, 1994. (Recent translation.)

—— (1445) *De quaerendo Deum* (On Seeking God), trans. J. Hopkins, *A Miscellany on Nicholas of Cusa*, Minneapolis, MN: Banning, 1994. (Recent translation.)

—— (1445) *De filiatione Dei* (On Being a Son of God), trans. J. Hopkins, *A Miscellany on Nicholas of Cusa*, Minneapolis, MN: Banning, 1994. (In Book 3, Nicholas likens all created beings to mirrors.)

—— (1445) *De geometricis transmutationibus* (On Geometrical Transformations), in the Paris edition of Collected Works, vol. II, 2, ff. 33^r–53^v. (Edition of mathematical work.)

—— (1445) *De arithmeticis complementis* (On Arithmetical Complements), in the Paris edition of Collected Works, vol. II, 2, ff. 54^r–58^v. (Edition of mathematical work.)

—— (1445–6) *De dato patris luminum* (The Gift of the Father of Lights), trans. J. Hopkins, *Nicholas of Cusa's Metaphysic of Contraction*, Minneapolis, MN: Banning, 1983. (Recent translation.)

—— (1446) *Coniectura de ultimis diebus* (A Surmise

Regarding the Last Days), in the Heidelberg Academy edition of Collected Works, vol. IV, *Opuscula*. (Reliable edition.)

—— (1447) *Dialogus de genesi* (On the Genesis [of All Things]), trans. J. Hopkins, *A Miscellany on Nicholas of Cusa*, Minneapolis, MN: Banning, 1994. (Nicholas' writings on creation.)

—— (1449) *Apologia doctae ignorantiae* (A Defense of Learned Ignorance), trans. J. Hopkins, *Nicholas of Cusa's Debate with John Wenck*, Minneapolis, MN: Banning, 1988. (Includes text and translation of Wenck's *De ignota litteratura* (On Unknown Learning).)

—— (1450) *Idiota de sapientia* (The Layman on Wisdom), trans. J. Hopkins, Nicholas of Cusa on Wisdom and Knowledge, Minneapolis, MN: Banning, 1996. (Further work on epistemology.)

—— (1450) *Idiota de mente* (The Layman on Mind), trans. J. Hopkins, Nicholas of Cusa on Wisdom and Knowledge, Minneapolis, MN: Banning, 1996. (Nicholas allows that the mind can make concepts of things whose forms are not found in nature.)

—— (1450) *Idiota de staticis experimentis* (The Layman on Experiments Done with Weight-Scales), trans. J. Hopkins, Nicholas of Cusa on Wisdom and Knowledge, Minneapolis, MN: Banning, 1996. (Edition of mathematical work.)

—— (1450) *De circuli quadratura* (On Squaring the Circle), Munich, Staatsbibliothek, Codex Latinus Monacensis 14213, ff. 101^r–104^v. (Edition of mathematical work.)

—— (1450) *Quadratura circuli* (Squaring the Circle), in the Basel edition of Collected Works, 1091–95. (Includes what the Basel edition entitles *De sinibus et chordis*.)

—— (1452) *Tres epistolae contra Bohemos* (Three Letters against the Hussites), in the Strasbourg edition of Collected Works, vol. II, 674–97. (The Strasbourg, Paris and Basel editions have the wrong ordering. Corrected order: Letter I is in the Strasbourg edition, vol. II, 675–9, and Paris edition, vol. II, 2, ff. 14^r–15^v. Letter II is the Strasbourg edition, vol. II, 679–82, and Paris edition, vol. II, 2, ff. 15^v–16^v. Letter III is in the Strasbourg edition, vol. II, 674–97, and Paris edition, vol. II, 2, ff. 13^v–22^r. Letter III contains, as inserted material, the first two letters. See H. Hallauer, 'Das Glaubengespräch mit den Hussiten', *Mitteilungen und Forschungsbeiträge der Cusanus-Gesellschaft* 9, 1971: 72–3.)

—— (1453) *De pace fidei* (On Peaceful Unity of Faith), trans. J. Hopkins, *Nicholas of Cusa's De Pace Fidei and Cribratio Alkorani*, Minneapolis, MN: Banning, 1994. (Recent translation.)

—— (1453) *De visione Dei* (The Vision of God), trans.

J. Hopkins, *Nicholas of Cusa's Dialectical Mysticism*, Minneapolis, MN: Banning, 1988. (Recent translation.)

—— (1453) *De mathematicis complementis* (On Mathematical Complements), in the Strasbourg edition of Collected Works, vpl. II, 388–430. (A second, fuller version was produced in 1454.)

—— (1453) *De theologicis complementis* (Complementary Theological Considerations), trans. J. Hopkins, *Nicholas of Cusa: Metaphysical Speculations*, Minneapolis, MN: Banning, 1997. (Recent translation.)

—— (1454?) *Declaratio rectilineationis curvae* (An Explication of the Straightening of a Curved Line), in the Basel edition of the Collected Works, 1100–1. (Edition of mathematical work.)

—— (1454?) *De una recti curvique mensura* (On a Single Measurement of the Straight and the Curved), in the Basel edition of the Collected Works, 1101–6. (Edition of mathematical work.)

—— (1457) *Dialogus de circuli quadratura* (Dialogue on Squaring a Circle), in the Basel edition of the Collected Works, 1095–8. (Pages 1099–1100 contain a letter from Master Paul to Nicholas.)

—— (1457) *De caesarea circuli quadratura* (The Imperial Squaring of a Circle), Milan, Biblioteca Ambrosiana, Codex Latinus Mediolanensis G 74 inf., ff. 3^r–4^r. (Edition of mathematical work.)

—— (1458) *De beryllo* (On [Intellectual] Eye-Glasses), trans. J. Hopkins, *Nicholas of Cusa: Metaphysical Speculations*, Minneapolis, MN: Banning, 1997. (Translation of mathematical work.)

—— (1458) *De mathematica perfectione* (On Mathematical Perfection), in the Strasbourg edition of Collected Works, vol. II, 698–709. (Edition of mathematical work.)

—— (1459) *De aequalitate* (On Equality), trans. J. Hopkins, *Nicholas of Cusa: Metaphysical Speculations*, Minneapolis, MN: Banning, 1997. (Recent translation.)

—— (1459) *De principio* (On the Beginning), trans. J. Hopkins, *Nicholas of Cusa: Metaphysical Speculations*, Minneapolis, MN: Banning, 1997. (Recent translation.)

—— (1459) *Aurea propositio in mathematicis* (The Golden Proposition in Mathematics), Milan, Biblioteca Ambrosiana, Codex Latinus Mediolanensis G 74 inf., ff. 2^v–3^r. (Edition of mathematical work.)

—— (1460) *De possest* (On Actualized-possibility), trans. J. Hopkins, *A Concise Introduction to the Philosophy of Nicholas of Cusa*, Minneapolis, MN: University of Minnesota, 1978; 3rd edn, Minneapolis, MN: Banning, 1986. (Reliable translation.)

—— (1461) *Cribratio Alkorani* (A Scrutiny of the Koran), trans. J. Hopkins, *Nicholas of Cusa's De*

Pace Fidei and Cribratio Alkorani, Minneapolis, MN: Banning, 1994. (Recent translation of Nicholas' writings against Islam.)

—— (1461 or 1462) *De li lon lliud* (On Not-other), trans. J. Hopkins, *Nicholas of Cusa on God as Not-other*, Minneapolis, MN: University of Minnesota, 1979; 3rd edn, Minneapolis, MN: Banning, 1987.

—— (1462) *De figura mundi* (On the Shape of the World). (No longer extant.)

—— (1462–3) *De ludo globi* (The Game of Spheres), trans. P. Watts, *Nicholas de Cusa. De Ludo Globi. The Game of Spheres*, New York: Abaris Books, 1986. (Translation of mathematical work.)

—— (1462 or 1463) *De venatione sapientia* (On the Pursuit of Wisdom), trans. J. Hopkins, *Nicholas of Cusa: Metaphysical Speculations*, Minneapolis, MN: Banning, 1997. (Recent translation.)

—— (1464) *Compendium*, trans. J. Hopkins, *Nicholas of Cusa on Wisdom and Knowledge*, Minneapolis, MN: Banning, 1996. (Recent translation.)

—— (1464) *De apice theoriae* (Concerning the Loftiest Level of Contemplative Reflection), trans. J. Hopkins, *Nicholas of Cusa: Metaphysical Speculations*, Minneapolis, MN: Banning, 1997. (Recent translation.)

References and further reading

Euler, W. (1990) *Unitas et Pax. Religionsvergleich bei Raimundus Lullus und Nikolaus von Kues* (Unity and Peace: Ramon Llull's and Nicholas of Cusa's Comparison of Religions), Würzburg: Echter Verlag. (A careful study of Llull's influence on Cusa.)

Hagemann, L. (1976) *Der Kur'ān in Verständnis und Kritik bei Nikolaus von Kues. Ein Beitrag zur Erhellung islamisch-christlicher Geschichte* (The Qur'an as Understood and Criticized by Nicholas of Cusa: A Contribution to the Illumination of Islamic-Christian History), Frankfurt: Knecht. (Major study of Nicholas' *Cribratio Alkorani* and of his approach to Islam.)

Harries, K. (1975) 'The Infinite Sphere: Comments on the History of a Metaphor', *Journal of the History of Philosophy* 13: 5–15. (Explores Nicholas' emphasis on perspective and his use of the metaphor of God as a sphere whose centre is everywhere and whose circumference is nowhere.)

Haubst, R. (1991) *Streifzüge in die cusanische Theologie* (Forays into Nicholas of Cusa's Theology), Münster: Aschendorff. (A collection of Haubst's major essays analyzing Nicholas' theological views.)

Haubst, R. *et al.* (eds) (1961–) *Mitteilungen und Forschungsbeiträge der Cusanus-Gesellschaft* (Reports and Research-Contributions of the Cusanus Society), Mainz: Mattias-Grünewald. (A continuing series; bibliographies in vols. I, III, VI, X, XV.)

Jacobi, K. (1969) *Die Methode der cusanischen Philosophie* (Cusanus' Philosophical Method), Munich: Alber. (An extensive survey of previous interpretations of Cusa; Jacobi himself is influenced by H. Rombach.)

* McTighe, T. (1964) 'Nicholas of Cusa and Leibniz's Principle of Indiscernibility', *Modern Schoolman* 42: 33–46. (Gives the gist of one competing interpretation of Nicholas' ontology.)

Meuthen, E. (1979) *Nikolaus von Kues, 1401–1464. Skizze einer Biographie* (Nicholas of Cusa 1401–1464: A Biographical Sketch), 4th edn, Münster: Aschendorff. (Provides, concisely, the essential facts about Nicholas' life.)

Meuthen, E. and Hallauer, H. (eds) (1976, vol. I, fascicle 1, and 1983, fascicle 2) *Acta Cusana. Quellen zur Lebensgeschichte des Nikolaus von Kues*, Hamburg: Meiner. (Other volumes in progress. A wealth of crucial details concerning Nicholas' life and works.)

* Rombach, H. (1965) *Substanz, System, Struktur. Die Ontologie des Funktionalismus und der philosophische Hintergrund der modernen Wissenschaft* (Substance, System, Structure: Functionalist Ontology and the Philosophical Background of Modern Science), vol. I, Freiburg: Alber. (Contains an extreme, but extremely intriguing, construal of Cusa's metaphysics as a metaphysics of functionalism.)

Sigmund, P. (1963) *Nicholas of Cusa and Medieval Political Thought*, Cambridge, MA: Harvard University Press. (A balanced examination of Nicholas' theory of conciliar and papal authority.)

Vansteenberghe, E. (1920) *Le Cardinal Nicolas de Cues* (Cardinal Nicholas of Cusa), Paris; repr. Frankfurt: Minerva, 1963. (An early monumental, pathbreaking work.)

JASPER HOPKINS

NICOLE, PIERRE *see* Arnauld, Antoine; Port-Royal (§2)

NIEBUHR, HELMUT RICHARD (1894–1962)

After early writings interpreting the social dimensions of US religious life from a Protestant point of view, Helmut Richard Niebuhr came increasingly to focus on theology, the interpretation of the Word and experience of God, and ethics, the attempt to live a responsible life grounded in the deepest values. More successfully than any contemporary, he brought into creative tension two major strands of modern Christian thought. From the liberal tradition, he came to stress the relativity of all statements about God and accented the situation of the believer who makes them. Niebuhr matched or countered this perspectival approach with an inheritance from 'neo-orthodoxy' which stressed the otherness of God, the distance between God and all human experiences, statements and perspectives. While preoccupied with witness to 'God beyond the gods', Niebuhr was also devoted to understanding the human in the light of the experience of God. He developed comprehensive views of the responsible self as the focus of ethics and emphasized the communal dimensions of human life.

1 The sovereignty of God
2 Social history and the kingdom of God
3 Theology and Jesus Christ
4 Theory of value and the responsible self

1 The sovereignty of God

Helmut Richard Niebuhr was born in Wright City, Missouri, on 3 September 1894. He acquired theological interests early as the son of a well-read small-town pastor; his brother, Reinhold NIEBUHR, also became a prominent theologian. The sermons he heard as a child reflected German Protestant traditions, which were nurtured in the college and seminary life of the Evangelical and Reformed tradition. After receiving a PhD at Yale in 1924 and studying at Berlin and Marburg in 1930, he taught at Yale Divinity School (adjacent to a secular university), where seminarians from many denominations studied. His thought was never devoted to sectarian interests, but reflected and kept in mind the ecumenical context, and addressed the world of those who cared little for the Christian faith. He died on 5 July 1962.

Despite the broadness of Niebuhr's thought, many of its accents are developments of the Reformed background. In the tradition associated with John CALVIN (§3), he witnessed to a God who is not the product of human imagination, not one among many deities, not merely immanent and able to be taken captive within human affairs, and not capable of compromising or being compromised. This is the 'God beyond the gods', not to be confused with the idols and deities manufactured by humans to justify their nations, Churches or other institutions. The ethical human being is to draw their values from reference to this sovereign God.

Niebuhr balanced this view of God, which in philosophical terms he called 'radical monotheism', with a very realistic view of the way human beings grasped the activity of God. God is indeed active in the world in a distinctive way through Jesus Christ; he is testified to in the Bible, engaged in human affairs through the life of the Church and manifestly holds humans responsible for actions that could be valued as good.

2 Social history and the kingdom of God

Not a biblical scholar, Niebuhr was frankly a philosophical theologian at a time when American Protestant elites often denigrated philosophy. He was not so much a precise or seminal philosophical thinker as someone who carried on a lifelong dialogue with philosophers, at first with social and political thinkers. This led him to write a sociological and then a historical interpretation of modern and especially American religious life. In *The Social Sources of Denominationalism* (1929), he displayed an almost deterministic view of what social class did to shape Churchly response. At that time he was strongly influenced by the German social philosopher Ernst TROELTSCH, who led Niebuhr towards relativism, or at least towards the need to see the relativity of all human witness to God. He later wrote his own critique of this sociological determinism, *The Kingdom of God in America* (1937). In it, he accented the way the experience of God and thinking about God shaped the life of the American nation.

A third historical work, *Christ and Culture* (1951), saw him move towards a classifying system for relating the believing community to the culture around it. He tended to favour two views: 'Christ Transforming Culture', in which responsible humans in community set out to realize something of the coming kingdom of God; and 'Christ and Culture in Paradox', a dialectical view which showed Christians at times affirming and at times negating the main elements of culture. These reflect Niebuhr's own view of the limits of human achievement, and his belief in the need to be responsible within culture.

3 Theology and Jesus Christ

While writing these three more or less historical works, Niebuhr came to favour a more abstract and philosophical approach to theology. Through it all, he kept two poles of thought in the front of his mind. One was witnessed to in *Radical Monotheism and Western Culture* (1960), a judgment upon all efforts to reduce God to a cultural artefact or to claim God for favoured human causes. His last book, *The Responsible Self* (published posthumously in 1963), demonstrated that he had never left behind his preoccupation with conscience, community and responsibility. He died before being able to complete a synthetic work. Yet his life and teachings were sufficiently consistent for one to be able to deduce the elements of a complete systematic theology. Two generations of Niebuhr students went from Yale to strategic positions in theological schools, there to develop these poles of his thought.

As a Christian philosophical theologian, Niebuhr naturally focused on the figure of Jesus Christ. He connected Jesus chiefly with the redeeming activity of God. Niebuhr spent little time revisiting ancient creedal categories, largely shaped under Greek influence, in order to deal with the ways the human Jesus is to be regarded as a distinctive expression of divine action. He chose historical more than philosophical language for this purpose. Jesus was first of all a pious Jew, a person of his times. He was a proclaimer of the sovereignty of God, of radical monotheism focused on the one he called 'Father'. He was also a mediator of faith, who proclaimed and brought about for human beings a new relation to God.

4 Theory of value and the responsible self

Rather than make original contributions to what Christians call Christology, Niebuhr related Jesus to Niebuhrian theories of values and valuation. Jesus embodied the revelation of God and used his situation to offer a new covenant with God, a revolutionary impulse that called others who saw him as an exemplar of faith to change the world around them. One of Niebuhr's students, Hans Frei, summarized well the way Niebuhr could speak of 'the teaching and acts of Jesus Christ, his moral virtues' as offering 'the direct clue to his being'. In these, one may find 'in faith, hope and love, the unique moral Sonship to God of one who is completely at one with men' (Frei 1957: 115).

Niebuhr is usually described as a confessional theologian, that is, a thinker about God who interprets the 'confessions' or creeds of the believing community. In fact, he presented two perspectives.

One is indeed 'internal', the 'we' language of the community. But there is also the perspective of the sociologist, historian or analyst, who looks at the community from the 'external' point of view and sees a very different sort of reality. It is this understanding that has led Niebuhr to be described, second, as a 'perspectival' thinker – not a mere relativist, but someone acutely conscious of the relativity of all human experience and discourse, the perspectives through which people interpret God's action.

On the basis of these interpretations, Niebuhr can be seen, third, as a philosophical theologian of 'value'. For him, the experience of God and the witness to God are not ends in themselves, having no connection with action in the public world. On the contrary, the witness to God should impel responsible selves to give expression to that which they value. God is the source and centre of value, and knowledge of God leads believers to patterns of loyalty that help them to develop appropriate scales of value with respect to the things of the world. For the believer, knowing is a matter that involves valuing. The act of valuing is not capricious, not a matter of mere preference, but is related to the deepest commitments of life. Being and value are inseparable in Niebuhr's thinking. While this could have meant 'Whatever is, is right', for Niebuhr it had to be 'Whatever is, is good', since 'Being' for him meant the Being of the creator God who is good and creates good. The person of faith becomes the one who knows, in a limited way at least, to trust Being, God, the source and centre of values. This view of values and valuation relates again to Niebuhr's lifelong interest in the God who holds human beings responsible, and in human beings who, for all their limits, should be responsive to God; this means that they should be bound in loyalty to the signals of the 'Creative Action of God', the 'Governing Action of God', and the 'Redemptive Action of God'.

Philosophers interested in thinkers who would prove the existence of God and describe the divine attributes would be frustrated upon encountering Niebuhr, who never tried to do either. In *The Meaning of Revelation* (1941), another major work, he describes the experience and confession of a revealing God who, in the ambiguities of history, summons people to trust and to responsible action. Niebuhr elaborated this perspective of the believing community and its 'internal' history as well as anyone in American Protestantism in his time, and remained a consistent witness to radical monotheism.

List of works

Niebuhr, H.R. (1929) *The Social Sources of Denomi-*

nationalism, New York: Holt. (More sociological than theological. A categorization of social contexts that shape religious responses.)

—— (1937) *The Kingdom of God in America*, New York: Harper & Row. (A theological interpretation of religion in the USA from a Reformed Protestant point of view.)

—— (1941) *The Meaning of Revelation*, New York: Macmillan. (Reflects on the way believers respond to what they regard as a transcendent message.)

—— (1951) *Christ and Culture*, New York: Harper & Bros. (A classic typology of the ways in which Christianity relates to its surrounding culture.)

—— (1960) *Radical Monotheism and Western Culture*, New York: Harper & Bros. (A collection of essays on faith and intellectual life, centring on a rigorous call to monotheistic expression.)

—— (1963) *The Responsible Self*, New York: Harper & Row. (An 'ethics of responsibility' for the individual in a complex society.)

References and further reading

* Frei, H. (1957) 'The Theology of H. Richard Niebuhr', in P. Ramsey (ed.) *Faith and Ethics*, New York: Harper Torchbooks, 115. (A compressed early critique, focusing on Niebuhr's methods and classic Christian doctrines.)

Fowler, J.W. (1985) *To See the Kingdom: The Theological Vision of H. Richard Niebuhr*, New York: University Press of America. (A clear elaboration of Niebuhr's main theological themes.)

Irish, J.A. (1983) *The Religious Thought of H. Richard Niebuhr*, Atlanta, GA: John Knox Press. (A reliable popular interpretation, and the best introduction to the main themes of Niebuhr's thought.)

Ramsey, P. (ed.) (1957) *Faith and Ethics*, New York: Harper & Bros. (A collection of critical essays by colleagues.)

MARTIN MARTY

NIEBUHR, REINHOLD (1892–1971)

Reinhold Niebuhr is widely regarded as the foremost public theologian in twentieth-century America. A 'public' theologian is one who is responsive to the biblical tradition and responsible to the Christian Church, but who also responds to the social and political concerns of the world and seeks to effect change in that world. In the case of Niebuhr, this meant being attuned to life in the USA as it passed through times of prosperity, depression, war, cold war and cultural complacency. It also meant that he had to be as alert to the secular philosophy and expression of the times as to the biblical and creedal traditions of the Church, and he managed to correlate and connect these in ever-changing ways.

Niebuhr is known as a developer of a school of thought often called 'Christian realism'. Though shaped first by the more optimistic liberal thought of his teachers' generation, which stressed the immanence of God and the potential for goodness in human beings, Niebuhr came to witness to the otherness of God and the drastic limits of human potential. He even helped resurrect the term 'original sin' to describe the human condition, well aware that the term was scorned by most philosophers of his time. Yet over the decades, his realism came to be seen as so appropriate to descriptions of human actions, especially in situations of power, that he attracted a following far beyond Church communities. Niebuhr thus influenced both domestic and international policies. He was seen both as a self-critical theologian who uttered judgments on the Christian Church and the American nation, and as a theologian of the Cold War who issued devastating critiques of Soviet Communism. In the time before the Second World War, when most of the more notable Protestant clerics leaned towards pacifism, Niebuhr let his realistic vision and his opposition to totalitarian powers lead him to argue for 'preparedness' for war and to scold those who refused to see with him a need for military response to the threat of dictators.

1   **A theology informed by public life**
2   **The witness to God**
3   **The nature of the human**
4   **Christian realism**

1   **A theology informed by public life**

Reinhold Niebuhr, brother of the equally notable theologian H. Richard NIEBUHR, was born in Wright City, Missouri, on 21 June 1892 and died in Stockbridge, Massachusetts, on 1 June 1971. He first learned Reformed Protestant theology from his German-born father, a small-town pastor. Schooled in the rather provincial sphere of his denomination's college and seminary, he moved on to Yale Divinity School and University and from there to a thirteen-year pastorate in industrial Detroit. His next move was to the interdenominational Union Theological Seminary in New York, where he taught from 1930 to 1960. During all these years, he expressed himself through thousands of editorials and articles in religious and secular publications alike, plunged actively into politics, and lectured and preached widely.

At the same time, Niebuhr kept schooling himself in theology and philosophy, though he made no secret of his limits as a philosopher or his lack of interest in its more abstract formulations. However, he was sufficiently disciplined and prestigious as a philosophical theologian to be invited to give the Gifford Lectures at the University of Edinburgh in 1939; these were published as his most systematic work, *The Nature and Destiny of Man* (1941, 1943). Yet for all the philosophical power and passion displayed in that work, Niebuhr came to be more noticed for his comments on the USA and world affairs. He made his mark with a contentious work published at the beginning of the Depression, *Moral Man and Immoral Society* (1932), a book that seemed to be intended to insult liberal theologians. For several years afterwards he was avowedly informed by Marxian critical ideas, though he never advocated radical socialist or communist programmes and soon passed critical judgment on those ideas as well. He developed his reasoned perspective on domestic and international affairs at mid-century in *The Irony of American History* (1952). Although hampered by the effects of a stroke, he continued to comment on the Cold War scene and on American culture for more than a decade after he could no longer teach.

2   The witness to God

The term 'theology' etymologically combines witness (*logos*) with God (*theos*). Theologians thus try to interpret the life of believing communities and the world around them not only in the light of experience, but also with reference to a transcendent God. Niebuhr conformed to this model, since his whole career was devoted to seeing public life, including that of the Churches, in the light of divine activity. His choice to be a theologian of the engaged sort showed an understanding of his own personality, talents and interests, but was also a sign of his limitations. He spent little or no energy on some classic philosophical themes such as the proofs for the existence of God.

Instead, Niebuhr's God was the God witnessed to in the Hebrew Scriptures and the New Testament, the Bible of the Christian world. Uncommonly informed by Jewish thought at a time when many Christians went their separate way, Niebuhr had identified with rabbis in Detroit who shared his concern for social justice. With them, he explored the tradition of the Hebrew prophets, who, also using the transcendent reference to God to judge human affairs, usually put more energy into confronting their rulers and the religious powers around them than their enemies. Niebuhr's God was therefore the God of the prophets, the one who measures human affairs and finds them wanting.

In *The Irony of American History*, Niebuhr defined the relation of God to human power and potential as succinctly as he did anywhere. It was a self-consciously ironic – as opposed to tragic, comic or pathetic – understanding. He liked to quote Psalm 2: 4, in which the transcendent God is pictured as laughing at and even holding in derision earthly rulers and powers when they are over-proud and unmindful of their limits. At the same time, according to Niebuhr, this God was not witnessed to as being above human affairs or eager to demean and annihilate people. Instead, this God honoured human aspirations and held people responsible.

Niebuhr was often criticized for refusing to do basic theological work. He shunned concepts associated with ontology, metaphysics and epistemology, took much for granted and spent his energies witnessing to the God revealed in the Bible. He was also criticized for not having developed a sustained and sophisticated hermeneutic. There was an often-expressed American pragmatic bent to his use of the Bible. Thus Niebuhr argued that one is drawn to the Bible in human affairs because it seems to represent the most accurate and appropriate description of human nature and the mortal plight. It was a profoundly relevant address to the world he and the realists around him perceived.

Niebuhr's God was active in creating the world and sustaining it, and in judging human pride and pretension. But the same God was also present in history through revelation in Jesus Christ. Again, Niebuhr avoided agendas common among theologians in that he spent little time expounding the natures of the divine and the human in Jesus. He focused on Jesus' ethical proclamation, which he saw to be severe, 'an impossible possibility'. And he saw in the figure of Jesus crucified not only a love that redeemed humans, but also a sign of the evil of a world that could not be just and did not welcome love. So he could say to the 'atheists for Niebuhr', as some of the people who did not share his theology but identified with his social and political outlook (such as Arthur Schlesinger and Hans Morgenthau) waggishly called themselves, that for a full understanding of him and his thought they had to know that he preached Christ crucified, Jesus on the cross.

3   The nature of the human

While God can only be witnessed to, humans are accessible to social scientists, ordinary people making observations, and theologians who use divine perspectives to study them. It was on these grounds that

Niebuhr suggested that 'original sin' was the only empirically observable Christian doctrine. However, after disagreements with philosophers such as John Dewey, who wanted to dismiss Niebuhr as a grouchy preacher of doom, he expressed regret for having retrieved the notion, or at least for having chosen the term 'original sin'. He did not want it to suggest how morally low humans could sink, or to shift responsibility from them to someone else (such as Adam in the Genesis myth). Instead, it was intended to signal that all humans have limits that cause them to express their pride and to rebel against God (see FEMINIST THEOLOGY §1). These limits were never fully explained; the question as to where evil comes from was of the sort that Niebuhr preferred to hand over to the philosophers, though expecting little yield from their answers. Instead, Niebuhr insisted, the limits are simply 'there' and have to be reckoned with. And though all that humans do is tainted, their evil inclinations and pride do not leave them free to be irresponsible.

If human nature is marked by the sin of pride, the evil effects are most noted in collective life; hence the title of Niebuhr's *Moral Man and Immoral Society*. Less concerned with petty vice or personal errancy than with public life – he believed redemptive love to be at its most effective in more intimate spheres – Niebuhr asked what the particular evils are to which Churches, corporations, political parties and especially nations are prone. He saw little possibility of large scale self-purification by societies and this led him to stress justice more than love in collective life. Societies have a way of turning even their good intentions into proud and self-interested purposes. For this reason, Niebuhr came to believe in balances of power, of checking the set of interests of one group by countering them with those of another. It was this pragmatic realism, with its blunt readiness to use power, that so offended Christian and other pacifists who opposed Niebuhr.

4 Christian realism

To those philosophical and cultural critics who thought Niebuhr simply wrong in his assessment of human nature and strategically misguided because his pessimism could lead to passivity, the adjective 'Christian' could be interpreted in either of two ways. To some it was the key to explaining why Niebuhr had gone wrong. The Bible, from which he drew so many ideas, saw human nature against a cosmic and mythic backdrop in which God warred against Satan, heaven was opposed to hell, and humans were utterly evil unless rescued by Christ; anyone bringing such a view to ordinary human affairs would inevitably distort them. On the other hand, fellow Christians often complained that Niebuhr did not do justice to the themes of redemption, love and peace. The central figure of the Christian faith, Jesus of Nazareth, represented and taught the way of peace and was an exemplar of love. In traditional creedal terms, Jesus Christ, as the divine Son of God, effected redemption and helped people begin to realize a new age, a new ordering of being. Why, these critics asked, did Niebuhr so often act and teach as if none of this had happened? Was not his Christianity mere realism, indeed, pessimism?

In the face of such criticisms Niebuhr spent many hundreds of pages pointing to what he thought were the specific Christian dimensions of his philosophy and action. Yes, he would be a realist, not hiding from view the excessively proud antisocial aspects of humans, especially in their collective actions. No, no efforts to educate or reform would bring people to a situation where they could live in an era of progress or move towards Utopia. But the word 'Christian' did signal a different interpretation of realism. Niebuhr liked to think in polar terms, and just as he set redemption against sin, and the kingdom of God against human striving, so he introduced a kind of idealistic note to counter ordinary realism. This ideal was not some abstract or remote notion. It had been present in the utterances of the prophets and embodied and proclaimed by Jesus, who presented humans with something of God's love and therefore of God's very nature. So Niebuhr could praise *agape*, the Greek New Testament's name for the spontaneous, unmotivated, generous and even reckless love of God, who showed concern for humans even in their waywardness and who made it possible for them to express such love.

The presence of *agape*, even if one cannot expect to see much of it in the spheres of human self-interest, is realized just often enough in personal affairs to inspire idealistic action in public ones. The ethical teachings of Jesus in the Gospels, for instance, expressed such idealism in the form of love. Niebuhr succinctly addressed the polarity between ideal and reality by observing that if realists are not idealists they are 'inclined to obscure the residual moral and social sense even in the most self-regarding men and nations'; on the other hand, idealists who are not realists 'are inclined to obscure the residual individual and collective self-regard either in the "saved" or in the rational individuals and groups' (1965: 31–2).

Niebuhr was criticized by many orthodox Christians for not revisiting classic ways of discussing the divine nature of Jesus Christ or the metaphysical aspects of the divine–human transaction in the death of Jesus on the cross. Other Christians accused him of drawing too severe a line between the potential for sacrificial love in personal life (a love transcending mere self-interest) and the self-interest that realists saw as marking human affairs so much that the love of Christ could hardly enter political and international transactions. But it is always the hazard of a dialectical thinker who tries to do justice to two contrasting, if not overtly contradictory, poles to be vulnerable from both sides. Niebuhr took this chance, for his worldview was so decisively shaped by such poles as 'idealism' and 'realism', and 'self-interest' and 'sacrificial love' that he could not have avoided dealing with them. In a lifelong devotion to this vision, applied to countless changing situations, Niebuhr left a stamp on American political and Church life deeper than that of any other religious thinker of his times.

List of works

Niebuhr, R. (1932) *Moral Man and Immoral Society: A Study in Ethics and Politics*, New York: Charles Scribner's Sons. (A strong indictment of liberal optimism in politics and religion.)

—— (1935) *An Interpretation of Christian Ethics*, New York: Harper & Bros. (Discusses the 'impossible possibility' of ethics based on the teachings of Jesus.)

—— (1941, 1943) *The Nature and Destiny of Man: A Christian Interpretation*, New York: Charles Scribner's Sons, 2 vols. (The author's most formal statement in theology, stressing human limitations and responsibility to the divine.)

—— (1949) *Faith and History: A Comparison of Christian and Modern Views of History*, New York: Charles Scribner's Sons. (Philosophy of history on a grand scale, stressing distinctively Christian aspects.)

—— (1952) *The Irony of American History*, New York: Charles Scribner's Sons. (A Cold War-era interpretation of US history, criticizing the pride of nations.)

—— (1955) *The Self and the Dramas of History*, New York: Charles Scribner's Sons. (Niebuhr confronts individualism, a neglected topic for him, and locates it in social processes.)

—— (1965) *Man's Nature and His Communities*, New York: Charles Scribner's Sons. (A late statement discussing pluralism and international affairs.)

References and further reading

Fox, R. (1985) *Reinhold Niebuhr: A Biography*, New York: Pantheon. (The most comprehensive biogra-

phy, essential for understanding the career, though criticized by some for slighting the theology.)

Harland, G. (1960) *The Thought of Reinhold Niebuhr*, New York: Oxford University Press. (A fair-minded synthesis of the main themes.)

Kegley, C. and Bretall, R.W. (eds) (1984) *Reinhold Niebuhr: His Religious, Social and Political Thought*, New York: Pilgrim Press. (A revised and expanded second edition of an extensive set of critiques first published in 1956.)

Rasmussen, L. (ed.) (1989) *Reinhold Niebuhr: Theologian of Public Life*, London: Collins. (A well-introduced collection of Niebuhr's writings.)

Richards, P. (1984) *Annotated Bibliography of Reinhold Niebuhr's Works*, Madison, NJ: American Theological Library Association. (Includes succinct and helpful comments on hundreds of works.)

Stone, R.H. (1972) *Reinhold Niebuhr: Prophet to Politicians*, Nashville, TN: Abingdon. (Stresses the political effects of Niebuhr's theological and philosophical career.)

MARTIN MARTY

NIETZSCHE, FRIEDRICH (1844–1900)

Appointed professor of classical philology at the University of Basel when he was just 24 years old, Nietzsche was expected to secure his reputation as a brilliant young scholar with his first book, Die Geburt der Tragödie (The Birth of Tragedy) *(1872). But that book did not look much like a work of classical scholarship. Bereft of footnotes and highly critical of Socrates and modern scholarship, it spoke in rhapsodic tones of ancient orgiastic Dionysian festivals and the rebirth of Dionysian tragedy in the modern world. Classical scholars, whose craft and temperament it had scorned, greeted the book with scathing criticism and hostility; even Nietzsche eventually recognized it as badly written and confused. Yet it remains one of the three most important philosophical treatments of tragedy (along with those of Aristotle and Hegel) and is the soil out of which Nietzsche's later philosophy grew. By 1889, when he suffered a mental and physical collapse that brought his productive life to an end, Nietzsche had produced a series of thirteen books which have left a deep imprint on most areas of Western intellectual and cultural life, establishing him as one of Germany's greatest prose stylists and one of its most important, if controversial, philosophers.*

Nietzsche appears to attack almost everything that has been considered sacred: not only Socrates and scholarship, but also God, truth, morality, equality, democracy and most other modern values. He gives a large role to the will to power and he proposes to replace the values he attacks with new values and a new ideal of the human person (the Übermensch meaning 'overhuman' or 'superhuman'). Although Nazi theoreticians attempted to associate these ideas with their own cause, responsible interpreters agree that Nietzsche despised and unambiguously rejected both German nationalism and anti-Semitism. Little else in his thought is so unambiguous, at least in part because he rarely writes in a straightforward, argumentative style, and because his thought changed radically over the course of his productive life. The latter is especially true of his early criticism of Socrates, science and truth.

Nietzsche's philosophizing began from a deep sense of dissatisfaction with modern Western culture, which he found superficial and empty in comparison with that of the ancient Greeks. Locating the source of the problem in the fact that modern culture gives priority to science (understood broadly, including all forms of scholarship and theory), whereas Presocratic Greece had given priority to art and myth, he rested his hopes for modern culture on a return to the Greek valuation of art, calling for a recognition of art as 'the highest task and the truly metaphysical activity of this life'.

He soon turned his back on this early critique of science. In the works of his middle period he rejects metaphysical truth but celebrates the valuing of science and empirical truth over myth as a sign of high culture. Although he had earlier considered it destructive of culture, he now committed his own philosophy to a thoroughgoing naturalistic understanding of human beings. He continued to believe that naturalism undermines commitment to values because it destroys myths and illusions, but he now hoped that knowledge would purify human desire and allow human beings to live without preferring or evaluating. In the works of his final period, Nietzsche rejects this aspiration as nihilistic.

In his final period, he combined a commitment to science with a commitment to values by recognizing that naturalism does not undermine all values, but only those endorsed by the major ideal of value we have had so far, the ascetic ideal. This ideal takes the highest human life to be one of self-denial, denial of the natural self, thereby treating natural or earthly existence as devoid of intrinsic value. Nietzsche saw this life-devaluing ideal at work in most Western (and Eastern) religion and philosophy. Values always come into existence in support of some form of life, but they gain the support of ascetic religions and philosophies only if they are given a life-devaluing interpretation. Ascetic priests interpret acts as wrong or 'sinful' because the acts are selfish or 'animal' – because they affirm natural instincts – and ascetic philosophers interpret whatever they value – truth, knowledge, philosophy, virtue – in non-natural terms because they share the assumption that anything truly valuable must have a source outside the world of nature, the world accessible to empirical investigation. Only because Nietzsche still accepted this assumption of the ascetic ideal did naturalism seem to undermine all values.

According to his later thought, the ascetic ideal itself undermines values. First it deprives nature of value by placing the source of value outside nature. Then, by promoting the value of truth above all else, it leads to a denial that there is anything besides nature. Among the casualties of this process are morality and belief in God, as Nietzsche indicated by proclaiming that 'God is dead' and that morality will gradually perish. Morality is not the only possible form of ethical life, however, but a particular form that has been brought about by the ascetic ideal. That ideal has little life left in it, according to Nietzsche, as does the form of ethical life it brought about. Morality now has little power to inspire human beings to virtue or anything else. There is no longer anything to play the essential role played by the ascetic ideal: to inspire human beings to take on the task of becoming more than they are, thereby inducing them to internalize their will to power against themselves. Modern culture therefore has insufficient defences against eruptions of barbarism, which Nietzsche predicted as a large part of the history of the twentieth and twenty-first centuries.

But Nietzsche now saw that there was no way to go back to earlier values. His hope rested instead with 'new philosophers' who have lived and thought the values of the ascetic ideal through to their end and thereby recognized the need for new values. His own writings are meant to exhibit a new ideal, often by exemplifying old virtues that are given a new, life-affirming interpretation.

1   Life

Nietzsche was born in Rocken, a small village in the Prussian province of Saxony, on 15 October 1844. His father, a Lutheran minister, became seriously ill in 1848 and died in July 1849 of what was diagnosed as 'softening of the brain'. His brother died the following year, and Nietzsche's mother moved with her son and daughter to Naumberg, a town of 15,000 people, where they lived with his father's mother and her two sisters. In 1858, Nietzsche was offered free admission to Pforta, the most famous school in Germany. After graduating in 1864 with a thesis in Latin on the Greek poet Theogonis, he registered at the University of Bonn as a theology student. The following year he transferred to Leipzig where he registered as a philology student and worked under the classical philologist Friedrich Ritschl. The events of his Leipzig years with the most profound and lasting influence on his later work were his discoveries of Schopenhauer's *Die Welt als Wille und Vorstellung* (*The World as Will and Representation*) and F.A. Lange's *Geschichte des Materialismus* (*History of Materialism*), and the beginning of a personal relationship with Richard Wagner (see SCHOPEN-HAUER, A. §§3–6; LANGE, F.A. §2). Nietzsche became Ritschl's star pupil, and on Ritschl's recommendation he was appointed to the Chair of Classical Philology at Basel in 1869 at the age of twenty-four. Leipzig proceeded to confer the doctorate without requiring a dissertation.

Basel's proximity to the Wagner residence at Tribschen allowed Nietzsche to develop a close relationship with Richard and Cosima Wagner. Sharing with the composer a deep love of Schopenhauer and a hope for the revitalization of European culture, he initially idealized Wagner and his music. His first book, *Die Geburt der Tragödie* (*The Birth of Tragedy*) (1872), used Schopenhauer's philosophy to interpret Greek tragedy and to suggest that Wagner's opera constituted its rebirth and thereby the salvation of modern culture. Torn between philology and philosophy since shortly after his discovery of Schopenhauer, Nietzsche devoted much of his teaching to the texts of ancient Greek and Roman philosophy and hoped that his first book would establish his credentials as a philosopher. Instead, its unorthodox mixture of philosophy and philology merely served to damage his reputation as a philologist.

In 1879, he resigned his chair at Basel because of health problems that had plagued him for years. In the meantime, he had become progressively estranged from Wagner, a process that culminated in the 1878 publication of the first volume of *Menschliches, Allzumenschliches* (*Human, All Too Human*), a positivist manifesto that praised science rather than art as indicative of high culture. The ten productive years left to him after his retirement were marked by terrible health problems and a near absence of human companionship. Living alone in Italian and Swiss boarding houses, he wrote ten books, each of which has at least some claim to being a masterpiece. His last seven books mark a high point of German prose style.

In January 1889, Nietzsche collapsed in Turin. He wrote a few lucid and beautiful (although insane) letters during the next few days, and after that nothing of which we can make any sense. Following a brief institutionalization, he lived with his mother and then his sister until his death in Weimar on 25 August 1900.

2 Writings and development

During the sixteen years between his first book and his last productive year, Nietzsche's thinking underwent remarkable development, usually with little notification to his readers. The traditional grouping of his writings into three major periods is followed here, although there is significant development within each period. In addition to *The Birth of Tragedy* his early work consists of four essays of cultural criticism – on David Strauss, history, Schopenhauer, and Wagner – published separately but linked together as *Unzeitgemäße Betrachtungen* (*Unfashionable Observations*) (1873–6), plus a number of largely finished essays and fragments that belong to the *Nachlaß* of the period. The most important of the essays are 'Über Wahrheit und Lüge im außermoralischen Sinne' ('On Truth and Lies in a Nonmoral Sense'), 'Homer's Wettkampf' ('Homer's Contest'), and 'Die Philosophie im tragischen Zeitalter der Griechen' ('Philosophy in the Tragic Age of the Greeks').

These early writings sound a note of great dissatisfaction with European (Enlightenment) culture, of which Socrates is taken as the earliest representative and continuing inspiration. At the base of Socratic culture Nietzsche finds the belief that life's highest goal is the theoretical grasp of truth at which science and philosophy aim. Theory's claim to provide truth has been undermined, he thinks, by the doctrine of Kant and Schopenhauer that discursive thought gives access not to things-in-themselves but only to 'appearance' (see KANT, I. §5; SCHOPENHAUER, A. §§2, 4). Nietzsche's suggestion for saving European culture is that art should replace theory as the most valued, the 'truly metaphysical', human activity. At first, his main argument for elevating art is that it is more truthful than theory. But he also suggests a very different argument: that theory is destructive of culture unless it is guided and limited by the needs of life which art serves. In his essay on history, the second argument has largely replaced the first. He argues that when practised as autonomous theory, devoted solely to truth, history destroys the limited and mythical horizons required by life and action. And if we emphasize for another generation the naturalistic understanding of human beings at which Socratic culture has now arrived (for example, the denial of a cardinal distinction between humans and other animals), we will only further our culture's disintegration into chaotic systems of individual and group egoism. Nietzsche suggests that history can be harnessed to serve the needs of life, for instance when it is written to emphasize great lives and other aspects that encourage individuals to set lofty and noble goals for themselves. Such history is as much art as it is theory or science.

Nietzsche turns decisively away from such criticism of pure theory in the writings of his middle period, *Human, All Too Human* (1878–80) and *Morgenröte* (*Daybreak*) (1881). He here celebrates as a sign of high culture an appreciation of the little truths won by rigorous method, and presents his own philosophy as a form of natural science that serves only truth. He also commits himself to the truth of the naturalism he earlier considered so dangerous: there is no cardinal distinction between humans and other animals; everything about human beings, including their values, can be explained as a development from characteristics found among other animals. At the beginning of this period Nietzsche struggles with how naturalism can be compatible with a commitment to values, for he sees it as exposing and thereby undermining the illusions that are needed in order to find value in life. In *Human*, his hope is that knowledge will gradually purify 'the old motives of violent desire' until one can live 'as in *nature*', without preferring or evaluating, but 'gazing contentedly, as though at a spectacle' (*Human* §34 [*Werke* IV.2: 50]). Nietzsche later has Zarathustra mock this spectator conception of knowledge and life as 'immaculate perception' (*Zarathustra* II: §15 [*Werke* V.1: 152–5]).

Nietzsche's final period begins with *Die Fröhliche Wissenschaft* (*The Gay Science*) (1882), which replaces the spectator conception with one in which the 'knower' belongs to the dance of existence and is one of its 'masters of ceremony' (*The Gay Science* §54 [*Werke* V.2: 90]). This formulation expresses his new confidence that naturalism, which he often calls 'knowledge', is compatible with commitment to values. In this period, Nietzsche once again celebrates art, criticizes Socrates and denies the autonomy of theory, suggesting to some that he has reverted to the viewpoint of his early period. Evidence is provided throughout this entry for an alternative interpretation: the later Nietzsche does not deny that theory can provide truth, and he remains as committed to the pursuit of truth as he was in his middle period. The

difference is that he now recognizes in even the apparently autonomous theory of his middle period a commitment to an ideal that is external to and served by theory, namely, the ascetic ideal. Nietzsche returns to the suggestion of his first book, that theory is not autonomous; however, he now objects not to theory, but only to the ideal that theory has served (see §§6 and 7 of this entry). The works of Nietzsche's final period are largely devoted to uncovering, criticizing and offering an alternative to that ideal.

Gay Science was followed by *Also Sprach Zarathustra* (*Thus Spoke Zarathustra*) (1883–5), a fictional tale used as a vehicle for Nietzsche's most puzzling and infamous doctrines, including the overhuman (*Übermensch*), will to power and eternal recurrence. He considered this to be the deepest work in the German language and suggested that chairs of philosophy might one day be devoted to its interpretation. Our surest guides to it at present are the other books of his final period, especially the two that followed it: *Jenseits von Gut und Böse* (*Beyond Good and Evil*) (1886) and *Zur Genealogie der Moral* (*On the Genealogy of Morality*) (1887). These masterpieces show Nietzsche at the height of his powers as a thinker, an organizer and an artist of ideas. Yet some prefer his last five books. At the beginning of 1888, Nietzsche published *Der Fall Wagner* (*The Case of Wagner*) and then composed four short books before the year was out: *Die Götzen Dämmerung* (*The Twilight of the Idols*), an obvious play on Wagner's *Götterdämmerung* (*Twilight of the Gods*), puts the finishing touches to his accounts of knowledge and philosophy and offers his final critique of Socrates; *Der Antichrist* (*The Antichrist*), a critique of Pauline Christianity, offers a relatively sympathetic portrait of Jesus; and *Ecce Homo*, Nietzsche's own portrait of his life and work under such chapter headings as 'Why I write such good books'. It is easy to hear signs of his impending insanity in the shrill tone and self-promotion that sometimes takes over in these books (although not in the very funny and brilliantly anti-Socratic chapter headings of *Ecce Homo*), and perhaps also in the fall-off in organizational and artistic power from the masterpieces of the previous two years. *Nietzsche Contra Wagner*, which he dated Christmas 1888, leaves a different impression. Nietzsche's shortest and perhaps most beautiful book, it is a compilation of passages from earlier works, with a few small improvements, as if aiming at perfection. He collapsed nine days later.

3 The *Nachlaß*

Nietzsche left behind a large body of unpublished

material, his *Nachlaß*, which technically should include *The Antichrist* and *Ecce Homo*, published by his sister in 1895 and 1908 respectively. However, Nietzsche had made arrangements for their publication and prepared a printer's copy of each. For purposes of understanding his philosophy, these are therefore accorded the same status as his earlier works and are not usually considered to be part of his *Nachlaß*. This entry gives a very secondary role to the remainder of Nietzsche's *Nachlaß*, which includes the relatively polished essays written in the early 1870s (mentioned in §2 of this entry). These essays are informative about Nietzsche's early views, and are sometimes also thought to provide a clearer statement of his later views of truth and language than do the works he published. The interpretation of Nietzsche's development offered here supports a very different view: that Nietzsche chose not to publish these essays because he soon progressed beyond them to quite opposed views.

Another issue that divides interpreters concerns the weight to give to the notes of Nietzsche's later years. Many treat them as material he would have published if he had remained productive for longer. But since he might instead have rejected and disposed of much of this material, others advise great caution in its use. Further, we often cannot determine the use Nietzsche had in mind for particular notes even when he wrote them. Nietzsche *composed* his books to lead prepared readers to certain views. The rich context and clues for reading supplied by his books, when they are attended to, provide a check on interpretive licence and a basis for getting at Nietzsche's own thinking that has no parallel in the case of the *Nachlaß* material. This applies to the entire contents of *Der Wille zur Macht* (*The Will to Power*), which some have regarded as Nietzsche's magnum opus. Although he did announce it as 'in preparation', there is evidence that he dropped his plans to publish a work of this title; the book we have is actually a compilation of notes from the years 1883–8 selected from his notebooks and arranged in their present form by his sister and editors appointed by her. Such notes may sometimes help in understanding what Nietzsche actually did publish. But it is difficult to justify giving them priority when they suggest views that differ from and are even contrary to those suggested by a careful reading of Nietzsche's books (see §§11–12 of this entry).

4 Truth and metaphysics

In the writings of his early and middle periods, Nietzsche often appears to deny that any of our theories and beliefs are really true. By the end of his final period, he denies only metaphysical truth. The rejection of metaphysics forms the cornerstone of his later philosophy.

What Nietzsche rejects as metaphysics is first and foremost a belief in a second world, a metaphysical or true world. *Human, All Too Human* offers a genealogy of this belief. Receiving their first idea of a second world from dreams, human beings originally share with 'everything organic' a belief in the existence of permanent things (substance) and free will. When reflection dawns and they fail to find evidence of these in the world accessible to empirical methods, they conclude that these methods are faulty, and that the real world is accessible only to non-empirical methods. They thus take the empirical world to be a mere appearance or distortion of a second world, which is thereby constituted as the true one. Metaphysics is purported knowledge of this non-empirical world. *The Birth of Tragedy* affirms metaphysics in this sense – 'an artists' metaphysics' he later called it – in the suggestion that perception and science confine us to mere appearance, whereas truth is accessible in the special kind of preconceptual experience characteristic of Dionysian art.

Human, All Too Human sets out to undermine metaphysics by showing that knowledge of a non-empirical world is cognitively superfluous. Nietzsche's Enlightenment predecessors had already established the adequacy of empirical methods to explain what goes on in the nonhuman world. However, belief in a metaphysical world persisted because that world is assumed to be necessary to account for the things of the highest value in the human world. Nietzsche sought to explain the origin of this assumption and to undermine it. The assumption was made, he claims, because thinkers were unable to see how things could originate from their opposites: disinterested contemplation from lust, living for others from egoism, rationality from irrationality. They could deny this origination only by positing for 'the more highly valued thing a miraculous source in the very kernel and being of the "thing-in-itself"'. Nietzsche offers a naturalistic account of higher things, which presents them as sublimations of despised things and therefore as 'human, all too human'. Once it is clear that we can explain their origin without positing a metaphysical world, he expects the interest in such a world to die out. We cannot deny the bare possibility of its existence, however, because 'we view all things through the human head and cannot cut this head off; yet the question remains what of the world would still be there if we had cut it off' (*Human* §§1, 9 [*Werke* IV.3: 19, 25]).

Nietzsche later goes a step further and denies the very existence of a metaphysical world. His history of the 'true' world in *Twilight of the Idols* offers a six-stage sketch of how the metaphysical world came to be recognized as a 'fable'. Stage Four corresponds to the position of *Human*: the 'true' world is cognitively superfluous. In Stage Five, its existence is denied. Stage Six adds that without a true world, there is no merely apparent world either: the empirical world originally picked out as 'merely apparent' is the only world there is. Nietzsche thus makes clear that he has moved beyond the assumption that there *might* be a metaphysical world to a positing of the empirical world as the only one. He dismisses the whole idea of a second world as unintelligible. The books after *Beyond Good and Evil* proceed on this assumption: they no longer claim that the empirical world is a mere appearance or, what amounts to the same thing, that empirical truths are illusions or falsifications.

5 Knowledge

The position on knowledge to which Nietzsche is led by his rejection of metaphysics is a combination of empiricism, antipositivism and perspectivism. Claiming in his later works that 'all evidence of truth comes only from the senses', and that we have science 'only to the extent that we have decided to *accept* the testimony of the senses – to the extent to which we sharpen them further, arm them, and think them through', he considers the rest of purported knowledge 'miscarriage and not yet science', or formal science, like pure logic and mathematics (*Beyond Good and Evil* §134 [*Werke* VI.2: 96]; *Twilight* III §3 [*Werke* VI.3: 69–70]). The latter, he now insists, departing from his earlier stand that they falsify reality, make no claim about reality at all. Nietzsche's empiricism amounts to a rejection of any wholesale disparaging of sense experience, an insistence that the only bases for criticizing or correcting particular deliverances of the senses are other sense experiences or theories based on them.

Nietzsche's antipositivism involves a rejection of two aspects associated with some other versions of empiricism. First, he rejects foundationalism. Anticipating many later critics of positivism, he denies that there is any experience that is unmediated by concepts, interpretation or theory. Sense experience, our only evidence of truth, is always already interpreted, and knowledge is therefore interpretation, as opposed to the apprehension of unmediated facts. Nietzsche also avoids the problem of needing an a priori theory to establish his empiricism, which he bases instead on his genealogy of the belief in a metaphysical world (a genealogy that is itself empirical in that it accepts the testimony of the senses) and a diagnosis and working-through of the intellectual confusions that have locked previous philosophers into that belief. Clearing away these confusions (especially pictures of knowledge that set the world's true nature over against its appearances) removes all intellectual basis for considering sense experience in principle problematic, and all intellectual motivation for pursuing a priori knowledge. Philosophers may, however, still have non-intellectual motives for this pursuit (see §6 of this entry). The upshot of Nietzsche's antipositivism is that what counts as knowledge is always revisable in the light of new or improved experience. This reinforces his empiricism, and in no way devalues empirical theories or denies that they can give us truth.

Nietzsche's perspectivism is often thought to imply that empirical knowledge offers us 'only a perspective' and not truth. But is perspectivism itself only a perspective? If not, it is false; if so, it is not clear why we should accept perspectivism rather than some other perspective. And Nietzsche himself puts forward as truths not only perspectivism, but also many other claims.

We can avoid saddling Nietzsche with these problems by recognizing that, at least in its mature and most important formulation (at *Genealogy* III §12 [*Werke* VI.2: 381–3]), perspectivism is a claim about knowledge; it is not a claim about truth, and it does not entail that truth is relative to perspective. Further, 'perspectives' are constituted by affects, not beliefs. The point is *not* that knowledge is always from the viewpoint of a particular set of beliefs and that there are always alternative sets that would ground equally good views of an object (see RELATIVISM). Such a view inevitably saddles perspectivism with relativism and problems of self-reference. Nietzsche's explicit point in describing knowledge as perspectival is to guard against conceiving of knowledge as 'disinterested contemplation'.

His early essay 'Truth and Lie' did use the impossibility of disinterested knowledge to devalue empirical knowledge, arguing that the latter was only a perspective and an illusion. But the point of the *Genealogy*'s claim that there is 'only a perspective knowing' is quite the reverse: to guard against using the idea of 'pure' knowing to devalue the kind of knowledge we have. The metaphor of perspective sets up disinterested knowing as the equivalent of the recognizably absurd notion of seeing something from nowhere. If the conception of knowledge ruled out by perspectivism really is absurd, however – and Nietzsche insists that it is – then it excludes only a kind of knowledge of which we can make no sense and which we could not really want. This explains why so many find perspectivism obvious and even self-evident; but so interpreted, it does nothing to devalue empirical knowledge.

Why does Nietzsche deny the possibility of disinterested knowledge? That surely does not follow from the impossibility of seeing something from nowhere. His early basis for this denial was Schopenhauer's doctrine that the intellect originates as servant to the will, but he accepted the same doctrine in later works on the basis of a thoroughgoing Darwinian naturalism. Human cognitive capacities exist because of the evolutionary advantage they confer on the species, and no such advantage is to be found in attending to any and all features of reality. The intellect must be directed to certain features – initially at least, those most relevant to human survival and reproduction. Affect – emotion, feeling, passion, value orientations – turns the mind in a particular direction, focusing its attention on certain features of reality and pushing it to register them as important; knowledge is only acquired when the intellect is so pushed and focused. Nietzsche's perspectivism is a metaphorical formulation of this naturalistic understanding of knowledge.

Because knowledge is always acquired from the viewpoint of particular interests and values, there are therefore always other affective sets that would focus attention on different aspects of reality. Nietzsche's use of the metaphor of perspective thus implies that knowledge is limited in the sense that there are always other things to know, but not that perspectives block our access to truth. Affects are our access, the basis of all access to truth. If its perspectival character raises any problems for knowledge, it is only because being locked into a particular perspective can make one unable to appreciate features of reality that are apparent from other perspectives. Nietzsche's solution is simple: the more affects we know how to bring to bear on a matter, the more complete our knowledge of it will be.

This does not mean that true knowledge requires assuming as many perspectives as possible. Knowledge does not require complete knowledge, and complete knowledge is not Nietzsche's epistemological ideal. In fact, he suggests that the greatest scholars tend to serve knowledge by immersing themselves deeply and thoroughly in some particular perspective, so much so that they damage themselves as human beings. The situation is different for philosophers because their ultimate responsibility is not knowledge, but values. To undertake the task to which Nietzsche assigns them, they need practice in shifting perspectives. This explains much that is distinctive about his way of writing philosophy: why it involves so much affect and seems so given to extremes of expression. He uses different affective stances – assuming them for a while – in order to show us features of reality

that are visible from them. More importantly, by moving from one perspective to another, he attempts to show philosophers the kind of 'objectivity' that is required for their task: objectivity understood not as disinterested contemplation, but as a matter of not being *locked into* any particular valuational perspective, as an ability to move from one affective set to another.

6 Philosophy and the ascetic ideal

According to Nietzsche, philosophy has been understood as an a priori discipline, a deliverance of pure reason. Given his empiricism, what role can he allow philosophy? In *Human, All Too Human* he claims to practise 'historical philosophy' and denies that it can be separated from natural science, suggesting that he counts empirical theories as philosophy if they illuminate topics of traditional philosophical concern. Attention to the more conceptual aspects of such theories might especially count as continuing the philosopher's traditional role (§§8–9 of this entry provide an example).

Further, Nietzsche's thinking on topics of traditional philosophical concern (§§4–5 of this entry) is philosophical in a more traditional sense, to the extent that it deals with conceptual as opposed to empirical matters. Such 'pure' philosophy is a matter of battling the images and pictures that beguile the mind and lead philosophers into thinking that there are purely philosophical questions to be answered concerning knowledge, truth and reality. Philosophy in this sense functions as therapy, and to the extent that Nietzsche practises it, he counts as a forerunner of Wittgenstein (see WITTGENSTEIN, L. §§9–12).

Like Wittgenstein, Nietzsche gives language a major role in generating the problems and confusions of previous philosophy. He sometimes seems to criticize language itself for falsifying reality, holding the subject–predicate structure of Indo-European languages responsible for philosophers' propensity to think that reality itself must consist of ultimate subjects that could never be part of the experienced world: God and the ego, or indivisible atoms of matter. But he would probably say of language what he ultimately says of the senses: only what we make of their testimony introduces error. Language misleads us into traditional philosophy only if we erroneously assume that linguistic structure offers us a blueprint of reality that can be used to challenge the adequacy of empirical theories. This is similar to Wittgenstein's diagnosis that philosophical problems arise when language is taken away from the everyday tasks for which it is suited and expected to play a different game. Nietzsche's philosopher forces language to play the 'game' of affording insight into a non-empirical world.

Unlike Wittgenstein, however, Nietzsche fights the confusions of traditional philosophy to free us not *from* the need to do philosophy, but *for* what he considers the true task of genuine philosophy. And this task is not a matter of offering empirical theories. In his later work, Nietzsche insists that philosophers should not be confused with scholars or scientists, that scholarship and science are only means in the hands of the philosopher. Gradually it has become clear to him, he says, that philosophers' values are the 'real germ' from which their systems grow. While pretending to be concerned only to discover truth, philosophers have actually been wily advocates for prejudices (values) they call 'truths'. They interpret the world in terms of their own values, and then claim that their interpretation, which they present as objective knowledge, gives everyone reason to accept these values – as the Stoics justified their ideal of self-governance on the grounds that nature itself obeys laws, an interpretation they arrived at by projecting their ideal of self-governance onto nature (*Beyond Good and Evil* §§1–9 [*Werke* VI.2: 207–16]).

Because Nietzsche believes that interpretations of the world in terms of values provide something that is as important as truth, he wants the philosophy of the future to preserve this function of traditional philosophy. He does not, however, wish to preserve two aspects of the way in which previous philosophers have gone about this task: the lack of courage evident in their failure to recognize that they were reading values into the world rather than discovering truth, and the particular values they read into the world.

These values, he claims, have been expressions of the ascetic ideal, the ideal that takes the highest human life to be one of self-denial, denial of the natural self. Behind this ideal, which he finds in most major religions, Nietzsche locates the assumption that natural or earthly existence (the only kind he thinks we have) is devoid of intrinsic value, that it has value only as a means to something else that is actually its negation (such as heaven or nirvana). He claims that this life-devaluing ideal infects all the values supported by most religions (although *The Antichrist* retracts this in the case of Buddhism). Having come into existence in support of some form of life, values gain the support of the ascetic priest only if they are given a life-devaluing interpretation. Acts are interpreted as wrong or 'sinful', for instance, on the grounds that they are selfish or animal, that they affirm natural instincts. Traditional ('metaphysical') philosophers are successors to the ascetic priest because they interpret what they value – truth, knowledge, philosophy, virtue – in non-natural terms.

In the background of their interpretations Nietzsche spies the assumption of the ascetic ideal: that whatever is truly valuable must have a source outside the world of nature, the world accessible to empirical investigation. What ultimately explains the assumption that philosophy must be a priori, and therefore concerned with a metaphysical world, is philosophers' assumption that nothing as valuable as philosophy or truth could be intimately connected to the senses or to the merely natural existence of human beings.

The philosophy of Nietzsche's early and middle periods can itself be diagnosed as an expression of the ascetic ideal. We can understand his devaluation of human knowledge in "Truth and Lie' (his claim that human truths are 'illusions') as a response to the recognition that knowledge is rooted in the world of nature and thereby lacks the 'purity' demanded by the ascetic ideal. And we can surmise that he considered Darwinian naturalism dangerous because he saw that it deprives human life of value – if one accepts the ascetic ideal (see DARWIN, C.). Indeed, when he embraced the truth of naturalism in *Human* (to the extent of accepting philosophy itself as an empirical discipline), he drew the conclusion that follows from the combination of naturalism and the ascetic ideal: that human life is without value. From the viewpoint of Nietzsche's later philosophy, it is hardly surprising that his early philosophy turns out to be another expression of the ascetic ideal. According to his *Genealogy*, the ascetic ideal is the only ideal of any widespread cultural importance human beings have had so far, it has dominated the interpretation and valuation of human life for millennia. To have escaped the ascetic ideal without having to work through its influence on him would have been impossible.

On the other hand, Nietzsche was also fighting the ascetic ideal. Naturalism works against the supernatural interpretation of human life that has been promoted by the ascetic ideal, and as modern science increasingly shows how much of the world can be understood in naturalistic terms, the influence of the ascetic ideal wanes. Or, rather, it goes underground. Nietzsche denies that science and the naturalism it promotes are themselves opposed to the ascetic ideal. The commitment to science is actually the latest and most noble form of the ascetic ideal, based as it is on the Platonic/Christian belief that God is truth, that truth is divine. This amounts to the assumption that truth is more important than anything else (for instance, life, happiness, love, power) an assumption Nietzsche traces to the ascetic ideal's devaluation of our natural impulses. Thus the development of science and naturalism has been promoted by inculcating the discipline of the scientific spirit – the willingness to give up what one would like to believe for the sake of what there is reason to believe – as the heir to the Christian conscience cultivated through confession. This has thereby worked against the exterior of the ascetic ideal, against the satisfaction it has provided – in particular, the sense that this life, and especially its suffering, has a meaning, that it shall be redeemed by another life. But to work against such satisfaction is not to oppose the ascetic ideal; it is simply to require more self-denial.

Nietzsche believes that we need a new ideal, a real alternative to the ascetic ideal. If philosophers are to remain true to the calling of philosophy and not squander their inheritance, they must create new values and not continue merely to codify and structure the value legislations of ascetic priests. To create new values, however, it will be necessary for philosophers to overcome the ascetic faith that truth is more important than anything else, for truth is not sufficient support for any ideal. Although they must therefore overcome the ascetic ideal to create a new one, undertaking this task responsibly requires the training in truthfulness promoted by the ascetic ideal. The overcoming of the ascetic ideal that Nietzsche promotes is thus a self-overcoming.

7 The 'death of God' and nihilism

Nietzsche is perhaps best known for having proclaimed the death of God. He does in fact mention that God is dead, but his fullest and most forceful statement to this effect actually belongs to one of his fictional characters, the madman of *Gay Science* 125 (*Werke* V.2: 158–60). Nietzsche's madman declares not only that God is dead and that churches are now 'tombs and sepulchres of God', but also that we are all God's 'murderers'. Although the madman may accept these statements as literally true, they clearly function as metaphors for Nietzsche. The 'death of God' is a metaphor for a cultural event that he believes has already taken place but which, like the death of a distant star, is not yet visible to normal sight: belief in God has become unbelievable, the Christian idea of God is no longer a living force in Western culture.

Nietzsche views all gods as human creations, reflections of what human beings value. However, pagan gods were constructed from the qualities human beings saw and valued in themselves, whereas the Christian God was given qualities that were the opposite of what humans perceived in themselves, the opposite of our inescapable animal instincts. Our natural being could then be reinterpreted as 'guilt before God' and taken to indicate our unworthiness. Constructed to devalue our natural being, the Christian God is a projection of value from the viewpoint of

the ascetic ideal (see §6 of this entry). That this God is dead amounts to a prediction that Christian theism, along with the ascetic ideal that forms its basis, is nearing its end as a major cultural force and that its demise will be brought about by forces that are already and irreversibly at work.

One such force, to which Nietzsche himself contributed, is the development of atheism in the West, a development that stems from Christian morality itself and the will to truth it promotes. The will to truth, a commitment to truth 'at any price', is the latest expression of the ascetic ideal, but it also undermines the whole Christian worldview (heaven, hell, free will, immortality) of which 'God' is the symbol. Inspired by the will to truth, philosophy since Descartes has progressively undermined the arguments that supported Christian doctrines, and science has given us reason to believe that we can explain all the explicable features of empirical reality without appealing to God or any other transcendent reality. Theism has thus become cognitively superfluous. In this situation we can justify atheism without demonstrating the falsity of theism, Nietzsche claims, if we also have a convincing account of how theism could have arisen and acquired its importance without being true. Even if there is no cognitive basis for belief in God, however, might not one still accept something on the order of William James' will to believe? (see WILLIAM J. §4). Nietzsche nowhere treats this option as irrational, but he does deny that it is now a serious option for those who have taken most strictly and seriously Christianity's ascetic morality. It may not be irrational, but it is psychologically impossible, Nietzsche thinks, to accept theism if the commitment to truthfulness has become fully ingrained, if hardness against oneself in matters of belief has become a matter of conscience. Atheism is 'the awe-inspiring catastrophe of a two-thousand year discipline in truth that finally forbids itself the *lie involved in belief in God*' (*Genealogy* III §27 [*Werke* VI.2: 427]).

Although atheism, especially among the most spiritual and intellectual human beings, undoubtedly weakens Christianity, depriving it of both creative energy and prestige, it does not bring about the death of God by itself. The modern world, as KIERKEGAARD had seen already, contains many other factors that weaken the influence of Christianity and its ideal; among these Nietzsche includes the development of money-making and industriousness as ends in themselves, democracy, and the greater availability to more people of the fruits of materialistic pursuits. Zarathustra's statement that 'when gods die, they always die several kinds of death' suggests that just as the ascetic ideal has been accepted by different kinds of people for different reasons, the death of God and the ascetic ideal is also brought about by a multiplicity of causes that operate differently on different kinds of people. What matters, says Zarathustra, is that 'he is gone' (*Zarathustra* IV §6 [*Werke* VI.1: 320]).

According to Nietzsche, the loss of belief in God will initiate a 'monstrous logic of terror' as we experience the collapse of all that was 'built upon this faith, propped up by it, grown into it; for example, the whole of our European morality' (*Gay Science* §343 [*Werke* V.2: 255]). In notes made late in his career (published in *The Will to Power*), Nietzsche calls this collapse of values 'nihilism', the 'radical repudiation of value, meaning, and desirability'. He predicts '*the advent of nihilism*' as 'the history of the next two centuries', and calls himself 'the first perfect nihilist of Europe'. However, he adds that he has 'lived through the whole of nihilism, to the end, leaving it behind' (*Will to Power* Preface [*Werke* VIII.2: 431–2]). Nihilism is therefore not his own doctrine, but one he diagnoses in others (including his own earlier self). He *does not* believe that nothing is of value (or that 'everything is permitted') if God does not exist, but that this form of judgment is the necessary outcome of the ascetic ideal. Having come to believe that the things of the highest value – knowledge, truth, virtue, philosophy, art – must have a source in a reality that transcends the natural world, we necessarily experience these things as devoid of value once the ascetic ideal itself leads to the death of God, to the denial that any transcendent reality exists.

8 Morality

Nietzsche's criticism of morality is perhaps the most important and difficult aspect of his later philosophy. Calling himself an 'immoralist' – one who opposes all morality – he repeatedly insists that morality 'negates life'. He turned against it, he claims, inspired by an 'instinct that aligned itself with life' (*Birth of Tragedy* Preface 5 [*Werke* III.1: 13]). Whatever Nietzsche might mean by suggesting that morality is 'against life,' his point is *not* that morality is 'unnatural' because it restricts the satisfaction of natural impulses. He finds what is natural and 'inestimable' in any morality in the hatred it teaches of simply following one's impulses, of any 'all-too-great freedom': it teaches 'obedience over a long period of time and in a single direction' (*Beyond Good and Evil* §188 [*Werke* VI.2: 110–11]). Nietzsche analyses the directive to 'follow nature' as commanding something that is either impossible (if it means 'be like the nonhuman part of nature') or inevitable (if it means 'be as you are and must be').

His objection to morality sometimes seems to be not that it is 'against life', but that it promotes and

celebrates a kind of person in which he finds nothing to esteem: a 'herd animal' who has little idea of greatness and seeks above all else security, absence of fear, absence of suffering. To complicate matters still further, he sometimes uses 'morality' to refer to what he approves of, for instance, 'noble morality' and 'higher moralities'.

The last of these interpretive problems can be resolved by recognizing that Nietzsche uses 'morality' in both a wider and a narrower sense. Every ethical code or system for evaluating conduct is 'a morality' in the wider, but not in the narrower sense. A system that determines the value of conduct solely in terms of 'the retroactive force of success or failure', for instance, is an instance of 'morality' in the wider sense, but Nietzsche counts it as 'pre-moral' in the narrower sense (*Beyond Good and Evil* §32 [*Werke* VI.2: 46–7]). And it is the narrower sense Nietzsche is using when he commits himself to 'the overcoming of morality' and claims that it 'negates life'. His immoralism does not oppose all forms of ethical life. Although he opposes morality in the narrower sense, Nietzsche accepts another ethical system in terms of which he considers himself 'bound' or 'pledged'. Indeed, he claims that, contrary to appearances, 'we immoralists' are human beings 'of duty', having 'been spun into a severe yarn and shirt of duties [which we] *cannot* get out of' (*Beyond Good and Evil* §226 [*Werke* VI.2: 168]).

Why didn't Nietzsche just say that he opposed *some* moralities and call his own ethical system his 'morality'? He undoubtedly thought that would be more misleading than his use of the term in a dual sense because it would trivialize the radical nature of his position. He called himself an 'immoralist' as a 'provocation' that would indicate what distinguishes him from 'the whole rest of humanity' (*Ecce Homo* IV: §7 [*Werke* VI.3: 369]). And it could so function, he thought, even though he actually opposes morality only in the narrower sense, precisely because this is the sense 'morality' has had until now. That word has been monopolized, he thinks, for a particular kind of ethical system on which all our currently available choices for an ethics are mere variations.

Genealogy provides a genealogy of morality in the narrower sense (the sense 'morality' will have hereafter in this entry) and a complex and sophisticated analysis of that concept of morality. Although there is no agreed-upon definition, we all have a feeling for what 'morality' in this sense means. But both the feeling and the 'meaning' are actually products of a complicated historical development that synthesized meanings of diverse origins into a unity, one that is difficult to dissolve or analyse and impossible to define. If conceptual analysis were a matter of formulating necessary and sufficient conditions for the use of a term, we might analyse the concept of morality by specifying the characteristics that are both necessary and sufficient to qualify a code of conduct as 'a morality'. But this approach has never delivered great clarification, and Nietzsche's understanding of concepts explains why: our concepts need clarification precisely because they are products of a complicated historical development. Different strands have been tied together into such a tight unity that they seem inseparable and are no longer visible as strands. To analyse or clarify such a concept is to disentangle these strands so that we can see what is actually involved in the concept. History can play a role in analysing a concept because at earlier stages the 'meanings' that constitute it are not as tightly woven together and we can still perceive their shifts and rearrangements. Looking at the history of the corresponding phenomenon can therefore make it easier for us to pick out the various strands that make up the concept and better able to recognize other possible ways of tying them together. Nietzsche's genealogy of morality aims to show that there are distinct aspects of morality, each with a separate pre-moral source, which makes the synthesis we call 'morality' something that can be undone, so that its strands might be rewoven into a different form of ethical life.

The three essays of *Genealogy* separate out for examination three main strands of morality: the good (in the sense of virtue), the right (or duty), and a general understanding of value. Each essay focuses on the development of one strand without paying much attention to the other two, even though any developed form of ethical life will actually involve all three aspects in some form and interconnection. The overall account of morality constitutes a 'genealogy' precisely because it traces the *moral* version of each strand back to pre-moral sources – thus *ancestors of morality*. Its upshot is that what we call 'morality' emerged from these pre-moral ancestors when the right and the good become tied together under the interpretation of value provided by the ascetic ideal. This explains why Nietzsche claims that morality 'negates life': morality is an ascetic interpretation of ethical life.

The first essay in *Genealogy* finds the central pre-moral ancestor of morality's idea of goodness among politically superior classes in the ancient world whose members called themselves 'the good' and used 'good' and 'virtue' as their marks of distinction, the qualities that distinguished them from commoners or slaves. 'Good' and 'virtuous' were the same as 'noble' in the sense of 'belonging to the ruling class'; their contrasting term was 'low-born' or 'bad' (the German, schlecht, originally meant 'simple' or 'common').

As Nietzsche uses 'bad' (he does not claim to reflect contemporary usage), it involves no connotation of blame, whether applied to the poor person or the liar. 'Bad' certainly expresses a value judgment: that the person so described is inferior. The nobles regard themselves as superior and look down on the bad (sometimes with contempt, sometimes with pity). But they do not blame them for being inferior, or think that the inferior ought to be good (much less that inferiority deserves punishment or goodness a reward). Such judgments make sense only if one is judging inferiority in moral terms – that is, if 'bad' has become 'morally bad' or 'evil'.

To explain the origin of the good/evil (the specifically moral) mode of valuation, Nietzsche postulates a 'slave revolt in morality', a revaluation inspired by *ressentiment* (grudge-laden resentment) against the nobles. Nietzsche does not claim that the nobles' actions were considered wrong because they were resented. He is dealing only with ideas of goodness or virtue in this essay; he seeks to explain how goodness became connected to praise and blame, reward and punishment. His postulated 'slave revolt' was led not by slaves but by priests, the 'great haters' in human history precisely because their spirituality is incompatible with the direct discharge of resentment and revenge. They hated the nobles not because they were oppressed by them but because the nobles considered themselves superior and had been victorious over them for the respect and admiration of the people. Because this hatred could not be expressed directly, it grew to monstrous proportions until it finally found an outlet in revaluing the nobles and their qualities as inferior. As a result, certain qualities – useful to those in a slavish or dependent position – were called 'good', not because anyone found them particularly admirable, but from a desire to 'bring down' people with the opposite qualities. Simply 'looking down' at the nobles and their qualities would not have done the trick, especially since the majority envied and admired them. Only through the transformation of bad into evil, of inferiority into something for which one could be blamed, could the revaluation succeed. Pent-up *ressentiment* could then be vented in acts of blaming and moral condemnation, which Nietzsche sees as acts of 'imaginary revenge' that 'bring down' hated opponents 'in effigy' and elevate those who do the blaming, at least in their own imagination. Blaming, for Nietzsche, evidently involves the judgment that the person blamed is deserving of punishment, in this case for their inferiority. Therefore, once 'bad' is transformed into 'evil', God and his judgment along with heaven and hell can be used to support the revaluation by winning over to it those who would not feel sufficiently elevated by mere moral condemnation of the nobles. Nietzsche suggests that this is how the issue of free will became connected to morality. Blaming or holding people responsible for their actions does not raise the issue; it is raised by holding them responsible for what they are. And that is precisely what was required for the revaluation of noble values.

9 Morality (cont.)

Priests did not invent the idea of 'evil' on the spot, however. The notion of blame required for the revaluation emerged in a quite different sphere, that of right conduct or duty, the development of which Nietzsche sketches in the second essay of *Genealogy*. The pre-moral ancestor to which this essay traces moral versions of right and wrong, duty or obligation, is the ethics of custom (*Sittlichkeit der Sitte*), an early system of community practices that gained the status of rules through the threat of punishment. These rules were perceived as imperatives, but not as moral imperatives: violation was punished, but not considered to be a matter of conscience or thought to incur guilt.

Nietzsche finds an ancestor of guilt in the realm of trade, in the creditor–debtor relation. Guilt arises, Nietzsche claims, when the idea of debt is put to the uses of the 'bad conscience', the sense of oneself as unworthy, which develops when the external expression of aggressive impulses becomes restricted to such an extent that they can be expressed only by being turned back against the self. This internalization does not take place automatically, however; human beings must learn techniques that promote it, and Nietzsche views priests as the great teachers in this field. One such technique exploits the idea that a debt is owed to ancestors (who eventually come to be perceived as gods) for the benefits they continue to bestow and for violations of community laws which represent their will. Priests use this idea to teach the people that they must make difficult sacrifices to the gods – for example, to sacrifice one's first-born – and that certain instances of apparent bad luck and suffering constitute the extraction of payment for violations of divine law, hence are deserved punishments.

So conceived, the debts are still mere debts, material rather than moral 'owings'. The moralization of debt (and thereby of duty) removes the idea that it can simply be paid off and connects it to one's worth or goodness. This moralization takes place by means of the third strand of morality analysed in Genealogy, the understanding of value, which in the case of morality is guided by the ascetic ideal. We enter what Nietzsche calls the 'moral epoch' only when the divine being to whom the debt is owed is considered the highest being and is conceived in non-naturalistic or ascetic terms, as a purely spiritual being and thus as a repudiation of the value of natural human existence (see §§6–7 of this entry). What must now be sacrificed to the divine is 'one's own strongest instincts, one's "nature"' (*Beyond Good and Evil* §55 [*Werke* VI.2: 72]). The affirmation of these instincts is conceived as rebellion against God, and the normal sufferings of human life as punishments for this rebellion. The debt is now owed precisely for what one is and continues to be, for being part of the natural world. This debt can no longer be considered material, a mere debt, for while it is owed and payment must be made, it can never be paid off. And the punishment one deserves is now completely bound up with one's (lack of) goodness or virtue, which is interpreted in ascetic terms as self-denial, the denial of one's natural impulses, or at least as selflessness.

The priest now has the notion of 'evil' required for the revaluation of the noble values: the moralized notion of virtue as self-denial provides the standard against which the nobles could be judged inferior, whereas the moralized notion of debt provides the basis for blaming the nobles for that inferiority. Both notions (of virtue and duty) were moralized by being tied together under the understanding of value provided by the ascetic ideal. Morality connects duty and virtue in such a way that blameable violations of duty are taken to show lack of virtue and lack of virtue is blameable (luck has nothing to do with it). Because he sees this connection as having been brought about by means of the ascetic ideal, Nietzsche regards that ideal as a major element of morality.

His own ideal is a very different one. Named after the Greek god Dionysus, Nietzsche's ideal celebrates the affirmation of life even in the face of its greatest difficulties, and thus gives rise to a doctrine and valuation of life that is fundamentally opposed to the one he finds behind morality. Committed to finding the sources of value in life, he rejects all non-naturalistic interpretations of ethical life, those that make reference to a transcendent or metaphysical world. It therefore seems likely that what he opposes in morality is not the idea of virtue, or standards of right and wrong, but the moralization of virtue and duty brought about by the ascetic ideal. Morality 'negates life' because it is an ascetic interpretation of ethical life. By interpreting virtue and duty in non-natural terms, it reveals the assumption of the ascetic ideal: that things of the highest value must have their source 'elsewhere' than in the natural world. This is why Nietzsche says that what 'horrifies' him in morality is 'the lack of nature, the utterly gruesome fact that *antinature* itself received the highest honours as morality and was fixed over humanity as law and categorical imperative' (*Ecce Homo* IV: §7 [*Werke* VI.3: 370]).

But how is this connected to Nietzsche's complaints against 'herd morality'? 'Herd' is his deliberately insulting term for those who congregate together in questions of value and perceive as dangerous anyone with a will to stand alone in such matters. He calls the morality of contemporary Europe 'herd animal morality' because of the almost complete agreement 'in all major moral judgments'. Danger, suffering, and distress are to be minimized, the 'modest, submissive, conforming mentality' is honoured, and one is disturbed by 'every severity, even in justice'. Good-naturedness and benevolence are valued, whereas the 'highest and strongest drives, if they break out passionately and drive the individual far above the average and the flats of the herd conscience,' are slandered and considered evil (*Beyond Good and Evil* §§201–2 [*Werke* VI.2: 123–7]).

This morality does not seem to involve the ascetic ideal. In fact, it is more likely to be packaged as utilitarianism, which offers a naturalistic, and therefore presumably unascetic, interpretation of duty and virtue, in terms of happiness (see UTILITARIANISM). We might, in fact, formulate Nietzsche's main objection to herd morality as a complaint that there is nothing in it to play the role of the ascetic ideal: to hold out an ideal of the human person that encourages individuals to take up the task of self-transformation, self-creation, and to funnel into it the aggressive impulses, will to power and resentment that would otherwise be expressed externally. Although it horrifies him, Nietzsche recognizes the greatness of the ascetic ideal. It is the only ideal of widespread cultural importance human beings have had so far, and it achieved its tremendous power, even though it is the 'harmful ideal *par excellence*', because it was necessary, because there was nothing else to play its role. 'Above all, a counterideal was lacking – until Zarathustra' (*Ecce Homo* III GM [*Werke* VI.3: 352]).

The problem is that the ascetic ideal is now largely dead (as part of the 'death of God'). Nietzsche thinks we need something to replace it: a great ideal that will inspire the striving, internalization, virtue, self-creation that the ascetic ideal inspired. 'Herd animal morality' is what we are left with in the absence of any such ideal. It is what morality degenerates into once the ascetic ideal largely withdraws from the synthesis it brought about. The virtuous human being no longer is anything that can stir our imagination or move us. For Nietzsche, this is the 'great danger' to which morality has led: the sight of human beings makes us weary.

10 The overhuman (*Übermensch*)

Nietzsche's apparent alternative to 'herd-animal morality' is his most notorious idea, the Übermensch. (There is no really suitable English translation for this term: 'overhuman' has been chosen instead of 'superman' or 'overman' because it seems best able to bring out the idea of a being who overcomes in itself what has defined us as human.) The idea actually belongs to the protagonist of *Thus Spoke Zarathustra*, Nietzsche's work of philosophical fiction, and it can never be assumed that Zarathustra's ideas are the same as those of Nietzsche. As the story opens, Zarathustra is returning from ten years of solitude in the wilderness, bringing human beings a gift: his teaching that humanity is not an end or goal, but only a stage and bridge to a higher type of being, the overhuman. He teaches that now that God is dead, it is time for humanity to establish this higher type as the goal and meaning of human life, a goal that can be reached only if human beings overcome what they now are, overcome the merely human.

The idea of becoming a higher kind of being by overcoming one's humanity can seem frightening. For some, it calls up images of Nazi stormtroopers seeking out 'inferior' human beings to annihilate. However, *Zarathustra* suggests that Nietzsche has something very different in mind. 'Zarathustra' is another name for Zoroaster, the founder of Zoroastrianism (see ZOROASTRIANISM). Nietzsche claims that the historical Zarathustra 'created the most calamitous error, morality', because his doctrine first projected ethical distinctions into the metaphysical realm (as a cosmic fight between good and evil forces). Nietzsche bases his character on Zarathustra because the creator of the error 'must also be the first to recognize it' (*Ecce Homo* IV §3 [*Werke* VI.3: 365]).

Zarathustra is thus the story of a religious leader, the inventor of one of the world's oldest religions, who comes to recognize the 'error' of traditional (moralized) religions. Far from turning against every aspect of traditional religion, however, Zarathustra commits himself to its central task: urging human beings to raise their sights above their usual immersion in materialistic pursuits to recognize the outlines of a higher form of being that calls them to go beyond themselves, to become something more than they are. Zarathustra's overhuman can thus be seen as a successor to the images of 'higher humanity' offered by traditional religions. His teaching is not intended to encourage human beings to throw off the constraints and shackles of morality (something Nietzsche sees as well underway without his help). Its point is, rather, to combat the forces of barbarism by encouraging us to take on a more demanding ethical task than modern morality requires: that of becoming what Nietzsche had earlier called a 'true human being'. When he used that phrase, however, Nietzsche believed it applied only to 'those no-longer animals, the philosophers, artists, and saints'. Animal (purely natural) existence was a senseless cycle of becoming and desire, and only those who escape it by extinguishing egoistic desire counted as truly human. The saint in particular counted as 'that ultimate and supreme becoming human', in which 'life no longer appears senseless but appears, rather, in its metaphysical meaningfulness' (*Unfashionable Observations* III §5 [*Werke* III.1: 371–9]). From the viewpoint of his later philosophy, early Nietzsche's conception of true humanity is an obvious expression of the ascetic ideal; it devalues natural existence relative to something that is its opposite. Once one recognizes this opposite as unattainable (as Nietzsche did in *Human*), the conception can be seen for what it really is: a devaluation and condemnation of human life.

Nietzsche never abandoned his early belief that the modern world is threatened by forces of both conformism and barbarism and that our great need is therefore for educators who will inspire human self-overcoming by the force of a lofty ideal. But since he rejects the ascetic ideal, he must abandon his earlier image of a true human being. At the end of *Genealogy's* second essay, Nietzsche suggests that what the overhuman overcomes is not the 'natural' inclinations against which the ascetic ideal has been directed, those that make apparent our connection to other animals, but rather the 'unnatural' inclinations, the aspirations to a form of existence that transcends nature and animality. In other words, the overhuman must overcome all the impulses that led human beings to accept the ascetic ideal, an ideal that has so far defined what counts as 'human'. As we will see in §2, however, Zarathustra's call for the overcoming of the human is still too bound up with the old ideal.

11 The will to power

Zarathustra teaches that life itself is will to power, and this is often thought to be Nietzsche's central teaching as well. However, will to power first appears in Nietzsche's work in *Daybreak* (1881), and there it is one human drive among others, the striving for competence or mastery. It is usefully thought of as a second-order drive or will: a need or desire for the effectiveness of one's first-order will. In *Daybreak*, Nietzsche finds this drive at work in large areas of human life: in asceticism, revenge, the lust for money, the striving for distinction, cruelty, blaming others, blaming oneself. He explains the drive's apparent omnipresence in human life by saying not that life is

will to power (or that power is the only thing humans want), but that power has a special relation to human happiness. He calls love of power a 'demon' because human beings remain unhappy and low-spirited if it is not satisfied even if all their material needs are satisfied, whereas power can make them as happy as human beings can be, even if everything else is taken away (*Daybreak* §262 [*Werke* V.1: 211]). In Genealogy (1887) he expresses a similar idea in more positive terms when he calls the will to power 'the most life-affirming drive', that is, the one whose satisfaction contributes most to finding life worth living (*Genealogy* III §18 [*Werke* VI.2: 383]).

Zarathustra claims that this 'will to be master' is found in all that lives, and that this explains why life is 'struggle and becoming', always overcoming itself, always opposing what it has created and loved: 'Verily, where there is perishing and a falling of leaves, behold, there life sacrifices itself – for power' (*Zarathustra* II §12 [*Werke* VI.1: 144– 5]). But this seems a clearly anthropomorphic conception of life, the projection of the human will to power onto nonhuman nature. Nietzsche rejects anthropomorphic conceptions of nature, insists that will is to be found only in beings with intellects, and complains that Schopenhauer's idea of will 'has been turned into a metaphor when it is asserted that all things in nature possess will' (*Human* II §5 [*Werke* IV.3: 18]).

Yet Nietzsche does say that life, and even reality itself, is will to power. The idea seems to be that reality consists of fields of force or dynamic quanta, each of which is essentially a drive to expand and thus to increase its power relative to all other such quanta. However, almost all the passages to this effect are found in Nietzsche's notebooks. He actually argues that reality is will to power in only one passage he chose to publish, and this passage gives us good reason to doubt that Nietzsche actually accepted the argument. He neither says nor implies that he accepts its conclusion, and he argues against its premises in earlier passages of the same book (*Beyond Good and Evil* §36 [*Werke* VI.2: 50–1]).

Why would Nietzsche construct a rather elaborate argument from premises he clearly rejects? Perhaps it was to illustrate the view of philosophy presented earlier in the same book. Philosophers' ultimate aim, he claims, is not to obtain knowledge or truth, but to interpret the world in terms of their own values (see §6 of this entry) – to 'create [in thought] a world before which [they] can kneel' (*Zarathustra* II §12 [*Werke* VI.1: 143]). Yet they present their interpretations as true, and argue for them on the basis of amazingly 'little': 'any old popular superstition from time immemorial', a play on words, a seduction by grammar, or 'an audacious generalization of very narrow, very personal, very human, all too human facts' (*Beyond Good and Evil* Preface [*Werke* VI.2: 3–4]). This seems an apt diagnosis of Nietzsche's own argument, since he elsewhere identifies its first premise as 'Schopenhauer's superstition' and the exaggeration of a popular prejudice, and its second and third premises as part of the 'primeval mythology' Schopenhauer 'enthroned' (*Beyond Good and Evil* §§16–19 [*Werke* VI.2: 22–6]; *Gay Science* §127 [*Werke* V.2: 160]). Furthermore, the effect of the argument is an 'audacious generalization' to the whole universe of the will to power, which Nietzsche originally understands as one human drive among others. In generalizing this drive, Nietzsche can be seen as generalizing and glorifying what he values, just as he claims philosophers have always done and must do. For Nietzsche's own answer to 'what is good?' is 'everything that heightens the feeling of power in human beings, the will to power, power itself' (*Antichrist* §2 [*Werke* VI.3: 168]).

Why does Nietzsche value the will to power? He certainly came to recognize it as responsible for the violence and cruelty of human life and as the prime ingredient in what he had earlier called the 'cauldron full of witches' brew' that threatens the modern world with 'horrible apparitions' (*Unfashionable Observations* III §4 [*Werke* III.1: 363]). But he also saw it as 'the most life-affirming drive' and as responsible for the great human accomplishments – political institutions, religion, art, morality and philosophy. His basic psychological claim is that human beings are subjected to intense experiences of powerlessness and that such experience leads to depression unless some means is found for restoring a feeling of power. What we call 'barbarism' is largely a set of direct and crude strategies for restoring the feeling of power by demonstrating the power to hurt others. What we call 'culture' is a set of institutions and strategies for achieving the same feeling in a sublimated or less direct fashion. The most important strategies have all involved directing the will to power back against the self. Such internalization is responsible for all the ethical achievements of human life, all the ways in which human beings have changed and perfected their original nature by taking on a new and improved nature. But the internalization of the will to power has been promoted by the ascetic ideal's condemnation of our original nature, especially of the will to power. This is what Zarathustra attempts to overcome with his overhuman teaching, which directs the will to power back against the self to overcome the inclinations that led to the old ideal. He therefore does not condemn the will to power, but celebrates it.

12 Eternal recurrence

Nietzsche identifies himself above all else as the teacher of eternal recurrence, which is often interpreted as a cosmological theory to the effect that the exact history of the cosmos endlessly repeats itself. Although he did sketch arguments for such a theory in his notebooks, he actually does not argue for or commit himself to a recurrence cosmology in any work he published. And, although he presents eternal recurrence as the 'basic conception' of *Zarathustra*, he does not commit its protagonist to a cosmology. He identifies this 'basic conception' not as a cosmology, but as 'the highest formula for affirmation that is at all attainable' (*Ecce Homo* III §1 [*Werke* VI.3: 335]).

As first articulated in *Gay Science*, eternal recurrence is a heuristic device used to formulate Nietzsche's Dionysian ideal (see §9 of this entry). How well disposed we are to life is to be measured by how we would react upon being told by a demon (in a manner designed to induce uncritical acceptance) that we will have to live again and again the exact course of life we are now living. Would we experience despair or joy, curse the demon or greet him as a god? Nietzsche's ideal is the *affirmation of eternal recurrence*, to be a person who would respond to the demon with joy. This is *not* equivalent to having no regrets, since it has no implication concerning how to respond if given the choice of variations on history. Nietzsche's ideal is to love life enough to be joyfully willing to have the whole process repeated eternally, including all the parts that one did not love and even fought against. Eternal recurrence gives him a formula for what it is to value the process of life as an end and not merely as a means.

Nietzsche's special self-identification with eternal recurrence can be explained in terms of his view regarding the importance of the ascetic ideal and his explanation of its power: 'a *counterideal* was lacking – until Zarathustra'. There are only two plausible candidates for the counterideal Zarathustra offers, the overhuman and the affirmation of eternal recurrence. The overhuman is one who overcomes the ascetic ideal. But, as Zarathustra first preaches it, the overhuman ideal can be seen as another variation on the ascetic ideal. Like the ascetic priest, Zarathustra treats our lives as valuable only as a means to a form of life that is actually their negation. Like the ascetic priest, he turns his will to power against human life and takes revenge against it (for the powerlessness it induces) by excluding it from what he recognizes as intrinsically valuable. The ideal of affirming eternal recurrence, in contrast, values the whole process of living, and thereby overcomes the ascetic ideal's devaluation of human life, even while pushing us to go beyond its present form. It provides us with the image of a higher form of human life, but does not take revenge against the latter by refusing to call its higher form 'human'. It therefore appears to be Zarathustra's true alternative to the ascetic ideal.

It may seem, however, that happy pre-moral barbarians should be able to affirm eternal recurrence. How then can it provide an image of a higher form of human life towards which to strive, one that could inspire internalization, virtue and self-creation comparable to that inspired by the ascetic ideal? One relevant factor is Nietzsche's hope for new philosophers who will create new values. Perhaps he did not expect his counterideal to provide the full content of new values, just as the ascetic ideal did not provide the full content of the old values. The ascetic priests did not create their values from scratch. They took over virtues, duties, forms of life that were already there and gave them a new interpretation, one that denied the value of natural human existence. Nietzsche seems to hope that new philosophers will do something comparable – that they will provide a new life-affirming interpretation of virtues, duties and forms of life that are already there. Eternal recurrence would function as the form of new values, a test that they must pass to count as non-ascetic or life-affirming. The test for teachers of new values would be: can you endorse and teach these values while affirming eternal recurrence?

If this suggestion is correct, Nietzsche's relation to the modern world is not quite as revolutionary as it sometimes appears. The role of his new philosophers is not to overturn everything, but to take what is in pieces due to the dissolution of the old interpretation of value and to provide a new interpretation. This kind of philosophizing is not just for the future, but is found in Nietzsche's own writings. He praises old virtues – justice and generosity, for instance – but gives us a new interpretation of them, a different way of seeing them as valuable. Generosity is valuable not because it is selfless, but because it exhibits the soul's richness and power. And justice is perhaps the greatest virtue not because it is disinterested or obeys a higher law, but because it is the rarest and highest mastery that is possible on earth. And Nietzsche does not merely talk about these matters. His writings show us a new kind of person and a new kind of philosopher in the virtues he exhibits in them, not least of all in the interpretations he gives of his virtues. Truthfulness or honesty, justice, generosity are all exhibited in his writings, but are given life-affirming interpretations that bring to our attention the role of the will to power in them.

This is not to say that Nietzsche's new values are simply repackaged old ones. Nietzsche's ideal leads

him to value qualities that he claims have never before been considered part of greatness, such as malice, exuberance and laughter. But even in their new interpretations of old values, the aim of Nietzsche's new philosophers is to push culture in new directions, for instance, towards giving explicit expression at the higher levels of culture to what the old ideal excluded from the highest forms of life. This is what Nietzsche exhibits, for instance, in the positive and negative emotion, the exuberance and malice, the aggression and eros, that permeates his writings. At this level, his philosophy is art, but it is an art that completes and is no longer used to devalue knowledge, which can now be recognized as its sometimes contentious partner in Nietzsche's soul and writings.

See also: GENEALOGY §2; NIETZSCHE: IMPACT ON RUSSIAN THOUGHT

List of works

Nietzsche, F. (1967–84) *Werke: Kritische Gesamtausgabe* (Complete critical works), ed. G. Colli and M. Montinari, Berlin: de Gruyter. (Now the standard German edition of Nietzsche's works. Volumes of the critical apparatus are still appearing, but the books and *Nachlaß* were completed by 1984. A paperback edition of the essentials appeared in 1980 as *Sämtliche Werke*.)

—— (1872) *Die Geburt der Tragödie*; trans. W. Kaufmann and R. Hollindale as *The Birth of Tragedy*, in *Basic Writings of Nietzsche*, New York: Modern Library, 1968. (Nietzsche's first book, written under the influence of Wagner and Schopenhauer, with 'Attempt at a Self-Criticism', a preface written for the second edition of 1886. Important source for Nietzsche's early views of art and of the Dionysian, but too bound up with the thesis that art is more truthful than science to represent Nietzsche's later view.)

—— (1873–6) *Unzeitgemäße Betrachtungen*; trans. R. Gray as *Unfashionable Observations*, Stanford, CA: Stanford University Press, 1995. (Four essays of cultural criticism from Nietzsche's early period, in which he is still trying to elevate art over science. These essays exhibit Nietzsche's early philosophy as a critique of modern culture, and the essays on history and Schopenhauer point forward to his later ideas of eternal recurrence and the overhuman. This work has also been translated as 'Untimely Meditations' and 'Unmodern Observations'.)

—— (1878–80) *Menschliches, Allzumenschliches*; trans. R. Hollingdale as *Human, All Too Human*, intro. R. Schacht, Cambridge: Cambridge University Press, 1996. (Represents the beginning of Nietzsche's middle period, his turn away from Wagner, art and metaphysics, and his embrace of science and a thoroughgoing naturalism. Contains his first, relatively crude, attempts at a naturalistic understanding of moral values.)

—— (1881) *Morgenröte*; trans. R. Hollingdale as *Daybreak*, ed. M. Clark and B. Leiter, Cambridge: Cambridge University Press, 1997. (The second work of Nietzsche's middle period, it represents the true beginning of Nietzsche's own way in philosophy. He called it the beginning of his 'campaign against morality,' and it contains much of his psychology of the will to power. This work has also been translated as 'Dawn'.)

—— (1882) *Die Fröhliche Wissenschaft*; trans. W. Kaufmann as *The Gay Science*, New York: Vintage, 1974. (The work that inaugurates Nietzsche's final period, it announces the 'death of God' and contains Nietzsche's first formulation of his idea of eternal recurrence. Book Five, added in the second edition of 1887, contains some of Nietzsche's most important reflections on science and its connection to democracy. This work has also been translated as 'Joyful Wisdom'.)

—— (1883–5) *Also Sprach Zarathustra*; trans. W. Kaufmann as *Thus spoke Zarathustra*, in *The Portable Nietzsche*, New York: Viking, 1954. (Nietzsche's work of philosophical fiction and the major source for the cosmological version of the will to power and the ideas of the overhuman and eternal recurrence. Not easily understood without knowledge of Nietzsche's other books.)

—— (1886) *Jenseits von Gut und Böse*; trans. W. Kaufmann and R. Hollingdale as *Beyond Good and Evil*, in *Basic Writings of Nietzsche*, New York: Modern Library, 1968. (Nietzsche at the height of his powers on philosophy and science, religion, morality, politics, nationality and nobility. A true masterpiece, but difficult.)

—— (1887) *Zur Genealogie der Moral*; trans. M. Clark and A. Swensen as *On the Genealogy of Morality*, Indianapolis, IN: Hackett Publishing Company, 1997. (Nietzsche's most detailed analysis of and most important treatment of morality, considered by him as probably the most accessible introduction to his work and the 'touchstone' of what 'belongs' to him. Contains his most sustained discussion of the ascetic ideal, and was intended to clarify the title and contents of *Beyond Good and Evil*. This work has also been translated as 'On the Genealogy of Morals'.)

—— (1888a) *Der Fall Wagner*; trans. W. Kaufmann and R. Hollingdale as *The Case of Wagner*, in *Basic Writings of Nietzsche*, New York: Modern Library, 1968. (Finished at the beginning of his final year,

this is an often very funny book, and a major source for Nietzsche's views of Wagner and art.)

—— (1888b) *Die Götzen-Dämmerung*, 1889; trans. W. Kaufmann as *The Twilight of the Idols*, in *The Portable Nietzsche*, New York: Viking, 1954. (Contains Nietzsche's final accounts of truth and knowledge, as well as important sections on morality and art. Fairly straightforward and more accessible than many of his other works.)

—— (1888c) *Der Antichrist*, 1895; trans. W. Kaufmann as *The Antichrist*, in *The Portable Nietzsche*, New York: Viking, 1954. (Nietzsche's version of 'Why I am not a Christian'. Distinguishes original Christianity from the Pauline version and gives a relatively sympathetic portrait of the former and of the one who lived it. Fairly straightforward and accessible.)

—— (1888d) *Ecce Homo*, 1908; trans. W. Kaufmann and R. Hollingdale in *Basic Writings of Nietzsche*, New York: Modern Library, 1968. (Nietzsche's autobiographical work, written in the middle of his final year, includes his own invaluable accounts of all his earlier works under the title 'Why I write such good books'. An important source for his view of art since the autobiography is clearly intended as a work of art.)

—— (1888e) *Nietzsche contra Wagner*, 1895; trans. W. Kaufmann in *The Portable Nietzsche*, New York: Viking, 1954. (Nietzsche's last and shortest book, this is a compilation of passages from earlier works designed to show that Nietzsche and Wagner are 'antipodes'. A source for Nietzsche's final view of art and of the ways in which the art he promotes differs from Wagner's.)

—— (1906) *Der Wille zur Macht*,; trans. W. Kaufmann as *The Will to Power*, New York: Viking, 1967. (Although treated by many, including Nietzsche's sister, as his magnum opus, this is not a book by Nietzsche. Rather, it is a collection of outlines, notes and jottings from his notebooks of 1883–8, selected and arranged by his sister and editors appointed by her.)

—— (1975–84) *Briefwechsel: Kritische Gesamtausgabe*, ed. C. Colli and M. Montinari, Berlin: de Gruyter. (An edition of the complete letters to and from Nietzsche (the Nietzsche side of the correspondence was published in 1986 as *Sämtliche Briefe*). A 1969 English edition of selected letters, translated by Christopher Middleton, is reprinted as *Selected Letters of Friedrich Nietzsche*, Indianapolis, IN: Hackett Publishing Company, 1996.)

—— (1979) *Philosophy and Truth: Selections from Nietzsche's Notebooks of the early 1870's*, trans. D. Breazeale, Atlantic Highlands, NJ: Humanities Press. (A valuable collection of material from the

Nachlaß of the period surrounding the publication of *The Birth of Tragedy*. Includes 'Über Wahrheit und Lüge im aussermoralischen Sinne', trans. as 'On Truth and Lies in a non-moral sense', a widely known essay in which Nietzsche argues that, except for tautologies, all truths are 'illusions'.)

References and further readings

Ansell-Pearson, K. (1994) *An Introduction to Nietzsche as Political Thinker*, Cambridge: Cambridge University Press. (A lively introduction to Nietzsche's political thought.)

Clark, M. (1990) *Nietzsche on Truth and Philosophy*, Cambridge: Cambridge University Press. (An account of the development of Nietzsche's thinking about truth which forms the basis of the present entry. Includes chapters on truth and the ascetic ideal, the will to power and eternal recurrence.)

Deleuze, G. (1962) *Nietzsche et la philosophie*; trans. H. Tomlinson as *Nietzsche and Philosophy*, New York: Columbia University Press, 1983. (A reading of Nietzsche as anti-Hegelian; known especially for its influential distinction between active and reactive forces. An often difficult read.)

Derrida, J. (1978) *Éperons: Les Styles de Nietzsche*; trans. B. Harlow as *Spurs: Nietzsche's Styles*, Chicago, IL and London: University of Chicago Press, 1979. (Responds to Heidegger's interpretation of Nietzsche as a metaphysician by playing with Nietzsche's texts rather than attempting to establish a truth about them. An example of philosophy as deconstruction. The translation is a French-English edition.)

Heidegger, M. (1961) *Nietzsche*, 2 vols; trans. D. Krell, San Francisco, CA: Harper & Row, 1979–82, 4 vols. (This interpretation of Nietzsche as a critic of metaphysics who was himself unable to avoid metaphysics has greatly influenced later Continental readings of Nietzsche; for advanced students who are as interested in Heidegger as in Nietzsche.)

Janz, C.P. (1978) *Friedrich Nietzsche Biographie*, Munich: Carl Hanser Verlag, 3 vols. (The standard biography; an English translation is in progress.)

Kaufmann, W. (1950) *Nietzsche: Philosopher, Psychologist, Antichrist*, Princeton, NJ: Princeton University Press, 4th edn, 1974. (A landmark study that went a long way towards destroying the picture of Nietzsche as a Nazi sympathizer and an anti-Socratic irrationalist that once dominated the English-speaking world. Still useful for this purpose.)

* Lange, F.A. (1866) *Geschichte des Materialismus und Kritik seiner Bedeutung in der Gegenwart*; trans. E.C. Thomas as *History of Materialism*, Boston, MA: Osgood, 1977, 3 vols. (A history of materialism from ancient Greece to 19th century Europe which Nietzsche read during his student days at Leipzig. A major influence on his views of science and knowledge.)

Morgen, G. (1941) *What Nietzsche Means*, New York: Harper & Row. (Still a valuable and very accessible introduction to all the main themes of Nietzsche's philosophy.)

Mueller-Lauter, W. (1971) *Nietzsche: Seine Philosophie der Gegensätze und die Gegensätze seiner Philosophie* (Nietzsche's philosophy of contradictions and the contradictions of his philosophy), Berlin: de Gruyter. (Perhaps the most important German work on Nietzsche written after the Second World War; distinguishes the apparent from the real contradictions of Nietzsche's philosophy of the will to power, and argues that Nietzsche's thinking leads him to two very different versions of the overhuman. English translation in progress.)

Nehamas, A. (1985) *Nietzsche: Life as Literature*, Cambridge, MA: Harvard University Press. (Important attempt to relate Nietzsche's philosophical views to his literary styles, and the most important examination of how Nietzsche's books *exhibit* what this entry calls Nietzsche's 'ideal'. Its accounts of the will to power and eternal recurrence are alternatives to those given above.)

Richardson, J. (1996) *Nietzsche's System*, Oxford: Oxford University Press. (A systematic, challenging account of Nietzsche's thought that provides a more metaphysical alternative to the naturalistic Nietzsche of this entry, especially in its accounts of the will to power and perspectivism. Influenced by Continental readings of Nietzsche, especially those of Heidegger and Deleuze.)

Schacht, R. (1983) *Nietzsche*, London: Routledge & Kegan Paul. (Careful and detailed survey of all the main themes of Nietzsche's philosophy. Its Nietzsche has a basically naturalistic orientation, but nevertheless accepts the will to power as the basic principle of life.)

* Schopenhauer, A. (1818) *Die Welt als Wille und Vorstellung*; trans. E.F.J. Payne as *The World as Will and Representation*, New York: Dover, 2 vols, 1969. (Perhaps the major philosophical influence on Nietzsche's thought and development.)

Young, J. (1992) *Nietzsche's Philosophy of Art*, Cambridge: Cambridge University Press. (Interesting account of Nietzsche's view of art; highly critical of Nietzsche *vis-à-vis* Schopenhauer.)

MAUDEMARIE CLARK

NIETZSCHE: IMPACT ON RUSSIAN THOUGHT

Nietzsche's thought had a massive influence on Russian literature and the arts, religious philosophy and political culture. His popularizers were writers, artists and political radicals who read his works through the prism of their own culture, highlighting the moral, psychological and mythopoetic aspects of his thought and their sociopolitical implications, and appropriating them for their own agendas. Literature addressed to a mass readership disseminated crude notions of a master morality and an amoral Superman.

Russians discovered Nietzsche in the early 1890s. His admirers regarded him as a proponent of self-fulfilment and an enemy of the 'slave morality' of Christianity. Two of them, Dmitri Merezhkovskii (1865–1941) and Maksim Gor'kii (real name Aleksei Peshkov, 1868–1936), were the progenitors of the two main streams of Nietzsche appropriation – the religious and the secular. Merezhkovskii was the initiator of Russian Symbolism. In 1896 he began trying to reconcile Nietzsche and Christianity; this attempt led him to propound an apocalyptic Christianity in 1900 and to found the Religious-Philosophical Society of St Petersburg (1901–3, 1906–17). Its members, the so-called God-seekers, included artists and intellectuals who were also attracted to Nietzsche. As for Gor'kii, his early short stories featured vagrant protagonists who personified crude versions of the slave and the master morality. In 1895 Gor'kii began to dream of a Russian Superman who would lead the masses in a struggle for liberation and imbue them with respect for Man, which he always wrote with a capital letter. During the Revolution of 1905, he and Anatolii Lunacharskii (1875–1933), a Bolshevik admirer of Nietzsche, constructed a Marxist surrogate religion to inspire heroism and self-sacrifice. They believed, as did most Symbolists and some philosophers, that art could transform human consciousness.

New literary schools emerged after 1909. The Futurists exaggerated Nietzsche's anti-rationalism, anti-historicism and cultural iconoclasm. The Acmeists propounded a non-tragic Apollonian Christianity and idealized classical antiquity and 'world culture'. After the Bolshevik Revolution, Nietzsche was considered an ideologue of reaction and his books were removed from the People's Libraries, but his ideas, not identified as such, continued to circulate and pervaded Soviet literature, the arts and political culture.

1 Symbolists
2 Philosophers
3 Bolsheviks
4 Futurists and Acmeists
5 The Soviet period

1 Symbolists

In Russia, literature and literary criticism were the venues for discussing social and political ideas in coded Aesopian language. This applied to Nietzsche as well. Successive generations of writers and critics developed their own interpretations of Nietzsche, polemicizing with their contemporaries and with preceding generations, and basing their arguments on different Nietzsche texts or on variant readings of the same text. Strictly speaking, Nietzsche had no Russian disciples. Rather, his ideas fructified various literary and artistic schools, religious philosophy and Bolshevik political culture. The early twentieth-century religious renaissance was in large part a response to Nietzsche, as was the Soviet obsession with creating a new culture and a new man (*chelovek*); the word is gender neutral but discussions focused on men.

For the Symbolists, the key Nietzsche text was *The Birth of Tragedy*. They were dazzled by Nietzsche's aesthetic justification of the world and human existence, his celebration of the Dionysian, and his belief that myth is essential to the health of a culture. Much of their imagery and their perception of Nietzsche as a mystic and a prophet, derived from *Thus Spoke Zarathustra*.

The first generation of Russian Symbolists – Merezhkovskii, his wife Zinaida Hippius (1869–1945), Konstantin Balmont (1867–1942), Valerii Briusov (1873–1924), N.M. Minskii (N.M. Vilenkin, 1855–1937) and their allies, the modernists of *Severnyi vestnik* (Northern Herald, 1885–98) and the aesthetes of *Mir iskusstva* (The World of Art, 1898–1904) – discovered Nietzsche at a time when the appeal of populism, the surrogate religion of the intelligentsia, was fading. Nietzsche's aestheticism helped fill the spiritual gap. Art became their religion. They saw themselves as warriors for culture and against arid rationalism and emotional repression, as creators who smashed the old 'tables of values' and inscribed their own values on new tables. Balmont regarded the artist as Superman. Later on, Merezhkovskii referred to the Symbolists of the 1890s, including himself, as Decadents.

In a famous 1892 essay on the causes of the decline of Russian literature, Merezhkovskii attacked positivism and populism for debasing and despiritualizing art and argued that Symbolism would lead to new truths (note the plural) that would unite the atheistic intelligentsia and the Christian people (*narod*). Unlike Nietzsche, most Russian Symbolists believed that higher truths did exist somewhere beyond the Dionysian flux. Only two years later, Merezhkovskii propounded an aesthetic individualism in which self-expression and the creation of beauty were the highest values. In essays and poems, and in his historical novel *Otverzhennyi* (The Outcast) (1895) later published as *Smert' bogov: Iulian Otstupnik* (*Death of the Gods: Julian the Apostate*), about the Roman Emperor who tried to restore paganism, he celebrated the liberation of the passions and instincts repressed by Christianity, sexuality in particular, and the Nietzschean theme of laughter. But Merezhkovskii's inordinate fear of death, together with other factors such as his discovery of the cruelty of Roman civilization, led him to reconsider Christianity. In 'Pushkin' (1896), he declared that Christianity articulated the 'truth of heaven' (love and personal immortality) and paganism (really Nietzscheanism), the 'truth of the earth' (enjoyment of worldly pleasures) – two truths that must be reconciled by an all-encompassing higher truth. Asserting that Pushkin had reconciled them unconsciously, Merezhkovskii set about trying to find Pushkin's 'secret'. In the same essay, he also stated that Pushkin was the perfect combination of Apollo and Dionysus, in other words, a Superman in the popular conception of the term. Nietzsche himself expected the Superman to emerge only in the remote Future. Merezhkovskii's essay stimulated new readings of Pushkin well into the Soviet period.

Merezhkovskii's equally seminal book *Tolstoi i Dostoevskii* (1900–2) compared the Russian writers with one another and with Nietzsche. This book was Merezhkovskii's response to Nietzsche's critique of Christianity, which Merezhkovskii now claimed applied only to 'historical Christianity' (Christianity as preached in the churches). A Third Testament or Third Revelation was forthcoming. Jesus Christ himself would show humankind how to reconcile Christianity and paganism. The Revolution of 1905 politicized Merezhkovskii. He regarded it as the beginning of the apocalypse and labelled the Autocracy, the Orthodox Church and middle-class philistinism (*meshchanstvo*) guises of the Beast. Nietzschean elitism helped this Russian aristocrat justify his contempt for the middle class. Like his fellow Symbolists, Merezhkovskii considered Nietzsche an anarchist.

A second generation of Symbolists – Viacheslav Ivanov (1866–1949), Andrei Belyi (1880–1934) and Aleksandr Blok (1880–1921) – emerged after 1900. Ivanov maintained, in 'Ellinskaia religiia stradaiiushchego Boga' (The Hellenic Religion of the Suffering God) (1904), that Dionysianism was an aesthetic-psychological-religious phenomenon, and that Dio-

nysus was a precursor of Christ. In subsequent essays, Ivanov renounced 'Nietzschean' individualism and the Superman ideal and urged the Symbolists become myth-creators – to articulate the myths around which Russians could unite and thereby end social conflict. During the Revolution of 1905, Ivanov supported a doctrine called Mystical Anarchism, the brainchild of Georgii Chulkov, an anarchist and a former editor of Merezhkovskii's revue *Novyi put'* (New Path, 1902–4). Mystical Anarchism demanded the abolition of all authorities external to the individual – government, law, morality and social custom. Post-apocalyptic society would be characterized by freedom, beauty and love (*eros*, not *agape*) and would be cemented by passion, myth and sacrifice. These invisible bonds would be forged in a theatre-temple modelled on the Theatre of Dionysus and devoted to myth-creation (*mifotvorchestvo*). The Symbolists would serve as high priests and the spectators would become a chorus and participate actively in the myth-creating process. In the orgiastic ecstasies of the rites, they would shed their separateness and become one, thereby bringing about the communitarian consciousness necessary for a society without coercion. Ivanov's ideas on a Dionysian theatre impressed his contemporaries, and were a major source of the mass festivals and political theatre of the early Soviet period. Ivanov's Christ/Dionysus archetype became a Symbolist trope.

One product of the post-1905 easing of the censorship laws was a vulgar Nietzscheanism (*Nitsheanstvo*) of pornography, nihilism and decadence in literature and in life. Appalled by this phenomenon, Ivanov and Merezhkovskii distanced themselves from Nietzsche. Nevertheless, his ideas continued to shape their thought, informing, for example, the Symbolist concept of life-creation (*zhiznetvorchestvo*) which exalted art as a theurgical activity that would transfigure man and the world. Different Symbolists had their own versions.

Nietzsche's ideas were an important component of a mystical revolutionism that associated the people with Dionysus and the intelligentsia with Apollo and bourgeois civilization. Blok predicted, even welcomed, the destruction of the intelligentsia by the enraged people. He, Belyi and a group called the Scythians perceived the Bolshevik Revolution as the beginning of a 'revolution of the spirit' that would engender a new culture and a new man – an artist (see RUSSIAN RELIGIOUS-PHILOSOPHICAL RENAISSANCE §5).

2 Philosophers

Philosophic debate on Nietzsche was initiated by the respected journal *Voprosy filosofii i psikhologii* (Questions of Philosophy and Psychology) and centred on his critique of Christian morality. In October 1892, the journal published 'Friedrich Nietzsche: The Critique of Altruism' by V.P. Preobrazhenskii (1864–1900) who praised Nietzsche as a moralist, a defender of freedom and an advocate of the elevation and strengthening of the human person. Three articles in the next issue (January 1893) attacked Nietzsche as an amoralist and a decadent. The discussion spilled over into other journals. Nikolai MIKHAILOVSKII (1842–1904), editor of the Populist journal *Russkoe bogatstvo* (Russian Wealth) and a long-time advocate of the efficacy of individual action, regarded Nietzsche as an ally in his struggle against Marxist collectivism and historical determinism, as an advocate of a higher morality. As a socialist, Mikhailovskii recognized and objected to the anti-democratic implications of the Superman ideal. Vladimir SOLOV'ËV (1853–1900), the most influential philosopher of this period, described Nietzsche's idea of the Superman as 'mangodhood', the obverse of his own idea of *Bogochelovechestvo* (*Godmanhood*). Decrying Nietzsche's separation of beauty and power from religion, Solov'ëv maintained that only religion can free beauty from death. He also argued that even though the Superman ideal was demonic, it was religiously significant because it expressed a desire for human perfection, a yearning to be more than human. The Symbolists combined Solov'ëv and Nietzsche in various ways, in the above-mentioned concept of life-creation for example.

Nietzsche was of central importance to Nikolai BERDIAEV (1874–1948), Semën FRANK (1877–1950) and Lev SHESTOV (1866–1938). Nietzsche confirmed and reinforced their objections to positivism and rationalism, and challenged them to think about goodness, truth and beauty in new ways.

In their contribution to the symposium *Problemy idealizma* (Problems of Idealism) (1902), Berdiaev and Frank, two former Marxists turned Neo-Kantians, tried to accommodate Nietzsche to Kant. Berdiaev wanted to replace Kant's 'morality of duty' with a higher Nietzschean morality of free desire, but in the same essay he declared that man had a duty to become a Superman. He regarded the Superman as a religious-metaphysical ideal and envisaged a spiritual aristocracy roughly comparable to Nietzsche's 'new nobility'. Frank interpreted Zarathustra's 'love for the most distant' as love for distant goals such as truth, justice and beauty, as opposed to love for the nearest, for one's neighbour. Frank also talked about a 'new nobility', a spiritual or cultural elite, that struggled to realize its ideals. Years later, Frank credited Nietzsche with revealing to him the reality of the psyche and of spiritual life.

Berdiaev came to consider Nietzsche the forerunner of a new religious anthropology and the unwitting prophet of a new Christianity of freedom ungrounded in material reality, of limitless creativity, unprecedented beauty, and self-overcoming. In *Smysl tvorchestva: opyt opravdanie cheloveka* (*The Meaning of the Creative Act: An Attempt at the Justification of Man*) (1916), he maintained that the Third Revelation will be about man and will be accomplished in a free creative act. Nietzsche's goal, he said, was 'not to justify creativity by life but to justify life by creativity' ([1916] 1954: 110). At a time when most of his contemporaries had distanced themselves from Nietzsche, Berdiaev lauded *Thus Spoke Zarathustra* as 'the most powerful human book without Grace; whatever is superior to Zarathustra is so by Grace from on high' ([1916] 1954: 90).

Shestov maintained that reason can neither explain nor assuage misfortune, suffering or ugliness. In *Dobro v uchenii gr. Tolstogo i Fr. Nitshe* (The Good in the Teaching of Tolstoi and Nietzsche) (1900) and *Dostoevskii i Nitshe – filosofiia tragedii* (Dostoevsky and Nietzsche: The Philosophy of Tragedy) (1903), he used Nietzsche to negate the 'rational morality' of self-renunciation preached by Kant and Tolstoi, and to argue against rational systems in general. Unlike the philosophers mentioned above, Shestov did not consider Nietzsche an advocate of a higher morality; rather Shestov insisted that Nietzsche was not a moralist at all, for he showed that people must seek God rather than 'the good'. In subsequent works, Shestov attacked philosophical systems that impose a non-existent unity on the world and gloss over the horrors of life. His religious existentialism reminds one of Kierkegaard's, whom he discovered in the late 1920s.

3 Bolsheviks

Nietzsche's most important Bolshevik popularizers – Gor'kii (even though he did not join the Party), Anatolii Lunacharskii and Aleksandr BOGDANOV (Aleksandr Malinovskii, 1873–1928) – wanted to restore heroism and voluntarism to Marxism and to supplement Marx's teachings with new findings in the social and the physical sciences. All of them maintained that under socialism, Kant's 'morality of duty' would be superseded by a morality of free desire, a 'master morality', so to speak, but for everyone. They invoked the power of creative will, emphasized the collective aspects of Dionysianism (self-forgetting) and quoted Zarathustra's dictum 'man is a bridge and not a goal'. Nietzsche's powerful future-orientation and his related espousal of instrumental cruelty (as distinct from sadism), were taken up without acknowledgement by the Leninist-Marxists, especially Trotsky.

Nietzsche helped Gor'kii substitute an ethos of self-development for the Populist dictum that the writer must serve the people. Later on, Gor'kii tried to develop a Nietzschean aesthetic for a socially committed literature that promoted reason and science as guides to life. After he allied with the Bolsheviks in 1905, he denounced what he took to be Nietzschean individualism as philistinism. Gor'kii's favourite Nietzsche text was 'On War and Warriors' in *Thus Spoke Zarathustra*, which includes the line 'man is something that must be overcome'. Also important to Gor'kii was Zarathustra's injunction 'be hard – all creators are hard'. For most of his life, Gor'kii regarded the masses as sources of Dionysian energy, to be channelled by an Apollonian elite.

Lunacharskii discovered Nietzsche in 1901. Nietzsche helped him reconcile his love of the arts with his commitment to revolution. He claimed that art is a powerful stimulus to revolutionary ardour, described the 'will to power' as the 'will to creativity' (including social creativity), and called the Marxist ideal of a just and harmonious society an aesthetic ideal.

During the Revolution of 1905, he and Gor'kii developed the Marxist surrogate religion of *Bogo stroitel'stvo* (God-building). It extolled the heroic proletariat as saviour of humanity, preached worship of collective humanity, and promised collective immortality to encourage people to risk death fighting for socialism. The basic texts of God-building are Lunacharskii's *Religiia i sotsializm* (Religion and Socialism) (2 vols, 1908, 1911), Gor'kii's novel *Ispoved'* (*Confession*) (1908) and his essay 'The Destruction of the Person' (1909), written against individualism. *Confession* includes a scene in which the energies of an assembled crowd raise a paralyzed girl; it also includes a Superwoman, aptly named Christina.

Strictly speaking, Bogdanov was not a God-builder, but he did try to create a new myth. He wrote the utopian novels *Krasnaia zvezda* (Red Star) (1908) and *Inzhener Menni* (Engineer Menni) (1913), about a perfected communist society on the planet Mars, to inspire the workers to continue their struggle by showing them what they were fighting for. Bogdanov's vision was based on an ultra-collective, ultra-egalitarian interpretation of Marxism which denigrated the individual as a 'bourgeois fetish'. Paradoxically, Bogdanov claimed that communism would facilitate self-development. He hated authoritarianism and militarism. His ideal world had no experts, no hierarchies and no would-be supermen. It was a world of proletarian renaissance persons (he

was a partisan of gender equality) who had conquered nature or at least kept it at bay. They were guided by 'expediency norms' that changed as conditions changed, as distinct from 'coercive norms' (absolute commandments) and eternal truths. Bogdanov's first 'expediency norm' was 'there shall be no herd instinct'.

Bogdanov maintained that the Revolution of 1905 failed because the workers were culturally and psychologically unprepared to assume power. Therefore, he argued, cultural revolution must precede and accompany political revolution. Lenin disagreed. In 1909, he had Bogdanov expelled from the Party. The expulsion gave Bogdanov time to develop his concept of cultural revolution, by which he meant: the psychological and spiritual emancipation of the proletariat from bourgeois dominance, systematic revaluation of the cultural legacy from a proletarian perspective, and the construction of a distinctively proletarian art and science. Bogdanov's views inspired Proletkult (proletarian culture), an extra-Party movement that he, Lunacharskii and others founded in October 1917. Gor'kii was not among them; he wanted culture to be above class. At its peak in 1921, Proletkult numbered half a million members and had an extensive network of schools, art studios and theatres. The movement collapsed after Lenin attacked it, but crude versions of Bogdanov's ideas were perpetuated by self-styled proletarian groups during the culture wars of the 1920s, and helped inspire Stalin's cultural revolution of 1928–31. Gor'kii championed Socialist Realism, the Stalinist form of myth-creation and the official aesthetic of the Soviet Union from 1934, when it was officially adopted by the first Congress of Soviet Writers, until well after Stalin's death. Lunacharskii was involved in preparatory activities but he died before the Congress met (see RUSSIAN EMPIRIOCRITICISM).

4 Futurists and Acmeists

To the Futurists, the key Nietzsche text was the madman's announcement of the death of God in *The Gay Science* (§125) and the chaotic, directionless, universe and infinite horizons that ensue. Their foundational myth was *Pobeda nad solntsem* (Victory Over the Sun) (1913), the title of an operetta about the capture of the sun (Apollo), which occurs offstage, by Futurist strongmen. These new people are male or androgynous, but definitely not female. They speak a new language – *zaum* – literally 'beyond the mind', a concept inspired, in part, by Nietzsche's attack on 'reason in language' and his association of language and power. The Futurists advocated a complete break with history, exaggerating the anti-historicism and

865

celebration of youth in Nietzsche's *The Advantage and Disadvantage of History for Life*, and they wished to jettison the cultural legacy. The bellicosity of their language and their aggressive masculinism echoed some of Nietzsche's most ferocious passages. Their unabashed primitivism and orientation to Asiatic Russia stemmed from a literal reading of Nietzsche's 'new barbarians' and indicated their desire to create *de novo*. Paradoxically, they were enthralled by technology, large cities and noisy crowds. *Pobeda nad solntsem* was performed together with *Vladimir Maiakovskii: Tragediia*, by Vladimir Maiakovskii (1893–1930), which was structured like a Dionysian dithyramb and included Maiakovskii's version of the Christ/Dionysus archetype. Maiakovskii knew *Thus Spoke Zarathustra* well; his pre-Revolutionary poetry is permeated with images and themes drawn from it. Many Futurists were also painters; their alogism was a pictorial counterpart to *zaum*.

The Futurists brought the issues of language and form to the centre of literary debates, where they remained for over two decades. Their cultural iconoclasm and anti-bourgeois stance were easily politicized. After the Bolshevik Revolution they achieved quasi-official status. They maintained that a 'revolution of the spirit' was needed to complete the political and social revolution and tried to establish their own dictatorship of taste.

The Acmeists, a short-lived group of poets that included Nikolai Gumilëv (1886–1921) and Osip Mandel'shtam (1891–1938), developed the concept of the Apollonian in a way that enabled them to reconcile Hellenism with Orthodox Christianity in a poetic exaltation of earthly reality. Rejecting theurgy and mysticism, their aesthetics emphasized clarity in language, concreteness and a visual orientation. They defended Christian ethical values (Apollo is the ethical deity), moral courage and 'manly will'. Gumilëv's warrior pose and conquistador persona stemmed from *Thus Spoke Zarathustra*; also important to him was Nietzsche's concept of *amor fati*. Mandel'shtam's statement that 'to remember also means to invent' encapsulated his own interpretation of Nietzsche's views on history and myth and affirmed past values and 'world culture'. The Acmeists were persecuted during the Soviet period. Gumilëv was executed for treason; Mandel'shtam died in the Gulag.

5 The Soviet period

Unacknowledged Nietzschean ideas (ideas mediated by Nietzsche's Russian popularizers) helped shape Soviet literature and culture, including political culture, in ways too numerous and complex to be detailed here. They inspired literary, artistic and architectural experimentation, a ruthless revolutionary morality and cultural construction. In addition, they underlay the Lenin Cult, the Stalin Cult, socialist realism and the grandiose projects of the first and second five-year plans. Nietzschean themes were taken up by now-forgotten poets and playwrights and by such Soviet luminaries as the writer Isaac Babel, the theatrical director Vsevolod Meierhol'd and the film director Sergei Eisenstein. The religious stream of Nietzsche appropriation was perpetuated by Boris Pasternak, Mikhail BAKHTIN and other disaffected intellectuals.

Nietzsche's name was linked with 'isms that the government denounced: bourgeois individualism and nihilism in the 1920s, fascism in the 1930s, and bourgeois hedonism in Brezhnev's time. The few books and articles about Nietzsche published after 1927 quoted *Beyond Good and Evil* and *The Will to Power* extensively, but his works remained inaccessible to ordinary readers. Under Gorbachev's policy of *glasnost'* Nietzsche's writings were reprinted in press runs of 100,000, which sold out immediately.

See also: NIETZSCHE, F.

References and further reading

For additional references see the entries RUSSIAN RELIGIOUS-PHILOSOPHICAL RENAISSANCE and SHESTOV, L.

* Berdiaev, N. (1916) *Smysl tvorchestva: opyt opravdanie cheloveka*, Moscow; trans. D. Lowrie, *The Meaning of the Creative Act: An Attempt at the Justification of Man*, New York: Harper, 1954.

  Clowes, E. (1988) *The Revolution of Moral Consciousness: Nietzsche and Russian Literature, 1890–1914*, De Kalb, IL: Northern Illinois University Press. (Treats popularizers and vulgarizers of Nietzsche, mystical Symbolists and revolutionary Romantics.)

* Gor'kii [Gorky], M. (1908) *Ispoved'*, St Petersburg: Znanie; trans. R. Strunsky, *Confession*, New York: Stokes, 1916.

  Gunther, H. (1993) *Der sozialist Übermensch: Maksim Gor'kij und der sovjetische Heldenmythos* (The Socialist Superman: Maksim Gorkii and the Soviet Hero-Myth), Stuttgart: Metzler. (Treats Gor'kii's changing perceptions and utilizations of Nietzsche.)

* Ivanov, V. (1904) 'Ėllinskaia religiia stradaiiushchego Boga' (The Hellenic Religion of the Suffering God), serialized in *Novyi put'*.

  Kline, G.L. (1968) '"The God-builders": Gorki and Lunacharsky', in *Religious and Anti-Religious Thought in Russia*, 103–27. (Traces the roots of

God-building to nineteenth-century Russian radicalism, Feuerbach and Nietzsche.)

—— (1969) '"Nietzschean Marxism" in Russia', in *Demythologizing Marxism*, ed. F. Adelmann, Boston, MA: Boston College Studies in Philosophy, vol. 2, 166–83. (Discusses Lunacharskii, Bogdanov, V.A. Bazarov and S. Volskii.)

* Lunacharskii, A. (1908, 1911) *Religiia i sotsializm* (Religion and Socialism), St Petersburg: Shipovnik, 2 vols.

Merezhkovskii, D. (1914) *Pol'noe sobranie sochinenii* (Collected Works), Moscow: D. Sytin, 24 vols. (Contains all Merezhkovskii's works listed in this entry.)

* —— (1895) *Otverzhennyi* (The Outcast), in *Severnyi vestnik*; subsequently retitled *Smert' bogov: Iulian Otstupnik*; trans. C. Johnson, *Death of the Gods: Julian the Apostate*, London: Constable. (This historical novel is the first of a trilogy of historical novels titled *Khristos i Antikhrist* (Christ and Antichrist).)

* —— (1896) 'Pushkin', in 'Filosofskie techeniia russkoi poèzii', ed. P.P. Pertsov, St Petersburg: Merkushev.

* —— (1900–2) 'Tolstoi i Dostoevskii', in *Mir iskusstva*; *Tolstoy as Man and Artist, with an Essay on Dostoievsky*, Westminster: Constable, 1902.

Rosenthal, B.G. (ed.) (1986) *Nietzsche in Russia*, Princeton, NJ: Princeton University Press. (Multi-author work. Chapters on Symbolism, religious philosophy, Bolshevism, popular literature, Bakhtin; list of publications by and about Nietzsche 1892–1919; historical introduction by the editor.)

—— (1991) 'A New Word for a New Myth: Nietzsche and Russian Futurism', in P.I. Barta (ed.) *The European Foundations of Russian Modernism*, Lewiston, NY: Mellen, 219–50. (The interconnection of word and myth.)

—— (ed.) (1994) *Nietzsche and Soviet Culture: Ally and Adversary*, Cambridge: Cambridge University Press. (Multi-author work. Chapters on Futurism, Acmeism, occult doctrines, Soviet literature, art and architecture; adaptations of Nietzsche in Soviet ideology; Nietzsche among disaffected writers and thinkers; his influence on Hebrew writers before the Revolution. Editor's introduction includes discussion of methodological problems of assessing a buried influence.)

BERNICE GLATZER ROSENTHAL

NIFO, AGOSTINO
(*c.*1470–1538)

Agostino Nifo was a university teacher, medical doctor and extremely prolific writer. His books included many commentaries on Aristotle's logic, natural philosophy and metaphysics, as well as original works on topics ranging from elementary logic to beauty and love. However, his most important works had to do with the human intellect, and with Averroes' view that there is just one intellect shared by all human beings. Although he never accepted Averroes' position as true, he did initially believe that Averroes correctly interpreted Aristotle on this point. He also entered into public controversy with Pomponazzi on the question whether human immortality could be proved. Nifo's Aristotelianism reflects his interest in many different traditions of commentary on Aristotle, including medieval Latin commentators, especially Thomas Aquinas, medieval Arab commentators and their Latin followers, especially John of Jandun, but most of all the Greek commentators. Here he shows the strong influence of Renaissance humanism, which made the Greek texts available. It was when Nifo himself learned Greek that he came to abandon the notion that Averroes was an accurate interpreter of Aristotle. Nifo was also very interested in Plato and Platonism, particularly as presented by Marsilio Ficino. His careful presentations of other people's doctrines were popular in university circles for much of the sixteenth century.

1   **Life and works**
2   **Natural philosophy**
3   **Psychology**
4   **Metaphysics**

1   Life and works

Agostino Nifo (Eutychus Augustinus Niphus Suessanus) was born at Sessa Aurunca, near Caserta in southern Italy. After studying the liberal arts at Naples, he went on to Padua, where he received his degree around 1492. During his stay at Padua he gained the enmity of the Franciscan theologian Antonio Trombetta, a Scotist. He also engaged in a dispute with his teacher, Nicoletto VERNIA, regarding the correct interpretation of Alexander of Aphrodisias' doctrine on the human soul (see ALEXANDER OF APHRODISIAS). Presumably he was also on poor terms with Pietro POMPONAZZI, who was his competitor by 1495. Pomponazzi scornfully criticizes Nifo in his own early questions on the soul.

Nifo left his post at Padua in 1499 and returned to his native town. There he witnessed the difficulties and trials resulting from the Spanish occupation. Nifo, who was also a practising medical doctor, was the personal physician of the Spanish Grand Captain in 1504. He seems to have taught at Naples in 1505 (where he moved in humanist circles), at Salerno in 1506–7, and again at Naples in 1507–8, when he unsuccessfully attempted to regain his post at Padua. In 1514 he taught at Rome. Subsequently he entered into controversy with his old rival Pomponazzi. Encouraged by Ambrogio Flandino to write a reply to Pomponazzi's *De immortalitate animae* (On the Immortality of the Soul), which had been published in 1516, Nifo wrote a work with the same title that appeared in 1518. Pomponazzi replied in turn with his *Defensorium* (1519).

Nifo taught at Pisa for the Florentines from 1519 to 1522. He seems to have then taught at Salerno from 1522 to 1526 and again from 1533 to 1535; there is evidence that he taught at Naples in 1531–2. In 1535 he declined Pope Paul III's invitation to teach natural philosophy at Rome. He was elected mayor of his native town and extended a formal welcome to the Emperor Charles V when he visited Sessa Aurunca on 24 March 1536.

Nifo was an extraordinarily prolific writer, though very little of his work is available in a modern edition. His first work was an edition of the works of Aristotle and Averroes that appeared at Venice in 1495 and 1496. In 1497 this was followed by his own commentary on the *Destructio destructionum* (the medieval Latin translation of Averroes' *Tahafut al-tahafut* (The Incoherence of Incoherence)) and a treatise on the agent sense. While at Padua, he apparently finished a commentary on a Latin translation of Aristotle's *On the Soul* that was published against his wishes in 1503, the same year that he published his own important treatise on the intellect (*De intellectu*), which differs significantly from the commentary. He wrote a long sequence of commentaries on Aristotle's logical works, on Aristotle's works in natural philosophy, and on Aristotle's *Metaphysics* (see ARISTOTLE). In 1520 he published a textbook in elementary logic, the *Dialectica ludicra* (Playful Dialectics). He paid some attention to political philosophy, and published *De regnandi peritia* (On the Practical Knowledge of Ruling) (1522), a free adaptation of Machiavelli's *Il principe* (The Prince) (see MACHIAVELLI, N. §2). He also wrote on humanist topics, including a work on beauty and love which he finished at his villa Niphanus in 1529. In them he attempted to give an Aristotelian theory of beauty and love in competition with that of Plato and his followers. He finished his commentary on Aristotle's books *On Animals* in 1534. Many of

Nifo's Aristotle commentaries continued to be published for at least three decades after his death.

2 Natural philosophy

Nifo showed an interest in natural philosophy from the beginning. In his early commentary on Averroes' *Destructio destructionum* he emphasizes that inasmuch as natural philosophy takes the senses as its starting point, it cannot reach a knowledge of God's act of creation, which is a form of making that is totally beyond sense knowledge. It was thus a grievous error on the part of the medieval Christian philosopher-theologians, the Latin Expositors (*expositores latini*), to have attributed a doctrine of creation to Aristotle. He was also concerned about the relationship between natural philosophy or natural science (*naturalis scientia*) and metaphysics, arguing that natural philosophy was subordinate to metaphysics. It is true that the existence of God and the separate substances (or purely immaterial beings) is demonstrated by natural philosophy on the basis of eternal motion. However, the existence of these beings is studied in a more complete fashion in metaphysics, which thus takes us beyond natural philosophy.

Nifo's commentary (1508) on Aristotle's *Physics* is remarkable for what it shows of his changing use of sources in response to a newly acquired mastery of Greek. Nifo openly admits that in his youth he asserted that the position of Averroes on the intellect is the same as that of Aristotle (see AVERROISM), but he explains that after having read and examined Aristotle's words in the Greek he came to see that Averroes' position is nonsense (*deliramentum*). Because Averroes, who did not know Greek, was working with erroneous translations which he could not correct, he misrepresents THEMISTIUS and generally acts like a drunkard. Nifo even stresses that he prefers himself to err with the Greeks in explicating a Greek author, rather than to think correctly with barbarians who lack command of the language. In the commentary, Nifo makes frequent reference to the Greek commentators on Aristotle, namely Alexander of Aphrodisias, SIMPLICIUS, Themistius and John PHILOPONUS, who are all mentioned in his preface. In the same place however, he states his strong commitment to AQUINAS, his 'trustworthy leader', to whom he gives, following JOHN OF JANDUN and others, the honorific title of 'the Expositor'.

In both the commentary on Averroes and the commentary on the *Physics*, Nifo also mentions the Oxford Calculators (see OXFORD CALCULATORS). In the earlier commentary, he dismisses their work on the grounds that they follow mathematical principles and not natural principles. In the later work, he remarks that the Peripatetics (see PERIPATETICS) never dreamed of such a doctrine as that of the intension and remission of forms; it is a new question invented by idle men who want to be noticed.

3 Psychology

Both of Nifo's earliest works, the treatise on the agent sense and the commentary on Averroes' *Destructio destructionum*, treat psychological topics. The first treatise takes up the question of whether an agent sense is required in the process of sensation. ARIS-TOTLE had argued that an agent intellect is required to initiate the process of understanding, and JOHN OF JANDUN had argued that, in a parallel manner, an agent sense is required to initiate the process of sense perception. The activity of external objects and their impact on our passive sense organs via the reception of sensible species is not enough to explain how perception can occur. Nifo argues that Jandun was wrong. In the second treatise, he argues that Averroes' doctrine of the unity of the intellect – which is that all human beings share one intellect – is the correct interpretation of Aristotle. He calls Averroes 'Aristotle transposed' and 'Aristotle's priest'.

In his early commentary (published in 1503) on Aristotle's *On the Soul*, Nifo continues his praise of Averroes, whom he calls 'the Arab Aristotle' (see IBN RUSHD), and his attacks on John of Jandun. This time he asserts that John of Jandun was wrong in believing that Averroes acknowledged the existence of intelligible species as part of the process of understanding. Other striking positions that Nifo adopts are his belief that according to philosophy one can achieve an intuitive knowledge of God during this life, and his insistence that according to Aristotle and Averroes there is no real distinction between psychological faculties, notably the intellect and the will. He uses the phrase 'potestative whole' (*totum potestativum*) of the human soul, thus emphasizing his view that it is a single power, and also reflecting the influence of ALBERT THE GREAT. In the commentary, Nifo shows a close knowledge both of Themistius' paraphrases on Aristotle's *On the Soul* in the translation of Ermolao Barbaro and of a now lost Latin translation of the commentary on *On the Soul* traditionally attributed to Simplicius. He compares both these sources to PLOTINUS, whom he knew from Marsilio Ficino's translation of the Enneads and commentary (see FICINO, M.).

In 1503 Nifo published *De intellectu* (On the Intellect), his major psychological work. Book I is divided into five treatises (*tractatus*) that are devoted to fundamental topics: the origin and immortality of the soul, the nature of the soul's separability from the

body, the unity of the soul, the agent and possible intellects, and the speculative and practical intellects. At the end of each treatise Nifo sets forth what he calls the 'true position'. In fact, these passages are borrowed word for word from Albert the Great's *De natura et origine animae* (On the Nature and Origin of the Soul). The same practice is continued in Book II, which concerns the felicity or 'state' (*status*) of the soul, a term found earlier in Albert and Jandun. While Nifo bases the 'true position' primarily on Albert the Great, it should be noted that Aquinas and Ficino play secondary roles. Nifo's remarks on individuation are basically Thomistic, and his emphasis on moral arguments for immortality seem to be inspired by his study of Ficino.

Some themes from Nifo's earlier writing reappear in *De intellectu*. He consistently attacks Jandun as misrepresenting Averroes' doctrines, especially by postulating that Averroes accepted intelligible species in his theory of intellectual cognition. He also rejects Aquinas' doctrine of a real distinction between the intellect and the will. But the most outstanding feature of *De intellectu* is Nifo's complete reversal of his position on Averroes. Although he spends much effort on determining the correct interpretation of Averroes' views on the soul and intellect, he now rejects Averroes as a true interpreter of Aristotle. He offers arguments against Averroes culled from Albert the Great, Thomas Aquinas and Marsilio Ficino, drawing especially on Aquinas' *De unitate intellectus contra Averroistas* (On the Unity of the Intellect Against the Averroists), and on Ficino's *Theologia platonica* (Platonic Theology). He states decisively that the immortality of the soul can be demonstrated, and he offers arguments drawn from Albert, Aquinas and Ficino. He attacks Alexander of Aphrodisias for denying immortality, and criticizes Vernia for proposing Alexander as a proponent of immortality. In like fashion, without mentioning him by name, he rejects Duns Scotus' view that immortality was a neutral topic because equally good arguments can be given for and against it (see DUNS SCOTUS, J.).

A remarkable feature of *De intellectu* is Nifo's command of the thought of Plotinus, Alexander, Themistius and Simplicius, and his attempt to delineate their positions on the different topics that he treats. He also summarizes the contents of Siger of Brabant's *De intellectu*, thus serving as the primary source for knowledge of that now lost work (see SIGER OF BRABANT).

4 Metaphysics

As early as his commentary on the *Destructio destructionum*, Nifo adopted a conceptual scheme of

869

the hierarchy of being and a participation metaphysics that reflected his dependence on the thought of AQUINAS (§9). God exists by virtue of his essence, and all other beings exist by virtue of their participation in God's existence. Moreover, this participation comes in degrees: higher creatures participate more fully in existence than do lower creatures, and so we get the hierarchically ordered system that has been called the Great Chain of Being. What is noteworthy about Nifo's position here is not so much the basic doctrines as his attribution of them to Averroes. In this attribution he was followed by others, such as Marcantonio Zimara.

Another of Nifo's early treatments of metaphysics is a commentary on Book XII of Aristotle's *Metaphysics*, published in 1505. Among the doctrines discussed by Nifo in his commentary are the movement of the heavenly bodies, the nature of divine cognition, the union of the human intellect with God, the infinity of God's power, and the relation of God and the Intelligences. Two constant themes are Aquinas' ability to interpret even corrupt texts correctly, and Averroes' misreadings, owing to his ignorance of Greek and consequent reliance on faulty translations. Nifo added that he was none the less forced to expound Averroes, since no one is considered an Aristotelian unless he is an Averroist. This early commentary was later incorporated into a commentary on the *Metaphysics* as a whole, published at Venice in 1547 after Nifo's death.

Nifo's own major work on metaphysics is his *Metaphysicarum disputationum dilucidarium* (Clarification of Metaphysical Disputations), completed at Naples in 1510. One of the themes that he takes up is that of the transcendentals, being (*ens*), good (*bonum*), one (*unum*) and true (*verum*), so-called because they transcend Aristotle's ten categories. Nifo argues that no order can be established among the transcendentals, since they are all equally convertible with being. Nifo also notes that he has never read Aristotle calling being and one transcendentals (*transcendentia*) at all. Another topic of discussion was the distinction between existence (*esse*) and essence (*essentia*) in created things. Nifo takes Aquinas to hold that in every caused thing existence and essence are really and simply distinct, principally on the grounds that that which participates is distinct from that in which it participates. Nifo argues that the Peripatetic position is that there can be no composition of essence and existence in the separate substances or in the heavenly bodies, but that Aquinas, as a Catholic though not as a natural philosopher, was forced to posit that essence and existence were distinct even in the Intelligences, since he considered them able not to exist. Nifo is quick to add that as a good Peripatetic, Aquinas

rarely if ever departs from the thinking of Aristotle, and he adds that he himself rarely if ever departs from Aquinas.

See also: ARISTOTELIANISM, RENAISSANCE; ARISTOTLE COMMENTATORS; AVERROISM; JOHN OF JANDUN; POMPONAZZI, P.

List of works

For details of the publication of Nifo's Aristotle commentaries, see Lohr (1988).

Nifo, A. (1495, 1497) *Destructiones destructionum Averroys cum Augustini Niphi de Suessa expositione. Eiusdem Augustini quaestio de sensu agente* (Agostino Nifo's Exposition of Averroes' *Destructio destructionum*. The Same Agostino's Question on the Agent Sense), Venice: Octavianus Scotus, 1497. (Nifo began his commentary on the medieval Latin version of Averroes' *Tahafut al-tahafut* (Incoherence of the Incoherence) in 1494 and finished it at Padua in 1497. He accepts Averroes' interpretation of Aristotle on the unity of the intellect and ascribes to him a participation metaphysics. His question on the agent sense, completed at Padua in 1495, was written to discredit Jandun's postulating such a faculty. God provides the spiritual factor needed for sensation to occur.)

—— (1503) *Super tres libros De anima* (On the Three Books *On the Soul*), Venice: Petrus de Quarengis. (Completed at Sessa in 1498 and published against Nifo's wishes. Although he knows Greek and cites Themistius and Simplicius, he considers Averroes to have correctly interpreted Aristotle on the unity of the intellect.)

—— (1503) *Liber de intellectu* (Treatise on the Intellect), Venice: Petrus de Quarengis. (Examination of such topics as immortality, unity of the intellect and cognitive union of humans to separate intellects and God. Rejects Averroes as reliable interpreter of Aristotle and gives arguments against unity of intellect and for personal immortality. True position on all major topics derived from Albert the Great.)

—— (1505) *In duodecim metà tà physiká seu metaphysices Aristotelis et Averrois volumen* (Volume on Book XII of the *Metaphysics* of Aristotle and Averroes), Venice: Alexander Calcedonius. (This is a commentary only on Book XII of Aristotle's *Metaphysics*. Nifo questions Averroes' interpretations.)

—— (1508) *Aristotelis physicarum acroasum liber interprete atque expositore Eutyco Augustino Nypho* (Aristotle's Book of Physical Discourses, Agostino

Nifo the Translator and Expositor), Venice: Octavianus Scotus, 1508. (Completed in 1506 after only one year of work, the commentary reveals particular interest in Themistius and Aquinas.)

—— (1510) *Metaphysicarum disputationum dilucidarium* (Clarification of Metaphysical Disputations), Naples: Sigismundus Mayr Alemanus, 1511. (Begun at Salerno in 1507 and finished at Naples in 1510. Studies such topics as metaphysical participation, distinction of essence and existence, transcendentals, individuation, divine infinity and intuitive knowledge of God. The Venice 1559 edition of the *Dilucidarium* was reprinted by Minerva in 1967.)

—— (1518) *De immortalitate animae libellus* (Small Book on the Immortality of the Soul), Venice: Heirs of Octavianus Scotus. (Written against Pietro Pomponazzi's work *De immortalitate animae* and dedicated to Pope Leo X. Insists that Aristotle held to personal immortality. Offers arguments for immortality from different traditions: from Plato and Plotinus but also from Albert the Great and Aquinas. Human free choice shows the soul to be immaterial and immortal.)

—— (1520) *Collectanea ac commentaria in libros de anima* (Collected Remarks and Commentaries on the Books on the Soul), Venice: Heirs of Octavianus Scotus, 1522. (The *Collectanea* are Nifo's early commentary published in 1503; the *Commentaria* are a later commentary completed at Pisa in May 1520. Nifo at this point considers Averroes' explications of Aristotle worthless since he used bad translations. He therefore follows Themistius and Simplicius.)

—— (1520) *Dialectica ludicra tyrunculis atque veteranis utillima* (Playful Dialectics Useful for Beginners and Veterans), Florence: Heirs of Philippus Juncta. (An introduction to logic expressly opposed to recent logicians and claiming to be in harmony with real Aristotelians, the Greek commentators. Refers the reader to his commentary on the *Prior Analytics* (1524).)

—— (1522) *De regnandi peritia* (On the Practical Knowledge of Ruling), Naples: Aedes Dominae Catherine de Silvestro, 1523; trans. S. Pernet-Beau, *Une réécriture du Prince de Machiavel: le De Regnandi Peritia de Agostino Nifo*, Paris: Université Paris X-Nanterre, 1987. (Completed at Sessa in 1522. Derivative from Machiavelli's *Il principe* (The Prince).)

—— (1524) *Prioristica commentaria* (Commentary on the *Prior Analytics*), Naples: Evangelista Papiensis, 1528. (Completed at Salerno in 1524 and dedicated to Cajetan, that is, Thomas de Vio. Heavily dependent on John Philoponus and overall critical

of Latin commentators with the exception of Aquinas.)

—— (1529) *De pulchro et amore liber* (On Beauty and Love), Rome: Antonius Bladus, 1531; trans. F. Sotas, *Sobre la belleza y el amor*, Seville: Secretariado de Publicaciones de la Universidad de Sevilla, 1990. (Completed at Niphanus, near Sessa, November 1529, this work attempts to construct a theory of beauty and love based on Aristotelian concepts and competing with the theory of Marsilio Ficino. Notable erotic element.)

—— (1534) *Expositiones in omnes Aristotelis libros: De Historia animalium lib. IX; De Partibus animalium et earum causis lib. IV; ac De Generatione animalium lib. V* (Expositions on All Aristotle's Books *On Animals*), Venice: Hieronymus Scotus, 1546. (Completed at Salerno in 1534 but published only after Nifo's death. Follows John Philoponus. Says Albert the Great 'babbled' and 'stuttered'.)

—— (1535) *Aristotelis Stagiritae Topica inventio a magno Augustino Nipho Medice interpretata atque exposita* (Aristotle's Invention, the *Topics*, Translated and Explained by Agostino Nifo Medici), Venice: Octavianus Scotus. (Completed at Niphanus in 1535. Considers it evil to attempt to explain Aristotle's works without knowing Greek and using the Greek commentators. Both Averroes and the Latins followed erroneous translations.)

—— (1547) *Expositiones in Aristotelis libros metaphysices* (Expositions on Aristotle's *Metaphysics*), Venice: Hieronymous Scotus. (A close textual study published posthumously. He cites his own Greek manuscripts and his *Dilucidarium* (1510), showing great esteem for Aquinas. Covers participation, analogy, infinity of God, divine Ideas and divine knowledge. The Venice 1559 edition of the *Expositiones* was reprinted by Minerva in 1967.)

References and further reading

Ashworth, E.J. (1976) 'Agostino Nifo's Reinterpretation of Medieval Logic', *Rivista critica di storia della filosofia* 31: 354–74. (A study of Nifo's logic textbook, the *Dialectica ludicra* (1520), and how it modified medieval doctrines.)

Lohr, C.H. (1988) *Latin Aristotle Commentaries. II. Renaissance Authors*, Florence: Olschki, 282–7. (Listing of all Nifo's Aristotle commentaries in various editions and where they are to be found. Publishers are not uniformly indicated.)

Mahoney, E.P. (1971) 'Agostino Nifo's *De Sensu Agente*', *Archiv für Geschichte der Philosophie* 53: 119–42. (Discusses Nifo on Averroes, Albert the Great, Giles of Rome and John of Jandun regarding the notion of an agent sense.)

—— (1983) 'Philosophy and Science in Nicoletto Vernia and Agostino Nifo', in A. Poppi (ed.) *Scienza e filosofia all'Università di Padova nel quattrocento*, Contributi alla storia dell'Università di Padova 15, Padua: Lint, 135–202. (Examines Nifo's early discussions on subalternation of the sciences, nature of matter, intension and remission of forms, composition of the heavenly bodies, and the velocity of their movement; pages 173–200 focus on Nifo rather than Vernia.)

—— (1986) 'Marsilio Ficino's Influence on Nicoletto Vernia, Agostino Nifo and Marcantonio Zimara', in G.C. Garfagnini (ed.) *Marsilio Ficino e il ritorno di Platone: Studi e documenti*, vol. 2, Florence: Olschki, 509–31. (Emphasizes Nifo's heavy use of Ficino's work, especially on the soul and the intellect.)

—— (1989) 'Plato and Aristotle in the Thought of Agostino Nifo (ca. 1470–1538)', in G. Roccaro (ed.) *Platonismo e aristotelismo nel mezzogiorno d'Italia (secc. XIV-XVI)*, Palermo: Officina di Studi Medievali, 81–102. (Complete survey of the role of Plato and Aristotle in Nifo's writings with a useful bibliography.)

—— (1993) 'Agostino Nifo and Neoplatonism', in P. Prini (ed.) *Il Neoplatonismo nel Rinascimento*, Rome: Istituto della Enciclopedia Italiana, 205–31. (Detailed examination of Nifo's works delineating his acquaintance with the writings of Plotinus and other Neoplatonists.)

Nardi, B. (1958) *Saggi sull'aristotelismo padovano dal secolo XIV al XVI* (Essays on Paduan Aristotelianism from the 14th to the 16th Century), Università degli Studi di Padova: Studi sulla tradizione aristotelica nel Veneto 1, Florence: Sansoni. (A series of studies on Aristotelianism at the University of Padua which help to place Nifo in context.)

Poppi, A. (1966) *Causalità e infinità nella scuola padovana dal 1480 al 1513* (Causality and Infinity in the Paduan School from 1480 to 1513), Padua: Antenore, 222–36. (Critical discussion of Nifo on God's infinity.)

EDWARD P. MAHONEY